The 1995
Good Pub Guide

Edited by Alisdair Aird

Deputy Editor: Fiona May

Research Officer: Robert Unsworth
Editorial Research: Karen Fick
Additional Research: Milly Taylor

VERMILION
LONDON

This edition first published in 1994 by Vermilion,
an imprint of Ebury Press,
Random House, 20 Vauxhall Bridge Road,
London SW1V 2SA

3 5 7 9 10 8 6 4 2

Managing editor for Ebury Press: Nicky Thompson
Proof-reading: Pat Taylor Chalmers

A catalogue for this book may be found in the British Library.

ISBN 0 09 178252 X

Typeset from authors disks by Clive Dorman & Co.
Printed and bound by Clays Ltd, St Ives plc.

Contents

Introduction

Where are the best pubs?

We have always been struck by the way that some parts of the country are full of good pubs, while others have very few. This year, we have worked out how many good pubs there are for each area, and compared that with the number of people living there. We added together the main entries and the starred Lucky Dip entries for each area, as we reckon these are generally up to main entry standard, at least for the qualities described for them. Then we divided that total by the number of people living in each area, to see how many good pubs there are per 100,000 people there.

Cornwall comes out top for good pubs, with about 30 for every 100,000 people living there. Next come Devon, Cumbria, Gloucestershire, Oxfordshire, Somerset and North Yorkshire, with about 25. Buckinghamshire, the Isle of Wight, Wiltshire and the Channel Islands have about 20. At the bottom of the league table are Merseyside, the West Midlands and Cleveland, with less than one good pub for every 100,000 people.

For good food in pubs, Cambridgeshire, Kent, Leicestershire, Oxfordshire, Shropshire, Suffolk, Yorkshire and Scotland have done best this year in our readers' reports and our own inspections. On the drinks side, Derbyshire/ Staffordshire, the Midlands, Sussex and Wales have cornered far more than their fair share of our Beer Awards; and a higher than average proportion of pubs in Cambridgeshire, Gloucestershire, Hereford & Worcester, Kent, Leicestershire and Oxfordshire now serve decent wine.

The cheapest areas for decent pub food are now the West Midlands, Nottinghamshire, Humberside, Lancashire and London. The most expensive are Berkshire, Cambridgeshire, Hampshire, Kent and Wiltshire – here the same sort of pub meal typically costs about a third as much again as in the cheapest areas.

For drinks, the cheapest areas are now (in rough order, starting with the cheapest) the Channel Islands, West Midlands, Humberside, Lancashire, Cheshire, Nottinghamshire, Cumbria, Hereford & Worcester, Yorkshire, Derbyshire/Staffordshire, Northumbria and Shropshire. The most expensive, starting at the top with the dearest, are Surrey, Kent, London, Buckinghamshire, Sussex, the Isle of Wight, Berkshire and Scotland. Typically, people in Surrey are now paying over 40p more for their pint than people in the West Midlands.

Natural cooking

Over the last year or two we've noticed the emergence of a style of pub food which seems to have inspired quite a number of pub cooks, all over the country, quite independently of each other. It's going down very well indeed with our readers. It seems to be searching out some sort of rewarding middle ground between the two main streams of pub food development: on the one hand, the use of bought-in freezer packs so well prepared that many people would think them home-made; and on the other hand, creative cooking by innovative chefs who find dining pubs suit their style better than restaurants – and often outclass them. We're perfectly happy with both these main streams. We're always delighted to discover pubs where imaginative cooking is setting top standards in taste. And at the other extreme there's no denying that catering suppliers are filling a real need; for example, even pubs committed to home cooking find it very helpful for their customers if they can keep a range of interesting prepacked vegetarian dishes and puddings as a back up.

What is breaking new ground now, though, is an approach which combines cooking that's not necessarily elaborate with the best ingredients available locally. The landlord (or landlady) takes real pride in tracking down sources of top quality supplies. If this means getting up at 5am to get to the markets, that's what he or she does. Pubs are discovering that customers come back if the meat they use has real flavour – from local butchers who can be trusted to supply properly reared and properly hung meat. Country game (increasingly, rabbit and pigeon as well as venison and pheasant) is being used much more now than a few years ago. Fish has been popular in pub cooking for some years. But increasingly landlords are taking real care over where it comes from. If it's possible, some go down to the coast to meet the boats; others get up early to get the freshest and best supplies from the markets; others arrange their own deliveries from the coast, usually two or three times a week. In areas where it's possible (mainly Scotland and Wales), some pubs are even using river trout and wild salmon instead of farmed fish, to get that extra flavour and texture. Pubs are finding the rewards of buying directly from source specially selected locally grown fresh-picked vegetables instead of produce which may well have been picked locally originally but has then been chilled and travelled a long way to a central wholesale market or depot and then a long way back. A few even grow some of their own vegetables now; more grow many of the herbs they use.

With such good ingredients, food can be really interesting without being too complicated – indeed, the simplest presentation is often the best for such fresh well flavoured food. At the same time, we're now finding this care over ingredients is inspiring quite a few pub chefs to develop really interesting dishes that are inventive without being too fancy.

This new approach to pub food is best described as 'natural cooking'. The exponents of natural cooking range from quite a few cheap and unpretentious real ale pubs (the Old Ale House in Truro, Cornwall, the Fat Cat in Sheffield and the Beer Engine in Wakefield, both Yorkshire, are the best examples) to pubs which still keep this natural unfussy approach but – at a cost – inject professional expertise of the highest order (the Fish at Sutton Courtenay in Oxfordshire stands out).

In between these extremes, really good natural cooking can now be found at a great many pubs. Apart from the three or four places we have already mentioned, the pubs in which we and readers have most enjoyed really refreshing natural cooking this year have been the Harrow at West Ilsley (Berkshire), the Sun at Newton Reigny (a new Cumbria entry), the Drewe Arms at Broadhembury and Castle at Lydford (both Devon), the Green Man at Gosfield (Essex), the Five Bells at Buriton (Hampshire), the Crown & Anchor at Lugwardine (a new Hereford & Worcester entry), the Blue Ball in Braunston, Martins Arms at Colston Bassett and Peacock at Redmile (all in our Leicestershire chapter), the Black Horse at Nassington (Midlands), the Saracens Head near Erpingham (Norfolk), the Milecastle near Haltwhistle, a new entry, and Warenford Lodge at Warenford (both Northumbria), the Abingdon Arms at Beckley, Angel in Burford and Clanfield Tavern at Clanfield (all Oxfordshire), the Stables at Hope (Shropshire), the Brewers Arms at Rattlesden (Suffolk), the Elsted Inn at Elsted and Crabtree at Lower Beeding (Sussex), the Foresters Arms at Carlton and Fox & Hounds at Carthorpe (both Yorkshire), the Kilberry Inn at Kilberry, Tayvallich Inn at Tayvallich and Morefield Motel in Ullapool (all Scotland), and the Armstrong Arms at Stackpole (a very promising new entry in Wales).

The Green Man, Brewers Arms, Elsted Inn and Crabtree all exemplify natural cooking at its very best. (In the Brewers Arms, among the other faces tucking in happily, you may well see a cooking face that's very well known indeed.) Of these three, it's the Elsted Inn at Elsted in Sussex which we name as **Natural Cooking Pub of the Year**: though the food in the other two pubs is every bit as good, the Elsted Inn is a charmingly unspoilt, interesting and unpretentious country pub which serves as the perfect showcase for this style of cooking.

Children in pubs

In the first few editions of this book, the proportion of pubs which allowed children in was so low that we listed them all at the back of the book. This proportion has increased dramatically in the last decade. Now, over five out of six main entries allow children into at least some part of the pub – in Scotland and northern England almost all do. Even in Hampshire, which is the least child-friendly county as far as pubs are concerned, two-thirds of them make some sort of provision for children.

This year the Government intends to introduce a system of Children's Certificates for English and Welsh pubs (Scotland already has such a system). This will replace the present widely evaded law which states that children under 14 are not allowed into any pub room in which there is a servery for alcohol. In so far as it will be at least a degree of rationalisation, we do welcome the proposal. We are particularly relieved that, as we had urged, the time-limit of 8pm which had been mooted seems to have been abandoned. However, as we go to press the current proposal is for a time-limit of 9pm. We believe that there should be no legal time-limit. As things stand, of the 1,060 main entries in England and Wales which do allow children, 87% do not set any time-limit: we have not heard of a single instance at any of these pubs where this has caused any problem. Much better to leave it flexible, so that landlords can decide for themselves what time-limit, if any, would suit their particular pub. Of the small minority who do at the moment set time-limits, just under a quarter allow children only at lunchtime. The rest set time-limits covering fairly evenly the wide range between 6 (common in Lancashire) and 9.30. In practice, these variations seem to suit local circumstances and the nature of the pubs concerned; and it's important to remember that barely more than 10% of landlords allowing children find any need to set a time-limit at all. It's difficult to see any sense in ruling that, in a sophisticated dining pub in a part of the country where people eat relatively late, a family having a celebratory bar meal with their early teenage children should have to be out by 9, say (which is what the current proposals would do).

So, if there must be regulation, it ought not to include any time-limit. But, watching the pub scene closely for many years, and monitoring reports from many thousands of readers over those years, we have come to be convinced that the best change of all would now be complete deregulation. We believe that it would now be right to remove entirely the prohibition on children with responsible adults, and to leave the question to be settled between landlords and their customers at least in pubs in which a significant amount of food is served. If a pub chooses to exclude children to preserve its character, then so be it: entirely understandable. If parents choose to keep their children away from another pub because it doesn't sound suitable, well and good. If yet another pub proves to be a source of potential danger or harm to children, then its landlord would be in trouble anyway, almost certain to lose his licence. But that should surely be the way it works, rather than a bench of licensing magistrates deciding whether or not a particular pub should be allowed to cater for children, and setting a curfew on them.

As we have said, the great majority of pubs in this edition do provide for children. Some provide much better than others. Particularly good for families are the Jervis Arms at Onecote (Derbyshire), the Otter at Weston (Devon), the Wight Mouse at Chale (Isle of Wight), and above all a new entry this year, the Coombe Cellars at Combeinteignhead (Devon). The Coombe Cellars, doing extremely well under a newish owner, is **Family Pub of the Year**.

Good news about wine and beer in pubs

In the last few years there has been a marked improvement in the standard of wine in pubs. This year, one in five of the main entries qualifies for our Wine Award – the wine-glass symbol which shows that a pub has decent wines by the glass. Admittedly, this is not a particularly high hurdle to jump, and the converse – the fact that four out of five pubs have not gained this award – still shows tremendous room for further improvement. However, many pubs do set an admirably high standard for the range and quality of their wines. A rapidly increasing number now use a vacuum pump or inert gas injection to keep opened bottles in unopened condition. This can allow a splendid choice of wines by the glass, with many pubs now doing a dozen or more; the Ship at Conyer Quay (Kent) now has up to 100 on the go, and the Crown at Colkirk (a new Norfolk entry) will open any of the bottles on their quite extensive list even if you want just a glass.

Quality is of course more important than sheer numbers of bottles. We have been particularly impressed this year by the quality and interest of the wines by the glass at the Five Arrows in Waddesdon (a new Buckinghamshire entry), the Knife & Cleaver at Houghton Conquest and Anchor at Sutton Gault (in our Cambridgeshire chapter), the Cholmondeley Arms near Bickley Moss (Cheshire), the Drewe Arms at Broadhembury, Nobody Inn at Doddiscombsleigh, Ley Arms at Kenn and Cridford Inn at Trusham (all Devon – the last two new entries), the Three Horseshoes at Powerstock (Dorset), the Green Man at Toot Hill (Essex), the Fox at Lower Oddington (Gloucestershire), the Wykeham Arms in Winchester (Hampshire), the Roebuck at Brimfield (Hereford & Worcester), the Red Lion at Steeple Aston (Oxfordshire), the Crown in Southwold (Suffolk), the Plough at Blackbrook (Surrey), the Angel at Hetton, George & Dragon at Kirkbymoorside and Kaye Arms at Grange Moor (Yorkshire – the last two are new entries). For the sheer exuberance of its changing choice, we name as **Wine Pub of the Year** the Crown at Southwold.

In the last year or two the changes introduced by the Beer Orders, designed to increase competition by weakening the monopoly of the big brewing combines, have really started to bite. The range of beers on offer has widened dramatically. And prices have at last started to stabilise.

In 1988, immediately before the original Monopolies & Mergers Commission Report which spurred the changes, we checked the beers on offer in 281 pubs tied to national brewers, and not subject to special arrangements. At that time, only about one in nine regularly offered a beer from a different brewer. Not one Courage pub in our sample offered competing beers, and hardly any Bass/Charrington pubs did. We have repeated the exercise this year, in a sample of 159 pubs tied to the big brewers. Now, 85% of the pubs tied to the four great brewing combines (Allied, Bass, Courage and Whitbreads) stock beers brewed by competing brewers; often, more than one at a time. The proportion is much the same with each of these English big brewers. Nearly half the pubs tied to Scottish & Newcastle also offer guest beers from other brewers (in 1988 virtually none did), though S&N have not been large enough to be fully subject to the Beer Orders.

This really is a tremendous change. Moreover, of pubs offering a guest beer, about one in three is now getting it direct from the independent brewer (rather than via the wholesaling arm of their parent brewery). This proportion has been rising each year since the introduction of the Beer Orders – and of these independent buyers, about one in three is now selling that independently bought beer more cheaply than any beer from its tied brewery.

The beers most commonly sold as guests are Morlands Old Speckled Hen, Marstons Pedigree and, particularly, Wadworths 6X. But the range which may crop up in tied pubs is now staggering. We found our small sample of 159 national-tied pubs stocking the products of over 60 different competing breweries.

This is the first year since we started monitoring prices that beer prices have not increased more than the rate of inflation. We compare this year's beer price with last year, within each pub. This is a much more accurate method of monitoring prices than using sample surveys in which the pubs vary from year to year. In this year's survey, we had data for both years for 1,150 pubs all over Great Britain. The average price of a pint at the time of our survey was £1.48 – an increase of 2.3% over the year. This is certainly no higher than the underlying rate of inflation (ie prices excluding mortgages), which over the same period was 2.4%. In pubs getting their beers from the national brewers and in those tied to the bigger regional brewers the price rise was fractionally higher. In pubs tied to smaller breweries prices rose by less than 1%, and in those tied to the regional chains which have now opted out of brewing and buy their beers in (Boddingtons and Greenalls), they have risen by very little more.

All this does suggest that the big breweries' stranglehold over beer prices has been dramatically weakened, with a wider choice of beers available to drinkers, more competition, and more stable prices.

We show below those breweries that came out cheapest of all in our survey. In each case we show how much you save in one of their tied pubs, compared with the typical pub tied to a big national brewer:

	saving per pint		saving per pint
Holts	57p	Donnington	27p
Clarks	55p	Hoskins	25p
Bathams	34p	Jennings	25p
Hydes	33p	Lees	25p
Everards	31p	Robinsons/Hartleys	25p
Banks's/Hansons	30p	St Austell	25p
Sam Smiths	29p	Thwaites	25p
Hardys & Hansons	28p	Timothy Taylors	25p
Hook Norton	27p		

Maclays generally show as cheap in our surveys, but we did not this year include any of their pubs. Pubs brewing their own beers on the premises typically save you 25p, compared with a national tied pub.

The great majority of the pubs in this book stock real ale, and keep and serve it at least reasonably well. This year we have introduced a Beer Award, shown by the tankard symbol, for those pubs which stand out either for keeping particularly interesting beers or for serving what they do keep in tip-top condition. These awards are based on our own inspections and the flow of reports from readers. One in five of the main entries has qualified for the award in this first year. Unlike the Wine Awards – which you could think of as a sort of pass mark – these new Beer Awards denote a very high standard of cellarmanship indeed. Pubs which we would currently single out for their beers are the Blackwood Arms on Littleworth Common (Buckinghamshire), the Golden Pheasant at Etton (Cambridgeshire), the Old Ale House in Truro (Cornwall), the Alexandra and the Brunswick in Derby, the Bridge at Topsham (Devon), the Queens Head at Littlebury and Plough at Navestock (Essex), the Boat at Redbrook (Gloucestershire), the Wine Vaults in Southsea (Hampshire), the Taps in Lytham and Marble Arch in Manchester (Lancashire), the Rose & Crown at Hose and Market in Retford (Leicestershire chapter), the Griffin at Shustoke and Vane Arms in Sudborough (Midlands), the Crown at Churchill (in our Somerset chapter), the Richmond Arms at West Ashling (Sussex) and the Athletic Arms in Edinburgh. But it is a new entry, the traditional gaslit Beer Engine in Wakefield (Yorkshire), which is our **Beer Pub of the Year**, for its changing choice of up to 20 extremely well kept beers all from small independent brewers, served in just the right sort of atmosphere.

As the Special Interest list at the end of the book shows, nearly three dozen of the main entries now brew their own beer – a huge increase from our first edition, when fewer than ten did. In general, these own-brews are good value on cost grounds. Often, they also represent a good buy because they taste so good. An outstanding example is the Plough at Wistanstow (Shropshire): as well as serving good food, it is the source of the excellent Woods beers which can be found in some other pubs in the area. The Plough at Wistanstow is the **Own-Brew Pub of the Year**.

The beer which has stood out this year has been Black Sheep, brewed in Masham (Yorkshire) by Paul Theakston – from the Theakstons brewing family, but not connected with the Theakstons brewery since its takeover by Scottish & Newcastle. Black Sheep Bitter is a very good value beer, beautifully balanced and quite distinctive: we have been struck by how quickly it has spread into so many Yorkshire pubs. Black Sheep Bitter is our **Beer of the Year**.

It's in London that we find our brewery of the year – though this year we have had reports from readers pleased to find its products in places as far apart as Canada, California and Finland. Fullers has a chain of generally rather small and interesting pubs – many of them main entries, many others in the Lucky Dip sections – which is gradually expanding out of London into the south east. As a result of deals with national brewers, its good beers have been turning up increasingly in pubs tied to those national brewers, as well as in free houses. Most importantly, Fullers has this year won our readers' gratitude, and our respect, for holding the price of its excellent Chiswick Bitter (not strong, but with a breadth of flavour that can put many stronger beers to shame) down to £1.29 in its London pubs. That's well below the normal level of London prices. Fuller Smith

& Turner (to give them their full name) is the **Brewer of the Year**.

It's very encouraging to see so many English pubs offering a decent choice of malt whiskies now. The Crown & Horns at East Ilsley (Berkshire), Quayside in Falmouth (Cornwall), King George IV at Eskdale Green (Cumbria), Smiths Tavern in Ashbourne (a new Derbyshire entry), Nobody Inn at Doddiscombsleigh (Devon), Wight Mouse at Chale (Isle of Wight), Ship at Conyer Quay (Kent), Bulls Head at Clipston (Midlands), White Horse at Pulverbatch (Shropshire), Haunch of Venison in Salisbury (Wiltshire), Kaye Arms at Grange Moor (a new Yorkshire entry), Cadeby Inn at Cadeby, Sandpiper in Leyburn and Pack Horse at Widdop (also Yorkshire) and Bulls Head in Barnes (London SW13) all have particularly wide ranges, and the Kings Arms at Stockland in Devon has an interesting specialist range of Island malts. The Cragg Lodge at Wormald Green (Yorkshire) has a fascinating and encyclopaedic range of nearly a thousand malt whiskies, many at cask strength and many of extreme rarity. In Wales the Dinorben Arms at Bodfari stands out with a very wide and interesting range. In Scotland, as might be expected, a good many pubs and inns have a very wide choice; for something special we'd recommend the Bow Bar in Edinburgh (lots at cask strength), the Eilean Iarmain at Isleornsay on Skye (an excellent local collection, especially of vatted malts) and the Glenisla Hotel at Kirkton of Glenisla (very strong on Island malts). It's extremely unexpected to find a really excellent range of malt whiskies in the Midlands, and it's for that reason that the Bulls Head at Clipston (Northamptonshire), with over 350 malts to choose from now, is the **Malt Whisky Pub of the Year**.

Awards for food and service

The number of pubs using fresh-caught fish is increasing. Because the fish is so fresh, pubs are able to exploit its natural taste, without the need for strong sauces. Pubs currently outstanding for fish cookery are the White Hart at St Keverne and Port William at Trebarwith (both Cornwall), the Drewe Arms at Broadhembury, the Anchor at Cockwood and Start Bay at Torcross (all Devon), the Crown at Blockley (Gloucestershire), Sankeys in Tunbridge Wells and Pearsons in Whitstable (both Kent), the Waterford Arms at Seaton Sluice (famed for its big helpings; Northumbria), the Fish at Sutton Courtenay (a new main entry in Oxfordshire) and the Tayvallich Inn at Tayvallich and Morefield Motel in Ullapool (Scotland). From among these we choose as **Fish Pub of the Year** the Fish at Sutton Courtenay.

Virtually all the main entries in this book now have some sort of dish vegetarians are happy with – a big change from just a few years ago, when pubs rarely considered vegetarians. Even if there isn't anything obvious on the menu, it's now always worth asking. Quite a few pubs now go out of their way to provide an inventive choice of vegetarian food that tempts even us hardened meat-eaters. Outstanding among them are the Royal Oak at Barrington (Cambridgeshire), the Drunken Duck near Hawkshead (Cumbria), the Pheasant at Gestingthorpe (Essex), the Black Boys at Aldborough (Norfolk), the Lincolnshire Poacher in Nottingham and the Malt Shovel at Brearton (Yorkshire). The Pheasant at Gestingthorpe – generally a choice of ten interesting dishes, and two weeks in the year devoted to vegetarian extravaganzas – is our **Vegetarian Pub of the Year**.

More pubs now are looking around for interesting local cheeses, and we mention a lot of these in the text. But none can match the Dukes 92, Mark Addy and Royal Oak in Manchester for their fabulous choice and huge helpings, and the careful and interesting selection at the Shepherds at Melmerby (Cumbria), Nobody Inn at Doddiscombsleigh (Devon) and Roebuck at Brimfield (Hereford & Worcester). The Royal Oak astounds us by the speed with which it has got back to normal after serious fire damage: not for the first time, it is our **Cheese Pub of the Year**.

A great many pubs now make first-class puddings – nursery puddings, rich chocolate ones, fruit pies and crumbles, pavlovas and brûlées, interesting ice creams; overall, this year's favourites seem to be sticky toffee pudding and banoffi pie. In a few pubs, the pudding has reached a high art. We'd defy even the most hardened slimmer to resist the choice at the Woodmans Cottage at Gorefield

(Cambridgeshire), the Duke of York at Berrow, the Sun at Winforton (both Hereford & Worcester) and the Bear at Crickhowell (Wales). For the luscious extravagance of its range (up to 50 at a time, all home-made), we choose as **Pudding Pub of the Year** the Woodmans Cottage at Gorefield.

For a really enjoyable meal out and a sense of special occasion, one wants a combination of an attractive and individual atmosphere with excellent imaginative cooking. Currently pubs which stand out for this are the White Hart at Hamstead Marshall (Berkshire), the Mole & Chicken at Easington (a new Buckinghamshire entry), the White Hart at Bythorn, Pheasant at Keyston, Three Horseshoes at Madingley and Anchor at Sutton Gault (Cambridgeshire), the Cholmondeley Arms near Bickley Moss (Cheshire), the Royal Oak at Appleby, Bay Horse at Ulverston and Brown Horse at Winster (Cumbria), the White Horse at Woolley Moor (Derbyshire), the Castle at Lydford (Devon), Three Horseshoes at Powerstock (Dorset), the Fox at Lower Oddington (Gloucestershire), the Bell at Alderminster and Black Horse at Nassington (Midlands), the Strode Arms at Cranmore (Somerset), the Angel at Stoke by Nayland (Suffolk), the White Hart at Ford (Wiltshire), the Crab & Lobster at Asenby (Yorkshire), the Wheatsheaf at Swinton (Scotland), the Walnut Tree at Llandewi Skirrid (Wales), and the Eagle in EC1, London. Some of these are more restauranty than others: but our **Dining Pub of the Year**, the Crab & Lobster at Asenby, is very decidedly a pub.

All too many town pubs take things too easy. Out in the country, few pubs can still rely on local custom to survive: they have to work hard to build up a regular trade with customers who come back again and again even from some distance, because they've enjoyed themselves once and know they'll enjoy themselves again. But in towns, surrounded by workers, shoppers and visitors, pubs have more of a captive market: they don't have to work so hard to keep their tills ringing. So it's a delight to find town and city pubs which stand out for character and atmosphere, such as the Free Press in Cambridge, the White Hart in Exeter (Devon), the Wykeham Arms in Winchester (Hampshire), the Cooperage in Newcastle and Chain Locker in North Shields (both Northumbria), the Adam & Eve in Norwich (Norfolk), the Highbury Vaults in Bristol (in our Somerset chapter), the Brewery Tap in Ipswich (a new Suffolk entry), the Cricketers in Dorking (Surrey), Blind Jacks in Knaresborough and Whitelocks in Leeds (both Yorkshire), the Lamb & Flag, WC2, Red Lion in Waverton Street W1 and Star, SW1 (Central London), and the Bow Bar in Edinburgh (Scotland). The Wykeham Arms has been the subject of so many enthusiastic reports from readers this year that it must be our **Town Pub of the Year**.

Some pubs and inns charm because of their unique atmosphere and character, above all else. Among these, pubs which currently stand out are the Bell at Aldworth (Berkshire), the Queens Head at Newton (Cambridgeshire), the White Lion at Barthomley (Cheshire), the White Hart at Ludgvan, Pandora near Mylor Bridge and Eliot Arms at Tregadillett (Cornwall), the Drewe Arms at Drewsteignton and Double Locks near Exeter (Devon), the Square & Compass at Worth Matravers (Dorset), the Boat at Ashleworth Quay (Gloucestershire), the Sun at Bentworth and White Horse near Petersfield (Hampshire), the Fleece at Bretforton (Hereford & Worcester – and for sheer oddity the quaint Monkey House near Defford in that county), the White Horse in Beverley (Humberside), the Case is Altered at Five Ways (Midlands), the Lifeboat at Thornham (Norfolk), the Lamb in Burford and Falkland Arms at Great Tew (Oxfordshire), the Tuckers Grave at Faulkland and George at Norton St Philip (Somerset), the Yew Tree at Cauldon (Staffordshire) and the Scarlett Arms at Walliswood (Surrey). You can't beat the very basic Yew Tree at Cauldon for its quirkiness and its extraordinary collections; the White Horse near Petersfield is a near-perfect example of a no-frills country local; and the Falkland Arms at Great Tew is most people's dream of a quaint and picturesque village pub. Overall, the 1995 title of **Character Pub of the Year** goes to the Fleece at Bretforton, marvellously preserved down the centuries and full of interest.

We have been in some extraordinarily friendly pubs this year, where the service is both good and extremely welcoming. We'd particularly pick out Doug and Mavis Hughes of the Spinner & Bergamot (Cheshire), Ann and Iain Cameron of the Old Inn at St Breward (Cornwall), Colin and Hilary Cheyne of the Royal Oak in Appleby and Alan Coulthwaite of the Watermill at Ings (Cumbria), Geraldine McDonald of the Lantern Pike, a new entry at Hayfield, and Bill and Jill Taylor of the White Horse at Woolley Moor (both Derbyshire), Kerstin and Nigel Burge of the Drewe Arms at Broadhembury and David and Susan Grey of the Cott at Dartington (Devon), Yuksel Bektas, the remarkably accommodating Turkish landlord of the Plough at Clifton Hampden and Val Baxter of the Plough at Finstock (Oxfordshire), Stephen Waring of the Wenlock Edge Inn in Shropshire, and Jerry O'Brien of the Churchill Arms in London W8. The Cott at Dartington is a lovely old place with excellent food, extremely well run, where the warmth of the welcome is almost palpable: its owners, David and Susan Grey, are our **Licensees of the Year**.

The pubs which at the moment are doing best for sheer all-round enjoyment – good food, drink, service, atmosphere and character – are the Harrow at West Ilsley (Berkshire), the Anchor at Sutton Gault (Cambridgeshire), the Cholmondeley Arms near Bickley Moss and Smoker at Plumley (Cheshire), the Royal Oak at Appleby, Masons Arms on Cartmel Fell and Drunken Duck near Hawkshead (Cumbria), the Coach & Horses at Buckland Brewer, Cott Inn at Dartington, Nobody Inn at Doddiscombsleigh, Castle at Lydford, Blue Ball at Sidford and Oxenham Arms at South Zeal (all in Devon), the Sailors Return at East Chaldon (Dorset), the Crown at Blockley, Bakers Arms at Broad Campden, New Inn at Coln St Aldwyns and Wild Duck at Ewen (Gloucestershire), the White Horse at Droxford (Hampshire), the Ringlestone Inn at Ringlestone (Kent), the Inn at Whitewell (Lancashire), the Wenlock Edge Inn on Wenlock Edge (Shropshire), the Royal Oak at Luxborough (Somerset), the Ship at Dunwich, Angel in Lavenham and Crown in Southwold (Suffolk), the White Hart at Ford (Wiltshire), the Blue Lion at East Witton, Angel at Hetton and Old Hall at Threshfield (Yorkshire), the Riverside at Canonbie (Scotland), and the Bear at Crickhowell (Wales). Though all of these are excellent, one currently stands out. The White Hart at Ford, with good food, great atmosphere and character, a welcome for all ages, and a bar that's a really pubby bar, separate from the food side, is our **Pub of the Year**.

This has been a vintage year for new entries. We don't remember any other in which the Lucky Dip section – relying as it does largely on hot tips from thousands of readers – has included so many promising pubs. And the new main entries include several dozen particularly rewarding pubs. Those which we have most enjoyed are the Mole & Chicken at Easington (Buckinghamshire), a very relaxed dining pub – very old-seeming, too, though in fact in its present guise it's relatively new; the Ley Arms at Kenn (Devon), beautifully restored and extended after fire damage and doing very well indeed under its new owner, and the altogether more idiosyncratic little Green Dragon at Stoke Fleming (also Devon), transformed under its new tenants; the lively and welcoming old Catherine Wheel in the picturesque village of Bibury (Gloucestershire); the pretty Crown & Anchor at Lugwardine (Hereford & Worcester), blossoming under its new owners; the Fur & Feather at Woodbastwick (Norfolk), a splendid renovation of an old building, now the tap for the excellent little Woodfordes brewery; the very warmly welcoming Milecastle in its isolated spot opposite the Roman Wall near Haltwhistle (Northumbria); the Plough at Kelmscot (Oxfordshire), lovingly refurnished by new owners in a style of which William Morris would have approved when he was the local squire; the rambling and very old-fashioned White Hart at Littleton upon Severn, Avon (in our Somerset chapter), a splendid new addition to the very small chain tied to Smiles of Bristol; and the Brewery Tap in Ipswich (Suffolk), a new offshoot from the independent Tolly brewery. The George & Dragon at Kirkbymoorside (Yorkshire) has impressed us even more than these: an attractive building taken in hand by enthusiastic new owners, with good natural cooking, excellent drinks and fine service in very pleasant civilised surroundings. The George & Dragon at Kirkbymoorside is our **Newcomer of the Year**.

What is a Good Pub?

The main entries in this book have been through a two-stage sifting process. First of all, some 2,000 regular correspondents keep in touch with us about the pubs they visit, and nearly double that number report occasionally. The present edition has used a total of 32,738 reports from readers. This keeps us up-to-date about pubs included in previous editions – it's their alarm signals that warn us when a pub's standards have dropped (after a change of management, say), and it's their continuing approval that reassures us about keeping a pub as a main entry for another year. Very important, though, are the reports they send us on pubs we don't know at all. It's from these new discoveries that we make up a shortlist, to be considered for possible inclusion as new main entries. The more people that report favourably on a new pub, the more likely it is to win a place on this shortlist – especially if some of the reporters belong to our hard core of about five hundred trusted correspondents whose judgement we have learned to rely on. These are people who have each given us detailed comments on dozens of pubs, and shown that (when we ourselves know some of those pubs too) their judgement is closely in line with our own.

This brings us to the acid test. Each pub, before inclusion as a main entry, is inspected anonymously by the Editor, the Deputy Editor, or both. They have to find some special quality that would make strangers enjoy visiting it. What often marks the pub out for special attention is good value food (and that might mean anything from a well made sandwich, with good fresh ingredients at a low price, to imaginative cooking outclassing most restaurants in the area). Maybe the drinks are out of the ordinary (pubs with several hundred whiskies, with remarkable wine lists, with home-made country wines or good beer or cider made on the premises, with a wide range of well kept real ales or bottled beers from all over the world). Perhaps there's a special appeal about it as a place to stay, with good bedrooms and obliging service. Maybe it's the building itself (from centuries-old parts of monasteries to extravagant Victorian gin-palaces), or its surroundings (lovely countryside, attractive waterside, extensive well kept garden), or what's in it (charming furnishings, extraordinary collections of bric-a-brac).

Above all, though, what makes the good pub is its atmosphere – you should be able to feel at home there, and feel not just that *you're* glad you've come but that *they're* glad you've come.

It follows from this that a great many ordinary locals, perfectly good in their own right, don't earn a place in the book. What makes them attractive to their regular customers (an almost clubby chumminess) may even make strangers feel rather out-of-place.

Another important point is that there's not necessarily any link between charm and luxury – though we like our creature comforts as much as anyone. A basic unspoilt village tavern, with hard seats and a flagstone floor, may be worth travelling miles to find, while a deluxe pub-restaurant may not be worth crossing the street for. Landlords can't buy the Good Pub accolade by spending thousands on thickly padded banquettes, soft music and luxuriously shrimpy sauces for their steaks – they can only win it by having a genuinely personal concern for both their customers and their pub.

Using the *Guide*

THE COUNTIES

England has been split alphabetically into counties, mainly to make it easier for people scanning through the book to find pubs near them. Each chapter starts by picking out the pubs that are currently doing best in the area, or specially attractive for one reason or another.

Occasionally, counties have been grouped together into a single chapter, and metropolitan areas have been included in the counties around them – for example, Merseyside in Lancashire. When there's any risk of confusion, we have put a note about where to find a county at the place in the book where you'd probably look for it. But if in doubt, check the Contents.

Scotland and Wales have each been covered in single chapters, and London appears immediately before them at the end of England. Except in London (which is split into Central, North, South, West and East), pubs are listed alphabetically under the name of the town or village where they are. If the village is so small that you probably wouldn't find it on a road map, we've listed it under the name of the nearest sizeable village or town instead. The maps use the same town and village names, and additionally include a few big cities that don't have any listed pubs – for orientation.

We always list pubs in their true locations – so if a village is actually in Buckinghamshire that's where we list it, even if its postal address is via some town in Oxfordshire. Just once or twice, while the village itself is in one county the pub is just over the border in the next-door county. We then use the village county, not the pub one.

STARS ★

Specially good pubs are picked out with a star after their name. In a few cases, pubs have two stars: these are the aristocrats among pubs, really worth going out of your way to find. In past editions two or three pubs have had three stars. This year we have amalgamated the three-star and two-star grades, so that the top grade is now two stars. The reason for this is that the general standard of pubs has been improving, and we now believe that it is difficult to maintain a distinction between the pubs which have had three stars in the past and many of the two-star entries. So this is not a demotion of the former three-star pubs: if anything, it is recognition that the two-star grade is even more special than it has been in the past. The stars do NOT signify extra luxury or specially good food – in fact some of the pubs which appeal most distinctively and strongly of all are decidedly basic in terms of food and surroundings. The detailed description of each pub shows what its special appeal is, and that is what the stars refer to.

FOOD AND STAY AWARDS 🍴 🛏

The knife-and-fork symbol shows those pubs where food is quite outstanding. The bed symbol shows pubs which we know to be good as places to stay in – bearing in mind the price of the rooms (obviously you can't expect the same level of luxury at £15 a head as you'd get for £30 a head). Pubs with bedrooms are now mapped and are marked on the maps as a square.

♀

This wine glass symbol marks out those pubs where wines are a cut above the usual run. This should mean that a glass of house wine will be at least palatable. The text of the entry will show whether you can expect much more than this; in some cases pubs are now treating wine drinkers very well indeed, and our hope is that the prospect of gaining our wine award will encourage many more to join this sadly small minority. We are particularly grateful for readers' reports on wine quality.

– NEW THIS YEAR

The beer tankard symbol shows pubs where the quality of the beer is quite exceptional, or pubs which keep a particularly interesting range of beers in good condition.

£

This symbol picks out pubs where we have found decent snacks at £1.10 or less, or worthwhile main dishes at £3.30 or less. This is the same limit as we set last year, on the grounds that overall price inflation over the year has been close to zero. However, pub food prices have in general increased by between 4% and 5% over the year (rather more than the rate of inflation), so pubs gaining the Bargain Award really are very cheap indeed.

RECOMMENDERS

At the end of each main entry we include the names of readers who have recently recommended that pub (unless they've asked us not to). Important note: the description of the pub and the comments on it are our own and *not* the recommenders'; they are based on our own personal inspections and on later verification of facts with each pub. As some recommenders' names appear quite often, you can get an extra idea of what a pub is like by seeing which other pubs those recommenders have approved.

LUCKY DIPS

We've continued to raise the standard for entry to the Lucky Dip section at the end of each county chapter. This includes brief descriptions of pubs that have been recommended by readers, with the readers' names in brackets. As the flood of reports from readers has given so much solid information about so many pubs, we have been able to include only those which seem really worth trying. Where only one single reader has recommended a pub, we have now not included that pub in the list unless the reader's description makes the nature of the pub quite clear, and gives us good grounds for trusting that other readers would be glad to know of the pub. So with most, the descriptions reflect the balanced judgement of a number of different readers, increasingly backed up by similar reports on the same pubs from different readers in previous years (we do not name these readers). Many have been inspected by us. In these cases, LYM means the pub was in a previous edition of the *Guide*. The usual reason that it's no longer a main entry is that, although we've heard nothing really condemnatory about it, we've not had enough favourable reports to be sure that it's still ahead of the local competition. BB means that, although the pub has never been a main entry, we have inspected it, and found nothing against it. In both these cases, the description is our own; in others, it's based on the readers' reports.

Lucky Dip pubs marked with a ☆ are ones where the information we have (either from our own inspections or from trusted reader/reporters) suggests a firm recommendation. Roughly speaking, we'd say that these pubs are as much worth considering, at least for the virtues described for them, as many of the main entries themselves. Note that in the Dips we always commend food if we have information supporting a positive recommendation. So a bare mention that food is served shouldn't be taken to imply a recommendation of the food. The same is true of accommodation and so forth.

The Lucky Dips (particularly, of course, the starred ones) are under consideration for inspection for a future edition – so please let us have any comments you can make on them. You can use the report forms at the end of the book, the report card which should be included in it, or just write direct (no stamp needed if posted in the UK). Our address is *The Good Pub Guide*, FREEPOST TN1569, WADHURST, East Sussex TN5 7BR.

MAP REFERENCES

All pubs are given four-figure map references. On the main entries, it looks like this: SX5678 Map 1. Map 1 means that it's on the first map at the end of the book. SX means it's in the square labelled SX on that map. The first figure, 5, tells you to look along the grid at the top and bottom of the SX square for the figure 5. The *third* figure, 7, tells you to look down the grid at the side of the square to find the figure 7. Imaginary lines drawn down and across the square from these figures should intersect near the pub itself.

The second and fourth figures, the 6 and the 8, are for more precise pin-pointing, and are really for use with larger-scale maps such as road atlases or the Ordnance Survey 1:50,000 maps, which use exactly the same map reference system. On the relevant Ordnance Survey map, instead of finding the 5 marker on the top grid you'd find the 56 one; instead of the 7 on the side grid you'd look for the 78 marker. This makes it very easy to locate even the smallest village.

Where a pub is exceptionally difficult to find, we include a six-figure reference in the directions, such as OS Sheet 102 reference 654783. This refers to Sheet 102 of the Ordnance Survey 1:50,000 maps, which explain how to use the six-figure references to pin-point a pub to the nearest 100 metres.

MOTORWAY PUBS
If a pub is within four or five miles of a motorway junction, and reaching it doesn't involve much slow traffic, we give special directions for finding it from the motorway. And the Special Interest Lists at the end of the book include a list of these pubs, motorway by motorway.

PRICES AND OTHER FACTUAL DETAILS
The *Guide* went to press during the summer of 1994. As late as possible, each pub was sent a checking sheet to get up-to-date food, drink and bedroom prices and other factual information. In the last year, we've found that many pubs have held their food and accommodation prices almost unchanged, but that others have increased them by up to 15% (or even more in a very few cases). In the country as a whole, food prices seem to have increased by about 4% to 5%. We think it would be prudent to allow for increases of around this rate for summer 1995. But if you find a significantly different price *please let us know*.

Breweries to which pubs are 'tied' are named at the beginning of the italic-print rubric after each main entry. That means the pub has to get most if not all of its drinks from that brewery. If the brewery is not an independent one but just part of a combine, we name the combine in brackets. Where a brewery no longer brews its own beers but gets them under contract from a different brewer, we name that brewer too. When the pub is tied, we have spelled out whether the landlord is a tenant, has the pub on a lease, or is a manager; tenants and leaseholders generally have considerably greater freedom to do things their own way, and in particular are allowed to buy drinks including a beer from sources other than their tied brewery.

Free houses are pubs not tied to a brewery, so in theory they can shop around to get the drinks their customers want, at the best prices they can find. But in practice many free houses have loans from the big brewers, on terms that bind them to sell those breweries' beers – indeed, about half of all the beer sold in free houses is supplied by the big national brewery combines to free houses that have these loan ties. So don't be too surprised to find that so-called free houses may be stocking a range of beers restricted to those from a single brewery.

Real ale is used by us to mean beer that has been maturing naturally in its cask. We do not count as real ale beer which has been pasteurised or filtered to remove its natural yeasts. If it is kept under a blanket of carbon dioxide to preserve it, we still generally mention it – as long as the pressure is too light for you to notice any extra fizz, it's hard to tell the difference. (For brevity, we use the expression 'under light blanket pressure' to cover such pubs; we do not include among them pubs where the blanket pressure is high enough to force the beer up from the cellar, as this does make it unnaturally fizzy.) If we say a pub has, for example, 'Whitbreads-related real ales', these may include not just beers brewed by the national company and its subsidiaries but also beers produced by independent breweries which the national company buys in bulk and distributes alongside its own.

Other drinks: we've also looked out particularly for pubs doing enterprising non-alcoholic drinks (including good tea or coffee), interesting spirits (especially malt whiskies), country wines (elderflower and the like) and good farm ciders. So many pubs now stock one of the main brands of draught cider that we normally mention cider only if the pub keeps quite a range, or one of the less common farm-made ciders.

Meals refers to what is sold in the bar, not in any separate restaurant. It means that pub sells food in its bar substantial enough to do as a proper meal – something you'd sit down to with knife and fork. It doesn't necessarily mean you can get three separate courses.

Snacks means sandwiches, ploughman's, pies and so forth, rather than pork scratchings or packets of crisps. We always mention sandwiches in the text if we know that a pub does them – if you don't see them mentioned, assume you can't get them.

The food listed in the description of each pub is an example of the sort of thing you'd find served in the bar on a normal day, and generally includes the dishes which are currently finding most favour with readers. We try to indicate any difference we know of between lunchtime and evening, and between summer and winter (on the whole stressing summer food more). In winter, many pubs tend to have a more restricted range, particularly of salads, and tend then to do more in the way of filled baked potatoes, casseroles and hot pies. We always mention barbecues if we know a pub does them. Food quality and variety may be affected by holidays – particularly in a small pub, where the licensees do the cooking themselves (May and early June seems to be a popular time for licensees to take their holidays).

Any separate *restaurant* is mentioned. We also note any pubs which told us they'd be keeping their restaurant open into Sunday afternoons (when, in England and Wales, they have had to close their bars up to now). But in general all comments on the type of food served, and in particular all the other details about meals and snacks at the end of each entry, relate to the pub food and not to the restaurant food.

Children under 14 are now allowed into at least some part of almost all the pubs included in this *Guide* (there is no legal restriction on 14-year-olds going into the bar, though only 18-year-olds can get alcohol there). As we went to press, we asked the main-entry pubs a series of detailed questions about their rules. *Children welcome* means the pub has told us that it simply lets them come in, with no special restrictions. In other cases we report exactly what arrangements pubs say they make for children. However, we have to note that in readers' experience some pubs make restrictions which they haven't told us about (children only if eating, for example), and very occasionally pubs which have previously allowed children change their policy altogether, virtually excluding them. If you come across this, please let us know, so that we can clarify the information for the pub concerned in the next edition. Beware that if children are confined to the restaurant, they may be expected to have a full restaurant meal. Also, please note that a welcome for children does not necessarily mean a welcome for breast-feeding in public. Even if we don't mention children at all, it is worth asking: one or two pubs told us frankly that they do welcome children but don't want to advertise the fact, for fear of being penalised. All but one or two pubs (we mention these in the text) allow children in their garden or on their terrace, if they have one. Note that in Scotland the law allows children more freely into pubs so long as they are eating (and with an adult); there are moves afoot to follow suit in England and Wales. In the Lucky Dip entries we mention children only if readers have found either that they are allowed or that they are not allowed – the absence of any reference to children in a Dip entry means we don't know either way.

Dogs, cats and other animals are mentioned in the text if we know either that they are likely to be present or that they are specifically excluded – we depend chiefly on readers and partly on our own inspections for this information.

Parking is not mentioned if you should normally be able to park outside the pub, or in a private car park, without difficulty. But if we know that parking space is limited or metered, we say so.

Telephone numbers are given for all pubs that are not ex-directory. We give the numbers with the extra 1 which British Telecom is now adding to the dialling codes: we have been assured by BT that all the numbers in the book will work with this extra 1 from the time this edition is published.

Opening hours are for summer weekdays; we say if we know of differences in winter, or on particular days of the week. In the country, many pubs may open rather later and close earlier than their details show unless there are plenty of customers around (if you come across this, please let us know – with details). Pubs are allowed to stay open all day Mondays to Saturdays, from 11am (earlier, if the area's licensing magistrates have permitted) till 11pm. However, outside cities most English and Welsh pubs close during the afternoon. Scottish pubs are allowed to stay open until later at night, and the Government has said that it may introduce legislation to allow later opening in England and Wales too, though we don't expect any change before late 1995 at the earliest. We'd be very grateful to hear of any differences from the hours we quote. You are allowed 20 minutes' drinking-up time after the quoted hours – half an hour if you've been having a meal in the pub.

Sunday hours are standard in law for all English and Welsh pubs that open on that day: 12-3, 7-10.30. But a few still stick to 2pm closing (we mention this when we know of it). As we went to press the Government announced that it was likely to introduce proposals allowing all-day opening on Sunday, though it is unlikely that any law to give effect to this welcome change would take effect until late in 1995 at the earliest. If a pub has a supper licence (granted to some pubs which function as restaurants or have separate restaurants), it is allowed to serve meals (with alcohol) right through Sunday afternoon; we mention the few that do. In Scotland, a few pubs close on Sundays (we specify those that we know of); most are open 12.30-2.30 and 6.30-11, and some stay open all day. In Wales, pubs in Dwyfor (from Porthmadog down through the Lleyn Peninsula) are not allowed to sell alcohol to non-residents on Sunday, and generally close then. If we know of a pub closing for any day of the week or part of the year, we say so. The few pubs which we say stay closed on Monday do open on bank holiday Mondays.

Bedroom prices normally include full English breakfasts (if these are available, which they usually are), VAT and any automatic service charge that we know about. If we give just one price, it is the total price for two people sharing a double or twin-bedded room for one night. Otherwise, prices before the / are for single occupancy, prices after it for double. A capital B against the price means that it includes a private bathroom, a capital S a private shower. As all this coding packs in quite a lot of information, some examples may help to explain it:

£30 on its own means that's the total bill for two people sharing a twin or double room without private bath; the pub has no rooms with private bath, and a single person might have to pay that full price

£30B means exactly the same – but all the rooms have private bath

£30(£35B) means rooms with private baths cost £5 extra

£18/£30(£35B) means the same as the last example, but also shows that there are single rooms for £18, none of which have private bathrooms

If there's a choice of rooms at different prices, we normally give the cheapest. If there are seasonal price variations, we give the summer price (the highest). This winter – 1994-95 – many inns, particularly in the country, will have special cheaper rates. And at other times, especially in holiday areas, you will often find prices cheaper if you stay for several nights. On weekends, inns that aren't in obvious weekending areas often have bargain rates for two- or three-night stays.

MEAL TIMES

Bar food is commonly served from 12-2 and 7-9, at least from Monday to Saturday (food service often stops a bit earlier on Sundays). If we don't give a time against the Meals and snacks note at the bottom of a main entry, that means that you should be able to get bar food at those times. However, we do spell out the times if we know that bar food service starts after 12.15 or after 7.15; if it stops before 2 or before 8.45; or if food is served for significantly longer than usual (say, till 2.30 or 9.45).

Though we note days when pubs have told us they don't do food, experience suggests that you should play safe on Sundays and check first with any pub before planning an expedition that depends on getting a meal there. Also, out-of-the-way pubs often cut down on cooking during the week, especially the early part of the week, if they're quiet – as they tend to be, except at holiday times. Please let us know if you find anything different from what we say!

NO SMOKING

We say in the text of each entry what, if any, provision a pub makes for non-smokers. Pubs setting aside at least some sort of no-smoking area are also listed county by county in the Special Interest Lists at the back of the book. The Plough at Clifton Hampden (Oxfordshire) and Free Press in Cambridge are completely no smoking.

CHANGES DURING THE YEAR – PLEASE TELL US

Changes are inevitable, during the course of the year. Landlords change, and so do their policies. And, as we've said, not all returned our fact-checking sheets. We very much hope that you will find everything just as we say. But if you find anything different, please let us know, using the tear-out card in the middle of the book (which doesn't need an envelope), the report forms at the back of the book, or just a letter. You don't need a stamp: the address is *The Good Pub Guide*, FREEPOST TN1569, WADHURST, East Sussex TN5 7BR.

Author's
Acknowledgements

This book would not be possible without the enormous volume of help we get from several thousand readers, who send us reports on pubs they visit: thanks to you all. Many have now been reporting to us for a good few years, often in marvellously helpful detail, and in some cases have now sent us several hundred reports – even, in two or three cases, a thousand or more. We rely heavily on this hugely generous help, all of it unpaid, to keep us up to date with existing entries, to warn us when standards start slipping, to build up a record of reports on the most promising Lucky Dip entries, and to uncover for us new gems that we'd otherwise never hear of.

For the exceptional help they've given us this last year, I'm specially grateful to Ian Phillips, Gwen and Peter Andrews, Gordon, George Atkinson, Richard Houghton, Jenny and Michael Back, C and J Whelan, Charles Bardswell, E G Parish, TBB, Susan and John Douglas, Derek and Sylvia Stephenson, Alan Risdon, Joan Olivier, Lynn Sharpless and Bob Eardley, Peter and Audrey Dowsett, Colin Laffan, Karen and Graham Oddey, Brian Jones, Thomas Nott, John Wooll, Walter Reid, Graham Reeve, Martin Kay, Andrea Fowler, Stephen and Julie Brown, Andrew and Ruth Triggs, Frank Cummins, Nigel Woolliscroft, Wayne Brindle, Basil Minson, Roger Huggins, Ewan McCall, Tom McLean, Dave Irving, John C Baker, Joy Heatherley, Joan and Michel Hooper-Immins, WHBM, HNJ, PEJ, Tony and Louise Clarke, Ann and Colin Hunt, Marjorie and David Lamb, Brian and Anna Marsden, Mr and Mrs A E McCully, Dave Braisted, R J Walden, Andy and Jill Kassube, David Hanley, Colin Roberts, Peter Neate, Ted George, Roger Berry, Jim and Maggie Cowell, Nick and Alison Dowson, Frank W Gadbois, D R Patey, Tim Barrow, Sue Demont, Simon Collett-Jones, Rita Horridge, Jim Farmer, Andy Thwaites, Andrew Stephenson, B M Eldridge, H K Dyson, Jenny and Brian Seller, David Wallington, Andy Hazeldine, Bill Ryan, David Hedges, A and R Cooper, Barry and Anne, Sue Holland, Dave Webster, Paul and Ursula Randall, Pat and John Millward, Mayur Shah, David and Shelia, Michael Butler, J Waller, Mark Walker, John Fazakerley, Mr and Mrs C H Stride, Don Kellaway, Angie Coles, John F Sanders, Neil and Anita Christopher, John and Joan Nash, Tina and David Woods-Taylor, Richard Waller, Tom Evans, P Boot, John Evans, W H and E Thomas, Pat and John Millward and Brian and Jill Bond.

Particular thanks too to the thousands of landlords, landladies and staff of Good Pubs who have made our year so enjoyable.

Alisdair Aird

England

Avon *see* Somerset

Bedfordshire *see* Cambridgeshire

Berkshire

Berkshire pubs are nowadays working harder for their living. This works well for customers. It shows up in three important ways. Drinks prices and food prices have been held down. We've noticed many already good pubs trying to do even better, for example by introducing tempting new food, by hunting down more interesting drinks, or by making distinct internal improvements. And more of the county's pubs than before are moving into the front rank – we have had to expand the Lucky Dip section here quite a bit to make room for them. Perhaps the brightest rising star in the Dip is the Red Lion at Upper Basildon, and we'd also pick out particularly the Stag & Hounds in Binfield, Hinds Head at Bray (promising new regime), Red Lion at Compton, Bunk at Curridge, Pheasant at Great Shefford, Fox at Hermitage, George in Holyport, Green Man at Hurst, Bird in Hand at Knowl Hill, Fox & Hounds at Peasemore, Sweeney & Todd in Reading, Walter Arms at Sindlesham, Duke of Edinburgh at Woodside and Rising Sun at Woolhampton. We have inspected almost all of these, so can vouch for their quality. Three newcomers have made it to the main entries this year: the cosy and unpretentious Uncle Toms Cabin at Cookham Dean Common, the Water Rat at Marsh Benham (inventive food and a lovely garden) and the fine old Bell at Waltham St Lawrence. We should also mention the friendly new licensees making a particularly good impression at the Swan at Great Shefford. Our new Beer Award goes to the marvellously unspoilt Bell at Aldworth (one of Britain's finest country pubs), the Pineapple at Brimpton Common (doing well under a new landlady), the friendly and very well run Blue Boar near Chieveley, the Crown & Horns at East Ilsley (a wonderful collection of whiskies, too), and the splendidly unchanging Pot Kiln at Frilsham. The Ibex at Chaddleworth gains a Wine Award this year for its interesting and well chosen collection of Australian wines by the glass. Our award for Berkshire Dining Pub of the Year goes to the White Hart at Hamstead Marshall – the food here with its Italian overtones has been going from strength to strength in the time we've known the inn, and very few restaurants in the area can now match Mr Aromando's cooking.

ALDWORTH SU5579 Map 2

Bell ★ £ ⚲ ▰

A329 Reading—Wallingford; left on to B4009 at Streatley

People queue outside this warmly welcoming 14th-c country pub before the doors open because it really is an outstanding example of a marvellously traditional, simple local. It has been in the same family for over 200 years and the cosy bar has beams in the shiny ochre ceiling, benches around its panelled walls, a woodburning stove, an ancient one-handed clock, and a glass-panelled hatch rather than a bar counter for service. The incredibly good value food is confined to the rolls (apart from winter home-made soup), filled with good cheddar (80p), ham or pâté (90p), roast turkey (£1), smoked salmon (£1.40), and salt beef or particularly good Devon crab in season (£1.50); very well kept and very cheap Arkells BBB and Kingsdown, Badger Best, Hook Norton Best and Morrells Mild on handpump (they won't stock draught lager); very good house wines. Darts, shove-ha'penny, cribbage, dominoes, chess, and Aunt Sally. The quiet, old-fashioned garden is lovely in summer, and the pub is handy for the Ridgeway, so popular with walkers on Sundays. Occasional Morris dancing; Christmas mummers. *(Recommended by A T Langton, J and P Maloney, Sheilah Openshaw, Ian and Nita Cooper, Michael Marlow, Brenda and Jim Langley, Mrs A Morrison, H Taylor, Maysie Thompson, D T Taylor)*

Free house ~ Licensee H E Macaulay ~ Real ale ~ Snacks (11-2.45, 6-10.45; not Mon) ~ Newbury (01635) 578272 ~ Well behaved children in tap room ~ Open 11-3, 6-11; closed Mon (open bank hols)

BRIMPTON COMMON SU5662 Map 2

Pineapple 🍺

B3051, W of Heath End

Under a friendly new licensee, this 900-year-old thatched pub has low and heavy black medieval beams, individual but comfortable furnishings in the quarry-tiled main bar – mainly hewn from elm – and polished and golden, and a buoyant, chatty atmosphere. On the left, beyond a divider of black standing timbers, a dining area has wheelback chairs around neat tables. Bar food now includes good sandwiches, ploughman's (£3.50), home-made chicken and mushroom or steak in ale pies and vegetable curry (£4.50), daily specials such as tuna bake or home-made quiches (£4.50), and evening dishes like spinach and cheese crêpes (£5.25), halibut and smoked salmon wellington (£6.25) and sizzling dishes such as Cantonese prawns or Texas-style beef (£6.25). The seven well kept real ales include Boddingtons, Brakspears, Flowers Original, Greene King Abbot, Morlands Old Speckled Hen, Wethereds, and Whitbreads Castle Eden; several malt whiskies, and piped music. Behind the main chimney on the right are sensibly placed darts, bar billiards, shove-ha'penny, table skittles, cribbage, dominoes, fruit machine and trivia. A well hedged side lawn has lots of picnic-table sets under cocktail parasols. *(Recommended by Ian and Nita Cooper, Gordon, R M Sparkes)*

Whitbreads ~ Manageress Mrs Angie Brockway ~ Real ale ~ Meals and snacks (midday-9pm) ~ Restaurant ~ Reading (01734) 814376 ~ Children in restaurant ~ Folk night 1st Sun in month, singer/guitarist Tues evening ~ Open 11-11

CHADDLEWORTH SU4177 Map 2

Ibex 🍷

Off A338 Hungerford—Wantage and take second left at top of hill; village is signposted also, off B4494

Very popular with the racing fraternity, this brick and flint pub has a fine rural atmosphere and cheerfully served, very popular daily-changing food: filled crusty bread, home-made soup (£2.25), chicken livers in marjoram and Dijon mustard sauce or egg and stilton bake (£3.50), home-made moussaka or lasagne (£5.50), seasonal game (£5.75), gammon with egg or pineapple (£5.95), lots of fresh fish (when available) like halibut in wine, mustard and horseradish sauce, swordfish in garlic, skate in brown butter sauce, and sea bass (from £6.95), consistently good steaks (from £8.45), and home-made puddings like fresh fruit brûlée or apple crumble (£2.50); roast Sunday lunch (£7.25). Well kept Morlands Original and Old Speckled Hen on handpump, and a guest beer such as Charles Wells Bombardier; lots of New World wines by the glass. There's a big winter log fire in the thoroughly traditional carpeted lounge, and properly old-fashioned bench seating and refectory-style tables. The public bar has low settles, and a games area with dominoes and fruit machine. More tables are set for evening meals in the sun lounge (and a snug little dining room); maybe piped music. Out on a sheltered lawn and on the floodlit terrace are some tables. The landlord is *the* Colin Brown, the former National Hunt jockey who was Desert Orchid's early partner, and this is very much a racing-country village: thatched cottages, narrow lanes, distant dog barks, signs saying 'Caution – Mares and Foals'. *(Recommended by HNJ, PEJ, Peter and Audrey Dowsett)*

Morlands ~ Lease: Colin Brown ~ Real ale ~ Meals and snacks (not Sun evening) ~ Restaurant ~ Chaddleworth (01488) 638311 ~ Children welcome ~ Open 11-3, 6.30-11

CHIEVELEY SU4774 Map 2

Blue Boar 🍺

4 miles from M4 junction 13: A34 N towards Abingdon, first left into Chieveley, left at Winterbourne, Boxford sign, and keep on until T-junction with B4494 – turn right towards Wantage, pub on right; heading S on A34, don't take first sign to Chieveley

Oliver Cromwell stayed here in 1644 on the eve of the Battle of Newbury – and it's still a warmly hospitable and well run inn. The three rambling rooms of the beamed bar are furnished with high-backed settles, Windsor chairs and polished tables, and decked out with a variety of heavy harness (including a massive collar); the left-hand room has a roaring log fire and a seat built into the sunny bow window. A lot of space is given over to eating the popular bar food: soup, sandwiches and ploughman's, as well as a generous helping of tasty deep-fried mushrooms with garlic dip, speciality sausages (£4.95), half char-grilled chicken (£6.50), good pies like beef in Guinness or lamb and mint (£6.95), and puddings; there's an even wider range in the civilised oak-panelled restaurant. Both have excellent, helpful service. Well kept Boddingtons, Fullers London Pride, Wadworths 6X and various guests; several malt whiskies; soft piped music. There are tables among tubs and flowerbeds on the rough front cobbles outside. *(Recommended by Mrs J Prior, Miss D P Barson, Gordon, Simon J Barber, Prof A N Black, TBB, Jeff Davies, F J W Hodgson)*

Free house ~ Licensee Peter Ebsworth ~ Real ale ~ Meals and snacks ~ Restaurant ~ Chieveley (01635) 248236 ~ Children in eating area of bar ~ Open 11-3, 6-11 ~ Bedrooms: £42B/£47B

COOKHAM SU8884 Map 2

Bel & the Dragon

High Street; B4447 N of Maidenhead

The three peaceful rooms in this beautifully preserved, civilised old place have pewter tankards hanging from heavy Tudor beams, deep leather chairs, and old oak settles; one room is no smoking. Service at the low zinc-topped bar counter is decorous and very much of the old school – and prices aren't cheap; well kept Brakspears PA tapped from the cask. A good choice of wines includes decent ports and champagne, and they have all the ingredients needed for proper cocktails, and freshly squeezed orange juice. There are often free home-made crisps, olives or gherkins, and bar food includes soup (£2.50), sandwiches (from £2.75, prawn and avocado £4.50, Scotch smoked salmon £5.75; toasties from £2.75), home-made quiche (£3.50), home-made cannelloni (£5), omelettes (from £5.25), home-made steak and kidney pie (£6.50), and home-made puddings (£2.50); the restaurant is also very popular. In summer and good weather snacks are also served in the garden or on the back terrace. The inn has no car park and street parking can be very difficult. The Stanley Spencer Gallery is almost opposite. *(Recommended by Mr and Mrs G D Amos, Russell and Margaret Bathie, Martin and Karen Wake, Charles Bardswell, Wayne Brindle, Nigel Norman, Doug Kennedy)*

Free house ~ Licensee F E Stuber ~ Real ale ~ Meals and snacks (served throughout opening hours; only sandwiches Sun evenings) ~ Restaurant (closed Sun evenings) ~ Bourne End (01628) 521263 ~ Children welcome ~ Open 11-2.30, 6-10.30(11 Sat)

COOKHAM DEAN SU8785 Map 2

Jolly Farmer

Off A308 N of Maidenhead, or from A4094 in Cookham take B4447 and fork right past
Cookham Rise stn; can be reached from Marlow – fork left after bridge

Just across the quiet lane from the little village green and church, this part brick,
part flint-faced village pub has three small, happily traditional rooms; one is the
attractive dining room at one end, with its starched pink and white tablecloths, and
the middle room is the main bar serving well kept Courage Best, Morlands Old
Speckled Hen and Wadworths 6X on handpump from a tiny counter. Bar food
includes home-made soup (£1.95), filled French bread (£2.95), pan-fried sardines
(£3.50), home-cooked gammon and two eggs (£3.75), home-made steak, kidney
and ale pie or cheesy haddock and egg crumble (£5.95), Dutch calf's liver (£8.95),
8oz fillet steak (£11.95), and puddings (£2.75). Though it's very quiet on weekday
lunchtimes, it does get busy at weekends; dominoes, cribbage, shove-ha'penny, and
piped music. You can eat outside at the red-and-white clothed tables in front of the
pub, there's a terrace, and a big play area on the very long side lawn with swings,
slides and a Wendy house. *(Recommended by George Atkinson; more reports please)*

*Free house ~ Licensees Simon and Tracey Peach ~ Real ale ~ Meals and snacks
(not Sun or bank holiday evenings) ~ Restaurant (not Sun evening) ~ Marlow
(01628) 482905 ~ Children in restaurant and eating area of bar (no babies in
restaurant) ~ Open 11.30-3, 5.30(6 Sat)-11; closed 25 Dec pm*

COOKHAM DEAN COMMON SU8785 Map 2

Uncle Toms Cabin

Hills Lane, Harding Green; village signposted off A308 Maidenhead—Marlow – keep on
down past Post Office and village hall towards Cookham Rise and Cookham

Yet another attractive pub in this favoured area, a pretty cream-washed cottage
with a tiled roof sweeping down in such a long cat's slide at the back that the
ceilings in that part slope. Inside is a friendly series of 1930s-feeling little rooms,
carpeted for the most part, with low beams and joists in the front ones, lots of
shiny dark brown woodwork, old-fashioned plush-cushioned wall seats, stools
and so forth, and a chattily informal, even gossipy atmosphere. Food includes
French bread or granary rolls with a wide choice of good fillings such as brie with
celery (£2.55), rare roast beef (£3.05), hot salt beef (£3.25) or bacon and onion
(£3.35), filled baked potatoes (£3.15-£4.95), ploughman's with a choice of
fillings (£3.95), and hot dishes all home-made from fresh ingredients from soup
such as chicken and leek (£2.50) through pizzas (£4.50), tangy vegetable kebabs
(£4.75), pasta with bacon and mushrooms (£4.95) and steak and mushroom pie
(£5.75) to 8oz rump steak (£8.75), with a special such as seafood kebab (£5.50),
several puddings (£2.50) and children's dishes (from £2.85). Well kept Benskins
Best and a weekly changing guest such as Ringwood Fortyniner or Shepherd
Neame Spitfire on handpump, sensibly placed darts, cribbage. Piped music, if on,
is well chosen and well reproduced (a small collection of framed golden discs runs
from Judy Garland to Culture Club). Oggie is the busy black-and-white dog, and
in winter the coal fire is much loved by Vivien the cat. There are picnic-table sets
and a climbing frame in an attractive and sheltered back garden. *(Recommended by
TBB, D Hayward, A Young, Nigel Norman)*

*Benskins (Allied) ~ Tenants Nick and Karen Ashman ~ Real ale ~ Meals and
snacks (12-2, 7-10; half-hour later Sat/Sun lunchtime, not Sun evening) ~ Marlow
(01628) 483339 ~ Children in eating area of bar ~ Open 11-3, 5.30-11*

CRAZIES HILL SU7980 Map 2

Horns

From A4, take Warren Row Road at Cockpole Green signpost just E of Knowl Hill, then
past Warren Row follow Crazies Hill signposts; from Wargrave, take A321 towards Henley,
then follow Crazies Hill signposts right at Shell garage, then left

There's a good pubby atmosphere in this friendly little tiled whitewashed cottage in the evenings, when no food is served and there are pub games and weekly live music. The bars have exposed beams, open fires and stripped wooden tables and chairs, the barn room has been opened up to the roof like a medieval hall, and there's a huge boar's head on the wall. Home-made bar food includes hot or cold filled rolls (from £1.50), crab salad (£4.65), honey-glazed bacon steaks, an enjoyable late breakfast, and excellent liver and bacon, Cumberland sausage or beef in ale (all £4.95); their half-helpings are a bargain, and on Friday and Saturday they serve brasserie-style food (bookings only); maybe summer Sunday barbecues. Well kept Brakspears PA, Mild, SB, Old and OBJ (new to us) on handpump, and lots of malt whiskies. Darts, shove-ha'penny, dominoes and cribbage; the popular, young St Bernard is called Queenie. There's a three-acre garden. *(Recommended by Gordon, TBB, Roy Smylie, Simon Collett-Jones, Martin Hill, Jane Jackman, Ted Brown)*

Brakspears ~ Tenants David and Patsy Robinson ~ Real ale ~ Lunchtime meals and snacks (not Sun or Mon) ~ Wargrave (01734) 401416 ~ Children in converted barn attached to pub ~ Jazz/blues Mon evenings ~ Open 11-2.30(3 Sat), 5.30-11

EAST ILSLEY SU4981 Map 2

Crown & Horns 🍴 🛏

Just off A34, about 5 miles N of M4 junction 13

The four interesting beamed rooms in this friendly and busy old pub have racing prints and photographs on the walls and a log fire – while the side bar may be busy with locals watching the latest races on TV. The very wide range of regularly changing real ales, all reasonably priced, might typically include Bass, Fullers London Pride, Morlands Original and Old Master, Theakstons Old Peculier and Wadworths 6X, with guests like Brakspears or King & Barnes Festive on handpump. There is also an impressive collection of 170 whiskies from all over the world – Morocco, Korea, Japan, China, Spain and New Zealand. Good, interesting bar food includes sandwiches (from £1.60), home-made soup (£2.45), ploughman's (from £3.25), lasagne or liver and bacon casserole (£4.75), good game and venison pie in season (from £4.75), chicken breast with stilton and mushroom sauce or duck in a port and black cherry sauce (£7.25), steaks (from £7.95), and puddings such as home-made treacle tart (£2.45); quick, cheerful staff – even when busy. Skittle alley, darts, pool, bar billiards, shove-ha'penny, dominoes, cribbage, fruit machine, juke box and piped music. The pretty paved stable yard has tables under two chestnut trees. *(Recommended by Susie Northfield, Marjorie and David Lamb, HNJ, PEJ, Geraint Roberts, K R Waters, Tom McLean, Dayl Gallacher, Stephen Brown, Ian Phillips, Roger Huggins, Tom McLean, Ewan McCall, Dave Irving, Jos Joslin)*

Free house ~ Licensees Chris and Jane Bexx ~ Real ale ~ Meals and snacks (12-2, 6-10) ~ East Ilsley (01635) 281205 ~ Children in eating area, restaurant and TV room ~ Open 11-3, 6-11; closed evening 25 Dec ~ Bedrooms: £30B/£38B

Swan 🛏

Some touches of character in the nooks and corners of the open-plan bar here include a clock made from copper and oak salvaged from HMS *Britannia* (the last wooden three-deck battleship, 1862-1916) and local photographs on the walls of the elegant main area. Down by a gracefully arched 1930s fireplace with some pub cartoons on the walls is where the drinkers sit. Generous helpings of popular food include sandwiches (from £1.50), ploughman's (from £2.95), macaroni cheese (£3.75), chicken curry (£4.65) and steak and kidney pie (£4.95), with specials such as prawns in filo pastry with soy and honey dip (£4.50), pork ribs in port wine sauce (£4.95) and seafood lasagne (£5.25); the dining area is no smoking. Well kept Morlands Original and guests like Bass or Charles Wells Bomardier on handpump. There are picnic-table sets on a prettily trellised back terrace, and on a sheltered lawn with a play area. *(Recommended by Don Kellaway, Angie Coles, J and P Maloney, Nick Wikeley, Michael Sargent, D Boyd)*

Morlands ~ Lease: Michael and Jenny Connolly ~ Real ale ~ Meals and snacks (12-2, 6-10) ~ East Ilsley (01635) 281238 ~ Children in eating area of bar ~ Open 10.30-2.30, 6-11 ~ Bedrooms: £21.50(£32.50B)/£38(£42B)

FRILSHAM SU5473 Map 2

Pot Kiln

From Yattendon take turning S, opposite church, follow first Frilsham signpost, but just after crossing motorway go straight on towards Bucklebury ignoring Frilsham signposted right; pub on right after about half a mile

It's the unspoilt and unchanging atmosphere that readers like so much here. And although basic, it's not unsmart, with wooden floorboards and bare benches and pews. Beer is served from a hatch in the panelled entrance lobby – which has room for just one bar stool; the good log fire keeps the atmosphere warm even when it's not busy. Bar food is fairly simple but good, and includes filled hot rolls (from 95p), home-made soup (£1.85), a decent ploughman's (£2.95), good vegetarian dishes such as lasagne and lentil crumble (from £3.55), hickory-smoked chicken (£4.95), and daily specials; no chips, and vegetables are fresh. Rolls only on Sundays and Tuesdays. Well kept Arkells BBB, Morlands Original and Old Speckled Hen, and Morrells Mild on handpump; informal yet effective service. The public bar has darts, dominoes, shove-ha'penny and cribbage. The back room/dining room is no smoking. There are picnic-table sets in the big suntrap garden with good views of the woods and countryside. It's a good dog-walking area and they are allowed in public bar on a lead. *(Recommended by TBB, Gordon, Roger Byrne, Mick Simmons, R M Sparkes, Mrs P A Carlisle)*

Free house ~ Licensee Philip Gent ~ Real ale ~ Meals and snacks (limited food Sun and Tues) ~ Hermitage (01635) 201366 ~ Well behaved children in dining room ~ Folk singing 3rd Sun of month ~ Open 12-2.30, 6.30-11

GREAT SHEFFORD SU3875 Map 2

Swan

2 miles from M4 junction 14; on A338 towards Wantage

Friendly new licensees have taken over this village pub and are hoping by the time this book is published, to have carefully refurbished the low-ceilinged rooms of the spacious bow-windowed lounge bar – though keeping the horse and jockey pictures on the walls and adding old pictures of the village; the public side has darts, pool, a fruit machine, and CD juke box; unobtrusive piped music. There's now a wide range of good home-made food which can be eaten anywhere in the pub: two soups (£1.95), filled baked potatoes (from £1.95), half an avocado baked with stilton and prawns or home-made crab pâté (£3.50), blazing red fish (£5.50), lots of vegetarian dishes like spicy bean burgers or crumbles (from £5.95), local trout (£6.95), highland chicken (£8.75), steaks (from £9.50), and home-made puddings like very popular banoffi pudding (£2.95); children's menu (£3.95). Well kept Boddingtons, Courage Best, Wadworths 6X and Whitbreads Pompey Royal on handpump, several malt whiskies, and decent coffee. In summer, it's lovely to sit in the relaxing garden with its sycamore and willow overhanging the ducks on the River Lambourn (the restaurant shares the same view). *(Recommended by John and Shirley Dyson, H D Spottiswoode, J S M Sheldon; more reports on the new regime, please)*

Courage ~ Licensee Kevin Maul ~ Real ale ~ Meals and snacks ~ Children welcome ~ Restaurant ~ Great Shefford (01488) 648271 ~ Open 11-3, 6-11

Please keep sending us reports. We rely on readers for news of new discoveries, and particularly for news of changes – however slight – at the fully described pubs. No stamp needed: *The Good Pub Guide*, FREEPOST TN1569, Wadhurst, E Sussex TN5 7BR.

HAMSTEAD MARSHALL SU4165 Map 2

White Hart 🍴 ⌘

Village signposted from A4 W of Newbury

Berkshire Dining Pub of the Year

The Italian licensee does much of the exceptional cooking at this pleasant and civilised Georgian country inn and the bar food includes quite a few distinctive dishes – they concentrate on meals rather than snacks: home-made cream of potato, courgette and lovage soup with home-made Italian bread (£2.75), specials such as stuffed field mushrooms with ham, herbs and garlic (£3.50), goat's cheese grilled with garlic and yoghurt (£4.50), fettuccine with mussels, saffron and cream (£7.50), turkey fillets rolled with herbs and mushroom stuffing and braised in wine, salmon and prawns with parsley sauce, pan-fried liver with onions and wine or fillet of pork with artichokes, mushrooms, white wine and cream (all £8.50), and puddings such as good tiramisu, strawberry pavlova and lemon cheesecake. The L-shaped bar has a good atmosphere, red plush seats built into the bow windows, cushioned chairs around oak and other tables, a copper-topped bar counter, and a log fire open on both sides. Badger Best and Wadworths 6X on handpump, lovely coffee, and politely friendly, quick service. No dogs (their own Welsh setter's called Sam, and the pony's called Solo). The interesting walled garden is lovely in summer, and the quiet and comfortable beamed bedrooms are in a converted barn across the courtyard. *(Recommended by Verity Kemp, Richard Mills, T R and B C Jenkins, Roger Byrne, JCW, Pippa Bobbett, June and Tony Baldwin, Bill and Edee Miller)*

Free house ~ Licensee Mr Nicola Aromando ~ Real ale ~ Meals and snacks (not Sun) ~ Partly no smoking restaurant (not Sun) ~ Kintbury (01488) 58201 ~ Children in eating area of bar ~ Open 12-2.30, 6-11; closed Sun ~ Bedrooms: £40B/£55B

HARE HATCH SU8077 Map 2

Queen Victoria

Blakes Lane, The Holt; just N of A4 Reading—Maidenhead, 3 miles W of exit roundabout from A423(M) – keep your eyes skinned for the turning

The sound of chat and laughter fills the two low-beamed rooms of this friendly local, which is sturdily furnished with strong spindleback chairs, wall benches and window seats, and decorations like a stuffed sparrowhawk, and a delft shelf lined with beaujolais bottles; the tables on the right are no smoking. Popular bar food might include winter soup, sandwiches, sautéed chicken livers with bacon and granary toast (£3.25), boar and apple sausages (£3.55), beef korma (£4.40), hot fresh crab with brandy and parmesan cheese (£4.95), and venison escalope in red wine (£6.95); vegetables are fresh. Well kept Brakspears PA, SB, Mild, Old and OBJ on handpump; shove-ha'penny, cribbage, dominoes, three-dimensional noughts and crosses, fruit machine, and video game. There's a robust table or two in front by the car park. *(Recommended by TBB, Andrew Brookes, D J and P M Taylor, S R Jordan, Dave and Louise Clark, Dr D C Deeing, R J Saunders)*

Brakspears ~ Tenant Ronald Rossington ~ Real ale ~ Meals and snacks (11.30-2.45, 6.30-10.45) ~ Reading (01734) 402477 ~ Children welcome ~ Open 11-3, 5.30-11

HOLYPORT SU8977 Map 2

Belgian Arms

1½ miles from M4 junction 8/9; take A308(M) then at terminal roundabout follow Holyport signpost along A330 towards Bracknell; in village turn left on to big green, then left again at War Memorial shelter

Sitting in the delightful garden, with plenty of tables looking over the flag-irises in the pond towards the village green and a pen with a goat and hens, you'd never believe this homely pub was so close to the M4. Inside, the L-shaped, low-ceilinged bar has framed postcards of Belgian military uniform and other good military prints on the walls, a china cupboard in one corner, a variety of chairs around a few small tables, and a winter log fire. Bar food includes sandwiches (from £1.20; the open prawn one at £3.75 is excellent, and the toasted 'special' is very well liked: ham, cheese, sweetcorn, peppers, onion and mushroom £1.85), pizzas with different toppings (ham, cheese and pineapple is popular, from £3.25), home-cooked ham and eggs (£4.95), a range of daily specials such as lamb casserole in a plate-sized Yorkshire pudding (£4.95), chicken tikka masala (£6.50), Japanese-style breaded deep-fried prawns (£6.75), steaks (from £9.95), and puddings (from £2.50). Well kept Brakspears PA, SB and in winter Old on handpump, and one or two good malts; friendly service. The pleasant conservatory is used as a restaurant in the evening (when the pub can get busy with locals), but at lunchtime you can take bar food there. *(Recommended by TBB, Graham and Karen Oddey, Simon Collett-Jones, DJW, George Atkinson, Martin and Karen Wake, Susan and John Douglas)*

Brakspears ~ Tenant Alfred Morgan ~ Real ale ~ Meals and snacks (not Sun evening) ~ Small conservatory restaurant (not Sun evening) ~ Maidenhead (01628) 34468 ~ Children in restaurant ~ Open 11-3, 5.30 (6 Sat)-11; closed evening 26 Dec

nr HURLEY SU8283 Map 2

Dew Drop

Just W of Hurley on A423 turn left (if coming from Maidenhead) up Honey Lane and keep going till get to T-junction, then turn right – the pub is down a right-hand turn-off at the first cluster of little houses

The same friendly landlord has run this unchanging isolated cottage for over 20 years. The main bar is simply furnished and has a log fire at each end (space is rather tight in the serving area) and at the back is a homely roughcast white room. Bar food includes filled french sticks (£1.75), ploughman's (£3.50), mushrooms on toast (£3.25), summer salads (from £3.50), gammon and eggs or curry (£5.50), and puddings (£1.50); maybe summer barbecues. Well kept Brakspears PA and Old on handpump, and some good malt whiskies; darts. From his conversation and from the pictures on the wall, it's not difficult to discover the landlord's passion – golf. The attractively wild sloping garden is ideal for a summer evening, and looks down to white doves strutting on the pub's red tiles, tubs of bright flowers and a children's play area. Popular with dog owners. *(Recommended by Neil and Jenny Spink, Mark Hydes, Simon Collett-Jones, G L Carlisle, Comus Elliott, M E and Mrs J Wellington, A W Dickinson)*

Brakspears ~ Tenant Michael Morris ~ Real ale ~ Meals and snacks (not Sun evening or Mon) ~ Children in eating area of bar ~ Littlewick Green (01628) 824327 ~ Open 11-2.30 (3 Sat), 6-11

INKPEN SU3564 Map 2

Swan

Lower Inkpen; coming from A338 in Hungerford, take Park Street (first left after railway bridge, coming from A4); Inkpen is then signposted from Hungerford Common

It's best to get here early to find a seat in this beamed country inn if you want to enjoy the popular Singaporean food: pork spare ribs (£2.75), good Singapore fried noodles or nasi goreng (£3.75), and curries with coconut milk, lime leaves, lemon grass and coriander (from £4.50). Also, spicy fish soup (£3.75), vegetarian dishes (£4.95), chicken with cashew nuts (£5.95), sweet and sour prawns (£6.75), and marinated and stir-fried prime Scotch beef (£8.95). Western-style dishes are also available. The Singapore connection shows in other ways, too: a wicked gin sling, for instance, and deeply chilled lagers from Singapore, Thailand and China (as well as well kept Brakspears PA, Marstons Pedigree, Ringwood Fortyniner and a guest beer on handpump). The rambling rooms are decorated in soft colours, with muted chintz, cosy corners, beams, fresh flowers, waxed furniture, etched brass table lamps and a woodburning stove and log fire (there's a big old fireplace with an oak mantelbeam between the bar counter and the restaurant area). Fruit machine, quiet piped music, and magazines in one snug alcove up a couple of steps. There are flowers out in front by the picnic-table sets, which are raised above the quiet village road. *(Recommended by Susan and John Douglas, Susie Northfield, Roger Byrne, Mr and Mrs T F Marshall, George Atkinson, Clifford Payton, Lynn Sharpless, Bob Eardley, A W Dickinson, Bill and Edee Miller, Gladys Teall)*

Free house ~ Licensee John Scothorne ~ Real ale ~ Meals and snacks ~ Restaurant (evenings and Sun lunchtime) ~ Inkpen (01488) 668326 ~ Children in restaurant and bottom end of bar lunchtime and early evening ~ Open 12-2.30, 6.30-11

MARSH BENHAM SU4267 Map 2

Water Rat
Village signposted from A4 W of Newbury

To eat outside this old thatched pub with its huge hanging baskets, you order food through the window and can then sit on the terrace or on the long lawns that slope down to water meadows and the River Kennet; there's a butterfly reserve, goldfish, and a play area with a climbing frame, sandpit and wooden playhouse for children. The comfortable, unpretentious bar has deeply carved Victorian gothick settles (and some older ones), and is attractively decorated with cheerful murals of *The Wind in the Willows* characters. Bar food is all home-made and includes soup (£2.50), filled French bread with chips (£2.95), lasagne (£5.95), vegetarian dishes (£6.95), Cantonese sizzling chicken (£7.95), sweet and sour char-grilled pork (£8.25), baked fillet of salmon in filo pastry with white wine cream and tarragon sauce (£8.95), guinea fowl salad, char-grilled rump steak (£9.75), and puddings like sticky toffee pudding or brandy-snap baskets with strawberries and raspberry coulis (£2.95). Well kept Marsh Rat Best and Toad's Tipple as well as Brakspears SB and Hook Norton Old Hookey on handpump: the funky house beer names give the clue that the pub is owned by David Bruce, who made his name in the 1980s with the London-based chain of Firkin own-brew pubs. *(Recommended by Jill Knox, T R and B C Jenkins, Brenda and Jim Langley, HNJ, PEJ, Neil Franklin)*

Free house ~ Licensee Ian Dodd ~ Real ale ~ Meals and snacks ~ Restaurant ~ Newbury (01635) 582017 ~ Well behaved children welcome ~ Open 11.30-3, 6-11

SONNING SU7575 Map 2

Bull
Village signposted on A4 E of Reading; off B478, in village

The two old-fashioned rooms in this charming and unpretentious pub have low ceilings and heavy beams, cosy alcoves, cushioned antique settles and low wooden chairs, newspapers on racks, inglenook fireplaces, and a penny-farthing. Well kept Boddingtons, Brakspears SB, Flowers Original, and Wethereds SPA on handpump, and food that consists of a lunchtime cold buffet (from £4.20); chatty staff; soft piped music. The courtyard is particularly attractive in summer with tubs of flowers and a rose pergola resting under its wisteria-covered, black and white timbered walls – though at busy times it may be packed with cars. If you bear left through the ivy-clad churchyard opposite, then turn left along the bank of the river Thames, you come to a very pretty lock. *(Recommended by Mr and Mrs G D Amos, TBB, Roy Smylie, P J Caunt, George Murdoch, Anthony Bradbury)*

Whitbreads ~ Tenant Dennis Catton ~ Real ale ~ Lunchtime meals and snacks ~ Evening restaurant ~ Reading (01734) 693901 ~ Children in restaurant ~ Open 10-2.30, 5.30-11; 11-11 summer Sats ~ Bedrooms: £30/£50

Pubs staying open all afternoon are listed at the back of the book.

STANFORD DINGLEY SU5771 Map 2

Bull

From M4 junction 12, W on A4, then right at roundabout on to A340 towards Pangbourne; first left to Bradfield, where left, then Stanford Dingley signposted on right

Even when busy, this attractive 15th-c pub remains very friendly. The home-made bar food – with prices unchanged since last year – is very good and often includes some unusual dishes such as highly recommended carrot and orange or stilton soups (from £2.20), drunken fish pie (£4.55), savoury pancake topped with peanuts, spinach and cheese (£4.60), and chocolate roulade with brandied cream (£2.10), as well as filled baked potatoes (from £1.85), ploughman's (from £2.75), chicken provençale (£6.45), steaks (from (£6.95), and puddings such as fruit crumble (£1.90) or toffee pudding with butterscotch sauce (£2.10). Under the dark beams in the middle of the tiny bar are two standing timbers hung with horse-brasses, firmly dividing the room into two parts. The first is comfortably arranged with red-cushioned seats carved out of barrels, a window settle, wheelback chairs on the red quarry tiles, and an old brick fireplace. The other is similarly furnished but carpeted, and decorations include an old station clock, some corn dollies and a few old prints. The main area has refectory-type tables and a very long oak pew and chairs on the rich persian rug on top of the polished wooden floor, half-panelled walls and a brick fireplace. There's also a bright, extended saloon bar. Well kept Archers, Bass, and Brakspears on handpump, and interesting non alcoholic drinks such as elderflower pressé; very pleasant, quick service. Ring-the-bull, occasional classical or easy listening music. In front of the building are some big rustic tables and benches, and to the side is a small garden with a few more seats. *(Recommended by Phil H Smith, Margaret Dyke, Gordon, Caroline Wright, Romey Heaton, Maureen Hobbs, Stephen, Julie and Hayley Brown)*

Free house ~ Licensees Patrick and Trudi Langdon ~ Real ale ~ Meals and snacks (till 10pm; not Mon lunchtime) ~ (01734) 744409 ~ Children in saloon bar; not after 8.30 pm; not Sat evening ~ Open 12-3, 7-11; closed Mon lunchtime – except bank hols

WALTHAM ST LAWRENCE SU8276 Map 2

Bell

In summer, the hanging baskets in front of this timbered black and white old pub are very pretty, and the well kept back lawn (sheltered by a thatched barn and shaded by small trees and flowering shrubs) is very popular with walkers. The lounge bar has finely carved oak panelling, a good antique oak settle among more modern furniture, a log fire, and a happy, chatty atmosphere. The public bar has heavy beams, an attractive seat in the deep window recess, and well kept Badgers Best, Brakspears PA, Wadworths 6X and a guest beer every two weeks on handpump; several malt whiskies. Bar food includes soup (£1.75), ploughman's (from £3.35), filled baked potatoes (from £3.65), home-made pies like steak and kidney or chicken and asparagus (£4.95), sizzling cajun-style chicken (£5.95), gammon with two eggs (£6.95), and evening extras like vegetarian dishes (£6.75) or salmon steak (£8.50). The 'no children' policy is strictly enforced here. *(Recommended by Amanda Hodges, TBB, Dawn and Phil Garside, David Warrellow, Paul and Janet Giles)*

Free house ~ Licensee S W Myers ~ Real ale ~ Meals and snacks (till 10pm; not Sun evening) ~ Restaurant ~ (01734) 341788 ~ Open 11.30-2.30(3 Sat), 6-11

WEST ILSLEY SU4782 Map 2

Harrow ★

Signposted at East Ilsley slip road off A34 Newbury—Abingdon

In summer, the big garden of this popular white tiled village inn really comes into its own, with picnic-table sets and other tables under cocktail parasols looking out over the duck pond and cricket green, a notable children's play area, and a collection of ducks, fowls, canaries, rabbits, goats, a donkey, and maybe even a horse; watch out for the stubborn goose that sits in the road and refuses to budge for passing traffic. Lots of walks nearby – the Ridgeway is just a mile away. The open-plan bar has a friendly, welcoming atmosphere, dark terracotta walls hung with many mainly Victorian prints and other ornaments, big turkey rugs on the floor, and a mix of antique oak tables, unpretentious old chairs, a couple of more stately long settles, and an unusual stripped twin-seated high-backed settle between the log fire and the bow window. Morlands, who started brewing in this village before they moved to Abingdon, supply the Original, Old Masters and Speckled Hen, kept well on handpump, and there's a guest beer as well; coffee and teas (decaffeinated as well). Very good bar food includes granary rolls filled with hot sausage with home-made chutney or stilton, celery and apple (from £1.90), fine home-made soups (£2.50), ginger stir-fried prawns with monkfish (£3.25), generous ploughman's (from £4.50), tasty tagliatelle with mushrooms, spiced lentil patties with tomato sauce (£4.65), very good pies such as local wild rabbit, lemon, bacon and herbs or tender venison with stout and juniper (from £4.85), home-baked gammon with plum sauce (£5.95), lamb's liver and bacon (£6.95), daily specials, and puddings like spiced oranges with brandy and treacle tart (£2.75); children's helpings. Theoretically, the dining area is no smoking at lunchtime, but disappointingly readers have found that in practice this may not be the case. Darts, cribbage, fruit machine, piped music and quiz teams. *(Recommended by Christopher and Sharon Hayle, Bob Riley, HNJ, PEJ, I E and C A Prosser, John and Christine Simpson, George Atkinson, Geraint Roberts, A T Langton, R C Morgan, Martin and Karen Wake, Don Kellaway, Angie Coles, DAV, Pippa Bobbett, Marjorie and David Lamb, Mrs A Storm, T R and B C Jenkins, Dr Andrew Brookes, TBB, Werner Arend, Dorothee and Dennis Glover, Roger Huggins, Tom McLean, Ewan McCall, Dave Irving)*

Morlands ~ Tenant Mrs Heather Humphreys ~ Real ale ~ Meals and snacks (12-2.15, 6-9.15; not Sun evening Jan-Easter) ~ East Ilsley (01635) 281260 ~ Children welcome ~ Open 11-3, 6-11; closed 25 Dec pm

WOOLHAMPTON SU5767 Map 2

Rowbarge

Turn S off A4 opposite the Angel (may be signposted Station)

Interesting bric-a-brac such as cricketing mementoes, model ships, 80 brass blow lamps, weighing scales, and so forth fill the beamed bar, adjoining panelled room and small no smoking snug in this friendly pub; there's also a conservatory at the back of the building. Cribbage, dominoes and piped music. Good waitress-served bar food changes daily and might include sandwiches, home-made pies and curries, salmon tagliatelle and vegetarian dishes, and cranberry and brie chicken or game pudding (all around £6.20); a good choice of puddings and four or five fresh vegetables and two kinds of potato or rice. Well kept Courage Best, Fullers London Pride, Morland Speckled Hen, Ruddles Best and County and Wadworths 6X on handpump, and several malt whiskies. The garden has a fish pond and lawns running down to the Kennet & Avon canal. *(Recommended by J S M Sheldon, Andrew Scarr, Rob and Helen Townsend, David Holloway, D G Clarke, Dave and Carole Jones, A W Dickinson, Dick Brown, Lyn and Bill Capper)*

Free house ~ Licensees Roger and Lyn Jarvis ~ Meals and snacks (till 10pm) ~ (01734) 712213 ~ Children in separate room (not Sat evening) ~ Open 11-2.30 (3 Sat), 5.30-11

YATTENDON SU5574 Map 2

Royal Oak ★ ⑪ 🛏 ♀

The Square; B4009 NE from Newbury; turn right at Hampstead Norreys, village signposted on left

Under a new manager this year – and with a new chef – this stylish, handsome inn remains mainly popular for its fine restaurant quality food: home-made soup

(£2.50), chicken liver pâté (£4.50), poached mussels with creamy garlic and chive sauce (£5), grilled sausages, Yorkshire pudding and onion gravy (£7.50), spiced vegetable and mushroom ravioli with yoghurt (£8.25), grilled cod in an orange and mushroom sauce (£8.75), confit of duck leg with Chinese honey and lemon oil salad (£9.75), and puddings such as lemon meringue pie or white chocolate beignets with apricot sauce (from £3.95); vegetables (£1.50). You must book a table for bar lunches. The comfortable lounge and prettily decorated panelled bar – it's through at the back – have a relaxed atmosphere, a marvellous winter log fire, and a mechanical wall clock behind the bar counter. Well kept Adnams, Badger Tanglefoot, and Wadworths 6X and Farmers Glory on handpump, and a carefully chosen wine list. The pretty garden is primarily for the use of residents and restaurant guests, but is available on busy days for those in the bar. The attractive village is one of the few still owned privately, and the pub itself used to be the site of the Yattendon Revels. *(Recommended by Paul A Kitchener, Ralf Zeyssig, Gordon, Stephen, Julie and Hayley Brown, A W Dickinson, Mark Shutler)*

Free house ~ Manager Jeremy Gibbs ~ Real ale ~ Meals and snacks (till 10pm) ~ No smoking restaurant (closed Sun evenings) ~ Hermitage (01635) 201325 ~ Children welcome ~ Open 12-3, 6.30-11 ~ Bedrooms: £60(£70B)/£70(£80B)

Lucky Dip

Besides the fully inspected pubs, you might like to try these Lucky Dips recommended to us and described by readers (if you do, please send us reports):

☆ **Aldermaston** [SU5965], *White Hart:* Recently refurbished and doing well, with good food, under new licensee who previously had enviable track record at the Walter Arms at Sindlesham; a good place to stay *(Sheilah Openshaw)*

Aldworth [Haw Lane; B4009 towards Hampstead Norreys; SU5579], *Four Points:* Thatched family pub popular at lunchtime for big helpings of straightforward food, friendly service, Morlands beer, big log fire, lots of tables, well kept garden with play area over road *(Paul S McPherson, Gordon, Margaret and Trevor Errington, LYM)*

☆ **Aston** [Ferry Lane; signed off A423 Henley—Maidenhead; SU7884], *Flower Pot:* Big unspoilt walkers' pub with great garden – views over meadows to cottages and far side of Thames; well kept Brakspears, reasonably priced food (no children's helpings), friendly young staff, bare-boards public bar, darts, unobtrusive piped music; popular Sun lunchtimes, handy for riverside strolls *(Doug Kennedy, David Warrellow, Mr and Mrs G D Amos)*

☆ **Bagnor** [SU4569], *Blackbird:* Popular Ushers pub with efficient, friendly service, Fullers London Pride, Marstons Pedigree, Ushers and Websters Yorkshire on handpump, wide range of decent well cooked straightforward food, attractively presented, and pleasing tables and chairs; quiet piped music; lovely quiet garden backing on to River Lambourn, nr Watermill Theatre *(Rona Murdoch, HNJ, PEJ, TBB)*

Beedon [Worlds End; 3 miles N of M4 junction 13, via A34; SU4878], *Coach & Horses:* Good honest straightforward food (maybe not Mon evening in winter), well presented, at attractive prices inc bargain specials and evening meals, in clean and tasteful homely lounge bar; subdued piped music; darts, fruit machine etc in spick and span public bar; largish back garden with play area, small terrace *(HNJ, PEJ)*

☆ **Binfield** [B3034 Windsor rd; SU8471], *Stag & Hounds:* Pleasant and comfortable 14th-c pub with low-beamed bars, open fires, antiques, brass, good value food in quite separate room from sandwiches up (menu spread over three blackboards), consistently affable landlord, free newspapers *(A M Pring, Gordon, Peter and Lynn Brueton, Julie and Mike Taylor)*

Binfield [Terrace Rd N], *Victoria Arms:* Neat and pleasant Fullers pub, one of their best, with good choice of seating areas, well kept real ales, reasonably priced bar food; children's room, summer barbecues in quiet garden *(Martin Kay, Andrea Fowler, LYM);* *Bottle & Glass:* Attractive inside and out; worth knowing *(Roy Smylie);* [Terrace Rd N], *Jack o' Newbury:* Roomy and comfortable, with warm welcoming atmosphere, good choice of interesting real ales such as Old Luxters Barn, Wychwood Dr Thirstys and their own Binfield, popular food; two friendly black standard poodles can spot crisps being opened from a long way off; skittles alley in former stables *(Mike Davies)*

☆ **Bracknell** [High St/Ring Rd; SU8769], *Old Manor:* Recently refurbished with care by Wetherspoons, keeping its character and going back to the original old oak beams; large open-plan bars with no smoking areas, several sensibly priced real ales inc Youngers Scotch, decent food; good for the area *(Peter and Lynn Brueton, T G Thomas)*

☆ **Bray** [2 miles from M4 junction 9; SU9079], *Hinds Head:* 16th-c inn with splendid pedigree, atmosphere building up again in its splendid old rooms under new regime, increasingly popular for reasonably priced bar food; Adnams, Brakspears and other real ales, upstairs restaurant; very promising *(TBB, Ian Phillips, LYM)*

☆ Bray, *Crown:* Recently redecorated 14th-c pub with low beams, timbers and panelling, leather seats, well kept Wadworths 6X, bar food, restaurant, piped music; well behaved children allowed, plenty of seating outside inc flagstoned vine arbour *(A Plumb, George Atkinson, TBB, LYM; more reports on new regime please)*

Bray [Old Mill Lane], *Albion:* Consistently clean, comfortable and friendly, with good food in bars and conservatory restaurant *(TBB)*

☆ Bucklebury [Chapel Row; SU5570], *Blade Bone:* Comfortable pub, good bar food inc interesting specials such as excellent sweetbreads or venison, service pleasant without being obsequious; piped music in public bar *(W L G Watkins)*

Burghfield [SU6668], *Hatch Gate:* Small and friendly, recently changed hands; Morlands on handpump; standard menu and imaginative daily specials prepared by the landlord *(D and J Johnson)*

☆ Compton [E end, just off Streatley rd; SU5279], *Red Lion:* Good range of most attractively priced home-cooked food a big draw in small country local with cosy but lively rural atmosphere, friendly efficient service, well kept Morlands; sizeable quiet garden with children's play area; children in eating area on right *(Colin Stamp, Paul S McPherson, BB)*

Compton, *Swan:* Well modernised, with good food in comfortable lounge bar or restaurant; bedrooms *(Stan Edwards, A T Langton)*

Cookham Dean [OS Sheet 175 map reference 872853; SU8785], *Inn on the Green:* Former Hare & Hounds, unspoilt rambling layout inc stripped beams and two-sided log fires, Swiss specialities inc fondues and Oberlander Kaiserschnitte (bread fried in wine and topped with crispy bacon); four real ales *(Prof Ron Leigh)*

Cookham Rise [The Pound; B4447 Cookham—Maidenhead; SU8984], *Swan Uppers:* Flagstones, low beams and friendly newish management in quaint and pleasant pub; good range of real ales, bar food, piped music *(Nigel Norman, Thomas Neate, TBB, Julian and Sarah Stanton, LYM)*

☆ Curridge [3 miles from M4 junction 13: A34 towards Newbury, then first left to Curridge, Hermitage, and left into Curridge at Village Only sign – OS Sheet 174 map ref 492723; SU4871], *Bunk:* Stylish dining pub with adventurous fairly priced food (not Sun evening) inc unusual things like grilled goat's cheese – not cheap, but good value if you like upmarket food; smart stripped-wood tiled-floor bar on left, elegant stable-theme bistro on right with wooded-meadow views and conservatory;

four well kept real ales, good atmosphere, cheerful efficient service, tables in neat garden *(A T Langton, R C Watkins, Mrs C Layton, Lyn and Bill Capper)*

Datchet [The Green; not far from M4 junction 5; SU9876], *Royal Stag:* Friendly place with large helpings of good value food and well kept Benskins, Friary Meux, Shipstones and guests *(Mr and Mrs G D Amos)*

Easthampstead [Crowthorne Rd; SU8667], *Green Man:* Friendly pub, well kept Courage Best and Directors on handpump, reasonably priced standard bar food *(Peter and Lynn Brueton)*

Eton [Main St; SU9678], *Hogs Head:* Friendly and efficent service, good range of food and real ales, rustic interior *(K Harvey)*; [Bridge St], *Watermans Arms:* Well used pub nr Thames with popular food inc vegetarian, conservatory full of H M Bateman cartoons, seats in sheltered yard; well kept Courage Best and Directors; parking can be very difficult *(TBB, A W Dickinson, LYM)*

Eton Wick [32 Eton Wick Rd; SU9478], *Pickwick:* Congenial straightforward pub with pleasant landlord and Malaysian wife who cooks wonderful Malay and English food Weds and Sat evenings, slightly shorter menu lunchtime; Youngs *(Bill and Jane Rees)*

Grazeley [3 miles SW of junction 11 of M4; SU6966], *Olde Bell:* Popular, with beams, brasses, wide choice of food inc daily specials, Whitbreads-related ales, large garden with parasols; friendly service; bedrooms *(Ralf Zeyssig)*

☆ Great Shefford [Shefford Woodland; less than ½ mile N of M4 junction 14 – B4000, just off A338; SU3875], *Pheasant:* Pleasant and civilised motorway break, relaxed atmosphere in four neat rooms, open fires, very wide choice of good food inc home-made dishes and Sun lunches, well kept Wadworths IPA and 6X, decent wines and coffee; public bar with games inc ring the bull; children welcome, attractive views from garden; under same ownership as Royal Oak at Wootton Rivers *(Dave Irving, Dr C E Morgan, Jeff Davies, S J Edwards, LYM)*

☆ Hermitage [Hampstead Norreys Rd; 2½ miles from M4 junction 13, B4009; SU5073], *Fox:* Useful motorway break with attractive garden and terrace for summer, cosy log fire winter, good well presented bar food served reasonably quickly inc children's menu, well kept real ales, quietly friendly landlord *(Mrs A Storm, Tom Evans, LYM)*

Hermitage, *White Horse:* Popular public bar with darts, quiet lounge nicely decorated with foreign banknotes, friendly staff and big alsatian, nice food *(Geraint Roberts)*

☆ Holyport [The Green; 1½ miles from M4 junction 8/9 via A308(M)/A330; SU8977], *George:* Useful for big helpings of reliable straightforward home-cooked food at sensible prices, in busy but neat open-plan bar with low ceiling, bay window-seats and nice old fireplace; friendly and efficient service, Courage real ales, picnic-table sets outside, lovely village green *(R B Crail, Peter Locke, Peter Fraser, TBB)*

☆ **Hungerford** [Charnham St; 3 miles from M4 junction 14; town signposted at junction; SU3368], *Bear:* Civilised old-fashioned hotel bar with wonderful Act of Parliament clock, open fires, well kept real ales such as Wadworths 6X, pleasant service; decent food in bar (maybe via open-air passageway from kitchen) and comfortably unhurried restaurant; bedrooms comfortable and attractive *(Gordon, DGC, LYM)*

Hungerford [Bridge St (A338)], *John o' Gaunt:* Well kept Morlands beers on handpump, friendly atmosphere, good range of bar food; bedrooms *(Ann and Colin Hart, LYM)*; [Church St], *Just William:* Formerly the Angel, now more bistro cum restaurant than pub but the ale is still real; light, airy atmosphere, attractive food *(Dr and Mrs A K Clarke)*

☆ **Hungerford Newtown** [A338 a mile S of M4 junction 14; SU3571], *Tally Ho:* Good well presented home-made food (fish, mushroom and camembert platter, ham and egg, fish pie all tipped, beautiful chips), well kept Wadworths, friendly staff, plenty of room; children if eating *(Rona Murdoch, K H Frostick, A G Roby, Dorothy Morley)*

Hurley [SU8283], *Olde Bell:* Civilised and old-fashioned bar and lounge in handsome and very extensive timbered inn, well worth a look for its character (inc Norman doorway and window) and fine gardens; restaurant; bedrooms *(Ian Phillips, LYM)*

☆ **Hurst** [Hinton Rd/Church Hill; SU7972], *Green Man:* Old-fashioned traditional low-ceilinged country local with congenial atmosphere, mixed clientele, basic though comfortable furnishings with wooden seats and tables, friendly landlord and staff, bar food (not Mon evening) inc good home-made soup, pies and puddings, well kept Brakspears, piped music, pub games; pleasant back garden; has lost its main-entry place only because of a lack of very recent reports *(Rob and Helen Townsend, H Tidbury, TBB, Dave and Louise Clark, Mike Davies, Dr Andrew Brookes, LYM)*

Hurst [opp church], *Castle:* Sold to Morlands by Courage and refurbished, with more emphasis on rather more upmarket food and less on local atmosphere, but still has character in its three cottagey rooms with open fire; picnic-table sets out overlooking own bowling green *(D J and P M Taylor)*

☆ **Kintbury** [SU3866], *Dundas Arms:* Clean and tidy with rather hotelish atmosphere and clientele, lots of antique blue and white plates in bar with food (not Mon evening or Sun) from sandwiches to quite sophisticated dishes, well kept real ales from smaller breweries, decent wines – remarkable range of clarets in evening restaurant; pleasant walks by Kennet & Avon Canal; children welcome; comfortable bedrooms opening on to secluded waterside terrace *(L Walker, G Berneck, C Herxheimer, Neil Franklin, LYM)*

Kintbury [Inkpen Rd, S of A4; formerly the Crossways Inn], *Bistro Roque:* Food-orientated, meals served in all three rooms with dishes listed on big blackboards, all well-cooked and presented and promptly served *(Roger Byrne)*

☆ **Knowl Hill** [A4 Reading—Maidenhead; SU8279], *Bird in Hand:* Notable lunchtime cold buffet and other good home-made food in spacious and attractive beamed main bar with relaxed civilised atmosphere, splendid log fire, cosy alcoves, much older side bar and comfortable back cocktail bar; well kept Brakspears and Fullers London Pride, wide choice of wines and other drinks, consistently good service, good side garden; no smoking buffet area – where children allowed *(Mrs M Bush, Clifford Payton, E N and I J Wilkinson, Simon Collett-Jones, LYM)*

☆ **Knowl Hill** [A4], *Seven Stars:* Civilised and relaxed, though not as smart as our other starred entry here; good old-fashioned friendly atmosphere, good range of simple bar food from sandwiches through vegetarian and other dishes to steaks, well kept Brakspears (full range), good choice of wines, a lot of panelling and attractive log fire; helpful professional service, fruit machine – no music; big garden with summer barbecue, though provision for children could perhaps be improved; a couple of friendly dogs and a cat *(TBB, Simon Collett-Jones, Nick and Alison Dowson, David and Gill Carrington, BB)*

Knowl Hill [A4], *Old Devil:* Dining pub now owned by Badger, wide choice of food inc quite imaginative dishes, friendly staff, good view from pleasant verandah high above attractive lawn with tables and colourful awnings, swings and slide for children; piped music *(TBB)*; [signed off A4], *Royal Oak:* Pleasant and relaxed open-plan pub, some emphasis on food but still good for a drink; well kept beer *(Richard Houghton)*

☆ **Littlewick Green** [3¾ miles from M4 junction 9; A423(M) then left on to A4, from which village signposted on left; SU8379], *Cricketers:* Clean, attractive and neatly kept village pub opp cricket green, happy atmosphere though can be very quiet midweek lunchtime; food quality and range has been improving, service good, lots of cricketing pictures; Brakspears and Flowers *(Clem Stephens, Mr and Mrs C Holmes, Dr C A Brace, Angela and Alan Dale, G B Longden, LYM)*

Maidenhead [Braywick Rd; SU8783], *Pig in Hiding:* Under friendly newish management, with Whitbreads-related and other ales, good food, pig ornaments everywhere, fruit and quiz machines *(Andrew Burke)*; [Lee Lane, Pinkneys Green, just off A308 N; SU8582], *Stag & Hounds:* Refurbished and shows it, but worth knowing for tasty bar snacks, well kept Courage Best and a genuine guest beer, pleasant garden (good for children) and no piped music! *(TBB)*; [Pinkneys Green, just off A308 N], *Wagon & Horses:* Pleasant and very popular, with good value food, friendly atmosphere, Morlands Bitter and pleasant garden; unusual in that it's like two pubs with very pubby working men's drinking bar and lounge bar with separate entrance *(TBB)*

Moneyrow Green [between Holyport and B3024 – OS Sheet 175 map reference 892774; SU8977], *White Hart:* Unpretentiously pubby old-fashioned local with beautiful panelling, log fire, traditional ales, good plain bar snacks, very down-to-earth prices, and a truly genuine welcome from cheerful staff and permanent core of games players in public bar; piped music but mercifully fairly quiet *(Peter W Jackling, TBB)*

Newbury [Bartholomew St; SU4666], *Dolphin:* Nicely upgraded smart town pub with emphasis on food; modest range of Courage beers *(Dr and Mrs A K Clarke)*; *Lock Stock & Barrel:* Well placed Fullers pub by canal towpath; coffee shop open all afternoon, large curved bar, wooden flooring and usual range of Fullers ales *(George Atkinson)*

☆ **Old Windsor** [17 Crimp Hill, off B3021 – itself off A308/A328; SU9874], *Union:* Tidy L-shaped bar with nostalgic show-business photographs, lots of banknotes on beams, woodburner in big fireplace, fruit machine; Courage, Flowers and Theakstons, good service, but maybe loud piped pop music; attractive copper-decorated restaurant, white plastic tables under cocktail parasols on sunny front terrace; comfortable bedrooms *(Ian Phillips, Mrs R Simons, George Atkinson, BB)*

Old Windsor [Crimp Hill], *Oxford Blue:* Good back children's play area, incredible collection of model airliners and related memorabilia, conservatory dining area with good value food, well kept Brakspears, Ind Coope Burton and Tetleys *(Brian and Anna Marsden)*

Padworth [Padworth Common; SU6166], *Round Oak:* Has emerged from various personnel changes with return of chef who has made this unpretentious place worth knowing for good value bar food in the past *(Dr and Mrs R E S Tanner)*

☆ **Paley Street** [3 miles SW of Bray; SU8675], *Bridge:* Small pleasant beamed pub with young cheerful staff, good generous home-made food reasonably priced, several real ales; get there early on Sun or book; large garden *(Jeff and Rhoda Collins, G Medcalf, R J Purser)*

Paley Street [B3024], *Royal Oak:* Very good Fullers pub *(Martin Kay, Andrea Fowler)*

Pangbourne [SU6376], *George:* More old inn and restaurant than pub, but well worth knowing for very good value carvery; nice staff *(Elizabeth and Klaus Leist)*; [Shooters Hill], *Swan:* Attractive riverside pub dating from 1642, good range of bar food all day 7 days a week, good wine list, tea and coffee, Morlands ales on handpump, unobtrusive piped music; picnic-table sets and moorings; balcony and conservatory reserved for diners *(Jim Penman)*

☆ **Peasemore** [signed from B4494 Wantage—Newbury; SU4577], *Fox & Hounds:* Excellent civilised country local tucked away in racehorse country, good imaginative food, well kept real ales, particularly good house wines, quietly friendly service, some interesting pictures; well worth a main entry – only an unaccountable dearth of recent reader reports keeps it out this year *(LYM)*

☆ **Reading** [10 Castle St; next to PO; SU7272], *Sweeney & Todd:* Good value food, esp superb range of adventurous generously served home-made pies such as hare and cherry, partridge and pear; upstairs has good choice of well kept ales eg Boddingtons, Fullers London Pride, Eldridge Pope Royal Oak and Marstons Pedigree; downstairs labyrinth of small and cosy if not smart rooms and cubby holes; very busy lunchtime *(Susan and John Douglas, Chris Warne, A Cunningham, Rob and Helen Townsend)*

☆ **Reading** [Kennet Side], *Fishermans Cottage:* Good spot by lock on Kennet & Avon Canal, lovely big back garden, relaxed atmosphere, modern furnishings of character, pleasant stone snug behind woodburning range, light and airy conservatory; traditional pub lunches (very popular then), evening food inc Mexican, well kept Fullers Chiswick, ESB and London Pride, small choice of wines, quick pleasant service, small darts room; popular with students *(Martin Kay, Andrea Fowler, Paul and Janet Giles)*

☆ **Reading** [Chatham St], *Butler:* Good Fullers pub with horseshoe bar, efficient service, usual bar food lunchtime and early evening, particularly well kept beer *(Rob and Helen Townsend, Martin Kay, Andrea Fowler)*

Reading [35 Blagrave St], *Blagrave Arms:* Interesting town-centre pub with reasonably priced Courage, good popular bar lunches *(Anna Marsh)*; [Southampton St], *Cambridge Arms:* Good cheap food, well kept beer, friendly bar staff; enormous pots of tea *(Anna Marsh)*; [Kates Grove Lane – off A4 Pell St/Berkley Ave, next to flyover inner ring rd], *Hook & Tackle:* Real ale pub with outstanding twice-yearly beer festivals – maybe 150 beers in a fortnight; pastiche traditional decor, good service, usual food, lively young atmosphere, maybe smoky *(Mark and Diane Grist)*; [St Marys Butts],

Horn: Friendly busy character pub, friendly landlord; well kept Courage *(Gordon)*; [London Rd (low number)], *Turks Head:* Busy young person's pub, plain decor – bare boards etc; well kept real ales, electronic games *(Dr and Mrs A K Clarke)*

☆ **Remenham** [A423, just over bridge E of Henley; SU7683], *Little Angel:* Old low-beamed and panelled food pub darkly done up in red and black, not cheap but good cooking and presentation, service very friendly and helpful; splendid range of wines by the glass, well kept Brakspears, piped music (can be loud), back fish restaurant, floodlit terrace *(J A Collins, Brian and Anna Marsden, Frank Cummins, LYM)*

Shurlock Row [SU8374], *White Hart:* Attractive panelled pub, warm, comfortable and relaxing, with inglenook fireplace dividing bar from other rooms; flying memorabilia inc squadron badges, old pictures and brasses; quietly attentive licensees and staff, Flowers Original, Marstons Pedigree, Wethereds Best, small but pleasant lunchtime menu *(Michael and Jenny Back, Gordon)*

☆ **Sindlesham** [Bearwood Rd; signposted Sindlesham from B3349; SU7769], *Walter Arms:* Three comfortable main rooms (one recently extended) each with a log fire, good range of reasonably priced food lunchtime and evening inc Suns, efficient service, no smoking area, well kept Courage Best and Directors; very popular; tables outside; unpretentious bedrooms, good breakfasts *(Paul and Janet Giles, Julie and Mike Taylor, LYM)*

Slough [Albert St; SU9779], *Wheatsheaf:* Good spacious oak-beamed Fullers pub, well kept beer, good value food, smallish suntrap garden *(Martin Kay, Andrea Fowler, A W Dickinson)*

☆ **Stanford Dingley** [SU5771], *Old Boot:* Neat beamed inglenook bar with old pews and other country furnishings, pleasant views from attractive suntrap garden, short choice of decent generous food, Fullers Chiswick, ESB and London Pride, adjacent restaurant area; exemplary lavatories *(Angela and Alan Dale, TBB, Jane and Jaz Bevan, LYM)*

Streatley [SU5980], *Bull:* Lively, friendly pub in lovely setting, worth knowing for good choice of real ales, nice gardens; piped music may be loud *(Mr and Mrs G D Amos)*

☆ **Theale** [Church St; SU6371], *Volunteer:* Recently reopened by Fullers, a success, with nice wooden furniture, well kept ales, good choice of bar meals; children at reasonable times *(D and J Johnson, Martin Kay, Andrea Fowler)*

Theale [Station Rd], *Fox & Hounds:* Friendly and busy, with good service, well kept Ansells Extra, Wadworths 6X and Farmers Glory, good food inc home-made steak and kidney pie and steaks with fresh veg, also vegetarian dishes and puddings

like rhubarb and ginger crumble *(Muriel and John Hobbs)*; [A4 opposite Sulhamstead turning], *Winning Hand:* Quiet and friendly, good choice of beers on handpump inc Brakspears SB and Marstons Pedigree; extensive menu chalked on wall, roast at the weekend *(Roderic Plinston)*

Tidmarsh [The Street; A340 S of Pangbourne; SU6374], *Greyhound:* Great value food, beer well kept, service polite and efficient; good walks nearby *(Mr Warwick)*

☆ **Upper Basildon** [Aldworth Rd; SU5976], *Red Lion:* Notable not as a building (it's Victorian brick) but as a really welcoming pub, small but uncrowded and comfortable, with good food from warm filled rolls through vast pies to Sun roasts, also vegetarian and vegan dishes, well kept ales eg Boddingtons, Brakspears PA, Fullers London Pride, Timothy Taylors Landlord and guests, decent house wines; very attentive discreet young staff; children not constrained *(John Miller, Clifford Payton, Carolyn Lainbeer, KC, Stan Edwards)*

Warfield [Church Lane/A3095; SU8872], *Plough & Harrow:* Cheerful and friendly two-bar local with warm comfortable lounge, well kept Morlands, bar food inc good fish and chips, lovely friendly landlady; piano music Fri nights *(Gordon)*

☆ **Wargrave** [High St; off A321 Henley—Twyford; SU7878], *Bull:* Low-beamed dining pub popular for good often unusual food esp fish, good value if not cheap; well kept Brakspears, good log fires, friendly quiet atmosphere; tables on pretty covered terrace; bedrooms *(Colin Pearson, S R Jordan, Gordon, LYM)*

☆ **Wargrave** [High St], *White Hart:* Clean and friendly low-beamed lounge bar of some character, good value bar food, well kept Whitbreads-related real ales; restaurant *(Sidney and Erna Wells, LYM)*

White Waltham [Waltham Rd; SU8577], *Beehive:* Small public bar and pleasant larger back saloon, very reasonably priced mostly home-made food, well kept Whitbreads-related beers *(G Medcalf, R J Purser)*

☆ **Wickham** [3 miles from M4 junction 14, via A338, B4000; SU3971], *Five Bells:* Friendly new licensees concentrating rather more on food (excellent ham) in neat and smart yet pleasantly homely racing-village inn with big log fire, Courage-related real ales, plain garden with good play area; children in eating area; good value bedrooms *(HNJ, PEJ, LYM)*

☆ **Windsor** [Datchet Rd – opp Riverside Stn, nr Castle; SU9676], *Royal Oak:* Big and busy, with quick friendly service, red plush and panelling, some fine stained glass, good choice of reasonably priced bar food from big food servery in airy eating area; white furniture on L-shaped terrace *(Mayur Shah, TBB, BB)*

Windsor [Thames St], *Donkey House:* Lovely riverside position with plenty of

outside seating and good bridge view, inside is dark wood and bare boards with well kept Ind Coope Burton, reasonably priced food; can be noisy *(A E and P McCully, TBB);* [St Leonards Rd], *Trooper:* Comfortable back-street pub with fairly extensive menu of wholesome bar food, very attentive friendly service *(Chris Cook)*
Winkfield [Windsor Rd; A332 one mile N of Ascot on junction with B3034; SU9272], *Crispin:* Attractive Morlands Artists Fayre pub with welcoming atmosphere, esp for families (even high chairs); food all day, conservatory, tables outside *(Peter Ashcroft, Kim Turner);* [Lovel Rd; A330 just W of junction with B3034, turning off at Fleur de Lis – OS Sheet 175 map reference 921715], *Slug & Lettuce:* Bare bricks, low beams, black oak timbers, cottagey furnishings, good bar food, well kept real ales *(TBB, LYM);* [A330, opp church], *White Hart:* Neatly modernised Tudor pub with ex-bakery bar and ex-courthouse weekend restaurant, decent bar food (at a price), real ale, sizeable garden *(TBB, LYM)*
Winnersh [B3030; SU7870], *Jolly Farmer:* Pleasant Morlands pub with well kept beers, home-cooked food and big garden *(Dr M Owton)*
Winterbourne [not far from M4 junction 13; formerly the New Inn; SU4572], *Winterbourne Arms:* Pretty black and white house in quiet village with play area in attractive garden; a main entry in previous editions, with a welcoming local atmosphere, but we can't yet say how the new licensees, who are putting more emphasis on the food side, are turning out *(LYM)*
☆ **Wokingham** [Gardeners Green, Honey Hill – OS Sheet 175 map reference 826668; SU8266], *Crooked Billet:* Well kept Brakspears in homely and popular country pub with pews, tiles, brick serving counter, crooked black joists; good simple cheap food, small restaurant area (not Sun – bar food very limited Sun evening) where children allowed; nice outside in summer *(D K Carter, Mrs C A Blake, Nick and Muriel Cox, LYM)*

Wokingham [Market Sq; SU8068], *Olde Rose:* Comfortable Beefeater coaching inn with enough wood to build a Spanish galleon; commercialised, but appealing *(Gordon);* [Plough Lane – nr Coppid Beech roundabout, London Rd], *Plough:* Pleasant typical Beefeater with good service, bar food, children's menu, separate dining room; live music Thurs, booking advisable Sat/Sun evening *(A M Pring);* [Market Sq], *Red Lion:* Old coaching inn with three cosy smallish bars, galleried dining room overlooking central one; some nice panelling; heavily beamed back bar used to be connected with shop next door via passage over coach entry *(Gordon);* [Peach St, opp All Saints Ch], *Ship:* Excellent Fullers pub *(Martin Kay, Andrea Fowler);* [222 London Rd], *Three Frogs:* Friendly Morlands local with pleasant atmosphere, sandwiches, ploughman's, usual hot dishes, good choice of ales inc an interesting guest beer *(Peter and Lynn Brueton, AMP)*
☆ **Woodside** [off A322 Windsor—Ascot – look for blue/gold board; SU9270], *Duke of Edinburgh:* Food's the main draw (not Sun evening), esp fish, in bar and restaurant of cosy and friendly pub with well kept Arkells, small garden; children welcome *(Pat Woodward, H F King, Peter Ashcroft, Kim Turner)*
☆ **Woolhampton** [A4; SU5767], *Rising Sun:* Plain, even spartan bar and functional lounge, but excellent atmosphere, plentiful home-made food inc huge reasonably priced sandwiches, good choice of at least six well kept real ales, friendly service *(Phil H Smith, Rob and Helen Townsend, Mark and Diane Grist, Eric J Locker, Roger Byrne, LYM)*
Woolhampton, *Angel:* Friendly well managed Whitbreads coaching inn with good Wayside Inn food *(Mr and Mrs A L Budden)*
Wraysbury [High St; TQ0174], *Perseverance:* Genuinely beamed old pub with warm welcome, good straightforward food and Courage-related beers; old-style bar, lounge and dining areas *(Ian Phillips)*

Post Office address codings confusingly give the impression that some pubs are in Berkshire, when they're really in Oxfordshire or Hampshire (which is where we list them).

Buckinghamshire

An interesting crop of new main entries here includes the cosy Five Bells tucked up a country lane at Botley (gaining our new Beer Award), the charming Mole & Chicken at Easington (notable food, good drinks), the Prince Albert at Frieth (a delightful little country pub, another Beer Award winner), the Red Lion at Stoke Green (friendly good value; back in these pages after a break) and the quite unclassifiable Five Arrows in Waddesdon (a Beer Award, a Wine Award, a Stay Award and good food). Other places we'd now pick out particularly for food here include the friendly Peacock at Bolter End, the restauranty Walnut Tree at Fawley, the Chequers in its lovely spot opposite the church at Fingest, the very friendly little Dinton Hermit at Ford (outstanding), the civilised Yew Tree at Frieth (especially for its Austrian dishes), the Pink & Lily at Lacey Green (doing very well at the moment, with Beer and Wine Awards, too), the very friendly Swan at Ley Hill, the Rising Sun at Little Hampden (one of the best), the Greyhound at Marsh Gibbon (Thai food), the relaxed old White Hart at Northend and the quaint Old Crown at Skirmett (another excellent dining pub). Even against this established competition, though, it's the Mole & Chicken at Easington which gains our award as Buckinghamshire Dining Pub of the Year. On the whole, food prices in the area though by no means low have been relatively stable recently. In fact it's rather easier this year to find a really good main dish for under £5 than it was here last year, though a ploughman's tends to be typically nearer £3.50 than £3. Our new Beer Award also goes to the Queens Head near Amersham, the Stag & Huntsman at Hambleden and the Blackwood Arms at Littleworth Common (staggering numbers of unusual guest beers). New beers that have been winning approval in the area this year include Brakspears OBJ (short for O Be Joyful), Rebellion (from Marlow) and Ridgeway and Old Icknield (from over at Tring); Chiltern Beechwood (brewed near Aylesbury) is also well worth looking out for. Buckinghamshire though is an expensive county for beer – nearly 10% more expensive than the national average. On the wine front, the Hare & Hounds in Marlow stands out, with a splendid choice by the glass. The pick of the Lucky Dips are probably the Blue Flag at Cadmore End, Fox at Ibstone, Crown at Little Missenden and Lone Tree at Thornborough, with other very strong contenders being the Bull & Butcher at Akeley, Bottle & Glass near Aylesbury, Black Horse near Chesham, Swan at Denham, Sir Francis Drake at Gayhurst, Hampden Arms at Great Hampden, Crooked Billet at Little Marlow, Red Lion at Little Tingewick, Red Lion at Marsworth, Stag at Mentmore, Old Hat at Preston Bissett, Polecat at Prestwood, Old Swan at The Lee and Chequers at Weston Turville. We have inspected most of these ourselves, so can vouch firmly for their quality.

Looking for a pub with a really special garden, or in lovely countryside, or with an outstanding view, or right by the water? They are listed separately, at the back of the book.

ADSTOCK SP7330 Map 4

Old Thatched Inn

Just N of A413, 4 miles SE of Buckingham

The comfortable beamed and timbered bar in this attractive and cosy thatched village inn has a relaxed atmosphere, flagstones by the bar counter, an open winter fire (with a log-effect gas fire in summer), wheelback chairs and bays of green plush button-back banquettes in carpeted areas leading off – one part is no smoking – and antique hunting prints, copper and brassware. Popular bar food includes soup (£2.50), sandwiches (from £2.50), good ploughman's, lasagne (£4.95), steak in Guinness pie (£6), and steaks (from £9), with daily specials such as smoked chicken and mushrooms in sherry sauce and puff pastry (£3.50), chicken, pork and bacon pie with red wine, herbs and suet stuffing (£6.50), and white chocolate truffle cake (£2.75). Well kept Adnams, Hook Norton Best, Morrells, Ruddles Best and County and Websters Yorkshire on handpump (light blanket pressure on some) and lots of malt whiskies; prompt, friendly service. There is a dining conservatory attached to the partly no smoking restaurant, and a sheltered garden at the back. *(Recommended by Mrs E Smith, Martin Janson, Graham and Karen Oddey, Ian Phillips)*

Free house ~ Licensee Tony McCoy ~ Real ale ~ Meals and snacks ~ Restaurant (not Sun evening) ~ Aylesbury (01296) 712584 ~ Children in restaurant and eating area of bar ~ Open 12-3, 6-11

nr AMERSHAM SU9495 Map 4

Queens Head ◨

Whielden Gate; pub in sight just off A404, 1½ miles towards High Wycombe at Winchmore Hill turn-off; OS Sheet 165 map reference 941957

There's a good pubby atmosphere in the bar of this unspoilt little 18th-c country pub – as well as low beams, traditional furnishings, horsebrasses, and lots of brass spigots; Monty the dalmatian may be wandering around. Flagstones surround the big inglenook fireplace (which still has the old-fashioned wooden built-in wall seat curving around right in beside the woodburning stove – with plenty of space under the seat for logs), a stuffed albino pheasant, old guns, and a good cigarette card collection. Home-made bar food – using home-grown vegetables from the garden – includes soup (£2.25), omelettes (£3.50), tagliatelle neapolitana (£3.95), lots of pizzas to eat here or take away (from £4), broccoli and stilton pancakes (£4.50), and pheasant casserole (£5.25); children's menu; summer barbecues. Well kept Adnams, Fullers ESB, the new Rebellion from Marlow, and a weekly guest beer on handpump; darts, shove-ha'penny, dominoes, cribbage, fruit machine, piped music, and Aunt Sally. The garden has swings, a climbing frame and slide, an aviary with cockatiels, a rabbit and a guinea pig in a large run, plus Desmond the duck. *(Recommended by J S M Sheldon, Mr and Mrs C Holmes; more reports please)*

Free house ~ Licensees Les and Mary Anne Robbins ~ Real ale ~ Meals and snacks (till 10pm); not Sun evening ~ Amersham (01494) 725240 ~ Children in family room and eating area of bar ~ Open 11-2.30(3 Sat), 5.30(6 Sat)-11

BEACONSFIELD SU9490 Map 2

Old Hare

A mile from M40 junction 2; 41 Aylesbury End, Old Beaconsfield

There's a good mix of people in the cosy, rambling and traditionally decorated rooms of this warmly friendly and busy old pub. The rooms by the odd-angled bar counter are decorated with prints of hares, photographs and prints of the pub, and to the right of the door a dimly lit end room has a big, very high-backed antique settle and a serving hatch; a lighter room has a big inglenook with a copper hood. Under the new manageress, the popular bar food includes filled baps and French bread, and daily specials like deep-fried brie (3.95), broccoli and leek bake (£4.45), chilli con carne (£4.95), steak in ale pie (£5.10), chicken curry madras (£5.50), and 8oz rump steak (£8.75); home-made puddings. Cheerfully helpful staff serve well kept Benskins Best, Ind Coope Burton and Tetleys Yorkshire on handpump, and guests like Marstons Pedigree; lots of malt whiskies, decent house wines, and good strong coffee; no machines or music. The big, sunny back garden has a new terrace and lots of extra seating. *(Recommended by Ron and Sheila Corbett, Mark J Hydes, Simon Collet-Jones, George Atkinson, T A Bryan, Dr Gerald W Barnett, Paul and Buck Shinkman)*

Allied ~ Manager Jill Tindall ~ Real ale ~ Meals and snacks (not Sun evening) ~ Beaconsfield (01494) 673380 ~ Children in eating area of bar ~ Open 11-3, 5.30-11; closed evening 10 May for annual street fair

BLEDLOW SP7702 Map 4

Lions of Bledlow

From B4009 from Chinnor towards Princes Risborough, the first right turn about 1 mile outside Chinnor goes straight to the pub; from the second, wider right turn, turn right through village

A fair number of walkers from nearby Bledlow Ridge and the Chilterns come to this mossy-tiled old pub to enjoy the sheltered crazy-paved terrace, series of neatly kept small sloping lawns, and marvellous views. Inside, the attractive low-beamed rooms – one with a woodburning stove – are full of character. The inglenook bar has attractive oak stalls built into one partly panelled wall, more seats in a good bay window, and an antique settle resting on the deeply polished ancient tiles; log fires. Bar food includes home-made soup (£1.80), big filled cottage rolls (from £2.75), steak in Guinness pie (£4.75) and maybe daily specials such as chicken and ham pie (£4.50), fresh sautéed monkfish (£4.95), roast chicken (£5.25) and fresh sea bass (£6.95). Well kept Courage Directors, Gales HSB, John Smiths, Tolly Cobbold and Wadworths 6X on handpump. One of the two cottagey side rooms has a video game, as well as dominoes and cribbage. *(Recommended by Tim and Ann Newell, Simon Collett-Jones, Helen Hazzard, P E Churchill; more reports please)*

Free house ~ Licensee F J McKeown ~ Real ale ~ Meals and snacks (not Sun evening) ~ Restaurant (Weds-Sat evenings) ~ Princes Risborough (01844) 343345 ~ Children in side rooms and restaurant ~ Open 11-3, 6-11; closed evening 25 Dec

BOLTER END SU7992 Map 4

Peacock

Just over 4 miles from M40 junction 5; A40 to Stokenchurch, then B482

After 15 years here, the friendly licensees are as enthusiastic as ever. They are planning to take on regular guest beers, new carpets are to be laid – and the bar food is as reliably good and popular as it's always been: ploughman's (from £3.25), pizzas (from £4.50), spicy home-made beef and bean chilli (£3.95), home-made lasagne (£5.10), home-made steak and kidney pie or local ham salad (£5.25), chicken breast in creamy cheese and asparagus sauce (£6.25), steaks (from £9.95; they only use Aberdeen Angus meat), and three daily specials and a special pudding; their poultry is free-range, their air-dried ham, cheddar cheese and blue vinney come from farms in Dorset, and fresh fish comes from Billingsgate on Fridays. Well kept ABC Bitter, Ansells Mild, Bass and Tetleys on handpump; decent wines and coffee, and freshly squeezed orange juice. The brightly modernised bar has a rambling series of alcoves, a good log fire, and a happy, bustling atmosphere; cribbage and dominoes. In summer there are seats around a low stone table and picnic-table sets in the neatly kept garden. The 'no children' is strictly enforced here. *(Recommended by Peter Plumridge, Dr Gerald W Barnett)*

Ind Coope (Allied) ~ Lease: Peter Hodges ~ Real ale ~ Meals and snacks (till 10pm; not Sun evening) ~ High Wycombe (01494) 881417 ~ Open 11.45-2.30, 6-11

BOTLEY SP9702 Map 3

Five Bells 🍺

Tylers Hill Road; coming from Chesham, the first right turn on entering Botley, opposite the
Hen & Chickens

Off the beaten track, this friendly country pub keeps a good range of real ales on
handpump, such as Brakspears PA, Fullers London Pride, Timothy Taylors
Landlord and Wadworths 6X and Farmers Glory. The home-made, daily-
changing bar food is popular too: soup (£2), one-and-a-half rounds of sandwiches
(£2.50), steak and kidney pie or quiche (£4), baked ham in parsley sauce or
poached salmon (£5), and puddings such as cherry pie (£2). There are two
attractive beamed inglenook fireplaces and a warm welcome to those who have
come from far and wide to enjoy the quiet, cosy atmosphere. Outside this small
house are some seats and attractive views – and tracks lead off into the woods.
(Recommended by Helen Hazzard, Adrian and Karen Bulley and others)

Free house ~ Licensees Mr and Mrs Wilkins ~ Real ale ~ Meals and snacks ~
(01494) 775042 ~ Well behaved children welcome ~ Open 11-2.30, 6-11

BRILL SP6513 Map 4

Pheasant

Windmill Rd; village signposted from B4011 Bicester—Long Crendon

One reader enjoys this 17th-c pub so much that he walked the 26-mile round trip
from his home – to celebrate his 60th birthday. The views are splendid, and it's
said on a clear day that you can see nine counties from this hilltop. The windmill
opposite is one of the oldest post windmills still in working order. Inside, the
quietly modernised and neatly kept beamed bar has comfortable russet leatherette
button-back banquettes in bays around its tables, a woodburning stove, and a
step up to a dining area which is decorated with attractively framed Alken
hunting prints – and which also benefits from the view. Bar food includes
sandwiches (from £1.80), vegetable or locally-made meaty burgers (£3.20),
ploughman's (£3.95), home-cooked honey-roast ham and eggs (£4.25), fillet of
plaice (£4.95), Thai chicken (£7.40), steaks (from £9.50), and daily specials such
as vegetarian curry (£4.95), steak and mushroom pie (£5.50), and fresh fish such
as brill, salmon or sea bass (from £8). They do summer afternoon cream teas at
weekends and on bank holidays (3-6pm, May-Oct). Well kept Marstons Pedigree,
Tetleys, and Wadworths 6X on handpump, with Chiltern Ale as a guest; decent
house wine; piped music. No dogs (they have three golden retrievers themselves).
Roald Dahl used to drink here, and some of the tales the locals told him were
worked into his short stories. There are picnic-table sets in the small, sheltered
back garden. *(Recommended by Michael Sargent, Gordon, D A Edwards, Graham and
Karen Oddey, Mrs J Oakes, Richard and Maria Gillespie)*

Free house ~ Licensee Mike Carr ~ Real ale ~ Meals and snacks (till 10pm in
summer); not 25 Dec ~ Restaurant ~ Kingston Blount (01844) 237104 ~
Children welcome ~ Open 11-3, 6-11; 11-11 summer Sats/bank hols; 12-10.30
summer Suns

CHALFONT ST PETER SU9990 Map 3

Greyhound

High Street; A413

The spacious open-plan bar of this attractive old coaching inn has low beams,
brasses on the lantern-lit dark panelling, plenty of deep red plush seats, and a
huge winter log fire in a handsome fireplace. Well kept Courage Best and
Directors, John Smiths, Marstons Pedigree, Ruddles County and Wadworths 6X
on handpump kept under light blanket pressure. Bar food includes sandwiches
(from £1.75; toasties from £2; hot carvery joint with chips as well £3.50),
ploughman's (from £2.75), filled baked potatoes (from £2.75), salads (from
£3.95), and a choice of three roasts from their carvery. The restaurant is partly no

smoking. Fruit machine. You can sit outside at tables in the pretty front courtyard, sheltered by two creeper covered wings of the building, or on a lawn by the little River Misbourne. *(Recommended by Dr Andrew Brookes, Peter Watkins, Pam Stanley, Klaus and Elizabeth Leist, Rosemary and Brian Wilmot)*

Courage ~ Lease: John Harriman ~ Real ale ~ Meals and snacks (till 10pm); not Sun evening ~ Restaurant ~ Gerrards Cross (01753) 883404 ~ Children in restaurant and in eating area of bar ~ Open 11-11 ~ Bedrooms: £39/£46

CHEDDINGTON SP9217 Map 4

Old Swan

58 High St

The quietly civilised right-hand bar rooms of this mainly thatched, friendly pub have old-fashioned plush dining chairs, a built-in wall bench, and a few tables with nice country-style chairs on the bare boards, a big inglenook with glass cabinets filled with brass on either side of it and quite a few horsebrasses, and little hunting prints on the walls. On the other side of the main door is a room with housekeepers' chairs on the rugs and quarry tiles and country plates on the walls, and a step up to a carpeted part with stripy wallpaper and pine furniture; TV. Bar food can be eaten in the bar or restaurant and might include filled baked potatoes or sandwiches (from £1.95), ploughman's (from £2.45), nut cutlets (£4.25), salads (from £4.30), gammon and egg (£4.60), puddings (£2.50), and daily specials such as steak and kidney pie or spicy pork and bean casserole (£4.50) and fish and chips (£5.15); children's meals (£2.60); 3-course Sunday roast (£8.75). Well kept ABC Best, Ridgeway Bitter (from a local brewery), Tetleys and Wadworths 6X on handpump, quite a few malt whiskies, and decent wines; very pleasant, efficient staff. Piped nostalgic pop, shove-ha'penny, table skittles, cribbage, darts, fruit machine, and trivia. The garden has colourful hanging baskets and tubs and a children's play area. *(Recommended by The Shinkmans, Brian and Anna Marsden, Russell and Margaret Bathie, Marjorie and David Lamb, Margaret and Trevor Errington)*

Ind Coope (Allied) ~ Lease: Paul Jarvis ~ Real ale ~ Meals and snacks (till 10pm); not Sun evening ~ Restaurant; not Sun evening ~ Cheddington (01296) 668226 ~ Children in eating area of bar and in restaurant ~ Occasional folk or jazz music ~ Open 11.30-2.30(3 winter Sats), 6-11; 11-11 summer Sats; closed evening 25 Dec

CHENIES TQ0198 Map 2

Red Lion

2 miles from M25 junction 18; A404 towards Amersham, then village signposted on right; Chesham Rd

The front of this relaxed brick pub has been repaired this year, and new windows and a new front door have been added. Popular food is still the main draw, and might include tasty soup (£2.35), prawn, leek and stilton ramekin (£3.95), salmon and tarragon pâté (£4.50), hake, tomato and mushroom bake (£5.25), pasta with mushrooms in garlic and herb sauce (£5.50), pies like cod, leek and cheddar or turkey sausage and onion pie (from £5.75), turkey and cranberry strudel (£5.95), pork rogan (£6.75), and venison escalope with port and mushroom sauce (£9.95); all meals are served with potatoes (no chips) and fresh vegetables. The L-shaped bar has built-in wall benches by the front windows with beige or plum-coloured cushions, wheelback chairs and plush stools around a mix of small tables, and photographs and prints of traction-engines, as well as advertising and other prints on the walls; there's also a small back snug and a dining room. Well kept Adnams, Benskins Best, two local beers – Rebellion (from Marlow) and Ridgeway (from Tring) – and Wadworths 6X on handpump; pleasant service, and no noisy games machines. It's quiet midweek lunchtimes but lively and busy at weekends. Nicely decorated with pretty hanging baskets and window boxes, the pub is convenient for Chenies Manor. *(Recommended by Lyn and Bill Capper, A W Dickinson, June and Charles Samuel, BKA, J Slaughter, Simon Collett-*

Jones, Iain Baillie, Pat and Derek Westcott, Ian Phillips, Tracey and Kevin Stephens)

Free house ~ Licensees Heather and Mike Norris ~ Real ale ~ Meals and snacks (till 10pm) ~ Rickmansworth (01923) 282722 ~ Open 11-2.30, 5.30-11; closed 25 Dec

DINTON SP7611 Map 4

Seven Stars

Stars Lane; follow Dinton signpost into New Road off A418 Aylesbury—Thame, near Gibraltar turn-off

In a quiet village, this pretty white-rendered tiled house is run by particularly friendly and attentive licensees. The characterful and welcoming public bar (known as the Snug here) is notable for the two highly varnished ancient built-in settles facing each other across a table in front of the vast stone inglenook fireplace. The spotlessly kept lounge bar, with its beams, joists and growing numbers of old tools on the walls, is comfortably and simply modernised – and although these rooms are not large, there is a spacious and comfortable restaurant area. Well kept ABC, Tetleys and Wadworths 6X on handpump or tapped from the cask, and very good, popular home-cooked bar food that includes sandwiches (from £1.45; toasties 25p extra), filled baked potatoes (from £2.55), ploughman's (£3.55), tasty ham and egg (£3.50), quiche lorraine (£3.65), vegetable lasagne (£3.85), beef bourguignon (£4.50), steaks (from £8.95) and good daily specials. Darts and Aunt Sally. There are tables under cocktail parasols on the terrace, with more on the lawn of the pleasant sheltered garden. Popular with older people on weekday lunchtimes.

(Recommended by Lyn and Bill Capper, George Atkinson, Michael Sargent, Margaret and Trevor Errington, Miss L Mott, Marjorie and David Lamb, Joan Olivier)

Free house ~ Licensees Rainer and Sue Eccard ~ Real ale ~ Meals and snacks (not Sun or Tues evenings) ~ Restaurant (not Sun evening) ~ Children in eating area of bar and in restaurant ~ Aylesbury (01296) 748241 ~ Special theme evenings with live music ~ Open 12-3, 6-11; closed Tues evening

EASINGTON SP6810 Map 4

Mole & Chicken 🍽 ♟

From B4011 in Long Crendon follow Chearsley, Waddesdon signpost into Carters Lane opposite the Chandos Arms, then turn left into Chilton Road

Buckinghamshire Dining Pub of the Year

Since reopening under new management in 1992 this country dining pub has quickly become so popular that even on a midweek lunchtime many of its tables are booked. It's not really a place you'd come to just for a drink, though they certainly don't discriminate against drinkers and have well kept Hook Norton Best, Tetleys and a guest such as Fullers London Pride on handpump, decent French house wines (and a good choice by the bottle), and a fine collection of malt whiskies and other worthy spirits. But virtually all the tables are set for meals, and there's no denying that the food's the main thing. The changing choice, freshly cooked using good ingredients, includes good soups (£2.50), a few starters that would do as a light lunch such as grilled prawns with garlic bread or chicken satay (£3.95), artichoke with bearnaise sauce (£4.50) or even home-grown asparagus (from £3.95), and very generously served main courses including interesting salads (from £5.95) such as crispy bacon and duck or smoked chicken with toasted pine nuts and banana, home-made pasta (£5.95), curries or a rack of spare ribs (£6.95), giant garlic prawns (from £7.50), calf's liver (£8.95), succulent steaks (from £9.95) and duck (£10.50); a good choice of puddings such as spotted dick with real custard. The beamed bar curves around the serving counter in a sort of S-shape – unusual, as is the decor of designed-and-painted floor, pink walls with lots of big antique prints, and even at lunchtime lit candles on the medley of tables to go with the nice mix of old chairs. Smiling young neatly dressed staff, a pleasant chatty and relaxed atmosphere with a good mix of different age-groups, unobtrusive piped music, good winter log fires, pistachio nuts and other nibbles on the counter; no dogs. There's a smallish garden with picnic-table sets under cocktail parasols, with an outside summer bar and lunchtime summer barbecues. *(Recommended by C A Hall, John, Graham and Karen Oddey, Michael Sargent)*

Free house ~ Licensee Johnny Chick ~ Real ale ~ Meals and snacks (midnight supper licence) ~ (01844) 208387 ~ Open 11-3, 6-11; all day Sun

FAWLEY SU7586 Map 2

Walnut Tree 🛏 ♉

Village signposted off A4155 (then right at T-junction) and off B480, N of Henley

Although people do come to this beautifully placed dining pub just for a drink, the emphasis is very much on the very good, high class food, which is served in the attractively furnished bars, no smoking conservatory, and restaurant: soup (£2.40), ploughman's (from £3.50), smoked salmon and trout mousse (£3.95), giant kiwi mussels in garlic, parsley and parmesan butter (£4.25), baked stuffed aubergine (£4.95), steak and kidney pie or curry of the day (£5.25), hot ham and parsley sauce (£5.95), chicken oriental (£6.25), and puddings like sherry, lemon and ginger cheesecake, sticky toffee pudding or hot apple pie (£2.50). Well kept Brakspears PA and SB on handpump, and a good range of wines (including local English ones); attentive service. The big lawn around the front car park has some well spaced tables made from elm trees, with some seats in a covered terrace extension – and a hitching rail for riders. *(Recommended by Gwen and Peter Andrews, Roger Byrne, Gordon, Ron and Val Broom, Doug Kennedy, Chris Cook)*

Brakspears ~ Tenant Ben Godbolt ~ Real ale ~ Meals and snacks ~ Restaurant ~ Turville Heath (01491) 638360 ~ Children in conservatory and in restaurant (must be over 5 in evening) ~ Open 12(11 Sat)-3, 6-11 ~ Bedrooms: £35S/£50S

FINGEST SU7791 Map 2

Chequers

Village signposted off B482 Marlow—Stokenchurch

Perfect for a summer's day, the big garden outside this white-shuttered brick and flint pub has lots of tables under cocktail parasols among flower beds and a view down the Hambleden valley; beyond this, quiet pastures slope up to beechwoods. Inside, the spotless old-fashioned rooms are warmed in winter by a huge log fire. The friendly central bar room has seats built into its black-painted wooden dado, chairs of varying ages from ancient to modern, and an 18th-c oak settle. On the walls are pistols, antique guns and swords, toby jugs, pewter mugs and decorative plates. A sunny lounge has comfortable easy chairs and french windows to the garden; there's also a small no smoking room for eating. Very good, popular bar food includes sandwiches (from £1.60), soup (£2.95), ploughman's (from £3.75), Greek meze (£3.50), seafood salad (£4.50), vegetarian dishes (from £4.95), roasts or liver and bacon (all £5.95), steak, kidney and mushroom pie (£6.50), freshly caught trout (£7.50), steaks (from £8.50), beef stroganoff or salmon steak (£10.50), and puddings like lovely Danish chocolate cake (£2.75); there's also a romantic restaurant, which you walk through part of the kitchen to get to. Well kept Brakspears PA, SB and Old Ale on handpump; dominoes, cribbage, backgammon. Over the road is a unique Norman twin-roofed church tower – probably the nave of the original church. *(Recommended by Simon Collett-Jones, LM, Gordon, John Waller, Andy Thwaites, Dr D C Deeing, R J Saunders, Rosemary and Brian Wilmot, Ron Fletcher, B R Greenfield, Nigel Norman, June and Tony Baldwin, Doug Kennedy)*

Brakspears ~ Tenant Bryan Heasman ~ Real ale ~ Meals and snacks (11-2.30, 6-9.45; not Sun evening) ~ Restaurant ~ Turville Heath (01491) 638335 ~ Children in eating area of bar and in restaurant ~ Open 11-3, 6-11; winter evening opening 7

FORD SP7709 Map 4

Dinton Hermit 🍴

Village signposted between A418 and B4009, SW of Aylesbury

In pretty countryside, this particularly friendly and characterful stone cottage has a lounge on the right with a log fire, red plush banquettes along the cream walls and red leatherette chairs around polished tables, and red leatherette seats built into the stripped stone walls of a small room leading off. The attractively traditional partly tiled public bar on the left has scrubbed tables, a woodburning stove in its huge inglenook, and prints of a lady out hunting. Mrs Tompkins does the cooking and at lunchtime (when they don't take reservations) this might include sandwiches (from £1.40), soup (£2), ploughman's (from £3), saucy mushrooms (£3.25), smoked haddock in mushroom and cheese sauce (£4.75), a vegetarian hotpot, kidneys in cognac sauce (£4.95) or home-made lasagne (£4.95), pancake with stilton and asparagus or curries (£5.75), cold roast chicken (£6.25), and puddings such as home-made fruit pie or bread pudding (£2.50); in the evening (when you must book), dishes are slightly more expensive and include more grills and fish. Darts, shove-ha'penny, cribbage and dominoes. Well kept ABC Best, Bass and Tetleys on handpump, and decent coffee. The sheltered and well planted garden opposite (they don't serve food out there in the evenings) has swings, a slide and a seesaw. *(Recommended by Graham and Karen Oddey, June and Charles Samuel, Michael Sargent, P Saville, Margaret and Trevor Errington)*

Free house ~ Licensees John and Jane Tompkins ~ Real ale ~ Meals and snacks (not Sun/Mon; not 6-20 July) ~ Aylesbury (01296) 748379 ~ Well behaved children welcome ~ Open 11-2.30, 6-11

FORTY GREEN SU9292 Map 2

Royal Standard of England

3½ miles from M40 junction 2, via A40 to Beaconsfield, then follow sign to Forty Green, off B474 ¾ mile N of New Beaconsfield

Until after the Battle of Worcester in 1651 (when Charles II hid in the high rafters of what is now its food bar), this ancient pub used to be called the Ship. There are interesting rambling rooms with roaring open fires and handsomely decorated iron firebacks – including one from Edmund Burke's old home nearby, huge black ship's timbers, finely carved old oak panelling and a huge settle; also, rifles, powder-flasks and bugles, lots of brass and copper, needlework samplers, ancient pewter and pottery tankards, and stained glass. Good bar food includes home-made soups (£2), sausages (£4.25), home-made pies such as chicken and mushroom, beef and oyster or venison in red wine (from £5.75), and good summer salads such as crab, salmon, prawn and cold pies (£6.25). Well kept Marstons Pedigree and Owd Rodger (the beer was originally brewed here, until the pub passed the recipe on to Marstons), Morlands Old Speckled Hen, and regular local guests on handpump; quite a few malt whiskies, several Irish ones, and fruit wines; friendly service. There are seats outside in a neatly hedged front rose garden, or in the shade of a tree. Perhaps at its best in winter when the summer crowds have gone. *(Recommended by Chris Warne, W L G Watkins, Andrew Stephenson, Susan and John Douglas, A W Dickinson)*

Free house ~ Licensees Philip Eldridge, Peter and Gill Carroll ~ Real ale ~ Meals and snacks (12-2, 7-10); not 25 Dec ~ Beaconsfield (01494) 673382 ~ Children in eating area of bar ~ Open 11-3, 5.30-11

FRIETH SU7990 Map 2

Prince Albert 🍷 🍺

Village signposted off B482 in Lane End; turn right towards Fingest just before village

A classic cottagey little Brakspears pub standing alone in peaceful wooded countryside: at lunchtime the regulars appear from nowhere, each automatically getting their usual – and remarkably esoteric usuals they are, some of them, considering how well kept is the Bitter, Special, Mild, Old and OBJ on handpump. But then the house wines are Georges Duboeuf, decent whiskies on optic include Smiths Glenlivet and Jamesons, and there's no shortage of surprises such as elderflower pressé. There's an excellent assortment of generous fillings for hot granary bread rolls with salad (around £2.90), such as cheese and onion, giant sausage, black pudding and bacon or pastrami and cucumber, with a handful of robust hot dishes from ham and eggs (£3.75) to fried Japanese prawns (£4.45). Furnishings are comfortably old-fashioned – high-backed settles on the left by the inglenook with its woodburner and looming bison's head, more a medley of chairs on the right with its big log fire. Pleasant soft lighting, no music, cribbage, dominoes and shove-ha'penny. The lovely dog's called Digby. A nicely planted informal side garden has views of woods and fields, and there are plenty of nearby walks. *(Recommended by Helen Hazzard, Revd L J and Mrs Melliss, TBB, Pete Baker, Gordon)*

Brakspears ~ Licensees Frank and Joss Reynolds ~ Real ale ~ Meals and snacks (lunchtime only) ~ Moor End (01494) 881683 ~ Open 11-3, 5.30-11; Mon opening hours are half-an-hour later

Yew Tree
In village

As the landlord of this civilised 400-year-old pub is from Austria, there are fresh fruit punches in summer and gluhwein and jaegertee in winter – as well as bratwurst sauerkraut, good ham strudel, home-made sausages (all £4.85), Tyrolean platter (£5.95), very popular pork schnitzel (£6.45), and Viennese cheesecake; also, tagliatelle Milannaise (£3.85), smoked haddock in parsley sauce or grilled sardines (£5.25), and puddings like plum crumble, banana charlotte or hot bread and butter pudding (£2.35). The comfortable bar has stripped beams and joists, animal and sporting pictures (look out for the entertaining fishing engravings by F Naumann), china and glass sparkling in corner cupboards, and horsebrasses and guns over the log fires at each end. Well kept Ringwood Old Thumper, Ruddles County, Websters Yorkshire, and a beer brewed by Chiltern Valley Wines called Luxters Barn on handpump, lots of malt whiskies; decent wine and coffee; excellent friendly service. The neat front garden has tables on its lawn and small terrace – they serve out here too; there's also tethering space for horseriding clubs. *(Recommended by Nigel and Sara Walker, Simon Collett-Jones, Peter Watkins, Pam Stanley, Dr Gerald W Barnett, Susan and John Douglas, Ron and Val Broom, Dick Brown)*

Free house ~ Licensee Franz Aitzetmuller ~ Real ale ~ Meals (12-3, 6-10.30) ~ Restaurant; closed Sun evening ~ High Wycombe (01494) 882330 ~ Children welcome ~ Open 10-2.30, 5.30-11; winter evening opening 6

GREAT BRICKHILL SP9030 Map 2
Old Red Lion
Off A5 just SE of Milton Keynes

The view over Buckinghamshire and far beyond can be enjoyed from the prettily kept peaceful walled garden here, with its picnic-table sets and children's play train, wooden climbing frame and swings. The two gently refurbished and carpeted bars – mainly set for eating – have a pleasant villagey atmosphere, dried flowers on the walls, a chiming grandfather clock, and a log fire in the smaller room. A good range of simple bar food includes sandwiches (from £1.50; chicken, bacon and mayonnaise in a crusty roll £2.90), ploughman's (£3), vegetarian chilli (£4.25), tagliatelle with ham and mushroom (£4.50), home-made steak and mushroom pie (£5.95), salmon fillet with herb butter (£6.95), and steaks (from £6.95). Well kept Boddingtons, Brakspears, Flowers Original and Youngs Special on handpump, decent wines and coffee; friendly service; darts, bar billiards, pinball, dominoes, fruit machine, and unobtrusive piped music. *(Recommended by CW, JW, KC, David and Mary Webb, Bob and Maggie Atherton, Rita Horridge, Ian Phillips)*

Whitbreads ~ Lease: Andrew McCollin ~ Real ale ~ Meals and snacks (not winter

Sun evenings) ~ (01525) 261715 ~ Children in eating area of bar ~ Open 11.30-2.30, 5.30(6.30 Sat)-11

GREAT MISSENDEN SP8900 Map 4

Cross Keys
High St

Wooden standing timbers divide the two genuinely friendly and atmospheric rooms of this old-fashioned little town pub. One half is quarry-tiled with high wooden bar stools, an aged leather chair, old sewing machines on the window sill, collectors' postcards, bar and small brewery mirrors on the walls, horse bits and spigots and pewter mugs on the beams by the bar. The other has a bay window with a built-in seat overlooking the street, a couple of housekeeper's chairs in front of the big open fire, and a high-backed settle. Well kept Fullers Chiswick, London Pride, ESB and Hock on handpump and very cheap for the area. The large waitress-served eating room is attractively furnished with captain's chairs and iron tractor seats, traps and boxing gloves on some beams, and an old kitchen range in the brick fireplace. Bar food includes home-made soup (£2.25), 3-egg omelettes (£4.25), pasta carbonara (£4.50), prawn thermidor (£4.95), puddings like chocolate mousse, and specials such as baked cod on spinach with a cream sauce or kidneys in madeira (from £3.50); good value set 3-course meals in the bistro (lunch £8.75, dinner £14). Piped music, cribbage, dominoes, shove-ha'penny, and fruit machine. The terrace at the back of the building has picnic-table sets with umbrellas – and you can eat out here, too (there's even a heater for chillier summer evenings). *(Recommended by Wayne Brindle, George Atkinson, Martin Kay, Andrea Fowler)*

Fullers ~ Tenants Richard and Frederika Ridler ~ Real ale ~ Meals and snacks ~ Bistro restaurant (not Sun) ~ Great Missenden (01494) 865373 ~ Well behaved children in dining area ~ Open 11-3, 5-11

George ★
94 High St

In 1483, this attractive and friendly old place was built as a hospice for the nearby Abbey. The cosy two-roomed bar has little alcoves (including one with an attractively carved box settle – just room for two – under a fine carved early 17th-c oak panel), timbered walls decorated with prints, attractively moulded heavy beams, and Staffordshire and other figurines over the big log fire. A snug inner room has a sofa, little settles and a smaller coal fire; shove-ha'penny. Bar food includes home-made soup (£2.25), onion bhajis or deep fried mushrooms (£2.95), fresh pasta with different sauces or vegetable au gratin (£4.95), fresh cod with herb butter, bacon pieces and cheese (£6.25), steak and kidney pie (£6.60), marinated chicken (£6.95), rump steak (£8.50), and puddings; huge Sunday roast (£6.25). Well kept Adnams, Wadworths 6X and two guests on handpump kept under light blanket pressure, sangria in summer, mulled wine in winter, and tea and coffee; prompt and cheerful service. The big summer garden area has a hatch from the bar and tables and seats on the pea shingle at the back of the pub (in winter this area is used for extra parking). *(Recommended by Wayne Brindle, Peter Watkins, Pam Stanley, Graham and Karen Oddey, Dr D C Deeing, R J Saunders, Mark J Hydes, Nigel Norman)*

Greenalls ~ Tenants Guy and Sally Smith ~ Real ale ~ Snacks (served all day) and meals; not evenings 25 and 26 Dec ~ No smoking restaurant ~ Great Missenden (01494) 862084 ~ Children in eating area of bar and in restaurant ~ Open 11-11; closed evenings 25 and 26 Dec ~ Bedrooms: £60.95B

HAMBLEDEN SU7886 Map 2

Stag & Huntsman ◀

Turn off A4155 (Henley—Marlow Rd) at Mill End, signposted to Hambleden; in a mile turn right into village centre

Opposite the church in a particularly pretty Chilterns village and with beechwoods backing directly onto the spacious and neatly kept country garden, this peaceful brick and flint house is a popular place. The compact L-shaped, half-panelled lounge bar has a pleasant atmosphere, low ceilings, a large fireplace, and upholstered seating and wooden chairs on the carpet. The attractively simple public bar has darts, shove-ha'penny, dominoes, cribbage and a fruit machine, and there's a cosy snug at the front too. Good home-made bar food includes soup (£2.45), excellent smoked fish pâté (£3.25), spinach enchilada (£4.50), chicken curry or tagliatelle pesto (£5.25), steak and kidney pie (£5.50), prawn and salmon pancake (£5.50), and steaks (from £10.50); a wide choice of puddings (£2.50). Well kept Brakspears PA and SPA, Luxters Barn Bitter, Wadworths 6X and Farmers Glory on handpump; good service, even when busy. The 'no children' policy is strictly enforced. *(Recommended by Frank Cummins, Barbara Houghton, Simon Collett-Jones, Peter Plumridge, Chris Warne, Andy Thwaites, Gwen and Peter Andrews)*

Free house ~ Licensee Mike Matthews ~ Real ale ~ Meals and snacks (not Sun evening except for residents) ~ Restaurant (not Sun evening) ~ Henley (01491) 571227 ~ Open 11-2.30(3 Sat), 6-11; closed 25 Dec ~ Bedrooms: £35.50S/ £48.50S

LACEY GREEN SP8201 Map 4

Pink & Lily ♀ ◗

Parslow's Hillock; from A4010 High Wycombe—Princes Risborough follow Loosley signpost, and in that village follow Great Hampden, Great Missenden signpost; OS Sheet 165 map reference 826019

This friendly and popular dining pub has a wide appeal among our readers – and Rupert Brooke liked it so much that he wrote about it at the start of one of his poems – the result is framed on the wall (and there's a room dedicated to him). The little taproom has been preserved very much as it used to be, with built in wall benches on the red flooring tiles, an old wooden ham-rack hanging from the ceiling and a broad inglenook with a low mantelpiece. Much of the building has been modernised and extended but has kept its welcoming atmosphere: the airy main bar has low pink plush seats, with more intimate side areas and an open fire, and there's a Spanish-style extension with big arches and white garden furniture. Two open fires in winter. Pleasantly served genuinely home-made food includes sandwiches, filled baked potatoes (from £3), vegetarian curry (£3.75), chicken, bacon and stuffing or steak and kidney pies (£3.95), a roast of the day (£4.95), plaice fillet (£5.95), 8oz Scottish sirloin steak (£7.95), good home-made puddings like bakewell tart, sponges and tarts (£2.25), and daily specials; vegetables are fresh. The good range of well kept real ales on handpump includes Boddingtons, Brakspears, Chiltern Beechwood, Courage Directors, Flowers Original, Glenny Hobgoblin, Wadworths 6X and a guest; seven decent wines by the glass. Dominoes, cribbage and piped music. The big garden has lots of rustic tables and seats. *(Recommended by Dave Carter, N and J Strathdee, Simon Collett-Jones, Peter Watkins, Pam Stanley, Lyn and Bill Capper, TBB, Nigel Norman, Ian Phillips)*

Free house ~ Licensees Clive and Marion Mason ~ Real ale ~ Meals and snacks (not Sun evenings) ~ Beaconsfield (01494) 488308 ~ Children over 5 if eating, in bottom bar only ~ Open 11.45(11 Sat)-3, 6-11

LEY HILL SP9802 Map 4

Swan

Village signposted from A416 in Chesham

You can expect a warm welcome from the friendly licensees at this cosy and old-fashioned pub. The rambling main bar has snugs and alcoves with cushioned window and wall seats, one of which is only just big enough for one person, low heavy black beams, black oak props, an old kitchen range, and collections of tobacco pipes and cricket bats. Popular bar food includes soup (£1.70), sandwiches (from £1.95; open sandwiches such as brie with apricot preserve

£4.50), ploughman's (£3.50), filled baked potatoes (from £3.50), fine steak and kidney pie (£4.30), tortelloni ricotta (£4.50), lamb and mango curry (£4.60), plaice grilled with oranges and lemons (£6.20), steaks with a choice of sauces (from £7.80), puddings (£2.20), and a very good, thoughtful children's menu (from 55p for soup); the restaurant is no smoking. Well kept Benskins Best, Ind Coope Burton and Tetleys on handpump; cribbage, dominoes, trivia and piped music. On the front and back terraces and side lawn are picnic-table sets, as well as pretty hanging baskets, tubs of flowers and a climbing frame and adventure bridge, and opposite the pub are a cricket field and a common. *(Recommended by Wyn Churchill, Brian and Anna Marsden, Helen Hazzard, Mr and Mrs J Sandison, Andrew Scarr, J Slaughter, Sara Price, Alison and Dave Cary, Dr Paul Kitchener)*

Benskins (Allied) ~ Managers Matthew and Theresa Lock ~ Real ale ~ Lunchtime bar meals and snacks ~ Evening restaurant ~ Chesham (01494) 783075 ~ Children in eating area of bar and in restaurant ~ Occasional jazz ~ Open 11-2.30, 5.30-11; 11-11 summer Sats

LITTLE HAMPDEN SP8503 Map 4

Rising Sun 🍺

Village signposted from back road (ie W of A413) Great Missenden—Stoke Mandeville; pub at end of village lane; OS Sheet 165 map reference 856040

It's the imaginative food that readers like so much at this smart, secluded dining pub: sandwiches (not evenings), home-made soup (£2.25), marinated lamb and pork kebab with satay sauce (£3.95), salmon rissoles with dill mayonnaise (£4.75), Portuguese fish stew with squid, monkfish and prawns (£6.75), roast rack of lamb with garlic and herb crust and red wine and black cherry sauce (£7.95), a vegetarian dish, daily specials like super poached salmon, and puddings (£2.95). Well kept Adnams, Brakspears, Hook Norton Mild, Marstons Pedigree and guest ales on handpump, with home-made mulled wine and spiced cider in winter and sangria in summer; good service. Part of the opened-up bar is no smoking. There are some tables on the terrace by the sloping front grass; tracks lead on through the woods in various directions. It's a delightful setting, and the pub is on *Good Walks Guide* Walk 71, which takes in Hampden House and Coombe Hill (National Trust – with fine views) – but muddy boots and dogs must be left outside. *(Recommended by Davd Carter, Michael Sargent, B D Jones, Mr and Mrs T F Marshall, John Waller, Nigel Norman, T A Bryan, Dave Carter)*

Free house ~ Licensee Rory Dawson ~ Real ale ~ Meals and snacks (not Sun evening, not Mon) ~ Restaurant ~ High Wycombe (01494) 488393/488360 ~ Children welcome ~ Speciality evenings with music during winter months ~ Open 11.30-2.30, 6.30-11; closed Sun evenings and Mon – except for bank hols ~ Bedrooms planned

LITTLE HORWOOD SP7930 Map 4

Shoulder of Mutton

Church St; back road 1 mile S of A421 Buckingham—Bletchley

This half-timbered partly thatched medieval pub, crowned by a striking arched chimney, is a friendly place, and the rambling T-shaped bar is attractively but simply furnished with sturdy seats around chunky rustic tables, quarry-tiles, a showcase of china swans, and a huge fireplace at one end with a woodburning stove; the alsatian is called Benjamin and there's a black cat as well. Well kept ABC Best and Flowers Original on handpump; shove-ha'penny, cribbage, dominoes, and fruit machine in the games area, piped music. Good value bar food includes sandwiches, hot snacks, and daily specials such as home-made steak and kidney pie, spicy garlic chicken or spare ribs (£4.90). French windows look out on the pleasant back garden with plenty of tables, and there's a quiet churchyard beside it. From the north, the car park entrance is tricky.
(Recommended by John Honnor, Graham and Karen Oddey, Bob Riley, John Hazel, Jean and Antony Lloyd, Marjorie and David Lamb)

Pubmaster (Allied) ~ Tenant June Fessey ~ Real ale ~ Meals and snacks (not Sun evening, not Mon) ~ Restaurant (not Sun evening) ~ Winslow (01296) 712514 ~ Children in restaurant ~ Open 11-2.30(3 Sat), 6-11; closed Mon lunchtime

LITTLEWORTH COMMON SP9487 Map 2

Blackwood Arms ◀

Common Lane; 3 m S of M40 junction 2

The knowledgeable landlord aims to have tried around 850 different beers this year – and tries to deal especially with little independent brewers. On the six handpumps they may have up to 60 different beers a week such as Black Sheep Special, Clarks Festival, Hambleton Goldfields, Hop Back Summer Lightning, Mauldens Black Adder, Orkney Skull Splitter, Timothy Taylors Landlord and Woodfordes Nelsons Revenge; they also serve Belgian draught and bottled beers, a constantly changing farm cider, maybe a perry, and good choice of malt whiskies. Dominoes, cribbage. There's a bustling, friendly atmosphere and home-made food such as long rolls (from £1.75), traditional ploughman's (£2.95), omelettes (£3.25), home-cured ham and egg or steak in ale pie (£3.95), and chicken with cider curry or fish pie (£3.95), with evening extras such as mushroom crêpes (£2.75), lamb with fine herbs (£4.95), salmon with champagne and cream sauce (£5.25), and steaks (from £6.95); Sunday roast lunch (£4.50); roaring winter log fire. There's a garden with a canopy for sitting under, and the pub makes an ideal spot for country walks. *(Recommended by Helen Hazzard, Bob and Maggie Atherton, Nick and Alison Dowson, Cindy and Chris Crow, D Carter, Julian and Sarah Stanton)*

Free house ~ Licensee Graham Titcombe ~ Real ale ~ Meals and snacks (12-2, 6-9.30) ~ (01753) 642169 ~ Children welcome if well behaved ~ Open 11-2.30, 5.30-11; 11-11 Fri and Sat

MARLOW SU8586 Map 2

Hare & Hounds ♀

Henley Rd (A4155 W)

Lots of carefully refurbished inter-connecting rooms and cosy corners make up this friendly, pretty and neatly kept ivy-clad cottage. There are comfortable armchairs, free newspapers, flowers on the tables, a log fire in the inglenook fireplace as well as two log-effect gas fires, and a big no smoking area. The generous helpings of good home-made food can be taken into any part of the pub and might include soup (£1.95), filled french bread or filled baked potatoes (from £3.50), excellent garlic mushrooms with bacon (£3.95), the house speciality – smoked chicken, bacon and croûtons with salad and creamy dressing (£4.50 or £8.95), lasagne or tortellini filled with chicken and cheese in a spinach sauce (£5.95), pie of the day (£6.95), salmon in chicory and sherry wine sauce (£9.95), and duck breast in a raisin and peppercorn sauce (£10.25), with puddings like chocolate torte truffle or home-made apple pie (£2.95), and children's menu; good coffee. Well kept Boddingtons, Brakspears and Marlow IPA (from the Rebellion Beer Company – a micro-brewery in Marlow), and all their 17 wines are available by the glass or goblet; good, attentive service; piped music. There's a small garden. *(Recommended by Susan and John Douglas, Janet Pickles, Simon Collett-Jones, George Jonas, Andy Thwaites, Susan Nichols, Ron and Val Bloom)*

Whitbreads ~ Lease: Gavin Dick ~ Real ale ~ Meals and snacks (till 10pm) ~ (01628) 483343 ~ Children welcome ~ Open 11-3, 5.30-11

MARSH GIBBON SP6423 Map 4

Greyhound

Back road about 4 miles E of Bicester; pub SW of village, towards A41 and Blackthorn

Attractively presented and very popular Thai food is the speciality in this friendly old stone pub: spring roll or spare ribs in a special sauce (£3.90), chicken satay or beef in oyster sauce (£6.20), fresh salmon with ginger in a black bean sauce or king prawn green curry (£7.20), hot and sour Thai soup (for 2 people – £7.50), and 8oz entrecote teriyaki (£8.50); half price for children. The pleasant bar is full of traditional charm, with stripped beams, comfortable heavy-armed seats, and tables on old Singer sewing machine bases. The walls are stripped back to golden-grey stone, unusual hexagonal floor tiles cover the floor, and there's a finely ornamented iron stove. Well kept Fullers London Pride, Greene King Abbot and IPA, Hook Norton Best, and McEwans 80/- on handpump; dominoes, cribbage, and classical piped music. There's a small but pretty front garden with picnic-table sets, and a more spacious garden at the back, too, with swings and a climbing frame tucked among the trees. *(Recommended by S Demont, T Barrow, Graham and Karen Oddey, N and J Strathdee, George Atkinson, T Henwood, Mr and Mrs A Varnom)*

Free house ~ Licensee Richard Kaim ~ Real ale ~ Meals and snacks (till 10pm) ~ Thai restaurant ~ Stratton Audley (01869) 277365 ~ Well behaved children allowed ~ Open 12-3, 6-11

MEDMENHAM SU8084 Map 2

Dog & Badger
A4155 Henley—Marlow

Nell Gwyn is supposed to have sold her wares at this welcoming 14th-c stone and brick timbered pub. The long, busy low-beamed bar is comfortably modernised and neatly kept, with banquettes and stools around the tables, an open fire (as well as an illuminated oven), brasses, a crossbow on the ceiling, and soft lighting. Well kept Boddingtons, Brakspears, Flowers Original, and Wadworths 6X on handpump, and freshly squeezed fruit juice; darts, shove-ha'penny, dominoes, and unobtrusive piped pop music; cheerful efficient service. Attractively presented bar food includes good sandwiches (from £1.85, open prawn £4.10), very good soup (£3.10), ploughman's (£4.80), filled baked potatoes (from £4.75), ham and egg (£4.95), salads (from £5.25), vegetarian savoury nutburger (£5.55), steak and kidney pie (£5.90), beef stir-fry (£6.85), and rump steak (£7.25). A Roundhead cannon ball from the Civil War was found during restoration – it's on a shelf above a table in the restaurant area. *(Recommended by S Brackenbury, TBB, Lyn and Bill Capper, S M Rowland, W K Hyde, M L Clarke, Wayne Brindle, Helen Frewer, James Rowlatt)*

Whitbreads ~ Lease: Bill Farrell ~ Real ale ~ Meals and snacks (till 10pm) ~ Restaurant ~ Henley-on-Thames (01491) 571362 ~ Children in small bar area and in restaurant ~ Open 11-3, 5.30(6 Sat)-11

NORTHEND SU7392 Map 4

White Hart
On back road up escarpment from Watlington, past Christmas Common; or valley road off A4155 Henley—Marlow at Mill End, past Hambleden, Skirmett and Turville, then sharp left in Northend itself

Although the food in this cosy little 16th-c pub is very good indeed, you will be made just as welcome by the charming licensee if you only want a drink. The quiet but friendly bar has good log fires (one in a vast fireplace), some panelling, very low handsomely carved oak beams, and comfortable window seats. Bar food – all home-made – includes soup (£2.25), ploughman's with home-made pickles (£3.75), chicken in cointreau pâté or Greek salad (£3.95), pasta with tomato, mushroom, parmesan cheese, basil and cream (£5.25), beef in ale pie or lasagne (£5.25), curry (£5.95), roast duckling in a raspberry sauce (£8.50), and home-made puddings (from £2.50); daily specials like avocado, bacon and stilton salad (£5.25) or calf's liver with sage butter (£8.50); well kept Brakspears PA, SB, Old and Mild on handpump. Hatch service in summer to the lovely garden, which also has a children's play area. The pub is popular with walkers exploring the surrounding beechwoods. *(Recommended by Dave Carter, Mr and Mrs A Atkinson, Gordon, Mrs R J Wyse, Dr Gerald W Barnett, Andy Thwaites, Jeff and Rhoda Collins, Dr Julie Hilditch, John Sheffield)*

Brakspears ~ Tenant Andrew Hearn ~ Real ale ~ Meals and snacks (not Sun evening) ~ Henley-on-Thames (01491) 638353 ~ Children in eating area of bar ~ Open 11.30-2.30, 6(6.30 winter)-11

nr PRINCES RISBOROUGH SP8003 Map 4

Red Lion

Upper Icknield Way, Whiteleaf; village signposted off A4010 towards Aylesbury; OS Sheet 165 map reference 817040

On a quiet village lane at the foot of the Chilterns, this welcoming 17th-c pub has a friendly, local atmosphere in the well kept and pleasantly old-fashioned bar. There's a log fire, an alcove of antique winged settles, lots of sporting, coaching and ballooning prints on the walls, and quite a collection of antiques. Good bar food includes sandwiches (from £1.95), very tasty filled baked potatoes (from £2.25), excellent omelettes (from £3.50), home-made curry (£4.50), home-made lasagne or steak and kidney pie (£4.75), and weekday lunchtime home-made daily specials (from £2.50); a popular Sunday lunch. Well kept Brakspears PA, Hook Norton Best, Morlands PA and Wadworths 6X on handpump; cribbage and piped music. Outside there are tables in a small front lawn surrounded by colourful window boxes and hanging baskets, with more on a most attractive large back garden; the pub is close to Whiteleaf Fields (National Trust). *(Recommended by Steve Webb, Marianne Lantree, Lyn and Bill Capper, Tom and Rosemary Hall, D Carter)*

Free house ~ Licensee Richard Howard ~ Real ale ~ Meals and snacks ~ Resaurant ~ Princes Risborough (01844) 344476 ~ Children in restaurant and must be over 5 ~ Open 11.30-3, 5.30(6 Sat)-11 ~ Bedrooms: £29.50B/£39.50B

SKIRMETT SU7790 Map 2

Old Crown 🍺

High St; from A4155 NE of Henley take Hambleden turn and keep on; or from B482 Stokenchurch—Marlow take Turville turn and keep on

Although this charming early 18th-c village pub has placed a lot of emphasis on the very good, popular food, there's still a relaxed pubby atmosphere in the three rooms. The small central room and larger one leading off have Windsor chairs and tankards hanging from the beams, and the little no smoking white-painted tap room has trestle tables and an old-fashioned settle; also, three open fires (two inglenooks), lots of beams, and over 700 bric-a-brac items, paintings, antiques, bottles and tools. The home-made waitress-served food includes very good soup (£2.95), fricassee of mixed mushrooms (£4.50), chicken liver pâté (£4), lunchtime ploughman's (£4.25), filled baked potatoes (from £4.25), steak, kidney and mushroom pie (£7.35), medallions of pork in apricot brandy or poached Scotch salmon with prawn and dill sauce (£9.50), pan-fried Dutch calf's liver (£9.75), grilled fresh sea bass (£13.25), and giant prawns in garlic and butter (£14.50). In the evenings and at weekends it's a good idea to book a table. Well kept Brakspears PA and SB are tapped from casks in a still room, and served though a hatch; good value wine; dominoes, cribbage and trivia. A sheltered front terrace has flower tubs, and old oak casks as seats; the pretty garden has picnic-table sets under cocktail parasols, and a fish pond. Note that children under 10 are not allowed. There are two pub alsatians. *(Recommended by Barbara Houghton, P Saville, Chris Warne, Dave Carter, Mike Tucker, Mr and Mrs David Harvey, Gordon, A W Dickinson, Dr Gerald W Barnett, Pippa Bobbett, Howard Gatiss, G D and M D Craigen, Mr and Mrs David Harvey, Nigel Norman)*

Brakspears ~ Tenant Peter Mumby ~ Real ale ~ Meals and snacks (not Mon, except bank hols) ~ Restaurant ~ Turville Heath (01491) 638435 ~ Open 11-2.30, 6-11; closed Mon except bank hols

STOKE GREEN SU9882 Map 2

Red Lion

1 mile S of Stoke Poges; on B416 come to roundabout and turn right for Wexham; pub is on left; OS Sheet 175 map reference 986824

This friendly rambling 17th-c place was a former farmhouse for Stoke Place Manor and is covered by one of the oldest wisterias in the county. The main bar has robust high-backed settles forming alcoves, inglenook seats, lots of bric-a-brac, and well kept Bass and two guests such as Fullers London Pride or Wadworths 6X on handpump from a chest-high bar counter; winter mulled wine and summer punch. Good value, cheerfully served home-made bar food includes sandwiches (from £1.35), ploughman's with five different cheeses (from £2.95), salads (from £4.35), and daily-changing hot dishes like broccoli and brie bake (£3.95), lots of pasta dishes (from £3.95), steak and kidney or fish pie (£4.30), steaks (from £5.99), and puddings like fruit pies or bread and butter pudding (£1.95); the back Stables restaurant is connected to the main pub by a covered walkway. One room is no smoking; the chocolate labrador is called Toby; dominoes, cribbage, fruit machine and piped music. On the roundel of lawn in front of this attractive tiled house are picnic-table sets under cocktail parasols, with more on the sheltered back terrace where they hold summer barbecues. *(Recommended by Nick and Alison Dowson, T I G Gray, D Chafer, Helen Hazzard, Simon Collett-Jones)*

Bass ~ Managers Michael and Lyn Smith ~ Real ale ~ Meals and snacks (not Sun evening) ~ Restaurant; closed Sat lunchtime and Sun evening ~ Slough (01753) 521739 ~ Children in eating area of bar ~ Open 11-3(2.30 in winter), 5.30-11; 11-11 Fri and Sat

TURVILLE SU7690 Map 2

Bull & Butcher

Valley road off A4155 Henley—Marlow at Mill End, past Hambleden and Skirmett

A new licensee has taken over this pretty black-and-white timbered pub in its lovely wooded Chilterns valley. The comfortable and atmospheric low-ceilinged bar is partly divided into two areas, with beams from ships seized from the Spanish Armada, cushioned wall settles, and an old-fashioned high-backed settle by one log fire. Good bar food includes smoked salmon pâté (£3), popular ploughman's (£3.25), beef in ale pie (£5.25), genuine curries or chicken Dijon tarragon (£6.45), and home-made puddings. Well kept Brakspears PA, SB, Old and Mild on handpump, and good house wines; darts, shove-ha'penny, dominoes, cribbage and piped music. It's a fine place to finish a walk, and the attractive garden has tables on the lawn by fruit trees and a neatly umbrella-shaped hawthorn; there may be summer barbecues. Once a month (Tuesday evenings) the MG car club meets here. *(Recommended by Ron and Sheila Corbett, T R and B C Jenkins, Dave Carter, Gordon, David Warrellow, Barbara Houghton, Andy Thwaites, Julian and Sarah Stanton)*

Brakspears ~ Tenant Nicholas Abbott ~ Real ale ~ Meals and snacks (possibly not Sun evenings) ~ Turville Heath (01491) 638283 ~ Children in eating area of bar ~ Open 11-3, 6-11

WADDESDON SP747 Map 4

Five Arrows 🛏 � 🍾

A41 NW of Aylesbury

From the roadside this solid brick-built small hotel owned by Lord Rothschild gives no clue to the pleasant informality you find inside, and the very reasonable prices. One surprise is to find so much care taken over the condition of the four well kept real ales – Chiltern Beechwood, Fullers London Pride and an unusual guest such as Archers Old Cobleigh on handpump, with Tring Old Icknield in a jacketed keg on the bar counter. This is a handsome affair, carved with the five arrows of the Rothschild crest which symbolise the dispersal of the five founding sons of the international banking business; there are also family portrait engravings, and lots of old estate-worker photographs. The neat recently refurbished bar, usually uncrowded at least on weekdays, is an open-plan series of light and airy high-ceilinged rooms, most with solid upright pub furnishings on parquet flooring but one with comfortably worn-in armchairs and settees. The regular bar menu includes staples such as sandwiches (from £2.25), burgers (£3.95) salads like home-cooked ham or grilled goat's cheese (from £3.75) and vegetarian stir-fry (£4.95) or french onion tart (£5.25), but the highlights tend to be found among the wide choice of daily-changing specials: on our early summer inspection including a hearty leek and potato soup (£2.50), rollmop or melon with strawberries (£3.50), asparagus (£3.95), spaghetti with pesto (£4.95), a very well flavoured game casserole (£6.95) and plump grilled scallops on a very fresh and pretty salad (£7.50); there are good puddings (£2.95). Besides a formidable wine list that naturally runs to Rothschild first-growth clarets, wines by the glass include excellent and often intriguingly unusual bargains as well as altogether less well known Rothschild estate wines such as Los Vascos Chilean cabernet sauvignon. Other drinks including many malt whiskies are exemplary. Friendly efficient service, unobtrusive piped pop music. The spacious sheltered back garden has attractively grouped wood and metal furnishings, with some weekend and bank holiday barbecues. *(Recommended by Margaret and Ron Erlick, Richard Ames, C Fletcher)*

Free house ~ Licensees Terry Jackson and Gaynor Hitchcock ~ Real ale ~ Meals and snacks ~ Waddesdon (01296) 651727 ~ Children welcome ~ Open 11-11 in summer; 11-3.30, 5.30-11 in winter ~ Bedrooms: £50B/£65B

WEST WYCOMBE SU8394 Map 4

George & Dragon
London Rd; A40 W of High Wycombe

There's a good old-fashioned atmosphere in the comfortable and rambling main bar of this striking 15th-c building, as well as massive beams, sloping walls, and a big log fire; the magnificent oak staircase is said to be haunted by a wronged girl. Popular bar food includes home-made soup (£1.75), ploughman's (from £2.95), sandwiches (from £3.25; toasties from £1.50), herby mushrooms (£3.45), macaroni and broccoli cheese (£3.65), very good home-made pies like sole and grape, chicken and asparagus or duck, pigeon and orange pies (from £5.25), beef curry (£5.55), 12oz sirloin steak (£9.95), and home-made puddings (from £1.95). Courage Best and Directors and a guest beer on handpump, decent wine list, and quite a few malt whiskies. The arched and cobbled coach entry leads to a spacious, peaceful garden with picnic-table sets, a climbing frame and slides. It gets crowded at weekends – so it's best to get there early for a seat. The pub is on *Good Walks Guide* Walk 70. Nearby you can visit West Wycombe Park with its fine furnishings and classical landscaped grounds. *(Recommended by TBB, Simon Collett-Jones, Clifford Payton, Barbara Houghton, Dr Andrew Brookes, Barbara Hatfield, George Atkinson, Steve Webb, Marianne Lantree, Chris Warne, Paul and Margaret Baker, Dr D C Deeing, R J Saunders, P and J Roberts, Nigel Norman)*

Courage ~ Lease: Philip Todd ~ Real ale ~ Meals and snacks (12-2, 6-9.30) ~ High Wycombe (01494) 464414 ~ Children in room set aside for them ~ Open 11-2.30, 5.30-11; 11-11 Sat ~ Bedrooms: £40B/£50B

WHITCHURCH SP8020 Map 4

White Swan ★
10 High Street; A413 Aylesbury—Buckingham

As we went to press, the Tuckers warned us that there was a risk they might be giving up the tenancy here before the end of 1994, and that they would definitely have left by May 1995. The pub's main entry and star do depend very much on them – so we are keeping our fingers crossed that by publication date there will still be at least a few months in which to enjoy their time here. There are two relaxed and comfortable bars with chunky elm tables, a few very old leather dining chairs and a carved Gothick settle in the oddly shaped saloon bar, seats built into squared honey-coloured oak panelling below a delft shelf, a longcase clock, fresh flowers, and a small open fire; Charlie the labrador or TC and Pi the cats will probably be there to greet you. Good value, tasty bar food includes a huge choice of sandwiches or french bread rolls (from £1.10; toasties from £1.20, triple deckers from £2), egg and chips (£1.70), lots of ploughman's (from £3.25), salads (from £3.75, ham and peach £5.25, mixed seafood £6.25), a variety of good omelettes (from £3.50), breakfast grill (£4.50), vegetable lasagne (£5), steak and kidney pie (£5.25), evening rump steak (£8), and a good choice of puddings; courteous and helpful service. Well kept Fullers ESB and London Pride on handpump, quite a few whiskies, and cheap help-yourself coffee; sensibly placed darts, shove-ha'penny, dominoes, cribbage and piped music. Behind the pub, a rambling informal garden has picnic-table sets under trees. *(Recommended by Janet Pickles, Mr and Mrs A Varnom, Dr and Mrs Rackow, Pat and Derek Westcott, TBB, George Atkinson, Lyn and Bill Capper, Mick and Mel Smith, M J Ridgway)*

Fullers ~ Tenants Rex and Janet Tucker ~ Real ale ~ Meals and snacks (12-2, 6-9.45; not Sun evening or bank hol evenings) ~ Restaurant ~ Aylesbury (01296) 641228 ~ Children in restaurant ~ Open 11-2.30, 6-11; closed Sun evenings

WORMINGHALL SP6308 Map 4

Clifden Arms

4½ miles from M40 junction 8: B4011 to Oakley off A41 S of Bicester, then minor rd to Worminghall and Wheatley; or from Oxford bypass (A4142) take minor rd to Wheatley and Worminghall

There have been a few changes to this very pretty pub since the welcoming new licensees took over – with more to come in early 1995. The lovely flower-filled garden with its ancient pump and well has been opened up, and the big children's play area with slides, log fort and so forth, has been safely railed-off from the car park; there are picnic-table sets in the orchard. Inside, one little room (which will eventually become the public bar) has had a partition-wall removed and an upright beam put back to create more space, old-fashioned seats, squint-timbered ochre walls, and a roaring log fire in the big fireplace. Hanging from the heavy beams is quite a forest of interesting bottles, brass powder-flasks, milk-yokes, black iron vices and tools. On the left, the beamed room (which will become the lounge bar) has a second fire (gas). A restaurant is to be opened up as well. Bar food includes sandwiches (from £1.65), filled baked potatoes (from £2.75), ploughman's (£3.50), all day breakfast (£3.50), salads or curries (from £4.50), potato, cheese and leek bake (£4.95), steak and kidney pie (£5.25), and daily specials like seafood creole, marinated chicken or game casserole (all under £9.95). Well kept Adnams Broadside, Bass, Fullers ESB and London Pride, Hook Norton and a guest beer every two weeks on handpump; Addlestones cider. Darts, dominoes and piped music. They have an active Aunt Sally team, weekend barbecues, and outside events like jazz or blues bands and Morris dancers. The picturesque village has almshouses built in 1675, and the Norman church has a 15th-c tower and 14th-c chancel. Nearby Waterperry Gardens are worth a visit. *(Recommended by Michael Sargent, Marjorie and David Lamb, Martin Jones, Simon Collet-Jones, Helen Hazzard, Gordon Smith, Alan Skull, Martin Richardson)*

Free house ~ Licensee Mick Gilbert ~ Real ale ~ Meals and snacks (11.30-2, 6.30-9.30) ~ Restaurant ~ Ickford (01844) 339273 ~ Children welcome ~ Open 11.30-2.30(3 Sat), 6.30-11; winter evening opening 7

Lucky Dip

Besides the fully inspected pubs, you might like to try these Lucky Dips recommended to us and described by readers (if you do, please send us reports):

☆ **Adstock** [Verney Junction, Addington – OS Sheet 165 map reference 737274; SP7327], *Verney Arms:* Tucked-away country inn with settees and motley furniture rather like private house, pictures, memorabilia, lots of local books, games inc Scrabble, warmly welcoming landlord with wickedly dry sense of humour, friendly labrador, good carefully presented bar food inc imaginative continental and spicy dishes, real ales such as Hook Norton Old Hookey; bedrooms *(George Atkinson)*

☆ **Akeley** [The Square; just off A413; SP7037], *Bull & Butcher:* Very good value lunchtime buffet (maybe only cold food; not Sun) inc wide range of help-yourself salads, several puddings, also evening steak bar (not Sun or Mon); three good fires in long open-plan beamed bar with red plush banquettes, well kept Fullers London Pride, Marstons Pedigree, Morlands Original and a guest beer, decent house wines, winter spiced wine, traditional games; children allowed in eating area, tables in attractive garden with notable flower beds and hanging baskets, occasional live entertainment; handy for Stowe Gardens *(Marjorie and David Lamb, Michael Sargent, Janet Pickles, JJW, CMW, LYM)*

☆ **Amersham** [High St, Old Town (A413); SU9597], *Kings Arms:* Wonderfully picturesque old building in charming street, lots of timbers, heavy beams and snug alcoves, big inglenook, high-backed antique settles and other quaint old furnishings (but rather too many stools), big inglenook; low-priced bar food inc vegetarian, restaurant, pleasant service, well kept Allied ales with a guest such as Tring Ridgeway, children in eating area; open all day, rather a young person's pub evening; nice garden *(E G Parish, Rosemary and Brian Wilmot, Ian Phillips)*

☆ **Amersham** [High St], *Eagle:* Friendly low-beamed old town pub, wide choice of good straightforward lunchtime food (not Sun) from sandwiches up inc good fish fresh daily (get there early or book); friendly, efficient service, Allied real ales with a guest beer, log fire, maybe soft piped music, fruit machine; more lively young person's pub evenings *(Lyn and Bill Capper, Wayne Brindle)*

Amersham [High St], *Elephant & Castle:* Popular and attractive food pub with low beams, china, velvet, brasses, fine U-shaped bar counter, piped music, well kept Morrells *(Steve Goodchild, LYM)*

☆ **Ashendon** [Lower End; between A41 and A418 W of Aylesbury; SP7014], *Red Lion:* Good interesting food (no sandwiches), well kept Adnams, Badger, Wadworths IPA and 6X and a monthly guest beer, decent range of wines, comfortable and well kept

bar, piped music; closed Sun evenings except bank hols and all day Mon; tables outside with pleasant views, children allowed at meal times; two comfortable bedrooms *(Lyn and Bill Capper)*

Asheridge [SP9404], *Blue Ball:* Good atmosphere in country pub, busy and lively weekends (no food Sun – good other times), well kept real ales, good play area; piped music *(MD)*

☆ **Aston Clinton** [SP8712], *Oak:* Good Fullers pub, attractively refurbished, big helpings of good food, decent wine list, no music or machines, obliging service *(Stephen King, Martin Kay, Andrea Fowler)*

Aston Clinton [Weston Rd], *Rothschild Arms:* Genuine local with friendly staff, lively dog and well kept Allied beers *(Dr and Mrs A K Clarke)*

☆ **Astwood** [off A422; SP9547], *Swan:* Refurbished and reopened 1993, attractive, clean, airy and spacious, furnishings traditional yet modern; well kept beers such as Federation and Thwaites, wine or port by the jug, good bar food esp pies, warm cosy atmosphere, friendly staff; shame about the piped music; side garden bar *(O J W Hunkin, Stephen G Brown, Mrs R Horridge, LYM)*

Aylesbury [1 Wendover Rd; A413 one-way; SP8213], *Aristocrat:* Well kept Fullers and good value food all day lunchtime onwards Tues-Sat, with afternoon break Mon, in neat and cosy pub with good service *(Mike Pugh)*

☆ nr **Aylesbury** [Gibraltar; A418 some miles towards Thame, beyond Stone – OS Sheet 165 map reference 758108; SP7501], *Bottle & Glass:* Low-beamed thatched pub doing very well under current tenant (same as Boot at Barnard Gate, Oxon), with attractively individual layout, wide choice of good imaginative food inc vegetarian dishes, warm and friendly atmosphere; Tetleys and Wadworths 6X tapped from the cask, neat garden *(Michael Sargent, LYM)*

☆ **Beaconsfield** [Windsor End; SU9490], *Greyhound:* Good bar food (same in bar and restaurant) and well kept Courage Best, Fullers London Pride and Wadworths 6X in pleasant and cosy coaching inn with good atmosphere, polite service *(Dr Gerald W Barnett, R Houghton)*

Beaconsfield [London rd], *Royal Saracens Head:* Perhaps most notable for its striking timbered façade; a bit too opened-up inside, but massive beams and timbers in one corner, a good atmosphere, well kept real ale, useful steak bar, attractive sheltered courtyard *(Graham and Belinda Staplehurst, LYM)*

☆ **Bourne End** [Hedsor Rd – former Old Red Lion; SU8985], *Masons:* Cheap bar lunches (good sandwiches and filled baked potatoes) and well kept Fullers in friendly and cosy local with pleasantly simple furnishings inc good plain wooden tables; piped music, two pool tables in separate annexe, fruit machines and juke box; must book evening restaurant (not Mon); tables outside, but traffic noise *(Simon Collett-Jones, Dr Gerald W Barnett, TBB, BB)*

Bourne End [Kiln Lane], *Chequers:* Lovely setting, well kept Eldridge Pope and good restaurant; good bedrooms inc 4-posters *(Mr and Mrs M J Martin)*

☆ **Brill** [Windmill St; SP6513], *Sun:* Cosy and welcoming village pub, pleasantly refurbished but unpretentious, with wide range of good food in bar and restaurant (butcher landlord), well kept beers *(Ian Phillips, N and J Strathdee)*

Bryants Bottom [4 miles N of High Wycombe; SU8599], *Gate:* Pleasant country pub with big basic bar (popular with walkers and cyclists) and comfortable and nicely furnished beamed lounge; wide range of food inc very cheap bar snacks, well kept beers, tables outside; no piped music *(Lyn and Bill Capper, Helen Hazzard)*

Buckingham [SP6933], *Whale:* Good Fullers pub, worth knowing in this relative pub desert *(Martin Kay, Andrea Fowler)*

☆ **Cadmore End** [B482 towards Stokenchurch; SU7892], *Blue Flag:* Old-fashioned beamed pub attached to small modern hotel, wide choice of good interesting generous food at most attractive prices, lots of proper big tables for comfortable eating; well kept changing real ales such as Fullers London Pride, Morlands Old Speckled Hen, Luxters Old Barn and Wadworths 6X, decent wines, good atmosphere, expert unobtrusive service, fascinating vintage MG pictures in side room; attractive little restaurant; bedrooms *(D C Bail, DJW, S J Patrick, Dr Gerald W Barnett, Mr and Mrs A Noke, BB)*

Cadmore End [B482], *Old Ship:* Tiny country local set back so that little more than the roof is visible from the road; two basic unspoilt bars, friendly unhurried atmosphere, well kept beers inc Brakspears brought up from the cellar on a tray; in same family – and unaltered – for decades *(Pete Baker)*

Chalfont St Giles [London Rd (A413) at junction with Pheasant Hill – continuation of High St; SU9893], *Pheasant:* Beams, cosy atmosphere, big garden with play area and summer barbecues, Tetleys and Greene King ales; has had good range of reasonably priced home-made food and good service, but no news yet of new licensees *(Lyn and Bill Capper)*

☆ **Cheddington** [Station Rd; by stn, about a mile from village; SP9218], *Rosebery Arms:* Very comfortable lounge with sofas by roaring log fire, pubbier seats by servery, old photographs on panelled walls, smart restaurant with no smoking area; good lunchtime food from sandwiches to

imaginative and original main courses, wide evening choice, Badger, Charles Wells Eagle and Bombardier, friendly service, piped music (turned down on request), well spaced picnic-table sets on back lawn with play equipment and Wendy house *(Michael Sandy)*

Cheddington [Station Rd], *Duke of Wellington:* Quiet but pleasant, with good generous food and special weekday rate for OAPs *(Graham and Karen Oddey, Margaret and Trevor Errington)*

☆ **Chesham** [Church St/Wey Lane; SP9501], *Queens Head:* Though extended, still small, cosy and friendly, full of interesting pictures and paraphernalia, and smart as a new pin, with coal fires in both fireplaces, scrubbed tables and sparkling brass; well kept Brakspears PA, SB and Old and Fullers London Pride, pleasant staff, friendly locals; tables in small courtyard *(DJW, Helen Hazzard)*

☆ **nr Chesham** [Chesham Vale – back rd to Hawridge, Berkhamsted and Tring, off A416 as you leave centre], *Black Horse:* Big helpings of good value straightforward food inc lots of good speciality home-made pies and now unusual sausages in quietly set and neatly extended country pub with black beams and joists, book-lined converted barn, exceptionally punctilious staff, well kept Allied ales and guests such as Adnams and Tring Ridgeway, unobtrusive piped music, lots of well spaced tables outside *(Paul Coleman, Nigel Norman, Helen Hazzard, LYM)*

☆ **Chicheley** [A422; quite handy for M1 junction 14; SP9045], *Chester Arms:* Cosy two-bar beamed pub, spotless and pretty after refurbishment, with log fire, comfortable settles and chairs, wide choice of generous and well presented home-made bar food from sandwiches to full meals, inc vegetarian dishes and children's helpings, friendly service, Greene King Abbot, darts, fruit machine, quiet piped music; sizeable evening restaurant, picnic-table sets in garden *(Paul and Maggie Baker, George Atkinson)*

☆ **Clifton Reynes** [no through road; off back rd Emberton—Newton Blossomville; SP9051], *Robin Hood:* Small friendly local with two attractive bars, nice conservatory and big garden, almost a field, with picnic-table sets, chickens and barbecue, leading to riverside walk from Olney; old dark beams, brasses, horns, inglenook and newspapers in lounge; open fire, table skittles and juke box in public bar; well kept Greene King, decent food (not Mon evening), no children inside *(Andrew Roberts)*

☆ **Colnbrook** [1¼ miles from M4 junction 5 via A4/B3378, 'then village only' rd; TQ0277], *Ostrich:* Striking Elizabethan pub with long and entertaining history, skilfully modernised to keep its old-fashioned character; good open fire, reasonably priced bar food, real ale, friendly service, restaurant *(Dr Andrew Brookes, LYM)*

Colnbrook [High St; nr M4 junction 5], *Olde George:* Very old coaching inn, lots of photographs of old Colnbrook, pleasant newish licensees, good food esp home-made pies, Courage-related ales, friendly atmosphere; upstairs restaurant *(Dr Andrew Brookes)*

Cuddington [village signposted from A418 Thame—Aylesbury; SP7311], *Crown:* Small and cosy, open fire, friendly service, interesting and unusual choice of good food, Fullers ESB, London Pride and Chiswick on handpump *(Nigel Pritchard)*

☆ **Denham** [¾ mile from M40 junction 1; follow Denham Village signs; TQ0486], *Swan:* Pretty pub in lovely village setting, comfortable inside, with friendly service, real ales, decent straightforward bar food inc tempting puddings, open fires, good atmosphere; big floodlit garden behind with play house *(Mark J Hydes, TBB, Martin and Jane Bailey, Helen Hazzard, LYM)*

Denham, *Falcon:* Open-plan but cosy and traditional with inglenook fireside seats; well kept Marstons Pedigree and Morlands Old Speckled Hen, good lunchtime bar food, friendly welcome *(Mr and Mrs M J Martin)*

☆ **Dorney** [Village Rd; SU9278], *Palmer Arms:* Efficient modern-style dining pub with lots of young staff, wide choice of above-average food inc good fish and skillet dishes, decent wine list, interesting well kept real ales; plenty of tables in pleasant garden *(C J Parsons, MMD)*

Downley [OS Sheet 165 map reference 849959; SU8594], *Le De Spencer:* Unpretentious Fullers pub hidden away on common, fairy-lit loggia overlooking lawn, friendly landlord, bar snacks *(Martin Kay, Andrea Fowler, LYM)*

Dunsmore [a mile off A413 Wendover—Gt Missenden – OS Sheet 165 map reference 862054; SP8605], *Fox:* Tucked-away Chilterns village pub with interesting old-fashioned garden, very good reasonably priced food; handy for good walks *(Gethin Lewis, LYM)*

Farnham Royal [Blackpond Lane; SU9583], *Emperor of India:* Small and pleasant open-plan pub with well kept garden and barn for summer eating, friendly landlord and wife, good food inc fresh fish, Whitbreads-related and a guest ale *(B E West)*

☆ **Flackwell Heath** [3½ miles from M40 junction 4; A404 towards High Wycombe, 1st right to Flackwell Heath, right into Sheepridge Lane; SU8988], *Crooked Billet:* Old-fashioned pub in lovely country setting, pleasant garden with quiet views, good value food, real ale *(Helen Hazzard, BB)*

☆ **Gayhurst** [B526; SP8446], *Sir Francis Drake:* Unusual Gothick traceried and pinnacled building, cosy and rather intimate inside, with good value home-made food inc some unusual dishes, very

friendly landlord, helpful staff, well kept real ales inc Fullers ESB, Mansfield and Wadworths Farmers Glory, good range of spirits; tables in small sheltered garden *(George Atkinson, LYM)*

Gerrards Cross [Packhorse Rd – OS Sheet 176 map reference 003885; TQ0088], *Packhorse:* Good honest pub worth knowing despite the loud music for good big helpings of attractively priced food *(Mr and Mrs J Back)*

☆ **Great Hampden** [corner of Hampden Common – OS Sheet 165 map reference 845015; SP8401], *Hampden Arms:* Good choice of outstanding freshly cooked food, charming efficient service, lovely location with good walks nearby, tables in sizeable and attractive peaceful garden (no swings and slides) by cricket-green common; cosy rather than distinguished inside, with big sensible tables in two small but friendly and comfortable rooms, very civilised and relaxed – they take bookings; real ales inc Greene King IPA and Abbot and Tetleys, efficient young licensees; well placed for walkers *(Margaret Drazin, R A Buckler, Chris Cook, BKA)*

Great Kimble [Risborough Rd (A4010); SP8206], *Bernard Arms:* Popular upmarket pub with wide choice of excellent imaginative bar food, four changing real ales, games room, well kept gardens, interesting food in restaurant ; six bedrooms with own bathrooms *(J W Joseph)*

Great Kingshill [A4128; SU8798], *Red Lion:* Small traditional two-roomed stone dining pub with good choice of wines, three real ales on handpump, freshly squeezed orange juice, young friendly landlord; good food inc lots of fish fresh daily from Billingsgate – with good chips *(Joseph Williams)*

☆ **Great Linford** [4½ miles from M1, junction 14; from Newport Pagnell take Wolverton Rd towards Stony Stratford; SP8542], *Black Horse:* Large rambling pub with good range of good value food inc pastas and help-yourself salads, well kept Allied and guest beers, friendly staff, good pubby atmosphere, upstairs restaurant; just below Grand Union Canal – drinks can be taken out on the towpath (good walks along here), and sizeable lawn with well spaced picnic-table sets and biggish play area; children allowed away from bar *(Michael, Alison and Rhiannon Sandy, Bob Riley, LYM)*

☆ **Great Missenden** [London Rd; old London rd, E – beyond Abbey; SP8901], *Nags Head:* Good straightforward food from sandwiches to wide choice of main dishes served quickly in cosy creeper-covered small pub; well kept Allied and guest real ales, big log fire, no piped music, picnic-table sets on back lawn; the dog's called Charlie *(John Waller)*

Great Missenden [Mobwell], *Black Horse:* Next to fields from which hot-air balloons take off in suitable conditions, nice garden, pleasant food, lots of photographs of balloons on walls *(Jane Greening)*

☆ **Haddenham** [Church End; SP7408], *Green Dragon:* Emphasis on good helpings of home-cooked food (not Sun evenings) in spacious and pleasantly decorated 17th-c pub nr village green and duck pond; well kept Marstons or Wadworths, decent house wines, attentive service, log fire, tables in quiet walled garden *(David Pither and others)*

Hawridge [The Vale; signed from A416 N of Chesham – OS Sheet 165 map reference 960050; SP9505], *Rose & Crown:* Wide choice of good value bar food, half a dozen or more real ales, quick welcoming service and big log fire in spacious open-plan bar, broad terrace with lawn dropping down beyond giving peaceful country views, play area; children allowed *(LYM)*

☆ **Hawridge Common** [off A416 N of Chesham; then towards Cholesbury; SP9505], *Full Moon:* Pretty and very popular little country pub with snugly comfortable low-beamed rambling bar and spacious common-edge lawn, with good friendly service by cheerful young staff, good choice of very reasonably priced food, wide choice of well kept real ales *(Nick Dowson, S T Whitaker, Rhoda and Jeff Collins, LYM)*

☆ **Hedgerley** [SE of M40 junction 2; SU9686], *White Horse:* Quaint and attractive old country local in immaculate village, small bar and larger lounge, up to seven well kept changing beers tapped from the cask inc ones from smaller independent brewers, relaxed atmosphere, very friendly service, good lunchtime sandwiches, ploughman's and a hot dish, limited evening snacks, occasional barbecues in pleasant back garden *(Julian and Sarah Stanton, Nick and Alison Dowson, Andrew Stephenson, Richard Houghton)*

☆ **Hedgerley** [One Pin Lane, towards Gerrards X; OS Sheet 175 map reference 968863], *One Pin:* Very much a family-run local, with good friendly atmosphere, Courage-related ales, log fires, decent food and well kept garden *(Nick and Alison Dowson, Cindy and Chris Crow)*

High Wycombe [Frogmore (A4128); SU8792], *Bell:* Useful for the area, with well kept Fullers *(Martin Kay, Andrea Fowler)*

Hyde Heath [Hyde Heath Rd; village signposted off B485 Great Missenden—Chesham; SU9399], *Plough:* Prettily placed homely and friendly village pub with three good real ales, good home-cooked food at reasonable prices, very cosy atmosphere *(Andrew Jollie, LYM)*

☆ **Ibstone** [follow signs for Ibstone from M40; SU7593], *Fox:* Good M40 recovery point, in attractive rural surroundings, with generous helpings of decent bar food (not cheap) inc good sandwiches, children's dishes and good home-made puddings, well kept real ales such as Brakspears, Tetleys and Luxters Old Barn, good range of wines

and some other rather upmarket trappings, polite service, restaurant, pleasant garden; can be busy on sunny days; comfortable bedrooms *(John Radford, Nigel Norman, Marjorie and David Lamb, Mark J Hydes, Mr and Mrs J W Allan, Duncan Redpath, Mark Whitmore, Peter Watkins, Pam Stanley, John Watson, David Wright, Sharon Hancock, LYM)*

☆ **Iver** [TQ0381], *Gurkha:* Gurkha paintings and trophies in pleasant sizeable bar, good intimate and individual atmosphere; ample helpings of consistently good home-cooked food, wide choice in big restaurant, over-60s club, friendly staff and locals *(Len and Fran Shaw)*

Iver Heath [Slough rd; TQ0282], *Black Horse:* Two-part bar with eating area, good mix of customers and pleasantly bustling atmosphere, service very pleasant, five real ales, mostly from smaller brewers; conservatory, garden *(Richard Houghton)*; [Swallow St], *Whip & Collar:* Small, friendly and relaxing, with pleasant landlord and well kept Courage Best *(Richard Houghton)*

Kingswood [A41; SP6919], *Crooked Billet:* Warm, welcoming and lively, with well kept Greene King, decent food, books and papers *(Tim and Ann Newell)*

Lacey Green [SP8201], *Whip:* Helpful and friendly service, Boddingtons ales, decent range of food in bar and light and airy dining area; garden *(Nigel Pritchard)*

☆ **Lane End** [B482 Marlow—Stokenchurch; SU7991], *Old Sun:* Wide choice of good value bar food (not Sun or Mon evenings) in nicely laid out and refitted old pub with winter log fires, well kept Whitbreads-related real ales, pleasant staff, unobtrusive piped music, pretty garden; children welcome unless too busy *(LYM)*

Little Kingshill [Hare La; SU8999], *Full Moon:* Picturesque pub doing well under new management, revitalising the food side; nice gardens *(J D T Andrews)*

☆ **Little Marlow** [Sheepridge Lane; off A4155 at Well End about 2 miles E of Marlow; SU8786], *Crooked Billet:* Pretty little low-beamed pub with lovely flower-filled garden and pleasant views; good choice of lunchtime food (not Sun), friendly and efficient service, well kept Brakspears and Whitbreads, good welcoming atmosphere, comfortable seating with separate eating area *(Richard Houghton, TBB)*

Little Marlow [Church Rd; pub signed off main rd], *Kings Head:* Cosy and ancient flower-covered free house with emphasis on good food in lounge bar, friendly landlord, four or five real ales inc Wadworths and Whitbreads *(Comus Elliott)*

☆ **Little Missenden** [signed off A413 W of Amersham; SU9298], *Crown:* Friendly, unspoilt old country local in same family for 80 years, spotless small bar with coal fires at each end, harness, farm tools, guns and old prints; well kept Hook Norton Best, Marstons Pedigree and Morrells

Varsity, cheerful, friendly landlord, good sandwiches and simple bar lunches, nice big flower-filled back garden with hatch service and country views – attractive and interesting village; very popular *(Ron and Val Broom, Julian and Sarah Stanton, DJW, Simon Collett-Jones, John Waller)*

Little Missenden, *Red Lion:* Pleasant and popular country pub with Allied beers and Wadworths 6X, good value bar sandwiches, garden being developed with children in mind – ducks and geese *(Julian and Sarah Stanton)*

☆ **Little Tingewick** [Mere Lane – off A421/B4031 SW of Buckingham; SP6432], *Red Lion:* Big divided bar and small dining area, piped Sibelius, well kept Fullers beers, wide choice of good bar food inc vegetarian, pleasant friendly staff *(George Atkinson, Martin Kay, Andrea Fowler)*

☆ **Long Crendon** [Bicester Rd (B4011); SP6808], *Angel:* More restaurant than pub, and not really a place for just a drink, but well worth knowing for good fresh well prepared food, esp fish, not cheap but good value and generous; partly 17th-c, stylishly refurbished, warm and clean, with conservatory dining room, friendly young staff, well kept Brakspears and Marstons Pedigree *(Michael Sargent, B R Shiner, Marjorie and David Lamb)*

☆ **Long Crendon** [Bicester Rd (B4011)], *Chandos Arms:* Handsome thatched pub with cheerful local atmosphere, tasty well presented food, log fire, real ales such as Fullers, Morrells and Whitbreads, pleasant low-beamed communicating bars, lots of brass and copper, friendly efficient service *(Marjorie and David Lamb, Tim and Ann Newell)*

Long Crendon, *Hen & Chicken:* Restaurant pub run with style and vigour; extensive choice of beautifully cooked food inc char-grills, in big helpings, well kept real ale; very busy weekends *(A M Pickup)*

☆ **Ludgershall** [off A41 Aylesbury—Bicester; SP6617], *Bull & Butcher:* Quiet little gently refurbished country pub with interesting collection of china jugs hanging from beams, good range of meals inc good well chosen meats and steaks served in bar or back dining room (where children allowed); efficient friendly service, unobtrusive piped music, front lawn facing green *(Marjorie and David Lamb, N and J Strathdee)*

☆ **Marlow** [St Peter St; first right off Station Rd from double roundabout; SU8586], *Two Brewers:* Good food served promptly even when very busy in attractive recently redecorated low-beamed bar with shiny black woodwork, nautical pictures, gleaming brassware, polite staff and Whitbreads-related real ales; sheltered back courtyard, glimpse of Thames from front benches; some concentration on restaurant (children allowed here if not too busy), piped music; parking nearby – a special bonus for Marlow *(TBB, Mrs S Smith, MJH, LYM)*

☆ **Marlow** [West St (A4155)], *Ship:* Fine collection of closely packed warship photographs and nautical equipment in low-beamed town local's small side-by-side bars, straightfoward bar lunches from sandwiches upwards, well kept Whitbreads-related real ales, good friendly service, piped music, tables on pleasant little back terrace, evening restaurant (children allowed here) *(John and Karen Day, LYM)*

☆ **Marlow** [Quoiting Sq, Oxford Rd], *Clayton Arms:* Classic unspoilt town pub with long-serving licensee, well kept Brakspears, welcoming atmosphere, motley collection of furnishings in tiny snug and bigger public bar with darts, cribbage and dominoes – no music, machines or food *(Pete Baker)*

☆ **Marsworth** [Vicarage Rd; village signed off B489 Dunstable—Aylesbury; SP9214], *Red Lion:* Good atmosphere in low-beamed partly thatched simple and unfussy old pub with well kept real ales inc Bass, Hook Norton Best and Wadworths 6X, decent wines, interesting, varied, good value food from doorstep sandwiches up inc real vegetarian food and particularly good curries, tiled-floor main bar with basic traditional furnishings, two open fires and lively games area, steps up to cosy parlour; friendly service; tables in front, and in small sheltered butterfly-friendly back garden; children in games area until 8.30; not far from impressive flight of canal locks *(Michael, Alison and Rhiannon Sandy, Russell and Margaret Bathie, Mrs M Lawrence, LYM)*

☆ **Marsworth** [Startops End (B489)], *White Lion:* Comfortably plush modernised pub notable for position by Grand Union Canal (pleasant walk from above entry), nicely planted garden with lily pond, and terrace with picnic-table sets; dining bar, small restaurant, well kept Greene King and guest ales, efficient polite service, good-sized children's room, unobtrusive piped music *(Sidney and Erna Wells)*

☆ **Mentmore** [SP9119], *Stag:* Small civilised lounge bar with low oak tables, attractive fresh flower arrangements, open fire; restaurant and public bar leading off; good value well presented bar food from sandwiches to main dishes, with wider evening choice; well kept Charles Wells Eagle, polite well dressed staff, charming sloping garden *(Maysie Thompson, BB)*

☆ **Milton Keynes** [Broughton Rd, Old Village; SP8938], *Swan:* Fine old thatched pub, rebuilt and extended after a fire some 20 years ago; big and spacious with big but cosy dining area, inglenook fireplace, dark beams, no smoking area; Boddingtons, Courage Best and Marstons Pedigree, vast choice of good if not cheap food inc vegetarian, generous helpings, attractive furnishings, very friendly attentive service, maybe piped pop music; popular with businesspeople lunchtime; picnic-table sets in back garden, footpaths to nearby lakes *(George Atkinson, Prof John White, Mrs*

Patricia White, Bob Riley)

Milton Keynes [Bradwell Common Bvd; SP8339], *Countryman:* Popular estate pub with half a dozen or more well kept changing real ales, reasonably priced home-cooked food, big back conservatory *(Bob Riley)*; [Woodstone; SP8938], *Cross Keys:* Thatched pub not over-modernised in untouched corner of an original village, well kept Charles Wells Eagle, bar snacks lifted out of the ordinary by good French-type bread baked here *(John C Baker)*

Naphill [100 Main Rd; SU8497], *Wheel:* Friendly old beamed local, pleasant garden with play area, inexpensive food, well kept beers *(DH)*

New Bradwell [2 Bradwell Rd; SP8341], *New Inn:* Cheerful busy pub by Grand Union canal, with lots of canal photographs and watercolours; competent food, particularly well kept Charles Wells Bombardier, Eagle and one or two guests *(John C Baker)*

New Denham [TQ0485], *Nine Stiles:* Well kept beer, plentiful sensibly priced good food, enthusiastic staff *(Mr and Mrs C Holmes)*

Newport Pagnell [SP8743], *Bull:* Really welcoming local with good plain food, wide range of real ales such as Hook Norton Best, Morlands Old Speckled Hen and Ruddles, softly lit low-ceilinged bar and lounge decorated with front pages on famous events; daily papers too; bedrooms *(Ian Phillips)*; [High St], *Dolphin:* Large pub just off town centre with Youngs Special and good coffee; very neat and comfortable with carpeted lounge, beams, piped music and good service; fruit machine *(George Atkinson)*

Newton Longville [Whaddon Rd; Westbrook End; SP8431], *Crooked Billet:* Good food and well kept beer in cool thatched half-timbered inn on the edge of council estate; Hook Norton and Tetleys beers *(Ian Phillips)*

Olney [Mkt Pl; SP8851], *Bull:* Spacious well placed pub, HQ of the town's famous Shrove Tuesday pancake race; food servery with good choice at one end, Charles Wells and other real ales such as Morlands Old Speckled Hen and Wadworths 6X, nice coffee, log-effect gas fires, very friendly chatty landlord *(George Atkinson)*

☆ **Penn** [Witheridge Lane; SU9193], *Crown:* Friendly and relaxed Country Carvery dining pub open all day, perched on high ridge with distant views, particularly attractive gardens with good play area; three low-ceilinged refurbished bars, one with medieval flooring tiles; weekend barbecues, well kept Courage-related ales, friendly service; popular at lunchtime with businessmen; children in eating areas *(Caroline Wright, LYM)*

Penn, *Horse & Jockey:* Good range of promptly served daily changing bar food, most home-made, good beers *(Dr Gerald Barnett)*

☆ **Penn Street** [SU9295], *Hit or Miss:* Comfortably modernised low-beamed, three-room pub with own cricket ground, good cricket memorabilia and interesting display of traditional local chair-bodging work; welcoming new landlord has introduced good choice of real ales; some emphasis on decent bar food (special diet needs accommodated), open fire, no piped music or machines, occasional live music *(Dave Carter, N E Bushby, W Atkins, D G Clarke, LYM)*

Penn Street, *Squirrel:* Properly pubby, a Greenalls pub but with well kept Adnams and Bass, food with emphasis on home cooking; handy for lovely walks *(BH)*

☆ **Preston Bisset** [SP6529], *Old Hat:* Beautifully old-fashioned village pub, basic but utterly charming and always spotless; quiet and relaxed cottage-parlour atmosphere, with old pew, built-in wall settle, open fire – servery behind hatch-type bar looks more like granny's kitchen; well kept Hook Norton on handpump, no food, well behaved children if early; licensees and their dogs friendly and welcoming *(Pete Baker)*

☆ **Prestwood** [Wycombe Rd (A4128); SP8700], *Polecat:* Roomy and civilised dining pub with good interesting food inc vegetarian and particularly good roasts and puddings, modest prices, friendly young staff, well kept Brakspears and Courage-related real ales, decent house wines; in fine old building with charming antique-style furniture, lots of stuffed animals and birds, soft piped classical music; big garden – handy for nice walks *(Rhoda and Jeff Collins, Barry Hancox, Dr Gerald W Barnett, SCCJ)*

Princes Risborough [SP8003], *Black Horse:* Worth knowing for well kept Fullers and pleasant atmosphere *(Martin Kay, Andrea Fowler)*

Saunderton [Wycombe Rd; SU8198], *Rose & Crown:* Handy hotel between Aylesbury and High Wycombe, comfortable coffee lounge, friendly staff, bar food *(George Atkinson)*

Slapton [SP9320], *Carpenters Arms:* Former Benskins pub, now free house with Greene King IPA and Rayments, reasonably priced popular food, cottage-style furnishings – pub doubles as antique/bric-a-brac shop; small garden *(Julian and Sarah Stanton)*

☆ **Speen** [Flowers Bottom Lane; road from village towards Lacey Green and Saunderton Stn – OS Sheet 165 map reference 835995; SU8399], *Old Plow:* Really restaurant not pub (they won't serve drinks unless you're eating, the bar's tiny compared with the dining room, and atmosphere's rather formal), but charmingly cottagey, with good open fires, well kept Adnams and Brakspears as well as good wines, fine Chilterns surroundings; food generally excellent if pricy (you can have just one course), fine service, children in eating area, pretty lawns; closed Sun evening and Mon *(Andrew Scarr, E G Parish, P Saville, Jeff and Rhoda Collins, David Wallington, LYM)*

☆ St Leonards [edge of Buckland Common – village signed off A4011 Wendover—Tring; SP9107], *White Lion:* No frills in simple but neat open-plan Chilterns pub with old black beams, cushioned seats, log-effect gas fire; good value simple home cooking (no hot main dishes Sat, no food Sun), well kept Allied ales with a guest such as Fullers, friendly service, unobtrusive piped music, separate darts room, attractive sheltered garden with good separate play area *(BB)*

☆ Stewkley [High St S, junction of Wing and Dunton rds; SP8526], *Carpenters Arms:* Big helpings of reasonably priced bar food, wide choice from sandwiches up, well kept Adnams, Hook Norton, Tetleys and Youngs beers, warm and friendly licensees, friendly alsatian called Boon; nice old building with bookcases in extended dining lounge, darts in jolly little public bar, subdued piped music *(Lyn and Bill Capper, LYM)*

☆ Stewkley [High St N], *Swan:* Old pub with tiled front public bar, comfortable lounge, nice dining area with huge log fire; well kept Courage-related real ales, good value food (sandwiches, fish, barbecued pork and children's dishes recommended), maybe piped pop music; children's room, extensive gardens inc big enclosed children's lawn with swing, climbing frame, Wendy-house and apple trees *(Graham and Karen Oddey)*

☆ Stoke Hammond [canal, outside village; SP8829], *Three Locks:* Busy canalside pub with wide range of bar food inc huge pizzas, quiet efficient service, Allied real ales, lots of evening events, case showing canal building techniques; can be very busy, best to get there early; very good glassed-in children's room *(Ian Phillips)*

☆ Stony Stratford [72 High St; SP7840], *Cock:* Quiet and comfortable old-fashioned hotel with warm welcome, well kept real ales such as Hook Norton Best, Morlands Old Speckled Hen and Theakstons, very tasty bar food, handsome old oak settles; bedrooms *(John and Joan Nash, LYM)*

☆ Taplow [Station Rd; SU9082], *Oak & Saw:* Interesting lunchtime food in cosy and welcoming open-plan local opp attractive village green, pleasant young Australian staff, interesting pictures, well kept Courage Best and Marstons Pedigree, piped music *(A W Dickinson, TBB)*

☆ The Lee [Swan Bottom; back rd ¾ mile N of The Lee – OS Sheet 165 map reference 902055; SP8904], *Old Swan:* Good imaginative food (quite a restauranty style, evenings), well kept interesting real ales inc guests from afar such as Butcombe, decent wines and attractive furnishings in four low-beamed interconnecting rooms, logs burning in cooking-range inglenook; spacious and prettily planted back lawns with play area *(Mr and Mrs K Box, LYM)*

☆ Thornborough [outside village, just off A421 4 miles E of Buckingham; SP7433], *Lone Tree:* Wide choice of interesting freshly cooked food in spotless and attractively furnished long bar with old-fashioned tables and chairs, nice fire, magazines and books in alcove, real fire in inglenook, good choice of wines and well kept beers (usually four guests), good coffee, polite service, unobtrusive classical music; garden with play area *(F M Bunbury, A Morgan, George Atkinson, E J and M W Corrin, JJW, CMW)*

☆ Twyford [Galncott Rd; SP6626], *Seven Stars:* Pleasant and friendly beamed country pub with varied and imaginative food in lounge bar and separate dining area, welcoming service, four well kept ales with two weekly changing guests such as Ridleys ESX and Thwaites, open fires, old farm tools, seats on pleasant lawn with animals for children *(Tim and Ann Newell, Dave Gabol)*

Wavendon [not far from M1 junctions 13 and 14; SP9137], *Leathern Bottel:* Charles Wells pub increasingly popular for good food; good service *(K H Frostick)*

Wendover [High St; SP8607], *Red Lion:* Wide choice of food inc Sun lunch in simple old-fashioned beamed bar with oak tables and restaurant adjacent, cheerful efficient service, several real ales inc Marstons Pedigree; walker-friendly – on Ridgeway Long Distance Path; bedrooms *(Neil and Anita Christopher)*

☆ West Wycombe [London Rd; SU8394], *Plough:* Good range of bar food, lots of old beams, blazing log fires, friendly staff, pool table in downstairs bar, upstairs lounge, restaurant, pretty little garden up behind *(Ian Phillips)*

☆ Weston Turville [Church Lane; SP8510], *Chequers:* Tucked away in attractive part of village, some tables outside; flagstone bars on two levels, open fire, stylish solid wooden furniture, attractive and characterful beamed restaurant off bar; three well kept real ales inc Allied, particularly wide choice of wines and spirits, wide choice of interesting food in bar and restaurant, often French-based – the tenant's French *(Michael Sargent, B D Jones)*

☆ Weston Underwood [off A509 at Olney; SP8650], *Cowpers Oak:* Charming old creeper-clad beamed pub in pleasant setting, big helpings of good reasonably priced bar food usually served in back restaurant area, friendly service, unobtrusive piped music, Hook Norton Best and Marstons Pedigree, tropical fish tank, games area with skittles and darts, rabbits in garden *(George Atkinson, Maysie Thompson)*

Whaddon [High St; SP8034], *Lowndes Arms:* Friendly L-shaped bar with limited choice of good value food (not Sun) from cheap sandwiches to good steaks, three ales on handpump, decent wines, comfortable atmosphere, beams, horsebrasses, bric-a-brac and cartoons; piped music, fruit machine, darts; open for breakfast 7.30-9; motel-style bedrooms *(JW, CW, George Atkinson)*

☆ **Wheelerend Common** [just off A40; SU8093], *Brickmakers Arms:* Friendly, roomy and comfortable, with nooks, panelling, low beams, armchairs and open fires; good changing food, decent range of beers and wines; play area in big garden, common opp for walks *(Wendy Arnold)*
Winslow [Market Sq; SP7627], *Bell:* Elegant black and white timbered inn under promising new management, with bar food and real ales in plush lounge, restaurant, bedrooms *(Dr Iain Clark, LYM)*; [Buckingham Rd], *Swan:* Amazingly updated in pretty pastel shades, impressively friendly atmosphere *(Dr and Mrs A K Clarke)*
Woburn Sands [High St (A5130); SP9235], *Swan:*Large Victorian-looking Beefeater pub/restaurant haunted by lady in green dress, old pictures and photographs, solid comfortable furniture in alcoves; good if not cheap standard food, Boddingtons and Flowers on handpump, newspapers, piped music, Tues quiz night; no smoking area

(JJW, CMW)
☆ **Wooburn Common** [Wooburn Common Rd; about 3½ miles from M40 junction 2; SU9387], *Royal Standard:* Busy pub with wide choice of good generous reasonably priced bar food, knowledgeable friendly staff, well kept Whitbreads-related beers, mix of old and brighter new decor with popular restaurant area; wide range of wines, tables outside *(Cindy and Chris Crow, Simon Collett-Jones, LYM)*
Wooburn Common [Kiln Lane], *Chequers:* Hotel bar with lots of character, smart customers, food inc exceptional sandwiches and superb interesting salads (service can slow at very busy times), good range of Eldridge Pope beers inc Porter, popular restaurant; attractive bedrooms furnished in stripped pine, good breakfasts *(Susan and John Douglas)*
Wooburn Green [SU9188], *Old Bell:* Light, airy and friendly free house with emphasis on home-made pies; five real ales *(Comus Elliott); Queen & Albert:* Newest pub on the green, but nicely old-faswhioned *(Comus Elliott); Red Cow:* Yet another good pub on this favoured green, old and snug with beams etc *(Comus Elliott)*

If you report on a pub that's not a main entry, please tell us any lunchtimes or evenings when it doesn't serve bar food.

Cambridgeshire and Bedfordshire

Pubs doing particularly well here at the moment include the very individual Millstone at Barnack (food on the up), the Three Tuns at Fen Drayton (consistently good food, but a good atmosphere for drinkers too), the Red Lion at Hinxton (its big new extension really works out very well indeed), and the Haycock at Wansford (consistently innovative in all sorts of ways). We'd certainly pick out both it and the Three Tuns for really good meals: other pubs outstanding for food here include the classy but very welcoming White Hart at Bythorn, the cheerful Woodmans Cottage at Gorefield (amazing choice of puddings), the consistently good Pheasant at Keyston, the very civilised Three Horseshoes at Madingley, and the Anchor up by the canal at Sutton Gault. The Chequers at Fowlmere has produced some marvellous meals this last year, and we'd give a special mention to the steaks at the Fox & Hounds at Riseley – one of the area's new main entries. Among all of these, we choose as the area's Dining Pub of the Year the White Hart at Bythorn. One shock here this last year was the area's most interesting brewer, Banks & Taylors in Shefford, going into receivership. In May 1994 the brewery restarted production under a new trading name, B & T Brewing, and in the summer as we went to press it did seem as if the beers were finding their way back into the area's pubs. Beer prices here have held very steady this last year, hovering around or a few pence more than the national average. The Live & Let Live in Cambridge has had some exceptionally low beer prices recently. Quite a few of the area's pubs stand out as exceptional for people who like good beer, with half a dozen gaining our new Beer Award. In the Lucky Dip section at the end of the chapter, some pubs to mention particularly include the Cock at Broom (lovely pub, but new regime so no firm verdict possible as we go to press), Racehorse at Catworth, White Swan at Conington, Kings Head at Dullingham, White Horse and other pubs in Eaton Socon, George & Dragon at Elsworth, Cutter outside Ely, both entries in Fen Ditton, Oliver Twist up at Guyhirn, Bell at Kennett (just reopened this year, very promising), Pike & Eel at Needingworth, Swan at Radwell, Rose & Crown at Ridgmont, Locomotive near Sandy, White Horse at Southill, Three Fyshes at Turvey, both entries in Wisbech and Tickell Arms at Whittlesford. There's a splendid choice in Cambridge.

BARNACK (Cambs) TF0704 Map 5

Millstone 🍺

Millstone Lane; off B1443 SE Stamford; turn off School Lane near the Fox

Readers feel the food in this friendly village pub seems to be getting better and might include soup (£1.50), toasties like bacon and egg (from £1.75), large plaited rolls (£2.45), ploughman's (£3.75), home-cooked ham with two eggs (£4.45), vegetable pie (£5.45), sweet and sour chicken or steak and kidney pie (£5.95), minted lamb bake (£6.50), spare ribs in barbecue sauce (£6.95) and home-made puddings (from £1.95). The atmospheric and comfortable bar has timbering and high beams hung with lots of harness, cushioned wall benches on the patterned carpet, and well kept Adnams Southwold, Everards Old Original and Tiger, Ridleys IPA and a guest beer on handpump; the little snug is decorated with the memorabilia of a former regular, including his medals from both World Wars. The snug and dining room are no smoking. *(Recommended by Wayne Brindle, R J Robinson, John C Baker, Richard Balls, WHBM, Tom Evans, M J Morgan)*

Everards ~ Tenant Aubrey Sinclair-Ball ~ Real ale ~ Meals and snacks (11.30-2, 6-9) ~ (01780) 740296 ~ Children in eating areas ~ Open 11-2.30, 5.30-11

BARRINGTON　(Cambs)　TL3949 Map 5

Royal Oak

From M11 junction 11, take A10 for Royston; village signposted on right after 3½ miles

Few pubs offer such a variety of interesting vegetarian dishes as this thatched and heavily timbered place: soup (£3.25), chestnut and cashew pâté (£3.95), nut and date curry, walnut spiral, or moussaka with yoghurt and mint dressing (£5.85), pecan, mango and mushroom stroganoff or leek, mushrooms, tomatoes and almond crumble (£6.25), pear and pasta au poivre or hazelnut, pineapple and pepper pancake (£6.45); also, sandwiches (from £1.95), omelettes (from £4.95), steak and kidney pie or smoked sea fish with mushrooms, sweetcorn and tomato sauce on tagliatelle (£5.85), prawn, ham and pepper pancake with yoghurt and mint dressing on the green salad (£6.45), sirloin beef in stout (£6.75), king prawns in garlic butter with hint of anise (£7.90), and puddings (from £3); there may be quite a wait if the pub is busy. Several rambling and comfortable tile-floored rooms are packed with brass, copper, antlers and harness and there is some fine Tudor brickwork above a mantelbeam in the large central chimney – opened up as a sort of connecting lobby. Well kept Greene King IPA and Abbot on handpump, a good few malt whiskies; fruit machine and piped music. There's a no smoking conservatory next to the restaurant, and outside seats and tables under cocktail parasols overlook one of the largest village greens in England. Opposite are some beautiful thatched cottages built by Oliver Cromwell. The pub is by no means lacking in character, but it just wouldn't be the same without its colourful landlady. *(Recommended by RJH, Nigel Gibbs, Susan and Nigel Wilson, Paul Cartledge, Dr and Mrs M Bailey, Charles Bardswell, Andrew Latchem, Helen Reed, Trevor P Scott, Stephen Brown, Gordon Mott, Gill Earle, Andrew Burton, Clare Dawkins, Gordon Phillips, Nigel Norman, Ian Phillips)*

Free house ~ Licensees Robert and Elizabeth Nicholls ~ Real ale ~ Meals and snacks (12-2, 6.30-10.30) ~ Restaurant ~ Cambridge (01223) 870791 ~ Children in old restaurant next to bar ~ Open 11.30-2.30, 6-11

BIDDENHAM　(Beds)　TL0249 Map 5

Three Tuns ◧

57 Main Road; village signposted from A428 just W of Bedford

There's a good mix of customers and a nice bustling atmosphere in this neatly kept thatched pub. The comfortable lounge has low beams and country paintings on the walls, and the public bar has table skittles as well as darts, dominoes, and fruit machine. Good bar food includes sandwiches (from £1.20), home-made soup (£1.40 – you can have it with a choice of any sandwich for £2.10), and pâté (£1.90), good, fresh ploughman's (£2.50), burgers (from £3), salads (£3.50), quiche or home-made chilli con carne (£4.20), home-made steak and kidney pie or chicken casserole (£4.80), and 8oz sirloin steak (£8); children's menu (£1.60). Very well kept Greene King IPA, Abbot and Rayments on handpump; cheerful, prompt service. The particularly attractive big garden is popular with families as it's very sheltered, there's a big terrace with lots of picnic-table sets and a very good separate children's play area with swings for all ages and a big proper wooden climbing frame – as well as doves and a dovecote. The village is pretty especially in spring. *(Recommended by Klaus and Elizabeth Leist, L Walker, Russell and Margaret Bathie, Bob and Maggie Atherton, Wayne Brindle, Dr and Mrs M Bailey, Simon Cottrell, Michael, Alison and Rhiannon Sandy)*

Greene King ~ Tenant Alan Wilkins ~ Real ale ~ Meals and snacks (not Sun or Mon evenings) ~ (01234) 354847 ~ Children in small dining room ~ Open 11.30-2.30, 6-11

BOLNHURST (Beds) TL0859 Map 5

Olde Plough
B660 Bedford—Kimbolton

Apart from two items, all the food in this pretty and friendly 500-year-old cottage is home-made – and the same menu is used in the upstairs restaurant and in the bar (and changes weekly): lunchtime filled rolls (£1.50), soup (£1.95), smoked fish pâté (£2.75), local sausages (£3.50), steak and kidney pie (£5.25), vegetarian pasta (£4.50), chicken breast (£6.50), fillet of salmon or fillet of perch in green peppercorn sauce (£7.50), 8oz fillet steak (£11.50), and puddings such as fruit crumble or sticky toffee pudding (£2.25). The upstairs restaurant has old beams and polished tables. Well kept Courage Directors, Ruddles Best, and John Smiths Magnet on handpump, and summer specials such as kir royale and buck's fizz. The spacious and comfortable carpeted lounge bar has a relaxed atmosphere, black beams, little armchairs around low tables, a leather sofa and armchair, and a log fire in the big stone fireplace. A dining room has seats around tables ingeniously salvaged from oak barn fittings; its wooden ceiling uses boards from a Bedford church. The public bar has a couple of refectory tables, settles and other seats on the flagstones, and a big woodburning stove; darts, pool, hood skittles, cribbage, dominoes, trivial pursuit and cards. The cats are called Blacky and Titch, the doberman Zeus and the other dog Lica – she likes to fall asleep under the tables; other dogs welcome. The lovely garden has an established rock bank (where there's the remains of a moat under trees), as well as rustic seats and tables, and a long crazy-paved terrace which looks on to the pond; they let you take cuttings. The landlady is a faith healer, gives healing free of charge, hopes to hold yoga lessons, and writes cheerful poems to put up on the pub walls. *(Recommended by Mrs Cynthia Archer, S Eldridge, John Fahy, Stephen Brown, Prof J V Wood, Wayne Brindle)*

Free house ~ Licensee M J Horridge ~ Real ale ~ Meals and snacks (till 10pm Sat) ~ Restaurant (Fri/Sat evenings and Sun lunch only) ~ (01234) 376274 ~ Well behaved children till 9pm ~ Open 12-2.30 (3 Sat), 7-11; closed 25/26 Dec

BYTHORN (Cambs) TL0575 Map 5

White Hart ⑪ ♀
Village signposted just off A604 Huntingdon—Cambridge
Cambridgeshire Dining Pub of the Year

Mr and Mrs Bennett work very hard to ensure that you always get a warm welcome in this civilised dining pub. The food is quite special, too – and is now served in the bar as well as the dining room or no smoking restaurant. The pub part, at the front, has a homely atmosphere and several linked smallish rooms with a real variety of styles giving lots to look at without being cluttered. In one bit you may find a big leather chesterfield and lots of silver teapots, in another wing armchairs and soft leather chairs and stools; also attractive tables, rugs on stripped boards, and a log fire in a huge brick fireplace. There are cookery books and plenty of magazines for reading, not just decoration. Imaginative and very popular, the bar food includes spicy fish soup with lemongrass or duck liver terrine with orange chutney (£4.50), ploughman's or confit of duck (£4.95), squid ink pasta with fresh scallops or toasted brie with bacon (£5.95), venison casserole (£6.95), sirloin steak (£10), and puddings like home-made rhubarb sorbet or toasted fresh fruit sabayon (£4.25). Well kept Greene King IPA and Abbot on handpump, a good, no nonsense, well chosen wine list including four by the glass, free nuts and spicy sausages, and pleasant staff. You might catch the Morris dancers on one of their visits. *(Recommended by Michael Sargent, Cdr Patrick Tailyour, Stephen, Julie and Hayley Brown, Rita Horridge, Mrs R Cotgreave)*

Free house ~ Licensees Bill and Pam Bennett ~ Real ale ~ No-smoking restaurant

*(not Sun evening, not Mon) ~ Bythorn (01832) 710226 ~ Children welcome ~
Open 11-3, 6-11; closed Sun evening, all day Mon*

CAMBRIDGE   TL4658 Map 5

Anchor 🍺

Silver St

In a marvellous setting right by the River Cam, this big lively pub has been
renovated this year. The area around the entrance has now been sectioned off to
create more of a cosy atmosphere, there's lots of bric-a-brac and seats are now
church pews; they still have a brick fireplace at each end. The upstairs bar has been
made more pubby with pews and wooden chairs and the ceiling has been lowered;
the windows here have good riverside views. Downstairs, the café-bar (open all
day) has enamel signs on the walls and a mix of interesting tables, settles,
farmhouse chairs, and hefty stools on the bare boards. Steps take you down to a
similar though simpler flagstoned room, and french windows lead out to the
terrace with picnic-table sets and some tubs of flowers. Bar food includes
sandwiches (from £1.75), ploughman's (from £2.90), hot dishes, and Sunday roast
(£4.50). Well kept Boddingtons, Flowers Original, Morlands Old Speckled Hen
and three changing guests on handpump, with a good range of foreign bottled
beers; cheerful young service, piped music, various trivia and fruit machines and a
juke box. *(Recommended by Nigel Woolliscroft, Ben Regan, Paul Cartledge, Tom Smith,
John Fahy, Steve Goodchild, Andrew and Ruth Triggs, Frank Cummins)*

*Whitbreads ~ Manager Alistair Langton ~ Real ale ~ Meals and snacks (12-6;
downstairs café bar 11-7) ~ (01223) 353554 ~ Children in eating area until 7pm
~ Open 11-11*

Eagle ♀

Bene't Street

Popular with young and older people alike, this lively central 16th-c inn has no
noisy fruit machines or juke box. The five individually furnished rambling bars still
have many of the original feature such as two fireplaces dating back to around
1600, two medieval mullioned windows, much of the original pine panelling and
the remains of two wall paintings, thought to be medieval. The high, dark red
ceiling has been left unpainted since the war to preserve the signatures of British
and American airmen worked in with 'Zippo' lighters, candle smoke and lipstick;
one room is no smoking. Bar food includes cold meats, cheeses, quiche and pasties
to have as ploughman's or salads (from £1.75), steak and kidney pie, chicken
korma or roast lamb in rosemary gravy (from £3.95), and evening burgers (from
£3.75) and roast chicken (£4.25). Well kept Greene King IPA and Abbot, and
Rayments on handpump, and up to 20 wines by the glass; good service. Hidden
behind a sturdy gate is a cobbled and galleried coachyard with heavy wooden seats
and tables. This was the local of Nobel Prize winning scientists Crick and Watson,
who discovered the structure of DNA. *(Recommended by Ben Regan, Barry and Anne,
Tom Smith, Rita Horridge, Julian Holland, Barbara Hatfield, Wayne Brindle)*

*Greene King ~ Licensees Peter and Carol Hill ~ Real ale ~ Meals and snacks
(12-2.30, 5.30-8; not Fri, Sat, Sun) ~ (01223) 301286 ~ Children welcome ~
Open 11-11*

Free Press

Prospect Row

Run by a particularly friendly landlord and his welcoming, efficient staff, this
ever-popular traditional pub is the only one we know of that is also registered as
a boat club – and one of the few totally no smoking pubs. It's fittingly decorated
with rowing blades and photographs (and other sportsmen pictures), and its
nicely unmodernised rooms are full of character; one is served from a hatch;
friendly cat. Good, wholesome bar food includes two soups each day, one of
which is always vegetarian, such as carrot and mustard or parsnip and ginger

(£1.95), hot chilli, lamb, apple and rosemary casserole or carrot, mushroom and stilton bake (£3.95) and puddings like toffee apple tart or chocolate, cherry and marzipan cake (£1.90); get there early if you want a seat. Well kept Greene King IPA and Abbot on handpump, with a good selection of malt whiskies and freshly squeezed orange juice; iced coffee in hot weather; cards, cribbage and dominoes behind the bar. The sheltered and paved garden at the back is quite a suntrap, and is home for some rabbits who have built their own burrows there.

(Recommended by Patricia and Tony Carroll, Frank W Gadbois, Paul Cartledge, Nigel and Sara Walker, William Pryce, John and Marianne Cooper, Frank Cummins)

Greene King ~ Tenant Christopher Lloyd ~ Real ale ~ Meals and snacks (12-2, 6.30-8.30) ~ (01223) 68337 ~ Well behaved children welcome ~ Open 12-2.30, 6-11; closed 25 Dec evening, 26 Dec

Live & Let Live 🍺

40 Mawson Road; off Mill Road SE of centre

The atmosphere in this unpretentious pub is chatty and friendly (no machines, piped music unobtrusive or absent) and the bar is very straightforward with a pleasantly relaxed feel, bare boards and brickwork, pale wood chairs around sturdy varnished pine tables, and heavy timber baulks; also, coming-events posters at one end and lots of interesting old country bric-a-brac. Equally basic generous bar food, all home-made (you can see the comings and goings in the kitchen), includes doorstep sandwiches, chicken in wine sauce, curry, chilli, stuffed mushrooms, and lots of other things with chips, beans and peas (from £3.50); the eating area is no smoking and the low prices attract many graduate students. Quick and friendly bar service, good table clearance, and well kept Adnams, Everards Tiger, Exmoor Stag, and Felinfoel Double Dragon on handpump.

(Recommended by Paul Cartledge, Frank Cummins, Michael Quine; more reports please)

Everards ~ Lease: Margaret Rose Holliday ~ Real ale ~ Meals and snacks (not Sun evening) ~ (01223) 460261 ~ Children in eating area if eating till 8.30 ~ Open 12-2, 6-11

Mill 🍺 £

Mill Lane

Eight handpumps in this popular riverside pub serve a constantly changing range of real ales, often including little-known brews: Banks & Taylors Dragonslayer, Cains Formidable, Coach House Coachmans, Mitchells Fortress, Nethergate Bitter, IPA and Old Growler, and Tolly Cobbold Original. They also get beers direct from local microbreweries, and have farm ciders and 21 English country wines. The simple bars have kitchen chairs, chunky stools, settles and a mix of wooden tables on bare boards and ancient quarry tiles, there are lots of display cases filled with clay pipes or brewery taps and slings, photographs of college games teams, and oars with names of past Pembroke College rowers; an open brick fireplace, too. Bar food includes sandwiches, filled baked potatoes (£2.75), vegetarian pasta bake (£3.50), and daily specials (from £3.50); fruit machine, piped pop music. The main punt station is next door. There are now a good few other pubs in this back-to-basics chain, mainly in the North of England.

(Recommended by Paul Cartledge, Julian Holland, Dr and Mrs M Bailey, James K McDonell, Bill Ryan, Marjorie and Bernard Parkin)

Pubmaster ~ Manager Christopher Spinks ~ Real ale ~ Lunchtime meals and snacks (till 3, except Sun 12-2) ~ (01223) 357026 ~ Children welcome until 7pm ~ Open 11-11

DUXFORD (Cambs) TL4745 Map 5

John Barleycorn

Moorfield Rd; village signposted off A1301; pub at far end of village

Most people coming to this pretty, thatched early 17th-c building do so for the popular – if not cheap – food: ploughman's (lunchtimes, from £3.50), unusual open sandwiches such as hot black pudding with gooseberries (lunchtimes, from £3.90), smoked haddock with poached eggs (£6.50), salads (from £6.50), ragout of lamb with parsley scones or steak, mushroom and vegetable pie (£6.90), and puddings like spiced apple and almond slice (£3.40); best to book in the evenings. Well kept Greene King IPA, Abbot and Dark Mild, decent wines, a range of brandies, and mulled wine in winter. Service is reserved but courteous. The friendly dimly lit bar is quietly chatty and attractively furnished, with high-backed booth-type oak settles, some wheelback chairs and chunky country tables, and autumnal-coloured curtains to match the cushions. A couple of standing timbers and a brick pillar break up the room, and below a shotgun on the wall there's a raised brick fireplace with horsebrasses hung along the mantelbeam, as well as a mix of old prints, decorative plates (including game ones), photographs of the pub, brass lamps, a ship's clock and some scales, and horse bits and reins; dominoes and piped music. The low building has exceptionally pretty hanging baskets, tubs and flowerbeds around picnic-table sets, and there are more tables in the colourful back garden surrounded by roses and flowering shrubs. There's also a converted barn with ancient timbers and some back-to-back seats, and a brick barbecue. *(Recommended by Patricia and Tony Carroll, Trevor P Scott, I S Thomson, Paul Cartledge, RJH, Martin and Pauline Richardson, Stephen, Julie and Hayley Brown, Gary Roberts, Clare Dawkins, Gordon Phillips, Caroline Wright, Bill and Beryl Farmer, Brian and Jill Bond, Bill and Edee Miller, David Carrington, R C Wiles, J E Rycroft)*

Greene King ~ Tenant Henry Sewell ~ Real ale ~ Meals and snacks (till 10pm) ~ (01223) 832699 ~ Open 12-2.30, 6.30-11; closed 25/26 Dec, 1 Jan

ELTISLEY (Cambs) TL2659 Map 5

Leeds Arms 🛏

The Green; village signposted off A45

Overlooking the large and peaceful village green, this pleasant and attractive tall white brick house has a comfortable and interesting bar made up of two rooms knocked together; there are red plush stools, pew-like cushioned wall benches, a huge winter log fire with brass hunting horns, and decorative plates on the mantelpiece. Down some steps a third room is dominated by tables with cushioned wheelback chairs. Popular and good value bar food includes home-made soup (£1.75), sandwiches (from £1.75), ploughman's or good spicy mushrooms (£2.75), seafood pancake (£3.50), lasagne (from £4.25), curries and vegetarian dishes (from £4.75), home-made steak and kidney pie (£5.50), steaks (from £9), and puddings such as lemon mousse or treacle tart (£2.20). Well kept Greene King IPA and Hook Norton Best on handpump; efficient service; darts, dominoes, cribbage, a fruit machine sensibly set aside in an alcove, and piped music. The pleasant garden has swings, slides and picnic-table sets among the silver birches on the lawn. The bedrooms, plainly furnished but comfortable and well equipped, are in a separate block beyond the garden. *(Recommended by P and D Carpenter, C Fisher, Fred Punter, Gwen and Peter Andrews)*

Free house ~ Licensee George Cottrell ~ Real ale ~ Meals and snacks (12-2, 7-9.45) ~ Restaurant (until 8.30 Sun) ~ Eltisley (01480) 880283 ~ Children over 6 in eating area of bar and in restaurant ~ Open 11.30-2.30, 6.30-11; closed 25 Dec ~ Bedrooms: £35B/£42.50B

ETTON (Cambs) TF1406 Map 5

Golden Pheasant 🍺

Village just off B1443, just E of Helpston level crossing; and will no doubt be signposted from near N end of new A15 Peterborough bypass

Seven real ales are kept on handpump all the time here, and at any one time they might include Bass, Batemans XXXB, Boddingtons, Greene King IPA, North Yorkshire Flying Herbert, Ruddles County, and Wadworths 6X; lots of malt whiskies. The comfortable bar has high-backed button-back maroon plush settles built against the walls and around the corners, an open fire, and prints on the walls; in the airy, glass-walled, no smoking side room are some Lloyd Loom chairs around glass-topped cane tables. At lunchtime, there are around 15 dishes under £4 – such as Cumberland sausage, chilli-stuffed peppers, home-made barbecued ribs, steak hogie, and turkey olives, as well as lots of fish like smoked fish pie, baked salmon in a cheese and chive sauce or halibut steaks with asparagus (from £8), and steaks (from £8.95); the golden labrador is called Bonnie. Pool, cribbage, dominoes, fruit machine, video game and piped music. The stone-walled garden, surrounded by tall trees, looks out across flat countryside, there's an aviary with 70 birds (golden pheasants, quail, cockatiels, rosella parakeets and budgerigars, and a big paddock. *(Recommended by Richard Balls, John C Baker; more reports please)*

Free house ~ Licensees Dennis and Hilary Wilson ~ Real ale ~ Meals and snacks (till 10pm) ~ Restaurant (not Sun evening) ~ Peterborough (01733) 252387 ~ Children in eating area of bar, in restaurant and family room ~ Open 11-11

FEN DRAYTON (Cambs) TL3368 Map 5

Three Tuns 🍴

High Street; village signposted off A604 NW of Cambridge

The friendly licensees have struck just the right balance in this thatched pub between providing consistently good food and having plenty of room to enjoy a drink. The cheerfully atmospheric bar has heavy-set moulded Tudor beams and timbers, two inglenook fireplaces (one of which is usually alight), cushioned settles and an interesting variety of chairs, big portraits and old photographs of local scenes, old song sheets of local folk songs, and brass plates on the timbered walls, fresh flowers, and old crockery in a corner dresser. The popular bar food – with prices unchanged since last year – includes sandwiches with a choice of brown, white or french bread (from £1.25), home-made soup (£1.80), home-made chicken liver and bacon pâté or Greek dips (£2.50), chicken satay with peanut sauce or ploughman's (£3), salads (from £3.50), home-made dishes such as lasagne (£4.25) or chicken curry (£4.50), gammon with pineapple (£5.50), chicken kiev (£6), and 8oz rump steak (£8); daily specials such as special macaroni cheese (£3.50), a pie such as rabbit, bacon and apple or pigeon breast, bacon and black cherry or bobotie lamb (£4.75) and breast of chicken in garlic butter (£5); excellent vegetarian options and puddings like home-made apple pie and good treacle tart. Helpful staff serve well kept Greene King IPA and Abbot and Rayments on handpump kept under light blanket pressure, as well as a range of malt whiskies. Sensibly placed darts, shove-ha'penny, dominoes, cribbage and fruit machine. A well tended lawn at the back has tables under cocktail parasols, apple and flowering cherry trees, and some children's play equipment. The pub can get very crowded, so it's best to arrive early if you want to eat. *(Recommended by Ian Phillips, Wayne Brindle, Maysie Thompson, Gordon Theaker, Mr and Mrs Powell, S Brackenbury, Nigel Foster, Prof John and Mrs Patricia White, Donald and Margaret Wood, Paul Cartledge, Bill and Edee Miller, Mr and Mrs B Hobden, Roger Bellingham, Sara Price, R C Wiles, Mary and Peter Clark)*

Greene King ~ Tenants Michael and Eileen Nugent ~ Meals and snacks (not evenings of 24/25 Dec or 1 Jan) ~ (01954) 230242 ~ Children in eating area of bar until 8pm ~ Open 11-2.30, 6.30-11; cl evening 25 Dec

FOWLMERE (Cambs) TL4245 Map 5

Chequers 🍴 🍷

B1368

Attentive black-and-white-dressed waiters serve the ambitious food in this civilised and upmarket coaching inn – though people do still drop in just for a drink. The unusual range may include curried parsnip soup (£2.80), English cheeses and walnut bread (£3), New Zealand mussels in garlic butter (£3.60), duck and pork pâté with truffles and pistachios (£4.90), cassoulet of pork and smoked sausage or vegetarian courgettes with cream almonds (£4.95), and puddings like date sponge with toffee sauce or treacle and orange tart (£2.80);

maybe nibbles on the bar. There are two warm and cosy comfortably furnished communicating rooms; upstairs there are beams, wall timbering and some interesting moulded plasterwork above the fireplace, and downstairs has prints and photographs of Spitfires and Mustangs flown from Fowlmere aerodrome, and an open log fire. Look out for the priest's hole above the bar. Well kept Tolly Original and Tetleys on handpump, freshly squeezed orange juice, a good choice of vintage and late-bottled ports and brandies by the glass, and an excellent choice of fine wines by the glass. The garden is particularly well looked after, with white tables under cocktail parasols among the flowers and shrub roses; a conservatory/function room overlooks the garden. *(Recommended by Martin and Pauline Richardson, Charles Bardswell, Stephen, Julie and Hayley Brown, Ian Phillips, Russell and Margaret Bathie, RJH, PACW, BHP, Gwen and Peter Andrews, R C Wiles)*

Pubmaster ~ Lease: Norman Rushton ~ Real ale ~ Meals and snacks (till 10, except Sun till 9.30) ~ Restaurant ~ Fowlmere (01763) 208369 ~ Children welcome ~ Open 12-2.30, 6-11; closed 25 Dec

GOREFIELD (Cambs) TF4111 Map 8

Woodmans Cottage 🍽

Main St

At the weekend, there may be over 50 puddings on offer at this cheerfully run, thriving village pub – which was recently featured on the Anglia TV food programme. These puddings include cheesecakes, roulées, flans, trifles – almost anything tempting, all £2.50. A wide choice of bar food includes toasties (from £1), ploughman's (from £3.50), omelettes (£4), steak and kidney pie (£5.50), a giant mixed grill (£8), and up to two dozen changing specials (£5.50); helpings are most generous. The spacious modernised bar, with leatherette stools and brocaded banquettes around the tables on its carpet, rambles back around the bar counter. A comfortable side eating area has a growing collection of china plates, as well as 1920s prints on its stripped brick walls, and there's space for non-smoking diners called 'the Cellar'. Beyond is an attractive pitched-ceiling restaurant so popular that it may be booked some three weeks ahead. At the other end of the pub, a games area has darts, pool and CD juke box. Well kept Adnams, Bass and Greene King IPA on handpump and several Australian wines (the sunny licensee is Australian); helpful waitress service, piped music, bridge school on Mondays. There are tables out in a sheltered back terrace, with a few more on a front verandah. *(Recommended by Mr and Mrs J Back, Wayne Brindle, Ian R Hydes, Gordon Theaker, Mark J Hydes, R F and M K Bishop)*

Free house ~ Licensees Lucille and Barry Carter ~ Real ale ~ Meals and snacks (till 10pm; not 25 Dec) ~ Restaurant (closed Sun evening) ~ Wisbech (01945) 870669 ~ Children welcome away from the bar counter ~ Open 11-3, 7-11; closed evenings 25/26 Dec

HINXTON (Cambs) TL4945 Map 5

Red Lion

2 miles from M11 junction 9, 3½ miles from junction 10; just off A1301 S of Great Shelford

The award-winning extension here has doubled the size of this bustling, friendly pub, and it has been carefully done in keeping with the original 16th-c building. The mainly open-plan bar has a charming village atmosphere, some grandfather and grandmother clocks, a barometer, some big prints and quite a lot of smaller rustic pictures on the walls, shelves of china in one corner, and a few beams and timbers hung with horsebrasses. As well as George the Amazon parrot (his repertoire is increasing), there's a stuffed tarantula, and an egret and guillemot near the entrance. Well kept Adnams, Bass, Boddingtons and Greene King IPA on handpump at the central bar counter, also a useful wine list. Good bar food includes sandwiches, soup (£1.95), ploughman's (£3.75), salmon and broccoli quiche or vegetable curry (£4.50), salads (from £4.50), lamb's liver and bacon or barbecue chicken (£4.95), and daily specials. Part of the restaurant is no smoking;

trivia and unobtrusive piped classical music. Outside the pretty white slightly jettied twin-gabled old building is a neatly kept garden with picnic-table sets and a paddock with a small pony and goat; there's an unusual heraldic roaring red lion face on the inn-sign. *(Recommended by Wayne Brindle, John Fahy, N M Gibbs, Paul Cartledge, Roger Bellingham, Martin and Pauline Richardson, Jane Kingsbury, K Stevens)*

Free house ~ Licensees James and Lynda Crawford ~ Real ale ~ Meals and snacks (till 10pm) ~ Restaurant ~ Saffron Walden (01799) 530601 ~ Children in eating area of bar and in restaurant ~ Open 11-2.30, 6-11; closed evenings 25/26 Dec

HOLYWELL (Cambs) TL3370 Map 5

Old Ferry Boat

Village and pub both signposted (keep your eyes skinned!) off A1123 in Needingworth

In a remote part of the fens, this thatched wisteria-covered old building is attractively set on the edge of the Great Ouse. The site was once that of a monastic ferry house, and a stone in the bar marks the ancient grave of the resident ghost Juliette, said to return every year on 17 March. The six open-plan bar areas have window seats overlooking the river, low beams, and timbered and panelled walls; one also has a pretty little carved settle. One of the four open fires has a fish and an eel among rushes moulded on its chimney beam, and two areas are no smoking. Good bar food might include home-made soup (£2.25), filled granary bread (from £2.50), lunchtime ploughman's (£4.50), omelettes (£5.50), deep-fried plaice (£6.50), cheese-topped turkey curry pancake or chicken breast strips with fresh chillis, peppers and oyster sauce (£6.95), cold poached salmon with vanilla vinaigrette (£7.50), and puddings (£2.25); weekly and weekend specials (from £6.50), and children's dishes (£3.50). Well kept Adnams Broadside, Courage Directors, Fullers London Pride, Nethergate Old Growler, and Websters Yorkshire on handpump; friendly, attentive service. Fruit machine and piped music. The front terrace has tables under cocktail parasols, with more on a side rose lawn along the river. *(Recommended by I E and C A Prosser, Gordon Theaker, Russell and Margaret Bathie, Ian Phillips, Basil J S Minson, Mr and Mrs D T Deas, Julian Holland, David and Michelle Hedges, Steve Oddy, Denise Plummer, Jim Frogatt, Brian and Jill Bond, Clare Dawkins, Gordon Phillips)*

Free house ~ Licensee Richard Jeffrey ~ Real ale ~ Meals and snacks (till 10pm) ~ St Ives (01480) 463227 ~ Children welcome ~ Open 11.30-3, 6-11 ~ Bedrooms: £39.99B/£49.50B

HORNINGSEA (Cambs) TL4962 Map 5

Plough & Fleece ★

Just NE of Cambridge: first slip-road off A45 heading E after A10, then left at T; or take B1047 Fen Ditton road off A1303

This small but rambling country pub is a welcoming place with a good homely atmosphere and a friendly black-beamed public bar with high-backed settles and plain seats on the red tiled floor, a stuffed parrot and a fox by the log fire, and plain wooden tables – the most interesting of which is an enormously long slab of elm (with an equally long pew to match). Lots of rumbustious locals keep the place lively. Bar food includes sandwiches (from £1.45), home-made soup (£1.75), ploughman's (£2.90), stilton and broccoli flan (£3.25), home-cooked ham and egg (£3.90), good omelettes (£4.90), Suffolk hotpot (£4.85), steak, kidney and mushroom pie (£6.25), honey-roast guinea fowl (£7.75), sirloin steak (£10), and lovely puddings (£2.30); prices are higher in the evening; prompt, cheerful service. There's a no-smoking dining room with lots of wood and old bricks and tiles, linked by a terrace to the garden. Well kept Greene King IPA and Abbot on handpump, half a dozen good malt whiskies and a couple of vintage ports; dominoes and cribbage. The mix of wild and cultivated flowers in the garden is a nice touch; picnic-table sets beyond the car park. *(Recommended by Wayne Brindle, Mike Pugh, A T Langton, Paul Cartledge, Iain Baillie, Mrs J Barwell, J Slaughter, Huw and Carolyn Lewis, P and D Carpenter, Jason Caulkin, Keith Symons, Dr and Mrs M Bailey, G W Ayres, Andrew Latchem, Helen Reed, Roy Bromell, Barry and Anne, Clare Dawkins, Gordon Phillips, Andrew and Ruth Triggs)*

Greene King ~ Tenant Kenneth Grimes ~ Real ale ~ Meals and snacks (not Sun or Mon evenings) ~ No-smoking restaurant (till 1.30 Sun) ~ (01223) 860795 ~ Children over 5 and only in restaurant ~ Open 11.30-2.30, 7-11; closed evenings 25/26 Dec

HOUGHTON CONQUEST (Beds) TL0441 Map 5

Knife & Cleaver ♀

Between B530 (old A418) and A6, S of Bedford

You can now choose from 25 good wines by the glass (or 50cl carafe) in this civilised 17th-c brick-built dining pub. They've also improved their cheeseboard to include even more British farmhouse cheeses, cheddar with fruitcake and a lovely Irish blue brie called Abbey, have extended their range of fresh fish, and use their local smokery for hickory smoked beef, venison sausages and so forth. The welcoming and comfortable bar has a blazing fire in winter, various maps, drawings and old documents on the walls, and a fine choice of well aged malt whiskies – besides well kept Banks & Taylors Shefford and Batemans on handpump, and Stowford cider. Very good bar food might include sandwiches (from £2.50), interesting home-made soups like chilled local asparagus or chicken and lettuce (£1.95), ploughman's (£3.50), baked goat's cheese (£4), crab tart (£4.50), stir-fry prawns (£4.25), a dish of the day such as wild boar and beef casserole, corn-fed chicken casserole with figs (£4.95), and home-made puddings such as brioche and butter pudding with apricots, banoffi pie or ice creams like apple and Calvados or white and dark chocolate chip (£2); friendly service, and maybe unobtrusive piped classical music. Quite a bit of attention is focused on the restaurant, with its airy conservatory – rugs on the tiled floor, swagged curtains, cane furniture and lots of hanging plants. There are tables out in the neatly kept garden. *(Recommended by Brian and Jill Bond, John C Baker, Joyce and Stephen Stackhouse, Philip Russell, Michael Sargent, Andrew Scarr, Nigel and Sara Walker, Margaret Watson, Maysie Thompson)*

Free house ~ Licensees David and Pauline Loom ~ Real ale ~ Meals and snacks (not Sun evening) ~ Restaurant (not Sun evening) ~ (01234) 740387 ~ Children in eating area of bar and in restaurant ~ Themed dinners with accompanying music some Fri evenings ~ Open 11-2.30(2 Sat), 6-10.30; closed Sun evening; 27-30 Dec ~ Bedrooms: £41B/£53B

KEYSOE (Beds) TL0762 Map 5

Chequers

B660 N of Bedford

An unusual stone-pillared fireplace divides the two comfortable beamed and neatly modernised rooms of this friendly village pub – which tend to fill up quickly with people keen to enjoy the consistently good food: sandwiches, interesting home-made soups, tasty garlic mushrooms, cauliflower and stilton quiche or mushroom and cashew nut roast (£4.75) good cottage pie, beef stew with caraway dumplings (£6), wing of skate or whole lemon sole, and puddings like treacle tart, orange cheesecake or fresh fruit pavlova; children's helpings; one bar is no smoking. Well kept Bass, Fullers London Pride and Hook Norton Best on handpumps on the stone bar counter; some malts. Darts, video game, piped music. The terrace at the back looks over the garden which has a wendy house, play tree, swings and a sand-pit. *(Recommended by Jenny and Michael Back, S Eldridge, S G Brown, Stephen Brown, Prof John White, Patricia White, Wayne Brindle)*

Free house ~ Licensee Jeffrey Kearns ~ Real ale ~ Meals and snacks (12-2, 7-9.45; not Mon) ~ (01234) 708678 ~ Children welcome ~ Open 11-2.30, 6.30-11; closed Tuesdays

---

The telephone numbers we give include the new British Telecom codes.

KEYSTON (Cambs) TL0475 Map 5

Pheasant 🍴 🍷

Village loop road; from A604 SE of Thrapston, right on to B663

One menu is offered throughout this pretty and characterful thatched house – the only difference being that the Red Room has linen napkins on bigger tables and is a no smoking area. There's a friendly and nicely civilised feel, with low beams, old photographs, leather slung stools and a heavily carved wooden armchair; the room that used to be the village smithy has a heavy-horse harness on the high rafters and an old horse-drawn harrow on the wall. Food is imaginative though not cheap – might include Tuscan bean soup (£3.25), wild mushroom risotto with parmesan cheese (£3.65), ceviche of salmon with orange and walnut salad (£4.85), seared chicken with daikon and teriyaki sauce (£5.25), wild boar sausages with Dijon and onion sauce (£6.25), poached fillet of hake with stir-fried vegetables (£7.25), lamb and vegetable suet pudding (£7.75), breasts of wood pigeon with swede purée, bacon and haricot beans (£8.75), marinated fillets of red mullet on a pasta cake with tomato and cumin sauce (£9.75), roast sirloin of beef (Sundays only, £9.95), and unpasteurised British cheeses (£4.25) and puddings like pecan and butterscotch pudding with toffee sauce (£3.65), honey and brandy ice cream (£3.85), and honey and walnut tart (£4). Well kept Adnams Best and three guest beers such as Felinfoel Double Dragon, Theakstons XB and Wadworths 6X on handpump, a superb selection of wines (including 14 by the glass), and coffee and herbal teas; very good friendly service. Some tables under cocktail parasols at the front are laid with tablecloths. No dogs. This is one of Ivo Vannocci's Poste Hotels. *(Recommended by Roger and Christine Mash, Martin and Pauline Richardson, Basil J S Minson, John and Tessa Rainsford, Gordon Theaker, Dr M V Jones, Michael Sargent, R C Wiles, Stephen Brown)*

Free house ~ Licensees John Hoskins, Roger Jones ~ Real ale ~ Meals and snacks (12-2, 6-10) ~ Restaurant ~ Bythorn (01832) 710241 ~ Children welcome ~ Open 12-3, 6-11; closed evening 25 Dec

MADINGLEY (Cambs) TL3960 Map 5

Three Horseshoes 🍴 🍷

Well run and comfortably furnished, this smart thatched white pub is well known for its very good, imaginative food. In the charming bar with its open fire, this might include soup (£2.50), risotto of oyster mushrooms and herbs (£3.50), tomato and basil tart with parmesan salad (£4), fresh crab salad with avocado, pink grapefruit and ginger vinaigrette (£4.50), wild mushroom ragout with char-grilled herb polenta (£7), roast cod fillet (£8.50), pan-fried duck breast with mint and baby caper dressing (£9.50), and puddings like lemon tart or soup of mango, papaya and passion fruit with coconut ice cream (£3.50). Very interesting and wide-ranging wine list and Adnams Best and two guest beers like Boddingtons or Morlands Old Speckled Hen on handpump. In summer it's nice to sit out on the lawn, surrounded by flowering shrubs, roses and trees. This is one of Ivo Vannocci's Poste Hotels. *(Recommended by B D Jones, Martin Copeman, Martin and Pauline Richardson, Maysie Thompson, Paul Cartledge, Michael Sargent, Nigel Gibbs, R C Wiles)*

Free house ~ Licensees R Stokes, John Hoskins ~ Real ale ~ Meals and snacks (till 10pm) ~ Restaurant (not Sun evening) ~ Madingley (01954) 210221 ~ Children welcome ~ Open 11.30-2.30, 6-11

NEWTON (Cambs) TL4349 Map 5

Queens Head ★ 🍺

2½ miles from M11 junction 11; A10 towards Royston, then left on to B1368

It's the old-fashioned and unspoilt charm that readers like so much about this delightful pub. The traditional main bar has a low ceiling and crooked beams, bare wooden benches and seats built into the walls and bow windows, a curved high-backed settle on the yellow tiled floor, a lovely big log fire, a loudly ticking clock, and paintings on the cream walls. The little carpeted saloon is broadly similar but cosier. Fine, simple bar food includes a good choice of sandwiches (from £1.50) and filled baked potato (£1.80) or superb home-made soup served in mugs; in the evening and on Sunday lunchtime they serve plates of excellent cold meat, smoked salmon, cheeses and pâté (from £2.75). Well kept Adnams Bitter and Broadside tapped from the cask, with Old Ale in winter and Tally Ho at Christmas; country wines including elderflower and strawberry and Crones cider. Darts in a side room, with shove-ha'penny, table skittles, dominoes, cribbage, fruit machine, and nine men's morris. There are seats in front of the pub, with its vine trellis and unusually tall chimney, or you can sit on the village green. Belinda the goose who used to patrol the car park now sits stuffed above the fruit machine, but lives on in the pub sign, painted by the licensee's father and son. *(Recommended by Norman Foot, J L Phillips, Susan and Nigel Wilson, Charles Bardswell, Paul Cartledge, Mr and Mrs G F Marshall, Tony Beaulah, William Pryce, Stephen, Julie and Hayley Brown, Bob and Maggie Atherton, RJH, David Hedges, Mike Simpson, Janet and Gary Amos, R D Greaves)*

Free house ~ Licensee David Short ~ Real ale ~ Snacks (12-2, 6-9.30) ~ (01223) 870436 ~ Well behaved children in games room ~ Open 11.30-2.30, 6-11; closed 25 Dec

ODELL (Beds) SP9658 Map 5

Bell

Horsefair Lane; off A6 S of Rushden, via Sharnbrook

The pleasant garden outside this pretty thatched village pub runs back to the Great Ouse, and is full of golden pheasants and cockatiels (and maybe canaries) – as well as a goose called Lucy who's rather partial to lettuce leaves. Inside, there's a warm and friendly atmosphere in the five linked rooms that loop around the central servery, as well as quite a few handsome old oak settles and more neatly modern furniture, a log fire in one big stone fireplace, two coal fires elsewhere, and low ceilings with black shiny beams over on the right. Popular bar food, using fresh local ingredients, includes sandwiches (from £1.65), ploughman's (from £2.70), omelettes or home-made flans (from £3), ham and egg (£3.50), savoury pancakes (from £4), home-made lasagne (£4.10), liver and bacon (£4.75), daily specials such as creamy fish pie (£4.50), steak and kidney pie (£5.25) or venison casserole (£5.85), and children's dishes (from £1.60). Well kept Greene King IPA and Abbot and Rayments on handpump, faint piped music, and good, friendly service. Further along the road is a very pretty church. No dogs. *(Recommended by Mr and Mrs Ray, Penny and Martin Fletcher, Rita Horridge, Mr and Mrs R C Allison, Maysie Thompson, Nick Bentley, John Fahy, Roy Y Bromell, T G Saul)*

Greene King ~ Tenant Derek Scott ~ Real ale ~ Meals and snacks (not Sun evening) ~ Bedford (01234) 720254 ~ Children in eating area of bar ~ Open 11-2.30, 6-11

RISELEY (Beds) TL0362 Map 5

Fox & Hounds

High St; village signposted off A6 and B660 N of Bedford

The long-standing speciality here is the cabinet of well hung steaks at one end of the bar counter: you choose which piece of meat you want yours cut from, say how much you want and how you want it cooked, and you're then charged by weight, say £8.80 for 8oz rump. We tried it as steak sandwiches: beautiful, tender slices of well flavoured meat in two big hot crusty rolls with a fresh salad garnish, two platefuls for a total of £3.50 – highly recommended. A wide choice of other food includes mushroom soup or garlic bread (£1.75), beef and garlic pâté (£2.75), ploughman's (£3.95), chilli con carne (£5.95), several vegetarian dishes such as nut roast (£6.25), chicken Monte Carlo (£6.75) and grilled trout (£8.25); children's dishes (£2.50), good nursery and other puddings. Plenty of tables spread under the heavy low beams and among timber uprights, with two candlelit side dining rooms. Well kept Charles Wells Eagle and Bombardier with regularly changing guests like Hook Norton Old Hookey or Marstons Pedigree on handpump, a decent collection of other drinks, unobtrusive piped Glen Miller or light classics, very friendly and helpful service. There are picnic-table sets in the huge garden. The landlord is great fun – a real personality. *(Recommended by T G Saul, Mr and Mrs P Watts, Dr M V Jones, Michael Sargent, George Atkinson, Prof J V Wood, Bill and Sylvia Trotter)*

Charles Wells ~ Manager Jan Zielinski ~ Real ale ~ Meals and snacks (12-1.45, 7-10) ~ Restaurant ~ Bedford (01234) 708240 ~ Children welcome ~ Open 11.30-2.30, 6.30-11

STILTON (Cambs) TL1689 Map 5

Bell 🍺 ♀

High Street; village signposted from A1 S of Peterborough

The famous cheese was never actually made here – but invented by Mrs Paulet, housekeeper at Quenby Hall in Leicestershire who supplied it to her brother-in-law, the 18th-c inn-keeper; the cheese gradually took on the name of the village as its fame spread. It is still much in evidence on the menu in the filled baguettes (£2.50), ploughman's (£3.95), lamb casserole and stilton dumplings (£6.85), and as an alternative to a pudding, blue stilton with plum bread (£3.95). Other interesting food includes home-made soup (£1.95), courgette and seafood creole (£4.95), sweet and sour stir-fried vegetables (£5.95), steak and kidney in ale pie (£6.95), 10oz sirloin steak (£9.75), puddings, and daily specials like ham hock with coarse grain mustard (£5.95); helpings are generous. Well kept Marstons Pedigree, Ruddles County, Tetleys and a guest beer on handpump, fine choice of wines by the glass, and good, friendly service. The two attractive rambling bar rooms have sturdy upright wooden seats, plush-cushioned button-back banquettes built around the walls and bow windows, big prints of sailing and winter coaching scenes on the partly stripped walls, and a large log fire in the fine stone fireplace; dominoes, cribbage, backgammon, Mastermind and Scrabble. Particularly striking is the sheltered cobbled and flagstoned courtyard, with picnic-table sets and a well believed to date back to Roman times. The inn sign is a stately affair – on a huge curlicued gantry by the coach-arch, with distances to cities carved on the courtyard side. *(Recommended by David and Ruth Hollands, Mr and Mrs Powell, Martin and Pauline Richardson, Neil Townend, Charles and Dorothy Ellsworth, Roy Smylie, John Fahy, Huw and Carolyn Lewis, F J Robinson, Wayne Brindle, David and Michelle Hedges, Janet and Gary Amos, Alan and Heather Jacques, Denise Plummer, Jim Froggatt)*

Free house ~ Licensees John and Liam McGivern ~ Real ale ~ Meals and snacks ~ Restaurant (not Sun evening) ~ Peterborough (01733) 241066 ~ Children in eating area of bar at lunchtimes ~ Open 12-2.30, 6-11 ~ Bedrooms: £59B/£64B

STRETHAM (Cambs) TL5072 Map 5

Lazy Otter

Cambridge Rd, Elford Closes; off A10 S of Stretham roundabout

The tables on a neat terrace in front of this popular family pub are a fine place to watch the boats on the River Great Ouse – and the garden runs down to the pub's own moorings; children's play area, too. Inside it's well kept, spacious and comfortable with a relaxed, informal atmosphere, friendly helpful staff, and lunchtime food (served all day in summer) that includes home-made soup (£2.20), big filled baps (from £2.85), ploughman's (from £3.50), burgers (from £4.25), ham and egg or chilli (£4.75), home-made vegetable loaf (£5.25), and steaks (from £6.75), with evening dishes such as pork with apple and cider (£6.75) or breaded lamb with mint and redcurrant sauce (£7.50), daily specials like fresh fish pie (£5.25) or hot sweet and spicy chicken (£6.75), and puddings (£2.25); the conservatory is no smoking. Well kept Courage Directors, Greene King IPA and

Abbot, Morlands Old Speckled Hen, and Wadworths 6X on handpump.
(Recommended by Dr Paul Kitchener, Julian Holland, Nigel and Sara Walker, Clare Dawkins, Gordon Phillips, Ian Phillips, R C Vincent, Dave Braisted)

Free house ~ Licensees Jim Hardy, Stephen Owen ~ Real ale ~ Meals and snacks (served all day in summer) ~ Restaurant ~ (01353) 649780 ~ Children in conservatory area ~ Open 11-11

SUTTON GAULT   (Cambs) TL4279 Map 5

Anchor 🍴 ♀

Village signed off B1381 in Sutton

Cosy in winter with gas lights and candles, it is most enjoyable in summer to sit outside this popular dining pub at the tables or on the bank of the Old Bedford River watching the swans and house martins; the river bank walks are lovely. Inside, the emphasis is very much on the delicious food such as home-made soup (£2.95), home-made chicken liver, brandy and hazelnut pâté (£4.25), fresh dressed Cromer crab (£5.25), curried nut loaf with yoghurt and mango dip or spicy Indonesian beef (£7.95), supreme of chicken in lemon and tarragon sauce (£8.95), freshly roasted French duck breast with Chinese spice sauce (£12.95), half helpings for children, lunchtime specials such as home potted shrimps (£4.25), medley of cheeses with tomato salad and home-made chutney (£4.50) and home-made spinach and bacon quiche (£5.50), and home-made puddings like rich chocolate and brandy pot (£3:45) or delicious Bailey's Irish Cream cheesecake (£3.75). The four heavily timbered rooms have a stylish symplicity with antique settles on the gently sloping floors, along with dining or kitchen chairs and well spaced, stripped and scrubbed deal tables, good lithographs and big prints on the walls, and three log fires; a family room is no smoking. Best to book. Well kept Greene King IPA and Ind Coope Burton tapped from the cask, very good wine list (including a wine of the week and 10 by the glass), winter mulled wine; they also do freshly squeezed orange juice (£1.75 a glass), and a choice of coffees or teas. Shove-ha'penny, dominoes, cribbage, well reproduced piped classical music. No dogs. *(Recommended by J S M Sheldon, John Fahy, Nicholas Law, Prof John and Mrs Patricia White, Gwen and Peter Andrews, Rita Horridge, Wayne Brindle, Ingrid Abma, Andrew Langbar, Paul and Janet Waring, Trevor Scott, Keith Symons, V and E A Bolton, Michael Sargent, Julian Holland, Dr and Mrs M Bailey, Clare Dawkins, Gordon Phillips, Basil J S Minson, Paul Cartledge, R C Wiles)*

Free house ~ Licensees Robin and Heather Moore ~ Real ale ~ Meals and snacks (till 10pm Sat) ~ Ely (01353) 778537 ~ Well behaved children in no-smoking room and one other eating area, but must leave by 8.30pm ~ Open 12-2.30, 6.30-11;.winter evening opening 7; closed 25 and 26 Dec and maybe Sun evenings Oct-Easter

SWAVESEY   (Cambs) TL3668 Map 5

Trinity Foot ♀

A604, N side; to reach it from the westbound carriageway, take Swavesey, Fen Drayton turnoff

Don't be put off by the busy trunk road, this is a really unexpected oasis of genuineness – in its welcome, pubby atmosphere and food. Fresh fish is delivered daily direct from the East Coast ports and is sold both in the pub and in their fish shop next door (open Tuesday-Saturday 11-2.30, 6-7.30). On the menu there might be smoked fish and fresh herb pâté (£3), herring roes on toast (£3.50), 6 oysters (£5), grilled butterfish, cod or plaice or tuna kebabs (all £6.75), dressed crab salad (£6.50), grilled fillet of turbot (£9.50), Dover sole (£11), and fresh lobster (£11.50); other dishes include sandwiches (from £1), ploughman's (£3), omelettes (£5.50), grills (from £5.50), and local seasonal things like samphire and soft fruits. Usually quite busy, it's pleasantly decorated with well spaced tables and fresh flowers, and there's a light and airy conservatory. Well kept Boddingtons and a guest beer on handpump, lots of wines including New World ones, freshly squeezed orange juice, and coffee that's constantly replenished at no extra charge; cheerful and efficient service. Big enclosed garden of shrubs, trees and lawns. *(Recommended by Gordon Theaker, Michael Sargent, Jane Kingsbury, David and Ruth Hollands, David Surridge)*

Whitbreads ~ Tenants H J and B J Mole ~ Real ale ~ Meals and snacks (12-2, 6-9.30; not Sun evening) ~ (01954) 230315 ~ Children welcome ~ Open 11-2.30, 6-11; closed Sun evenings

UFFORD (Cambs) TF0904 Map 5

Olde White Hart

From A15 N of Peterborough, left on to B1443; village signposted at unmarked road on left after about 4 miles

The three acres of gardens around this friendly 17th-c pub have been carefully reworked this year and there are now rose arbours, steps and various quiet corners, as well as the sunny terrace with its white metal seats and canopy, and the children's play area. It's a good stop for walkers and cyclists; you can camp on the paddock. The comfortable and welcoming lounge bar is divided in two by an attractive stone chimney, and has wheelback chairs around dark tripod tables, pewter tankards hanging from the beam over the bar counter, and Boris the stuffed tarantula. The carpeted public bar has old-fashioned settles and dark tables, and the refurbished snug is furnished with wooden settles made by the landlord's father, who also crafted the outdoor benches. Popular bar food includes sandwiches and light lunchtime snacks, as well as daily specials such as pancakes stuffed with three cheeses, onions, mushrooms and peppers (£4.50), home-made steak in ale pie (£4.95), breast of lemony chicken in sherry sauce (£6.50) and sizzling 8oz rump steak in garlic sauce (£8.95), puddings like summer pudding and Sunday hot beef rolls and roast lunch. Well kept Theakstons Best, XB and Old Peculier, and guests like Home Bitter on handpump, lots of bottled beers from all over the world, several wines by the glass, and farm ciders. Darts, cribbage, and dominoes, ring-the-bull and captain's mistress. *(Recommended by Wayne Brindle, Stephen, Julie and Hayley Brown, David and Michelle Hedges, M Morgan, Mark J Hydes)*

Youngers ~ Tenants Chris and Sally Hooton ~ Real ale ~ Meals and snacks (not Sun evening or Mon) ~ Restaurant (not Sun evening) ~ Stamford (01780) 740250 ~ Children in eating area of bar and in restaurant ~ Folk/blues/cajun/comedy Sun evenings ~ Open 11-2.30(3 Sat), 6-11; closed 25 Dec

WANSFORD (Cambs) TL0799 Map 5

Haycock ★ 🍽 🛏 ♀

Village clearly signposted from A1 W of Peterborough

One of the nice things about this particularly well run and marvellously civilised golden stone inn is the staff – who are friendly, very efficient and seem to put a genuine enjoyment into their work. It's a thriving place with plenty of character and an appealing atmosphere, and the fine flagstoned main entry hall has antique hunting prints, seats and a longcase clock, and leads into the lively panelled main bar with dark terracotta walls, a sturdy dado rail above mulberry dado, and old settles. Through two handsome stone arches is another attractive area, while the comfortable front sitting room has some squared oak panelling by the bar counter, a nice wall clock, and a big log fire. There's an airy stripped brick eating bar by the garden with dark blue and light blue basketweave chairs around glass-topped basket tables, pretty flowery curtains and nice modern prints of sunny conservatory or garden scenes; doors open on to a big terrace with lots of tables. There are two no smoking areas. Fine bar food includes home-made soup (£2.95), soused mackerel with apple chutney (£3.25), grilled sardines in garlic butter (£3.55), three cheeses with ciabatta bread and pickles (£4.95), vegetable stroganoff (£5.95), open sandwiches (from £5.95), grilled gammon and egg (£6.95), lamb's liver and bacon (£7.95), steak and kidney pie (£8.45), grilled salmon fillet with thyme and parsley butter (£9.45), home-made puddings (from £3.50), and summer barbecues (from £8.95); weekday three-course lunch £14.50. The outdoor eating area with its big cream Italian umbrellas is very popular. Well kept Adnams, Banks & Taylors Shefford, Bass, Ruddles Best and County, and a guest beer on handpump, a range of around 11 good house wines by the glass from an exceptional list, and properly mature vintage ports by the glass; freshly squeezed juices. The spacious walled formal garden has boules and fishing as well as cricket (they have their own field). One of Ivo Vannocci's Poste Hotels. *(Recommended by Wayne Brindle, Michael Sargent, Martin and Pauline Richardson, Linda Norsworthy, Mrs F M Halle, Mrs R Cotgreave, Frank Gadbois, Keith and Margaret Kettell, June and Malcolm Farmer, Comus Elliott, R C Wiles, Maysie Thompson, Gwen and Peter Andrews)*

Free house ~ Licensee Richard Neale ~ Real ale ~ Meals and snacks (served all day) ~ Restaurant ~ Stamford (01780) 782223 ~ Children welcome ~ Open all day from 10.30 ~ Bedrooms: £60B/£90B

WOODDITTON   (Cambs) TL6659 Map 5

Three Blackbirds

Village signposted off B1063 at Cheveley

The two comfortably snug bars in this pretty and friendly thatched village pub have high winged settles or dining chairs around fairly closely spaced neat tables, cigarette cards, Derby-Day photographs, little country prints, and winter fires – the room on the left has the pubbier atmosphere. Well kept Greene King IPA and Ind Coope Burton on handpump; service remains cheerful and efficient even when busy; piped music. A wide choice of bar food includes home-made soup (£2.10), vegetarian or duck liver pâté (£2.60), home-cooked ham (£5.25), lasagne (£5.55), escalope of pork in cream and mushroom sauce (£6.75), fish pot (£6.95), venison casserole (£8.25), steaks (from £8.50), and puddings (from £1.95); good Sunday roasts; the menu is the same in the restaurant. The attractive front lawn, sheltered by an ivy-covered flint wall, has flowers, roses, and a flowering cherry, with a muted chorus of nearby farm noises. *(Recommended by Brian and Jill Bond, Martin and Pauline Richardson, Paul and Janet Waring, John Fahy, Dr and Mrs M Bailey, Wayne Brindle, Trevor Scott)*

Pubmaster ~ Tenant Edward Spooner ~ Real ale ~ Meals and snacks (11.30-2, 6.30-10) ~ Partly no smoking restaurant ~ Newmarket (01638) 730811 ~ Children in restaurant ~ Open 11.30-2.30, 6.30-11

Lucky Dip

Besides the fully inspected pubs, you might like to try these Lucky Dips recommended to us and described by readers (if you do, please send us reports). Pubs are in Cambs unless we list them as in Beds.

Arrington [TL3250], *Hardwicke Arms:* Attractive creeper-covered coaching inn with pleasant beamed and panelled lounge, next to Wimpole Hall; a main entry before being closed early 1992, but reopened under new ownership 1994 *(Reports please)*
Babraham [just off A1307; TL5150], *George:* Useful pleasantly unpretentious pub with decent food in bar and restaurant, well kept real ale, friendly efficient service *(Nigel and Helen Aplin, John Fahy)*
☆ **Bartlow** [TL5845], *Three Hills:* Family pub with long spacious bar, well kept Greene King IPA, subdued pipe music, bar food, evening restaurant, Sun lunches; interesting hill forts nearby *(Wayne Brindle, Paul Cartledge, Brian and Jill Bond)*

Bedford, Beds [Union St; TL0449], *Foresters Arms:* A useful find for the town, with well kept Charles Wells Eagle and Bombardier, guests such as Boddingtons, Badger Tanglefoot, Wadworths 6X, two well furnished rooms, friendly staff, tables on terrace; bedrooms *(Bob Hurling, Rosalind Hodges)*
☆ **Bourn** [TL3256], *Duke of Wellington:* Good range of generous imaginative bar food cooked to order, attractive interior (former private house), pleasant attentive staff, well kept Greene King *(Maysie Thompson, Geoff Lee, R C Wiles)*
Boxworth [TL3463], *Golden Ball:* Clean and pleasant, with attractive garden and setting, Courage-related beers, good

friendly service, decent food *(Gordon Theaker, EHS, David Bundock)*

☆ **Brampton** [Bromholme Lane; signed off A141 Huntingdon Rd opp Hinchingbrooke House; TL2170], *Olde Mill:* Popular Beefeater in old converted mill with working waterwheel, in beautiful riverside spot, attractively floodlit at night; good value bar food, upper restaurant, Whitbreads-related real ales *(Julian Holland)*
Bromham, Beds [Bridge End; nr A428, 2 miles W of Bedford; TL0050], *Swan:* Comfortable beamed village pub with pleasant atmosphere, quick friendly service, open fires, lots of pictures, well kept Greene King IPA and Abbot, decent coffee, popular food inc carvery and salad bar; public bar with darts and fruit machine, pleasant garden *(T G Saul, George Atkinson)*

☆ **Broom**, Beds [23 High St; TL1743], *Cock:* Attractive and unusual old-fashioned small-roomed pub which has had well kept Greene King ales and a guest such as Wadworths 6X tapped from the cask for corridor servery, wide range of food, friendly service and fine atmosphere; has been very good indeed, but no reports yet on new 1994 regime *(LYM – news please)*
Burrough Green [TL6355], *Bull:* Attractive, with cricketing decor, separate dining area; friendly landlord, well kept ales *(Frank W Gadbois)*
Caddington, Beds [1 Luton Rd; TL0619], *Chequers:* Very friendly cosy village pub with low-priced real ales and cheap but good food *(Jacqueline Walshe)*

☆ **Cambridge** [14 Chesterton Rd], *Boathouse:* Open all day, L-shaped main room with varnished wood tables and framed prints, carpeted extension with verandah overlooking river, eight or so well kept beers such as Brakspears and Boddingtons, good chocie of ciders, decent coffee, generous food, unspoilt relaxed atmosphere, pleasant service; juke box; children welcome *(Frank Cummins, Kate and Robert Hodkinson, Mr and Mrs B Hobden, Lorrie and Mick Marchington, Paul Cartledge, Ian Phillips, P and D Carpenter, LYM)*

☆ **Cambridge** [85 Gwydir St], *Cambridge Blue:* Well kept Mauldons, Nethergate and other real ales, good food (not Sun evening) inc home-made pies and vegetarian dishes, small and simply furnished – one of its two rooms no smoking; university sports photographs, local paintings, friendly pubby atmosphere, sheltered terrace with children's climbing frame *(Bill Ryan, Paul Cartledge, Susan and Nigel Wilson, Frank W Gadbois, LYM)*

☆ **Cambridge** [Ferry Path; car park on Chesterton Rd], *Old Spring:* Good individual atmosphere, cosy old-fashioned furnishings and decor, bare boards, gas lighting, lots of old pictures, decent straightforward bar food inc Sun roasts, well kept Greene King real ales, two open fires, back conservatory, summer barbecues; children till 8, has been open all day Sat *(Pauline and Martin Richardson, Stephen, Julie and Hayley Brown, Paul Cartledge, Trevor P Scott, LYM)*

☆ **Cambridge** [Midsummer Common], *Fort St George:* Particularly good in summer for its charming waterside position on Midsummer Common, overlooking boathouses; extensive but with interesting old-fashioned Tudor core, good bar food, well kept Greene King real ales, games in public bar, intriguing display of historic boating photographs *(Dr and Mrs P J S Crawshaw, Paul Cartledge, LYM)*

☆ **Cambridge** [King St], *Champion of the Thames:* Small and cosy town pub with welcoming landlord, pleasant young staff and good mix of students and others; sensitively preserved, with padded walls and seats, painted embossed wallpaper on the ceiling, lots of woodwork, no music, well kept Greene King IPA and Abbot; one of the best in the city for atmosphere *(Frank Cummins, William Pryce)*

☆ **Cambridge** [Clarendon St; TL4658], *Clarendon Arms:* Very popular local with well kept Greene King ales, wide choice of good cheap but adventurous bar lunches inc giant crusty sandwiches; open all day; bedrooms clean and comfortable *(I S Thomson, Paul Cartledge, Noel Jackson, Louise Campbell)*

☆ **Cambridge** [Tenison Rd/Wilkin St], *Salisbury Arms:* It's the dozen or so well kept and well priced real ales which bring crowds of mainly young customers to this spacious high-ceilinged main bar, renovated in fine style; good no-smoking area, decent basic lunchtime bar food from separate counter inc vegetarian dishes, games room, TV, farm cider, maybe jazz Sun lunchtime; can get very busy *(Frank Cummins, Paul Cartledge, Wayne Brindle, LYM)*

☆ **Cambridge** [Dover St (off East Rd)], *Tram Depot:* Bustling town pub with bare bricks, flagstones, old furniture, unconventional layout (light and airy upper area, glazed mezzanine – converted tram stables); well presented reasonable bar food (not Sat evening), pleasant service, well kept Everards and wide range of other changing ales; seats out in courtyard *(Wayne Brindle, Julian Holland, Bill Ryan, Frank Cummins)*

☆ **Cambridge** [Newmarket Rd], *Wrestlers:* Good cheap Thai food the main draw (inc take-aways); good choice of well kept Charles Wells and guest real ales, pool table, student atmosphere and simple furnishings; lively evenings (free live music Thurs-Sat), quieter lunchtime *(Dr R M Williamson, Anna Marsh, Paul Cartledge)*
Cambridge [Napier St; next to Grafton Centre], *Ancient Druids:* Big bright air-conditioned modern pub notable for Kite, Merlin and Druids Special ales brewed on premises; tapes playing in lavatories not to everyone's taste *(Bill Ryan, Ben Regan)*; [19 Bridge St], *Baron of Beef:* Small, friendly and traditional, lots of old photographs, panelling, Greene King ales from

uncommonly long counter, buffet food inc very tasty hot roast beef sandwich *(D K Carter, Paul Cartledge)*; [Newmarket St], *Bird in Hand:* Doing well under new landlord, with good food *(Dr R M Williamson)*; [4 King St], *Cambridge Arms:* Spacious and unusual bare-brick modern pub (former brewery) with several different areas and levels inc sheltered courtyard, Greene King IPA and Abbot, rather good food, lively evenings – maybe jazz nights *(Frank Cummins, Julian Holland, LYM)*; [18 Melbourne Pl], *Cricketers:* Good value food *(P Carpenter)*; [Barton Rd, corner Kings Rd], *Hat & Feathers:* Enjoyable local with well kept Tetleys, good value bar food *(Paul Cartledge)*; [King St], *Horse & Groom:* Well kept real ales not common around here such as Banks's, Morlands, Timothy Taylors; popular with young people, piped music *(Frank W Gadbois)*; [17 Bridge St, opp St Johns Coll], *Mitre:* Plain wooden floors with Victorian-style furnishing, welcoming staff, good food (no smoking area), good choice of well kept ales such as Adnams, Greene King Abbot, Ind Coope Burton, Marstons Pedigree, Tetleys and Wadworths 6X, Addlestone's cider *(David and Gill Carrington, Barbara Hatfield)*; [110 Water St, Chesterton], *Pike & Eel:* Worth knowing for pleasant and peaceful riverside setting *(Paul Cartledge)*; [Barton Rd], *Red Bull:* Plenty of bare boards in old-style town pub with good if often studenty atmosphere, wide choice of real ales tapped by jug from the cask, juke box (can be loud), helpful pleasant staff; can get crowded, seating limited *(Trevor P Scott)*

☆ **Catworth** [High St; B660 between A45 (Kimbolton) and A604; TL0873], *Racehorse:* Rather elegant village pub with lots of racing memorabilia, doing well under new licensees whom we reckoned to produce easily the best food at any of the Midlands 'Little' pubs in their time there – their seafood pie is particularly good, ditto puddings; well kept Theakstons Bitter, XB and Old Peculier, log fire games in public bar, tables outside; children welcome *(Howard and Margaret Buckman, LYM)*

☆ **Chatteris** [Pickle Fen, B1050 towards St Ives; TL3986], *Crafty Fox:* Wide choice of generous well presented food inc excellent Sun lunches in unpretentious but distinctive roadside pub with warm welcome and obliging landlord; small bar area with adjacent country-kitchen lounge, big back glass-covered summer eating area with fountain, fish pond and mature vines; well kept ales such as Morlands Old Speckled Hen and John Smiths on handpump, piped music *(Wayne Brindle, Julian Holland, John Beeken, Bill and Edee Miller, Frank W Gadbois, LYM)*
Chatteris [Bridge St], *Walk the Dog:* Adnams, Bass, Charringtons IPA and guest beer such as Greene King Abbot *(Paul Sutton)*

☆ **Clayhithe** [TL5064], *Bridge:* Pretty garden

by River Cam, good log fire in cosy beamed and timbered bar; good value bar food, restaurant, pleasant staff, well kept Everards Tiger; comfortable bedrooms in motel extension; staff pleasant *(Wayne Brindle, Martin and Pauline Richardson, LYM)*

☆ **Conington** [Boxworth Rd; TL3266], *White Swan:* Welcoming country pub very popular for good range of consistent well served bar food, good service, lovely big garden, well kept Greene King IPA and Abbot tapped from the cask, games room; restaurant *(Wayne Brindle, Martin and Pauline Richardson)*
Coton [quite handy for M11, junction 13: 2 miles W of Cambridge off A1303; TL4058], *John Barleycorn:* Very cheerful local atmosphere, Greene King IPA and Abbot on handpump, bar food; unpretentious place with old local photographs, garden with play area *(Keith and Janet Morris)*; *Plough:* Useful good value Whitbreads food pub with cleanly modern spacious back bar, front restaurant, good big garden; good service *(Dr and Mrs M Bailey, LYM)*

☆ **Croydon** [TL3149], *Queen Adelaide:* Sizeable beamed dining bar with standing timbers dividing off separate eating area, comfortable sofas, banquettes and stools, good choice of waitress-served food, well kept Mansfield Riding and Rayments *(Denise Plummer, Jim Froggatt, Keith Morris, D J Bundock)*

☆ **Downham** [Main St; sometimes known as Little Downham – the one near Ely; TL5283], *Plough:* Good basic home cooking at low prices in welcoming little fenland village local with lots of old photographs and bric-a-brac, Greene King ales under light top pressure, good choice of malt whiskies, tables outside; bustling atmosphere *(Basil Minson, Wayne Brindle)*

☆ **Dry Drayton** [off Park St, opp church; TL3862], *Black Horse:* Unspoilt 17th-c local with big helpings of good food inc wide vegetarian choice, wide range of beers inc weekly changing guests, friendly prompt service, pleasant atmosphere, central fireplace, games area, garden; camping/caravanning in field behind *(Keith and Janet Morris, Dr and Mrs M Bailey, E Robinson, P and D Carpenter)*

☆ **Dullingham** [50 Station Rd; TL6357], *Kings Head:* Cosy dining pub, popular for a wide range of food from sandwiches to interesting main dishes (inc German specialities) and lots of puddings at very reasonable prices; open fires, well kept Tolly and Original, good choice of fairly priced wines, friendly staff, fairy-lit seats out above the broad village green; children in family room – does not feel part of pub *(Mr and Mrs J Back, John Fahy, Gwen and Peter Andrews, Nigel and Sara Walker, LYM)*
Dunstable, Beds [High St N; TL0221], *Old Sugarloaf:* Three busy and hospitable bars, quick friendly mainly Antipodean staff,

good range of real ales, good food in bar and restaurant *(W J Albone, L K Edlin)*

Eaton Bray, Beds [SP9620], *White Horse:* Wide choice of generous good food and great country atmosphere in rambling old low-beamed dining pub with timbered dividers, suit of armour in one room, Greene King real ales; ranks of tables on back lawn, good walking nearby *(Ian, Kathleen and Helen Corsie)*

Eaton Socon [Old Great North Rd; village signposted from A1 nr St Neots; TL1658], *White Horse:* Good value freshly prepared bar food and well kept Whitbreads-related and guest real ales in interesting series of rambling and attractively furnished low-beamed rooms, very friendly helpful service and relaxing atmosphere, nice high-backed traditional settles around fine log fire in end room; play area in back garden; children in eating areas; bedrooms *(George Atkinson, Dave Irving, LYM)*

Eaton Socon, *Crown:* Comfortable little old inn, refurbished but not over-heavily, with wide and interesting choice of perfectly kept real ales served in the frothy W Yorks style; two cosy low-beamed bars, friendly service, moderately priced bar food (not Sun), open fire, nostalgic piped music, restaurant (good steaks); no T-shirts *(John C Baker, Denise Plummer, Jim Froggatt, S Eldridge, M C Jeanes)*

Eaton Socon, *Waggon & Horses:* Attractive and popular yet unsmoky old open-plan low-beamed bar with good value plain food inc copious fresh veg, delicious home-made puddings, good Sun lunches; Allied ales, welcoming landlord, restaurant doing lots of steaks *(Mrs L E Baker, H Bramwell, Denise Plummer, Jim Froggatt, S Eldridge)*

Elsworth [TL3163], *George & Dragon:* Attractively furnished and decorated panelled main bar and quieter back dining area, plenty of character and atmosphere, wide choice of decent food inc good Sun carvery, Courage-related ales, open fire, unhurried pleasant service; nice terraces, play area in garden, restaurant; attractive village *(Martin and Pauline Richardson, LYM)*

Elton [Village St; TL0893], *Black Horse:* Low stone building in bypassed village, with lounge, bar, games room and restaurant, wide choice of reasonably priced straightforward bar food, Adnams and Wadworths Farmers Glory (rare in this area); tables out under chestnut trees; very handy for Elton Hall *(Mr and Mrs J Back)*

Ely [Annesdale; off A10 on outskirts; TL5380], *Cutter:* Comfortable and friendly series of relatively unspoilt bars and a genuine welcome for children, but the undoubted draw is the riverside setting – lovely in summer, with plenty of tables outside; decent food, real ales *(W H and E Thomas, Steve Goodchild, Nigel and Sara Walker, Wayne Brindle, Clive Petts, LYM)*

Ely [Silver St], *Prince Albert:* Cheerful local with well kept real ales, good atmosphere and smashing cathedral-side garden *(Wayne Brindle)*

☆ **Fen Ditton** [High St; TL4860], *Ancient Shepherds:* Generous helpings of good food in comfortable lounge (with settees) and (not Sun) restaurant; excellent housekeeping, no music or fruit machines *(Dr and Mrs M Bailey, Paul Cartledge, Trevor P Scott)*

☆ **Fen Ditton** [Green End], *Plough:* Big busy riverside Brewers Fayre pub with promptly served food inc good specials, fresh appetising puddings and children's menu, friendly staff, well kept Whitbreads beers at reasonable prices; nice walk across meadows from town *(Roy Y Bromell, Julian Holland, LYM)*

Fen Drayton [TL3368], *Black Horse:* Worth knowing for good value unpretentious well cooked food *(P Carpenter)*

Fenstanton [High St; off A604 near St Ives; TL3168], *King William IV:* Civilised low-beamed pub with wide choice of above-average food inc good ploughman's and help-yourself salad bar, also good restaurant; well kept Greene King ales, good range of spirits, pretty outside *(C J Westmoreland)*

☆ **Fowlmere** [High St; TL4245], *Swan House:* Friendly and comfortable local with enormous log fire, wide and interesting choice of reasonably priced good bar food, good choice of well kept real ales, attentive landlord, piano *(John Fahy)*

Fowlmere [Long Lane], *Queens Head:* Simple beamed family lounge and larger low-ceilinged bar in pretty 17th-c thatched cottage, nice garden with boules pitch, well kept Greene King beers, friendly landlady; more orthodox hot dishes tending to replace the splendid range of unusual cheeses and home-made breads which won it so many friends under the previous regime, but still worth knowing *(Stephen, Julie and Hayley Brown, LYM)*

Grafham [TL1669], *Montagu Arms:* Well kept Bass and Greene King ales, decent range of bar food, restaurant serving locally-caught trout, weekday OAP bargains, Fri evening fish and chips, good value Sun lunch; bedrooms *(J E Brown)*

☆ **Grantchester** [TL4354], *Green Man:* Attractively laid out and welcoming, with individual furnishings, lots of beams, good choice of food, Adnams and Tetleys on handpump, extremely pleasant licensees, no music; nice village, a short stroll from lovely riverside meadows; children welcome *(Paul Cartledge, Andrew and Ruth Triggs, LYM)*

Grantchester, *Red Lion:* Spacious, airy and comfortable food pub with sheltered terrace and good-sized lawn (animals to entertain the many children); well kept Real ales, staff helpful even when busy; restaurant *(Neil and Angela Hunter, LYM)*; [junction Coton rd with Cambridge—Trumpington rd], *Rupert Brooke:* Renovated, but traditional beamed rooms, pleasant, friendly and cosy, with coal fire, Whitbreads-related ales, wide choice of usual food inc vegetarian, discreet piped music *(R I and E B Page)*

Great Abington [off A604 Cambridge—Haverhill, and A11; TL5348], *Three Tuns:* Lovely setting, friendly bar staff *(John and Elspeth Howell)*

☆ **Guyhirn** [High Rd (off A47); TF3903], *Oliver Twist:* Particularly good choice of reasonably priced food, lots of real ales and dozens of other beers, good atmosphere, big open fire; very popular as lunchtime business meeting place *(E Robinson, Dr Sherriff, G D Lee)*

Hail Weston [just off A45, handy for A1 St Neots bypass; TL1662], *Royal Oak:* Picturesque thatched and beamed pub in quiet village nr Grafham Water; good value food inc sandwiches and vegetarian dishes, cosy fire, well kept Charles Wells, pleasant service, family room with bar billiards, nice big garden with good play area which children can use even if pub's shut *(Bob and Maggie Atherton, Andy and Jill Kassube)*

Harlington, Beds [High St; TL0330], *White Hart:* Large very well renovated Fullers pub, good atmosphere, well kept beers *(Martin Kay, Andrea Fowler)*

☆ **Harston** [48 Royston Rd (A10); nr M11 junction 11; TL4251], *Queens Head:* Consistently generous decent food (not Sun evening) inc very nice well presented pies, well kept Greene King IPA and Abbot, quick friendly service, no smoking area; tables outside *(Jim Farmer, Trevor P Scott)*

Hemingford Abbots [High St; TL2870], *Axe & Compass:* Old pub nr interesting church, reasonably priced food, Greene King and Courage-related ales *(CW, JW)*

Henlow, Beds [TL1738], *Five Bells:* Comfortable one-bar pub with restaurant opp church, very wide range of reasonably priced home-made food inc good value lunchtime specials, well kept Greene King beers, occasional live music Sun lunchtimes *(G R Weaver)*

☆ **Hexton,** Beds [Pegsdon; B655 a mile E of Hexton; TL1230], *Live & Let Live:* Very snug and traditional, with two rooms opening off tiled and panelled taproom, good cheap food inc vegetarian, Greene King and other real ales kept well, good service, entertaining parrot, lovely garden below Chilterns *(Jim Farmer, LYM)*

☆ **Heydon** [off A505 W of M11 junction 10; TL4340], *King William IV:* Extraordinary collection of furniture and bric-a-brac, English and continental, in rambling attractively lit partly 16th-c beamed and timbered rooms; tables in garden, paddock with animals; several real ales, bar food, friendly service, central log fire, interesting parrot, piped music; bedrooms *(P Carpenter, LYM)*

☆ **Hildersham** [High St; TL5448], *Pear Tree:* Busy old-fashioned local atmosphere, very obliging licensees, huge woodburner, comfortable seats, big helpings of very good straightforward home cooking (they give

lessons), inc children's helpings, home-made bread and ice creams; well kept Greene King IPA and Abbot, exceptionally clean; tables in back garden with aviary *(Jenny and Michael Back, Nick and Mary Baker)*

Histon [High St; TL4363], *Red Lion:* Local with good atmosphere, good choice of well kept beers such as Boddingtons, Hook Norton Old Hookey and Wadworths 6X, reasonably priced food *(Paul Cartledge, Ian Hydes)*

Horningsea [TL4962], *Crown & Pheasant:* Recently refurbished in excellent style, well kept Elgoods on handpump, very friendly service, pleasant food; quite atmospheric; bedrooms superb *(Wayne Brindle)*

Houghton [TL2872], *Jolly Butchers:* Beams and brasses; quiet family atmosphere, good bar food inc Sun lunches, tables outside, occasional barbecues; children's play area *(Julian Holland)*

☆ **Huntingdon** [TL2371], *Old Bridge:* Civilised hotel by River Great Ouse, with superb gardens, terraces and landing stage; good imaginative food – not cheap, but very popular, inc great cold table; good wine by the glass, fine coffee, afternoon teas, good waitress service, charming plush lounge; monthly jazz nights; bedrooms excellent, if expensive *(George Atkinson, R C Wiles, Julian Holland)*

☆ **Huntingdon** [Victoria Sq], *Victoria:* Cosy and welcoming local in pretty part of town, wide choice of generous good food and of well kept real ales; Sun lunch particularly popular *(Wayne Brindle)*

☆ **Ireland,** Beds [off A600 Shefford—Bedford – OS Sheet 153 map reference 135414; TL1341], *Black Horse:* Very pleasant isolated pub, extended into big dining area with brick pillars, beamery and log-effect gas fire; generous helpings of good reasonably priced food (not Sun evening), good friendly staff, Bass and Stones real ale, tables in garden; closed Mon *(George Atkinson, Richard Holloway, S Eldridge)*

☆ **Kennett** [Bury Rd; TL7066], *Bell:* Delightful old heavy-beamed and timbered inn closed in 1992 but reopened under new management 1994, after sympathetic refurbishment – now plusher and neater: good food (dining area already so popular booking may be needed), well kept Bass, Greene King IPA, Abbot and Rayments and Marstons Pedigree on handpump, rather a county atmosphere *(Frank W Gadbois, John C Baker, LYM)*

Kensworth, Beds [B4540, Whipsnade end; TL0318], *Farmers Boy:* Fine village pub with well kept Fullers, good lounge bar, excellent old-fashioned dining room (more restaurany evenings and Sun); play area and rabbit hutches in fenced-off garden by fields; children very welcome *(Michael and Alison Sandy and family)*

☆ **Kimbolton** [20 High St; TL0968], *New Sun:* Recently reopened, more bistro than pub but pleasant atmosphere, good if not cheap food and good range of well kept real ales such as Hook Norton *(Prof J V Wood, Stephen Brown)*

Linslade, Beds [SP9225], *Globe:* Very popular, even midweek, for promptly served good food; pleasant walks nearby *(Bill Sykes)*

Linton [TL5646], *Dog & Duck:* Picturesque traditional thatched pub with decent beers, friendly staff and you can feed the ducks outside *(Bill and Lydia Ryan)*

Luton, Beds [TL0921], *Brewery Tap:* Nice atmosphere, good range of ales, reasonably priced lunchtime food; packed Thurs-Sat evenings *(Andrew Jeeves, Carole Smart);* [Latimer Rd], *Mother Redcap:* Well kept Greene King IPA and Abbot in open-plan pub with screen between bar and door, lots of seats and round tables, sensibly placed darts and pinball behind end fireplace; plush but not too smart, welcoming and comfortable *(Michael Sandy); Wigmore Arms:* Big smart steak pub, good value, with big leather chesterfields in eating area, Allied ales inc Mild, no under-21s in lounge (separate games bar with pool tables) *(Phil and Heidi Cook)*

☆ **Marholm** [TF1402], *Fitzwilliam Arms:* Thatched stone-built inn, cheerful atmosphere in attractively refurbished and comfortable rambling three-room bar, good value food, efficient service, well kept Allied real ales; good big garden *(David and Michelle Hedges)*

Moggerhanger, Beds [TL1449], *Guinea:* Lively and popular two-bar pub with Charles Wells Eagle and a guest beer, interesting food; no children *(S Eldridge)*

☆ **Needingworth** [Overcote Lane; pub signposted from A1123; TL3472], *Pike & Eel:* Marvellous peaceful riverside location, with spacious lawns and marina; two separate eating areas, one a carvery, in extensively glass-walled block overlooking water, boats and swans; easy chairs and big open fire in room off separate main plush bar, well kept Adnams, Bass, and Greene King Abbot, friendly and helpful staff, provision for children; clean simple bedrooms, good breakfasts *(Brian and Jill Bond, Julian Holland, Clare Dawkins, Gordon Phillips, LYM)*

☆ **Odell, Beds** [Little Odell; SP9657], *Mad Dog:* Cosy and friendly old beamed and thatched Greene King pub with wide choice of good value food from sandwiches to local venison, inc several vegetarian dishes and popular Sun lunch; three well kept real ales, open fire in inglenook, quiet piped music, good service, no dogs or children; pleasant garden with miniature fairground roundabout; handy for Harrold-Odell Country Park *(T G Saul, Dr M V Jones)*

☆ **Old Warden, Beds** [TL1343], *Hare & Hounds:* Cosy and unpretentious old local with wide choice of generously served fresh bar food, welcoming efficient staff, well kept Charles Wells beers, comfortable lounge, character public bar, separate dining room (shame about the smokers), garden with children's play area; beautiful village, handy for Shuttleworth collection; very popular in summer *(the Shinkmans, Sue Holland, Dave Webster, Bob Hurling, Rosalind Hodges, Denise Plummer, Jim Froggatt)*

Orton Longueville [part of Orton Hall Hotel; TL1696], *Old Ramblewood:* Recently converted stable block, sympathetically done with stripped woodwork and stone; pleasant atmosphere, real ales inc Adnams Bitter and Broadside, Bass, Fullers London Pride, Greene King IPA and Youngs Special, wide range of food from soup or ploughman's to steak diane *(Peter and Pat Frogley)*

☆ **Peterborough** [465 Oundle Rd – off A605 in Woodston; TL1999], *Botolph Arms:* Attractive ivy-covered flagstone-floored Sam Smiths pub, popular with business people at lunchtime; good facilities for disabled visitors, safe play area *(David Hedges, David and Michelle Hedges)*

Peterborough [North St], *Bogarts:* Basic pub with several good real ales and simple snacks and meals; handy for the Westgate shopping centre *(Tony Gayfer);* [Town Bridge], *Charters:* Converted Dutch barge with particularly good range of beers – Adnams Broadside, Bass, Fullers London Pride, three guest beers and a Mild, at reasonable prices; bar down in former hold, with restaurant on deck overlooking river *(David and Michelle Hedges)*

☆ **Potton, Beds** [TL2449], *Royal Oak:* Good choice of lunchtime food, esp remarkable value roasts with plenty of fresh local vegetables; warm welcome, pleasant dining room *(Maysie Thompson)*

☆ **Radwell, Beds** [TL0057], *Swan:* Attractive thatched pub in small quiet village, roomy and cosy inside, two rooms joined by narrow passage, beams, woodburner, lots of prints, maybe piped classical music, good choice of delicious food from soup and sandwiches up inc good puddings, Charles Wells Eagle on handpump, decent coffee, hospitable landlord, popular evening restaurant; pleasant garden *(George Atkinson, Derek and Sylvia Stephenson, Olivier Carr-Forster, RH)*

☆ **Ridgmont, Beds** [SP9736], *Rose & Crown:* Consistently good all round, with good sensible pub food, warm welcome, choice of well kept real ales, good coffee, interesting collection of *Rupert Annual* covers in well laid out lounge; low-ceilinged traditional public bar with open fire, games inc darts and pool; piped music, stables restaurant (not Mon or Tues evenings); long and attractive suntrap sheltered back garden; children allowed in bar eating area; easy parking, good wheelchair access *(A T Langton, L M Miall, LYM)*

Roothams Green, Beds [TL1057], *Wheatsheaf:* Six real ales, decent averagely priced food *(Chris Aslett)*

☆ **nr Sandy, Beds** [Deepdale; B1042 towards

Potton and Cambridge; TL2049],
Locomotive: Reliable pub nr RSPB HQ,
very reasonably priced food nicely prepared
and presented, friendly staff, well kept
Charles Wells Eagle and Bombardier, no
smoking area, lots of railway pictures and
signs, attractive and sizeable garden with
views; piped radio, good service; can be
busy weekends; children allowed in eating
area *(George Atkinson, Dono and Carol
Leaman, Denise Plummer, Jim Froggatt, Ian
Phillips)*

☆ **Sawston** [High St (Cambridge Rd);
TL4849], *Greyhound:* Cosy, clean, friendly
and comfortable, with open fire,
Whitbreads-related real ales, good choice of
generously served food inc vegetarian,
obliging staff; restaurant area, good big
garden, good facilities for children *(Martin
and Pauline Richardson, E M Goodman-
Smith, Nigel Gibbs)*

Sharnbrook, Beds [Templars Way, SE of
village; SP9959], *Fordham Arms:* Quick,
polite and friendly service in well kept pub,
main bar laid out for food service – very big
helpings of lasagne, gammon and so forth;
well kept Boddingtons and Marstons
Pedigree, decent house wines; local
paintings, copper pans and nick-nacks on
walls, smaller bar with darts and pool
table, big garden with play area *(Joyce and
Stephen Stackhouse); Swan With Two Nicks:*
Well kept Charles Wells beers and guests
such as Adnams Broadside and Morlands
Old Speckled Hen; adventurous menu, esp
Central American dishes *(John C Baker)*

☆ **Sharpenhoe**, Beds [Harlington Rd;
TL0630], *Lynmore:* Huge helpings of
reasonably priced food inc children's dishes
in recently extended spacious and friendly
beamy family lounge and back dining area
(good views), well kept Boddingtons,
Morlands Old Speckled Hen and Tetleys,
generous wine glasses; new public bar,
good garden for children, big Wendy house;
popular with walkers *(Michael and Alison
Sandy)*

☆ **Shefford**, Beds [2 North Bridge St, Clifton
Rd; TL1438], *White Hart:* Genuine-feeling
old coaching inn, friendly rather than
smart, with interesting local ales such as
Banks & Taylors Dragon Slayer and hefty
Old Bat, superbly kept, very respectable
food inc some interesting dishes, friendly
landlady, locals and boxer dogs, pleasant
lounge, dining room, basic public bar; four
bedrooms *(Frank W Gadbois, Roz and Bob
Hurling, Derek and Sylvia Stephenson, John
and Shirley Barrett, John C Baker, Buck and
Gillian Shinkman, BB)*

☆ **Shepreth** [12 High St; just off A10 S of
Cambridge; TL3947], *Plough:* Bright and
airy local, very neatly kept, with modern
furnishings, bow-tied staff, Adnams
Broadside, Boddingtons, Greene King IPA
and Tetleys on handpump kept well, decent
wines, popular and well presented home-
cooked food from sandwiches up in bar
and side dining room, piped music; pleasant

back garden with fairy-lit arbour, summer
barbecues and play area *(Trevor Scott, Susan
and Nigel Wilson, BB)*

☆ **Silsoe**, Beds [TL0835], *George:* Large
pleasant open-plan hotel bar with public
end, good bar meals (high chairs provided),
restaurant, well kept Greene King IPA and
Abbot, big garden with aviary, rabbits and
play equipment; organist Sat evening;
bedrooms *(Phil and Heidi Cook, Michael,
Alison and Rhiannon Sandy)*

☆ **Southill**, Beds [off B658 SW of
Biggleswade; TL1542], *White Horse:*
Delightful big garden with children's rides
on diesel-engine 7in railway, separate
sheltered lawn with bird feeders, garden
shop and good play area; well decorated
comfortable main lounge, dining room with
spotlit well, small public bar with prints,
harness and big woodburner; good value
food (not Sun evening, and polystyrene
plates for outside) inc wide choice of
sandwiches and snacks, Whitbreads-related
real ales; children in eating areas *(JJW,
CMW, Joyce and Stephen Stackhouse, Denise
Plummer, Jim Froggatt, Michael, Alison and
Rhiannon Sandy, LYM)*

Stapleford [TL4651], *Rose:* Comfortable,
friendly and well run, in pretty village
setting; generous good fresh food, friendly
service, good range of beers, log fire *(Mr
and Mrs M A Judson)*

Steppingley, Beds [TL0135], *French Horn:*
18th-c former bakery, olde-worlde with
brass and oak beams; Spanish chef does
good bar food, popular restaurant with
good very varied menu inc seasonal game;
well kept beers on handpump *(Ron and Val
Broom)*

Stow Cum Quy [Newmarket Rd (old A45);
TL5260], *Prince Albert:* Basic roadside pub
with five changing well chosen and well
kept complementary beers, good
atmosphere, cheerfully enthusiastic staff
(John C Baker)

☆ **Stretham** [High St – OS Sheet 154 map
reference 535745; TL5174], *Red Lion:*
Tastefully rebuilt and refurbished, with well
kept real ales such as Greene King IPA and
Nethergate Old Growler, good bar food inc
vegetarian dishes, popular restaurant, solid
pine furniture, conservatory, separate
attractive upstairs games room, friendly
staff *(Caroline and Gerard McAleese, John C
Baker)*

☆ **Studham**, Beds [TL0215], *Red Lion:*
Comfortable, friendly pub in attractive
setting below grassy common, good range
of well kept beers and good generous food
(not Sun), cheerful modernish decor, chatty
helpful staff; tables outside, handy for
Whipsnade Zoo *(Mr and Mrs McDougal,
George Atkinson, Michael, Alison and
Rhiannon Sandy, LYM)*

Studham, Beds [Dunstable Rd; TL0215],
Bell: 17th-c village pub doing well under
welcoming newish management, with
plates, brass and prints in lounge and
restaurant behind, flame-effect gas fire,

darts, pool and juke box in public bar; well kept Bass, Charrington IPA, Ind Coope Burton and Tetleys on handpump; good value generous home-made bar food; good no smoking evening restaurant (not Sun/Mon); big back garden *(Phil and Heidi Cook)*

☆ **Sutton**, Beds [village signposted off B1040 Biggleswade—Potton; TL2247], *John o' Gaunt:* Cosy and cottagey low-beamed lounge bar, very relaxing, with easy chairs and low settles around copper-topped tables, newspapers, open fire, simple bar food, well kept Greene King IPA; traditional public bar with hodd skittles; close to fine 14th-c packhorse bridge – you have to go through a shallow ford to reach the pub *(Joyce and Stephen Stackhouse, LYM)*

☆ **Swaffham Prior** [B1102 NE of Cambridge; TL5764], *Red Lion:* Welcoming and attractive village local with well kept Tolly Original, maybe Old Strong, wide range of food from sandwiches and ploughman's to steaks, dining area divided into several separate spaces, quick cheerful service; unusually plush gents' *(Margaret and Trevor Errington, J N Child)*

Swavesey, Cambs [TL3668], *White Horse:* Over last three years or so enthusiastic owners have converted this tucked-away village pub into a good welcoming place with bar food (not Sun evening) from sandwiches to steaks inc vegetarian dishes, all home-cooked using fresh ingredients; three real ales, good choice of other drinks *(Anon; more reports please)*

Tebworth, Beds [The Lane; SP9926], *Queens Head:* Exceptionally cheap straightforward food inc perfect chips in light and airy lounge bar with old plush banquettes, helpful landlord, well kept Charles Wells Eagle and a guest such as Adnams Broadside; well spaced picnic-table sets in tree-sheltered garden, sheep in nearby fields *(Michael and Alison Sandy)*

☆ **The Turves** [W of March; TL3396], *Three Horseshoes:* Good food esp fish and shellfish in friendly extended pub with family conservatory; well kept real ales *(John C Baker, Richard Balls)*

☆ **Thorney** [A47/B1040; TF2804], *Rose & Crown:* Wide range of well presented reasonably priced plentiful food, good service, pleasant surroundings; good family pub *(Eustace A Turner, C and J M Day)*

Tilsworth [SP9724], *Anchor:* Opened out a little and brightened up, food inc set Sun lunch, warm welcome, well kept Fullers; side lawn with picnic-table sets on paving stones, more paddock part with wooden climber and slide *(Michael Sandy)*

☆ **Toddington**, Beds [19 Church Sq; handy for M1 junction 12; TL0028], *Sow & Pigs:* Good value freshly prepared food (be prepared to wait a bit; evening meals must be booked) inc vegetarian, banquettes, pews and bare boards, amusing pig motifs, well kept Greene King Abbot and Raymonts on handpump, good coffee, two

real fires, friendly black labrador and landlord; books for sale for charity and board games piled up on piano; back pool room now a 'Victorian' dining room for parties; small garden with benches *(JJW, CMW)*

Toddington [64 High St], *Bedford Arms:* Pleasant well preserved beamed Tudor pub with big back garden/orchard, split bar/lounge areas, decent straightforward food inc vegetarian and good baked potatoes, Charles Wells Eagle and Bombardier, pleasant friendly service, family area beyond standing timbers *(George Atkinson)*; [Longer Lane], *Oddfellows Arms:* Small bars, beams and stripped pine, warm and pleasant, Allied real ales, short choice of reasonably priced weekday food, helpful landlord *(Dr and Mrs M Bailey)*

☆ **Turvey**, Beds [Bridge St; A428 NW of Bedford, at W end of village; SP9452], *Three Fyshes:* No frills but full of character, with flagstones, early 17th-c beams, inglenook fires, good beer brewed there, several well kept ales from other breweries, farm ciders; welcoming staff; good value food from sandwiches and big crusty rolls to substantial hot dishes inc vegetarian; newspapers, traditional games, no music (but maybe TV); relaxed family atmosphere in garden with access to Great Ouse, summer barbecues, dogs, cats and rabbits; open all day Sat; children and dogs welcome, can get crowded *(Roger Danes, Stephen, Julie and Hayley Brown, LYM)*

☆ **Turvey** [off A428, by church], *Three Cranes:* Modern-feeling clean two-level bar, efficient and pleasant, with simple, generous and reliable bar food from good sandwiches and ploughman's to mixed grills, well kept real ales such as Hook Norton Best, Fullers London Pride, decent wines and whiskies, pleasant staff, unobtrusive piped music; distinctive portico with jettied upper storey; restaurant, garden with climbing frame and occasional jazz evenings or barbecues; children welcome; bedrooms *(Clare Dawkins, Gordon Phillips, Maysie Thompson, Stephen and Julie Brown, BB)*

Upper Dean, Beds [TL0467], *Three Compasses:* 350-year-old thatched pub with authentic beams, friendly, caring landlord and good choice of inexpensively priced food (Sun lunch bookings only); shame about the piped music *(Hilary Aslett)*

☆ **Upware** [off A1123 W of Soham; (full name Five Miles From Anywhere, No Hurry); TL5370], *Five Miles From Anywhere:* Friendly service and decent if not cheap food in remarkably sited spacious modern riverside free house – its name means what it says *(P and D Carpenter, LYM)*

Wansford [TL0799], *Paper Mills:* Modernised old pub with two Allied real ales, good food – big dining room very popular for Sun lunch *(Frank Gadbois)*

Waterbeach [A10; TL4965], *Slap Up:* Wide choice of generous food inc popular carvery and Sun lunch, about 30 home-made puddings in cold cabinet *(John Whittaker, Andrew Latchem, Helen Reed)*

Westoning, Beds [High St/Greenfield Rd; 1½ miles from M1, junction 12: SP0332], *Bell:* Friendly 15th-c pub with lots of oak beams, copper, brass, cuckoo clock, spinning wheel, needlework and painting; comfortable settles and chairs, inglenook fireplace separating two rooms, good food inc vegetarian and children's, Greene King IPA, Abbot and Rayments on handpump, split-level garden with play area and boules; weekday bargains for over-55s *(CMW, JJW)*

☆ **Whipsnade**, Beds [B4540 E; TL0117], *Old Hunters Lodge:* Pleasant snug area on right, plusher modernised main lounge, wide range of attractively priced good generous food from sandwiches up esp fish with some children's helpings, roaring fire, good friendly service, well kept Greene King or Websters, oil paintings and castle prints, subdued piped music; spacious old-world restaurant; handy for zoo *(Brian and Anna Marsden, David Shillitoe)*

☆ **Whittlesford** [off B1379 S of Cambridge; handy for M10 junction 10, via A505; TL4748], *Tickell Arms:* Very individual, ornate and theatrical, with heavy furnishings, dim lighting, lovely log fires, attractive flower-filled conservatory, beautiful formal garden, wide range of imaginative bar food which though not cheap can be good value, friendly service (can slow when busy), well reproduced classical music; closed Mon (except bank hols); the wines often a better bet than the beers; no credit cards *(P and D Carpenter, Bob and Maggie Atherton, John and Beverly Bailey, P I Burton, Barbara Hatfield, LYM)*

☆ **Wingfield**, Beds [SP9926], *Plough:* Low-beamed but spacious, with good atmosphere, friendly staff, well kept ales such as Adnams, Banks & Taylors and unusual guests; usual food all day from sandwiches up inc good fresh chips, picnic-table sets out on grass – dogs allowed out in front *(the Shinkmans)*

☆ **Wisbech** [North Brink; TF4609], *Red Lion:* Friendly, comfortable and civilised long front bar in lovely Georgian terrace on River Nene, nr centre and NT Peckover House; wide choice of good value well presented home-cooked food inc vegetarian, fish and good salad bar, good range of beers inc local Elgoods *(Dr Sherriff, J M Wooll)*

☆ **Wisbech** [53 North Brink], *Rose:* Cosy, friendly and popular little pub in same splendid riverside spot, notable for exceptional choice of well kept real ales such as Badger, Butterknowle, Cains, Clarks, Daleside, Smiles and Thwaites; good value filled french bread, no juke box or pool tables *(L Priest, R Martin, Julian Holland)*

Witcham [Silver St; TL4679], *White Horse:* Relaxed and very friendly, with good value food running up to steaks (not Mon or Sun evening) *(Audrey and Dennis Nelson)*

☆ **Woburn**, Beds [SP9433], *Bell:* Consistently well prepared food inc lunchtime buffet and evening restaurant, well kept Greene King Abbot and friendly service in restored old inn's small but comfortable bar and dining area; lots of Spy cartoons, piped music, tables outside; bedrooms *(Ted Corrin, Peter and Jean Brooks, George Atkinson)*

Woburn, *Birchmoor Arms:* Cosy and pleasant country pub doing well now it's a free house, with well kept range of beers and decent food in separate eating area *(Mr and Mrs K H Frostick);* [1 Bedford St], *Black Horse:* Spacious and cheery open-plan food pub with wide choice from sandwiches and baked potatoes to moderately priced steaks, also children's and vegetarian dishes; jolly chef and good service, well kept real ales inc Nethergate on handpump, quick service; open all day summer Sat and bank hols, lots of summer barbecues in pleasant sheltered garden; children in eating areas *(Andrew Jeeves, Carole Smart, Ron and Sheila Corbett, LYM)*

Post Office address codings confusingly give the impression that some pubs are in Cambridgeshire, when they're really in the Leicestershire or Midlands groups of counties (which is where we list them).

Cheshire

Value is clearly what Cheshire people look for in their pubs: big helpings of decent food, well kept drinks and low prices. This makes it one of the best parts of the country for brewery-chain dining pubs, with the regional brewers (or in the last two cases ex-brewers) Marstons, Boddingtons and the locally based Greenalls all having some of their very best dining pubs in this county. As so often, though, it's in the more independently run places (whether or not they're tied to a brewery) that the value for money equation is given a real quality lift – with the bonus of a good bit of character on top. Places we'd pick out for particular food value include the Jolly Thresher at Broomedge, the Alvanley Arms at Cotebrook, the Sutton Hall Hotel near Macclesfield, the Swan at Marbury (the very long-serving licensees now joined by their son), the Dog at Peover Heath, the Smoker at Plumley (more and more popular these days), the Rising Sun at Tarporley and the canalside Dusty Miller at Wrenbury. Shining above even these is the splendid Cholmondeley Arms near Bickley Moss: almost unique in being chosen by us for the second year running as its county's Dining Pub of the Year. The White Lion at Barthomley, an unspoilt thatched gem, and the very pleasantly relaxed and traditional Ring o' Bells at Overton both notch up an enviable record for serving decent food at remarkably low prices. Throughout the county, pub food prices stand out as being much lower than the national average, given equivalent quality: Cheshire pub diners are typically saving between £1 and £2 on a good main dish, compared with diners down south. Perhaps because of the area's relative prosperity, though, pub food prices have started to drift up here, and you should keep a beady eye on menu prices here over the next few months. Drinks prices have been holding relatively steady over the last few years, and now average about 15p a pint lower than the national norm. Two Sam Smiths pubs, the Bird in Hand at Mobberley and Whipping Stocks at Over Peover, stand out for particularly low beer prices, and we found pubs tied to Hydes and Robinsons very good value on the drinks side, too. Four pubs in the area this year win our new Beer Award for the quality of their offerings: the White Lion at Barthomley, the friendly Irish-run Ryles Arms at Sutton, the George & Dragon in the pretty village of Great Budworth, and the Leathers Smithy up at Langley. These two last pubs are newly back among the main entries this year, after an absence. Other newcomers are the canalside Barbridge Inn at Barbridge (a family pub currently doing well under a new manager), and – quite a find in a county we thought we knew really well – the charming Boot & Slipper at Wettenhall. Sadly, we have to warn that the licensees who have made the Stanley Arms at Bottom of the Oven such a nice pub (with really good home cooking) will definitely be leaving, though as we went to press they hoped that they would still be there for at least the early months of this new edition's currency. There are some strong contenders for joining the main entries in the Lucky Dip at the end of the chapter, including particularly the Grosvenor Arms at Aldford (a definite comer), Bhurtpore at Aston (new to us, but very promising indeed), Beeston Castle at Beeston, Vale in Bollington, quite a few pubs of considerable character in Chester, the Copper Mine at Fullers Moor, Birch & Bottle at

Higher Whitley, Chetwode Arms at Lower Whitley, an interesting choice of pubs in both Mobberley and Nantwich, the Olde Park Gate at Over Peover, Golden Pheasant at Plumley, Highwayman at Rainow, Swettenham Arms at Swettenham (new licensees with a good track record) and reopened Ferry outside Warrington. As we have inspected virtually all of these we can firmly vouch for their quality.

BARBRIDGE   SJ6156 Map 7

Barbridge Inn

Village signposted just off A51 N of Nantwich; OS Sheet 118 map reference 616566

For those arriving by boat, there is easy canalside mooring at the bottom of the big garden here – or you can just sit at the picnic-table sets (some under cover) and watch the narrow-boats; also, a play house, climber, swings and slide, and summer Sunday lunchtime barbecues. It's very friendly and has been a particularly well run pub (it's under new management this year), comfortably modernised and open-plan, and serving a wide choice of good, popular bar food: filled baked potatoes (from £1.75), sandwiches (from £1.85), ploughman's (from £3.45), steak and kidney pie (£3.95), gammon and egg (£4.45), spinach and ricotta cannelloni (£4.65), seafood crêpes (£4.85), farmhouse grill (£6.95), daily specials, puddings (£1.95), and roast Sunday lunch (£4.95); the balustraded restaurant area (part of which is no smoking), up steps, overlooks the canal. Well kept Boddingtons and Cains on handpump and decent wines; rack of daily papers, darts, dominoes, fruit machine, video game, and piped music. There's a side conservatory, and children's area (the children's menu has a colouring page, with crayons from the bar; also, baby-changing facilities). Good disabled facilities. *(Recommended by Brian and Anna Marsden, Richard Lewis, Patrick and Mary McDermott; more reports on the new regime, please)*

Boddingtons (Whitbreads) ~ Manager W H Eyre ~ Real ale ~ Meals and snacks ~ Restaurant ~ Wettenhall (01270) 73443 ~ Children welcome ~ Jazz Thurs evenings ~ Open 11.30-11; 11.30-3, 5.30-11 in winter

BARTHOMLEY   SJ7752 Map 7

White Lion   ★   £   ◧

A mile from M6 junction 16; take Alsager rd and is signposted at roundabout

Very much part of the local community and popular with a good mix of people, this black and white timbered pub is one of the most attractive buildings in a pretty village. There's a fine, unspoilt atmosphere and the simply furnished main room has attractively moulded black panelling, and heavy oak beams dating back to 1614 (one big enough to house quite a collection of plates). On the walls are Cheshire watercolours and prints, and there's also a lovely open fire, and latticed windows. Up some steps, a second room has another open fire, more oak panelling, a high-backed winged settle, a paraffin lamp hinged to the wall, and sensibly placed darts, shove-ha'penny, cribbage and dominoes. This year they've opened up a third room by altering the kitchen. Very cheap lunchtime bar food includes soup (£1), filled french sticks (£1.20), hot beef sandwiches (£1.50), popular pies like steak and kidney, and cheese and onion oatcake or Cornish pasties (£1.30), and home-made hotpot (£2); on Saturday and Sunday pies and rolls only are available. Well kept Burtonwood Bitter, Forshaws, Dark Mild and Top Hat on handpump; the cats have their admirers too. It can get very busy at weekends. The early 15th-c red sandstone church of St Bertiline across the road is worth a visit. *(Recommended by Barbara Houghton, Nigel Woolliscroft, DAV, D Cox, Dick Brown, John Fazakerley, Barbara Hatfield, E G Parish, Sue Holland and Dave Webster, Dave Irving, P Bromley, Chris Cook, Brian and Anna Marsden, David and Sheila, Nick and Alison Dowson)*

Burtonwood ~ Tenant Terence Cartwright ~ Real ale ~ Lunchtime meals and snacks ~ Crewe (01270) 882242 ~ Children welcome except in main bar – must be gone by 8.30pm ~ Spontaneous folk music first Sunday lunchtime and fourth Tuesday evening of each month ~ Open 11.30-11 – though they were undecided on their winter opening times as we went to press; closed Thurs lunchtime ~ Bedrooms: £20S/£35S

BICKLEY MOSS SJ5549 Map 7

Cholmondeley Arms ★ ⑪ ⇌ ♀

Cholmondeley; A49 5½ miles N of Whitchurch; the owners would like us to list them under Cholmondeley Village, but as this is rarely located on maps we have mentioned the nearest village which appears more often

Cheshire Dining Pub of the Year

This year, we have had more enthusiastic praise about this light and airy converted Victorian schoolhouse than for almost any other pub in the country. For the excellence of the food and wine (which many readers feel would put a lot of restaurants to shame), the friendly but not intrusive service, and for the interesting furnishings. The cross-shaped and high-ceilinged bar has a range of seating from cane and bentwood to pews and carved oak, masses of Victorian pictures (especially portraits and military subjects), patterned paper on the shutters to match the curtains, an open fire, and a great stag's head over one of the side arches; some of the old school desks are above the bar on a gantry. Daily specials are especially popular and might include carrot and fennel or leek soup, nicely presented fresh asparagus, good leeks wrapped in ham in a cheese mornay sauce, Thai pork and crab toast (£3.85), smoked kassler loin of pork with silver onions and gherkins or hot baked prawns in sour cream and garlic (£3.95), terrific salmon fishcakes, leek and mushroom gratin with sesame seed topping (£6.50), pies such as chicken, cheese and bacon, excellent chilli, fillet of whitby cod (£6.95), cassoulet (£7.95), fillets of lemon sole with prawns in a lobster mornay sauce (£8.75) and puddings like baked jam sponge or strawberry pavlova; children's dishes. An old blackboard lists ten or so interesting and often uncommon wines by the glass; well kept Boddingtons, Flowers IPA and Original and a weekly changing guest beer on handpump; big (4 cup) pot of cafetière coffee, teas, and hot chocolate. There are seats out on a sizeable lawn, and Cholmondeley Castle and gardens are close by. *(Recommended by R Ward, Roger and Christine Mash, Nigel Woolliscroft, L W Baal, Lynn Sharpless, Bob Eardley, Martin Aust, M G Hart, John and Christine Simpson, G E Stait, Sue Holland, Dave Webster, Barry Hankey, Andrew Stephenson, Gill and Mike Cross, Mr and Mrs W J A Timpson, Mr and Mrs J Furber, Julian Jewitt, Maysie Thompson, George Jonas, A R and B E Sayer, Julie Peters, J and P Maloney, David R Shillitoe, Basil Minson, Peter and Jenny Quine, G B Rimmer, E Riley, Mr and Mrs Alex Williams, W C M Jones, J E Rycroft, Mrs J Oakes, Roger and Christine Mash, Brian Kneale, Hugh and Toni Saddington, Mr and Mrs D E Connell, Richard Dolphin, Mr and Mrs C J Frodsham, Hugh Chevallier, W K Struthers)*

Free house ~ Licensees Guy and Carolyn Ross-Lowe ~ Real ale ~ Meals and snacks (till 10pm) ~ Cholmondeley (01829) 720300 ~ Children in eating area of bar till 8pm ~ Open 12-3, 7(6.30 Sat)-11; closed 25 Dec ~ Bedrooms: £34S/£46S

BOTTOM OF THE OVEN SJ9872 Map 7

Stanley Arms

From A537 Buxton—Macclesfield heading towards Macclesfield, take first left turn (not signposted) after Cat & Fiddle; OS Sheet 118 map reference 980723

This year, this unspoilt and isolated moorland pub was in the running for a star award as it has been well worth knowing for its three warmly friendly and cosy rooms, lovely fresh flowers bought by Mrs Harvey from the market, and very good home-made food – but as we went to press the licensees thought they were probably leaving; they'll be a hard act to follow, so we're keeping our fingers crossed. Two of the rooms have lots of shiny black lacquered woodwork, subdued red and black flowery plush wall settles and stools, some dark blue seats, and low dimpled copper tables on the grey carpets; the third is laid out as a dining room, with pretty pastel tablecloths; open winter fires. The fine, very popular food has included sandwiches, garlic mushrooms, home-made soup, ploughman's, omelettes, lamb's liver and onions, lasagne, salads, freshly roasted duckling, and fish and vegetarian dishes. Well kept Marstons Burton and Pedigree on handpump. There are picnic-table sets on the grass behind. *(Recommended by Ian and Val Titman, Jill and Peter Bickley, Nigel Woolliscroft, F C Johnston, Mr and Mrs B Hobden, Basil J S Minson, Mr and Mrs J Furber; if Mr and Mrs Harvey have left, we'd be grateful for reports on the new regime, please)*

Marstons ~ Real ale ~ Meals and snacks (till 10pm) ~ Restaurant ~ Sutton (01260) 252414 ~ Children in eating area of bar ~ Open 11.30-3, 7-11; closed 25 Dec

BRERETON GREEN SJ7864 Map 7

Bears Head 🛏

1¾ miles from M6, junction 17; fork left from Congleton road almost immediately, then left on to A50; also from junction 18, via Holmes Chapel

Though there is quite an emphasis on the popular restaurant in this civilised and quietly friendly timber-framed old pub – and the staff are smartly uniformed – the neatly kept rambling open-plan rooms have a relaxed, old-fashioned feel and are popular with locals who pop in for a drink and a chat, as well as those wanting to eat. There are masses of heavy black beams and timbers, some traditional oak panel-back settles and a corner cupboard full of Venetian glass, and a section of wall in one room (under glass for protection) has had the plaster removed to show the construction of timber underneath. There are two serving bars, though only one is normally in use. Popular bar food consists of home-made soup (£1.75), sandwiches (from £1.95, excellent steak and onion £5.95), home-made pâté (£3.25), splendid home-made lasagne (£4.95), salads (from £4.25), hot dishes such as gammon and egg, roast chicken with home-made stuffing or grilled fillet of plaice with banana, lemon and butter sauce (from £5.25) and rump steak (£7.95); also daily specials such as very good moules marinières and haddock; very good chips and super home-made puddings from the pudding trolley. Bass, Burtonwood Bitter and Courage Directors on handpump, kept in fine deep cellars, a good range of blend and malt whiskies, fine brandies and liqueurs and decent wines (especially Italian); trivia machine, soothing piped music. Outside a pretty side terrace has white cast-iron tables and chairs under cocktail parasols, big black cast-iron lamp clusters and a central fountain; barbecues are held outside on the terrace in the summer. *(Recommended by Douglas and Patricia Gott, C H Stride, Mr and Mrs John Smyth, Neale Davies, Mr and Mrs A F Walters, Dick Brown; more reports please)*

Free house ~ Licensee Roberto Tarquini ~ Real ale ~ Meals and snacks (till 10pm) ~ Restaurant (not Sun evening) ~ Holmes Chapel (01477) 535251 ~ Children welcome ~ Trad folk music every other Weds evening ~ Open 11.30-3, 6-11 ~ Bedrooms: £25(£35B)/£49.50(£52.50B)

BROOMEDGE SJ7085 Map 7

Jolly Thresher

A56 E of Lymm

Very popular locally, this welcoming 16th-c pub is spaciously open-plan with fresh flowers, two open fires, stripped wood country chairs and tables on stripped boards, prints of some of Lowry's less well known paintings on the papered walls, and swagged curtains. Good value, popular bar food (prices are unchanged since last year) includes lovely soup (£1.15), sandwiches (from £1.60), toasties (£1.75), chilli con carne (£3.25), southern fried chicken (£4.25), Barnsley chop (£6.25), good sirloin steak in Dijon sauce (£7.95), and daily specials like roast rack of lamb in rosemary, good fresh fish or chicken in leek and stilton sauce; well kept Hydes Bitter and Mild on handpump; darts, dominoes, fruit machine and piped music. There are tables out behind, looking over the pub's neat bowling green to the Bridgewater Canal. *(Recommended by John Broughton, Andy and Jill Kassube, Judith Mayne)*

Hydes ~ Tenant Peter McGrath ~ Real ale ~ Meals and snacks (not Sun evening or Mon) ~ (01925) 752265 ~ Children in eating area of bar until 7pm ~ Open 11.30-3(4 Sat), 5.30-11

BURLEYDAM SJ6143 Map 7

Combermere Arms
A525 Whitchurch—Audlem

This 16th-c pub is a lovely place which is still popular for its well kept real ales: Bass, Highgate Dark, Worthington Bitter and guest beers on handpump. They also hold a beer festival at the end of October with around 30 real ales. The traditionally furnished bar has horsebrasses and tankards on the beams, fox masks on standing timbers, and an unusal circular oak bar. Generous helpings of popular bar food include very good soup (£1.30), sandwiches (from £1.40), burgers (from £1.60), ploughman's (from £2.75), salads (from £4.25), steak, kidney and mushroom pie in ale (£4.50), home-made lasagne (£4.60), ricotta cheese and spinach cannelloni (£4.65), Turkish lamb (£5.25), poached tuna steak (£5.45), okra and vegetable balti or lamb and spinach balti served with nan bread (from £5.45), steaks (from £7.95), puddings such as jam roly poly, strawberry and Cointreau gateau and apple pie (£1.95), and specials like fresh Welsh mussels in white wine, cream and garlic (£2.95), monkfish in Pernod sauce (£5.95), whole grilled red snapper with garlic (£6.45) and giant whole lemon sole (£7.95); children's menu. Welcoming staff; darts, shove-ha'penny, dominoes, video game and piped music. There's a children's adventure play complex. *(Recommended by Paul Boot, Martin Aust, Kate and Robert Hodkinson, Basil Minson, David and Sheila)*

Free house ~ Licensee Neil Murphy ~ Real ale ~ Meals and snacks (served all day)~ Restaurant ~ (01948) 871223 ~ Children welcome ~ Open 11-11

CHURCH MINSHULL SJ6661 Map 7

Badger
B5074 Nantwich—Winsford

New licensees are now running this listed building, and have taken on the whole family to help – brother, sister and parents. It's in a pleasant setting with the Shropshire Union Canal 250 yards away and picnic-table sets under cocktail parasols in the neat garden below the handsome village church, sheltered by shrubs and a flowering cherry; more seats on a back verandah, and children's play area. The friendly bar with its straightforward, largely modern furnishings is decorated with lots of stuffed animals lurking in nooks and crannies. Quite a few pop up around the bar counter, with a badger peering out of a hole in a big wooden cask; some open fires. Bar food now includes soup (£1.25), open batches (from £1.25; hot ones from £1.75), omelettes (£3.95), braised liver and onions (£4.25), chicken curry (£4.50), salmon and prawn pasta bake (£4.95), steaks (from £6.95), and puddings (£1.50); there's a special OAP lunch menu during the week. Part of the restaurant is no smoking. Burtonwood Bitter, Forshaws and Top Hat on handpump. The bare-boards public bar has pool, sensibly placed darts, dominoes, fruit machine, video game, juke box, Monday evening quizzes and piped music. *(Recommended by Mr and Mrs R J Phillips, Kate and Robert Hodkinson, P Boot, D J Underwood, H Hazzard; more reports on the new regime, please)*

Burtonwood ~ Lease: Andrew Webb ~ Real ale ~ Meals and snacks ~ Restaurant ~ Church Minshull (01270) 522607 ~ Children welcome ~ Piano in restaurant Tues-Sun lunchtime and evening ~ Open 11-11

Pubs in outstandingly attractive surroundings are listed at the back of the book.

COMBERBACH SJ6477 Map 7

Spinner & Bergamot

Village signposted from A553 and A559 NW or Northwich; pub towards Great Budworth

The friendly licensees and their staff seem to enjoy looking after the customers at this very neatly kept pub. The front bar has toby jugs hanging from the beams, one or two hunting prints on the cream textured walls, red plush button-back built-in wall banquettes, and a warming log fire. The softly lit back dining room has country-kitchen furniture (some of oak), pretty curtains, and a big brick inglenook with a stripped high mantelbeam; brocaded wall seats in the neat red-tiled public bar. Lunchtime bar food includes home-made soup (£1.80), sandwiches (from £2.80; toasties or open sandwiches from £2.50), filled baked potatoes (from £3), cottage pie (£3.20), salads (from £4.50), home-made steak and kidney pie or gammon and egg (£4.80), with evening extras like potted shrimps (£3), jumbo scampi in home-made batter (£6.60), and steaks (from £9); daily specials like chicken curry (£6), fresh grilled halibut with lemon and lime sauce (£7) or steak au poivre (£9), and there's a separate Sunday menu as well; vegetables are fresh. You can eat outside, as a hatch in the front lobby serves the white tables on the sloping lawn. Well kept Greenalls on handpump; darts, dominoes and piped music, and a bowling green outside at the back – bowls can be hired. Assorted rabbits and birds in the garden, along with swings and a climber (children not allowed inside), and lots of flowering tubs and hanging baskets. Good pubs run in the family; the landlady's sister is the landlady at the Bells of Peover in Lower Peover. *(Recommended by Roger and Christine Mash, John Broughton, Mr and Mrs C J Frodsham, Simon J Barber, George Jonas, S R and A I Ashcroft, Olive and Ray Hebson, RJH, Chris Walling, Mrs A M Hays, Sue and Alan Gallagher)*

Greenalls (Allied) ~ Tenants Doug and Mavis Hughes ~ Real ale ~ Meals and snacks (not Sun evening) ~ Restaurant; not Sun evening ~ (01606) 891307 ~ Open 11.30-3.30(3.50 Sat), 5.30(6 Sat)-11; closed evening 25 Dec

COTEBROOK SJ5765 Map 7

Alvanley Arms 🍺

Forest Rd; Junction A49/B5152, N of Tarporley

Popular with locals and visitors, this handsome 16th-c creeper-covered farmhouse has a main bar with neat high beams, fairly close-set tables (dining-height by the red plush wall banquettes around the sides and lower ones with plush stools in the middle), a few hunting and sporting prints, brasses, and a big open fire. Well kept Robinsons Mild and Best on handpump from the solid oak bar counter; several malt whiskies; prompt and friendly service. On the other side of a pleasantly chintzy small hall is a quieter but broadly similar room with more interesting prints and a delft shelf of china. Very generous helpings of waitress-served food include sandwiches (from £1.75), salads (from £4.15), steak pie (£4.75), seafood lasagne (£5.05), chicken breast in a provençale sauce (£5.80), honey-glazed lamb steak (£6.80), halibut or monkfish tails (£6.95), rump steak (£7.20), local venison steak (£7.95), puddings (£2.25), daily specials like hotpot (£4.15) or pigeon in port (£6.95), and children's meals (£2.65). A fruit machine is tucked away in a lobby. The very pleasant garden looks out towards rolling fields, and has a pond with geese, and fairy-lit picnic-table sets under a small cedar, where food is served during the summer; swings. *(Recommended by Paul Boot, Olive and Ray Hebson, Graham Reeve, G B Rimmer, E Riley, Roger and Christine Mash, George Jonas)*

Robinsons ~ Tenants Mr and Mrs J White ~ Real ale ~ Meals and snacks ~ Candlelit restaurant (evening only Sun; closed bank holiday Mon) ~ Little Budworth (01829) 760200 ~ Children in lounge ~ Open 11.30-3, 5.30(6 Sat)-11 ~ Bedrooms: £25B/£50B

Pubs with particularly interesting histories, or in unusually interesting buildings, are listed at the back of the book.

DELAMERE SJ5669 Map 7

Fishpool

A54/B5152

As this attractive and comfortable pub is so well placed near the pike-haunted lake and Delamere Forest it can be particularly busy at weekends – best to go early, then. It's run by friendly and welcoming licensees, and the four small room areas (watch out, one of the doors between them is very low) are bright with polished brasses and china. They keep a decent range of wines as well as well kept Greenalls Bitter, Mild and Original on handpump, and good, home-made food includes sandwiches, pies like chicken and ham or beef and mushroom (from £4.35), Cumberland sausage in mustard and whisky sauce (£4.75), fresh salmon (£5.25), steaks, and puddings such as delicious hot chocolate fudge cake. *(Recommended by Steve and Karen Jennings, Olive and Ray Hebson, A Craig, Mrs Ann-Marie Colligan, Geoffrey and Brenda Wilson)*

Greenalls (Allied) ~ Tenants Michael and Kathleen Melia ~ Real ale ~ Meals and snacks (11.30-2, 6-9.30) ~ (01606) 883277 ~ Children in eating area ~ Open 11-3, 6-11 ~ Bedrooms: £17.50/£35

FADDILEY SJ5953 Map 7

Tollemache Arms

A534 Nantwich—Wrexham

The rooms inside this friendly, thatched and timbered 15th-c pub have a very cosy cottagey feel to them, particularly the two on the right with their dark glossy beams, upholstered, built-in wall settles and leatherette-cushioned cask seats around gleaming copper tables. They also have copper utensils, houseplants and an open fire; the inner room, up a couple of steps, is the snugger of the two. The room on the left is laid out more conventionally, but like the others has lots of brass and copper, and shiny beams. The Tap Room – where children are allowed – houses the landlord's collection of frogs; it's joined to the rest of the pub via an archway knocked in the wall and looks out over the fields at the back of the building. Good bar food includes sandwiches, sautéed liver, bacon and mushrooms (£4.35), braised steak in red wine (£4.95), poached salmon in Pernod and fennel (£5.25), duck in orange and port (£5.55) and mixed grill (£6.95). Well kept Burtonwood Bitter and Foreshaws on handpump; cheery service. Darts and dominoes in the back public bar; piped music. The neat small lawn, with a couple of substantial yew trees guarding the gate in its picket fence, has picnic-table sets and a black-and-white children's playhouse with lots of toys, and there are pretty hanging baskets. The fields that surround the pub were once the site of a fierce battle between the Mercians and the Welsh. *(Recommended by Paul Boot, Martin Aust, Margaret Mason, David Thompson, Sue Holland, Dave Webster)*

Paramount/Burtonwood ~ Tenants Janice Brindley and Andy Bebbington ~ Real ale ~ Meals and snacks (not Mon; except bank hols) ~ (01270) 74223 ~ Children welcome ~ Open 12-2.30(3 Sat), 7-11; closed Mon except bank hols

GREAT BUDWORTH SJ6778 Map 7

George & Dragon 🍺

4½ miles from M6, junction 19; from A556 towards Northwich, turn right into B5391 almost at once; then fork right at signpost to Aston-by-Budworth, Arley Hall & Gardens

In a very pretty village, this friendly 17th-c pub is popular with a good cross-section of people – though walkers must leave their muddy boots in the porch. The rambling panelled lounge is filled with plenty of nooks and alcoves, copper jugs hang from the beams, a fine big mirror has horsebrasses on the wooden pillars of its frame, and there are red plush button-back banquettes and older settles; one area is no smoking at lunchtimes. The public bar has plenty of room for traditional pub games such as darts and pool, and there's also dominoes, a fruit machine, trivia and piped music. At busy times families can use the upstairs restaurant, which is no smoking on Sunday lunchtimes. Bar food includes soup (£1.50), sandwiches (from £1.95), dim sum (£2.90), ploughman's (£3.95), salads (from £4.50), vegetarian curry (£4.75), fresh fillet of cod or gammon and egg (£4.95), steaks (from £7.50), daily specials such as liver and onions (£3.95), home-made steak in ale pie (£4.25) or lamb with orange and ginger (£4.75), and puddings (£2); children's menu (£1.95). Well kept Tetleys and two weekly changing guests on handpump, quite a few malt whiskies, and Addlestones cider. Opposite the fine wrought-iron gantry that serves for an inn sign is an 11th-c church and the village stocks. *(Recommended by Tony and Lynne Stark, E G Parish, Peter and Lynn Brueton, S R and A I Ashcroft, Bill and Lydia Ryan, Mrs J M Bell, Simon J Barter, Barbara Hatfield)*

Tetleys (Allied) ~ Lease: Malcolm and Lynne Curtin ~ Real ale ~ Meals and snacks ~ Upstairs restaurant ~ Comberbach (01606) 891317 ~ Children in eating area of bar ~ Open 11.30-3, 6(6.30 in winter)-11; all day summer Sats

HIGHER BURWARDSLEY   SJ5256   Map 7

Pheasant 🛏

Burwardsley signposted from Tattenhall (which itself is signposted off A41 S of Chester) and from Harthill (reached by turning off A534 Nantwich—Holt at the Copper Mine); follow village signpost down hill from Post Office; OS Sheet 117 map reference 523566

From the windows in the attractive bar, the picnic-table sets in the garden, and from the bedrooms, you can enjoy one of the county's most magnificent views overlooking the Cheshire Plain and the Wirral. The landlord's previous career was as a ship's pilot and some of the decorations in the bar are associated with this, such as his Merchant Navy apprenticeship papers, some ship photographs, and a brass ship's barometer – though there's also a parrot, big colour engravings of Victorian officials of the North Cheshire Hunt, a stuffed pheasant (as well as a picture of one), and a set of whimsical little cock-fighting pictures done in real feathers. Over the high stone mantelpiece of the see-through fireplace – said to house the biggest log fire in the county – are some plates, and around the fire is a tall leather-cushioned fender (in front of it Thomas the cat may be sitting). Other seats range from red leatherette or plush wall seats to one or two antique oak settles. Good bar food includes home-made soup (£1.80), sandwiches (from £1.80), home-made chicken liver pâté (£2.80), ploughman's or home-made vegetarian quiche (£3.75), daily curry (£4.50), home-made beef and Guinness pie (£4.80), whole rack of hill lamb with redcurrant and rosemary sauce or breast of duckling sliced and served with orange sauce (£9), steaks (from £9.50), home-made puddings (£2), and daily specials; the pleasant conservatory is no smoking in the daytime and is useful for families. The dining room specialises in game and beef dishes and is decorated with pictures and rosettes won by the pub's own Highland cattle herd. Well kept Bass and a guest such as Fullers London Pride or Morlands Old Speckled Hen on handpump, a choice of over 40 malts and quite a few wines; friendly staff. Dominoes, fruit machine (not in main bar) and piped music. The bedrooms are in an attractively and very comfortably converted sandstone-built barn, and all have views. Picnic-table sets on a big side lawn. The pub is well placed for walks along the Peckforton Hills, situated at the start of *Good Walks Guide* Walk 72 and is half a mile from Tattenhall Fly Fisheries. *(Recommended by Lynn Sharpless, Bob Eardley, L M Miall, David Goldstone, Sue Holland, John Watson, Andrew Stephenson, Barbara Hatfield, Ian Sharp)*

Free house ~ Licensee David Greenhaugh ~ Real ale ~ Meals and snacks ~ Restaurant ~ Tattenhall (01829) 70434 ~ Children in conservatory till 8pm ~ Horses welcomed, and horse-and-trap rides can be arranged ~ Open 12-3, 7-11 ~ Bedrooms: £40B/£60B

Most of the big breweries now work through regional operating companies, with different names. If a pub is tied to one of these regional companies, we put the parent company's name in brackets – in the details at the end of each main entry.

LANGLEY SJ9471 Map 7

Leathers Smithy 🍺

From Macclesfield, heading S from centre on A523 turn left into Byrons Lane at Langley, Wincle signpost; in Langley follow main road forking left at church into Clarke Lane – keep on towards the moors; OS Sheet 118 map reference 952715

The room that readers like the best in this friendly old-fashioned pub is the lively, partly flagstoned right-hand bar with its bow window seats or wheelback chairs, and gin traps, farrier's pincers, a hay basket and other ironwork on the roughcast cream walls. On the left, there are more wheelback chairs around cast-iron-framed tables on a turkey carpet, little country pictures and drawings of Cheshire buildings, Wills steam engine cigarette cards and a locomotive name-plate curving over one of the two open fires; faint piped music. The family room is no smoking. Ind Coope Burton, Jennings Bitter and Snecklifter, Tetleys Bitter and occasional guest beers on handpump, as well as Addlestones cider. Gluhwein in winter from a copper salamander, and a decent collection of spirits, including around 80 malt whiskies and 10 Irish; dominoes, fruit machine. Hearty bar food includes sandwiches (from £1.70), black pudding and mushy pieas (£3.40), ploughman's (from £3.70), lasagne (£4.50), vegetarian dishes such as spinach and walnut pancake or cheese and onion quiche (£4.45), good salads (£4.50), home-made steak pie (£4.85), halibut or gammon and egg (£6), steaks (from £8), and delicious puddings such as butterscotch and walnut fudge cake (£2.50). A couple of benches in front look across to the Ridgegate Reservoir, and as the pub is backed by the steep mass of Teggs Nose (a country park), it's popular with walkers. *(Recommended by Wayne Brindle, Andrew Stephenson, Dave Irving)*

Tetleys (Allied) ~ Tenant Paul Hadfield ~ Real ale ~ Meals and snacks 12-2, 7-8.30 (9.30 Fri and Sat, not Mon evening) ~ (01260) 252313 ~ Children in own room Sat & Sun lunchtime only ~ Occasional pianola music ~ Open 12-3, 7-11

nr LANGLEY SJ9471 Map 7

Hanging Gate

Higher Sutton; follow Langley signpost from A54 beside Fourways Motel, and that road passes the pub; from Macclesfield, heading S from centre on A523 turn left into Byrons Lane at Langley, Wincle signpost; in Sutton (half-mile after going under canal bridge, ie before Langley) fork right at Church House Inn, following Wildboarclough signpost, then 2 miles later turning sharp right at steep hairpin bend; OS Sheet 118 map reference 952696

The windows from the three snug little rooms in this low-beamed old drovers' pub look out beyond a patchwork of valley pastures to distant moors (and the tall Sutton Common transmitter above them). They are simply and traditionally furnished and there are big coal fires, a stuffed otter, and some attractive old photographs of Cheshire towns; down stone steps an airier garden room has been redecorated this year and has much the same view from its picture window. Dominoes, juke box. Reasonably priced bar food includes soup (£2), sandwiches (£2.50), and baskets meals (from £4.20), with daily specials such as steak and kidney pie, chicken in tarragon wine, beef roghan josh or drunken bull (all £5.50). Well kept Courage Directors, Ruddles County and John Smiths on handpump, mulled wine in winter; friendly service. There is a crazy-paved terrace outside. *(Recommended by Nigel Woolliscroft, Andy Petersen, Mike and Wendy Proctor; more reports please)*

Free house ~ Licensees John and Lyn Vernon ~ Real ale ~ Meals and snacks ~ (01260) 252238 ~ Children welcome and in two special rooms ~ Open 12-3, 7-11

LOWER PEOVER SJ7474 Map 7

Bells of Peover ★

The Cobbles; from B5081 take short cobbled lane signposted to church

The setting here is lovely: a sheltered crazy-paved terrace in front of this wisteria-covered pub faces a beautiful black and white timbered church, mainly 14th-c, with lovely woodwork inside, and a spacious lawn beyond the old coachyard at the side spreads down through trees and rose pergolas to a little stream. Inside, it's spotlessly kept, and the little tiled bar has side hatches for its serving counter, toby jugs, and comic Victorian prints, while the original lounge has antique settles, antique china in the dresser, high-backed Windsor armchairs, a spacious window seat, pictures above the panelling and two small coal fires. There's a second similar lounge. Good waitress-served bar food includes soup (£1.85), sandwiches with home-cooked meats (from £1.85; open sandwiches from £3.20), filled baked potatoes (mostly £3.95), home-made quiche (£4.85), attractive salads (from £4.85), home-made pies (£5.25), good daily specials, and several puddings (£2.50). Most people wear a jacket and tie in the restaurant. Well kept Greenalls Best on handpump and several wines, and warmly welcoming staff – even when very busy. The landlady's great grandfather ran this fine old-fashioned pub for half a century, and also gave it its name. *(Recommended by P D and J Bickley, Dono and Carol Leaman, S R and A I Ashcroft, George Jonas, G B Rimmer, E Riley, David and Sheila, Gill and Mike Cross, Carl Travis)*

Greenalls (Allied) ~ Lease: Dave Barker ~ Real ale ~ Meals and snacks (not Sat or Sun evening) ~ Restaurant; closed Sat lunchtime, Sun evening, Mon/Tues ~ Lower Peover (01565) 722269 ~ Children in restaurant ~ Open 11.30-3, 5.30(6 Sat)-11

MACCLESFIELD SJ9271 Map 7

Sutton Hall Hotel ★ 🛏

Leaving Macclesfield southwards on A523, turn left into Byrons Lane signposted Langley, Wincle, then just before canal viaduct fork right into Bullocks Lane; OS Sheet 118 map reference 925715

Readers are fond of this warmly welcoming and secluded 16th-c baronial hall. It's a very civilised place to spend time and the bar – divided into separate areas by tall black timbers – has some antique squared oak panelling, lightly patterned art nouveau stained-glass windows, broad flagstones around the bar counter (carpet elsewhere), and a raised open fire. The furnishings are mainly straightforward ladderback chairs around sturdy thick-topped cast-iron-framed tables, but there are a few unusual touches such as an enormous bronze bell for calling time, a brass cigar-lighting gas taper on the bar counter itself, a suit of armour by another big stone fireplace, and a longcase clock. The menu is not unusual but the food is excellently cooked and presented, and there's friendly waitress service; the range includes home-made soup (£1.45), open sandwiches (from £2.65), home-made pâté (£3.25), home-made lasagne (£4.95), home-made steak and kidney pie or spinach pancakes filled with ratatouille with a sour cream dressing (£5.25), and puddings (£2). Well kept Bass, Marstons Bitter, Stones Best and a guest beer on handpump, 40 malt whiskies, freshly squeezed fruit juice, and decent wines. There are lovely grounds, with tables on a tree-sheltered lawn. They can arrange clay shooting, golf or local fishing. *(Recommended by Nigel Woolliscroft, Mr and Mrs B Hobden, S G Brown, Basil J S Minson, S R and A I Ashcroft, Mike and Wendy Proctor, Dr S W Tham, David Heath, Mr and Mrs D E Connell)*

Free house ~ Licensee Robert Bradshaw ~ Real ale ~ Meals and snacks (till 10pm) ~ Restaurant ~ Sutton (01260) 253211 ~ Children allowed weekends and bank hol lunchtimes only ~ Open 11-11 ~ Four-poster bedrooms: £68.95B/£85B

MARBURY SJ5645 Map 7

Swan

NNE of Whitchurch; OS Sheet 117 map reference 562457

George and Ann Sumner have been at this creeper-covered white pub for 24 years and have now been joined by their son Mark. The neatly kept, partly panelled lounge has upholstered easy chairs and other country furniture, a grandfather clock, a copper-canopied fireplace with a good winter fire (masses of greenery in summer), discreet lighting and piped music. Most of the imaginative food is listed on a board and changes daily to include half-a-dozen starters and main courses and up to a dozen puddings: fine soups, chicken liver pâté or cheese and bacon toastie (£2.50), garlic mushrooms (£2.95), Italian mushroom hotpot with char-grilled polenta (£4.50), good spinach and garlic mushroom pancake, tasty fish pie, ragout of beef with smoked bacon and baby onions (£5.75), fresh fillet of plaice stuffed with prawns and mushrooms baked in a cheese sauce (£6.25), steaks (from £7.30), and puddings like fresh fruit pavlova or chocolate and almond torte (£2.25); chips are home-made. Well kept Greenalls Bitter and Original on handpump, forty malt whiskies, and friendly service; darts, dominoes and piped music. The pub, rebuilt in 1884, is in a quiet and attractive village, a half-mile's country walk from the Llangollen Canal, Bridges 23 and 24. The church is worth a visit. *(Recommended by Nigel Woolliscroft, Mr and Mrs R J Phillips, Kate and Robert Hodkinson, Gill and Keith Croxton, Sue Holland, Dave Webster, Barbara Hatfield)*

Greenalls (Allied) ~ Lease: George, Ann and Mark Sumner ~ Real ale ~ Meals and snacks (not Mon lunchtime; till 10pm Sat) ~ Partly no smoking restaurant ~ (01948) 663715 ~ Children in eating area of bar ~ Open 12-3, 7-11; closed Mon lunchtime (except bank hols) and 25 Dec

MOBBERLEY SJ7879 Map 7

Bird in Hand

B5085 towards Alderley

The simple, relaxed atmosphere and warm coal fires in each of the cosy low-ceilinged rambling rooms are quite a draw to this friendly partly 16th-c pub. There are comfortably cushioned heavy wooden seats, small pictures on the attractive Victorian wallpaper, toby jugs and other china on a high shelf, and wood panelling in the little snug; the top dining area is no smoking. Good bar food ranges from sandwiches (from £1.85; open sandwiches such as home-roasted ham with peach £3.50), home-made soup (£1.70), and ploughman's (£3.75), good value salads (from £4.75), home-made steak and onion pie or fresh battered haddock (£4.65), gammon with two eggs (£4.95), to puddings like home-made fruit pie (£1.95); daily specials such as giant Yorkshire pudding filled with spicy sausage and onion gravy (£5.25), and roast Sunday lunch. Well kept Sam Smiths OB and Museum on handpump and lots of malt whiskies; professional, cheery service; darts, dominoes, and fruit machine. It can get crowded, but there are seats outside. *(Recommended by Jill and Peter Bickley, Janet Naylor, Mr and Mrs D E Connell; more reports please)*

Sam Smiths ~ Manager Andrew Towers ~ Real ale ~ Meals and snacks ~ Mobberley (01565) 873149 ~ Children in eating area of bar no later than 8.30pm ~ Open 11-3, 5.30-11; 11-11 Sat

OVER PEOVER SJ7674 Map 7

Whipping Stocks

Stocks Lane; just off and easily seen from A50 S of Knutsford

Surrounded by attractive, level countryside, this welcoming 17th-c pub has a comfortably relaxed atmosphere. Several rooms open off the spacious central bar area – each with a distinct style of its own. There's a good deal of fine old oak panelling, including the determinedly oaken bar counter with its interesting elbow and foot rests, and seats range from small linenfold wooden chairs to sturdy wall settles upholstered in a rather 1930s plush fabric; most rooms have neat fireplaces, and one is no smoking. Popular waitress-served home-made bar food at lunchtime includes soup, sandwiches (from £1.70), filled baked potatoes (£2.90), ploughman's (from £3.80), salads (from £4.10), home-made quiche (£4.25), a home-made pie of the day (£4.45), puddings like treacle or chocolate sponge or banoffi pie, and daily specials such as haddock and prawn pasta, vegetable lasagne or goulash, with evening extras such as gammon and pineapple (£5.25) and sirloin steak (£7.25). Well kept Sam Smiths OB on handpump, with Museum kept under light blanket pressure; fruit machine, trivia, and well chosen and reproduced piped music. The grey and white cat is called Smudge. The countryside around the pub is attractive and level, with a pretty walk through to the church and hall; there are picnic-table sets in quite a spacious tree-sheltered garden with a safe play area. *(Recommended by DC, Mr and Mrs K H Frostick, Carl Travis; more reports please)*

Sam Smiths ~ Managers John and Johanne Eadie ~ Real ale ~ Meals and snacks 12-2, 6.30-9) ~ (01565) 722332 ~ Children in eating area of bar – but must be gone by 8pm ~ Open 11.30-3, 5-11; closed evening 25 Dec

OVERTON SJ5277 Map 7

Ring o' Bells £

Just over 2 miles from M56, junction 12; 2 Bellemonte Road – from A56 in Frodsham take B5152 and turn right (uphill) at Parish Church signpost

Apart from a little decorating, we're happy to say that things are unchanged at this friendly early 17th-c local. The landlady is keen to welcome visitors and make them feel at ease – and it's very much the sort of place where people tend to talk to each other. There are a couple of little rambling rooms with windows giving a view past the stone church to the Mersey far below; one at the back has some antique settles, brass-and-leather fender seats by the log fire, and old hunting prints on its butter-coloured walls. A beamed room with antique dark oak panelling and stained glass leads through to a darts room (there's also shove-ha'penny, dominoes and cribbage, but no noisy games machines). Good value waitress-served home-made bar food is served at lunchtime only and includes sandwiches and toasties (from £1.30), vegetarian dishes, hotpot or curries (£3.35), a big breakfast (£3.50), steak and mushroom pie or various fish dishes (£3.75), and nursery puddings (£1.40). Well kept Greenalls Bitter and Original on handpump or tapped from the cask and no less than 80 different malt whiskies served from the old-fashioned hatch-like central servery; cheerful helpful service; piped music. The cats are called Blackberry India (who is particularly friendly) and Lottie, and they were about to have tabby twins from a rescue home. *(Recommended by G Kelsall and others; more reports please)*

Greenalls (Allied) ~ Tenant Shirley Wroughton-Craig ~ Real ale ~ Lunchtime meals and snacks ~ Children welcome until 8pm (not in bar itself) ~ Frodsham (01928) 732068 ~ Open 11.30-3(4 Sat), 5.30(6 Sat)-11

PEOVER HEATH SJ7973 Map 7

Dog

Off A50 N of Holmes Chapel at the Whippings Stocks, keep on past Parkgate into Wellbank Lane; OS Sheet 118 map reference 794735; note that this village is called Peover Heath on the OS map and shown under that name on many road maps, but the pub is often listed under Over Peover instead

The emphasis in this busy rambling pub is very much on the popular and generously served home-made food. This includes home-made soup (£2.20), a big choice of sandwiches (from £2.35), starters like mushrooms in beer batter with garlic dip or duck and port pâté (£3.85), ploughman's (from £4.45), salads (from £5.70), and daily specials such as rack of lamb with apricots and ginger, braised oxtail, poached salmon in cucumber sauce or rabbit in herbs and mustard (from £6.45), and puddings such as fruit pies, cheesecakes and pavlovas (£2.20); booking is essential. There's an engaging series of small areas around the main bar with seats ranging from a comfortable easy chair, through wall seats (one built into a snug alcove around an oak table), to the handsome ribbed banquettes in the quiet and spacious no smoking dining room on the left; logs burn in one old-fashioned black grate and a coal fire opposite it is flanked by two wood-backed built-in fireside seats. Well kept Flowers, Jennings Mild and Tetleys on handpump, Addlestones cider, lots of malt whiskies, decent wine list, freshly squeezed orange juice and espresso and cappuccino coffee; darts, pool, dominoes, video game, quiz night Thursdays, and piped music. There are picnic-table sets out on the quiet lane, underneath the pub's pretty hanging baskets and an attractive beer garden which is lit in the evenings. The bedrooms have been upgraded this year and have thoughtful extras included, and the licensees have just taken over the attractive Swettenham Arms at Swettenham. *(Recommended by S·Ashcroft, Jill and Peter Bickley, Tim Galligan, L Walker, Richard Lewis, Brian Kneale, Helene Thompson, Dr R H M Stewart, F C Johnston, RJH, Chris Walling, Dave Thompson, Margaret Mason, Carl Travis)*

Free house ~ Licensee Frances Cunningham ~ Real ale ~ Meals and snacks ~ Chilford (01625) 861421 ~ Well behaved children welcome ~ Pianist Tues, Country & Western/60s music alternate Weds ~ Open 11.30-3, 5.30-11 ~ Bedrooms: £38B/£58

PLUMLEY SJ7175 Map 7

Smoker

2½ miles from M6 junction 19: A556 towards Northwich and Chester

Well run and very popular – best to get here early if you want a table – this thatched 16th-c inn has three well decorated connecting rooms with open fires in impressive period fireplaces, comfortable deep sofas, cushioned settles, Windsor chairs, and some rush-seat dining chairs. As well as the collection of copper kettles and the military prints on dark panelling, there's a glass case containing an interesting remnant from the Houses of Parliament salvaged after it was hit by a bomb in World War II. The Edwardian print by Goodwin Kilburne of a hunt meeting outside shows how little the pub's appearance has changed. Good, swiftly served home-made bar food includes soup (£1.60), sandwiches (from £1.70), starters such as home-made savoury pancakes or pâté (£2.95) or macaroni with stilton and port (£3.15), main courses like salads (from £4.95), kofta curry, turkey fricassee or lasagne (£5.15), fine fresh plaice, home roast sirloin of beef or halibut steak mornay (£5.95), and steaks (from £7.95); children's dishes (£1.95). Well kept Hartleys XB and Robinsons Best and Mild on handpump; 30 malt whiskies and a good choice of wines; friendly service. Outside there's a sizeable side lawn with roses and flowerbeds. *(Recommended by D Newth, Bronwen and Steve Wrigley, J and PM, Gary Roberts, Bill and Lydia Ryan, M V and J Melling, George Jonas, Dick Brown, F A Noble, Paul and Sue Merrick, Nick and Meriel Cox, J E Hilditch, Kate and Robert Hodkinson, W C M Jones, A R and B E Sayer, Simon J Barber, Neville Kenyon, Roger Sherman, Ron Gentry, Paul and Margaret Baker, Peter Burton, Geoffrey and Brenda Wilson, C Roberts, P Boot, G B Rimmer, E Riley, John Heath)*

Robinsons ~ Tenants John and Diana Bailey ~ Real ale ~ Meals and snacks (11-2, 6.30-10) ~ Restaurant (not Sun evening) ~ Lower Peover (01565) 722338 ~ Children in eating area of bar and in restaurant ~ Open 11-3.30, 5.30-11

SUTTON SJ9469 Map 7

Ryles Arms 🍺

Off A54 Congleton—Buxton, 2¾ miles E of A523 – signposted Sutton 2¾, or coming into Sutton from Macclesfield, fork right after going under aqueduct; OS Sheet 118 map reference 942694

The success of this pleasant slated white stone local owes a lot to the attentive and warmly friendly Irish landlord. It's very much a dining pub with big helpings of hearty food – though people do drop in for a drink. The menu and prices are unchanged from last year and include soup (£1.50), sandwiches (from £2), ploughman's (£3.50), tuna and courgette quiche or chicken curry (£5), steak and kidney pie or a good lasagne (£5), gammon and egg or roast beef (£6), and grilled halibut steak (£7.50). The section of the pub by the bar is basically two rooms knocked together, with comfortable seats and french windows leading to a terrace with metal and plastic chairs. On the right is a dining area (no smoking at eating times), with some attractively individual furnishings; the family room is no smoking too. Well kept Marstons Pedigree, Ruddles Best and County and a guest beer on handpump, a good choice of whiskies; fruit machine. *(Recommended by Peter and Jill Bickley, John Watson; more reports please)*

Free house ~ Licensee Frank Campbell ~ Real ale ~ Meals and snacks (till 10pm) ~ Sutton (01260) 252244 ~ Children in family room till 8pm ~ Open 11.30-3, 7-11; closed 25 Dec

TARPORLEY SJ5563 Map 7

Rising Sun

High St; village signposted off A51 Nantwich—Chester

Warmed in winter by three open fires and pretty in summer with its mass of hanging baskets and flower tubs, this village pub is very popular with locals and has a bustling, friendly atmosphere. Well chosen tables are surrounded by character seats including creaky 19th-c mahogany and oak settles, and there's also an attractively blacked iron kitchen range, sporting and other old-fashioned prints on the walls, and a big oriental rug in the back room. Good value lunchtime bar food includes sandwiches (from £1.60), filled baked potatoes (from £1.95), home-made cottage pie (£2.55), home-made steak and kidney pie (£3), gammon and egg or pork and apple in cider (£4.75), beef in ale (£4.95), and more elaborate dishes in the evening from the restaurant menu; helpful, friendly and prompt service. Well kept Robinsons Best and Mild on handpump; fruit machine, maybe unobtrusive piped music. *(Recommended by David and Sheila, Andrew Shore, Paul Boot, Brian Wainwright, A R and B E Sayer, Brian Kneale, John Heath, G B Rimmer, E Riley; more reports please)*

Robinsons ~ Tenant Alec Robertson ~ Real ale ~ Meals and snacks ~ Restaurant ~ Tarporley (01829) 732423 ~ Open 11.30-3, 5.30-11

WESTON SJ7352 Map 7

White Lion 🏠

3½ miles from M6 junction 16; A500 towards Crewe, then village signposted on right

From the road all you can see is the pretty black and white timbered old inn, as the comfortable hotel part is discreetly hidden away at the back. The busy low-beamed main room is divided up into smaller areas by very gnarled black oak standing timbers, and has a friendly, relaxing atmosphere, a varied mix of seats from cushioned modern settles to ancient oak ones, and plenty of smaller chairs. The best settles though are in a smaller room on the left – three of them, well carved in 18th-c style. Popular bar food includes home-made soup (£1.40), good sandwiches or batch cakes (from £1.50), chicken liver or smoked salmon pâté (£2.75), vegetarian quiche or a daily special (£3.75), ploughman's (from £4.15), daily roast (£4.25), poached local Dee salmon (£6.20), steak (£7.95), and big home-made puddings (£1.55). Well kept Bass, Boddingtons, Highgate Dark and Worthingtons on handpump; piped music, very friendly service by smartly dressed staff; the restaurant is no smoking – as are some bar areas. Picnic-table sets shelter on neat grass behind, by the pub's own bowling green. *(Recommended by E G Parish, Martin Aust, C H and P Stride, Miss D P Barson, John Evans, J H Walker)*

Free house ~ Licensee Mrs A J Davies ~ Real ale ~ Meals and snacks (not 25 or 26 Dec or 1 Jan evenings) ~ Restaurant (not Sun evening) ~ Crewe (01270) 500303 ~ Children in eating area of bar and in restaurant ~ Open 11-3, 5-11; closed evening 25 Dec ~ Bedrooms: £47B/£57B

WETTENHALL SJ6261 Map 7

Boot & Slipper 🏠

From B5074 on S edge of Winsford, turn into Darnhall School Lane, then right at Wettenhall signpost: keep on for 2 or 3 miles

There's a nice chatty and relaxed atmosphere in this attractively refurbished tucked-away country pub – the lane it's on, once a coaching highway, doesn't go anywhere much nowadays, so the people who track it down are really those in the know. The main bar has dark beams, three old shiny dark settles and more straightforward chairs, white walls, and a big log fire in the deep low fireplace with a fishing rod above it. The modern bar counter also serves the left-hand communicating beamed room with its shiny pale brown tiled floor, cast-iron-framed long table, panelled settle and bar stools; darts, dominoes and piped music. An unusual trio of back-lit arched fireplaces form one stripped-brick wall and there are two further rooms on the right, as well as a back restaurant with big country pictures. Good bar food includes sandwiches (from £1.10; steak batch £2.50), home-made soup (£1.40), home-made steak pie (£3.95), salads (from £4), gammon and egg (£5.50), daily specials such as spare ribs (£3.85), peppered cider pork (£4.50) or lamb rogan josh (£4.75), puddings (£1.75), and children's dishes (£2). Well kept Highgate Mild, and Marstons Bitter and Pedigree on handpump, and a decent wine list. Outside a few picnic-table sets sit on the cobbled front terrace by the big car park. *(Recommended by Mr and Mrs G R Smith-Richards, Nancy Griffiths)*

Free house ~ Licensee Rex Challinor ~ Real ale ~ Meals and snacks ~ Restaurant ~ (01270) 73238 ~ Children welcome ~ Open 11.30-3, 5.30-11 ~ Bedrooms: £26S/£40S

WINCLE SJ9666 Map 7

Ship

Danebridge

One of the oldest pubs in Cheshire, this quaint 16th-c place has old-fashioned little rooms with a nice atmosphere, very thick stone walls, a coal fire and well kept Boddingtons Bitter and a weekly changing guest beer on handpump, served through a hatch; decent wines. Good bar food includes soup (£1.50), sandwiches, toasties (from £1.80), ploughman's or home-made steak and kidney pie (£3.75), grilled Dane Valley trout (£4.75), sirloin steak (£7.95), delicious venison casserole, puddings such as brown bread ice cream, and children's meals (£1.95); fondue bourguignon is the house speciality for two people and includes a litre of house red wine (£17.50); dominoes, chess, draughts, Monopoly and cards – and games for children. The pub is tucked away in scenic countryside with fine walks all round. *(Recommended by Nigel Woolliscroft, Roger and Christine Mash, Dave Braisted, G B Rimmer, E Riley)*

Free house ~ Licensees Andrew Harmer and Penelope Hinchcliffe ~ Real ale ~ Meals and snacks (till 10pm; not winter Mon) ~ (01260) 227217 ~ Well behaved children in family room ~ Open 12-3, 7-11; closed Monday Nov-Mar ~ One bedroom: £20/£30

WRENBURY SJ5948 Map 7

Dusty Miller

Village signposted from A530 Nantwich—Whitchurch

You're sure of a warm, friendly welcome from the licensees at this handsome converted 19th-c mill, and it's in a lovely spot by the Llangollen branch of the Shropshire Union Canal and next to a striking counter-weighted drawbridge. Picnic-table sets stand on a gravel terrace among rose bushes by the water, and they're reached either by the towpath or by a high wooden catwalk above the River Weaver; in summer they hold regular barbecues including whole hog roasts. Inside, the main area is comfortably modern, and has a series of tall glazed arches with russet velvet curtains facing the water, long low hunting prints on the white walls, and tapestried banquettes and wheelback chairs flanking dark brown rustic tables. Further in, there's a quarry-tiled standing-only part by the bar counter, which has well kept Robinsons Best, Frederics and Hartleys XB on handpump; good, friendly service; the right-hand side of the lounge bar is no smoking. Dominoes, cribbage, shove-ha'penny, piped music. A wide choice of imaginative, popular bar food – using local produce where possible – includes sandwiches (lunchtimes), filled french bread, salads and steaks, as well as daily changing dishes such as fresh squid deep fried in sweet Japanese breadcrumbs and served with hot Thai sauce (£3.45), trout stuffed with hummus and fresh coriander or chicken cooked in grated parmesan cheese, orange and cream (£6.95), pork Normandy with Calvados, cream and mushroom sauce or salmon and monkfish roulade with seafood sauce (£7.95), and lamb cutlets with hazelnuts and served with a puree of aubergine (£8.35); separate children's menu. *(Recommended by John Andrew, Nigel Woolliscroft, Paul Noble, Patrick and Mary McDermott, H Hazzard, Graham Bush, Jennifer Sapp, David and Sheila)*

Robinsons ~ Licensee Robert Lloyd-Jones ~ Real ale ~ Meals and snacks ~ Upstairs restaurant (closed Sun evening) ~ Nantwich (01270) 780537 ~ Children in restaurant ~ Open 12-3, 6-11; closed evening 25 Dec

---

Lucky Dip

Besides the fully inspected pubs, you might like to try these Lucky Dips recommended to us and described by readers (if you do, please send us reports):

☆ **Acton Bridge** [Hilltop Rd; B5153 off A49 in Weaverham, then right towards Acton Cliff; SJ5975], *Maypole*: Landlord formerly at White Lion in Alvanley now doing big helpings of varied good value food in this spacious and civilised beamed dining pub very popular Sun lunchtime; some antique settles as well as more modern furnishings, friendly service, Greenalls Bitter and Mild on handpump, two coal fires, gentle piped music; seats in well kept garden with orchard behind *(Graham and Lynn Mason, LYM)*

☆ **Aldford** [Chester Rd; B5130 Chester—Wrexham; SJ4259], *Grosvenor Arms*: Large and lofty country pub, cleanly refurbished with imaginative layout and interesting decor; efficient friendly service, wide choice of generous food with speciality ice creams, five real ales inc a guest, fine wines by the glass, library, conservatory, cosy games room with bar billiards; pleasant terrace and garden behind, popular summer barbecues *(Chris Walling, John Heath, Mr and Mrs J Williams, Mr and Mrs W J A Timpson, W C M Jones)*

Alsager [Crewe Rd; SJ7956], *Lodge*: Small friendly two-room local popular with students; bar food, well kept Tetleys and guests, darts, dominoes, pool *(Sue Holland, Dave Webster)*; [Crewe Rd], *Old Mill*: Very popular for efficiently served good food from sandwiches to steaks; children's parties booked; bedrooms all with own bathrooms *(Richard Lewis)*

Alvanley [Manley Rd – OS Sheet 117 map reference 496740; SJ4974], *White Lion*: Busy and comfortable dining pub with extremely wide choice of generous and popular food from sandwiches up inc vegetarian and children's dishes, soft plush seats in low-ceilinged lounge, games in smaller public bar, Greenalls Mild, Bitter and Original, tables and play area outside *(Mr and Mrs B Hobden, Olive and Ray Hebson, Graham and Lynn Mason, LYM)*

Anderton [just NW of Northwich; SJ6575], *Stanley Arms*: Overlooking Anderton boat lift, very welcoming pub with friendly landlord, well kept beer, reasonably priced basic food; overnight mooring *(Patrick and Mary McDermott)*

Aston [Wrenbury Rd (off A530); SJ6147], *Bhurtpore*: Up to nine well kept and quickly changing real ales on handpump inc a Porter and a Mild, also a German beer and a Belgian dark beer, and farm cider; cosy former farmhouse with comfortable assortment of old chairs and tables, very friendly staff, good food esp curries, some unusual dishes such as wild mushrooms with raspberry vinaigrette, duck breast with apple and brandy sauce *(Richard Lewis, Jill and Peter Bickley)*

☆ **Audlem** [Audlem Wharf – OS Sheet 118 map reference 658436; SJ6543], *Shroppie Fly*: Fine spot looking out over one of the long flight of locks here; mainly modern furnishings, one bar shaped like a barge, good canal photographs, collection of brightly painted bargees' china and bric-a-brac, seats on waterside terrace; usual food, well kept Boddingtons, friendly staff, children in room off bar and restaurant; open almost all day summer, closed winter lunchtimes *(Jason Caulkin, Julian Jewitt, Nigel Woolliscroft, LYM)*

Audlem [A525, Audlem Wharf], *Bridge*: Particularly well kept real ales, esp Marstons Pedigree, in plain and spotless pub with coal fire, tiled floor, friendly staff; quite a good choice of food inc good sandwiches, darts, pool, juke box and games machines; seats out by canal *(Paul and Gail Betteley, Margaret and Allen Marsden)*

Barton [A534 E of Farndon; SJ4554], *Cock*: Handsome sandstone country pub with log fires, traditional furnishings inc high-backed built-in settles, black beams, snug alcoves, hunting and ornamental fowl prints, great collection of whiskies, well kept McEwans 80/- and Youngers Scotch, bar food from soup and sandwiches to steak; tables outside with separate summer soft drinks snack servery; closed Mon lunchtime *(LYM; more reports please)*

☆ **Beeston** [Bunbury Heath; A49 S of Tarporley; SJ5459], *Beeston Castle*: Clean, comfortable, well restored and very hospitable, with good range of unusual and ample reasonably priced food from huge open sandwiches to restaurant dishes, mouth-watering puddings, prompt service even when busy, short but well chosen wine list, well kept beers; children until 8 *(D T Taylor, Don Kellaway, Angie Coles, R A Chesher, Mrs A Bradley, Mrs H Jack, Mr and Mrs D Conroy)*

☆ **Bell O Th Hill** [just off A41 N of Whitchurch; SJ5245], *Blue Bell*: Attractive two-roomed heavily beamed country pub with log fire (could perhaps be lit more often), quite a wide choice of generous well prepared food (worth waiting for), Sun papers, well kept real ales inc local Hanby, piped music, pleasant American landlord and cheerful service; nice garden, attractive surroundings *(J Roy Smylie, Gill and Maurice McMahon, Catherine and Andrew Brian, LYM)*

☆ **Bollington** [29 Adlington Rd, heading N off B5091 by railway viaduct – OS Sheet 118 map reference 931781; SJ9377], *Vale*: Pleasantly modernised local nr canal walks, comfortable and spotless, with good home-cooked bar food, well kept Thwaites Bitter and Mild and Timothy Taylors Landlord on handpump, very friendly staff, log fire, neat woodside lawn with good play area; closed Mon lunchtime except bank hols, jazz Mon evening *(PACW, A F C Young, LYM)*

☆ **Bollington** [Church St], *Church House*: Small corner terrace pub very popular lunchtime for excellent range of good quickly served food with wide choice of veg, well kept Tetleys and Theakstons, furnishings inc pews and working sewing-machine treadle tables, separate dining room, piped music in both rooms, friendly staff *(Bill Sykes, PACW)*

☆ **Bollington Cross** [SJ9277], *Cock & Pheasant*: Pleasantly cool and comfortable family lounge bar, beams, dark wood, old prints, log fire; promptly served good value food inc children's dishes in attractive little dining room, conservatory, Boddingtons, plenty of tables in garden, back playground *(PACW, C Roberts, Marjorie M Roberts)*

Bosley [Leek Rd (A523); SJ9266], *Harrington Arms*: Genuinely home-made food inc freshly cooked veg *(K H Frostick)*

☆ **Broxton** [A41/A534; SJ4754], *Egerton Arms*: Spacious black and white pub with well polished old furniture in roomy and attractive dark-panelled bar, stained glass lights above, old plates and prints, discreet piped music, partly no smoking dining area off; good variety of well prepared bar food inc lots for children, helpful efficient staff, Burtonwood Forshaws and Top Hat, decent wines; tables under cocktail parasols on balcony terrace with lovely views to River Dee; children very welcome, colouring materials, play area with Wendy house; bedrooms *(Mr and Mrs R Phillips, E G Parish, Jeanne and Tom Barnes)*

☆ **Broxton** [Nantwich Rd; A543, nr junction with A41], *Durham Heifer*: Very good food in welcoming and comfortable beamed dining pub, reasonable prices, interesting specials, unobtrusive piped music, good range of drinks; pleasant country views *(Mr and Mrs R D Bromley, Kenneth and Joyce Houghton, Paul Boot)*

☆ **Bunbury** [SJ5758], *Dysart Arms*: Old farmhouse converted into attractive pub with lots of antique furniture, generally old-fashioned atmosphere, Tetleys and Thwaites ales, tables in lovely big garden *(Mr and Mrs J H Adam, G T Jones)*

☆ **Burton Wood** [Alder Lane; 3 miles from M62 junction 9, signed from A49 towards Newton-le-Willows – OS Sheet 108 map reference 585930; SJ5692], *Fiddle i'th' Bag*: Tucked away in peace and quiet by the waterside, with tables outside, friendly, comfortable and spacious inside – plenty of alcoves, brassware, pottery and stuffed animals; popular lunchtime for good food *(D Grzelka, LYM)*

☆ **Butley Town** [A523 Macclesfield—Stockport; SJ9177], *Ash Tree*: Popular dining pub with wide choice of good bar food, three attractive rooms, good coal fires, well kept Boddingtons/Whitbreads ales, friendly atmosphere *(C A Wilkes, LYM)*

☆ **Chester** [Park St, off Albion St)], *Albion*: Distinctive backstreet local under city wall, masses of WWI memorabilia in three carefully refurbished Victorian rooms, also 40s and 50s things; big helpings of good value home-cooked chip-free lunchtime food inc massive sandwiches and unusual main dishes, Cains and Greenalls beers, quick friendly service *(Peter and Jenny Quine, Andy and Jill Kassube, Mary Ann Cameron, Brian Kneale, Tony and Lynne Stark, Sue Holland, Dave Webster, Mike and Pam Simpson, Wayne Brindle)*

☆ **Chester** [Watergate St], *Watergate*: Wide range of quickly served delicious food from ploughman's up in lovely medieval crypt dating from 1270; a wine bar, with candlelit tables and good wine choice, but also well kept Cains real ale *(Jenny Penn, Geoff and Angela Jaques, David Hanley)*

☆ **Chester** [Lower Bridge St], *Falcon*: Striking building with beams, handsome stripped brickwork, well kept Sam Smiths OB and Museum, usual lunchtime bar food (not Sun), uniformed staff, fruit machine, piped music; children allowed lunchtime (not Sat) in quiet and airy upstairs room, other times under-18s may be kept out; jazz Sat lunchtime, open all day Sat; can get very crowded Fri/Sat *(H K Dyson, Tony and Lynne Stark, George Atkinson, Mary Ann Cameron, J and P Maloney, LYM)*

☆ **Chester** [Watergate St], *Custom House*: Popular old pub with lots of brass in three character rooms, good bar lunches, good range of Marstons ales inc Mild, efficient service, good evening atmosphere, fruit machine in lounge *(David and Rebecca*

Killick, Mary Ann Cameron, D Hanley)

☆ Chester [Eastgate Row N], *Boot*: Included for its atmosphere and fine position on The Rows, with heavy beams, lots of old woodwork, oak flooring and flagstones, black-leaded kitchen range in lounge beyond food servery, no smoking oak-panelled upper room; efficient friendly service, cheap Sam Smiths beer; children allowed *(Andy and Jill Kassube, D R Shillitoe, J and P Maloney, H K Dyson, LYM)*

☆ Chester [1 Russell St, down steps off City Rd], *Old Harkers Arms*: Lofty Victorian canalside building full of bric-a-brac, with four well kept changing real ales inc Cains, interesting malt whiskies, good choice of varied and unusual food, nicely presented in generous helpings, efficient staff; quiet lunchtime, very lively evening *(David and Judith Woodcock, J L Moore, Peter Pocklington)*

☆ Chester [Tower Wharf, Raymond St; behind Northgate St, nr rly], *Telfords Warehouse*: New owners doing well in converted warehouse overlooking canal basin, with good unusual food in pub, cellar wine bar and upper restaurant; blond furniture, well kept real ales, nightly live music; children welcome *(Mary Ann Cameron)*

Chester [Garden Lane (off A540)], *Bouverie*: Bustling, friendly local, Greenalls beers on handpump, good bar lunches *(J L Moore)*; [city centre], *Chester Bells*: Pleasant city pub with good choice of beers, well priced varied food, friendly service *(Julian Jewitt)*; [Westgate Row N/Watergate St], *Deva*: 17th-c oak-beamed Greenalls pub upstairs in one of the Rows; long carpeted bar with dining section, longish reasonably priced menu; Greenalls and Stones on handpump; busy at lunchtime *(Mr and Mrs C Roberts)*; [1 Liverpool Rd], *George & Dragon*: Pleasant atmosphere, well kept Boddingtons and Whitbreads Castle Eden, welcoming staff *(D Halford)*; [St John St], *Marlborough Arms*: Pleasant town pub with racing memorabilia, straightforward lunchtime food, Whitbreads-related beers, good staff *(George Atkinson)*; [Bridge St], *Olde Vaults*: Decent Greenalls pub, heavily panelled, with leaded lights, upstairs lounge, downstairs bar *(D Hanley)*

☆ Childer Thornton [from A41 heading S, turn right at PO on to new rd, straight on at crossroads – OS Sheet 117 map reference 365784; SJ3678], *White Lion*: A bit like someone's living room with winter fire and framed matchbooks on the walls, friendly and welcoming staff, well kept Thwaites Mild and Bitter, small garden with picnic-table sets and small swing and slide for children; good basic, reasonably priced food; no music or machines *(David and Rebecca Killick)*

☆ Churton [Farndon Rd (B5130); SJ4256], *White Horse*: Very good home-cooked food, superb service and attractive atmosphere in small village pub with three connecting bars, copper-topped tables, lots of polished bric-a-brac, real ales such as Bass and Burtonwood; pool *(P Mattinson, Michael Back)*

nr Congleton [Timbersbrook; E, off A54 or A527; SJ8961], *Coach & Horses*: The views make this isolated pub well worth finding; excellent simple home-cooked food, friendly staff *(Ian Phillips)*

☆ Crewe [Nantwich Rd (A534) opp rly stn; SJ7056], *Crewe Arms*: Warmly comfortable spacious lounge with Victorian pictures, marble-topped tables, alabaster figurines, curtained alcoves, ornate ceiling; good pubby public bar; well kept Tetleys, good value attractive bar meals, helpful friendly staff, good parking; open all day; bedrooms *(E G Parish)*

Crewe [58 Nantwich Rd, nr stn], *British Lion*: Known locally as the Pig, well run, with good atmosphere, mixed customers, Allied and guest real ales *(Sue Holland, Dave Webster)*; [Broad St], *Cross Keys*: Large, well established and expertly run, with wide choice of bar food from huge meat-filled baps up to popular Sun lunches; Allied real ales *(E G Parish)*

Crowton [SJ5875], *Hare & Hounds*: Friendly and comfortable tucked-away pub with well kept Greenalls, big helpings of varied food *(Nick Cox)*

Daresbury [Old Chester Rd; SJ5983], *Ring o' Bells*: Comfortable, with good choice of reasonably priced good food, well kept Greenalls Original and Mild on handpump, garden; short walk from canal; village church has window showing all the characters in *Alice in Wonderland*; bedrooms *(H Hazzard, E G Parish)*

Dean Row [102 Adlington Rd; SJ8781], *Unicorn*: Good value generous home-cooked food inc Sun breakfast in nicely refurbished pub with no smoking room; friendly staff, Whitbreads-related real ales, lots of tables in pleasant garden; children allowed, no dogs *(Mr and Mrs B Hobden)*

Eaton [A536 Congleton—Macclesfield; SJ8765], *Plough*: Warm welcome, attentive landlord, very good food, well kept beer, decent wine, functional refurbishment *(Anon)*

☆ Fullers Moor [A534 – OS Sheet 117 map reference 500542; SJ4954], *Copper Mine*: Friendly landlady in comfortable dining pub with lovely views, esp from well laid out spacious garden with barbecues; interesting copper-mining memorabilia, bright and airy low-ceilinged rooms with stripped beams and timbering, generous helpings of popular good value bar food, restaurant (must book Sat evenings); well kept Bass and Burtonwood Best, good waitress service, children welcome; handy for Sandstone Trail *(G Hallett, Pat Neate, W C M Jones, G B Rimmer, E Riley, C F Walling, LYM)*

☆ **Goostrey** [Station Rd (towards A535); SJ7870], *Red Lion*: Comfortable and attractive modernised open-plan bar and family restaurant with friendly efficient service, Robinsons and Tetleys on handpump, piped music and fruit machines, restaurant, nice garden with play area; children welcome *(LYM)*

Goostrey [111 Main Rd; off A50 and A535], *Crown*: Well kept Marstons and good atmosphere in brewery-chain dining pub, recently extended and renovated without losing original character; bedrooms *(Mr and Mrs G D Amos, LYM)*

Grappenhall [nr M6 junction 20; A50 towards Warrington, left after 1½ miles – OS Sheet 109 map reference 638863; SJ6486], *Parr Arms*: Good bar food (lunchtime only), tables outside by church *(John Watson)*

Guilden Sutton [SJ4568], *Bird in Hand*: Some concentration on restaurant food, well presented with fresh veg; smiling service, pleasant atmosphere; well kept beer, though could do with more room; children welcome *(Mary Ann Cameron, John Hillyer, Peter E Morris; more reports please)*

Hassall Green [SJ7858], *Romping Donkey*: Small picturesque cottage pub nr Shropshire Union Canal, immaculately furnished in authentic country-pub style, pleasant countryside with canal walks; Ansells real ales, good bar food *(E G Parish, LYM)*

☆ **Hatton** [Warrington Rd; on B5356; SJ6082], *Hatton Arms*: Cottagey 18th-c country pub on cobbled pavement, small snug warm rooms, welcoming landlord, bar lunches and sandwiches, real ales on handpump *(E G Parish, Andy and Jill Kassube)*

☆ **Heatley** [Mill Lane; SJ7088], *Railway*: Old original railway pub with four distinct rooms, good cheap bar food inc excellent barm cakes, superbly kept Boddingtons and guest beers, friendly licensees and Welsh terrier *(Eileen and Alan Gough)*

☆ **Higher Whitley** [1¼ miles from M56 junction 10; A559 towards Northwich; SJ6280], *Birch & Bottle*: Good value food in civilised and attractively decorated pub with good log fires, well kept Greenalls Mild, Bitter and Original, decent wines; attractively furnished conservatory; children allowed if eating, till 8.30 *(John Watson, LYM)*

Holmes Chapel [Knutsford Rd; SJ7667], *Old Vicarage*: A hotel, but well worth knowing for good reasonably priced food and very friendly service; no food Sat lunchtime; bedrooms comfortable and good value *(J R Smylie)*

Houghton Green [Ballater Dr; SJ6292], *Millhouse*: Thoughtfully laid out with cosy bar area, well kept beers; attractively named village *(R Houghton)*

Kirkleyditch [Mottram St Andrew; SJ8778], *Bulls Head*: Good food esp steaks in Beefeater restaurant, well kept Boddingtons and Wadworths 6X on handpump, quick cheerful service; pub part comfortable, nothing brash or modern, with sensibly priced varied food *(Mr and Mrs C Roberts)*

Langley [SJ9471], *Lamb*: Superbly good value *(Wayne Brindle)*

☆ **Little Bollington** [the one nr Altrincham, 2 miles from M56 junction 7: A56 towards Lymm, then first right at Stamford Arms into Park Lane – use A556 to get back on to M56 westbound], *Swan With Two Nicks*: Wide choice of food with some evening concentration on fish in beamed village pub full of brass, copper, bric-a-brac and cabaret memorabilia; snug alcoves, antique settles in back room, log fire, well kept Whitbreads-related real ales, friendly staff, tables outside; attractive surroundings inc Dunham Hall deer park *(Bill and Lydia Ryan, C A Wilkes, Dennis Jones, LYM)*

Little Bollington [A56, about 3 miles E of Lymm], *Olde No 3*: Cosy old pub by Bridgewater Canal, good atmosphere, reasonably priced food, John Smiths beer, coal fire *(Bill and Lydia Ryan)*

Little Leigh [A49, just S of A533; not far from M56 junction 10; SJ6276], *Holly Bush*: The future of this interesting former farm-pub still uncertain; sold by Greenalls, new owners plan changes with link to 16th-c barn as potential added restaurant *(D Grzelka, LYM; news please)*; [A49 by swing bridge], *Legh Arms*: Riverside setting with large garden and play area, Burtonwood ales, good value bar food – big helpings, some imaginative dishes inc vegetarian, early-evening bargains, also full restaurant menu; always a friendly welcome *(Alan Spence, Suzi Curtis)*

☆ **Lower Peover** [Crown Lane; B5081, off A50; SJ7474], *Crown*: Lots of bric-a-brac inc interesting gooseberry championship memorabilia in attractive and relaxing L-shaped bar with two rooms off, very friendly good service, Boddingtons on handpump, bar food, relaxing atmosphere, dominoes *(C Roberts, Carl Travis)*

☆ **Lower Whitley** [SJ6179], *Chetwode Arms*: Very popular Greenalls Millers Kitchen dining pub with traditional layout, good solid furnishings, warm coal fires, good service and own immaculately kept bowling green; children in eating area, open all day Sat *(Roger and Christine Mash, Gary Roberts, LYM)*

☆ **Lymm** [Eagle Brow, nr M6 junction 20; SJ6787], *Spread Eagle*: Character beamed village pub with three well furnished distinct areas inc small snug, cheery atmosphere, well kept Lees on handpump, good home-made bar food, juke box *(Alan Gough)*

Lymm, *Church Garden*: Pleasant atmosphere, good esp home-made apple pie, well kept Greenalls *(M A Robinson)*

☆ **nr Macclesfield** [A537 some miles out

towards Buxton – OS Sheet 119 map reference 001719; SK0071], *Cat & Fiddle*: Britain's 2nd-highest pub, surrounded by spectacular moorland (though on a trunk road), with magnificent views; spacious spotlessly kept lounge, roomy flagstoned public bar, Robinsons real ales, decent bar food; busy lunchtime in summer *(LYM)*

Marford [SJ4166], *Trevor Arms*: Lovely place to stay for Chester and surrounding area; Stones beer, good restaurant – must book; bedrooms *(Julian Jewitt)*

Mickle Trafford [Chester Rd; A56; SJ4569], *Shrewsbury Arms*: Good friendly staff, guest beers inc Flowers IPA, Morlands Old Speckled Hen and Wadworths 6X on handpump, good food inc delicious puddings; tables outside; children welcome *(Steve and Karen Jennings)*

☆ **Mobberley** [Mobberley Rd; opp church; SJ7879], *Church*: Friendly and comfortable pub notable for big helpings of very good food from longish menu (increasingly popular, may have to book), well kept Greenalls, cheerful young service; tables in courtyard, big garden with play area, own bowling green; children welcome *(C and Marjorie Roberts, Bill and Lydia Ryan)*

☆ **Mobberley** [Town Lane; down hill from sharp bend on B5185 at E edge of 30mph limit], *Roebuck*: Spacious and pleasant open-plan bar with long pews on polished floorboards, solid panelling, well kept Courage-related real ales, generously served bar food from lunchtime sandwiches to delicious main dishes, attentive service, upstairs restaurant, seats in cobbled courtyard and garden behind, play area; children welcome *(Pauline Crossland, Dave Cawley, Bill and Lydia Ryan, LYM)*

Mobberley [Wilsons Mill Lane], *Bulls Head*: Friendly and comfortable low-beamed open-plan village local with good value food, well kept Boddingtons, central open fire, plusher furnishings than previously, soft lighting; another with own immaculate bowling green *(Bill and Lydia Ryan, DI, BB)*; [Ashley Rd, nr stn – towards Altrincham], *Chapel House*: Friendly and homely, real fire and lap-loving cat in cosy and relaxing panelled lounge; particularly well kept Boddingtons, small games room with darts, seats in courtyard, outside lavatories; nr stn *(Bill and Lydia Ryan)*

☆ **Nantwich** [Hospital St – by side passage to central church; SJ6552], *Lamb*: Hotel bar with leather chesterfields and other comfortable seats, well kept Burtonwood Forshaws, decent wines and malt whiskies from modern bar counter, good value nicely presented home-cooked bar food inc outstanding fish in bar and traditional upstairs dining room, generous helpings, attentive staff, flowery wallpaper and long russet velvet curtains; piped music may be rather obtrusive; bedrooms – hotel backs

on to parish church, has useful car park *(W C M Jones, Nick and Alison Dowson, Nigel Pritchard, BB)*

Nantwich [97 Welsh Row], *Oddfellows Arms*: Cosy, with friendly service, well kept Burtonwood, reasonably priced food inc vegetarian, pub games; very attractive street *(Sue Holland, Dave Webster)*; [51 Beam St], *Red Cow*: Former 15th-c farmhouse, very rare for a pub in being Grade I listed – Robinsons the brewery spent three years taking the building apart beam by beam, treating them and putting them back; comfortable with pleasant decor, lively but not overcrowded on a weekend evening, well kept Best, Mild, Old Tom and Hartleys XB *(Nick and Alison Dowson)*; [Hospital St], *Vine*: Long and narrow with quiet corners, lots of nick-nacks, friendly service, good atmosphere; varied menu with daily specials, real ale such as Marstons Pedigree *(Sue Holland and Dave Webster, Nick and Alison Dowson)*

Neston [19 Quayside, SW of Little Neston – OS Sheet 117 map reference 290760; SJ2976], *Harp*: Charming tiny old pub in marvellous spot by ruined quay on the Burton Marshes looking out over the River Dee to Wales; one cosy and friendly room, the other workingman's-club-style; well kept Whitbreads and Timothy Taylors Landlord, basic cheese or ham sandwiches *(Tony and Lynne Stark)*

Ollerton [A537; – OS Sheet 118 map reference 775769; SJ7877], *Dun Cow*: Comfortable and traditional small-roomed country pub with attractive and individual furnishings, two fine log fires, well kept Greenalls Cask and Original, drinkable wine, dominoes, shove-ha'penny and darts in small taproom, interesting bar food from sandwiches up inc vegetarian; open all day (inc restaurant in summer), children in snug and restaurant *(Paul Wreglesworth, JHMB, Olive and Ray Hebson, LYM)*

☆ **Over Peover** [off A50 S of Knutsford; SJ7674], *Olde Park Gate*: Splendid collection of Macclesfield chairs in attractive small panelled rooms, busy and friendly atmosphere, very welcoming licensee, big helpings of good straightforward food reasonably priced and promptly served, well kept Sam Smiths; family room, tables outside *(Carl Travis, BB)*

☆ **Parkgate** [The Parade; SJ2878], *Boathouse*: Wide choice of good food inc good-value dinner, attractive furnishings, well trained friendly young staff, relaxing atmosphere, Allied ales; great view of Welsh hills from conservatory restaurant; trad jazz Tues *(Douglas Copeland, Mrs D Craig)*

☆ **Parkgate** [The Parade], *Red Lion*: Another comfortable Allied pub on this attractive waterfront, Victorian, with good value sandwiches, 19th-c paintings and beer-mug collection *(Anon)*

Parkgate, *Old Quay*: Comfortable Whitbreads seafront pub, modern decor, reasonably priced Brewers Fayre food *(Fred Collier)*

Pickmere [B5391 NE of Northwich; SJ6977], *Red Lion*: Beautiful decor, helpful friendly staff, good well served food, three different types of cider *(Susanne Bertschinger)*

☆ **Plumley** [Plumley Moor Lane; off A556 by the Smoker; SJ7175], *Golden Pheasant*: Generous helpings of attractive bar food inc good value OAP and 'junior adults' menus, well kept Lees Bitter and Mild, very pleasant and welcoming newish management, spacious series of comfortably modernised rooms inc pool room and roomy conservatory overlooking back children's garden, pub gardens and bowling green; excellent well equipped bedrooms *(R H Jones, Simon J Barber, Bill and Lydia Ryan, LYM)*

☆ **Pott Shrigley** [towards Rainow, off Spurley Lane – OS Sheet 118 map reference 945782; SJ9478], *Cheshire Hunt*: Comfortable and friendly small-roomed country dining pub with decent food, well kept Boddingtons, good open fires, friendly staff, piped music; tables on flagstoned terrace with pasture views, play area; good walks *(Alan and Heather Jacques, LYM)*

Poynton [Shrigley Rd N; Higher Poynton, off A523; SJ9283], *Boars Head*: Nr canal and bridleway converted from railway, good value low-priced food, horsey theme with rosettes on walls and even real horses behind; popular midweek lunchtime with pensioners from nearby golf club *(Andrew and Ruth Triggs)*

Prestbury [London Rd; A523 towards Adlington stn; SJ9077], *Ash Tree*: Locally popular for wide choice of good bar food; good atmosphere *(B C Armstrong)*

☆ **Rainow** [NE of village on A5002 Whalley Bridge—Macclesfield; SJ9576], *Highwayman*: Early 17th-c small-roomed low-beamed moorland pub, a favourite for all who put character and atmosphere first and certainly main-entry quality on that score; well kept Thwaites, good fires, bar food, rather late opening *(Keith W Mills, Dr Roy Partington, LYM)*

Sandbach [Sweettooth Lane; SJ7661], *Limes*: Elegant and imposing Victorian pub overlooking bowling green, friendly and helpful staff *(Dr and Mrs A K Clarke)*; [Newcastle Rd, 1¼ miles from M6 junction 17], *Old Hall*: Handsome Jacobean hotel with fine panelling and spreading lawns; Ruddles Best in small bar, good restaurant meals, excellent service, agreable atmosphere; bedrooms comfortable and well equipped *(E G Parish, LYM)*

Scholar Green [off A34 N of Kidsgrove; SJ8356], *Rising Sun*: Well run by welcoming new owners, good choice of well kept ales inc Marstons Bitter and Pedigree, Robinsons, Tetley-Walkers Dark Mild and Thwaites; bright comfortable recently refurbished restaurant, imaginative

home-cooked food, family room; unobtrusive piped music *(Maeve and Peter Thomson)*

☆ **Smallwood** [Newcastle Rd; A50 N of Alsager; SJ8160], *Bulls Head*: Attractive interestingly decorated dining pub with lots of space and particularly good garden with play area; well kept Burtonwood and Tetleys, decent house wines, imaginative range of well presented generous food inc good puddings, good service; piped pop music, children welcome; quite handy for Biddulph Grange (NT) *(R C Vincent, Keith Plant, LYM)*

☆ **Styal** [Altrincham Rd; B5166 nr Ringway Airport; SJ8383], *Old Ship*: Friendly pub in attractive NT village with nice walks in riverside woods and seats out in front; wide choice of copious food all day, well kept Courage-related real ales, cheerful service; children allowed, though perhaps the pub's rather small for them *(Mr and Mrs A F Walters, Terry Buckland, Andrew and Ruth Triggs)*

☆ **Swettenham** [off A54 Congleton—Holmes Chapel or A535 Chelford—Holmes Chapel; SJ8067], *Swettenham Arms*: Prettily placed village pub tucked away behind church, big beamed family bar divided into several sections, all sparkling, with log fires, efficient friendly service, good sensibly priced food, well kept beer; no gaming machines, seats in spacious garden; recently taken over by licensees of the Dog at Over Peover (see main entries), making a chain of three good pubs *(A Lomas, LYM)*

Tarporley [High St; SJ5563], *Foresters Arms*: Friendly pub in bypassed village, very good bar food, immaculate surroundings, very pleasant no smoking area refurbished with pine furniture, four Boddingtons beers on handpump, quick pleasant service *(E G Parish)*

☆ **Thelwall** [B5157, nr M6 junction 20; SJ6587], *Pickering Arms*: Fine atmosphere in attractive low-beamed village pub with cobbled forecourt, good reasonably priced bar food lunchtime and evening, friendly service, Greenalls Bitter and Mild and Stones on handpump; children allowed if eating *(H Hazzard)*

Tilston [SJ4652], *Fox & Hounds*: First-class friendly service, well presented good food *(D Ellis)*

☆ **nr Tiverton** [Wharton's Lock; Bates Mill Lane – OS Sheet 117 map reference 532603; SJ5660], *Shady Oak*: Beautifully placed canalside Chef & Brewer pub with fine views of Beeston Castle, airy lounge opening into small carpeted conservatory, well kept Courage-related ales, plenty of seats and good play area in waterside garden and terrace, summer barbecues, moorings *(M A Cameron, LYM)*

Walgherton [A51 between Bridgemere Gdn Centre and Stapeley Water Gdns; SJ6949], *Boars Head*: Country-pub atmosphere, good food quickly served, very friendly staff, reasonably priced beer; TV in lounge, children's play area; bedrooms *(Sue Badel)*

☆ **Walker Barn** [A537 Macclesfield—Buxton; SJ9573], *Setter Dog*: Remote but civilised extended moorland dining pub with fine bleak and windswept view, well kept Marstons, good if not cheap food in small bar and restaurant, good service, roaring fire; handy for Teggs Nose Country Park *(Mike and Wendy Proctor)*

☆ **Walleys Green** [Minshull Lovell; off A530 Middlewich—Crewe – OS Sheet 118 map reference 684621; SJ6861], *Verdin Arms*: Friendly and attractive mock-Tudor canalside pub in quiet countryside, good fresh home-cooked food, well kept Robinsons, big play area *(H Hazzard, E G Parish)*

☆ *nr* **Warrington** [Fiddlers Ferry; leave A562 in Penketh – park in Station rd off Tannery Lane – OS Sheet 108 map reference 560863; SJ5686], *Ferry*: Picturesquely isolated between Manchester Ship Canal and Mersey, now reopened after refurbishment following fire damage, with four well kept real ales inc weekly guest and a Mild, over 50 whiskies, decent food in nice upstairs dining room (not Sun or Mon) as well as Sun breakfast, provision for children; tables outside; traditional bagatelle table lost after last high tide flood *(D Grzelka, LYM)*

Wheelock [Mill Lane; A534 Sandbach—Crewe; SJ7559], *Nags Head*: Inviting black and white façade, secluded walled garden, well furnished bars, good bar food (tables at a sensible height for eating), cottagey atmosphere, brass artefacts, Boddingtons on handpump; good canalside and country walks *(E G Parish)*

Whiteley Green [OS Sheet 118 map reference 924789; SJ9278], *Windmill*: Spacious and attractive garden with summer bar and barbecues, roomy modernised lounge, good lunchtime bar food, well kept Whitbreads-related real ales; provision for children; in attractive countryside nr Middlewood Way *(C A Wilkes, BB)*

Willaston [Newcastle Rd, Blakelow – OS Sheet 118 map reference 680517; SJ6851], *Horseshoe*: Panelled lounge with fire, dining room, public bar; friendly service, Robinsons Bitter and Best on handpump (sometimes Mild too) *(Sue Holland)*

Willaston [Wistaston Rd – OS Sheet 117 map reference 329777; SJ3378; not the same as the one above], *Pollards*: Wide choice of good bar food inc comfortable partly 14th-c beamed and flagstoned bar, unusual cushioned wall seats with some stone armrests, Greenalls real ales, conservatory/lounge extension overlooking sizeable pleasant garden; striking building; bedrooms *(Mr and Mrs A Craig)*

Wilmslow [Altrincham Rd (A538); SJ8481], *Boddingtons Arms*: Large modern pub, well furnished and comfortable, with good cheap menu in Henry's Table restaurant, very good simple reasonably priced bar food; Boddingtons and Theakstons on handpump, speedy reasonably friendly service *(Mr and Mrs C Roberts)*; [just off A34], *King William*: Refurbished Robinsons pub with cosy alcoves opening off bar, well kept real ales, lunchtime snacks inc wide range of burgers, friendly atmosphere; children welcome *(Dave Irving)*; [Old Wilmslow Rd (B5166 N, nr Manchester Airport)], *Romper*: Quietly popular, with well kept beer, good value food, pleasant garden, efficient staff *(Terry Buckland)*

Wincham [A559; SJ6775], *Black Greyhound*: Spaciously plush lounge, children made most welcome with one menu for 12s and under and another for 6s and under, also generous adult food; well kept Greenalls Bitter and Original, large lawn with picnic-table sets and a few tyre swings, welcoming service *(Brian and Anna Marsden)*

Winterley [Crewe Rd; nr Sandbach on A534; SJ7557], *Holly Bush*: Attractive and comfortable black and white pub with wide choice of bar food, large garden, play area; handy for canal *(E G Parish)*

Withington [Lower Withington, off B5392; SJ8169], *Red Lion*: Good varied bar food, Robinsons real ale, tables outside; handy for Jodrell Bank *(J M Watson, Andrew Wilson)*

Wybunbury [Main Rd (B5071); SJ6950], *Swan*: Recently refurbished, with well kept beer, really home-made bar food inc excellent Cumberland sausage, seats in garden – charming spot by churchyard, with antique shop behind car park *(Catherine and Andrew Brian, LYM)*

Post Office address codings confusingly give the impression that some pubs are in Cheshire, when they're really in Derbyshire (and therefore included in this book under that chapter) or in Greater Manchester (see the Lancashire chapter).

Cleveland *see* Northumbria

Cornwall

Cross the Tamar from Devon, and one immediate benefit is lower drinks prices – around 10p a pint cheaper for beer here in Cornwall, on average. Drinks prices in the county have hardly changed at all this last year – what increase there has been is only about half as much as what we've found elsewhere. It's in pubs getting their supplies locally (usually from the St Austell brewery) that prices have generally been held down best, with significant savings over pubs supplied by the national breweries. Though far fewer Cornish pubs are now tied to the relatively high-priced big national breweries, many which used to be tied to the more local Devenish (or its alter ego Cornish Brewery) are now tied to Greenalls. This Cheshire-based ex-brewer as a rule supplies its pubs with beers produced in distant breweries by Whitbreads (typically Flowers and/or Boddingtons). Moreover, many of the county's free houses get their beers from the big nationals rather than smaller or more local breweries, and in these too drinks prices tend to be higher than in locally-supplied pubs. There are exceptions – the nationally-supplied Port Gaverne Hotel near Port Isaac, for instance, deserves credit for keeping its drinks prices down to very local levels. But the general rule must be: for good drinks prices, look for local supplies. Local supplies should be something here to look out for on the food side, too. Considering the county's great fishing tradition, and the fact that such a high proportion of its good pubs are on or close to the coast, you'd expect most to do good fresh local fish and seafood. Alas, not so. As the detail of the individual entries shows, only about one in five of even the better pubs here takes the trouble to find and prepare significant quantities of fresh local fish or seafood. Among these, the new licensees at the Maltsters Arms at Chapel Amble are now specialising in good fresh fish; the Port William at Trebarwith can firmly be recommended for a good choice of interesting fish dishes (and what a marvellous seaside spot to eat them in); and our tastebuds are still resonating happily to seafood memories from our anonymous inspection meal at one of our new entries here, the White Hart at St Keverne. Both entries on the Isles of Scilly, the idyllically placed Turks Head on St Agnes and particularly the very friendly New Inn on Tresco (a good new licensee this year), make tempting use of local seafood. These five pubs now come closest of any here to attaining our Food Award. Of the other two new entries, the Quayside in Falmouth has as interesting a choice of beers as its sister pub the Old Ale House in Truro (with the bonus of an outstanding collection of malt whiskies, and a good waterside position), and the Ship at Lerryn (back in these pages after a break) is also one of very few pubs here to gain our new Beer Award. Another is the wonderfully unchanging Bush at Morwenstow (bargain snacks, too), and the Blue Anchor at Helston gains one for the interesting beers from its old-established in-house brewery. The newish landlord at the Roseland at Philleigh is going from strength to strength, and besides a wonderful atmosphere the food there is increasingly attractive. Other pubs here currently doing particularly well include the intriguing Cobweb in Boscastle, the Trengilly Wartha near Constantine (good food, interesting beers), the beautifully placed Pandora near Mylor Bridge (lots of wines by the glass now), the Ship at Porthleven (another marvellously placed waterside pub), and the fascinating Eliot Arms at Tregadillett. Strong contenders this year in the Lucky Dip at the end of the chapter include the Old Ferry at Bodinnick, Jamaica Inn at Bolventor, Napoleon in Boscastle, Gurnards Head Hotel, Halzephron near Helston (promising new owners), Lamorna Wink, Crown at Lanlivery, Top House at Lizard, Mexico at Longrock, Royal Oak in Lostwithiel, Heron at Malpas, New Inn at Manaccan (again, good new owners), Red Lion at Mawnan Smith, Royal Oak at Perranwell, Lugger at Portloe, Plume of Feathers at Portscatho, Who'd Have Thought It at St Dominick, Tree at Stratton and Tinners Arms at Zennor; as we have already inspected the great majority of these we can vouch for their quality. There is also a useful choice, again mostly inspected, in Falmouth, Kingsand, Padstow, Polperro and Truro.

BOSCASTLE   SX0990 Map 1

Cobweb

B3263, just E of harbour

One reader was pleased to find the welcome he received here was as warm as the one he'd had nine years ago. It's very popular with both locals and visitors – thanks to the hard-working and cheerful licensee and his staff. Hundreds of old bottles hang from the heavy old beams in the lively bar and there's a cosy log fire, two or three curved high-backed winged settles against the dark stone walls, and a few leatherette dining chairs. Well kept Bass, Exmoor Gold, St Austell Tinners, HSD, XXXX on handpump, with occasional guest beers. The quickly served, good value bar food includes sandwiches (from £1.30, crab or prawn £3), soup and baked potatoes, fine pasties, sausage, egg and chips (£3; the chips are very good), lasagne and vegetarian meals (£4), gammon steak (£6.50), and steaks (£8.50); daily specials and some vegetarian dishes. Good, if obtrusive, juke box, darts, pool (keen players here), video game, fruit machine, dominoes and cribbage; the big communicating family room has an enormous armchair carved out of a tree trunk as well as its more conventional Windsor armchairs, and another cosy winter fire. Opening off this a good-sized children's room has a second pool table, and more machines. The pub's position near the tiny harbour can mean crowds in the holiday season. *(Recommended by S Demont, T Barrow, Richard Dolphin, Mrs Ann Saunders, Jack and Philip Paxton, N and J Strathdee, Steve and Liz Tilley, Roy and Margaret Randle, K R Flack, Alec and Marie Lewery, Janet C M Pickles, Rob and Helen Townsend, Rita Horridge)*

Free house ~ Licensee Ivor Bright ~ Real ale ~ Meals and snacks (till 10pm) ~ Restaurant (not Sun evening) ~ (01840) 250278 ~ Children in own room ~ Live entertainment Sat evening ~ Open 11-3, 6-11 (midnight Sat)

CHAPEL AMBLE   SW9975 Map 1

Maltsters Arms ♀

Village signposted from A39 NE of Wadebridge; and from B3314

Friendly new licensees, their daughters and son-in-law have taken over this popular early 16th-c pub – and although there is emphasis on the good food, they hope the atmosphere is now more pubby. The attractively knocked together rooms (one is no smoking) have black oak joists in the white ceiling, partly panelled stripped stone walls, heavy wooden tables on the partly carpeted big flagstones, and a large stone fireplace; there's also a side room with Windsor chairs. Fresh fish is the speciality now and you might find char-grilled sardines or chilli prawns (£5.50), oysters in season, squid, good bream, delicious skate,

Fowey sea trout, 1lb in weight, and grilled (£9.50), fillet of sea bass with saffron sauce (£10.50), and paella (£17.50 for two people); also, lunchtime sandwiches, spaghetti bolognese (£5), chicken in ginger (£5.50), steaks from the local butcher, and puddings such as fruit crumbles, bread and butter pudding with brandy and cream, and lemon tart; lots of clotted cream. Well kept Bass, Flowers IPA, Ruddles County and a guest beer on handpump kept under light blanket pressure; varied wine list with quite a few from Australia, and several malt whiskies. Darts, winter pool, cribbage, dominoes, video game, and piped music. Benches outside in a sheltered sunny corner. The local hunt meets here twice a year. *(Recommended by Jennifer Tora, Simon and Natalie Forster, Margaret Mason, David Thompson, Steve and Liz Tilley, Nick Wikeley, S R Chapman, Ted George)*

Free house ~ Licensees David and Marie Gray ~ Real ale ~ Meals and snacks (till 10pm) ~ Wadebridge (01208) 812473 ~ Children in restaurant and family room ~ Open 10.30-2.30, 6-11; winter weekday closing 10.30

CONSTANTINE SW7229 Map 1

Trengilly Wartha 🛏 🍺 🍴

Constantine signposted from Penryn—Gweek rd (former B3291); in village turn right just before Minimarket (towards Gweek); in nearly a mile pub signposted left; at Nancenoy, OS sheet 204, map reference 731282

An unexpected find down these narrow lanes, this busy pub is popular with all age groups. The low-beamed main bar has a woodburning stove and modern high-backed settles boxing in polished heavy wooden tables, and there's a no smoking conservatory family room; darts, pool, bar billiards, shove-ha'penny, dominoes, shut-the-box, backgammon, fruit machine, and video and trivia machines. A lounge has machine-tapestried wall benches, a log fire and some harness. Up a step from the bar an eating area with some winged settles and tables. Good, home-made bar food includes soup (£1.95), filled baked potatoes (from £2.50), smoked fish or chicken liver pâtés (£3), a home-made sausage and a guest one (£3.30), raised vegetable pie or lasagne (£4), lunchtime ploughman's with home-made pickles (from £4), salads (from £4.50), 10oz sirloin steak (£9.50) and puddings (£2), with daily specials such as fresh tagliatelle with watercress and yoghurt sauce (£3.30), light beef curry (£4.80), smoked chicken and tomato strudel (£5.40), and half a fresh lobster (£9.50); children's menu (from £2). Regular festivals are held throughout the year like the summer Sausage Festival, a fish one in November, and a Pudding Week in January. They keep an unusually wide choice of drinks for the area, such as well kept Fergusons Dartmoor, Tetleys and St Austell XXXX Mild on handpump with regularly changing ales from smaller brewers tapped from the cask such as Ash Vine, Berrows, Cotleigh Tawny, Exmoor Gold, Gibbs Mew Bishops Tipple, Hadrian's Emperior, and so forth. Also, two farm ciders, over 35 malt whiskies (including 10 extinct ones), over 10 interesting wines by the glass (a fine choice by the bottle, too) and country wines. The pretty landscaped garden has some picnic-table sets around the vine-covered pergola, an international sized piste for boules, and a lake garden next door to the inn. *(Recommended by John and Sally Clarke, Charles Lovedale, Andy and Jill Kassube, Jack and Philip Paxton, Mr and Mrs W J A Timpson, S R Chapman, Pat and John Millward, Margaret Kemp, David and Michelle Hedges, Ian Phillips, David Carrington, Stephen Oxley, Anna Cwajna)*

Free house ~ Licensees Nigel Logan, Michael Maguire ~ Real ale ~ Meals and snacks ~ Restaurant ~ Falmouth (01326) 40332 ~ Children welcome ~ Occasional live music ~ Open 11-2.30 or 3, 6-11; winter evening opening 6.30 ~ Bedrooms: £36(£42B)/£48(£59B)

CROWS NEST SX2669 Map1

Crows Nest

Signposted off B3264 N of Liskeard; or pleasant drive from A30 by Siblyback/St Cleer rd from Bolventor, turning left at Common Moor, Siblyback signpost, then forking right to Darite; OS Sheet 201 map reference 263692

Once the pay office/company store where tin and copper miners were paid, this old-fashioned and friendly 17th-c pub has an interesting table converted from a huge blacksmith's bellows (which still work), an unusually long black wall settle by the big log fire as well as other more orthodox seats and polished tables, and lots of stirrups, bits and spurs hanging from the bowed dark oak beams. On the right, and divided by a balustered partition, is a similar area with old local photographs and maybe flowers on the tablecloths. Good value bar food includes soup (£1.35), stilton, leek and potato bake or lasagne (£3.50), home-cooked ham (£3.95), prawn and mushroom bake (£4.50), whole boneless lemon sole (£5.25), sizzling cajun or texas beef (£6), chicken steaks (from £7), and puddings (from £1.50). Well kept St Austell Tinners and HSD on handpump kept under light blanket pressure; euchre, juke box, fruit machine and piped music; helpful, friendly service, gets slower when busy. On the terrace by the quiet lane there are picnic-table sets. No children. *(Recommended by R L Turnham, R and S Bentley, Jack and Philip Paxton, S Brackenbury, Ted George)*

St Austell ~ Tenant T W C Rosser ~ Real ale ~ Meals and snacks ~ Liskeard (01579) 345930 ~ Open 11.30-3, 6-11; closed evening 25 Dec

FALMOUTH   SW8032 Map 1

Quayside
ArwenackSt/Fore St

If you enter this pub from the attractively bustling street you walk into the lounge bar with its comfortable, if rather ancient, armchairs and sofas – there are more straightforward tables and chairs at the other end – picture windows overlooking the harbour, and huge range of over 180 whiskies (most of them single malts). Downstairs the subterranean-feeling simple public bar has malt sacks tacked into the counter, lots of beer mats on the panelled walls, book matches on the black ceiling, a big red ensign, a mix of ordinary pub chairs on the bare boards, a log-effect gas fire in the stripped stone fireplace, and a fine range of beers such as Bass, Boddingtons, Flowers IPA and Original, Ruddles County on handpump, with guests tapped from the cask like Batemans XXXB, Cotleigh Old Buzzard, Gibbs Mew Bishops Tipple, and Wadworths 6X; Inch's cider and a big barrel of free peanuts (which gives an individual touch to the floor covering). Bar food includes specials such as oriental prawns, chilli con carne, grilled plaice and fresh prawns (£7.95), and Sunday roast (£3.50). There are picnic-table sets on the tarmac by the Custom House Dock and next to the handsome Georgian harbour-master's office. *(Recommended by John Lansdown, John Wooll, David and Michelle Hedges, Nigel Woolliscroft, P and M Rudlin)*

Free house ~ Licensees David Patterson and Derrick Smith ~ Real ale ~ Meals and snacks (not Sun evening) ~ (01326) 312113 ~ Children in top lounge ~ Duo Fri and Sat evenings, folk alternate Sun ~ Open all day – at least in summer

HELFORD   SW7526 Map 1

Shipwrights Arms
The draw to this thatched pub is its lovely position above a beautiful wooded creek – best enjoyed in summer when you can sit on the terraces; the top part of the terrace is roofed over with Perspex. Inside there's quite a nautical theme with navigation lamps, models of ships, sea pictures, drawings of lifeboat coxwains and shark fishing photographs – as well as a collection of foreign banknotes behind the bar counter. A dining area has oak settles and tables; winter open fire. Well kept Flowers, Whitbreads Castle Eden and a guest beer on handpump, and straightforward bar food; piped music. It does get crowded at peak times. *(Recommended by Gwen and Peter Andrews, Martin and Penny Fletcher, Jack and Philip Paxton, Margaret Kemp, David and Michelle Hedges, D and H Broodbank, Bill and Edee Miller, Stephen Oxley, Anna Cwajna, Stephen C Harvey)*

Greenalls ~ Lease: Brandon Flynn and Charles Herbert ~ Real ale ~ Meals and snacks (not Sun or Mon evenings in winter) ~ (01326) 231235 ~ Children in eating area of bar ~ Parking only right outside the village in summer ~ Open 11-2.30, 6-11(10.30 in winter)

HELFORD PASSAGE SW7627 Map 1

Ferryboat

Signed from B3291

New licensees have taken over this pub – which is popular with families as just ten yards from the terrace (where summer barbecues are held) is a sandy beach with safe swimming and where you can hire small boats and arrange fishing trips; there's also a ferry across to Helford village (again, summer only). The big spacious bar has well kept St Austell BB, Tinners and HSD on handpump, and home-made bar food like good soup, sandwiches (£2), locally-made Cumberland sausage (£2.50), filled baked potatoes (from £2.70), ploughman's (from £3), salads (from £5), fresh fish dishes, and barbecues and summer afternoon cream teas. Darts, pool, fruit machine, video game, juke box and piped music. They hold their own regatta on the second Sunday of August. *(Recommended by Mr and Mrs W J A Timpson, Gwen and Peter Andrews, Nigel Woolliscroft, Mr and Mrs C R Little, Martyn and Mary Mullins, Stephen and Jean Curtis; more reports on the new regime, please)*

St Austell ~ Manager Steven Brown ~ Real ale ~ Meals and snacks ~ Restaurant ~ (01326) 250625 ~ Children welcome ~ Live entertainment twice a week in summer ~ Open 11-11; 11-3, 6-11 in winter

HELSTON SW6527 Map 1

Blue Anchor £ 🍺

50 Coinagehall Street

This thatched town pub dates back to the 15th c when it was a monks' rest house – and it's probably the oldest brewing house in the country. Brewing continued after the dissolution of the monasteries, and today they still produce their Medium, Best, 'Spingo' Special (the name comes from the Victorian word for strong beer) and Extra Special ales. At lunchtimes you can usually go and look round the brewery and the cellar; they also sell farm cider. Opening off the central corridor, the series of small, low-ceilinged rooms look their age, with simple old-fashioned furniture on the flagstones, interesting old prints, some bared stone walls, and in one room a fine inglenook fireplace. A family room has video game, fruit machines, darts, dominoes and cards. Bar food includes rolls (£1.10), pasties (£1.50), and some pot meals. Past an old stone bench in the sheltered little terrace area is a skittle alley. The pub is very popular with locals (mainly men), and gets quite busy. The nearby Flambards Triple Theme Park has a lot of family attractions, and Godolphin House is well worth visiting. *(Recommended by Jack and Philip Paxton, Mark Walker, Sue Holland, Dave Webster, David and Michelle Hedges)*

Own brew ~ Licensees Kim and Simon Corbett ~ Real ale ~ Snacks ~ Helston (01326) 562821 ~ Children in family room ~ Live bands Fri evenings ~ Parking sometimes difficult ~ Open all day

LANNER SW7240 Map 1

Fox & Hounds

Comford; junction A393/B3293; OS sheet 204 map reference 734399

In summer, the colourful hanging baskets and tubs of flowers here are pretty, and there are picnic-table sets on the sheltered and neatly kept back lawn; swings and climber for children. Inside, the rambling bar has black beams and joists, stripped stonework and dark panelling, some comical 1920s prints by Lawson Wood, greeny gold plush or deep pink cloth banquettes on the red carpet, and a relaxed atmosphere. One granite fireplace has a woodburning stove, another has a good log fire, and there may be cheerful summer flowers to brighten up the tables. Bar food includes sandwiches, ploughman's, soup (£1.65; the stilton and celery is good), cashew nut paella (£4.35), Cumberland sausages (£4.95), seafood mornay (£6.50), steaks (from £9.25), honey roast duck (£10.25), puddings (£1.95), children's menu (from £1.50), and daily specials. Well kept Bass and St Austell Tinners and HSD tapped from the cask. Pool, shove-ha'penny, cribbage, dominoes, fruit machine and piped music. Part of the restaurant is no smoking. *(Recommended by Tom Evans, RB, Andy and Jill Kassube, S Brackenbury, Jack and Philip Paxton)*

St Austell ~ Tenants Mike and Sue Swiss ~ Real ale ~ Meals and snacks ~ Restaurant ~ St Day (01209) 820251 ~ Children in eating area of bar ~ Open 11-3, 6-11

LERRYN SX1457 Map 1

Ship

Village signposted from A390 in Lostwithiel

On the walls of this pleasant village pub are photographs of the small seagull-engined craft race, held in December – the winner is the first back to the pub to ring the ship's bell. There are photographs of this event around the pub (as well as some old village ones), brasses on beams, and a locally made grandfather clock; part of the lounge bar is no-smoking. A separate room has sensibly placed darts, pool, dominoes, fruit machine and piped music. Well kept ales might include Bass, Boddingtons, Cotleigh Old Tawny, Courage Best, Exmoor Gold, Fullers London Pride, Morlands Old Speckled Hen, and Otter Ale on handpump, and local farm cider and wine, and fruit wine. Bar food includes sandwiches and lots of pies like venison, pheasant and cranberry, pumpkin, homity, and steak and oyster pie (all £5.50). In front of the stone building by the flower borders, tubs and hanging baskets there are some picnic-table sets, with more on a sheltered back lawn which also has a children's play area. You can walk along the bank of the River Lerryn or through the National Trust woodland nearby. There is a self-catering flat for rent. *(Recommended by Gerry Hollington, A N Ellis, Nick Wikeley, Jack and Philip Paxton, S Brackenbury, R L Turnham, Dave Braisted)*

Free house ~ Licensee Howard Packer ~ Real ale ~ Meals and snacks ~ Restaurant ~ Bodmin (01208) 872374 ~ Well behaved children welcome ~ Open 11.30-3(2.30 in winter), 6-11 ~ Bedrooms: £40

LUDGVAN SW5033 Map 1

White Hart

Churchtown; off A30 Penzance—Hayle at Crowlas – OS Sheet 203 map reference 505330

Carefully furnished and with a timeless and relaxed atmosphere, this friendly 14th-c village local is a marvellously unspoilt place with no noisy machines or piped music. The small and snug beamed rooms have soft oil-lamp-style lighting, masses of mugs and jugs glinting in cottagey corners, bric-a-brac, pictures and photographs (including some good ones of Exmoor), stripped boards with attractive rugs on them, and a fascinating mix of interesting old seats and tables; the two capacious woodburning stoves run radiators too. Good simple low-priced bar food includes sandwiches (from £1.10), home-made soup or village-made pasties (£1.50), ploughman's (£2.50; good stilton), sausage and egg (£3), salads (from £3.50), omelettes (£3.75), home-made vegetable or meaty lasagne (£4), steaks (from £7.75), puddings (£1.50), and daily specials such as delicious fresh mackerel (£3), toad in the hole (£3.75), or rabbit casserole (£4.50). Well kept Devenish Cornish Original, Flowers IPA, and Marston Pedigree tapped from the cask; part of the eating area is reserved for non-smokers. *(Recommended by R and S Bentley, Dr R J Rathbone, Peter Neate, Anthony Barnes, Andy and Jill Kassube)*

Devenish (Greenalls) ~ Tenant Dennis Churchill ~ Real ale ~ Meals and snacks (not Mon evening end Oct-May) ~ (01736) 740574 ~ Children in restaurant ~ Open 11-2.30, 6-11

METHERELL SX4069 Map 1

Carpenters Arms

Village signposted from Honicombe, which is signposted from St Ann's Chapel, just W of Gunnislake on A390; pub signposted in village, OS Sheet 201, map reference 408694

Cheerfully presented and popular, the wide choice of home-made bar food in this old-fashioned little place includes sandwiches (from £1.70), home-made soup (£1.90), excellent omelettes (from £3.50), vegetable curry (£4.50), steak and kidney pie (£5.50), good chicken kiev (£6.90), puddings like home-made blackcurrant cake (£1.95), traditional Sunday lunch (£4.75), and children's dishes (£1.70). Well kept Bass, Ruddles County, St Austell HSD and a guest beer on handpump, as well as good farm ciders and decent house white wine. Heavy black beams hang from the ceiling, supported by massive stone walls, and there are huge polished flagstones, and tiny windows. Plants and brasses decorate the walls, and the various alcoves are furnished with winged high-backed red leatherette settles; one end of the pub is reserved for non-smokers. Piped music, sensibly placed darts, and fruit machine; landlord of distinctive character. Outside, by an old well, there are some sheltered tables. Cotehele, the lovely National Trust Tudor house by the head of the Tamar estuary, is a couple of miles further on through these narrow lanes. *(Recommended by A N Ellis, S Brackenbury, J M Hill, Ted George, John Kirk, Roy and Margaret Randle, Phil and Anne Smithson, Michael Pritchard)*

Free house ~ Licensees Douglas and Jill Brace ~ Real ale ~ Meals and snacks (12-1.45, 6.30(7 winter)-9.30) ~ Liskeard (01579) 50242 ~ Children welcome ~ Open 11.30-2.30, 6.30-11 (winter 12-2.30, 7-11); closed lunchtime 25 Dec

MITHIAN SW7450 Map 1

Miners Arms ★

A new back terrace has been built here this year where there are seats – with more on the sheltered front cobbled forecourt. Inside this 16th-c pub are several cosy little rooms and passages warmed by winter open fires. The atmospheric little back bar has an irregular beam and plank ceiling, wood block floor and bulging squint walls (one with a fine old wall painting of Elizabeth I), and another small room has a decorative low ceiling, lots of books and quite a few interesting ornaments; the new oak bar has stained glass panels. Popular bar food includes sandwiches, soup (£1.80), good ploughman's (from £3.40), crab bake with walnut bread (£3.50), lasagne (£4.80), beef curry or steak and kidney pie (£5.20), and daily specials; puddings like bread and butter pudding or toffee apple fudge cake (£2.10) and children's dishes (£2); the plump spaniel might be walking around with his 'please don't feed me' notice around his neck. Well kept Boddingtons and Marstons Pedigree on handpump kept under light blanket pressure; friendly service. Darts, dominoes, shove-ha'penny and piped music. *(Recommended by Tim and Chris Ford, Mr and Mrs K C Wood, Peter Cornall, Margaret Mason, David Thompson, S Brackenbury, Mark and Nicola Willoughby, A L Winkley, Mr and Mrs W J A Timpson, Jack and Philip Paxton, S R and A J Ashcroft, R L Turnham, Les King)*

Greenalls ~ Tenant David Charnock ~ Real ale ~ Meals and snacks (served throughout opening hours) ~ Restaurant ~ St Agnes (01872) 552375 ~ Children welcome ~ Open 12-2.30(3 Sat), 6.30-11; winter evening opening 7

MORWENSTOW SS2015 Map 1

Bush £ ◧

Village signposted off A39 N of Kilkhampton

With few concessions to modern ideas, this unchanging little pub is one of the oldest pubs in Britain – part of it dates back over 1000 years and a Celtic piscina carved from serpentine stone is still set in one wall. There are ancient built-in settles, flagstones, and a big stone fireplace, and a cosy side area with antique seats, a lovely old elm trestle table, and a wooden propeller from a 1930 De

Havilland Gipsy Moth. An upper bar, opened at busy times, is decorated with antique knife-grinding wheels, miners' lamps, casks, funnels, and so forth. Well kept St Austell HSD and Winter Brew (December and January only) both on handpump, and guest beers such as Cotleigh Old Buzzard, Wadworths 6X and Farmers Glory tapped from the cask behind the wood-topped stone bar counter (with pewter tankards lining the beams above it); quite a few malt whiskies and Inches cider. Simple lunchtime bar food includes sandwiches, good, proper home-made soup (£1.50), good locally-made pasties (£1.60), ploughman's with a bowl of home-made pickle (£2), delicious home-made stew (£3), crab and coleslaw (£3.50), various daily specials, and puddings like spotted dick or apple pie. No chips. Darts, dominoes and two friendly cats. Seats outside shelter in the slightly sunken yard. Opposite is an interesting church, with a wrecked ship's figurehead as a gravestone for its crew, and Vicarage Cliff, one of the grandest parts of the Cornish coast (with 400-ft precipices) is a ten-minute walk away. The landlord is firmly against piped music, and children and dogs are not allowed. *(Recommended by Patricia Nutt, A N Ellis, Jack and Philip Paxton, Rita Horridge, LM, Ian and Nita Cooper, P C Russell, S Demont, T Barrow, David Holloway, Basil Minson, S H Godsell, Joan and Gordon Edwards, Werner Arend)*

Free house ~ Licensee J H Gregory ~ Real ale ~ Lunchtime snacks (not Sun) ~ Morwenstow (01288) 331242 ~ Open 12-3, 7-11; closed Mon Oct-Apr, except bank hols

MOUSEHOLE   SW4726 Map 1

Ship

In a lovely village right by the harbour, this very relaxed place is a traditional fisherman's local. The opened-up main bar has genuine character, black beams and panelling, built-in wooden wall benches and stools around the low tables, sailors' fancy ropework, granite flagstones, and a cosy open fire. Bar food (with prices unchanged since last year) features fresh fish specials every day as well as sandwiches (fresh local crab £3.50), home-made lasagne or prawn curry (£4.40), smoked fish or chicken (from £4.95), crab salad (£7), steaks (from £7), seafood platter (£8.50). On 23 December they bake Starry Gazy pie to celebrate Tom Bawcock's Eve, a tradition that recalls Tom's brave expedition out to sea in a fierce storm 200 years ago. He caught seven types of fish, which were then cooked in a pie with their heads and tails sticking out. Well kept Bosuns, Tinners and HSD on handpump, and several malt whiskies; friendly staff; darts, dominoes, cribbage, and fruit machine. The village does get packed in summer and over the Christmas period (when people come to visit the elaborate harbour lights). *(Recommended by Lynn Sharpless, Bob Eardley, DAV, Dr and Mrs A K Clarke, John and Vivienne Rice, Mark Walker, Richard Dolphin, Gwen and Peter Andrews, Mr and Mrs John Gilks, Roy and Bettie Derbyshire, Pete and Rosie Flower, Mark Walker)*

St Austell ~ Tenants Michael and Tracey Maddern ~ Real Ale ~ Meals and snacks (12-2.30, 6-9.30) ~ Restaurant ~ Penzance (01736) 731234 ~ Children welcome if kept away from bar ~ Summer parking can be difficult ~ Open 10.30am-11pm ~ Bedrooms: £40B

nr MYLOR BRIDGE   SW8036 Map 1

Pandora ★ ★ ♀

Restronguet Passage: from A39 in Penryn, take turning signposted Mylor Church, Mylor Bridge, Flushing and go straight through Mylor Bridge following Restronguet Passage signs; or from A39 further N, at or near Perranarworthal, take turning signposted Mylor, Restronguet, then follow Restronguet Weir signs, but turn left down hill at Restronguet Passage sign

After a lovely waterside walk, what could be nicer than to sit outside this pretty medieval thatched pub at the picnic-table sets in front or on the long floating jetty and enjoy a leisurely drink. Quite a few people arrive by boat and there are showers for visiting yachtsmen. Inside is splendidly atmospheric, and the several rambling, interconnecting rooms have beautifully polished big flagstones, low wooden ceilings (mind your head on some of the beams), cosy alcoves with leatherette benches built into the walls, a kitchen range, and a log fire in a high hearth (to protect it against tidal floods); two no smoking areas. Bar food includes home-made soup (from £1.80), sandwiches (from £2.50), burger (£3.95), wholemeal pancakes (£4.50), fish pie (£4.75), crab thermidor (£7.75), daily specials, puddings like home-made treacle tart (£2), and children's dishes (from £1.50). Bass, St Austell Tinners, HSD and Tinners' and Bosun's on handpump from a temperature controlled cellar, several malt whiskies, and forty-two wines and bin ends – with 18 by the glass; dominoes and winter pool. It does get very crowded in summer, and parking is difficult at peak times. *(Recommended by Gwen and Peter Andrews, P M Lane, Susan and Nigel Wilson, Lynn Sharpless, Bob Eardley, Jim and Maggie Cowell, Nigel Flook, Betsy Brown, Don Kellaway, Angie Coles, Penny and Martin Fletcher, Mr and Mrs B Hobden, S R and A J Ashcroft, Andy and Jill Kassube, Jack and Philip Paxton, Mr and Mrs W J A Timpson, Dr and Mrs Jack Davies, S Demont, T Barrow, C A Foden, G Atkinson, Peter and Rose Flower, K Harvey, Stephen Oxley, Anna Cwajna)*

St Austell ~ Tenants Roger and Helen Hough ~ Real ale ~ Meals and snacks (till 10pm in summer) ~ Evening restaurant; closed winter evenings and winter Sun ~ Falmouth (01326) 372678 ~ Children in eating area of bar ~ Open 11-11; 12-2.30(3 winter Sun), 7-11 in winter

PELYNT SX2055 Map 1

Jubilee 🛏

B3359 NW of Looe

An inner area of the relaxed lounge bar in this smart and comfortable old place is decorated with mementoes of Queen Victoria, such as a tapestry portrait, old prints, and Staffordshire figurines of the Queen and her consort; there's also an early 18th-c Derbyshire oak armchair, brown leather and red fabric cushioned wall and window seats, Windsor armchairs, magazines stacked under the oak tables, and a good winter log fire in the stone fireplace under the neatly squared oak beams; gleaming brass and fresh flowers. The flagstoned entry is separated from this room by an attractively old-fangled glass-paned partition. Good, popular food, quickly served by cheery waitresses, includes home-made soup (£2), a good choice of sandwiches (from £1.60; local crab £3.50), ploughman's (from £2.80), good barbecued spare ribs (£4.50), salads (from £4.80), tasty smoked haddock with poached eggs or mixed grill (£4.90), local seafood mornay (£5.40), fresh cod (£5.60), gammon and egg (£6.50), sirloin steak (£9.80), and puddings (from £1.80). Well kept Furguson Dartmoor Strong and Tetleys on handpump, several malt whiskies, and quite a few wines. The quite separate public bar has sensibly placed darts, pool, cribbage, dominoes, fruit machine, juke box and piped music. A crazy-paved central courtyard has picnic-table sets with red and white striped umbrellas, pretty tubs of flowers, and barbecues (weather permitting), and there's a well equipped children's play area. *(Recommended by James Morrell, K and R Beaver, John and Tessa Rainsford, David Burnett, Donna Lowes, Jack and Philip Paxton, Buffy and Mike Adamson)*

Free House ~ Licensee Frank Williams ~ Real ale ~ Meals and snacks ~ Restaurant (not Sun evening) ~ (01503) 220312 ~ Children welcome ~ Open 11-3, 6-11 ~ Bedrooms: £35B/£60B

PENDOGGETT SX0279 Map 1

Cornish Arms

B3314

Tables on the terrace outside this 16th-c pub give a pleasant view down the valley to the beach. The two attractive panelled rooms of the front bar (one of which is no smoking at lunchtime) have high-backed built-in oak settles surrounding solid old wooden tables on the Delabole slate floor, and the big, lively locals' bar has high-backed settles around stripped deal tables, a sturdy woodburning stove, and darts, dominoes, fruit and trivia machines, and piped music; the coffee room/children's area is also no smoking. Bar food includes sandwiches (from £1.70), ploughman's (£2.95), locally-made pasty (£3.75), salads (from £4.95), beef in ale casserole (£6.25), locally caught lemon sole (£9.50), and puddings like treacle tart and fruit crumble (£2.85); popular Sunday lunch. Well kept Bass, Flowers IPA and a beer named for the pub on handpump, and a decent range of cognac, armagnac and malt whiskies. *(Recommended by Helen Taylor, Jack and Philip Paxton, S Brackenbury, Andrew Low, Graham Tayar, D L Barker, Dave Thompson, Margaret Mason)*

Free house ~ Licensees Mervyn Gilmour, Tim Tolhurst ~ Real ale ~ Meals and snacks (12-2, 6-9.30) ~ Restaurant ~ Bodmin (01208) 880263 ~ Children in eating areas away from main bar ~ Live entertainment in summer ~ Open 11-11 ~ Bedrooms: £49B/£78B

PENELEWEY   SW8240 Map 1

Punch Bowl & Ladle

Feock Downs, B3289

Near the King Harry ferry and Trelissick Gardens, this quaint and thatched pub has been extended inside to create several comfortably furnished, attractive rooms – though the cosy ones in the original part have lots of shipwreck paintings and farm implements around the walls, and an open fire. Well kept Bass, Boddingtons, Flowers Original and Whitbreads Best on handpump, fine bloody marys, and bar food such as sandwiches, soup (£2.50), crab bake (£3.50), chicken teriyaki (£5.25), vegetarian dishes, steaks (from £7.75), and home-made daily specials; friendly, helpful staff. Darts, shove-ha'penny, cribbage, dominoes, fruit machine and piped music. *(Recommended by Jim and Maggie Cowell, John Wooll, R and S Bentley, E M Hughes, Alec and Marie Lewery)*

Greenalls ~ Manager Richard Rudland ~ Real ale ~ Meals and snacks (11.30-2.30, 6.30-10) ~ Restaurant ~ (01872) 862237 ~ Children in eating area of bar and in restaurant ~ Open 11-3, 5.30-11

PENZANCE   SW4730 Map 1

Turks Head

At top of main street, by big domed building (Lloyds Bank), turn left down Chapel Street

There has been a Turks Head here for over 700 years – though most of the original building was destroyed by a Spanish raiding party in the 16th-c. The relaxed and chatty main bar is interestingly decorated with old flat irons, jugs and so forth hanging from the beams, pottery above the wood-effect panelling, wall seats and tables, and a couple of elbow rests around central pillars. The menu has quite an emphasis on seafood, with crab soup (£1.60), crab salad (mixed meat £6.70, white meat £7.25), cold seafood platter (£8.95), and daily specials such as home-made fish pie (£5.25), home-made salmon, cod and mushroom bake (£5.95), mussels in wine, tomato and garlic, and crevettes; also, soup (£1.40), sandwiches (from £1.40), filled baked potatoes (from £1.90), ploughman's (from £3.20), ratatouille topped with cheese (£2.95), meaty or vegetarian lasagne (£4.35), popular steak and kidney pie (£4.60), gammon and egg or 8oz rump steak (£6.50), and puddings. Boddingtons, Flowers Original and Marstons Pedigree on handpump, and friendly helpful service; fruit machine, piped music. The suntrap back garden has big urns of flowers. *(Recommended by Mark Walker, RB, David Yandle, Neil and Anita Christopher, David Dimock, S Brackenbury, Gill Earle, Andrew Burton, Peter and Rose Flower, Alec and Marie Lewery, Bill and Edee Miller)*

Greenalls ~ Tenant William Morris ~ Real ale ~ Meals and snacks (11-2.30, 6-10) ~ Restaurant ~ Penzance (01736) 63093 ~ Children in cellar dining room ~ Open 11-3, 5.30-11

There are report forms at the back of the book.

PHILLEIGH SW8639 Map 1

Roseland ★

Very much a focus for the local community, this little 17th-c pub is headquarters to the Roseland Rugby club in winter and to a syndicate which has just purchased a traditional gaff-rigged oyster dredger, built in 1898; she will be raced locally during the summer. There are new inside lavatories this year, a new cellar and the kitchen has been extended – plans for a children's play area are to follow. They still firmly stick to the relaxed and old-fashioned atmosphere by banning video games, juke boxes and piped music. The low beamed bar has a nice oak settle and antique seats around the sturdy tables on the flagstones, an old wall clock, a good winter fire, and lots of rugby and rowing prints – the landlord's sports. Popular home-made bar food includes pasties (£1.75), home-made soup (£1.95), sandwiches (from £2.50), ploughman's (from £3.75), filled oven-baked potatoes (from £2.25), ratatouille au gratin (£4.25), vegetarian stuffed pepper (£4.50), steak and mushroom pie (£4.75), fresh cracked crab claws (£5.95), with evening dishes such as gammon with mustard (£7.25), whole fresh local lemon sole (£8.75), sirloin steak with rich cream and whisky sauce (£8.95), and seafood platter (24 hours' notice, £25 for two people); children's dishes (£2.50). Well kept Devenish Cornish Original, Flowers Original, and Marstons Pedigree on handpump, farm cider from the barrel (summer only), and an increasing range of malt whiskies; dominoes, cribbage, shove-ha'penny. The pretty paved front courtyard is a lovely place to sit in the lunchtime sunshine beneath the cherry blossom; the birds are unusually tame. The furniture here too is interesting – one table made from a converted well. When you leave it's best to check your car in case the pub cat is on (or even in) it. The quiet lane leads on to the little half-hourly King Harry car ferry across a pretty wooded channel, with Trelissick Gardens on the far side. *(Recommended by Lynn Sharpless, Bob Eardley, Peter and Audrey Dowsett, R and S Bentley, S R Chapman, Liz Wakley, Glen Weston, BHP, Brian Whittaker)*

Greenalls ~ Tenant Graham Hill ~ Real ale ~ Meals and snacks ~ Portscatho (01872) 580254 ~ Children welcome ~ Open 11-3, 6-11; winter openings half-an-hour later

PILLATON SX3664 Map 1

Weary Friar 🛏

Best reached from the good Callington—Landrake back road; OS Sheet 201 map reference 365643

With pleasant views over the gentle hills and the church spire behind it, this 12th-c pub is a pretty sight. The four characterful and tidy knocked-together rooms (one is no smoking) have beam-and-plank ceilings, comfortable seats around sturdy wooden tables, easy chairs by a little coal fire at one end, and a much grander old stone fireplace at the other. Good, popular bar food includes lunchtime sandwiches (£2.50) or ploughman's (from £3.25), as well as soup (£2.50), basket meals or salads (from £4), vegetable or steak in ale pies (£5.50), chicken Maryland (£7.50), steaks (from £8.50), and puddings (from £2.50). Well kept Bass, Ushers Founders, and Wadworths 6X on handpump, and country wines; piped music. There are old-fashioned slatted teak seats outside, in the angle of the L-shaped black-shuttered building and over the quiet lane. *(Recommended by P J Caunt, Bronwen and Steve Wrigley, Ian and Deborah Carrington, Vernon Crockett, Linda and Brian Davis, R L Turnham, M and R Hepburn, J and J O Jones, Mayur Shah, Mr and Mrs V Edmunds)*

Free house ~ Licensees Mr and Mrs R Sharman ~ Real ale ~ Meals and snacks (till 10pm) ~ Restaurant (closed Mon) ~ (01579) 50238 ~ Children in eating area of bar ~ Open 11.30-3, 6.30-11; closed 25 Dec to non-residents ~ Bedrooms: £30B/£15

It is illegal for bar staff to smoke while handling your drink.

POLKERRIS   SX0952 Map 1

Rashleigh

Even in winter you can still enjoy the fine views towards the far side of St Austell and Mevagissey bays from the stone terrace here, and the isolated beach – without the crowds. Inside, the front part of the bar has comfortably cushioned seats, with local photographs on the brown panelling of a more simply furnished back area; friendly staff and locals, and winter log fire. Good food includes soup (£1.95), sandwiches (from £1.65; open ones from £4.25), ploughman's (from £3.80), pasta and mushroom bake (£4.50), fish, steak or rabbit and bacon pies (£5.50), popular lunchtime cold buffet (from £5.50), local sea trout or steaks (£9.50), and puddings (£1.95). Furgusons Best and Dartmoor, St Austell HSD, and occasional guest beers on handpump, decent wine list and fine choice of whiskies and brandies; shove-ha'penny, dominoes, cribbage, trivia and piped classical music. Though parking space next to the pub is limited, there's a large village car park, and there are safe moorings for small yachts in the cove. This whole section of the Cornish coast path is renowned for its striking scenery. *(Recommended by John and Tessa Rainsford, A N Ellis, Mr and Mrs C R Little, Peter and Lynn Brueton, Jack and Philip Paxton, S Brackenbury, Dave Braisted, R L Turnham, P and K Lloyd, D P Pascoe, Denis and Margaret Kilner)*

Free house ~ Licensees Bernard and Carole Smith ~ Real ale ~ Meals and snacks (till 10pm in summer) ~ Restaurant ~ (01726) 813991 ~ Well behaved children in eating area of bar ~ Classical pianist Fri and Sat evenings ~ Open 11-3(4.30 Sat), 6(5.30 Sat)-11; 11.30-3, 6.30-11 in winter

POLRUAN   SX1251 Map 1

Lugger

Reached from A390 in Lostwithiel; nearby parking expensive and limited, or steep walk down from village-edge car park; passenger/bicycle ferry from Fowey

There are fine views of the little harbour and across to Fowey from this friendly local – and if you arrive by boat, there are steep stone steps leading up to the pub. The left-hand bar is a small, traditional lino-floored locals' bar, while the main bar on the right is more geared to visitors. There's a fairly nautical theme in this beam-and-board ceilinged room, with big model boats, local boat photographs, and a fish tank; also, colourful window-boxes, high-backed wall settles, and plush-cushioned wheelback chairs on the turkey carpet. Half the family room is no smoking. Good bar food includes sandwiches, ploughman's, vegetarian dishes and steaks, with summer specials like fresh local whole plaice (from £5.25) or home-made seafood pie (£5), and fresh local shark steaks (£6.25). St Austell BB, Tinners, HSD and XXXX on handpump; darts, pool (winter only), cribbage, dominoes, trivia and piped music. Good surrounding walks. *(Recommended by P and J Shapley, David Rule, Peter and Audrey Dowsett, Gerry Hollington, Bronwen and Steve Wrigley, Martyn and Mary Mullins, Roy and Margaret Randle, Peter Neate, Norman Constable, Bjanka Kadic, Charles Turner)*

St Austell ~ Manager Terry Jones ~ Real ale ~ Meals and snacks (all day in summer; 12.30-2, 7-8.30 in winter – though best to check)~ Children in family room ~ (01726) 870007 ~ Local singer/comedian or middle of road singing duo Fri evenings ~ Open 11-11; 11-3, 6.30-11 in winter

PORT ISAAC   SW9980 Map 1

Golden Lion

Fore Street

You can sit at the windows of the handsome, cosy rooms in this bustling, friendly pub and look down on the rocky harbour and lifeboat slip far below. There's a fine antique settle among other comfortable seats, decorative ceiling plasterwork, perhaps the pub dog Hollie, and a relaxed, friendly atmosphere – despite the summer crowds. Good home-made food includes double decker crab sandwich

(£3.75), ploughman's (from £3.75), steak, sausage or bacon crusties (from £3.95), fish pie (£4.95), tasty seafood lasagne (£5.25), lovely crab thermidor or mixed grill (£8.50), and fresh seafood platter (£12.75); during the summer, evening meals are served in the bistro. Well kept St Austell Tinners and HSD on handpump and 23 malts. Darts, shove-ha'penny, dominoes, cribbage, a fruit machine in the public bar, and piped music. The very steep narrow lanes of this working fishing village are most attractive. *(Recommended by Lynn Sharpless, Bob Eardley, Margaret Mason, David Thompson, David and Julie Glover, Graham Tavar, Keith and Janet Morris, M Veldhuyzen, Rita Horridge, Martyn and Mary Mullins)*

St Austell ~ Tenants Mike and Nikki Edkins ~ Real ale ~ Meals and snacks ~ Bistro restaurant ~ (01208) 880336 ~ Children in eating area of bar and in bistro ~ No parking nearby ~ Folk music Weds evenings ~ Open 11-11; closed evening 25 Dec

nr PORT ISAAC SX0080 Map 1

Port Gaverne Hotel ★ ⇔ ♀

Port Gaverne signposted from Port Isaac, and from B3314 E of Pendoggett

This is a lovely, peaceful place to stay with marvellous clifftop walks all round and a fine view from the raised terrace outside (you can't actually see the sea from the bar). Inside, the well kept bars have low beams, flagstones as well as carpeting, big log fires, some exposed stone, a collection of antique cruets, and an enormous marine chronometer. In spring the lounge is filled with pictures from the local art society's annual exhibition in aid of the Royal National Lifeboat Institution (they also take part in the annual costumed four-legged race in aid of the same organization); at other times there are interesting antique local photographs. Simple but popular bar food includes sandwiches (from £1.50, excellent crab £3.50), home-made soup (£2.25, crab £2.75), ploughman's (from £2.75), vegetarian spicy bean casserole (£2.75), home-made cottage pie (£2.95), salads (from £3.75, half a lobster £8.50), and deep-fried local plaice (£4.50). There may be nibbles on the bar counter. During the season lunchtime food is served buffet-style in the dining room, as it is on Sunday throughout the year (when food stops at 2 sharp). The rest of the time it's served in the bar or 'Captain's Cabin' – a little room where everything except its antique admiral's hat is shrunk to scale (old oak chest, model sailing ship, even the prints on the white stone walls). Well kept Bass, Flowers IPA and St Austell HSD on handpump, a good bin-end wine list with 60 wines, a very good choice of whiskies and other spirits such as ouzo and akvavit, and around 38 liqueurs; tea and coffee; quick, efficient service. Dominoes, cribbage and piped music, with darts, pool and a fruit machine in the renovated Green Door Club across the lane, which also has a big diorama of Port Isaac. *(Recommended by S Demont, T Barrow, R L Turnham, Rita Horridge, Brian and Jill Bond, J L Hall, Margaret Dyke, A E and P McCully, Norma and Keith Bloomfield, Nigel Flook, Betsy Brown, Pippa Bobbett, Vernon Crockett, Peter and Lynn Brueton, E Money, Mr and Mrs J V Wild, David and Ann Stranack, Mrs Brenda Morgan)*

Free house ~ Licensee Mrs M Ross ~ Real ale ~ Meals and snacks (till 10pm) ~ No smoking restaurant ~ Bodmin (01208) 880244 ~ Children in restaurant (must be over 7) and in Captain's Cabin in evening (served at 7pm; no children after 9pm) ~ Open 11-3(2.30 in winter), 6-11; closed 7 Jan to 18 Feb ~ Bedrooms: £47B/£94B; restored 18th-c self-contained cottages

PORTHALLOW SW7923 Map 1

Five Pilchards

SE of Helston; B3293 to St Keverne, then village signposted

Right on the beach with boats anchoring in the small bay, this robustly stone-built old place has been in the same family for the last 29 years. Inside, it's small and cosy with an abundance of salvaged nautical gear, lamps made from puffer fish, and interesting photographs and clippings about local shipwrecks (even one boat is said to have been washed up on the beach as the helmsman had been drinking here). Well kept Devenish Cornish Original, Greene King Abbot, John Smiths, and Whitbreads Pompey Royal on handpump; also country wines, wines by the bottle to take away (and they'll fill beer flagons for sailors and others to take on board). Lunchtime food includes home-made soup (£1.50), ploughman's (from £3), crab sandwiches (£3.50), daily specials (from £2.25), and prawn platter (£6.95); darts in winter, dominoes and a fruit machine. The attractive cove is largely protected against unsightly development by being owned by its residents. Tides and winds allowing, you can park on the foreshore. No children under 18. *(Recommended by Gwen and Peter Andrews, John and Sally Clarke, Andy and Jill Kassube, Stephen C Harvey, Eric and Shirley Broadhead; more reports please)*

Free house ~ Licensee David Tripp ~ Real ale ~ Lunchtime snacks ~ (01326) 280256 ~ Open 12-2.30(3 Sat), 6(7.30 in winter)-11; closed Mon from Jan-Whitsun ~ Self-contained flat sleeps 6

PORTHLEVEN SW6225 Map 1

Ship ★

To get to this old fisherman's pub you have to climb a flight of rough stone steps – it's actually built onto the steep cliffs. There are marvellous views over the pretty working harbour and out to sea, both from the window seats in the friendly bar and from the candlelit dining room. The knocked-through bar has log fires in big stone fireplaces and some genuine character, and well kept Courage Best and Directors and Ushers Best and Founders on handpump; dominoes, cribbage, fruit machine and piped music. Nicely presented, popular bar food (with prices unchanged since last year) includes sandwiches (from £1.55; fine toasties from £2.25; excellent crusty loaf from £1.95), filled oven-baked potatoes (from £2.30), ploughman's (from £3.95), vegetable curry or steak and kidney pudding (£4.95), seafood lasagne (£5.25), sweet and sour chicken (£6.95), mussels in garlic butter (£7.50), interesting daily specials like chicken casserole in orange and Cointreau, and sirloin steak (£8.50); puddings like home-made apple torte (from £1.95), evening extras such as an excellent big bowl of mushrooms in garlic (£3.95), and children's meals (£1.95). Terraced garden. The harbour is interestingly floodlit at night. *(Recommended by DAV, John and Sally Clarke, Peter and Lynn Brueton, Sue Holland, Dave Webster, Mark Walker, Mr and Mrs C R Little, Martin and Penny Fletcher, Andy and Jill Kassube, David and Michelle Hedges, E A George, K Harvey, Roy and Bettie Derbyshire, Martin Cooke, S Howe)*

Ushers ~ Tenant Colin Oakden ~ Real ale ~ Meals and snacks ~ (01326) 572841 ~ Children in family room ~ Parking can be difficult in summer ~ Open 11.30-3, 6.30-11; 11.30-2.30, 7-11 in winter

SCORRIER SW7244 Map 1

Fox & Hounds

Village singposted from A30; B3298 Falmouth road

By the time this book is published, the brewery will have made some changes to this pleasant long white cottage. A restaurant is to be added, new kitchens built, and the lavatories upgraded. The long bar, which is divided into sections by a partition wall and low screens, will remain largely unchanged, with its creaky joists, vertical panelling, stripped stonework, hunting prints, comfortable furnishings and big log fires, as well as a stuffed fox and fox mask; there's also more seating in a no-smoking front extension, formerly a verandah. Popular bar food served by uniformed waitresses includes home-made soup (£1.95), doorstep or open sandwiches (from £2.80), filled baked potatoes (from £2.85), ploughman's (from £3.15), ratatouille au gratin (£3.40), omelettes (from £3.95), Lebanese kofta or chicken tikka masala (£4.40), moussaka (£4.45), cold prawns in curried mayonnaise (£4.95), spicy sausage and pasta bake (£5.25), sirloin steak (£8.25), daily specials such as giant steak and kidney pie (£4.85), deep-fried giant mussels in light crispy batter with a choice of dip (£4.95) or cod and prawn sunrise (£5.95), and lots of puddings. Well kept Boddingtons, Flowers IPA and Wadworths 6X on handpump; piped nostalgic music. The long, low white building – well set back from the road – is prettily decorated outside with hanging baskets and window boxes, and has picnic-table sets under cocktail parasols in front. No children. *(Recommended by S Brackenbury, Ian Phillips, E M Hughes; more reports please)*

Greenalls ~ Tenants David and Linda Halfpenny ~ Real ale ~ Meals and snacks (till 10pm; and see below) ~ (01209) 820205 ~ Open 11.30-2.30, 6.30-11; closed Mon evenings Jan-Mar, 25/26 Dec

ST AGNES SW7250 Map 1

Railway

10 Vicarage Rd; from centre follow B3277 signs for Porthtowan and Truro

Almost like a museum, this lively and friendly little terraced pub has some splendid brasswork that includes one of the finest original horsebrass collections in the country, and a remarkable collection of shoes – minute or giant, made of strange skins, fur, leather, wood, mother-of-pearl, or embroidered with gold and silver, from Turkey, Persia, China or Japan and worn by ordinary people or famous men. As if this wasn't enough to look at, there's also a notable collection of naval memorabilia from model sailing ships and rope fancywork to the texts of Admiralty messages at important historical moments, such as the announcement of the ceasefire at the end of the First World War. Bar food includes home-made soup (£1.80), sandwiches (from £1.80), ploughman's or filled baked potatoes (£3.50), home-made daily specials (£4.25),fresh plaice or lemon sole (£4.65), and puddings. Well kept Boddingtons Best, Flowers IPA, and Marstons Pedigree on handpump; darts, pool, cribbage, pinball, dominoes, fruit machine and juke box. *(Recommended by S R and A J Ashcroft, R and S Bentley, Andy and Jill Kassube, Paul Cartledge, Jack and Philip Paxton)*

Greenalls ~ Tenant Christopher O'Brien ~ Real ale ~ Meals and snacks (12-2.30, 6-10) ~ (01872) 552310 ~ Children in eating area of bar ~ Open 11-3, 6-11; 11-11 Sat

ST AGNES (Isles of Scilly) SV8807 Map 1

Turks Head

The Quay

It's an easy boat trip to reach this marvellously peaceful little slate-roofed white cottage from St Marys. It's Britain's most south-westerly pub and sits just above the sweeping bay, with gorgeous sea views. Across the sleepy lane are a few tables on a patch of lawn above the water, with steps down beside them to the slipway – you can walk down with your drinks and food and sit right on the shore. The simply furnished but cosy and very friendly pine-panelled bar is attractively decorated with maritime photographs and model ships, and the extension is no smoking. First-class bar food includes legendary huge locally made pasties (though they do sell out; £2.65), soup (£1.50), open rolls (from £1.65; crab £3.15), ploughman's (from £3), ham or beef and chips or cajun vegetable casserole (£4.75), with evening gammon in port wine sauce (£5.25), fresh fish of the day, and sirloin steak (£7.35); children's meals (from £1.75). Ice cream and cakes are sold through the afternoon, and in good weather they do good evening barbecues (£3-7 Tuesday, Thursday and Sunday, July/August only), arranging special boats from St Marys – as most tripper boats leave by 5-ish. Remarkably, they also have real ale which arrives in St Agnes via a beer supplier in Truro and two boat trips: Furgusons Dartmoor and Ind Coope Burton, in good condition on handpump, besides decent house wines, a good range of malt whiskies, and hot chocolate with brandy. Unobtrusive piped music, with a piano for impromptu evening sessions; darts, dominoes, cribbage, and trivia out of season. In spring and autumn hours may be shorter, and winter opening is sporadic, given that only some 70 people live on the island; they do then try to open if people ask, and otherwise tend to open on Saturday night, Sunday lunchtime (bookings only, roast lunch), over Christmas and the New Year, and for a Wednesday quiz night. *(Recommended by P and M Rudlin, Peter and Rose Flower, H A P Russell, David Mead, Mark Walker, Ken Moreman; more reports please)*

Free house ~ Licensees John and Pauline Dart ~ Real ale ~ Meals and snacks ~ Scillonia (01720) 422434 ~ Well behaved children welcome ~ Open 11-11 summer (see text for winter) ~ Bedrooms: £38B

ST BREWARD SX0977 Map 1

Old Inn

Old Town; village signposted off B3266 S of Camelford, also signed off A30 Bolventor—Bodmin

It's the warmly friendly welcome that readers like so much about this small old country pub. The two roomed bar has fine broad slate flagstones, banknotes and horsebrasses hanging from the low oak joists that support the ochre upstairs floorboards, and plates on the stripped stonework. The inner room has a good log fire, cushioned wall benches and chairs around its tables, naif paintings on slate by a local artist (for sale cheaply), and a glass panel showing a separate games room with pool table, juke box and fruit machine, where children are allowed; cribbage, dominoes. The outer room has fewer tables (old ones, of character), an open log fire in big granite fireplace, a piano and sensibly placed darts. Popular home-made bar food includes good soup, sandwiches (from £1.50), ploughman's (£2.75), fresh plaice (£4.75), a pie of the day (£4.50), vegetarian dishes (from £4.50), two sizes of huge mixed grill (from £6.75), and puddings like sticky toffee pudding or banoffi pie (£1.95); big helpings. Well kept Bass, John Smiths Best, Ruddles County, and a guest such as Exmoor Stag on handpump; the landlord is from the West Highlands and his range of thirty-eight malt whiskies reflects this – only coming from the Highlands and Islands; cheap but decent coffee. Picnic-table sets outside are protected by low stone walls. There's plenty of open moorland behind, and cattle and sheep wander freely into the village. In front of the building is a very worn carved stone; no-one knows exactly what it is but it may be part of a Saxon cross. *(Recommended by Jennifer Tora, David Burnett, Donna Lowes, Dave Thompson, Margaret Mason, Ted George, John Woodward, Edward and Grace Wauton, Jane and Charlie Ritchie, Iain and Penny Muir)*

Free house ~ Licensees Ann and Iain Cameron ~ Real ale ~ Meals and snacks (not 25 Dec) ~ Restaurant ~ Occasional live groups ~ Bodmin (01208) 850711 ~ Children in eating areas, children's room and one of bars ~ Open 12-3, 6-11; winter closing may be 2.30

ST EWE SW9746 Map 1

Crown

Village signposted from B3287; easy to find from Mevagissey

The same warmly welcoming family has run this unspoilt village cottage for 38 years. The traditional bar has 16th-c flagstones, a very high-backed curved old settle with flowery cushions, long shiny wooden tables, and an ancient weight-driven working spit (though the fire is now log-effect gas); the fireside shelves hold plates, and a brass teapot and jug. The eating area has a burgundy coloured carpet, velvet curtains and matching cushions to go on the old church pews. Good, popular food includes good, fresh pasties (95p), sandwiches (from £1.55, local crab in season £3.45, open sandwiches £3.65), tasty soup (£1.65; the french onion is recommended), ploughman's or filled baked potatoes (from £2.95), salads (from £4.50, lovely fresh crab in season £6.95), gammon with egg or pineapple (£7), tasty steaks (from £7.95), grilled lemon sole (£9.45; evenings only), daily specials such as steak and kidney pie or fresh trout, and puddings like home-made fruit or very good mincemeat and brandy pies (from £1.65) and their special Green Mountain ice cream (£3). Well kept St Austell Tinners and HSD on handpump, several malt whiskies and local wine; fruit machine and piped music. Several picnic-table sets on a raised back lawn. *(Recommended by Colin Harnett, J C Simpson, Peter Cornall, Richard Dolphin, Gwen and Peter Andrews, P and J Shapley, BHP, David Watson, P and M Rudlin, Brian Whittaker)*

St Austell ~ Tenant Norman Jeffery ~ Real ale ~ Meals and snacks ~ Restaurant ~ Mevagissey (01726) 843322 ~ Children in eating area of bar ~ Open 11-2.30, 6-11; closed evening 25 Dec ~ Bedrooms: £34

ST JUST IN PENWITH SW3631 Map 1

Star ⌂

Fore Street

There's a very relaxed, friendly atmosphere in this interesting and unchanging old inn – helped by the characterful regulars with their dark faces, long curls, beards, and colourful clothes. The dimly lit L-shaped bar has tankards hanging over the serving counter, some stripped masonry, appropriately old-fashioned furnishings, and a good many mining samples and mementoes; it opens through into a separate snug. Good value bar food includes soup (£1.50), pasties (from £1.50), french bread covered with chilli pickle or garlic mushrooms and melted cheese with herbs (from £1.90), filled baked potatoes, ploughman's (£2.50), vegetable curry (£3.20), and daily specials such as crab sandwich or chicken in wine and cornish cream sauce (£3.20), and steak and mushroom pie (£3.90); no chips. Well kept St Austell Tinners, HSD and XXXX Mild tapped from the cask, with farm cider in summer, mulled wine in winter, old-fashioned drinks like mead, lovage and brandy or shrub with rum, and decent coffee or hot chocolate with rum and cream; shove-ha'penny, cribbage, dominoes, table skittles, euchre, shut-the-box, chess, Scrabble, fruit machine and juke box. Attractive back yard with roses, a gunnera, and tables. The bedrooms are simple but comfortably furnished in period style, with notable breakfasts; the pub's not far from the coast path. *(Recommended by DAV, Andy and Jill Kassube, Margaret Mason, David Thompson, Mick Hitchman, K R Flack, Bill Sharpe)*

St Austell ~ Tenants Rosie and Peter Angwin ~ Real ale ~ Meals and snacks (between 3pm and 6pm pasties and rolls only, otherwise food served all day) ~ (01736) 788767 ~ Children in snug with toy box ~ Celtic folk music on Mon evenings and impromptu entertainment any time ~ Open 11-11 ~ Bedrooms: £15/£25(£35B)

ST KEVERNE SW7921 Map 1

White Hart

The Square; at the end of B3293 SE of Helston – the village is well signposted

If you're after fresh fish treated really well by a sympathetic cook, then this friendly pub is the place to come to. Chalked up on a blackboard, there might be crab cocktail (£4.50), good plump scallops au gratin or mussels (£6), delicious and very generous crab claw salad (£9), king prawns in garlic butter (£7), plaice (£10), bass with ginger and spring onions (£13), and half a lobster (£13.75); also, soup (£2), sandwiches (from £2), filled baked potatoes (from £2.50), ploughman's (£4.50), and lasagne (£5). Well kept Devenish Cornish Original and Flowers IPA and Original on handpump. There are three fireplaces, decorative plates, ship's and carriage lamps, black beams hung with horsebrasses, some comfortable fabric-covered wall seats as well as mate's chairs and some heavy rustic small wooden seats around sturdy tables, and a relaxed, chatty atmosphere; on the left is an area with a pool table, angel fish in an inset aquarium, and a free CD juke box; winter darts, euchre. Outside are some picnic-table sets under umbrellas on a narrow front terrace, with more on a side lawn with an elephant slide and tree swing. Dogs are allowed if on a lead. We have not yet heard from readers who have stayed here, but would expect it to qualify for our Stay Award. *(Recommended by E A George, Dave Braisted, John and Christine Deacon)*

Greenalls ~ Tenant Vicki Blake ~ Real ale ~ Meals and snacks (not winter Sun

*evenings) ~ Restaurant ~ (01326) 280325 ~ Children welcome ~ Open 11-3,
6.30-11 ~ Bedrooms: £40B/£55B*

ST KEW   SX0276 Map 1

St Kew Inn
Village signposted from A39 NE of Wadebridge

As well as a big peaceful garden with plenty of space for children to play (and a
usually friendly goat called Aneka), there are picnic-table sets on the front cobbles,
sheltering between the wings of this rather grand-looking stone building. The
atmosphere is charming and unspoilt (no noisy machines or piped music) and
there's a friendly welcome, as well as very popular food: sandwiches, home-made
soup (£1.50; the crab is good), ploughman's (£3), leeks and bacon in cheese sauce
(£3.50), lasagne (£4.95), highly praised steaks (£8.95), and evening extras like
chicken tikka (£3.25), mixed bean casserole or fish pie (£4.95), king prawns in
garlic (£6.25), and hot smoked salmon steak (£6.95); children's menu (£2.75) and
Sunday roast (£3.95). There are winged high-backed settles and varnished rustic
tables on the lovely dark Delabole flagstones, black wrought-iron rings for lamps
or hams hanging from the high ceiling, a handsome window seat, pretty fresh
flowers, and an open kitchen range under a high mantelpiece decorated with
earthenware flagons. Well kept St Austell Tinners and HSD tapped from wooden
casks behind the counter (lots of tankards hang from the beams above it); good
service. Parking is in what must have been a really imposing stable yard. The
church next door is lovely. *(Recommended by Nick Wikeley, R and S Bentley, Graham
Tayar, Jack and Philip Paxton, Sheilah Openshaw, Paul Adams, Simon and Natalie Forster, A
E and P McCully, C J Parsons, Ian and Val Titman, E Money, David Heath)*

*St Austell ~ Tenants Steve and Joan Anderson ~ Real ale ~ Meals and snacks (not
25 Dec) ~ Restaurant ~ St Mabyn (01208) 841259 ~ Well behaved children in
restaurant and own room, though no children under 6 in evenings ~ Open 11-
2.30, 6-11; closed 25 Dec*

ST MAWGAN   SW8765 Map 1

Falcon
NE of Newquay, off B3276 or A3059

In a lovely village setting, this wisteria-covered old stone pub has a peaceful
pretty garden with plenty of seats, its own wishing well, play equipment for
children, and stone tables in a cobbled courtyard. Inside the big friendly bar has a
log fire, small modern settles and large antique coaching prints on the walls, and
there's plenty of space for eating the well-presented food, which might include
sandwiches (lunchtime only), good crab soup (£2.20), garlic mushrooms (£2.95),
home-made curry (£4.85), home-made steak and kidney pie (£4.95), and steak
(from £8.50), with evening dishes such as an Indian and Chinese platter, lamb
and cranberry casserole and lemon chicken (£5.95); on summer evenings
barbecues are held in the garden. The restaurant is no smoking and there are lots
of paintings by two local artists for sale. Well kept St Austell Tinners, HSD and
XXXX Mild on handpump; cheery service; darts, dominoes, euchre, trivia and
piped music. The bedrooms have been upgraded this year. A handsome church is
nearby. *(Recommended by Ian and Deborah Carrington, D Stokes, Don Kellaway, Angie
Coles, Simon and Natalie Forster, Mr and Mrs W J A Timpson, Steve and Liz Tilley, B J
Woodford, David Holloway, Dave Thompson, Margaret Mason)*

*St Austell ~ Tenant Andy Banks ~ Real ale ~ Meals and snacks ~ Restaurant ~ St
Mawgan (01637) 860225 ~ Children in restaurant ~ Live jazz or brass bands
summer Sun evenings ~ Open 11-3, 6-11 ~ Bedrooms: £15/£34(£42S)*

Please let us know what you think of a pub's bedrooms. No stamp needed:
The Good Pub Guide, FREEPOST TN1569, Wadhurst, E Sussex TN5 7BR.

ST TEATH SX0680 Map 1

White Hart

B3267; signposted off A39 SW of Camelford

Sailor hat-ribands and ships' pennants from all over the world as well as swords and a cutlass decorate this friendly village pub. A coin collection is embedded in the ceiling over the serving counter in the main bar, which also has a fine Delabole flagstone floor. Between the counter and the coal fire is a snug little high-backed settle. Leading off is a carpeted room, mainly for eating, with modern chairs around neat tables, and brass and copper jugs on its stone mantelpiece; piped music. Generous helpings of simple but popular well presented bar food include sandwiches (from £1.50), filled baked potatoes (from £3), ploughman's (£3.50), salads (from £3.50), plaice in breadcrumbs (£4.25), half a chicken or scampi (£4.95), chicken kiev (£5.95), trout (£9.50), steak (£7.95), puddings (£2.25), and Sunday roasts (£4). Well kept Ruddles County and Ushers Best on handpump. The games bar has darts, two pool tables, dominoes, fruit machine, table football, space game and satellite TV with three screens. *(Recommended by Simon Pyle, David and Julie Glover, John Whiting, Barry and Anne, Mr and Mrs David Silcox, Iain and Penny Muir, Julian and Sarah Stanton; more reports please)*

Free house ~ Licensees Barry and Rob Burton ~ Real ale ~ Meals and snacks (12-2, 6.30-till late) ~ (01208) 850281 ~ Children welcome ~ Open 11-2.30, 6-11 ~ Bedrooms: £20/£40

TREBARWITH SX0585 Map 1

Port William

Trebarwith Strand

The views over the beach and out to sea from the picnic-table sets on the terrace in front of this converted old harbourmaster's house are glorious – and the sunsets are even better. Inside, there's quite a nautical theme with fishing nets and maritime memorabilia decorating the walls, a separate gallery area with work by local artists, and the 'captain's cabin' which has a full-size fishing dinghy mounted on the wall; part of the bar is no smoking. There's quite an emphasis on fish, with eight different fresh dishes daily, such as home-made smoked mackerel pâté (£2.95), fried john dory (£5.50), skate wings in black butter with capers (£5.75), halibut in a mustard, cheese and cream sauce (£7.75), turbot in herb and lemon butter (£9), and whole oven-baked brill (£8.50); also, home-made soup (£1.95), filled rolls (from £1.75), steak £3.50), home-made pasties (£2.35), salads (from £4.25), lasagne (£5.25), and evening steaks (from £8.95), as well as non-fishy specials like vegetable curry (£4.25), tagliatelle with seafood sauce (£4.95) or home-made steak and kidney pie (£5.25); children's menu (from 75p). Well kept St Austell HSD and Tinners and John Smiths with guests like Courage Directors, Marstons Pedigree, Ruddles County and Ushers on handpump; jugs of sangria and rum punch. Darts, pool, cribbage, fruit machine, video game, trivia and piped music. Dogs welcome and bowl of water provided for them. *(Recommended by Jeff Davies, S Brackenbury, Margaret Mason, David Thompson, David Heath, Ann Reeder, K R Flack, C J Parsons)*

Free house ~ Licensees Peter and Gillian Hale ~ Real ale ~ Meals and snacks ~ Restaurant ~ (01840) 770230 ~ Children in eating area of bar ~ Live music Fri and Sat plus spontaneous sessions during the week ~ Open 11-11 ~ Self-catering holiday flat

TREEN SW3824 Map 1

Logan Rock

Just off B3315 – the back road Penzance—Lands End

After a walk along the wild cliffs – or just to see the nearby Logan Rock (an 80-ton boulder from which the pub takes its name) – you can work up an appetite to enjoy the popular bar food in this friendly and relaxed pub. This might include sandwiches (from £1.40, local crab when available £4), good pasties (£1.30), wholesome soup (£1.75), vegetarian quiche (£3.75), salads (from £3.95, crab £6.75), a popular fish and egg dish they call the Seafarer (£3.75), lasagne (£4.25), scampi (£4.95), very good charcoal-grilled steaks (from £6.95), and puddings like home-made fruit pie or crumble (£1.80); children's dishes (from £1.20) and afternoon cream teas. They will heat baby foods on request. The low-beamed main bar has a series of old prints telling the story of the rock, high-backed modern oak settles, wall seats, a really warm coal fire, and well kept St Austell Tinners and HSD on handpump. Lots of games such as darts, dominoes, cribbage, fruit machine, video games, winter pool and another fruit machine in the family room across the way; juke box, piped music. Dogs are allowed in if on a lead. There are some tables in a small wall-sheltered garden, looking over fields, with more in the front court. *(Recommended by DAV, Dr and Mrs A K Clarke, Anthony Barnes, Alan Castle, Andy and Jill Kassube, Mark Walker, K R Flack, E J Locker, Peter and Rosie Flower, David Mead)*

St Austell ~ Tenants Peter and Anita George ~ Real ale ~ Meals and snacks (from June-Sept all day, otherwise 12-2, 7-9) ~ Restaurant ~ St Buryan (01736) 810495 ~ Well behaved children in family room ~ Open 10.30am-11pm; 10.30-3, 5.30-11 in winter

TREGADILLETT SX2984 Map 1

Eliot Arms ★ ★ ♀

Village signposted off A30 at junction with A395, W end of Launceston bypass

Readers remain delighted with this creeper-covered old house – for its generous helpings of good food, friendly, genuinely welcoming staff, and quietly cosy atmosphere. The charming series of little softly lit rooms has a fine old mix of furniture, from high-backed built-in curved settles, through plush Victorian dining chairs, armed seats, chaise longues and mahogany housekeeper's chairs, to more modern seats, and the walls seem to be covered with hundreds of horsebrasses, old prints, old postcards or cigarette cards grouped in frames, and shelves of books and china. There's also a collection of 72 antique clocks including 7 grandfathers – don't worry when they don't all strike the right number of times. As well as all this, there are open fires, flowers on most tables, and a lovely ginger cat called Peewee; inoffensive piped music. The good home-made food comes in very big helpings, and might include several ploughman's, daunting open sandwiches including a massive slab of rib of beef, home-made soup (£1.65), pork and pineapple crunch, fish pie, vegetarian moussaka, spicy lamb kofta, and honeyed beef casserole (all £4.95); daily specials and lovely puddings. Well kept Flowers Original, Marstons Pedigree, Wadworths 6X and a summer guest beer on handpump, a fine choice of wines, and excellent friendly service; darts, shove-ha'penny, table skittles and fruit machine. A garden beyond the car park has picnic-table sets, a good climbing frame, swing and playhouse. *(Recommended by Paul Weedon, Mrs Patricia Nutt, Lynn Sharpless, Bob Eardley, Jeff Davies, S Brackenbury, Brian Jones, Nigel Flook, Betsy Brown, Dr and Mrs R Neville, F J Robinson, Mr and Mrs D T Deas, Graham Tayar, Sue Anderson, Phil Copleston, Mrs J Barwell, Phil and Anne Smithson, Rita Horridge, Peter and Lynn Brueton, David and Ann Stranack, John Fazakerley, Elaine Meredith, Ron Tennant, Stephen and Jean Curtis)*

Free House ~ Licensees John Cook and Lesley Elliott ~ Real ale ~ Meals and snacks (not 25 Dec) ~ (01566) 772051 ~ Children in eating area of bar ~ Open 11-2.30, 6-11; closed 25 Dec ~ Bedrooms: £20/£38

TRESCO (Isles of Scilly) SV8915 Map 1

New Inn 🍽 🛏 ♀

New Grimsby

Once a row of fishermen's cottages, this was converted in the last c into Nowlans Hotel, and when Mrs Nowlan retired it became Tresco New Inn; in the 1890s it was briefly known as The Canteen (a name which, oddly, has stuck among the island's older locals), and then in the 1900s became the New Inn; it incorporated the island's Stores until the 1960s. Above the front window there's a small sign saying For Ready Money Only (dating back to Great War, when sailors based here were refused credit. The light and airy bar – with picture windows looking out over the swimming pool – has been completely refurbished this year using driftwood and has a much more atmospheric, pubby feel. Bar lunches, of remarkable quality considering the supply difficulties, might include under the friendly new licensee, soups that are virtually meals in themselves (£1.90; wonderful fish soup with lobster, scallops, a bowl of cheese and so forth £4.40), sandwiches (from £1.80; crab £3.65), lots of pasta and pizza dishes at lunchtime (from £2.90), filled french bread (from £3.50; local lobster £9), salads with mozzarella, avocado, egg and fresh basil and their own gravadlax or marinated fish (from £3.40), pheasant chasseur (£4.10), beef kromeskis (minced steak with Dijon mustard, wrapped in smoked bacon and dipped in beer batter £4.40), local monkfish kebabs (£6.10), and local hake steaks steamed in a champagne and lobster sauce (£8.40), with evening starters (from £1.90) and lots of char-grilled meat and fish (from £5.80). The well regarded restaurant also has a separate children's menu. Boddingtons, Flowers IPA and Original, Marstons Pedigree, and Whitbreads Castle Eden and Pompey Royal tapped from the cask or on handpump (kept under light blanket pressure); well kept interesting wines and a good range of malt whiskies. Darts, cribbage, dominoes and juke box (rarely played); enthusiastic service. There are white plastic tables and chairs in the garden. Many of the people staying here are regular return visitors. *(Recommended by Bill Sykes, Desmond Curry; more reports please)*

Free house ~ Licensee G T Shone ~ Real ale ~ Meals and snacks ~ Restaurant ~ Scillonia (01720) 422844 ~ Children welcome till around 9.30 ~ Live music twice a month ~ Open 11-11; 12-2.30, 7.30-11 in winter ~ Bedrooms: £70B inc dinner

TRESILLIAN SW8646 Map 1

Wheel

A39 Truro—St Austell

The distinctive wheel worked into the thatch of the roof of this friendly pub makes it instantly recognisable. The two cosy and traditional original room areas (watch for the low door as you go in) have some timbering and stripped stonework, as well as low ceiling joists, soft lighting, and plush wall seats on the carpet. There are steps from one part to another, though access for the disabled is quite reasonable. Generous helpings of good value bar food include soup (£1.50), large filled rolls (from £1.95; open sandwiches from £2.75), ploughman's (from £2.75), vegetarian crumble (£3.65), salads (from £3.50), good gammon (£5.25), steaks (from £9.25), home-made daily specials, and puddings (from £1.70); children's dishes (from £1.50). Well kept Devenish Royal Wessex and a changing guest beer on handpump, coffee and tea; piped music. The neat garden stretches down to a tidal stretch of the River Fal, and has a play area. The pub was used as the headquarters of General Fairfax in the closing stages of the Civil War. *(Recommended by P M Lane, Peter Cornall, J I Fraser, Mr and Mrs Barker, Jack and Philip Paxton, E M Hughes, Phil and Heidi Cook)*

Greenalls ~ Tenant David Hulson ~ Real ale ~ Meals and snacks (till 9.30pm most nights, till 10pm Fri and Sat) ~ Truro (01872) 520293 ~ Children in room with no bar ~ Open 11-2.30(3 Sat), 6-11

TRURO SW8244 Map 1

Old Ale House £ ◀

7 Quay St/Princes St

Particularly friendly and full of character, this old fashioned, back to basics style pub is popular with a good mix of people. There's some interesting 1920s bric-a-brac, an engagingly old-fashioned diversity of furnishings that would do credit to any small-town auction room, and newspapers and magazines to read. But for many people, it's the fact that there are fifteen well kept, constantly changing real ales tapped from the cask that is the draw here: Bass, Brakspears Best, Cotleigh Tawny, Courage Best and Directors, Crown Buckley Reverend James, Fullers London Pride, Greene King Abbot, Palmers Tally Ho!, Shepherd Neame Bitter, Smiles Exhibition, Theakstons Best, and Woodfordes Nog, and interesting country wines such as damson and birch. What comes as more of a surprise is the enterprising and varied choice of good food, freshly prepared in a spotless kitchen in full view of the bar, such as doorstop sandwiches (from £2.15; hot baked garlic bread from £1.25), filled oven baked potatoes (£2.85), ploughman's (£3.25), hot meals served in a skillet pan like oriental chicken, sizzling beef or liver, bacon and onions (small helpings from £3.25, big helpings from £4.50), lasagne or steak and kidney pie (£3.95), daily specials like crab bake, mussels in white wine or beef and stilton pie, and puddings (from £1.65). Altogether, an excellent departure for Cornwall. No dogs, clean lavatories. *(Recommended by Ted George, Susan and Nigel Wilson, Jeff Davies, Steve and Sue Noakes, P and M Rudlin, E Howe)*

Greenalls (Devenish) ~ Manageress Mandy Keir ~ Real ale ~ Lunchtime meals and snacks ~ (01872) 71122 ~ Live music two nights a week ~ Open 11-2.30, 5.30-11(Sat 7-11)

Lucky Dip

Besides the fully inspected pubs, you might like to try these Lucky Dips recommended to us and described by readers (if you do, please send us reports):

☆ **Albaston** [OS Sheet 201 map reference 423704; SX4270], *Queens Head*: Pub's heart is vast but consistently welcoming public bar with changing displays of local industrial memorabilia; well kept Courage, good pasties, friendly traditional landlord, low prices; handy for Cotehele House and Tamar Valley railway *(Phil and Sally Gorton, John and Tessa Rainsford)*

☆ **Altarnun** [just N, OS Sheet 201 map reference 215825; SX2182], *Rising Sun*: Appealingly ordinary isolated pub just outside pretty village, flagstoned bar, six well kept real ales, good lunchtime and evening food; popular with local farmers as well as visitors *(Richard Houghton, Tom Evans)*

☆ **Bodinnick** [across the water from Fowey; SX1352], *Old Ferry*: Lovely situation with hotel part looking over water, character back flagstoned public bar partly cut into rock, lots of boating pictures, bar snacks, summer evening restaurant, well kept Flowers Original, St Austell Tinners and a guest ale at least in summer; pool table in games room where children allowed; bedrooms comfortable and roomy, with super views; can go very quiet out of season *(Jack and Philip Paxton, Margaret and Roy Randle, Peter Neate, Gerry Hollington, R and S Bentley, D and H Broodbank, Lynn Sharpless, Bob Eardley, LYM)*

☆ **nr Bodmin** [Dunmere, A389 NW; SX0467], *Borough Arms*: Neatly redecorated and spacious, with stripped stonework, open fire, side room packed with old railway photographs and posters (children particularly welcome here), well kept Bass, Boddingtons and Whitbreads, decent wines, friendly atmosphere, big helpings of good value straightforward food (no sandwiches), unobtrusive piped music, fruit machine; picnic-table sets out among shady apple trees, can get very busy lunchtime in season *(C J Parsons, BB)*

☆ **Bolventor** [signed just off A30 on Bodmin Moor; SX1876], *Jamaica Inn*: Despite the tourist commercialism is welcoming and interesting, with lots of character in clean, comfortable and cosy oak-beamed pub part, log fire, parrot, well kept Whitbreads ales, reasonably priced food, lovely cream teas; pretty secluded garden with play area, impressive moorland setting – all the better for the new bypass *(Mark and Jill Schmitz, D K Carter, Richard Houghton, Bronwen and Steve Wrigley, R F and J L Howard)*

☆ **Boscastle** [upper village – steep toil up from harbour, drive if you can; SX0990], *Napoleon*: Small-roomed low-beamed 16th-c pub, quiet and interesting, with fine collection of Napoleon prints, bar food inc vegetarian dishes, well kept Bass and St Austell real ale, decent wines, polished slate floor, big open fire; piped music, maybe folk music; sheltered terrace; children allowed in eating area *(Alan Mills, Roy and Margaret Randle, LYM)*

Bude [Falcon Terrace; SS2005], *Falcon*: Former coaching inn overlooking canal and town, popular with locals, wide range of quickly served good value food, well kept St Austell Tinners and HSD, friendly staff and cat; bedrooms *(Dr and Mrs Nigel Holmes, David Whalley)*

Cadgwith [SW7214], *Cadgwith Cove*: Worth knowing that this famously photogenic village does have a pub, useful for basic food, Whitbreads real ale, seats in pleasant front courtyard; but very much a local *(David and Michelle Hedges, Nigel Woolliscroft, Sue Holland, Dave Webster)*

☆ Camborne [Pendarves Rd; B3303 towards Helston; SW6440], *Old Shire*: Comfortable, homely family pub with good value interesting bar food, friendly staff, good range of beers; garden with summer barbecues, five bedrooms *(P and M Rudlin, Roy and Bettie Derbyshire)*

Camelford [Main St (A39); SX1083], *Masons Arms*: Heavy-beamed old stone building with local photographs and old advertising mirrors, friendly staff, good menu inc children's dishes, well kept St Austells, reasonable prices; pool table and juke box in one bar; children welcome *(Keith and Janet Morris)*

☆ Cargreen [the Quay; off A388 Callington—Saltash; SX4362], *Spaniards Arms*: Superb setting on Tamar with tables on terrace – always some river activity, esp at high tide; at least five real ales, very friendly staff, small panelled bar, huge fireplace in another smallish room, big restaurant with super food *(Ted George, M W Edwards)*

Charlestown [SX0351], *Rashleigh Arms*: Good value straightforward food esp steaks and fish, good range of reasonably priced real ales inc changing guests, very professional service, large comfortable lounge, good canalside family room; piped music may obtrude; big restaurant, seats out by tiny harbour; good value bedrooms *(Mayur Shah, Keith and Janet Morris)*

Coverack [SW7818], *Paris*: Good old-fashioned weatherbeaten pub open for good teas, Sun lunches, lovely views over sea and harbour, friendly staff *(Margaret Cadney)*

☆ Crackington Haven [SX1396], *Coombe Barton*: Good sea view from big welcoming comfortable bar, friendly service, very wide choice of good nicely presented bar food, four well kept ales such as Furgusons Dartmoor and St Austell Tinners, good coffee; other bars inc back family room and public bar with pool tables; bedrooms *(D Millichap, C J Westmoreland, Rita Horridge)*

☆ Crafthole [SX3654], *Finnygook*: Much modernised spacious lounge bar with wide choice of good value straightforward food, quick good service, Whitbreads-related beers, pleasant restaurant, good sea views from residents' lounge; bedrooms small but clean, comfortable and beautifully warm – good value *(BB)*

☆ Crantock [SW7960], *Old Albion*: Pleasantly placed thatched village pub doing well under friendly newish tenants, with old-fashioned tastefully decorated bar, good range of generously served home-cooked food *(Mark and Nicola Willoughby, LYM)*

Devoran [SW7939], *Old Quay*: Pleasant and friendly local, licensees work hard to please visitors, generous cheap food, well kept beers *(Simon Evans)*

Dobwalls [SX2165], *Highway*: Good food

inc well filled sandwiches and lots of specials; good choice of local ales *(John Kirk)*

Duloe [B3254 N of Looe; SX2358], *Olde Plough House*: Large refurbished L-shaped room with log fires at each end, cushioned settles and sewing-machine tables on big polished flagstones, two good open fires, good well presented reasonably priced food inc vegetarian, well kept Bass, attentive friendly staff; locals' end with darts and pool *(Maureen Hobbs, Martyn and Mary Mullins)*

☆ Egloshayle [Wadebridge—Bodmin; SX0172], *Earl of St Vincent*: Attractive furnishings and decor inc interesting antique clocks, good value freshly cooked food, well kept St Austell Tinners and HSD, good staff; colourful flowers in summer *(Buffy and Mike Adamson)*

☆ Falmouth [Maenporth Beach – round Falmouth Bay towards Mawnan; SW8032], *Seahorse*: Smooth smoked-glass café/bar, part of holiday complex, virtually on beach with super view over Fal estuary; wide range of good bar food inc fresh fish and some unusual dishes, well kept Ansells and Ruddles County, chilled foreign beers, good friendly service, upstairs restaurant, tables on terrace with boules – busy on barbecue nights; children very welcome *(John Wooll, Alec and Marie Lewery, Adrian Acton, E M Hughes)*

☆ Falmouth [The Moor], *Seven Stars*: Unchanging town local, rather tatty but warmly welcoming, with well kept Bass, Flowers Original and St Austell HSD tapped from the cask, minimal food, tables on roadside courtyard; landlord doubles as local vicar *(John Wooll, PA, Rob Weeks, BB)*

Falmouth [Docks], *Admiral Nelson*: Free house with fisherman's-bar atmosphere, friendly service, good food, well kept beers *(Michael Witte)*; [Prinslow Lane, Swanvale], *Boslowick*: Black and white beamed former manor house with generous good value straightforward bar food, well kept real ale, pleasant friendly staff, plenty of seats inc plush sofas, log-effect gas fires, family room with games machines; children's play area *(John Wooll)*; [Custom House Quay], *Chain Locker*: Same excellent harbourside position as Quayside (see main entries), with interesting nautical decor in roomy bare-boards bar, decent straightforward food from side servery, well kept Whitbreads-related ales *(LYM)*; [Church St], *Grapes*: Nice range of food, lovely harbour views *(Alec and Marie Lewery)*; [Church St], *Kings Head*: Rambling old-world bar with lots of pictures and bric-a-brac, soft settees, easy chairs and firmer dining chairs, old china and engravings, well kept Whitbreads-related ales, bar food, winter log fire, piped music; perhaps less atmosphere than some pubs here *(John Wooll, Mike Hallewell, LYM)*

Flushing [SW8033], *Royal Standard*:

Traditional unspoilt little friendly free house in fishing village, simple well cooked reasonably priced food inc good baked potatoes, tables in front overlooking water *(Margaret Cadney)*

☆ Fowey [SX1252], *Ship*: Good atmosphere, friendly service and good value usual food from sandwiches up through local fish to steak; comfortable cloth-banquette main bar with coal fire, pool/darts room off on left, steps up to family dining room on right with big stained-glass window; well kept St Austell HSD and other real ales, juke box; very popular though away from the water and back by the shops, dogs allowed; bedrooms old-fashioned, some oak-panelled *(Roy and Margaret Randle, Rita Horridge, S Brackenbury, Ann and Bob Westbrook)*

Fowey [Town Quay], *King of Prussia*: Good value side family food bar, upstairs bay windows overlooking harbour, well kept St Austell ales, efficient cheerful service, seats outside; bedrooms *(E H and R F Warner, LYM)*

☆ Golant [off B3269; SX1155], *Fishermans Arms*: Superb position by estuary, with good waterside garden, lovely views from terrace and window; a plain local with rather plain food, but friendly to all, with good sandwiches, generous helpings, well kept Courage-related real ales, log fire, interesting pictures, tropical fish *(Phil and Susanne Gullen, Nick Wikeley)*

Goldsithney [B3280; SW5430], *Crown*: Friendly local, has been praised for generous straightforward bar food, well kept St Austell beers inc good Mild, and very pretty suntrap glass-roofed front loggia, but no recent reports *(News please)*

Gorran Haven [SX0141], *Llawnroc*: Friendly atmosphere in village pub adjoining hotel overlooking harbour and fishing village; good value well cooked bar food, Flowers IPA, Morlands Old Speckled Hen and Whitbreads Pompey Royal on handpump; very convenient for the Lost Gardens of Heligan; bedrooms *(Norma and Keith Bloomfield)*

Grampound [A390 St Austell—Truro; SW9348], *Dolphin*: Friendly service, good fairly priced meals, unusual lounge with really comfortable easy chairs *(C May)*

Gulval [SW4832], *Coldstreamer*: Unusual high-ceilinged pub in quiet, pleasant village, very friendly staff, restaurant busy and cosy, with very good if not cheap food, Whitbreads-related real ales, resident cat *(Jo Rees, DAV)*

☆ Gurnards Head [SW4338], *Gurnards Head*: Good pubby atmosphere in big, comfortable bar with open fires at each end; varied and interesting food inc unusual fish dishes and local specialities using local produce (served all day at least in summer), friendly efficient service, good wine; bedrooms *(LM, Stephen Gibbs)*

Hayle [Bird Paradise Park; SW5536], *Bird in Hand*: Listed for its good own-brewed beers – a busy barn-like place geared to

families visiting the Bird Park, with food to match, four-table upstairs pool room, play area in garden *(David and Michelle Hedges)*

Helston [Coinagehall St; SW6527], *Fitzsimmons Arms*: Comfortable and loungey, varied menu, a safe place to eat *(Sue Holland, Dave Webster)*

☆ nr Helston [Gunwalloe; signposted off A3083, S; SW6522], *Halzephron*: Experienced new owners doing good real food, generous and satisfying, in clean and comfortable traditional pub looking over clifftop fields to sea; well kept Furgusons Dartmoor Strong, splendid fire, gleaming copper, quietly welcoming bar staff, tables outside; children welcome; comfortable bedrooms *(Alan Castle, G Atkinson, Paul Weedon, Gwen and Peter Andrews, LYM)*

☆ Hessenford [A387 Looe—Torpoint; SX3057], *Copley Arms*: Comfortable pub in lovely spot by river, good reasonably priced food in bar and restaurant, well kept St Austell Tinners, big family room, play area and seats in waterside garden; bedrooms *(Jenny and Neil Spink, Bronwen and Steve Wrigley)*

Kilkhampton [SS2511], *New Inn*: Spacious well kept local with rambling interconnecting rooms, some traditional furnishings, fine woodburner, decent bar food inc good home-cooked ham, well kept Bass, some tables out in front; children in good games room, handy for Pixieland Fun Park *(LM, LYM)*

☆ Kingsand [Fore St; towards Cawsand – OS Sheet 201 map reference 434505; SX4350], *Halfway House*: Smart but welcoming, with cosy softly lit low-ceilinged bar around huge central fireplace, neat simple furnishings, wide choice of food inc well presented fresh local fish, Bass, Charrington and Worthington real ales, decent wines, good staff, unobtrusive piped music, restaurant; comfortable well equipped bedrooms, handy for Mount Edgcumbe and marvellous cliff walks on Rame Head *(Dr K T Nicolson, Mike and Heather Barnes, A Kingstone)*

☆ Kingsand [village green], *Rising Sun*: Friendly old single-bar local with massive helpings of good food from sandwiches, pasties and burgers up inc plenty of local fish and incredibly long sausage, good choice of well kept beer and wine, open fire, casual atmosphere; small, so worth booking *(Derek and Rosemary King, Mike and Heather Barnes, Ann and Bob Westbrook)*

☆ Lamorna [off B3315 SW of Penzance; SW4424], *Lamorna Wink*: Lots of beautifully kept naval memorabilia and pictures in simply furnished friendly country local a short walk from pretty cove with good coast walks; decent food served efficiently from hatch inc huge baked potatoes, good pasties and plenty of fish, Whitbreads-related and Devenish real ales *(Shirley Pielou, LYM)*

Lands End [SW3425], *State House*: Admission charged, as part of extensively developed Lands End complex, but decent food in big conservatory extension housing bars and pretty bistro-style dining area; obliging staff, tables on terrace; bedrooms priced by view *(Mark Walker, David Carrington)*

☆ **Lanlivery** [SX0759], *Crown*: Cosy traditional atmosphere and plenty of space in interconnected rooms of friendly village pub said to date from 12th c; pews, painted settles, armchairs and sofas, flagstones and carpets, ornate stained-glass window in lounge; very accommodating staff, well kept Bass and Hancocks HB on handpump, no music or games machines, good reasonably priced waitress-served lunchtime bar food, evening restaurant; bedrooms in separate accommodation by garden (no dogs allowed in these) *(Phil and Susanne Gullen, S Brackenbury, John and Valerie Martin, Michael and Joan Johnstone)*

Launceston [SX3384], *White Hart*: Good value reasonably priced bar food inc sandwiches, help-yourself salads and hot dishes in big pub with log fire and dining room *(John and Christine Vittoe, Mr and Mrs J V Wild)*

☆ **Lizard** [SW7012], *Top House*: Lots of interesting local sea pictures and fine shipwreck relics in extensive well kept bar with well kept Cornish Original, Flowers IPA and Marstons Pedigree on handpump (serpentine handpulls in public bar), good choice of other drinks, generous helpings of usual bar food with good local fish and seafood specials and some interesting vegetarian dishes, friendly efficient service, roaring log fire, darts, fruit machine; more local serpentine craft in passage to lavatories, striking local granite porch; tables on terrace; dull village *(Ian Phillips, John Tyler, Gwen and Peter Andrews, Sue Holland, Dave Webster, BB)*

☆ **Longrock** [old coast rd Penzance—Marazion; SW5031], *Mexico*: Remarkably wide choice of food from traditional pub dishes to Far Eastern things served generously at sensible prices, cheerfully relaxed local atmosphere, genuinely welcoming licensees; former office of Mexico Mine Company, with massive stone walls *(J M Bowers, Mark Walker)*

Looe [Fore St, East Looe; SX2553], *Ship*: Very welcoming, with good choice of competitively priced food, highly efficient service *(Miss E S Draper)*

☆ **Lostwithiel** [Duke St (behind Talbot Hotel off A390); SX1059], *Royal Oak*: Friendly and busy pub dating from 13th c, with spacious comfortable lounge, flagstoned back public bar, good staff, good value food from lunchtime sandwiches to steaks inc children's and vegetarian dishes, unusually good choice of real ales such as Bass, Fullers London Pride, Marstons Pedigree, Whitbreads and two or three guests, lots of bottled beers, decent wines; restaurant, some tables on terrace; parking may be difficult; bedrooms *(E M Hughes, Richard*

Houghton, Dr John Lunn, LYM)

Lostwithiel [North St], *Globe*: Traditional pub worth noting for marvellous variety of pies (not Mon) *(J Fletcher)*

Mabe Burnthouse [SW7634], *New Inn*: Tasty well presented food in good helpings and reasonably priced, lounge and separate locals' bar, good service *(Mr and Mrs B Hobden)*

☆ **Malpas** [off A39 S of Truro; SW8442], *Heron*: Wonderful setting above wooded creek, big helpings of reasonable bar food served quickly, St Austell Tinners and HSD; rectangular bar with good Truro photographs, log fire, pool, machines, piped music, suntrap slate-paved terrace; children welcome, parking may be difficult *(Eric and Shirley Broadhead, S Brackenbury, R L Turnham, Helen Taylor, LYM)*

☆ **Manaccan** [down hill signed to Gillan and St Keverne; SW7625], *New Inn*: Friendly new licensees doing well in unspoilt and character-filled old pub, good bar food, well kept Whitbreads/Devenish tapped from the cask, individual furnishings, lots of atmosphere; big garden with swing, attractive waterside village *(E Money, John and Sally Clarke, LYM)*

Marazion [The Square; SW5231], *Cutty Sark*: Very good food esp fresh Newlyn fish in bar and restaurant, Flowers ale, open fire, some stripped stone and nautical bric-a-brac; not far from beach, overlooking St Michaels Mount; bedrooms good value *(Richard Bamford)*

Marhamchurch [off A39 just S of Bude; SS2203], *Bullers Arms*: Big rambling L-shaped bar with half a dozen well kept real ales, limited but fresh and tasty food served quickly and generously, good puddings, friendly staff and locals, darts in flagstoned back part, pool room, piped pop music, restaurant; children welcome; tables and play area in sizeable garden, a mile's walk to the sea; bedrooms *(LM, LYM)*

☆ **Mawgan** [St Martin; SW7323], *Old Courthouse*: Particularly well kept Whitbreads/Devenish beers in open-plan split-level pub beautifully placed down leafy lane, very spacious, clean and comfortable, with good choice of food, very friendly service, pleasant garden; children encouraged *(Nigel Woolliscroft)*

☆ **Mawnan Smith** [W of Falmouth, off Penryn—Gweek rd – old B3291; SW7728], *Red Lion*: Good atmosphere and lots of bric-a-brac, plates, china, brasses etc in thatched pub's cosy series of varied interconnecting rooms inc no smoking room behind restaurant, generous helpings of usual food from sandwiches to steaks, well kept Bass and Devenish, friendly helpful service, children welcome *(E M Hughes, Paul Weedon, Mr and Mrs W J A Timpson, Stephen and Jean Curtis, S R Chapman, Mrs J Barwell, Gwen and Peter Andrews, LYM)*

☆ **Menheniot** [off A38; SX2862], *White Hart*: Friendly and relaxing, well kept Bass and Boddingtons, wide choice of very generous good food (though little for vegetarians) which can be taken away, one old fireplace now a shrine to brassware; bedrooms well equipped and neatly modernised *(David Burnett, Donna Lowes)*

☆ **Mevagissey** [Fore St, nr harbour; SX0145], *Ship*: 16th-c pub with big helpings of good food esp low-priced local fish, full range of well kept St Austell beers, welcoming licensees; big comfortable room divided into small interesting areas, ships' memorabilia, big open fire, friendly cat; fruit machines, music can rather obtrude; bedrooms *(P and K Lloyd, Ann and Bob Westbrook, P and M Rudlin)*

Mevagissey [Fore St], *Fountain*: Tucked away up narrow lane by post office, great friendly atmosphere, well kept beer, decent food, plenty of summer visitors; both bars clean and tidy, piano music some evenings *(Ted George, Paul Cartledge)*; [Polkirt Hill], *Harbour Lights*: Hilltop pub's straightforward but large and comfortable bar has panoramic views over harbour and bay; good value straightforward food, well kept Bass, very helpful, friendly and efficient service; trad jazz Sun lunchtime, tables outside, car park; bedrooms *(Roy and Margaret Randle, P and M Rudlin)*

☆ **Mitchell** [off A30 Bodmin—Redruth; SW8654], *Plume of Feathers*: Rambling comfortable bar with lots of bric-a-brac, huge open fire, good choice of home-made food from sandwiches to hearty grills from open-plan back kitchen, Whitbreads/Devenish real ales on handpump; piped music, darts and winter pool; tables outside, with adventure playground and farm animals; children welcome *(Jim and Maggie Cowell, Gwen and Peter Andrews, LYM)*

☆ **Mullion** [SW6719], *Old Inn*: Thatched village pub extended and given thoroughly nautical refurbishment, lots of intimate nooks and crannies, plenty of atmosphere and interest, big inglenook fireplace, friendly welcome, well kept Bass and Whitbreads-related ales, good straightforward bar food inc grills and specials, efficient service; piped music; bedrooms, and self-catering cottages *(Andy and Jill Kassube, David and Michelle Hedges, Gwen and Peter Andrews, S R Chapman, LYM)*

Newbridge [A3071 Penzance—St Just – OS Sheet 203 map reference 424316; SW4232], *Fountain*: Recently completely refurbished, though still unspoilt; current management doing delicious food *(Robin and Molly Taylor)*

☆ **Newquay** [Station Approach; SW8161], *Cavalier*: Friendly and comfortable, with good bar food from sandwiches to steaks inc interesting snacks and evening dishes, well kept real ales, good service; open all day *(Eric and Shirley Broadhead)*

Newquay, *Central*: Heavily refurbished with some interesting photographs of old Cornwall, separate dining area, good range

of food inc vegetarian, St Austell ales; adjoining disco; children in dining room *(Gill Earle, Andrew Burton)*

Newtown [Newtown in St Martin; the one off B3293, SE of Helston; SW7423], *Prince of Wales*: Small stone pub with welcoming young licensees, Whitbreads ales, bar food, popular restaurant, pool table; piped radio *(E A George, Gwen and Peter Andrews)*

Notter [Notter Bridge; just off A38, Saltash—Liskeard, 10 miles from Plymouth; SX3861], *Notter Bridge*: Attractive spot in wooded valley with big picture windows overlooking river, simple decor, wide choice of good value generous basic food, cheerful holidaytime atmosphere, tables on terrace *(Bronwen and Steve Wrigley)*

☆ **Padstow** [Lanadwell St; SW9175], *Golden Lion*: Friendly local with pleasant black-beamed front bar, high-raftered back lounge with russet plush banquettes against ancient white stone walls; reasonably priced simple lunches, evening steaks and fresh seafood; well kept Whitbreads and Cornish Original on handpump, piped music, juke box, fruit machines; bedrooms *(Keith and Janet Morris, BB)*

☆ **Padstow** [Lanadwell St], *London*: Shiny red and cream decor for sprucely cottagey fishermen's local which has long been the best pub here, with good atmosphere, well kept St Austells and decent food, but sadly the long-serving tenants have both died this last year; bedrooms *(News please)*

☆ **Padstow** [South Quay], *Old Custom House*: Comfortably refurbished open-plan bar with sensibly priced food inc vegetarian, comfortable chesterfields around open fire, prints of old harbour, big beams and timbers; attentive helpful staff, well kept St Austell real ales, restaurant; attractive spot by harbour, with conservatory; bedrooms very pretty and comfortable *(S A Boulter, John and Vivienne Rice, Phil and Heidi Cook, BB)*

Padstow [North Quay – was the Blue Lobster], *Shipwrights*: Stripped brick, flagstones, lobster pots and nets in big popular quayside bar with St Austell Bosuns and Tinners on handpump; very much a young person's pub evenings – when juke box takes over *(Phil and Heidi Cook, John and Vivienne Rice, BB)*

Paul [SW4627], *Kings Arms*: Good beer and extensive choice of decent value food, pleasant atmosphere; a little off the beaten track so useful alternative to Mousehole in the tourist season; bedrooms *(Colin Pearson)*

Pendeen [SW3834], *Radjel*: Cosy stripped-stone bar handy for walkers, big wood-panelled lounge with old local photographs, well kept St Austells beers, friendly staff, good food; children in eating area *(Eric and Shirley Broadhead, LYM)*

☆ **Penzance** [Barbican; Newlyn rd, opp harbour after swing-bridge; SW4730], *Dolphin*: Good harbour views, welcoming atmosphere, attractive nautical decor, quickly served bar food inc good big pasties, St Austell ales, competitive prices, great fireplace, helpful service, big pool room with juke box etc; children in room off main bar; no obvious nearby parking *(LM, Mark Walker, LYM)*

Penzance [Chapel St], *Admiral Benbow*: Nautical decor perhaps overdone, but fun – figureheads, even a pirate on the roof; handy for a quiet lunch, with friendly staff, decent food, Courage-related ales, children allowed, downstairs restaurant; open all day summer *(Mark Walker, LYM)*; [Quay], *Yacht*: Friendly, with quick reasonably priced food, St Austells beers, area for children *(Mark Walker)*

☆ Perranarworthal [A39 Truro—Penryn; SW7839], *Norway*: Elaborately tricked out as small-roomed country pub, lots of country bygones, rustic bric-a-brac, stuffed birds and fish; big helpings of popular lunchtime bar food, restaurant, Whitbreads/Devenish real ales, tables outside *(Jim and Maggie Cowell, BB)*

☆ Perranuthnoe [signed off A394 Penzance—Helston; SW5329], *Victoria*: Good atmosphere, well kept Courage-related ales, small choice of good generous food and cheerful service in comfortable L-shaped bar with coastal and wreck photographs, some stripped stonework, neat coal fire, booth seating in family area, games area; sheltered picnic-table sets outside, handy for Mounts Bay beaches; bedrooms *(RB, LYM)*

☆ Perranwell [off A393 Redruth—Falmouth and A39 Falmouth—Truro; SW7839], *Royal Oak*: Welcoming and relaxed black-beamed village pub, cosy and comfortable, with good bar food inc sandwiches and attractive lunchtime cold table, sensible prices, well kept Whitbreads-related ales, good winter fire, provision for children, garden with picnic-table sets; piped music *(E M Hughes, Gwen and Peter Andrews, LYM)*

☆ Polgooth [SW9950], *Polgooth*: Much modernised country local with good big family room and (up steep steps) outside play area; popular food, St Austell real ales, pleasant atmosphere *(LYM)*

☆ Polperro [The Quay], SX2051], *Blue Peter*: Cosy and unpretentious little low-beamed wood-floored harbourside local with well kept St Austell Tinners and HSD and guest beers, strong farm cider, normally bar food from sandwiches up (though sometimes unexpectedly not available this last year), traditional games, piped music (may be loud), some seats outside; family room, open all day *(K R Flack, Roy and Margaret Randle, Peter Neate, S R and A J Ashcroft, Norma Constable, Bjanka Kadic, D Cox, LYM)*

☆ Polperro [Quay], *Three Pilchards*: Low-beamed and dim-lit local, particularly well kept Courage beers, good value quick simple food inc good prawn sandwiches, open fire, friendly staff; open all day *(Denis and Margaret Kilner, Norma Constable, Bjanka Kadic, Nigel and Teresa Blocks)*

☆ Polperro [Old Mill; top of village nr main car park], *Crumplehorn Mill*: Friendly atmosphere and generous reasonably priced food in attractive pub, separate areas inc atmospheric beamed upper bar with stripped stone, flagstones, curtains between simple tables; log fire, Bass and St Austell HSD and XXXX, farm cider; pool area, piped music (can be loud when the teenagers are there in force); bedrooms *(Norma Constable, Bjanka Kadic, J H Bell)*

Polperro [bear R approaching harbour], *Noughts & Crosses*: Cosy little bar, upper family room and softly lit lower riverside bar with comfortable banquettes, pool table and fruit machines; cheerful busy atmosphere, Courage beers, piped music, good value usual bar food inc good crab sandwiches *(Nigel and Teresa Blocks, Bronwen and Steve Wrigley)*

Polruan [West St; SX1251], *Russell*: Friendly, lively and without frills, reasonable food and beer, piped pop music (may be loud) *(Martyn and Mary Mullins, Steve and Liz Tilley)*

Polzeath [SW9378], *Oyster Catcher*: Bright and cheerful, with spectacular bay views from bow window, spacious eating area, limited but well cooked tasty food, helpful staff; games machines *(A E and P McCully, L Powys-Smith)*

Port Isaac [SX0080], *Slipway*: Built into cliff on several floors, pleasant decor, particularly helpful staff, well kept beer, good food inc excellent seafood in restaurant; bedrooms *(S R Chapman)*

☆ Porthleven [Peverell Terr; SW6225], *Atlantic*: Has been praised for stunning setting overlooking sea, well kept Bass and Whitbreads/Devenish real ales on handpump, wide choice of good value bar food esp local seafood; big open-plan lounge with well spaced seating and cosier alcoves, good log fire in granite fireplace; but no recent reports *(News please)*

☆ Portloe [SW9339], *Lugger*: Well presented bar lunches inc children's dishes, with comfortable armchairs, two fires, good evening restaurant, decent wines, friendly service, tables on terrace, pretty setting in attractive village above cove; comfortable bedrooms (not all with sea view); restaurant licence – you can't just go for a drink – otherwise clear main entry *(Brian Whittaker, Mr and Mrs C R Little, Miss R M Tudor, Dr R J Rathbone, Mr and Mrs W J A Timpson, P and J Shapley, S Brackenbury, P M Lane, S R Chapman, LYM)*

Portmellon Cove [closed Oct-Mar; SX0144], *Rising Sun*: Superb setting overlooking small small cove nr Mevagissey, small bar, dining area, family/games room upstairs, good bar food inc vegetarian and children's dishes; St Austell tapped from the cask, Wadworths 6X on handpump, seats outside; bedrooms *(P and K Lloyd, LYM)*

Portreath [SW6545], *Basset Arms*: Very

welcoming village pub, comfortable and well decorated, with well kept beers, varied food, unobtrusive piped music *(S Howe)*

☆ **Portscatho** [SW8735], *Plume of Feathers*: Friendly and comfortable, with good thriving atmosphere, popular good value food in main bar or small eating area, side locals' bar, well kept St Austell Tinners, well reproduced loudish pop music, good staff; in pretty fishing village, very popular with summer visitors, on South Cornwall Coastal path; dogs allowed *(E M Hughes, R and S Bentley, Eric and Shirley Broadhead, LYM)*

☆ **Poughill** [SS2207], *Preston Gate*: Friendly and busy welcoming local with pews and long mahogany tables on flagstones, log fires, well kept Courage-related real ales and St Austell Tinners, darts, locals at the bar, some seats outside; children welcome, dogs looked after well, bar food *(Richard Cole, Brian Jones, LYM)*

Probus [Fore St; A390; SW8947], *Hawkins Arms*: Warmly welcoming local, good helpings of well priced food esp home-made pizzas, well kept St Austell beers, toby jug collection; bedrooms *(Andy and Jill Kassube, DH)*

☆ **Quintrel Downs** [East Rd; SW8560], *Two Clomes*: Attractive largely unspoilt old converted cottage with open fire, aptly-chosen furnishings, nice mix of customers, beers well kept by knowledgeable and pleasant landlord, reasonably priced food; family room *(Tom Evans)*

☆ **Redruth** [Tolgus Mount; SW6842], *Tricky Dickies*: Well converted tin mine's blacksmith's shop with interesting local industrial relics, good food inc lots of pizzas (booking advised weekends), changing range of well kept beers such as Boddingtons, Greene King Abbot, Hook Norton and Wadworths 6X, knowledgeable and enthusiastic owner; partly covered terrace, summer barbecues, trad jazz Tues, other live music Thurs *(P and M Rudlin, Andy and Jill Kassube)*

☆ **Roche** [just off A30; SW9860], *Victoria*: Snug low-ceilinged bar with woodburner, antique oak settles, oak panelling and a carved doorway, lots of interesting sea relics and pictures among other bric-a-brac, small lounge, big restaurant with open fire, panelled family room; popular food inc good home-made pasties, well kept St Austell ales, panelled children's room, cheery service; garden with outside summer servery *(Phil and Heidi Cook, LYM)*

☆ **Ruan Lanihorne** [off A3078 St Mawes rd; SW8942], *Kings Head*: Good standard home-made food inc good sandwiches and fine Sun roast in attractive pub beautifully placed overlooking Fal estuary; Allied real ales, quick friendly service, pleasant atmosphere, china hanging from beams, cigarette cards, no smoking area; suntrap sunken garden and seating area with beautiful view; children welcome; bedrooms *(BHP, S Brackenbury)*

Saltash [off A38 towards Liskeard, about two miles into Cornwall; SX4258], *Crooked*: Newish pub in lovely setting, popular and happy, huge sloping garden with big play area overlooking road and valley, Vietnamese pot-bellied pig; decent food; good reasonably priced bedrooms in separate building *(Bronwen and Steve Wrigley)*

Seaton [B3247 Downderry—Looe; SX3054], *Old Smugglers*: Ancient free house in small village, well kept Bass, Wadworths 6X, Whitbreads and a distant guest such as Woodfordes Nog, farm cider; good helpings of reasonably priced standard food inc fresh fish *(Ann and Bob Westbrook)*

☆ **Sennen Cove** [SW3526], *Old Success*: 17th-c inn, perhaps best out of season, in glorious spot by big beach with magnificent view along Whitesand Bay; small bar with seafaring decorations, courteous staff, quickly served generous reasonably priced bar food inc fresh seafood and good triple-decker sandwiches, well kept real ales inc Bass, piped music; carvery restaurant; gents' past car park; attractive bedrooms – good breakfasts, good value winter weekends *(LM, N and J Strathdee, Alan Castle, Mr and Mrs R Head)*

☆ **St Dominick** [Saltash; a mile E of A388, S of Callington – OS Sheet 201 map reference 406674; SX3967], *Who'd Have Thought It*: Very different from your usual Cornish pub – flock wallpaper, tasselled plush seats, Gothick tables, gleaming pottery and copper; consistently good food inc interesting dishes and fresh fish (lunch orders may stop 1.30), well kept Bass and Whitbreads/Devenish, decent wines, charming waitresses, impeccable lavatories; no children; quiet countryside nr Cotehele House *(Geoffrey Thompson, Ted George, Mrs C Watkinson, John Kirk, S R Chapman)*

St Erth [1 Church St; SW5535], *Star*: Deceptively spacious low-beamed 17th-c pub, lots of collections eg brasses, radios, snuffs; very wide choice of food inc delicious bread, melt-in-the-mouth local steak in madeira sauce, several specials such as seafood pasta packed with prawns, squid and fish in superb tomato, garlic and herb sauce; Boddingtons, Marstons Pedigree and a weekly changing summer guest beer *(Keith Denton)*

☆ **St Issey** [SW9271], *Ring o' Bells*: Neatly modernised village inn with good cheerful atmosphere, consistently good food inc children's helpings, well kept Courage, friendly staff, open fire; bedrooms *(J W Patrick, Mr and Mrs R J Phillips, LYM)*

St Ive [A390 Liskeard—Callington; SX3167], *Butchers Arms*: Two tastefully furnished rooms with substantial helpings of good value food and well kept beers; quiet and pleasant with lots of plants and flowers in all sorts of containers *(Ted George)*

☆ **St Ives** [Fore St; SW5441], *Castle*: Bar food inc well priced substantial open sandwiches and five Whitbreads-related ales and other real ales in comfortable and friendly local, roomier than seems at first, with original pine panelling, old local photographs, maritime memorabilia, good service and atmosphere, unobtrusive piped music; best out of season *(Shirley Pielou)*

St Keverne [The Square; SW7921], *Three Tuns*: Cheery local by church with big helpings of cheap straightforward bar food inc good seafood and excellent steaks (landlord was a butcher), well kept Flowers IPA and Original, decent whiskies, woodburner, darts, some nautical decorations, picnic-table sets out by square; bedrooms *(Peter and Lynn Brueton, Sue Holland, Dave Webster, John and Sally Clarke, BB)*

St Mabyn [SX0473], *St Mabyn*: Atmospherically refurbished by new owners, banishing pool table – much less a local now, but more for visitors, inc much more interesting food; darts *(Margaret Mason, David Thompson)*

☆ **St Mawes** [SW8433], *Rising Sun*: Just across village lane from harbour wall, with pubby little front locals' bar, plush hotel bar, attractive conservatory, slate-topped tables on terrace, lunchtime bar food, evening restaurant and Sun lunches, well kept St Austell BB and HSD on handpump, decent wine list, good service; open all day summer; prettily furnished if expensive bedrooms with good estuary views *(Les King, N and J Strathdee, P and K Lloyd, Helen Taylor, E M Hughes, LYM)*

St Mawes [Tredenham Rd (harbour edge)], *Idle Rocks*: Terrace overlooking the bay wonderful on a fine day; bedrooms *(Nick Barber, Ann Jacklin)*; *Victory*: Lots of sailing and other sea photographs in unpretentious and friendly bar with well kept Whitbreads, good value standard bar food inc some unusual puddings; piped music; seats out in the alley, a few steep yards up from the harbour; bedrooms *(Keith and Janet Morris, N and J Strathdee, LYM)*

☆ **St Merryn** [SW8874], *Farmers Arms*: Big, busy and extensively refurbished, with decent food from sandwiches to steaks inc vegetarian dishes, also carvery, in bright and spacious no smoking dining area, St Austell HSD and Tinners on handpump, good value house wine, floodlit well, children's games room with videos and so forth, family room, tables on back terrace; bedrooms *(Don Kellaway, Angie Coles)*

St Merryn [Church Town (B3276 towards Padstow)], *Cornish Arms*: Well kept St Austell Tinners and BB and straightforward bar food from pasties to steak in simply furnished local with fine Delabole flagstones and some 12th-c stonework; good games room, picnic-table sets outside; children over 6 may be allowed in eating area *(LYM)*

St Minver [SW9677], *Four Ways*: Straightforward and likeable, with pleasant garden, friendly service, food inc wonderful shark steaks *(Margaret Mason, David Thompson)*

☆ **St Neot** [N of A38 Liskeard—Bodmin; SX1867], *London*: Good imaginative home-made food, well kept real ales, cheerful service, beams and two open fires; attractive village tucked away down tricky roads in wooded valley *(Mr and Mrs W J A Timpson)*

St Tudy [off A39 nr Wadebridge; SX0676], *Cornish Arms*: Good food esp steaks and particularly well kept Whitbreads-related ales in friendly pub with enthusiastic landlord; restaurant, quiet village (birthplace of Captain Bligh of the *Bounty*) *(David Borthwick, DH)*

☆ **Stratton** [SS2406], *Kings Arms*: Lovely old well kept three-room 17th-c free house, six or more regularly changed real ales such as Batemans, Fullers London Pride and Ind Coope Burton, varied tempting food; children welcome *(P and M Rudlin, David Holloway)*

☆ **Stratton**, *Tree*: Rambling old pub built around coachyard with massive ancient gate, very friendly landlord, staff and locals, well kept St Austell Tinners, varied bar food, good evening meals in character restaurant; family room, lounge and public bar; bedrooms *(LM, Peter and Lynn Brueton, David Holloway, BB)*

☆ **Tintagel** [Tregatta (B3263 S); SX0588], *Min Pin*: Simple modern bar and dining area in converted farmhouse brewing its own beers, at least in the tourist season; bar food, piped music, restaurant doing evening steaks, trout and so forth, tables in attractive garden; children allowed if eating though not welcome to stay; bedrooms clean, tidy and well equipped; open weekends only in winter, except Christmas/New Year *(Margaret and Roy Randle, Gerald Cleaver, David and Gill Carrington, LYM)*

Tintagel [Fore St], *Tintagel Arms*: Good generous food inc children's and some Greek dishes, spacious yet cosy plush bar, restaurant; good bedrooms *(Mr and Mrs M Lewis, Mrs A Derham)*

Trebarwith [signed off B3263 and B3314 SE of Tintagel – OS Sheet 200 map reference 058865; SX0585], *Mill House*: Marvellous spot in own steep streamside woods above sea; has had its ups and downs, but recent reports suggest putting it back on the list, with decent food inc children's dishes in very quiet main bar with fine Delabole flagstones, real ales, friendly service, comfortable bedrooms *(Peter and Lynn Brueton, Mark and Nicola Willoughby, Stephen and Jean Curtis; more reports please)*

Trebetherick [SW9377], *Carpenters Arms*: Doing well under newish but experienced landlord, with well kept Courage Directors and St Austell HSD, reasonably priced bar food; children welcome *(C J Parsons)*

Treburley [A388 Callington—Launceston; SX3477], *Springer Spaniel*: Cheerful free house with emphasis on good food at modest prices, carefully chosen wines, well kept beers, good welcoming service; handsome springer spaniel *(John and Tessa Rainsford)*

☆ Treleigh [A3047 just outside Camborne, handy for A30; SW7043], *Inn for all Seasons*: Spacious, stylish and relaxing modern bar, part no smoking, which has been a worthy main entry, with good interesting food and friendly unobtrusive service; also restaurant and comfortable well equipped bedrooms; but in receivership summer 1994, though still open *(News please)*

Trelights [signposted off B3314 Wadebridge—Delabole; SW9979], *Long Cross*: Useful coastal hotel with fine restored Victorian garden, now settling down under friendly new owner; well kept St Austell Tinners and good value bar food in modern bar with plush-and-varnish furnishings, stained-glass panels, unusual heptagonal bench around small central fountain; family room, further dining bar, good play area; bedrooms comfortable and well furnished, many with good views *(Graham Tayar, BB)*

☆ Trevaunance Cove [The Beach; SW7251], *Driftwood Spars*: Good nicely presented quickly served food using fresh ingredients from sandwiches up in former tin-mine store nr beach with huge beams, thick stone walls and log fires, atmospheric decor reflecting smuggling and lifeboat influences; reasonable prices, big family room, attractive restaurant, well kept ales, lots of malt whiskies; bedrooms comfortable *(W S Shields, Mark and Nicola Willoughby, Alan Wheatley)*

☆ Trevaunance Cove, *Trevaunance Point*: Popular dining pub in clifftop former customs house, fine sea and cliff views, huge beams, log fires, well kept beers; owned by colourful Cornish ex-Rugby football player; garden; good value well equipped bedrooms, good breakfasts *(Tony Eberts)*

☆ Truro [Frances St/Castle St], *Wig & Pen*: Generous helpings of good reasonably priced bar food with interesting specials in big unpretentious L-shaped pub, well spaced comfortable chairs and tables, newspapers to read, unobtrusive piped music, pleasant service, well kept St Austell HSD and Tinners; tables out on busy street *(Keith and Janet Morris, John Wooll)*

☆ Truro [Frances St], *Globe*: Good value generous home-made bar food inc self-service lunchtime salad bar, well kept Whitbreads-related ales, comfortable mix of furnishings inc leather armchairs and sofas in several attractively contrived rooms radiating from central serving area; old panelling and beamery, bottle-glass screens, taxidermy, old prints *(D P Pascoe, Paul Cartledge, E M Hughes)*

☆ Truro [Kenwyn St], *William IV*: Good value buffet food inc some daily hot specials (very busy, so some things may run out) in elegantly tiled two-level conservatory dining room opening into flowery garden with plenty of tables; dark-panelled bar with slightly secluded raised areas and lots of bric-a-brac, well kept St Austell beers *(Anon)*

Truro [Lemon St], *Daniell Arms*: Wide range of good food lunchtime and evening inc lots of home-made pies; friendly landlord, attractive and welcoming interior *(Shirley Pielou)*; [Lemon Quay, by central car park], *Market*: Friendly and simply furnished town local with home-made food inc good Cornish pasties, well kept beer *(Eric and Shirley Broadhead, Mark Walker, LYM)*; [Little Castle St], *Onion*: Strictly a wine bar, but has Flowers IPA and quite pubby feel, as well as good range of wines and increasing range of tasty well cooked food *(John Wooll)*

☆ Veryan [SW9139], *New Inn*: Good value bar food in neatly kept village pub with friendly landlord, well kept St Austell tapped from the cask, quiet seats out behind; bedrooms *(P and K Lloyd, E M Hughes)*

☆ Zennor [SW4538], *Tinners Arms*: Good basic bar food, well kept St Austell real ales from barrels behind bar and decent coffee in plain but comfortable pub with lots of granite and stripped pine, dark, friendly and intimate; friendly cats, no music, tables outside; beautiful windswept setting nr coast path *(Gerald Cleaver, Brian and Jill Bond, Peter and Lynn Brueton, Gwen and Peter Andrews)*

Isles of Scilly

☆ St Marys – Hugh Town [The Strand; SV9010], *Atlantic*: The local favourite, with good cheery atmosphere, substantial helpings of unassuming but reliable bar food, well kept St Austell Tinners and HSD, great assortment of customers; big low-beamed L-shaped harbourside bar full of interesting nautical bric-a-brac, wreck salvage and photographs; piped music (may be obtrusive); family room, restaurant; good views, esp from small back jetty/terrace; bedrooms in adjacent hotel *(P and M Rudlin, BB)*

Tresco [SV8915], *Island*: Friendly hotel in beautiful location, with excellent reasonably priced food in very comfortably furnished bar areas; grounds superb except when it's raining, tables out on terrace by grass (with badminton); right by shore with sweeping sea and island views *(P and M Rudlin, BB)*

If we know a pub has an outdoor play area for children, we mention it.

Cumbria

For the second year running, this favoured county has quite a clutch of good new main entries: the civilised and individual Dukes Head at Armathwaite, the Royal at Dockray (recently very thoughtfully modernised, with particularly good wines and beers), the very characterful George & Dragon at Garrigill (very well kept beers) and the Sun at Newton Reigny (excellent food). All these have bedrooms – as do a very high proportion of existing main entries here; this is one of the best areas in Britain for finding friendly inns to stay at, often in lovely scenery. Drinks prices are well below the national average; the very traditional Golden Rule in Ambleside (tied to the regional brewer Robinsons) and the Blue Bell in Heversham (tied to Sam Smiths from Yorkshire) stand out as particularly cheap for drinks. In general, as elsewhere, we have found pubs supplied locally charge less for drinks than those relying on the national brewery chains, and it's always worth looking out for beer from Jennings and Yates. In the last few years a surprising number of Cumbrian pubs have started brewing their own beers, and the Sun at Dent (currently doing very well indeed), Cavendish Arms in Cartmel (lots of other real ales, too), the homely and idiosyncratic Old Crown at Hesket Newmarket and the Masons Arms on Cartmel Fell can all be recommended for their own brews. The Masons Arms is the region's best pub – immensely popular, and remarkable in this meat-loving part of the world for doing about 50% vegetarian food. Other pubs currently on top form here include that marvellous all-rounder the Royal Oak at Appleby, the friendly and relaxed Punch Bowl at Askham (good interesting food), the chatty old Hole in t' Wall at Bowness, the Pheasant at Casterton (doing really well under its fairly new Scottish owners), the extremely well run Drunken Duck near Hawkshead (its immense popularity with readers this year gaining it a star), the Watermill at Ings (exceptionally welcoming owners), the warmly friendly Shepherds at Melmerby (good food, outstanding cheeses), and the Queens Head at Troutbeck (this year joining the county's elite Food Award pubs). With several pubs serving outstanding food, it's the Royal Oak at Appleby which we choose as the county's Dining Pub of the Year, for its exhilarating combination of excellent atmosphere with lovely food. Among Lucky Dips currently showing well, we'd mention particularly the Turks Head in Alston, St Patricks Well at Bampton, Burnmoor at Boot, Engine at Cark in Cartmel, Butchers Arms at Crosby Ravensworth, Old Posting House at Deanscales, Sawrey at Far Sawrey, Howtown Hotel, Kings Arms in Kirkby Stephen, Abbey Bridge at Lanercost, both Middleton entries, Black Swan at Ravenstonedale, Queens Head at Tirril, Church House at Torver, Mortal Man at Troutbeck and Bay Horse at Winton. We've inspected most of these, so can certainly vouch for their quality; many are over in the Pennines, much less visited than the Lakes, so in most cases all that's keeping them out of the main entries is a relative shortage of reader reports. There's quite a varied choice in both Grasmere and Keswick.

ALSTON NY7246 Map 10

Angel

Front Street (A689)

Half way up the steep cobbled main street, sits this friendly 17th-c stone pub. The black-beamed and timbered L-shaped bar has logs burning in a big stone fireplace, wheelback chairs and traditional black wall seats around dimpled copper tables, horsebrasses on the beams, and brass pans and a coach-horn on the walls. Good value bar food, quickly served, includes sandwiches (from £1.20), home-made soup (£1.30), ploughman's (£2.80), salads (from £3.10), good Cumberland sausage (£3.45), mushroom and nut fettucini (£3.95), excellent Japanese prawns (£4.65), 12oz gammon and egg (£5.50), 8oz sirloin steak (£7.25), and puddings like sticky toffee or pavlova (£1.50); good Sunday roast, children's meals. Well kept Flowers IPA and Tetleys on handpump, and darts, dominoes, cribbage and piped music. A sheltered back garden has some picnic-table sets and umbrellas. *(Recommended by Jim and Maggie Cowell, H K Dyson, G W Lindley, Leonard Dixon, Bill Sharpe, Keith Croxton, JJW, CMW)*

Free house ~ Licensees Nicky and Sue Ashcroft ~ Real ale ~ Meals and snacks (not Tues evening) ~ Alston (01434) 381363 ~ Children welcome until 9pm ~ Open 11-4.30, 7-11 ~ Bedrooms: £13/£26

AMBLESIDE NY3804 Map 9

Golden Rule

Smithy Brow; follow Kirkstone Pass signpost from A591 on N side of town

After a trek over the fells, you can be sure of a friendly welcome from the landlord – even if your boots are a bit muddy. It's a traditional pub, popular with locals, with lots of local country pictures and a few fox masks decorating the butter-coloured walls, horsebrasses on the black beams, built-in leatherette wall seats, and cast-iron-framed tables. The room on the left has darts, a fruit machine and dominoes; the one down a few steps on the right is a quieter sitting room. Well kept Hartleys XB and Robinsons Bitter and Mild on handpump; some meals; friendly dog. There's a back yard with tables, a small pretty summer garden, and wonderfully colourful window boxes. The golden rule referred to in its name is a brass measuring yard mounted over the bar counter. *(Recommended by Helen Hazzard, H K Dyson, David Lewis, Mike and Jo, David Lands, John and Marianne Cooper, Tim Heywood, Sophie Wilne, Andrew Sykes)*

Hartleys (Robinsons) ~ Tenant John Lockley ~ Real ale ~ Meals and snacks ~ (015394) 33363 ~ Children welcome ~ Nearby parking virtually out of the question ~ Open 11-11

APPLEBY NY6921 Map 10

Royal Oak ★ ⑪ ⇌ ♀ ◧

Bongate; B6542 on S edge of town

Cumbrian Dining Pub of the Year

One of the nicest things about this very popular old-fashioned coaching inn is the licensees' happy knack for treating everyone as an individual. And that despite people flocking here from far and wide, the locals still feel very much at home. Part of the long, low building dates back to the 14th century, and the beamed lounge has old pictures on the timbered walls, some armchairs and a carved settle, and a panelling-and-glass snug enclosing the bar counter; there's a good open fire in the smaller, oak-panelled public bar; dominoes. From an imaginative and most comprehensive menu, the excellent home-made food might include superb soup with home-made bread (£1.50), lunchtime sandwiches such as home-cooked ham and beef (from £1.40), traditional lunchtime ploughman's (£2.50), green pancakes (£2.95), Cumberland sausage (made by hand by the local butcher's wife, £3), crab, prawn and cheese crêpes (£3.45), delicious brown

Lancashire shrimps (£3.75), vegetarian dishes, English gammon and egg, chicken breast with spinach and apple (£6.95), pork fillet with mushrooms, madeira and cream (£7.95), simply cooked fresh fish such as baby Dover sole, cod, halibut or baby sea bass (from £5.95), and steaks; adventurous daily specials, children's meals, and puddings. One of the dining rooms is no smoking. They keep a marvellous range of around eight real ales on handpump: Bongate Special Pale Ale (their own beer made locally), Jennings Cumberland, McEwans 70/-, Scottish Oatmeal Stout, Theakstons Best, Yates Bitter and Premium, Youngers Scotch, and regular guests; several malt whiskies, and a carefully chosen wine list with 10 by the glass and quite a few half bottles. In summer the outside is very colourful, with seats on the front terrace among masses of flowers in tubs, troughs and hanging baskets. You can get here on the scenic Leeds/Settle/Carlisle railway. *(Recommended by Luke Worthington, BDA, Jan and Dave Booth, S R and A J Ashcroft, Gwen and Peter Andrews, Geoffrey and Brenda Wilson, Mike and Ann Beiley, H K Dyson, Mr and Mrs R Head, Jane Kingsbury, Lucy James, Dr RKP, Jeff Davies, Angela Steele, David Heath, David and Margaret Bloomfield, Simon Watkins, Jill Bickerton, Malcolm Taylor, P Boot, Steve and Julie Cocking, Gill and Maurice McMahon, Alan Wilcock, Christine Davidson, Roger and Jillian Shaw, R D Greaves)*

Free house ~ Licensees Colin and Hilary Cheyne ~ Real ale ~ Meals and snacks (12-2, 6-9; not 25 Dec) ~ Restaurant ~ (017683) 51463 ~ Well behaved children welcome ~ Open 11-3, 6-11; closed 25 Dec ~ Bedrooms: £26.50(£39.75B)/ £57.50B

See also entry under nearby BRAMPTON

ARMATHWAITE NY5146 Map 10

Dukes Head 🛏

Off A6 a few miles S of Carlisle

In a quiet Eden Valley village below the Pennines, this well kept inn has a civilised lounge bar with oak settles and little armchairs among more upright seats, oak and mahogany tables, antique hunting and other prints, and some brass and copper powder-flasks above its coal fire. Good home-cooked bar food includes soup (£1.80), warmed potted shrimps (£2.95), vegetarian dishes such as leek and cheese quiche (£4.50) or pasta parcels (£5.90), omelettes (£4.75), gammon and egg (£5.90), trout fillets with nut butter or wild salmon (£6.95), venison (£7.80), sirloin steak (£8.30), and their particular pride, roast duck (£8.50), with children's dishes (£3.20) and old-fashioned puddings. The breakfasts are huge. Well kept Tetleys and Whitbreads Castle Eden on handpump, decent wines, welcoming licensees, nostalgic piped music; separate public bar with darts and pool, two games machines and juke box in back lobby. There are tables out on the lawn behind. *(Recommended by G R Prest, John Oddey, William Osborn-King, Richard Holloway, Jean and Douglas Troup, David Heath, Paul and Ursula Roberts)*

Free house ~ Licensee Peter Lynch ~ Real ale ~ Meals and snacks ~ Restaurant ~ (0169 74) 72226 ~ Children welcome ~ Open 11-3, 6-11; closed 25 Dec ~ Bedrooms: £20(£25B)/£35(£40B)

ASKHAM NY5123 Map 9

Punch Bowl

Village signposted on right from A6 4 miles S of Penrith

Warmly welcoming and relaxed, this well run pub is quietly set facing the lower village green. Interesting furnishings in the rambling bar include Chippendale dining chairs and rushwork ladder-back seats around the sturdy wooden tables, well cushioned window seats in the white-painted thick stone walls, an antique settle by an open log fire, coins stuck into the cracks of the dark wooden beams (periodically taken out and sent to charity), and local photographs and prints of Askham. The old-fashioned woodburning stove, with its gleaming stainless chimney in the big main fireplace, is largely decorative. Big helpings of interesting bar food include home-made soup (£2.10), fine lunchtime sandwiches with side salad (£2.50), pork and bacon pâté (£2.70), pies like pork and apple or venison with red wine and mushrooms (from £4.95), chicken biryani (£5.85), chicken fritters (£5.95), delicious beef casserole or good spare ribs (£6.10), Mexican bean pot (£6.80), fisherman's pot (£7.50), and steaks (from £6.90); children's dishes (£2.80). Some dishes may run out on busy evenings. A well kept monthly guest beer like Morlands Old Speckled Hen, Timothy Taylors Landlord, and Whitbreads Castle Eden on handpump kept under light blanket pressure; several malt whiskies and wines; cribbage and piped pop music, and in the separate, recently decorated public bar darts, pool, juke box and fruit machine. There are tables out on a flower-filled terrace. *(Recommended by Malcolm Phillips, Ian and Deborah Carrington, S and D Shaw, Kathryn and Brian Heathcote, Lucy James, Dr RLP, H K Dyson, N H and A G Harries, Tony Walker, Graham Fogelman, George Dundas, TBB)*

Whitbreads ~ Lease: David and Frances Riley ~ Real ale ~ Snacks (lunchtime) and meals ~ Restaurant ~ Hackthorpe (01931) 712443 ~ Children welcome until 9pm ~ Open 11.30-3, 6.30-11; 12-3, 7-11 in winter ~ Bedrooms: £18.50/£37

Queens Head

Village crossroads by lower green

Under a new licensee, this well kept, friendly pub has two comfortably furnished lounge rooms with an open fire, beams hung with gleaming copper, and brass and horsebrasses. Decent bar food includes lunchtime sandwiches (from £1.50), soup (£1.60), ploughman's (from £3.25), salads (from £4.10), good steak in ale pie (£4.45), steaks (from £8.25), and puddings. Well kept Wards Sheffield Best on handpump; darts, dominoes and piped music. The garden has a waterfall, fountain and fish, and the pub is handy for the Lowther Wildlife Park. *(Recommended by H K Dyson, Roger Berry, David Cooke, Dr Sherriff; more reports please)*

Vaux ~ Tenant Sylvia Anderson ~ Real ale ~ Meals and snacks ~ Restaurant ~ (01931) 712225 ~ Children in back bar and in dining room ~ Open 11.30-3, 6.30-11 ~ Bedrooms: £18.50/£37

BARBON SD6383 Map 10

Barbon Inn 🛏

Village signposted off A683 Kirkby Lonsdale—Sedbergh; OS Sheet 97 map reference 628826

The lovely sheltered garden here is very prettily planted and neatly kept, and nicely floodlit at night, and there are tracks and paths leading up to the fells. Pony trekking and golf nearby. Inside, several small rooms lead off the main bar, each individually and comfortably furnished: carved 18th-c oak settles, deep chintzy sofas and armchairs, a Victorian fireplace, and lots of fresh flowers. Decent bar food includes sandwiches (from £1.75), excellent soup (£1.75), tasty Morecambe Bay potted shrimps (£4.25), duck and chicken liver pâté (£3.25), Cumberland sausage (£4.50), platters and salads (from £4.75), home-roasted ham (£4.95), home-made steak and kidney pie (£5.75), sirloin steak (£9.50), and puddings like home-made fruit pie (from £2.25). Well kept Theakstons Best and Old Peculier on handpump, and quite a few wines; polite, helpful service; dominoes and piped music. *(Recommended by Wayne Brindle, A P Jeffreys, L Grant, H K Dyson, Sue Holland, Dave Webster, Barbara Wensworth, Kim Schofield, BDA, Gill and Mike Cross, Denis and Margaret Kilner, Malcolm Taylor, R J Herd, Alan Wilcock, Christine Davidson, Gill and Maurice McMahon)*

Free house ~ Licensee Lindsey MacDiarmid ~ Real ale ~ Meals and snacks ~ No smoking restaurant ~ Barbon (0152 42) 76233 ~ Children welcome ~ Open 12-3, 6.30-11 ~ Bedrooms: £32/£55(£66B)

BASSENTHWAITE NY2332 Map 9

Sun

Village itself, signposted off A591 a few miles NW of Keswick

In a charming village, this pleasant former farmhouse is popular for its generously served food. The landlady is from the Lakes, while her husband is Italian, and the surprisingly wide ranger of dishes draws on both their backgrounds: minestrone soup (£1.50), squid in batter (£2.50), ploughman's (£3.50), Lancashire hotpot (£4), salads (from £4.50), steak and kidney pie, good vegetarian or meaty lasagne with garlic bread (£5), pork steaks in mushroom sauce (£5), sirloin steak (£8), and puddings such as syrup sponge or sticky toffee pudding (£2). Well kept Jennings on handpump. Though the inn looks tiny from outside, its bar rambles around into areas that stretch usefully back on both sides of the servery. There are low 17th-c black oak beams, lots of brasses, built-in wall seats and plush stools around heavy wooden tables, and a good stone fireplace with big logs burning in winter; fruit machine; no dogs. A huddle of white houses looks up to Skiddaw and other high fells, and you can enjoy the view from the tables in the pub's front yard, by a neighbour's blackberry bush. *(Recommended by David Heath, Nick Cox, N H White, Brian and Jill Bond, Peter and Lynn Brueton, Michael Wadsworth, A Preston, Mr and Mrs L D Rainger, John Allsopp, D T Taylor, Mike Muston, H K Dyson)*

Jennings ~ Tenants Giuseppe and Josephine Scopelliti ~ Real ale ~ Meals and snacks (12-1.30, 6.30-8.30ish; not Sun evening) ~ Keswick (0176 87) 76439 ~ Children in side rooms whenever possible ~ Open 12-2.30, 6-11; may close earlier winter lunchtimes if very quiet; closed Mon lunchtimes Nov-Mar

BASSENTHWAITE LAKE NY1930 Map 9

Pheasant ★ 🛏

Follow Wythop Mill signpost at N end of dual carriageway stretch of A66 by Bassenthwaite Lake

The pubby little bars in this rather smart civilised hotel are surprisingly old-fashioned and relaxed, with drinks served from a hatch at a low serving counter, and furnishings like rush-seat chairs, library seats and cushioned settles, and hunting prints and photographs on the fine ochre walls. Well kept Bass and Theakstons Best on handpump, lots of malt whiskies, and elderflower, raspberry and strawberry wines. Good, freshly made lunchtime bar food includes soup (£1.40), ploughman's or Cumberland pork and ham pie (£3.50), salmon mousse (£3.70), smoked local Herdwick lamb with melon (£3.90), vegetable and nut terrine with minted yoghurt dressing (£4.40), sweet smoked chicken (£4.70), and smoked venison, duck and Cumberland sauce (£4.90); there's a wider range of very good food in the elegant no-smoking restaurant. If the bars are full, you might want to move to the large and airy beamed lounge at the back, which has easy chairs on its polished parquet floor and a big log fire on cool days; there are also some chintzy sitting rooms with antique furniture (one is no smoking). The hotel is surrounded by very attractive woodlands, with beeches, larches and Douglas firs, and you can walk into them from the garden. This is a very good walking area. *(Recommended by V and E A Bolton, Jerry and Alison Oakes, Lynn Sharpless, Bob Eardley, P D and J Bickley, Cath and John Howard, WAH, N H White, Nigel Woolliscroft, John Allsopp, John Evans, Mr and Mrs D E Powell, H K Dyson, J E Rycroft, John Allsopp, Stephen Newell, Heather M N Robson; also recommended by The Good Hotel Guide)*

Free house ~ Licensee W E Barrington Wilson ~ Real ale ~ Lunchtime snacks (no bar food Sun evening) ~ Restaurant ~ Bassenthwaite Lake (0176 87) 76234 ~ Children welcome (not Sun) ~ Open 11(11.30 in winter)-3, 5.30-10.30(11 Sat); closed 24/25 Dec ~ Bedrooms: £52B/£70B

BEETHAM SD5079 Map 7

Wheatsheaf 🛏

Village (and inn) signposted just off A6 S of Milnthorpe

Built in 1609, this fine old building was a coaching inn for travellers on the main London to Scotland road. It's still popular with those seeking a rest from what is now the A6, and there's a chatty, relaxed atmosphere in lounge bar – as well as lots of exposed beams and joists, attractive built-in wall settles, tapestry-cushioned chairs, a massive antique carved oak armchair, and a cabinet filled with foreign costume dolls. Beyond a little central snug is a tiled-floor bar with darts and dominoes. Good, reasonably priced home-made bar food includes soup (£1.30), sandwiches (from £1.70), home-made hotpot (£3.10), ploughman's (£3.75), home-made pies like cheese or steak and kidney (from £3.20), sausage, liver and bacon (£3.40), salads (from £3.60), steaks (from £6.75), daily specials, and puddings (from £1.50); courteous, friendly staff. If the bar is too crowded, you can eat in the upstairs dining room for the same price. Well kept Boddingtons and Thwaites Bitter on handpump, and quite a few malt whiskies. *(Recommended by Mr and Mrs K H Frostick, R D Knight, Cath and John Howard, Derek and Margaret Underwood, Anthony Barnes, Miss D P Barson, A T Langton)*

Free house ~ Licensee Mrs Margaret Shaw ~ Real ale ~ Meals and snacks (11.45-1.45, 6-8.45; not evenings 25/26 Dec, 1 Jan) ~ Restaurant ~ Milnthorpe (0153 95) 62123 ~ Children welcome till 8.30 ~ Open 11-3, 6-11; closed evenings 25/26 Dec ~ Bedrooms: £30B/£40B

BOWLAND BRIDGE SD4289 Map 9

Hare & Hounds 🛏

Village signposted from A5074; OS Sheet 97 map reference 417895

Quietly set in the Winster Valley, this popular and friendly Lakeland pub is pretty in summer with climbing roses, window boxes and hanging baskets; there are picnic-table sets in the spacious garden at one side, with more by the road. The comfortably modernised bar, divided into smaller areas by stone walls, has oak beams, ladder-back chairs around dark wood tables on the spread of turkey carpet, Liverpool and England team photographs and caps (the landlord used to play for both), reproduction hunting prints, a stuffed pheasant, and open fires. Good helpings of bar food include soup (£1.40), sandwiches (from £1.50), pizzas (from £3.95), salads (from £4.25), Cumberland sausage or filled Yorkshire puddings (£4.50), coq au vin (£5.50), steaks (from £8.95), and daily specials like home-made steak and mushroom pie (£5.75) and fresh poached salmon (£6.25); very good, prompt service. Well kept Tetleys on handpump, from a long bar counter with a cushioned red leatherette elbow rest for people using the sensible backrest-type bar stools. Dominoes, fruit machine and piped music. The pub is by the bridge itself. *(Recommended by Mark Bradley, Colin and Shirley Brown, LM, Margaret and Arthur Dickinson, S R and A I Ashcroft, Malcolm Taylor, Tony Bland, Denis and Margaret Kilner)*

Free house ~ Licensee Peter Thompson ~ Real ale ~ Meals and snacks ~ Restaurant (residents only) ~ Crosthwaite (0153 95) 68333 ~ Children welcome ~ Open 11-3, 5.30-11; winter evening opening 6pm ~ Bedrooms: £33/£46 (not all have bathrooms)

BOWNESS ON WINDERMERE SD4097 Map 9

Hole in t' Wall 🍺

Full of interest and character, this is the sort of place where locals and visitors mingle. The atmosphere is lively and chatty and the licensees friendly and caring. The bar has lots to look at such as giant smith's bellows, and old farm implements and ploughshares, and a room upstairs has handsome plasterwork in its coffered ceiling. On cool days a splendid log fire burns under a vast slate mantelbeam. The tiny flagstoned front courtyard (where there are sheltered seats) has an ancient outside flight of stone steps to the upper floor. Good bar food includes sandwiches (from £1.80), vegetarian ratatouille with cheese topping and garlic bread (£4.50), chicken and leek lasagne, home-made fish pie with tuna, prawns and haddock or steak and kidney pie (£4.85), and popular whole roast pheasant with red wine sauce (£5.95). Hartleys XB and Robinsons Frederics, Best, Old Stockport, and Old Hutters Mild on handpump in excellent condition; darts, pool, fruit machine and juke box upstairs. If you'd rather catch it on a quiet day, it's better to visit out of season. *(Recommended by Elizabeth and Anthony Watts, John and Marianne Cooper, Alan and Ruth Woodhouse, Richard Lewis, Chris Cook, David Lands, P Barnsley, Andrew Hazeldine, John Evans)*

Hartleys (Robinsons) ~ Tenants: Andrew and Audrey Mitton ~ Real ale ~ Meals and snacks (not Sun evening) ~ (0153 94) 43488 ~ Children in family room off taproom until 9pm ~ Parking nearby can be difficult ~ Open 11-11

BRAITHWAITE NY2324 Map 9

Coledale Inn

Village signposted off A66 W of Keswick; pub then signed left off B5292

Mr and Mrs Mawdsley's two sons now run this popular, cream-coloured house. The left-hand bar has fine views of Skiddaw and the much closer bracken-covered hills from the window seats, a winter coal fire, and little 19th-c Lakeland engravings; the green-toned bar on the right, with a bigger bay window, is more of a dining bar. Simple, reliable food includes home-made soup (£1.30), sandwiches (from £1.60), filled baked potatoes (from £2.70), platters (from £3.20), ploughman's (from £4), Cumberland sausage (£4.80), gammon and egg (£5.30), 14oz steak (£11.50), and puddings with custard or cream (£1.75); daily specials and several children's dishes (£1.75). Well kept Jennings, Theakstons, Yates and Youngers Scotch on handpump, and coffee, tea and hot chocolate; winter darts, dominoes, trivia and piped music, friendly service. The dining room is partly no smoking. The pub is perfectly placed at the foot of the Whinlatter Pass, and walkers can start their hike straight from the door. On a sunny day it's hard to beat sitting in the quiet garden, with its tables and chairs on the slate terrace beyond the sheltered lawn. *(Recommended by V and E A Bolton, Nick Cox, WAH, Dave Davey, Sarah Bertram, D Hanley, Adrian and Gilly Heft, David Cooke, H K Dyson, Tim Gilroy, Mr and Mrs D E Powell)*

Free house ~ Licensees Geoffrey and Michael Mawdsley ~ Real ale ~ Meals and snacks ~ Braithwaite (017687) 78272 ~ Children welcome until 9.30pm ~ Open 11-11 ~ Bedrooms: £25S/£50S

BRAMPTON NY6723 Map 10

New Inn

Note: this is the small Brampton near Appleby, not the bigger one up by Carlisle. Off A66 N of Appleby – follow Long Marton 1 signpost then turn right at church; village also signposted off B6542 at N end of Appleby

The two cosy little rooms of the bar in this 18th-c black-and-white slated building have a good range of local pictures (mainly sheep and wildlife), and a medley of seats including panelled oak settles and a nice little oak chair; a stuffed fox is curled on top of the corner TV, and a red squirrel pokes out of a little hole in the dividing wall. The particularly interesting flagstoned dining room has horsebrasses on its low black beams, well spaced tables, and a splendid original black cooking range at one end, separated from the door by an immensely sturdy old oak built-in settle. Good bar food includes lunchtime sandwiches (from £1.20), home-made soup (£1.50), home-made chicken liver pâté with gooseberry sauce (£2.50), Morecambe Bay shrimps (£2.95), pizzas (from £3.60), Cumberland sausage and egg (£3.60), vegetable curry (£4.50), steak and kidney pie (£4.60), chicken and cheese crunch (£4.95), spicy stroganoff (£6.95), sirloin steak (£7.95), and puddings like fruit crumble or treacle sponge (£2); 3-course Sunday lunch (£6.50, children £3). Well kept Boddingtons, Theakstons Best, Whitbreads Castle Eden and Youngers Scotch on handpump, and a good choice of whiskies with some eminent malts; friendly service, darts, cribbage and dominoes. No dogs in bedrooms. In June, the Appleby Horse Fair tends to base itself here. Incidentally another Brampton near Chesterfield has a pub of the same name. *(Recommended by Dave Davey, Graham and Belinda Staplehurst, Neil and Jenny Spink, Gill and Maurice McMahon)*

Free house ~ Licensees Roger and Anne Cranswick ~ Real ale ~ Meals and snacks ~ Restaurant ~ Kirkby Thore (0176 83) 51231 ~ Children welcome ~ Open 12-3, 6-11 ~ Bedrooms: £18/£36

BUTTERMERE   NY1817 Map 9

Bridge Hotel 🛏

Many walkers make their way to the friendly comfortable lounge bar here after enjoying some of the best steep countryside in the county, and Crummock Water and Buttermere are just a stroll away. In the summer food is served all day, starting with breakfast in the lounge bar between 9 and 10, and they do afternoon tea and have a high tea menu too. The beamed bar is divided into two parts and furnished with settles and brocaded armchairs around copper-topped tables, a panelled bar counter, and some brass ornaments; the flagstoned area is good for walking boots. Good bar food includes home-made soup (£1.90), open sandwiches or ploughman's (£3.60), leek and onion tart (£4.80), Cumbrian hotpot (£5.30), salads (from £5.90), hare, venison and rabbit pie (£6), gammon with an egg and pineapple or poached Borrowdale trout (£6.20), steaks (from £8.70), and puddings (£2.30); Sunday lunch (£5.20); the restaurant is no smoking. Well kept Black Sheep Best and Special, Theakstons XB and Old Peculier and Youngers No. 3 on handpump, a large wine list, over 20 malt whiskies, and tea, coffee and hot chocolate; dominoes, cribbage. Outside, a flagstoned terrace has white tables by a rose-covered sheltering stone wall. *(Recommended by Dave Lands, J B Neame, Bronwen and Steve Wrigley, S and D Shaw, Sara Geyer, Mick Whelton, Mr and Mrs S Ashcroft, Tim Gilroy, Mike Muston, Elizabeth and Anthony Watts, John and Diana Elsy)*

Free house ~ Licensee Peter McGuire ~ Real ale ~ Meals and snacks (12-2.30, 3-5.30, 6-9.30) ~ Evening restaurant ~ (0176 87) 70252 ~ Children welcome ~ Open 10.30-11 ~ Bedrooms: £35B/£70B; also, self-catering apartments

CARTMEL   SD38879 Map

Cavendish Arms

Off main sq

As we went to press, Nick Murray told us they were hoping to open their own brewery here, brewing two bitters to start with. They also keep up to eight other real ales on handpump – such as Ballards Wild, Bass, Butterknowle Bitter, Harviestoun 80/-, Ruddles County, John Smiths, and Stocks Select. Bar food includes lunchtime things such as open sandwiches (£2.50; hot beef and onion £2.95), home-made burgers (from £2.50), good filled baked potatoes (from £2.95), and filled pancakes (£3.75), as well as home-made soup (£1.75), home-made chicken liver pâté (£2.95), home-made plaice goujons (from £3.85), vegetable stir-fry (£4.75), steak and kidney pie (£4.95), mixed grill (£5.75), chicken with a lemon and coriander sauce (£7.95), steaks using Aberdeen beef (from £9.75), and venison steak (£10.95); they hold regular food theme nights including a popular medieval one; helpful staff and a very nice atmosphere. Darts, cribbage, dominoes. There are tables in front of the pub, with more at the back by the stream, and their flower displays tend to win awards. The landlord will take inexperienced fell walkers on guided treks over the mountains. *(Recommended by Janis and Neil Hedgecock, Mrs C Thexton, A T Langton, Gill and Maurice McMahon, Malcolm Taylor)*

Free house ~ Tom and Nick Murray ~ Real ale ~ Meals and snacks (12-2.15, 6-9.30) ~ Restaurant ~ (0153 95) 36240 ~ Children welcome until 8.30pm in bar ~ Open 11.30-11 ~ Bedrooms: £20B/£40B

Kings Arms

The Square

The rambling bar in this rather grand little black and white pub has handsome heavy beams, a mixture of seats including old country chairs, settles and wall banquettes, a fox's mask and small antique prints on the walls, and tankards hanging over the serving counter. Bar food includes open sandwiches (from £2.20), filled baked potatoes (from £2.90), Cumberland sausage (£4.85), lasagne (£5.10), roast beef and Yorkshire pudding (£6.50), and a big mixed grill

(£10.95), with daily specials such as steak and kidney pie or Chinese-style turkey steak (£5.50); they also have a tea shop (open all day) with home-made cakes. The restaurant is no smoking. Well kept Flowers IPA and Wards Darleys Thorne; darts, fruit machine, piped music. Seats outside make the most of the lovely square. This ancient village has a grand priory church, and close to the pub is a fine medieval stone gatehouse; the race track is 200 yards away. Coach parties are welcome. *(Recommended by Elizabeth and Anthony Watts; more reports please)*

Whitbreads ~ Lease: Graham Hamlett ~ Real ale ~ Meals and snacks (all day) ~ Restaurant (open all day) ~ (0153 95) 36220 ~ Children welcome ~ Open 10.30-11

CARTMEL FELL SD4288 Map 9

Masons Arms ★ ★ 🍺

Strawberry Bank, a few miles S of Windermere between A592 and A5074; perhaps the simplest way of finding the pub is to go uphill W from Bowland Bridge (which is signposted off A5074) towards Newby Bridge and keep right then left at the staggered crossroads – it's then on your right, below Gummer's How; OS Sheet 97 map reference 413895

Nigel Stevenson has done a great deal for beer lovers in the North West. The 24-page booklet in which he clearly describes hundreds of imported beers, most stocked and some even imported by him, is now in its 14th edition and, considering its scale, is unique. You can be sure of finding some beers here that simply don't exist anywhere else in the country. He does a brisk trade for instance in Liefmanskriek and Liefmansframbozen (cherry and raspberry beer from Belgium), has two authentic German beers (Furstenberg Export from the Black Forest and St Georgen Dunkel, a dark lager from Franconia), a genuine Dutch Trappist beer, La Trappe Blonde, on draught (very rarely on draught even in Holland itself), Bitburger Pils on draught, and a tap for wheat beers which he is finding remarkably popular. Many of the beers have their own particular-shaped glasses. On the five handpumps he includes two beers he brews himself – Amazon (light and hoppy but quite strong), Big Six or Great Northern, and usually Black Sheep Special, Thwaites Bitter, and a guest. He usually makes his own damson beer (depending on the fruit crop), has recently made Morocco Ale to an ancient recipe for a local stately home, and makes cider using mainly local apples, calling it Knickerbocker-breaker. As well as house wine, the Stevensons keep two white and two red guest wines, often from Australia and Chile. Popular wholesome food (lots of vegetarian choices) includes soup (from £2.25), sandwiches (from £2.95), hot stuffed vine leaves with a sun-dried tomato sauce (£3.95), hazelnut and lentil pâté (£4.95), ploughman's (£5.25), pasta al pesto (£5.95), fisherman's pie (£6.25), Cumberland sausage and cider casserole or rogan josh (£7.25), home-made puddings (£2.50), and daily specials such as spicy vegetable garlic crumble (£5.95), roasted Mediterranean vegetable strudel (£6.25), brazil nut and almond roast layered with cranberries (£6.50), and Flemish beef carbonnade (£7.50); quick service. The main bar has low black beams in the bowed ceiling, country chairs and plain wooden tables on polished flagstones, and a grandly Gothick seat with snarling dogs as its arms. A small lounge has oak tables and settles to match its fine Jacobean panelling, and a plain little room beyond the serving counter has pictures and a fire in an open range; the family room has an old-parlourish atmosphere. This year, they've opened an upstairs room which helps at peak times. The setting overlooking the Winster Valley to the woods below Whitbarrow Scar is unrivalled and a good terrace with rustic benches and tables makes the most of the dramatic view. They sell leaflets outlining local walks of varying lengths and difficulty. As it's such a favourite with so many people, don't be surprised if the bar is extremely crowded; it's often much quieter mid-week. *(Recommended by Paul McPherson, P Barnsley, Ewan and Moira McCall, Mike and Wendy Proctor, LM, Sharron Thompson, Lucy James, Dr RKP, Lynn Sharpless, Bob Eardley, Mick Hitchman, Cath and John Howard, TBB, Karen Eliot, Helen Hazzard, Derek and Margaret Underwood, Tina and David Woods-Taylor, Mr and Mrs Rankine, John Scarisbrick, John and Marianne Cooper, S R and A I Ashcroft, Nigel Woolliscroft, Mark Bradley, Julie and Andy Hawkins, David Lands, Colin Davies, D Grzelka, Philip Dixon, M Hitchman, Dr David Webster, Sue Holland, John and Diana Elsy, Mr and Mrs J Denham-Vaughan, David Wallington, Gill and Maurice McMahon)*

Own brew ~ Licensees Helen and Nigel Stevenson ~ Real ale ~ Meals and snacks (12-2, 6-8.45) ~ Crosthwaite (0153 95) 68486 ~ Children welcome till 9.30pm ~ Open 11.30-3, 6-11 ~ Four self-catering flats and two self-catering cottages available

CASTERTON SD6279 Map 7

Pheasant 🛏 ♀

A683 about a mile N of junction with A65, by Kirkby Lonsdale; OS sheet 97 map reference 633796

Doing very well under the present licensees, this civilised white-painted inn has a relaxed and warmly friendly atmosphere. The two comfortably modernised, beamed rooms of the main bar have padded wheelback chairs, plush wall settles, newspapers and magazines to read, an open log fire in a nicely arched bare stone fireplace with polished brass hood, and souvenir mugs on the mantelpiece; there's a further room across the passage. Well kept Jennings, Ind Coope Burton and Tetleys on handpump, a small but good wine list from Corney & Barrow, and an increasing range of malt whiskies. Good, popular bar food includes home-made soup (£2.25), sandwiches (from £2.25), prawn and gruyère pot (£4.50), salads (from £4.50), omelettes (£4.75), mixed chilli bean casserole or locally-made black pudding and bacon grill (£4.95), good mince collops or home-made fish cakes (£5.25), home-made steak and kidney pie (£5.50), daily specials like Thai prawns, lamb balti (£6.95) and langoustine salad or fish mixed grill (£7.95), and puddings (£2.50); hearty breakfasts; they have a new char-grill this year. The restaurant and garden room are no smoking; darts, dominoes and piped music. There are some tables with cocktail parasols outside by the road. The nearby church (built for the girls' school of Brontë fame here) has some attractive pre-Raphaelite stained glass and paintings. *(Recommended by Frank Cummins, Les and Jean Scott, Kim Schofield, W G Burden, Neil Townend, John Allsopp, Dr J A Caldwell, H K Dyson, K H and P C Richards, R J Herd, Robert Neill, Dr I M Ingram)*

Free house ~ Licensees Melvin and May Mackie ~ Real ale ~ Meals and snacks ~ Restaurant ~ Kirkby Lonsdale (0152 42) 71230 ~ Children welcome ~ Open 11-3, 6-11; closed one week Jan ~ Bedrooms: £32B/£40B

CHAPEL STILE NY3205 Map 9

Wainwrights

B5343

There are lots of good walks around this white-rendered Lakeland house, and you can enjoy its lovely fellside position from the picnic-table sets out on the terrace. Inside, there's a comfortable welcoming atmosphere and plenty of room in the characterful slate-floored bar with its old kitchen range and cushioned settles; half the pub is no smoking. Good food includes soup (£1.80), sandwiches (from £1.95), filled baked potatoes (from £2.75), children's dishes (£2.45; free lollipop and children's cocktails, too), and changing daily specials such as battered cod (£5.25), baked stuffed local rainbow trout or vegetarian kebabs with mild korma sauce (£5.95), and seafood medley (£6.95); good, prompt service. Well kept Theakstons Best, XB and Old Peculier with a summer guest beer like Marstons Pedigree or Morlands Old Speckled Hen on handpump and a decent wine list; dominoes, fruit machine, trivia and piped music. *(Recommended by Roger and Christine Mash, Sara Geyer, Mick Whelton, V and E A Bolton, Ewan and Moira McCall, Philip Orbell, John E Crowe)*

Matthew Brown (S & N) ~ Manager Christopher Gibson ~ Real ale ~ Meals and snacks (12-2, 6-9.30) ~ (0153 94) 37302 ~ Children welcome ~ Quiz night Weds evening, Folk music Thurs evening ~ Open 11.30-11; 11-3, 6-11 in winter

---

It's very helpful if you let us know up-to-date food prices when you report on pubs.

COCKERMOUTH NY1231 Map 9

Trout 🛏

Crown St

This bustling 17th-c inn – next to William Wordsworth's birthplace – is well run and friendly, and the comfortable bar has low pink plush sofas and captain's chairs around dark polished tables, some patterned plates on the walls, pot plants, and an open fire in the stone fireplace; the coffee lounge and restaurant are no smoking. Well kept Bass, Jennings Cumberland, Morlands Old Speckled Hen and Worthington Best on handpump, over 50 malt whiskies, wines of the month, and freshly squeezed orange or grapefruit juices; piped music. Bar food includes home-made soup such as lettuce and curry cream (£1.40), soup and a sandwich (from £3.60), chicken pâté with cognac and fresh basil (£2.50), ploughman's or vegetable tandoori (£4.50), Cumbrian tattie pot or gammon and egg (£4.95), home-made steak, kidney and mushroom pie (£5.45), Cantonese prawns (£6.70), 8oz sirloin steak (£8.95), daily specials like poached delice of Lakeland salmon or roast rib of English beef with Yorkshire pudding (£5.95), and puddings like golden crunchy syrup tart or fresh fruit salad (£2.25); prompt, courteous staff. In summer you can eat in the pretty gardens, next to the River Derwent. There are private fishing rights for guests, and the hotel runs fly fishing courses. Dogs welcome. *(Recommended by Ian Fraser, I H Rorison, David Gittins, Mr and Mrs L D Rainger)*

Free house ~ Licensee Gill Blackah ~ Real ale ~ Meals and snacks ~ Restaurant ~ Cockermouth (01900) 823591 ~ Children welcome ~ Open 10.30-3, 5.30-11 ~ Bedrooms: £54.95B/£69.95B

CONISTON SD3098 Map 9

Sun 🛏

Inn signposted from centre

At the foot of the mountains with tracks from the lane leading straight up to the Old Man of Coniston, this substantial stone inn doubles as a mountain rescue post. There are white tables out on the terrace, and a big, tree-sheltered garden; fishing, riding and shooting can all be arranged for residents. Inside, the back bar has cask seats (one pair remarkably heavy), spindleback chairs and brown plush built-in wall benches around the traditional cast-iron-framed tables, and a small but very warm log fire. The floors are part carpeted, part handsome polished flagstones, and the walls are covered wth lots of Lakeland colour photographs and some recalling Donald Campbell (this was his HQ during his final attempt on the world water speed record). Home-made bar food includes a good soup of the day (£1.50), sandwiches (from £1.80; toasties from £2.50), filled baked potatoes (from £2.65), omelettes (£2.95), lamb curry (£4), fried fish (from £4.25), meat or fish pies (from £4.95), gammon and egg (£5.95), sirloin steak (£8.25), and puddings like sticky toffee (£2.25). The restaurant is no smoking. Jennings, Tetleys and a guest like Black Sheep Bitter on handpump, from the deep 16th-c granite cellar; friendly staff; darts, dominoes, piped music. As we went to press, we heard that the inn was up for sale. *(Recommended by Mr and Mrs Rankine, John Allsopp, David Heath, D J and P M Taylor, L Grant, V and E A Bolton, David Lands, GSB, Tina and David Woods-Taylor, Stephen Newell, Greg Parston, Andrew Hazeldine, Mike and Jo, Roy and Bettie Derbyshire, J E Rycroft)*

Free house ~ Licensees Richard, Philip and Stephen Elson ~ Real ale ~ Meals and snacks; not 24-26 Dec ~ Restaurant ~ Coniston (0153 94) 41248 ~ Children in restaurant and eating area of bar till 9pm ~ Open 11-11 ~ Bedrooms: £35B/£70B

DENT SD7187 Map 10

Sun

Village signposted from Sedbergh; and from Barbon, off A683

This pretty pub's own Dent Brewery is set up in a converted barn some three miles up in the dale, and produces their Bitter, Ramsbottom and T'Owd Tup – which they also supply to other pubs all over the country. They also keep Tetleys Bitter on handpump. The friendly bar, busy with walkers and motorists, has a pleasant traditional atmosphere, fine old oak timbers and beams studded with coins, as well as dark armed chairs, brown leatherette wall benches, lots of local snapshots and old Schweppes advertisements on the walls, and a coal fire; one of the areas is no smoking. Through the arch to the left are banquettes upholstered to match the carpet (as are the curtains). Good value, straightforward bar food includes home-made soup (£1.25), sandwiches (from £1.45), ploughman's (£2.95), home-made pasties or chilli con carne (£3.05), home-made steak and kidney pie (£3.65), Cumberland sausage (£3.95), gammon and pineapple (£4.55), rump steak (£5.15), puddings (£1.60), and children's helpings (£2); pleasant, prompt service; good breakfasts. Darts, pool, dominoes, cribbage, fruit machine, and juke box (in the pool room). There are rustic seats and tables outside. *(Recommended by Richard Lewis, Tina and David Woods-Taylor, CW, JW, David Eberlin, Derek and Margaret Underwood, Richard Houghton, Kim Schofield, H K Dyson, Paul McPherson, Dono and Carol Leaman, Peter and Lynn Brueton, Julie and Andy Hawkins, Mary Moore, David Wallington, J Dearn, David Varney, A T Langton)*

Own brew ~ Licensee Martin Stafford ~ Real ale ~ Meals and snacks (not 25 Dec) ~ Dent (0153 96) 25208 ~ Children welcome until 9pm ~ Open 11-11; 11-3, 7-11 in winter; closed 25 Dec ~ Bedrooms: £16/£32

DOCKRAY NY3921 Map 9

Royal 🛏 ♀ 🍺

A5091, off A66 W of Penrith

Among lovely low hills above (though not in sight of) Ullswater, this carefully renovated inn has an unusually spacious, airy and light open-plan bar, with comfortable new built-in bays of olive-green herringbone plush button-back banquettes and a spread of flowery pink and blue carpet. For walkers, an area of more traditional seating has stripped settles on flagstones, with darts, cribbage and dominoes, and there are unusual leatherette-topped sewing-machine tables throughout. Two dining areas (one no smoking) spread beyond the bar, and a wide choice of good home-cooked food includes soup (£1.75), filled rolls (from £2.30) or baked potatoes (from £2.50), a choice of lunchtime ploughman's (£4.40), omelettes (£4.95), salads (from £5.25), steak and kidney pie, ham and egg or mushroom and garlic feuilleté (£5.50), grilled Barnsley chop (£7.25), 8oz sirloin steak (£8.50), and with particularly good dishes of the day such as very fresh seafood lasagne, chicken breast stuffed with smoked cheese, maybe even delicious roast Herdwick mutton (£5.75); they use herbs from a good-sized herb garden beyond the car park. Well kept Boddingtons Bitter and Mild, Hartleys XB, Marstons Pedigree, Morlands Old Speckled Hen, Whitbreads Castle Eden and a couple of own-brews from the Old Crown at Hesket Newmarket on handpump, a decent range of malt whiskies, unusually good wines by the glass for this area, quite a few country wines; helpful friendly staff, unobtrusive piped music. There are picnic-table sets on a tree-sheltered lawn. *(Recommended by David Heath, Caroline and John Smith, Jacquie and John Payne, P D Harrop, R L Anderson, Ann and Bob Westbrook, G R Prest, H K Dyson, Roger Berry, Kathryn and Brian Heathcote, Mr Callard)*

Free house ~ Licensees James and Sarah Johnson ~ Real ale ~ Meals and snacks (12-2.30, 6-9) ~ Restaurant ~ (0176 84) 82356 ~ Children welcome if supervised ~ Open 11-11 ~ Bedrooms: £25B/£48B

ELTERWATER NY3305 Map 9

Britannia Inn ★ 🛏 🍺

Off B5343

It's not a surprise to find that this unpretentious little pub is so popular with walkers as it's right in the heart of the Lake District and close to Langdale and the central lakes, with tracks over the fells to Grasmere and Easedale. At the back is a small and traditionally furnished bar, while the front bar has settles, oak benches, Windsor chairs, winter coal fires, and a couple of window seats looking across to Elterwater itself through the trees on the far side; there's also a comfortable no smoking lounge. It's best to arrive early at peak times. Well kept Boddingtons Bitter, Jennings Bitter and Mild, Marstons Pedigree and guest beers on handpump, quite a few malt whiskies, and a well chosen, good value wine list. Bar food includes home-made soup or lunchtime filled wholemeal baps (£1.30), filled baked potatoes (from £2), lunchtime ploughman's (£3.85), pizzas (from £3.85), vegetable tikka masala (£5.20), local trout or steak in ale pie (£5.50), children's dishes (from £2.10), and puddings like home-made sticky toffee pudding (£2.10). The restaurant is no smoking; darts, dominoes and cribbage. The front terrace has chairs and slate-topped tables. In summer, people flock to watch Morris and Step and Garland dancers on the pretty village green opposite. *(Recommended by Lynn Sharpless, Bob Eardley, Michael and Harriet Robinson, Phil and Heidi Cook, H K Dyson, John Atherton, Mr and Mrs Ray, Paul and Sue Merrick, V and E A Bolton, Lorrie and Mick Marchington, Ian and Val Titman, Ewan and Moira McCall, Helen Hazzard, Simon Watkins, David Heath, Mr and Mrs S Ashcroft, G and M Stewart, Mr and Mrs J Denham-Vaughan, Dr D C Deeing, R J Saunders, Barry and Diana Powderhill, Bob Hurling, Roz Hodges, Trickie Hirst, Philip Orbell)*

Free house ~ David Fry ~ Real ale ~ Meals and snacks ~ Restaurant ~ Langdale (0153 94) 37210 ~ Children welcome ~ Summer parking may be difficult ~ Open 11-11; closed 25 Dec and evening 26 Dec ~ Bedrooms: £23.50/£47(£53S)

ESKDALE GREEN NY1400 Map 9

Bower House 🛏

½ mile W of village towards Santon Bridge

Alongside the village cricket field (summer Sunday matches), this old stone-built inn has a quietly relaxed, chatty atmosphere with no noisy machines or piped music. The lounge bar has cushioned settles and Windsor chairs that blend in well with the original beamed and alcoved nucleus around the serving counter, and there's a good winter fire; also, a separate lounge with easy chairs and sofas. Popular, good value food includes big helpings of sandwiches (from £1.60), home-made soup (£1.75), Cumberland sausage (£4), lasagne (£4.50), salads (from £4.75), gammon and egg or steak and kidney pie (£4.95), nut roast with fresh tomato sauce (£5.50), sirloin steak (£9.50), and daily specials (which can run out quite quickly) such as guinea fowl with cranberry sauce or venison in red wine (£6.25), and puddings like sticky toffee pudding (£2). The restaurant is no smoking. Well kept Courage Directors, Hartleys XB, Theakstons Best and Youngers Scotch on handpump, a reasonably priced wine list, and quite a few malt whiskies; friendly staff; dominoes. There's a neatly tended sheltered lawn and garden. Some of the comfortable bedrooms are in the annexe across the garden. *(Recommended by John Allsopp, J Weeks, Andy and Julie Hawkins, V and E A Bolton, Mr and Mrs Rankine, Andrew Sykes)*

Free house ~ Licensee Derek Connor ~ Real ale ~ Meals and snacks (12-2, 6.30-9.30) ~ Restaurant ~ Eskdale (0194 67) 23244 ~ Children welcome lunchtime and early evening ~ Open 11-11 ~ Bedrooms: £42B/£53.50B

King George IV

E of village at junction of main rd with rd up to Hard Knott Pass

Even when busy, this Georgian-looking pub (it's actually a good deal older) remains relaxed and friendly. Though there's been some refurbishment this year, the bar still has traditional wall seats for its handful of tables, giving plenty of space out in the room, there's a comfortable lounge, and a back games room with darts, pool, dominoes, fruit machine and piped music; warming winter log fire. A wide choice of generously served good bar food includes home-made soup (£1.50), excellent sandwiches (from £1.60), black pudding in a cider sauce (£4.25), ploughman's (£3.95), stir-fried vegetables (£5.25), omelettes such as salmon and prawn (£4.95), steaks (from £8.50), daily specials such as fried liver and onions (£4.95), large juicy tuna steak in herb butter, chicken kiev or evening steaks (from £8.25), with children's dishes (£2); quick, welcoming staff. The restaurant is no smoking. Well kept Bass, Marstons Pedigree, Morlands Old Speckled Hen and Theakstons Best and XB on handpump, and over 160 malt whiskies. The Eskdale views, from inside and from the tables in the garden, are charming. *(Recommended by Andrew Stephenson, Tina and David Woods-Taylor, Tim Heywood, Sophie Wilne, J Weeks, Peter Watkins, Pam Stanley, Paul and Maggie Baker, Andrew and Ruth Sykes)*

Free house ~ Licensees Harry and Jacqui Shepherd ~ Real ale ~ Meals and snacks ~ Restaurant ~ (0194 67) 23262 ~ Children welcome ~ Open 11-3, 5.30-11; 12-2.30, 6-11 in winter; closed 25 Dec ~ Bedrooms: £19.50/£39

FAUGH NY5155 Map 9

String of Horses 🛏

From A69 in Warwick Bridge, turn off at Heads Nook, Castle Carrock signpost, then follow Faugh signs – if you have to ask the way, it's pronounced Faff

The open-plan bar in this attractive 17th-c coaching inn is made up of several cosy communicating beamed rooms with some interesting carved furniture including fine old settles and elaborately carved Gothick seats and tables; there are also simpler Windsor and other chairs, panelling, brass pots, warming pans and antique prints about the walls and log fires in cool weather. Good bar food consists of sandwiches, home-made soup (£1.75), shrimps in a mild curry mayonnaise (£2.75), Cumberland sausage (£4.25), mushroom and nut fettucini (£4.95), honey-roast ham and parsley sauce or chicken Malaysian (£5.25), steak and kidney pudding (£5.50), 8oz sirloin steak (£7.95), daily specials like beef bourguignon (£5.50) or fresh trout fillet (£5.75), and puddings like bread and butter pudding (£1.95). Several malt whiskies and an extensive wine list; darts, pool, dominoes, fruit machine, video game and piped music. Residents have the use of a jacuzzi, sauna, solarium and small outdoor heated pool. There are pretty hanging baskets amongst the dutch blinds and lanterns outside, and lanterns and neat wrought iron among the greenery of the sheltered terrace. *(Recommended by Tim Heywood, Sophie Wilne, Dr R H M Stewart, Mr and Mrs C Roberts, R E and P Pearce)*

Free house ~ Licensee Mrs Anne Tasker ~ Meals and snacks ~ Restaurant ~ Hayton (01228) 70297 ~ Children welcome ~ Jazz 1st Fri of month; karaoke on certain nights ~ Open 11.30-3, 5.30-11 ~ Bedrooms: £58B/£68B

GARRIGILL NY7441 Map 9

George & Dragon 🍺

Village signposted off B6277 S of Alston

In a pretty village of stonebuilt houses clustered together in a high Pennine valley, this small inn is a famous stop for walkers on the Pennine Way which passes its door. It too is stonebuilt, part of a largely 17th-c terrace with massively heavy stone slates, and on the right the bar has very broad polished flagstones, a lovely stone fireplace with a really good log fire, good solid traditional furnishings and a cosy and relaxed atmosphere; there's a separate tartan-carpeted games room with sensibly placed darts, pool and dominoes. The very friendly landlord's wife prepares the good value generous bar food, such as soup (£1.30), sandwiches (£1.35), filled Yorkshire puddings (from £1.30) and baked potatoes (from £2.10), Cumberland sausage and egg (£3.95), gammon and egg (from £3.95), chicken (£4), cod (£4.10), vegetarian dishes such as spinach and mushroom lasagne (£4.15), home-made steak pie (£4.25) and sirloin steak (£7.25), with sticky toffee pudding (£1.70), children's dishes (from £1.25) or maybe just a bowl of chips (85p). Well kept McEwans 70/-, Theakstons Best, XB and Old Peculier and changing guest beers on handpump, decent malt whiskies, very friendly service; maybe unobtrusive piped music. *(Recommended by Gill and Maurice McMahon, Alan Risdon, N P Cox, Dr Sherriff, G W Lindley, David and Margaret Bloomfield)*

Free house ~ Licensees Brian and Jean Holmes ~ Real ale ~ Meals and snacks ~

Restaurant ~ (01434) 381293 ~ Children welcome ~ Open 11-3.30(4 Sat), 6-11;
winter opening 12 and 7 ~ Bedrooms: £15/£30, also very cheap small bunkhouse

GRASMERE NY3406 Map 9

Travellers Rest

Just N of Grasmere on A591 Ambleside—Keswick rd; OS sheet 90 map reference 335089

There are fine views of the wonderful surrounding scenery from this homely little
16th-c pub – and from the side garden with its picnic-table sets and stream; good
nearby walks. The comfortable, beamed lounge bar has a friendly atmosphere,
bluey-grey banquettes and cushioned wooden chairs around varnished wooden
tables, local watercolours, suggested walks and coast-to-coast information on the
walls, some horsebrasses by the bar counter, and piped classical music; just inside
the door is a large, warming log fire. The no smoking dining room is similarly
furnished, as is the games room which is popular with families; pool, darts, fruit
machine, juke box and piped music. Good bar food includes home-made soup
(£1.50), local trout pâté (£2.95), ploughman's (£4.50), open sandwiches (from
£3.95), 6oz char-grilled burger (£4.75), local Cumberland sausage and apple
sauce (£4.85), vegetable brochette (£4.95), steak and kidney pie (£5.55), chicken
chasseur (£5.95), steaks (from £8.25), children's menu (£2.95), daily specials, and
puddings (£2.35). Well kept Jennings Bitter, Cumberland and Sneck Lifter on
handpump, and at least a dozen malt whiskies. *(Recommended by Simon Watkins,*
Derek and Margaret Underwood, Paul Boot, Neil Townend, H K Dyson, Mr and Mrs G R
Smith-Richards, WAH, Tina and David Woods-Taylor, Susan and Alan Buckland, David
Lands, Paul and Sue Merrick, Mr and Mrs C Roberts, C A Wilkes, Miss D P Barson, John
and Diana Elsy, Lorrie and Mick Marchington, Roger and Christine Mash, Dave and Jules
Tuckett)

Free house ~ Licensees Lynne, Derek and Graham Sweeney ~ Real ale ~ Meals
and snacks (12-3, 6-9.30) ~ Grasmere (0153 94) 35604 ~ Children welcome ~
Open 11-11 ~ Bedrooms: £22/£43

HAWKSHEAD SD3598 Map 9

Kings Arms 🛏 🍺

The lovely terrace outside this pretty old inn with its old-fashioned teak seats and
oak cask tables around the roses, overlooks the central square of this delightful
Elizabethan village. The low-ceilinged bar is popular with locals and has a cosy
traditional feel with most tables designed to suit drinkers rather than eaters, but
there are also comfortable red-cushioned wall and window seats and red plush
stools on the turkey carpet, and an open fire. Popular good-value food includes
home-made soup (£1.50), sandwiches (from £1.40), ploughman's, local
Cumberland sausage with spicy apple sauce, home-made steak and mushroom pie
or lasagne (£5.50), and 8oz sirloin steak, puddings, and Sunday roast beef and
Yorkshire pudding (£5.25). The restaurant is no smoking. Very well kept
Greenalls, Tetleys and Theakstons Best and Old Peculier on handpump and a
good choice of malt whiskies. Darts, dominoes, fruit machine and piped pop
music. In keeping with the atmosphere of the rest of the place, the bedrooms
(refurbished this year) have coins embedded in the old oak beams. The village car
park is some way away, but if you're staying at the inn, you'll get a free permit.
(Recommended by H K Dyson, Richard Lewis, Mr and Mrs R Head, D Cox, John Allsopp,
Linda Norsworthy, Neil and Jenny Spink)

Free house ~ Lease: Rosalie Johnson ~ Real ale ~ Meals and snacks (12-2.30, 6-
9.30) ~ Restaurant ~ Hawkshead (0153 94) 36372 ~ Well behaved children
welcome ~ Occasional live folk music ~ Open 11-11; closed 25 Dec ~ Bedrooms:
£27(£32B)/£44(£54B); 2 self-catering cottages closeby

It's against the law for bar staff to smoke while handling food or drink.

Queens Head

The comfortable, low-ceilinged open-plan bar in this attractive black-and-white 16th-c timbered pub has heavy bowed black beams, red leatherette wall seats and plush stools around heavy traditional tables on the discreetly patterned red carpet, some decorative plates on one panelled wall, and an open fire; a snug little room leads off. Popular bar food includes lunchtime sandwiches, soup (£2.25), bruchetta (garlic bread with tomato, onion, herbs, garlic and olive oil, £2.95), ploughman's (£5), home-made pancakes with nuts and vegetables in a creamy white sauce or steak pie (£6.50), devilled lamb's kidneys (£6.75), kedgeree (£7.50), pork fillet topped with mozzarella cheese and wrapped in bacon (£8.50), seafood dishes, and 9oz sirloin steak (£10.95). The restaurant is no smoking. Well kept Hartleys XB and Robinsons Bitter, Frederics, and Mild on handpump, and quite a few whiskies; dominoes and piped music. Walkers must take their boots off. In summer, the window boxes are pretty. The village is a charming and virtually car-free network of stone-paved alleys winding through huddles of whitewashed cottages. *(Recommended by H K Dyson, Richard Lewis, Simon J Barber, D J and P M Taylor, D Cox, Wayne Brindle, D J Underwood, C Roberts)*

Hartleys (Robinsons) ~ Tenant Tony Merrick ~ Real ale ~ Meals and snacks (12-2.30, 6.15-9.30) ~ Restaurant ~ Hawkshead (0153 94) 36271 ~ Children in restaurant if eating ~ Occasional live jazz ~ Open 11-11 ~ Bedrooms: £35(£45)/£53(£59.50B)

nr HAWKSHEAD NY3501 Map 9

Drunken Duck ★ ⑪ ◗

Barngates; the hamlet is signposted from B5286 Hawkshead—Ambleside, opposite the Outgate Inn; or it may be quicker to take the first right from B5286, after the wooded caravan site; OS Sheet 90 map reference 350013

Despite its immense popularity, the staff at this attractive and friendly old pub manage to cope with the crowds with cheerful efficiency. There are several cosy and traditionally pubby beamed rooms with good winter fires, tub chairs, cushioned old settles, blond pews, ladderback country chairs, and wheelbacks on the fitted turkey carpet, and maybe the multi-coloured cat and small elderly dog. Around the walls are pictures, cartoons, cards, fox masks and cases of fishing flies and lures. Imaginative and changing daily, the very good food might include filled rolls (£1.75), pâté such as mushroom and nut or cream cheese and chive (£2.95), ploughman's (£3.95), ricotta tortelloni in tomato and herb sauce or fennel, orange and butterbean bake (£4.95), chilli con carne (£5.50), creamy garlic chicken, leeks and cashew nuts (£5.75), beef and vegetables in ale or Cumberland sausage casserole (£5.95), and curried prawn and apple pasta or game pie (£6.25). The dining room is no smoking. Well kept Boddingtons Bitter, Jennings Bitter and Cumberland, Mitchells ESB, Theakstons Old Peculier, and Yates Bitter on handpump or tapped from the cask, and over 60 malt whiskies; darts. Seats on the front verandah look across to Lake Windermere in the distance; to the side there are quite a few rustic wooden chairs and tables, sheltered by a stone wall with alpine plants along its top, and the pub has fishing in a private tarn behind. *(Recommended by Neville Kenyon, H K Dyson, LM, Frank Cummins, V and E A Bolton, David Wright, Tina and David Woods-Taylor, Walter and Susan Rinaldi-Butcher, Simon and Amanda Southwell, C A Wilkes, Michael and Rachael Dunlop, John Scarisbrick, Dr B and Mrs P B Baker, Bronwen and Steve Wrigley, Mike and Jo, Phil and Heidi Cook, Bill and Lydia Ryan, M V Fereday, Linda Norsworthy, Helen Hazzard, Kate and Robert Hodkinson, Mr and Mrs G R Smith-Richards, Jerry and Alison Oakes, Mark Bradley, Andrew Scarr, N H White, Paul and Sue Merrick, S R and A I Ashcroft, John and Marianne Cooper, Andrew and Ruth Triggs, Dick Brown, David Wallington, Mark Howell, Caroline Poupart, Greg Parston, Mr and Mrs J Denham-Vaughan, R E Rhodes, Denis and Margaret Kilner)*

Free house ~ Licensee Stephanie Barton ~ Real ale ~ Meals and snacks ~ Hawkshead (0153 94) 36347 ~ Children in eating area of bar ~ Open 11.30-3, 6-11; closed 25 Dec ~ Bedrooms: £50B/£69B

HESKET NEWMARKET NY3438 Map 9

Old Crown ♦

Village signposted from B5299 in Caldbeck

It's the warmly friendly and homely atmosphere – as well as the own-brewed beers – that readers like so much about this cosy, old-fashioned pub. The little bar has a pile of teddy bears in a corner, just four tables, comfortably serviceable chairs, a coal fire, shelves of well thumbed books (they have a lending library with a small donation to charity), a sleepy ginger cat and a friendly orangeman labrador called Blot ('as in on the landscape'). You can book up to have a tour around the brewery and inspect the Skiddaw Special (light and refreshing), Blencathra (darker and hoppier, though no stronger), Old Carrock (strong), Doris's 90th (named for the landlady's mother's birthday in 1989),Old Carrock Strong Ale, Catbells Bitter, and Great Cockup Porter; a good few malt whiskies. At lunchtime (apart from Sunday) they only do good stock-pot soup and robust sandwiches, but in the evening there's quite an emphasis on Indian dishes such as chicken korma or vindaloo and rogan josh or kheema matar (£4.50), and local trout with almonds (£5); Sunday lunch. The no smoking side dining room is small and simple, with a nice little upright stove. A public bar on the right has pool; darts, shove-ha'penny, dominoes, cribbage and juke box. Though the bedrooms are simple, they are good value – especially considering the excellent breakfasts. The pub is part of a stone terrace facing a long narrow green, with Caldbeck Fells rising behind. *(Recommended by P and M Rudlin, Lucy James, Dr RKP, Ian Woodhead, Gayle Butterfield, John and Maggie Churcher, Tina and David Woods-Taylor, S R and A J Ashcroft, Malcolm Taylor)*

Own brew ~ Licensees Liz Blackwood and Jim Fearnley ~ Real ale ~ Meals (evening, Sun lunchtime) and snacks ~ Caldbeck (0169 74) 78288 ~ Children welcome until 8.30pm ~ Open 12-3, 5.30-11; closed winter weekday lunchtimes ~ Bedrooms in next door cottage: £15/£30

HEVERSHAM SD4983 Map 9

Blue Bell

A6 (now a relatively quiet road here)

Comfortably civilised, this partly timbered old country inn was once a vicarage. The bay-windowed lounge bar has an antique carved settle, comfortable cushioned Windsor armchairs and upholstered stools on the flowery carpet, pewter platters hanging from the beams, and small antique sporting prints on the partly panelled walls; there's a particularly warm atmosphere in winter when the fires are lit. One big bay-windowed area has been divided off as a children's room, and the long, tiled-floor, quieter public bar has darts and dominoes. Good bar food based on fresh local produce includes sandwiches, home-made soup, lovely Morecambe Bay potted shrimps, smoked haddock mornay (£3.95), local game casserole (£4.25), roast lamb (£4.95), and sizzling sirloin steak platter (£6.75); also, morning coffee, afternoon teas high teas and good Sunday lunch. The restaurant is no smoking. Well kept Sam Smiths OB on handpump, with Museum kept under light blanket pressure, several malt whiskies, a decent wine list, and their own cider; helpful staff. Darts, pool, cribbage, dominoes, fruit machine, piped music and Sky TV (in the public bar). Crossing over the A6 into the village itself, you come to a picturesque church with a rambling little graveyard; if you walk through this and on to the hills beyond, there's a fine view across to the estuary of the River Kent. The estuary itself is a short walk from the pub down the country road that runs by its side. Pets welcome by arrangement. *(Recommended by Mr and Mrs C Roberts, Wayne Brindle, Malcolm Taylor, David Wallington, Anthony Barnes, Roger and Christine Mash, Alan Wilcock, Christine Davidson, D C Holt)*

Sam Smiths ~ Manager Richard Cowie ~ Real ale ~ Meals and snacks (11-2.30, 6-9.30) ~ Restaurant ~ Milnthorpe (0153 95) 62018 ~ Children welcome ~ Jazz and folk music Thurs and Fri evenings ~ Open 11-3, 6-11; all day Sat ~ Bedrooms: £34.50B/£60B

INGS SD4599 Map 9

Watermill 🛏 🍺

Just off A591 E of Windermere

Within minutes of arriving at this warmly friendly family-run inn you'll be on first name terms with the licensee and treated as friends for the rest of your stay, and it's the sort of place where locals pop in for early morning coffee and a chat. The bars have a happy mix of chairs, padded benches and solid oak tables, bar counters made from old church wood, open fires, and amusing cartoons by a local artist on the wall; one area is no smoking. The spacious lounge bar has been refurbished this year in much the same traditional style as the other rooms, and has rocking chairs and a big open fire. Walkers, their muddy boots and their dogs (on leads) are welcome. Bar food includes home-made soup (£1.50), lunchtime sandwiches (from £1.95), lunchtime ploughman's (£3.40), local Cumberland sausage (£3.90), salads (from £4.10), home-made curry (£4.60), Whitby scampi (£5.50), local grilled gammon (£5.80), and steak (£8.95); they specialise in real ale casseroles and pies; children's meals (from £2). Well kept Theakstons Best, XB and Old Peculier and Lees Moonraker and eight other regularly changing guest ales from around the country; continental and English bottled beers, farm cider and growing selection of malts. Darts, table skittles and dominoes. The inn is in a lovely spot with the River Gowan bordering the garden and lots of climbing, fell-walking, fishing, boating of all kinds, swimming and pony-trekking within easy reach. *(Recommended by Graham and Lynn Mason, Paul Boot, Sharron Thompson, Dick Brown, John and Marianne Cooper, John Scarisbrick, Mr and Mrs Ashcroft, D Hanley, Wayne Brindle, Barbara McHugh, A Preston, C F Walling)*

Free House ~ Licensee Alan Coulthwaite ~ Real ale ~ Meals and snacks (not 25 Dec) ~ (01539) 821309 ~ Children in lounge ~ Open 12-2.30(3 Sat), 6-11; closed evening 25 Dec ~ Bedrooms: £21.25S/£38.50S

KIRKBY LONSDALE SD6278 Map 7

Snooty Fox

Main Street (B6254)

On Thursdays – market day – this rambling pub gets even more crowded than usual, so it's best to arrive early then if you want a seat. The various rooms are full of lots of things to look at, such as stage gladiator costumes, horse-collars and stirrups, mugs hanging from beams, eye-catching coloured engravings, stuffed wildfowl and falcons, mounted badger and fox masks, guns, a powder-flask and so forth. The bar counters are made from English oak, as is some panelling, and there are also country kitchen chairs, pews, one or two high-backed settles and marble-topped sewing-trestle tables on the flagstones, and two coal fires. Under the new chef, the good home-made food now includes sandwiches, soup (£1.75), mushrooms in a marjoram and garlic sauce (£2.95), filled baked potatoes (from £2.95), Cumberland sausage with onion gravy (£4.25), fruity chicken curry (£4.95), steak and kidney pudding (£5.25), ragout of Scottish salmon in lemon and oyster sauce (£6.50), haunch of venison in elderberry sauce (£7.75), 12oz T-bone steak (£9.95), and puddings such as sticky toffee pudding with butterscotch sauce, steamed raspberry sponge or chilled Belgian chocolate mousse with caramel and orange sauce (from £2.25). Well kept Hartleys XB, Theakstons Best, and Timothy Taylors Landlord on handpump, several malt whiskies, and country wines; dominoes, fruit machine and good juke box. There are tables out on a small terrace beside the biggish back cobbled stableyard, with more in a pretty garden; small play area for children. *(Recommended by Paul McPherson, David and Ruth Hollands, Neville Kenyon, Sue Holland, David Webster, J Weeks, Mr and Mrs C J Frodsham, Roger and Jillian Shaw, Brian and Jenny Seller, Andrew Sykes, Dr David Webster, Sue Holland)*

Free house ~ Licensee Jack Shone ~ Real ale ~ Meals and snacks (all day) ~ Restaurant ~ Kirkby Lonsdale (0152 42) 71308 ~ Children in eating area of bar ~ Open 11-11 ~ Bedrooms: £21(£26B)/£36(£46B)

Sun 🛏

Market St (B6254)

This year, a stone barn, with lovely views across the Barbon Fells, has been converted to create additional bedrooms. And the rest of this atmospheric and lively little pub has been refurbished too. The low beamed, rambling rooms are filled with a collection of some 500 banknotes, maps and old engravings, and the walls – some of which are stripped to bare stone or have panelled dados – are hung with battleaxes and other interesting antiques, and even a fireplace. Furnishings include window seats and cosy pews and there are good winter fires. Well kept Boddingtons, and Dent Bitter (from the Sun in Dent) and Youngers No. 3 on handpump, and 50 malt whiskies; dominoes, cribbage, trivia and piped music. Good food includes sandwiches, vegetarian dishes, and pork and stilton sausage or bubble and squeak (£3.95), beef and Guinness casserole (£4.50), and Chinese lemon chicken or Indian chicken jalfreizi (£5.50). There's an unusual pillared porch; the steep cobbled alley is also attractive. Lady Anne Clifford stayed here in 1649, as did Turner in 1818, while painting *Ruskin's View*. *(Recommended by David and Ruth Hollands, Kim Schofield, Mike and Wendy Proctor, Michael Marlow, Anthony Barnes, Sue Holland, David Webster, Jenny and Steve Corrigan, Paul Boot, Wayne Brindle, J B Thackray)*

Free house ~ Licensee Andrew Wilkinson ~ Real ale ~ Meals and snacks (11-2, 6-10) ~ Restaurant ~ Kirkby Lonsdale (0152 42) 71965 ~ Children welcome ~ Open 11-11 ~ Bedrooms: £22(£25B)/£39(£48B)

LANGDALE NY2906 Map 9

Old Dungeon Ghyll 🛏

B5343

Not surprisingly, this dramatically set inn is very popular with fell walkers and climbers. It's at the heart of the Great Langdale Valley and surrounded by fells including the Langdale Pikes flanking the Dungeon Ghyll Force waterfall – and there are grand views of the Pike of Blisco rising behind Kettle Crag from the window seats cut into the thick stone walls of the bar. Furnishings are very simple, and the whole feel of the place is basic but cosy, and full of boisterous atmosphere. Well kept Broughton Oatmeal Stout, Jennings Cumberland, Theakstons XB, Old Peculier and Mild, and a guest beer on handpump, Westons cider, and a fair range of malt whiskies; darts and dominoes. Straightforward good value food includes lunchtime sandwiches, soup (£1.50), Cumberland sausage, chicken nuggets, scampi, local trout, steaks (all around £5), and home-made puddings (£1.50); if you are not a resident and want to eat in the no smoking restaurant you must book ahead. It can get really lively on a Saturday night (there's a popular National Trust campsite opposite). *(Recommended by Nigel Woolliscroft, Bronwen and Steve Wrigley, H K Dyson, Sara Geyer, Mick Whelton, John and Marianne Cooper, Lynn Sharpless, Bob Eardley, Lorrie and Mick Marchington, V and E A Bolton, Andrew McKeand, Andrew Sykes)*

Free house ~ Licensee Neil Walmsley ~ Real ale ~ Meals and snacks (12-2, 6-9) ~ Evening restaurant ~ Langdale (0153 94) 37272 ~ Children welcome ~ Spontaneous live music ~ Open 11-11; closed 24-26 Dec ~ Bedrooms: £28.50(£30B)/£57(£60B)

LEVENS SD4886 Map 7

Hare & Hounds

Village signposted from A590; since completion of dual carriageway link, best approach is following route signposted for High Vehicles

The low-beamed, carpeted lounge bar of this very attractive little village pub is furnished with a wicker-backed Jacobean-style armchair and antique settle on its sloping floor, as well as old-fashioned brown leatherette dining seats and red-cushioned seats built into the partly panelled walls. There's an interesting display of old fire-engine artefacts. Generously served food includes soup (£1.20), lunchtime sandwiches (from £1.45; toasties from £1.55), filled baked potatoes (from £2.95), ploughman's (£3.60), salads (from £3.60), battered cod (£3.95), broccoli and cream cheese bake (£4.05), Cumberland sausage (£4.15), steak and kidney pie (£4.25), puddings (£1.90), and children's meals (from £2.40); friendly service. At the front is a snug tap room, with darts, cribbage and dominoes; also golden-oldie juke box in the separate pool room, down some steps. Well kept Vaux Samson and Wards Thorne on handpump. The pub is also close to Sizergh Castle. *(Recommended by Mike and Wendy Proctor, Paul McPherson, A T Langton, David Wallington, Stephen Newell, Brian Jones, C Roberts)*

Vaux ~ Tenants Pat and Maggie Dolan ~ Real ale ~ Meals and snacks (not Mon or Tues evenings Nov-Mar) ~ (0153 95) 60408 ~ Children in all areas except Tap Room until 8pm ~ Open 11-3, 6-11

LITTLE LANGDALE　NY3204 Map 9

Three Shires 🛏

From A593 3 miles W of Ambleside take small road signposted The Langdales, Wrynose Pass; then bear left at first fork

Run by the same family for 20 years, this pleasant stone-built inn has lovely views over the valley to the partly wooded hills below Tilberthwaite Fells; there are seats on the terrace with more on a well kept lawn behind the car park, backed by a small oak wood. Inside, the comfortably extended back bar has antique oak carved settles, country kitchen chairs and stools on its big dark slate flagstones, stripped timbers and a beam-and-joist stripped ceiling, a modern stone fireplace and chimney piece with a couple of recesses for ornaments, and Lakeland photographs lining the walls; an arch leads through to a small, additional area. Bar food includes soup (£1.60), lunchtime sandwiches (from £1.70), ploughman's (from £3.85), salads (from £4.50), home-made steak and kidney pie (£5.25), whitby scampi (£6), daily specials like vegetable goulash (£4.95) or sauté chicken in lemon and tarragon sauce (£5.50), puddings (£2.25), and children's meals (£2.85); good breakfasts. The restaurant and small public bar are no smoking. Marstons Pedigree, Morlands Old Speckled Hen, Ruddles County, and Websters Yorkshire on handpump, and lots of malt whiskies; darts, dominoes and cribbage. *(Recommended by V and E A Bolton, David Goldstone, Tina and David Woods-Taylor, G C Brown, Ron Gentry, Dr J P Cullen)*

Free house ~ Licensee Ian Stephenson ~ Real ale ~ Meals and snacks (no evening food Dec and Jan) ~ Restaurant ~ Langdale (0153 94) 37215 ~ Children welcome until 9pm ~ Open 11-11; 11.30-2.30, 8-10.30 in winter; closed 25 Dec ~ Bedrooms: £30B/£60B)

LOWESWATER　NY1222 Map 9

Kirkstile

From B5289 follow signs to Loweswater Lake; OS Sheet 89 map reference 140210

The very attractive covered verandah here is a fine place to sit and admire the spectacular surrounding peaks and soaring fells. There's been some redecoration this year which has brightened up the public areas, and the low-beamed and carpeted bar has comfortably cushioned small settles and pews, partly stripped stone walls, and a big log fire; there are fine views from the big bow windows in one of the rooms off here. Decent bar food includes home-made wholemeal filled rolls (from £1.80), good home-made soup (£1.95), filled baked potatoes (from £3.25), home-made pasty (£3.50), ploughman's (£4.15), bean and tomato casserole (£4.50), omelettes (from £4.75), Cumberland sausage and egg (£5), sirloin steak (£9.25), and puddings; big breakfasts, lovely high teas, morning coffee. Well kept Jennings Bitter and Cumberland on handpump, a fair choice of malt whiskies, and decent wine list; darts, dominoes, cribbage and a slate shove-ha'penny board; a side games room called the Little Barn has pool, fruit machine, video game and juke box. There are picnic-table sets on the lawn. *(Recommended by H K Dyson, Roger and*

Christine Mash, Nigel Woolliscroft, Dave Lands, Mike and Ann Beiley, John Allsopp, V and E A Bolton, D Baker, Michael Wadsworth, Heather M N Robson, Peter and Lynn Brueton)

Free house ~ Licensees Ken and Shirley Gorley ~ Real ale ~ Meals and snacks (12-2.30, 6-9) ~ Restaurant ~ (01900) 85219 ~ Children welcome ~ Open 11-11 ~ Bedrooms: £31(£40B)/£40(£50B)

LOWICK GREEN   SD2985 Map 9

Farmers Arms

A590 N from Ulverston, then left on to A5092 after about 4 miles

A few miles south of Conison Water, this rambling old hotel has an unchanging and civilised public bar with huge flagstones, dark heavy beams, and a handsome fireplace with a big open fire; some seats are in cosy side alcoves. The hotel itself is across the yard, with its own plusher lounge bar, and a preserved spinning gallery. Bar food includes sandwiches and daily specials such as prawn and sweetcorn parcels (£2.50), stilton and walnut pâté (£3.75), hotpot (£4.95), and chicken kiev (£5.25). Theakstons XB and Youngers IPA and No. 3 on handpump, and a good choice of spirits. Darts, pool, cribbage, dominoes, fruit machine, trivia and piped music. *(Recommended by Paul J Bispham, Dr R H M Stewart, Chris Cook, W Mecham, Nora Poolman)*

Scottish & Newcastle ~ Manager Ron Maxfield ~ Real ale ~ Meals and snacks (12-2, 6-9.30) ~ Restaurant ~ (01229) 861376/861277 ~ Children welcome ~ Open 11-11; 11-3, 6-11 in winter ~ Bedrooms: £25(£40B)/£49B

MELMERBY   NY6237 Map 10

Shepherds 🍽 ♉

About half way along A686 Penrith—Alston

Readers continue to be delighted with the warm, friendly welcome and very good home-made food in this sandstone village pub. As well as their fine range of cheeses – 10 North Country cheeses, 6 other English cheeses, and European Community cheeses of the month – you might find soup like chicken and leek or creamed parsnip (£1.80), ploughman's with home-made roll (from £3.30), pork and port pâté (£3.40), cod fillet with home-made batter (£4.50), ham and chicken cobbler (£5), delicious Cumberland sausage and white onion casserole (£4.90), tagliatelle garniture forestière (£5.40), steak and kidney pie (£5.95), Calcutta beef curry (£5.90), a mountain of spare ribs (£6.20), Italian baked chicken (£6.40), very tender spiced lamb with yoghurt (£6.80), chicken breast Leoni (£6.70), venison and roquefort crumble (£7.20), and steaks (from £9.60); lots of daily specials, Sunday roast lunch (£4.80), and delicious puddings such as superb ginger surprise, lemon meringue pie or rich chocolate torrone (£2.15); part of the main eating area is no smoking; quick, friendly table service. Although it's a spacious place, it's best to get there early. Well kept Greene King IPA, Jennings Cumberland and Sneck Lifter, Marstons Pedigree, and a guest beer on handpump, as well as over 45 malt whiskies, a good wine list, and quite a few bottled continental beers. Lots of pot plants brighten up the bar, which also has cushioned wall seats, sunny window seats, sensible tables and chairs, light-panelling, and an open fire. A games bar has darts, pool, shove-ha'penny, dominoes, fruit machine and juke box. During the winter they have league quiz, darts (men and ladies), and pool teams. Hartside Nursery Garden, a noted alpine and primula plant specialist, is just over the Hartside Pass, and there are fine views across the green to the Pennines. *(Recommended by Jerry and Alison Oakes, Frank Davidson, T M Dobby, Paul and Janet Waring, Joe and Carol Pattison, Mrs D M Dunne, Mr and Mrs C Roberts, Dr A and Dr A C Jackson, Kathryn and Brian Heathcote, Michael Sargent, Paul A Kitchener, F J Robinson, Stephen Savill, I MacG.Binnie, Gill and Maurice McMahon, Malcolm Taylor, Keith Croxton, Dr Sherriff)*

Free house ~ Licensees Martin and Christine Baucutt ~ Real ale ~ Meals and snacks (11-2.30, 6-9.45) ~ Langwathby (01768) 881217 ~ Children in eating area of the bar till 8.30pm ~ Open 11-3, 6-11; closed 25 Dec ~ Several holiday cottages

NEAR SAWREY SD3796 Map 9

Tower Bank Arms

B5285 towards the Windermere ferry

As it backs on to Beatrix Potter's Hill Top Farm (owned by the National Trust) this cream-and-green place can get very busy – but the landlord is very welcoming and there's a lovely traditional atmosphere in the low-beamed main bar. Emma or Maxwell the pub's labradors may be sitting in front of the big cooking range with its fine log fire, there are high-backed settles on the rough slate floor, local hunting photographs and signed photographs of celebrities, and a grandfather clock. Lunchtime bar food includes soup (£1.50), filled brown rolls (from £1.90), ploughman's (from £3.60), home-made quiche (£4.25), and a home-made pie of the day (£4.50); more substantial evening main meals such as grilled gammon and eggs or Esthwaite trout (£6), venison or duckling (£7) and good, sticky puddings; quick, friendly service. Well kept Theakstons Best, XB and Old Peculier, and Mild, and a weekly changing guest beer on handpump, as well as 28 malt whiskies, Belgian fruit beers and other foreign beers, and wine bottled for the pub; darts, shove-ha'penny, table skittles, cribbage, dominoes, backgammon and Connect 4. Seats outside have pleasant views of the wooded Claife Heights. This is a good area for golf, sailing, birdwatching, fishing (they have a licence for two rods a day on selected waters in the area), and walking, but if you want to stay at the pub, you'll have to book well in advance. *(Recommended by P Barnsley, David Wright, S R and A I Ashcroft, Mike and Jo, Tina and David Woods-Taylor, Helen Hazzard, Sara Geyer, Mick Whelton, J Jones, Simon and Amanda Southwell, Mrs J Jones, H K Dyson, D Cox, Peter and Pat Frogley, Andrew Sykes, A T Langton, Jane Thompson, I MacG.Binnie)*

Free house ~ Licensee Philip Broadley ~ Real ale ~ Meals and lunchtime snacks (not 25 Dec) ~ Restaurant ~ Hawkshead (0153 94) 36334 ~ Children in eating area of bar at lunchtime, in the restaurant in evening ~ Open 11-3, 5.30(6 in winter)-11; closed evening 25 Dec ~ Bedrooms: £30B/£40B

NEWTON REIGNY NY4382 Map 9

Sun 🍴

Under 2 miles from M6 junction 41; B5305 W, then first left through Catterlen, then left at T-junction

This is one of Britain's best motorway-break pubs for a really good meal at sensible prices. Besides good home-made vegetable soup (£1.75), sandwiches (from £1.95) and Morecambe Bay shrimps (£2.95), the menu changes day by day to take advantage of fresh supplies, and might include lasagne or broccoli and tomato pancake (£4.95), wholetail Whitby scampi (£5.25), local gammon and egg (£5.75), grilled bass with orange and marjoram (£5.95), and puddings such as pancake with Calvados or sticky toffee (£1.95); they have good local ice creams. The carpeted open-plan bar has plush seats around its black tables, red crushed velvet curtains, some brass platters, some stripped stone and wrought iron, and a good coal fire in a central hearth. Well kept Courage Directors, John Smiths Magnet, Websters Yorkshire and Yates on handpump (they change weekly), decent malt whiskies, friendly landlord; darts and a small pool table at one end, piped music. *(Recommended by John Oddey, Richard Holloway)*

Free house ~ Licensee Barry Pickles ~ Real ale ~ Meals and snacks ~ (01768) 67055 ~ Children welcome away from bar ~ Open 11-3, 6-11; all day Sat ~ Bedrooms: £14/£36B

OUTGATE SD3699 Map 9

Outgate Inn 🍺

B5286 Ambleside—Hawkshead

This bustling and neatly kept early 18th-c pub has three comfortably modernised communicating areas with decor and furnishings varying from each to each:

button-back wall banquettes or country-kitchen and housekeeper's chairs, exposed joists rather than plaster ceiling, and carefully-lit local photographs or drawings of jazz musicians or a cabinet of bottles on the walls. One cosy corner has shelves of books and oddments, another has big windows looking out through the beech trees to steep pastures, and there are open fires; the lounge area is no smoking during eating hours. Efficiently served bar food includes home-made soup (£1.50), sandwiches (from £1.50), home-made Scottish salmon pâté (£2.95), filled baked potatoes (from £2.75), ploughman's (from £4.50), salads (from £5.25), mushroom and lentil moussaka or home-made steak and kidney pie (£5.50), mixed grill (£5.95), Esthwaite trout (£6.50), 8oz sirloin steak (£9.25), puddings, and children's dishes (from £2.50); prompt, friendly service. Well kept Hartleys XB and Robinsons Best and Frederics on handpump, and dominoes, and maybe restrained piped music. In summer there are tables and umbrellas outside, and this year there's a new big car park. *(Recommended by Frank Cummins, H K Dyson, Tina and David Woods-Taylor, D Cox, Wayne Brindle, and Mr and Mrs S Ashcroft, Ron Gentry, Andrew Hazeldine)*

Hartleys (Robinsons) ~ Tenant Ian Kirsopp ~ Real ale ~ Meals and snacks ~ (0153 94) 36413 ~ Children in eating area of bar till 9pm ~ Jazz Fri evenings 8.30 ~ Open 11-3, 6-11 ~ Bedrooms: /£35

SCALES NY3427 Map 9

White Horse ♀

A66 1½ miles NE of Threlkeld: keep your eyes skinned – it looks like a farmhouse up on a slope

This isolated old farmhouse has warm winter fires burning in the comfortable beamed bar, hunting pictures and local hunting cartoons on the walls, and a growing range of locally mounted animals and birds native to the area. It extends into the old kitchen (no smoking) which has dark oak high-backed settle-style seating upholstered in deep red, an unusual textured wall hanging showing a white horse on the fells, and candles and flowers on the tables; a cosy little snug is installed in what used to be the dairy. At lunchtime, the good popular bar food might include home-made carrot and courgette soup (£1.75), ploughman's (£4.25), potted shrimp salad with hot garlic bread (£4.50), chicken and mushroom filo parcels (£4.95), gammon with two eggs (£5.50), and puddings like sticky toffee ginger pudding or baked fresh strawberry pudding (£2.75); in the evenings there's a shorter fixed menu as well as daily specials like smoked salmon pâté (£3.95), tagliatelle with walnuts and mushroom sauce (£5.95), beef olives in red wine (£7.50), chicken breast with tarragon and cream sauce (£8.50), and blueberry and apple crumble (£2.75). Well kept Jennings Bitter, Cumberland and Sneck Lifter on handpump, and a decent wine list; dominoes. There are wooden settles, flower boxes and tubs outside. From the cluster of pub and farm buildings, tracks lead up into the splendidly daunting and rocky fells around Blencathra – which have names like Foule Crag and Sharp Edge. The newly opened pretty bedroom has a view of the fells. *(Recommended by WAH, N H White, Tina and David Woods-Taylor, Gill and Mike Cross, Simon and Louise Chappell, Neil Townend, Miss J F Reay, H K Dyson, Roger and Christine Mash, V and E A Bolton, R E and P Pearce, Mike Muston, Martin, Jane, Simon and Laura Bailey)*

Free house ~ Licensees Larry and Judith Slattery ~ Real ale ~ Meals and lunchtime snacks; no evening meals winter weekdays ~ Threlkeld (0176 87) 79241 ~ Children in eating area of bar ~ Open 11-3, 6-11; 12-2.30, 6-11 in winter; closed 25 Dec ~ One bedroom: /£35

SEATHWAITE SD2396 Map 9

Newfield

Duddon Valley, nr Ulpha (ie not Seathwaite in Borrowdale)

Despite its weekend and holiday popularity with walkers and climbers, this cottagey 16th-c inn has managed to keep a relaxed and genuinely local atmosphere. There's a big round table among others in the slate-floored main bar, a comfortable side room, a games room with pool, darts and dominoes. Generously served and freshly prepared, the good bar food includes proper home-made soup (£1.65), sandwiches (£1.35), ploughman's (£3.75), Cumberland sausages that are a real challenge (£4.50), home-made steak pie or a vegetarian dish (from £4), huge gammon steaks with local farm eggs (£5.85), and good steaks (from £8); the choice is bigger in the evening. The restaurant is no smoking. Well kept Theakstons Best, XB and Old Peculier and a guest such as Marstons Pedigree, Morlands Old Speckled Hen or Youngs Special on handpump, a dozen malt whiskies, and good service. Well behaved dogs allowed. Tables out in the nice garden have good hill views. The pub owns and lets the next-door cottages. *(Recommended by I H Rorison, J Jones, DC, Andrew Sykes, C Roberts)*

Free house ~ Licensee Chris Burgess ~ Real ale ~ Meals and snacks ~ Restaurant ~ Seathwaite (01229) 716208 ~ Well behaved children welcome ~ Occasional folk music ~ Open 11-3, 6-11; 11-11 Sat ~ Self-catering flats available

SEDBERGH SD6692 Map 10

Dalesman 🛏

Main St

There's a real mix of styles and decorations in this popular and nicely modernised old pub. The stripped stone and beams are surrounded by houseplants, tropical fish, a blunderbuss, horsebrasses and spigots, various stuffed animals including a badger and a greater spotted woodpecker, and Vernon Stokes gundog pictures. A raised stone hearth has a log-effect gas fire and there are cushioned seats around dimpled copper tables. Through stone arches on the right a buttery area serves popular food such as soup (£1.50), filled rolls and toasties (from £2), filled baked potatoes, ploughman's or salads (from £4), steak and kidney pie (£4.95), and daily specials like gammon and egg (£5.95), venison casserole (£6.50), fresh poached salmon (£6.95), and half a roast duckling (£8.95); Sunday lunch; friendly service. Well kept Ind Coope Burton, Tetleys Bitter and Dark Mild, Theakstons, and an interesting beer brewed for the pub by Tetleys (nut-brown, slightly fuller-flavoured and less bitter than the regular brew) on handpump; dominoes, fruit machine and piped music. There are some picnic-table sets out in front; small car park. *(Recommended by Simon and Louise Chappell, Paul McPherson, B Horner, H K Dyson, Neil and Anita Christopher)*

Free house ~ Licensees Barry and Irene Garnett ~ Real ale ~ Meals and snacks ~ Restaurant ~ Sedbergh (0153 96) 21183 ~ Children in eating area of bar until 9.30pm ~ Open 11-11; 11-2.30, 6-11 in winter ~ Bedrooms: £33(£36B)/ £44(£48B)

STAINTON NY4928 Map 10

Kings Arms

1¾ miles from M6 junction 40: village signposted from A66 towards Keswick, though quickest to fork left at A592 roundabout then turn first right

Very popular locally, this pleasant, modernised old pub also offers a good welcome to visitors too. Reasonably priced traditional bar food includes soup (£1.30), sandwiches (£1.80, open sandwiches from £3), filled baked potatoes (from £2.30), home-made minced beef pie (£3.40), home-made steak and kidney pie (£3.60), breast of chicken with sage and onion stuffing (£4.20), salads (from £4.20), local trout (£4.50), delicious farmhouse gammon with egg (£5), and sirloin steak (£7.20); children's dishes (£2.50), puddings (from £1.40), and roast Sunday lunch; there may be quite a wait for food when the pub is busy. The roomy open-plan bar has leatherette wall banquettes, stools and armchairs, wood-effect tables, brasses on the black beams, and prints and paintings of the Lake District on the swirly cream walls; piped music. Well kept Flowers IPA, Whitbreads Castle Eden, and Worthington on handpump. Sensibly placed darts, dominoes, fruit machine and piped music. There are tables outside on the side terrace and a small lawn. *(Recommended by Duncan Redpath, Lorraine Milburn, N H White, Gary Roberts, Ian and Deborah Carrington, Robert and Gladys Flux, David Heath, Roy Y Bromell, Dorothy and David Young, R E Pearce)*

Pubmaster ~ Tenant Raymond Tweddle ~ Real ale ~ Meals and snacks ~ Penrith (01768) 62778 ~ Children allowed if eating ~ Open 11-3, 6.30(6 Sat)-11; winter weekday evening opening 7pm

THRELKELD NY3325 Map 9

Salutation

Old main rd, bypassed by A66 W of Penrith

Walkers are fond of this unpretentious little village local after a day on the fells and the tiled floor is used to walkers' muddy boots. The several simply furnished connecting rooms can get quite crowded in summer, but even then there's a good atmosphere and the staff are welcoming. The home-made food is generous and hearty, including sandwiches (from £2.15), soup (£2.25), large ploughman's (from £4.35), Hungarian goulash, sweet and sour pork or good steak and mushroom pie (£4.95), jumbo Cumberland sausages made in Keswick to the pub's own recipe (not for the faint hearted! £5.85), daily specials like mushroom stroganoff, beef curry madras, or lamb provençale, and puddings (from £1.85). Well kept Theakstons Best, XB and Old Peculier and guests like Boddingtons Bitter or Jennings Bitter on handpump. The spacious upstairs children's room has a pool table and juke box (oldies); there are also darts and trivia. The owners let a couple of holiday cottages in the village; we have no experience of the one by the pub but can recommend the one up the hill. *(Recommended by V and E A Bolton, I E and C A Prosser, Nigel Woolliscroft, Paul and Sue Merrick, Nick Cox, David Heath, M and J Back, G and M Stewart)*

S & N ~ Tenants Ken and Rose Burchill ~ Real ale ~ Meals and snacks (not 25 Dec) ~ Children welcome (must be in family room after 9pm) ~ Threlkeld (0176 87) 79614 ~ Open 11-3, 5.30-11; 12-2, 6-11 in winter

TROUTBECK NY4103 Map 7

Queens Head 🍴 🛏

A592 N of Windermere

Readers have enjoyed the imaginative food here so much over the last year that we have decided to give this friendly 17th-c coaching inn a food award. All dishes are freshly prepared to order and they use no frozen products at all – and although this can mean a wait at busy times people tell us it is well worth it. You can also have only a starter or pudding if you want and they will serve half helpings for children (no special menu). Good soup like celery and apple or mushroom and tarragon with home-made brown bread (£1.95), lunchtime filled french bread (from £2.50), chorizo sausage, black pudding and sauté potatoes (£3.50), at least four vegetarian dishes such as canelloni filled with ricotta cheese and spinach with a cheese and nutmeg sauce (£5.95), Indonesian chicken with spicy banana and sultana sauce (£6.95), fillet of salmon poached with white wine, cream, sun-dried tomatoes and fresh herbs (£7.95), and lamb shank braised with root vegetables, red wine, redcurrants and rosemary (£8.95), with lovely puddings such as delicious Baileys crème brûlée, white chocolate and praline truffle cake or walnut and maple syrup sponge; good vegetables. The bright bar has cushioned antique settles among more orthodox furniture, a massive Elizabethan four-poster bed as the basis of its serving counter, other fine antique carving, and two roaring log fires in imposing fireplaces. The bar rambles through some half-dozen attractively decorated rooms, including an unusual lower gallery, a comfortable dining area and lots of alcoves and heavy beams. Well kept Boddingtons, Mitchells ESB, and Tetleys and weekly changing guest beers on handpump; friendly service; darts, dominoes, chess and cards. Plenty of seats outside have a fine view over the Trout valley to Applethwaite moors. *(Recommended by H K Dyson, WAH, Lynn Sharpless, Bob Eardley, Sara Geyer, Mick*

Whelton, Phil and Heidi Cook, Philip Saxon, A Preston, Mike and Jo, R E and P Pearce, John Norris, Bob Hurling, Roz Hodges, Trickie Hirst)

Free house ~ Licensees Mark Stewardson and Joanne Sherratt ~ Real ale ~ Meals and snacks ~ Restaurant ~ Ambleside (0153 94) 32174 ~ Children welcome ~ Open 11-11; closed 25 Dec ~ Bedrooms: £37.50B/£55B

ULVERSTON SD2978 Map 7

Bay Horse 🍴 ♀

Canal Foot signposted off A590 and then again by the large factory

The delicious food here is so beautifully presented that it almost seems a shame to eat it. In the bar it might include home-made baps (£1.35), home-made soup (£1.85), home-made herb and cheese pâté with cranberry and ginger purée (£4.50), smoked venison sausage with sage and apple stuffing, fried onions and sun-dried tomatoes (£6.75), layers of beef tomato, aubergine and red peppers in a rich savoury egg custard with emmental cheese and fresh basil (£6.95), courgettes stuffed with mushroom and onion pâté wrapped in Cumbrian air-dried ham, baked on bed of sliced leek with cheese and peanut butter sauce (£7.25), slices of salami and red kidney beans baked in a tomato provençale on fresh pasta (£7.50), and home-made puddings (£2.95). There's also the grill with well hung Scotch steaks, and three-course set lunch in the no-smoking conservatory restaurant (£14.50). There's a steady flow of real ales on handpump which might include Hook Norton Old Hookey, Timothy Taylors Landlord, Marstons Pedigree, Mitchells ESB, Wadworths 6X and so forth, a decent choice of spirits, and an impressive and interesting New World wine list, tea, coffee, hot chocolate and home-made shortbread. The restaurant has exceptional views across to Morecambe Bay. The bar has a pubby atmosphere and a huge stone horse's head, as well as attractive wooden armchairs, some pale green plush built-in wall banquettes, glossy hardwood traditional tables, blue plates on a delft shelf, and black beams and props with lots of horsebrasses. Magazines are dotted about, there's a handsomely marbled green granite fireplace, and decently reproduced piped music; darts, bar billiards, shove-ha'penny, cribbage and dominoes. Out on the terrace are some picnic-table sets. The owners also run a very good restaurant at their Miller Howe hotel on Windermere. *(Recommended by Christopher Mobbs, Philip Vernon, Kim Maidment, Jack Morley, Ian Morley, A and M Dickinson, Brian Jones, Neville Kenyon, Stephen Newell, Greg Parston; also recommended by* The Good Hotel Guide*)*

Free house ~ Licensee Robert Lyons ~ Real ale ~ Lunchtime bar meals and snacks (not Mon) ~ Restaurant (not Sun or Mon lunchtimes) ~ Ulverston (01229) 53972 ~ Children in eating area of bar ~ Open 11-11 ~ Bedrooms: £80B/£140B inc dinner

WASDALE HEAD NY1808 Map 9

Wasdale Head Inn 🛏

To NE of lake; signposted from Gosforth

The marvellous steep fellside setting of this busy gabled old pub has the added advantage of being well away from the main Lakeland tourist areas; it makes an excellent base for walking and climbing. The high-ceilinged, spacious main bar has shiny panelling, cushioned settles on the polished slate floor, fine George Abraham photographs on the walls, and a log-effect gas fire; there's an adjoining pool room, as well as a panelled and comfortably old-fashioned residents' bar and lounge. The snug, restaurant and children's room are no smoking. Popular bar food includes home-made soup (£2.10), home-made shepherd's pie (£4.50), home-made steak and kidney pie (£4.75), cold platters (from £4.90), Cumberland sausage or cheese and onion flan (£6.25), and puddings. Well kept Jennings, Theakstons Best and Old Peculier and Yates on handpump, a decent choice of malt whiskies, and good wine list; dominoes, cribbage. If you're in the car, the drive along the screes by the lake is pleasant. *(Recommended by David Wright,*

Andrew Stephenson, Nigel Woolliscroft, Dr R H M Stewart, D Baker, Brian and Jill Bond, H K Dyson, E A George, Peter and Lynn Brueton; also recommended by The Good Hotel Guide*)*

Free house ~ Licensee Jaspar Carr ~ Real ale ~ Meals and snacks (11-3, 6.30-9.45 ~ Restaurant ~ Wasdale (0194 67) 26229 ~ Children in own room ~ Open 11-11; closed mid-Nov-28 Dec, mid-Jan-mid-Feb ~ Bedrooms: £25B/£50B; also, self-catering cottages

WINSTER SD4293 Map 9

Brown Horse 🍴
A5074 S of Windermere

The food in this popular dining pub would put many restaurants to shame – indeed Steven Doherty spent many years working for the Roux brothers. Using fresh produce and totally home-made, the menu might include excellent soup such as cream of tomato with basil and pesto sauce (£2), creamed chicken and mushrooms gratinated with parmesan cheese (£3.50), hors d'oeuvres or vegetarian aubergine and polenta (£4.50), crêpe fruits de mer (£5.50), fillet of prime plaice (£6), jumbo prawns in crispy batter with a remoulade sauce (£6.50), and puddings like chocolate and praline mousse or apple strudel (from £2.20); they will do sandwiches if they are not too busy. You must book to be sure of a table. Well kept Jennings and Marstons Pedigree on handpump, and short but thoughtful wine list; cheerful, helpful service. The big open-plan light and comfortable main room has plenty of room between tables on the red carpeted floor and a blazing winter log fire. No games machines or piped music. *(Recommended by G R Prest, A L Strange, WHBM, Mr and Mrs S Ashcroft, Dick Brown, P Barnsley)*

Free house ~ Licensees Rudolf Schaefer, Steven Doherty ~ Real ale ~ Meals and snacks ~ (0153 94) 43443 ~ Children welcome ~ Open 12-3, 6-11

Lucky Dip

Besides the fully inspected pubs, you might like to try these Lucky Dips recommended to us and described by readers (if you do, please send us reports):

☆ **Alston** [Main St; NY7246], *Turks Head*: Spotless and charming little pub in corner of square at top of steep cobbled street, extremely well priced if limited menu, well kept Boddingtons and Theakstons on handpump, friendly landlord and staff, convivial atmosphere, bar counter dividing big front room into two areas, back lounge with cosy fire and small tables, friendly landlord *(Jim and Maggie Cowell, H K Dyson, Frank Davidson)*
Ambleside [Market Sq; NY3804], *Queens*: Recently refurbished bar with pleasant staff, big helpings of good value bar food, Boddingtons, Hook Norton, Jennings, Oatmeal Stout and Theakstons XB; red-cushioned wall seats and stools matching the padding on the modern bar counter, swagged floral curtains, flowery patterned wallpaper, log fire with ornamental mirrored chimneypiece; separate cellar bar with pool room, real ale; bedrooms all with own bathrooms *(H K Dyson, Pat Woodward)*; [Lake Rd], *Royal Oak*: Very busy and pubby local with good log fire, well kept Theakstons *(H K Dyson)*
☆ **nr Ambleside** [A592 N of Troutbeck; NY4007], *Kirkstone Pass*: Lakeland's

highest inn, with fine surrounding scenery and best of all out of season; snug and cheery inside with lots of bric-a-brac, wide choice of whiskies, well kept Tetleys, popular coffee, open fire, lively amusements, simple food; bedrooms, all with four-posters *(Brian and Jenny Seller, H K Dyson, LYM; more reports on new regime please)*
Appleby [Boroughgate; NY6921], *Crown & Cushion*: Busy pub in main square, good mixture of enlarged rooms and rambling passageways; appealing food *(Dave Braisted)*; [25 Clifford St], *Midland*: Clean, friendly and cosy pub next to Settle—Carlisle rly stn up above town; now owned by Jennings, with reasonably priced usual bar food in separate small dining area, well kept Jennings and Marstons on electric pump, dogs welcome *(Alan and Eileen Gough)*
☆ **Bampton** [NY5118], *St Patricks Well*: Pretty little village local in stonebuilt terrace, well kept Jennings Bitter and Mild on handpump, good malt whiskies (welcoming Scots landlord), good bar food inc wonderful steaks and fresh veg (not Mon lunchtime in winter), real fire, friendly

locals, pool room, darts, juke box (may be loud), TV; a couple of seats outside; bedrooms simple, good value and clean, with good breakfasts *(Anne and Chris Norman, H K Dyson, David Heath, David Cooke, BB)*

Bampton Grange [NY5218], *Crown & Mitre*: Enthusiastic welcoming landlady, simple cheap food, real ale, darts and quiz teams; bedrooms simple and cheap *(D J Cooke)*

☆ **Bardsea** [SD3074], *Bradylls Arms*: Wide choice of good food from sandwiches to fresh seafood and duck in plushly refurbished old village inn, some stripped stone, lovely Morecambe Bay views from well furnished back conservatory restaurant; Boddingtons and Theakstons real ale, very friendly landlady; garden with play area *(C Roberts, Peter and Lynn Brueton)*

☆ **Beckermet** [NY0207], *White Mare*: Big pub with well furnished connecting rooms, good home-cooked bar food inc delicious puddings, well kept Theakstons, friendly landlord; tables in streamside garden, attractive village *(Chris and Anne Fluck, Irene Shuttleworth)*

☆ **Biggar** [Isle of Walney, opp Barrow; SD1965], *Queens Arms*: Snug little bar with lots of woodwork, good home-made bar food from sandwiches up, high-backed settles in family eating room, restaurant, Hartleys on handpump, open fire, tables in courtyard; piped music may be loud; fine windswept surroundings, nr sandy beaches and nature reserve; closed Mon exc bank hols *(LYM)*

☆ **Blencow** [NY4633], *Clickham*: Comfortable, with real fires, quaint alcoves, good efficient service, good food, Whitbreads-related real ales *(D T Taylor)*

☆ **Boot** [just off Wrynose/Hardknott Pass rd – OS Sheet 89 map reference 175010; NY1701], *Burnmoor*: Well used friendly walkers' inn beautifully placed below the fells, generous quickly served standard bar food with one or two Austrian dishes, maybe their own veg and eggs, good puddings; well kept Jennings Bitter and Cumberland on handpump, pool room, juke box; children welcome till 9; comfortable bedrooms *(Paul S McPherson, John Evans, LM, Richard Waller, Peter and Lynn Brueton, A Preston, Russell and Margaret Bathie, Elizabeth and Anthony Watts, Helen Hazzard, John and Marianne Cooper, LYM)*

Bouth [off A590 nr Haverthwaite; SD3386], *White Hart*: In good South Lakes walking country, friendly Australian managers, good food inc barbecues behind, come-as-you-are atmosphere; bedrooms *(Sally Edsall)*

Bowness on Windermere [SD4097], *Royal Oak*: Comfortable, clean and friendly local; limited menu, well kept Whitbreads-related ales *(D J Underwood)*

Braithwaite [NY2324], *Royal Oak*:

Jennings ales, bar meals, pool in back room, piped music *(D Hanley)*

Brampton [Market Pl; the one just off A69 E of Carlisle; NY5361], *Nags Head*: Friendly pub with Whitbreads beers, bar food, dogs; open afternoons *(Roger Berry)*; [old A69, Newcastle Rd], *Sands*: Well kept Jennings, good plentiful food *(David and Margaret Bloomfield)*

nr **Brampton** [Roweltown, several miles N – off B6318 and W of Stapleton; NY4971], *Drove*: Very remote, good food inc speciality steaks (booking advised), real ale, bar full of splendid characters who might still be reavers *(David and Margaret Bloomfield)*

Brigsteer [OS Sheet 97 map reference 481896; SD4889], *Wheatsheaf*: Welcoming and attractively placed Whitbreads pub with particularly well kept Boddingtons and Theakstons, usual bar food *(A T Langton, R D Knight, David Wallington)*

Brothers Water [NY4013], *Brothers Water*: Full of campers from nearby sites having a great time on all the games, bunk-bed accommodation for those not hardy enough for tents; rather different, worth a look *(H K Dyson)*

Brough [Main St; NY7914], *Golden Fleece*: Huge helpings of good food like trout and almonds or mixed grill with lots of veg or salad; Boddingtons and guest beers on handpump *(Michael and Rachael Dunlop)*

Brough Sowerby [A685; NY7913], *Black Bull*: Locally popular for wide choice of beautifully presented food; atmosphere perhaps not its strongest suit *(L Heethfield)*

☆ **Broughton in Furness** [Church St; SD2187], *Old Kings Head*: Big helpings of good moderately priced food from sandwiches and children's dishes up in smart but relaxed old-world pub with stone fireplace, chintz and nick-nacks, prompt friendly service; bedrooms *(Geoff Lee, Linda White, Jason Macniven)*

Buttermere [NY1817], *Fish*: Spacious bar area with well kept Theakstons Best, XB and Old Peculier and bar food from sandwiches up in smartly refurbished former coaching inn between Buttermere and Crummock Water; bedrooms *(H K Dyson, BB)*

Caldbeck [NY3039], *Oddfellows Arms*: Large recently updated village pub with Jennings and Tetleys ales, good wide-ranging menu, pleasant staff and relaxed atmosphere *(Peter and Pat Frogley)*

☆ **Cark in Cartmel** [B5278; follow Holker Hall signs; SD3776], *Engine*: Newish owners going from strength to strength in comfortably refurbished pub with good value food inc good soups, delicious lunchtime sandwiches and pies, enormous meat platter, Theakstons Best and XB and Youngers, very friendly obliging staff, open fire; restaurant, tables out by little stream; self-contained holiday flats *(M and J Back, A T Langton, Louise and Simon Chappell, BB)*

Cark in Cartmel [SD3776], *Cavendish Arms*: Homely old-fashioned pub with good food, good choice of beers, friendly staff and customers *(Alan G Moore)*; *Pheasant*: South Lakes real ale pub with interesting guest beers, small open-plan dining room/lounge, games room; food inc Indian and Chinese take-aways *(John Scarisbrick)*

Carlisle [Lowther St], *Howard Arms*: Well kept Theakstons on handpump, food inc ploughman's, baked potatoes, steak sandwiches at lunchtime; crowded, can be smoky *(Ian and Gabrielle)*; [Milbourne St], *Woolpack*: Well kept Jennings on handpump in big clean open rooms with dance floor (jazz and disco, can get loud and smoky later), food lunchtime and evening; bedrooms basic but clean *(Ian and Gabrielle)*

☆ **Cockermouth** [Main St; NY1231], *Bush*: Recently refurbished to high standard, but still keeping tradition and character; well kept Jennings Bitter and Cumberland, usually two guests, friendly atmosphere and staff, good food *(Ian Woodhead, Gayle Butterfield, Stephen Crothers)*

Coniston [SD3098], *Black Bull*: Big 16th-c pub with separate rooms appropriate to walkers and to better-dressed trippers, two log fires, piped baroque and classical music, relaxed atmosphere, usual bar food promptly served, well kept S&N ales, restaurant, tables in enclosed courtyard *(Linda White, Jason Macniven, David Heath, I H Rorison)*; [Bowmanstead, behind Broughton rd], *Ship*: Popular with campers from lakeside campsites for good-sized helpings of good value food, well kept Hartleys, pool room; children in evenings if eating *(Michael A Butler)*

Cowgill [nr Dent Station, on Dent—Garsdale Head rd; SD7587], *Sportsmans*: Fine Dentdale location with good nearby walks; home-made bar food lunchtime and evening, real ale, log fires, bar/lounge with darts in snug at one end and pool room at the other; bedrooms all overlooking river *(E G Parish)*

☆ **Crosby Ravensworth** [NY6215], *Butchers Arms*: Good value simple food, well kept S&N beers on handpump, friendly young licensees, simple but comfortable furnishings, interesting mountain photographs, pretty village and countryside; children welcome; closed winter weekday lunchtimes *(BB)*

☆ **Crosthwaite** [off A5074 Levens—Windermere; SD4491], *Punch Bowl*: Interestingly rambling many-roomed modernised dining bar with upper galleries, usual food, helpful smartly dressed staff, well kept S&N ales, separate games area, some tables outside; children and dogs allowed, restaurant; pleasant roomy bedrooms (readers prefer nos 2 and 3), attractive quiet location *(Jane Thompson, Michael Butler, Roy and Bettie Derbyshire, LYM)*

Cumwhitton [some way outside village; NY5152], *Pheasant*: Goes from strength to strength, good food and atmosphere, changing guest beers; booking essential at weekends *(David and Margaret Bloomfield)*

☆ **Dean** [just off A5086 S of Cockermouth; NY0825], *Royal Yew*: Good range of particularly good value food rather than atmosphere is what puts the pressure on table space in this friendly comfortably modernised dining pub; well kept Stones *(Elizabeth and Anthony Watts, D Boyd, Tim Gilroy)*

☆ **Deanscales** [A5086 S of Cockermouth; NY0927], *Old Posting House*: Very welcoming and comfortable food pub, good value from sandwiches through generous home-made stews and pies to steaks and mixed grill, enough chips to feed an army; modernised split-level bar with some stripped stonework, interesting old fittings surviving from posting and coaching days, Lakeland and heavy-horse prints; well kept Jennings Bitter and Cumberland *(Jacquie and Jon Payne, M E A Horler, Elizabeth and Anthony Watts, Tim Gilroy, BB)*

Durdar [NY4151], *Black Lion*: Handy for Carlisle racecourse and not far from M6 junction 42; just taken over by landlord with good track record, particularly for robust good value food and good staffing – so should be worth knowing *(Anon)*

Ennerdale Bridge [NY0716], *Fox & Hounds*: Attractive and cosy local, well kept Jennings, reasonably priced traditional bar meals; popular with walkers, quiet village *(Neil and Elaine Piper)*

☆ **Far Sawrey** [SD3893], *Sawrey*: Simple stable bar with tables in wooden stalls, harness on rough white walls, big helpings of good simple lunchtime bar food, well kept Black Sheep Bitter and Special and Jennings, pleasant staff; separate hotel bar, evening restaurant; seats on nice lawn look up to Claife Heights, which have good views of Lake Windermere; dogs allowed, and they're kind to children; bedrooms *(J E Rycroft, H K Dyson, Greg Parston)*

☆ **Glenridding** [back of main car park, top of road; NY3917], *Travellers Rest*: Well kept Flowers and Whitbreads Castle Eden now in homely unpretentious bar (known as the Jerry from the days when it was used by local lead miners); big helpings of good simple food for hungry walkers, simple newish decor, everyone friendly *(David Lewis, H K Dyson, Russell and Margaret Bathie)*

☆ **Grasmere** [main bypass rd; NY3406], *Swan*: A Forte hotel but very individual and distinctive, with relaxed atmosphere, friendly service even when busy, lively little public bar, quieter old-fashioned up-market lounge popular with older people, oak beams, armchairs, velvet curtains, prints and swords, inglenook log fires; well prepared bar food, keg beer but good malt whiskies, tables in garden, picturesque surroundings, drying room for walkers; easy parking; comfortable bedrooms *(John

Evans, John Atherton, Elizabeth and Anthony Watts, LYM)

☆ **Grasmere** [in village], *Red Lion*: Ideal spot in lovely village, very friendly staff, good bar food in pleasing hotel lounge and conservatory, well priced restaurant meals, well kept beers, good range of malt whiskies; bedrooms spotless *(Andy and Jill Kassube, W H and E Thomas)*

☆ **Grasmere** *Wordsworth*: Well kept and stylish hotel; its popular down-to-earth separate Dove & Olive Branch bar does good cheap bar food, with cheerful barmaid, log fire and well kept Bass Special; good light lunches in conservatory, nice garden, comfortable bedrooms *(Peter and Pat Frogley, LYM)*

Grasmere, *Tweedies*: Comfortable lounge bar with good, though not cheap, standard bar food – very tasty; well kept Boddingtons and Theakstons on handpump, good service, tartan displays, restaurant *(Chris Cook, Simon Watkins)*

Haweswater [NY4914], *Haweswater Hotel*: Lovely spot, and handy for walkers; bedrooms *(H K Dyson)*

Hawkshead [SD3598], *Red Lion*: Friendly modernside village pub with some old-fashioned touches (and interesting carved gables), good log fire, Courage-related ales, bar food, piped music; bedrooms *(H K Dyson, Jean and Douglas Troup, LYM)*; *Sun*: Newish landlord making headway in pleasant pub with sizeable eating area, simple well prepared food; bedrooms *(D J and P M Taylor)*

☆ **Howtown** [NY4519], *Howtown Hotel*: Restful hotel in stunning setting nr Ullswater, small cosy lounge bar and public bar with lunchtime food inc good ham sandwiches for hungry walkers, morning coffee or afternoon tea; very welcoming, well kept Theakstons Best, sound wines by the glass, pleasant garden; bedrooms *(David Cooke, Lucy James, RKP)*

☆ **Ireby** [NY2439], *Sun*: Attractive, unspoilt country local, clean and friendly, with good plentiful food, well kept Jennings, woodburning stove, beams, brasses and harness, red plush seats and polished tables; no meals Tues lunch; no meals Mon (winter) *(A Preston, John and Maggie Churcher)*

Kendal [SD5293], *Globe*: Civilised and popular beamed and carpeted split-level bar, pleasant decor, cheerful atmosphere, good cheap bar food, quick friendly service, separate dining-room upstairs (where children welcome); has had loud music at night *(Mr and Mrs C Roberts)*; [Stramongate], *Phoenix*: Very clean, with Vaux ales, usual food but good and cheap, inc children's dishes *(Mrs L H Lever)*; *Riverside*: Praised in previous editions as the best place here for good bar food, well kept Tetleys and comfortable bedrooms, but alas now converted into an insurance company training centre

☆ **Keswick** [Lake Rd, off top end Mkt Sq; NY2624], *Dog & Gun*: Unpretentious town local, friendly, busy and lively, with some high settles, low beams, partly slate floor (rest carpeted or boards), fine Abrahams mountain photographs, log fire; well kept Theakstons Best, XB and Old Peculier, open fires, good helpings of popular bar food from sandwiches up (hot ham with Cumberland sauce, filled baked potatoes, goulash generally recommended), nostalgic piped music; children if eating, no dogs *(WAH, Dave and Jules Tuckett, V and E A Bolton, D Hanley, Andrew Sykes, Mark Bradley, Paul and Gail Betteley, Philip Saxon, H K Dyson, P and M Rudlin, LYM)*

☆ **Keswick** [Crosthwaite Rd; by A66, a mile out], *Pheasant*: Delightful atmosphere in cosy beamed pub decorated with amusing country prints by local artist, big helpings of reasonably priced usual food promptly served, outstandingly friendly and helpful staff; children if eating; bedrooms *(WAH, P and M Rudlin)*

☆ **Keswick** [St John's St], *George*: Attractive black-panelled side room with good log fire where the poet Southey used to wait for Wordsworth to arrive from Grasmere, also open-plan main bar with old-fashioned settles and modern banquettes under Elizabethan beams; bar food, well kept Theakstons and Yates, smartish restaurant; bedrooms comfortable *(P and M Rudlin, H K Dyson, LYM)*

Keswick [Lake Rd], *Four in Hand*: Cosy and smart, wide choice of good reasonably priced food, full range of Jennings ales on handpump, friendly staff; go early for a seat *(Paul and Gail Betteley, Dave and Jules Tuckett)*; [Market Pl], *Keswick Lodge*: Comfortable free house with pubby atmosphere, well kept beers, good reasonably priced food, pleasant service *(Ian Fraser)*; *Oddfellows Arms*: Busy but cheerful, big helpings of varied food, particularly well kept Jennings *(Mike Appleton)*

☆ nr **Keswick** [Newlands Valley – OS Sheet 90 map reference 242217], *Swinside*: Lovely spot in peaceful valley surrounded by marvellous crags and fells; cleanly modernised, with well kept Jennings Bitter, Cumberland and Sneck Lifter, decent house wine, open fires, usual bar food, restaurant; tables outside with best view; dogs allowed, open all day Sat and summer, may not open winter lunchtimes; bedrooms *(WAH, H K Dyson, V and E A Bolton, LYM)*

☆ **Kirkby Stephen** [NY7808], *Kings Arms*: Solidly comfortable old-fashioned oak-panelled lounge bar, good home cooking inc good sandwiches, popular lunchtime cold table, meals in decent-sized dining room (where children allowed), well kept Whitbreads-related beers, friendly and helpful owners, darts and dominoes in easy-going main bar, tables in walled garden; bedrooms *(H and M Steavenson, Dono and Carol Leaman, LYM)*

☆ **Lanercost** [(attached to New Bridge Hotel); NY5664], *Abbey Bridge*: Delightful conversion of old forge, stone walls, high rafters, spiral stairs to minstrel gallery restaurant above, four real ales on handpump, warm welcome, and some concentration on good food, with lively mix of diners and locals; pretty riverside position; bedrooms *(John Oddey, J E Rycroft, Barry and Anne, R E and P Pearce)*

☆ **Langdale** [by car park for Stickle Ghyll; NY2906], *Stickle Barn*: Well placed for walkers and mountaineers (and very popular with them), in lovely setting with good walk (not as hard as it looks) past waterfall to Stickle Tarn high above; lively and well kept, good choice of food, well kept Courage-related beers, fruit machines and so forth; big pleasant terrace, open all day in summer; bunkhouse accommodation *(Philip Orbell)*
Laversdale [N of Carlisle airport; NY4762], *Sportsman*: Enormous mixed grills and steaks superbly cooked and presented; booking essential at weekends *(David and Margaret Bloomfield)*

☆ **Lazonby** [NY5539], *Joiners Arms*: Small and simply refurbished, very friendly licensees, well kept Bass and Stones, good food; comfortable bedrooms *(Robert and Susan Phillips, Dr Sherriff)*

☆ **Levens** [Sedgwick Rd, by Sizergh Castle gates – OS Sheet 97 map reference 500872; SD5087], *Strickland Arms*: 16th-c pub owned by National Trust, standard breweryised internal refurbishment but clean and comfortable, with well kept Theakstons, wide choice of good value popular bar food, friendly staff, log fire; beer mats over bar, dried flowers, prints and plates; piped music, children allowed, good garden *(Mr and Mrs C Roberts, David Wallington, A T Langton)*

☆ **Lindale** [B5277 N of Grange-over-Sands – OS Sheet 97 map reference 419805; SD4280], *Lindale*: Big helpings of good reasonably priced food from sandwiches to huge steaks and Sun roast in comfortable spacious bar with nice oak-beamed dining area (children welcome here); well kept Whitbreads Castle Eden, good friendly service; bedrooms *(Janis and Neil Hedgecock, Mr and Mrs C Roberts)*

☆ **Little Bampton** [NY2755], *Tam o' Shanter*: Out-of-the-way village pub with spacious modernised plush lounge, neat and attractive communicating dining area, neatly carpeted games area; has gone through some recent foodless interregnums, but we are hoping the present new management will re-establish its reputation for civilised good value food *(W S Purslow, L D Rainger, LYM)*
Lorton [on Buttermere-Cockermouth Rd; NY1525], *Wheat Sheaf*: Doing well under newish management, spacious new restaurant with central open fire, bar with log fire, a few books to read, darts, new

juke box, quiet fruit machine; well kept Jennings, pleasant atmosphere and staff *(Tim Heywood, Sophie Wilne)*

☆ **Lowick Bridge** [just off A5084; SD2986], *Red Lion*: Cheerful, attractive and cosy, with two spacious and comfortable areas, well kept Hartleys XB and Robinsons, good choice of inviting food from sparkling kitchen; charming location – not too touristy, but pub can get very busy *(David Heath, JCW)*
Lupton [A65, nr M6 junction 36; SO5681], *Plough*: Good food under new young and enthusiastic management *(Jean and Douglas Troup)*

☆ **Middleton** [A683 Kirkby Lonsdale—Sedbergh; SD6386], *Swan*: Simple and quaint very old two-roomed pub, clean, friendly and great on character – mainly through the two sisters who run it; keg beer, but open fire in bar, small but varied choice of good food in second room; particularly good steaks *(David Heath, Mike and Wendy Proctor, LYM)*

☆ **Middleton** [A683 Kirkby Lonsdale—Sedbergh; SD6288], *Middleton Fells*: Comfortably plush open-plan oak-beamed bar with lots of brasswork (some made by the landlord), open fire, good choice of popular home-made food, friendly service, well kept Boddingtons and Tetleys; games room, juke box; very attractive garden, charming countryside; children welcome *(David Heath, LYM – deserves more customers)*

☆ **Mungrisdale** [village signed off A66 Penrith—Keswick, a bit over a mile W of A5091 Ullswater rd – OS Sheet 90 map reference 363302; NY3731], *Mill Inn*: Simple pub in lovely valley hamlet, tasty bar food, S&N real ale, lots of malt whiskies, maybe a table reserved for local dominoes players, plain extension with pool table, separate restaurant; children welcome, tables on gravel forecourt and neat lawn sloping to little river, can arrange salmon and sea trout fishing on River Eden; warm pleasant bedrooms (note that there's a quite separate Mill Hotel here) *(V and E A Bolton, LYM)*
Nateby [B6259 Kirkby Stephen—Wensleydale; NY7807], *Black Bull*: Popular but relaxed; genuine country pub with friendly atmosphere and locals, roaring log fire, pleasant layout with nice decorations and beams, Theakstons and Youngers beers; big helpings of good food inc imaginative meat and vegetarian dishes, children's dishes, delicious puddings; good service, ramblers very welcome; bedrooms good value, superb breakfasts *(Anon)*
Nenthead [NY7843], *Miners Arms*: Basic family-run pub with friendly welcome, some choice of beers, reasonably priced home-cooked food; children welcome *(Edward Watson)*

☆ **Nether Wasdale** [NY1204], *Strands*: Lovely spot below the remote high fells around Wastwater, good range of generous bar food, well kept Hartleys XB and Robinsons, run by friendly family; bedrooms *(Peter and Lynn Brueton)*

Nether Wasdale [OS Sheet 89 map reference 125041], *Screes*: Big friendly bar, well kept ales, reasonably priced food, interesting piped music; five bedrooms, great views *(Peter and Lynn Brueton)*

Newbiggin [B6413; NY5649], *Blue Bell*: Small, cramped and friendly, very busy bar and kitchen staff, good food esp Cumberland sausage *(David and Margaret Bloomfield)*

Newby Bridge [SD3786], *Newby Bridge*: Revamped and redecorated panelled hotel bar, friendly service, decent beer, food limited but good value; bedrooms *(LM)*; *Swan*: Fine setting next to river with waterside picnic-table sets by old stone bridge; bedrooms *(LM)*

☆ **Oxenholme** [½ mile up hill, B6254 towards Old Hutton – OS Sheet 97 map reference 536900; SD5390], *Station*: Tidy, clean and comfortable breweryised country pub with good generous straightforward food, well kept S&N and Whitbreads-related beers, very friendly staff, log fire, garden; name dates from coaching rather than railway era *(David Wallington, Mr and Mrs C Roberts)*

Patterdale [NY3916], *White Lion*: Long, narrow pub popular with walkers, open all day with something to eat all day in summer, S&N and Whitbreads real ale, comfortable banquettes; cheery, but bar staff may change too often to be consistently helpful; piped music even in the lavatories; parking 100 yards away across road; bedrooms basic, but good views *(Peter and Lynn Brueton, H K Dyson, A Preston, Philip Crawford)*

☆ **Penrith** [NY5130], *George*: Handsome old-fashioned beamed and oak-panelled hotel lounge hall with fine plasterwork, oak settles and easy chairs around good open fire, big bow windows; short choice of reasonably priced lunchtime bar food, well kept Marstons Pedigree, lively back bar, restaurant; bedrooms *(LYM)*

Penrith [Cromwell Rd/Castlegate; first roundabout coming from M6], *Agricultural*: Doing well since sale by Marstons to Jennings, with their ales kept well, good service and wide choice of good inexpensive food *(J M Potter)*

Pooley Bridge [NY4724], *Swiss Chalet*: Free house with choice of real ales, wide choice of very popular bar meals, separate dining room, friendly staff; bedrooms comfortable and well equipped *(Margaret and Fred Punter)*

Portinscale [off A66 at Grane/Newlands Valley sign; NY2523], *Farmers Arms*: Very generous food, well kept Jennings, comfortable seats, very welcoming landlord; lots of locals and visitors *(H K Dyson, V and E A Bolton)*

☆ **Ravenstonedale** [signed off A685 Kirkby Stephen—M6; NY7204], *Black Swan*: Sedately comfortable hotel bar with open

fire, polished copper-topped tables, some stripped stonework and panelling-effect wall finish, tables in pretty tree-sheltered streamside garden over road; good bar food with interesting specials, well kept Hartleys XB, Robinsons, Theakstons, Worthington, Youngers and a changing guest, lots of country wines, good service, welcoming licensees, evening restaurant; dogs welcome; comfortable well equipped bedrooms, inc some for disabled *(John Allsopp, Malcolm Phillips, BB)*

Ravenstonedale, *Kings Head*: Currently under same management as above entry; neat comfortable beamed bar, log fires, well kept Bass Special and S&N beers, good bar food and evening meals (booking suggested); children welcome; bedrooms *(John Allsopp, LYM)*

☆ **nr Ravenstonedale** [Crossbank; A683 Sedbergh—Kirkby Stephen], *Fat Lamb*: Remote friendly inn recently extended to give more bar space (and residents' lounge and TV lounge); brightly modernised bar with pews, piped music, log fire in traditional black kitchen range, good photographs of steam trains and local beagles; cheerful service, usual bar food, keg beers, maybe piped classical music, restaurant, seats out by sheep pastures; comfortable bedrooms with own bathrooms *(WAH, Malcolm Phillips, BB)*

Red Dial [NY2546], *Sun*: Clean and comfortable functional main-road pub/restaurant with well kept ales such as Hesket Newmarket, Jennings and Theakstons, wide choice of very generous food, polite quite speedy service; piped pop music *(Mr and Mrs C Roberts, Mr and Mrs L D Rainger)*

☆ **Rockcliffe** [NY3661], *Crown & Thistle*: Comfortable and clean, modern but not too much so, wide choice of attractively priced good food in huge helpings, very fast friendly service even when busy, well kept Theakstons Bitter and Mild; locally popular games bar *(Mr and Mrs C Roberts)*

☆ **Rosthwaite** [NY2615], *Scafell*: Purpose-built basic flagstoned walkers' bar, very popular with them for short choice of good value lunchtime food, full range of Theakstons ales kept well, quick friendly service; glassed-in verandah overlooking river, subdued piped proper music, wider range of food in smart hotel's sunlounge bar; bedrooms *(H K Dyson, Tim Gilroy, Simon Watkins, D Boyd, I H Rorison, Joe and Carol Pattison)*

☆ **Sandside** [B5282 Milnthorpe—Arnside; SD4781], *Ship*: Spacious modernised pub with glorious view of estuary and mountains beyond; bar food, well kept S&N real ales, decent wines, summer barbecues, tables out on grass by good children's play area; children allowed in eating area *(Michael Butler, LYM)*

Santon Bridge [NY1102], *Bridge*: Doing well under new management, modernised hotel bar with imaginative varied choice of good food; bedrooms *(Neil Townend)*

Satterthwaite [SD3492], *Eagles Head*: Friendly and unpretentious village pub with good value generous home-cooked food from soup and sandwiches up (no meals winter evenings), good service, well kept Thwaites on handpump, pool, darts; papers and guidebooks for sale; handy for Grizedale Forest; bedrooms comfortable and clean, shared bathroom *(Sue Holland, David Webster, LM, Sara Geyer, Mick Whelton, Margaret and Roy Randle)*

Seascale [The Banks; NY0401], *Scawfell*: Attractive and comfortable lounges in early Victorian hotel overlooking sea, good range of well kept S&N beers, good value bar food; bedrooms *(B M Eldridge)*

Seatoller [NY2414], *Yew Tree*: Good low-ceilinged restaurant at foot of Honister Pass in area short of good pubs, with well presented and imaginative food inc local specialities, efficient friendly staff; you can get just a drink at the bar, but may have to sit out in the garden with it *(Barry and Diane Powderhill, Bill Sykes)*

Sedbergh [Main St; SD6692], *Bull*: Quiet bar in rather rambling hotel, reasonable choice of beers and food; bedrooms *(B Horner)*; [Finkle St (A683)], *Red Lion*: Cheerful and comfortable local with stuffed gamebirds and sporting prints, full range of Jennings ales kept well, fair range of food, good friendly service *(Richard Houghton, D T Taylor, BB)*

Shap [A6, S end; NY5615], *Greyhound*: Friendly and unpretentious, with wide range of generous good value traditional food, Tetleys real ale; popular with coast-to-coast walkers; bedrooms *(Neil and Elaine Piper)*

St Bees [Main St; NX9712], *Queens*: Simple three-room bar, well kept Boddingtons, Theakstons Best and Youngers Scotch, friendly service and big helpings of good home-made bar food in dining area with big tables; good start or finish for Wainwright's coast-to-coast walk; bedrooms *(Chris Fluck, M E A Horler)*

St Bees [Main St], *Manor House*: Lots of 18th-c beams, nicely upholstered seats, exceptionally friendly service, well kept S&N beers, good choice of food, unobtrusive fruit machine, games room with darts, dominoes and TV football; restaurant; bedrooms *(Geoff Lee)*; [Main St], *Oddfellows Arms*: Little terraced local with well kept Jennings, quiet friendly service, very reasonably priced bar food inc huge helpings of chips, piped music, darts *(Geoff Lee)*

Staveley [SD4798], *Eagle & Child*: Friendly and helpful newish licensees doing good value home-cooked bar food with fresh veg, with well kept Tetleys and Theakstons, in bright but comfortable little modern front lounge and more spacious carpeted bar; well kept, with small neat garden; bedrooms inexpensive, good breakfast *(Dr B and Mrs P B Baker, David Lands, BB)*

Stonethwaite [Borrowdale; NY2613], *Langstrath*: Neat and friendly recently decorated small carpeted bar, good proper fresh bar food, very welcoming staff; delightful village *(Sara Price, H K Dyson)*

☆ **Talkin** [village signed off B6413 S of Brampton; NY5557], *Blacksmiths Arms*: Welcoming and cheerful, recently redecorated with local photographs and paintings of Cumbria; good generous quick food in bar or dining room, Sun lunch very popular (booking advisable); well kept Boddingtons and Theakstons Best on handpump, open fire; unobtrusive piped music, fruit machine; five well appointed bedrooms, prettily set village *(Graham and Lynn Mason, Mr and Mrs C Roberts)*

Talkin, *Hare & Hounds*: Improving under new landlord, with good range of changing real ales such as Eldridge Pope Blackdown Porter and Morlands Old Speckled Hen alongside Jennings; decent food; neat simple bedrooms *(RRD, LYM)*

Tebay [very handy for M6 junction 38; NY6204], *Cross Keys*: Friendly local with pleasant staff, good food in separate eating area, coal fire, darts, pool, cribbage; bedrooms *(C M Charlton, N K Musgrave, Roy and Bettie Derbyshire)*

☆ **Tirril** [3½ miles from M6 junction 40; A66 towards Brough, A6 towards Shap, then B5320 towards Ullswater; NY5126], *Queens Head*: Important change of direction for this useful staging-post off the road to Scotland, with its attractively quaint front core of low beams, black panelling, old-fashioned settles and inglenook fireplace; the new Italian landlord (an experienced restaurateur) has quietened the juke boxes, and the spacious well decorated back restaurant now has great atmosphere (a lot of lamp-cooking) and superb fresh pasta; well kept Theakstons, smart service; lovely unpretentious individually refurbished bedrooms *(Jan and Dave Booth, T S O'Brien, Nick Haslewood, Ilona Pocsik, H K Dyson, Lee Goulding, David Whitehead, LYM)*

☆ **Torver** [A593 S of Coniston; SD2894], *Church House*: Imaginative reasonably priced proper food in small clean tidy low-beamed bar and attractive evening restaurant, splendid hill views, good fire, well kept Whitbreads Castle Eden, very obliging landlord, big garden; children welcome; open all day at least in summer; spacious, airy bedrooms *(W Mecham, Dr and Mrs P B Baker)*

☆ **Troutbeck** [Upper Rd, nr High Green – OS Sheet 90 map reference 411035; NY4103], *Mortal Man*: Comfortable rather modern hotel bar popular for good sandwiches and meals (not Mon evening), well kept S&N beers, good log fire, friendly staff, darts in winter, children welcome; restaurant, comfortable bedrooms, attractive village in spectacular setting; weekend opening (and not bedrooms) Dec, cl Jan-mid Feb *(Mike* *and Wendy Proctor, I H Rorison, H K Dyson, Derek and Margaret Underwood, D J and P M Taylor, Gill and Mike Cross, LYM)*

Troutbeck [the other one, nr Penrith, off A5091/A66; NY3926], *Troutbeck*: Clean, pleasant decor, good choice of straightforward food, pleasant friendly service *(Mr Callard)*

Ulverston [King St; SD2978], *Rose & Crown*: Good friendly traditional pub atmosphere, good food inc interesting seafood, well kept Hartleys XB, Robinsons Best Mild and Bitter, quick service even when busy on Sat market day *(Roy and Bettie Derbyshire, Margaret and Roy Randle)*

☆ **Warwick on Eden** [2 miles from M6, junction 43; A69 towards Hexham, then village signposted; NY4657], *Queens Arms*: Well kept Ind Coope Burton, Tetleys and Greenalls Original, some interesting wines and farm cider in friendly two-room bar with good log fires, model cars, trains and vintage car pictures; good basic food (not winter Sun evening); tables in side garden with bright play area; open all day Sat; children welcome; clean but modest

bedrooms *(John and Diana Elsy, Julian Holland, R E and P Pearce, LYM)*

Whitehaven [Hensingham; NY0017], *Richmond*: Beautifully served attractively priced home-made food in well kept clean surroundings *(Irene Shuttleworth)*

☆ **Winton** [just off A685 N of Kirkby Stephen; NY7810], *Bay Horse*: Friendly little inn in lovely moorland setting, two unpretentious welcoming low-ceilinged rooms decorated with Pennine photographs and local fly-tying, big helpings of good reasonably priced home-cooked food inc fresh veg, well kept Theakstons Best, Jennings Bitter and Cumberland and Youngers Scotch with summer guest beers, pool in games room; may close Tues-Thurs lunchtimes in winter; clean good value bedrooms *(LYM)*

Yanwath [B5320 S of Penrith; NY5128], *Gate*: Good unusual reasonably priced home-made food in welcoming well furnished pub with open fire in old range, well kept Theakstons Best and Yates, friendly service; restaurant *(John D Savage, Bruce Dean)*

Derbyshire and Staffordshire

This area holds the country's brewing capital, Burton on Trent, which produces the two great national beers Bass and Ind Coope Burton, and houses Marstons the regional brewer – whose flagship beer Pedigree is now almost as well known. On an altogether smaller scale Burton also has a good interesting brew pub, the Burton Bridge Brewery. So it's hardly surprising that beer in the area's pubs tends to be better than average – and drinks prices are well below the national average, too. The Brunswick in Derby, brewing its own, is outstandingly cheap, as is that marvellous odd pub the Yew Tree at Cauldon (which sells Burton Bridge even more cheaply than the brew pub itself). Other good pubs standing out for low-priced beer are the Abbey in Derby (tied to Sam Smiths), the Barley Mow at Kirk Ireton (an interesting new entry, a free house), and the John Thompson near Melbourne and Rising Sun at Shraleybrook (both brewing their own). Many of these gain our new Beer Award for the quality of their beer, as do the Alexandra in Derby, the well placed Monsal Head Hotel, the friendly Jervis Arms at Onecote (a good family pub), the Old Crown in Shardlow, the unspoilt Three Stags Heads at Wardlow, the Olde Royal Oak at Wetton, and – doing so well now that it's pushing towards a star award too – the White Horse at Woolley Moor. The Horseshoe at Tatenhill also gains a Beer Award – but its real forte is perhaps wine – the only pub in the area to gain our Wine Award this year. Food prices in the area are rather lower than average, though the area has very few pubs in which food quality stands out as the main draw. Those with better than average food include the Druid at Birchover (huge choice), the Izaak Walton at Cresswell (perhaps the best pub meals in the area), the Miners Arms at Eyam (good home cooking), the Barrel at Foolow (remarkable value), the Robin Hood at Holmesfield (this dining pub, long a bastion of keg beer, is now installing real ale), the civilised Hardinge Arms at Kings Newton, the Jervis Arms at Onecote, the Crown at Rushton Spencer (still a lot of Greek food though the former Greek licensees have gone), the Old Crown in Shardlow (interesting specials), the Olde Dog & Partridge in Tutbury (very popular carvery), the Three Stags Heads at Wardlow, the Greyhound at Warslow (good specials) and the White Horse at Woolley Moor. Because of its enjoyable combination of thriving atmosphere with good often interesting food, it's the White Horse which we choose as the area's Dining Pub of the Year. It's worth noting that Marstons' chain of Tavern Table dining pubs, generally reliable, normally stay open for food all through Sunday afternoon. There's good value food too at two new main entries here: the interestingly old-fashioned Smiths Tavern in Ashbourne, and the exceptionally friendly and welcoming Lantern Pike at Hayfield. New licensees at the Chequers on Froggatt Edge are doing well, gaining it a new Place to Stay Award this year. The Lucky Dip section includes a great many worthwhile pubs – more starred entries than for most areas. Among them we'd particularly pick out the George & Dragon at Alrewas, Derwent at Bamford, Devonshire Arms at Beeley, Albion in Burton on Trent,

Navigation at Buxworth, a choice of several in Castleton, Bluebell at
Farnah Green, Hardwick Inn by Hardwick Hall, George and others in
Hathersage, Slaters at Hill Chorlton, Raddle at Hollington, Cheshire Cheese
at Hope, Worston Mill at Little Bridgeford, Red Lion at Litton, Colvile
Arms at Lullington, Greyhound at Penkhull, Little Mill at Rowarth, Seven
Stars at Sandonbank, Malt Shovel in Shardlow, both Ticknall entries,
George at Tideswell, Derby Tup at Whittington Moor and Crown at
Wrinehill. We have inspected the great majority of these, so can firmly
vouch for them as being well worth using.

ACTON TRUSSELL (Staffs) SJ9318 Map 7

Moat House

Village signposted from A449 just S of Stafford; the right turn off A449 is only 2 miles
(heading N) from M6 junction 13

This year, there are mooring facilities for narrowboats on the Staffordshire and
Worcestershire Canal – which runs along one side of this fine 14th-c timbered
building, and you can wander around the six acres of lovely landscaped grounds.
As the family have a 400-acre farm they are able to supply some of the produce
for the enjoyable food (the rest comes daily from the markets). In the charming
oak-beamed and comfortable bar this includes six home-made daily specials
(from £4.50), as well as home-made soup (£1.50), filled french bread (from
£1.95), home-made duck liver pâté (£2.25), ploughman's (£2.95), filled home-
grown potatoes (from £2.95), omelettes (£3.75), gammon and egg (£4.60),
broccoli cream cheese bake (£4.75), and sirloin steak (£7.95). Part of the
restaurant is no smoking. Well kept Banks's Bitter and Mild, Camerons
Strongarm and Marstons Pedigree on handpump, a good wine list, and decent
range of spirits; helpful, friendly service. Fruit machine, piped music. The house
has been in the Lewis family for nearly 50 years and they have carefully restored
the east wing to its former glory. *(Recommended by Dorothee and Dennis Glover, G J
Parsons, John and Christine Simpson, Graham Reeve, David Heath, Basil J S Minson, D
Cox, R T and J C Moggridge, Peter and Jenny Quine, Dorothy and David Young, M A
Watts, Chris Hackett)*

*Free house ~ Licensees John and Mary Lewis ~ Real ale ~ Meals and snacks (no
bar food Sat evening or Sun) ~ Restaurant ~ (01785) 712217 ~ Children welcome
~ Open 11-3, 6-11; 11-11 Sat; closed 25/26 Dec*

ALSTONEFIELD (Staffs) SK1355 Map 7

George

Village signposted from A515 Ashbourne—Buxton

Nicely set by the village green, this 16th-c stone inn has foreign banknotes on the
low beams, a fine collection of old photographs and pictures of the Peak District,
and pewter tankards hanging by the copper-topped bar counter – where you may
also find a box of greeting cards reproducing paintings by a local artist. A
spacious family room is full of wheelback chairs around tables. Bar food is
ordered at the kitchen door: big helpings of promptly served soup or sandwiches
(£1.60), ploughman's (from £3.45), meat and potato pie, lasagne or home-made
Spanish quiche (£4.85), and 5oz fillet steak (£7.20). Well kept Burtonwood
Bitter, Forshaws and Top Hat on handpump; dominoes and piped music. The big
sheltered stableyard behind the pub has a pretty rockery with picnic seats, and
there are some stone seats beneath the attractive inn sign at the front; you can
arrange with the landlord to camp on the croft. Useful walking country.
*(Recommended by Peter Marshall, Nigel Woolliscroft, Jack and Philip Paxton, Jeanne and
Tom Barnes, Ian and Emma Potts, S R Howe, Dawn and Phil Garside)*

Burtonwood ~ Tenants Richard and Sue Grandjean ~ Real ale ~ Meals and snacks (till 10pm) ~ (0133 527) 205 ~ Children in dining room ~ Open 11-2.30, 6-11

Watts Russell Arms

Hopedale

New licensees have taken over this late 18th-c pub and as we went to press, had made few changes. The furniture is elegantly comfortable, with brocaded wall banquettes and wheelback chairs and carvers, there's an open fire below a copper hood, a growing collection of blue and white china jugs hanging from the ceiling, bric-a-brac around the roughcast walls, and an interesting bar counter made from copper-bound oak barrels. Bar food includes home-made soup (£1.75), filled baps (from £1.85), sausage and egg (£3.75), ploughman's (£3.95), lasagne or chicken curry (£4.25), home-made chilli (£4.25), rump steak (£8), and puddings (from £1.85). Well kept Mansfield Old Baily and Riding Bitter on handpump; darts, table skittles, dominoes. Outside there are picnic-table sets on its sheltered terrace, with more tables behind. Situated in the Peak District National Park, close to Dovedale and the Manifold Valley, it's popular with walkers and busy at weekends. *(Recommended by Joan and John Calvert, Jeanne and Tom Barnes, Eric J Locker, Catherine and Andrew Brian)*

Free house ~ Licensees Frank and Bridgette Lipp ~ Real ale ~ Meals and snacks (not winter Sun evenings, not winter Mon lunchtimes) ~ (0133 527) 271 ~ Children in eating area of bar (must be over 5) ~ Open 12-2.30, 7-11; closed winter Mon lunchtimes

ASHBOURNE (Derbys) SK1846 Map 7

Smiths Tavern

St Johns St; bottom of market place

This attractive and original three-room pub starts by the door as an archetypal well cared for old-fashioned town tavern, with horsebrasses and tankards hanging from heavy black beams, a delft shelf of antique blue and white china, old cigarette and drinks advertisements, and a black leatherette wall seat facing the bar counter. This has well kept Marstons Pedigree, Merrie Monk and maybe a special brew such as Iron Founders, with a particularly good and growing selection of many dozen malt whiskies. Steps take you up to a middle room with leatherette seating around barrel tables, a log-effect gas fire and piano, and beyond that to a light and airy end room with three nice antique settles among more ordinary seats around simple dining tables. Good value bar food includes soup (£1.25), sandwiches or burgers (from £1.50), steak cob £1.75), filled baked potatoes (from £2.75), and lots of main dishes, many home-made, such as beef curry or several vegetarian dishes (£4.95), steak and kidney pie (£5.25), gammon and egg (£5.50) and steaks (from £7.50), with children's dishes (from £2.50). Good friendly service and atmosphere; darts, cribbage, fruit machine and well chosen and reproduced if not quiet piped pop music. *(Recommended by Roger Taylor, H K Dyson, CW, JW, Mr and Mrs D Lawson, Wayne Brindle)*

Marstons ~ Tenants François and Christine Prados ~ Real ale ~ Meals and snacks (11-2.30, 5.30-9) ~ (01335) 342264 ~ Children welcome ~ Maybe piano singalongs Fri, Sun ~ Open 11-3, 5-11 (winter opening 12, 6; cl 25 Dec); all day Sat

ASHFORD IN THE WATER (Derbys) SK1969 Map 7

Ashford Hotel 🛏 ♀

Church Street; village signposted just off A6 Bakewell—Buxton

Comfortable and relaxing, this handsome stone-built inn has lots of gleaming brass and copper on the stripped brick of the broad stone inglenook fireplace, plush seats and stools around its traditional cast-iron-framed tables on the patterned carpet, and an imposing bar counter; there are some no-smoking areas. Friendly neatly dressed staff serve well kept Bass, Stones, a beer brewed for them (Ashford Best and brewed by Coach House) from handpump, and a guest beer such as Morlands Old Speckled Hen or Everards Tiger, decent wines and lots of malt whiskies. Big helpings of decent freshly cooked bar food include sandwiches (from £1.95, not after 5pm), filled baked potatoes (from £2.50), ploughman's (£4.50), vegetable pancakes or steak, kidney and mushroom pie (£4.95), gammon and egg (£5.35), trout fillets in a wine and parsley sauce (£5.75), and children's menu (£1.95); Sunday lunch (£8.95). Cribbage, dominoes, fruit machine, maybe unobtrusive piped music. There are tables out in the garden. The village is remarkably pretty and the packhorse bridge is lovely. *(Recommended by David and Michelle Hedges, Brian and Anna Marsden, Pat and Tony Young, G J Parsons, Mr and Mrs R F Wright, J Weeks, Ann and Colin Hunt, Mr and Mrs A F Walters)*

Free house ~ Licensees John and Sue Dawson ~ Real ale ~ Meals and snacks (midday-9pm; not 25 Dec) ~ Restaurant ~ Children in eating area of bar ~ (01629) 812725 ~ Open 11-11 ~ Bedrooms: £50B/£70B

BIRCHOVER (Derbys) SK2462 Map 7

Druid

Village signposted from B5056

This must have the widest choice of good food of any pub in Derbyshire. There are over 100 popular dishes every day which might include soup (£1.70), devilled mushrooms with chilli and cream (£3.60), potted prawn, apple and celery with garlic butter (£3.95), dim sum with apricot dip or ploughman's (£4.20), steak and mushroom pie (£4.70), fruit and vegetable curry (£5.30), Somerset pork with cider, honey and cream (£6.90), Siam chicken with lime, lemon, ginger and banana (£7.50), chicken tikka masala or steamed trout with a sauce of orange, garlic, honey and ginger (£8.40), steaks (from £10.50), and puddings (from £2.30); half price helpings for children. Not surprisingly, it's very popular, and bookings are advisable for evenings and weekends. The bar itself is small and plain, with plush-upholstered wooden wall benches around straightforward tables, and a big coal fire; the Garden Room is reserved for non-smokers. The spacious and airy two-storey dining extension, candlelit at night, has pink plush seats on olive-green carpet and pepper-grinders and sea salt on all the tables. Well kept Adnams, Mansfield Riding and Charles Wells Bombardier on handpump, and a good collection of malt whiskies, as well as cafetière coffee and a selection of teas; very good friendly service. A small public bar has dominoes; well reproduced classical music. There are picnic-table sets in front. *(Recommended by Catheryn and Richard Hicks, Sue Grossey, Mrs M A Kilner, Nigel Woolliscroft, Jim Farmer, Pauline Crossland, Dave Cawley, Stephen, Julie and Hayley Brown, Roger and Christine Mash, Neville Kenyon, Mr and Mrs G Turner, Mrs C Heaps, Stephen Newell, Caroline Midmore, Derek and Sylvia Stephenson, Dr and Mrs Richard Neville, L S Manning, N Clack)*

Free house ~ Licensees Brian Bunce and Nigel Telford ~ Real ale ~ Meals and snacks ~ Winster (01629) 650302 ~ Children welcome if eating but must be gone by 8pm ~ Open 12-3, 7-11; closed 25 Dec, 26 Dec pm

BRASSINGTON (Derbys) SK2354 Map 7

Olde Gate

Village signposted off B5056 and B5035 NE of Ashbourne

Built in 1616 from timbers salvaged from Armada wrecks, this unspoilt and traditional country pub is quiet and relaxing – no piped music or noisy games machines. The public bar has a lovely old kitchen range with lots of gleaming copper pots, pewter mugs hang from a beam which also has embossed Doulton stoneware flagons on a side shelf, and there's an ancient wall clock and traditional furnishings such as rush-seated old chairs and antique settles (one ancient, partly reframed, black oak solid one); stone-mullioned windows look across the garden to small silvery-walled pastures. On the left of a small hatch-served lobby, another beamed room has stripped panelled settles, tables with scrubbed tops, and a fire under a huge mantelbeam. Bar food changing day by day includes big open sandwiches such as prawns or crab (£4.95), home-cooked meat salads, big American-style burgers (£5.25), home-made curries (£6.50), winter roast (£6.25), cajun chicken (£6.95), balti curries (£7.50), and T-bone steak (£12.50); good puddings; no chips. The dining room is no smoking. Well kept Marstons Pedigree and winter Owd Rodger on handpump, and 24 malt whiskies; cribbage and dominoes. The Carsington reservoir is five minutes' drive from the pub and is ideal for water sports and so forth. No children under 10. *(Recommended by J and P M, David Eberlin, Mike and Wendy Proctor, Alan and Judith Gifford, Jack and Philip Paxton, Ann and Colin Hunt, John Beeken, Peter Marshall, Norma and Keith Bloomfield, David Ing, Mr and Mrs S Price, Andy and Jill Kassube, C Roberts, J and D Boutwood)*

Marstons ~ Tenant Paul Burlinson ~ Real ale ~ Meals and snacks (not Mon) ~ (0162 985) 448 ~ Children in dining room – but must be over 10 ~ Open 12-2.30(3 Sat), 6-11; closed Mon lunchtimes

BURTON-ON-TRENT (Staffs) SK2423 Map 7

Burton Bridge Inn £ 🍺
24 Bridge St (A50)

A new upstairs dining room with wooden panelling has been opened up in this friendly basic local this year. But downstairs, the place to head for is the little front bar, which is where the beers the pub brews itself are beautifully kept on handpump: Burton Bridge Bitter, Burton Bridge XL, Porter and Festival in the little front bar; in winter they also serve Top Dog Stout and Old Expensive and in summer, Summer Ale. The brewery is at the back in a long old-fashioned yard, and you can go round it on Tuesdays if you book in advance; a growing choice of malt whiskies, and fruit wines. The plain walls are hung with notices, awards and brewery memorabilia, simple furnishings include pews and plain tables; even when it's quiet people tend to spill out into the corridor. Bar snacks such as chip butties (£1), good filled cobs (from £1.45), cheese-filled oatcakes (£2.25), and giant filled Yorkshire puddings with ratatouille, faggots and mushy peas, a roast of the day or sausages (from £2.40); upstairs there's a skittle alley, with gas lighting and open fires, which can be hired for the evening, with a pie and pea supper or buffet if required; country wines, dominoes. *Recommended by Barbara Hatfield, Wayne Brindle, Graham Reeve; more reports please)*

Own Brew ~ Tenant Kevin McDonald ~ Real ale ~ Lunchtime meals and snacks (filled cobs Sun) ~ (01283) 36596 ~ Children in eating area of bar and in upstairs dining room, until 8pm ~ Open 11.30-2.15, 5.30-11; closed bank hol lunchtimes – except Easter ~ annual beer festival

BUTTERTON (Staffs) SK0756 Map 7

Black Lion ★ 🛏
Village signposted from B5053

In a conservation village, this warmly friendly old inn has picnic-table sets and rustic seats on a prettily planted terrace looking up to the tall and elegant spire of the local church. It's not far from the Manifold Valley, there are pleasant views over the Peak National Park, and plenty of sports such as watersports, shooting and fishing. Inside, there's a series of homely rambling rooms, one of which has a low black beam-and-board ceiling, lots of brassware and china, a fine old red leatherette settle curling around the walls, well polished mahogany tables, and a good log fire. Off to the left, there are red plush button-back banquettes around sewing-machine tables and Victorian prints, while an inner room has a parakeet called Sergeant Bilko who squawks loudly at regular intervals, and a fine old kitchen range; the lounge is no smoking. Bar food includes sandwiches, home-made soup (£1.40), ploughman's (£3.75), steak and kidney pie or battered cod (£4.45), lasagne (£4.55), 10oz gammon steak (£5.25), mixed grill (£7.45), daily specials such as Cumberland sausage bake, ham and egg or lamb's liver and bacon, and puddings like plum pudding (£1.95); there's also a carvery with a separate menu. The four real ales on handpump might include Bass, McEwans 70/-, Morlands Old Speckled Hen, Theakstons Best and Old Peculier or Youngers No.3; several malt whiskies; a cocktail bar is open weekend evenings. Darts, bar billiards, shove-ha'penny, dominoes, cribbage, table football, table skittles, and separate well lit pool room; piped music. *(Recommended by David and Shelia, Jed and Virginia Brown, Peter Marshall, Eric and Jackie Robinson, Mike and Wendy Proctor, Nigel Woolliscroft, TBB, Jack and Philip Paxton, Paul and Karen Mason, Jenny and Roger Bell, PACW, Jennie and Malc Wild, V Ogden, R Rayner, Sean Bathe, Dr R S K Barnes, S Howe, Colin Steer)*

Free house ~ Licensee Ron Smith ~ Real ale ~ Meals and snacks (not Weds lunchtime) ~ Restaurant (only open Fri/Sat evenings, Sun lunchtime) ~ Onecote (01538) 304232 ~ Children welcome ~ Impromptu live music monthly Thurs ~ Open 12-3, 7-11; closed Weds lunchtime ~ Bedrooms: £29.38B/£47B

nr BUXTON (Derbys) SK0673 Map 7

Bull i'th' Thorn

Ashbourne Road (A515) six miles S of Buxton, nr Hurdlow; OS Sheet 119 map reference 128665

Handy for the High Peak Trail, this solid old place does look a bit uninspiring from outside. Inside, however, is a fascinating medieval hall with fine long settles and panelled window seats in the embrasures of the thick stone walls, an ornately carved hunting chair, handsome panelling, a massive central beam among a forest of smaller ones, and old flagstones stepping gently down to a big open fire, as well as a longcase clock, a powder-horn, and armour that includes 17th-c German helmets, swords, blunderbusses and so forth. Straightforward bar food such as sandwiches, soup (£1.10), plaice (£3.50), steak and kidney pie or roast beef (£3.80), sirloin steak (£6.50), and puddings (£1.40); Sunday roast (£4.50). An adjoining room has darts, pool, dominoes, fruit machine, juke box and piped music; well kept Robinsons Best on handpump. The rather unprepossessing family room opens on to a terrace and big lawn, with swings, and there are more tables in a sheltered angle in front. There's a holiday flat and adjacent field for caravans and camping. The pub is handy for the High Peak Trail. Coach parties are welcome. *(Recommended by Sarah and Steve de Mellow, Jack and Philip Paxton, Ann and Colin Hunt)*

Robinsons ~ Tenant George Haywood ~ Real ale ~ Meals and snacks ~ Restaurant (only used for big parties) ~ (01298) 83348 ~ Children in family room ~ Occasional karaoke evenings and weekend cabarets ~ Open 11.30-3.30, 6.30-11 ~ Two bedrooms: £32

CAULDON (Staffs) SK0749 Map 7

Yew Tree ★ ★ £

Village signposted from A523 and A52 about 8 miles W of Ashbourne; OS Sheet 119 map reference 075493

Tucked inpropitiously between enormous cement works and quarries, this plain roadside local doesn't from outside suggest any reason for stopping. When we add to this the fact that it does only the most basic snacks, that its seats are somewhat shabby, and that a good spring-clean wouldn't come amiss (one of its greatest supporters is plagued by a recurring nightmare in which the public health inspectorate shuts it down), you'll wonder why it has any place in this book – let alone our top star rating. It's because shining through all that is the character of its landlord Alan East and above all the unique fascination of the profusion of bizarre mainly Victorian objects that he's crowded into the pub's dimly lit rooms. Perhaps the most impressive are the working Polyphons and Symphonions – 19th-c developments of the musical box, often taller than a person, each with quite a repertoire of tunes and elaborate sound-effects; go with plenty of 2p pieces to work them. But there's also two pairs of Queen Victoria's stockings, ancient guns and pistols, several penny-farthings, an old sit-and-stride boneshaker, a rocking horse, swordfish blades, and even a fine marquetry cabinet crammed with notable early Staffordshire pottery. 18th-c settles mingle with soggily sprung sofas, and a four-person oak church choir seat with carved heads which came from St Mary's church in Stafford, and above the bar is an odd iron dog-carrier (don't ask how it works!) As well as all this there's an expanding set of fine (and vociferous) longcase clocks in the gallery just above the entrance, a pianola with an excellent collection of piano rolls, a working vintage valve radio set, a crank-handle telephone, a sinuous medieval wind instrument made of leather, and a Queen Elizabeth I four poster dated from about 1690 which was once owned by Josiah Wedgwood and still has the original wig hook on the headboard. Remarkably cheap simple snacks like hot pork pies (60p), meat and potato pies or steak pies (65p), big filled baps (from 75p), and quiche or smoked mackerel (£2.20). Beers include Bass, Burton Bridge and M & B Mild on handpump or tapped from the cask, and there are some interesting malt whiskies such as overproof Glenfarclas; drinks prices are very low indeed. Darts, shove-ha'penny, table skittles (taken very seriously here), dominoes and cribbage. Hiding behind a big yew tree, the pub is difficult to spot – unless a veteran bus is parked outside. Dovedale and the Manifold Valley are not far away. In past editions this pub has had three stars. This year, as explained at the start of the book, we have revised the star grading system to amalgamate the two-star and three-star grades – the change in rating does not reflect any lowering of our exceptionally high opinion of the Yew Tree. *(Recommended by Ann and Colin Hunt, John and Marianne Cooper, Sue Hollands, David Webster, Jim and Maggie Cowell, Nigel Woolliscroft, David and Ruth Hollands, Martin Aust, Tom McEwan, Roger and Jenny Huggins, J amd P M, Brian and Anna Marsden, Paul and Gail Betteley, Mike and Wendy Proctor, John Scarisbrick, Wayne Brindle, Stephen, Julie and Hayley Brown, Barbara and Norman Wells, Jack and Philip Paxton)*

Free house ~ Licensee Alan East ~ Real ale ~ Snacks (11-3, 6-9.30 but generally something to eat any time they're open) ~ (01538) 308348 ~ Children in Polyphon room ~ Pianola most nights – played by the landlord ~ Open 10-3, 6-11

CRESSWELL (Staffs) SK9739 Map 7

Izaak Walton ⊕
Village signposted from Draycott in the Moors, on former A50 Stoke—Uttoxeter

It's the daily specials that readers like best in this smart dining pub: lamb and apricot curry (£5.95), prawns filled with spinach and bacon, dipped in batter and fried and served with a curry sauce, or chicken supreme filled with blue cheese and served with stilton sauce (£6.95), and beef wellington; there are also lunchtime snacks like filled omelettes (from £1.50), baked potatoes (from £1.60), filled cobs (from £1.95), sausage and egg (£2.25), and salads with home-made quiche and so forth (from £3.50), as well as home-made soup (£1.95), home-made pâté (£2.95), home-made steak and kidney pie (£4.50), beef bourguignon (£5.95), mushroom crumble (£5.95), halibut poached in wine with breval sauce (£6.50), and steaks with a choice of sauces (from £7.95). The two neatly kept rooms of the bar have little country pictures, dried flowers on walls and beams, pastel flowery curtains, and gentle lighting, and although there's a little settee in one window, furnishings are mainly uniform solid country-kitchen chairs and tables in polished pale wood, going nicely with the fawn carpet. You can only smoke in the bar area now – the rest of the pub is no smoking. Well kept Marstons Pedigree on handpump; piped music. The licensees have just opened another dining pub, the George in Waterhouses. *(Recommended by Sue Holland, David Webster, Eric J Locker, Paul and Maggie Baker, John Scarisbrick; more reports please)*

Free house ~ Licensees Anne and Graham Yates ~ Real ale ~ Meals and snacks (till 10pm Sat; no snacks Sun lunchtime) ~ Restaurant ~ (01782) 392265 ~ Children in restaurant ~ Open 12-2.30, 7-11; closed 25/26 Dec

---

Pubs brewing their own beers are listed at the back of the book.

DERBY SK3438 Map 7

Abbey Inn

Darley Street; coming in from A38/A6 roundabout, take first left signposted Darley Abbey, then left into Old Road signposted to toll bridge, turning right just before the bridge itself

Part of this little pub is all that remains of a once-powerful 11th-c monastery that covered much of this area. The old stonework is most visible in the bigger upstairs bar, especially in the windows. There are handsome reconstructed high oak rafters and trusses, and neat cushioned pews built into stalls around the tables – and the bow of a Viking longship built into the wall. You can join the pub's Viking Association, which gives you the opportunity to take part in occasional mock battles. Down the stone spiral staircase, the other bar has some massive stonework (leaning, in the case of the outer wall), a refectory table and some shiny elm ones, William Morris-ish brocaded stools and benches, a long pew, a big brick inglenook with stone chimneypiece, a brick floor, and studded oak doors. Decent lunchtime bar food includes filled rolls (£1.55), ploughman's (£2.95), hot dishes (from £3.55), and Sunday roast lunch (£3.50). Well kept Sam Smiths Museum and Old Brewery on handpump; darts, cribbage, dominoes and Wednesday evening quiz night. Besides a couple of sturdy teak seats outside, there are stone side-steps to sit on, and a stone well-head. You can walk into the park opposite, by a weir on the Derwent. *(Recommended by Alan and Eileen Bowker; more reports please)*

Sam Smiths ~ Licensees Christine and Simon Meyer ~ Real ale ~ Lunchtime meals and snacks ~ (01332) 558297 ~ Children allowed up to 8pm ~ Folk singing/guitarist lat Fri in month ~ Open 11.30(12 Sat)-2.30, 6-11; closed 25 Dec

Alexandra 🍺

Siddals Rd, just up from station

Last year this well managed and lively pub sold 619 different beers – and as well as the five ever-changing guests on handpump, they keep Batemans XB and Mild, Courage Bitter and Marstons Pedigree; rare farm ciders, country wines, and several changing malt whiskies. The pub had been redecorated this year, but still has railway pictures and shelves of bottles around its walls (they stock a good range of Belgian beers), and good heavy traditional furnishings on its dark-stained floorboards. It has strong railway connections, and Mr Robins is an enthusiast. Popular food varies from day to day and shows a good deal more thought than you might expect from the style of the pub, with a range of carefully chosen English cheeses (different every week) and cooking based on naturally reared meats and organically-grown vegetables rather than chips. It includes filled rolls (from 95p), a range of ploughman's (£2.55), good chilli con carne (£2.30), spaghetti bolognese (£2.30), liver and bacon casserole (£2.95) and a vegetarian Gloucester pie (£2.50). Quick cheery service, dominoes, a soundless fruit machine, piped music. *(Recommended by Jack and Philip Paxton; more reports please)*

Free house ~ Licensee Mark Robins ~ Real ale ~ Meals and snacks (12-2, 4.30-7; not Sun) ~ (01332) 293993 ~ Open 11-2.30, 4.30(6 Sat)-11; closed 25 Dec

Brunswick £ 🍺

1 Railway Terrace; close to Derby Midland railway station

Apart from the almost bewildering range of very well kept beers here it's the very friendly atmosphere and enjoyable food that add to this pub's popularity. Including their own brew, from the fourteen handpumps and six more ales tapped from the cask there might be Bass, Batemans Mild, Greene King Abbot, Hook Norton Old Hookey, Marstons Pedigree, Theakstons XB and Best, Timothy Taylors Landlord, and Wards Sheffield. Their own brews include First Brew, Recessionale Second Brew, Railway Porter, Old Accidental and Owd Abusive. As if this choice wasn't enough, they hold a beer festival over four days around 3 October (anniversary of their opening), with many more ales on offer. Draught farm cider, too. The high-ceilinged serving bar has heavy, well padded real leather seats, whisky-water jugs above the dado, and a dark blue ceiling and upper wall, with squared dark panelling below. The no-smoking room is decorated with little old-fashioned prints and swan's neck lamps, and has a high-backed wall settle and a coal fire; behind a curved glazed partition wall is a quietly chatty family parlour narrowing to the apex of the triangular building. Darts, cribbage, dominoes, fruit machine; good friendly service. Good bar food includes pork pies (75p), filled salad rolls with turkey, beef and ham (90p), home-made soup (£1.25), hot beef, hot turkey or hot traditional sausage-beef cobs (£1.30), home-made beef and onion pie (£1.70), cauliflower cheese (£2.50), and beef and mushroom pie in home-brewed porter (£3.50). There are seats in the terrace area behind. *(Recommended by Andrew Stephenson, Luke Hundleby, D W Gray, Jack and Philip Paxton, Derek and Sylvia Stephenson, John Scarisbrick, Wayne Brindle, David Gray, David and Sheila)*

Free house ~ Licensee Trevor Harris ~ Real ale ~ Lunchtime meals and snacks (rolls only Sun) ~ Restaurant (not open Sun) ~ Derby (01332) 290677 ~ Children in family parlour ~ Jazz Thurs evenings, folk club last Sun in month ~ Open 11-11

EYAM (Derbys) SK2276 Map 7

Miners Arms 🛏

In 1684 the local parson came to this traditional pub to baptise a sick child. He drank so much ale afterwards that when he finally came round he found himself married to the landlord's daughter Anne. His former fiancée sued him for such swingeing damages that it's said he had to abandon the vicarage and set up house with Anne in the church crypt. So watch your consumption here in these three little plush rooms with their pleasant restful atmosphere (no noisy games machines or piped music), beams, and stone fireplaces. The emphasis is very much on the popular, fresh home-made bar food – no frozen food is used at all. At lunchtime this might include home-made soup or sandwiches, ploughman's, lamb and mint sausages in onion gravy (£3.95), braised ox tails (£4.95), crispy roast duck or cod mornay (£5.50), chicken breast in mushroom and madeira sauce (£5.25), fettucine with mushrooms in a white wine sauce (£4.25), and puddings; good Sunday roast (no bar food then). Well kept Boddingtons on handpump; friendly service. *(Recommended by M G Hart, W H and E Thomas, M Baxter, Anne Wren, David William Taylor, Ian Sharp*

Free house ~ Licensees Nicholas and Ruth Cook ~ Real ales ~ Lunchtime meals and snacks (not Sun or Mon) ~ Evening restaurant – though they do Sun lunch (not Sun evening, not Mon) ~ (01433) 630853 ~ Children welcome ~ Open 12-3, 7-11; closed Sun night and Mon lunchtime and first 2 weeks Jan ~ Bedrooms: £25B/£40B

FENNY BENTLEY (Derbys) SK1750 Map 7

Coach & Horses

A515 N of Ashbourne

In winter, the two log fires in this comfortable coaching inn are very welcoming after a walk – muddy boots must be left outside though. It's a quietly friendly place, with ribbed green built-in wall banquettes and old prints and engravings on the dark green leafy Victorian wallpaper of the pleasant little back room. There are more old prints in the front bar, which has flowery-cushioned wall settles and library chairs around the dark tables on its turkey carpet, waggonwheels hanging from the black beams, horsebrasses and pewter mugs, and a huge mirror; no-smoking area. Popular bar food includes soup (£1.20), baps and sandwiches (from £1, toasties from £2.30), filled baked potatoes (mostly £2.90), sausage, egg and chips (£3.55), salads (from £3.95), filled Yorkshire puddings or vegetarian broccoli and cream cheese (£4.95), grilled trout (£5.25), lamb's liver and onions (£5.50), steak and kidney pie (£5.95), 12oz steaks (from £9.25), children's menu (from £2.25), and puddings (£1.95). Well kept Black Bull Bitter (brewed in the village) and Hartington Bitter on handpump, good coffee, and pleasant service; darts, dominoes and piped music; picnic-table sets on the back grass by an elder tree, with rustic benches and white tables and chairs under cocktail parasols on the terrace in front of this pretty rendered stone house. *(Recommended by Wayne Brindle, Eric J Locker, David and Shelia, T I G Gray, D Hanley, Frank Cummins, Ann and Colin Hunt, J E Rycroft, P and M Rudlin)*

Free house ~ Licensee Edward Anderson ~ Real ale ~ Meals and snacks (till 10pm) ~ Restaurant ~ Thorpe Cloud (0133 529) 246 ~ Children welcome ~ Open 11.30-2.30, 6-11; closed 25 Dec

nr FOOLOW (Derbys) SK1976 Map 7

Barrel £

Bretton; signposted from Foolow which itself is signposted from A623 just E of junction with B6465 to Bakewell

There are fine views from this warmly friendly pub, perched on the edge of an isolated ridge, over the pastures below and way past the county borders. Inside, stubs of massive knocked-through stone walls divide up the cosy beamed bar into several areas – the snuggest is at the far end with an open wood fire, a leather-cushioned settle, and a built-in corner wall-bench by an antique oak table. Decorations on the cream walls include local maps and history, an aerial photograph, a rack of clay pipes, poems about the pub and a clock which moves in an anti-clockwise direction; a delft shelf has lots of old glass and china bottles, and there's a mix of seats including converted wooden barrels. Good, cheap bar food includes sandwiches (from £1.10; double decker 80p extra, toasties from £1.70), soup (£1.25), filled baked potatoes (from £1.95), open wholemeal baps (from £2.40), good salads (from £2.40), ploughman's (£3), and daily specials like stilton toastie or pork pie sandwich (£1.80) and home-made steak and kidney pie (£3.20); Bass and Boddingtons on handpump, and a good choice of whiskies. Darts, cribbage, dominoes. There are seats on the breezy front terrace, and the pub is popular with walkers. *(Recommended by I H Rorison, Geoffrey and Irene Lindley, Sarah and Gary Goldson, Mrs F M Halle, Nigel Woolliscroft, Pauline Crossland, Dave Cawley, John Cadman, Derek and Sylvia Stephenson, M G Hart, John Burdett)*

Free house ~ Licensee Derek Smith ~ Real ale ~ Meals and snacks ~ (01433) 630856 ~ Children welcome ~ Open 12-3, 6.30-11; 12-11 summer Sats; winter evening opening 7pm

FRADLEY (Staffs) SK1414 Map 7

Swan

Off A38 Burton—Lichfield, signposted Fradley Park; after a mile turn right at Fradley Junction sign, then left at T-junction, then left along far bank of canal; OS Sheet 128, map reference 140140

On summer evenings you can sit outside this cheery old brick building at the tables by the water (the pub is attractively set at the junction of the Trent—Mersey Canal and the Birmingham Navigation System), or take a stroll to the pretty bridge nearby. Inside, the room on the right is a traditional lino-floored public bar. The lounge on the left is rather smarter, with canal photographs and painted ware, red plush banquettes and dimpled copper tables; it leads down into a low vaulted Cellar Bar with more plush banquettes in its alcoves, and old waterway maps and photographs. A back food servery (with fruit machine) dispenses big helpings of food including sandwiches, wrapped filled rolls (85p), salads (from £2.95), lunchtime late breakfast, steak and kidney pie (£3.90), grills (from £5.80), and good value Sunday lunch – which the landlord carves between noon and 2pm; well kept Ansells Bitter and Mild and Ind Coope Burton on handpump and a wide range of malt whiskies; cribbage, dominoes, and piped music. *(Recommended by Ian and Emma Potts, Nigel Hopkins, Karen Phillips, T Henwood, Graham Reeve, Mr and Mrs A F Walters, Dave Braisted)*

Ansells (Allied) ~ Lease: Bill Smith ~ Real ale ~ Meals and snacks (not 25/26 Dec ~ (01283) 790330 ~ Children if eating in Cellar Bar till 8.30pm ~ Open 11-3, 6-11; closed evening 25 Dec

FROGGATT EDGE (Derbys) SK2477 Map 7

Chequers 🛏

B6054, off A623 N of Bakewell; Ordnance Survey Sheet 119, map reference 247761

Helpful new licensees have taken over this comfortable, old-fashioned inn and early reports from readers suggest that things are looking very promising. There are antique prints on the white walls (partly stripped back to big dark stone blocks), library chairs or small high-backed winged settles on the well waxed floorboards, an attractive, richly varnished beam-and-board ceiling, and a big solid-fuel stove; one corner has a nicely carved oak cupboard. Well kept Vaux Samson and Wards Best and Thorne on handpump, and a good wine list. Popular bar food now includes home-made soup (£1), big sandwiches served with chips (from £2.80), mushroom and hazelnut fettucini (£3.85), superb rabbit and vegetable casserole (£4.55), home-made chicken and mushroom lasagne (£4.70), chicken and coconut curry (£4.90), pan-fried calf's liver (£4.95), scallops of salmon (£5.45), and puddings (from £1.40); very efficient service. The restaurant is no smoking; piped music. A relaxing place to stop if out walking for the day and you can enjoy views over the attractive valley from white benches at the front; there are also tables on the back terrace. The Edge itself is up through the woods behind the inn. *(Recommended by Peter Marshall, David and Michelle Hedges, M G Hart, CW, JW, Ann and Colin Hunt, Dawn and Phil Garside, Dr M V Jones, Bob Riley, Neville Kenyon, Leonard Robinson, Margaret and Paul Digby, Pauline Crossland, Dave Cawley, Sue Holland, David Webster, Mark Hydes, V Ogden, R Rayner)*

Free house ~ Lease: E and J Bell ~ Real ale ~ Meals and snacks ~ Restaurant ~ Hope Valley (01433) 630231 ~ Children in restaurant ~ Open 11-3, 5-11 ~ Bedrooms: £38B/£48B

GRINDLEFORD (Derbys) SK2478 Map 7

Maynard Arms 🛏

B6521 N of village

After a walk on Froggatt Edge and down Padley Gorge you can relax on the seats in the neatly kept hotel garden here. The big smart high-ceilinged main bar has some dark panelling, tapestry wall hangings, comfortable blue-coloured plush seats on the blue patterned carpet, and silver tankards above the bar. Off the hall there's a smaller green plush bar for restaurant diners only which is no smoking. Good bar food now includes sandwiches (from £1.95; open sandwiches from £2.75), lamb lasagne (£4.25), all-day breakfast (£4.50), stir-fry chicken or mackerel fillets (£4.75), baked loin of bacon (£5.50), 8oz rump steak (£8.95), and home-made puddings (£1.75). Well kept Boddingtons and Whitbreads Castle Eden on handpump; piped music. *(Recommended by John Fahy, G W H Kerby, Peter Marshall, David and Fiona Easeman, Helen Crookston, Roger and Christine Mash, Anthony John)*

Free house ~ Manager Edward Gallagher ~ Real ale ~ Meals and snacks ~ Restaurant ~ Hope Valley (01433) 630321 ~ Children in restaurant and eating area of bar ~ Open 11-3, 6-11; 11-11 Sat ~ Bedrooms: £39.50B/£49.50B

nr HARTINGTON (Derbys) SK1561 Map 7

Jug & Glass

Newhaven; on A515 about 1 mile N of junction with A5012; OS Sheet 119 map reference 156614

The cosy bar in this remote and unpretentious moorland pub has a relaxed atmosphere, simple furnishings, lots of flowery china hanging from low beams, and winter coal fires. There's another room with flock wallpaper, and an attractive no-smoking dining room has a stone-pillared fireplace with an old oak mantelbeam. Bar food includes sandwiches, home-made curries (£4.25), home-made steak and kidney pie (£4.50), 14oz gammon steak (£6.75), grilled halibut and salmon steaks (£7.95), sirloin steak (£8.95), and home-made puddings (£1.65). The restaurant is no smoking. Bass, Marstons Pedigree and a guest beer on handpump. Darts, dominoes, fruit machine and piped music. There are seats and parasols on the terrace. *(Recommended by S Howe; more reports on the new regime please)*

Free house ~ Licensee C J Bettaney ~ Real ale ~ Meals and snacks (11-3, 7-10) ~ Restaurant ~ Hartington (01298) 84224 ~ Children welcome ~ Open 11-3, 6.30(6 Sat)-11

HAYFIELD (Derbys) SK0388 Map 7

Lantern Pike 🛏

Little Hayfield; A624 towards Glossop

On a dismally wet and cold November day of pub inspections when our efforts to get something to eat had been frustrated by other pubs around here curtly saying their kitchen had just closed, it was a delight to be given an immediate welcome here, with the fire stoked up for us, and the spontaneous offer of whatever we wanted to eat. Readers uniformly confirm that outstandingly warm and friendly service from the landlady and her team is the pub's hallmark. It's unpretentious but cosy, comfortable, and spick and span, with plush seats, flowers on the tables, lots of brass platters, china and toby jugs; well kept Boddingtons, Flowers IPA, Timothy Taylors Landlord and a guest such as Chesters Best Mild on handpump, a good selection of malt whiskies. Good well presented home-made bar food includes soup (£1.95), sandwiches (from £2.25, with an excellent steak and onion muffin £2.75), plaice (£4.60), curry (£4.70), steak and kidney pie (£4.95) and steak (£7.25), with several vegetarian dishes (£4.95), good children's dishes (£1.95) and puddings (£1.95); darts, dominoes, piped nostalgic pop music. Tables on a two-level stonewalled back terrace, served from a window, look over a big-windowed weaver's house to the Lantern Pike itself, and the pub's very well placed for walkers. *(Recommended by Gary Williams, A N Ellis, Tony Short, Jack Morley, Mr and Mrs J Ireland)*

Free house ~ Licensee Gerry McDonald ~ Real ale ~ Meals and snacks (12-2.30, 6-9.30) ~ Restaurant open all day Sun ~ (01663) 747590 ~ Open 11.30-3, 6-11; all day Sat ~ Bedrooms: £25B/£35B

HOLMESFIELD (Derbys) SK3277 Map 7

Robin Hood

Lydgate; just through Holmesfield on B6054

Served by friendly staff, the wide choice of food in this pleasant, rambling old place might include home-made soup (£1.95), sandwiches (from £1.95), filled jacket potatoes (from £2.25), ploughman's (£4.25), lasagne (£4.95), honey-glazed ham (£5.25), home-made steak, ale and mushroom pie (£5.95), tandoori chicken (£6.50), gammon and egg (£6.95), 10oz sirloin steak (£10.95), daily specials such as vegetable lasagne (£5.65), lamb steak with rosemary and redcurrant sauce (£8.95), home-made puddings (from £2.25), and children's dishes (£2.25). Best to book at weekends. By the time this book is published, they hope to be serving real ale – Bass and Stones; piped music. The neat extended lounge area has exposed beams, chintz and paisley curtains, plush button-back wall banquettes around wood-effect tables, partly carpeted flagstone floors, and open fires; piped music. Outside on the cobbled front courtyard there are stone tables, and opposite the pub are a number of footpaths into the famous Cordwell valley – the views over Chesterfield and Sheffield are fine. They are hoping to add a conservatory. *(Recommended by Sarah and Steve de Mellow, Mr and Mrs W Normington, Andrew Stephenson, Mrs Williams, Mrs F M Halle)*

Free house ~ Licensees Chris and Jackie Hughes ~ Real ale by 1995 ~ Meals and snacks (11.30-2.30, 6-9.30; all day Sun) ~ Sheffield (01742) 890360 ~ Children in eating area of bar ~ Open 11.30-3, 6-11; 11.30-11 Sat

---

We say if we know a pub has piped music.

HOPE (Derbys) SK1783 Map 7

Poachers Arms 🛏

Out towards Castleton

There are several interconnecting bars here with beamed doorways, traditional furnishings, and a pleasant, relaxed atmosphere. Served by friendly staff, the wide choice of popular food might include a mug of home-made soup (£1.40), ploughman's (£3.50), locally-made black pudding in cider and apple sauce (£3.35), noodle and ratatouille bake or fruit and nut vegetable risotto (£4.75), rabbit casserole (£5.10), steak and kidney pie (£5.30), a roast of the day (from £5.40), grilled whole lemon sole (£7), curried prawns (£7.50), grilled sirloin steak (£8), daily specials such as barbecued pork (£5.50) or swordfish (£5.65), children's dishes (from £2.50), and puddings (£2). Well kept Courage Directors, Marstons Pedigree and John Smiths on handpump; darts, dominoes and piped music; the two dogs are called Barney and Tina. As it's in the Peak District National Park there are lots of walks, riding and cycling nearby. *(Recommended by M G Hart, Jim Farmer, B M Eldridge, Mr and Mrs A F Walters*

Free house ~ Licensee Gladys Bushell ~ Real ale ~ Meals and snacks (till 10pm; not evening 25 Dec) ~ Restaurant ~ (01433) 620380 ~ Children in restaurant and eating area of bar ~ Open 12-2.30, 6-11 ~ Bedrooms: £39B/£52B

KINGS NEWTON (Derbys) SK3826 Map 7

Hardinge Arms

5 miles from M1 junction 24; follow signs to E Midlands airport; A453, in 3 miles (Isley) turn right signed Melbourne, Wilson; right turn in 2 miles to Kings Newton; pub is on left at end of village

There's a rather civilised atmosphere in this friendly well run place, and the rambling front bar has open fires, beams, fine panelled and carved bar counter, and blue plush cushioned seats and stools – some in a pleasantly big bow window. There's also a stately and spacious back lounge. Good bar food includes home-made soup, sandwiches, stilton ploughman's (£3), home-made steak and kidney pie (£5), and roast beef and trimmings (£6). Well kept Bass and Ind Coope Burton on handpump, and several malt whiskies; table skittles (Sunday evening only), dominoes and juke box. *(Recommended by George Atkinson; more reports please)*

Free house ~ Licensee Michael Johnson ~ Real ale ~ Meals and snacks (not Mon evenings) ~ (01332) 863808 ~ Children in eating area of bar until 8pm ~ Open 11-2.30, 6-11

KIRK IRETON (Derbys) SK2650 Map 7

Barley Mow 🛏 🍴

Signposted off B5023 S of Wirksworth

A handsome three-storey twin-gabled Jacobean stone house, this can hardly have changed inside or out since it was built. It's how one imagines the better country pubs should have been like a century or more ago. The small main bar has antique settles on the tiled floor or built into the panelling, a coal fire, old prints, shuttered mullioned windows – and a simple wooden counter behind which reposes a tempting row of casks of real ales, kept well and sold cheaply. On our inspection visit these included Batemans XXX, Hook Norton Best and Old Hookey, Marstons Pedigree and Timothy Taylors Landlord; they may rotate these with Adnams, Courage Directors, Greene King IPA and Wadworths 6X, and Thatcher's farm cider. Another room has cushioned pews built in, oak parquet flooring and a small woodburner, and a third has more pews, tiled floor, beams and joists, and big landscape prints. Filled lunchtime rolls; good value evening meals, but only for residents. Civilised old fashioned service, a couple of friendly pugs and a somnolent newfoundland, dominoes and cribbage. There's a good-sized garden, as well as a couple of benches out in front; the village is quiet, and most attractive. *(Recommended by Frank Peakall, Michel Hooper-Immins, David Eberlin, JM, PM)*

Free house ~ Licensee Mary Short ~ Real ale ~ Lunchtime snacks ~ (01335) 370306 ~ Children may be allowed by arrangement ~ Open 12-2, 7-11; closed 25 Dec, 1 Jan ~ Bedrooms: £25.50B/£37.75B

LITTLE HUCKLOW (Derbys) SK1678 Map 7

Old Bulls Head

Pub signposted from B6049

Kept absolutely spic and span, this friendly little village pub has two atmospheric rooms with old oak beams, thickly cushioned built-in settles, interesting collections of locally mined semi-precious stones, antique brass and iron household tools, and a coal fire in a neatly restored stone hearth. One room is served from a hatch, the other over a polished bar counter. Bar food includes sandwiches (£1.80), ploughman's or filled Yorkshire puddings (£3), omelettes (£3.50), lasagne (£4.50), peppered pork or steak and kidney pie (£4.75), poached salmon in a rich asparagus sauce (£5), gammon with pineapple (£5.45), 8oz sirloin steak (£6.95), and puddings (£1.95). Well kept Stones Best and Worthingtons from carved handpumps; a good range of well reproduced piped classical music, dominoes. There are tables in the neatly tended garden, which is full of an unusual collection of well restored and attractively painted old farm machinery. *(Recommended by Basil J S Minson, Peter Marshall, Susan Boyle, Eugene Wills, Jack and Philip Paxton, Ann and Colin Hunt)*

Free house ~ Licensee George Saxon ~ Real ale ~ Meals and snacks ~ (01298) 871097 ~ Children welcome ~ Open 12-3, 7-11

LITTLE LONGSTONE (Derbys) SK1971 Map 7

Packhorse

Monsal Dale and Ashford Village signposted off A6 NW of Bakewell; follow Monsal Dale signposts, then turn right into Little Longstone at Monsal Head Hotel

Warmly welcoming to locals and visitors alike, this traditional 16th-c cottage has two rooms simply furnished with country kitchen chairs, cloth-cushioned settles and a more unusual almost batwinged corner chair under the beam-and-plank ceiling. Around the walls are a collection of prettily hung decorative mugs, brass spigots, attractive landscape photographs by Steve Riley, blow-ups of older local photographs and the odd cornet or trumpet. Good, popular bar food includes soup or baps spread with dripping and generously filled with hot well hung beef or with hot pork, apple sauce and stuffing (£1.75), starters like spare ribs (which are a meal in themselves) or stilton garlic mushrooms (£2.75), ploughman's (£3.95), cheese and spinach cannelloni or very tasty, filling steak and kidney pie (£4.60), lamb steak in stilton sauce (£6.60), steaks (£7.95), and puddings like brandy roulade or steamed puddings (£1.75); bookings are preferred in the restaurant (which is also used as an overflow for the bar at busy times). Well kept Marstons Best or Pedigree on handpump; darts, dominoes, cribbage. In the steep little garden there's a new terrace, goats and rabbits. *(Recommended by Mrs D Craig, Derek and Sylvia Stephenson, L S Manning, Michael and Hilary Rooke, Andy Stone, P S McPherson, Gill and Maurice McMahon, Mr and Mrs J E Rycroft, Allan and Heather Jacques, Nigel Wooliscroft)*

Marstons ~ Tenants Lynne and Mark Lythgoe ~ Real ale ~ Meals and snacks (12-2, 7-9) ~ Restaurant ~ (01629) 640471 ~ Well behaved children in eating area lunchtime and perhaps early eve ~ Live music alternate Weds nights ~ Open 11-3, 5(6 on Sat)-11; closed 25 Dec evening

nr MELBOURNE (Derbys) SK3825 Map 7

John Thompson 🍺

Ingleby; village signposted from A514 at Swarkestone

As well as being very cheap, the beers brewed here by Mr Thompson are also very good – and extremely popular. Brewing was started to commemorate the

Queen's Silver Jubilee, and you can also buy the pub's own home-brew kits: Summer Gold, JTS Bitter, and winter Porter; Bass is also available on handpump; friendly efficient service. The big, pleasantly modernised lounge has ceiling joists, some old oak settles, button-back leather seats, sturdy oak tables, antique prints and paintings, and a log-effect gas fire; a couple of smaller cosier rooms open off, with pool, a fruit machine, and a juke box in the children's room, and a no-smoking area in the lounge. Good but straightforward bar food consists of sandwiches (nothing else on Sundays; the beef is excellent), or a set meal of soup, a cold buffet with very good meats or excellent hot roast beef (£5, not Mondays) and well liked puddings. The setting is lovely – well kept lawns and flowerbeds running down to the rich watermeadows along the River Trent, lots of tables on the upper lawn, and a partly covered outside terrace with its own serving bar. *(Recommended by Cdr Patrick Tailyour, Dorothee and Dennis Glover, John and Christine Simpson, Russell Edwards)*

Own brew ~ Licensee John Thompson ~ Real ale ~ Lunchtime meals and snacks (snacks only Sun; cold buffet only, Mon) ~ (01332) 862469 ~ Children in separate room ~ Open 10.30-2.30, 7-11

MONSAL HEAD (Derbys) SK1871 Map 7

Monsal Head Hotel 🛏 🍺

B6465

Perched high above the steep valley of the River Wye, this comfortable hotel with its fine views has a lively Stable Bar – popular with readers. There is still a somewhat horsey theme, with stripped timber horse-stalls, harness and brassware, as well as flagstones, a big warming woodburning stove in an inglenook, cushioned oak pews around flowery-clothed tables, farm tools, and railway signs and lamps from a local disused station; steps lead up into a crafts gallery. The spacious high-ceilinged main front bar is set out more as a wine bar, with dining chairs around big tables; it's partitioned off from the no-smoking restaurant area. Well kept Courage Directors, Marstons Pedigree, Ruddles Best and County, and Theakstons Old Peculier on handpump; helpful staff; darts. Bar food includes sandwiches (from £1.50), home-made vegetable soup (£1.75), onion bhajis (£1.85), garlic mushrooms (£2.25), scampi (£4.50), home-made leek and mushroom au gratin (£4.75), home-made steak and kidney pie (£5.75), gammon and egg (£7.25), steaks (from £7.95), duckling with orange and Grand Marnier sauce or rabbit pie (£8.95), and children's menu (from £1.95). The back garden has a play area. *(Recommended by David and Michelle Hedges, John Fahy, K Flack, Gwen and Peter Andrews, A Preston, Mike and Wendy Proctor, Phil and Heidi Cook, Carolyn Eaton, Mark Watkins, Sarah and Gary Goldson, Derek and Sylvia Stephenson, E N and I J Wilkinson, M Joyner, David Atkinson)*

Free house ~ Licensee Nicholas Smith ~ Real ale ~ Meals and snacks (12-2.30, 6-9.30) ~ Restaurant ~ Great Longstone (01629) 640250 ~ Children welcome, but not after 7 in Stable Bar ~ Open 11-11; closed 25 Dec ~ Bedrooms: £22.50 (£32.50B)/£45(£65B)

ONECOTE (Staffs) SK0555 Map 7

Jervis Arms 🍺

B5053, off A523 Leek—Ashbourne

In a lovely moorland setting on the banks of the River Hamps, this bustling 17th-c pub is a friendly place – with a positive welcome for families. As well as play trees, slides and swings in the garden, there are two family rooms with high chairs, and a mother and baby room. On the lawn are some picnic-table sets under cocktail parasols with a little shrubby rockery behind, and lots of sheltering ash trees; a footbridge leads to the car park. Inside, the irregularly shaped main bar has white planks over shiny black beams, window seats, wheelback chairs, two or three unusually low plush chairs, little hunting prints on the walls, and toby jugs and decorative plates on the high mantelpiece of its big stone fireplace.

A similar if slightly simpler inner room has a fruit machine. Generous helpings of good bar food include soup (£1.20), filled rolls (£1.60), filled baked potatoes (from £3.50), home-made chilli or cottage pie (£3.75), ploughman's (from £3.95), home-cooked ham or roast topside of beef (£4.25), curried nut fruit and vegetable pie or savoury cheesecake (£4.50), steaks (from £7.95), puddings (£1.75), and children's meals (from £1.25). Very well kept Bass, Marstons Pedigree, Ruddles County, Theakstons XB, Old Peculier and Mild, Websters Yorkshire Bitter and Worthington Bitter on handpump, a fair range of malt whiskies, and Scrumpy Jack cider; friendly service. Darts, dominoes, cribbage, fruit machine, and piped music. A spacious barn behind the pub has been converted to self-catering accommodation. *(Recommended by Richard Lewis, Martin Aust, Eric and Jackie Robinson, Susan Boyle, John Beeken, Myke and Nicky Crombleholme, Peter and Lynn Brueton, Sidney and Erna Wells, Paul and Margaret Baker)*

Free house ~ Licensees Robert and Jean Sawdon ~ Real ale ~ Meals and snacks (till 10pm) ~ Onecote (01538) 304206 ~ Children welcome, three family rooms ~ Open 12-2.30, 7-11; closed 25/26 Dec ~ Self-catering barn (with two bedrooms); £125 a week for the whole unit

OVER HADDON (Derbys) SK2066 Map 7

Lathkil 🛏

Village and inn signposted from B5055 just SW of Bakewell

The little hamlet of Over Haddon has one of the finest sites of any Derbyshire village, perched as it is on a hillside looking steeply down into Lathkil Dale – one of the quieter dales, with an exceptionaly harmonious spread of pastures and copses. Paths from the village take you straight into this tempting landscape, which has a lot to interest the nature lover. So it's a delight to find a good pub making the most of the views, and welcoming walkers (there's a place for muddy boots in the lobby) despite offering a good range of civilised comforts. The airy room on the right has a warming fire in the attractively carved fireplace, old-fashioned settles with upholstered cushions or plain wooden chairs, black beams, a delft shelf of blue and white plates on one white wall, original prints and photographs, and big windows. On the left is the spacious and sunny family dining area, which doubles as a restaurant in the evenings; at lunchtime the bar food is served here and includes home-made soup (£1.40), filled cobs (from £1.70), salads (from £4), beef curry (£4.65), lasagne (£4.75), steak and kidney pie (£5.25), smoked trout (£5.30), and home-made puddings (from £1.80). Well kept Thornes Best, Thornes Best Mild, and Wards Best on handpump; piped classical music or jazz, shove-ha'penny, dominoes, cribbage. Best to get here early in good weather. *(Recommended by W H and E Thomas, Mike and Wendy Proctor, Bob Riley, L W Baal, Simon Morton, Roger and Christine Mash, Barbara Hatfield, Mrs F M Halle, Ann and Colin Hunt, John Fahy, Sarah and Garry Goldson, Sue Holland, Dave Webster, Donald Clay, A M McCarthy, Nigel Woolliscroft, Andrew Stephenson, J E Rycroft, Brian Kneale, John Voos, Jonathan and Nicky Teare, Mr and Mrs A F Walters, E N and I J Wilkinson)*

Free house ~ Licensee Robert Grigor-Taylor ~ Real ale ~ Lunchtime meals and snacks ~ Evening restaurant (residents only Sun) ~ Bakewell (01629) 812501 ~ Children in eating area of bar at lunchtime and in restaurant in evening – but must eat a meal ~ Open 11.30-2.30, 6.30-11; closed 25 Dec evening ~ Bedrooms: £32.50S/£60B

RUSHTON SPENCER (Staffs) SJ9462 Map 7

Crown

Congleton Rd; off A523 Leek—Macclesfield at Ryecroft Gate

The outside of this pub has been considerably smartened up by its new owners who have also repainted the children's slide and swings, and replaced the inn signs with more traditional ones; the pretty back garden and barbecue area have had a lot of work spent on them too. But many of the popular Greek dishes on the menu have stayed: tzatziki (Greek yoghurt with cucumber and garlic), stuffed vine leaves or keftedes (all £1.95), beef stiffado or chicken with marjoram and tomatoes (£6.25) or marinated lamb kebabs (£6.50); also, sandwiches (from £1.65; open ones £3.25), ploughman's (£4.25), chicken curry (£4.50), vegetable and asparagus pancakes (£5.25), gammon steak (£5.50), steaks (from £7.50), and children's dishes (£1.95). There's a lively smallish front bar with well kept Bass, Theakstons Best and XB and weekly guest beers on handpump. The simply furnished but comfortable back lounge extension is roomier, with picture windows giving a fine view over the steep countryside. A plain games room has cribbage, darts and trivia; piped music. *(Recommended by C A Wilkes, Nigel Woolliscroft, Mike and Wendy Proctor, Jim and Maggie Cowell, John Scarisbrick; more reports please)*

Free house ~ Licensee Anthony Ansell ~ Real ale ~ Meals and snacks ~ (01260) 226231 ~ Children in eating area of bar ~ Open 12-3, 6-11

SHARDLOW (Derbys) SK4330 Map 7

Hoskins Wharf

3½ miles from M1 junction 24; A6 towards Derby, pub on left

One branch of the canal actually flows through a sweeping arch in the middle of the bar here – and to reach the pub (a converted 18th-c warehouse) you have to go across a counter-weighted drawbridge. There are picnic-table sets outside among the weeping willows between the canal branches, and more by a children's play area on a bigger lawn behind. The smallish bar has picture window overlooking the canal basin, stripped brickwork, heavy beams, brick flooring, simple furniture, and some colourful narrowboat nameplates. Bar food includes home-made soup (£1.25), filled french sticks (from £1.35), filled baked potatoes (from £1.65), ploughman's (£3.75), home-made hotpot (£4.25), poached salmon salad (£5.50), and steaks (from £7.25). The restaurant is no smoking. Well kept Hoskins Beaumanor, Churchills Pride and Penns, and several guest beers on handpump or tapped from the cask; fruit machine and piped music. *(Recommended by Mayur Shah, Geoffrey and Irene Lindley, Alan and Eileen Bowker, David and Sheila; more reports please)*

Hoskins ~ Tenant David Holmes ~ Real ale ~ Meals and snacks (not Sat evening) ~ Restaurant ~ Derby (01332) 792844 ~ Children in restaurant ~ Open all day; 11.30-3, 5-11 in winter

Old Crown 🍺

Cavendish Bridge

Going from strength to strength, this fine and friendly old place has an interesting choice of daily-changing specials on the menu. These might include liver with sweetbreads casseroled in mushroom sauce (£4.50), steak and kidney pudding (£4.75), pork in pernod and cream (£5.50), lamb with mint and rochefort cheese potroasted in port (£5.75), mediterranean chicken (£6.25), and beef fillet in black bean sauce (£7.25). They also have sandwiches or rolls (from £1.40), sausage and egg (£3.95), basket meals (from £4), ploughman's and salads (from £4.25), home-made steak and kidney pie (£4.50), vegetable tikka masala (£5.25), steaks (from £7.50), puddings (£1.75), and children's dishes (from £3). Well kept Bass and Marstons Pedigree with changing guests like Exmoor Gold, Greene King Abbot, Hadrian Centurion and Woods Bitter on handpump, and a nice choice of malt whiskies. The friendly beamed bar is full of interesting bric-a-brac such as lots of jugs and mugs hanging from the beamed ceiling, brewery and railway memorabilia, and lots of pictures. Cribbage and piped music. The garden has a children's play area. *(Recommended by Andrew Stephenson, Wayne Brindle, A and R Cooper, Jack and Philip Paxton, Harry and Irene Fisher, Stephen Newell)*

Free house ~ Licensees Peter and Gillian Morton-Harrison ~ Real ale ~ Lunchtime meals and snacks ~ (01332) 792392 ~ Children allowed lunchtime only ~ Open 11.30-3, 5-11; closed evenings 25/26 Dec

---

There are report forms at the back of the book.

SHRALEYBROOK (Staffs) SJ7850 Map 7

Rising Sun ◗

3 miles from M6 junction 16; from A500 towards Stoke take first right turn signposted
Alsager, Audley; in Audley turn right on the road still shown on many maps as A52, but now
in fact a B, signposted Balterley, Nantwich; pub then signposted on left (at the T-junction
look out for the Watneys Red Barrel)

This was the winner of the 1994 Own Brew Pub of the Year award – and the
beers are still as impressive as ever. They are produced in the brewery behind the
pub and currently include five bitters – Rising, Setting, Sunlight, Sunstroke, Solar
Flare – and a stronger brew fittingly called Total Eclipse. Guest beers might
include Adnams, Ashvine, Badger, Batemans XXXB, Courage Directors, Eagle,
Hadrian Gladiator and Centurion, Mansfield, Oakhill, Pitfield Dark Star,
Robinwood Old Fart, Sarah Hughes and Titanic. As well as these, there are
around 125 malts, 12 cognacs and 100 liqueurs; foreign beers from Belgium,
Germany, Singapore, Spain and Australia. Food is mostly simple with sandwiches
(from £1.35), soup (£1.50), burgers (from £1.95 as a snack, £3.50 as a main
meal), filled jacket potatoes (from £2.30), a wide range of very good home-made
pizzas (from £3), omelettes (from £3.85), salads (from £4), vegetarian dishes like
adzuki bean bake with tomato sauce, country lentil crumble or leek and butter
Dijonnaise (from £6.50), and steak (from £7.50); friendly service. The bar has
shiny black panelling and beams and timbers in the ochre walls, red leatherette
seats tucked into the timberwork and cosy alcoves, brasses and some netting, dim
lighting, curtains made from beer towels sewn together, and a warm open fire.
Dominoes, fruit machine and piped music. *(Recommended by Dave Braisted, John
Scarisbrick, David and Shelia, Bill and Lydia Ryan, Peter and Lynn Brueton, M S and M
Imhoff, Sue Holland, Dave Webster, Mark and Diane Grist, Andrew Stephenson, Paul and
Gail Betteley, Peter and Jenny Quine, Roger and Christine Mash, JJW, CMW)*

*Own brew ~ Licensee Mrs Gillian Holland ~ Real ale ~ Meals and snacks (12-
2.30, 6.30-10.30) ~ Restaurant ~ (01782) 720600 ~ Children welcome ~ Blues
and ballads Thurs evenings in upstairs function room ~ Open 12-3.30, 6.30-11;
midday-11 Sat*

TATENHILL (Staffs) SK2021 Map 7

Horseshoe ♀ ◗

Off A38 at A5121 Burton exit – then signposted; OS Sheet 128 map reference 203217

At lunchtime this carefully modernised and well run old pub is popular with
businessmen from Burton. There are several cosy communicating areas such as
the tile-floored Tab Bar with booth seats and some standing timbers, and a back
area with wheelback chairs, flowery wallpaper and a pleasant garden view
through picture windows; the square-panelled front part has a flowery carpet, a
delft shelf with antique bottles and pictorial plates, and on the left is a smallish
self-contained area with a woodburning stove and wheelback chairs around a few
tables divided off from the rest by timber and wrought iron. Very quickly served
good value bar food includes home-made soup (£1.10), rolls and sandwiches
(from £1.15, a generous steak one £4.80), burgers (from £2.25), omelettes (from
£3.15), filled baked potatoes (from £3.25), ploughman's (from £3.50), home-
made steak and kidney pie (£4.10), salads (from £4.25), steaks (from £5.95), and
children's dishes (from £2.30); you must book for the Sunday lunch in the cosy
pitched-roof two-level restaurant. Well kept Marstons Pedigree on handpump
and Owd Roger in winter, and wines from all ten beaujolais village appellations,
direct from growers; dominoes, cribbage, fruit machine, piped music. The garden
has plenty of tables either on the terrace or among small trees, and an ambitious
play area including a fort and a huge timber climber. *(Recommended by Ian and
Emma Potts, Dave Braisted, Dorothee and Dennis Glover, Alan Wright)*

*Marstons ~ Tenant Michael Bould ~ Real ale ~ Meals and snacks (not Sun
evening) ~ Burton upon Trent (01283) 564913 ~ Children in family room and, if
over 10, in restaurant ~ Open 11.30-3, 5.30-11; closed evening 25 Dec*

TUTBURY (Staffs) SK2028 Map 7

Olde Dog & Partridge 🛏

A444 N of Burton on Trent

The excellent carvery in this 15th-c civilised dining pub has been warmly praised by readers this year (roast of the day £6.95, prime sirloin of beef with big Yorkshire pudding £7.75). A wide choice of other good food includes home-made soup (£1.50), sandwiches (from £1.75), ploughman's (£2.75), vegetarian stroganoff (£5.50), steak and kidney pie (£5.75), a fish of the day, and puddings (from £2.15). The stylish bar has two warm turkey-carpeted rooms, one with red plush banquettes and rather close-set studded leather chairs, sporting pictures, stags' heads and a sizeable tapestry, the other with a plush-cushioned oak settle, an attractive built-in window seat, brocaded stools and a couple of Cecil Aldin hunting prints; a pianist plays each evening. Much of the extensive carvery is no smoking. Well kept Marstons Pedigree and a guest beer from the small oak bar counter, freshly squeezed orange, and decent wines; friendly efficient service. The hanging baskets are very pretty and the neat garden has white cast-iron seats and tables under cocktail parasols, with stone steps between its lawns, bedding plants, roses and trees. The pub is near Tutbury Castle, where Mary Queen of Scots was imprisoned on the orders of Elizabeth I. *(Recommended by Ralph and Lorna Lewis, Mrs S Beniston, G J Parsons, David Wright, Peter and Audrey Dowsett, Wayne Brindle, J and P M)*

Free house ~ Licensee Mrs Yvette Martindale ~ Real ale ~ Meals and lunchtime snacks (not Sun) ~ Carvery ~ (01283) 813030 ~ Children welcome ~ Evening and Sunday lunch pianist ~ Open 11-2.30, 6-11; closed 25/26 Dec ~ Bedrooms: £52.50B/£72.50B

WARDLOW (Derbys) SK1875 Map 7

Three Stags Heads 🍺

Wardlow Mires; A623 by junction with B6465

As well as being delightfully unspoilt, this simple and very friendly little white-painted cottage has a relaxed and unchanging atmosphere. Walkers, their boots and dogs are welcome – and the pub has four dogs (and some cats) of its own. The tiny parlour bar has old leathercloth seats, a couple of antique settles with flowery cushions, two high-backed Windsor armchairs and simple oak tables on the flagstones, and a cast-iron kitchen range which is kept alight in winter; one curiosity is the petrified cat in a glass case. Tables in the small, no-smoking dining parlour – where there's an open fire – are bookable. Food is served all day and served on home-made plates (the barn is a pottery workshop): leek and potato soup (£1.75), spinach and chick pea curry (£5), vegetable and apricot casserole (£5.50), steak and kidney pie (£7), guinea fowl with fruity red wine sauce (£8.50), and fillet steak with garlic butter (£10); friendly service. Hoskins & Oldfields Navigation and Ginger Tom, Kelham Island Pale Rider (they also brew a wheat beer which this pub serves), and Springhead Bitter from the little Springhead brewery in Sutton-on-Trent on handpump, and large range of continental and British bottled beers. Cribbage and dominoes. The front terrace outside looks across the main road to the distant hills. The car park is across the road by the petrol station. *(Recommended by Bill and Lydia Ryan, Nigel Woolliscroft, John Fahy, Mike and Wendy Proctor, Peter Lecomber, Andrew Stephenson, E N and I J Wilkinson, David Atkinson)*

Free house ~ Licensees Geoff and Pat Fuller ~ Real ale ~ Meals and snacks (12.30-10pm – but see winter opening times below) ~ Restaurant ~ (01298) 872268 ~ Children welcome until 8.30pm ~ Live folk/blue grass/traditional blues Sat evening and Sun lunch ~ Open 12-11; winter weekday opening 7pm

Children welcome means the pub says it lets children inside without any special restriction; readers have found that some may impose an evening time limit – please tell us if you find this.

WARSLOW (Staffs) SK0858 Map 7

Greyhound 🛏

B5053 S of Buxton

Pretty countryside surrounds this warmly friendly plain slated stone building and there are picnic-table sets under ash trees in the side garden, with rustic seats out in front. The long beamed bar has cushioned oak antique settles (some quite elegant), a log fire, houseplants in the windows, and quietly restrained landscapes on the cream walls. Big helpings of good home-made bar food include filling soup (£1.60), sandwiches (from £1.75), ploughman's (£4.20), home-made steak, mushroom and ale pie or home-made vegetarian chilli (£4.75) and steak (from £6.90), while daily specials might include chicken curry or chilli (£4.75), a trio of sausages in onion gravy, chicken in a leek and cream sauce, Somerset pork or minted lamb casserole (all £4.95), and roast Sunday lunch (£4.95); children's meals (from £1.50) and good breakfasts. Well kept Marstons Pedigree and two guest beers such as Burton Bridge Bitter, Everards Tiger, Jennings Cumberland, and Timothy Taylors Landlord on handpump. Pool room, with darts, dominoes, cribbage and fruit machine; piped classical music at lunchtimes. The simple bedrooms are comfortable and clean. The pub takes its name from the Buxton to Uttoxeter coach which used to stop here, and is handy for the Manifold Valley, Alton Towers and Dovedale. The licensees also run the Devonshire Arms in Hartington. *(Recommended by Derek and Sylvia Stephenson, Mike and Wendy Proctor, Mr and Mrs H Brierly, R H and V A Rowley, Paul Dunaway, Tim Britton, G B Rimmer, E Riley, A Preston, E P Jobling, Vickie Blake)*

Free house ~ Licensees David and Dale Mullarkey ~ Real ale ~ Meals and snacks (not Mon except bank hols and school summer hols) ~ Buxton (01298) 84249 ~ Children in tap room until 9pm ~ Live 60s/rock and roll music Sat ~ Open 12-2.30, 7-11; closed Mon lunchtime except bank hols (and then closed the following Tues lunchtime) ~ Bedrooms: £16/£32

WETTON (Staffs) SK1055 Map 7

Olde Royal Oak 🍺

The first official world championship for toe wrestling was held at this white-painted and shuttered stone village pub in June 1994 – it seems regulars are keen on the sport. The older part of the building has black beams supporting the white ceiling boards (to which a collection of golf clubs has been attached), small dining chairs sitting around rustic tables, a piano surrounded by old sheet music covers, an oak corner cupboard, and a log fire in the stone fireplace; this room extends into a more modern-feeling area with another fire which in turn leads to a carpeted sun lounge looking out onto the small garden. A room out there has been opened up for families which has taken some of the pressure off the bar; much needed as it does get very busy. Popular bar food includes sandwiches (from £1.20), filled baked potatoes (from £1.50), ploughman's (from £3.60 – the cheese for the stilton version is made in nearby Hartington), salads (from £4.25), omelettes (£3.85), ham and egg (£4.25), lasagne (£4.25), local trout or cream cheese and broccoli bake (£4.95), steak (£7.95), puddings (from £1.70), and children's meals (from £1.70). Well kept Eldridge Pope Royal Oak, Ruddles County and Rutland, Theakstons XB, and a weekly guest beer on handpump, 17 malt whiskies, and Addlestones cider; darts, dominoes, cribbage, shove-ha'penny and piped music. Places like Wetton Mill and the Manifold Valley are nearby, and behind the pub is a croft suitable for caravans and tents. *(Recommended by Paul Perry, Frank Cummins, Jeanne and Tom Barnes, George Atkinson; more reports please)*

Free house ~ Licensee George Burgess ~ Real ale ~ Meals and snacks (not winter Sun evenings) ~ (01335) 310287 ~ Children in family room ~ Open 11.30-2.30(3 Sat), 6.30-11; 12-2, 7.30-11 in winter ~ Bedrooms: £38S

If we know a pub has a no-smoking area, we say so.

WOOLLEY MOOR (Derbys) SK3661 Map 7

White Horse ◀

Badger Lane, off B6014 Matlock—Clay Cross

Derbyshire Dining Pub of the Year

The original tap room is where the cheerful locals gather to organise their two football teams, two boules teams, darts, dominoes and quiz teams – and to enjoy the well kept Bass and Highgate Dark and two guest beers on handpump. Several beer festivals are held during the year, with eight real ales and usually a skiffle or jazz group. And from November until Easter they organise special food nights cooking dishes from around the world (£9.95 for four courses, including drinks). Bar food, eaten in the cottagey beamed dining lounge, is popular and good value and uses meat from the local butcher, bread from the local baker and vegetables grown by a villager in an allotment across the road. From a choice of a dozen daily specials there might be spinach and bacon tagliatelle (£2.25), prawns in a herb and garlic batter with home-made garlic mayonnaise (£2.50), celery, almond and stilton quiche or wild mushroom ragout (£4), pepperoni and pasta bake (£4.50), lamb in honey with hazelnuts or very popular pies such as steak and kidney (£4.95), and fresh salmon and leek fricassee (£5.25); also, soup, sandwiches, filled baked potatoes and ploughman's and so forth; decent wines. Another little dining room is no smoking. There are picnic-table sets in the garden and a very good children's play area with wooden play train, climbing frame and swings for all ages. A local has just written a booklet which includes eight walks from the pub – and the landlord is a keen walker. The pub is handy for Ogden Reservoir. *(Recommended by Norma and Keith Bloomfield, John Honnor, Alan and Judith Gifford, CW, JW, Derek and Syliva Stephenson, Pat and Tony Young, G P Kerman, Geoffrey and Irene Lindley, Pat Woodward)*

Free house ~ Licensees Bill and Jill Taylor ~ Real ale ~ Meals and snacks (11.30-2, 6.30-9; not Sun evening) ~ Restaurant (not Sun evening) ~ (01246) 590319 ~ Children in eating area of lounge bar if eating and in restaurant ~ Open 11.30-2.30(3 Sat), 6.30-11

Lucky Dip

Besides the fully inspected pubs, you might like to try these Lucky Dips recommended to us and described by readers (if you do, please send us reports):

☆ **Abbots Bromley**, Staffs [High St; SK0724], *Coach & Horses*: Attractive Tudor village pub doing well under pleasant new landlord, good helpings of well prepared food in refurbished beamed bar, well kept beers, fresh flowers, friendly staff; comfortable bedrooms *(Roy Hutchinson, M A Robinson, H and T Dyal, Tim and Sarah Bucknall)*

☆ **Abbots Bromley** [Bagot St], *Royal Oak*: Wide choice of good partly Dutch-inspired food in clean, comfortable and attractive dining lounge with efficient polite service, well kept Marstons and a guest real ale, extensive wine list, interesting restaurant *(Nigel Hopkins, S Howe)*

Alfreton, Derbys [High St; SK4155], *Olde McDonalds Farm*: Extreme farm theme – moving sheep heads, parachuting chickens, talking horses – but traditional atmosphere, real fires, friendly staff; Theakstons Best and XB on handpump, imaginative menu, games area with pool; open all day, facilities for the disabled *(Russell Allen)*

☆ **Alrewas**, Staffs [High St; off A38 – OS Sheet 128 map reference 172150; SK1714], *George & Dragon*: Consistently well kept Marstons, good generous cheap bar food (not Sun) inc children's dishes, efficient staff and friendly atmosphere in three low-beamed areas recently partly knocked together; attractive paintings, piped music; pleasant partly covered garden with good play area, children welcome in eating area *(Graham Richardson, Mr and Mrs A F Walters, Dave Braisted, B M Eldridge, Gordon Smith, G P Kernan, G E Stait, LYM)*

☆ **Alton**, Staffs [SK0742], *Talbot*: Warmly welcoming stone-built pub, small and cosy, with well kept beer, good interesting food, good staff *(Mike and Wendy Proctor)*

Apperknowle, Derbys [High St; SK3878], *Travellers Rest*: Pleasant stone-built pub in farmland setting, good food from sandwiches to good value Sun lunchtime carvery, well kept Wards *(John Goodwin)*

☆ **Ashbourne**, Derbys [Ashbourne Green (A515 towards Matlock); SK1846],

Bowling Green: Straightforwardly comfortable lounge bar with well kept Bass, Worthington and two other changing ales, wide choice of well priced tasty bar lunches inc plenty for vegetarians, good friendly atmosphere; comfortable bedrooms (*M D Farman, Philip da Silva*)

Ashbourne, [Victoria Sq], *Horns*: Attractive recently refurbished old pub with bay window overlooking steep cobbled street, welcoming newish young licensees, olde-worlde atmosphere, good value if not cheap straightforward bar food, well kept Bass, decent coffee (*F A Ward*)

☆ **Ashford in the Water**, Derbys [SK1969], *Black Bull*: Smartly comfortable lounge with good service, friendly local atmosphere, decent food and well kept Robinsons (*Brian and Jill Bond, S Howe*)

☆ **Ashley**, Staffs [signposted from A53 NE of Market Drayton; SJ7636], *Peel Arms*: Almost surgically clean village local, plush furnishings but olde-worlde touches such as warming old kitchen range; good friendly licensees, well kept Marstons; lovely big garden with swings (*Tom and Jeanne Barnes, Nigel Woolliscroft*)

☆ **Ashley**, *Meynell Arms*: Very much a village local, but decent range of good value bar food (not Mon evening) inc popular Sun lunches and take-aways, well kept Bass, M&B Mild and Theakstons, deep sofa, cast-iron range, timbering, panelling and stripped stone; games in comfortable public bar, children in eating area; vintage tractors in yard (*Tom and Jeanne Barnes, Catherine and Andrew Brian, LYM*)

☆ **Ashover**, Derbys [SK3564], *Red Lion*: Tasteful turn-of-the-century decor with comfortable settees and banquettes, imaginative choice of food, cheerful fire, small dining area; friendly service, S&N real ales, quiet piped music, darts, piano; bedrooms (*JJW, CMW*)

Aston, Staffs [A34 Stafford—Stone; SJ9131], *Crown*: Decorative plates, Bass and Worthington, good old-fashioned steak pudding (*Dave Braisted*)

Bakewell, Derbys [Bridge St; SK2168], *Castle*: Good value food, newspapers to read, smart wine-bar feel, friendly staff (*Mrs C McAleese, Pauline Crossland, Dave Cawley*)

☆ **Bamford**, Derbys [Main St; A6013; SK2083], *Derwent*: Unusual layout with varied separate rooms off central hall-servery, big pictures and windows, friendly landlord, good value bar food inc vegetarian and giant Yorkshire puddings, well kept Boddingtons, Stones Best, Wards Sheffield Best and guests, decent wines, restaurant, open all day; children welcome, seats in garden; comfortable bedrooms (*Lynn Sharpless, Bob Eardley, Barbara and Norman Wells, M Joyner, LYM*)

Barlborough, Derbys [Church St; junction A616/A619; SK4777], *De Rodes Arms*: Old but modernised Brewers Fayre pub, pleasant friendly atmosphere, good value

food, Whitbreads-related beers on handpump, benches outside; children away from bar (*CW, JW*)

Barton under Needwood, Staffs [Main St; SK1818], *Shoulder of Mutton*: 17th-c, with pleasant rooms, oak beams, pictures and memorabilia, relaxing seating, well kept Bass, wide range of food; garden with play area (*B M Eldridge*); [leaving village westwards], *Top Bell*: Regular live music, well kept ale inc Ind Coope Burton, Marstons Pedigree and guests (*T G Thomas, B M Eldridge*)

☆ **Baslow**, Derbys [Nether Rd; SK2572], *Devonshire Arms*: Small hotel in pleasant surroundings, comfortably refurbished corner bar, wide choice of usual food inc fresh veg, evening restaurant, Marstons Pedigree and Tetleys, quiet piped music, footpath to Chatsworth; bedrooms (*C J Westmoreland, Mr and Mrs A F Walters, Mrs F M Halle*)

☆ **Beeley**, Derbys [SK2667], *Devonshire Arms*: Good range of well kept real ales inc Black Sheep, Theakstons and Marstons Pedigree, quite a bit of atmosphere with black beams, stripped stone, flagstones and big log fires, wide range of decent bar food from sandwiches up, nice dining room; attractive rolling scenery nr Chatsworth – can get very busy; children welcome, with upstairs family room and own menu (*Geoffrey and Irene Lindley, E D Bailey, W H and E Thomas, Ian and Val Titman, Dr and Mrs D E Awbery, Barbara Hatfield, Dr Keith Bloomfield, D C Alcock, LYM*)

☆ **Biggin**, Derbys [W of A515; SK1559], *Waterloo*: Wide choice of good value generous mostly home-cooked food inc children's dishes in welcoming pleasant bars overlooking dales, friendly and efficient service, Bass real ale (*Neil and Daphne McAdam*)

☆ **Birch Vale**, Derbys [Sycamore Rd; from A6015 take Station Rd towards Thornsett; SK0287], *Sycamore*: Wide-ranging good reasonably priced food inc children's dishes and rich puddings in four busy connecting eating rooms, well kept real ales, friendly helpful service, piped music, fountain in downstairs drinking bar; spacious streamside gardens with good play area, pets' corner and summer bar; restaurant open all day Sun, children welcome, pleasant nearby walk on Sett Valley trail; bedrooms (*John Burdett, LYM*)

Bonsall, Derbys [SK2858], *Kings Head*: Very child-friendly, with efficient, helpful and friendly landlord, good value food inc good vegetarian menu; handy for Limestone Way and other walks (*Mark and Mary Fairman*)

Boylestone, Derbys [Harehill; signed off A515, N of A50; SK1735], *Rose & Crown*: Oak-beamed tile-floored country local with enthusiastic regulars, landlord doing lively piano/vocals Fri and Sun, well kept beers inc guests (*Anon*)

Brackenfield, Derbys [A615 Matlock—

Alfreton, about a mile NW of Wessington – OS Sheet 119 map reference 360587; SK3658], *Plough*: Much modernised but welcoming oak-beamed 18th-c former farmhouse in lovely setting, cosy three-level bar, cheerful log-effect gas fire, well kept Bass, Mansfield Old Baily, Tetleys and Worthington, sensibly priced food; big beautifully kept gardens with play area *(Derek and Sylvia Stephenson, Wendy Arnold)*

Bradwell, Derbys [B6049 S of Hope; SK1781], *Valley Lodge*: Comfortable big lounge bar with good guest beers, attentive friendly staff *(David and Michelle Hedges)*

Brassington, Derbys [SK2354], *Miners Arms*: Very welcoming, with good food, good-humoured landlord; children welcome; bedrooms *(Dr Roy F Stark)*

☆ **Burton on Trent**, Staffs [Shobnall Rd (B5234 towards Abbots Bromley); SK2423], *Albion*: Particularly well kept Pedigree on handpump in showpiece pub nr Marstons brewery, spacious, comfortable and attractive, with generous good value lunchtime bar food and carvery, good service, family conservatory, roomy separate public bar with games and juke box; big fairy-lit garden with good play area, children's bar, barbecues *(Mike and Di Saxby, Ian and Emma Potts, LYM)*

Burton on Trent [Tutbury Rd (A50)], *Beacon*: Spacious and comfortable, well kept Bass, friendly staff, good value bar food inc three-course bargains; has had free pick-up service for parties of four and over *(B M Eldridge)*; [The Dingle, Stapenhill; SK2521], *Boat House*: Well kept Greene King Abbot, Marstons, Morlands Speckled Hen, Ruddles, and Theakstons, good food from bar and upstairs restaurant looking over river and wetlands *(Alan R Woolley)*; [27/28 Victoria St], *Duke of York*: Particularly well kept beer in small very friendly backstreet local, clean, comfortable and carefully renovated *(T W Roulstone, Alistair Kennedy)*; [349 Anglesey Rd], *New Talbot*: Bright, spacious and plush, with well kept Marstons (often inc trial new brews), good bar food inc OAP bargain lunches, popular Sun carvery; comfortable separate bar with pool *(B M Eldridge)*; [Station St], *Roebuck*: Very friendly, good beer inc changing guests, well presented good food *(Alistair Kennedy)*; [Anglesey Rd], *Thomas Sykes*: In former stables and waggon shed of ex-Everards brewery (latterly Heritage Brewery Museum), two rooms with breweriana, wood benches, cobbled floors, well kept Bass, Ind Coope Burton and Marstons Pedigree, good bar food inc home-made pies *(B M Eldridge)*

☆ **Buxton**, Derbys [Bridge St; SK0673], *Railway*: Varied well cooked food inc imaginative salads and home-made puddings in popular railway theme food pub with good welcoming service *(C J Westmoreland)*

Buxton, *Old Clubhouse*: Spacious comfortable lounge on several levels, polished floorboards, armchairs, good decoration, cheerful staff, nice atmosphere, Ind Coope Burton and Tetleys; opp opera house *(Peter Childs)*

☆ **nr Buxton**, [Hurdlow Town; A515 Ashbourne Rd about half a mile from the Bull i'th' Thorn; SK1166], *Duke of York*: Clean and comfortable, with Robinsons real ale, good generous food inc children's dishes (all day Sun), coal fire, pleasant staff; lovely views, well spaced tables outside *(Janet Brown)*

☆ **Buxworth**, Derbys [Silkhill, B6062; off A6 at Furness Vale – OS Sheet 110 map reference 022821; SK0228], *Navigation*: Welcoming village local overlooking historic canal basin, lots of atmosphere in individual rooms each dedicated to a theme – local history, canals, music; real coal and log fires, flagstone floors, plentiful pleasantly served food with up to ten puddings, four well kept Courage-related and other ales such as Timothy Taylors Landlord, enthusiastic staff; separate eating area, darts, pool, piped music; occasional outdoor events; bedrooms *(Bill Sykes, David Ball, John Derbyshire, Peter Yearsley)*

Carsington Reservoir, Derbys [S side, NE of Atlow, down short track off rd along dam bottom – OS Sheet 119 map reference 246496; SK2449], *Millfield*: Lots of potential for interesting building with flagstones, heavy stripped beams, lots of stripped stone inc massively sarsenish fireplace, conservatory restaurant with pasture view, darts in quite separate pool room *(BB; news please)*

☆ **Castleton**, Derbys [Cross St; SK1583], *Olde Nags Head*: Plenty of character and good feel in comfortably renovated village inn's smallish bar, open fires, antique furniture, well presented traditional bar food, attractive service, Bass, restaurant; no boots or backpacks; bedrooms warm and comfortable, interesting village *(C J Westmoreland, JM, PM, M Joyner, J F M West)*

☆ **Castleton** [High St at junction with Castle St], *Castle*: Plushly comfortable hotel bars with handsome flagstones, beams, stripped stonework, open fires, decent bar food though keg beers; open all day in summer, tables outside; bedrooms well equipped if not cheap *(C J Westmoreland, B M Eldridge, LYM)*

☆ **Castleton**, *George*: Good atmosphere and good value simple hot fresh food in roomy bars with friendly helpful staff, well kept Bass; tables on wide forecourt; popular with young people – nr YHA; dogs welcome *(John Burdett, JM, PM, Stephen Brown)*

☆ **Cauldon Lowe**, Staffs [Waterhouses; A52 Stoke—Ashbourne; SK0748], *Cross*: Good range of well kept beers and of decent food in several attractive rooms around central bar, charming service, reasonable prices, scenic setting *(Derek Manning, Tom and Jeanne Barnes)*

Chapel en le Frith, Derbys [SK0680], *Cross Keys*: Good food (all day Sun) in old pub under imposing railway viaduct, one room smartly decorated and even more smartly decorated restaurant; well kept beers, very friendly service; children welcome *(Lee Goulding, Jack Morley)*

☆ **Cheddleton**, Staffs [Basford Bridge Lane, off A520; SJ9651], *Boat*: Cheerful local overlooking canal with narrow neatly furnished bar, low plank ceilings, well kept Marstons, simple choice of generous cheap food; handy for North Staffs Steam Railway Museum *(LYM)*

☆ **Chinley**, Derbys [off A624 towards Hayfield; SK0482], *Lamb*: Profusely decorated stone-built three-room roadside pub with friendly atmosphere, well prepared reasonably priced bar food served quickly once you order (though you may have to wait a while for a table, and weekday lunchtime food stops 2 sharp), well kept Marstons and other real ales on handpump; children allowed till 8.30; lots of tables out in front *(Lorrie and Mick Marchington, JM, PM, Mike and Wendy Proctor, BB)*

Chinley, *Crown & Mitre*: Good food and welcome *(Pauline Crossland, Dave Cawley)*; *Oddfellows Arms*: Clean and popular, esp with walkers, with well kept Marstons Pedigree *(Chris Elias, Stephen, Julie and Hayley Brown)*; *Old Hall*: Friendly family-run 16th-c inn with choice of real ales, home-made bar food; four good bedrooms, self-catering cottage *(Dr J Morley)*

Chunal, Derbys [A624 a mile S of Glossop; SK0391], *Grouse*: Usual bar food with some good interesting specials such as game pie and venison, good value above-average wine by glass, friendly caring attentive staff, attractive personal atmosphere *(Gwen and Peter Andrews)*

☆ **Clifton Campville**, Staffs [SK2510], *Green Man*: New licensees in attractive low-beamed 15th-c village pub with character public bar, airy modernised lounge, good family atmosphere, well kept Bass, good value bar food; children in family room, garden with swings *(Michael Back, Graham Richardson, George Atkinson, LYM)*

Colton, Staffs [Bellamour Way; SK0520], *Greyhound*: Really welcoming new licensees, good reasonably priced food *(Nigel Hopkins)*

☆ **Consall**, Staffs [Consallforge; best approach from Nature Pk, off A522 – OS Sheet 118 map reference 000491; SJ9748], *Black Lion*: Big helpings of cheap individually prepared food (may be delays even for snacks when busy) in basic unspoilt tavern isolated in very old-fashioned canalside settlement; free-speaking landlady, good coal fire, well kept Marstons Pedigree and Ruddles County on handpump, traditional games, piped music; children welcome;

busy weekends, good walking area on edge of country park, with nice towpath walk from Froghall picnic area – muddy boots OK on quarry-tiled floor *(Bill Sykes, G B Rimmer, E Riley, LYM)*

☆ **Copmere End**, Staffs [W of Eccleshall; SJ8029], *Star*: Classic simple two-room country local overlooking mere, Bass and guest ale, surprisingly good home-made food from sandwiches to duck breast or seafood tagliatelle, very friendly service, picnic-table sets in beautiful back garden full of trees and shrubs; local horticultural society produce for sale Sun lunchtime; children very welcome *(Nigel Woolliscroft)*

Coton in the Elms, Derbys [Coalpit Lane; SK2415], *Queens Head*: Pleasant modern lounge bar, friendly staff, well kept Marstons Pedigree and related beers, good value bar food and Sun lunches; Weds show night, Fri maybe karaoke; attractive small village *(B M Eldridge)*

Cromford, Derbys [SK2956], *Boat*: Comfortable bar with warm welcome from friendly staff, Bass and Mansfield ales kept well, varied menu, garden *(S Howe)*

Cutthorpe, Derbys [NW of Chesterfield; B6050 W of village; SK3473], *Gate*: Free house in lovely isolated spot, good views over moorland and to Chesterfield, comfortable bar areas, dining room with good reasonably priced food (very popular summer evenings), real ales such as Boddingtons, Flowers, Stones and Mansfield, friendly service *(Alan and Heather Jacques, S E Paulley)*

Darlaston, Staffs [A34, just S of A51; SJ8835], *George & Dragon*: Big but surprisingly cosy, quite a bit of stained glass, Burtonwood real ale, usual bar food with more interesting specials; restaurant *(Dave Braisted)*

☆ **Derby** [Queen St, nr cathedral], *Olde Dolphin*: Fine 16th-c beamed pub, cosy and civilised, with several rooms around central bar inc tiny snug, well kept Bass, Worthington BB and an interesting guest beer, with cheap beer Mon night, good value food, upstairs no smoking dining area (children allowed here), prompt friendly service; newspapers, board games, even a ghost *(Brian Jones, Andrew Stephenson)*

☆ **Dovedale**, Staffs [Thorpe—Ilam rd; Ilam signposted off A52, Thorpe off A515, NW of Ashbourne; SK1452], *Izaak Walton*: Sizeable hotel out on the sheep pastures, with pleasant and relaxing low-beamed bar, some distinctive antique oak settles and chairs, good log fire in massive central stone chimney; Ind Coope Burton on handpump, bar food and restaurant, morning coffee and afternoon tea; seats out on lawn; bedrooms comfortable *(Mike and Wendy Proctor, LYM)*

Doveridge, Derbys [SK1134], *Cavendish Arms*: Well kept Marstons Pedigree on handpump, home-made food, friendly regulars and dogs, open fire *(David and Shelia)*

☆ **Eccleshall**, Staffs [Castle St; SJ8329], *St George*: Traditional beamed decor and plenty of atmosphere in attractive modernised bar with well kept Bass, Boddingtons and Tetleys, good wines, good home-cooked food, friendly landlord; elegant yet welcoming restaurant;, comfortable individually decorated bedrooms *(A Shropshall, R Clark)*

Edale, Derbys [SK1285], *Old Nags Head*: Useful for walkers, with substantial basic food, open fire, well kept Marstons and S&N ales, character high-raftered room which was once a barn; children in airy back family room with video games; open all day summer *(Ann and Colin Hunt, LYM)*

Elton, Derbys [SK2261], *Duke of York*: Unusual local in delightful village, like stepping back in time; nothing fancy, back-to-basics small bar in little back room, darts in one of two front rooms; closed lunchime, open 8-11 *(Ann and Colin Hunt)*

Endon, Staffs [Denford; byroad some way E; SJ9553], *Holly Bush*: Good setting, wide range of well kept beers, friendly staff and welcoming atmosphere, good value well prepared food *(Patrick and Mary McDermott)*

Eyam, Derbys [SK2276], *Bulls Head*: Smallish old pub with good freshly prepared food (so may be a wait), good attentive service, open fire, stained glass, ornamental teapots, friendly dog, quiet piped music; lounge, smoke room, games area with pool, darts, TV, juke box; bedrooms *(JJW, CMW)*

☆ **Farnah Green**, Derbys [follow Hazelwood signpost off A517 in Blackbrook, W edge of Belper; SK3346], *Bluebell*: Plush well kept dining pub with particularly attentive service, good food promptly served in relaxing small rooms; sturdy tables out on terrace and in quiet gently sloping spacious side garden, restaurant with inventive cooking, well kept Bass; may be closed Mon *(Peter Marshall, Mike and Jo, BB)*

Foolow, Derbys [SK1976], *Bulls Head*: Reports please on this attractive moorland village pub, very popular indeed as a main entry under its previous name of Lazy Landlord, but now under new ownership and being refurbished 1994 *(LYM)*

Glossop, Derbys [Charlestown Rd; SK0394], *Whitely Nab*: Good value above-average food *(Pauline Crossland, Dave Cawley)*

Great Chatwell, Staffs [SJ7915], *Red Lion*: Friendly village pub with good atmosphere and helpful staff, very nice Sun lunch; no food Mon *(Jean and Douglas Troup)*

☆ **Great Hucklow**, Derbys [SK1878], *Queen Anne*: New licensee doing good range of food esp big helpings of fish, also some unusual dishes, in comfortable beamed bar with open fire and two other rooms, one with french windows on to small terrace and pleasant garden with lovely views; children welcome *(Roger A Mash)*

Grindleford, Derbys [B6001; SK2478], *Sir William*: Relaxed local atmosphere, good value food, pool table in spacious room; splendid view, walking nearby *(Dr Paul Kitchener)*

☆ **Grindon**, Staffs [signed off B5033 N of A523; SK0854], *Cavalier*: 16th-c traditional stonebuilt country pub with well kept Wards Best, usual food maybe inc late-night bargains Fri/Sat or Sun happy hour with free sandwiches, pleasant service; smallish front bar with larger room behind and separate games room, good mix of locals and visitors; pleasant informal garden, has been closed Mon lunchtime and maybe other lunchtimes *(Frank Cummins, Nigel Woolliscroft, Dr and Mrs B Baker, LYM)*

☆ **Hanley**, Staffs [65 Lichfield St; SJ8747], *Coachmakers Arms*: Character unspoilt friendly town pub, three small rooms and drinking corridor, particularly well kept Bass and M&B Mild, skittles; exemplary outside lavatories *(Nigel Woolliscroft)*

Hanley [Albion Sq, Lichfield St/Old Hall St], *Albion*: Big turn-of-century city corner pub, busy but quick and obliging service, good value basic lunchtime meals and snacks in no-smoking dining area, interesting photographs *(CW, JW)*; [Derby St], *New Inn*: Friendly and attentive staff in spacious bar and lounge, noteworthy range of wines by the glass, good food *(Malcolm and Penny Locker)*; [Tontine St], *Tontine Alehouse*: City-centre pub with generous tasty lunchtime food, well kept Tetleys and Marstons Pedigree *(Dr and Mrs B Baker)*

☆ **Hardwick Hall**, Derbys [Hardwick Park; from M1 junction 29 take A6175 towards Clay Cross, but turn off first left and keep along parallel with M-way, passing Stainsby – pub by third entry to Hardwick; SK4663], *Hardwick Inn*: Quietly traditional 17th-c National Trust inn in delightful setting, several separate rooms, big helpings of generous food (not Sun evening) from sandwiches and burgers to carvery, also vegetarian; well kept Marstons Pedigree and S&N beers, generally quick service, big dogs, children allowed; tables outside with nice view *(Andy and Jill Kassube, D W Crossley, A W Dickinson, Ann and Colin Hunt, Barry and Anne, Stephen Jones, Mayur Shah, J F M West, LYM)*

☆ **Hartington**, Derbys [The Square; SK1360], *Devonshire Arms*: Doing well under welcoming current management, good well priced food, well kept beer, very efficient service, cheerful welcome; bedrooms comfortable *(M P Jefferson, Mr and Mrs Dolby)*

Hartington, *Minton House*: Outstandingly clean hotel with good beautifully presented bar snacks; bedrooms *(W H and E Thomas)*

Hartshill, Staffs [296 Hartshill Rd (A52); SJ8545], *Jolly Potters*: Traditional, with four little rooms off a drinking corridor, well kept Bass and M&B Mild, simple snacks *(Nigel Woolliscroft)*

Hassop, Derbys [SK2272], *Eyre Arms*: Delightful 17th-c inn with good bar food, small dining area, cosy atmosphere, courteous friendly landlord; good walks nearby *(F J Lascelles Pallin)*

☆ **Hathersage**, Derbys [A625; SK2381], *George*: Limited good value bar food, well kept Boddingtons, decent wine in substantial comfortably modernised old inn, picturesque outside; popular lunchtime bar food, neat flagstoned back terrace by rose garden; a nice place to stay (the back bedrooms are the quiet ones) *(Margaret and Paul Digby, David Eberlin, LYM)*

☆ **Hathersage** [A625], *Hathersage*: Comfortable and friendly inn, modernised with restraint, with good value food in spacious bar and lounge, well kept Courage-related ales, log fires; bedrooms good value *(Dr Paul Kitchener, Mrs F M Halle)*

Hathersage [Leadmill Bridge; A622 (ex B6001) towards Bakewell – OS Sheet 110 map reference 235805], *Plough*: Good food using fresh produce, friendly landlord, good choice of beers in former farm with Derwent-side garden *(Bill and Beryl Goddard)*; [Church Lane], *Scotsmans Pack*: Attractive 17th-c stonebuilt pub doing well under current warmly welcoming landlord, good choice of generous nicely presented food, well kept Burtonwood, decent wines; comfortable in quasi-archaic 1930s style, good walking area; some seats outside; now does bedrooms *(Margaret and Paul Digby)*

☆ **Hatton**, Derbys [Station Rd (A50); by Tutbury rly stn; SK2130], *Castle*: Family-run coaching inn, warm and friendly, with wide choice of good home-cooked food inc duck and wild boar in lounge bar, well kept Bass, Theakstons and Worthington, reasonably priced food; restaurant from vegetarian to steaks; handy for glassworks, castle and antique shops; bedrooms *(B M Eldridge, G A Clark)*

Haughton, Staffs [SJ8620], *Bell*: Good atmosphere, lovely open fires in both bars, good value snacks, well kept guest beer; landlord of laconic charm *(John and Frances Stott)*; [A518], *Shropshire*: Very welcoming landlord, quick obliging service, good range of usual food inc hefty steak and kidney pudding; relaxed atmosphere, pleasant garden *(Cyril Burton)*

Hayfield, Derbys [Church St, off A624 Glossop—Chapel-en-le-Frith; SK0387], *George*: Red plush lounge with coal fire in big black range, flagstones and black beams in central area, pool, electronic football, juke box and fruit machine in games bar on left; Burtonwood on handpump, piped pop music; some seats outside – pretty village; bedrooms *(H K Dyson, Jack Morley, Mr and Mrs A E McCully, Pauline Crossland, Dave Cawley, BB)*; [Market St], *Pack Horse*: Busy but welcoming dining pub, good proper food at close-set tables

(Pauline Crossland, Dave Cawley); *Royal*: Cheerful 18th-c local, interesting and well run, popular for a drink; bedrooms *(H K Dyson, JM, PM)*; *Waltzing Weasel*: Recently redone as traditional pub, bar with farmhouse chairs, delft shelves, warming pan, grandfather clock, well kept real ales, good wines and food *(Jack Morley)*

Heath, Derbys [just off M1 junction 29; A6175 towards Clay Cross, then first right; SK4466], *Elm Tree*: Friendly atmosphere, simple food at very reasonable prices, well kept Mansfield ales *(R A Hobbs)*

Hednesford, Staffs [Mount St; SJ9913], *West Cannock*: Cosy Victorian-style pub, bar recently extended and turned into second comfortable lounge, widening range of good value food, extremely friendly staff; well kept real ales – now a free house *(John and Christine Simpson)*

☆ **High Offley**, Staffs [towards High Lea – Bridge 42, Shrops Union Canal; SJ7826], *Anchor*: Unspoilt canal pub, two simple homely rooms, basic sandwiches, well kept Marstons Pedigree and Owd Rodger and Wadworths 6X brought up from cellar, lots of Weston's farm ciders; in same family for over a century; children welcome, impromptu folk music, cl Mon-Weds winter; caravan/campsite *(Nigel Woolliscroft)*

Higham, Derbys [Main St; A61 N of Alfreton; SK3959], *Greyhound*: A Marstons Tavern Table with good friendly service, nice interior, good food inc interesting specials, well kept real ales; can get busy *(J Finney)*

☆ **Hill Chorlton**, Staffs [Stone Rd (A51); SJ7939], *Slaters*: Comfortable newish beamed bar in former farm buildings, attractive decor, good tasty standard bar food from sandwiches up inc Sun roasts and limited selection for vegetarians, well kept Banks's, Boddingtons and Marstons Pedigree, decent wines, upstairs restaurant, children's room; tables out in attractive garden, animals in barn – still a true working farm; bedrooms *(Mayur Shah, Mike and Wendy Proctor, Paul and Gail Betteley, Peter and Jenny Quine, LYM)*

Hilton, Derbys [Main St; SK2430], *Kings Head*: 17th-c coaching inn, now dining pub with good value Sun lunch, well kept Marstons Pedigree, pleasant surroundings *(B M Eldridge)*

☆ **Hoar Cross**, Staffs [off A515 Yoxall—Sudbury; SK1323], *Meynell Ingram Arms*: Unspoilt traditional country pub with log fires, good varied reasonably priced food, well kept Marstons Pedigree, warm and friendly atmosphere *(Mrs R Cotgreave, Mr and Mrs Tom Chetwynd, M A Robinson)*

Hognaston, Derbys [SK2350], *Red Lion*: Particularly well kept Marstons Pedigree, good value food, real old-fashioned atmosphere *(D W Gray)*

☆ **Holbrook**, Derbys [14 Chapel St; SK3644], *Wheel*: Friendly local with range of well kept ales, wide choice of imaginative home-cooked food *(S M McDonough, M E Harold)*

☆ **Hollington**, Staffs [the one between Alton and Uttoxeter; SK0538], *Raddle*: Attractively placed extended country pub popular for big helpings of good bar food inc vegetarian and children's dishes, five well kept real ales on handpump, neatly modernised rambling bar, sizeable upstairs family room with own servery, helpful young staff; great views from tables in recently improved garden with big play area *(John Scarisbrick, BB)*

Hollington, Derbys [the one off A52 Derby—Ashbourne; SK2239], *Red Lion*: Genuine rustic atmosphere, relaxed and friendly, with popular food, tables in garden; children welcome, cl Mon lunchtime *(Graham Richardson)*

☆ **Hope**, Derbys [Edale Rd; SK1783], *Cheshire Cheese*: Interesting good value home cooking, welcoming helpful staff and cosy little up-and-down oak-beamed rooms in down-to-earth 16th-c stonebuilt pub with well kept Stones and Wards, lots of old local photographs and prints, abundant coal fires; attractive village setting, children allowed in eating area, walkers welcome; bedrooms *(Sue Demont, Tim Barrow, Sarah and Steve de Mellow, LYM)*

Hope [1 Castleton Rd], *Woodroffe Arms*: New regime doing well in tastefully redeveloped inn, warren of rooms off main bar, wide-ranging choice of well prepared and presented food at very reasonable prices, numerous guest beers; bedrooms *(Geoffrey and Irene Lindley)*

☆ **Huddlesford**, Staffs [off A38 2 miles E of Lichfield – OS Sheet 139 map reference 152097; SK1509], *Plough*: Huge helpings of good plain food esp filled rolls, pies and casseroles in pleasant old brick pub alongside canal and railway, particularly well kept Ind Coope Burton and Theakstons on handpump, tables out by water *(Dorothee and Dennis Glover, Peter Wilcox)*

☆ **Hulme End**, Staffs [SK1059], *Manifold Valley*: Good generous bar food and well kept Wards in country pub nr river, spacious lounge bar with good atmosphere and open fire, Sun lunches in separate dining room; provision for children *(Peter Marshall, BB)*

☆ **Kinver**, Staffs [A449; SO8483], *Whittington*: Genuine Dick Whittington connection with striking black and white timbered Tudor house, full of character; interesting old-fashioned bar with attentive staff and roaring fire, conservatory opening on to fine garden; taken over by Banks's 1994, with good value straightforward food and well kept real ale *(Philip and Julie Grosset, LYM)*

Knighton, Staffs [B5415 Woore—Mkt Drayton; SJ7240], *White Lion*: Large beamed bar with two log fires, smaller side room, dining area, conservatory, well kept

Marstons and guests like Adnams and Morlands Old Speckled Hen, good food, good bar nibbles; restaurant (not Mon or Sun evening); large adventure playground *(Nigel Woolliscroft, David Hanley)*

Knockerdown, Derbys [1½ miles S of Brassington; SK2352], *Knockerdown*: Pleasant small pub nr Carsington reservoir, well kept Marstons Pedigree, good value Sun lunch, friendly local atmosphere *(David Eberlin)*

☆ **Ladybower Reservoir**, Derbys [A57 Sheffield—Glossop, at junction with A6013; SK1986], *Ladybower*: Fine views of the attractively set reservoir from clean, spacious and comfortable open-plan stone pub with red plush seating, discreet piped music, reasonably priced popular food, Allied ales etc; stone seats outside, good walks *(Pauline Crossland, Dave Cawley, P Corris, DC)*

Leek, Staffs [St Edward St; SJ9856], *Swan*: Old pub across from church, with reasonably priced food, range of Bass beers and regular guests, plenty of malt whiskies, no-smoking room, tables in courtyard; service can sometimes slow *(John Scarisbrick)*

Leek, Staffs [Blackshaw Moor; A532 NNW; SK0059], *Three Horseshoes*: Large, well appointed, well run, clean and welcoming *(W H and E Thomas)*

Lees, Derbys [Long Lane; SK2637], *Three Horseshoes*: Owned by village shareholders, with well kept Marstons Pedigree and a changing guest beer, good value traditional food (now has small restaurant), open fire, welcoming service, no juke box *(Andrew Stephenson, Martin Grundy)*

☆ **Lichfield**, Staffs [Market St; one of the central pedestrian-only streets; SK1109], *Scales*: Long dark oak-panelled bar recently carefully refurbished to keep old-fashioned feel, with big etched window, wooden flooring, screens, immitation gas lights, sepia photographs of old Lichfield; meals and snacks, well kept Bass, Batemans XXXB, Highgate Mild and Lichfield Inspired and Steeplejack on handpump, darts, uniformed bar staff; suntrap back courtyard *(Luke Hundleby, T G Thomas, LYM)*

☆ **Lichfield** [Tamworth St], *Pig & Truffle*: Good range of well presented reasonably priced food in nicely decorated newish dining pub with panelled bar, attentive service, well kept real ales, good coffee, seats in sunny back yard; shame about the piped music; no food Fri-Sun evenings when more a younger person's preserve *(T G Thomas, David and Valerie Hooley, William and Dilys Cliffe)*

Lichfield [Bird St], *Kings Head*: Family courtyard conservatory, traditional front rooms, good bar food, well kept Marstons Pedigree and Best, tables outside *(T G Thomas)*; [Stafford Rd], *Little Barrow*: Plushly comfortable and spacious hotel bar with Theakstons beers, good bar food, good service; children welcome; bedrooms *(T G Thomas)*; [Lombard St, off Tamworth St], *Propino Bibo:* Newish, with bar counter made from butcher's block, Latin theme with mottos and so forth, well reproduced music, windows looking on to side street; regular comedy evenings, good for the young at heart *(T G Thomas)*

☆ **Little Bridgeford,** Staffs [nr M6 junction 14; turn right off A5013 at Little Bridgeford; SJ8727], *Worston Mill:* Very popular Marstons family dining pub in interesting and very comfortably converted former watermill, with wheel and gear still preserved, ducks on millpond and millstream in attractive garden with adventure playground and nature trail, attractive conservatory; well kept ales, wide choice of reasonably priced good food, friendly staff, children welcome *(Michael and Rachel Brookes, Paul and Gail Betteley, Richard Lewis, LYM)*

☆ **Litton,** Derbys [off A623; SK1675], *Red Lion:* Cosy and pretty village pub/restaurant disqualified as a main entry because you have to have a meal, not just a drink, but well worth knowing for well above-average food esp game in intimate low-ceilinged partly panelled front rooms or bigger back room with stripped stone and antique prints; huge log fires, good friendly service, well kept Boddingtons, decent wine, quiet piped classical music; dogs allowed; cl weekday lunchtimes, Sun/Mon evenings *(Mrs D M Everard, Mr and Mrs David Lee, G W Lindley, JJW, CMW, LYM)*

Longdon, Staffs [off A51 Rugeley—Stafford; SK0714], *Swan With Two Necks:* In lovely village, with well kept real ale, generous home-cooked food *(Nigel Hopkins)*

☆ **Lullington,** Derbys [SK2513], *Colvile Arms:* Choice 18th-c village pub with basic panelled bar, plush lounge, pleasant atmosphere, friendly staff, piped music, well kept Bass and Marstons Pedigree on handpump, good value snacks, tables on small sheltered back lawn overlooking bowling green; cl weekday lunchtimes *(George Atkinson, David Gaunt, LYM)*

Makeney, Derbys [Holly Bush Lane; A6 N, cross river Derwent, before Milford turn right, then left; SK3544], *Holly Bush:* Popular and down-to-earth old-fashioned pub with three roaring open fires, good choice of beers brought from cellar in jugs; children allowed in conservatory *(Andrew Stephenson)*

Mapleton, Derbys [SK1648], *Okeover Arms:* Small comfortable bar with well kept real ale, decent bar food, restaurant; good walking country *(S Howe)*

Marston Montgomery, Derbys [SK1338], *Crown:* Well kept Bass and imaginatively presented bar food inc excellent sandwiches, friendly staff, cheerful atmosphere with open fire (even at

breakfast), good garden; bedrooms large and comfortable with easy chairs and televisions *(JM, PM)*

☆ **Melbourne,** Derbys [SK3825], *White Swan:* Carefully and interestingly restored 15th-c pub with good value imaginative food, friendly owners, well kept Marstons Pedigree; pleasant narrow garden; children welcome *(Richard and Maria Gillespie, LYM)*

☆ **Melbourne** [222 Station Rd, towards Kings Newton/Islay Walton], *Railway:* Good value food in attractive dining room, traditional bar with well kept Marstons Pedigree, Timothy Taylors Landlord, Wards and guest beers, tiled and wooden floors, cast-iron gas fireplaces; well behaved children allowed *(Derek and Sylvia Stephenson)*

Millers Dale, Derbys [SK1373], *Anglers Rest:* Good friendly atmosphere in attractively placed village pub with well kept Tetleys and Worthington and great value food – good choice inc vegetarian; cosy lounge with fire, pool room, very friendly staff; good walks *(Rupert Lecomber, Susan Boyle, Eugene Wills)*

☆ **Millthorpe,** Derbys [Cordwell Lane; SK3276], *Royal Oak:* Cosy snug with real fire, another in stripped-stone oak-beamed main bar, inexpensive simple but interesting home-made lunchtime food, well kept Wards on handpump, helpful licensees, tables outside in pleasant surroundings; good walks nearby, cl Mon lunchtime exc bank hols *(E W Scott, LYM)*

Milton, Derbys [Main St; just E of Repton; SK3126], *Swan:* Well kept Marstons in pleasant smart lounge, good friendly staff, good range of good value bar food (not Mon); garden with play area, attractive village *(B M Eldridge)*

Milwich, Staffs [Smallrice; B5027 towards Stone; SJ9532], *Red Lion:* Also known as the Romping Cat, farmhouse with one pub room at the end, Bass tapped from the cask, friendly welcome, log fire *(Nigel Woolliscroft)*

☆ **Monyash,** Derbys [OS Sheet 119 map reference 153665; SK1566], *Bull:* Good well presented home-cooked food inc vegetarian in quiet village pub; Ind Coope Burton and Tetleys Bitter and Mild on handpump, friendly efficient staff, quiet piped music, dining room, pool room off larger bright public bar, coal fire; children and muddy dogs welcome *(Phil and Heidi Cook, Mrs R S Rotbart)*

Moorwood Moor, Derbys [nr South Wingfield; SK3656], *White Hart:* Country pub smartened up by newish owners, with emphasis now on good choice of reasonably priced food, spacious and comfortable new dining area; booking needed Fri/Sat evening, Sun lunchtime; tables in garden *(A Preston)*

Muckley Corner, Staffs [A5/A461 (Walsall Rd); formerly Muckley Corner Hotel; SK0806], *Olde Corner House:* Recently extensively refurbished on the hotel side yet unpretentious, with good value restaurant-style food, well kept Marstons Pedigree and other real ales, friendly atmosphere, pleasant decor; comfortable bedrooms *(M S and M Imhoff, M V Fereday)*

Needwood, Staffs [SK1724], *New Inn*: Good reasonably priced food, friendly and helpful licensees *(Sue Badel, B M Eldridge)*

New Mills, Derbys [Mellor Rd; 1/2 way between New Mills & Mellor; SJ9886], *Pack Horse*: Popular and friendly local with plentiful good value food, lovely views *(Mr and Mrs A E McCully, J F M West)*

Newborough, Staffs [SK1325], *Red Lion*: Unpretentious Marstons pub reopened after a closure, with well kept Pedigree and good choice of wines and spirits in comfortable modern lounge, good value traditional food; facing church in quiet village *(B M Eldridge, LYM)*

☆ **Newcastle under Lyme,** Staffs [High St; SJ8445], *Golden Lion*: Good value cheap and simple home cooking in comfortably modernised but old-fashioned pub with well kept Bass; handy for open market *(Nigel Woolliscroft)*

Newcastle under Lyme, Staffs [Etruria Rd], *New Victoria*: Two theatre bars (one opening even on non-performance nights) with good choice of well kept real ales inc uncommon guest beers, nice atmosphere, bar snacks *(Mike and Wendy Proctor)*

Newton Solney, Derbys [Repton Rd; SK2825], *Unicorn*: Busy, with well kept Bass, fairly big bar opened up from smaller rooms, pleasant small lounge with no serving bar, easy disabled access *(B M Eldridge)*

Norbury Junction, Staffs [off A519 Eccleshall—Newport via Norbury; SJ7922], *Junction*: Busy canalside local in pleasant setting, wide range of good reasonably priced home-cooked bar food, good value carvery, well kept beer, friendly efficient service *(Sandra Iles, DC)*

Oakerthorpe, Derbys [SK3955], *Butchers Arms*: Welcoming atmosphere, log fire, good food, red tablecloths and waitress service, well kept Hardys & Hansons *(Nan Axon)*

Old Brampton, Derbys [Wigley; off A619 Chesterfield—Baslow at Wadshelf; SK3171], *Fox & Goose*: Recently refurbished hilltop pub overlooking Chesterfield and towards Sheffield, roomy pleasant low-ceilinged main bar with big stone fireplace, two smaller side rooms, friendly welcome, interesting sandwiches, good range of Whitbreads-related beers *(Andrew Turnbull)*

Padfield, Derbys [SK0396], *Peels Arms*: Smartly decorated yet homely stonebuilt village pub with split-level lounge and cosy public bar, three real fires, games room, well kept Youngers real ales, good food, pleasant views *(Pauline Crossland, Dave Cawley, Lee Goulding)*

☆ **Penkhull,** Staffs [Manor Court St – OS Sheet 118 map reference 868448; SJ8644], *Greyhound*: Remarkably good value filling snacks and well kept Marstons Pedigree and Tetleys in relaxed and traditional two-room pub with friendly villagey feel; children in eating area, picnic-table sets on back terrace *(David and Shelia, LYM)*

☆ **Penkridge,** Staffs [Market Pl – handy for M6 junctions 12/13; SJ9214], *Star*: Open-plan, with lots of black beams and button-back red plush, good value generous lunchtime food (extended hours Weds and Sat) with gingham tablecloths in dining area, well kept cheap Banks's ales with a guest such as Marstons Pedigree, cheery landlord; piped music, open all day *(Dorothy and David Young, John and Christine Simpson, Graham Reeve)*

☆ **Pilsley,** Derbys [off A619 Bakewell—Baslow; SK2471], *Devonshire Arms*: Cosy and welcoming local with limited good value food using fresh Chatsworth ingredients lunchtime and early evening, Mansfield Riding and Old Baily, Stones and Whitbreads Castle Eden on handpump; lovely village within walking distance of Chatsworth Farm and Craft Shops *(DC)*

Ripley, Derbys [Buckland Hollow; A610 towards Ambergate, junction B6013 – OS Sheet 119 map reference 380510; SK3851], *Excavator*: Modern open-plan Marstons Tavern Table dining pub, very popular for good reasonably priced food (all day Sun) inc good specials and vegetarian dishes; Pedigree and Best on handpump *(Mark Bradley)*

Rolleston on Dove, Staffs [Station Rd; SK2427], *Jinnie*: Pleasant and attractively set Banks's pub with lovely comfortable seats, friendly staff and customers, well kept ales inc Marstons Pedigree, home-cooked lunchtime food running up to steaks; picnic-table sets on small lawn *(B M Eldridge)*

☆ **Rowarth,** Derbys [off A626 in Marple Bridge at Mellor sign, sharp left at Rowarth sign, then follow Little Mill sign; OS Sheet 110 map reference 011889 – but need Sheet 109 too; SK0189], *Little Mill*: Beautiful tucked-away setting, unusual features inc working waterwheel, voluble parrot, vintage Pullman-carriage bedrooms, pretty garden dell across stream with good play area; wide choice of cheap plentiful bar food all day, dark open-plan bar crowded with little settees, armchairs and small tables, Banks's, Hansons, Robinsons Best Mild and Bitter and a guest beer, hospitable landlord, pub games, juke box, busy upstairs restaurant (wide choice of Sun roasts); live music Weds, children welcome *(Trevor Scott, Mrs J Barwell, Lorrie and Mick Marchington, C Findell, John Burdett, Bill and Lydia Ryan, LYM)*

☆ **Rowsley,** Derbys [SK2566], *Peacock*: Decent unpretentious lunchtime bar food (not Sun) in civilised small hotel's spacious and comfortable lounge, interestingly old-fashioned inner bar, real ales, friendly efficient staff, attractive riverside gardens, trout fishing; bedrooms comfortable, big and well furnished *(Doug Kennedy, LYM)*

Rowsley [A6], *Grouse & Claret*: Comfortably refurbished and spacious Mansfield Landlords Table family restaurant, good choice of food from carvery counter, efficient service *(Tim and Lynne Crawford, A Preston)*

Salt, Staffs [signposted south of Stone on A51; SJ9527], *Holly Bush*: Very friendly partly thatched 14th-c village pub with extraordinarily wide choice of good generous home-cooked food in bar and restaurant; occasional live music summer Sats *(Pat Bromley, Kate and Harry Taylor)*

☆ **Sandonbank**, Staffs [SJ9428], *Seven Stars*: Wide choice of good value food from sandwiches to as-much-as-you-want carvery inc vegetarian dishes in big busy dining pub with several cosy corners and two big open fires; well kept Burtonwood, two pool tables (winter only), piped music; restaurant, children welcome, seats out behind *(Paul and Gail Betteley, David and Shelia, LYM)*

☆ **Shardlow**, Derbys [The Wharf; SK4330], *Malt Shovel*: Good changing lunchtime food and well kept Marstons and changing guest ales in attractively set former 18th-c canalside maltings with odd-angled walls, good open fire heating two rooms, friendly atmosphere, pleasant service; seats out by water *(Andrew Stephenson, David and Shelia, Bill Sykes, A and R Cooper, LYM)*

Shebden, Staffs [N of Newport, nr Harpur Adams Ag Coll; SJ7626], *Wharf*: Below canal embankment, with big garden and playground; wide choice of good value simple food, guest beers such as Eldridge Pope Royal Oak and Morlands Old Speckled Hen, bar billiards, games machines; children very welcome *(Nigel Woolliscroft)*

Shenstone, Staffs [SK1004], *Black Bull*: Recently refurbished Bass pub, keeping flagstones, bare brick walls and panelling; big helpings of good food; children welcome *(G McGarry)*; [Main St], *Railway*: Friendly, with varied choice of nicely cooked lunchtime food, well kept Marstons ales inc Union Mild, leather chesterfields in high-ceilinged lounge; barbecue and picnic-table sets in garden *(Mr and Mrs H S Hill)*

Shenstone Woodend, Staffs [Birmingham Rd, nr Lichfield; SK1101], *Highwayman*: Friendly staff, lounge bar with well kept Bass, pleasant Toby carvery restaurant *(Russell Allen)*

Shottle, Derbys [A517 Belper—Ashbourne; SK3149], *Hanging Gate*: Good variety of reliable food inc vegetarian, friendly service; nice spot in summer; children welcome *(B B Watling, Mr and Mrs J Fowden)*

Smalley, Derbys [A608; SK4044], *Bell*: Three small rooms around servery, cushioned wall settles, bric-a-brac, friendly staff, good helpings of straightforward food, well kept Ansells, Marstons Pedigree

and Ruddles County, decent wines, lovely garden *(Mark Bradley, Sue Badel)*

☆ **Sparrowpit**, Derbys [nr Chapel en le Frith; junction of A623 – B6061; SK0980], *Wanted Inn*: Friendly and attractive stonebuilt 16th-c inn, central bar for two rooms each with real fire, good value home-cooked food, well kept Robinsons Bitter and Mild on handpump, lots of copper, piped music, picnic-table sets by car park; beautiful countryside *(JJW, CMW, D W Gray, Susan Boyle, Eugene Wills)*

Stableford, Staffs [A51 towards Nantwich; SJ8138], *Cock*: Charming 17th-c stonebuilt pub, recently refurbished without being spoilt; generous helpings of good food from sandwiches up, very reasonable prices, good service, charming restaurant, real fire *(Mrs D Raper)*

☆ **Stafford** [turn right at main entrance to station, 100 yards down], *Stafford Arms*: Friendly real ale pub recently taken over by Titanic, with their Best, Capt Smiths and changing guest beer kept well; good reasonably priced food, comfortable seats, wide range of customers of all ages – but no under-21s *(Richard Lewis, John and Christine Simpson, Ken Wright)*

Stafford [A34/A449 central roundabout; take Access Only rd past service stn], *Malt & Hops*: Rambling pub with splendid choice of very cheap real ales, big helpings of bargain lunchtime food, good friendly service, provision for children; evenings esp Thurs-Sat becomes lively young person's place *(Mr and Mrs J C Burton, LYM)*; [Mill St], *Nags Head*: Good town pub with loud juke box (good music), silent TV, extremely well kept Bass, Highgate Mild and Worthington Best; mixed customers, with young people taking over later in evening *(Graham Reeve)*; [7 Lichfield Rd, Forebridge, opp Borough Library], *Sun*: Friendly, well furnished and clean, good range of good cheap home-made food *(Mrs D Jones)*

Stanton, Derbys [A444; SK2719], *Gate*: Recently well refurbished Marstons pub, busy at lunchtime (when service can slow), fairly imaginative good value food inc children's dishes, well kept Pedigree, friendly staff *(Graham Richardson, B M Eldridge)*

Stanton by Dale, Derbys [three miles from M1 junction 25; SK4638], *Stanhope Arms*: Attractive rambling pub in unspoilt village, friendly staff, well kept Shipstones and Tetleys on handpump, well cooked standard bar food reasonably priced, upstairs dining room converted from adjoining cottage *(Dr and Mrs J H Hills)*

Stoke on Trent, Staffs [Hill St; SJ8745], *Staff of Life*: Classic Potteries local with lots of character, often heaving but still friendly and welcoming with good mix of locals and visitors; three rooms and drinking corridor, decor unchanged for years *(Pete Baker)*

☆ **Stone**, Staffs [21 Stafford St (A520);

SJ9034], *Star*: Simple 18th-c canalside pub with canal photographs and exposed joists in intimate public bar, snug lounge and family room; well kept Banks's real ales, friendly welcome, good value snacks, open fire in one room *(DC, LYM)*

Stone [Lichfield Rd, Little Stoke; SJ9132], *Three Crowns*: Welcoming staff in spotless and comfortable character local with good generous food inc Sun lunch; children welcome *(Ron Jones, Jean Macdonald, Keith Plant)*

☆ **Stourton**, Staffs [Bridgnorth Rd; SO8585], *Fox*: Comfortable, friendly and peaceful, with remarkable value food, lovely log fires, Bathams beer *(Sally M Rowland, William K Hyde)*

Stowe, Staffs [off A518 Stafford—Uttoxeter; SK0027], *Cock*: Village pub with good changing food in upstairs eating area, two small and friendly bars, cricketing pictures, beermat ceiling decorations *(Peter and Jenny Quine)*

Stretton, Staffs [A5, not far from M6 junction 12; SJ8811], *Bell*: Banks's beer, good food in bar and restaurant, children's area, garden with barbecue *(David Hanley)*

Stretton, Staffs [Craythorne Rd – the one nr Burton on Trent; SK2525], *Craythorne*: Unusual pub functioning as golf clubhouse but open to all, with friendly atmosphere, good food in bar and restaurant, well kept Marstons Pedigree *(EAW)*

Sudbury, Derbys [A515, about 2 miles S; SK1632], *Boars Head*: A hotel, but with good range of beer and wines, efficient service, well presented bar food; bedrooms *(K H Frostick)*

Swanwick, Derbys [The Delves; off A61 at The Green; SK4053], *Gate*: Open-plan village pub with good value food esp steaks, friendly licensees, well kept Courage-related ales, small back dining room *(Michel Hooper-Immins)*

Taddington, Derbys [SK1472], *Queens Arms*: Attractively furnished and decorated, welcoming landlord and staff, wide choice of generous food inc good children's dishes *(Mrs Elizabeth Howe)*

☆ **Tansley**, Derbys [A615 Matlock—Mansfield; SK3259], *Tavern*: Very wide choice of good reasonably priced food inc nice unusual puddings and home-made ice cream, friendly and relaxed atmosphere, well kept beer *(Pat Woodward, Mrs C Heaps)*

☆ **Ticknall** [7 High St; SK3423], *Staff of Life*: Very neat food-oriented pub with very wide choice of good popular inexpensive food, yet also excellent choice of real ales such as Bass, Marstons Pedigree, Theakstons and several guests on handpump or tapped from the cask; good atmosphere, restaurant, good wine list *(George Atkinson, Dr Keith Bloomfield, Alan and Heather Jacques, Derek and Sylvia Stephenson)*

☆ **Ticknall** [B5006 towards Ashby de la Zouch], *Chequers*: Stronger on character

than our other entry here, memorably big inglenook fireplace (maybe with winter roast chestnuts) in simple, cosy 16th-c pub, bright brass, old prints, well kept Marstons Pedigree and Ruddles, very welcoming landlady, good lunchtime filled baps and ploughman's (not Sun), seats in sizeable garden *(Alan and Heather Jacques, George Atkinson, LYM)*

☆ **Tideswell**, Derbys [SK1575], *George*: Welcoming village inn with big helpings of good value straightforward home-cooked food, simple traditional decor and furnishings in various rooms inc little tiled-floor snug, velvet-cushioned no smoking room, games room with pool and juke box; well kept Hardys & Hansons on handpump, friendly landlord, open fire, soppy Dulux dog, weekly folk bands; tables in front overlooking pretty village and in sheltered back garden; children welcome; good value bedrooms *(Sarah and Gary Goldson, W H and E Thomas, A F C Young, K Flack, Susan Boyle, Eugene Wills, BB)*

Tunstead, Derbys [nr Whaley Bridge; SK1175], *Rose & Crown*: Rose-clad pub with three rooms, small restaurant area, good food esp shepherd's pie *(John Derbyshire)*

☆ **Uttoxeter**, Staffs [High St, opp cinema; SK0933], *Wellington*: Unusual though not unique in being kept by a clergyman – *Church Times* as well as local papers for customers; long menu written out in copperplate on the blackboard, inc top quality home-made continental dishes at reasonable price; Belgian beer and Spanish brandy among more usual drinks *(Pat Bromley)*

nr **Uttoxeter**, Staffs [Dove Bank; SK1361], *Roebuck*: Welcoming small-roomed traditional pub with good substantial cold meals and snacks, hot dishes cooked to order; well kept Theakstons and guest beers, separate bar with pool and games, dogs allowed *(Alf and Shirley Dobson, BB)*

Walton upon Trent, Derbys [Main St; SK2118], *White Swan*: Recently refurbished Marstons Tavern Table, friendly atmosphere, Victorian styling, varied food inc vegetarian and steaks, well kept Pedigree and other ales; open for food all day Sun; children's play area *(B M Eldridge)*

☆ **Wardlow**, Derbys [B6465; SK1874], *Bulls Head*: Has been popular as plushly comfortable and reliable dining pub with Wards real ale, helpful landlord, provision for children and simple bedrooms, but no reports since early spring 1994 *(Geoffrey and Irene Lindley, Mrs D Craig, Dr and Mrs D E Awbery, LYM; news please)*

Waterhouses, Staffs [SK0850], *George*: Recently opened as a food pub by the licensees of the Izaak Walton at Cresswell, on similar lines to it – see main entries; should be good

Wensley, Derbys [B5057 NW of Matlock;

SK2661], *Three Stags*: Small local in delightful countryside, clean, bright and comfortable, with friendly landlord, Hardys & Hansons real ale, big helpings of good value lunchtime food inc home-made steak and kidney pie *(Pat and Tony Young, A Preston)*

☆ **Weston**, Staffs [The Green; off A518 – OS Sheet 127 map reference 978268; SJ9726], *Woolpack*: Extensively modernised open-plan pub, but keeping character with separate areas inc small dining room, cosy corners, antique furniture inc high-backed settle and well polished brassware; unusual reasonably priced good fresh pub food, well kept Marstons, friendly attentive staff, lovely relaxed well tended gardens by village green *(Peter and Jenny Quine, Bill Sykes)*

Wheaton Aston, Staffs [Canalside, Tavern Br; SJ8412], *Hartley Arms*: Canalside pub with bar food, Banks's beers, seats outside; service can slow if busy *(David Hanley)*

Whiston, Staffs [the one nr Penkridge; SJ8914], *Swan*: Good home-made food at low prices, well kept Bass *(Nigel Hopkins)*

☆ **Whitmore**, Staffs [3 miles from M6 junction 15 – A53 towards Mkt Drayton; SJ8141], *Mainwaring Arms*: Friendly and welcoming series of rambling interconnected oak-beamed rooms, stone walls, four open fires, antique settles among more modern seats; well kept Bass, Boddingtons, Marstons Pedigree, wide range of foreign bottled beers and ciders, lunchtime bar food from sandwiches up, seats outside, children in eating area; open all day Fri/Sat *(Roger Sherman, Peter and Jenny Quine, Gary Roberts, D W Gray, Catherine and Andrew Brian, David Lewis, LYM)*

Whittington, Derbys [Old Whittington; SK3874], *White Horse*: Well refurbished village inn with big lounge, good value food (not Sun evening), well kept Whitbreads-related ales *(Andy and Jill Kassube)*

☆ **Whittington Moor**, Derbys [387 Sheffield Rd (B6057), off A61 1½ miles N of Chesterfield centre; SK3873], *Derby Tup*: Pleasantly spartan ale-drinkers' pub with superb range of well kept constantly changing real ales – every week seems a beer festival; staff efficient and courteous even when busy, decent wholesome pubby food inc vegetarian lunchtime and early evening, minimal decor, small snug, spacious lounge; very friendly dog called Hoskins *(Joan and Michel Hooper-Immins, Peter Marshall, Mark and Mary Fairman, Margaret and Paul Digby, Andy and Jill Kassube)*

Winshill, Staffs [Newton Rd; off A50; SK2623], *Royal Oak*: Well modernised riverside pub with Marstons beers on handpump, extensive menu; can get very busy *(Ian and Emma Potts)*

☆ **Winster**, Derbys [B5056 above village; SK2460], *Miners Standard*: Good local feel, well kept Marstons Pedigree, Theakstons XB and a guest such as Black Sheep, good filled rolls and other food, well placed darts, attractive view from garden; children allowed away from garden *(Jack Morley, Barbara Hatfield, Brian and Anna Marsden)*

Wirksworth, Derbys [B5036; SK2854], *Red Lion*: Old town pub with big split-level L-shaped bar, pool, TV, piped pop, fruit machine; separate quiet lounge with tables set for good value food, high chair, attentive service, well kept Bass, Marstons Pedigree and Tetleys *(CW, JW)*

Wombourne, Staffs [High St; SO8792], *Vine*: Locally popular for well presented standard bar food with interesting specials and puddings, Bass and related ales on handpump, friendly service and atmosphere; can get busy Fri/Sat evening *(Paul and Sue Merrick)*

☆ **Wrinehill**, Staffs [Den Lane; pub signed just off A531 Newcastle—Nantwich; SJ7547], *Crown*: Thriving atmosphere in neat and attractively refurbished pub with good helpings of decent bar food (not Sun evening) inc good vegetarian choice, plush seats, interesting pictures, two open fires, friendly efficient service, well kept Bass and Marstons Pedigree, well reproduced pop music; children allowed lunchtime, early evening; closed weekday lunchtimes exc bank hols *(Colin and Shirley Brown, David and Sheila, LYM)*

Wrinehill, *Bluebell*: Specialising in good value generous grills, with quick friendly service, sensibly sized tables, well kept Greenalls *(Paul and Gail Betteley)*

☆ **Youlgreave**, Derbys [High St; nr Bakewell; SK2164], *Farmyard*: Extended village pub with low ceilings and flagstones, open stone fireplace, old farm tools, character landlord, well kept Mansfield Mild and Riding on handpump, good reasonably priced food up to steaks, big upstairs restaurant; children welcome *(Alan and Heather Jacques, R W Grey)*

Youlgreave, Derbys [Church St], *George*: Pleasant, friendly stonebuilt local under new management, handy for walkers with one flagstoned bar; good value bar food, well kept Home and Theakstons on handpump, quick service, pictures and comfortable banquettes; games room, juke box, outside benches *(JJW, CMW, Dave Braisted)*

☆ **Yoxall**, Staffs [Main St; SK1319], *Crown*: Relaxed atmosphere thanks to the friendly (but efficient) landlord, local produce making for good value tasty food, also generous puddings, particularly well kept Marstons Pedigree, cosy refurbished lounge with log-effect gas fire, separate raised dining room; children welcome lunchtime *(Norma and Keith Bloomfield, B M Eldridge)*

Sunday opening is generally 12-3 and 7-10.30 throughout England.

Devon

We have no hesitation in saying that a high proportion of the entries in the Lucky Dip section at the end of the chapter – probably higher than in any other part of the country – are now well up to main entry standard. Virtually all the starred Lucky Dip entries have been either inspected by us or approved and described to us in some detail by a number of trusted reader-reporters. So we are confident that, for the qualities described, they are well worth seeking out (subject of course to the usual caveat about the risk of any pub changing, especially with a change of management). Indeed, the only thing that stops most of these pubs being given a full main entry is that there simply wouldn't be room in the book. And there are certainly too many to pick out individually in this Introduction. But the strength of the Lucky Dip section in this county, coupled with the great wealth of pubs in the main entry section, does underline the fact that Devon is the best part of Britain for good pubs. Two things seem to us to make it so. One is that a great many pub buildings here are interesting in themselves – old places, often pubs for centuries, which seem to have acquired extra layers of atmosphere as the years have passed. The other more important factor is that so many of the county's pubs are run with genuinely welcoming individuality. And what's shown by the Dips is shown even more clearly by the main entries – nearly a hundred in this county, this year, and the richest choice of anywhere in Britain: a great many buildings of considerable character, often ancient and in charming surroundings, with licensees who stand out for their friendly, caring and hard-working attitude. There's a good deal of excellent food, especially fresh fish, with no less than twelve pubs here gaining our Food Award – a very high proportion. Our search for the county's best dining pub left us with a shortlist of six: the Drewe Arms at Broadhembury (exceptional fish in charming cosy surroundings, and last year's winner); Floyds Inn (Sometimes) at Tuckenhay (as the new name for what was the Maltsters Arms suggests, the main food effort here goes into the restaurant rather than the pub side); and four pubs which all combine very good food with interesting surroundings, full of character and atmosphere – the Cott at Dartington, the Castle at Lydford, the Cridford Inn at Trusham and the Otter at Weston. Though the Otter has the additional advantage of being particularly good for families with young children, we choose from all of these, as Devon Dining Pub of the Year, the Castle at Lydford. We should add that the Cott at Dartington has been doing so well all round recently that this year we have awarded it a star. Other pubs here of exceptional all-round quality include the Coach & Horses at Buckland Brewer (another to gain a star this year – what many think of as a perfect village pub), the Nobody Inn at Doddiscombsleigh (incredible choice of drinks, and of West Country cheeses – among many other virtues), the Tally Ho in Hatherleigh (character Italian landlord, fine own-brewed wines, even unusual delicatessen takeaways), the Masons Arms at Knowstone (idiosyncratic, not smart, but the many people who do fall in love with it see no faults), the Oxenham Arms at South Zeal (lovely unhurried calm atmosphere), and the Church House at Stoke Gabriel (lots *of character and warmth, good choice of sandwiches). Entirely new main entries here, or pubs back in these pages after an absence, are the Court Farm at Abbotskerswell (attractive dining pub), the Coombe Cellars at Combeinteignhead (good family pub, lovely spot), the Mildmay Colours at Holbeton (friendly local brewing its own good beers), the Ley Arms at Kenn (beautifully restored dining pub, excellent wines), the White Hart at Moretonhampstead (a civilised refuge from Dartmoor), the Green Dragon at Stoke Fleming (lots of individuality) and the Cridford Inn at Trusham – as we've said, a great place for eating out, but also plenty of character. Pubs gaining our new beer award here are the London in Ashburton, Fountain Head at Branscombe, Tally Ho in Hatherleigh, Mildmay Colours, Royal at Horsebridge, Castle at Lydford and Beer Engine at Newton St Cyres, all brewing their own on the premises; and the Anchor at Cockwood, Kingfisher at Colyton, Nobody at Doddiscombsleigh, Double Locks just outside Exeter, Elephants Nest at Horndon, Blue Ball at Sidford, Tower at Slapton and Bridge at Topsham (up to 18 beers on at a time in this unusual old place). Devon beer prices are very slightly higher than the national average: pubs with particularly attractive drinks prices include the Pyne Arms at East Down, the Tally Ho, the Drewe Arms at Drewsteignton, the Kings Arms at Stockland, the Old Thatch at Cheriton Bishop, the Beer Engine at Newton St Cyres, the Bridge at Topsham and the Normandy Arms at Blackawton.*

ABBOTSKERSWELL SX8569 Map 1

Court Farm

Off A381 just S of Newton Abbot; in Wilton Way – look for the church tower

Once a farmhouse, this attractive red granite 17th-c pub has polished crazy flagstones, a woodburning stove in a stripped red granite fireplace, ladderback chairs, some with arms, around solid tables with fresh flowers on them, button-backed red plush banquettes, a nice big round table by an angled black oak screen, a turkey rug in one alcove formed by a low granite wall with timbers above, and a long rough-boarded bar counter; a further small room is broadly similar with stripped kitchen tables and more spindleback chairs. On the right of the entrance is the two-roomed public bar with red plush cushioned small settles facing each other, a woodburning stove, fruit machine, and a simple end room with darts, cribbage and dominoes; they also have their own cricket team. Popular bar food includes home-made leek and potato soup (£1.50), doorstep sandwiches (from £1.95), filled baked potatoes (from £2.75), moules marinières (£3.25 starter, £5.95 main course), ploughman's (from £3.25), home-made pasty (£3.95), popular fry-up (£4.25), home-cooked ham and egg (£4.50), steak and kidney pie or liver and bacon (£5.50), and specials such as tagliatelle pesto (£4.25), grilled skate wing and capers or braised venison (£5.95), steaks (from £7.95), and puddings like rhubarb crumble or treacle tart (£2). Well kept Bass, Boddingtons and a weekly changing guest beer like Flowers IPA on handpump; pleasant, friendly service, well produced piped mainstream jazz. The pretty garden has a Wendy house full of bikes and toys to ride for children, and Muffy the elderly alsatian may be sunning herself on the lawn; big car park. Mrs Mogford's brother runs the Sea Trout at Staverton, another of our Devon main entries. *(Recommended by Steve Huggins, A E and P McCully, Peter and Jenny Quine, Joan and Gordon Edwards, N King, Mrs Marian Greenwood)*

Heavitree (who no longer brew) ~ Tenant Nicky Mogford ~ Real ale ~ Meals and snacks (till 10pm) ~ (01626) 618666 ~ Children welcome ~ Live music every two weeks at weekends ~ Open 11-3, 6-11; maybe all day in high season

ASHBURTON SX7569 Map 1

London Hotel 🍺

11 West St

In the village centre stands this rather grand but friendly coaching inn with its good own-brewed beers on handpump: Bitter, Figurehead, Man o' War and Porter. The spacious turkey-carpeted lounge has little brocaded or red leatherette armchairs and other seats around the copper-topped casks they use as tables, stripped stone walls, and a central fireplace; the room spreads back into a softly lit dining area. Bar food includes home-made soup, sandwiches, ploughman's, steak and kidney pie (£3.75), 8oz rump steak £4.95), puddings like home-made apple pie, and daily specials; farm ciders; darts, dominoes, cribbage and piped music. *(Recommended by Cdr Patrick Tailyour, Mr and Mrs McDougal, R J Walden, Nigel and Teresa Brooks, Alan and Heather Jacques, Jim and Maggie Cowell, Marian Greenwood)*

Own brew ~ Licensee M Thompson ~ Real ale ~ Meals and snacks ~ Restaurant ~ Ashburton (01364) 652478 ~ Children welcome ~ Open 11-3, 5.30-11 ~ Bedrooms: £27B/£35B

ASHPRINGTON SX8156 Map 1

Durant Arms 🍽

Village signposted off A381 S of Totnes; OS Sheet 202 map reference 819571

Handy for Totnes, this friendly and neatly kept gable-ended dining pub is popular both locally and with visitors for its very good food. At lunchtime there might be sandwiches, ploughman's (£3), stilton and asparagus flan (£3.50), haddock and broccoli bake (£3.95), casserole of lamb cutlets (£4.20), big brown pot or good chicken curry with pots of mango chutney, banana and coconut, and crisp poppadum (£4.25), venison casserole (£4.75) and cashew nut paella (£4.95), with evening dishes such as tomato and basil soup (£1.75), baked avocado and crab (£2.75), baked skate in tarragon butter (£7.15), excellent veal marsala, generous rack of lamb, pork tenderloin with cider and apple sauce (£7.95), monkfish in cream and garlic (£8.50), and roast duckling with orange and brandy sauce (£10.95); very good puddings include lemon meringue pie and crème brûlée; best to book to be sure of a seat. The two rooms of the bar have a nice mix of wooden tables and chairs as well as unusual cutaway barrel seats on the red turkey carpet, water colours by local artists on the wall, and Bass, Exmoor, and Palmers IPA on handpump from a temperature controlled cellar, 12 malt whiskies and decent wines; good service. The lower carpeted lounge – where families are allowed – is furnished with settles, tables, chairs, red velvet curtains and a winter fire (there are two others as well); darts, dominoes and piped music. The dog, George II, is a real favourite among customers – particularly children. Tables in the sheltered back garden. *(Recommended by Dr P R Davis, P R Ferris, T Aldworth, Mrs Margaret Barker, Gordon, Marian Greenwood, S V Bishop, David Wallington, D I Baddeley, Steve Huggins, E Money)*

Free house ~ Licensees John and Gill Diprose ~ Real ale ~ Meals and snacks ~ (01803) 732240 ~ Children in restaurant – not Sat evening after 7pm ~ Open 11.30-2.30, 6-11

Watermans Arms 🛏

Bow Bridge, on Tuckenhay road; OS Sheet 202 map reference 812565

On the bank of the River Harbourne at the head of Bow Creek, this bustling, friendly inn has picnic-table sets in the flower-filled garden and more by the river where you can watch the ducks (or even swans and kingfishers). Inside, the quarry-tiled bar area has heavy beams, high-backed settles, built-in wall benches, rustic seats, and candles in bottles, and the comfortable eating area has Windsor chairs on its red carpet, more beams, and stripped stone walls; log fires. Good bar food includes home-made soup (£1.95), sandwiches (from £2.25; fresh crab £3.95), pasties (£3.50), ploughman's (£3.95), cold platters (from £6.25), home-made steak and kidney pie (£6.95), Thai chicken curry (£7.50), freshly-made pasta with riccotta cheese and sauce of mushrooms, white wine and cream and herbs or fresh fillet of plaice (£6.95), roasted rack of Devon lamb (£7.95), daily specials, and children's dishes (£2.50); part of the restaurant is no smoking. Bass, Furgusons Dartmoor, Palmers and Tetleys Bitter on handpump, with Addlestones cider, a farm cider called Pigsqueal, and Luscombe real apple juice; good, quick service. Dominoes and piped music. *(Recommended by Steve Huggins, Jim and Maggie Cowell, M V and J Melling, T Aldworth, A Plumb, Mrs J Barwell, Alan and Heather Jacques, Paul Boot, John Wilson, S V Bishop, David Surridge, P and J Shapley, David and Ann Stranack)*

Free house ~ Licensee Trevelyan Illingworth ~ Real ale ~ Meals and snacks ~ Restaurant ~ Harbertonford (01803) 732214 ~ Children in eating area of bar and in restaurant ~ Open 11-3, 6-11 ~ Bedrooms: £34.50S/£59S

AXMOUTH   SY2591   Map 1

Harbour

B3172 Seaton—Axminster

Before enjoying a drink in this thatched stone pub, it's worth nipping across to the handsome church to look at the fine stone gargoyles. The Harbour Bar has fat pots hanging from pot-irons in the huge inglenook fireplace, black oak beams and joists, brass-bound cask seats, a high-backed oak settle, and an antique wall clock. A central lounge has more cask seats and settles, and over on the left another room is divided from the no smoking dining room by a two-way log fireplace. At the back, a big flagstoned lobby with sturdy seats leads on to a very spacious and simply furnished family bar. Well kept Boddidngtons, Devenish Royal Wessex and Flowers IPA and Original on handpump; darts and pool. Bar food includes sandwiches (from £1.50), ploughman's (from £3), vegetarian dishes (from £4.50), and fresh fish (from £4.75); roast Sunday lunch (£4.50); friendly, cheerful service. They have a lavatory for disabled people, and general access is good. There are tables in the neat flower garden behind. *(Recommended by A Plumb, Brian A Websdale, Liz and John Soden, M E and Mrs J Wellington, JM, PM)*

Free house ~ Licensees Dave and Pat Squire ~ Real ale ~ Meals and snacks (not winter Sun evenings) ~ (01297) 20371 ~ Children in family room in summer, in eating area of bar in winter ~ Open 11-2.30, 6-11

BANTHAM   SX6643   Map 1

Sloop 🛏 ♀

Off A379/B3197 NW of Kingsbridge

Only a few hundred yards over the dunes is one of the best beaches for surfing on the south coast – so this 16th-c building does get extremely busy in summer. The black-beamed bar has country chairs around wooden tables, stripped stone walls and flagstones, and easy chairs in a quieter side area with a nautical theme. Bar food includes home-made soup, pasties (from £1.15), sandwiches (from £1.65), basket meals (from £2.20), ploughman's (£3.60), salads (from £5.20; fresh crab £8.25), steaks (from £8.35), daily specials like hot potted shrimps (£3.20), scallop mornay (£4.65), skate or roast pheasant (£7.40), and john dory with orange sauce (£7.85); hearty breakfasts; there may be delays at busy times. Well kept Bass, Blackawton Bitter, Ushers Best and a guest beer on handpump, Churchward's cider from Paignton, 25 malt whiskies, and a very good wine list; tea, coffee and hot chocolate. Darts, dominoes, cribbage, table skittles, fruit machine, and trivia. There are some seats at the back. The bedrooms in the pub itself have the most character. *(Recommended by Mr and Mrs C R Little, John and Vivienne Rice, P and J Shapley, Bill Edwards, Mrs J Barwell, T Aldworth, Marion and John Hadfield, Barry and Ann, Tim and Pam Moorey, Roger White, John Bowdler, Andrew and Teresa Heffer, Nick Wikeley, John and Suzanne McClenahan, David and Ann Stranack)*

Free house ~ Licensee Neil Girling ~ Real ale ~ Meals and snacks (till 10pm; not 25/26 Dec) ~ Restaurant ~ Kingsbridge (01548) 560489/560215 ~ Children in eating area of bar and in restaurant ~ Open 11-2.30, 6-11; winter evening opening 6.30 ~ Bedrooms: £52B; they also have self-catering cottages

BERRYNARBOR SS5646 Map 1

Olde Globe ★

Village signposted from A399 E of Ilfracombe

Even when this characterful old pub is really busy, service remains quick and cheerful. The atmospheric series of dimly lit homely rooms have curved deep-ochre walls, bulging unevenly in places, low ceilings, floors of flagstones or of ancient lime-ash (with silver coins embedded in them) and old high-backed oak settles (some carved) and plush cushioned cask seats around antique tables. Decorations include a profusion of genuinely old pictures, priests (fish-coshes), thatcher's knives, sheep shears, gin traps, pitchforks, antlers, copper warming pans and lots of cutlasses, swords, shields and fine powder flasks. Well kept Courage Directors and Ushers Best on handpump, and several country wines; sensibly placed darts, skittle alley, pool, dominoes, cribbage, rather noisy fruit machine, and piped music. Bar food includes soup (£1.20), sandwiches (from £1.20), pasties (£2.40), ploughman's (£2.50), salads (from £3.10), lasagne or good chilli con carne (£3.70), steaks (from £6.95), daily specials, puddings (from £1.40), children's dishes (£1.80), and popular main course Sunday lunch (£3.70; 3-course in restaurant £5.90 – best to book). In high season the restaurant is used as a no smoking room for bar rather than restaurant meals. There's now a children's activity house in the garden and the crazy-paved front terrace has some old-fashioned garden seats. The village is pretty. Dogs are welcome. *(Recommended by Dave and Moyra Burley, Dorothee and Dennis Glover, Jim and Maggie Cowell, S R and A J Ashcroft, R J Walden, Andy and Jackie Mallpress, John Sanders, Michael and Harriet Robinson, Bob Smith, Carol and Mike Muston, Clare Carpenter, Dennis and Janet Johnson, Mr and Mrs Moody)*

Courage ~ Lease: Phil and Lynne Bridle ~ Real ale ~ Meals and snacks (till 10pm) ~ Gaslit restaurant ~ Combe Martin (01271) 882465 ~ Children in own room with toys ~ Live entertainment Thurs evenings mid-July-1st week Sept ~ Open 11.30-2.30, 6-11; winter evening opening 7pm

BISHOPS TAWTON SS5630 Map 1

Chichester Arms

Pub signposted off A377 outside Barnstaple

Even though this carefully restored thatched pub is on the edge of Barnstaple, Bishops Tawton itself is a pleasantly quiet village. There's a rather smart bar with low heavy beams, plush wall banquettes and cushioned wheelback chairs on its patterned carpet, a solid old bar counter, uneven sloping floors, stout supporting timbers, and an open fire. The family room has its own bar: darts, pool, alley skittles, cribbage, dominoes, fruit machine, video game, table football, piped music, and doors out to barbecue area. Both the bar and restaurant have no smoking areas. All the meat, game, fish and vegetables are delivered fresh daily, and dishes might include sandwiches, soup, filled baked potatoes, and ploughman's, as well as fresh pasta carbonara or home-made sausages like venison, pork and garlic or Cumberland (£3.95), and lamb and stilton hotpot (£4.75). Well kept Bass, Morlands Old Speckled Hen and Worthingtons on handpump. There are picnic-table sets on a flagstoned front terrace, with more in a sheltered back area. The licensees also run the Old Barn at Bickington. *(Recommended by R J Walden, E H and R F Warner, P and J Shapley, B M Eldridge, Mr and Mrs Moody, Michael and Alison Sandy, David Wallington)*

Free house ~ Lease: Hugh and Gay Johnston ~ Real ale ~ Meals and snacks (till 10pm) ~ Restaurant ~ Barnstaple (01271) 43945 ~ Children welcome ~ Occasional live entertainment ~ Open 11.30-2.30, 5.30-11; all day Sat

BLACKAWTON SX8050 Map 1

Normandy Arms 🛏

Signposted off B3207 W of Dartmouth; OS Sheet 202 map reference 807509

Interesting for World War II veterans, this solid old inn still carries some of the bullet scars from when this whole village was commandeered as a training ground to prepare for the Normandy landings and inside there's an interesting display of battle gear of that time. The quaint and cosy main bar has a good log fire and a warmly welcoming atmosphere, as well as bar food such as sandwiches (from £1.80, crab £2.85), home-made soup (£1.90), home-made chicken liver pâté or ploughman's (£3.75), home-made steak and kidney pie (£4.75), and whole lemon sole (£7.95), pork in cider and cream (£8.45), steaks (from £8.95), and home-made puddings like luscious lemon cake or apple pie (from £2.50). Well kept Blackawton Bitter and in winter Forty-Four from the nearby brewery, as well as Bass and Ruddles on handpump, decent wines, good coffee and tea. Sensibly placed darts, shove-ha'penny, cribbage and dominoes; well behaved dogs welcome; tables out in the garden, where there's a gaggle of elderly tractors. *(Recommended by Paul and Janet Waring, J L Hall, Dennis Heatley, D G King, David Holloway, J H Bell, E Money)*

Free house ~ Licensees Jonathan and Mark Gibson ~ Real ale ~ Meals and snacks (not Sun evenings Nov-Mar) ~ Restaurant ~ (01803) 712316 ~ Children in family room and in restaurant ~ Open 11.30-2.30, 6.30-11; 12-2.30, 7-11 in winter; closed 25 Dec ~ Bedrooms: £30B/£48B; not 24-26 Dec

BRANSCOMBE SY1988 Map 1

Fountain Head ◖

Upper village, above the robust old church; village signposted off A3052 Sidmouth—Seaton

The beer festival last year was such a success, that this old tiled stone house is now making it an annual event with lots of different ales, live bands, folk music, Morris men, and a spit-roast. Their own-brewed beers – Branoc, Jolly Geff (named after Mrs Luxton's father, the ex-licensee), and Olde Stoker – will naturally head the cast; Green Valley farm cider. The room on the left – formerly a smithy – has a log fire in the original raised firebed with its tall central chimney, forge tools and horseshoes on the high oak beams, and cushioned pews and mates' chairs around wooden tables and walls of stripped uncoursed stone. On the right, an irregularly shaped, more orthodox snug room has another log fire, white-painted plank ceiling with an unusual carved ceiling-rose, brown-varnished panelled walls, and rugs on its flagstone-and-lime-ash floor; the children's room is no smoking, and the airedale is called Oscar. Bar food includes cockles or mussels (£1.25), soup (£1.25), sandwiches (from £1.50; fresh crab £2.25), ploughman's (£3.25), home-made shepherd's pie or lasagne (£3.95), salads (from £4, fresh crab £6.50), home-made steak and kidney pie (£4.50), kebabs (£5.75), steaks (from £7.95), and daily specials like fried sardines (£3.50) or salmon steaks poached with fresh herbs, with children's dishes (from £1.95), and roast Sunday lunch (£4.50). They also hold speciality food nights throughout the year, and Friday night is fresh fish and chips night (£4.50); darts, cribbage, dominoes. There are seats out on the front loggia and terrace, and a little stream rustling under the flagstoned path. *(Recommended by J I Fraser, R J Walden, Mike and Terri Richards; more reports please; also recommended by* The Good Hotel Guide*)*

Free house ~ Licensee Mrs Catherine Luxton ~ Real ale ~ Meals and snacks (not 25 Dec) ~ Branscombe (0129 780) 359 ~ Children in own small room at lunchtimes; over 10 in evening in eating area of bar ~ Monthly folk group last Sun of month ~ Open 11.30-2.30, 6.30-11; 11.30-2, 7-11 in winter ~ Self-catering available

Masons Arms ♀ ⇌

At the bottom of an unusual village scattered along its sheltering combe, this 14th-c inn is only half a mile from the sea. The rambling low-beamed bar has a massive central hearth in front of the roaring log fire where there's a roasting spit (used on Thursday lunchtimes and/or evenings to spit-roast beef and lamb, and once a month on a Friday evening to spit-roast a whole pig), Windsor chairs and settles, and a relaxed atmosphere. Home-made bar food using the best local produce includes soup (£1.60), sandwiches (from £1.85; crab £2.80), tagliatelle with smoked salmon (£4.50), ploughman's (from £3.25), deep-fried local fillet of plaice (£5.50), chicken, stilton and walnut strudel (£5.95), steak and kidney pudding (£6.25), half a roast duckling with orange sauce (£9.50), daily specials such as mushrooms baked with spinach, peppers and cheese (£3.45), duck and bacon pie (£6.20), grilled red mullet (£6.80) or sea bass (£7.50), and puddings such as nutty toffee tart or apple strudel (£2.50); on Sunday lunchtimes there are sandwiches, ploughman's, one hot dish or a roast only. One of the three rooms of the restaurant is no smoking. Well kept Bass, Eldridge Pope Hardy and Furgusons Dartmoor, and occasional guest beers such as Morlands Old Speckled Hen; good wine list, several malt whiskies, freshly squeezed orange juice, and Jack Rat or Luscombe ciders. Darts, shove-penny, skittle alley and dominoes. Well behaved dogs welcome (you may see Sam, the rhodesian ridgeback, wandering the corridors). Outside, the quiet flower-filled front terrace has tables with little thatched roofs, extending into a side garden. *(Recommended by J I Fraser, W F C Phillips, M Owton, Mrs J M Corless, B D Jones, Mark and Heather Williamson, J D Maplethorpe, Nan and David Johnson, Tom Evans, E and Mrs J Wellington, Chris and Chris Vallely)*

Free house ~ Licensee Janet Inglis ~ Real ale ~ Meals and snacks ~ Restaurant ~ (0129 780) 300 ~ Well behaved children may be allowed well away from bar ~ Jazz/cajun and other music most Fris in Waterfall Room ~ Open 11-3, 5.30-11; 11-2.30, 6-11 in winter ~ Bedrooms (some in cottage across road): £22.50 (£28B)/£44(£54B)

BRAYFORD SS6834 Map 1

Poltimore Arms £

Yarde Down – 3 miles from village, towards Simonsbath; OS Sheet 180 map reference 724356

This is a genuine, friendly local with a good pubby atmosphere. The main bar has a woodburning stove in the inglenook fireplace, old leather-seated chairs with carved or slatted backs, cushioned wall settles, a little window seat, some interesting tables, and a beam in the slightly sagging cream ceiling with another over the small serving counter; there are photos of hunt meetings and hunting cartoons on the walls. The lounge bar has a mix of chairs and a settle, Guinness and Fry's Chocolate prints, plants and a small brick open fire; pool, darts, dominoes, fruit machine and juke box in the plainly decorated games room. The decent range of bar food includes sandwiches (from £1.10), soup (£1.20), chicken and chips (£2), ham and two eggs (£3), locally made jumbo sausages and egg (£3.30), ploughman's (from £3.25), cashew and mixed nut paella (£3.90), home-made steak and kidney pie (£3.90), rump steak (£5.80), children's dishes (from £1.20), and puddings (from £1.20). Well kept Courage Directors and Cotleigh Tawny tapped from the cask, and Inch's cider. In the side garden there are picnic-table sets and a grill for barbecues. *(Recommended by Gethin Lewis, R J Walden, Anthony Barnes, B M Eldridge, Mrs C A Blake, Mr and Mrs Moody, David Wallington, Jerry and Alison Oakes, Dave and Louise Clarke)*

Free house ~ Licensees Mike and Mella Wright ~ Real ale ~ Meals and snacks (12-2, 6-9.30; not 25 Dec) ~ Restaurant ~ (01598) 710381 ~ Children in games room and restaurant ~ Open 11.30-2.30, 6.30-11

BROADHEMBURY ST1004 Map 1

Drewe Arms ★ 🍴 🍷

Signposted off A373 Cullompton—Honiton

It's not just the superb, really fresh fish that readers love so much here, but the fact that all the staff are so friendly and welcoming. And the pretty village with its cream-coloured thatched cottages is worth a stroll around, too. To get a seat you have to get here early – even midweek. There's fresh scallops, half a fresh lobster, excellent turbot, John Dory, wonderfully fresh lemon sole, Dover sole, fillet of sea trout, fresh Lyme Bay plaice, brill, fresh red mullet griddles with garlic, smoked eel, spider crabs and so forth (from around £6); also, really wonderful tomato soup, very satisfying open sandwiches (from £3.95), lovely baby lobster ploughman's, daily specials that includes two meat dishes, and lovely puddings. Well kept Otter Bitter, Ale, Bright and Head (from a tiny brewery a few miles from the pub in Luppitt) tapped from the cask, a very good wine list (with good value house wine and four by the glass), local cider, and tea and coffee. The bar has neatly carved beams in its high ceiling, and handsome stone-mullioned windows (one with a small carved roundabout horse). On the left, a high-backed stripped settle separates off a little room with three tables, a mix of chairs, flowers on sturdy country tables, plank-panelled walls painted brown below and yellow above with attractive engravings and prints, and a big black-painted fireplace with bric-a-brac on a high mantelpiece. The flagstoned entry has a narrow corridor of a room by the servery with a couple of tables, and this year they've opened up a cellar bar; dominoes, cribbage and skittle alley. There are some interesting pottery clocks for sale. A flower-filled lawn with picnic-table sets and cocktail parasols stretches back under the shadow of chestnuts towards a church which has a singularly melodious hour-bell. *(Recommended by Tim and Chris Ford, Eric and Patricia King, Howard and Margaret Buchanan, John and Fiona Merritt, Ian Phillips, Trevor Leary, David Eberlin, John and Vivienne Rice, Mr and Mrs J Brown, J I Fraser, John and Tessa Rainsford, M V and J Melling, Jason Caulkin, B and K Hyper, Pat and John Millward, Gordon, G Pugh, John and Sally Clarke, Basil Minson, H G Robertson, BHP, David Shillitoe, Graeme Jameson, Martyn John, Mrs M C Barrett)*

Free house ~ Licensees Kerstin and Nigel Burge ~ Real ale ~ Meals and snacks (till 10pm; not Sun evening) ~ Restaurant (not Sun evening; no cigars or pipes allowed) ~ (01404) 841267 ~ Well behaved children in eating area of bar and in restaurant ~ Open 11-3, 6-11

BUCKLAND BREWER SS4220 Map 1

Coach & Horses ★ 🍺

Village signposted off A388 S of Bideford; OS Sheet 190 map reference 423206

Readers have enjoyed this carefully preserved 13th-c thatched pub so much that this year we have given it a star. It's very much as you'd hope a village pub would be – warmly friendly with a good pubby atmosphere, cheerful locals, and very good food. The attractively furnished bar has heavy oak beams, comfortable seats including an attractive antique settle, and a woodburning stove in the inglenook; a good log fire also burns in the big stone inglenook of the cosy lounge. A small back room serves as a children's room. A skittle alley was just opening as we went to press. Food in the bar, with the more elaborate dishes served in a cosy little restaurant, includes home-made soup (£1.60), sandwiches (from £1.50), burgers (from £1.60), popular home-made pasties (£1.95), good ploughman's (from £3), cheesy lentil and vegetable pie (£4.25), salads with home cooked meats (from £4.50), liver and bacon casserole (£4.50), home-made steak and kidney pie or home-made curries (£5.25), daily specials such as Normandy pork, venison casserole or beef bourguignon, and puddings like banoffi pie or treacle tart with lemon and ginger (£2.20), and children's menu (from £1). Sunday lunch (£4.50) – bookings preferred but not essential. Well kept Flowers IPA and Original and a guest beer such as Fullers London Pride or Morlands Old Speckled Hen on handpump. Pool, darts, dominoes, shove-ha'penny, cribbage, fruit machine, video game and trivia. The two cats are called Amos and Benson. There are tables on a terrace in front, and in an attractive side garden with benches, swings and slides. *(Recommended by Michael and Joan Johnstone, R J Walden, Mrs Ann Saunders, A E and P McCully, Alan Carr, Alan and Julie Wear, Roderic Plinston, Les and Mavis Law, Nigel Chapman, Derek and Margaret Underwood, Rita Horridge, Peter J Moore, Chris and Pauline Ford, Nigel and Lindsay Chapman, Gerry Hollington, Alan and Eileen Bowker, Mr and Mrs J D Marsh, David Heath, Jane Thompson, John and Beryl Knight, Clare Carpenter)*

Free house ~ Licensees Kenneth and Oliver Wolfe ~ Real ale ~ Meals and snacks ~ Restaurant ~ Horns Cross (01237) 451395 ~ Well behaved children welcome ~ Occasional Morris dancers ~ Open 11.30-3, 6-11; closed evening 25 Dec ~ Bedrooms: £22/£36

BUDLEIGH SALTERTON SY0682 Map 1

Salterton Arms

Chapel Street

The very pretty flowering tubs and hanging baskets here have won this pub an award for the 6th consecutive year. But it's the wide choice of generously served food that readers like so much: sandwiches (from £1.35, steak £3.95), maybe a good crab soup (£2), several interesting vegetarian dishes such as aubergine bake or vegetable and nut curry (£4.50), chicken curry (£4.50), monumental salads such as local crab (£6.75), steaks (from £6.95), and ten or so specials. In the evening these might include lamb noisettes, chicken breast filled with mushrooms or baked crab (£6.95) and a good choice of fresh fish such as grilled red mullet (£7); at lunchtime they tend to be simpler and cheaper – mainly £4-5. Fresh properly cooked vegetables, and sautéed potatoes, may come in their own separate bowls; tempting home-made puddings include a heady chocolate mousse (£2). The L-shaped bar has dark green plush wall seats and solid chairs around plain pub tables on the new dark red carpet, lots of prints on the walls, small open fires; a very comfortable upper gallery serves as restaurant. Well kept Bass, John Smiths and a guest beer like Morlands Old Speckled Hen or Wadworths 6X on handpump, a good few Irish whiskeys, and efficient neatly uniformed staff; darts, cribbage, dominoes, fruit machine and piped music. *(Recommended by Mrs J M Corless, Mark and Heather Williamson, Gethin Lewis, George Atkinson, Howard and Margaret Buchanan, B D Jones, Peter Richards, Marian Greenwood)*

Free house ~ Licensees Steve and Jennifer Stevens ~ Real ale ~ Meals and snacks (till 10pm; not 25 Dec) ~ Restaurant ~ (01395) 445048 ~ Children welcome ~ Jazz some Sun evenings ~ Open 11-3, 5.30-11

BURGH ISLAND SX6443 Map 1

Pilchard

Park in Bigbury-on-Sea and walk about 300 yds across the sands, which are covered for between six and eight hours of the twelve-hour tide; in summer use the Tractor, a unique bus-on-stilts which beats the tide by its eight-foot-high 'deck'.

It's the unique isolated island location that makes this ancient smuggler's and fisherman's pub so special. The small L-shaped bar has storm-shuttered windows giving a snug view of the tide inching across the sands, lots of bare wood and stripped stone, and low chairs, settles edged with rope, and others with high backs forming cosy snug booths; it is lit by big ships' lamps hanging from the beam-and-plank ceiling, and there's a good – though not always lit – log fire. The white-plastered back bar has darts, dominoes, cards and backgammon. Straightforward bar food includes pasty (£2), filled baked potatoes (£3), and ploughman's (£3.50). John Smiths and Ushers Best on handpump and Wadworths 6X tapped from the cask; piped music. Children may be expected to sit in the downstairs bistro. The licensees actually own the island, and the art deco hotel nearby has been patronised by Agatha Christie (who used to write here) and the Duke of Windsor and Mrs Simpson. It can be very popular in season and there's an outside terrace overlooking the beach. *(Recommended by Paul McPherson, Tim and Lynne Crawford, Gordon, Natalie Spencer, Simon Forster, David and Ann Stranack, Barry and Anne)*

Free house ~ Licensee Tony Porter ~ Real ale ~ Meals and snacks (11-9 in summer; lunchtime only in winter) ~ Kingsbridge (01548) 810344 ~ Children welcome ~ £1.50 car parking in Bigbury; cheaper by the Bay Café ~ Open 11-11; 11-3, 7-11 in winter (depending on weather)

BUTTERLEIGH SS9708 Map 1

Butterleigh Inn 🍺

Village signposted off A396 in Bickleigh; or in Cullompton take turning by Manor House Hotel – it's the old Tiverton road, with the village eventually signposted off on the left

The food in this friendly 16th-c village pub is very good indeed and might include filled rolls (lunchtimes £1.25), home-made soup (£2.25), clam fries with garlic mayonnaise (£2.95), ploughman's or salads (£3.25), venison sausages with a hot chilli pepper sauce, crispy mushroom layer or spinach, walnut and feta cheese pancakes (£4.25), bacon chops with plum sauce or marinated lamb kebab (£6.50), steaks (from £8.95), daily specials (including a vegetarian one) and puddings like chocolate and rum pot, pear and almond crumble or iced apricot mousse (£1.95). An unpretentious series of little rooms are decorated with pictures of birds and dogs, topographical prints and water colours, a fine embroidery of the Devonshire Regiment's coat-of-arms and plates hanging by one big fireplace. One room has a mix of Edwardian and Victorian dining chairs around country kitchen tables, another has an attractive elm trestle table and sensibly placed darts, and there are prettily upholstered settles around the three tables that just fit into the cosy back snug. Well kept Cotleigh Tawny, Harrier and Old Buzzard on handpump; darts, shove-ha'penny, cribbage, dominoes and piped music; jars of snuff on the bar. Outside are tables on a sheltered terrace and neat small lawn, with a log cabin for children; children are not allowed inside the pub. *(Recommended by Bill and Beryl Farmer, Mr and Mrs B Hobden, Nigel and Teresa Brooks, John Hazel, Mrs J Horsthuis, Jim and Maggie Cowell, Steve Dark, Alan Carr, Eric and Patricia King, David Eberlin, John Horsthuis, David Wallington, P H Spray, Marian Greenwood, Rita Horridge, Nick Wikeley)*

Free house ~ Licensees Mike and Penny Wolter ~ Real ale ~ Meals and snacks ~ Bickleigh (01884) 855407 ~ Open 12-2.30(3 Sat), 6-11 ~ Bedrooms: £20/£34

CHAGFORD SX7087 Map 1

Ring o' Bells

Off A348 Moretonhampstead—Whiddon Down

Close to some good moorland walks, this big, friendly old pub has an oak-panelled bar with comfortable seats, photographs of the village and local characters on the walls, a log-effect gas fire, and Tabbie the pub cat. Good bar food (the same menu is used in the restaurant) includes sandwiches (from £2.50), soup (£1.60), basket meals (from £3), home-made steak and kidney pie (£4.50), salads (from £4.75), tomato and vegetable tagliatelle (£5.75), daily lunchtime specials (from £3.50), chicken tikka (£6.20), evening gammon steak (£6.30), half a fresh roast duck with orange liqueur sauce (£9.95), 8oz sirloin steak (£10.25) or home-made puddings (from £1.75), and Sunday roasts. Well kept Eldridge Pope Hardy, Exmoor Best, Furgusons Dartmoor, Ind Coope Burton, and changing guests on handpump, Addlestones cider, and decent wines; darts, shove-ha'penny, cribbage, dominoes, fruit machine, trivia and piped music. *(Recommended by John and Christine Vittoe, Patrick Clancy, A N Ellis, C A Hall, P and M Rudlin, John Wilson)*

Free house ~ Licensee Mrs Judith Pool ~ Real ale ~ Meals and snacks ~ Restaurant ~ (01647) 432466 ~ Children in eating area of bar and in restaurant ~ Open 11-3, 6-11

CHARDSTOCK ST3004 Map 1

George 🛏

Village signposted off A358 S of Chard

The two-roomed original bar in this neatly thatched 13th-c inn is mainly set out for dining, but has massive beams, ancient oak partition walls, character furnishings, two good log fires, stone-mullioned windows, and well converted old gas lamps. It's quietly chatty as the piped music is confined to an interestingly laid out two-level back bar. Good food includes sandwiches, kedgeree or breaded plaice (£4.95), home-made steak and kidney pie or devilled kidneys (£5.25), local trout with lemon butter and almonds (£7.25), gammon hock with honey and mustard (£7.95), pheasant breasts with a mushroom and madeira sauce (£8.95), and home-made puddings such as sticky toffee pudding with butterscotch sauce or apple fritters with Drambuie syrup (£2.75). Well kept Boddingtons, Flowers

Original, Whitbreads Castle Eden, and a guest beer on handpump; several wines and ciders. Darts and alley skittles. There are some tables out in a back loggia by a flint-cobbled courtyard sheltered by the rather attractive modern extensions to the ancient inn, with more in a safely fenced grass area with a climber and swings. The four bedrooms are in a well converted back stable block. The inn has an interesting booklet about its history. Excellent walks nearby. *(Recommended by R M Bloomfield, Alan and Judith Gifford, J E Davies, David Eberlin, Gordon, M E and Mrs J Wellington, Jim Cowell, Robin and Janice Dewhurst, Mr and Mrs D V Morris)*

Free house ~ Licensee John Hall ~ Real ale ~ Snacks (not Sat evening or Sun lunchtime) and meals ~ Restaurant ~ South Chard (01460) 220241 ~ Children in eating area of bar and in top bar ~ Open 11.30-3, 6-11; cl Mon lunchtime 2 Jan-31 Mar ~ Bedrooms: £35B/£42.50B

CHERITON BISHOP SX7793 Map 1

Old Thatch

Village signposted from A30

To enjoy the large choice of food in this 16th-c pub it's best to get here early to make sure of a seat: sandwiches, home-made soup (£1.45), home-made pâté (£2.25), ploughman's (£2.60), sautéed lamb's kidneys (£2.75), gammon and egg (£4.65), steak and kidney pudding (£4.80), a curry of the day (£5.95), pork tenderloin in a sour cream and mustard sauce (£6.95), 8oz sirloin steak (£7.50), daily specials like kedgeree, vegetable risotto, beef olives or stuffed hearts, and puddings (from £2.35). The rambling, beamed bar is separated from the lounge by a large open stone fireplace (lit in the cooler months); pleasant, friendly service. Well kept Cotleigh Tawny, Ruddles County and Wadworths 6X on handpump; tea and coffee. Dominoes, cribbage and piped music. No children. *(Recommended by Dennis Heatley, R J Walden, TOH, Betty Laker, David Burnett, Donna Lowes, Don Kellaway, Angie Coles, John Hazel, Robert and Gladys Flux, E H and R F Warner)*

Free house ~ Licensee Brian Bryon-Edmond ~ Real ale ~ Meals and snacks ~ Cheriton Bishop (01647) 24204 ~ Open 12-3, 6.30-11; 11.30-3, 6-11 Sat; winter weekday opening 7; closed first two weeks Nov ~ Bedrooms: £32B/£44B

CHITTLEHAMHOLT SS6521 Map 1

Exeter Inn 🛏

Village signposted from A377 Barnstaple—Crediton and from B3226 SW of South Molton

This friendly old inn – close to Exmoor National Park – has cushioned mate's chairs and stools, settles, and a couple of big cushioned cask armchairs, an open woodburning stove in the huge stone fireplace, and an interesting collection of matchboxes, bottles and foreign banknotes. In the side area there are seats set out as booths around the tables under the sloping ceiling. Good bar food served by attentive staff includes sandwiches (from £1.40), home-made soup (£1.45), filled baked potatoes (from £2.25), ploughman's (from £3.75), hog pudding (like a haggis, £4.95), salads (from £3.65), vegetarian cheese and nut croquettes (£5.95), local trout (£5.95), excellent local steaks (£8.95), daily specials, children's meals (from £2.75), and home-made puddings with clotted cream (£2); Sunday roast (£4.50). Well kept Furgusons Dartmoor, Ind Coope Burton, Tetleys and Wadworths 6X on handpump or tapped from the cask and changing guests, freshly squeezed orange juice, and local cider; darts, dominoes, shove-ha'penny, fruit machine and piped music. The dog is called Alice and the cat, Clyde. The terrace has benches and flower baskets. Local facilities for fishing, golf and horse riding nearby; the pub's cricket team play on Sundays. *(Recommended by R J Walden, Alan and Heather Jacques, Mr and Mrs J Westlake; more reports please)*

Free house ~ Licensees Norman and Margaret Glenister ~ Real ale ~ Meals and snacks (11.30-2, 6-9.30) ~ Restaurant ~ Chittlehamholt (01769) 540281 ~ Children in eating area of bar ~ Open 11.30-2.30, 6-11 ~ Bedrooms: £17S/£34S; self-catering available

CHURCHSTOW SX7145 Map 1

Church House

A379 NW of Kingsbridge

There's a good villagey atmosphere in the long and cosy characterful bar of this fine medieval pub – as well as cushioned seats cut into the deep window embrasures of the stripped stone walls, an antique curved high-backed settle and lots of smaller red-cushioned ones, a line of stools – each with its own brass coathook – along the long glossy black serving counter, and low and heavy black oak beams; a great stone fireplace has a side bread oven. The carvery is very good indeed – and so popular that you might need to book in advance (£7.75 for 2 courses; Wednesday-Saturday evenings and Sunday lunch). Other good bar food, served at the curtained-off end of the bar, includes sandwiches (from £1.75), home-made soup (£1.95), ploughman's (£2.95), fresh haddock (from £3.75), home-made cottage pie (£3.95), home-made steak and kidney pie (£4.45), salads (from £4.25), gammon and pineapple (£5.95), mixed grill (£6.95), and home-made fruit pies or wonderful banana cheesecake (£2.10); the restaurant is no smoking. Well kept Bass and Furgusons Dartmoor on handpump, and local Loddiswell wine; hardworking, friendly staff; cribbage, dominoes, euchre and fruit machine. Just inside the back entrance there's a conservatory area with a floodlit well in the centre, and there are seats outside. *(Recommended by Alan and Heather Jacques, T Aldworth, Gordon, C and Marjorie Roberts, David Eberlin, Jim and Maggie Cowell, M E and Mrs J Wellington, Graham and Sharon Stevenson, Margaret and Trevor Errington)*

Free house ~ Licensees Nick and Vera Nicholson ~ Real ale ~ Meals and snacks (12-1.30, 6.30-9) ~ Restaurant (not Sun evening) ~ Kingsbridge (01548) 852237 ~ Children welcome ~ Open 11-2.30, 6-11; closed first Mon in Feb

COCKWOOD SX9780 Map 1

Anchor 🍺

Off, but visible from, A379 Exeter—Torbay

There are 30 different ways of serving mussels in this busy, attractively set pub (£5.50 normal size helping, £9.75 for a large one) and other fresh fish dishes might include fried shark steak or locally caught cod (£5.50), whole grilled plaice (£6.50), local crab platter (£6.95), red mullet, john dory or sea bass, and halibut steak (£7.50); also, sandwiches (from £1.95), soup (£2.30), home-made chickenb liver pâté (£3.85), salads (from £3.65), ratatouille (£3.95), home-made cottage pie (£4.50), 8oz rump steak (£8.95), and children's dishes (£1.95). The restaurant is no smoking. The small, low-ceilinged, rambling rooms have black panelling, good-sized tables in various alcoves, and a cheerful winter coal fire in the snug. Well kept Bass, Boddingtons, Eldridge Pope Royal Oak, Flowers, Marstons Pedigree and several guests on handpump or tapped from the cask, with rather a good wine list, country wines, and 40 malt whiskies; dominoes, cribbage, fruit machine and piped music. On the sheltered verandah are some tables – and over the road there are yachts and crabbing boats in the landlocked harbour. Nearby parking may be difficult if it's busy. *(Recommended by Jim and Maggie Cowell, P M Lane, Jon and Julie Gibson, A E and P McCully, S R and Mrs A J Ashcroft, David and Fiona Easeman, John and Vivienne Rice, Dr and Mrs R E S Tanner, David Carrington, P Corris, George Jonas, Graham Reeve, Michael Woodhead)*

Heavitree (who no longer brew) ~ Tenants T Morran, Miss A L Sanders, Mrs I Wetton ~ Real ale ~ Meals and snacks ~ Restaurant ~ Starcross (01626) 890203 ~ Children in eating area of bar and in restaurant ~ Open 11-2.30 6-11; 11-11 Sat

---

The 🍺 symbol indicates pubs which keep their beer unusually well or have a particularly good range.

COLEFORD SS7701 Map 1

New Inn 🛏 ♀

Just off A377 Crediton—Barnstaple

At 600 years old, this must be the oldest 'new' inn in the country. It's set in a quiet valley by the side of a stream – where there are some benches and seats for outside eating. Inside, four interestingly furnished areas spiral around the central servery with paraffin lamps, antique prints and old guns on the white walls, landscape plates on one of the beams and pewter tankards on another, and ancient and modern settles, spindleback chairs, low dark green velour armchairs, plush-cushioned stone wall seats, some character tables – a pheasant worked into the grain of one – and carved dressers and chests; the resident parrot is chatty and entertaining. The servery itself has modern settles forming stalls around tables on the russet carpet, and there's a winter log fire. Good food might include sandwiches, soup (£2.10), stilton and walnut pâté (£3.30), Greek salad (£3.50), creamy fish pie (£4.85), chilli con carne (£4.95), fresh pasta with blue cheese and mushrooms (£4.80), Mediterranean lamb (£7.50), chicken breast in wine, cream and sorrel sauce (£8.30), roast duck with apple sauce (£9.50), and puddings like treacle tart (£2.40); friendly, helpful staff. Well kept Boddingtons, Otter Ale, Robinsons and Wadworths 6X on handpump, an extensive wine list, quite a range of malt whiskies, and port; fruit machine (out of the way up by the door), darts and piped music. Big car park. *(Recommended by Liz and Jake Nelson, David Watson, R J Walden, Mike Cargill, Graham and Karen Oddey, J L Cox, Steve Williamson, John Hazel, John and Vivienne Rice, N P Cox)*

Free house ~ Licensees Paul and Irene Butt ~ Real ale ~ Meals and snacks (till 10pm) ~ Restaurant ~ Copplestone (01363) 84242 ~ Children in eating area of bar ~ Open 11.30-2.30, 6-11; closed evening 25 Dec, all day 26 Dec ~ Bedrooms: £30B/£48B

COLYTON SY2493 Map 1

Kingfisher 🍴

Dolphin St; village signposted off A35 and A3052 E of Sidmouth, in village follow Axminster, Shute, Taunton signpost

This homely and friendly local has blue plush cushioned window seats, stools, sturdy elm wing settles and rustic tables, a big open fireplace and walls stripped back to stone. Glasses slotted into the two waggon-wheels hanging above the bar swing in unison when someone in the upstairs family room walks above the beamed ceiling; sensibly placed darts, dominoes, cribbage, fruit machine, video game and skittle alley. Well kept Badger Best and Tanglefoot and Charles Wells Bombardier with guests like Eldridge Pope Royal Oak, Gribble Bitter or Wiltshire Old Grumble on handpump; they also have farm cider. Bar food includes sandwiches (from £1.50, speciality prawn £2.75), filled baked potatoes (from £2.80), plaice (£4.25), local gammon (£4.75), a winter daily special, and home-made cheesecakes and fruit pies (from £1.80); children's menu. There are tables under cocktail parasols on the terrace, and a lawn with pergola, flowerbeds and water features. *(Recommended by Mrs Ann Saunders, Helen Flaherty, H G Robertson, JM, PM, Nick Wikeley)*

Free house ~ Licensees Graeme and Cherry Sutherland ~ Real ale ~ Meals and snacks (till 10pm) ~ (01297) 552476 ~ Children in family room ~ Open 11-2.30, 6-11

COMBEINTEIGNHEAD SX9071 Map 1

Coombe Cellars

Pub signposted off B3195 Newton Abbot—Shaldon

Children are very welcome at this waterside pub. As well as a huge play galleon and fenced-in playground in the garden, there are baby-changing facilities, a nappy machine, nursing chair, highchairs, a children's room, and half-helpings or their own menu. The long beamed bar has one area with old photographs and pictures of the pub, another with hunting, shooting and fishing items, and yet another with nautical bric-a-brac; there are sofas at one end and two easy chairs at the other, dark wooden upholstered chairs, and a woodburning stove and two log-effect gas fires. You can book tables in the dining area with its very large windows superb view up the River Teign, or in the bar – the menu is the same, and the food very good: soup (£1.95), filled rolls (from £1.95), ploughman's (from £3.95), cannelloni stuffed with ricotta cheese with a tomato and herb sauce (£5.75), home-made steak in ale pie (£5.95), chicken with onions, tomatoes and peppers in a white wine and cream sauce (£6.95), and good fresh local fish such as cod in parsley sauce or Teign salmon with local crab in a white wine and cream sauce (from around £5.95), with puddings (from £2.50). Well kept Bass, Boddingtons, and Flowers Original on handpump. The pub cat is called Emma. The estuary setting here is really lovely and at low tide you can watch innumerable wading birds on the mudflats. Pontoons and jetties with tables overlook the water, and there are more tables on big terraces. Lots of water-sports facilities, too – the pub is the base for the South Devon Water Sports Association. There's a pleasure trip service from Teignmouth that takes in this pub. *(Recommended by D Cox, Marian Greenwood, Neville Kenyon, Heather and Howard Parry, Michael A Butler, George Atkinson, Tom Evans, D I Baddeley, George Smaylen, Mrs J Rogerson, Tony Triggle, DPB, M and C McRum, Mr and Mrs W H Crowther, Joan Harris, M J Brooks)*

Free house ~ Licensee John Haworth ~ Real ale ~ Meals and snacks (11.30-2.15, 6.30-9.30) ~ Restaurant ~ Newton Abbot (01626) 872423 ~ Children welcome ~ 6-piece trad jazz group Weds evening, jazz duo (and impromptu players) Sun lunchtime ~ Open 11-3, 6-11; may stay open longer in summer if trade demands

CORNWORTHY SX8255 Map 1

Hunters Lodge

Off A381 Totnes—Kingsbridge ½ mile S of Harbertonford, turning left at Washbourne; can also be reached direct from Totnes, on the Ashprington—Dittisham road

Friendly, helpful staff serve the generous helpings of popular food in this simple local. This might include fresh basil and tomato soup (£1.80), home-cooked honey roast ham (£4.95), home-made steak and kidney pie (£5.25), chicken maryland (£5.95), grilled sardines, tandoori halibut or guinea fowl (£8.75), and seafood grill (£8.25); three course Sunday roast (£6.75). As the two rooms of the little low-ceilinged bar have only around half a dozen red plush wall seats and captain's chairs around heavy elm tables, it can get crowded at holiday times. There's also a small and pretty cottagey dining room with a good log fire in its big 17th-c stone fireplace. Well kept Blackawton Special and Forty-four and Ushers Best on handpump and local Pigsqueal cider; darts, dominoes, shove-ha'penny, children's games, puzzles and colouring place-mats, trivia and piped music; they have four dogs (only let loose after closing time). There are picnic-table sets on a big lawn stretching up behind the car park, with swings, a climbing frame and summer barbecues, and closer to the pub is a new terrace with flowering tubs and more seats. Several walks start from the pub and dogs are welcome in the bar. *(Recommended by Dennis Heatley, David and Tina Woods-Taylor, Gordon, Paul Boot, David Wallington, E Money, Marian Greenwood, David and Ann Stranack, John Evans, J Rees, Jane Palmer)*

Free house ~ Licensee Robin Thorns ~ Real ale ~ Meals and snacks (till 10pm) ~ Cottagey restaurant ~ Harbertonford (01803) 732204 ~ Children welcome ~ Open 11-3, 6.15-11; closed evening 25 Dec

DALWOOD ST2400 Map 1

Tuckers Arms

Village signposted off A35 Axminster—Honiton

In a neatly kept village, this thatched longhouse has original 800-year-old stripped beams and original flagstones in the bar – as well as a random mixture of dining chairs, window seats, a pew, a high-backed winged black settle, and oak stripped beams; it's kept warm by a woodburning stove and a log fire in the inglenook fireplace. A side lounge with shiny black woodwork has a couple of cushioned oak armchairs and other comfortable but unpretentious seats. Good bar food includes home-made soup (£1.75), filled french sticks (from £2.55), potato skins with interesting dips (from £2.65), the notably popular 'tiddy' (a big puff pastry with a changing home-made filling; £6.95), rack of lamb with lemon, herbs and garlic or fresh local trout with lemon butter (£7.55), speciality rib-eye steaks (from £8.25), and puddings (from £2.55). Well kept Boddingtons and Otter Ale on handpump, quite a few malt whiskies, and coffee; darts, shove-ha'penny, table skittles, dominoes, fruit machine, piped music and skittle alley. Outside, there are some picnic-table sets and pretty summer hanging baskets and big pots of flowers. *(Recommended by Pat and Robert Watt, Paul Boot, John and Fiona Merritt, Gordon, R J Walden, Mrs J M Corless, Desmond and Pat Morris, TOH, J L Hall, Denzil Taylor, David Eberlin, M E and Mrs J Wellington, Maj D A Daniels)*

Free house ~ Licensees David and Kate Beck ~ Real ale ~ Meals and snacks (till 10pm) ~ Stockland (0140 488) 342 ~ Children in family room ~ Open 11.15-3, 6.30-11 ~ Bedrooms: £25S/£40S

DARTINGTON SX7762 Map 1

Cott ★ 🍽 🛏 🍷

In hamlet with the same name, signposted off A385 W of Totnes opposite A384 turn-off

Reports from readers over the past year have been so warmly enthusiastic that we have decided to award this ancient inn a star. There's always a friendly welcome – either from the Greys or their hard-working staff – and the food, beer and wines have come in for special praise. The communicating rooms of the traditional, heavy-beamed bar have big open fires, some flagstone flooring, lots of polished brass and horse-harnesses on the whitewashed walls, and traditional carved cast-iron, copper-topped round tables in front of sturdy high-backed settles, some elaborately carved; one area is no smoking. At lunchtime, there's a hot and cold buffet (£5.50) with six home-made salads, home-cooked ham, roast sirloin of beef, turkey, local Dart salmon, three different quiches (two vegetarian), and mushroom and cream cheese roulade. Evening specials might include Mediterranean vegetable crumble, salmon and sole pie, steak and kidney pie, lamb casserole with rosemary and orange dumplings (all £5.50), braised duck in juniper and bramble jelly sauce (£6.75), fillets of john dory with aoili (£6.95), fillets of Torbay sole stuffed with local crab and lobster sauce (£8.75), rib steak with mushrooms and red wine sauce (£11.75), and puddings like fresh gooseberry tart, chocolate and brandy mousse or banana and caramel flan (£3). Part of the restaurant is no smoking. Well kept Bass, Blackawton Forty-four (in summer), Fullers London Pride – and Cotts Wallop (see if you can guess what it really is) – on handpump; Inch's cider, eight wines by the glass, and a good selection of malt whiskies. Darts on Tuesday evenings (Nov-March) and pub cricket team – they'd welcome enquiries from visiting teams. Harvey the cat likes to creep into bedroom windows in the middle of the night, and Minnie and Podge the Jack Russells are keen to greet visitors. There are benches and attractive buckets of flowers in the crazy-paved courtyard. Good walks through the grounds of nearby Dartington Hall, and it's good touring country – particularly for the popular Dartington craft centre, the Totnes-Buckfastleigh steam railway and one of the prettiest towns in the West Country, Totnes. *(Recommended by Mrs S Segrove, David and Tina Woods-Taylor, M V and J Melling, Jim and Maggie Cowell, David Cundy, Bryan Polley, A Plumb, T A Bryan, D G King, Patrick Clancy, Neil and Anita Christopher, Peter and Lynn Brueton, A E and P McCully, David Wallington)*

Free house ~ Licensees David and Susan Grey ~ Real ale ~ Meals and snacks (12-2.15, 6.30-9.30) ~ Restaurant ~ Totnes (01803) 863777 ~ Children in restaurant ~ Open 11-2.30, 5.30-11; closed evening 25 Dec ~ Bedrooms: £40(£45B)/£40(£50B)

DARTMOUTH SX8751 Map 1

Cherub ★

Higher St

Mr and Mrs Hill have retired this year but their son Steven has now taken over the running of this lovely 14th-c Grade I listed building. It's a very friendly place and the comfortable little bar is full of locals enjoying the relaxed atmosphere. There are tapestried seats under creaky heavy beams, red-curtained leaded-light windows and an open stove in the big stone fireplace. Each of the two heavily timbered upper floors juts further out than the one below. Good bar food includes sandwiches, soup (£1.95), filled baked potatoes (from £3.50), ploughman's (from £3.75), ratatouille (£4.95), beef in ale stew (£4.95), seafood pasta or smoked chicken with broccoli and ham (£5.95), daily specials like poached scallops in dill sauce or venison sausage casserole (£5.95) or tiger prawns in filo pastry (£6.25), and puddings such as bread and butter pudding or treacle tart (£2.75). Well kept Flowers Original, Morlands Old Speckled Hen, Wadworths 6X and a guest beer on handpump, Addlestones cider, 52 malt whiskies, and English wines. In summer, the flower baskets are very pretty. *(Recommended by W H Bruton, Gordon, R W A Suddaby, Pat and John Millward, Mr and Mrs A K McCully, Paul and Janet Waring, Steve Goodchild, John Evans, Wayne Brindle, Joy Heatherley, George Jonas, Nigel Gibbs, Gerard Paris)*

Free house ~ Licensees Steven Hill ~ Real ale ~ Meals and snacks (till 10pm) ~ Restaurant ~ Dartmouth (01803) 832571 ~ Children in restaurant until 8.30pm ~ Open 11-3, 5-11

Royal Castle 🛏

11 The Quay

Full of character, this bustling harbourside hotel has a lively, left-hand, local bar decorated with navigation lanterns, glass net-floats and old local ship photographs, a mix of tables from scrubbed deal to polished mahogany, and stripped pine country kitchen chairs and stools, mate's chairs and a couple of interesting old settles; one wall is stripped to the original stonework and there's a big log fire. On the right in the more sedate, partly no smoking carpeted bar, they spit-roast joints from October to April over the open range (pork over apple wood on Monday lunchtime, lamb over sycamore on Tuesday evening and beef over oak Wednesday lunchtime); there's also a Tudor fireplace with copper jugs and kettles (beside which are the remains of a spiral staircase) and plush furnishings, including some Jacobean-style chairs, and in one alcove swords and heraldic shields on the wall. Well kept Bass, Boddingtons, John Smiths and a local guest beer on handpump; quite a few malt whiskies; welcoming staff. Dominoes, fruit machine, trivia, pinball and piped music. The range of generously served bar food includes lunchtime sandwiches (from £1.45, good crab £2.75) and a choice of ploughman's (from £2.45), as well as home-made soup (£1.65), baked potatoes with hot or cold fillings (from £2.70), cauliflower cheese and bacon (£3.25), home-made steak and kidney pie or smoked haddock and mushroom crumble (£4.50), curry of the day or whole plaice (£4.95), steaks (from £9.95), daily specials like Cumberland sausage or half-a-dozen local oysters (£4.50) or lobster (£12), and puddings (£2.45); maybe evening bar nibbles. *(Recommended by Mr and Mrs A K McCully, Pat and John Millward, George S Jonas, Mr and Mrs R Head, P and J Shapley, A Craig, David and Anne Stranack)*

Free house ~ Licensee Nigel Way ~ Real ale ~ Meals and snacks (till 10pm) ~ Restaurant ~ Dartmouth (01803) 833033 ~ Children in first-floor library ~ Live entertainment in public bar Tues and Thurs ~ Open 11-11 ~ Bedrooms: £40B/£80B

If you enjoy your visit to a pub, please tell the publican. They work extraordinarily long hours, and when people show their appreciation it makes it all seem worth while.

DODDISCOMBSLEIGH SX8586 Map 1

Nobody Inn ★ ★ 🛏 ♗ 🍺

Village signposted off B3193, opposite northernmost Christow turn-off

Mr Borst-Smith keeps in his remarkably popular 16th-c pub what is perhaps the best pub wine cellar in the country – 800 well cellared wines by the bottle and 20 by the glass kept oxidation-free; there's also properly mulled wine and twice-monthly tutored tastings (they also sell wine retail, and the good tasting-notes in their detailed list are worth the £3 it costs – anyway refunded if you buy more than £20-worth); there's also a choice of 250 whiskies, Gray's and Inch's farm ciders and well kept Bass, Branscombe Vale Branoc and a beer brewed by Branscombe Vale especially for the pub called Nobodys, and guest beers on handpump or tapped straight from the cask. The two atmospheric rooms of the lounge bar are attractively furnished with carriage lanterns hanging from the beams (some of which are original), handsomely carved antique settles, Windsor and wheelback chairs, and benches, and guns and hunting prints in a snug area by one of the big inglenook fireplaces. Bar food includes home-made soup (£1.95), sandwiches (from £1.75; made to order), cheesy pasta with walnuts and celery (£2.65), good sausage and mash (£2.90), coarse home-made duck's liver pâté with port (£3.10), chicken and apricot pie (£3.90), daily specials like tuna loaf with cucumber sauce, chicken parmesan, peanut and spinach loaf or pork cassoulet, puddings such as warm treacle tart or home-made spiced bread pudding (from £2.25), and a marvellous, constantly changing choice of 40 west country cheeses (a choice of six £2.90); they sell clotted Jersey cream to take away. The restaurant is no smoking. There are picnic-table sets on the terrace, with views of the surrounding wooded hill pastures. The medieval stained glass in the local church is some of the best in the West Country. No children except in the restaurant Tues-Sat evenings – and accommodation is not suitable for them. *(Recommended by Jim and Maggie Cowell, John Waller, Joan and Gordon Edwards, J L Cox, John and Vivienne Rice, S Demont, T Barrow, Paul Harrison, Peter West, D K Carter, J E Parry, R J Walden, Don Kellaway, Angie Coles, S R and A J Ashcroft, Dennis Dickinson, DAV, Mike Cargill, Steve Huggins, James Nunns, Mr and Mrs R P Begg, E B Davies, Lynn Sharpless, Bob Eardley, A Young, D Hayward, Gerry Hollington, Victor Sunderland, A P Jeffreys, Peter and Lynn Brueton, John Wilson, David Gittins, Mr and Mrs B H Robinson, Clare Carpenter, E V M Whiteway, J E Davies, Bill and Edee Miller, Simon and Caroline Turner, David and Ann Stranack, Ian Sharp)*

Free house ~ Licensee Nicholas Borst-Smith ~ Real ale ~ Meals and snacks (till 10pm) ~ Evening restaurant (not Sun) ~ Christow (01647) 52394 ~ Open 12-2.30, 6-11; winter evening opening 7; closed evening 25 Dec ~ Bedrooms (some in distinguished 18th-c house 150yds away: £23(£33B)/£33(£53B)

DREWSTEIGNTON SX7390 Map 1

Drewe Arms

Signposted off A382 NW of Moretonhampstead

A must for people who like absolutely unspoilt basic locals, this marvellous old thatched place has simple built-in wooden benches facing each other across plain tables, ochre walls with local team photographs and advertisements tacked to them, an open fire, and no serving counter – the well kept real ale (typically Flowers IPA) and draught cider, which you can draw yourself, are kept on racks in the tap room at the back. A third room, used occasionally, has a notable herringbone-pattern Elizabethan brick floor. Ham or cheese sandwiches (£1.25); darts, dominoes, cribbage and chess. Mabel Mudge is 99 now and has held the licence nearly 76 years – though it's Dorothy, her barmaid for 41 years, who does all the work. Castle Drogo nearby (open for visits) looks medieval, though it was actually built earlier this century. *(Recommended by Frank Cummins, Lynn Sharpless, Bob Eardley, George Atkinson, J I Fraser, Brian A Websdale, Patrick Clancy, Barbara and Norman Wells, Gordon, John Hazel, Pat and Robert Watt, Phil and Sally Gorton, E Money)*

Whitbreads ~ Tenant Mabel Mudge ~ Real ale ~ Lunchtime snacks ~ Drewsteignton (01647) 21224 ~ Children welcome ~ Open 10.30-2.30, 6-11

EAST DOWN SS5941 Map 1

Pyne Arms ♀

Off A39 Barnstaple—Lynton; OS sheet 180 map reference 600415

There are lots of nooks and crannies in the low-beamed bar here, with a very high-backed curved settle by the door (as well as more ordinary pub seating), a woodburning stove with horse harness and farm tools on the wall above it, horse-racing prints and Guinness and Martell placards on the red walls, and some copper jugs and big barrels; up some steps is a small, no smoking galleried loft with more tables and chairs. A flagstoned games area has pine-plank wall benches, and pool, darts, shove-ha'penny, table skittles, fruit machine and trivia; juke box. Good food from a wide menu includes sandwiches (from £1.55), delicious home-made soup (£1.75), ploughman's (£2.85), home-made pâté (£3.35), home-cooked ham and egg (£4.65), mussels in season prepared in four different ways (£6.25), scampi provençal (£7.25), several veal dishes (£8.35), beef stroganoff (£9.65), steaks (from £9.65), and a range of puddings; food service stops promptly at 2pm. Well kept Courage Directors and John Smiths on handpump and four wines by the glass, tea and coffee. The boisterous doberman is popular with visitors, though he isn't allowed in the bar. No children. The Black Venus at Challacombe, White Hart at Bratton Fleming, and Station House at Blackmoor Gate are under the same management. Arlington Court is close by. *(Recommended by Andy and Jackie Mallpress, R J Walden, S R and A J Ashcroft, Steve and Carolyn Harvey, Clare Carpenter, Chris Philip, Dave Braisted)*

Free house ~ Licensees Jurgen and Elisabeth Kempf ~ Real ale ~ Meals and snacks (till 10pm) ~ (01271) 850207 ~ Open 11-2.30, 6-11; closed 25 Dec

EXETER SX9292 Map 1

Double Locks ★ 🍺

Canal Banks, Alphington; from A30 take main Exeter turn-off (A377/396) then next right into Marsh Barton Industrial Estate and follow Refuse Incinerator signs; when road bends round in front of the factory-like incinerator, take narrow dead end track over humpy bridge, cross narrow canal swing bridge and follow track along canal; much quicker than it sounds, and a very worthwhile diversion from the final M5 junction

Very popular with lively people of all ages (though a large percentage are, of course, students), this busy and friendly lockside pub keeps a fine range of beers on handpump or tapped from the cask: Adnams Broadside, Batemans XXXB, Blackawton Headstrong, Branscombe Vale Branoc, Eldridge Pope Royal Oak, Everards Old Original, Gibbs Mew Bishops Tipple, Greene King Abbot, Morlands Old Speckled Hen, Smiles Bitter and Exhibition, Wadworths 6X and guests; Grays farm cider and some Irish whiskies as well as Scottish malts. Popular bar food includes soup (£1.50), sandwiches (from £1.80), a generous mushrooms on toast (£2.90), filled baked potatoes (from £3), ploughman's (£3.75), salads (£4.70), hot dishes such as feta cheese and spinach pie or ham and eggs (£3.60), ratatouille crêpe (£4.10), breakfast special (£4.50), and home-made puddings like chocolate biscuit cake or sticky toffee pudding (£2.40); summer barbecues. There's quite a nautical theme in the bar – with ship's lamps and model ships – and notably friendly service. Darts, dominoes and cribbage in the main bar, bar billiards in another; piped music and trivia. There are picnic-table sets, a well provisioned play area, and volley ball – and cycle paths along the ship canal. *(Recommended by Victor Sunderland, P M Lane, Dr M V Jones, J I Fraser, Pat and John Millward, A P Jeffreys, Linda and Brian Davis, Susie Northfield)*

Free house ~ Licensee Jamie Stuart ~ Real ale ~ Meals and snacks (11-10.30) ~ Exeter (01392) 56947 ~ Children welcome away from main bar ~ Jazz 1st and 3rd Thurs of month and live entertainment Weds evenings ~ Open 11-11; closed evening 25 Dec

---

Most pubs in the *Guide* sell draught cider. We mention it specifically only if they have unusual farm-produced 'scrumpy' or even specialise in it.

White Hart ★ 🛏 ♀

66 South St; 4 rather slow miles from M5 junction 30; follow City Centre signs via A379, B3182; straight towards centre if you're coming from A377 Topsham Road

People have been meeting in the atmospheric, rambling bar of this well run inn for six centuries. There are big Windsor armchairs and built-in winged settles with latticed glass tops to their high backs, oak tables on the bare oak floorboards (carpet in the quieter lower area) and a log fire in one great fireplace with long-barrelled rifles above it. In one of the bay windows is a set of fine old brass beer engines, big copper jugs hang from heavy bowed beams in the dark ochre terracotta ceiling, the walls are decorated with pictorial plates, old copper and brass platters (on which the antique lantern lights glisten), and a wall cabinet holds some silver and copper. From the latticed windows, with their stained-glass coats-of-arms, one can look out on the cobbled courtyard – lovely when the wisteria is flowering in May. The Tap Bar, across the yard, with flagstones, candles in bottles and a more wine-barish feel, serves soup (£1.80), sandwiches (from £2.30), baked potato with cheese and anchovy topping (£2.50), cold meats (from £4.75), steak and kidney pudding or chicken and chestnut pie (£5.95), and charcoal-grilled rib of beef steak (£9.50). There is yet another bar, called Bottlescreu Bill's, even more dimly candlelit, with bare stone walls and sawdust on the floor. It serves much the same food, as well as a respectable range of Davy's wines and pint jugs of vintage port from the wood or tankards of bucks fizz, and in summer does lunchtime barbecue grills in a second, sheltered courtyard. On Sundays both these bars are closed. Bass, Davy's Old Wallop (served in pewter tankards in Bottlescreu Bill's) and John Smiths on handpump or tapped from the cask; piped music. Bedrooms are in a separate modern block. *(Recommended by R J Walden, Wayne Brindle, B A Ferris Harms, John and Vivienne Rice, Barry and Anne, Patrick Clancy, David and Fiona Easeman, Jim and Maggie Cowell, E V M Whiteway, Peter and Audrey Dowsett, J I Fraser, E Money, Robert and Gladys Flux, H G Robertson, M E and Mrs J Wellington)*

Free house ~ Licensee Graham Stone ~ Real ale ~ Meals and snacks (till 10pm) ~ Restaurant ~ Exeter (01392) 79897 ~ Children in eating area of bar and in lounges ~ Open 11.30-3, 5-11; 11.30-11 Sat; closed evening 25 Dec ~ Bedrooms: £54.50B/£78B

EXMINSTER SX9487 Map 1

Turf ★

Follow sign to Swan's Nest signposted from A379 S of village, then continue to end of track, by gates; park, and walk right along canal towpath – nearly a mile

Both the inside and outside of this attractively isolated pub have been redecorated this year, the garden has been considerably smartened up and the children's play area extended. The pleasantly airy, high-ceilinged rooms of the bar have fine views from the bay windows out to the mudflats – which are full of gulls and waders at low tide – mahogany decking and caulking tables on the polished bare floorboards, church pews, wooden chairs and alcove seats, fresh flowers, big bright shorebird prints by John Tennent and pictures and old photographs of the pub and its characters over the years on the walls, and a woodburning stove and antique gas fire. Bar food includes sandwiches (from £2), home-made soup (£2.25), lots of toasties (from £2.35), cheesy nut roast or ploughman's (£4.50), lasagne and garlic bread (£5.75), daily specials like bobotie (£5.95) or fresh Exe salmon salad (£6.50), and puddings like apple crumble or sticky toffee pudding (from £1.75). Well kept Eldridge Pope Royal Oak, Furgusons Dartmoor, and Tetleys Bitter on handpump, and a short but thoughtful good value wine list; darts, shove-ha'penny, cribbage, dominoes, trivia, volley ball and piped music; friendly, efficient service. The dining room is no smoking. Well behaved dogs welcome. To reach the pub you can either walk (which takes about 20 minutes along the ship canal) or take a 40-minute ride from Countess Wear in their own boat, the Water Mongoose (bar on board; £3 adult, £2 child return, charter for up to 56 people £110 – free a couple of winter evenings a week). They also operate a 12-seater and an 8-seater boat which bring people down the Exe estuary from Topsham quay (15-minute trip, adults £2, child £1.50). For those arriving in their own boat there is a large pontoon as well as several moorings. *(Recommended by J I Fraser, Mike Cargill, Robin and Peter Etheridge, Keith Stevens)*

Free house ~ Licensees Clive and Ginny Redfern ~ Real ale ~ Meals and snacks ~ Restaurant (Fri/Sat evenings only) ~ Exeter (01392) 833128 ~ Children welcome ~ Open 11-11 June-Aug; 11-2.30 (11-11 Sat) Mar-May and Sept-Oct (closed weekday evenings then); closed 5 Nov-beg Mar ~ Bedrooms: £17.50/£45

HARBERTON SX7758 Map 1

Church House ♀

Village signposted from A381 just S of Totnes

Readers report that the food here seems to be on the up this year – they now have a chef from Madeira, and lunchtime specials might include deep-fried banana wrapped in bacon with a mild curry mayonnaise dip (£2.95), fresh battered cod and chips (£3.95), steak and kidney pie (£4.95), and fillet of plaice marinated in white wine, garlic and lemon juice, dipped in egg and fried (£5.95), with evening dishes such as scallops and prawns au gratin (£3.95), mushroom stroganoff (£4.95), seafood piri-piri (£6.95), and char-grilled leg of lamb steak with pork, rosemary and redcurrant sauce (£7.95); also, sandwiches (from £1.75), home-made soup such as stilton and broccoli (£1.85), three locally-made sausages (£3.25), ploughman's (£3.50), fry-up (£4.95), curries (from £5.25), gammon and egg (£5.95), grills (from £6.50), and puddings (from £1.95); children's dishes (from £1.85). There's some magnificent medieval oak panelling – and the latticed glass on the back wall of the open-plan bar is almost 700 years old and one of the earliest examples of non-ecclesiastical glass in the country (it had been walled off until Victorian times). Furnishings include attractive 17th- and 18th-c pews and settles and there's a large inglenook fireplace with a woodburning stove; one half of the room is set out for eating. Bass and Courage Best and two weekly-changing guest beers such as Brakspears Best, Eldridge Pope Royal Oak, Hook Norton Old Hookey, Marstons Pedigree, Smiles Best and Exhibition, and Wadworths 6X and winter Old Timer on handpump, and decent wines; darts and dominoes. The pub is in a steep little twisting village, pretty and surrounded by hills. *(Recommended by T Aldworth, David Holloway, Gordon, Alan and Brenda Holyer, Jim and Maggie Cowell, Marion and John Hadfield, Thomas Neate, Steve Huggins, Michael and Joan Johnstone, R W A Suddaby, P and J Shapley, Mrs Ann Roberts and family, M E and Mrs J Wellington)*

Free house ~ Licensee Mrs Jennifer Wright ~ Real ale ~ Meals and snacks (not 25 Dec) ~ Restaurant ~ Totnes (01803) 863707 ~ Children in family room and eating area of bar ~ Occasional jazz or folk; Morris men in summer ~ Open 12(11.30 Sat)-2.30(3 Sat), 6-11; closed evenings 25/26 Dec and 1 Jan

HATHERLEIGH SS5404 Map 1

George ♀

A386 N of Okehampton

This is a friendly place, popular with locals and visitors, and the little front bar in the original part of the building has huge oak beams, stone walls two or three feet thick, an enormous fireplace, and easy chairs, sofas and antique cushioned settles. The spacious L-shaped main bar was built from the wreck of the inn's old brewhouse and coachmen's loft, and has more beams, a woodburning stove, and antique settles around sewing-machine treadle tables; a quieter no-smoking extension, with more modern furnishings, leads off this; darts, pool, fruit machine and piped music. Well kept Bass, Boddingtons, Otter Ale, and Summerskills Whistle Belly on handpump, Inch's cider, wines and champagnes by the glass, several malt whiskies, and home-made lemonade in summer. Generous helpings of good, tasty bar food include sandwiches on ciabatta bread, home-made soup (£2), fried halloumi with lime and caper vinaigrette (£2.75), ploughman's using local cheeses, local chutney and home-baked rolls (£3.25), steak and kidney pie (£4.75), mediterranean prawns with garlic mayonnaise, a fresh fish dish and several pasta dishes; they also hold summer hog roasts. In the flood-lit courtyard there are very pretty hanging baskets and window-boxes on the black and white timbering, and rustic wooden seats and tables on its cobblestones; there's also a walled cobbled garden. *(Recommended by John and Vivienne Rice, Les and Mavis Law, Rita Horridge, R J Walden, Derek and Margaret Underwood, Alan and Eileen Bowker, Wm H Mecham)*

Free house ~ Licensees Veronica Devereux and John Dunbar-Ainley ~ Real ale ~ Meals and snacks (12-2, 6-9.30) ~ Restaurant (closed Sun) ~ Okehampton (01837) 810454 ~ Children in eating area of bar ~ Open 11-3.30, 6-11 ~ Bedrooms: £28(£48B)/£49.50(£69.50B)

Tally Ho

Market St (A386)

There's now a cabinet in this warmly friendly bustling pub which displays take-away wines, grappas (of which there are a staggering 22), and delicatessen items, and the own-brewed beers can also be purchased in swing-top bottles (conditioned). The opened-together rooms of the bar have heavy beams, two woodburning stoves (an armchair by one, the other in a very high-manteld smoking-chamber of a hearth), sturdy old oak and elm tables on the partly carpeted wooden floor, fresh flowers, decorative plates between the wall timbers, candles in bottles, and shelves of old bottles and pottery. Lovely food (with Italian touches, of course) includes sandwiches (from £2.95), ploughman's (from £3.20), omelettes (from £2.40), good sausages (£2.75), salami platter (£3.70), local devilled crab (£3.95), Wednesday evening pizzas, daily changing pasta dishes, a vegetarian dish, fritto misto (£8.75), sirloin steak (£9.45), and puddings (from £1.75); very good continental breakfasts. They have a rather good voucher system on food and drinks (about 5% of the bill) that can be used at any time as valid currency here. The restaurant is no smoking. Through a big window in one building of the former back coach yard you can see the spotless copper brewing equipment where they brew deep-coloured quite strongly hopped Potboiler with its sturdily appetising finish, Tarka Tipple, Thurgia, Nutters, and Dark Mild; also, a fine range of Italian wines, 16 malt whiskies, and freshly squeezed orange juice and other fresh seasonal fruit. Darts, shove-ha'penny, dominoes, cribbage, chess, bridge, trivia and piped music. The friendly boxer is called Boris. There are tables in the sheltered garden. The atmospheric little back dining room specialises in Italian dishes. Mr Scoz is a keen fisherman and fishing can be arranged on about 8 miles of the Torridge. *(Recommended by M J Gardner, Ron and Sheila Corbett, R J Walden, Joan and Gordon Edwards, John and Marianne Cooper, Alan and Eileen Bowker, Christian Farmer, Mrs L Powys-Smith, E Money)*

Own brew ~ Licensees Gianni and Annamaria Scoz ~ Real ale ~ Meals and snacks (not Sun lunchtime) ~ Evening restaurant; closed Sun, Weds and Thurs ~ Hatherleigh (01837) 810306 ~ Well behaved children in eating area of bar and in restaurant ~ Open 11-2.30, 6-11 ~ Bedrooms: £28B/£40B

HAYTOR VALE SX7677 Map 1

Rock ★

Haytor signposted off B3344 just W of Bovey Tracey, on good moorland road to Widecombe

Friendly and rather civilised, this Dartmoor inn has candlelit, polished antique tables in its two communicating, partly panelled rooms, as well as easy chairs, oak Windsor armchairs and high-backed settles, old-fashioned prints and decorative plates on the walls, and good winter log fires (the main fireplace has a fine Stuart fireback). The ground floor dining room is no smoking – as is the restaurant. A wide choice of good bar food includes home-made soup (£1.75), sandwiches (from £2.35), ploughman's (from £3.95), filled baked potatoes (from £3.95), lasagne (£4.35), 3-egg omelettes using free range eggs or tagliatelle with garlic and tomato sauce (£4.95), curries (£5.25), steak and kidney pie (£5.35), local rabbit in mustard sauce (£5.55), poached Devonshire salmon with orange and coriander butter (£8.95), steaks (from £7.95), daily specials like fillet of sea bass with gooseberry and nutmeg, and puddings such as apple bread and butter pudding (£2.45) or banoffi pie (£2.95); Sunday roast; there may be delays during busy periods. Well kept Bass and Eldridge Pope Dorchester, Hardy, and Royal Oak on handpump, and several malt whiskies; courteous service. In winter you pay for a meal for two in the restaurant and get free overnight accommodation. In summer, the pretty, well kept large garden opposite the inn is a popular place to sit and there are some tables and chairs on a small terrace next to the pub itself. The village is just inside the National Park, and golf, horse riding and fishing (and walking, of course) are nearby. *(Recommended by David and Tina Woods-Taylor, Dennis Heatley, David Holloway, Jon and Julie Gibson, A Plumb, T Aldworth, Mark and Heather Williamson, Steve Huggins, Colin Pearson, P M Lane, B A Ferris, Patrick Clancy, W F C Phillips, Tim Barrow, Sue Demont, S V Bishop, P Boot, Brian and Gill Hopkins, Dave and Jules Tuckett, Mrs Ann Roberts and family, Denis Korn)*

Free house ~ Licensee Christopher Graves ~ Real ale ~ Snacks (not Sun or bank hol) ~ Restaurant ~ Haytor (01364) 661305 ~ Children in eating area of bar ~ Open 11-3, 6-11; 11-11 Sat ~ Bedrooms: £29.95(£39.95B)/£50(£63B)

HOLBETON   SX6150 Map 1

Mildmay Colours 🍺
Off A379 Plymouth—Kingsbridge

In a very pretty old-fashioned village on a quiet little road, it's quite a surprise to find this neat and friendly pub brewing its own well hopped and fruity beers – Colours Best, SP, 50/1, and Old Horse Whip on handpump, as well as Bass and Flowers Original; you are very welcome to look at the brewery. Lots of named tankards hang over the bar counter and there are plenty of bar stools as well as cushioned wall seats and wheelback chairs on the turkey carpet, various horse and racing pictures on the partly stripped stone and partly white walls, and a tile-sided woodburning stove; an arch leads to a smaller, similarly decorated family area. The separate plain back bar has pool, sensible darts, dominoes, cribbage, backgammon, euchre, juke box, fruit machine and Sky TV. Good, popular bar food includes sandwiches (from £1.80), half pint of garlic prawns (£2.75), ploughman's or vegetarian nut roast (£3.95) and Mexican dishes such as huevos rancheros (£4.25) or enchiladas (£5.35), with specials like tomato and bacon soup (£2.25), beef in ale or steak and stilton pie (£4.50), whole plaice (£6.95), skate wings with capers and black butter (£7.25), and puddings (£2.50); helpful service. The well kept back garden has picnic-table sets, a swing and some guinea pigs and rabbits in a big cage, and there's a small front terrace. *(Recommended by J C Hathaway, Geoff and Marianne Millin, David Lewis, John and Suzanne McClenahan)*

Own brew ~ Licensee Andrew Patrick ~ Real ale ~ Meals and snacks (till 9.45pm) ~ Upstairs carvery restaurant (closed Mon-Thurs) ~ (01752) 830248 ~ Children welcome ~ Open 11-3, 6-11; occasional all day opening in summer ~ Bedrooms in two cottages opposite: £20B/£40B

HOLNE   SX7069 Map 1

Church House 🛏️
Village signed off B3357 2 or 3 miles W of Ashburton

People come to this friendly and well run country inn to enjoy the well kept beers and very good home-made food in a relaxed and quietly chatty atmosphere – no piped music, noisy machines or pool tables. The lower bar has stripped pine panelling and an 18th-c curved elm settle, and is separated from the atmospheric carpeted lounge bar by a 16th-c heavy oak partition; open log fires in both rooms. There are fine moorland views from the pillared porch (where regulars tend to gather). They take great care in preparing their food – using local fresh produce and even growing some of their own organic vegetables; fish comes from Brixham, meat from two local butchers: lunchtime sandwiches, soup (£1.75), mushrooms in garlic butter (£3.50), filled baked potatoes (from £3.25), lunchtime ploughman's (from £3.50), 3-egg omelettes (from £3.75), a vegetarian dish

(£4.75), excellent steak and kidney in ale pie (£4.95), Devon lamb in cider (£5.25), grills (from £5.25), daily specials such as pasta in a ham, leek and cream sauce (£3.95), lamb's liver in sherry and cream sauce (£5.75), grilled Torbay sole on the bone (£6.25), and venison in red wine (£6.75), and puddings like fruit crumble or sherry trifle with clotted cream (from £1.95). The restaurant is no smoking. Well kept Furgusons Dartmoor and Palmers IPA, and two guest beers like Blackawton Bitter, Furgusons Strong, Morlands Old Speckled Hen or Wadworths 6X on handpump, Greys farm cider, and decent house wines; darts, dominoes, cribbage and table skittles in the public bar. The quarter-hour walk from the Newbridge National Trust car park to the pub is rather fine, and there are many other attractive walks nearby, up on to Dartmoor as well as along the wooded Dart valley. Charles Kingsley (of *Water Babies* fame) was born in the village. Dogs on a lead are welcome. *(Recommended by Simon Evans, R J Walden, T Aldworth, D Goodger, P R Ferris, A Plumb, Simon and Natalie Forster, David Eberlin, Mrs Ann Roberts and family, Alison Jill Trace)*

Free house ~ Lease: N E and W J Bevan ~ Real ale ~ Snacks (not evening) and meals ~ Restaurant ~ Poundsgate (0136 43) 208 ~ Well behaved children in eating area of bar; over 7 (except residents) in restaurant in evening ~ Occasional local musicians or Morris dancers ~ Open 11.30-3, 6.30-11; winter opening 12 and close 10.30 Sun-Thurs ~ Bedrooms: £22(£27.50B)/£39(£50B)

HORNDON SX5280 Map 1

Elephants Nest ★ ♀ 🍺

If coming from Okehampton on A386 turn left at Mary Tavy Inn, then left after about ½ mile; pub signposted beside Mary Tavy Inn, then Horndon signposted; on the Ordnance Survey Outdoor Leisure Map it's named as the New Inn

The name of the pub is written up on the beams in the bar here in 60 languages, and there are cushioned stone seats built into the windows, captain's chairs around the tables, large rugs and flagstones, a beams-and-board ceiling, an amusing elephant mural in the bar, and a good log fire on cool days. Another room – created from the old beer cellar and with views over the garden and beyond to the moors – acts as a dining or function room or an overspill from the bar on busy nights. Good home-made bar food at lunchtime includes home-made soup (£1.30), good granary rolls, ploughman's or home-made pâté (from £2.80), chilli con carne (£3.30), steak and kidney pie (£4), tandoori chicken (£5), Aberdeen Angus steaks (from £9.45), daily specials such as ham and leek lasagne (£4), lamb and cashew nut korma (£4.10) or guinea fowl with port and red wine gravy (£5.50), and puddings served with clotted cream like treacle and walnut tart or apricot crumble (£1.90); fresh vegetables are £1 extra. Well kept Boddingtons Bitter, Palmers IPA, St Austells HSD, and a local and another guest on handpump (around 130 guests each year); farm cider, and a weekly guest wine; friendly service. Sensibly placed darts, cribbage, dominoes and piped music. Outside on the spacious, flower-bordered lawn are some wooden benches and tables that look over the walls to the pastures of Dartmoor's lower slopes. You can walk from here straight on to the moor or Black Down, though a better start (army exercises permitting) might be to drive past Wapsworthy to the end of the lane, at OS Sheet 191 map reference 546805. They have three dogs, two cats, ducks, chickens, rabbits, and horses; customers' dogs are allowed in on a lead. Please note – they are not doing bedrooms this year. *(Recommended by Andy and Jackie Mallpress, R J Walden, Paul Boot, Mrs S Segrove, A N Ellis, Dr N Holmes, Frank Cummins, E Money, Caroline and Simon Turner, Peter and Lynn Brueton)*

Free house ~ Licensee Nick Hamer ~ Real ale ~ Meals and snacks (until 10pm) ~ Mary Tavy (01822) 810273 ~ Children welcome in two rooms ~ Folk music 2nd Tues evening of month ~ Open 11.30-2.30, 6.30-11

We checked prices with the pubs as we went to press in summer 1994. They should hold until around spring 1995 – when our experience suggests that you can expect an increase of around 10p in the £.

HORSEBRIDGE SX3975 Map 1

Royal ★ 🍺

Village signposted off A384 Tavistock—Launceston

Besides the beers brewed on the premises – Tamar, Horsebridge Best and the more powerful Heller – this prettily-set pub also keeps Bass, Boddingtons, and Marstons Pedigree on handpump, and country wines. The rooms are simple and old-fashioned and the one on the right has vertically panelled cushioned stall seats around neat old tables, some mate's and wheelback chairs, and harness and brasses on the stripped stone walls; the one on the left has cushioned casks and benches around three tables on the slate floor, and bar billiards, sensibly placed darts, and dominoes; piped music and a cage with cockatiels. There's another small room, called the Drip Tray, for the overflow at busy times. The good variety of freshly cooked bar food at lunchtime includes soup, lots of ploughman's (from £2.95), and cottage pie or fisherman's pot; also, ricotta cheese and spinach cannelloni, steak and kidney pie, vegetable tikka masala, venison in wine, sherried kidneys, prawn cantonese, and salads (from £5.50-£6.25), and puddings like treacle pudding or nutty apple and caramel strudel (£2.10); no chips or fried food. The covered area in the garden, presided over by Fred, the resident jackdaw, also has budgies, finches and so forth, and a big terrace with seats, a rose arbour and hanging baskets. The pub was originally called the Packhorse, and got its present name for services rendered to Charles I (whose seal is carved in the doorstep). The nearby bridge, painted by Turner, is lovely. No children. *(Recommended by Peter Taylor, R J Walden, John Hazel, Mayur Shah, John and Tessa Rainsford, A N Ellis, Paul and Heather Bettesworth, John Wilson, P and M Rudlin)*

Own brew ~ Licensees T G and J H Wood ~ Real ale ~ Snacks (lunchtime) and meals (not Sun evening) ~ (01822) 87214 ~ Open 12-2.30, 7-11

IDDESLEIGH SS5708 Map 1

Duke of York

B3217 Exbourne—Dolton

Very much the social centre of the village and filled with chatty regulars, this largely 14th-c thatched, white stone pub has rocking chairs by the roaring log fire, cushioned wall benches built into the wall's black-painted wooden dado, stripped tables, and other homely country furnishings. Bar food includes sandwiches, home-made soup (£1.50), lasagne (£3.95), ham and egg, local sausages, and steaks. Well kept Cotleigh Tawny and Hook Norton Old Hookey tapped from the cask, Inch's farm ciders, and bottled beers from Czechoslovakia. Shove-ha'penny, cribbage, dominoes and sensibly placed darts. Through a small coach arch is a little back garden with some picnic-table sets under cocktail parasols. Good fishing nearby. *(Recommended by Gwen and Peter Andrews, R J Walden, Anthony Barnes, Steve Dark, David Watson, Joan and Gordon Edwards, J R Williams, Philip and Bronwen Parr, E Money, Carol and Mike Muston, Alan and Heather Jacques)*

Free house ~ Licensees Diane and Andrew King ~ Real ale ~ Meals and snacks (not winter Mon) ~ Restaurant ~ Hatherleigh (01837) 810253 ~ Children in eating area of bar and in restaurant ~ Open 11.30-3, 6.30-11 ~ Bedrooms: £20/£40B

KENN SX9285 Map 1

Ley Arms ♀

Signed off A380 just S of Exeter

Very pretty outside with its newly thatched roof and hanging baskets and close to an attractive church and churchyard, this busy pub has been carefully refurbished (after a fire) by the helpful landlord who took over in Janury 1994. The bustling public bar, popular with cheery locals, has a fine polished granite floor, black beams, blue plush cushioned sturdy wooden wall seats, red plush stools, an elbow rest round a central timber, and tall cast-iron cushioned bar stools. Good, popular home-made bar food includes soup (£1.95), open sandwiches (from £1.95), ploughman's with a good choice of cheeses (from £2.95), fresh fish, as available, collected from Brixham Quay (from £3.50), lasagne (£4.50), the house special, steak and kidney pie (£4.75), tiger prawns or Greek salad (£4.95), kidneys, shallots and crispy bacon (£6.50), pork in soy and ginger (£7.75), sirloin steak (£8.50), and puddings such as cheesecakes and pancakes with maple syrup. Well kept Bass, Boddingtons, Flowers IPA and Original, and Whitbreads Summer on handpump, and a good, interesting choice of 5 red and 5 white wines – from France, California, Australia and Germany; quick service; piped music. The lounge has nice black applied panelling, red, green and gold plush small chairs, a glass-topped carved table and other plain black tables, a button-backed brocaded wall settle, dried flowers and brass ornaments in the windows, and a woodburning stove in the big red granite fireplace; a big expanse of red flowery carpet leads past a cosy area with chesterfields used for pre-restaurant drinks and past a neat inner no-smoking family room, to the rather smart restaurant. Dogs are allowed in the public bar. An extension will be built by the time this book is published, with a skittle alley, pool, darts, and fruit machine; winter whist and euchre. *(Recommended by Graham Reeve, Annette Stewart, Gordon, E V M Whiteway, A E and P McCully)*

Free house ~ Licensee Trevor Keary ~ Real ale ~ Meals and snacks ~ Restaurant ~ (01392) 832341 ~ Well behaved children welcome ~ Live music Sun evening ~ Open 11-11; 11-3, 6-11 in winter but open all day winter Sats; closed evening 25 Dec ~ Bedrooms planned Spring 1995

KILMINGTON SY2797 Map 1

Old

A35

It's always a good sign when locals like a pub – but this thatched white pub is popular with visitors as well. There's a characterful, traditionally furnished main bar, comfortable lounge with leather armchairs and sofa around the inglenook fireplace, well kept Bass and Worthington Best on handpump, and darts, dominoes, cribbage and fruit machine. Good value food includes sandwiches, home-made soup (£2), basket meals (from £3.25), salads (from £4.50), home-made steak, mushroom and Guinness pie (£4.95), and specials like ribbons of steak marinated in Pernod with rich tomato sauce and served with tagliatelle (£5.95), chicken breast flamed in brandy with Dijon mustard sauce (£6.95), rack of lamb or half a roast duck with spiced peach or honey and black cherry sauce (£8.95), and steaks (from £9.50); their little no-smoking restaurant is doing very well. There are two gardens – a big one by the car park and a more secluded one behind. *(Recommended by N Bushby, W Atkins, M E and Mrs J Wellington, David Gaunt; more reports please).*

Free house ~ Licensees Carol and Jeff Little ~ Real ale ~ Meals and snacks ~ Restaurant ~ (01297) 32096 ~ Children in eating area of bar and in restaurant ~ Open 11-2.30(3 in winter), 5.30-11; winter evening opening 6

KINGSKERSWELL SX8767 Map 1

Barn Owl 🛏

Aller Mills; just off A380 Newton Abbot—Torquay – inn-sign on main road opposite RAC post

Run by helpful and friendly licensees, this 16th-c inn places a lot of emphasis on its good, popular food. This might include home-made soup (£1.75), big sandwiches with interesting side salad (from £2.70, crab £3.75), filled baked potatoes (from £2.95), delicious garlic mushrooms (£3.25), generous ploughman's (from £3.75), quite a few salads (from £5.50; home roast loin of pork £5.95; fine fresh local salmon £7.95), fresh fillet of plaice (£5.25), fresh fillet of sole (£5.95), gammon (£6.25), steaks (from £9.75), mixed grill (£10.95), puddings (£2.25), and specials like pork madeira with prunes or Danish-style chicken (£5.50) or game casserole (£5.95). Well kept Furgusons Dartmoor, Ind Coope Burton and Wadworths 6X on handpump, 15 malt whiskies, and several wines by the glass. There are some grand furnishings in one room such as a couple of carved oak settles and old-fashioned dining chairs around the handsome polished tables on its flowery carpet, antique dark oak panelling, a decorative wooden chimney piece, and an elaborate ornamental plaster ceiling. Three other rooms (one was being refurbished as we went to press) have low black oak beams, with polished flagstones and a kitchen range in one; four log fires. There are picnic-table sets in a small sheltered garden. No children. *(Recommended by Steve Goodchild, C and Marjorie Roberts, Peter Pocklington, Tom Evans, John Dowell, Steve Huggins, A E and P McCully, Michael A Butler, Jim and Maggie Cowell)*

Free house ~ Licensees Derek and Margaret Warner ~ Real ale ~ Meals and snacks (till 10pm) ~ Evening restaurant (not Sun) ~ Kingskerswell (01803) 872130 ~ Open 11.30-2.30, 6-11; winter evening opening 6.30; closed evening 25 Dec, closed 26/27 Dec ~ Bedrooms: £47.50B/£60B

KINGSTEIGNTON SX8773 Map 1

Old Rydon ★ ⑪

Rydon Rd; from A381/A380 junction follow signs to Kingsteignton (B3103), taking first right turn (Longford Lane), go straight on to the bottom of the hill, then next right turn into Rydon Rd following Council Office signpost; pub is just past the school, OS Sheet 192 map reference 872739

Readers think the food here is the best for miles around – and most efficiently served, too. Constantly changing and imaginative, it might include cream of cauliflower and fresh lovage soup (£1.85), deep-fried butterfly prawns with soy, ginger and sherry sauce (£2.95), home-made leek and garlicky mushroom quiche (£3.95), vegetarian ricotta tortelloni (£4.25), grilled venison sausages on a bed of bubble-and-squeak in rich onion, red wine and rosemary sauce (£4.65), oxtail and vegetable casserole (£5.45), terrific roast guinea fowl, fisherman's crumble with cod, prawns, mushrooms and spinach (£5.85), and puddings served with clotted cream like German apple cake, summer pudding or chocolate nut fudge flan (£2.25); vegetables are imaginative. Well kept Bass, Wadworths 6X, and a changing guest ale on handpump. The small, cosy bar has a big winter log fire in a raised fireplace, cask seats and upholstered seats built against the white-painted stone walls, and a heavy beam-and-plank ceiling with lots of beer mugs hanging from it. There are a few more seats in an upper former cider loft facing the antlers and antelope horns on one high white wall; piped music. There's also a prettily planted dining conservatory. Seats in a nice biggish sheltered garden, which has also has a swing. *(Recommended by B A Ferris Harms, Steve Huggins, Thomas Neate, Steve Dark, George Atkinson, P and J Shapley, D I Baddeley, Peter and Jenny Quine, John and Vivienne Rice, Paul and Janet Waring, Jim and Maggie Cowell, Joy Heatherley, Ian and Nita Cooper, E Money, David Wallington)*

Free house ~ Licensees Hermann and Miranda Hruby ~ Real ale ~ Meals and snacks ~ Restaurant (closed Sun) ~ Newton Abbot (01626) 54626 ~ Children in conservatory or upstairs, but no under 8s after 8pm ~ Open 11-2.30, 6-11

KINGSTON SX6347 Map 1

Dolphin

Off B3392 S of Modbury (can also be reached from A379 W of Modbury)

As you approach this peaceful 16th-c inn, there's a sign saying 'Please drive slowly through the pub' – it has buildings on both sides of the narrow lane. There's a warmly welcoming atmosphere in the several knocked-through beamed rooms with rustic tables and cushioned seats and settles around their bared stone walls; one small area is no smoking. Very good home-made bar food includes sandwiches (from £1.50), ploughman's (from £3.50), crab bake (£3.95), Mississippi chicken (£4.75), vegetarian moussaka or ginger beef (£4.95), gammon and egg (£5.95), steaks (from £7.25), freshly poached salmon (£7.50), puddings like treacle tart or apple and cherry crumble (£2.25), and children's meals (from £1.50). Well kept Courage Best and Ushers Founders on handpump. Outside, there are tables and swings. There are several tracks leading down to the sea about a mile-and-a-half away. *(Recommended by David Cundy, Gordon, T Aldworth, Maurice Ingram, Lorraine Flanagan, David Goldstone, Roger Berry, Dr and Mrs B D Smith, John Wilson, E Money)*

Ushers ~ Tenants Neil and Annie Williams ~ Real ale ~ Meals and snacks (till 10pm) ~ (01548) 810314 ~ Children in eating area of bar and in family room ~ Open 11-3, 6-11 ~ Bedrooms: £30B/£40B

KNOWSTONE SS8223 Map 1

Masons Arms ★ 🛏 🍷

Village signposted off A361 Bampton—South Molton

There's a great deal of individual character and a marvellously relaxed and informal atmosphere in this unspoilt rural pub. It's run in a very personal way by the warmly welcoming licensees and the small untampered main bar always has a good mix of chatty locals and visitors. Ancient bottles of all shapes and sizes hang from the heavy medieval black beams, there are farm tools on the walls, substantial rustic furniture on the stone floor, and a fine open fireplace with a big log fire and side bread oven. A small lower sitting room has pinkish plush chairs around a low table in front of the fire and bar billiards. Bar food can be very good indeed: widely praised home-made soup (£1.50) and pâté (£2.25), ploughman's with proper local cheese and butter in a pot (£3.25), salads (from £3.50), fried plaice or home-made pies, varying from day to day, like venison, cheese and leek or rabbit (£3.95), home-made curry (£5.25), good fritto misto (£5.95), and home-made puddings like strawberry shortcake (£1.75); specials such as pasta bows with courgettes, garlic and parmesan (£3.25), liver and bacon hotpot (£3.95) or sweet and sour pork (£4.25); good value Sunday lunch, a popular Thursday curry night, and theme nights about once a month, usually with live music, a special menu and a special drink. The restaurant is no smoking. They often sell home-made marmalades, fruit breads or hot gooseberry chutney over the counter. Well kept Badger Best and Cotleigh Tawny tapped from the cask, farm cider, a small but well chosen wine list, and coffee and teas; several snuffs on the counter; shove-ha'penny, bar billiards, dominoes, cribbage, board games (on request), and general knowledge quiz on the last Sunday of the month (proceeds to charity). In the back garden they hold Friday and Saturday evening barbecues in summer (weather permitting). Charlie, the engaging bearded collie, likes to join you on a walk – at least part of the way; the cats are called Archie and Allie. *(Recommended by Robin and Molly Taylor, Jed and Virginia Brown, D B Delany, Patricia Nutt, Jim and Maggie Cowell, A E and P McCully, John Wootten, David Saunders, Tim Barrow, Sue Demont, Christine Hodgson, Martin Jones, R J Walden, Lyn Sharpless, Bob Eardley, Paul and Heather Bettesworth, David Wilkinson, David Stanley, Sue Garner, Brian and Gill Hopkins, Jerry and Alison Oakes, The Umbrella Club, Hugh Chevalier)*

Free house ~ Licensees David and Elizabeth Todd ~ Real ale ~ Meals and snacks (not evenings 25/26 Dec) ~ Restaurant ~ Anstey Mills (0139 84) 231/582 ~ Children welcome away from bar ~ Occasional live music ~ Open 11-3, 7(6 summer Sats)-11; closed evenings 25/26 Dec ~ Bedrooms: £40S/£55S; dogs £1.50

LITTLEHEMPSTON SX8162 Map 1

Tally Ho!

The bare stone walls in the cosy low-beamed rooms of this friendly old pub are covered with growing collections of porcelain, brass, copperware, mounted butterflies, stuffed wildlife, old swords, shields, hunting horns and so forth; there's also an interesting mix of chairs and settles (many antique and with comfortable cushions), candles on the tables, fresh flowers, panelling, and two ornamental woodburning stoves. The relaxed, chatty atmosphere is helped by the fact that there are no noisy machines or piped music. Bar food, using only the best ingredients, is very good indeed and as well as the very popular daily specials (including vegetarian dishes), there are starters like delicious soup, sandwiches, home-made chicken liver pâté, and mussels in cream and white wine (all from £2.45), fresh Brixham fish dishes (from £6.75), Aberdeen Angus steaks (from £7.95), fresh roast duckling (£10.95) and home-made puddings with clotted cream (£2.45). Well kept Bass, Furgusons Dartmoor, and Wadworths 6X on handpump from a temperature controlled cellar. The terrace is a mass of flowers in summer. *(Recommended by Ian Phillips, Steve Huggins, Alan and Brenda Holyer, Margaret and Trevor Errington, Jane Palmer)*

Free house ~ Licensees Alan Hitchman and Dale Hitchman ~ Real ale ~ Meals and snacks (till 10pm; not 25 Dec) ~ (01803) 862316 ~ Children in eating area of bar ~ Open 12-2.30, 6-11; closed 25 Dec

LUSTLEIGH SX7881 Map 1

Cleave

Village signposted off A382 Bovey Tracey—Moretonhampstead

This thatched 16th-c pub has a neat, sheltered and pretty garden – very popular in summer. Inside, the cosy, low-ceilinged lounge bar has fresh summer flowers and big winter log fires, and attractive antique high-backed settles, pale leatherette bucket chairs, red-cushioned wall seats, and wheelback chairs around the tables on its patterned carpet. The second bar has large dresser, harmonium, an HMV gramophone, prints, and other similar furnishings. Tasty bar food includes home-made soup (£1.95), sandwiches (£2.65), pasta with pesto (£3.60), ploughman's (from £3.95), home-made chicken curry (£5.45), home-made steak, kidney and Guinness pie or roast beef and Yorkshire pudding (£5.75), daily specials, puddings like warm treacle tart or gooseberry and almond pie (£2.25), and children's dishes (from £2.95); friendly service. Well kept Bass, Boddingtons, Flowers Original and Whitbreads Pompey Royal on handpump, several malt whiskies, and farm ciders; good tea, coffee and hot chocolate. Please note – they no longer do bedrooms. *(Recommended by David and Tina Woods-Taylor, Joan and Gordon Edwards, Patrick Clancy, Steve Huggins, P M Lane, Alan and Brenda Holyer, R J Walden, David and Celia Burke, John Knighton, E Money)*

Heavitree (who no longer brew) ~ Tenant A Perring ~ Real ale ~ Meals and snacks ~ Lustleigh (0164 77) 223 ~ Open 11-3, 6-11; 11-11 Sat ~ Children in no smoking family area ~ Parking may be difficult

LUTTON SX5959 Map 1

Mountain

Off Cornwood—Sparkwell road, though pub not signposted from it

From the window seat in the beamed bar of this unspoilt and friendly pub there's a fine view over the lower slopes of Dartmoor; the same view is shared by the terrace. The bar has a high-backed settle by the log fire, some walls stripped back to the bare stone, and Windsor chairs around old-fashioned polished tables in a larger connecting room. Well kept Furgusons Dartmoor, Ind Coope Burton, Wadworths 6X and a guest beer on handpump, several malt whiskies, and farm cider; darts, cribbage, dominoes and liar dice; three very friendly dogs, and cats. Generous helpings of good straightforward bar food include good pasties (£1), sandwiches (from £1.60), soup (£1.70; with a hunk of cheese as well £3), sausage and chips (£2.60), cottage pie (£3.50), ploughman's or ham cooked in cider (£3.80), and chicken kiev. *(Recommended by J H Bell, J S Poulter, E Money, Romey Heaton)*

Free house ~ Licensees Charles and Margaret Bullock ~ Real ale ~ Meals and snacks (till 10 evening) ~ Cornwood (0175 537) 247 ~ Children in eating area of bar and in own room ~ Open 11-3, 6-11; winter Mon-Weds evening opening 7

Waterside pubs are listed at the back of the book.

LYDFORD SX5184 Map 1

Castle ★ 🛏 🕼 ♈ 🍺

Signposted off A386 Okehampton—Tavistock

Devon Dining Pub of the Year

An extension is to be added to this charming pink-washed Tudor inn which will create a family restaurant and lounge area, and two new family bedrooms. As well as a cosy atmosphere and particularly friendly staff, it's the food that readers like so much here. From an interesting menu, there might be soups like stilton and asparagus or Thai curry (£2.20), ploughman's (from £3.35; assorted Devon cheese platter £4), leek, cream cheese and sweetcorn roulade (£4.95), seafood risotto (£5.15), pork and apple cobbler (£5.25), pies like steak and kidney or local venison with dried fruit (from £5.35), hot and sour sizzling prawns (£5.75), spicy Moroccan chicken with dates, lemon grass and fresh coriander (£5.95), delicious puddings such as old-fashioned English trifle or rum and raisin chocolate crunch cake, and children's helpings (from £3.60). Part of the restaurant is no smoking. Well kept Bass, Furgusons Dartmoor, Palmers IPA and up to three weekly guest beers on handpump or tapped from the cask, and around 13 wines by the glass, as well as a sparkling wine and bucks fizz. One of the rooms of the twin-roomed bar (where the bar food is served) has low lamp-lit beams, a sizeable open fire, masses of brightly decorated plates, some Hogarth prints, an attractive grandfather clock, and, near the serving-counter, seven Lydford pennies hammered out in the old Saxon mint in the reign of Ethelred the Unready, in the 11th-c; the second room has an interesting collection of antique stallion posters, and both rooms are furnished with country kitchen chairs, high-backed winged settles and old captain's chairs around mahogany tripod tables on big slate flagstones. Unusual stained-glass doors; sensibly placed darts, cribbage and dominoes. The terrace in the well kept garden has a pets corner for resident's children with goats, rabbits, hens and a Shetland pony called Wanda. The pub is next to the village's daunting, ruined 12th-c castle and close to a beautiful river gorge (owned by the National Trust; closed Nov-Easter); the village itself was one of the four strong-points developed by Alfred the Great as a defence against the Danes. *(Recommended by J R Williams, Frank Cummins, R J Walden, John and Christine Vittoe, Mick Gray, Alan and Brenda Holyer, Richard Davies, P and M Rudlin, Peter and Lynn Brueton, Patrick Clancy, Werner Arend, Derrick and Karen McClelland, Steven Tait, Susie Lovie, John Evans, M Veldhuyzen, A E Brace, P Bell, Alan Mills, John Fazakerley)*

Free house ~ Licensees Clive and Mo Walker ~ Real ale ~ Meals and snacks ~ Restaurant ~ Lydford (0182 282) 242/252 ~ Children in eating area of the bar (lunchtime only), in restaurant and in snug ~ Open 11.30-3, 6-11 ~ Bedrooms: £27.50(£37.50B)/£40(£49.90B)

LYNMOUTH SS7249 Map 1

Rising Sun 🛏

Mars Hill; down by harbour

This is the sort of place that to make the most of, you should spend the night, when you can enjoy the views over the little harbour after the crowds have left, you'd be more likely to make friends with the landlord (who is not always around in the bar) and quite likely to eat in the attractive no-smoking restaurant where the food is very good. Indeed, most people staying here would recommend the inn for a star award. The modernised panelled bar usually has a good atmosphere due to the friendly Antipodean staff, as well as cushioned built-in stall-seats on the uneven oak floors, black beams in the crooked ceiling, some stripped stone at the fireplace end, and latticed windows facing the harbour; piped music. Well kept Courage Directors and John Smiths on handpump, and decent lunchtime bar food such as home-made soup (£1.95), filled rolls (from £2.45; crab £3.50), filled baked potatoes (£3.25), ploughman's (£3.95), chilli con carne (£4.25), bacon lardons and crispy croutons on mixed leaves with a walnut dressing (£4.50), and steak, mushroom and Guinness pie (£4.75). There's a charming terraced garden behind the inn, cut into the hillside. Shelley reputedly spent his honeymoon with his 16-year-old bride, Harriet, in one of the cottages here. The steep walk up the Lyn valley to Watersmeet (National Trust) and Exmoor is particularly pleasant. *(Recommended by Bill and Beryl Farmer, M D Beardmore, E B Davies, John and Christine Vittoe, John and Vivienne Rice, Paul Randall, Mr and Mrs M Brown, R J Walden, Dorothee and Dennis Glover, D R Tyler, B M Eldridge, Dr and Mrs Paveley; also recommended by The Good Hotel Guide)*

Free house ~ Licensee Hugo Jeune ~ Real ale ~ Lunchtime meals and snacks ~ Restaurant ~ Lynton (01598) 53223 ~ Children restaurant if over 5 ~ Open 11-3, 5.30-11; 11-2.30, 6.30-11 in winter ~ Bedrooms:£39.50B/£79B

LYNTON SS7249 Map 1

Rockford

Lynton—Simonsbath rd, off B2332

Small, homely and friendly 350-year-old inn by the East Lyn river with its good salmon, brown trout and sea trout fishing; Watersmeet is close by, riding can be arranged, and there are lots of fine walks. The original stables and hay loft have been converted into bars and there are lots of old photographs on the walls (which the landlord is happy to describe to you). Bar food includes lunchtime dishes like home-made cottage pie (£2.65), smoked trout (£3.50), or home-made chicken and mushroom pie (£3.95), with evening things such as gammon home-braised in ale with honey glaze (£5.95), and lamb in redcurrant and port or chicken supreme stuffed with prawns (£6.95); well kept Cotleigh Tawny, and Courage Best and Directors on handpump, and decent wines. Darts, pool, shove-ha'penny, cribbage and dominoes. *(Recommended by Dorothee and Dennis Glover, Peter and Audrey Dowsett, Mr and Mrs Moody, C A Blake)*

Free house ~ Licensees D W Sturmer and S J Tasker ~ Real ale ~ Meals and snacks ~ (01598) 7214 ~ Children welcome in eating area of bar ~ Local folk every 3rd Sat evening of month ~ Open 12-2.30(2 in winter), 7-11; closed weekday lunchtimes 2 weeks Nov and 2 weeks Feb ~ Bedrooms: £18/£36

MEAVY SX5467 Map 1

Royal Oak

This traditional old place is one of only a handful of pubs still owned by the parish council. The L-shaped bar has pews from the next door church, red plush banquettes and old agricultural prints and church pictures on the walls, and a smaller bar – where the locals like to gather – with a big fireplace and side bread oven, and red-topped barrel seats. Bar food includes sandwiches (from £1.80), soup (£1.90), filled baked potatoes (£2.75), ploughman's (£3.25), cheesy cottage or fisherman's pies or sweet and sour chicken (£3.95), chicken tikka masala (£4.25), steak and kidney pie (£4.50), puddings like spotted dick or apple pie (£1.95), and roast Sunday lunch. Well kept Bass, Blackawton Headstrong, Courage Best, and Eldridge Pope Royal Oak on handpump or tapped from the cask; good service from the hard-working licensees. Darts, dominoes, euchre and piped music. There are benches and picnic-tables outside the pub by the village green (where the 500-year-old oak tree once had nine men eating inside its trunk). No children. *(Recommended by A N Ellis, Paul Redgrave, Frank Cummins, David Whalley, R J Walden, E Money, John Wilson)*

Free house ~ Licensees Roger and Susan Barber ~ Real ale ~ Meals and snacks ~ (01822) 852944 ~ Open 11-3, 6-11

MILTONCOMBE SX4865 Map 1

Who'd Have Thought It ★

Village signposted from A386 S of Tavistock

A good place for lunch before a visit to the lovely gardens of the Garden House at

Buckland Monachorum or for Buckland Abbey, this attractive 16th-c pub has an atmospheric, black-panelled bar with cushioned barrel seats and high-backed winged settles around solid, polished wooden tables, a woodburning stove in the big stone fireplace, rapiers, sabres and other weapons on its walls, and colourful plates on a big black dresser; two other rooms (one is no smoking) have seats made from barrels. Generous helpings of popular bar food include sandwiches, home-made soup (£2.25), pâté (£3.25), chicken or vegetable curry (from £3.50), tasty steak and kidney pie (£4.50), rabbit casserole or lamb steak in orange and ginger (£5.25), grilled trout (£6.95), sirloin steak (£8.50), and puddings like cherry and almond strudel or chocolate fudge cake (£2.10); on Sunday lunchtime the food is a bit more restricted but also includes two roasts (£4.25). Well kept Bass, Blackawton Headstrong, Eldridge Pope Royal Oak, Hook Norton Best, and Wadworths 6X on handpump, and Bulmers and Inch's ciders; efficient staff; dominoes, fruit machine. There are picnic-table sets on a terrace with hanging baskets, by the little stream. No children. *(Recommended by Frank Cummins, R J Walden, Jim and Maggie Cowell, Andy and Jill Kassube, A N Ellis, Caroline and Simon Turner, Joan and Tony Walker, John Fazakerley, P Boot, Robert and Gladys Flux)*

Free house ~ Licensees Keith Yeo and Gary Rager ~ Real ale ~ Meals and snacks (restricted Sun lunchtime) ~ Yelverton (01822) 853313 ~ Folk club Sun evening in lower bar ~ Open 11.30-2.30(3 Sat), 6.30-11

MORETONHAMPSTEAD SX7585 Map 1

White Hart 🍽

Once people have discovered this civilised place, they tend to make regular return visits. The friendly licensee has now been here for 17 years and has been a hotelier in Devon for over 30. The large lounge bar is furnished with oak pews from the parish church, armchairs, plush seats and stools, the hall has a splendidly large-scale 1827 map of Devon by Greenwood, and in the lively public bar there are leatherette seats and settles under a white beam-and-plank ceiling; log fires – and the friendly standard poodles are called Poppy and Rosie. A wide choice of promptly served, popular bar food includes soup (£2.25), sandwiches (from £2.25), egg and chips (£3), ploughman's or broccoli and cheese quiche (£4.35), steak and kidney or lamb, leek and apricot pie (£5.45), and puddings like treacle tart or bread pudding (£2.25), with evening extras like a daily roast (£6.75), grilled local trout (£8.50), and half a duckling with orange sauce (£10.25); daily specials, cream teas from 3pm, and Sunday roast; no children's helpings but an extra plate is available. The restaurant is no smoking. Well kept Bass and Smiles on handpump, and Luscombe farm cider; darts and fruit machine. You can sit on a pew among the flowers in the small back courtyard. Well placed for Dartmoor and good for nearby walks, riding, golf and fishing. *(Recommended by Lynn Sharpless, Bob Eardley, Ernie and Joan Potter, Paul Randall, D Goodger, David Crossley)*

Free house ~ Licensee Peter Morgan ~ Real ale ~ Meals and snacks ~ Restaurant and evening grill room ~ Moretonhampstead (01647) 40406 ~ Children in eating area of bar ~ May have to park in the public car park, a short walk away ~ Open 11-11 ~ Bedrooms: £43B/£63B

NEWTON ST CYRES SX8798 Map 1

Beer Engine 🍺

Sweetham; from Newton St Cyres on A377 follow St Cyres Station, Thorverton signpost

This friendly old station hotel brews its own beer and from the downstairs cellar bar you can see the stainless brewhouse: Rail Ale, Piston Bitter, and the very strong Sleeper. The spacious main bar has partitioning alcoves, Windsor chairs and some button-back banquettes around dark varnished tables on its red carpet. Good, reasonably priced bar food includes speciality sausages like pork and garlic or oriental (£3.65), a choice of three vegetarian dishes or lasagne (£3.95), and cod and parsley pie (£4.25); darts, shove-ha'penny, dominoes and cribbage; fruit machine and video game in the downstairs lobby. There's a large sunny garden on several interesting levels with lots of sheltered seating; you can eat out here, too. *(Recommended by Mike Cargill, Peter and Lynn Brueton, Jim and Maggie Cowell, R H Martyn, Graham Reeve)*

Own brew ~ Licensee Peter Hawksley ~ Real ale ~ Meals and snacks (till 10pm) ~ (01392) 851282 ~ Children in eating area of bar ~ Rock and blues Fri and Sat evenings and folk and jazz Sun lunchtimes ~ Open 11.30-2.30, 6-11; 11.30-11 Sat (cellar bar open till midnight Fri/Sat)

NOSS MAYO SX5447 Map 1

Old Ship

In a charming village, this 16th-c pub is popular with yachtsmen who (at high tide) can get here by boat – and there are tables on the terrace overlooking the water. Inside, the two thick-walled bars have a warm, friendly atmosphere and reliably good bar food that includes sandwiches, good pasties, home-made daily specials, locally caught fish grilled on the bone, steaks, and nice puddings with clotted cream; 3-course Sunday carvery (£7.50). The restaurant is no smoking. Well kept Bass, Flowers Original, Furgusons Dartmoor and Wadworths 6X on handpump, local farm cider, and several malt whiskies; swift, helpful service; darts, cribbage, fruit machine, video game and piped music. *(Recommended by Steve Huggins, Marion and John Hadfield, David and Ann Stranack, Roy and Margaret Randle, A E Brace, P Boot, John and Suzanne McClenahan)*

Free house ~ Licensees Norman and Val Doddridge ~ Real ale ~ Meals and snacks (till 10.30pm) ~ Restaurant ~ (01752) 872387 ~ Children welcome ~ Open 11-3, 6-11

PLYMOUTH SX4755 Map 1

China House ★

Marrowbone Slip, Sutton Harbour, via Sutton Road off Exeter Street (A374)

Overlooking Sutton Harbour, this marvellously positioned and carefully converted 17th-c waterside pub is Plymouth's oldest warehouse. It's lofty and very spacious but partitioned into smaller booth-like areas, with bare slate and stone walls, great beams, flagstone floors, and is strung with nets, kegs and fishing gear; there's even a clinker-built boat; no-smoking areas. On the left is the main bar with plain wooden seats around dark tables in front of a good log fire – all very chatty, comfortable and relaxed. Good home-made food includes lunchtime doorstep sandwiches (from £2.45), home-made soup with garlic bread (£2.50), baked potatoes with crispy bacon, tomatoes and sour cream (£2.95), a daily vegetarian dish (£4.35), and steak and stilton pie, chicken and celery curry or lemon sole and prawn mornay (£4.95), with evening dishes like pork and apple en croute, fresh fish of the day or chicken breasts with cream cheese, broccoli and pine nuts (£9.95); puddings (£2.75). The upstairs restaurant is no smoking. Well kept Furgusons Dartmoor Best and Strong, and Wadworths 6X on handpump; two fruit machines, piped music. In front of the pub are some picnic-table sets, with benches on the verandah. The view from the Barbican across to the pub is lovely. *(Recommended by Brian and Anna Marsden, Brian Jones, Shirley Pielou, Mark Walker, Paul Redgrave, S M P Elford, Caroline and Simon Turner, Dorothee and Dennis Glover, Carol S Addison, Andy McGoldrick, Margaret and Michael Woodhead)*

Ansells (Allied) ~ Manager Mo Law ~ Real ale ~ Lunchtime bar meals and snacks ~ Plymouth (01752) 260930 ~ Children in restaurant ~ Live jazz Sun lunchtime and evening and Thurs evenings, and blues Weds ~ Open 11.30-3, 5-11

Stars after the name of a pub show exceptional quality. One star means most people (after reading the report to see just why the star has been won) would think a special trip worth while. Two stars mean that the pub is really outstanding – many that for their particular qualities cannot be bettered.

nr POSTBRIDGE SX6780 Map 1

Warren House

B3212 1¼ miles NE of Postbridge

Right in the middle of Dartmoor, this remote place has a fire at one end of the bar that is said to have been kept almost continuously alight since 1845, simple furnishings such as easy chairs and settles under a beamed ochre ceiling, wild animal pictures on the partly panelled stone walls, and dim lighting (fuelled by the pub's own generator); even in high season there's quite a local atmosphere as the pub is something of a focus for this scattered moorland community. Bar food includes sandwiches, home-made soup (£1.80), filled baked potatoes (from £2.25), good ploughman's (£3.50), a home-made vegetarian dish (£3.75), home-made pies like steak in ale or chicken (from £5.50), and scampi (£5.75). Well kept Butcombe Bitter, Flowers Original, Gibbs Mew Bishops Tipple, and a guest beer on handpump, farm cider and a range of country wines. Darts, pool, cribbage, dominoes, fruit machine, video game and piped music. This road is worth knowing, as a good little-used route westward through fine scenery. Dogs allowed. *(Recommended by John and Marianne Cooper, John Hazel, R J Walden, Frank Cummins, Mrs Ann Roberts and family, David Gittins)*

Free house ~ Licensee Peter Parsons ~ Real ale ~ Meals and snacks (noon-9.30 in summer) ~ Tavistock (01822) 88208 ~ Children in family room ~ Open 11-11; 11-2.30, 5.30-11 in winter

POUNDSGATE SX7072 Map 1

Tavistock

Off B3380 at SW end of Ashburton; or from central Dartmoor follow B3357 E, keeping on to bear right past Corndon Tor

Over 700 years old, this friendly slated white house has some interesting old features like the narrow-stepped granite spiral staircase, original flagstones, and ancient fireplaces – one with a woodburning stove, the other with logs. Bar food includes home-made soup like lentil, onion and lemon or bean and bacon (£1.70; they always have a vegetarian one), bacon and eggs (£2.25), all-day breakfast (£3.45), hot, spicy beanburger (£2.45), ploughman's (from £2.95), grilled swordfish (£4.95), beef curry (£5.25), lamb steak (£6.45), puddings (from £1.60), and daily specials such as Lyme Bay crab flan or chicken breast stuffed with stilton and bacon and covered with puff pastry. Well kept Courage Best and Ushers Best and Founders from a temperature-controlled cellar, local farm cider, elderflower pressé, and mulled wine and brandied hot chocolate in winter; good welcoming service; darts and fruit machine. The family room was once the stable. In summer the lovely garden behind the pub is a big draw, with prize-winning displays of bedding plants; also, picnic-table sets on the front terrace just above the quiet lane and lots of hanging baskets. *(Recommended by P R Ferris, Derek and Margaret Underwood, Dr and Mrs R E S Tanner, Joan and Gordon Edwards, Jane Palmer, Les and Mavis Law, Derrick and Karen McClelland)*

Ushers ~ Lease: Ken and Janice Comer ~ Real ale ~ Meals and snacks (11.30-2.30, 6-9.30; not 25 Dec) ~ (0136 43) 251 ~ Children in family room ~ Open 11-3, 6-11

RATTERY SX7461 Map 1

Church House

Village signposted from A385 W of Totnes, and A38 S of Buckfastleigh

The spiral stone steps behind a little stone doorway on your left as you go into this ancient place probably date from about 1030. And there are massive oak beams and standing timbers in the homely open-plan bar, as well as large fireplaces (one with a little cosy nook partitioned off around it), Windsor armchairs, comfortable leather bucket seats and window seats, and prints on the plain white walls; the dining room is separated from this room by heavy curtains.

Shandy the golden labrador is very amiable and there's a nice black cat with two white paws. Good bar food includes home-made soup, filled rolls, excellent home-made quiche or home-cooked ham in cider with an egg, smoked salmon platter or chicken Wensleydale (£5.50), Algerian lamb or Indonesian beef (£6.25), home-made puddings and children's dishes. Well kept Furgusons Dartmoor, Ind Coope Burton, and a weekly guest beer on handpump, a range of malt whiskies (up to 40 years old), decent wines, and farm cider; friendly staff and locals. Outside, there are peaceful views of the partly wooded surrounding hills from picnic-table sets on a hedged courtyard by the churchyard. *(Recommended by Neil and Anita Christopher, John and Vivienne Rice, Steve Huggins, Paul and Janet Waring, T Aldworth, Mark and Diane Grist, D J Elliott, A Plumb, Gordon, Alan and Brenda Holyer, John Evans, Dr and Mrs Rackow, Mrs Ann Roberts and family, R W Brooks, Brian Whittaker, John Fazakerley, S V Bishop, C A Hall, Jim and Maggie Cowell)*

Free house ~ Licensees Mr B and Mrs J J Evans ~ Real ale ~ Meals and snacks ~ Buckfastleigh (01364) 642220 ~ Children in dining room and eating area of bar ~ Open 11-2.30, 6-11

SHEEPWASH SS4806 Map 1

Half Moon 🛏 ♀

Off A3072 Holsworthy—Hatherleigh at Highampton

Fishermen enjoy staying in this buff-painted, civilised inn as they have 10 miles of private fishing on the River Torridge (salmon, sea trout and brown trout) as well as a rod room, good drying facilities and a small shop stocking the basic things needed to catch fish. There are lots of fishing pictures on the white walls of the neatly-kept and friendly carpeted main bar, solid old furniture under the beams, and a big log fire fronted by slate flagstones. Lunchtime bar food is attractively straightforward and good, including sandwiches (£1.50, toasties £1.75), home-made soup (£1.75), home-made pasties (£2.50), ploughman's (£2.90) and home-cooked ham salad (£3.50). Well kept Bass, Courage Best, and Worthingtons Best on handpump (well kept in a temperature-controlled cellar), a fine choice of malt whiskies, and an extensive wine list; darts, fruit machine, and separate pool room. *(Recommended by Andrew Low, John and Vivienne Rice, R J Walden, David Gittins, Mr and Mrs J D Marsh)*

Free house ~ Licensees Benjamin Robert Inniss and Charles Inniss ~ Real ale ~ Snacks (lunchtime)~ Evening restaurant ~ Black Torrington (0140 923) 376 ~ Children welcome lunchtime only ~ Open 11.30-2.30, 6-11 ~ Bedrooms: £36.50B/£73.50B

SIDFORD SY1390 Map 1

Blue Ball ★ 🛏 ◧

A3052 just N of Sidmouth

Tables on a terrace outside this 14th-c thatched inn look out over a colourful walled front flower garden, and there are more seats on a bigger back lawn – as well as in a covered area next to the barbecue; safe swing, see-saw and play house for children. Inside, there's a bustling, cheerful atmosphere and quickly served, popular food: sandwiches (from £1.50, good crab £2.30), a generous ploughman's (from £3), omelettes (£4), cheese and asparagus flan (£4.50), salads (from £4.50), home-made steak and kidney pie or beef curry (£5), very good fish pie, daily specials like salmon and prawn thermidor, lamb Dijonnaise or chicken Normandy (from £3.25), and good steaks (from £8.75); puddings (£2), and very good breakfasts (with free papers); cheerful service. The low, partly-panelled well kept lounge bar has heavy beams, upholstered wall benches and Windsor chairs, a lovely winter log fire in the stone fireplace (there are two other open fires as well), and Boddingtons, Devenish Royal Wessex, Flowers IPA, Marstons Pedigree, and a guest beer on handpump, kept well in a temperature-controlled cellar. A plainer public bar has darts, cribbage and a fruit machine; piped music. *(Recommended by Paul and Janet Waring, E V N Whiteway, Eric and Patricia King, Brian A*

Websdale, TOH, David Holloway, Wally Huggins, John and Vivienne Rice, Denzil T Taylor, Wayne Brindle, Deborah and Ian Carrington, B D Jones, Shirley Pielou, Gordon, Helen Flaherty, J L Alperin, D S Beeson, JM, PM, Pat and Roger Fereday, Dr and Mrs Frank Rackow, W T Healey, Marian Greenwood, E M Hughes, Nick Wikeley, Werner Arend, Chris and Chris Vallely)

Devenish ~ Tenant Roger Newton ~ Real ale ~ Meals and snacks (till 10pm; not 25 Dec) ~ Well behaved children in dining room and in family room ~ Sidmouth (01395) 514062 ~ Open 10.30-2.30, 5.30-11 ~ Bedrooms: £22/£36

SLAPTON SX8244 Map 1

Tower 🍺

Signposted off A379 Dartmouth—Kingsbridge

Originally three cottages, this atmospheric old place is run by a knowledgeable landlord who always has time for his customers. There are two open log fires in the low-ceilinged bar, small armchairs, low-backed settles and some furniture made from casks on the flagstones, and evening candlelight; piped music. A good range of real ales might include Badger Tanglefoot, Boddingtons, Gibbs Mew Bishops Tipple, Exmoor Bitter, Wadworths 6X, and Whitbread Castle Eden on handpump, Stancombe cider, good Italian wine by the glass, and malt whiskies. The Italian licensee's pasta dishes are popular – spaghetti bolognese (£4.95), excellent pizzas (from £4.95), broccoli pasta (£5.20), saltimbocca (chicken breast with bacon and cheese, £6.95), steaks, and spaghetti in seafood sauce with crab claws, king prawns and mussells (£11.50). There are picnic-table sets on the neatly kept back lawn, which is overhung by the ivy-covered ruin of a 14th-c chantry. The lane up to the pub is very narrow. *(Recommended by Gordon, A Plumb, David Holloway, Pat and John Millward, W Fletcher, Alan and Heather Jacques, John A Barker, David and Ann Stranack, Natalie Spencer, Simon Forster, Nigel Gibbs, Paul and Gail Betteley, E Money)*

Free house ~ Licensees Keith and Kim Romp, Jan Khan, Carlo Cascianelli ~ Real ale ~ Meals and snacks (not winter Mon) ~ Restaurant ~ Kingsbridge (01548) 580216 ~ Children in family rooms ~ Open 11-2.30(3 Sat), 6-11; closed Mon lunchtime in winter ~ Bedrooms: £17/£34

SOURTON SX5390 Map 1

Highwayman ★

A386 SW of Okehampton; a short detour from the A30

If you let your imagination run riot and tried to dream up a cross between a pub, a fairy-tale and a pirate adventure, you might come up with a pale imitation of this extraordinary place. It doesn't have a lot of the things that people expect from a pub – no real ale and virtually no food – but what it does have is a marvellously well executed fantasy decor that the owners have over the years put great enthusiasm and masses of hard work into. The porch (a pastiche of a nobleman's carriage) leads into a warren of dimly lit stonework and flagstone-floored burrows and alcoves, richly fitted out with red plush seats discreetly cut into the higgledy-piggledy walls, elaborately carved pews, a leather porter's chair, Jacobean-style wicker chairs, and seats in quaintly bulging small-paned bow windows; the ceiling in one part, where there's an array of stuffed animals, gives the impression of being underneath a tree, roots and all. The separate Rita Jones' Locker is a make-believe sailing galleon, full of intricate woodwork and splendid timber baulks, with white antique lace clothed tables in the embrasures that might have held cannons. They only sell keg beer, but specialise in farm cider, and food is confined to a range of meaty and vegetarian pasties (£1); service is warmly welcoming and full of character; old-fashioned penny fruit machine, and 30s, 40s and 50s piped music. Outside, there's a play area in similar style for children with little black-and-white roundabouts like a Victorian fairground, a fairy-tale pumpkin house and an old-lady-who-lived-in-the-shoe house. You can take children in to look around the pub but they can't stay inside. *(Recommended by John Hazel, Paul Weedon, John and Vivienne Rice, Mr and Mrs A K McCully, Barbara and Norman Wells, Jim and Maggie Cowell, Steven Tait, Susie Lovie)*

Free house ~ Licensees Buster and Rita Jones and Sally Thomson ~ Snacks (11-1.45, 6-10) ~ Bridestowe (0183 786) 243 ~ Open 11-2, 6-10.30; closed 25/26 Dec ~ Bedrooms: £36

SOUTH POOL   SX7740   Map 1

Millbrook

Off A379 E of Kingsbridge

When the tide comes in, this tiny pub (one of the smallest in this book) is popular with boating people who make the most of the mooring facilities, and there are seats on the terrace by the stream with its Aylesbury ducks. Inside, the charming little back bar has handsome Windsor chairs, a chintz easy chair, drawings and paintings (and a chart) on its cream walls, clay pipes on the beams, and fresh flowers. Bar food includes home-made soup (£1.65), sandwiches (from £1.90, excellent crab £4), filled baked potatoes (from £2.75), ploughman's (from £3.50), cottage pie (£3.75), vegetable lasagne (£3.85), chilli con carne (£3.85), fish pie (£5.25), and puddings (£2.25). Bass tapped from the 9-gallon cask on the bar, Ruddles Best and John Smiths on handpump, and Churchwards farm ciders; good, friendly service even when busy. Darts and euchre in the public bar. *(Recommended by Mrs J Barwell, Bill Edwards, Mrs Romey Heaton, Natalie Spencer, Simon Forster, E Money, Margaret and Trevor Errington, David and Ann Stranack; more reports please)*

Free house ~ Licensees Arthur and Cindy Spedding ~ Real ale ~ Meals and snacks ~ (01548) 531581 ~ Children in eating area of bar ~ Open 11-3, 5.30-11; 11.30-2.30, 6.30-11 in winter; may open longer in summer to cover high tide; closed evening 25 Dec

SOUTH ZEAL   SX6593   Map 1

Oxenham Arms   ★ ⌂ ♀

Village signposted from A30 at A382 roundabout and B3260 Okehampton turn-off

There's a fine unhurried atmosphere in this friendly, historic inn. It was first licensed in 1477 and has grown up around the remains of a Norman monastery, built here to combat the pagan power of the neolithic standing stone that still forms part of the wall in the family TV room behind the bar (there are actually twenty more feet of stone below the floor). It later became the Dower House of the Burgoynes, whose heiress carried it to the Oxenham family. The beamed and partly panelled front bar has elegant mullioned windows and Stuart fireplaces, and Windsor armchairs around low oak tables and built-in wall seats. The small family room has beams, wheelback chairs around polished tables, decorative plates, and another open fire. Good bar food includes tasty soup (£1.85), sandwiches (from £1.95; the rare roast beef are particularly good), a generous ploughman's (£3.15), fish and chips (from £3.75), salads (from £3.95), tasty home-made steak, kidney, mushroom and Guinness pie (£4.95), grilled local trout (£5.75), and good daily specials such as mixed bean casserole (£3.25), lamb, onion, apple and sultana pie or fresh salmon and broccoli mornay (£4.75). Bass and Furgusons Dartmoor tapped from the cask, and an extensive list of wines including good house claret; darts, shove-ha'penny, dominoes and cribbage. Note the imposing curved stone steps leading up to the garden where there's a sloping spread of lawn. *(Recommended by Myroulla West, Denzil T Taylor, John and Christine Vittoe, Peter and Lynn Brueton, John and Vivienne Rice, Mr and Mrs C R Little, Mike Dickerson, Joan and Gordon Edwards, Mr and Mrs R Copeland, Patrick Clancy, David Holloway, Steve Goodchild, David Gittins, Marion and John Hadfield, DAV, Gordon, Mr and Mrs C R Little, Nigel Flook, Betsy Brown, P and K Lloyd, Heather Robson, W T Healey, Derrick and Karen McLelland; also recommended by The Good Hotel Guide)*

Free house ~ Licensee James Henry ~ Real ale ~ Meals and snacks ~ Restaurant ~ Okehampton (01837) 840244 ~ Children welcome away from bar ~ Open 11-2.30, 6-11 ~ Bedrooms: £40B/£50B

STAVERTON SX7964 Map 1

Sea Trout 🛏

Village signposted from A384 NW of Totnes

Although this well run white-painted country inn is a comfortable place to stay and both the bar and restaurant food is good, it is also very much somewhere that locals like to gather for just a drink and a chat – a good sign. The main bar has low banquettes, soft lighting and an open fire, and the neatly kept rambling beamed lounge bar has cushioned settles and stools, a stag's head above the fireplace, and sea trout and salmon flies and stuffed fish on the walls. There's also a public bar with a pool table, darts, fruit machine and juke box. Reasonably priced, bar food includes home-made soup (£1.50), sandwiches (from £2.10), ploughman's (from £3.25), home-cooked ham and egg (£4.50), mixed grills (from £4.75), smoked haddock and prawn crumble (£4.95), home-made steak and kidney pie (£5.25), local trout (£5.50), salads (from £5.50), and steaks (from £7.95); daily specials, puddings, and good Sunday lunch. Well kept Bass, Furgusons Dartmoor, and Wadworths 6X on handpump or tapped from the cask with guests like Brakspears, Fullers London Pride and Palmers IPA; friendly, attentive staff. There are seats under parasols in the garden. The Mogford family now also run Court Farm, Abbotskerswell. A station for the Torbay Steam Railway is not far away. *(Recommended by Alan and Brenda Holyer, Joan and Gordon Edwards, Mr and Mrs A K McCully, J H Bell, Dennis Heatley, Quentin Williamson, Doug Kennedy, Don and Thelma Beeson, Robert and Gladys Flux, June and Tony Baldwin)*

Free house ~ Licensees Andrew and Pym Mogford ~ Real ale ~ Meals and snacks ~ Restaurant ~ Staverton (01803) 762274 ~ Children in eating area of bar if over 6 ~ Open 11-3, 6-11 ~ Bedrooms: £39.50B/£48B

STOCKLAND ST2404 Map 1

Kings Arms 🍴 🛏 🍷

Village signposted from A30 Honiton—Chard

People come from miles around to this friendly 16th-c pub to enjoy the first-class, home-made food served in the dark beamed, elegant dining lounge with its solid refectory tables, attractive landscapes, medieval oak screen (which divides the room into two), and great stone fireplace across almost the whole width of one end. At lunchtime, bar food includes sandwiches (from £1.50), soup (£2), burgers (from £1.75), ploughman's or sausage and mash with onion gravy (£3.50), omelettes or pancakes (from £3.50), steak and kidney pie (£4.50), salads (from £5), gammon and egg (£5.50), and children's dishes (from £1.25); in the evening there might be moules marinières (£3.50), pacific prawns in garlic sauce (£4.50), tandoori chicken masala (£7.50), rack of lamb (£8.50), fillets of dab with crabmeat (£9.50), and half a roast duck (£10.50), and puddings or cheese (£3); booking is essential; hearty breakfasts. Well kept Badger Best, Exmoor Bitter, Ruddles County, and John Smiths on handpump, imported lager on draught, over 40 island malt whiskies, and a good wine list that includes house wines and special offers by the bottle or glass chalked up on a board. At the back, a flagstoned bar has leatherette chairs and seats built into the stripped high dado of its bare stone walls; it leads on to a carpeted darts room with two boards, another room with dark beige plush armchairs and settees (and a fruit machine), and a neat ten-pin skittle alley; table skittles, cribbage, dominoes, video game, and mainly piped classical music. They have tug-of-war training night on Sunday (they are county champions at top weight), ladies' league skittles/quiz evening on Monday (for the 2nd year running they are county champions), occasional skittles on Tuesday, and men's league skittles Wednesday, Thursday and Friday; the Stockland Fair is held on Whitsun Bank Holiday Monday. There are tables under cocktail parasols on the terrace in front of the white-faced thatched pub. Well behaved dogs allowed. *(Recommended by John and Fiona Merritt, Mr and Mrs D T Deas, R James, Mrs J M Corless, Marion and John Hadfield, Gordon, LJBH, Pat and Robert Watt, J Dobson, J I Fraser, Michael A Butler, R J Walden, Steve Tasker, Eric and Patricia King, Mrs K Jeal, Chris and Eleri Richards, Lawrence Pearse)*

Free house ~ Licensees Heinz Kiefer and Paul Diviani ~ Real ale ~ Snacks (lunchtime) and meals; not Sun lunchtime ~ Restaurant ~ Stockland (01404) 881361 ~ Well behaved/supervised children in eating area of bar and in restaurant ~ Lyme Bay folk club first Sat in month, varied music every Sun ~ Open 12-3, 6.30-11; on 25 Dec only open 11-1 ~ Bedrooms: £20B/£30B

STOKE FLEMING SX8648 Map 1

Green Dragon ♀

Church Rd; turning off A379 in village, which is S of Dartmouth

This relaxed and very informal pub is run by Peter Crowther the successful long-distance yachtsman – now a bit closer to the sea than when he was making the Weld Arms, East Lulworth (Dorset) so popular with readers. The beamed main part of the bar, busy with young locals on our visit, has two small settles, bay window seats, boat pictures, and maybe Electra or Maia the young Burmese cats, while down on the right is an area with throws and cushions on battered sofas and armchairs, a few books (20p to RNLI), adult board games, fruit machine, the case of a grandfather clock, a wringer, and cuttings about the landlord and maps of his races on the walls. Down some steps is the Mess Deck decorated with lots of ensigns and flags, and there's a playbox of children's games. Home-made bar food includes soup (£1.70), sandwiches (from £1.80), ploughman's with three cheeses (£3), chicken and mushroom pancakes, pasta au gratin or Italian meatloaf (£4.50), salmon roulade (£5.10), and puddings like chocolate whisky cake or treacle tart (£2.20); they do Sunday breakfasts between 9 and 11am. Well kept Bass, Boddingtons, Eldridge Pope Royal Oak, and Flowers IPA on handpump, big glasses of six good house wines from Australia, California, France and Germany, Addlestones cider, and a good range of spirits; you can take the beer away with you. There's a back garden with swings, a climbing frame and picnic-table sets and a front terrace with some white plastic garden tables and chairs. The tall church tower opposite is interesting. *(Recommended by A Plumb)*

Heavitree (who no longer brew) ~ Tenants Peter and Alix Crowther ~ Real ale ~ Meals and snacks (not winter Sun evenings) ~ (01803) 770238 ~ Children welcome ~ Open 11-2.30, 5.30-11; closed evening 25 Dec

STOKE GABRIEL SX8457 Map 1

Church House ★

Village signposted from A385 just W of junction with A3022, in Collaton St Mary; can also be reached from nearer Totnes; nearby parking not easy

Full of warmth and character, this popular early 14th-c pub is still leased from the church. The lounge bar has window seats cut into the thick butter-coloured walls, a black oak partition wall, an exceptionally attractive medieval beam and plank ceiling, a huge fireplace still used in winter to cook the stew, and decorative plates and vases of flowers on a dresser. The mummified cat in a case, probably about 200 years old, was found during restoration of the roof space in the verger's cottage three doors up the lane – one of a handful found in the West Country and believed to have been a talisman against evil spirits. Home-made bar food includes soup (£1.45), a huge choice of sandwiches and toasties (from £1.65; local drab £3.25), filled baked potatoes (from £2.35), ploughman's (from £3.25), daily specials like fresh Dart salmon, various platters, and steak and kidney in ale pie, and puddings (from £1.95); well kept Bass and Worthington Best on handpump, quite a few malt whiskies, and farm cider. Darts, cribbage and fruit machine in the little public locals' bar; piped music. There are picnic-table sets on the little terrace in front of the building. No children. *(Recommended by Mr and Mrs A K McCully, Bill and Beryl Farmer, E B Davies, T Aldworth, June and Tony Baldwin, Barry and Anne, E Money)*

Free house ~ Licensee Glyn Patch ~ Real ale ~ Meals and snacks (11-2.30, 6.30-9.45) ~ Stoke Gabriel (01803) 782384 ~ Open 11-3.30, 6-11; 11-11 Sat

STOKENHAM SX8042 Map 1

Church House ♀

Just off A379 Dartmouth—Kingsbridge

This well-run spacious pub – in lovely countryside – is a good place for families. The family room is well stocked with books and toys, and the carefully planted, attractive garden has a play area, swings, a slide and tame chipmunks (Alvin, Theodore and Simon); there are lots of tables and a fish pond, and they play aunt sally (very far from its Oxfordshire home). Three rambling open-plan areas connected by archways have a bustling atmosphere and bar food such as seven fresh local fish dishes (from £4.75), lasagne or steak and Guinness pie (£4.95), monkfish thermidor (£8.95), and fruits de mer with mussels, crab, shrimps, prawns and salmon (£9.95). Their curries are hot, and they use good fresh vegetables, including some own-grown ones. Booking's essential for the popular Sunday roast; part of the restaurant is no smoking. Well kept Bass, Eldridge Pope Hardy and Flowers Original on handpump, kept under light blanket pressure, Paington farm cider, and decent house wines; friendly and helpful staff, under the amiable eye of the caring landlord; darts, fruit machine and unobtrusive piped music. *(Recommended by T Aldworth, P and J Shapley, Norman Evans, Andrew and Teresa Heffer)*

Heavitree (who no longer brew) ~ Tenants Jon and Christine Godfrey ~ Real ale ~ Meals and snacks (all day in summer; 11-2.30, 6-9.30 in winter) ~ Restaurant ~ (01548) 580253 ~ Children in family room and eating area of bar, and in restaurant (where under 8s must be gone by 7pm) ~ Open 11-11; 11-3, 6-11 in winter

TIPTON ST JOHN SY0991 Map 1

Golden Lion 🛏

Pub signposted off B3176 Sidmouth—Ottery St Mary

The friendly licensees have been running this bustling village pub for 24 years now. It's a popular place with locals and visitors, and the softly-lit bar is decorated with lots of guns, little kegs, a brass cauldron and other brassware, bottles and jars along a delft shelf, and plenty of fresh flowers; there's also a comfortable old settee, red leatherette built-in wall banquettes, an attractive gothick carved box settle, a carved dresser, a longcase clock, and an open fire. Good bar food includes soup (£1.40), sandwiches (from £2.20), ploughman's (from £3.25), vegetarian chilli (£3.95), home-made dishes such as quiche (£3.95) or lasagne (£4.30), salads (from £4.65; seafood £7.95), steak and kidney pie (£4.85), tipsy pork with mushrooms and cream sauce (£7.25), steaks (from £7.95), and puddings like excellent gooseberry and apple crumble with clotted cream (from £2); daily specials like chicken livers with bacon (£3.15), wild rabbit in grain-mustard pie (£4.75), marinated fillet of lamb (£7.95), fresh fish dishes, and breast of duck with chestnuts (£9.25). The restaurant and children's area are no smoking. Well kept Bass, Boddingtons, Eldridge Pope Hardy and Whitbreads Castle Eden on handpump, Inch's cider, fresh local apple juice, a comprehensive wine list, and fruit wines; darts, dominoes, shove-ha'penny, and piped music. There are pretty summer hanging baskets, a few picnic-table sets on the side lawn, a pretty walled area, and a terrace. *(Recommended by Mark and Heather Williamson, B D Jones, Alan A Newman, Denzil T Taylor, J I Fraser, Eric and Patricia King, David Holloway, Mrs J M Corless, Derek Clarke, E H and R F Warner, Keith Stevens, Robert and Gladys Flux, Dr P D Putwain)*

Heavitree (who no longer brew) ~ Tenants Colin and Carolyn Radford ~ Real ale ~ Meals and snacks ~ Small restaurant ~ Ottery St Mary (01404) 812881 ~ Children in small area next to bar; must be over 7 in evening ~ Open 11-3(4 Sat), 6-11 ~ Two bedrooms: £20.56S/£41.12S

Please let us know up-to-date food prices when you report on pubs.

TOPSHAM SX9688 Map 1

Bridge 🍺

2¼ miles from M5 junction 30: Topsham signposted from exit roundabout; in Topsham follow signpost (A376) Exmouth on the Elmgrove Road

Tapped from the cask in the cosy no-smoking inner sanctum where only the most regular of regulars sit, the marvellous choice of real ales in this unchanging ex-maltings might include Adnams Broadside, Badger Tanglefoot, Barrons Devon Glory, Bass, Branscombe Vale Branoc (see Fountain Head, Branscombe), Eldridge Pope Royal Oak, Gibbs Mew Bishops Tipple, Marstons Owd Rodger, Theakstons Old Peculier, and Wadworths 6X. The little no-smoking parlour, partitioned off from an inner corridor with leaded lights let into the curved high back of one settle, is decorated with a booming grandfather clock, crossed guns, swords, country pictures and rowing cartoons, and mugs hanging from the beams; a bigger room is opened at busy times. Food is confined to pasties (90p), sandwiches (£1.40) and ploughman's (from £2.50). *(Recommended by J I Fraser, Jim and Maggie Cowell, Wayne Brindle, Mark Grist, W T Healey, Graham Reeve, Phil and Sally Gorton; more reports please)*

Free house ~ Licensee Mrs Phyllis Cheffers ~ Real ale ~ Lunchtime snacks ~ (01392) 873862 ~ Children in eating area of bar ~ Open 12-2, 6-10.30 (11 Fri and Sat)

Passage

2 miles from M5 junction 30: Topsham signposted from exit roundabout; in Topsham, turn right into Follett Road just before centre, then turn left into Ferry Road

In a delightful waterside setting, this attractive pub is an enjoyable place to enjoy very good fresh local fish: fresh mussels (in season, £3.50), pollock, grilled monkfish, lemon sole, Dover sole, turbot, cod, halibut, crab and so forth (£4.95-£10); other food includes filled rolls (from £1.50), ploughman's (£3.50), platters (from £3.75; crab and prawn £3.75), ham and eggs or vegetable lasagne (£3.95), 4oz rump steak (£5.95), and puddings. Well kept Bass, Eldridge Pope Hardy, Flowers IPA, and Marstons Pedigree on handpump. The traditional bar has leatherette wall pews and bar stools and is decorated with electrified oil lamps hanging from big black oak beams in the ochre ceiling; plank panelling and crazy-paving flagstones in one room; fruit machine and piped music. The front courtyard has benches and tables, and there are more seats down on the quiet shoreside terrace. No children. *(Recommended by Howard and Margaret Buchanan, Eric and Patricia King, John and Vivienne Rice, A E and P McCully, Wayne Brindle, Marian Greenwood, Werner Arend)*

Heavitree (who no longer brew) ~ Licensee David Evans ~ Real ale ~ Meals and snacks (till closing time) ~ Restaurant (not Sun evening) ~ Topsham (01392) 873653 ~ Parking can be a problem ~ Open 11-11

TORBRYAN SX8266 Map 1

Old Church House

Most easily reached from A381 Newton Abbot—Totnes via Ipplepen

The bar on the right of the door in this atmospheric and ancient inn is particularly attractive, and has benches built into the fine old panelling as well as the cushioned high-backed settle and leather-backed small seats around its big log fire. On the left there are a series of comfortable and discreetly lit lounges, one with a splendid deep Tudor inglenook fireplace with a side bread oven. There's quite a lot of emphasis on the large choice of bar food – which might include sandwiches, home-made soup (£1.95), prawn and mushroom crêpe (£3.25), whole plaice (£4.95), mixed cold meat platter (£5.95), fresh local trout and seafood or gammon and sweet and sour sauce (£6.95), seafood platter (£7.45), local pheasant (£8.65), and daily specials such as liver and bacon, steak and kidney pie or breast of chicken in blue cheese sauce (£4.95). Well kept Brains Dark Mild, Flowers IPA and Original, maybe two beers named for the pub on handpump or tapped from the cask, and fruit wines; piped music. *(Recommended by Ian Phillips, Patrick Clancy, Gordon, Steve Huggins, P and J Shapley)*

Free house ~ Licensee Eric Pimm ~ Real ale ~ Meals and snacks (till 10pm) ~ Restaurant ~ Ipplepen (01803) 812372 ~ Children welcome away from bar ~ Open 12-2.30, 6-11; winter evening opening 7pm ~ Bedrooms: £30B/£55B

TORCROSS SX8241 Map 1

Start Bay ⊕

A379 S of Dartmouth

It would be hard to find fresher fish than that served in this extremely popular thatched 14th-c pub. Often caught by the landlord and manager, there might be lovely cod and haddock in three sizes – medium (£3.70), large (£4.80) and jumbo (£5.90 – truly enormous), plaice in two sizes – medium (£3.70) and large (£4.95), and there's also skate (£4.95), excellent crab (from £6.75), giant prawns in garlic butter, and superb lemon sole. Other food includes sandwiches, burgers or sausages, gammon (£5.25), T-bone steaks (£9.95), puddings (from £1.75), and daily specials; they warn of delays at peak times (and you will probably have to wait for a table), though service is organised and efficient. Well kept Bass and Flowers IPA and Original on handpump, Addlestones cider, and Luscombe's fresh apple juice. The unassuming – and often very busy – main bar has photographs of storms buffeting the pub and country pictures on its cream walls, wheelback chairs around plenty of dark tables or (round a corner) back-to-back settles forming booths, and a winter coal fire; a small chatty drinking area by the counter has a brass ship's clock and barometer; one area is no smoking as is part of the family room. The good winter games room has pool, darts, shove-ha'penny, dominoes, fruit machine, video game and juke box; there's more booth seating in a family room with sailing boat pictures. Fruit machine in the lobby. On the terrace are some picnic-table sets looking out over the three-mile pebble beach. The freshwater wildlife lagoon of Slapton Ley is just behind the pub. *(Recommended by Alan and Brenda Holyer, C J Pratt, John and Vivienne Rice, Paul and Gail Betteley, Alan and Heather Jacques, Mrs M C Barrett, Stephen and Jean Curtis, Nigel Gibbs, Natalie Spencer, Simon Forster, Brian and Gill Hopkins, Don and Thelma Beeson, David and Ann Stranack, M V and J Melling, Jo Rees, Andrew and Teresa Heffer, David Wallington)*

Heavitree (who no longer brew; Whitbreads tie) ~ Tenant Paul Stubbs ~ Real ale ~ Meals and snacks (11.30-2, 6-10; not evening 25 Dec) ~ (01548) 580553 ~ Children in family room ~ Open 11.30-2.30, 6-11; closed evening 25 Dec

TORRINGTON SS4919 Map 1

Black Horse ⇔ £

High St

One of the oldest inns in North Devon, this pretty twin-gabled place is popular for its generously served, good value food: sandwiches (from £1; triple decker with toasted bread and chips £2.45), filled baked potatoes (from £1.50), ploughman's (from £2.65; the stilton is excellent), salads (from £2.65), good home-made chicken and mushroom pie (£2.95), vegetable lasagne (£3.40), chilli con carne or home-made steak and kidney pie (£3.45), steaks (from £6.85), good value daily specials, children's dishes (from £1.70), promptly served Sunday roast lunch, and good vegetables. Well kept Courage Directors, John Smiths, Ushers Best, Wadworths 6X and a regular changing guest beer. The bar on the left has an oak counter, a couple of fat black beams hung with stirrups, a comfortable seat running right along its full-width window, and chunky elm tables; on the right, a lounge has a striking ancient black oak partition wall, a couple of attractive oak seats, muted plush easy chairs and a settee. The restaurant is oak-panelled; darts, shove-ha'penny, cribbage, dominoes, fruit machine, trivia, and well reproduced piped music; friendly cat and dogs. Handy for the RHS Rosemoor garden and Dartington Crystal. *(Recommended by R J Walden, K H*

Frostick, Gerry Hollington, Nigel Chapman, Joy Heatherley, David Holloway, Rita Horridge, Carol and Mike Muston, David Watson, C J Westmoreland, Clare Carpenter, Nicholas H Smith)

Ushers ~ Lease: David and Val Sawyer ~ Real ale ~ Meals and snacks (not Sun evening) ~ Restaurant (not Sun evening) ~ Torrington (01805) 22121 ~ Children in lounge and in restaurant ~ Open 11-3, 6(6.30 Sat)-11 ~ Bedrooms: £16B/£28B

TOTNES SX8060 Map 1

Kingsbridge Inn 🍴 ♀

9 Leechwell St; going up the old town's main one-way street, bear left into Leechwell St approaching the top

Mentioned in Domesday Book, this ancient pub is popular for its good, often interesting home-made bar food – they use fresh local produce, and the only frozen things are chips and peas: sandwiches (from £1.75), soup such as chicken, leek and celery or gazpacho (from £1.50), sesame-topped french sticks (from £2), very good Welsh rarebit (£2.50), excellent platters with home-made pickle (from £3.75), Turkish-style stuffed aubergine or sweet and sour pork (£4.95), local wild rabbit and prune pie (£5.95), chicken breast with hazelnut cream sauce (£6.75), evening dishes like nut roast with peanut and ginger sauce (£4.95), trout teryaki (£6.25), and steaks (from £8.80), and puddings like summer pudding or lemon meringue pie (£2.30); they have home-pickled free range eggs on the bar. Bass, Courage Best, Furgusons Dartmoor, Theakstons Old Peculier, and a guest beer on handpump, up to a dozen good wines by the glass, Luscombe cider, organic apple juice, fresh orange juice, summer coolers and winter mulled wine, herbal teas and cappuccino or espresso coffee; pleasant service. The low-beamed rambling bar has an elaborately carved bench in one intimate little alcove, comfortable peach plush seats and wheelbacks around rustic tables on the clover and peach carpet, broad stripped plank panelling, and bare stone or black and white timbering; also, an antique water pump, a log-effect gas fire, and magazines and newspapers to read; shove-ha'penny. A small area above the bar (usually reserved by diners) is no smoking. Nearby ancient Leechwells is worth the walk down and back up steep hill (reputed to have healing properties). Dogs allowed (on a lead). *(Recommended by C J Pratt, Paul Newman, June and Tony Baldwin, Joy Heatherley, Alan and Brenda Holyer, P and·J Shapley, Peter Pocklington, John Wilson, D I Baddeley, Gordon, S V Bishop, E Money, Rita and David Simons, David Wallington, Barry and Anne, Nigel Gibbs)*

Free house ~ Licensees Rosemary Triggs, Martyn and Jane Canevali ~ Real ale ~ Meals and snacks (not 25 Dec or evening 31 Dec) ~ (01803) 863324 ~ Children in eating area of bar ~ Local groups Weds evening ~ Open 11-2.30, 5.30-11; closed 25 Dec

TRUSHAM SX8582 Map 1

Cridford Inn 🍴 ♀ 🛏

Village and pub signposted from B3193 NW of Chudleigh, just N of big ARC works; 1½ very narrow miles

During recent renovations, the licensees have discovered quite a lot about this friendly pub's history. It was originally built in 825 and rebuilt as a safe religious house in 1081, and mentioned in Domesday Book as belonging to Buckfast Abbey in the Manor of Trusham. During rethatching the original Norman roof was discovered, which is possibly the only one in England – and the very early medieval transept window in the bar is said to be the oldest domestic window in Britain and is Grade I listed. The atmospheric bar has cushioned window seats, pews and chapel chairs around kitchen and pub tables, stout standing timbers, natural stone walls, flagstones, and a big woodburning stove in the stone fireplace. Bar food (all home-made and using no frozen or pre-cooked food) is very good – fish comes from Brixham, cheeses from Ticklemoor, the game is local, and they have their own smokehouse. Mr Hesmondhalgh does the cooking which might include lunchtime sandwiches (from £1.85), delicious orange and parsnip or cauliflower and stilton soup (£2), lovely smoked salmon, pâté like chicken and pork with Cumberland sauce or marvellous cream cheese and walnut (£3.85), lovely pasta with a rich garlic, tomato and mushroom sauce or excellent tuna, prawn and pasta bake (£4.50), fresh fish and chips (£4.75), ploughman's (£4.95), steak and kidney pie (£5.50), cajun chicken (£6.75), sirloin steak (£9.75), puddings (£3), and daily specials such as lentil and mushroom bake, chicken with apricots and cider, and fresh fish as available (mullet, bream, sole, monkfish); children's meals (£3.75). They hold theme evenings in winter (October-March), and summer barbecues with a Sunday evening accordionist; the no-smoking restaurant has a mosaic date stone showing 1081 and the initials of the then Abbot of Buckfastleigh. Well kept Adnams Broadside, Bass, Cotleigh Old Buzzard, and a beer they call Trusham Bitter on handpump, a good wine list as well as wines of the month, local Brimblecombe cider, and country wines. The cats are called Smudge and Sophie, the Jack Russells Patch and Jack, and the 20-year-old labrador, Sam; piped music. The suntrap front terrace has some seats. *Recommended by Joan and Gordon Edwards, Miss A Battye, John Allsopp, Richard Armstead, Alan and Rose Hogg, R Rawlings, Steve Huggins, Mr and Mrs R P Begg, Dr Monica Nurnberg, Mrs N Mendelssohn, B M J Ambrose)*

Free house ~ Licensees David and Sally Hesmondhalgh ~ Real ale ~ Meals and snacks (not Mon – except bank holidays) ~ Evening restaurant (closed Sun and Mon) ~ Chudleigh (01626) 853694 ~ Children in top bar but must be gone by 8.30pm ~ Open 11.30-2.30, 6.15-11; closed Mon (except bank holidays, when they then close the following Weds) and 25 Dec ~ Bedrooms: £35B/£50B

TUCKENHAY SX8156 Map 1

Floyds Inn (Sometimes) 🍴

Take Ashprington road out of Totnes (signed left off A381 on outskirts), keeping on past Watermans Arms

By a peaceful wooded creek, this well known dining pub is obviously popular for its excellent food – which to make the most of, you would really have to eat in the light and airy downstairs restaurant. In the bar there might be a choice of cheeses (£8.50), corned beef hash with poached egg (£9.50), fish and chips with mushy peas or poached salmon (£10.50), liver and bacon or Thai red duck curry (£12.50), squid ink pasta with seafood (£13), grilled sirloin steak (£16), and puddings like sticky toffee pudding, tiramisu or bakewell tart (from £5). While prices might strike some as outlandish, others feel the cooking's good enough to justify it. Bass, Blackawton, Exmoor Bitter, and Furgusons Dartmoor on handpump, decent wines, over 60 malt whiskies, and Luscombe farm cider. The long, narrow bar with its stools, fishing rods on the ceiling, and jars of cockles, pickled eggs, mint imperials and jelly babies on the counter links the two other rooms. At one end is a snug little room with a couple of fat leather armchairs, a sofa, other chairs and small tables, some stuffed fish and fish prints, fishing books, and a fire. At the other end (on the left of the door as you go in) there are red-painted vertical panelled seats and stripped kitchen tables on the wooden floor, more fish prints, and a model sailing ship over the log fire; juke box. There are creekside tables and popular summer barbecues, and you can reach the pub by boat. *(Recommended by Mrs J Barwell, Mrs S Smith, Jim and Maggie Cowell, A Plumb, Mrs S Segrove, John and Fiona Merritt, David Wallington, S V Bishop, Brian and Gill Hopkins, Richard Carpenter)*

Free house ~ Licensee Keith Floyd ~ Real ale ~ Meals and snacks ~ Restaurant ~ Harbertonford (01803) 732350 ~ Live music Sun evening ~ Children in eating area of bar ~ Open 10.30-3.30, 5.30-11

The knife-and-fork symbol distinguishes pubs where the food is of exceptional quality.

UGBOROUGH SX6755 Map 1

Anchor

Off A3121 – village signposted from A38 W of South Brent

The good, popular food plays an important role in this friendly village pub. As well as holding theme nights for Halloween, Beaujolais Nouveau, an Autumn game festival and so forth, bar food might include tasty home-made soup (£2), filled long hot crusty rolls (from £2.25), omelettes (from £3), ploughman's (from £2.85), pizzas (from £4), pasta dishes (from £3.80), salads (from £3.85), vegetarian dishes (£4.65), good pork fillet in stilton sauce, steak and kidney pie (£5.30), gammon (£5.80), and children's dishes (from £2.25). The oak-beamed public bar has wall settles and seats around the wooden tables on the polished woodblock floor, and a log fire in its stone fireplace; there are Windsor armchairs in the comfortable dining lounge. Well kept Bass, Wadworths 6X and guests like Eldridge Pope Royal Oak or Fullers London Pride on handpump or tapped from the cask, several malt whiskies, 8 ports, and a decent wine list; courteous service. Darts, shove-ha'penny, cribbage, dominoes, fruit machine, trivia and piped music. There are seats in the garden. This is an attractive village, unusual for its spacious central square. *(Recommended by Mr and Mrs Hart, Garth Redgrave, A E Brace, Roger Berry, Gordon, John A Barker)*

Free house ~ Licensees Sheelagh and Ken Jeffreys-Simmons ~ Real ale ~ Meals and snacks (till 10pm) ~ Restaurant ~ Plymouth (01752) 892283 ~ Children welcome ~ Live folk/jazz/70s music Mon/Thurs/some Sats ~ Open 11-3, 6-10.30; 10-3.30, 6-11 Sat ~ Bedrooms: £25B/£40B

WELCOME SS2217 Map 1

Old Smithy

Village signposted from A39 S of Harland; pub signposted left at fork; in hamlet of Darracott

Off the beaten track in a lovely rural setting, this friendly pub has a pretty, terraced, sheltered garden with plenty of seats, as well as three kinds of owls (they participate in an owl rescue service, for rehabilitation and release), chickens, ducks, horses, sheep and goats; the lane going past leads eventually to parking down by Welcombe Mouth, an attractive rocky cove. The open-plan bar has log fires at both ends of the room, button-back banquettes and wheelback chairs and little snug windows; the restaurant was once the old forge; piped music. Quickly served, straightforward food includes sandwiches, lasagne (£4.25), vegetarian dishes (£4.95), and steaks (£7.50); they also have a no-smoking tea shop (12.30-6.30) and a gift shop. Well kept Butcombe and Marstons Pedigree on handpump. Darts, fruit machine and piped music. *(Recommended by Robin and Molly Taylor, R J Walden, S R and A J Ashcroft, Jeff Davies, Dave Braisted, John LeSage, Tim Barrow, Sue Demont, Mrs Ann Saunders, Derrick and Karen McClelland)*

Free house ~ Licensees Geoff and Sandra Marshall ~ Real ale ~ Meals and snacks ~ Morwenstow (01288) 331305 ~ Children welcome ~ Open 11-11; 12-3, 7-11 in winter; closed Tues and Weds Nov-March ~ Bedrooms: £20(£20B)/£35(£39B)

WESTON ST1200 Map 1

Otter 🍽 ♀

Village signposted off A30 at W end of Honiton bypass

There's a good relaxed atmosphere in the very low-beamed main bar of this attractive white-painted, black-shuttered pub – as well as chamberpots and jugs hanging from beams, comfortable chairs by the log fire that stays alight right through from autumn to spring, an interesting mix of polished wooden antique tables and wooden chairs, handsome chapel pews, and candles in bottles; each day a page of the Bible on the lectern that ends one pew is turned, and there's lots of attractive bric-a-brac such as some formidable arms and armour, horse collar and bits, quite a few pictures, and an old mangle; a veritable library leads off, with quite a few readable books and magazines, as well as board games, darts, shove-ha'penny, cribbage, dominoes, pinball, a fruit machine, video game, trivia and piped music; pool and skittle alley, too. Good value food includes home-made soup (£1.85), sandwiches (from £1.70), filled baked potatoes (from £2.35), creamy cheese terrine with fresh home-made cranberry and orange chutney (£2.90), pancake filled with duck and asparagus with a Grand Marnier glaze (£3.80), magnificent ploughman's or local sausages (£3.95), honey-roast chicken (£4.15), spinach, cheese and almond flan (£4.65), steak and kidney pudding (£4.95), and daily specials such as superb rack of lamb or excellent roast guinea fowl, fresh brill fillet with chive and lime sauce (£8.50), beef olives in a mustard and mushroom sauce (£8.75), and pan-fried fresh venison in a peppered sauce (£9.50). They're good to children, with high chairs, a children's menu (£2.50) with a picture to colour and free lollipop, a box of toys, rocking-horse, and a bike. Well kept Bass, Boddingtons, Flowers IPA, and Eldridge Pope Hardy on handpump, good inexpensive wines, and farm cider. There are pretty climbing plants, hanging baskets and flowering tubs, and the sizeable lawn, with picnic-table sets and swings, runs down to the little River Otter which is quite safe for paddling in the summer; lots of ducks congregate at feeding time and the animal sanctuary has free-ranging cockerels, hens, rabbits and guinea-pigs. *(Recommended by Desmond and Pat Morris, Mrs J Blake, E V M Whiteway, T Buckley, L Knight, Peter and Audrey Dowsett, Richard Dolphin, Gordon, Mr and Mrs P J Murphy, Graham Reeve, David Carrington, R M Sparkes)*

Free house ~ Lease: Brian and Susan Wilkinson ~ Real ale ~ Meals and snacks (till 10pm; not 25 Dec) ~ (01404) 42594 ~ Children welcome ~ Occasional live entertainment ~ Open 11-3, 6-11; only 11-1 on 25 Dec

WOODBURY SALTERTON SY0189 Map 1

Diggers Rest ★

3½ miles from M5 junction 30: A3052 towards Sidmouth, village signposted on right about ½ mile after Clyst St Mary; also signposted from B3179 SE of Exeter

This used to be called the Salterton Arms, but when WWII Australian troops were stationed nearby and used it as their local, the name was changed. It's a very welcoming and cosy thatched village pub that has been run by the present licensees for over 21 years. There are comfortable old-fashioned country chairs and settles around polished antique tables, a dark oak Jacobean screen, a grandfather clock, heavy black oak beams, plates decorating the walls of one alcove, and a log fire at one end of the bar with an ornate solid fuel stove at the other. The big skittles alley is popular with families and is open for them in July and August, and there's a games room with pool. Well kept Bass, Furgusons Dartmoor, and Tetleys on ancient handpumps, and local farm ciders; sensibly placed darts and dominoes in the small brick-walled public bar. Good bar food includes home-made soup (£1.55), sandwiches with home-cooked meats (from £2.75; local crab £3.25), ploughman's (£4.25), home-made curry or home-cooked beef with chips (£4.25), salads (from £5.95), steaks (from £8.45), daily specials such as cod and prawn crêpes or liver and bacon (£4.25), steak and kidney pie (£4.75), gammon and egg (£6.95), and puddings (£2.25); vegetables are fresh. The terrace garden has views of the countryside. *(Recommended by John and Vivienne Rice, B D Jones, E V M Whiteway, Peter and Lynn Brueton, J E Davies, Helen Flaherty, John Beeken, J I Fraser, Anthony Barnes, Robert and Gladys Flux, E Money)*

Free house ~ Licensee Sally Pratt ~ Real ale ~ Meals and snacks (12-1.45, 7-10) ~ (01395) 232375 ~ Well behaved children in family area ~ Open 11-2.30, 6.30-11; closed evenings 25/26 Dec

---

Ideas for a country day out? We list pubs in really attractive scenery at the back of the book – and there are separate lists for waterside pubs, ones with really good gardens, and ones with lovely views.

Lucky Dip

Besides the fully inspected pubs, you might like to try these Lucky Dips recommended to us and described by readers (if you do, please send us reports):

Abbotskerswell [SX8569], *Butchers Arms*: Relaxing old pub with well kept Eldridge Pope and Whitbreads, pleasant nooks and corners *(Steve Huggins, P Corris)*

☆ **Appledore** [Irsha St; SS4630], *Royal George*: Fantastic views over Taw/Torridge estuary in homely pub with understated emphasis on good fresh food inc local fish, good value Sun roasts; welcoming local atmosphere in unspoilt old bars, well kept Bass and Wadworths 6X, attractive pictures *(Mr and Mrs J D Marsh, David Avery, Chris Westmoreland, Nigel and Lindsay Chapman, Mr and Mrs N Hazzard)*

Appledore [Irsha St], *Beaver*: Superb setting overlooking Taw/Torridge estuaries, friendly professional staff, well kept beers, good food, separate games room *(A Cull)*; *Seagate*: Friendly, good food, fantastic views; bedrooms pretty and good value *(Mary Reed, Rowly Pitcher)*

☆ **Ashburton** [West St; SX7569], *Exeter*: Friendly old-fashioned pub with well kept Courage-related ales, good value food *(John and Tessa Rainsford)*

Ashburton [East St], *Red Lion*: Taken over towards the end of 1993 by promising landlord with good track record at other Devon pubs which have done well in the GPG; should be one to watch

☆ **AvonWick** [B3210 ½ mile from A38; SX7157], *Mill*: Pretty converted mill with play area in big lakeside garden, popular carvery restaurant, friendly service, wide choice of good value bar food in big helpings inc children's helpings (they have high chairs), Bass on handpump *(John Evans)*

☆ **Axmouth** [SY2591], *Ship*: Very civilised and comfortable, with pleasant service, nice atmosphere, lovely fresh local fish and game, good wine and coffee, well kept Whitbreads-related real ales, friendly staff and samoyeds, lots of embroidered folk dolls; attractive garden with sanctuary for convalescent owls *(W C M Jones, LYM)*

Aylesbeare [SY0393], *Aylesbeare Inn*: Friendly local with rabbit-filled garden, friendly staff, well kept Ushers and big helpings of food *(Nick Barber, Ann Jacklin)*

Babbacombe [112 Babbacombe Rd; A379 Torquay—Teignmouth; SX9365], *Masons Arms*: Atmospheric 3-room bar with stripped stone and panelling, good food from talented young chef, well kept Boddingtons, Theakstons XB and Wadworths 6X; very busy evenings *(John Allsopp)*

nr Barnstaple [Pilton; SS5433], *Ring of Bells*: Small, cosy village pub off main tourist path, very handy for Marwood Hill Gardens; relaxing dining area, good food and service, sensible prices, good friendly landlord *(K R Harris, J M Pyle)*

☆ **Beer** [Fore St; ST2389], *Anchor*: Busy and friendly village pub with concentration on well presented food inc wide choice of fresh fish, big helpings; well kept ales inc Wadworths, garden looks over cove – delightful on a sunny day; bedrooms *(Dennis Dickinson, Alan A Newman, Mrs V Rollo, Mr and Mrs D S Beeson)*

Beesands [SX8140], *Cricket*: Plain pub in good spot on beach with tables outside, particularly good crab sandwiches, Whitbreads-related real ales *(Alan and Heather Jacques)*

Belstone [SX6293], *Belstone Inn*: Simple Dartmoor inn with most friendly atmosphere, well kept beer and good reasonably priced food inc well filled sandwiches *(Mr and Mrs G Williams)*; *Tors*: Imposing granite-built hotel in attractive village, popular with locals and tourists alike, good choice of reasonably priced generous food, wide range of well kept beers; bedrooms *(J L Jones)*

Bickington [A383 Ashburton—Newton Abbot; SX7972], *Dartmoor Half Way*: Big helpings of well cooked food, wide range to choose from *(Steve Huggins)*; *Old Barn*: Bought by tenants of Chichester Arms at Bishops Tawton (see main entries), and being run on similar lines; should be well worth knowing. *Toby Jug*: Distinctive, full of toby jugs (one 3ft tall), good food; friendly if not always swift service *(Jon and Julie Gibson)*

☆ **Bickleigh** [SS9406], *Fishermans Cot*: Fishing hotel by weir and ancient bridge over Exe, with beautiful views; has had nice atmosphere and good reasonably priced carvery, but reported to have been on market – news please *(E V M Whiteway, Jim and Maggie Cowell, Mr and Mrs R Head, Mrs J M Corless)*; [A396, N of junction with A3072], *Trout*: Another pub we'd like news on, as no reports since in receivership and for sale spring 1994 – has been well worth knowing as comfortable, spacious and attractively furnished dining pub with good range of food, tables on pretty lawn, and good-sized well equipped bedrooms *(LYM)*

Bideford [The Quay; SS4526], *Kings Arms*: Friendly, welcoming and popular pub nr quay, good range of reasonably priced food inc good Sun lunches, alcovey front bar *(Nigel and Lindsay Chapman, C J Westmoreland)*

☆ **Bigbury** [St Anns Chapel – B3392 N; SX6647], *Pickwick*: Rustic-look traditional main bar, good choice of bar food, well kept real ales such as Bass and Flowers, local farm cider, very friendly staff, piped music; plainer family extension with pool and other games children treated very well; carvery restaurant, bedrooms *(David*

Cundy, LYM)

☆ **Blackmoor** [SS6443], *Old Station House*: Big dining pub in same local chain as Pyne Arms, East Down (see main entries), with similar food, Marstons Pedigree; churchy pews, plush dining chairs, soft red lighting, character no-smoking area with grandfather clock; good pub for just a drink too, spacious games area with two well lit pool tables, darts and juke box; picnic-table sets on terrace, lovely views; skittle alley; children allowed (but under-5s in small family room only) *(C J Westmoreland, BB)*

☆ **Bovey Tracey** [SX8278], *Riverside*: Attractive cottagey hotel on River Bovey, good value food, real ales, children welcome; very comfortable bedrooms *(Mrs C Heaps, Mrs S N James, E G Parish)*

☆ **Brampford Speke** [off A377 N of Exeter; SX9299], *Agricultural*: Good friendly food pub in same stable as Salterton Arms, Budleigh Salterton (see main entries), with wide choice of good home cooking inc interesting puddings, attractive prices, well kept Courage, prompt service, gallery restaurant where children allowed; picnic-table sets on sheltered terrace *(Philys A L Cooper, Mrs E McFarland)*

☆ **Brandis Corner** [A3072 Hatherleigh—Holsworthy; SS4103], *Bickford Arms*: Well kept ales inc Bass and Flowers, good service and remarkable choice of well presented generous food at reasonable prices esp fresh fish and steaks, in simple 17th-c beamed village local; log fires, games room, restaurant, garden, attractive countryside; bedrooms *(Joan and Gordon Edwards, Roderic Plinston, A B Agombar)*

Bratton Fleming [SS6437], *White Hart*: Alcovey village pub with big inglenook fire, lots of alcoves, big helpings of good value bar food (not Sun lunchtime), Exmoor ale and farm cider, large tables, traditional games in one side area, video games in small family room, piano; dogs allowed, some seats outside *(Dave and Louise Clark, LYM)*

☆ **Bridestowe** [SX5189], *White Hart*: Consistently good generous food in bar and pleasant panelled restaurant inc excellent steaks, sauces and veg, in ancient whitewashed local, cosy, friendly and unpretentious bar, with thick walls, low ceilings, old village photographs, well kept Palmers on handpump, good friendly service; peaceful, unspoilt Dartmoor village; bedrooms *(Paul and Heather Bettesworth, Chris and Pauline Ford, Dr and Mrs N Holmes)*

Bridestowe [A386 Okehampton—Tavistock], *Fox & Hounds*: Welcoming basic pub on main road, simple food very popular with locals; bedrooms *(Dr and Mrs N Holmes)*

☆ **Bridford** [off B3193 Dunsford—Chudleigh; SX8186], *Bridford Inn*: Tucked away in peaceful village with pretty valley views, dark beams inside, with some well polished antique furnishings, turkey carpet, big stone fireplace, consistently good food esp interesting soups and popular Sun lunch (worth booking), well kept beers and local cider; cl Tues, does not open till 12 and 7 (6.30 Sat); tables on fairylit terrace, well behaved dogs allowed *(Hugh and Peggy Holman, Robert and Gladys Flux, S G N Bennett, Peter Whittle, Claire Harding, BB)*

Brixham [SX9255], *Manor*: Old-fashioned unpretentious local, happy and friendly, worth knowing for particularly well kept Ruddles County *(Tom Evans)*; *Quayside*: Tasty food, particularly friendly and efficient service; bedrooms good value, attractively quaint *(Ron and Sheila Corbett)*

☆ **Broadclyst** [B3121, on green; SX9897], *Red Lion*: Attractive beamed local in pleasant surroundings nr interesting church, with wide range of good generous food – excellent value; well kept real ales inc Bass, decent wines, quick friendly service, stripped brickwork, fresh flowers, open fire; back skittles bar, great children's area, seats outside; not far from Killerton (NT) *(P and M Rudlin, Desmond and Pat Morris, E V M Whiteway, Graham Reeve, Eric and Patricia King, J I Fraser, Mrs J M Corless, Canon and Mrs M A Bourdeaux, Denzil T Taylor)*

☆ **Broadclyst** [Whimple Rd], *New Inn*: Friendly country pub doing well under efficient and very welcoming current management, with good range of reasonably priced food esp fish, well kept Whitbreads-related ales, decent wine; stripped-brick bar with boarded ceiling, low doorways, roaring log fires, country and horsey bygones – used to be a farmhouse; small restaurant, skittle alley *(Eric Whiteway, E H and R F Warner, A E Brace)*

☆ **Broadhempston** [SX8066], *Coppa Dolla*: Traditional country inn in lovely remote village, currently doing well with friendly efficient service, wide choice of good value food and of real ales, decent reasonably priced wines, big garden with pleasant views; two apartments *(Harry and Irene Fisher, Mrs Y Yates, Steve Huggins, Joan and Gordon Edwards)*

Broadhempston [The Square], *Monks Retreat*: Enjoyable 14th-c village pub with home-made food (not Mon), welcoming fires in big fireplace, very friendly landlord, attentive service *(P Freeman, Gordon)*

☆ **Buckfastleigh** [SX7366], *White Hart*: Reopened fairly recently, attractive comfortable bar with generous helpings of good value home-cooked food and well kept Furgusons Dartmoor and Ind Coope Burton; woodburner one end, huge log fire the other, stone walls, lots of pictures, horsebrasses, plates, jugs and so forth; friendly licensees, dogs and children welcome – even have some toys; tables in pretty back courtyard *(Nigel and Teresa Brooks)*

☆ **Buckland Monachorum** [SX4868], *Drakes*

Manor: Well kept Courage and John Smiths, good friendly service, good value food inc good Sun lunches, beams and oak panelling; public bar with games machines *(John A Barker)*

☆ Chagford [Mill St; SX7087], *Bullers Arms*: Friendly local with very wide range of interesting dishes inc good vegetarian choice, reasonable prices, three changing real ales, log fires, collection of militaria, darts, very friendly licensees; summer barbecues *(John Hazel, John Wilson, John and Christine Vittoe, LYM)*

Chagford, *Three Crowns*: Lovely medieval atmosphere in thatched stone hotel with mullioned windows, said to be based on part of 13th-c monks' hospice; bar with big fire, good food, service and beer (and modern furnishings), coffee all day, restaurant; bedrooms old, with lots of atmosphere and some four-posters *(E G Parish, Ted George, John and Christine Vittoe, Gordon)*

☆ Challacombe [B3358 Blackmoor Gate—Simonsbath – OS Sheet 180 map ref 695411; SS6941], *Black Venus*: Snug low-beamed pub in attractive scenery, with good range of generous reasonably priced home-cooked food inc delicious puddings, well kept real ales and good friendly service; pews, decent chairs, stuffed birds, woodburning stove and big open fire, separate games room, attractive restaurant; children allowed in eating area (not under 5), dogs maybe by arrangement; in same local chain as Pyne Arms, East Down – see main entries; seats in garden; bedrooms *(M C and S Jeanes, H and D Cox, H F Cox, Mrs C A Blake, BB)*

☆ Chillington [SX7942], *Chillington Inn*: Friendly village local with old settles, benches and low tables in front bar, motley collection of good chairs in back bar, good bar food often inc local seafood, well kept Bass, Palmers and guests on handpump; restaurant; may be closed winter lunchtimes Mon-Thurs; bedrooms *(Alistair Stanier, P Bass)*

Chip Shop [OS Sheet 201 map ref 436752; SX4375], *Chip Shop*: Good value wholesome straightforward food in friendly local with welcoming service, well kept Bass, Exmoor and Marstons Pedigree, and lots of mirrors, unobtrusive piped music, garden with play house; well placed darts *(Chris and Debra, John Hazel)*

☆ Christow [Village Rd; SX8385], *Artichoke*: Good range of food from sandwiches and basic pub food to more elaborate dishes, and lovely warm village atmosphere, in thatched 16th-c local with big log fire in quaint stepped open-plan bar, second fire in back dining room, cheerful service, Boddingtons and Flowers IPA on handpump; tables outside, pretty hillside village nr Canonteign Waterfalls and Country Park *(P and M Rudlin, Mr and Mrs A K McCully)*

☆ Clayhidon [ST1615], *Half Moon*:

Welcoming old village pub, pleasantly restored, popular in the area for imaginative choice of home-cooked food; well kept Bass and Cotleigh, good house wine; in nice spot *(Richard Dolphin, John and Fiona Merritt)*

☆ Clearbrook [off A386 Tavistock—Plymouth; SX5265], *Skylark*: Particularly well kept beer and generous good value food in big, busy pub with children's room; good Dartmoor views *(Derrick and Karen McClelland, John A Barker)*

Clyst Hydon [B3176, not far from M5 junction 28; ST0301], *Five Bells*: 16th-c thatched former farmhouse doing very well under newish owners, decor reflecting their previous involvement in antiques trade, wide range of tasty food with fresh veg, very friendly atmosphere and good family feel, well kept Flowers IPA, Furgusons Dartmoor, Wadworths 6X, farm cider and wines, log fires, pleasant efficient staff, colourful garden with play area *(Denzil T Taylor, J E Davies, R M Sparkes, Eric and Patricia King, Marian Greenwood, Timothy Gee)*

Clyst St Mary [nr M5 junction 30; SX9790], *Half Moon*: Friendly old two-bar village pub, well kept Bass tapped from the cask, good value generous bar food, good sturdy tables; bedrooms *(Mike Dickerson, C J Westmoreland)*

Cockington [SX8963], *Drum*: Spacious and well decorated beamed pub in keeping with this showpiece thatched village just outside Torquay, Allied real ales inc Furgusons, wide choice of food inc lots of pizzas, juke box or piped music, two children's eating areas; seats on terrace and in attractive back garden *(Michael A Butler, Steve Huggins)*

☆ Cockwood [SX9780], *Ship*: Comfortable and welcoming 17th-c inn overlooking estuary and harbour, good seafood menu from open crab sandwiches up, Ushers beer, reasonable prices, pleasant quick service, good steep hillside garden *(Peter and Jenny Quine, Jim and Maggie Cowell, Ian Phillips)*

☆ Coffinswell [SX8968], *Linny*: Very pretty 14th-c thatched country pub with cosy window seats and alcoves, good value usual food in bar and restaurant, cheerful atmosphere; well kept Bass, Ind Coope Burton and Morlands Old Speckled Hen, open fires, friendly professional service, children's room; picturesque village *(Peter and Jenny Quine, John Wilson, Jim and Maggie Cowell, T A Bryan, Mr and Mrs A K McCully)*

Colyford [A3052 Sidmouth—Lyme Regis – OS Sheet 192 map ref 253925; SY2492], *Wheelwright*: Welcoming and civilised 17th-c pub with well kept Bass and a guest such as Shepherd Neame Spitfire, wide choice of really good freshly cooked food – not for those in a hurry but worth the wait *(Gwen and Peter Andrews)*

Combe Martin [Seaview Hill; SS5847],

Dolphin: Pleasant spacious bar well patronised by locals, good reasonably priced food, Worthington BB, lots of whiskies, friendly licensee, unobtrusive piped music *(John Sanders)*

☆ **Combeinteignhead** [SX9071], *Wild Goose*: Fine 17th-c beamed pub, very spacious, with central bar area and separate food servery, lots of hanging jugs and teapots, wide choice of good food, good range of real ales such as Barrons Exe Valley and Dobs Best, Janners Mill and Wadworths 6X, good friendly service, pool room, darts *(George Atkinson, D Cox)*

☆ **Countisbury** [A39, E of Lynton – OS Sheet 180 map ref 747497; SS7449], *Exmoor Sandpiper*: Well placed for Exmoor, with attractive rambling layout, black beams, antique furniture, no fewer than five fireplaces; usual bar food from sandwiches to steaks, well kept Flowers Original and Greene King Abbot, restaurant; children in eating area, open all day; comfortable bedrooms *(Don and Thelma Beeson, Dave Braisted, Dave and Louise Clark, LYM)*

Crediton [SS8300], *Crown*: Small simple pub with friendly Chinese landlord, Worthington BB, local bar leading to good Cantonese restaurant *(John and Vivienne Rice)*

☆ **Croyde** [B3231 NW of Braunton; SS4439], *Thatched Barn*: Friendly and lively rambling thatched inn nr surfing beach, good range of generous bar food (some not cheap) inc local fish, well kept Allied ales, morning coffee, teas, mostly young staff, piped music (can be a bit loud), tables outside; restaurant, children in eating area, open all day; bedrooms *(K Harvey, P Butler, Jo Rees, Mr and Mrs M P Aston, A M Pring, R J Walden, LYM)*

☆ **Croyde** [off B3231 NW of Braunton], *Whiteleaf*: a guest house not a pub, but a firm recommendation for a peaceful and comfortable break, with truly imaginative fresh food and good wines; previously the owners made the Rhydspence at Whitney on Wye (H&W) one of Britain's top dining pubs; dogs allowed

☆ **Dartmouth** [Smith St; SX8751], *Seven Stars*: Lively beamed and panelled bar local with efficiently served and well priced popular food, Courage-related beers, piped pop music and fruit machine; upstairs restaurant, children's room *(Barry and Anne, BB)*

Dawlish Warren [SX9979], *Mount Pleasant*: Heavitree pub with some interesting bar food; good views on the way *(A Craig)*

☆ **Denbury** [The Green; SX8168], *Union*: Beautifully kept low-beamed local on edge of old village green, simple food from excellent sandwiches to steaks inc vegetarian and lots of puddings, Whitbreads-related real ales, very good coffee, charming landlady; tables in garden, quietly pretty sheltered village *(Bill Sharpe, Joan and Gordon Edwards, Steve Huggins, BB)*

☆ **Devonport** [6 Cornwall St; SX4555], *Swan*: Lively and friendly riverside local notable for a dozen or more well kept real ales; enormous good value doorstep sandwiches, home-made pasties and other generous food, roaring fire, live music most nights with extended opening till midnight *(W Fletcher)*

☆ **Dittisham** [The Level; SX8654], *Red Lion*: Welcoming local with well kept Bass, hard-working staff and reasonably priced food; family room; in attractive village *(Belinda Mead, Norman Evans)*

☆ **Dittisham**, *Ferry Boat*: Lovely peaceful position down by the water, with big windows overlooking the boats; well kept Courage, bar food inc good pasties (service may stop rather early) *(Jim and Maggie Cowell, Steve Huggins, LYM)*

☆ **Dog Village** [B3185 S – ½ mile off A30 opp airport; SX9896], *Hungry Fox*: Spacious and comfortable mock-Tudor dining pub with wide choice of good value home-cooked bar food, wide range of beers inc well kept Flowers, and of wines and spirits; efficient friendly service *(E V M Whiteway)*

Dousland [SX5368], *Burrator*: Jovial landlord is ex-Smithfields butcher and ex-farmer, so always has fresh produce for bar and restaurant; big Victorian place with two bars, pool room, big lounge with live music two or three times a week, real ales and lots of facilities (in and out) for children; good value bedrooms *(Paul Redgrave)*

☆ **Down Thomas** [SX5050], *Langdon Court*: Interesting country-house hotel (Edward VII stayed) whose lounge bar and children's room are very popular with non-residents for good food, some unusual, at reasonable prices; ornate servery, good fire, country views, Whitbreads-related ales, picnic-table sets outside; dogs allowed; comfortable bedrooms *(Susan Cody, Geoffrey Thompson)*

☆ nr **Drewsteignton** [Fingle Bridge – leave A38 at Crockernwell, narrow lanes via Preston or Drewsteignton; OS Sheet 191 map ref 743899; SX7390], *Anglers Rest*: Sprucely airy and spacious bar in idyllic Teignside setting – wooded valley by 16th-c packhorse bridge, with lovely walks; café rather than pub feel, lots of light woodwork and tourist souvenirs, but has well kept Cotleigh and Courage real ales and reliable food inc children's meals (not Sun); welcoming efficient service, tables outside *(John Wilson, T H G Lewis, E Money, Jim and Maggie Cowell, LYM)*

☆ **Dunsford** [just off B3212 NE of Moretonhampstead – OS Sheet 191 map ref 813891; SX8189], *Royal Oak*: Friendly and relaxed village inn with light and airy lounge bar around servery with good choice of half a dozen well kept real ales and farm cider, good food (soup, starters, sandwiches, pies and puddings all praised), friendly family service; steps down to games room, provision for children, Fri barbecues in sheltered tiered garden; good value bedrooms *(David Burnett, Donna Lowes, LYM)*

East Prawle [SX7836], *Pigs Nose*: Lots of piggy things in cheery low-beamed pub with well cooked straightforward food inc children's helpings, open fire, Whitbreads-related ales, easy chairs and sofa, pool, darts, several tables outside; small family area by kitchen, dogs on leads allowed *(Mrs S Burrows-Smith, Mr and Mrs A Jacques)*; *Providence*: Welcoming 18th-c village pub with convivial landlord, Fergusons Dartmoor Best and Wadworths 6X on handpump, generous helpings of good value bar food, basic bar area with brass plates and displays of knots and old photographs *(John Beeken)*

☆ **Ermington** [SX6353], *Crooked Spire*: Good fresh generous food esp local fish and puddings in clean and tasteful open-plan bar; friendly and efficient service, good local atmosphere; bedrooms comfortable, with washbasin, TV, shared clean bathroom *(Jane Palmer, John A Barker, John Evans, Alan and Brenda Holyer)* **Ermington**, *First & Last*: Good beers, esp Bass, and good bar food *(K H Frostick)*

☆ **Exeter** [Cowick Lane; between A377 and B3212], *Cowick Barton*: Friendly and comfortable pub in 17th-c former red sandstone farmhouse, wide choice of good hot and cold food in big helpings, Bass, Courage Best and Ruddles County on handpump, lots of country wines, good service, log fire; new small restaurant behind *(Eric Whiteway, Jim and Maggie Cowell)*

☆ **Exeter** [The Quay], *Prospect*: Welcoming and relaxing waterside pub handy for Maritime Museum, in former 17th-c cottages; beams, settles and panelling, old safari pictures and prints of old Exeter; currently doing well, with wide range of reasonably priced freshly cooked food inc good fish in big dining area up a few steps, well kept Bass and Charrington IPA, helpful staff *(Jim and Maggie Cowell, John and Vivienne Rice, Peter Churchill, E V M Whiteway, Mr and Mrs David Lee, June and Tony Baldwin, Wayne Brindle)*

☆ **Exeter** [Martins Lane – just off cathedral close], *Ship*: Photogenic 14th-c pub with heavy-beamed atmospheric bar, well kept Bass and Boddingtons on handpump, big helpings of decent food maybe inc good fish, upstairs restaurant *(E V M Whiteway, C J Westmoreland, John and Vivienne Rice, Paul Randall, Barry and Anne, LYM)*

☆ **Exeter** [The Close; actually bar of Royal Clarence Hotel], *Well House*: Big windows looking across to cathedral in open-plan bar divided by inner walls and partitions; lots of Victorian prints, well kept changing real ales such as Bass, Fullers London Pride, Wadworths 6X, limited choice of popular bar lunches inc good salads, good service; Roman well beneath (can be viewed when pub not busy); piped music, plastic glasses for outside drinking, rather trendy customers at night *(M E and Mrs J Wellington, PC, C J Westmoreland, Paul Randall, Wayne Brindle, Graham Reeve, BB)*

Exeter [Mary Arches St], *Butlers*: Very good value food, good cheerful service, very pleasant atmosphere *(B J B Lunn)*; [High St], *Chaucers*: Busy lunchtime, with good interesting food, well kept Bass and Tetleys; evening doorman *(Graham Reeve)*; [North St], *Crown*: Limited weekend food but super value, inc gigantic pasties *(Ian, Janet and Joanne James)*; [Mary Arches St], *Exchange*: Wooden-floor pub with food inc good filled french bread, Whitbreads-related and other ales, good attentive service; piped music could be quieter *(Joan and Michel Hooper-Immins)*; [St Davids Hill], *Great Western*: Busy and comfortable, with pleasant lounge, locals' bar with satellite TV, reasonably priced bar food, well kept Bass, Greene King Abbot, Stones and Worthington *(Graham Reeve)*; [St Davids Hill], *Jolly Porter*: Lively and attractive multi-roomed traditional pub popular with students and locals, several Courage-related ales and other well kept changing guests such as Marstons Pedigree and Robinsons Best, good cheap plentiful food, snooker room, bric-a-brac and books; jazz Weds *(Chris and Debra, Jim and Maggie Cowell, Graham Reeve)*; [Bonhay Rd], *Mill on the Exe*: Comfortable St Austell pub recently rebuilt with old bricks and timbers, riverside terraces, good food, quick friendly service *(Eric Whiteway, Wayne Brindle, BB)*; [6-10 Southern Warehouse], *On the Waterfront*: Recently enlarged by Forte, bar and pizza restaurant now more separate; in superb spot by river, extremely busy (worth booking); very filling giant pizzas, well kept Courage; children in restaurant *(Graham Reeve)*; [Heavitree], *Ship & Pelican*: Comfortable traditional local with Devenish and Wadworths 6X *(Nigel Gibbs)*

☆ **Exminster** [just off A379 on outskirts; SX9487], *Swans Nest*: Very popular high-throughput food pub, handy for M5, with attractive medley of furniture inc many pieces of real character in inviting and well thought-out rambling dining bar; no-smoking areas, Bass and Furgusons Dartmoor, helpful staff, huge choice of reasonably priced honest self-service food from sandwiches up inc attractive carvery, salads and children's dishes; especially good for family groups with children *(Desmond and Pat Morris, Mr and Mrs C R Little, R L Turnham, D S Beeson, Mrs J M Corless, B D Jones, Mr and Mrs K C B Box, LYM)*

☆ **Filleigh** [off A361 N Devon link rd; SS6627], *Stags Head*: Attractive 16th-c thatched pub with lake, friendly and neatly furnished with good range of generous food, well kept Bass and wide range of other beers, cheerful efficient service; bedrooms comfortable and good value, good breakfasts *(Dave and Louise Clark, N Beesley)*

Fremington [B3233 Barnstaple—Instow; SS5132], *New Inn*: Family-run, long popular for good food and well kept beer *(Mr and Mrs D S Beeson)*

Frithelstock [just W of Torrington; SS4619], *Clinton Arms*: Excellent choice of bar food, Bass tapped from the cask; friendly welcome to children *(Nigel Chapman)*

Frogmore [A379 E of Kingsbridge; SX7742], *Globe*: Character pub with two bars and restaurant, wide choice of good value food, well kept beers, decent wines, pleasant setting; bedrooms bright, clean and comfortable *(Anon)*

☆ **George Nympton** [SS7023], *Castle*: Good range of food inc various vegetarian dishes and lots of specials, comfortably stylish surroundings; bedrooms comfortable too, fishing rights *(Mrs A Hallworth)*

☆ **Georgeham** [Rock Hill; above village – OS Sheet 180 map ref 466399; SS4639], *Rock*: Cheerful character oak-beamed pub, lively in summer, with old red quarry tiles, open fire, pleasant mix of country furniture inc traditional wall seats, lots of nick-nacks; well kept reasonably priced Courage-related real ales, local farm cider, usual bar food but well done, with interesting specials and well filled french bread; piped music, darts, fruit machine, pool room, tables under cocktail parasols on front terrace, pretty hanging baskets *(Jim and Maggie Cowell, E J Locker, B M Eldridge, BB)*

☆ **Hartland Quay** [at the end of toll rd; SS2522], *Hartland Quay*: Marvellous location at bottom of cliff road, handy for exhilarating rugged coast walks – both it and museum opp feature local shipwrecks; good menu, comfortable furnishings, quick pleasant service, lots of tables outside; bedrooms *(Dave Braisted, Carol and Mike Muston, John Sanders)*

Hemyock [ST1313], *Catherine Wheel*: Popular local with warm welcome and good food *(Ron Shelton)*

☆ **Hexworthy** [village signed off B3357 Tavistock—Ashburton, 3¾ miles E of B3212; SX6572], *Forest*: Good solid Dartmoor hotel snugly set in fold of the moors, comfortable and spacious open-plan bar and back walkers' bar, welcoming new management, good range of beers, good bar food; good-sized bedrooms *(Julian and Sarah Stanton, J R Williams, Joan and Gordon Edwards, LYM)*

☆ **Highampton** [A3072 W of Hatherleigh; SS4804], *Golden*: Attractive and homely 16th-c thatched free house, low-beamed lounge with alcoves, padded barrel stools, long high-backed upholstered settle among other seats, brasses, watercolours, farm tools, stove in big stone fireplace; good value food, well kept Bass tapped from the cask, pool room, back garden with view of Dartmoor Tors; well behaved children allowed *(R J Walden, Chris and Pauline Ford)*

Holbeton [Fore St], *Dartmoor Union*: Tastefully modernised, clean and friendly, with good fresh fish and well kept Bass; picturesque village *(A E Brace)*

☆ **Holcombe Rogus** [ST0518], *Prince of Wales*: Full range of Cotleigh (and other) beers kept well in the local brewery's first tied pub; spacious and comfortable, with big fireplaces, no machines or music, friendly atmosphere, good honest food (not Mon/Tues); occasional jazz Sun evening *(Gerald Cleaver)*

Holsworthy [Town Sq; SS3408], *Kings Head*: Traditional Victorian town pub with etched windows, coal fires, 40s and 50s advertisements, lots of optics behind ornate counter, Whitbreads-related ales and particularly well kept Bass and Wadworths 6X *(Roderic Plinston)*

☆ **Honiton** [43 High St; ST1500], *Red Cow*: Busy town pub with plenty of atmosphere, log fires, Courage-related and local ales, good value food inc some unusual dishes, very pleasant helpful staff *(George Mitchell, K R Harris, Mrs J Blake)*

☆ *nr* **Honiton** [Fenny Bridges – A30 4 miles W; SY1198], *Fenny Bridges*: Has been reliable A30/A303 break, spacious bar with big helpings of good standard food, well kept local beer, good wines by the glass, good quick service; restaurant, tables in garden; but no news of new regime *(June and Tony Baldwin; reports please)*

☆ **Horns Cross** [A39 Clovelly—Bideford – OS Sheet 190 map ref 385233; SS3823], *Hoops*: Attractive thatched building dating from 13th c, much modernised inside though still has big inglenook log fires; best thought of as an eating place, with new eating area in central courtyard as well as cosy restaurant and bar; fresh bar food inc good puddings; Whitbreads-related real ales, decent wines, provision for children and disabled; comfortable bedrooms; new landlady May 1994, too soon for us to judge results *(LYM)*

Hunters Inn, *see Lynton*

☆ **Ideford** [SX8977], *Royal Oak*: Tiny thatched village local, friendly, dark and cosy, with lots of Victorian, Edwardian and World War regalia, flags and so forth; particularly well kept Bass, sandwiches, character landlord, raised log fire *(Barry and Anne, Steve Huggins)*

☆ **Ilfracombe** [Bicclescombe Park Rd (off A361); SS5147], *Coach House*: Doing well under newish landlord who previously saw the Ebrington Arms at Knowle into the main entries: extensively restored and spotless, with pleasant bar and family room, beamed upstairs restaurant; good food and service *(A J D Hale)*

☆ **Ilfracombe** [Broad St], *Royal Britannia*: Old-fashioned hotel, friendly and sedately comfortable, in attractive spot above harbour; low seats, armchairs, copper tables and lots of prints in series of connecting rooms; wide choice of good value bar food inc local fish, well kept Courage-related beers; bedrooms *(Chris*

Westmoreland, Reg Nelson, B M Eldridge)
Ilfracombe, *George & Dragon:* Lots of local and other bric-a-brac, well kept Courage, bar food, piped music *(B M Eldridge)*; [Hillsborough Rd], *Thatched*: Attractive thatched pub, good range of well kept beers, pleasant and comfortable lounge bar, colourful garden with plenty of tables; handy for Chambercombe Manor *(B M Eldridge)*

Ivybridge [Western Rd; SX6356], *Imperial*: Small, friendly pub catering well for families with good, reasonably priced food; helpful staff *(Robert and Gladys Flux, Mr and Mrs Barker)*

Kennford [just off A38; SX9186], *Gissons Arms*: Good carvery *(David Bloomfield)*; *Seven Stars*: Farm cider, interesting choice of food *(Dave Braisted)*

☆ **Kentisbeare** [3½ miles from M5 junction 28, via A373; ST0608], *Wyndham Arms*: Bustling village local with comfortable armchairs and sofas, big log fire, tables tucked into walls of long beamed main bar and out in sheltered courtyard; big helpings of very varied good value bar food, well kept Flowers IPA and Original, polite service, daily papers; games room, candlelit restaurant, skittle alley *(Robert and Eve Butler, Muriel and Bryan Harris, BB)*

Kenton [SX9583], *Dolphin*: Very good food with fresh veg and well kept beer *(W H Brooks)*

☆ **Kings Nympton** [SS6819], *Grove*: Pretty thatched and beamed local in picturesque village with well kept Ushers and local cider; pleasant licensee, enjoyable friendly atmosphere, good range of reasonably priced food (esp Tues cheap fish-and-chips night, Weds steak night, puddings); very popular with families, lots of games and skittle alley *(D B Delany, Mr and Mrs J D Marsh, LYM)*

☆ **Kingsbridge** [quayside, edge of town; SX7344], *Crabshell*: Famous old pub long popular for lovely waterside position with fine view over moorings – gets the evening sun; wide choice of bar food inc lunchtime crab sandwiches and, at a price, ambitious hot dishes esp local fish; quick friendly staff, well kept Bass and Charrington IPA, decent choice of wines, good farm cider, good fire *(Gethin Lewis, D M Shalit, Natalie Spencer, Simon Forster, Bill Edwards, Michele and Mike Zinopoulos, Dorothee and Dennis Glover, BB)*

Kingsbridge [Church St, Dodbrooke], *Dodbrooke Inn*: Friendly staff in busy but comfortable local serving good value food inc good steaks, nice range of puddings and good Sun lunch, well kept beers inc good Boddingtons and Bass-related beers *(Alan and Heather Jacques, Peter and Annette Wright)*; [Mill St], *Seven Stars*: Simple town pub with good value home-cooked food at very reasonable prices, Bass and Wadworths 6X on handpump; near quay, but quieter than some others here *(Alan and Heather Jacques)*

☆ **Kingskerswell** [Torquay Rd; SX8767], *Hare & Hounds*: Busy food pub with carvery/dining room extension, carvery and salad bar both praised for value and choice; good service *(Mrs Jean Knight, D J Knight, Mrs M A Brasher)*

Kingskerswell [outside town], *Bickley Mill*: Big rambling former flour mill, alcoves for good interesting bar food inc several vegetarian dishes, restaurant (Weds—Sat evenings); good pubby atmosphere in bar with several well kept real ales inc Bass, professional but very friendly staff; bedrooms comfortable *(John Wilson, Mr and Mrs V Edmunds)*

Kingswear [Higher St; SX8851], *Ship*: Not particularly stylish, but cosy and welcoming, with good mix of locals and visitors, generous well priced food inc imaginative dishes served quickly, one table with Dart views, a couple outside, warm and friendly atmosphere; restaurant *(Joy Heatherley)*

☆ **Knowle** [just off A361 2 miles N of Braunton; SS4938], *Ebrington Arms*: Friendly pub with attractive candlelit dining area as well as two comfortable opened-up rooms with lots of bric-a-brac; good value varied meals, well kept Bass, friendly service, piped music; pool room, separate snug bar *(Steve and Carolyn Harvey, Ian and Nita Cooper, R J Walden, S R and A J Ashcroft, LYM)*

Landkey [SS5931], *Ring o' Bells*: Small village pub with well cooked and presented food, friendly staff and range of real ales; interesting main bar *(K R Harris)*

☆ **Landscove** [Woolston Green – OS Sheet 202 map ref 778662; SX7766], *Live & Let Live*: Friendly, homely and spotless open-plan bar with popular bar food, well kept Ind Coope Burton, woodburner, tables in small orchard facing over moors to Dart valley *(E Money, LYM)*

☆ **Lee** [SS4846], *Grampus*: Pleasant atmosphere in attractive 14th-c pub well placed for superb coastal walks; lots of seats in quiet sheltered garden, wide range of basic but good well presented home-made food, well kept Whitbreads-related ales, maybe piped classical music or jazz; two bedrooms *(Sue Demont, Tim Barrow, LYM)*

☆ **Loddiswell** [SX7148], *Loddiswell Inn*: Busy and neatly kept little local with well kept Ushers, good choice of freshly cooked food inc local lamb, fresh fish and fine veg, generous helpings, good service, friendly licensees, log fire *(Alan and Heather Jacques, Ian Langmead, John A Barker)*

☆ **Longdown** [B3212 W of Exeter; SX8690], *Lamb*: Recently redecorated, with one side of open-plan bar given over to restaurant dining area, settees in one front alcove, Exmoor Gold, Furgusons Dartmoor, Ind Coope Burton and Morland Old Speckled Hen, wide choice of imaginative reasonably priced home-made food *(David Burnett, Donna Lowes, John Stoner)*

☆ **Lower Ashton** [off B3193; SX8484], *Manor*: Wide choice of good generous interesting food (not Mon) in small unspoilt two-bar country pub with four or five real ales tapped from the cask, very loyal friendly group of locals; garden overlooking Teign Valley *(Marion and John Hadfield)*

Luppitt [OS Sheet 192 map ref 169067; ST1606], *Luppitt*: Real throwback to what pubs used to be like, friendly and chatty landlady who keeps the pub open because she likes the company – one cosy room by farm kitchen, a second sparser games room, lavatories across the yard *(Gordon)*

☆ **Luton** [Haldon Moor; SX9076], *Elizabethan*: Low-beamed pub of some character, doing well under current owners, with wide range of good cheap generous food inc lots of pies and fish; well kept beer, friendly staff *(Julie A Bennett, A P Jeffreys)*

Lydford [A386; SX5184], *Dartmoor*: Pleasant atmosphere, generous helpings of good food; bedrooms *(P and M Rudlin)*; [off A386], *Manor*: Also known as Mucky Duck, with partitioned bar open all day, well kept ales such as Bass, Hook Norton Old Hookey, Greene King Abbot and St Austells Tinners, wide range of generously served food; pool table and games machines in separate room, tables and grassy play area outside; live music Sun evening; bedrooms *(P and M Rudlin)*

☆ **Lympstone** [Exmouth Rd (A376); SX9984], *Nutwell Lodge*: Particularly good friendly service in spacious and attractive dining pub with pleasant variety of different areas and seating, big helpings of decent straightforward home-cooked food inc good carvery at sensible prices (maybe bargains for early lunchers), well kept Bass and Furgusons Dartmoor, decent wines; children welcome *(Don and Thelma Beeson, Dr P R Davis, John and Vivienne Rice, B D Jones, J I Fraser, LYM)*

Lympstone, *Globe*: Popular two-room pub, simply furnished and easy-going, with quick friendly service, small pleasant restaurant, good seafood salads and sandwiches; in centre of attractive coastal village *(Shirley Pielou, C J Westmoreland, BB)*

Lynmouth [harbour; SS7249], *Rock House*: Small bar with good food, fine restaurant, very friendly staff, good choice of beers and wine; good bedrooms, lovely spot *(John and Christine Vittoe)*

Lynton [Market Pl; SS7249], *Crown*: Pleasant welcome and service – this hotel's bar used to be the village's alehouse; decent beer and cider, very acceptable food; bedrooms *(Dorothee and Dennis Glover)*; [Castle Hill], *Royal Castle*: The views are the really striking thing here, and this comfortable Edwardian-style hotel has well kept real ales, good value bar food and friendly staff; bedrooms *(Mrs C A Blake)*; [North Walk, Lynbridge (B3223); SS7248], *Olde Cottage*: Well placed overlooking

river gorge nr stone bridge, lots of potential in attractive beamed interior with Victorian churchy windows; Whitbreads-related ales, bar food inc baked potatoes, glorious coast views from terrace; bedrooms *(Anon)*

☆ **nr Lynton** [Martinhoe, towards Heddon's Mouth – OS Sheet 180 map ref 654482; SS6548], *Hunters Inn*: Big rambling pub among lovely NT hills and woodland, with wonderful walks nearby (half an hour to the sea); some emphasis on good food inc vegetarian and children's dishes in bar or restaurant, but also surprising number of real ales such as Boddingtons, Courage Directors, Eldridge Pope Royal Oak, Exmoor, Flowers, Fullers London Pride, Morlands Old Speckled Hen, Tetleys, Theakstons XB and Wadworths 6X, good farm cider; cream teas; attractive bedrooms *(Alan and Brenda Holyer)*

☆ **Maidencombe** [Steep Hill; SX9268], *Thatched*: Wide choice of cheap and plentiful good food in bar and restaurant of picturesque extended thatched pub with lovely coastal views, attractive garden with small thatched cabañas (dogs allowed out here but not in pub); Allied real ales, quick friendly service, big family room, no-smoking areas; children allowed; bedrooms in adjacent building, small attractive village *(John and Joanne Parsonage, Julie Bennett)*

☆ **Malborough** [SX7039], *Old Inn*: Unpretentious country pub notable for good choice of reasonably priced but really good bar food (esp mussels and puddings); charming quick service, good house wine, pleasant children's room *(Gethin Lewis, Tim and Lynne Crawford, Karen Sims)*

☆ **Manaton** [SX7581], *Kestor*: Clean and cheerful modern Dartmoor-edge inn in splendid spot nr Becky Falls, with wide range of good value, wholesome and original home cooking, well kept changing real ales, farm cider, various alcoves, open fire, helpful service; attractive bedrooms *(C A Hall, Mr and Mrs C T Alcock, Denzil Taylor, Denis Korn)*

☆ **Marsh** [signed off A303 Ilminster—Honiton; ST2510], *Flintlock*: Welcoming, well kept and comfortable 17th-c inn with wide choice of attractively served good bar food inc vegetarian, well kept beer and cider, armoury and horsebrasses *(Neil Kellett, Mrs J M Corless)*

Mary Tavy [A386 Tavistock—Okehampton; SX5079], *Mary Tavy*: Small and unpretentious, with attractive bar, welcoming licensees, Bass, St Austell Tinners and a guest ale such as Wadworths 6X, well prepared range of modest food *(John Wilson)*

☆ **Meeth** [A386 Hatherleigh—Torrington; SS5408], *Bull & Dragon*: Old-fashioned thatched village pub with 16th-c beams, very welcoming to families, well priced real ales inc Ushers, decent wines, wide range of good value generous food using local produce, friendly staff and locals, unobtrusive piped music; exemplary lavatories; bedrooms *(A J Blackler, Gill Earle, Andrew Burton)*

☆ **Merrivale** [B3357; 4 miles E of Tavistock – OS Sheet 191 map ref 459752; SX5475], *Dartmoor*: Welcoming licensees and good value generous basic lunchtime food (esp pasties, gammon, mixed grill and ice-cream specials) in recently refurbished pub with Dartmoor views, nr Bronze Age hut circles, stone rows, pretty river, good walks; well kept Courage and another real ale on handpump, water from their 120-ft well, good choice of country wines, open fire, friendly cat, efficient service, tables outside – very popular summer evenings; surcharge for low-bill credit cards *(Frank Cummins, Margaret and Trevor Errington, Alec and Marie Lewery, Dr and Mrs N S Holmes, Mr and Mrs K C B Box)*

Molland [SS8028], *London*: Totally unspoilt and quite extraordinary olde-worlde basic pub in Exmoor-edge village, with Bass and Worthington BB tapped from casks behind bar, big dining room, welcoming landlord, good food inc good value huge gammon steaks and children's meals, log fire, dim lighting; drawings in gents' not to everyone's taste; next to one of the most unspoilt churches in the country *(S G N Bennett, T J H Bodys, Dave Lands, Robin and Molly Taylor)*; *Black Cock*: Cotleigh beers, usual bar food but good home cooking, friendly atmosphere, good family room with pool table, heated indoor swimming pool *(Doug and Gill Green, Dave Lands)*

☆ **Monkton** [A30 NE of Honiton; ST1803], *Monkton Court*: Imposing stone house with neatly kept spacious main bar with beams, panelling and stone or slate walls, snug side areas, well kept Courage, log fire, wide choice of straightforward bar food, restaurant (children allowed till 7), spacious relaxing garden; bedrooms *(Mayur Shah, A Craig, Nick Wikeley, LYM)*

☆ **Moreleigh** [B3207; off Kingsbridge—Totnes in Stanborough, left in village – OS Sheet 202 map ref 767527; SX7753], *New Inn*: Unrestored traditional country pub with character old furniture, big inglenook, nice pictures, candles in bottles; limited choice of good wholesome home-cooked food served generously at low prices, well kept Palmers; may be closed on race days *(David Wallington, R W A Suddaby, Jim and Maggie Cowell, Andy and Jill Kassube, LYM)*

☆ **Mortehoe** [off A361 Ilfracombe—Braunton; SS4545], *Ship Aground*: Massive rustic furnishings in open-plan village pub by church, lots of nautical brassware, log fire, well kept Boddingtons, Whitbreads Castle Eden and a guest beer, Hancock's cider in summer, bar food; big family room, pool, skittles and other games; piped music *(Mr and Mrs Moody, D P and M E Cartwright, Sarah Elliott, Gary Goldson, Susan and Nigel Wilson, Ian and Nita Cooper, S R and A J Ashcroft, LYM)*

☆ **Mortehoe**, *Chichester Arms*: Warm, welcoming, friendly, helpful service, standard hot and cold bar meals *(P and J Shapley)*

☆ **Newton Abbot** [East St; SX8671], *Olde Cider Bar*: Basic, old-fashioned and very local, with no-nonsense stools and wall benches and pre-war-style decor; superb choice of farm ciders and perries from fat casks behind bar, good country wines, cheap snacks inc venison pasties, very low prices; small games room with machines *(Peter Hitchcock)*

Newton Abbot, *Jolly Farmer*: Well kept Courage, decent bar food, barn theme, skittle room, juke box *(Steve Huggins)*

☆ **nr Newton Abbot** [A381 2 miles S, by turn to Abbotskerswell], *Two Mile Oak*: Doing well under new landlord, attractively quiet and old-fashioned, with secluded candlelit alcoves, good log fire, black panelling, low beams, stripped stone, lots of brasses; wide choice of well prepared reasonably priced bar food, cosy little dining room, well kept Bass, Flowers IPA, Eldridge Pope Royal Oak and guest beers, seats on back terrace and nicely planted garden *(Peter and Jenny Quine, Steve Huggins, Joan and Gordon Edwards, LYM)*

☆ **Newton Ferrers** [Riverside Rd East; SX5448], *Dolphin*: In lovely village overlooking yachting harbour, good value food, very friendly landlord *(Margaret and Roy Randle, David Lewis, David Goldstone)*

☆ **Newton St Cyres** [SX8798], *Crown & Sceptre*: Former tenants of Royal Oak at Meavy doing good imaginative home-made food; pleasant character and decor, Bass and Boddingtons, family area, splendid lawn with trees and stream *(Paul Redgrave, John and Vivienne Rice)*

☆ **Newton Tracey** [5 miles S of Barnstaple on B3232 to Torrington; SS5226], *Hunters*: Decent range of good reasonably priced bar food and four real ales in friendly old pub with log fire, juke box, fruit machines; tables outside, play area, evening restaurant; children in eating part of bar or in skittle alley/games room *(Mr and Mrs N Hazzard)*

☆ **No Mans Land** [B3131 Tiverton—South Molton; SS8313], *Mount Pleasant*: Good atmosphere in genuine traditional country pub with wide range of good inexpensive home-made food from huge sandwiches through imaginative pastas and seafood to superb steaks in cosy bars or ex-forge restaurant (usually an exhibition of local crafts); good wine list, real ales such as Bass, Butcombe and Devenish, friendly knowledgeable staff, open fires, informal live folk music; children's room, tables outside *(C Roberts, Mr and Mrs T B Mills)*

☆ **North Bovey** [SX7483], *Ring of Bells*: 13th-c Dartmoor thatched inn on edge of lovely tree-covered village green, simple bulgy-walled main bar with well kept Furgusons Dartmoor, Ind Coope Burton,

Marstons Pedigree and Wadworths 6X, Gray's farm cider, games etc, good log fire, straightforward bar food (good value), restaurant, friendly staff, seats outside; children welcome; big bedrooms with four-posters *(Denzil T Taylor, Steve Huggins, J L Hall, C A Hall, M Veldhuyzen, R H Martyn, George Atkinson, D Cox, Steve Huggins, LYM)*

North Tawton [SS6601], *Copper Key*: Particularly welcoming landlord in neat thatched pub, cosy and comfortable, with decent food, well kept Marstons Pedigree *(R J Walden)*

☆ **Noss Mayo** [SX5447], *Swan*: Newish management doing well in small waterside pub with charming views over creek, good range of bar food inc fresh fish, well kept Courage Best and Directors on handpump, old beams, open fire; children welcome, tables outside – peaceful picturesque village *(Romey Heaton, Margaret and Roy Randle, David Lewis, Shirley Pielou)*

Otterton [SY0885], *Kings Arms*: Good choice of food, real ale and pleasant service in popular but roomy pub, comfortably refurbished; charming village *(Mrs J M Corless, J I Fraser)*

Ottery St Mary [Gold St; SY0995], *London*: Cosy little pub with wide range of reasonably priced food *(Sarah and Gary Goldson, Eric Whiteway; more reports on new regime please)*

☆ **Paignton** [27 Esplanade Rd; SX8960], *Inn on the Green*: Decidedly not a quiet and personal local – very big and brightly comfortable family bar open all day, and well worth knowing for enormous choice of popular sensibly priced quick food, good facilities for children, well kept Courage-related ales (and good soft and hot drinks), friendly service; out-of-the-way family room, live music and dancing nightly, restaurant, big terrace looking out over green to sea *(C Roberts, Marjorie Roberts, George Atkinson, Mrs J M Corless, LYM)*

Paignton [Torquay Rd, nr Oldway Museum], *Half Moon*: Popular roadhouse under enterprising new management *(Tom Evans)*

☆ **Parkham** [SS3821], *Bell*: Good value freshly cooked food and pleasant atmosphere in spacious and comfortably refurbished thatched village pub with lots of nooks and crannies, log fire, old-fashioned furnishings, choice of real ales *(Mr and Mrs J D Marsh, R J Walden, LYM)*

☆ **Peter Tavy** [signed off A386 N of Tavistock, nr Mary Tavy; SX5177], *Peter Tavy*: Has been an outstanding Dartmoor-edge pub for years, with an atmospheric low-beamed bar with old-fashioned settles, flagstones and good log fire, its notable good value home-made food (especially unusual vegetarian dishes), and its ten or so well kept real ales tapped from the cask, allowing children in dining extension; though still of great appeal, it has run into recent management problems which we

hope will be a temporary glitch *(Bill and Edee Miller, G A McConnell, Peter and Audrey Dowsett, Alec and Marie Lewery, David and Tina Woods-Taylor, Romey Heaton, N P Cox, R J Walden, Ian and Val Titman, Mrs C Watkinson, LYM; more reports please)*

☆ **Plymouth** [Saltram Pl – back of Plymouth Hoe, behind Moat House], *Yard Arm*: Carefully done out as series of naval-theme semi-snugs on three levels, with intimate friendly atmosphere, attractive woodwork and some really interesting nautical bric-a-brac, in fine spot overlooking the Hoe; well kept Courage-related ales and a guest such as Bass, well presented straightforward food inc children's dishes, good prices, friendly service; subdued piped music, children allowed in bottom area, tables outside *(Brian and Anna Marsden, Ian Phillips, Denis and Margaret Kilner, Alan and Maggie Telford)*

☆ **Plymouth** [Old George St; Derrys Cross, behind Theatre Royal], *Bank*: Busy and interesting three-level pub beautifully converted from former bank, dark wood balustrades, conservatory area upstairs (children allowed here) leading to tables outside; good service, wide choice of good value food all day (queue while it's done, take it on tray – busy at lunchtime for this), well kept Allied ales; music nights, lively young evening atmosphere *(W Fletcher, Andy and Jill Kassube, Geraldine Berry, Steve Howe)*

Plymouth [Borringdon Terr; Turnchapel signs off A379 Kingsbridge rd], *Borringdon Arms*: An adventure to find – down increasingly steep and narrow lane that leads to dead end with Royal Marines gate and public car park; real unchanging local with yellowing ceiling, peeling wall paper, worn carpet, but clean and friendly, with back conservatory, five good beers at low prices, occasional real ale festival week, good value food *(B and K Hypher, R Houghton)*; [Barbican], *Dolphin*: Frequently busy and boisterous, with inimitable style, well kept beer straight from the barrel, Beryl Cook paintings (you may see her here) *(J S Poulter)*; [Breton Side], *Kings Head*: No special merit, anonymous rectangle with long bar down one side and nicotine-effect decor, spit-and-sawdust-style atmosphere; but welcoming pub worth knowing for well kept beers such as Marstons Pedigree, Morlands Old Speckled Hen, Ruddles County, Wadworths 6X and their excellent value Kings Ransom own brew; opens 10am, occasional folk music *(BM, AM, M J Manuel, J Harris)*; [Barbican], *Mermaid*: Friendly and lively spit-and-sawdust-style pub with particularly well kept Bass at very reasonable price tapped from the cask *(Brian and Anna Marsden)*; [13 Sutton Rd], *Shipwrights Arms*: Simple good value food in open-plan Courage local with welcoming fire; kind staff *(C W Jenkins)*; [West Hoe

Rd, corner of Millbay Rd], *Sippers*: Small split-level theme pub with centre bar done out as street scene; friendly and efficient service, well kept beer, good value food, triangular snooker table and bar billiards *(Brian Jones)*; [50 Eastlake St], *Unity*: Efficient service, Furgusons Dartmoor Best and Ind Coope Burton, good range of food from pasties and doorstep sandwiches to sensibly priced main dishes; open 9am for coffee *(Brian and Anna Marsden)*; [Grand Parade, West Hoe], *Waterfront*: Good spot by Plymouth Sound, more café/cocktail bar than pub, but pleasant and enjoyable; big restaurant areas, strict dress code, good choice of beers and other drinks *(Mayur Shah)*

☆ **Postbridge** [B3212; SX6579], *East Dart*: central Dartmoor hotel by pretty river, with cheerful open-plan bar largely given over to efficiently served good value bar food, well kept Exmoor and other real ales, farm cider, good fire, pool room; children welcome; bedrooms, some 30 miles of fishing *(C Roberts, BB)*

☆ **Princetown** [SX5873], *Plume of Feathers*: Popular hikers' pub, unchanging atmosphere despite big recent extension; good value food inc good pasties, friendly efficient service, well kept Bass and St Austell HSD and Tinners, two log fires, solid slate tables, live music Fri night, Sun lunchtime – can be lively then; children welcome, play area outside; good value bedrooms, also bunkhouse and camping *(Y Cotterill, John Hazel, David Holloway)*
Princetown, *Prince of Wales:* Friendly no-nonsense local, wide choice of good value straightforward food, Flowers and Wadworths 6X on handpump, large dog and two cats; two huge open fires, granite walls and dusty wall hangings give atmosphere *(John Wilson, E Money, BB)*
Pyworthy [SW of Holsworthy; SS3102], *Molesworth Arms*: Popular country pub with attractively priced food inc good curries in bar or restaurant, well kept Bass with a guest such as Morlands Old Speckled Hen, friendly staff *(Dr and Mrs Holmes)*

☆ **Rackenford** [off A361 NW of Tiverton; SS8518], *Stag*: Lots of character and atmosphere in ancient and interesting low-beamed thatched pub, one of England's oldest (probably Devon's oldest), with original flagstoned and cobbled entry passage and huge fireplace flanked by ancient settles; good daily-changing fresh and imaginative food, friendly service, well kept real ales such as Cotleigh and Exmoor Gold; bedrooms *(Elizabeth Beresford, K Flack, Eric and Patricia King, BB)*

☆ **Ringmore** [SX6545], *Journeys End*: Atmospheric old village inn doing well under new management, character panelled lounge, well kept real ales such as Butcombe, Exmoor, Otter and St Austell HSD and Tinners tapped from casks in back room, local farm cider, log fires;

varied interesting food inc good fresh fish, helpful welcoming service, pleasant big terraced garden, sunny well furnished conservatory; provision for children, attractive setting nr thatched cottages, not far from the sea; bedrooms antique but comfortable and well equipped *(E Money, M D Hare, David Lewis, David Burnett, Donna Lowes, Tim Brierly, Gordon, Lynn Sharpless, Bob Eardley, LYM)*

☆ **Rockbeare** [SY0295], *Jack in the Green*: Cheerful staff in clean and pleasant pub doing well under current ownership; wider choice of particularly good interesting food in back restaurant *(Mrs E Punchard, E V M Whiteway)*
Salcombe [off Fore St nr Portlemouth Ferry; SX7338], *Ferry*: Fine spot overlooking water, bottom stripped-stone bar giving on to sheltered flagstoned waterside terrace, top one opening off street, middle one now an enjoyable Mediterranean-style bistro; well kept Palmers real ales *(Stephen and Jean Curtis, Tim and Lynne Crawford, Alan and Brenda Holyer, LYM)*; [Fore St], *Victoria*: Nice position, and attractive building and furnishings, with comfortable lounge, pleasant eating area and generally well kept Bass; segregated children's room, bedrooms *(Tim and Lynne Crawford, Mr A Craig)*

☆ **Sampford Courtenay** [B3072 Crediton—Holsworthy; SS6301], *New Inn*: 16th-c thatched pub with well kept Bass and Flowers and big helpings of good food in low-beamed open-plan bar, open fires, nice garden with children's play area and playhouse *(David and Julie Glover, E Money)*

☆ **Sampford Peverell** [16 Lower Town; a mile from M5 junction 27, village signed from Tiverton turn-off; ST0214], *Globe*: Spacious and comfortably modernised, handy for good generous home cooking inc tasty Sun lunch and puddings; cheerful attentive staff, well kept Whitbreads-related real ales, piped music, games in public bar, pool room, skittle alley, tables in front; open all day; children allowed in eating area and family room *(Mr and Mrs A E Barrey, Ron Shelton, Mrs J M Corless, LYM)*

☆ **Sandy Park** [SX7189], *Sandy Park*: Thatched country tavern with austerely old-fashioned small bar, stripped old tables, built-in high-backed wall seats, big black iron fireplace, decent changing choice of wines, real ales such as Cotleigh Tawny, Eldridge Pope Hardy and Palmers IPA – well liked for its unspoilt feel; bar food (not winter Sun/Mon evenings), children in eating area, has been open all day Sat; simple bedrooms *(R J Walden, E Money, S M Rowland, W K Hyde, Steve Huggins, LYM)*
Seaton [Marine Cres; SY2490], *Fishermans*: Decent food all day at least in summer, and very low prices, in basic but welcoming pub with Irish undertone, open fire *(Brian Websdale)*

Scorriton [SX7068], *Tradesmans Arms*: In attractive countryside, unpretentious extremely clean Dartmoor-edge open-plan local, friendly licensees, good value simple home-cooked food, real ale, farm cider, big children's room; bedrooms *(John Wilson)*

Shaldon [The Ness; SX9372], *Ness House*: Hotel on Ness headland, with comfortable bar areas, good range of food and beer inc Furgusons Dartmoor and Eldridge Pope Hardy County; splendid setting, superb on a summer evening (when can get busy); bedrooms *(George Atkinson)*; [Ringmore Rd (B3195 to Newton Abbot)], *Shipwrights Arms*: Friendly village local worth knowing for nice river views esp from back garden; reasonably priced simple food, Courage Directors; parking can be difficult – just a few spaces on the quayside *(George Atkinson, LYM)*

Shillingford [SS9823], *Barleycorn*: Restaurancy feel, though locals do drink here; decent food inc good local lamb chops *(Pete and Rosie Flower)*

☆ **Shiphay** [off A380/A3022, NW edge of Torquay; SX8865], *Devon Dumpling*: Good range of Courage and other well kept beers and wide choice of good reasonably priced food inc vegetarian, plenty of space inc upper barn loft, friendly staff, good atmosphere; aquarium, occasional live music; no dogs inside *(Wally Huggins, John Wilson)*

☆ **Sidmouth** [Old Fore St; SY1287], *Old Ship*: Partly 14th-c, with shiny black woodwork, ship pictures, wide choice of fair-priced food inc good ploughman's, local fish and provision for vegetarians, well kept real ales such as Boddingtons, Marstons Pedigree, Wadworths 6X; close-set tables but roomier raftered upstairs bar, dogs allowed; just moments from the sea, so can get crowded in summer, but service good and friendly *(Jason Caulkin, Jim and Maggie Cowell, Sarah and Gary Goldson, C J Westmoreland, E V M Whiteway, Eric and Patricia King, M E and Mrs J Wellington, BB)*

☆ **Sidmouth** [High St], *Tudor Rose*: Nostalgic bric-a-brac from copper kettles to a penny-farthing, good value straightforward food, happy atmosphere, soft lighting, low ceilings, good staff, comfortable seats, well kept Bass on handpump, quiet piped music *(C J Westmoreland, Brian A Websdale, Robin and Janice Dewhurst, J I Fraser)*

Sidmouth [opp Radway Cinema], *Radway*: Good value food inc vegetarian, good choice of beers, very friendly; live music during Sidmouth Folk Week *(Brian Websdale)*

☆ **Silverton** [14 Exeter Rd; SS9502], *Three Tuns*: Good choice of good value food in 17th-c inn; old-fashioned bar or cosy restaurant, Courage real ale, friendly staff, good value bedrooms in new block *(Denzil Taylor)*

Slapton [SX8244], *Queens Arms*: Comfortable old inn re-opened by new licensees; well served and reasonably priced food, good real ales inc Bass, Exmoor and Palmers, lovely suntrap garden with plenty of tables *(Alan and Heather Jacques)*

South Molton [High St; SS7125], *Old Coaching Inn*: Clean, comfortable and pleasant bar, local real ales, a relaxing atmosphere, good food; bedrooms – good touring centre *(K R Harris)*

☆ **South Tawton** [off A30 at Whiddon Down or Okehampton, then signed from Sticklepath; SX6594], *Seven Stars*: Quietly placed and unpretentious, with good helpings of simple decent bar food, well kept Ind Coope Burton, Palmers and Wadworths 6X, farm cider; pool and other bar games, folk club last Sun in month; restaurant (closed Sun and Mon evenings winter); children welcome; bedrooms *(Derrick and Karen McClelland, LYM)*

South Zeal [SX6593], *Kings Head*: Excellent bar food *(David Holloway)*

☆ **Spreyton** [SX6996], *Tom Cobbley*: imaginative home-made food and well kept Cotleigh Tawny and occasional guest beers in friendly village local, busy at weekends; darts, cards, attractive garden with summer barbecues; bedrooms clean and comfortable, but share bath *(R J Walden)*

☆ **Sticklepath** [off A30 at Whiddon Down or Okehampton; SX6494], *Devonshire*: 16th-c thatched village inn with good low-priced snacks, fine evening meals on request, friendly and cosy low-beamed slate-floored bar, big log fire, some nice old furniture, comfortable armchairs in room off, St Austell Tinners and HSD, farm cider, magazines to read; open all day Fri/Sat *(A R Pike, N P Cox, LYM)*

Stoke Gabriel [SX8457], *Castle*: More modern-seeming than the Church House, big carpetted bar with rough stone walls, good low-priced food, friendly quick service *(C Roberts, Marjorie Roberts)*

☆ **Stokeinteignhead** [SX9170], *Chasers Arms*: A restaurant not a pub (you can't go just for a drink), but this 16th-c thatched place is very popular for well served good food, esp soups, steaks and puddings – also does ploughman's; well kept Eldridge Pope Dorset, fine range of house wines, quick friendly service; lovely unspoilt village *(Mrs K Buchanan, Tom Evans)*

☆ **Stokeinteignhead**, *Church House*: Picturesque 13th-c thatched dining pub, restored and reopened after 1993 fire – if anything even more attractive, with extra fireplace and delightful spiral staircase; good value food in character bar, dining lounge or restaurant area, friendly chatty staff, well kept Bass, Flowers IPA and Marstons Pedigree on handpump, farm cider, good coffee; nice back garden with little stream *(John Wilson, George Atkinson, Jim and Maggie Cowell, Gethin Lewis, Gordon)*

☆ **Stokenham** [just off A379 Dartmouth—Kingsbridge; SX8042], *Tradesmans Arms*:

Tranquil 15th-c newly rethatched cottage with plenty of antique tables neatly set for good simple bar food esp fresh seafood; well kept Bass, good malt whiskies, very friendly staff; restaurant, children allowed in left-hand bar, picnic-table sets outside (nice surroundings); tiny car park *(E Money, John Allsopp, Gordon, Steve Huggins, LYM)*

Swimbridge [nr Barnstaple; SS6130], *Jack Russell*: Named after the famous hunting parson and his terriers, with good bar food inc children's dishes, well kept Courage-related ales; Sat restaurant, children's room, terrace *(B M Eldridge)*

Tavistock [SX4874], *Ordulph Arms*: Recently refurbished local, friendly welcome and well kept Bass *(A E and P McCully)*

☆ **Tedburn St Mary** [village signposted from A30 W of Exeter; SX8193], *Kings Arms*: Pleasant old inn doing well under new management, with good choice of competitively priced food (all day Sun), attractive and comfortable open-plan bar with big log fire and lots of brass, end games area, well kept real ales, local cider; children in eating area; bedrooms *(J A Kempthorne, E V M Whiteway, LYM)*

Teignmouth [Quayside; SX9473], *Ship*: Quayside setting, good value bar food, well kept beers, pleasant staff, friendly atmosphere *(A Cull)*

☆ **Topsham** [Fore St; 2 miles from M5 junction 30; SX9688], *Globe*: Good solid traditional furnishings, log fire and plenty of character in heavy-beamed bow-windowed bar of friendly and relaxed 16th-c inn; low-priced straightforward home-cooked food, well kept Bass, Ushers Best and Worthington BB on handpump, decent reasonably priced wine, civilised locals, snug little bar-dining room, separate restaurant; seats in sheltered courtyard, children in eating area, open all day; good value attractive bedrooms *(C J Westmoreland, Gordon, E H and R F Warner, LYM)*

☆ **Topsham**, *Lighter*: Former harbour-master's/customs house, right on old quay, spacious and plushly refurbished, with well kept Badger ales, good friendly staff, decent quickly served bar food, panelled alcoves and tall windows looking out over tidal flats; good choice of board games, children in eating area; big good value bedrooms, but (contrary to our previous information) share bathroom *(Ian Lock, Gabrielle Coyle, C J Westmoreland, E V M Whiteway, BB)*

☆ **Topsham** [High St], *Lord Nelson*: Well priced generously served food inc giant open sandwiches, pleasant atmosphere, attentive service *(Alan A Newman, C J Westmoreland)*

Topsham [Monmouth Hill], *Steam Packet*: Olde-worlde free house with flagstones, scrubbed boards, panelling, stripped stonework and brick, bar food in lighter eating room, good choice of well kept real ales; on boat-builders' quay *(C J Westmoreland, LYM)*

☆ **Torquay** [Park Lane; SX9264], *Hole in the Wall*: Very friendly new licensees in small dark flagstoned bar nr clock tower by harbour, Courage beers on handpump, lots of character, much Naval memorabilia, old local photographs, chamberpots; open all day *(Peter and Jenny Quine, Jim and Maggie Cowell)*

Torquay [Babbacombe Beach], *Cary Arms*: Cheerful service, reasonable atmosphere, decent straightforward food, well kept beers, views of cliffs around bay *(John Evans, Les Gee)*

Torrington [SS4919], *Puffing Billy*: Well kept real ales, decent wines and sensible choice of food in former station building, full of train memorabilia and pictures; pleasant family atmosphere *(Susan and Nigel Wilson)*

Totnes [Fore St, The Plains; SX8060], *Royal Seven Stars*: Hotel rather than pub, but delightful, friendly place with fascinating history; bedrooms *(Ian Jones)*

Upottery [ST2007], *Sidmouth Arms*: Attractive pub in pleasant village setting, efficient staff, decent beer; small restaurant; bedrooms *(Paul and Heather Bettesworth, Gordon)*

☆ **Ugborough** [SX6755], *Ship*: Open-plan extended and modernised dining pub with remarkably wide choice of really good food inc lots of fresh fish, interesting specials and outstanding veg; pleasant efficient waitresses, well kept Bass and Wadworths 6X *(John A Barker, C A Hall)*

Umberleigh [SS6023], *Rising Sun*: Neatly kept pub at crossroads by River Taw with well kept beer and reasonable choice of bar food *(Alan Castle)*

☆ **Weare Giffard** [SS4721], *Cyder Press*: More restaurant than pub, but very homely, clean and welcoming, with wide choice of good yet inexpensive food inc lots of fish; at lunchtime starters can be had as light meals on their own; calm, clean and welcoming – no children in bar; beautiful countryside *(Richard Dutton, Peter and Rose Flower)*

☆ **Wembworthy** [Lama Cross; SS6609], *Lymington Arms*: Big helpings of good food inc vegetarian and good value Sun lunch, in clean, bright and cosy beamed pub with well kept Eldridge Pope and Palmers beer and Inch's cider; garden; children welcome *(Caroline and Peter Warwick, R J Walden)*

☆ **West Charleton** [A379; SX7542], *Ashburton*: Interesting history on wall of clean and friendly main bar, well kept Bass, Fergusons Dartmoor and Wadworths 6X, good value wines, good food inc fresh local crab, also self-cook 'sizzler' dishes; small pleasant dining area *(Alan and Heather Jacques, Andrew and Teresa Heffer)*

☆ **West Down** [the one up nr Ilfracombe; SS5142], *Crown*: Good value generous food inc children's and vegetarian cooked to order by welcoming landlord, in nice village pub with alcovey lounge, little red plush dining room, family room, discreet back pool/darts room; Flowers Original and other real ales, superb big garden behind with play areas and good shelter *(Michael, Alison and Rhiannon Sandy, D P and M E Cartwright, Mr and Mrs Moody)*

Westleigh [½ mile off A39 Bideford—Instow; SS4628], *Westleigh*: Friendly old village pub with old pictures in smallish lounge, well kept Courage-related beer, usual food inc good cheap home-made burgers, gorgeous views down over the Torridge estuary from spacious neatly kept hillside garden, good play area *(Chris Westmoreland, Michael, Alison and Rhiannon Sandy, Mr and Mrs N Hazzard, LYM)*

☆ Whiddon Down [off A30; SX6992], *Post*: Friendly local with decent food, nice atmosphere, well kept Whitbreads-related ales, lots of horsebrasses and china; low-key family room, skittle alley, small garden *(Paul and Heather Bettesworth, W T Healey, P and M Rudlin; reports on new management please)*

Whimple [off A30 Exeter—Honiton; SY4097], *New Fountain*: Pleasant and attractive village local that turns its hand to food; friendly landlord *(Gordon, LYM)*

☆ Widecombe [SX7176], *Olde Inne*: Quaintly rebuilt pub with stripped stonework, big log fires in both bars, dining room with wide choice of reasonably priced food (nothing very cheap for children, and they reserve the right to refuse just starters if busy), Ushers and other beers, friendly service; in pretty moorland village, very popular with tourists – some say the pub's at its best out of season; restaurant area, good big garden *(Philip and Debbie Haynes, J Harris, Michael A Butler, N P Cox, Patrick Clancy, John Hazel, LYM)*

☆ Widecombe [turning opp Old Inne, down hill past long church house – OS Sheet 191 map ref 720765], *Rugglestone*: Unspoilt and welcoming traditional alehouse (no spirits licence) in beautiful streamside setting, well kept cheap Bass *(Phil and Sally Gorton)*

☆ Winkleigh [off B3220; SS6308], *Kings Arms*: Quaint beamed and flagstoned bar with scrubbed pine tables, woodburner and big separate log fire, interesting aquariums, even a parrot, good home-cooked food (light snacks Sun evening), Courage-related real ales, good efficient service, well reproduced piped music, no smoking restaurant; small sheltered side courtyard with pool; children over 6 allowed, cottage to let by the week;

closed Mon *(Andrew and Teresa Heffer, Jim and Maggie Cowell, LYM)*

☆ Winkleigh, *Winkleigh Inn*: Fairly spartan but recently redecorated pub with well kept real ale such as John Smiths or Wadworths 6X, Inch's farm cider, commendable menu with interesting and original dishes yet very reasonable prices, lovely garden with view of church tower *(David Burnett, Donna Lowes, Derrick and Karen McClelland)*

☆ Wonson [Throwleigh – OS Sheet 191 map ref 673897; SX6789], *Northmore Arms*: Ancient little one-bar pub, unpretentious and relaxed, with stripped stonework, low beams, two stone fireplaces; reasonably priced well kept beers inc Adnams, Ash Vine and Flowers, simple good value bar food, friendly Jack Russell called Basher, picnic-table sets in garden; open all day; well behaved children welcome; two modest bedrooms – beautiful remote walking country *(John Wilkinson, Chris and Debra, Sean and Wendy McGeeney, John Wilson)*

☆ Woodbury [3½ miles from M5 junction 30; A376, then B3179; SY0187], *White Hart*: Pleasant and attractive, with comfortable lounge bar, small homely restaurant, wide range of good generous home-cooked food changing daily, good friendly service, well kept Bass and Worthington BB; good locals' bar with many characters, skittle alley with own buffet, peaceful village *(Mr and Mrs D Moon, Richard Armstead, Jeanne and George Barnwell, Robert and Gladys Flux)*

Woodbury Salterton [Sidmouth Rd; A3052 Exeter—Sidmouth; SY0189], *White Horse*: Modern and spacious, with wide range of good reasonably priced food in big but comfortably sectioned dining areas (booking essential Sat), choice of real ales, cheerful obliging young staff, good children's room and play area; bedrooms *(J I Fraser, Robert and Gladys Flux)*

Woolacombe [Ossaborough; unclassified rd signed off B3343 and B3231; SS4543], *Mill*: Welcoming 17th-c mill conversion, long narrow bar with flagstone floor and pool table, separated from second bar by large woodburner; friendly chatty landlord, well kept Courage Directors, good choice of generous if not cheap food inc local specialities, good service; tables in walled courtyard *(A M Pring)*

☆ Woolfardisworthy [SS3321], *Farmers Arms*: Small and cosy thatched village pub with warm welcome, good food, spotless housekeeping, well kept Northern guest beers *(David Heath, David Field)*

Real ale may be served from handpumps, electric pumps (not just the on-off switches used for keg beer) or – common in Scotland – tall taps called founts (pronounced 'fonts') where a separate pump pushes the beer up under air pressure. The landlord can adjust the force of the flow – a tight spigot gives the good creamy head that Yorkshire lads like.

Dorset

Several changes here include new licensees at the New Inn in Cerne Abbas (still doing an excellent range of wines by the glass), the Red Lion there (they've kept the same chef and seem to be enhancing its civilised character), the Elm Tree at Langton Herring, the Ilchester Arms at Symondsbury (rather less specialisation in fish; they're letting bedrooms now), and the Langton Arms at Tarrant Monkton (in just the few weeks before this edition went to press keen new owners here were winning warm support, with good food, well kept beer and promising refurbishments). Another pub where recent refurbishment is working out well is the friendly New Inn at Church Knowle, and extensive refurbishment at the Pilot Boat in Lyme Regis has given a fresh look to this bustling and popular place. That fine idiosyncratic old pub the Square & Compass at Worth Matravers has shed its brewery tie now, so looks set to preserve its quite unspoilt character: it gains one of our new Beer Awards this year, as do the Museum at Farnham (where food is in fact the main thing) and the Fox in Corfe Castle. Entirely new main entries here, or pubs back in these pages after an absence, are the individual old Royal Oak in Cerne Abbas (a thriving free house now, and a change of landlord since we last knew it – but in fact the new landlord Mr Holmes, a warm-hearted ex-merchant seaman, was at the helm here some years back, and the pub's never been better than when it was under his hand), the well run Smugglers in its snug spot by the sea at Osmington Mills, and the Masons Arms at Upwey, a friendly and welcoming unpretentious village pub. Our other entry in that village, the Old Ship, is quite a contrast, with stylish food and wines – doing very well currently. The Brace of Pheasants at Plush and the Three Horseshoes at Powerstock are also doing particularly well on the food side at the moment: the Three Horseshoes gains a Food Award this year, and we choose it as our Dorset Dining Pub of the Year. In general prices for both food and drink tend to be slightly higher than the national average in the county's pubs, though pubs tied to local breweries, particularly Palmers of Bridport, generally offer worthwhile savings on the drinks side. In the Lucky Dip section at the end of the chapter particularly promising entries include Pickwicks in Beaminster, the Gaggle of Geese at Buckland Newton, Winyards Gap near Chedington, Chetnole Arms at Chetnole, Fox at Corscombe, Loders Arms at Loders, Crown at Marnhull, Haven House at Mudeford, Halfway at Norden Heath, Inn in the Park in Poole, Digby Tap and Skippers in Sherborne and Dormers in Wimborne Minster.

ABBOTSBURY SY5785 Map 2

Ilchester Arms 🛏

B3157

In an interesting and picturesque old village, this bustling and handsome stone inn is a good base for exploring the area. The nearby swannery has been famous for centuries for its hundreds of nesting pairs, and in season there are pochard, tufted duck, goldeneye, brent geese and widgeon; the inn is very handy for the abbey, and its sheltered 20-acre gardens (closed in winter) with unusual tender plants and peacocks. There are rambling beamed rooms with a good, cosy atmosphere, and the main bar has over 1,000 prints on the walls, many depicting swans from the nearby abbey, as well as red plush button-back seats and spindleback chairs around cast-iron-framed and other tables on a turkey carpet, and some brocaded armchairs in front of the open log fire. Hunting horns hang from the beams along with stirrups and horsebrasses, there's a stag's head, and some stuffed fish. Popular bar food includes soup (£1.50), Dorset sausage baguette (£2.60), cottage pie (£3), jacket potato with cheese and bacon (£3.95), home-made steak and ale pie (£4.95), roast beef and Yorkshire pudding (£5.95), daily specials including lots of seafood such as tuna or salmon steaks or local lemon sole (around £6.50), and home-made puddings (all £2); children's menu (from £1.95). Big breakfasts are served in the sizeable and attractive no-smoking conservatory restaurant, and there are afternoon teas in the bar. Well kept Flowers Orginal, John Smiths, and Wadworths 6X on handpump, with a few malt whiskies; friendly service; darts, dominoes, cribbage, fruit machine, and piped music. You can see the sea from the comfortable back bedrooms, and lanes lead from the back of the building into the countryside, with other scenic walks along the coastal path. *(Recommended by David Brokensha, Bill and Beryl Farmer, Myroulla West, Dr and Mrs J H Hills, Sue Holland, David Webster, Peter Neate, Susan Cody, A Plumb, C J Pratt, Denise Plummer, Jim Froggatt, Dr and Mrs D M Gunn, Neil and Jenny Spink, Chris and Chris Vallely)*

Greenalls ~ Managers Mike and May Doyle ~ Real ale ~ Meals and snacks ~ Restaurant ~ Dorchester (01305) 871243 ~ Children in eating area of bar and in restaurant ~ Open 11-11 ~ Bedrooms: £35B/£55B

ASKERSWELL SY5292 Map 2

Spyway ★ ♀ £

Village signposted N of A35 Bridport—Dorchester; inn signposted locally; OS Sheet 194 map reference 529933

There's a fine choice of drinks in this simple and friendly country inn. As well as Ruddles County, Ushers Best, and Wadworths 6X on handpump, the particularly helpful licensee keeps 18 wines by the glass, 23 country wines, around 40 whiskies and a big choice of unusual non-alcoholic drinks. The cosy and characterful little rooms have old-fashioned high-backed settles, cushioned wall and window seats, fine decorative china, harness and a milkmaid's yoke, and a longcase clock; there's also a no-smoking dining area decorated with blue and white china, old oak beams and timber uprights. Shove-ha'penny, table skittles, dominoes and cribbage. Promptly served and reasonably priced, the good bar food usually includes a range of generous ploughman's such as hot sausages and tomato pickle or home-cooked ham with pickle (from £2.95), and lots of salads (from £3.75), as well as three-egg omelettes (£2.95), sausages and chips (£3.25), haddock or plaice (£3.50), evening extras like gammon and egg (£5.75) or 8oz steak (£7.95), and daily specials like mushroom, leek and courgette bake (£3.50), chicken, mushroom and sweetcorn crumble (£3.75), rabbit or steak and onion pies (£3.95), and pork steak in barbecue sauce (£4.50). In the pretty little back garden are ducks and other pets, and nearby are plenty of paths and bridleways for exploring the area more closely. Eggardon Hill, which the pub's steep lane leads up, is one of the highest in the region, with lovely views of the downs and to the coast. No children. *(Recommended by Huw and Carolyn Lewis, Mr and Mrs C R Little, Jim and Maggie Cowell, Paul Harrison, Jason Caulkin, S R Chapman, TOH, Ron Shelton, Chris Warne, Richard Dolphin, Mr and Mrs P B Dowsett, Roger and Sheila Thompson, John Sanders, Wayne Brindle, John Beeken, Pauline Bishop, Ian and Deborah Carrington, D S Beeson, Galen Strawson, Dr and Mrs D M Gunn, J H Bell, Mr and Mrs Moody, Major D A Daniels, M E A Horler, Mr and Mrs Michael Howl, M Dyer)*

Free house ~ Licensees Don and Jackie Roderick ~ Real ale ~ Meals and snacks ~ (01308) 485250 ~ Open 10.30-2.30(3 Sat), 6-11

BISHOPS CAUNDLE ST6913 Map 2

White Hart

A3030

There's plenty of space in the big, irregularly-shaped bar in this busy grey slate dining pub – as well as handsomely moulded low beams, ancient panelling, a good variety of seats and tables in decent wood, dark red curtains, and nice lamps. The walls are attractively decorated with brass trays and farming equipment. Good mostly home-made bar food includes french sticks, a wide range of ploughman's, salads, a smaller-appetite menu (from £2.95) such as cottage pie, sweet and sour chicken or lasagne, vegetarian dishes (£4.75), and gammon topped with hard-boiled egg and cheese sauce (£5.95); they grow their own herbs and some vegetables, and do afternoon teas in summer. Well kept Badger Best and Tanglefoot on handpump, and they are hoping to stock guest ales; friendly helpful service; darts, alley skittles, fruit machine and piped music. The biggish garden is floodlit at night, and is ideal for families – its children's play area has trampolines, a playhouse with slides, and a sandpit. *(Recommended by H D Wharton, J Muchelt, Don and Thelma Beeson, PWV, Major and Mrs E M Warrick, Guy Consterdine, Mrs C Archer, Romey Heaton)*

Badger ~ Managers Gordon and Joyce Pitman ~ Real ale ~ Meals and snacks (till 10pm) ~ (01963) 23301 ~ Children in eating area of bar and in skittle alley/playroom ~ Open 11-2.30(3 Sat), 6-11 ~ Bedrooms: £12.50/£25.00

BRIDPORT SY4692 Map 1

George

South St

Full of old-fashioned charm and lots of genuine character, this friendly and busy town local has two sizeable bars divided by a coloured tiled hallway one is served by a hatch from the main lounge. There are nicely spaced old dining tables and country seats and wheelback chairs, big rugs on tiled floors, a mahogany bar counter, fresh flowers, and a winter log fire. A wide range of carefully cooked good food (you can watch the licensee at work preparing your meal) using only fresh local produce, might include soup (£1.80), sandwiches (from £1.60), home-made pâté (£2.75), chicken in cream, mushroom and Calvados sauce (£3), Welsh rarebit and bacon (£3.25), ploughman's (from £3.50), over a dozen omelettes (£3.75), home-made pies such as ham, chicken and mushroom, vegetarian meals, whole grilled plaice (£4.75) and puddings such as home-made apple tart; you order at the bar and there is table service. You can only have an evening meal out of season if you make a reservation. Well kept Palmers 200, Bridport, IPA and Tally Ho on handpump, up to seven brands of Calvados, freshly squeezed orange, and an espresso coffee machine; an ancient pre-fruit-machine ball game and Radio 3 or maybe classical, jazz or opera tapes. *(Recommended by Brenda and Rob Fincham, Jeremy Williams, Anne Hyde, Jim and Maggie Cowell, R Wilson, Jane Pendock)*

Palmers ~ Tenant John Mander ~ Real ale ~ Meals and snacks (not Sun lunch – and see note above about evening meals) ~ Bridport (01308) 423187 ~ Children in family room ~ Open 10am-11pm (8.30am for coffee every day); closed 25 Dec ~ Bedrooms: £18.50/£37

BURTON BRADSTOCK SY4889 Map 1

Three Horseshoes

Mill St

You're sure of a warm welcome in this attractive thatched inn – either from the friendly landlord (who has been here for 16 years) or from the chatty locals. The pleasant roomy bar has an enjoyable atmosphere, an open fire, comfortable seating, and Palmers 200, Bridport, IPA and Tally Ho! on handpump. Popular, quickly served food from a menu with lots of jokes includes burgers (from £2.15), good crab sandwich (£2.75), several ploughman's (from £3.20), steak and kidney pie (£3.65), fish and chips (£3.75), vegetarian pie (£4.20), lasagne (£4.50), grilled gammon (£5.40), crab salad (£7.50), puddings (from £2.05), and evening extras like beef curry (£5.70), Cantonese prawns (£5.70), and sirloin steak (£8.95); the dining room is no-smoking; karum (a mix of shove-ha'penny and snooker) and piped music. There are tables on the lawn, and Chesil beach and cliff walks are only 400 yards away. The pretty village is worth strolling around. *(Recommended by Mark and Toni Amor-Segan, Rona Murdoch, Mr and Mrs Red Shimwell, Eric J Locker, Mrs J A Powell, M E A Horler, Andy and Jill Kassube, R Wilson, David Gray)*

Palmers ~ Tenant Bill Attrill ~ Real ale ~ Meals and snacks ~ Partly no-smoking restaurant ~ (01308) 897259 ~ Children in eating area of bar and in dining room ~ Open 11-2.30, 6-11; closed evening 25 Dec ~ Bedrooms: /£31

CERNE ABBAS ST6601 Map 2

New Inn ⇔ ♀

14 Long Street

Once again, this 15th-c inn – built as a guest house for the nearby Benedictine abbey – is under new management. The comfortable L-shaped lounge bar has oak beams in its high ceiling, seats in the stone-mullioned windows with a fine view down the main street of the attractive stone-built village, and a warm atmosphere. At lunchtime, bar food now includes sandwiches (from £1.75), ploughman's (£3.50), filled baked potatoes (from £3.50), fish and chips (£4.50), a cold carvery (from £5.50), and home-made specials like steak and kidney pie (£5.50) or three-fish grill in sorrel sauce (£6.95); in the evening there might be soup (£1.90), herb and garlic mushrooms (£2.75), mussels in cider (£3.50), oriental stir-fry (£4.95), Scottish salmon in a herb and garlic sauce (£7.50), skate with black butter and capers (£9), char-grilled steaks (from £9.50), and puddings such as summer pudding (£3.40). Well kept Eldridge Pope Best, Hardy and Royal Oak on handpump, a good wine list with around 10 by the glass, and several malt whiskies; piped music. The old coachyard still has its old pump and mounting block, and behind it there are tables on a big sheltered lawn. A good track leads up on to the hills above the village, where the prehistoric (and rather rude) Cerne Giant is cut into the chalk. *(Recommended by Geoff Butts, Polly Marsh, Joan and Michel Hooper-Immins, Lynn Sharpless, Bob Eardley, David Holloway, J L Aperin, Andy and Jill Kassube, Major and Mrs E M Warrick, WHBM, Joy and Arthur Hoadley, Major T C Thornton, Paul Boot)*

Eldridge Pope ~ Managers Paul and Vee Parsons ~ Real ale ~ Meals and snacks ~ Cerne Abbas (01300) 341274 ~ Children in eating area of bar ~ Open 11-3, 6-11 ~ Bedrooms: £25/£30

Red Lion

Long St

As we went to press, we heard that this friendly and neatly-kept pub had just changed hands – though the new licensees were planning to make few changes, and they've even kept the same chef and many of the same dishes: sandwiches, home-made soup, filled baked potatoes (from £3.40), ploughman's (from £3.80), omelettes (from £4), and grills (from £7.50), with daily specials such as fresh vegetable cannelloni (£4.95), whole breast of chicken with cranberry stuffing and served with lemon and tarragon sauce (£6.70), fresh fish such as grilled halibut (£6.40) or poached fresh salmon steak with hollandaise sauce (£6.80), and lovely puddings like hot apple pancakes with butterscotch sauce or peanut and chocolate mousse on biscuit base (£2.70); some of the vegetables come from local gardeners and allotments. Well kept Wadworths IPA and 6X and two changing guests beers like Bass or Ringwood Fortyniner on handpump, and a decent wine list. The bar has a handsome wooden counter, wheelback chairs on the green patterned carpet, and two little areas leading off; skittle alley and piped music. The secluded little garden is full of pretty cottagey flowers. *(Recommended by Joy and Arthur Hoadley, Sally Edsall, Jason Caulkin, David Holloway, Geoff Butts, Polly Marsh, Rona Murdoch; more reports on the new regime, please)*

Free house ~ Licensees Brian and Jane Cheeseman ~ Real ale ~ Meals and snacks ~ (01300) 341441 ~ Children in eating areas off main bar ~ Open 11.30-3, 6.30-11

Royal Oak
Long Street

Now a free house, this friendly 500-year-old pub has a row of three communicating rooms with sturdy oak beams, flagstones, neat courses of stonework decked out with antique china, brasses and farm tools, lots of shiny black panelling, and open fireplaces filled with fresh flowers. Well kept Flowers IPA, Morlands Old Speckled Hen and a changing guest like Wadworths 6X on handpump from the uncommonly long bar counter, and 6 wines by the glass. Bar food includes sandwiches (from £1.50), winter soup, ploughman's (from £3.75), fried brie with cranberry sauce (£3.95), lasagne (£4.50), steak and kidney pie or fried lemon sole (£4.95), Portland crab salad (£5.50), steaks (from £6.25), gammon and egg (£6.75), and puddings such as Jamaican crunch (£2.50); classical piped music. There are seats in the big garden. *(Recommended by David Holloway, Rona Murdoch, Joy and Arthur Hoadley, G U Briggs, Brig T I G Gray, B B Morgan, Gwyneth and Salvo Spadaro-Dutturi)*

Free house ~ Licensee Barry Holmes ~ Real ale ~ Meals and snacks ~ Children in eating area of bar (must be over 5) ~ (01300) 341797 ~ Open 11-2.30, 6-11

CHESIL SY6873 Map 2

Cove House
Entering Portland on A354, bear right following Chiswell Only signs: keep eyes skinned for pub, on right

Only about 30 or 40 metres from the edge of the water, this simple old place has super views out to sea. The pebbly Chesil beach seems to go on for miles along the coast, and parts of it have been known to come down the pub's chimney in particularly violent storms. The bar on the right is modestly furnished, with polished floorboards and local shipwreck photographs gently underlining the maritime feel; it opens into a dining room on the left. Under the new licensee good value bar food might include sandwiches (from £1.40), daily soups (£1.65), four or five types of ploughman's (from £3.20), and main courses like chilli or lasagne (£3.75), scampi (£4.50) and steaks (from £8.25). Well kept Boddingtons, Flowers Original, Marstons Pedigree and maybe a guest on handpump; helpful service and piped music. If you go out by the gents', at the back you can see the massive masonry which has let it stand up to the storms. No dogs. *(Recommended by A G Drake, Gwyneth and Salvo Spadaro-Dutturi, David Eberlin, David Brokensha, Dave and Jules Tuckett, Derek R Patey, Rich and Pauline Appleton; more reports please)*

Greenalls ~ Tenant Steve West ~ Real ale ~ Meals and snacks ~ Portland (01305) 820895 ~ Well behaved children allowed in main bar ~ Open 11.30-2.30, 6-11

nr CHIDEOCK SY4292 Map 2

Anchor
Seatown; signposted off A35 from Chideock

This welcoming pub is well placed for walks – it almost straddles the Dorset Coast Path and the 617 foot Golden Cap pinnacle is just behind the building. The two small bars have cosy winter fires, some sea pictures and interesting old photographs of local scenes, simple but comfortable seats around neat tables, and low white-planked ceilings; the family room is no-smoking, and there are friendly animals (especially the cat). Good bar food includes home-made soup (£1.95), sandwiches (from £1.65, crab £3.25), filled jacket potatoes (from £2.65), ploughman's (£3.45), curry (£3.95, with a larger version for £6.45), pizzas (from £4.50), home-made steak and kidney pie (£4.95), local crabmeat salad (£8.45), children's dishes (from £1.95), daily specials such as stuffed peppers (£4.45), Mexican pork (£4.95), seafood casserole (£5.25), lemon and turmeric chicken (£5.45), and turkey in hazelnut and cream sauce (£6.45); afternoon clotted cream teas in summer. Well kept Palmers 200, Bridport, IPA and Tally Ho on handpump, under light top pressure during the winter; freshly squeezed orange juice, and a decent little wine list; friendly service whatever time of year you go. Darts, shove-ha'penny, table skittles, cribbage, dominoes, fruit machine (summer only), a carom board, shut-the-box, and piped, classical music. As the pub is beside a seaside cove, it can get very busy indeed during high season. If you stay here, you can eat your breakfast in the bedroom if you want so you can have it overlooking the sea. *(Recommended by Mr and Mrs M P Aston, Andy and Jill Kassube, Marjorie and David Lamb, Dr R J Rathbone, Eric J Locker, D L Barker, Wayne Brindle, E M Hughes, Gwyneth and Salvo Spadaro-Dutturi, J E and A G Jones, Clem Stephens, Denise Plummer, Jim Froggatt)*

Palmers ~ Tenants David and Sadie Miles ~ Real ale ~ Meals and snacks (12-9.30 in summer; not winter Sun evenings) ~ (01297) 89215 ~ Well behaved children welcome ~ Folk, blues or jazz most Sat evenings ~ Open 11-11; 11-2.30, 7-11 in winter ~ Bedrooms: £16.50/£33

CHILD OKEFORD ST8313 Map 2

Saxon

Gold Hill; village signposted off A350 Blandford Forum—Shaftesbury and A357 Blandford—Sherborne; from centre follow Gillingham, Manston signpost

After walking on the nearby neolithic Hambledon Hill, this welcoming old farmhouse is a very cosy place to rest. The bar is a quietly clubby room with a log fire, and leads through a lethally low-beamed doorway into a rather more spacious side room with a mix of tables including an attractive mahogany one in the centre, plank-panelled dado, and a big woodburning stove in its brick and stone fireplace. The food is simple but neatly presented and good value (prices are the same as last year), including lots of sandwiches (from £1.25, prawn £3.50), toasties (from £1.50), filled baked potatoes (from £2.10), ploughman's (from £3.35), a wide choice of hot dishes such as a daily curry (£3.85), home-cooked ham or shepherd's pie (£3.95), cod in batter (£4.50), chicken kiev (£5.25), home-made steak and kidney pie (£5.50) and 8oz rump steak (£8.95), with several dishes of the day including a vegetarian dish; puddings such as raspberry and redcurrant pie or meringue surprise (£2.50), and children's menu (from £1.60). Well kept Bass, Butcombe Bitter and a guest beer on handpump; maybe quite well reproduced piped music, shove-ha'penny, cribbage and dominoes. Dry dogs are welcome on a lead. They still have their menagerie in the attractive back garden: dogs (Bass, a golden retriever and Sebastian, a bearded collie), cats (William, Henry, and Thomas), contented rabbits in neat hutches, goldfish, an entertainingly wide variety of fowls from khaki campbells to vociferous geese, two goats called Polly and Thea and, of course, George, the Vietnamese pot-bellied pig. Please note, they no longer do bedrooms. *(Recommended by Andy and Jill Kassube, Douglas Adam, Brian Chambers, Marjorie and David Lamb, H D Wharton, John Hazel, Harriet and Michael Robinson, WHBM, Rev A Nunnerley, M E A Horler)*

Free house ~ Licensees Roger and Hilary Pendleton ~ Real ale ~ Meals and snacks; not Sun or Tues evenings ~ Child Okeford (01258) 860310 ~ Children welcome in top bar ~ Open 11.30-2.30(3 Sat), 7-11

nr CHRISTCHURCH SZ1696 Map 2

Fishermans Haunt

Winkton: B3347 Ringwood road nearly 3 miles N of Christchurch

Close to weirs on the River Avon, this very relaxing creeper-covered hotel has tables among the shrubs, roses and other flowers in the back lawn – a very tranquil spot, and perhaps more so at night when the building is decked with fairy lights. The modernised and extended series of interconnecting bars have a variety of furnishings and moods: stuffed fish and fishing pictures, oryx and reindeer heads, some copper, brass and plates, and even a spring water well. At one end of the chain of rooms big windows look out on the neat front garden, and at the other there's a fruit machine and video game; there's a small no-smoking area. Good value, straightforward bar food includes sandwiches (from £1.50; toasties from £2.10), soup (£1.60), sausages, onion rings and chips (£3.20), chicken nuggets (£3.70) and scampi (£4.50), with specials chalked on a board and a popular cold carvery. Well kept Bass, Ringwood Best and Fortyniner, and Wadworths 6X on handpump, cheerful staff; piped music. *(Recommended by David Sweeney, J Muckelt, Andy and Jill Kassube, Iris and Eddie Brixton, C J Westmoreland, Mr and Mrs Moody; more reports please)*

Free house ~ Licensee James Bochan ~ Real ale ~ Meals and snacks (not 25 Dec) ~ Restaurant ~ Children in eating area of bar and in restaurant ~ (01202) 484071 ~ Open 10-2, 6-11; closed 25 Dec ~ Bedrooms: £28(£36B)/£54(£59B)

CHURCH KNOWLE (Isle of Purbeck) SY9481 Map 2

New Inn

Careful refurbishment here has included the linking of the two bars with an arch, and the knocking down of the wall between the lounge bar and the restaurant, creating a less formal dining lounge. New carpets have been laid and new farmhouse chairs and dining tables added, and a new skittle alley is to be built. And the gents' lavatory has been upgraded, giving access from inside the pub. It's a comfortable and relaxed place with warm coal and log fires, and good, popular food: sandwiches, home-made soup (£2, the Dorset blue vinny is much enjoyed), grilled sardines (£4.50), moules marinières or steak and kidney pie (£5), home-made lasagne (£5.50), fresh fillet of deep-fried plaice (£6), fisherman's pie (£6.50), rump steak in brandy and pepper sauce (£11), and they specialise in fresh fish like cod (£4.50), haddock (£5.50), and skate wings (£6.50), as well as smoked wild Scottish venison (£4.85), roast leg of Dorset lamb (£5), and puddings with clotted cream or custard such as spotted dick, lemon brûlée and summer pudding. Well kept Boddingtons, Devenish Royal Wessex, Flowers Original and a summer guest, and several wines by the glass. There are fine views of the Purbeck hills from the garden. *(Recommended by J L Alperin, David Eberlin, Mrs C Watkinson, Jason Caulkin, Charles Bardswell, Dr and Mrs R E S Tanner, Wayne Brindle, Trevor P Scott, Harriet and Michael Robinson, Dr N Holmes, A E and P McCully, G R Sunderland, R H Brown, John and Joan Nash, Romey Heaton, Julian and Sarah Stanton, Jerry and Alison Oakes, Marjorie and David Lamb)*

Greenalls (Whitbreads) ~ Tenants Maurice and Rosemary Estop ~ Meals and snacks ~ Restaurant ~ Corfe Castle (01929) 480357 ~ Children in eating area of bar ~ Open 11-3, 6-11; winter evening opening 7

CORFE CASTLE (Isle of Purbeck) SY9681 Map 2

Fox 🍺

West Street, off A351; from town centre, follow dead-end Car Park sign behind church

In summer, the very pleasant suntrap back garden here, reached by a pretty flower-hung side entrance and divided into secluded areas by flowerbeds and a twisted apple tree, really comes into its own – and you can sit and look at the dramatic ruins of the castle. Inside, the cosily traditional feel owes a lot to the fact that it's been run by the same family for over 50 years, who despite alterations and additions, have managed to preserve its character very well. The tiny front bar has small tables and chairs squeezed in, a painting of the castle in its prime among other pictures above the panelling, old-fashioned iron lamps, and hatch service. An ancient well was discovered in the lounge bar during restoration, and it's now on display there under glass and effectively lit from within. There's also a pre-1300 stone fireplace and another alcove has further ancient stonework and a number of fossils. Enjoyable bar food includes sandwiches (from £1.70), home-made soup (£1.80), filled baked potatoes (from £3), well presented ploughman's (from £3.20), ham, egg and chips (£4), home-made steak and kidney pie or plaice (£4.50), daily specials like cauliflower cheese (£4.20), walnut and lentil bake (£4.50), and sirloin steak au poivre (£8.20), and puddings (from £1.95). Well kept Eldridge Pope Royal Oak, Gibbs Mew Bishops Tipple, Greene King Abbot, Ind Coope Burton, and Wadworths 6X tapped from the cask; good dry white wine. The surrounding countryside is worth exploring and there's a local museum opposite. No children. *(Recommended by Geoff Butts, Polly Marsh, Andy and Jill Kassube, David Eberlin, Paul Boot, John Honnor, James Skinner, David Holloway, D G Clarke, Wayne Brindle, Dr and Mrs D M Gunn, David Gray, Alison Burt, Graham and Karen Oddey)*

Free house ~ Licensees Miss A L Brown and G B White ~ Real ale ~ Meals and snacks ~ (01929) 480449 ~ Open 11-3(2.30 winter), 6(6.30 winter)-11; closed 25 Dec

Greyhound
A351

The setting here is very striking as this busy pub is set directly underneath the battlements of the castle. The three small low-ceilinged areas of the main bar have mellowed oak panelling, old photographs of the town on the walls, a collection of old bottles, and flowers on each table; there's also a no-smoking family area. They specialise in seafood such as Mediterranean prawns sautéed in garlic (£4.75), good fresh crab salad, mixed seafood platter (£9) or lobster salad with prawns and crab (£12). Other bar food includes large filled rolls (from £1.30), home-made winter soup, generously filled baked potatoes (from £2.50), ploughman's, home-made chilli con carne (£3.50), and mushroom and nut fettucini (£3.95); prompt friendly service. Well kept Boddingtons, Flowers Original, and a guest beer on handpump; friendly service; darts sensibly placed in the back room, pool (winter), cribbage, dominoes, fruit machine and juke box. There are benches outside, and – given its position – the pub does get very crowded. *(Recommended by Steve Huggins, Dave Braisted, Alastair Campbell, Romey Heaton; more reports please)*

Whitbreads ~ Lease: A P and P C Southwell ~ Real ale ~ Meals and snacks ~ (01929) 480205 ~ Children in family room ~ Open 11-11; 11-3, 6.30-11 in winter ~ Bedrooms: £20/£30

CRANBORNE SU0513 Map 2

Fleur-de-Lys 🛏
B3078 N of Wimborne Minster

Readers very much enjoy staying at this friendly inn, and tell us that the rooms are most comfortable, spacious, and well equipped, and that the breakfasts are good. Thomas Hardy also stayed here while writing *Tess of the D'Urbervilles* – and if you fork left past the church you can follow the pretty downland track that Hardy must have visualised Tess taking home to 'Trentridge' (actually Pentridge), after dancing in what's now the garage. Rupert Brooke liked the pub so much he wrote a poem about it (displayed above the fireplace), though this was inspired too by his visit to a duller place in the same area by mistake. The oak-panelled lounge bar is attractively modernised, and there's also a more simply furnished beamed public bar with well kept Badger Best and Tanglefoot on handpump, farm cider, and some good malt whiskies. Popular bar food includes sandwiches, good soup, lots of main courses like aubergine bake, tagliatelle carbonara or smoked haddock fish pie with a crunchy nut topping (£4.75) and steak and kidney pudding (£4.95), with puddings such as various pavlovas or banoffi pie; good value Sunday lunch – best to arrive early. Darts, shove-ha'penny, dominoes, cribbage, fruit machine and piped music. There are swings and a slide on the lawn behind the car park. *(Recommended by Sue Holland, David Webster, C J Pratt, Nigel Clifton, H D Wharton, Alan and Eileen Bowker, John Hazel, Keith Symons, Michael and Harriet Robinson, CG, Mrs C A Blake, Dorothy Pilson, Paul S McPherson, Andy and Jill Kassube)*

Badger ~ Tenant Charles Hancock ~ Real ale ~ Meals and snacks (not 25 Dec or evening 26 Dec) ~ Cranborne (01725) 517282 ~ Children in eating area of bar and dining room ~ Open 10.30-2.30, 6-11 ~ Bedrooms: £24(£29B)/£36(£42B)

DORCHESTER SY6890 Map 2

Kings Arms 🍺 🛏
High East St

This rather elegant Georgian inn has long played a central role in Dorset history – there are strong links with Nelson, and the handsome first-floor bow window is memorable from Thomas Hardy's *Mayor of Casterbridge*. The spacious and comfortable bar has a civilised yet bustling atmosphere and some interesting old maps and pictures – including a historic photograph of Thomas Hardy himself with a 1915 film crew. The most popular tables are those around the capacious fireplace, full of eaters enjoying the bar food: soup (£1.95), well-served sandwiches (from £2.25), steak and kidney pie (£4.95), chicken stir-fry or beef stroganoff (£6.95), steaks (from £7.65) and poached salmon (£7.95); they also have evening grills and a coffee shop; neatly dressed obliging staff. Well kept Bass, Boddingtons, Courage Directors, Flowers Original, Marstons Pedigree, Morlands Old Speckled Hen, John Smiths, and Ruddles County on handpump, freshly squeezed fruit juice and a range of malt whiskies from the long mahogany bar counter; pool, fruit machine, piped music. (Recommended by Andy and Jill Kassube, Barbara Hatfield, Peter Neate, Sue Holland, David Webster, Julian Bessa, Steve and Carolyn Harvey, W H and E Thomas, John A Barker)

Free house ~ Licensee Richard Lowe ~ Real ale ~ Meals and snacks ~ Restaurants ~ (01305) 265353 ~ Children in eating area of bar and in separate restaurants ~ Jazz every Tues evening, weekend discos ~ Open 11-3, 6-11; 11-11 Sat ~ Bedrooms: £42.95B/£46.40B

EAST CHALDON SY7983 Map 2

Sailors Return

Village signposted from A352 Wareham—Dorchester; from village green, follow Dorchester, Weymouth signpost; note that the village is also known as Chaldon Herring; Ordnance Survey sheet 194 map reference 790834

If you want to enjoy the generous helpings of very good food here, you must arrive early to be sure of a seat. It's a warmly friendly place too, and in an isolated tranquil spot near Lulworth Cove, with benches, picnic-table sets and log seats on the grass in front looking down over cow pastures to the village. It's the daily specials that readers like best – which might include chicken, ham and stilton pie (£4.75), jugged steak (£5.50), fisherman's pie or braised oxtails (£5.75), good smoked haddock with cheese sauce, delicious fresh whole mackerel, whole local plaice or tasty whole gammon hock (£6.25), vegetarian dishes, grills, and puddings such as good apricot-filled pancakes; also, sandwiches, home-made soup, burgers, filled baked potatoes, ploughman's and so forth, children's meals, and good value Sunday lunch. The restaurant is no-smoking. The welcoming bar still keeps much of its original character, and the low-ceilinged stone-floored core now serves as a coffee house. The newer part has open beams showing the roof above, uncompromisingly plain and simple furnishings, and old notices for decoration; the dining area has solid old tables in nooks and crannies. Well kept Wadworths 6X, Whitbreads Strong Country and a guest beer on handpump, country wines, farm cider, and malt whiskies. Darts, shove-ha'penny, table skittles, dominoes and piped music. From nearby West Chaldon a bridleway leads across to join the Dorset Coast Path by the National Trust cliffs above Ringstead Bay. (Recommended by Mr and Mrs B Hobden, Mrs M A Mees, Jason Caulkin, Roger and Jenny Huggins, Charles Bardswell, David Mead, Dr Andrew Brookes, Neil Hardwick, V Regan, D Baker, Frank W Gadbois, John and Joan Nash, Eric J Locker, Stephen and Jean Curtis)

Free house ~ Licensees Bob and Pat Hodson ~ Real ale ~ Meals and snacks ~ Restaurant ~ Dorchester (01305) 853847 ~ Children in small family room and in restaurant ~ Open 11-2.30, 6.30-11; closed evening 25 Dec

EAST KNIGHTON SY8185 Map 2

Countryman 🛏 ♀

Just off A352 Dorchester—Wareham; OS Sheet 194 map reference 811857

You can still make out some of the original shape of the two old cottages that once made up this comfortable and friendly pub. The main bar is a long carpeted room with plenty of character and atmosphere, a fire at either end, and a mixture of tables and wheelback chairs with cosier sofas. It opens into several other areas, including a no-smoking family room, a games bar with pool and darts, and a carvery. Quickly served and in big helpings, the wide range of food might include well filled sandwiches (from £1.50), soup (£1.80), omelettes (from £2.95), ploughman's (from £3.20), a good few vegetarian meals like vegetable pie (from £4.25), whitebait (£4.50), salads (from £5.50), sardines (£5.25), prawns or scampi (£5.75), lemon sole (£5.95), and specials like fish mornay (£4.25) or liver and bacon casserole (£4.50), with home-made puddings (£2.20) and children's dishes (from £1.95). Well kept Courage Best and Directors, Ringwood Best and Old Thumper and Wadworths 6X on handpump, Addlestones cider, a good choice of wines, and courteous well trained staff; piped music. Well behaved dogs allowed. There are tables and children's play equipment out in the garden. *(Recommended by Martyn Kearey, Stan Edwards, Marjorie and David Lamb, John and Joan Nash, Steve Webb, Marianne Lantree, Keith Houlgate, Mrs M A Mees)*

Free house ~ Licensees Jeremy and Nina Evans ~ Real ale ~ Meals and snacks (till 10) ~ Restaurant (closed Sun evening, all day Mon, Tues lunchtime) ~ (01305) 852666 ~ Children welcome ~ Open 11-3, 6-11; closed 25 Dec ~ Bedrooms: £32B/£45B

FARNHAM ST9515 Map 2

Museum 🛏 ♀ ◖

Village signposted off A354 Blandford Forum—Salisbury

It's the food that is the main draw to this smart and friendly old inn. From a wide range of changing dishes, there might be home-made tomato and basil soup (£2.50), sandwiches (from £3.25 with very lavish salad), ploughman's (£3.95), potted shrimps (£4.25), vegetable curry (£5.25), venison sausages with red cabbage (£5.50), home-made steak and kidney pie (£5.75), English breakfast (£5.95), gammon and eggs (£6.50), and daily specials such as scrambled eggs and anchovies (£4.75), mouclade of mussels (£5.50), home-made pigeon pie (£6.50), salmon and crab fishcakes (£6.95), and baked monkfish with Pernod and lime (£9.95), with puddings such as chocolate profiteroles or fresh strawberry pancakes (from £2.75). There's a calmly civilised feel to the Coopers Bar, which has green cloth-cushioned seats set into walls and windows, local pictures by Robin Davidson, an inglenook fireplace, and piped classical music. Very well kept Adnams, Batemans, Shepherd Neame Spitfire, and Wadworths 6X on handpump, as well as a large range of decent wines, local country wines, and twenty-six malt whiskies; darts, pool, trivia machine and juke box. There's a most attractive small brick-walled dining conservatory, leading out to a sheltered terrace with white tables under cocktail parasols, and beyond an arched wall is a garden with swings and a colourful tractor. Good value, simple bedrooms in converted former stables. The rustic village is largely thatch and flint. *(Recommended by DC, KC, Bernard and Kathleen Hypher, D and B Carter, K E Wohl, John Hazel, C Fisher, Lynn Sharpless, Bob Eardley, R Aldworth, W K Struthers; also recommended by* The Good Hotel Guide*)*

Free house ~ Licensee John Barnes ~ Real ale ~ Meals and snacks (service stops at 1.45 lunchtime) ~ Restaurant ~ Tollard Royal (01725) 516261 ~ Children in eating area of bar and in restaurant ~ Live entertainment on 3rd Thurs in month ~ Open 11-3, 6-11; closed 25 Dec ~ Bedrooms: £35B/£50B

GODMANSTONE SY6697 Map 2

Smiths Arms £

A352 N of Dorchester

Charles II is supposed to have stopped to have his horse shod at this tiny 15th-c thatched place – it was originally a smithy. Inside, the little bar has some antique waxed and polished small pews hugging the walls (there's also one elegant little high-backed settle), long wooden stools and chunky tables, National Hunt racing pictures and some brass plates on the walls, and an open fire. Well kept Ringwood Best tapped from casks behind the bar; friendly, helpful staff (the landlord is quite a character); piped music. Good home-made food (with prices unchanged since last year) includes sandwiches (from £1.35), ploughman's (from £2.90), jumbo sausage (£2.40), quiche (£3.25), chilli con carne (£3.30), a range of salads (from £3.55), home-cooked ham (£4.25), and scampi (£4.90), with daily specials such as broccoli au gratin, curried prawn lasagne or topside of beef; puddings like treacle tart or strawberry flan (from £1.50). It's very pleasant to sit outside, either on a crazy-paved terrace or the grassy mound by the narrow River Cerne – and from here you can walk over Cowdon Hill to the River Piddle. No children. (Recommended by Ted George, J Muckelt, V G and P A Nutt, David Holloway, John and Joan Nash, Stephen George Brown)

Free house ~ Licensees John and Linda Foster ~ Real ale ~ Meals and snacks (till 9.45) ~ (01300) 341236 ~ Open 11-3, 6-11; winter evening opening 6.30

KINGSTON (Isle of Purbeck) SY9579 Map 2

Scott Arms

B3069

After a good walk (there are plenty around here) you can sit in the garden outside this fine creeper-clad stone house and enjoy the superb views which take in the Purbeck Hills, Corfe Castle, and even distant Poole Harbour. Inside, there are lots of rambling rooms – all with old panelling, stripped stone walls and some fine antique prints; an attractive room overlooks the garden, and there's a decent extension well liked by families. It gets very busy indeed at times, but everyone seems to be absorbed into the space without it seeming too crowded. Popular bar food might include home-made soup (£2.25), deep-fried calamari with lemon and garlic dip (£2.75), ploughman's (£3.25), salads or fillet of plaice (£4.75), vegetarian dishes, steak and Guinness pie (£5.50), gammon and pineapple (£5.95), 6oz sirloin steak (£6.95), lots of daily specials, puddings (£2.20), and children's menu; the dining room is no smoking. Well kept Courage Best, Ringwood Best and Fortyniner, and Wadworths 6X on handpump, kept under light blanket pressure, and country wines; efficient, pleasant service; darts and quiet piped music. (Recommended by Trevor P Scott, Charles Bardswell, John Wheeler, James Skinner, David Mead, Peter Churchill, Romey Heaton, Derek R Patey, Andy and Jill Kassube, Mrs J Oakes)

Free house ~ Lease: Mike and Wendy Ralph ~ Real ale ~ Meals and snacks (not Sun evenings or Mondays in winter) ~ (01929) 480270 ~ Children in eating area of bar ~ Local singer alternate Thurs evenings ~ Open 11-2.30, 6-11

LANGTON HERRING SY6182 Map 2

Elm Tree

Village signposted off B3157

As we went to press, new licensees had just taken over this thatched cottage and had not really sorted out their menu. As well as sandwiches, ploughman's and salads (from £3.95), there are fresh fish dishes such as moules marinières (£5.25), baked mackerel (£5.95) and whole plaice or haddock (£7.95), as well as prawn tagliatelle or lasagne (£5.95), and puddings like summer pudding (£3.50). Boddingtons and Whitbreads Pompey Royal on handpump. The main carpeted rooms have beams and walls festooned with copper, brass and bellows, cushioned window seats, red leatherette stools, Windsor chairs, and lots of tables; there is a central circular modern fireplace in one room, and an older inglenook (and some old-fashioned settles) in the other. The traditionally furnished extension gives more room for diners. Outside in the pretty flower-filled sunken garden are colourful hanging baskets, flower tubs, and tables; a track leads down to the Dorset Coast Path, which here skirts the 8-mile lagoon enclosed by Chesil Beach. (Reports on the new regime, please)

Greenalls ~ Tenants Roberto D'Agostino, L M Horlock ~ Real ale ~ Meals and snacks (till 10pm) ~ (01305) 871257 ~ Children welcome ~ Open 11-3, 6.30-11

If you know a pub's ever open all day, please tell us.

LYME REGIS SY3492 Map 1

Pilot Boat ♀

Bridge Street

Deservedly popular, both in summer and winter, this bustling pub – undergoing extensive refurbishment – is full of diners happily choosing their good, waitress-served food: sandwiches (from £1.35, delicious crab £2.95), home-made soup (£1.95; the fish one is wonderful), very good huge ploughman's (£3.25), excellent crab pâté (£3.50), quite a few fish dishes (from £4.75, local trout £7.50, whole grilled lemon sole £9.50), avocado and sweetcorn bake (£5.50), steak and kidney pie (£5.95), salads (from £5.25, home-cooked ham £5.75, local crab £7.25), steaks (from £9.50), specials such as plaice fillets stuffed with asparagus (£7.50), salmon in lemon sauce (£9.50) and sea bass, and children's dishes (from £1.95 – including some proper food which is nice to see). The restaurant is no smoking. Well kept Palmers Bridport, IPA and Tally Ho on handpump, and a decent wine and liqueur list. The light, airy and comfortable bar is interestingly decorated with local pictures, Navy and helicopter photographs, lobster-pot lamps, sharks' heads, an interesting collection of local fossils, a model of one of the last sailing ships to use the harbour, and a notable collection of sailors' hat ribands. At the back, there's a long and narrow lounge bar overlooking the little River Lym; darts, dominoes and cribbage. There's a terrace outside and the pub is not far from the sea and beaches. The licensees run another Lyme Regis pub, the Cobb Arms. *(Recommended by TOH, Chris Thomas, C J Pratt, Myroulla West, Joan and Michel Hooper-Immins, Liz and John Soden, Steve Huggins, Stan Edwards, Jason Caulkin, Julian Bressa, A Craig, Ian Phillips, John and Suzanne McClenahan, Chris and Chris Vallely)*

Palmers ~ Tenants Bill and Caroline W C Wiscombe ~ Real ale ~ Meals and snacks (till 10 in summer) ~ Restaurant ~ Lyme Regis (0129 74) 43157 ~ Children welcome ~ Occasional live entertainment ~ Open 11-3, 6.30-11 (winter 11-2.30, 7-11)

MARNHULL ST7718 Map 2

Blackmore Vale ♀

Burton Street; quiet side street

For around 200 years, this welcoming and atmospheric place has been an ale house – though parts of the building are over 400 years old. It was supposed to have started as a brewhouse and bakehouse for the Strangeways Estate, and the entrance to the old bake oven can still be seen at one of the bar, near the fireplace. The home-made bar food is good and very popular and includes sandwiches (from £1.40), soup (£1.50), ploughman's (from £3.45), ham and egg (£4.40), mushroom and nut fettucini (£4.55), pies like steak and kidney or game (from £4.80), whole grilled plaice (£5.80), chestnut patties in red wine sauce (£6.85), tipsy crab pie (£7.95), steaks (from £7.95), and daily specials; Fridays is fish night, they do three roasts on Sundays, and have lots of home-made puddings. They will bring your food to the garden, where one of the tables is thatched. The comfortably modernised lounge bar is decorated with fourteen guns and rifles, keys, a few horsebrasses and old brass spigots on the beams, and there's a log fire. Well kept Badger Best, Hard Tackle and Tanglefoot on handpump, farm cider and a good wine list. Darts, cribbage, dominoes, shove-ha'penny, fruit machine, piped music and a skittle alley. There's an extensive range of purpose-built wooden children's play equipment. The pub was used by Thomas Hardy in *Tess of the D'Urbervilles* as the model for Rollivers. *(Recommended by Keith Stevens, Dr and Mrs J H Hills, WHBM, Major T C Thornton)*

Badger ~ Tenants Roger and Marion Hiron ~ Real ale ~ Meals and snacks (till 10pm) ~ (01258) 820701 ~ Children in eating area of bar ~ Open 11.30-2.30, 6.30-11

Soup prices usually include a roll and butter.

MILTON ABBAS ST8001 Map 2

Hambro Arms 🍺

This neatly kept and pretty pub is set in a beautiful 1770s landscaped village, its gently winding lane lined by lawns and cream-coloured thatched cottages. The beamed front lounge bar, reached through a maze of stone corridors, has a bow window seat looking down over the houses, captain's chairs and round tables on the carpet, and in winter an excellent log fire. Bar food includes sandwiches, soup, ploughman's, broccoli mornay, fresh fish like halibut, sole or haddock, and quite a few daily specials; roast Sunday lunch. Well kept Boddingtons and Flowers IPA on handpump; darts, juke box and fruit machine in the cosy back public bar. The outside terrace has some tables and chairs. No children. *(Recommended by WHBM, J Muckelt, Andy Jones, Andy and Jill Kassube, John Honnor, M V and J Melling, Dr and Mrs Nigel Holmes, Mrs J Oakes, Galen Strawson, Ann Reeder, Dave Craine)*

Greenalls ~ Tenants Ken and Brenda Baines ~ Real ale ~ Meals and snacks ~ Milton Abbas (01258) 880233 ~ Open 11-2.30, 6.30-11 ~ Bedrooms: £30B/£50B

OSMINGTON MILLS SY7341 Map 2

Smugglers

Village signposted off A353 NE of Weymouth

The sea is just moments away from this partly thatched stone-built pub – a stroll down through the pretty combe. It's a well run and spacious place, with shiny black panelling and woodwork dividing the bar into lots of cosy, friendly areas. There are stormy sea pictures, big wooden blocks and tackle, soft red lantern-light and logs burning in an open stove; some seats are tucked into alcoves and window embrasures, and one is part of an upended boat. Served by friendly staff, the good bar food includes home-made soup (£2), filled french bread (from £3.25), ploughman's (£4), pasta of the day or baked potato with pork in a creamy mushroom and cider sauce (£4.75), Thai chicken curry (£5), home-made steak, kidney and mushroom pie (£5.50), wild mushroom and nut fettucine (£7.50), and fresh fish dishes; they hold theme nights like cajun, French or medieval. Half the restaurant area is no smoking. Well kept Courage Best and Directors, Morlands Old Speckled Hen, Ringwood Old Thumper, and Wadworths 6X on handpump, and a fine choice of wines by the glass. Darts, pool and fruit machine are well segregated, dominoes, shut-the-box and piped music. There are picnic-table sets out on crazy paving by a little stream, with a thatched summer bar and a good play area over on a steep lawn. It gets very busy in high season (there's a holiday settlement just up the lane). *(Recommended by Mrs B M Fyffe, Charles Bardswell, John and Joan Nash, Peter and Lynn Brueton, Andy and Jill Kassube, Tony and Val Marshall, Alan Kilpatrick)*

Free house ~ Licensee Bill Bishop ~ Real ale ~ Meals and snacks ~ Restaurant ~ (01305) 833125 ~ Children welcome ~ Occasional jazz, blues and steel bands ~ Open 11-11; 11-3, 6-11 in winter ~ Bedrooms: £28B/£55B

PIDDLEHINTON SY7197 Map 1

Thimble

B3143

In the heart of the countryside, this pretty thatched pub has been extended this year. It's very neatly kept and friendly, with beams, attractive furnishings, an open stone fireplace, a newly discovered deep well which has a glass panel over it, and well kept Badger Best and Hard Tackle, Eldridge Pope Hardy, and Ringwood Old Thumper on handpump, farm cider, quite a few malt whiskies, and helpful, efficient service. Well presented good value food includes sandwiches (from £1.60), home-made soup (£2.10), home-made pâté (£2.80), filled baked potatoes (from £2.40), ploughman's (from £3.75), lasagne (£4.60), broccoli and mushroom mornay (£4.65), scampi en croute (£5.50), steak and oyster pudding (£5.95), gammon and egg (£6.95), steaks (from £9.50), and puddings (£2.25), with weekly specials like chicken stir-fry (£5.20), beef, venison and strong ale pie (£5.70), and fresh fish such as bream, skate or sea bass (as available); roast beef Sunday lunch (£5.35). There are masses of flowers in the garden and a little bridge over the stream running alongside. *(Recommended by David Dimock, K E Wohl, R A F Montgomery, G U Briggs, Bronwen and Steve Wrigley, Jason Caulkin, John A Barker, Nicholas H Smith, M D Donovan, Mrs C J Mason, A W Spicer, M W Young, Andy and Jill Kassube)*

Free house ~ Licensees N R White and V J Lanfear ~ Real ale ~ Meals and snacks ~ (01300) 348270 ~ Children in eating area of bar ~ Open 12-2.30, 7-11

PLUSH ST7102 Map 2

Brace of Pheasants

Village signposted from B3143 N of Dorchester at Piddletrenthide

Originally a row of cottages that included the village forge, this long, low 16th-c thatched pub is charmingly placed in a fold of the hills surrounding the Piddle Valley, and lies alongside Plush Brook; an attractive bridleway behind goes to the left of the woods and over to Church Hill. Behind the pub is a decent-sized play garden with swings, an aviary, a rabbit in a cage and a lawn sloping up towards a rookery. Inside, the beamed bar has good solid tables, some oak window seats as well as the Windsor chairs, fresh flowers, a heavy-beamed inglenook at one end with cosy seating inside the old fireplace, and a good log fire at the other. A very wide choice of deservedly popular and imaginative home-made bar food includes soup (£1.85), crab savoury (£3), ploughman's (from £3.50), soft herring roes with garlic butter or excellent smoked pheasant pâté (£3.50), salads (from £5.95), steak, kidney and mushroom pie or liver, bacon and onion (£5.95), gammon and pineapple (£6.50), steaks (from £9.25), lamb in blackcurrant and cassis sauce (£9.75), duck with apple and calvados (£11.25), daily specials like rabbit stew (£5.95), chicken and prawn stir-fry (£6.50), local crab salad (£6.95), and grilled lemon sole with parsley and lemon butter (£9.50); children's menu (from £1.75 – good to see some proper dishes offered). The restaurant and the family room are no smoking. Well kept Exmoor Bitter, Greene King IPA, Hook Norton Old Hookey, Smiles Best and Wadworths 6X on handpump, and they do country wines; darts, alley skittles and dominoes. The golden retriever is called Scallywag and the labradors Becky and Bodger. *(Recommended by H D Wharton, Bronwen and Steve Wrigley, John and Tessa Rainsford, Dr and Mrs J H Hills, Julian Bessa, Chris and Sue Heathman, Frank Cummins, Mr and Mrs Michael Howl, Nicholas H Smith)*

Free house ~ Licensees Jane and Geoffrey Knights ~ Real ale ~ Meals and snacks ~ Restaurant ~ (01300) 348357 ~ Children in family room and restaurant ~ Open 11.30(12 in winter)-2.30, 7-11

POWERSTOCK SY5196 Map 2

Three Horseshoes 🍽 🍷

Can be reached by taking Askerswell turn off A35 then keeping uphill past the Spyway Inn, and bearing left all the way round Eggardon Hill – a lovely drive, but steep narrow roads; a better road is signposted West Milton off the A3066 Beaminster—Bridport, then take Powerstock road

Dorset Dining Pub of the Year

This popular dining pub is a perfect base for fishing – either at the nearby trout ponds, from the beach, or you can book a six-hour trip out to sea. And fresh fish, landed daily at Weymouth, features strongly on the menu. Depending on availability, there might be Lyme Bay plaice or skate wing with capers (£8.95), fillet of brill with onions, wine and cream (£9.50), monkfish tail provençale (£10.50), local scallops sautéed with chopped shallot, garlic and parsley or char-grilled sea bass (£12.50), and a seafood grill (£17.50); there are also filled french sticks, vegetable soup (£2.50), spinach pancake with cheese sauce (£4.50), moules marinières (£4.95), pasta pesto (£5.50), chicken in tomato, basil and tarragon sauce (£7.50), wild rabbit casserole (£8.50), venison in a red wine sauce (£10.50), and puddings like sunken chocolate soufflé, summer berry tart or sticky toffee pudding (from £3). Good breakfasts with home-made marmalade. The restaurant is no-smoking. Well kept Palmers 200, Bridport, IPA and Tally Ho on handpump, quite a few wines by the glass, and freshly-squeezed fruit juice. The comfortable L-shaped bar has country-style chairs around the polished tables, pictures on the stripped panelled walls, and warm fires; Daisy the friendly retriever may be wandering round. The garden has swings and a climbing frame, and from the neat lawn rising steeply above the pub, there are lovely uninterrupted views towards the sea. *(Recommended by Huw and Carolyn Lewis, Mrs Margaret Barker, J L Alperin, Gethin Lewis, Barbara Hatfield, J Muckelt, C J Pratt, DC, Mr and Mrs J A Wilson, Dr R J Rathbone, Desmond L Barker, Rev A Nunnerley, Mrs J Oakes, Jane Pendock, TOH)*

Palmers ~ Tenant P W Ferguson ~ Real ale ~ Meals and snacks ~ Restaurant ~ Powerstock (01308) 485321 ~ Children welcome ~ Open 11-3, 6-11 ~ Bedrooms: £24(£30B)/£40(£45B)

SHAFTESBURY ST8622 Map 2

Ship

Bleke Street; you pass pub on main entrance to town from N

There's a lovely old-fashioned and friendly atmosphere in this handsome and unpretentious 17th-c stone inn. One of the cosiest parts is the snug black-panelled alcove facing the main bar counter, with built in seats and a striking old oak staircase behind it; on the left there's a panelled similarly furnished room, and the eating area is on the right. Well kept Badger Best and Tanglefoot on handpump, and traditional farm cider; darts, pool, cribbage, dominoes, juke box and an outdoor boules court. Bar food includes sandwiches (from £1.25), home-made soup (£1.45), pâté or garlic mushrooms (£1.95), quite a few vegan dishes like pasta in a red pepper sauce, nut roast or lentil and tomato savoury (£3.50), meaty dishes such as lasagne or beef in Guinness (£4.50), daily specials like middle eastern tomatoes (£3.50) or Spanish pork or Taunton chicken (£4.50), and puddings (£1.95). No dogs in the flower-filled lounge. The little garden has white tables and chairs on the terrace. Behind the Town Hall round the corner is Golden Hill, the steep terraced street of the nostalgic Hovis TV advert. *(Recommended by Gordon, Barbara Hatfield, Kevin Booker, Jim and Maggie Cowell, Stephen Brown)*

Badger ~ Tenants Steve Marshall, Pam Tait ~ Real ale ~ Meals and snacks ~ (01747) 853219 ~ Children in eating area of bar ~ Open 11-3, 5-11; all day Thurs-Sat

SHAVE CROSS SY4198 Map 1

Shave Cross Inn ★

On back lane Bridport—Marshwood, signposted locally; OS Sheet 193 map reference 415980

This friendly and partly 14th-c thatched inn got its name from the style of haircut given to monks on the last stage of their pilgrimage to the shrine of St Wita at Whitchurch Canonicorum. You can try and follow their route along the path that starts opposite the pub. The pretty flower-filled sheltered garden has a thatched wishing-well, a goldfish pool, a children's adventure playground, and a small secluded campsite for touring caravans and campers. Inside, the original timbered bar is a lovely flagstoned room, surprisingly roomy and full of character, with one big table in the middle, a smaller one by the window seat, a row of chintz-cushioned Windsor chairs, and an enormous inglenook fireplace with plates hanging from the chimney breast. The larger carpeted side lounge has a dresser at one end set with plates, and modern rustic light-coloured seats making booths around the tables. Popular, promptly served bar food includes fine ploughman's (from £2.75), good sausages (£2.75), steak sandwich (£3.95), mushroom and spinach lasagne (£3.95), salads (from £3.75), vegetable tikka masala (£5.25), kebabs of sweet and sour pork and spicy lamb (£5.95), mixed grill (£7.95), daily specials like tiger prawns in filo pastry (£4.35), chicken, ham and mushroom pie (£4.45), and char-grilled shark or swordfish steak (£7.45), puddings such as crêpes in orange sauce, flamed with cointreau (from £1.85), and children's meals (from £1.95). Well kept Badger Best, Bass and Eldridge Pope Royal Oak on handpump, and local cider in summer; friendly, polite staff; darts, alley skittles, dominoes and cribbage. *(Recommended by Marjorie and David Lamb, D L Barker, Mrs A R E Bishop, David Holloway, Chris Warne, David Eberlin, TOH, D Boyd, M E and J Wellington, Clem Stephens, R W Brooks)*

Free house ~ Licensees Bill and Ruth Slade ~ Real ale ~ Meals and snacks (not Mon, except bank holidays) ~ (01308) 868358 ~ Children in lounge bar ~ Open 12-2.30(3 Sat), 7-11; closed Mon (except bank holidays)

SYMONDSBURY SY4493 Map 1

Ilchester Arms

Village signposted from A35 just W of Bridport

New licensees have taken over this pretty old thatched inn and have introduced a new menu: home-made soup or fish mousse (£1.75), filled baked potatoes (from £1.95), ploughman's or filled rolls (from £2.50), gammon steak or pork Dijon (£4.25), vegetarian dishes (from £4.25), mince and tatties (£4.75), whole plaice (£5.75), whole lemon sole (£6.25), crab mornay (£6.75), and daily specials such as liver and onions, beef teriyaki or beef and dumplings. Well kept Palmers Bridport, IPA, and Tally Ho on handpump or tapped from the cask. One side of the open-plan bar has rustic benches and tables, seats in the mullioned windows, and a high-backed settle built into the bar counter next to the big inglenook fireplace; the other side, also with an open fire, has candlelit tables and is used mainly for dining in the evening and at weekends. Darts, pool, shove-ha'penny, dominoes, cribbage, and a separate skittle alley (with tables); piped music. There are tables outside in a quiet back garden by a stream. The high-hedged lanes which twist deeply through the sandstone behind this village of pretty stone houses lead to good walks through the wooded low hills above the Marshwood Vale. *(Recommended by Gwyneth and Salvo Spadaro-Dutturi, Dr R J Rathbone, Reg and Carrie Carr, TOH, R M Bloomfield; more reports on the new regime, please)*

Palmers ~ Tenants Dick and Ann Foad ~ Real ale ~ Meals and snacks (not winter Mon) ~ Restaurant ~ Bridport (01308) 422600 ~ Children welcome ~ Open 11-3, 6.30-11; 12-2.30, 7-11 in winter ~ Bedrooms: £12.50/£25(family room)

TARRANT MONKTON ST9408 Map 2

Langton Arms

Village signposted from A354, then head for church

Some careful changes to this attractive 17th-c thatched inn this year include the redecoration of the skittle alley (which is also now a welcoming family room with an indoor play area), the refurbishment of the no-smoking restaurant which has become more of a bistro, and the building of a new and safe play area outside for under 8s. Very good bar food now includes cream of Poole Bay crab soup (£2.30), wild boar and venison sausages in red wine gravy or pasta parcels filled with spinach and ricotta cheese with a creamy onion and garlic sauce (£4.25), sweet and sour prawn fritters, breast of chicken in a creamy cheese and bacon sauce, fillet of salmon in a prawn and white wine sauce, and puddings like coffee and tia maria cheesecake or apple and strawberry crumble (£1.95); they also have Monday fish and chips (£2.95), Tuesday pizza and pasta (from £3.50), Thursday steaks (from £4.25), and children's dishes (2 courses £1.99). Well kept Exmoor Stag, Hook Norton Best, Morlands Old Speckled Hen, Ringwood Fortyniner, and Shepherd Neame Spitfire, and decent wines – some by the glass. The comfortable beamed main bar has settles that form a couple of secluded booths around tables at the carpeted end, window seats, and another table or two at the serving end where the floor's tiled. The public bar, with a big inglenook fireplace, has darts, pool, shove-ha'penny, cribbage, dominoes, fruit machine, juke box and piped music. There are some seats in the pretty garden. Tracks lead up to Crichel Down above the village, and Badbury Rings, a hill fort by the B3082 just south of here, is very striking.

(Recommended by Richard Dolphin, John Hazel, Phil and Heidi Cook, Gary Roberts; more reports please)

Free house ~ Licensees Philip Davison, James Cossins, Michael Angel ~ Real ale ~ Meals and snacks (till 10pm) ~ Restaurant (not Sun evening or Mon) ~ Tarrant Hinton (01258) 830225 ~ Children in family room ~ Open 11.30(11 Sat)-11; 11.30-3, 6-11 winter ~ Bedrooms: £35B/£48B

UPWEY SY6684 Map 2

Masons Arms

B3159, nr junction A354

The friendly considerate landlady contributes a great deal to the relaxèd pleasant atmosphere in this plain brick roadside pub. One of the two small rooms is decorated with lots of china pigs, 1930s Grants whisky playing cards, match books, tea-towels and carved walking sticks on the ceiling, policemen's helmets and sailors' caps, and pictures of the pub and other local scenes; brocaded wall benches and chunky tables. The other room, no-smoking and set out for eating, has more tea-towels on the ceiling, plates and display of bomber-command sheets, photographs of Lancasters and more pictures. Bar food includes winter soup (£1.50), sandwiches (from £1.50), lots of omelettes (from £3), award-winning ploughman's with fruit, salad, a piece of cake, pickles and an egg (from £3.50), filled giant Yorkshire puddings or spaghetti bolognese (£4), and ham and egg (£4.75). Well kept Marstons Pedigree on handpump; CD player, skittle alley, darts, cribbage, dominoes and fruit machine. Outside in the garden there are wooden tables and white chairs under umbrellas, with more in a larger back part where there's a playhut, climber, swings, see-saw and small chicken run.

(Recommended by J Soden, E Hobday, D Newton, S Place, Stan Edwards, Eric J Locker)

Greenalls ~ Tenants Wally and Ann Tanner ~ Real ale ~ Meals and snacks (not Sun evening or winter Mon-Thurs evenings) ~ (01305) 812740 ~ Children welcome ~ Open 11.30-2.30, 6-11

Old Ship ♀

Ridgeway; turn left off A354 at bottom of Ridgeway Hill into old Roman Rd

Doing very well indeed, this pretty little whitewashed cottagey pub with its colourful hanging baskets has a lovely tranquil atmosphere, good, popular food, a fine choice of 12 wines by the glass, well kept real ales, and a warmly friendly atmosphere. There are several interconnected rooms with a mix of sturdy chairs, some built-in wooden wall settles, beams, an open fire with horsebrasses along the mantelbeam, fresh flowers on the solid panelled wood bar counter and tables, china plates, copper pans and old clocks on the walls, and a couple of comfortable armchairs. Bar food includes home-made soup (£1.95), very good garlic mushrooms (using proper field mushrooms), sandwiches (from £2.25), 3-egg omelettes (from £3.10), cheese and broccoli quiche (£3.95), ploughman's (from £3.95), ham and egg (£4.75), battered cod fillet (£5.95), lamb with garlic and cream or cajun-style chicken (£7.95), steaks (from £8.95), and daily specials like pork cutlet au poivre or fillet of bream Bretonne (£6.25), and lovely venison steak chasseur (£9.50); two or three course Sunday lunches (from £6.10). Well kept Boddingtons Bitter, Flowers Original and weekly guest beers on handpump); skittle alley. Outside, there are picnic-table sets and umbrellas in the garden. *(Recommended by Michel and Joan Hooper-Immins, Andy and Jill Kassube, TOH)*

Greenalls ~ Tenant Paul Edmunds ~ Real ale ~ Meals and snacks (not 25 Dec) ~ (01305) 812522 ~ Children in eating area of bar ~ Open 11-2.30(3 Sat), 6-11

If we don't specify bar meal times for a main entry, these are normally 12-2 and 7-9; we do show times if they are markedly different.

EST BEXINGTON SY5387 Map 2

Manor Hotel ⏚ 🛏

Village signposted off B3157 SE of Bridport, opposite the Bull in Swyre

This is a particularly pleasant place to spend a few days – and you can see the sea from the bedrooms and from the garden, where there are picnic-table sets on a small lawn with flowerbeds lining the low sheltering walls; a much bigger side lawn has a children's play area. Inside, a handsome Jacobean oak-panelled hall leads down to the busy pubby cellar bar, actually on the same level as the south-sloping garden. Small country pictures and good leather-mounted horsebrasses decorate the walls, and there are red leatherette stools and low-backed chairs (with one fat seat carved from a beer cask) under the black beams and joists, as well as heavy harness over the log fire. A smart no-smoking Victorian-style conservatory has airy furnishings and lots of plants. A wide choice of very good, popular bar food, including lots of fish dishes, might consist of sandwiches (from £2.15), soup (£2.25), ploughman's (£4.25), devilled crab or lobster roulade (£4.65), bangers and mash (£5.95), salads (from £6.05; crab £7.35), brazil nut loaf (£6.75), lasagne (£6.85), rabbit or steak and kidney pies (£6.95), grey mullet (£7.95), rack of lamb (£8.65), lemon sole caprice (£9.95), monkfish au poivre (£11.45), puddings (£2.95), and children's dishes (£3.25); good breakfasts. Well kept Eldridge Pope Royal Oak, Palmers Bridport (which here carries the pub's name) and Wadworths 6X on handpump, and quite a few wines by the glass; helpful, courteous service; alley skittles. *(Recommended by Mrs J A Powell, Eric and Patricia King, John Coatsworth, Jacqueline White, J Muckett, KC, Basil Minson, W C M Jones, Mr and Mrs M P Aston, J L Alperin, David Brokensha, P J Hanson, R Wilson, Brian and Jill Bond, Chris and Chris Vallely, E H George, John and Suzanne McClenahan, Marjorie and David Lamb)*

Free house ~ Licensee Richard Childs ~ Real ale ~ Meals and snacks (till 10pm) ~ Restaurant (not Sun evening) ~ Burton Bradstock (01308) 897616 ~ Children welcome ~ Open 11-11; closed evening 25 Dec ~ Bedrooms: £46B/£76B

WEST LULWORTH SY8280 Map 2

Castle 🛏

B3070

This very popular and friendly thatched white inn is in a lovely spot close to Lulworth Cove (best to walk down there from here as the car park at the bottom is expensive); there are good walks each way from the cove, and on the coastal path by Old Harry Rocks. The award-winning garden has giant chess boards, boules, hopscotch, steeply terraced rose beds, a barbecue area, and good views. Inside, the lively public bar has polished flagstones and button-back leatherette seats forming a maze of booths around the tables, and the comfortably furnished lounge, though more modern-feeling, is still cosy, with blue banquettes under the countryside prints on the walls, and pewter tankards hanging from one beam. A wide choice of good bar food includes home-made soup (£1.80), filled rolls (from £1.80), ploughman's (from £3), salads (from £5), vegetable and cheese bake or liver and bacon casserole (£4.50), steak and kidney or chicken, ham and mushroom pies (£4.90), swordfish (£5.90), salmon steak (£6.50), beef stroganoff (£8.50), seafood stew (£10), puddings (£1.50), and children's meals (from £2.50); excellent breakfasts. Well kept Devenish Wessex, Flowers Original and Marstons Pedigree on handpump, farm cider, and welcoming helpful staff; darts, shove-ha'penny, table skittles, dominoes, cribbage, fruit machine, trivia, backgammon, Scrabble and other board games, outdoor chess, and piped music. *(Recommended by Martyn Kearey, W H and E Thomas, Trevor Scott, J L Alperin, Gill Earle, Andrew Burton, Neil and Jenny Spink, Mrs C A Blake)*

Greenalls ~ Lease: Graham Halliday ~ Real ale ~ Meals and snacks (11-2.30, 7-10.30) ~ Restaurant ~ West Lulworth (01929) 400311 ~ Children in eating area of bar and in restaurant ~ Occasional live music/Morris dancing ~ Open 11-2.30, 7-11 ~ Bedrooms: £20(£25B)/£35(£41B)

WORTH MATRAVERS SY9777 (Isle of Purbeck) Map 2

Square & Compass £ ◀

At fork of both roads signposted to village from B3069

As we went to press we heard that Mr Newman – the fourth generation of the family that has run this delightfully unchanging pub for nearly 90 years – had just bought the freehold from the brewers. It is a genuinely and determinedly unspoilt place with an almost unique atmosphere – no plush furnishings or decor, noisy modern machines or big imaginative menus here – just an old-fashioned main bar with wall benches around the elbow-polished old tables on the flagstones, and interesting local pictures under its low ceilings. Well kept Badger Tanglefoot, Flowers Original, Marstons Pedigree, Ringwood Fortyniner, and Whitbreads Castle Eden and Strong Country tapped from a row of casks behind a couple of hatches in the flagstoned corridor (local fossils back here, and various curios inside the servery), which leads to a more conventional summer bar; Bulmers and Inch's ciders. Bar snacks consists of pasties (80p); cribbage, shove ha'penny and dominoes. On a clear day the view from this peaceful hilltop setting is hard to beat, looking down over the village rooftops to the sea between the East Man and the West Man, the hills that guard the sea approach, with on summer evenings the sun setting out beyond Portland Bill. There are benches outside to admire the view, or to watch the assorted birds that roam freely and happily in front of the building. The pub is at the start of an OS Walkers Britain walk; dogs welcome. *(Recommended by Gwyneth and Salvo Spadaro-Dutturi, David Warrellow, D G Clarke, David Mead, Geoff Butts, Polly Marsh, Geraint Roberts, A Plumb, R H Brown, Lynn Sharpless, Bob Eardley, Peter Pocklington, Jerry and Alison Oakes, Andy and Jill Kassube, Derek R Patey, Mr and Mrs Moody, David Gray, Denise Plummer, Jim Froggatt, Nigel Norman, R Wilson)*

Free house ~ Licensee Charlie Newman ~ Real ale ~ Lunchtime snacks ~ (01929) 439229 ~ Children welcome ~ Occasional live music ~ Open 11-3, 6-11; all day summer Sats

---

Lucky Dip

Besides the fully inspected pubs, you might like to try these Lucky Dips recommended to us and described by readers (if you do, please send us reports):

☆ **Almer** [just off A31; SY9097], *Worlds End*: Extensive L-shaped open-plan thatched family pub with well kept Badger Best and Tanglefoot, jolly atmosphere, almost too wide a choice of bar food (no sandwiches), well trained staff; picnic-table sets out in front and behind, plenty of space with good big well equipped play area and pets *(Andy and Jill Kassube, Will Podmore, Mr and Mrs P D Prescott, Anthony Willey, BB)*

☆ **Beaminster** [The Square; ST4701], *Pickwicks*: Good atmosphere and friendly landlord in quaint but comfortable 16th-c pub with interesting real ales, wide choice of outstanding value well presented home-cooked food inc good vegetarian dishes – more restaurant than pub evenings; piped opera; bedrooms *(David Brown, A J Peile, Mr and Mrs Michael Howl, R MacDonald, Chris Woodward)*

☆ **Beaminster** [The Square], *Greyhound*: Small and homely 18th-c pub, locally very popular for uncommonly wide choice of reasonably priced food inc interesting vegetarian dishes served promptly; well kept Palmers IPA and BB, friendly staff; small family room *(C J Pratt)*

☆ **Bere Regis** [West St; SY8494], *Royal Oak*: Well kept open-plan modernised local with very friendly licensees, well kept Flowers Original and Whitbreads Strong Country on handpump, good value food, pleasantly busy atmosphere, woodburner, sensibly placed darts, cribbage, fruit machine; dining room; open all day Fri and Sat; bedrooms *(John and Joan Nash, Nicholas H Smith, BB)*

Bournemouth [165 Old Christchurch Rd; SZ0991], *Botlers Crab & Ale House*: Well placed, clean and well furnished in wine-bar style, with decent food running up to steaks, friendly service, Boddingtons from attractive central bar *(Mr and Mrs A R Hawkins, Anna and Steven Oxley)*; [423 Charminster Rd], *Fiveways*: Wide choice of usual pub food, Eldridge Pope real ales, no-smoking area, friendly local atmosphere, good games room popular with young people *(WHBM, George Murdoch)*

Bourton [off A303 – Mere exit westbound, Wincanton eastbound; ST7430], *Red Lion*: Badger pub with good Malaysian/Chinese cooking though no separate dining room *(R H Martyn)*; *White Lion*: This attractive and interesting coaching inn has been a very popular main entry, with good food, an interesting range of real ales, and friendly service, but after a brewery/tenant dispute followed by an interregnum was closed and boarded up spring 1994 (the former tenants can be found at Skippers in Sherborne); we hope the pub will eventually reopen *(LYM; news please)*

Bridport [34 East St; SY4692], *Knights Bull*: Hotel rather than pub, but has decent bar snacks and Wadworths 6X, Worthington BB; good bedrooms *(Jim and Maggie Cowell)*; [West Bay; SY4690], *West Bay*: Notable for wide choice of perfectly cooked and presented food inc lots of seafood fresh off local boats, with superb sauces, fine meat, game and veg, lovely puddings *(Chris Warne)*

☆ **Buckhorn Weston** [ST7524], *Stapleton Arms*: Friendly and spacious, doing well under current management, with wide choice of food inc fresh fish Thurs, steaks Fri, good puddings; pleasant surroundings *(Brian Chambers, Brig T I G Gray)*

☆ **Buckland Newton** [ST6904], *Gaggle of Geese*: Attractive L-shaped bar with comfortably solid furnishings, pleasant decorations, good licensees, several friendly dogs and a cat, well kept Bass, Badger Best, Wadworths 6X and a guest such as Fullers London Pride, decent wines and spirits, usual bar food, smartish restaurant; spacious pool/snooker and skittle rooms, sizeable grounds *(Maj T C Thornton, R J Herd, BB)*

☆ **Charlton Marshall** [A350 Poole—Blandford; ST9003], *Charlton Inn*: Smart and tidy food pub with wide choice of generously served good food from sandwiches and lots of baked potatoes up, well kept Badger Best and Tanglefoot, well chosen wine list, quick friendly service, attractively furnished oak-beamed bars, unobtrusive piped music, small garden *(WHBM, Alan Kilpatrick)*

☆ *nr* **Chedington** [A356 Dorchester—Crewkerne; ST4805], *Winyards Gap*: Spectacular view from tables in front of tastefully modernised pub with wide choice of traditional food inc lots of home-made puddings, children's and vegetarian dishes, popular Sun lunch; well kept Exmoor Stag, Flowers Original, Wadworths 6X and a guest ale, country wines, no-smoking area, skittle alley, also darts, pool etc; children in dining area, live music Sun evening, self-catering in converted barn; pleasant walks nearby *(A D Marsh, Steve Huggins, Nicholas H Smith, Ron Shelton, John and Suzanne McClenahan, Marjorie and David Lamb, E A George, LYM)*

☆ **Chetnole** [ST6007], *Chetnole Arms*: Wide choice of good food cooked by licensee's mother in very welcoming pub with lively mix of customers, well kept changing ales such as Adnams, Exmoor Gold, Fullers London Pride and Morlands Old Speckled Hen, good range of local ciders, log fires, cheerful staff; nice garden *(Tim Wilde, Dr and Mrs N Holmes, Dorothy Pilson)*

☆ **Chideock** [A35 Bridport—Lyme Regis; SY4292], *George*: Thatched 17th-c pub with wide choice of bar food, well kept Palmers real ales, efficient staff, neat rows of tables in simple front bar, big log fire in dark-beamed plush lounge, restaurant, tables in back garden; bedrooms *(Stephen Bayley, Andy Jones, R A F Montgomery, Mrs J M Corless, LYM)*

Christchurch [Bure Lane, Friars Cliff; SZ1593], *Sandpiper*: Attractive modern family pub, open all day, with bar café, lunchtime bar food, evening restaurant *(E G Parish)*

nr **Christchurch** [Ringwood Rd, Walkford; just off A35 by Hants border – OS Sheet 195 map ref 222943], *Amberwood Arms*: Eye-catching red and cream pub festooned with flowers, imaginative food, picnic-table sets; open all day *(E G Parish)*

see also **Mudeford, Winkton**

☆ **Colehill** [off A31 E of Wimborne; down hill N of village, right at bottom into Long Lane – OS Sheet 195 map ref 032024; SU0201], *Barley Mow*: Very popular thatched 16th-c country dining pub, recently very much extended around its attractive beamed and panelled core; extremely wide range of food always promptly served even when busy, at very reasonable prices; well kept Best and Tanglefoot and a guest such as Charles Wells, good log fires; provision for children, folk music Fri, nice garden with play area *(Maurice Southon, Mr and Mrs J E C Hobbs, P and H Douglas, John Hazel, Alan and Eileen Bowker, LYM)*

Corfe Castle [SY9681], *Bankes Arms*: Large welcoming ex-coaching inn with Whitbreads-related real ales, decent food; can get very busy in holiday period *(R H Brown, Gwyneth and Salvo Spadaro-Dutturi)*

Corfe Mullen [A31 W of Wimborne Minster; former Coventry Arms; SY9798], *Famous Old Trout*: Done up old-style, five spacious intercommunicating bars and two restaurant areas popular for good food changing each day, Whitbreads-related real ales *(John Hazel)*

☆ **Corscombe** [off A356 Dorchester—Crewkerne; outskirts, towards Halstock; ST5105], *Fox*: Short choice of good fresh food from sandwiches up (no microwaves, so can sometimes be a real wait) in very pretty 17th-c thatched pub, idiosyncratic but generally warm and welcoming, with well kept real ales such as Exmoor and Fullers London Pride tapped from the cask, farm cider, obvious horse and hunting connections, friendly greyhound called Katie, old-fashioned furnishings, stuffed birds and so forth, log fires; seats across quiet lane on streamside lawn, good walks; children welcome *(John and Suzanne McClenahan, Alice Valdes-Scott, Marcus Corah, LYM)*

Dorchester [1 Alexandra Rd], *Cornwall*: Good choice of food inc particularly good two-course Sun lunch at bargain price, friendly landlord and staff *(K D Corbett)*; [Weymouth Ave; by Dorchester Sth Stn], *Stationmasters House*: Busy railway-theme pub with friendly service, notable for well kept Eldridge Pope ales straight from the handsome adjacent brewery; can be noisy, esp weekend evenings *(Barbara Hatfield, Stan Edwards)*; [40 Allington Ave; A352 towards Wareham], *Trumpet Major*: Wide choice of food inc good two-course Sun lunch, well kept Eldridge Pope ales, good service, two spacious, bright and airy newish bars, big family dining conservatory, adjacent play area *(K D Corbett, Joan and Michel Hooper-Immins; other useful pubs here include Bakers Arms, Junction, Old Ship, Royal Oak, Tom Browns)*

East Lulworth [SY8581], *Weld Arms*: The tenants who made this a popular main entry in previous editions can now be found at the Green Dragon at Stoke Fleming (see Devon main entries)

☆ **East Stour** [A30, E towards Shaftesbury; ST7922], *Kings Arms*: Good generous freshly prepared bar food inc interesting specials and good range of puddings, well kept real ales inc Bass, good family service in friendly, comfortable and attractively refurbished pub with local paintings and drawings, no piped music; restaurant (not Mon) beyond tanks of catfish, public bar with darts and fruit machine; tables outside; children welcome *(Lt Cdr G J Cardew)*

☆ **Evershot** [off A37 8 miles S of Yeovil; ST5704], *Acorn*: Helpful polite staff and wide choice of generous bar food from sandwiches to steaks inc good salads in comfortable L-shaped bar with stripped stone, fine old fireplaces; changing real ales such as Palmers, Wadworths 6X, decent wines, games in public bar, piped music; pretty village in attractive Hardy walking country; children in skittle alley and restaurant; bedrooms comfortable *(Maj and Mrs J A Gardner, LYM)*

Fiddleford [A357 Sturminster Newton—Blandford Forum; ST8013], *Fiddleford Inn*: Comfortably revamped in old-fashioned style, keeping some broad flagstones and log fire; wide choice of food from sandwiches up inc wonderful puddings and good fresh veg in sizeable dining area, well kept Courage-related ales, tables on terrace and in pleasant spacious garden with play area *(Helen Morton, LYM)*

Furzehill [SU0101], *Stocks*: Big busy thatched dining pub, attractive interior with copper and brass, old prints and even a lobster pot and fishing net, extensive range of food, attentive young staff; spacious back restaurant *(Brian Chambers)*

☆ **Gillingham** [Peacemarsh; ST8026], *Dolphin*: Good friendly pub with new landlord cooking particularly good value food, wife runs the bar; well kept Badger ales *(R A Cullingham, Jeanne and Tom Barnes)*

Gillingham, *Red Lion*: Old stone building with big fireplace, good range of Badger beers, reasonable range of generous sensibly priced bar food *(Roderic Plinston)*; *Unicorn*: One to watch, as being taken over by licensees who made a name for themselves running the Bull at Hardway (Somerset) as a civilised and popular dining pub *(RHM)*

☆ **Gussage All Saints** [SU0010], *Drovers*: Big helpings of solid basic well presented food, well kept Bass, Marstons Pedigree and Ruddles County on handpump, country wines, in country local turned dining pub, sturdy furnishings in two main no-frills areas divided by big brick fireplace, pleasant views, tables out on terrace, good play area; children in eating area, in summer has been open all day Sat (service can slow then) *(Andy and Jill Kassube, Neil Hardwick, Michael and Rachel Brookes, Phil and Heidi Cook, Sue Holland, Dave Webster, Peter Churchill, LYM)*

Highcliffe [SZ2193], *Globe*: Large but cosy recently refurbished Brewers Fayre pub with good value food, Courage-related and other real ales; open all day inc Sun *(David Cundy)*

Horton [B3078 Wimborne—Cranborne; SU0207], *Horton*: Good food in bar and restaurant, Courage Directors and Ringwood Best, lots of locals, busy weekends; dogs allowed on lead; bedrooms *(W W Huggins)*

☆ **Hurn** [village signed off A338, then follow Avon, Sopley, Mutchams sign – OS Sheet 195 map ref 136976; SZ1397], *Avon Causeway*: Spacious and civilised hotelish lounge with interesting railway decorations and very wide choice of quickly served bar food inc children's dishes; though nominally tied to Wadworths manager has wide ale-buying discretion and gets several interesting changing guest beers such as Elgoods Black Dog, Hook Norton Old Hookey, Moles Brew 97; dining-car restaurant, piped music, open all day; bedrooms *(Alastair Campbell, WHBM, LYM)*

Kingstag [ST7210], *Green Man*: Very pleasant licensees, reasonably priced food *(John Hazel)*

Little Canford [Fox Lane; off A31 Wimborne—Ferndown; SZ0499], *Fox & Hounds*: Extended thatched country pub with extensive lawns, two big comfortable eating areas, Whitbreads-related ales, limited range of good food; good staff, pleasant walks *(Bernard and Kathleen Hypher)*

☆ **Loders** [SY4994], *Loders Arms*: Wide choice of good original food such as smoked pheasant with mango and mint or duck breast with anchovy sauce, lots of fish, excellent veg, fine puddings, in attractive thatched village pub with friendly licensees, well kept Palmers BB and IPA, good choice of wines, restaurant area; bedrooms comfortable and well equipped

(Nigel and Bridget Pullan, H G Robertson, Nigel Gibbs, Patrick McGrath)

☆ **Longham** [A348 Ferndown—Poole; SZ0698], *White Hart*: Small traditional pub with pine furniture, log fire, good range of food from sandwiches and baked potatoes up, Badger Best and Tanglefoot with an interesting guest beer, friendly staff; soft piped music, dogs allowed *(George Murdoch)*

Longham, *Angel*: Wide choice of food inc traditional puddings, friendly prompt service, well kept Badger Best and Tanglefoot, unobtrusive piped music; big garden with lots of play facilities for children *(R Wilson, A Plumb)*

Lower Burton [Old Sherborne Rd; SO4257], *Sun*: Cleverly converted 18th-c farmhouse with wide range of good generous food inc superb home-made puddings, efficient friendly service, real ales inc Smiles, Hook Norton and Wadworths 6X *(Ian and Deborah Carrington)*

Lyme Regis [25 Marine Parade, The Cobb; SY3492], *Royal Standard*: Cosy and friendly low-ceilinged bar with well kept Palmers, bar food, floodlit terrace leading to beach *(Julian Bessa, Jim and Maggie Cowell)*

Lytchett Matravers [High St; SY9495], *Chequers*: Low-beamed and cosy, with good straightforward bar food, big family room, good-sized separate restaurant *(Gorden Theaker)*

☆ **Marnhull** [B3092 (Crown Rd); ST7718], *Crown*: Charming thatched pub opp church with log fire in huge fireplace warming simple but attractive beamed and flagstoned public bar, recently refurbished lounge/dining area, well kept Badger Best, Hard Tackle and Tanglefoot on handpump, warmly welcoming newish tenants, usual food; children in eating area; three comfortable bedrooms, good breakfasts *(Dr and Mrs J H Hills, Graham and Lynn Mason, LYM)*

☆ **Marshwood** [B3165 Lyme Regis—Crewkerne; SY3799], *Bottle*: Simple old thatched country local with well kept Hook Norton and Wadworths 6X, reasonably priced bar food, traditional games and skittle alley; handy for pretty walking country *(Marjorie and David Lamb, LYM)*

Martinstown [SY6488], *Brewers Arms*: Friendly village pub with Flowers tapped from the cask, a vegan dish as well as a vegetarian one *(Rona Murdoch)*

Melbury Osmond [Roman Rd, Drive End; ST5707], *Rest & Welcome*: Welcoming and cottagey, full of nick-nacks, with Whitbreads-related real ales, bar food *(Gwyneth and Salvo Spadaro-Dutturi)*

Morden [off B3075, between A35 and A31 E of Bere Regis; SY9195], *Cock & Bottle*: Recently extended Badger food pub, lots of newly installed beamery to match original traditional front part, much enlarged choice of ambitious bar food; getting very popular, welcoming staff *(WHBM, David Dimock)*

Moreton [SY8089], *Frampton Arms*: Pleasant atmosphere, welcoming landlord, good range of reasonably priced bar food, locomotive pictures and 50s photographs of local station; bedrooms *(Mrs K E Neville-Rolfe)*

☆ **Mosterton** [High St; ST4505], *Admiral Hood*: Neat and civilised dining pub which has been good for wide range of reliable and quickly served food at reasonable prices, esp fish, well kept real ales, friendly service and good coal fire, but no recent reports *(BB; news please)*

Motcombe [just NW of Shaftesbury; ST8425], *Coppleridge*: Former 18th-c farmhouse in good-sized grounds, well cooked and presented food in bar and restaurant, good wines, welcoming service; bedrooms big and airy *(Jack R Gerber, HDW)*

☆ **Mudeford** [beyond huge seaside car park at Mudeford Pier – OS Sheet 195 map ref 182916; SZ1891], *Haven House*: Much-extended seaside pub, blissfully quiet in its quaint old part-flagstoned heart in winter, service fast and efficient when the summer crowds come; Whitbreads-related ales, bar food from sandwiches up, family cafeteria, tables on sheltered terrace right on beach – from here you can walk for miles by the sea *(Alan and Maggie Telford, Mr and Mrs Berner, WHBM, LYM)*

Nettlecombe [SY5195], *Marquis of Lorne*: Attractively placed country pub-with-bedrooms now reopened under new tenants after 1994 refurbishment *(Reports please)*

☆ **Norden Heath** [Furzebrook; A351 Wareham—Corfe Castle; SY9483], *Halfway*: Unpretentious thatched main-road pub with enterprising very reasonably priced home-made food from traditional favourites to interesting Greek-Cypriot specialities and imaginative puddings – Cypriot landlord; well kept Ringwood, Whitbreads Strong Country and a couple of guest beers, unspoilt exterior, outside gents' – very smart new ladies' *(Bernard and Kathleen Hypher, John and Christine Simpson, Derek R Patey, D G Clarke, Nigel and Bridget Pullan)*

☆ **Poole** [Pinewood Rd, Branksome Park; off A338 on edge of Poole, towards Branksome Chine – via The Avenue; SZ0590], *Inn in the Park*: Friendly small hotel bar well off the tourist beat in quiet pine-filled residential area, nice steep walks down to sea; consistently well kept Adnams, Ringwood and Wadworths real ales, good value generous bar food (not Sun evening), attractive dining room (children allowed), log fire, very friendly licensee, tables on small sunny terrace; very popular weekends; comfortable bedrooms *(Peter Churchill, J Muckell, Mark Hydes, LYM)*

☆ **Poole** [88 High St; SZ0190], *Old Harry*: Very busy city local in main shopping area, good range of good value food esp fish, big raised and balustraded dining area, good welcoming service, Bass and Charrington real ale *(K R Harris, Basil J S Minson)*

Poole [Sandbanks Rd, Lilliput], *Beehive*: Large conservatory-style no-smoking family eating area with popular indoor barbecue and other food, well kept Eldridge Pope beers, garden – play area replaced by picnic-table sets *(Mr and Mrs A P Reeves, Andy and Jill Kassube)*; *Helmsman*: Simple pub food, helpful and friendly staff, Eldridge Pope Hardy *(Sue Holland, David Webster)*; [The Quay], *Portsmouth Hoy*: Spotless, with naval memorabilia, charming Irish licensee, Eldridge Pope beers and good choice of bar food; nice back dining area, separate no-smoking area; handy for boat trips *(W H and E Thomas)*

☆ **Portesham** [Front St; SY6086], *Kings Arms*: Sympathetically extended pub with good choice of generous food inc some unusual dishes, welcoming service, very pleasant sizeable garden with play area and trout stream *(Stan Edwards, Ken and Liz Draper)*

☆ **Portland Bill** [SY6870], *Pulpit*: Wonderful location nr Pulpit Rock, short stroll to lighthouse and cliffs; comfortable food pub with local shellfish as well as usual bar and restaurant food inc vegetarian, well kept Gibbs Mew real ales, friendly efficient staff; piped music *(Stan Edwards, Eric J Locker)*

☆ **Puncknowle** [Church St; nr Dorchester; SY5388], *Crown*: 16th-c beamed and thatched flint inn prettily set opp church, carefully renovated open-plan lounge, good home-cooked food esp pies and steak sandwiches, good vegetarian choice, well kept Palmers, decent wines, lots of country wines, very friendly staff; family room, locals' bar; attractive garden; bedrooms *(Neil Hardwick, Deborah and Ian Carrington, Mr and Mrs J E C Hobbs)*

Pymore [SY4694], *Pymore Inn*: Well appointed and friendly village pub with cosy winter coal fires, good well priced food done by landlord, tables on sheltered lawn *(Chris and Joan Woodward, Maj D A Daniels)*

☆ **Sandford Orcas** [off B3148 and B3145 N of Sherborne; ST6220], *Mitre*: Tucked-away country local with a good deal of unpretentious character, decent food, good service, well kept beer, hard-working newish owners; bedrooms *(A G Drake, SRC, LYM)*

☆ **Shaftesbury** [St James St; 150 yds from bottom of Gold Hill; ST8622], *Two Brewers*: Charming town pub down famously photogenic Gold Hill, pleasant lounges, good choice of reasonably priced bar food (maybe free chocolate for children), very friendly quick service, well kept real ales *(Mrs A E Sargent, Christopher and Sharon Hayle, Andy and Jill Kassube)*

☆ **Shaftesbury** [High St], *Mitre*: Wide range of quickly served good generous food from sandwiches up inc vegetarian dishes and cheap OAP specials in simply but attractively refurbished pub with wonderful Blackmore Vale views from back dining room; well kept Eldridge Pope beers, good choice of malt whiskies and wines, daily papers, good sprinkling of local characters; bedrooms *(A E and P McCully, Marjorie and David Lamb, LYM)*

☆ **Shaftesbury** [The Commons], *Grosvenor*: Good local atmosphere in warm and comfortable lounge bar of photogenic wisteria-covered Forte hotel, good genuine fair-priced bar snacks, well kept beers; ask Reception if you can see the magnificently carved oak 19th-c Chevy Chase sideboard in the first-floor lounge (not always possible as used for private meetings); good bedrooms, wonderful breakfasts *(W H and E Thomas, Mrs J A Powell, Dr and Mrs A K Clarke)*

☆ **Sherborne** [Cooks Lane (nr abbey); ST6316], *Digby Tap*: Good atmosphere in character flagstoned pub, unpretentious and simple, with up to four interesting well kept ales, farm cider, huge helpings of bar food, considerate staff, pub games; thriving atmosphere, with older customers early on, younger ones later; seats outside *(Andy and Jill Kassube, Mr and Mrs A P Reeves, Ron Shelton)*

☆ **Sherborne** [Horsecastles], *Skippers*: Marvellous little pub just out of main town, pleasant local bustle, welcoming landlord, good food, particularly well kept Bass and several other real ales *(Andy and Jill Kassube, John and Joan Nash, John Hazel)*

Sherborne [Oborne Rd, Newland], *Black Horse*: Praised in previous editions for good food and good value bedrooms, but closed and for sale 1994 *(News please)*; [Westbury; off Acreman St opp Cooks Lane], *Britannia*: Relaxed and comfortable local with basic but ample good value bar snacks, obliging landlord, well kept beers; pool table, juke box; bedrooms comfortable *(Alistair Harris, Gordon)*; [Cheap St], *Cross Keys*: Busy but friendly town pub, handy for the Abbey and shopping; Eldridge Pope beers, good club sandwiches, tasty hot dishes; friendly staff *(John and Joan Nash)*; [4 miles out; A352 towards Dorchester, then first left at top of hill], *Plume of Feathers*: Super country setting, good range of beers inc Smiles and Boddingtons, wide choice of good value food *(Alistair Harris)*; [Swan Passage], *Swan*: Good lunchtime bar food and evening meals (esp soup), warmly welcoming atmosphere and staff *(Mr and Mrs Norman Davies, F J Willy)*

Southbourne [Overcliff Dr; about 2 miles W of Hengistbury Head; SZ1591], *Commodore*: Sea view from clifftop hotel bar with good choice of usual food in clean and airy surroundings, several Whitbreads-related real ales, family area *(WHBM, Mr and Mrs A P Reeves)*

Southover [SY6294], *Dove*: Friendly staff, character cosy bars, log fires, well kept ales and cider, interesting choice of reasonably priced food, restaurant; children's room; bedrooms *(Geoff Payne)*

☆ **Stoke Abbott** [off B3162 and B3163 2 m W of Beaminster; ST4500], *New Inn*: Attractive 17th-c inn with welcoming staff and enterprising varied menu, wide range of beers, picturesque garden; comfortable bedrooms *(John Fisher, J L Alperin, R Wilson, LYM)*

☆ **Stour Provost** [just off B3092 Sturminster Newton—Gillingham; ST7921], *Royal Oak*: Pleasant atmosphere in entirely no-smoking pub with good fresh food inc wide vegetarian choice, spotless housekeeping, welcoming service, well kept Badger ales, log fires *(C and J M Watson)*

☆ **Studland** [SZ0382], *Bankes Arms*: Wonderful peaceful spot above one of England's best beaches, giving good views of Poole Harbour and Bournemouth Bay; friendly and easy-going, generous helpings of simple bar food (no lunchtime sandwiches), well kept Whitbreads-related ales maybe with unusual local guests, attractive log fire, pool table; nr Coast Path; can get trippery in summer; bedrooms *(Denise Plummer, Jim Froggatt, Barbara Hatfield, Geoff Butts, Polly Marsh)*
Studland [Beach Rd], *Manor House*: Very good bar food, a hotel rather than a pub (you can't just have a drink) but still very pleasant; bedrooms *(Derek R Patey)*

☆ **Sturminster Marshall** [A350; SY9499], *Black Horse*: Smart but welcoming, with above-average bar food, well kept Badger beers, restaurant *(Paul S McPherson)*
Sturminster Marshall [High St], *Red Lion*: Clean, pleasant and tastefully furnished open-plan bar with log fire, wide choice of food, skittle alley doubles as family room *(John McMullen)*

☆ **Sturminster Newton** [Market Cross (B3092); ST7814], *White Hart*: Homely 18th-c thatched inn with eager-to-please new landlord, warm cosy bar with well kept Badger and friendly locals, reasonably priced varied bar food, morning coffee, afternoon teas, garden beyond cobbled coach entry; bedrooms comfortable, though road not quiet *(Graham and Lynn Mason)*

☆ **Sutton Poyntz** [off A353 SE of Weymouth; SY7083], *Springhead*: Large Victorian building in pretty village opp stream, with comfortable spacious bar, well kept Eldridge Pope and other ales, log fires, welcoming attentive staff, newspapers, bar billiards, good food from an unusual and interesting menu; good play area in big garden *(Gwyneth and Salvo Spadaro-Dutturi)*
Swanage [Ulwell Rd; SZ0278], *Ferryboat*: An oasis of tranquillity, with decent Tetleys and speciality pancakes – even a Mars Bar one; not luxurious, but lovely view over bay *(Joan and Michel Hooper-Immins)*; [1 Burlington Rd], *Pines*: Big hotel bar popular at lunchtime for good choice of food esp starters and puddings, well kept beers; excellent views from garden (a long way from bar); bedrooms good *(Bernard and Wendy Brookes)*

Swanage [The Square; SZ0278], *Ship*: Reliable well run pub with good atmosphere; bedrooms *(Dave Braisted)*

☆ **Tarrant Gunville** [ST9212], *Bugle Horn*: Attractive and comfortable country pub with good value ploughman's and wide choice of other usual pub food, welcoming licensees, well kept Ringwood and Wadworths 6X; seats in garden *(John Hazel)*
Tarrant Keynston [ST9304], *True Lovers Knot*: Good atmosphere in traditional village pub with usual food, children in eating area, big garden *(John Hazel)*
Three Legged Cross [113 Ringwood Rd; SU0904], *Old Barn Farm*: Large family pub with good reasonably priced food, pleasant restaurant, efficient friendly service, fair range of beers; lots of seating outside, some children's amusements *(Phyl and Jack Street, Alan and Julie Wear)*

☆ **Tolpuddle** [SY7994], *Martyrs*: Pleasantly welcoming, with decent food, well kept Badger beers, nice garden with ducks, hens and rabbits, friendly Highland terrier *(Mr Gilmore)*

☆ **Trent** [ST5918], *Rose & Crown*: Wide choice of consistently good quickly served food in old-fashioned bar, relaxed and comfortable, with log fire, flagstone floors, good oak settles, nice pictures, fresh flowers, books, no piped music; decent choice of real ales, dining conservatory; picnic-table sets behind; children welcome *(LM)*
Verwood [Station Rd (B3081); SU0808], *Albion*: Good food with proper chips and well kept Gibbs Mew Salisbury and Bishops Tipple in welcoming pub with pictures of former nearby railway *(David Eberlin, Andy and Jill Kassube)*

☆ **Wareham** [South St; SY9287], *Quay*: Bright and roomy stripped-stone bars in excellent quayside position, bar food from soup and sandwiches up, open fire, well kept Boddingtons and Ringwood real ales; children allowed away from main bar; parking nearby can be difficult *(David Dimock)*

☆ **Wareham** [41 North St; A351, N end of town], *Kings Arms*: Friendly traditional thatched town pub with back serving counter and two bars off flagstoned central corridor, well kept Flowers Original and Whitbreads Pompey Royal, reasonably priced bar food (not Fri—Sun evenings), back garden *(Nicholas H Smith, R H Brown, LYM)*
Wareham [14 South St], *Black Bear*: 18th-c inn, all rooms leading off central passage, particularly well kept Eldridge Pope Royal Oak on handpump, comprehensive choice of good value food inc vegetarian; bedrooms *(Joan and Michel Hooper-Immins)*

☆ **Waytown** [between B3162 and A3066 N of Bridport; SY4697], *Hare & Hounds*: 17th-c pub refurbished and transformed under very friendly newish licensees, good mix of customers, Palmers ales, wide range of excellently cooked reasonably priced food inc OAP bargains, simple garden with rabbits and chickens *(Dr David Evans, R E Goldsmith)*

West Bay [SY4590], *George:* Popular and unassuming harbourside inn in Bridport's seaside holiday village, small bar with well kept Palmers real ales, food which has included carefully prepared fresh local fish and good value carvery; comfortable bedrooms *(R Wilson, Joan and Michel Hooper-Immins)*

☆ **West Knighton** [off A352 E of Dorchester; SY7387], *New Inn:* Neatly refurbished bar with good range of home-cooked food inc fine steaks, reasonably priced small restaurant, quick friendly staff, real ales, country wines, skittle alley, good provision for children, parrot; colourful garden, pleasant setting in quiet village with wonderful views *(Mrs J Oakes, Stan Edwards)*

West Moors [195 Station Rd; SU0802], *Old Tap House:* Unusual pub with well kept beers, reasonably priced food and lots of toby jugs *(Bernard Phillips)*

☆ **West Stafford** [SY7289], *Wise Man:* More toby jugs here in this thatched and beamed 16th-c pub, attractive and comfortable, with wide choice of good value generous food, friendly staff, well kept Whitbreads-related ales, decent wines and country wines, public bar with darts; nr Hardy's cottage *(R J Walden)*

☆ **West Stour** [ST7822], *Ship:* Good carefully prepared food cooked by young landlady's father (ex-naval chef) in bar and intimate split-level restaurant, clean, fresh, delightfully furnished, with big log fire; well kept real ales, good range of wines, caring service; garden behind; comfortable bedrooms *(Brig T I G Gray, R A F Montgomery)*

☆ **Weymouth** [Trinity Rd; SY6778], *Old Rooms:* Lovely harbour views over part-pedestrianised street from benches in front of low-beamed fisherman's pub, well priced straightforward lunchtime food with plenty of fresh fish and good sandwiches in character bar and unpretentious restaurant, quick friendly staff, well kept Whitbreads-related ales; seats outside with lovely views *(Shirley Pielou, Stephen and Anna Oxley, Stan Edwards)*

☆ **Weymouth** [Barrack Rd], *Nothe Tavern:* Good food inc fresh fish, obliging and friendly service, well kept Eldridge Pope Royal Oak and Hardy and decent wines in spacious and popular local with glimpses of harbour from garden *(Jonathan Beard, Emma Clarke, Joan and Michel Hooper-*

Immins, C J Pratt, BB)

Whitchurch Canonicorum [SY3995], *Five Bells:* Uncommercialised, unpretentious simple village local, friendly landlord, Palmers ale, basic bar food; lovely views, attractive village with fine church, good walking country; interesting pottery for sale *(Richard Burton, Marjorie and David Lamb)*

☆ **Wimborne Minster** [Hanham Rd, East Borough; SZ0199], *Dormers:* Partly 17th-c with handsome panelling and ceilings, not a conventional pub though does have a spacious pubby bar, linking with conservatory-feel coffee shop and with restaurant; good food, helpful staff, well kept Badger Best and Tanglefoot, piped classical music, boxed games; garden runs down to small river *(WHBM, Geoffrey Heron)*

☆ **Wimborne Minster** [Corn Mkt], *White Hart:* Old-fashioned low-beamed bar in pedestrian precinct a few steps from minster, unpretentious and friendly, with well kept Eldridge Pope Dorset, Dorchester and Royal Oak on handpump, wide range of good fresh reasonably priced bar food in eating area *(A P Reeves, Iris and Eddie Brixton)*

Wimborne Minster [Victoria Rd, W of town], *Lost Keys:* Friendly, good food esp filled rolls and salads, chatty staff *(Sally Edsall)*

Wimborne St Giles [SU0212], *Bull:* Clean and comfortable, with particularly good food esp fish fresh daily from Cornwall; Badger ales *(W Mecham, John Hazel)*

Winfrith Newburgh [A352 Wareham—Dorchester; SY8084], *Red Lion:* Useful roadside eating place with quickly served reasonably priced generous food, Badger beers; piped music; tables outside behind; bedrooms *(John and Joan Nash, Ann Reeder, Dave Craine, Mrs M A Mees)*

☆ **Winkton** [Bockhampton Rd, via Burley Rd, off B3347 – OS Sheet 195 map ref 166962], *Lamb:* Particularly good range of well kept real ales (esp late October beer festival) in bustling country pub with reasonably priced good food in bar and restaurant, pleasant decor, good friendly service; good garden for children with play area, nice setting *(C J Westmoreland, Andy and Jill Kassube, WHBM)*

☆ **Winterbourne Abbas** [A35 W of Dorchester; SY6190], *Coach & Horses:* Big roadside pub with extensive lounge bar and long side dining area, cold food counter and hot carvery service, well kept Bass, Eldridge Pope Thomas Hardy and Royal Oak, efficient service; particularly good well equipped outside play area; bedrooms *(Stan Edwards, F H Swan, T A Bryan, BB)*

Post Office address codings confusingly give the impression that some pubs are in Dorset, when they're really in Somerset (which is where we list them).

Durham *see* Northumbria

Essex

Pubs currently doing particularly well here include the Swan at Chappel (great fish dishes in a lovely friendly setting), the Cricketers at Clavering (especially popular for food), the Black Bull at Fyfield (another place that's good for fish, though getting perhaps a little restauranty for our tastes), the very friendly Pheasant at Gestingthorpe (good for vegetarians), the friendly Green Man at Gosfield (such good home cooking that we choose it as Essex Dining Pub of the Year), the White Hart at Great Yeldham (back in these pages after a break – good food and atmosphere), the Cock & Bell at High Easter (friendly new licensees), the friendly and busy Bell at Horndon on the Hill, the warmly welcoming old Red Lion at Lamarsh, the Shepherd & Dog at Langham (big helpings of good food), the Eight Bells in Saffron Walden (very good fish and other food), the Cap & Feathers at Tillingham (excellent old-fashioned atmosphere), the Green Man at Toot Hill (glowing praise from readers for food and wines), the unpretentious and civilised Bell at Wendens Ambo (an entirely new main entry) and the Bell at Woodham Walter (friendly newish licensees proving popular). A higher proportion of pubs here than in most areas have qualified for our new Beer Award: the Pheasant at Gestingthorpe, Cock & Bell at High Easter, Crooked Billet at Leigh on Sea, Queens Head at Littlebury (exceptional range, with a very low-priced bargain offer), Plough at Navestock, Hoop at Stock, Cap & Feathers at Tillingham and Cats at Woodham Walter. Although Essex beer prices are slightly higher than the national average, they have been held down in many pubs this year: pubs getting their beers from Greene King the regional brewer now tend to be considerably cheaper than in those getting their beers from national brewers, and prices tend to be even lower in pubs supplied by the local brewers Crouch Vale and Ridleys. It's unusual to find a good main dish in a pub here for under £5 now: the Ferryboat at North Fambridge and Hoop at Stock stand out for their low food prices. In the Lucky Dip section at the end of the chapter, we'd particularly pick out the Compasses near Coggeshall, Three Ashes at Cressing, Anchor in Danbury, Sun at Dedham, Swan near Great Henny, Gardeners Arms in Loughton, Station Buffet in Manningtree, Volunteer near Waltham Abbey and Green Dragon at Youngs End; as we have inspected most of these, we can vouch for their quality.

ARKESDEN TL4834 Map 5

Axe & Compasses ★ ♀

Village signposted from B1038 – but B1039 from Wendens Ambo, then forking left, is prettier; OS Sheet 154 map reference 482344

Blending in very well with the attractive village, this is a lovely rambling thatched country pub, well liked for its comfortably old-fashioned feel and friendly welcome. Service is efficient and attentive, with the Greek licencees really working hard to make you feel at home. A comfortable carpeted saloon bar has pastel-green-cushioned oak and elm seats, quite a few easy chairs, old wooden tables, lots of brasses on the walls, a bright coal fire, and maybe a friendly cat called Spikey. The smaller public bar, with cosy built-in settles, has sensibly placed darts and dominoes. The popular meals can be eaten in the bar or the restaurant, from a daily changing menu that might include soup (£1.90), good sandwiches (from £2.10), and steak and kidney pie (£5.95), as well as more elaborate choices like chicken, leek and bacon crumble or wild mushroom pancakes in a cheese sauce (£5.95), and grilled skate with mustard sauce (£6.75); Tuesday night is fish night, with several extra fresh fish dishes. Well kept Greene King IPA and Abbott on handpump under light blanket pressure, a very good wine list, and several malts. There are seats outside, on a side terrace with colourful hanging baskets, where there may be barbecues in summer. The village is very pretty. *(Recommended by E A George, K and B Moore, Gwen and Peter Andrews, Martyn Kearey, D K Carter, Caroline Wright, Penny and Martin Fletcher, John Fahy, Adrian Kelly, R A Buckler, E Money, J S Frost, D Cox, Marjorie and David Parkin)*

Greene King ~ Lease: Themis Christou ~ Real ale ~ Meals and snacks ~ Restaurant (not Sun evening) ~ Saffron Walden (01799) 550272 ~ Children in restaurant ~ Open 11-2.30, 6-11

CASTLE HEDINGHAM TL7835 Map 5

Bell

B1058 E of Sible Hedingham, towards Sudbury

There's a good log fire in each of the rooms at this fascinating old coaching inn, creating the kind of cosy atmosphere in which people wind down and secrets come out. Perhaps this explains why Disraeli regularly leaked his legislative plans to the Hinkford Hundred Conservative Club in an assembly room upstairs, and it's especially true of the beamed and timbered saloon bar. Jacobean-style seats and Windsor chairs stand guard around sturdy oak tables, and beyond the standing timbers left from a knocked-through wall, some steps lead up to a little gallery. Behind the traditionally furnished public bar a games room has dominoes and cribbage; piped pop music. One bar is now completely no smoking. A particular highlight is the fine big walled garden behind the pub – an acre or so, with grass, trees and shrubs; you can play croquet out here. Promptly served bar food includes home-made soup (£2), ploughman's (£3), half pint of smoked prawns with garlic dip (£3.50, a pint is £6.50), ham and broccoli bake (£4), steak and Guinness pie, Thai chicken curry or haddock and prawn gratinée (£4.50), rainbow trout (£5.50) and treacle tart (£2); Greene King IPA and Abbot tapped from the cask, with occasional guest beers like Morlands Old Speckled Hen, and local farm ciders. As well as in the garden, there are seats on a small terrace in the car park. Lucia the Great Dane may be ambling around or taking a break in front of the fire – best not to bring your own dog. The nearby 12th-c castle keep is worth a visit. *(Recommended by Barbara and Norman Wells, John Fahy, Anthony Barker, Wayne Brindle, Mrs P R M Barker)*

Grays (who no longer brew) ~ Tenant Sandra Ferguson ~ Real ale ~ Meals and snacks (till 10pm; not Mon evening, except bank holidays) ~ (01787) 460350 ~ Well behaved children welcome, except in public bar ~ Jazz last Sun lunchtime of month, acoustic guitar group Fri evening ~ Open 11.30-3, 6-11; closed evening 25 Dec

CHAPPEL TL8927 Map 5

Swan

Wakes Colne; pub visible just off A604 Colchester—Halstead

Most of the patio at this timbered 14th-c pub is now covered by a canopy, so there are far more opportunities to sit outside and admire the wonderful setting. Of course you may choose to venture outside only when the weather is at its least capricious, on the kind of day when it's almost impossible to resist basking in the sheltered suntrap cobbled courtyard, where parasols, big tubs overflowing with flowers, and French street signs create something of a continental feel. Inside, the relaxed and friendly bar area is a spacious, rambling and low-beamed affair, with one or two swan pictures and plates on the white and partly panelled walls, banquettes around lots of dark tables, and red velvet curtains on brass rings hanging from wooden curtain rails. Standing oak timbers divide off side areas, and there are a few attractive tiles above the very big fireplace, filled in summer with lots of plants. It's the sort of friendly, warmly-welcoming place that people like to come back to time and time again. Popular and good value bar food includes filled french rolls (from £1.30), sandwiches (from £1.40; the rare beef is excellent), ploughman's (from £2.95), chicken curry, gammon steak or first class home-made steak and kidney or chicken and mushroom pie (all £3.95), cod or rock eel (£4.45), smoked salmon salad (£4.95 or £6.95 depending on size) and good puddings such as apricot and coffee soufflé made by the landlady's mother. The landlord has connections with a wholesale fish company so the seafood side of the menu is generally a good bet. Well kept Boddingtons and Greene King IPA and Abbot on handpump, a good selection of wines by the glass, and very nice coffee, all served by notably cheery helpful staff; cribbage, faint piped music. The public bar has been converted to a no-smoking lounge and no longer has pool or any games and machines. The River Colne runs down the garden to a splendid Victorian viaduct below; train buffs won't get too exited by the BR line that goes over it, but should find plenty to interest them at the Railway Museum just a few minutes' walk from the pub. *(Recommended by Gwen and Peter Andrews, Professor S Barnett, Russell and Margaret Bathie, Barbara and Norman Wells, R A Quantock, Basil J S Minson, Margaret Drazin, Anthony Barker, Wayne Brindle)*

Free house ~ Licensees Terence Martin and M A Hubbard ~ Real ale ~ Meals and snacks (till 10.15) ~ Restaurant ~ Earls Colne (01787) 222353 ~ Children over 5 in restaurant and eating area of bar ~ Open 11-3, 6-11

CLAVERING TL4731 Map 5

Cricketers

B1038 Newport—Buntingford, Newport end of village

Very much the kind of place to come to when you feel like spoiling yourself, this pretty and comfortably modernised 16th-c dining pub is drawing plenty of praise at the moment for its imaginative home-made food. Tasty dishes on the regularly changing menu might include sandwiches (from £2), soup (£2.75), chicken and duck liver pâté with hot toast and redcurrant sauce (£3.65), avocado pear grilled with king prawns and garlic butter (£3.75), wholemeal blinis topped with shredded smoked salmon and dill yoghurt sauce (£3.95), salads (from £6), steak and kidney pie (£7.95), sautéed lamb's kidneys with smoked bacon, mushrooms and tarragon vinegar sauce (£8.50), veal with tomato concasse and melted stilton (£9.25), scallops, scampi and monkfish with timbale of wild rice, celery and thermidor sauce (£10.25), several daily specials, home-made puddings (£2.75), and children's dishes (£2.25). The Wednesday night Pudding Club menu features steak and kidney pudding, roast beef and Yorkshire pudding and various sweeter members of the genre. The roomy L-shaped bar has lots of beams and standing timbers, pale green plush button-backed banquettes, stools and Windsor chairs around shiny wooden tables, gleaming copper pans and horsebrasses, dried flowers in the big fireplace (open fire in colder weather), and fresh flowers; one area is no smoking. Well kept Wethereds, Boddingtons and Flowers IPA on handpump; unobtrusive piped music. The front terrace has picnic-table sets and umbrellas and colourful flowering shrubs. They hope to have bedrooms ready this year. *(Recommended by Adrian M Kelly, Gwen and Peter Andrews, Gordon Theaker, Mrs Gwyneth Holland, Bernard and Marjorie Parkin, P Carpenter, RJH, Maysie Thompson, P C H Ablitt)*

Free house ~ Licensees Trevor and Sally Oliver ~ Real ale ~ Meals and snacks (till 10pm) ~ Restaurant (not Sun evening) ~ Saffron Walden (01799) 550442 ~ Children in eating area of bar and in restaurant ~ Open 10.30-2.30, 6-11

Post Office address codings confusingly give the impression that some pubs are in Suffolk, when they're really in Essex (which is where we list them).

COGGESHALL TL8522 Map 5

Fleece

West Street, towards Braintree

The glorious heritage of this handsome old inn is evident as soon as you walk in, but while such a history might encourage some pubs to become rather snooty, the atmosphere here remains surprisingly unpretentious – it's a real local, with a refreshingly friendly welcome. There are plenty of original Tudor fittings, as well as exposed brickwork, a grand fireplace and interesting plasterwork, while a well kept and comfortably refurbished lounge bar has fine carved beams, lots of horsebrasses, maybe piped music, and in a separate area darts, table skittles, dominoes, shove-ha'penny, cribbage and fruit machine; it can get a little smoky at busy periods. Very well kept Greene King IPA and Abbot on handpump, good wine by the glass, coffee all day and popular cocktails with the kind of colourfully saucy names such concoctions usually attract; notably cheery service. Straightforward bar food includes sandwiches (from £1.30), soup (£1.55), filled baked potatoes (from £1.60), breaded mushrooms (£2.60), ploughman's (£3.65), and scampi, steak and kidney pie or curry (£3.95), with fresh fish on Thursdays, specials on Saturdays and traditional Sunday lunch (£4.25); on Sunday lunchtime there are often nibbles on the bar counter. The garden behind is spacious and well protected, with swings and trampolines for children. The pub is part of the same striking terrace as Paycocke's, one of the loveliest timber-framed houses in Britain (open Tuesday, Thursday and Sunday afternoons from March to September). Coggeshall used to be full of pubs, and a couple more of the survivors, listed in the Lucky Dip section, are in similarly aged buildings. *(Recommended by D P Pascoe, Gwen and Peter Andrews, Mike Simpson, Ernest Hofer, Anthony Barker)*

Greene King ~ Tenant Alan Potter ~ Real ale ~ Meals and snacks (not Tues or Sun evenings) ~ (01376) 561412 ~ Children in eating area ~ Open 10-11; closed evening 25 Dec

DEDHAM TM0533 Map 5

Marlborough Head 🛏

Parts of this nicely old-fashioned inn date back to the 15th c and it had a rather varied history before becoming a pub in 1704, the year of the Duke of Marlborough's victory at Blenheim. Comfortable and atmospheric, it's long been a popular place for eating, but without losing its pubby feel at all – you're as likely to find yourself sitting next to country ladies taking tea as anything else. There's a smartly relaxed feel throughout, with a couple of roaring log fires, lots of beams and pictures and a wealth of finely carved woodwork in the cheerful central lounge; the refurbished beamed and timbered bar is well-liked for dining and has lots of tables (which have a numbered pebble for ordering food) in wooden alcoves around its plum-coloured carpet. An imaginative choice of reliable bar food might include sandwiches (from £1.65), soup (£1.85), jacket potato with cheese (£2), baked garlic mushrooms (£2.95), tiger prawns (£3.35), bacon, mushroom and tomato quiche (£4.15), asparagus pancakes or creamy bean and spring onion bake (£4.50), cold smoked duckling or wing of skate (£5), steak and kidney pie, loin of pork with apricot and brandy sauce or lamb and spring onions au gratin (£5.85), half a pheasant in red wine and mushroom sauce (£6.45) and very good home-made puddings such as oranges in caramel with cream and brandy snaps (from £2.75); get there early for a table, it does get busy. They also have menus for morning coffee and afternoon tea. Ind Coope Burton and Worthingtons under light blanket pressure, freshly squeezed orange juice. Seats on the patio or in the garden at the back (part of which is now the car park). The pub is right in the heart of Constable's old town, directly opposite the artist's school, and the handsome flushwork church tower that features in a number of his paintings. *(Recommended by Andrew Jeeves, Carole Smart, Ian Phillips, George Atkinson, David and Ruth Hollands, M J Morgan, D J Underwood, Y Cotterill, Maysie Thompson, Bill and Beryl Farmer, Anthony Barker, Jennie and Malc Wild)*

Ind Coope (Allied) ~ Lease: Brian and Jackie Wills, Linda Mower ~ Real ale ~ Meals and snacks (not 25 Dec) ~ Colchester (01206) 323250 or 323124 ~ Children in family room only ~ Open 10-11; closed 25 Dec ~ Bedrooms: £32.50S/£50S

FYFIELD TL5606 Map 5

Black Bull
B184, N end of village

Very good food is the main draw at this enjoyable 15th-c pub, and at lunchtimes especially you'll usually find a varied mix of businessmen and older people enjoying the wide range of well-priced meals. Popular dishes include stockpot soup (£1.35), sandwiches (from £1.60), filled baked potatoes (from £2.25), ploughman's (£2.40), ratatouille with garlic bread or soft roes (£2.95), chilli con carne or flaked smoked haddock in cheese and wine sauce (£3.25), spinach and mushroom lasagne (£3.35), chicken roasted with cider, mustard, ginger and spices (£6.10), wing of skate with lemon butter (£6.95) and escalope of veal (£7.50); the vegetables are nicely cooked. On Thursday evenings a separate fresh fish menu includes sole, plaice and more exotic choices like red snapper. Under an arbour by the car park is an aviary with budgerigars and cockatiels, and there are picnic-table sets on a nearby stretch of grass, as well as to the side of the building. Inside, the series of communicating rooms have low ceilings, big black beams, standing timbers, and cushioned wheelback chairs and modern settles on the muted maroon carpet. Well kept Courage Best and Directors and Wadworths 6X on handpump under light blanket pressure, darts, dominoes, cribbage, piped music, fruit machine. *(Recommended by Mrs Gwyneth Holland, John Fahy, Beryl and Bill Farmer, Wayne Brindle, Robert Turnham, Caroline Shearer, Stephen and Jean Curtis, Mr and Mrs Chris Thorn, George Atkinson, D Cox, Shirley Gofford, Quentin Williamson)*

Free house ~ Licensee Alan Smith ~ Real ale ~ Meals and snacks (12-1.45, 7-9.30) ~ Restaurant ~ (01277) 899225 ~ Children in restaurant ~ Open 11-2.30 (3 Sat), 6.30-11

GESTINGTHORPE TL8138 Map 5

Pheasant 🍺
Village signposted from B1058; pub at Audley End end

Vegetarians tell us they feel unusually welcome here – as well as a good choice of meat-free meals there are two weeks a year devoted to vegetarian specialities. Dog owners feel at ease, as even though the cheery licensees have their own friendly hounds they make a fuss of those that drop in to visit. And beer drinkers too find themselves rather well catered for. In fact most people seem to feel at home as soon as they walk through the door of this simple country pub, thanks to its lovely old-fashioned air and uncommonly congenial atmosphere. The little lounge bar has a big pheasant-print-cushioned bow window seat looking out over the quiet lane to gently rising fields, a raised log fire, and interesting old furnishings: a grandfather clock, arts-and-crafts oak settle, and a pew. The red-walled public bar, with more orthodox pub furniture, has another winter log fire, and sensibly placed darts; also dominoes, cribbage and shove ha'penny. There's a family room available. Big helpings of reasonably priced home-made food, including sandwiches (from £1.50), soup (£1.75 – the french onion soup is almost a meal on its own), smoked pheasant and fresh mango or mushrooms in tarragon cream sauce (£2.95), shepherd's pie or ploughman's (£3.75), fisherman's pie (£4.25), vegetarian dishes such as aubergine layer bake, cider bean casserole or leek croustade (£5.25), beef bourguignon (£6.50), and scampi in brandy cream sauce (£6.95), with puddings like their popular treacle tart or home-made ice cream (from £1.95); no chips or deep-fried meals. A wide range of well kept real ales on handpump includes Adnams Southwold and Broadside, Greene King IPA, Nethergate Bitter and a couple of regularly changing guests, usually tracked down from rather more obscure local breweries; also several malt whiskies, bottled

European fruit beers, country wines, popular cocktails and an extremely strong local cider. The garden has picnic-table sets looking over the fine views of the countryside, and you can play pétanque out here. *(Recommended by Gwen and Peter Andrews, Miss D Morrison, A Kemp, Ian Phillips, Sue Holland, Dave Webster)*

Free house ~ Licensees Adrian and Tricia McGrillen ~ Real ale ~ Meals and snacks (11.30-2.15, 6.30-9.45, though they try to be flexible) ~ Halstead (01787) 461196 ~ Well behaved children welcome ~ Live music one Tues a month, fortnightly Sun quiz nights ~ Open 11-3, 6-11

GOSFIELD TL7829 Map 5

Green Man 🍴 ⚲

A1017 N of Braintree

Essex Dining Pub of the Year

No matter how long you take over your meal at this warmly friendly pub they never seem to hurry you, and no wonder – food this good really needs to be savoured. It's already a firm favourite with plenty of readers, many of whom have this year particularly enjoyed the lunchtime cold table, with a splendid help-yourself choice of home cooked-ham, tongue, beef and turkey (all carved by the landlord), dressed salmon or crab (in season), game pie, salads and home-made pickles (£6.95). Other really excellent dishes include good leek and potato or superb game with sherry soups (£1.90), lovely soft roes on toast with bacon, fresh battered cod (£5.35), delicious liver and bacon, faultless ragout, braised oxtail (£5.95), really good rare lamb chops, cider-baked hot ham or hot sirloin of beef (£6.25), tender roast shoulder of wild boar (£6.50), pheasant in red wine or roast duck with gooseberry sauce (£7.95), fresh scallops mornay (£8.20), 20oz T-bone steak (£13.50), and well made home-made puddings like treacle pudding or spotted dick (£2.25); the vegetables are fresh and the chips home-made. They have regular curry evenings and occasional highly praised Italian meals; the dining room is no-smoking. The first-class staff are welcoming to locals and visitors alike, and there's a fine atmosphere in the two little bars. Well kept Greene King IPA and Abbot on handpump, and decent nicely priced wines, many by the glass; darts. *(Recommended by Gwen and Peter Andrews, Paul and Ursula Randall, Bernard Phillips)*

Greene King ~ Lease: John Arnold ~ Real ale ~ Meals and snacks (not Sun evening) ~ Restaurant (not Sun evening) ~ (01787) 472746 ~ Well behaved children in eating area ~ Open 11-3, 6.30-11 (midnight supper licence)

GREAT YELDHAM TL7638 Map 5

White Hart

Poole Street; A604 Halstead—Haverhill

Lots of fervently enthusiastic reports over the last few months deservedly earn this attractive Tudor house a return to the main entries. Originally built as a cell for prisoners on their way to Chelmsford Jail, it became a pub in the late 17th c – its original licence apparently endorsed by Samuel Pepys. The black-and-white building and well-kept garden are very attractive, with white cast-iron tables among a variety of trees and shrubs on the lawns. Inside, the smart yet cosy bar has heavy beams and oak-panelling, winged easy chairs, settees and wall settles, attractive antique Morland prints and a log fire; it opens into an extension, giving the feel of three separate room areas. The unusual food is very highly regarded, with an interesting choice including sandwiches, soup (£2.50), field mushrooms baked with stilton and herb butter (£4), green lipped mussels in a herb crust with cheese (£4.50), roast duck in orange sauce (£9.50) and five freshwater crayfish in shrimp sauce (£11.50); they also do two-course meals for £7.99 or three for £11.99, with dishes like venison terrine or chicken breast with cream and tarragon. Well kept Nethergate Bitter and IPA on handpump, coffee and tea; very friendly service and atmosphere, no juke box or games, two friendly dogs, Darby and Beauty. *(Recommended by Barbara and Norman Wells, Paul Dodds, J L Knight,*

Gordon Theaker, C O Day, V E Hinton, Paul and Ursula Randall, Wayne Brindle)

Free house ~ Licensee David Smillie ~ Real ale ~ Meals and snacks (not Sun evening or Mon) ~ Restaurant (not Sun evening or Mon) ~ Great Yeldham (01787) 237250 ~ Children welcome ~ Open 11.30-3, 6.30-11; closed Sun evening, all day Mon (except bank holidays)

HATFIELD BROAD OAK TL5416 Map 5

Cock

High St

The genuinely old-fashioned atmosphere is what most people notice first at this characterful 15th-c village pub, with its beams, wide-planked wooden floors, tap room with open fire (there's a woodburning stove in another room), and lots of fresh flowers. The walls are decorated with the title sheets of Victorian and Edwardian music hall songs and old advertisements, and there's an untouched Victorian brass railed bar; the tap room is no-smoking. Popular bar food includes home-made soup (£2.25, unusual flavours like chilli vegetable), home-made chicken liver pâté or pasta, onion and tarragon salad (£2.95), fresh asparagus in hot butter or beef tomato stuffed with prawns and egg (£3.75), home-cooked gammon and egg (£3.95), pheasant casserole (£4.50), pork chop in cider sauce or pasta, chilli and salad (£5.50), giant Yorkshire pudding filled with mushrooms and beanshoots (£5.95), plaice with lemon grass (£6.25), grilled wing of skate (£6.95) and sirloin steak with grain mustard (£8.95); Sunday roast and children's dishes (£2.50); good, attentive staff. Well kept Adnams Bitter and Broadside and a couple of changing guest beers, several malt whiskies, various ciders, maybe nibbles on the bar at weekends; darts, bar billiards, dominoes, fruit and trivia machines, and piped music. *(Recommended by Gwen and Peter Andrews, L V Nutton, David H Stevens, R Shelton)*

Free house ~ Licensees Patrick Dick and Andrew Stock ~ Real ale ~ Meals and snacks (till 10pm; not Sun evening) ~ Restaurant (not Sun evening) ~ (01279) 718273 ~ Children in eating area of bar ~ Open 12-3, 5.30(6 Sat)-11

HIGH EASTER TL6214 Map 5

Cock & Bell ◖

The Easters are signposted from the Rodings, on B184/A1060

Friendly new licensees have taken over this handsomely timbered 14th-c pub since our last edition. It's very much the focal point of the village, and probably has been for centuries – heavy oak beams fill the rooms, and the dragon-beamed ceiling is the oldest in Essex. The comfortable and atmospheric lounge bar has cushioned Windsor chairs and vases of fresh flowers, and a cheerful second bar has a log fire. There's still the same wide range of regularly changing beers as before, with ales like Batemans Valiant, Crouch Vale IPA, Flowers Original, Gibbs Mew Bishops Tipple and Salisbury Bitter on handpump, and a decent choice of wines; darts, piped music. Bar food includes home-made dishes such as lasagne or their delicious steak, ale and mushroom pie (£4.95); they make their own chips. There's a terrace and garden with a play area outside. Note they once again offer bedrooms: we'd be interested to hear if they deserve our place to stay award. *(Recommended by Sandra Iles, Roxanne Chamberlain, Caroline Wright; more reports please)*

Free house ~ Licensees Ann and Alan Steel ~ Real ale ~ Meals and snacks ~ ~ Restaurant ~ Chelmsford (01245) 231296 ~ Children welcome ~ Open 12-3, 7-11 ~ Bedrooms: £29.50B/£39.50B

HORNDON ON THE HILL TQ6683 Map 3

Bell ♀

M25 junction 30 into A13, then left into B1007 after 7 miles, village signposted from here

It's business as usual at this popular partly-medieval timbered and panelled pub, but don't think that means there's even a hint of complacency. Another year at the Bell means more prizes won for (amongst other things) their superb food, and their profuse flowers and countless hanging baskets – not to mention the successes of the pub's various sporting teams. After years of training in the monthly Fun Run (every second Wednesday in summer, 7pm start) one of their regulars recently won the London Marathon, while others successfully try their hand at cricket, skiing, or the London to Brighton cycle ride. Even the oldest person in the village plays their part, summoned each Good Friday since 1905 to hang a hot cross bun from one of the beams in the open-plan bar. Seats in a bow window at the back of here have views over the fields, and there are some antique high-backed settles, plush burgundy stools and benches on the flagstones or highly-polished oak floorboards. The excellent and very unusual bar food might typically include sandwiches, ploughman's, soup such as broccoli (£2.10) or mussel with vegetables and saffron (£2.50), chicken livers with black pudding (£2.95), red mullet and orange salad (£3.25), rabbit and bacon terrine (£3.95), smoked chicken and vegetable strudel (£3.75), deep-fried aubergine with tofu (£6.50), steak and kidney pudding (£7.10), chicken breast with prosciutto ham and polenta (£8.50), lamb cutlets in pastry with haggis (£8.95), roast pheasant with bacon and game chips (£10.20), grilled salmon with mussels and chives (£10.50), and puddings such as lemon soufflé with almond biscuits or date and ginger pudding with vanilla custard (£3.50). Many of the starters can be had as a main course. Well kept Bass, Charrington IPA and Fullers London Pride on handpump, with weekly changing guest beers; service is friendly and efficient. They have a huge selection of over 100 well chosen wines from all over the world (several by the glass or half bottle), listed on a blackboard with notes on what to drink with your food; you can also buy them off-sales. On the last weekend in June the High Road outside is closed (by Royal Charter) for period-costume festivities and a crafts fair; the pub holds a feast then. There may be a barbecue other summer weekends. The Verekers have converted a house two doors away into a busy little hotel, Hill House, and from this year you can stay in a room in the pub itself, with its original Tudor beams and windows. (*Recommended by Mrs Gwyneth Holland, Gwen and Peter Andrews, D Cox, S Howe, John Whitehead, David Bridge, Jennie and Malc Wild, M L Clarke, Graham Bush, Mr and Mrs Chris Thorn, Professor John White, Patricia White, J S Frost*)

Free house ~ Licensee John Vereker ~ Real ale ~ Meals and snacks (not Sun lunch) ~ Restaurant ~ Stanford-le-Hope (01375) 673154 ~ Children in restaurant and eating area of bar ~ Open 11-2.30(3 Sat), 6-11; closed evenings 25 and 26 Dec ~ Bedrooms in house two doors away: /£55B

LAMARSH TL8835 Map 5

Red Lion

From Bures on B1508 Sudbury—Colchester take Station Road, passing station; Lamarsh then signposted

A real favourite with some of our most-travelled readers, this is a warmly friendly old place, full of character and atmosphere, and very hard to beat for its service and setting. It's especially attractive on a summer evening, when you can look out over the river and hills and contentedly watch the daylight drift away. Inside the flower arrangements dotted all around reflect the licensees' carefully attentive style of management, and there are fine views of the fields and colour-washed houses of the Stour Valley from the tables and small pews by the front windows, in stalls with red velvet curtain dividers; also abundant timbering, local scenes on the walls, and unobtrusive piped music. They never quite know what's going to be on the menu, the very good chef pretty much deciding on the spur of the moment the meals she wants to cook that day; current favourites include excellent soups such as carrot and orange, huge filled rolls with a very flexible range of fillings (£3.35), stilton and walnut bake (£4.95), chicken, ham and broccoli pie (£4.95), well-liked salads such as Greek-style tuna with feta cheese (£5.25), good rare roast beef on Sundays (£4.95), and home-made puddings such as cherry pie (£1.65). Part of the eating area is no-smoking. Well kept Courage Directors, Greene King IPA, John Smiths, Marstons Pedigree and Wadworths 6X on handpump, a range of malt whiskies, and decent dry white wine by the glass; very friendly staff. Pool, darts, cribbage, fruit machine, video game and trivia. There are swings in the biggish sheltered sloping garden, looking particularly good at the moment after some recent landscaping. *(Recommended by Gwen and Peter Andrews, D Cox, Basil J S Minson, Professor S Barnett, Anthony Barker)*

Free house ~ Licensees John and Angela O'Sullivan ~ Real ale ~ Meals and snacks (till 10.30) ~ Restaurant ~ Bures (01787) 227918 ~ Children in eating area ~ Very occasional live music ~ Open 11-3, 6-11; 11-11 Sat

LANGHAM TM0233 Map 5

Shepherd & Dog ♀

Moor Rd/High St; village signposted off A12 N of Colchester

An engaging hotch-potch of styles, this good-natured and warmly friendly local might not look old but its history goes back some 300 years or so. The licensees put a lot of trouble into the housekeeping, food and drink and it seems to be paying off – the pub is deservedly popular at the moment for its welcoming atmosphere and in particular the big helpings of extremely tasty and well-served home-made food. One reader saw a lady at the next table gasp aloud when she saw the size of her meal. Favourite dishes on the menu include the big doorstep sandwiches (from £1.60), thick flavoursome soups such as broccoli and almond or a filling bouillabaisse (from £1.75), vegetable samosas (£2.25), ploughman's (from £2.50), vegetable pie or feta and cheddar cheese in filo pastry (£4.50), lamb chops (£4.75), wing of skate or Dover sole (£6.25), chicken breast stuffed with lobster (£7.25), fillet of lamb with fresh apricots (£7.50) and puddings such as raspberry bavarois or chocolate mousse (£1.95); it's worth getting there early as they do get busy. Their Greek, Chinese and other speciality restaurant evenings are still very popular. Well kept Greene King IPA, Abbot and Rayments Special and a guest such as Nethergate Old Growler on handpump, decent wines; unobtrusive piped music. The L-shaped bar, with an interesting collection of continental bottled beers, is kept spick and span, and there's often a sale of books for charity. Tables outside. *(Recommended by Jeff Davies, Barbara and Norman Wells, Gwen and Peter Andrews, D and B Carter, M A and C R Starling, R G Smedley)*

Free house ~ Licensees Paul Barnes, Jane Graham ~ Real ale ~ Meals and snacks (12-2.30, 6-10) ~ Restaurant ~ (01206) 272711 ~ Children welcome ~ Open 11-3, 5.30(6 Sat)-11; closed 26 Dec

LEIGH ON SEA TQ8385 Map 3

Crooked Billet ◀

51 High St; from A13 follow signpost to station, then cross bridge over railway towards waterside

Recalling the glory days of the great English seaside, this is a chummily inviting old place, bracingly set right by the sea wall. It's older than was originally thought; restoration work uncovered Tudor beams and plasterwork and it's reckoned to have started off as a 16th-c farmhouse. The seats in the unspoilt and homely lounge bar are built around the walls so that they face into the room rather than looking at other chairs or tables – perhaps this is why there's such a friendly atmosphere. There's a solid fuel stove in here too, as well as two big bay windows with good views out to sea, and photographs of local cockle smacks on the shiny, yellowing walls. On the left, the bare-floored public bar has a huge log fire, more photographs, and sensibly placed darts, shove-ha'penny and cribbage. In the winter there's an incredible range of real ales, with at least 12 different beers served from barrels behind the bar, but this is reduced to about six in summer, usually including well kept Adnams, Ind Coope Burton, Taylor-Walker, and Tetleys on handpump, with weekly changing guests like Robinsons or Hartleys. Straightforward snacks such as filled rolls (from £1.50), ploughman's

(£3), chilli con carne and hotpots (around £3.50). The big terrace has an outside servery used on fine afternoons when the pub is closed. They don't mind you eating cockles, shrimps or jellied eels out here, from Ivy Osborne's marvellous stall, just down the lane (it shuts at 10pm). No children inside. Their colourful window boxes and hanging baskets have won local prizes, and sitting underneath them is a good place from which to watch the shellfish boats in the old-fashioned working harbour. *(Recommended by Trevor P Scott, Nigel Norman, D Cox, A Plumb, Mr and Mrs A N Piper, Ian Bourne)*

Ind Coope (Allied) ~ Manager Alan Downing ~ Real ale ~ Lunchtime meals and snacks (not Sun) ~ Southend on Sea (01702) 714854 ~ Open 11-11

LITTLE BRAXTED   TL8314 Map 5

Green Man

Kelvedon Road; village signposted off B1389 by NE end of A12 Witham bypass – keep on patiently

Considering how tucked away this lovely unspoilt place is, it's good to see how many people take the trouble to track it down. In fact its comparative isolation adds very much to the appeal, helping to preserve the delightfully cosy atmosphere; it's an idyllic spot for a quiet drink. Simple and snug, the traditional little lounge has an interesting collection of bric-a-brac, including 200 horsebrasses and some harness, mugs hanging from a beam, a lovely copper urn, and an open fire. Well kept Ridleys IPA and ESX (cheaper in the public bar) is dispensed from handpumps in the form of 40mm brass cannon shells, and there are several malt whiskies; piped music. The tiled public bar leads to a games room with darts, shove-ha'penny, dominoes, cribbage, fruit machine, trivia and several board games like Scrabble. All the bar food is home-made, often even the bread, and though the range isn't enormous, it's wholesome and tasty – and generally very good value; the choice typically includes stuffed mushrooms, crab and salmon pot (£3.95), steak and ale pie or fidget pie (an East Anglian recipe involving onion, apple, bacon and cider – £4.75) and, more unusually, authentic-tasting haggis. It's worth arriving early for a table. Readers this year have been very impressed with the welcoming, friendly service, and in fact the licensees recently won a brewery award for customer care. There are picnic-table sets in the sheltered garden behind, extended in the year since the Wileys took over. *(Recommended by John C Baker, George Atkinson, David Cardy, Mrs Gwyneth Holland, Hazel Morgan, Bernard Patrick, Gwen and Peter Andrews, S J Barney, R C Morgan, Derek and Sylvia Stephenson, Ian Phillips)*

Ridleys ~ Tenants Tony and Andrea Wiley ~ Real ale ~ Meals and snacks ~ (01621) 891659 ~ Children welcome ~ Open 11-3, 6-11; closed evening 25 Dec

LITTLEBURY   TL5139 Map 5

Queens Head ♀ ⇦ ◖

B1383 NW of Saffron Walden; not far from M11 junction 9, but exit northbound only, access southbound only

Food and beer continue to be the main attractions at this engaging no-nonsense old inn. The range of well kept real ales is exceptional, with generally up to eight at a time such as Bass, Courage Best and Directors, John Smiths, Theakstons Best, Worthington BB and Youngers IPA, and the landlord's tasting notes chalked up to stimulate your appetite. An added bonus is that on weekdays they usually have beer at the bargain price of £1 a pint. They hold an annual real ale festival with over 60 different beers, and once a month they have a small brewery week; also interesting bottled beers, and a decent recently expanded wine list. As for the delicious food, the excellent menu changes every day, with lunchtime sandwiches joined by very popular dishes such as chicken and pearl barley soup (£1.80), filled baked potatoes (from £2.20), baked avocado with stilton butter (£2.80), trio of poached fish salad (£3), ploughman's (£3.85), peppers stuffed with pulse casserole (£4.80), provençal tarts with garlic pastry (£5.20), gammon with cider and apple (£5.90), skate with capers or dressed crab salad (£6.40), chicken stuffed with rhubarb (£6.40), pheasant with cranberries (£8) and puddings like walnut treacle tart or banoffi pie (£2.50). Also Sunday lunches and regular food festivals with maybe Indian, French and Italian themes. The unusual herbs you'll immediately notice come straight from the garden, and they also grow their own vegetables and soft fruit. The pub has been carefully refurbished to make the most of its unpretentious appeal – flooring tiles, beams, simple but attractive wooden furniture, and snug side areas leading off the bar; a part near the restaurant is no smoking. The atmosphere's vibrant and friendly; darts, shove-ha'penny, cribbage, dominoes and maybe piped music. Tables out in a nicely planted walled garden, and swings, stepping stumps, a climbing frame and slide for children. *(Recommended by Ben Grose, Ian Phillips, John Fahy, Alan and Ruth Woodhouse, John C Baker, Trevor P Scott, Tony Gayfer, Gwen and Peter Andrews, Chris Dewhurst, Nigel Gibbs)*

Free house ~ Licensees Deborah and Jeremy O'Gorman ~ Real ale ~ Meals and lunchtime snacks ~ Restaurant (not Sun evening) ~ Saffron Walden (01799) 522251 ~ Children in eating area and restaurant ~ Open 12-11; limited opening 25 and 26 Dec ~ Bedrooms: £29.95B/£44.95B

MILL GREEN TL6400 Map 5

Viper 🍺

Mill Green Rd; from Fryerning (which is signposted off north-east bound A12 Ingatestone bypass) follow Writtle signposts; OS Sheet 167 map reference 640019

One reader was pleasantly surprised to see that this homely little place hasn't really changed since his last visit – some time in the 1950s. The setting is ideal for a summer day, with the pub nestling in a lovely oak wood, a bank of sweet chestnuts behind; it's a popular stop for walkers. Tables on the neat lawn look over wonderfully cared-for gardens, a mass of nasturtiums, foxgloves, geraniums and lathyrus, and the pub itself is all but hidden by honeysuckle, overflowing hanging baskets and window boxes. There are more fresh flowers in vases on the tables inside. For many people the main attraction is the monthly changing choice of three impeccably kept ales from all around the country (including some rare in this area) that might include Cains Traditional, Cotleigh Rebellion, Eldridge Pope Royal Oak, Gales Best, Morlands Original, Smiles Best and Robinsons, all served from the oak-panelled counter. The two little rooms of the lounge have pale hessian walls (the log fireplace is in a stripped brick wall), spindleback seats, armed country kitchen chairs, and tapestried wall seats around neat little old tables. The parquet-floored taproom (where booted walkers are directed) is more simply furnished with shiny wooden traditional wall seats, and beyond there's another room with country kitchen chairs and sensibly placed darts; shove-ha'penny, dominoes, cribbage and a fruit machine. Bar snacks include soup (£1.30), good sandwiches (from £1.25, toasties from £1.35), Hawaiian toast (£2.20), ploughman's (from £2.70), and chilli con carne (£2.80). *(Recommended by George Atkinson, D Cox, S J Barney, Peter Baggott, Derek R Patey)*

Free house ~ Licensee Fred Beard ~ Real ale ~ Lunchtime snacks ~ Ingatestow (01277) 352010 ~ Open 11-2.30(3 Sat), 6-11

NAVESTOCK TQ5397 Map 5

Plough 🍺

Sabines Rd, Navestock Heath (off main rd at Alma Arms)

There are fine views of open country from the front garden of this neatly kept pub, deservedly popular with beer drinkers for its outstanding choice of real ales. There may be up to 13 of them on handpump or tapped from the cask at any one time, typically including brews such as Archers Village, Ash Vine Challenger, Banks & Taylors Mild, Brains Bitter, Gibbs Mew Bishops Tipple, Greene King Abbot, Mitchells ESB and Fortress, Moorhouses Mild, and Timothy Taylors Landlord; also, three cask ciders. Several interconnecting rooms have a mix of dark wooden solid chairs with flowery-cushioned seats around polished wooden tables, horsebrasses and dried flowers on the beams, and an open fire. Bar food includes sandwiches, home-made hot dishes (from around £3.95), steaks (from £7.95), weekend barbecues, and a favourite dish called snob's chicken. Darts, cribbage, dominoes and piped music. *(Recommended by George Atkinson, D Cox, Derek R Patey)*

Free house ~ Licensee Ros Willson ~ Real ale ~ Meals and snacks (not Sun evenings) ~ (01277) 372296 ~ Children in eating area of bar ~ Trad jazz every 2nd Sun evening, country music on 1st and 3rd Weds of month ~ Open 11-4 (5 Sat), 6-11

NORTH FAMBRIDGE TQ8597 Map 5

Ferryboat £

The Quay; village signposted from B1012 E off S Woodham Ferrers; keep on past railway

Apart from a few floods over the years very little disturbs the peaceful atmosphere at this unspoilt waterside pub, tucked away at the end of the lane down by the River Crouch, with good lonely walks around. It's a lovely unassuming spot, attracting a good few yachtsmen in summer, and the 15th-c weatherboarded pub is decorated in a similarly simple style: traditional wall benches, settles and chairs on its flooring tiles, nautical memorabilia, old-fashioned lamps, a few historic boxing-gloves. There's a log fire at one end, and a woodburning stove at the other, and a dining conservatory for families. There's some emphasis on food, all very good value, with a catholic menu where sausage, egg and chips (£2.70) rub shoulders with venison cooked in port (£6); other well-priced dishes include sandwiches (from £1), french onion soup (£1.50), fried clams or pâté (£2.20), plaice or cod and chips (£2.50), very popular ham and eggs or good salt beef salad (£3), scampi (£3.50), swordfish (£5), and deep-fried turkey stuffed with asparagus and ham (£6); vegetables are fresh. On Sundays they do roasts, and there may be fewer other meals available then. Well kept Flowers IPA and two guests on handpump, one of which is usually Morlands Old Speckled Hen, decent wine, dry-witted landlord, friendly attentive service; shove ha'penny, cribbage, trivia and Wednesday quiz nights; seats outside. *(Recommended by Myroulla West, Gwen and Peter Andrews, Russell and Margaret Bathie, K and B Moore, George Atkinson)*

Free house ~ Licensees William Boyce, Roy Maltwood ~ Real ale ~ Meals and snacks ~ Restaurant ~ (01621) 740208 ~ Children in family conservatory ~ Open 11-3, 6(7 winter)-11; closed evening 25 and 26 Dec

PELDON TL9916 Map 5

Rose

B1025 Colchester—Mersea, at junction with southernmost turn-off to Peldon

Especially busy in fine weather, this partly 14th-c pink-washed house is a nicely old-fashioned place. Creaky close-set tables and antique mahogany fill the cosy, cream-walled bar and one or two standing timbers support the low ceiling with its dark bowed 17th-c oak beams. The mantelpiece of the gothick-arched brick fireplace is decorated with brass and copper, and there are chintz curtains in the leaded-light windows; the large conservatory with its white tables and chairs and potted plants is no-smoking. The spacious garden is very relaxing, and as well as its good teak seats and occasional wild rabbit has two ponds with geese and ducks – some of whom have been known to wander round the tables looking for food. In summer there may be Morris dancers out here. The food servery, beside a stripped pine dresser on an old-fashioned brick floor, does sandwiches (from £1.95), salads (£4.95), lasagne (£5.50), beef bourguignon (£5.75), Sunday roasts (£6.75), and various fish; children's helpings. It's worth getting there early if you're planning to eat. They do cream teas every afternoon in summer and weekends in winter. Well kept Boddingtons, Flowers Original and IPA and maybe a guest on handpump, quite a few wines; well organised service. *(Recommended by*

Chris Harrison, Barbara and Norman Wells, Professor John and Mrs Patricia White, Les
Downes, Hazel Morgan)

*Free house ~ Licensees Alan and Ariette Everett ~ Real ale ~ Meals and snacks
(until 10) ~ Restaurant; only Fri and Sat evening ~ Peldon (01206) 735248 ~
Children welcome away from main bar ~ Open 11-2.30, 5.30-11 ~ Bedrooms:
£25S/£35S*

PLESHEY TL6614 Map 5

White Horse

Signposted with Howe Street off A130 Dunmow—Chelmsford

An attractive place with a cheery atmosphere, this 15th-c pub rarely seems
crowded even when busy, its fascinating nooks and crannies effortlessly able to
absorb the steady stream of diners and drinkers. There's plenty to look at, and
almost every available space is filled with jugs, tankards, antlers, miscellaneous
brass, prints, books, bottles – even an old ship's bell. The rooms have a genuinely
friendly feel and are furnished with wheelback and other chairs and a mix of dark
wooden tables; one fireplace has a woodburning stove, another big brick one has
horse-brasses along the mantelbeam, and yet another has an unusual curtain-like
fireguard. The snug room by the tiny bar counter has brick and beamed walls, a
comfortable sofa, some bar stools and a table with magazines to read, as well as a
sonorous clock. A constantly changing range of well kept beers might include
such brews as Boddingtons, Courage Directors, Crouch Vale Woodham, Jennings
Cumberland, Nethergate Best, Ridleys IPA or Tolly Original on handpump; by
the time this edition is published they plan to have a new bar, with a greater
range of beers on at any one time. The eating area will then become no-smoking,
and there should be a new enclosed children's play area. The emphasis continues
to shift towards food, with a good value range that includes huffers (from £2.50),
soup (£2 – their carrot and marrow is good), filled baked potatoes or
ploughman's (from £3.50), breaded plaice or scampi (£4.50), curry and rice (£5),
steak and kidney pie with Guinness (£5.50), grilled rainbow trout (£8.50), lemon
sole (£9.50), rack of lamb (£10.50), fillet steak (£12.50), daily specials and
puddings like spotted dick and custard (£2.50). Decent wines, good cheery
service; fruit machine. Glass cabinets in the big dining room are filled with 1500
miniatures and the room also has sturdy furniture, lots of plants, and an old-
fashioned stove in the brick fireplace. Doors from here open on to a terrace with
white plastic garden furniture, a grass area with similar seating and a few picnic-
table sets, and a children's play area with slide, swings and a see-saw. The
hanging baskets and flowering tubs are lovely – and the cat is called Tigger.
*(Recommended by Mike Beiley, Dorothy Pilson, Tony Beaulah, Gwen and Peter Andrews,
Professor John White, Patricia White, Paul and Ursula Randall, Roger Danes, Stephen and
Jean Curtis, D P Pascoe, D Cox)*

*Free house ~ Licensees John and Helen Thorburn ~ Real ale ~ Meals and snacks
(till 10pm) ~ Restaurant ~ Pleshey (01245) 237281 ~ Children welcome ~ Open
11-3, 7-11*

RICKLING GREEN TL5029 Map 5

Cricketers Arms 🍴

Just off B1383 N of Stansted Mountfitchet

Instantly friendly and delightfully pubby, this is becoming a real favourite with
some readers, mainly because everyone always looks so cheerful. The Proctors
really go out of their way to make visitors feel at home, and the whole family
seem to muck in and cheerfully turn their hand to almost anything. Essex CC
play on the village green outside every year, and there are certainly enough
cricketing mementoes to make them feel at home. Masses of cricket cigarette
cards are displayed on the walls of the softly lit and comfortable saloon bar, the
two bays of which are divided by standing timbers; in winter chestnuts are
roasted on the log fire. Well kept Flowers IPA and a monthly changing strong

bitter such as Felinfoel Double Dragon or Courage Directors, unlimited coffee (served with a jug of cream), efficient service; maybe unobtrusive piped music. Well priced bar food, all home-made using fresh ingredients, might include sandwiches, soup (£1.75), soft roes (£2.25), garlic sausage platter (£2.45), choice of ploughman's, black pudding with mustard sauce (£4.25), mussels done in various ways such as marinière or a lightly curried version of mouclade (from £4.95), cod mornay or chilli con carne (£5.25), home baked gammon or steak and kidney pie (£5.95), crab and prawn thermidor (£7.50), sirloin steak (£8.95), and tempting puddings; Wednesday night is fish and chips night. There's a very heavily beamed little stone-floored side family dining area (no smoking), a separate front bar with pool, darts, cribbage, dominoes, fruit machine and juke box, and a modern back restaurant (usefully they do a second sitting at 3 for their genuinely no-rush Sunday lunch – booking only). A sheltered front courtyard has picnic-table sets overlooking the cricket green. The bedrooms are in a modern block behind – handy for Stansted Airport, with a courtesy car for guests. *(Recommended by K and B Moore, George Atkinson, Hugh and Peggy Colgate, Wayne Brindle, Dr Andrew Brookes, Gwen and Peter Andrews, the Pollard family, Bill and Edee Miller, H O Dickinson, Prof John White, Patricia White)*

Free house ~ Licensees Tim and Jo Proctor ~ Real ale ~ Meals and snacks (till 10) ~ Restaurant ~ Rickling (01799) 543210 ~ Children in eating area and family room ~ Open 11-3, 6-11; all day Sat ~ Bedrooms: £50B/£60B

SAFFRON WALDEN   TL5438 Map 5

Eight Bells ♀

Bridge Street; B184 towards Cambridge

The fresh fish from Lowestoft or Billingsgate continues to attract a good many people to this handsomely timbered black and white Tudor inn, with tasty dishes like dressed crab, wing of skate with capers (£6.35), wholemeal scampi (£6.30), or prawns baked in cheese and white wine sauce (£6.50). The other home-made meals are just as popular, with the interesting daily changing menus typically including soup (£1.90), ploughman's (from £3.45), good omelettes (£4.40), cheese, leek and potato pie or mushroom thermidor (£5.75), steak, kidney and mushroom pie or saffron-gilded chicken (£6.25), roast quail with peppercorn sauce (£7.15), venison in blackcurrant and red wine sauce (£9.90), char-grilled steaks (from £10.20), puddings including chocolate brandy pot or toffee apple fudge cake (£2.25), children's menu (from £1.65) and daily specials; prompt, attentive and friendly service. Well kept Adnams, Friary Meux, Ind Coope Burton, Marstons Pedigree, Tetleys and a changing guest on handpump, decent wines by the glass (with a choice of glass size), and coffee. Partly no-smoking, the restaurant is in a splendidly timbered hall with high rafters, tapestries and flags, and the neatly kept open-plan bar is divided by old timbers, its modern oak settles forming small booths around the tables. There's a family room in the carpeted old kitchen with an open fire. There are seats in the garden. Nearby Audley End makes a good family outing, and the pub is close to some good walks. *(Recommended by John Fahy, Judith Mayne, Gwen and Peter Andrews, K and B Moore, Mr and Mrs W R R Bruce, D K Carter, David and Ruth Hollands, Professor John White, Patricia White, Bill and Edee Miller)*

Ind Coope (Allied) ~ Manager David Gregory ~ Real ale ~ Meals and snacks (till 10 Sat) ~ Restaurant ~ Saffron Walden (01799) 522790 ~ Children in restaurant and family room ~ Open 11-3, 6-11

STOCK   TQ6998 Map 5

Hoop £ 🍺

B1007; from A12 Chelmsford bypass take Galleywood, Billericay turn-off

You might expect a landlord with a name like Kitchin to pay a good deal of attention to his food, but it's still a surprise to find that the meals at this cheerfully unsophisticated and homely old place are such good value. Once again fish is the speciality, with dishes often including green-lipped mussels in parsley and white wine sauce (£3), grilled monkfish or skate (£4), swordfish with ginger and lime butter (£4.50), trout florentine with dill sauce (£5) and paella (£7.50), but the all-day menu also includes soup (£1), sandwiches (from £1, toasties from £1.20), jacket potatoes (from £1.10), omelettes (from £2.50), sausage pie (£2.75), ploughman's or cottage pie (£3), hotpot, steak and kidney or vegetable pie (all £3.50), daily specials like rabbit stew (£3.50) or pheasant en croute (£4.50) and puddings such as home-made cheesecake or various strudels (£1.50). The bustling bar has a friendly and traditional atmosphere, as well as brocaded wall seats around dimpled copper tables on the left, a cluster of brocaded stools on the right, and a coal-effect gas fire in the big brick fireplace. An outstanding range of real ales on handpump or more likely tapped from the cask includes Adnams and Nethergate and a variety of changing beers such as Crouch Vale, Exmoor Gold, Fullers ESB, and Wadworths 6X, with several from smaller independent breweries; the range is even bigger over the May Day week when there's a choice of around a hundred. They also have farm cider, decent wines by the glass, country wines in summer, and mulled wine in winter; staff are smiling and efficient. Sensibly placed darts (the heavy black beams are studded with hundreds of darts flights), cribbage and dominoes. Lots of picnic-table sets in the big sheltered back garden, prettily bordered with flowers where they have occasional summer barbecues and maybe croquet (or boules on the front gravel). The dog is called Misty and the cat Thomas. *(Recommended by Mike and Pam Simpson, Gwen and Peter Andrews, Jennie and Malc Wild, D Cox; more reports please)*

Free house ~ Licensee Albert Kitchin ~ Real ale ~ Meals and snacks all day ~ Stock (01277) 841137 ~ Children in eating area of bar ~ Open 11-11

TILLINGHAM TL9903 Map 5

Cap & Feathers ★ ◗

B1027 N of Southminster

A quaint and characterful old tiled house, what really makes this traditional village pub stand out is its lovely old-fashioned atmosphere. You could easily be forgiven for thinking you'd gone back 40 years or more, and once ensconced in its warmly snug low-beamed and timbered rooms it's often rather difficult to leave. Divided into three cosy little areas, the crookedly creaky bar has sturdy wall seats (including a venerable built-in floor-to-ceiling settle), a homely dresser and a formidable woodburning stove, as well as little wheelback chairs with arms and etched-glass brass-mounted lamps; one parquet-floored part has bar billiards (operated by an old shilling, provided at the bar), sensibly placed darts, and table skittles – there's another set in the attractive no-smoking family room, and they have shove-ha'penny, cribbage and dominoes. Daily changing bar food features the succulent and distinctively flavoured products of their own smokery, such as smoked fillet of beef (£5.95) or trout (£6.75), as well as their own beef and venison pies, soup (£1.75), lasagne (£4.95), sirloin steak (£10.50), and home-made puddings like apple pie or ice cream. A fine range of drinks includes well kept Crouch Vale Woodham, Best, SAS, and winter Willie Warmer, a guest beer, Thatcher's farm cider, and English fruit wines. Service is friendly and efficient; last year's manager has recently taken over the tenancy. A small side terrace has picnic-table sets under birch trees. Just down the lane is the village cricket pitch, and the pub fields its own team. *(Recommended by A Plumb, Gwen and Peter Andrews, Evelyn and Derek Walter, D Cox, Derek and Sylvia Stephenson, Jennie and Malc Wild, Brian Horner, Brenda Arthur)*

Crouch Vale ~ Tenant John Moore ~ Real ale ~ Meals and snacks ~ Tillingham (01621) 779212 ~ Children in no-smoking family room ~ Open 11.30-3, 6-11 ~ Three bedrooms: £25/£30

TOOT HILL TL5103 Map 5

Green Man ♀

Village signposted from A113 in Stanford Rivers, S of Ongar; and from A414 W of Ongar

A country dining pub far more unusual than its simple furnishings might suggest, partly because of the imaginative food but mainly due to an extraordinarily civilised attitude to wines. There are usually around 100 different well chosen bottles on the list (as well as several half bottles), carefully selected from five different merchants, with a special offer wine of the week and over 30 different champagnes by the bottle (many pinks, including their *doyenne,* Veuve Clicquot), one sold by the glass; they do regular tastings. The daily changing menu offers soup and ploughman's as well as more unusual dishes such as spinach noodles with salmon flakes and cucumber dressing or quail wrapped in smoked bacon with red wine sauce (£3), baked avocado and crab in stilton sauce (£3.95), steak and kidney pie (£5.95), braised duck casserole (£6), pork tenderloin with apricot and chillis (£7.50), honey grazed lamb with toasted almonds in a tangy orange sauce (£8), fish dishes like pink trout or lemon sole (£8.50) and home-made puddings (£2.50); four-course Sunday roasts; welcoming, flexible service. There may be nibbles of cheddar and cheesy biscuits on the bar. Well kept Adnams and two weekly changing guest beers on handpump. The main emphasis is on the neatly looked after long dining lounge, with its candlelit tables, fresh flowers, and attractively figured plates on a delft shelf. In the evenings they take bookings for tables in here, but only for 7.30; after that, when you turn up they put you on a queue for tables that come free. A smallish and simply furnished area by the bar has mushroom plush chairs and pale mustard leatherette stools and settles, one or two hunting prints above the dark varnished wood dado, brass platters on a shelf just below the very dark grey-green ceiling, and an open fire; darts around the other side, shove-ha'penny, dominoes, cribbage and piped music. In summer, there's a lovely mass of colourful hanging baskets, window boxes and flower tubs, prettily set off by the curlicued white iron tables and chairs – there may be Morris dancers out here then; more tables behind. A couple of miles through the attractive countryside at Greensted is St Andrews, the oldest wooden church in the world. *(Recommended by D A Edwards, Mick Hitchman, K and B Moore, Adrian M Kelly, C Slack, J H Gracey, Eric and Jackie Robinson, Helen Morton, Gwen and Peter Andrews, H O Dickinson, Professor John White, Patricia White, Graham Bush, Derek R Patey)*

Free house ~ Licensee Peter Roads ~ Real ale ~ Meals and snacks (not 25 Dec) ~ Restaurant (not Sun evening) ~ North Weald (01992) 522255 ~ Children over 10 only ~ Open 11-3, 6-11; closed 25Dec

WENDENS AMBO TL5136 Map 5

Bell

B1039 just W of village

Handy for Audley End, and just a short stroll through a pleasant village from Audley End Station, this is a proper old-fashioned country pub, small and welcoming. It used to be tied to Allied but is now a free house, and its liberation from the tie seems to have breathed new life into it. It's cottagey outside and in, with patterned red carpet in small rooms that ramble engagingly round to the back, quite a lot of pictures on cream walls, brasses on ancient timbers, wheelback chairs around neat tables, and comfortably cushioned seats worked into snug alcoves; there are good open fires. Everything glistens with cleanliness and care, and there's good friendly service and a warm atmosphere. Good straightforward bar food includes filled home-baked rolls (from £1.65), ploughman's (from £3.50), moussaka or chilli con carne (£4.95), beef and ale pie or cajun chicken (£5.75), mixed grill (£6.25), good puddings (£2) such as treacle pie and summer pudding, and (Oct-May) a popular Sunday lunch (four courses, £9.75); there's a quaintly pretty dining room. Well kept Adnams, Ansells Dark Mild, Greene King IPA and a guest beer on handpump. The very extensive back garden's quite special: an informal layout with a big tree-sheltered lawn, lots of flower borders, unusual plant-holders, plenty of amusements for children (even a goat called Gertie, and a sort of mini nature-trail wandering off through the shrubs). The lively dog's called Kate. *(Recommended by A Langan, A M Pring, Gwen Andrews, Neil Barker, Ian Phillips, Trevor Scott)*

Free house ~ Licensees Geoffrey and Bernadette Bates ~ Real ale ~ Meals and snacks (not Mon evening) ~ Children in family dining room ~ Saffron Walden (01799) 540382 ~ Open 11.30-3, 6-11; cl evening 25/26 Dec

WIDDINGTON TL5331 Map 5

Fleur de Lys

High Street; signposted off B1383 N of Stansted

The sort of quietly welcoming dining pub where the staff smile even at their busiest, and the atmosphere always stays comfortably restful and unhurried. Though the emphasis is pretty much on the food, drinkers are far from neglected, and the landlord takes time to elucidate the seven well kept real ales on handpump, which generally include Adnams, Bass, Courage Directors, Timothy Taylors, Wadworths IPA and 6X and Whitbread Castle Eden. The varied menu includes bulging weekday sandwiches, enterprising home-made soups such as the enduringly popular authentic gazpacho or shellfish soup (£1.95), garlic mushrooms (£3.50), various curries or steak and kidney pie (£5.75), a wide range of fish such as grilled sardines, cod, halibut or scampi (from £5.50; the crisply fried mixed seafood malaguena has been well liked), venison and local game, vegetarian and children's dishes, and delicious puddings. For Sunday lunch there's a choice of fish or paella as well as a choice of roasts (from £5.45), and there may be a tapas buffet on Sunday night. The low-beamed and timbered L-shaped bar has brocaded small settles and mates' chairs, and red tiles by its inglenook log fire; a simple sturdily furnished back bar has darts, dominoes and games machines. There are picnic-table sets out on the side lawn. *(Recommended by Caroline Wright, Audrey and Dennis Nelson, John Fahy, Gwen and Peter Andrews)*

Free house ~ Licensee Richard Alder ~ Real ale ~ Meals and snacks ~ Restaurant (not Sun evening) ~ Saffron Walden (01799) 540659 ~ Children in restaurant and no-smoking family room ~ Folk music Friday night ~ Open 12-3, 6-11

WOODHAM WALTER TL8006 Map 5

Bell £

A414 E from Chelmsford; village signposted on left after about 6 miles

Increasingly popular under its newish licensees, this is a strikingly attractive Elizabethan house facing a group of oak trees in a pretty hollow, its prominent jettied upper storey standing out immediately as you drop down towards it. Very friendly and welcoming, the relaxed and neatly kept lounge bar is divided into irregularly-shaped alcoves on various levels, with old timbers and beams, comfortable seats and a log fire. A changing range of decent bar food includes a very wide choice of well-priced sandwiches (from £1.05), soup (£1.75), real ale pâté (£2.35), plaice or fried egg and sausages (£3.75), steak and kidney pie (£4.95), salmon and broccoli pie (£5.25), prawn curry (£5.50), duck in orange sauce (£7.95) and rump steak (from £7.95) as well as specials and vegetarian dishes. There's a prettily decorated dining room in a partly panelled gallery up steps from the main bar. Adnams, Benskins Best and a changing guest like Eldridge Pope Hardy or Marstons Pedigree on handpump. This was one of the many buildings that tried to avoid paying the window tax in the mid 18th c by plastering up half their windows. *(Recommended by Quentin Williamson, Gwen and Peter Andrews, Paul and Ursula Randall, J S Frost, Bill and Beryl Farmer, D Cox)*

Free house ~ Licensees Alan and Margaret Oldfield ~ Real ale ~ Meals and snacks (not evening Mon and poss Sun) ~ Danbury (01245) 223437 ~ Children in eating area or separate lounge ~ Open 12-3, 6.30(7 Sat)-11

Cats 🍺

Back road to Curling Tye and Maldon, from N end of village

Tucked well away from the village, this attractively timbered old building has a truly rural feel, and the conversation often turns towards farming and livestock. The roof is constantly patrolled by prowling stone cats, and the feline theme is continued inside where there are shelves of china cats. The atmosphere is very relaxed, especially in summer, when you can sit in the delightful garden with its views of peaceful hills. The rambling low-ceilinged bar is full of interesting nooks and crannies and traditionally decorated, with low black beams and timbering set off well by neat white paintwork, and a warming open fire. The simple food is straightforward and enjoyable, and the Adnams Southwold and Broadside, Greene King IPA and Abbot and Rayments Special on handpump particularly well kept; friendly service. The pleasantly chatty landlord would rather we didn't include his pub in the *Guide*, but letting licensees decide for us which pubs *not* to include would damage our independence almost as much as allowing other landlords to pay for their inclusion, so we have, quite deservedly, included it once more. *(Recommended by Paul and Ursula Randall, Gwen and Peter Andrews, Lynn Sharpless, Bob Eardley, D Cox)*

Free house ~ Real ale ~ Snacks ~ Open 11-2.30ish, 6.30ish-11; may close if not busy in winter

---

Lucky Dip

Besides the fully inspected pubs, you might like to try these Lucky Dips recommended to us and described by readers (if you do, please send us reports):

☆ **Abridge** [Market Pl (A113/B172); TQ4696], *White Hart*: Large refurbished pub with wide range of reasonably priced food and beers and Charrington IPA on handpump in friendly and spacious open-plan refurbished bar, RAF fighter-bomber pictures, riverside garden; young people and piped pop music evenings – live jazz Mon-Weds *(Robert Lester)*
Abridge [London Rd (A113)], *Maltsters Arms*: Friendly two-bar 16th-c pub with open fires, beams, Greene King IPA and Abbot on handpump; popular with young people evenings *(Robert Lester)*
Althorne [TQ9199], *Huntsman & Hounds*: Country pub with lovely garden, Greene King ales, good food and coffee, good friendly service; piped music *(George Atkinson, LYM)*
Aythorpe Roding [B184; TL5815], *Axe & Compasses*: Decent food esp Sun lunches in beamed bar with big compass dividing it from restaurant; well kept Greene King and other ales, courteous landlord, subdued piped music, darts *(P and H Douglas)*
☆ **Battlesbridge** [Hawk Hill; TQ7894], *Barge*: Attractive weatherboarded inn by art and craft centre nr Crouch estuary, old-fashioned, low-ceilinged and cosy, with good value limited but generous bar lunches, well kept Allied ales and a guest such as Adnams, good coffee, good service, barge pictures; children's room; can get busy summer weekends *(George Atkinson)*
Billericay [TQ6794], *Quilters*: Seems like a converted church, with huge conservatory on one side; busy and trendy, with Courage Directors *(Graham Bush)*

☆ **Blackmore** [Blackmore End; nr church; TL6001], *Bull*: Doing well under new licensees, pleasant rural ambience in long bar with lots of beams, family room one end, attractive restaurant the other; really good interestingly cooked food inc bargain lunches, well kept Adnams, Bass, Greene King IPA, Mauldons White Adder and a guest such as Batemans, good house wines; closed Mon exc bank hols *(Gwen and Peter Andrews)*
Blackmore [The Green], *Prince Albert*: Spacious three-sided bar, beams and walls hung with mugs, brass and copper, big stove, pleasant staff, well kept Bass and Worthington BB on handpump, decent wine, good value food, darts *(Gwen and Peter Andrews)*
Broomfield [160 Main Road; TL7010], *Angel*: Busy main-road pub, attractively restored (dates from 14th c), with well kept Allied ales and guests such as Adnams, good wholesome reasonably priced straightforward food, old prints and posters, pretty flowers outside *(Paul and Ursula Randall, Dave Braisted)*; [off A130 N of Chelmsford], *Kings Arms*: Warm welcome, good helpings of good value interesting changing specials, well kept Greene King IPA and Original on handpump *(D M Green)*
☆ **Broxted** [TL5726], *Prince of Wales*: Big helpings of consistently good food in friendly L-shaped bar with restaurant and conservatory dining areas, particularly good choice of wines by the glass, Courage-related real ales with a guest such as Wadworths 6X, attentive welcoming

service; good garden with play area *(Gwen and Peter Andrews, Mr and Mrs Blake)*

☆ **Burnham on Crouch** [The Quay; TQ9596], *White Harte*: Two high-ceilinged panelled bars in old-fashioned yachting inn overlooking anchorage, very busy weekends and in season; oak tables, polished parquet, sea pictures, panelling and stripped brickwork; straightforward good value food from sandwiches up, restaurant, well kept Adnams and Tolly, friendly staff, terrace above river; children allowed in eating area; bedrooms *(George Atkinson, LYM)*

Castle Hedingham [B1058, Sible Hedingham side; TL7835], *Wheatsheaf*: Unassuming local with jolly licensees, generous helpings of well cooked food inc Sun lunches, well kept Greene King IPA and Abbot on handpump, decent coffee; darts and pool in public bar; piped music (live some nights) *(Gwen and Peter Andrews)*

☆ **Chelmsford** [Roxwell Rd, about 2 miles from centre; TL7006], *Horse & Groom*: Popular and attractive mock-Tudor pub just out of town, country views from nicely furnished conservatory; friendly, welcoming and efficient staff, well kept Courage-related real ales (pub bought by S&N, so this may change), decent wines, good value food inc Sun lunch in big no-smoking dining area, unobtrusive piped music; tables outside *(Paul and Ursula Randall, Gwen and Peter Andrews, John and Beryl Kersey)*

nr **Chelmsford** [Cooksmill Green; A414 5 miles W – OS Sheet 167 map ref 638052; TL6305], *Fox & Goose*: Spaciously extended well kept pub with lots of tables, well kept real ale, decent quick food, lively but not boisterous evening atmosphere, matey efficient service *(PR, LYM)*

☆ **Chigwell** [High Rd (A113); TQ4693], *Kings Head*: Magnificent 17th-c building with strong Dickens connections, lots of memorabilia, some antique furnishings; good value standard Chef & Brewer bar food, friendly staff, well kept Courage-related real ales (may change to S&N), good coffee, first-floor restaurant; very spacious and quiet weekday lunchtimes, can get extremely crowded weekend evenings; in pretty part, with neat attractive garden *(George Atkinson, D Cox, C H and P Stride)*

Chipping Ongar [TL5502], *Kings Head*: Large comfortable town pub with panelling, reproduction oil paintings, good value food inc Sun roast in big back dining area, Courage-related ales; piped music; floodlit terrace *(Sandra Iles)*

☆ **Coggeshall** [Main St; TL8522], *White Hart*: Good pubby atmosphere in bar of 15th-c inn, lots of low dark beams, library chairs and one or two attractive antique settles around oak tables, bow window seats, flower prints and fishing trophies on cream walls, wide choice of food inc authentic pasta, well kept Adnams, decent wines and

coffee; bedrooms comfortable *(Gwen and Peter Andrews, BB)*

Coggeshall, *Chapel*: Genuine 19th-c woodwork, old beams, fascinating prints, good simple food *(Ernest Hofer)*; [91 Church St; turn off main st opp Post Office and Barclays Bank], *Woolpack*: Photogenic timber-framed Tudor pub with attractive unassuming period lounge bar, usually good value sandwiches and a few home-cooked hot dishes, good value Sun roast, well kept Adnams, log fire; shame about the piped music *(Anthony Barker, G Neighbour, LYM)*

☆ *nr* **Coggeshall** [Pattiswick (signed from A120 just W of Coggeshall bypass – OS Sheet 168 map ref 820247)], *Compasses*: Spotless country pub, spacious and attractive, with warm and friendly staff, wide choice of generous food in big helpings cooked to perfection with veg or salad and potatoes cooked four ways, good choice of vegetarian dishes; Greene King IPA and Abbot, Ridleys and Tetleys, log fire, tiles and beams, quick courteous service; spreading lawns with play area and orchard – in May 1994 a reader saw ten fallow deer in neighbouring wheatfield *(G Neighbour, LYM)*

☆ **Colchester** [Castle St, off Roman Rd; TM0025], *Forresters Arms*: Remarkably good varied lunchtime food inc imaginative fillings for sandwiches and baked potatoes, unusual soups, quail's-egg salads in friendly town local with well kept Whitbreads-related and accompanying ales on handpump; good prices, live folk music Tues *(Colin Keane, Dagmar Junghanns, Anthony Barker)*

☆ **Colchester** [East St], *Rose & Crown*: Carefully modernised handsome Tudor inn, timbered and jettied, parts of a former gaol preserved in its rambling beamed bar, good value bar food, real ale; comfortable bedrooms *(Anthony Barker, Barbara and Norman Wells, LYM)*

Colchester [Nayland Rd], *Dog & Pheasant*: Clean and spacious, with good food, hospitable landlord *(J W Cockerton)*; [Lexden Rd], *Tap & Spile*: Good range of changing real ales, cases of rugby club ties, cricketer photographs, some flagstone flooring; tables in small back courtyard, busy but efficient and pleasant staff *(Anthony Barker, Barbara and Norman Wells)*

Colne Engaine [signed off A604 in Earls Colne; TL8530], *Five Bells*: Warmly welcoming, with Greene King ales, no music *(Gwen and Peter Andrews)*

Coopersale Common [TL4702], *Theydon Oak*: Welcoming pub with pleasant service, well kept real ales, varied bar food, separate restaurant menu, nice atmosphere – popular with all ages; tables in garden with play area *(Mrs C A Miller)*

Coxtie Green [Coxtie Green Rd; TQ5695], *White Horse*: Six real ales and good value food in quiet country pub with big garden

(N Mortlock, D Cox)

☆ **Crays Hill** [London Rd; TQ7192], *Shepherd & Dog*: Well renovated and much improved recently by Mancunian licensees, who have tamed and enhanced the large garden; well kept Allied ales with a guest such as Wadworths 6X, well cooked nicely presented food (OAP bargains Tues/Thurs) in oak-beamed horseshoe bar or more formally in newish conservatory, friendly service, big log fire; fruit machines, quiet piped music, live music Sun pm; good walks; children in conservatory *(Tony Burke, Mike Beiley)*

☆ **Cressing** [TL7920], *Three Ashes*: Good value low-priced food inc good veg, bargain suppers Mon-Thurs and OAP lunches some weekdays, well kept Greene King IPA and Abbot, friendly landlord; spotless and unpretentiously charming bar with copper jugs, brasses and china cabinet; obliging service, restaurant a couple of steps down from bar; no music; unspoilt garden *(Gwen and Peter Andrews)*

☆ **Danbury** [Runsell Green; N of A414, just beyond green; TL7905], *Anchor*: New licensees spring 1994 doing generous helpings of promising food (they both cook) in welcoming timbered pub with gleaming brass, log fires, warm atmosphere, attractive conservatory, generous showing of malt whiskies, well kept Adnams and Extra and Ridleys IPA on handpump, decent wine, chatty and welcoming staff; mussel chowder planned as a winter speciality *(Prof John White, Patricia White, Gwen and Peter Andrews)*

☆ **Danbury** [TL7805], *Griffin*: Quiet and spacious Chef & Brewer pub, very well run, with good pubby atmosphere, 16th-c beams and some older carved woodwork, decent food, Courage-related and Greene King real ales (may switch to S&N) *(Mrs Gwyneth Holland)*

Debden [High St; TL5533], *Plough*: Quite big, with good range of straightforward home-cooked food inc vegetarian and children's dishes, very friendly customers and staff, welcoming atmosphere, Greene King IPA, Abbot and Rayments, decent house wines; children welcome, fair-sized garden behind *(Sandra Iles, Gwen and Peter Andrews)*

☆ **Dedham** [TM0533], *Sun*: Spacious and comfortably refurbished Tudor pub opposite the church seen in so many of Constable's paintings; cosy panelled rooms with log fires in huge brick fireplaces, handsomely carved beams, well kept beer, good range of generous reasonably priced food, friendly staff; tables on back lawn, car park behind reached through medieval arch, wonderful wrought-iron inn sign; modestly luxurious old panelled bedrooms with four-posters *(Quentin Williamson, Ian Phillips, Anthony Barker, Mrs Gwyneth Holland, LYM)*

Downham [TQ7295], *De Beauvoir Arms*: Recently renovated free house retaining much character; frequently changing guest beers, good value bar food; big garden, close to Hauningfield reservoir, popular for trout fishing and bird watching *(Mike Beiley)*

Dunmow [W of centre; TL6221], *Queen Victoria*: Pleasant thatched and beamed local with hardworking, welcoming landlord and staff, good food inc fresh fish in bar and restaurant, well kept Courage Best, Greene King and Mauldons *(Robert Bardell)*

☆ **Duton Hill** [off B184 Dunmow—Thaxted, 3 miles N of Dunmow; TL6026], *Three Horseshoes*: Very welcoming new licensees transforming this free house with its central log fire and their growing collection of social-history memorabilia (landlord was an actor); several well kept Whitbreads-related and other ales such as Ridleys IPA, decent bar food, dining room, games area with pool and juke box; lovely view from informal garden which already has a stage – plans for terrace and play area; one to watch *(Gwen and Peter Andrews)*

East Hanningfield [signed from A130; TL7601], *Three Horseshoes*: Opened-up beamed pub with plenty of tables, back restaurant, jolly atmosphere, usual bar food, Courage-related ales, tables outside looking down green-lined village street *(Gwen and Peter Andrews)*

Epping [High St; TL4602], *Black Lion*: Good choice of well priced food in nicely set-out pub with beams and horsebrasses; dogs in bar but not eating area *(Mr and Mrs N A Spink)*; [26 High St, opp water tower], *Half Moon*: Clapboarded pub with impressive window boxes, partly beamed inside, wonderful log fire, welcoming landlord, flexible straightforward food, good coffee, Bass and Worthington beers *(Ian Phillips)*

Feering [3 Feering Hill; TL8720], *Sun*: Five perfectly kept real ales, two Courage-related, Wadworths 6X and guests, interesting menu; despite refurbishment much of the pubby atmosphere has been kept *(John C Baker)*

Felsted [Station Rd; TL6721], *Swan*: Central log fire in saloon bar, games room beyond public bar, nice little restaurant (can eat here at no extra charge if saloon is full); well presented reasonably priced varied food (not Sun evening) inc Italian dishes, carefully cooked steaks, old-fashioned puddings, filled huffers; Adnams and Ridleys, decent house wines; bedrooms *(Tony Beaulah)*

☆ **Fiddlers Hamlet** [Stewards Green Rd, a mile SE of Epping; TL4700], *Merry Fiddlers*: Attractive 17th-c country pub with lots of beer mugs hanging from ceiling, no pub games or loud music, well kept Adnams and Courage-related ales, sensibly short choice of good value generous food; big garden with play area *(Robert Lester, A L Turnbull)*

Finchingfield [Mill End, N of village;

TL6833], *Green Man*: Quietly welcoming spacious beamed 15th-c pub with well kept Adnams and Greene King IPA tapped from the cask, decent wine, enjoyable standard food; just outside the picture-book village *(Gwen and Peter Andrews)*

Fingringhoe [TM0220], *Whalebone*: Family-run pub with good food, friendly service, changing real ales, pool; spacious garden; a former landlord built a bicycle-powered punt he used to pedal to Colchester *(C M F Harrison)*

Fordham Heath [TL9426], *Cricketers*: Popular for good value substantial bar and restaurant food *(Barbara and Norman Wells)*

Fordstreet [A604 W of Colchester; TL9126], *Shoulder of Mutton*: Picturesque old riverside pub with beams, log fire and country prints; friendly welcome, well kept Flowers on handpump, good choice of bar food inc good fresh veg, piped music *(Alan and Jill Stanford)*

Fryerning [Mill Green; TL6400], *Cricketers*: Greene King IPA and Abbot, straightforward lunchtime food, interesting cricketing memorabilia, friendly Jack Russell; country views *(D Cox, John Fahy)*

☆ **Fuller Street** [The Green; off A131 Chelmsford—Braintree, towards Fairstead; TL7416], *Square & Compasses*: Delightful little beamed cottage pub with good reasonably priced home-cooked bar food inc lunchtime filled rolls, well kept Ridleys, lots of brasses; seats in small garden overlooking fields, lovely spot (on Essex Way); piped folk music (live last Fri of month) *(Shirley Pielou)*

☆ **Furneux Pelham** [TL4327], *Brewery Tap*: Friendly refurbished bar, good reasonably priced traditional pub food, well kept Greene King and Rayments; back garden room and terrace overlooking attractive lawns and flower beds *(Sidney and Erna Wells)*

Goldhanger [TL9009], *Chequers*: Amazingly extensive reasonably priced menu, charming licensee and staff *(Trevor Leary)*

☆ **Great Baddow** [Galleywood Rd; or off B1007 at Galleywood Eagle; TL7204], *Seabrights Barn*: Family pub in rustic raftered barn conversion, with lots for children inc spacious enclosed play area and good pets' corner; upper gallery one end, partly no smoking restaurant/conservatory (open for meals all day Sun); wide choice of usual bar food, well kept Adnams Best and Broadside, Greene King IPA, Abbot and Rayments, decent wines; tables on terrace, barbecues, open all day Sat *(Derek R Patey, Les Downes, LYM)*

Great Easton [2 miles N of Dunmow, off B184 towards Lindsell; TL6025], *Green Man*: Good value pleasantly served food from sandwiches up inc Sun lunch in welcoming 15th-c pub with well kept Adnams, Greene King IPA and Ridleys,

cribbage; fine views, good big garden *(Gwen and Peter Andrews, Derek R Patey)*; [2 miles N of Dunmow, off B184 – signed by Anglo garage], *Swan*: Small cosy pub in attractive village street with country bygones, comfortable furnishings, warm atmosphere and pleasant staff; Charringtons and Websters Yorkshire on handpump, big choice of bar food *(GA, PA)*

☆ nr **Great Henny** [Henny Street; a mile or so E, on Sudbury—Lamarsh rd; TL8738], *Swan*: Tables on lawn by quiet river and pond beside cosy little well furnished L-shaped timbered lounge with partly no-smoking conservatory restaurant, decent bar food (not Sun evening) from sandwiches to steaks, garden barbecues, well kept Greene King IPA and Abbot, children allowed, maybe piped music *(Prof S Barnett, Bill and Wendy Burge, A Plumb, LYM)*

Great Horkesley [Nayland Rd; TL9730], *Rose & Crown*: On two floors with three bars and restaurant; very welcoming reception, Greene King beers, good range of food *(N Bushby, W Atkins)*

☆ **Great Saling** [village signposted from A120; TL7025], *White Hart*: Friendly and attractive Tudor village pub with easy chairs in unusual upper gallery, ancient timbering and flooring tiles, lots of plates, brass and copperware, good speciality giant sandwiches and other snacks served till late, well kept Adnams Extra and Ridleys on handpump, good service, restaurant Tues-Sat evenings, well behaved children welcome; seats outside *(LYM)*

☆ **Great Stambridge** [1 Stambridge Rd; TQ9091], *Cherry Tree*: Comfortable and cosy dining pub with big circular conservatory dining room, big bar/lounge area with beams and rough plaster, Courage Directors and Flowers IPA; good if not cheap fish from wide restaurant menu, reasonably priced more basic dishes; garden; very popular, but can get crowded *(George Atkinson)*

Great Stambridge [Stambridge Mills], *Royal Oak*: Locals' dining pub, food from good well filled sandwiches up, food service good *(George Atkinson)*

Great Wakering [TQ9487], *Exhibition*: Pleasant terrace and garden area with waterfalls, small pond and gnomes, friendly staff, good value food *(George Atkinson)*; [High St], *Red Lion*: Well kept real ale such as Crouch Vale IPA, Morlands Old Speckled Hen, John Smiths, Wadworths 6X and Websters, huge log fire, good friendly atmosphere, fresh home-cooked food, free bar nibbles; jazz Weds *(B A Crawley)*; [High St], *White Hart*: Attractive beamed bar with lots of brasses, cosy seating, friendly staff – very hospitable; piped local radio; seats in courtyard *(George Atkinson)*

☆ **Great Waltham** [old A130; TL6913], *Beehive*: Quietly welcoming new landlords, substantial improvements to bars, wider choice than before of decent straightforward food, well kept Ridleys, quite a few malt whiskies, decent wine, good log fire; subdued piped music; tables outside *(Gwen and Peter Andrews, Mike Barry)*

Great Warley Street [TQ5890], *Thatchers Arms*: Pretty Chef & Brewer pub by village green, helpful service, decent food and drink *(Norman Foot)*

Halstead [Hedingham Rd; TL8130], *Dog*: Well kept Adnams and Nethergate, good value bar food, friendly landlord; bedrooms good *(Mike and Pam Simpson)*; [15 High St], *White Hart*: Very attractive eclectic exterior with bay windows between twin steep gothic gables; decor inside doesn't do justice to the good timbering, but has real ales, well priced usual bar food, very helpful friendly staff *(Ian Phillips)*

Hatfield Heath [TL5215], *White Horse*: Old-fashioned place on edge of county's biggest village green, friendly attentive licensees, freshly cooked food *(Harold Curry)*

Hatfield Peverel [TL7911], *William Boosey*: Long split-level bar with food counter at one end, quiet restaurant with good value steaks *(G Boyes)*

☆ **Herongate** [Dunton Rd – turn off A128 Brentwood—Grays at big sign for Boars Head; TQ6391], *Old Dog*: Good choice of well kept local and other real ales and of lunchtime bar food (only snacks weekends) in long traditional dark-raftered bar, open fire, comfortable back lounge, friendly relaxed atmosphere; dogs allowed; picnic-table sets on front terrace and in neat sheltered side garden *(D Cox, LYM)*

Herongate [Billericay Rd; A128 Brentwood—Grays], *Green Man*: Useful pub with several rooms, Adnams and Allied ales, friendly chatty staff; children allowed in back rooms *(George Atkinson)*

☆ **Heybridge Basin** [TL8707], *Old Ship*: Lovely views of the Blackwater saltings and across to Northey Island from clean and spruce pub with well kept Adnams Bitter, Extra and Broadside, eating area one end with reasonably priced food, blond wooden furniture, unobtrusive piped music; can be very busy, esp in summer when parking nearby impossible (but public park five mins' walk) *(Gwen and Peter Andrews, Margaret and Trevor Errington)*

High Ongar [King St, Nine Ashes; TL5603], *Wheatsheaf*: Very comfortable, good variety of good value food, friendly staff *(G Boyes)*

☆ **High Roding** [The Street (B184); TL6017], *Black Lion*: Attractive low-beamed bar dating from 15th c, Italian landlord doing good food esp minestrone, authentic pasta, vegetarian dishes; comfortable relaxed surroundings, cheerful staff, well kept Adnams and Ridleys *(E J Cutting, Paul and Ursula Randall)*

Hockley [Main Rd; TQ8293], *Bull*: Family local on edge of woods so very popular with walkers, vast car park, stable area with well, very hospitable; well kept beers; big garden with own servery, animals, pond and play area *(George Atkinson)*

Howe Street [TL6914], *Green Man*: Pleasant and spacious old timbered two-bar pub with comfortably plush lounge, nice brass and prints, well kept Adnams Extra and Ridleys IPA on handpump, welcoming newish licensees, bar food and restaurant; unobtrusive piped music; garden with play area *(Gwen and Peter Andrews)*

☆ **Little Baddow** [North Hill; towards Hatfield Peverel; TL7807], *Rodney*: Friendly low-beamed country local full of nautical brasswork and Nelson memorabilia, well kept Greene King and Rayments Special, decent food, welcoming staff; pool room with unobtrusive piped music, terrace and garden with well equipped play area *(Gwen and Peter Andrews)*

Little Bentley [TM1125], *Bricklayers Arms*: Small welcoming country local with enjoyable good value home cooking running up to speciality steaks; real ale, friendly obliging staff *(Jim Kinnear, Beryl and Bill Farmer)*

Little Hallingbury [Hall Green; TL5017], *Sutton Arms*: Nice beamed and carpeted thatched pub with good food, very nice atmosphere and friendly and attentive staff; close to M11, can get very busy *(George Atkinson)*

Little Oakley [B1414 Harwich—Clacton; TM2129], *Olde Cherry Tree*: Friendly and unpretentious, long bar divided by real log fire in open grate, Adnams and Broadside on handpump, simple cheap food inc vegetarian, piped music, quieter dining room *(Nigel Norman)*

Little Walden [B1052; TL5441], *Crown*: Fine choice of good food in enormous helpings, three real ales, in spacious low-beamed open-plan bar; peaceful area, handy for Linton Zoo *(Bill and Lydia Ryan)*

☆ **Loughton** [103 York Hill; just off A121 High Rd; TQ4296], *Gardeners Arms*: Quietly attractive traditional low-ceilinged bar with surprising views towards Epping Forest from side terrace; Adnams and Courage-related real ales, two open fires, friendly service, good value straightforward lunchtime bar food (not Sun) from sandwiches up with hot dishes all fresh-cooked (so can be delays), children in restaurant *(Quentin Williamson, Joy Heatherley, J S Frost, John Fahy, LYM)*

Loughton [227 High Rd], *Last Post*: Good 1993 addition to Wetherspoon chain, expensively converted former post office with good warming atmosphere, decent food, good service; Courage Directors, Theakstons, Wadworths 6X and Youngers Scotch *(Robert Lester)*; [165 Smarts Lane], *Victoria*: Traditionally furnished with separate dining area, three real ales inc Greene King IPA, good value home-made food; pleasant garden with aviary *(Richard M Brady)*

☆ **Manningtree** [Manningtree Stn; out towards Lawford; TM1031], *Station Buffet*: Early 1950s feel, esp on cold days when the heavily steamed etched windows make a sort of cocoon against the outside world; long marble-topped bar, three little tables and a handful of unassuming seats; wide range of properly kept real ales inc Adnams, Greene King, Mauldons and unusual guests such as Mitchells ESB or Summerskills Best, big helpings of good low-priced simple food all home-cooked, friendly service *(John C Baker, Graham Reeve)*

Marden Ash [Brentwood Rd (A128); TL5502], *Stag*: McMullens pub with AK Mild, Country, Special Reserve and winter Stronghart and a guest like Wadworths Farmers Glory; food, pleasant garden *(D Cox)*

Margaretting [B1002; TL6701], *Spread Eagle*: Clean and spacious, with Bass, Charrington IPA and Highgate Mild on handpump, bar food, attentive staff, fairly unobtrusive piped music, live jazz Tues *(Gwen and Peter Andrews)*

☆ **Margaretting Tye** [TL6800], *White Hart*: Good summer pub with lots of tables in attractive garden by quiet village green, good walks nearby, wide choice of good value promptly served food, well kept Adnams and Broadside, Mauldons, Greene King IPA and a guest beer on handpump, friendly staff; piped music; barbecue *(G Leibou, Mike Beiley, S Howe, Gwen and Peter Andrews)*

☆ **Mashbury** [TL6411], *Fox*: Friendly character pub in quiet countryside, beamed and flagstoned lounge, old-fashioned long tables, little or no music, huge helpings of homely food, well kept Adnams and Ridleys tapped from the cask, decent wine; dominoes, cribbage, skittles *(Gwen and Peter Andrews, Jennie and Mack Wild)*

Moreton [TL5307], *Moreton Massey*: Enormous choice of food in sizeable open-plan bar and small restaurant, inc bargain meals Mon-Thurs; friendly and comfortable, winter log fire giving a homely feel, well kept Bass, Greene King IPA and John Smiths on handpump, darts area, unobtrusive piped music *(D Cox, Gwen and Peter Andrews)*; *White Hart*: Very welcoming local with lovely log fire, good genuine home-cooked food and real ales such as Adnams, Courage Best, Greene King Abbot or Theakstons XB; bedrooms *(Alan and Ruth Woodhouse, E J Cutting)*

☆ **Navestock** [Huntsmanside, off B175; TQ5397], *Alma Arms*: Huge helpings of good value food esp steak and kidney pie in comfortable low-beamed pub's spacious and popular dining area; well kept ales such as Adnams, Greene King Abbot and Rayments BBA, decent wines; good service, no children *(G Leibou, Miss Sandra Iles)*

☆ **Paglesham** [TQ9293], *Plough & Sail*: Beautifully kept dining pub with good flower arrangements, aviary in pleasant garden, wide and attractive menu from sandwiches up, warm and friendly atmosphere, well kept Courage-related beers, quick helpful service even when busy; carvery; very popular on warm summer evenings, in pretty spot nr marshes *(Mrs P J Pearce)*

☆ **Peldon** [TL9916], *Plough*: Pretty tiled and white-boarded village local, small, simple and warmly welcoming; good home-cooked food to order (so not instant) inc fresh fish and seafood, well kept Crouch Vale IPA, pool, quiz and fruit machine *(ABS, Chris Harrison)*

☆ **Pilgrims Hatch** [Ongar Rd; TQ5895], *Black Horse*: Particularly good home cooking at sensible prices inc fresh veg and huge puddings; friendly service *(Geo Rumsey, K and B Moore)*

☆ **Purleigh** [by church; TL8401], *Bell*: Cosy rambling hilltop pub, black beams and timbers, enticing nooks and crannies, cushioned wall banquettes, tables and chairs, maybe a big log fire, well kept Adnams and Greene King IPA on handpump, good reasonably priced home-made lunchtime food, welcoming landlord; picnic-table sets on side grass, views over Blackwater estuary *(Gwen and Peter Andrews, LYM)*

☆ **Radwinter** [B1053 E of Saffron Walden – OS Sheet 154 map ref 612376; TL6137], *Plough*: Out in the country, very attractive terrace and garden behind neatly kept red plush open-plan black-timbered beamed bar with central log fire and separate woodburner; good choice of popular bar food inc vegetarian, well kept Greene King IPA, Nethergate and Charles Wells Bombardier on handpump, decent wine, piped music; bedrooms *(Gwen and Peter Andrews, Brian and Jill Bond, John and Karen Day, BB)*

☆ **Rayleigh** [14 High Rd; TQ8190], *Paul Pry*: Good Chef & Brewer pub with character, decent food, well kept Courage-related ales (maybe S&N), friendly efficient service; nice big gardens with tuck-shop in summer *(Margaret and Trevor Errington)*

☆ **Ridgewell** [A604 Haverhill—Halstead; TL7340], *Kings Head*: Much modernised unpretentious local with good value bar food inc some enterprising dishes, some signs of Tudor origins, interesting local World War II memorabilia, well kept Greene King IPA and Abbot on handpump, decent wines; pool and other games in airy public bar, subdued piped music, a few tables in roadside garden *(Gwen and Peter Andrews, BB)*

☆ **Rochford** [35 North St (one-way); TQ8790], *Golden Lion*: Pretty white clapboard cottage with lots of real ales, mostly changing guests, such as Greene King Abbot, Eldridge Pope Hardy Country, Fullers London Pride, McEwans 80/-,

Palmers Bridport and even Zum Zum; good range of extremely reasonably priced lunchtime snacks inc seven styles of sausage; friendly landlord, wonderful atmosphere, though not smart *(Ian Phillips)*

☆ **Rowhedge** [Quay; TM0021], *Anchor*: Wonderful spot overlooking River Colne with its swans, gulls and yachts; Courage-related real ales, fishing bric-a-brac, good atmosphere, ample helpings of good value food such as fresh plaice, restaurant; gets very busy *(Roxanne Chamberlain)*

☆ **Shalford** [TL7229], *George*: Genuine home cooking (be prepared to wait) at attractive prices in pleasantly refurbished L-shaped bar and eating area, lots of exposed brickwork, log fire in enormous fireplace, well kept Greene King IPA and Rayments with a guest such as Adnams Broadside, young smiling staff, plenty of dark wood tables and chairs, real family atmosphere with lots of children at weekends, no music; new terrace *(Gwen and Peter Andrews)*

☆ **South Weald** [Weald Rd (off A1023); TQ5793], *Tower Arms*: Consistently well kept real ales, Courage-related up till now, in pleasant unpretentious 18th-c bar, decent Chef & Brewer food in attractive conservatory restaurant (not Sun-Tues evenings) overlooking nice secluded garden with boules; picturesque village; friendly staff, children allowed away from bar *(Derek R Patey)*

Stanway [London Rd; TL9324], *Swan*: Friendly refurbished pub with wide choice of food inc good roasts, good service, winter log fire, Greene King Abbot and Rayments on handpump; nice verandah, terrace and children's play area *(Mrs Cooke, N E Bushby, W Atkins)*

Stapleford Tawney [TQ5098], *Mole Trap*: Welcoming small country pub, simple bar food at reasonable prices, McMullens AK and County on handpump; very popular summer evenings *(D Cox, H O Dickinson)*

☆ **Stock** [B1007 towards Galleywood – OS Sheet 167 map ref 704004; TQ6998], *Ship*: Extremely friendly and welcoming, with good food inc delicious sandwiches, efficient service, well kept local real ales; old plastered building tucked behind trees, oak furniture in beamed bar and modern extension, restaurant; children welcome *(Caroline Wright)*

Stock [The Square], *Bear*: Lovely old building with cosy restaurant, good well cooked and presented food, Adnams and Tetleys *(Graham Bush, Mrs Gwyneth Holland, A Morgan, Les Downes)*

☆ **Stow Maries** [TQ8399], *Prince of Wales*: Nice bare-boards atmosphere, with several unspoilt rooms, particularly well kept Crouch Vale and other changing ales generally from interesting distant small breweries, country wines and decent real wine, log fire, friendly service, good popular food inc vegetarian and children's dishes *(Derek and Sylvia Stephenson)*

☆ **Sturmer** [The Street; A604 SE of Haverhill;

TL6944], *Red Lion*: Warm and welcoming thatched and beamed pub, tastefully decorated, with good choice of generous reasonably priced good food (starters in dining room only – where it pays to book), some home-made – esp filling steak and kidney pie; helpful service, convenient layout if you don't like steps; children in dining room and conservatory *(Mrs Carol Canter, W T Aird)*

☆ **Thaxted** [Mill End; TL6130], *Star*: Cheerful old beamed pub with wide choice of good food even on Sun, well kept Ind Coope Burton, good service *(Joanne Suter, John Fahy)*

Thaxted [Bullring], *Swan*: Comfortable and friendly four-gabled Tudor pub with views to church and almshouses; good choice of food; bedrooms *(John Fahy)*

☆ **Theydon Bois** [Station Rd (off B172); TQ4599], *Railway Arms*: Small but comfortable refurbished village local nr shopping centre, with prints of old steam engines, well kept Theakstons XB, cheap food from sandwiches up, decent coffee, good friendly service, garden *(Geo Rumsey, George Atkinson)*

Theydon Bois, *Bull*: Friendly, quite interesting, with good beer and bar food – popular half-price days for OAPs *(Joy Heatherley)*

Thornwood Common [TL4705], *Blacksmiths Arms*: Good family pub, with well kept outdoor adventure play area and indoor children's area which can be seen from eating area; wide choice of Allied ales, good value food esp mixed grill £6.95 and old-fashioned puddings *(R C Vincent)*

☆ **nr Waltham Abbey** [very handy for M25 junction 26; A121 towards Waltham Abbey, then follow Epping, Loughton sign from exit roundabout], *Volunteer*: Large open-plan McMullens pub distinguished by Chinese landlady (unless away on Mar/Apr holiday) doing lots of chow mein dishes and big pancake rolls as well as usual things from generous filled rolls up, in massive helpings; attractive conservatory, guest beer, some tables on side terrace, pretty hanging baskets; nice spot by Epping Forest, can get very busy weekends *(J S Frost, Joy Heatherley, Dave Braisted, John and Elspeth Howell, BB)*

Weeley [TM1422], *Black Boy*: Very well run, with good range of well kept beers, friendly service, good food in pleasant dining room *(John McGee)*

West Mersea [TM0514], *Fox*: Well placed pub, an oasis for this area, with well kept Adnams, varied range of good meals cooked by landlady, cheerful landlord; bar billiards in separate room *(Bernard Phillips)*

Wethersfield [High St; TL7131], *Dog*: Fine Georgian building, Adnams, Ridleys and Charles Wells on handpump, good authentic Italian food in two big bars and restaurant, welcoming service *(E J Cutting)*

☆ **White Roding** [TL5613], *Black Horse*: Friendly staff, good interesting home cooking (real custard), well kept Ridleys beers, pleasant pub atmosphere in well kept building (*J Kruger, Mrs M Handley*)

☆ **Wickham Bishops** [TL8412], *Mitre*: Very well kept Adnams Extra and Ridleys IPA and decent food and wine in cosy pub with snug bars and spacious family dining area, friendly service, good fire (*Gwen and Peter Andrews*)

☆ **Wivenhoe** [Black Buoy Hill, off A133; TM0321], *Black Buoy*: Well kept beers inc Adnams in spacious and charming open-plan bar, good food, river views, restaurant (*A Barker, Dr D C Deeing, R J Saunders*)
Wivenhoe, *Rose & Crown*: Friendly quayside pub with good river views, jovial licensee, warm fire (*Les Downes*)
Woodham Ferrers [Main Rd; TQ7999], *Bell*: Much expanded attractive L-shaped beamed lounge/dining area with lots of exposed brickwork, friendly chatty staff, cheap straightforward food, well kept Adnams and Ridleys IPA, good coffee; piped music not too obtrusive, pool, fruit machine; restaurant; nice sheltered garden with well and pond (*George Atkinson, Gwen and Peter Andrews*)
Woodham Mortimer [TL8104], *Hurdlemakers Arms*: Quiet tucked-away local, open fire in simply furnished flagstoned lounge with cushioned settles, low ceiling and timbered walls, well kept Greene King IPA and Abbot, good darts alley in public bar; picnic-table sets well spaced among trees and shrubs outside, barbecues; outdoor children's room with video games (*M J Murphy, BB*); [A414 Danbury—Maldon], *Royal Oak*: New management doing huge helpings of good value food; well kept Adnams, piped music (*Gwen and Peter Andrews*)

☆ **Wormingford** [B1508; TL9331], *Crown*: Reasonably priced food and well kept Greene King ales in pleasant and relaxing old pub, no music, friendly service; good big garden (*Anthony Barker, Gwen and Peter Andrews*)

☆ **Youngs End** [A131 Braintree—Chelmsford, nr Essex Show Ground; TL7319], *Green Dragon*: Friendly modernised 17th-c pub, very well run, with neat attentive staff, lots of small tables, well kept Greene King ales, good house wines, remarkably wide choice of food, often interesting, in generous helpings, attractive and spacious barn restaurant; piped music (*Gwen and Peter Andrews, L V Nutton, B R Shiner, Basil Minson*)

People don't usually tip bar staff (unlike in a really smart hotel). If you want to thank a barman – dealing with a really large party say, or special friendliness – offer him a drink. Common expressions are: 'And what's yours?' or 'And won't you have something for yourself?'.

Gloucestershire

What a mixture of pubs this county has, from unspoilt and relaxed places like the Boat at Ashleworth Quay, the Tunnel House at Coates, the Hobnails at Little Washbourne (great filled rolls) and Boat at Redbrook (up to ten real ales), to sophisticated dining pubs like the Crown at Blockley, the New Inn at Coln St Aldwyns (doing very well indeed at the moment), the Lamb at Great Rissington, and the Kilkeney Inn at Kilkenny (calling itself a brasserie these days). Quite a few pubs manage to combine the two ends of this range, doing good interesting food in civilised surroundings, preserving a great deal of individual character and run by really friendly people. The top examples of these are currently the New Inn at Coln St Aldwyns, the Wild Duck at Ewen and the Fox at Lower Oddington – of these, it's the Fox which we choose as Gloucestershire Dining Pub of the Year (excellent wines here, too). Given the stylish nature of so many pubs here (and indeed the fact that so many can rely on a steady flow of often well heeled visitors to the Cotswolds), it's quite a surprise to find that prices in the area are by no means high. Indeed, drinks prices tend to be rather lower than the national average, particularly in pubs supplied by local small breweries such as Archers, Donnington, Hook Norton and Smiles – all of which have been doing their bit to keep prices here down. And price is by no means related to quality of surroundings here – the lowest beer price we found was at the stylish and comfortable Wyndham Arms at Clearwell. Beer quality is often excellent: more than a dozen pubs here gain our new beer award. Some changes to note here include the new bedrooms at the Bear in Bisley, the new barn extension at the Golden Heart at Brimpsfield, extensions proceeding at the very popular Bakers Arms in Broad Campden, the Brockweir Inn being taken back into the hands of owners who have been away for a couple of years, and new licensees at the Olde Inne at Guiting Power. Interesting new entries include the Farmers Arms at Apperley (brewing its own beers, though mainly a food place), the very welcoming and attractive Catherine Wheel in the lovely village of Bibury, and the Fox at Great Barrington, a simple riverside pub doing very well under new tenants. In the Lucky Dip section at the end of the chapter there are a great many worthwhile pubs: some to mention particularly include the Gardeners Arms at Alderton, several in Chipping Campden, Slug & Lettuce in Cirencester, Highwayman at Elkstone, Glasshouse at Glasshouse, Harvest Home at Greet, Farmers Boy at Longhope (a real comer, this), Egypt Mill at Nailsworth, Royal Oak in Painswick, Snowshill Arms at Snowshill, Crown in Tetbury, Bell in Tewkesbury, Bell at Willersey and Corner Cupboard in Winchcombe.

AMBERLEY SO8401 Map 4

Black Horse ♀

Village signposted off A46 Stroud—Nailsworth; as you pass village name take first very sharp left turn (before Amberley Inn) then bear steeply right – pub on your left

Very popular locally – in fact, a syndicate of locals owns it – this bustling and friendly place has a fine range of well kept real ales on handpump: Archers Best, Fullers London Pride, Furgusons Dartmoor, Hartleys XB, Hook Norton, Moorhouses Pendle Witches Brew, Smiles Exhibition, Tetleys, Timothy Taylors Landlord, and Youngs. There are marvellous views from both the conservatory and dining bar – which has wheelback chairs, green-cushioned window seats, a few prints on the plain cream walls, and a fire in a small stone fireplace; the family bar is no smoking. Bar food includes sandwiches and other straightforward bar meals, as well as Indian baltis, steak, Guinness and mustard pie and chicken piri-piri (£5.95). Teak seats and picnic-table sets on a back terrace (with barbecue) share the same glorious view as the bars, and on the other side of the building, a lawn with pretty flowers and honeysuckle has more picnic-table sets. (*Recommended by Dave Irving, Tom McLean, Roger Huggins, Ewan McCall, Michael Marlow, Tony and Wendy Hobden, Richard and Janice Searle*)

Free house ~ Licensee Patrick O'Flynn ~ Real ale ~ Meals and snacks (till 10.30) ~ Amberley (01453) 872556 ~ Children welcome ~ Open 12-3, 6-11

AMPNEY CRUCIS SP0602 Map 4

Crown of Crucis

A417 E of Cirencester

In summer, it's most pleasant to sit outside at the many tables on the back grass by a stream with ducks and maybe swans, and enjoy the very popular, good value food – best to get there early if you want a seat. As well as lunchtime things like soup (£1.30), sandwiches (from £1.45), ploughman's (£2.95), and a home-made dish of the day (from £3.20), there might be sausages and chips (£3.30), broccoli, almond and cream cheese crêpes (£4.75), salmon fishcakes or steak and kidney pie (£4.95), gammon and egg (£5.10), mixed grill (£6.95), steaks (from £8.95), daily specials such as tasty lamb and aubergine stew, good puddings (£1.80), and children's menu (£2.10); the restaurant is no smoking. The spacious and tastefully modernised bar has a cheery welcoming feel, and some character, and service is efficient and very friendly. Well kept Archers Village, Ruddles County and Theakstons XB on handpump, and elderflower drinks and apple juices. (*Recommended by Peter Pocklington, Mrs S Smith, Gwen and Peter Andrews, Neil and Anita Christopher, Jan and Dave Booth, E A George, The Monday Club, Dave Irving, Roger Huggins, Ewan McCall, Tom McLean, Mrs J Oakes, Dr and Mrs R E S Tanner*)

Free house ~ Licensee R K Mills ~ Real ale ~ Meals and snacks (11.45-2.30, 5.45-10) ~ Restaurant ~ Poulton (01285) 851806 ~ Children welcome; no under 6s in restaurant in evening ~ Open 11-11 ~ Bedrooms: £31B/£48B

APPERLEY SO8628 Map 4

Farmers Arms 🏮

Off B4213, which is off A38 N of Gloucester

Extended but cosy, this friendly beamed pub brews its own good Mayhems Oddas Light and Sundowner Heavy in a thatched brewhouse by the car park (you can usually look round from its upper viewing gallery); it also keeps Boddingtons, their own cider, decent wines and a fair range of malt whiskies. Yet the main draw is the good straightforward food, and though there's plenty of room at the bar it tends to be the comfortable and spacious dining lounge which is the focus of attention. We'd put their fresh fish at the top of the list, fresh daily and including plump scallops (£3.95), cod or haddock (£4.25/£4.95 depending on how hungry you are), plaice (£4.95) and salmon (£6.50), served with real chips. A wide choice of other food includes sandwiches (£1.50), ploughman's (from £3.25), ham and egg (£4.50), lots of vegetarian dishes (£5.25), beef pie (£5.95) and several steaks (from £6.75), with children's dishes (£3.25 inc sundae) and a wide variety of puddings (£2.50). Service is prompt and very friendly even when they're busy; open fires. The neat garden has picnic-table sets by a thatched well, with a Wendy house and play area. (*Recommended by Mrs M Haggie, Dr Vivien Bull,*

Kathryn and Brian Heathcote, John Miles, D Irving, R Huggins, E McCall, T McLean, Derek and Sylvia Stephenson, Mike Pugh)

Own brew ~ Licensees Geoff and Carole Adams ~ Real ale ~ Meals and snacks (12-2, 6.30-10) ~ Restaurant ~ (01452) 780307 ~ Children welcome ~ Occasional live music ~ Open 11-2.30, 6-11

ASHLEWORTH QUAY SO8125 Map 4

Boat

Ashleworth signposted off A417 N of Gloucester; Quay signed from village

Up a secluded lane on the banks of the Severn River sits this friendly and uncomplicated 15th-c cottage. Charles II granted the licence (allowing them to run a ferry across the Severn), and astonishingly it's been run by the same family ever since. This probably accounts for its rather special timeless feel, as the charming landladies really do work hard at preserving its unique character. The front parlour has a great built-in settle by a long scrubbed deal table that faces an old-fashioned open kitchen range with a side bread oven and a couple of elderly fireside chairs; there are rush mats on the scrubbed flagstones, houseplants in the window, fresh garden flowers, and old magazines to read. A back parlour with rugs on its red tiles has plump overstuffed chairs and a sofa, a grandfather clock and dresser, a big dog basket in front of the fire, and shove-ha'penny, dominoes and cards (the front room has darts and a game called Dobbers). A pair of flower-cushioned antique settles face each other in the back room where Arkells BBB and Smiles Best and a summer guest like Crown Buckley Reverend James or Oakhill Yeoman are tapped from the cask, along with a full range of Westons farm ciders. They do lunchtime rolls (£1.20) or ploughman's with home-made chutney (£2.50) during the week, and groups of walkers can book these or afternoon teas. In front, there's a suntrap crazy-paved courtyard, bright with plant tubs in summer, with a couple of picnic-table sets under cocktail parasols; more seats and tables under cover at the sides. The medieval tithe barn nearby is striking. *(Recommended by Dave Irving, Roger Huggins, Tom McLean, Ewan McCall, Derek and Sylvia Stephenson, Ted George, Richard and Janice Searle, Jed and Virginia Brown, P Neate, K Baxter, Leonard Dixon, R H Martyn, Roger Sherman)*

Free house ~ Licensees Irene Jelf and Jacquie Nicholls ~ Real ale ~ Lunchtime snacks ~ Painswick (01452) 700272 ~ Children welcome ~ Open 11-3, 6-11; 11-2.30, 7-11 in winter

AWRE SO7108 Map 4

Red Hart

Village signposted off A48 S of Newnham

Tucked away in a remote Severnside farming village, this red-tiled 16th-c pub is surprisingly tall – with a chimney to match. The L-shaped main part of the bar has a deep glass-covered well, a grand piano, and an upholstered wall settle and wheelback chairs, and the end area has plates on a delft shelf, a gun and a stuffed pheasant over the stone fireplace, big prints on the walls, and a bale of straw swinging from pitched rafters; there's a pleasant mix of locals and visitors. Bar food includes home-made soup (£2), home-made chicken liver pâté (£3.50), ploughman's (£3.75), home-made burger (£4.50), home-baked ham with egg (£4.95), home-made steak and kidney pie (£5.25), chicken curry (£5.75), seafood pancake (£6.25), and 10oz sirloin steak (£8.75). Well kept Bass and Wadworths 6X on handpump, and several malt whiskies; darts, fruit machine and piped music. In front of the building are some picnic-table sets. *(Recommended by Paul Boot, Paul Weedon; more reports please)*

Free house ~ Licensee Patrick Purtill ~ Real ale ~ Meals and snacks (not Sun evenings) ~ Restaurant (not Sun evenings) ~ (01594) 510220 ~ Children in eating area of bar until 9pm ~ Open 11-2.30, 7-11; closed Mon exc bank holidays

BARNSLEY SP0705 Map 4

Village Pub

A433 Cirencester—Burford

After a visit to Rosemary Verey's garden, which is in the village, it's well worth stopping at this friendly and bustling stone pub to enjoy the promptly served, good food. This might include open sandwiches (from £1.75, prawn £2.95), filled baked potatoes (from £2.25), mushroom and hazelnut pâté or vegetable samosas (£2.75), ploughman's (£3.35), nut and lentil cutlet (£4.60), salads (from £4.75), steak and kidney pie (£4.75), chicken cordon bleu or smoked salmon and dill quiche (£5), and daily speicals such as lasagne (£4.60) or seafood risotto. Well kept Flowers IPA and Wadworths 6X on handpump, country wines, and farm cider. The walls of the comfortable low-ceilinged communicating rooms are decorated with gin-traps, scythes and other farm tools, and there are several winter log fires, as well as plush chairs, stools and window settles around the polished tables; cribbage, shove ha'penny and dominoes. The sheltered back courtyard has plenty of tables, and its own outside servery. *(Recommended by Dave Irving, Roger Huggins, Tom McLean, Ewan McCall, Paul McPherson, Maysie Thompson, Roger Byrne, K H Frostick, J Weeks, Brian Whittaker, Alastair Campbell, Carol and Mike Muston, John Knighton, Mrs S Gillotti, George Dundas)*

Free house ~ Licensee Mrs Susan Wardrop ~ Real ale ~ Meals and snacks (not 25 Dec) ~ Restaurant ~ (01285) 740421 ~ Children welcome ~ Open 11-2.30(3 Sat), 6-11; closed 25 Dec ~ Bedrooms: £29B/£44B

BIBURY SP1106 Map 4

Catherine Wheel

Arlington; B4425 NE of Cirencester

Beautifully placed in a famously pretty village, this low-beamed Cotswold stone pub has a promising lobby opening into the main front bar, welcoming, with lots of old-fashioned dark wood furniture, a good log fire, gleaming copper pots and pans around the fireplace, and papers to read beside it – at its best perhaps on a winter weekday evening. On summer weekends when the village swarms with visitors, you may be more comfortable at a table in one of the other two rooms – generally quieter. There's also a good-sized and well kept garden behind with picnic-table sets among fruit trees (and a play area), and some seats out in front. A good choice of substantial straightforward well presented bar food includes sandwiches (£2), filled baked potatoes (from £3.25), ploughman's (£3.50), liver and bacon (£4.50), vegetarian dishes (£5.25), lamb chops or steak and kidney pie (£5.75), and many puddings (£2.50); besides special dishes (£2.50), they'll usually do a small helping of anything else for children, and their Sunday lunch is good. Well kept Courage Best, Tetleys, Whitbreads Best and West Country PA on handpump, and changing guests such as Archers and Bass; soft drinks prices have been very fair here. Helpful and friendly service, shove-ha'penny, cribbage, fruit machine, piped music; dogs welcome if well behaved – maybe even given Bonios. New bedrooms should be ready by the time this edition comes out: we'd expect this to be a nice place to stay. *(Recommended by George Atkinson, M Joyner, Gordon, Neil and Anita Christopher, R Huggins, D Irving, T McLean, E McCall)*

Free house ~ Licensee Carol Parmer ~ Real ale ~ Meals and snacks throughout the day ~ (01285) 740250 ~ Well behaved children welcome ~ Open 11-11; cl evening 25 Dec ~ Bedrooms: (see above) /£45B

BISLEY SO9005 Map 4

Bear

Village signposted off A419 just E of Stroud

New licensees have taken over this elegantly gothic 16th-c inn and have introduced a menu using fresh local produce. Changing daily and all home-made, there might be specials such as cod marinated in olive oil, coriander and lime juice or chicken liver, spinach and bacon salad (£3.95), asparagus, mussels and prawn parcels with garlic and gin (£5.95), and Chinese trout (£6.25); also, filled french sticks (from £1.95; melted cheddar and bacon £2.50, 4oz rump steak £3.50), fried potatoes with garlic and herb butter (£3.25) or bacon and sausage (£3.75), burgers (from £3.50), vegetable pasty filled with fennel, mushrooms and pine kernels in white wine and cream sauce (£4.25), home-made steak and kidney pie (£5.45), and popular home-made puddings; on Mondays they do bubble and squeak with a roast; no chips. The tropical fish tank has gone, as has the piped music and games machine. The meandering L-shaped bar has a long shiny black built-in settle and a smaller but even sturdier oak settle by the front entrance, an enormously wide low stone fireplace (not very high – the ochre ceiling's too low for that), and a lovely atmosphere; a separate stripped-stone area is used for families. Well kept Bass, Flowers Original and Tetleys on handpump; table skittles and dominoes. A small front colonnade supports the upper floor of the pub, and the sheltered little flagstoned courtyard made by this has a traditional bench; as well as the garden, there's quite a collection of stone mounting-blocks and quoits. The steep stone-built village is attractive. *(Recommended by Martyn Kearey, Roger Huggins, Ewan McCall, Tom McLean, Dave Irving, Paul Weedon, Dr Vivien Bull, P Freeman)*

Pubmaster ~ Tenant N S Evans ~ Real ale ~ Meals and snacks (not evenings Sun or Mon) ~ (01452) 770265 ~ Children in own room ~ Open 11-3, 6-11; closed evening 25 Dec ~ Bedrooms: £15/£34

BLEDINGTON SP2422 Map 4

Kings Head ♀ ⇔ ◖
B4450

Attractively set by the village green, this 15th-c inn has a relaxed, cosy, pleasantly up-market atmosphere and extremely popular, often imaginative food. The smart but welcoming main bar is full of ancient beams and other atmospheric furnishings, such as high-backed wooden settles, gateleg or pedestal tables, and a warming log fire in the stone inglenook (which has a big black kettle hanging in it); the lounge looks on to the garden. At lunchtime, bar food might include home-made soup (£1.95), sandwiches (£2.95), spiced sausages with cherry tomatoes, olives and bacon or squid pockets stuffed with lemon, garlic and tomato (£3.25), salad platters (from £3.25), lamb's liver in red wine (£3.95), savoury chicken crêpes or grilled red mullet and avocado salsa (£4.25), a vegetarian dish of the day (£4.50), pasta with smoked salmon and dill (£4.95), minted lamb, aubergine and artichoke fritters (£4.95), home-made steak and mushroom pie (£5.50), local jugged hare (£5.95), pork cooked with sherry, mushrooms and cream (£7.95), baked whole sea bass (£10.95), puddings such as lovely fruit pavlova (£2), and children's dishes (from £1.50); evening dishes are just as interesting, with grills as well. An antique bar counter has well kept Adnams Broadside, Hook Norton, Shepherd Neame Spitfire, Stanway Old Eccentric, Uley Old Spot and Pigs Ear, Wadworths 6X and two monthly changing guest beers on handpump, local ciders in summer, a comprehensive wine list (with eight by the glass), and 30 malt whiskies. They are often very busy, but service is usually prompt, efficient and friendly. Part of the restaurant area is no-smoking; piped music. The public bar has darts, pool, shove-ha'penny, dominoes, fruit machine, trivia, and juke box. The back garden is being redeveloped to include a terrace, water garden, and children's 'bunny' park; Aunt Sally. There are also tables that look over to a little stream with lots of ducks that locals often greet by name. *(Recommended by Mr and Mrs Butler, Stephen Guy, Ted George, Andrew Shore, Neil and Anita Christopher, Graham Reeve, Fred Collier, Gwen and Peter Andrews, Pat and John Millward, John Waller, M A Watts, Maysie Thompson, Basil Minson, Mr and Mrs Gorton, John and Marianne Cooper, Ann and Bob Westerook, W C M Jones, T and D Borneo, E J and M W Corrin, Alan Skull, Mrs B Lawton, Alan and Jane Clarke, Dr and Mrs Peter Simpson, S J Isles, T W Miller-Jenn, Jo Rees, John Bowdler, F Armitage, Jane and Calum Maclean, Dorothee and Dennis Glover, C F Walling, P R Cowan)*

Free house ~ Licensees Michael and Annette Royce ~ Real ale ~ Meals and snacks ~ Restaurant ~ Kingham (01608) 658365 ~ Children in restaurant and garden room extension ~ Open 11-2.30, 6-11; closed 25 Dec ~ Bedrooms: £32B/£55B

BLOCKLEY SP1634 Map 4

Crown ★ 🍴 ♟ 🛏 🍺

High Street

The wide choice of very good food can be enjoyed in three different places in this smartly civilised golden stone Elizabethan inn. They have a back bistro and a hotel-ish restaurant, both specialising in fresh fish – which might include sea bream, mackerel, halibut, herring, sprats, whitebait, whiting, salmon, Dover sole, skate, plaice, monkfish, eel, red and grey mullet, sardines, trout, shark, lobster, moules, swordfish and crab. In the bar there may be soup (£2.50), one-and-half rounds of sandwiches (from £2.50), mushrooms in garlic and herbs or chicken and ham pie (£3.95), delicious Teignmouth oysters, fillets of fresh trout marinated in an orange and Cointreau pickle or fresh sardines (£4.50), good cod in beer and chive batter (£4.95), very good steak and Guinness pie or chicken breast with grilled bacon and cheese (£5.95), moules marinières or poached salmon salad (£5.95), and sirloin steak (£9.95). Well kept Bass, Donnington BB, Fullers London Pride, Hook Norton, Wadworths 6X, and a guest beer on handpump, and a large choice of wines; particularly friendly staff. The bustling bar itself has a slightly more pubby atmosphere, and an antique settle as well as the more recent furnishings. Off this is the snug carpeted lounge with an attractive window seat, Windsor chairs around traditional cast-iron-framed tables, a winter log fire; steps lead up into a little sitting room with easy chairs. This in turn leads through to another spacious dining room. The terraced coachyard is surrounded by beautiful trees and shrubs, and there's a hatch to hand drinks down to people sitting out in front, by the lane. Close to Batsford Park Arboretum. *(Recommended by Dr David Clegg, Andy Petersen, George Atkinson, Andrew and Ruth Triggs, John Waller, Pat and John Millward, D Grzelka, P D and J Bickley, J and S E Garrett, Richard Osborne, Leith Stuart, John and Shirley Dyson, Michael Sullivan, Dorothee and Dennis Glover, Graham and Karen Oddey, Susan and John Douglas, Gwen and Peter Andrews, Mrs J Oakes, Gabrielle and John Clezy, D J Williams, M Joyner)*

Free house ~ Licensees John and Betty Champion ~ Real ale ~ Meals (not in bar on Sat) and snacks ~ Restaurant ~ Blockley (01386) 700245 ~ Well behaved children welcome ~ Open 11-3, 6-11 ~ Bedrooms: £53B/£79B

BRIMPSFIELD SO9312 Map 4

Golden Heart 🍺

Nettleton Bottom; A417 Birdlip—Cirencester, at start of new village bypass

The extension into the adjoining barn has now been completed at this busy country pub, which has added another bar and lots more seating; they also have a marquee which can be set up on the terrace. The main low-ceilinged bar is divided into three cosily distinct areas with a huge stone inglenook fireplace in one, and traditional built-in settles and other old-fashioned furnishings throughout. A comfortable parlour on the right has another decorative fireplace, and leads into a further room opening on to a suntrap gravel terrace, where hens and plump geese wander among rustic cask-supported tables. Bar food includes good sandwiches, vegetarian pancakes (£5.75), fresh lemon sole (£6.25), steak and mushroom pudding (£6.50), salmon with cucumber and dill (£6.95), and venison (£7.50). Well kept Adnams, Bass, Hook Norton, Ruddles Best, and weekly changing guest beers on handpump or tapped from the cask, Scrumpy Jack cider, and several wines by the glass; cribbage and dominoes. Good walks nearby. *(Recommended by Steve Goodchild, D C King, P Neate, Jeff Davies, Martyn Kearey, R M Bloomfield, Dave Irving, Ewan McCall, Roger Huggins, Tom McLean, G W A Pearce, Dr Vivien Bull)*

Free house ~ Licensee Catherine Stevens ~ Real ale ~ Meals and snacks (till 10pm) ~ (01242) 870261 ~ Children welcome ~ Open 12-2.30, 6-11

Please let us know of any pubs where the wine is particularly good.

BROAD CAMPDEN SP1637 Map 4

Bakers Arms ★ £ ▧

Village signposted from B4081 in Chipping Campden

There's a good mix of visitors and locals in this enjoyably bustling pub – and despite the fact that the extension and new lavatories are still on-going, the licensees have worked hard to ensure the atmosphere remains friendly and cosy. There are always at least five real ales on handpump or tapped from the cask and all come from small independent brewers: Donnington, Morlands Old Speckled Hen and Stanway (a tiny brewery in Stanway House, Winchcombe), and changing guests such as Glenny Wychwood Best, Hook Norton, Uley, Wickwar Brand Oak, Woods Wonderful, and lots more, and up to 21 during their beer festivals over the spring and August bank holiday weekends; farm ciders, too. Good, very reasonably priced popular food includes specials such as cheese and ale soup (£1.75), tagliatelle bolognese (£2.95), smoked haddock bake (£3.50), meatloaf and vegetables (£3.95), tasty beef in beer casserole (£4.25), chicken tikka masala (£4.50), and puddings such as apple and blackberry crumble or steamed treacle sponge (£1.50); also, ploughman's (from £1.95), omelettes (from £2.35), macaroni cheese (£2.85), chilli con carne (£3.25), steak and kidney pie (£3.75), and for children or those with smaller appetites there are dishes like cottage pie, pizza or lasagne (from £1.75). The beamed bar has a pleasantly mixed bag of tables and seats around the walls (which are stripped back to bare stone), a log fire under a big black iron canopy at one end with a rocking chair beside it, and another at the other end; the friendly cats may already be occupying the best chairs. The oak bar counter is attractive, and there's a big framed rugwork picture of the pub; darts, cribbage and dominoes. There are white tables under cocktail parasols by flower tubs on a side terrace and in the back garden, some seats under a fairy-lit arbour, and a play area, with Aunt Sally and Tippit. The tranquil village is handy for the Barnfield cider mill. *(Recommended by J and S E Garrett, Ann and Bob Westerook, L Walker, Mrs S Smith, Derek and Sylvia Stephenson, BKA, Roy Smylie, Mrs Pat Crabb, H O Dickinson, Simon and Amanda Southwell, E V Walder, Leith Stuart, Mr and Mrs K H Frostick, Mr and Mrs P B Dowsett, David Heath, Douglas Adam, Basil Minson, Paul Boot, Gwen and Peter Andrews, John and Audrey Davidson, John Bowdler, Rosemary and Brian Wilmot, Mrs K Cattermoul, Dorothy Pilson, Peter and Erica Davis, N W Penney, John and Barbara Gibson, Mrs J Oakes, Jenny and Neil Spink)*

Free house ~ Licensees Carolyn and Tony Perry ~ Real ale ~ Meals and snacks ~ (01386) 840515 ~ Children welcome ~ Folk night 3rd Tues of month ~ Open 11.30-3.30, 5.30-11; 11.30-2.30, 6.30-11 in winter; closed 25 Dec, evening 26 Dec and lunchtime first Sat after spring bank hol, for local 'Scuttledown Wake'

BROCKHAMPTON SP0322 Map 4

Craven Arms ♀

Village signposted off A436 Andoversford—Naunton – look out for inn sign at head of lane in village; can also be reached from A40 Andoversford—Cheltenham via Whittington and Syreford

Originally a 17th-c farmhouse, this picturesque Cotswold inn is in a lovely setting with gorgeous views. Inside, there are low beams, thick roughly coursed stone walls and some tiled flooring, and though much of it has been opened out to give a sizeable (and spotlessly kept) eating area off the smaller bar servery, it's been done well to give a feeling of several communicating rooms; the furniture is mainly pine, with some wall settles, tub chairs and a log fire. Well kept Butcombe Best, Hook Norton Best and Wadworths 6X on handpump. Home-made bar food includes soup (£1.95), giant sausage (£2.50), big ploughman's (£3.50), steak sandwich (£4.95), beef curry (£4.95), home-made steak and kidney pie (£5.75), broccoli and walnut quiche or gammon and egg (£5.95), cold poached salmon (£8.50), char-grilled sirloin steak (£9.95), and good puddings like sherry trifle or sticky toffee pudding; people like the 'real' chips. Darts and shove-ha'penny. There are swings in the sizeable garden. *(Recommended by Dave Irving, Ewan McCall, Roger Huggins, Tom McLean, Mr and Mrs P R Bevins, Mr and Mrs W W Swaitt, John and Joan Wyatt, Derek and Sylvia Stephenson)*

Free house ~ Licensees Dale and Melanie Campbell ~ Real ale ~ Meals and snacks ~ Restaurant ~ (01242) 820410 ~ Children welcome ~ Open 11-3, 6-11

BROCKWEIR SO5401 Map 4

Brockweir

Village signposted just off A466 Chepstow—Monmouth

Mr and Mrs Jones have now come back to run their 17th-c pub – they had leased it out since 1991. They have redecorated throughout and added new carpets and curtains, and re-opened and tidied up the garden, where there are picnic-table sets under umbrellas. The bare-stone-walled and beamed main bar has sturdy settles on quarry tiles in the front part, a winter open fire, and brocaded seats and copper-topped tables in a series of carpeted alcoves at the back, and the bare-floored and traditionally furnished public bar has pool and trivia; piped music. The characterful trailhound is called Monty. Well kept Freeminer Bitter (brewed only 4 miles away) and Hook Norton Best with a changing guest such as Smiles Exhibition on handpump; Bulmers farm cider. Bar food now includes sandwiches (from £1.30), soup (£1.70), ploughman's (£2.80), pork in cider or chicken tikka (£4.50), and puddings such as pecan pie or chocolate fudge cake (£1.60). A covered courtyard at the back opens into a sheltered terrace. As the pub is not too far away from the steep sheep-pastures leading up to Offa's Dyke Path and the Devil's Pulpit, with views over the Wye and Tintern Abbey, it's understandably a popular stop with walkers. Canoeing, horse riding and salmon fishing are available locally. Dogs welcome. *(Recommended by N C Walker, Bob Riley, Andrew and Liz Roberts; more reports please)*

Free house ~ Licensees George and Elizabeth Jones ~ Real ale ~ Meals and snacks ~ (01291) 689548 ~ Children in family room ~ Open 12-2.30(3 Sat), 6-11 ~ Bedrooms: £20/£35

CHEDWORTH SP0511 Map 4

Seven Tuns

Queen Street, Upper Chedworth; village signposted off A429 NE of Cirencester; then take second signposted right turn and bear left towards church

In attractive surroundings, this friendly and pleasantly remote Cotswold pub has two bars with completely different characters. On the right, the smarter but cosily atmospheric lounge has sizeable antique prints, tankards hanging from the beam over the serving bar, comfortable seats, decent tables, a partly boarded ceiling, a good winter log fire in the big stone fireplace, and a relaxed, quiet atmosphere. The basic public bar on the left is more lively, and opens into a games room with darts, pool, fruit machine, video game and trivia; there's also a skittle alley (which can be hired). Generous helpings of freshly-made bar food under the new chef might include soup (£1.50), sandwiches (from £1.50), pâtés such as stilton and herb or liver and brandy (£2.95), basket meals (from £2.40), ploughman's (£3.25), spinach and mushroom lasagne, vegetable tagliatelle or steak in ale pie (£3.85), evening dishes like duck and bacon pie (£7.25) and steaks (from £8.50), and puddings such as jam roly-poly, apple and blackberry pie and profiteroles (from £1.95); good curry night on Fridays (£5.25), other themed evenings throughout the year (such as the August bank holiday Monday pig roast and a live band), roast Sunday lunch (£5), and children's meals. Well kept Courage Best, John Smiths Bitter, Morlands Old Speckled Hen, and a changing guest like Theakstons Best on handpump; mulled wine in winter, kir and sangria in summer; welcoming, hard-working staff. Across the road is a little walled raised terrace with a stream running through it forming a miniature waterfall. There are plenty of tables both here and under cocktail parasols on a side terrace – perfect for relaxing after a walk through the valley. The famous Roman villa is a pleasant walk away. *(Recommended by Tom McLean, Roger Huggins, Ewan McCall, Dave Irving, Gordon, Audrey and Peter Dowsett, D G King, Dorothy Pilson, Dr Vivien Bull, Alastair Campbell, Jo Rees)*

Free house ~ Licensees Barbara and Brian Eacott ~ Real ale ~ Meals and snacks (not winter Mon lunchtime, not 25 Dec) ~ (01285) 720242 ~ Children in eating area of bar until 9pm ~ Open 12-2.30, 6.30-11; 11.30-3, 6.30-11 Sat; closed Mon lunchtime

CHIPPING CAMPDEN SP1539 Map 4

Kings Arms ♀

This civilised little 16th-c hotel overlooking the market square offers a genuinely warm welcome, not just to grown ups, but to children (who are given crayons and colouring books) and to dogs (who are given bowls of water). The comfortably old-fashioned bar has handsomely carved black beams, a fine stone inglenook fireplace (there are log fires throughout winter), maybe fresh flowers, and some big bay window seats. Very popular bar food includes lunchtime sandwiches, soup (£1.75), country pâté (£3.30), pasta provençale (£4.50), generous gammon with pineapple, lamb's kidneys (£5), steak and kidney pie (£6), and hot game pie (£6.75), with puddings (all £2.20) such as sherry trifle or lemon and kiwi flummery; best to get there early. They have a very extensive wine list – almost 100 by the bottle and 10 by the glass. There are seats in the gardens behind, and the hotel is handy for the attractive nearby gardens of Hidcote and Kiftsgate Court. *(Recommended by Malcolm Davies, Leith Stuart, Derek Allpass, Jill White, Gordon Mott, Peter Lloyd, Kathryn and Brian Heathcote, John Bowdler, E G Parish, Prof John and Patricia White, C Turner, H O Dickinson, Andrew and Ruth Triggs, Peter Lloyd, JF, Mr J Brown, R C Smail, Mr and Mrs G J Rice)*

Free house ~ Licensee Stan Earnshaw ~ Meals and snacks (12-3, 6-9.30; all day in summer) ~ Restaurant ~ (01386) 840256 ~ Children welcome ~ Open 11-11 ~ Bedrooms: £30B/£60B

Noel Arms 🛏 ♀

Very well run and rather smart, this bustling inn is said to have been licensed since 1360. The interesting and welcoming bar is decorated with casks hanging from its beams, farm tools, horseshoes and gin traps on the bare stone walls, armour, and old oak settles, attractive old tables, seats and newer settles among the Windsor chairs; there's a winter coal fire, and a conservatory behind. The small lounge areas are comfortable and traditionally furnished with coach horns, lantern lighting, and some stripped stonework, and the reception area has its quota of pikes, halberds, swords, muskets and breastplates. Well kept Bass and Hook Norton on handpump, with guest ales such as Benskins, Brains, Crown Buckley Reverend James, Thwaites Craftsman, and Woods Wonderful, and a good choice of malt whiskies, brandies, and around 150 wines. Generously served, good big helpings of good home-made lunchtime bar food include soup (£1.95), filled french bread (from £3), ploughman's (£3.75), chicken and leek pie (£4.35), soup and sandwich (£4.50), good salads (from £4.15), lamb's liver and bacon (£4.50), vegetables au gratin (£4.75), tandoori chicken or cajun prawns (£4.95), and puddings like steamed sponge pudding (£2.20); friendly service; dominoes, and piped music. There are seats in the old coachyard. *(Recommended by C Turner, John Waller, Col A H N Reade, Andrew and Ruth Triggs)*

Free house ~ Licensee Neil John ~ Real ale ~ Lunchtime meals and snacks ~ Restaurant ~ Evesham (01386) 840317 ~ Children welcome ~ Open 11-3, 6-11; all day Thurs/Fri/Sat ~ Bedrooms: £58B/£78B

CLEARWELL SO5708 Map 4

Wyndham Arms 🛏 ♀

B4231, signposted from A466 S of Monmouth towards Lydney

For over 21 years the friendly licensee has run this neatly kept and civilised country inn, set near the Wye Valley and the Forest of Dean. The smart and comfortable beamed bar has red plush seats and velvet curtains, a collection of flat-irons by the log-effect gas fire in its spacious stone fireplace, and two big unusual patchwork pictures on its bared stone walls; cribbage and dominoes. Well kept Bass and Hook Norton on handpump, lots of malt whiskies, a very good range of generously served wines by the glass or half bottle – and gherkins, onions and olives on the counter. Good, well presented food includes home-made soup (£3), sandwiches (from £3.50; open ones from £4), ploughman's (£4.50), home-made pâtés like cheese and fresh herb or chicken liver (£4.55), sausages and egg or smoked haddock with poached egg (£4.95), a daily pasta dish (£5.95), mixed hors d'oeuvres (£6.25), a vegetarian dish of the day (£6.75), prawn or vegetable curry (£7), deep-fried lemon sole with home-made tartare sauce (£7.50), liver and bacon (£7.75), steaks (from £8.25), and puddings (£2.50); excellent breakfasts. Seats out on the neat patios, and two friendly and characterful flat-coated retrievers – Sam and his son Theo; other dogs welcome. *(Recommended by Martyn Kearey, M Lithgow, Bob Riley, C W Channon, David and Mary Webb, Tom McEwan, Roger Huggins, Dr and Mrs K Hofheinz, Nick Cox, Ron Corbett, Robin and Val Rowland, G W H Kerby, JM, PM, Barry Roe, Wendy Mogose)*

Free house ~ Licensees John and Rosemary Stanford ~ Real ale ~ Meals and snacks ~ Restaurant ~ Dean (01594) 833666 ~ Children welcome ~ Open 11-11; closed 25 Dec ~ Bedrooms: £35B/£60B

COATES SO9600 Map 4

Tunnel House

Tarlton Rd; village signposted off A419 W of Cirencester; in village follow Tarlton signposts, turning right then left; pub up track on right just after railway bridge; OS Sheet 163 map reference 965005

Very relaxed and informal – and often full of students from the Royal Agricultural College in Cirencester – this rather eccentric bow-fronted stone house guards one entrance to the derelict tunnel of the old Thames and Severn Canal – another main entry, the Daneway at Sapperton, is at the other end; both were built for the 'leggers' who worked the barges through the tunnels. When there's enough water, they organise boat trips into the tunnel. The pub has a happy mix of furnishings such as easy chairs, a sofa, massive rustic benches and seats built into the sunny windows, and little spindleback seats; there are lots of enamel advertising signs, stuffed otters and weasels, race tickets and air travel labels, dried flowers hanging from the beams, and some friendly dogs and cats; several open fires. Bar food includes bacon or sausage butties, burgers, lasagne (£3.75), ploughman's with home cooked ham (£3.80) and chilli (£4); barbecues on summer Sundays. Well kept Archers Best, Smiles, Theakstons Best and Wadworths 6X on handpump; darts, shove ha'penny, pinball, dominoes, cribbage, fruit machine and huge, often noisy, juke box. They have camping facilities. *(Recommended by P and M Rudlin, Ewan McCall, Tom McLean, Roger Huggins, Dave Irving, Pat and John Millward, Mike Davies, Peter and Janet Race, John Bowdler, Alastair Campbell)*

Free house ~ Licensee Chris Kite ~ Real ale ~ Meals and snacks (till 10) ~ (01285) 770 280 ~ Children welcome ~ Open 11-3, 6(7 winter)-11; 11-11 Sat

COLD ASTON SP1219 Map 4

Plough

Village signposted from A436 and A429 SW of Stow-on-the-Wold; beware that on some maps the village is called Aston Blank, and the A436 called the B4068

'A gem of a pub' is how some readers describe this marvellously unspoilt and tiny 17th-c pub. Standing timbers divide the bar into snug little areas, one of which has a built-in white-painted traditional settle facing the stone fireplace. There's an old photograph of the pub on the mantelpiece, low black beams, simple old-fashioned seats on the flagstone and lime-ash floor, and a happy mix of customers. Warmly friendly staff serve big helpings of good bar food, including home-baked filled rolls (from £2.25), ploughman's, nicely filled baked potatoes (from £3.50), vegetarian meals like delicious cauliflower cheese (from £3.50), home-made pies or chilli (£4.95), and popular puddings. Well kept Theakstons

Best and XB and a guest beer on handpump, and mulled wine in winter; darts, cribbage, dominoes, shove-ha'penny, quoits and piped easy-listening music. The small side terraces have picnic-table sets under parasols, and there may be Morris dancers out here in summer. *(Recommended by Dave Irving, Ewan McCall, Roger Huggins, Tom McLean, Tim Brierly, Gordon, John and Joan Wyatt, Neil and Anita Christopher, George Atkinson, Dorothy Pilson, Wayne Brindle, Julian and Sarah Stanton)*

Free house ~ Licensee J A King ~ Real ale ~ Meals and snacks (12-1.45, 7-9; till 1.30 Sun) ~ Cotswold (01451) 821459 ~ Children in tiny dining room ~ Open 11-2.30, 6.30-11

COLN ST ALDWYNS SP1405 Map 4

New Inn ⍟ 🛏 ♀

On good back road between Bibury and Fairford

Prettily placed and quietly civilised, this popular country inn has a genuinely old-fashioned atmosphere and, readers tell us, particularly good, imaginative food from a reassuringly short menu. Changing regularly, dishes might include soup (£2.50), doorstep sandwiches (£2.95), pheasant and lentil terrine with a blueberry dressing (£3.50), tortellini of spinach and ricotta with a mushroom cream sauce (£3.75), ploughman's (£4.50), provençale vegetables with pasta bows baked under a herb cheese crust (£4.90), steak and kidney in stout pie or braised oxtail with roasted shallots and red cabbage (£5.25), breaded collops of salmon with lemon and tartar sauce (£5.75), 6oz rump steak with an onion confit (£6), and puddings like honey and walnut cheesecake with a mango coulis or baked banana sponge with a caramel sauce (from £3); carefully prepared vegetables £1.50 extra; children's meals. The two main rooms are most attractively furnished and decorated, and divided by a central log fire in a neat stone fireplace with wooden mantelbeam and willow-pattern plates on the chimney breast; also, oriental rugs on the red tiles, low beams, some stripped stonework around the bar servery and hops above it, and a mix of seating from library chairs to stripped pews. Down a slight slope, a further room has a log fire in an old kitchen range at one end, and a stuffed buzzard on the wall. Well kept Hook Norton, John Smiths and Wadworths 6X as well as guest beers on handpump, half-a-dozen good wines by the glass, and several malt whiskies; very good, friendly service. Cribbage, dominoes, cards, chess and draughts. Lots of seats under umbrellas in the split-level terraced garden; popular sunny weekend barbecues. The peaceful Cotswold village is pretty, and this is good walking country. *(Recommended by Tom McLean, Dave Irving, Ewan McCall, Roger Huggins, Gordon, J and S Askin, Ivor Hockman, Joan Olivier, S J Pearson, George and Heather Tucker, Dr John Evans, Claire and Michael Willoughby, D M St G Saunders, Pat and John Millward, Paul Harrison, Paul McPherson)*

Free house ~ Licensee Brian Evans ~ Real ale ~ Meals and snacks ~ Restaurant ~ (01285) 750651 ~ Children in eating area only ~ Open 11-2.30, 5.30-11; 11-11 summer Sats ~ Bedrooms: £45B/£60B

EBRINGTON SP1840 Map 4

Ebrington Arms

Signposted from B4035 E of Chipping Campden; and from A429 N of Moreton-in-Marsh

Since 1764, this unpretentious local has been an ale house and there are some fine old low beams, stone walls, flagstoned floors and inglenook fireplaces – the one in the dining room still has the original iron work. The little bar has sturdy traditional furnishings – including seats built into the airy bow window, and a slightly raised woodfloored area. A lower room, also beamed and flagstoned, has stripped country-kitchen furnishings. Decent, simple bar food, generously served, might include sandwiches (£1.95, sirloin steak baguette £4.25), egg and chips (£2.25), ploughman's, ratatouille (£3.75), omelettes (from £3.55), lasagne (£3.95), cottage pie, fresh cod, gammon and eggs and pies such as chicken, ham and tarragon or a good steak and kidney pie (£5.95) and steaks (from £8.50); tasty breakfasts; good service. Allow yourself plenty of time to read the menu –

it's often chalked up on the beams and stretches on for what seems like miles. Mr Richards has a pottery in the courtyard where he hand throws and fires the crockery used in the restaurant. Well kept Donnington SBA, Hook Norton Best and regular guest beers on handpump, and Bulmer's farm cider; absolutely no piped music or games machines – just an old-fashioned harmonium. There are plenty of trophies around won by the enthusiastic dominoes team, and you can also play cribbage and darts. An arched stone wall shelters a terrace with picnic-table sets under cocktail parasols. No dogs at least at mealtimes, when even the licensees' friendly Welsh springer is kept out. Handy for Hidcote and Kiftsgate. One or two readers have suggested that more attention might be paid to the housekeeping. *(Recommended by Graham Reeve, P D and J Bickley, D A Edwards, Richard Osborne, David and Helen Wilkins, Leith Stuart, Pam Adsley, E V Walder, M A and C R Starling, M L Clarke, Andy and Ali Sweetman, Gwen and Peter Andrews, H O Dickinson, Mrs J Oakes, Jason Caulkin, R D Greaves)*

Free house ~ Licensees Gareth Richards and Andrew Geddes ~ Real ale ~ Meals and snacks (not Sun evening) ~ Paxford (0138 678) 223 ~ Children in dining room ~ Open 11-2.30, 6-11; closed 25 Dec ~ Bedrooms: /£35B

EWEN SU0097 Map 4

Wild Duck ★ 🍴 🍷 🍺

Village signposted from A429 S of Cirencester

Readers are very fond of this lovely 16th-c inn – and we feel it has earned a star this year. It has a particularly warm and cosy atmosphere, consistently friendly service, and a wide range of very popular food. The high-beamed main bar has an nice mix of comfortable armchairs and other seats, candles on the tables, a fine longcase clock, a talking grey parrot in a cage near the bar, paintings on the coral walls, crimson drapes, magazines to read, and an open winter fire, and another bar has a handsome Elizabethan fireplace and antique furnishings and looks over the garden. The menu is extensive and imaginative and usually includes around 16 fish dishes like john dory (£7.50), tuna loin or red snapper (£7.95), red bream (£8.95), and sea bass (£12.95), as well as soup (£2.50), delicious deep-fried brie with redcurrant sauce, ploughman's (£3.95), enjoyable Japanese prawns with mint dip (£4.50), red bean, cashew and beanshoot salad (£4.95), smoked salmon filled with prawns in a curry mayonnaise (£5.50), steaks (from £5.95), mushrooms stroganoff (£6.50), fried loin of pork with a Dijon mustard sauce (£8.25), rack of lamb with mustard and herb crust (£9.50), half a Thai-style chicken on a sizzle platter (£9.95), and specials such as sizzling garlic sardines (£4.95), dressed crab salad (£5.95) or beef Wellington (£9.95). A good range of beers too, with Fullers London Pride, McEwans, Theakstons XB and Old Peculier, Wadworths 6X, Youngs Special, and Duckpond, a beer brewed for them by Archers, and good wines; shove-ha'penny, gentle piped music. There are teak tables and chairs in the sheltered and well kept garden. On the edge of an attractive village, the pub is handy for Cirencester. *(Recommended by Dave Irving, Roger Huggins, Tom McLean, Ewan McCall, Susan and John Douglas, A C W Boyle, D G King, Dr and Mrs James Stewart, Jan and Dave Booth, Pat and John Millward, F J Robinson, P Neate, Dave Braisted, W C M Jones, John Oddey, John and Pat Smyth, Neil and Anita Christopher, John, Janet and Dominic Naylor)*

Free house ~ Licensees Brian and Tina Mussell ~ Real ale ~ Meals and snacks (till 10pm) ~ Restaurant ~ Kemble (01285) 770310 ~ Children welcome ~ Open 11-11 ~ Bedrooms: £48B/£65B

FORD SP0829 Map 4

Plough

B4077

The old 'Step in and quaff my nut-brown ale' sign outside this unchanging pretty stone pub has been cleaned up this year. The beamed and stripped-stone bar has old settles and benches around the big tables on its uneven flagstones, oak tables in a snug alcove, racing prints and photos on the walls (the gallops for local stables are opposite), log fires, and a warmly welcoming atmosphere; darts, dominoes, cribbage, shove-ha'penny and several board games. Bar food includes good sandwiches, home-made pâtés (£3.45), garlic mushrooms (£3.75), ham and egg (£5.45), trucker's breakfast (£5.50), local trout (£5.75), game casserole, knuckle of lamb or steak and kidney pie (£6.50), and home-made puddings (£2.35); good big helpings. Traditional asparagus feasts are held every April-June, when the first asparagus spears to be sold at auction in the Vale of Evesham usually end up here. Well kept Donnington BB and SBA served on handpump by obliging staff; also freshly squeezed orange juice, and a range of wines and champagnes. There are benches in front, with rustic tables and chairs on grass by white lilacs and fairy lights. Dogs are welcome. It used to be the local court house, and what's now the cellar was the gaol. Look out for the llama farm between here and Kineton. *(Recommended by Gwen and Peter Andrews, Roger Byrne, Lawrence Pearse, Dave Irving, Roger Huggins, T McLean, Ewan McCall, John and Shirley Dyson, E V Walder, Andy and Jill Kassube, Gordon, Kathryn and Brian Heathcote, Roger Taylor, David Crane, Jed and Virginia Brown, Roger Taylor)*

Donnington ~ Tenant Andrew Porter ~ Real ale ~ Meals and snacks (till 10pm at weekends; not winter Sun evenings) ~ (01386) 584215 ~ Children welcome ~ Jazz 2nd Tues in month ~ Open 11-11 ~ Bedrooms: £25/£35

GREAT BARRINGTON SP2013 Map 4

Fox

Village signposted from A40 Burford—Northleach; pub between Little and Great Barrington

Doing very well under its friendly new young licensees, this simple Cotswold inn is attractively set by the River Windrush where they have private fishing, summer barbecues, and seats (with more seats near the landscaped pond in the orchard). The low-ceilinged little bar has stripped-stone walls, two roaring log fires, rustic wooden chairs, tables and window seats, and well kept Donnington BB and SBA on handpump, and Addlestones cider; sensibly placed darts, pool, shove-ha'penny, dominoes, cribbage, fruit machine, video game, trivia and piped music. The pub dog is called Bruiser (though he's only little). Bar food includes pâté (£2.95), beef in ale pie or home-made lasagne (£5.50), very good steaks supplied by the landlord's father, and giant breakfasts; they have a senior citizens' special lunch on Mondays. There's a skittles alley out beyond the sheltered yard. *(Recommended by Gordon, Martin and Karen Wake, David Holloway, Bronwen and Steve Wrigley, Chris and Annie Clipson, Peter and Audrey Dowsett)*

Donnington ~ Tenants Paul and Kate Porter ~ Real ale ~ Meals and snacks ~ (01451) 844385 ~ Children welcome ~ Open 11-11; closed evening 25 Dec ~ Bedrooms: £20/£35

GREAT RISSINGTON SP1917 Map 4

Lamb ♀ 🛏

This is a nice, civilised place to stay for a few days – and one of the chintzy bedrooms in the warren of small stairs and doors has a four-poster carved by the landlord; there's an indoor swimming pool. The cosy two-room bar has a good pubby atmosphere, wheelback and tub chairs with cushioned seats grouped around polished tables on the light brown carpet, a nook under the stairs with a settle and table, and a log-effect gas fire in the stone fireplace. On the walls are photographs of the guide dogs the staff and customers have raised money to buy (over 20), as well as a history of the village, plates, pictures, and an interesting collection of old cigarette and tobacco tins. Bar food includes sandwiches (they tell us they do them, but readers have found differently sometimes), home-made soup (£2.75), mushrooms stuffed with stilton or deep-fried brie with redcurrant jelly (£3.95), vegetables en croute (£6.95), local trout with apricot and almond stuffing (£8.75), Scotch sirloin steak with tomato and herb sauce (£9.50), half a roast duckling with orange sauce (£10.95), daily specials like tuna and anchovy pâté (£3.25), home-made sausages with onion sauce (£4.25), and lasagne (£4.95), and home-made puddings (£2.25); the restaurant is no smoking. Well kept Hook Norton, Morlands Old Speckled Hen, and John Smiths on handpump; a decent wine list (with highly praised and well-served wines by the glass), country wines, and farm cider. You can sit out in the sheltered hillside garden, or really take advantage of the scenery and walk, via gravel pits now used as a habitat for water birds, to Bourton on the Water. *(Recommended by P D and J Bickley, D Walker, Marjorie and David Lamb, D A Edwards, Dr C B Cohen, T and D Archer, Peter and Janet Race, Neil and Anita Christopher, Peter and Rosemary Ellis, Leith Stuart, John and Annette Derbyshire, C F Walling, Barry and Anne)*

Free house ~ Licensees Richard and Kate Cleverly ~ Real ale ~ Meals and snacks (till 1.45 lunchtime) ~ Restaurant ~ (01451) 820388 ~ Well behaved children welcome ~ Open 11.30-2.30, 6.30-11; closed 25/26 Dec ~ Bedrooms: £32B/£48B

GRETTON SP0131 Map 4
Royal Oak

Village signposted off what is now officially B4077 (still often mapped and even signed as A438), E of Tewkesbury; keep on through village

In summer, the garden here is very popular, with picnic-table sets on the flower-filled terrace and under a giant pear tree, a neatly kept big lawn running down past a small hen-run to a play area (with an old tractor and see-saw), and even a bookable tennis court. There's a very friendly atmosphere in the series of bare-boarded or flagstoned rooms – the pub was once a pair of old stone-built cottages – all softly lit (including candles in bottles on the mix of stripped oak and pine tables), and with dark ochre walls, beams (some hung with tankards, hop bines and chamber-pots), old prints, and a medley of pews and various chairs. The no-smoking dining conservatory has stripped country furnishings, and a broad view over farmland to Alderton and Dumbleton Hills. Well kept John Smiths, Marstons Pedigree, Morlands Old Speckled Hen, Ruddles County and Wadworths 6X on handpump, around 70 whiskies, and decent wines. Bar food includes a good few starters and main courses like mackerel with yoghurt and french mustard sauce (£4.95) and Normandy chicken (£5.95); darts, shove-ha'penny, fruit machine, and piped music. At weekends, bank holidays and two weeks in summer, the Great Western Steam Railway that runs from Toddington to Winchcombe station stops at the bottom of the garden here. *(Recommended by Derek and Sylvia Stephenson, Roger Huggins, Tom McLean, Dawn and Phil Garside, Dr Vivien Bull; more reports please)*

Free house ~ Licensees Bob and Kathy Willison ~ Real ale ~ Meals and snacks ~ Restaurant ~ Cheltenham (01242) 602477 ~ Well behaved children may be allowed ~ Folk/blues Weds evening ~ Open 11-2.30(3 Sat), 6-11; closed 25/26 Dec

GUITING POWER SP0924 Map 4
Olde Inne

Village signposted off B4068 SW of Stow-on-the-Wold (still called A436 on many maps)

New licensees had just taken over this snug old cottage as we went to press. They were planning to refurbish and redecorate, without too much change, and to introduce gourmet nights throughout the winter (they had recently held an Indonesian/Burmese/Thai/Vietnamese fortnight). The welcoming beamed and gently lit bar has a winter log fire in an unusual pillar-supported fireplace, attractive built-in wall and window seats (including one, near the serving counter, that's the height of the bar stools), and small brocaded armchairs. The public bar is similarly furnished but also has flagstones and stripped masonry, as well as sensibly placed darts. Bar food includes home-made soup (£2.25), chilli con carne (£4.75), steak and kidney pie (£4.95), ham and chips (£5.50), spicy eastern lamb (£7.25), rump steak (£7.95), daily specials, puddings like apple and walnut crumble or banoffi pie, and children's menu (£2.50). Well kept Hook Norton and Theakstons Best and guests like Bass, Exmoor Gold and Marstons Pedigree on handpump, and several malt whiskies. From the pleasant garden behind are views towards the peaceful sloping fields. *(Recommended by A Y Drummond, John and Shirley Dyson, Gordon, Andy and Jill Kassube, George Atkinson, Dr Vivien Bull, Mr and Mrs P B Dowsett; more reports on the new regime, please)*

Free house ~ Licensees Bill and Julia Tu ~ Real ale ~ Meals and snacks (not 25 Dec) ~ Restaurant ~ (01451) 850392 ~ Children in eating area of bar and in restaurant ~ Open 11.30-3, 5.30-11; 11.30-2.30, 6-11 in winter

HYDE SO8801 Map 4

Ragged Cot ♀ 🍺

Burnt Ash; Hyde signposted with Minchinhampton from A419 E of Stroud; or (better road) follow Minchinhampton, Aston Down signposted from A419 at Aston Down airfield; OS Sheet 162 map reference 886012

In the heart of the Cotswolds, this attractive cottage with its stone-slab roof is always friendly and chatty. The relaxed and rambling bar has lots of stripped stone and black beams, as well as a traditional dark wood wall settle by the end fire, cushioned wheelback chairs and bar stools, and cushioned window seats; off to the right is a no-smoking restaurant area. A good choice of popular home-made bar food includes onion soup (£1.50), pizzas or cauliflower cheese (£3.25), pâté (£3.50), omelettes (from £3.25), several vegetarian meals (£4.50), fresh fish (from £4.50), steak and kidney pie or salads (£4.95), gammon (£5.95) and steaks (from £8.95). Well kept Marstons Pedigree, Theakstons Best, Uley Old Spot, Wadworths 6X and Youngs Special on handpump, and several malt whiskies and wines; good service; darts, cribbage, and fruit machine. There are picnic-table sets in the garden, and bedrooms in an adjacent converted barn. The pub is nicely set beside a row of chestnut trees, and the garden has an interesting pavilion (now used as a conference or function room). *(Recommended by Dave Irving, Roger Huggins, Tom McLean, Ewan McCall, John and Shirley Dyson, R C Watkins, John and Joan Wyatt)*

Free house ~ Licensees Mr and Mrs M Case ~ Real ale ~ Meals and snacks ~ Restaurant (closed Sun evening) ~ (01453) 884643 ~ Children in eating area of bar and in restaurant ~ Open 11-2.30, 6-11 ~ Bedrooms: £35B/£50B

KILKENNY SP0018 Map 4

Kilkeney Inn 🍴 ♀

A436 nr Cheltenham – OS Sheet 163 map reference 007187; if this hamlet is not shown on your map look for Dowdeswell

This is almost more of a smart restaurant now – and even calls itself a brasserie – and not surprisingly, most of the readers' comments are to do with the food. To be sure of a table it's best to book in the evenings, especially at weekends and in the winter when they run mid-week special events. Changing every two months, the menu includes lunchtime things like sandwiches (from £2.50), ploughman's (from £3.25), salads (from £6.45) and tandoori chicken (£4.50), as well as all-day dishes such as soup (£2.10), home-cured gravadlax (£3.50), diced steak and kidney in red wine sauce with puff pastry top (£5.95), mixed vegetable and pine-nut hotpot or lamb and vegetable casserole (£6.25), pork, apple and smoked bacon roulade with apricot brandy sauce (£8.10), provençale-style fish and seafood bake (£8.45), steaks (from £10.25), and puddings like raspberry romanoff shortcake, toffee pudding with caramel sauce or orange and Cointreau mousse (£2.50); efficient service. Quite widely extended and modernised in recent years, the airily spacious, bright and open bar has neatly alternated stripped Cotswold stone and white plasterwork, gleaming dark wheelback chairs around the tables and an open fire. Up at the other end of the same long bar is more of a drinking area, with well kept John Smiths, Ruddles Best, and Wadworths 6X on handpump, an excellent range of decent wines and lots of malt whiskies. At the back, it opens into a comfortable dining conservatory. Attractive Cotswold views, good parking. *(Recommended by Wyn Churchill, R M Bloomfield, Neil and Anita Christopher, Mrs K E Neville-Rolfe, Andy Petersen, Philip Brown, Mrs Jackson, Frank W*

Gadbois, Don Kellaway, Angie Coles, Paul Boot, Victoria Logue, Jo Rees, Viv Middlebrook, Lt Col E H F Sawbridge, S V Bishop, TOH, Mr and Mrs J Brown, Martin G Richards)

Free house ~ Licensees John and Judy Fennell ~ Real ale ~ Meals and lunchtime snacks ~ (01242) 820341 ~ Well behaved children in eating areas ~ Open 11.30-2.30, 6.30-11; closed 25/26 Dec, and Sun evenings Jan-March

KINGSCOTE ST8196 Map 4

Hunters Hall ★ ♀

A4135 Dursley—Tetbury

There's plenty of atmosphere in this civilised, creeper-covered old inn – which has held a licence for 500 years. The connecting rooms have fine high Tudor beams, a lovely old box settle, sofas and miscellany of easy chairs by the stone walls and velvet curtains, and sturdy settles and oak tables on the flagstones in the lower-ceilinged public bar. Decent bar food, generally served from a buffet in an airy end room, includes sandwiches (not Sunday lunchtime), soup (£2.20), chicken and pork liver pâté (£2.95), vegetable and cream cheese pancake (£4.95), home-made steak and kidney pie (small £4.95, large £5.45), sweet and sour pork or lamb and red wine casserole (£5.45), trout with almonds (£6.25), peppered rump steak (£8.65), home-made puddings (£2.30), and children's menu (£1.85); there's more space to eat in the no-smoking Gallery upstairs. Well kept Bass, Hook Norton, Uley Old Spot, and Wadworths 6X on handpump, around ten wines by the glass, several malt whiskies and elderberry punch in winter. A back room – relatively untouched – is popular with local lads playing pool; darts and juke box. The garden is very much geared towards families, with the highpoint a fortress of thatched whisky-kegs linked by timber catwalks; also a climber and some swings. *(Recommended by Brad and Joni Nelson, MM, Nick and Meriel Cox, Dave and Jules Tuckett, MS, Margaret Dyke, Paul McPherson, Peter Neate, Nick Cox, Mrs M Hurst, Dave Irving, Roger Huggins, Tom McLean, Ewan McCall, Alastair Campbell, Carol and Mike Muston, Leonard Dixon, Richard Carpenter, Paul Weedon)*

Free house ~ Licensee David Barnett-Roberts ~ Real ale ~ Meals and snacks (no sandwiches Sun) ~ Restaurant ~ (01453) 860393 ~ Children welcome ~ Open 11-3.30, 6-11 ~ Bedrooms: £41B/£54B

nr LECHLADE SU2199 Map 4

Trout

St John's Bridge; 1 mile E of Lechlade on A417

On a sunny day after a walk along the Thames Footpath, the big garden – with plenty of space to sit either under the old walnut tree or by the side of the river – really comes into its own; boules and Aunt Sally, a summer bar and marquee for families, and fine views over the meadows. Inside this ancient place (first an inn in 1472), the atmospheric low beamed partly-panelled main bar is decorated with various stuffed trout and pike, and a flagstoned part by the serving counter has Courage Best, John Smiths Yorkshire, and Wadworths 6X on handpump; obliging service. Opening off here is a snug area, once the ground-floor cellar, with wooden tables and settles, and fishing prints on the walls. A third bar leads to the garden. Popular bar food includes home-made soup (£2.95), home-made chicken liver pâté (£4.30), ploughman's (from £4.30), locally made sausages (£5.30), macaroni cheese (£5.50), bean curry (£5.95), pizzas (from £6.20), gammon steak (£6.35), salads or seafood crumble (£6.50), rump steak (£9.95), and home-made puddings and daily specials; there may be queues; part of the restaurant is no smoking. Darts, shove-ha'penny, and video game; the amiable pointer is called Blucher. On the second weekend in June they hold a steam engine and tractor meet, on the last weekend in June there is a musical event, and there's a big party on bonfire night. *(Recommended by Peter and Audrey Dowsett, Sue Cubitt, Gwen and Peter Andrews, Jenny and Brian Seller, Mrs C Archer)*

Courage ~ Lease: Bob and Penny Warren ~ Real ale ~ Meals and snacks (until 10pm) ~ Restaurant ~ Faringdon (01367) 252313 ~ Children in eating area of bar ~ Trad jazz Tues evenings, modern jazz Sun evenings ~ Open 10-3, 6-11; all day summer Sats

LITTLE WASHBOURNE SO9933 Map 4

Hobnails

B4077 (though often mapped still as the A438) Tewkesbury—Stow-on-the-Wold; 7½ miles E of M5 junction 9

You can be sure of a cheerful welcome from the friendly licensees here (it's been run by the same family for 250 years now) – even when the pub is busy. The snug and welcoming little front bar has old wall benches by a couple of tables on its quarry-tiled floor, low sway-backed beams hung with pewter tankards, and lots of old prints and horsebrasses, and there's a more modern, carpeted back bar with comfortable button-back leatherette banquettes; open fire. The speciality here is the enormous choice of large and generously filled baps, ranging from egg and mushroom (£2.25), through cider cake and cheese (£2.40), liver and onions (£3.15) and chicken and mushroom in creamy sauce (£4.90), to steak with egg and mushrooms (£6.25). Also, a choice of soups (£2.10), macaroni cheese (£4.80), vegetarian dishes like filo pastry parcels with leeks and stilton cheese or lentil curry (all £5), lasagne (£5.30), curries (£5.55), lamb casserole (£5.65), and a wide range of big home-made puddings such as treacle and lemon tart, tyrolean chocolate gateau or french fruit flan (£2.60); half the restaurant is no smoking. Well kept Boddingtons, Flowers Original, Wadworths 6X, and Whitbreads West Country PA on handpump; darts, shove-ha'penny, fruit machine, piped music. A separate skittle alley (with tables) is for hire Monday to Friday evenings. Between the two buildings, and beside a small lawn and flowerbed, there's a terrace with tables, and children's playground. *(Recommended by R J Herd, David Cooke, Neil and Anita Christopher, Derek and Sylvia Stephenson, Graham and Belinda Staplehurst, J D Maplethorpe, David Heath)*

Whitbreads ~ Lease: Stephen Farbrother ~ Real ale ~ Meals and snacks (till 10pm; not 25/26 Dec) ~ Restaurant ~ Alderton (01242) 620237 ~ Children in skittle alley/family room and restaurant ~ Open 11-2.30, 6-11

LOWER ODDINGTON SP2325 Map 4

Fox 🍴 ♟

Nr Stow-on-the-Wold

Gloucestershire Dining Pub of the Year

This carefully restored, rather elegant place is doing very well at the moment – and readers have particularly commented on the relaxed, country house atmosphere, warmly friendly service, imaginative food – and, of course, the exceptionally good choice of wines – the owners are in partnership with a very hightly regarded wine guru as shippers. The carefully restored, simply and spotlessly furnished rooms have fresh flowers, flagstones and an open fire, a lovely dining room, and very nice customers; piped classical music. From a changing menu, the popular food might include brie and broccoli soup (£2.25), french bread sandwiches (from £2.25), chicken liver pâté (£2.95), mushrooms in stilton sauce with puff pastry (£3.50), spinach and ricotta cheese cannelloni (£4.95), moussaka (£5.50), steak, kidney and mushroom pie (£6.50), guinea fowl in a green peppercorn sauce (£6.95), fillet of salmon in filo pastry with fresh herb sauce (£7.50), rack of Cotswold lamb with onion sauce (£7.95), sirloin steak (from £8.25), and puddings like chocolate terrine with white chocolate sauce, lemon crunch or rhubarb fool (£2.25); roast Sunday lunch (£7.95). Well kept Hook Norton Best, Marstons Pedigree and a guest such as Adnams, Boddingtons or Timothy Taylors Landlord on handpump, several malt whiskies, sloe gin, elderflower pressé, fresh orange juice, Pimms in a jug, and so forth. *(Recommended by Graham Reeve, Gordon, Stephen Guy, Paul Boot, E J and M W Corrin, Pat and John Millward, Mr and Mrs Michael Heald, Anna and Bob Westbrook)*

Free house ~ Licensees Nick and Vicky Elliot ~ Real ale ~ Meals and snacks (till

10pm; not 25 Dec) ~ (01451) 870888 ~ Children in eating area of bar ~ Open 12-2.30, 6.30-11; closed evening 25 Dec

NAILSWORTH ST8699 Map 4

Weighbridge ♀

B4014 towards Tetbury

What readers like about this bustling stone pub is the unchanging relaxed and friendly atmosphere. The three little nicely old-fashioned rooms all have antique settles and country chairs, some have stripped-stone walls and window seats and one even has a bell to ring for prompt service. The one on the left has its black beam-and-plank ceiling thickly festooned with black ironware – sheepshears, gin traps, lamps, cauldrons and bellows – while up some steps a raftered loft has candles in bottles on an engaging mix of rustic tables, as well as unexpected decorations such as a wooden butcher's block. Good bar food includes filled rolls (from £1.40), ploughman's (from £2.80), shepherd's pie (£3.60), meaty or vegetarian lasagne (£3.95), a very popular two-in-one pie with cauliflower cheese in one half and steak and mushroom in the other (small £4.30, big £5.40), and puddings like treacle tart or banoffi pie (from £1.80). Well kept Marstons Pedigree, John Smiths, Ushers Best and Wadworths 6X on handpump, and 18 wines by the glass (or bottle). Behind is a sheltered garden with swings and picnic-table sets under cocktail parasols. *(Recommended by Neil and Anita Christopher, Mrs M C Barrett, Dave Irving, Roger Huggins, Tom McLean, Ewan McCall, Richard and Janice Searle, Paul Weedon)*

Free house ~ Licensee Janina Kulesza ~ Real ale ~ Meals and snacks ~ (01453) 832520 ~ Children in two rooms away from bar ~ Open 11-2.30, 7(6.30 Sat)-11; closed 25 Dec

NAUNTON SP1123 Map 4

Black Horse 🛏 ♀

Village signposted from B4068 (shown as A436 on older maps) W of Stow-on-the-Wold

Very popular locally, this busy village inn has a comfortable bar with simple country-kitchen chairs, built-in oak pews, and polished elm cast-iron-framed tables, black beams and stripped stonework, and a big woodburning stove. Good food includes home-made soup (£2), lunchtime ploughman's (from £3), chicken liver pâté (£3.50), ham and egg (£5), salads (from £5), salmon and broccoli fishcake (£6), steaks (from £9), daily specials like ham and mushroom tagliatelle (£4), lamb and apricot curry (£5) or pork chop valentine (£7), and puddings like apple crumble flan or treacle sponge (£2); last orders for lunch at 1.30 prompt, and service can be slow. Well kept Donnington BB and SBA on handpump, a choice of wines by the glass and malt whiskies; sensibly placed darts. Some tables outside. No children. *(Recommended by John and Marianne Cooper, D A Edwards, Alex and Beryl Williams, Andy and Jill Kassube, Andrew and Catherine Brian, Mr and Mrs J Brown, Neil and Anita Christopher, D Grzelka, Paul Boot, Wayne Brindle, Julian and Sarah Stanton, Lynn Sharpless, Bob Eardley, Helen Chalmers, John Bowdler, Mrs J Oakes, Gwen and Peter Andrews)*

Donnington ~ Tenants Adrian and Jennie Bowen-Jones ~ Real ale ~ Meals and snacks (stop at 1.30 lunchtime; not 25 Dec) ~ Restaurant ~ Guiting Power (01451) 850378 ~ Open 11-2.30, 6-11; closed evening 25/26 Dec ~ Two bedrooms: £20/£30

NEWLAND SO5509 Map 4

Ostrich ♀ 🍺

B4231 Lydney—Monmouth, OS Sheet 162 map reference 555096

In a pretty Forest of Dean village, this friendly, partly 13th-c inn has a delightfully informal – though rather civilised – atmosphere. There may be unobtrusive classical piped music, current affair magazines lying around for people to read, and candles on the tables, and the spacious but cosily traditional low-ceilinged bar has huge logs burning in a fine big fireplace decorated with a very capacious copper kettle and brass-bound bellows; comfortable furnishings include cushioned window seats and wall settles and rod-backed country-kitchen chairs. Interesting home-made bar food might include good soup, wild mushrooms or moules marinières (£3.50), lunchtime specials like avocado, bacon and mushrooms in cream or mussels provençale (£4.50), steak and oyster pie (£7), very good rack of lamb, roast Banbury duck in port wine (£8), and venison medallions in wild mushroom sauce (£10); good vegetables, and they bake all their own bread. Eight well kept real ales on handpump such as Exmoor Gold, Marstons Pedigree, Ringwood Old Thumper, Ruddles Best, Shepherd Neame Spitfire and Wadworths 6X; also, farm cider, seven or eight wines by the glass, and over 20 malt whiskies. Tables out in the small garden, and walkers are welcome if they leave their muddy boots at the door. No children. *(Recommended by Martyn Kearey, Dawn and Phil Garside, Keith J Willoughby, JCT, Sue Demont, Tim Barrow, Phil and Heidi Cook, Mr and Mrs G J Snowball, R G and M P Lumley, Mrs Pat Crabb, Roger Huggins, Dave Irving, Tom McLean, Ewan McCall, Leslie and Dorothy Pilson, Neil and Anita Christopher, John Bowdler, Mr and Mrs D E Connell, Mr and Mrs Peter B Dowsett, Jane and Ian Williams)*

Free house ~ Licensees Richard and Veronica Dewe ~ Real ale ~ Meals and snacks (not 25 Dec) ~ (01594) 833260 ~ Children in dining room ~ Open 12-2.30(3 Sat), 6.30-11; closed 25 Dec ~ Bedrooms: £25/£40

NORTH CERNEY SP0208 Map 2

Bathurst Arms

A435 Cirencester—Cheltenham

The beamed and black-panelled bar here has a nice easygoing and comfortable atmosphere, a collection of high-backed antique settles and snug window seats, Windsor chairs on the turkey carpet, pewter tankards hanging above the serving counter, and a splendid stone fireplace. A good choice of bar food might include sandwiches, home-made pâté (£2.85), various pasta dishes (£4.95), home-made pies (£5.25), and fresh salmon fillet in Pernod sauce (£6.95). Well kept Archers, Boddingtons, Tetleys and Wadworths 6X on handpump, and decent wines; good friendly service. The Stables Bar has darts, pool, dominoes, video game, juke box and piped music; quiz nights every other month, on Sundays. The attractive flower-filled front lawn runs down to the River Churn, and there are summer barbecues in good weather. *(Recommended by Neil and Anita Christopher, D G King, T and D Archer, Dave Irving, Roger Huggins, Tom McLean, Ewan McCall, M A and C R Starling, Mrs M C Barrett)*

Free house ~ Licensees Mr and Mrs F A C Seward ~ Real ale ~ Meals and snacks ~ Restaurant ~ (01285) 831281 ~ Children welcome ~ Occasional live music Sat/Sun evenings ~ Open 11-2.30(3 Sat), 6-11; closed 25 Dec ~ Bedrooms: £35B/£45B

NORTH NIBLEY ST756 Map 4

New Inn ★ 🛏 🍺

Waterley Bottom, which is quite well signposted from surrounding lanes; inn signposted from the Bottom itself; one route is from A4135 S of Dursley, via lane with red sign saying Steep Hill, 1 in 5 (just SE of Stinchcombe Golf Course turn-off), turning right when you get to the bottom; another is to follow Waterley Bottom signpost from previous main entry, keeping eyes skinned for small low signpost to inn; OS Sheet 162 map reference 758963; though this is the way we know best, one reader suggests the road is wider if you approach directly from North Nibley

This is very much a pubby pub and the characterful landlady tells us she has every intention of keeping it that way. The beer is particularly well kept and either tapped from the cask or served from antique beer engines – one is called Barmaid's Delight and another is 160 years old: Cotleigh Tawny and WB (a beer brewed specially for the pub), Greene King Abbot, Smiles Best and Exhibition, and Theakstons Old Peculier. Good value bar food includes filled brown baps (from 80p), toasties (from £1.30), ploughman's (from £2.80), home-made egg and bacon quiche (£3.85), home-made lasagne (£4), plaice (£4.95), daily specials such as home-made fish pie or mushroom bake, and puddings like home-made sherry trifle (£1.50). The carpeted lounge bar has cushioned Windsor chairs and varnished high-backed settles against the partly stripped stone walls, and sensibly placed darts, dominoes, shove-ha'penny, cribbage and trivia in the simple public bar; piped music. Also Inch's cider and over 50 malt whiskies. It's in a beautiful setting in the heart of pleasant walking country; outside is a beautifully kept terrace, with the garden beyond, and then a bowl of quiet pastures, rising to a fringe of woods (worth exploring). At the far end of the garden is a small orchard with swings, slides and a timber tree-house. To stay here you have to book a long way ahead – and best not to arrive outside opening hours. No children inside. *(Recommended by P M Lane, Dave Davey, T M Dobby, Patrick Clancy, D Baker, Dono and Carol Leaman, Jeff Davies, Nigel and Teresa Blocks)*

Free house ~ Licensee Ruby Sainty ~ Real ale ~ Meals and snacks ~ (01453) 543659 ~ Open 12-2.30, 7-11; closed evening 25 Dec ~ Two bedrooms: £20/£35

OAKRIDGE LYNCH SO9102 Map 4

Butchers Arms

Village signposted off Eastcombe—Bisley road, E of Stroud; or steep lanes via Frampton Mansell, which is signposted off A419 Stroud—Cirencester

Not easy to find – but worth it when you do – this well run pub has three warming log fires and lots of good food. The spacious rambling bar has a few beams in its low ceiling, some walls stripped back to the bare stone, and comfortable, traditional furnishings like wheelback chairs around the neat tables on its patterned carpet. Lunchtime bar food might include sandwiches, ploughman's (from £3.25), cauliflower cheese (£3.50), home-made cottage pie (£3.75), omelettes or brunch (£4.95), beef and stout pie (£5.50), rib steak (from £6.95), with evening dishes such as bacon and black pudding with mustard sauce (£3.95), deep-fried baked potato wedges with spicy chicken tikka (£4.95) or haddock and prawns in cheese sauce (£5.50), orange pork stroganoff (£8.95), and lamb cutlets mornay (£9.50). The prominence given to food hasn't in any way made this less of a drinker's pub – in the evening, food is only served in the Stable Room (just off the main bar area) which keeps the atmosphere warm and lively – and diners can enjoy a drink at the bar before or after their meal. Well kept Archers Best, Bass, Butcombe, Ruddles County, Tetleys and Theakstons Best on handpump; darts, dominoes, fruit machine, trivia and alley skittles. The hanging baskets in summer are pretty, and from the picnic-table sets on a stretch of lawn there are good views over the village and the valley dropping beyond, and you can really appreciate the village's rather odd remote setting. Usefully, the pub's car park is up on the level top road, so you don't have to plunge into the tortuous network of village lanes. *(Recommended by Paul Weedon, Peter and Audrey Dowsett, Dave Irving, Tom McLean, Ewan McCall, Roger Huggins, Dr Vivien Bull, Mrs M C Barrett)*

Free house ~ Licensees Peter and Brian Coupe ~ Real ale ~ Meals and lunchtime snacks ~ Restaurant (Weds-Sat evenings, Sun lunch) ~ (01285) 760371 ~ Children in small anteroom only ~ Open 12-3, 6-11

ODDINGTON SP2225 Map 4

Horse & Groom 🛏

Upper Oddington; signposted from A436 E of Stow-on-the-Wold

Set in a quiet Cotswold village, this very friendly pub has a warm local atmosphere, pale polished flagstones, a big log fire, a handsome antique oak box settle among other more modern seats, some horsebrasses on the dark 16th-c oak beams in the ochre ceiling, and stripped-stone walls with some harness and a few brass platters; the family room has a fruit machine. Reasonably priced bar food includes soup (£1.65), sandwiches (from £1.80), filled baked potatoes (from £3.10), ploughman's (£3.50), mushroom and nut fettucine or beef curry (£4.75), steak and kidney pie or gammon and egg (£5.40), steaks (from £7.45), several specials such as rabbit and groundnut stew with a very hot sauce (in a separate bowl), puddings, and children's meals (£2.40); the candlelit dining room is pretty. Well kept Hook Norton Best, Wadworths 6X and a guest beer on handpump. A quarry-tiled side area with a fine old polished woodburner has pool; also darts and piped music. The lovely garden has picnic-table sets on the neat lawn below the car park, apple trees, and a fine play area including an enormous log climber, a budgerigar aviary, a hut housing fat rabbits, and Aunt Sally. Beyond a rose hedge is a pretty water-garden where there are large trout. The bedrooms are not large, but quaint and comfortable. *(Recommended by George Atkinson, Roger Huggins, Dave Irving, Tom McLean, Ewan McCall, Mike and Jill Steer, Fred Collier, Graham Reeve, Mr and Mrs P B Dowsett, Paul Boot, Sir Nigel Foulkes, I MacG Binnie, C F Walling)*

Free house ~ Licensees Russell and Stephen Gainford ~ Real ale ~ Meals and snacks ~ Restaurant ~ (01451) 830584 ~ Children welcome ~ Open 11-2.30, 6-11; winter evening opening time 6.30 ~ Bedrooms: £31S/£50S

PARKEND SO6208 Map 4

Woodman

Just off B4234 N of Lydney

The popular, well presented bar food is the reason many people come to this Forest of Dean pub. As well as house specialities like nut roast (£4.50), good chicken breast in stilton sauce (£5.50), roast duck with teryaki sauce (£7) and giant rack of ribs with barbecue sauce (£8.50), there might be soup (£1.70), ploughman's (£3.75), rump steak sandwich (£4), steak and mushroom pie or home-cooked ham and egg (£4.50), seafood curry (£5) and children's meals (£1.95); three-course Sunday lunch (£8.95; under 7s £3.50); the restaurant is no smoking. The long heavy-beamed and carpeted bar is spacious and comfortable without being at all plush, with two open fires, and wall settles and wheelback chairs around gleaming copper-topped tables. The walls are stripped back to stone in some places, and decorated with monster two-handed saws and some unusual carvings of hounds and badgers. Well kept Bass and Boddingtons on handpump, and maybe darts, fruit machine, video game and juke box. There are picnic-table sets out on the front terrace, facing the village green. *(Recommended by MJ, Dave Irving, P G Brown, David and Mary Webb; more reports please)*

Whitbreads ~ Lease: Pat Buckingham ~ Real ale ~ Meals and snacks (until 10pm) ~ Small evening restaurant ~ (01594) 563273 ~ Children welcome ~ Open 11-3, 6-11; 11-11 Sat; 11.30-2.30, 7-11 in winter ~ Bedrooms: £12.50/£25(£30B)

REDBROOK SO5410 Map 4

Boat 🏴

Pub's car park is now signed in village on A466 Chepstow—Monmouth; from here 100-yard footbridge crosses Wye (pub actually in Penallt in Wales – but much easier to find this way); OS Sheet 162 map reference 534097

The car park in this marvellously located pub is in England, but the pub itself is in Wales. It's really worth a walk over the old railway bridge to look at the curve of the River Wye with the woods above, and down at the little pub with smoke curling up from the chimney; no wonder it's a popular place with walkers. You can sit in the garden (prettily lit at night) with the sound of the water spilling down the waterfall cliffs into the duck pond below. Inside, the cosy bar is cheery and full of character, with lots of pictures of the pub during floods, landscapes, a wall settle, a grey-painted piano, and a woodburning stove on the tiled floor. A fine choice of between eight and ten well kept beers, tapped straight from casks behind the bar counter might include Bass, Batemans XXXB, Brains SA, Boddingtons, Butcombe Bitter, Fullers London Pride, Hook Norton Best and Old Hookey, Shepherd Neame Spitfire, Smiles Best and Exhibition, Theakstons Best,

XB and Old Peculier, Thwaites Best and Craftsman, and Charles Wells Bombardier; also, a good range of country wines. Big helpings of good bar food include filled baked potatoes (from £1.50), soup (£1.55), ploughman's (£3.20), cauliflower and broccoli cheese (£3.60), vegetable curry (£3.80), chilli (£4), cidered pork (£4.25), brie and haddock pie (£4.70), and puddings like gooseberry tart or bread and butter pudding (from £1.65). Darts, shove-ha'penny, table skittles, cribbage, dominoes and trivia.

(Recommended by Robin Cordell, Ted George, Tony and Lynne Stark, Simon and Amanda Southwell, David Lewis, Roger Huggins, Dave Irving, Tom McLean, Ewan McCall, Alan and Eileen Bowker, R G and M P Lumley, Steve and Liz Tilley, PW, P M Lane, John and Helen Thompson, Gwynne Harper, Paul Boot, Paul Williams, Mr and Mrs D E Connell, Dave and Jules Tuckett, Dave Thompson, Margaret Mason, Robert Powell)

Free house ~ Licensees Steffan and Dawn Rowlands ~ Real ale ~ Meals and snacks ~ (01600) 712615 ~ Children welcome ~ Folk music Tues evening, jazz or blues Thurs evenings ~ Open 11-3, 6-11; 11-11 Sat

SAPPERTON SO9403 Map 4

Bell

Village signposted from A419 Stroud—Cirencester; OS Sheet 163 map reference 948033

Surrounded by good walks, this well run pub serves consistently reliable and good value straightforward food: sandwiches (from £1.40), soup (£1.50), ploughman's (from £2.85), good Gloucester sausages and chips (£3), salads (from £3.15), smoked haddock pasta (£4.15), half chicken (£4.80), grilled gammon and pineapple (£4.95), steaks (from £7.40). The spacious but warm and cosy carpeted lounge has stripped-stone walls and a good log fire; an extension up a couple of steps makes it L-shaped, with sturdy pine tables and country chairs. Well kept Bass, Flowers Original, Wadworths 6X and Whitbreads West Country PA on handpump, and generally friendly service. The large public bar has some old traditional wall settles, and well placed darts, cribbage, fruit machine and trivia; separate skittle alley/function room. There are tables out on a small front lawn.

(Recommended by Ewan McCall, Tom McLean, Dave Irving, Roger Huggins; more reports please)

Free house ~ Licensees Gordon and Violet Wells ~ Real ale ~ Meals and snacks (till 10pm) ~ (01285) 760298 ~ Children in eating area of bar ~ Open 11-2.30, 6-11; closed evening 25 Dec

Daneway

Village signposted from A419 Stroud—Cirencester; from village centre follow Edgeworth, Bisley signpost; OS Sheet 163 map reference 939034

Bustling and friendly, this pub is popular with both locals and visitors (many are walkers) – and it's worth the short stroll to the entrance of the Sapperton Tunnel which was used at the end of the 18th-c by the 'leggers', men who lay on top of the canal boats and pushed them through the two-and-a-half mile tunnel with their feet. The bar has a good welcoming atmosphere and a remarkably grand and dominating fireplace, elaborately carved oak from floor to ceiling, and racing and hunting prints on the attractively papered walls. Lunchtime bar food includes good value filled rolls (from 90p, not Sundays), burgers (£1.95), filled baked potatoes (£2.40), ploughman's (from £2.60), lasagne (£3.60), beef and Guinness pie (£4.50), and chicken tikka (£4.95), with evening extras like gammon steak (£5.50) and rump steak (£7.25) and occasional specials like almond nut roast (4.95); puddings such as hot apple pie (£1.50). Well kept Archers Best, Bass, Wadworths 6X, a beer brewed for the pub (from a local brewery) and a weekly changing guest on handpump or tapped from the cask, and local farm cider. Darts, dominoes, shove-ha'penny and ring-the-bull in the public bar, which has a big inglenook fireplace, quoits. The lovely sloping lawn is bright with flowerbeds and a rose trellis, and lots of old picnic-table sets look down over the remains of the Thames and Severn Canal and the valley of the little River Frome. There may be a vintage motor cycle club meeting in the car park on some summer

Wednesdays. The pub's car park is built over what used to be one of the canal locks – you can still see the corner-stone of the lock gates. *(Recommended by Roger Huggins, Tom McLean, Ewan McCall, Dave Irving, Mike Davies, Dave and Jules Tuckett, P and M Rudlin, D A Edwards, Neil and Anita Christopher, Mrs P Biles, Brian Whittaker, George Atkinson, Tracey and Kevin Stephens, Alastair Campbell, Ron Corbett)*

Free house ~ Licensees Liz and Richard Goodfellow ~ Real ale ~ Meals and snacks ~ (01285) 760297 ~ Children in small no-smoking family room off lounge ~ Open 11-2.30(3 Sat), 6.30-11

SHEEPSCOMBE SO8910 Map 4

Butchers Arms ♀

Village signposted from B4070 NE of Stroud, and A46 N of Painswick (narrow lanes)

Very much the centre of village activity – with frequent visits from local singing organisations and country dancing clubs – this friendly pub has a good chatty atmosphere and no fruit machines, juke boxes or piped music. The bar is decorated with lots of interesting oddments like assorted blow lamps, irons, and plates, and there are seats in big bay windows, and flowery-cushioned chairs and rustic benches. From a wide menu, the good food includes soup (£1.50), filled baguettes (from £2.50; brie and redcurrant £2.75, steak £4.75), ham and cheese crêpes (£3.50), ploughman's (from £3.50), leek and broccoli bake (£4.25), steak and kidney pie or gammon and pineapple (£4.95), mixed grill (£7.50), evening poached salmon with prawn sauce (£6.50) or steaks (from £8.75), specials such as swordfish steak (£6.50), half rack of ribs (£7.75) or half roast duck with Grand Marnier and citrus fruit sauce (£9.50), and puddings like home-made banoffi pie (£2). Well kept Bass, Boddingtons, and Hook Norton Best and Old Hookey on handpump, farm ciders, and a good wine list; darts, cribbage, and maybe winter quiz evenings. There are teak seats below the building, tables on the steep grass behind, and dramatic views over the valley. *(Recommended by Mr and Mrs W J Walford, Neil and Anita Christopher, Peter Neate, Paul Weedon, Nick and Meriel Cox, Roger Huggins, Dave Irving, Tom McLean, Ewan McCall, Lawrence Pearse, Gwen and Peter Andrews)*

Free house ~ Licensees Johnny and Hilary Johnston ~ Real ale ~ Meals and snacks ~ Restaurant ~ Painswick (01452) 812113 ~ Children in eating area of bar and in restaurant ~ Open 11-11; 11-2.30, 6-11 in winter

SIDDINGTON SU0399 Map 4

Greyhound

Ashton Rd; village signposted from industrial estate roundabout in Cirencester through-traffic system; and from A419 (northbound only)

There's a particularly good atmosphere in this friendly, characterful pub and the biggish lounge bar has two big warming log fires, a happy mix of high-backed winged settles, high dining chairs, chapel seats and so forth on the old herringbone brick floor, and good tables – mainly stripped pine, but one fine circular mahogany one. Lots of copper and brass cover the beams and ochre walls, as well as a few hunting prints, Edwardian hat feathers, some black-lacquered farm tools, and china and other bric-a-brac. Good, popular bar food includes sandwiches or rolls (from £1.95), soup (£2.15), garlic mushrooms (£2.45), ploughman's (from £3.55), salads (from £4.75), cauliflower and broccoli bake (£4.60), tuna and pasta (£5.20), steak and kidney pudding (£5.55), chicken and cashew nut curry (£5.95), lamb casserole (£6.25), steaks (from £10.45), and puddings like blackberry and apple crumble or banoffi pie (from £1.85). Well kept Wadworths IPA and 6X, Badger Tanglefoot and a fortnightly changing guest on handpump; the public bar has darts, table skittles, shove-ha'penny, cribbage, dominoes, fruit machine and piped music. There are picnic-table sets and older seats among lilacs, apple trees, flower borders and short stone walls behind the car park. Dogs allowed. *(Recommended by Dave Irving, Roger Huggins, Ewan McCall, Tom McLean, Dave Braisted, Jan and Dave Booth, A Maundrell, Nick Dowson, Lyn and Bill Capper, Peter Pocklington, Alastair Campbell, Brian Whittaker)*

Wadworths ~ Tenants Bob and Elaine Flaxman ~ Real ale ~ Meals and snacks
(till 10pm, 10.30pm Fri and Sat) ~ (01285) 653573 ~ Children in eating area of
bar ~ Open 11.30-2.30(3 Sat), 6.30(7 Mon and Sat)-11; closed 25 Dec and
evenings 26 Dec, 1 Jan

SOUTHROP SP2003 Map 4

Swan ♀

Village signposted from A417 and A361, near Lechlade

In a pretty village (the spring daffodils are lovely), this rather civilised creeper-
covered old pub is popular for its interesting food. The home-made ice creams
have come in for special praise this year: orange and marmalade, apple, ginger
and Calvados, white chocolate, mint and meringue, and lime and pistachio, with
sorbets like passion fruit, orange and Cointreau. Also, stilton and onion soup
(£2.80), cottage pie (from £3.25), smoked haddock and prawns in a creamy sauce
(£3.50), tiger prawns in filo pastry (£4.95), and buckwheat pancake filled with
chicken, bacon and mushrooms (£5.25), with evening extras like sirloin steak
(£8.75) or beef Wellington (£9.65). Morlands Original and guest beers such as
Archers Golden and Oakhill Bitter on handpump or tapped from the cask, and a
good wine list; the small restaurant is no smoking. The extended low-ceilinged
front lounge has cottagey wall seats and chairs, and winter log fires, and beyond
it is a spacious stripped-stone-wall skittle alley, well modernised, with plenty of
tables on the carpeted part, and its own bar service at busy times; piped music.
There are tables in the sheltered garden behind. *(Recommended by Mike and Jo, Pat
and John Millward, Mrs K E Neville-Rolfe, Mrs S Smith, Dave Braisted, Patrick Freeman,
Maysie Thompson, Bill and Edee Miller, Brian Whittaker, John Bowdler)*

*Free house ~ Licensees Patrick and Sandra Keen ~ Real ale ~ Meals ~ Restaurant
(not Sun evening) ~ Southrop (0136 785) 205 ~ Children welcome ~ Open 12-
2.30, 7-11; closed Mon evening in winter*

ST BRIAVELS SO5605 Map 4

George 🛏

Lots of local atmosphere and warmly friendly service are what people like about
this historic pub – it has its own ghost, and a Celtic coffin lid dating from 1070,
discovered when a fireplace was removed and now mounted next to the bar
counter. The three rambling rooms have old-fashioned built-in wall seats, some
booth seating, green-cushioned small settles, toby jugs and antique bottles on black
beams over the servery, and a large stone open fireplace. A dining area is no-
smoking. Well presented and tasty home-made bar food includes ploughman's
(from £3.95), chilli or lasagne (£5.50), steak and kidney pie or beef curry using
fresh spices (£6.95), fresh local rainbow trout or salmon (from £6.95), char-grilled
steaks (from £8.95; 16oz T-bone £12.95), and specials such as hock of ham
(£5.75), poussin (£7.95), and duck à l'orange (£8.95). Well kept Bass, Boddingtons,
Marstons Pedigree, and Wadworths 6X on handpump, kept under light blanket
pressure; a good range of malt whiskies, good wines, and Scrumpy Jack cider;
cribbage, dominoes and piped music. Tables on a flagstoned terrace at the back
overlook the grassy former moat of a silvery stone 12th-c castle built as a fortifica-
tion against the Welsh, and later used by King John as a hunting lodge (it's now a
Youth Hostel); there are more tables among roses and shrubs and an outdoor chess
board; lots of walks start nearby. *(Recommended by V G and P A Nutt, Dave and Jules
Tuckett, H Anderson, Andrew and Liz Roberts, Andy and Jill Kassube, P J F Westlake, Simon
and Amanda Southwell, F C Wilkinson, Simon Collett-Jones, Maureen Hobbs)*

*Free house ~ Licensee Bruce Bennett ~ Real ale ~ Meals and snacks ~ Dean
(01594) 530822 ~ Children welcome (no crying babies) ~ Occasional live jazz ~
Open 11.30-2.30, 6.30-11 ~ Bedrooms: £20B/£40B*

Pubs with outstanding views are listed at the back of the book.

STANTON SO0634 Map 4

Mount

Village signposted off B4632 (the old A46) SW of Broadway; Old Snowshill Road – take no-through road up hill and bear left

A new no-smoking extension has been built onto this busy pub, which in winter is a restaurant and in summer, more of an informal eating bar. The atmospheric original bar has black beams, cask seats on big flagstones, heavy-horse harness and racing photographs, and a big fireplace. An older spacious extension, with some big picture windows, has comfortable oak wall seats and cigarette cards of Derby and Grand National winners. Well kept, and very reasonably priced for the area, Donnington BB and SBA on handpump, and farm cider; friendly staff. Darts, dominoes, cribbage, fruit machine, video game and piped music. Bar food includes sandwiches (from £2, tasty toasties £3.30), good ploughman's (£3.80), chicken and broccoli lasagne (£4.70), daily specials like hickory smoked chicken (£4.70), and puddings (£1.80); at busy times a PA announces when your food is ready. You can play boules on the lawn, and there are seats on the terrace. The view is superb, looking down from its steep tranquil lane onto the picture-postcard golden stone village, and on a clear day beyond to the Welsh mountains; popular summer Sunday barbecues. *(Recommended by P M Lane, Andrew and Ruth Triggs, E G Parish, Peter and Audrey Dowsett, Michael and Margaret Norris, John and Joan Wyatt, A Y and JM Drummond, David Campbell, Vicki McLean, Miss P Adsley, Peter and Erica Davies, Dr Vivien Bull)*

Donnington ~ Tenant Colin Johns ~ Real ale ~ Meals and snacks (not Sun evening) ~ (01386) 584316 ~ Children welcome if well behaved ~ Open 11-3, 6-11; 11-11 Sat; closed 25 Dec

STOW-ON-THE-WOLD SP1925 Map 4

Queens Head 🍺

The Square

In a village of charming buildings, this characterful old local, with its colourful climbing rose and hanging baskets, is a bustling place with a friendly landlord. The most atmospheric part is the traditional flagstoned back bar, with lots of beams and a couple of interesting high-backed settles as well as wheelback chairs, public school football team colours on a back wall, a big log fire in the stone fireplace – and the landlord's coffin (installed for use at some later date, he tells us!). He's also quite a racing buff, and there are horse prints on the walls. The music is piped classical or opera (not in front), and there's also darts, shove-ha'penny and a fruit machine. The busy stripped-stone front lounge is packed with small tables, little Windsor armchairs and brocaded wall banquettes. Bar food includes sandwiches (from £1.50), very good soup or filled baked potatoes (from £1.75), popular ploughman's (£3.25), broccoli flan or faggots (£3.50), cottage pie or lasagne (£4.50), steak and kidney or cheese and potato pie (£4.75), specials such as asparagus in season (£5.25) and puddings like delicious apricot crumble or toffee pudding (£1.75); they may not do food some winter evenings. Donnington BB and SBA are particularly well kept on handpump; they do mulled wine in winter, and service is quick and helpful. A green bench in front has a pleasant view, and in a back courtyard there are some white tables, and perhaps their two dogs. *(Recommended by Tom Mclean, Ewan McCall, Roger Huggins, Dave Irving, Andy and Jill Kassube, Joan and Michel Hooper-Immins, Mrs B Sugarman, D L Barker, John Waller, Ralf Zeyssig, J Weeks, Gordon, Richard Lewis, M L Clarke)*

Donnington ~ Tenant Timothy Eager ~ Real ale ~ Meals and snacks (not Sun) ~ (01451) 830563 ~ Children in back bar ~ Occasional jazz Sun ~ Open 11-2.30, 6(6.30 Sat)-11

Post Office address codings confusingly give the impression that some pubs are in Gloucestershire, when they're really in the Midlands (which is where we list them).

nr STOW-ON-THE-WOLD SP1729 Map 4

Coach & Horses £ 🍺

Ganborough; A424 2½ miles N of Stow; OS Sheet 163 map reference 172292

The Donnington XXX, BB and SBA on handpump are well kept in this friendly little stone Cotswold building – as well they should be, this being the nearest pub to the Donnington brewery. The bar area is decorated with good wildlife photographs on the walls and coach horns on its ceiling joists, there's a winter log fire in the central chimney-piece, and leatherette wall benches, stools and Windsor chairs on the flagstone floor; steps lead up to a carpeted part with high-backed settles around the tables. Tasty bar food includes home-made game soup (£1.75), sandwiches (from £1.80; toasties from £1.95), macaroni cheese (£1.95), cottage pie (£2.50), filled baked potatoes (from £2.95), ploughman's (from £3.25), lasagne (£3.50), curried chicken (£3.75), home-made steak and kidney pie (£5.35), grilled Donnington trout (£5.95), mixed grill (£7.50), and puddings (£1.90); the dining area is no smoking. Darts, dominoes, fruit machine and juke box, and a popular skittle alley. There are seats outside, on a terrace and a narrow lawn. The attached field where the three pub dogs play (one an enormous wolfhound) also has a goat and maybe an occasional horse, and is a site for Caravan Club members; slide and swings for children, and they are still planning to add a bouncy castle. (*Recommended by A Wallbank, Andy and Jill Kassube, Michael and Margaret Norris, W C M Jones, Bronwen and Steve Wrigley, Philip Brown, E V Walder, Paul Weedon, Adrian Zambardino*)

Donnington ~ Tenant Andy Morris ~ Real ale ~ Meals and snacks ~ (01451) 830208 ~ Children in eating area of bar ~ Occasional duo/jazz ~ Open 11-3, 6-11; closed 25 Dec

WOODCHESTER SO8302 Map 4

Ram 🍺

South Woodchester, which is signposted off A46 Stroud—Nailsworth

You can rely on this bustling country pub for a lively atmosphere and a fine choice of real ales – which at any one time might include Archers Best, Boddingtons, Courage Directors, Fullers London Pride, Ruddles Best and County, Uley Bitter and Old Spot, and Wickwar Coopers. The attractive L-shaped beamed bar has three open fires, some stripped stonework, country-kitchen chairs, several cushioned antique panelled settles around a variety of country tables, and built-in wall and window seats; sensibly placed darts. From a menu that changes constantly, bar food might include sandwiches, various ploughman's, mixed bean lasagne, Greek-style potato and olive stew or pork and pineapple curry (all £4.95), and venison and apricot pie or Maryland crab and prawn cakes (£5.95); fresh vegetables and a choice of potatoes. From the picnic-table sets on the terrace there are spectacular views down the steep and pretty valley. (*Recommended by Roger Huggins, Tom McLean, Ewan McCall, Dave Irving, Paul Boot, Anne Morris, Leonard Dixon, Steve and Alison Ray, Richard Carpenter*)

Free house ~ Licensees Michael and Eileen McAsey ~ Real ale ~ Meals and snacks ~ Restaurant (not Sun evening) ~ (01453) 873329 ~ Children welcome ~ Open 11-3, 5.30-11; 11-11 Sat

---

Real ale to us means beer which has matured naturally in its cask – not pressurised or filtered. We name all real ales stocked. We usually name ales preserved under a light blanket of carbon dioxide too, though purists – pointing out that this stops the natural yeasts developing – would disagree (most people, including us, can't tell the difference!).

Lucky Dip

Besides the fully inspected pubs, you might like to try these Lucky Dips recommended to us and described by readers (if you do, please send us reports):

☆ **Alderton** [off B4077 Tewkesbury—Stow – OS Sheet 150 map ref 999334; SP0033], *Gardeners Arms*: Fine atmosphere in thatched Tudor pub in lovely quiet spot, well prepared fresh food in evening restaurant (not Sun evening; booked up Cheltenham week, and weekends when open lunchtime too), limited but interesting lunchtime bar menu, well kept Hook Norton Best and Wadworths 6X, log fire, good antique prints and high-backed settles in civilised old-fashioned bar, friendly licensees and labrador, tables on sheltered back terrace by well kept garden; basic lavatories; children allowed *(D Grzelka, Derek and Sylvia Stephenson, R J Herd, Nick Cox, LYM)*

☆ **Aldsworth** [A433 Burford—Cirencester; SP1510], *Sherborne Arms*: Unusual, thoroughly modernised and extended from original stone cottage, almost a winebar atmosphere with beams, bric-a-brac and spacious and attractive no-smoking conservatory dining area, good food esp fish, Whitbreads-related ales, log fire, friendly helpful service, lovely garden; lavatory for disabled *(Dr Vivien Bull, A J Madel, Paul McPherson, Mark Bradley, E Prince)*

Amberley [SO8401], *Amberley Inn*: Delightful panelled and carpeted lounge bar in small hotel with beautiful views, sparkling brass, riding whips, standard food at reasonable prices; bedrooms *(Dono and Carol Leaman)*

☆ **Ampney St Peter** [A417, ½ mile E of main village – OS Sheet 163 map ref 089013; SP0801], *Red Lion*: Quietly relaxing 17th-c village local, very traditional and completely unspoilt, with much character; no real bar counter, just a serving area in main lounge, in a gap between a settle and the wall; old-fashioned seats around big central table, friendly chatty crowd who welcome strangers; separate games room across the corridor with darts, cards and dominoes; well kept Whitbreads on handpump *(Pete Baker, Roger Huggins, Dave Irving, Tom McLean, Ewan McCall)*

☆ **Andoversford** [SP0219], *Royal Oak*: Windowless area behind big central open fire has unusual upper gallery with almost medieval feel; particularly well kept Bass, wide choice of good straightforward food, friendly licensees, games room with darts and pool *(Dr Vivien Bull, D Irving, E McCall, R Huggins, T McLean, Philip Brown)*

Apperley [SO8628], *Coalhouse*: Splendid riverside inn with wide choice of food, at end of long cul-de-sac from village; especially nice in summer *(Derek and Sylvia Stephenson)*

Arlingham [SO7111], *Red Lion*: Pleasant village pub nr Severn, friendly welcome, well kept real ale *(Neil and Anita Christopher)*

Ashleworth [village signposted off A417 at Hartpury; SO8125], *Arkle*: Fairly modern-looking brick house with relaxed homely atmosphere (except when skittles match is on, when it's very lively), sofas and comfortable seats as well as the usual pub furniture, attractively priced Donnington ales, pleasant landlord *(D Irving, R Huggins, T McLean, E McCall)*

Berry Hill [SO5713], *Kings Head*: Refurbished friendly pub with good food inc bargain Weds OAP lunch *(David and Mary Webb)*

Birdlip [A417/A436 roundabout – OS Sheet 163 map ref 935162; SO9316], *Air Balloon*: Good chain-brewery-style eating house with choice of real ales *(DI)*; *Royal George*: Good atmosphere in hotel's pubby part, well kept Whitbreads-related ales, huge helpings of decent food inc special Tues/Thurs suppers (must book); bedrooms *(the Monday Club)*

Bisley [SO9005], *Stirrup Cup*: Bustling friendly local, genuine and comfortable *(Neil and Anita Christopher, T McLean, R Huggins, E McCall, D Irving)*

☆ **Blaisdon** [off A48 – OS Sheet 162 map ref 703169; SO7017], *Red Hart*: Very brightly lit beamed and flagstone-floored village local with interconnecting bars, wide range of interesting well kept real ales such as Pickled Priest, good value food (not Sun evening) inc home-cooked dishes, pretty separate eating area, friendly service; dogs allowed; tables under cocktail parasols on attractive terrace and in nice garden *(Mr and Mrs D Johnson, Ian Phillips, Ted George)*

Blockley [Station Rd; SP1634], *Great Western Arms*: Typical Cotswolds stone pub in attractive village with small comfortably modernised relaxing lounge, back window has lovely view; good range of basket meals, well kept Flowers and Hook Norton, games bar *(B M Eldridge)*

☆ **Bourton on the Hill** [A44 W of Moreton-in-Marsh; SP1732], *Horse & Groom*: Easy chairs, low tables, big log fire and steeplechasing pictures in small but high-ceilinged stripped-stone lounge, bigger more local bar with games; usual bar food, Bass on handpump, decent restaurant (not Sun or Mon evenings), no under-10s; bedrooms good value, quiet and comfortable though sparsely equipped *(AB, CB, John Le Sage, LYM)*

Bourton on the Water [Bridge End Walk; SP1620], *Old Manse*: Courage-related and Hook Norton ales, bar food, front garden overlooking River Windrush, separate restaurant; bedrooms *(David Hanley)*; *Old*

New Inn: Old hotel next to 1:9 scale model of village built in 1930s by previous landlord, comfortably worn and welcoming, with history; parrot in fireplace *(R Huggins, D Irving, T McLean, E McCall)*

☆ **Broadwell** [off A429 2 miles N of Stow-on-the-Wold; SP2027], *Fox*: Pleasant village local attractively placed opp big village green, doing well under current welcoming licensees, with well kept Donnington beer, good choice of good value food served in small eating areas from ploughman's to well cooked main dishes with good fresh veg and delicious puddings, quick service even when crowded at weekends; bedrooms *(G W A Pearce, Sue and Vic North, Ted George, Marjorie and David Lamb)*

Cerney Wick [SU0796], *Crown*: Spacious village pub, conservatory beyond lounge with comfortable banquettes, woodburner, lots of brasses and rocking-horse, plain old public bar with pool, TV and log fire; Whitbreads-related ales, fair choice of well presented food; good-sized garden with swings; bedrooms *(Neil and Anita Christopher, R Huggins, D Irving, E McCall, T McLean)*

Chalford [SO9002], *Neighbourhood*: New terrace and smartly polished tables outside are indicative of the attention the owners are paying to detail; inside beginning to age nicely; very cheap beers *(T McLean, R Huggins, E McCall)*

☆ **nr Chalford** [France Lynch – OS Sheet 163 map ref 904036], *Kings Head*: Attractive old country local doing well under new management, with great views, friendly atmosphere, well kept beer, wide range of good bar food, no juke box or fruit machine, garden *(Roger Entwistle, Mrs P A Orr)*

Charlton Kings [Cirencester Rd; A435; SO9620], *Little Owl*: Attractive Whitbreads pub with other beers too and a good wine list, well run by friendly couple, good range of bar food, good meals in dining room inc lots of seafood *(Mr and Mrs W J B Walford)*

Cheltenham [Bath Rd; SO9422], *Bath*: Classic basic unspoilt two-room local with well kept Bass and Uley Bitter *(E McCall, D Irving, R Huggins, T McLean)*; [Portland St], *Cotswold*: Welcoming Regency pub, well preserved but up-to-date, tastefully and comfortably furnished with Victorian prints on flock-papered walls; well kept Wadworths, good simple food from good sandwiches to Sun lunches, obliging staff; open all day *(Paul Weedon)*; [Benhall Ave], *National Hunt*: Modern chalet-style pub with big but comfortable and pleasant lounge, good friendly staff, well kept Whitbreads-related ales, good value bar food *(B M Eldridge)*; [High St], *Restoration*: Long dimly lit bar, lots of beams, bric-a-brac etc, plenty of seats, good atmosphere, adjoining real ale bar with five or more well kept and reasonably priced

beers, attractively presented American-style fast food *(Steve Goodchild)*; [Montpellier Walk], *Rotunda*: Particularly well kept Allied ales and Wadworths 6X, good service, friendly atmosphere *(K D Graham)*

☆ **Chipping Campden** [Church St; SP1539], *Eight Bells*: Ancient flagstoned and heavy-beamed pub by church, recently refurbished by enthusiastic newish owners, enormous log fire, cushioned pews, lots of dark wood tables and chairs for diners, interesting food using fresh local ingredients, plenty of choice from sandwiches to steaks, big helpings, friendly staff, well kept Allied and guest beers, decent wines; picnic-table sets in courtyard; bedrooms *(Peter and Jenny Quine, Martin Jones, J G Quick, Charles and Lesley Knevitt, David and Anne Smith)*

Chipping Campden [High St], *Lygon Arms*: Well worn-in stripped-stone bar, separate eating room and raftered evening restaurant, well kept Donnington SBA, Hook Norton Best and Wadworths 6X, friendly staff; tables in sheltered courtyard, skittle alley, darts; children welcome, open all day exc winter weekdays; decent bedrooms *(Andrew and Ruth Triggs, Richard Waller, LYM)*; [Sheep St], *Red Lion*: Refurbished with plenty of character, newish local owners extending small menu of good home-cooked simple food, well priced beer – definitely on the up *(E V Walder, Martin Jones)*; *Volunteer*: Good friendly atmosphere, good range of beers and of good food, military memorabilia *(Steve Bowser, Jim Love)*

☆ **Cirencester** [W Market Pl; SP0201], *Slug & Lettuce*: Flagstones, bare boards, lots of woodwork, attractive mix of furnishings inc good big tables, hearty log fires; Courage real ales, good coffee, bar food inc unusual dishes, friendly helpful staff, piped music (live jazz some Suns), children welcome; tables in inner courtyard; can get packed with agricultural college students or the like evenings *(J Boylan, George Atkinson, D Irving, H Huggins, T McLean, E McCall, LYM)*

Cirencester [Dyer St], *Bear*: Friendly stone-floored old pub with well kept Courage and Smiles *(Dr and Mrs A K Clarke, RH, DI)*; [Market Pl], *Fleece*: Wide choice of good reasonably priced food, flagstones and stripped wood; also plusher hotel bar; bedrooms *(W H and E Thomas, BB)*; [Blackjack St; between church and Corinium Museum], *Golden Cross*: Busy rather basic but very friendly local with very cheap food, well kept Arkells BB, BBB and Mash Tun Mild on handpump; skittle alley *(George Atkinson, Nick Dowson, D Irving, H Huggins, T McLean, E McCall)*; [Gloucester St], *Nelson*: Interesting bar modelled on HMS *Victory*, well kept beers *(Dr and Mrs A K Clarke)*; [10-14 Chester St], *Oddfellows Arms*: Recently refurbished cosy backstreet local with decent range of strong real ales *(Nick Dowson)*; *Twelve Bells*: Reopened after open-plan refurbishment, pleasant mix of olde-worlde English with country French, red chalk-board menus, some continental prints *(Tom McLean)*; [Chesterton Lane], *Woodbine*: Straightforward pub vitalised by hardworking newish landlord, with decent food inc notable bargains, well kept Courage-related and good guest beers *(D Irving, R Huggins, T McLean, E McCall)*

☆ **Cliffords Mesne** [out of Newent, past Falconry Centre – OS Sheet 162 map ref 699228; SO6922], *Yew Tree*: Good choice of good value food (not Mon) in comfortable beamed lounge bar of welcoming well laid out country pub, clean and quiet, on slopes of May Hill (local landmark, NT); well kept Courage-related ales and Wadworths 6X, friendly service; restaurant, children welcome, pool table in separate area, tables out on terrace *(Neil and Anita Christopher, Alan and Jane Clarke, R G and M P Lumley, John and Shirley Dyson)*

☆ **Coberley** [A436 Brockworth—Andoversford, just SW of junction with A435 Cheltenham—Cirencester; SO9516], *Seven Springs*: Spacious and airy dining pub with very lofty ceiling, big windows, snugger side areas and sloping pond-side garden; generous food inc good value OAP lunch, Courage beers, cheery piped music; children allowed daytime – has been open all day *(Dorothy and Leslie Pilson, LYM)*

☆ **Coleford** [Joyford; best approached from Christchurch 5-ways junction B4432/B4428, by church – B4432 towards Broadwell, first left signed Joyford, then lane on right beyond hamlet; OS Sheet 162 map ref 580134; keep your eyes skinned for pub sign hidden in hedge; SO5813], *Dog & Muffler*: Prettily set country pub with log-effect gas fire in cosy lounge bar, good range of reasonably priced generous bar food in long back conservatory dining room overlooking verandah, old well in foyer, well kept Ruddles County and Sam Smiths on handpump, very pleasant service, pool and skittles in big recent games-room extension; high-hedged lawn with picnic-table sets, some under thatched conical roofs, 18th-c cider press by path from car park *(Phil and Heidi Cook)*

☆ **Colesbourne** [A435; SO9913], *Colesbourne Inn*: Friendly and comfortable panelled inn, quite imposing from outside, with huge log fire, hunting prints, settles and oak tables, masses of mugs on beams; well kept Wadworths real ales inc Old Timer, good range of bar food, smart waitresses, tables in back garden; comfortable bedrooms *(Mr and Mrs P B Dowsett, Neil and Anita Christopher, N Cox, W H and E Thomas, Debby Hawkins, T McLean, R Huggins, E McCall, D Irving)*

Coln St Aldwyns [SP1405], *Red Lion*: Good French cooking *(SC)*

☆ nr **Cowley** [Cockleford, signed off A435 S of junction with A436; SO9614], *Green Dragon*: Attractive two-room country pub

with flagstones and bare boards, which has changed hands yet again (it would have been a main entry but for the new people's couldn't-care-less attitude to our repeated requests for information); good choice of good food, big stone fireplace and woodburner, Smiles and other well kept real ales; skittle alley, tables out on terrace with pretty view *(Paul Boot, Martin Kearey, M L and B S Rantzen, Frank Gadbois, D Cox, LYM)*

☆ **Cranham** [nr church – OS Sheet 163 map ref 897129; SO8912], *Black Horse*: Unpretentious and friendly old-fashioned local, small and cosy, with open fire in attractive quarry-tiled public bar, sensibly limited choice of good very British food such as game pie and pheasant, generous helpings and marvellous value, also good inexpensive sandwiches; Hook Norton and Whitbreads-related ales, Stowford Press cider; a magnet for walkers; car park rather tricky *(Margaret Drazin, Nick and Meriel Cox, A Y Drummond)*

Didmarton [ST8187], *Kings Arms*: New owners doing good food from good slightly upmarket menu; well kept Smiles and Theakstons, daily papers *(Paul Weedon)*

☆ **Duntisbourne Abbots** [A417 N of Cirencester – OS Sheet 163 map ref 978091; SO9709], *Five Mile House*: Small old unspoiled country local, all sit companionably around the single table in the tiny bay-windowed flagstoned bar, or in the even tinier snug formed from two huge and ancient high-backed settles; well kept Courage tapped from cask behind perfunctory counter, relaxed atmosphere, home-made pickled eggs (sometimes goose eggs) as well as crisps *(Pete Baker, E McCall, D Irving, R Huggins, T McLean)*

Eastleach Turville [off A361 S of Burford; SP1905], *Victoria*: Attractive lounge/dining area, good pianist most Sat nights (when juke box off), locals' bar with pool; well kept Arkells, good rather than quick food, nice views *(Gordon, Paul McPherson)*

☆ **Edge** [A4173 N of Stroud; SO8509], *Edgemoor*: Modernised food pub, clean and tidy, with good imaginative well served food from new chef, no-smoking restaurant, spectacular valley views through big picture windows, industrious landlord, Smiles, Tetleys and Uley Old Spot on handpump, little or no piped music; provision for children, tables in garden; virtually on Cotswold Way *(Paul Weedon, John and Joan Wyatt, LYM)*

☆ **Elkstone** [Beechpike; A417 6 miles N of Cirencester – OS Sheet 163 map ref 966108; SO9610], *Highwayman*: Surprising quality for a busy trunk road, well kept Arkells real ales, good house wines, decent food from lunchtime sandwiches to steaks, good friendly staff, and considerable character in rambling warren of low beams, stripped stone, alcoves, antique settles among more modern furnishings, log fires; piped music;

outside play area, good indoors provision for children *(Chris and Sue Heathman, D Irving, R Huggins, T McLean, E McCall, BHP, LYM)*

Forest of Dean, see Berry Hill, Coleford, Lower Lydbrook, and main entries for Clearwell, Newland, Parkend and St Briavels

☆ **Fossebridge** [A429 Cirencester—Stow-on-the-Wold; SP0811], *Fossebridge*: Handsome Georgian inn with attractive lakeside lawns and terrace by River Coln, interesting heavy-beamed side Tudor bar with massive fireplace, traditional furnishings, rugs on flagstones; food (not Sun evening) expensive but good; children in eating area; comfortable bedrooms *(George Jonas, D Grzelka, Alan Carr, Jan and Dave Booth, Mr and Mrs R Leeds, Paula Harrison, I E and C A Prosser, LYM)*

☆ **Frampton Mansell** [off A491 Cirencester—Stroud – OS Sheet 163 map ref 923027; SO9102], *Crown*: Quiet pub in lovely setting above village and steep wooded valley, decorous stripped stone lounge bar with dark beam-and-plank ceiling, darts in public bar, well kept ales such as Archers Village, Oakhill Farmers, Wadworths 6X, good bar food and good Sun lunch, friendly service, restaurant; children in eating area, teak seats outside; comfortable bedrooms *(Paul Weedon, D Irving, E McCall, R Huggins, T McLean, Mr and Mrs LaFayette Noah, Mrs M C Barrett, LYM)*

☆ **Glasshouse** [by Newent Woods; first right turn off A40 going W from junction with A4136 – OS Sheet 162 map ref 710213; SO7122], *Glasshouse*: Carefully preserved small country tavern with interesting decor, changing well kept real ales tapped from the cask, open fire in cavernous fireplace, good value straightforward food, helpful landlady, seats on fenced lawn with big weeping willow loved by children; fine nearby woodland walks *(Michael, Alison and Rhiannon Sandy, LYM)*

☆ **Gloucester** [Bristol Rd about 1½ miles S of centre, opp Lloyds Bank], *Linden Tree*: Lively and attractive local with good varied straightforward food, three Wadworths ales and three interesting guests such as Smiles Exhibition, Morland Old Speckled Hen and Hardy Country tapped from casks particularly well kept in temperature-controlled cabinet behind false wooden barrel ends; new back skittle alley *(Joan and Michel Hooper-Immins, Paul Weedon)*

Gloucester [Llanthony Rd; off Merchants Rd, S end of Docks], *Waterfront*: Nr canal, with 12 real ales inc interesting brews tapped from the cask in bare-boards black-beamed bar with scrubbed tables, tin helmets, barrels you can chalk on, free peanuts (shells go on the floor); pool, bar billiards, table football, ninepins, chess, dominoes, draughts and scrabble; food very substantial and cheap, eating area up a step with back-to-back cubicle seating; piped music, fruit machine, TV *(Ted George, Roger Huggins)*

☆ **Greet** [Evesham Rd; B4078 N of Winchcombe; SP0230], *Harvest Home*: Simple village pub transformed by current tenants, German chef-patron does lovely fresh food esp fish, vegetarian and delicious puddings as well as wide choice of more straightforward dishes; reasonable prices, bright unpretentious atmosphere, warm welcome, Hook Norton Best, Wadworths 6X and Whitbreads-related ales; restaurant evenings and Sun lunchtime *(Lorraine Gwynne, Michael Green, Ian and Sheila Richardson, Brian and Genie Smart)*

Guiting Power [SP0924], *Farmers Arms*: Friendly licensees, well kept Donnington, good generous home-made food, prompt service; bedrooms *(Robert Huddleston)*

Hardwicke [Sellars Bridge; SO7912], *Pilot*: Well kept Whitbreads-related ales, decent food, lovely canalside setting overlooking lock; good children's facilities inc nappy-changing room *(P J and S E Robbins)*

Hartpury [Ledbury Rd (A417); SO7924], *Canning Arms*: Cosy and distinctive, lots of nick-nacks – red bows, horsebrasses on beams, gin traps, old farm tools, prints; log fire, Ind Coope Burton, Tetleys and Theakstons Old Peculier, decent genuine bar food in eating area with bright tartan tablecloths; live jazz some nights, big car park *(Neil and Anita Christopher, Jo Rees)*; *Royal Exchange*: Cheery atmosphere and furnishings, well kept John Bull and Oak Hill, tasty food, friendly staff and locals *(Ron and Sheila Corbett)*

☆ **Hillesley** [ST7689], *Fleece*: Busy and attractive local with friendly landlord, interesting bar food inc good specials and steaks and fresh, no-smoking upper dining bar; well kept Whitbreads-related real ales, decent wines and malt whiskies, friendly service; small Cotswolds village surrounded by lovely countryside, nr Cotswold Way; bedrooms *(Carol and Mike Muston, Paul Weedon, Robert Huddleston)*

Kemble [outside village; A433 Cirencester—Tetbury – OS Sheet 163 map ref 981986; ST9897], *Thames Head*: A lot of stripped stone now and some black-painted timbering, pews and log-effect gas fire in big fireplace of cottagey back bar, country-look dining room with another big gas fire, real fire in front room; well kept Arkells Bitter, 2B and 3B on handpump, good value straightforward food, seats outside, children welcome *(J M and K Potter, D Irving, R Huggins, T McLean, E McCall, LYM)*

Kempsford [SU1597], *Axe & Compass*: Simple pleasant old local with warmly welcoming licensees and good reasonably priced food *(Klaus and Elizabeth Leist)*

☆ **Kineton** [signed from B4068 and B4077 W of Stow-on-the-Wold; SP0926], *Halfway House*: True country local, unpretentiously traditional, with well kept cheap Donnington from nearby brewery, simple sensibly priced food from sandwiches up, friendly staff, pub games (and juke box), tables on narrow front terrace and sheltered back lawn, restaurant; children allowed lunchtime, no visiting dogs; simple but comfortable bedrooms *(Nick and Meriel Cox, Lawrence Pearse, LYM)*

☆ **Lechlade** [SU2199], *Red Lion*: Traditional village local with wide range of attractively priced well prepared food inc good puddings and Sun lunches, friendly helpful service, well kept Arkells, restaurant with log fire *(Marjorie and David Lamb, D Irving, R Huggins, T McLean, E McCall)*

☆ **Little Barrington** [A40 W of Burford; SP2012], *Inn for All Seasons*: Despite trunk-road location feels like quiet country pub inside, very old with plenty of character, big log fire, comfortable wing armchairs, magazines; friendly helpful staff, good extensive choice of generous bar food esp fish, informal restaurant; local beers such as Wychwood Best, piped classical music; tables in garden; bedrooms; may be closed Mon winter *(Martin and Karen Wake, Mr and Mrs Peter Dowsett)*

☆ **Longhope** [Ross Rd (A40); SO6919], *Farmers Boy*: Good wholesome food inc same two-in-one pies as at Weighbridge nr Nailsworth (see main entries) in three big carefully refurbished rooms, one with running water in covered well; farm tools, log fire, relaxed atmosphere, very helpful and welcoming service, well kept Courage Directors and Wadworths 6X, no juke boxes or machines; well tended gardens *(Neil and Anita Christopher, Pam Bentley, Mrs Pat Crabb, Joy Raymond, Mr and Mrs K Box, T Buckley, L Knight)*

☆ **Lower Lydbrook** [Vention Lane; pub signposted up single-track rd from B4228 NE of village – OS Sheet 162 map ref 604167; SO5916], *Royal Spring*: Very prettily placed Forest of Dean pub, simple and quiet, with pews and high-backed settles in long beamed lounge looking down valley, wide range of well presented straightforward bar food, good Sun lunch, friendly chatty licensees, log fire, well kept Worthington; pretty garden built around stream dropping down steep coombe, play area, pets' corner; children very welcome *(J Fortey, Robert Huddleston, Geoff and Eileen Keeling, LYM)*

☆ **Lower Swell** [B4068 W of Stow-on-the-Wold; SP1725], *Golden Ball*: Welcoming local with particularly well kept Donnington BB and SBA from the pretty brewery just 20 mins' walk away, good range of ciders and perry, cheery landlord, generous wholesome bar food, evening restaurant (no food Sun evening); simple bar with log fire, games area behind big chimneystack, pleasant streamside garden with occasional barbecues, Aunt Sally and quoits; clean simple bedrooms, good value *(D Grzelka, T McLean, E McCall, R Huggins, D Irving, LYM)*

☆ **Lower Wick** [ST7196], *Pickwick*: Bright clean dining pub very popular (particularly with older people) for good range of reasonably priced straightforward home-cooked food; Bass, John Smiths and Theakstons, rather close-set tables; wonderful countryside, but M5 and railway nearby; children welcome *(A D Shore, Margaret Dyke, C H and P Stride)*

☆ **Meysey Hampton** [SU1199], *Masons Arms*: Extensively renovated handsome small inn with good freshly cooked reasonably priced food, fine range of beers and French wines by the glass, hospitable atmosphere, big open fire at one end; comfortable bedrooms of considerable character, very good breakfasts *(Patricia and Tony Carroll, Paul McPherson)*

Minchinhampton [SO8600], *Halfway House*: Enthusiastic and very friendly new management, good food and beer, marvellous views; gardens improved *(Roger Entwistle)*

☆ **Minsterworth** [A48 S of Gloucester; SO7716], *Apple Tree*: Wide choice of well presented straightforward food in attractive and comfortable Whitbreads dining pub based on extended oak-beamed 17th-c farmhouse; open fires, friendly service, unobtrusive piped music, well kept real ales, wide choice of usual food presented well, big garden ideal for children with safe enclosed play area; open all day – lane beside leads down to the Severn, a good way of avoiding east bank crowds on a Bore weekend *(Lt Col E H F Sawbridge)*

☆ **Moreton in Marsh** [High St; SP2032], *White Hart Royal*: Busy and comfortable traditional inn, partly 15th-c, with big inglenook fire in lounge area just off main bar, friendly helpful staff, well kept Bass from the cask, good choice of decent food inc good fish and Sun lunches in bar and simple but pleasant restaurant; can get crowded; good value bedrooms *(Derek Allpass, Jill White, George Atkinson, A E and P McCully)*

☆ **Moreton in Marsh** [Market Pl], *Black Bear*: Good value enterprising food served with a smile in busy, clean and welcoming pub with warm, comfortable and peaceful lounge overlooking road, livelier public bar; full range of well kept local Donnington ales *(Joan and Michel Hooper-Immins, John and Barbara Gibson, B M Eldridge)*

Moreton in Marsh [High St], *Redesdale Arms*: Decent straightforward food in comfortably old-fashioned panelled bar and attractive restaurant, good log fires, well kept Bass and Courage Directors; good well equipped bedrooms *(M Watson, Fred Collier)*

☆ **Nailsworth** [coming from Stroud on A46, left and left again at roundabout; ST8499], *Egypt Mill*: Unusual and interesting, attractively converted three-floor mill with working waterwheel in one room, static machinery in second area, Ind Coope Burton and Wadworths 6X on handpump, wide choice of good generous bar food inc fresh veg, quick service, good value meals in civilised upstairs restaurant; can get crowded weekends, occasional loud karaoke or jazz evenings; children welcome, no dogs; lovely gardens, good bedrooms *(Mrs M C Barrett, Roger Entwistle, Dr and Mrs A K Clarke, Mr and Mrs J Brown)*

☆ **Nether Westcote** [SP2120], *New Inn*: Good value home-cooked food in warmly welcoming pub, pleasantly unpretentious but cosy, clean and homely; particularly well kept Morrells, attractively priced Sun roast *(Michael and Merle Lipton, T McLean, E McCall, R Huggins, D Irving)*

☆ **North Nibley** [B4060; ST7496], *Black Horse*: Good atmosphere and wide range of generous fresh home-made bar food from ploughman's up in straightforward village pub, comfortably old-fashioned, with efficient friendly staff, well kept Whitbreads-related real ales and an interesting guest beer, good log fire, maybe piped music; popular restaurant Tues-Sat evenings, Sun lunchtime, tables outside; good value cottagey bedrooms, good breakfasts *(Paul Weedon, Mrs Anne Parmenter, T and D Archer, LYM)*

☆ **Northleach** [Market Pl; SP1114], *Red Lion*: Good value generous food from good sandwiches to Sun roasts in straightforward bar with open fire, well kept Courage-related real ales, decent coffee, very friendly service; piped music and fruit machines *(Joan Olivier, Lt Col E H F Sawbridge)*

☆ **Northleach** [Cheltenham Rd], *Wheatsheaf*: Clean and comfortable, almost more hotel than pub, with pleasant rather upmarket atmosphere, quiet piped classical music, very polite and friendly unflappable staff; particularly good reasonably priced lunchtime bar food, two real ales, a German beer on tap, efficient friendly staff; restaurant, lovely terraced garden; well equipped modern bedrooms *(J R Smylie, John Honnor)*

☆ **Norton** [Wainlode Hill; SO8523], *Red Lion*: Cosy isolated fishermen's pub on River Severn, stuffed fish, good range of reasonably priced bar food, Whitbreads-related real ale; plenty of seats outside, views to Malvern Hills *(S H Godsell)*

☆ **Nympsfield** [SO8000], *Rose & Crown*: Wide choice of real ales such as Bass, Theakstons, Uley Bitter and Old Spot and Wadworths 6X in pretty village local nr Coaley Peak viewpoint over Severn Valley; with cosy and pleasant partly stripped-stone lounge, big helpings of reasonably priced well cooked hot food, friendly landlord; separate public bar; clean and comfortable bedrooms sharing bath and lavatory, big breakfasts *(T M Dobby)*

☆ **Painswick** [St Mary's St; SO8609], *Royal Oak*: Busy and attractive old town local with bubbly atmosphere, interesting layout and furnishings inc some attractive old or antique seats, good value honest food (bar nibbles only, Sun) from sandwiches to changing hot dishes inc Thurs fresh fish, well kept Whitbreads-related ales, friendly

family service, small sun lounge by suntrap pretty courtyard; children in eating area; can get crowded, nearby parking may be difficult *(Mrs M C Barrett, David Gray, D Irving, E McCall, R Huggins, T McLean, Paul Weedon, Martyn Kearey, Michael Marlow, LYM)*

Parkend [SO6208], *Fountain*: Friendly and efficient landlord, lots of interesting bric-a-brac, log fires, varied well kept beers; good value usual food *(J Deave, David and Mary Webb)*

☆ **Prestbury** [Mill St; SO9624], *Plough*: Vast helpings of good bar food in well preserved thatched village pub's small but cosy and pleasant oak-panelled front lounge, very local atmosphere and lots of regulars in basic but roomy flagstoned back taproom with grandfather clock and big log fire, well kept Whitbreads-related ales tapped from casks (cheapest prices from hatch in hall), pleasant back garden *(B M Eldridge, Lt Col E H F Sawbridge, E McCall, D Irving, R Huggins, T McLean)*

☆ **Purton** [just upstream from Sharpness village on left bank of Severn estuary – ie not pub of this name in nearby Berkeley; SO6904], *Berkeley Arms*: Basic rustic pub-cum-farm on banks of the Severn with wonderful estuary view, two character flagstoned rooms with plain high-backed settles, well kept Wadworths 6X, food confined to pickled eggs, crisps, maybe ploughman's, no noise; you can walk for miles; summer caravanning allowed when there's no risk of flooding *(Paul and Gail Betteley)*

☆ **Quenington** [SP1404], *Keepers Arms*: Cosy, clean and tidy stripped-stone pub, popular and very comfortable, with traditional settles, lots of mugs hanging from low beams, good coal fire, decent food in both bars and restaurant, Whitbreads-related real ales, very friendly licensees, no piped music; bedrooms *(Audrey and Peter Dowsett)*

Quenington, *Earl Grey*: Extraordinarily small bar, slightly bigger lounge with brass ornaments and massive Welsh dresser, very welcoming landlord, remarkably low-priced well kept Wadworths 6X, open fires *(T McLean, R Huggins, E McCall, D Irving)*

☆ **Redmarley** [Playley Green; A417 just off M50 exit 2; SO7531], *Rose & Crown*: Generous helpings of good reasonably priced food in good-sized lounge with exposed walls or big attractive restaurant (was skittle alley), well kept beers, quick service; beautiful countryside *(Neil and Anita Christopher)*

Rodborough [SO8404], *Bear*: Very comfortable and well appointed Forte hotel, separate-entrance bar with flagstoned floor, pleasant window seats, welcoming log fire, good range of bar food, well kept Courage; children welcome; comfortable bedrooms – good base for touring Cotswolds *(W H and E Thomas, Dave Irving)*; [Rodborough Common], *Black*

Horse: Good view, attractive building, good choice of beer *(D Irving, E McCall, R Huggins, T McLean)*

Sandhurst [SO8223], *Globe*: Under new ownership, with extended dining room, good choice of well cooked and presented straightforward food, frequent special offers, cosy lounge bar with open fire, Banks's, Camerons and John Smith; views from garden with plans for adventure play area *(Neil and Anita Christopher)*

Selsley [just SW of Stroud; SO8304], *Bell*: Very wide range of reasonably priced home-cooked bar food, well kept Whitbreads-related real ales and Uley Old Spot, friendly landlord and staff in attractive little 17th-c village pub perched on hillside common overlooking Stroud, popular with Cotswold Way walkers *(Robert Huddleston)*

Shipton Moyne [off B4040 Malmesbury—Bristol; ST8989], *Cat & Custard Pot*: Consistently well kept Whitbreads-related ales, well presented food inc good sandwiches; unassuming village local, dogs welcome *(J Wedel, BB)*

☆ **Slad** [SO8707], *Woolpack*: Thriving village local in beautiful valley, very welcoming landlord, traditional furnishings, good straightforward food, well kept Whitbreads-related real ales and a guest such as Uley Old Spot; great views *(Rosemary and Brian Wilmot, I H Rorison, E McCall, D Irving, R Huggins, T McLean)*

☆ **Slimbridge** [Shepherds Patch, by swing bridge across ship canal OS Sheet 162 map ref 728042; SO7303], *Tudor Arms*: Welcoming and popular straightforwardly comfortable pub, very handy for Wildfowl Trust and canal, with good value home-cooked food in bar and evening restaurant, children's room; bedrooms in small building next door *(Pauline Crossland, Dave Cawley, Paul Weedon)*

☆ **Snowshill** [SP0934], *Snowshill Arms*: Good popular chippy food served most efficiently in friendly, spruce and airy bar with charming village views from bow windows and from big back garden; well kept Donnington BB and SBA (but no coffee unless you've eaten), log fire; skittle alley, good play area; children welcome if eating; handy for Snowshill Manor (which closes lunchtime), can get very busy *(John and Audrey Davidson, Mr and Mrs P B Dowsett, D Grzelka, D Hanley, Maysie Thompson, Joan and John Calvert, Patrick Freeman, Andrew and Ruth Triggs, Richard Lewis, LYM)*

Somerford Keynes [OS Sheet 163 map ref 018954; SU0195], *Bakers Arms*: Welcoming village local with well kept real ales such as Bass, Courage Best, Marstons Pedigree and Wadworths 6X on handpump, pleasantly traditional partly stripped-stone lounge bar, food inc good specials; big garden *(Alastair Campbell, R Huggins, D Irving, E McCall, T McLean, Dr and Mrs A K Clarke)*

☆ **South Cerney** [SU0497], *Eliot Arms*: Smart pub/hotel, clean and tidy but full of relaxed and comfortable little rooms; some emphasis on attractive choice of reasonably priced food, good range of well kept Whitbreads-related and other ales, interesting foreign bottled beers, fast service *(D Irving, E McCall, R Huggins, T McLean, Dr and Mrs A K Clarke, Nick Dowson)*

South Cerney, *Walter Mittys*: Formerly the Old George, extraordinary bar with model trains on the ceiling, posters and a parrot – you name it, it's there; beer well kept, welcome friendly *(Dr and Mrs A K Clarke)*

Stonehouse [High St; SO8005], *Woolpack*: Friendly old town pub with low ceilings, lots of interesting prints, well kept beer *(Dr and Mrs A K Clarke)*

☆ **Stow-on-the-Wold** [The Square; SP1925], *Old Stocks*: Well run simple hotel with cosy, clean and welcoming small bar and dining room, decent food and wines, well kept real ale, friendly staff; subdued piped music; seats on pavement and in sheltered garden; good value bedrooms *(Wayne Brindle, BB)*

Stow-on-the-Wold [The Square], *Talbot*: Popular pub with wide choice of good food inc Sunday, Wadworths ales, friendly staff *(Richard Lewis)*; [The Square], *White Hart*: Decent food in cheery and cosy old small front bar or more orthodox plush back dining lounge; bedrooms *(Paul McPherson, BB)*

☆ **Stroud** [1 Bath Rd; SO8504], *Clothiers Arms*: Recently extended 18th-c pub with interesting and beautifully presented food in pleasant airy dining room, four well kept real ales inc Tetleys in busy bar with old Stroud brewery decorations, popular Italian landlord; garden *(Neil and Anita Christopher, Dave Irving)*

☆ **Stroud**, *Seven Stars*: Unusual and comfortable recently refurbished triangular bar around circular servery, good interesting bar food, well kept Greene King IPA and Abbot and Wadworths 6X, attractive pictures, jovial landlord, newish restaurant; exemplary lavatories; bedrooms *(C O Day, Gwen and Peter Andrews)*

Stroud [opp rly stn], *Imperial*: Popular and comfortable Chef & Brewer with good straightforward food, good service, Courage-related ales *(Geoff Summers, Paul Weedon)*; [Stratford Rd], *Nelson*: Recently renovated and converted former private school named after former headmaster, gaining popularity for food in bar and restaurant *(Anon)*; [Rooksmoor (A46 a mile S); SO8403], *Old Fleece*: Old stone pub with lively log fire and dark panelling in open-plan bar, well kept Bass and Whitbreads-related ales, dining room with attractive food inc interesting light meals as well as more expensive main dishes; landlord has collected and returned local evening customers (not Tues or Sun) *(Dave Irving)*; [off High St], *Retreat*: Basic pub with surprisingly interesting good value food (*Dave Irving*)

Teddington [Stow Rd, 3½ miles from M5 junction 9; SO9632], *Teddington Hands*: Very welcoming simply modernised pub with wide choice of good value food esp fresh fish, good choice of Whitbreads-related and other ales, decent house wines; handy for Cheltenham Races, very busy then (*Norma and Keith Bloomfield, George S Jonas*)

☆ **Tetbury** [Gumstool Hill, Mkt Pl; ST8893], *Crown*: Warm and friendly 17th-c town pub, popular with business people weekday lunchtimes for wide choice of decent food from sandwiches up inc interesting home-made pies, well kept Hook Norton Best and Whitbreads-related ales; log fires in carpeted oak-beamed lounge, attractive medley of tables, efficient courteous service, unobtrusive piped music; back family dining conservatory with lots of plants, picnic-table sets on back terrace; comfortable bedrooms (*Lyn and Bill Capper, P and J Shapley, Alastair Campbell, Graham and Karen Oddey, Roger Huggins*)

*nr***Tetbury** [A433 towards Cirencester, nr Cherington], *Trouble House*: Pretty 17th-c pub with no music, well kept Wadworths beers, open fire, small lounge (quiet unless children around), small bar with bar billiards and darts in room off, usual food (*Roger Huggins*)

☆ **Tewkesbury** [52 Church St; SO8932], *Bell*: Plenty of armchairs and settees in hotel's plush and interesting bar, very clean but not intimidatingly smart, with some neat William and Mary oak panelling, black oak beams and timbers, medieval leaf-and-fruit frescoes, tapestries and big log fire; good choice of decent bar food from sandwiches up, restaurant, well kept Banks's, Bass and Wadworths 6X on handpump, friendly helpful service; garden above Severnside walk, nr abbey; comfortable bedrooms (*David Mair, David Rogers, Adrian and Gwynneth Littleton, Ted George, Gordon Mott, LYM*)

Tewkesbury, *Berkeley Arms*: Fine medieval timbered inn best seen from narrow passageway outside lounge with jettied windows above, welcoming landlord, full range of Wadworths ales and Badger Tanglefoot, good value food; bedrooms (*Joan and Michel Hooper-Immins*); [High St], *Black Bear*: Extremely picturesque timbered pub, said to be county's oldest, with rambling heavy-beamed rooms off black-timbered corridors, real ales, limited bar food, riverside lawn (*Pat Bromley, LYM*); [Barton St], *Duke of York*: Heavy accent on jazz with imaginative decor, well kept beer, good service (*Dr and Mrs A K Clarke*); [High St], *Lloyds*: Popular black and white gabled local nr market cross, perky friendly landlord, food low-key and fairly priced (*Margaret Cadney*)

Todenham [SP2436], *Farriers Arms*:

Cotswold pub in quiet village with good straightforward bar food inc Sun lunch (must book for this), Whitbreads-related ales, friendly staff; bedrooms (*C F Walling, Michael Heald*)

☆ **Twyning** [Twyning Green; SO8936], *Fleet*: Star is for superb setting, with good river views from big popular welcoming open-plan bar, variety of seating areas inside and out, well kept Whitbreads-related ales, access for the disabled, bar food, boat shop (*DAV, Dr and Mrs A K Clarke*)

Twyning, *Village Inn*: Welcoming village pub with good atmosphere, helpful staff, good bar food (may be limited Mon and Tues), well kept beer, decent wines; dogs allowed, pretty garden (*DAV*)

☆ **Uley** [The Street; ST7898], *Old Crown*: Recently refurbished to give much more space but as welcoming as ever; good value generous bar food inc good toasties and children's dishes, well kept Uley and Pigs Ear with a couple of Whitbreads-related ales, darts and fruit machine, unobtrusive piped music, attractive garden; bedrooms (*Alastair Campbell*)

Uley [The Street], *Kings Head*: Attractive Cotswold village inn in deep valley with nice views from long comfortable beamed lounge with dark red walls, smaller public bar down some steps; has had well kept Wadworths beers, good wines and good food, but no news yet on tenants who took over in 1994 (*June and Tony Baldwin*)

Upper Framilode [Saul Rd, not far from M5 junction 13; SO7510], *Ship*: Attractive and relaxing setting by disused canalside offshoot from Severn with ducks and swans, neat and nicely decorated cricket-theme lounge, good waitress-served food at low prices (service, normally prompt, can occasionally slow), enjoyable atmosphere (*Rona Murdoch, PN*)

☆ **Wanswell Green** [SO6901], *Salmon*: Good fair-priced food from soup and sandwiches up, two attractive candlelit back dining rooms, busy front bar (esp Fri/Sat night), well kept Whitbreads-related real ales, decent wines and cider, good friendly staff helpful with children; big front play area; nr Berkeley Castle and Severn walks (*Andrew Shore, Mr and Mrs J Brown, Paul Weedon*)

☆ **Westbury on Severn** [Bell Lane (A48 Gloucester—Chepstow); SO7114], *Red Lion*: Tiled and timbered pub on lane with footpath to Severn, next to churchyard and close to NT gardens; good generous food esp specials and puddings and well kept ales inc Hook Norton Best in small comfortable bar with coal stove and separate back dining room, decent wine, very friendly landlord and staff (*Mr and Mrs W A Poeton, Philip Lake*)

☆ **Westonbirt** [A433 SW of Tetbury — OS Sheet 162 map ref 863904; ST8690], *Hare & Hounds*: Comfortable and relaxed old-fashioned hotel bar with decent reasonably priced lunches esp salad bar and puddings,

Wadworths IPA and 6X, helpful staff, pleasant gardens; handy for Arboretum; limited space for families; bedrooms *(D G Clarke, Mr and Mrs J Brown, W H and E Thomas)*

☆ **Whitminster** [A38 1½ miles N of M5 junction 13; SO7708], *Old Forge*: Small and happily unpretentious old beamed pub with welcoming attentive staff, home-made bar food, small restaurant, good choice of beers and wines; children welcome *(Joan Olivier, D G Clarke, P J and S E Robbins, Paul Weedon)*

☆ **Willersey** [nr Broadway – OS Sheet 150 map ref 106396; SP1039], *Bell*: Good choice of food, good value though not cheap, from sandwiches to inventive main dishes cooked by landlord in smart and civilised 14th-c golden stone dining pub overlooking picturesque village green and duck pond; spotless housekeeping, comfortable tasteful furniture, three Whitbreads-related ales, friendly attentive service; already very popular – have to wait for tables unless you book; tables in garden *(John Williams, Pam Adsley, Roderic Plinston, Peter Lloyd, R and J Fitzpatrick)*

☆ **Winchcombe** [High St; SP0228], *Corner Cupboard*: Relaxed atmosphere and traditional layout in local at top of attractive village, with hatch-service lobby, small smoke room, pleasant armchair lounge with beams, stripped stone and good inglenook log fire, attractive small back garden; well kept Hook Norton, Marstons Pedigree and three Whitbreads-related ales, well presented usual bar food from quite a few sandwiches and good ploughman's up, friendly landlord, board games; bedrooms in self-contained wing *(Neil and Anita Christopher, Roger Huggins, Tom McLean, Michael and Derek Slade, Richard and Janice Searle, R A Baker)*

Winchcombe [High St, nr church], *Plaisterers Arms*: Friendly pub with good generous promptly served food from big sandwiches up inc vegetarian dishes and good traditional puddings, well kept real ales such as Bass, Ind Coope Burton, Tetleys and Wadworths, lots of seating inc comfortably worn settles, two bars and dining area, lots of exposed stonework, beams, copper and brass; pleasant garden, long and narrow; comfortable bedrooms *(Alain and Rose Foote, Peter and Janet Race, Debby Hawkins, Mrs M Hamilton, Neil and Anita Christopher)*

☆ **Withington** [signed off A436, A40; from church go S, bearing left – OS Sheet 163 map ref 032153; SP0315], *Mill*: Fine mossy-roofed old stone building, an old favourite for its character and position, with rambling, higgledy-piggledy beamed bar and cosy little side rooms, interesting antique seats, good log fire and lovely streamside gardens (summer barbecues) in peaceful valley; gets very busy weekends, service can sometimes slow, and piped music may intrude; children allowed, Sam Smiths real ales, usual bar food from ploughman's to steaks, games bar; bedrooms *(Greg Kilminster, John and Joan Wyatt, R Huggins, T McLean, E McCall, Rebecca Mortimer, Gordon, GM, CM, LYM)*

Woodmancote [Stockwell Lane; SO9727], *Apple Tree*: Spacious and popular local with well kept Whitbreads-related and guest ales such as Bass and Wadworths 6X, wide range of usual bar food inc Sun roasts, bar billiards, big garden with children's play area *(Lawrence Pearse, Mr and Mrs J Brown, D Walker)*

Children welcome means the pubs says it lets children inside without any special restriction. If it allows them in, but to restricted areas such as an eating area or family room, we specify this. Places with separate restaurants usually let children use them; hotels usually let them into public areas such as lounges. Some pubs impose an evening time limit – let us know if you find this.

Hampshire

Quite an expensive area for pubbing, this, with good main dishes often costing over £5 and even a ploughman's tending to be nearer £4 than £3. Drinks prices are rather higher than the national average, too, particularly in pubs tied to the big national brewers. There are worthwhile savings in pubs supplied by the area's smaller breweries, and occasional real bargains: we found drinks prices much lower than average in the White Horse at Droxford (doing extremely well at the moment, with good food and a great atmosphere) and the unspoilt Flower Pots at Cheriton (brewing its own good beers). Some changes to note include a change from tenancy to leasehold at the busy and friendly Horse & Groom in Alresford, our grant of a Food Award to the unpretentious Five Bells at Buriton (doing really well these days), new management at the prettily placed Jolly Sailor at Bursledon and at the Coach & Horses at Rotherwick (lots of unusual beers now), and the departure of the Emberleys from the New Forest Inn at Emery Down where they've been so popular (and indeed from their satellite pubs); they've opened a new place at Cadnam (in the Lucky Dips – it was still under wraps as we went to press in the summer of 1994). Several newcomers to the main entries, or pubs back in these pages after a gap, include the stylish Fox & Hounds at Crawley, the Still & West in its superb position by Portsmouth Harbour, and the Plough at Sparsholt, doing very well under newish licensees. Other pubs currently doing particularly well at the moment include the Milbury's at Beauworth, the the Sun at Bentworth, the Red Lion at Boldre, the Bush at Ovington, the White Horse near Petersfield, the Tichborne Arms at Tichborne, and the Wykeham Arms in Winchester. From a shortlist of superb dining pubs which also includes the Red Lion at Boldre, the Bush at Ovington, theRose & Thistle at Rockbourne and the Wykeham Arms (last year's winner), we choose as Hampshire Dining Pub of the Year the little Five Bells at Buriton – for really good English home cooking in relaxed and unpretentious surroundings. There is such a wealth of good pubs among the starred Lucky Dips at the end of the chapter that it might help if we picked out some (most inspected) of special note: the Globe in Alresford, Three Tuns at Bransgore, Chairmakers Arms at Denmead, Hampshire Bowman at Dundridge, George at East Meon, Olde Whyte Harte in Hamble (or for more comfort the Bugle there), Yew Tree at Highclere, Boot at Houghton, Trout at Itchen Abbas, Ship at Langstone, Plough at Longparish, Peat Spade at Longstock, Ship at Owslebury, Good Intent in Petersfield, Alice Lisle at Rockford, Filly at Setley, White Hart at Sherfield on Loddon, Cricketers at Steep, Grosvenor and White Hart in Stockbridge, Three Lions at Stuckton, Thomas Lord at West Meon, White Lion at Wherwell and Cartwheel at Whitsbury; there are several useful places in Portsmouth.

ALRESFORD SU5832 Map 2

Horse & Groom

Broad St; town signposted from new A31 bypass

Busy and welcoming, the carefully renovated open-plan layout has several
rambling nooks and crannies to suit different moods. The tables in the three bow
windows on the right, looking out over the broad street, are an enjoyable place to
sit. There's quite a smart feel and a notably pleasant atmosphere, along with neat
settles and Windsor chairs, black beams and timbered walls partly stripped to
brickwork, old local photographs and shelves of earthenware jugs and bottles.
Big helpings of tasty home-made dishes like sandwiches (from £1.75, club
sandwiches are something of a speciality), soup (£1.95), ploughman's (from
£2.75), very popular warm salads (from £3.95) and changing daily specials like
beef korma, honey glazed lamb chops in rosemary or pies such as steak and
kidney or game (£4.95); puddings include Belgian biscuit cake (£2.25). Well kept
Bass, Boddingtons, Fremlins, Marstons Pedigree and Whitbreads Castle Eden and
Strong Country on handpump; coal-effect gas fire, unobtrusive piped music.
Service can slow down at busy periods, but always remains friendly.
(*Recommended by KCW, Lynn Sharpless, Bob Eardley, Dawn and Phil Garside, Martin and
Karen Wake, J Muckelt, Peter and Doreen Wilson, Hilary Edwards*)

*Whitbreads ~ Lease: Robin and Kate Howard ~ Real ale ~ Meals and snacks ~
(01962) 734 809 ~ Children welcome ~ Open 11-2.30, 6-11*

BATTRAMSLEY SZ3099 Map 2

Hobler ♀

A337 a couple of miles S of Brockenhurst; OS Sheet 196 map reference 307990

Not all visitors to this lively 16th-c pub appreciate or even understand the
landlord's idiosyncratic sense of humour, but those that do say it really adds to
the character and good-humoured atmosphere of the place. He also runs the local
butcher's shop, supplying meat to around 40 other pubs and hotels in the area, so
you can rely on the meat in the well-praised food being just right. The very good
meals are often rather unsual, and the frequently changing choice might include
filled rolls (from £1.95), several soups (from £2.50, fish soup at £3.95), snails in
garlic, a good hearty ploughman's with home-made pickle (£3.75), hot goat's
cheese salad (£4.95), tagliatelle (£5.95), game pie (£6.95), hot beef curry (£7.95),
baked red snapper with cajun spices (£8.95), duck breast stuffed with
strawberries and bacon (£10.95), and their popular 'Hot Rocks', a hot stone on a
plate upon which you cook your own chicken, steak and quail's eggs (£9.95);
they don't do chips. It is very popular, so get there early for a table in the main
building (many are booked in the evening). Divided by the massive stub of an
ancient wall, the black-beamed bar has a very relaxed feel, and is furnished with
lots of tables with red leatherette bucket seats, pews, little dining chairs and a
comfortable bow-window seat. Guns, china, New-Forest saws, the odd big
engraving, and several customer photographs decorate the walls, some of which
are stripped back to timbered brick. The cosy area on the left is black-panelled
and full of books. Well kept Flowers Original, Wadworths 6X and a high-gravity
guest such as Bunces Old Smokey on handpump, and a good range of malt
whiskies (over 60) and wines (including some expensive bargains by the bottle).
In summer a spacious forest-edge lawn has a summer bar, a huge timber climbing
fort in the good play area, and picnic-table sets, beside a paddock with ponies,
pigs, donkeys, a peacock and hens. The landlord now also runs the slightly bigger
Turf Cutters Arms, East Boldre, near Bealieu; this has a similar atmosphere and
menu. (*Recommended by Jenny and Brian Seller, Mr and Mrs G P Tobin, Andrew Scarr,
Don Kellaway, Angie Coles, Stephen and Anna Oxley, F Hutchinson, Sheila Edwards*)

*Whitbreads ~ Licensee Pip Steven ~ Real ale ~ Meals and snacks (till 10) ~
(01590) 23291 ~ No children inside and no dogs ~ Jazz Tues ~ Open 11-2.30, 6-
11; closed evening 25 Dec*

BEAUWORTH SU5624 Map 2

Milbury's ♀ 🍺

Turn off A272 Winchester—Petersfield at Beauworth ¾, Bishops Waltham 6 signpost, then continue straight on past village

Full of character and instantly welcoming, this wonderfully aged inn is doing rather well at the moment, earning high praise in particular for its genuinely old-fashioned and civilised atmosphere. It's quite a remote place, and until the 1940s the 600-year-old well that still opens into a side area of the bar was the pub's only supply of water. Drop an ice cube into the spotlit shaft and it takes about five full seconds to reach the bottom, which apparently means the depth is 300 feet; it used to take the landlord (or his donkey) 678 paces to wind up the original water cask. Sturdy beams, stripped masonry, panelling and massive open fireplaces (with good winter log fires) offer reminders of the building's years, and there are suitably old furnishings inside and out. A very good range of drinks takes in well kept Ansells Best, Courage Directors, Greene King Abbot, Tetleys and local King Alfred and Pendragon on handpump, as well as farm cider, some malt whiskies, over 100 wines, and plenty of country wines. Tasty bar food, largely home-made using local ingredients, includes home-made soup (£1.95), sandwiches (from £2.35), a choice of ploughman's (£2.95), spinach, cottage cheese, and mushroom pancake (£3.95, £4.95 with prawns), salads (from £4.20), steak and kidney pie or leeks with ham and cheese sauce (£4.95), gammon (£5.95), and steak (from £7.80), with children's dishes (£2.75), home-made puddings such as apple pie or hazelnut meringue (from £1.80) and Sunday roasts. Sunday brunch (£4.95, served 9.30-11.15) comes with Sunday papers; service is prompt, efficient and cheerful. It's a popular place, so booking is more or less essential at weekends; there may be summer barbecues. Darts, video game, skittle alley. The garden has fine views, and there are good walks nearby. Dogs welcome. Milbury's was at first only a nickname, coming from the Millbarrow, a Bronze Age cemetery surrounding it, briefly famous back in 1833 when a Norman hoard of 6,000 silver coins was found here. (*Recommended by W J Wonham, Dave Braisted, KCW, Ann and Colin Hunt, Mayur Shah, Ron Shelton, Lynn Sharpless, Bob Eardley, J S M Sheldon, Linda and Brian Davis, Mr and Mrs P B Dowsett, DC, Mr and Mrs A F Walters*)

Free house ~ Licensees Jan and Lenny Larden ~ Real ale ~ Meals and snacks (till 10) ~ Restaurant ~ (01962) 771248 ~ Children welcome, except main bar ~ Open 11-2.30(3 Sat), 6-11 ~ Bedrooms: £22.50/£38.50

BENTLEY SU7844 Map 2

Bull

A31 Farnham—Alton, W of village and accessible from both directions at W end of dual carriageway Farnham bypass

In summer the approach to this warmly welcoming little tiled white pub is a real treat, with colourful hanging baskets and tubs of flowers making the building look especially attractive. Inside is relaxed and cosy, with the friendly landlady and staff really going out of their way to make everyone feel at home. Traditionally furnished with tapestried wall seats and stools, the low-beamed rooms have plenty of interesting local prints, pictures and photographs on the walls, especially in the snug left-hand room, which also has a dimly lit back alcove with a tapestried pew built around a nice mahogany table, and a log-effect gas fire in a big old fireplace. The restaurant area has several comical pre-war Bonzo prints. Attractively-presented bar food includes sandwiches (from £1.95), soup (£1.95), ploughman's (from £3.95), lasagne (£5.45), salads (from £5.45), home-made steak, kidney and mushroom pie (£5.95), steaks (from £8.95) and seven or eight changing daily specials such as lamb steaks, chicken supreme, sea bass, a well-liked salmon and broccoli bake or a vegetarian dish; puddings (£2.25). They specialise in Pimms, attracting quite a lot of attention for it, and also have Courage Best, Fullers London Pride and Wadsworth 6X on handpump, and a large range of malt whiskies; darts, fruit machine, piped music. There are tables on the side terrace, by a fairy-lit Wendy house on stilts. It's very well placed for Alice Holt Forest. (*Recommended by John and Vivienne Rice, A D Marsh, Mrs B G Laker, Michael A Butler, Ian and Wendy McCaw, WHBM, Peter and Doreen Wilson*)

Inntrepreneur (Courage) ~ Lease: Mary Holmes and Bill Thompson ~ Real ale ~ Meals and snacks (11.30am till 10.30pm) ~ Restaurant ~ Bentley (011420) 22156 ~ Children in restaurant ~ Occasional pianist Tues, monthly jazz Sun lunch ~ Open 11-11

BENTWORTH SU6740 Map 2

Sun ◥

Sun Hill; from the A339 coming from Alton the first turning takes you there direct; or in village follow Shalden 2¼, Alton 4¼ signpost

Exceptionally well received by readers over the last few months, this lovely unspoilt cottage always seems splendidly relaxed and at ease with itself, if anything getting better as it gets older. All is traditional and old-fashioned, but at the same time feels cheery and very much alive; it's the kind of atmosphere that would be impossible to imitate – unless you had three or four hundred years to spare. We like it best in winter, when there aren't quite so many people and you can really enjoy the unique character of the two tiny communicating rooms. Both have open fires in the big fireplaces, a mix of seats like high-backed antique settles with pews and schoolroom chairs, olde-worlde prints and blacksmith's tools, and bare boards and scrubbed deal tables on the left; lots of fresh flowers dotted around and newspapers and magazines to read. An arch leads to a new brick-floored room with another open fire and hanging baskets, incorporating what used to be the outside lavatories. Generously served bar food includes sandwiches, home-made soup (£2), ploughman's, filled baked potatoes, spinach roulade with bacon and cream cheese (£4.50), giant Yorkshire pudding and beef or salmon fishcakes and crab sauce (£4.95), steak and kidney pie or sweet and sour chicken (£6.50), fillet pork stroganoff (£7.50), lovely summer salads and home-made puddings like white and dark chocolate mousse, pear honey and almond tart or sponge puddings (from £2); booking may be advisable at weekends. Well kept Bass, Courage Best, Marstons Pedigree, Ringwood Best and 49er, Ruddles Best, Wadworths 6X and Worldham Old Dray on handpump; also a full range of Gales country wines; dominoes. Service is quick and friendly – as are the three dogs, Snuff, Honey and Ruddles. Several picnic-table sets under cocktail parasols look over the quiet lane. (*Recommended by Susan and John Douglas, J S M Sheldon, Guy Consterdine, Lynn Sharpless, Bob Eardley, Julia Stone, Alan and Margot Baker, David Sweeney, G B Longden, Martin and Karen Wake, Brenda and Jim Langley, Phil and Sally Gorton, John and Joan Nash, Andrew Scarr, Betty Laker, Christopher Kilburn, Denis J McLaughlin, TBB*)

Free house ~ Licensees Richard and Jan Beaumont ~ Real ale ~ Meals and snacks (not Sun evening Nov-Feb) ~ (01420) 562338 ~ Children allowed in new garden room, no under 10s after 8pm ~ Occasional Morris dancers (26 Dec and odd Fri nights in summer) ~ Open 12-3, 6-11; closed 25 Dec

BOLDRE SZ3298 Map 2

Red Lion ★ ⊕ ♟

Village signposted from A337 N of Lymington

The good, thoughtfully-prepared food is what draws the crowds to this perennially popular old pub, nicely set just on the edge of the New Forest. This is especially true in summer, when the flowerbeds in front are a riot of colour and there may even be queues before opening time. The four warmly atmospheric black-beamed rooms are filled with a bewildering variety of ephemera from heavy urns and platters to needlework and rural landscapes, taking in farm tools, heavy-horse harness, needlework, gin traps and even ferocious-looking man traps along the way; the central room with its profusion of chamber-pots is no smoking. An end room has pews, wheelback chairs and tapestried stools, and a dainty collection of old bottles and glasses in the window by the counter. The menu really is impressive, with a typical choice including home-made soup (£2.20), good sandwiches (from £2.40), various ploughman's (£3.90), potted shrimps or avocado and prawns (£3.90), unusual and well liked basket meals ranging from sausages to duck with wine-soaked orange slices (from £4.20), leek and broccoli bake or vegetable casserole (£4.60), chicken and tarragon risotto (£5.20), fish creole or plaice stuffed with prawns and mushrooms (£5.90), lamb paprika (£6.50), steak and kidney pie (£6.90), and an interesting range of ice creams (£2.90) such as chocolate dream (with maple syrup and walnut) or coupe Jaques (lemon, cassis and mandarin sorbets). Do get there early, some days tables go within minutes. Well kept Eldridge Pope Dorchester, Hardy Country and Royal Oak on handpump; a good range of up to 20 wines by the glass, with more by the bottle including changing guests; prompt and friendly service. (*Recommended by Jean-Bernard Brisset, Miss E Evans, Gill and Mike Cross, Martin and Pauline Richardson, Martin, Jane, Simon and Laura Bailey, J Watson, Keith and Margaret Kettell, Andrew Scarr, John and Christine Simpson, Jason Caulkin, Mr and Mrs A R Hawkins, J L Hall, Lynn Sharpless, Bob Eardley, Stephen Brown, Keith Stevens, P and R Wayth*)

Eldridge Pope ~ Lease: John and Penny Bicknell ~ Real ale ~ Meals and snacks (11-2.15, 6-10.15) ~ Restaurant ~ Lymington (01590) 673177 ~ No children under 14 inside ~ Open 11-3, 6-11; cl 25 Dec

BRAMDEAN SU6128 Map 2

Fox ♀

A272 Winchester—Petersfield

Again it's the food that stands out at this welcoming 350-year-old dining pub, and though the fish is a particularly good bet, the whole range is very satisfying, and far more unusual than first sight of the building might suggest. Favourite dishes include sandwiches (from £2.25, the beef or pork are excellent), good soup (£2.50), ploughman's (£3.95), a fine locally smoked trout (£4.50), king prawns with mayonnaise or mussels and prawns in sherry and garlic butter (£5.50), cauliflower cheese (£6.25), battered cod (£6.95), beef stroganoff (£7.95), and usually lots of fresh fish dishes such as skate, halibut, lobster or salmon steak in lime butter (£10.95). If you're not sure which wine to choose from the extensive wine list, they're quite happy to open a bottle to taste. The much modernised and neatly cared for open-plan bar has black beams, tall stools with proper backrests around its L-shaped counter, and comfortably cushioned wall pews and wheelback chairs; the fox motif shows in a big painting over the fireplace, and on much of the decorative china. Well kept Marstons Burton and Pedigree on handpump, an extensive wine list and decent coffee; piped music. At the back of the weatherboarded house is a walled-in patio area, and a spacious lawn spreading among the fruit trees, with a really good play area – trampoline as well as swings and a see-saw. Please note they don't allow children inside. (*Recommended by Peter and Audrey Dowsett, Colin Laffan, Ann and Colin Hunt, Betty Laker, R K F Hutchings, R B Crail, Mr and Mrs A F Walters, B J P Edwards, Peter and Doreen Wilson*)

Marstons ~ Tenants Jane and Ian Inder ~ Real ale ~ Meals and snacks ~ (01962) 771363 ~ Open 10.30-2.30(3 Sat), 6-11; closed 25 Dec

BURITON SU7420 Map 2

Five Bells 🍴

Village signposted off A3 S of Petersfield
Hampshire Dining Pub of the Year

Cosy and characterful, this unpretentious old country local is the kind of place it's easy to take to straight away. Not surprisingly it has an enviable reputation at the moment, mainly for its excellent range of superb food. Typically well prepared and tasty dishes might include soup (£2.25), sandwiches, ploughman's, filled jacket potatoes or filled croissants (£3.50), several vegetarian dishes such as courgette and aubergine lasagne (£4.75), devilled kidneys or various curries (£5.50), pork, apple and cider casserole or steak and kidney pie (£6.50), steaks, and lots of seasonal fish and game like scallops in wine and cream or crab and sherry bake (£7.50) and partridge stuffed with haggis and blackcurrant sauce (£8.95); puddings include New Orleans bread pudding with whisky sauce or treacle tart (£2.25). The pub is attractive and genuinely welcoming, with wood and flowers everywhere, and a mixture of simple relaxing furniture. The low-beamed lounge on the left is dominated by the big log fire, and has period photographs on its partly stripped brick walls, as well as a rather worn turkey carpet on oak parquet, while the public side has some ancient stripped masonry, a woodburning stove, and old-fashioned tables. An end alcove with cushioned pews and old fishing prints has board games such as Scrabble (sensibly issued with a referee dictionary). The good choice of well kept beers generally features Ballards Best, Friary Meux Best, Ind Coope Burton, Ringwood Old Thumper, Tetleys and an often unusual guest on handpump. Service is prompt and friendly. Cribbage, shove ha'penny, darts, dominoes. There are a few tables on sheltered terraces just outside, with many more on an informal lawn stretching back above the pub. (*Recommended by Ted Burden, Paula Harrison, John and Joy Winterbottom, Barry and Anne, G B Longden, Mike and Jo, Lynn Sharpless, Bob Eardley, Jack Taylor, Gwen and Peter Andrews, John Carter, Rona Murdoch, J S M Sheldon, Ian and Wendy McCaw, Brian Kneale, Beryl and Bill Farmer, Peter and Doreen Wilson, W K Struthers, Mr and Mrs Simon Turner, John and Chris Simpson*)

Free house ~ Licensee John Ligertwood ~ Real ale ~ Meals and snacks (till 10) ~ Restaurant (not Sun evening) ~ (01730) 263584 ~ Children in restaurant and snug ~ Jazz last Mon in month, folk or blues each Weds ~ Open 11-2.30(3 Fri and Sat) 5.30-11

BURSLEDON SU4809 Map 2

Jolly Sailor

2 miles from M27, junction 8; follow B3397 towards Hamble, then A27 towards Salisbury, then just before going under railway bridge turn right towards Bursledon Station; it's best to park round here and walk as the lane up from the station is now closed to cars

A charmingly unspoilt seaside pub, perfectly positioned on the waterfront. Tables in the garden under a big yew tree, and even on the wooden jetty, are just right for watching all the goings on in the rather pretty yachting harbour. The nautical theme continues inside, with ship pictures, nets and shells in the airy front bar, as well as Windsor chairs and settles on its floorboards. The atmospheric beamed and flagstoned back bar, with pews and settles by its huge fireplace, is a fair bit older. Lots of beers including Badger Best and Tanglefoot, Gales HSB, Gribble Bitter, Reg's Tipple and Jolly Sailor and Wadworths 6X on handpump, with an extensive range of country wines; darts, fruit machine and piped music. Under the new managers' home-made bar food includes soup (£1.85), sandwiches (from £1.95), ploughman's (from £3.65), devilled whitebait (£3.75), filled jacket potato or grilled sardines (£3.95), salads (from £4.75), moules marinières, smoked haddock paella with pasta (£4.95), fish and chips or beef and mushroom pie (£5.25) and a catch of the day. The restaurant is no smoking. (*Recommended by Dawn and Phil Garside, Susan and John Douglas, David Lewis, John Atherton, Eamon Green, S Eldridge*)

Badger ~ Managers Stephen and Kathryn Housley ~ Real ale ~ Meals and snacks ~ Restaurant ~ Bursledon (01703) 405557 ~ Children in eating area and restaurant ~ Open 11-11(11-2.30, 6-11 winter weekdays); closed 25 Dec

CHALTON SU7315 Map 2

Red Lion ♀

Village signposted E of A3 Petersfield—Horndean

Hampshire's oldest pub, a really lovely-looking thatched house overlooking the South Downs, first licensed in 1503 though apparently dating back in part to 1150 when a workshop here was site office for the rebuilding of the Norman church opposite. It's far from being undiscovered, but it is worth braving the crowds for the very impressive food, rapidly becoming the centre of attention. Big helpings of sandwiches (from £2), deep fried brie with redcurrant jelly (£3), filled baked potatoes (from £3.20), ploughman's (£3.75) and delicious daily changing specials like chicken in avocado sauce, baked rabbit in lemon sauce or beef casserole (£4.95), grilled trout with clotted cream or salmon steak with lime and pine nuts (£5.50); always a couple of vegetarian meals, as well as children's dishes (£2.95), and a good choice of puddings and ice creams (from £2.25). Food can be eaten anywhere in the pub, though families are usually directed to a modern restaurant extension; service is efficient and friendly. The heavy-beamed and panelled bar has an ancient inglenook fireplace with a frieze of burnished threepenny bits set into its mantelbeam, and is furnished with high-backed traditional settles and elm tables. Gales BBB, Best, HSB and Winter Brew on handpump, along with a changing guest like Morlands Old Speckled Hen; also a good few wines by the glass, over 50 malt whiskies, a variety of country wines (many of which are used in the cooking), coffee, and ten teas ranging from Earl Grey to mango, peppermint and strawberry. Fruit machine, piped music. They run cricket and football teams. Popular with walkers and riders, the pub is fairly close to the extensive Queen Elizabeth Country Park and about half a mile down the lane from a growing Iron Age farm and settlement, and it's only about 20 minutes to the car ferry. (*Recommended by Eileen Akehurst, Penny and Peter Keevil, Theo Schofield, Lynn and Bill Capper, Jack Taylor, Peter and Doreen Wilson, Y M Healey, Lt Cdr L R Ball, John Sanders*)

Gales ~ Managers Mick and Mary McGee ~ Real ale ~ Meals and snacks (till 10; not Sun evening) ~ (01705) 592246 ~ Children in no-smoking family dining room ~ Open 11-2.30(3 Sat), 6-11; closed 25 Dec evening

CHERITON SU5828 Map 2

Flower Pots 🍺

Pub just off B3046 (main village road) towards Beauworth and Winchester; OS Sheet 185 map reference 581282

A flourishing family-run village local with a notably friendly welcome; for many years a popular stop thanks to its simple unspoilt character, it's now winning new support for the range of beers from their micro-brewery, the Cheriton Brewhouse. Current flavoursome and extremely well-priced brews include Cheriton Best, Diggers Gold and Pots Ale. The dedication and enthusiasm of the licensees is evident throughout, and the two little rooms have a really pleasant atmosphere that readers appreciate very much. The quiet and comfortable one on the left has pictures of hounds and ploughmen on its striped wallpaper, bunches of flowers, and a horse and foal and other ornaments on the mantelpiece over a small log fire. Behind the servery there's disused copper filtering equipment, and lots of hanging gin traps, drag-hooks, scaleyards and other ironwork. The range of bar food includes well-priced dishes such as sandwiches (from £1.50, toasted from £1.75), filled jacket potatoes (from £2.50), ploughman's (from £2.75), chilli (£3.50) and beef stew (£3.75); good efficient service. Darts in the neat plain public bar, also cribbage, shove-ha'penny and dominoes; the family room has a TV, board games and colouring books. There are old-fashioned seats on the pretty front and back lawns – very useful in fine weather as they can quickly fill up inside. Near the site of one of the final battles of the Civil War, the pub was built in 1840 by the retired head gardener of nearby Avington Park, which explains the unusual name. As we said last year, the Bartletts aren't ones for standing still – they've recently purchased another pub at Broughton, near Stockbridge, which, after sprucing up, they plan to run along the same lines. (*Recommended by A R and B E Sayer, Ann and Colin Hunt, Lynn Sharpless, Bob Eardley, Phil and Sally Gorton, Ron Shelton, Tom Espley, Graeme Jameson, A Stone, Dr M I Crichton*)

Own Brew ~ Licensees Patricia and Joanna Bartlett ~ Real ale ~ Meals and snacks (till 8.30 Sun evenings, not at all winter Sun evenings) ~ Bramdean (01962) 771318 ~ Children in family room ~ Open 11.30-2.30, 6-11 ~ Bedrooms: £23B/£42B

CRAWLEY SU4234 Map 2

Fox & Hounds 🛏

Village signposted from A272 Winchester—Stockbridge and B3420 Winchester—Andover

A well-deserved return to the main entries for this meticulously run pub, a bizarre-looking building that conjures up a marriage of 1880s Tudor and Sound-of-Music Bavarian. With each timbered upper storey successively jutting further out, lots of pegged structural timbers in the neat brickwork (especially around the latticed windows), and elaborately carved steep gable-ends, it's a striking sight. The scrupulous workmanship continues inside, with oak parquet, latticed windows, and an elegant black timber arch in the small lounge, and neatly panelled black wall benches around the polished copper tables of the beamed main bar. There are fires in both spotlessly maintained rooms – real logs in the lounge, log-effect gas in the other. The regularly changing choice of superbly cooked and presented bar food might include sandwiches, home-made soup or feta cheese and olive salad (£2.25), chicken liver and brandy pâté or prawn-filled avocado pear (£3.50), hot stilton, celery and apple bake (£3.60), various salads (from £4.95), spinach and mushroom pancake or mixed bean casserole (£5.75), steak and kidney pie (£5.95), stuffed courgettes with salmon and prawns or fillets of plaice (£6.25), pan fried black sea bream (£6.50) and minted lamb chops (£6.75); friendly, careful service. Well kept Gales BBB and Wadworths 6X on handpump. The pub's architectural qualities are maintained in the rest of the village, which also has a pretty duckpond. *(Recommended by J N Tyler, Peter and Susan Maguire, Professor H G Allen, Guy Consterdine, Julia Stone, Gill and Brian Pacey, Peter and Doreeen Wilson, Lynn Sharpless, Bob Eardley)*

Free house ~ Licensees Doreen and Luis Sanz-Diez ~ Real ale ~ Meals and snacks ~ Restaurant (not Sun evening) ~ Sparsholt (01962) 72285 ~ Children in restaurant and eating area ~ Open 11.30-2.30(3 Sat), 6.30-11 ~ Bedrooms: £40B/£55B

DROXFORD SU6018 Map 2

White Horse

4 miles along A32 from Wickham

The marvellous atmosphere at this rambling 16th-c coaching inn is much more relaxed than it was in those turn-of-the-century days when they ran dancing classes; a strictly-enforced policy prevented anyone from having a partner unless could do all the steps on their own. Run by a particularly friendly and attentive family, it's very popular indeed at the moment, with the character and food the features people seem to like best. The atmospheric lounge bar is made up of a series of small intimate rooms with attractive furnishings, low beams, bow windows, alcoves and log fires, while the public bar is larger and more straightforward; cribbage, dominoes, pool, shove ha'penny, table football and CD juke box. One of the cubicles in the gents' overlooks an illuminated well. Well kept Burts Bitter, Hartridges Nipper, Morlands Old Speckled Hen, Wadworths 6X and guest on handpump – they're about 5p cheaper in the public bar – and a wide range of country wines; prompt professional service. Popular and generously served bar food includes excellent filling sandwiches (from £1.40, toasted £1.65), home-made soup (£2), green-lipped mussels (£2.50), hot crusty french sticks (from £2.55), ploughman's (from £3), barbecue ribs (£3.65), salads (from £4.05), vegetarian dishes like tomato and vegetable tagliatelle (£4.95), gammon steak (£5.35), rainbow trout and almonds (£5.40), brace of smoked quail (£5.65), steak (from £9.15), well-liked daily specials such as sardines in garlic (£3.95) and steak and Guinness pie (£7.95), and puddings like fruit filled pancakes or Spanish ice cream (from £2.25); children's menu (from £1.80). The landlord's son likes to go deep-sea fishing, so the menu may feature conger eel or skate that he's brought back with him, and it's not uncommon for breakfasts to include mushrooms picked that morning. The restaurant is no smoking. There are tables in a secluded flower-filled courtyard comfortably sheltered by the building's back wings. It's handy for Portsmouth and even Southampton. *(Recommended by John and Joan Nash,*

*Mr and Mrs R J Foreman, Eileen Akehurst, Lynn Sharpless, Bob Eardley, Lt Col E H F
Sawbridge, Professor H G Allen, Peter and Audrey Dowsett, Simon Collett-Jones, Mayur
Shah, G B Longden, B S Bowden, I E and C A Prosser, Betty Lakert, Ann and Colin Hunt,
Mr and Mrs B Salter, Brian Kneale, Barry and Anne, P R Cobb)*

*Free house ~ Licensee Sidney Higgins ~ Real ale ~ Meals and snacks (till 9.45) ~
Restaurant (not Sun evening) ~ (01489) 877490 ~ Children in family room and
restaurant ~ Live bands most bank hol Mons and some Tues evenings ~ Open 11-
3, 6-11; all day Sat in back bar ~ Bedrooms: £25(£40B)/£35(£50B)*

DUMMER   SU5846   Map 2

Queen

Half a mile from M3, junction 7; take Dummer slip road

Much bigger than it looks from the outside but somehow still having an almost
cosy feel, this traditional tiled cottage is a very handy food stop for travellers on
the M3, filling up quite quickly with satisfied diners. Meals are well thought out
and good value, with the menu including warming home-made soup (£2.50),
magnificent sandwiches (from £2.75), potato skins with dips (from £2.95),
omelettes (from £4.95), salads such as tuna, avocado and feta cheese (from
£6.50), generous helpings of hot dishes such as chilli con carne or lasagne
(£5.95), char-grilled steaks (from £9.95), plenty of popular daily specials like
seafood mornay or bangers and mash (£6.50) and pigeon pie (£7.95), Sunday
lunch, and puddings. Service is notably cheery and friendly. The bar is open-plan,
but has a pleasantly alcovey feel, with a liberal use of timbered brick and plaster
partition walls, as well as beams and joists and an open fire. There are built-in
padded seats, cushioned spindleback chairs and stools around the tables on the
dark blue patterned carpet, and pictures of queens, old photographs, small
steeplechase prints and advertisements. Well kept Courage Best and Directors and
Fullers London Pride on handpump, freshly squeezed fruit juice; darts, fruit
machine in one corner, well reproduced pop music. Picnic-table sets under
cocktail parasols on the terrace and in a neat little sheltered back garden.
*(Recommended by J S M Sheldon, Tina and David Woods-Taylor, KC, Tony and Louise
Clarke, Patrick Clancy, Chris Warne, Tony and Wynne Gifford, John Evans, D Cox)*

*Grand Met (Courage) ~ Lease: John and Jocelyn Holland ~ Real ale ~ Meals and
snacks (till 10) ~ Restaurant (not Sun evening) ~ Dummer (01256) 397367 ~
Children over 14 welcome ~ Live entertainment Sun evenings ~ Open 11-3.30,
5.30-11*

IBSLEY   SU1509   Map 2

Old Beams

A338 Ringwood—Salisbury

A steady stream of summer diners flows through this pretty thatched cottage.
Promptly served and well presented, the wide range of tasty home-cooked meals
includes an appetising cold buffet, soup, sandwiches, ploughman's, curries (£5),
braised oxtail (£5.10), quiche (£5.30), steak and kidney pie (£5.85), beef
bourguignon (£6.30), venison in red wine (£6.50), Dover sole (£7.60), char-grilled
scotch steaks (£9), and lots of daily specials; they announce when food is ready
over an intercom. An excellent range of real ales such as Bass, Eldridge Pope Royal
Oak, Gales HSB, Gibbs Mew Bishops Tipple, Ringwood Best and Old Thumper,
and Wadworths 6X on handpump, as well as decent wines by the glass, country
wines and some foreign bottled beers. The main room is divided by wooden
panelling and a canopied log-effect gas fire, and there are lots of varnished wooden
tables and country-kitchen chairs under the appropriately aged oak beams. It's
spacious and comfortable, with more room inside than you might expect – just as
well as it can get very full. Part of the eating area and half the restaurant are no-
smoking. The garden behind has picnic-table sets among its trees, and a
trampoline; as we went to press they were planning to add a conservatory.
(Recommended by Colin Barnett, Ruth Trott, John Watson, RH, Mr and Mrs Hawkins, S

Eldridge, D Baker, Basil J S Minson, Dr Gerald W Barnett, M J D Inskip, M Veldhuyzen)

Free house ~ Licensees R Major and C Newell ~ Real ale ~ Meals and snacks (till 10pm) ~ Restaurant (not Sun evening) ~ Ringwood (01425) 473387 ~ Children in eating area, restaurant and family room ~ Open 10.30-2.30, 6-11(10.30 winter)

LANGSTONE SU7105 Map 2

Royal Oak

High Street; last turn left off A3023 (confusingly called A324 on some signs) before Hayling Island bridge

Most people come to this delightfully-placed old pub in the summer, but it can be just as satisfying in the winter, when through the windows in the bar you can watch the afternoon sun slowly slip away over Hayling Island. The pretty building is right on the edge of a landlocked natural harbour, and the garden has good views of the water too, as well as a pets' corner with goats, rabbits and a pot-bellied pig. At high tide swans come right up to here, much as they must have done when it was a landing point for the 18th-c Langstone Gang, a notorious group of smugglers. Unhurried and peaceful, even in summer, the spacious flagstoned bar is simply furnished with Windsor chairs around old wooden tables on the wooden parquet and ancient flagstones, and two open fires in winter. Bar food is much what you'd find in other Whitbreads Wayside Inns, including home-made soup (hearty here, £1.45), french bread well filled with ham or cheese (from £2.15), ploughman's (£3.55), vegetarian dishes like ratatouille or macaroni cheese and celery bake (from £3.75), steak and kidney pie (£4.25), lasagne (£4.85), roast of the day (£5.50), a good choice of fresh local fish (from £5.95) and rump steak (£7.50); the service is very well organised. Well kept Boddingtons, Flowers Original, Gales HSB, Morlands Old Speckled Hen and Wadworths 6X on handpump, as well as Bulmer's cider; welcoming smartly dressed staff. Though this is part of a chain, it is an individual place, and readers continue to be impressed with the personal service. (*Recommended by Brenda and Jim Langley, Ted Burden, Viv Middlebrook, Richard and Maria Gillespie, David Eberlin, Wayne Brindle, A Craig, J E Hilditch, Ian Phillips, R C Vincent, Mrs D Craig, Lawrence Pearse*)

Whitbreads ~ Manager Paul Clarke ~ Real ale ~ Meals and snacks (12-9.30) ~ Portsmouth (01705) 483125 ~ Children in eating area ~ Parking at all close may be very difficult ~ Open 11-11

LYMINGTON SZ3194 Map 2

Chequers ♀

¾ mile down Ridgeway Lane; marked as dead end just south of A337 roundabout in Pennington W of Lymington, by White Hart; please note this pub was listed under Pennington in some previous editions

Very well run by the Jamiesons, this pleasantly tucked away yachtsmen's local is simple but stylish, with a good range of home-made bar food that always seems to have had plenty of thought put into it. The blackboard menu changes daily but might typically include lunchtime filled french sticks (from £1.50), home-made soup (£2), asparagus salad, moules marinières or ploughman's (from £3.50), garlic bread with cheese and prawns (£3.50), half rack barbecue ribs (£4.75), a vegetarian meal, pork in cider with apples, lamb cassoulet or steak gigot in orange and redcurrant sauce (from £6.95), fish dishes like cod mornay, Dover sole, trout with prawns and almonds, steaks (from £8.95), and puddings; Sunday roasts (£5.50). Well kept Bass, Wadworths 6X, Whitbreads Strong Country and two changing guests like Devonish Cornish Original, Gales HSB, Greene King Abbot and Morlands Old Speckled Hen on handpump; Whitbreads own the freehold but it's run as a free house. Also lots of wines, and various rums, whiskies and brandies. The bar has a nice old-fashioned feel with polished floorboards and crisp quarry-tiles, a cannon by the fireplace, attractive local landscapes and townscapes above the green dado, and plain chairs and wall pews around wooden or cast-iron-framed tables; the atmosphere may be smoky. Very friendly service; well chosen and reproduced piped pop music, cribbage, dominoes and darts. There are picnic-table sets out in its neat sheltered garden, with teak tables on a terrace below, and more tables in an inner courtyard; there may be barbecues out here in summer. They tell us rules for dogs are the same as for children. (*Recommended by Bernard Phillips, E G Parish, Martin, Jane, Simon and Laura Bailey, W K Struthers, Peter and Doreen Wilson*)

Whitbreads ~ Lease: Michael and Maggie Jamieson ~ Real ale ~ Meals and snacks (till 10, 9.30 Sun) ~ Restaurant ~ Lymington (01590) 673415 ~ Well behaved children welcome ~ Open 11-3, 6-11; closed 25 Dec

MATTINGLEY SU7357 Map 2

Leather Bottle

3 miles from M3, junction 5; in Hook, turn right-and-left on to B3349 Reading Road (former A32)

A riot of colour in summer, this cosy brick and tiled pub has lots of tubs and baskets of bright flowers, and wisteria, honeysuckle and roses both at the front and in the attractive tree-sheltered garden. The busy beamed main bar is friendly and relaxed, and has some inglenook fireplaces (one with a ticking metal clock over it), brocaded built-in wall seats, little curved low-backed wooden chairs, red plush bar stools, some sabres on the cream wall, and a good local atmosphere. At the back is the characterful cottagey second bar with lots of black beams, an antique clock, country pictures on the walls (some stripped to brick), lantern lighting, sturdy inlaid tables with seats, and a red carpet on bare floorboards. Good value bar food includes sandwiches (from £1.60, toasted ham, mushroom and egg – named a Tom Special for one of the regulars – £3.20, steak £4.50), soup (£1.95), various ploughman's (from £3.75), salads (from £5), vegetable balti (£5.80), lasagne (£6.50), prawn curry (£6.90), char-grilled salmon, halibut and monkfish (£8.50), and roast duckling with orange sauce (£11.80); puddings like lemon brûlée (£2.30). Well kept beers on handpump or tapped from the cask include Courage Best and Directors and interesting guest beers bought direct from small breweries, such as Glenny Hobgoblin and Moles Bitter; also coffee; prompt friendly service; trivia machine, maybe unobtrusive piped music. (*Recommended by TBB, David Warrellow, Theo Schofield, J N Tyler, D A Edwards, Chris Warne, KC, Tony and Val Marshall, Stephen Brown, Lynn Sharpless, Bob Eardley*)

Courage ~ Lease: Richard and Pauline Moore ~ Real ale ~ Meals and snacks (till 10) ~ (01734) 326371 ~ Children in eating area ~ Open 11-2.30, 6-11

OVINGTON SU5531 Map 2

Bush ★ ♀

Village signposted from A31 on Winchester side of Alresford

Civilised and quietly upmarket, this charming little tucked-away cottage remains a firm favourite with readers, many of whom find it hard to resist a post-prandial stroll along the banks of the River Itchen. It gets very busy in summer, when there are seats running down to the water, and more on a tree-sheltered pergola dining terrace with a good-sized fountain pool. We like it best though on chilly winter weekdays when the atmosphere is undisturbed by lots of people, and the low-ceilinged bar has a warmly cosy feel that immediately makes you feel at home. There's a roaring fire on one side with an antique solid fuel stove opposite, as well as cushioned high-backed settles, elm tables with pews and kitchen chairs, and masses of old pictures in heavy gilt frames on the green walls. Very tasty home-made bar food includes sandwiches (from £1.75), home-made soup (£1.95), ploughman's (from £3.50), spinach and cream cheese roulade (£3.25), brie croquettes with gooseberry sauce (£3.75), macaroni cheese with walnuts and grapes (£5.25), summer vegetable pie (£5.75), chilli (£5.95), good green-lipped mussels in garlic butter (£6.75), daily specials, puddings (from £1.50) and children's dishes (from £2.50); the restaurant meals are very elaborate. Service is friendly and prompt, even at their busiest. Well kept Badger Tanglefoot, Flowers Original, Gales HSB, Wadworths 6X and Whitbreads Strong Country on handpump; a good choice of wines and country wines. It's handy for the A31, and there are nice walks nearby. (*Recommended by Lynn Sharpless, Bob Eardley, David Rule, John Le Sage, Tom Espley, Martin and Pauline Richardson, Roy Smylie, Derek and Margaret Underwood, KCW, Jenny and Brian Seller, J L Hall, Mike Davies, J S M Sheldon, A Honigmann, J L Archambault, Peter and Doreen Wilson, Mayur Shah, Ian Jones*)

Free house ~ Licensees Geoff and Sue Draper ~ Real ale ~ Meals and snacks ~ Evening restaurant (not Sun) ~ Alresford (01962) 732764 ~ Nearby parking may be difficult ~ Children in eating area of bar lunchtimes and restaurant evenings ~ Open 11-2.30, 6-11

nr PETERSFIELD SU7423 Map 2

White Horse ★ ★ ◖

Priors Dean – but don't follow Priors Dean signposts: simplest route is from Petersfield, leaving centre on A272 towards Winchester, take right turn at roundabout after level crossing, towards Steep, and keep on for 4 miles or so, up on to the downs, passing another pub on your right (and not turning off into Steep there); at last, at crossroads signposted East Tisted/Privett, turn right towards East Tisted, then almost at once turn right on to second gravel track (the first just goes into a field); there's no inn sign; alternatively, from A32 5 miles S of Alton, take road by bus lay-by signposted Steep, then, after 1¾ miles, turn off as above – though obviously left this time – at East Tisted/Privett crossroads; OS Sheet 197 coming from Petersfield (Sheet 186 is better the other way), map reference 715290

Tracking down this wonderfully unchanging old farmhouse is half the fun, its apparent reluctance to be found adding to the feeling that this is a place from another era, a place the rest of the world has left far behind. For many people it's all a traditional country pub should be, and the good-hearted landlord tells us he runs it in the style of the pubs he used to look for 40 years ago. Of course pubs have changed a lot since then, and so have their customers, so if you come here looking for elaborate meals, smart decor and family play areas then you're going to be disappointed. It's the unique atmosphere and character that earn the White Horse its continued high rating, and both of these owe a lot to the licensee, who for the past 20 years has offered the same down-to-earth Lancashire welcome to locals and visitors alike. One of the things readers find most endearing is the – (how can we put it?) – somewhat lived-in look of the place, but recent years have seen a few concessions to modernity: new covers, fresh paint, and now the threat of a new carpet. The two charming and highly idiosyncratic parlour rooms are full of a relaxing mix of furnishings and bric-a-brac: old pictures, farm tools, drop-leaf tables, oak settles, rugs, stuffed antelope heads, longcase clock, and a fireside rocking-chair to name a few. An excellent and well-priced range of a dozen or so beers on handpump includes the very strong No Name Bitter, as well as Ballards Best, Courage Best and Directors, John Smiths, King & Barnes Sussex Bitter and Sussex Mild, Ringwood Fortyniner, and Theakstons Old Peculier. Around 26 country wines, some sparkling, are tapped from small china kegs and may be mulled in the winter; they also have a wine from a local vineyard. Shove-ha'penny, dominoes, cribbage. Bar food generally includes sandwiches, good thick soup (£2.10, winter only, as it's done overnight on the Aga), ploughman's (from £2.95), and a few daily changing home-made meals such as spinach and mushroom lasagne (£3.75), chicken, ham and leek pie (£4.95) and gammon, chicken and mushroom pie (£5.25); the menu is usually rather limited on winter Sunday lunchtimes. They've usually got local eggs for sale, including organic free range ones, and in season pheasants too. There are of course times (not always predictable, with Sundays – even in winter – often busier than Saturdays) when the place does get packed. Rustic seats (which include chunks of tree-trunk) and a terrace outside; as this is one of the highest spots in the county it can be quite breezy. A nearby field has caravan facilities, and is regularly used for pony club meetings – as well as a landing place for the odd Tiger Moth plane or hot-air balloon. If trying to find it for the first time, keep your eyes skinned – not for nothing is this known as the Pub With No Name. In past editions this pub has had three stars. This year, as explained at the start of the book, we have revised the star grading system to amalgamate the two-star and three-star grades – the change in rating does not reflect any lowering of our exceptionally high opinion of the White Horse. *(Recommended by J S M Sheldon, Lynn Sharpless, Bob Eardley, David and Michelle Hedges, Ann and Colin Hunt, Julie Munday, Martin Robinson, John and Christine Simpson, Owen Upton, Mark and Diane Grist, Gordon, R J Walden, Don Kellaway, Angie Coles, Jason Caulkin, Peter and Lynn Brueton, James Nunns, Wayne Brindle, KCW, Steve Tasker, Stephen, Julie and Hayley Brown, Mr and Mrs Simon Turner, Nigel Norman, Barbara Hatfield, Peter and Doreen Wilson, Barry and Anne, Wendy Arnold)*

Free house ~ Licensee Jack Eddleston ~ Real ale ~ Meals and snacks (not Sun lunchtime) ~ (0142 058) 387 ~ Children not allowed in ~ Open 11-2.30(3 Sat), 6-11

PILLEY SZ3298 Map 2

Fleur de Lys

Village signposted off A337 Brockenhurst—Lymington

The landlord who took over this pretty thatched house just as we were going to press seems to share the same pub philosophy as his predecessor, so hopefully things should remain much the same. Of course a change of licensee means another name added to the list in the entrance-way, which traces back the holders of this position over the last 500 years. In fact this isn't the whole story, as there's evidence that an inn of some sort existed here in Norman times, making this the oldest pub in the New Forest. There's plenty of character in the heavy-beamed lounge bar, with lots of bric-a-brac and a huge inglenook log fire. Bar food currently includes sandwiches, and hot dishes like rabbit in spring onion and ginger sauce (£6.50), honey roast barbecue ribs (£7.25), and pheasant in whisky and raspberry sauce (£8.25). Brakspears, Flowers Original, Morlands Old Speckled Hen and Marstons Pedigree on handpump, Gales country wines, and Scrumpy Jack cider; fruit machine. There are tables and swings out in quite an individual garden (with a grinder pressed into service as a flowerpot, for instance), where there's also a dovecote whose inhabitants can be fed by hand. *(Recommended by A D Marsh, Lynn Sharpless, Bob Eardley, Andrew Shore, Michael Leigh, Mrs P MacFarlane, Stephen Oxley, Dr M Onton, Julia Stone, Sally Edsall, Gill and Mike Cross; reports on the new regime please)*

Whitbreads ~ Lease: Craig Smallwood ~ Real ale ~ Meals and snacks ~ Restaurant ~ (01590) 672158 ~ Children welcome ~ Open 11-2.30, 6-11 (10.30 winter)

PORTSMOUTH SZ6501 Map 2

Still & West

Bath Square; follow A3 and Isle of Wight Ferry signs to Old Portsmouth water's edge

The ships that pass by the terrace and upstairs restaurant of this wonderfully positioned waterside pub are so close you could almost reach out and touch them. Such unrivalled views mean it does get busy, especially on fine days, but it's a friendly, cheery place and the extra people rather add to the atmosphere. The bar is comfortably decorated in nautical style, ship models, an early brass submarine periscope and so forth, and has very well kept Gales BBB and HSB on handpump or electric pump, with a guest like Everards Tiger, Morlands Old Speckled Hen or Morrells Varsity, along with some aged whiskies and the full range of Gales country wines. Popular bar food here includes traditional fish and chips (wrapped in newspaper ready to take away if you want, £2.95), a proper ploughman's (£3.95) and around 10-15 cheeses from around the world. A wider range of meals in the upstairs restaurant features plenty of fresh fish dishes like haddock gratinée (£5.50) or halibut Véronique (£7.95). Parking can be quite difficult. The pub is quite near to HMS *Victory*. *(Recommended by D Grzelka, Alan Bunt, Peter and Audrey Dowsett and others)*

Gales ~ Managers Mick and Lynn Finnerty ~ Real ale ~ Meals and snacks ~ Restaurant ~ (01705) 821567 ~ Children in restaurant ~ Live music evenings Sun and maybe Mon ~ Open 10-11

ROCKBOURNE SU1118 Map 2

Rose & Thistle ♀

Village signposted from B3078 Fordingbridge—Cranborne

The smartly civilised atmosphere at this attractive thatched 17th-c pub is well liked, but perhaps the feature praised most highly is the extremely good (though not always cheap) bar food. Typical dishes might include sandwiches, soup (£2.45), soft herring roes on toast or avocado topped with stilton cheese (£3.95), ploughman's (£4.25), scrambled egg with smoked salmon and prawns or Welsh rarebit (£5.25), tagliatelle with mushrooms, ham and cream (£5.75), daily specials like chicken stuffed with stilton and walnuts in a creamy cheese sauce, quail in pastry with spinach, apricot and brandy sauce or Dover sole, and puddings such as chocolate roulade or their deliciously rich sticky toffee pudding (£3.25); on some Sundays they may only do a three-course set meal (£12). Friendly service. Well kept Butcombe Bitter, Courage Best, Gales HSB, Hopback Summer Lightning, Marston's Pedigree and Wadworths 6X on handpump, with a good range of wines from around the world, some by the glass. The public bar has tables arranged like booths, old engravings, sparkling brass and a good log fire, as well as new furnishings such as lovely polished tables and carved benches; darts, cribbage, shove ha'penny, dominoes, shut the box and boules. There are tables by a thatched dovecote in the neat front garden, and the charming village has the excavated remains of a Roman villa. (*Recommended by Dave Braisted, Joe Jonkler, Jerry and Alsion Oakes, Jason Caulkin, J H L Davis and others*)

Free house ~ Licensee Tim Norfolk ~ Real ale ~ Meals and snacks ~ Restaurant ~ (017253) 236 ~ Children in separate restaurant only ~ Open 11-3, 6-11; winter 12-3, 7-10.30

ROTHERWICK SU7156 Map 2

Coach & Horses ◀

4 miles from M3, junction 5; follow Newnham signpost from exit roundabout, then Rotherwick signpost, then turn right at Mattingley, Heckfield signpost; village also signposted from A32 N of Hook

Thanks mainly to its wonderfully relaxed and away-from-it-all feel, this creeper-covered 16th-c pub is a pleasant place to spend an evening. It's always spotless, and everything seems to be done with an air of efficiency, while the staff are consistently friendly and helpful. A fine choice of unusual well kept real ales on handpump dispensed at the servery in the parquet-floored inner area includes Badger Best, Hard Tackle and Tanglefoot, Charles Wells Eagle, Gribble Black Adder and Wadworths 6X; pleasant service. The two small beamed front rooms each have a stripped brick open fireplace, oak chairs and other interesting furniture, and a fine assortment of attractive pictures; one is tiled, the other flagstoned, and one is no-smoking. The menu usually includes around five speciality sausages, served with well-chosen sauces and vegetables (£5.45), as well as sandwiches (from £1.50), chilli or mushroom stroganoff (£4.25), stilton and broccoli pasta (£4.95), various pies (£5.25 – the steak and kidney is good), boozy beef stew (£5.35) and steaks (from £5.75); children's menu (£2.95), Sunday roasts. They do sandwiches and soup all day. Cribbage, dominoes, backgammon, Connect Four and Scrabble, and a Sunday night quiz. In summer it's surrounded by tubs and baskets of flowers, and there are rustic seats and picnic-table sets under cocktail parasols. (*Recommended by Martin Jones, Chris Warne, KC, Derek and Sylvia Stephenson, D A Edwards, D Cox, Chris and Anne Fluck, Roger and Jenny Huggins, Ron Corbett, Stephen, Julie and Hayley Brown, Dr Paul Kitchener, Nigel Norman, Mark Every, Lynn Sharpless, Bob Eardley*)

Badger ~ Manager Albert Rhodes ~ Real ale ~ Meals and snacks (till 10, 9.30 Sun) ~ Restaurant ~ Rotherwick (01256) 762542 ~ Children in eating area ~ Open 11-11

Sunday opening is generally 12-3 and 7-10.30 throughout England.

SOPLEY SZ1597 Map 2

Woolpack

B3347 N of Christchurch; village signposted off A338 N of Bournemouth

This friendly waterside pub is a busy place – in fact tables often fill up so quickly they've had to add a couple extra in a little tent at the side of the conservatory. On fine days though there should be plenty of space in the garden, an ideal spot to watch the ducks dabbling about on the little chalk stream under the weeping willows, by the little bridge that leads over to a grassy children's play area with a swing and climbing frame. The rambling low-beamed open-plan bar has a good local atmosphere, and very good, attentive service. It's furnished with red leatherette wall seats and simple wooden chairs around heavy rustic tables, and has both a woodburning stove and a small black kitchen range. A wide choice of good-value bar meals includes filled rolls (from £2.95), and well-liked main courses like cod wrapped in newspaper, Thai-style chicken curry or gammon hock in cider sauce (all around £5.95); some dishes may be slightly more expensive in the evenings. Well kept Flowers Original, Ringwood Best, Wadworths 6X on handpump, maybe under light blanket pressure; boules pitch outside, piped music. Short-sighted readers should note that the bird on the thatched roof is made of straw too. (*Recommended by Anna and Steven Oxley, Andy and Jill Kassube, Peter and Doreen Wilson, J Morris, C J Westmoreland*)

Whitbreads ~ Lease: Barbara and Dick Goemaat ~ Real ale ~ Meals and snacks ~ (01425) 672252 ~ Regular piano or pianola nights ~ Open 11-11

SOUTHSEA SZ6498 Map 2

Wine Vaults £ ◗

Albert Rd, opp Kings Theatre

Though this is a very simple place, there's a rather unusual atmosphere that makes it something more, and it's especially nice to see how visitors of quite different ages immediately feel comfortable and welcome. The main attraction is the beer, with at least 10 different real ales on handpump at any one time. These might include Ballards Best, Bass, Exe Valley, Exmoor Stag, Harveys Best, Hop Back Summer Lightning and GFB, Otter Ale and Bitter, Ringwood Fortyniner, Best, and Old Thumper, and Smiles Bitter; they have special offers for cheap beer on Monday evenings, and hold beer festivals in March and November. The bar has wood-panelled walls, a wooden floor, Wild West saloon-type swing doors, and an easy-going, chatty feel. Mainly straightforward but very well priced bar food comes in big helpings, from a range that includes sandwiches, soup such as well-liked potato and watercress, tasty home-made vegetarian meals (£2.75) and meat dishes like chicken and walnut lasagne (£2.95). The one-eyed black labrador is called Ziggy. No noisy games machines or piped music, and no children. Dogs welcome. (*Recommended by Graham Brooks, Sue Anderson, Phil Copleston, John Beeken, Andy and Jill Kassube, Bill Sykes, Ann and Colin Hunt, Lynn Sharpless, Bob Eardley, J Boylan, James K McDonell*)

Free house ~ Licensee M R A Hughes ~ Real ale ~ Meals and snacks (12-2, 5.30-9.30 9 weekends) ~ (01705) 864712 ~ Open 11.30-3.30, 5.30-11; 11-11 Sat

SPARSHOLT SU4331 Map 2

Plough ♀

Village signposted off A272 a little W of Winchester

Enlarged and opened up under go-ahead new licensees, the Plough's doing very well, popular with older people on weekday lunchtimes, and with families at weekends. The main draw is now the food, from good doorstep sandwiches or filled baguettes (£2.25), interesting soups such as carrot and cranberry or brie with cucumber (£3), ploughman's (from £3.75), vegetarian dishes such as tagliatelle with tomato and chilli (£4.95) or courgettes and fennel in filo pastry (£5.25), curries with real spices, unusual smoked and other sausage dishes (£6.50), and a tasty lemon chicken casserole (£6.75). There's a changing choice of good puddings (£2.25), and as well as specific children's dishes they'll do small helpings for children. Besides generous measures of decent house wines, with a choice of six by the glass, they have well kept Wadworths IPA and 6X and a guest beer changing fortnightly such as Everards Tiger. The main bar area, with plenty of tables and comfortable seats, has been extended into what was the next-door cottage, and is a pleasant and airy mix of cream paintwork, stripped brick and some panelling. The side bar has bar billiards, cribbage and dominoes, and there may be unobtrusive piped radio. There are tables outside, with a climbing frame, and even donkeys and hens. *(Recommended by Lynn Sharpless, Bob Eardley, Peter and Doreen Wilson, John and Joy Winterbottom, Alan and Julie Wear, John and Joan Calvert)*

Wadworths ~ Tenants Bernie Startup and Sarah Hinman ~ Real ale ~ Meals and snacks (till later evening Fri/Sat) ~ (01962) 776353 ~ Well behaved children allowed ~ Occasional informal music ~ Open 11-3, 6.30(7 Sat); cl evening 25 Dec

STEEP SU7425 Map 2

Harrow

Take Midhurst exit from Petersfield bypass, at exit roundabout first left towards Midhurst, then first turning on left opposite garage, and left again at Sheet church; follow over motorway bridge to pub

Another claimant for the title of the Pub That Time Forgot, a charmingly old-fashioned family-run place with a remarkably homely atmosphere, where only the gentle ticking of the clock reminds you it will soon be time to leave. The little public bar is perhaps the nicest, with its tiled floor, built-in wall benches around scrubbed deal tables, a good log fire in the big inglenook, stripped pine wallboards, and dominoes or cribbage. Hops and dried flowers hang from the beams. Enormous helpings of good simple home-cooked bar food such as home-made scotch eggs (£1.30), sandwiches (from £1.70), excellent soups overflowing from old-fashioned bowls, huge ploughman's (from £3.40), various quiches, home-cooked ham, lasagne or cauliflower cheese (£4.90), and salads served on a gigantic carving plate (from £6.50); puddings include a delicious treacle tart. Boddingtons, Flowers Original and Whitbread Strong Country tapped from casks behind the counter, country wines, Bulmers cider; polite and friendly staff, even when under pressure. The big garden is left free-flowering so that goldfinches can collect thistle seeds from the grass. There are lots of tables out here, and it's the only part children are allowed in. Lavatories are outside, but very clean. The Petersfield bypass doesn't intrude on this idyll, though you will need to follow the directions above to find it. *(Recommended by Nick Twining, B S Bowden, Mrs B M Spurr, Professor A N Black, Lynn Sharpless, Bob Eardley, Mark and Diane Grist, R C Watkins, Anna Marsh, W T Healey, Phil and Sally Gorton, Susan and John Douglas, Sheila Edwards, C H Stride, Julia Stone)*

Free house ~ Licensee Edward C McCutcheon ~ Real ale ~ Snacks (till 10) ~ Petersfield (01730) 262685 ~ Children in garden only ~ Open 11-2.30(3 Sat), 6-11

STOCKBRIDGE SU3535 Map 2

Vine

High St (A30)

Though there's still a distinctive pubby feel to this popular old coaching inn, the emphasis is very much on eating, with readers this year picking out as favourite dishes the sandwiches, soup (£2.15), tagliatelle with walnuts, grapes and sour cream (£3.45), ploughman's (£3.55), Norwegian green-lipped mussels with smoked halibut (£3.75), grilled salmon and monkfish brochette on a bed of wild rice (£9.95) and 12oz T-bone steak (£11.25). There's also a good range of fish dishes, with trout fresh from the stream at the end of the garden. They warn of delays with some meals, and booking is advisable at weekends. They also do summer barbecues. The open-plan bar is comfortably pleasant, with an interesting combination of woodwork, brickwork and papered walls, a delft shelf of china and pewter, and old-gold velvet curtains. Boddingtons, Morlands Old Speckled Hen, Ringwood Best and Wadworths 6X on handpump, maybe under light blanket pressure; a small but decent wine list. Very good obliging service; darts, dominoes, maybe piped music. (*Recommended by J F Burness, Dr and Mrs Nigel Holmes, Ann and Colin Hunt, Mr and Mrs G P Tobin, A R and B E Sayer, John Sanders, Mr and Mrs A Craig, D A Edwards, Mr and Mrs R J Foreman, R Hepburn, Peter and Doreen Wilson, Mr and Mrs M Bullivant*)

Whitbreads ~ Tenant John Green ~ Meals and snacks (12-2.30, 6.30-10) ~ Restaurant (teas 3.30-5.30) ~ Andover (01264) 810652 ~ Children in restaurant ~ Open 11-2.30(3 Sat), 6-11; may be all day summer Sats ~ Bedrooms: £22.50/£37.50

TICHBORNE SU5630 Map 2

Tichborne Arms

Village signed off A31 just W of Alresford

Never failing to please, this attractive thatched pub is a firm favourite with a good many readers, none of whom could this year voice even the slightest criticism. It's the food they like best of all, with a very good, often imaginative, range of home-made bar meals, particularly praiseworthy for excellent use of fresh ingredients. On a typical day the choice might include soup (£2, the stilton and celery is recommended), sandwiches (from £1.30, prawn £2.75, lots of interesting toasties from £1.95), liver and bacon nibbles with a home-made dip (£2.25), ploughman's (from £3.30 – the ham version is especially good), baked potatoes with a fine range of fillings (from £3.50), salads (from £4.75), daily specials such as liver, bacon and onion casserole or well-liked turkey curry (£4.95), steak and mushroom pie (£5.25), chicken breasts with apricot and brandy (£5.75), and puddings like meringues with ice cream, fudge and walnut flan or lemon sponge (£2); they warn of delays at busy times. The comfortable, square-panelled room on the right has pictures and documents on the walls recalling the bizarre Tichborne Case, when a mystery man from Australia claimed fraudulently to be the heir to this estate, as well as a log fire in an attractive stone fireplace, wheelback chairs and settles (one very long), and latticed windows with flowery curtains. On the left, a larger and livelier room, partly panelled and also carpeted, has sensibly placed darts, cribbage, shove-ha'penny, dominoes and a fruit machine; well kept Boddingtons, Flowers IPA and Original and Wadworths 6X tapped from the cask, and country wines; excellent friendly service. There are picnic-table sets outside in the big well kept garden. Dogs are made very welcome, but please note they don't allow children under 14 into the bars. (*Recommended by Lynn Sharpless, Bob Eardley, A N Black, Phil and Sally Gorton, Ron Shelton, Paul Adams, Ewa Sawicka, Martin and Karen Wake, J L Hall, Mayur Shah, Rita and Derrick Barrey, Julia Stone, P J Guy, R Wilson, Marjorie and David Lamb, A N Black, Harriet and Michael Robinson, Dr and Mrs R E Tanner, Peter and Doreen Wilson*)

Free house ~ Licensees Chris and Peter Byron ~ Real ale ~ Meals and snacks (12-1.45, 6.30-9.45) ~ (01962) 733 760 ~ Open 11.30-2.30, 6-11

UPHAM SU5320 Map 2

Brushmakers Arms

Shoe Lane; village signposted from Winchester—Bishops Waltham downs road, and from B2177 (former A333)

Regular visitors say this comfortably modernised pub keeps getting better, and they particularly like the chatty, welcoming atmosphere. The L-shaped bar, extended in the late 1980s, is divided into two by a central brick chimney, the raised two-way fireplace filled by a round woodburning stove, and has a few beams in its low ceiling, comfortably cushioned wall settles and chairs, and a variety of tables including some in country-style stripped wood; there's quite a collection of ethnic-looking brushes. Well kept Bass, Ringwood Best and a guest like Ruddles County or Ringwood 49er on handpump, Gales country wines and several malt whiskies. Good reasonably priced bar food includes sandwiches, leeks wrapped in ham and covered in cheese sauce or pasta with stilton and bacon (£3.95), turkey and cranberry pie (£4.25), braised beef in mustard sauce (£4.50), duck à l'orange (£7.95), 8oz sirloin steak with boursin (£8.75), and Sunday roasts (£4.95). Sensibly placed darts, dominoes, cribbage and video game; the friendly dog is called Rosie. There are picnic-table sets on a sheltered back terrace among lots of tubs of flowers, and on the tidy tree-sheltered lawn. There's not much parking nearby. (*Recommended by A R and B E Sayer, John and Joan Nash, Lynn Sharpless, Bob Eardley, Peter and Doreen Wilson*)

Free house ~ Licensees Sue and Andy Cobb ~ Real ale ~ Meals and snacks all day ~ (01489) 860231 ~ Children allowed away from bar ~ Open 11-2.30, 6-11, all day Sat

VERNHAM DEAN SU3456 Map 2

George

On the old coach road going NW from Hurstbourne Tarrant; follow Upton signpost from A343; or from A338 5 miles S of Hungerford follow Oxenwood signpost and keep on

Popular with all ages, this charming old-fashioned village pub is one of those places where you know everything is going to be just right. The atmosphere is relaxed, the food good and reasonably-priced, the staff friendly – and the garden behind can be a joy in summer. Well run and spotless, the rambling open-plan beamed bar has a lovely polished elm table, traditional black wall seats built into the panelled dado, some easy chairs, and a log fire in its big inglenook fireplace. Tasty and generously served home cooking includes toasted sandwiches (including Mary's Scraps with a bit of everything), soup with home-made stock, various ploughman's, gently garlicky mushrooms with a bacon and cheese topping (£3.75), good corned beef hash pie or a layered cheese, bacon and onion pie (£3.90), seasonal game dishes such as winter rabbit stew or pheasant and pigeon, and puddings like good treacle tart with ice cream; vegetables now come from the pub's own garden, and its flowers adorn the tables. Service is slower at busy periods. Well kept Marstons Best and Pedigree on handpump; dominoes, cribbage and trivia machine. There are tables in the pretty garden behind. (*Recommended by Colin and Ann Hunt, Lynn Sharpless, Bob Eardley, Professor A N Black, Brenda and Jim Langley, Alan and Julie Wear, I E and C A Prosser, Basil Minson, E H George, Peter and Doreen Wilson, Jeff Davies, C G T Herbert*)

Marstons ~ Tenants Mary and Philip Perry ~ Real ale ~ Meals and snacks (not evenings Sun or Weds) ~ (01264) 87 279 ~ Well behaved children in family area ~ Open 11-2.30(3 Sat), 6-11; closed evening 25 Dec

WELL SU7646 Map 2

Chequers

5 miles W of Farnham; off A287 via Crondall, or A31 via Froyle and Lower Froyle (easier if longer than via Bentley); from A32 S of Odiham, go via Long Sutton; OS Sheet 186 map reference 761467

A smart but relaxing and ever so English country pub, delightful on a summer day. It's run by the people who own the excellent Sporting Page and Front Page in London, and the style is very much the same. The spotlessly kept snug rooms, full of alcoves, have low beams, wooden pews and old stools, books on a shelf for reading (not just show), GWR carriage lamps, a few horsebrasses, panelled walls with lots of 18th-c country-life prints, and old sepia photographs of locals enjoying a drink. As with the London pubs, the food is just that bit different, with enterprising home-made dishes like soup (£2.50), pâté or cheese and bacon potato skins (£3.50), ploughman's or avocado and prawn salad (£4.25), pasta of the day (£4.95), coronation chicken (£5.25), seafood vol au vents or smoked salmon and scrambled eggs (£5.50), dressed crab salad (£7.95), grilled monkfish tails (£8.25), and puddings such as white chocolate cheesecake; good prompt service. Well kept

Boddingtons, Fremlins and Flowers Original on handpump, and decent wines. In the back replanted and tidied-up garden are some chunky picnic-table sets; at the front, there's an interesting looking vine-covered arbour (they sometimes make wine for cooking from the grapes) – though it doesn't look quite so idyllic in winter. (*Recommended by John and Christine Simpson, Keith Widdowson, Julia Stone, J A Stein, Susan and John Douglas, Martin and Karen Wake, Ian Phillips, Dr and Mrs R E S Tanner, A and A Dale, Simon Collett-Jones, Lynn Sharpless, Bob Eardley*)

Free house ~ Licensees Christopher Phillips, Rupert Fowler ~ Real ale ~ Meals and snacks (till 10) ~ Restaurant (not Sun) ~ Basingstoke (01256) 862605 ~ Children welcome ~ Open 11-3, 5.30-11

nr WHERWELL SU3839 Map 2

Mayfly

Testcombe; A3057 SE of Andover, between B3420 turn-off and Leckford where road crosses River Test; OS Sheet 185 map reference 382390

It's well worth getting here in good time if you're planning to eat, as the lovely riverside setting is something of a magnet, and on a sunny day they do get busy. The wide range of cheeses really stands out, with a choice of around three dozen served with fresh crusty wholemeal bread (£2.95); other popular meals include home-made quiche (£2.95), smoked trout (£3), chicken tandoori (£3.60), unusual salads, and a selection of cold meats such as topside of beef (from £3.60), served with big helpings from eight or so attractive salads (70p extra each). The buffet-style system can lead to queues at busy periods. In the winter they add hot dishes such as braised oxtail or steak and vegetable pie. The spacious, beamed and carpeted bar has fishing pictures and bric-a-brac on the cream walls above a dark wood dado, Windsor chairs around lots of tables, two woodburning stoves, and bow windows overlooking the water. Well kept Boddingtons, Flowers Original, Morlands Old Speckled Hen and Wadworths 6X on handpump, in winter sensibly kept under light blanket pressure; good range of country wines and malt whiskies; fruit machine and piped music. There's a conservatory over on the right. Plenty of tables run down to the trout stream, and you can watch the swirls and eddies made by the fish as they're carried along by the fast-flowing tide. (*Recommended by L Grant, M Moore, A R and B E Sayer, C H and P Stride, R J Herd, Gill and Mike Cross, Mrs C Archer, T Aldworth, Stephen and Jean Curtis, Professor H G Allen, Ian and Liz Phillips, H D Spottiswoode, LM, Christopher Gallop, W K Struthers, Romey Heaton, George Murdoch, Sheila Edwards, Peter and Doreen Wilson, Bernard Phillips*)

Whitbreads ~ Managers Barry and Julie Lane ~ Real ale ~ Meals and snacks (12-9) ~ (01264) 860 283 ~ Children welcome ~ Open 11-11

WINCHESTER SU4829 Map 2

Wykeham Arms ★ ⑪ 🛏 ♉

75 Kingsgate Street (Kingsgate Arch and College Street are now closed to traffic; there is access via Canon Street)

How things have changed since Anthony Trollope described this splendid place as 'a very ancient but then third rate hostelry.' Today it stands unrivalled amongst the town pubs we know, hard to beat for all-round comfort and hospitality. The list of names below is testament to its enduring popularity, but rather than rest on his laurels, (something you could well excuse in this instance), the enterprising landlord is constantly trying new things and making improvements – he really works hard to create an atmosphere in which everyone feels at home. One recent innovation is what they call the Alternative Beverage list, an eclectic range of non-alcoholic drinks taking in Horlicks, Ovaltine and Bovril. The drinks that really stand out though are the wines, an excellent seasonally-changing list including over 20 by the glass, several half-bottles, and helpful tasting notes. Also well kept Eldridge Pope Dorchester, Hardy and Royal Oak on handpump, and a number of cognacs and liqueurs. There's quite an emphasis on the excellent food, with lunchtime dishes like good sandwiches (from £2.25, toasted from £2.75), delicious soups (£2.25), spinach roulade with smoked ham and tarragon (£3.50), stilton and quince pâté (£3.65), ploughman's (from £3.95, the beef one is very highly praised), seafood and leek pasta bake (£4.95), and Moroccan lamb meatballs with noodles or pork, sage and apple casserole (£5.25); in the evening they do meals such as asparagus and tomato tartlet (£8.25), beef, orange and tarragon casserole (£9.25), plaice fillets rolled with a smoked salmon, lemon and chive mousseline (£10.75), roast duck breast with butter beans, olives and smoked bacon (£10.85) and rack of lamb roasted wth rosemary-scented dauphinoise and a redcurrant and port wine glaze (£11.25); puddings (from £2.95) might include chocolate and ratafia biscuit cake or lemon and ginger cheesecake. The menu changes every day; even on a weekday you may find it useful to book a table, or at least get there early. Rather smart and stylish, the busy rooms radiating from the central bar are furnished with 19th-c oak desks retired from nearby Winchester College (the inkwells imaginatively filled with fresh flowers), a redundant pew from the same source, kitchen chairs and candlelit deal tables and big windows with swagged paisley curtains; all sorts of collections are dotted around. A snug room at the back, known as the Watchmakers, is decorated with a set of Ronald Searle 'Winespeak' prints, a second one is panelled, and all of them have a log fire; several areas are no-smoking. Service is welcoming and friendly. There are tables on a covered back terrace, with more on a small but sheltered lawn. The lovely rooms are thoughtfully equipped, and residents have the use of a sauna. The landlord has pledged to raise £60,000 over four years for the nearby Cathedral Appeal Fund; they're well on the way but it's worth popping in to help. (*Recommended by Tim Galligan, Gwen and Peter Andrews, John and Joy Winterbottom, Caroline Raphael, Lynn Sharpless, Bob Eardley, Anthony and Freda Walters, Mr and Mrs Hawkins, Nic Armitage, Wim Kock, Willem-Jan Kock, Hans Chabot, Mayur Shah, K E Wohl, Brenda and Jim Langley, Phil and Sally Gorton, Mr and Mrs A Craig, Gill and Mike Cross, Ted Burden, Paula Harrison, Julia Stone, Mr and Mrs Stewart, Jo Rees, JM, PM, Jenny and Brian Seller, J L Hall, Dr and Mrs R E S Tanner, Martyn and Mary Mullins, R C Morgan, P Corris, J W and S B McClenahan, Heather M N Robson, Gordon Mott and others*)

Eldridge Pope ~ Lease Mr and Mrs Graeme Jameson ~ Real ale ~ Meals and snacks (12-2.30, 6.30-8.45; not Sun) ~ Evening restaurant; not Sun ~ (01962) 853834 ~ If the small car park is full local parking may be difficult – don't be tempted to block up Kingsgate Street itself ~ Open 11-11 ~ Bedrooms: £65B/£75B

Lucky Dip

Besides the fully inspected pubs, you might like to try these Lucky Dips recommended to us and described by readers (if you do, please send us reports):

☆ **Alresford** [The Soke, Broad St (extreme lower end); SU5832], *Globe*: Wide choice of good cheapish popular food, Courage-related ales with a guest such as Wadworths 6X, lots of decent wines by the glass, free Sun bar nibbles, big open fire each end, uncluttered decor with quite a lot of local history – esp about the 12th-c ponds which make for lovely view from back windows and garden; piped music; open all day, nearby parking can be difficult (*Martin and Karen Wake, Peter and Doreen Wilson, J Muckelt, KCW; more reports on new tenants please*)
Alresford [West St], *Bell*: Friendly good value Georgian coaching inn with 17th-c origins, good food and beer; comfortable bedrooms (*Sarah Webb, Jenny Spohn, Tony Gayfer*)
☆ **Ampfield** [off A31 Winchester—Romsey;

SU4023], *White Horse*: Wide choice of good food in comfortably done-up extended dining pub with welcoming service, period-effect furniture, log fire, well kept Wadworths 6X, decent wine (*Joan and John Calvert, A Craig, KCW*)
☆ **Avon** [B3347; SZ1498], *New Queen*: Well managed and attractive Badger dining pub with atmospheric different areas and levels, low pitched ceiling, good range of popular food, friendly service, well kept Best and Tanglefoot; bedrooms (*Alastair Campbell, WHBM*)
☆ **Basing** [Bartons Lane (attached to Bartons Mill Restaurant), Old Basing; SU6653], *Millstone*: Decent good value food and good choice of well kept real ales tapped from the cask in simply decorated converted mill in lovely spot by River Loddon; good service, big garden (*Brenda and Jim Langley,*

Stephen, Julie and Hayley Brown)

☆ **Beaulieu** [almost opp Palace House; SU3802], *Montagu Arms*: Civilised and comfortable hotel in attractive surroundings; entirely separate less upmarket Wine Press bar, open all day, has basic lunchtime bar food, well kept Whitbreads-related real ales, decent wines, lots of malt whiskies, quick friendly service, picnic-table sets out on front courtyard, piped pop music (can be obtrusive); children welcome; comfortable but expensive bedrooms *(John Woodward, E G Parish, Mr and Mrs Moody, Mrs J Styles, LYM)*

Bentworth [signed off A339 Alton—Basingstoke; SU6640], *Star*: Completely refurbished under new licensee, promising food in bar and brasserie, lots of wines, four changing real ales *(Anon; more reports please)*

☆ **Bighton** [off B3046 in Alresford just N of pond; or off A31 in Bishops Sutton – OS Sheet 185 map ref 615344; SU6134], *Three Horseshoes*: Good simple lunchtime food in plain but friendly village local with open fire in small lounge (unusual thatched cover over fireplace), police memorabilia (ex-police landlord), well kept Gales in Dark Mild and Winter, lots of country wines, fresh flowers in spotless lavatories; children welcome, geese in garden *(Lynn Sharpless, Bob Eardley, Peter and Doreen Wilson)*

☆ **Bishops Sutton** [former A31 Alresford—Alton; SU6031], *Ship*: Friendly and pleasantly relaxed local which has had good quickly served bar food; for sale 1994 – news please *(Peter and Doreen Wilson, LYM)*

Bishops Waltham [Church St; SU5517], *Bunch of Grapes*: Simple friendly village local in same family for many years, two old-fashioned small rooms, bar food, well kept Courage-related and Ushers ales, no music; opens 10 most mornings, small garden *(Ann and Colin Hunt)*; *White Swan*: Cosy and homely little village local, welcoming licensees, lounge with good coal fire, plates, picture mirrors and old pictures, well kept Courage ales, good choice of straightforward bar food from sandwiches up inc bargain special *(Colin and Ann Hunt)*

☆ **Bishopstoke** [Fairoak Rd; SU4619], *River*: Spacious family pub with good reasonably priced food, interesting things to look at; big safe riverside garden with swings, trampolines; some live music *(Dr and Mrs A K Clarke, John and Christine Simpson, Mrs D Brown, Martyn Yates)*

Blacknest [OS Sheet 186 map ref 798416; SU7941], *Jolly Farmer*: Good value generous quick food inc children's dishes in modern, light and airy dining pub with good open fire, big bay window, family room; tables on sheltered terrace and in garden *(J and D Lloyd-Lewis, G B Longden)*

Botley [The Square; SU5112], *Bugle*: Attractive beamed pub with popular bar

food inc good fresh fish, Whitbreads-related real ales, quick pleasant service; restaurant *(Peter and Doreen Wilson)*

Botley [Botley Rd; close to railway stn], *Railway*: Recent comfortable railway-theme refurbishment, popular good value generous food, fresh veg, quick cheerful service, Marstons real ales with a guest such as Banks's Mild *(Peter and Doreen Wilson, John and Christine Simpson, John Sanders)*

☆ **Braishfield** [Newport Lane; SU3725], *Newport*: Friendly, very popular and scruffily comfortable unreconstructed two-bar village local with simple good value food inc huge sandwiches, well kept Gales HSB, country wines, decent coffee, down-to-earth landlord, weekend singsongs; good summer garden with geese, ducks and chickens *(Lynn Sharpless, Bob Eardley, John and Christine Simpson)*

Bramshill [SU7561], *Hatch Gate*: Free house with big garden, good food, pleasant service *(Ian Phillips)*

☆ **Bransgore** [Ringwood Rd; off A35 N of Christchurch; SZ1897], *Crown*: Clean and comfortable Brewers Fayre pub with quick friendly service, good value generous food from sandwiches up inc children's dishes and lots of puddings, Whitbreads-related real ales (may change to S&N), big garden with good play area maybe inc bouncy castle *(D Baker, DWAJ)*

☆ **Bransgore** [Ringwood Rd], *Three Tuns*: Picturesque thatched pub with flower-festooned forecourt, tables out on well kept back lawn with play area, backed by open fields; roomy low-beamed bar, clean and comfortable, with Windsor chairs and fresh flowers, Whitbreads-related and other ales such as Ringwood Fortyniner and Wadworths 6X, wide range of good well presented food inc good vegetarian choice, welcoming service, small restaurant; bedrooms *(C A Hall, Anthony and Freda Walters, Mr and Mrs George Clarke, D Baker, C J Westmoreland, E G Parish)*

Bridgemary [just off A32 Gosport—Fareham; SU5803], *Bridgemary Manor*: Tastefully modernised and enlarged hotel bar, collection of chamber pots, usual bar food; well priced Courage Best, Marstons Pedigree and other real ales; bedrooms *(Ann and Colin Hunt)*

Brockenhurst [Lyndhurst Rd; SU2902], *Snakecatcher*: Long narrow dining pub with children's dishes too, well kept Eldridge Pope Royal Oak, good choice of wines by the glass, good service *(K R Flack, C J Westmoreland)*

Brook [B3078 NW of Cadnam; SU2714], *Green Dragon*: Recently very much enlarged New Forest pub with good range of quick food in big dining area, well kept Whitbreads-related ales, tables inc big garden with good enclosed play area, often ponies and donkeys nearby *(Jack Taylor)*

☆ **Burghclere** [off A34 – OS Sheet 174 map ref 462608; SU4761], *Carpenters Arms*: Superb country views from attractively laid-out dining conservatory, good genuine thriving pub atmosphere in bar, big helpings of reasonably priced bar food, well kept real ales such as Archers Village, Fullers London Pride, the newish local Hampshire King Alfreds and Morlands Old Speckled Hen, unobtrusive piped music; garden, maybe live music Sat; handy for Sandham Memorial Chapel (NT) *(Lyn and Bill Capper)*

☆ **Burley** [back rd Ringwood—Lymington; SU2003], *Queens Head*: Done-up Tudor pub but still with some flagstones, beams, timbering and panelling, wide choice of good generous straightforward bar food, well kept Whitbreads-related real ales on handpump, maybe piped music; gift/souvenir shop in courtyard – pub and New Forest village can get packed in summer; children welcome *(K R Flack, M Veldhuyzen, Sheila Edwards, LYM)*

☆ **Burley** [Bisterne Close, ¾ mile E], *White Buck*: Big helpings of good reasonably priced food esp fish in plush and elegant well furnished high-ceilinged pub/restaurant, friendly service, good choice of well kept beers, separate dining room, children's room; dogs allowed; tables on spacious lawn; well equipped bedrooms *(A D Marsh, S H Godsell)*

☆ **Bursledon** [Hungerford Bottom; SU4809], *Fox & Hounds*: Cheery rustic atmosphere in handsomely rebuilt ancient Lone Barn behind with immense refectory table, lantern-lit side stalls, lots of interesting farm tools and equipment, wide choice from food bar, well kept Courage-related real ales, country wines; children allowed only in conservatory connecting it to original pub *(Eamon Green, LYM)*

☆ **Cadnam** [off M27 junction 1; SU2913], *White Hart*: Taken over, refurbished, and reopened summer 1994 by the Emberleys who had formerly made the New Forest Inn at Emery Down and Fleur de Lys at Pilley popular main entries; early to tell yet, but seems to have the sort of food that did so well there; Flowers Original, Gales HSB, Ringwood Best and Wadworths 6X on handpump, no games *(Reports please)*

Cadnam [by M27, junction 1], *Sir John Barleycorn*: Decent bar food inc generous puddings in pretty thatched pub's cosily divided open-plan bar and attractive restaurant area; two big log fires, pot plants, hunting and game prints, well kept Whitbreads-related real ales on handpump, good coffee; garden with barbecue *(Anthony and Freda Walters, Keith and Margaret Kettell)*

☆ **Canterton** [Upper Canterton; off A31 W of Cadnam follow Rufus's Stone sign; no right turn Wbound; SU2613], *Sir Walter Tyrell*: Big but pretty New Forest pub by lovely clearing often with ponies, ideal base for walks; restaurant, wide choice of good value bar food inc good steaks, well kept Courage-related ales, friendly atmosphere; big play area, sheltered terrace *(K Flack, Colin Barnett, Ruth Trott)*

☆ **Chandlers Ford** [Valley Park; SU4320], *Cleveland Bay*: Comfortable big well laid-out family pub, recently built and open-plan but with attractively old-fashioned feel; wide range of real ales inc well kept guests, good food inc trad favourites, friendly service; garden with stream and picnic-table sets; dogs allowed on lead *(Jon and Jane Fawbert)*

Chilbolton [OS Sheet 185 map ref 394398; SU3939], *Abbots Mitre*: Fair-sized friendly Test Valley village local with good furniture and decor, Whitbreads-related ales and a guest such as Ringwood Best on handpump, wide choice of food in bars and restaurant, terrace and decent garden with play area; handy for Chilbolton Common *(Jim Penman)*

☆ **Chilworth** [A27 Romsey Rd; SU4018], *Clump*: Doing well under newish landlord, popular and comfortable for decent straightforward business lunches from sandwiches up, big brocaded settles and chairs, conservatory, tables in garden; prompt service, well kept Whitbreads-related and other ales *(John and Christine Simpson, Ian Phillips, A Craig)*

Chineham [Hanmoor Rd, just NE of Basingstoke; SU6554], *Chineham Arms*: Good newish country-style Fullers pub with good value food and big garden *(Martin Kay, Andrea Fowler)*

Clanville [SU3149], *Red Lion*: Updated pub with increased emphasis on food, well kept Bunces at very low price; very friendly *(Dr and Mrs A K Clarke)*

Crawley [A272 Stockbridge—Winchester, about 5 miles N of Winchester; SU 4234], *Rack & Manger*: Useful main-road managed Marstons pub with decent reasonably priced food, nice garden with good children's facilities *(KCW)*

☆ **Crondall** [SU7948], *Castle*: Unpretentious village local with good unusual choice of fresh bar food and good Sun lunch; garden, skittle alley, Fullers real ales, jazz evenings *(J S M Sheldon, Pat and Tony Martin)*

☆ **Denmead** [Forest Rd, Worlds End; SU6211], *Chairmakers Arms*: Welcoming staff and good value well presented food from separate counter in simple but spacious and comfortable country pub with well kept Gales BBB, HSB and XXXL; no music, surrounded by paddocks and farmland *(Lt Cdr L R Ball, John Sanders, LYM)*

Denmead [Southwick Rd, Bunkers Hill; SU6611], *Harvest Home*: Friendly and popular country pub with one long bar, separate eating area off, Gales ales, straightforward food; guinea pig compound in car park *(Colin and Ann Hunt)*

Dibden Purlieu [B3054/A326; SU4106], *Heath*: Useful family pub with some quiet corners, reasonably priced food, Whitbreads-related ales; swings outside *(E G Parish)*

Dogmersfield [SU7853], *Queens Head*: Attractive country setting, friendly atmosphere, tasty well priced food *(Christof F Niklaus)*

☆ Downton [A337; SZ2793], *Royal Oak*: Eye-catching main-road country pub, quiet, immaculate and half no smoking, with consistently above-average genuinely home-made bar food inc excellent pies, friendly landlady (pub been in family for long time), half-panelling, no machines, unobtrusive music, well kept Whitbreads-related ales, decent wines, family atmosphere; huge well kept garden with good play area *(John Cromar, E G Parish)*

☆ Droxford [SU6018], *Hurdles*: Not at all pubby, but locally very popular for big helpings of good simple home cooking; friendly prompt service, well kept real ales *(John Beeken, Brian Bowden, Mr and Mrs J E C Hobbs)*

Dunbridge [Barley Hill; SU3126], *Mill Arms*: Really good food, all home-made – even the bread *(Jo Goldsmith)*

☆ Dundridge [Dundridge Lane; off B3035 towards Droxford, Swanmore, then right towards Bishops Waltham – OS Sheet 185 map ref 579185; SU5718], *Hampshire Bowman*: Tucked-away unspoilt downland pub, friendly and cosy, with well kept Archers Village and King & Barnes Old, Festive and Mild tapped from the cask, decent red wine, country wines; good value straightforward food from sandwiches to venison inc vegetarian dishes; children welcome, tables on spacious and attractive lawn *(Peter and Doreen Wilson, Colin and Ann Hunt)*

Durley [Heathen St – OS Sheet 185 map ref 516160; SU5116], *Farmers Home*: Wide choice of good varied reasonably priced bar food, relaxed, friendly atmosphere, efficient obliging staff, well kept beers; garden with swings, trampoline, rabbits and goat *(Richard Burton)*

☆ East Boldre [SU3700], *Turf Cutters Arms*: Dimly lit but spacious New Forest pub with good original atmosphere and very enjoyable food – if the Hobler at Battramsley appeals to you (see main entries), so will this; bedrooms *(Gill and Mike Cross, Andrew Scarr)*

☆ East Meon [Church St; signed off A272 W of Petersfield, and off A32 in West Meon; SU6822], *George*: Attractive rambling beamy country pub in lovely setting, cosy areas around central bar counter, scrubbed deal tables and horse tack; wide choice of good food, Badger Tanglefoot, Ballards, Boddingtons, Flowers and Gales HSB, welcoming atmosphere, log fire; good outdoor seating arrangements; bedrooms *(Mr and Mrs A B Cassells, G B Longden, Peter and Doreen Wilson, Wendy Arnold, Nic Armitage, R L Martin, LYM)*

☆ East Tytherley [SU2929], *Star*: Charming country pub in lovely surroundings, well priced Courage-related, Gales and Ringwoods ales, decent food from sandwiches up, no-smoking lounge bar and restaurant, courteous service, relaxing

pubby atmosphere; giant chess and draughts games on forecourt *(Ann and Colin Hart, Peter and Doreen Wilson)*

☆ Easton [SU5132], *Chestnut Horse*: Cosy, comfortable and spacious dining pub, popular with a wide age-range of locals; wide choice of good imaginative food, Bass, Charrington IPA, Courage Best, Fullers London Pride; said to date from 16th c, with beams, good log fire, smart prints and decorations *(Lynn Sharpless, Bob Eardley, KCW, Brenda and Jim Langley)*

Easton [OS Sheet 185 map ref 511321], *Cricketers*: Doing well under newish licensees, simple but well-prepared food, Whitbread-related beers *(KCW)*

Ecchinswell [SU4959], *Royal Oak*: Unchanging carefully kept country local with well kept beer *(Sheilah Openshaw)*

☆ Emery Down [off A35 just W of Lyndhurst; SU2808], *New Forest*: Excellent position in one of the nicest parts of the Forest, with good walks nearby, tables out on three-level back lawn; attractive softly lit open-plan lounge with log fires, Whitbreads-related real ales, bar food, children welcome, bedrooms; has been a starred main entry, very popular indeed with readers, but the family who made it so have now moved to the White Hart at Cadnam and we have not yet built up a sufficient dossier of favourable reports under the new regime to be sure of its still deserving a main entry *(LYM; news please)*

Emsworth [29 South St; SU7406], *Blue Bell*: Warm atmosphere, good smiling service, Ringwood Old Thumper and Ruddles, good choice of food inc children's *(John Sanders)*; [South St], *Coal Exchange*: Simple, with good atmosphere, Gales real ales (happy hour most evenings), food inc good value Sun lunch; open all day Sat *(Ann and Colin Hunt)*; [High St], *Crown*: Spacious low-beamed bar in small hotel, good choice of real ales inc Courage, Marstons Pedigree, Wadworths 6X, good range of very reasonably priced bar food inc children's dishes, two cosy coal fires, prompt service; separate eating area; bedrooms *(Ann and Colin Hunt, A J Blackler)*; *Lord Raglan*: Small simple chatty Gales pub with log fire, popular newish licensees, wide range of reasonably priced bar food, restaurant, children welcome *(Ann and Colin Hunt)*

Enborne [W, towards Hamstead Marshall; SU4365], *Craven Arms*: Very well kept Wadworths ales and guest beers on handpump, reasonably priced varied food, spacious bars and grounds *(Adrian Kelly)*

☆ Everton [3 miles W of Lymington; SZ2994], *Crown*: Warm and friendly traditional pub with good cheap food in relaxing bar with log fire, well kept Bass and Whitbreads-related ales, second lively bar with pool, darts, table football, Sky TV and juke box (not loud, classical and rock music); welcoming chatty locals and ex-Navy landlord; picnic-table sets outside, quite handy for New Forest *(Christopher L*

Francis, C J Westmoreland, WHBM)

Ewshot [SU8149], *Windmill*: Well kept Ind Coope Burton on handpump, enormous garden with putting green and Sunday lunchtime barbecues *(M M Matthews)*

Exton [signposted from A32; SU6121], *Shoe*: Very attractive outside, bright, clean and comfortable in, with well kept Bass, friendly barman, attractive food, lovely grassed area across road *(John and Joan Nash)*

Faccombe [SU3858], *Jack Russell*: Comfortable country pub with attractive dining conservatory opp pond in hilltop village, lovely views nearby, bedrooms; has been popular for good food, but no news yet of new licensees *(HNJ, PEJ, Peter and Doreen Wilson; reports please)*

☆ **Fair Oak** [Winchester Rd (A3051); SU4918], *Fox & Hounds*: Busy, comfortable and attractive open-plan dining pub with exposed brickwork, beam-and-plank ceilings, soft lighting; wide choice of reasonably priced food in old-world bar and separate modern family area, friendly service, Courage-related ales, decent wines; children's play area by car park *(John and Joan Nash, Mr and Mrs A Craig, Lynn Sharpless, Bob Eardley, Colin and Ann Hunt)*

Fareham [Lower Quay, Old Gosport Rd; was Coal Exchange; SU5706], *Castle in the Air*: Refurbished as spacious open-plan bar with separate raised eating area, big fireplace, Flowers Original and Wadworths 6X, usual food from good doorstep sandwiches up, tables outside, good views over Fareham Creek *(Ann and Colin Hunt)*; [1 Wallington Shore Rd], *Cob & Pen*: Keenly priced good food in pleasant eating area, well kept beers *(Thomas Neate)*; [Porchester Rd, just off A27 nr M27 junction 11], *Delme Arms*: Well kept Bass on handpump, pleasant bar and nice lounge with emphasis on ships, bar food; can get busy weekends, children welcome *(Colin and Ann Hunt)*

☆ **Farnborough** [Rectory Rd; nr Farnborough North stn; SU8753], *Prince of Wales*: Lvely and friendly local with three small connecting rooms, ten well kept real ales inc several guests, decent malt whiskies, popular well presented lunchtime food, good service; can get very crowded *(Dr W M Owton, KC)*

Farnborough [Southwood], *Monkey Puzzle*: Open-plan roadside pub with good choice of Whitbreads-related and other ales, good value food from sandwiches up, picnic-table sets out by big lawn with striking eponymous araucaria *(Chris Warne)*

☆ **Farringdon** [off A32 S of Alton; Crows Lane, Upper Farringdon; SU7135], *Rose & Crown*: Generous helpings of good value food in clean, bright and friendly local doing well under very welcoming newish landlord, with neat back dining room, Marstons and other well kept real ales, decent wines; tables and playthings in well kept back garden *(Rob and Doris Harrison,*

C H Stride, BB)

☆ **Fawley** [Ashlett Creek, off A326; SU4703], *Jolly Sailor*: Splendid waterside position by dinghy club overlooking busy shipping channel, plushly modernised, with promptly served good value food, Whitbreads-related real ales, friendly landlord, restaurant, good liner pictures; piped music, children welcome; handy for the Rothschild rhododendron gardens at Exbury *(Hugh Spottiswoode, Mr and Mrs P B Dowsett, LYM)*

Fishers Pond [B3354/B2177; SU4820], *Queens Head*: Completely refurbished and very popular big Marstons dining pub, nicely divided into groups of a few tables; children's play facilities, handy for Marwell Zoo *(Joan and John Calvert)*

Fordingbridge [14 Bridge St; SU1414], *George*: Outstanding waterside position, with tables out on pleasant terrace and in sun lounge; bar food inc good open sandwiches *(Anon)*

☆ **Freefolk** [N of B3400; SU4848], *Watership Down*: Friendly and cosy partly brick-floored bar with simple but pretty wall seats, lounge and games areas off, interesting real ales such as Archers Best, Brakspears Bitter and Mild, Chatford Clout and Hampshire Pendragon on handpump, cheap cheerful food with good specials; piped music *(Peter Churchill, Andy Jones)*

☆ **Fritham** [SU2314], *Royal Oak*: Unspoilt and basic thatched New Forest pub, Whitbreads-related ales tapped from the cask, high-backed settles, pots and kettles hanging in wide old chimney; tables in garden with climbing frame, anything from ponies to piglets wandering past; no food beyond pickled eggs and occasional barbecues, bring your own sandwiches; children in back room *(Andy and Jill Kassube, LYM)*

☆ **Frogham** [Abbotswell Rd, off A338/B3078 SE of Fordingbridge; SU1713], *Foresters Arms*: Another New Forest pub though a good deal less basic, with fine walks, Bass, Boddingtons and three well kept changing guest beers, decent wines, usual food from sandwiches to steaks, restaurant, games room, tables on front verandah; children welcome, open all day Sat *(Andy and Jill Kassube, LYM)*

☆ **Froxfield Green** [Alton—Petersfield rd; SU7025], *Trooper*: Well kept Bass, Ringwood and guest beers such as Wadworths, interesting good value wines, simple bar food inc good evening steaks, candlelight and bare boards *(Philip Puddock)*

☆ **Froyle** [Upper Froyle; A31 Alton—Farnham; SU7542], *Hen & Chicken*: Attractive 16th-c pub with oak beams and pillars, antique settles, oak tables, huge fireplace among more orthodox furnishings; under cheerful and helpful newish management, with wide choice of generous food from sandwiches up esp fish, good range of well kept real ales; unobtrusive piped music, tables outside, play area *(Hazel Morgan, Guy Consterdine, LYM)*

Goodworth Clatford [SU3542], *Royal Oak*: Pleasant sheltered quiet garden outside comfortable pub with good service, nicely presented usual bar food from sandwiches up inc vegetarian and Sun lunch, restaurant *(Colin Brown and others)*

Gosport [Hardway; formerly the Jolly Roger; SZ6199], *Hogshead & Halibut*: Big flagstoned bar and rooms off, superb views of Portsdown Hill and Portsmouth Harbour, Whitbreads-related real ales and others such as Smiles and Wadworths 6X, bar food inc fish, good service, real fire; open all day *(Ann and Colin Hunt)*; [Queens Rd], *Queens*: Particularly well kept Archers Village, Fullers London Pride and Greene King Abbot on handpump, with two interesting weekly-changing guest beers; not much in the way of food *(B S Bowden)*

nr **Gosport** [Alverstoke; SZ6099], *Old Lodge*: Comfortable Courage local in pretty village nr sea, friendly landlord, good inexpensive bar snacks, good food in restaurant, no piped music; nice bedrooms *(Peter and Audrey Dowsett)*

☆ **Hamble** [3 miles from M27 junction 8; SU4806], *Olde Whyte Harte*: Friendly welcome, blazing inglenook log fire, low beams and massive masonry in down-to-earth yachtsmen's pub with cheap bar food, Gales Best, BBB and HSB, lots of country wines, seats outside; children in eating area *(Dave Braisted, John Atherton, Ian Phillips, LYM)*

☆ **Hamble**, *Bugle*: Good reasonably priced food in improved river-view restaurant of spaciously extended rambling pub, neat, tidy and comfortable, with some character, Courage-related real ales; tables on terrace *(Peter and Doreen Wilson, M J D Inskip, Lyn and Bill Capper, LYM)*

☆ **Hambledon** [West St; SU6414], *Vine*: Good simple home cooking (not Tues evening) in attractive traditional beamed pub with old prints, china, ornaments, farm tools, high-backed settles, lounge with open fire; warm and comfortable atmosphere, well kept Gales and other real ales, country wines, shove-ha'penny, darts *(Lynn Sharpless, Bob Eardley)*

Hambledon [West St], *New Inn*: Typical village local with public bar, separate room for pool and darts, good choice of real ales such as Ringwood Fortyniner and Old Thumper (well priced), quieter back lounge; friendly landlord *(Colin and Ann Hunt)*

Hartley Wintney [SU7656], *Lamb*: Popular but rarely crowded, decent food, friendly feel, reasonable prices, cheery landlord and staff; comfortable bedrooms *(Christof F Niklaus)*; [High St], *Waggon & Horses*: Good friedly local, well priced generous helpings of well presented food, well kept Courage Best and a guest *(Anna Marsh)*

Havant [South St; SU7106], *Old House At Home*: Carefully enlarged and much modernised Tudor pub, with well kept

Gales BBB and HSB, good value bar food *(Tony and Wendy Hobden, LYM)*

☆ **Hawkley** [Pococks Lane – OS Sheet 186 map ref 746292; SU7429], *Hawkley*: Warm welcome, good value food, well kept beers inc guests, decent choice of wines, no-smoking area, juke box, back restaurant, tables in pleasant garden behind; lovely countryside, lots of walks *(David Martin, Nigel Norman)*

Hayling Island [Ferry Rd – OS Sheet 196 map ref 689000; SU7201], *Ferry Boat*: Friendly pub with nice atmosphere, views across Portsmouth harbour, good puddings; pool, fruit machines *(Sue Anderson, Phil Copleston)*

Hazeley [B3011 N of H Wintney – OS Sheet 186 map ref 742591; SU7459], *Shoulder of Mutton*: Popular if not cheap dining pub with good fire in cosy lounge, no smoking area, Courage-related ales, quiet piped music *(Chris Warne, A J Madel)*

☆ **Heckfield** [B3349 Hook—Reading; SU7260], *New Inn*: Efficient food service with good choice in extensive rambling open-plan bar with lots of well spaced dining tables, some traditional furniture in original core, two good log fires, well kept ales such as Badger Tanglefoot, Courage Directors, Fullers London Pride, unobtrusive piped music; restaurant (not Sun); bedrooms in comfortable and well equipped extension *(Chris Warne, LYM)*

☆ **Highclere** [Andover Rd; A343 S of village; SU4360], *Yew Tree*: Plush L-shaped dining bar with big log fire, tasty and enterprising food, friendly licensees, good unobtrusive waitress service, well kept real ales inc Brakspears, Ringwoods Fortyniner, Wadworths 6X, decent wines, some attractive decorations; restaurant; four comfortable bedrooms *(Mr and Mrs I Langrish, Maureen Hobbs, Peter and Doreen Wilson, David Storey, G Shannon, LYM)*

☆ **Hill Head** [Cliff Rd; SU5402], *Osborne View*: Good bar food inc Sun roasts and well kept Badger Best and Tanglefoot in clean and modern pub with lovely Solent views (right by bird reserve) and good service; evening restaurant *(Mr and Mrs A Craig, John Sanders)*

Hill Top [B3054 Beaulieu—Hythe; SU4003], *Royal Oak*: Big, clean, well decorated bar, friendly staff, bar food inc good baked potatoes *(Geraint Roberts)*

Holybourne [SU7341], *White Hart*: Friendly local with wide choice of home-made food inc very tasty bread and butter pudding *(Linda and Brian Davis)*

☆ **Hook** [London Rd – about a mile E; SU7254], *Crooked Billet*: Warm welcome and wide choice of good food from sandwiches to good home-made pies and steaks all day in spacious pub with good service, homely open fires, Courage Best, good range of soft drinks; attractive garden with stream, ducks, even bats; children welcome, dogs may be allowed *(Anna*

Marsh, D Conquer)

☆ **Horndean** [London Rd; SU7013], *Ship & Bell*: Comfortable and cosy relaxed local with well kept Gales beers from the next-door brewery; good choice of reasonably priced bar lunches; bedrooms *(John Sanders, Penny and Peter Keevil, John and Christine Simpson)*

☆ **Horsebridge** [about a mile SW of Kings Somborne – OS Sheet 185 map ref 346303; SU3430], *John o' Gaunt*: Consistently good unpretentious food, well kept Adnams, Palmers and Ringwood beers and attractive prices in friendly L-shaped bar welcoming walkers and dogs; by mill on River Test, very popular weekends *(Peter Churchill, Dr and Mrs N Holmes)*

☆ **Houghton** [S of Stockbridge; SU3432], *Boot*: Wide range of tasty well presented food in friendly and well run dining pub, well kept beer, popular restaurant; bar tables rather low, simple decor; closed Mon *(Peter and Doreen Wilson, J F Burness, A D Marsh, DP)*

☆ **Hursley** [in village; SU4225], *Kings Head*: Decent open-plan pub with good friendly service, wide range of reasonable food, well kept Bass, Charrington IPA and Wadworths 6X on handpump *(Gordon B Mott)*
Hursley [A31 Winchester—Romsey], *Dolphin*: Welcoming ex-seagoing steward at bar, good imaginative freshly prepared food from the hatch; popular with local forestry workers and Sparsholt Agricultural Coll students *(KCW)*

Hurstbourne Tarrant [A343; SU3853], *George & Dragon*: Old posting inn in attractive village, low beams and inglenook, separate rooms and eating area leading off, real ales inc Wadworths 6X, reasonably priced bar food; bedrooms *(Colin and Ann Hunt, LYM)*

Hythe [Hythe Marina; SU4207], *Lock n Quay*: Overlooking marina, attractive and modern; Ringwood *(Dave Braisted)*

Itchen Abbas [B3047; SU5333], *Trout*: Simple but comfortable character bars being gradually and carefully done up, bar food from sandwiches up imaginative and good value – can be excellent when the friendly landlord's present, well kept Marstons, pleasant garden; spacious new bedrooms with big breakfasts, on the way to a main entry *(W J Wonham, Dennis H Phillips, KCW, Paul and Fiona Hutt, Lynn Sharpless, Bob Eardley, Jenny and Brian Seller, BB)*

☆ **Keyhaven** [SZ3091], *Gun*: Lots of character in 17th-c nautical-theme beamed pub overlooking boatyard, popular at lunchtime particularly with older people for wide choice of good value simple bar food (tables rather small and close), well kept Whitbreads-related real ales; garden with swings, rabbits and fish pond; children welcome *(Lynn Sharpless, Bob Eardley, Stephen Savill, Mr and Mrs A Craig, Jeff Davies, GSS)*

☆ **Kings Worthy** [A3090 E of Winchester, just off A33; SU4933], *Cart & Horses*: Big rambling Marstons family dining pub with softly lit alcoves, lots of well spaced tables, conservatory, reasonably priced home-cooked food, efficient service system, well kept Pedigree, tables in pleasant garden with marvellous play houses *(R T and J C Moggridge, Stephen, Julie and Hayley Brown, Nick Wikeley, Peter and Doreen Wilson, LYM)*

Kingsclere [Swan St; SU5258], *Swan*: Popular local with decent food esp burgers *(Sheilah Openshaw)*

☆ **Langstone** [A3023; SU7105], *Ship*: Waterside pub with lovely view from spacious bar and upstairs restaurant; cheerful log fire, wide choice of generous food cooked within sight inc good fresh fish, well kept Gales, country wines; children's room, seats outside *(John Sanders, David Eberlin, John and Christine Simpson, Penny and Peter Keevil, R K F Hutchings)*

Lasham [SU6742], *Royal Oak*: Friendly welcome, real log fire, good atmosphere, well kept beers and fine home-made food *(John Castelete)*

Lee on the Solent [Crofton Ave/Sea Lane, off Stubbington Lane; SU5600], *Swordfish*: Big comfortable pub notable for outstanding position with Solent views; big family room, usual pub food, Courage-related real ales *(Ann and Colin Hunt)*; *Wyvern*: Managed by ex-Pompey footballer, food varied and good; getting popular *(John and Joy Winterbottom)*

☆ **Linwood** [signposted from A338 via Moyles Court, and from A31; keep on – OS Sheet 195 map ref 196107; SU1910], *High Corner*: Marvellous New Forest position for extensive pub with rambling series of rooms inc family room and no-smoking verandah lounge, big neatly kept lawn with sizeable play area; decent straightforward bar food from sandwiches to steaks, quick friendly service even when busy, restaurant carvery open all day Sun, Whitbreads-related real ales; open all day Sat, very popular on fine days; bedrooms *(Iris and Eddie Brixton, Dono and Carol Leaman, Joan and John Calvert, Lynn Sharpless, Bob Eardley, Jacquie and Jon Payne, LYM)*
Linwood [up on heath – OS Sheet 195 map ref 186094], *Red Shoot*: Pleasantly modernised using old furniture and rugs on the floorboards, generous decent food inc good sandwiches, well kept Wadworths IPA, 6X and Morrells Varsity on handpump, friendly staff, nice New Forest setting *(Pat and Tony Martin, WHBM)*
Locks Heath [Fleet End Rd, nr M27 junction 9; SU5207], *Jolly Farmer*: Lots of character inside and lots of flowers in baskets outside, friendly attentive staff, good attractively presented food *(Mrs P McFarlane)*

☆ **Longparish** [B3048 off A303 just E of Andover; SU4344], *Plough*: Good service and nice atmosphere in neat open-plan pub/restaurant with good food from good sandwiches to steaks, well kept Whitbreads-related real ales, good value wine, restaurant allowing children over 4; piped music, can be crowded weekends; attractive garden *(J H Walker, John Evans, Keith Symons, LYM)*

☆ **Longstock** [SU3536], *Peat Spade*: Bright, airy and elegant high-ceilinged bar with adjoining dining room, pot plants and central table with books, well kept Hampshire ales, unusually wide choice of wines by glass, really good food inc shellfish all cooked by landlady (so be prepared to wait); no dogs *(Martin and Karen Wake, Dr and Mrs A K Clarke, BB)*

☆ **Lower Froyle** [SU7544], *Anchor*: Clean and brightly lit yet keeping a warm and attractive atmosphere, wide range of well cooked and presented standard food inc sandwiches, cheerful informal service, well kept ales, well in bar, restaurant; piped music; seats outside *(Peter and Doreen Wilson, Lynn Sharpless, Bob Eardley, R B Crail, John and Vivienne Rice, KC)*

☆ **Lower Wield** [SU6340], *Yew Tree*: Welcoming dining pub, consistently good well priced food, well kept beer; closed Mon *(Betty Laker, Mr and Mrs A Craig)*

☆ **Lymington** [Southampton Rd (A337); SZ3295], *Toll House*: Wide choice of consistently good sensibly priced food (not Sun or Mon evening) inc children's dishes, and good friendly atmosphere, in oak-beamed bar with well kept Ringwood, Wadworths 6X and several guest beers; pleasant efficient staff, good-sized children's room *(D J Underwood, A D Marsh)*

Lymington [High St], *Angel*: Spacious and comfortable dark-decor modernised hotel bar with largely home-made bar food, Eldridge Pope real ales on handpump; children in buffet bar, tables in attractive inner courtyard; reputed ghosts include one of the very few naval ones; clean bedrooms *(Peter and Doreen Wilson, Stephen Savill, LYM)*; [The Quay], *Ship*: Waterfront family pub, spacious and well decorated, open all day from breakfast on, reasonably priced usual food, Whitbreads-related ales, some seating outside with boating views *(D H T Dimock, Hugh D Spottiswoode)*; *Crown*: Hotel with good range of reasonably priced tasty bar food, Courage-related real ales; bedrooms *(H Croft, Hugh Spottiswoode)*; [Swan Green (A35 SW)], *Swan*: Attractive hotel with usual pub meals, cream teas; open all day, tables under cocktail parasols on lawn, wooded surroundings *(E G Parish)*; [Pikes Hill], *Waterloo Arms*: 17th-c thatched food pub with pleasant furnishings, log fire, four Whitbreads-related ales on handpump, unusually good wine list; dogs welcome, properly pubby atmosphere *(WKS)*

☆ **Mapledurwell** [off A30 Hook—Basingstoke; SU6851], *Gamekeepers*: Upmarket restaurant with wide choice of good generous food inc game, well made sauces

and al dente veg, more limited but well presented good value snacks in interesting old bar with well, Eldridge Pope ales well kept, good value wines, farm cider, friendly smart service; piped music; in lovely thatched village with duckpond *(Simon Collett-Jones, G B Longden, J S M Sheldon, KC)*

Meonstoke [SU6119], *Bucks Head*: Well kept Bass and Morlands Old Speckled Hen, country wines, good bar food with fresh veg, lovely village setting with river nr garden *(Terry and Eileen Stott, John Sanders)*

☆ **Micheldever** [Winchester Rd; SU5142], *Dever Arms*: Attractive village pub recently renovated by new owners; plenty of beams and chintzy curtains, good food inc excellent bouillabaisse, well kept frequently changing beers inc Flower Pot, Gales HSB, Hop Back Summer Lightning and Smiles, decent wines, good service *(J I Conville, Mr and Mrs Stewart)*

Milford on Sea [SZ2891], *Smugglers*: Efficient service, well priced plentiful good food; small children's area with slide and climbing frame *(R S and M P Dauncey)*

Minley [from A30 take B3013 towards Fleet, then first left; SU8357], *Crown & Cushion*: Attractive small traditional pub with separate raftered and flagstoned 'meade hall' behind, frightfully rustic – lunches there impressive in a mass-produced sort of way (very popular weekends), evenings more a young people's meeting place; huge log fire, children in eating area, piped music may be too obtrusive, keg beers now *(Dick Brown, Anna Marsh, Marjorie and David Lamb, LYM)*

☆ **Minstead** [SU2811], *Trusty Servant*: Friendly old-fashioned country pub, beautifully placed, with very wide-ranging menu – not cheap, but generous; smart candlelit dining room, three or four guest beers; comfortable bedrooms *(R C Davis, S Eldridge, David Wallington)*

☆ **Mortimer West End** [off Aldermaston rd at Silchester sign; SU6363], *Red Lion*: Welcoming country dining pub with good range of Badger and other well kept real ales, lots of beams, stripped masonry and woodwork, good log fire; quiet piped music; seats on small flower-filled terrace by quiet road *(KC, LYM)*

☆ **Nether Wallop** [village signed from A30 or B2084 W of Stockbridge; SU3036], *Five Bells*: Simple welcoming country local with well kept Marstons real ales on handpump inc Mild, long cushioned settles and good log fire in beamed bar, bar billiards and other traditional games in locals' bar, small restaurant, provision for children; seats outside, well equipped play area *(RA, EA, LYM)*

Netley Marsh [A336, 2 miles from M27 junction 1; SU3313], *White Horse*: Recently refurbished village local on edge of New Forest, good range of real ales, standard choice of good reasonably priced bar food

(Chris and Kim Elias)

Newnham [nr M3 junction 5; SU7054], *Old House At Home*: Peaceful bay-windowed house in secluded hamlet tucked up cul de sac, attractive frontage with flower tubs and carriage blocks; friendly welcome, real ales, country food; pleasant walks nearby; car park full of status cars Sun lunchtime *(E J Parish)*

Newtown [A34/A339 2 miles S of Newbury; SU4764], *Swan*: Beefeater steak house with attractive flagstoned bar, real ales tapped from the cask, old photographs *(Dr and Mrs A K Clarke)*

☆ North Gorley [Ringwood Rd, just off A338; SU1611], *Royal Oak*: 17th-c thatched pub in lovely New Forest situation nr pond, shiny planked ceiling and panelled dado, comfortable furnishings, generous helpings of reasonably priced usual food from sandwiches to steaks inc children's dishes, Whitbreads-related ales, welcoming young staff; children in family room, big back garden with swings and climber *(Jeanne and Tom Barnes, Lynn Sharpless, Bob Eardley)*

☆ North Warnborough [near M3 junction 5; SU7351], *Swan*: Good variety of well priced good food in friendly canalside village pub, well kept Courage Best, Marstons Pedigree, Wadsworth 6X on handpump *(P J Caunt, Mark Every)*

☆ Odiham [High St (A287); SU7450], *George*: Short choice of imaginative daily-changing home-cooked food in old-fashioned inn with nice garden outlook from small and comfortable back bar, well kept Courage-related ales, decent wines by the glass, pleasant staff; bedrooms *(Maysie Thompson, F C Johnston, LYM)*

Odiham [Church Sq], *Bell*: Welcoming local in pretty square opp church, well kept Courage-related ales, limited choice of good food, friendly service *(J S M Sheldon)*; [Colt Hill Wharf, signed off main st], *Water Witch*: Garden with extensive children's facilities, Courage-related ales, usual pub food; very busy weekends *(Dr M Owton)*

Over Wallop [SU2838], *White Hart*: Pretty little thatched pub with ducks on the lawn and cats round the open fire *(MR, HR)*

☆ Owslebury [SU5123], *Ship*: Small updated village local with lots of character, good tasty home cooking, quick friendly service even when busy, well kept Marstons; magnificent downland views from two garden areas, children's play area, goat, maybe even bowls practice and cricket net *(M J B Inskip, John and Joan Nash, Lt Cdr L R Ball, Mark Hydes, Peter and Doreen Wilson, LYM)*

Pennington [North St; SZ3194], *Musketeer*: Popular ale-drinkers' local, several from distant small breweries *(A D Marsh)*

☆ Petersfield [College St; SU7423], *Good Intent*: Neat, comfortable and spotless, with remarkable range of good reasonably priced well presented home-cooked food (not Mon) from sandwiches to steaks, real ales such as Bass, Marstons Pedigree and

Ringwood Fortyniner, good cappuccino, efficient friendly service; a relatively modern feel despite its 16th-c beams and timbers and good log fires; cosy restaurant *(Ian Phillips, S C Harvey, Ron Shelton, Richard and Maria Gillespie)*

Porchester [SU6105], *Cormorant*: Whitbreads pub in pleasant close handy for the castle, not smartly furnished, with good value food; children in dining area, seats outside *(David Dimock)*

☆ Portsmouth [High St, Old Town; SU6501], *Sally Port*: Spick-and-span, brightly modernised but still interesting, with reasonably priced good bar food, well kept Marstons, good friendly staff, upstairs restaurant; as with other pubs here, nearby parking may be difficult; comfortable bedrooms *(M J D Inskip, Ann and Colin Hunt)*

☆ Portsmouth [High St, Old Town], *Dolphin*: A dozen or more real ales from the Whitbreads family to Ringwood Fortyniner and Old Thumper and the like in big spacious well refurbished pub with wide range of food, friendly cat, attractive fires, cosy snug, nice warm atmosphere; video games; open all day Sat *(Ann and Colin Hunt, J Boylan, Mr and Mrs Dara de Cogan)*

☆ Portsmouth [Bath Sq, Old Town], *Spice Island*: Big modernised two-floor Whitbreads pub newly fitted with nicely worked seafaring theme, big windows and outside seats overlooking passing ships, good atmosphere, well kept ales, food all day inc vegetarian, friendly staff, family room (one of the few in Portsmouth), upstairs restaurant *(Julie Mundy, Martin Robinson, Lyn and Bill Capper, Penny and Peter Keevil)*

Portsmouth [The Wharf, Camber Dock], *Bridge*: Good views over the water, furnished with barrels and smart tables and chairs, bar food esp fresh fish, Whitbreads-related ales *(Colin and Ann Hunt, Sue Anderson, Phil Copleston)*

☆ Ringwood [The Bridges, West St, just W of town – OS Sheet 195 map ref 140050; SU1505], *Fish*: Friendly and comfortably modernised pub doing well under current management, open all day, with wide choice of good value straightforward food, eating area allowing children, clean and pleasant bar with log fire, good obliging service; no dogs, some live music; tables on riverside lawn *(A P Reeves, S and J Moate, Wally Huggins, J H L Davis, Ian Phillips, LYM)*

☆ Rockford [OS Sheet 195 map ref 160081; SU1608], *Alice Lisle*: Friendly open-plan pub attractively placed on green on edge of New Forest, wide choice of reliable generous bar food inc good sandwiches and children's helpings in big conservatory-style family eating area, pleasant bar, well kept Gales and guest beers, country wines, attentive obliging staff, baby-changing facilities; garden with good play area and pets' corner; handy for Moyles Court

(WHBM, W H and E Thomas, S Eldridge, Tony Tucker, Charles Owens, Catherine Almond, BB)

☆ nr **Romsey** [Botley Rd; A27 towards N Baddesley – handy for M27 junction 3; SU3521], *Luzborough House*: Extensively developed Whitbreads family dining pub with interesting series of smaller rooms leading off high-raftered main bar (newly restored to flagstones), very generous food from sandwiches to chicken kiev all day, well kept real ales, big log fire, cheerful staff; piped pop music may be loud; children welcome away from bar, tables and play area in spacious walled garden *(Lt Cdr L R Ball, Nick Wikeley, Basil Minson, John Watson, LYM)*

nr **Romsey** [Greatbridge (A3057 towards Stockbridge); SU3522], *Dukes Head*: Well kept old Whitbreads pub festooned with flowering baskets in summer; inglenook eating places, wide range of good bar food, Strong Country tapped from the cask, garden behind; one to watch *(David Dimock, D Illing)*; [Woodley (A31 towards Winchester – OS Sheet 185 map ref 373221)], *Hunters*: Extended managed Whitbreads pub with good range of food served all day inc home-made puddings, friendly staff, pleasant atmosphere, well kept ales *(KCW, Dennis H Phillips)*

Rotherwick [High St; SU7156], *Falcon*: Well kept local beers, friendly licensees, good cheap food *(Anna Marsh)*

Selborne [SU7433], *Queens*: Very welcoming young landlord in well decorated pub with interesting pictures and local memorabilia, well kept beer, good food esp seafood platter; bedrooms *(Michael Jefferson, LYM)*

☆ **Setley** [A337 Brockenhurst—Lymington; SU3000], *Filly*: Two contrasting and attractive bars handy for New Forest walks, wide choice of generous well presented food inc vegetarian (call your name when it's ready), well kept Bass, Ringwood Old Thumper and Wadworths 6X, decent wines, friendly landlord, quick service – very popular with older people (and children) lunchtime; some tables outside *(Mrs C A Blake, D J Underwood, Joan and John Calvert, Derek and Margaret Underwood, R M Leonard, A D Marsh, R Ward, Anna and Steven Oxley, Dave Braisted, LYM)*

Sherfield English [SU2822], *Hatchet*: Well prepared food, seven real ales, attentive staff; need to book in restaurant area *(Dr and Mrs N Holmes)*

☆ **Sherfield on Loddon** [SU6857], *White Hart*: Wide choice of generous decent fresh food prepared to order (so can be a wait if busy) in quietly welcoming pub, clean and tidy, with interesting relics of coaching days, huge inglenook fireplace, friendly efficient service, well kept Courage ales with a guest such as Brakspears, good choice of wines, tables outside; soft piped music; handy for The Vyne *(Rosalie Watkins, K D and C M Bailey, Marjorie and David Lamb, Chris*

Warne, Simon Collett-Jones, LYM)

☆ **Soberton** [signed off A32 S of Droxford; SU6116], *White Lion*: Charmingly simple country pub with scrubbed tables and woodburner in rambling lounge bar, irregularly shaped public bar and quiet views from sheltered garden (with play area and suntrap fairy-lit terrace); has had good value food, well kept real ales, a welcome for children, and earliest reports on new regime are promising *(J S M Sheldon, John Sanders, G B Longden, John and Joy Winterbottom, LYM; news please)*

Soberton Heath [SU6014], *Bold Forester*: Traditional country pub in small village, well kept Morlands, good wide choice of cheap food inc bargain Sun lunch; attractive play area *(Colin and Ann Hunt, Jill Bickerton, JW)*

Southampton [55 High St, off inner ring rd; SU4212], *Red Lion*: Included for its surprising genuine galleried medieval hall under lofty rafters, timbered walls decorated with arms and armour, Tudor panelling; Courage-related real ales, open all day; piped music can be loud, and evenings young people can take over *(A P Reeves, Mr and Mrs A Craig, LYM)*

Southsea [Delamere Rd; SZ6498], *Golden Eagle*: Clean pub with well kept beer, good welcoming service *(M P Jefferson)*; *Western*: Old-fashioned attentive landlord, good food, cheerful atmosphere *(P Neate)*

☆ **St Mary Bourne** [SU4250], *Coronation Arms*: Friendly and neatly kept village local with well kept Marstons, usual pub food, Sun lunches, good summer barbecues; handy for Test Way walks; bedrooms *(Peter and Doreen Wilson, BB)*

St Mary Bourne, *George*: Unpretentiously friendly old village local with very relaxed 1950s feel, big helpings of good food in bar and bookable evening restaurant food, polite service *(HNJ, PEJ)*

☆ **Steep** [Church Rd; Petersfield—Alton, signposted Steep off A325 and A272; SU7425], *Cricketers*: Big helpings of good interesting well prepared food inc several unusual dishes in clean, spacious and airy bare-boards lounge with pews, good solid benches and heavy wooden tables, lots of cricket prints on the panelling, well kept Gales real ales, decent wines and malt whiskies; restaurant, picnic-table sets on back lawn with swings and play-house; comfortable good value bedrooms *(Martin and Karen Wake, B S Bowden, John Sanders, LYM)*

☆ **Stockbridge** [High St; SU3535], *Grosvenor*: Good atmosphere and helpful cheerful service in pleasant and comfortable old country-town hotel, scrupulously clean, with well cooked reasonably priced food in both rather small bars and dining room; large attractive garden behind; bedrooms good value – a friendly and homely place to stay *(Bernard Phillips, Brig D B Rendell, W and S Jones, BB)*

☆ **Stockbridge** [bottom end of High St;

A272/A3057], *White Hart*: Cheerful and welcoming bar divided into lots of small areas, oak pews and other seats, antique prints, shaving-mug collection, lots of china on beams of comfortable small side restaurant with its own blazing log fire; reasonably priced usual bar food, Sun lunches, Bass and Charrington IPA on handpump, country wines, courteous service; children allowed in restaurant; bedrooms *(Peter and Doreen Wilson, Wim Kock, Willem-Jan Kock, Hans Chabot, J V Dadswell, Ann and Colin Hunt)*

☆ **nr Stockbridge** [Leckford (A30 E) – OS Sheet 185 map ref 404367], *Leckford Hutt*: Comfortable settles, easy chairs and settees in welcoming main bar with good fire, lots of mugs and tankards, friendly licensees, extraordinarily deep much-photographed well, good value simple food from sandwiches to steaks inc children's and some imaginative specials, well kept Marstons Best and Pedigree, good coffee, enterprising evening events; public bar with table games, quoits, quiet fruit machine and lots of chamber-pots; children in lunchtime family area, friendly dogs allowed later; garden behind *(Lynn Sharpless, Bob Eardley, Charles Bardwell, KCW)*

☆ **Stratfield Saye** [signed off A33 Basingstoke—Reading; SU6861], *New Inn*: Cheerful staff and decent bar food inc children's dishes, tasty barbecues and good puddings in open-plan rather 1950s-style country pub in pleasant surroundings; several semi-detached areas inc lounge with log fires, nice prints and plates, well kept Badger beers and guests, children and dogs welcome; attractive garden with swings and slides *(Klaus and Elizabeth Leist)*

Stubbington [Stubbington Lane; SU5503], *Golden Bowler*: Former country club, now free house with big comfortable bar and restaurant, good friendly staff, Bass, Stones Best, Wadworths 6X on handpump *(Ann and Colin Hunt)*

☆ **Stuckton** [village signposted S of Fordingbridge, by A338/B3078 junction; SU1613], *Three Lions*: Too restaurant for the main entries, but excellent, with wide choice of generous, interesting and unusual wholesome food (not Mon) inc good old-fashioned puddings in neat and airy bar, with good welcoming service, warm atmosphere, lots of fresh flowers, well kept Allied and other ales on handpump, decent wines; closed Sun evening and Mon in winter, maybe two weeks' summer hol *(David Cundy, LYM)*

Swanmore [Hill Grove – OS Sheet 185 map ref 582161; SU5716], *Hunters*: Good spacious family dining pub with playpacks for sale, big family room besides two other bars, big well equipped play area and plenty of picnic-table sets, some shaded, reasonably priced children's food; main menu with vegetarian and champion sausages, Courage Directors, good house wine, cheerful attentive staff; very busy weekends *(Mr and*

Mrs A McCall, Mr and Mrs J E C Hobbs, Miss D J Hobbs, John Sanders); *Rising Sun*: Good pub atmosphere, good log fires – nice place for a drink in comfortable surroundings *(TBB)*

Swanwick [Swanwick Lane (A3051); handy for M27 junction 9 – OS Sheet 196 map ref 515097; SU5109], *Elm Tree*: Neat and comfortably refurbished three-room local with Courage-related ales, good bar food, tables in garden, children welcome; handy for new Hampshire Wildlife Reserve *(John and Joy Winterbottom)*

Sway [SZ2798], *Hare & Hounds*: Well spaced tables in pleasant and comfortable New Forest pub with very nice staff, good range of generous bar food inc delicious rich puddings, real ales, garden *(June M Drummond)*

☆ **Tangley** [SU3252], *Fox*: Warm welcome, good service, generous helpings of good value imaginative well prepared food inc home-made puddings, well kept Courage-related ales with a guest such as Eldridge Pope Royal Oak and good choice of wines in small, smart pub with two big log fires, pleasant restaurant; landlord's own honey for sale *(Mr and Mrs John Hobbs)*

☆ **Thruxton** [from A303 eastbound follow Thruxton village signs, then go under A303 towards Cholderton; westbound, follow signs, then left at T-junction towards Thruxton, then left into car park before pub and A303 bridge; SU2945], *White Horse*: Very friendly 16th-c low-beamed thatched local with well kept Bunces, Wadworths 6X and guest beers, decent food inc good sandwiches, separate dining area, log fire *(Mrs B M Spurr)*

Thruxton [just off A303], *George*: Generous food inc good home-made pies, big eating area with well spaced tables *(Mrs M Campbell)*

☆ **Timsbury** [Michelmersh; A3057 towards Stockbridge; SU3424], *Bear & Ragged Staff*: Spacious but cosily refurbished and comfortable Whitbreads country dining pub, wide choice of decent food all day from separate counter (very popular lunchtime with older people), several well kept ales inc guests from the Whitbreads portfolio, country wines, tables out in garden, good play area; children in eating area *(Anthony and Freda Walters, A Craig, P J Caunt, S Eldridge, Andrew Brookes, LYM)*

☆ **Titchfield** [Mill Lane, Segensworth; off A27 at Titchfield Abbey; SU5305], *Fishermans Rest*: In pleasant spot opp Titchfield Abbey with tables out behind overlooking river, refurbished as Whitbreads pub/restaurant – most feel it has not been spoilt; proper bar, nice separate eating area, good choice of well kept real ales from the Whitbreads portfolio, reasonable wine, pleasant atmosphere, open fire *(Ann and Colin Hunt, John and Christine Simpson, A E Green, Sue Anderson, Phil Copleston, Anthony and Freda Walters, M J D Inskip)*

☆ **Titchfield** [East St, off A27 nr Fareham], *Wheatsheaf*: Friendly new landlord keen on real ales, with guest beers as well as Courage, Marstons Pedigree, Morlands Old Speckled Hen and Wadworths 6X on handpump; reasonably priced food, tables outside behind *(Ann and Colin Hunt, David Lewis)*

☆ **Totton** [Eling Quay; SU3612], *Anchor*: Nautical photographs and good value basic food in interestingly placed creekside pub, no frills but friendly *(Dave Braisted)*

☆ **Turgis Green** [A33 Reading—Basingstoke; SU6959], *Jekyll & Hyde*: Enjoyable atmosphere in rambling black-beamed pub with five changing real ales, some interesting furnishings and prints particularly in back room, quick friendly service, wide range of food (can be good) from sandwiches up, all day inc breakfast; piped music; lots of picnic-table sets in good sheltered garden (some traffic noise) with play area and various games; lavatories for the disabled, children allowed *(Chris Warne, KC, Dr Paul Kitchener, Stephen Brown, LYM)*

☆ **Twyford** [SU4724], *Bugle*: Friendly newish management in open-plan pub done up in rich post-Victorian style, wide choice of generous reasonably priced good food inc good value Sun lunch, well kept Eldridge Pope ales, decent wines by the glass *(J L Hall, Prof A N Black)*

Upton [(the one near Hurstbourne Tarrant); SU3555], *Crown*: Comfortable little country pub with home-cooked bar food, well kept real ales *(GSS, BB)*

☆ **Upton Grey** [SU6948], *Hoddington Arms*: Consistently good bar food at attractive prices inc interesting dishes and good fresh veg in friendly unpretentious two-bar village local; well kept Morlands and other real ales, Australian wines by glass, family room, bar billiards; piped music; garden *(Mrs B M Spurr, G B Longden)*

Wallington [nr M27 junction 11; SU5806], *White Horse*: Small cosy village pub, good lunchtime bar food, particularly well kept Bass tapped from the cask, guest ales *(Terry and Eileen Stott)*

☆ **Warnford** [A32; SU6223], *George & Falcon*: Popular generous food in spacious and comfortable softly lit country pub with wide range of beers and quick friendly service, piped light classical music, Courage-related real ales *(Miss D J Hobbs, Sue Anderson, Phil Copleston)*

☆ **Warsash** [Fleet End Rd, Locks Heath – OS Sheet 196 map ref 509062; SU4906], *Jolly Farmer*: Welcoming extended dining pub full of rustic memorabilia and bric-a-brac, fine old-fashioned farm furniture, very quickly served popular food, reasonable prices, well kept Whitbreads-related ales; sheltered seats outside with lots of flowers and play area; bedrooms *(Ian Phillips, Alan Reid)*

☆ **West Meon** [High St; SU6424], *Thomas Lord*: Popular and attractive cricket-theme village pub, good food inc superbly cooked fish (tables may all be booked esp at weekends), well kept Whitbreads-related real ales, friendly helpful staff; growing collection of club ties in lounge, landlord keeps interesting book of episcopal signatures; tables in garden *(KCW)*

☆ **West Wellow** [nr M27 junction 2; A36 2 miles N of junction with A431; SU2919], *Red Rover*: Wide range of good value food in extensive partly no-smoking dining area, friendly staff *(Peter and Doreen Wilson, K R Harris)*

West Wellow [Canada Rd; off A36 Romsey—Ower at roundabout, signposted Canada], *Rockingham Arms*: Plush beamed 19th-c pub on edge of New Forest with good food and drinks, friendly atmosphere and service, open fire; dogs on leads allowed, pool and darts, restaurant; children welcome; garden with play area, small caravan park *(A D Marsh)*

☆ **Weyhill** [A342, signed off A303 bypass; SU3146], *Weyhill Fair*: Well kept Gales HSB, Marstons and Morrells on handpump, weekly guest beers tapped from the cask in the cellar, wholesome generous food at fair prices in spacious solidly furnished lounge with easy chairs around woodburner and old advertisements, smaller family room; children welcome *(Andy and Jackie Mallpress, LYM)*

Weyhill, *Star*: Tidy Gales pub with all their ales kept well, nice choice of malt whiskies, wide choice of good value food in big dining area; no machines in lounge *(Patrick Godfrey)*

☆ **Wherwell** [B3420; SU3941], *White Lion*: Friendly and genuine village pub with particularly helpful service, good cosy atmosphere in beamed bar with log fire, fresh flowers, polished brass, shelves of plates, good value food esp sandwiches and ploughman's in bar or dining room, Whitbreads-related real ales *(Dr H C Mackinnon Elmdon, R A Dean, Colin Laffan, P J S Mitchell)*

☆ **Whitsbury** [follow Rockbourne sign off A354 SW of Salisbury, turning left just before village; or head W off A338 at S end of Breamore, or in Upper Burgate; SU1219], *Cartwheel*: Low-beamed country pub with wide choice of well presented reasonably priced food inc good sandwiches, good range of changing real ales, horse-racing decorations, good friendly service; dogs allowed, weekly barbecue in attractive secluded sloping garden with play area; steep walk through fields behind for good views; children allowed in restaurant when not in use *(A Stone, W K Struthers, WHBM, Dennis H Phillips)*

Wickham [Kingsmead; A30 towards Droxford; SU5711], *Roebuck*: Pleasantly divided pub with decent generous home cooking, no piped music *(John Sanders)*; [Botley Rd], *Wheatsheaf*: Comfortable little two-bar pub, well kept Marstons Best and Pedigree on handpump, usual food, friendly service *(Ann and Colin Hart)*

Winchester [St Cross; SU4727], *Bell*: Very good fresh sandwiches and omelette served quickly and graciously *(Gethin Lewis)*; [Broadway (E end)], *Crown & Anchor*: Pleasant pub with nice decor, well kept Marstons; games machines *(JM, PM)*; [The Square, between High St and cathedral], *Eclipse*: Picturesque little partly 14th-c pub with heavy beams, timbers and oak settles, very handy for cathedral, with Whitbreads-related real ales, well done lunchtime bar food, seats outside *(JM, PM, A E Green, Stephen, Julie and Hayley Brown, A Craig, R Kelly, LYM)*; [Alresford Rd], *Golden Lion*: Big pub on outskirts, friendly service, 1950s decor and GWR posters, well kept Wadworths beers *(Dr and Mrs A K Clarke)*; [40 Bar End Rd], *Heart in Hand*: Lovely garden, friendly service, lots of games, electronic and traditional, good range of well kept beers *(Dr and Mrs A K Clarke)*; [Saxon Rd], *King Alfred*: Good friendly panelled Marstons local away from centre *(Dr and Mrs A K Clarke)*; [Morn Hill, Alresford Rd; Winchester exit off A31], *Percy Hobbs*: Intimate little cubbyholes, well presented if not cheap food, pervasive piped music and air conditioning; efficient if not exactly personal service *(Anon)*

Winchfield [Winchfield Hurst; SU7753], *Barley Mow*: Straightforward two-bar pub with wide choice of good value generous home-cooked food from sandwiches up (bookable tables), friendly staff, well kept Courage-related real ales, unobtrusive piped music; nr Winchfield wharf of Basingstoke canal *(G B Longden)*

Wolverton [Towns End, off A339; SU5558], *George & Dragon*: Pleasant country pub a bit off the beaten track with wide range of well kept beers and good value bar food; big garden area with a horse in the next field *(J V Dadswell)*

☆ **Woodgreen** [OS Sheet 184 map ref 171176; SU1717], *Horse & Groom*: Atmospheric and friendly beamed local, good genuinely home-cooked food with plenty of choice at reasonable prices, excellent veg, lovely puddings; real ale, log fire, eating area off bar *(M J Clenshaw, Harriet and Michael Robinson, Joan and John Calvert)*

Yateley [Vigo Lane; off Cricket Hill Lane; SU8161], *Anchor*: Decent food and well kept Courage-related ales in small friendly two-bar pub with very pleasant staff and locals *(R Houghton, Anna Marsh)*

Bedroom prices normally include full English breakfast, VAT and any inclusive service charge that we know of. Prices before the '/' are for single rooms, after for two people in double or twin (B includes a private bath, S a private shower). If there is no '/', the prices are only for twin or double rooms (as far as we know there are no singles). If there is no B or S, as far as we know no rooms have private facilities.

Hereford & Worcester

New entries in this interesting area, or pubs reinstated after a break, are the friendly Crown & Trumpet in Broadway (wonderfully untouristy, considering the surroundings), the unusual and very individual Talbot at Knightwick, and the attractive Crown & Anchor at Lugwardine (another very friendly place, extremely well run). Other pubs currently doing particularly well here include the Slip at Much Marcle (outstanding gardens, and very pleasant inside), the Crown & Sandys Arms in Ombersley, the Olde Salutation at Weobley and the Butchers Arms (a very nice place to stay in) and Crown, both in Woolhope. All these are popular for food; other pubs where food is a particularly strong point are the Duke of York at Berrow, the Bear & Ragged Staff at Bransford and Roebuck at Brimfield (both of these rather restauranty, both with outstanding cooking), the Pandy at Dorstone, the Feathers in Ledbury, the Ancient Camp at Ruckhall, the Lough Pool at Sellack and the Sun at Winforton. Taking both food and atmosphere into account, for an enjoyable meal in memorable surroundings we choose the Ancient Camp at Ruckhall as Hereford & Worcester Dining Pub of the Year. Food prices are around the national average: the Green Man at Fownhope and particularly the idiosyncratic Three Castles at Hanley Castle deserve credit for their unusually low prices. Drinks prices, on the other hand, are clearly below the national average – very cheap beer indeed at the Talbot at Knightwick, and very low prices too at the Green Man at Fownhope and in both Woolhope pubs. Hook Norton is the beer to go for here, for sheer value. Of course, this area's great speciality is farm cider, and most of the pubs we include have at least one example: the Monkey House at Defford is remarkable as an utterly unchanging cider house. In the Lucky Dip section at the end of the chapter, we'd particularly pick out the Green Dragon at Bishops Frome, March Hare at Broughton Hackett, Fox at Chaddesley Corbett, Old Chequers at Crowle, Trotter Hall at Droitwich (a fine new example of the area's eccentric 'Little' pubs), Firs at Dunhampstead, White Swan at Eardisland, Old Bull at Inkberrow, Huntsman at Kempsey, Talbot in Leominster, Hope & Anchor in Ross on Wye, Ship in Tenbury Wells, recently reopened Swan in Upton upon Severn, Coach & Horses at Weatheroak Hill, Rhydspence at Whitney on Wye and Jolly Roger and Cardinals Hat in Worcester.

BERROW SO7934 Map 4

Duke of York

A438 Tewkesbury—Ledbury, just E of junction with B4208

A lot older than it looks, this friendly place was originally a much-needed refreshment stop for 15th-c pilgrims going from Tewkesbury to Hereford. Since then the pub has become something of a centre of pilgrimage itself, with sweet-toothed food lovers travelling from all over the area to gaze upon the choice of up to 20 home-made puddings, ranging from bread and butter pudding through treacle tart, fruit pies and crumbles to lovely gooey gateaux. Other good and popular bar food includes sandwiches, home-made soup (£1.50), ploughman's

(from £2.50), spinach filo triangles or Cumberland sausage and black pudding
with a mild mustard sauce (£3.25), bouillabaisse (£3.95), salads (from £4.50),
several vegetarian dishes such as broccoli and cream cheese bake (£4.95) or
cashew nut nuggets in a mushroom and sherry sauce (£5.60), steak and kidney
pie or filled Yorkshire pudding (£5.25), rabbit pie (£5.95), speciality fritto misto
(a mixture of fried fish, £5.95 as a main course, £2.95 starter) and other Italian
dishes, cajun spiced chicken breast (£6.50), duck in red wine and plum sauce
(£6.75), deep fried butterfly prawns with barbecue sauce (£6.95) and various
steaks (from £7.25); Sunday roast. The two connected rooms of the comfortable
bar have beams, nooks and crannies and a good log fire, and there's a small back
restaurant; dominoes, cribbage, maybe a couple of cheery dogs. Well kept
Boddingtons, Flowers Original and Whitbreads West Country on handpump;
decent wines, local farm cider, good service, piped music. A spacious garden
behind has picnic-table sets and a slide. The pilgrims' cross in the nearby church
is thought to have stood originally in front of the pub. Good walking in the
nearby Malvern Hills. *(Recommended by Anthony and Freda Walters, Graham Reeve, B
Walton, G and M Hollis and others)*

*Whitbreads ~ Lease: Pam Harber ~ Real ale ~ Meals and snacks ~ Restaurant ~
(01684) 81449 ~ Children in eating area ~ Open 11-3, 6.30-11*

BEWDLEY SO7875 Map 4

Little Pack Horse

High Street; no nearby parking – best to park in main car park, cross A4117 Cleobury road,
and keep walking on down narrowing High Street; can park 150 yds at bottom of Lax Lane

Look around the bustling, characterful rooms here and you'll quickly see that
though this looks like an old-fashioned traditional local, it's full of the
eccentricities and oddities that have become the hallmark of the 'Little' chain. The
walls are covered with various clocks, wood-working tools, Indian clubs, a
fireman's helmet, an old car horn, lots of old photographs and advertisements,
and even an incendiary bomb; a wall-mounted wooden pig's mask is used in the
pub's idiosyncratic game of swinging a weighted string to knock a coin off its ear
or snout. There are pews, red leatherette wall settles, a mixed bag of tables on the
red-tiled floor, roughly plastered white walls, and low beams. Good, reasonably
priced bar food includes home-made soup (£1.75), very substantial sandwiches
(weekdays only), filled baked potatoes (£2.95), lasagne or chilli (£3.95), gammon
with pineapple or home-baked ham salad (£4.25), the hefty Desperate Dan pie
(£4.75), and sirloin steak (£5.95); with puddings such as jam roly poly with
custard (£1.95). A changing range of well kept beers such as Holt Plant &
Deakins Entire, Ind Coope Burton, Marstons Pedigree or Tetleys, along with the
good value strong Lumphammer ale that's brewed for the chain (even non-beer-
drinkers seem to like it), house wine, and well made coffee; woodburning stove;
fruit machine, video game. No dogs. You can buy a mug in each of the 'Little'
pubs and at the end of your tour you get a bonus one free. This quiet riverside
town is full of attractive buildings. *(Recommended by Jenny and Brian Seller, Stephen,
Julie and Hayley Brown, S P Bobeldijk, Patrick and Mary McDermott, David and Shelia,
Pete Yearsley, P M Lane, Bill and Beryl Farmer, W A Wheeler, Roger Taylor)*

*Free house ~ Licensees Peter and Sue D'Amery ~ Real ale ~ Meals and snacks ~
(01299) 403 762 ~ Children in back bar or stable room ~ Open 11-3, 6-11 (all
day summer Sats)*

BIRTSMORTON SO7935 Map 4

Farmers Arms

Off B4208

A really pleasant old-fashioned rural atmosphere radiates through this attractive
black-and-white timbered village pub. On the right a big room rambles away
under low dark beams, with some standing timbers, and flowery-panelled
cushioned settles as well as spindleback chairs; on the left an even lower-beamed

room seems even snugger, and in both the white walls have black timbering. Service is quick and friendly. Popular, good value home-made bar food includes filled sandwiches (from £1.10), ploughman's (from £2.20), summer salads (from £2.50), macaroni cheese (£2.60), sausage and chips (£2.95), chicken and vegetable curry (£3.65), steak and kidney pie (£4.75), trout and almonds (£5.50), rump steak (£7.25), and puddings (from £1.40). Well kept Courage Best, Hook Norton Old Hookey, Ruddles Best, and John Smiths on handpump; darts in a good tiled area, shove-ha'penny, cribbage and dominoes. There are seats out on the grass. Plenty of walks nearby. *(Recommended by Ted George, Rebecca Mortimer, Mrs C Archer)*

Free house ~ Licensee Colin Moore ~ Real ale ~ Meals and snacks (11-2, 6-10) ~ (01684) 833308 ~ Children welcome ~ Open 11-2.30(3 Sat), 6-11 ~ Self-catering cottage from £110 per week

BRANSFORD SO7852 Map 4

Bear & Ragged Staff 🍴 ♉
Powick Rd; off A4103 SW of Worcester

The excellent changing daily specials are the highlight at this very foody place, close to a restaurant in style and quality but happily not so much in price. Current favourites include the very popular sirloin strips in black pepper, cream and brandy on a bed of rice (£5.95), creamy chicken and tarragon, an excellent fish pie with halibut, sea bass, prawns, crab, salmon and tuna (£6.10), or smoked ham and asparagus, and the menu also includes lovely soup (£2.10), ploughman's (from £4.95), mushroom and watercress pancake with yoghurt dip or lentil and cider roast with garlic spicy tomato sauce (£5.25), faggots and peas (£5.30), beef in red wine (£5.65), grilled sirloin steak (£7.60) and puddings like lemon meringue pie or old-fashioned trifle (from £2.10); vegetables are extra (£1.85). Booking is advisable, both for the waitress-served bar food (actually served in one of the restaurants) and the dearer à la carte menu. The freshly decorated interconnecting rooms have a cheery and chatty feel, an open fire, well kept Boddingtons and Flowers Original on handpump kept under light blanket pressure, and a good range of wines; friendly good-humoured service; darts, cribbage, dominoes and piped music. *(Recommended by Graham Reeve, A Preston, W H and E Thomas, Mrs C A Blake)*

Free house ~ Licensee John Owen ~ Real ale ~ Meals and snacks (till 10pm) ~ Restaurant ~ (01886) 833399 ~ Well behaved children welcome ~ Piano Fri and Sat evenings, other music Thurs evening ~ Open 12-3, 6-11

BREDON SO9236 Map 4

Fox & Hounds
4½ miles from M5 junction 9; A438 to Northway, left at B4079, then in Bredon follow To church and river signpost on right

Recently refurbished to create more space, this neat thatched pub continues to elicit warm praise for its range of tasty home-made bar food. Well served by friendly staff, popular dishes include home-made soup (£1.95), leeks and ham in cheese sauce (£2.75), broccoli and almond bake or mushroom stroganoff (£4.95), chicken breast in a mushroom, onion and white wine sauce (£6.75), steaks (from £7.95), roast salmon with a creamy watercress sauce (£8.50), half a shoulder of lamb with mint and honey glaze (£8.95), roast duck in orange sauce (£9.95), daily specials including seasonal fish and game dishes, Sunday lunch, and good puddings such as butterscotch and walnut meringue; you can eat from the same menu anywhere in the pub. The comfortable and well-modernised carpeted bar has dressed stone pillars and stripped timbers, a central wood-burning stove, maroon plush and wheelback chairs around attractive mahogany and cast-iron-framed tables and elegant wall lamps. There's a large rooflight and a clever mirror-like window. A smaller side bar has assorted wooden kitchen chairs, wheelbacks and settles, and an open fire at each end. Well kept Boddingtons, Wadworths 6X and Hook Norton Best on handpump, also freshly squeezed fruit juice and several malt whiskies. Prompt friendly service; darts, cribbage, shove-ha'penny, dominoes and piped music. The pub is perhaps prettiest in summer with its colourful hanging baskets, and there may be barbecues in the garden then; unusually some of the picnic-table sets are under Perspex so you can still eat outside in the rain, and there's a thatched Wendy house. The landlord has recently taken on another pub, the Royal Oak, about 400 yards up the road. *(Recommended by E A George, Alan and Jane Clarke, John Kirk, Mr and Mrs A K McCully, Brad and Joni Nelson, George Atkinson, Michael A Butler, Chris Heathman, W H and E Thomas, Derek and Sylvia Stephenson, Alan and Heather Jacques, Jill and Peter Bickley)*

Whitbreads ~ Lease: Michael Hardwick ~ Real ale ~ Meals and snacks (till 10) ~ Restaurant ~ (01684) 72377 ~ Children welcome ~ Open 10.30-2.30, 6.30-11; closed evening 25 Dec ~ Bedrooms in adjacent private house: £15

BRETFORTON SP0943 Map 4

Fleece ★ ★

B4035 E of Evesham: turn S off this road into village; pub is in centre square by church; there's a sizeable car park at one side of the church

One reader was lucky enough to visit this unique medieval house while it was being used for filming a new TV adaptation of *Martin Chuzzlewit;* all the visible electric fittings were removed so the only light came from the fire and candles, giving him a rare chance to experience the place just as it must have been when it first opened as a pub in 1848. Until then it was a private house, with the same family living here from the 15th-c right up to 1977, when the last of the line bequeathed it to the National Trust. Nothing whatsoever has changed since, and it's still the same astonishing assemblage of antiquities it's been for centuries, quite unlike any other pub you'll ever see. All the furnishings are original, many of them heirlooms: a great oak dresser holds a priceless 48-piece set of Stuart pewter, there's a fine grandfather clock, ancient kitchen chairs, curved high-backed settles, a rocking chair, and a rack of heavy pointed iron shafts, probably for spit roasting, in one of the huge inglenook fireplaces. There are massive beams and exposed timbers, worn and crazed flagstones (scored with marks to keep out demons), and plenty of oddities such as a great cheese-press and set of cheese moulds, and a rare dough-proving table; a leaflet details the more bizarre items, and there are three warming winter fires. The room with the pewter is no-smoking. What's particularly nice is that despite the amazing surroundings this is very much a thriving local, with a good, chatty atmosphere. Well kept Hook Norton Best, M & B Brew XI and Uley Old Spot and Pigs Ear – from the Jolly Roger in Worcester (see Lucky Dips); country wines and farm ciders. Bar food includes sandwiches (from £1.30), ploughman's (from £2.80), Gloucester sausages (£3.30), lasagne (£3.80), steak and kidney pie (£4.15), locally cured gammon (£4.95), and steak (£6.25); they do barbecues; friendly obliging staff. Darts, cribbage, dominoes, shove-ha'penny. In summer, when it gets very busy, they make the most of the extensive orchard, with seats on the goat-cropped grass that spreads around the beautifully restored thatched and timbered barn, among the fruit trees, and at the front by the stone pump-trough. There's also an adventure playground, a display of farm engines, an aviary, and maybe anything from Morris dancing, a vintage car rally, and sheep-shearing or spinning and weaving demonstrations to the merriment of their Friday-to-Sunday festival on the second weekend in July, with up to 30 real ales, bands and pony-rides. They also hold annual asparagus auctions at the end of May. No dogs (they have their own). It may be hard to find a table at lunchtime. *(Recommended by Gordon, Mrs M A Kilner, Ted George, Arthur Frampton, D Baker, Kathryn and Brian Heathcoate, Andy and Jill Kassube, Jean-Bernard Brisset, Gordon Mott, Andrew and Ruth Triggs, Leith Stuart, P J Hanson, P D and J Bickley, David R Shillitoe, Brad and Joni Nelson, John and Marianne Cooper, Dr S J Parkinson, CW, JW, Peter and Erica Davies, Phil and Sally Gorton, Roderic Plinston, John and Beverley Bailey, Derek and Sylvia Stephenson, Mr and Mrs P B Dowsett, Mrs C A Blake)*

Free house ~ Licensee N J Griffiths ~ Real ale ~ Meals and snacks (not Mon evening, or Sun evening in Jan and Feb) ~ (01386) 831173 ~ Children welcome ~ Occasional live entertainment ~ Open 11-2.30, 6-11

BRIMFIELD SO5368 Map 4

Roebuck 🍽 ⇔ ♈

Village signposted just off A49 Shrewsbury—Leominster

The beautifully presented meals at this smartly civilised dining pub aren't cheap but considering the exceptional quality are still good value; it's an ideal place to come and pamper yourself. The licensee really is a wonderful cook, and one of her imaginative recipes deservedly found a place in a recent book highlighting the country's best women chefs. The bar menu changes regularly, but might include dishes like good soups (£2.70), ploughman's with home-made pickles (£4.50), crab pot with melba toast or warm smoked chicken salad (£5), spinach and pine-kernel pie (£6.25), pies such as steak and kidney or lamb and apricot (£7), baked queen scallops stuffed with mushroom and garlic butter (£7), Shetland salmon on a bed of hop shoots (£7.50), lots of tempting puddings like home-made ice creams (unusual flavours like prune and Armagnac) or bread and butter pudding with apricot sauce (£4.50). There's an excellent range of unusual British farmhouse cheeses served with home-made oat cakes and walnut and sultana bread, with some really lovely varieties (£5); vegetables are nicely cooked and they use organic produce whenever possible. The meals are very much the focus of the place now, though it's not lacking in other more traditionally pubby features. The quiet and old-fashioned snug has an impressive inglenook fireplace unearthed by chance last year, another panelled bar has dimpled copper-topped cask tables, decorative plates mounted over dark ply panelling and a small open fire, and the public bar has cribbage and dominoes; the popular big-windowed side restaurant is elegant and modern. The caring, pleasant staff serve olives and friandises (good ones) before your bar meal comes. The wine list is enormous and remarkably good, particularly strong on the better burgundy and rhone growers and éleveurs, and New World wines; also Morlands Old Speckled Hen and Woods Parish on handpump, a range of malt whiskies, farm cider and good coffee. Incidentally, there's a family connection with the Walnut Tree at Llandewi Skirrid. *(Recommended by JT, W H and E Thomas, R M Bloomfield, The Monday Club, Mr and Mrs S Price, Neville Kenyon, Pat and John Millward)*

Free house ~ Licensee Carole Evans ~ Real ale ~ Meals and snacks (till 10pm; not Sun or Mon or 25 and 26 Dec) ~ Restaurant (closed Sun, Mon and two weeks Feb) ~ Brimfield (01584) 711230 ~ Children welcome (there's a highchair) ~ Open 12-2.30, 7-11; closed Sun, Mon, two weeks Feb, one week Oct ~ Bedrooms: £45B/£60B

BROADWAY SP0937 Map 4

Crown & Trumpet 🍺

Church St, just off High St

Prettily set behind a green, this ancient place is a down-to-earth real pub patronised by real locals, especially at night, with a quiz night on Thursdays, Saturday sing-alongs, and pool, bar billiards, darts, shove-ha'penny, ring the bull and shut the box at one end; they also play Evesham quoits here. The beamed and timbered bar is cosily unpretentious, with dark high-backed settles and a blazing log fire; in the last few months the well worn seats have been re-covered, and there's been some fresh painting. They keep a guest beer such as local Stanway alongside Boddingtons, Flowers IPA and Original and Morlands Old Speckled Hen or Wadworths 6X on handpump, all in good condition. A wide choice of homely food, low-priced for the area and often using local ingredients, includes sandwiches (£2), ploughman's or vegetable lasagne (£3.95), steak and kidney pie (£4.35) and a variety of other pies, children's dishes and home-made puddings (£1.95); they now do Sunday lunches, and in season there's an asparagus menu (£6) with five variations. Service is quick and friendly, and the atmosphere thriving and cheerful; seats out on the front terrace. *(Recommended by Sheila Keene, Andrew and Ruth Triggs, Pam Adsley, John and Marianne Cooper, Jill and Peter Bickley, Paul Boot, Peter and Erica Davis, Neil and Anita Christopher, D Hanley, T M Dobby)*

Whitbreads ~ Lease: Andrew Scott ~ Real ale ~ Meals and snacks ~ (01386) 853202 ~ Children in eating area ~ Sing-along duo Sat ~ Open 11-3(2.30 winter), 5-11 ~ Bedrooms: £23.50B/£43B

CAREY SO5631 Map 4

Cottage of Content ★ 🛏 ♀

Village, and for most of the way pub itself, signposted from good road through Hoarwithy

One reader took his ten grandchildren to this very pretty and out-of-the-way medieval country cottage and was delighted to find them all made welcome. It's peacefully set by a stream in a quiet little lane, and picnic-table sets on the flower-filled front terrace let you wallow in the charming and refreshingly unspoilt setting; a couple more on a back terrace look up a steep expanse of lawn. The main bar is a lovely light, airy room with a happy, chatty atmosphere, stripped pine tables and country kitchen chairs on the old flagstones, lots of hops hanging from the beams and over the bar counter, a brick fireplace, and through a partly knocked-through timbered wall on the left, a big table with long pews on either side. An alcove with just one table connects this room with a second bar which has a small wood-planked bar counter, a brick fireplace with pewter tankards and champagne bottles on the mantelpiece above it, copper jugs and more hops hanging from the beams, and a few tables and chairs; standing timbers lead to the end dining room with elegant spindleback chairs around a mix of old-fashioned tables, a big rug on the stripped wooden floor, and fish prints on the walls. Popular well-presented bar food includes soup (£1.50), ploughman's (£3.95), king prawns in garlic butter (£3.75), lasagne or cannelloni (£4.50), breaded plaice (£4.95), home-made pie of the day such as steak and kidney or lamb and apricot (£5.25), steaks (from £6.95), and salmon steak (£7.50), as well as seasonally changing specials and puddings like lovely bread and butter pudding; decent breakfasts. Well kept Bass, Hook Norton Best and Old Hookey, and Worthingtons on handpump, with 60 wines, 30 single malt whiskies and Old Rosie's cider; darts, dominoes, and cribbage, and TV in main bar. *(Recommended by TBB, R G and M P Lumley, Andy and Jill Kassube, Dorothy Pilson, R M Bloomfield, Mr and Mrs W W Swaitt, Ted George, Marian Greenwood, Nick and Alison Dowson, David and Mary Thomas, Graham Reeve, Mrs C A Blake)*

Free house ~ Licensee Mike Wainford ~ Real ale ~ Meals and snacks (till 10pm Fri and Sat; not Tue and Thur lunch Jan and Feb) ~ Carey (01432) 840242 ~ Children welcome ~ Open 12-2.30(3 Sat), 7(6 summer Sats)-11; closed 25 Dec ~ Bedrooms: £30B/£48B

DEFFORD SO9143 Map 4

Monkey House

Woodmancote; A4104 towards Upton – immediately after passing Oak public house on right, there's a small group of cottages, of which this is the last

A very special though highly unusual place, this pretty black-and-white cottage is one of the few remaining absolutely traditional cider-houses, a charming example of unspoilt rustic simplicity. Set back from the road behind a small garden with one or two fruit trees, you might at first think it just a private house – there's no inn-sign, or even a bar counter. Instead there's a hatch beside the door where very cheap Bulmer's Medium or Special Dry cider, tapped from wooden barrels, is poured by jug into pottery mugs. Beer is sold in cans – a concession to modern tastes. They don't do food (except crisps and nuts), but allow you to bring your own. In good weather, you can stand outside with Tess the bull terrier and Tapper the Jack Russell, and hens and cockerels that wander in from an adjacent collection of caravans and sheds; they now have two horses called Murphy and Mandy. Or you can retreat to a small side outbuilding with a couple of plain tables, a settle and an open fire; darts and dominoes. The name came from a drunken customer some years ago who fell into bramble bushes and insisted he was attacked by monkeys. *(Recommended by Derek and Sylvia Stephenson, Graham*

Reeve, W A Wheeler and others; more reports please)

Free house ~ Licensee Graham Collins ~ (01386) 750234 ~ Open 11-2.30, 6-10.30 (11 Fri and Sat); closed Mon evening, all day Tues

DORSTONE SO3141 Map 6

Pandy 🍺

Pub signed off B4348 E of Hay-on-Wye

The oldest pub in the county, a cosy and atmospheric half-timbered place built in 1185 by Richard de Brico to house workers constructing a chapel of atonement for his part in the murder of the murder of Thomas à Becket. It's very relaxed and friendly, with really very good bar food, from a changing menu that might include sandwiches, soup, warm chicken liver salad with raspberry dressing (£3.75), vegetarian dishes like moussaka or nut roast, popular pies such as pheasant and pigeon, steak and Guinness or wild rabbit (from £5.45), chicken tikka masala (£5.95), venison and steak ragout with simmal dumplings (£6.95), and lots of home-made puddings like treacle and walnut tart or locally-made sheep's milk ice cream; most dishes come in big helpings. There's also a sandwich and snack menu, and maybe occasional Indian themed evenings (the licensee went on an Indian cookery course). The obviously well-cared for main room – on the right as you go in – has heavy beams in the ochre ceiling, stout timbers, upright chairs on its broad worn flagstones and in its various alcoves, and a vast open fireplace with logs – you may see a couple of slumbering cats in front of here. They usually have three beers on handpump at a time, maybe four in summer, such as very well kept Bass and Hook Norton alternated with a guest like Gales Pompey Royal or Woods Parish; lots of Scotch whiskies and all major Irish ones, and unlimited coffee. A games area with stripped stone walls and a big woodburning stove has pool, darts, dominoes, quoits, old-fashioned juke box, video and fruit machine, and they hold quiz evenings; a side extension has been kept more or less in character. There are picnic-table sets and a play area in the neat side garden, and the pub is in a lovely setting, surrounded by most attractive, partly wooded gentle hills. *(Recommended by P A Clark, Huw and Carolyn Lewis, K R Wood, Ted George, Sue Demont, Tim Barrow, A K Thorlby, BKA, Chris and Chris Vallely, Gwen and Peter Andrews)*

Free house ~ Licensees Chris and Margaret Burtonwood ~ Real ale ~ Meals and snacks (winter not Mon lunchtime or all day Tues) ~ (01981) 550273 ~ Children welcome ~ Visiting Morris dancers and ceilidh band in summer, occasional jazz, folk nights or piano sing-alongs ~ Open 12-3, 7-11; winter closed Mon lunchtime and all day Tues

FOWNHOPE SO5834 Map 4

Green Man 🛏 £

B4224

One of the more famous landlords of this striking black and white inn was Tom Spring, the champion bare-knuckle fighter born in the village in 1795; the lounge is named after him. In fact the hotel has had quite an interesting history since it opened in the late 15th c, providing shelter for Colonel Birch and his Roundhead forces the night before they recaptured Hereford in the Civil War, and later used as a Petty Sessions Court; you can still see the iron bars to which prisoners were chained, the cell, and the judge's bedroom with a special lock on the door. These days it's well-liked for its generously served good value food, from a range that includes very good sandwiches (from £1.35), soup (£1.65), ploughman's or deep fried plaice (£3.30), roast local chicken (£3.50), salads (from £3.95), lasagne (£4.30), home-made steak pie or trout with almonds (£5.10), rump steak (£7.25), specials such as beef, mushroom and ale casserole or smoked cod crumble (£4.50), puddings (£1.75) and children's meals (from £2.80); they do a Sunday carvery in one of the restaurants. Well kept and very attractively priced Boddingtons, Courage Directors, Hook Norton Best, Marstons Pedigree and Sam

Smiths OB on handpump, some under light blanket pressure, and Weston's farm ciders; helpful staff. Standing timbers create the feel of several separate rooms, and the nicest bar, on the left as you come in from the road, has a big log fire, comfortable armchairs under its high oak beams, long cushioned settles agains the timbered ochre walls (hung with small pictures and brasses), and seats set into tall latticed windows; fruit machine. The residents' lounges and the main restaurant are no-smoking. The quiet garden behind has robust benches and seats around slatted tables among the trees and flowerbeds of the big lawn, where they serve coffee and afternoon tea in good weather; there's also a play area. They do get very busy indeed, especially at weekends – you'll find its original atmosphere best at other times. *(Recommended by Mr and Mrs B Hobden, Andy and Jill Kassube, Veronica Purcocks, Jane and Calum McLean, N Hardyman, Gwen and Peter Andrews, Mr and Mrs A F Walters, N P Cox, Graham Reeve; more reports please)*

Free house ~ Licensees Arthur and Margaret Williams ~ Real ale ~ Meals and snacks (12-2, 6-10) ~ Two restaurants ~(01432) 860243 ~ Children welcome ~ Open 11-3, 6-11 ~ Bedrooms: £31B/£49B

HANLEY CASTLE SO8442 Map 4

Three Kings £ ◧

Pub signposted (not prominently) off B4211 opposite Manor House gates, N of Upton upon Severn, follow Church End signpost

Very restful and unhurried, this unspoilt old place has been in the same family for 80 years now, and you get the feeling nothing much has changed for most of that time. The little rooms have a genuinely old-fashioned atmosphere, and an air of cosy intimacy that readers really like. The little tiled-floor taproom on the right is separated off from the entrance corridor by the monumental built-in settle which faces its equally vast inglenook fireplace. A hatch here serves very well kept Butcombe Bitter, Thwaites and usually three guest beers on handpump, and a good range of malt whiskies and farm cider. On the left, another room is decorated with lots of small locomotive pictures, and has darts, dominoes, shove-ha'penny and cribbage. A separate entrance leads to the comfortable timbered lounge with a neatly blacked kitchen range, little leatherette armchairs and spindleback chairs arounds its tables, and another antique winged and high-backed settle. Bar food includes a number of remarkably low-priced dishes such as soup (75p), sandwiches (from 80p, toasties £1.00), omelettes (from £1.50), ploughman's (from £1.95), sausage, egg and chips, plaice or burgers (£2), as well as changing specials like provençale nut Wellington (£5.75), salmon en croûte (£6), beef Wellington (£6.75), or grilled fillet steak (£8.50); be warned that they say that the specials may take at least half an hour to prepare, and a couple of readers have had to wait slightly longer. Bow windows in the three main rooms and old-fashioned wood-and-iron seats on the front terrace look across to the great cedar which shades the tiny green. *(Recommended by John and Marianne Cooper, Derek and Sylvia Stephenson, DAV, P and M Rudlin, Mike Dickerson, Ian and Nita Cooper, A R Pike, Bill Edwards, W A Wheeler, P J Hanson, Jed and Virginia Brown, Peter Lloyd)*

Free house ~ Licensee Mrs Sheila Roberts ~ Real ale ~ Meals and snacks (not Sun evening) ~ Upton upon Severn (01684) 592686 ~ Children in family room, maybe elsewhere if not busy ~ Live music every Sun and alternate Sat evenings, folk club alternate Thurs ~ Open 11-3, 7-11; closed evening 25 Dec ~ Bedrooms: £27.50B/£45B

KIDDERMINSTER SO8376 Map 4

Little Tumbling Sailor

42 Mill Lane; from Mill St, which is signposted off ring road by A442 Bridgnorth exit, fork right at General Hospital up narrow lane

Lots of the places we recommend seem to be quite hard to track down, but you shouldn't have any trouble with this vibrant themed pub – if you do get stuck, it's the one with the big mock-up lighthouse on top. It's another of Mad O'Rourke's idiosyncratic Little chain, this one done up in seafaring style but with the usual unpretentious cheery bustle. Inside the rooms meander right the way around a central servery, every inch of the navy-blue walls and ceilings packed with a particularly rich collection of naval photographs, attended by the relevant sailor's hat riband for each ship. Dotted around are masses of other seafaring pictures, model ships, ships' wheels and badges, nautical brassware, net-floats, hammocks, anchors, oars, a naughty figurehead, and rope fancywork; also, red and blue leatherette seats around cast-iron-framed tables. Reliable home-made bar food includes sandwiches (weekday lunchtimes only), soup (£1.75), filled baked potatoes (from £2.50), calamari (£3.25), a wide choice of vegetarian meals on a separate menu (from £3.95 – all with interesting salads), herby chicken pasty, lasagne or chilli (£4.25), fisherman's pie (£4.50), the old favourite, their Desperate Dan pie (£4.95), and poached salmon (£6.95), with daily changing specials and home-made puddings such as sticky toffee pudding or tumbling sailor ice cream (all £1.80). Well kept Holt, Plant and Deakins Entire and Mild, and the chain's own Lumphammer on handpump, and house wine; fruit machine, and piped popular music. They sell their own pink seaside rock, key rings, printed T-shirts, and edited paper *The Lark*. The little sheltered garden has a trawler's deckhouse and a sand pit. *(Recommended by S P Bobeldijk, Pete Yearsley, Stephen, Julie and Hayley Brown, David and Shelia, Peter Burton)*

Free house ~ Licensee Sharon Moffitt ~ Real ale ~ Meals and snacks (till 10) ~ (01562) 747 527 ~ Well behaved children welcome ~ Music night Mon (from 50s and 60s to Folk and Irish) ~ Open 12-3, 6-11

KNIGHTWICK SO7355 Map 4

Talbot 🛏 🍷

Knightsford Bridge; B4197 just off A44 Worcester—Bromyard

Back on top form again, this rambling 14th-c inn has a range of food that's by no means cheap but really is impressive – imaginative, well presented and full of flavour. A typical day's menu might feature sandwiches, soup (from £1.50 for pea and lovage, £1.75 for the delicous filling chicken), fresh asparagus, blue cheese pancake or pork, orange and cognac pâté (£4.25), gravadlax or king prawns and garlic noodles (£4.95), liver and bacon (£6.50), steak and kidney pie (£7.25), ratatouille and falafel (£7.95), herb-crusted pork with shallots (£8.50), lamb noisettes with orange and cinnamon (£8.25), casseroled hare with noodles (£9.50), steamed monkfish on a bed of leeks and bulb fennel (£11.95), turbot in a pernod, cream and chive sauce (£12.95) and puddings like rhubarb and ginger pavlova or Italian poached pear pudding (from £3); several readers feel the helpings could sometimes be bigger. Bass, Hobsons Bitter and Worthingtons on handpump, all well kept and, with the latter two at times just £1 a pint, exceptionally well priced; also good wines by the glass and freshly squeezed orange juice. The lounge has a variety of interesting seats from small carved or leatherette armchairs to the winged settles by the tall bow windows, heavy beams, entertaining and rather distinguished coaching and sporting prints and paintings on its butter-coloured walls, and a vast stove which squats in the big central stone hearth; there's another log fire, too, though it's not always lit. The well furnished back public bar has darts, pool on a raised side area, fruit machine, video game and juke box. Well behaved dogs welcome. There are some old-fashioned seats outside, in front, with more on a good-sized lawn over the lane (they serve out here too). Some of the bedrooms are above the bar; if you're staying, expect good breakfasts. *(Recommended by Alan Skull, Thomas Low-Beer, P Hunter, R G and M P Lumley, Mr and Mrs Sean Crampton, Rebecca Mortimer, Mr and Mrs Bryn Gardner, Mrs S le Bert-Francis, Ian Jones)*

Free house ~ Licensees Annie and Wiz Clift ~ Real ale ~ Meals and snacks ~ Restaurant ~ (01886) 21235 ~ Children in eating area until 7.30 ~ Folk night alternate Fri, Morris dancers every winter Weds ~ Open 11-11; closed 25 Dec evening ~ Bedrooms: £24.50(£31B)/£42(£56.50B)

Sunday opening is generally 12-3 and 7-10.30 throughout England.

LEDBURY SO7138 Map 4

Feathers 🍺 ♀

High Street, A417

The Prince of Wales whose heraldic feathers give this striking and familiar old building its name was Prince Arthur, who, if he had lived, would have become king in 1509 instead of his brother, Henry VIII. The elaborate timbering of the elegant black and white frontage dates back mainly to about this period, though the top floor was added a century later; if you look closely from across the road you should be able to spot the join. Readers this year have been particularly enthusiastic about the bar food, imaginative and tasty, and served on hand-made pottery; the choice includes good soup (£2.95), starters like gratin of roast Mediterranean vegetables or fettucini with prawns and pesto (£3.95), asparagus timbale with coriander and crème fraîche (£4.65), and fillet of trout with dill cream and pumpernickel (£4.95), main courses such as spicy fishcakes (£5.85), spinach and ricotta cheese filo tart with a sweet pepper salad (£7.50), venison sausages with braised red cabbage and apple (£7.95), turkey schnitzel with noodles (£9.45), and grilled salmon topped with brie on watercress sauce (£9.85), and puddings including hot rum and raisin cheesecake or passion fruit syllabub (£3.25); friendly, attentive service. They do good afternoon teas. Often very busy, the popular and quite atmospheric Fuggles Bar – broken up into areas by attractive brick pillars – has one or two old oak panelled settles, comfortable upholstered seats, pleasantly individual cloth banquettes built into bays, beams and timbers as well as some blond squared panelling, and fresh flowers on a variety of solid tables. Decorations include 19th-c caricatures, fowl prints on the stripped brick chimney breast, hop bines draped liberally over the beams, some country antiques, and soft lighting from picture lamps, one or two table lamps and old-fashioned wall lamps. Big curtained windows look over the rather narrow coachyard. There's also a more formal lounge by the reception area with high-sided armchairs and settees. Well kept Bass, Courage Directors, Crown Buckley Reverend James, Worthington BB and maybe a guest beer on handpump, a 70 bin-end wine list, various malt whiskies, farm cider. They have their own squash courts. *(Recommended by Gordon Theaker, TBB, Alan Skull, Mike Beiley, R G and M P Lumley, Tony and Wynne Gifford, AT, J Weeks, Derek and Cerys Williams, Graham Reeve, Dr M I Crichton, John Bowdler, Tony and Lynne Gifford)*

Free house ~ Licensee D M Elliston ~ Real ale ~ Meals and snacks (till 10pm Fri and Sat) ~ Restaurant (not Sun evening) ~ Ledbury (01531) 635266 ~ Children in eating area ~ Live music Thurs and alternate Tues ~ Open 11-11 ~ Bedrooms: £59.50B/£78.50B

LUGWARDINE SO5541 Map 4

Crown & Anchor ♀

Cotts Lane; just off A438 E of Hereford

This attractive old black-and-white timbered inn, in what's become a dormitory village for Hereford with quite a lot of stylish mainly modern houses, used to be a Whitbreads pub and stood closed for some time, until the Squireses bought it just before it went to auction. Many readers will recognise them from the Butchers Arms at Woolhope, where Mr Squires was for some time the mainstay barman. They've made the Crown & Anchor smart and comfortable inside, with an interesting mix of furnishings in its several smallish character rooms (one suitable for families), and as those who knew them at the Butchers would expect, a friendly and very pleasant atmosphere. A wide choice of food includes interesting dishes such as herring with tomato (£2.75), rabbit with garlic, ginger and soy (£5.50), a remarkable pie made with local eel, sherry and nutmeg (£6.20) and pork baked with spinach and mozzarella (£6.50), besides staples such as sandwiches (from £1.25), ploughman's (£3.50), good cold platters (meat £4.50, smoked fish or seafood £5.50) and several vegetarian dishes such as courgette and ricotta lasagne (£5.20); besides usual children's dishes (£2.40), they will do small helpings of some other main courses, and main dishes come with a choice of accompaniments – chips, salad, vegetables, rice, even paella. Well kept Bass, Hook Norton Best, Worthington BB, M&B Mild or Highgate Mild and a weekly guest beer such as Sam Powells Old Sam on handpump, decent wines including a clutch of usefully priced bin ends; big log fire. *(Recommended by Lynn Sharpless, Bob Eardley, J H C Peters, Paul Merrick, Susan Martin)*

Free house ~ Licensees Nick and Julie Squires ~ Real ale ~ Meals and snacks (till 10) ~ (01432) 851303 ~ Children welcome ~ Open 11.30-11

MUCH MARCLE SO6633 Map 4

Slip Tavern

Off A449 SW of Ledbury; take Woolhope turning at village stores, then right at pub sign

Just one of the things that stands out about this quiet country pub is the truly welcoming and hospitable atmosphere; several readers turning up late have been delighted to find the friendly staff still happy to whip something up from the kitchens. Perhaps the most immediately arresting feature though is the dazzling gardens stretching out behind. The landlord used to be a nurseryman, which explains the quality of the interestingly laid out plantings, and the handsome displays in hanging baskets and big urns in front. There's a well separated play area out here, and maybe summer barbecues. Inside is cosy and chatty, with ladderback and wheelback chairs around the black tables of the immaculately kept lounge bar, angling around the counter to a similar family area. A good point is that the public bar (carpeted too) is divided off only by the bar counter itself – so in the lounge the atmosphere is warmed by the true country voices from over on the other side. Well kept Boddingtons and Hook Norton on handpump, with local farm ciders (the pub is surrounded by Weston's cider-apple orchards), and several wines; pleasant service, muted piped music. Nicely presented reasonably priced food includes sandwiches, soup (£1.40), ploughman's (from £3.50), filled jacket potatoes (£4.15), vegetarian meals like mushroom and nut fettucine (£4.95), steak pie (£4.75), a good choice of daily specials such as chicken with broccoli in a creamy sauce, cod cooked in cider or pork casserole with leek and onions (all £5.10) and puddings like strawberry and apple crumble (£2.10). There's more space for eating in the new conservatory (again attractively planted), though you may still at times find it helpful to book. The pub is named after a nearby hillside landslip in the last century (there was another in 1988). *(Recommended by AT, Mr and Mrs J Brown, Mrs Pat Crabb, Mr and Mrs W W Swaitt, Neil and Anita Christopher, Mr and Mrs J Back, Barbara Wensworth, Alan Illidge, Margaret Drazin, Graham Reeve, G and M Hollis)*

Free house ~ Licensee Gilbert E Jeanes ~ Real ale ~ Meals and snacks ~ Restaurant (not Sun) ~ (01531) 660246 ~ Children welcome ~ Open 11.30-2.30, 6.30-11

OMBERSLEY SO8463 Map 4

Crown & Sandys Arms ⇐ ♀

Coming into the village from the A433, turn left at the roundabout, into the 'Dead End' road

This pretty Dutch-gabled white inn is doing very well at the meoment, with the civilised meals still what seems to be drawing most people in. The choice generally includes generously-filled sandwiches (from £1.60), very good soups (£1.50), popular salmon terrine (£2.50), ploughman's (from £2.75), avocado pear with prawns and crabmeat (£3.15), home-made curry (£4.95), steak and kidney pie (£5.15), gammon (£6.25), 10oz local sirloin steak (£8.55), very well praised and imaginative daily specials (the wild boar with mead and apricots and the turkey and langoustine kebabs have been favourites), several local game and fish dishes, and evening meals like monkfish and black tiger prawn tails in vermouth and peppercorn sauce (£8.50), pan-fried venison in gin and juniper sauce, and roast duck with savoury onion marmalade (£8.95); lots of home-made puddings (£2.25), and children's dishes (£1.50). Try and get here early for lunch, they do get busy. Hook Norton Best and Old Hookey and a range of guest beers like

Bass, Butcombe Bitter, Shepherd Neame Spitfire or Woods Special on handpump, an extensive wine list with a range of country wines, and coffee, tea and hot chocolate with whipped cream and chocolate flakes; very good efficient service. The lounge bar has comfortable Windsor armchairs, antique settles, a couple of easy chairs and plush built-in wall seats, black beams and some flagstones, old prints, maps and ornamental clocks (which are for sale) on its timbered walls, log fires and maybe daily newspapers; half is no smoking. There are picnic-table sets in the garden behind the building, where in summer they may have miniature golf. No dogs except guide dogs. *(Recommended by M G Hart, Mr and Mrs J Brown, Alan Skull, E H and R F Warner, Thomas Low-Beer, Michael and Margaret Norris, George Atkinson, A R and B E Sayer, Steve and Jill Taylor, DAV, R M Bloomfield, Neville Kenyon, J Weeks, Dr M I Crichton, Marian Greenwood, Graham Reeve, Ian Smith, P Boot, Dr P D Putwain, Paul and Margaret Baker)*

Free house ~ Licensee R E Ransome ~ Real ale ~ Meals and snacks (till 9.45) ~ Restaurant ~ Worcester (01905) 620252 ~ Well behaved children allowed until 7pm (no prams, push-chairs or carrycots) ~ Open 11-2.30, 5.30-11; closed 25 Dec, and evenings 26 Dec and 1 Jan ~ Bedrooms: £25S/£35S

Kings Arms

They've been busy at this bustling black-beamed and timbered Tudor pub over the last year, transforming the old kitchen into a new lounge to create more space for dining. At the same time the whole place was sympathetically refurbished, and building work turned up a hitherto forgotten inglenook fireplace, bringing the total number of fireplaces in the building to four. The comfortable, informal rooms ramble around various nooks and crannies full of stuffed animals and birds and a collection of rustic bric-a-brac; one room has Charles II's coat of arms moulded into its decorated plaster ceiling – he's reputed to have been here in 1651. It's a very popular place for tasty home-made food, with the changing menus frequently adapted to suit new tastes and trends; well-liked dishes include sandwiches (not evenings or Sun), soup (£1.95), spicy chicken wings, garlic mussels or one of several French cheeses covered in sesame seeds then deep-fried (£4.95), steak and kidney pie (£5.25), fennel and potato hotpot (£5.45), salmon and cod fishcakes or cold roast meat platter (£5.75), seafood tagliatelle (£5.95), chicken, ham and leek pie (£6.25), steak (£8.95), and puddings (£2.45); it can get very busy at lunchtimes. Well kept Bass, Boddingtons and Flowers Original on handpump, maybe under light blanket pressure, with a decent range of malt whiskies; quick cheerful service. No dogs inside. A tree-sheltered courtyard has tables under cocktail parasols, and colourful hanging baskets and tubs in summer. *(Recommended by Jack Barnwell, Basil J S Minson, John Radford, David Mair, David Rogers, Brian Kneale, Dorothee and Dennis Glover, Dr S J Parkinson, Graham Reeve, J Barnwell, Patrick and Patricia Derwent, Tony and Pat Martin, Mrs R Smyth, W C M Jones, Steve de Mellow, Alan Sherman, S J Cutforth)*

Free house ~ Licensees Chris and Judy Blundell ~Real ale ~ Meals and snacks (till 10, all day Sun) ~ (01905) 620315 ~ Children over 8 in eating area if eating, up to 8.30pm ~ Open 11-2.45, 5.30-11; 12-10.30 Sat

PEMBRIDGE   SO3958   Map 6

New Inn

Market Square; A44

Despite the name, the massive stones below the black and white timbered walls of this beautiful village inn date back to 1311, and the building used to house the Petty Sessions court and jail. Simple, but comfortable and atmospheric, the three little rooms of the aged bar have oak peg-latch doors, elderly traditional furnishings including a fine antique curved-back settle on the worn flagstones, and a substantial log fire. Good honest home cooking includes sandwiches, tasty soup (£2), stilton and pork pâté (£3.50), leek and mushroom croustade or warm smoked turkey and avocado salad (£4.25), chicken and apricot casserole (£5), pork fillets in mustard and cream or trout with lime and fennel (£6), duckling in apple and cider sauce (£8.75), and puddings like bananas baked in cider or lemon fudge tart (£2); efficient, friendly service. John Smiths and Ruddles Best and County on handpump or tapped from the cask, wines from Australia, Chile and Greece and 30 malt whiskies; cribbage, shove-ha'penny, dominoes, darts and quoits. Lavatories are outside. There are some tables on the cobblestones between the pub and the open-sided 16th-c former wool market behind it, with good views of the neighbouring church with its unusual detached bell-tower. The pub's regulars apparently include the ghost of a redcoat soldier and the similarly spectral presence of a wronged girl, who, not one to fall for the same flannel twice, appears to women but never to men. *(Recommended by Steve Goodchild, A E and P McCully, Kevin and Katharine Cripps, M G Hart, P A Clark and others, Margaret and Roy Randle, Nick and Alison Dowson, Andy Stone, Peter Rees; more reports please)*

Free house ~ Licensee Jane Melvin ~ Real ale ~ Meals and snacks ~ Restaurant (not Sun evening) ~ Pembridge (0154) 4388427 ~ Children in eating area until 9pm ~ Monthly jazz ~ Open 11-3, 6(6.30 winter)-11 ~ Bedrooms: £17.50/£35

RUCKHALL SO4539 Map 4

Ancient Camp 🛏 ♀

Ruckhall signposted off A465 W of Hereford at Belmont Abbey; from Ruckhall pub signed down private drive; can reach it too from Bridge Sollers, W of Hereford on A438 – cross Wye, then after a mile or so take first left, then left again to Eaton Bishop, and left to Ruckhall

Hereford & Worcester Dining Pub of the Year

In any weather the peaceful rustic views from this stylish country inn are quite magnificent, but it's on sunny days you appreciate them properly, sitting out on the terrace among the roses, and looking down to the river and beyond. If you're staying try and get the front bedroom which has the same view, as does the bar. Inside it's well kept and rather smart, the central beamed and flagstoned bar simply but thoughtfully furnished with comfortably solid green-upholstered settles and library chairs around nice old elm tables. On the left, a green-carpeted room has matching sofas around the walls, kitchen chairs around tripod tables, a big Victorian architectural drawing of the imposing Ram Mills in Oldham (the family firm), and a good few sailing pictures. On the right, there are simple dining chairs around stripped kitchen tables on a brown carpet, and stripped stonework; nice log fire. Good quality, home-made food includes sandwiches, soup (£2.25), garlic mushrooms (£3.70), taramasalata or ploughman's (from £3.95), black-eyed bean and mushroom casserole (£4.95), spaghetti with chicken and pine nuts in basil sauce (£5.75), baked red peppers with mozzarella and anchovies (£5.95), and beef in Guinness or oxtail casserole (£6.95); another menu has more elaborate dishes like pears in roquefort cheese and watercress sauce (£4.25), moules marinières (£9.75), and poached chicken in lemon and black pepper sauce with asparagus (£10.25). Well kept Whitbreads West Country PA and Woods Parish on handpump, decent wines and spirits, and prompt friendly service; good log fires, maybe unobtrusive piped music. Take care when parking at night – one reader felt he was going to topple into the Wye. *(Recommended by Mr and Mrs W W Swaitt, John Bowdler, R G and M P Lumley, Martin Richards, P A Clark, Mrs S Wright, Peter Yearsley, Chris and Chris Vallely)*

Free house ~ Licensees David and Nova Hague ~ Real ale ~ Meals and snacks (not Sun evening, not Mon) ~ Restaurant – closed Sun and Mon ~ Golden Valley (01981) 250449 ~ Children in eating area lunchtime only; only residential if over 8 ~ Very occasional jazz ~ Open 12-2.30, 6-11; closed Mon lunchtime, all day Mon in winter ~ Bedrooms: £35B/£48B

SELLACK SO5627 Map 4

Lough Pool Inn ★ ♀

Back road Hoarwithy—Ross on Wye; OS Sheet 162 map reference 558268

The esteem in which readers hold this attractive black and white timbered cottage is clear to us from the way several of them recommend we award it one of our place to stay awards – even though the pub doesn't do bedrooms: obviously they feel, like us, that it's the sort of place you don't really want to leave. The cosy atmosphere and friendly welcome both stand out, but what most people seem to like best of all is the excellent range of very tasty home-made food. Consistently reliable meals include soup (£1.90), stilton and port pâté (£2.75), moules marinières (£2.80), jumbo sausages (£3.50), ploughman's (£3.75), ribs in spicy sauce or especially highly praised vegetarian dishes like bean and vegetable goulash or Caribbean fruit curry (£5.75), steak and kidney pie (£5.95), plaice (£6.50), chicken korma (£6.75), steaks, salmon in prawn, mushroom and white wine sauce (£8.45) and the much-loved Greek-style goat casserole (£8.50); prices are unchanged from last year. Service may slow down at busy periods (weekdays are quieter). The beamed central room has a log fire at each end, kitchen chairs and cushioned window seats around plain wooden tables, sporting prints and bunches of dried flowers, and a mainly flagstoned floor. Other rooms lead off, with attractive individual furnishings and nice touches like the dresser of patterned plates; piped classical music. Well kept Bass, John Smiths and Wye Valley Hereford on handpump, as well as a good range of malt whiskies, local farm ciders and a well-chosen wine list. No dogs inside (except guide dogs). The neat front lawn has plenty of picnic-table sets, and the surrounding countryside is lovely. The lough pool from which the pub takes its name, over the road by an ancient redwood, has long since dried to mud. *(Recommended by P Brown, Alan and Ruth Woodhouse, Roger Byrne, Ted George, Mr and Mrs W W Swaitt, Bill and Edee Miller, David and Mary Thomas, M A Watkins, Marian Greenwood, J E and A G Jones, Neil and Anita Christopher, N P Cox, Pat and John Millward)*

Free house ~ Licensees Philip and Janet Moran ~ Real ale ~ Meals and snacks ~ Restaurant ~ Harewood End (01989) 730236 ~ Children in restaurant and snug ~ Open 12-3, 6.30-11; closed 25 Dec

ST OWENS CROSS SO5425 Map 4

New Inn 🛏

Harewood End

Fine views over rolling countryside to the distant Black Mountains from this lovely timbered 15th-c coaching inn, known locally as 'the pub with the hanging baskets' (the pub is festooned with them) or 'the pub with the three dobermans (Baileys and her two daughters Tia Maria and Ginnie). Inside, there are lots of nooks and crannies, settles, old pews, beams, timbers, huge inglenook fireplaces in both lounge bar and restaurant, a happy mix of drinkers and diners, and a lively, cheerful atmosphere. Bar food is home-made using only local seasonal produce, and a typical day's choice might include sandwiches (from £1.75), soup (£1.95), chicken liver and brandy pâté (£2.95), vegetarian lasagne (£4.25), salads (from £4.50), home-made steak and kidney pie or Mexican chicken (£5.50), daily specials like beef in red wine or smoked haddock and prawn bake (£5.95) and poached lemon sole in prawn and white wine sauce (£6.25), char-grilled swordfish (£6.95), steaks (from £8.95), puddings (£2.25), and children's dishes (from £1.75); the same menu is available in the restaurant. Well kept Bass, Courage Directors, Hook Norton Old Hookey, Smiles Best, Tetleys, and Wadworths 6X on handpump, a good choice of malt whiskies, local ciders, and decent choice of wines including English ones; darts, pool, shove-ha'penny, dominoes, and piped music. The two bedrooms have four-posters and lots of beams. *(Recommended by John Dowsett, George Atkinson, J E and A G Jones; more reports please)*

Free house ~ Licensee Nigel Donovan ~ Real ale ~ Meals and snacks (till 10pm Sat) ~ Restaurant ~ (01989) 730274 ~ Children welcome ~ Occasional live entertainment ~ Open 12-2.30(3 Sat), 6-11 ~ Bedrooms: £30B/£50B

WEOBLEY SO4052 Map 6

Olde Salutation 🛏 ♀

Village signposted from A4112 SW of Leominster; and from A44 NW of Hereford (there's also a good back road direct from Hereford – straight out past S side of racecourse)

Looking straight down the broad main street of a picture-book village, this spotless and carefully run 500-year-old pub seems to get more popular every year. Most people come to eat, but despite the emphasis on food the atmosphere is relaxed, friendly and traditionally pubby. Excellent bar food such as soup (£2.10), deep-fried brie with blackcurrant dip (£3.75), smoked chicken crêpe (£3.85), first-class filled baguettes (from £3.20 – all the bread is home-made), sautéed lamb's kidneys (£5.50), steak and Guinness pie (£5.75), salmon and broccoli gratin (£5.95), and lots of daily specials like lentil terrine with red pepper sauce (£5.50), fillet of plaice with prawns and mussels or venison sausage with redcurrant sauce (£6.25) and grilled sirloin steak (£10.25); three-course Sunday lunch (£8.75); big breakfasts. The no-smoking restaurant has a more elaborate menu. The two areas of the quiet, comfortable lounge – separated by a few steps and standing timbers – have brocaded modern winged settles and smaller seats, a couple of big cut-away cask seats, wildlife decorations, a hop bine over the bar counter, and logs burning in a big stone fireplace; it's divided by more standing timbers from the neat restaurant area, and there's a separate smaller parquet-floored public bar with sensibly placed darts, and a fruit machine; dominoes, cribbage, draughts and chess. Well kept Bass, Boddingtons and Hook Norton Best on handpump, Weston's ciders, over 100 interesting wines and quite a good collection of whiskies; cheery, interested service. On a sheltered back terrace are tables and chairs with parasols. The prettily decorated bedrooms are clean and comfortable – there may even be flowers in the bathroom. *(Recommended by Mr and Mrs R Sparham, A P Jeffreys, Cath and John Howard, W H and E Thomas, DAV, the Monday Club, A Preston, P A Clark, Simon and Amanda Southwell, R J Walden, P Boot)*

Free house ~ Licensees Chris and Frances Anthony ~ Real ale ~ Meals and snacks ~ Restaurant (not Sun evening) ~ (01544) 318443 ~ Children in eating area of bar and restaurant ~ Open 11-3, 7-11; closed 25 Dec ~ Bedrooms: £32B/£54B

WINFORTON SO2947 Map 6

Sun

The chief draw at this neatly kept little pub has to be Mrs Hibbard's quite exceptional home-cooked meals; you'll often find bigger menus, but rarely one with so much imagination put into it. Not surprisingly we know of several people who find it impossible to drive past without stopping. The choice changes every day but might include dishes like spinach and fennel soup (£2.25), smoked salmon ravioli with chive sauce (£2.85), Thai-style chicken in filo pastry with a lemon and ginger sauce (£3.50), warm pigeon breast and wild mushroom salad (£3.50), mussels in coconut cream sauce (£3.95), various ploughman's with some unusual cheeses (£3.99), chicken and leek pie (£5.99), ragout of shellfish (£7.99), lamb with cider sauce, saffron and applemint or quail en croute with quince sauce (£8.99), wild boar casserole (£9.25), and a choice of up to ten exquisite puddings such as tipsy bread and butter pudding with nutty toffee sauce or chocolate and ginger cheesecake (£3.50). There's a really friendly feel to the two beamed areas on either side of the central servery, with an individual assortment of comfortable country-kitchen chairs, high-backed settles and good solid wooden tables, heavy-horse harness, brasses and old farm tools on the mainly stripped-stone walls, and two log-burning stoves. Well kept Felinfoel Double Dragon, Hook Norton Best and Woods Parish on handpump, and a dozen or so malt whiskies; sensibly placed darts, cribbage, dominoes, maybe piped music. The neat garden, with some sheltered tables, also has a good timbery play area. *(Recommended by Peter Yearsley, A K Thorlby, Mrs B Sugarman, P A Clark, Mrs C H Thompson, Pat and Paul Munday, Dr I W M Roper)*

Free house ~ Licensees Brian and Wendy Hibbard ~ Real ale ~ Meals and snacks (not winter Tues) ~ Eardisley (01544) 327677 ~ Children in eating area of bar ~ Open 11.30-3, 6.30-11; closed winter Tues

We say if we or readers have seen dogs or cats in a pub.

WOOLHOPE SO6136 Map 4

Butchers Arms ★ 🛏 🍷

Signposted from B4224 in Fownhope; carry straight on past Woolhope village

A friendly family-run black-and-white 14th-c pub, where everything seems to blend together naturally and they always seem pleased to see you. The food, setting and service have all come in for high praise, and in the last year or so readers have particularly enjoyed staying here, some regularly returning for an overnight break. The two welcoming bars are filled with flowers, and one has old-fashioned built-in seats with brocaded cushions, captain's chairs and stools around small tables, very low beams decorated with hops, old photographs of country people on the walls, and a brick fireplace filled with dried flowers. The other, broadly similar though with less beams, has a large built-in settle and another log fire. The very good bar food, usually served in generous helpings, might include lunchtime sandwiches (from £1.75), soup (£1.95), ploughman's with home-made chutney (£3.25), leek and hazelnut terrine wrapped in vine leaves (£3.25), salads (from £4.25), mushroom, butterbean and basil stew (£4.50), spinach and mushroom pancake (£4.95), wild rabbit cooked in local cider or steak and kidney pie (£5.25), lamb and cranberry casserole (£5.95), and a big range of puddings such as frozen ginger and coffee meringue cake and chocolate cup with cream; very good, hearty breakfasts; an à la carte menu is available on Saturday nights only. Well kept and very well priced Hook Norton Best and Old Hookey, Marstons Pedigree and a guest beer on handpump, local farm cider and wines, selection of malt whiskys, decent coffee. Friendly cat – dogs not welcome. Sliding french windows lead from the bar to a little terrace with teak furniture, a few parasols and cheerful flowering tubs; there's also a tiny willow-lined brook. The spotless bedrooms have welcome touches like a bowl of fruit and chocolates by the bed. The countryside around is really lovely – to enjoy some of the best of it, turn left as you come out of the pub and take the tiny left-hand road at the end of the car park; this turns into a track and then into a path; the view from the top of the hill is quite something. They tell us unruly children will be captured and sold as slaves. (*Recommended by Andy and Jill Kassube, C L Metz, the Monday Club, Mrs B Sugarman, Paul and Karen Mason, Roy Smylie, Lynn Sharpless, Bob Eardley, Mr and Mrs W W Swaitt, Ian Jones, C J Westmoreland, John Bowdler, Andrew and Barbara Sykes, Mr and Mrs D E Connell*)

Free house ~ Licensees Charlie Power and Lucinda Matthews ~ Real ale ~ Meals and snacks ~ Restaurant Sat only ~ (01432) 860281 ~ Well behaved children in eating area at landlord's discretion, up to 8pm ~ Occasional Morris dancing ~ Open 11.30-2.30, 6.30(7 Mon-Thurs in winter)-11; closed 25 Dec ~ Bedrooms: £25/£39

Crown ♀

In village centre

It's nice to see both our Woolhope pubs doing so well at the moment; this warmly welcoming old place in the heart of the village is still extremely popular, its spotless rooms and relaxing atmosphere worthy of note, but perhaps most appreciated for its range of often imaginative food. The choice generally includes soup (£1.65), potted stilton and mushrooms or grilled sardines with garlic (£2.75), avocado with prawns or crab or lunchtime ploughman's (£3.50), cauliflower and potato bake or mushroom and cashew nut roast (£4.75), chicken and asparagus lasagne, smoked salmon quiche or steak and kidney pie (£5.20), grilled trout with almonds (£5.75), lemon sole (£9.75), and excellent home-made puddings like chocolate and Cointreau mousse or crème brûlée with oranges and Grand Marnier (£2); children's meals (£2.50). One of the two bars is bookable (and no smoking). It can get busy, and service can slow right down then. Well kept Bass, Hook Norton Best, Smiles Best and two guests like Bass or Woods Bitter on handpump, priced below the regional average; Weston's and Stowford Press farm cider, a good range of wines; helpful service. The lounge bar is light and airy with dark burgundy plush button-back built-in wall banquettes and stools, a timbered divider strung with hop bines, good wildlife photographs and little country pictures on the cream walls, and open fires; very quiet piped music. There are picnic-table sets under cocktail parasols on the neat front lawn; darts, summer quoits. *(Recommended by Mrs Pat Crabb, Mr and Mrs W W Swaitt, Derek and Sylvia Stephenson, R G and M P Lumley, Peter Lloyd, Alan Skull, the Monday Club, W F C Phillips, Andy and Jill Kassube, W L Congreve, W H and E Thomas, C J Westmoreland)*

Free house ~ Licensees Neil and Sally Gordon ~ Real ale ~ Meals and snacks (till 10) ~ Restaurant ~ Fownhope (01432) 860468 ~ Well behaved children allowed till 8, though customers with under 10s are asked to check with licensee to avoid there being too many at one time ~ Open 12-2.30, 6.30(7 winter Mon-Thurs)-11; closed evening 25 Dec

WYRE PIDDLE SO9647 Map 4

Anchor

B4084 NW of Evesham

Customers are as likely to arrive by boat as by car at this relaxing 17th-c place, for many people the archetypal summer pub. A spacious lawn runs down to the River Avon, and on fine days the tables out here are a wonderful place to relax and take in the view, spreading out over the Vale of Evesham as far as the Cotswolds, the Malverns and Bredon Hill. They also offer ringside seats for the kind of blissfully unspectacular activities that on a lazy day seem so compelling: summer barges tying up on the moorings alongside, or ducks scuttling about on the water. In winter the setting takes on a new mood, just as impressive, but better appreciated then from the big airy back bar inside. The friendly and well kept little lounge has a good log fire in its attractively restored inglenook fireplace, comfortably upholstered chairs and settles, and two beams in the shiny ceiling. Very popular bar food includes good helpings of soup (£1.95), open filled baps (from £1.95), ploughman's (from £3.20), moules marinières (£4.50), spinach cannelloni (£4.60), home-made pies like steak and kidney or chicken, ham and mushroom (£4.90), changing specials such as chicken and mushroom curry (£5.25) or a good tagliatelle (£6.25), steaks (from £9), and puddings like good home-made meringue concoctions (from £2); three-course Sunday lunch. Friendly, obliging service. Well kept Boddingtons, Flowers IPA, Marstons Pedigree and Morlands Old Speckled Hen on handpump or tapped from the cask, and several malt whiskies, bottled beers and fruit wines; fruit machine. They can get busy, but no wonder – several readers feel that sitting outside here is hard to beat. *(Recommended by Michael and Margaret Norris, Peter Pocklington, R J Herd, Simon and Louise Chappell, D R Shillitoe, John and Marianne Cooper, Alan and Jane Clarke, Bronwen and Steve Wrigley, Brad, Joni and Kristin Nelson, Bill Sykes, Simon Parkinson, George Murdoch, Mike Whitehouse, Basil Minson, Iris and Eddie Brixton)*

Whitbreads ~ Lease: Michael Senior ~ Real ale ~ Meals and snacks (not Sun evening) ~ River-view lunchtime restaurant ~ Pershore (01386) 552799 ~ Children welcome ~ Open 11-2.30(12-3 Sat), 6-11

> Post Office address codings confusingly give the impression that some pubs are in Hereford and Worcester, when they're really in the Midlands, Shropshire, Gloucestershire or even Wales (which is where we list them).

Lucky Dip

Besides the fully inspected pubs, you might like to try these Lucky Dips recommended to us and described by readers (if you do, please send us reports):

Abberley [SO7667], *Manor Arms*: Comfortable village pub in quiet backwater, good lunchtime bar food, well kept beers, interesting collection of toby jugs and coats of arms; bedrooms *(Nick Cox)*

☆ **Abbey Dore** [SO3830], *Neville Arms*: Pleasant unpretentious and welcoming atmosphere, good bar food such as local brook trout with good veg, well kept beers; beautiful Golden Valley views, friendly landlord, good coffee; interesting façade *(Derek Allpass, Jill White)*

☆ **Allensmore** [SO4735], *Three Horseshoes*: Good range of value for money food inc good puddings in attractive and beautifully placed 17th-c timbered pub with a good deal of character; well kept Bass *(Dr S Bhattacharya, Mr and Mrs E Burton)*

☆ **Aston Crews** [SO6723], *Penny Farthing*: Partly 15th c, interesting good value food, roomy and relaxing bar with easy chairs, two restaurant areas, one with pretty valley and Forest of Dean views from its picture windows; well kept Bass and Hook Norton on handpump, decent wines, cheerful owner; garden tables, bedrooms *(Mr and Mrs J Back, BB)*

Badsey [2 miles E of Evesham on B4035 ; SP0743], *Round of Gras*: Popular fresh-cooked food, esp asparagus, in straightforward pub with Whitbreads-related ales and log fire *(Dave Braisted, Kathryn and Brian Heathcote, BB)*

☆ **Barnards Green** [junction B4211 to Rhydd Green with B4208 to Malvern Show Ground – OS Sheet 150 map ref 793455; SO7945], *Blue Bell*: Well laid-out, comfortably and attractively refurbished Marstons dining pub in pleasant setting, wide choice of reasonably priced standard food from sandwiches to steaks inc vegetarian dishes, well kept Best and Pedigree and maybe Banks's Mild, friendly quick service, small no-smoking area, lavatories for the disabled; children allowed till 8, nice garden *(Frank Cummins, Mr and Mrs A F Walters, Graham Reeve, Dave Braisted)*

Barnt Green [SP0173], *Victoria*: Two-level brick-built pub, food inc decent sandwiches *(Dave Braisted)*

Belbroughton [High St (off A491); SO9277], *Queens*: Friendly local in quiet village, under new management but no major changes, simple food, well kept beer *(Andy Petersen)*

☆ **Bishops Frome** [just off B4214 Bromyard—Ledbury; SO6648], *Green Dragon*: Good interesting range of well kept beers inc five northerners in attractive unspoilt flagstoned pub with plenty of character, good choice of reasonably priced standard bar food inc good home-made pasta, fine log fire, games

room, seats outside; children welcome, no dogs; open all day Sat (and can get crowded and noisy) *(D L Gordon, Hugh Spottiswoode, Rebecca Mortimer, LYM)*

Bishops Frome [B4214; SO6648], *Chase*: Simple friendly village local opp green, seats on terrace, children welcome; three comfortable bedrooms *(Jill Easty, Graham Laylee)*

Bredenbury [A44 Bromyard—Leominster; SO6156], *Barneby Arms*: Locally popular for wide range of generously served food inc Sun carvery and vegetarian dishes in large hotel bar, bright and clean, with lots of old woodworking tools; well kept beers, friendly staff; comfortable bedrooms *(Peter Collins, W H and E Thomas)*

☆ **Broadway** [Collin Lane; marked Gt Collin Farm on OS Sheet; follow Willersey sign off A44 NW – OS Sheet 150 map ref 076391; SP0739], *Collin House*: Good bar lunches inc interesting freshly cooked main courses and good traditional puddings in lovely bar of small country hotel, very relaxed and civilised – good log fires, no machines or piped music (but no sandwiches or ploughman's either), very accommodating; nice restaurant not overpriced, good wine list, local beers, proper coffee, pleasant staff; tables outside; comfortable bedrooms *(Lawrence Bacon, Peter Lloyd, W H and Mrs E Thomas, W C M Jones)*

☆ **Broadway** [Main St (A44); SP0937], *Lygon Arms*: Srikingly handsome Savoy-group stately hotel, with interesting old rooms rambling away from attractive if pricey oak-panelled bar; sandwiches all day; imaginative reasonably priced bar food in adjoining more intimate Goblets wine bar, with decent wines, wooden tables and pleasant service – does get busy in holiday season; tables in prettily planted courtyard, well kept gardens; children allowed away from bar; bedrooms *(J and D Boutwood, D Hanley, Mrs V Nolan, LYM)*

Broadway [Main St (A44)], *Horse & Hound*: Whitbreads-related ales with guests such as Hook Norton Best and Wadworths 6X, bar meals, quick service even when busy; china cabinets and Sun magazines in bay-windowed L-shaped room with dining end *(D Hanley)*; [Main St (A44)], *Swan*: Beefeater with well kept real ale, decent food, good service *(Andrew and Ruth Triggs)*

Brockhampton [Bringsty Common; down track off A44 Bromyard—Worcester; SO6955], *Live & Let Live*: Rustic and basic, down rough track over bracken-covered common – only the sign is visible from the road; black and white half-timbered cottage with consistently friendly service and well kept beers *(Rebecca Mortimer)*

☆ **Bromyard** [Sherford St; SO6554], *Crown & Sceptre*: 17th/18th-c family pub with ever-changing guest beers, wide choice of good generous simple food inc good veg and children's dishes, day's newspapers, plain decor with big woodburner in inglenook; popular at weekends, good dining room; bedrooms *(Rebecca Mortimer, P Bromley, Douglas and Patricia Gott)*

Broughton Hackett [A422 Worcester—Alcester – OS Sheet 150 map ref 923543; SO9254], *March Hare*: Individual dining pub with good range of good food, rustic decor inc huge stuffed fish, well cushioned stripped pews, country-kitchen chairs and tables, rugs on tiled floor, glass-covered deep floodlit well; Marstons Bitter and Pedigree, efficient friendly service; tables in garden with play area *(Graham Reeve, C E Power, Tony Walker, BB)*

Castlemorton [B4208, 1¼ mile S of Welland crossroads; SO7937], *Robin Hood*: Charming old beamed country pub with upholstered pews, big brick fireplace, lots of horsebrasses, hops, jugs, etc, interesting menu, Flowers and Theakstons ales, local Weston's cider; area with fruit machine and darts, separate small dining room; big lawns and space for caravans behind *(Neil and Anita Christopher)*

☆ **Chaddesley Corbett** [off A448 Bromsgrove—Kidderminster; SO8973], *Fox*: Particularly good value carvery (not Mon/Tues lunchtime), wide range of other good home-cooked bar food; welcoming atmosphere, friendly staff, well kept Theakstons, good service, nice dogs *(W H and E Thomas, David G Pearce)*

Charlton [the one nr Evesham – OS Sheet 150 map ref 012458; SP0145], *Gardeners Arms*: Amiable pub in attractive village, spartan public bar with darts and personable lounge with lots of tables; good atmosphere, food inc superb ploughman's *(A Y Drummond)*

☆ **Claines** [3 miles from M5 junction 6; A449 towards Ombersley, then leave dual carriageway at second exit for Worcester; village signposted from here, and park in Cornmeadow Lane; SO8558], *Mug House*: Outstanding unique setting in churchyard by fields below the Malvern Hills, ancient basic country tavern with low doorways, heavy oak beams, well kept cheap Banks's Bitter and Mild, minimal choice of basic but generous snacks (not Sun), children allowed in snug away from servery *(John and Phyllis Maloney, LYM)*

Clent [A491 Bromsgrove—Stourbridge; SO9279], *Holly Bush*: Popular and pleasant country pub, Holt Plant & Deakins Bitter and Entire on handpump, good range of freshly cooked bar food (may be a wait) inc genuinely fresh fish *(Jack Barnwell)*

Clifford [B4350 N of Hay-on-Wye; SO2445], *Castlefield*: A surprise find in the middle of nowhere, wide choice of bar food inc good moules marinières, well kept

Whitbreads-related ales *(J M Potter)*

☆ **Clows Top** [A456 Bewdley—Tenbury – OS Sheet 138 map ref 717719; SO7171], *Colliers Arms*: Welcoming service in civilised and comfortably modernised spacious dining pub with wide choice of food inc vegetarian dishes, log fires, well kept Allied real ales, unobtrusive piped music; no dogs *(Frank Cummins)*

☆ **Crowle** [SO9256], *Old Chequers*: Refurbished and extended pub very popular for wide changing range of good food; has kept some character, with good prompt service, well kept Bass *(Dr S J Parkinson, W H and E Thomas, Mrs Nicola Holden, Dave and Jane Lee, Graham Reeve)*

☆ **Doverdale** [off A449 Kidderminster—Worcester; SO8665], *Ripperidge*: Good food from filled baked potatoes to enormous mixed grill inc good fish and puddings, separate restaurant, pleasant service and surroundings *(W H and E Thomas, Mrs C J Richards)*

☆ **Droitwich** [Copcut Elm (A38 Worcester rd); SO9063], *Trotter Hall*: A 'little' pub in all but name, gloriously dotty invention of a piggy stately home with appropriate ceiling paintings, waxwork boar musicians, statues and portraits of noble pigs, but also tasty food in the two big basic but comfortable rooms, well kept beers inc Bass and Thwaites Craftsman, friendly manager; children welcome *(David and Shelia, Graham Reeve, Dave Braisted)*

Droitwich [Hanbury Rd; SO8861], *Eagle & Star*: Pleasant pub with friendly staff, wide choice of food inc some unusual dishes *(Paul Boot)*; [Kidderminster Rd], *Railway*: Traditional local with Banks's Mild and Marstons Pedigree on handpump, limited lunchtime food, friendly landlord and customers, pub games; open all day Fri/Sat *(Dr and Mrs B Baker)*

☆ **Dunhampstead** [just SE of Droitwich; pub towards Sale Green – OS Sheet 150 map ref 919600; SO9160], *Firs*: Relaxing country local with helpful prompt service and good home cooking inc doorstep sandwiches and some unusual dishes, civilised furnishings, friendly dogs, comfortable conservatory; well kept Bass, popular restaurant, tables in garden – a nice spot in summer, nr canal *(Mr and Mrs N C Shaw, Mr and Mrs R Phillips, LYM)*

☆ **Eardisland** [A44; SO4258], *White Swan*: Very welcoming interesting old oak-beamed pub, cosy armchairs, books and magazines, good log fires, gleaming copper, wide choice of nicely prepared generous food inc huge Sun lunches, well kept Marstons Pedigree, proper coffee with warmed milk, attentive but unobtrusive staff; dining room, good garden behind with retired tractor for children; lovely black-and-white village *(Nick and Alison Dawson, D Green, Mrs K Williams)*

Eardisley [SO3149], *Tramway*: Another very welcoming pub, with particularly well kept Ansells, good choice of food, very nice garden *(David Gittins, Peter Yearsley)*

Egdon [B4084 2 miles S of A422; or off A44 at Windmill Hill – OS Sheet 150 map ref 918513; SO9151], *Berkeley Arms*: Wide choice of usual reasonably priced food inc imaginatively filled soft baps in big pub, very simply furnished but comfortable and not breweryised; well kept Ansells *(Tony Walker, Steve and Lynda Corrigan)*

☆ **Elmley Castle** [village signed off A44 and A435, not far from Evesham; SO9841], *Queen Elizabeth*: Cheap farm cider and well kept Marstons in ancient tavern in pretty village below Bredon Hill, attractive old-fashioned tap room, haphazard medley of periods in decoration and furnishings, friendly licensee and locals, maybe piped classical music *(Derek and Sylvia Stephenson, LYM)*

Elmley Castle [Mill Lane], *Old Mill*: Good value lunchtime specials and lovely secluded garden looking over village cricket pitch to Bredon Hill, well kept Whitbreads-related ales, children allowed in eating area *(Pam Adsley, LYM)*

Evesham [Vine St; SP0344], *Royal Oak*: Comfortable timbered town pub with Worcs CCC cricket memorabilia, good choice of Whitbreads-related and other ales, good range of food inc extravagant ploughman's, prompt service *(A W Dickinson)*

Fairfield [A491 Stourbridge—Bromsgrove, outside village; SO9475], *Bell*: Pleasantly refurbished Toby inn, limited range of bar food *(Dave Braisted)*

Far Forest [A4117 Bewdley—Ludlow, just W of junction with A456 – OS Sheet 138 map ref 730745; SO7374], *Plough*: Clean, bright and cosy, centred on beamed dining area with woodburner in big open hearth; good value nicely cooked food inc ploughman's, steak and kidney pie, vegetarian dishes and big steaks, pleasant friendly service, well kept Bass, Boddingtons BB, M&B Mild and a guest such as Ruddles; picnic-table sets on neat lawn, subdued piped pop music; children allowed if eating; good walks from here *(Frank Cummins)*

Felton [SO5848], *Crozen*: Dining pub with very good value food esp roast beef with help-yourself veg, good puddings *(Dorothy and Leslie Pilson)*

☆ **Fladbury** [Chequers Lane – OS Sheet 150 map ref 996461; SO9946], *Chequers*: Peaceful, friendly and comfortable, dating back to 14th c, with good value food inc good Sun carvery, well kept Banks's real ale, good service; beamed restaurant, comfortable bedroom extension *(Mr and Mrs B H Robinson)*

☆ **Gorcott Hill** [off A435 3 miles S of M42 junction 3; SP0868], *Hollybush*: Quietly located country pub with big car park, busy with office people weekday lunchtime; good choice of home-made bar food esp crayfish (Tues/Thurs), crab salad and steaks, competitive prices, well kept Bass,

good service, lively atmosphere *(Ralf Zeyssig, Graham Reeve, F A J Dent)*

Hadley [Hadley Heath; A4133 Droitwich—Ombersley; SO8664], *Bowling Green*: Lovingly refurbished three-roomed inn with UK's oldest bowling green, well kept Banks's Bitter and Mild, Marstons Pedigree and Hook Norton, good choice of reasonably priced food; comfortable bedrooms *(G Reeve)*

☆ **Hanbury** [Woodgate; SO9663], *Gate Hangs Well*: Well kept Whitbreads-related ales, good food with particularly good carvery in much extended friendly and popular pub *(Mr and Mrs George Snowball, Dave Braisted)*

Harewood End [A49 Hereford—Ross; SO5327], *Harewood End*: Welcoming and attentive service, pleasant atmosphere (quiet and not smoky), good food *(C J Parsons)*

Hereford [Broad St], *Green Dragon*: Good bar food and decent wines in comfortable hotel bar; bedrooms *(BHP)*; [nr Cathedral], *Spread Eagle*: Old pub down side alley, some eccentric decorations, well kept Morlands Old Speckled Hen and Wadworths *(Dave Braisted)*

☆ **Hoarwithy** [signed off A49 Hereford—Ross on Wye; SO5429], *New Harp*: Well kept and friendly basic local with good simple well priced food, well kept Whitbreads-related real ales, decent wines, games area; picnic-table sets on yew-sheltered lawn beside pretty flower garden; children welcome; in attractive village nr River Wye; bedrooms good value, in cottage across road *(N Hardyman, BB)*

☆ **Holt Heath** [A443/A4133; SO8162], *Red Lion*: Long bar decorated with cigarette cards and team photographs, wide choice of good value home-cooked food esp puddings, generous chips, children's menu, real ales such as Ind Coope Burton and Ruddles; restaurant *(Dave Braisted, Graham Reeve)*

Honeybourne [SP1144], *Thatched Tavern*: Real English country local with character, homely, comfortable and relaxing; two bar areas with real fires, end games area with machines, bar food, dining area *(Gordon)*

☆ **Howle Hill** [coming from Ross fork left off B4228 on sharp right bend, first right, then left at crossroads after a mile – OS Sheet 162 map ref 603204; SO6121], *Crown*: Delightful pub in a maze of lanes, friendly landlord and even more friendly labradors (no visiting dogs), good range of well priced tasty food (not Sun evening, Mon; no sandwiches), well kept Whitbreads-related ales, padded pews; bar skittles, tables in garden; winter opening may be limited *(Colin Laffan, R G and M P Lumley)*

☆ **Inkberrow** [A422 Worcester—Alcester; set well back – OS Sheet 150 map ref 015573; SP0157], *Old Bull*: Photogenic Tudor pub, striking inside, with huge inglenooks, flagstones, oak beams and trusses, and some old-fashioned high-backed settles among more modern furnishings; lots of Archers memorabilia (it's the model for the Ambridge Bull), regimental coats of arms; good range of Whitbreads-related real ales, limited good value bar food, friendly service; children allowed in eating area, tables outside *(Alan and Eileen Bowker, Gordon, Peter and Jenny Quine, LYM)*

☆ **Kempsey** [Green Street – a village, signed off A38 in Kempsey itself; SO8649], *Huntsman*: Out-of-the-way local with horsey and hunting prints, Worcs CCC cricket memorabilia, simple furnishings, short choice of food (not Sun/Mon evenings) inc very good help-yourself lunchtime cold table, well kept Banks's Mild and Bitter on electric pump and Everards Tiger on handpump, friendly, landlord, daughter and locals, the jet-black Great Dane called Sam is friendly too; children welcome *(Mike Tucker, Maj T C Thornton, Derek and Sylvia Stephenson, FC, LYM)*

☆ **Kidderminster** [Comberton Hill, in stn; SO8376], *King & Castle*: Good setting on Severn Valley Rly with steam trains outside, beautiful replica of smart Edwardian refreshment rooms; good range of well kept changing real ales, wide choice of basic good value food; pleasant atmosphere, very busy bank hols and railway gala days *(Patrick and Mary McDermott, Nick and Alison Dowson, B M Eldridge)*

☆ **Kingsland** [SO4561], *Angel*: Unpretentious roadside pub with big helpings of good often unusual food, decent sensibly priced wines, prompt friendly service, attractive restaurant *(Frank Davidson, Anthony Barnes)*

☆ **Kington** [Church Rd (A44); note this is the Herefs one, handy for Hergest Croft Garden, Hergest Ridge and Offa's Dyke Path, at SO3057], *Swan*: Cosy but airy bar overlooking square, friendly helpful staff, good value food, well kept ales; restaurant; children welcome; bedrooms clean and simple *(James Skinner, Dorothy and Leslie Pilson)*

Kington [Victoria Rd], *Olde Tavern*: Wonderful time-warp old place, very idiosyncratic, with plain parlour, dark brown woodwork, commemorative china; good range of well kept ales, friendly service *(Tim Locke)*

☆ **Ledbury** [New St; SO7138], *Olde Talbot*: 16th-c timbered inn, cheerful and comfortable, with two bars and a restaurant, brass and copper hanging from the beams, well kept beers, wide range of good value food, open fire; decent bedrooms sharing bath *(Mrs S Wright)*

☆ **Leintwardine** [SO4174], *Sun*: Remarkable and memorable survivor, more private house than pub, three tables and benches in red-tiled bar with faded blue wallpaper and roaring fire, lounge with small settee and a couple of chairs is octogenarian landlady's own sitting room, Pitfield PA and Mild real ale drawn from casks in her kitchen *(Roger Huggins, Tom McLean)*

☆ **Leominster** [West St; SO4959], *Talbot*: Comfortable and attractive old coaching inn with polished floors, heavy beams, gleaming copper, armchairs, antique settles and handsome log fires in delightful bay-windowed entrance bar; bar food inc good sandwiches and ploughman's, efficient cheerful service; bedrooms *(Derek Clarke, A K Thorlby, Paul Neate, BHP)*

☆ **Leominster** [South St], *Royal Oak*: Big busy Georgian hotel, unspoilt, clean and comfortable, good atmosphere, good home-made bar food esp generous sandwiches, real ales such as Woods; spotless genuine Edwardian gents'; simple bedrooms *(W F C Phillips)*

Lindridge [set well back from A443; SO6869], *Nags Head*: Friendly welcome, good straightforward food, well kept beers, nice setting overlookinng hop yard *(Dave Braisted, Mr and Mrs K H Frostick)*

☆ **Lingen** [OS Sheet 149 map ref 367670; SO3767], *Royal George*: Doing well under new management, in beautiful country setting nr Kim Davis's renowned alpine nursery and garden; own big garden has attractive views of hills, play area, fenced-off water garden, plenty of tables; Bass, Hook Norton and Morlands Old Speckled Hen, good value bar food *(T G Thomas, A K Thorlby)*

☆ **Little Cowarne** [off A465 S of Bromyard; SO6051], *Three Horseshoes*: Wide choice of good reasonably priced food (all home-made, even ices), well kept ales, pleasant staff, spacious restaurant with lunch carvery, disabled access; juke box, pool, darts and fruit machine; comfortable bedrooms *(David and Julie Glover, Mr and Mrs W W Swaitt)*

☆ **Longdon** [B4211 S; SO8336], *Hunters*: Wide choice of good often imaginative food from sandwiches up inc children's dishes in rather upmarket but relaxed pub with beams, flagstones, log fires, brass, copper and bric-a-brac; real ales, decent wines, good views *(John and Joan Wyatt)*

Malvern [British Camp, Wynds Pt; formerly the British Camp; SO7641], *Malvern Hills*: Well kept Bass and Woods Parish, filling food, friendly service, welcoming panelled plush lounge bar with open fire; good position high in the hills, former owners include Jennie Lind, and the Cadbury brothers); bedrooms comfortable *(Derek and Sylvia Stephenson, Anthony and Freda Walters)*; [SO7845], *Morgan*: Customers are young, mainly students, but it does have decent real ales and a very good value happy hour – so worth an earbashing *(Steve Goodchild)*; [Belle Vue Terr], *Mount Pleasant*: Edwardian hotel with glorious views, bar with log fire, enthusiastic local following for bar food and restaurant with Spanish dishes; bedrooms *(Anon)*

☆ **Mathon** [SO7345], *Cliffe Arms*: Enormous helpings of food inc good open sandwiches in small low-beamed rooms, lots of nooks and crannies, pleasant young landlord, well kept Wadworths 6X and Websters Yorkshire on handpump; evening restaurant with small band in minstrels' gallery; streamside garden, lovely setting; children welcome *(Mr and Mrs G Taylor)*

☆ **Michaelchurch Escley** [OS Sheet 161 map ref 315341; SO3134], *Bridge*: Remote but lovely setting, two bars with good generous reasonably priced home-made food in dining room, well kept Bass and Wye Valley on handpump, obliging staff, friendly atmosphere; terrace overlooking stream, good walks nearby *(Patrick Freeman, C J Parsons)*

☆ **Monnington on Wye** [A438 Hereford—Hay; SO3744], *Portway*: Pleasantly refurbished 16th-c pub, quite roomy and comfortable, doing well under welcoming new management; elegant oak-beamed lounge, good atmosphere, wide range of good nicely served imaginative home-cooked bar food inc vegetarian, using local produce; restaurant *(Dr Michael Smith, C E Power, P Hogger)*

Much Cowarne [A4103, between A417 and B4214 junctions; SO6247], *Fir Tree*: Good food, good friendly service *(Dave Braisted)*

Newbridge Green [B4211, off A4104 just W of Upton upon Severn; SO8439], *Drum & Monkey*: Has been popular for well prepared reasonably priced food and good range of well kept beers, but found closed spring 1994 *(News please)*

Oldfield [SO8464], *Reindeer*: Comfortably refurbished Milestone Tavern food pub, good value, with well kept Banks's Bitter and Mild, interesting miniatures of bridges *(Graham Reeve, Dave Braisted)*

☆ **Pensax** [B4202 Abberley—Clows Top; SO7269], *Bell*: Friendly newish landlord keen to talk about the art of beerkeeping, changing range of well kept ales such as Enville, Hook Norton Best, Timothy Taylors Landlord, wide choice of good sensibly priced food esp home-made puddings, decent coffee, open fires; simple comfortable bar, dining extension opening on to wooden sun deck looking out to Wyre Forest, small garden; children welcome *(Andy Petersen, Alan Skull)*

☆ **Pershore** [Bridge St; SO9445], *Millers Arms*: Good value home cooking (no starters or puddings), friendly atmosphere in spacious but cosy beamed bar, well kept Wadworths and guest beers; more of a young people's pub in the evening *(Derek and Sylvia Stephenson)*

Pershore [High St], *Angel*: Formidable plain square exterior, parking down coach entry, panelled lounge with comfortable benches and chairs, friendly quick service, wide choice of bar food, well kept real ales such as Theakstons and Whitbreads Castle Eden; bedrooms *(Anon)*

☆ **Radford** [Alcester Rd; S of A422 Worcester—Stratford; SP0055], *Wheelbarrow Castle*: Busy beamed pub with new extension, wide choice of good

generous reasonably priced food served in unusual china, fish specialities, friendly service, well kept Banks's, Hook Norton and Theakstons *(Peter Lloyd, John and Shirley Dyson)*

Redditch [Dagnall End Rd; SP0064], *Meadow Farm*: New pub, the open spaces of Banks's typical Swiss-chalet-style architecture filled with cleaned-up farm tools; usual decent Milestone food *(Dave Braisted)*

☆ **Ross on Wye** [Riverside; coming in from A40 W side, 1st left after bridge; SO6024], *Hope & Anchor*: Notable for its position by the river, with big-windowed family extension looking out on flower-lined waterside lawns; boating theme in cheery main bar, cosy upstairs parlour bar and Victorian-style dining room, popular bar food inc wider choice for children than usual, well kept Bass and Whitbreads, silver band outside summer Sun evenings; open all day, very popular weekends *(Steve Thomas, N Hardyman, I H Rorison, the Sandy family, LYM)*

☆ **Ross on Wye** [High St], *Rosswyn*: Well kept Courage-related beers, friendly staff and wide choice of reasonably priced bar food in 15th-c inn with curious 17th-c carvings in back bar, fruit machines round corner, open fire; restaurant, beautiful garden; bedrooms *(Mr and Mrs Dara de Cogan)*

Ross on Wye [Wilton], *Hereford Bull*: Nice relaxing pub, formerly the White Lion; good range of food, real ales, outbuilding for children; prettily placed in small hamlet just outside, lovely view of river, french windows to garden sloping gently down to it; bedrooms *(Mrs M M Westwood, Steve Thomas)*

☆ **Severn Stoke** [A38 S of Worcester; SO8544], *Rose & Crown*: Courage-related and other real ales in well modernised low-beamed black and white pub, big helpings of good food inc children's dishes, character front bar with nick-nacks and good fire, back room where children allowed; huge garden with picnic-table sets, playhouse and play area *(Dr and Mrs A K Clarke)*

Severn Stoke, *Bull*: Good food, choice of real ales, open fires in little Victorian grates, pleasant service *(D C Alcock)*

☆ **Shatterford** [Bridgnorth Rd; SO7981], *Red Lion*: Spotless and popular olde-worlde pub with good atmosphere, good value well cooked food, courteous service, fine views *(B Carter, W H and E Thomas)*

☆ **Shobdon** [OS Sheet 149 map ref 405625; SO4062], *Bateman Arms*: Good food and choice of well kept real ales in comfortable and friendly two-bar local; restaurant; bedrooms *(A Barker, Ralph and Lorna Lewis)*

Spetchley [SO8953], *Berkeley Knot*: Wide choice of good generous bar food in extended renovated pub, well kept Bass, attentive staff; well placed for Spetchley

Gardens *(K H Frostick, Dave Braisted)*

Staunton on Wye [SO3645], *New Inn*: Roomy well run 16th-c village local with cosy alcoves, good range of generous home-cooked food inc vegetarian, Courage Directors and Smiles; quiz team, boules club *(Denis and Kate Dighton, Nigel Foster)*

☆ **Stiffords Bridge** [A4103 W of Gt Malvern; SO7348], *Red Lion*: Interesting menu inc good sandwiches – very busy with enthusiastic eaters weekend evenings; well kept Marstons Pedigree (though a Banks's pub), local farm cider, pleasant service and garden *(Dr David Clegg, Steve and Cherri Griffiths)*

☆ **Stockton Cross** [SO5161], *Stockton Cross*: Wide range of imaginative good reasonably priced food in welcoming and beautifully kept squat black and white building, well kept beers, decent wines; attractive garden *(Dave Braisted, Penny and Ray Perry, John and Diane Elphinstone, K Baxter)*

Stoke Prior [Hanbury Rd (B4091); the one nr Bromsgrove, SO9468;], *Country Girl*: Good choice of beers, speedy and efficient service, big helpings of beautifully cooked food, reasonable prices *(A J Goring)*

☆ **Stoke Works** [Shaw Lane; a mile from M5 Junction 5 – OS Sheet 150 map ref 938656; SO9365], *Bowling Green*: Attractive building revitalised by friendly new landlord, caringly and comfortably refurbished; good value food inc children's dishes, well kept Banks's Bitter and Mild, good atmosphere; big garden with beautifully kept bowling green; handy for Worcs & Birmingham Canal *(Graham Reeve, Dave Braisted)*

Storridge [A3103 W of Leigh Sinton; SO7448], *New Inn*: Pleasant pub with small garden, well kept Marstons, some unusual and tasty food *(Dave Braisted)*

Stourport on Severn [Hartlebury Rd; SO8171], *Bay Horse*: Good value food, special offers most nights, well kept beer on handpump, very friendly staff *(D Cockroft)*

☆ **Tenbury Wells** [Teme St; SO5968], *Ship*: Fine old pub with lots of dark wood, popular locally for good imaginative bar food and Sun lunch in bright dining room with fresh flowers, lots of puddings, reasonable prices, friendly landlord and staff, good relaxed atmosphere; immaculate lawn on site of former stables; comfortable bedrooms *(George Atkinson, S M Rowland, W K Hyde, Graham Reeve, Roy and Mary Roebuck, Michael and Barbara Chance)*

☆ **Tenbury Wells** [A4112 just outside], *Fountain*: Comfortable and attractive lounge bar with good choice of well home-cooked food inc some unusual dishes, friendly and courteous service, attractively arranged restaurant; tables on front terrace and in back garden *(W W Swait, W H and E Thomas)*

Tillington [SO4645], *Bell*: Good well presented food in recently extended lounge,

real ales inc Smiles, friendly landlady *(J Penford)*

Ullingswick [SO5949], *Three Horseshoes*: Friendly licensees, good food, pleasant surroundings, nice view from terrace *(J Penford)*

☆ **Uphampton** [SO8364], *Fruiterers Arms*: Small country pub brewing its own Arrowhead, Buckshot and good strong Mild, also has well kept Donnington Best and John Smiths; woodburner and comfortable armchairs in lounge, lunchtime food; brothers who run the pub collect old local memorabilia *(Anon)*

Upper Arley [nr stn; off B4194 NW of Bewdley; or off A442 then footbridge; SO7680], *Harbour*: Pleasant old-fashioned pub in delightful countryside, limited choice of bar food, restaurant; children's play area *(DAV)*

Upper Wyche [Chase Rd off Walwyn Rd; off B4218 Malvern—Colwall, 1st left after hilltop on bend going W; SO7643], *Chase*: Fine views from charming lounge of small quietly appealing country pub on Malvern Hills, well kept real ales, straightforward bar food; under new management *(Anthony and Freda Walters)*

Upton Snodsbury [Worcester Rd (A422); SO9454], *Coventry Arms*: Well kept Whitbreads-related ales, wide choice of good value food, pleasant atmosphere *(Andy and Maureen Pickering, F Tomlin)*

☆ **Upton upon Severn** [Riverside; SO8540], *Swan*: At last reopened 1994 after long closure, completely redone inside with very attractive new dining areas; good value interesting food inc fresh shellfish and weekend buffets, well kept Banks's real ales; lovely waterside position, summer barbecues *(Derek and Sylvia Stephenson, Jo Rees, Mike Dickerson, LYM)*

☆ **Upton upon Severn** [High St], *Olde Anchor*: Very obliging service in picturesque 16th-c pub with old-fashioned furnishings, old black timbers propping its low ceiling, lots of copper, brass and pewter, good fire in unusual central fireplace; well kept Courage-related real ales, straightforward low-priced food; has been open all day summer, can get crowded evenings then *(D Godden, C H and P Stride, J and S Gregory, LYM)*

Upton upon Severn, *Kings Head*: Good riverside setting, smart furnishings, Whitbreads-related real ales, several different areas inc separate eating area *(P and M Rudlin)*; [Old St – far end High St], *Little Upton Muggery*: Basic pub with massive collection of mugs hanging from ceiling or framed on walls; generous food, well kept real ales *(Brian Wainwright, Brian Jones, Bill Sykes)*; *Plough*: Friendly service, well kept Marstons, good value bar food; children welcome *(P and M Rudlin)*; [High St], *Star*: Attractive and comfortable partly panelled lounge bar, interesting reasonably priced bar food inc vegetarian, real ales on handpump; well equipped bedrooms *(P and M Rudlin)*

☆ **Upton Warren** [SO9367], *Swan*: Good value and friendly Greenalls Millers Kitchen dining pub, well kept beers *(Graham Reeve, Dave Braisted)*

Walterstone [OS Sheet 161 map ref 340250; SO3425], *Carpenters*: Good food and beer at reasonable prices in tasteful country-style pub, clean and friendly *(Mr and Mrs S Price)*

Warndon [Berkeley Way – not far from M5; SO8856], *Poachers Pocket*: Refurbished Banks's pub with well kept ale, big helpings of reasonably priced food, good chips; skittle alley *(Graham Reeves)*

☆ **Weatheroak Hill** [Icknield St – coming S on A435 from Wythall roundabout, filter right off dual carriageway a mile S, then in village turn left towards Alvechurch; not far from M42, junction 3; SP0674], *Coach & Horses*: Notable range of nine interesting well kept real ales, most from small breweries, in chatty and spacious country pub with plush-seated low-ceilinged two-level lounge bar, tiled-floor public bar, dining room, and plenty of seats out on lawns and upper terrace; piped music, cheap straightforward bar food; children allowed in eating area *(Mr and Mrs C Roberts, Dave Braisted, Cathy Scott, Richard Baker, Graham Reeve, Lawrence Bacon, Mrs M Cadney, George Atkinson, LYM)*

☆ **Wellington Heath** [SO7141], *Farmers Arms*: Spacious, comfortable and friendly, with consistently good food and service; tables on sunny terrace overlooking pretty wooded valley *(Anthony and Freda Walters)*

West Malvern [SO7646], *Brewers Arms*: Refurbished pub with welcoming landlord, well kept beers, good food *(A R Pike)*

☆ **Whitney on Wye** [SO2747], *Rhydspence*: Immensely picturesque country inn with appropriately old-fashioned furnishings in rambling beamed and heavily timbered rooms, pretty dining room, well kept Bass, Hook Norton Best and Robinsons Best, a welcome for children, tables in attractive garden with fine views over Wye valley, comfortable bedrooms; has been a starred main entry with good interesting food, and still well worth a visit, but one or two hiccoughs in the last few months *(Dave Braisted, N W Kingsley, S Demont, T Barrow, John F Shapley, Peter Yearsley, LYM)*

Wickhamford [Pitchers Hill; SP0641], *Sandys Arms*: Family pub with well kept Theakstons, decent food – even taking time to make sandwiches in the bustle of serving Sun lunch *(G and M Armstrong)*

Wolverley [B4189 N of Kidderminster; SO8279], *Lock*: Superb setting with outside tables by a lock on the quaint Staffs & Worcs Canal as it negotiates a red sandstone bluff into which the pub is set, one well furnished canalia-decorated room with bay window overlooking lock, straightforward food, Banks's and Camerons real ales *(Bill Sykes)*

☆ **Worcester** [50 Lowesmoor], *Jolly Roger*: Lively and down-to-earth pub with good low-priced beers brewed on the premises, very interesting guest beers, good helpings of straightforward cheap food inc big sandwiches, basic barrel furniture, well spaced tables, bar crafted to look like galleon, beams, lots of dried hops, live music Fri and Sat evenings; piped music can be very loud; unassuming surroundings *(P Butler, David Campbell, Vicki McLean, Graham Reeve, Nick and Alison Dowson, Sue Anderson, Phil Copleston)*

☆ **Worcester**, *Cardinals Hat*: The town's oldest pub, with its own-brewed Jolly Roger (see pub of that name, above), Shipwrecked and Flagship, also guest beers; panelled back room, open fires, decent food esp home-made soups, good coffee, warming log-effect gas fire, piped blues music, staff very cheerful; jug-and-bottle off licence next door, brewery visits can be arranged *(Graham Reeve, Frank W Gadbois, David and Shelia)*

☆ **Worcester** [London Rd, about ½ mile from centre], *Little Worcester Sauce Factory*: Fun pub with tiled walls advertising sauces, superb tiled map of Britain filling ceiling of largest room, lots of stripped pine and sawdust – and lots more sauce; hearty good value food, beers inc Lumphammer *(Bill and Beryl Farmer, Andrew Jeeves, Carole Smart, Brian Jones, David and Shelia, Paul Weedon)*

Worcester [Angel Passage, Broad St], *Crown*: Good food and beer, very welcoming landlord, all clean and inviting *(M Borg)*; [Fish St], *Farriers Arms*: Nona Pettersen, who made this pleasantly furnished city pub a popular main entry, with relaxed atmosphere, interesting decorations and unusual food, left in autumn 1994 *(LYM)*

☆ **Yarpole** [SO4765], *Bell*: Substantial timbered pub, smart and clean, with comfortable banquettes, lots of brass and bric-a-brac, Hobsons real ales, good straightforward food, skittle alley; tables in sunny garden, very handy for Croft Castle *(T G Thomas, Alan Skull)*

We mention bottled beers and spirits only if there is something unusual about them – imported Belgian real ales, say, or dozens of malt whiskies; so do please let us know about them in your reports.

Hertfordshire

On the whole this is a county where pub food scores on straightforward good value rather than on great individuality: food prices are lower than in many places, and have been virtually static this last year (unlike the rises we've seen in most areas). The pubs currently doing best for food here are the Jolly Waggoner at Ardeley, the Bull at Cottered (a new main entry this year), the old-fashioned Bricklayers Arms at Flaunden, the smoothly run Green Man at Great Offley, the unpretentious Moon & Stars at Rushden (outstanding for simple home cooking), the George & Dragon at Watton at Stone (restaurant and bar menus have been combined now – not cheap but very good) and the Sword in Hand at Westmill (its new bedrooms have now been completed). From among these the George & Dragon really does stand out, so for the second year running we choose it as Hertfordshire Dining Pub of the Year. There's decent food in the Salisbury Crest at Essendon, another main entry. A high proportion of the area's pubs have excellent beer. Drinks prices are around the national average, with the Valiant Trooper at Aldbury selling Sam Smiths remarkably cheaply, and low prices too in the Fox & Hounds at Barley (sometimes brewing its own) and the Garibaldi in St Albans (tied to Fullers). Among Lucky Dip entries at the end of the chapter, we'd particularly pick out the three pubs in Ashwell (and be very interested to know which readers prefer), Farmers Boy at Brickendon, Two Brewers at Chipperfield, Horns near Datchworth, Green Dragon at Flaunden, Alford Arms at Frithsden, Fox in Harpenden, Silver Fox at Hertford Heath, Three Horseshoes at Hinxworth, Farmers Boy at Langley, Five Horseshoes at Little Berkamstead, Nags Head at Little Hadham, both pubs at Much Hadham, Holly Bush at Potters Crouch, Cabinet at Reed and Eagle & Child at Whitwell.

ALDBURY SP9612 Map 4

Valiant Trooper ◖

Village signposted from Tring and under a mile E of Tring railway station; Trooper Road (towards Aldbury Common)

A pint of John Smiths is cheaper here than it was last year. They call it a 'walker's special' and it's only £1, on offer all day, every day. They also have well kept Bass, Fullers London Pride, Greene King Abbot, Marstons Pedigree and a guest on handpump. During their popular happy hours (12 to 2pm and 5 to 7pm) one of their ales and one of their lagers is only £1.20. Their spirits are only £1.50 for a double and they do farm cider. Inside this characterful, friendly, family run, partly pink-painted, tiled and brick-built free house the furniture is rustically basic, it's clean and tidy, and there's a cosy fire in winter. The lively first room, beamed and tiled in red and black, has built-in wall benches, a pew and small dining chairs around the attractive country tables, and a woodburning stove in the inglenook fireplace. In the brown-carpeted middle bar there's some exposed brickwork and spindleback chairs – and some easily missed signs warning you to 'mind the step'. The far room has nice country kitchen chairs around individually chosen tables, and a brick fireplace; decorations are mostly antique cavalry prints. A new chef is doing simple but excellent, well presented bar food, including a popular range of open sandwiches or filled baked potatoes (from £2.75), cottage pie (£4.20), liver and bacon casserole (£4.70), and mixed grill (£4.90). The lounge bar is no-smoking at lunchtime; super, friendly service. The friendly big black dog is called Alexander. There are some tables in the small, prettily flowered garden at the back, and the concrete terrace has been reduced and laid to grass. Shove-ha'penny, dominoes, cribbage, bridge on Monday nights; other dogs welcome. The village itself is fascinating, and handy for some of the very best Chilterns scenery – particularly nice views can be had from around the monument to the Duke of Bridgewater, and the woods close to the pub are very good for walking. *(Recommended by Lyn and Bill Capper and Ted George; more reports please)*

Free house ~ Licensee Dorothy Eileen O'Gorman ~ Real ale ~ Meals and snacks (not Sun or Mon evenings) ~ Restaurant (not Sun evening) ~ (0144 285) 1203 ~ Children in eating area of bar until 9pm ~ Open 11.30-11

ARDELEY TL3027 Map 5

Jolly Waggoner

Readers describe the food here as unbelievably wonderful, superbly presented, and served with real flare. The licensee makes nearly all the home-made dishes using fresh produce from local suppliers. The bar menu has sandwiches, various home-made burgers (£4.25), their special Arnold Bennett omelette filled with smoked haddock and topped with light cheese béchamel (£5.50), prawn salad, vegetable salad with sharp tangy dressings, chilli con carne with an imaginative tomato salad – sounding straightforward enough, but in fact cooked with real thought and care; delicious puddings. The small pretty building is tucked out of the way in a nice quiet village, and has been sensitively refurbished by Greene King without losing too much of its character or charm. There's lots of open woodwork in the bar and in the restaurant which has been extended into the cottage next door and is decorated with modern prints. There's a good atmosphere and service is brisk and friendly. Well kept Greene King IPA and Abbot tapped from the cask; good range of wines; cribbage, dominoes, fruit machine and piped music; the garden has matured and is looking very pretty; they play boules on Monday evening; must book Sunday lunch. *(Recommended by Charles Bardswell, David Surridge, Andrew Scarr, Bill Brown, Martyn Kearey, Prof John and Mrs Patricia White)*

Greene King ~ Tenant: Darren Perkins ~ Real ale ~ Meals and snacks ~ Restaurant ~ (01438) 861350 ~ Well behaved children welcome (must stay seated); no babies ~ Open 12-2.30(3 Sat), 6-11; closed Mon lunchtime

AYOT ST LAWRENCE TL1916 Map 5

Brocket Arms ★ ◀

B651 N of St Albans for about 6 miles; village signposted on right after Wheathampstead and Marshall's Heath golf course; or B653 NE of Luton, then right on to B651

Set well off the beaten track in lovely countryside and down some very narrow lanes, this white-painted and tiled 14th-c brick pub is a traditional place – full of individuality and atmosphere, steadily running at its own pace. It's even said to be haunted by the ghost of a Catholic priest who was tried and hanged here during the Reformation when it was the monastic quarters for the nearby romantically ruined Norman church. Its two well cared for bustling rooms are genuinely old-fashioned and reeking with character. Orange lanterns hang from the sturdy oak beams in the low-ceilinged bars. There's a big inglenook fireplace (often too hot to sit in), a big coal fire in the back room (which can be a bit cold in winter if the fire isn't lit), a fishtank in the dining room fireplace, magazines to read, and a long built-in wall settle in one parquet-floored room. Some of the pictures by a local artist are for sale. The very good range of beers on handpump includes Greene King Abbot and IPA, Gibbs Mew Deacon, Hook Norton Old Hookey, Theakstons Best and Wadworths 6X, with two weekly changing guests such as Batemans XXXB, Gibbs Mew Bishops Tipple, Eldridge Pope Royal Oak or Everards Old Original; Rosie's farm cider. We've noticed that the very reasonable bar food prices have stayed the same this year – soups such as stilton and onion (£1), ploughman's (£3), summer buffet lunches such as beef salad (from £3, fresh salmon salad £5.50) and home-made hot dishes such as chilli con carne or cottage pie (£4.75); there's a daily changing blackboard with seasonal dishes. Afternoon cream teas are served at weekends and bank holidays: it can get very crowded at weekends when the service might suffer a little. The extensive suntrapping walled garden has a summer bar and a children's play area; darts and dominoes. Nearby is the house of George Bernard Shaw, also reputedly haunted – not by Shaw, but his friend T E Lawrence. *(Recommended by Nigel Norman, G D and M D Craigen, Martin and Pauline Richardson, JJW, CMW, Clare Dawkins, Gordon Phillips, Chris Mawson, Andy Thwaites, JMB, J A Boucher, J and P Maloney, Wayne Brindle)*

Free house ~ Lease Toby Wingfield Digby ~ Real ale ~ Meals and snacks ~ Partly no-smoking restaurant (not Sun or Mon evening, 10% service) ~ Stevenage (01438) 820250 ~ Children welcome away from bar ~ Open 11-2.30(Sat 3), 6-11 ~ Bedrooms: £40/£55(£60B)

BARLEY TL3938 Map 5

Fox & Hounds ★ 🍺

Junction 10 of M11 then A505 towards Royston, then left on to B1368 after 4 miles

The licensee tells us she tried to increase her handpumps to twelve, but there just wasn't enough space – she's settled for ten, which still means an excellent choice of very well priced real ale. The pub brews its own Nathaniels Special and the somewhat stronger Flame Thrower, as well as having Theakstons Best, XB and Old Peculier (they are trying to get the new Mild) and up to four varied guest beers with lots more during their real ale festivals. They also have farm ciders, a good range of wines by the bottle or glass, and several malt whiskies. The enormous menu of carefully prepared, good value food is on a blackboard that covers an entire wall and has dishes like leek and potato soup (£1.30), chestnut and wine pâté (£2.95), generous whitebait (£3.25), spare ribs (£3.45), a good selection of pies and casseroles like steak and kidney pie or cassoulet (£5.25), lots of seafood like seafood lasagne (£5.55), king prawns fried with tomato, onion and mushroom (£5.95) and salmon steak in hollandaise (£7.65); very good selection of vegetarian food with dishes like celery and nut risotto, vegetable goulash with sour cream (£4.95) and cashew nut paella (£5.75); children's menu. Originally called the Waggon & Horses, this was a favourite with James I when he was hunting from Royston, and is hard to miss thanks to its unusual sign. The attractive 15th-c interior has low-ceilinged and alcovey rambling rooms, well furnished, with substantial log fires on both sides of a massive central chimney. The dining area with its odd-shaped nooks and crannies was originally the kitchen and cellar; half of it is now no smoking. The garden has a barbecue area, and this is a pub where children's fizzy drinks are cheap. The staff, locals and cat are friendly. There's a fine range of games, from darts (two teams), bar billiards and dominoes (two schools), to shove-ha'penny, cribbage, fruit machine and juke box; also a league cricket team and skittle alley; minibus service for customers; disabled lavatories and ramp access to dining room at the back. *(Recommended by Werner Arend, Prof John White, Patricia White, Rita Horridge, Nigel Gibbs, Sarah and Jamie Allan, Alison McCarthy, Mick Hitchman, Mrs M C Barrett, D A Edwards, Adrian Pitts, Dr S W Tham, Charles Bardswell, SJC, Nick and Alison Dowson)*

Own brew ~ Licensee Rita Nicholson ~ Real ale ~ Meals (evenings only) and snacks ~ Restaurant ~ Royston (01763) 848459 ~ Children welcome (not too late Sats) ~ Open 12-2.30, 6-11 (12-11 Sat in summer)

BERKHAMSTED SP9807 Map 5

Boat 🍷 🍺

Gravel Path

The energetic landlord here tells us he's going to landscape the towpath – he's just taken over its care from British Waterways. At its best in summer, this is already a lovely canalside setting with abundant colourful flowers, so it should soon be glorious. Guests are instantly relaxed by the easy welcome and pleasant atmosphere. The bar is full of plants and fresh flowers, and there are little touches like home-made chutneys, pickled onions and butter in pots (rather than horrid little packets). Bar food under a new chef includes vegetarian dishes, and, all at £4, steak pie, pork and apple pie, curry and fisherman's pie, and maybe more adventurous dishes such as chicken breast in Calvados cream; puddings like chocolate tart with cinnamon crust or summer pudding (£1.50). Well kept and very reasonably priced Fullers Chiswick, London Pride, ESB and Hock on handpump or tapped from the cask, and quite a few wines by the glass. Cribbage, dominoes, trivia, fruit machine and piped music. *(Recommended by Lesley Johnson, Comus Elliott, Richard Church, Alan Stourton, Stephen King and Clive Fry)*

Fullers ~ Tenant Chris Elford ~ Real ale ~ Meals and snacks (not Sun or evenings) ~ (01422) 877152 ~ Children in eating area, lunchtime only ~ Open 11-3, 5.30-11

BOURNE END TL0206 Map 5

Three Horseshoes

Winkwell; narrow lane just off A41 Berkhamsted—Hemel Hempstead

This pretty little tiled black and white pub with shuttered windows is a good deal older than most canal pubs: it's said to date back to the 16th c. There are three cosy and homely rooms with low ceilings, three roomy inglenook fireplaces (one still with its side bread oven) and an Aga. It's warm and welcoming in winter when they get the good log fires going. Under oak beams, the furnishings are comfortable and traditional, there are gleaming horsebrasses and harness, and the lighting is soft. A recent extension directly overlooks the canal through bay windows. Tables on the terrace and more tables out among tubs of flowers by the water look down to the nearby narrowboat basin. There's an interesting swing bridge over the canal. Food is fairly well priced for the area. There is a cold menu with for example three cheese ploughman's (£3.95), and 14 daily specials (of which seven are home-cooked) which might be chicken and ham lasagne (£4.45), Persian lamb or chilli con carne (£4.55), steak and ale pie or chicken, ham and leek pie or crab platter (£4.60), fresh fish and three vegetarian dishes such as vegetarian lasagne (£4.05) or vegetarian platter (£4.15); Sunday roast (£5.35). They have seven real ales: Benskins Best, Ind Coope Burton, Marstons Pedigree, Tetleys and sometimes Wadworths 6X on handpump and two guests, one of which changes weekly – the other, Eldridge Pope Royal Oak, is more or less fixed because it's so popular; friendly and relaxed staff. It can sometimes be difficult to find a seat inside – though that tends to be in fine weather, when the outside tables come into play anyway; piped music; trivia machine and lots of board games like chess and draughts. *(Recommended by Stephen King, John Whitehead, G Keating, Peter Watkins, Pam Stanley, Chris Hackett, Mr and Mrs R V Bathie)*

Allied ~ Manager Cilla Palmer ~ Real ale ~ Meals and snacks (not Sun evening)~ Restaurant ~ (01442) 862585 ~ Children welcome ~ Open 11-11; closed evening 25 Dec

COTTERED TL3129 Map 5

Bull

A507 W of Buntingford

This attractive and pleasantly lit pub, in a pretty setting among trees and green, is increasingly popular for well presented fair-priced tasty food with lots of vegetables – they've been enlarging the restaurant and putting in a conservatory beyond, so as to make more space for diners. Besides sandwiches (£2.50), dishes which have recently been well supported include vegetarian lasagne (£5.50), lamb casserole (£5.95), steak and kidney pie (£6.50) and fresh halibut or grilled monkfish (£7.95); you can choose between chips and boiled potatoes, vegetables and salad. There's a daily pasta dish, home-made puddings (£2.20) are good, and they'll do children's helpings. The low-beamed front lounge is roomy and comfortable, with lots of horsebrasses, a formidable collection of cream jugs hanging from the beams and around the walls, and a good fire; the piped music is not obtrusive. A second bar has darts, pool, dominoes, fruit machine and trivia; well kept Greene King IPA, Abbot, XX Dark Mild and Rayments SB, decent wines, quick pleasant service. The well reworked sizeable garden has boules and a play area. *(Recommended by Bob and Maggie Atherton, Charles Bardswell, Phil and Heidi Cook, George Atkinson)*

Greene King ~ Licensee Robin Wilson ~ Real ale ~ Meals and snacks (12-2.30, 6-9.30; not Sun evening) ~ Restaurant (not Sun evening) ~ (01763) 281243 ~ Children in restaurant ~ Open 12-3, 6-11; cl evening 25/26 Dec

ESSENDON TL2708 Map 5

Salisbury Crest

West End; off B158 Hertford—Potters Bar

A proper pub this, with a fine sense of continuity – despite a change of landlord not long ago one reader was recently served by the same waiter who served him on his first visit 30 years earlier. The chatty smallish bar on the right has green plush cushions on traditional vertical-panelling wall seats, beams with brasses and coach horns, and an open fire, and good value changing straightforward bar food might include soup and other starters (£2.25), sandwiches (from £1.75), good fresh mussels or ploughman's (£3.75), chilli con carne, lamb cutlets in tomato and garlic or chicken with smoked sausage in garlic and mushroom sauce (all £5.95), with good home-made puddings such as pecan pie or fresh fruitcake (£2.50). Well kept Ansells and Greene King IPA and Abbot, a good range of spirits, decent house wines. The cosy and stylish two-room restaurant has a cheerful and relaxed atmosphere, too, despite its smartness. The back terrace has pleasant country views. *(Recommended by Gordon Pitt, Margaret and Allen Marsden, Jeremy Williams, Anne Hyde, Michelle and Iain Ferguson)*

Free house ~ Licensee Ray Curson ~ Real ale ~ Meals and snacks ~ Restaurant (not Sun evening) ~ (01707) 261267 ~ Children in restaurant ~ Open 11-2.30(3.30 Sat), 5.30-11

FLAUNDEN TL0100 Map 5

Bricklayers Arms

Village signposted from A41; Hogpits Bottom – from village centre follow Boxmoor, Bovingdon road and turn right at Belsize, Watford signpost

This is a peaceful, inviting spot, especially in summer when the picnic-table seats and tables with cocktail umbrellas in the lovely old-fashioned garden are surrounded by foxgloves against sheltering hawthorn and ivy hedges, and the low cottagey tiled pub is covered with Virginia creeper. The emphasis is very much on the wonderful and often unusual good value bar food, served in good generous helpings. On weekday lunchtimes the bar menu is used throughout the whole pub, and includes sandwiches (from £1.70), soup (£1.80), filled baked potatoes (from £2.95), ploughman's (from £3.50), prawn stroganoff (£3.45), prawn and halibut roll (£3.95), cottage pie (£4.50), vegetable bake (£4.75), curried chicken breast (£5.70), fish pie and vegetables and pasta capsicum (£5.95), bricklayer's feast – ribs, chicken wings, potato skins piled high and coated with barbecue sauce and garlic dip (£6.45), beef in ale pie and vegetables (£6.95), steaks (from £9.45), and daily specials; puddings; the evening and Sunday lunch menu used in the back dining room is broadly similar. There may also be nibbles on the bar, and a summer salad bar in the garden. The warmly decorated friendly and busy low-beamed bar has buff leatherette armchairs and dark brown-painted traditional wooden wall seats, open winter fires, and stubs of knocked-through oak-timbered walls that give a snug feeling to the three original rooms. There's a back dining room. Well kept not cheap Adnams, Chiltern Beechwood, Fullers London Pride and three guests on handpump; prompt professional service from welcoming staff. It gets packed at the weekends, so arrive early for a table. Just up the Belsize road there's a path on the left, through woods, to more Forestry Commission woods around Hollow Hedge. *(Recommended by Mrs J A Blanks, Lyn and Bill Capper, Dave Carter, G D and M D Craigen, H Hazzard, J E Stanton, David Shillitoe, BKA, D B Delany, David Surridge)*

Free house ~ Licensees R C Mitchell and Stuart Lawson ~ Real ale ~ Meals and snacks (no sandwiches Sun) ~ Restaurant ~ (01442) 833322 ~ Children in restaurant ~ Open 11-2.30(3 Sat), 6-11

GREAT OFFLEY TL1427 Map 5

Green Man ★ ♀

Village signposted off A505 Luton—Hitchin

There's an impressive sweeping view from the spacious and elegant conservatory with its massive flagstoned floor, tall pillars, white cast-iron furniture and tall gracious plants, across the picturesque garden, pond and waterfall, and beyond to the flatter land below which stretches for miles to the east. Around three sides of the conservatory the flagstoned terrace has plenty of chairs and tables with a profusion of flowers in hanging baskets and tubs. The immaculate but relaxed rambling bars have low moulded beams, lots of antique farm-tool illustrations, wheelback and spindleback chairs around simple country pine scrubbed tables, some stripped brick, a lovely open fire and a woodburning stove. The larger and more airy right-hand room has lots of little countryside prints and one or two larger pictures, a cabinet of trophies, cushioned built-in wall seats as well as the chairs around its tables, and another big woodburner with a row of brass spigots decorating the chimneypiece. It's efficiently but comfortably run with tremendous attention to detail, and the feeling comes across that the staff are involved and take pleasure and pride in their work. In the gents' you will find a shoeshine kit and nailbrush and in the ladies' tissues, brushes and a settee. The fairly priced lunchtime food comes in satisfying helpings of well presented dishes including soup (£1.25), well filled sandwiches and large filled rolls (from £2), filled baked potatoes (from £2.05), ploughman's (from £2.50), tasty steak and kidney or chicken, ham and leek pies (£4.50), a good lunchtime spread of help-yourself salads (from £5.50), gammon (£5.75), and puddings like apple pie (from £2). They do a daily carvery with either roast beef or honey roast ham (£5.95) and the hot salt beef sandwiches with dill, pickles and garnish are very well liked. It's a popular place which can get very busy. Well kept Boddingtons, Courage Directors, Ruddles County and Websters on handpump under light blanket pressure; decent choice of wines by the glass; friendly cat; piped music, fruit machine; it's best if children play at the front where there are some swings and a slide. *(Recommended by Clare Dawkins, Gordon Phillips, G L Tong, Andrew Jeeves, Carole Smart, Sue Grossey, M L Clarke, Michael, Alison, Rhiannon and Stuart Sandy, Lyn and Bill Capper, Susan and Nigel Wilson, Bob and Maggie Atherton, K and B Moore, Mrs C Watkinson, Jim Cowell, Nic Armitage, Steve and Carolyn Harvey)*

Free house ~ Licensee Raymond H Scarbrow ~ Real ale ~ Meals and snacks (cold food all day; no food Sun afternoon) ~ Restaurant (open all day Sun) ~ Offley (01462) 768256 ~ Children welcome ~ Open 10.30am-11pm

RUSHDEN TL3031 Map 5

Moon & Stars

Village signposted from A507 Baldock—Buntingford, about 1 mile W of Cottered

This unspoilt and characterful pretty tiled row of country cottages has a good villagey feel. Staff and customers in the small unmodernised bar are friendly and welcoming, and there's an intimate atmosphere under its heavy-beamed low ceiling with its vast inglenook fireplace; it connects at the front with the table-filled no-smoking lounge bar. The simple straightforward bar food is very highly praised by readers (one regularly does a hundred mile round trip to come here) who make particular mention of the very fresh vegetables that are cooked exactly right, and the delicious fresh fish and chips on Thursday evenings (£3.95). On Friday and Saturday evenings there is a special menu, and the Davidsons take great pride in their home-made puddings. They do sandwiches, home-made stilton pâté with Abbot ale (£2.95), ploughman's (from £3.50), ham and egg (£3.95), home-made steak and kidney pie (£5) steak (from £8.75) Sunday roast (£5) and cream teas on summer Sunday afternoons. Well kept Greene King IPA and Abbot on handpump; a small, decent wine list; very friendly service; darts, dominoes, shove-ha'penny, cribbage, a fruit machine and pétanque; piped music. Fred the splendid friendly labrador and friend Lucy are still around. There are good views from the tables on the rolling lawns that extend up the hillside, and benches at the front. This is another of those pubs where not all the spirits are drinkable – the ghost here has apparently been known to turn off the gas in the cellar. *(Recommended by John Whitehead, G L Tong, Charles Bardswell, D A Edwards, Robert Turnham, Martyn Kearey, David and Ruth Hollands, Diane Foster, Martin Danzebrink, Paul Kitchener, R A Buckler)*

Greene King ~ Tenants Robbie and Gill Davidson ~ Real ale ~ Meals and snacks (cold food Sun and Mon evening) ~ (01763) 88330 ~ Children over 5 in eating area ~ Occasional live entertainment ~ Open 12-2.30, 6(7 Sat)-11; closed Mon lunchtime

ST ALBANS TL1507 Map 5

Fighting Cocks

Off George Street, through abbey gateway (you can drive down, though signs suggest you can't)

Following ancient tradition things are still changing at this enchanting spot. This year they have almost doubled the size of the family room, and there's been another change of management. When it first opened as an alehouse about 400 years ago it was called the Round House because of its rather odd shape. It later became known as the Fisherman before it took its present name – a reference to the modernised Stuart cock-fighting pit that is still evident as a sunken area (now with nice seating) below the much-modernised bar. Some sort of building is said to have been here since the foundation of the Abbey in 793, and the years before it became an inn are filled with periods as a battlemented gatehouse, a mill and a boathouse. Though it's changed a good deal since then, heavy low beams still give a trace of its heritage, and a good log fire in the inglenook fireplace, a stuffed cock in a cabinet, some pleasant window alcoves, and other nooks and corners add to the atmosphere. Well kept Ansells Mild, Benskins Best, Ind Coope Burton, Tetleys and up to three changing guests like Allsopps IPA (another Allied ale despite its small-brewery sound), Eldridge Pope Royal Oak or Wadworths 6X on handpump; farm cider. The sensibly limited bar food menu includes popular filled wholemeal baps (from £2.35), excellent ploughman's (from £3.40), cottage or steak and kidney or fighting cock pie (£4.25), vegetarian dishes (from £3.50) like vegetable bake (£3.95), daily specials like spinach quiche salad (£3.95), good fish dishes and good home-made puddings; friendly service; fruit machine, pinball and piped music. It's an attractive spot, with lots of ducks on the river which runs beyond the colourful garden with its seats, and further still are the Roman remains of Verulamium. *(Recommended by John Boylan, Stephen Brown, H Hazzard, David Goldstone, Belinda and Graham Staplehurst)*

Ind Coope (Allied) ~ Managers John Middleton and Carole Taylor ~ Real ale ~ Meals and snacks (has had very limited menu Sat and Sun evenings) ~ (01727) 865830 ~ Children in family room ~ Occasional winter entertainment ~ Open 11-11 in summer, 11-3 and 6-11 in winter; closed 25 Dec

Garibaldi 🚩

61 Albert Street; off Holywell Hill below White Hart Hotel – some parking at end of street

The exterior of this town pub has been smartly rejuvenated over the last year. Its refurbished Victorian-style interior is bigger than its façade suggests. Readers have particularly praised the friendly interesting bustling atmosphere, and while it's largely popular with a youngish crowd, older readers rate it very highly as well. The well kept bar angles around the central island servery, and there's a little tiled-floor snug up some steps; a separate food counter on a lower level opens out into a neat and cosy little no-smoking conservatory. Victorian and Edwardian theatrical prints decorate the walls. Its cheerful, well run and very popular with locals, many of them here for the good value home-made food (chip-free, they boast). The menu is still mostly Mexican – enchiladas (£3.75), along with sandwiches and a comprehensive range of more established favourites such as steak and ale pie (£4.20) and vegetarian dishes. Very cheap well kept Fullers Chiswick, London Pride, ESB and Hock on handpump; cribbage, dominoes, trivia, fruit machine, decent piped pop music; they have their own cricket team; a few picnic-table sets in the side yard. *(Recommended by J A Boucher, Stephen Brown, D J Saunders, BKA, George Atkinson, J Carroll, Chris Cook, Nick and Alison Dowson)*

Fullers ~ Manager Paul McFarlane ~ Real ale ~ Meals and snacks (12-9 except Sundays when 12-2) ~ Restaurant (closed Sun evening) ~ (01727) 855046 ~ Children in eating area of bar until 8.30 ~ Live blues music at least once a month ~ Open 11-11

Goat ◀

Sopwell Lane; a No Entry beside Strutt and Parker estate agents on Holywell Hill, the main southwards exit from town – by car, take the next lane down and go round the block

There is a new licensee at this historic inn which can trace its landlords as far back as at least 1686, although the attractive building has changed enormously since then. It's justifiably still a popular place, especially with students so there's usually a cheery boisterous atmosphere, even more lively when there's well-received live jazz. The several characterful areas rambling around the central bar contain a profusion of eye-catching decorations – stuffed birds, chamber pots, books and prints. Blackboards display a good range of beers and food, with real ales such as Boddingtons, Abbot, Gales Pompey Royal, Hook Norton Best, Marstons Pedigree and Wadworths 6X on handpump; good range of malt whiskies. Home-made bar food includes good value doorstep sandwiches (from £1.80), seafood pasta, home-made steak and oyster pie or oriental skillets (£3.50) and daily specials (from £3.95) like seafood salad, curries and fresh fish; some of the puddings are home-made; fruit machine and piped music. There are tables on the neat lawn-and-gravel smallish back garden, and may be barbecues out here in summer. *(Recommended by John Boylan, Stephen Brown, Brian Marsden, Susan and Nigel Wilson; more reports please)*

Devenish ~ Managers Robin Hamill and Wanda Nightingale ~ Real ale ~ Meals and snacks (not Sun evening and possibly not all day Sat in winter) ~ (01727) 833934 ~ Children in eating area ~ Jazz Sun lunchtime, live music Mon evening ~ Nearby parking may be rather difficult ~ Open 11-2.30, 5.30-11 (all day Sat); closed evening 25 Dec

Rose & Crown

St Michaels Street; from town centre follow George Street down past the abbey towards the Roman town

There's a relaxed, friendly and rather civilised atmosphere behind the elegant façade here, and it's far too traditional for games machines of any kind. The beamed public bars have unevenly timbered walls, old-fashioned wall benches, a pile of coffee-table magazines, chintzy curtains and cushions, and black cauldrons in a deep fireplace. In winter there's a large fire. Service is never less than efficient. They specialise in very filling tasty American-style sandwiches which can be quite straightforward like cheese, apple and lettuce (£2.25) or more adventurous concoctions such as ham, salted peanuts, red leicester, tomato and mayonnaise or roast beef, honey-roast ham, Swiss cheese, tomato, onion, watercress, lettuce and french mustard. They're attractively served with home-made potato salad, sweet pickled cucumber and Kettle crisps – decidedly the aristocrat of the potato crisp world. They also do standard sandwiches (from £1.35), chilli con carne (£3.75), chicken paprika (£4.95) and various pasta dishes (from £4.35). Well kept

Adnams, Greenalls Original, Morlands Old Speckled Hen, Tetleys and Wadworths 6X on handpump, and farm ciders, lots of malt whiskies, winter hot punch and tea or coffee; darts (placed sensibly to one side); dominoes. Lots of tables and benches along the side and at the back of the pub, with shrubs and roses, flowerbeds and hanging baskets. *(Recommended by Stephen Brown, Russell and Margaret Bathie, Michael and Alison Sandy, Brian Marsden)*

Greenalls (Allied) ~ Tenant Neil Dekker ~ Real ale ~ Lunchtime meals and snacks (not Sun) ~ (01727) 51903 ~ Children in eating area ~ Blues Mon eve, Irish and Scottish folk Thurs eve, occasional Morris dancers in summer ~ Open 11-3, 5.30(6 Sat)-11

WADESMILL TL3517 Map 5

Sow & Pigs

Thundridge (the village where it's actually situated – but not marked on many road maps, which is why we list it under nearby Wadesmill); A10 just S of Wadesmill, towards Ware

As the name suggests, there's quite a porcine theme, and the comfortable and traditionally furnished bar has lots of little piggies in a glass cabinet, and amusing pictures in this vein on the wall. The natural focus of this cheerful, unassuming, well run and comfortable village pub of considerable character is the small central serving bar. There's plank-panelling, a small ship's wheel and a binnacle, and a rustic table supported by two barrels in the bay of the cosy window seat. More spacious rooms lead off on both sides – the dining room on the right has dark beams and massive rustic tables, while the area on the left has a timber part divider, and a couple of steps halfway along, helping to break it up. The landlord is very friendly and the staff refreshingly polite and attentive. Excellent bar food in good helpings includes sandwiches (from £1.50), soup (£1.75), ploughman's (from £3.25) and mixed grills (£7.50) and various daily specials (from £4.75) like beef in Guinness or liver and bacon or hock of ham with honey glaze (£4.95) and pigeon pie (£5.25). Their speciality is what they call Yorkshire fish and chips – haddock in an unusual batter (£4.75); lots of puddings. Well kept, cheaper than last year, Adnams, Shipstones and Wadworths 6X on handpump, and two guests like Bass, Greenalls Original or Worthington Best. There are picnic-table sets under cocktail parasols, with their own service hatch, on a smallish fairylit grass area behind by the car park, sheltered by tall oaks and chestnut trees. Access directly onto the A10 can be difficult. *(Recommended by Martyn Kearey, John Whitehead, Sue Grossey, G L Tong, R C Vincent, K and B Moore, S M Wallace, Geoffrey and Eddi Cowling)*

Greenalls ~ Tenant Chris Severn ~ Real ale ~ Meals and snacks 11.30-2.30, 6-10 ~ Restaurant ~ Ware (01920) 463281 ~ Children welcome ~ Open 11-3, 6.30(6 Sat)-11

WATTON AT STONE TL3019 Map 5

George & Dragon ★ 🍴 🍷

Village signposted off A602 about 5 miles S of Stevenage, on B1001; High St
Hertfordshire Dining Pub of the Year

The bar menu which has always been imaginative has been further improved in its amalgamation with the dining room menu while keeping some sensibly simple dishes. Food is of a very high standard (although not cheap) and includes first courses like home-made soup (£1.45), pickled herring salad (£3.85), flaked smoked haddock with tomato concassé, gratinéed and finished under the grill (£4.25). The deep-fried brie with apricot sauce and the home-made pâté are wonderful. Superb main courses include blintzes (pancake filled with creamy mushroom and wine sauce) or fresh mushrooms covered with savoury mince topped with cheese and finished under the grill (£4.50), diced beef cooked in red wine and garlic (£4.75), darne of fresh salmon poached in white wine and fennel (£6.25), seafood thermidor in sauce of cream and brandy with a little mustard and topped with cream (£6.50), and medallions of fillet steak cooked in the pan with a Drambuie and cream sauce (£12.50); sandwiches (from £1.10), salads (from £4.25). On the daily specials board they might have lovely things like fresh asparagus (£3.85), fresh dressed crab (£5.85) or fillet of beef en croûte. Home-made puddings change daily; the apple and raspberry tart is said to have excellent pastry. There's a really sophisticated feel to this enjoyable old place (first licensed in 1603) with its proper napkins, antiques and daily newspapers – not a place for sleeveless shirts. Service is always friendly and efficient, no matter how busy they are – it's likely to be crowded by 12.30. Well kept Greene King Abbot and IPA on handpump, under light blanket pressure; several malt whiskies and good house wines by half-pint or pint carafes, and a house claret. The carpeted main bar has country kitchen armchairs around attractive old tables, dark blue cloth-upholstered seats in its bay windows, an interesting mix of antique and modern prints on the partly timbered ochre walls, and a big inglenook fireplace. A quieter room off, with spindleback chairs and wall settles cushioned to match the green floral curtains, has a hunting print and old photographs of the village above its panelled dado. The splendid restaurant with some no-smoking tables doesn't impinge on the pub itself. Fruit machine, popular boules and pétanque area. The pretty extended shrub-screened garden has picnic-table sets; handy for Benington Lordship Gardens; credit cards on bills over £10 only. *(Recommended by Patricia White and Prof John White, Nigel Norman, Chris Mawson, Huw and Carolyn Lewis, G D and M D Craigen, Hazel Morgan, Bernard Patrick, J A Boucher)*

Greene King ~ Lease: Kevin Dinnin ~ Real ale ~ Meals and snacks (till 10; not Sun evening) ~ Restaurant (not Sun eve) ~ Ware (01920) 830285 ~ Children in small family room and restaurant ~ Occasional live entertainment on theme nights ~ Open 11-2.30, 6-11(11-11 Sat); closed evening 25 Dec

WESTMILL TL3626 Map 5

Sword in Hand

Village signposted W of A10, about 1 mile S of Buntingford

Next to the church of a particularly beautiful village with its old water pump on the village green, this colour-washed local stands out among the pretty cottages and houses – especially if you go during one of the classic car shows organised by the landlord in the big garden. Photographs on the cream and brown timbered walls inside reflect this interest, with other pictures and photographs of old local scenes. The comfortable beamed bar also has elaborate furnishings, cushioned seats on the turkey carpet, good log fires, a friendly traditional atmosphere and Scruffy, the playful little dog. It's best to get here early if you want to sample the popular bar food. The fixed menu has starters like soup of the day (£2.25), whitebait (£2.95) and oriental king prawns (£3.65), and main courses that include a selection of salads from (£4.50), egg and chips (£4.50), lamb rosemary, lasagne or steak pie (£5.25), steaks from (£6.95) and two vegetarian dishes – mushroom and nut fettucini (£5.25) and broccoli and cream cheese bake (£5.95). A specials board normally has four or more dishes; puddings like treacle pudding or banoffi pie (£2.25), crêpe in a Cointreau and orange sauce (£2.75) and several ice creams. You will need to book to eat in the restaurant. Well kept Greene King IPA, Abbot and a guest on handpump. There are tables in the happy, relaxed, partly crazy-paved side garden that extends to the edge of fields, and a bouncy castle (with a fairly audible compressor) at the back, so it's popular with families. The sword in hand comes from the crest of Thomas Greg, a local landowner, for whom the pub's first landlord (also the village blacksmith) made the tools used on his Caribbean sugar plantations; darts, cribbage, shove-ha'penny and piped music; nice walks nearby. *(Recommended by Maysie Thompson, Mrs R Smith, G Keating, D A Edwards, Mr and Mrs G Walfish, S J Edwards)*

Free house ~ Licensees David and Heather Hopperton ~ Real ale ~ Meals and snacks ~ Restaurant ~ Royston (01763) 271356 ~ Well behaved children allowed ~ Open 12-3, 6.30-11; closed evening 25 Dec ~ Bedrooms: /£50

Post Office address codings confusingly give the impression that some pubs are in Hertfordshire, when they're really in Bedfordshire or Cambridgeshire (which is where we list them).

Lucky Dip

Besides the fully inspected pubs, you might like to try these Lucky Dips recommended to us and described by readers (if you do, please send us reports):

Aldbury [SP9612], *Greyhound*: Attractive old pub by village duckpond below Chilterns beechwoods, warm, welcoming and very hospitable; children allowed *(Mr and Mrs W R R Bruce, LYM)*

☆ **Amwell** [village signposted SW from Wheathampstead; TL1613], *Elephant & Castle*: Secluded and spacious floodlit garden behind low-beamed ancient pub with inglenook fireplace, panelling, stripped brickwork, 200-ft well shaft in bar – which can have decidedly local atmosphere; bar food (not Sun), well kept Benskins, Ind Coope Burton and guest beers on handpump; restaurant; children in eating area *(John Whitehead, Nigel Norman, J and P Maloney, Phil and Heidi Cook, George Atkinson, Mr and Mrs N Hazzard, HM, LYM)*

☆ **Ashwell** [TL2639], *Bushel & Strike*: Charming dining pub by church in attractive village, food slightly different and very good value, inc good Sun lunchtime buffet; good welcoming service – landlord very much in charge but obviously has heart of gold; well kept Fullers and Wethereds, cask seats, restaurant with old farm tools, good garden seating *(H Bramwell, N S Holmes, Ann and John Peacock, Susan and Nigel Wilson)*

☆ **Ashwell** [High St], *Three Tuns*: 18th-c Greene King hotel, masses of flowers and hanging baskets outside, atmospheric lounge full of pictures, stuffed pheasants and antiques – opulent Victorian feel; good range of very quickly served food, good coffee, pleasant atmosphere, friendly staff; more modern public bar with IPA and Abbot, pool *(George Atkinson, R Humphrys, Susan and Nigel Wilson)*

☆ **Ashwell** [69 High St], *Rose & Crown*: Clean and comfortable 16th-c open-plan beamed local, refurbished but keeping its log fire, with good freshly cooked food inc vegetarian dishes in bar and restaurant (children allowed); Greene King Abbot, IPA and Rayments on handpump, pleasant service, darts and machines at plainer public end; tables in big pretty country garden *(Prof John White, Patricia White, Phil and Heidi Cook)*

☆ **Ayot Green** [off B197 S of Welwyn, nr A1(M) – OS Sheet 166 map ref 222139; TL2213], *Waggoners*: Friendly, busy and efficient, with good well presented bar food, three cosy well kept areas, lots of mugs hanging from low ceiling, separate eating area, good range of real ales, good atmosphere, quiet suntrap back garden with swings, wooded walks nearby *(G D and M D Craigen, Paul and Fiona Hutt, Hazel R Morgan)*

Batford [Lower Luton Rd; B653, S of B652 junction; TL1415], *Gibraltar Castle*: Large

Fullers pub renovated well in smart old-fashioned mode, low beams, sparkling crystal, brass etc, nice cosy window alcoves, interesting militaria; well kept beers, food (not Sun – bar nibbles then), friendly staff and locals, some tables on front roadside terrace *(Michael Sandy, Dr and Mrs A K Clarke)*

☆ **Benington** [just past Post Office, towards Stevenage; TL3023], *Bell*: Lovely old pub in secluded village, unusual wall painting of stag hunt over big fireplace; generous helpings of food, efficient service, well kept beer *(Charles Bardswell, M L Clarke)*

Bennett End [Radnage; SP7897], *Three Horseshoes*: Old beamed local tucked away in pretty countryside, well worth tracking down; good traditional food, also Chinese and Indian dishes cooked by landlord *(Henry Oliphant)*

☆ **Brickendon** [1 Brickendon Lane; S of Hertford – OS Sheet 166 map ref 323081; TL3208], *Farmers Boy*: Recently reopened and refurbished village pub with emphasis on food that's good value though not cheap, but keeps country-pub atmosphere (and sandwiches); roomy, with dining area, Greene King ales, friendly service, seats in back garden and over road *(Martyn Kearey, Chris Mawson, A C Morrison, K C Phillips)*

☆ **Burnham Green** [OS Sheet 153 map ref 263167; TL2516], *White Horse*: Friendly oak-beamed village pub with banquettes and other seats, log-effect gas fire in old fireplace, increasing emphasis on good well presented if not cheap food in bar and busy restaurant, generous helpings; good service, well kept Adnams, Ind Coope Burton and Theakstons; tables and chairs in back garden and on big village green *(Phil and Heidi Cook, Chris Mawson, Martyn Kearey)*

Bushey [25 Park Rd (off A411); TQ1395], *Swan*: Homely and friendly atmosphere in rare surviving example of old-fashioned single-room backstreet terraced pub, reminiscent of 1920s; well kept Benskins Best and Ind Coope Burton on handpump; darts, cribbage and dominoes *(Pete Baker, BB)*

Chandlers Cross [TQ0698], *Clarendon Arms*: Lively traditional country pub with well kept Courage-related and unusual guest ales, attractive verandah, lots of tables and cocktail umbrellas; simple bar lunches (not Sun) *(R Houghton)*

☆ **Chipperfield** [The Common; TL0401], *Two Brewers*: Warmly relaxed atmosphere in pubby dark-beamed main bar with cushioned antique settles, well kept Bass, Greene King IPA and Abbot, Marstons Pedigree and a guest beer; popular lunchtime bar food in bow-windowed lounge with comfortable sofas and easy chairs, good restaurant; overlooks pretty tree-flanked cricket green; children allowed in lounge and restaurant, open all day Sat; comfortable bedrooms – it's an untypical Forte country hotel *(Peter Watkins, Pam Stanley, Richard Houghton, J S M Sheldon, Janet Pickles, Neil O'Callaghan, LYM)*

☆ Chorleywood [The Swillet; from M25 junction 17 follow Heronsgate signpost; TQ0295], *Stag*: Neat dining lounge with popular small restaurant area at end, good often imaginative food (not Sun evening) from sandwiches up inc imaginative dishes and lovely puddings, Allied real ales, no piped music or fruit machines, friendly staff, tables on back lawn, children's play area; busy weekends *(Lyn and Bill Capper)*
Cole Green [towards Letty Green; TL2811], *Cowper Arms*: Pleasant setting, speedy and efficient service, decent Brewers Fayre food, Whitbreads-related ales *(Charles Harvey)*

☆ nr Datchworth [Bramfield Rd, Bulls Grn; TL2717], *Horns*: Relaxed and pretty 15th-c country pub with a good deal of character inside, good sensibly priced straightforward food, well kept Whitbreads-related ales, beams and inglenook, attractive decorations, small snug, good cider and coffee, log fire; seats among rocks on crazy paving overlooking green *(Ann and John Peacock, George Atkinson, LYM)*
Digswell [Digswell Hill; TL2314], *Red Lion*: Large and attractive, very popular with business people from Welwyn with wide choice of food from soup and snacks through steak sandwich to pies, scampi, gammon and so forth *(Charles Bardswell)*

☆ Flamstead [High St; TL0714], *Three Blackbirds*: Cosy low-beamed pub with quick friendly service, well kept Courage-related real ales, good value food, two open fires; good walks nearby *(Clare Dawkins, Gordon Phillips)*

☆ Flaunden [TL0100], *Green Dragon*: Attractive and comfortable Chilterns pub with well kept real ales such as Charles Wells Bombardier, Greene King IPA, Marstons Pedigree and Union Mild, Moorhouses Pendle Witches Brew; good-sized partly panelled extended lounge with small back restaurant area, blue and red flooring tiles, pottery dragons behind bar, darts and shove-ha'penny in traditional 17th-c small tap bar; reasonably priced straightforward food, friendly service, fruit machine; very popular Sun lunchtime; charming well kept garden with summer-house and aviaries *(Simon Collett-Jones, R and S Kreloff, Marjorie and David Lamb, LYM)*

☆ Frithsden [from Berkhamsted take unmarked rd towards Potten End, pass Potten End turning on right then take next left towards Ashridge College; TL0110], *Alford Arms*: A Whitbreads country local, but usually brews its own real ales in tiny

brewhouse; good choice of bar food from filled rolls up, pleasant old-world atmosphere, good service even when busy, open all day Sat; darts, bar billiards, fruit machine; in attractive countryside, picnic-table sets out in front *(Clare Dawkins, Gordon Phillips, Lyn and Bill Capper, Nigel Chapman, LYM)*

☆ Graveley [TL2327], *Waggon & Horses*: Unspoilt former Great North Road coaching inn with lots of comfortable seating in beamed and timbered lounge with big open fire, very approachable landlord, good choice of tasty straightforward food, Whitbreads-related real ales; locals' snug by door where Brin the pub's terrier can be found; big terrace by village duckpond with trellises, summer lunchtime barbecues *(Charles Bardswell, Denise Plummer, Jim Froggatt)*
Great Amwell [TL3712], *George IV*: Quiet spot by church and river, good range of reasonably priced food inc fish and vegetarian dishes, Adnams ales *(Audrey and Dennis Nelson)*
Great Offley [towards Kings Walden; TL1427], *Red Lion*: Simple and cosy 16th-c country inn, log fire in small low-ceilinged central bar, good choice of bar food, restaurant, Whitbreads-related ale; piped music; bedrooms *(Steve and Carolyn Harvey, Jim Cowell)*

☆ Halls Green [NW of Stevenage; TL2728], *Rising Sun*: Charming 18th-c beamed country pub with big open fire in small lounge, darts area behind fireplace, newish dining conservatory, decent food inc doorstep sandwiches and popular Sun lunch, well kept McMullens Country, AK Mild and a guest beer on handpump; huge garden with big children's play area, terrace and barbecue *(Norman and Gill Fox, Phil and Heidi Cook)*

☆ Harpenden [Kinsbourne Green; 2¼ miles from M1 junction 10; A1081 towards town, on edge; TL1015], *Fox*: Pews, antique panelling, two log fires, lots of toby jugs, tankards, bottles, plates, vases, carvings, foxes' masks and masses of prints in big but cosy and relaxing extended lounge bar, good value food inc big starters, smaller public bar; very friendly efficient staff, good choice of well kept ales such as Benskins, Burton Bridge, Eldridge Pope Royal Oak and Thomas Hardy, Marstons Pedigree, Tetleys Bitter and Imperial, Youngs Special; March real ale festival, good coffee; children welcome, play area in big garden *(Phil and Heidi Cook, G L Tong, Mayur Shah, Ian Phillips, BB)*
Harpenden, *Gibraltar Castle*: One of the better Fullers pubs *(Martin Kay, Andrea Fowler)*; [High St/Station Rd], *Harpenden Arms*: Nice old pub, now Fullers, opened out inside but old fireplaces still separate the rooms; not over-smart but clean and neat; bar part with pinball machine, comfier lounge area, end Thai restaurant

with bar-food prices and some English dishes too (not weekend evenings); well kept London Pride, ESB and Hock *(Michael Sandy, Martin Kay, Andrea Fowler)*; [East Common], *Three Horseshoes*: Pleasant country pub tucked away on quiet common, with tables outside, good bar food, decent range of changing Whitbreads-related ales; can get crowded weekend lunchtimes but tables can be reserved; children welcome *(Andrew Jeeves, Carole Smart, LYM)*

☆ Hatfield [Park St, Old Hatfield; TL2308], *Eight Bells*: Quaint and attractive old beamed pub with Dickens connections, pleasantly restored, well kept Allied and a guest real ale, decent reasonably priced bar food, tables in back yard, friendly service, piped music; open all day, occasional live music; best at quiet times *(Nick Dowson, Miss Woodsend, John Boylan)*

Hemel Hempstead [A41, 2 miles W of centre, opp Hemel Hempstead Moat House; TL0506], *Anchor*: Warmly welcoming local, good range of beers, remarkable choice of good value food for such a small place, inc thoughtfully presented puddings; fortnightly jazz, landlady joining in *(Steve Torrance)*

☆ Hertford [Fore St], *Salisbury Arms*: Relaxing lounge in traditional English country-town hotel with cheerful service, decent food (not Sun evening), well kept McMullens ales inc AK Mild; splendid Jacobean staircase to bedrooms

Hertford [The Folly], *Old Barge*: Long low canalside pub, relaxing atmosphere but can get busy, usual Allied ales kept well, decent food inc wide vegetarian choice *(P Corris, LYM)*

☆ Hertford Heath [OS Sheet 166 map ref 353110; TL3510], *Silver Fox*: Lively friendly atmosphere in well laid out pub with sensibly priced well presented straightforward food from sandwiches up inc good range of puddings, quick service (new licensees who used to run the Barge in Hertford), good choice of well kept real ales, reasonable house wines; fills quickly lunchtime; relaxing courtyard *(A C Morrison, Chris Mawson, G L Tong, Neil O'Callaghan, Audrey and Dennis Nelson, Martyn Kearey)*

☆ Hinxworth [Main St, just off A1(M); TL2340], *Three Horseshoes*: Charming and popular old thatched, beamed and timbered dining pub with wide daily-changing choice of good food (not Sun evening, Mon) inc children's dishes and good veg; big brick inglenook, small dining extension, Greene King IPA and Abbot, friendly licensees, no juke box or piped music, Weds singalong; big garden with swings, climbing frames and maybe friendly wandering pig *(G L Tong, Neil O'Callaghan, Joyce and Stephen Stackhouse)*

Hunsdon [OS Sheet 167 map ref 417143; TL4114], *Fox & Hounds*: Smart village pub with Greene King ales, very popular weekends for good choice of good generous food inc lots of daily specials; friendly atmosphere, attentive staff; big garden, pretty village *(Martyn Kearey, Mrs M C Barrett)*

☆ Knebworth [Park Lane, Old Knebworth; TL2320], *Lytton Arms*: Friendly and comfortable, with interesting bric-a-brac, though most notable for eight or so weekly changing real ales (more in spring beer festival); decent bar food inc good mixed grill, espresso coffee, efficient staff, open fire; fruit machines; well kept garden, barbecues and play area *(P Neate, Denise Plummer, Jim Froggatt, Sir John Stokes)*

☆ Langley [off B656 S of Hitchin, on edge of Knebworth Park; TL2122], *Farmers Boy*: Charming smallish local, big inglenook fire in lounge with lots of low 15th-c beams, exposed woodwork, brasses, country prints, well kept Greene King IPA and Abbot on handpump; good quite adventurous food (not Sun), very friendly and homely atmosphere; end family room with piano, darts, TV; back garden *(Phil and Heidi Cook, D Pugh, J B Moizer, Michael Stringfellow, Peter Watkins, Pam Stanley, Tony Crump)*

☆ Lemsford [TL2111], *Sun*: Comfortable, welcoming and rather smart low-beamed and timbered pub nr River Lea, several well kept real ales inc Theakstons, good value generous bar food; can be busy evenings *(A W Dickinson, LYM)*

nr Lemsford [A6129 towards Wheathampstead], *Crooked Chimney*: Spacious and popular open-plan country dining pub with central feature fireplace, several well kept real ales inc Greene King, comfortable restaurant, young staff; garden by fields *(Clare Dawkins, Gordon Phillips, Martyn Kearey, LYM)*

☆ Letchmore Heath [2 miles from M1 junction 5; A41 towards Harrow, first left towards Aldenham, then signed right; TQ1597], *Three Horseshoes*: Pretty and cottagey little flower-decked local nicely placed opp duck pond on tree-shaded green, wide choice of standard weekday lunchtime bar food (snacks Sat), well kept Allied ales, maybe faint piped music, white tables outside; can get crowded *(Barry Roe, Wendy Mogose, LYM)*

☆ Little Berkamstead [1 Church Rd; TL2908], *Five Horseshoes*: Genuinely old-feeling 17th-c village pub with beams, stripped brickwork, two log fires, well kept Greene King and Tetleys ales, decent wines, good reasonably priced generous bar food from sandwiches to unusual main dishes inc vegetarian, quick responsive service; good restaurant; garden with picnic-table sets, busy in summer *(Martyn Kearey, Colin Quille, A C Morrison)*

☆ Little Hadham [The Ford; TL4422], *Nags Head*: Cosy series of beamed interconnecting rooms in clean and comfortable 16th-c country pub increasingly popular for notable yet reasonably priced food using fresh ingredients, inc lots of fish, Sun roast (must be booked); well kept Greene King and Rayments Special, very friendly attentive staff, relaxed atmosphere; restaurant; children welcome *(George Atkinson, J D Patrick, Martyn Kearey, LYM)*

Little Heath [Heath Rd; TL0108], *Builders Arms*: Friendly atmosphere in largish McMullens pub with lovely floral decorations, good reasonably priced bar food – must book Sun lunch *(J D Patrick)*

☆ **Little Wymondley** [by Stevenage/Hitchin bypass, nr Hitchin; TL2127], *Plume of Feathers*: Nice friendly refurbished pub where they'll try and suit your tastes even if what you want's not on the menu; the big alsatian's called Leah *(Charles Bardswell)*

Little Wymondley, *Bucks Head:* Small, cosy and chintzy, with brasses, beams, wooden settles, cushioned seats; well kept Whitbreads-related ales, popular lunchtime food, attractive garden *(Denise Plummer, Jim Froggatt, LYM)*

☆ **London Colney** [Waterside; just off main st by bridge at S end; TL1704], *Green Dragon*: Attractive setting with riverside tables for friendly and immaculate pub with good value generous food (not Sun) inc good sandwiches and some unusual main dishes, lots of beams and brasses, soft lighting, well kept Allied and guest real ales, palatable food *(Mrs C Archer, LYM)*

☆ **Much Hadham** [Hertford Rd, about ¼ mile outside; TL4319], *Jolly Waggoners*: Good all-round country pub concentrating on attractive home-cooked food inc children's dishes and superb puddings, pleasant efficient service, Greene King real ales, good choice of malt whiskies, nice window seats; huge garden with friendly animals *(David Surridge, Martyn Kearey)*

☆ **Much Hadham** [B1004 – OS Sheet 167 map ref 428197], *Bull*: Attractive old pub reopened not long ago, with comfortable banquettes in lounge, simple character inglenook public bar, back family dining room, wide choice of slightly unusual food well cooked and presented at sensible prices, Allied real ales; children welcome, unusually big garden *(Dr Ronald Church, Martyn Kearey, PACW, LYM)*

☆ **Newgate Street** [1 mile N of Cuffley; TL3005], *Coach & Horses*: Civilised old country pub with heavy beams, flagstones, built-in black wall pews, lots of brasses, two open fires; bar food inc vegetarian, well kept Allied and guest real ales, efficient friendly service; picnic-table sets in sheltered garden, good walks nearby *(J Giles Quick, John Whitehead, Nigel Norman, Norman Foot, LYM)*

Nuthampstead [TL4034], *Woodman*: Character thatched pub of real individuality, well kept real ales, inglenook log fire with cats dreaming inscrutably, locals include everyone in their conversations *(David Surridge)*

Park Street [Smug Oak Lane; TL1403],

Moor Mill: Spectacular old mill done up with skill, attractive atmosphere and gardens *(Douglas Bail)*

☆ **Pirton** [Great Green; TL1431], *Cat & Fiddle*: Well kept Adnams Broadside and Charles Wells Eagle and friendly landlord in homely and comfortable pub facing village green, swing on back lawn *(Clare Dawkins, Gordon Phillips, LYM)*

☆ **Potters Crouch** [leaving St Albans on Watford rd via Chiswell Green, turn right after M10 – OS Sheet 166 map ref 116052; TL1105], *Holly Bush*: Highly polished biggish tables and other dark wood furniture, lots of pictures, plates, brasses and antlers, old-fashioned lighting, good helpings of simple well presented food, efficient service, particularly well kept Fullers Chiswick, London Pride and ESB, reasonable wines; busy weekends; good big garden with picnic-table sets *(A C Morrison, Martin Kay, Andrea Fowler, S J Edwards, Roy and Mary Roebuck)*

☆ **Puckeridge** [TL3823], *White Hart*: Pleasant and cosy rambling dining pub with lots of wooden armchairs as well as button-back banquettes, tremendously wide choice of food esp fish, well kept McMullens Bitter, AK Mild and a guest beer, good tables outside; has been open all day Sat *(PACW, J A Boucher, Wayne Brindle, M L Clarke, D A Edwards, LYM; more reports please)*

Radlett [14 Cobden Hill (Watling St); TL1600], *Cat & Fiddle*: Interesting building converted from cottages, cat theme throughout, lots of china ones; well kept beers, wide choice of good food *(M T Carpenter)*

Redbourn [Redbourn Rd (A5183); nr M1 junction 9; TL1012], *Chequers*: Friendly refurbished Chef & Brewer, good service, well kept real ales, good array of food *(John Whitehead)*

☆ **Reed** [High St; TL3636], *Cabinet*: Current landlord making the most of this ancient tiled and weatherboarded pub, with its charmingly parlourish little rustic public bar and pleasant lounge; five well kept real ales, welcoming log fire, good generous food, helpful staff, tables in big garden with pond and flowers *(Simon Watkins, Joyce and Stephen Stackhouse, LYM)*

☆ **Rickmansworth** [Scots Hill Rd; off Park Rd (A412) towards Watford; TQ0594], *Scotsbridge Mill*: Rambling and comfortable former water mill with good value food in bar and Beefeater restaurant, Whitbreads-related real ales; River Chess runs through building and under narrow bridges outside, with well spaced tables *(Lyn and Bill Capper)*

Rickmansworth [High St], *Coach & Horses*: Greene King pub dating back in part to 16th c, log fire, lots of farm tools, friendly service, good food with different evening menu *(Mr and Mrs N Hazzard)*

Royston [Kneesworth St; TL3541], *Coach & Horses*: Friendly town pub with two comfortable bar areas, cheery locals inc bellringers and church choir, good home-made food *(Owen Davies)*

☆ **Sandridge** [High St; TL1610], *Rose & Crown*: Comfortable dining pub with wide range of generous changing food inc five rich soups and lots of main courses, good service, several Whitbreads-related and other real ales *(J A Boucher)*

Sarratt [The Green; TQ0499], *Cricketers*: Very welcoming new licensees, tasty well presented food, tables outside *(Douglas C Bail); Cock:* This attractive country pub is now closed, with plans for conversion to a private house

Shenley [37 London Rd; TL1800], *White Horse*: Comfortably refurbished lounge, well kept beers, nice garden, good food *(Michael and Alison Sandy, Ken Smith)*

South Mimms [off B556; TL2201], *Black Horse*: Beams, decorations from champagne bottles to polished brass skillets, well kept Greene King beer and low-cost food inc good avocado and bacon sandwich *(Dave Irving)*

☆ **St Albans** [Holywell Hill; TL1507], *White Hart*: Comfortable and civilised if a bit formal, two small bar areas opening into larger one with tables; antique panelling, handsome fireplaces and furnishings, courteous helpful service, some bar food bargains esp Weds lunchtime businessman's special, food all day Sat; restaurant, Allied and guest real ales; bedrooms *(Michael, Alison and Rhiannon Sandy, Brian Marsden, LYM)*

St Albans [2 Keyfield Terr; off London Rd], *Beehive*: Recently refurbished sawdust-style pub with good lively atmosphere, well kept Whitbreads-related ales, decent food Sun-Thurs; piped music may be loud, live music Thurs, lots of young people Fri/Sat *(Nick Dowson, John Boylan);* [Fishpool St], *Black Lion:* Genteel and restful hotel lounge with discreet piped music, Bass, Charrington IPA, Fullers London Pride *(Brian Marsden);* [Fishpool St], *Blue Anchor:* Perhaps the cheapest pub here, busy and friendly, with small warmly welcoming locals' bar on left, newspapers to read, well kept real ales inc Mild, sensibly placed darts, friendly alsatian, real fire; comfortable lounge opening on to sizeable garden, good value bar food (not Sun evening) from sandwiches up, coffee, wines; handy for Roman remains *(Brian Marsden, JJW, CMW)*

Please keep sending us reports. We rely on readers for news of new discoveries, and particularly for news of changes – however slight – at the fully described pubs. No stamp needed: *The Good Pub Guide*, FREEPOST TN1569, Wadhurst, E Sussex TN5 7BR.

Humberside

This is one of Britain's best value areas for pubs. Given equal quality, the cost of eating out in a pub here is well below the national average. A decent main dish which in most places elsewhere would cost over £5 can generally be found here for £4 or less. The same goes for drinks. On average, a pint of beer here costs about 20p below the national norm. In the St Vincent Arms, Sutton upon Derwent, we found we could get a whole pint of beer for little more than the price of just a half in many equivalently civilised pubs down in the south of England! What an excellent choice of beers in that pub, too – new to the main entries this year after an absence of some years. Another remarkably cheap pub, for both drinks and food, is the very traditional White Horse in Beverley: quite a surprise to find this extraordinarily old-fashioned pub to be one of the first in the area to have a no-smoking room. Other changes to mention here include the decision at the Dacre Arms at Brandesburton to have just a single menu for both bar and restaurant – in effect, a wider choice now at this pleasant dining pub. The Seabirds at Flamborough, which has always had decent wine to go with its excellent fish, has at last put in real ales. That comfortable meeting place, the Feathers in Pocklington, has new licensees who are keeping it open all through Sunday afternoon for food. Some things fortunately don't change here: perhaps most notably the wonderfully old-fashioned character of the handsome Olde White Harte in Hull, but also the consistently excellent Yorkshire puddings in the Half Moon at Skidby – the first pub to show how splendid this could be as a pub meal. In the Lucky Dip section at the end of the chapter, we'd particularly mention the Boot & Shoe at Ellerton (character), Light Dragoon at Etton (good family pub), Brewers Arms in Snaith (brewing its own excellent beers) and, for decent food in civilised surroundings of character, the Londesborough Arms in Market Weighton and Star at North Dalton.

ALLERTHORPE SE7847 Map 7

Plough

Off A1079 nr Pocklington

This is one of the few pubs in the area to have a chef/patron as landlord, and readers confirm that the results are very appetising. It's the popular daily specials which are his real showcase: big helpings of much-praised venison in red wine sauce, for instance, or poached fresh salmon with a prawn sauce, rack of lamb in honey, mint and currant sauce, braised dishes like English lamb's liver and onions, steak and onions or lamb's kidneys. More usual bar food includes soup (£1.50), sandwiches (from £1.75), ploughman's (from £3.50), home-made pâté (£3.65), lasagne (£4.95), scampi (£5.10), steaks (from £8.50); vegetarian dishes are available on request; the usual children's meals and a selection of puddings (from £1.95). It's best to book for Sunday roast lunch (£4.75). It's pleasant to relax on the seating in the garden at the front of this idyllic little village pub, and inside the pretty white house the friendly two-room lounge bar has snug alcoves (including one big bay window), hunting prints, some wartime RAF and RCAF photographs (squadrons of both were stationed here), and open fires; the games –

pool, dominoes, shove-ha'penny, cribbage, fruit and video machine and juke box – are in an extension. Well kept reasonably priced Theakstons XB and Old Peculier and Tetleys on handpump. The pub is handy for the attractive lily-pond gardens and stuffed sporting trophies of Burnby Hall. *(Recommended by Roger A Bellingham, Lee Goulding, Miss J F Reay, Allan and Ruth Sharp)*

Free house ~ Licensees David and Janet Booth ~ Real ale ~ Meals and snacks ~ Restaurant ~ Pocklington (01759) 302349 ~ Children in eating area, games room and restaurant ~ Open 12-3, 7-11

BEVERLEY TA0340 Map 8

White Horse ('Nellies') £

Hengate, close to the imposing Church of St Mary's; runs off North Bar Within

This wonderfully unspoilt pub saw John Wesley preach in the back yard in the mid 18th c, and the building – which actually dates from 1425 – has barely changed since that time. Now you'll find it bustling with locals, some of whom might still recall its determinedly traditional former landlady Nellie Collinson (she's still remembered in the pub name), who didn't even have a bar counter and was one of the very last to enforce a men-only rule. Readers love this place for the basic but very atmospheric little rooms, huddled together around the central bar, with antique cartoons and sentimental engravings on the nicotine-stained walls, brown leatherette seats (with high-backed settles in one little snug), basic wooden chairs and benches, a gaslit pulley-controlled chandelier, bare floorboards, a deeply reverberating chiming clock, and open fires – one with an attractively tiled old fireplace. Well kept cheap Sam Smiths OB and Museum on handpump. There's a daily changing menu with very cheap, simple, quickly served food which might include sandwiches (£1), filled baked potatoes (£1.50), a vegetarian dish like vegetable lasagne, lasagne or steak and kidney pie (£3.25); Sunday roast (£3.65). What used to be a restaurant has now been converted to a games room with darts, dominoes, trivia and two pool tables – these and the no-smoking room behind the bar are the only modern touches. *(Recommended by A W Dickinson, A Craig, David and Ruth Hollands, Annette Moore, Chris Pearson, John Honnor; more reports please)*

Sam Smiths ~ Lease John Southern ~ Real ale ~ Lunchtime meals and snacks ~ Hull (01482) 861973 ~ Children welcome (not in bar Sun) ~ Folk music Mon, Jazz Weds nights ~ Open 11-11 (cl 25 Dec)

BRANDESBURTON TA1247 Map 8

Dacre Arms

Village signposted from A165 N of Beverley and Hornsea turn-offs

On 28 February 1844 the Franklin Dead Brief Society was formed here by a horse dealer, who, while visiting the annual Brandesburton horse fair, was moved to hear that a friend could not afford to bury his wife. The society with approximately 270 members is still pooling money for funerals today, and still has its annual meeting here on the first Wednesday in February; the landlord of the pub is Treasurer by tradition. There has been an inn on this site since the 16th c, with stabling for up to 50 horses around a cobbled yard; it was once one of the most important posting stations in the East Riding. The present structure dates from 1806. Roomy and comfortable, the rambling rough-plastered modernised bar is vividly furnished with plenty of tables, and the snug area on the right once housed the local Court of Justices. The restaurant has been redecorated this year, and of course you can still book a table in here, but they are now serving the same menu throughout the pub. The consequence is that the good value varied bar menu now includes more vegetarian and seafood dishes as well as soup (£1.40), large filled Yorkshire puddings (from £3.95), smoked salmon tagliatelle (£4.25), lasagne (£4.75), southern fried chicken (£4.95), the popular 'taste of 45' (strips of fillet steak, cooked with Drambuie and cream on a bed of rice, £5.25), seafood thermidor (£5.95) and steaks (from £6.85); puddings like hot apple pie, tiramisu or sticky toffee meringue (from £1.95); freshly ground coffee; reasonably priced well kept Boddingtons, Tetleys, Theakstons Old Peculier and guests on handpump; lots of malt whiskies; darts, dominoes, fruit machine, trivia and piped music. *(Recommended by Ivor Maw, Anthony Barnes; more reports please)*

Free house ~ Licensee Martin Rowe ~ Real ale ~ Meals and snacks (12-2, 6.30-10.30; not 25 Dec, no sandwiches Sun) ~ Restaurant ~ Hornsea (01964) 542392 ~ Children in eating area of bar and restaurant ~ Open 11-2.30(3 Sat), 6.30(5 Sat)-11

FLAMBOROUGH   TA2270   Map 8

Seabirds ♀

Junction of B1255 and B1229

The excellent fresh fish and the very good home cooking attract holidaymakers and locals to this straightforward village pub above the cliffs of Flamborough Head. The fish and chips really is something, with extraordinarily light and crispy batter. Other reasonably priced bar food from the daily changing specials board includes very good fresh crab or salmon salads, lobster thermidor (in season), mince and onion pie and smoked haddock mornay. The regular menu has soup of the day (£1.60), sandwiches, prawns in tangy dressing (£3.60), salads, home-made steak and kidney pie (£4.60), sirloin steak (£9.75), and many additional dishes in the evening like fillet of pork in white wine with whole grain mustard sauce (£7.65) and rack of lamb (£7.95); two vegetarian dishes, lasagne and broccoli and cream cheese bake. This year they have introduced real cask conditioned ales and have John Smiths and a weekly changing guest on handpump; there's a good well priced wine list, hot mulled wine and a large choice of whiskies and liqueurs. The cheerful public bar is full of shipping paraphernalia and old framed photographs of Flamborough. Leading off this is the lounge, with pictures and paintings of the local landscape, a mirror glazed with grape vines, and a woodburning stove; there's also a whole case of stuffed seabirds along one wall; hardworking staff; piped music; family room in the garden. *(Recommended by Alan Wilcock, Christine Davidson, R M Macnaughton, Mark Bradley, Roger and Christine Mash, Martin and Pauline Richardson, Joy Heatherley, Lawrence Bacon, Jean Stott, Eric J Locker, Ann and Bob Westbrook)*

Free house ~ Licensee Jean Riding ~ Meals and snacks (not Sun or Mon evenings in winter) ~ Restaurant (not Sun evening in winter) ~ Bridlington (01262) 850242 ~ Children in eating area of bar and restaurant ~ Open 11-3, 7(6.30 Sat)-11

HULL   TA0927   Map 8

Minerva

From A63 Castle Street/Garrison Road, turn into Queen Street towards piers at central traffic lights; some metered parking here; pub is in pedestrianised Nelson Street, at far end

Near the attractive restored waterfront and bustling marina, this picturesque Georgian pub in the heart of the old harbour really does reflect the atmosphere of Hull. The floor is raised a few feet above ground level though the windows are down at normal height, so the views over the Humber are unusually good. Several thoughtfully refurbished rooms ramble all the way round a central servery and are filled with comfortable seats, interesting photographs and pictures of old Hull (with two attractive wash drawings by Roger Davis) and a big chart of the Humber. There is a tiny snug with room for just three people, and a back room (which looks out to the marina basin, and has darts) with a profusion of varnished woodwork. Besides very reasonably priced well kept Arrols 80/-, Ind Coope Burton, Marstons Pedigree and Tetleys Bitter and Mild on handpump, the pub brews its own Pilots Pride (a throwback to the days when the town was renowned for its beer, and the expression eating Hull Cheese was a euphemism for having a bit to drink) – you can see into the microbrewery from the street. Straightforward bar food in really healthy portions – the reader who says they are reminiscent of school lunches must have gone to a more generous school than your Editor – includes hot or cold filled baguettes (from £1.85), soup (99p), burgers (£1.90), filled baked potatoes (from £1.85), ploughman's (£3.25), salads (from £3.25), fried haddock (£3.60), steak and kidney pie or lasagne (£3.95), mixed grill (£6.95) and at least five daily specials, two of which are vegetarian; traditional hot puddings daily. Piped music from the fine reproduction Wurlitzer juke box (the real 'works', with the records, are actually in a completely different place); darts, dominoes fruit and video machines, trivia; small lounge is no smoking. *(Recommended by J S M Sheldon, Miranda Hutchinson; more reports please)*

Own brew (Tetleys) ~ Manager John Harris McCue ~ Real ale ~ Meals and snacks (not Sun evenings) ~ (01482) 26909 ~ Children in eating area of bar ~ Open 11-11; 11-3, 5-11 in winter; cl 25 Dec

Olde White Harte ★ £

Off 25 Silver Street, a continuation of Whitefriargate; pub is up narrow passage beside the jewellers' Barnby and Rust, and should not be confused with the much more modern White Hart nearby

Tucked away in a cosy little courtyard among little alleyways, this beautifully preserved ancient tavern is best appreciated on a quiet weekday evening when you can gently absorb the fascinating interior. In fact history was made in the heavily panelled room up the oak staircase on St George's Day 1642, when Sir John Hotham, the town's Governor, made the decision to lock the nearby gate against the king, Charles I, depriving him of Hull's arsenal. It didn't do him much good, as in the Civil War that followed, Hotham, like the king, was executed by the parliamentarians. In the downstairs bar attractive stained-glass windows look out above the bow window seat, carved heavy beams support black ceiling boards, and two brocaded Jacobean-style chairs sit in the brick inglenook with its frieze of delft tiles. The curved copper-topped counter serves well kept Youngers IPA and No 3, Theakstons Old Peculier and XB and a guest on handpump, and 14 malt whiskies. Otherwise very similar, the second bar has a turkey carpet. Resting on the zigzagging old stairs which go up to the dining area is a fine longcase clock. Very reasonably priced simple, traditional bar food includes sandwiches (from £1.10), made to order salads (from £2.20), lasagne (£2.50) and a pie of the day (£2.65), with changing specials such as toad in the hole (£1.30); traditional puddings like jam roly poly or bread and butter pudding (£1.40); the weekday lunchtime atmosphere is vibrant and bustling. They also do Sunday lunch; courteous, excellent friendly service; seats in the courtyard outside; dominoes, fruit machine. *(Recommended by C A Hall, Stephen E Millard, J S M Sheldon, Martyn and Mary Mullins; more reports please)*

Youngers (S & N) ~ Managers Brian and Jenny Cottingham ~ Real ale ~ Lunchtime meals and snacks ~ Lunchtime restaurant ~ Hull (01482) 26363 ~ Children in restaurant ~ Quiz nights Mon ~ No nearby parking ~ Open 11-11

LOW CATTON SE7053 Map 7

Gold Cup

Village signposted with High Catton off A166 in Stamford Bridge or A1079 at Kexby Bridge

You can rely on a straightforward warm welcome and good home-cooked food at this friendly, comfortable white-rendered house where the cheery locals might be eating or just having a drink. The licensees tell us that prices of the good, popular bar food have not changed since last year – soup (£1.50), lunchtime sandwiches (from £1.45), crusty rolls (from £2.30), and ploughman's (£3.25), chicken curry or deep-fried battered vegetable platter (£4.35), steak and mushroom pie (£4.40), fisherman's pie (£4.95) and more elaborate dishes in the evening like trout wrapped in bacon and stuffed with spinach and hazelnuts, or lamb in Cumberland sauce; Tuesday-Friday they also have a two-course roast lunch (£3.50). The fat geese in the back paddock originally came from the farm next door, and now Shetland ponies and goats keep them company. Inside, the three communicating rooms of the lounge have a very relaxed atmosphere, with open fires at each end, red plush wall seats and stools around good solid tables, flowery curtains, some decorative plates and brasswork on the walls, all bathed in a soft red lighting. Well kept reasonably priced John Smiths and Tetleys on handpump, good coffee, decent wines; congenial service. The back games bar is comfortable too, with a well lit pool table, darts, dominoes, quiz game, fruit machine and well reproduced music. *(Recommended by Bill and Beryl Farmer; more reports please)*

Free house ~ Licensees Ray and Pat Hales ~ Real ale ~ Snacks and meals ~ Restaurant ~ Stamford Bridge (01759) 371354 ~ Children welcome ~ Open 12-3, 7-11; cl Mon lunch (exc bank holidays)

POCKLINGTON SE8049 Map 7

Feathers 🛏

56 Market Place; sigposted off A1079 York—Hull

Thankfully it's more welcoming here than in days gone by when public hangings took place in the yard – one room is even said to be haunted by chilling breathing and dragging sounds thought to be linked to the 1810 murder of a maid by a highwayman who was later put to death outside. The spreading open-plan lounge has comfortable banquettes and a cheerful market-town atmosphere (especially on market day itself, Tuesday), while the separate timbered restaurant and some other parts predate the 19th-c rebuilding. Under the new licensees they are now open all day for food on Sunday. Decent bar meals include sandwiches (from £1.40, hot beef and onion £1.95), soup (£1.55), filled Yorkshire puddings (from £2.75), salads (from £4.50), gammon (£4.95), lasagne, chilli con carne and pie of the day (£4.25), a choice of four roasts (from £4.75), fresh haddock, fillet or cod (£4.95), chicken kiev (£5.95); puddings; good breakfasts. Well kept Theakstons Best and Youngers Scotch on handpump, and over 25 malt whiskies; good service from friendly staff; fruit machine and piped music; no-smoking conservatory. *(Recommended by Steve Merson; more reports please)*

Pennine Inns (Scottish & Newcastle) ~ Manager Shane Wragg ~ Real ale ~ Meals and snacks ~ Restaurant ~ Pocklington (01759) 303155 ~ Children welcome ~ Jazz Weds evening ~ Open 10.30-11 ~ Bedrooms: £39.50B/£49.50B

SKIDBY TA0133 Map 8

Half Moon

Main Street; off A164

Once again it's quite clear that this pub is still cooking the best Yorkshire puddings in the country, and a tremendous number too. Their unique speciality loaf-sized but feather-light Yorkshire puddings with various fillings are so popular that their creation involves some 70,000 eggs and 7,000lb of flour a year – and of course a closely guarded secret ingredient. The choice runs from onion gravy made the traditional way with no artificial thickeners (£2.60, or £3 with vegetarian gravy), chilli and curry (£4.55) to roast beef (£4.90); other efficiently served dishes include soup (£1.60), burgers (from £2.55) and superb home-made steak and kidney pie with suet pastry or a quarter chicken (£4); lots of these dishes, including the Yorkshire puddings, are available in small helpings for children. The decor throughout is new this year; it's bright and cheerful – like the landlord and staff – but there's still a homely atmosphere in the old-fashioned partly panelled front tap-room with long cushioned wall benches, old elm tables, a little high shelf of foreign beer bottles and miniatures, a tiled floor, and a fire. The more spacious communicating back rooms have a lighter and airier atmosphere, and an unusually big clock. Darts, bar billiards, shove ha'penny, dominoes, cribbage, fruit machine, piped music; John Smiths and Marstons Pedigree on handpump, with a wide range of malt whiskies and an Irish gin. The landscaped garden area beside the car park has a children's play area with a suspended net maze, and in summer a bar with sweets, ice cream and fizzy drinks; part no-smoking restaurant. A black and white windmill is nearby. *(Recommended by David Gray, Stephen G Brown, Jane Kingsbury, D Fell, Joy Heatherley, Alan Burt, J S M Sheldon, J L Phillips, John Hazel)*

John Smiths (Courage) ~ Lease Peter Madeley ~ Meals and snacks (noon till 10) ~ (01482) 843403 ~ Children in eating area of bar; no under 14s after 8.30 ~ Live music Tues, rock'n'roll first Fri of month ~ Open 11-11; cl evening 25 Dec

SUTTON UPON DERWENT SE7047 Map 7

St Vincent Arms 🍺

B1228 SE of York

Last a main entry in the 1990 edition of *The Guide,* this cosy old family-run pub with its friendly atmosphere and unbeatable service is named after the Admiral who was given the village and lands at the nation's bequest for his successful commands, and for coping with Nelson's infatuation with Lady Hamilton. Equally popular for the good food and good beer, the parlour-like, panelled front bar has traditional high-backed settles, a cushioned bow-window seat, Windsor chairs and a coal fire. Another lounge and separate dining room open off here, and what was the games room is now a restaurant. The landlord's son is a chef and the excellently presented first-class bar food in generous portions is all home-made, and includes sandwiches (from £1.55), steak and kidney pie and lasagne (£5.20), steaks from (£9) and changing dishes of the day such as fresh fish, sausage and mash (£2.75), pork stroganoff (£7), a daily stir-fry (£7.50) and duck breast in orange (£8.50); traditional home-made puddings like treacle tart. It's best to book a table if you want a full meal, especially at weekends. The landlord is well known for his excellent range of at least nine or more very cheap well kept real ales with resident Boddingtons, John Smiths, Mansfield Riding and Timothy Taylors Landlord, and regulary changing guests which might be Adnams, Courage Directors, Fullers London Pride, Shepherd Neame Spitfire, Theakstons XB and Whitbreads Castle Eden all on handpump; very reasonably priced spirits; piped music; large handsome garden with tables and seats; no-smoking room at the back. *(Recommended by Dr P R Davis, Geraldine Liddell; more reports please)*

Free house ~ Licensee Phil Hopwood ~ Real ale ~ Meals and snacks ~ Restaurant ~ (01904) 608349 ~ Children welcome (must be well behaved in restaurant) ~ Open 11-3, 6-11; closed eve 25 Dec

---

Lucky Dip

Besides the fully inspected pubs, you might like to try these Lucky Dips recommended to us and described by readers (if you do, please send us reports):

Airmyn [89 High St; half a mile from M62 junction 36; SE7225], *Percy Arms*: Useful motorway break, well kept Courage-related beers *(Mrs J Barwell)*

Beverley [TA0340], *Woolpack*: Very small, well run and spotlessly clean, with tiny snug, not much bigger lounge, small back garden; well kept Burtonwood Bitter and Mild, very friendly service *(Richard Houghton)*

Burton upon Stather [N of Scunthorpe; SE8717], *Sheffield Arms*: Wide choice of generous food in attractively furnished old-fashioned stone pub with well kept ales, genial landlord, old photographs *(J L Phillips)*

☆ **Cleethorpes** [Kingsway; TA3008], *Willys*: Own good beers brewed behind modern bistro-style pub with good basic reasonably priced lunchtime food, quiet juke box, good views of Humber estuary *(Alf and Jane Ludlam)*

☆ **Ellerton** [signed off B1228 – OS Sheet 105 map ref 705398; SE7039], *Boot & Shoe*: Cottagey and comfortable, with low 16th-c beams, cosy corners, decent food at reasonable prices, friendly service, restaurant, garden behind *(I A McCaskey, LYM)*

☆ **Etton** [3½ miles N of Beverley, off B1248; SE9843], *Light Dragoon*: Wide range of decent bar food in roomy, comfortable and atmospheric country local, inglenook fireplace, pleasant service, well kept Youngers Scotch and IPA on handpump, garden with play area *(Roger A Bellingham, LYM)*

Flamborough [Dog & Duck Sq; junction B1255/B1229; TA2270], *Royal Dog & Duck*: Friendly local with pleasant layout, well kept real ale, usual food *(Martin and Pauline Richardson, LYM)*

Grimsby [Victoria St; TA2609], *Hope & Anchor*: Good real ale pub, basic and traditional, with lunchtime food inc huge Yorkshire puddings *(Alf and Jane Ludlam)*

☆ **Hull** [Land of Green Ginger, Old Town; TA0927], *George*: Good choice of cheap, generous and tasty lunchtime food inc good fish in handsomely preserved traditional long Victorian bar, lots of oak, mahogany and copper, well kept Bass and Stones on handpump, good service, piped music; can get very busy – get there early; handy for the fine Docks Museum; children allowed in plush upstairs dining room; open all day *(J S M Sheldon, LYM)*

Hull [193 Collingham Rd], *Newland Park*:

Straightforward 1930s hotel, updated and modernised over the years, with good standard pub food inc lunchtime carvery at reasonable prices, reasonable beers, good service and pleasant atmosphere *(Roger Bellingham)*

☆ **Kirkburn** [signed off A163 SW of Great Driffield; SE9855], *Queens Head*: Clean, airy and welcoming, with well kept Courage-related ales, good value bar food, good staff, galleried evening and weekend restaurant; tables among flowers and fruit-trees in pretty garden; children welcome *(Steve and Julie Cocking, LYM)*

☆ **Market Weighton** [SE8742], *Londesborough Arms*: Good food in elegant and comfortable lounge bar and restaurant, nice wine, friendly staff; bedrooms good value and comfortable *(B Gee, Roger A Bellingham, BB)*

☆ **North Dalton** [SE9352], *Star*: Decent bar food from soup and generous open sandwiches up in comfortably refurbished lounge bar with welcoming coal fire, obliging young staff, well kept real ales, character restaurant; a striking sight, one wall rising straight from sizeable pond; comfortable bedrooms *(P J Keen, BB)*
Shiptonthorpe [A1079 Mkt Weighton—York; SE8543], *Crown*: Good food inc Sun lunch, good service, well kept beer *(Roger Bellingham)*

☆ **Snaith** [10 Pontefract Rd; SE6422], *Brewers Arms*: Good beers – Old Mill, Bullion, Mild – brewed at this attractive converted mill, with exposed joists, brick and timber bar counter, light conservatory-style dining area with pine ceiling, green plush chairs, turkey carpet, lots of plants; good bar food esp sandwiches, good value restaurant; bedrooms *(Thomas Nott)*

☆ **South Dalton** [OS Sheet 106 map ref 964454; SE9645], *Pipe & Glass*: Some high-backed settles, old prints, log fires, beams and bow windows for very quiet dining pub with good choice of decent wines, well kept John Smiths, Theakstons Best and Whitbreads Castle Eden, friendly if not always speedy service, conservatory, tables in garden with play area; restaurant, children welcome, lovely setting by Dalton Park; closed Mon *(J S M Sheldon, Mrs M S Black, Eric J Locker, M and J Back, LYM)*

South Ferriby [set back from A1077; SE9921], *Nelthorpe Arms*: Old-established, comfortable, unhurried sort of place with big square lounge, decent food esp steak and kidney pie, Tetleys and related beers; welcoming atmosphere *(J L Phillips)*

☆ **Walkington** [B1230; SE9937], *Dog & Duck*: Popular Mansfield dining pub with good bar food esp steak and kidney pie in long lounge or small restaurant; well kept Mansfield and Riding ales, decent wine, pleasant atmosphere, good service *(C A Hall, Roger Bellingham)*

☆ **Walkington** [B1230], *Ferguson Fawsitt Arms*: Mock-Tudor bars in 1950s style, with good choice of properly cooked good value food and good puddings from airy no-smoking flagstone-floored self-service food bar, very popular lunchtime with older people; friendly cheerful service, decent wine; tables out on terrace, games bar with pool table *(Roger Bellingham, John Bestley, LYM)*

Walkington [B1230 Beverley—South Cave], *Barrel*: Completely refurbished local by village duckpond, no loss of character from changes, the place sparkles and the welcome is as big as the landlord; four magnificently kept real ales, good basic cheap unfussy food *(C A Hall, Thomas Nott)*

Wilberfoss [off A1079 E of York; SE7351], *Oddfellows Arms*: Very friendly newish landlord doing good generous food inc vegetarian in dining room at end of spacious bar, Bass and Stones beers, interesting pictures, delft shelf *(K J Hillier)*

Winteringham [off A1077; SE9322], *Bay Horse*: Roomy open-plan refurbished lounge split into big alcoves, with carefully arranged brasses and ornaments, very welcoming landlord, Whitbreads-related and guest beers, freshly prepared and therefore not speedy bar food; children welcome *(J L Phillips)*

Bedroom prices normally include full English breakfast, VAT and any inclusive service charge that we know of. Prices before the '/' are for single rooms, after for two people in double or twin (B includes a private bath, S a private shower). If there is no '/', the prices are only for twin or double rooms (as far as we know there are no singles).

Isle of Wight

Food in the island's pubs is rather good value by mainland standards – similar dishes tend to cost nearly £1 less than across the Solent in Hampshire, for example. For eating out, we'd mention particularly the unusual Bonchurch Inn in Bonchurch (new to the main entries this year after a break, Italian-run), the Red Lion at Freshwater (making the most of its re-equipped kitchen), the Seaview Hotel in Seaview (its front dining lounge is very much as you'd expect from a small hotel in this decorous Victorian resort, but it also has a surprisingly pubby bar of great character), the Crown prettily tucked away at Shorwell, and the Wheatsheaf in Yarmouth. Under its current management the Red Lion has such a happy combination of welcoming unpretentious surroundings with careful home cooking that we choose it as Isle of Wight Dining Pub of the Year. By contrast with food, drinks prices on the island are in general higher than the national norm, with supply here dominated by the national brewers, particularly Whitbreads. Locally produced beers from first Hartridges and now Goddards don't yet seem to have had a moderating influence on island drinks pricing in the way that Burts did before the demise of that brewery. However, they certainly add to choice, and in general the choice of real ales available on the island is a good deal wider than it was a few years ago: the Buddle at Niton has an excellent variety, and this year gains our new Beer Award. In the Lucky Dip section at the end of the chapter we'd particularly pick out the Chequers at Rookley and New Inn at Shalfleet; and the Eight Bells at Carisbrooke looks to be a very promising main-entry candidate.

ARRETON SZ5486 Map 2

White Lion

A3056 Newport—Sandown

Still one of the most popular on the island, this cream-painted village pub is one of the few that has managed to stay relatively unspoilt and keep much of its original character. Cosy and relaxing, the roomily comfortable beamed lounge bar has guns, shining brass and horse-harness on the partly panelled walls, and cushioned Windsor chairs on the brown carpet. Excellent value home-made food includes sandwiches (from £1.70), winter soup, ploughman's (from £2), salads (£3) and various home-baked meals such as fresh fish, chicken, ham and leek and daily specials (from £2.25 to around £5); good English cheeses and no fried food. The smaller, plainer public bar has dominoes, cribbage and winter darts. Well kept Bass and Whitbreads Strong Country tapped from casks behind the bar, with an interesting cask-levelling device; good service; piped music. There's a family Cabin Bar (full of old farm tools) in the pleasing garden, and you can also sit out in front by the tubs of flowers – you may need to as it does get very busy. The village church is 12th c and houses the Isle of Wight Brass Rubbing Centre; a craft village nearby. *(Recommended by Bill Edwards, David P Sweeney, M and A Cook, Martyn and Mary Mullins, Theo Curtis, HNJ, PEJ, J M Campbell)*

Whitbreads ~ Tenants David and Maureen James ~ Real ale ~ Meals and snacks (till 10.30) ~ Isle of Wight (01983) 528479 ~ Children in family room and eating area ~ Open 11-4(3 winter), 6.30(7 winter)-11

BONCHURCH SZ5778 Map 2

Bonchurch Inn

Bonchurch Shute; from A3055 E of Ventnor turn down to Old Bonchurch opposite
Leconfield Hotel

The greeting you get here is likely to be an exuberant succession of warmly
welcoming handshakes from the Italian landlord. Then perhaps you'll bask in the
continental atmosphere while seated at a table in the flower-filled cobbled
courtyard which is enclosed by buildings worked into the steep rock slope, and
sample the good Italian cooking. The licensees tell us that because there are only
the two of them in the kitchen they can be a bit flexible about what they cook and
it's possible they'll do special requests – in fact all vegetarian customers are served
on this basis. It's certainly the mixture of good well priced Italian and English
cooking, alongside the rather different atmosphere, that attracts readers here. The
menu includes minestrone soup (£1.50), pizza (£3), spaghetti bolognese (£3.95),
canelloni with spinach or seafood risotto (£4), antipasto or fettuccine alla
carbonara or vegeteriana (£4.25); puddings (£2), zabaglione (£2.50); children can
eat anything in half portions; there's a small cosy dining room. Boddingtons and
Flowers Original tapped from the cask; fresh orange juice squeezed to order;
Italian wines by the glass and a few bottled French wines and coffee. At its best
when it's busier, the high-ceilinged and friendly public bar is partly cut into the
steep rocks of the Shute, and conjures up an image of salvaged shipwrecks with its
floor of narrow-planked ship's decking, and seats of the sort that old-fashioned
steamers used to have; there's also a smaller saloon; darts, bar billiards, shove-
ha'penny, table tennis, dominoes and cribbage. *(Recommended by Michael and Harriet
Robinson, Martyn and Mary Mullins, Lynn Sharpless, Bob Eardley; more reports please)*

*Free house ~ Licensees Ulisse and Aline Besozzi ~ Real ale ~ Meals and snacks
(11.30-2.15, 6-10.30) ~ Restaurant ~ Ventnor (01983) 852611 ~ Children in
family room ~ Open 11-3, 6.30-11; closed 25 Dec ~ Bedrooms: £15/£30*

CHALE SZ4877 Map 2

Clarendon / Wight Mouse ★ ♀

In village, on B3399, but now has access road directly off A3055

With its lively bustling holiday atmosphere, varied entertainments and delightful
rural situation this is perhaps the complete family place. Small children can ride
Arthur, the friendly new Shetland pony, visit the pets' corner, swings and
climbing frames in the spacious sheltered back garden, or watch regular Punch
and Judy shows. More restful souls can soak up the lovely views out towards the
Needles and Tennyson Downs. Inside it's an extended, rambling, atmospheric
place, the original core hung thickly with musical instruments, and with guns,
pistols and so forth hanging over an open log fire. At one end, it opens through
sliding doors into a pool room with dark old pews and large antique tables, video
game and juke box. At the other end is an extension with more musical
instruments, oars and even part of a rowing eight hanging from its high pitched
ceiling, lots of china mice around a corner fireplace, big decorative plates and
other bric-a-brac; there are modern pine pews and blond kitchen chairs here. The
turkey-carpeted family room extends beyond a two-way coal-effect gas fire, with
quite close-set pews around its tables, hunting prints and more decorative plates.
A very good range of drinks includes well kept Batemans XB, Boddingtons,
Marstons Pedigree, Morlands Old Speckled Hen, Wadworths 6X and Whitbreads
Castle Eden and Strong Country on handpump, an outstanding choice of around
365 whiskies, nearly 50 wines, and some uncommon brandies, madeiras and
country wines. Big helpings of home-made bar food, often made from local
produce, include sandwiches (from £1.60, fresh crab £3.10, toasties 25p extra),
home-made soup (£1.70), salads or burgers (from £3.80), ham and eggs (£3.80),
wiener schnitzel (£4.40), home-made pizzas (from £4.70), Mexican hot chilli con
carne in taco shells (£5.10), fisherman's platter or gravadlax (£6.80), giant mixed
grill (£7.20) and steaks (from £8.80), a range of vegetarian dishes (from £3.50),
usual straightforward children's menu (from £1.40) and daily specials; puddings

include knickerbocker glory, home-made gateaux and a Christmas pudding ice cream, made in a nearby dairy which you can visit. Darts at one end, dominoes, fruit machine, pinball, piped music. Live music every evening is never too loud for conversation. Mini-bus service for four or more people (£3 a person).

(Recommended by Paul and A Sweetman, John Farmer, Nigel Gibbs, Chris and Kim Elias, J M Campbell, Mr and Mrs D E Powell, John and Christine Simpson, Phil and Heidi Cook, Paul Cartledge, Andrew Stephenson, Sue Anderson, Phil Copleston)

Free house ~ Licensees John and Jean Bradshaw ~ Real ale ~ Meals and snacks 11.30-10 (not Sun) ~ Restaurant (closed Sun eve) ~ Isle of Wight (01983) 730431 ~ Children in eating areas and three family rooms ~ Live music every night ~ Open 11am-midnight (12-3, 7-10.30 Sun, all day bank holidays and school holidays) ~ Bedrooms: £25(£28B)/£50(£56B)

nr COWES (EAST) SZ5092 Map 2

Folly

Folly Lane – which is signposted off A3021 just S of Whippingham

In a superb setting on the river bank of the estuary, this efficiently run nautically themed pub has big windows overlooking boats on the water, and is an ideal spot for a quiet drink on a winter's afternoon, or to sit out on the water's edge terrace in summer. The maritime connections go back a long way. The original building was based around a beached sea-going barge, and the roof still includes part of the deck. Today, altogether more modern, it's especially well liked by yachtsmen, who not only have their mail collection boxes and showers here, but their own mooring pontoon. The nautical theme is evident in the recently opened-out bar, where there's a wind speed indicator, a barometer and chronometer. Around the old timbered walls are venerable wooden chairs and refectory-type tables, shelves of old books and plates, railway bric-a-brac and farm tools, old pictures, and brass lights. Good bar food includes generously filled sandwiches (from £2.15), soup (£1.75), potato skins (£2.25), mushroom provençale (£2.45), home-made chilli (£4.25), steak and kidney pie (£4.65), steaks (£8.55) and fresh fish daily from (£4.50); children's menu. Well kept Boddingtons, Flowers Original, Morlands Old Speckled Hen, Wadworths 6X and Whitbreads Strong Country on handpump under light blanket pressure, several rums such as West Indian Amber and Gales country wines; darts, pool, video game, fruit machine and piped music. There's a bouncy castle in the landscaped garden. Close to Osborne House; if you're coming by land, watch out for the sleeping policemen along the lane. *(Recommended by A E R Albert, Martyn and Mary Mullins, Derek and Margaret Underwood, John Watson, Bill and Beryl Farmo, Martin, Jane, Simon and Laura Bailey and Chris and Kim Elias)*

Whitbreads ~ Managers John and Christine Pettley ~ Real ale ~ Meals and snacks (all day)~ Isle of Wight (01983) 297171 ~ Children in eating area of bar ~ Keyboard player Thurs, Sat, Sun night ~ Open 11-11 (9 for breakfast)

FRESHWATER SZ3487 Map 2

Red Lion

Church Place; from A3055 at E end of village by Freshwater Garage mini-roundabout follow Yarmouth signpost and brown sign to Hill Farm Riding Stables, then take first real right turn signed to Parish Church

Isle of Wight Dining Pub of the Year

Reports suggest that the recently extended and re-equipped kitchen is producing better and better food. They're certainly making all sorts of weird and wonderful ice creams like avocado or melon and port sorbet with their new machine. On their good value traditional menu they have sandwiches (from £1.35), baked potatoes (from £2.95), ploughman's (from £2.50) and things like lasagne, macaroni cheese or cottage pie (£3.75). It's the sizeable daily specials board which tends to show the chef's imagination, with starters like curried parsley and apple soup (£1.70), dim sum with sweet and sour sauce (£1.95) and hot shell-on prawns with garlic, herbs, wine and cream (£3.95) and main courses such as fish pie, steak and kidney pie, chicken curry (£5.25), sirloin steak (£7.95) and fresh whole lobster salad (£10.50). Fresh vegetables (they hope to grow a lot of their own this year) are cooked just right. Lots of puddings (all £1.95) include spotted dick, treacle pudding and apple and pecan pie. They do a superb Sunday roast. It's a charming friendly place in a picturesque setting at the heart of the local community, and under the newish landlord there is a caring, attentive and thoughtful atmosphere. Quite smart with open fires, comfortable seats and sturdy country-kitchen style furnishings on mainly flagstoned floors with bare boards at one end, and a good mix of pictures and china platters on the walls. Well kept Boddingtons, Flowers Original, Goddards Best (brewed on the island) and Morlands Old Speckled Hen; White Monk cider (cask-conditioned on the island for three years in an oak barrel to a Carthusian monks' recipe); small but good range of carefully chosen wines by the bottle and glass; unobtrusive mainly classical piped music, fruit machine, darts, shove-ha'penny, dominoes, bardo, jenga and shut the box. There are picnic-table sets on a sheltered back lawn edged by neat flowerbeds. The church next door has a Norman tower, and there are good walks for nature lovers nearby, especially around the River Yar. *(Recommended by Lynn Sharpless, Bob Eardley, Theo Curtis, HNJ, PEJ, Michael and Harriet Robinson, John Beeken, Alison Bond, Bill Edwards, Robert and Gladys Flux, M and A Cook, Barry Hall, John Watson, Nigel Gibbs)*

Whitbreads ~ Lease: Michael Mence ~ Real ale ~ Meals and snacks (not Sun eve in winter) ~ Isle of Wight (01983) 754925 ~ Well behaved supervised children welcome ~ Open 11.30-3(11-4 Sat), 5.30(6 Sat)-11

NITON   SZ5076   Map 2

Buddle ◖

From A3055 in extreme S of island, take village road towards coast

From the well cared for garden, with its tables spread over the sloping lawn and stone terraces, you can look out over the cliffs and St Catherine's lighthouse, and at night watch its beam sweep around the sea far below. It doesn't take much to imagine the days when this friendly old house, nicely off the tourist track, was the haunt of notorious local smugglers. The modernised characterful bar – which can get busy – still has its heavy black beams and big flagstones, a broad stone fireplace with a massive black oak mantelbeam, and old-fashioned captain's chairs around solid wooden tables; pewter mugs and so forth hang on the walls. Decent bar food includes sandwiches in winter, soup (£1.95), garlic mushrooms (£2.75), vegetable samosas (£2.95), chilli con carne (£4.25), breaded plaice fillet (£4.35), steak (from £8.75), well cooked chips; big helpings of very nice home-made puddings (from £1.95) on the specials board and a few on the menu like banana split (£2.25); usual children's menu; the dining area is no smoking. Always at least six real ales from a changing range including Adnams, Bass, Boddingtons, Clarks, Flowers Original, Greene King and Morlands Old Speckled Hen on handpump or tapped from the cask, as well as a range of wines by the bottle or the glass and local wines and ciders; good service. Along one side of the lawn, and helping to shelter it, is what they call the Smugglers' Barn, being renovated as we go to press. When it's finished they hope to have lots more live music. Pool, shove ha'penny, fruit machine, trivia, video game and juke box. The cat is called Marmaduke and there are friendly dogs. Good walks nearby. *(Recommended by Bill Edwards, Phil and Heidi Cook, John Beeken; more reports please)*

Whitbreads ~ Lease John and Pat Bourne ~ Meals and snacks (11.30-3, 6-9.45) ~ Niton (01983) 730243 ~ Children in eating area ~ Occasional live music in summer ~ Open 11-11 (winter Mon-Thurs 11-3, 6-11)

SEAVIEW   SZ6291   Map 2

Seaview Hotel ⇐

High Street; off B3330 Ryde—Bembridge

Apart from the very different atmosphere, they sometimes have a better range of beers in the old fashioned cosy back bar – which can be busy with young locals –

than in the airy front bar, so it's worth checking in both. Located in a timeless Victorian resort, this is an immaculate and pleasantly restrained little hotel, relaxing and friendly and full of suitably nautical pictures and memorabilia. The surprisingly pubby back bar is a dimly lit room with quite a bit of marine bric-a-brac like oars, a ship's wheel, porthole cover and block and tackle around its ochre walls, as well as traditional pub furnishings on the bare boards, and a log fire. The particular point of interest in the bay-windowed front bar is the splendid array of naval and merchant ship photographs, as well as Spy nautical cartoons for *Vanity Fair,* and original receipts fom Cunard's shipyard payments for the *Queen Mary* and the *Queen Elizabeth;* it has a line of close-set tables down each side on the turkey carpet, and a pleasantly chatty relaxed atmosphere. Particularly praised dishes among the good freshly made bar food are sandwiches (from £1.95; tasty prawn and fresh local crab when available), soup (£2.20), ploughman's or crispy chicken wings (£3.65), roasted pepper and bacon salad with black olives and sun dried tomatoes (£4.95), seafood quiche with mussels, prawns, cream, fresh herbs and cheese (£5.95), entrecote steak (£9.95) and whole or half lobster salads (from £10.95); puddings like treacle sponge pudding (£2.75). Herbs come from the garden, and there are good crusty rolls; Sunday roast; good restaurant. Flowers IPA and local Goddards on handpump, decent little wine list, local apple juice; darts, cribbage and dominoes and piped music. Tables on the front terrace and in the sun porch have a view of the sea and across to the south coast; there are more tables in a sheltered inner courtyard. *(Recommended by J M Campbell, Jack Barnwell, Andrew Stephenson, Shirley Pielou, John Watson, Mr and Mrs D E Powell)*

Free house ~ Licensees Nicholas and Nicola Hayward ~ Real ale ~ Meals and snacks ~ No-smoking restaurant (not Sun evening, except bank holidays) ~ Seaview (01983) 612711 ~ Children in eating area of bar ~ Open 10.30-3, 6-11 ~ Bedrooms: £40B/£60B

SHANKLIN SZ5881 Map 2

Fishermans Cottage

Bottom of Shanklin Chine

A lovely walk along the zigzagged path down the steep and sinuous Chine, the beautiful gorge that was the area's original tourist attraction (there may be a charge for this route in summer), takes you down to tables on the terrace looking towards the beach and sea – a delightful setting for a meal and a beer, with the sound of the surf in the background and certainly a refreshing change from the usual seaside bustle. It's best to go during the day, as the terrace does lose the sun in the evening. Inside the unpretentious thatched cottage the clean low-beamed and flagstoned rooms are still cosy after a recent refurbishment, with photographs, paintings and engravings on the stripped-stone walls. Good bar food includes sandwiches (from £1.70), sausage and chips (£2.70), ploughman's (from £2.90), salads (from £3.70, crab and prawn £5.90) scampi (£4.90) and a pint of shell-on prawns (£5.80); Courage Directors; coffee all day and a range of local country wines; polite and friendly bar staff; fruit machine and piped music; wheelchair access. *(Recommended by Mr and Mrs P C Clark, John and Christine Simpson, Bill Edwards, Nigel Gibbs, Reg Nelson, Sarah Bullard; more reports please)*

Free house ~ Licensees Mrs A P P Springman and Miss M L Prince ~ Meals and snacks (11-3, 6-9, not Sun) ~ Isle of Wight (01983) 863882 ~ Children welcome ~ Occasional live entertainment in summer ~ Open 11-11; cl Nov-Feb

SHORWELL SZ4582 Map 2

Crown

B3323 SW of Newport; OS Sheet 196 map reference 456819

Really popular with readers – one of whom says it's their first choice on this side of the island for food and hospitality – this civilised pub remains a real local, in spite of the holidaymakers. A friendly, chatty place, slightly off the beaten track, where you can sit in a charming garden: picnic-table sets and white garden chairs and tables look over a little stream that broadens out into a wider trout-filled pool with prettily planted banks. The front entry to the pub is over a footbridge and through a little garden with a pump. The small warm and cosy beamed two-room lounge bar has blue and white china in a carved dresser, old country prints on the stripped-stone walls, other character furnishings, a cabinet of model vintage cars, and a winter log fire with a fancy tilework surround. Black pews form bays around tables in a stripped-stone room off to the left, with another log fire; the stone window ledges are full of houseplants. Lots of people come here for the consistently good bar food which includes sandwiches, chilli bean and vegetable pot (£3.95), steak and kidney pie (£4.95) and chicken breast in cider sauce (£5.95); Badger Best, Hardtackle and Tanglefoot, Flowers Original and Hampshire Pendragon tapped from the cask, local apple juice, cider and country wines; chatty staff and landlord; darts, trivia, boules; faint piped music. *(Recommended by HNJ, PNJ, DJW, Phil and Heidi Cook, M Powys-Smith, Nigel Gibbs, Martyn and Mary Mullins, Andrew Stephenson)*

Whitbreads ~ Tenant Mike Grace ~ Real ale ~ Meals and snacks (till 10pm) ~ Isle of Wight (01983) 740293 ~ Children in eating area of bar ~ Open 10.30-3.30, 6-11

VENTNOR SZ5677 Map 2

Spyglass

Esplanade, SW end; road down very steep and twisty, and parking can be difficult

Set behind its own spacious sunny terrace that's perched on top of the sea wall with views along the bay is this superb rambling pub. The cheery landlord has filled it with a genuinely interesting jumble of memorabilia that just keeps growing and growing. Wrecked rudders, ships' wheels, old local advertisements, stuffed seagulls, an Admiral Benbow barometer and an old brass telescope among much else – the snug separate areas that the bar is cleverly divided into seem to be full of such nautically-themed memorabilia. Locals crowd into the carefully refitted place, giving it a friendly, thriving atmosphere. Most is quarry-tiled, with pews around traditional pub tables, with a carpeted no-smoking room at one end and a family area (with piped pop music) at the other. Bar food includes sandwiches (from £1.80), filled baked potatoes (£2.75), ploughman's (£3.25), salads (from £4.25; seafood with lobster £13.95), chilli con carne or seafood lasagne (£4.25), home made cottage pie (£4.50), crab (£5.95), a whole fresh local lobster (£11.75), daily specials like ham and leek bake (£4.95), fresh Ventnor Bay plaice, crab and prawn or asparagus mornay (£5.25), beef beaujolais (£5.95); vegetarian dishes like potato skins filled with tortellini or vegetable chilli (£4.75). Well kept Benskins and Ind Coope Burton on handpump, with maybe changing guest beers tapped from the cask; on special occasions such as a lifeboat support week there may be half a dozen or more; efficient staff. Fruit machine, video game, piped music and there's a boat rocker for children. They have no objection to dogs or muddy boots. *(Recommended by P Neate, Sue Anderson, Phil Copleston, Reg Nelson; more reports please)*

Free house ~ Licensees Neil and Steph Gibbs ~ Real ale ~ Meals and snacks; afternoon tea in summer ~ Isle of Wight (01983) 855338 ~ Children in family room ~ Live traditional Irish or jazz every night ~ Open 11-11; 11-3, 7-11 in winter ~ Bedrooms:/£35B

YARMOUTH SZ3589 Map 2

Wheatsheaf

Bridge Rd

It's the wide choice of reasonably priced good food in generous helpings that's the main draw here. From the menu this might include soup of the day (£1.50), sandwiches (from £2), filled baked potatoes (from £2.20), crusty rolls (£2.30), particularly good value ploughman's (from £2.75), burgers (from £3.20), smoked trout fillet (£3.25), four giant garlic mussels (£3.45), salads (from £3.50), home-cooked gammon (£4.50), trout with stilton sauce or almonds (£5.25), steaks (from £7), puddings (from £1.90), and good daily specials from the blackboard like Japanese king prawns (£3.25), fresh black bream with grape and wine sauce (£5.45), game pie (£5.95), fresh local lobster salad (from £7.95), fresh dressed crab platter (£8.95) and the impressive lobster platter with prawns, garlic mussels and smoked trout (£10.95); puddings on menu and blackboard. When you arrive don't be put off by the slightly unprepossessing street frontage – once inside, it's comfortable and spacious with four eating areas including a light and airy conservatory and the service is very quick and friendly. Well kept Boddingtons, Flowers, Gales HSB, Goddards and Morlands Old Speckled Hen and other guests on handpump; fruit machine, pool (winter only) and juke box (in public bar); piped music. *(Recommended by Martyn and Mary Mullins, HNJ, PEJ, Tony Triggle)*

Whitbreads ~ Lease: Anthony David and Mrs Suzanne Keen ~ Real ale ~ Meals and snacks (11-2.30, 6-9.30) ~ (01983) 760456 ~ Children in Harbour lounge and conservatory ~ Open 11-3, 6-11

Lucky Dip

Besides the fully inspected pubs, you might like to try these Lucky Dips recommended to us and described by readers (if you do, please send us reports):

☆ **Bembridge** [Station Rd; SZ6487], *Row Barge*: Open-plan pub nr harbour with well kept real ales such as Flowers, Eldridge Pope Hardy, Theakstons and Whitbreads Pompey Royal, farm cider, very good pizzas and other food, friendly landlord, unpretentious nautical decor; service can sometimes slow when busy; bedrooms *(David White, N Mortlock, Martyn and Mary Mullins)*

☆ **Brading** [56-57 High St; A3055 Sandown—Ryde; SZ6086], *Bugle*: Three comfortable and spacious though not pubby connecting rooms popular for very big helpings of good straightforward bar and restaurant food inc children's dishes and good value Sun lunch, pretty floral wallpaper, service welcoming and quick even when busy, well kept Flowers IPA, Goddards Special, Wadworths 6X, exemplary lavatories; piped music; restaurant, supervised children's room with lots of games and videos, garden *(Shirley Pielou, Mr and Mrs J Beere, Mark King)*

☆ **Brighstone** [Limerstone Rd (B3399 E); SZ4482], *Countryman*: Large brightly lit high-ceilinged open-plan bars and restaurant area, mock dark beams, white paintwork, horse/farming equipment and pictures, lots of tables with candles and flower decorations, usual bar food from filled rolls to steaks, friendly attentive staff, Ind Coope Burton and Wiltshire on handpump; moderate piped music; front garden with sea view *(Phil and Heidi Cook, HNJ, PEJ)*

☆ **Carisbrooke** [Calbourne Rd (B3401 1½ miles W)], *Blacksmiths Arms*: Pleasantly quiet roadside pub with panoramic views, friendly helpful landlord, Bass on handpump, good value bar food, terraced back garden *(John Beeken)*

Carisbrooke [High St; SZ4888], *Eight Bells*: Spotless refurbished dining pub well set at foot of castle, bigger than it looks from outside, with Whitbreads-related and other beers such as the well priced local Goddards, good range of good value generously served bar food inc tasty specials like dressed crab; friendly staff; beautifully kept lawns and gardens behind running down to swan-filled lake, also play area *(HNJ, PEJ, Mr and Mrs M Farmer, Martyn and Mary Mullins)*

Cowes [The Parade; SZ4996], *Globe*: Good food with lots of seafood, helpful young staff *(HNJ, PEJ)*; [Newport Rd], *Kingston Arms*: Well kept beer, cheap food, character landlady *(Martyn and Mary Mullins)*

Downend [A3056; SZ5387], *Hare & Hounds*: Thoroughly and comfortably refurbished spring 1994 as extended dining pub in tasteful cream-and-stripped-brick style, lots of beams, several areas inc original core with open fire and flagstones, two serving bars, usual food inc vegetarian dishes, young staff, well kept Flowers and Goddards, tables on terrace with wide views over pleasant countryside; under same ownership as Blackgang Chine theme park and adjacent Robin Hill Country Park which has good play area *(Simon Collett-Jones, BB)*

Havenstreet [off A3054 Newport—Ryde; SZ5690], *White Hart*: Really pubby atmosphere in one of the village's oldest buildings, two clean and comfortable bars with well kept real ales, varied generous food esp home made pies with fresh veg and splendid salads, reasonable prices; interesting beer-bottle collection *(F D Wharton, Rozelle Say, David P Sweeney)*

☆ **Hulverstone** [B3399 – OS Sheet 196 map reference 398840; SZ3984], *Sun*: A sunny-day star, for the attractive garden outside this thatched pub, with profusion of roses, geraniums and nemesias, good sea views, even village stocks for fun photographs; pubby inside, with well kept Gales BB and HSB tapped from the cask, cheerful pleasant service, usual bar food esp basket meals *(John Beeken, Adrian Stopforth)*

☆ **Newchurch** [OS Sheet 196 map reference 562855; SZ5685], *Pointer*: Friendly and unassuming genuine village local next to photogenic church, good generous straightforward country cooking (little for vegetarians) at fair prices, well kept Gales BBB and HSB, good range of country wines; brightly lit plush lounge, flame-effect fires, old photographs, L-shaped games bar on right, spotty dogs, pleasant back garden with floodlit boules area *(Bill Edwards, David P Sweeney, HNJ, PEJ, BB)*

Newport [centre; SZ4988], *Calvert*: Hotel bar with very ornate frontage, genuine character and atmosphere, fine choice of real ales, maybe blues band; bedrooms *(Reg Nelson)*; [High St], *Castle*: Ancient stone-floored pub with relaxed if slightly staid atmosphere, good choice of real ales, bar nibbles *(Reg Nelson)*; [1 Sea St, off High St], *Railway Medina*: Good feel in corner pub next to old station, lots of railway photographs and memorabilia; real ales *(Reg Nelson)*; [St Thomas Sq], *Wheatsheaf*: Inn dating back to 17th c, its big public bar looking as a typical bar did 40 years ago; friendly helpful staff, good generous reasonably priced food, children welcome; bedrooms *(HNJ, PEJ, Colin Harnett)*

Ningwood [A3054 Newport—Yarmouth, a mile W of Shalfleet – OS Sheet 196 map reference 399892; SZ3989], *Horse & Groom*: Old rather rambling pub with usual range of Whitbreads-related beers, wide choice of bar food *(HNJ, PEJ)*

☆ **Niton** [off A3055; SZ5076], *White Lion*: Clean and comfortable refurbished spacious pub with warmly welcoming landlord, well kept Whitbreads-related real ales, good value usual food inc children's dishes, exotic puddings, Sun lunches; children welcome *(J M Campbell, Adrian Stopforth, Theo Curtis, David P Sweeney)*

☆ **Northwood** [85 Pallance Rd; off B3325 S of Cowes; SZ4983], *Travellers Joy*: Ten or so real ales inc several rare visitors in pleasantly busy local with roomy L-shaped bars, good range of generous reasonably priced simple bar food, friendly staff, old island prints; fruit machine, subdued piped music; family room, garden behind with swings and lots of rabbits; open all day Fri/Sat and summer *(Nigel Gibbs)*

☆ **Rookley** [Niton Rd; pub signed off A3020; SZ5183], *Chequers*: Wide range of good straightforward bar food inc vegetarian dishes and good veg served separately, personal service and well kept Courage-related real ales on handpump in spacious plush refurbished lounge bar looking over road to rolling downland; small log fire, livelier partly flagstoned games area on left; Lego in family room, picnic-table sets out on grass, realistic play house in safely fenced play area *(Jack Barnwell, J H Peters, Martyn and Mary Mullins, BB)*

Ryde [164 High St; SZ5992], *Castle*:

Vibrant one-bar pub full of character with Gales ales, notable etched windows, associations with bikers and heavy-metal cults *(Reg Nelson)*; [Union St], *Redan*: Unusual quietly atmospheric pub with fine collection of bric-a-brac, real ales *(Reg Nelson)*

Seaview [Esplanade; B3340, just off B3330 Ryde—Brading; SZ6291], *Old Fort*: Spacious, light and airy pub in commanding position nr Yacht Club, good choice of beers, separate cold buffet area at one end, prompt efficient service, wide choice of good value usual bar food in big helpings, natural wood furnishings; fine sea views from inside and tables outside *(Jack Barnwell, HNJ, PEJ)*

☆ **Shalfleet** [OS Sheet 196 map reference 414893; SZ4189], *New Inn*: Popular seafood in small tastefully refurbished pub/restaurant with roaring log fire in engagingly traditional panelled and flagstoned bar, more orthodox stripped stone dining lounge, restaurant, no-smoking family area; well kept Gales HSB, Hartridges Nipper and NBB on handpump, decent wines and coffee, cheerful service, children in eating area, open all day summer *(Alison Bond, P Neate, DJW, Robert and Gladys Flux, LYM)*

Shanklin [High St Old Town; A3055 towards Ventnor – OS Sheet 196 map reference 584812; SZ5881], *Crab*: Thatched pub making a lovely picture from outside, with tables outside too; nothing special inside, with a brisk trade in family food, well kept Whitbreads-related real ales; open all day *(Bill Edwards, Reg Nelson, David P Sweeney, LYM)*; [The Esplanade – OS Sheet 196 map reference 585812], *Longshoreman*: Right on seafront with wonderful view of one of island's best beaches; comfortable, with low beams, old island photographs *(David P Sweeney, Reg Nelson)*; [Old Village], *Village Pub*: Picturesque thatched pub, attractive inside too, with well kept beers, daily fish specials, pleasant talkative bar staff *(Anon)*

Ventnor [Sandown rd; SZ5677], *Landsdowne Arms*: Very efficiently run, with cheap Allied ales, friendly landlord, unusual pipe collection, old advertisements, nicely segregated food and games areas; no machines *(Reg Nelson)*

☆ **Whitwell** [High St; SZ5277], *White Horse*: Well furnished big interconnected beamed bars, Gales HSB, Best, BBB and XXXD on handpump, wide range of food inc vegetarian, cheerful quick service, horse brasses, log fire; muted piped music *(Martyn and Mary Mullins)*

Wootton Bridge [A3054 Ryde—Newport; SZ5492], *Sloop*: Good reasonably priced food, real ale and friendly staff in simple main bar done out boat-style with panelling, port-holes and curved ceiling, games room with darts and billiards, plainer dining room overlooking river, children's room; nice setting, riverside garden with galleon for children to climb on *(Barry Hall)*

☆ **Yarmouth** [St James' Sq; SZ3589], *Bugle*: Dark-panelled rooms inc peaceful lounge and friendly and lively bar with counter like galleon stern, food from well filled sandwiches to grills, seafood salads and children's dishes, well kept Whitbreads-related real ales; piped music can be rather loud; restaurant, children's room with pool and video game, sizeable garden, summer barbecues and Sat jazz; good big airy bedrooms – make sure you get one that's not over the bar *(A E R Albert, Chris and Kim Elias, M and A Cook, LYM)*

☆ **Yarmouth** [Quay St], *George*: Good atmosphere and food esp seafood in unspoilt and relaxing nautical-theme bar, quick friendly service, well kept Hartridges Nipper, decent wine, maybe pianist; big garden running down to sea shore with outside summer bar, big barbecue area and lovely view; bedrooms comfortable *(Bill Edwards, K Flack, Ian Pickard)*

Children welcome means the pubs says it lets children inside without any special restriction. If it allows them in, but to restricted areas such as an eating area or family room, we specify this. Places with separate restaurants usually let children use them, hotels usually let them into public areas such as lounges. Some pubs impose an evening time limit – let us know if you find this.

Kent

As we'd feared, we have to report that the Mounted Rifleman near Luddenham – one of Kent's most interestingly unspoiled pubs – has now closed down. But there are a good many other pubs here of considerable character. Standing out among them are the Three Chimneys near Biddenden (good food too, and a lovely garden), the unpretentious Gate at Boyden Gate (almost as chatty as the millions of ducks on the marshes behind), the ancient Woolpack at Brookland on Romney Marsh (a new main entry this year), the George at Newnham (another pub combining good food with a lovely atmosphere), the timeless Ringlestone Inn at Ringlestone, the ancient Bell near Smarden, and the Compasses at Sole Street up on the downs above Wye (another new entry, very good for children in summer). Drinks prices here have been rising quite sharply in the last few months – considerably more than elsewhere, particularly in pubs getting their beers from national brewers. Overall, drinks prices in the county are now markedly higher than the national average. The cheapest beer we found was in the Dove at Dargate and the Woolpack at Brookland – both tied to the local brewer Shepherd Neame, whose beers do generally offer worthwhile savings here. Their new Porter has gone down well, too. Beer quality is generally good in the county, with half a dozen pubs here gaining our new Beer Award. Eating out in Kent tends to be a pricey business. Food prices here are now among the highest in Britain, so it's doubly important to make sure you're getting quality for your money. Notable dining pubs here include the Three Chimneys near Biddenden, both Ivy Hatch entries, the George at Newnham, the Spotted Dog at Penshurst, Sankeys in Tunbridge Wells, the Pepper Box at Ulcombe and Pearsons in Whitstable. A special mention too for the White Lion at Selling, always willing to do cut-price smaller helpings of its good food for older customers. From among all of these, it is Sankeys in Tunbridge Wells which we choose as Kent Dining Pub of the Year – excellent seafood, and they now do the seafood in the busy downstairs bar as well as letting you have their bar food in the calmer surroundings upstairs. An important change to note this year is that the Meers who've been so popular at the Bottle House near Penshurst have now also taken on the grand old George & Dragon at Speldhurst – quite a handful for them, though early signs are that the George & Dragon is benefiting without spreading their energies too thin. In the Lucky Dip section at the end of the chapter, pubs to mention particularly include the Little Gem in Aylesford, Canterbury Tales in Canterbury, Elephant in Faversham, Four Elms at Four Elms, Red Lion at Hernhill, King William IV in Littlebourne, reopened Shipwrights Arms at Oare, Black Lion at Southfleet, Harrow at Warren Street, Tickled Trout at West Farleigh and Bull at Wrotham. There are several good possibilities in Otford, and the only reason the attractive Tiger at Stowting misses the main entries this year is a relative shortage of recent readers' reports.

Tipping is not normal for bar meals, and not usually expected.

nr BIDDENDEN TQ8538 Map 3

Three Chimneys ★ 🍴 🍷 📕

A262, a mile W of village

Nestling into the ground with its tiny windows and entrance this lovely old building has been here so long it has a slightly organic appearance. At the back the lusciously growing garden with nut trees at the end (probably the habitat of the very boistrous grey squirrels) has densely planted curving borders with flowering shrubs and shrub roses, that seem to permeate the garden room. Always cheerfully busy, the rambling series of small, very traditional rooms are huddled under low oak beams with simple wooden furniture and old settles on flagstone and coir matting, some harness and sporting prints on the exposed brick walls, and good winter log fires. The simple public bar has darts, shove-ha'penny, dominoes and cribbage. For many people the main draw is the very good food. Their seasonal repertoire of meals is amazing but there's always a choice of four starters (with a hot or cold soup according to the season), four main courses and four puddings. Current favourites include starters like tomato and celeriac soup or avocado and mint soup (£2.50 and £2.70), eggs benedict (£2.75) stilton and pear mousse (£3.10) and ham and parmesan pancake (£3.75) and main courses such as broccoli quiche (£4.75), Kentish lamb pie (£6.20), steak and oyster pie (£6.25), lamb and almond curry (£6.30) and salmon and dill filo tart (£6.50), fricassee of veal (£6.60) and venison steak in rob roy sauce (£6.75), all served with well cooked baked or new potatoes, rice, salad or fresh vegetables; delicious traditional and French puddings like treacle tart (£2.65), ginger pudding, blackberry and almond crunchy pie and date and walnut pudding (£2.70), brown bread ice cream, summer pudding, pear frangipane and prune and apple meringue (£2.75), sugar plum flan and chocolate and orange mousse (£2.85), all served with fresh Jersey cream. You can book tables in the Garden Room which is popular with families (it isn't licensed so you have to carry your drinks in from the main bar). A good range of well kept real ales tapped from the cask: Adnams Best, Brakspears, Harveys Best (and Old in winter), Marstons Pedigree, Morlands Old Speckled Hen and Wadworths 6X, along with a very dry Biddenden local cider, and a sensible wine list including several half bottles (as well as local wine) and about 20 malt whiskies. Sissinghurst gardens are just down the road. *(Recommended by Mike and Joyce Bryant, Mr and Mrs Hillman, Paul Adams, G Futcher, Simon Morton, N M Gibbs, C P and M G Stent, Gordon, Ian Sharp, K Flack, Andrew and Ruth Triggs, Tim Galligan, Sean and Sharon Pines, M A and C R Starling, George Moore, Colin Laffan, L G Milligan, N H and A H Harries)*

Free house ~ Licensees C F W Sayers and G A Sheepwash ~ Real ale ~ Meals and snacks (till 10pm) ~ Restaurant ~ Biddenden (01580) 291472 ~ Children in restaurant ~ Occasional live entertainment ~ Open 11-2.30, 6-11; closed 25 and 26 Dec

BOUGH BEECH TQ4846 Map 3

Wheatsheaf

B2027, S of reservoir

Locals believe this sturdy handsome old inn was once a hunting lodge belonging to Henry V. The variety of heads and horns on the walls and above the massive stone fireplaces certainly indicate that someone has been hunting during its long history but the additional curiosities like a war sword from Fiji, crocodiles, stuffed birds, squirrels and even an armadillo suggest a wider ranging field than that provided by the chase around Tudor Hever. It's in a lovely spot, with pretty, sheltered lawns to the side and stretching behind filled with flowerbeds, fruit trees, roses, flowering shrubs, and a children's rustic cottage and boat. Inside there's a congenial atmosphere, the landlord is in the old tradition and the mature bar staff are really friendly. The neat central bar has unusually high ceilings with lofty oak timbers and divided from this by standing timbers – formerly an outside wall to the original building – is the snug. Other similarly aged features include a piece of 1607 graffiti, '*Foxy Galumpy*', thought to have been a whimsical local squire; also cigarette cards, swordfish spears and the only matapee in the south of England. The public bar has an attractive old settle carved with wheatsheaves; shove-ha'penny, dominoes, cribbage, fruit machine, trivia and sensibly placed darts and other board games. The very good bar food in hefty helpings includes curries and chillies made with freshly ground spices (from £4.50), home-cooked meat pies (from £4.95) and a variety of fish dishes, pasta, salads, ploughman's and local pheasant and wild duck when in season; home-made puddings (from £1.50). Well kept Boddingtons, Fremlins, Flowers Original and Morlands Old Speckled Hen on handpump, a variety of malts; piped music. *(Recommended by Wayne Brindle, Mrs J E Hilditch, A E Brace, Roy Y Bromell, TBB)*

Whitbreads ~ Lease: Elizabeth and Peter Currie ~ Real ale ~ Meals and snacks (till 10pm) ~ (01732) 700254 ~ Children in eating area of bar ~ Folk music Weds eve ~ Open 11-3, 6-11(11-11 Sat)

BOUGHTON ALUPH   TR0247   Map 3

Flying Horse 🛏

Boughton Lees; just off A251 N of Ashford

You can sit outside this marvellously Kentish, civilised and friendly place in summer and watch cricket on the broad village green. The particularly warm welcome and happy atmosphere probably haven't changed much since the 15th c when it's thought the pub was built to catch the hungry pilgrim traffic on its way to Canterbury. A few clues to its age still remain, mainly in the shiny old black panelling and the arched windows (though they are a later Gothic addition). This year they've opened a new bar in what was once the old brewing area. In uncovering the original brick floor they discovered two ancient wells, both of which have spring water. These have been illuminated and covered at ground level with walk-over glass. The open-plan bar has lots of standing room so although it does get very busy it never seems too crowded. It also has comfortable upholstered modern wall benches, fresh flowers on many tables, hop bines around the serving area, horsebrasses, and stone animals on either side of the blazing log fire. Large doors open out onto the spacious rose filled garden (with seating) from the back room. The pleasant and not over expensive bar food from the lengthy menu might include sandwiches, liver and bacon (£4.50), fresh grilled fish (£5), paprika chicken (£5.25) and fillet of duck (£6.50); barbecues; good breakfasts. Well kept Courage Best, John Smiths, Morlands Old Speckled Hen, Ruddles County, Shepherd Neame and Wadworths 6X on handpump; a good wine list that includes their own labelled house wine and a good selection of malts. Darts, shove-ha'penny, cribbage, fruit machine and piped music. *(Recommended by Mrs B F Benson, Theo Curtis, Werner Arend, Mrs C Greener, J Jay, D K and H M Brenchley, Peter Middup, N and M Foster, John McGee, Darryl Greer, C H Garnett, June and Tony Baldwin)*

Courage ~ Lease: Howard and Christine Smith ~ Real ale ~ Meals and snacks ~ Restaurant ~ (01233) 620914 ~ Children in restaurant ~ Occasional live music ~ Open 11-3, 6-11 (11-11 Sat) ~ Bedrooms: £20/£30S

BOYDEN GATE   TR2265   Map 3

Gate Inn ★ 🍺

Off A299 Herne Bay—Ramsgate – follow Chislet, Upstreet signpost opposite Roman Gallery; Chislet also signposted off A28 Canterbury—Margate at Upstreet – after turning right into Chislet main street keep right on to Boyden; the pub gives its address as Marshside, though Boyden Gate seems more usual on maps

Unpretentious and charming, this two-room inn seems to be the perfect combination of unspoilt traditional atmosphere, friendly good-humoured service and very good value meals. With the additional consideration of the well regarded landlord – he's published his own cook booklet and the tomato soup is said to be excellent – its not surprising that they can get quite busy here at the weekends. In fact it's a focus for many activities and 'MCC' here stands for Marshside Cricket Club. Distinctly pubby, the bar has pews with flowery cushions around tables of considerable character, hop bines hanging from the beam, a good winter log fire (which serves both quarry-tiled rooms), and attractively etched windows; there are photographs on the walls – some ancient sepia ones, others new. Unfussy but tasty, the well prepared food includes enterprising sandwiches with lots of pickles (black pudding £1.35), jacket potatoes (from £1.10), home-made vegeburger (£1.60), garlic mushrooms (£1.75), ploughman's (£3.50), home-made flan (£3.50), bean and pepper hotpot or spicy sausage hotpot (£4), and puddings like lovely bread pudding (95p); they use organically grown local produce where possible, and encourage children to share their parents' food (with their own cutlery and plate provided). The eating area is no smoking at lunchtime. Well kept and reasonably priced for the area Shepherd Neame Bitter, Spitfire, and Bishops Finger tapped from the cask, with local apple juice and coffee; they take care to give individual service. Sensibly placed darts, as well as shove-ha'penny, bar billiards, dominoes and cribbage. On a fine evening, it's extraordinary to sit at the picnic-table sets on the sheltered side lawn listening to the contented quacking of what seems like a million happy ducks and geese (they sell duck food inside – 5p a bag). *(Recommended by Kathy O'Donoghue, Mr and Mrs Joseph Williams, Michael Sargent, Louise Weekes, Jacquie and Jon Payne, Martin and Pauline Richardson, Stephen Brown, W Walters)*

Shepherd Neame ~ Tenant Christopher Smith ~ Real ale ~ Meals and snacks (till 10) (01227) 860498 ~ Children in eating area of bar and in family room ~ Piano Sun evening, jazz Tues, folk Friday ~ Open 11-2.30(3 Sat), 6-11

BROOKLAND TQ9926 Map 3

Woolpack

Just out of village; off A259

Huddling low against the flat landscape and swathed in the marsh mists, this crooked white early 15th-c cottage with steep pitched peg-tiled roof and inevitable smuggling connections was once the beacon keeper's house. Its tremendous age is immediately apparent in the ancient entrance lobby with uneven brick floor and black painted pine-panelled walls. On the right is a simple but homely low-beamed and softly lit main bar with basic cushioned plank seats in a massive inglenook fireplace, and a painted wood-effect bar counter hung with plenty of water jugs. On the new quarry-tiled floor is a long elm table with shove-ha'penny carved into one end, other old and new wall benches (a lazy cat sleeps on one), chairs at mixed tables around the walls, and engaging photographs of the locals (and perhaps their award-winning sheep). To the left of the lobby is a tiny room sparsely furnished with what looks like a 1950s lounge suite, and through this is the open-plan games room with central chimney stack, modern bar counter, and young locals playing pool. Very well priced real ales well kept on handpump are Shepherd Neame Best, Bishops Finger and Spitfire. The straightforward well priced bar food, served very generously, includes sandwiches (from £1.40, home-cooked ham £1.80, crab or prawn £2.30), soup (£2.25), shepherd's pie (£2.75), filled baked potatoes (from £2.95), cod (£3.25), ham, egg and chips or ploughman's (£3.50), a generous pint of prawns (£3.95), lasagne, chilli (£3.95), trout (£5.95) and a huge mixed grill or sirloin steak (£7.25); vegetarian lasagne and chilli (£3.95). Tables outside; fishing rights – the stream runs past the bottom of the garden. *(Recommended by Simon Morton, Geoff and Sarah Schrecker, Mike and Joyce Bryant, Richard Gibbs; more reports please)*

Shepherd Neame ~ Tenants John and Pat Palmer ~ Real ale ~ Meals and snacks ~ (01797) 344321 ~ Children in eating area of bar ~ Open 11-2.30, 6-11

CHIDDINGSTONE TQ4944 Map 3

Castle ♀

Village signposted from B2027 Tonbridge—Edenbridge

Set amidst some lovely countryside, this rambling old inn – with seats outside opposite the church – forms part of a wonderfully picturesque cluster of unspoilt National-Trust-owned Tudor houses and buildings. Until it became a pub in 1730, it was a private house, and could perhaps have been where Anne Boleyn found shelter when she was stranded in a terrible blizzard on her way to nearby Hever. Inside, the handsome, carefully modernised beamed bar has an attractive mullioned window seat in one small alcove, latticed windows, well made settles forming booths around the tables, and cushioned sturdy wall benches; a recent redecoration has left it with a much lighter atmosphere. It does get very busy with visitors to the area in the summer so it's worth getting there early. Bar food (which isn't cheap) includes home-made soup (£2.55), home-made pâté (£3.65), half a dozen giant snails (£5.30), open sandwiches (from £3.45; filled giant wholewheat french bread £4.15), filled baked potatoes (from £4.05), ploughman's (from £4.90), very hot chilli con carne (£5.15), a daily pasta dish (£4.80), salads (from £6.95) and a changing two or three course meal (from £9.95), with starters like moules marinières, marinaded prawns, and main courses like rack of lamb, salmon in caper and parsley sauce, Chiddingstone pigeon casseroled in real ale or fillets of grey mullet with a dill and chive sauce; puddings such as Cointreau ice cream, chocolate torte or home-made cheesecake (£2.45). Well kept Harveys Sussex, Larkins Sovereign and Shepherd Neame Bitter on handpump; an excellent choice of over 150 wines (including house wines), a good range of malt whiskies, coffee, liqueur coffees and tea. The public bar – popular with locals – has darts, shove-ha'penny, dominoes and cribbage. The friendly chatty landlord has been here for more than twenty years. The pretty back garden has a small pool and fountain set in a rockery and tables on a brick terrace and neat lawn. *(Recommended by J G Smith, M Veldhuyzen, Susan and John Douglas, Andy Stone, David and Ruth Hollands, Brian and Jenny Seller, Chris Fluck, Anne Phelan)*

Free house ~ Licensee Nigel Lucas ~ Real ale ~ Meals and snacks (until 15 minutes before closing time) ~ Restaurant ~ Penshurst (01892) 870247 ~ Children welcome ~ Open 11-3, 6-11; all day Sat

CONYER QUAY TQ9665 Map 3

Ship ♀ 🍺

From A2 Sittingbourne—Faversham turn off towards Deerton St (signposted) then at T-junction turn left signposted Teynham, Sittingbourne; Conyer signposted from Teynham

The 'beer stalker's trail' is popular here at the moment and guaranteed to get you into the swing of things. Customers have an official card which is kept behind the bar and signed by the bar staff each time one of the 60 bottled beers from any of 30 countries is tried and there are prizes for completed cards. There seems to be a different 'liquid' trail each year and it all rather reflects the speciality of this lively old creekside smuggling pub. It's difficult to know where to begin describing the vast range of drinks they keep, every year it gets still more incredible. Perhaps most impressive is the number of wines, with over 300 different bottles (100 more than last year) and 40 half bottles from 15 countries, and thanks to a nifty preservation system about 100 of these can now be sold by the glass or carafe. New wines are introduced at their regular tastings. There's also a choice of more than 20 malt wines, 175 malt whiskies plus a further 75 blended scotches, Irish whiskies and bourbons, over 150 liqueurs, 50 rums (fitting in nicely with the pub's nautical connections), 25 ports, 50 cognacs, armagnacs and brandies. Five handpumps serve a constantly changing selection of well kept real ales such as Adnams Broadside, Courage Directors, Ind Coope Burton, Nethergate Old Growler and Whitbreads Trophy, but again the list is endless – they got through 250 different beers last year, many of them during their regular autumn and spring beer festivals; Biddenden farm cider and local country wines. There's a happy hour every night between 6 and 7 (7-8 Sundays) when doubles are priced as singles and pints of beer or cider are 10p cheaper. The rambling and cosy little rooms have various pieces of maritime memorabilia: fishing nets hanging from low planked ceilings, wooden floors, wall boards, and a notice-board with boating advertisements. Bar food (which you may have to wait for if it's busy) includes toasties (from £1.60), ploughman's (from £3.30), home-made steak and kidney pies (£4.85), vegetarian dishes like broccoli and almond lasagne (£4.95), cod and chips (£4.95), local oysters (£5.25), moules marinières (£6.25) and daily specials. Dominoes, cribbage, shove-ha'penny, various board and card games, and a quiz each Tuesday evening at 8.30; piped music. Used paperbacks are sold and exchanged – proceeds to charity – and there are reference books and magazines for use whilst in the pub; the lavatory walls are covered with plaques of printed graffiti and there's a blackboard and chalk to write your own. Tables on a narrow gravel terrace face the boat-packed water – you can get here by boat up the quiet back water off the Swale. The atmosphere is jolly and friendly with quite a local bent and the enthusiastic landlord loves talking about his collection. *(Recommended by E D Bailey, Dr J P Cullen, Jim Smallcraft, J E Lloyd, Miss M Byrne, Brent and Diane Hanger, Neil Hardwick, J and M Baker-Dalton)*

Free house ~ Licensee Alec Heard ~ Real ale ~ Meals and snacks (till 10.30pm) ~ Restaurant ~ Teynham (01795) 521404 ~ Children in restaurant (because they are small it's best to ring first) ~ Occasional live entertainment ~ Open 11-3, 6-11; midnight supper licence

DARGATE TR0761 Map 3

Dove

Village signposted from A299

Old-fashioned honeysuckle-clad brick house in a quiet hamlet surrounded by strawberry fields and orchards that started life as a home brewhouse 150 years ago and now serves well kept (and very well priced for the area) Shepherd Neame Bitter and Spitfire on handpump, with a winter Porter; unusual strong local cider. Simple but tasty good value home-made bar food in big helpings from the daily changing blackboard includes a soup (winter only) like celery and stilton or oxtail (£1.95), ploughman's (all £3.25), lasagne (£5.25), vegetable curry (£5.95), steak and kidney pie, or chicken, mushroom and asparagus pie (£6.50); puddings. They also do full English breakfast (£3.75) from 9-11 on Sunday mornings, for which booking is essential. The basic old-fashioned rambling rooms are carefully refurbished and there's a good winter log fire and pictures of the pub in former days; darts. The rather lovely garden has roses, lilacs, paeonies and many other flowers, picnic-table sets under pear trees, a dovecote with white doves, a rockery and pool, and a swing; there may be summer barbecues; bridlepath leads up from the pub (along the charmingly-named Plumpudding Lane) into Blean Wood. *(Recommended by Ian Phillips, Mr and Mrs J Back, D K Carter, Simon Small; more reports please)*

Shepherd Neame ~ Tenant Simon Blount ~ Real ale ~ Meals and snacks (not Sun evening) ~ Canterbury (01227) 751360 ~ Well behaved children welcome ~ Open 11-3, 6-11 (closed evening 25 Dec)

GROOMBRIDGE TQ5337 Map 3

Crown ♀

B2110

This quaint, carefully preserved tile-hung Elizabethan inn with seats at the front is set at the end of a horseshoe shaped row of pretty cottages, surrounding a lovely steep village green with views to the village below. Its series of snug, atmospheric rooms decorated with various antique bottles – many accompanied by an anecdote the landlord is only too happy to share – were once the haunt of smugglers en route between London and Rye. It's a relaxed and chatty place, with a cheery bustle around the long copper-topped serving bar, and logs quietly burning in the big brick inglenook; lots of old teapots and pewter tankards on the walls. The end room, normally for eaters, has fairly close-spaced tables with a variety of good solid chairs, a log-effect gas fire in a big fireplace, and an arch through to the food ordering area. The walls, mostly rough yellowing plaster with some squared panelling and some timbering, are decorated with small topographical, game and sporting prints (often in pretty maple frames), and a circular large-scale map with the pub at its centre; some of the beams have horsebrasses. A pretty little parlour serves as an overflow for eaters, and is bookable too. Quickly served on an entertaining assortment of plates old and new, the tasty food includes seafood risotto (£5), honey roast ham (£4.80), salads (£5), duck with cherry brandy sauce (£7.50) and tasty steak and mushroom pie; most served with beautifully cooked vegetables; Sunday roast. Well kept Courage Directors, Harveys IPA, Ruddles Best and Theakstons Best, good value house wines (by the glass as well), and local Biddenden cider; shove-ha'penny, cribbage and backgammon. There are picnic-table sets on the sunny front brick terrace or on the green. Across the road is a public footpath beside the small chapel which leads, across a field, to moated Groombridge Place (the gardens of which are now open to the public) and fields beyond. *(Recommended by A Jarvis, P Bell, Wayne Brindle, K R Flack, Heather Martin, Mrs C Hartley, Dr and Mrs P Dismorr, JM, PM, R Hughes, Adrian Pitts, Emma Lake, J A Snell)*

Free house ~ Licensees Bill and Vivienne Rhodes ~ Real ale ~ Meals and snacks (not Sun evening) ~ Evening restaurant ~ (01892) 864742 ~ Children in snug and restaurant ~ Occasional Morris dancers in summer ~ Open 11-2.30(3 Sat), 6-11; 11-11 Sat in summer ~ Bedrooms: £19/£35

nr HADLOW TQ6352 Map 3

Artichoke

Hamptons; from Hadlow-Plaxtol road take second right (signposted West Peckham – the pub sign on the oak tree has gone, but they hope to have added a new one soon); OS Sheet 188 map reference 627524

It's rather lovely in summer to sit outside this isolated little cottage on the fairy-lit front terrace under a striped awning or on the wooden seat built around the lime tree, and look out across the surrounding countryside. Two atmospheric little rooms are warmed in winter by a woodburning stove and an inglenook fireplace filled with tree trunk sized logs. These often very busy bars are filled with fairly closely-spaced cushioned high-backed wooden settles, wooden farmhouse-kitchen chairs, upholstered wrought-iron stools matching unusual wrought-iron, glass-topped tables on the turkey carpet, and beams in the low ceilings; lots of gleaming brass, some country pictures (mainly hunting scenes), antique umbrellas, old storm lamps, and a fox mask. Home-made bar food such as quiche lorraine (£4.95), lasagne or cannelloni (£5.50), cod fillet, steak and kidney or vegetable pies (from £5.75), lamb chop (£6.95), Mediterranean king prawns (from £8.50) and sirloin steak (from £8.95); specials like casseroles, stews, curries and fisherman's pie; puddings could include home-made apple crumble or tiramisu (£2.50). Fullers London Pride, Greene King Abbot, and Youngs Special on handpump, with a good range of spirits. *(Recommended by A Church, E D Bailey, L M Miall, Gail and Trevor Cargill, Andy Stone, Anthony Barnes)*

Free house ~ Licensees Terence and Barbara Simmonds ~ Real ale ~ Meals ~ Restaurant (not Sun eve) ~ Plaxtol (01732) 810763 ~ Children in eating area of bar ~ Open 11.30-2.30, 6.30-11; closed winter Sun evenings

IVY HATCH TQ5854 Map 3

Plough 🍽 ♀

Coach Rd; village signposted off A227 N of Tonbridge

The fastidious French chef at this civilised and friendly inn is also the manager and this really reflects the emphasis on the cooking here. This is a place for those who enjoy excellent food and wine, the best ingredients, and professional service – go in a restaurant mood rather than a pub one, and you'll feel happier about the prices. There is a bar menu with soup (£2.50), warm stilton tart with wild garlic mushrooms or warm duck liver salad (small or large from £3.50), ratatouille (£4.75), crab and smoked salmon roulade (£4.95), seafood tagliatelle (£5.25), mushroom and seafood pie (£5.95), steamed chicken with a crème fraîche and chive sauce (£8.25) and char-grilled rump steak (£9.50) or you can eat from the restaurant menu which changes twice a day and might include cream of asparagus and celery (£3), puff pastry parcels filled with crab or smoked trout and smoked chicken and stilton salad (£4.95), grilled fresh sardines with thyme (£6.95), roast poussin with plum sauce or venison casserole (£9.95) and escalope or roast guinea fowl (£10.95); some home-made puddings from the blackboard like apricot or French apple tart (£3); Sunday roasts. Well kept but expensive Brakspears and Marstons Pedigree on handpump, an interesting selection of fine wines and some very good house wines; very efficient service. The simple candlelit bar (you can now book early tables) has several cosy room areas with soft banquettes in a snug off on the left, small well cushioned settles and attractive country chairs around good solid tables in the main part, and round behind on the right another snug area – which leads on through to the elegant and comfortable back conservatory restaurant; piped music. There are picnic-table sets on gravel in front, and in a fairy-lit sloping back garden with its own summer bar and barbecue. Walkers should leave muddy boots outside. *(Recommended by J LeSage, Maysie Thompson, D L Barker, A Church, Mrs P MacFarlane, D C Eastwood, E D Bailey, Simon Small, TOH, C P and M G Stent, Tina and David Woods-Taylor, R C Morgan, J G Smith, John Archer, David Wright, E D Bailey, Dr and Mrs J W McClenahan, Chris and Anne Fluck, E G Parish, D A Edwards, M Veldhuyzen, Darren Ford, Tom and Rosemary Hall)*

Free house ~ Manager: Daniel Humbert ~ Real ale ~ Meals and snacks (not Sun evening) ~ Restaurant ~ Plaxtol (01732) 810268 ~ Children in eating area of bar and restaurant only ~ Live entertainment on Bastille night ~ Open 11-3, 6.30-10.30

nr IVY HATCH TQ5754 Map 3

Rose & Crown

Stone Street; signposted from Ivy Hatch

Behind this straightforward country pub in quiet countryside are plenty of picnic tables in a wonderfully unpretentious garden surrounded by gnarled old trees, lilac and fig trees, rhododendrons and shrubs, a good-sized children's play area and barbecues on Friday evenings in summer. You get quite a good view of the building from here too, its higgledy piggledy stone walls looking much older than their 300 years. Inside, the pleasant bar has some stripped masonry and lots of jugs hanging from the ceiling, with a friendly dog and well kept Harveys and Wadworths 6X. Very popular home-cooked specials include plenty of Italian meals (the licensee is from Italy), as well as dishes like mushrooms piccanti (£2.85), pasta of the day or smoked salmon maison (£3.95), guinea fowl (£7.95), scotch fillet steak au poivre (£10.50) and Dover sole (£10.95) and seasonal game like jugged hare; efficient speedy service. The restaurant overlooks an orchard, and a barn has been converted to a children's room; they can get booked up at weekends. There is good woodland walking to the south: Bitchet Common just along the road past the pub, then One Tree Hill (National Trust). Ightham Mote, signposted from Ivy Hatch, is an attractive moated manor house, well worth visiting. *(Recommended by L M Miall, Ian Phillips, Tim and Pam Moorey, Richard Atkinson)*

Free house ~ Licensee Luigi Carugati ~ Real ale ~ Meals and snacks ~ Restaurant (not Sun evening) ~ (01732) 810233 ~ Children in eating area of bar ~ Open 12-3, 7-11

LAMBERHURST TQ6635 Map 3

Brown Trout ♀

B2169, just off A21 S of village nearly opposite entrance to Scotney Castle

Immensely popular for its fresh fish (the licensee goes to Billingsgate twice a week), this busy, cheerfully run pub might have starters such as soft roes on toast (£3.50) or a heap of mussels (Sept-March £3.50), six oysters (£3.95), and Mediterranean prawns in garlic butter (£4.95), and main courses like a 10oz fresh fillet of plaice (£4.95), wing of skate (£6.95), dressed crab with prawns (£7.50), and whole lobster (£13.95); there are non-fishy dishes like soup (£1.95), pork chops (£6.25) and steaks (from £8.95). Good value daily specials (all £4.95) may include fresh huss, lasagne and prawn or smoked salmon salads; service is consistently welcoming and friendly. You usually have to book ahead – on Saturday evenings this may mean weeks in advance. The small bar has a big central bar counter surrounded by russet hessian walls with small country prints, glowing copper and brass hanging thickly from the beams, and eight or nine tables – most people tend to eat in the biggish extension dining room which has many closely set tables and a fish tank. Adnams and King & Barnes Bitter on handpump, a large choice of wines and freshly squeezed fruit juices; side fruit machine, faint piped music. Picnic-table sets under cocktail parasols on the sloping front grass to the road and a large, safe garden behind with swings, slides and trampolines. The densely hung vermillion hanging baskets stand out against the white-painted façade (even in winter the show is marvellous with baskets and tubs of pansies). The licensee also runs the Rainbow Trout in Rotherfield. *(Recommended by Jim and Maggie Cowell, Martin Jones, E D Bailey, Maysie Thompson, Brian Kneale, Ian Phillips, Paul and Margaret Baker, K Flack)*

Whitbreads ~ Lease: Joseph Stringer ~ Real ale ~ Meals and snacks (till 10) ~ Restaurant ~ Tunbridge Wells (01892) 890312 ~ Children welcome ~ Open 10.30(11 in winter)-3.30, 6-11; closed evening 25 Dec

NEWNHAM TQ9557 Map 3

George ★ ♀

44 The Street; village signposted from A2 just W of Ospringe, outside Faversham

Readers love both the Dickensian atmosphere and the delicious food at this distinctive 16th-c village pub which is obviously very well cared for, with tremendous attention to detail, from the beautiful flower arrangements, through the furnishings and decor to the excellent, imaginative bar food. The meals are particularly popular at the moment, with a choice from the menu that might include sandwiches (from £1.20), delicious soup (£2), moules marinières (£3.75), cheese topped cottage pie (£3.80), a good variety of ploughman's and salads (from £4.25, avocado and prawns £6), pasta of the day or chilli con carne (£4.60), vegetarian parcel (£5.30), steak and kidney pie or pudding (£5.95 or £6.25), fillets of sole Dieppoise (£8.30), memorable rack of lamb (cooked pink £8.50), fillet steak with port and cream sauce (£11.95), puddings (not served on Sundays) such as chocolate roulade or an old-fashioned suet pudding (£2.50), and specials such as pheasant eggs florentine (£3.25), courgettes bolognese (£3.75), fried plaice and chips or baked potatoes filled with liver and bacon and topped with mozzarella (£4.95), game pie (£6.30), lemon and ginger poussin on a bed of caramelised onions (£8.40) and pot roast half shoulder of lamb glazed with mint jelly (£10.75) and puddings like bananas with caramel sauce (£2) or bread pudding (£2.20); game in season, local fruit and vegetables used as much as possible, and they try to cater for those with special diets. At lunchtime they may not always do grills or some of the more expensive dishes. It's important to get there well before 1.30 on a Sunday (when they don't serve puddings) as service stops promptly. Most of the larger tables are usually shared but they take reservations for parties of six or more; no credit cards. The spreading series of atmospheric rooms have prettily upholstered mahogany settles, dining chairs and leather carving chairs around candlelit tables, table lamps and gas-type ceiling chandeliers, rugs on the waxed floorboards, early 19th-c prints (Dominica negroes, Oxford academics, politicians), a cabinet of fine rummers and other glassware, and a collection of British butterflies and moths; hop bines hang from the beams and there are open fires. Well kept Shepherd Neame Bitter, Best, Bishops Finger and Spitfire on handpump, four wines by the glass and more by the bottle, and unobtrusive, well reproduced and interesting piped music; shove-ha'penny, cribbage, dominoes, fruit machine. There are picnic-table sets in a spacious sheltered garden with a fine spreading cobnut tree, below the slopes of the sheep pastures. Dogs allowed (drinking bowl in lobby). *(Recommended by June and Tony Baldwin, P M Lane, M W Atkinson, Stephen and Julie Brown, Derek R Patey, Brian Kneale, Tina and David Woods-Taylor, Miss M Byrne, Ben Regan, Tim and Pam Moorey)*

Shepherd Neame ~ Tenant Simon Barnes ~ Real ale ~ Meals and snacks (till

10pm, till 1.30 sharp Sun; not Sun evening, not Mon) ~ (01795) 890237 ~
Children welcome ~ Open 10.30-3, 6-11; they close at 2 Sun lunchtimes

PENSHURST TQ5243 Map 3

Bottle House ◖

Coldharbour Lane, Smarts Hill; leaving Penshurst SW on B2188 turn right at Smarts Hill
signpost, then bear right towards Chiddingstone and Cowden

The long imposing exterior offers only a few clues to the great age and
friendliness of this relaxed, low beamed family run free house dating from the
15th c. Readers particularly tell us how instantly comfortable they feel in the care
of the pleasant, affable and attentive licencees (although they're spending a lot of
time at the George and Dragon in Speldhurst which they have recently taken
over) and how much they enjoy the extensive choice of excellent food. Particular
favourites from the wide bar menu are the soup (£2.95), filled jacket potatoes and
ploughman's (from £4.25), breaded lemon sole, braised liver and bacon,
vegetable madras or spaghetti bolognese (£5.95), whole grilled trout (£7.95), fillet
of pork marsala (£8.50), grilled monkfish with garlic and lemon or rack of
hickory smoked ribs (£8.95) and steaks (from £10.95); good puddings and
Sunday lunch. It soon fills up, but even when busy service remains efficient and
notably friendly. Through the main entrance the bar floor, smoothed with age, is
exposed brick extending to behind the polished copper-topped bar counter. Light
and bright – the large windows look out to a patio area with climbing plants and
hanging baskets around picnic-table sets under cocktail parasols, and beyond to
the quiet fields and oak trees – the unpretentious main red carpeted bar down a
step has massive behopped supporting beams, two large stone pillars with a small
brick firplace inbetween with a copper hood and stuffed turtle to one side and old
paintings and photographs on mainly plastered walls. To the far right, an isolated
extension forms a small pine panelled snug hung with part of an extensive
collection of china pot lids, the rest are in the low ceilinged, well appointed dining
room. Scattered throughout the pub is the licencees' collection of old sewing
machines. Well kept Harveys, Ind Coope Burton and Larkins from nearby
Chiddingstone on handpump (they've won awards for their cellar), cider from
Chiddingstone too, and local wine; unobtrusive piped music. *(Recommended by E D
Bailey, R and S Bentley, Mr and Mrs R W Hawley, Mary Defer, A Church, Colin Laffan,
Tim and Pam Moorey, P J Guy, Mr and Mrs M C Westley, T O Haunch, G T White, G
Leibou, P Neate, A Jarvis, Comus Elliott, Mark and Nicola Willoughby)*

*Free house ~ Licensees Gordon and Val Meer ~ Real ale ~ Meals and snacks (till
10) ~ Restaurant (not Sun evening) ~ (01892) 870306 ~ Children in eating area
of bar and in restaurant ~ Open 11-2.30, 6-11*

Spotted Dog ♀

Smarts Hill; going S from village centre on B2188, fork right up hill at telephone box: in just
under ½ mile the pub is on your left

You go down some steps to enter this quaint tiled house that's perched on the
side of a hill with an idyllic summer view from the greatly extended terraces –
there's now lots of room outside for children to play – over more than 20 miles of
countryside, with the lush upper Medway valley curling round below towards
medieval Penshurst. First licensed in 1520, it's very popular indeed at the
moment, with plenty of readers impressed with the way staff stay organised and
keep smiling amidst the cheery bustle. The neatly kept and heavily beamed and
timbered bar has some antique settles as well as wheelback chairs on its rugs and
tiles, a fine brick inglenook fireplace, and attractive moulded panelling in one
alcove. They are producing some wonderful food at the moment, some from the
bar menu which includes soup (£1.95), garlic mushrooms (£2.95), ploughman's
(£4.05) filled baked potatoes (from £4.95), but most from the five blackboards
that are changed twice a day and might have starters like guacamole, gravadlax
or pan fried tiger prawns and main courses like smoked chicken and avocado
salad (£6.45), lots and lots of fresh fish like tuna, red snapper and parrot fish and
seasonal meat dishes like lamb oregano, fresh tomato, garlic and black olive

casserole (£6.95, summer) and venison with wild mushroom and port pie (£6.95, winter) and a very popular and extensive range of vegetarian dishes like fresh aubergines stuffed with chilli vegetables and cheese (£4.95), spinach and blue cheese roulade (£5.95) and wild mushroom and cashew nut stroganoff (£5.45); puddings from the board made with Devon clotted cream and seasonal fruits like summer pudding, fresh cherry strudel with filo pastry, chocolate truffle, treacle tart or spotted dick. Well kept Adnams, Eldridge Pope Hardy, King & Barnes Sussex, Wadworths 6X on handpump, and Old Spotty – actually Courage Best. The wine list is good (lots from the New World, even some from Penshurst); unobtrusive piped music. *(Recommended by Richard Waller, Paul McKeerer, David Wright, P Neate, Comus Elliott, Simon Morton, J Muckelt, Wayne Brindle, S R Howe, J G Smith, Colin Laffan, R C Morgan, Nick Wikeley)*

Free house ~ Licensee Andy Tucker ~ Real ale ~ Meals and snacks ~ Restaurant ~ (01892) 870253 ~ Children welcome away from bar area ~ Open 11.30-2.30, 6-11; closed 25 Dec

PLUCKLEY TQ9243 Map 3

Dering Arms 🛏 🍷

Near station, which is signposted from B2077 in village

Strikingly handsome and architecturally unique among Kent pubs, the imposing castle-like exterior has Dutch gables cleanly cut against the skyline, topping the massive grey stone blocked walls with heavy studded oak doors and unusual arched mullioned 'Dering' windows. These took the family name after one of the clan escaped through one from the Roundheads and afterwards decreed that all houses built on the estate should have similar fenestration – you can still see lots locally. Inside in the unusually high ceilinged echoing baronial bar it's not hard to imagine huge dogs lounging on the wood and stone floors in front of the great log fireplace in the days when it was built as a hunting lodge for the Dering estate. Stylishly simple decorations with a variety of good solid wooden furniture – the smaller bar is similar. The food is very popular, with the fish dishes especially highly praised and featuring strongly in the beautifully presented specials: potted crab, good monkfish with bacon and orange sauce or whole crab salad (all £9.65), and fillet of halibut meunière (£10.65), as well as mussels in cider and cream or quail's eggs on onion croutons (£3.95), chicken and banana pie or pie of the day (£6.95), skate with caper butter (£8.45), fillet of salmon with pernod and lemon butter or local trout with hazelnuts and lemon (£9.65), medallions of fillet steak in green peppercorn sauce (£10.45) and Jim's seafood special for two people, but they need 24 hours' notice; all-day breakfast (£3.95), and puddings like chestnut and chocolate slice with cointreau (£2.45) or banana pancake (£2.95); cafetière of coffee with almond shortbread (£1.20). Every six weeks they have gourmet evenings, elaborate black-tie affairs with seven courses. Well kept Goachers Maidstone Light, Mild, Gold Star (summer), Porter (winter) and Dering ale, a beer they brew for the pub, on handpump; a big range of decent wines, local cider, log fires, and shove-ha'penny and dominoes. There's a vintage car rally once a month, and in summer garden parties with barbecues and music from jazz to classical string quartets. *(Recommended by Andrew and Ruth Triggs, Miss M Byrne, Mr and Mrs Scholey, Viv Middlebrook, C T Laffan, Dave Braisted, Nigel Gibbs, Nicola Thomas, Paul Dickinson, Gregg Davies)*

Free house ~ Licensee James Buss ~ Real ale ~ Meals and snacks (till 10pm; not Sun evening) ~ Restaurant; closed Sun evening and 26 Dec ~ (01233) 840371 ~ Children in eating area and restaurant ~ Folk music every third Sun ~ Open 11-3, 6-11 (closed 26 and 27 Dec) ~ Bedrooms: £28/£36

RINGLESTONE TQ8755 Map 3

Ringlestone ★ 🍷 🍴

M20 Junction 8 to Lenham/Leeds Castle; join B2163 heading N towards Sittingbourne via Hollingbourne; at water tower above Hollingbourne turn right towards Doddington (signposted), and straight ahead at next crossroads; OS Sheet 178 map reference 879558

There's a well documented history to this lovely timeless old inn which was built in 1533 as a hospice for monks and became an ale house in 1615. In more recent history it was taken over by Charles Alfred Rayfield, the father of Charles 'Gunner' Rayfield – the man who fired the first artillery shot against the enemy in WW1. On a worn brick floor, the central room has farmhouse chairs, cushioned wall settles and tables with candle lanterns and on the exposed brick and flint walls old-fashioned brass and glass lamps; a woodburning stove and small bread oven in an inglenook fireplace. An arch from here through a wall – rather like the outside of a house, windows and all – opens into a long, quieter room with cushioned wall benches, tiny farmhouse chairs, three old carved settles (one rather fine and dated 1620), similar tables, and etchings of country folk on its walls (bare brick too). Regulars tend to sit at the wood-panelled bar counter, or liven up a little wood-floored side room. The food is a big draw here, especially the help-yourself hot and cold lunchtime buffet – well worth the queues for meals like herrings in madeira or mussels provençale (£2.95), garlic chicken, steak, kidney or leek pie or beef goulash (£4.25) and a choice of 9 salads; puddings like home-made brandy bread pudding or fruit crumble (all £2.85). Other food includes a thick vegetable and meat soup (£2.75), liver and apple pâté or melon cocktail ploughman's (£3.95), lasagne or chilli con carne (£4.95), many pies such as beef and beer pie, lamb and apricot pie or chicken and bacon pie (£6.85), trout (£7.95) and rump steak (£8.95); vegetables and potatoes of the day £2.35 extra; no chips or fried food. Changing well kept real ales tapped from casks behind the bar or on handpump and chalked up on a board might include Brains, Burton, Boddingtons, Fullers London Pride, Gibbs Mews Bishops Tipple, Greene King IPA, Marstons Pedigree, Morlands Old Speckled Hen, Shepherd Neame Spitfire, Wadworths 6X, and over 24 country wines (including sparkling ones); hard-working, friendly staff. There are picnic-table sets on the two acres of beautifully landscaped lawns with shrubs, trees and rockeries and a water garden with four pretty ponds linked by cascading waterfalls, a delightful fountain and troughs of flowers along the pub walls. Well behaved dogs welcome. *(Recommended by Jim Cowell, Beverley James, Mrs P J Pearce, Dr G M Regan, Miss M Byrne, Nicola Thomas, Paul Dickinson, E D Bailey, A B Dromey, Dr S R Dando, Stephen Brown, Professor J R Leigh, D A Edwards, Evelyn and Derek Walter, Tina and David Woods-Taylor)*

Free house ~ Licensee Michael Millington-Buck ~ Real ale ~ Meals and snacks ~ Restaurant (not Sun eve) ~ (01622) 859900 ~ Children welcome (under gentle supervision) ~ Open 12-3, 6(6.30 in winter)-11; closed 25 Dec

SELLING TR0456 Map 3

White Lion ♀

3½ miles from M2 junction 7; village signposted from exit roundabout; village also signposted off A251 S of Faversham

Tucked away in a small village among hop gardens this 300-year-old coaching inn is a mass of colour in the summer with riotous hanging baskets. The historically atmospheric interior is decorated with moss and dried flowers. Two huge brick fireplaces (with a spit over the right-hand one) warm the bar in winter, and there are pews on stripped floorboards, and an unusual semi-circular bar counter. Bar food comes normally in generous helpings, though unusually smaller helpings are available here for older as well as for younger customers. Served with very accurately cooked vegetables, the range includes sandwiches (from £1.25), home-made soup (£2.25), garlic and herb pâté or smoked salmon mousse (£2.95), ploughman's (from £3.50), salads (from £4.75), several vegetarian meals like mushrooms in a provençal spicy sauce with cheese topping (£5.75), steaks (from £7.50), lunchtime specials such as traditional beef pudding or steak and kidney pie (£4.95) or curries including chicken and coconut (£5.95); Monday is curry night; Sunday roasts; a wide range of home-made puddings like banoffi pie, mousses and lemon meringue pie. Prices are higher in the restaurant, where there are also more unusual dishes. Well kept Shepherd Neame Mild, Best and Spitfire on handpump, several decent wines, some by the glass and a range of malt whiskies. Maybe quiet piped music – the landlord's a trumpet-player, and may even play on jazz nights. *(Recommended by Nigel Foster, June and Tony Baldwin, Stephen Brown, Evelyn and Derek Walter, D K Carter, L M Miall)*

Shepherd Neame ~ Tenant Anthony Richards ~ Real ale ~ Meals and snacks ~ Restaurant (not Sun evening) ~ (01227) 752211 ~ Children welcome (in family room) ~ Jazz every Mon in bar and during candlelit dinner last Tues evening of the month; 60s music second Tues evening of the month ~ Open 11-3, 6.30-11; closed 25 Dec

nr SMARDEN TQ8842 Map 3

Bell ★ ♀ ◖

From Smarden follow lane between church and The Chequers, then turn left at T-junction; or from A274 take unsignposted turn E a mile N of B2077 to Smarden

Built as a farm dwelling in 1536, the earliest recorded occupant was Matthew Stronge – thought to have been a blacksmith – who's mentioned in a document dated 1583 which describes the inn as a forge. The last known blacksmith to have shoed a horse at the inn was George Port, keeper and blacksmith of the Bell from 1903 to 1907. In 1630 the inn was granted an ale and cider licence and from thenceforth doubled as an inn and forge. It's easy to look back on these bygone days sitting in the dusky snug little low beamed back rooms (one is no smoking) with bare brick or rough ochre plastered walls, brick or flagstone floors, pews and the like around simple tables (candlelit at night), and inglenook fireplaces. The larger airy white painted and green matchboarded bar has a beamed ceiling and quarry tiled floor, large fireplace with woodburning stove, a family area, and a games area with darts, pool, dominoes, fruit machine and juke box at one end. The building has a typical Wealden peg tiled roof and massive brick chimneys, and rose-covered tile hung upper half and brick or weatherboard lower halves. It's pleasant to sit in the garden amongst the mature fruit trees and shrubs although you need to get there early for a seat outside at weekends, particularly when the gathering of vintage and classic cars takes place on the second Sunday of each month. Bar food includes home-made soup (£1.70), sandwiches or toasties (from £2, rump steak £3.30), home-made pâté (£2.35), pizza (from £2.75), ploughman's (from £3.25), shepherd's pie (£3.45), salads (from £4.50), plaice (£4.95), scampi (£5.25), steaks (from £7.95), and one or two daily specials such as fish mornay or Cumberland pie; puddings like home-made chocolate crunch cake and spotted dick (£1.80); usual children's and vegetarian menu. Well kept Flowers Original, Fremlins, Fullers London Pride, Goachers Maidstone, Harveys, Shepherd Neame, and Ringwood Old Thumper on handpump; also, eight wines by the glass, and local Biddenden cider. Breakfasts with cereal and toast. *(Recommended by M W Young, A H Denman and others; more reports please)*

Free house ~ Licensee Ian Turner ~ Real ale ~ Meals and snacks (till 10pm, 10.30 Fri and Sat) ~ Smarden (0123 377) 283 ~ Children in family room ~ Open 11.30-2.30(3 Sat), 6-11; closed 25 Dec ~ Bedrooms: £20/£32

SOLE STREET TQ6567 Map 3

Compasses

Back lane between Godmersham (A28) and Petham (B2068); OS Sheet 189 map reference 095493

Well preserved 15th-c family run brick tavern standing almost alone on its quiet lane over the scenic North Downs. A little room at the back of this atmospheric pub has narrow wooden wall benches round the big kitchen table on the polished flagstone floor, a carefully restored massive brick bread oven, and enamelled advertisement placards on the walls; also a Cresset Auto Machine, an entertaining and far more skill-demanding forerunner of the fruit machine. The front bar is a long, narrow room with beams in the shiny ochre ceiling, simple antique tables on its polished bare boards, rows of salvaged theatre seats along some walls, and a log fire in winter. Bar food from the menu includes filled rolls freshly baked on the premises daily (from £1.80), large filled french sticks (from £2.95), soup

(£1.95), dim sum (£3.65), ploughman's (from £3.70), chilli con carne (£5.20), lasagne (£5.40), steak and kidney or steak and mushroom pie or chicken and sweetcorn in herb, mushroom, onion and wine sauce (£5.90) and salmon, cod and mushroom pie (£6.30). They do quite a few very popular dishes en croûte like chicken breast, stilton and bacon in puff pastry or puff pastry parcel filled with prawns and cheese (£6.95) and chicken breast wrapped in pâté in puff pastry (£7.25). There's a specials board that's changed a couple of times a week; lots of ice cream, rich sundaes and puddings like jam roly poly and custard (£2.50), champagne and orange mousse cake with strawberry mousse (£2.95), trifle (£2.95); children's menu. Well kept Boddingtons, Fullers London Pride and ESB on handpump; Biddenden local cider and fruit wines. Children will love the large garden with its fruit trees, well stocked aviaries, goats and sheep, wooden play house with slide and swing and steel climbing frame, and on fine summer lunchtimes the landlady might bring out her cockatoo named B Bob. The area is good for walking, and cobwebbed with footpaths. *(Recommended by P Butler, David Bloomfield, Peter Hitchcock, Ron and Sheila Corbett, Paul Adams; more reports please)*

Free house ~ Licensees John and Sheila Bennett ~ Real ale ~ Meals and snacks (till 10 at weekends) ~ (01227) 700300 ~ Children in Garden Room ~ Open 11-3, 6.30-11 all year

SPELDHURST TQ5541 Map 3

George & Dragon ♀

Village signposted from A264 W of Tunbridge Wells

A marvellously distinguished black and white half timbered medieval building, based on a manorial great hall dating back to 1212 and known to be one of the oldest pubs in the south of England. As with so many ancient places there have been a few changes, with the addition of heavy oak beams during modernisation – although to be fair this was in 1589. It's got some of the biggest flagstones you can find anywhere, and it's said that Kentish archers returning from their victory at Agincourt rested on them in 1415. On arrival through an oak panelled entrance lobby there is a carpeted bar on the left with a comfortable sofa and padded banquettes, exposed beams, rough plaster, a grandfather clock that marks the half hour and a small fireplace. Inside the spacious open plan public bar – part panelled and plastered – seating is on high backed wooden benches at several old wood topped cast iron tables. The undoubted centre point of the bar is the vast sandstone fireplace with a vast iron fireback that's over three hundred years old. Recently taken over by the couple who've made a great success of the Bottle House near Penshurst, it's possible that we could see this already tremendous inn improve further. Popular and well served bar food includes filled baked potato (from £4.25), taramasalata with pitta bread and salad or Speldhurst sausages (£4.95), chilli con carne or vegetable and onion pie or battered squid (£5.50), lasagne or vegetable lasagne (£5.95), steak, kidney and Guinness pie or chicken madras (£6.95), dressed crab (£7.50), hot or cold poached Scotch salmon or smoked salmon salad or cajun chicken or lamb steak with green pepper sauce (£7.95), rack of hickory smoked ribs or king prawns (£8.95); service is friendly and attentive. Well kept Fullers London Pride and Harveys Armada, BB and IPA on handpump, with lots of malt whiskies and a large wine cellar of around 140 bins; darts and fruit machine. The striking first-floor restaurant under the original massive roof timbers serves good à la carte food and has a quite splendid wine cellar – a place for special occasions. There are white tables and chairs on the neat little lawn, ringed with flowers, in front of the building. It can get busy at weekends, especially at night. *(Recommended by A Kilpatrick, Peter Neate, Gwen and Peter Andrews, R and S Bentley, J G Smith, Colin Laffan, Thomas Nott, M E A Horler)*

Free house ~ Licensees Gordon and Val Meer ~ Real ale ~ Meals and snacks (till 10pm; not Sun evening) ~ Restaurant (not Sun evening) ~ Langton (01892) 863125 ~ Children in eating area ~ Open 11-11

TUNBRIDGE WELLS TQ5839 Map 3

Sankeys 🍴 🍷

39 Mount Ephraim (A26 just N of junction with A267)

Kent Dining Pub of the Year

The downstairs cellar bar has proved incredibly popular since it opened a couple of years ago and in order to cope with the overflow the bar menu is now available (Monday to Friday) in the redecorated upstairs restaurant. The really good news is that they now offer the full seafood menu in the lively relaxed gas-lit, York-stoned bar. It's decorated with old mirrors, prints, enamel advertising signs, antique beer engines and other bric-a-brac (most of which has been salvaged from local pub closures) and there are french windows leading to a sun-trap walled garden with white tables and chairs under cocktail parasols. The four rooms upstairs have Spy prints on the walls, plush dining chairs and old pews; the two back rooms are no smoking. The wide choice of excellent meals from both menus includes starter and main courses like filled baguettes (£2.75), taramasalata (£3.50), pâtés and terrines or spaghetti con cozze (£4), salads, fish soup with rouille and gruyere, grilled sardines or a very good value charcuterie with Bayonne ham (£4.50), Belgian moules with chips or stuffed Cornish clams or moules marinières (£5), scallops grilled with garlic and breadcrumbs or leek en croûte with mushroom sauce (£5.50), fillets of witch sole with shrimp sauce (£7), cajun cod (£8), seafood paella (£9), lemon sole fillets with spinach, nutmeg and red pepper sauce (£11), halibut grilled with fresh herbs (£12.50), medley of fish with tarragon cream (£13.50), plateau de fruits de mer (£16) and lobster (from £18); home-made puddings (all £3). Some combination of Harveys, King & Barnes or Shepherd Neame from an antique beer engine, though most people seem to be taking advantage of the superb wine list; you need to get there early in the evening for a table in the bar. *(Recommended by Father D Glover, G L Tong, J A Snell, E D Bailey; more reports please)*

Free house ~ Licensee Guy Sankey ~ Real ale ~ Meals and snacks 12-3, 7-10 ~ No-smoking restaurant (not Sun) ~ (01892) 511422; closed Sun ~ Children in eating area of bar ~ Live music Sun evenings ~ Open 10-11; 10-3, 6-11 Sat; closed 25 Dec

ULCOMBE TQ8550 Map 3

Pepper Box

Fairbourne Heath (signposted from A20 in Harrietsham; or follow Ulcombe signpost from A20, then turn left at crossroads with sign to pub)

The name of this unassuming, relaxed and cosy old country inn dating from 1665 derives from the pepperbox pistol – an early type of revolver with numerous barrels. At one time the pub was used as a clearing house for smuggled spices and until faily recently was also the village shop, bakery and butcher. It's situated on high ground above the weald, looking out over a great plateau of rolling arable farmland. The friendly, homely bar has standing timbers, low beams hung with hops, copper kettles and pans on window sills, some very low-seated Windsor chairs, wing armchairs, and a sofa and two armchairs by the splendid inglenook log fire. A side area is more functionally furnished for eating. There is a very snug little dining room that's ideal for dinner-parties. If you're in the garden, with its small pond, swing and tables among trees, shrubs and flowerbeds, you may catch a glimpse of the deer that sometimes come up, but if not you're quite likely to meet Jones the tabby tom, the other two cats, or Boots the plump collie. The good value well presented home-cooked food includes lunchtime sandwiches, home-made fish pie (£5), home-made steak and kidney pudding (£5.90), breaded huss (£6.50), roast duck in honey (£8) and delicious poached salmon in orange sauce; good puddings; Sunday lunches. Well kept Shepherd Neame Bitter and Bishops Finger on handpump or tapped from the cask; fruit wines and malt whiskies; piped music. *(Recommended by A Church, Werner and Karla Arend, Evelyn and Derek Walter, Chris and Pauline Ford, M A and C R Starling; more reports please)*

Shepherd Neame ~ Tenants Geoff and Sarah Pemble ~ Real ale ~ Meals and snacks (till 10, not Sun evening) ~ Restaurant ~ (01622) 842558 ~ Children in dining room, lunchtimes only ~ Guitarist/vocals Sun evening ~ Open 11-3, 6.30-11

WHITSTABLE TR1166 Map 3

Pearsons 🍴

Sea Wall; follow main road into centre as far as you can, turning L into Horsebridge Rd; pub opposite Royal Free Fishers & Dredgers; parking limited

Still very popular with diners for its delicious fresh seafood, this friendly busy pub has fine sea views, best seen inside from the upstairs restaurant – downstairs you may just get the sea wall. The choice of well served good food includes cockles (£1.50), delicious crab sandwiches (£2.25, or peeled prawn £2.40), grilled king prawns (from £5.25), six local oysters in season (£6), seafood platter (£9.25), Pearson's paradise – a huge meal for two involving lobster, crab, prawns, oysters, mussels and more (£32) and changing fresh fish (excellent plaice) or shellfish specials; also, other sandwiches (from £1.70) and ploughman's (£3.10); vegetarian meals (all £5.95) like mushroom and nut fettucine or vegetable lasagne; usual children's food from (£3.25). Small areas in the downstairs bar are divided by stripped brickwork and decorated with sea paintings, old local photographs, a ship's wheel, and lobster pots; a lower flagstoned part gets most of its submarine light from a huge lobster tank, filled with small lobsters and other creatures. Well kept Boddingtons, Flowers Original, Fremlins, Morlands Old Speckled Hen and Whitbreads under light blanket pressure; decent house wines; piped pop music, fruit machine. Upstairs, in two or three pleasantly close-packed dining rooms (with no-smoking area) there's a wider choice of meals; there are some picnic-table sets outside between the pub and the sea.

(Recommended by Tracy Lovatt, E D Bailey, John Watson, Thomas Nott, Mr and Mrs Barnes, Ted George; more reports please)

Whitbreads ~ Lease: Linda and Michael Wingrove ~ Real ale ~ Meals and snacks (till 10, not Fri or Sat evening) ~ Restaurant (till 10) ~ Whitstable (01227) 272005 ~ Children in eating area of bar ~ Open 11-3, 6-11

Lucky Dip

Besides the fully inspected pubs, you might like to try these Lucky Dips recommended to us and described by readers (if you do, please send us reports):

Addington [just off M20, junction 4; TQ6559], *Angel*: Nice big bar with plenty of well spaced tables, fast friendly food service, reasonable prices; Courage-related ales *(L M Miall)*
Aldington [TR0736], *Good Intent*: Good village local, decent beer, nice decor *(Comus Elliott)*
Ash [South Ash Rd; the one nr Brands Hatch; TQ6064], *Anchor & Hope*: Cosy 16th-c weatherboarded pub with two log fires, well kept Bass, Charrington IPA and a guest ale; good range of generous food (not Sun lunchtime), barbecues in big garden with swings, climbing frame, owls, ducks and goats *(M Thorley, K Brown)*
Ashurst [A264 next to railway station; TQ5038], *Bald Faced Stag*: Recently redecorated with emphasis on food inc cheap Sun lunch; Harveys on handpump, decent coffee; garden with play area, pleasant walks nearby *(E G Parish)*
✰ **Aylesford** [handy for M2 junction 3 or M20 junction 6, via A229; 19 High St;

TQ7359], *Little Gem*: Ancient little pub, very cosy and quaint, with good range of interesting real ales, lots of atmosphere, interesting upper gallery; bar lunches (can be a wait) and evening snacks, flame-effect gas fire, children welcome, piped radio *(N and M Foster, E D Bailey, LYM)*
Badgers Mount [London Rd (old A21) opp Polhill Garden Centre; TQ4951], *Badgers Mount*: Expensively refurbished Brewers Fayre family dining pub, big indoor play area, children's videos in eating area, high chairs; can get very busy at peak times; good choice of food inc children's and puddings, well-meaning young staff; busy at peak times *(A M Pring)*
✰ **Barham** [The Street; TR2050], *Duke of Cumberland*: Big helpings of good value straightforward lunchtime food in pleasant open-plan local with Whitbreads-related real ales, bedrooms, caravan site *(L M Miall)*
✰ **Barham** [Elham Valley Rd (B2065)], *Dolls House*: Unusual pub in beautiful Elham

Valley, wide choice of well cooked food inc some interesting dishes and good vegetarian choice, good range of real ales inc Morlands Old Speckled Hen, very good service; large unexpected dolls sitting around, doll pictures; has been closed Tues, can be very quiet indeed other weekday lunchtimes *(Pat and Andy Veitch, Louise Weekes)*

☆ **Biddenden** [High St; TQ8538], *Red Lion*: Plush but friendly old inn in lovely village, good straightforward food, well kept Whitbreads-related ales *(Andy and Jackie Mallpress, Gordon)*

Bishopsbourne [signed off A2; TR1852], *Mermaid*: Traditional welcoming country pub in lovely unspoilt Kentish village, lunchtime food inc good filled rolls, well kept Shepherd Neame Bitter and Porter *(Andy and Jill Kassube)*

Bodsham [TR1045], *Timber Butts*: Attractive building in lovely setting, very wide range of varied food, good service *(Mrs J A Trotter)*

Botolphs Bridge [Lower Wall Rd; TR1233], *Botolphs Bridge*: Handsome Edwardian local with airy and chatty open-plan bar, very friendly licensees, big helpings of home-made food with real chips; wide choice of beers under light CO2 blanket, traditional games, no juke box, occasional barbecues in small garden; children in restaurant *(Mr and Mrs Joseph Williams)*

☆ **Boughton Street** [¾ mile from M2 junction 7, off A2 – most people just call it Boughton; TR0559], *White Horse*: Good attentive service and decent food all day inc early breakfast in cosy and interesting dark-beamed bars and timbered dining room, well kept Shepherd Neame inc Porter on handpump, good tea and coffee; tables in garden, children allowed; bedrooms comfortable and well equipped – back ones quiet; handy for Canterbury *(Miss M Byrne, Jim Cowell)*

Boxley [TQ7759], *Kings Arms*: Pleasant pub most notable for really good sandwiches alongside other good value straightforward food *(Dr T E Hothersall)*

☆ **Brasted** [High St (A25), 3 miles from M25 (Sevenoaks junction) – OS Sheet 188 map reference 469550; TQ4654], *Bull*: Friendly local with well kept Shepherd Neame ales inc Porter, intimate dining lounge, separate public bar with darts and maybe skittles; tables in garden *(Comus Elliott, B B Morgan, the Pollard family, Paul McKeerer)*

☆ **Brasted** [A25], *White Hart*: Spacious relaxing lounge and extension sun lounge, interesting Battle of Britain bar with signatures and mementoes of Biggin Hill fighter pilots, well kept Bass and Charrington IPA; children welcome, big neatly kept garden; food in bar and restaurant, can get very busy weekends; bedrooms clean if rather old-fashioned *(Andrew and Teresa Heffer, Gordon Smith,*

Sandra Iles, M E A Horler, C O Day, Rob and Doris Harrison, LYM)

Brenchley [TQ6741], *Rose & Crown*: Sturdily timbered Tudor village inn with comfortable and friendly feel, home-made bar food, good choice of real ales; restaurant, provision for children, tables outside; bedrooms comfortable, all with private bath *(Susan Elliott, LYM)*

☆ **Bridge** [53 High St, off A2; TR1854], *White Horse*: Smartly comfortable dining pub, former coaching inn, doing well under current management, with wide range of good reasonably priced well presented fresh food in snug series of rooms inc civilised restaurant, several real ales on handpump, good choice of wines, very pleasant service; attractive village *(Mrs Hilarie Taylor, R F and M K Bishop, J F Webley)*

Brook [not far from M20 junction 10, via Willesborough Lees; TR0644], *Honest Miller*: Welcoming small pub in surprisingly remote-feeling village with Whitbreads-related ales, food inc vegetarian meals, steaks to cook yourself on sizzle stones, children's dishes; bat and trap *(John Watson)*

☆ **Canterbury** [12 The Friars; just off main St Peters St pedestrian area], *Canterbury Tales*: Relaxing and civilised, with good range of changing real ales such as Fullers London Pride, cheap Goachers, Shepherd Neame Bishops Finger and Belgian cherry beer, decent bar food, smart helpful staff, clean and airy lounge – popular lunchtime with local businesspeople; opp Marlow Theatre *(Robert Gomme, Malcolm Wight, David Dimock, Mark Thompson, Julian Holland)*

Canterbury [St Peters St], *Cricketers*: Interesting cricketing memorabilia in well run traditional pub with well kept Shepherd Neame beers, quickly served wholesome meals *(J and P Maloney)*; [London Rd], *Eight Bells*: Cheerful friendly local, well kept Bass and Fremlins *(David Bloomfield)*; [Upper Bridge St], *Flying Horse*: Well kept beers, good helpings of tasty food, friendly efficient service *(W Bailey, Julian Holland)*; [Castle Row, opp tree-shaded square off Castle St], *White Hart*: Unusually good bar food inc interesting specialities and some good puddings; one of the only pub gardens here *(J R Biesmans)*

Capel [Alders Rd; SE of Tonbridge; TQ6344], *Dovecote*: Attractive village local with big dovecote in garden; regulars enthusiastic about pub food, range of Allied and other ales and welcoming staff

☆ **Challock** [Church Lane; TR0050], *Chequers*: 17th-c beamed pub overlooking village green, straightforward bar food inc some bargain hot dishes, Courage-related ales, friendly helpful service *(N and M Foster, J H L Davies)*

☆ **Chiddingstone Causeway** [Charcott; off back rd to Weald; TQ5355], *Greyhound*: Unchanging country local, very unpretentious, with good choice of cheap beer and food inc outstanding value cheese and pickle sandwich; bar games *(Comus Elliott)*

Chiddingstone Causeway [B2027; TQ5146], *Little Brown Jug*: Popular Victorian country pub extensively and comfortably modernised in olde-brick-and-beam style, good choice of real ales such as Adnams and local Larkins, wide range of promptly served reasonably priced bar food, friendly welcome, restaurant; attractive garden with play area and maybe geese; bedrooms *(Jason Reynolds, Angela and Alan Dale, Colin Laffan)*

☆ **Chilham** [off A28/A252; TR0753], *White Horse*: Outstanding position on prettiest village square in Kent; food from sandwiches up in comfortably modernised beamed bar (has been available all day in summer exc Tues evening, maybe lunchtimes only winter), Whitbreads-related ales, good winter log fire, restaurant *(Stephen Brown, LYM)*

☆ **Chilham**, *Woolpack*: Good range of reasonably priced bar food inc vegetarian, cheerful service, pews, sofa, little armchairs, inglenook fires, well kept Shepherd Neame ales; restaurant (children allowed till early evening), unobtrusive piped music; bedrooms *(Stephen Brown, Mrs C Greener, J Jay, LYM)*

☆ **Chillenden** [TR2653], *Griffins Head*: Attractive beamed, timbered and flagstoned 14th-c pub with decent if not cheap food, good range of beers, three comfortable rooms, big log fire; pleasant small garden surrounded by wild roses *(M Veldhuyzen, Phil Godwin)*

Chipstead [39 High St; nr M25 junction 5; TQ4956], *George & Dragon*: Heavy black beams and standing timbers, usual bar food inc good Sun lunch, well kept Courage-related and guest ales, unobtrusive piped music; tables in pleasant garden *(Tim and Pam Moorey, LYM)*

☆ **Cliffe** [TQ7376], *Black Bull*: Friendly cosy village pub with good choice of well kept real ales, good authentic Malaysian bar food, weekday evening basement restaurant (ingeniously heated by heat-exchange from keg beer and soft drinks dispenser); darts/pool room, quiet juke box, no machines, very welcoming to children *(James Curran, Margaret Hung)*

☆ **Cobham** [B2009, handy for M2 junction 1; TQ6768], *Leather Bottle*: Beautifully laid-out extensive colourful garden with fishpond and play area, and masses of interesting Dickens memorabilia inside, are the attractions at this pub, with ancient beams and timbers but extensive modernisation; usual brewery-chain bar food and real ales; quiet, pretty village; bedrooms *(Jim Cowell, Ian and Nita Cooper, E D Bailey, George Atkinson, Thomas Nott, LYM)*

☆ **Cowden** [Cowden Pound; junction B2026 with Markbeech rd; TQ4642], *Queens Arms*: Splendid landlady, well kept Whitbreads and delightful pre-war atmosphere in clean and friendly two-room country pub, unaltered for decades and very old-fashioned; darts *(Sarah Webb and Jenny Spohn, Pete Baker)*

☆ **Cowden** [Holtye Common; A264 S of village – actually just over border in Sussex; TQ4539], *White Horse*: Pleasant old village pub with good range of generous low-priced food inc lots of fresh fish in spacious dining room, carp swimming under glass panels in its floor; barbecues *(R D Knight)*

Darenth [Darenth Rd; TQ5671], *Chequers*: Old-fashioned warm and friendly local with well kept beers and lots of lunchtime diners (good steak and kidney pie) *(Comus Elliott, Jim Smallcraft)*

☆ **Dunks Green** [Silver Hill; TQ6152], *Kentish Rifleman*: Early 16th-c, with short but sensible choice of good bar food, pleasant genuinely pubby atmosphere, Larkins and Whitbreads-related ales, decent wine, no machines *(L M Miall)*

East Sutton [TQ8349], *Shant Hotel*: Characterful pub/hotel facing cricket green, much emphasis on good value food; real ales inc Youngs Special; bedrooms *(Chris and Pauline Ford)*

Eastling [off A251 S of M2 junction 6, via Painters Forstal; TQ9656], *Carpenters Arms*: Pretty and cottagey oak-beamed pub with big fireplaces front and back, welcoming Irish licensees, decent food, well kept Shepherd Neame, some seats outside; children allowed in restaurant; small but attractive bedrooms in separate building *(Paula Harrison, A N Ellis)*

Edenbridge [74–76 High St; TQ4446], *Old Crown*: Cheerful local with Tudor origins, reopened 1994 after closure for refurbishment: good well priced food, good value fixed-price evening meals, four real ales; one of the last pubs to have kept its 'gallows' inn-sign stretching right across the road *(John A Archer)*

Elham [St Marys Rd; TR1743], *Kings Arms*: Consistently well run, very attractive bar, steps down to big dining area with interesting choice of good reasonably priced food; good open fire, pool table in public bar *(Ian Phillips, L M Miall)*

☆ **Eynsford** [TQ5365], *Malt Shovel*: Spacious dining pub with wide range of bar food from ploughman's or well filled prawn sandwiches up inc lots of seafood in big helpings; real ales inc Boddingtons, Morlands Old Speckled Hen, Wadworths 6X, friendly staff, nice atmosphere, pleasant if not smart furnishings; wine pricey; handy for castle and Lullingstone Roman villa *(Nigel Gibbs, Martyn Hart, G Futcher, D W Welton)*

☆ **Faversham** [31 the Mall, handy for M2 junction 6; TR0161], *Elephant*: Pretty pub doing well under welcoming go-ahead newish licensees, good range of ambitious food inc imaginative vegetarian dishes, good choice of changing real ales, prompt service, simple but attractive furnishings;

summer barbecues *(Pat and Andy Veitch, Mrs K E Neville-Rolfe, C J Parsons, Louise Weekes)*

☆ **Finglesham** [The Street; just off A258 Sandwich—Deal; TR3353], *Crown*: Pleasant 16th-c country pub, attractively refurbished without losing its charm, with wide choice of reasonably priced good food in bar and popular olde-worlde restaurant with inglenook fireplace and flagstones; good friendly service, lovely garden *(Alan and Edwina Prior)*

☆ **Fordwich** [off A28 in Sturry; TR1759], *Fordwich Arms*: Generous helpings of decent plain cooking inc fresh veg in civilised and handsome pub with open fire in attractive fireplace, Whitbreads-related real ales, discreet piped music; spacious garden by River Stour *(Russell and Margaret Bathie, LYM)*

☆ **Four Elms** [B2027/B269 E of Edenbridge; TQ4648], *Four Elms*: Popular dining pub, clean, homely and comfortable, with two big open fires, deep carpet, lots of interesting pictures and wall ornaments, with very wide choice of generous reasonably priced food inc good fish and veg, well kept Courage Directors and Harveys, decent wine, good service; children allowed; handy for Chartwell *(Colin Laffan, Rhoda and Jeff Collins, David and Michelle Hedges, Alan Kilpatrick)*

☆ **Frittenden** [TQ8141], *Bell & Jorrocks*: Traditional timber-framed village local, well kept Whitbreads-related ales, Battle of Britain memorabilia, good food *(Ian Sharp, Comus Elliott)*

☆ **Goudhurst** [TQ7238], *Star & Eagle*: Outstanding Wealden views esp from tables out behind this striking medieval inn with settles and Jacobean-style seats in heavily beamed open-plan bar, well kept Whitbreads-related ales, decent bar food, polite staff; children welcome; bedrooms comfortable *(G Leibou, Ralph A Raimi, LYM)*

☆ nr **Goudhurst** [A262 W], *Green Cross*: Good genuinely home-cooked bar food at attractive prices, good choice of real ales inc distant rarities, enjoyable though not exactly pubby atmosphere with open fires and friendly staff; beamed dining room for residents; bedrooms light and airy, good value *(A Preston)*

Gravesend [26 Wrotham Rd; TQ6473], *Prince Albert*: Genuine lively street-corner pub, well kept Shepherd Neame beers, traditional games *(Dr and Mrs A K Clarke)*

☆ **Great Chart** [Chart Rd; TQ9842], *Hooden Horse*: Six changing well kept real ales and local farm cider in flagstoned pub with friendly staff, short but interesting choice of generously served food, occasional Morris dancers *(Comus Elliott)*

Greenhill [TR1666], *Share & Coulter*: Traditional country pub with cosy relaxed atmosphere, Shepherd Neame Bishops Finger on handpump, friendly service

(Louise Weekes)

☆ **Hadlow** [Ashes Lane (off A26 Tonbridge Rd); TQ6349], *Rose Revived*: Friendly and attractive 16th-c pub with well kept beers inc Harveys and King & Barnes, good bar food inc well filled fresh sandwiches *(Andrew and Teresa Heffer, D and B Carter)*

Hastingleigh [TR0944], *Bowl*: Traditional village pub, friendly landlord, good choice of real ale inc some barrels on counter; in lovely countryside *(Comus Elliott)*

☆ **Hawkhurst** [Pipsden – A268 towards Rye; TQ7730], *Oak & Ivy*: Good pub atmosphere in comfortable and attractive old panelled inn with well kept Whitbreads-related real ales, friendly staff, generous good value home cooking inc popular Sun roasts, roaring log fires; attractive restaurant *(E G Parish)*

Hawkhurst [Rye Rd], *Queens Head*: Decent food inc good Sun lunch, attractive surroundings; bedrooms *(Mr and Mrs B W West)*

☆ **Heaverham** [Watery Lane – OS Sheet 188 map reference 572587; TQ5658], *Chequers*: Good choice of good food and friendly service in attractive two-bar country pub with well kept range of beers; lots of birds both caged and free in big garden *(L M Miall)*

Herne [TR1865], *Smugglers*: Cosy and busy old traditional village local with loads of atmosphere; well kept Shepherd Neame ales, friendly efficient service *(Louise Weekes)*

☆ **Hernhill** [2 miles from end of M2; TR0660], *Red Lion*: Generous helpings of well prepared and served home-cooked food inc children's dishes in 14th-c tiled and timbered building, olde-world without being twee – lots of old beams, log fires, flagstones; decent house wine, tea and coffee, very welcoming service; jazz nights, children allowed, heavily beamed upstairs restaurant; charming village setting by church and small daffodil-covered green *(Miss M Byrne, Peter Hitchcock, F Tomlin)*

☆ **Hever** [TQ4744], *Henry VIII*: Very handy for visitors to Hever Castle, with lots of Henry VIII items and motifs (even woven into the carpet); fine panelling (even in the ladies') and beams, friendly and comfortable feel, inglenook fireplace, good food from ploughman's to restaurantish dishes, well kept local and other beers, decent wines, good service; pondside lawn *(Paul and Sue Davis, LYM)*

Hodsoll Street [TQ6263], *Green Man*: Lovely country pub on green, lots of flowers inside and out, big garden with aviary and pet's corner; winter log fires, good choice of quality food lunchtimes and evenings (not Sun/Mon pm), pleasant staff *(Sandra Powell, E D Bailey)*

☆ **Hollingbourne** [Eyhorne St; B2163, off A20; TQ8354], *Dirty Habit*: Attractive old pub on Pilgrims Way with good choice of reasonably priced interesting food and of well kept real ales, decent house wines, flame-effect gas fire in big fireplace, games area, unobtrusive juke box *(Comus Elliott)*

Hollingbourne [Eyhorne St – OS Sheet 188 map reference 833547], *Windmill*: Great for summer eating, with play area in sunny garden; well kept Whitbreads-related ales, comfortable and interesting split-level bar with alcoves around central servery *(Jim Smallcraft)*

Horsmonden [TQ7040], *Gun & Spitroast*: Old-fashioned pub on village green, good range of Allied beers *(Comus Elliott)*

Horton Kirby [TQ5668], *Fighting Cocks*: Friendly helpful staff, good choice of food inc well presented sandwiches; big garden with bat and trap and boules *(Patricia Nutt)*

Hythe [Saltwood – OS Sheet 189 map reference 155358; TR1535], *Castle*: Good food such as grilled fresh sprats, pleasant service *(Derek Howse)*; [High St; TR1634], *White Hart*: Good food, small interesting wine list *(Margaret Lennard)*

☆ **Ide Hill** [off B2042 SW of Sevenoaks; TQ4851], *Cock*: Pretty old pub on charming village green, neatly modernised, with well kept Greene King ales, good range of straightforward bar food (not Sun evening, only snacks Sun lunchtime), fine log fire, bar billiards, piped music, some seats out in front; handy for Chartwell and nearby walks – so gets busy, with nearby parking sometimes out of the question *(Colin Laffan, David Dimock)*

Ightham [TQ5956], *Chequers*: Very comfortable oldish pub with discreet piped music, good range of hot and cold meals (no sandwiches); service can sometimes slow when busy *(M D Hare)*; [Crown Point (off A25)], *Crown Point*: Welcoming big place set back from road, handy for Ightham Mote; five different real ales, good value food, play area *(Colin Harnett)*

☆ **Ightham Common** [Common Rd; TQ5755], *Harrow*: Small, cosy and unsmart but very welcoming indeed in its individual way, with roaring log fire, papers to read, games, great fresh bar food, well kept real ales; restaurant evenings and Sun; bedrooms *(Paul and Sue Davis, Ingrid Abma, Andrew Langbar, David Wright)*

☆ **Kingsdown** [Cliff Rd; TR3748], *Rising Sun*: Small friendly 17th-c pub with decent food, well kept real ales, open fire, lovely cottage garden; nr beach *(Margaret Lomax)*

☆ *nr* **Lamberhurst** [Hook Green; B2169 towards T Wells; TQ6535], *Elephants Head*: Ancient country pub with rambling opened-up bar, heavy beams, some timbering, brick or oak flooring, log fire and woodburner, plush-cushioned pews etc; well kept Harveys ales, bar food; darts and fruit machine in small side area, picnic-table sets on back terrace and grass with play area (peaceful view), and by front green; nr Bayham Abbey and Owl House, very popular with families weekends *(C P and M G Stent, Anthony John, BHP, LYM)*

Langton Green [A264; TQ5538], *Hare*: Friendly pub with attractive decor, enjoyable food in room with long tables and books around the walls, well kept Greene King IPA and Abbot, good current management *(Mr and Mrs Bishop, Mr and Mrs T Hancock)*

☆ **Leigh** [Powder Mills; the village is pronounced Lye – OS Sheet 188 map reference 568469; TQ5446], *Plough*: Busy, rambling and well kept timbered country pub with good atmosphere, huge log fire, well kept ales inc Harveys, King & Barnes and Youngs, good value generous straightforward food from sandwiches up, Sun lunches in capacious old barn carvery, quick friendly service; juke box; tables in well kept big garden *(H H Denman)*

☆ **Littlebourne** [4 High St; TR2057], *King William IV*: Good freshly prepared food cooked by landlord's New Zealand wife, bright friendly service, good range of well kept real ales, interesting wines inc New World ones; bedrooms *(S D Samuels, Mr and Mrs Blake, Desmond and Gillian Bellew)*

Lower Hardres [TR1552], *Three Horseshoes*: Happy country pub with old-fashioned furnishings, good range of beers, bar food, classical piped music *(Gillian Fisher, LYM)*

Luddenham [TQ9862], *Mounted Rifleman*: With the retirement of its long-serving landlord this utterly unspoilt country pub – long a main entry – has closed

Lympne [Aldington Rd; TR1235], *County Members*: Comfortable, with wide choice of reasonably priced bar food and well kept real ales *(Desmond and Gillian Bellew)*

Maidstone [Weavering St; TQ7656], *Fox & Goose*: The pub this reader – who holds the record for the number he's been to – uses as his local; four well kept Courage-related ales, reasonable food inc most evenings *(Comus Elliott)*; [Havock Lane, opp central library and museum], *Royal Albion*: Good live music most nights, friendly atmosphere, lots of games inc pinball and table football *(John Brundrett)*

Martin [TR3346], *Old Lantern*: Old-world 17th-c pub beautifully placed in a quiet cul-de-sac in peaceful village; spotless comfortable lounge, good log fire, plenty of tables in attractive gardens, food inc good value prawn sandwiches; several red wines by glass *(Geoff Lindley)*

☆ **Meopham** [Meopham Green; A227 Gravesend—Wrotham; TQ6466], *Cricketers*: Good value imaginative food, cricket memorabilia, Allied ales and friendly service in 17th-c pub with tasteful modern restaurant extension; nice village-green setting *(Dave Braisted)*

Meopham, *George*: Hard-working new licensee, well kept beers, good food *(H E Prime)*

☆ **Mersham** [OS Sheet 179 map reference 049341; TR0539], *Farriers Arms*: Former early 17th-c forge, now an attractive and rather upmarket three-roomed local with good value straightforward bar food, well kept Allied ales, good friendly service; exceptionally well kept pleasant gardens behind; bedrooms *(Duncan Redpath, Comus Elliott)*

☆ Minster [42 Station Rd; the one nr Ramsgate; TR3164], *Mortons Fork*: Attractive country-style small bar and linked dining area in well kept small hotel, log fire, helpful friendly staff, good choice of varied reasonably priced unusual bar food inc good puddings, decent wine, good housekeeping; restaurant, tables outside; three luxurious bedrooms *(Michael Sargent)*

☆ Molash [TR0251], *George*: Interesting food inc outstanding sandwiches and enormous ploughman's in pleasant 16th-c character country pub, friendly helpful service, well kept Whitbreads Castle Eden; pleasant garden, plenty of pets *(John Whitehead)*

Nettlestead [B2015 Pembury—Maidstone; TQ6852], *Hop Pole*: Good atmosphere and fresh flowers in recently extended pub among the orchards, good food, well kept beer, decent wine, central fire; courteous and friendly staff *(Mr and Mrs A P Reeves)*

☆ Oare [Ham Rd, Hollowshore; 1/2 mile track off Faversham—Oare road, on E side of Oare Creek – OS Sheet 178 map reference 016635; TR0163], *Shipwrights Arms*: Good relaxed atmosphere in remote and ancient traditional tavern, superb shoreside location, lots of old-fashioned character, interesting decorations, log fire, well kept Shepherd Neame, good chippy food inc popular pizzas; down daunting bumpy track to nowhere through marshes – not a journey to take if you want more sophistication *(Louise Weekes, Susan Elliott, LYM)*

☆ Offham [TQ6557], *Kings Arms*: Warm welcome, well kept Courage Best, good range of bar food, reasonable prices, log fire, lots of interesting ancient tools; good draught beer, piped music; attractive village *(K Flack)*

☆ Otford [High St; TQ5359], *Crown*: Pretty pub opp pond in delightful village, character beamed bar, friendly staff, well presented reasonably priced food from good sandwiches through imaginative main dishes to Sun lunch, well kept Allied ales, decent house wines, good mix of age-groups, nice setting; occasional jazz evenings, lovely garden behind *(Mrs S J Findlay, Russell and Margaret Bathie, Jan and Colin Roe, Thomas Nott)*

☆ Otford [High St], *Bull*: Limited range of decent bar food inc sandwiches, well kept Courage-related real ales, helpful service, attractive garden, good family room *(Thomas Nott)*

☆ Otford [High St], *Horns*: Very attentive friendly service and good if not cheap food in well kept and cosy 15th-c beamed pub with several well kept real ales inc Harveys and King & Barnes; log fire in big inglenook *(Alan Jarvis)*

Paddock Wood [Matfield—Tonbridge; TQ6745], *Dovecote*: Pretty and well run pub with flowers and baskets outside, friendly obliging landlord *(Heather Martin)*

Pembury [TQ6240], *Black Horse*: Small pleasantly modernised pub with well kept real ales, friendly staff, quick food, tidy little restaurant/carvery; children's garden neat and well kept *(Thomas Nott)*

☆ Penshurst [centre; TQ5243], *Leicester Arms*: Wide choice of good bar food, surprisingly reasonably priced, in well kept undaunting hotel bar with extended eating area, quiet corners, prompt friendly service; in charming village by Penshurst Place; decent bedrooms *(W J Wonham, P Neate, Tim and Pam Moorey)*

☆ Penshurst [Hoath Corner – OS Sheet 188 map reference 497431], *Rock*: Good atmosphere in ancient beamed pub tucked out in the country, good straightforward generous home-made food, well kept local Larkins and other ales, inglenook, ring the bull; tables outside *(Comus Elliott, J A Snell, R and S Bentley)*

Petteridge [TQ6740], *Hopbine*: King & Barnes and other ales, very friendly atmosphere, good generous home-made food, folk night every third Sun *(Gillian and Tony Betts)*

☆ Plaxtol [Sheet Hill; TQ6054], *Golding Hop*: Secluded little country pub with sun-trap streamside lawn, real ales such as Adnams Broadside tapped from the cask, choice of ciders (sometimes even their own), limited bar food (not Mon evening), straightforward country furniture, woodburner – but rather a take-it-or-leave-it atmosphere *(L M Miall, LYM)*

☆ Pluckley [TQ9245], *Black Horse*: Cosy and attractive, with vast inglenook, comfortable furnishings with something of the feel of a good city pub, big restaurant area popular for business lunches, good choice of well cooked and presented if not cheap generous food (esp puddings); friendly staff and black cat, well kept Whitbreads-related real ales; pleasant orchard garden *(Mr and Mrs Taylor, G Futcher, Andrew and Ruth Triggs)*

☆ Pluckley [Munday Bois], *Rose & Crown*: Small pub with good varied food at reasonable prices, well kept real ales, imaginative wines, nice atmosphere in restaurant, good service; friendly dog *(A Honigmann, D K and H M Brenchley)*

☆ Rochester [10 St Margarets St; TQ7467], *Coopers Arms*: Very friendly licensees in comfortable and neatly kept old local, said to be Kent's oldest; quaint and interesting, with good value bar lunches, well kept Courage-related ales; handy for castle and cathedral *(Elizabeth and Klaus Leist)*

☆ Rolvenden Layne [TQ8530], *Another Hooden Horse*: Recent addition to small chain (see Great Chart entry), already very popular for good reasonably priced home-made food, good range of beers and local ciders and wine, good friendly staff; beams, hops and candlelight, no music or machines *(Peter and Vivian Symes, Paul Adams, Ewa Sawicka)*

Ruckinge [B2067 1½ miles E of Ham Street; TR0233], *Blue Anchor*: Good value, well kept and friendly, with Whitbreads-related and guest ales, home-cooked food inc good big all-day breakfast; tastefully furnished conservatory, garden with pretty pond *(Rob and Doris Harrison)*

☆ **Sandgate** [Brewers Lane – main rd towards Hythe, then 100 yds or so after it emerges on to sea front park opp telephone box on R (beware high tides) and walk up steep cobbled track beside it; TR2035], *Clarendon*: Relatively cheap well cooked food inc delicious clams in fine low-beamed simply furnished backstreet local, marvellous Kent CC cricket memorabilia, friendly licensees, consistently well kept Shepherd Neame esp Spitfire, splendid dog *(L M Miall, Terry Buckland)*

Sandgate [High St], *Ship*: Usually eight changing well kept real ales, cheap and cheerful home-made bar food, good service, character landlord, seafaring theme, genuinely old furnishings; seats outside *(A B Dromey)*

☆ **Sarre** [TR2565], *Crown*: Comfortable and carefully restored old pub with good range of reasonably priced home-cooked food, well kept Shepherd Neame; bedrooms *(Jim and Maggie Cowell)*

☆ **Sevenoaks** [London Rd, nr stn; 2½ miles from M25 junction 5;TQ5355], *Halfway House*: Quiet and friendly partly 16th-c local with well kept Greene King IPA, Abbot and Rayments, wide range of reasonably priced home-made food inc good fresh veg, good service, very accommodating landlord, oak beams and horsebrasses *(Miss J C Drumey, Pam and Tim Moorey, K Widdowson, Ian Phillips)*

Sevenoaks [Bessels Green, just off A21], *Kings Head*: Popular for food inc good range of good value Sun roasts; well kept Allied ales *(David Dimock)*; [A225 just S], *Royal Oak Tap*: Quite independent of neighbouring Royal Oak Hotel, with well kept Boddingtons, Fremlins, Wadworths 6X and Websters, interesting food such as hot salt beef sandwich with dill pickle, two real fires, big conservatory *(Ian Phillips)*; [Tonbridge Rd – A225 S, past Knole], *White Hart*: Recently refurbished and comfortable, with some old settles, two bars, two dining areas, Friary Meux real ale, pleasant lawns with well established shrubs *(Ian Phillips)*

☆ **nr Sevenoaks** [Godden Green, off B2019 just E;TQ5555], *Bucks Head*: Cheery and quaint old village-green local in pretty spot by duckpond, surrounded by cherry blossom in spring; particularly well kept Courage-related and guest beers, friendly atmosphere, interesting normally good bar food, cosy furnishings; in attractive walking country nr Knole *(Tony Gayfer, Comus Elliott, David Wright)*

☆ **Shipbourne** [Stumble Hill; TQ5952], *Chaser*: Clean and well run hotel in lovely spot by village church and green, friendly service, ploughman's and home-made meals in bar and restaurant, decent wines, tables outside; bedrooms *(Tim and Pam Moorey, Andrew and Teresa Heffer, Christopher H Dent, R C Morgan)*

☆ **Shoreham** [TQ5161], *Kings Arms*: Pretty and popular little pub in picturesque village on River Darent; good food inc good value ploughman's, Ruddles beer, interesting decorations inc waxwork ostler relate to pub's coaching days; free Sun bar nibbles, tables outside, good nearby walks *(Jenny and Brian Seller, K R Flack)*

☆ **Sissinghurst** [TQ7937], *Bull*: Very welcoming airily modernised pub with good pleasant dark-beamed restaurant area specialising in generous Italian food inc good pizzas and pasta, also bar food from sandwiches and ploughman's up, quick willing service, Whitbreads-related ales, quiet piped music, fruit machine; good garden *(Joan and Gordon Griffes, C P and M G Stent, A N Black, Mr and Mrs F G Browning)*

☆ **Smarden** [TQ8842], *Chequers*: Welcoming and comfortable olde-worlde pub, cosy and relaxed, with plenty of character, beams, log fire, varied choice of really good and generous food inc vegetarian dishes, lots of seasonal veg and real puddings, well kept Courage ales, big cat, no music or machines; pleasant tables outside; bedrooms simple (and some within earshot of bar) but good value, with exceptionally good breakfasts *(J Biesmans, Gordon)*

Snargate [Romney Marsh; B2080 Appledore—Brenzett – OS Sheet 189 map reference 990285; TQ9828], *Red Lion*: Wonderfully unspoilt 19th-c pub with well kept Adnams and Batemans; no food *(Phil and Sally Gorton)*

☆ **Southfleet** [off A2 via A227 S towards Southfleet; or from B262 turn left at Ship in Southfleet then sharp right into Red St – pub about half-mile on right;TQ6171], *Black Lion*: Very friendly staff in cheerful and well run character two-room local with good barbecue in big shrub-sheltered garden, good generous bar food from ploughman's up (not cheap), well kept Adnams, Greene King Abbot and Courage-related beers, helpful staff, friendly airedale; handsome no-smoking restaurant; children in eating area *(E J and J W Cutting, Darren Ford, Ian and Nita Cooper, Michael and Jenny Back, LYM)*

☆ **St Margarets at Cliffe** [High Street; TR3644], *Cliffe Tavern Hotel*: Attractive clapboard-and-brick inn opp church, with pleasantly decorated bar and larger open-plan lounge, secluded back walled garden, several well kept real ales, decent wines, often imaginative bar food from sandwiches up using fresh local produce, bedrooms mostly in cottages across yard; has open all day Sat, allowing well behaved children; as the large number of recommenders shows, is very popular indeed with a great many readers, but some recent disappointments (often with service – normally a strong point here) *(Dr C A Brace, Mr and Mrs Moody, Hazel Morgan, Michael Butler, Jay Voss, Dorothee and Dennis Glover, Phil Godwin, Richard Waller, M Veldhuyzen, Mr and Mrs S McQuade, Walter Reid, D A Edwards, LYM)*

☆ **St Margarets Bay** [on shore below Nat Trust cliffs; TR3844], *Coastguard*: Remarkable views from modernised pub by sea; current management doing well, with well kept sensibly priced real ales, good range of food esp vegetarian; lots of tables outside *(J Watson, Mark Thompson, J Ryeland, LYM)*

☆ **St Mary in the Marsh** [TR0628], *Star*: Most enjoyable for friendly relaxed atmosphere, remote situation and quietness (at least at lunchtime – piped music may be noticeable evenings); well kept Shepherd Neame inc Mild tapped from the cask, run by friendly family; bedrooms attractive, with views of Romney Marsh *(A Preston, BB)*

St Nicholas at Wade [just off A299; TR2666], *Bell*: Olde-worlde, with four separate beamed rooms, friendly staff, winter open fire, good seafood and good puddings *(Judy Booth)*

☆ **Stalisfield Green** [off A252 in Charing; TQ9553], *Plough*: Pretty pub in charming setting, good choice of well presented home-cooked food inc good fish, friendly service, big but tasteful side extension, tables in large garden, good view *(Miss M Byrne, Evelyn and Derek Walter)*

☆ **Staplehurst** [Chart Hill Rd – OS Sheet 188 map reference 785472; TQ7847], *Lord Raglan*: Charming new licensees doing good interesting food (husband cooks) in 17th-c beamed pub with three open fires, well kept real ales, good coffee, no piped music; picnic-table sets outside *(R D Knight)*

Stockbury [Stockbury Green; TQ8361], *Harrow*: Good food on big platters, esp prawn and pineapple curry, Shepherd Neame ales with a guest beer, good choice of wines, friendly new landlord *(R Owen)*

☆ **Stowting** [off B2068 N of M20 junction 11; TR1242], *Tiger*: Charming country pub of considerable individuality, with attractive unpretentious furniture, candles on tables, faded rugs on bare boards, good bar food from sandwiches to steaks, well kept Adnams, Boddingtons, Everards Tiger, Ind Coope Burton, Tetleys, Wadworths 6X and guest beers, Biddenden farm cider, good log fire, tables outside with occasional barbecues; well behaved children allowed, jazz Mon *(P Butler, A B Dromey, Ian Phillips, Dave Braisted, Comus Elliott, LYM)*

Sutton Valence [TQ8149], *Swan*: Usual food inc various ploughman's and salads, Whitbreads-related and other ales such as Wadworths 6X; pretty village nr Leeds Castle *(MAS, CRS)*

Tankerton [TR1267], *Tankerton Arms*: Friendly and busy pub overlooking sea, good food inc good vegetarian and vegan range, well kept beer inc Fullers London Pride, farm cider; pool, jazz Tues; summer entertainer outdoors *(Louise Weekes)*

☆ **Tenterden** [High St; TQ8833], *Woolpack*: Good generous home-cooked food inc good value specials in striking and attractive 15th-c inn, several oak-beamed rooms inc family dining room, inglenook log fires, pleasant atmosphere, friendly efficient staff, well kept Whitbreads-related and other ales, decent coffee; open all day; comfortable bedrooms *(Andrew and Ruth Triggs, J Watson)*

Tenterden [St Michaels; 3/4 miles towards Biddenden; TQ8835], *Man of Kent*: Nice friendly pub with small eating area serving sensibly priced bar food inc good pies and Sun lunch; garden with play area for children *(A M Pring)*

Toys Hill [OS Sheet 188 map reference 470520; TQ4751], *Fox & Hounds*: Small, dark, old-fashioned and full of domestic furniture – a bit like going into someone's (rather dusty) back room; well kept Greene King beers, lovely display of photographs *(Phil and Sally Gorton, Jenny and Brian Seller)*

☆ **Tunbridge Wells** [High Rocks; actually just over the Sussex border; TQ5638], *High Rocks*: Extensively refurbished pub in beautiful gardens with attractive views opp sandstone climbing rocks (small fee), good reasonably priced food in big restaurant and smaller bar area, hard-working continental staff, jazz some evenings; open all day, children welcome *(P Gillbe, Simon Small)*

Tunbridge Wells [Tea Garden Lane, Rusthall], *Beacon*: Good food under new licensee in pub/restaurant with plenty of comfortable sofas, jazz and theatre events *(Peter Neate)*; [St Johns Rd], *Flute & Flypaper*: Deceptive pub with shopfront-style entrance, comfortable top bar, cellar games bar with beams and tiled floor, good atmosphere *(Phil)*; [29 Mount Ephraim], *George*: Unpretentious local, good value straightforward food freshly cooked to order, interesting range of beers *(Dr G M Regan)*; [Mount Edgcumbe Hotel], *La Galoche Bar*: Has been a popular main entry for its good food (inc outstanding cheeses) and wines, making it a good civilised lunch stop, but the owners who'd put so much thought into this sold the hotel in 1994; comfortable bedrooms *(LYM)*

☆ **Warren Street** [just off A20 at top of North Downs – OS Sheet 189 map reference 926529; TQ9253], *Harrow*: Quiet and comfortable extended dining pub on Pilgrims Way, 16th-c low-beamed core, neat furnishings, flowers and candles, faint piped music, big woodburner; attentive service, generous helpings of well cooked food, well kept Shepherd Neame and a guest beer on handpump, sensible prices; restaurant (not Sun evening) with attractive conservatory extension; good bedrooms *(J A Snell, Comus Elliott, BB)*

☆ **West Farleigh** [B2010 off A26 Tonbridge—Maidstone; TQ7152], *Tickled Trout*: Attractively renovated old pub with Medway views (esp from garden), well kept Whitbreads-related ales, good food in bar and restaurant with good choice of vegetarian and fish dishes, fast friendly service; path down to river with good walks in either direction *(C P and M G Stent, Comus Elliott, Robert Hurling, LYM)*

West Malling [High St; TQ6857], *Bear*: Good choice of good home-made food, well kept beer, friendly efficient service; plenty of room *(J W Joseph)*

☆ **West Peckham** [TQ6452], *Swan*: Wonderful country setting, popular on summer weekends, with wide range of good food, Harveys on handpump *(K Flack, C O Day)*

Westerham [Grays Rd, Hawley Corner; A233 to Biggin Hill; TQ4454], *Spinning Wheel*: Particularly well appointed Brewers Fayre pub-restaurant, open all day, with good food, pleasant waitresses, family dining room, facilities for disabled *(E G Parish)*

Whitstable [seafront; TR1166], *Old Neptune*: Seafront pub, busy, friendly and relaxed, real ales inc Morlands Old Speckled Hen; good food inc vegetarian, dogs and children welcome; tables out on beach *(Louise Weekes)*

Wingham [Canterbury Rd; TR2457], *Dog*: Dating from 13th c, with lots of character, exposed beams etc; Whitbreads-related ales, good food; good value bedrooms *(P G Hicks)*

☆ **Wingham Well** [Mill Rd; TR2356], *Eight Bells*: Friendly and comfortably modernised late 18th-c pub with unusual split-level bar area, restaurant and play area; good food

inc vegetarian choice and good steaks, well kept real ale *(S J Raine, Pat and Andy Veitch, BB)*

Woodlands [nr Otford; TQ5560], *Rising Sun*: Good choice of food and Whitbreads-related ales with a guest such as Larkins in old-world pub with main bar, small games room, family room and dining area; large front garden with picnic-table sets, handy for North Downs Way walkers *(Ian S Morley)*

☆ **Worth** [The Street; TR3356], *St Crispin*: Lovely gardens, lovely village position not far from beach, eight well kept ales inc four changing guests, wide range of good value fresh food eg home-made soup, local asparagus, crab, steak and kidney pie, duck breast in gooseberry sauce, 16oz T-bone, seafood platter; busy but very friendly and relaxed refurbished bar, restaurant; comfortable bedrooms *(A B Dromey, C P and M G Stent, Russell and Margaret Bathie)*

☆ **Wrotham** [signposted 1¾ miles from M20, junction 2; TQ6159], *Bull*: 14th-c inn in attractive village, friendly licensee, attractive bar, good food, log fires, well kept Whitbreads-related ales, decent wines, friendly staff; children welcome, separate restaurant; comfortable bedrooms, huge breakfasts *(P Walker, LYM)*

☆ **Wye** [signed off A28 NE of Ashford; TR0546], *Tickled Trout*: Pleasant riverside lawn, spacious conservatory/restaurant, bar done out in rustic style, straightforward bar food, Whitbreads-related ales on handpump; children allowed *(E D Bailey, LYM)*

☆ **Yalding** [Yalding Hill; TQ7050], *Walnut Tree*: Well kept Fremlins and Wadworths 6X in attractive beamed bar with inglenook and interesting pictures, good friendly new licensees, bar food and restaurant; bedrooms *(John and Elspeth Howell, Jenny and Brian Seller)*

Real ale to us means beer which has matured naturally in its cask – not pressurised or filtered. We name all real ales stocked. We usually name ales preserved under a light blanket of carbon dioxide too, though purists – pointing out that this stops the natural yeasts developing – would disagree (most people, including us, can't tell the difference!).

Lancashire (including Greater Manchester and Merseyside)

Pubs here offer better value than anywhere else in Britain. The price of drinks is well below the national average – so far below that drinkers here typically pay 40p less for a pint of beer than drinkers in much of the south-east of England. The main reason for these low prices is the fact that thriving competing regional and local brewers here have a significant share of the market. This has broken the monopoly grip of the national brewing chains, so that they can't get away with charging the high prices that they do elsewhere – either in their own pubs or in chains which are now more or less exclusively supplied by them such as Boddingtons and Greenalls. A symptom of this vigorous price competition is that in this area we have found that there isn't such a wide variation between individual pubs as we tend to find elsewhere: prices are spread over quite a tight range. Even so, it's in pubs supplied by regional brewers (Robinsons, Thwaites) and local ones (Holts, Hydes, J W Lees; and Sam Smiths and maybe Timothy Taylors from Yorkshire) that prices do tend to be lowest – Holts in particular is an outstandingly cheap brewer. Pub food prices too are much lower than the national average: a good main dish typically costs £1 or £1.50 less than in the south – and probably comes in a more generous helping. The best pub food we've found here is in the Moorcock up at Blacko (even using their own lamb raised on the surrounding moors), the Dog & Partridge at Chipping (excellent choice of wines, too), the Bushells Arms at Goosnargh (another with good wines), the Romper in its superb setting above Marple, the Devonshire Arms in Mellor (not sophisticated but all home-made – stands out for the Stockport area), the friendly Parkers Arms at Newton in the Forest of Bowland, and the New Inn at Yealand Conyers up near the Lake District, doing well under its new licensees. Of these pubs, we choose the Moorcock at Blacko as Lancashire Dining Pub of the Year, for its winning combination of very good often inventive food with most attractive surroundings. Three Manchester pubs, the Mark Addy, its new-entry sister pub the Dukes 92, and above all the Royal Oak in Didsbury (heroically restored after a serious arson attack), stand out for a fine choice of tremendous value cheeses. Other pubs currently doing particularly well here include the amazingly cheap Black Dog at Belmont, Owd Nells at Bilsborrow (very commercialised but particularly good for families), the very friendly Old Rosins near Darwen (a good place to stay), the Philharmonic in Liverpool (wonderful building, very cheap food), the Taps in Lytham (recently successfully done out as a thorough-going real ale pub), the vibrant and atmospheric (if sometimes studenty) Lass o' Gowrie in Manchester, the Red Lion at Newburgh (a new main entry, very useful for all-day food), the White Bull in Ribchester (another new main entry, a good value family food pub), the Waterside at Summerseat (yet another new entry, *a most interesting building in unexpected surroundings), the cosy Rock at Tockholes (winning a Wine Award for the first time this year), and above all the Inn at Whitewell, with loads of character in a lovely setting – especially well liked as a place to stay in. Some pubs to pick out in the Lucky Dip section at the end of the chapter are the Coach & Horses at Bolton by Bowland, Black Lion at Croston (perhaps our favourite real ale pub in the area, with good home-made food), Rams Head at Denshaw, Assheton Arms at Downham, Strawbury Duck at Entwistle, Golden Ball at Heaton with Oxcliffe, Egerton Arms near Heywood, Water Witch in Lancaster, Ship at Lathom, Kettledrum at Mereclough, Hark to Bounty at Slaidburn, Red Bull in Stockport, Seven Stars at Thornton Hough, Old Sparrow Hawk at Wheatley Lane and Freemasons Arms at Wiswell: we have inspected virtually all of these so can vouch for their quality. There is a fine choice of interesting pubs in Manchester (much less so in Liverpool). Note that we include the Wirral and the area around Stockport to the south of Manchester in this chapter as they are officially part of Merseyside and Greater Manchester respectively (and have been for the last 20 or so years), though many of their inhabitants still think of them as being in Cheshire.*

---

nr BALDERSTONE (Lancs) SD6332 Map 7

Myerscough Hotel

Whalley Rd, Salmesbury; A59 Preston—Skipton, over 3 miles from M6 junction 31

The character of this 18th-c pub might vary according to the time of day, but the atmosphere is always welcoming and friendly. At lunchtime it's a popular food stop and feels quite bustling, usually busy with businessmen, families or workers from the British Aerospace plant across the road; it's very handy for the M6. In the evening the emphasis is less on food and more on the pub side, with the mood becoming more relaxed. At times like these the softly-lit bar has a pleasant cottagey feel and appearance, and under its beams are a number of well made and comfortable oak settles around dimpled copper or heavy cast-iron-framed tables, as well as nice ink and pen drawings of local scenes, a painting of the month by a local artist, and lots of brass and copper. The serving counter has a nice padded elbow rest, and dispenses well kept Robinsons Best and Mild and Hartleys XB on handpump, and several malt whiskies; shove-ha'penny, dominoes, and fruit machine. At lunchtime, good bar food includes home-made soup (£1.20), sandwiches (from £1.50; the open ham is good), ploughman's or steak escalopes on granary barm cake (£3.20), chilli or home-made curry (£3.50), steak and kidney pie (£3.95), gammon (£4.50), braised steak (£4.95), specials like grilled liver and bacon or fish (from £3.95), and puddings; prices are unchanged from last year. Service is obliging and friendly. There are picnic-table sets, bantams and their chicks, and rabbits in the garden. *(Recommended by Russell and Margaret Bathie, Phil and Dilys Unsworth, P Boot; more reports please)*

Robinsons ~ Tenant John Pedder ~ Real ale ~ Meals and snacks (12-2, 6.30-8.30) ~ Mellor (01254) 812222 ~ Well behaved children in front room till 8.30 ~ Weds quiz night ~ Open 11.30-3, 5.30-11

BELMONT (Lancs) SD6716 Map 7

Black Dog

A675

Cosy is the word that everyone uses to describe this characterful 18th-c farmhouse, an unpretentious little place that's still a real favourite with readers, not least because of the very good value food and drinks. As we went to press the Holts Mild was on sale for just 92p a pint and the well kept Bitter didn't cost much more, at around half what you'd expect to pay for a pint in most southern pubs, and nearly 20p less than the county average. The original cheery and traditional small rooms are packed with antiques and bric-a-brac, from railwaymen's lamps, bedpans and chamber-pots to landscape paintings, as well as service bells for the sturdy built-in curved seats, rush-seated mahogany chairs, and coal fires. The atmosphere is perhaps best on a winter evening, especially if you're tucked away in one of the various snug alcoves, one of which used to house the village court. The landlord may be happily whistling along to the piped classical music, and they have occasional orchestral concerts. Popular and good value bar food includes home-made soup (£1.20; they do a winter broth with dumplings), sandwiches (from £1.30; steak barm cake £1.70), ploughman's (from £2.90), steak and kidney pie, gammon, lamb cutlets or scampi (£3.60), curry (£3.80), well liked salads with various fruits like grape, banana and strawberry, steaks (from £5) and daily specials like pork in stilton and celery sauce, braised steak in red wine or pepperoni, pasta and chilli bake. There may be some delays to food service at busy times (they fill up quite quickly), but it is generally worth the wait. An airy extension lounge with a picture window has more modern furnishings; morning coffee, darts, pool, shove-ha'penny, dominoes, cribbage, and fruit machine. From two long benches on the sheltered sunny side of the pub there are delightful views of the moors above the nearby trees and houses; there's a track from the village up Winter Hill and (from the lane to Rivington) on to Anglezarke Moor, and paths from the dam of the nearby Belmont Reservoir. *(Recommended by JJW, CMW, Comus Elliott, Bill and Lydia Ryan, S R and A I Ashcroft, Wayne Brindle, R B Berry, G L Tong, Richard Davies, Patrick Clancy, Andy and Julie Hawkins, Mayur Shah, MMD, Mr and Mrs John Gilks, P Boot)*

Holts ~ Tenant James Pilkington ~ Real ale ~ Meals and snacks (not Mon or Tues evenings except for residents) ~ Belmont (01204) 811218 ~ Children welcome away from bar ~ 9-piece orchestra four times a year ~ Open 12-4, 7-11 ~ Bedrooms: £29.50B/£38B

BILSBORROW (Lancs) SD5139 Map 7

Owd Nells 🍺

Guy's Thatched Hamlet, St Michaels Road; at S end of village (which is on A6 N of Preston) take Myerscough College turn

Not at all the kind of place you'd come to for a quiet drink, but ideal as part of a family day out, this is part of a thriving little complex that's transformed a previously neglected stretch of canal; as well as the pub there's an expanding hotel with indoor pool and gym and various craft and tea shops. All quite artificial of course (cynics would say gimmicky) but none the worse for that, and they do a good range of popular well priced food; it's especially welcoming to children. Good helpings of bar meals such as home-made soup (£1.20), cheese and pickles (£2.70), local potted shrimps (£3), burgers or steak sandwich (£3.85), steak and kidney pudding or big fish and chips (£4.60), barbecue chicken (£4.50) and minute steak (£6.25), with afternoon sandwiches (from £2.30), and useful late-evening snacks such as deep-fried courgette strips (£2), buffalo wings (£3.10) and fresh prawns (£4); waitress service is prompt and slickly professional even under pressure – it often gets busy, especially in school holidays. The three or four spacious communicating rooms have a mix of brocaded button-back banquettes, stable-stall seating, library chairs and other seats, high pitched rafters at either end, and lower beams (and flagstones) by the bar counter in the middle; a couple of areas are no smoking. Well kept Boddingtons, Whitbreads Castle Eden and an interesting choice of weekly changing guests like Dents Bitter, Flowers Original, Mitchells, Moorhouses Pendle Witches Brew, Robinsons Best and a couple of local brews on handpump, several wines including a bargain house champagne, tea and coffee; video game, fruit machine, Connect Four, and unobtrusive piped pop music. Children are made especally welcome; there may be free lollipops and they'll give you bags of bread for feeding the ducks. Colourful seats out on the terrace, part of which is covered by a thatched roof; a small walled-in play area has a timber castle, and you can play cricket or boules. There may be Morris dancers out here on summer weekends. More bedrooms are under construction. *(Recommended by Gill and Keith Croxton, Brian and Jill Bond, John Atherton, Sarah Elliott, Gary Goldson, Bronwen and Steve Wrigley, Jim and Maggie Cowell, Fred Collier, D Grzelka, Alan Reid, Chris Heathman, Carl Travis, Michael Butler, Andy and Julie Hawkins, D C Holt, Eric Locker)*

Free house ~ Licensee Roy Wilkinson ~ Real ale ~ Meals (11-9) and snacks (all day) ~ Next-door restaurant; open all day inc Sun ~ (01995) 640010/640020 ~ Children welcome ~ Morris dancing in square, craft demos ~ Open 11-11; closed 25 Dec ~ Bedrooms: 37B/£42B

BLACKO (Lancs) SD8541 Map 7

Moorcock

A682; N of village towards Gisburn

Lancashire Dining Pub of the Year

It's the excellent food that quite deservedly brings most people to this well placed old stone inn. All home-made by the landlady, well presented bar meals might typically include soup (£1.75), a substantial ploughman's (from £4.95, with proper little pots of butter), pâté (£1.95), chilliburger or savoury pancakes (£4.95), steak and kidney pie or a good few vegetarian dishes such as wheat and walnut bake, vegetable biriani or stuffed peppers (£4.95), unusual continental specialities like splendid bratwürst (£4.50) and schweinschnitzel (£5), whole ham shank in a light mustard sauce (£5.50), salmon in maybe a scallop, prawn and mussel sauce (£5.95), halibut mornay (£6.50), steaks (from £6.50 for minute steak), first-rate specials such as pork fillet in a Calvados, apple and raisin sauce or roast duckling in black cherry and brandy, and puddings like strawberry and white chocolate cheesecake, Irish coffee meringue or good fruit pies (£2.15); Sunday roasts. They do a number of lamb dishes, with the meat coming from their own flock. The bar is spaciously comfortable, with breath-taking views from the big picture windows, a lofty ceiling, and cream walls hung with brass ornaments. Well kept Thwaites Bitter and Best Mild on handpump; friendly sheepdog. Service is efficient and cheery. The attractively landscaped back garden is very busy at weekends, though quieter during the week; there's usually a retired collie out here along with a goat, a couple of lambs, game cocks, and lots of white doves. The pub used to be a farmhouse and the landlord maintains the tradition, often out with his sheep around the Blacko Tower a mile or so across the moors. His collie puppies go to other working farms as far afield as Ireland, Canada and America. *(Recommended by Gwen and Peter Andrews, Roger and Christine Mash, Paul McPherson, G L Tong, Michael Butler, Olive Carroll, Brian Kneale)*

Thwaites ~ Tenant Elizabeth Holt ~ Meals and snacks (till 10) ~ Nelson (01282) 614186 ~ Children welcome ~ Open 11.30-2.30, 7-11; open all day Sun; closed 25 Dec

BLACKSTONE EDGE (Gtr Manchester) SD9716 Map 7

White House

A58 Ripponden—Littleborough, just W of B6138

The Pennine Way crosses the road outside this imposing old pub, high up on the bleak and moody moors with panoramic views stretching for miles into the distance. Even in summer it somehow manages to seem windswept up here, and the cosy rooms of the 17th-c building seem especially appealing. The cheery main bar has a large-scale map of the area and a turkey carpet in front of a blazing coal fire; the snug Pennine Room opens off here, with brightly coloured antimacassars on its small soft settees, and there's a new extension. A spacious room on the left has a big horseshoe window looking over the moors, as well as comfortable seating and coloured pins on a map of the world showing where foreign visitors have come from. Good helpings of homely bar food include sandwiches, home-made vegetable soup, very popular garlic mushrooms, Cumberland sausage with egg (£3.25), quiche lorraine, lasagne or home-made steak and kidney pie (£3.50), salads, and 8oz sirloin steak (£7.50); also, daily specials and home-made apple pie (£1.25); children's meals. Good friendly service. Well kept beers on handpump such as Black Sheep Bitter, Marstons Pedigree, Moorhouses Pendle Witches Brew and Theakstons Best, farm cider, and malt whiskies; trivia, fruit machine. It's a popular stop for walkers, whose muddy boots can be left in the long, enclosed porch. *(Recommended by Paul Wreglesworth, G W Lindley, Ian and Emma Potts, M L Clarke, Mr and Mrs John Gilks)*

Free house ~ Licensee Neville Marney ~ Real ale ~ Meals and snacks (till 10) ~ Restaurant ~ Littleborough (01706) 378456 ~ Children welcome ~ Open 11.30-3, 7-11

BRINDLE (Lancs) SD6024 Map 7

Cavendish Arms

3 miles from M6 junction 29; A6 towards Whittle-le-Woods then left on B5256

Some of the woodwork partitions in this snugly civilised old pub have fascinating stained-glass scenes with lively depictions of medieval warriors and minstrels. Many of them commemorate the bloody battle of Brundenburg, a nasty skirmish between the Vikings and Anglo-Saxons on the Ribble estuary. Quite a cheery place, several cosy little rooms ramble around a central servery, each with quite a distinct character and filled with comfortable seats, little partitions, discreet flowery curtains, and lots of pictorial plates and Devonshire heraldic devices in plaster on the walls. Well kept Burtonwood Best and Mild on handpump, and a good choice of malt whiskies; if it's quiet the friendly licensees are very happy to chat about the pub's history. There are white metal and plastic tables and chairs on a terrace by a rockery with a small water cascade, with another table on a small lawn behind. Simple, straightforward bar food includes soup (£1.50), home-made beef or chicken pie (£4), seafood platter (£4.75), home-made lasagne or crispy battered cod (£5), grilled salmon (£5.25) and roast beef and Yorkshire pudding (£5.50), daily specials, and puddings (from £1.50). The pub takes its name from William Cavendish, who in 1582 was sold the village of Brindle so that the previous owner could buy his way out of the Tower. It's nicely set in a tranquil little village, and there's a handsome stone church across the road. *(Recommended by G McKaig, Mr and Mrs J H Adam, Peter and Lynn Brueton, Paul Boot, Helen Hazzard, Phil and Dilys Unsworth)*

Burtonwood ~ Tenant Peter Bowling ~ Real ale ~ Meals and snacks (11-2, 5.30-9; not Sun evening) ~ Restaurant ~ (0125) 485 2912 ~ Children in eating area and restaurant ~ Open 12-3, 5.30-11; closed 25 Dec

nr BROUGHTON (Lancs) SD4937 Map 7

Plough at Eaves

4½ miles from M6, junction 32: take M55 turn-off, then A6 N, then after about 1 mile N of Broughton traffic lights, first left into Station Lane; then carry on for 2 miles and pub on the right; OS Sheet 102 map reference 495374

A change of licensee at this unfussy old country pub since our last edition, but that doesn't seem to have affected the really friendly and cosy feel of the place. The two homely low-beamed bars are neatly but traditionally furnished with a mixture of wooden chairs, tables and upholstered seats, and there are three aged guns over one good copper-hooded open fire with a row of Royal Doulton figurines above another, and little latticed windows. Popular bar food such as club sandwiches (from £1.95), soup (£1.35), prawn platter (£2.95), quiche of the day (£3.25), ploughman's (from £3.55), cheese, potato and leek bake £3.75), beef ragout, roast of the day or fisherman's pie (£4.25), mushroom, peanut and pepper strogonoff (£4.75), lasagne or salmon and broccoli pie (£5.25), steak (£7.95) and various daily specials; children's helpings. Well kept Thwaites Bitter and Craftsman on handpump and lots of malt whiskies; darts, pool, dominoes, cribbage, fruit machine and piped music. There's a well equipped children's play area at the back, and metal and wood-slat seats and cast-iron-framed tables running along the front by the quiet lane. *(Recommended by Mr and Mrs R J Phillips,*

Dave Braisted, Miss D P Barson, Sarah Elliott, Gary Goldson; more reports please)

Thwaites ~ Tenant Geoff Moss ~ Real ale ~ Meals and snacks (not Mon or Tues) ~ Restaurant ~ Catforth (01772) 690233 ~ Children welcome ~ Weds quiz night ~ Open 12-3, 7-11; closed Mon and Tues lunchtime

CHIPPING (Lancs) SD6243 Map 7

Dog & Partridge ♀

Hesketh Lane; crossroads Chipping—Longridge with Inglewhite—Clitheroe, OS Sheet 103 map reference 619413

Set in very attractive countryside between Longridge and Wolf Fell, this is a very comfortable and relaxed dining pub, well worth a visit for its good home-cooked food. Parts of the building date back to 1515, though it's been much modernised since, spreading over into a nearby stable, now used mainly for extra eating space. Bar food usually includes dishes like sandwiches (from £2), home-made vegetable soup (£1.80), duck and orange pâté (£2.50), ploughman's, and highly praised hot dishes such as a vegetarian meal (£5), roast chicken (£6), scampi or duckling (£7) and steaks (£7.50); the home-made chips are particularly well liked and they do various fish and game specials. The main lounge, quite snug and with rather a genteel feel, is comfortably furnished with small armchairs around fairly close-set low wood-effect tables on a blue patterned carpet, brown-painted beams, a good winter log fire, and multi-coloured lanterns; service is friendly and helpful. Tetleys on handpump, over 60 wines, and a good range of malt whiskies; easy listening music. *(Recommended by Dr T E Hothersall, Peter Churchill; more reports please)*

Tetleys ~ Licensee Peter Barr ~ Real ale ~ Meals and snacks (12-1.45, 7-9.45; not Sat evening, Sun lunchtime) ~ Restaurant (not Sun evening) ~ Chipping (01995) 61201 ~ Children welcome ~ Open 11.45-3, 6.45-11

nr DARWEN (Lancs) SD6922 Map 7

Old Rosins 🛏

Pickup Bank, Hoddlesden; from B6232 Haslingden—Belthorn, turn off towards Edgeworth opposite the Grey Mare – pub then signposted off to the right; OS Sheet 103 map reference 722227

One of those places that despite its moves towards a hotel still keeps a good pubby atmosphere, this attractively-set inn has particularly friendly staff, with several readers saying they've never had such congenial service. We've often commented on the good views over the moors and down the wooded valley, but the pub is perhaps at its most atmospheric when you can't see anything at all, on one of those famous foggy days when the moorland mists obscure what can seem like everything except the welcoming lights inside. The open-plan bar is comfortably furnished with red plush built-in button-back banquettes, and stools and small wooden chairs around dark cast-iron-framed tables. Lots of mugs, whisky-water jugs and so forth hang from the high joists, while the walls are decorated with small prints, plates and old farm tools; there's also a good log fire. Parts of the bar and restaurant are no smoking. Well kept Boddingtons, Flowers Original, Marstons Pedigree and Theakstons Old Peculier on handpump or tapped from the cask, plenty of malt whiskies and coffee; fruit machine, maybe piped music. Generously served good value bar food, usefully available all day, ranges from good home-made soup (£1.30), sandwiches (from £1.85; open sandwiches from £3) and ploughman's (£3.25), through pork satay (£2.50), vegetable spring rolls (£3.50), salads (£3.60), and home-made pizzas (from £3.75), to freshly battered plaice (£3.95), delicious beef in Old Peculier or chicken tikka (£4.25), and sirloin steak (£7.25); puddings (£1.75), and children's meals. There are picnic-table sets on a spacious crazy-paved terrace. Readers have enjoyed their murder weekends and other themed evenings. *(Recommended by Tim Galligan, RJH, Sarah and Gary Goldson, Brian Horner, Brenda Arthur, David Eberlin, Bronwen and Steve Wrigley, Andy Hazeldine, Harry Stirling)*

Free house ~ Licensee Bryan Hankinson ~ Meals and snacks (noon-10.30) ~

Restaurant ~ Darwen (01254) 771264 ~ Children welcome ~ Open 12-11 ~ Bedrooms: £39.50B/£49.50B

DUNKINFIELD   SJ9497 Map 7

Globe

Globe Sq

Friendly and well run by a hardworking all-muck-in family, this pleasant pub is reputed to be the oldest in Dunkinfield. There's a welcoming atmosphere, solid dark wooden chairs around shiny wooden tables, comfortable wall banquettes, and several prints on the walls. Good home-cooking includes hot sandwiches (from 90p for chip butty; £1.45 for bacon and egg, £1.65 for liver and bacon), omelettes (£3), vegetable chilli (£3.75), garlic king prawns (£4.20), ploughman's or salads (from £4.25), gammon and egg (£5), sirloin steak (£7.50), 22oz T-bone steak (£12.90) and blackboard specials; delicious three-course Sunday lunch (£5.25). Well kept Boddingtons and Whitbreads Bentleys Yorkshire on handpump, several malt whiskies and brandies; pool, shove-ha'penny, cribbage, dominoes, fruit machine, triva and piped music. The pub is just 50 yards from the Lower Peak Forest Canal. *(Recommended by Ian and Emma Potts, Graham Reeve, Pauline Crossland, Dave Cawley, Neville Kenyon)*

Free house ~ Licensee Gary Mallinder ~ Real ale ~ Meals and snacks (not evenings Mon or Tues) ~ 0161-330 5561 ~ Children welcome ~ Open 11-11; 11.30-3, 7-11 Sat ~ Bedrooms: £29.37S/£41.12S

GARSTANG (Lancs) SD4845 Map 7

Th'Owd Tithebarn ★ ♀

Signposted off Church Street; turn left off one-way system at Farmers Arms

Parts of this converted, creeper-covered canalside barn seem more like a farmhouse kitchen parlour than anything else; it's a unique building to visit, the old-fashioned surroundings and atmosphere creating a curiously timeless feel. Looking round the low-beamed bar and dining area you could be forgiven for thinking the interesting museum upstairs had extended – there's an old kitchen range, prints of agricultural equipment on the walls, masses of antique farm tools, stuffed animals and birds, and pews and glossy tables spaced out on the flagstones under the high rafters. Waitresses in period costume with mob-caps complete the vintage flavour. Sitting on the big stone terrace is particularly pleasant, with plenty of ducks and boats wending their way along the water. Straightforward bar food includes home-made vegetable soup (£2.20), ploughman's (£3.50), meat and baked potato pie (£4.25), salads (from £4.25), steak pie (£4.55), a choice of roast meats (£4.95) and ham and eggs (£5.40); there's a new ice cream menu (from £1.75), and a good choice of meals for children (from £1.75). Lots of country wines, and a fine antique bar billiards machine. It can get busy. You may be lucky enough to be there when teams of Morris dancers are performing, and it really is the sort of place where you just want to relax and watch what's going on. *(Recommended by Mike and Wendy Proctor, Fred Collier, Lynn Sharpless, Bob Eardley, Andy and Julie Hawkins, A R Sayer and Barbara Sayer, TBB)*

Free house ~ Licensees Kerry and Eunice Matthews ~ Meals and snacks (not Mon) ~ Restaurant ~ (01995 604486) ~ Children welcome till 6pm ~ Open 11-3, 7(6 Sat)-11; closed Mon (though not lunchtime bank hol Mons)

GOOSNARGH (Lancs) SD5537 Map 7

Bushells Arms ⊕ ♀

4 miles from M6 junction 32; A6 towards Garstang, turn right at Broughton traffic lights (the first ones you come to), then left at Goosnargh Village signpost (it's pretty insignificant – the turn's more or less opposite Whittingham Post Office)

Really thoughtfully prepared food is still the reason most people come to this bustling place. The constantly changing menu often has a number of exotic and imaginative dishes from the Mediterranean or further afield, and everything is home-made using fresh, local ingredients. As well as a number of unusual soups like lovage or Dutch pea with ham and garlic sausage (£1.30), there are dishes like falafel or vegetable samosas (£2.50), spicy chicken wings (£2.50), good vegetable pasties (£4.50), steak and kidney pie (£5), stifatho (a Greek beef stew), or chicken with asparagus, cheese and bacon wrapped in puff pastry (£6), changing specials such as Cumberland sausage casserole or Lancashire hotpot (£5), delicious vegetarian Mediterranean beanpot casserole or rabbit pie (£5.50) and kleftico (lamb baked with potatoes and spices, £6), fresh fish from Fleetwood, and delicious puddings like chocolate, vanilla and strawberry roulade, apricot and rhubarb crumble, or Danish spice cake (all £2); also children's dishes (£1.75), and traditional local shortbread flavoured with caraway seeds and known as Goosnargh cakes (the place is pronounced Goozner, incidentally). Crisp and fresh vegetables include tasty potatoes, done with garlic, cream, peppers and parmesan. They do a good value set lunch including three courses and local cheeses (not Sun) for £5. There may be delays at peak periods (mainly evenings and weekends), but service is friendly, and they're still happily serving lunches not long before closing time. The spacious, modernised bar has lots of snug bays, each holding not more than two or three tables and often faced with big chunks of sandstone (plastic plants and spotlit bare boughs heighten the rockery effect); also soft red plush button-back banquettes, with flagstones by the bar; fruit machine. Two areas are no smoking. The well chosen and constantly developing range of wines is excellent, with some New World ones and several half bottles, as well as changing wines of the month; the list gives useful notes to help you choose. Also well kept Boddingtons and Tetleys on handpump, and several malt whiskies. Tables in a little back garden, and hanging baskets at the front. The signal for opening the doors at lunchtime is the tolling of the church clock, and haunted Chingle Hall is not far away. *(Recommended by Paul Boot, Tom Ross, Fred Collier, Andy and Julie Hawkins, E J and M W Corrin, Dave Braisted, Mr and Mrs A Cook, John Watson, J and P Maloney, Sue Holland, Dave Webster, Mike and Jo, Michael A Butler, D Grzelka, Ron Gentry, Colin and Shirley Brown, Martin, Jane, Simon and Laura Bailey, Anthony John, Paul and Margaret Baker, Graham Bush, Brian Kneale, David Poole, Mrs Jean Dundas, Mr and Mrs John Gilks)*

Whitbreads ~ Tenants David and Glynis Best ~ Meals and snacks (till 10pm) ~ (01772) 865235 ~ Well behaved children in eating area of bar until 9pm ~ Open 12-3, 6-11; may close some Mondays

Horns ♀

Pub signed from village, about 2 miles towards Chipping below Beacon Fell

Readers who have praised the puddings at this nicely-set former coaching inn will be delighted to know you can buy them to take away. Much older than you'd expect from the building's brightly mock-Tudor façade (over 200 years old, in fact), the polished but snug rooms haven't changed much since they were built, and all have log fires in winter. Dotted around are a number of colourful flower displays – a good indication of the care and effort the friendly licensees put into running the place. Beyond the lobby, the pleasant front bar opens into attractively decorated middle rooms with antique and other period furnishings, and there's a thriving, enjoyable atmosphere. Tasty bar food includes wholesome soups (£1.50), beautifully presented sandwiches (from £1.95), plaice, roast pheasant or steak and kidney pie (£4.95), gammon and egg (£5.50), and specials nicely served with freshly cooked, piping hot chips; home-made puddings like sherry trifle or an excellent sticky toffee pudding (£2.50). The civilised, intimate restaurant is good, with a set lunch (£9.50) or dinner (£17); the speciality is still the popular and tasty roast duckling. A very good range of up to ten or so wines by the glass, a fine choice of malt whiskies, but the Tetleys is keg; cheerful and helpful young staff, background music. *(Recommended by Mr and Mrs S Ashcroft, J A Boucher, Andy and Julie Hawkins, John Atherton)*

Free house ~ Licensees Elizabeth Jones and Mark Woods ~ Meals and snacks (not Sat evening or Sun lunch) ~ Restaurant ~ Broughton (01772) 865230 ~ Children welcome if dining ~ Open 11.30-3, 6.30-11; closed Mon lunchtime ~ Bedrooms: £40B/£65B

LIVERPOOL SJ4395 Map 7

Philharmonic ★ £ ▨

36 Hope Street; corner of Hardman Street

Hard to beat for atmosphere and style, this grand late Victorian gin palace (more properly the Philharmonic Dining Rooms), is an incredible, exquisitely decorated place, with charm and character at every turn. It may look like you've stumbled into a fine arts museum, but it never feels that way, the opulent fittings a wonderful backdrop to the workaday bustle and chat you'll usually find going on around. At its heart is a mosaic-faced serving counter, from which heavily carved and polished mahogany partitions radiate under the intricate plasterwork high ceiling. The echoing main hall is decorated with stained glass including contemporary portraits of Boer War heroes such as Baden-Powell and Lord Roberts, rich panelling, a huge mosaic floor, and copper panels of musicians in an alcove above the fireplace. More stained glass in one of the little lounges declares *Music is the universal language of mankind* and backs this up with illustrations of musical instruments. Well kept Cains Traditional, Ind Coope Burton, Jennings Bitter and Walkers Bitter and Best on handpump, and some malt whiskies; fruit machine, piped music. Good value home-made bar food includes sandwiches, soup (95p), vegetarian quiche (£2.50), and various well priced dishes like lasagne, curry, steak and kidney pie or chilli con carne (all £2.95) and gammon or haddock (£3.25), and is usually served in a splendid Grecian room decorated with half-naked art nouveau plaster goddesses reclining high above the squared panelling. There are two plushly comfortable sitting rooms, and a function room on the first floor. Lavatory devotees may be interested to know that the famous gents' are original 1890s Rouge Royale by Twyfords. All red marble and glinting mosaics, many readers feel that these alone earn the pub its star. *(Recommended by Ian G T White, Jonathan Mann, Abagail Regan, Geraint Roberts, Mr and Mrs S Ashcroft, Ian Phillips)*

Walkers (Allied) ~ Manager Phil Ross ~ Real ale ~ Lunchtime meals and snacks ~ Restaurant ~ 0151-709 1163 ~ Children in restaurant only ~ Weds quiz night ~ Metered parking nearby ~ Open 11.30-11 weekdays; 11.30-3, 6-11 Sat

LYTHAM (Lancs) SD3627 Map 7

Taps £ ▨

A584 S of Blackpool; Henry Street – in centre, one street in from West Beach

The landlord of this cheery place is something of a real ale enthusiast and obviously really enjoys tracking down and trying out unusual brews from all around the country. Every time he changes a barrel he puts on something different, and in the last year alone his handpumps have got through 1,000 different beers – that's a third of the total number currently available. We have a feeling he'll get round to all the rest eventually. The well kept range can be different every day, but might typically include Boddingtons, Clarks Rams Revenge, the award winning Coach House Blunderbuss from not far away, Marstons Pedigree, Mitchells ESB, Moorhouses Bitter or Pendle Witches Brew, Oaks Wobbly Bob and Whitbreads Castle Eden and Trophy; you'd think it was a freehouse rather than tied to one of the big brewers. Friendly and unassuming, the Victorian-style bare-boards bar has plenty of stained-glass decoration in the windows and the solid wood screens that divide up the central area, with depictions of fish and gulls reflecting the pub's proximity to the beach. Well chosen pictures of local boats and the like continue this theme, and there are also captain's chairs in bays around the sides, open fires, and a coal-effect gas fire between two built-in bookcases at one end; TV for special sporting events, piped music. Still the same good value prices as last year, simple lunchtime bar food includes soup (85p), filled baked potatoes (from 90p), sandwiches (from £1.40, toasties from £1.70), and cold platters (from £2.95), with hot home-made daily specials like cottage pie, steak and ale pie, chicken curry and lasagne (£3.25); the ham and beef is home-cooked. There are no meals on Sunday, but instead they have free platters of food laid out, with tasty morsels like black pudding, chicken wings or minted lamb. *(Recommended by Andy and Julie Hawkins, Fred Collier, Alan and Eileen Bowker, Kevin Potts, Graham Bush, Karen Simpson, Paul Williams, Robert Brock, Simon Bates)*

Whitbreads ~ Manager Ian Rigg ~ Real ale ~ Lunchtime meals and snacks (not Sun, 25 or 26 Dec or 1 Jan) ~ (01253) 736226 ~ Children in eating area during meal times ~ Open 11-11

MANCHESTER SJ8498 Map 7

Dukes 92 £

Castle Street, below the bottom end of Deansgate

Right in the heart of Manchester by the site of the original Roman fort, this has been something of a lost area, with the hulking old warehouses of the Castle Field Wharves, smoky railway viaducts and disused canals. On your way past industrial dereliction you may have your doubts, but once here in this focus of vigorous redevelopment you'll be well rewarded. This lively place has been beautifully converted from canal-horse stables, with black wrought-iron work contrasting boldly with whitewashed bare plaster walls, a handsome marble-topped bar, and an elegant spiral staircase to an upper room and balcony. Up here are some modern director's chairs, but down in the main room the fine mix of furnishings is mainly rather Edwardian in mood, with one particularly massive table, and chaises-longues and other comfortable seats. The pub is under the same ownership as the well established Mark Addy (see below) and has a similar excellent choice of splendid value cheeses and pâtés, served in huge helpings with granary bread (£2.80). Well kept Boddingtons, Marstons Pedigree and a changing guest beer on handpump, decent wines, friendly staff; piped music. There are some tables out by the canal basin which opens into the bottom lock of the Rochdale Canal, and events in the forecourt may include jazz and children's theatre. *(Recommended by Brian Wainwright, Dr M Bridge, Carl Travis, Rupert Lecomber, Liz, Wendy and Ian Phillips, P M Mason, Margaret and Allen Marsden)*

Free house ~ Licensee Thomas Joyce ~ Real ale ~ Snacks (11.30-9, Sun 12-3) ~ 0161-839 8646 ~ Children welcome away from bar till 7pm ~ Open 11.30-11

Lass o' Gowrie £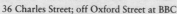

36 Charles Street; off Oxford Street at BBC

Simple and characterful, this lively place is a favourite with students, especially on a Friday or Saturday night when it seems like the entire university is here to sample the excellent own-brew beer; it's quieter at other times, though you'll never have it to yourself. The simple appearance of the long bar with its gas lighting and bare floorboards is one of the distinctive things about the pub, but it's the malt-extract beers that people like best. Named for their original gravity (strength), LOG35 is quite lightly flavoured and slips down very easily, while LOG42 is a little meatier. Seats around a sort of glass cage give a view of the brewing process in the micro-brewery downstairs in the cellar. There's also well kept Whitbreads Castle Eden on handpump, and Biddenden cider; it might take some while to get served at busy periods. Hop sacks drape the ceiling, and the bar has big windows in its richly tiled arched brown façade, as well as mainly stripped walls and a vibrantly friendly atmosphere. Good value bar food includes sandwiches (from £1.25) and big filled baps (from £1.45), vegetable lasagne or moussaka (£3), cottage pie (£3.20) and chicken curry (£3.30); efficient, cheery service. The volume of the piped pop music really depends on the youth of the customers – so it may be at its loudest in term-time; fruit machine, video game, trivia. *(Recommended by Bill and Lydia Ryan, Andy and Julie Hawkins, Terry Buckland, Paul Jones, Neil H Barker, Bill Ryan)*

Own brew (Whitbreads) ~ Manager Joe Fylan ~ Real ale ~ Lunchtime meals and snacks ~ 0161-273 6932 ~ Children over 2 in small side room and raised area until 6pm ~ Open 11.30-11; closed 25 Dec

Marble Arch £ 🍴

73 Rochdale Rd (A664), Ancoats; corner of Gould St, just E of Victoria Station

There's an incredible range of 12 well kept beers on handpump at this striking Victorian place, with several of them rather unusual in this part of the country. The choice changes regularly but typically takes in brews like Fullers London Pride (they were the first pub in the North to keep it regularly), Goachers, Hydes Anvil, Marstons Pedigree and Owd Roger, Mitchells, Oak Wobbly Bob, Titanic Captain Smith and Lifeboat, and Youngs Special. They also keep a good choice of bottled beers (including Belgian Trappist beers) and a selection of country wines. The style and appearance are still very much those of a late Victorian drinking house, with extensive marble and tiling (particularly the frieze advertising various spirits, and the chimney breast above the carved wooden mantelpiece), a sloping mosaic floor, rag-rolled walls, magnificently restored lightly barrel-vaulted high ceiling, and walls partly stripped back to the glazed brick. Bar food, served in the lounge extension at the back, includes huge filled barm cakes (from £1), and hot dishes like curries, casseroles and pies (around £2.95); bar billiards, dominoes, cribbage, pinball, fruit machine and juke box. On the third Wednesday of the month the Laurel and Hardy Preservation Society, the Sons of the Desert, meet here, and show old films. The pub's original name was the Elephant's Head, and the Marble Arch was a nickname inspired by its porphyry entrance pillars; the name was formally changed in the 1970s. *(Recommended by Bill and Lydia Ryan, Brian Wainwright, Simon J Barber, P Boot, Stephen Brown, Andrew Hazeldine)*

Free house ~ Managers John and Janet Oshey ~ Real ale ~ Snacks and lunchtime meals (not Sun) ~ 0161-832 5914 ~ Children in eating area of bar ~ R & B, jazz or folk Fri and Sat evenings ~ Open 12-11; closed Sun, maybe bank hol lunchtimes, and all day 25 and 26 Dec

Mark Addy ♀ £

Stanley Street, Salford, Manchester 3; look out not for a pub but for what looks like a smoked glass modernist subway entrance

If during long nights you too dream of cheeses, this smart pub is a good place to head for – they usually have a choice of up to 50 different varieties at any one time, from all over Britain and Europe. Served with granary bread (£2.80), it comes in such big chunks you might not be able to finish your helping – a doggy-bag is thoughtfully provided; there's also a good range of pâtés including a vegetarian one (£2.80), and maybe winter soup. Well converted from waiting rooms for boat passengers, it has quite a civilised atmosphere, especially in the flower-filled waterside courtyard from where you can watch the home-bred ducks. Inside, the series of barrel-vaulted red sandstone bays is furnished with russet or dove plush seats and upholstered stalls, wide glassed-in brick arches, cast-iron pillars, and a flagstone floor. Well kept Boddingtons, Marstons Pedigree and fortnightly changing guests on handpump, quite a few wines; piped music. They get very busy, so it is worth getting there early, and they prefer smart dress. It's named after a 19th-c man who rescued over 50 people from drowning in the River Irwell outside – praiseworthy enough at the best of times, but when you remember the stretch of water in those days was a sluggish open sewer he seems a hero indeed. *(Recommended by Dawn and Phil Garside, Caroline Wright, Stephen Brown, Dr M Bridge; more reports please)*

Free house ~ Licensee Sara Louise Ratcliffe ~ Real ale ~ Snacks (11.30-8, Sun 12-3) ~ 0161-832 4080 ~ Children welcome away from bar till 8pm ~ Open 11.30-11

Royal Oak 🍴 £

729 Wilmslow Road, Didsbury, Manchester 20

Manchester's most famous cheese pub was badly damaged in an arson attack in spring 1994, but the dedicated landlord had rebuilt and reopened again by the summer, and things are now pretty much back to normal. Very well liked indeed, the Royal Oak looks ordinary from the outside, but has the biggest choice of cheeses we've ever come across, in, as one reader puts it, what still looks like a cross between Harrods cheese counter and a theatre bar. Though in the fire Mr Gosling sadly lost the great collection of theatrical memorabilia which he'd built up over the last few decades, he has started afresh even on this. Over the last 30-odd years, he has been enthusiastically tracking down cheeses from all over the place, and you'd be hard pushed to think of one he doesn't keep. It seems unusual to be served with much less than a pound of even the rarer ones, with a substantial chunk of bread, salad and extras such as beetroot and pickled onions (£2.80 for a choice of two cheeses, take-away bags provided); there are also pâtés and winter soup. Particularly well kept Batemans Mild, Marstons Burton and Pedigree and guests on handpump, and some sherries and ports from the wood; efficient, friendly service. There are some seats outside. *(Recommended by Stephen, Julie and Hayley Brown, Patrick Clancy, Martin Richards, Bill and Lydia Brown, Simon J Barber, Ian Phillips)*

Marstons ~ Tenant Arthur Gosling ~ Real ale ~ Lunchtime snacks (not weekends or bank holidays) ~ 0161-445 3152 ~ Open 11-11; closed evening 25 Dec

Sinclairs Oyster Bar £

Shambles Square, Manchester 3; in Arndale Centre between Deansgate and Corporation Street, opposite Exchange Street

Wonderful though it is for shopping, the city's Arndale Centre is probably the last place you'd look for interesting old buildings, so it comes as quite a shock to find this timeless 18th-c pub incongruously set in the middle. And perhaps still more surprising is the way it's kept its old-fashioned style and atmosphere intact. Split up into lots of snugs and (partly no smoking) dining areas, the interesting rooms have low ceilings, squared oak panelling, and traditional furnishings such as small-backed stools that run along a tall old-fashioned marble-topped eating bar. The larger room upstairs has low old-fashioned wall settles, a scrolly old leather settee, pictures of old Manchester, and good lunchtime bar food such as sandwiches (from £1.10), ploughman's (£2.50), vegetarian or meaty lasagne or chilli con carne (£3), beef and oyster pie (£3.80), seafood platter (£4.20), and half-a-dozen oysters (£4.80); prices are unchanged from last year. Friendly service from neatly-uniformed barmaids. Very well kept Sam Smiths OB (priced well below the regional average) and Museum on handpump, chess, dominoes, cribbage, draughts, fruit machine and piped music. There are picnic-table sets outside in the pedestrians-only square. *(Recommended by Bill and Lydia Ryan; more reports please)*

Sam Smiths ~ Manager Darren Coles ~ Real ale ~ Lunchtime meals and snacks (till 3 Sat and Sun) ~ 0161-834 0430 ~ Children in eating area till 6pm ~ Nearby parking difficult ~ Open 11-11; closed 25 and 26 Dec, 1 Jan

MARPLE (Gtr Manchester) SJ9588 Map 7

Romper

Ridge End; from A626 Stockport Road in Marple, coming in from Manchester side, look out for Church Lane on your right (third turning after railway bridge and just after a garage); once in Church Lane, follow The Ridge signposts; OS Sheet 109 map reference 965966

Still popular for its good range of lunchtime food, this comfortably busy country pub is in a superb setting, standing alone on the steep side of the Goyt Valley, with good views down it. There's a pretty walk down towards the Peak Forest Canal from a car park attractively set in hilly common, 100 yards along the Marple road. Big helpings of reliable home-made dishes such as soup (£1.75), filled jacket potatoes (from £2), garlic mussels (£3.15), ploughman's (£4.50), prawns served in a variety of ways such as with paprika sauce (£4.95), meat salads (£5.50), several vegetarian dishes like leek and mushroom crumble (£5.75), steak, kidney and mushroom pie, lasagne or moussaka (£5.95), spicy Mexican chicken (£6.95), steaks (£8.50), and various daily specials. The four knocked-through oak-beamed rooms have soft blue corduroy seats and some antique settles around the many tables; there's soft lighting and gentle piped music. Well kept Flowers IPA, Marstons Pedigree, Theakstons Old Peculier and Timothy

Taylors Landlord on handpump, with 38 malt whiskies and a developing wine list; efficient service from friendly staff. The pub was once a row of hatters' cottages, and there are some pretty door arches linking them. *(Recommended by Peter Childs, Ian and Emma Potts, Pauline Crossland, Dave Cawley, Estelle Budge; more reports please)*

Free house ~ Licensees Geoff and Patty Barnett ~ Real ale ~ Meals and snacks (all day Sun) ~ Children in eating area, no under-7s after 7pm ~ Open 12-2.30(3 Sat), 6-11 all year; closed 25 Dec

MELLOR (Gtr Manchester) SJ9888 Map 7

Devonshire Arms

Longhurst Lane; follow Mellor signpost off A626 Marple—Glossop and keep on up hill

An unpretentious place with a good friendly feel, this engaging pub stands out for its good and often unusual lunchtime food. Everything is home-made and has obviously had plenty of thought put into it, and though the menu frequently changes, it's particularly strong on curries and other spicy dishes. A typical choice might take in soups such as pea and ham or carrot and mint (£1.45), potted shrimps (£2.75), steamed fresh mussels (£2.95), a very popular mussel chowder (£3.25), ploughman's (£3.95), smoked sausage (£4.25), vegetarian dishes like tortellini (£4.50), lots of curries like egg, lamb and almond or prawns and ginger (from £4.75), diced chicken and peppers in a spicy sherry sauce or lamb's kidneys in a red wine and mushroom sauce (£4.95), pan fried trout or home-cured gravadlax with dill sauce (£5.25), steaks, and puddings like crêpes with orange and Grand Marnier (£2.45). They may do more evening meals in future. Readers appreciate the pleasant service and excellent welcome – the Harrisons take a great pride in their pub and do their best to make sure strangers feel at home. The cheerful little front bar has a couple of old leather-seated settles among other seats, lots of old local and family photographs, and a sizeable Victorian fireplace with a deep-chiming clock above it. A couple of small back rooms, attractively papered and with something of a period flavour, both have their own Victorian fireplaces – the one on the right including an unusual lion couchant in place of a mantelpiece. Robinsons Best, Mild and tasty new Frederic's Premium on electric pump, a decent collection of spirits including 50 malt whiskies, several New World wines, and good coffee (which comes with a little pot of fresh cream); cribbage, shove-ha'penny and dominoes. There are picnic-table sets out in front, and behind, where an attractively planted terrace leads back to a small tree-sheltered lawn. Walkers are welcome if they take their boots off. *(Recommended by Roger and Christine Mash, John and Annette Derbyshire, David Heath, TBB, Mrs J Ellis, D R Shillitoe; more reports please)*

Robinsons ~ Tenant Brian Harrison ~ Real ale ~ Meals and snacks every lunchtime and Mon evening ~ 0161-427 2563 ~ Well behaved children in eating area ~ Trad jazz Thurs evenings ~ Open 11-3, 5.30-11; they may stay open longer in fine weather; closed evening 25 Dec

NEWBURGH (Lancs) SD4710 Map 7

Red Lion

A5209 Standish—Ormskirk

Long a popular dining pub, this extensive old place with lions and Tudor roses worked into stained glass in its windows has a comfortable main bar, almost an ante-room for its big downstairs dining area, with plush built-in seats and an attractive old-fashioned coal fire with a pot and kettle stand beside it. The long part-panelled dining area opening off here has lots of heavy black beamery and standing timbers, and there's a separate upstairs restaurant. A very wide choice of good value food served all day, from sandwiches up, has included all the usual things and (from £5.50) a semi-set meal with soup to start, main courses such as beef and mushroom pie, chicken chasseur or spaghetti carbonara, and fruit cocktail as pudding, but we were warned as we went to press that the menu was likely to change, with a new manager (and some refurbishment). A good relaxed atmosphere, piped music, well kept Burtonwood Bitter and Forshaws, cheerful and efficient service. *(Recommended by D Grzelka, J A Boucher, Dilys Unsworth, Comus Elliott)*

Burtonwood ~ Real ale ~ Meals and snacks ~ Restaurant ~ (01257) 462336 ~ Children in eating area ~ Open 11-11 ~ Bedrooms: £25/£50

NEWTON (Lancs) SD6950 Map 7

Parkers Arms

B6478 7 miles N of Clitheroe

An imposing building clearly visible as you approach from Clitheroe, this pretty black and white pub is a popular place at the moment, largely thanks to its friendly atmosphere and range of good home-made food. The very well liked and generously served bar food changes regularly but might include soup (£1.60), sandwiches (from £1.80, the salmon are recommended), barbecue ribs (£2.95), steak and kidney pie (£4.75) and a big choice of daily blackboard specials like trout stuffed with crab and basil or prawn and salmon pancakes (£4.95); excellent service. There's a particularly warm welcome in the bar, some of the joists in which are from the same oak used to repair the Blitz-damaged Houses of Parliament. Plenty of stuffed animals and paintings on the walls in here, as well as red plush button-back banquettes and a mix of new chairs and tables. Beyond an arch is a similar area with sensibly placed darts, pool, dominoes, fruit machine, video game and discreet piped music. Boddingtons, Flowers IPA and Black Sheep Bitter on handpump. They have a friendly black labrador (who has been known to bring customers a stick to throw) and Jack Russell. Well spaced picnic-table sets on the big lawn look down towards the village's river, and beyond to the hills. It's a really attractive spot, between Waddington and Beatrix Fell, with the building standing right in the middle of a cluster of neat stone cottages. *(Recommended by Fred Collier, John Broughton, Mr and Mrs S Ashcroft, Kevin Potts, Gwen and Peter Andrews, Bob Riley, Mrs F M Halle, Sarah Elliott, Gary Goldson, Eric Locker, C J Parsons)*

Whitbreads ~ Tenant Nicholas Hardman ~ Real ale ~ Meals and snacks ~ Restaurant ~ Slaidburn (01200)446 236 ~ Children welcome ~ Open 11-3, 6-11; all day summer Sundays; closed 25 Dec ~ Bedrooms: £20/£35

RABY (Merseyside) SJ3180 Map 7

Wheatsheaf

The Green, Rabymere Road; off A540 S of Heswall

A traditional local through and through, this attractive timbered old place (known locally as 'The Thatch') is the only real country pub of its type in the area. Readers like it mainly for the very good range of changing real ales, but this year we've had a lot of praise for the huge range of toasted sandwiches, which often extends to unusual kinds such as black pudding. Beers on handpump might include Cains Traditional, Courage Directors, Ind Coope Burton, Tetleys, Theakstons Best, XB and Old Peculier, Thwaites and Youngers Scotch, and there's also a good choice of malt whiskies. The little rooms are simply furnished and characterful, with an old wall clock and homely black kitchen shelves in the central bar, and a nice snug formed by antique settles built in around its fine old fireplace. A second, more spacious room has upholstered wall seats around the tables, small hunting prints on the cream walls and a smaller coal fire. As well as the sandwiches, lunchtime snacks may include hot dishes like steak and kidney pie, gammon, scampi and plaice. The old-fashioned feel extends to the service and opening hours, and under 18s are strictly excluded. If you visit this pub, we'd be very grateful for up-to-date news on the beers on offer and on food (with prices if possible) as the landlord consistently refuses to give us details. *(Recommended by Mr and Mrs C Roberts, Basil Minson, Brian Kneale, Don Kellaway, Angie Coles, Mr and Mrs Sean Crampton, Fred Collier, Tony and Lynne Stark, Gill and Mike Cross, P and K Lloyd)*

Free house ~ Licensee Ian Cranston ~ Real ale ~ Lunchtime meals and snacks (not Sun) ~ Open 11.30-3, 5.30-10.30

RIBCHESTER (Lancs) SD6435 Map 7

White Bull

Church Street; turn off B6245 at sharp corner by Black Bull

The pillars of the entrance porch at this friendly 18th-c dining pub are Tuscan, and have stood here or nearby for nearly 2,000 years. It's a popular stop for lunchtime food and can get busy, so it's worth getting there early for a table. Good value bar meals includes soup (£1.30), open sandwiches (from £1.70), black pudding (£1.75), stuffed mushrooms or lightly battered and fried prawns (£2.45), salads (from £3.95), steak and kidney pie (£4.15), lasagne, chilli or an honest ploughman's (£4.25), various steaks with a choice of toppings (from £6), and changing specials such as fisherman's pie or pork and apricot pie; children's menu. Service is caring and attentive, even during busy periods, and children are made particularly welcome. The spacious and attractively refurbished main bar has comfortable old settles, and is decorated with Victorian advertisements and various prints, as well as a stuffed fox in two halves, arranged to look as if it goes through the wall; most areas are set out for eating during the day, and you can also eat out in the garden behind. Well kept Boddingtons, Chesters Best, Hartleys and a monthly changing guest on handpump, occasionally kept under light blanket pressure, good range of malt whiskies, several wines by the glass; darts, dominoes, piped music. Behind the pub are the remains of a Roman bath house, and there's a small explanatory museum close by. Just up the road is an excellent Museum of Childhood. *(Recommended by Paul McPherson, W Bailey, Phil and Dilys Unsworth)*

Whitbreads ~ Lease: Marilyn and Bob Brooks ~ Real ale ~ Meals and snacks (not Mon evening) ~ Children welcome ~ Occasional jazz or folk night ~ Open 11.30-3, 6.30-11; all day Sun and bank holidays

SUMMERSEAT (Gtr Manchester) SD7814 Map 7

Waterside

Kay Bridge, Waterside Road; ½ mile from M66 junction 1 (northbound exit only); just north of the exit traffic-lights turn off A56 Walmersley Road/Manchester Road into Bass Lane, turn right into Cliffe Avenue, then bear right

One block of a huge 19th-c stonebuilt cotton mill (the separate main block is now flats), this is one of those attractive places which has an interesting atmosphere with plenty to look at when it's fairly empty in the early evening, yet keeps an enjoyably welcoming feel when busy later on. It's well converted, a big square room with punkah fans in its high barrel-vaulted brick ceiling, tall windows looking out to the mill race, and well divided seating on the flagstone and tiled floor. There's some fine well restored mill machinery (not originally on this site). A good range of bar food includes soup (£1.75), sandwiches (from £2), giant sausage in french bread (£2.60), a huge piece of gammon with an egg in a round roll (£2.90), ploughman's (£4.25), steak and kidney pie (£4.80), rabbit pie (£4.90), calf's liver (£5.20) and a massive mixed grill (£8.50), with vegetarian dishes (from £4.10), several fish dishes and children's dishes. Well kept Boddingtons, Moorhouses Pendle Witches Brew, Theakstons Best, XB and Old Peculier and Youngers IPA on handpump, decent wine; fruit machine, trivia, piped music (the Eagles and similar on our inspection visit). There are picnic-table sets out on the terrace where a fountain may play; it's a quiet spot. *(Recommended by Peter Butler, Dr M Bridge, Carol and Richard Glover; more reports please)*

Free house ~ Licensee Bernard Grogan ~ Real ale ~ Meals and snacks (5.30-9.30; Sat/Sun 12-9.30) ~ (01706) 822065 ~ Children welcome ~ Live music Weds ~ Open 5.30-11 (12-11 Sat)

TOCKHOLES (Lancs) SD6623 Map 7

Rock ♀

Village signposted from A666 S of Blackburn; OS Sheet 103 map reference 663233

Like a reassuring number of other Lancashire pubs, this warmly welcoming moorland inn is one where the licensees take a great pride in their business, really working hard to ensure they're offering what people want. But at the same time they make it seem a pleasure rather than a chore, happy to chat about things or whip up something that's not on the menu. The recently redecorated two-room beamed bar is cosy, with wall banquettes, moiré curtains, brass ornaments around the neat fireplace, old sporting prints on the cream-coloured walls and plates on a delft shelf. On the left by the bar counter (which has unusually comfortable swivel bar stools) there's some dark brown panelling. Well kept Thwaites Bitter, Craftsman and Mild on handpump, a variety of malt whiskies and some unusual liqueurs; they keep around 30 wines, several by the glass, but you won't find them on a written list – the very agreeable landlord likes to vary them all the time. The bar food is cooked by the landlady, with big helpings of reasonably priced dishes like soup (£1.25), sandwiches (from £1.55), ploughman's (£2.25), home-made steak pie (£3.85), roasts, gammon or chicken baked in wine (£4.50), sirloin steak (£7.95), changing specials like beef in ale or pork baked in cider, tarragon and herbs (£5.50) and puddings (from £1.75); occasional flambé evenings. Unobtrusive piped music, darts, fruit machine. There are tables out on a small terrace. On a clear day from the back dining area you may be able to see not only rolling well wooded pastures, but the coast some 20 miles away – look out for Blackpool Tower. *(Recommended by G L Tong, John Fazakerley, Jim and Maggie Cowell and others)*

Thwaites ~ Tenants Dominic and Maureen Gallagher ~ Real ale ~ Meals and snacks (not Mon lunchtime, except bank holidays) ~ (01254) 702733 ~ Children welcome until 8.45pm ~ Open 12-2, 7-12 (supper licence); closed Mon lunchtime

UPPERMILL (Gtr Manchester) SD9905 Map 7

Cross Keys £

Runninghill Gate; from A670 in Uppermill turn into New Street, by a zebra crossing close to the chapel; this is the most practical-looking of the lanes towards the high moors and leads directly into Runninghill Gate, but is still steep and more than a mile long

This lively old place is very much at the heart of the local community: every Monday night you can watch the the Saddleworth Clog and Garland Dancers practising their clog dancing on the old flag floor in the kitchen, there are various clubs and teams (including the Gun Club, which meets for clay pigeon shooting every other Sunday at 10 am), and the pub each year sponsors the road running or fell races in the first week in June and on the last Saturday in August. It's also the headquarters of the Oldham Mountain Rescue Team, and they even have a bridge school Monday and Friday evenings and Saturday lunchtimes. Even when there's nothing going on the atmosphere in the several connecting low-beamed rooms is friendly and chatty, and at lunchtimes especially you can start to feel quite at home, particularly if you're sitting on one of the comfortable old settles. One room has an original cooking range, another, overlooking Saddleworth church, has local prints and drawings for sale. Good value bar food includes soup (90p), sandwiches (from £1.10, toasted from £1.20), lasagne or sausage, chips and peas (£2.85), steak and kidney pie, chicken tikka, lemon sole, or plaice (all £3.50), balti curries (£3.75), and puddings like apricot crumble (£1.20). Well kept Lees Bitter and Mild on handpump, lots of malt whiskies; darts, dominoes, cribbage and fruit machine. There's a side terrace and a stylish flagstoned back terrace with bright flowers sheltered by a dry stone wall; there's a new adventure playground out here. The setting is lovely, and tracks from behind the pub lead straight up towards Broadstone Hill and Dick Hill. *(Recommended by G J Parsons, Andrew and Ruth Triggs, Bronwen and Steve Wrigley, Neil H Barker)*

Lees ~ Tenant Philip Kay ~ Real ale ~ Meals and snacks ~ (01457) 874626 ~ Children in two side rooms till 8pm ~ Clog dancing Mon evenings, folk Weds evenings ~ Open 11-11; winter 11-4, 6.30-11, all day Sat and bank holidays

Post Office address codings confusingly give the impression that some pubs are in Lancashire when they're really in Yorkshire (which is where we list them).

WHARLES (Lancs) SD4435 Map 7

Eagle & Child

Church Road; from B5269 W of Broughton turn left into Higham Side Road at HMS Inskip sign; OS Sheet 102 map reference 448356

Quiet, friendly, and snugly traditional, this thatched country pub is a very special place, particularly worth a look for its lovely antique furnishings. The landlord has amassed a fine collection of venerable oak seats, and the most interesting can be seen in the L-shaped bar, where a beamed area round the corner past the counter has a whole group of them. One of the highlights is a magnificent, elaborately carved Jacobean settle which originally came from Aston Hall in Birmingham, carrying the motto *exaltavit humiles*. There's also a carved oak chimneypiece, and a couple of fine longcase clocks, one from Chester, and another with a nicely painted face and an almost silent movement from Manchester. The plain cream walls are hung with modern advertising mirrors and some older mirrors, and there are exotic knives, carpentry tools and so forth on the plastered structural beams; even when it's not particularly cold, there should be a good fire burning in the intricate cast-iron stove. Well kept Boddingtons and three regularly changing guests such as Cains Traditional, Wadworths 6X or Wards on handpump; darts in a sensible side area, friendly cat. One or two picnic-table sets outside. Do please note it's closed on weekday lunchtimes, and there is no food. The nearby forest of radio masts clearly belongs to another, more complicated age. *(Recommended by John Atherton, Mr and Mrs G Goldson, Graham Bush)*

Free house ~ Licensees Brian and Angela Tatham ~ Real ale ~ No food ~ (01772) 690312 ~ Open 7-11 (and 12-3 Sat; usual Sun hours)

WHITEWELL (Lancs) SD6546 Map 7

Inn at Whitewell ★ ★ ⇔ ♀

Most easily reached by B6246 from Whalley; road through Dunsop Bridge from B6478 is also good

Deep in the Forest of Bowland, surrounded by well wooded rolling hills set off against higher moors, this enduringly popular hotel is one of those rare places that just seems to have everything going for it. This year we've had more reports about it than any other pub in Lancashire, and its fans are united in declaring it a quite exceptional place to stay. The atmosphere is so civilised and the furnishings so elegant that at times it feels almost like a stately home, and there's always plenty going on. The inn also houses a wine merchant (hence the unusually wide range of around 180 wines available – the claret is recommended), an art gallery, and a shop selling cashmere, shoes and so forth, and owns several miles of trout, salmon and sea trout fishing on the Hodder; with notice they'll arrange shooting. A real bonus is that although it gets very busy, there's plenty of room inside and out, so its popularity doesn't cause any problems to either space or service, and it usually remains peaceful and relaxing. The old-fashioned bar has antique settles, oak gateleg tables, sonorous clocks, old cricketing and sporting prints, log fires (the lounge has a very attractive stone fireplace), and heavy curtains on sturdy wooden rails; one area has a selection of newspapers, local maps and guide books. The public bar has darts, pool, shove-ha'penny, dominoes and juke box, with a 1920s game-of-skill slot machine; there's a piano for anyone who wants to play. Down a corridor with strange objects like a stuffed fox disappearing into the wall is the pleasant sun-trap garden, with wonderful views across the River Hodder and down to the valley. Popular lunchtime bar food includes soup (£1.60), big sandwiches (from £2.50), spinach, mushroom and potato pie (£4.80), Cumberland sausage, salads or ploughman's (from £5), steak and kidney pie (£5.20), fisherman's pie (£5.60), weekend oysters, steaks (£8.50), home-made puddings like chocolate roulade (£2) and British hand-made cheese (from £2.50); there's an à la carte menu and slightly different evening dishes, and they serve coffee and cream teas all day. Well kept Boddingtons and Marstons Pedigree on handpump. Some readers feel that the pictures in the gents' don't really fit in with the otherwise ultra-stylish feel of the place. *(Recommended by Jim and Maggie Cowell,*

Jonathan Mann, Abagail Regan, John and Phyllis Maloney, Bob and Janet Lee, Nic Armitage, Geoff and Sue Abbott, S R and A I Ashcroft, L P Thomas, Neville Kenyon, J Roy Smylie, Paul McPherson, Barry and Lindsey Blackburn, Nigel Woolliscroft, Andy and Julie Hawkins, Mr and Mrs John Gilks, C J Parsons, Andrew Sykes, Hugh Chevallier, Mrs E Wareing, Jill and Peter Bickley; also recommended by The Good Hotel Guide)

Free house ~ Licensee Richard Bowman ~ Real ale ~ Meals and snacks (not Sat evening if a big function is on) ~ Restaurant (not Sun lunchtime) ~ Dunsop Bridge (0120 08) 222 ~ Children welcome ~ Pianist Fri evening ~ Open 11-3, 6-11 ~ Bedrooms: from £45B/£59.50B

YEALAND CONYERS (Lancs) SD5074 Map 7

New Inn

3 miles from M6 junction 35; village signposted off A6 N

Dating back to 1600, this simple ivy-covered stone pub has proved a welcome stop for generations of tired and hungry walkers fresh from the fells. It's an atmospheric old place, with a genuinely old-fashioned feel and a good friendly reception. On the left is a simply furnished little beamed bar with a log fire in the big stone fireplace, and on the right are two communicating cottagey dining rooms with black furniture to match the shiny beams, an attractive kitchen range and another winter fire. As we mentioned last year the new licensees have brought with them considerable catering experience, and their very good bar food is already proving popular, the menu displaying some unusual touches; favourites this year have included chicken breast stuffed with cheese and herb pâté (£5.95), and beef marinated in red wine and beer (£6.50). The restaurant is no smoking. Well kept Hartleys XB and Robinsons Best on handpump, a good choice of malt whiskies, home-made lemonade. Dominoes, cribbage, piped music. A sheltered lawn at the side has picnic-table sets among roses and flowering shrubs.

(Recommended by Rev J E Cooper, Derek and Margaret Underwood, David Bloomfield, Brian Kneale, Olive Carroll, P Barnsley, Michael A Butler, Colin and Shirley Brown, Wayne Brindle, Paul McPherson, Martin, Jane, Simon and Laura Bailey, Mike Tucker, I H Rorison, D L and E L Keech, Basil J S Minson, D C Holt and others)

Hartleys (Robinsons) ~ Tenant Annette Dutton ~ Real ale ~ Meals and snacks (all day till 9.30) ~ Restaurant ~ (01524) 732938 ~ Children in restaurant if over 14 ~ Open 11-11

Lucky Dip

Besides the fully inspected pubs, you might like to try these Lucky Dips recommended to us and described by readers (if you do, please send us reports):

Abbey Village [SD6422], *Hare & Hounds*: Popular chatty local with big beamed main bar, toby jugs, plates, brasses and animal heads, food inc good cheeses; machines, juke box, pool room, can be smoky; good views of Darwen tower; live music and quiz nights *(Phil and Dilys Unsworth)*

☆ **Adlington** [5A Market St (A6); SD5912], *White Bear*: Popular unpretentious town local with wide choice of good value cheap food, turkey-carpeted dining areas, five S & N real ales kept well, quick cheery service, pool table in back bar; safely enclosed back terrace with lots of play equipment *(Greenwood and Turner, Mr and Mrs John Gilks, Richard Davies, BB)*

☆ **Altrincham** Gtr Man [Navigation Rd, Broadheath; junction with Manchester Rd (A56); SJ7689], *Old Packet House*: Now under same ownership as Dog at Peover Heath (see Cheshire main entries), easily

overlooked as tucked almost under canal bridge by busy traffic lights in office building area; well restored, its small rooms knocked together but still with an intimate feel, open fires, some dark panelling and stripped brickwork; good bar food inc lots of sandwiches and well presented salads, some fresh-cooked hot dishes; well kept Boddingtons, friendly prompt service; enclosed garden, well equipped bedrooms *(Ian Phillips, Brian Jones)*

Altrincham [Old Market Pl], *Orange Tree*: Nice atmosphere in cosy bar with side rooms, Courage-related and guest real ales; good value upstairs bistro *(Bill and Lydia Ryan)*; [Tipping St], *Tatton Arms*: Basic local with well kept Boddingtons *(Bill and Lydia Ryan)*; [Hale Rd, Halebarns – nr M56 junction 6], *Unicorn*: Large hotel, but bar has genuine local atmosphere and is good value; bedrooms *(Bob and Janet Lee)*

Appley Bridge Gtr Man [Station Buildings; SD5210], *Old Station House*: Interesting conversion of station buildings, extensive and imaginative range of bar food, restaurant; six real ales on handpump *(Paul Boot)*

☆ **Ashton under Lyne** [152 Old St; SJ9399], *Witchwood*: Live bands virtually every night (worth the admission), great atmosphere, well kept real ales such as Boddingtons, Courage Directors and John Smiths, lunchtime snacks (not Sun), low prices *(Pauline Crossland, Dave Cawley, Graham Reeve)*

Ashton under Lyne [Mossley Rd; SJ9399], *Hartshead*: Brewers Fayre dining pub in former farmhouse, good views over Manchester, standard food, garden with playground and picnic-table sets; can get very busy summer weekends and bank hols, open all day *(Ian and Emma Potts)*; [Mossley Rd], *Heroes of Waterloo*: Good straightforward food from sandwiches up, good service *(Bill Ryan, C J Westmoreland)*

Aughton [L'pool Rd (A59); SD3905], *Royal Oak*: Good decor, well lit bar, beers well kept *(Colin Trowler)*

Bamber Bridge [Lostock Lane; A582 W of M6 junction 29; SD5728], *Poachers*: Excellent provision for families, relaxed family area with own entrance discreet distance from main bar, playroom and outdoor play area; wide choice of enterprising food inc vegetarian, good service *(Alan Griffiths)*

☆ **Barnston** Mer [Barnston Rd (A551); SJ2883], *Fox & Hounds*: Interesting long lounge bar, half flagstoned and half carpeted, with plates, prints, brasses, fox masks and brushes, even decorative clothes rack over kitchen range; reasonably priced well presented good straightforward food from ploughman's up inc very popular Sun lunch, several Courage-related ales and Marstons Pedigree, brisk businesslike service; pretty summer courtyard and garden with outside bar; by farm and lovely wooded dell *(Mr and Mrs C Roberts, Paul Boot, A Craig)*

Bartle [Rosemary Lane; SD5033], *Sitting Goose*: Pleasant relaxed country pub with small dining area, well kept Thwaites ales, remarkably good value food *(Dr and Mrs D E Awbery)*

Barton [A6 Preston—Garstang; SD5137], *White Horse*: Decent food, well kept Theakstons ales, small garden; can get crowded lunchtimes *(Jim and Maggie Cowell)*

☆ **Bashall Eaves** [SD6943], *Red Pump*: Lovely old pub in very rural spot (can be very quiet out of season) with two log fires, restaurant, welcoming bar/snug area; newish young licensees doing good home-made food, all fresh, presentation well above average; Whitbreads-related ales; two bedrooms, own fishing on River Hodder *(A and M Dickinson, Paul McPherson)*

☆ **Birkenhead** Mer [Claughton Firs, Oxton;

SJ3289], *Shrewsbury Arms*: Particularly well kept Cains and Whitbreads-related real ales in friendly and bustling pub, spacious lounge recently refurbished with extension in character, good bar food, hard-working landlord; tables on terrace *(Tony and Lynne Stark)*

☆ **Blackpool** [204 Talbot Rd; opp Blackpool North stn; SD3035], *Ramsden Arms*: Well kept Boddingtons, Jennings and Tetleys with guests such as Cains and Robinsons, over 40 whiskies, cheap food, attractive country-style decor, ornaments and pictures, CD juke box, games; good value bedrooms *(Andy Hazeldine, Bill and Lydia Ryan)*

☆ **Bolton** Gtr Man [606 Halliwell Rd; SD7108], *Ainsworth Arms*: Unpretentious and friendly, with particularly well kept Allied beers and an interesting guest, basic good value food, quick service, pub games, old-fashioned smoke room; busy evenings, helpful attitude to wheelchairs *(Bill and Lydia Ryan)*

☆ **Bolton** [36 Pool St], *Howcroft*: Newish landlord in well preserved friendly old local with lots of small screened-off rooms, good cheap lunches, well kept Allied ales, Addlestone's cider, plenty of games inc pintable, darts, bar billiards; bowling green; live music weekends *(Andy Hazeldine, Bill and Lydia Ryan)*

☆ **Bolton** [52 Junction Rd, Deane], *Kings Head*: Attractive local with central servery for flagstoned bar and two lounges, well kept Walkers Bitter, Mild, Best and Winter Warmer, massive stove, good reasonably priced lunchtime food, pleasant atmosphere; seats out overlooking church or back bowling green *(Andy Hazeldine, Lyn and Bill Capper)*

Bolton [94 Newport St], *Clifton Arms*: Good local feel, beers consistently well kept (with occasional festivals), reasonably priced lunches, quiet front snug *(Andy Hazeldine, Bill and Lydia Ryan)*; [Churchgate], *Man & Scythe*: Interesting old pub with lively corridor-style drinking area, two quieter rooms popular for lunchtime meals, Flowers or Holts real ale, several farm ciders, limited range of popular food; handy for shopping area *(Brian Wainwright)*; *Queens Moat House*: Worth knowing that this hotel's restaurant is very well converted from old church – interesting eating in such surroundings; good value food, but limited choice of expensive beers; bedrooms *(G L Tong)*; [127 Crook St], *Sweet Green*: Four small rooms off central bar, green decor, well kept Hydes, Tetleys and guests, basic lunchtime food, friendly staff, good local atmosphere; darts, pool, seats out overlooking station and clocks *(Andy Hazeldine, Bill and Lydia Ryan)*

☆ **Bolton by Bowland** [SD7849], *Coach & Horses*: Good fresh well presented food inc imaginative dishes in bar and restaurant of clean, comfortable and welcoming pub with coal fires and pleasantly untouristy traditional decor – get there early weekends

for a table; well kept Whitbreads-related beers, children may be allowed in dining room; lovely village with stream and pretty church *(Paul McPherson, Jim and Maggie Cowell, J A Boucher, Roger Berry, GTW)*
Bredbury Gtr Man [Stockport Rd, next to stn; SJ9391], *Rising Sun*: Good value lunchtime meals, Courage-related ales; clean and tidy *(P Corris)*

☆ **Brierfield** [Burnley Rd (A682), just off M65 junction 12; SD8436], *Waggon & Horses*: Lovingly restored late Victorian local, beautiful fittings and decor in bar and small rooms leading off; well kept Thwaites Bitter, Craftsman and Mild on handpump, good malt whiskies, warm fires; bar food (not evenings Sun-Weds), children allowed away from servery, open all day Fri/Sat *(J E Hilditch, LYM)*

Bury Gtr Man [36 Manchester Old Rd – OS Sheet 109 map reference 836125; SD8312], *Tap & Spile*: Unpretentious and cheery, notable for wide and swiftly changing choice of well kept real ales, often interesting; old railway signs, limited bar food lunchtime and from 5; can get crowded evenings *(Andy Hazeldine, Brian Wainwright, Bill and Lydia Ryan)*

☆ **nr Bury** [Nangreaves; off A56/A666 N, down cobbled track; SD8115], *Lord Raglan*: Lovely location up on the moors, great views on bright days, desolate in winter, but warm and snug inside; lots of bric-a-brac in traditional front bar, big open fire in back room, plainer blond-panelled dining room (where children allowed); well kept S&N real ales, interesting foreign bottled beers, hearty bar food *(LYM)*

nr Bury [Woodhill Rd, Burrs Country Park; SD8313], *Brown Cow*: Garden a paradise for train buffs with the steam East Lancs Light Railway running by; simple, quiet and respectable pub, very out of the way, with Boddingtons ale; reasonably priced food *(Brian Wainwright)*

Chipping [SD6243], *Star*: Old-fashioned, very unmodernised, well kept Boddingtons, short range of very cheap local food such as meat and potato pie and mushy peas *(Bob Riley)*

☆ **Chorley** [Friday St, behind stn; SD5817], *Malt 'n' Hops*: Wide range of well kept changing real ales such as Hydes, Moorhouses Pendle Witches Brew and Timothy Taylors Landlord in friendly and comfortable newish pub done out well in old-fashioned style; bar food *(Mary Moore)*

☆ **nr Chorley** [White Coppice; 2 miles from M61 junction 8; signposted from A674 towards Blackburn; SD6118], *Railway*: Friendly country local by recreational park, with well kept S&N ales, big helpings of bar food with children's helpings; fine cigarette-card collection, Sat evening live entertainment (monthly in summer); cricket on green, may be closed winter lunchtimes, at least on Mon *(Mr and Mrs John Gilks)*

☆ **Churchtown** Mer [off A565 from Preston, taking B5244 at Southport; SD3618],

Hesketh Arms: Good value freshly prepared food from chip butties to roast beef inc children's helpings in spacious and very popular dining pub, bright and lively, with smart Victorian-style decor; Tetleys Bitter and Mild on handpump from central servery, open fires, Weds jazz; attractive partly thatched village nr Botanic Gardens *(BB)*

☆ **Churchtown** , the different Lancs one [nr church, off A586 Garstang—St Michaels-on-Wyre; SD4843], *Punchbowl*: Good choice of good food in attractive mock-Tudor beamed pub/restaurant with panelling, stained glass, lots of stuffed animals; friendly staff, well kept Tetleys and Dark Mild, good fires; lavatory for disabled people; lovely village *(J A Boucher)*

Clitheroe [Castle St; SD7441], *Starkie Arms*: Low-priced beer on handpump, good choice of bar food, efficient service, table football; handy for castle *(Sarah Elliott, Gary Goldson)*

☆ **nr Clitheroe** [Higher Hodder Bridge; nr Chaigley on old Clitheroe—Longbridge high rd parallel to B6243 – OS Sheet 103 map reference 699412], *Hodder Bridge*: In lovely country spot, with spacious pleasantly decorated panelled bar, family restaurant and terraces looking down to pretty River Hodder, quiet comfortable bedrooms, own fishing; but found closed early 1994 *(LYM; news please)*

Cowan Bridge [Burrow-by-Burrow; A65 towards Kirkby Lonsdale; SD6277], *Whoop Hall*: Spacious, spruce and comfortable open-plan bar with interesting quick food all day from 8am from popular buttery on left, beyond that a pleasant restaurant; well kept Boddingtons and Theakstons Best and XB, decent wines, tables outside with play area; children allowed in eating area; well appointed bedrooms *(Frank Cummins, Sue Holland, David Webster, LYM)*

Croston [Westhead Rd (A581 Chorley—Southport), OS Sheet 108 map reference 486187; SD4818], *Black Horse*: Good value bar food served all day inc good hefty hot beef or steak sandwiches, generous gammon and eggs, good Cumberland sausage and puddings, though main draw in this relaxed unpretentious place is fine range of interesting well kept changing beers usually inc Black Country Milds; small restaurant (closed Tues), friendly landlord, darts, hexagonal pool table, cribbage, CD juke box, own bowling green; ambitious beer festivals, occasional folk music; resident cats, can be smoky *(John Fazakerley, Jim and Maggie Cowell, John Scarisbrick, BB)*

Croston [Station Rd], *Crown*: Old-fashioned beamed village pub with well kept beers, good home-cooked specials competitively priced *(Mr and Mrs J Jones)*; *Grapes*: Good range of good freshly made food in dining room off bar area, booking advisable weekends; friendly staff *(D Grzelka)*; [Out Lane (off A581) – OS Sheet 108 map reference 486187], *Lord Nelson*: Old-fashioned local with lots of little rooms, well kept Boddingtons and tasty cheap bar food, nice relaxed atmosphere *(Andy and Julie Hawkins, F A Noble)*

nr **Darwen** [Roman Rd, Grimehills; SD6922], *Crown & Thistle*: Country pub with good food, well kept Thwaites Bitter and Mild *(Neville Kenyon)*

☆ **Denshaw** Gtr Man [2 miles from M62 junction 2; A672 towards Oldham, pub N of village on Ripponden Rd; SD9710], *Rams Head*: Traditional settles in comfortable small-roomed moorland farm/pub with well kept Theakstons, Timothy Taylors and maybe a guest beer, choice of handpump or tapped from cask, bric-a-brac on beams and panelling, log fires, unobtrusive piped music; simple food weekend lunchtimes, lovely scenery, good walking; closed Mon-Fri lunchtimes, sometimes Sat lunchtime too *(Andy and Jill Kassube, LYM)*

Denshaw Gtr Man [SD9710], *Junction*: Good reasonably priced food inc sandwiches and children's dishes, well kept Lees; dogs welcome in tap room *(Stanley Ward and friends)*; [Oldham Rd], *Printers Arms*: Open fire in lounge, no-smoking room near bar, good reasonably priced home-made food with interesting specials, well kept Courage-related ales and Marstons Pedigree *(S E Paulley)*

☆ **Diggle** Gtr Man [Diglea Hamlet, Sam Rd; village signed off A670 just N of Dobcross; SE0008], *Diggle Hotel*: Modernised three-room hillside pub with emphasis lunchtime and early evening on good food from sandwiches to reasonably priced steaks, inc children's dishes; well kept Boddingtons and Timothy Taylors Golden Best and Landlord, decent wines, good choice of malt whiskies, good coffee, friendly service, soft piped music, rustic fairy-lit tables among the trees, nice spot just below the moors; opens noon *(Andy and Jill Kassube, BB)*

☆ **Downham** [OS Sheet 103 map reference 785443; SD7844], *Assheton Arms*: Exceptionally pretty village draws many at weekends to this attractive rambling beamed pub with its wide range of generous reasonably priced food inc children's dishes, well kept Whitbreads-related ales, decent wines, and piped music that for once draws plaudits; a welcome for children, too; still strongly recommended, though recently service has sometimes been a bit too unbending for a main entry listing *(J R Henderson, Brian Kneale, Robert Gartery, Gwen and Peter Andrews, Julie and Andy Hawkins, Bronwen and Steve Wrigley, Wayne Brindle, LYM)*

Dunham Woodhouses Gtr Man [B5160 – OS Sheet 109 map reference 724880; SJ7288], *Vine*: Reliable food (not Sun-Weds evenings) in carefully refurbished village pub with fires in its four cosy rooms; seats outside *(John Watson, Bill Ryan)*

☆ **Eccles** Gtr Man [33 Regent St (A57 – handy for M602 junction 2); SJ7798], *Lamb*: Large Edwardian pub, imposing but down to earth despite its splendid etched windows, fine woodwork and furnishings; cheap well kept Holts from unusual bar counter, full-size snooker table *(Bill and Lydia Ryan)*

Eccles [146 Church St], *Wellington*: More cheap well kept Holts in small main-st pub with pleasant unpretentious but comfortable lounge, friendly staff; pool in adjacent bar *(B M Eldridge)*; [133 Liverpool Rd, Patricroft, a mile from M63 junction 2; SJ7698], *White Lion*: Good Holts yet again, at the same low price, in fine multi-roomed character pub with games-oriented tap room, quiet lounge, smoke room with old-fashioned weekend sing-songs *(Pete Baker)*

Eccleston [Towngate; B5250, off A581 Chorley—Southport; SD5117], *Farmers Arms*: Food all day in big Whitbreads pub/restaurant with black cottagey furniture, red plush wall seats, low beams, rough plaster covered with plates, pastoral prints, clocks and brasses; good range of well kept ales inc guests, darts; bedrooms *(John Fazakerley)*

☆ **Edgworth** [Bury St; B6391, off A676 N of Bolton – OS Sheet 109 map reference 742168; SD7416], *White Horse*: Pleasantly informal local feel, not too organised, despite lots of highly polished carved dark oak panelling, log fires, copper beams, antique clocks, plush banquettes; five well kept S&N real ales, good value freshly cooked bar food (not Sat evening), friendly quick service; children welcome, tables outside; open all day summer *(LYM)*

☆ **Entwistle** [Overshores Rd, by stn; village signed off Blackburn Rd N of Edgworth – OS Sheet 109 map reference 726177; SD7217], *Strawbury Duck*: Lots of character in cosy dim-lit beamed and flagstoned pub tucked away in attractive West Pennine walking country – occasional trains from Blackburn and Bolton; good value bar food (all day Sat and Sun) from sandwiches to authentic curries and good steaks inc children's dishes, well kept Boddingtons, Marstons Pedigree and Timothy Taylors Best and Landlord with a weekly guest beer; games room, restaurant, live music Thurs, tables outside; children till 8.30; closed Mon lunchtime; bedrooms *(Andy Hazeldine, Mr and Mrs Ashcroft, Bronwen and Steve Wrigley, Bill and Lydia Ryan, LYM)*

☆ **Fence** [300 Wheatley Lane Rd; SD 8237], *White Swan*: Up to a dozen or more well kept real ales and good choice of whiskies in friendly and lively three-room pub with roaring fires, horsey decorations inc jockeys' silks, good quietly pubby atmosphere; no food *(David Poole, LYM)*

☆ **Freckleton** [off A584 opp The Plough; towards Naze Lane Ind Est, then right into Bunker St; SD4228], *Ship*: Oldest pub on the Fylde, big windows looking out over the watermeadows from roomy nautical-theme main bar, good value bar food (not Mon evening) from sandwiches to bargain big steaks, Boddingtons on handpump, airy upstairs carvery and buffet, tables outside;

children provided for *(Jim and Maggie Cowell, J A Boucher, LYM)*

☆ **Garstang** [northbound section of one-way system; SD4845], *Wheatsheaf*: Good range of well priced freshly cooked food inc notable specials (esp fish) and good duck and steak in small and cosy low-beamed pub, very well kept, with gleaming copper and brass, little plush-cushioned black settles and dining chairs; good service, good collection of malt whiskies *(Robert and Gladys Flux, J Roy Smylie, BB)*

Goosnargh [SD5537], *Grapes*: Welcoming local with cosy little low-beamed areas, lots of brass around central fireplace separating bar from restaurant, collection of whisky-water jugs and old telephones, reasonably priced generous standard food inc good Sun roast, well kept Boddingtons on handpump *(Peter Churchill)*

Grindleton [SD7545], *Buck*: Bright, cheerful and popular well run country pub in nice village; good attractively priced home-made food, well kept Vaux beers *(M V and J Melling)*

Hambleton [off A588 towards Poulton – OS Sheet 102 map reference 370412; SD3741], *Shard Bridge*: Attractive whitewashed pub on Wyre estuary by former toll bridge; small lounge with restaurant tables beyond, wide choice of reasonably priced waitress-served food from soup and ploughman's to main courses and puddings, Boddingtons, Ind Coope Burton, Tetleys Bitter and Dark Mild and Walkers Best kept well *(M and J Back)*

Haskayne [Rosemary Lane, just off A567; SD3507], *Ship*: Refurbished canalside pub with interesting canalia in two cosy rooms and two more airy ones; good reasonably priced food, well kept beers *(Fred Collier, Ian Hughson)*

☆ **Haslingden** [Grane Rd (B6232) – OS Sheet 103 map reference 767228; SD7522], *Duke of Wellington*: Reasonably priced food in well designed and run Brewers Fayre dining pub, lovely views over attractive countryside by Rossendale reservoirs; comfortable softly lit main room, polished dark woodwork, bookcases, corner cabinets; good efficient service, well kept Whitbreads-related ales, children in restaurant, big garden with good playground; open all day, good walks *(Mayur Shah, Carl Travis, LYM)*

☆ **Hawk Green** [SU9687], *Crown*: Wide choice of food in lively and spacious bar and well laid out restaurant in barn extension (weekend booking suggested; open all day Sun); well kept Robinsons, good friendly service *(Anon)*

☆ **Heaton with Oxcliffe** [shd be signed Overton off B5273 Lancaster—Heysham; SD4460], *Golden Ball*: Unique isolated setting by River Lune, road sometimes cut off at high tide; three cosy little traditional rooms with very friendly staff, antique settles, low beams, parrot, good winter fires, well kept Mitchells served from a hatch, reasonably priced food, evening restaurant; seats outside; children welcome; open all day Sat

in summer *(S R and A I Ashcroft, LYM)*

Heswall Mer [SJ2782], *Dee View*: Good plain food at sensible prices served briskly in small straightforward pub, unobtrusive piped 60s pop music *(Mr and Mrs C Roberts)*

☆ **nr Heywood** Gtr Man [off narrow Ashworth Rd; pub signed off B6222 on Bury side of N Heywood; SD8513], *Egerton Arms*: Super setting alone by moorland church (pub known as Chapel House), lovely views esp from terrace; comfortable sofas and easy chairs in plush lounge by smart restaurant (huge steaks), simpler bar with cosy coal fire even in summer, big-windowed small extension, good bar food from sandwiches up inc imaginative main dishes, old farm tools on walls; keg beer, huge car park *(Graham Reeve, BB)*

Horton [A59 Skipton—Gisburn; SD8550], *Coronation Arms*: Unpromising exterior but pleasant and spacious inside, Theakstons on handpump, good value bar food all day inc children's and vegetarian; exceptionally helpful friendly service, fine walking country *(D Stokes)*

Irby Mer [Thurstaston Rd; SJ2684], *Anchor*: Comfortable and pleasant Brewers Fayre dining pub extended around original part, Whitbreads-related ales, extensive reasonably priced quick food *(Mr and Mrs C Roberts)*;[Irby Mill Hill, off Greasby rd; SJ2684], *Irby Mill*: Warm red sandstone country pub formerly attached to long-demolished windmill, flagstoned bar with carpeted side room, well kept Boddingtons, Cains and two regularly changing guests, open fire; good lunchtime food (not Sun), though not a dominant feature *(Tony and Lynne Stark, Gill and Maurice McMahon, E G Parish, Paul Boot)*

☆ **Lancaster** [Canal Side; parking in Aldcliffe Rd behind Royal Lancaster Infirmary, off A6 – cross canal by pub's footbridge], *Water Witch*: Good straightforward food in bar (inc summer lunchtime barbecues) and upstairs restaurant of cheerful canalside pub attractively converted from 18th-c barge-horse stabling – flagstones, stripped stone and rafters, pitch-pine panelling, simple furniture; real ales, games room, juke box; children allowed in eating areas, open all day Sat; barbecues *(Brian Kneale, LYM)*

Lancaster [centre], *John of Gaunt*: Well kept Jennings and Tetleys and quite a lot of wines by the glass in Victorian pub with old-fashioned kitchen chairs, plain tables and leather wall settles, immense beermat collection, longish menu of good cheap food; piped jazz, can get smoky *(Mr and Mrs C Roberts)*

☆ **Lathom** [Wheat Lane; Parbold Rd after Ring o' Bells heading into Burscough; off A5209; SD4512], *Ship*: Six well kept and presented changing real ales, often interesting, with occasional real stouts or porters, in comfortable canalside pub, extended but pleasantly cottagey, with painted canal boat utensils in one room, naval memorabilia elsewhere, good value lunchtime food, friendly staff; games room *(S R and A I Ashcroft, John Fazakerley, D Grzelka)*

Lathom, *Briars Hall*: Good food, well kept beer, very friendly; bedrooms *(Fred Collier)*

Leyland [Ulnes Walton (A581 S); SD5422], *Rose & Crown*: Friendly little pub with Burtonwood Mild and Bitter on handpump, basic food lunchtime and early evening; tables outside, aviary where landlord breeds parakeets and other birds *(R B Berry)*

Little Eccleston [by toll bridge; off A586 Garstang—Blackpool; SD4139], *Cartford*: Very busy esp weekend lunchtimes, good range of beers, tasty food; bedrooms *(Andy and Julie Hawkins)*

☆ **Liverpool** [Albert Dock Complex], *Pump House*: Some comfortable seating in multi-level conversion of dock building, lots of polished dark wood, bare bricks, mezzanine and upper gallery with exposed roof trusses; marble counter with bulbous beer engines and brass rail supported by elephants' heads, tall chimney; wide choice of generous cheeses, some hot food, friendly efficient service; waterside tables, boat trips in season, busy weekend evenings *(Geraint Roberts)*

Liverpool [A5036 continuation S; promenade drive by former Garden Festival site], *Britannia*: Good setting on Mersey, wonderful views of shipping and across to the Wirral *(Brian Kneale)*; *Cain Brewery Tap*: Friendly refurbished pub – a place to try these good beers at their best – cheaply, too *(Stephen and Jean Curtis)*; [Score Lane], *Childwall Abbey*: Good lunchtime food inc inventive puddings *(R H Sawyer)*; [Hope St], *Everyman Bistro*: Not a traditional pub, but has well kept Marstons Pedigree and often guest beers; good well priced food inc amazing puddings *(Steve and Karen Jennings)*; [Mathew St], *Flanagans Apple*: Good atmosphere, live music *(Anon)*; [195 County Rd, Walton; SJ3694], *Glebe*: Extensively refurbished Hogshead Ale House – Whitbreads pub mimicking the back-to-basics bare wood and brickwork independent alehouses, with good range of interesting beers from small breweries alongside their own; open all day, lunchtime food, piped music, darts *(Duncan Redpath, Lorraine Milburn)*; [Roscoe St], *Roscoe Head*: Small friendly city pub with particularly well kept Jennings and maybe Jennings, immaculate tie collection *(Steve and Karen Jennings)*

Longridge [Longridge Fell; off B6243 Longridge—Clitheroe above Ribchester – OS Sheet 103 map reference 644391; SD6037], *New Drop*: In lovely countryside, big room overlooking Ribble Valley; family run, decent bar food *(Ada Bradley)*

☆ **Lowton** Gtr Man [443 Newton Rd (A572 1½ miles S of A580; SJ6297], *Travellers Rest*: Popular for good range of tasty food in bar and restaurant, friendly staff, relaxed atmosphere in small cosy rooms off main area – based on four 16th-c cottages, tap room once a mortuary (perhaps explaining

the tale that an unseen ghostly hand sometimes forces staff across the room); Greenalls ales, clocks, tapestry of pub; tables outside *(D Grzelka, J M Watson, Olive and Ray Hebson)*

Luzley Gtr Man [Luzley Rd off A670; SD9601], *Hare & Hounds*: Village local feel, open fire, maps on walls, good lunchtime food *(Ian and Emma Potts)*

☆ **Manchester** [127 Gt Bridgewater St, Oxford St side], *Peveril of the Peak*: Busy lunchtime, but homely local atmosphere evenings in three rooms looping around central servery, lots of mahogany and stained glass, sturdy furnishings, interesting pictures; well kept Courage-related real ales, cheap basic lunchtime food (not Sun), good service, pub games inc table football; lovely external tilework, seats outside; children welcome *(Andy Hazeldine, Bill and Lydia Ryan, Terry Buckland, LYM)*

☆ **Manchester** [50 Great Bridgewater St; corner of Lower Mosley St], *Britons Protection*: Friendly genuine feel in well run small pub with fine tilework and solid woodwork in rather plush front bar, attractive softly lit inner lounge with coal-effect gas fire, battle murals in passage leading to it; well kept though not cheap Ind Coope Burton, Jennings and Tetleys, good bar lunches inc unusual fish, quiet and relaxed evenings; handy for GMEX centre *(Lorrie and Mick Marchington, Terry Buckland, Bill and Lydia Ryan, BB)*

☆ **Manchester** [Shambles Sq; behind Arndale off Market St in centre], *Old Wellington*: Genuinely ancient, with flagstones, gnarled oak timbers, oak panelling; well kept Bass and Stones on handpump, bar food (from noon, not Sun) esp hot beef sandwiches, small upstairs carvery (cl Mon-Weds evenings and all day Sun); often packed lunchtime *(Neil H Barker, BB)*

☆ **Manchester** Gtr Man [Honey St; off Red Bank, nr Victoria Stn], *Queens Arms*: Eye-opening views of Manchester across the Irk Valley and its railway lines from pleasant garden behind cosy and welcoming pub hidden among railways viaducts, scrapyards and industrial premises; well kept Batemans, Timothy Taylors and lots of changing guest beers, simple but often unusual lunchtime and evening bar food, bar billiards, good juke box, bottle collection *(Andy Hazeldine, D W Gray, P Boot, Brian Wainwright, Bill and Lydia Ryan)*

☆ **Manchester** Gtr Man [4a Helmshaw Walk; nr Upper Brook St (A34), off Kincardine Rd/Whitekirk Cl], *Kings Arms*: Worth penetrating the decaying 1960s council estate around it to try its good cheap own-brewed West-Coast-style Yakima Grande Pale Ale, Ginger Beer (the real thing, packs a punch), and Old Soporific (stupefyingly strong); good value unusual lunchtime food (inc good Caribbean chicken); friendly staff, sparse furnishings, good-natured no-frills atmosphere *(John C Baker, Bill and Lydia Ryan)*

☆ **Manchester** [6 Angel St; off Rochdale Rd], *Beer House*: Fine interesting range of ten or so well kept changing real ales maybe inc Belgian Kriek, also farm ciders and good range of bottled foreign beers, in utterly basic pub; outstanding juke box, lively atmosphere, robust cheap bar snacks *(Brian Wainwright, Bill and Lydia Ryan)*

☆ **Manchester** [86 Portland St], *Circus*: Quaint chatty charm, entertaining landlord, two tiny unspoilt panelled rooms with just two pumps both serving particularly well kept Tetleys Bitter – everything else by bottle or can; has always tended to keep door closed to discourage big groups (you have to knock) but has recently seemed more resolutely closed *(Stephen Brown, Bill and Lydia Ryan, Andy Hazeldine; news please)*

Manchester [centre], *Athenaeum*: Quiet pub with brass and mahogany fittings, high ornate ceilings, good real ales, quite a few wines *(A Barker)*; [Hodson St, Salford – off Blackfriars Rd], *Braziers Arms*: Basic and unspoiled, warm friendly atmosphere, two small rooms and big lounge which can be noisy; particularly well kept Boddingtons *(Brian Wainwright)*; [Kennedy St], *City Arms*: Popular bar lunches and well kept Allied and guest ales; may be closed much of weekend *(Bill and Lydia Ryan)*; [71 Old Bury Rd; Whitefield, opp Piccadilly Stn], *Coach & Horses*: Multi-room coaching inn built around 1830, little changed, very popular and friendly, with well kept Holts – maybe table service; darts, cards *(Pete Baker)*; [Windsor Cres, Salford; opp Salford University], *Crescent*: Lively studenty pub with terrific juke box, well kept Holts and excellent choice of guest ales, three separate rooms, spit-and-sawdust mood, comfortable if unsmart; parking behind *(Rupert Lecomber, Bill and Lydia Ryan, Andy Hazeldine)*; [95 Cheetham Hill Rd (A665)], *Derby Brewery Arms*: Huge showpiece for nearby Holts Brewery, their well kept beer, reasonably priced lunchtime food from hatch; mixed clientele *(Brian Wainwright)*; [Oldham St], *Dry 201*: Trendy modern bar, attractive minimalist pillared design, smart staff, up-to-date piped dance music, well kept Marstons Pedigree, continental lagers, real vodkas; over-35s may feel unwanted *(P M Mason)*; [Park St, Strangeways], *Dutton Arms*: Welcoming backstreet pub in shadows of prison, remarkable parrot repeats what you say, Hydes beers *(Brian Wainwright)*; [Oxford Rd; by Polytechnic], *Flea & Firkin*: Very studenty, often packed though big; well kept beer, live entertainment *(Bill and Lydia Ryan)*; Gtr Man [Ontario Basin; Salford Quays], *Flying Dutchman*: Busy one-time working Dutch barge converted to pub/restaurant, decent food *(Jim Sargeant)*; [47 Ducie St], *Jolly Angler*: Friendly smallish backstreet Irish pub very popular with lovers of good beer (Hydes Best and Mild); informal folk music Mon *(Andy Hazeldine, Pete Baker, Bill and Lydia Ryan, Brian Wainwright,*

BB); [52 Cross St], *Mr Thomas Chop House*: Popular city-centre pub reopened after closure 1994, with popular food from fresh hot beef sandwiches to steaks in busy oak-panelled front bar and especially in tiled back dining room with shellfish bar too; well kept Whitbreads-related real ales; open all day but cl from early evening and Sun *(Stephen Brown, Bill and Lydia Ryan)*; [Greenside Lane, Droylsden], *Pig on the Wall*: Big Boddingtons country-style pub in the middle of an estate, lunchtime food Mon-Fri, well kept Mild and Bitter and Theakstons Best; children allowed in TV room *(Graham Reeve)*; [Wilmslow Rd, Withington], *Red Lion*: Old-fashioned front rooms, spacious two-level plusher back bar, food area (no food Sun evenings) and conservatory; well kept Marstons Pedigree, bowling green *(Bill and Lydia Ryan)*; [Granada Studios], *Rovers Return*: Replica of the TV set, just three walls in a larger building, and only accessible on studio tour, but works well – interesting experience, with well priced 'Newton & Ridley' real ale (is it Holts?) *(John Honnor)*; [Church St], *Unicorn*: Well kept Bass, Stones, Worthington and a guest beer on handpump; handy for shopping area, popular with older men *(Brian Wainwright)*; [Gt Ancoats St], *White House*: Well kept beers inc Coach House and Holts, good local atmosphere *(Bill and Lydia Ryan)*; [Liverpool Rd, Castlefield], *White Lion*: Busy but friendly, with good inexpensive food in nicely decorated dining area, four Whitbreads-related ales, interesting local history around the walls; very handy for GMEX and Castlefield *(Paul and Karen Mason, Brian Wainwright)*; [Eccles], *White Lion*: Classic Edwardian layout favoured by Holts but so often destroyed by other brewers, with drinking corridor, usual games in lively vault, quiet lounge, smoke room with weekend singsongs; extremely friendly, well kept beer *(Peter Baker)*

Marple Bridge Gtr Man [Brabyns Brow; SJ9689], *Midland*: Good atmosphere, good friendly service, good value Brewers Fayre food, generous helpings *(Karen Phillips)*; [Compstall Rd], *Spring Gardens*: Good food freshly made and reasonably priced, friendly atmosphere and staff; good for families *(John Fitzpatrick)*

☆ **Mawdesley** [Bluestone Lane; Croston—Eccleston road, N of village – keep going; OS Sheet 108 map reference 505164; SD4915], *Robin Hood*: Good helpings of good value home-cooked food with fresh veg in busy dining pub with open-plan well refurbished rooms inc small pretty upstairs restaurant (often booked well ahead), good atmosphere, cheap children's helpings, several well kept Whitbreads-related real ales, decent wines, quick friendly service, children's room; pleasant countryside *(Keith Croxton, Fred Collier, Jim and Maggie Cowell)*

Mawdesley [Mawdesley—Parbold], *Eagle &*

Child: Nice choice of beers and good value home-made food in beamed partly flagstoned bar; fast friendly service *(Keith Croxton)*

☆ **Mereclough** [302 Red Lees Rd; off A646 Burnley—Halifax – OS Sheet 103 map reference 873305; SD8730], *Kettledrum*: Wide choice of good value genuine home cooking in friendly, cosy and pleasantly individual country local with good views, extraordinary collections esp gruesome knives, partly no-smoking gaslit upstairs dining room, five well kept Courage and Theakstons real ales, good service; children allowed away from main bar till 9, seats outside *(Andrew Stephenson, LYM)*

Morecambe [Paulton Sq; SD4565], *New Inn*: Simple old pub, superb beers, no juke box – where to see the town's real old characters *(Anon)*

Mossley Gtr Man [Manchester Rd (A635 N); SD9802], *Roaches Lock*: Welcoming, with massive helpings of good value food (not Sun evening) *(Roy Cove, Pauline Crossland, Dave Cawley)*

☆ **Mottram** Gtr Man [off A57 M'ter—Barnsley; at central traffic lights turn opp B6174 into Broadbottom Rd; SJ9995], *Waggon*: Reliably good generous food served very promptly all day in comfortable open-plan local, sensible prices, well kept Robinsons Best and Best Mild on electric pump, friendly waitresses, big central fire, good wheelchair access; picnic-table sets and good play area outside *(Pauline Crossland, Dave Cawley, Michael and Janet Hepworth, BB)*

☆ **Much Hoole** [Liverpool Old Rd; SD4723], *Rose & Crown*: Family local, nothing much to look at from outside, but word's getting around about its good food (not Sun), all home-cooked, fairly priced and often imaginative; good service, Greenalls beer, pool, satellite TV; known locally as the Hangmans – Pierrepoint was once the landlord *(Bob and Janet Lee, Jim and Maggie Cowell)*

Nelson [Manchester Rd; SD8638], *Clayton Arms*: Local with good food, well kept beer, real fire *(Colin Trowler)*

New Hey Gtr Man [113 Huddersfield Rd; SD9311], *Bird in the Hand*: Quiet local with particularly well kept Sam Smiths; note the street number – there's another similarly named pub near here *(Bill and Lydia Ryan)*

☆ **Parbold** [Alder Lane; SD4911], *Stocks*: Particularly friendly and obliging service in cosy and warm pub/restaurant popular for good value home-cooked food (not Sun evening) inc vegetarian dishes; main part of pub is a restaurant; well kept Tetleys, busy evenings *(Andy Hazeldine, Rona Murdoch)*

Pleasington [Victoria Road – OS Sheet 103 map reference 642266; SD6426], *Butlers Arms*: Comfortable, with friendly new landlord, good flexible bar menu and interesting specials, games room, bowling green at back *(Sarah Elliott, Gary Goldson)*

Preston [Liverpool Rd, Penwortham Hill; SD5326], *Fleece*: Recently well refurbished, worthwhile food *(Mrs A Bradley)*; [Aqueduct St], *Mill*: Converted cotton mill with club-like studenty atmosphere, live entertainment most evenings (pay at the door); basic bar food, well kept Jennings and Tetleys *(Graham Bush)*; [114 Church St], *Olde Blue Bell*: Large but cosy old pub now run by Peter Sayer, former Welsh International footballer, with good choice of good lunchtime food inc Sun, cheap well kept Sam Smiths from long bar *(Jim Cowell)*

Rawtenstall [SD8123], *Old Cobblers*: Comfortable well furnished pub newly built from local stone, with lots of antique advertisements for fashion shoes, pre-Raphaelite prints; wide choice of well priced food from fresh sandwiches up; nr steam railway *(Ian Phillips)*

☆ **Riley Green** [A675/A6061; SD6225], *Royal Oak*: Cosy three-room pub with ancient stripped stone, low black beams, open fires, seats from high-backed settles to red plush armchairs, turkey carpet, soft lighting; good range of bar food from generous ploughman's up, Thwaites Bitter and Mild on handpump, friendly efficient service; can be packed weekends; interesting model steam engines *(John Fazakerley, BB)*

Riley Green [A675 Preston—Bolton, N of A674 junction], *Boatyard*: Attractively designed newish Thwaites dining pub, good food all day every day, on mound by canal with plenty of narrowboat activity to watch and a beached barge in the grounds; good prices, well kept real ales, tables outside *(Jim Cowell)*

Ringley [right off A667 at sign for Kidds Garden Centre; SD7605], *Horseshoe*: Pleasant, civilised and hospitable, three areas off main bar, good value lunchtime food inc nice puddings, interesting local pictures, pleasant garden behind; well behaved children at lunchtime; can get busy; small village with old stocks and ancient bridge over river Irwell *(Bronwen and Steve Wrigley)*

Sabden [SD7737], *Wellsprings*: By dry ski slope in wonderful position on Pendle Hill with panoramic views over Ribble Valley, pleasant open-plan pub around log-effect gas fire with good straightforward food; local bands Fri *(Bronwen and Steve Wrigley)*

Salterforth [High Lane; B6251 Barnoldswick—Foulridge; SD8845], *Fanny Grey*: Good varied choice of good food inc vegetarian; bedrooms *(David Templar)*

☆ **Salwick** [Treales Rd; N of Salwick Stn, towards Inskip; SD4535], *Hand & Dagger*: New licensees in pleasant old stonebuilt country pub, well kept Boddingtons or Greenalls, food in bar and back restaurant; unspoilt country by Lancaster Canal; children welcome *(Comus Elliott)*

Scarisbrick [535 Southport Rd; SD3813], *Master McGraths*: Single-storey modern pub with imaginative impressive interior – beams, leaded lights, soft piped music, good hot food inc good choice of children's dishes, efficient service, Burtonwood beers *(M and J Back)*

Shuttleworth Gtr Man [Twine Valley; signed off A56 N of Bury; SO8017], *Fishermans Retreat*: Well named as surrounded by well stocked trout lodges; good interesting well presented reasonably priced food, good choice of beers; open all day from 8am *(W Greenhalgh)*

☆ **Slaidburn** [B6478 N of Clitheroe; SD7152], *Hark to Bounty*: Attractive and interesting country inn in pretty village nr Trough of Bowland, decor a pleasant mix of old and new, open fire, brasses, lots of tables (food generally good value, with some summer barbecues); relaxed country atmosphere, friendly staff – a nice place to stay; afternoon teas, restaurant; S&N real ales *(Dr C A Brace, Andrew Sykes, C J Parsons, Comus Elliott, Fred Collier, D Grzelka, Paul McPherson, Sarah and Gary Goldson, J A Boucher, M G Lavery, Bronwen and Steve Wrigley, LYM)*

Southport Mer [Stanley St; SD3316], *Oast House*: New landlord keeps good Bass, iced schnapps; generous cheap food *(W W Alters)*; [Seabank Rd], *Windmill*: Real fires, lots of small areas, good atmosphere, good cheap food *(Andy and Julie Hawkins)*

Stacksteads Gtr Man [SD8522], *Rose & Bowl*: Large and comfortable, in attractive spot; good choice of well served food, good reasonably priced carvery, wide choice of beers, decent wine, cheerful helpful staff; well maintained floodlit bowling green *(W Greenhalgh)*

Stalmine [SD3745], *Seven Stars*: Very welcoming and comfortable, good pub atmosphere, good value food; bedrooms good *(Mrs R Humphrey)*

Stalybridge Gtr Man [Stalybridge Stn; SJ9698], *Station Buffet*: This wonderful private-enterprise place with its excellent changing real ales, good cheap snacks and fine nostalgic decor and atmosphere seems at last to have lost its battle against BR to stay open *(LYM)*; *White House*: Friendly mix of customers, Marstons Pedigree, Theakstons Best and XB, traditional decor with pews, red letterbox for weekly tote, cheap meals *(Andy Hazeldine, Rupert Lecomber)*

Standish Gtr Man [Platt Lane, Worthington – OS Sheet 108 map reference 575114; SD5711], *Crown*: Comfortable panelled bar with chesterfields, armchairs, fresh flowers and open fire, well kept real ales such as Bass and Bass Mild and Boddingtons on rather splendid handpumps, wide range of good value tasty food in pleasantly bright and airy restaurant extension; children allowed away from bar *(Paul Boot, D Grzelka, LYM)*; [very handy for M6 junction 27/28], *Beeches*: Spacious upmarket modern steakhouse-style dining pub, partly flagstoned, in refurbished extended Victorian house; decent food, Walkers real ale, good value wines, friendly efficient service; bedrooms *(Comus Elliott, D Grzelka)*; [Almond Brook], *Charnley Arms*: Modern

more conventional Greenalls family dining pub also well placed for M6, very tidy; reasonable prices, open all day *(TN)*

☆ **Stockport** Gtr Man [14 Middle Hillgate; SJ8991], *Red Bull*: Robinsons Best and Best Mild at their best from nearby brewery in very friendly well run beamed and flagstoned local with substantial settles and seats, open fires, lots of pictures and brassware, and traditional island servery; good value bar lunches (not Sun) inc good hot beef sandwich; quiet at lunchtime, can get crowded evening *(Alan and Lesley Holden, Bill and Lydia Ryan, Brian Wainwright, LYM)*

☆ **Stockport** [12 Little Underbank; can be reached by steps from St Petersgate], *Queens Head*: Handsomely restored late Victorian pub, long and narrow, snug with daily papers, old posters and adverts, back dining area; good bustling atmosphere, reasonable bar food, well kept Sam Smiths on handpump, rare brass cordials fountain; some live jazz, otherwise piped; famous narrow gents' *(S Demont, T Barrow, Bill and Lydia Ryan)*

☆ **Stockport** [552 Didsbury Rd (off A5145), Heaton Mersey; SJ8691], *Griffin*: Thriving unspoilt local with well kept Holts Bitter and Mild in four unpretentiously Victorian rooms off central servery with largely original curved-glass gantry, basic furnishings, no piped music, lunchtime food, seats outside *(BB)*

Stockport [23 Millgate St; behind Asda], *Arden Arms*: Traditional, with old-fashioned snug, extended bar area, lunchtime bar food, well kept Robinsons, several grandfather clocks *(Bill and Lydia Ryan)*; [Brinksway Bridge], *Olde Woolpack*: Two constantly changing interesting guest beers as well as Theakstons, Tetleys and Marstons Pedigree, good value home-made food *(David Ball)*; [82 Heaton Moor Rd, Heaton Moor; SJ9090], *Plough*: Cheap pleasant food and well kept Tetleys and Jennings in big open-plan pub with numerous dark little corners, Zippo lighter collection, character landlady *(Lee Goulding)*; [Buxton Rd], *Red Lion*: Busy bar area surrounded by dining tables, decent food all day inc breakfast, well kept Robinsons; big no smoking area *(Keith Mills)*; [41 Wellington Rd S (A6)], *Unity*: Open-planned Victorian pub, comfortable, cosy and warm; friendly hard-working landlady and staff, well kept Robinsons Best Mild and Bitter on handpump, bar food *(Alan Gough)*

☆ **Tarleton** [70 Church Rd; off A59/A565 Preston—Southport; SD4420], *Cock & Bottle*: Pleasant dining pub, very busy weekend evenings, good value if not cheap, with wide choice inc interesting starters, lots of game and fish; Thwaites Best Bitter and Mild on handpump, friendly service, separate public bar; very busy weekend evenings *(John and Jane Horn, Jim and Maggie Cowell, K R and I Hall)*

☆ **Thornton Hough** Mer [Church Rd (B5136);

SJ3081], *Seven Stars*: Civilised two-room dining pub especially popular with older people, with easy chairs and sofa as well as banquettes and wheelback chairs, usual bar food from sandwiches to steaks inc Sun roasts, well kept Whitbreads-related ales with guests such as Cains, cheerful service, tables outside; bedrooms *(Don Kellaway, Angie Coles, P and K Lloyd, Olive and Ray Hebson, Mr and Mrs C Roberts, John Allsopp, LYM)*

Thurstaston Mer [A540; SJ2484], *Cottage Loaf*: Fairly recently converted from a restaurant, comfortable, friendly atmosphere, professional service, four real ales, good food *(E G Parish)*

☆ **Tockholes** [Brokenstones Rd, Livesey – towards Blackburn – OS Sheet 103 map reference 666247; SD6624], *Black Bull*: Very friendly licensee, well kept Thwaites Bitter and Mild and good reasonably priced straightforward food in friendly modernised pub with good views over moors and Blackburn from big windows and some seats outside; side room with fine snooker table, dogs and children allowed lunchtime; good walks *(Andy Hazeldine, LYM; the Royal Arms and Victoria up here are also good)*

Unsworth Gtr Man [Hollins Lane; not far from M66 junction 3; SD8207], *Queen Anne*: Well kept Thwaites and reasonably priced evening bar food *(Brian Wainwright)*

☆ **Uppermill** Gtr Man [Runninghill Gate, nr Dick Hill; SD9905], *Church*: Clean and comfortable partly stripped-stone old pub on steep moorland slope by isolated church, good value straightforward food, well kept Theakstons and other real ales *(Pauline Crossland, Dave Cawley, LYM)*

Uppermill [A670], *Navigation*: Bright modernised pub with comfortable alcoves, some big modern chairs and tables, Theakstons ales, friendly efficient staff *(Andrew and Ruth Triggs)*

☆ **Waddington** [SD7243], *Lower Buck*: Very genuine and traditional, with hatch service to lobby and front bar with built-in dresser, plain back room, pool room; friendly busy atmosphere evenings and weekends, popular food, Theakstons and other well kept ales; pretty village *(Wayne Brindle, J A Boucher, Andrew Stephenson, BB)*

☆ **Westhoughton** Gtr Man [490 Wigan Rd; SD6505], *Hart Common*: Three-roomed traditional local with basic decor, well kept Theakstons XB and Best; pub games, friendly landlord *(Bill and Lydia Ryan)*

Westhoughton Gtr Man [2 Market St (A58); SD6505], *White Lion*: Traditional hatch-service pub with well kept Holts, several separate small rooms *(Andy Hazeldine, Bill and Lydia Ryan)*

☆ **Wheatley Lane** [off A6068, on the old road parallel to and just N of it between Fence and Barrowford; SD8338], *Old Sparrow Hawk*: Comfortable, civilised and well run country pub with good food, atmosphere, service and wines, well kept Bass, Bass Special and Mild, dark oak panelling, stripped stonework, mock-Tudor carvery; tables out on roomy terrace with views to the moors beyond Nelson and Colne; open all day, food all day, children allowed in eating areas *(C J Parsons, LYM)*

Wheelton [Blackburn Rd (A674); Higher Wheelton – OS Sheet 103 map reference 609223; SD6022], *Golden Lion*: Small stone-built pub recently refurbished in subdued Victorian style, dark furniture, sepia local photographs; well kept Thwaites on handpump, shortish menu but food nicely cooked with fresh veg, attentive landlord *(John Fazakerley)*

White Stake [Wham Lane; not far from M6 junction 29; SD5126], *Farmers Arms*: Popular straightforward Whitbreads food pub now benefiting hugely from massive influx of competitively priced constantly changing guest beers *(Jim and Maggie Cowell, Fred Collier)*

☆ **Whittle le Woods** [Preston Rd (A6); not far from M61 junction 7; SD5721], *Sea View*: This comfortable inland pub really does have a sea view (from upstairs); spacious but cosy and friendly, with decent bar food, Theakstons ales, dining rooms (one no smoking), beams, horsebrasses and coach horns, big stone fireplace in extension; piped music *(Andrew Sykes, Mr and Mrs John Gilks)*

Wigan Gtr Man [Frog Lane; SD5805], *Old Pear Tree*: Friendly cosy local with decent lunchtime food inc vegetarian, well kept Burtonwood beers, beams, brasses, old plates and pictures, and comfortable homely settees *(D Grzelka)*; [Wigan Pier], *Orwell*: Good range of beers inc Timothy Taylors Landlord and an unusual Tetleys Mild, quick food inc pizzas from separate counter *(A Preston)*

Wiswell [just NE of Whalley; SD7437], *Freemasons Arms*: Good well presented interesting food esp starters and puddings, wide choice and attractive prices – so popular Sat evening there's no chance in the restaurant without booking; pleasant and cosy pub in lovely village setting below Pendle Hill, friendly efficient service, good range of beers, lots of malt whiskies *(Joan Fenlon, A and M Dickinson)*

Worsley Gtr Man [not far from M62 junction 13; SD7400], *Duke of Bridgewater*: Good atmosphere in huge pub facing village green, helpful staff *(D Grzelka)*

Wrea Green [Station Rd; SD3931], *Grapes*: Large refurbished open-plan local with well kept Boddingtons, Marstons Pedigree and Theakstons, decent bar food, open fire; tables out overlooking village green, picturesque neighbouring church *(Graham Bush)*

Wrightington Bar [Whittle Lane, High Moor; 2 miles from M6 junction 27; SD5313], *Rigbye Arms*: Tasty good value bar food, nice relaxed atmosphere, pleasant country setting *(D Grzelka)*

Leicestershire, Lincolnshire and Nottinghamshire

New entries here, or pubs back in these pages after an absence, include the civilised Griff Inn at Drakeholes, the friendly Monckton Arms at Glaston, the attractively set Red House at Knipton (good food – all these three places are comfortable to stay in), the Swan in the Rushes in Loughborough (excellent real ales, and good simple food), the French Horn at Upton (increasingly popular for food) and the Pear Tree at Woodhouse Eaves (good wines, imaginative food). As these new entries suggest, this is a good area for pub food, quite reasonably priced – with some real bargains here and there. Leicestershire has the best choice of first-class pubs for dining out in: the cosy old Blue Ball in Braunston, the White Horse at Empingham, the very individual Old Barn at Glooston, the Red House at Knipton, the engagingly small-roomed Crown at Old Dalby, the relaxed and attractive Peacock at Redmile, the hard-to-classify Ram Jam Inn at Stretton (there are those who say it's too continental in style to count as a pub, but we'd say it's an admirable style of wayside coaching inn for the 1990s), and the Pear Tree at Woodhouse Eaves. Of these, we name the Blue Ball in Braunston as Leicestershire Dining Pub of the Year – a very-close run thing between it, its sister pub the Peacock, which won the title last year, and the Crown at Old Dalby. The best Lincolnshire dining pubs are the unassuming Hare & Hounds at Greatford, the stylish Wig & Mitre in Lincoln, the attractive Red Lion at Newton, and the grand old George in Stamford. Of these, we choose the Red Lion at Newton as Lincolnshire Dining Pub of the Year, for its splendid buffet. In Nottinghamshire, the most notable dining pubs are the Martins Arms at Colston Bassett, and the comfortable French Horn at Upton: it's the Martins Arms which we choose as Nottinghamshire Dining Pub of the Year, for the second year in succession. On average, food prices tend to be lower in Nottinghamshire than in the rest of the area, and in comparison with the other two counties it's fair to say that Nottinghamshire pub food scores more on price and value than on sheer quality. In Nottinghamshire, too, beer prices tend to be lower than in the rest of this area; overall, beer prices in the three counties are clearly lower than the national average, and particularly so in pubs supplied by the local brewer, Hardys & Hansons (own brews from the Fellows Morton & Clayton in Nottingham were the cheapest beers we found). Beer quality is uniformly high in the area, one of the best in Britain for good ales as witnessed by the relatively high proportion of pubs here gaining our new Beer Award. In the Lucky Dip section at the end of the chapter, we'd particularly mention the White Horse in Alford, Tally Ho at Aswarby, Five Horseshoes at Barholm, Priest House near Castle Donington, Leagate near Coningsby, Chequers at

Gedney Dyke, Black Horse at Grimston, Bell at Halton Holegate, Fox &
Goose at Illston on the Hill, Three Horseshoes at Kibworth Harcourt,
George at Leadenham, Welford Place in Leicester, Softleys in Market
Bosworth, Bull at Market Deeping, Full Moon at Morton, Old Kings Arms
in Newark, Vine in Skegness, Finches Arms at Hambleton, Cross Keys at
Upton, Black Horse at Walcote and Abbey Lodge at Woodhall Spa; as we
have inspected most of these, we can vouch for their quality.

BRAUNSTON   (Leics)   SK8306 Map 4

Blue Ball ⊕ ♀

Village signposted off A606 in Oakham

Leicestershire Dining Pub of the Year

Said to be Rutland's oldest pub, this carefully refurbished place is under the same
ownership as the extremely popular Peacock at Redmile, and run along similar
lines, with an emphasis on the very good and rather unusual food. First-rate
dishes might include sandwiches (from £1.80), home-made soup (£1.90; they
always use vegetarian stock), a platter of French cheeses (£3.50), guinea fowl
gallantine (£3.85), wild mushroom and artichoke salad (£4.20), tagliatelle
(£4.75), lasagne (£4.95), free-range chicken with a changing sauce (£6.50), pork
in mustard sauce (£6.95), excellent bream in basil sauce or red mullet in garlic
sauce, grilled salmon in honey and lime sauce (£8.40), fillet of steak with stilton,
wrapped in bacon with a port sauce (£11.95), and puddings like profiteroles in
hot chocolate sauce or millefeuille (£2.50). The main area preserves its original
form of separate rooms, and has quite a cosy and informal atmosphere, while the
furnishings and decorations – not too fussy – are individual and interesting. The
staff are cheerful; efficient and warmly welcoming atmosphere. A fine choice of
real ales on handpump such as Bass, Greene King Abbot, Ind Coope Burton,
Marstons Pedigree and Tetleys, and up to 8 wines by the glass (including one
sparkling). Dominoes, shove-ha'penny (not much used), and piped music; one
room is no smoking. (*Recommended by Brian and Jill Bond, Jim Farmer, Stephen Brown,
Dr M Bridge, Brian Atkin, Robert Gower, Margaret Mason, David Thompson, Mike and Jo,
Rona Murdoch*)

*Free house ~ Licensees Colin and Celia Crawford ~ Real ale ~ Meals and snacks
(12-2, 6.30-10) ~ Restaurant (closed Sun-Tues evenings) ~ (01572) 722135 ~
Children welcome ~ Open 12-3, 6-11*

Old Plough ♀

One reader tells us he's had many a happy Sunday at this popular old inn. It's
becoming very foody, but the meals are well worth sampling, with real effort put
into their preparation and presentation. A good choice of attractively served
wholesome meals includes dishes like soup (£1.85), filled rolls (from £2.25),
hoagies (£2.50), king prawn kebab (£4.25), feta cheese salad (£5.75), chicken,
tomato and garlic tortellini, vegetable and oyster strudel or steak and kidney pie
(£6.95), fettucini with prawns, smoked salmon, mushroom and chives (£7.95),
chicken wrapped in bacon with a creamy leek and pepper sauce (£8.95) and steaks
(from £9.50); also good specials, interesting ice creams and other puddings like
lemon and kiwi mousse torte or toffee apple bakewell (£2.50). They mark
healthier dishes on the menu with a special symbol. Booking is recommended for
their Sunday lunch. There's a nice pubby feel in the traditional bars, with
upholstered seats around cast-iron-framed tables under the heavy and irregular
back beams, and plenty of brass ornaments on the mantelpiece. At the back is a
stylish modern conservatory dining room, with cane furniture, neat tiles, cream-
painted brickwork and frilled and swagged pastel curtains. The lounge bar has
well kept John Smiths, Marstons Pedigree, Theakstons Old Peculier and XB on
handpump, with Pimms by the jug in summer, and a very good range of wines that

includes several half bottles (though not all the wines on the list may be available). The carpeted public bar has darts in winter; maybe piped music. Beside the no-smoking conservatory picnic-table sets shelter among fruit trees, and there's a boules pitch out here. The inn-sign is attractive. (*Recommended by Paul Cartledge, Jim Farmer, L Walker, David and Gillian Phillips, J D Cloud, Paul J Skeldon, Joan and Michel Hooper-Immins, Paul and Janet Wareing, G E Power, Ralph Holland*)

Free house ~ Licensees Andrew and Amanda Reid ~ Real ale ~ Meals and snacks (till 10) ~ Restaurant ~ Oakham (01572) 2714 ~ Children in restaurant and eating area of bar ~ Open 11-3, 6-11; closed 25 Dec

BURROUGH ON THE HILL (Leics) SK7510 Map 7

Stag & Hounds

Village signposted from B6047 in Twyford, 6 miles S of Melton Mowbray

It is worth tracking down this friendly little village pub – the licensees work really hard to make everything just right, and brought with them to the pub considerable catering experience. The current selection of meals includes dishes like sandwiches (from £1.25, one reader who ordered too many was happily provided with a doggy bag), soup (£1.75), garlic mushrooms with stilton or ploughman's (£2.50), pork chops or moules marinières (£3.95), chicken curry (£4.25), steak pie, stew and dumplings or chilli (£4.95), chicken curry (£4.25), steak pie (£4.95), trout with prawns and flaked amonds (£6.25), steaks (from £7.50), and several more fish specials; children's meals (from £1.50). They do good theme nights, with a recent French evening particularly well received; as well as excellent French dishes they decorated the pub specially and had an accordion player going from table to table. Well kept Courage Directors, John Smiths, Marstons Pedigree, the local Parish Bitter (which several years ago used to be brewed here), and summer guests on handpump. The bar has been tidied up since the Moores took over, and has traditionally pubby furnishings and good open fires; darts, pool, fruit machine, juke box. There are seats in the garden, with a children's play area, and a new pétanque court. (*Recommended by David and Shelia, Brian Atkin, J D Cloud, Stephen Brown, Derek and Sylvia Stephenson, E J Locker, Paul and Margaret Baker, P J Caunt*)

Free house ~ Licensees Peter and Lynn Moore ~ Real ale ~ Meals and snacks (till 10 Fri and Sat); not Sun evening) ~ Somerby (01664) 77375 ~ Children welcome ~ Open 11-2(3 Sat), 6-11; closed winter weekday lunchtimes

COLEBY (Lincs) SK9760 Map 8

Bell £

Far Lane; village signposted off A607 S of Lincoln, turn right into Far Lane

New licensees have taken over this welcoming and reliable dining pub since our last edition but they're no strangers to the Bell, with Sara having spent the last few years working in the restaurant. Usually busy at lunchtimes, it's a cosy place, with a roaring log fire at each end of the main bar, and American and Canadian car licence plates hanging on the wall. Newly redecorated, the three communicating carpeted rooms also have low black joists, pale brown plank-panelling, a variety of small prints, and open fires. Generously served food includes soup (from £1.50), garlic mushrooms in tomato and basil sauce (£2.50), cauliflower and broccoli au gratin (£4.75), mushroom stroganoff (£4.95), plaice stuffed with prawns and mushrooms (£5.50), beef, mushroom and Guinness pie (£5.95), slices of beef wrapped around a minced pork and cheese stuffing in a tomato and basil sauce (£6.95), chicken en croûte (£7.95), steak with a choice of sauces (from £8.75), and daily specials; Wednesday night is fish night. They also have a range of cheaper snacks in the bar and pool room like burgers, local sausage and chicken nuggets (£3.25). Well kept Bass, Marstons Pedigree and Tetleys on handpump, lots of malt whiskies; friendly service. There's a quite separate pool room, satellite TV, and a couple of picnic-table sets outside. (*Recommended by Lawrence Pearse, Roger A Bellingham, M and J Back, Mike and Maggie Betton, Drs N R and A de Gay, Jeff Davies*)

Pubmaster ~ Tenants Robert Pickles and Sara Roe ~ Real ale ~ Meals and snacks (till 10) ~ Restaurant ~ Lincoln (01522) 810240 ~ Children welcome ~ Jazz every Fri ~ Open 11-3, 7(6 summer Sats)-11 ~ Bedrooms: /£29.50B, plus £3 breakfast

COLSTON BASSETT (Notts) SK7033 Map 7

Martins Arms 🍴 ♀

Signposted off A46 E of Nottingham

Nottinghamshire Dining Pub of the Year

A very popular place for a civilised meal – not cheap, but with a good deal of style and imagination put into the unusual dishes that easily merits the extra pound or so: soup (£2.75), well made sandwiches (from £2.75), Welsh rarebit or potato cake filled with cheese made in the village (£4.95), chicken sausages with a leek salad, vegetable filled filo parcels or Melton Mowbray pork pie with local ham and cheeses (£6.95), fish hotpot with a fennel sauce and topped in puff pastry or sauté of duck and rabbit with figs and thyme (£8.95), sirloin steak with a black pepper sauce (£11.95), and puddings such as baked banana in puff pastry with vanilla and Malibu sauce or a good sticky toffee pudding (£3), with extra dining room meals like grilled breast of pheasant with cranberry sauce (£11.50) or pan-fried sea bass on a bed of caramelised onions with Noilly Prat sauce (£12.95). They have occasional gourmet or wine tasting evenings. Uniformed staff give a slight air of formality but the bar part has kept a good deal of homely charm (though it's certainly not the sort of place you'd start a knees-up in) and has a good choice of well kept real ales such as Adnams, Bass, Batemans XB and XXXB, Fullers London Pride, Greene King Abbot, Marstons Best and Pedigree and Morlands Old Speckled Hen, a good range of malt whiskies, lots of wines, some by the glass, an open fire, and a proper snug. Furnishings are a comfortable lived-in mix. No music, just the murmur of conversation. The well laid out restaurant is decorous and smart, with well spaced tables. There's a nice little garden behind, and they can arrange croquet, riding and ballooning. The pub is run by the same people as that enduring favourite, the Crown at Old Dalby, also a main entry in this chapter. (*Recommended by Roy Bromell, R K Wright, B D Atkin, Ian and Val Titman, Stephen Newell, Jane and Brian Bird, Mike and Jo, F and M Brightman, Elizabeth and Anthony Watts*)

Free house ~ Licensees Lynne Strafford Bryan and Salvatore Inguanta ~ Real ale ~ Meals and snacks (till 10; not Sun or Mon evening) ~ Restaurant (not Sun evening) ~ Kinoulton (01949) 81361 ~ Children in garden ~ Open 12-3, 6-11

DONINGTON ON BAIN (Lincs) TF2382 Map 8

Black Horse

Between A153 and A157, SW of Louth

Well worth knowing about in an area short of decent places to eat, this bustling village pub always seems terribly well organised – one reader reports how even at their busiest they effortlessly handled a big group that included seven children. The emphasis is very much on the food (to the extent they might assume you want to eat before you've really made your mind up), but it also has a great deal of character and atmosphere, and the staff often go out of their way to ensure everybody is happy. A softly lit little inner room has some unusual big murals of carousing Vikings, while the snug back bar, with cushioned seats by the log fire in the reconstructed brick inglenook, has very low black beams, and antlers around the wall lanterns. There's more room in the main bar area, popular with locals, and with some heavy-horse prints and harness, a very twisty heavy low beam under its ceiling joists, and a big woodburning stove; the public bar (another log fire) has a games room off, with darts, pool, dominoes, trivia machine, video game and juke box. The good value bar food includes soup (£1.95), filled baked potatoes (from £1.95), ploughman's (£2.95), fresh cod (Friday and Saturday), cottage pie (£4.50), a good steak and kidney pie with a huge puff pastry top (£4.75), vegetarian dishes such as vegetable nut bake (£4.75), gammon and egg

(£5.25), steaks (from £5.95), a huge mixed grill (£10.25), children's dishes (£1.50) and specials such as ham with cider sauce (£5.25), chicken with sherry sauce, almonds and courgettes or fillet of plaice with creamy tarragon sauce (£5.95); pizzas are served till they close, and they do take-aways. Well kept Adnams, Courage Directors, John Smiths, Ruddles Best and a guest like Morlands Old Speckled Hen on handpump; friendly service; maybe unobtrusive piped music. No dogs. There are heavy picnic-table sets in the back garden, where there may be barbecues in summer. The pub is on the Viking Way and looks across the rolling Wolds. (*Recommended by Stephen Brown, Paul S McPherson, Nigel and Lindsay Chapman, Anthony Barnes, Dr C A Brace, Derek and Sylvia Stephenson, Wayne Brindle*)

Free house ~ Licensees Tony and Janine Pacey ~ Real ale ~ Meals and snacks (till 10, 9.30 Sun) ~ (01507) 343640 ~ Children in eating area, not late evening if under 11 ~ Open 11.30-3(12-2.30 winter), 7-11(midnight supper licence) ~ Bedrooms: £25S/£40S

DRAKEHOLES (Notts) SK7090 Map 7

Griff Inn 🛏

Village signposted from A631 in Everton, between Bawtry and Gainsborough

A handsome and imposing brick hotel built originally to serve the increased traffic brought about by the new Chesterfield canal. The waterway passes under the road through a long tunnel, but has been restored and is navigable; a map in the lounge shows the route. In summer people flock to the neatly kept landscaped gardens from where you can look down over the canal basin and the flat valley of the River Idle. Inside, the civilised and carefully colour-matched main lounge bar has small plush seats around its tables, and little landscape prints on silky-papered walls. It's a busy place, well liked as a place to stay but also popular as a lunch stop, with a choice of bar food like soup (£1.75), sandwiches (from £2), ploughman's (£3.50), salads (from £3.50), sweet and sour pork or several vegetarian main meals such as lentil crumble (£4.50), steak pie (£4.75), seafood platter (£5.95), garlic prawns (£6), and fillet steak (£7.50); children's meals (£2.35), and a good bookable carvery. If you're staying, they do substantial breakfasts, said by one reader to be the best they'd ever had. Besides the very good main restaurant (which is no smoking), there's a more airy brasserie-style summer restaurant and a cosy cocktail bar. Boddingtons, Tetleys and Whitbreads Castle Eden on handpump; very friendly helpful service; trivia and piped music. (*Recommended by Mrs M J Aston, June and Tony Baldwin, Simon Collett-Jones, Paul Cartledge, ILP, Dr C A Brace*)

Free house ~ Licensees Michael and Barbara Edmanson ~ Meals and snacks (till 10) ~ Restaurant ~ Retford (01777) 817206 ~ Children welcome ~ Open 11.30-3, 5.30-11; maybe closed winter Mons (except for residents) ~ Bedrooms: £35B/£50B

DYKE (Lincs) TF1022 Map 8

Wishing Well

21 Main Street; village signposted off A15 N of Bourne

Highly thought of by people in the area, this friendly village inn continues to have a reliable reputation for tasty home-cooked food. Well-served dishes include sandwiches (from £1.75), cheddar ploughman's (£3.50), Lincolnshire sausages (£3.75), a selection of home-made pies (from £4), vegetarian feuilleté, prawn salad or lemon sole (£4.50) and daily specials; popular Sunday lunch (£8.50) for which booking is essential, huge puddings, children's dishes, and sometimes even complimentary fried potato slices with cheese and onion. Service can slow right down during busy periods. At the dining end of the long, rambling front bar there is indeed a wishing well, as well as lots of heavy beams, dark stone, brasswork, candlelight and a cavern of an open fireplace. The carpeted lounge area has green plush button-back low settles and wheelback chairs around individual wooden tables. A regularly changing range of well kept beers on handpump might include

Greene King Abbot, Palmers Tally Ho, Ruddles County, Tetleys and Theakstons Best. The quite separate public bar, smaller and plainer, has sensibly placed darts, pool, shove-ha'penny, dominoes, fruit machine and juke box. There's a play area by the garden. (*Recommended by M and J Back, Alice Wooledge Salmon, M J Morgan*)

Free house ~ Licensee Barrie Creaser ~ Real ale ~ Meals and snacks ~ Restaurant (closed Sun evening) ~ Bourne (01778) 422970 ~ Children welcome ~ Open 11-11 ~ Bedrooms: £19.50S/£39S

EMPINGHAM (Leics) SK9408 Map 4

White Horse 🛏

Main Street; A606 Stamford—Oakham

Whatever time you're passing this well-run and consistently popular old inn it's worth popping in for something to eat – even if it's 8 o'clock in the morning. They do lovely morning coffee, afternoon tea and excellent lunches and evening meals, all of which are warmly praised by readers. The landlord works very hard to make sure he's offering what people want, and all the meals make good use of seasonal local ingredients. The main bar menu generally features tasty dishes like soup (£1.95), wholemeal hoagie (£2), ploughman's, shepherd's pie or a tasty chicken bake (£4.95), stir-fried chicken (£5.25), home-baked ham or steak and kidney pie (£5.50), vegetable enchilada or fish pancakes (£5.50), moules marinières (£5.95), sirloin steak (£8.55), daily specials such as lamb's liver in onion and red wine gravy (£5.35) or grilled trout with dill and almonds (£5.95), and a good selection of huge home-made puddings like spotted dick and custard or jam roly poly; children's menu. You can also choose from the à la carte restaurant menu (3 courses from £16). Helpings are big, and vegetables are served separately in a little dish. They've totally refurbished and redecorated since our last edition, but all in keeping with the building's original character. The open-plan lounge bar has a big log fire below an unusual free-standing chimney-funnel, lots of fresh flowers, and a very relaxed and comfortable atmosphere; one eating area is no smoking. Well kept Courage Best and Directors, John Smiths, Ruddles County and Wadworths 6X on handpump, perhaps under light blanket pressure, and good wines; fruit machine and piped music. Bedrooms include some in a delightfully converted back stable block away from the main road and a 4-poster honeymoon suite. Outside are some rustic tables among urns of flowers – a popular stop for cyclists. The pub is on the edge of Europe's largest man-made lake, with good water-sports facilities. (*Recommended by A M McCarthy, H Bramwell, Rita Horridge, V and E A Bolton, Philip da Souza, Father D Glover, RJH, John Knighton, Gordon Theaker, Barry Roe, Wendy Mogose, G and M Brooke-Williams*)

Courage ~ Lease: Roger Bourne ~ Real ale ~ Meals and snacks (till 10) ~ Restaurant (closed Sun evening) ~ Empingham (01780) 460221 ~ Well behaved children allowed ~ Open 11-11, open from 8am for breakfast etc; closed except for residents evening 25 Dec and 26 Dec ~ Bedrooms: £30(£40B)/£40(£52B)

EXTON (Leics) SK9211 Map 8

Fox & Hounds

Signposed off A606 Stamford—Oakham

The unusual village green makes a fine setting for this strikingly tall stone building, handy for walkers on the Viking Way. The elegant high-ceilinged lounge bar is particularly attractive, with some dark red plush easy chairs as well as wheelback seats around lots of dark tables, hunting and military prints on the walls, brass and copper ornaments, and a winter log fire in a large stone fireplace. Popular bar food includes soup (£2.20), sandwiches, ploughman's (from £3.25), excellent liver, bacon and onions (£4.95), chilli con carne, lasagne or home-made pies such as steak and kidney (£5.25), big salads, and the ever popular local-water trout (£7.25) at lunchtime, with scampi or gammon (£5.95), rump steak (£9.50) and duckling breast (£9.95) in the evenings. On Sundays at lunchtime there's a choice between ploughman's and a traditional roast lunch (£9.20). Well kept Greene King IPA, Marstons Pedigree and Sam Smiths OB on handpump; piped music. The lively and quite separate public bar has darts, pool, cribbage, dominoes, juke box, fruit machine and video game. There are seats among large rose beds on the well kept back lawn, overlooking paddocks. Rutland Water is about 2 miles away. Though the road outside is now usually quiet, the size of the building is a reminder of the days when it was the main coach route to Oakham – and indeed coming here some lunchtimes you could be forgiven for thinking it still is; service can slow down if coach parties are in. (*Recommended by Stephen Brown, Tony Gayfer, Michael Betton, Jim Farmer, WHBM, H Bramwell, L Walker, C E Power, R T Moggridge, G B Gibson*)

Free house ~ Licensee David Hillier ~ Real ale ~ Meals and snacks ~ Restaurant (not Sun evening) ~ Oakham (01572) 812403 ~ Children welcome ~ Open 11-2.30(3 Sat), 6-11 ~ Bedrooms: £22/£36

GLASTON (Leics) SK8900 Map 4

Monckton Arms 🛏

A47 Leicester—Peterborough, E of Uppingham

An attractive old stone roadside inn with a sizeable modern extension, this has three small and spotless rooms grouped around the bar servery, giving it a happy and friendly feel; service too is very friendly, attentive and quick. The nicest seats are by a big woodburner in an inglenook fireplace. A very wide choice of good value bar food, all freshly prepared and strong on local ingredients, includes filled rolls (£1.95), home-made soup (£2), filled baked potatoes (from £3), burgers (£3.50), good salty smoked salmon (£3.65), prawns and mushrooms in garlic (£3.75), omelettes or ploughman's (£3.95), tandoori chicken or vegetable pie (£4.95; there are usually lots of other vegetarian dishes, too), pasta (from £4.95), mint-marinated lamb (£5.50), curry (£5.65), steak pie (£6.25), grilled halibut (£6.50) and specials such as baked avocado, liver and bacon or game casserole. Well kept Bass, Marstons Pedigree and Tetleys on handpump, good coffee, a decent choice of wines; maybe piped music. There are picnic-table sets on a sheltered terrace, where a friendly collie-cross is often to be found. The inn is quite handy for Rutland Water. (*Recommended by George Atkinson, K Harvey, Nan Axon, D Goodger, Rona Murdoch, Ruth and Alan Cooper*)

Free house ~ Licensees John and Shirley Hibbitt ~ Real ale ~ Meals and snacks ~ Restaurant ~ (01572) 822326 ~ Children welcome ~ Open 11-3, 6-11 ~ Bedrooms: £32B/£40B

GLOOSTON (Leics) SP7595 Map 4

Old Barn ★ 🛏 ♀ 🍴

From B6047 in Tur Langton follow Hallaton signpost, then fork left following Glooston signpost

Driving down the narrow country lanes that lead to this carefully restored 16th-c pub is very pleasant, encouraging just the right relaxed frame of mind to best appreciate the building and its charms. It's a tasteful place, and the atmospheric old rooms have a definite civilised feel. Steep steps lead down from the small and charming front restaurant with its attendant bar to the lower beamed main bar behind it, which has stripped kitchen tables and country chairs, pewter plates, Players cricketer cigarette cards, and an open fire; up steps, a snug corner has easy chairs and attractive country prints. A varied range of often unusual food can include home-made soup (£1.85), sautéed avocado, mushrooms and peppers on granary toast (£3.75), hot roast beef sandwich (£4.75), ham hock in mustard sauce, well-liked pasta dishes, supreme of chicken with lemon and walnut glaze (£7.20), fillet of plaice in dry vermouth and kiwi sauce (£7.95), roast duck with croutons in a black olive sauce (£9.50), and puddings like jam roly poly and custard; vegetarians are catered for – especially if they ring ahead. Good breakfasts may include local ham. Four well kept real ales on handpump rotated from a wide choice of beers like Adnams Broadside, Bass, Batemans XB,

Fullers London Pride, Greene King Abbot, Hook Norton Old Hookey, Morlands Old Speckled Hen, Theakstons Best and XB, Wadworths 6X and so forth; foreign bottled beers, decent wines, several by the glass. There are a few old-fashioned teak seats in front, with picnic-table sets by roses under the trees behind. The French-style shower-and-wash cabinets please readers, but might perhaps suit best those with at least a modest degree of mobility. (*Recommended by Stephen, Julie and Hayley Brown, Joan and Michel Hooper-Immins, Gwen and Peter Andrews, Eric J Locker, R K Wright, Jim Farmer, David Hedges, Lucy Alexander, Brian Atkin, Derek and Sylvia Stephenson*)

Free house ~ Licensees Charles Edmondson-Jones and Stewart Sturge ~ Real ale ~ Meals and snacks (12-1.45, 7-9.30) ~ Restaurant (not Sun evening) ~ East Langton (01858) 545215 ~ Well behaved children welcome ~ Open 12-2, 7-11; closed Sun evening and Mon lunchtime ~ Bedrooms: £37.50B/£49.50B

GRANTHAM (Lincs) SK9135 Map 7

Beehive £

Castlegate; from main street turn down Finkin Street opposite St Peter's Place

This simple no-frills pub has two claims to fame. The first is its remarkable sign – a hive full of living bees, mounted in a lime tree. Happily they're kept 25 feet up. It's been here since at least 1830, and probably the 18th-c, making this one of the oldest populations of bees in the world. The second distinction is that the father of the current very English-sounding landlord was probably the first to use the name 'ploughman's' for the lunches he served here in the early 1960s. Bar food still includes a good value basic ploughman's with cheddar or stilton (from £2.25 – or a small version from just £1.60), as well as a wide choice of freshly cut sandwiches or filled jacket potatoes, soups like carrot and coriander (£1.45), home-made chilli con carne (£2.30), gammon (£2.95), changing daily specials (from £2.25) and home-made puddings (from £1.35); cheerful service. The bar itself is comfortably straightforward, with Adnams Broadside, Boddingtons and a guest on handpump, maybe kept under light blanket pressure, and a few malt whiskies; fruit machine, trivia, video game, good juke box and satellite TV. The back bar is no smoking at lunchtime. (*Recommended by RB, Ian Phillips, Dr C A Brace and others; more reports please*)

Free house ~ Licensees John Bull and S J Parkes ~ Real ale ~ Lunchtime meals and snacks ~ Grantham (01476) 67794 ~ Children in eating area lunchtimes only ~ Open 11-3, 5(7 Sat)-11; closed lunchtime Sun and bank hols

GREATFORD (Lincs) TF0811 Map 8

Hare & Hounds

Off A15 at Baston N of Market Deeping, or (via Barholm) off A16 Stamford—Market Deeping; signposted off A6121 Stamford—Bourne

It's the current licensees and their culinary skills that lift this little village pub firmly out of the ordinary. All the delicious food is home-made and cooked by the landlord using the best local produce (the meat is naturally reared and comes from a local farmer). Good value and very well liked dishes have included sandwiches (the home-cooked ham are particularly good), soup, chicken breast fried in garlic butter, steak and kidney pudding, carbonnade of beef, pork cooked in cream and Calvados, fresh fish dishes, venison, noisettes of lamb in red wine and shallot sauce, and excellent steaks; good French cheeses and special themed evenings. They may also have a three-course set menu. The homely bar has two rooms, one small (with darts and cribbage), and the other a bit bigger – a cosy dining lounge with four double tables and a roaring winter log fire. The dining room is no-smoking. Well kept Adnams Broadside, Morlands Speckled Hen, and Charles Wells IPA and Bombardier on handpump, decent wines; piped music. There are tables out in the garden; it's a pretty village. (*Recommended by Michael Morgan, Madeline Fuller*)

Charles Wells ~ Tenants Olga and Ricky Payne-Podmore ~ Real ale ~ Meals and

snacks ~ (01778) 560332 ~ Children in eating area of bar and in dining room lunchtime only ~ Open 12-2.30, 5(7 Sat)-11

HALLATON (Leics) SP7896 (Map 4)

Bewicke Arms ★ 🍺

On good fast back road across open rolling countryside between Uppingham and Kibworth; village signposted from B6047 in Tur Langton and from B664 SW of Uppingham

An old thatched inn beside the village green, this friendly pub is a real favourite with some readers, who particularly enjoy the unchanging and traditional feel of the place. It's consistently welcoming to locals and visitors alike and on the rare occasions when there may be slight cause for complaint the obliging staff immediately do all they can to put it right. The unpretentious beamed main bar has two small oddly shaped rooms with farming implements and deer heads on the walls, pokerwork seats, old-fashioned settles (including some with high backs and wings), wall benches, and stripped oak tables, and four copper kettles gleaming over one of the log fires; the bottom room is no smoking during the week. Big helpings of well liked bar food including sandwiches (from £1.40), a huge crock of help yourself home-made soup (£1.95), ploughman's (£3.60), haddock (£4.20), breaded scampi or a choice of salads (£5.20), half roast chicken (£5.50), gammon with pineapple or egg (£6.60), 5oz sirloin steak (£6.80), puddings like lemon cheesecake or pavlovas (£2.25), and daily specials such as spinach and mushroom pancake (£5.85), burgundy beef cooked in red wine with onions, or fresh trout (£7.20), or good Thai chicken served on a bed of pilau rice (£8.20); children's menu or half helpings. Bar meals can be booked on Saturday evening, otherwise get there early as tables fill up very quickly, and meals can stop quite promptly. Service is charming and flexible. Very well kept Marstons Pedigree, Ruddles Best and County and Websters Yorkshire on handpump; coffee; darts, dominoes and a fruit machine in the side corridor; piped music. Picnic-table sets on a crazy-paved terrace behind the whitewashed pub look over the ex-stableyard car park to the hills behind. And from the front you can watch the various activities on the village green, especially entertaining on Easter Monday when there's a 'bottle-kicking' race (they actually use miniature barrels), or in the summer when there may be Morris dancing. No dogs. (*Recommended by Eric J Locker, Rona Murdoch, Mr and Mrs J Back, P G Plumridge, Stephen, Julie and Hayley Brown, WHBM, David and Shelia, D Goodger, Jim Farmer, Anthony John, David Hedges, Alan and Eileen Bowker, Brian and Jill Bond*)

Free house ~ Licensee Neil Spiers ~ Real ale ~ Meals and snacks (till 9.45) ~ Restaurant ~ Hallaton (0185) 889217 ~ Well behaved children welcome ~ Open 12-2.30, 7-11 ~ Big self-catering flat for up to 8 people from £220 per week

HECKINGTON (Lincs) TF1444 Map 8

Nags Head ♀

High Street; village signposted from A17 Sleaford—Boston

Quite a jolly place this, a late 17th-c village pub that wears its years rather well, especially popular at the moment for its warm welcome, friendly atmosphere, and wide choice of well-cooked food. Favourite dishes on the satisfying and enterprising menu have this year included well filled sandwiches (from £1.60), liver and bacon, avocado and prawn hotpot or an unusual potato, onion, cheese and herb pie (£4.50), and smoked haddock and broccoli lasagne or cheese soufflé and prawns (£4.95); also Sunday roasts and puddings such as a well-liked lemon and sultana cheesecake. Comfortable and rather cosy, the left-hand part of the snug two-roomed bar has a coal fire below the shiny black wooden chimney-piece in what must once have been a great inglenook, curving into the corner and taking up the whole of one end of the small room – it now houses three tables, one of them of beaten brass. On the right there are red plush button-back built-in wall banquettes, small spindleback chairs, a clock and an attractive bronze statuette-lamp on the mantelpiece of its coal fire; also, a lively watercolour of a horse-race finish (the horses racing straight towards you), a modern sporting print of a problematic gun dog, and newspapers and magazines set out to read. The good-humoured landlord tells us there may be a few improvements to the decor and furnishings this year. Well kept Vaux Double Maxim and Wards Sheffield Best and Kirby Strong on handpump, with a choice of wines by the glass and cheery, efficient service; pool, shove-ha'penny, dominoes, fruit machine, video game and juke box. They may charge for using credit cards. The garden behind has picnic-table sets, and it's not far to an unusual eight-sailed windmill. (*Recommended by Owen Davies, Susan and John Priestley, Noel Jackson, Louise Campbell, F J and A Parmenter, Alan Mills, Nick Dowson, Wayne Brindle*)

Wards ~ Lease: Bruce and Gina Pickworth ~ Real ale ~ Meals and snacks (till 10) ~ Sleaford (01529) 460218 ~ Children welcome ~ Sun quiz night ~ Open 11-3, 5-11 ~ Bedrooms: £22/£32

HOSE (Leics) SK7329 Map 7

Rose & Crown ⬤

Bolton Lane

Most people come to this atmospheric pub in the sleepy Vale of Belvoir for its really excellent range of well kept beers, but the majority of letters we've had about it over the last few months have also made a point of praising the particularly friendly welcome they've had from the cheery licensees. One reader tells how they insisted he bring his children in, another how they quite happily let him order from the lunch menu in the evening. Mr Routh is quite clearly an expert on beer, and the wide choice he offers on handpump usually includes brews you won't often find in this area, from smaller breweries in the west country or in the north; forthcoming beers are posted up on the walls. There are usually eight on handpump at a time, and over the past year these have included Arhvine Tanker and Hop and Glory, Exmoor Gold, Fullers London Pride, Hadrian Gladiator and Centurion, Hanby Treacle Miner, Hardingtons Best and Old Lucifer, Harviestoun Manor, Moorhouse Pendle Witches Brew, Oakhill Yeoman and Wickwar Brand Oak to name just a few. They also stock several malt whiskies. The wall between the two bars has been knocked down and the place is now much more open plan, with more space and new soft red furnishings; pool, cribbage, dominoes, a fruit machine and juke box. The restaurant and part of the lounge bar are no smoking. Bar food includes filled rolls (from £1.50), soup (£1.75), smoked mackerel or garlic mushrooms (£1.80), ploughman's (from £3.95), vegetarian mushroom stroganoff or home-made pies (£5.50), fresh seafood platter (£5.75), lots of steaks (from £6.55), various fresh salads including chicken and ham or trout (from £7.75), puddings such as cheesecake or apple pie and cream, and various daily specials like pan-fried duck in orange and Cointreau sauce (£8.50); service can slow down at busy times. There are tables on a fairy-lit sheltered terrace behind the building and a fenced family area at the rear of the car park. Campers and caravanners are welcome. (*Recommended by D C Roberts, Andrew Stephenson, June and Malcolm Farmer, J D Cloud, Stephen Brown, R M Taylor, Joan and Michel Hooper-Immins, Elizabeth and Anthony Watts, Simon and Angela Taylor*)

Free house ~ Licensees Carl and Carmel Routh ~ Meals and snacks (till 10, 9 Sun) ~ Restaurant ~ (01949) 60424 ~ Children in bar and eating area till 9pm ~ Open 12-2.30, 7-11; closed 25 Dec

KEGWORTH (Leics) SK4826 Map 7

Cap & Stocking ★ £ ⬤

Under a mile from M1 junction 24: follow A6 towards Loughborough; in village, turn left at chemists' down one-way Dragwall opposite High Street, then left and left again, into Borough Street

New licensees again at this smashing little pub, a genuinely old-fashioned place that never seems to change, whoever's name is above the door. Indeed a visit here is like stepping back in time, the notably friendly atmosphere free from any music or distractions and Bass served the traditional way in a jug direct from the cask. They also rotate well kept beers like Hancocks HB, Smiles Exhibition, Stones Best, Timothy Taylors Landlord and Wadworths Farmers Glory on handpump and electric pump; farmhouse cider, and a developing range of wines. Each of the two determinedly simple front rooms has a coal fire, and on the right there's lots of etched glass, big cases of stuffed birds and locally caught fish, fabric-covered wall benches and heavy cast-iron-framed tables, and a cast-iron range; the back room has french windows to the garden. Good value bar food includes filled cobs, home-made soup (£1.20), ploughman's, Melton pork pie (£3), good chilli con carne (£3.50), beef in cider (£4.25), a selection of vegetarian dishes including curries and lasagne and home-made specials like lamb curry or steak and kidney cobbler (£4.50). Dominoes, cribbage and boules on a sheltered terrace are the only games you'll come across. (*Recommended by Stephen Brown, Karen Eliot, John and Carol Holden, Mike and Kathleen York, Norma and Keith Bloomfield, Paul Wreglesworth, Wayne Brindle, Mrs Elizabeth Howe, Derek and Sylvia Stephenson, Mayur Shah, David and Ruth Hollands, David and Shelia, N P Cox, Stephen Newell, Richard Waller, Jim Farmer, TBB, Russell Dawson, Brian Jones*)

Bass ~ Lease: Graham and Mary Walsh ~ Real ale ~ Meals and snacks ~ Kegworth (01509) 674814 ~ Children welcome ~ Open 11.30-3, 6-11

KIMBERLEY (Notts) SK5044 Map 7

Nelson & Railway £ ◗▮

2 miles from M1 junction 26; Kimberley signposted from exit roundabout, pub in Sation Rd, on right from centre

Last year's managers of this cheery village local have now taken on the tenancy. It's directly opposite the Hardys & Hansons brewery, so has their Bitter and Classic on handpump, consistently well kept. The beamed bar and lounge have a friendly and welcoming atmosphere, as well as an attractive mix of period Edwardian-looking furniture, and are interestingly decorated with brewery prints and railway signs; it can get busy. The food's good value (some dishes even more so than last year), with dishes like sandwiches (from 95p), burgers (from £1.50), filled baked potatoes (from £1.75), crispy deep-fried camembert, or cottage pie (£2.25), several popular vegetarian meals like tomato and vegetable tagliatelle or spinach and mushroom lasagne (from £3.25), ploughman's or steak and kidney pie (£3.75), chicken curry (£4.50), farmhouse grill (£4.75), sirloin steak (£5.95), and specials such as fresh fish, pheasant, or plaice with crab and prawns; children's meals (from £1.50). Good housekeeping, efficient service; darts, skittles, dominoes, cribbage, fruit machine, chess, Scrabble and juke box. There are tables and swings out in a good-sized cottagey garden. The unusual name comes from the days when it was just yards away from two competing railway stations. (*Recommended by Jack and Phillip Paxton, CW, JW, Stephen and Brenda Head, Derek and Sylvia Stephenson, Barbara Wensworth, Mark Bradley, Ian and Nita Cooper, Gary Roberts, Stephen Brown, Professor Ron Leigh, Roger A Bellingham, David Gray*)

Hardys & Hansons ~ Tenants Harry and Pat Burton ~ Real ale ~ Meals and snacks (12-2.30, 5-9) ~ (0115) 938 2177 ~ Children in eating area ~ Open 11-3, 5-11 Mon-Weds, all day Thurs-Sat ~ Bedrooms: £18/£31S

KNIPTON (Leics) SK8231 Map 7

Red House ♀ ⇦

Village signposted off A607 Grantham—Melton Mowbray

Truly red, this beautifully proportioned three-storey former hunting lodge stands on a knoll in the Vale of Belvoir, looking down over a cricket field (hockey in winter) to the attractive village. In the hall you may be welcomed by friendly dogs and cats – a bit like a private house. The roomy turkey-carpeted bar, divided by a central hearth with a woodburning stove, has sturdy old-fashioned furnishings, hunting pictures, and a delft shelf of sporting or game bird decorative plates. A neatly furnished conservatory opens off the airy no-smoking restaurant (good value interesting menus including one for OAPs), and a good choice of rewarding bar food might include cream of stilton soup (£2.25), wild mushroom risotto (£3.25), Rutland pie (£4.65), good smoked salmon, or avocado and wild mushrooms in filo pastry on ratatouille (£4.95) and chicken breast with a stilton and tarragon sauce (£6.95), beautifully served with good often interesting fresh vegetables; they do sandwiches (not Sunday lunchtime), and in winter there's often game from the Duke of Rutland's estate. Well kept Marstons Pedigree, Tetleys and a guest beer changing weekly such as Thwaites Craftsman, a good choice of wines including several dozen changing bin-end selections and good house wines by the glass, decent malt whiskies and brandies, and the best range of ports by the glass that we have seen this year. The public bar area has darts, cribbage, dominoes and fruit machine; there may be unobtrusive piped music. Service is friendly and obliging. *(Recommended by RJH, R A Hobbs, Elizabeth and Anthony Watts, R M Taylor)*

Free house ~ Lease: Robin Newport ~ Real ale ~ Meals and snacks ~ Restaurant ~ (01476) 870352 ~ Children welcome ~ Occasional trad or Dixieland jazz ~ Open 11-3, 6-11 ~ Bedrooms: £21.50(£32.50B)/£32.50(£46.50B)

LAXTON (Notts) SK7267 Map 7

Dovecote

Signposted off A6075 E of Ollerton

Next to this redbrick house are three huge medieval open fields, and this is one of the only parts of the country still to be farmed using this historic method. Every year in the third week of June the grass is auctioned for haymaking, and anyone who lives in the parish is entitled to a bid – as well as to a drink. A former stable block behind the pub has a visitor centre explaining it all. Parts of the pub hgave been refurbished in the last year, but a window in the central room by the bar still looks out over the village to the church tower, and there are brocaded button-back built-in corner seats, stools and chairs, and a coal-effect gas fire; it opens through a small bay which was the original entry into another similar room. Around the other side a simpler room with some entertaining Lawson Wood 1930s tourist cartoons leads through to a pool room with darts, juke box, fruit machine, cribbage and dominoes. Home-cooked bar food includes sandwiches (from £1.50), soup (£1.70), ploughman's (£3.75), steak and kidney pie (£3.90), lasagne or several vegetarian dishes such as mushroom stroganoff (£3.95), salads (from £4), scampi (£4.50), daily specials like roast rib of beef with Yorkshire puddings, fresh fish or chicken breast fillet in a honey and mustard sauce (£4.25), and home-made puddings such as jam roly-poly (around £2.20); pleasant, welcoming service. Well kept Bass, Mansfield Riding and Traditional and Worthingtons on handpump or electric pump; helpful service. There are white tables and chairs on a small front terrace by a sloping garden with a disused white dovecote, and a children's play area. *(Recommended by P J and S E Robbins, F J Robinson; more reports please)*

Free house ~ Licensees Stephen and Betty Shepherd ~ Real ale ~ Meals and snacks ~ (01777) 871586 ~ Children in eating area ~ Open 11-3(4 Sat), 6.30(6 Sat)-11

LINCOLN SK9872 Map 8

Wig & Mitre ★ ⑪ ♀

29 Steep Hill; just below cathedral

You wonder how they ever find time to draw breath at this very civilised and welcoming old town pub – they're on the go non-stop from 8 o'clock in the morning to around midnight, serving a bewildering variety of food and drink from what seems to be countless different menus, some of them changing as often as twice a day. They're happy to let you mix and match items from the various lists, and however rushed or busy they are service always stays cordial and efficient – in fact they were the first pub in the country to receive a commendation from the Polite Society. On a very pretty steep street running down from the cathedral, the attractively-restored building is well worth a look in its own right, and still has some of its original 14th-c features, such as exposed oak rafters and part of the medieval wattle-and-daub by the stairs. Downstairs, the cheerful, simple bar has pews and other straightforward furniture on its tiles, and a couple of window tables on either side of the entrance; the upstairs dining room has settees, elegant small settles, Victorian armchairs, shelves of old books, and an open fire. It's decorated with antique prints and more modern caricatures of lawyers and clerics, with plenty of smart magazines and newspapers lying about – it's the kind of place you'd feel comfortable in on your own. The several menus vary in style and price but a rough selection of dishes might include sandwiches (from £2.75), soups such as pea and watercress (£3), broccoli and cauliflower bake (£5), a full English breakfast (£5, available most of the day), smoked trout, quail's eggs and green bean salad (£5.25), chicken and mushroom pie (£5.75), lamb braised with chillies, ginger and mixed peppers (£6), rabbit with red wine, mushrooms and smoked bacon (£6.50), boneless guinea fowl baked in filo pastry with cabbage and black pudding or pan-fried rib eye steak with cracked black peppercorns, brandy and cream (£10.95), and excellent puddings like warm banana and almond loaf with crème anglaise or chocolate and amaretti biscuit cake (£2.95). It's all very tasty, and understandably very popular, attracting a wonderful mix of customers. There's an excellent and extensive, if somewhat pricey, selection of over 95 wines, many of them available by the glass, with an emphasis on South African, Australian, Chilean or other regional wines. Sam Smiths OB and Museum on handpump, lots of liqueurs and spirits, freshly squeezed orange juice and good coffee. The Hopes run a similar establishment in Leicester, Welford Place. (*Recommended by A M McCarthy, Graham and Karen Oddey, Michael Sargent, P Neate, Rita Horridge, Mrs A Loxley, M Baxter, B R Shiner, Mike and Maggie Betton, J E Rycroft, David and Shelia, Drs N R and A de Gay*)

Sam Smiths ~ Tenants Toby and Michael Hope ~ Real ale ~ Meals and snacks (8am-11pm) ~ Restaurant ~ Lincoln (01522) 535190/523705 ~ Children in eating area and restaurant ~ Open 8am-11pm, including Sun; closed 25 Dec

LOUGHBOROUGH (Leics) SK5319 Map 7

Swan in the Rushes £ 🍺

The Rushes (A6)

Behind its grey-green tiled façade, this chatty pub has several neatly kept separate room areas, each with its own style – though the overall character is lively down-to-earth informality. The seats are most comfortable in the left-hand bay-windowed bar (which has an open fire) and in the snug back dining room. It can get very crowded, but service is good. The main draw is the fine collection of beers – interesting German, Belgian and other bottled beers, and on handpump well kept Archers Golden, Boddingtons, Exmoor, Marstons Pedigree, Theakstons Old Peculier, three changing guests such as Batemans XXXB, Bunces Benchmark and Fullers London Pride, and a changing Mild such as Thwaites. They keep country wines, a good range of malt whiskies, and a couple of changing farm ciders or perries. Bar food (considering the prominence of beers here) is surprisingly good, genuine home cooking using good fresh ingredients, and includes filled rolls (from 80p, hot bacon or sausage ones £1.30), a variety of ploughman's (from £2.95), a couple of vegetarian dishes, chilli con carne or good fresh pasta (£2.75), and beef in Pedigree (£3.75). Shove-ha'penny, cribbage, dominoes, trivia, juke box, and they're licensed for backgammon. The simple bedrooms (a 10% discount for members of the Campaign for Real Ale) are clean and cosy; breakfasts are said to be informal but excellent – just what's wanted after an evening of good beers. (*Recommended by Joan and Michel Hooper-Immins, Stephen Brown, Jim Farmer, Tony and Pat Martin, Miss J Hutchinson, D Wilson*)

Free house ~ Licensee Andrew Hambleton ~ Real ale ~ Meals and snacks (12-2, 6-8.30; not Sat-Mon evenings) ~ Children in dining room ~ Blues or R&B Sat, occasional folk ~ Open 11-2.30, 5-11; all day Fri/Sat ~ Bedrooms: £25(£30B)/ £35(£40B)

LYDDINGTON (Leics) SP8797 Map 4

Marquess of Exeter

Village signposted off A6003 N of Corby

Just as we were going to press we heard that this warmly welcoming and handsome stone hotel had been seriously damaged in a fire and was likely to be closed for several months. Thanks to the age and special character of the building (not to mention the thatch) repair work is likely to be quite a painstaking job, but they hope to have it restored to its former glory by early 1995. Other pubs that have suffered similar setbacks generally do manage to finish rebuilding on schedule, but it is worth phoning to check they're open before setting off to visit. We don't expect things will be much different; it has been very well liked for its friendly atmosphere, and they do good bar food such as sandwiches (from £1.50), soup (£1.75), lemon chicken stir fry (£3.25), several vegetarian dishes such as spinach and almond cannelloni (£4.55), liver and sausage casserole (£4.95), tagliatelle carbonara or tuna and pasta gratinée (£5.10), salmon and feta cheese pancake (£5.35), a pie of the day (£5.95), various specials and home-made puddings (£1.75); they also have a three course fixed price menu (£16.95). Good service from neatly welcoming staff. Well kept Batemans XXB and Theakstons XB on handpump, some malt whiskies; piped music. The pub is named after the Burghley family, who have long owned this charming village. (*Recommended by Stephen, Julie and Hayley Brown, Peter Dowd, Rona Murdoch, Peter and Pat Frogley, Jean and Antony Lloyd; more reports please*)

Free house ~ Licensee L S Evitt ~ Real ale ~ Meals and snacks (till 10) ~ Restaurant (not Sun evening) ~ Uppingham (01572) 822477 ~ Children in family room ~ Open 11.30-11 ~ Bedrooms: £40B/£55B

MEDBOURNE (Leics) SP7993 Map 4

Nevill Arms 🛏

B664 Market Harborough—Uppingham

Nicely placed just over a little footbridge in the centre of the village, this is a brightly bustling and handsome old mullion-windowed inn, with an immediately friendly welcome. The attractive main bar has an especially cheerful atmosphere, as well as two winter log fires, chairs and small wall settles around its tables, a lofty, dark-joisted ceiling and maybe a couple of dogs or a cat. A spacious back room by the former coachyard has pews around more tables (much needed at busy times), but in summer most people prefer eating at the tables outside on the grass by the dovecote; they may give you bread for the noisy ducks in the stream out here. Well kept Adnams, Ruddles Best and County and now two fortnightly changing guests on handpump, country wines, and freshly squeezed orange juice – but they're quite happy to serve you just coffee; good service. Good value bar food includes sandwiches (from £1.45, they do some good open sandwiches like cream cheese and asparagus), peppered mackerel (£2.75), ploughman's (£2.95), spicy chicken wings (£4.25), seafood platter (£4.45) and daily specials like chicken in orange and tarragon sauce, lamb and apricot casserole, pork in apple and brandy sauce or salmon in dill sauce (all £4.95); puddings such as home-made treacle tart or bread and butter pudding (£1.95). Darts, fruit machine and piped music, with carpet bowls, table skittles, Devil Among the Tailors, and Captain's Mistress available for organised functions. Readers this year have particularly enjoyed staying here, and they do big breakfasts, which several people tell us should keep you going all day. (*Recommended by R K Wright, Eric J Locker, P G Plumridge, Douglas and Patricia Gott, Mr and Mrs Ray, WHBM, Ian and Sue Mackenzie, Jim Farmer, K H Frostick*)

Free house ~ Licensees E F Hall and Partners ~ Real ale ~ Meals and snacks (till 9.45) ~ Medbourne Green (0185) 883 288 ~ Children welcome ~ Open 12-2.30, 6-11 ~ Bedrooms: £40B/£50B, cheaper weeeekends

---

Pubs staying open all afternoon are listed at the back of the book.

NEWTON (Lincs) TF0436 Map 8

Red Lion ★ 🍴

Village signposted from A52 E of Grantham; at village road turn right towards Haceby and Braceby; pub itself also discreetly signed off A52 closer to Grantham

Lincolnshire Dining Pub of the Year

As one reader put it recently, nothing changes here, thank heavens. It's a civilised old place, full of charm and character, and still extremely popular for the really very good food; the licensee used to be a butcher, and it does show – the meat and fish could hardly taste better. Still liked best of all is the range of excellent imaginatively displayed salads. You choose as much as you like, with six different types of fish such as fresh salmon, nine cold meats, and pies; a small helping is £6.95, normal £7.95, and large £8.95, with children's helpings £3.50. Their prices are unchanged from last year. The home-made soups are also very good (£1.90), and there's a choice of hot dishes in the winter months including one or two local specialities such as stuffed chine of pork or spicy Lincolnshire sausages; they also do rich puddings, a Sunday carvery, and sandwiches on request. Spotless and welcoming, the communicating rooms have old-fashioned oak and elm seats and cream-rendered or bare stone walls covered with farm tools, malters' wooden shovels, a stuffed fox, stag's head and green woodpecker, pictures made from pressed flowers, a dresser full of china, and hunting and coaching prints. Very well kept Bass and Batemans XXXB on handpump, good coffee and mints and good value champagne. Fresh flowers, unobtrusive but well reproduced piped music, friendly, relaxed service, and nice dogs. Pool, fruit machine and video game; during the day and at weekends two squash courts run by the pub can be used by non-members. The neat, well sheltered back garden has some seats on the grass and on a terrace, and a good play area. The countryside nearby is ideal for walking, and acccording to local tradition this village is the highest point between Grantham and the Urals. (*Recommended by June and Malcolm Farmer, Malcolm Phillips, Brian and Jill Bond, RB, Chris Walling, M E A Horler, Roy Briggs, Barbara Taylor, John C Baker, Dr C A Brace, Howard and Margaret Buchanan, Caroline Wright, M J Morgan, Drs N R and A de Gay, David and Ruth Hollands, David and Shelia, Peter Dowd, David Atkinson*)

Free house ~ Licensee Graham Watkin ~ Real ale ~ Meals and snacks (till 10) ~ Sleaford (01529) 497256 ~ Children welcome ~ Open 11.30-3, 6-11; closed 25 Dec

NORMANTON ON TRENT (Notts) SK7969 Map 7

Square & Compass £

Signposted off B1164 S of Tuxford

Very restful and cosy, this friendly village pub is the kind of place where the landlord always finds time to talk to strangers. The bar has has an attractive grandfather clock in one corner, and is divided by an enormous woodburning stove in a central brick fireplace. There are several more or less separate snug areas, alcoves and bays, mainly with green plush furnishings, farming photographs, a flowery red carpet, red curtains and roughcast shiny cream walls. Big helpings of good value home-cooked bar food such as well-filled sandwiches (from £1.10), soup (£1.10), burgers (from £1.40), pâté made with local game (£1.95), lunchtime snacks like sausage, egg, chips and beans (£2.45), steak and kidney pie or barbecued spare ribs (£3.75), vegetable lasagne (£4.25), and specials like devilled kidneys or chicken in whisky sauce (£3.95); the restaurant has a wider range; children's meals (£2.95). On Sundays they only do a traditional roast lunch (two courses £5.50, three courses £6.50). The public side has pool, table skittles, dominoes, juke box, and a new children's play area with wendy house, swings, Mother Hubbard boot house and tables and chairs for parents. They usually have up to five frequently changing well kept real ales such as Adnams, Black Sheep Bitter, Hull Brewery Bitter, Shepherd Neame Best, Stones and Theakstons Best on handpump, as well as lots of malt whiskies and a carefully chosen wine list; efficient cheery service. (*Recommended by Mrs M Littler, John Honnor, Jean-Bernard Brisset, Eamon Green, Wayne Brindle, G L Tong, Derek and Sylvia Stephenson*)

Free house ~ Licensee Janet Lancaster ~ Real ale ~ Meals and snacks (till 9.45) ~ Restaurant (not Sun evening) ~ (01636) 821439 ~ Children welcome ~ Open 12-3, 6-11, 12-11 Sat ~ Family bedroom: £20B, plus £3 each breakfast

NOTTINGHAM SK5640 Map 7

Fellows Morton & Clayton £ 🍺

54 Canal Street (part of inner ring road)

The delicious own brew beers are still the main attraction at this carefully converted canal building, and a big window in the quarry tiled glassed-in area at the back lets you see into the little brewery that makes them. The creamily malty, gently hopped Samuel Fellows is especially tasty, while the Matthew Claytons is stronger; both are well kept on handpump and very reasonably priced. They also have a range of more familiar ales such as Boddingtons, Fullers Chiswick, Wadworths 6X, Whitbreads Castle Eden and guests like Timothy Taylors Landlord. The building only took on its current appearance a few years ago, but there's such a warmly pubby and traditional feel you'd think it had been here for much longer. It's a softly lit place, with screens of wood and stained glass, dark blue plush seats built into its alcoves, copper-topped tables, some seats up two or three steps in a side gallery, and bric-a-brac on the shelf just below the glossy dark green high ceiling; a sympathetic new extension provides extra seating. They may be busy at lunchtime, when the range of good value bar food includes filled cobs (from 80p), home-made soup (90p), ploughman's (from £2.10), vegetarian dishes such as lasagne (from £3.25), home-made steak and kidney pie or curry (from £2.95), fish and chips (the house special, £3.65), and rump steak (£4.95); prompt, friendly service. Decent wines. Well reproduced nostalgic pop music, trivia, fruit machine and maybe newspapers on a rack. There's a terrace with seats and tables. In the evening (when, as we say, they don't do food) it seems to aim more at young people. The canal museum is nearby, and Nottingham station is just a short walk away. (*Recommended by Norma and Keith Bloomfield, BKA, David and Shelia, R M Taylor*)

Own brew (Whitbreads) ~ Tenant Les Howard ~ Real ale ~ Lunchtime meals and snacks ~ Restaurant (not Sun evening) ~ Nottingham (0115) 950 6795 ~ Children in restaurant ~ Open 11-11; cl 25 Dec

Lincolnshire Poacher

Mansfield Rd; up hill from Victoria Centre

Cooked mainly by the landlord or his brother, the thoughtfully chosen bar food at this cheery town pub can be rather unusual – not least because around half of it is generally vegetarian. Produced using fresh local ingredients, the choice of tasty meals changes every day, but might include leek and potato soup (£2.25), cheese, leek and spinach bake, grilled aubergine and goat's cheese croûtons with pesto or vegetable galette (£3.95), sausage and bean casserole (£4.25), ham and asparagus au gratin (£4.50), smoked salmon and prawn lasagne (£4.75) and braised rabbit chasseur (£4.95); in summer they may serve gazpacho or other seasonal dishes. Helpings are generous, and service pleasant and efficient. They have a splendid arrangement with Batemans under which the pub can serve several interesting changing guest beers and Marstons Pedigree, alongside perfectly kept Batemans XB and XXXB on handpump; also good ciders, mass of whiskies, fruit beers, a wine of the week and an interesting clutch of continental lagers. The big wood-floored front bar has wall settles and plain wooden tables, and is decorated with breweriana; it opens on to a plain but lively room on the left, from where a corridor takes you down to the chatty panelled back snug. It's very popular with young people in the evenings and can get smoky, though less so in the conservatory overlooking tables on the terrace behind. (*Recommended by Mr and Mrs B F Condon, David and Shelia, Geoffrey and Irene Lindley, Dr Keith Bloomfield, Andrew Stephenson, Derek and Sylvia Stephenson*)

Batemans ~ Lease: Neil Kelso and Laurence McDowall ~ Real ale ~ Meals and snacks (12-3, 5-8; not evenings Sat or Sun) ~ (0115) 941 1584 ~ Children in eating area until 8 ~ Occasional impromptu local bands ~ Open 11-3, 5(6 Sat)-11

Olde Trip to Jerusalem ★ £

Brewhouse Yard; from inner ring road follow The North, A6005 Long Eaton signpost until you are in Castle Boulevard then almost at once turn right into Castle Road; pub is up on the left

Easily the city's best-known pub, but it's good to see its appeal extends far beyond the architecture – this unique old building is a good pub too. Deceptively normal-looking from the outside, it's built onto caverns burrowing into the sandstone rock below the castle, some of which have been unusually converted into cellarage and bars. The upstairs bar is the most impressive, the walls, panelled at the bottom, soaring steeply up into remote and shadowy heights, with cosy and simply furnished hollowed-out side alcoves. Unfortunately, this part is often closed at lunchtime. The friendly downstairs bar is also mainly carved from the rock, with leatherette-cushioned settles built into the dark panelling, barrel tables on tiles or flagstones, and more low-ceilinged rock alcoves. Ghostly footsteps heard in the cellar may belong to some ancient cellarman, though he probably wouldn't recognise the current well kept ales: Hardys & Hansons Classic and Best, and Marstons Pedigree, all served on handpump – and quite reasonably priced. Home-made bar food includes cobs and sandwiches (from 80p), filled baked potatoes (from £1.50), giant Yorkshire puddings with 12 different fillings such as beef and vegetables or pork and stuffing (£3.80), and daily specials such as steak and kidney pie or a mixture of traditional English, Chinese and Mexican meals, with a few vegetarian dishes always available (up to £3.95). Several whiskies and wines, cribbage, dominoes, chess, fruit machine, ring-the-bull; seats outside. The pub dates back much earlier than the current building, and in the late 12th-c a previous one was a meeting place for Crusaders on the way to the Holy Land. *(Recommended by Mark and Diane Grist, Richard Houghton, David and Shelia, Paul and Ursula Randall, D Cox, Keith Mills)*

Hardys & Hansons ~ Manager Patrick Dare ~ Real ale ~ Lunchtime meals and snacks ~ Nottingham (0115) 947 3171 ~ Open 11-11 Weds-Sat, 11-3, 6-11 Mon and Tues; closed 25 Dec

Sir John Borlase Warren £

1 Ilkeston Rd; Canning Circus (A52 towards Derby – pub faces you as you come up the hill from city centre)

Attractively placed opposite Georgian almshouses and now smartened up outside to more accurately reflect the internal character, this traditional local is probably the city's most civilised pub. It takes its name from the distinguished naval commander who in 1798 defeated an attempted French invasion of Ireland off Kilkenna, and there are plenty of prints commemorating his career on the walls of the half-dozen communicating rooms. Other pictures range from early humorous advertisements and Victorian sentimental engravings to a big chromolithograph of Queen Victoria's Diamond Jubilee procession, as well as etched mirrors, engraved glass, comfortable parlourish seating, swirly Victorian acanthus-leaf wallpaper, dark brown Anaglypta dado, sturdy brass lamps, a delft shelf, and swagged russet curtains with net lower curtains in the three big bay windows. Well kept Greenalls Original, Shipstones Bitter and Tetleys on handpump; good friendly service. Well-priced and popular home-made bar food, from a counter in the downstairs room, includes filled cobs (from 95p), filled baked potatoes, ploughman's (from £2.40), and hot meals like chilli con carne, nut and mushroom fettucine, meat or vegetable lasagne, steak and kidney pie or fisherman's hotpot (all £2.95); Sunday lunch (£4.25). The eating area is no smoking at lunchtime; fruit machine, trivia game and piped music. At the back a garden has tables sheltering under an old tree, and there may be barbecues out here in summer. *(Recommended by David and Shelia, Eric Locker and others; more reports please)*

Greenalls ~ Manager Ian Haldane ~ Real ale ~ Lunchtime meals and snacks ~ Restaurant (not Sun evening) ~ Nottingham (0115) 947 4247 ~ Children welcome ~ Mon quiz night ~ Open 11(12 Sat)-3, 5-11, all day Fri

OLD DALBY (Leics) SK6723 Map 7

Crown ★ ⑪ ♀

By school in village centre turn into Longcliff Hill then left into Debdale Hill

The excellent and ambitious food at this converted farmhouse is all home-made, right down to the bread, sausages, oil and vinegar; even the herbs are grown in the garden. Meals are quite pricey but very imaginative, tasty and completely fresh (the pub is free from microwaves or chips), and they generally come in big helpings. With lots more lighter meals added to the menu this year the choice might include soup (£2.75), sandwiches and rolls (from £2.75), Welsh rarebit or a vegetarian sausage on a bed of pickled red cabbage (£4.95), vine leaf parcels filled with rice, wild mushrooms and courgettes or shallow fried scallops and mussels in a cream and mushroom sauce (£5.95), stuffed quail (£6.95), baked aubergine (£7.90), beef and oyster pie or chicken breast filled with julienne of carrots and spinach with a watercress sauce (£8.50), salmon in seaweed and puff pastry (£10.50), fillets of sea bass on Chinese-style noodles with lemon, lime and ginger sauce (£10.95), and puddings like pear and almond flan or crème brûlée (£3). The restaurant now has the same menu with an additional £1 surcharge; Sunday lunch; no credit cards. A very wide range of real ales tapped from the cask includes beers like Adnams Broadside, Brakspears, Batemans XXXB, Fullers London Pride, Greene King Abbot, Hook Norton Best, Marstons Pedigree, Morlands Old Speckled Hen, Timothy Taylors Landlord and Woodfordes Wherry and Baldric; also a reasonably priced wine selection, 20 malt whiskies and several brandies and Italian liqueurs served by staff wearing black-and-white uniforms and bow ties. Despite the emphasis on food, the pub still keeps much of its original layout and feel, and the three or four little rooms have black beams, one or two antique oak settles, William Morris style armchairs and easy chairs, hunting and other rustic prints, fresh flowers, and open fires; the snug and large dining room are no smoking. One room has darts, dominoes, and cribbage. Morris dancing once a year. There are plenty of tables on a terrace, with a big, sheltered lawn (where you can play boules and croquet) sloping down among roses and fruit trees. It can get very full (especially in the evenings and at weekends), and service can slow down then. The licensees run another main entry, the Martins Arms at Colston Bassett. (*Recommended by Paul and Sue Merrick, D K Carter, Stephen Brown, Martin Janson, David and Helen Wilkins, V and E A Bolton, Sue and Brian Wharton, Ted George, Brian and Jane Bird, David and Shelia, Martin Cooke, Drs N R and A de Gay, Comus Elliott, George Atkinson, PACW*)

Free house ~ Licensees Lynne Strafford Bryan and Jack Inguanta ~ Real ale ~ Meals and snacks (till 10) ~ Restaurant (not Sun evening) ~ Melton Mowbray (01664) 823134 ~ Occasional Morris dancers ~ Children welcome away from bar and Tap Room ~ Open 12-2.30, 6-11

OLD SOMERBY (Lincs) SK9633 Map 7

Fox & Hounds

B1176 E of Grantham

The seafood stands out at this attractive creeper-covered country pub, but the rest of the tasty, promptly served food is well liked too. You might find dishes like home-made soup (£1.60), sandwiches or spectacular jumbo rolls (from £1.95; ham, banana and grilled cheese £2.35, steak £3.95), home-made pâté (£2.95), ploughman's (£3.45), home-made lasagne (£4.50), salads with home-cooked meats (from £4.95), freshly-battered Grimsby haddock, plaice or halibut (from £5.25), steaks (from £8.75), and daily specials like cream cheese and broccoli bake (£4.50), home-made chicken and ham pie (£4.75) or smoked cod en croûte (£5.50); Sunday roast lunch (£4.95). There's a warming, friendly atmosphere in the several little rooms, as well as some copper-topped tables, comfortable seats including some banquettes and stools upholstered in a hunting-print fabric, and pictures on the same theme. One room is no smoking. Well kept Marstons Pedigree, Ruddles County and guests like Theakstons Old Peculier or Timothy Taylors Landlord on handpump or electric pump. There's a large garden with plenty of tables and chairs, and a big car park. *(Recommended by Stephen Brown, Derek and Sylvia Stephenson, RB, Carl Day, Bernard and Wendy Brookes, Mrs S Wilbram, R Simmons)*

Free house ~ Licensees Tony and Karen Cawthorn ~ Real ale ~ Meals and snacks (not Mon) ~ Restaurant (not Sun evening) ~ (01476) 64121 ~ Children in eating area of bar ~ Occasional live entertainment ~ Open 11.30-2.30, 7-11, all day Sat; closed Mon (except bank hols)

REDMILE (Leics) SK7935 Map 7

Peacock 🍴 ♉

Off A52 W of Grantham at Belvoir Castle, Harlby, Melton signpost, then right at crossroads signposted Redmile

Once again the reports we've had over the last few months on this friendly village house have been full of unstinting praise for the distinguished bar food. It seems they can't put a foot wrong at the moment, with readers astonished at the amount of care taken with the texture, flavour and presentation of all their dishes. In particular one family were delighted to see they took the same care preparing a tiny helping of pork for their one-year old daughter. They aim for a French flavour with the excellent, generously served meals, which might include dishes like lunchtime sandwiches, watercress soup (£1.90), baked avocado and stilton (£3.50), tagliatelle with a sauce of smoked bacon, onion, mushroom, tomato and basil (£4.75), poached eggs with mushrooms and bacon in red wine sauce, king prawns provençale (£5.15), chicken Dijon or delicious red mullet baked with tomato and basil, sirloin steak or pan-fried slices of duck with a blackcurrant sauce (both £8.50), and lots of perfect puddings such as caramelised apple tart; vegetables are very good, while service is prompt and efficient. There's also a pretty little no-smoking restaurant, with a three course set menu for £12.95. It can get busy at lunchtimes and they recommend booking. The range of well kept beers on handpump includes Bass, Greene King Abbot, Marstons Pedigree, Tetleys, and Timothy Taylors Landlord, and they have decent wines including fairly priced bottles and some by the glass; occasional special events such as cookery demonstrations or wine tastings. Despite the emphasis on eating, the spotless beamed rooms have an easy-going pubby feel, as well as pews, stripped country tables and chairs, the odd sofa and easy chair, some stripped golden stone, old prints, chintzy curtains for the small windows, and a variety of wall and table lamps; several areas are no-smoking. Open fires, darts, cribbage, dominoes, maybe unobtrusive piped music, and tables outside. There's a newish conservatory, the Green Room. The pub is in an extremely pleasant tranquil setting near Belvoir Castle. *(Recommended by David and Helen Wilkins, David Atkinson, Michael Lyne, Roxanne Chamberlain, Nigel Hopkins, T Whitford, Mike and Jo, Mark and Mary Fairman, Sue and Brian Wharton, Wendy Arnold, Dr Sheila Smith, Derek and Sylvia Stephenson, E D Bailey, Dave Thompson, Margaret Mason, Drs N R and A de Gay, Keith Stevens, D S and J M Jackson)*

Free house ~ Licensees Celia and Colin Craword ~ Real ale ~ Meals and snacks (12-2, 6-10) ~ Restaurant ~ Bottesford (01949) 42554 ~ Children welcome ~ Open 11-3, 6-11

RETFORD (Notts) SK 6980 Map 7

Market £ 🍺

West Carr Road, Ordsall; follow Retford Leisure Centre sign off A620 W, then after West Carr Road Industrial Estate sign on your right take first left turning up track which – if you look closely – is signed for the pub; or, on foot, from Retford Rly Stn follow footpath under S of frontage, turn R at end

A surprising find amongst the factories of a light industrial estate, this unexceptional-looking place turns out to be rather friendly and comfortable, and has a range of around 14 well kept beers that lifts it firmly out of the ordinary. With helpful notes detailing each brew, the choice typically includes such ales as Bass, Boddingtons, Fremlins, Fullers Chiswick, Kelham Pale Rider, Marstons Pedigree, Morlands Old Speckled Hen, Theakstons Best, Old Peculier and XB, Youngers No 3 and IPA and Youngs Special, all on handpump; they also have farmhouse cider. Very good value and tasty home cooked bar food includes soup (£1.25), burgers (from £1.40), filled baked potatoes (from £1.75), sausage, egg, chips and peas (£3), lasagne, curry or mushroom and nut fettucini (£3.95), steak and kidney pie (£4.25), scampi (£4.50), mixed grill (£4.95), steaks, their popular fresh Scarborough haddock weighing over one pound (£8.50) and children's meals (£2); they're quite happy to provide dishes not on the menu wherever possible. They do a carvery (£5.95 help-yourself main course) on Sunday lunchtimes and some winter evenings, and have recently introduced a take-away service between 10.30 and 11.30 pm; cheery and obliging service. The cosy bar has green plush wall banquettes and dimpled copper or dark wood tables, and pantiles over the bar servery, with an open fire at one end and a little blue plush snug at the other. A spacious conservatory dining room opens off (it can get very warm on a sunny summer's day), and in turn gives on to a small terrace with white tables. They may have theme nights like Bavarian or Italian. *(Recommended by Alan and Eileen Bowker, Peter Marshall, John C Baker and others)*

Free house ~ Licensee Raymond Brunt ~ Real ale ~ Meals and snacks (till 10) ~ Restaurant ~ Retford (01777) 703278 ~ Children in eating area ~ Jazz monthly Sunday lunchtimes, occasional music Fri or Sat night ~ Open 11-4, 5.30-11; all day Sat

SIBSON (Leics) SK3500 Map 4

Cock

A444 N of Nuneaton

The outside of this thatched and timbered country pub is especially attractive, and best of all in summer when there may be colourful hanging baskets standing out starkly against the whitewashed walls. It dates back to the 13th c, with proof of its age in the unusually low doorways, ancient wall timbers, heavy black beams, and genuine latticed windows. An atmospheric room on the right has comfortable seats around cast-iron tables, and more seats built in to what was once an immense fireplace, which they like to say provided sanctuary for Dick Turpin when his pursuers got too close. His horse, apparently, would hide out in the cellars. The room on the left has country kitchen chairs around wooden tables. Good value generously served bar food includes excellent sandwiches (from £1.40), home-made soup (£1.40), salads (from £4), a good home-made steak and kidney pie or lasagne (£4.75), honey roast ham with fried egg (£5.25), steaks (from £7), children's dishes (£2.50), six or so home-cooked daily specials such as 8oz smoked bacon steak with parsley sauce (£5.50), Cantonese prawns or cajun fish fillet (£5.75) and puddings like home-made pavlova (£1.85); they have regular gourmet evenings. It can seem cramped at times but that just adds to the cosy atmosphere. Well kept Bass and M & B Brew XI on handpump; excellent service; bar billiards, fruit machine and piped music. A little garden and courtyard area has tables and a new barbecue. The restaurant (in a former stable block) is popular, and they have a caravan field (certified with the Caravan Club). *(Recommended by Stephen Brown, Julie Peters, Dennis and Dorothee Glover, John Cadman, Graham and Karen Oddey, Graham Bush, Geoff Lee)*

Bass ~ Lease: Graham and Stephanie Lindsay ~ Real ale ~ Meals and snacks (till 9.45; not Sun lunchtime) ~ Restaurant (not Sun evening) ~ Tamworth (01827) 880357 ~ Children in eating areas and games room ~ Open 11.30-2.30, 6.30(6 Sat)-11

Sunday opening is generally 12-3 and 7-10.30 throughout England.

STAMFORD (Lincs) TF0207 Map 8

Bull & Swan

High St, St Martins; B1081 leaving town southwards

The first of our two main entries in Stamford is a good, solid, traditional old place – quite a contrast to the elegant George across the road. The three interesting low-beamed connecting rooms generally have a cosy and friendly feel, as well as shallow steps and wooden partition walls creating a split-level effect, lots of highly polished kettles and other brassware, wheelback chairs, and log-effect gas fires. Generously served bar food includes lunchtime sandwiches, starters like deep-fried brie or prawn cocktail, main courses such as lasagne, a good steak and mushroom pie or rack of lamb (£7.95), and a big mixed grill (steak, kidney, gammon, sausage, liver, lamb chop – £8.25); several readers have found they may have special offers on food prices some evenings. Very well kept Bass and Tetleys; lots of malt whiskies, a number of bottled beers, and decent house wine; pleasant service, unobtrusive piped music. An arched passageway leads back to the old coachyard, with tables. *(Recommended by Simon Collett-Jones, Stephen and Julie Brown, Norma and Keith Bloomfield, Paul Baxter, George Atkinson, Janet and Gary Amos)*

Pubmaster ~ Tenant Ricky Emerson ~ Real ale ~ Meals and snacks (till 10.15) ~ Restaurant ~ Stamford (01780) 63558 ~ Children in eating area of bar ~ Open 11-2.30, 6.30-11 ~ Bedrooms: £35B/£45B

George ★ ★ ⊞ 🛏 ♀

71 High St, St Martins

Hard to miss thanks to the at once welcoming and daunting gallows sign stretching across the road, this beautifully preserved old coaching inn is a remarkable place, reeking of history and full of character. Despite its elegance it always keeps a warmly pubby flavour and relaxed feel, and you feel as welcome coming for a drink as you do coming to stay for a week. The current building dates from 1597 when it was built for Lord Burghley, but there are still parts of a much older Norman pilgrims' hospice, and a crypt under the cocktail bar that may be 1000 years old. In the 18th and 19th c it was a bustling coaching inn, with 20 trips a day each way from London and York, and two of the front rooms are still named after these destinations. They have a medley of seats ranging from sturdy bar settles through leather, cane and antique wicker to soft settees and easy chairs, while the refurbished central lounge has sturdy timbers, broad flagstones, heavy beams, and massive stonework. The atmosphere is warm and friendly even on the coldest winter's day. The nicest place for lunch (if it's not a warm sunny day) is the indoor Garden Lounge, with well spaced white cast-iron furniture on herringbone glazed bricks around a central tropical grove, and a splendidly tempting help-yourself buffet (from £9.50). Other bar food includes soup (£3.25), chicken liver pâté (£4.95), toasted club or Danish open sandwiches (from £6.45), pasta dishes like fettucini with fresh and smoked salmon in cream sauce or pasta parcels filled with ricotta cheese and mushrooms (£6.95), gruyère cheese fritters with a quince jelly, seafood pancake or fish and chips (£7.25), local sausages (£7.95), escalopes of turkey with pasta and a tomato and basil sauce or chicken supreme filled with swiss cheese on mushroom tagliatelle (£9.95), whole grilled plaice (£10.45), char-grilled sirloin steak with onion rings and chips (£10.95), and puddings (£3.45). The food is rather more expensive than you might expect, but the quality is exceptional so it's worth saving up for; they do a range of cheaper sandwiches in the York bar (from £2.75), as well as a ploughman's (£3.95) and soup. Adnams and Ruddles Best on handpump, but the best drinks are the Italian wines, many of which are good value and sold by the glass; also freshly squeezed orange juice, filter, espresso or cappuccino coffee. Welcoming staff. The cobbled courtyard at the back is lovely in summer, with comfortable chairs and tables among attractive plant tubs and colourful hanging baskets; waiter drinks service. Besides the courtyard, there's a neatly maintained walled garden, with a sunken lawn where croquet is often played. This is the headquarters of Ivo Vannocci's small but reliably good chain of Poste Hotels. *(Recommended by Graham and Karen Oddey, Mr and Mrs T F Marshall, Michael Sargent,*

J F M West, Thomas Nott, WHBM, Paul Cartledge, Dr C A Brace, M E A Horler, Bill and Edee Miller, T G Thomas, R C Wiles; also recommended by The Good Hotel Guide)

Free house ~ Licensees Ivo Vannocci and Chris Pitman ~ Real ale ~ Meals and snacks (till 11) ~ Two restaurants ~ Stamford (01780) 55171 ~ Children welcome ~ Open 11-11 ~ Bedrooms: £75B/£100B

STRETTON (Leics) SK9416 Map 7

Ram Jam 🛏 ♉

Great North Rd (A1)

Rather like a continental coffee house or smart wine bar (though looking like a traditional coaching inn from the outside), this is a very civilised and relaxed place, with an efficient little all-day snacks bar proving food and drinks from breakfast-time on. Meals are consistently good and imaginatively presented, and might include soup (£1.99), vegetarian tortilla chips with melted cheese and tomato salsa (£3.50), poached Polish sausage with shallot and watercress salad and Dijon mustard dressing (£4.50), Egyptian-style falafel or brunch (£4.95), minced steak burger or pasta linguini (£5.75), stir-fried duck with oriental vegetables in honey and ginger or farmhouse platter with home-made chutney (£5.95), and puddings like warm treacle tart or French-style lemon tart with blackcurrant coulis (£3.50); daily fresh fish (not Monday) and Sunday roast (£6.95); friendly, efficient service, even under pressure. The comfortably airy modern lounge bar has Mexican hand-made tiles, sofas around turkey carpets, old breadboards and modern china on the cream walls, and neat contemporary seats; it opens out at the rear to a leisurely no-smoking restaurant. Good wines, freshly squeezed orange juice, fresh-ground coffee and so forth. There are teak seats on the terrace at the back looking up to the orchard behind (some traffic noise here, of course, though the bedrooms are surprisingly quiet); big car park. *(Recommended by Geoffrey and Irene Lindley, Michael Sargent, Simon Collett-Jones, Anthony John, C J Westmoreland, J Butler, Roxanne Chamberlain)*

Free house ~ Licensee Tim Hart ~ Meals and snacks (till 10pm) ~ Restaurant ~ (01780) 410361 ~ Children welcome ~ Open 11-11 (snack bar open earlier for breakfast); closed 25 Dec ~ Bedrooms: £39B/£49B

UPTON (Notts) SK7354 Map 7

French Horn ♉

A612

Back as a main entry again, thanks to a number of enthusiastic reports about the food, drinks, service and atmosphere; for several readers this friendly place is something of a favourite. It's well regarded locally for eating, and at lunchtimes you may find most tables set out ready for meals. Favourite dishes this year have included sandwiches (from £1.25), soup (£1.35), mushrooms stuffed with stilton in a port and redcurrant sauce (£2.65), steak and kidney pie, fresh fish and very good specials like pork in sweet and sour sauce, guinea fowl in an apricot and brandy sauce or baked salmon (around £5.50); there's a massive list of puddings like coffee meringue or white chocolate profiterole gateau (£2.25), with a variety of ice creams. Usefully they also do a range of sandwiches and hot snacks all afternoon. The neat and comfortable open-plan bar has a nicely relaxed feel, as well as cushioned captain's chairs, wall banquettes around glossy tables, and watercolours by local artists on the walls; it's just been repainted. You may also spot the cat in here. Well kept Vaux Double Maxim and Extra Special and Wards Bitter and Thorn on handpump, and a good choice of a dozen decent wines by the glass; staff are amiable and efficient. The big sloping back paddock, with picnic-table sets, looks over farmland. *(Recommended by Ian and Val Titman, ILP, David and Shelia, Rev Tim Haggis and others)*

Wards ~ Licensee Joyce Carter ~ Real ale ~ Meals and snacks ~ Restaurant ~ Southwell (01636) 812394 ~ Children welcome ~ Occasional live music ~ Open 11-11

WELLOW Notts SK6766 Map 7

Olde Red Lion

Eakring Road; pub visible from A616 E of Ollerton

However much the world changes you can still rely on Wellow having its famous May Day celebrations, and windows in the low-beamed front room of this satisfying 16th-c pub look out on their centrepiece, a tremendously tall brightly spiral-painted maypole. The series of rooms have recently been refurbished, with a new bar and different seating arrangements and furnishings, though all in a sympathetic traditional style. There are photographs tracing the building's development on the partly panelled walls. The food has a great local reputation for value – a combination of low prices and big helpings – so it's best to get here early if you want to eat: good sandwiches (from £1.40), vegetarian meals such as mushroom and nut fettuccine (from £3.25), steak and kidney pie (£3.95), lasagne (£4.95), halibut steak or salmon fillet (£5.95), mixed grill (£9.95), daily specials and children's menu (£1.95). Booking is recommended for the 3-course Sunday lunch; part of the dining area is no smoking. Well kept John Smiths Magnet, Marstons Pedigree, Morlands Old Speckled Hen, Ruddles Best and County, and guest beers on handpump; quick service; dominoes, table skittles and fairly unobtrusive piped pop music. An L-shaped strip of grass above the car park has picnic-table sets under cocktail parasols, and a set of swings. The original deeds for the pub set out what really was just a peppercorn rent, one peppercorn per year to be precise; you can still see the deeds on the wall of one of the bars. *(Recommended by David and Shelia, L Grant, G B Rimmer, E Riley; more reports please)*

Free house ~ Licensee Richard Henshaw ~ Real ale ~ Meals and snacks (till 10) ~ Restaurant ~ Mansfield (01623) 861000 ~ Children in eating area and restaurant ~ Weds quiz night ~ Open 11.30-3, 5.30-11, all day summer Sats; closed 25 Dec

WOODHOUSE EAVES (Leics) SK5214 Map 7

Pear Tree ♀

Church Hill; main street, off B591 W of Quorndon

The lower part of this pub is a straightforward comfortable turkey-carpeted local, with well kept Ansells, Ind Coope Burton, Marstons Pedigree and Tetleys on handpump, decent wines, and an open fire. It's the upper flagstoned food area which is special, with pews forming booths around the walls, flagstone floor, and a pitched roof giving a pleasantly airy and open feel at lunchtime; at night, despite low lighting, the atmosphere is pleasantly lively. The end food servery looks straight through into the kitchen, which does generous helpings of good food such as up to five ploughman's (£3.75), salmon fishcakes, smokies en cocotte done with wine and cream, deep-fried chicken tikka, spit-roast chicken (£5.25), with interesting soups (cauliflower and stilton, aubergine and rosemary, £1.85), a few specials such as savoury mince, sweet and sour chicken and char-grilled swordfish, and puddings like spotted dick, summer pudding or cheesecakes (£2). As the food's all fresh, service can sometimes be slow. There's a log fire in an attractive Victorian fireplace; dominoes, cribbage, fruit machine, and piped music. Outside there are a few picnic-table sets under cocktail parasols, with a summer bar by an arbour of climbing plants. There are good walks nearby. *(Recommended by Bill Edwards, H Paulinski, George Atkinson, Andrew Stephenson)*

Ansells ~ Tenants Mr and Mrs Dimbleby ~ Real ale ~ Meals and snacks (till 10pm); not Sun evening ~ (01509) 890243 ~ Children welcome ~ Open 11-3, 6-11; closed 25 Dec

---

Post Office address codings confusingly give the impression that some pubs are in Leicestershire, when they're really in Cambridgeshire (which is where we list them).

Lucky Dip

Besides the fully inspected pubs, you might like to try these Lucky Dips recommended to us and described by readers (if you do, please send us reports):

Acresford, Leics [A444 Burton—Nuneaton; SK3113], *Cricketts*: Pleasant lounge with Bass, Marstons Pedigree and regional guest beers, good range of other drinks, good home-cooked food inc vegetarian, kind service; attractive garden *(B M Eldridge, Graham Richardson)*

☆ **Alford**, Lincs [29 West St (A1004); TF4576], *White Horse*: Thatched and gabled, neatly kept inside with dark green plush and dimpled copper; well kept Bass, Batemans XB and Worthington Best, excellent range of Polish vodkas, wide range of good value fresh-cooked bar food from interesting sandwiches to steak with stilton wrapped in bacon, comfortable restaurant, quietly friendly unflappable service; bedrooms *(George and Sheila Edwards, LYM)*

Alford [Mkt Sq], *Windmill*: Big inn overlooking square with ancient stocks, recently thoroughly refurbished, good reasonably priced food, decent beers; bedrooms *(Gordon B Thornton)*

☆ **Allington**, Lincs [The Green; SK8540], *Welby Arms*: Good range of reasonably priced straightforward home-cooked food inc fresh fish and vegetarian, particularly well kept ales inc guests such as Morlands Old Speckled Hen and Timothy Taylors Landlord; clean and welcoming, tastefully but subtly refurbished, no-smoking section in eating area; friendly landlord and standard poodles *(Stuart and Alison Exley, John C Baker, Tony Gayfer)*

Appleby Parva, Leics [A444, nr Measham and M42 junction; SK3109], *Appleby Inn*: Good range of reasonably priced straightforward food, red plush furnishings, olde-worlde effects; spotless *(Graham Richardson, F J Robinson)*

☆ **Ashby Folville**, Leics [SK7011], *Carington Arms*: Good country atmosphere in attractively placed spacious and comfortable Tudor-style country pub, substantial straightforward home-cooked food using local produce from filled rolls and enormous ploughman's up; jovial obliging landlord, Adnams, Everards Old Original and Tiger and interesting changing guest beer; children welcome, nice garden, maybe calves or horses in back paddock *(O K Smyth, Jim Farmer)*

Ashby Parva, Leics [off A426 N of Lutterworth; not far from M1 junction 20; SP5288], *Holly Bush*: Largish lounge divided up into smaller cosy areas, friendly staff, reasonable cheap food, piped music *(George Atkinson)*

☆ **Aswarby**, Lincs [A15 Folkingham—Sleaford; TF0639], *Tally Ho*: Neatly kept and civilised oak-beamed country pub with big log fire and woodburning stove, simple traditional furnishings, affable newish landlord; well kept Adnams, Batemans XB and a guest beer on handpump, welcoming service, decent bar food esp game and home-made puddings, imaginative menu in smart restaurant with piped classical music; tables and timber play fort on grass behind, by sheep meadow; bedrooms comfortable and well equipped, in neatly converted block behind; nearby church worth a visit *(Chris Walling, LJBH, Sqdn Ldr and Mrs P A Bouch, BB)*

Awsworth, Notts [quite handy for M1 junction 26, via A610/A6096; SK4844], *Hog Head*: Very good value food, good Sun lunch, good drinks and helpful staff in separate restaurant; children's adventure playground, waterfall and pool with fish (fenced off) *(R V Saynor)*

☆ **Barholm**, Lincs [TF0810], *Five Horseshoes*: Well kept Adnams, Batemans and interesting guest beers in old-fashioned and easy-going village local, clean and cosy, with old farm tools, stuffed birds; tables in garden, paddocks behind *(David and Michelle Hedges, LYM)*

Barkston, Lincs [The Green; SK9241], *Stags Head*: Good bar, decent food in separate dining area *(K H Frostick)*

Barnby in the Willows, Notts [Front St; SK8652], *Willow Tree*: Well kept Batemans XB, better than average food, friendly and efficient service; children in games room or lobby *(JCB)*

☆ **Barrow upon Soar**, Leics [Mill Lane, off South St (B5328); SK5717], *Navigation*: Attractive and comfortable two-roomed extended split-level pub based on former barge-horse stabling, lovely view of Grand Union Canal from small back terrace with moorings; small selection of good value straightforward bar food, interesting bar top made from old pennies, central open fire, friendly landlord; well kept Courage Directors, Marstons Pedigree and Shipstones, skittle alley, piped music (may be a bit loud) *(Stephen Brown, Dr K Bloomfield)*

Bleasby, Notts [SK7149], *Hazleford Ferry*: Beautifully refurbished old waterside inn with good bar food, well kept beers, lovely dining room and conservatory *(Ian and Val Titman)*

Blidworth, Notts [B6020; SK5956], *Little John*: Clean and friendly converted farmhouse with two big carpeted and comfortable rooms, pictures, quiet piped pop, well kept Mansfield Riding and Old Baily on handpump, wines, tea, coffee, reasonably priced bar meals; garden with picnic-table sets, climber and swing *(JJW, CMJ)*

☆ **Blyth**, Notts [SK6287], *White Swan*: Well kept Whitbreads-related real ales and good food from sandwiches up inc good fresh fish in cosy and friendly neatly kept pub with big open fires, good service; may be piped music; good A1 break *(E J Cutting, Paul Cartledge)*

Boston, Lincs [Horncastle Rd (B1183); TF3244], *Kings Arms*: Clean and unpretentious brickbuilt pub by canal opp striking tall working windmill, well kept Batemans Mild, XB and XXXB, friendly efficient landlady, bar food from sandwiches to steak; bedrooms modern and comfortable with cheery furnishings *(Frank W Gadbois, BB)*; [Wormgate], *Goodbarns Yard*: Former Wormgate Inn tastefully restored as modern pub and restaurant, renamed for medieval yard behind; well kept Courage and weekly guest real ales, bar food from sandwiches, baked potatoes and burgers to lasagne, steak pie, catfish fillets and steak, with various more or less spicy snacks *(Bill Isaac, Frank W Gadbois)*

☆ **Brandy Wharf**, Lincs [B1205 SE of Scunthorpe; TF0197], *Hankerin*: Not the smartest pub but very interesting, landlord full of enthusiasm for cider (over 60 varieties kept), intriguing decor inc all sorts of cider items from posters to drinking pots, odd foot poking through ceiling of dim-lit lounge; lovely open fire, good value generous plain food inc wonderful real chips, summer cider shop; riverside setting with good moorings, slipways; cl Christmas, New Year, Mon winter lunchtimes *(Jane Kingsbury)*

Branston, Leics [Main St; SK8129], *Wheel*: Classic unpretentious country local with well kept Batemans, friendly service *(Simon Collett-Jones)*

☆ **Breedon on the Hill**, Leics [A453 Ashby—Castle Donington; SK4022], *Holly Bush*: Very red-plush-and-turkey-carpet, with lots of brass, sporting plates etc, very low 16th-c beams; well kept Marstons Pedigree and Tetleys, popular bar food (stops early lunchtime; not Sun), restaurant (can be fully booked Sat, cl Sun), no-smoking area, friendly efficient service; piped music (live Mon, or maybe karaoke); some tables outside, nice bedrooms; interesting village with hilltop church above huge limestone face *(Gordon Theaker, Norma and Keith Bloomfield, George Atkinson, Nan Axon, Spider Newth, A and R Cooper, Rona Murdoch, BB)*

Breedon on the Hill, Leics, *Lime Kiln*: Nice clean country pub with friendly atmosphere, good choice of well cooked and presented lunchtime bar food at reasonable prices *(G Neighbour)*; *Three Horse Shoes*: Separate bars, popular restaurant with good value carvery, well kept Marstons Pedigree; motel-style bedrooms *(Norma and Keith Bloomfield)*

Bunny, Notts [Nottingham—Loughborough; SK5728], *Rancliffe Arms*: Doing well under current licensee, beautifully kept beers, good reasonably priced food, happy relaxed atmosphere *(Anon)*

Castle Donington, Leics [90 Bondgate; B6504; SK4427], *Cross Keys*: Low-ceilinged snug litle pub with very friendly landlord, popular at lunchtimes for food; good range of well kept beers *(Dr and Mrs A K Clarke)*; [Hillside], *Jolly Potters*: Genuine unspoilt town pub, very basic but friendly, with good real ale *(Dr and Mrs A K Clarke)*; [Station Rd], *Lamb*: Small two-roomed Victorian pub with particularly well kept Marstons beers *(Dr and Mrs A K Clarke)*; [A453, S end], *Nags Head*: Old beamed pub which has recently been concentrating more on good food; well kept beer, decent wine, very friendly service *(Dr and Mrs A K Clarke, Stephen Newell)*

☆ nr **Castle Donington** [Kings Mills], *Priest House*: Watermill turned hotel, with medieval tower, beautifully set in 50 acres of wooded grounds by River Trent; good food and atmosphere in rambling beamed dining bar, friendly helpful staff, a real ale brewed for the pub, children really welcome; fishing, canoeing and occasional clay pigeon shoots; bedrooms excellent *(George Atkinson, Dr and Mrs A K Clarke, Michael and Margaret Norris, Ruth and Alan Cooper, LYM)*

Catthorpe, Leics [just off A5 S of Gibbet Island; SP5578], *Cherry Tree*: Attractive country local, friendly, cosy, clean and warm, with pleasant atmosphere, dark panelling, profusion of plates and pictures, coal-effect fire, very attentive landlord, good value bar food, well kept Hook Norton Best; piped radio; cl Mon/Tues lunchtimes *(George Atkinson, Ted George)*

Chapel St Leonards, Lincs [St Leonards Drive; TF5572], *Trafalgar*: Simple pub with good well cooked reasonably priced meals in big helpings; piped pop music may be intrusive *(Geoffrey and Irene Lindley)*

Chilwell, Notts [Swiney Way; SW edge of Nottingham; SK5135], *Corn Mill*: Newish pub with good choice of generous food inc vegetarian and good puddings, great value coffee, family room with children's menu *(Derek and Iris Martin)*

Church Langton, Leics [B6047 about 3 miles N of Mkt Harborough; just off A6; SP7293], *Langton Arms*: Wide choice of good interesting reasonably priced meals inc vegetarian in smartly extended popular country pub, welcoming and relaxing, with helpful friendly staff, candlelit dining area, well kept Marstons Pedigree and other ales; weekly OAP bargain lunch *(Rona Murdoch, Jim Farmer)*

Claypole, Lincs [SK8449], *Five Bells*: Clean and welcoming village pub, busily cheerful, with well kept Batemans and Wards, simple wholesome food at reasonable prices inc real chip butties, good friendly service, games; well equipped play area *(P White, John C Baken)*; [Main St], *Woolpack*: Wonderfully unspoiled, with superb friendly local atmosphere, perfectly kept real ale inc guest such as Timothy Taylors Landlord, interesting but uncomplicated food *(John C Baker)*

Clipsham, Leics [SK9616], *Olive Branch*: Relaxed village local with changing food inc local game, trout and veg, well kept beers, friendly welcoming licensees, open fires; children in restaurant *(David and Michelle Hedges, BB)*

Clipstone, Notts [Old Clipstone; B6030 Mansfield—Ollerton – OS Sheet 120 map ref 606647; SK6064], *Dog & Duck*: Good value basic home cooking in three-roomed pub with comfortable blue plush seating, amazing teapot collection, family dining room, well kept Home ales and Theakstons XB, very friendly landlord *(Norma and Keith Bloomfield, M and J Back)*

Coleorton, Leics [SK4017], *Angel*: Friendly modernised old inn with attractive oak beams, coal fires and somewhat wonky floor; well kept Marstons beers *(Dr and Mrs A K Clarke)*

☆ **Coningsby**, Lincs [Boston Rd (B1192); ½ mile NW of village - OS Sheet 122 map ref 242588; TF2458], *Leagate*: Old heavy-beamed fenland pub with three linked dim-lit areas, ageing medley of furnishings inc great high-backed settles snugged around the biggest of the three log fires, run by genuine local; prompt attractively priced straightforward food, several well kept Courage-related and maybe other ales; piped jazz or pop music, fruit machine; rustic garden with play area and koi carp centre; children if eating *(P R Morley, K D Day, F Armitage, Maxine Larkin, Robin Etheridge, Mark Hydes, Alan Wilcock, Christine Davidson, LYM)*

Copt Oak, Leics [nr M1 junction 22; A50 towards Leics, then B587; SK4812], *Copt Oak*: Comfortable Marstons Tavern Table dining pub with good views over Charnwood Forest, useful for quick friendly food service even all day Sun; well kept real ale, very busy Sat lunchtime *(M and J Back)*

☆ **Cottesmore**, Leics [Main St; SK9013], *Sun*: Good sensibly priced food served well by friendly staff in attractive bar with decent sporting prints, plush button-back banquettes, blazing fire in stone inglenook; quieter side rooms, piped music and fruit machine; tables in garden; children welcome *(Michael Butler, F J Robinson, BB)*

☆ **Cowbit**, Lincs [Barrier Bank; A1073 S of Spalding; TF2618], *Olde Dun Cow*: Wide choice of good value bar food inc some bargains in split-level bar with restaurant off one end, games area at the other, real ales such as Batemans XXXB, Boddingtons, Morlands Old Speckled Hen, Theakstons Best and XB; pleasant black and white decor with old oak beams and old notices, friendly waitress service; bedrooms *(Mr and Mrs J Back)*

Cropston, Leics [15 Station Rd (B5328); SK5510], *Bradgate Arms*: Wide choice of decent food (not Sun evening) in very much modernised extended village pub, separate servery for sunken dining area, preserved

snug, well kept Banks's Bitter and Mild; family area, biggish garden, good friendly service; can get crowded *(George Atkinson, Mr and Mrs A Cooper, LYM)*

Crowland, Lincs [The Common; B1166 towards Market Deeping; TF2310], *Olde Bridge*: Welcoming bar glittering with brass and copper on walls mixing new brick and old plaster, ceiling decorated with young beams; well kept Wards Sheffield Best *(Tom Evans)*

Deeping St James, Lincs [Church St; TF1609], *Waterton Arms*: Good reasonably priced food inc delicious puddings, prompt service even when busy *(David and Tricia Lunn)*

Denton, Lincs [SK8632], *Welby Arms*: Cosy and comfortable Mansfield pub, good range of reasonably priced bar food, separate dining room; walkers welcome even with dogs, reasonable wheelchair access *(Elizabeth and Anthony Watts)*

Diseworth, Leics [down street opp churchyard; nr East Midlands Airport, and M1 junction 23A; SK4524], *Plough*: Good value food and well kept Bass in well run rather middle-class pub; big garden *(Dr and Mrs A K Clarke)*

Dry Doddington, Lincs [1 mile off A1 Newark—Grantham; SK8446], *Wheatsheaf*: Small village pub with very welcoming landlord who cooks unexpectedly wide range of well presented bar meals to order; Marstons Pedigree *(Gordon Smith)*

☆ **East Bridgford**, Notts [Kneeton Rd, off A6075; can also be reached from A46; SK6943], *Reindeer*: Comfortable village pub with several eating areas, good generous food cooked to order (so may be a wait) esp fish, quick pleasant service, changing real ales such as Charles Wells Bombardier, open fire; need to book at weekends; attractive village *(G Mitchell, Derek and Sylvia Stephenson)*

East Langton, Leics [signed off B6047; the Langtons also signed off A6 N of Mkt Harborough; SP7292], *Bell*: More pubby than previously; decent food in attractive surroundings with stripped stone walls and good log fire, though the beams are a bit bright; piped radio may be rather loud *(George Atkinson, LYM)*

☆ **Edenham**, Lincs [A151; TF0621], *Five Bells*: Wide choice of generous usual bar food well served in busy but spacious modernised dining lounge with neatly ranged tables, flying waitress; well kept Marstons Pedigree, Tetleys and Tolly Original, generous coffee, two log fires, piped music, lots of foreign banknotes, soft lighting; back restaurant/function room, tables in garden with good play area; children welcome *(M and J Back, LYM)*

☆ **Elkesley**, Notts [just off A1 S of Blyth; SK6975], *Robin Hood*: Big helpings of good reasonably priced food inc good specials esp fish in well furnished traditional lounge/dining room and well kept basic public bar; well kept Whitbreads-related real ales, service usually good (KC, Gordon Smith)

☆ **Elston**, Notts [A46 SW of Newark; SK7548], *Coeur de Lion*: Extraordinary building like a small Iberian summer palace – pinnacles, domes, lancet windows, steep roofs, tall chimneys, elevated terraces; decorous panelled bar with soft russet plush seats, country prints and engravings, neat accommodating staff; good bar food from chips and sandwiches up, well kept Bass, two candlelit dining rooms, one upstairs with soaring pitched and raftered ceiling (David and Ruth Hollands, BB)

Elton, Notts [A52 Nottingham—Grantham; SK7638], *Manor Arms*: Mansfield pub with simple good value bar food and friendly welcome (Norma and Keith Bloomfield)

Enderby, Leics [7 Mill Hill Lane; SP5399], *Plough*: Unprepossessing exterior belied by cosy, spacious interior, separate eating area, home-made food inc late breakfasts and always a vegetarian dish, good range of puddings, Marstons Pedigree and Chestnut Ale (Nan Axon)

Epperstone, Notts [SK6548], *Cross Keys*: Popular traditional village pub in pleasant countryside, lounge fills lunchtime for usual good value bar food from sandwiches up, but normally space in public bar; friendly landlord, Hardys & Hansons ale (Norma and Keith Bloomfield)

Fiskerton, Notts [SK7351], *Bromley Arms*: Popular Trentside pub just NE of Nottingham, interesting food, Hardys & Hansons ales; can be busy in summer (D W Gray)

Foxton, Leics [Foxton Locks; off A6 3 miles NW of Mkt Harboro (park by bridge 60/62 and walk) – OS Sheet 141 map ref 691897; SP7090], *Bridge 61*: In good setting by locks, rather café-like interior, quickly served food, lots of old tools and implements, friendly service (George Atkinson)

Frampton, Lincs [signed off A16 S of Boston; TF3239], *Moores Arms*: Pleasant pub with character and friendly atmosphere, well kept Bass, good food, popular lunchtime with Boston businessmen; pretty Fenland village (V and E A Bolton, Peter Burton)

☆ **Frisby on the Wreake**, Leics [Main St; SK6917], *Bell*: Friendly pine-beamed pub with brass, oil paintings and real fire in big bar, seven well kept real ales on handpump at sensible prices, fair range of wines, decent coffee, extensive if fairly straightforward lunch menu, different evening choice – good value and quality; smaller back family room; piped music, smart dress required; tables outside (CMW, JJW, RJH)

☆ **Gedney Dyke**, Lincs [TF4125], *Chequers*: The wide choice of good freshly cooked food inc vegetarian dishes, lots of fresh fish and seafood and enjoyable puddings is winning very warm approval from many readers for this welcoming village pub, small

and spotless – good value in both bar and restaurant; well kept Adnams Bitter and Mild, Bass, Batemans XXXB and Greene King Abbot on handpump, well served coffee, attentive staff, open fire, picnic-table sets in garden (Maysie Thompson, F J and A Parmenter, Joan and Michel Hooper-Immins, John Honnor, Peter Hann, G P Kernan, R and L Scrimshaw)

☆ **Grantham**, Lincs [High St; SK9135], *Angel & Royal*: Forte hotel extending behind original very interesting small front core unique 14th-c carved stone façade, ancient oriel window seat in upstairs plush bar on left, massive inglenook in high-beamed main bar opp (has had spit-roasts); well kept Bass and occasional guest beers, bar food; bedrooms comfortable (Neville Kenyon, LYM)

Grantham [Vine St], *Blue Pig*: Characterful beamed Tudor pub with well kept Greene King Abbot, welcoming service, usual bar food reasonably priced; punks and machines in front bar, young professionals in back lounge, pretty parlour with glazed pottery show cupboard (Ian Phillips, RB); [Bridge End Rd], *White Lion*: Friendly local with Courage-related ales and guests such as Morlands Speckled Hen, cheap food; bedrooms (Phil and Anne Smithson)

☆ **Great Casterton**, Lincs [village signed off A1; TF0009], *Crown*: Good value home-cooked bar food and good range of well kept real ales in neat stripped-stone bar with high booth seating and inglenook log fire, simpler back bar, friendly landlord, good atmosphere; old-fashioned seats in pretty little garden opp attractive church (Christopher Turner, DC, BB)

Great Dalby, Leics [B6047 S of Melton Mowbray; SK7414], *Royal Oak*: Low-beamed pub with farm tools, good popular bar food inc wide evening choice and Sun lunch, quick service, Ruddles ales, tables in garden with play area (V and E A Bolton)

Great Glen, Leics [off A6 Leicester—Mkt Harboro; SP6597], *Greyhound*: Particularly good interesting home-cooked food in friendly informal pub with good bar and lounge and comfortable snug (Mr and Mrs M Steane)

☆ **Greetham**, Leics [B668 Stretton—Cottesmore; SK9214], *Wheatsheaf*: Simple but welcoming L-shaped communicating rooms with good choice of good value generous bar food inc lots of char-grills and tasty puddings served till 11; coal fire, nautical charts, well kept Tetleys and Whitbreads on handpump, attentive staff; pool and other games in end room, restaurant, tables on side grass; some live entertainment/discos Sun (M and J Back, Jim Farmer, BB)

☆ **Grimston**, Leics [off A6006 W of Melton Mowbray; SK6821], *Black Horse*: Remarkable collection of cricket memorabilia in spick and span comfortable pub with consistently good imaginatively presented straightforward bar food –

always freshly cooked, so takes time; well kept Marstons Pedigree, open fire, discreet piped music; no food Sun, cl Sun evening and Mon exc bank hols; attractive village with stocks and 13th-c church *(RJH, J H Gracey, David and Shelia, Patrick Clancy, LYM)*

Hagworthingham, Lincs [A158 Horncastle—Skegness; TF3469], *George & Dragon*: Two comfortable and friendly low-beamed bars with decent food, Courage-related ales; big lawn with swings; children welcome *(Mike and Maggie Betton)*

Halam, Notts [SK6754], *Waggon & Horses*: Busy dining pub with good value food, Marstons Pedigree on handpump, quick efficient service; attractive exterior *(George Mitchell, Paul Gretton)*

Haltham, Lincs [A163 Horncastle—Coningsby; TF2463], *Marmion Arms*: Friendly licensees, good freshly prepared food, particularly well kept Batemans *(D Lawson)*

☆ **Halton Holegate**, Lincs [B1195 E of Spilsby; TF4165], *Bell*: Friendly welcome and wide choice of decent home-made food from soup and sandwiches to steaks inc outstanding fish and chips, vegetarian dishes and Sun lunches in pretty village local, simple but comfortable furnishings, aircraft pictures (the Lancaster bomber flying over the pub on the inn-sign commemorates 207 and 44 Squadrons, stationed nearby), well kept Bass, Batemans and Mansfield Old Baily, pub games, maybe piped music; children in eating area and restaurant *(Derek and Sylvia Stephenson, D W Gray, LYM)*

☆ **Hayton**, Notts [Main St (B1403) – OS Sheet 120 map ref 728852; SK7384], *Boat*: Good range of reasonably priced bar food from sandwiches up inc children's dishes, evening and Sun lunchtime carvery (booking suggested), quite cosy, welcoming and comfortable, big log fire, well kept Bass, Stones and Whitbreads Castle Eden on handpump; garden with play area and summer help-yourself barbecue; good value bedrooms in separate cottage block with good breakfasts; on quiet stretch of Chesterfield Canal (moorings) *(Derek and Sylvia Stephenson, Ian Phillips)*

Hemington, Leics [21 Main St; SK4528], *Jolly Sailor*: Friendly village local with beautiful hanging baskets; well kept Marstons Pedigree and three guest ales, bar food inc good fresh rolls; coal fire, table skittles *(Jack and Philip Paxton)*

Hinckley, Leics [Watling St (A5); SP4294], *Lime Kilns*: Tranquil canal flowing past big garden with play area, good choice of food inc reasonably priced ploughman's, efficient service, Marstons Pedigree, comfortable furnishings; some moorings *(George Atkinson)*; [Derby Rd], *Weavers Arms*: Genuine, friendly, full range of Marstons beers, nice outside area, neat and tidy with an emphasis on pub games *(Dr and Mrs A K Clarke)*

Hoby, Leics [SK6717], *Blue Bell*: Very big helpings of good value usual pub food Weds-Sat, Everards Old Original on handpump; classic car meetings summer *(Jim Farmer)*

Horncastle, Lincs [North St; TF2669], *Old Nicks*: Pleasant, warm and friendly atmosphere, reasonably priced carvery, no-smoking dining area *(Gordon B Thornton)*

☆ **Hough on the Hill**, Lincs [SK9246], *Brownlow Arms*: Attractive 17th-c pub in peaceful picturesque village, wide range of good value well cooked and presented food (not weekday lunchtimes), relaxing lounge with sofas and comfortable chairs, pubby separate bar, good restaurant; well kept Marstons Pedigree and changing guest beers, decent wines, friendly efficient service; pretty and good value bedrooms, good breakfasts *(Norman and Gill Fox, RB, R A Hobbs, V and E A Bolton)*

Hoveringham, Notts [SK6946], *Reindeer*: Particularly well kept Marstons Pedigree; bar food *(Peter Hann)*

Husbands Bosworth, Leics [A427 Market Harborough—Lutterworth, junction A50; SP6484], *Bell*: Genuine and unpretentious local with a welcome for visitors, decent food *(G D Lee)*

☆ **Illston on the Hill**, Leics [off B6047 Mkt Harboro—Melton; SP7099], *Fox & Goose*: Friendly newish licensees in welcoming Everards pub full of interesting decorations, well kept Mild, Beacon, Old Original and Tiger, good coal fires *(Jim Farmer, J D Cloud, LYM)*

☆ **Ingham**, Lincs [High St; SK9483], *Inn on the Green*: Wide choice of quickly served good home-made food inc interesting dishes and Sun lunch in well modernised pub on village green; lots of brass and copper in spacious beamed lounge bar, good fire, upstairs dining room; children welcome *(Mike and Maggie Betton)*

Kegworth, Leics [towards West Leake – OS Sheet 129 map ref 501268; SK5026], *Station*: Good value well served food, well kept Bass and Worthington, pleasant atmosphere; bedrooms starting *(David Eberlin)*

Kibworth Beauchamp, Leics [Leicester Rd; SP6893], *Coach & Horses*: Warm and friendly, with log fires, pleasant staff, well kept Bass, popular food *(Eric J Locker)*

☆ **Kibworth Harcourt**, Leics [Main St (just off A6); SP6894], *Three Horseshoes*: Unassuming but civilised village pub, quiet and relaxing, with well cooked and presented straightforward food (not Sun evening) in generous helpings, well kept Bass and Marstons Best and Pedigree, friendly service, comfortable plush seating with side eating areas; piped music, children welcome; tables on attractive back terrace *(Stephen Brown, PC, Rona Murdoch, Alan and Jackie Stuart, Eric J Locker, Gwen and Peter Andrews, LYM)*

☆ **Kilby Bridge**, Leics [A50 S of Leicester; SP6097], *Navigation*: Straightforward pub nicely placed by Bridge 87 of Grand Union Canal's Leicester arm, usual food inc hefty hot meat baps, garden overlooking canal, Allied real ales and Marstons Pedigree on handpump; huge fish in tank in lounge, piped pop music, busy bookable restaurant; children welcome, no dogs inside *(Jim Farmer, P G Topp)*

Kirby Muxloe, Leics [Main St; SK5104], *Royal Oak*: Deceptive modern exterior hides pleasant pub with wide range of filled french sticks and sandwiches, several good value hot dishes, full range of Everards beers and one or two guests, efficient service; piped music *(Derek and Sylvia Stephenson, Joan and Michel Hooper-Immins)*

☆ **Knossington**, Leics [off A606 W of Oakham; SK8008], *Fox & Hounds*: Unspoilt small village pub of vanishing type, comfortable seats, open fires, friendly licensees, real ale, excellent choice of malt whiskies at fair prices, reasonably priced food inc unusual new dishes as well as old favourites, summer barbecues in big garden *(Dave and Pat Heath, J D Cloud)*

Langham, Leics [Bridge St; SK8411], *Noel Arms*: Comfortable and attractively furnished low-ceilinged lounge, smart covered terrace, well kept beers inc Ruddles from nearby brewery, usual bar food *(Jim Farmer, LYM)*

Langworth, Lincs [A158 Lincoln—Wragby; TF0676], *New Station*: New station is long gone, although railway still there to add interest; well kept Courage-related beers, food inc superb fish and chips, fresh, properly fried in big helpings *(John C Baker)*

☆ **Leadenham**, Lincs [High St; A17 Newark—Sleaford; SK9552], *George*: Friendly and unaffected old inn with several hundred whiskies, good choice of wines by the glass inc their own direct German imports, well kept Greene King IPA, Ruddles County and Theakstons Old Peculier on handpump; straightforward bar, generous good value straightforward food, friendly service and customers, piped music, side games room, restaurant; bedrooms basic but clean and comfortable; good breakfasts, for non-residents too *(Robert Cowan, LYM)*

Leasingham, Lincs [Lincoln Rd; TF0548], *Duke of Wellington*: Friendly village pub with good range of beers, decent food and warm welcome *(A E Potter)*

☆ **Leicester** [9 Welford Pl; corner Newarke St/Welford Rd], *Welford Place*: Good if pricey changing food all day in spacious semicircular Victorian bar overlooking busy streets, quiet and comfortable almost clubby feel, with Ruddles Best and County, good choice of reliable though not cheap wines and other drinks, good friendly and obliging service; palatial stone stairs to good restaurant, quiet, tasteful and elegant; under same management as main-entry Wig & Mitre in Lincoln *(O K Smyth, Susan and Nigel Siesage, Julie Peters)*

☆ **Leicester** [Silver St/Carts Lane], *Globe*: Old-fashioned three-room pub with stone-mullioned windows, lots of woodwork, gas lighting, coal fire – and the juke box seems quieter under the new manager; more peaceful upstairs dining room with good value simple lunchtime food served piping hot; well kept Everards and guest beers such as Felinfoel Double Dragon and Wadworths Farmers Glory *(Joan and Michel Hooper-Immins, Paul Cartledge, LYM)*

☆ **Leicester** [Charles St], *Rainbow & Dove*: Big open-plan unplush bar nr station with well kept Banks's Mild and Bitter, Hansons Mild, Camerons Strongarm, Marstons Pedigree and two changing guest beers, good service, plain well cooked food weekday lunchtimes inc good filled rolls and scotch eggs; students evening, professionals too lunchtime, live music Sun evening *(Joan and Michel Hooper-Immins, J D Cloud, Paul Cartledge)*

☆ **Leicester** [131 Beaumanor Rd; off Abbey Lane (A5131), rt fork S from A6 at Red Hill Circle], *Tom Hoskins*: Tap for Hoskins small brewery – group brewhouse tours can be arranged; flagstones, floorboards, panelling, varnished pews, brewery memorabilia; well kept cheap Hoskins and guest real ales, limited but good value lunchtime food (not Sun), traditional games and fruit machine; can get smoky *(Jim Farmer, A G Roby, LYM)*

Leicester [Belgrave Gate nr flyover], *Black Swan*: Welcoming young licensees, well kept Bank's Bitter and Mild, Camerons Strongarm and Marstons Pedigree, cheap food *(Joan and Michel Hooper-Immins)*; [Pocklingtons Walk], *Lamplighters*: Big new pub handy for shoppers, unusual decor and stained-glass round roof in former Gas Board offices; usual food reasonably priced, Mansfield Bitter, Riding and Old Baily; music can be obtrusive *(Joan and Michel Hooper-Immins)*; [139 London Rd], *Marquis of Wellington*: Well restored Edwardian pub, busy and lively, popular with accountants and solicitors lunchtime, lots of students evening, swift professional service, friendly concerned licensees, good filled lunchtime rolls and simple changing hot dishes inc evening pot meals, well kept Adnams, Everards and guest beers; pleasant and peaceful back courtyard with colourful murals, cheerful flowers *(Joan and Michel Hooper-Immins, J Weeks, Paul Cartledge, JCW)*; [London Rd, opp Victoria Pk], *Old Horse*: Good mix of people, good value usual bar food, well kept Everards and guest beers, games area with pool, airy conservatory, big garden; may be live music some evenings *(Rona Murdoch, Paul Cartledge)*; [Market St], *Wilkies*: Bare yet cheerful, with imaginative lunchtime food reflecting German landlady; splendid choice of bottled beers, well kept Flowers Original, Theakstons and Thwaites Mild *(Joan and Michel Hooper-Immins)*

Leicester Forest West, Leics [Hinckley Rd (A47); SK5001], *Bulls Head*: Food that's notable for its variety in popular timbered Everards pub, some alcove seating; can get rather smoky when crowded *(C J Pratt, RM)*

Leire, Leics [Main St; SP5290], *Queens Arms*: Decent food inc good pie-and-pint bargain offer; no loud music *(Cdr Patrick Tailyour)*

☆ **Lincoln** [Steep Hill], *Browns Pie Shop*: Not a pub (restaurant licence only), but does have Everards Tiger and Ruddles Best as well as the wide choice of good food inc spectacular pies which consistently pleases readers; good choice of wines, comfortable seats, friendly staff, pleasant traditional atmosphere *(M J Morgan, ILP, David and Shelia)*

Lincoln [Waterside North], *Green Dragon*: Noble waterside Tudor building – carved 16th-c façade gave its homelier name 'The Cat Garret'; downstairs bar with character timbers, beams and flagstones may be closed; quick bar food, well kept beers, friendly staff, restaurant *(Mike and Maggie Betton, LYM)*; [Rasen Lane], *Lord Tennyson*: Good honest pub food served on hot plates, very reasonable prices and smiling service *(Mrs Aldred)*; [1 Exchequer Gate], *Magna Carta*: In the heart of tourist area, a stone's throw from the cathedral and castle; wide variety of food (not Fri-Sun evenings) inc children's dishes, breakfast and afternoon teas; Mansfield ales *(Gordon B Thornton)*; [Burton Lane End, off A57 Saxilby rd SW], *Woodcocks*: Modern family pub, well built and tastefully decorated, each dining area with a different decorative theme like the Civil War or hunting; varied reasonably priced menu inc children's dishes, pleasant friendly staff, Marstons real ales, extensive facilities for children – outside playground, supervised indoor play area, plenty of high chairs in dining areas; in pleasant grassy area with trees nr canal walk *(David and Ruth Hollands, Gordon B Thornton)*

Littlethorpe, Leics [Station Rd; not far from M1 junction 21; off B4114; SP5496], *Plough*: 16th-c thatched pub; bar, dining room and smoke room with darts, copper tabletops and kettles, silver cabinet, good food lunchtime and evenings, Adnams, Everards, Wadworths Farmers Glory and a guest ale, quiet piped pop, benches outside; dogs and children allowed *(JJW, CMW)*

Long Bennington, Lincs [SK8344], *Reindeer*: Consistently good choice of good food, good wines, friendly welcoming and efficient service *(Donald and Margaret Wood)*

Long Sutton, Lincs [Main St; off bypass A17 Kings Lynn—Holbeach; TF4222], *Crown & Woolpack*: Busy and unpretentious pub with really good generous simple home cooking (sandwiches only, Mon-Weds) at low prices, inc good Sun lunch; panelled back dining room, Bass, Highgate Mild, Greene King Abbot and Worthington BB *(Mr and Mrs J Back)*

☆ **Loughborough**, Leics [The Rushes (A6); SK5319], *Black Lion*: Wide range of Hoskins and other beers in welcoming and widely appealing pub with lots of stripped pine and pews, bare boards and sawdust in front bar area, cosier back lounge; very helpful bar service, good value simple food, peaceful at lunchtime but noisy evenings; handy for canal basin *(Joan and Michel Hooper-Immins, Dr and Mrs A M Evans, Mr and Mrs A Cooper)*

Loughborough [about ¼ mile from Loughborough Wharf; SK5319], *Albion*: Down-to-earth canalside local with emphasis on good choice of changing well kept real ales inc Milds; cheap straightforward bar food, occasional barbecues, budgerigar aviary in big courtyard; children welcome *(Norma and Keith Bloomfield)*; [Wards End], *Blacksmiths*: Newly renovated, huge range of beers *(Alan and Kristina Thorley)*; [Canal Bank, Meadow Lane], *Boat*: Picturesque recently refurbished canalside pub with good atmosphere, friendly staff, good food at reasonable prices, good range of beers, boating memorabilia *(Ruth and Alan Cooper)*; [The Rushes (A6)], *White Lion*: Warmly welcoming licensees, Hoskins Bitter, Penns and in winter Old Nigel, guest such as Eldridge Pope Royal Oak; peaceful lunchtime, can be crowded and noisy evening; straightforward lunchtime food inc good filled rolls *(Joan and Michel Hooper-Immins)*

Louth, Lincs [Cordeaux Corner; Brackenborough – off new bypass; TF3289], *Brackenborough Arms*: Welcoming local meeting-point with Marstons and Stones on handpump, wide choice of bottled beers, food inc good generous home-cooked pies and fresh Grimsby fish and chips; good bedrooms in new wing *(W and P J Elderkin)*

Lowdham, Notts [Main St; nr A612/A6097; SK6646], *Old Ship*: Comfortable beamed split-level bar/lounge area, very friendly and relaxed, with copper-topped tables and red plush seating; helpful staff, good reasonably priced food from newish chef, well kept Courage-related ales and Marstons Pedigree, separate public bar; pleasant walks nearby *(Alan and Eileen Bowker, Linda Norsworthy)*

Lubenham, Leics [SP7087], *Coach & Horses*: Straightforward pub with coal fire, pictures and jugs etc in quiet lounge bar, good value bar food from toasted sandwiches up, friendly staff, well kept Everards ales with guests such as Wadworths Farmers Glory *(George Atkinson, Cdr P Tailyour)*

☆ **Lutterworth**, Leics [34 Rugby Rd (A426 S); very handy for M1 junction 20; SP5484], *Fox*: Straightforward, clean and welcoming, with good food (dish of proper butter for ploughman's, for instance), well kept Whitbreads-related ales, good coffee, open

fires; fruit machine but no piped music;
very friendly and accommodating landlord,
tables in garden *(George Atkinson, Frank
Davidson, Cdr Patrick Tailyour)*
Lutterworth [Market St], *Cavalier*: Good
atmosphere, genuinely home-cooked food,
good range of beers *(Cdr Patrick Tailyour)*;
Red Arrow: Recently refurbished, decent
food *(Cdr Patrick Tailyour)*

☆ **Lyddington**, Leics [SP8797], *Old White
Hart*: Consistently good value bar food (not
Sun evening) with fresh veg in clean and
popular traditional village inn, two small
character flagstoned bars and adjoining
restaurant, well kept Flowers IPA; safe and
pretty summer garden *(Stephen, Julie and
Hayley Brown, Brian and Jill Bond)*
Mansfield, Notts [Stockwell Gate;
SK5561], *Stockwells*: Traditional town
pub, real fires, Theakstons Best, XB and
Old Peculier, good value food inc very
cheap breakfast, games area, occasional live
music upstairs; open all day *(Russell J
Allen)*
Manton, Leics [SK8704], *Horse & Jockey*:
Good range of promptly served food, can
get busy even in winter; bedrooms *(Anon)*

☆ **Maplebeck**, Notts [signpost on A616 /
A617; SK7160], *Beehive*: Snug little
unspoiled beamed country tavern,
traditional furnishings, open fire, free
antique juke box, Mansfield real ale, tables
on small terrace with grassy bank running
down to small stream – very peaceful
(Eamon Green, LYM)

☆ **Mapperley**, Notts [Plains Rd (B684);
SK6043], *Travellers Rest*: Friendly and
popular road house, open all day, with well
kept Theakstons Best, Mild, XB and Old
Peculier, Youngers IPA and No 3 and a
guest like Jennings Cumberland, wide
choice of good value food all day (not after
2 Sun/Mon) inc vegetarian and children's
dishes, sensible write-your-own-order
system; new back family building with
adjacent play area *(Alan & Eileen Bowker,
David Gray, Bruce Bird)*

☆ **Market Bosworth**, Leics [Mkt Pl; SK4003],
Softleys: Describes itself as wine
bar/restaurant but has well kept Hook
Norton Best and Wadworths 6X in nice
beamed bar with mug collection overhead,
fine old fireplace and interesting brasses;
good food inc sandwiches and changing hot
dishes, some interesting, very friendly
service, spotless housekeeping, attractive
upstairs dining room; closed Mon;
bedrooms *(George Atkinson, Dorothee and
Denis Glover, P J Caunt)*

☆ **Market Bosworth** [The Square], *Black
Horse*: Locally popular for wide choice of
reasonably priced food, with good friendly
service and well kept Marstons Pedigree
and Tetleys *(Jim Farmer, the Monday Club,
David Atkinson)*
Market Bosworth [Rectory Lane], *Inn on
the Park*: Rather austere-looking pub in
beautiful big grounds, good value reliable
food in restaurant, tasteful bar, polite

welcoming staff *(C J Pratt, K Walton)*

☆ **Market Deeping**, Lincs [Market Pl;
TF1310], *Bull*: Rambling character pub
with low-ceilinged alcoves, little corridors,
interesting heavy-beamed medieval Dugout
Bar; well kept Adnams, Everards Tiger and
Old Original and a guest beer, good value
bar food (not Sun or Mon evening) inc
tempting puddings in attractively decorated
eating area, no piped music lunchtime,
helpful friendly service, restaurant; seats in
pretty coachyard; children in eating areas;
open all day Fri, Sat *(Norma and Keith
Bloomfield, LYM)*

☆ **Market Harborough**, Leics [High St;
SP7388], *Three Swans*: Fine range of bar
food inc good ploughman's and fish in
handsome coaching inn's plush lounge bar,
fine conservatory or attractive suntrap
courtyard, decent wines, good coffee, very
friendly and helpful staff; Courage-related
ales; bedrooms *(George Atkinson, Stephen
Brown, M J Morgan)*
Market Harborough [Church St], *Nags
Head*: Clean and well run, with pleasant
courteous staff, good honest simple food
cooked as you want it at low prices, well
kept Banks's and other beers, quiet bar
virtually reserved for oldies with log-effect
gas fire *(Cdr Patrick Tailyour)*
Market Rasen, Lincs [King St; TF1189],
Chase: Pleasant and comfortable family-run
free house with good range of food, cosy
cheery atmosphere; busy Tues market day
(Gordon B Thornton); [Queen St], *Gordon
Arms*: Quiet local, very friendly, with good
basic food; bedrooms simple, clean and
tidy, with good breakfast; share bathroom
(David Whitehead)
Markfield, Leics [Markfield Ln; SK4810],
Field Head: Recently comfortably
refurbished; very generous food, real ale,
decent wine; bedrooms *(the Monday Club)*

☆ **Marston**, Lincs [2 miles E of A1 just N of
Grantham; SK8943], *Thorold Arms*:
Refurbished by excellent new licensees,
doing well now, with well kept ales, good
food, friendly service and pleasant
atmosphere *(Jeanne and Tom Barnes, Peter
Burton)*
Moira, Leics [1 Shortheath Rd; SK3115],
Rawdon Arms: Good value food *(Michael
D Hurd)*

☆ **Morton**, Notts [SK7251], *Full Moon*: Good
food inc fish, vegetarian and Indian
specialities and lots of puddings in rambling
and welcoming 16th-c inn, comfortably
enlarged but not spoilt; well kept
Theakstons and guest beers, prompt
service; children welcome *(John C Baker,
Ian and Val Titman, A Douglas)*

☆ **Mountsorrel**, Leics [Loughborough Rd; off
A6; SK5714], *Swan*: Good unusual home-
made food, log fires and red banquettes in
two simple whitewashed bars with well kept
Batemans and Theakstons, wide choice of
wines by the glass, friendly service, walled
back garden leading down to canalised
River Soar; bedrooms *(A and R Cooper)*

Mountsorrel [Sileby Rd], *Waterside*: Comfortable modern split-level lounge and dining area overlooking busy lock on the Soar, well kept Everards, good range of bar meals, friendly staff; picnic-table sets outside *(B M Eldridge)*

Muston, Leics [off A52 W of Grantham; SK8237], *Muston Gap*: Good food, well kept ales; wheelchair access *(Elizabeth and Anthony Watts)*

☆ **Navenby**, Lincs [High St; car park behind is off East Rd; SK9858], *Kings Head*: Clean and friendly little village pub with welcoming new licensees, decent food inc vegetarian and bouillabaisse speciality, interesting nick-nacks, books, quick courteous service, well kept Bass, no-smoking area *(Roger and Linda Nicklin, P Neate)*

Nettleham, Lincs [A46 N of Lincoln; TF0075], *Brown Cow*: Comfortable lounge bar without fruit machines, good varied reasonably priced food, friendly service; Sun lunch very popular *(Gordon B Thornton)*

☆ **Newark**, Notts [19 Kirkgate; SK8054], *Old Kings Arms*: Simply furnished vaulted-ceiling bar with good choice of notably well kept Marstons real ales on handpump, unusual bottled beers, upstairs partly no-smoking eating area open all day (Sat afternoon closure) for good value often interesting home-cooked food with fresh veg (children allowed here), good service; trad jazz Mon, can be busy and noisy weekends *(David and Shelia, LYM)*

☆ **Newark** [London Rd, nr Beaumond Cross], *Mail Coach*: Fine atmosphere and interesting subtle decor in comfortable communicating areas, friendly service, generous reasonably priced lunchtime food (not Sun), well kept Allied ales with one or two guest beers, decent wines *(Drs N R and A de Gay, Paul Gretton, Lorna and Bill Tyson)*

☆ **Newark** [Northgate], *Malt Shovel*: welcoming and comfortably refurbished old-fashioned local with good doorstep sandwiches and well served lunchtime hot dishes inc fresh veg, well kept Timothy Taylors Landlord, Wards Sheffield Best and regular guest beers, choice of teas, very friendly staff; outside green tilework *(Derek and Sylvia Stephenson, Lorna and Bill Tyson)*

Newark [Jersey St; Hawton Rd Estate], *Cardinals Hat*: Large estate pub with friendly games area, good live entertainment, well kept Home ales *(Russell Allen)*

☆ **Newton Burgoland**, Leics [Main St; off B586 W of Ibstock; SK3708], *Belper Arms*: Good reasonably priced food and friendly atmosphere in interesting pub said to date back to 13th c, full of bric-a-brac; roomy lounge and low-beamed areas off, well kept Marstons, restaurant; big garden with play area *(Julie Peters)*

No Mans Heath, Leics [SK2808], *Four*

Counties: Popular food, Ind Coope Burton, Marstons Pedigree and Everards Original on handpump, welcoming service, witty pictures, friendly atmosphere *(Gwen and Peter Andrews)*

Normanton on Soar, Notts [Main St – OS Sheet 129 map ref 518230; SK5123], *Plough*: Popular mock-Tudor waterside pub in picturesque spot, nice atmosphere and decorations, good value food, well kept Marstons Pedigree and Tetleys, attentive friendly staff; children's playground *(A and R Cooper, George Atkinson)*

☆ **North Muskham**, Notts [Ferry Lane; village signed just off A1 N of Newark; SK7958], *Muskham Ferry*: Has changed hands since our main-entry recommendation, but still worth knowing for delightful Trent-side location – one of surprisingly few pubs on this noble river; well kept Courage-related ales and a guest such as Elgoods Cambridge, some home-made food inc fresh chips and salads, good puddings, attentive staff, children very welcome *(D Grzelka, David and Shelia, JF, D and B Carter, Malcolm Phillips, Mary Moore, LYM)*

North Scarle, Lincs [off A1133 Newark—Gainsborough; SK8567], *White Hart*: Friendly village local with well kept Whitbreads-related ales, generous good value bar food inc fresh specials, small restaurant, live music Sun evenings *(David and Ruth Hollands)*

☆ **Norton Disney**, Lincs [Main St; off A46 Newark—Lincoln; SK8859], *St Vincent Arms*: Attractive and comfortable country village pub with well kept Batemans Mild and XXXB, Marstons Pedigree, three interesting guest beers from afar, open fire, good value plain food from sandwiches up, pleasant landlord; tables and big entertaining adventure playground out behind *(Drs N R and A de Gay, Derek, Sylvia and Andrew Stevenson, O K Smyth)*

☆ **Nottingham** [18 Angel Row; off Market Sq], *Bell*: Georgian façade masking quaint 15th-c pub, low beams, timbers and panelling in three bustling downstairs bars (very crowded and maybe smoky late evening), nice window seats in calmer raftered upstairs bar used as lunchtime family restaurant – good value simple lunchtime food; Bass, Eldridge Pope Royal Oak, Jennings Bitter, Marstons Pedigree and Theakstons XB and a guest like Mansfield Old Baily kept well in extraordinarily deep sandstone cellar, good value wines, quick friendly service; trad jazz Sun lunchtime (rolls only then), Mon and Tues evenings; open all day weekdays *(Joan and Michel Hooper-Immins, Norma and Keith Bloomfield, Eamon Green, David and Shelia, LYM)*

Nottingham [Wellington Circus], *Limelight*: Restaurant and bar attached to the Playhouse theatre, full of life, with well kept real ales such as Adnams, Marstons Pedigree, Theakstons XB and Old Peculier, occasional modern jazz *(David and Shelia, Derek and Sylvia Stephenson)*; *Old Vic*: Former warehouse converted into Victorian-style pub, good period atmosphere and furnishings, smartly dressed staff, good value basic pub food, very varied entertainment *(R M Taylor)*; [Mansfield Rd], *Peacock*: Traditional, with Marstons Pedigree, Theakstons Best and XB and guests on handpump, pleasant bar, lounge with waitress bells, food inc big pies; licensed for backgammon, open all day *(Russell Allen)*; [Maid Marion Way], *Salutation*: Ancient back part with beams and flagstones, plush modern front, cheap and cheerful food, up to a dozen changing Whitbreads-related and other real ales inc interesting ones such as Batemans Salem Porter or Marston Moor Cromwell *(George Atkinson, David and Shelia, BB)*; [Sheriff's Way], *Tom Hoskins*: Plain alehouse with well kept Hoskins and Penns, Batemans Mild and a guest beer *(Joan and Michel Hooper-Immins, David and Shelia)*

Oakham, Leics [out nr Rutland Water; SK8508], *Normanton Park*: This hotel's Sailing Bar has interestingly varied choice of good food; well kept Ruddles County; bedrooms *(G Hadnam)*

Old Brampton, Notts [6 Fairview Rd; SK3372], *Royal Oak*: Good range of inexpensive bar food, separate dining room; friendly efficient service, well kept M & B and Tetleys on handpump *(Anne and Ian Fleming)*

Papplewick, Notts [SK5451], *Burnstump*: Good value Mansfield Landlords Table family dining pub in country park, tables on terrace, Riding on handpump; children welcome *(J Finney)*

Pinchbeck, Lincs [Glenside S; West Pinchbeck; TF2425], *Packing Shed*: Cosy and friendly pub with beautiful fire and horsebrasses, wide choice of good food *(Simon and Louise Chappell)*; [Northgate], *Ship*: Friendly atmosphere, obliging service, good value bar food, comfortable small lounge and dining area, Courage-related real ales *(Michael Brook-Lawson)*

☆ **Pleasley**, Notts [handy for M1 junction 29; A617 Mansfield—Chesterfield, just inside county boundary; SK5064], *Old Plough*: Attractively refurbished and comfortably extended, wide range of good value food from sandwiches to well priced steaks, well kept Ind Coope Burton, Tetleys, Mansfield Old Baily and guests such as Thwaites Craftsman *(Andy and Jill Kassube, Derek and Sylvia Stephenson)*

Plumtree, Notts [just off A606 S of Nottingham; SK6132], *Griffin*: Big helpings of good food in tastefully refurbished pub with comfortable conservatory, well kept beers *(Mrs J Barwell, Ruth and Alan Cooper)*

Plungar, Leics [SK7633], *Belvoir*: Plain and simple but welcoming, with consistently well kept Batemans *(Elizabeth and Anthony Watts)*

Preston, Leics [Uppingham Rd; SK8602], *Kingfisher*: Good home-cooked food, attentive service, open fires, comfortable seating *(Cdr Patrick Tailyour)*

Quorndon, Leics [46 High St; SK5616], *Bulls Head*: Handsome three-storey Georgian inn newly refurbished in traditional style, very tastefully, with reasonably priced good food from sandwiches up inc vegetarian and children's, very friendly staff, Bass, Stones and a guest beer, big back garden; open all day every day, food whenever open *(A and R Cooper)*; [Main St (A6)], *White Hart*: Unusual for being listed as Grade I, recently very carefully refurbished to retain original character; friendly atmosphere and staff, good value food *(A and R Cooper)*

Radcliffe on Trent, Notts [Main Rd; SK6439], *Black Lion*: Pleasant Tudor village pub, friendly staff, bar food (not Sun), real ale, separate games bar; back garden with play area; facilities for the disabled, children welcome; traction engine fair first week Oct *(Russell J Allen)*; [Main St], *Royal Oak*: Wide range of Whitbreads-related ales, friendly service; recently enlarged *(Andrew Wilson)*

☆ **Ranby**, Notts [just off A1 by A620 Worksop—E Retford; SK6580], *Chequers*: Well placed by canal, with waterside terrace, some mooring, weekend boat trips; good value plain generous food inc vegetarian served noon-10, well kept beer, cheerful service; attractive and comfortable renovation, dining room pleasantly decorated with farm tools and bric-a-brac; open all day *(Mrs D Dabinett, Neville Kenyon)*

☆ **Redmile**, Leics [off A52 Grantham—Nottingham; SK8036], *Olde Windmill*: Welcoming and comfortable lounge and dining room, well kept Adnams, Everards and other real ales, good range of generous good value bar food; less crowded than our main entry here; tables on terrace and in garden *(Elizabeth and Anthony Watts, Dr and Mrs J H Hills)*

☆ **Rothwell**, Lincs [Caistor Rd (A46); TF1599], *Nickerson Arms*: Refurbished as attractive open-plan bar under newish landlord, good range of food with some emphasis on fish, well kept ales such as Batemans, Tetleys, Timothy Taylors Landlord, friendly and relaxed atmosphere; children welcome, tables outside *(Nigel and Lindsay Chapman)*

Sandilands, Lincs [off A52 nr Sutton on Sea; TF5280], *Grange & Links*: A hotel, but good bar food and well kept beer; fine gardens some 200 yds from good beach; bedrooms *(Gordon B Thornton)*

☆ **Shawell**, Leics [not far from M6 junction 1; village signed off A5/A427 roundabout – turn right in village; SP5480], *White Swan*: Tucked-away creeper-covered dining pub with good fresh fish Thurs and other well presented food in roomy dining room; pub with coal fire and two log-effect gas fires in bar, oak-panelled lounge, separate bar and games room, open fires, well kept real ales such as Adnams Broadside, Banks's, Shipstones, friendly careful service; tables in garden *(George Atkinson, Frank Albrighton)*

☆ **Shearsby**, Leics [A50 Leicester—Northampton; SP6290], *Chandlers Arms*: Small stonebuilt pub with well kept Marstons Pedigree and other ales such as Adnams and Greene King, relaxing atmosphere, good food inc Indian, several vegetarian, even vegan dishes, Dutch landlady, very welcoming barman, well chosen piped music; attractive back terrace garden, picturesque village; children allowed in one room for lunch, no motorcyclists *(Jim Farmer, George Atkinson, Rona Murdoch)*

☆ **Sheepy Magna**, Leics [Main St (B4116); SK3201], *Black Horse*: Straightforward village pub, very well kept, with good generous attractively priced food from filled rolls up, friendly licensees, well kept Ansells Mild and Marstons Pedigree on handpump, games in lively public bar, family area, tables on pleasantly arranged back terrace *(George Atkinson, M and J Back, LYM)*

☆ **Sibson**, Leics [A444 N; SK3500], *Millers*: Large hotel around converted bakery and watermill, mill wheel and stream nr entrance, even a small fountain in flagstoned corridor to low-beamed lounge bar with Courage-related ales and good range of good value popular food, one table made from old millstone; afternoon teas, handy for Twycross Zoo and Bosworth Field; bedrooms good *(Christopher Bearfoot, George Atkinson)*

☆ **Sileby**, Leics [Swan St; SK6015], *White Swan*: Simple exterior, so a surprise to find such interesting good value food (not Sun eve or Mon) inc several vegetarian dishes in generous helpings; comfortable and welcoming dining lounge, well kept Marstons Pedigree, entertaining boxer dogs, small tasteful restaurant; children's playroom in converted back bowling alley with closed-circuit TV *(Rona Murdoch, Jim Farmer, Ruth and Alan Cooper)*

☆ **Skegness**, Lincs [Vine Rd, Seacroft (off Drummond Rd); TF5660], *Vine*: Dating mainly from late 18th c and peacefully set in decorous suburb away from the holiday crowds, comfortable well run bar overlooking drive and own bowling green, imposing antique seats and grandfather clock in turkey-carpeted hall, juke box in inner oak-panelled room; three well kept Batemans real ales, good if limited bar food, restaurant, tables on big back sheltered lawn with swings; bedrooms *(Denise Plummer, Jim Froggatt, Norma and Keith Bloomfield, Derek and Sylvia Stephenson, Ruth and Alan Cooper, Peter Burton, LYM)*

Skendleby, Lincs [Spilsby Rd; off A158 about 10 miles NW of Skegness – OS Sheet 122 map ref 433697; TF4369], *Blacksmiths Arms*: Old-fashioned cosy bar with open fire, Batemans real ale, limited range of reasonably priced food in big helpings; busy *(Bill Isaac)*

☆ **Somerby**, Leics [High St; SK7710], *Old Brewery*: Good Parish ales brewed in the yard behind this roomy carefully renovated two-bar pub, often all five on handpump with interesting guest beer; good value home-cooked food inc wonderful steaks from local butcher, roaring open fires, pleasant service; groups can see brewery, have buffet supper and drink as much as they like for set price; tables in garden, with boules and play area *(A and R Cooper, Joan and Michel Hooper-Immins, J D Cloud)*

South Kilworth, Leics [Rugby Rd (B5414); SP6081], *White Hart*: Friendly, pleasant atmosphere in very old village pub with quaint little dining room and larger bar with real fire, and skittles, darts and fruit machine; well kept Banks's Bitter on handpump, freshly cooked bar food inc cheap Sun lunch; piped pop music *(CW, JW)*

☆ **South Luffenham**, Leics [10 The Street; off A6121 at Halfway House, then first right; SK9402], *Boot & Shoe*: Homely village inn with comfortable rambling stripped-stone bar, good log fire, four or more well kept real ales, usual bar food from sandwiches to steaks, no-smoking eating area, evening restaurant; seats in neat small garden, pool in public bar; children welcome; four simple bedrooms, sharing two bathrooms – good breakfasts *(LYM)*

South Thoresby, Lincs [(about a mile off A16); TF4077], *Vine*: Large inn with small pub part – tiny bar, steps up to three-table lounge, wide choice of food in nicely panelled dining room, separate pool room; Batemans XB and Valiant and Vaux, good choice of whiskies; bedrooms *(M and J Back)*

☆ **Southwell**, Notts [Church St (A612); SK6953], *Bramley Apple*: Friendly pub with attractively worked Bramley apple theme, generous good value food inc fresh fish, eating area separated by stained-glass screens; well kept Batemans XB, Marstons Pedigree and a guest beer *(TOH, Mrs J Barwell, Andy and Jill Kassube, BB)*

Southwell, *Saracens Head*: Interesting old Forte hotel (where Charles I spent his last free night), with well kept Courage-related ales, good value bar lunches in beamed and panelled character bar, good service; children in eating area or restaurant; bedrooms comfortable *(Andy and Jill Kassube, LYM)*

Spalding, Lincs [town centre, next to river; TF2618], *Lincolnshire Poacher*: Good range of real ales, friendly attentive service, good home-made food, slow to come but worth the wait; several bars, tables out opp river *(George and Sheila Edwards)*; [Pinchbeck Rd], *Royal Mailcart*: Reasonably priced bar food, several

Courage-related ales, bar and games room, lounge with nicely decorated back eating area, separate restaurant *(MB, JB)*

Spilsby, Lincs [High St; TF4066], *White Hart*: Well kept Hardys & Hansons, good friendly service, good home cooking *(Ruth and Alan Cooper)*

☆ **Stamford**, Lincs [Broad St; TF0207], *Lord Burghley*: Jess the huge Great Dane rules the roost in this welcoming old character pub, with good long-serving landlord, well kept Greene King IPA and Abbot and several guest beers such as Fullers, a Marstons special brew, Ridleys or Youngs, wide choice of attractively priced good bar lunches, filled rolls other times; piped jazz, pleasant small walled garden with summer barbecues *(T G Thomas, David Surridge, Joan and Michel Hooper-Immins, Simon Collett-Jones)*

Stamford [All Saints Pl], *Crown*: Large rambling stonebuilt pub with good range of food in panelled bar and no-smoking dining room, quick friendly service, several real ales inc Ruddles; bedrooms *(K D Day)*; [St Peters St], *St Peters*: Good home-cooked food at reasonable prices, but main emphasis on well kept real ales – Marstons Best and Pedigree and four or five guests a week *(R Matthew)*

Stathern, Leics [Red Lion St; SK7731], *Red Lion*: Recently freed of tie, extensively renovated under new owners and now very busy; well kept sensibly priced beers, warm homely atmosphere *(Anon)*

Stow, Lincs [SK8882], *Cross Keys*: Prettily set village pub with attractive new dining area, interesting reasonably priced food, well kept Theakstons *(Dorothy and Leslie Pilson)*

Stragglethorpe, Notts [off A52 Nottingham—Radcliffe-on-Trent; SK6437], *Shepherds*: Big thatched Brewers Fayre dining pub with usual menu, Whitbreads-related ales, very good facilities for children *(Mrs J Barwell)*

Stretton, Leics [signed off A1; SK9416], *Jackson Stops*: Thatched pub very handy for A1, yet tucked away in quiet village; informal and homely small bar with well kept Ruddles Best and County and Sam Smiths OB on handpump, decent wines, open fires, RAF memorabilia, foreign car licence plates *(RB, LYM)*

Susworth, Lincs [Main St; SE8302], *Jenny Wren*: Overlooking River Trent, lots of character, nooks and crannies exposing various antiques, good food – why don't we hear more of this? *(Michael Swallow)*

☆ **Sutton Cheney**, Leics [Main St – off A447 3 miles S of Mkt Bosworth; SK4100], *Royal Arms*: Friendly and attractive dining pub, lots of tables in three smallish low-ceilinged rooms around central bar, wide choice of food inc lots of unusual changing specials, two open fires, well kept Marstons on handpump with changing guest beers; upstairs restaurant, family conservatory with wishing well, lots of picnic-table sets

in big garden with good children's play area; handy for Bosworth Field and Mallory Park, can get busy *(Roy Y Bromell, Jim Farmer)*

☆ **Sutton in the Elms**, Leics [Coventry Rd; B4114, just S of B581 – quite handy for M69 junction 2, and M1 – OS Sheet 140 map ref 509937; SP5194], *Mill on the Soar*: Bustling local atmosphere in substantial converted watermill – stripped brickwork, some rugs and carpet on the flagstones, brown beams and joists festooned with china and copper, conservatory area, river views from upstairs restaurant, quickly served good value bar food, Everards and guest ales; children welcome; good value bedrooms in separate comfortably modern block *(T M Dobby, LYM)*

Swinderby, Lincs [A46 Newark—Lincoln; SK8663], *Half Way House*: Good reasonably priced food in friendly, roomy and comfortable lounge, good staff, well kept Lorimers and Wards; piped music *(R A Hobbs, Dorothy Pilson)*

Swithland, Leics [SE end of village; between A6 and B5330, between Loughborough and Leicester; SK5413], *Griffin*: Very much a local, so some may not feel entirely at home here, but current landlady proving popular, with growing range of Everards and other well kept beers, reasonable choice of food, pleasant new decor and good family room; gardens by stream with horses, nice setting *(Tony and Joan Walker, Andrew Stephenson, Mr and Mrs A Cooper, LYM)*

☆ **Tetford**, Lincs [OS Sheet 122 map ref 333748; TF3374], *White Hart*: Interesting early 16th-c pub under new management since Easter 1994, old-fashioned settles, slabby elm tables and red tiled floor in pleasant quiet inglenook bar, bigger more straightforward extension, no-smoking snug; well kept Batemans, interesting reasonably priced food with good options for children; seats and swings on sheltered back lawn, simple bedrooms *(Mike and Maggie Betton, LYM)*

Thorpe Langton, Leics [SP7492], *Bakers Arms*: All that's left of the station is a pair of automatic level crossing barriers, but this unspoilt local recalls its railway associations with pre-1923 Hamilton Ellis prints from former LMS carriages; particularly well kept Mansfield Riding and Old Baily, friendly atmosphere *(John Baker)*

Thurgarton, Notts [Southwell Rd; A612; SK6949], *Red Lion*: Pleasant surroundings, friendly licensee, well kept Mansfield Riding and Marstons Pedigree on handpump, good reasonably priced bar food *(Elizabeth and Anthony Watts)*

Tilton on the Hill, Leics [B6047; SK7405], *Rose & Crown*: Characterful Ansells pub with friendly service, well kept beers and good reasonably priced food *(J V Dadswell)*

☆ **Timberland**, Lincs [Station Rd; TF1258], *Penny Farthing*: Pleasant and spacious stripped-stone beamed lounge, big helpings of good food (evening dining room), Tetleys and Youngers Scotch, decent house wine, unobtrusive piped music, local paintings for sale; bedrooms *(W and P J Elderkin)*

☆ **Tugby**, Leics [Main St; village signposted off A47 E of Leicester, bear right in village; SK7600], *Black Horse*: Wide choice of good generous home-made evening meals in cosy, quaint and attractive black-and-white thatched village pub with small rooms, well kept Ansells and Tetleys on handpump, friendly service, log fire; can get a bit smoky if crowded, esp small back drinkers' room; children welcome; cl lunchtime *(Stephen, Julie and Hayley Brown, JF, LYM)*

Tur Langton, Leics [off B6047; follow Kibworth signpost from village centre; SP7194], *Crown*: Well kept Bass and Marstons Pedigree, attractive furnishings from antique curved settle to chintzy easy chairs; tables on pleasantly planted terraces and in sheltered back courtyard; restaurant; cl weekday lunchtimes *(Paul Cartledge, LYM)*

Twyford, Leics [SK7210], *Saddle*: Old country pub with firearms above open fire, food inc good big freshly filled rolls, well kept Mansfield Riding *(Stephen, Julie and Hayley Brown)*

Ullesthorpe, Leics [SP5087], *Chequers*: Wide choice of reasonably priced food, popular evenings and Sun; good attentive service; bedrooms *(Miss D P Barson)*

☆ **Upper Hambleton**, Leics [village signposted from A606 on E edge of Oakham; SK9007], *Finches Arms*: Fine position high over Rutland Water, great views from tables on back gravel terrace and picture-window restaurant extension; good choice of well prepared food from sandwiches up, some interesting main dishes with particularly good veg, built-in button-back leatherette banquettes and open fire in knocked-through front bar, well kept Bass and other ales on handpump; friendly and entertaining licensees *(Joan and Michel Hooper-Immins, Eric J Locker, M J Morgan, David and Michelle Hedges, Mr and Mrs Peakman, BB)*

☆ **Uppingham**, Leics [High Street W; SP8699], *White Hart*: Old pub doing well under new licensees, wide choice of well priced attractively presented simple tasty food using local produce in front lounge with panelling and inglenook and back restaurant, two well kept Courage-related ales with a guest such as Morlands Speckled Hen, uncomplicated wine list chalked on blackboard; bedrooms *(O K Smyth, Eric J Locker, R H Jones)*

Uppingham [Market Sq], *Vaults*: Attractive pub overlooking square, tables outside; well kept Marstons Pedigree; bedrooms *(Jim Farmer)*

☆ **Upton**, Notts [Main St (A612); SK7354], *Cross Keys*: A favourite for atmosphere, and highly recommended for this; rambling

heavy-beamed bar with good welcoming service, lots of alcoves, central log fire, masses to look at from sporting cartoons and local watercolours to decorative plates and metalwork, interesting medley of furnishings; well kept Batemans XXXB, Boddingtons, Brakspears, Marstons Pedigree and guest beers on handpump, decent wines; friendly dog, unobtrusive piped music; children in back extension with carved pews or dovecote restaurant *(Derek and Sylvia Stephenson, Norma and Keith Bloomfield, John Fahy, K H Frostick, John C Baker, Brian and Jill Bond, David Gray, Stephen Newell, Gwen and Peter Andrews, David and Shelia, George Mitchell, Lorna and Bill Tyson, LYM)*

☆ **Walcote**, Leics [Lutterworth Rd (A427); 1½ miles from M1 junction 20 towards Market Harborough; SP5683], *Black Horse*: Almost the reverse of the above pub, in that the big draw here is the food – good authentic Thai dishes (not Mon or Tues lunchtime) cooked by the landlady, in good value big helpings; by contrast the pub itself is straightforward and housekeeping standards have not been all that one would wish; well kept Hook Norton Best and Old Hookey, Judges, Timothy Taylors Landlord and guest beers, interesting bottled beers and country wines; no-smoking restaurant *(Stephen, Julie and Hayley Brown, Graham Reeve, David and Shelia, Mayur Shah, P Butler, Cathy Scott, Richard Baker, Andy and Jill Kassube, Dr and Mrs D E Awbery, LYM)*

Walton on the Wolds, Leics [Loughborough Rd; SK5919], *Anchor*: Good if not cheap food, esp steak and kidney pie, in long rambling open-plan pub, popular with lunching businessmen; Allied ales on handpump *(Norma and Keith Bloomfield, A and R Cooper)*

☆ **Watnall Chaworth**, Notts [3 miles from M1 junction 26: A610 towards Nottingham, left on to B600, then keep right; SK5046], *Queens Head*: Tastefully extended old pub with beams and pine, snug bar and dining area, and coal fires; wide range of good value food, Home Bitter and Mild and Theakstons XB and Old Peculier on handpump, efficient friendly service; fruit machine, piped pop music; big back garden with benches and big play area; open all day Fri and Sat *(JJW, CMW, Mike and Penny Sanders, Jack and Philip Paxton)*

Welby, Lincs [Main St; SK9738], *Crown & Anchor*: Attractive village pub with homely atmosphere in spacious bar area and dining room, pictures and bric-a-brac, well kept Batemans and guest beers on handpump, good reasonably priced food *(AG)*

Wellingore, Lincs [High St; SK9856], *Marquis of Granby*: Aluring atmosphere, pleasant food service, good value for money, log fire, good range of beers *(P Neate)*

West Markham, Notts [close to A1/A57/A638 roundabout, just N of

Tuxford, S on B1164; SK7272], *Royal Oak*: Mansfield Landlords Table dining pub with standard menu, modern bar areas; open all day, real ales inc Dark Mild; useful journey respite *(Thomas Nott)*

☆ Whitwell, Leics [A606 Stamford—Oakham; SK9208], *Noel Arms*: Two tiny welcoming unpretentious rooms with good cheerful local atmosphere, spacious plush and decorous back extension; wide choice of good generous waitress-served home-cooked food (till 10), afternoon teas (not Mon), Ansells and Ruddles Best and County, efficient service, tables outside with occasional barbecues; piped music; handy for Rutland Water, children welcome; bedrooms *(G Olive, Prof John and Mrs Patricia White, LYM)*

☆ Whitwick, Leics [B587 towards Copt Oak; quite handy for M1 junction 22; SK4514], *Bulls Head*: Highest pub in Leics, nicely decorated, cosy and welcoming, with splendid views over Charnwood Forest; well kept Ansells, Ind Coope Burton and Tetleys, maybe Marstons Pedigree, quickly served home-cooked food (lunchtime, not Sun) using good ingredients, big garden with menagerie of farm animals; children very welcome away from bar *(E G Wright, A and R Cooper, J D Cloud, George Atkinson)*

Wigston, Leics [Bull Head St; SK5900], *Horse & Trumpet*: Everards pub with generous home-made cheap food lunchtime – popular with local workers then, more of a local evenings; skittle alley, friendly staff *(Rona Murdoch)*

Wilford, Notts [Main Rd; SK5637], *Ferryboat*: Clean traditional pub with genuine furnishings, two snugs, dining lounge with lofted roof and imposing fireplace; well kept real ales, tidy back terrace, garden with play area, view over river to Nottingham Castle *(Mrs J Barwell)*

☆ Wing, Leics [Top St; signed off A6003 S of Oakham; SK8903], *Kings Arms*: Well kept Bass, Ruddles County and Stones from rare cash-register handpumps in attractively restored early 17th-c inn, very welcoming, cosy, clean and quiet, with stripped stonework, roaring log fires; good generous home-cooked straightforward food at sensible prices in bar or separate spacious restaurant; attractive village; comfortable well equipped bedrooms in modern annexe, also cottage to let *(Peter Dowd, David and Michelle Hedges, LYM)*

☆ Woodhall Spa, Lincs [Kirkstead; Tattersall Rd (B1192 Woodhall Spa—Coningsby); TF1963], *Abbey Lodge*: Attractively and discreetly decorated food pub, warm, cosy and always popular, with some antique furnishings, good welcoming service, good-sized tasty bar meals and good Sun lunches, well kept real ale, RAF memorabilia *(P R Morley, Dr J Lunn)*

☆ Woodhouse Eaves [Brand Hill; beyond Main St, off B591 S of Loughborough – OS Sheet 129 map ref 533148], *Wheatsheaf*: Plushly civilised open-plan country pub with good log fires, good if pricy home-cooked food inc vegetarian, up to ten or so well kept real ales, decent wines, good friendly service – a popular business meeting place; tables out in floodlit former coachyard *(Norma and Keith Bloomfield, Drs N R and A de Gay, Dr J Gardner, Jack and Philip Paxton, A and R Cooper, Andrew Stephenson, LYM)*

Woodhouse Eaves, *Bulls Head*: Congenial pub with country-house-type decor, book-lined walls, beams, old Singer sewing machines etc, relaxed atmosphere; good home-cooked food, friendly and helpful young staff *(Roy Briggs, Barbara Taylor, Mr and Mrs A Cooper)*

☆ Woolsthorpe, Lincs [the one nr Belvoir, signed off A52 Grantham—Nottingham; SK8435], *Rutland Arms*: Comfortable and relaxed country pub with good reasonably priced bar food esp fish, welcoming service, lounge with some high-backed settles, hunting prints and brasses, family extension with old furniture, open fire, video juke box, bric-a-brac, separate dining room; well kept Whitbreads-related ales on handpump, two pool tables in annexe; play equipment on big lawn, quiet spot *(Norma and Keith Bloomfield, Elizabeth and Anthony Watts)*

Worksop, Notts [Chesterfield Rd; Whitwell; SK5879], *Half Moon*: Warm friendly atmosphere, good varied menu for vegetarians, slimmers and hearty eaters alike, reasonable prices, special offers between 5 and 7 *(C E Ilett)*; [Carlton Rd, nr stn], *Newcastle Arms*: Deceptively spacious, good value bar food, variety of real ales, games room *(Tony and Wendy Hobden)*

☆ Wymeswold, Leics [A6006; SK6023], *Hammer & Pincers*: Well refurbished, very clean and bright, with pine furniture in four or five rooms on several levels, interesting varied good value food, well kept Bass, Ruddles County, Stones, Theakstons Old Peculier and guest beers; tables on terrace, neat garden *(Andrew Stephenson, Ruth and Alan Cooper, Alan and Eileen Bowker, Stephen Brown)*

☆ Wymondham, Leics [Edmonthorpe Rd; off B676 E of Melton Mowbray; SK8518], *Hunters Arms*: Cosy two-bar pub with restaurant, French chef/patron, friendly atmosphere, well kept real ales such as Bass, Batemans, Greene King IPA and Abbot; good French-influence dishes such as lamb and haricot casserole or beef medaillons in mustard sauce, also cheaper staples such as steak and kidney pie; very popular weekends *(Norma and Keith Bloomfield, V and E A Bolton)*

Wysall, Notts [off A60 at Costock, or A6006 at Wymeswold; SK6027], *Plough*: Attractive place with well kept Bass, friendly staff, nice mix of furnishings and gentle lighting; tables in good garden; no cooked lunches on Sun *(Dr and Mrs J H Hills, A and R Cooper)*

Lincolnshire *see* Leicestershire

Midlands (Northamptonshire, Warwickshire and West Midlands)

Pubs currently doing particularly well for food here include the restauranty Bell at Alderminster, the Ferry at Alveston, the idiosyncratic Olde Coach House at Ashby St Ledgers, the peaceful Red Lion at East Haddon, the civilised Falcon at Fotheringhay, the smart Howard Arms at Ilmington, the Black Horse at Nassington, the Falcon at Priors Marston, the Blue Boar at Temple Grafton, the Old Friar at Twywell, the Pheasant at Withybrook and (a new entry this year) the Bulls Head at Wootton Wawen. From among these, we choose as Midlands Dining Pub of the Year the Black Horse at Nassington. Pub food prices in the area are among the lowest in the country – especially so in the West Midlands, where there are some remarkable bargains (the interesting Old Windmill in Coventry, a new entry, is an outstanding example). Beer prices too are generally low in the area – again, particularly so in the West Midlands, where the cheapest pubs we found were the Brewery in Langley (the very local Holt Plant & Deakins brewery of the Allied brewing empire) and the extraordinary Crooked House in Himley (tied to the regional brewer Banks's); beers from the distant Yorkshire brewer Sam Smiths were also very cheap indeed in the Old Windmill in Coventry, and the wonderfully old-fashioned Case is Altered at Five Ways. We have mentioned one or two new entries; others here include two very sharply contrasting pubs, the outrageously entertaining Pie Factory in Tipton, and the very civilised Bulls Head at Wootton Wawen. In the Lucky Dip section at the end of the chapter, pubs we'd particularly mention include the Kings Head at Aston Cantlow, Great Western at Deppers Bridge (for families), Eastcote Arms at Eastcote (if it should reopen), Castle on Edge Hill, Butchers Arms at Farnborough (which has reopened), White Lion at Hampton in Ardern, Greyhound in Hawkesbury, Red Lion at Hellidon, Crewe Arms at Hinton in the Hedges, Saracens Head at Little Brington, Snooty Fox at Lowick, Waggon & Horses in Oldbury, Boat at Stoke Bruerne, Old Washford Mill at Studley, Heart of England at Weedon, Bell at Welford on Avon, Royal Oak at Whatcote, and Great Western in Wolverhampton; there are several good pubs in both Kenilworth and Stratford.

Post Office address codings confusingly give the impression that some pubs are in the Midlands, when they're really in the Derbyshire, Leicestershire or Shropshire areas that we list them under.

ALDERMINSTER (Warwicks) SP2348 Map 4

Bell 🍴 ♈

A3400 Oxford—Stratford

Hardly your average local, this rather civilised place reminds some readers more of a restaurant, but the informal and relaxed atmosphere is very much that of a pub. Most people come for the food, which though quite pricey is really thoughtfully prepared and very tasty – we know of several people who would rather eat here than anywhere else they've ever been to. Using fresh produce (no fried food at all), the range of meals changes every day but might include dishes such as soups like courgette and stilton (£2.50), sausages in mustard and honey or half a pint of prawns (£3.95), chicken liver and Cointreau pâté or ploughman's (£4.25), mushroom and smoked haddock scallop (£4.75), smoked salmon ravioli or asparagus and prawn quiche (£6.75), dressed crab salad (£7.75), beef, orange and brandy casserole (£8.95), steak, kidney and oyster pie (£9.25), whole lemon sole (£9.50), turbot steak with watercress sauce (£10.95), and several good puddings like peach and almond tart or lemon and orange Boodles fool (£3.95); also two-course business lunch available weekdays (£5.75). They do a number of themed evenings with special menus, like French or Indian; the Symphony Suppers and Calypso Dinners are especially entertaining. The communicating areas of the spacious bar have a panelled oak settle and plenty of stripped slatback chairs around wooden tables on the flagstones and wooden floors, little vases of flowers, small landscape prints and swan's-neck brass-and-globe lamps on the cream walls, and a solid fuel stove in a stripped brick inglenook; dominoes. Most of the restaurant is no smoking. Flowers Original and Marstons Pedigree on handpump, and a good range of wines (from Berry Bros & Rudd); obliging, friendly service. There are tables under cocktail parasols on the sheltered grass, and a large car park. It's just 4 miles from Stratford. (*Recommended by Stephen Richards, David and Ruth Hollands, Mrs R Bennett, Peter Lloyd, A Cowell, Peter Neate, the Monday Club, Mrs J Oakes, Clare Dawkins, Gordon Phillips, Peter and Erica Davis, H R Bevan, Olive Carroll, S V Bishop, John and Annette Derbyshire, Mr and Mrs G J Rice*)

Free house ~ Licensees Keith and Vanessa Brewer ~ Real ale ~ Meals and snacks ~ Restaurant ~ Alderminster (01789) 450414 ~ Children welcome ~ Open 12-2.30, 7-11; closed evening 25 Dec, maybe other evenings between Christmas and New Year

ALVESTON (Warwicks) SP2356 Map 4

Ferry ♈

End of village; off B4086 Stratford—Wellesbourne – OS Sheet 151 map reference 236565

Tucked away in an attractive spot, with a path leading off along the River Avon, this comfortable village pub is proving rather popular at the moment, and once again the main attraction is the very good range of often imaginative food. The choice changes all the time, but favourite dishes over the last few months have included soup (£1.95), generously-filled rolls and baguettes (from £2.25), garlic mushrooms (£3.25), avocado, crab and prawn salad or fresh peaches filled with cottage cheese (both £4.95), good Thai-style king prawns in filo pastry, a big filled Yorkshire pudding (£5.50), trout in soy and oyster sauce or baked chicken and asparagus pancake au gratin (£6.50), stir-fry chicken kung po (£6.95), poached salmon with hollandaise (both £7.95), steaks (from £8.95) and good home-made puddings like treacle sponge or excellent banoffi pie; helpings are usually generous. They don't accept bookings, so get there early, as it can get busy and if you time it wrong you may have to wait. Well kept Hook Norton Best, Marstons Pedigree and Theakstons Best and XB on handpump, a particularly good choice of wines by the bottle or glass, and good coffee; notably well trained friendly and always cheerful staff. Three rooms are knocked into one long single bar and have comfortable newish brocaded seating and a low-key decor – cream walls, fish prints, very clear lighting; piped music, log fire. (*Recommended by Geoff and Angela Jaques, Helen Hazzard, Steve and Liz Tilley, Andrew Shore, David and Ruth Hollands, the Monday Club, Mrs B Sugarman, Thomas Nott, Simon Morton, John Bowdler, George Atkinson, H R Bevan, Tony Walker*)

Trent (S & N) ~ Tenants David and Sarah Russon ~ Real ale ~ Meals and snacks (not Sun evening) ~ (01789) 269883 ~ Well behaved children over 5 in eating area ~ Open 11-2.30, 6-11; closed 25 Dec

ASHBY ST LEDGERS (Northants) SP5768 Map 4

Olde Coach House ★ 🛏 ♀ ◖

4 miles from M1 junction 18; A5 S to Kilsby, then A361 S towards Daventry; village is signposted left. Alternatively 8 miles from M1 junction 16, then A45 W to Weedon, A5 N to sign for village.

One of those remarkable pubs that just seems to get better and better all the time, this thriving ivy-covered inn has a wonderful traditional feel that everyone who goes really seems to like. It's been getting quite a lot of national attention recently, what with awards and gushing newspaper articles, but it's not the kind of place to be spoiled by success; you'll find the charming atmosphere the same as it ever was. The several comfortable, rambling little rooms have harness on a few standing timbers, hunting pictures (often of the Pytchley, which sometimes meets outside), Thelwell prints, high-backed winged settles on polished black and red tiles, old kitchen tables, and a big winter log fire. A front room has darts, pool, trivia, video game and piped music. Good waitress-served bar food includes filled rolls (£1.50), tasty home-made soup (£1.95), jacket potatoes with various fillings (from £1.95), vegetable pie (£4.25), home-made lasagne, chilli con carne or curry (£4.75), venison sausages with stilton, salad and bread (£4.95), tagliatelle in a tomato and mixed pepper sauce (£5.95), steaks (from £8.95), grilled salmon with a dill mayonnaise (£9.25), daily specials like steak, kidney and mushroom pie (£6.95) or cajun chicken (£7.25), puddings, and children's dishes (from £1.95); popular daily cold buffet, winter Sunday lunch. Most of the recently refurbished dining room is no smoking. Well kept Boddingtons, Everards Old Original, Flowers IPA, Morrells Varsity, and Jennings Cumberland on handpump, with lots more during their spring beer festivals, fresh orange juice, decent wine list with several by the glass, and some malt whiskies. Service is always smiling. There are seats among fruit trees and under a fairy-lit arbour, and there may be barbecues in summer; a children's play area is planned. They've just added a new entrance for disabled visitors and they have baby-changing facilities. The pub is well placed in an attractive village full of thatched stone houses, and the nearby manor house was owned by one of the gunpowder plotters. (*Recommended by Graham and Lynne Mason, Cathy Scott, Richard Baker, Simon Marsden, John and Elliott Gwynne, Miss D P Barson, Julie Peters, G P Kernan, KC, Natalie Spencer, Mr and Mrs Spencer, Stephen, Julie and Hayley Brown, Greg Parston, C H Stride, D Cox, Comus Elliott, John Bowdler*)

Free house ~ Licensees Brian and Philippa McCabe ~ Real ale ~ Meals and snacks ~ Rugby (01788) 890349 ~ Children welcome ~ Open 12-2.30, 6-11; 12-11 Sat ~ Bedrooms: £40B/£48B

BADBY (Northants) SP5559 Map 4

Windmill 🛏 ♀

Village signposted off A361 Daventry—Banbury

Rather popular at the moment, this thatched coaching inn is a good mixture of old-fashioned charm and tasteful modernisation. The emphasis is very much on family dining, and although they have a good range of beers they're just as happy to serve tea, coffee or other non-alcoholic drinks, giving it something of the feel of a continental-style brasserie. There's a good friendly feel in the thriving bars, both of which have beams, flagstones and lace, cricketing pictures and appropriately simple country furnishings in good solid wood; there's an enormous inglenook fireplace in one area and a cosy and comfortable lounge. They plan to create a new bar in the restaurant and add another lounge area. Very well liked tasty bar food includes sandwiches (from £1.50), home-made soup (£1.75), filled baked potatoes (from £3.25), a continental platter (£3.75), good home-made vegetarian dishes (£4.50), home-made chicken and ham pie in herb pastry (£6.25), char-grilled cajun chicken (£7.25), bargain daily specials, steaks with their own stilton sauce (from £7.25), children's dishes (from £1.75), a popular three-course Sunday lunch (£8), and home-made puddings such as treacle tart and banoffi pie; they do occasional themed evenings and special events. Well kept Bass, Boddingtons, Flowers Original, Morlands Old Speckled Hen and Wadworths 6X on handpump; decent wines. Service is generally efficient and welcoming, though a couple of readers this year seem to have caught them on off days. Dominoes, video game, piped music. There are tables outside, with a children's play area beyond the car park. *(Recommended by Sheila and Terry Wells, George Atkinson, Paul Burdett, Christopher and Sharon Hayle, Stephen, Julie and Hayley Brown, Gunnar Arholt and family, Michael Marlow, John Fahy, CW, JW, R A Buckler)*

Free house ~ Licensees John Freestone and Carol Sutton ~ Real ale ~ Meals and snacks ~ Restaurant (Fri and Sat; Sun lunchtime) ~ (01327) 702363 ~ Children welcome ~ Live music and dancing every Sat ~ Open 11.30-3, 5.30-11; all day summer Sats ~ Bedrooms: £30B/£40B

BRIERLEY HILL (W Midlands) SO9187 Map 4

Vine £ ◀

Delph Rd; B4172 between A461 and A4100, near A4100

As this lively place is right next to the brewery, the beer is very well kept and priced: Bitter and Mild (dark, unusually full-flavoured with a touch of hops, and outstanding value) on handpump, with Delph Strong in winter. It's known in the Black Country as the Bull & Bladder, from the good stained-glass bull's heads and very approximate bunches of grapes in the front bow windows. The front bar has wall benches and simple leatherette-topped oak stools, a snug on the left has solidly built red plush seats, and the back bar has brass chandeliers and more seats. Good, fresh lunchtime snacks include old-fashioned sandwiches (£1), faggots and peas (£1.50) and marvellous-value salads (from £1.70). Darts, cribbage, dominoes, fruit machine, video game and trivia. It can get crowded. Plans are in the pipeline for extensions to the pub over the next year or so. *(Recommended by Graham Reeve, Dr Bill Baker; more reports please)*

Bathams ~ Manager Melvyn Wood ~ Real ale ~ Lunchtime snacks (not Sun) ~ (01384) 78293 ~ Children in own room ~ Blues Sun, jazz or folk Mon ~ Open 12-11

CLIPSTON (Northants) SP7181 Map 4

Bulls Head ◀

B4036 S of Market Harborough

A friendly and very relaxed slate-roofed local, with a good welcome to visitors. Countless coins glisten in the black beams, carrying on an odd tradition started by US airmen based nearby in World War II – they used to wedge the money waiting for their next drink in cracks and crannies of the ancient woodwork. It's cosily divided into three snug areas leading down from the servery, with comfortable seats, sturdy small settles and stools upholstered in red plush, a grandmother clock, some harness and tools and a log fire. Well kept Bass, Batemans, Boddingtons, Flowers Original, Fullers Chiswick, Greene King IPA, Hook Norton Old Hookey and Marstons Pedigree on handpump, and a very impressive choice of malt whiskies – they had 366 varieties at the last count. The long back games bar, lively in the evenings, has darts, pool, table skittles, dominoes, shove-ha'penny, fruit machine, video game, trivia, juke box and piped music. Decent bar food includes sandwiches and other light snacks, and daily specials such as Drunken Bull pie (£4.50), poached salmon in cream and dill sauce, Dijon chicken or local trout poached in white wine (£4.95), and T-bone steak topped with stilton (£8.95); a couple of readers have found on Sundays most tables may be reserved for lunch. Outside, a terrace has a few white tables under cocktail parasols, and there may be barbecues out here in summer. *(Recommended by L Walker, J Cox, Stephen, Julie and Hayley Brown, Wayne Brindle, Eric J Locker, Mr and Mrs K H Frostick, Ron Fletcher; more reports please)*

Free house ~ Licensees Colin and Jenny Smith ~ Real ale ~ Meals and snacks (not evening Sun or Mon) ~ Clipston (01858) 525268 ~ Children in eating area of bar and back games room ~ Occasional live entertainment ~ Open 11.30-2.30, 6.30-11; closed 25 Dec ~ Bedrooms: £29.50B/£35.50B

COVENTRY (W Midlands) SP3379 Map 4

Old Windmill £

Spon Street

Known locally as Ma Brown's after a former landlady, this attractive timber-framed 16th-c pub is unlike most other buildings in this picturesque medieval street – it has always been here, whereas most of the other neighbouring survivors of wartime bombing have been moved here from other parts of the city. But it is in its own right, as a pub, that it really scores. There's a good thriving atmosphere in its rambling series of tiny cosy old rooms, one little more than the stub of a corridor, another with carved oak seats on flagstones and a woodburner in a fine ancient inglenook fireplace, another with carpet and more conventionally comfortable seats. There are exposed beams in the uneven ceilings, and a back room preserves some of the equipment which used to be used for brewing here. Nowadays the beers are well kept Ruddles Best and County, John Smiths Magnet, Wadworths 6X and Websters Yorkshire, with very cheap Sam Smiths. At lunchtime you order food at the kitchen door, and that's where it's handed to you: generous extraordinarily cheap soup (70p), filled rolls (from £1), vegetarian quiche (£1.70), steak and kidney pie, curries, lamb or pork chops or lasagne (all £2) – chips and beans loom large – and apple pie and custard, cooked by the landlady. Very friendly staff, unpretentious atmosphere; popular with students, extremely busy on Friday and Saturday evenings; dominoes, fruit machine and piped music. Handy for the Belgrave Theatre. *(Recommended by Ann Griffiths, Graham Reeve, Alan and Maggie Telford, Geoff Lee, George Atkinson)*

Courage ~ Tenant M Blackburn ~ Real ale ~ Lunchtime meals and snacks (not Sun or bank hol Mon) ~ (01203) 252183 ~ Children in eating area of bar at lunchtime ~ Open 11.30(11 Sat)-2.30, 5.30(7 Sat)-11; closed evening 25 Dec, 1 Jan

CRICK (Northants) SP5872 Map 4

Red Lion ◖

A mile from M1 junction 18; A428

This comfortable old thatched pub is very useful as a lunchtime stop if travelling up (or down) the M1. Readers like it best in winter when it takes on a fairly cosy air, but it's good in summer too when you can eat on a Perspex-roofed sheltered terrace in the old coach yard, with lots of pretty hanging baskets. There are a few picnic-table sets under cocktail parasols on grass by the car park. The low-ceilinged bar is a pleasant place to while away a couple of hours, with its two winter roaring log fires (filled in summer with big, bright copper dishes and brassware), stripped stonework, soft lighting and a notably relaxed chatty air; it's quietest and snuggest in the inner part of the bar. Good value lunchtime snacks include filled rolls and ploughman's, steak and kidney pie or roast of the day (£3.50), with dishes such as chicken kiev, gammon, stuffed plaice, roast duck, trout and different steaks (between £5 and £8.50), available in the evening; only filled rolls and ploughman's Sunday lunchtimes. Well kept Hook Norton Best, Courage Directors, John Smiths and Websters Yorkshire on handpump; friendly service. No piped music. *(Recommended by Mayur Shah, Stephen, Julie and Hayley Brown, D P Marson, Gwyneth Holland, Cathy Scott, Richard Baker, Stephen R Holman, Barbara and Norman Wells, Mr and Mrs K H Frostick, Mrs J Barwell, Ted George, Steve de Mellow, Mrs F Hart, F J Robinson, David C Alcock)*

Free house ~ Lease: Tom and Mary Marks ~ Real ale ~ Meals and snacks (12-1.45, 7-9, 9.30 Sat; not Sun evenings) ~ Crick (01788) 822342 ~ Children in family room lunchtime only ~ Open 11.30-2.30, 6.30-11

EAST HADDON (Northants) SP6668 Map 4

Red Lion 🛏 🍺

High St; village signposted off A428 (turn right in village) and off A50 N of Northampton

With so many interesting old objects dotted around, walking into this rather smart substantially-built golden stone hotel is rather like going to an antique shop. It's a popular old place, with most people coming for the high quality daily changing bar food: a typical menu might include sandwiches or soups (£2.95), ploughman's, home-made pâté (£4.95), dressed crab salad or fish cake with tomato and basil sauce (£5.95), good steak and kidney pie (£6.50), fillet of cod with lobster sauce, avocado pear stuffed with mushrooms and topped with stilton or asparagus and smoked salmon flan (£6.95), beef provençale (£7.95), poached salmon with hollandaise sauce (£9.95) and tempting puddings like chocolate terrine or apple and strawberry pie (£3.25); they do a three-course set lunch for £13.95. It's worth booking – quite understandably they do get busy. The discreetly well kept lounge bar has oak panelled settles, library chairs, soft modern dining chairs, and a mix of oak, mahogany and cast-iron-framed tables. Also, white-painted panelling, recessed china cabinets, old prints and pewter, and little kegs, brass pots, swords and so forth hung sparingly on a couple of beams; it's all been redecorated since our last edition. The small public bar has sturdy old-fashioned red leather seats. The pretty separate restaurant is good, as are the breakfasts. Very well kept Adnams Broadside, Charles Wells Eagle and Bombardier, and Morlands Old Speckled Hen on handpump, several New World wines on the wine list; attentive, friendly service; piped music. The walled side garden is very attractive, with lilac, fruit trees, roses and neat little flowerbeds; it leads back to the bigger lawn, where there are well spaced picnic-table sets. There are more tables under cocktail parasols on a small side terrace, and a big copper beech shades the gravel car park. They've recently upgraded the bedrooms, all of which are now en suite. *(Recommended by Mayur Shah, R H Jones, Mark and Toni Amor-Segan, Mrs Gwyneth Holland, Howard and Margaret Buchanan, Mrs B Sugarman, Maysie Thompson, Ian Fordham, G L Tong, D Jackson, Stephen George Brown, Martin and Sarah Crossley, Mrs D J Restall)*

Charles Wells ~ Tenants Mr and Mrs Ian Kennedy ~ Real ale ~ Meals and snacks (till 9.45; not Sun evening) ~ Restaurant (not Sun evening) ~ Northampton (01604) 770223 ~ Children in eating area and restaurant ~ Open 11-2.30, 6-11 ~ Bedrooms: £45B/£59B

ETTINGTON (Warwicks) SP2749 Map 4

Chequers

A422 Banbury—Stratford

As we hoped last year, the Deacons haven't done anything to change the atmosphere of this traditional village inn, though there have been alterations to the decor and furnishings. In particular the main lounge at the back has been refurbished to provide more comfort for people eating; it still has the attractive Ros Goody Barbour-jacket-era sporting prints on the walls. The front bar is more straightforward, and has sensibly placed darts, shove-ha'penny, dominoes, fruit machine and piped music. The chef has been here several years now, and produces light snacks and sandwiches, daily specials like braised liver and onions or steak and kidney pie (£3.50), fresh salmon and trout, maybe dishes using his speciality game, such as rabbit casserole or pigeon pie, and delicious home-made puddings like treacle tart and banoffi pie (£2); they have occasional themed evenings such as Chinese or Italian. Changing beers such as Bass, Hook Norton Best and Brew XI on handpump (cheaper than last year); pool room, and a spacious conservatory with garden tables and chairs. There are tables out on the neat back lawn and on an awninged terrace, with lots of hanging baskets. *(Recommended by Dennis H Phillips, Dorothy and David Young, Mr and Mrs Dara de Gogan; more reports please)*

Free house ~ Licensees Mike and Kay Deacon ~ Real ale ~ Meals and snacks (not Monday evenings) ~ (01789) 740387 ~ Children over 5 in dining area if eating ~ Open 11-3, 5.30-11

FIVE WAYS (Warwicks) SP2270 Map 4

Case is Altered ◀

Follow Rowington signposts at junction roundabout off A4177/A4141 N of Warwick

It was about 300 years ago that this wonderful place first got its licence, and changes since have been kept strictly to a minimum. It's one of those rare places that really is truly unspoilt, and is especially pleasant to visit for the delightfully warm welcome from the landlady, cheery staff and regulars. The small and unchanging simple main bar is decorated with a fine old poster showing the Lucas Blackwell & Arkwright brewery (now flats) and a clock with its hours spelling out Thornleys Ale, another defunct brewery; there are just a few sturdy and old-fashioned tables, with a couple of leather-covered sturdy settles facing each other over the spotless tiles. From this room you reach the homely lounge (usually open only weekend evenings and Sunday lunchtime) through a door lit up on either side. A door at the back of the building leads into a modest little room, usually empty on weekday lunchtimes, with a rug on its tiled floor and a bar billiards table protected by an ancient leather cover (it takes pre-decimal sixpences). Well kept Ansells Mild and Traditional, Flowers Original, and very well priced Sam Smiths OB served by rare beer engine pumps mounted on the casks that are stilled behind the counter. Behind a wrought-iron gate is a little brick-paved courtyard with a stone table under a chestnut tree. No food. *(Recommended by J Dwane, Michael and Derek Slade, Ted George, Pete Baker, the Monday Club, Wayne Brindle, Andy and Jill Kassube, R J Herd, E M Davies)*

Free house ~ Licensee Gwen Jones ~ Real ale ~ (01926) 484206 ~ Open 11.30-2.30, 6-11 (closed evening 25 Dec)

FOTHERINGHAY (Northants) TL0593 Map 5

Falcon ★

Village signposted off A605 on Peterborough side of Oundle

Judging by the reports we've had over the last year, this stylish old place never fails to please, and it's the kind of pub where, as they say on the menu, they're happy to serve just a cup of coffee if that's what you want. It's atmospheric, friendly and comfortable, but for many people the main attraction must be the very good, imaginative home-made bar food, with a choice of dishes like french onion soup or iced gazpacho (£2.70), pâtés like chicken or cream cheese and cashew nut (£2.90), a really excellent ploughman's (£3), herrings in a curry sauce or sweet spicy salad (£3.40), vegetable salad (£4.40), quail's eggs with smoked salmon (£4.50), steak and kidney pie or West African baboti (£4.60), cold tiger prawn salad (£5.50), grilled lemon sole fillets with asparagus (£6.80), roast duckling with apple and rosemary stuffing (£7), chicken in burgundy sauce with mushrooms (£7.20), venison cutlet in port wine sauce with oranges (£8.20), steak (£8.50) and puddings; in summer you can eat on the terrace. As well as the simpler public bar which the landlord prefers to keep for the locals, there's a comfortable lounge with cushioned slatback armchairs and bucket chairs, antique engravings on its cream walls, winter log fires in stone fireplaces at each end, and a hum of quiet conversation. Well kept Adnams Bitter, Elgoods Cambridge, Greene King IPA and Abbot, Nethergate and Ruddles County on handpump; excellent service; darts, shove-ha'penny, cribbage and dominoes. Behind is a well liked neat garden. Customers are asked not to smoke in the restaurant while others are still eating. The vast church behind is worth a visit and the site of Fotheringhay Castle is nearby (where Mary Queen of Scots was executed in 1587). *(Recommended by Dr Paul Kitchener, Roy Bromell, Ted George, Thomas Nott, David and Mary Webb, Brian and Jill Bond, Alain and Rose Foote, Gordon Theaker, Maysie Thompson, Tom Evans, Graham and Karen Oddey, Brian and Jill Bond, R C Wiles, Jim Farmer, Rita Horridge, E D Bailey, Andy and Jill Kassube)*

Free house ~ Licensee Alan Stewart ~ Real ale ~ Meals and snacks (till 9.45; not Mon) ~ Restaurant ~ Cotterstock (01832) 226254 ~ Children in eating area and restaurant ~ Open 10-3, 6(7 winter Mons)-11

GREAT WOLFORD (Warwicks) SP2434 Map 4

Fox & Hounds 🍺

Village signposted on right on A3400 3 miles S of Shipston on Stour

New licensees purchased this unspoilt and characterful 16th-c local just as we went to press, but they plan to do all they can to maintain its special character. It's the kind of place you can come back to after a gap of many years and find nothing much has changed, and there's usually an interesting mix of people in its little beamed rooms, all blending in perfectly with the cheery, chatty feel. The old-fashioned open-plan bar is rather cosy, with a pair of high-backed old settles and other comfortable seats around a nice collection of old tables, well cushioned wall benches and a window seat, old hunting prints on the walls, flagstones and low beams. There's an inglenook fireplace with a good winter log fire by the fine old bread oven. A small tap room serves eight weekly changing beers like Boddingtons, Flowers IPA, Greene King Abbot, Hook Norton Best, Morlands Old Speckled Hen, Wadworths 6X, and Whitbreads Castle Eden on handpump, as well as up to 35 malt whiskies and a selection of country wines; darts, shove-ha'penny, dominoes, cribbage, piped music. Bar food might include soup (£1.50), garlic mushrooms (£2), smoked salmon and prawn platter (£2.95), chicken balti (£3.95), rabbit in white wine, game pie, fillet steak (£8.25), and puddings. On the terrace outside is a well. *(Recommended by Gordon, Michael Sargent, Martin Jones, John Bowdler, Peter and Erica Davis, H O Dickinson; reports on the new regime please)*

Free house ~ Licensees Graham and Anne Seddon ~ Real ale ~ Meals and snacks ~ Restaurant ~ Barton-on-the-Heath (01608) 674220 ~ Children in restaurant ~ Open 12-3, 6-11

HIMLEY (W Midlands – though see below) SO8889 Map 4

Crooked House ★ 🍺

Pub signposted from B4176 Gornalwood—Himley, OS Sheet 139 map reference 896908; readers have got so used to thinking of the pub as being near Kingswinford in the Midlands (though Himley is actually in Staffs) that we still include it in this chapter – the pub itself is virtually smack on the county boundary

The name says everything about this quirky and disconcertingly wonky place, and it's almost impossible to adequately describe the feeling of disorientation you'll get when you go in. In fact even getting the doors open is an uphill struggle, and on one table a bottle on its side actually rolls 'upwards' against the apparent direction of the slope. For a 10p donation you can get a big ball-bearing from the bar to roll 'uphill' along a wainscot. There's still a room with no food for locals and the atmosphere throughout is very relaxed. At the back is a large, level and more modern extension with local antiques. Well kept and extremely well priced Banks's Bitter and Mild, and Marstons Pedigree (on electric pump); dominoes, fruit machine and piped music. Good value bar food includes sandwiches (£1.20, not Sun), spicy sausage with a cheese filling or home-made faggots (both £2.75), a seafood platter, ploughman's (£3.20), home-made steak and kidney pie (£3.50), and daily specials like chicken tikka masala and chicken kiev; Saturday evening barbecues in the summer. It can get busy if there's a local clay-pigeon shoot outside. The conservatory is no smoking at lunchtimes and there's a spacious outside terrace. *(Recommended by Andrew Jeeves, Carole Smart, Graham Reeve, John Hazel, the Monday Club, David and Shelia)*

Banks's ~ Manager Gary Ensor ~ Real ale ~ Meals and snacks (lunchtimes and Sat evenings) ~ (01384) 238583 ~ Children in food area at lunchtime only, no under 3s ~ Open 11-11; 11.30-2.30, 6.30-11 in winter

Pubs staying open all afternoon are listed at the back of the book.

ILMINGTON (Warwicks) SP2143 Map 4

Howard Arms ♀

Village signposted with Wimpstone off A34 S of Stratford

Everyone at this smart and very neatly kept golden-stone pub seems to be eating, and who can blame them – meals are attractively served, good value and well cooked. Favourite dishes include lunchtime sandwiches (not Sun), soup (£2), smoked halibut with horseradish or deep-fried brie with redcurrants (£3.50), battered cod (£5), canelloni with ricotta cheese and spinach or lamb and rosemary pie (£5.25), seafood croissant (£6), rib eye beef steaks with bacon and madeira sauce (£8), barbary duck with orange and Cointreau (£8.25) and puddings like tiramisu or strawberry crème brûlée (£2.50). Despite the emphasis on food, this still feels very much like a pub, and an atmospheric one at that, with the heavy-beamed bar often full of drinkers; it also has rugs on polished flagstones, comfortable seats, highly polished brass, and open fires (one is in a big inglenook, screened from the door by an old-fashioned built-in settle). A snug area off from here is no-smoking. Well kept Boddingtons and Marstons Pedigree on handpump, decent wines, and excellent freshly pressed apple juice; friendly, polite service. Friendly labrador; piped music. The sheltered lawn has fruit trees, a colourful herbaceous border and well spaced picnic-table sets, and there are tables on a neat gravel terrace behind. It's nicely set beside the village green, and there are lovely walks on the nearby hills. *(Recommended by P J Hanson, E V Walder, Mrs Nicola Holden, Ann and Bob Westbrook, Kathryn and Brian Heathcote, John and Marianne Cooper, Andrew Shore, Peter Lloyd, Margaret and Allan Marsden, Pam Adsley, Colin Mason, Martin Jones, John Bowdler, Peter and Erica Davis, Mr and Mrs G J Rice, B J P Edwards, K H Frostick, Sheila Keene, Roy Bromwell, S V Bishop, Hope Chenhalls, Peter Lloyd)*

Free house ~ Licensee Alan Thompson ~ Real ale ~ Meals and snacks ~ Restaurant (not Sun evening) ~ Ilmington (01608) 682226 ~ Well behaved children welcome ~ Open 11-2.30, 6.30(7 winter)-11 ~ Bedrooms: £30B/£50B

KENILWORTH (Warwicks) SP2871 Map 4

Virgins & Castle £

High St; opposite A429 Coventry Rd at junction with A452

New managers took over this nice old-fashioned town pub in February and it looks as if they're bringing some much-needed stability to the place. They've introduced a weekly changing guest beer and extended the range of food (both popular moves), and have more plans that should see the atmospheric building coming back towards its full potential again. Several separate rooms open off the inner flagstones-and-beams servery and there's a couple of simply furnished small snugs (one with flagstones and the other with rugs on its bare boards) flanking the entrance corridor; down a couple of steps, a large room has heavy beams, a big rug on ancient red tiles, and matching seat and stool covers. Also, a carpeted lounge with more beams, some little booths, hatch service, and a good warm coal fire; darts, cribbage, dominoes, video game and fruit machine (there's another in a lobby). They hope to have a range of board games soon. Bar food includes good value sandwiches (from 90p), soup (£1.75), Greek dips (£2.65), ploughman's (£2.75), vegetarian meals like mushroom stroganoff (£3.65), and daily changing hot dishes like steak and kidney pie or beef bourguignon (all £3.95); Sunday lunch (£4.60). Well kept Davenports, Greenalls Original, Wadworths 6X and a guest like Adnams or Gales BB on handpump. Seats outside in a sheltered garden. *(Recommended by Dr M V Jones, Michael and Derek Slade, George Atkinson, Steve and Karen Jennings, Dave and Jules Tuckett, Geoff Lee and others)*

Davenports (Greenalls) ~ Managers Alan and Sue Gregory ~ Real ale ~ Meals and snacks ~ Restaurant ~ Kenilworth (01926) 53737 ~ Children in all rooms without bar ~ Traditional jazz summer Suns, folk muusic Tues ~ Open 11-3, 5-11, all day Sat

---

Pubs with attractive or unusually big gardens are listed at the back of the book.

LANGLEY (W Midlands) SO9788 Map 4

Brewery ★ £ ◖

1½ miles from M5, junction 2; from A4034 to W Bromwich and Oldbury take first right turn signposted Junction 2 Ind Estate then bear left past Albright & Wilson into Station Rd

Perhaps more astonishing than the way this atmospheric place looks just like a typical Victorian pub is how they've managed to create an almost genuine period feel too; it was actually built no earlier than the mid-1980s. Very well liked by readers and with a good cheery air, the Parlour on the left has plates and old engravings on the walls, a corner china cabinet, brass swan's-neck wall lamps, a coal fire in a tiled Victorian fireplace with china on the overmantel, and dining chairs or sturdy built-in settles around four good solid tables. A red-tiled kitchen, divided off by shelves of Staffordshire pottery and old books, is similarly furnished, with the addition of lots of copper pans around its big black range; darts, cribbage, dominoes, fruit machine, trivia and piped music. Tractor seats in a back corridor give a view through a big picture window into the brewhouse, a charmingly think-small subsidiary of Allied Breweries, the Ind Coope empire, where they produce their Entire – full-flavoured, quite strong and much loved by beer-drinkers. The simple Tap Bar serves this and the ordinary Holt, Plant and Deakins Bitter, brewed up in Warrington, as well as a weekly changing guest; it has lots of plates and Staffordshire pottery, and a coal-effect gas fire. Straightforward bar food (written up rather waggishly on a blackboard) includes very good value doorstop sandwiches with hot roast beef, roast ham and cheese, roast pork and stuffing, even black pudding and onion (£1.50), ploughman's (£1.85) and a home-made dish of the day such as steak and kidney pie, macaroni cheese or Cornish pasties (£1.85); friendly service. Don't be fooled by the sign on a door saying Billiards Room – it's really the manager's office. *(Recommended by John and Christine Simpson, Brian and Anna Marsden, Ian and James Phillips, Stephen G Brown, Mike and Wendy Proctor, John Atherton, Neale Davies, Mayur Shah, Brian Jones)*

Holt, Plant & Deakins (Allied) ~ Manager Tony Stanton ~ Real ale ~ Lunchtime meals and snacks (not Sun) ~ Birmingham (0121) 544 6467 ~ Children in eating area lunchtimes and early evenings ~ Fortnightly Tues quiz ~ Open 11-2.30, 6-11

LAPWORTH (Warwicks) SP1670 Map 4

Navigation ◖

Old Warwick Rd (B4439 Warwick—Hockley Heath)

What really makes this bustling local special is its canalside setting, and in summer it comes into its own, when you can sit at tables on a back terrace or on the sheltered flower-edged lawn running down to the water. There may be barbecues, Morris dancers or even travelling theatre companies out here then, there's outside hatch service and it's all prettily lit at night. Inside, the bustling flagstoned bar is decorated with brightly painted canal ware (you can buy horseshoes in this style here, in aid of cot death research), and cases of stuffed fish, and has high-backed winged settles, seats built around its window bay and a coal fire in its high-manteled inglenook. A second quieter room has tables on its board-and-carpet floor – and a dresser with dominoes, shut-the-box and board games. Pleasantly-served straightforward bar food includes well filled cottage rolls (lunchtime, £1.40), cauliflower, broccoli and cheese bake (£4.25), lasagne, various curries or home-made lamb balti (£4.50), beef, Guinness and mushroom pie, gammon and egg or cod and chips, rump steak and puddings such as sherry trifle (£1.75); service can slow down when busy – as it often is on sunny days – but stays friendly and obliging. Well kept Bass, M&B Brew XI, and a daily changing guest beer such as Hadrian Gladiator or Morlands Old Speckled Hen on handpump; they also do various guest ciders in summer; fruit machine. Parties can book a pig or lamb roast in the garden anytime during the summer *(Recommended by Richard Lewis, Brian Jones, Graham Reeve, Mark Grist, Dennis H Phillips, Gary Roberts, Derek and Sylvia Stephenson, Dr H R Long, Bill Sykes, N and M Foster, Andy and Jill Kassube, Tom McLean)*

M&B (Bass) ~ Lease: Andrew Kimber ~ Real ale ~ Meals and snacks (not winter Sun and Mon evenings) ~ Lapworth (01564) 783337 ~ Children in eating area before 9pm ~ Occasional Morris dancing, folk music ~ Open 11-2.30, 5.30-11 (Sats in winter 11-3, 6-11, all day summer)

LITTLE COMPTON (Warwicks) SP2630 Map 4

Red Lion 🛏 ♀

Off A44 Moreton-in-Marsh—Chipping Norton

A simple but civilised low-beamed stone inn, the kind of friendly place where the landlord always likes to chat, and summer days drift lazily past your table in the garden. The comfortable lounge has snug alcoves, a couple of little tables by the log fire, with a settee facing it, and attractive etchings on the stripped stone walls. A dining area leading off has good generously served home cooked food such as large filled granary rolls (from £2.25), ploughman's (from £3.50), celery, apple and prawn salad (£3.75), lasagne (£5.50), fisherman's pie or lamb casserole (£5.95), chicken with sherry and mushroom cream sauce and garnished with asparagus (£6.50), rump steak (£8.60), rack of lamb with port, redcurrant and orange sauce (£8.95) and puddings like toffee pecan cheesecake (£2.25); Sunday roasts. Booking is recommended on Saturday evenings especially. The plainer public bar has another log fire, and darts, pool, dominoes, cribbage, fruit machine, video game, juke box and Aunt Sally. Well kept Donnington BB and SBA on handpump and extensive wine list; good service; piped music. The bedrooms are good value. No dogs – even in garden (where there's a children's play area with climbing frame). It's a handy base for touring the Cotswolds. *(Recommended by Marion and John Hadfield, Chris Warne, Mrs A Binns, Gordon, H M C Quick, H O Dickinson, Mrs B J Reynolds)*

Donnington ~ Tenant David Smith ~ Real ale ~ Meals and snacks ~ Restaurant ~ Barton-on-the-Heath (01608) 674397 ~ Children in eating area of bar ~ Occasional folk or country music ~ Open 11-2.30, 6-11; closed evening 25 Dec ~ Bedrooms: £24/£36 (not 24-26 Dec, no under 8s)

LOWSONFORD (Warwicks) SP1868 Map 4

Fleur de Lys ♀

Village signposted off B4439 Hockley Heath—Warwick; can be reached too from B4095 via Preston Bagot

Readers with children like coming to this quite civilised canalside pub, as the family room is unusually elegant and very well equipped: plush dining chairs, a white-ceilinged raftered upper gallery, a rocking horse, and wooden toys. In fact there's quite an individual feel to the whole place, and you'd never think it was part of a chain. The smart spreading bar has lots of low black beams in the butter-coloured ceiling, brocade-cushioned mate's, wheelback and dining chairs around the well spaced tables, and rugs on the flagstones and antique tiles; it's at its most parlourish on the left, with a sofa and some bookshelves, and at its most dining-roomish down steps on the right, where there are polished tables, and built-in wall banquettes. Often unusual bar food might include whole sardines in a herby sauce (£2.75), seafood pancakes (£2.95), seafood platter salad (with squid, plaice and scampi, £5.45), half a roast guinea fowl or lamb and mint pie (£5.95), Chinese rabbit in celery sauce (£6.25), and puddings; meals can take a while to arrive at times, with delays of up to 45 minutes not uncommon. Extensive children's menu. Well kept Boddingtons, Flowers Original, and two regularly changing guests on handpump, decent wines including good New World ones (lots by the glass), malt whiskies, several open fires, newspapers and magazines, unobtrusive piped classical music. Service is generally friendly but can be erratic. Down on the grass among tall weeping willows by the Stratford-upon-Avon Canal are picnic-table sets, with a very good safely fenced and well equipped play area. *(Recommended by G B Longden, John Fahy, Nigel Flook, Betsy Brown, Don Kellaway, Angie Coles, Dorothy and Leslie Pilson, David Heath, P J F*

Westlake, Mr and Mrs R J Phillips, John Bowdler, Dorothee and Dennis Glover, Brian and Anna Marsden, Wendy Arnold, Graham Reeve, Bill and Edee Miller, Susan and John Douglas, P Boot, M Hitchman, Neale Davies, Bill Sykes, Sheila Keene)

Whitbreads ~ Manager Russell Proctor ~ Real ale ~ Meals and snacks (12-3, 6-9.30, 12-9.30 summer) ~ (01564) 782431 ~ Children in eating area ~ Open 11-11

NASSINGTON (Northants) TL0696 Map 5

Black Horse 🍴 ♉

Off A47 and A605 W of Peterborough; can be reached off A1 via Wansford turn-off

Midlands Dining Pub of the Year

Readers this year have all used the word 'excellent' to describe the food at this civilised 17th-c pub, and it really is well chosen; meals are very cosmopolitan and often rather elaborate, with the emphasis firmly on fresh local produce. A wide choice might include soup (£2.45), home-made pâté (£2.85), prawns and scallops in a creamy cheese sauce (£3.25), Spanish-style tortilla (£4.20), whole prawns in garlic butter garnished with lime and watercress (£4.25), steak sandwich (£4.85), seafood pancake (£5.95), lots of vegetarian dishes such as mushroom and edam pie or vegetable and cream cheese crumble (both £6.25), imaginative fish dishes such as poached fillets of lemon sole in an orange, grapefruit, cream and white wine sauce (£8.45), pork sautéed with walnuts and apples served with a marsala wine sauce, or strips of turkey in an almond, hazelnut, pinenut and coriander sauce (£8.95), rich game casserole marinated in herbs and wine (£9.15), breast of duck with a sauce of black cherries, brandy and raisins (£9.95), puddings (£2.75) and children's meals (£2.25); vegetables are very good, as are sauces, a speciality of the chef. Imaginative monthly theme evenings make good use of their international recipes, with food and entertainment from countries like Spain, Italy and Mexico, and they even do wine tutoring nights. A splendid big stone fireplace in the lounge bar is thought to have come from Fotheringhay Castle (which had been destroyed some time earlier) when the pub was built. There are easy chairs and small settees, a beamed ceiling, and a pleasant, relaxed atmosphere. The bar servery, with panelling from Rufford Abbey, links the two comfortable rooms of the restaurant. Bass, Tetleys and two changing guests on handpump, a very good varied wine list, with several half bottles, and a good few malt whiskies; service is efficient and friendly. You can sit out on the very well tended attractive sheltered lawn, with plenty of flowers and plants. *(Recommended by Mrs J M Day, Andy Thwaites, Roger Bellingham, C Day, D H Buchanan, G E Power)*

Free house ~ Licensees Ron Orchard and Roland Cooke ~ Real ale ~ Meals and snacks (till 9.45) ~ Restaurant ~ Stamford (01780) 782324 ~ Children welcome ~ Monthly theme nights with music ~ Open 12-2.30, 7-11; closed evening 25 and 26 Dec

NETHERTON (W Midlands) SO9387 Map 4

Little Dry Dock

Windmill End, Bumble Hole; you really need an A-Z street map to find it – or OS Sheet 139 map reference 953881

We recommend several canalside pubs in this book but none are as bizarre as this tiny eccentric place, which somehow has an entire narrowboat squeezed into the right-hand bar and used as the servery (its engine is in the room on the left). There's also a huge model boat in one front transom-style window, winches and barge rudders flanking the door, marine windows, and lots of brightly coloured bargees' water pots, lanterns, jugs and lifebuoys; fruit machine and trivia. They have their own Little Lumphammer ale as well as Holt, Plant & Deakins Entire and a guest, and they do their own wine: Chateau Ballykilferret; friendly service. Bar food includes their Desperate Dan Pie, complete with horns (£4.95), and other dishes like soup (£1.65), sandwiches, black pudding thermidor (£1.95), lasagne or faggots and peas (£4.25), steak and mushroom pie or gammon (£4.95), big mixed grill (£6.95) and puddings like treacle roly-poly (£1.60). Others in Mr O'Rourke's small chain of Black Country pubs include main entries in Bradley Green and Kidderminster (Hereford and Worcester), and several in the Lucky Dips. There are pleasant towpath walks nearby. *(Recommended by Andrew Jeeves, Carole Smart, Basil J S Minson, Pete Yearsley, Patrick and Mary McDermott, James and Ian Phillips, Ron Fletcher, Stephen, Julie and Hayley Brown, David and Shelia, Dave Irving)*

Free house ~ Manager Frank Pearson ~ Real ale ~ Meals and snacks (12-2.30, 6-10) ~ (01384) 235369 ~ Children welcome ~ Irish folk music Mon evenings ~ Open 11-3, 6-11

NEWBOLD ON STOUR (Warwicks) SP2446 Map 4

White Hart

A34 Shipston on Stour—Stratford

Regular visitors to this consistently friendly and welcoming pub say it's as good now as it's ever been. Partly divided by stub walls and the chimney, the airy, beamed main bar has fresh white walls, gleaming copper-topped tables, modern high-backed winged settles, seats set into big bay windows, a fair amount of brass, and a gun hanging over the log fire in one big stone fireplace. A wide range of good, reasonably priced food includes home-made soup, ploughman's, garlic mushrooms in cream and white wine (£2.95), deep-fried brie with cranberry sauce (£4.25), lamb braised in wine and herbs or venison casserole (£5.50), chicken, salami and prawn paella (£5.85), poached salmon in a herby cream sauce (£6.95), daily specials and puddings like coffee sponge with hot fudge sauce; Sunday lunch. Booking is advisable Friday or Saturday evenings and Sunday lunch. The roomy back public bar has pool, dominoes, fruit machine, trivia and juke box; Bass and Worthingtons Best on handpump. There are some picnic-table sets under cocktail parasols in front of the pub, with its well tended hanging baskets. *(Recommended by Derek Allpass, Jill White, C Fisher, Marion and John Hadfield)*

M & B (Bass) ~ Lease: Mr and Mrs J C Cruttwell ~ Real ale ~ Meals and snacks (not Sun evening) ~ Restaurant (not Sun evening) ~ Stratford upon Avon (01789) 450205 ~ Children welcome ~ Open 11-2.30(3 Sat), 6-11

OUNDLE (Northants) TL0487 Map 5

Mill

Barnwell Rd out of town; or follow Barnwell Country Park signs off A605 bypass

This imposing old mill building was rebuilt in 1746 but actually dates back to the early 16th c. It's been interestingly converted to a pub and restaurant, and is proving quite popular for eating, with a very wide choice of well served meals including sandwiches (not Sun), soup (£2.75), chicken liver, port and brandy pâté (£3.55), ploughman's (from £3.75), lots of pizzas (from £4.10), salads (from £5.95), beef and mushroom pie or chicken marinated Portuguese-style with hot peppers (£6.95), several Mexican dishes like chicken chimichangas (£7.95) or beef fajitas (£9.95), T-bone steak (£12.75), and puddings. Stairs outside take you up to the most popular part, the Trattoria, which has stalls around tables with more banquettes in bays, stripped masonry and beams, and a millstone feature; its small windows looks down over the lower millpond and the River Nene. A rather dimly lit ground floor bar has red leatherette button-back built-in wall banquettes against its stripped-stone walls; on the way in a big glass floor panel shows the stream race below the building. Two-thirds of the bar is no smoking. Courage Best and Directors on handpump; top-floor restaurant (more beams, and the corn hoist); bar billiards. There are picnic-table sets under cocktail parasols among willow trees by the pond, with more on side grass and some white cast-iron tables on a flagstoned terrace. It's very well liked by young people in the evening. *(Recommended by Mr and Mrs G Hart, Peter Watkins, Pam Stanley, Rita Horridge, Wayne Brindle, David Hedges)*

Free house ~ Licensees Noel and Linda Tulley ~ Real ale ~ Meals and snacks (till 10pm) ~ Restaurant (not Sun evening) ~ (01832) 272621 ~ Children in eating area ~ Open 12-3, 6.30-11

Ship £ 🍺

West St

Brightly cheerful and genuinely welcoming, this is a well worn and unpretentious local that keeps its companionable feel however busy it might get. Leading off the central corridor on the left are the three rooms of the very heavily beamed lounge bar: up by the street there's a mix of leather and other seats including a very flowery piano stool (and its piano), with sturdy tables and a log fire in a stone inglenook, and down one end a panelled snug has button-back leather seats built in around it. This is no smoking – if you light up you have to donate £1 to the RNLI. Well kept Bass, Marstons Pedigree, Tetleys, Wadworths 6X and a guest on handpump. Bar food includes sandwiches (from £1.20), soup (£1.50), ploughman's (£2.50), peppered smoked mackerel with horseradish sauce (£2.75), salads (from £3.50), a wide choice of simple but well priced main courses like sausage and egg (£2.50), fried cod (£3) and haddock (£3.20), steak and kidney pie or lasagne (£4.25), beef curry (£5) and specials (around £3); Sunday lunchtimes they just do a roast and pies. Smiling, efficient service from the landlord and his sons, though it may slow down when thy're pushed; dominoes, maybe free Sunday nuts and crisps on the bar. The tiled-floor public side has darts, pinball, dominoes, juke box or piped music and fruit machine. A series of small sheltered terraces strung out behind has wooden tables and chairs, lit at night. Several of the bedrooms are in a new extension. *(Recommended by Tom Evans; more reports please)*

Free house ~ Licensee Frank Langridge ~ Real ale ~ Meals and snacks (till 10pm) ~ Oundle (01832) 273918 ~ Children welcome ~ Live music Fri or Sat ~ Open 11-3, 6-11; 11-11 Sat ~ Bedrooms: £20(£27.50B)/£35(£45B)

PRIORS MARSTON (Warwicks) SP4857 Map 4

Falcon

Hellidon Rd; village signposted off A425 Daventry Rd in Southam; and from A361 S of Daventry

A handsome pub dating back several hundred years, this is a spotlessly kept and civilised old place with a friendly, welcoming atmosphere. The main bar rambles around into an L beyond the log fire in the big high-manteled stone fireplace, with well padded high-backed winged settles on its cheerfully patterned carpet; a couple of big framed mirrors alongside the country pictures give a feeling of extra space. Popular well presented bar food, usually served in generous helpings, includes soup (£2.25), made to order sandwiches (from £1.95), salads (from £5.75), fisherman's platter (£6.25), barbecued pork ribs or steak and stout pie (both £6.45), sweet and sour chicken (£6.95), stir-fried vegetables (£7.45), steaks using prime Scottish beef (from £8.25), and puddings (all £2.25); there's a range of daily specials and two international theme nights such as Spanish or Indian every month. Well kept ABC Best, Everards Beacon and Old Original, Marstons Pedigree and a monthly changing guest on handpump; piped music. Note they now do bedrooms. *(Recommended by P J Caunt, Jill and Peter Bickley, Stephen, Julie and Hayley Brown, John and Marianne Cooper, Clive Watkins, John Fahy, David Mervin, George Murdoch)*

Free house ~ Licensees Stephen and Jane Richards ~ Real ale ~ Meals and snacks (till 10pm) ~ Daventry (01327) 60562 ~ Well behaved children allowed until 9pm ~ Open 12-3, 6(7 winter)-11 ~ Bedrooms: £25S/£35S

Holly Bush

From village centre follow Shuckburgh signpost, but still in village take first right turn by telephone box, not signposted

In winter the three open fires at this characterful refurbished golden stone building make it seem especially welcoming and cosy, but it's a friendly place all year round, with the chatty landlord working very hard to please. Home-made bar food includes sandwiches (from £1.75), filled baked potatoes (£2.95, with beef and Guinness or chicken), Cumberland sausage and egg (£3.25), chilli con carni, omelette or ploughman's (£3.95), lasagne or plaice (£4.95), salads (from £4.95), beef and Guinness or chicken, ham and leek pie (£5.95), sirloin steak (£7.95), and puddings like banoffi pie or sherry trifle; also a more comprehensive restaurant menu and occasional pig roasts. Well kept Bass, Boddingtons, Hook Norton Best, Marstons Pedigree and Theakstons Old Peculier on handpump. The small beamed rambling rooms have old-fashioned pub seats and stripped-stone walls; darts, pool, video game, trivia and piped music. The building was originally the village bakehouse, and there are similarly attractive stone houses nearby. (*Recommended by Stephen, Julie and Hayley Brown, Jill and Peter Bickley, Clive Watkins, George Murdoch, Roy Bromell*)

Free house ~ Licensee Mark Hayward ~ Real ale ~ Meals and snacks ~ Restaurant ~ Byfield (01327) 60934 ~ Children welcome ~ Open 12-3, 5.30 (6 Sat)-11

SAMBOURNE (Warwicks) SP0561 Map 4

Green Dragon

A435 N of Alcester, then left fork onto A448 just before Studley; village signposted on left soon after

Prettily covered with climbing roses in summer, this friendly village-green pub with its shuttered and timbered façade has long been a popular stop for good value lunchtime food. The modernised beamed communicating rooms have a good cheery atmosphere as well as little armed seats and more upright ones, some small settles, and open fires; piped music. Bar meals include sandwiches (from £1.95), home-made soup (£1.95), ploughman's (£3.50), steak and Guinness pie (£4.75), curry, fresh fish of the day or liver, bacon and onion (£4.95), vegetarian dishes like vegetable crêpe (£5.50), rack of lamb (£7.95), chicken supreme filled with smoked bacon and broccoli (£8.50), home-made puddings like treacle sponge or apple and blackberry crumble (£1.95), and children's meals (from £2.50). Well kept Bass, M & B Brew XI and Tetleys on handpump; cheerful, attentive service. There are picnic-table sets and teak seats among flowering cherries on a side courtyard, by the car park. (*Recommended by Jerry and Alison Oakes, John Radford, Dr S J Parkinson, Graham Reeve, Tony Walker*)

M & B (Bass) ~ Lease: Phil and Pat Burke ~ Real ale ~ Meals and snacks (till 10pm); not Sun ~ Restaurant (not Sun) ~ Astwood Bank (0152) 789 2465 ~ Children welcome ~ Open 11-3, 6-11

SHUSTOKE (Warwicks) SP2290 Map 4

Griffin 🍺

5 miles from M6, junction 4; A446 towards Tamworth, then right on to B4114 and go straight through Coleshill; pub is at Furnace End, E of Shustoke

Simple unfussy village pubs like this much-loved old place are becoming increasingly few and far between, more's the pity. For many years the Griffin has been quite a draw for beer drinkers, with an astonishing range of well kept ales from all around the country, and by the time this edition is published they should have their own microbrewery up and running. Known as the Church End brewery, it's located in an old barn beside the pub, traditionally used by the landlord as a base for a second occupation; one apparently made coffins in here, most of which no doubt ended up in the church yard opposite. As well as their as yet un-named bitter, the dozen or so handpumps will carry on dispensing beers like Bathams, Fullers London Pride, Hook Norton Old Hookey, Judges Barrister, Marstons Pedigree, Moorhouses Pendle Witches Brew, Orkney Skull Splitter, Theakstons Old Peculier and Wadworths 6X, all from a servery under a very low, thick beam; farm ciders also. The low-beamed, L-shaped bar has an old-fashioned settle and cushioned café seats (some quite closely packed), sturdily elm-topped sewing trestles, lots of old jugs on the beams, log fires in both stone fireplaces (one's a big inglenook), and a good, friendly atmosphere. The roomy conservatory is popular with families, there are old-fashioned seats and tables on the back grass, a children's play area, and a large terrace with plants in raised beds. Good value lunchtime bar food such as sandwiches (from £1.20), home-made steak and ale pie (£4), lemon sole with crabmeat (£4.20), cod or haddock (£5) and 12oz sirloin steak (£5.50); they sell local fresh eggs, and leeks and cauliflower in season. A couple of readers suggest the unspoilt feel extends to the lavatories. (*Recommended by Stephen Brown, Mrs Gwyneth Holland, Mark Whitmore, C Fisher, J Dwane, the Monday Club, Andrew Jeeves, Carole Smart, CW, JW, Richard Lewis, Graham Reeve, Roger and Christine Mash, David and Shelia*)

Own brew ~ Licensees Michael Pugh and Sydney Wedge ~ Real ale ~ Lunchtime meals and snacks (not Sun) ~ (01675) 481205 ~ Children in conservatory ~ Open 12-2.30, 7-11; closed evenings 25 and 26 Dec

SOUTHAM (Warwicks) SP4161 Map 4

Old Mint

Coventry Street; A423, towards Coventry

A former monk's hospice, this 14th-c pub is a nice place in summer, when you can go through the medieval arch of the back door to a sheltered, extended garden, with tables and chairs; there are more seats on the cobbles and laid bricks of a yard, which has clematis on a side wall and is fairy-lit at night. Inside the walls of the two-roomed bar are peppered with antique guns, powder flasks, rapiers, sabres, cutlasses and pikes, and there are heavy beams, sturdy old seats and settles, masses of toby jugs behind the serving counter, an open fire, and two cosy little alcoves; darts, fruit machine and piped music. Well kept Bass, Hook Norton Best, Marstons Pedigree, Timothy Taylors Landlord, Wadworths 6X and two regularly changing guests on handpump; country wines, mead, and hot punch in winter. Promptly served straightforward bar food includes soup (£1.25), baguettes (£1.50), filled baked potatoes (from £2.20), filled Yorkshire puddings (from £3.15), ploughman's (£3.60), home-made steak and kidney pie (£4.45), several vegetarian meals like vegetable lasagne (£4.55), steaks (from £7.65) with a choice of three sauces, a selection of puddings and traditional Sunday lunch (three courses, £7.25). The restaurant is no smoking. Permanent bouncy castle. The pub is named for the fact that in the Civil Wars it was used to melt down commandeered silver for coin to pay King Charles' troops before the Battle of Edge Hill. Though, as we say, they generally open at 11, there may be times when they don't open until 12. (*Recommended by Nigel Foster, Steve and Liz Tilley, Geoff Lee, John and Marianne Cooper, Dave Braisted, A H Thomas, George Murdoch, Chris Raisin, Graham and Belinda Staplehust, Brian Jones*)

Free house ~ Licensee Sylvia Wright ~ Real ale ~ Meals and snacks (till 10) ~ Restaurant ~ Southam (01926) 812339 ~ Children welcome ~ Open 11-2.30, 6.30-11; 11-11 Sat

STRATFORD UPON AVON (Warwicks) SP2055 Map 4

Slug & Lettuce ♀

38 Guild Street, corner of Union Street

A pleasantly bustling place, particularly just after work in the early evenings, when there's usually a good mix of people here to sample the tasty food (it's very handy if you're going on to the theatre). You can see some of the meals being prepared at one end of the long L-shaped bar counter, and there are dishes like home-made orange and basil soup (£2.35), hot spicy Hungarian style mushrooms (£4.25), baked chicken pieces in various sauces, delicious pork spare ribs or baked courgettes topped with tuna fish, sweetcorn, tomato and cheese (£5.45), tandoori style pork or vegetable kebabs (£6.25), chicken breast baked with avocado and garlic (£9.25), fillet steak topped with stilton in a brandy and mushroom sauce (£12), and lovely puddings like home-made chocolate mousse and banoffi pie (all £2.95). The bar has pine kitchen tables and chairs on rugs and flagstones, a few period prints on stripped squared panelling, a newspaper rack, and a solid fuel fire; piped music. Well kept beers such as Ansells, Ind Coope Burton, and Tetleys on handpump, and decent wine. There's a small flagstoned back terrace, floodlit at night, with lots of flower boxes and sturdy teak tables under cocktail parasols, with more up steps. As the evening goes on the pub becomes a favourite with younger customers. *(Recommended by Peter Neate, K Baxter, Cdr Patrick Tailyour, Brian Jones, David and Sheila, D C Eastwood)*

Ansells (Allied) ~ Manager Neil Miller ~ Real ale ~ Meals and snacks (5.30-9pm, all day Thurs-Sat) ~ (01789) 299700 ~ Open 11-3, 5.30-11; all day Thurs-Sat

SUDBOROUGH (Northants) SP9682 Map 4

Vane Arms 🍺 🍴

High St; A6116 Corby—Thrapston

The range of beers at this picturesque and popular thatched inn varies so much it's almost like they have a continuous beer festival. They usually have nine well kept and often rare brews on at a time, such as Adnams Tally Ho, Banks and Taylor Old Bat, Hop Back Summer Lightning, Mauldon Suffolk Comfort, Morlands Old Speckled Hen, Nene Valley Rawhide, Robinsons Old Tom, or Wards Kirby Strong. If you're not sure which to have, they do a sample tray for about £5, with around a third of a pint of each; they also keep a couple of Belgian fruit beers, farm cider and lots of country wines. The pub looks at its best on one of the summer days when the Morris men are dancing outside, but is always attractive and welcoming inside. The comfortable main bar has some stripped stonework, and good inglenook fireplaces with open fires in winter (and perhaps Nelson the dog in front of one of them); there's a small public bar with darts, pool, table skittles, fruit machine and piped music. A wide range of freshly cooked food includes sandwiches, home-made soup (£1.60), mushrooms in stilton sauce (£2.40), mozzarella cheese fingers (£2.50), lasagne (£4.50), good steak and kidney pie (£4.75), breast of chicken with stilton wrapped in bacon and encased in puff pastry (£6), venison steak (£6.50), beef Wellington (£8.20), steak (from £8.25), good puddings, a weekly changing fresh fish dish, and an increasingly popular separate Mexican menu featuring dishes like spicy chicken wings (£2.50), tacos (£5) and fajitas (£6.75). Service is always friendly and helpful, though may slow down at busy times. *(Recommended by David and Michelle Hedges, Derek and Sylvia Stephenson, Joan and Michel Hooper-Immins, D H and M G Buchanan, Stephen, Julie and Hayley Brown, R C Wiles)*

Free house ~ Licensees Tom and Anne Tookey ~ Real ale ~ Meals and snacks (12-1.45, 7-9.45; not Mon or Sun evening except for residents) ~ Restaurant (not Sun evening) ~ (01832) 733223 ~ Children in eating area and restaurant ~ Open 11.30-3.30, 5.30(6 Sat)-11; closed Mon lunchtime ~ Bedrooms: £30B/£45B

TEMPLE GRAFTON (Warwicks) SP1255 Map 4

Blue Boar £ ♀

Off A422 W of Stratford; a mile E, towards Binton

A well run place standing out for its excellent food and drink, this popular beamed dining pub is very highly regarded at the moment, and despite its emphasis on food has a good pubby feel throughout. Unusually for the area, it still preserves much of the more traditional appeal of the early 17th-c country tavern on which it's based. The good, fresh, home-cooked meals come from a menu that includes a choice of soups (£1.50), sandwiches (from £1.65), filled baked potatoes (from £2), ploughman's (from £2.95), canelloni or seafood crêpes (£3.15), and a range of hot dishes such as vegetable crêpes (£3.95) or mushroom stroganoff (£4.75), fresh fish (the grilled plaice is well liked), or a fine steak and kidney pie (£4.95), as well as notable puddings such as banana crunch, and chocolate whisky cake (£2.50). Vegetables are fresh, helpings are generous, and they employ a pastry chef. Well kept Donningtons BBA, Flowers Original, Hook Norton Best and Wadworths 6X on handpump, and nearly 40 different wines. There are several good log fires, cast-iron-framed tables and built-in wall and bow-window seats, and cribbage, dominoes, and sensibly placed darts in a flagstoned side room stripped back to golden Binton stone. The comfortable stripped-stone restaurant, with its own log fire and a glass-covered old well, is very popular (good Sunday lunches), and there are picnic-table sets outside. Service is excellent (as are the Christmas decorations). *(Recommended by Andrew Shore, Philip and Trisha Ferris, George Atkinson, Mr and Mrs C Moncreiffe, Peter Lloyd, Lindsley Harvard, Margaret Whalley, Dorothee and Dennis Glover, Dr S J Parkinson)*

Free house ~ Licensee Adrian Parkes ~ Real ale ~ Meals and snacks (till 10) ~ Restaurant ~ (01789) 750010 ~ Children welcome ~ Open 11.30-2.30, 6-11

THORNBY (Northants) SP6775 Map 4

Red Lion ♀

Welford Road; A50 Northampton—Leicester

A reliable old favourite, this friendly cream-painted slated brick roadside pub is a stylish place, but always manages to feel very welcoming. The bar has pewter tankards hanging from a beam, decorative plates densely covering the walls, china jugs and steins on a shelf and hanging over the bar, and logs burning in an open stove. Carefully chosen furnishings include individual old-fashioned lamps, a lovingly polished big golden table that sits between a couple of pews in one of the bay windows, and deep leather armchairs and sofa in one of two smallish areas opening off; shove-ha'penny, cribbage, dominoes, piped music, and three friendly dogs. Good home-made bar food includes sandwiches, soup (£2.25), garlic mushrooms (£2.95), lasagne (£5.50), home-made steak in ale pie or well liked curry (£5.95), cornet of smoked salmon filled with prawns (£7.25), steaks (£8.95), lunchtime burgers, sausages and jacket potatoes, several home-made puddings and at least eight evening specials such as marinated chicken and lamb kebab or half a roast duckling in an orange sauce. The restaurant is recommended. Well kept Batemans XB, Greene King Abbot, Marstons Pedigree and Robinsons Best on handpump, decent wines, and good coffee; friendly service. There are some seats outside. *(Recommended by George Atkinson, Roger and Christine Mash, Miss D P Barson, Cdr Patrick Tailyour, Tim Gilroy)*

Free house ~ Licensee Caroline Baker ~ Real ale ~ Meals and snacks ~ Small restaurant ~ Northampton (01604) 740238 ~ Well behaved children welcome ~ Open 12-2.30, 7-11

TIPTON (W Midlands) SO9592 Map 4

M A D O'Rourkes Pie Factory

Hurst Lane, Dudley Rd towards Wednesbury (junction A457/A4037) – look for the Irish flag

Even people who normally dislike theme pubs quickly develop a soft spot for this one – partly because it hasn't forgotten its primary purpose of serving good beer and tasty reasonably priced food, but also because the theme itself has been executed with such verve. It's a pastiche of a 1940s pork butcher's, with all sorts of meat-processing equipment from the relatively straightforward butcher's blocks to the bewilderingly esoteric (part of the fun is trying to guess what it's all for), not to mention strings of model hams, sausages and so forth hanging from the ceiling. Labels for pigs' heads mounted on the walls tell you about the dogs and abbots that are alleged to go into their recipes, and the menu tends to canter through fishy mermaid pie, gerbil giblet pie, baby seal pie and so forth. In fact the food's good solid value (and does include a vegetarian pie, £4.35); favourite items include black pudding thermidor (£1.95), shepherd's pie, the gargantuan Desperate Dan cow pie complete with pastry horns (£5.25), and sweet puddings such as spotted dick and jam roly poly (£1.95); there are lunchtime sandwiches (from £1.85), vegetable baltis (£4.75), and specials such as faggots and peas or pork pepperpot (around £4.45). The atmosphere is buoyant, and service is very friendly. They have their own variable but generally good Lumphammer ale, and Holt Plant & Deakins Mild and Entire and Tetleys; fruit machine, trivia and piped music. Though it's roomy, with more space upstairs, it can get very busy (packed on Friday and Saturday evenings), especially if there's a party from a Black Country coach tour wandering around in a state of tickled shock; piped music, car park. *(Recommended by Mike and Wendy Proctor, Mr and Mrs D T Deas, Stephen and Julie Brown, David and Shelia, Brian Jones)*

Free house ~ Licensee David Henaghan ~ Real ale ~ Meals and snacks (12-2.30, 6-10) ~ 0121-557 1402 ~ Children welcome ~ 60s singer Mon evening, Irish duo Weds evening ~ Open 11-3, 6-11; closed 25 Dec

TWYWELL (Northants) SP9478 Map 4

Old Friar

Village signposted from A14 about 2 miles W of Thrapston

The beams and the brick fireplaces at this bustling well run pub have wooden carvings of friars on them. It's a very foody place, with most of the tables set for eating and the dining area now completely no smoking, but despite this emphasis there's still a genuinely cheery atmosphere. There's a good hot and cold carvery (£6.95), as well as filled rolls and sandwiches, soup (£1.95), spring rolls (£3.25), chicken satay (£3.45), tuna risotto or primavera (£5.75), home-made pies including an excellent steak and kidney (£5.95), vegetarian dishes like nut en croûte provençal or macaroni cheese crumble (£7.95), chicken kiev (£8.50), venison steak (£9.50), puddings (£2.55) and children's menu (£3.55). Well kept Adnams Best, Ansells Best, Buchanan Federation, Marstons Pedigree and Tetleys on handpump served from the brick bar counter; hard-working helpful staff. The bar is attractively furnished with plain wooden tables, tub chairs and settles, and has shove-ha'penny, cribbage, dominoes, fruit machine and piped music. No dogs. The garden has tables and a children's play area, with a bouncy castle on Sundays. *(Recommended by Richard W Chew, David Hedges, Maysie Thompson; more reports please)*

Grand Met ~ Lease: Yvonne Joan Crisp ~ Real ale ~ Meals and snacks (till 9.45) ~ Restaurant ~ Thrapston (01832) 732625 ~ Children welcome ~ Open 11-2.30(3 Sat), 6-11

WARMINGTON (Warwicks) SP4147 Map 4

Plough £

Village just off B4100 N of Banbury

However busy this early 17th-c golden ironstone pub gets it rarely seems crowded, and the atmosphere is always relaxed and friendly. Nicely set in a delightful village a few yards up the quiet lane from a broad sloping green, it looks especially pretty in the autumn, when the creeper over the front of the building turns a striking crimson colour. The cosy bar has old photographs of the village and locals, an old high-backed winged settle, cushioned wall seats and lots of comfortable Deco small armed chairs and library chairs, and good winter log fires. Well kept Hook Norton Best and Marstons Pedigree on handpump, a regular guest beer and several malt whiskies; darts, dominoes and piped pop music. Straightforward but very generously served bar food includes good minestrone soup, sandwiches, cottage pie or chilli (£3.50), flavoursome home-baked ham (£4.95), home-cooked daily specials (from £3) and a popular Sunday lunch; pleasant service by cheery licensees. Charles I marched through the village towards Edge Hill with 18,000 men in October 1642, and some of those men are buried in the churchyard. *(Recommended by John Atherton, Bob and Maggie Atherton, Alan and Jane Clarke, Martin and Karen Wake, N and J Strathdee, Steve and Karen Jennings, J E Rycroft, Sir Nigel Foulkes, Ian, Janet and Joanne James)*

Free house ~ Licensee Denise Willson ~ Real ale ~ Meals and snacks (service stops at 8.30 in evenings); not Sun evening ~ (01295) 89666 ~ Children in eating area ~ Occasional live music ~ Open 12-3, 6-11; closed evening 25 Dec

---

The ▓ symbol indicates pubs which keep their beer unusually well or have a particularly good range.

WEST BROMWICH (W Midlands) SP0091 Map 4

Manor House

2 miles from M6, junction 9; from A461 towards Wednesbury take first left into Woden Rd East; at T-junction, left into Crankhall Lane; at eventual roundabout, right into Hall Green Rd. Alternatively, 5 miles from junction 7

This small 14th-c manor house is a remarkable place: you enter through the ancient gatehouse, across the moat, and inside, the main room is actually a great flagstoned hall, where massive oak trusses support the soaring pitched roof (the central one, eliminating any need for supporting pillars, is probably unique). This is now mainly an eating area (no smoking), and around the walls are a few lifesize medieval effigies, with as a centrepoint a rather unusual knight in armour, every 40 minutes or so turning round on his horse – which even neighs. A fine old sliding door opens on to stairs leading up to a series of smaller and cosier timbered upper rooms, including a medieval Solar Bar, which again have lovely oak trusses supporting their pitched ceiling beams. There are blue carpets and plenty of tables, and comfortably cushioned seats and stools around small tables, with the occasional settle; a snug Parlour Bar is tucked in beneath the Solar. The emphasis is pretty much on eating, and they do now call themselves a restaurant, but it is all rather jolly, and families are made especially welcome. Their meals are styled as feasts (and helpings are huge), with mostly char-grilled dishes like chicken or steak or a pound of cod with plenty of chips (£3.95), though they also do a well liked steak and kidney pie and good value Sunday lunch; they put sparklers in their home-made ice cream for children. Well kept Banks's Bitter and Mild on electric pump; trivia and fruit machines. Efficient, courteous staff. A broad stretch of grass leads away behind the moat, towards the modern houses of this quiet suburb; a car park is sensitively tucked away behind some modern ancillary buildings. *(Recommended by M Joyner, Stephen, Julie and Hayley Brown, Steve and Liz Tulley, Mayur Shah)*

Banks's ~ Managers Les and Rose Millard ~ Real ale ~ Meals and snacks (12-2.30, 6-9.30) ~ Restaurant ~ Birmingham (0121) 588 2035 ~ Children welcome ~ Medieval banquets Fri, quiz night Sun ~ Open 11.30-3, 6-11

WITHYBROOK (Warwicks) SP4384 Map 4

Pheasant ♀

4 miles from M6, junction 2; follow Ansty, Shilton signpost; bear right in Shilton towards Wolvey then take first right signposted Withybrook – or, longer but wider, second right into B4112 to Withybrook

Very nicely set beside the brook from which the village takes its name, this bustling well kept place is especially welcome in an area quite short of good pubs, and continues to be well liked for its wide choice of reliable food. A typical day's choice includes home-made soup (£1.25), sandwiches (£1.50), ploughman's (£4.75), omelettes (£4.95), home-made steak and kidney pie, braised liver and onions or a range of vegetarian dishes such as lentil and mushroom au gratin or spinach and mushroom lasagne (all £5.25), seafood salads (from £5.95), fisherman's pie or seafood vol-au-vent (£6.25), half a duck in orange sauce or braised pheasant(£7.25), steaks (from £7.50), fresh fish like plaice, lemon sole or sea bass, sizzling skillets like cajun chicken or Cantonese prawns, daily specials, and a choice of tempting puddings like raspberry and redcurrant pie (£2); Sunday roast (£5.95). They no longer have a restaurant so bar food can be eaten anywhere in the pub. The spacious lounge has a serving counter flanked by well polished rocky flagstones, lots of plush-cushioned wheelback chairs and dark tables on the patterned carpet, a few farm tools on its cream walls, and good winter fires. Well kept Courage Directors and John Smiths on handpump and a good range of wines, many available by the half-bottle; fruit machine in the lobby, and piped music. Friendly service. There are tables under lantern lights on a brookside terrace, and the bank opposite is prettily planted with flowers and shrubs. Parking can be difficult at busy times. *(Recommended by Cath and John Howard, G L Tong, Stephen, Julie and Hayley Brown, Ian and Nita Cooper, Paul and Sue*

Merrick, Cathy Scott, Richard Baker, D Cox, Harry Stirling, Roy Bromell, Geoff Lee)

Free house ~ Licensees Derek Guy, Alan and Rene Bean ~ Real ale ~ Meals and snacks (till 10pm) ~ Hinkley (01455) 220480 ~ Children welcome ~ Open 11-3, 6.30-11; closed 25 and 26 Dec

WOOTTON WAWEN (Warwicks) SP1563 Map 4

Bulls Head

Stratford Road; A3400 N of Stratford

Formerly a Bass Toby Inn, this has blossomed since its sale to new owners in 1992. A charming black and white timbered building, heavily beamed inside, it may date back to the 16th c, certainly to the 17th. Immaculately redecorated by the new people, it's still full of atmosphere, with pews and a sawdusted floor in rather an austere taproom, rugs setting off the good flagstones in the attractive low-ceiling L-shaped lounge with its massive timber uprights, decorations and furnishings that go well with the building, and a handsome newly done restaurant. There are fresh flowers, and service by the notably friendly and welcoming young staff is quick. Generous helpings of good often unusual food include wild mushrooms (£3.50), goat's cheese grilled in bacon, leek and cheese tart, pork and sage sausages (£6.95), and calf's liver and bacon (£10.50); the fish and seafood such as brill, salmon and crayfish is particularly good here (from around £8.95), and they don't overcook the asparagus when it's in season. Well kept Fullers London Pride, Greene King Abbot, Marstons Pedigree, Morlands Old Speckled Hen and Wadworths 6X served with a good head; decent wines, and coffee is served with proper cream. There are tables out in the garden, with some in a vigorous young vine arbour. It's handy for walks by the Stratford Canal. *(Recommended by Mrs Gladys Teall, Pat and Roger Fereday, the Monday Club, Dr S J Parkinson, Dr H R Long, B S Bourne, Joyce and Stephen Stackhouse, John Clements, Dr Vanessa Potter)*

Free house ~ Licensee John Willmott ~ Real ale ~ Meals and snacks (till 10pm) ~ Restaurant ~ (01564) 793511 ~ Well behaved children welcome ~ Open 12-3, 6-11; closed 25 Dec

Lucky Dip

Besides the fully inspected pubs, you might like to try these Lucky Dips recommended to us and described by readers (if you do, please send us reports):

Abthorpe, Northants [Silver St; SW of Towcester; SP6446], *New Inn*: Hidden up a cul-de-sac in quiet village, a local but welcoming to visitors, with beams, stone walls, inglenook log fire, lots of old pictures; simple good value food served by Liverpool landlady, lower dining area; well kept Hook Norton Best and Old Hookey; quiet piped radio; children welcome, big garden *(George Atkinson, JJW, CMW)*
Alcester, War [A435; SP0857], *Roebuck*: Old but much altered, with Theakstons Best and XB, wide choice of good value nicely cooked food in generous helpings; friendly landlord *(Mr and Mrs C Roberts)*; [High St], *Three Tuns*: Former wine bar, now with plenty of real ales and cheery customers, armchairs and low ceilings *(Graham Reeve)*
☆ **Allesley**, W Mid [off A45 E towards Birmingham; SP2981], *Windmill*: Hotel with 18-hole golf course and eight snooker tables, no piped music, ten or so real ales in cellar bar, good reasonably priced home-

grown food, warm welcome; live music some nights; comfortable bedrooms *(F T Wigley)*
Allesley [village centre], *Rainbow*: Busy and friendly unpretentious local, food plentiful and cheap *(Geoff Lee)*
☆ **Amblecote**, W Mid [Collis St; SO8985], *Robin Hood*: Friendly cosy open-plan local, good range of ales such as Badger Tanglefoot, Banks's Mild, Bathams, Enville, Everards Tiger and two guests such as Felinfoel and Fullers ESB, also ciders; reasonably priced food in dining area, children allowed till 8.30 if eating; comfortable bedrooms *(Paul Noble, Richard Houghton, Graham Reeve)*
Apethorpe, Northants [High St; TL0295], *Kings Head*: Recently reopened, with cosy bar, spacious lounge, arch to dining area; good choice of food, real ales inc Theakstons XB, Old Peculier *(Julian Holland)*
☆ **Ardens Grafton**, War [on edge of village, towards Wixford – OS Sheet 150 map ref

114538; SP1153], *Golden Cross*: Very
welcoming staff, food-oriented but plenty
of scope for just a drink and a chat;
pleasant L-shaped room with lots of
antique dolls in cabinets, also teddy bears,
toy rabbits etc, photographic magazines
(local society meets here), and
Shakespearean murals; generous helpings of
good bar food, well kept Whitbreads-
related real ales, efficient service,
unobtrusive piped music, fruit machine;
dolls-house restaurant, seats outside, nice
views *(John and Marianne Cooper, George
Atkinson)*

Arthingworth, Northants [SP7581], *Bulls
Head*: Refurbished, with good food inc
bargain three-course OAP lunch Tues-Sat;
open all day summer, has also been open all
day with food all day on spring bank hol
weekends *(Stephen, Julie and Hayley
Brown)*

☆ **Ashton**, Northants [the one NE of Oundle,
signed from A427/A605 island; TL0588],
Chequered Skipper: Attractive little pub on
green of thatched Tudor-style village, well
kept Adnams, Marstons Pedigree and two
other real ales, friendly staff, open fire, fish
tanks, stuffed birds, butterflies and so forth;
peacocks outside, on Nene Way footpath;
can get crowded; unusual inn sign using
different coloured nails; children welcome
*(JJW, CMW, Stephen, Julie and Hayley
Brown, Alan and Heather Jacques)*

Ashton [the other one, off A508 S of M1
junction 15; SP7850], *Old Crown*: Friendly
and welcoming Charles Wells pub, Eagle,
Bombardier and Boddingtons well kept on
handpump, decent food inc takeaways;
cosy and modernised, keeping some
character (beams, nick-nacks like muskets);
back bar with pool and darts, front lounge
allowing children; big back garden with
picnic-table sets *(Brian and Anna Marsden)*

☆ **Aston Cantlow**, War [SP1359], *Kings
Head*: Pretty timbered village pub not far
from Mary Arden's house in Wilmcote,
flagstones, inglenook, cheery log fire and
well used old furniture inc settles;
grandfather clock in low-beamed room on
left, snug on right, good prompt
straightforward food (not Sun or Mon
evenings) from sandwiches to steaks, well
kept Whitbreads-related ales with a guest
such as Morlands Old Speckled Hen,
friendly landlord and cat *(Peter and Erica
Davis, John and Marianne Cooper, Dr S J
Parkinson, Jerry and Alison Oakes, Mr and
Mrs C Roberts, LYM)*

Austrey, War [Church Lane; SK2906], *Bird
in Hand*: Olde-worlde thatched village pub,
recently extended and refurbished; bar
meals weekday lunchtimes, evening
restaurant, Marstons ales *(Graham
Richardson)*

☆ **Aynho**, Northants [SP5133], *Cartwright
Arms*: Neatly modernised lounge and bar in
16th-c former posting inn, friendly staff
and customers, good home-made bar food,
Bass, Hook Norton Best and Morlands Old

Speckled Hen, reasonably priced restaurant,
a few tables in pretty corner of former
coachyard; bedrooms comfortable and
attractive *(Margaret and Roy Randle,
Maxine Coleman, Dave Braisted, LYM)*

☆ **Aynho** [Wharf Base, B4031 W], *Great
Western Arms*: Pleasant and unpretentious,
by Oxford Canal, with good cheap bar
food from very good value sandwiches up
in roomy informal dining areas, log fire
inset into interior wall heating lounge and
bar, well kept Hook Norton Bitter and
Mild, GWR memorabilia; bar billiards,
video game, children's room; big garden
with moorings *(George Atkinson, Frank
Gadbois)*

☆ **Badby**, Northants [SP5559], *Maltsters
Arms*: Pleasant village pub with roaring
fires, good reasonably priced food in
intimate dining room; darts, pool, skittles,
nice licensees; well placed for walks on
nearby Knightley Way; bedrooms *(Wayne
Brindle)*

Balsall Common, W Mid [SP2377],
Saracens Head: Refurbished as Maltster
dining pub, good straightforward bar food
in roomy series of interconnecting rooms
some with 16th-c beams and flagstones but
the old character rather masked by the new
Victorianisation and video games; well kept
Allied ales inc Holt Plant & Deakins Entire,
muted piped music, friendly service,
restaurant *(the Monday Club, Dave
Braisted, Roy Bromell)*

Barnacle, War [village signed off B4029 in
Shilton, nr M6 junction 2; SP3884], *Red
Lion*: Good range of generous good value
food (not Sun lunchtime) in quiet two-room
pub with Bass and M&B real ales; seats out
in covered front area *(John and Marianne
Cooper)*

☆ **Barnwell**, Northants [TL0484], *Montagu
Arms*: Delightfully old-fashioned village
pub with well kept Batemans XXXB, Hook
Norton Old Hookey and Courage
Directors, food inc good Sun lunch, nice
atmosphere, friendly staff *(David Hedges,
Frank W Gadbois)*

Barston, W Mid [Barston Ln; SP2078],
Bulls Head: Attractive country pub with
two small rooms, partly dating from 1490;
oak beams, log fires, friendly bar staff,
good food, well kept Bass, secluded garden,
hay barn behind *(Richard Waller, L
Harvard, K Warren, M Whalley)*

Berkswell, W Mid [Spencer Lane, signed
from A452; SP2479], *Bear*: Rambling
timbered Chef & Brewer dining pub with
tables on pleasant tree-sheltered back lawn,
Crimean War cannon in front; usual bar
food from brightly lit servery in open-plan
bar, well kept Courage-related real ales,
separate restaurant; village church worth a
visit *(Roy Y Bromell, George Atkinson,
Roger and Christine Mash, C F Walling,
LYM)*

☆ **Birmingham** [Cambridge St], *Prince of
Wales*: Fine traditional local in lovely old
building, long-serving Irish landlord,

genuine hatch-served snug, two quiet and comfortable back parlours one of them frozen in 1900, ochre walls, bare floors, lively friendly atmosphere, welcoming service, particularly well kept real ales such as Ansells Bitter and Mild, Ind Coope Burton, Marstons Pedigree and Tetleys; wide choice of good food, piped Irish music, can get packed *(Cdr P Tailyour, Brian and Anna Marsden)*

☆ Birmingham [36 Winson St, Winson Green], *Bellefield*: Unspoilt sidestreet pub with Georgian smoking room, beautiful Victorian tiles, notable bar ceiling, framed tile pictures in lounge; Everards Mild, Tiger and Old Bill, Morlands Old Speckled Hen and two guest beers, other interesting bottled beers and occasional beer festivals; pizzas, samosas, patties, sandwiches and hot dishes such as speciality curried mutton – good value; bar games, music, friendly locals, terrace for children *(Richard Lewis, J W Busby)*

☆ Birmingham [St Pauls Sq, Hockley], *Rope Walk*: Comfortable pastiche of Edwardian pub with lots of glass, wood and elegant period prints, snug with TV, two-level lounge with full range of well kept Banks's beers, good coffee and service, food from separate servery; piped music, fruit machine; tiny outside verandah, opp attractive churchyard; open all day *(J Barnwell)*

Birmingham [Stephenson St; in Midland Hotel, off New St], *Atkinson Bar*: Recently redecorated, with good range of real ales (not cheap) tapped from the cask and kept under light blanket pressure inc Bass, Boddingtons, Flowers Original, Holdens Golden, Marstons Pedigree, Theakstons Old Peculier; served in lined mugs; always busy, good french bread sandwiches; bedrooms *(Brian Jones, Brian and Anna Marsden, Graham Reeve)*; [St Margarets Rd], *Barley Mow*: Typical Birmingham 1930s-type pub, can be loud and brash; cowboy and indian gunfight Fri; Ansells *(Dave Braisted)*; [144 High St, Aston], *Bartons Arms*: Still worth a look for its spectacular turn-of-the-century architecture, but does need taking in hand *(Graham Reeve, LYM)*; [Factory Rd, Hockley], *Black Eagle*: Good range of home-cooked food. friendly atmosphere and well kept beers *(J Dwane)*; [Ravenhurst St, Camp Hill, by roundabout A41/Middle Ring Rd; SP0786], *Brewer & Baker*: Friendly Banks's local worth knowing for well kept cheap Bitter and Mild, good value food *(Brian and Anna Marsden, Brian Jones)*; [Proctor St, Aston], *Britannia*: Backstreet town pub notable for its hot pork rolls *(Dave Braisted)*; [1320 Stratford Rd, Hall Green], *Bulls Head*: Recently pleasantly refurbished, good beer, friendly staff *(Richard Waller)*; [176 Hagley Rd, Edgbaston], *Hagley Duck*: Perhaps even a surfeit of bric-a-brac in front bar, wide choice in back real ale bar, also farm cider;

smart dress required *(Graham Reeve)*; [Tyburn Rd, Bromfield], *Navigation*: Good value food in one of the better standard Ansells pubs *(Dave Braisted)*; [Curzon St, just off the middle ring], *O'Neills Ale House*: Homely pub in industrial environment, candles, very cheap changing food, Ansells *(Graham Reeve)*; [Dudley Rd, Winson Green], *Old Windmill*: Unspoilt town pub, small, cosy, friendly and busy – good for drinkers *(Comus Elliott)*

Bishops Itchington, War [Fisher Rd; 2 miles from M40 junction 12; SP3857], *Malt & Shovel*: Reasonable range of cheap food inc bargain Sun lunch in cosy and friendly pub with small dining room, quick service, interesting things to look at; tiny bar and lounge do get packed at lunchtime, scarcely room to use the hexagonal swivelling pool table; music can be loud *(TBB, Tony and Wynne Gifford, D J Roberts, Ian Phillips, A H Thomas)*

Bishops Tachbrook, War [nr M40 junction 13, via A452; SP3161], *Leopard*: Well kept beer inc guests like Morland Old Speckled Hen, good value bar food inc well presented curry, faggots, pies, good steaks *(Steve and Liz Tilley)*

☆ Blakesley, Northants [High St (Woodend rd); SP6250], *Bartholomew Arms*: Short choice of good bar food inc vegetarian and good value rolls in authentic country pub with two pleasantly cosy beamed bars cluttered with nick-nacks; friendly staff, well kept Marstons Pedigree, pleasant enclosed back garden with summerhouse; children welcome in one bar *(Christopher and Sharon Hayle, Ted Corrin)*

Blisworth, Northants [former A43 S of Northampton; SP7253], *Royal Oak*: Nr Grand Union Canal with Courage-related beers and reasonable food at fair prices (all day inc Sun); coffee and tea; pool table, piped music, garden *(N and J Strathdee)*

Brackley Hatch, Northants [A43; SP6644], *Green Man*: Large Henry's Table dining pub on busy dual carriageway nr Silverstone; welcoming staff, comfortable beamed lounge area and conservatory, separate restaurant; lots of motor racing memorabilia and stuffed birds; cheap food, Boddingtons ales, open fires; big garden with play area; bedrooms *(George Atkinson)*

☆ Braunston, Northants [on canal, about a mile towards tunnel; SP5466], *Admiral Nelson*: Popular former 1730 farmhouse in lovely setting by lock and hump bridge, with pleasant waterside garden and towpath walks; currently doing well under newish licensees, well kept Batemans and Courage-related real ales, quick service, reasonably priced straightforward food, restaurant *(George Atkinson, John and Elizabeth Gwynne, George Murdoch)*

Bretford, War [A428 Coventry—Rugby – OS Sheet 140 map ref 431772; SP4377], *Queens Head*: Big airy refurbished dining pub with good food at reasonable prices inc good choice for children; big play area *(Roy Bromell, the Monday Club)*

Brigstock, Northants [SP9485], *Olde Three Cocks*: Large and very friendly, lovely fire, wide choice of good value food, Courage Directors and Marstons Pedigree; piped music, restaurant *(George Atkinson)*

☆ **Brinklow**, War [Fosse Way; A427, fairly handy for M6 junction 2; SP4379], *Raven*: Friendly old Marstons pub with 15th-c beams and open fire in dark-panelled lounge, more basic bar with alcoves and plants, collection of mugs and frog curios, good range of usual food inc vegetarian, three well kept real ales, good friendly service; piped local radio; tables on raised lawn with geese, rabbits and friendly Vietnamese pot-bellied pig; said to be haunted *(George Atkinson, CW, JW)*

Brixworth, Northants [SP7470], *George*: Interesting old local in a variety of styles from ironstone and tiles to corrugated iron, with real ales inc Adnams, Marstons and Charles Wells, bar food inc good value sandwiches; nearby Saxon church (one of the oldest in England) well worth a visit *(Norma and Keith Bloomfield)*

Broom, War [High St; SP0853], *Broom Tavern*: Attractive timbered pub, comfortable and relaxing, with some concentration on food; Shakespeare connections *(Gordon)*

Broughton, Northants [High St; SP8375], *Sun*: Friendly local with Charles Wells Eagle and Bombardier and a guest such as Morlands Old Speckled Hen, generous helpings of good value well served simple bar food, cosy central fire, good landlord; small garden *(M and J Back)*

Bugbrooke, Northants [14 Church St; SP6757], *Five Bells*: Small busy old-fashioned pub with low ceilings, friendly staff, good reasonably priced food esp good value steaks, pleasant garden, one dining area no smoking; games room; attractive village *(Mr and Mrs S Forster, Keith Croxton)*

Charlton, Northants [Main St; SP5236], *Rose & Crown*: Quiet thatched pub with attractive and individual furnishings, well kept Morlands Original and Old Masters, good range of good value bar food *(Derek and Sylvia Stephenson, C L Hicks, LYM)*

☆ **Churchover**, War [handy for M6 junction 1, off A426; SP5180], *Haywaggon*: Carefully modernised old pub, reopened after a closure, with good range of reasonably priced food in two snug eating areas, friendly atmosphere, Courage Best and Directors; on edge of quiet village with beautiful views over Swift valley *(Alain and Rose Foote, LYM)*

☆ **Claverdon**, War [SP1964], *Red Lion*: Food home-cooked but quickly served, with good veg, in pleasant village pub with helpful friendly service and well kept Whitbreads-related real ales; clean and spacious back saloon (where children allowed) opening on to sheltered terrace, garden and play area

with country views – garden not always open; small plush front L-shaped lounge, log fire; may not open until after noon some days *(Roy Bromell, Margaret Cadney, BB)*

Claverdon [Henley Rd], *Crown*: Pleasant and friendly, with good choice of generous good value food esp specials, fish and roasts; Ansells *(Dave Braisted, A H Thomas)*

☆ **Clay Coton**, Northants [off B5414 nr Stanford Hall; SP5977], *Fox & Hounds*: Popular, friendly and relaxed, with two log fires, well kept real ales such as Hook Norton and Wadworths, nice range of reasonably priced well prepared generous food inc good sandwiches in dining area; simple but comfortable furnishings, pleasant garden, dogs and cats, chatty licensees, interesting music – landlord chooses by clientele; skittle alley *(Ted George)*

Collingtree, Northants [High St; by M1 junction 15; SP7555], *Wooden Walls of Old England*: Doing well under newish landlord, good range of well kept beers inc guests, friendly atmosphere, good range of well priced food; one bar has hood skittles; garden with play area and tuck shop *(Mark and Toni Amor-Segan)*

☆ **Cosgrove**, Northants [Thrupp Wharf, towards Castlethorpe; SP7942], *Navigation*: Lovely canalside setting, good range of beers, usual pub food, friendly service, building itself of some character; children welcome *(C Driver, BB)*

☆ **Coventry** [1059 Foleshill Rd, handy for M6 junction 3; SP3379], *William IV*: Typical Midlands prewar pub notable for wide range of totally authentic Indian food at most attractive prices; well kept M&B ales *(Dave Thompson, Margaret Mason, John Allsopp)*

Cranford St Andrew, Northants [SP9277], *Woolpack*: Beautifully run and completely unspoilt country pub, good Flowers, garden area and no music or juke box; authentic games room and very friendly welcome *(Simon Green, Audrey Furnell)*

Cranford St John, Northants [42a High St; 3 miles E of Kettering just off A14; SP9277], *Red Lion*: Nice stone pub in quiet village with warm lounge and bar, friendly staff, changing food inc Tues bargain OAP lunch, Flowers Original and Tetleys, good house red; pleasant garden *(David and Mary Webb)*

Deanshanger, Northants [just off A422 W of Stony Stratford; SP7639], *Fox & Hounds*: Two bars with log fire and TV in lounge, pictures, pub mirrors, darts and fruit machines in public bar; quiet piped pop music, well kept Flowers and Greene King on handpump, good value food (not Sun evening); separate dining room; bedrooms *(CW, JW)*

Denford, Northants [High St; S of Thrapston; SP9976], *Cock*: Friendly and pleasant Elizabethan pub, dark beams, cosy areas; real fire in bar, woodburner in lounge/restaurant, good value food inc vegetarian and children's, six well kept real ales on handpump inc own brew, attentive service; quiet piped music; tables in garden, River Nene walks nearby; no food Sun/Mon evenings *(CMW, JJW)*

☆ **Deppers Bridge**, War [4 miles N of M40 junction 12; B4451; SP4059], *Great Western*: Real family pub, with good service, generous helpings of promptly served food inc lots of children's specials, good choice of beers and wines, fascinating train photographs and a non-stop working model train clattering round overhead; Ansells and Holt Plant & Deakins Entire; play area, tables on terrace *(Margaret Cadney, George Atkinson)*

☆ **Dorridge**, W Mid [Four Ashes Rd; SP1775], *Drum & Monkey*: Spacious Greenalls Millers Kitchen dining pub recently comfortably and attractively refurbished, wide choice of reliable good value food, well kept Allied ales, no-smoking dining area, efficient friendly service even when busy; big garden with play area *(Mrs M Cadney, Michael and Margaret Norris)*

☆ **Dorridge**, *Railway*: Small friendly local, largely unspoiled, with well kept Bass, family service and limited choice of good value food; small garden *(Brian Jones, Martin Richards)*

Dudley, W Mid [Blowers Green Rd; A461/A454; SO9390], *Lamp*: Extended pub with well kept Bathams, exceptional range of malt whiskies for this area, buzz of friendly conversation, surprisingly good view from the upstairs Panorama room, good value food in homely restaurant area; newly built bedrooms *(David and Shelia)*

☆ **Easenhall**, War [SP4679], *Golden Lion*: Big helpings of good value food inc good Sun carvery, pleasant atmosphere and efficient welcoming service even when busy in 16th-c inn with tasteful two-part oak-beamed lounge, dark panelling, comfortable seating; Boddingtons, Flowers Original and Theakstons Best on handpump, log fire; spacious attractive garden with terrace, barbecue, donkey called Charlotte; well equipped bedrooms *(George Atkinson, Mark and Toni Amor-Segan)*

☆ **Eastcote**, Northants [Gayton Rd; village signed off A5 3 miles N of Towcester; SP6753], *Eastcote Arms*: Long a popular main entry for its attractive unspoilt traditional layout, with a good choice of well kept real ales, simple cheap lunchtime food, log fires and a pretty garden, this was closed in 1994, though we hear that new owners hope to reopen it *(LYM; news please)*

☆ **Edge Hill**, War [SP3747], *Castle*: Fabulous views through trees from garden of renovated battlemented folly perched over steep slope of Edge Hill, recently very well refurbished, with friendly efficient staff, good value proper pub food, well kept Hook Norton ales; children welcome; even the lavatories are turreted *(N and J Strathdee, Margaret Dyke, LYM)*

☆ **Ettington**, War [Banbury Rd (A422 towards Stratford); SP2749], *Houndshill*: Neat and well organised dining bar/restaurant with good value food in pleasant surroundings, very popular with families and OAPs; Theakstons and Youngers beers, stripped stone and beams, good service, tables in big pleasant garden, good views from front; good well equipped bedrooms *(I R Hewitt, Mr and Mrs R Head, Dorothy and David Young, George Atkinson)*

Ettington, War [A429 Warwick—Moreton-in-Marsh], *White Horse*: Pretty building, very friendly atmosphere, helpful staff, good well presented good value food *(Sally and Bill Hyde)*

Evenley, Northants [The Green; SP5834], *Red Lion*: Clean friendly cricketing pub, real ale, good food at reasonable prices *(B A Ford)*

☆ **Farnborough**, War [off A423 N of Banbury; SP4349], *Butchers Arms*: Attractive country pub reopened after a year or two's closure, refurnished with period oak furniture to suit its old-fashioned layout and flagstone floor; good interesting food from proper thick sandwiches to steaks chosen by customer and charged by the ounce; well kept Adnams, Flowers IPA and Original and Marstons Pedigree, enthusiastic and talkative new landlord from Blackpool, good log fire, children welcome *(Jim Sargeant, Paul Haworth, Steve Williamson, LYM)*

☆ **Farthingstone**, Northants [SP6155], *Kings Arms*: Comfortable 18th-c village pub, well kept Hook Norton, wide choice of decent home-cooked food, games room with darts and skittles, friendly service; children allowed *(CW, JW)*

Fenny Compton, War [Wharf; SP4152], *George & Dragon*: Convenient canalside pub, friendly staff, good value food, well kept beer; gardens with aviary and rare poultry, moorings nearby; children in dining area *(Hazel Morgan)*; [High St], *Merrie Lion*: Friendly little neatly divided local, particularly well kept Banks's beers, usual bar food *(George Atkinson)*

Gayton, Northants [High St; SP7054], *Eykyn Arms*: Cheerful and friendly stonebuilt pub keeping much of its original style; plush lounge almost an aviation museum, perfectly kept Charles Wells Eagle *(John C Baker)*; *Queen Victoria*: Refurbished village pub, very popular weekends, with some emphasis on wide range of food from modern servery area, hunting prints in comfortable back lounge, well kept real ales inc Hook Norton, pleasant staff, darts and hood skittles in lively front public bar, piped music, pool room; bookable cheap transport for locals *(Mr and Mrs S Forster, LYM)*

Geddington, Northants [Bridge St; just off

A43 Kettering—Corby; SP8983], *Star*: Attractive setting not far from much-photographed packhorse bridge, food very much above average but still a real pub with properly separate restaurant *(WHBM)*

Glapthorn, Northants [off A427, N of Oundle; TL0290], *Crown*: Village local with comfortable homely atmosphere, beams, exposed brickwork, log fire, Boddingtons and Greene King beers on handpump *(David Hedges)*

Gornalwood, W Mid [Summit Pl, just off B4176; SO9190], *Bush*: Nicely decorated in unusual style, well kept beer, pleasant staff *(Richard Waller)*

☆ **Great Brington**, Northants [SP6664], *Fox & Hounds*: Low-beamed local with limited range of good reasonably priced food, six interesting changing real ales kept well, very friendly staff, two log fires, flagstones and bare boards, stone walls, newspapers to read, games room with table skittles, juke box or eclectic piped music (may be loud), quaint outside gents'; garden with play area, charming village nr Althorp House; children welcome *(George Atkinson, JW, CW)*

☆ **Great Oxendon**, Northants [SP7383], *George*: Stylish and civilised, with consistently good restaurant and bar food inc some imaginative dishes, obliging attentive service, pleasant no-smoking conservatory *(CW, JW, Cdr Patrick Tailyour, Mr and Mrs P Wilkinson)*

☆ **Halesowen**, W Mid [Cowley Gate St; just off A458 to Stourbridge, at Cradley Heath – OS Sheet 139 map ref 941847; SO9683], *Little Chop House*: Huge helpings of good solid food inc nursery puddings in good friendly 'Little' pub, relatively straightforward, with good friendly service, well kept Allied real ales inc Mild, and Little Lumphammer; can get crowded weekends *(Richard Waller)*

Hall End, W Mid [SP0093], *Old Blue Ball*: Small, very popular and friendly, with genial landlords, lunchtime sandwiches, summer barbecues, well kept Stones and Banks's beers, good garden with climbing frame, beautiful array of hanging baskets; can get very busy at night *(Mr and Mrs P Roberts)*

☆ **Hampton in Arden**, W Mid [1½ miles from M42 junction 6 via village slip rd from exit roundabout; SP2081], *White Lion*: Ancient unpretentious pub with unusual mid 20th-c feel in unfussy beamed lounge with real fire and plenty of room for the locals, surprising ship theme inc navigation lights, friendly staff, promptly served good value bar food (not Sun) from sandwiches to steaks inc children's dishes, well kept Bass, M&B Brew XI and John Smiths, decent wine, public bar with cribbage and dominoes, back dining room; handy for NEC, children allowed; bedrooms *(T Hurst, Thomas Nott, Graham Reeve, Roy Bromell, J D Rundle, George Atkinson, Jenny Huggins, Neville Kenyon, L Harvard,*

K Warren, M Whalley, John Fahy, LYM)

☆ **Hampton Lucy**, War [E of Stratford; SP2557], *Boars Head*: Convivial old beamed pub, traditional decor, log fire, brasses, popular for simple good value lunches but has kept a friendly local atmosphere, with well kept Whitbreads-related ales, prompt service; small garden, pretty village nr Charlcote House *(D Stokes)*

Handsworth, W Mid [Heathfield Rd; SP0490], *Stork*: Friendly, well kept beer, good value food, friendly staff *(Lisa Snell)*

Harbury, War [just off B4451/B4452; S of A425 Leamington Spa—Southam; SP3759], *Shakespeare*: Good atmosphere in popular dining pub with linked beamed rooms, reliable well served food inc Sun lunch, well kept Whitbreads-related ales with guests such as Adnams and Marstons Pedigree, separate pool room; children allowed in one area; tables in back garden with pets corner *(Mr and Mrs J Back)*

Hardingstone, Northants [57 High St; SP7657], *Crown*: Two-bar Chef & Brewer with hard-working new management, Courage-related ales, good value food, separate games room; picnic-table sets in sizeable garden with play area, dovecote and pets' corner *(JJW, CMW)*

☆ **Harpole**, Northants [High St; nr M1 junction 16; SP6860], *Bull*: Comfortable old pub with reliably good value generous food, well kept Courage-related ales, friendly service, real fire in big inglenook, games room, small terrace; no dogs *(K H Frostick, Dr M V Jones)*

Harpole, [Weedon Rd; A45], *Turnpike*: Beefeater pub/restaurant with split-level hotchpotch of old timber and brick, lamp post and fountain; good if not cheap food; garden *(JJW, CMW)*

☆ **Harrington**, Northants [High St; off A508 S of Mkt Harboro; SP7779], *Tollemache Arms*: Fine Tudor beamed stonebuilt pub in isolated village, very attractive when virginia creeper turns red; Charles Wells ales, very friendly staff, civilised atmosphere, good home-cooked fresh food inc unusual dishes and good soup, open fires, small back garden; children welcome; clean and attractive bedrooms *(George Atkinson, K H Frostick)*

Harringworth, Northants [Seaton Rd; SP9197], *White Swan*: Interesting carpenter's tools, good service, good food, well kept beers *(Mr and Mrs J F Batstone)*

☆ **Hawkesbury**, W Mid [close to M6 junction 3, exit past Moat House northwards on Longford Rd (B4113), 1st right into Black Horse Rd, cross canal and into Sutton Stop; SP3684], *Greyhound*: Idyllic summer location, with tables and safe play area in delightful garden by junction of Coventry and N Oxford Canals; good interesting pies and other generous food with delicious proper chips, good puddings with custard, well kept Bass and Banks's Mild, lots of nick-nacks (ties, beer labels, foreign banknotes, toby jugs etc), coal-fired stove, unusual tiny snug; firm service; booking essential for the Pie Parlour – lots of canalia and quite private olde-worlde atmosphere; children welcome *(Geoff Lee, D W Gray, Graham Reeve, the Monday Club)*

☆ **Hellidon**, Northants [off A425 W of Daventry; SP5158], *Red Lion*: Welcoming landlord, good well served reasonably priced food in bar and restaurant, well kept real ales inc Bass, clean, cosy and comfortable lounge and bars with woodburning stove, games room; beautiful setting overlooking village green, tables outside, pleasant walks nearby; bedrooms *(David Mervin, Mr and Mrs K H Frostick, Hilary Aslett, George Atkinson)*

Higham Ferrers, Northants [SP9668], *Green Dragon*: Good choice of real ales on handpump, food that's been on something of an upswing esp steaks bought by weight and char-grilled in restaurant *(Stephen, Julie and Hayley Brown)*

☆ **Hillmorton**, War [Crick Rd; outskirts, where A428, railway and canal intersect; SP5274], *Old Royal Oak*: Recently refurbished and extended as a Marstons Tavern Table with vast family dining area, carpeted lounge, flagstoned bar, terrace with tables spreading down to canal side, good value food, real ales; good play areas inside and out, nappy-changing facilities, lavatories for the disabled; piped music; open all dat Sat *(George Atkinson, Alain and Rose Foote)*

☆ **Hinton in the Hedges**, Northants [off A43 W of Brackley; SP5536], *Crewe Arms*: Good friendly family atmosphere in popular 17th-c pub, two roomy old-fashioned alcovey bars and modern extension, good choice of reasonably priced good food from sandwiches up, well kept beers such as Boddingtons, Hook Norton Best, Marstons Pedigree and Morlands Old Speckled Hen, good coffee, good service, games room, some picnic-table sets outside *(George Atkinson, Dr and Mrs James Stewart, Julian and Sarah Stanton, Mark and Diane Grist)*

☆ **Hockley Heath**, W Mid [Stratford Rd (A34 Birmingham—Henley-in-Arden); SP1573], *Wharf*: Friendly modernised Chef & Brewer, quick good value generous straightforward food inc Sun roasts (and has had Tues bargains), Courage-related real ales, plenty of seats; darts, TV, games machines, piped pop music; children welcome; attractive garden with adventure playground by Stratford Canal, interesting walks on renovated towpath *(Dennis H Phillips, JJW, CMW)*

Holcot, Northants [Main Street; SP7969], *White Swan*: Pleasant two-bar village local with reasonably priced food (not Sun-Weds evenings), Morlands Old Speckled Hen, Tetleys, Wadworths 6X and Courage-related ales, friendly service, no music, fresh flowers, corn dollies, old advertising mirrors, games room with skittles, pool and

darts, two fruit machines; picnic-table sets in garden; children welcome; bedrooms *(JJW, CMW, Eric J Locker)*

Iron Cross, War [A435 Evesham—Alcester; SP0552], *Queens Head*: Lots of antiques, warm friendly welcome, good value food inc good Sun lunch, Flowers and Theakstons real ales; open all day *(Patrick Godfrey, Mr and Mrs Berner, Graham Reeve)*

☆ **Kenilworth**, War [Castle Hill; SP2871], *Clarendon Arms*: Busy dining pub with good value food in several rooms off long partly flagstoned bar and in largish upstairs dining room; reductions for children and over-55s, efficient staff, Courage-related ales; opp castle *(TN, Colin Mason, Geoff Lee)*

☆ **Kenilworth** [High St], *Clarendon House*: Welcoming and civilised old hotel with well kept Flowers IPA and Original and Hook Norton Best and Old Hookey and good value simple bar food with interesting restaurant specials in partly panelled bar, antique maps, prints, copper, china and armour, decent wines, pleasant helpful staff; bedrooms comfortable and good value *(George Atkinson, Tony and Joan Walker)*

Kenilworth [Castle Green], *Queen & Castle*: Beefeater popular for its excellent position opp Castle; quaint corners, lots of pictures and beams, Whitbreads-related ales, wide food choice (shame about the piped pop music and games machines); tables on extensive lawns, good play apparatus *(Graham and Belinda Staplehurst, Bill Sykes, Geoff Lee, George Atkinson)*; [68 Warwick Rd], *Tut 'n' Shive*: Ales such as Badger Tanglefoot, Batemans XXB, Exmoor Gold, Hook Norton Old Hookey, Marstons Pedigree, Morlands Old Speckled Hen, Robinsons Best and Theakstons Old Peculier and XB in fun pub with zany decor – crooked mirrors, holes and corrugated iron in ceiling, old doors hanging crazily, painted slogans, bits of carpet scattered around, wheelbarrow in roof joist, odds and ends of seats inc garden chairs, a bed, even a sit-in bath, and a train going round; friendly attentive staff, limited food, rather loud piped rock music *(George Atkinson, Basil J S Minson)*

Kettering, Northants [off A43; SP8778], *Star*: Good menu at reasonable prices, attractive bar and sitting-out area *(K H Frostick)*

Kingswinford, W Mid [SO8888], *Court House*: Variety of real ales, good range of food served in bistro-style conservatory *(DAV)*; [Cot Lane], *Park*: Friendly two-room local with well kept real ales such as Bathams, Holt Plant & Deakins Entire and Ind Coope Burton *(DAV, G Fisher)*

Knowle, W Mid [High St; SP1876], *Red Lion*: Large busy beamed pub with good atmosphere, well kept real ales, friendly welcome *(Dr and Mrs A K Clarke)*

☆ **Lamport**, Northants [Harborough Rd

(A508); SP7574], *Lamport Swan*: Wide range of good value food in bar and cosy restaurant of large, busy and attractive straightforward pub with well kept Courage Directors and warm Canadian welcome, good views over Welland Valley; children welcome *(Stephen, Julie and Hayley Brown, Paul Amos, Mr and Mrs B Verlander, Mr and Mrs G Hughes, Mrs E Laughton, Cathy Scott, Richard Baker, Mr and Mrs S Forster)*

☆ **Leamington Spa**, War [Radford Rd; SP3165], *Red House*: Old-fashioned and individual, with friendly service and chatty customers, well kept Bass, no piped music – quiet and very relaxing; garden *(Graham and Belinda Staplehurst)*

☆ **Leamington Spa** [Campion Terr], *Somerville Arms*: Tiny unspoilt Victorian back lounge in neat and cosy local with well kept Ansells Bitter and Mild, Ind Coope Burton, Marstons Pedigree and Tetleys, friendly staff and locals, some memorabilia; no food *(Steve and Liz Tilley)*

Leamington Spa [Adelaide Rd], *Cricketers Arms*: Friendly town local with central bar, comfortable banquettes, well kept Flowers Original; next to bowling green *(Graham and Belinda Staplehurst, Michael and Derek Slade)*

Leek Wootton, War [Warwick Rd; SP2868], *Anchor*: Limited but good choice of very popular reasonably priced lunches (not Sun) in welcoming village pub close to Kenilworth; particularly well kept Bass, obliging service *(Andy and Jill Kassube, the Monday Club, Kate and Harry Taylor)*

☆ **Lighthorne**, War [a mile SW of B4100 N of Banbury; SP3355], *Antelope*: Pleasant 17th-c stonebuilt dining pub in attractive village, two comfortable and clean bars (one old, one new) with Cromwellian theme, wide choice of good reasonably priced food inc old-fashioned puddings, separate dining area; well kept Flowers IPA and Wadworths 6X, pleasant service; piped music; little waterfall in banked garden *(Jill and Peter Bickley, George Atkinson, Mr and Mrs R C Allison)*

☆ **Lilbourne**, Northants [Rugby Rd; 4 miles from M1 junction 18; A5 N, then 1st right; SP5677], *Bell*: Spaciously comfortable modern lounge bar, very neatly kept, popular for low-priced quickly served good value simple bar food; seats outside; children welcome *(Ted George, LYM)*

Litchborough, Northants [just off former B4525 Banbury—Northampton; SP6353], *Old Red Lion*: Simple village local with well kept Marstons Pedigree, reasonably priced sandwiches, scampi and so forth; attractive inglenook *(Tom Evans)*

☆ **Little Brington**, Northants [also signed from A428; 4½ miles from M1 junction 16; first right off A45 to Daventry; SP6663], *Saracens Head*: Sparklingly kept old-fashioned village pub with particularly good value well cooked and presented straightforward food, Courage-related real

ale, friendly staff and locals, log fires; cosy bar with masses of brass, clocks, an old store till, framed advertisements, and an aquarium; separate games bar, tables in neat back garden overlooking quiet fields; piano singalong Sat evening; afternoon teas, handy for nearby Althorp House or Holdenby House *(K H Frostick, L Walker, LYM)*

☆ **Little Harrowden**, Northants [Main St; SP8771], *Lamb*: Good range of reasonably priced home-cooked food (not Sun evening) inc fresh veg in pleasant 17th-c pub, three-level lounge with log fire, brasses on beams, quiet piped music, intimate dining area, well kept Charles Wells and a guest real ale, decent coffee, friendly helpful service; public bar, games room with hood skittles; garden; children welcome *(JJW, CMW, N E Johnson, M E Lane, Andrew Wood)*

☆ **Long Itchington**, War [Church Rd; SP4165], *Harvester*: Clean pub with straightforward furnishings, well kept cheap Hook Norton and Wadworths 6X, good value bar food, reasonably priced meals in small, relaxed restaurant, friendly staff *(George Atkinson)*

☆ **Long Itchington** [off A423], *Two Boats*: Neat pub with views of busy Grand Union Canal from alcove window seats, generous reasonably priced food, well kept ales such as Bass, Boddingtons, Hook Norton, Whitbreads West Country PA, pleasant 60s piped music, live music Fri/Sat; open all day *(Bill Sykes)*

Long Lawford, War [SP4776], *Sheaf & Sickle*: Usually at least five well kept beers, recently opened small restaurant with good food at reasonable prices, friendly staff *(Alain and Rose Foote)*

☆ **Lower Brailes**, War [SP3039], *George*: Pleasant old pub in lovely village setting, oak-beamed restaurant and bars, well kept Hook Norton beers, good Sun lunch and other reasonably priced food, piped classical music *(J H Peters, Graham Reeve, H D Spottiswoode)*

☆ **Lower Quinton**, War [off A46 Stratford—Broadway; SP1847], *College Arms*: Imposing building pleasantly set on green of pretty village, wide range of generous fresh bar food inc good Sun roasts, well kept Whitbreads-related real ales, warm welcome, efficient service; spacious open-plan lounge with stripped stone and heavy beams, unusual highly polished tables inc one in former fireplace, leather seats, partly carpeted parquet floor; games in public bar *(Mrs J Oakes, Martin Jones)*

☆ **Lowick**, Northants [off A6116; SP9780], *Snooty Fox*: Spacious two-room open-plan beamed lounge with stripped stonework, old-fashioned prints, big log fire, Courage-related and guest ales from massive dark wood counter with a stuffed snooty fox behind it; good value bar food esp fish, decent wines, good fresh coffee, piped music; popular restaurant around central open fireplace; jazz Thurs, rock/Irish folk

Fri *(Penny and Martin Fletcher, Darren Ford, Hilary Edwards, Richard W Chew, R Hughes, Natalie Spencer, Simon Forster, David Shillitoe, LYM)*

Loxley, War [signed off A422 Stratford—Banbury; SP2552], *Fox*: Pleasant friendly atmosphere, sandwiches and wide choice of freshly cooked meals inc good range of puddings, settles, brocaded banquettes, Whitbreads-related ales with guests such as Bass and Hook Norton Best *(A H Thomas, Dorothee and Dennis Glover)*

Mappleborough Green, War [Alcester Rd; SP0866], *Dog*: Modern Toby grill/restaurant and bar with consistently good food *(Michael and Margaret Norris)*

☆ **Marston St Lawrence**, Northants [off A422 Banbury—Brackley; SP5342], *Marston Inn*: Welcoming little village pub with good food inc generous sandwiches, children's and vegetarian dishes, and elaborate evening choice (not Sun or Mon evening); open fire, oak beams, good dining room, well kept Hook Norton; big garden, traditional games inc Aunt Sally *(G T O'Connell, LYM)*

☆ **Marston Trussell**, Northants [SP6985], *Sun*: Doing well under current owners, with good home-made food, decent house wines, helpful staff; bedrooms comfortable *(Cdr Patrick Tailyour, Mrs Davidge)*

☆ **Middleton**, War [OS Sheet 139 map ref 175984; SP1798], *Green Man*: Busy extended beamed family dining pub with good standard food, M&B beers *(J Barnwell, David Hanley)*

☆ **Monks Kirby**, War [Bell Lane, just off A427 W of Pailton; SP4683], *Bell*: Quiet open-plan beamed and timbered bar divided into separate areas, beautiful slabbed and cobbled floor, yet despite this classic English look Spanish landlord makes for a refreshingly different atmosphere – Spanish music sometimes, Spanish influences on the good generous food (esp fish); separate area for diners, woodburner, relaxed service, interesting wines *(Graham and Belinda Staplehurst, the Monday Club, John and Marianne Cooper)*

Moreton Pinkney, Northants [SP5749], *Olde House At Home*: Former Red Lion carefully converted into attractive pub, interesting food in bar and back restaurant, well kept Bass, Whitbreads Strong Country and Wychwood Best; seating outside; handy for Canons Ashby House and Sulgrave Manor *(George Atkinson)*

☆ **Napton**, War [Folly Lane; off A425 towards Priors Hardwick; SP4661], *Folly*: Beamed canalside pub in lovely spot by Napton locks, attractive collection of furnishings inc antiques, big helpings of good straightforward food inc lots of pies, well kept ales such as Boddingtons, Courage Directors, Eldridge Pope Dorchester and Theakstons, log fires, no piped music; provision for children indoors and out, good garden with wishing well, summer marquee and fine views (also all-

day shop); very busy weekends *(Graham Bush, Bill Sykes)*

Nassington, Northants [Station Road; TL0696], *Queens Head*: Good food, good value, esp tasty Sun roast; friendly feel and welcoming landlord *(Dr Andrew Brookes)*

Nether Whitacre, War [SP2292], *Dog*: Good balti food from Kashmiri chef in busy restaurant or in bar of 16th-c pub with Bass, M&B Brew XI and Mild and a guest beer; garden; children welcome *(Richard Lewis)*; [OS Sheet 139 map ref 220928], *Gate*: Lived-in feel, with cheap bar food, M&B ales, chickens in yard on the way to the gents', free range eggs for sale *(Dave Braisted)*

☆ **Netherton**, W Mid [89 Halesowen Rd; A459 just S of centre, towards Halesowen; SO9387], *Old Swan*: Friendly and traditional, with good cheap beer brewed at the pub, also guest real ales, limited but cheap food, nice old solid fuel stove, fine mirrors, decorative swan ceiling, matching extension; disco upstairs *(David and Shelia, Graham Reeve, LYM)*

Netherton [Baptist End Rd], *White Swan*: Well kept Ansells Mild, Holt Plant & Deakins Entire, Woods Best and guest beers such as Burton Bridge, cheap food inc hot pork sandwiches, lounge and games bar *(Graham Reeve)*

☆ **Newbold on Avon**, War [SP4777], *Barley Mow*: Good value promptly served straightforward food inc children's dishes in conservatory eating area of busy extended pub by Oxford Canal, well kept beer, good friendly service; pretty waterside terrace and garden with play area *(Alain and Rose Foote, Cathy Scott, Richard Baker)*

Newton Bromswold, Northants [SP9965], *Swan*: Homely and clean, with open fire, well kept Greene King *(Michael Marlow)*

☆ **Northampton** [Wellingborough Rd], *Abington Park*: Big Victorian town pub brewing its own good beers, brewery tours by arrangement; several bars, lunchtime bar food inc OAP and children concessions, friendly helpful staff, restaurant, family room; piped pop music, games machines; picnic-table sets outside; handy for cricket ground *(Cathy Scott, Richard Baker, JW, CW)*

Northampton [College St], *Newt & Cucumber*: Good choice of beers on handpump eg Hook Norton Best, Theakstons XB, Worthington BB and a bargain guest; sandwiches and good value quick hot dishes such as pizzas, in large comfortable split-level bar with pictures and alcoves, unobtrusive piped pop music, half a dozen games machines, coffee with real milk; closed Sun *(CW, JW, Susan and Nigel Wilson)*

nr Northampton [3½ miles from M1 junction 15 via A508, A428 then right turn into trading estate], *Britannia*: Rambling pub with massive beams, flagstones, attractive 18th-c kitchen, Courage-related

real ales, straightforward lunchtime bar food, carvery, conservatory; juke box may be loud, disco some nights; picnic-table sets by River Nene *(Julian Holland, LYM)*
Norton, Northants [off A5 N of Weedon; SP6063], *White Horse*: Old Charles Wells village local, obliging service, good rotation of well kept ales, good food inc take-aways *(Peter Phillips)*

☆ **Offchurch**, War [off A425 Radford Semele; SP3565], *Stags Head*: Good value straightforward food inc help-yourself salads and vegetarian dishes in friendly old low-beamed thatched dining pub with good service, well kept Ansells, unobtrusive piped music; good garden with play area *(Richard and Maria Gillespie, the Monday Club)*

☆ **Old Hill**, W Mid [Waterfall Lane; off Station Rd, between A4099 Gorstyhill Rd and A459 Halesowen Rd; SO9685], *Wharf*: Well worn in and chatty, with eight or so well kept largely S&N real ales, cheap food (not Sun) inc children's dishes, pool, juke box, pinball and other games, family area, tables in canalside garden with play area; occasional live music *(LYM)*

☆ **Old Hill** [132 Waterfall Lane], *Waterfall*: Genuine down-to-earth local with three or four interesting well kept guest beers and Bathams, Everards and Hook Norton; farm cider, popular plain food from good filled rolls to Sun lunch, tankards and jugs hanging from boarded ceiling; piped music *(Dave Braisted, Graham Reeve)*

☆ **Oldbury**, W Mid [Church St, nr Savacentre; SO9888], *Waggon & Horses*: Thriving town pub with good range of well kept changing beers such as Bathams, Boddingtons, Everards and Maclays, wholesome quite adventurous food in bar and upstairs restaurant, friendly staff, impressive Edwardian tilework, simple furnishings, old-fashioned Black Country memorabilia *(Chris Wrigley, Andy Petersen, Graham Reeve)*
Orlingbury, Northants [signed off A43 Northampton—Kettering, A509 Wellingborough—Kettering; SP8572], *Queens Arms*: Fine free house, beautifully clean and well looked after, with six well kept real ales inc unusual ones such as Oak Wobbly Bob, welcoming staff, food inc super sandwiches, cheap coffee, occasional live music; play area *(George Atkinson)*

☆ **Oundle**, Northants [52 Benefield Rd; TL0388], *Black Horse*: Good popular straightforward simple food from reasonably priced sandwiches up, usually more choice evenings inc good mixed grill, and good Sun lunch, in bright clean bar with comfortable dining room, changing ales such as Bass, John Smiths and Crown Buckley Revd James, roaring fire, friendly landlord and staff, games room, unobtrusive piped music; 10ft model black horse outside *(Mr and Mrs J Back, David and Mary Webb)*

☆ **Pailton**, War [A427 Coventry—

Lutterworth; SP4781], *White Lion*: Biggish nicely furnished 18th-c pub/restaurant popular for wide range of reasonably priced wholesome food inc two-sitting Sun lunch and children's dishes, good service, good range of wines, well kept beers; play area in garden; closed Mon; bedrooms *(Alain and Rose Foote, George Atkinson)*
Pailton [B4027 Lutterworth—Coventry], *Fox*: Good straightforward food inc lots of steaks, also vegetarian and children's dishes, attractive prices, well kept M&B Brew XI; bedrooms *(Geoff Lee)*

☆ **Preston Bagot**, War [B4095 Henley-in-Arden—Warwick; SP1765], *Crabmill*: Comfortable old low-beamed and timbered Brewers Fayre family dining pub with good value standard food (not Sun evening), lots of nooks and crannies, three log fires, old prints; some interesting furniture inc carved settles, but rather organised; well kept Whitbreads-related real ales, family area; seats in big garden with play area; open all day *(Peter Dowd, Dawn and Phil Garside, P G Clissett, Margaret and Michael Norris, LYM)*
Princethorpe, War [High Town; junction A423/B4453; SP4070], *Three Horseshoes*: Friendly and popular old roadside coaching inn with brasses and beams, four Whitbreads-related and other real ales, good food (OAP bargains), no-smoking eating area, open fires, pleasant garden with play area *(Richard Waller)*; [B4453 towards Cubbington], *Woodhouse*: Pleasantly placed hotel with good but pricy food inc carvery some days, cold table, exquisite puddings; Boddingtons and Ruddles County, espresso coffee, decent wines, good service; lawns with play area (and maybe white peacock); bedrooms *(George Atkinson, Roy Bromell)*
Priors Hardwick, War [SP4756], *Butchers Arms*: Good food and wines in friendly pub-restaurant with medieval oak beams, flagstones, panelling, antiques, inglenook bar, country garden – it advertises in upmarket Portuguese taxis *(Nicholas H Smith, Jill and Peter Bickley)*
Quarry Bank, W Mid [Saltwells Lane; signed off Coppice Lane, off A4036 nr Merry Hill Centre – OS Sheet 139 map ref 934868; SO9386], *Saltwells*: At end of rough lane past factory through nature reserve, popular with OAPs for good value lunches inc steak bargains; main lounge with bookshelves, family room, garden with play area; bedrooms *(Dave Braisted, Graham Reeve)*
Radford Semele, War [A425 2 miles E of Leamington Spa – OS Sheet 151 map ref 343645; SP3464], *White Lion*: Recently smartly refurbished as big Greenalls Millers Kitchen dining pub, good range of cheap food, Allied ales, garden *(George Atkinson, Steve and Liz Tilley)*
Roade, Northants [1 High St; just off A508 S of M1 junction 15; SP7551], *Cock*: Good solid lunchtime bar food in enormous

helpings, huge evening steaks and other food, Marstons Pedigree and Theakstons beers, piped music *(Penny and Martin Fletcher)*

☆ **Rockingham**, Northants [SP8691], *Sondes Arms*: Nicely set civilised beamed pub, recently extended and completely refurbished, with welcoming service, quiet piped music, good if not cheap home-made food inc some really unusual dishes, well kept Charles Wells Bombardier and Eagle; super views *(Alain and Rose Foote, CW, JW, D W Gray)*

☆ **Rowington**, War [Old Warwick Rd (B4439); SP2069], *Cockhorse*: Little cottage-style Edwardian pub in pleasant rural setting, fairly basic inside and decorated in slightly dated style but very homely; simple tasty pub food inc nice big hand-cut chips, friendly attentive staff, small bar with inglenook and fruit machine, second room with tables; picnic-table sets and flower tubs in front, cages of wildfowl, rabbits and guinea pigs behind; dogs allowed *(Susan and John Douglas, Dave Braisted)*

☆ **Rowington** [Finwood Rd; off B4439 N of Rowington, following Lowsonford sign], *Tom o' the Wood*: Extensively refurbished in formal green plush and mahogany, with Whitbreads-related real ales, wide choice of quickly served generous straightforward bar food; conservatory, picnic-table sets on terrace and neat side lawn, some provision for children lunchtime; handsome Elizabethan ceiling in upstairs restaurant *(A C Morrison, LYM)*

Rugby, War [Newbold Rd; SP5075], *Peacock*: Banks's pub with well kept beers, Victorian woodwork, lots of pictures of peacocks, quiet friendly atmosphere *(Cathy Scott, Richard Baker)*

☆ **Sedgley**, W Mid [Bilston St (A463); SO9193], *Beacon*: Unspoilt local brewing its own good well priced Sarah Hughes Surprise Bitter and Dark Ruby Mild in restored tower brewery, also two or three other well kept ales from tiny circular serving area with hatches to several Victorian rooms, family room and conservatory; seats on terrace *(John Scarisbrick)*

Sedgley [George St, Woodsetton], *Park*: Several excellent ales at low prices from next-door Holden's brewery, good lunchtime crowd and atmosphere, good range of good value bar snacks, no food evenings *(D W Gray)*

☆ **Shipston on Stour**, War [Church St; SP2540], *Horseshoe*: 17th-c timbered coaching inn with attractive modern pine interior, lots of nick-nacks, comfortable window seats, big fireplace, restaurant; Ruddles beer, good food with emphasis on fish in bar and chintzy restaurant; very welcoming service, pleasant atmosphere, no piped music; bedrooms pretty, bright and clean *(Diane Percivall, I R Hewitt)*

Shipston on Stour [Station Rd (off A3400)],

Black Horse: Nice pubby atmosphere in ancient thatched and beamed inn with small restaurant, good value bar food inc excellent char-grilled burgers and real chips, well kept Home, Ruddles, Theakstons XB, Websters and a guest beer, friendly staff and locals, log fire, back garden with terrace and barbecue, newfoundland dog and a couple of cats *(Jason Caulkin, Margaret Dyke, Chris and Anne Fluck)*; [High St], *White Bear*: Massive settles, good range of beers and cheerful atmosphere in traditional front bar, simpler but comfortable back lounge, interesting good value menu, tables in small back yard and benches on street; bedrooms *(J and D Boutwood, A Cowell, LYM)*

Shirley, W Mid [Farmhouse Way; SP1078], *Shelly Barn*: Pleasant converted barn with well kept beers; open till 2 am Sat *(Stephen Crothers)*

Shottery, War [Hathaway Lane; SP1755], *Bell*: Friendly, with well kept Whitbreads-related ales; on way to Anne Hathaway's cottage, but not on main tourist run *(Arthur and Annette Frampton)*

Shrewley, War [off B4439 Hockley Heath—Warwick; SP2167], *Durham Ox*: Small country pub under friendly new managment, good reasonably priced food from wide-ranging menu. real ale, spacious garden *(Roy Bromell, Dave Braisted, LYM)*

Shuttington, War [SK2505], *Wolferstan Arms*: Good family pub with imaginative bar meals, panoramic views from restaurant *(Graham Richardson)*

☆ **Sibbertoft**, Northants [SP6782], *Red Lion*: Huge range of good generous food inc vegetarian in small and civilised pub with welcoming landlord, well kept ales such as Adnams, Tetleys and Timothy Taylors, decent wines, piano, magazines, lovely big tables, comfortable seats *(Rona Murdoch)*

☆ **Slipton**, Northants [Slipton Ln; SP9479], *Samuel Pepys*: Attractively refurbished 16th-c two-bar pub with beams, exposed stonework, open fire, watercolours and decorative plates (and useful if not exactly matching new conservatory); five well kept real ales on handpump, decent wines, excellent coffee, good choice of somewhat upmarket meals, prompt service; good views from garden with play area; ; children allowed in restaurant *(CMW, JJW, Jeremy Wallington, D Howitt)*

Snitterfield, War [SP2159], *Snitterfield Arms*: Friendly local with good straightforward food, well kept Whitbreads-related ales, chatty smiling landlord, spacious but quite homely open-plan bar with open fire, shelves of china *(George Atkinson, Brian Jones)*

Stoke Albany, Northants [1 Harborough Rd; SP8088], *White Horse*: Very welcoming new young licensees, decent food inc very generous starters and wide choice of vegetarian dishes, Bass *(Eric Locker)*

☆ **Stoke Bruerne**, Northants [3½ miles from

M1 junction 15 – A508 towards Stony
Stratford then signed on right; SP7450],
Boat: Ideal canal location by beautifully
restored lock opp British Waterways
Museum and shop; little character bar by
canal, more ordinary back lounge without
the views (children allowed in this bit),
tables by towpath; well kept Marstons Best
and Pedigree, Sam Smiths OB and
Theakstons XB; food and service not its
strongest points; no-smoking restaurant
(not Mon lunchtime) and all-day tearooms,
pub open all day summer Sats *(Roger
Sherman, George Atkinson, Mr and Mrs
Moody, BM, A R Sayer and Barbara Sayer,
Mrs J Barwell, Martin, Jane, Simon and
Laura Bailey, Barry and Anne, Ian Phillips,
Rita Horridge, LYM)*

☆ **Stoke Doyle**, Northants [S of Oundle;
TL0286], *Shuckborough Arms*: Good
choice of food, esp vegetarian, lots of fresh
and varied veg, in peaceful and welcoming
L-shaped panelled bar or dining room; log
fires, comfortable chesterfields, no music or
fruit machines, games room with hood
skittles, well kept ales inc guests, helpful
landlord; picnic-table sets in garden with
play area; bedrooms good, with own
bathrooms *(CW, JW, Erica Head, N S
Smith)*

Stourbridge, W Mid [SO8984], *Retreat*:
Unpretentious bar-cum-bistro with simple
red drapes, black venetian blinds, candles in
plant pots, good value bar food (not Sun),
clean simple restaurant, well kept
Whitbreads-related ales *(Graham Reeve)*;
[Brook Rd, nr stn], *Seven Stars*: Large
Victorian pub with impressive wooden
carved bar, decorative tiles, well kept beers
inc Bathams and Theakstons, and wide
range of good bar food (big helpings); very
busy, friendly atmosphere *(Dr Bill Baker)*

☆ **Stratford upon Avon**, War [Southern Way;
SP0255], *Black Swan*: Great atmosphere,
mildly sophisticated, in neat 16th-c pub nr
Memorial Theatre – rather thespy, with lots
of signed RSC photographs; plainly served
bar food at moderate prices, Whitbreads-
related ales, friendly service, open fire,
children allowed in restaurant; attractive
terrace looking over the riverside public
gardens; known as the Dirty Duck
*(Graham and Belinda Staplehurst, Susan
and John Douglas, Dorothy and David
Young, LYM)*

☆ **Stratford upon Avon** [High St, nr Town
Hall], *Garrick*: Elaborately timbered lop-
sided pub with lots of character, also a bit
theatrical in the evening but a younger
more informal set than the Black Swan;
engaging sawdust-floor and stripped-stone
decor, cosy front bar, busier back one, well
kept Whitbreads-related real ales, sensibly
priced bar food (popular with office
workers lunchtime), friendly service,
thoughtfully chosen piped music; children
allowed in dining room when food being
served, service can falter when busy *(Dave
and Jules Tuckett, B Carter, Olive Carroll,*

George Atkinson, LYM)

☆ **Stratford upon Avon** [Chapel St],
Shakespeare: Our smartest
recommendation here, Forte hotel based on
handsome lavishly modernised Tudor
merchants' houses, with settles and
armchairs in comfortable Froth & Elbow
bar (though this may not always now have
real ale), limited but attractive and
reasonably priced hot and cold buffet
served promptly; tables in back courtyard,
also tea or coffee in peaceful armchairs or
plush settees by blazing log fires; bedrooms
comfortable and well equipped, though not
cheap *(J M Wooll, George Atkinson, LYM)*

Stratford upon Avon [Rother St, opp
United Reform Church], *Lamplighters*:
Spacious and welcoming, with alcoves,
brick pillars, well kept Courage-related
beers, wide choice of cheapish generous
food, relaxed atmosphere, a few guns on
walls and beams *(George Atkinson, John
Whitehead, Patrick Godfrey)*; [Bridgefoot],
Pen & Parchment: L-shaped split-level
lounge, big open fire in one room,
Whitbreads-related beers, bar meals and
breakfasts, fruit machine *(David Hanley)*;
[Ely St], *Queens Head*: Display of old
strong-beer bottles in lounge, decent food
inc Sun lunch, M&B and guest beers
(David Hanley); [Rother St], *White Swan*:
Another Forte hotel, with friendly old-
fashioned heavy-beamed bar, leather
armchairs, ancient settles and fine oak
panelling, lunchtime bar snacks, good
morning coffee and teas, quick friendly
service; 16th-c mural of Tobias, the Angel
and the Fish; children in eating area;
bedrooms *(George Atkinson, G S and A
Jaques, LYM)*; [Church St], *Windmill*:
Whitbreads-related and other real ales,
wide choice of good food inc vegetarian,
good atmosphere; very busy *(Richard
Lewis)*

Stretton on Dunsmore, War [off A45 and
A423; SP4172], *Shoulder of Mutton*:
Character friendly village pub with tiny
snug panelled public bar unaltered since
Victorian times, particularly well kept M &
B Mild and Brew XI on handpump, cards
and dominoes, pictures of old Coventry,
spotless furniture; also spacious lounge
built in the 50s with appropriate decor and
two darts boards; closed Mon-Thurs
lunchtime *(Ted George, Pete Baker)*

Stretton on Fosse, War [off A429; SP2238],
Plough: Large lounge and smaller bar with
darts and fruit machine, good value pub
food, Flowers Original and Theakstons Old
Peculier *(Graham Reeve)*

☆ **Studley**, War [Icknield St Dr; left turn off
A435, going N from B4093 roundabout;
SP0763], *Old Washford Mill*: Lots of
variety in attractive converted watermill,
old mill machinery, different levels, quiet
alcoves, good value food in varying styles
from pubby through pizzas and wine bar to
restaurant, provision for children, real ales
tapped from the cask, country wines; pretty

waterside gardens with good play area, ducks and black swan *(Karen Simpson, Paul Williams, Dave and Jane Lee, LYM)*
Studley [Alcester Rd (A435)], *Little Lark*: Friendly bustle in good 'Little' pub, more of a true local than most, well kept Lumphammer, good Yorkshire pudding, lots of printing equipment (this is where they do the group's newsletter) *(David and Shelia)*

☆ **Sulgrave**, Northants [Manor Rd; SP5545], *Star*: Lots of curios in cosy and spotless rambling inn with inviting range of good reasonably priced straightforward bar food, particularly well kept Hook Norton Best and other real ales, good interesting wines, inglenook with log fire (and skeleton), piped modern jazz, friendly staff; pleasant village dominated by manor – home of George Washington's forebears; bedrooms with own bathrooms *(Steve Goodchild, Heather Couper, Nigel Herbert, G T O'Connell)*

☆ **Sutton Bassett**, Northants [SP7790], *Queens Head*: Warm Irish welcome in peaceful village pub now doing really good if not cheap food using herbs from own garden – ploughman's, ham, chicken and cheese pancake, beef in mustard sauce, steaks all praised; expanding collection of changing well kept ales such as Marstons Pedigree, Hardys & Hansons, Shepherd Neame Spitfire, Smiles Bitter and Exhibition, Tetleys and Wadworths 6X, upstairs restaurant; some seats out beyond car park *(Joan and Michel Hooper-Immins, Stephen and Julie Brown)*
Syresham, Northants [off A43 Brackley—Towcester; SP6241], *Kings Head*: Quaint old pub with restaurant and two bars, dark beams, brasses, pictures, real fire; quiet piped pop music, fruit machine, pool and darts; Banks's, food inc vegetarian dishes, polite service, garden; children welcome *(Mark and Diane Grist)*
Sywell, Northants [Overstone Rd; off A43 NE of Northampton; SP8167], *Horseshoe*: Modern Chef & Brewer pub with central lounge bar and areas off inc a no-smoking one; reasonably good value food (high chairs provided), fresh flowers, Ruddles; darts, pool, fruit machine, juke box or piped pop music; largish garden with picnic-table sets and slide *(CW, JW)*

☆ **Thorpe Mandeville**, Northants [former B4525; SP5344], *Three Conies*: Attractive 1622 creeper-clad pub with lots of seats in big garden, lounge with brasses and beams, some stripped stonework, gin trap over inglenook fireplace, horse-racing photographs and conversation, furnishings to suit the old building; well kept Hook Norton and Old Hookey on handpump, good choice of wines and spirits, friendly service, games room, usual bar food, restaurant; children welcome *(Mrs M Shannon, George Atkinson, Graham and Karen Oddey, L Walker, JJW, CMW, Joan and Ian Wilson, LYM)*

☆ **Thorpe Waterville**, Northants [A605 Thrapston—Oundle; TL0281], *Fox*: Friendly old pub with wide range of enjoyable generous food inc huge steaks, reasonable prices, coal fire, Charles Wells ales, log-effect fire, quiet piped music, weekend restaurant, welcoming prompt service; children allowed, no dogs, small garden with play area *(Mr and Mrs J Back, Mrs Meg Hamilton, John and Pam Adams, David and Michelle Hedges)*
Tipton, W Mid [Lower Church Lane; opp Police Stn; SO9592], *Old Court House*: Large well renovated open-plan pub with wide range of beers like Home Bitter, Marstons Pedigree and Theakstons XB, Old Peculier and Mild and tasty food from simple menu; friendly and comfortable *(Graham Reeve, T Henwood)*

☆ **Titchmarsh**, Northants [village signed from A604 and A605, just E of Thrapston; TL0279], *Wheatsheaf*: Popular and comfortably extended evening dining pub, good local atmosphere, good home-made bar food, Hook Norton and Marstons Pedigree, lots of exposed stonework, golfing memorabilia, pool room, restaurant, cat and dogs, piped music; children allowed in eating areas; closed Mon evening, weekday lunchtimes *(Richard W Chew, George Atkinson, LYM)*

☆ **Towcester**, Northants [Watling St; SP6948], *Saracens Head*: Attractive coaching inn expansively refurbished to emphasise its old features, short but good range of food, Victorian dining room, Charles Wells Eagle and Bomardier, interesting *Pickwick Papers* connections; well equipped bedrooms *(Ian Phillips, Brig J S Green, LYM)*
Towcester [104 Watling St], *Brave Old Oak*: Just reopened, beautifully restored with panelling, heraldic shields, carpets and nice furnishings, very friendly service, decent food, Banks's real ales; family room; fruit machine, piped music and lots of shields on walls; bedrooms *(George Atkinson)*; [Watling St; A5 S, opp racecourse], *Folly*: Thatched pub with decent cheap food, well kept Charles Wells ales, friendly staff; new play equipment in back garden *(Christopher and Sharon Hayle, Helen Jeanes)*

☆ **Ufton**, War [White Hart Lane; just off A425 Daventry—Leamington, towards Bascote; SP3761], *White Hart*: Improved choice of good value food inc fine curry, lots of vegetarian dishes, good steaks and puddings, in 400-year-old beamed pub with good views from hilltop garden (hatch service out here); well kept Davenports and Tetleys, good friendly service; boules – Mon is beginners' night *(K R Flack, Steve and Liz Tilley, W H and E Thomas)*
Wakerley, Northants [Main St; SP9599], *Exeter Arms*: Former hunting lodge nr Wakerley Woods, with good views and walks over Welland Valley, two connecting rooms with woodburner, local

photographs, friendly black labrador, Adnams Broadside, Batemans XB and Marstons Pedigree on handpump, good value food (not Mon); piped music, fruit machine, occasional live music *(CMW, JJW)*

Walgrave, Northants [Zion Hill; off A43 Northampton—Kettering; SP8072], *Royal Oak*: Old ironstone building with hardworking newish tenants, bar and dining lounge split into smaller areas, Morrells, Wadworths 6X, good coffee, wide choice of good food; piped music, pictures for sale; children welcome *(George Atkinson)*

Walsall, W Mid [John St; properly the New Inn; SP0198], *Pretty Bricks*: Useful economical food served promptly in pleasant Victorian backstreet local, well kept Ansells Bitter and Mild, Ind Coope Burton and a guest such as Wadworths 6X, unobtrusive piped music; children may be allowed *(Graham Reeve, Ross Lockley)*

Warmington, Northants [off A605 NE of Oundle; TL0791], *Red Lion*: Shiny and welcoming, affable landlord, well kept beers inc guest, good food at good prices *(John Dyer)*

☆ **Warwick** [Guy's Cliffe; A429 just N], *Saxon Mill*: Converted mill with long history, wheel turning slowly behind glass, mill race under glass floor-panel, tables in pleasant setting outside looking out to the weir; inside is straightforward Harvester family eating pub, well kept Courage-related ales, summer weekend barbecues, good play area; open all day *(Graham and Belinda Staplehurst, LYM)*

☆ **Warwick** [11 Church St], *Zetland Arms*: Friendly newish licensees in pleasant no-frills town pub with limited choice of cheap bar food (not weekend evenings), well kept Davenports and Tetleys, quick service, newly decorated functional lounge bar; sheltered garden surprisingly good – secluded, interestingly planted, lovingly kept; children may be allowed; bedrooms, sharing bathroom *(Michael and Derek Slade, Brad and Joni Nelson, LYM)*

Warwick [11 Market Pl], *Tilted Wig*: Very popular, with imaginative range of real ales such as Ansells, Arrols 80/-, Judges Barristers and Tetleys; extensive range of food (not Sun evening), very friendly licensees; live jazz and folk Sun evening *(Richard Lewis)*

Wednesbury, W Mid [Myvod Rd, off A461; SP0095], *Myvod*: Large busy pub with attractive lounge, traditional bar, welcoming staff, reasonably priced lunchtime bar meals, well kept Bass, Hook Norton Old Hookey, Theakstons XB and Wadworths 6X, children's room; terrace and garden with rubber-floored play area; unobtrusive piped music; open all day *(Mr and Mrs P Roberts)*

☆ **Weedon**, Northants [3 miles from M1 junction 16; A45 towards Daventry; SP6259], *Heart of England*: Particularly

well kept Theakstons Bitter and XB with several often interesting guest beers in attractively refurbished pub with busy bar, well served reasonably priced good food inc some unusual dishes in panelled lounge/eating area, restaurant with new conservatory, good friendly easy-going service, picnic-table sets in garden with access to Grand Union Canal; piped music, children welcome; good value pine-furnished bedrooms *(George Atkinson, Robin Tillbrook, Peter Phillips, CW, JW, Peter J Kearns)*

Weedon [Stowe Hill; A5, S – OS Sheet 152 map ref 641589], *Narrow Boat*: Spacious terrace and big garden sweeping down to Grand Union Canal, warm atmosphere in busy well worn-in main bar, good range of bar food in high-raftered ex-kitchen family dining room, summer barbecues, well kept Charles Wells ales with a guest such as Adnams; good generous Cantonese restaurant, spacious and airy, with canal and country views (booking advised Sat); very busy in summer; bedrooms in recent motel extension *(David Tonkin, Bill Sykes, LYM)*; [A45/A5], *Crossroads*: Spacious and smartly refurbished Greenalls pub with useful bar food, Greenalls Original and Tetleys, light and airy separate all-day coffee bar, restaurant; bedrooms comfortable and attractive *(George Atkinson, LYM)*

☆ **Welford**, Northants [SP6480], *Shoulder of Mutton*: Arches between open-plan bar areas in friendly and well kept 17th-c inn with sensibly priced straightforward food (not Thurs) inc children's dishes, Batemans XB and Ruddles Best, good coffee, piped music; skittle room, good back garden with play area, lovely village nr canal marina *(George Atkinson)*

Welford, *Wharf*: Castellated folly by marina with good well served food and friendly staff – very pleasant place; bedrooms *(George Atkinson)*

☆ **Welford on Avon**, War [High St (Binton Rd); SP1452], *Bell*: Convivial pub with dark-timbered low-beamed lounge, flagstoned public bar with darts, pool and so forth, open fires, friendly service, well kept Flowers IPA and Original, generous straightforward food from sandwiches to steaks, conservatory; piped music; tables in pretty garden and back courtyard; children allowed in conservatory or restaurant; attractive riverside village *(John Radford, Dorothee and Dennis Glover, Bob and Maggie Atherton, R A Gabriel, George Atkinson, LYM)*

☆ **Welford on Avon** [Maypole], *Shakespeare*: Newish licensees doing well in comfortable dining pub with generous food inc good home-made puddings, well kept Whitbreads-related real ales, good choice of wines by the glass, attractive garden *(Peter Lloyd, A H Thomas)*

Welford on Avon [Binton Bridges; SP1455], *Four Alls*: Huge helpings of waitress-served food in Whitbreads dining pub with nice garden *(Steve and Liz Tilley)*

West Bromwich, W Mid [High St – pedestrianised part; SP0091], *Great Western*: Pleasant interior with plenty of room to sit down, friendly staff, good value cheap food, Holt Plant & Deakins ales *(Richard Waller)*; [High St], *Wheatsheaf*: Fairly basic popular pub with particularly well kept Holdens beers on handpump, good value if limited food inc good hot pork sandwiches *(Keith and Ann Dibble)*

☆ **Whatcote**, War [SP2944], *Royal Oak*: Extremely quaint and attractive partly 12th-c low-ceilinged local with huge inglenook, small rooms, vivid Civil War connections, lots to look at, animal skins on wall; wide choice of decent straightforward bar food, two or more real ales such as Marstons Pedigree, picnic-table sets outside; children in eating area; service can slow *(Mrs J Oakes, L Walker, Dorothy and David Young, Ann and Bob Westbrook, LYM)*

Wicken, Northants [Deanshanger Rd; SP7439], *Wicken Arms*: Pleasant little pub, rather plain inside, with mix of new pine and ancient beams; very laid-back atmosphere, friendly chatty staff, decent bar food inc Sun lunch, Greene King IPA and Abbot on handpump, two dogs and a cat; piped music, darts; children welcome; picnic-table sets in garden; bedrooms *(George Atkinson, JJW, CMW)*

Willenhall, W Mid [Wolverhampton St; SO9698], *Brewers Droop*: Fine choice of interesting changing well kept ales, good value simple lunches, evening meals Fri/Sat; folk music upstairs Thurs *(Graham Reeve)*; [Wolverhampton Rd, very close to M6 Junction 10], *Bridge*: Simple place with warm log fire, very cheap bar food and drinks *(TBB)*; [Upper Lichfield St], *M A D O'Rourkes Kipper House*: Enjoyable 'Little' pub with really friendly locals; open all day Fri/Sat *(David and Shelia)*

☆ **Willey**, War [just off A5, N of A427 junction; SP4984], *Old Watling*: Attractive layout with plenty of cosy corners in neatly kept rooms around bar, good furnishings, polished flagstones, stripped masonry, open fire, quick friendly service, generous good value enterprising bar food, well kept Adnams's, Banks's and Courage-related beers *(Mrs P J Pearce, Ted George, Geoff Lee)*

☆ **Wilmcote**, War [The Green; 3 miles NW of Stratford, just off new A46 bypass;

SP1657], *Swan House*: Genteel country hotel with front terrace overlooking Mary Arden's cottage, glass-topped well in 18th-c beamed lounge, good home-made food inc sizzle steaks in bar and restaurant, well kept Hook Norton Best and Theakston XB, quick friendly service; tables in back garden; comfortable bedrooms *(C H and P Stride, Joan and Michel Hooper-Immins, Bill Sykes)*

Wilmcote [Aston Cantlow Rd], *Masons Arms*: Friendly local, neat and snug, with good generous lunches – can eat in restaurant for same price as bar; well kept Whitbreads-related ales *(Peter Lloyd, A H Thomas)*

☆ **Wixford**, War [SP0954], *Three Horseshoes*: Good value generous food inc good home-made soups, casseroles, pasta dishes and home-made puddings, good service under friendly and hardworking new landlord *(Peter Lloyd, John Close)*

Wollaston, Northants [off A509 S of Wellingborough; SP9163], *Nags Head*: Huge choice of well cooked food and puddings cooked to order *(Mrs Meg Hamilton)*

☆ **Wolverhampton**, W Mid [Sun St; SO9198], *Great Western*: Lively backstreet pub with very promptly served good value plain food inc huge cheap filled cobs, lots of railway memorabilia, up to six well kept real ales inc Bathams and Holdens, three bar areas, smart but friendly staff, tables in yard with good barbecues; parking limited lunchtime *(Ross Lockley, DAV, J Dwane, Graham Reeve, Mr and Mrs H S Hill)*

Wolvey, War [nr M65 junction 1; SP4287], *Blue Pig*: Pleasantly unpretentious Chef & Brewer with friendly helpful staff, good range of standard sensibly priced food, series of small areas separated by stone pillars *(George Atkinson, Geoff Lee)*

Wolvey Heath, War [SP4390], *Axe & Compass*: Popular for big helpings of good food from sandwiches up, well kept Bass, Hook Norton Best, Brew XI and decent wines, good neat staff – friendly even on busy evenings; restaurant *(Steve de Mellow, the Monday Club)*

Yelvertoft, Northants [49 High St; SP5975], *Knightley Arms*: Decent food in small dining area with plates, brasses and pictures, log fire, two very friendly Hungarian viszlas, Courage-related ales and Marstons Pedigree, good coffee; tables in garden *(George Atkinson)*

The letters and figures after the name of each town are its Ordnance Survey map reference. *How to use the Guide* at the beginning of the book explains how it helps you find a pub, in road atlases or large-scale maps as well as in our own maps.

Norfolk

The Saracens Head near Erpingham stands out for inventive food in civilised but very individual and friendly surroundings – and walks away with our award as Norfolk Dining Pub of the Year for the second year running. But quite a few other pubs here are also very good for enjoyable meals out, and are currently doing very well in readers' reports: the Black Boys at Aldborough, the Ratcatchers at Cawston, the Adam & Eve in Norwich (tremendous character for a city pub), the Hare Arms at Stow Bardolph, the Red Lion at Stiffkey, and Darbys at Swanton Morley. It's important to underline this quality aspect, as the cost of eating out in Norfolk pubs tends to be rather on the high side. Beer prices are around the national average – higher in pubs getting their beers from the national chains, lower in pubs supplied by the regional brewer Greene King, or other more or less local brewers (we found the cheery Ferry in its lovely position on the River Yare at Reedham selling Charles Wells from Bedfordshire relatively very cheaply). Particularly good local beers are those from Woodfordes, and their new pub the Fur & Feather at Woodbastwick, right by the brewery, is a fine place to try them. It's a new main entry; another here is the Crown at Colkirk – an unpretentious place with a splendid approach to wines by the glass. Other places doing particularly well at the moment are the Kings Arms in Blakeney, the Rose & Crown at Snettisham, the Chequers at Thompson, the Lifeboat at Thornham, the Old Ram at Tivetshall St Mary and the Fishermans Return at Winterton on Sea. In the Lucky Dip at the end of the chapter, pubs currently showing well include the White Horse in Blakeney, Jolly Sailors at Brancaster Staithe, both entries at Cley next the Sea, the Ugly Bug at Colton, Crown at Gayton, Hill House at Happisburgh, Hare & Hounds at Hempstead, Swan at Hilborough, Nelsons Head at Horsey, Crown at Mundford, Barton Angler at Neatishead, Sculthorpe Mill at the village of that name, and Crown in Wells next the Sea. Norwich has a very wide variety of worthwhile pubs.

ALDBOROUGH TG1834 Map 8

Black Boys

Signposted off A140 S of Roughton

Nicely set beside the broad village green where there is summer cricket and winter football, this friendly and pretty pub places quite an emphasis on the popular food. All the meals are home-made using fresh produce: sandwiches, seafood, cheddar and garlic or chicken, mushroom and stilton pies (£5.95), vegetarian dishes like cheddar, spinach and walnut crêpes or sweet and sour avocado on noodles, gammon with banana, honey and cider or chicken or pork and prawn stir-fry (£6.20), beef and Guinness or kidney, bacon and liver steamed puddings (£6.95), and fresh whole plaice (£7.95); there are bar snacks at lunchtime, a Sunday roast, and winter game dishes (the game pudding is marvellous); particularly good vegetables. The neatly-kept and comfortable bar has pleasantly low-key furnishings such as brocaded chairs, green leatherette button-back wall banquettes and cast-iron-framed tables, as well as old local photographs, a log fire and lots of fresh flowers; two friendly cats. Well kept Ind Coope Burton and Tetleys on handpump, decent wines. There are tables outside in the little courtyard and colourful flowering tubs and hanging baskets. *(Recommended by Mrs E Stratton, Sheila and Brian Wilson, R C Vincent, A E Barwick, Rita Horridge, Frank Davidson)*

Pubmaster ~ Tenants Ron and Margaret McDermid ~ Real ale ~ Meals and snacks (not Mon) ~ Restaurant ~ (01263) 768086 ~ Children in eating area of bar ~ Open 12-3, 7-11; all day in summer

BLAKENEY TG0243 Map 8

Kings Arms
West Gate St

The friendly licensees in this characterful white cottage work hard to create a relaxed and welcoming atmosphere in the three simply furnished, knocked-together rooms – two of which are no smoking; there are baby-changing facilities, too. The smallest cartoon gallery in England is in what used to be a telephone kiosk, and other interesting pictures include work by local artists and some interesting photographs of the licensees' theatrical careers. A wide range of bar food at lunchtime includes tasty dishes like soup (£1.70), sandwiches (from £1.10), filled baked potatoes (from £2.60), ploughman's (from £3.50), vegetable lasagne (£3.90), fresh local fish like mussels (winter only), crab (summer only), haddock or cod (£4.90), or grilled trout (£6, evenings only), evening salads (from £6.50), steaks (£9.50), daily specials, puddings such as home-made crumble (from £2.20), children's menu (£2.75). Well kept Morlands Old Speckled Hen, Ruddles County, Websters Yorkshire and Woodfordes Wherry and Nog on handpump; freshly squeezed fruit juice. Darts, dominoes and fruit machine. The large garden has lots of tables and chairs and a separate, equipped children's area. The date 1760 is picked out in black tiles on the red roof. As it's not far from the harbour, this pretty white cottage can get crowded at peak times. *(Recommended by Thomas Nott, David and Michelle Hedges, L Walker, Bill Edwards, Peter and Pat Grogley, Sue Demont, Tim Barrow, Charles Bardswell, Riley and Jean Coles, John Beeken, Dr N Hardwick, Anthony Barnes)*

Free house ~ Licensees Howard and Marjorie Davies ~ Real ale ~ Meals and snacks (all day weekends and school holidays) ~ (01263) 740341 ~ Children welcome ~ Open 11-11 ~ Self-catering flatlets available upstairs

BLICKLING TG1728 Map 8

Buckinghamshire Arms
Off B1354 N of Aylsham

Often busy in summer – this Jacobean inn stands at the gates of Blickling Hall – with picnic-table sets under cocktail parasols on the lawn (they serve food from an out-building here in summer), and a climbing frame, slide and swing. Inside, the small front snug is simply furnished with fabric cushioned banquettes, and has pictures and memorabilia of bare knuckle fighters (especially Jem Mace the Norfolk-born world champion), while the bigger lounge has neatly built-in pews, stripped deal tables, and landscapes and cockfighting prints. Bar food includes home-made soup (£1.95), sandwiches (from £1.85), a good, proper ploughman's (£4.50), game, pork and port wine pie (£4.75), home-made specials such as baked gammon in madeira sauce (£5.25), baked spiced crab au gratin (£5.75), steak and mushroom crumble in Adnams ale (£6.75), and home-made puddings (£2.30). Well kept Adnams Best and Broadside, Everards Tiger, Sam Smiths Museum, and Woodfordes Wherry and Baldric on handpump; good selection of wines. Blickling Hall is open from April to mid-October only, and closed Mondays and Thursdays, though you can walk through the park at any time. *(Recommended by Peter Plumridge, Paul Cartledge, Sue Demont, Tim Barrow, Thomas Nott, Frank Cummins, Heather M N Robson)*

Free house ~ Licensees Danny and Wendy Keen ~ Real ale ~ Meals and snacks (11.30-2.30, 6-9) ~ Restaurant ~ Aylsham (01263) 732133 ~ Children in restaurant ~ Open 11-3, 6-11 ~ Three double bedrooms: £45S/£60S

BURNHAM MARKET TF8342 Map 8

Hoste Arms 🛏️
The Green (B1155)

In an attractive village, this rather civilised and handsome 17th-c hotel has a couple of convivial bars with massive log fires; the panelled bar on the right has a series of watercolours showing local scenes of what you might see on various walks from the hotel, and there's a bow-windowed bar on the left. At the back there's a new conservatory bar where the good bar food is served: home-made soup (£2), home-made pâté (£2.95), half-a-dozen local oysters (£4.25), pasta with creamy pesto sauce or ham hock with a grainy mustard sauce (£5.25), home-made crabcakes with a bigerade sauce (£5.50), venison, smoked bacon and mushroom pie (£6.50), chicken stir-fry (£6.75), steaks (from £8.95), daily specials, puddings (£2.50), and children's meals (£2.95); non-resident breakfast (£6.75), morning coffee, afternoon tea, and various themed food evenings. In the partly no-smoking restaurant, the owner may play the grand piano. Well kept Woodfordes Wherry and guest beers, good wine list, good choice of malt whiskies, and fresh orange juice; nice sitting room, and professional service by friendly staff. At the back is a pleasant garden with tables on a terrace. It can be busy at weekends. *(Recommended by Iain Baillie, Charles Bardswell, Peter and Pat Frogley, Mrs F M Halle, John Wooll, Mrs R Cotgreave, Alan Reid, Andrew Preston, John Whitehead)*

Free house ~ Licensees Pauline Osler, Paul Whittome ~ Real ale ~ Meals and snacks (till 10pm summer; set lunch only 25 Dec) ~ Restaurant ~ (01328) 738257 ~ Children welcome ~ Jazz or R&B Mon and Fri ~ Open 11-11; 11-3, 6-11 in winter ~ Bedrooms: £47B/£72B

BURNHAM THORPE TF8541 Map 8

Lord Nelson
Village signposted from B1155 and B1355, near Burnham Market

Enthusiastic new licensees have taken over this genuinely unspoilt and untouched pub, but are very keen that any original features should remain. They have re-opened the 'Ward Room' which has been closed for around 20 years and has flagstones, an open fire, and Nelson pictures, and will be used as a no-smoking eating room. The original bar – there's no bar counter and they certainly don't plan to install one – is just a small room with well waxed antique settles on the worn red flooring tiles and interesting Nelson pictures; the original fireplace is to be opened up with its three original smoke ovens, and the Nelson memorabilia will continue to grow. Straightforward bar food includes home-made soup (£1.50), sandwiches (from £1.70), sausage and egg (£2.90), ploughman's or English breakfast (£3.50), salads or omelettes (from £3.50), home-made daily specials like a pie of the day or lasagne, and children's meals. Well kept Greene King IPA, Abbot and Mild is tapped from the cask in a back stillroom, and there's an unusual rum concoction called Nelson's Blood; darts, shove-ha'penny, dominoes, and piped music. Inside lavatories are planned, they hope to convert the existing barn into a restaurant, and aim to make families more welcome; the children's big play area is to be developed; boules. *(Recommended by Alan Reid, Huw and Carolyn Lewis, Charles Bardswell, Bill Edwards, P G Plumridge, Peter and Pat Frogley; more reports on the new regime, please)*

Greene King ~ Lease: Lucy Stafford ~ Real ale ~ Meals and snacks ~ (01328) 738241 ~ Children welcome ~ Live music once a month ~ Open 11-4, 5.30-11

CASTLE ACRE TF8115 Map 8

Ostrich £
Stocks Green; village signposted from A1065 N of Swaffham; OS Sheet 144 map reference 815153

On the tree-lined green, this mainly 18th-c inn still has some signs of its older origins, with exposed 16th-c masonry and beams and trusses in the high ceiling. The L-shaped, low-ceilinged front bar has a huge old fireplace with a swinging potyard below its low mantelbeam (which may be used in winter for cooking soups and hams), straightforward furnishings, and big photographs of the local sights on the walls. Bar food includes sandwiches (from £1), various basket meals (from £1.50), pizzas (from £1.70), several ploughman's (from £2.50), and grills (from £5); children's meals (from £1). Well kept Greene King IPA, Abbot, Mild and Rayments on handpump; dominoes, cribbage, fruit machine, and piped music; picnic-table sets in the sheltered garden. There's a Cluniac monastery in the village, as well as the remains of a Norman castle. *(Recommended by Peter and Pat Frogley, J R Williams, Charles Bardswell, Dr and Mrs M Bailey, Sue Anderson, Phil Copleston, Wayne Brindle, R C Vincent, Michael Sargent, D Goodger, Mr and Mrs Ray, John and Elizabeth Gwynne, Rita Horridge, John Wooll)*

Greene King ~ Tenant Ray Wakelen ~ Real ale ~ Meals and snacks (till 10.30pm; not 25/26 Dec) ~ Swaffham (01760) 755398 ~ Children in decent family room only ~ Jazz every 2nd and 3rd Weds of month, folk last Weds of month ~ Open 12-2.30, 7-11 ~ Bedrooms: £15S/£30S

CAWSTON TG1323 Map 8

Ratcatchers ♀

Eastgate, 1 mile S of village; heading N from Norwich on B1149 turn left towards Haveringland at crossroads ½ mile before the B1145 turn to Cawston itself

The friendly licensees in this busy dining pub are working hard to make their pub even more appealing to customers. They've replaced their furniture with interesting solid wood tables and dining chairs bought at local auctions, are hoping to increase their real ale range, and have improved their wine list. The food continues to be the main draw, though, and regularly wins national awards. They bake their own bread, make their own herb oils, chutney, purées and stocks, pickle their own samphire and use no bought-in frozen dishes at all – there may be a 30-40 minute wait as everything is cooked to order: soups (£1.95), sandwiches (from £1.95), Norfolk mushrooms in garlic, basil and tomatoes with garlic bread (£4.25), local butcher's sausages and mash with rich onion and red wine gravy (£4.65), omelettes using three free-range eggs (from £4.65), ploughman's (£4.95), salads (from £4.95), vegetable pie (£5.45), Indonesian vegetarian stir-fry (£5.75), steak and kidney pie or lasagne (£5.95), steaks (from £9.35; various sauce from £1.95), big mixed grills (from £11.65; they need 24 hours' notice), puddings like rum baba or summer pudding (from £2.85), children's meals (£3.45), and daily specials such as pike, salmon and prawn in a herb pancake with Noilly Prat sauce (£2.95), Cromer crab with cheese, English mustard and cream and their own pickled samphire (£3.85), osso bucco (£7.85), sautéed monkfish, flamed in vodka, with pink peppercorns and cream (£8.65), braised veal (£9.65), and half a Norfolk duckling with orange and Cointreau sauce (£11.95); British cheese menu. It's pretty much essential to book most evenings, as they get very busy – service may slow down then. Well kept real ales on handpump such as Hancocks HB, Shepherd Neame Spitfire, and Wadworths 6X; open fires and piped music. As well as the L-shaped beamed bar, there's a quieter and cosier no-smoking, candlelit dining room on the right. *(Recommended by Patrick Clancy, Mrs M E Parry-Jones, K D Day, Mr and Mrs J F Baskerville, John and Christine Simpson, Dr G W Barnett, Paul Cartledge, Frank Cummins, Mike and Wendy Proctor, Werner Arend)*

Free house ~ Licensees Eugene and Jill Charlier ~ Real ale ~ Meals and snacks (till 10pm) ~ Restaurant ~ (01603) 871430 ~ Children in eating area and restaurant ~ Open 11.45-2.30, 6-11; closed 25/26 Dec

COLKIRK TF9126 Map 8

Crown ♀

Village signposted off B1146 S of Fakenham; and off A1065

By its own neat bowling green in an attractive and peacefully prosperous village, this unpretentious red-brick building has a wide choice of good food including some original dishes, but has kept its identity as a true village pub rather than becoming just another dining pub. It's comfortable and welcoming, with solid straightforward country furniture, rugs and flooring tiles, open fires in both public bar and the small lounge (the dining room off is pleasantly informal), and sympathetic lighting. There's a really friendly atmosphere. Very quickly served, good, straightforward, well presented food includes soup (£1.65), pâté (£2.80), mushrooms and prawns in garlic (£3), minute steak with peppercorns (£5.50), chicken in Thai or stilton sauces or gammon and egg (£5.75), and daily specials such as devilled kidneys (£5.25), fresh fish like trout fillets with mustard sauce, grilled lemon sole, crab or lobster salads (from £6.50), and various alcoholic puddings. Friendly and helpful landlord, well kept Greene King IPA, Abbot and Rayments on handpump; they'll open any bottle of wine you want from their list of several dozen – even for just a glass; malt whiskies; darts, table skittles, dominoes, fruit machine. There are tables out behind. *(Recommended by E M Goodman-Smith, Michael Sargent, Sue Anderson, Phil Copleston, Gwen and Peter Andrews, Frank Davidson)*

Greene King ~ Tenant P Whitmore ~ Real ale ~ Meals and snacks (service stops at 1.30 on Sunday); not 25/26 Dec ~ (01328) 862172 ~ Children in lounge and dining area ~ Open 11-3, 6-11

DERSINGHAM TF6830 Map 8

Feathers 🍺

Manor Road; B1440 towards Sandringham

In summer, the friendly licensee here keeps six real ales on handpump (three in winter). As well as their Adnams and M & B Brew XI, they keep a changing range of real ales such as Robinwood Old Fart, Titanic Premium, Uley Pigs Ear and Woodfordes Baldrick, Nelsons Revenge or Wherry. The two relaxed and welcoming bars are comfortably furnished with soft plush seats, wall settles, carved wooden chairs, and dark panelling and carving, and one of the fireplaces is still dominated by the Prince of Wales' feathers (Edward VII used to visit here), flanked by two brass warming pans. The main room opens on to a small terrace overlooking the neatly landscaped garden, which has a play area with swings, slide, and sand-pit; the garden has recently had lots more seats added. Bar food includes sandwiches (from £1.20), soup (£1.50), smoked mackerel or ploughman's (£3.25), turkey and ham pie (£3.75), daily specials such as beef curry or liver and onions (around £3.95), puddings (from £1.50) and children's meals (£1.60). Dominoes, cribbage, fruit machine, piped music. They can get busy in summer. *(Recommended by Mrs F M Halle, John Wooll, Mr and Mrs Ray, Eric Locker, Charles Bardswell, Rita Horridge, Mark J Hydes, R C Vincent, George Atkinson)*

Charringtons ~ Lease Tony and Maxine Martin ~ Real ale ~ Meals and snacks (till 10pm) ~ Restaurant (not Sun evening) ~ Dersingham (01485) 540207 ~ Children welcome ~ Open 11-2.30, 5.30-11; closed evening 25 Dec ~ Bedrooms: £25/£40

ERPINGHAM TG1631 Map 8

Saracens Head 🍽️ 🛏️ 🍷

Address is Wolterton – not shown on many maps; Erpingham signed off A140 N of Aylsham, keep on through Calthorpe, then where road bends right take the straight-ahead turn-off signposted Wolterton

Norfolk Dining Pub of the Year

Run by a helpful and amusing landlord, this rather remote and certainly civilised redbrick inn is doing very well at the moment. The two-room bar is simple and stylish, with high ceilings and tall windows giving a feeling of space, though it's not large, and around the terracotta walls are a mix of seats from built-in leather wall settles to wicker fireside chairs, solid-colour carpets and curtains, log fires and flowers on the mantelpieces. It looks out on a charming old-fashioned gravel stableyard with picnic-table sets. There's a pretty little four-table parlour on the right – cheerful nursery colours, and another big log fire, and this year they've improved their eating area at the back of the building. Much of the emphasis here is on the extremely good food – booking is virtually essential. Changing regularly, there might be gutsy tomato soup (£2.50), stilton and orange pâté (£3.50), very good vignotte cheese tartlets and real tomato sauce, Morston mussels in cider and cream or yummy deep-fried brie and apricot sauce (£3.95; £6.50 main course), grilled fillet of large Bure Valley trout (£6.50), filo parcels of spinach and stilton with pear sauce (£6.95), grilled fresh halibut fillet with fresh fennel (£7.25), pot roast tender leg of lamb with herbs and cream (£7.70), sirloin steak (£10.25), and puddings like sticky brown bread and butter pudding or lemon tart (£2.50); two-course lunches (£4.50), two-course Sunday supper (£5.50), and three-course monthly feasts (£11.50). Very well kept Adnams Bitter and Broadside and a guest beer such as Batemans XXXB, Courage Directors and Elgoods Greyhound on handpump, decent whiskies, good wines; friendly service. *(Recommended by John and Tessa Rainsford, Peter and Pat Frogley, John and Christine Simpson, BHP, Rita Horridge, Mrs D Morton, Sue Demont, Tim Barrow, Dr and Mrs M Bailey, Charles Bardswell, Thomas Nott, Nick and Carolyn Carter, Frank Cummins, Phil and Sue Pearce, Anthony Barnes, WAH, John Wooll, JM, PM, C R Whitham)*

Free house ~ Licensee Robert Dawson-Smith ~ Real ale ~ Meals and snacks (till 10pm) ~ (01263) 768909 ~ Well behaved children welcome ~ Open 11-3, 6-11; closed 25 Dec ~ Bedrooms: £30B/£45B

HOLKHAM TF8943 Map 8

Victoria

A149 on Burnham Overy Staithe—Wells-next-the-Sea rd; near Holkham Hall

Handy for both Holkham Hall and the sandy shores and nature reserves, this pleasant and neatly kept brick-and-flint inn has several homely communicating rooms: simple furnishings, leatherette wall banquettes, stools and dining chairs, plants and paintings, and in one room some easy chairs; a separate comfortable lounge has seats in bay windows. Well kept Bass, Adnams Bitter and Mild, Greene King Abbot and IPA on handpump. Bar-bar food includes sandwiches, plough-man's (from £3.50), steak and kidney pie or fresh crab salad (£4.95), Holkham fish pie (£5.25), fresh fish like sole, cod, halibut or plaice (from £5.95), and steaks (from £8.95); dominoes, cribbage, piped music. There are tables behind in the former tiled stableyard, with more on a front corner terrace, looking across the neat flower-fringed front lawn to rich coastal pastures beyond the road. *(Recommended by Peter and Pat Frogley, S G MacSwiney, Charles Bardswell, Peter Griffiths, BHP, John Wooll)*

Free house ~ Lease: Victor Manning ~ Real ale ~ Meals and snacks ~ Restaurant ~ Fakenham (01328) 710469 ~ Children in eating area of bar ~ Open 11-3, 6-11; winter evening opening 7 ~ Bedrooms: £27.50B/£50B

HUNWORTH TG0635 Map 8

Hunny Bell

Village signposted off B roads S of Holt

This pleasant pub overlooks the village green and has a rather unusual sign outside. Inside, the cosy L-shaped bar has Windsor chairs around dark wooden tables, comfortable settees (some of which are grouped around the log fire) and Norfolk watercolours and pictures for sale hanging above the panelling dado. Well kept Adnams Best and Greene King IPA and Abbot, and Woodfordes Wherry on handpump, quite a few malt whiskies, and decent wines. Bar food includes sandwiches (from £1.75), soup (£1.85), home-made pasty (£2.25), ploughman's (£3), sausage and egg (£3.50), home-cooked ham (£4.50), salads (from £4.25; local crab £4.50), home-made steak and kidney pie (£4.50), vegetable lasagne (£4.75), evening steaks (from £8.50), puddings (from £2), and children's meals (£2.50). Darts, dominoes, cribbage and piped music. The garden is an especially pleasant place to sit on a nice day, when there's bar service to the tables on the lawn; children's play area and maybe weekend barbecues. Sally King's father runs the Kings Head at Letheringsett. *(Recommended by John and Elizabeth Gwynne, Peter and Pat Frogley, David and Michelle Hedges, Wayne Brindle,*

George Atkinson, Geoff Lee, Frank Davidson, John Whitehead)

Free house ~ Lease: Sally King ~ Real ale ~ Meals and snacks ~ Restaurant ~ (01263) 712300 ~ Children in own small area and in restaurant ~ Open 10.30-3, 5.30-11

KINGS LYNN TF6220 Map 8

Tudor Rose 🛏

St Nicholas St (just off Tuesday Market Place – main square)

A nunnery in the 15th c, this attractive half-timbered pub has two relaxed bars with friendly staff and chatty locals. The front one is quieter and quite small and snug, with high beams, reproduction squared panelling and a big wrought-iron wheelrim chandelier; the quite separate back bar is more spacious, with sturdy wall benches, video games, trivia, fruit machine and juke box. Good value home-made bar food includes soup (£1.60), sandwiches or home-made hoagies (from £1.50), stilton and leek bake (£2.75), ploughman's (£3.75), home-made chilli (£3.95), Greek salad (£4.95), home-cooked ham and egg (£3.50), steak and kidney or rabbit pies (£5.50), sirloin steak (£7.50), and puddings like delicious treacle tart. Well kept Bass, Boddingtons, Woodfordes Wherry and a guest beer on handpump, a fine choice of whiskies, and decent wines; the upstairs raftered restaurant is no smoking. There are seats in the garden. Bedrooms are simple and modern but comfortable, and some have a pretty view of St Nicholas's Chapel. *(Recommended by Anna Marsh, R C Vincent, Rita Horridge, John Wooll)*

Free house ~ Licensees John and Andrea Bull ~ Real ale ~ Meals and snacks ~ Restaurant ~ Kings Lynn (01553) 762824 ~ Children in eating area of bar and in restaurant ~ Maybe summer live music every two weeks ~ Open 11-11 ~ Bedrooms: £38.50B/£40(£50B)

LETHERINGSETT TG0538 Map 8

Kings Head

A148 just W of Holt

On a fine summer's day, the attractive garden with its ample seating is quite a bonus for this friendly country pub. Inside, the walls of the bar are decorated with interesting prints, pictures and other items, and a signed poem by John Betjeman, and there's a talking parrot in the entrance hall and two decorative cats (the white one is called Harrold). There's also a small plush lounge, and a separate games room with darts, pool, dominoes, cribbage, fruit machines and piped music. Reasonably priced bar food includes good helpings of sandwiches (from £1.75, toasties £2.50), ploughman's (£3), home-made pasty (£4), salads (from £4.25, local crab in season £4.50), home-cooked ham or home-made steak and kidney pie (£4.50), evening steaks (from £8.50), vegetable quiche (£4.75), and a good Sunday lunch. Well kept Adnams, Bass, and Greene King IPA and Abbot on handpump, a dozen malt whiskies, and good service. The spacious lawn has plenty of tables. The pub is in a very pleasant setting opposite a church with an unusual round tower and is near Letheringsett's interesting water mill. Dogs allowed. *(Recommended by Bill Edwards, Rita Horridge, John Wooll, R C Vincent, George Atkinson, Frank Cummins)*

Free house ~ Lease: Thomas King ~ Real ale ~ Meals and snacks ~ Restaurant (not Sun evening) ~ (01263) 712691 ~ Children welcome ~ Middle-of-the-road live music Mon ~ Open 11-3, 5.30-11

NORTH CREAKE TF8538 Map 8

Jolly Farmers

B1355 N of Fakenham

Both locals and visitors are fond of this pleasant, welcoming village pub. The two little bars are spotlessly kept, and have a chatty atmosphere (no piped music), and an open winter fire; in summer there's a display of dried flowers and around 40 gnomes, stealthily imported by customers who know that the landlord cannot stand the sight of them. Fresh fish is supplied locally (some comes direct from the fishermen at Wells, from £4.95), and most other dishes are home-made: lunchtime filled rolls (from £1.75), home-made pâté (£2.60), ploughman's (£3.75), steak, kidney and ale pie (£4.95), chicken breast with mushrooms, onions and garlic (£6.50), pork in cider and cream (£6.95), sirloin steak (£8.25), and specials such as king prawn curry or chicken in red wine (£5.50); they have been doing Thai food on Wednesday and Friday evenings. Well kept Bass and Greene King Abbot and IPA and Ind Coope Burton on handpump or tapped from the cask, decent wines; bar billiards, cribbage, dominoes and fruit machine; tables in sheltered garden. The flintstone village is charming. *(Recommended by John Wooll, John Beeken, Charles Bardswell, J L Raker)*

Pubmaster (Allied) ~ Tenant Peter Whitney ~ Real ale ~ Meals and snacks ~ Restaurant ~ (01328) 738185 ~ Children in restaurant ~ Open 11.30-2.30(3 Sat), 6-11

NORWICH TG2308 Map 8

Adam & Eve ♀

Bishopgate; follow Palace Street from Tombland N of the Cathedral

At lunchtime, this striking Dutch gabled pub – the city's oldest – is at its bustling best, and it is very pretty in summer with award-winning colourful flowers in tubs and hanging baskets, and seats out on the terrace. Inside, the downstairs bar is thought to date back some 700 years when it was an alehouse for the men building the cathedral, and the traditionally furnished bars have old-fashioned high-backed settles, one handsomely carved, cushioned benches built into partly panelled walls, and tiled or parquet floors; the snug room is no smoking. Big helpings of good value food include sandwiches, granary baps or filled french bread (from £1.65, excellent prawn £2.50), cheese and ale soup with a pastry top (£2.60), ploughman's (from £3), salads (from £3.40), shepherd's pie (£3.60), vegetable bake (£3.70), pork casseroled in cider and rosemary (£3.95), game pie (£4.10), puddings like home-made spicy bread and butter pudding (from £1.70), and daily specials such as steak and kidney pie, liver and bacon or cod Wellington (£4.10), and Sunday roast – pork, beef, lamb, chicken and vegetarian nut roast and five vegetables. Well kept Adnams Best, Ruddles County, and Wadworths 6X, with guest like Morlands Old Speckled Hen or John Smiths on handpump or tapped from the cask from a serving counter with a fine range of pewter tankards, a wide range of malt whiskies, several decent wines by the glass or bottle, and Addlestones cider. *(Recommended by R C Morgan, Andrew and Catherine Brian, Ian Phillips, Pat Carlen, Michael Badcock, John Wooll, Thomas Nott, Anthony Barnes, Brian Wainwright, D J and P M Taylor, Hazel Morgan, J Cox)*

Courage ~ Lease: Colin Burgess ~ Real ale ~ Meals and snacks (12-7) ~ Norwich (01603) 667423 ~ Children welcome ~ Open 11-11

REEDHAM TG4101 Map 5

Ferry

B1140 Beccles—Acle; the ferry here holds only two cars but goes back and forth continuously till 10pm, taking only a minute or so to cross – fare £2 per car, 25p pedestrians

It's fun to arrive at this popular pub by boat – either on the interesting working chain ferry or on a holiday hire boat; there are very good moorings and the fee is refundable against what you buy in the pub. Plenty of well spaced tables on the terrace look out over the River Yare and all its traffic, whether that be colourful yachts, graceful swans or even the occasional wherry. Inside, the secluded and relaxing back bar has some traditional character, antique rifles, copper and brass, and a fine log fire. The long front, partly no-smoking bar has comfortable banquettes lining the big picture windows, robust rustic tables carved from slabs of tree-trunk, and video game and fruit machines; cribbage and dominoes.

Generous helpings of good bar food include sandwiches (from £1.40), ploughman's (from £3.95), vegetarian dishes (from £5.50), home-made pies like steak and kidney (from £5.65), fresh fish (from £6.95), delicious braised boeuf bourguignon, and steaks (from £8.95). Children's dishes and arrangements for baby food (and changing facilities in the ladies' lavatory). Well kept Adnams Bitter, Charles Wells Eagle, Woodfordes Nelsons Revenge and guest beers on handpump, quite a few malt whiskies, country wines, and good cheerful staff. Showers in the lavatories for the boaters moored here. The woodturner's shop next door is interesting. *(Recommended by Bronwen and Steve Wrigley, Tina and David Woods-Taylor, Mrs D Morton, Dennis and Margaret Kilner, J E Rycroft)*

Free house ~ Licensee David Archer ~ Real ale ~ Meals and snacks (till 10pm) ~ Restaurant ~ (01493) 700429 ~ Children welcome to 9pm ~ Open 11-3, 6.30-11; 11-2.30, 7-11 in winter

RINGSTEAD TF7040 Map 8

Gin Trap

Village signposted off A149 near Hunstanton; OS Sheet 132 map reference 707403

Very neatly kept and friendly, this attractive white-painted pub has copper kettles, carpenters' tools, cartwheels, and bottles hanging from the beams in the lower part of the bar, toasting forks above an open fire (which has dried flowers in summer), a couple of man-traps ingeniously converted to electric candle-effect wall lights, and captain's chairs and cast-iron-framed tables on the green-and-white patterned motif carpet. A small no-smoking room laid out for eating has quite a few chamber pots hanging from the ceiling and high-backed pine settles; you can book a table in here. Decent home-made bar food includes lunchtime sandwiches (£1.75), ploughman's (from £3), nut cutlet (£3.95), home-made steak and kidney pie or lasagne (£5), steaks (from £8.25), mainly home-made puddings (£2.20), children's dishes (from £1.75), and daily specials such as the ever-popular Norfolk pie (£4.45), home-made quiches (from £4.50), and local trout (£5.95); the dining room is no smoking. There are free nibbles on the bar counter on Sunday lunchtimes. Well kept Adnams Bitter, Bass, Greene King Abbot, Woodfordes Nog and a beer brewed by Woodfordes for the pub on handpump; freshly squeezed orange juice; efficient happy staff. The walled back garden has seats on the grass or small paved area and pretty flowering tubs. The pub is close to the Peddar's Way and hikers and walkers are welcome (but not their muddy boots). There's an art gallery next door and a handsome spreading chestnut tree in the car park; boules. *(Recommended by John Beeken, Peter and Pat Frogley, R C Vincent, L Walker, John Wooll, Charles Bardswell, Dave Braisted, Denise Plummer, Jim Froggatt, Anthony Barnes, Chris Mawson, Wayne Brindle, M J Morgan)*

Free house ~ Licensees Brian and Margaret Harmes ~ Real ale ~ Meals and snacks (not winter Sun evenings) ~ (01485) 25264 ~ Well behaved children welcome away from bar ~ Occasional piano player ~ Open 11.30-2.30, 7(6.30 summer Sats)-11; closed evenings 25 and 26 Dec

SCOLE TM1579 Map 5

Scole Inn ★ 🛏

A140 just N of A143

This stately building, with its magnificently rounded Dutch gables, was once an important coaching inn with up to 40 horse-drawn coaches a day – and famous for its enormous round bed that could sleep up to 30 people at one time. Today, the magnificent fireplaces are just as welcoming (there's even one in the ladies' lavatory), and the high-beamed lounge bar has a 17th-c iron-studded oak door, antique settles, and leather-cushioned seats and benches around oak refectory tables on its turkey carpets. The bare-boarded public bar has stripped high-backed settles and kitchen chairs around oak tables. Under the new licensee, bar food includes sandwiches (steak £4), grilled sardines (£4.25), lasagne or vegetable curry (£4.50), grilled trout (£5.25), steak and kidney pie (£5.50), and game pie

(£5.95). Well kept Adnams Best and Broadside, and Bass on handpump; cribbage, dominoes and piped music. *(Recommended by V and E A Bolton, Rita Horridge, Derek and Sylvia Stephenson, Eric and Jackie Robinson, Ian Phillips, Anne Reeder, Dave Craine, Anthony Barnes, Marjorie and Bernard Parkin, Denise Plummer, Jim Froggatt)*

Free house ~ Licensee Norman Jones ~ Real ale ~ Meals and snacks (till 10pm) ~ Restaurant ~ (01379) 740481 ~ Children welcome ~ Open 11-11 ~ Bedrooms: £49B/£63B

SNETTISHAM　TF6834　Map 8

Rose & Crown ★ ♀

Village signposted from A149 bypass S of Heacham; pub in Old Church Rd just S of centre

In summer, the hanging baskets and flowering tubs in front of this white cottage are very pretty, and there are picnic-table sets on a neat sheltered lawn and terrace, and a children's play area with a tree house, log cabin, climbing frame and swings. Inside, of the four bustling bars, the cosy locals' bar at the back has perhaps the nicest atmosphere: tapestried seats around cast-iron-framed tables, and a big log fire. At the front is an old-fashioned beamed bar with lots of carpentry and farm tools, cushioned black settles on the red tiled floor, and a great pile of logs by the fire in the vast fireplace (which has a gleaming black japanned side oven). There's also an airy carpeted room with plush seats around tables with matching tablecloths, and pictures for sale on the wall, and an extensive family room with a clean Scandinavian look, bentwood chairs and tractor seats on its tiled floor, bare brick walls, and narrow-planked ceilings. Generous helpings of quickly served bar food such as soup (£1.75), ploughman's (£3.50), sandwiches (£3.95; home honey roast ham or excellent rare topside of beef), savoury pancakes or vegetable curry (£6.50), salads (mostly £6.95), lamb chops with mint jelly (£7.95), steaks (from £8.75), puddings like home-made apple pie (£2.25), daily specials like fresh Cromer crab (£3.50), pork and apple burgers (£4.95) or rump steak in cream and brandy sauce (£9.50), children's meals (from £2.25), and a barbecue menu (from £4.95). Adnams Bitter, Bass, Greene King IPA and Abbot, and a couple of guest beers on handpump; freshly squeezed orange juice; friendly service, even when pushed; shove-ha'penny, dominoes. No dogs. *(Recommended by D Grzelka, John Wooll, Neil and Ruth Walden, Margaret and Roy Randle, Andrew and Catherine Brian, Charles Bardswell, Mrs J Barwell, Wayne Brindle, David Hedges, Basil J S Minson, Rita Horridge, Beryl and Bill Farmer, Bill and Edee Miller, George Atkinson, John Wooll, Phil and Sue Pearce, I MacG. Binnie, Mr and Mrs J D Cranston)*

Free house ~ Licensee Margaret Goddard ~ Real ale ~ Meals and snacks (till 10pm) ~ Restaurant ~ (01485) 541382 ~ Children in eating areas and in own room ~ Open 11-3, 5.30-11; 11-11 summer Sat ~ Bedrooms: £25/£30(£40B)

STIFFKEY　TF9743　Map 8

Red Lion

A149 Wells—Blakeney

There's a happy, chatty atmosphere in this well run and friendly village pub. The oldest parts have a few beams, aged flooring tiles or bare floorboards, open fires, a mix of pews, small settles, built-in wooden wall seats and a couple of stripped high-backed settles, a nice old long deal table among quite a few others, and oil-type or lantern wall lamps. Good attractively presented bar food includes sandwiches (the crab is generous), soup (£2.25), good soft herring roes or deep-fried local sand eels (£2.75), salmon and ginger terrine with pepper mayonnaise (£3.25), baked Cromer crabs with cheese sauce (£5.50), grilled whole plaice with garlic butter or chicken in pimento sauce (£6.20), and pork fillet in a spinach and stilton sauce (£6.35). Well kept Greene King IPA and Abbot on handpump, Woodfordes Wherry and Mild, and guest beers on handpump or tapped from the cask; good service; games room, detached from the main building, with darts, cribbage and dominoes. The back restaurant leads into a conservatory, and there are wooden seats and tables out on a back gravel terrace, and on grass further up beyond. Some pleasant walks nearby. *(Recommended by Sarah King, Patrick Forbest, Charles Bardswell, Peter and Pat Frogley, BHP, Walter Reid, Roy Bromell, John Wooll, Wayne Brindle, Dr Sherriff, Bryan and Joan Osborne, Denise Plummer, Jim Froggatt, Rita Horridge, Robert Gomme)*

Free house ~ Licensee Adrienne Cooke ~ Real ale ~ Meals and snacks ~ Restaurant (closed Sun) ~ (01328) 830552 ~ Children welcome ~ Open 11-3(2.30 in winter), 6(5.30 Sat)-11

STOW BARDOLPH TF6205 Map 5

Hare Arms ♀

Just off A10 N of Downham Market

Readers are fond of this bustling country pub – for its lovely happy atmosphere, quick, friendly service (the licensees have now been here for 18 years), and good, popular food. The comfortable bar, decorated with old advertising signs and fresh flowers, has plenty of tables around its central servery, and a good log fire. It opens into a spacious heated and well planted no-smoking conservatory, and that in turn opens into a garden with picnic-table sets under cocktail parasols. Bar food includes sandwiches, very good prawn mousse, proper tomato soup, broccoli pasta and mixed cheese bake (£4.95), Cromer crab salad, chicken breast filled with garlic cream cheese in hollandaise sauce, braised beef bourguignon, pigeon breast cobbler, and plaice fillet rolled and stuffed with spinach and prawns in white wine sauce (all £5.25), delicious bream with dill and lemon sauce, and salmon fillets with lemon and tarragon sauce (£6.95); local game such as pheasant in winter, and good puddings. Well kept Greene King Abbot, IPA and Rayments on handpump, and there may be cockles and whelks on the bar counter; fruit machine. Chickens and peacocks wander around outside and there are two ginger cats and a sort of tabby. *(Recommended by Basil J S Minson, Alan Reid, Rita Horridge, John and Sally Clarke, S G MacSwiney, John Wooll, Charles Bardswell, V and E A Bolton, Thomas Nott, Brian and Jill Bond, Irene and Derek Cranston)*

Greene King ~ Tenants Trish and David McManus ~ Real ale ~ Meals and snacks (till 10pm) ~ Restaurant (not Sun evening) ~ (01366) 382229 ~ Children in conservatory ~ Open 11-2.30, 6-11; closed 25/26 Dec

SWANTON MORLEY TG0117 Map 8

Darbys ◖

B1147 NE of Dereham

Full of friendly locals, this cosy beamed country pub keeps a fine range of eight real ales on handpump: Adnams Bitter and Broadside, Badger Tanglefoot, Woodfordes Wherry and Mardlers Mild, and three changing guest beers, kept in perfect condition. The owners' farming background shows in the agricultural equipment, gin traps and so on, and in the tractor seats which line the long, attractive serving counter. There are fresh flowers on the pine tables, and a good log fire (with the original bread oven alongside). Generous helpings of enjoyable bar food include filled rolls, home-made soups such as cream of broccoli and stilton (£1.95; shellfish chowder with coconut £2.25), devilled whitebait with lime (£2.25), sweet and sour pork or barlotti bean and vegetable goulash (£4.75), sautéed kidneys and chipolatas in sherry gravy (£5.25), whole plaice with parsley butter (£5.50), lamb casserole (£5.75), baked Cromer crab thermidor or baked bacon steak (£5.95), and puddings like chocolate, fruit and nut slice or lemon crunch flan (£2.25); staff stay friendly even when they're busy; a couple of relaxed labradors; occasional background music, darts, dominoes, cribbage, children's room with toy box, and challenging play area out in the garden. Bedrooms in the farmhouse. *(Recommended by J Cox, Mr and Mrs J Back, R C Vincent, JMG, John O Baker, Ian Matthews, W F C Phillips)*

Free house ~ Licensee John Carrick ~ Real ale ~ Meals and snacks 12-2, 7-9.45 ~ Restaurant ~ (01362) 637647 ~ Children welcome ~ Occasional singer or disco ~ Open 11-2.30, 6-11; 11-11 Sat ~ Bedrooms: £17(£19B)/£34(£38B)

THOMPSON TL9196 Map 5

Chequers

Griston Road; village signposted off A1075 Thetford—Watton; OS Sheet 144 map reference 923969

Originally several cottages, this charming 14th-c thatched inn is quietly set near woodland and field walks, and has benches, flower tubs and wall baskets, and a large garden with picnic-table sets and a children's play area. Inside, the three main rooms, each with their own bar (though not all are staffed), have crooked oak wall timbers completely covered with original brass and copper artefacts, farming tools, Victorian corkscrews and boot-scrapers and so forth, uncommonly low doors and ceilings (one is only five feet high so do watch your head), plenty of exposed beams, genuinely old wheelback and spindleback chairs, and a warm and relaxing atmosphere. One also has a woodburning stove. At one end there's a dining bar with a high gabled ceiling and lots of antiques on the walls, hanging from the ceiling and in the inglenook fireplace; the small snug is a family room. The well presented bar food can be eaten anywhere in the pub and includes sandwiches (from £1.75), soup (£1.95), filled baked potatoes (from £2.75), home-made mackerel pâté (£3), big ploughman's (from £3.50), vegetable chilli (£3.75), salads (from £3.75), big mixed grill or large rack of spare ribs (£7.50), steaks (from £7.50), and puddings (£1.95). Well kept Adnams Best and Broadside, Bass, Fullers London Pride, and guest beers on handpump; local farm cider; dominoes, cribbage and piped music. *(Recommended by G E Rich, L Walker, Margaret Drazin, Mrs D Morton, Mick Hitchman, Frank Cummins, M and J Back, Derek and Sylvia Stephenson, V and E A Bolton, WAH, George Atkinson, Mrs Susan Gillotti)*

Free house ~ Licensee Bob Rourke ~ Real ale ~ Meals and snacks (till 10pm) ~ (01953) 483360 ~ Children welcome ~ Open 11-3, 6-11

THORNHAM TF7343 Map 8

Lifeboat ★ 🛏

Turn off A149 by Kings Head, then take first left turn

It's the tremendous atmosphere that readers like so much here – perhaps at its best in winter, when the rooms are moodily lit with antique paraffin lamps and five warming fires keep out the chill. The relaxed and chatty main bar has low settles, window seats, pews, and carved oak tables on the rugs on the tiled floor, panelling, great oak beams hung with traps and yokes, shelves of china, and masses of guns, swords, black metal mattocks, reed-slashers and other antique farm tools. A simple conservatory (popular with families) has benches and tables, an old-fashioned stove, a flourishing vine, and a food hatch. Tasty bar food includes home-made soup (£2.25), sandwiches (from £2.25), ploughman's or home-made coarse-chopped pork and chicken liver pâté (£4.50), cold buffet (from £6.25), 6oz burger (£6.50), half chicken with barbecue sauce (£7.25), breast of duck with warm syrup of fresh kumquats and kiwi fruit (£7.95), fish kebab (£8.50), 12oz rib-eye steak (£9.95), specials such as spinach and feta cheese pie with tomato and basil sauce (£5.95), mussels with wine and cream (£6.25) or fish pie with cheesy mash (£6.50), and children's dishes (£2.50). Well kept Adnams Best, Greene King IPA and Abbot, Woodfordes Wherry and two guests on handpump or tapped from the cask, farm cider, freshly squeezed orange juice, decent wines, and several malt whiskies; good service. Shove-ha'penny and an antique penny-in-the-hole bench. Up some steps from the conservatory is a terrace with picnic-table sets, a climbing frame, and a slide. The pub can get very busy. Large car park. *(Recommended by Alastair Campbell, Alan Reid, Sarah King, Patrick Forbest, Charles Bardswell, Les and Jean Scott, John Wooll, Col A H N Reade, Ingrid Abma, Andrew Langbar, Dave and Carole Jones, Peter and Pat Frogley, Dave Braisted, Mr and Mrs Graham, Mrs J Barwell, M J Morgan, Nic Armitage, D Fell, David Hedges, Dr Sherriff, Irene Cook, Rita Horridge, George Atkinson, R Spens)*

Free house ~ Licensees Nicholas and Lynn Handley ~ Real ale ~ Meals and snacks (till 10pm) ~ Restaurant ~ (01485) 512236 ~ Children welcome ~ Folk/jazz/country Fri and Sun evenings ~ Open 11-11 ~ Bedrooms: £40B/£65B

TITCHWELL TF7543 Map 8

Manor Hotel 🛏

A149 E of Hunstanton

Looking over the coastal flats to the sea, and very handy for the nearby RSPB reserve, this comfortable hotel has a tranquil lounge with chintzy sofas, magazines, an open fire, and a good naturalists' record of the wildlife in the reserve. A small bar opening off this has attractive patterned beige wallpaper, grey plush wall banquettes, small round tables, Impressionist prints, and another open fire. Over on the right is a room rather like a farmhouse kitchen with pine furniture, a Welsh dresser with unusual mustards and pickles on it, and a collection of baskets and bric-a-brac; children are allowed in here. There's also a pretty no-smoking restaurant with french windows that open on to a sizeable and sheltered neatly kept lawn with sturdy white garden seats. Bar food, served in the pine room, includes sandwiches, soup (£2.25), very good oysters (85p each, or in winter poached with white wine, garlic and cream (£5.95), salads, home-made chicken, mushroom and ham pie or prawn curry (all £5.95), steak and kidney pie or crab and prawn salad (£6.95), andsteaks (from £9.95); specials usually include fresh fish dishes, and there are summer Sunday buffets; puddings (from £2). Greene King IPA and Abbot on handpump; helpful pleasant staff. *(Recommended by Charles Bardswell, Les and Jean Scott, John and Sally Clarke, R C Vincent, John Wooll, Phil and Sue Pearce)*

Free house ~ Licensees Ian and Margaret Snaith ~ Real ale ~ Meals and snacks ~ Restaurant ~ (01485) 210221 ~ Children welcome ~ Open 12-2, 6.30-11 ~ Bedrooms: £39B/£78B

TIVETSHALL ST MARY TM1686 Map 5

Old Ram ♀

Ipswich Rd; A140 15 miles S of Norwich

Especially popular at weekends, this well run and carefully refurbished 17th-c inn serves huge helpings of good food from a large menu: filled rolls (from £1.95), ploughman's (£4.50), burgers (from £4.50), aubergine and mushroom bake (£5.95), salads (from £5.95), home-made steak and kidney pie or moussaka (£6.50), jumbo cod fillet in home-made golden batter (£6.95), gammon and pineapple (£7.50), steaks (from £9.95), and formidable puddings (from £2.75); also daily specials such as pork ribs (£7.50), pasta with fresh cod, haddock and salmon with prawns and mussels (£8.50) or fresh lemon sole (£8.95). Well kept Adnams, Ruddles County, Websters Yorkshire and Woodfordes Ram, decent house wines, several malt whiskies, and freshly squeezed orange juice; unobtrusive fruit machine, piped music. The spacious main room, ringed by cosier side areas, has standing-timber dividers, stripped beams and brick floors, a longcase clock, antique craftsmen's tools on the ceiling, and a huge log fire in the brick hearth; other rooms ramble off and there are pretty lamps and fresh flowers. An attractive, no-smoking dining room with pews, an open woodburning stove and big sentimental engravings leads up to a gallery with Victorian copper and brassware and comfortable sofas; another dining room is no smoking. There are seats on the sheltered, flower-filled terrace and lawn behind. No dogs. *(Recommended by B Horner, Evelyn and Derek Walter, V and E A Bolton, Frank Davidson, Jan and Peter Shopland, John C Baker, J E Rycroft, Beryl and Bill Farmer)*

Free house ~ Licensee John Trafford ~ Real ale ~ Meals and snacks (from 7.30 for breakfast – non-residents welcome – till 10pm); not 25 or 26 Dec ~ (01379) 676794 ~ Children in eating area of bar but under 7s must leave by 8pm ~ Open 11-11; closed 25/26 Dec ~ Bedrooms: £39.95B/£59.90B

Ring the Bull is an ancient pub game – you try to lob a ring on a piece of string over a hook (occasionally a bull's horn) on the wall or ceiling.

UPPER SHERINGHAM TG1441 Map 8

Red Lion

B1157; village signposted off A148 Cromer—Holt, and the A149 just W of Sheringham

New licensees have taken over this little flint cottage and while trying to change things as little as possible, are redecorating the bars and have turned the snug into a no-smoking room with families in mind. Bar food uses home-grown herbs and fruit, fish is local, and the rabbits and pheasant are caught in the woodland behind the pub: home-made soup (from £1.80), home-made pâté (£2.95), ploughman's (£3.95), mushroom stroganoff (£4.75), Cromer crab salad or filled Yorkshire pudding (£4.95), lamb's kidneys (£5.75), chicken breast with bacon and onion cream sauce (£5.95), and huge fresh lemon sole (£6.95); Sunday roast (£5.75) and three-course Wednesday evening suppers (£7.95). Well kept Adnams Best and Greene King Abbot on handpump, with Adnams Broadside and Greene King IPA occasionally, and several malt whiskies. The two quiet small bars have stripped high-backed settles and country-kitchen chairs on the red tiles or bare boards, plain off-white walls and ceiling, a big woodburning stove, and maybe several cats; dominoes and cribbage. *(Recommended by John and Tessa Rainsford, Rita Horridge, Peter and Pat Frogley, K D Day, Sue Demont, Tim Barrow, Lorna and Bill Tyson, Mrs R Cotgreave, J S M Sheldon; more reports on the new regime, please)*

Free house ~ Licensee Jason Baxter ~ Real ale ~ Meals and snacks ~ Sheringham (01263) 825408 ~ Children in eating area of bar ~ Open 11-3, 7-11; closed winter Sun evenings ~ Bedrooms: £18/£36

WARHAM TF9441 Map 8

Three Horseshoes 🛏

Warham All Saints; village signposted from A149 Wells-next-the-Sea—Blakeney, and from B1105 S of Wells

The three friendly and unspoilt rooms in this old-fashioned local have gas lights, a sturdy red leatherette settle built around the yellowing beige walls, stripped deal or mahogany tables (one marked for shove-ha'penny), an antique American Mills one-arm bandit still in working order (it takes the new 5p pieces), a big longcase clock with a clear piping strike, a Norfolk twister on the ceiling (you give it a twist and according to where it ends up you pay for the next round), and a log fire. Generous helpings of good bar food include sandwiches (from £1.80), home-made soup such as smoked haddock and fennel (£2), soused local herrings (from £2.50), potted smoked fish (£2.80), local mushrooms in cheese sauce (from £3.50), fisherman's pie (£4.90), good rabbit pie (£5.25), children's dishes (from £2), and puddings like spotted dick or apple and blackberry pie (£2.20). Decent house wines and home-made lemonade as well as the notably well kept Greene King IPA and Abbot on handpump with guests like Woodfordes Nelsons Revenge and Wherry tapped from the cask. Shove-ha'penny, dominoes and fruit machine, and one of the outbuildings houses a wind-up gramophone museum opened on request. There are rustic tables out on the side grass, and the lavatories are outside. *(Recommended by Laura Ballantyne, Eric J Locker, Sarah King, Patrick Forbest, G E Stait, Ian Louden, Tim Bishop, John Wooll, John C Baker, Derek and Sylvia Stephenson)*

Free house ~ Licensee Iain Salmon ~ Real ale ~ Meals and snacks (not 25 and 26 Dec) ~ No-smoking restaurant ~ Fakenham (01328) 710547 ~ Children in eating area of bar ~ Occasional pianola Sat evenings ~ Open 11-3, 6-11 ~ Bedrooms: £20/£40(£44B)

WINTERTON-ON-SEA TG4919 Map 8

Fishermans Return 🛏

From B1159 turn into village at church on bend, then turn right into The Lane

Several readers have very much enjoyed their stay here this year, and the characterful bedrooms – up the steep curving stairs – have low doors and uneven floors. The white-painted, panelled lounge bar has a good, relaxed atmosphere and neat brass-studded red leatherette seats and a winter log fire, while the panelled public bar has low ceilings and a glossily varnished nautical air. Good, popular home-made bar food includes toasties (from £1.20), filled baked potatoes (from £2), cottage pie (£3.25), ploughman's (£3.50), meaty, vegetable and prawn burgers (from £4), omelettes (from £4.50), steaks (from £9.50), daily specials such as crab mornay (£4.75), medley of poached salmon and skate fillet in creamy dill sauce or spiced beef pie (£5.50), puddings like fruit crumble or home-made cheesecake (£2), and children's dishes (£2.50); good breakfasts. Well kept Adnams, Bass, Elgood Cambridge and Greyhound, John Smiths and guests on handpump, own label wine as well as a guest wine, and around 30 malt whiskies; darts, dominoes, cribbage, pool, fruit machine and piped music. Seats in the quiet lane have nice views, as do the sheltered garden and terrace, which opens out from the back bar. *(Recommended by Andrew and Catherine Brian, Michael Badcock, G E Stait, Paul Harrison, J Soden, E Hobday, D Newton, S Place, Sue and Dominic Dunlop, Peter Dowd, I Andre, John Allsopp, Mrs M C Barrett)*

Free house ~ Licensee John Findlay ~ Real ale ~ Meals and snacks ~ (01493) 393305 ~ Well behaved children in small dining room in winter, in family garden room in summer ~ Open 11-2.30, 6-11; 11-11 summer Sats ~ Bedrooms: £28/£40

WOODBASTWICK TG3315 Map 8

Fur & Feather 🍺

Village signposted from Horning off A1062; or off B1140

In that part of Norfolk north-east of Norwich which we have always found less productive of really good pubs than other parts of the county, this new development is very good news indeed. It was opened at the end of 1992, a careful conversion of thatched cottage buildings in the picturesque estate village where the small Woodfordes Brewery is now housed. But you'd imagine it had always been a pub, so carefully has the work been done. It's olde-worlde in style without being overdone, comfortable and roomy. For many people the main draw will be the full range of well kept good interesting ales from the next-door brewery, increasingly cropping up individually elsewhere (sometimes as other Norfolk pubs' unnamed house brews), but very rarely found all together: Broadsman, Wherry, Mardlers Mild, Baldric, perhaps Phoenix or XXX, Nog (a strong dark ale, good for keeping out the winter cold), very strong Headcracker, Pride, and the relatively new Nelsons Revenge and Porter. There is also a good choice of generous food using fresh ingredients (even in the burgers), such as sandwiches, a truly giant sausage, filled large Yorkshire puddings (from £4.50), home-made lasagne (£4.95), beef in ale pie (£5.50), vegetarian dishes, and puddings; the restaurant is no smoking. The staff stay friendly and helpful even when busy; piped music. There are tables out in the garden, with jazz and barbecue evenings in summer. *(Recommended by Susan Kerner, John C Baker, Jonathan and Gillian Shread, Mr and Mrs B Heath, Adrian Pearce, Bryan Hay, Brian Horner, Brenda Arthur, Mrs Meg Hamilton)*

Woodfordes ~ Licensee John Marjoram ~ Real ale ~ Meals and snacks ~ Restaurant (Tues-Sat evenings) ~ (01603) 720003 ~ Open 11-3, 6-11; closed evening 25 Dec

Post Office address codings confusingly give the impression that some pubs are in Norfolk when they're really in Suffolk (which is where we list them).

Lucky Dip

Besides the fully inspected pubs, you might like to try these Lucky Dips recommended to us and described by readers (if you do, please send us reports):

Aylsham [TG1926], *Greens*: Good value home cooking in spacious converted barn with cheery attentive service, pleasant lawns *(Mr and Mrs A R Hawkins)*

Bawburgh [TG1508], *Kings Head*: Very good choice of good bar food inc some oddities, good range of real ales, friendly service; lively place with lots of tables and small restaurant *(Dr G W Barnett, Sue Anderson, Phil Copleston)*

Binham [B1388 SW Blakeney; TF9839], *Chequers*: Very old and unimproved with huge fireplace at one end and smaller one at the other, fine choice of well cooked promptly served food inc imaginative dishes; outside lavatories; commanding position in pretty village *(CB, Alastair Campbell)*

Bircham [TF7732], *Kings Head*: Roomy local used as lunch place by Sandringham shooting parties, good open fire, friendly welcome, good food and atmosphere *(Charles Bardswell, John Wooll)*

☆ **Blakeney** [TG0243], *White Horse*: Good choice of well kept Adnams and Courage-related real ales and good food esp fish in lively bar, successfully refurbished but pleasantly pubby; efficient new licensees, elegant restaurant, good reasonably priced wines; suntrap courtyard; comfortable bedrooms *(Charles Bardswell, Susan and John Priestley, Mick Hitchman, Andy Whitaker, Frank Davidson)*

Bramerton [TG2904], *Woods End*: Much modernised, with big windows overlooking bend of River Yare, big L-shaped extension with pool table; wide choice of bar food up to char-grills *(Sheila and Brian Wilson)*

Brancaster [A149; TF7743], *Ship*: Comfortable and relaxing old country inn, big coal fires, reasonably priced bar food inc good ploughman's and good range of hot dishes, well kept beers, no music, obliging staff, restaurant; three good bedrooms *(Robert Gomme, Mr and Mrs Ray)*

☆ **Brancaster Staithe** [A149; TF7743], *Jolly Sailors*: Stylishly simple and old-fashioned pub with enjoyable if not cheap food, well kept Greene King and decent wines, upmarket customers; provision for children, log fire, attractive dining room, sheltered tables in nice garden with enclosed play area *(Charles Bardswell, LYM)*

☆ **Bressingham** [A1066 Thetford—Diss; TM0781], *Garden House*: Particularly well kept ales such as Adnams, Butcombe and Woodfordes Wherry and good food inc vegetarian in thatched pub's beamed and timbered bar and popular restaurant; opp steam museum, handy for Bressingham Garden; tables in garden *(John C Baker)*

☆ **Briston** [B1354, Aylsham end of village; TG0532], *John H Stracey*: Clean and well run country dining pub with wide choice of well cooked and presented reasonably priced bar food, fresh fish Tues, other speciality evenings, friendly young licensees, well kept ales such as Ind Coope Burton, Morlands Old Speckled Hen and Ruddles County, comfortable seats, log fire, dog and cat; popular restaurant; good value bedrooms with good breakfasts – nice for people who like being part of family *(John Beeken, C H Stride, R C Vincent, G E Rich)*

Brundall [Station Rd – OS Sheet 134 map ref 328079; TG3208], *Yare*: Busy, popular pub nr river; navigation lamps and other nautical bric-a-brac, good boat photograph, generous well presented food, real ales such as Boddingtons, Sam Smiths and Woodfordes, splendid log fire; children's room *(Mrs M A Kilner)*

Burnham Market [B1155; TF8342], *Lord Nelson*: The Jordans who made this unpretentious local popular for its good fresh fish and even a wild mushroom bar have left, and we've not yet had reports on the new regime; Courage-related and other ales, tables outside, and there has been a good range of pub games *(LYM)*

Buxton [off B1354; TG2322], *Buxton Mill*: Rather smart, with good well served bar food, decent wines, attractive setting *(Frank Davidson)*

☆ **Caistor St Edmunds** [Caistor Lane; TG2303], *Caistor Hall*: Pleasant public areas inc unusual bar with 18th-c shop-front counter, comfortable lounge and library, bar food from good sandwiches up, decent wine; lovely grounds, nr Roman camp; good well furnished bedrooms *(Ian Phillips)*

☆ **Cantley** [TG3805], *Cock*: Wide choice of snacks and other good value bar food in friendly pub with Woodfordes Wherry and several guest beers, conservatory, garden; dogs and children welcome *(F Shadbolt, Mrs M A Kilner)*

☆ **Carleton St Peter** [N of village; up track off lane Claxton—Langley Green, by River Yare – OS Sheet 134 map ref 350044; TG3402], *Beauchamp Arms*: Big homely Edwardian pub with moorings on Yare, good food, real ales inc Adnams and Woodfordes, armchairs, pool table, restaurant *(David and Kate Smith, Mrs M A Kilner)*

☆ **Castle Rising** [TF6624], *Black Horse*: Popular Beefeater family dining pub in pleasant village setting, good value food, Whitbreads-related real ales, highly organised for the weekend crowds; no dogs, tables out under cocktail parasols *(R C Vincent, M J Morgan, Charles Bardswell)*

Caston [TL9597], *Red Lion*: Bar food inc good sandwiches, well kept John Smiths, good coffee *(BHP)*

Cawston [High St; TG1323], *Bell*: True village local with cheapish straightforward food from huge filled rolls to steaks, noisy with conversation and laughter; teams for darts, pool, bowls, etc *(Geoff Lee)*

Chedgrave [TM3699], *White Horse*: Under newish management, with six real ales inc two brewed for them by Tolly and Milners Mild, best sampled in the panelled tap room; bar food inc bargain hot beef roll with roast potatoes on Sun *(Mrs M A Kilner)*

☆ **Cley next the Sea** [Holt Rd, nr church; TG0443], *George & Dragon*: Bird-watchers' haunt, diary on lectern to record sightings, well kept Greene King Abbot, reasonably priced good food inc winter Sun roast, attentive staff, friendly locals, stained-glass window of St George and the dragon; peaceful well screened garden over road with boules pitch, car park exit a bit unnerving; bedrooms overlooking St George's Scrape and Cley Marshes bird sanctuary, inc four-poster *(George Atkinson, Noel Jackson, Louise Campbell, Peter and Pat Frogley, S G MacSwiney)*

☆ **Cley next the Sea** [The Green, nr church], *Three Swallows*: On quietly attractive village green, with barbecues in big garden; two bars, one rather bare, the other with banquettes around long high leathered tables, decent generous home cooking, well kept Greene King IPA, good wines, good views – the magnificent church looks lovely from the garden; bedrooms simple but clean and comfortable, handy for the salt marshes *(BHP, S G MacSwiney, Mrs M A Mees, Geoff Lee)*

Cockley Cley [TF7904], *Twenty Churchwardens*: Attractive home-cooked bar food inc filled rolls, ploughman's, omelettes, salads and main dishes eg churchwarden pie (sausage, tomato and chilli), well kept Adnams, courteous landlord, pleasant waitresses; beams, darts alcove, simple furnishings; handy for Iceni village, Saxon church, medieval cottage museum across rd, Oxburgh Hall (NT) *(Frank Cummins, Patrick Godfrey)*

☆ **Coltishall** [Church St (B1354; TG2719], *Red Lion*: Good modernised family pub in pleasant setting, big helpings of decent straightforward food with some imaginative touches, Whitbreads-related ales and one brewed for them by Woodfordes, friendly helpful staff, several attractive split-level rooms, restaurant; tables out under cocktail parasols, good play area; shortish walk from staithe; bedrooms *(P Corris, S Kerner, R C Vincent, M Berry)*

☆ **Colton** [TG1009], *Ugly Bug*: Friendly and attractive family-run barn conversion with extensive lakeside gardens, separate dining area with good choice of consistently good straightforward food at reasonable prices from sandwiches to steak, inc vegetarian dishes; well kept real ale inc Adnams Old, sensible choice of wines, good atmosphere

and service, fishing day tickets; children in conservatory; two comfortable bedrooms *(Michael Bardsley, Mr R C Vincent, K Fisher, Frank Davidson)*

☆ **Cromer** [Promenade; TG2142], *Bath House*: Really welcoming seafront inn with lots of dark wood, well kept Greene King Abbot and guest beer, standard bar food inc good lunchtime sandwiches, dining room; plenty of tables out on prom; bedrooms *(Michael Butler, G D Lee)*

Denver Sluice [TF6101], *Jenyns Arms*: Pleasant modernised pub by River Ouse and locks, waterside lawns, friendly staff, big helpings of good food inc vegetarian; handy for Welney wildfowl reserve *(David and Mary Webb)*

Deopham [Church Lane; TG0500], *Victoria*: Well kept Adnams, Bass, Hook Norton and guest beers on handpump, good food at sensible prices *(Mr and Mrs J E Barnard)*

Dereham [High St; TF9913], *Bull*: Yet another change of ownership but still a reasonable range of bar food and affable service *(Frank Davidson)*; [Swaffham Rd], *George*: Good cheap home-cooked bar lunches, good carvery in bar or dining room, Courage-related and other real ales, carefully attentive landlord; bedrooms good *(Frank Davidson, Mary Moore)*

Dersingham [nr church; TF6830], *Gamekeepers Lodge*: Opened a few years ago in old buildings tastefully and comfortably refurbished, reasonable choice of well cooked and presented food in good helpings, pleasant dining room (children welcome here) off bar; tables outside *(John Wooll)*

☆ **Docking** [High St; TF7637], *Pilgrims Reach*: Good generous straightforward food in small bar and restaurant, friendly staff, Adnams Bitter and Broadside; tables on attractive sheltered back terrace, children's room *(M J Morgan, Mrs M A Mees, John Wooll)*

Docking, *White Horse*: Old coaching inn with Dickens connections, spacious bar, no smoking restaurant, pleasant staff, afternoon tea; bedrooms *(C R and M A Starling)*

East Barsham [B1105 3 miles N of Fakenham; TF9133], *White Horse*: Friendly welcome, well kept real ales such as the formidable Woodfordes Headcracker, very wide range of decent bar food inc fresh veg, long main bar with big log fire, pleasant dining alcove and restaurant, pork scratchings on counter; piped music, darts; children welcome; bedrooms *(Alastair Campbell)*

☆ **East Harling** [High St (B1111); TL9986], *Nags Head*: Plush seats in three bars and no-smoking tiled-floor dining room, neat white decor with black beams, wide range of good food inc Sun lunch, prompt friendly service, John Smiths and Whitbreads ales; juke box; children in restaurant area, big garden with boules, aviary and rabbits; not far from Snetterton Motor Racing Circuit *(Jenny and Michael Back, N F Ollerenshaw)*

☆ **East Ruston** [Oak St; back rd Horning—Happisburgh, N of Stalham; TG3427], *Butchers Arms*: Well run comfortable village pub with good range of well kept ales, good food in bar and restaurant, attractive garden, lots of hanging baskets *(Graham Reeve)*

Edgefield [TG0934], *Three Pigs*: Unpretentious and extremely friendly, with limited choice of good home-cooked straightforward food (not Mon evening), well kept Woodfordes Wherry; attractive and secluded site for a few caravan tourers at the back *(Geoff Lee, George Atkinson)*

Erpingham [OS Sheet 133 map ref 191319; TG1931], *Spread Eagle*: Well kept Woodfordes Norfolk Nog, Baldrics and Headcracker, cheerful friendly staff, usual ploughman's and salads, pool table, well kept garden *(D W Gray)*

Fakenham [Market Pl; TF9229], *Crown*: Friendly unpretentious Elizabethan inn with cosy front snug, nice carved oak furniture, well kept Whitbreads-related ales, limited choice of decent food, pleasant prompt service; interesting former gallery staircase; bedrooms *(Alastair Campbell, LYM)*

Foulsham [TG0224], *Queens Head*: Smallish village pub, very friendly and welcoming licensees, Adnams and guest real ales, reasonable well priced food; children welcome – family room, big back garden *(S Holder)*

☆ **Framingham Earl** [B1332; TG2702], *Railway*: Modern food pub, locally very popular with good friendly atmosphere, well kept beer, good service, reasonable prices *(Mike and Wendy Proctor)*

Garboldisham [TM0081], *Fox*: Popular food inc fresh tasty sandwiches and well kept Adnams and Woodfordes beers, in sympathetically modernised pub with many original beams and much charm *(John C Baker)*

☆ **Gayton** [TF7219], *Crown*: Attractive flower-decked pub, simple yet stylish inside, with some unusual old features, increasingly popular for consistently good food in bars and restaurant inc self-service roasts, well kept Greene King beers, friendly efficient service, comfortable seats, games room; tables in sheltered garden *(John Wooll, Sheila and Brian Wilson, G E Rich, LYM)*

Great Bircham [Main Rd; TF7632], *Kings Head*: Good atmosphere in neat, tidy and comfortable country inn with good choice of well cooked tasty food, plenty of room, Bass and Charrington IPA; bedrooms *(John Wooll, Charles Bardswell)*

☆ **Great Cressingham** [Water End; just off A1064 Swaffham—Brandon – OS Sheet 144 map ref 849016; TF8501], *Windmill*: Cosy and roomy family pub with nooks and crannies in three beamed bars, huge log fireplace, masses of farm tools,

conservatory, games room; good value standard food, quick service, well kept Adnams, Batemans, Bass, Charrington, Sam Smiths and guest beers; well kept big garden, dogs allowed *(WAH, Marjorie and Bernard Parkin)*

Great Ryburgh [TF9527], *Boar*: Pleasant pub and management, good food in restaurant *(R Joyce)*

☆ *nr* **Great Yarmouth** [St Olaves; A143 towards Beccles, where it crosses R Waveney – OS Sheet 134 map ref 458994; TM4699], *Bell*: Busy riverside pub, attractive Tudor brickwork and heavy timbering but extensively modernised, with straightforward bar food, Whitbreads-related ales from long bar counter, decent wines, games and juke box on public side, restaurant where children allowed; garden with good play area and barbecues *(George Atkinson, Mrs M A Kilner, LYM)*

nr **Great Yarmouth** [Berney Arms Stn – OS Sheet 134 map ref 464049], *Berney Arms*: Accessible only by boat, 8-min train ride or long walk across fields; usually busy, as is the last staging post for boats going through Gt Yarmouth; limited basic food, well kept Adnams and Courage, friendly atmosphere, few creature comforts but atmospheric when quiet – flagstones, woodburner, ex-cask settles; closed winter *(Denis and Margaret Kilner)*

☆ **Hainford** [TG2218], *Chequers*: Cottagey thatched pub with imaginative choice of well cooked and presented food, real ales such as Adnams, Hook Norton Old Hookey and Morlands Old Speckled Hen, big airy bar area and rooms off, pleasant staff, very friendly atmosphere; well laid-out gardens with play area, delightful setting; children welcome *(Dr S R Dando, Ian Phillips)*

☆ **Happisburgh** [by church; TG3830], *Hill House*: Friendly welcome, pleasant setting, well kept Adnams, Marstons Pedigree, Tetleys and Woodfordes Wherry, good helpings of tasty food from good sandwiches up, comfortable furnishings in long bar with fireplace each end, good staff, restaurant Sun lunch; well equipped children's room; tables outside front and back (can get breezy if the wind comes in off the sea); bedrooms *(DC, Charles Bardswell, John Burdett, Alastair Campbell)*

Harpley [off A148 Fakenham—Kings Lynn; TF7825], *Rose & Crown*: Unassuming country pub in quietly attractive village, small comfortable lounge, interesting reasonably priced food inc unusual vegetarian dishes, decent wine, friendly hard-working landlord; high chairs provided *(John Wooll, R C Vincent)*

Heacham [TF6737], *West Norfolk*: Unpretentious pub serving nearby big caravan park; cheap and cheerful food inc all-day breakfast, friendly staff, Bass *(S G MacSwiney)*

☆ **Hempstead** [signed from A148 in Holt, pub

towards Baconsthorpe; TG1137], *Hare & Hounds*: Relaxed atmosphere in unspoilt country pub with tiled floor, big woodburner, mix of old-fashioned furnishings, home-cooked bar food such as pies, casseroles and salads, interesting decorations, well kept Adnams, Bass, Greene King Abbot and a good beer brewed for them by Woodfordes – like Phoenix XXX in style; much enjoyed by those who like things simple and genuine, with no music or machines; a couple of geese patrolling the informal garden, with a pond, rockery and play area *(R C Vincent, Geoff Lee, George Atkinson, Mrs R Cotgreave, Peter and Pat Frogley, LYM)*

☆ Hethersett [Old Norwich Rd; TG1505], *Kings Head*: Cheerful and homely atmosphere in interesting old pub with decent lunchtime bar food, well kept Courage-related real ales and a changing monthly guest, comfortable carpeted lounge, obliging staff, traditional games in cosy public bar, attractive and spacious back lawn *(WAH, LYM)*

☆ Heydon [village signposted from B1149; TG1127], *Earle Arms*: The pub, like the forgotten-seeming village around it, is like stepping back into the early 1950s – flagstones, bare boards, plastic seats, maybe a roll or basic sandwich, well kept Adnams tapped from the cask and served through a hatch, stables still in use behind; bedrooms (cheap and simple) *(LYM)*

☆ Hilborough [A1065; TF8100], *Swan*: Welcoming early 18th-c two-room pub with well kept ales such as Bass, Fullers ESB, Greene King IPA and Abbot, Woodfordes Norfolk Nog and interesting guest beers, plenty of old-fashioned pub and board games, friendly landlord, good simple bar food prepared to order (so may be a wait) inc sandwiches, generous ploughman's, well served steak and kidney pie; picnic-table sets on pleasant sheltered lawn *(Frank Cummins, BB)*

Hillington [TF7225], *Ffolkes Arms*: Large and comfortable, with wide range of beers, popular Sun carvery, good choice of bar food, garden behind; reasonably priced bedrooms in former barn *(M J Morgan)*

Hockwold [B1112 N of Lakenheath; TL7388], *New Inn*: Friendly thatched village pub with three real ales on handpump inc changing guests; inexpensive food, good service *(Frank W Gadbois)*

☆ Holme next the Sea [Kirkgate St; TF7043], *White Horse*: Limited choice of good generous reasonably priced food in rather basic but very welcoming local, busy in season; big garden *(George Atkinson, Charles Bardswell, John and Sally Clarke)*

Holt [Bull St; TG0738], *Kings Head*: Pleasantly cheerful, with good home cooking inc children's and OAPs' menus, small restaurant, Theakstons *(John Wooll, PDM)*

Horning [Lower St; TG3417], *Swan*: Whitbreads Brewers Fayre dining pub on River Bure, wide range of reasonably priced food, good service, popular cream teas; bedrooms *(A H Denman)*

☆ Horsey [just visible down lane 'To The Sea' from B1159 in S bends; TG4522], *Nelsons Head*: Good range of bar food inc vegetarian and Austrian dishes in isolated pub kept carefully simple, very welcoming and obliging service, real ales such as Adnams, Flowers and Woodfordes Wherry, unobtrusive piped classical music, local paintings, some nautical touches, darts, fruit machine; children allowed in family room; restaurant, small but attractive garden; quiet spot nr coast, handy for Horsey Mill and Mere's Staithe *(Ann Reeder, Nigel and Sara Walker, BB)*

Hoveton [B1150; TG3018], *Recruiting Sergeant*: Good atmosphere and service, food inc good starters and well served roast beef *(Anon)*

☆ Ingham [B1151 E of Stalham; TG3826], *Swan*: Charmingly done olde-worlde low-beamed thatched inn, carefully furnished to suit, interesting corners in rambling rooms on two levels; good range of beers inc guests such as Elgoods and Felinfoel Double Dragon, interesting ciders, good reasonably priced pub food; family room by small enclosed garden; bedrooms in detached block *(Derek and Sylvia Stephenson, Walter Reid, Ian Richardson, Mr and Mrs R Huhndorf)*

Itteringham [TG1430], *Walpole Arms*: Warm, welcoming and lively old-fashioned village pub on River Bure with decent food and well kept beer *(John and Elizabeth Gwynne)*

Kings Lynn [Tuesday Mkt Pl/King St; TF6220], *Globe*: Wide range of good value bar meals inc fresh veg in town hotel, prompt and pleasant service, comfortable surroundings; changes character evenings; pleasant bedrooms *(R C Vincent)*: [Gayton Rd], *Wildfowler*: Busy former farmhouse now overtaken by the suburbs, increasingly popular for wide range of cheap and tasty food; Ind Coope Burton, friendly staff *(John Wooll)*

Little Snoring [TF9532], *Green Man*: Straightforward modern-styled pub with friendly music-free beamed lounge, prompt good value well prepared basic bar food, good choice of well kept beers, friendly licensees, log fires; more basic public games bar popular with younger people, children welcome; bedrooms *(John Wooll, Alastair Campbell)*

Marsham [Norwich Rd; TG1924], *Flags*: Beautifully renovated 18th-c pub with split-level open-plan bar serving Adnams, Greene King and Woodfordes real ales, decent food; friendly staff; bedrooms *(Mrs Redstone)*

☆ Middleton [off A47 Kings Lynn—Norwich; TF6616], *Gate*: Good unpretentious creeper-covered village local with well kept Greene King, good straightforward bar food, cosy beamed bar with horsebrasses, lots of bric-a-brac, pews, cushioned settle and milk churns, open fire; games bar with pool and machines, pretty side garden *(R D Greaves)*

☆ **Mundford** [Crown St, off A1065 Thetford—Swaffham; TL8093], *Crown*: Pleasant local atmosphere in 17th-c former coaching inn, interesting decorations and big open fire in cosy beamed bar, spiral staircase to club room, separate bar with games and juke box; good modestly priced food in bar and delightful upstairs restaurant from sandwiches to steaks inc some unusual recipes, well kept Websters Yorkshire and Woodfordes Nelsons Revenge on handpump, cheerful service, recently redone terrace and lawn; good bedrooms *(Frank Cummins, WAH, Andy Mottram, Marjorie and Bernard Parkin, Sue Demont, Tim Barrow, C E Power, Frank Davidson, BB)*

☆ **Neatishead** [Irstead Rd; TG3420], *Barton Angler*: Welcoming landlady cooking good reasonably priced straightforward food for pleasant comfortable and homely bar or friendly well furnished no-smoking restaurant; well kept Greene King beers, friendly staff, lovely quiet gardens; comfortable bedrooms, two with four-posters – a nice place to stay *(JM, PM, Myra and Keith Massey, Ann and Bob Westbrook, Michael and Lorna Helyar, G E Rich)*

New Buckenham [Chapel St (B1113); TM0890], *George*: Unpretentious village-green pub with small choice of good generous food, well kept Courage Directors, Greene King IPA and Tolly Original, lively games area with juke box *(Sue Anderson, Phil Copleston)*: [Market Pl], *Kings Head*: Plain unmodernised pub wth pleasant back room, three well kept beers on handpump, friendly landlord, good food *(Sue Anderson, Phil Copleston)*

Newton [A1065 by Castle Acre; TF8315], *George & Dragon*: Pleasant roadside pub with good choice of beers, long restaurant menu, good shorter choice of bar food inc home-made dishes *(Prof H G Allen)*

☆ **North Elmham** [B1110 N of E Dereham; junction with B1145; TF9820], *Kings Head*: Simple quite old-fashioned hotel, delightfully neat and tidy, with a welcome for all, good well presented food from sandwiches up served quickly in lounge with log fire or lovely small dining room; public bars, Courage-related ales and Greene King IPA; nr interesting ruins; bedrooms *(John and Elizabeth Gwynne, Gordon Mott, Marjorie and Bernard Parkin)*

☆ **Norwich** [Wensum St], *Rib of Beef*: Now a free house, with wide choice of real ales such as Adnams, Boddingtons Mild, Flowers IPA, Flying Herbert, Marstons Pedigree, Reepham, Woodfordes Wherry and one brewed for the pub, farm cider, friendly informal atmosphere; comfortable and very pleasant main room upstairs,

attractive smaller downstairs room with river view and some original local river paintings, short but well thought-out choice of lunchtime food from filled baps up; can be studenty evenings, but without deafening music *(Thomas Nott, Ian Phillips, Robert Gomme, Mrs M A Kilner)*

☆ **Norwich** [10 Dereham Rd], *Reindeer*: No-frills bare-boards home-brew pub just outside centre, good atmosphere, about five well kept guest beers as well as its own (you can see the brewery), dining area with reasonable range of generous food, plenty of friendly staff, occasional folk bands; not crowded outside University terms *(P Corris, Jim Cowell, Dave Thompson, Margaret Mason, Sue Anderson, Phil Copleston, Richard Houghton)*

☆ **Norwich** [King St], *Ferryboat*: Pleasant riverside Greene King pub with a good deal of character, stepped down from traditional beamed old-fashioned front part through spacious raftered and flagstoned back dining area to riverside garden with play area and barbecue *(Mrs M A Kilner, Thomas Nott, LYM)*

Norwich [Prince of Wales Rd, by stn], *Compleat Angler*: Chef & Brewer right on the bridge, with pleasant conservatory overlooking river (not very special here), riverside terrace; no evening food *(Ian Phillips)*; [Tombland], *Edith Cavell*: Light and airy big-windowed former teashop named for the gallant Norfolk nurse; comfortable, friendly and lively, with Courage-related real ales, good value food till 7 – after then young people and the CD juke box take over; facing Erpingham Gate into cathedral green *(John Wooll, Thomas Nott)*; [Duke St – N of bridge, on corner with Colegate], *Golden Star*: Small pleasant corner local with old-fashioned decor, basic furniture, brown varnished paper ceiling, green woodwork, Greene King Dark Mild, Abbot and Rayments, limited food *(Thomas Nott)*; [St John Maddermarket], *Ironmongers Arms*: Lively atmosphere, old-fashioned decor and basic furniture in L-shaped corner pub with Whitbreads-related ales; events most evenings *(Thomas Nott)*; [Orford Pl, off SE end of Haymarket], *Lamb*: Attractive open-plan pub with pleasant sheltered outside area, standard food with nursery puddings, Courage-related ales, satellite TVs *(Thomas Nott)*; [Spixworth Rd, Old Catton; TG2312], *Maids Head*: Former coaching inn now a Queens Moat House thoroughly refurbished to a high standard – a sober, solid and attractive design in keeping with the general run of hotel modernisations; good range of lunchtime food in courtyard bar, two comfortable drinking bars; not really a pub, but useful to know; bedrooms *(Anon)*; [Cowgate], *Plasterers Arms*: No frills, lots of local characters and colour, pleasing range of ales inc guests, very cheap food *(John Burdett)*; [Thorpe St Andrew; TG2609], *Red Lion*: Unsmart but cosy, good fresh daily specials, well kept beers, regular jazz, Glaswegian landlord who may start playing Scottish reels and swinging the lights around *(S Kerner)*; [Rosary Rd], *Rosary*: Small crowded but friendly backstreet pub notable for 10 to 12 real ales inc its own brew; good value home-made specials *(P Corris, Brian Wainwright)*; [centre], *St Andrews*: Simply furnished big panelled room with friendly service, tasty basic food inc wide range of sandwiches, six well kept real ales, pleasant conservatory leading to tables in small back yard *(Alastair Campbell)*; [St Andrews Hill], *Take Five*: Not a pub by any stretch of the imagination (in the evenings you can only get in through Cinema City for which it serves as the cafeteria), but does have Adnams and farm cider, besides good value health-and-trend-conscious food, relaxed atmosphere, interesting surroundings, piped classical music *(Tim Barrow, Sue Demont)*; [Crostwick], *White Horse*: More restaurant than pub with long menu of good value generously served bar food, friendly service *(Alan Prine)*; [Oak St], *White Lion*: Traditional pub in Tap & Spile style, lots of bare wood, good choice of real ales, simple cheap bar food; lively in the evening, quieter lunchtime; darts and bar billiards in smaller bar *(S Demont, T Barrow)*; [St George St], *Wild Man*: Thriving lunchtime atmosphere in open-plan room with good value straightforward food esp roasts served promptly, Tolly real ales; very quiet evening *(R C Vincent, K D Day)*

☆ **Old Hunstanton** [part of Le Strange Arms Hotel, Golf Course Rd; TF6842], *Ancient Mariner*: Good value straightforward food inc generous ploughman's and up to half a dozen well kept ales inc Adnams and Broadside, Bass and Charrington IPA in comfortable and interesting old bar with lots of dark wood, bare bricks and flagstones, several little areas inc upstairs gallery, friendly staff; bedrooms *(Dr Sherriff, D E Cattell, Denise Plummer, Jim Froggatt, Les and Jean Scott)*

Reepham [Market Sq; TG0922], *Old Brewery House*: Warm welcome in attractive Georgian house with big sundial over two-columned porch, decent food in roomy eating area, well kept ales inc Adnams in small cosy inner bar, friendly service, restaurant; comfortable attractive bedrooms *(John and Elizabeth Gwynne)*

☆ **Rollesby** [A149; TQ4416], *Horse & Groom*: Good value generous home-made food, esp fish and seafood, in otherwise straightforward pub, clean, comfortable and friendly, with well kept beer, good service; restaurant, decent wines *(Mr and Mrs M Bailey, Susan Kerner)*

Roydon [the one nr Kings Lynn; TF7022], *Three Horseshoes*: Comfortable and unpretentious two-bar local with good value food, pleasant restaurant, Flowers Original, Greene King IPA and Abbot *(John Wooll)*

Salthouse [A149 Blakeney—Sheringham; TG0743], *Dun Cow*: Warmly welcoming straightforward old country pub nicely set on the edge of the salt marshes, popular with ramblers and bird-watchers; decent bar food inc good soup, ploughman's and crab salad, Flowers Original and Tolly, tables outside *(Geoff Lee, Peter and Pat Frogley)*

☆ **Sculthorpe** [off S side of A148 2 miles W of Fakenham; TF8930], *Sculthorpe Mill*: Nicely placed old mill recently extensively but sympathetically restored, beamed bar and restaurant, open fires, lots of nooks and crannies; new owners but still good friendly service as before, wide choice of well presented bar food inc good home-made puddings, well kept beers such as Brakspears and Greene King IPA, restaurant; picnic-table sets in spacious waterside garden *(H Jones, Anthony Barnes, John Wooll, R C Vincent, Alastair Campbell, Mrs J Barwell)*

☆ **Sedgeford** [B1454, off A149 Kings Lynn—Hunstanton; TF7136], *King William IV*: Particularly friendly, with good quick reasonably priced simple bar food inc Sun roast with good veg, well kept Bass and Worthington, restaurant; children allowed in lounge if eating *(John Wooll)*

☆ **Sheringham** [on promenade; TG1543], *Two Lifeboats*: Busy and pleasant seafront pub, lovely view from comfortable lounge, big helpings of good bar food inc fresh fish (no-smoking dining area), well kept Greene King ales, friendly efficient service; bedrooms *(Peter and Pat Frogley, Michael Badcock)*

Sheringham, *Crown*: Two big bars, huge helpings of good home-cooked food inc vegetarian, friendly staff, pool table; plenty of tables on attractive terrace overlooking sea, open all day summer, handy for coast walks *(Mrs Jackie Deale, Geoff Lee)*

Skeyton [Falconry Centre signed off A140 N of Aylsham; TG2425], *Goat*: Old thatched pub with three low-beamed bars, real fires, well cooked and served straightforward food, attentive service, piped music; major attraction is adjacent Falconry Centre and sanctuary for injured owls, demonstrations every two hours in summer *(Dr C Harper-Bill, Dr R Harvey, Nigel and Sara Walker)*

Smallburgh [A149; TG3225], *Crown*: Attractive small 15th-c thatched and beamed village inn, welcoming landlord, well kept Greene King, Tolly and guest ales, good value simple home-made food, big log fires in winter; restaurant; tables in neat attractive garden; bedrooms *(Dr M V Jones, Roger and Pam McIntee)*

☆ **South Creake** [B1355 Burnham Mkt—Fakenham; TF8535], *Ostrich*: Pleasantly homely with pine tables in long bar, good range of food cooked to order (so can be delays) using fresh ingredients, well kept Adnams, Charrington IPA, Greene King IPA and Woodfordes, friendly young landladies *(Bryan and Joan Osborne, Charles Bardswell)*

South Walsham [TG3713], *Ship*: Small friendly pub, good freshly cooked non-standard food inc good puddings and fish and chips nights, well kept Woodfordes Wherry, informative staff *(Susan Kerner, Eric J Locker)*

☆ **South Wootton** [Nursery Lane; TF6422], *Swan*: Good value home-made straightforward food in small old-fashioned two-bar pub overlooking village green, duckpond and bowling green; conservatory dining area, well kept Courage-related ales and Greene King IPA, small enclosed garden with slide and swing *(John Wooll)*

Stanhoe [Main St (B1155); TF8036], *Crown*: Good home cooking in straightforward small village pub; well behaved children allowed *(Ian Langmead, Mrs S R Waite)*

☆ **Stokesby** [TG4310], *Ferry House*: Generous helpings of usual food and well kept ales in traditional character pub on River Bure, very popular with boating people (free moorings) so can feel touristy; family room, tables out by water *(Ann Reeder, Dave Craine, Denise Plummer, Jim Froggatt)*

☆ **Surlingham** [from village head N; pub on bumpy track to which both village roads fork; TG3206], *Ferry House*: Spaciously comfortable modernised bar, friendly and unpretentious, in lovely setting by River Yare and rowing-boat ferry, very busy with boats and visitors in summer – free mooring; sensibly priced standard bar food inc vegetarian and Sun roasts, Courage-related real ales, central woodburner, traditional pub games, restaurant; children welcome, with own menu; winter evening opening may be restricted; handy for RSPB reserve *(John Beeken, Ian Phillips, LYM)*

Swaffham [1 Station St; TF8109], *George*: Comfortable and friendly small-town hotel, busy on market-day Sats, with small choice of good value food inc some good dishes, Greene King IPA and Abbot; children welcome; bedrooms *(John Wooll)*

Swainsthorpe [A140 just S; TG2201], *Wig & Dickle*: Friendly bar with restaurant area, wide range of reasonably priced food from sandwiches to three-course meals, traditional Sun lunches, Allied and Tolly Mild ales, big garden with children's play area *(Neil Calver)*

Tasburgh [A140; TM1996], *Countryman*: Main-road pub strong on bar food, willing service, three well kept ales inc Adnams, decent wine *(Frank Davidson)*

☆ **Thetford** [White Hart St; TL8783], *Thomas Paine*: Wide choice of reliably good value bar food from fine range of sandwiches up and consistently good service in friendly and roomy hotel bar, well kept Adnams and Tolly Original, decent wines, open fire; children welcome; bedrooms *(Phil and Sue Pearce, Sheila and Brian Wilson, LYM)*

☆ **Thornham** [Church St; TF7343], *Kings Head*: Two low-beamed attractive bars

with generous decent food inc children's helpings, open fire, banquettes in well lit bays, lots of brass, no-smoking and darts areas; quick friendly service, Greene King IPA and Abbot, Marstons Pedigree and Tetleys; three bedrooms *(M and J Back)*

Thursford [TF9833], *Crawfish*: Small intimate bar with good home-made food inc fresh veg, open fire, friendly welcome, well kept Flowers Original on handpump; unobtrusive piped music *(Alastair Campbell, John Wooll)*

☆ **Titchwell** [A149; TF7543], *Three Horseshoes*: Good range of generous bar food and well kept Adnams and Bass in popular bar with rough walls, exposed wood, beams and struts, log fires; friendly attentive staff, family room, restaurant; garden with play area; peaceful and comfortable bedrooms pleasantly furnished in antique pine, handy for beach and RSPB reserve *(John Beeken, Dr P Mummery, Mrs M A Mees, R B Berry)*

☆ **Walsingham** [Common Place/Shire Hall Plain; TF9236], *Bull*: Particularly good friendly atmosphere and interesting simply furnished interior, with well kept Ind Coope Burton and Tolly Original, decent food, tables out in the busy village square; much used by pilgrims and normally all the better for that – though, as in any pub suddenly flooded by a big group not particularly interested in the pub itself, the atmosphere may temporarily be eclipsed *(Walter Reid, Alastair Campbell)*

Walsingham [Friday Market Pl], *Black Lion*: Dates back to 14th c, with three panelled rooms, cast-iron stove in one, open fire in another; well kept beers, wide choice of well presented bar food; comfortable bedrooms *(Alastair Campbell)*; *Robin Hood*: Basic friendly bar, separate room with juke box, fruit machine and pool table, open fire and TV in lounge, good value freshly prepared generous food *(Alastair Campbell)*

☆ **Wells next the Sea** [The Buttlands; TF9143], *Crown*: Bustling heavy-beamed Tudor bar and quieter back rooms behind three-storey Georgian façade, interesting pictures inc Nelson memorabilia, generally good service and bar food inc sandwiches and children's dishes, good log fire, well kept Adnams, Marstons Pedigree and Tetleys, piped music, popular restaurant, children allowed in small back conservatory; bedrooms; charming setting *(Sue Demont, Tim Barrow, Denise Plummer, Jim Froggatt, Peter and Pat Frogley, Gordon A C Pitt, George Atkinson, M J Morgan, John Townsend, Charles Bardswell, LYM; more reports please)*

☆ **West Beckham** [Bodham Rd; TG1339], *Wheatsheaf*: Limited but good reasonably priced food esp pies and casseroles in very friendly comfortable beamed pub with cottagey doors and banquettes, feature log fire, well kept Greene King ales; children's room, garden; bedrooms clean, comfortable and cheap, with good breakfasts *(John and Tessa Rainsford, Dr and Mrs M Bailey, Geoff Lee)*

West Runton [TG1842], *Village Inn*: Superb summer seafood buffet lunch *(Paul Cartledge)*

☆ **West Walton** [School Rd; N of Wisbech; TF4713], *King of Hearts*: Smart, attractive and comfortable dining pub with wide choice of good honest food in well furnished bar and restaurant, full range of Elgoods and a guest; holds key for lovely next-door church *(J Scotney, Sheila and Brian Wilson, S G Boswell, A J T Evans)*

Weston Longville [signed off A1067 Norwich—Bawdswell in Morton – OS Sheet 133 map ref 114158; TG1115], *Parson Woodforde*: Clean and roomy straightforward beamed pub, friendly and comfortable, with decent standard bar food, well kept ales inc Bass and Woodfordes Wherry *(Frank Davidson, Mr and Mrs J Back)*

Wighton [The Street; TF9340], *Sandpiper*: Good home cooking, well kept beer, friendly service; bedrooms *(R Aley)*

Wiveton [TG0342], *Bell*: Attractive old pub by green and church with roomy gently lit bar, pine tables in big glass extension, pleasant garden beyond; has had decent food, Adnams and Woodfordes Wherry, friendly staff and labrador called Jasper, but no news since found closed spring 1994 *(Reports please)*

☆ **Wreningham** [TM1598], *Bird in Hand*: Good varied reasonably priced food inc tasty and unusual vegetarian dishes and well kept Whitbreads-related and Woodfordes real ales in tastefully refurbished pub with cosy Victorian-style panelled dining area, local bygones and Lotus car photographs; good friendly service *(Sue Anderson, Phil Copleston, Andy Whitaker, Ian Taylor)*

Wroxham [Rackheath; A1151 towards Norwich; TG2814], *Green Man*: Notable for its beautifully kept bowling green, but well kept and comfortable inside too – easy chairs, plush banquettes and other seats in open-plan bar, log fires, popular bar food, Courage-related real ales, piped music; children allowed in eating area *(Peter Dowd, LYM)*

Wymondham [Market Pl; TG1101], *Cross Keys*: Attractive and welcoming old pub with friendly staff and locals, well kept real ales such as Sam Smiths, usual food from sandwiches up; piped music; bedrooms simple but clean and reasonably priced *(Ian Phillips)*: [Town Green], *Feathers*: Pleasant service, decent cheap food, usually five well kept beers on at a time *(Richard Houghton)*

Yaxham [TG0010], *Crow*: Unpretentious local reopened after about three years, above-average food, sensibly priced mainly New World wines, Bass and Greene King IPA on handpump; children give it a domestic atmosphere *(Frank Davidson)*

If a service charge is mentioned prominently on a menu or accommodation terms, you must pay it if service was satisfactory. If service is really bad, you are legally entitled to refuse to pay some or all of the service charge as compensation for not getting the service you might reasonably have expected.

Northamptonshire *see* Midlands

Northumbria (including Durham, Northumberland, Cleveland and Tyne & Wear)

This area has a lot of very enjoyable and friendly pubs with a good mix of customers, and food that's often good without being too pretentious; helpings tend to be more generous than down in the south, and food prices are on average rather lower than the national norm – though there are tremendous variations from pub to pub here. The most enjoyable pubs for eating out in are currently the very friendly Manor House at Carterway Heads, the civilised Fox & Hounds at Cotherstone (nice to stay at), the Cook & Barker Arms at Newton on the Moor (for the first time gaining a Food Award this year), the charmingly set Rose & Crown at Romaldkirk and the Warenford Lodge at Warenford. The Cook & Barker Arms is doing so well at the moment that we choose it as Northumbria Dining Pub of the Year. A new main entry, the Milecastle Inn near Haltwhistle, joins this select band: good interesting home-made food with a really delightful pubby atmosphere – it's already very popular locally, and by no means roomy. Other places well worth knowing for decent bar food include the Wheatsheaf in Corbridge, the homely and relaxed Dipton Mill at Diptonmill, the Tankerville Arms at Eglingham, the Feathers at Hedley on the Hill (meals weekends only), the Black Bull at Matfen, the Chain Locker in North Shields (cheap fresh local fish), the George at Piercebridge, the Masons Arms at Rennington, the Waterford Arms at Seaton Sluice (massive helpings of local fish), and another new entry, the Pheasant up near Kielder Water at Stannersburn (a nice friendly place to stay). The Lord Crewe Arms at Blanchland is certainly worth a visit if you're passing, a wonderful ancient building; and the old-fashioned character of the civilised old Morritt Arms at Greta Bridge is also well worth sampling. Beer in the area is notably cheaper than the national average – particularly so in the case of the Tap & Spile in Newcastle. It's frequently very well kept, too, as shown by the high proportion of pubs here qualifying for our new Beer Award. And aside from the regional brewers Camerons and Vaux, there are interesting beers to be found from local brewers such as Big Lamp, Butterknowle, Hadrian and Hexham. As well as our clutch of good interesting main entries in Newcastle, there are quite a few worthwhile prospects there in the Lucky Dip section at the end of the chapter; Durham too has some useful entries there, though nothing outstanding. Other Dip entries to note particularly include the Lord Crewe Arms at Bamburgh, Shepherd & Shepherdess in Beamish, Blue Bell at Belford, Black Bull at Etal, Duke of York at Fir Tree, Queens Head at Whittington, General Havelock at Haydon Bridge, Kings Head at Newton, Ship in Saltburn by the Sea, Ridley Arms at Stannington and Tynemouth Lodge in Tynemouth; as we have inspected almost all of these we can vouch for their quality.

BLANCHLAND (Northumberland) NY9750 Map 10

Lord Crewe Arms

In a lovely moorland village near the Derwent Reservoir, this historic inn is popular with a good mix of people – locals, walkers, and those enjoying the rather smart restaurant. Built in 1235, it was originally attached to the guest house of a monastery and was, remarkably, untouched for centuries. The cosy and simply furnished barrel-vaulted crypt bar has plush bar stools, built-in wall benches, ancient flagstones and walls that are eight feet thick in some places. Upstairs, the Derwent Room has low beams, old settles, and sepia photographs on its walls, and the Hilyard Room has a striking 13th-c fireplace where the Jacobite Tom Forster (part of the family who had owned the building before it was sold to the formidable Lord Crewe, Bishop of Durham) is said to have hidden after escaping from prison in London, on his way to exile in France. His loyal sister still haunts the place, asking guests to deliver a message to her long dead brother. Simple bar food includes soup (£1.80), filled rolls (mostly £2.50), pasta shells with tomatoes, mushrooms, butter beans and cheese (£3.75), ploughman's (£4.35), salads (from £4.35), fish cakes (£4), minced lamb kebab (£4.50), wild boar and pheasant pie (£5.10), sautéed minute steak (£5.65), and puddings (£2.20). Sunday lunch and afternoon teas with home-made cakes. Vaux Samson on handpump; darts, dominoes and cribbage. There's a pleasant enclosed garden. *(Recommended by R J Walden, Peter Race, John Fazakerley, Gill and Maurice McMahon, Mrs D Craig, Alan Wilcock, Chrsitine Davidson, Jennie and Malc Wild)*

Free house ~ Licensees A S Todd, Peter Gingell, Ian Press ~ Real ale ~ Meals and snacks ~ Evening restaurant, though they do Sun lunch ~ (01434) 675251 ~ Children welcome ~ Open 11-3, 6-11 ~ Bedrooms: £70B/£93B

CARTERWAY HEADS (Northumberland) NZ0552 Map 10

Manor House ♀ ◖

A68 just N of B6278, near Derwent Reservoir

Very popular for miles around, this simple slate-roofed stone house is a particularly friendly place with well kept beer and very good food. Changing daily and generously served, the choice might typically include sandwiches, soup such as leek and potato (£1.80), dill herrings with crème fraîche or grilled Craster kippers (£3.55), creamy pasta with leeks and cheese sauce or warm red onion and stilton tart (£4.60), honey-roast ham with mango chutney (£5.85), grilled lamb chops with haricot beans provençal (£6.60), cold rare roast beef with pepper confit (£6.85), monkfish fricasee with courgettes and dill (£6.95), sirloin steak (£8.60), and puddings like pear crumble or marmalade and sultana sponge (£2.35). The table d'hôte menu is no less interesting, with gnocchi with baked tomatoes and parmesan cheese, roast breast of guinea fowl with braised lentils, and Norwegian Jarger cake (£15 including coffee). Both menus are available throughout the building, lunchtime and evenings, seven days a week, with bookable waiter-served tables in the no-smoking restaurant end. A changing range of well kept beers such as Burton Bridge Porter, Butterknowle Bitter, Greene King IPA, Hadrian Centurion and North Yorkshire Flying Herbert on handpump, a farm cider or perry, up to 20 malt whiskies, and decent wines. The comfortable refurbished lounge bar has picture windows with fine views looking south over moorland pastures and a woodburning stove, and the beamed locals' bar is furnished with pine tables, chairs and stools, old oak pews, and a mahogany bar. Darts and piped music. Rustic tables out on a small side terrace and lawn. *(Recommended by John Fazakerley, Graham and Karen Oddey, R J Walden, John Oddey, Kay and Mark Denison, Roger Bellingham, Paul Boot, Alan Wilcock, Christine Davidson, John Whitehead, GSB)*

Free house ~ Licensee Anthony Pelly ~ Real ale ~ Meals and snacks ~ Restaurant ~ (01207) 55268 ~ Children in eating areas until 8pm ~ Open 11-3, 6-11; closed 25 Dec ~ Bedrooms: £20/£35

CHATTON (Northumberland) Map 10

Percy Arms 🛏

B6348 E of Wooler

Popular for its good, reasonably priced bar food, this cheerful and friendly stone inn is also a nice place to stay – and has 12 miles of private fishing for residents; fine breakfasts. At lunchtime, there might be home-made soup (£1.50), sandwiches (from £1.50), home-made pâté (£2.75), ploughman's (£3.85), home-made shepherd's pie (£3.95), salads (from £4.45; fresh local crab £6.25), fresh local cod or home-made steak and kidney pie (£4.55), a vegetarian dish (£4.75), children's dishes (£2.50), and puddings like home-made trifle (from £1.85). The bar is clean, comfortable and spacious, with wooden wall seats upholstered in pale brocade, studded chairs and stools around the dark tables in the carpeted main lounge area, an armchair or two among other seats in a family area through a stone-faced arch, and round on the other side a similarly furnished tiled-floor section leads through to a stripped-stone eating area. Well kept Theakstons XB on handpump, a fine selection of malt whiskies, open fire, unobtrusive piped music; public bar with darts, pool, dominoes, fruit machine, video game and juke box. There are picnic-table sets on its small front lawn above the village road, and a holiday cottage is available. No dogs in public areas. *(Recommended by Jeanne and Tom Barnes, Neil Townend, Chris and Anne Fluck, Mr and Mrs C Brown, Thomas Nott, John Allsopp, Les and Jean Scott, Jennie and Malc Wild, R M Macnaighton, Barry and Anne, Neil and Angela Huxter, Bob Shand)*

Free house ~ Licensees Pam and Kenny Topham ~ Real ale ~ Meals and snacks (lunchtime service stops at 1.30) ~ Restaurant ~ (0166 85) 244 ~ Children welcome ~ Open 11-3, 6-11 ~ Bedrooms: £20B/£40B

CORBRIDGE (Northumberland) NY9964 Map 10

Wheatsheaf 🛏

Watling St (former A69, just N of centre)

At lunchtime, this busy place is popular for its wide range of good food. The lounge bar on the left has comfortable ribbed wall banquettes and cushioned chairs, pink patterned wallpaper above a darker toning dado and below a delft shelf packed with china, some old-fashioned pictures, and roughened burnt orange paintwork between the beams. It opens through a chubby balustrade into a dining area with lots of little china bells on a delft shelf, and a similarly furnished conservatory section. Bar food includes soup (£1.65), home-made pâté (£3.25), home-made vegetarian dish (£3.95), salads (from £3.95), home-made beef casserole (£4.25), grilled gammon (£4.50), sirloin steak (£8.50), puddings (£1.85), and children's meals (from £2.50), with evening dishes such as New Zealand mussels (£3.25), lamb and apricot casserole (£6.50), and chicken breast in a port, dill and basil sauce or poached salmon steak with cucumber, prawns and white wine (£6.95); roast Sunday lunch (£4.50). Well kept Vaux Durham Cathedral, Darleys Thorne, and Wards on handpump, and a good choice of wines and malt whiskies; prompt friendly service. Darts, dominoes, fruit machines and piped music; some picnic-table sets out on the side grass. Out in the stableyard are a couple of strange stones, thought to be of Roman origin, and said to represent the gods Janus and Ceres. *(Recommended by Paul Boot, A Craig, Margaret and David Bloomfield, John Oddey, R M Macnaughton, Ian Phillips, Graham and Lynn Mason, Graham and Karen Oddey, Pauline Crossland, Dave Cawley, Roger Bellingham)*

Vaux ~ Lease: Gordon Young ~ Real ale ~ Meals and snacks ~ Restaurant ~ (01434) 632020 ~ Children welcome ~ Live entertainment Sat evenings, once monthly ~ Open 11-11 ~ Bedrooms: £37.50B/£49.50B

All main entries have been inspected anonymously by the Editor or Deputy Editor. We accept no payment for inclusion, no advertising, and no sponsorship from the drinks industry – or from anyone else.

COTHERSTONE (Durham) NZ0119 Map 10

Fox & Hounds ♨ ⇌ ♉

B6277 – incidentally a good quiet route to Scotland, through interesting scenery

It would be a shame to miss this white-painted dining pub if you are in this part of the country and want a very good meal. There might be particularly good home-made beef and vegetable broth (£2.50), black pudding with apple and garlic sauce (£3.65), lunchtime ploughman's (£3.95) and platters (from £4.95), fresh fillet of haddock deep fried or vegetable pancake (£6.45), salads (from £6.50), steak and kidney pie (£6.95), grilled gammon (£8.25), chicken with bacon, cheese and mushrooms (£9.75), half roast duckling with bilberry and red wine sauce (£10.95), medallions of fillet steak with madeira and mushroom sauce (£14.95), and puddings such as chocolate cream crunch, hot mixed fruit crumble or knickerbocker glory (from £2.45); children's dishes and three-course Sunday lunch (from £11.45); one restaurant is no smoking. It's not just the food that people like here though, as the lovely setting and the attractive building itself blend together to make it a charming and very well liked place to stay. The cosy beamed bar has various alcoves and recesses, with comfortable furnishings such as thickly cushioned wall seats, local photographs and country pictures on the walls, and a winter open fire. The food is served in the L-shaped lounge bar, and service is efficient and courteous. Well kept Hambleton Best, White Boar (from the same supplier as Hambleton) and John Smiths Bitter on handpump, a fair choice of malt whiskies, and good wines. The pub overlooks the picturesque village green and is handy for various walks and attractions. No pets. *(Recommended by Susan and Rick Auty, Mrs J R Thomas, B D Atkin, Peter and Lynn Brueton, Leonard Dixon, Stephen Savill, Anthony Barnes, Iain and Penny Muir, Robert and Susan Phillips, Phil and Heidi Cook)*

Free house ~ Licensees Patrick and Jenny Crawley ~ Real ale ~ Meals and snacks (lunchtime service stops at 1.45) ~ Restaurant ~ (01833) 650241 ~ Children in restaurant ~ Open 11.30-2.30, 6.30-11; closed 25 Dec ~ Bedrooms: £40B/£55B – children must be over 9 to stay here

CRASTER (Northumberland) NU2620 Map 10

Jolly Fisherman £

Off B1339 NE of Alnwick

A fine base for walkers (the splendid clifftop walk to Dunstanburgh Castle is close by), this unpretentious local is at its best on a clear day when you can enjoy the lovely position overlooking the harbour and out to sea – either from the little garden or from the big picture window in the airy extension. The relaxed and atmospheric original bar (particularly the snug by the entrance) is popular with workers from the kippering shed opposite and from the harbour. Cheap, simple food such as burgers (£1), home-made pizzas (£1.25), and local crab and salmon sandwiches (£1.50); obliging service. Well kept Wards Sheffield Bitter on handpump; darts, shove-ha'penny, dominoes, cribbage, juke box, fruit machine and trivia. *(Recommended by David Pither, D Devine, D Irving, Thomas Nott, June and Tony Baldwin, Mr and Mrs C Brown, P D and J Bickley, Jonathan Mann, Abigail Regan, Verity Kemp, Richard Mills, Julie Munday, Martin Robinson, Stephen Brown, Mr and Mrs Moody, P K Eames, Neil and Angela Huxter, Ben Grose, Barry and Anne, Denis and Margaret Kilner)*

Vaux ~ Lease: A George ~ Real ale ~ Snacks (available during opening hours) ~ (01665) 576461 ~ Children welcome ~ Open 11-3, 6-11

DIPTONMILL (Northumberland) NY9361 Map 10

Dipton Mill

Off B6306 S of Hexham at Slaley, Blanchland and Dye House, Whitley Chapel signposts and HGV route sign

This smashing little pub is the sort of place you don't want to leave once you've settled in. It's run by a friendly, helpful landlord who knows his beers and has a cheerful, relaxed atmosphere in its homely bar, which has dark ply panelling, red furnishings and open fires, and is popular with locals in the evening. Good value, reliable lunchtime bar food includes soup (£1.30), nicely presented sandwiches (from £1.50, the thick rare beef are recommended), ploughman's (£2.75), smoked salmon and prawn flan (£3.50), salads (from £3.50), steak, kidney and oyster pie or chicken breast in cream and cherry sauce (£4), puddings like lime cheesecake or chocolate sponge (£1.25), and good cheeses or home-made cakes and coffee (£1.30); no evening food. Well kept Hadrian Gladiator and Theakstons Best, as well as Hexhamshire Bitter, Devils Water and Whap Weasel from a local brewery about two and half miles from the pub; quite a few malt whiskies; darts, bar billiards, shove ha'penny and dominoes. The garden is a particularly nice place to unwind, perhaps on the sunken crazy-paved terrace by the restored mill stream, or by the pretty plantings and aviaries. There may be barbecues here on summer weekends. Easy-walking footpaths nearby. *(Recommended by Stephen Brown, Edward Watson, Dr R H M Stewart, John Oddey, Duncan Small, Graham and Karen Oddey, A S Clarke, Alan Wilcock, Christine Davidson, Leonard Dixon, JJW, CMW)*

Free house ~ Licensee Geoff Brooker ~ Real ale ~ Lunchtime meals and snacks ~ (01434) 606577 ~ Children in games room ~ Open 12-2.30, 6-11; closed 25 Dec

EGLINGHAM (Northumberland) NU1019 Map 10

Tankerville Arms

B6346 NW of Alnwick

A new licensee has taken over this busy village pub, which has been popular for its good, well presented food. The long stone building has coal fires at each end, black joists, some walls stripped to bare stone and hung with brassware, and plush banquettes and captain's chairs around cast-iron-framed tables on the turkey carpet; there's a snug no-smoking lounge. Bar food includes home-made soup (£1.50), sandwiches (from £1.75), steak in ale pie (£4.95), local game pie or minute steak (£5), whole tail scampi (£5.50), mushroom stroganoff (£6.95), and puddings (£2.50); four-course Sunday roast beef lunch (£8.25). Well kept Theakstons XB and Stones Bitter with a guest like Moorlands Old Speckled Hen on handpump; decent selection of wines and malt whiskies; fruit machine and piped music. There are seats in the garden. *(Recommended by GSB, Mr and Mrs C Brown, J and M Falcus, Thomas Nott, June and Tony Baldwin; more reports on the new regime, please)*

Free house ~ Licensee Edward Sweeney ~ Real ales ~ Meals and snacks ~ Restaurant ~ (01665) 578444 ~ Children welcome ~ Open 11-3, 6-11

GRETA BRIDGE (Durham) NZ0813 Map 10

Morritt Arms 🍺

Hotel signposted off A66 W of Scotch Corner

Charles Dickens stayed in this characterful and rather smart old coaching inn on the way to Barnard Castle in 1838 to start his research for *Nicholas Nickleby*, and one of the characterful unchanging bars is named after him. The rather jolly Dickensian mural that runs all the way around the walls was painted in 1946 by J V Gilroy, more famous for his old Guinness advertisements – six of which are displayed on the wall. There are also big Windsor armchairs and sturdy green-plush-seated oak settles clustered around traditional cast-iron-framed tables, and big windows that look out on the extensive lawn. The adjacent green bar has dark grey leatherette wall seats, a stag's head and a big case of stuffed black game; there's also a fine big model traction engine in one of the lounges. Flowers brighten up the rooms, open fires warm them, and the cheery twin brothers who run the place make sure there's always a friendly reception. Well kept Butterknowle Conciliation on handpump. A proper old shove-ha'penny board, with raisable brass rails to check the lie of the coins, and in the separate public bar – darts, dominoes and a juke box. Bar food includes soup (£2.10), a selection of sandwiches and salads, Yorkshire pudding filled with minced beef (£4.00), ploughman's (£4.50), seafood pancake (£5.95) and roast pigeon in a red wine game sauce (£6.25). In the nice garden are some picnic-table sets, teak tables in a pretty side area looking along to the graceful old bridge by the stately gates to Rokeby Park, and swings, slide and rope ladder at the far end.

(Recommended by Nicholas Law, Noel Jackson, Louise Campbell, B D Atkin, Maysie Thompson, M A E Symonds, Heather M N Robson, Roxanne Chamberlain, Colin and Caroline Maxwell)

Free house ~ Licensees David and John Mulley ~ Real ale ~ Meals and snacks (lunchtime; sandwiches and soup in evening) ~ Restaurant ~ (01833) 627232 ~ Children welcome, but 6s must be gone by 7pm ~ Open 12-3, 6-10.30(11 Sat) ~ Bedrooms: £45B/£68B

nr HALTWHISTLE (Northumberland) NY7164 Map 10
Milecastle 🍺
Military Rd; B6318 NE – OS Sheet 86 map reference 715660

Alone on the remote moorland road running alongside Hadrian's Wall, this cosily refurbished 17th-c pub is a particularly welcoming refuge from driving rain, or on a cold winter's night. It combines really good food with warm and genuine hospitality. The good value very generous food includes a lot of good game such as venison, hare, grouse, guinea fowl and pigeon. Dishes that we or readers have specially enjoyed are splendid home-made sausages, particularly venison (£4.75) and Cumberland (£5.95) ones, also sausage swirls – sausage meat in flaky pastry like a Swiss roll), and interesting pies (around £5.95) such as beef and venison, wild boar and duckling, turkey, ham and chestnut, pheasant and claret, or coulibiac pie – salmon with rice, mushroom and parsley. There are half a dozen or so good dishes of the day. Meat (local, well chosen and well hung) and vegetables (fresh, also local) are good, as are soups (£1.75) such as spiced tomato and puddings such as chocolate and orange cake or treacle tart (£2). Sandwiches (from £2.35) and ploughman's (from £3.95) tend to be dressed up with a great deal of salad. Well kept changing real ales such as Whap Weasel and Devils Water (from a local Hexham brewery), Black Sheep, Jennings Snecklifter and Tetleys on handpump; a decent collection of malt whiskies in ¼-gill measures, good wine list. The snug small rooms of the beamed bar, decorated mainly with brasses, horsey and local landscape prints and attractive dried flowers, do get very busy in season (or when two dozen local farmers arrive in force); there's a lunchtime overflow into the small comfortable restaurant. Good friendly chatty service; a splendid coal fire, with a welcome for walkers (but no rucksacks allowed); some white plastic seats and tables outside, by the moorland pastures.

(Recommended by Julia Stone, Roger Berry, Dr A M Rankin, John Honnor, R T and J C Moggridge, Gill and Maurice McMahon, Alan Wilcock, Christine Davidson)

Free house ~ Licensees Ralph and Margaret Payne ~ Real ale ~ Meals and snacks ~ Restaurant (not Sun-Tues evenings) ~ (01434) 321372 ~ Children over 5 if eating ~ Open 12-2.30, 6.30-11

HEDLEY ON THE HILL (Northumberland) NZ0859 Map 10
Feathers
Village signposted from New Ridley, which is signposted from B6309 N of Consett; OS Sheet 88 map reference 078592

Every Easter Monday, this friendly and traditional little stone local holds a barrel race – which ends a weekend mini beer festival with around 20 real ales to choose from. The three well kept turkey-carpeted bars have beams, woodburning stoves, stripped stonework, solid brown leatherette settles, country pictures, and a relaxed atmosphere. Well kept Boddingtons and two continuously changing guest ales on handpump with favourites such as Butterknowle Bitter, Hexhamshire Devils Water and Yates Bitter, and around 25 malt whiskies; darts, shove-ha'penny, and dominoes. The popular food is restricted to weekends only (apart from evening sandwiches) as the landlady does not want to turn the pub into an eating house: sandwiches (from £1.45), soups such as pea and mint (£1.65), peppered steak in french bread (£3.25), ploughman's (£3.45), watercress and smoked salmon roulade (£3.50), increasingly popular vegetarian meals like feta tart with sun-dried tomatoes, onions, olives and basil (£3.45) or fennel, tomato, aubergine and mozzarella with french bread (£3.50), chicken with tarragon and mushrooms or salmon with parsely butter (£4.75), beef with spices and apricots (£4.95), and puddings like pear and ginger pudding or sticky toffee pudding (£1.95); children's meals (£1.25). *(Recommended by GSB, Andrew O'Doherty and others; more reports please)*

Free house ~ Licensees Marina and Colin Atkinson ~ Real ale ~ Weekend meals and snacks (though they do weekday evening sandwiches) ~ (01661) 843607 ~ Children in eating area and family room till 8.30pm ~ Irish/Northumbrian folk night (bring your own instruments) 2nd Tues of each month ~ Open 6-11 weekdays; 12-3, 6-11 Sat; closed lunchtimes Mon-Fri except bank holidays

MATFEN (Northumberland) NZ0372 Map 10

Black Bull

Village signposted off B6318 NE of Corbridge

A lot of hard work has gone into the terrace in front of this charming old creeper-covered long stone inn this year and there are pretty hanging baskets, shrubs and bedding plants, as well as plenty of seats. Also, the bedrooms now have their own private bathrooms – and a golf course is opening nearby. The spacious turkey-carpeted main bar has Windsor chairs, copper-topped tables, and steeplechasing pictures, and there's a side room with red plush button-back built-in wall banquettes, and attractive 1940s photographs. Good, fresh, well presented bar food includes home-made soup (£1.50), duck liver pâté with Cumberland sauce (£3.75), filled Yorkshire puddings (from £4), herb pancake filled with spiced prawns (£4.25), battered haddock (£4.25), salads (from £4.45), home-made steak and kidney in ale pie or honey-glazed breast of chicken with toasted almonds (£4.50), home-made game pie (£6.40), steaks (from £10.95), and puddings (£2.95); good, fresh vegetables. They will do sandwiches, and in addition you can order off the seasonally varying, and very good, restaurant menu; part of the restaurant is no smoking. Well kept Theakstons Best and XB with guests like Morlands Old Speckled Hen and Smiles Exhibition on handpump, a good choice of malt whiskies, log fires, sensibly placed darts, dominoes, fruit machine and juke box. The pub faces the green of an attractive and well kept 18th-c stone-built estate village. No dogs. *(Recommended by T M Dobby, John Allsopp, Derek Robb, John Oddey, R Deeming, Mrs A Gray, R and G Underwood, Lomas family, Leonard Dixon, JJW, CMW)*

Free house ~ Licensees Colin and Michele Scott ~ Real ale ~ Meals and snacks ~ Restaurant ~ (01661) 886330 ~ Children in eating area of bar ~ Open 11-3, 6-11; 11-11 Sat ~ Bedrooms: £32.50B/£55B

NEW YORK (Tyne & Wear) NZ3370 Map 10

Shiremoor House Farm ★

Middle Engine Lane/Norham Road; from A1 going N from Tyne Tunnel, right into A1058 then next left signposted New York, then left at end of speed limit (pub signed); or at W end of New York A191 bypass turn S into Norham Road, then first right (pub signed)

Marvellously transformed from derelict farm buildings, this enjoyable and smartly relaxed place has several well divided areas with a real mix of interesting and extremely comfortable furniture, and in one place there's a big kelim on the broad flagstones; also, warmly colourful farmhouse paintwork on the bar counter and several other tables, as well as conical rafters of the former gin-gan, a few farm tools, and good rustic pictures such as mid-West prints, big crisp black-and-white photographs of country people and modern Greek bull sketches. Bar food includes soup (£1.35), potted cheese and walnuts (£2.75), roast duck julienne with cold Cumberland sauce (£3.95), breast of chicken with garlic, brandy and prawn sauce (£7.25), ragout of lamb (£7.95), venison steak in red wine sauce

(£9.90), beef stroganoff (£10.50), steaks (from £11.25), daily specials like spaghetti bolognese (£3.80), chicken chasseur (£3.95) or Chinese chicken (£5.95), and home-made puddings (£2.50). The granary extension is good for families with high chairs, and bottle or baby food warmed on request. Well kept Stones Best, Theakston's Best and Old Peculier, Timothy Taylors Landlord and a guest beer on handpump, decent wines by the glass, polite and efficient young staff. No music or games machines; Monday evening quiz. A separate bar serves the equally attractive rather smart restaurant. It can get crowded at weekday lunchtimes. There are picnic-table sets on neat grass at the edge of the flagstoned farm courtyard, by tubs and a manger filled with flowers. *(Recommended by Neil Townend, John Coatsworth, Jacqueline White, Trevor Scott, John Oddey, Chris and Anne Fluck, Barbara and Norman Wells, Bob Shand)*

Sir John Fitzgerald Ltd ~ Licensees M W Garrett and C W Kerridge ~ Real ale ~ Meals and snacks (all day Sun) ~ Restaurant ~ 0191-257 6302 ~ Children in eating area of bar and in restaurant ~ Open 11-11

NEWCASTLE UPON TYNE (Tyne & Wear) NZ2266 Map 10

Bridge Hotel £ 🍺

Castle Square (in local A-Z street atlas index as Castle Garth); right in centre, just off Nicholas St (A6215) at start of High Level Bridge; only a few parking meters nearby, but evening parking easy

At lunchtime, this bustling and chatty Victorian pub is full of businessmen, shoppers and lawyers from the Crown Court next door, and in the evening it's popular with younger people. The imposing, neatly kept old-fashioned lounge has high ceilings, a bar counter equipped with unusual pull-down slatted snob screens, decorative mirrors, brown leather banquettes and elegant small chairs on its rust carpet, and a massive mahogany carved fireplace. In the public bar, which has some cheerful stained glass, there's a good (sometimes loud) jukebox, pool, pinball, dominoes, a video game and fruit machine. Well kept Theakstons Best and XB and two weekly changing guest beers on handpump; simple bar snacks include toasted sandwiches (90p) and wholemeal stottie cakes with meat and salad (£1.10); friendly service. Tables on the flagstoned back terrace are by the remains of the city wall that look down over the Tyne and its bridges. *(Recommended by GSB, Julian Holland, Graham and Karen Oddey, Stephen and Julie Brown)*

Sir John Fitzgerald Ltd ~ Licensee M W Garrett ~ Real ale ~ Snacks ~ 0191-232 7780 ~ Over 18s only ~ Folk and blues club Mon, other live music Thurs and occasional Fri ~ Open 11-3, 5.30(6 Sat)-11; closed 25 Dec

Cooperage £ 🍺

32 The Close, Quayside; immediately below and just to the W of the High Level Bridge; parking across road limited lunchtime, easy evening

With the exception of the castle and keep, this bustling Grade 2* listed pub is the city's oldest secular building. It's best known for its seven real ales on handpump including regulars such as Ind Coope Burton (they are the second biggest seller of Burton ale in the country), Hadrian Centurion, Marstons Owd Rodger and Tetleys, and three guests from an extremely extensive list, like Ansells Mild, Benskins Best, Flowers Original, Friary Meux Best, Fullers ESB, Marstons Pedigree or Timothy Taylors Landlord. They're so busy with locals, businessmen and students that they'll generally get through about 15 beers a week; also hand-pulled Addlestone's and Bulmer's ciders. The bustling bar has heavy Tudor oak beams and exposed stonework, and there's extra seating in the lounge area by the pool room; fruit and trivia machines and a juke box. Very good value bar lunchtime food might include pea and ham soup or scotch broth (both £1.10), hot roast beef stottie (£2.55), grilled North Shields kipper fillet (£2.20), a vegetarian dish like mushrooms and leeks in garlic and herb butter with noodles (£2.90), steak and Guinness pie (£3), sliced pork with Dijon mustard (£3.25), and puddings like brandy bread and butter pudding or baked apple sponge (both £1.20). An extension to the upstairs function room is planned. The pub, near the waterfront, is close to the Sunday outdoor market. *(Recommended by Noel Jackson, Louise Campbell, John Oddey, Julian Holland, Ross Lockley, G Taylor, Gill and Maurice McMahon)*

Free house ~ Licensee Michael Westwell ~ Real ale ~ Meals and snacks (11-7) ~ Restaurant (not Sun evening) ~ Newcastle 0191-232 8286 ~ Children in eating area of bar and in restaurant lunchtime only ~ Open 11-11

Crown Posada £ 🍺

31 The Side; off Dean Street, between and below the two high central bridges (A6125 and A6127)

This is the city's second oldest pub and has not changed for decades. There are lots of architectural charm and oddities such as an elaborate coffered ceiling in cream and dusky pink, a line of gilt mirrors each with a tulip lamp on a curly brass mount matching the great ceiling candelabra, stained glass in the counter screens, and Victorian flowered wallpaper above the brown dado (with its fat heating pipes along the bottom – a popular footrest when the east wind brings the rain off the North Sea). It's a very long and narrow room, making quite a bottleneck by the serving counter, and beyond that, a long soft green built-in leather wall seat is flanked by narrow tables. Well kept Bass, Boddingtons, Butterknowle Conciliation, Hadrian Gladiator, Theakstons Best, and a weekly changing guest beer on handpump; lunchtime sandwiches and toasties (£1); friendly barmen, chatty customers; fruit machine. On some weekday evenings you can find it quiet, with regulars reading the papers put out in the front snug, but by Friday it should be quite packed. Note they don't allow children. *(Recommended by Noel Jackson, Louise Campbell, Thomas Nott, Dr and Mrs A K Clarke, Denis and Margaret Kilner, Ross Lockley, Stephen Brown)*

Free house ~ Manager Malcolm McPherson ~ Real ale ~ Lunchtime snacks (not Sun) ~ 0191-232 1269 ~ Open 11-11; 11-4, 7-11 Sat

Tap & Spile £ 🍺

33 Shields Road, Byker; from central motorway (A6127(M)) take A193/A187 Wallsend road, then fork off left into Shields Road Shopping Centre

A wide and rapidly changing choice of interesting and well kept real ales from around the country is kept in this simply but comfortably furnished place. All nicely priced, the regulars include Hadrian Gladiator, Jennings Cumberland, Marstons Pedigree, Ruddles Best and Thwaites Craftsman with up to nine others such as Badger Best, Bull Mastiff, Glenny Witney, Harviestoun Waverley, Mitchells ESB and Timothy Taylors Landlord. They also keep Westons Old Rosie farm cider and country wines. The nicer room is at the back, and has a quiet, relaxed atmosphere, bare boards, big modern windows, stripped brickwork, sturdy built-in wall seats, stripped chairs, and even tractor seats around one corner table. There are lots of old brewery pictures, cases of taps and spiles, models of cask slings and so forth. The front bar has pool, darts and fruit machine. Lunchtime sandwiches (£1). *(Recommended by Ross Lockley; more reports please)*

Pubmaster ~ Manager Kevin Watson ~ Real ale ~ Lunchtime snacks ~ 0191- 276 1440 ~ Live jazz Mon ~ Open 12-3, 6-11; all day Fri and Sat

NEWTON ON THE MOOR (Northumberland) NU1605 Map 10

Cook & Barker Arms 🍴 🛏

Village signposted from A1 Alnwick—Felton

Northumbria Dining Pub of the Year

Readers have been so pleased with the food at this carefully refurbished old pub this year that we have decided to give it a food award. Generously served and very good, there might be soup (£1.25), sandwiches like hot beef and onion or prawn and avocado with lime (from £2.95), pitta bread with pork and shrimp stir-fry or with prawns, smoked fish and tuna with salads and seafood sauce (from £3.50), walnut, peach and cottage cheese crunch or penne carbonara

(£3.95), salads (from £4.50), lamb's liver or a daily pie (£4.65), chicken cooked in wine with prawns and asparagus (£6.95), a duo of rainbow trout (£7.95), steaks (from £7.95), hearty grill (£8.50), and several puddings (from around £2.30). Well kept Boddingtons, Jennings Cumberland, Theakstons Best and XB, and Timothy Taylors Best and Landlord on handpump, 30 good malt whiskies, and decent wines; hardworking, friendly licensees and good prompt service – even when busy. The long beamed bar has a coal fire at one end with a coal-effect gas fire at the other, stripped, partly panelled walls, brocade-seated settles around oak-topped tables, framed banknotes and paintings by local artists on the walls, brasses, and a highly polished oak servery. What was the old storeroom now has tables, chairs and an old settle, and darts – it's popular with locals – and the games room has scrubbed pine furniture, french windows leading on to the terrace, and darts, dominoes, fruit machine and juke box. The popular restaurant was a blacksmith's shop and dates in part back to the 1700s. The pub has been calling itself Cook & Barker for some time now, like so many other pubs dropping its 'Arms'. *(Recommended by Les and Jean Scott, Julia Stone, June and Tony Baldwin, G A Pearce, Reg and Carrie Carr, John Allsopp, Mike Eeckelaers, Jack Morley, Gerald and Su Mason, B B Pearce, Roger A Bellingham)*

Free house ~ Licensees Lynn and Phil Farmer ~ Real ale ~ Meals and snacks ~ Evening restaurant ~ Shilbottle (01665) 575234 ~ Children in eating area of bar ~ Open 11-3, 6-11 ~ Bedrooms: £30B/£60B

NORTH SHIELDS (Tyne & Wear) NZ3468 Map 10

Chain Locker £ 🍺
New Quay

As this welcoming turn-of-the-century Tyneside pub is close to the pedestrian ferry landing area, there's quite a nautical theme, with seafaring pictures and navigational charts and maps on the walls (some giving a detailed account of the Falklands campaign). Also, local literature and arts information, stools and wooden wall benches around small tables (the one on your left as you go in, built over a radiator, is prized in winter) and an open fire. Four impeccably kept real ales on handpump (two are weekly changing guests) such as Bass, Ind Coope Burton, Tetleys, and Timothy Taylors Landlord; malt whiskies, farm ciders. Dominoes, fruit machine and piped music. Bar food, with prices unchanged since last year, includes lunchtime sandwiches, chilli con carne (£3.25) and steak in ale (£3.65), with a large amount of local fresh fish such as garlic mussels (£2.50), rock turbot in cider, smoked fish pie (£3.25) or cod and chips (£3.50); Sunday lunch. They may have free biscuits and cheese on a Sunday, when they sometimes organise boat trips. *(Recommended by Mrs M A Kilner, Jonathan Mann, Abigail Regan, John Oddey, Leonard Dixon, JJW, CMW; more reports please)*

Free house ~ Licensee Wilfred Kelly ~ Real ale ~ Meals and snacks (12-2.30, 6-9.30) ~ Restaurant (Thurs-Sat evening, and Sun lunch) ~ 0191-258 0147 ~ Children welcome ~ Folk music Fri evening ~ Open 11-11; 11.30-4, 6-11 Mon-Thurs in winter

Wooden Doll 🍺

103 Hudson Street; from Tyne Tunnel, follow A187 into town centre; keep straight ahead (when the A187 turns off left) until, approaching the sea, you can see the pub in Hudson Street on your right

There's a fascinating seagull's-eye view from the covered glassed-in verandah here down on the bustling boats and warehouses of the Shields Fish Quay, with the derricks and gantries beyond. Past them is the sweep of the outer harbour with its long piers, headlands and low Black Middens rocks. It's an unpretentious place with three simple and unassuming bars, a couple of chesterfields, red plush seats and Formica-topped cast-iron tables, and a coal-effect gas fire. A fine range of well kept real ales on handpump might include Courage Directors, Ind Coope Burton, Marstons Pedigree, Tetleys, Theakstons Best and Old Peculier, and Timothy Taylors Landlord; friendly service. Home-made bar food includes open baps (from

£2.45), cod or prawn bake (£4.50), seafood platter (£6.75), sirloin or T-bone steaks (from £7.95), puddings (from £1.55) and Sunday roasts (£4.50); not altogether surprisingly there may also be a number of fresh fish specials; much of the eating area is no smoking. Dominoes, fruit machine and piped music. Photographs and paintings by local artists are for sale. *(Recommended by JJW, CMW, Leonard Dixon, Graham and Karen Oddey, John Oddey, Dennis and Margaret Kilner)*

Free house ~ Licensee Colin Michael Pitman ~ Real ale ~ Meals and snacks (not Sun evenings) ~ 0191-257 3747 ~ Children in eating area of the bar ~ Live music Sat evening ~ Open 11-3, 6-11.30; all day Sat

PIERCEBRIDGE (Co Durham) NZ2116 Map 10

George 🛏

B6275 over bridge just S of village

During the five years that the friendly licensees have been at this busy old coaching inn, they have been carefully redecorating and refurbishing throughout – they tell us that they have now almost finished. It's in a fine setting by the River Tees, and the riverside gardens have several pleasant eating areas surrounded by colourful flowerbeds; you may see herons and even kingfishers. This is also where the clock *stopped short, never to go again, when the old man died,* and the venerable timepiece still stands silently in the hallway. The three bars have no fewer than five open fires in one room or another and solid wood furniture, and it's well worth a visit to the Ballroom Bar – just that, a bar inside a fully-fitted ballroom (open only for special functions or during barbecues); piped music. A wide choice of popular bar food includes sandwiches (£1.75), quite a few starters like good soup, tuna and cucumber savoury or pâté (all £1.95), vegetarian dishes such as fruit, vegetable and nut curry, apricot stuffing tartlet and orange sauce or stroganoff (all £4.65), huge salads (£4.65), and a wide selections of meat and fish dishes including steak and kidney pie (£4.65), cod in mushroom sauce (£4.65), pork in oyster sauce (£5.75), Roman chicken with mozzarella (£6.50), poached salmon in hollandaise (£8.45), good steaks (from £8.95), or half duckling in orange (£10.50); puddings such as sherry trifle, raspberry cheesecake or apple pie (£1.95), four course breakfasts (£5.50), afternoon tea, and Sunday lunch; attentive service. John Smiths, Theakstons Best and Websters Yorkshire on handpump, malt whiskies, and decent wines; to save staff, they often close the bars in the afternoon, but continue to serve beers in the tea room; piped music. The bedrooms are in the converted stables. Attractively positioned on the alternative, scenic route between Scotch Corner and Edinburgh, the inn is handy for various Roman remains. A fort once stood just over the bridge and there are some interesting excavations on display. *(Recommended by J M Turner, Brian Webster, Verity Kemp, Richard Mills, Mr and Mrs N Bogg, G and B Hartley, R T and J C Moggridge, J S Poulter, Mrs Cook, George Morrison, N R Beer, R J Walden, Maysie Thompson, David Varney, Joan and Tony Walker)*

Free house ~ Licensee John Wain ~ Real ale ~ Meals and snacks ~ Restaurant ~ (01325) 374576 ~ Children in eating area of bar and in restaurant ~ Open 11-11 ~ Bedrooms: £45B/55B

RENNINGTON (Northumberland) NU2119 Map 10

Masons Arms

Stamford Cott; B1340 NE of Alnwick

This friendly and well-run old coaching inn has an attractive lounge bar with ceiling beams, wheelback and mate's chairs around solid wooden tables on the patterned carpet, plush beige bar stools, lots of brass, pictures and photographs on the walls, and a relaxed atmosphere; the family room has pine panelling and wrought-iron wall lights. Boddingtons, Courage Directors, and Ruddles Best on handpump, and piped music but no noisy games machines. Popular bar food includes sandwiches, home-made soup (£1.50), home-made chicken liver and brandy pâté (£3.45), fried haddock or vegetable provençale (£4.95), game casserole (£5.50), gammon or chicken chasseur (£5.95), steaks (from £8.55), a choice of daily specials, and children's meals. There are sturdy rustic tables on the little front terrace, surrounded by lavender. The bedrooms are in recently converted stables. *(Recommended by Duncan Redpath, Lorraine Milburn, Les and Jean Scott, P D and J Bickley, Mark Bradley, Mrs M Armstrong, P G Jones, Jennie and Malc Wild, Revd L J and Mrs Melliss)*

Free house ~ Licensees Frank and Dee Sloan ~ Real ale ~ Meals and snacks ~ Restaurant ~ (01665) 577275 ~ Children in restaurant up to 8pm; no infants in evening ~ Open 12-2, 6.30-11 ~ Bedrooms: £33B/£43B

ROMALDKIRK (Durham) NY9922 Map 10

Rose & Crown ⑪ 🛏

Just off B6277

For over 250 years, people have been meeting at this rather smart old coaching inn with its relaxed and peaceful atmosphere. The beamed traditional bar has old-fashioned seats facing the log fire, a Jacobean oak settle, cream walls decorated with lots of gin traps, some old farm tools and black and white pictures of Romaldkirk at the turn of the century, as well as a grandfather clock, and lots of brass and copper. The smart Crown Room, where bar food is served, has more brass and copper, original coloured etchings of hunting scenes, and farm implements; the hall is hung with wine maps and other interesting prints. Very good – and popular – bar food includes home-made soup (£2.25), lunchtime filled brown baps (from £2.50), rich chicken liver pâté (£3.50), fresh pasta with blue Wensleydale cheese in fresh tomato sauce (£3.75), sausages, black pudding and onion confit (£3.95), lunchtime ploughman's with their own pickled onions and chutney (£4.95), smoked Loch Fyne salmon with scrambled eggs (£4.75), sautéed chicken livers, bacon and walnuts with fresh pasta (£5.25), steak, mushroom and ale pie (£7.50), 8oz sirloin steak (£10.50), evening dishes like pork fillet in sherry and cream sauce with fresh pasta (£7.95) or chicken breast with garlic butter (£8.50), daily specials like moules marinières baked with cream and Cotherstone cheese (£3.85), rabbit with grain mustard sauce (£6.50), baked fillets of whiting with oyster mushrooms and chives (£6.95), and char-grilled rump of venison with madeira sauce (£8.95), and home-made puddings like hot apple and Calvados tart or sherry and almond trifle (£2.75). The no-smoking oak-panelled restaurant has been completely refurbished this year. Theakstons Best and Old Peculier on handpump and several wines by the glass; good service. In the summer, the tables outside look out over the village green, still with its original stocks and water pump. The village is close to the superb Bowes Museum and the High Force waterfall, and has an interesting old church. *(Recommended by Paul and Janet Waring, Catheryn and Richard Hicks, Leonard Dixon, Maysie Thompson, Noel Jackson, Louise Campbell, John Honnor, Peter Race, John Fazakerley, Mavis and John Wright, John Cadman, R J Walden, Peter and Heidi Cook, Anthony Barnes, Mary and Peter Clark, Roger Bellingham, Gill and Maurice McMahon, Stephen Savill, R J Herd; also recommended by* The Good Hotel Guide*)*

Free house ~ Licensees Christopher and Alison Davy ~ Real ale ~ Meals and snacks ~ Restaurant (not Sun evening) ~ (01833) 560213 ~ Children welcome ~ Open 11-3, 5.30-11; closed 25/26 Dec ~ Bedrooms: £52B/£74B

SEAHOUSES (Northumberland) NU2232 Map 10

Olde Ship ★ 🛏

B1340 coast road

Although this marvellously atmospheric pub is very popular with the friendly local shipping fraternity, it's warmly welcoming to visitors too. And even those who are not particularly nautical could not fail to enjoy this treasure-trove of seafaring memorabilia. Everywhere you look in the small rooms there are shiny brass fittings, sea pictures and model ships, including a fine one of the North Sunderland lifeboat and a model of Seahouses' lifeboat *The Grace Darling*, as well as ships' instruments and equipment and a knotted anchor made by local fishermen; all the items are genuine. Even the floor of the saloon bar is scrubbed ship's decking, and if it weren't for the view through the one clear window, you could be almost forgiven for thinking you really were on a boat. The window looks out over the harbour to the Farne Islands (the rest have stained-glass sea pictures). There is another low-beamed snug bar, and a family room at the back. Popular bar food includes sandwiches, home-made soups such as vegetable or delicious crab (£1.50), steak and kidney pie, beef olives, liver and onions, beef and rabbit pie or cheesy baked haddock (all £4), puddings such as bakewell tart, chocolate trifle or raspberry pie (£1.50), and evening extras like roast leg of lamb, a vegetarian dish or fisherman's pie using local cod (all £5.50). Five real ales on handpump might include Longstone Bitter (from a micro-brewery just along the road at Belford), Morlands Old Speckled Hen, McEwans 70/-, Theakstons Best, XB and Old Peculier, and Youngs No 3 and Special, some kept under light blanket pressure; they also serve several malt whiskies, a hot toddy and mulled wine in winter, and some uncommon bottled beers. Open fire, dominoes, trivia and piped music. Pews surround barrel tables in the back courtyard, and a battlemented side terrace with a sun lounge looks out on the harbour. An anemometer is connected to the top of the chimney. This year, two of the bedrooms have been upgraded, the hotel frontage has been smartened up, they are hoping to add a conservatory on to the Ward Room function room, and bar meals have been extended to include evenings. You can book boat trips to the Farne Islands Bird Sanctuary at the harbour, and there are bracing coastal walks, particularly to Bamburgh, Grace Darling's birthplace. *(Recommended by A Craig, June and Tony Baldwin, Julie Munday, Martin Robinson, Julie Peters, Stephen and Julie Brown, Trevor and Christine Millum, Thomas Nott, D Devine, Penny and Peter Keevil, George and Chris Miller, Michael A Butler, Duncan Redpath, Lorraine Milburn, D Maplethorpe, Nigel and Teresa Blocks, Penny and Peter Keevil, P K Eames, Olive Carroll, Barry and Anne)*

Free house ~ Licensees Alan and Jean Glen ~ Real ale ~ Meals and snacks ~ Restaurant (not Sun evening) ~ (01665) 720200 ~ Children in restaurant until 8.30pm ~ Open 11-3, 6-11 ~ Bedrooms: £33B/£66B

SEATON SLUICE (Northumberland) NZ3477 Map 10

Waterford Arms

Just off A193 N of Whitley Bay

The emphasis in this comfortably modernised pub is very much on the big helpings of fresh fish from the nearby fish market. A big choice of seafood dishes might include battered cod or haddock (priced according to size – small, medium or large from £4.50 to £9), crab and prawn salad (£4.95), a generous seafood platter (£6.75), halibut with a prawn and lobster sauce or swordfish florentine (£6.95); also other food such as soup (90p), hot or cold sandwiches (from £1.95), garlic mushrooms (£2.50), mushroom and nut fettucine or vegetable Mexicana (£4.50), good steaks (from £7.95), daily specials, and puddings (from £1.95); part of the restaurant is no smoking. Well kept Vaux Bitter, Double Maxim, and Wards Best and Thorne on handpump; pool in the back lobby. The bar has spacious green plush banquettes in its roomy bays, bright paintings in one high-ceilinged room, and brown plush furnishings in another; darts, dominoes, fruit machine, juke box and piped music. *(Recommended by John Oddey, Mrs M A Kilner, Wendy Arnold, M G Hart, R T Moggridge)*

Vaux ~ Tenant Christopher Hall ~ Real ale ~ Meals and snacks (all day summer Suns but not winter Sun evenings) ~ Restaurant (not winter Sun evenings) ~ 0191-237 0450 ~ Children welcome ~ Open 11-3, 7-11

STANNERSBURN (Northumberland) NY7286 Map 10

Pheasant 🍺

Kielder Water road signposted off B6320 in Bellingham

Just below Kielder Water, this friendly and pleasantly unpretentious inn is in a very peaceful valley, with picnic-table sets out in the streamside garden, a pony-paddock behind, and quiet forests all around. The red-carpeted largely stripped-stone lounge is traditional, comfortable and attractive, and the separate public bar, similar but simpler, opens into a games room with darts, pool and dominoes; in the evenings there's a happy mix of locals and visitors. There is a no-smoking carpeted country dining room; besides sandwiches, good home-cooked bar food with fresh vegetables includes lasagne, seafood pasta, haddock, garlic chicken and pies such as chicken and leek or steak and kidney (all £4.95 at lunchtime). Prices are a bit higher in the evening, with extra dishes such as sole filled with crab, cider-baked gammon with Cumberland sauce (£5.75) and steaks (from £9.75). Well kept Ind Coope Burton, Tetleys and Theakstons Best and XB on handpump, a good collection of malt whiskies, decent wines, good welcoming service. Breakfasts are good. *(Recommended by J S Poulter, Ian and Sue Stratford, John Allsopp, Denis and Margaret Kilner, Pauline Crossland, Dave Cawley)*

Free house ~ Licensees Walter and Irene Kershaw ~ Real ale ~ Meals and snacks ~ Restaurant ~ (01434) 240382 ~ Children in eating area lunchtime and early evening ~ Open 11-3, 6-11 (winter 12-2, 6.30 or 7-11) ~ Bedrooms: £30B/£52B

WARENFORD   (Northumberland) NU1429 Map 10

Warenford Lodge
Just off A1 Alnwick—Belford, on village loop road

It's easy to drive straight past this pub as there is no pub sign – and it does look like an ordinary small stone house from the outside. Inside, the bar looks modern with cushioned wooden seats around pine tables, some stripped stone walls, and a warm fire in the big stone fireplace; steps lead up to an extension which has comfortable easy chairs and settees around low tables, and a big woodburning stove. Attractively presented, often imaginative home-made bar food might include home-made soup or creamed mushroom canapé (£1.95), spinach and cheese pancakes (£2.90), a pan of grilled herbed mussels (£3.50), tagliatelle with fresh tomato and rosemary sauce topped with pecorino cheese (£3.90), cold roast pork with a fruit and crumb stuffing (said to have been Oliver Cromwell's favourite meal, £5.20), chicken with lemon grass and ginger (£6.50), pepperpot of beef with cinnamon, cloves, sugar and chilli (£6.90), halibut baked with a crunchy topping (£7.20), Italian shank of pork (£10.65), grilled sirloin steak (£11.60), and puddings like jam roly poly or home-made ginger ice cream (from £1.95); decent selection of wines. *(Recommended by Trevor and Christine Millum, Jill and Peter Bickley, Les and Jean Scott, Thomas Nott, Penny and Peter Keevil, G A Peace, Anthony John, John Coatsworth, P R Williams, Dr P D Smart)*

Free house ~ Licensee Raymond Matthewman ~ Meals and snacks (not Mon, not lunchtimes except weekends when lunchtime service stops 1.30) ~ Evening restaurant ~ (01668) 213453 ~ Children in restaurant ~ Open 7-11 (closed weekday lunchtimes), plus 12-2 Sat and Sun; closed Mon except bank holidays

---

Stars after the name of a pub show exceptional character and appeal. They don't mean extra comfort. And they are nothing to do with food quality, for which there's a separate knife-and-fork symbol. Even quite a basic pub can win stars, if it's individual enough.

Lucky Dip

Besides the fully inspected pubs, you might like to try these Lucky Dips recommended to us and described by readers (if you do, please send us reports):

Acomb, N'land [NY9366], *Miners Arms*: Small 18th-c pub, up to seven real ales, good coffee, comfortable settles, huge fire in stone fireplace, advertising mirrors, brass plates, Formica-top sewing-machine tables; attractive garden behind; children in dining room *(JJW, CMW)*

☆ **Allendale**, N'land [NY8456], *Golden Lion*: Friendly old pub with two or three changing real ales, lots of country wines, wide choice of good value food (not Mon) inc several vegetarian dishes and cheap Tues-Sat afternoon menu, partly no-smoking dining area with more room upstairs, two real fires, pictures, old bottles, willow-pattern plates; games area with pool and darts, piped music; children welcome; bedrooms *(JJW, CMW, Adrian Dodd-Noble)*

Allendale [B6295], *Hare & Hounds*: Chatty landlord, cheap Websters and hot pies, pleasant atmosphere, nice 18th-c building (modernised); bedrooms *(JJW, CMW, Adrian Dodd-Noble)*; [B6295], *Hotspur*: Roomy, with friendly service, three real ales, wide choice of food, low prices; unusual bow windows and carvings, piped music, pool etc; children welcome; bedrooms *(JJW, CMW, Adrian Dodd-Noble)*; [Market Pl, B6295], *Kings Head*: S&N ales with guests such as Butterknowle, Marstons Pedigree, Morlands Old Speckled Hen and Youngs Special, no games machines or music, newspapers, big log fire, darts, dominoes, chess and outdoor quoits, friendly helpful service; bar food inc good value sandwiches, specials, children's dishes and puddings; Fri evening live music, children welcome; comfortable bedrooms *(JJW, CMJ, Edward Watson, Adrian Dodd-Noble)*

☆ **Allenheads**, N'land [just off B6295; NY8545], *Allenheads*: Treasurehouse of antiques and bric-a-brac (esp in pool room), very friendly, entertaining landlord, huge helpings of good cheap food, well kept Tetleys and occasional guests such as Morlands Old Speckled Hen, decent coffee; dining room; tables outside, with more machinery; bedrooms *(David and Margaret Bloomfield, JJW, CMJ)*

☆ **Alnmouth**, N'land [N'land St; NU2511], *Saddle:* Enormous helpings of well cooked fresh food inc fresh veg and fesh fruit puddings in clean and friendly old pub rambling through several rooms, unpretentious and homely; well kept S&N and local ales, helpful staff, paintings for sale *(Nigel and Teresa Brooks, Penny and Peter Keevil, CW, JW)*

☆ **Alnwick** N'land [Fenkle St; NU1913], *Market Tavern*: Popular basic no-frills pub with good value food, huge helpings at really bargain prices, friendly and efficient service, warm friendly atmosphere *(Chris and Anne Fluck, Duncan Redpath, Lorraine Milburn)*; [Narrowgate], *Olde Cross*: Pleasant well kept pub with well kept ale, bar food, interesting window display, games room *(D Devine)*

Anick, N'land [signed NE of A69/A695 Hexham junction; NY9665], *Rat*: Friendly nicely refurbished pub overlooking magnificent north Tyne valley, good home-cooked meals from hot counter, esp Sun roasts and home-made puddings like lemon meringue, apple crumble and blackberry and raspberry pie with custard, well kept Courage-related ales, friendly cat; children welcome, lovely garden *(Penny and Peter Keevil)*

☆ **Bamburgh**, N'land [NU1835], *Lord Crewe Arms*: Small hotel with interesting bric-a-brac and good log fire in back cocktail bar, serviceable side bar (children, can get noisy), usual bar food, restaurant with good service, tables outside; main draw is great position below magnificent castle by coast; dogs allowed; bedrooms comfortable, good breakfasts esp kippers *(Thomas Nott, D T Deas, Mr and Mrs Moody, Catheryn and Richard Hicks, Julia Stone, LYM)*

☆ **Barnard Castle**, Dur [Market Pl; NZ0617], *Golden Lion*: Warm welcome, generous good value home-cooked lunchtime food inc children's helpings in two roomy bars, unpretentious but comfortable, well kept Bass and Youngers Scotch, children's room; rather small but decent bedrooms *(Penny and Peter Keevil, Brian Kneale, John Fazakerley, BB)*

☆ **Barrasford**, N'land [NY9274], *Barrasford Arms*: Friendly country local, lovely sandstone building, with blazing fires, good generous straightforward home cooking at sensible prices; keg beer and can be smoky; dining room, residents' lounge, children's room; good value bedrooms *(John Oddey)*

Beadnell, N'land [NU2329], *Craster Arms*: Good bar food and Sun lunch, plenty of room with lots of tables, friendly service; games room; children welcome *(Philip and Helen Heppell)*

☆ **Beamish**, Dur [NZ2254], *Shepherd & Shepherdess*: Very useful for its position nr outstanding open air heritage museum; wide choice of cheap quick straightforward food with good puddings, rather standard layout with tables around walls, but comfortable, with good service, well kept Vaux Samson and Wards Sheffield Best; can get crowded, piped music; children welcome, tables and play area with fibreglass monsters out among trees; has been open all day *(Derek and Sylvia Stephenson, Mrs D Craig, Mr and Mrs C*

Brown, Anthony John, Trevor Scott, Mrs
M A Kilner, LYM)

Beamish, Dur [off A693 signed No Place
and Cooperative Villas, S of museum;
NZ2254], *Beamish Mary*: Friendly down-
to-earth 1960s pub with Durham NUM
banner in games room, very assorted
furnishings and bric-a-brac in bar with Aga;
Hartleys, Theakstons, a beer brewed for
them by Big Lamp and maybe a guest beer,
piped music; quiet lunchtime, lively evening
with live music in converted stables concert
room; bedrooms *(JJW, CMJ)*; [far side of
Beamish Open Air Museum – entry fee],
Sun: Part of the museum; very basic, with
well kept McEwans 80/- and Youngers No
3, black pudding nibbles and filled barm
cakes, real turn-of-the-century feel – before
the days when you could expect ice and
lemon in your gin; it does get packed
(LYM)

☆ **Belford**, N'land [Market Pl; village signed
off A1 S of Berwick; NU1134], *Blue Bell*:
Distinctive traditional-feeling family stable
bar (the Belford Tavern) with plentiful bar
food (maybe not on bank hols) inc
children's dishes and cut-price OAPs'
helpings, keg beer, darts, pool and piped
music, also separate comfortable, stylish
and relaxing hotel lounge, pleasantly old-
fashioned restaurant; children in eating
areas; comfortable bedrooms *(Thomas
Nott, LYM)*

Bellingham, N'land [NY8483], *Cheviot*:
Decent food inc sandwiches and well kept
ales in cosy pleasantly redecorated bars;
bedrooms *(Mr and Mrs R J Foreman)*

Belsay, N'land [NZ1079], *Highlander*:
Good range of food in bar and restaurant,
reasonable prices, cheerful welcome, well
kept Youngers No 3 on handpump, good
log fire *(Mrs M A Kilner)*

☆ **Berwick upon Tweed**, N'land [Spittal Rd,
Tweedmouth; NU0053], *Rob Roy*:
Outstanding local fish a speciality in quiet
and cosy seaview pub with roaring fire and
polished wood floor, fishing theme, friendly
landlord; keg beers but good fresh coffee;
bedrooms *(Jim and Maggie Cowell,
Thomas Nott)*

Berwick upon Tweed [A1 N of town, nr
Safeways], *Meadow House*: Tidy little pub,
the most northerly in England *(Thomas
Nott)*

☆ **nr Berwick upon Tweed** [West Allerdean; 5
miles S – B6354 towards Duddo, Etal – OS
Sheet 75 map ref 965465], *Plough*:
Cheerful homely country local out by farm,
chapel and sheep fields, good value
straightforward food in pine-furnished back
dining room, woodburner in understated
traditional lounge, bar done out with lots
of standard rustic memorabilia, back games
bar; Allied beers, Burmese cats, pleasant
garden with splendid Cheviot views and
play area *(Les and Jean Scott, Jean and
Douglas Troup, Roger Berry, Thomas
Nott)*

Bowes, Dur [A66 about 4 miles W;

NY9212], *Bowes Moor*: One of England's
highest hotels, oasis on this bleak dual
carriageway; breakfast for passing reps, bar
food, restaurant, very welcoming licensees;
good value wine by glass; bedrooms *(Frank
Davidson)*

Butterknowle, Dur [off B6282; NZ1126],
Malt Shovel: Isolated extended stonebuilt
country pub known as the Wham, well kept
local Butterknowle ales and Boddingtons,
reasonable choice of good value bar food 5-
11 and Sat lunchtime, good value Sun
lunch, attentive waitresses, pictures in long
bar with open fire and horse tack, fruit
machines, piped pop music; children very
welcome *(Duncan Small, JJW, CMW)*

☆ **Catton**, N'land [B6295 N of Allendale;
NY8358], *Crown*: Good value home-
cooked food till 10 inc children's dishes, lots
of sandwiches and take-aways in friendly
and cosy traditional pub with big log fire,
Theakstons and other beers, specialist teas
and coffee with real milk, jovial landlord,
pool, darts, juke box, piped music; small
garden; children and dogs welcome *(JJW,
CMW, Adrian Dodd-Noble)*

Chester le Street, Dur [A167 just S – OS
Sheet 88 map ref 267493; NZ2752],
Chester Moor: Rather townified pub with
wide range of cheerfully served good value
food – even a 7-course Greek menu *(Prof
Ron Leigh)*

☆ **Coatham Mundeville**, Dur [Brafferton
Lane; off A68, ¼ mile from A1(M);
NZ2920], *Foresters Arms*: Big helpings of
good reasonably priced food and well kept
Black Sheep, John Smiths Magnet and
Theakstons Best; pleasant helpful staff *(R J
Walden, Norman Beer)*

☆ **Coatham Mundeville** [part of Hallgarth
Hotel; from A1(M) turn towards Brafferton
off A167 Darlington rd on hill], *Stables*:
Good choice of well prepared bar food and
Sun lunches in enjoyable and roomy
converted high-ceilinged stone outbuildings
with no-smoking eating area, four well kept
S&N real ales; side conservatory for
families; bedrooms *(R J Walden)*

☆ **Corbridge**, N'land [Middle St; NY9964],
Black Bull: Roomy old-fashioned pub, open
all day and doing well under newish
management; low ceilings, stone floor,
traditional settles, mix of comfortable
chairs, roaring fire; wide range of ales with
well kept guest beers, lots of country wines,
good choice of wines, big helpings of good
food, nice friendly atmosphere; popular
with young people evenings *(Graham and
Lynn Mason, Jane, Stuart and Caroline,
Noel Jackson, Louise Campbell)*

Corbridge [Station Rd], *Dyvels*:
Unassuming old stonebuilt Bass pub nr
railway station with well kept beer inc
unusual guests, good atmosphere, tables in
pleasant outside area; bedrooms well
furnished, super value *(Paul Boot)*

☆ **Cornforth**, Dur [Metal Bridge; off B6291
N; NZ3134], *Wild Boar*: Comfortable L-
shaped main bar with boar's head, pictures,

brasses, horse tackle, farm tools, sewing-machine tables; big friendly family room with overhead model train, canaries in cage; good value generous fresh food inc takeaways and upstairs bistro, real ales such as Bass, Big Lamp Blackout and Stocks Old Horizontal, prompt obliging service; garden with big play area and rides on miniature railway; BR intercity trains run by *(CW, JW, M P Wood)*

☆ **Cramlington**, N'land [NZ2777], *Plough*: Good value bar food and wide choice of well kept real ales in big open-plan pub attractively converted from farm buildings; good friendly service, nice setting *(Mike Simpson)*

Crookham, N'land [A697 Wooler—Cornhill; NT9238], *Blue Bell*: Smart small pub with jolly atmosphere, Bass tapped from the cask, decent straightforward food, efficient service *(Thomas Nott)*

Cullercoats, T&W [NZ3771], *Queens Head*: Recently refurbished local with good food, well kept Bass on handpump, friendly efficient local; very popular with locals *(John Oddey)*

Darlington, Dur [NZ2915], *Kings Head*: Immaculate old-fashioned county hotel with charming obliging waitresses, civilised food and drink; bedrooms *(SS)*

Dunstan, N'land [NU2520], *Cottage*: Long low cottage-row conversion, low-beamed and softly lit, with smart staff, pleasant back conservatory, usual food; partly covered sheltered arbour full of flowers, huge lawn; new bedrooms *(RC, Dave Irving, GSB)*

☆ **Durham** [Sadler St, between Market Sq and cathedral], *Shakespeare*: Particularly well kept S&N real ales with a guest such as Marstons Pedigree, busy unpretentious front bar, charming panelled snug, back room with signed actor photographs; lots of malt whiskies, simple cheap bar snacks, efficient service; children welcome, open all day – convenient for castle, cathedral and river *(John Fazakerley, LYM)*

Durham [84 New Elvet], *City*: Originally 17th-c, with spacious series of knocked-through much refurbished rooms, comfortable banquettes, bric-a-brac; wide range of food, well kept Tetleys and Imperial; bedrooms *(Walter Reid, John Fazakerley)*; [A167 N of Nevilles Cross], *Duke of Wellington*: Useful for wide range of decent food inc lots for vegetarians; well kept Bass, pleasant staff *(GSB, John Allsopp)*; [New Elvet], *Half Moon*: Mainly a drinking pub but does some food like toasted sandwiches on Sun; well kept real ale, comfortable lower bar, bare-boarded top one *(Mrs M Kilner)*; [Market Sq], *Market*: Recently refurbished, traditional wooden furniture, two levels, good atmosphere, friendly efficient staff, limited food, well kept S&N ales with a guest such as Jennings Cumberland *(Mark Fawcitt)*; [Elvet Bridge], *Swan & Three Cygnets*: Brightly refurbished Victorian pub in good

bridge-end spot, reasonably priced bar food kept warm at servery, Sam Smiths ales, good river and city views from big windows *(Derek and Sylvia Stephenson, Walter Reid)*

East Cramlington, N'land [NZ2876], *Bay Horse*: Smartly refurbished with comfortable dark red banquettes, good well presented bar food, particularly well kept Bass; friendly helpful staff *(John Oddey)*

Edmondbyers, Dur [NZ0250], *Punch Bowl*: Plain free house with good home cooking – sausage and onion pudding highly recommended *(Dave Braisted)*

☆ **Eggleston**, Dur [off B6278 N of Barnard Castle; NY9924], *Three Tuns*: Charming spot by broad sloping Teesdale village green, log fire and some interesting furniture in relaxing traditional beamed bar, warm welcome, generous straightforward food (not Sun evening) in big-windowed back room, Whitbreads Castle Eden and an occasional guest beer; tables on terrace and in garden; children welcome, cl Mon lunchtime exc bank hols *(WAH, Stephen Savill, LYM)*

Ellingham, N'land [signed off A1 N of Alnwick – OS Sheet 75 map ref 167257; NU1726], *Pack Horse*: Decent bar food in friendly well run bar and two rooms off *(Philip and Helen Heppell)*

Elwick, Clvd [¼ mile off A19 W of Hartlepool; NZ4532], *McOrville*: Recently taken over by ex-brewery man, warm cosy atmosphere, friendly service, good basic food cooked by his wife *(Mrs P Heslop, JHBS)*

☆ **Etal**, N'land [off B6354 SW of Berwick; NT9339], *Black Bull*: Pretty thatched local in attractive village by ruins of Etal Castle, straightforward food inc good sandwiches in modernised lounge, well kept Lorimers Scotch, Tetleys and Wards Sheffield Best; nice walks, nr steam railway; can get a bit crowded *(CW, JW, Roger Berry, D Cox, GSB, F A Noble, LYM)*

Felling, T&W [Whitemore Pool, Wardley; just off A1(M) – OS Sheet 88 map ref 310614; NZ3161], *Green*: Large lounge, separate bar, restaurant area, Bass, Ruddles County, Theakstons Best and XB and a couple of guest beers, pleasant atmosphere; light piped music *(Mrs M Kilner)*; [Carlisle St, handy for Metro], *Wheatsheaf*: Cheap well kept Big Lamp ales in clean and comfortable basic backstreet pub, real fire, snacks *(JW, CW)*

☆ **Fir Tree**, Dur [A68 West Auckland—Tow Law; NZ1434], *Duke of York*: Wide choice of reliable food served cheerfully in comfortable roadside pub with dining room off cosy wing-chair bar; real ale, racing prints, children welcome, tables outside *(Mrs K I Burvill, Caroline Shearer, BB)*

☆ **Framwellgate Moor**, Dur [Front St; NZ2745], *Tap & Spile*: Good range of well kept beers, decent food at low prices; children really welcome, one room with board games, another with pool and fruit machine *(Mark Havers)*

☆ **Great Stainton**, Dur [useful detour from A1; NZ3422], *Kings Arms*: Wide range of consistently good attractively priced food, well kept Whitbreads Castle Eden, friendly and comfortable; restaurant *(M E A Horler)*

☆ **Great Whittington**, N'land [NZ0171], *Queens Head*: Friendly old stone pub now moving into a different league under new management: two comfortably rustic refurbished beamed rooms opened together with log fires, mural over fireplace, carved oak settles, key collection, prints; good food here and in attractive new restaurant, well kept Marstons Pedigree, Tetleys and two guest beers such as Hambleton, attentive service; tables out on small front lawn; has been closed Mon lunchtime *(Philip and Helen Heppell, JJW, CMJ, GSB, John Oddey)*

Haltwhistle, N'land [Castle Hill; NY7164], *Spotted Cow*: Central bar, dining and games areas (pool, darts, TV) off, five real ales, wide choice of reasonably priced food inc lots of pizzas, vegetarian dishes, Fri/Sat evening bargains; open all day Sat, cl Tues lunch; fruit machine, juke box; seats out in front *(CW, JW)*; [Rowfoot, Featherstone Pk – OS Sheet 86 map ref 683607], *Wallace Arms*: Pleasant rambling old former farmhouse with barn dining room, attractive grounds and bedrooms, which has been popular for good value food, real ales; but found closed spring 1994 *(News please)*

Hamsterley, Dur [nr Witton-le-Wear; NZ1231], *Cross Keys*: Generous helpings of good value food, John Smiths real ale; good walking in nearby Hamsterley Forest *(Mrs M Kilner)*

Hartlepool, Clvd [Stranton; formerly Tap & Spile; NZ5133], *Causeway*: Decent Camerons pub right by the brewery *(JHBS)*; [Wooler Rd], *White House*: Former school, particularly well kept Tetleys *(JHBS)*

☆ **Haydon Bridge**, N'land [NY8464], *General Havelock*: Limited choice of lunchtime bar food (not Sun) and good interesting if rather pricy full evening meals (not Sun) and full Sunday lunch in civilised and individually decorated pub with atmospheric Tyne-view stripped stone restaurant (not Sun evening); well kept Tetleys, good wines by the glass, pleasant service, friendly local atmosphere, children and dogs allowed; closed Mon/Tues, also early Jan and Sept, also week after Easter *(Mr and Mrs C Brown, B B Pearce, LYM)*

☆ **Hexham**, N'land [Priestpopple; E end of main st, on left entering from Newcastle; NY9464], *County*: Reliably good straightforward lunches from particularly good sandwiches up in cosy hotel lounge, good friendly waitresses, proper coffee; bedrooms *(Dr R H M Stewart)*

Hexham, N'land [East Wallhouses, Military Rd (B6318)], *Robin Hood*: Friendly welcome, good food *(John Oddey)*

☆ **High Force**, Dur [B6277 about 4 miles NW of Middleton-in-Teesdale; NY8728], *High Force*: A mountain rescue post, perfectly placed for the high moors (and England's highest waterfall, for which it's named); good service, straightforward food from sandwiches to steaks (not winter Mon evenings), good range of malt whiskies; children allowed; new owners with ambitions for the hotel side *(JRL, Mrs D Craig)*

☆ **Holy Island**, N'land [NU1343], *Lindisfarne*: Friendly owners and locals, lots of whiskies, very well prepared straightforward food from local crab sandwiches up in bar and simple dining room, morning coffee, teas and high teas; children welcome, well kept garden; bedrooms good value *(Scott and Ann Foringer, John Hazel, A Craig, Julia Stone)*

Holy Island, *Northumberland Arms*: Small welcoming local, friendly cockatoo called Cocky (a sucker for toast crusts), well kept Border ale, open fire, very limited food; bedrooms *(Olive Carroll, John Hazel, Mrs M A Kilner)*

Horsley, N'land [B6528; just off A69 Newcastle—Hexham; NZ0966], *Crown & Anchor*: Friendly pub doubling as a post office; comfortable banquettes and high-backed carvers in L-shaped bar with big bay window, pictures and fish tank, chatty landlord, three real ales, good generous food, high chair provided, picnic-table sets in garden with benches, play area and lovely Tynedale views *(JJW, CMW)*; *Lion & Lamb*: Efficient 18th-c pub with lounge and larger restaurant, stove and log-effect gas fire in lounge, good value lunchtime bar meals, Whitbreads Castle Eden, wines on tap *(JJW, CMW, Leonard Dixon)*

Houghton le Spring, T&W [NZ3450], *Burn*: Good food, friendly atmosphere *(Norman Beer)*

Humshaugh, N'land [off B6320 N of Hexham; NY9272], *Crown*: Basic old village local with woodburner, food (not Fri evening) inc good home-made shepherd's pie, Belhaven 80/- and Boddingtons on handpump; bedrooms *(CW, JW)*

Lamesley, T&W [minor rd S of Gateshead western bypass, A1, Team Valley junction; NZ2558], *Ravensworth Arms*: Large S&N dining pub with good value bar food from servery, well kept Theakstons Best and XB, good coffee, games machines, lots of piped music; children welcome, play area and picnic-table sets outside; open all day *(JJW, CMW)*

☆ **Lanchester**, Dur [NZ1647], *Queens Head*: Good generous often interesting food, well kept Vaux beers, decent wines and friendly and attentive Swedish landlady in comfortable high-ceilinged village pub *(Pat Woodward)*

Longframlington, N'land [NU1301], *Granby*: Comfortably modernised two-room bar very popular for generous food from sandwiches to steaks, good collection of malt whiskies, restaurant; service generally welcoming but can be offhand (the Editor's favourite band from the 1970s, coming from their luxury touring bus parked some way off, were refused admission on the grounds that they were a coach party – just six of them); bedrooms in main building good, with big breakfasts *(R C Lewis, Roger A Bellingham, Mr and Mrs Moody, LYM)*

☆ **Longhorsley**, N'land [Linden Hall Hotel, a mile N of village; NZ1597], *Linden Pub*: Sprucely converted ex-granary pub behind country house conference hotel in extensive grounds; briskly served limited but generous bar food, a couple of well kept real ales such as Boddingtons and Whitbreads Castle Eden, upper gallery restaurant, quite a few old enamel advertising signs; children welcome, bedrooms in main hotel *(GSB, A Craig, Dave Irving, Thomas Nott, LYM)*

☆ **Lowick**, N'land [2 Main St (B6353); off A1 S of Berwick upon Tweed – OS Sheet 75 map ref 013396; NU0139], *Black Bull*: Comfortable and attractive main bar and small back bar in pleasant country pub on edge of small pretty village, popular dining room with good choice of food inc vegetarian, McEwans ale, friendly attentive staff *(D Maplethorpe, Les and Jean Scott, P and J Daggett)*

☆ **Marsden**, T&W [signposted passage to lift in A183 car park, just before entering Marsden coming from Whitburn; NZ4164], *Grotto*: Uniquely built into seaside cliff caverns, with lift down to two floors – upper pink plush, lower brown varnish; Vaux Samson real ales, food in bar and restaurant, good sea views *(Pauline Crossland, Dave Cawley)*

Mickleton, Dur [NY9724], *Rose & Crown*: Good value bar food, character landlord, cheap and cheerful place to stay – bedrooms remarkably inexpensive *(G W Lindley)*

☆ **Middleton in Teesdale**, Dur [Mkt Pl; NY9526], *Teesdale*: Well furnished if rather brightly lit hotel lounge bar with very attentive service, good value if not cheap food, well kept Tetleys, log fire; comfortable bedrooms *(Phil and Heidi Cook)*

Morpeth, N'land [Manchester St; NZ2086], *Tap & Spile*: Cosy little two-room pub, comfortable and friendly, seven real ales on handpump, farm cider, good value food; service can slow when busy; children welcome, open all day *(JJW, CMW)*

☆ **Newcastle upon Tyne** [High Bridge], *Duke of Wellington*: Small and comfortable, with well kept cheap real ales inc Marstons Pedigree, Tetleys and Timothy Taylors, good range of reasonably priced bar food till it runs out; lots of 19th-c prints and documents, many connected with Wellington; open all day, next to market so gets very busy *(Denis and Margaret Kilner,*

Dr and Mrs A K Clarke)

Newcastle upon Tyne [St Peters Basin], *Fog on the Tyne*: Comfortable new pub overlooking marina, maritime pictures, piped music, four or five well kept real ales on handpump, welcoming helpful staff, changing choice of good bar food *(John Oddey)*; [off Stowell St, between Percy St and Gallowgate], *Newcastle Arms*: Smart pub with traditional fittings, old photographs, well kept Ind Coope Burton *(Dr and Mrs A K Clarke)*; [44 The Side, Quayside], *Off Shore*: Good value lunchtime food esp carvery in well converted warehouse with low-ceilinged dark-panelled front bar linking back through to room with flagstones and sawdust, loft ceilings supported by old oak columns, stone and brick walls; some tables and stools wound with rope to look like capstans, bits of rigging and nautical items, well kept Courage Directors and other ales, friendly atmosphere; younger crowd evenings *(John Oddey, Graham and Karen Oddey)*; [Quayside], *Red House*: Stone-walled bar with two rooms off, generous helpings of good cheap food 11-6 from doorstep sandwiches up, Courage-related and S&N beers, jukebox *(D Harrison)*; [Stowell St], *Rosies*: Bustling, friendly, eccentric city centre pub, interesting decor with weird and wonderful objects hanging from ceiling, good juke box with folksy Irish feel reflected in music; eclectic mix of people, well kept beer, friendly staff *(Jane, Stuart and Caroline)*

Newton, Clvd [A173; the one in Cleveland, at NZ5713], *Kings Head*: Good value food from wide range of excellent attractively presented unusual sandwiches to Sun lunch, good friendly attentive service, wide choice of beer and real cappuccino coffee in spruce modernised dining pub, pleasant surroundings nr Roseberry Topping; tables out on terrace *(D P Wilcox, G K and D M Holden)*

☆ **Newton by the Sea**, N'land [The Square, Low Newton; NU2426], *Ship*: Quaint and cosy pub tucked into top corner of courtyard of old cottages facing beach and sea, with tables out on green; good snacks, keg beers, coffee, tea and ices; pool table, children welcome *(Andrew and Susan Field, R and G Underwood)*

North Shields, T&W [Camden St; NZ3470], *Magnesia Bank*: Big brightly lit bar in Victorian pub with well kept real ale; pleasant atmosphere *(GSB)*; [Bell St], *Prince of Wales*: Three well refurbished differently decorated smallish rooms inc lounge with black and red tiled floor, dark red leather settle, stained wood, polished brass, old photographs of Tyne ships, coal fire; cheap well kept Sam Smiths OB and Museum, usual bar food *(John Oddey)*

Otterburn, N'land [NY8992], *Percy Arms*: Useful hotel with coal fires in both lounge bars, Theakstons Best and XB, decent range of well priced spirits, good value bar food (may be a wait), friendly staff, juke box in back bar; comfortable bedrooms *(Andrew and Susan Field, Denis and Margaret Kilner)*

Ovington, N'land [signposted off A69 Corbridge—Newcastle; NZ0764], *Highlander*: Village pub with bar, games room (pool and darts) and restaurant, good value food, three S&N real ales on handpump, TV, quiet piped music, garden with play area; open all day summer; bedrooms *(JJW, CMW)*

Penshaw, T&W [nr Monument; NZ3254], *Grey Horse*: Welcoming, well kept Tetleys on handpump, low-priced good simple lunchtime food (not Sun) *(Mrs M A Kilner)*

Ponteland, N'land [North Rd; NZ1773], *Blackbird*: Lovely old pub being carefully redone by new licensee, stone-vaulted ceiling, well kept Theakstons on handpump, good value straightforward food *(John Oddey)*; [Main St], *Seven Stars*: Well refurbished in old-fashioned style, S&N beers, efficient friendly service, good value food *(John Oddey)*

Portobello, T&W [just SE of Birtley; NZ2855], *Board*: Comfortable and friendly old pub, games room with darts and dominoes, split-level beamed extension bar with plate collection, old photographs, fruit machines and TV; wide choice of reasonably priced food, well kept Boddingtons on handpump; children under supervision *(JJW, CMW)*

Riding Mill, N'land [NZ0262], *Wellington*: Large S&N dining pub with standard good value meals, two Theakstons ales, piped pop music; children welcome, disabled access; play area and picnic-table sets outside *(JJW, CMJ)*

Ridsdale, N'land [A68 S of Otterburn; NY9184], *Gun*: Friendly helpful staff, well kept Castle Eden, fine views from the restaurant, wide range of reasonably priced food; bedrooms *(Dr A and Dr A C Jackson)*

Rochester, N'land [NY8398], *Redesdale Arms*: This hotel, recommended by us in previous editions for its usefulness in this bare area, was devastated a year ago by an explosion and fire; some readers staying the night report that they were lucky to escape with their lives, but did lose all their luggage including their *Good Pub Guide;* we do not know whether rebuilding is planned

☆ **Romaldkirk**, Dur [NY9922], *Kirk*: Cosy and friendly little two-room pub, well worn but clean, doubling as Post Office in attractive moorland village, 18th-c stonework around bar, good log fire, wide choice of interesting good value food (not Tues), good coffee, well kept Black Sheep, Butterknowle and Whitbreads-related beers on handpump, darts, piped popular classics, outside picnic-table sets on expanse of grass, Weds quiz nights *(JJW, CMW, John Fazakerley)*

Rothbury, N'land [NU0602], *Anglers Arms*: Fine pub in splendid location with decent beer and good food; restaurant booked well ahead *(Noel Jackson, Louise Campbell)*

Rothbury, N'land [NU0602], *Queens Head*: Big bar in stonebuilt village pub with friendly service, wide choice of decent food from soup and sandwiches up, well kept Lorimers Scotch and Vaux Samson; good value bedrooms *(George and Chris Miller, C J Parsons)*

Ryton, T&W [Ryton Old Village; NZ1564], *Half Moon*: Most welcoming new tenants, well kept Bass, M&B Brew XI and Worthington BB on handpump, chain of connecting rooms; good food contracted out to firm that does Newcastle's TV stations *(John Oddey)*

☆ **Saltburn by the Sea**, Clvd [A174 towards Whitby; NZ6722], *Ship*: Beautiful setting right on shore among beached fishing boats, sea views from tasteful nautical-style black-beamed bars and big plainer summer dining lounge; Tetleys on handpump now, with good range of bar food, quick friendly service, good evening restaurant (not Sun), children's room and menu, seats outside; busy at holiday times *(Graham Bassett, Ken Smith, LYM)*

☆ **Seahouses**, N'land [NU2232], *Lodge*: Scandinavian-style hotel with lots of stripped pine, nice atmosphere, good bar food inc seafood, friendly staff, keg beer, restaurant; pleasant chalet-style bedrooms behind *(D Maplethorpe)*

☆ **Sedgefield**, Dur [Front St; NZ3629], *Dun Cow*: Large attractive village inn popular for wide choice of good value interesting bar food in two bars and restaurant, welcoming service, S&N real ales with guests such as Jennings and Ridleys, good range of malt and other whiskies; children welcome; bedrooms sharing bathrooms *(Geoff Hughes, J L Adamson)*

☆ **Shincliffe**, Dur [A177 S of Durham, three buses an hour from the door; NZ2941], *Seven Stars*: Good choice of substantial food from bar snacks to restaurant meals in small but quietly smart inn, traditionally furnished in one half, with remarkable fireplace in the other; friendly staff, well kept Vaux ales, some seats outside; attractive village; nice well equipped spotless bedrooms, good breakfasts (they don't let children stay) *(Derek and Sylvia Stephenson)*

Slaley, N'land [NY9858], *Rose & Crown*: Good straightforward bar food, wider choice in restaurant, good value Sun lunch, four real ales, friendly service, dark-beamed lounge with hanging mugs, public bar with fruit machine, juke box, darts; bedrooms attractive and well equipped *(Bernard and Margaret Pascoe, Alan Wilcock, Christine Davidson, JJW, CMW)*

South Hylton, T&W [OS Sheet 88 map ref 351569; NZ3556], *Golden Lion*: Big popular Tetleys steak house overlooking River Wear, well kept beer, good value food, tables out on terrace *(Mrs M Kilner)*

☆ **South Shields**, T&W [South Foreshore; beach rd towards Marsden; NZ3766], *Marsden Rattler*: Real ale and basic food served in central seafront bar area or in two railway carriages with original seats, windows and curtains, conservatory with plants; all-day tea, coffee and cakes, evening restaurant; pleasant and friendly *(GSB)*

South Shields [Ferry St (B1344)], *Alum House*: Honest, basic 18th-c pub with friendly relaxed atmosphere, big bars with real fire, pictures and newspaper cuttings, good value basic lunchtime bar food, well kept Banks's, Camerons Strongarm and Butterknowle Festival and Conciliation, piped music, two games machines, weekly entertainment; children welcome *(JJW, CMW)*; [137 Commercial Rd (B1301/B1302)], *Dolly Peel*: Six real ales in friendly and busy local named after legendary local fishwife; two rooms with old photographs, nautical and railway mementoes, good variety of filled rolls, bar billiards, local radio or piped pop; children welcome *(JJW, CMW, Pauline Crossland, Dave Cawley)*; *Eureka*: Comfortable, smallish old-fashioned pub with lots of photographs, friendly staff, well kept competitively priced beers; juke box *(J Thompson, Pauline Crossland, Dave Cawley)*; [Beacon St/Lawe Rd], *Harbour Lights*: Near river mouth, friendly, honest, basic three-room local with games and dining areas; good value limited very cheap fresh-cooked food, Theakstons on handpump, piped pop music *(CW, JW)*; [Mill Dam Bank], *Railway*: Well kept real ales in brightly lit two-roomed pub with shipping theme in public bar and sort of railway theme in lounge *(J Thompson)*; [51 Coronation St, Mill Dam], *Steamboat*: Said to be oldest pub here, full of interesting nautical bits and pieces; doing well under friendly landlord, five real ales on handpump; usually open all day, nr river and market place *(CW, JW)*

Springwell, T&W [off Springwell Rd (B1288 W of A194(M)); NZ2959], *Guide Post*: Modern estate-type pub in old village with big split-level lounge and games room, piped music, Sun evening quiz, and Theakstons on handpump; wide choice of good value food, freshly cooked so a wait *(CW, JW)*

St Johns Chapel, Dur [Market Pl, A689 Alston—Stanhope; NY8838], *Golden Lion*: Large, unusual village pub, comfortable and friendly, with stuffed animals and birds, horsebrasses, cigarette cards, ornaments etc; jovial landlord, two real ales on handpump, good value food inc Sun lunch; pool, fruit machine; open all day, tea, coffee; bedrooms *(JJW, CMJ)*

☆ **Stannington**, N'land [just off A1; NZ2279], *Ridley Arms*: Good straightforward food at reasonable prices in spacious open-plan main bar, pleasant and cosy in rustic style,

efficient helpful staff, quiet lounge, restaurant; well kept Whitbreads Castle Eden *(Mary and Peter Clark, GSB, T M Dobby, Mrs M A Kilner, LYM)*

Summerhouse, Dur [B6279 7 miles NW of Darlington – OS Sheet 93 map ref 201191; NZ2019], *Raby Hunt*: Well appointed old inn with burgundy upholstered seats, old wooden settle, antique prints with local connections, stuffed Lady Amherst pheasants; well kept Marstons ales and one named for the pub, good imaginative food; tables in back yard and in front *(John Fazakerley)*

☆ **Sunderland**, T&W [Hanover Pl, S bank of R Wear; NZ4057], *Saltgrass*: Friendly and relaxed nautical-theme Victorian pub with welcoming lively staff, good fires, decent bar food inc good lunchtime sandwiches and Sun lunches, well kept Vaux and Wards ales; quiz nights *(David Caslaw)*

☆ **Thro)pton**, N'land [NU0302], *Cross Keys*: Traditional stonebuilt three-roomed village local, good basic pub food, open fires in cosy beamed main lounge, attractive garden looking over village to the Cheviots, well kept Bass and a guest beer *(Mary and Peter Clark, LYM)*

☆ **Tynemouth**, T&W [Tynemouth Rd (A193); ½ mile W of Tynemouth Metro stn; NZ3468], *Tynemouth Lodge*: Particularly well kept real ales such as Bass, Belhaven 80/-, Ruddles County and Theakstons Best, farm ciders, and cheap lunchtime filled rolls in friendly and quiet little Victorian-style pub; coal fire, women's magazines, open all day *(JJW, CMW, LYM)*

Tynemouth [Front St], *Fitzpatricks*: Beautifully refurbished in mahogany, red leather and cast iron, cosy open-plan rooms on split levels, good mix of low and tall tables, settles, armchairs and so forth; six perfectly kept real ales on handpump, huge helpings of usual bar food, friendly helpful staff *(John Oddey)*

☆ **Wall**, N'land [NY9269], *Hadrian*: Some interesting reconstructions of Romano-British life in solidly cushioned two-room bar with good bar food using fresh local ingredients, well kept Vaux ESB and Samson, decent wines and whiskies, friendly staff; darts, fruit machine; Victorian dining room; children welcome; bedrooms – back ones quieter, with good views *(BB)*

☆ **Warden**, N'land [½ mile N of A69; NY9267], *Boatside*: Pleasant friendly dining pub, good range of good food, good service *(Catheryn and Richard Hicks)*

Waren Mill, N'land [nr Budle Bay campsite; NL1535], *Burnside*: Very reasonably priced food, friendly atmosphere; beaches nearby *(Mr and Mrs J Lisowski)*

☆ **Warkworth** [23 Castle St; NU2506], *Hermitage*: Clean, friendly and well run typical small-town pub below the castle, generous well served food from sandwiches up, well kept Courage Directors, John

Smiths and a guest such as Theakstons XB, cheerful obliging staff, small plush upstairs restaurant *(Mrs J Boyt, Neil and Angela Huxter, BB)*

☆ **Warkworth** [3 Dial Pl], *Masons Arms*: Cosy central local, good friendly service, big helpings of good value food, well kept S&N beers *(Jim and Maggie Cowell, John Watson)*

West Pelton, Dur [NZ2353], *Highwayman*: Good value food esp generous mid-week meals inc carvery; usually busy – worth booking *(Pat Woodward)*

☆ **West Woodburn**, N'land [NY8987], *Bay Horse*: Simple open-plan bar with red plush banquettes and other seats, open fire, well kept Theakstons XB, standard bar food inc vegetarian and children's dishes and helpings, games room, singer Sat evening; children welcome, airy dining room, a couple of picnic-table sets in riverside garden; only roasts, Sun lunch; closed Mon/Tues lunchtime in winter; bedrooms spick and span, modernised, uncluttered, comfortable *(Roger Berry, Dr and Mrs P J S Crawshaw, LYM)*

☆ **Whalton**, N'land [NZ1382], *Beresford Arms*: Genuine home cooking nicely presented at reasonable prices in pleasant civilised bar or dining room, welcoming staff, well kept Vaux Lorimers Scotch and Wards; attractive village *(Mrs Marian Rae, R and G Underwood)*

Whitburn, T&W [East St/Front St (A183); NZ4261], *Jolly Sailor*: Old village local with bar and rooms off, well kept Bass on handpump, cheap daily specials *(CW, JW)*

Whitfield, N'land [Blue Black Bridge; off A686 SW of Haydon Bridge; NY7858], *Elks Head*: Good value plain food and helpful service in friendly basic pub with tiny dining room, three Courage-related real ales, lots of country wines, usual bar games; seats outside with quoits and barbecue, lovely scenic area *(JJW, CMW, GSB)*

Whitley Bay, T&W [Old Hartley; NZ3672], *Delaval Arms*: Good home cooking inc pies and daily specials, well kept McEwans 80/- and Theakstons *(R J Archbold)*

Wolsingham, Dur [Market Pl; NZ0737], *Black Bull*: Small choice of standard food nicely presented from good sandwiches up, very good value; Vaux Samson on handpump, lounge on right, public bar with games room on left *(M and J Back)*

☆ **Wooler**, N'land [Ryecroft Way, off A697; NT9928], *Ryecroft*: Friendly family hotel under new ownership, Marstons Pedigree, Theakstons Best, Yates and a changing guest beer in relaxing lounge and conservatory-style bar, decent whiskies, open fire, food in bar and restaurant; bedrooms comfortable and good value *(Anon)*

☆ **Wylam**, N'land [Station Rd; NZ1265], *Boathouse*: Very friendly pub with good range of well kept real ales, decent food *(Leonard Dixon)*

Real ale to us means beer which has matured naturally in its cask – not pressurised or filtered. We name all real ales stocked. We usually name ales preserved under a light blanket of carbon dioxide too, though purists – pointing out that this stops the natural yeasts developing – would disagree (most people, including us, can't tell the difference!).

Nottinghamshire *see* Leicestershire

Oxfordshire

For the second year running, Oxfordshire has a fairly massive influx of new entries, or pubs here gaining a main entry after an absence of some years. They are the welcoming Red Lion up on the downs at Blewbury, the most enjoyable Pear Tree just a stroll from the Hook Norton brewery, the attractively refurbished ancient Plough at Kelmscot, the grand old Shaven Crown at Shipton under Wychwood, the Perch & Pike at South Stoke (its hardworking new licensees doing good innovative food and lots of decent wines by the glass), the unspoilt North Star at Steventon, and the Fish at Sutton Courtenay (the best of this bunch for a meal out – first-class food, especially fish, and good wines). In this county really good pub food is expensive, but there are plenty of places where it's well worth while: the Abingdon Arms by its attractive gardens at Beckley (gaining our Food Award this year), the very popular Lord Nelson at Brightwell Baldwin, the Angel and perhaps the Lamb at Burford (the Angel has lots of nicely presented unusual things, the Lamb more traditional food in delightful old-fashioned surroundings), the very civilised Sir Charles Napier near Chinnor, the cottagey Clanfield Tavern (another pub gaining our Food Award this year, for its imaginative cooking), the Five Horseshoes in its clearing in the Chilterns woods at Maidensgrove (yet another to qualify now for our Food Award, excellently chosen and prepared ingredients), the civilised but expensive Beetle & Wedge on the Thames at Moulsford, the friendly Nut Tree at Murcott, the Crown at Nuffield (doing very well at the moment), the pretty and individual Home Sweet Home at Roke (another pub that's doing really well currently – so much so that this year it gains a star award), the Bell at Shenington (the village school, which they cater for, must be the best-fed in the country), the smart Lamb at Shipton under Wychwood, the upmarket Feathers in Woodstock, and the Kings Head at Wootton. From among all these, for its winning combination of good food with a lovely atmosphere, we choose the Clanfield Tavern at Clanfield as Oxfordshire Dining Pub of the Year. However, you'd also be sure of a really special evening at the entirely no-smoking Plough at Clifton Hampden, whose Turkish landlord is quite extraordinarily accommodating. Some pubs where value for money comes first include the Romany at Bampton and the Elephant & Castle at Bloxham – both very cheap indeed by local standards (for beer too – the beers at the Romany are well worth a special look). Other pubs here gaining our new Beer Award are the comfortable old Highwayman at Exlade Street (expensive for food), and the handsome White Hart at Fyfield. Beer is in general more expensive than average in Oxfordshire, but pubs supplied by the local Hook Norton brewery are generally a good deal cheaper than average – this brewery's good beers have increasingly been helping to bring prices down in pubs much further afield, too. Of the other two prominent local brewers, Morlands prices are around the area average, Brakspears are generally higher than average (though not in the King William IV at Hailey or Fox & Hounds on Christmas Common, both lovely unspoilt country taverns). The cheapest place we found for drinks here is the Trout at Tadpole Bridge; besides the Romany and the Elephant & Castle, other pubs with low bar prices are the Wykham Arms at Sibford Gower, both Hook Norton entries, the Plough at Finstock, the Duke of Cumberlands Head at

Clifton, the Crown at Toot Baldon and the Red Lion at Steeple Aston (a lovely pub, that). In the Lucky Dip section at the end of the chapter, pubs we'd particularly commend include the Boot at Barnard Gate, Bull in Burford, Bell at Charlbury, Fleur de Lys in Dorchester, White Horse at Duns Tew, King Charles Head at Goring Heath, Dog & Duck at Highmoor, New Inn at Kidmore End, Maybush at Newbridge and Plough at Noke, with quite a collection of worthwhile pubs in Oxford.

ADDERBURY SP4635 Map 4

Red Lion 🛏 ♀

A423 S of Banbury

This carefully refurbished and comfortable old stone inn seems to appeal to quite a wide mix of our readers who enjoy the restful atmosphere, friendly, helpful staff, and good, if pricey, food. The right-hand bar has high stripped beams, quotations (and prints) written on the terracotta walls and on the beams behind the bar, comfortable chairs, and a lovely big inglenook; there's a list of all the landlords since 1690. The left-hand bar is more for eating, with cosy floral tablecloths, and leads through to the comfortable and prettily decorated residents' lounge; there's also an attractive back dining room; one room is no smoking. Good, well presented home-made bar food includes sandwiches, garlic mushrooms or duck liver pâté (£3.25), ravioli or tortellini (£3.50; main course £6.50), vegetarian dishes (£5.95), salmon burger in leek sauce (£6.75), beef bourguignon (£8.95), chicken Italian-style (£9.95), duck breast in orange and port sauce (£10.95), and rack of lamb with rosemary and garlic sauce (£11.95); three-course Sunday lunch (£10.95). Well kept Hook Norton Best and Old Hookey, Ruddles and Websters, and eight white and red wines available by the glass or bottle. Tables out on the well kept garden terrace. *(Recommended by Chris Cook, P D and J Bickley, Gordon, Roger Huggins, Dave Irving, Tom McLean, Ewan McCall, John Waller, Neil and Susan Spoonley, Graham Reeve, The Monday Club, Dr and Mrs D E Awbery, Mayur Shah, Mark Shutler, Chris Raisin)*

Free house ~ Licensees Michael and Andrea Mortimer ~ Real ale ~ Meals and snacks (till 10pm) ~ Restaurant ~ (01295) 810269 ~ Children welcome ~ Open 11-3, 5-11 ~ Bedrooms: £39.95B/£49.95B

BAMPTON SP3013 Map 4

Romany £ 🍺

Bridge St; off A4095 SW of Witney

You can expect wonderful value for money in this balconied 17th-c building – the beer is very cheap for the area and you would be pushed to find food at lower prices. The comfortable bars have plush cushioned Windsor chairs and stools around wooden tables, plates and prints on the partly stripped stone walls, and a winter open fire. The popular food includes sandwiches (from 95p; toasties from £1.20), home-made soup (£1.25), home-made pâté (£1.55), filled baked potatoes (from £1.85), sausage, egg, beans and chips (£2.20), salads (from £2.65), lamb's liver and onions or home-made lasagne (£2.70), home-made pies like steak and kidney or chicken and mushroom (£2.90), tomato, celery and cashew nut risotto or vegetable chilli (£2.95), braised pork chop (£3.65), fried haddock (£3.75), steaks (from £4.35 for 6oz sirloin), and puddings (£1.05); 3-course meals (£5.25), and very popular Sunday lunch; friendly, hard-working licensees. The restaurant is no smoking. Well kept Archers Village, Hook Norton Best and Mild, Morlands Original and two guest beers, handpumped from the Saxon cellars below the bar; cribbage, dominoes, fruit machine, Aunt Sally and piped music. The big garden has picnic-table sets and a children's play area with tree house, see-saw, and mushroom slide and house. *(Recommended by Sue Anderson, Phil Copleston, Marjorie and David Lamb, Mrs L Lailey, Harold and Alys Daubney, Stephen, Gaynor and Jasper Cooper)*

Free house ~ Licensees Bob and Ursula Booth ~ Real ale ~ Meals and snacks (11-2.30, 6-9.30) ~ Restaurant ~ (01993) 850237 ~ Well behaved children welcome ~ Open 11-11 ~ Bedrooms: £21B/£30B

BARFORD ST MICHAEL SP4332 Map 4

George

Lower Street, at N end of village: coming from Bloxham, take first right turn

A large painting of the Battle of Agincourt, using many of the locals as the soldiers, has been placed over the fireplace in this pretty 17th-c thatched pub – and seems to have attracted quite a lot of media attention. And by the time this book is published, a new steak and fish restaurant should have opened. The three rambling modernised rooms have cushioned rustic seats and captain's chairs around the dark wood tables, open fires, and a growing collection of company and regimental ties hanging from the beams, most donated by customers over the last few years; darts, pool, shove-ha'penny, pinball, cribbage, dominoes, fruit machine, video game and piped music. Promptly served, good value bar food includes sandwiches and very good value hot dishes like chilli con carne or steak and kidney pie (£3.95); well kept Adnams, Wadworths 6X and guest beers on handpump, and lots of country wines. The plump and friendly Staffordshire bull terrier is called Jay-Jay. The garden with picnic-table sets and views over fields is very pleasant, and indeed from outside the whole building is attractive with its golden stone and mullioned windows. *(Recommended by Wayne Brindle, Marjorie and David Lamb, George Atkinson, Lyn and Bill Capper; more reports please)*

Free house ~ Licensees Spencer and Theresa Richards ~ Real ale ~ Meals and snacks (not evenings Sun and Mon) ~ Restaurant ~ (01869) 38226 ~ Children in games room ~ Blues or folk Mon evenings ~ Open 12-3, 6(7 Sat)-11

BECKLEY SP5611 Map 4

Abingdon Arms 🍴 ♈

Village signposted off B4027

Unusually, this stone-built pub has separate winter and summer menus though readers enjoy the imaginative dishes from both. In winter, there might be Cumberland sausage and mashed potato (£3.75), french bread with cheddar, hard-boiled egg, an apple, a tomato, crudités and chutney or with brie, pickled vegetables, grapes, a tomato salad and hard-boiled egg (from £3.75), smoked salmon pâté (£4.25), baked aubergine stuffed with lentils and apricots with a tomato sauce or chicken and mushroom curry (£5.50), sliced, smoked chicken, served warm with apple, yoghurt and nutmeg sauce and salad or delicious bouillabaisse (£5.75), a two or three course supper (from £9.75) and themed evenings every alternate Friday – Spanish, regional French, Indian and so forth; in summer, maybe marinated anchovies (£3.75), Greek salad with feta cheese, taramasalata and olives (£5.25), ham with grain mustard sauce and potato salad (£5.95), fresh crab with a ginger dressing (£7.25), and a seafood salad for two people (£18.50); puddings include home-made truffled ice cream or apple and almond tart (£2.25). No credit cards. Well kept Adnams and Wadworths 6X on handpump, a good range of wines, and quite a few malt whiskies; helpful service. The comfortably modernised simple lounge has cloth-cushioned seats built around the wall, and a smaller public bar on the right has a couple of antique carved settles (one for just one person), and bar billiards; dominoes, shove-ha'penny. Outside, there's a gently floodlit terrace and formal flower-edged lawn dropping quietly and spaciously away into the shadows of groves of fruit trees, willows and other shrubs and trees, with well spaced tables, a summer-house, and a little fountain. No children. *(Recommended by Adam and Elizabeth Duff, Michael Sargent, A M Rankin, L Walker, Terry and Eileen Stott, Walter Reid, Dave Braisted, T G Brierly, TBB, A T Langton, Sir Nigel Foulkes, G D and M D Craigen)*

Free house ~ Licensee Hugh Greatbatch ~ Real ale ~ Meals and snacks (not Sun evening) ~ (01865) 351311 ~ Open 11.30-2.30, 6.30-11; Sunday opening 8

BINFIELD HEATH SU7478 Map 2

Bottle & Glass ★

Village signposted off A4155 at Shiplake; from village centre turn into Common Lane – pub at end, on Harpsden Road (Henley—Reading back road)

This thatched and black and white timbered 15th-c building has a neatly kept, low-beamed bar with scrubbed, ancient tables, a bench built into black squared panelling, spindleback chairs, attractive flagstones, and a roaring log fire in the big fireplace. The side room, similarly decorated, has a window with diamond-scratched family records of earlier landlords; Brakspears Bitter, SB and Old on handpump and quite a few malt whiskies. A good choice of bar food includes sandwiches (lunchtime only), Cumberland sausages with egg (£4.25), mussels in garlic and herb butter or lamb's kidneys in a brandy sauce (£4.50), steak and kidney or chicken and ham pies (£5.75), steak and apricot casserole (£5.95), fresh trout (£6.50), fresh salmon fillets (£6.95), 10oz rump steak (£8.95); friendly staff. The garden has old-fashioned wooden seats and tables under little thatched roofs (and an open-sided shed like a rustic pavilion). No children. *(Recommended by Clifford Payton, TBB, Elizabeth and Klaus Leist)*

Brakspears ~ Tenants Mike and Anne Robinson ~ Real ale ~ Meals and snacks (lunchtime service stops 1.45); not Sun evening ~ (01491) 575755 ~ Open 11-3, 6-11

BIX SU7285 Map 2

Fox

On A423 Henley—Wallingford

In the middle of the week this is a lovely peaceful place to come – it's much busier at weekend lunchtimes. The two interconnecting panelled rooms are warmly welcoming, and the L-shaped lounge bar has beams, armchairs and settles making the most of the big log fires, and gleaming brasses. There's another log fire and some settles in the wood-floored farmers' bar, with darts, dominoes and fruit machine. Quickly served, good value bar food includes sandwiches (from £1.55), pasties (£1.95), popular soup (£1.95), ploughman's (from £3.05), lasagne or steak and kidney pie (£4.55), beef and venison burgers (£4.75), daily specials like winter game dishes, vegetarian bean pot, sausages, beans and egg, and casseroles, puddings (£1.75), and Sunday roast lunch (£5.50). Well kept Brakspears PA and Old (in winter) on handpump, picnic-table sets in the good-sized garden behind. The friendly dog is called Henry, and there's a much-used hitching rail for horses outside. No children. *(Recommended by David Wright, TBB, P J Caunt, David Warrellow, Bill Ingham, N and J Strathdee, Frank Cummins, Jack Barnwell, R and H Townsend)*

Brakspears ~ Tenants Richard and Sue Willson ~ Real ale ~ Meals and snacks (not Mon evening) ~ (01491) 574134 ~ Open 11-3, 7-11

BLEWBURY SU5385 Map 2

Red Lion

Chapel Lane, off Nottingham Fee; narrow turning northwards from A417

This year, a new kitchen has been added to this welcoming 18th-c pub, and the old kitchen has been converted into a no-smoking bar where children are welcome. The garden now has a terrace with quite a few seats and tables and has been enlarged. But it's the engaging beamed bar that has the most atmosphere – upholstered wall benches and armed seats on its scrubbed quarry tiles, brewing tools, cupboards and miniature cabinets filled with ornaments, a steadily ticking station clock, foreign banknotes and a stuffed partly albino pochard; in winter you can roast chestnuts over the big open fire. Good value bar food includes carrot and orange or nettle soup (£2), fresh plaice or trout fillets (£5.25), beef in ale (£5.50), pork tenderloin with ginger (£5.95), and puddings like treacle tart (£2.30). Well kept Boddingtons and Brakspears PA, SB and Old on handpump, and decent wines. *(Recommended by R C Watkins, Marjorie and David Lamb, Geraint*

Roberts, Susie Northfield, A T Langton, Mr and Mrs Peter Dowsett)

Brakspears ~ Licensee Roger Smith ~ Real ale ~ Meals and snacks (not 25/26 Dec) ~ (01235) 850403 ~ Children in eating area of bar ~ Open 11-2.30, 6-11; closed evening 25 Dec

BLOXHAM SP4235 Map 4

Elephant & Castle £

Humber Street; off A361

You'll find marvellously good value beer and food at this warmly welcoming Cotswold stone local, and from a straightforward range, there might be soup (90p), decent sandwiches (from £1.50), ploughman's (from £1.75), steak and kidney pie, lasagne, haddock or plaice (all £3), excellent scampi, and rump steak (£5.95). Well kept Hook Norton Best, Old Hookey, summer Haymaker, and monthly guest beers from small independent brewers; lots of malt whiskies. The relaxed and elegantly simple public bar has a striking 17th-c stone fireplace and a strip wood floor, and the comfortable lounge, divided into two by a very thick wall, has a good winter log fire in its massive fireplace too. Sensibly placed darts, dominoes, cribbage, a fruit machine, trivia and shove-ha'penny – the board is over a century old. The flower-filled yard has Aunt Sally in summer and there are barbecues on Saturday evenings and Sunday lunchtimes. *(Recommended by Tom Evans, David Campbell, Vicki McLean, Basil Minson, Alan Skull)*

Hook Norton ~ Tenant Chas Finch ~ Real ale ~ Lunchtime meals and snacks (not Sun) ~ Restaurant ~ (01295) 720383 ~ Children in restaurant ~ Open 10-3, 6(5 Sat)-11

BRIGHTWELL BALDWIN SU6595 Map 4

Lord Nelson 🍴 ♀

Brightwell signposted off B480 at Oxford end of Cuxham or B4009 Benson—Watlington

Relaxed and civilised, this 17th-c pub places quite a bit of emphasis on its good and very popular food – and most tables (especially at weekends) are laid out for eating and usually reserved. Nelson's presence is still very much felt – particularly in the bar on the left, where the plain white walls are decorated with pictures and prints of the sea and ships, there are some ship design plans, and a naval sword hangs over the big brick fireplace in the wall (which divides off a further room). At the moment, some of the most popular dishes are mixed leaves with avocado, parmesan cheese, bacon and croûtons (£4.25), sauté of lamb's liver and bacon (£7.50), pork fillet with sage and stilton (£9.75), and roast guinea fowl with a creamy cider and onion sauce or seafood casserole (£10.95); other dishes include soups like courgette and peanut or cabbage and smoked bacon (£2.95), marinated herring fillets with crème fraîche (£4.25), ploughman's (£4.75), grilled tuna with chilli dressing (£6.50), chicken curry (£7.50), steak and kidney pie in red wine and Guinness (£7.95), grilled sirloin steak with bearnaise sauce (£11.75), and puddings such as chocolate and orange trifle cake or raspberry and apple crumble (from £3.25); they do a two or three course Sunday lunch (from £11.50); friendly, helpful service (Maureen has been here for over 20 years). Brakspears PA on handpump, a good wine list, including unusual bottles such as Lebanese burgundy and a good choice of French country wines. Furnishings are comfortably modernised, with wheelback chairs (some armed), country kitchen and dining chairs around the tables on its turkey carpet, candles in coloured glasses, orange lanterns on the walls, and pretty fresh flowers; piped music. There's a verandah at the front, and tables on a back terrace by the attractive garden or under its big weeping willow, beside the colourful herbaceous border. The village church is worth a look. *(Recommended by Gordon, Joan Olivier, C Moncreiffe, Michael Sargent, Margaret Dyke, M A and C R Starling, TBB)*

Free house ~ Licensees Peter Neal, Richard Britcliffe ~ Real ale ~ Meals and snacks ~ Restaurant (not Sun evening) ~ (01491) 612497 ~ Children over 8 only ~ Open 12-3, 6.30-11; closed Sun evening

BURCOT SU5695 Map 4

Chequers

A415 Dorchester—Abingdon

Readers enjoy this pretty black and white thatched pub for its friendly welcome and lovely relaxed atmosphere. The smartly comfortable beamed lounge seems more spacious than you might have expected from outside, and has an open fire, and a pretty no-smoking art gallery at one end (with some decent work). Well kept Ruddles County, Ushers Best and a guest beer on handpump, with some good whiskies and unusual spirits. Good home-made food includes their own freshly baked breads, garlic mushrooms with melted cheese (£3.15), deep-fried cambazola and fruit dressing (£3.25), nice vegetarian dishes, steak and kidney pudding (£5.30), pan-fried chicken in wine and cream with stilton and walnuts, and puddings like ginger meringues. There are tables among roses and fruit trees on the neatly kept roadside lawn. There's good access for wheelchairs. *(Recommended by Mrs H D Astley, Geraint Roberts, Ian Phillips, Marjorie and David Lamb, Hazel Astley)*

Free house ~ Lease: Mary and Michael Weeks ~ Real ale ~ Meals and snacks (not Sun evening) ~ Restaurant ~ (01865) 407771 ~ Children in eating area of bar and in gallery (until 9pm) ~ Grand piano Fri and Sat evenings; brass band concerts ~ Open 11-2.30, 6-11

BURFORD SP2512 Map 4

Angel ♀

14 Witney St, just off main street; village signposted off A40 W of Oxford

The layout of the long panelled bar has been improved this year by opening it onto the terrace and pretty walled garden and creating a sunny drinking corner – but it still has attractive old tables on its flagstones, with cushioned wall settles, wheelback chairs and an open fire; steps lead up to a partly no-smoking dining room – and there's another behind, charming and cosy, with a huge log fire and stripped stone walls. Enjoyable and popular bar food includes sandwiches (lunchtime), chicken liver pâté (£3.95), lovely avocado stuffed with tuna and prawn mayonnaise, grilled goat's cheese salad with raisins, marinated peppers and olive oil, ploughman's or tagliatelle with pesto, cream and fresh parmesan (all £4.95), liver, bacon and mushroom pie (£5.95), marinated seafood salad on spiral pasta with black olives (£6.25), honey-roast Cotswold ham (£6.95), sirloin steak (£9.95), daily specials such as fresh fish delivered twice a week from Cornwall – dressed crab, scallops, red snapper, lemon sole and so forth – and puddings like home-made ice cream, apple and cinnamon crumble or walnut fudge tart (£2.50). Well kept Flowers IPA and Marstons Pedigree with a guest like Shepherd Neame Spitfire on handpump, good wines by the glass, and friendly and considerate service; dominoes and trivia. *(Recommended by Michael Sargent, Paul McPherson, Stephen Brown, Mark Bradley, Marion and John Hadfield, Viv Middlebrook, David Holloway, Ian and Freda Millar, Mr and Mrs M A Thorpe)*

Free house ~ Licensee Mrs Jean Thaxter ~ Real ale ~ Meals and snacks 12-2, 7-9.30 ~ Restaurant ~ (01993) 822438 ~ Children in eating area of bar ~ Open 11-2.30(3 Sat), 6.30-11; closed Sun evening Nov-Mar ~ Bedrooms: £35B/£45B

Lamb ★ ★ 🛏

Sheep Street; A40 W of Oxford

As one reader told us, for the 40 years he and his wife have known this civilised 500-year-old Cotswold inn it has remained a real oasis of tranquillity with an air of old-fashioned dignity and character – and it's still very much somewhere that people wander in for a drink and a chat with the friendly long-standing staff. The spacious beamed main lounge has distinguished old seats including a chintzy high winged settle, ancient cushioned wooden armchairs, easy chairs, and seats built into its stone-mullioned windows, bunches of flowers on polished oak and elm tables, oriental rugs on the wide flagstones and polished oak floorboards, and a winter log fire under its elegant mantelpiece. Also, attractive pictures, shelves of plates and other antique decorations, a grandfather clock, and a writing desk. The public bar has high-backed settles and old chairs on flagstones in front of its fire. Good, promptly served and nicely presented bar lunches might typically include sandwiches (from £2.50), home-made soups like cream of parsnip and coriander (£2.50), ploughman's or coarse pigeon pâté (£4.25), fresh herb pancake filled with salmon and prawns (£4.95), sautéed chicken livers with crispy bacon (£5.25), pan-fried minute steak (£5.65), lamb curry (£5.95), grilled gammon and pineapple or steak and kidney pie (£6.25), and puddings like bakewell tart or strawberry shortcake (£2.50); free dips at Sunday lunchtime; the restaurant is no smoking. Well kept Wadworths IPA, 6X and winter Old Timer are dispensed from an antique handpump beer engine in a glassed-in cubicle. A pretty terrace leads down to small neatly-kept lawns surrounded by flowers, flowering shrubs and small trees, and the garden itself can be really sunny, enclosed as it is by the warm stone of the surrounding buildings. Dogs welcome. The bedrooms are simple, old-fashioned and chintzy. *(Recommended by Adam and Elizabeth Duff, Lynn Sharpless, Bob Eardley, M V and J Melling, David Holloway, John Bowdler, David Mair, Dr H Y Chan, A Cowell, Stephen Brown, Jean-Bernard Brisset, Paul McPherson, Leith Stuart, Gordon Theaker, Gordon, Michael Marlow, Mrs J M Bell, John and Marianne Cooper, J Weeks, Mike and Jo, Mark Bradley, Brian Jones, Michael and Alison Sandy, Marjorie and Bernard Parkin, C and A Moncreiffe, Basil Minson, Maysie Thompson, M L Clarke, Wayne Brindle, Roger Huggins, Tom McLean, Ewan McCall, Dave Irving; also recommended by* The Good Hotel Guide)

Free house ~ Licensee Richard de Wolf ~ Real ale ~ Lunchtime bar meals and snacks ~ Restaurant ~ (01993) 823155 ~ Children welcome ~ Open 11-2.30, 6-11; closed 25/26 Dec ~ Bedrooms: £35(£50B)/£80B

Mermaid ♀

High St

The handsome Tudor-style frontage of this busy dining pub juts out onto the broad pavement of this famously picturesque sloping Cotswold street, and there are picnic-table sets under cocktail parasols. Inside, the attractive if rather dark flagstoned bar is long and narrow, with brocaded seats in bays around the single row of tables down one side – each softly lit by a red-fringed lamp. The inner end, with a figurehead over the fireplace and toby jugs hanging from the beams, is panelled, the rest has stripped stonework; there's also a no-smoking dining conservatory. Bar food includes good sandwiches, Cumberland sausage wrapped in bacon with fried onions on hot garlic bread, mushroom omelette or home-baked ham with pickles (all £4.95), half a roast chicken (£5.50), and roast beef salad (£5.95). Well kept Morlands Original, Old Masters and Speckled Hen on handpump; friendly and helpful service. *(Recommended by Gordon, Mrs L Lailey, Stephen Brown, Mark Bradley, David Hanley, David Holloway, Ian and Freda Millar, Robert Gomme, Wayne Brindle)*

Morlands ~ Lease: John Titcombe ~ Real ale ~ Meals and snacks (all day) ~ Restaurant ~ (01993) 822193 ~ Children in restaurant and conservatory; no facilities for small children ~ Pianist Fri and Sat evenings ~ Parking may be difficult ~ Open 10am-11pm; 11-11 Sundays and winter; closed 25 Dec

nr CHINNOR SU7698 Map 4

Sir Charles Napier 🍴 ♀

Spriggs Alley; from B4009 follow Bledlow Ridge sign from Chinnor; then, up beech wood hill, fork right (signposted Radnage and Sprigg Alley) then on right; OS Sheet 165 map reference 763983

During the week when this decidedly civilised place is relatively quiet, you can find room in the original small front bar to enjoy a straightforward drink and very good food from the short bar menu; at other times you may find the whole place is virtually dedicated to the stylish back restaurant, and there's little point coming at weekends unless you want to eat there. The comfortable rooms have a great deal of character, homely, simple furnishings, a good winter log fire, a smartly relaxed feel and friendly staff. Delicious bar food could include spinach and nutmeg soup (£3.50), oeufs benedict (£4.50), poached mussels with shallots and cream (£5), home-made sausages with pork, cider and coriander, and mash (£7.50), pasta with artichokes, lemon and parmesan (£8.50), and chicken with rosemary and garlic or baked cod with boulangere potatoes (£9). Sunday lunch is distinctly fashionable – in summer it's served in the crazy-paved back courtyard with rustic tables by an arbour of vines, honeysuckle and wisteria (lit at night by candles in terracotta lamps). Well kept Wadworths IPA or 6X tapped from the cask, champagne on draught, an enormous list of well chosen wines by the bottle, freshly squeezed orange and pink grapefruit juice, Russian vodkas and a few malt whiskies; piped music well reproduced by the huge loudspeakers. The back restaurant is decorated with sculpture by Michael Cooper. The croquet lawn and paddocks by the beech woods drop steeply away to the Chilterns, and there's a boules court out here too. *(Recommended by R C Smail, E G Parish; more reports please)*

Free house ~ Licensee Julie Griffiths ~ Real ale ~ Bar meals (not Sat evening or Sun lunch) ~ Restaurant (not Sun evening) ~ (01494) 483011 ~ Children welcome lunchtimes; in evenings if over 8 ~ Open 12-3, 6.30-11; closed Sun evening and all day Mon

CHRISTMAS COMMON SU7193 Map 4

Fox & Hounds £

Hill Rd from B4009 in Watlington; or village signposted from B480 at junction with B481

In lovely Chilterns countryside – and a favourite place for local walkers to end up in, especially during the bluebell season – this simple and old-fashioned pub is always welcoming and friendly. On the left, the cosy beamed bar is plainly furnished with three tables and wooden wall benches or bow-window seats, a little carpet down on the red-and-black flooring tiles, two sturdy logs to sit on in the big inglenook – which has a fire burning even in summer – and a framed Ordnance Survey walker's map on one cream wall; the room on the right is popular with locals and pretty much for drinking only, though you may also see the three cats and a friendly alsatian. Lunchtime food such as soup (£1; winter only), sandwiches (from £1), ploughman's (£2.50; summer only) and sausage and eggs (£3.50) – sandwiches only on Sundays and Mondays; good coffee. Well kept Brakspears Old, PA, SB and OBJ tapped from the cask in a back still room; darts, shove-ha'penny, dominoes, cribbage. There are old-fashioned garden seats and sitting-logs by the roses and buddleia on the front grass beyond a small gravel drive, with picnic-table sets beside the house. *(Recommended by Jamie and Sarah Allan, Gordon, Peter Baker, P J Hanson, TBB, Julian and Sarah Stanton)*

Brakspears ~ Tenant Kevin Moran ~ Real ale ~ Lunchtime snacks (service stops 1.45) ~ (01491) 612599 ~ Children allowed in games room until 9pm ~ Open 12-2.30, 6-11

CHURCH ENSTONE SP3724 Map 4

Crown 🛏

From A34 take B4030 turn-off at Enstone

The comfortable beamed bar in this creeper-covered Cotswold stone inn has a friendly atmosphere, brown plush button-back wall banquettes and Windsor chairs on the brown patterned carpet, and prints on the bare stone walls; the dining area extends into the conservatory; part of the upper bar is no smoking. Good bar food includes ploughman's (from £2.95), Cumberland sausage and egg or cheese and onion flan (£3.95), lasagne (£4.25), steak, kidney and mushroom pie or beef and Guinness casserole (£4.95), fisherman's pie (£5.25), and steaks (from £7.95); good traditional breakfast. Well kept Bass, Boddingtons, Flowers Original and Marstons Pedigree on handpump from the horseshoe bar; piped music. There are some white metal tables and chairs in front of the pub, a little back garden, and the River Glyme flows just below the building. *(Recommended by C A Hall, Wayne Brindle, Lynn Sharpless, Bob Eardley, H O Dickinson, Bruce Coles, B J P Edwards)*

Free house ~ Licensees Peter Gannon and Jean Rowe ~ Real ale ~ Meals and snacks ~ Restaurant ~ (01608) 677262 ~ Children in eating area of bar ~ Open 12-3, 7-11; closed evening 25 Dec ~ Bedrooms: £28(£30B)/£38(£42B)

CLANFIELD SP2802 Map 4

Clanfield Tavern 🍴 ♀

A4095 5 miles S of Witney
Oxfordshire Dining Pub of the Year

Served by pleasant welcoming staff, the food here is so good that we have decided to give this pretty village inn a Food Award this year – and you can't now find a more enjoyable place in Oxfordshire for a good meal out without spending the earth. From a daily changing menu, there might be sandwiches (from £1.75), soup (£1.95) and ploughman's (£3.75), and imaginative dishes like smoked brie-filled mushrooms with barbecue sauce (£5.75), breast of chicken with tarragon, tomatoes, cream and white wine (£6.50), smoked haddock goujons (£6.95), escalope of pork Dijonnaise (£7.45), grilled monkfish with a light fennel sauce (£7.45), delicious lamb cutlets in red wine and rosemary sauce (£7.75), superb trout fillets with king prawn and leek sauce, and lovely puddings such as fresh strawberry shortbread, lemon and ginger cheesecake, butterscotch and toffee ice cream wrapped in filo pastry and deep-fried and served with a raspberry coulis (£2.25); excellent vegetables and good Sunday lunch. Several flagstoned, heavy-beamed and stone-walled small rooms (one is partly no smoking) lead off the main bar furnished with settles and various chairs and seats cut from casks, as well as brass platters, hunting prints, and a handsome open stone fireplace with 17th-c plasterwork panel above it; the restaurant is partly no smoking. Boddingtons, Hook Norton Best and Flowers Original on handpump, and quite a few bin-end wines; dominoes, shut-the-box, shove-ha'penny, cribbage and piped music. It's pretty in summer, with tiny windows peeping from the heavy stone-slabbed roof and tables on a flower-bordered small lawn that look across to the village green and pond. *(Recommended by Sheila Keene, Joan and Ian Wilson, John Waller, Paul Perry, Dr Sheila Smith, Tom McLean, Ewan McCall, Roger Huggins, Dave Irving, Mr and Mrs P B Dowsett)*

Free house ~ Licensee Keith Gill ~ Real ale ~ Meals and snacks (11.30-2, 6-10) ~ Cottagey restaurant ~ Clanfield (0136 781) 223 ~ Children welcome ~ Open 11.30-2.30, 6-11 ~ Bedrooms: £40/£50B

CLIFTON SP4831 Map 4

Duke of Cumberlands Head ♀ 🛏

B4031 Deddington—Aynho

A new licensee had just taken over this thatched old village pub as we went to press, and was just beginning to find his feet. But he plans to change very little in the coming year. There's still quite an emphasis on eating, though the relaxed atmosphere in the spacious and simply but stylishly refurbished lounge with its lovely log fireplace should still attract drinkers. Bar food includes sandwiches, soup like broccoli and ginger (£1.95), garlic mushrooms (£2.50), vegetable quiche (£3.95), oriental king prawns, beef bourguignon, stifado, and steak in stout pie (all £4.75), grilled plaice (£5.25), and puddings (£1.95); roast Sunday lunch. Well kept Adnams Best, Batemans XXXB, Hook Norton Old Hookey, and Wadworths 6X on handpump, and good wines by the glass. There are tables out in the garden; the canal's a short walk away. Bedrooms are in a new but sympathetic extension – you drive under it to park. *(Recommended by Eric Locker, V G and P A Nutt, S Demont, T Barrow, G E Stait, Simon Stern, J Dawe, Gordon Theaker, N J Clifton, E A George, R G and M P Lumley, Gordon, David and Mary Webb, John C Baker; more reports on the new regime, please)*

Free house ~ Licensee Nick Huntington ~ Real ale ~ Meals and snacks (not Sun evening) ~ Restaurant (not Sun or Mon evenings) ~ (01869) 38534 ~ Children welcome till 9 ~ Open 12-2.30, 6.30-11; closed Sun evening ~ Bedrooms: £22.50S/£37.50S

CLIFTON HAMPDEN SU5495 Map 4

Plough 🛏 ♀

N of A415 towards Long Wittenham

There can be few landlords as genuinely warmly friendly and accommodating as Mr Bektas – you can't miss him when you go in, he'll be the one wearing tails or an evening suit. He's quite happy to serve any meal at any time – even if that means a full breakfast at five o'clock in the afternoon, will drive you home if you've indulged too much, give you a free bedroom if you have a party of 8 for a meal in the restaurant, will offer his wife and daughter as babysitters in their own quarters – and may even clean your car! The pub is totally no smoking and the emphasis is very much on the popular food. The opened-up bar area has beams and panelling, black and red floor tiles, antique furniture, attractive pictures, and a friendly, relaxed atmosphere; it's said to be haunted by a benign presence that neatly upturns empty glasses. Bar food includes home-made soup (£2.45), sandwiches (from £2.75), good oak-smoked fish platter (£4.25), pasta with chicken, vegetables, and hazelnuts or with sun-dried tomatoes, parmesan, prawns and basil (£3.85; main course £5.25), steak in beer pie (£5.95), lovely chicken stir-fry (£6.25), sautéed lamb's liver and bacon (£8.50), salmon with pommary mustard and white wine sauce (£10.25), puddings (£2.50), and three-course meal (£16.50); the several varieties of coffee come with the cream in a pewter cup and the sugar in a silver-plated bowl. Well kept Courage Best and Directors and Websters Yorkshire, plenty of wines and malt whiskies. Some tables and seats outside. *(Recommended by Bob Rendle, Miss J F Reay, Stephen Brown, Eamon Green, Susie Northfield, D R Stevenson, Ian Phillips, David Wright, T A Bryan, Paul McPherson, Simon and Caroline Turner, B Pennell, Marjorie and David Lamb, Martine Cooke, Joan Olivier)*

Courage ~ Lease: Yuksel Bektas ~ Real ale ~ Meals and snacks (served all day) ~ No-smoking restaurant ~ (01865) 407811 ~ Children welcome ~ Open 11-11 ~ One bedroom (4-poster): £55B

CROPREDY SP4646 Map 4

Red Lion

Off A423 4 miles N of Banbury

Canal boaters enjoy strolling to this pretty thatched 15th-c pub from the nearby Oxford Canal. There have been some subtle changes to the decor this year, but the simply furnished and old-fashioned bar still has high-backed settles under its ancient low beams, seats in one of the inglenooks, quite a lot of brass, plates and pictures on the walls, and winter open fires; the two rooms on the right are more for eating. Popular home-made bar food includes sandwiches, specials such as vegetarian moussaka or gammon and pineapple (£4.50), chicken maribu or home-made steak and kidney pie (£4.95), evening grills, and puddings; children's menu (from £1.95), and Sunday roasts (from £4.50). Well kept Courage Directors, John Smiths, Ruddles Best, and Websters Yorkshire; darts, pool, cribbage, fruit machine and piped music. The pub is part of a row of pretty cottages and set opposite a handsome old church with raised churchyard; seats in the small back garden. *(Recommended by Dr D K M Thomas, Graham and Belinda Staplehurst, Chris Raisin, Peter and Jenny Coombs, Mr and Mrs Moody, George Murdoch, JJW, CMW; more reports please)*

Courage ~ Lease: John Dando ~ Real ale ~ Meals and snacks (not every night in winter – best to check) ~ (01295) 750224 ~ Children in dining area only ~ Parking may be difficult in summer ~ Open 12-3, 6-11; all day Sat

CUDDESDON SP5903 Map 4

Bat & Ball

S of Wheatley

There's a huge collection of cricketing memorabilia in this pleasant pub – programmes, photographs, porcelain models of cricketers in well-lit cases, score books, cigarette cards, pads, gloves and hats, and signed bats, bails and balls. The

L-shaped bar also has low ceilings, beams, a partly flagstoned floor, and a cheery, straightforward atmosphere. Good bar food includes doorstep sandwiches (£2), soup (£2.50), meaty or spicy bean burgers (£3.75), cajun chicken or drunken prawns (£4.75), rack of ribs with barbecue sauce (£6.50), fillet of lamb with mustard sauce (£7), 12oz sirloin steak (£9.75), and puddings (£2.50); Sunday roasts. Well kept Boddingtons Bitter, Brakspears Bitter, and Morlands Old Speckled Hen; shove-ha'penny, dominoes and piped music; Aunt Sally. The conservatory at the back leads on to the terrace which has fish ponds, seats, and good views over the Oxfordshire plain. *(Recommended by LM, Derek and Sylvia Stephenson, Marjorie and David Lamb, Richard Atkinson, Joan Olivier, G L Furguson, B Pennell, Gill and Andrew Simpson)*

Free house ~ Licensee David Sykes ~ Real ale ~ Meals and snacks ~ (01865) 874379 ~ Children welcome ~ Open 12-2.30, 6-11 ~ Bedrooms: £35S/£40S

CUMNOR SP4603 Map 4

Bear & Ragged Staff

19 Appleton Road; village signposted from A420: follow one-way system into village, bear left into High St then left again into Appleton Road signposted Eaton, Appleton

As we went to press, we heard that this rather civilised old place was about to have a change of management. The comfortably rambling, softly lit bar has a relaxed and cosy atmosphere, easy chairs, sofas and more orthodox cushioned seats and wall banquettes, a log fire, and polished black flagstones in one part, with turkey carpet elsewhere; one of the eating areas is no smoking. The emphasis has been on eating, with food such as sandwiches, moules marinières, sautéed liver and bacon, rack of lamb in garlic with redcurrant, sirloin steak, daily specials and good puddings; roast Sunday lunch. Morrells Bitter and Varsity and guest on handpump, a decent wine list, cognacs and malt whiskies. At the back a garden in summer has its own bar and barbecue. The building is named for the three-foot model of a Warwick heraldic bear which guards the large open fire. *(Recommended by Sue Demont, Tim Barrow, Peter and Audrey Dowsett, Lynn Sharpless, Bob Eardley, D C T and E A Frewer; more reports on the new regime, please)*

Morrells ~ Real ale ~ Meals and snacks ~ Restaurant ~ (01865) 862329 ~ Children in eating area of bar and restaurant ~ Open 11-11

DEDDINGTON SP4631 Map 4

Kings Arms ♀

Horsefair, off A423 Banbury—Oxford

There's a happy, bustling atmosphere in this attractive 16th-c coaching inn, and a friendly welcome from the licensees. The bar, full of cheery locals, has black beams and timbering and white-painted stone walls, and one stone-mullioned window in the front has a good sunny window seat. The carpeted lounge has attractive settles and other country furnishings, and a side bar has darts, shove-ha'penny, table skittles, cribbage, dominoes and trivia; Tuesday evening quiz. There's a good fire in the old stone hearth, and well chosen piped music from 1930s big bands to Handel or Vivaldi. Well presented bar food includes sandwiches (lunchtime only), steak in ale pie (£4.85), gammon steak with onion sauce (£5.75), chicken breast in a cherry and wine sauce (£6.90), fillet steak on pâté with a redcurrant wine sauce (£10.95), and Friday evening balti nights (£6.95). Well kept Adnams, Bass, Eldridge Pope Hardy, Greene King IPA and Abbot, and Tetleys on handpump, ten wines by the glass from an interesting list, and 22 malt whiskies. *(Recommended by M Joyner, Dr Stern, Miss Dawe, Frank Gadbois, Eric Locker, John Bowdler, George Atkinson)*

Free house ~ Licensees Susan and Nigel Oddy ~ Real ale ~ Meals and snacks ~ (01869) 38364 ~ Children allowed away from main bar ~ Occasional folk and jazz ~ Open 11.30-3, 6-11; all day Sat; closed evening 25 Dec

DORCHESTER SU5794 Map 4

George 🛏 ⚥

High St; village signposted just off A423 Maidenhead—Oxford

First used as a brewhouse for the Norman abbey which still stands opposite, this lovely timber and tile house later flourished as a posting and then a coaching inn. The civilised beamed bar is comfortably old-fashioned with an open fire in the big fireplace, cushioned settles and leather chairs, Brakspears and guest beers on handpump, and good wine by the glass from a quite exceptional wine list of over 130 bin-ends. Good lunchtime food includes open sandwiches (from £3.50), mozzarella, beef tomatoes and avocado salad (£3.95), omelettes using free range eggs, a cheese platter with home-made pickles (£5), salmon with a cucumber and avocado sauce (£6.50), sirloin steak with a pâté of shallots and mushrooms with bone-marrow sauce (£7.75), and puddings like home-made ice creams and sorbets and grilled fruit brûlée (£3.50); roast Sunday lunch. *(Recommended by P L Warwick, Susie Northfield, John Waller, TBB, Adam and Elizabeth Duff; also recommended by* The Good Hotel Guide*)*

Free house ~ Licensee Brian Griffin ~ Real ale ~ Meals and snacks ~ Restaurant ~ Oxford (01865) 340404 ~ Children welcome ~ Open 11-3, 6-11; closed Christmas week ~ Bedrooms: £55B/£70B

EAST HENDRED SU4588 Map 2

Wheatsheaf ⚥

Chapel Square; village signposted from A417

Most attractive 16th-c black and white timbered pub just below the downs, and very much the heart of this fine village. There are high-backed settles and stools around tables on quarry tiles by a log-burning stove, some wall panelling, cork wall tiles, and a tiny parquet-floored triangular platform by the bar; low, stripped deal settles form booths around tables in a carpeted area up some broad steps. Promptly served, rather good bar food might include sandwiches, filled baked potatoes (from £2.95), curry or chicken tikka (£4.75), very good home-made steak and kidney pie (£4.95), and daily specials like vegetable moussaka (£4.95), steak mexican (£5.95), local trout or medallions of lamb in a rich port and mint sauce (£6.95), breast of duck in a madeira sauce (£7.25), sirloin steak chasseur (£8.95), and puddings; three-course Sunday lunch (£6.95). Darts, Aunt Sally and dominoes. Well kept Morlands Bitter, Old Speckled Hen and Old Masters on handpump, a few malt whiskies, and wines by the glass; piped music, and maybe Bonnie, the golden labrador. The garden behind is colourful with roses and other flowers beneath conifers and silver birch; out here too is a budgerigar aviary, a play area for children with swings and so forth, and barbecues on summer Sunday evenings. The nearby church is interesting – its Tudor clock has elaborate chimes but no hands. *(Recommended by A T Langton, Geraint Roberts, Tom McLean, A E and P McCully, Marjorie and David Lamb, Nigel Norman, Roger Huggins, Ewan McCall, Dave Irving, Giles Bullard, TBB)*

Morlands ~ Tenants John and Maureen Donohue ~ Real ale ~ Meals and snacks (till 10pm) ~ Restaurant ~ (01235) 833229 ~ Children welcome ~ Open 11-3, 6-11

EXLADE STREET SU6582 Map 2

Highwayman 🛏 ⚥ 🍴

Signposted just off A4074 Reading—Wallingford

Although most of this comfortable and cosy rambling inn is 17th c, some parts go back another 300 years or so. The two beamed rooms of the bar have quite an unusual layout, with an interesting variety of seats around old tables and even recessed into a central sunken inglenook; there's also an airy conservatory dining room. The emphasis is very much on the wide choice of popular home-made bar food: sandwiches, soup (£2.95), garlic mushrooms with bacon and white wine

(£4.95), lasagne (£6.50), steak, Guinness and mushroom pie or seafood pancake (£6.95), steaks (from £9.50), mixed grill (£9.75), and weekly changing, rather pricey specials such as game consomme (£5.75), devilled kidneys (£5.95), saddle of rabbit in cider and cream (£12.95), grilled Dover sole (£13.95), and salmon and monkfish oriental (£14.95). Well kept Boddingtons, Brakspears, Fullers London Pride, Gibbs Mew Bishops Tipple, and changing guests like Hook Norton Old Hookey and Shepherd Neame Spitfire on handpump; decent wines, winter mulled wine, Pimms in summer; piped music in restaurant. The attractive garden has tables with fine views, and the friendly mongrel is called Willie and the black and white spaniel, Saigon. *(Recommended by Brian and Anna Marsden, SD, JD, Mike Beiley, Chris Warne, Marjorie and David Lamb, Martin and Sarah Crossley, Jeremy Kessell)*

Free house ~ Licensees Carole and Roger Shippey ~ Real ale ~ Meals and snacks (11-2.30, 6-10.30) ~ Restaurant ~ (01491) 682020 ~ Children in restaurant ~ Open 11-3, 5-11 ~ Bedrooms: £45S/£55S

FARINGDON SU2895 Map 4

Bell

Market Place; A420 SW of Oxford, then right into A417 – the village is now by-passed

The wide gates at the front entrance of this friendly 16th-c inn are a reminder of the days when this was a favourite stop on the stagecoach route. An ancient glazed screen through which customers would have watched the coaches trundling through the alley to the back coachyard is now the hallway. The old-fashioned and atmospheric bar has comfortable red leather settles, some unusual fragments of a very old mural, Cecil Aldin hunting prints, and, notably, a 17th-c carved oak chimney-piece over the splendid inglenook fireplace. Well kept Badger Tanglefoot, Wadworths 6X and Farmers Glory, and a guest beer every two weeks on handpump (kept under light blanket pressure); several malt whiskies; piped music. Good bar food, with prices unchanged since last year, includes sandwiches, baked potatoes (£2.75), ploughman's (from £3.50), filled Yorkshire puddings (£3.50), omelettes (from £3.80), vegetarian dishes, salads (from £4.25), steaks (£7.95), daily specials and puddings; the dining room is no smoking. The cobbled and paved yard, sheltered by the back wings of the pub, has wooden seats and tables among tubs of flowers. *(Recommended by Barry and Anne, Gordon, Peter and Audrey Dowsett, P Freeman, Roy and Margaret Randle)*

Wadworths ~ Tenants Malcolm and Brenda Bourton ~ Real ale ~ Meals and snacks ~ Restaurant ~ (01367) 240534 ~ Children in eating area of bar and in restaurant ~ Live entertainment winter Sat evening ~ Open 10.30-11; closed 25 Dec ~ Bedrooms: £35B/£35B

FERNHAM SU2992 Map 4

Woodman ★

A420 SW of Oxford, then left into B4508 after about 11 miles; village a further 6 miles on

In winter, you can mull your own beer or wine over the big log fire in this atmospheric 17th-c country pub – or enjoy the real ales such as Bass, Fullers London Pride, Marstons Pedigree, Morlands Old Speckled Hen, and Theakstons Old Peculier tapped from the casks behind the bar; plenty of fruit wines. With a snugly cosy feel, the heavily beamed rooms have cushioned benches, pews, Windsor chairs, and candlelit tables made simply from old casks – and an amazing assortment of old objects like clay pipes ready-filled for smoking, milkmaids' yokes, leather tack, coach horns, an old screw press, some original oil paintings and good black and white photographs of horses; over the bar there's a collection of over a hundred hats; another bar area is in what was the barn. Bar food changes regularly but might include liver and bacon casserole, spicy sausages, home-made cottage or steak and kidney pies (all £4.50), curries (from £5.40), Chinese prawns (£5.50), and puddings like chunky apple flan or treacle sponge (£2). OAPs who visit regularly get a very substantial discount; fruit machine, piped music, friendly dog and two entertaining cats. *(Recommended by Bill Bailey, Peter and Audrey Dowsett,*

Mr and Mrs J Brown, June and Tony Baldwin, S H Godsell)

Free house ~ Licensee John Lane ~ Real ale ~ Meals and snacks (not Mon) ~ (01367) 820643 ~ Children in eating area of bar ~ Open 11-3, 6.30-11; closed Mon lunchtime

FINSTOCK SP3616 Map 4

Plough 🛏 ♀

The Bottom; just off B4022 N of Witney

The licensees here are particularly cheerful and friendly which creates a nicely relaxed atmosphere in this neatly refurbished thatched 18th-c pub. The clean and comfortable long, rambling bar is nicely split up by partitions and alcoves, with an armchair by the open log-burning stove in the massive stone inglenook, tiles up at the end by the servery (elsewhere is carpeted), and a cosy feel under its low oak beams. Generous helpings of good bar food include filled baps, crab terrine with scallions or pan-fried scallops and mangetout (£3.95), Chinese peking duck with pancakes (£4.50), vegetarian pie with mustard and dill dip (£6.25), salmon and asparagus quiche (£6.50), rack of lamb with rosemary gravy (£7.95), and strips of fillet steak with shallots in a port and stilton sauce (£8.95). A comfortable low-beamed stripped-stone no-smoking dining room is on the right. Well kept Adnams Broadside, Hook Norton Best and Old Hookey, and a weekly changing guest on handpump, farm cider in summer, and a decent choice of wines and malt whiskies; maybe unobtrusive piped music. A separate games area has darts, bar billiards, cribbage, dominoes, fruit machine and trivia. There are tables (and Aunt Sally) in the good, sizeable garden. *(Recommended by Peter and Audrey Dowsett, John Waller, D Bryan, S Demont, T Barrow, David Heath, JM, PM, Brian Kneale, H T C Daubney)*

Free house ~ Licensee Val Baxter ~ Real ale ~ Meals and snacks ~ Restaurant ~ (01993) 868333 ~ Children welcome ~ Open 12-3, 6-11; all day Sat ~ One bedroom: £32B/£45B

FYFIELD SU4298 Map 4

White Hart 🍺

In village, off A420 8 miles SW of Oxford

An impressive medieval building – built to house priests who would pray for the soul of its rather modest proprietor – with soaring eaves, huge stone-flanked window embrasures, and an attractive carpeted upper gallery make up the main room (actually a hall), while a low-ceilinged side bar has an inglenook fireplace with a huge black urn hanging over the grate, and a framed history of the pub on the wall. The priests' room and barrel-vaulted cellar are dining areas; three areas are no-smoking. Well kept real ales might include Boddingtons, Fullers London Pride, Gibbs Mew Bishops Tipple, Hook Norton Best, Theakstons Old Peculier and Wadworths 6X on handpump or tapped from the cask; country wines and Weston's cider. Bar food includes sandwiches (lunchtime), soup (£1.95), home-made pâté (£2.75), vegetable curry or cheese pie (£4.95), home-made steak and kidney pie (£5.25), local trout (£5.95), steaks (from £7.95), and daily specials; pleasantly welcoming service. Shove-ha'penny, dominoes, darts, cribbage, trivia and piped music. A heavy wooden door leads out to the rambling, sheltered and flowery back lawn, which has a children's playground. *(Recommended by NN, Audrey and Peter Dowsett, M Lithgow, Gordon, Jon Carpenter, D C T and E A Frewer, Basil Minson)*

Free house ~ Licensee John Howard ~ Real ale ~ Meals and snacks (till 10pm) ~ (01865) 390585 ~ Children allowed in several rooms ~ Open 11-3, 6.30-11; closed 25/26 Dec

Food details, prices, timing etc refer to bar food – not to a separate restaurant if there is one.

GODSTOW SP4809 Map 4

Trout

Follow Wolvercote signpost from roundabout at N end of Woodstock Road

It's the lovely position that makes this pretty medieval pub so special – best enjoyed on a sunny day. Sitting at the sturdy oak tables on the cobbled waterside terrace watching the plump trout in the clear stream really is delightful, and there are peacocks, rabbits and guinea pigs in the grounds, and you can hand feed the chub and bream in the water. The beamed main bar has cushioned old settles on the flagstones and bare floorboards, old Oxford views and sporting prints on the walls, and a weight-driven spit in front of one of the big stone fireplaces; an old visitors' book recalls some of its more distinguished customers from the 1920s, and there's piped classical music. There's a separate beamed and partly no-smoking restaurant, and a more modern extension bar where you can eat ploughman's or salads (from £4), and hot dishes such as steak and kidney pie, toad in the hole or macaroni cheese (all £4.95). Well kept Bass, Charrington IPA and Fullers London Pride on handpump. The pub is, naturally, popular with tourists. *(Recommended by Lynn Sharpless, Bob Eardley, Jim and Maggie Cowell, Prof A N Black, Julie Munday, Martin Robinson, T A Bryan, Tim and Ann Newell, Julian Bessa, Ann and Bob Westerook, Wayne Brindle, Jenny and Brian Seller, Stephen Savill, Nigel Norman)*

Bass ~ Manager Russell Harding ~ Real Ale ~ Meals and snacks ~ Restaurant ~ (01865) 54485 ~ Children welcome ~ Open 11-11

GREAT TEW SP3929 Map 4

Falkland Arms ★ ★ 🛏

Off B4022 about 5 miles E of Chipping Norton

In a beautiful untouched village full of golden stone thatched cottages, this delightful place is many people's idea of the perfect English pub. The partly panelled bar has a wonderful inglenook fireplace, high-backed settles and a diversity of stools around plain stripped tables on flagstones and bare boards, one, two and three handled mugs hanging from the beam-and-board ceiling, dim converted oil lamps, and shutters for the stone-mullioned latticed windows. The bar counter, decorated with antique Doulton jugs, mugs and tobacco jars, always serves around five or so reasonably priced and well kept guest beers, as well as the regular Badger Tanglefoot, Donnington BB, Hook Norton Best and Wadworths 6X; also country wines, 50 malt whiskies, a couple of farm ciders, hot punch in winter, clay pipes filled ready to smoke, some 50 different snuffs, and tankards, a model of the pub, and handkerchiefs for sale; the snug is no-smoking at lunchtime. Darts, shove-ha'penny, dominoes, cribbage and table skittles. Straightforward lunchtime food usually includes sandwiches, sausage and pickle (£4.80), and beef and pâté pie or gingered lamb casserole (£5). There are tables outside in front of the pub, with picnic-table sets under umbrellas in the garden behind – where there's a dovecote. The lavatories continue to be a let-down. Perhaps best visited on a weekday lunchtime – it does get extremely crowded at other times. The licensees also run the Reindeer in Banbury, which has been very attractively restored. *(Recommended by Graham and Lynn Mason, Leith Stuart, Christopher and Sharon Hayle, Ewan McCall, Dave Irving, Roger Huggins, Tom McLean, Gordon, N and J Strathdee, John Waller, Jim and Maggie Cowell, WHBM, John and Christine Simpson, J Wedel, Roy Smylie, John and Shirley Dyson, Michael Marlow, The Monday Club, Paul Boot, S Demont, T Barrow, Wayne Brindle, Frank Gadbois, Ted George, Paul and Tony Martin, Lynn Sharpless, Bob Eardley, Basil Minson, Tom Evans, Hugh Chevallier, Phil and Sally Gorton, Marjorie and Bernard Parkin, Steve Goodchild, John and Annette Derbyshire, I R Hewitt, John Bowdler)*

Free house ~ Licensees John and Hazel Milligan ~ Real ale ~ Lunchtime meals and snacks (not Sun and Mon, except bank holidays) ~ (01608) 68653 ~ Children in eating area of bar at lunchtime ~ Folk music Sun evening ~ Open 11.30-2.30, 6-11; closed Mon lunchtime except bank holidays ~ Bedrooms: £25(£30S)/ £40(£45S)

HAILEY SU6485 Map 2

King William IV ★ £

Note – this is the hamlet of Hailey, near Ipsden (not the larger Hailey over in west Oxon); signposted with Ipsden from A4074 S of Wallingford; can also be reached from A423; OS Sheet 175 map reference 641859

A perfect way to reach this charming old-fashioned pub is by Ian Smith's horse and wagon service; he arranges rides from Nettlebed to the pub where you then have a ploughman's or supper and gently return through the woods and via Stoke Row back to Nettlebed (£10 a head; 01491-641324 to book). And on a summer evening you can sit among the smartly-painted old farm equipment on the lawn behind the pub and look across to peaceful, rolling pastures. Inside, the relaxed beamed bar has some good sturdy furniture on the tiles in front of the big winter log fire, and so many well restored farm implements that it could almost be a museum; the timbered bare brick walls are covered with root cutters, forks, ratchets, shovels, crooks, grabbers, man-traps, wicker sieves, full-size carts, ploughs, and a pitching prong, all with details of their age, use and maker – there's even a couple of dried bladders. Two broadly similar carpeted areas open off. Well kept and reasonably priced Brakspears PA, SB, and XXXX Old tapped from casks behind the bar, and farm ciders; popular filled rolls such as ham, cheese and pickle, and corned beef (from 60p – the only evening food), and lunchtime pies, pasties or ploughman's with home-made soup (from £3). They've happily got another Shire horse – Duke – who's already a favourite with customers (and with their children). *(Recommended by Adrian Pearce, Roderic Plinston, Steve Goodchild, Giles Bullard)*

Brakspears ~ Tenant Brian Penney ~ Real ale ~ Snacks ~ (01491) 680675 ~ Children in eating area at lunchtime ~ Open 11-2.30, 6-11

HENLEY-ON-THAMES SU7682 Map 2

Besides Lucky Dip entries listed under this town, you might like to see the entries listed under Remenham – just over the Thames bridge, and therefore in Berkshire

Three Tuns

5 Market Place

This welcoming traditional little place has a much-loved old-fashioned appeal. The heavily beamed front bar has pine furnishings, a log-effect gas bar central chimney, and pre-nationalisation railway company notices on the panelled walls. A stable bar with pinball, fruit machine and juke box leads off the terrace. Popular home-made bar food includes sandwiches, home-made chicken and leek broth (£2.25), filled baked potatoes and pancakes (from £2.50), pasta dishes and grills (from £3.50), and fresh fish (from £4.50). Well kept Boddingtons and Brakspears PA, SB and Old on handpump, and reasonably priced doubles from an old-fashioned central servery. The back garden is floodlit at night. No children. *(Recommended by Andy Thwaites, David Warrellow, Graham and Karen Oddey, Brian and Anna Marsden, Gordon, P J Caunt, Andy Stone, Mr and Mrs Simon Turner, Elizabeth and Klaus Leist, Susan and John Douglas)*

Brakspears ~ Tenant Robin Gladman ~ Real ale ~ Meals and snacks (10-9.30); not Sun evening ~ (01491) 573260 ~ Live entertainment every fortnight ~ Open 10am-11pm

HOOK NORTON SP3533 Map 4

Pear Tree ◖

Village signposted off A361 SW of Banbury

This attractive pub has always been a beer-drinkers' paradise, with well kept Hook Norton Best and Old Hookey in perfect condition from the brewery barely 100 yards down the lane. Though it remains an honest unspoiled village local, its appeal has been broadened in the last few years. Two previously separate small rooms have been refurbished and knocked together to make room for country-kitchen furniture, including long tables as if for communal eating. (The only out-of-place element has been the pair of Colt and Fillies signs for the lavatories.) There's a rather wider choice nowadays of very good value food including generous sandwiches (from £1.60), a fine baked potato topped with ham and cheese (from £1.85), ploughman's (from £3.35), and well cooked main dishes such as cottage pie, vegetable curry or lasagne (£3.95), beef in ale casserole (£4.90), and daily specials such as smoked haddock and broccoli bake (£3.95), ginger spiced pork (£4.35), lamb casserole (£5.45), and puddings like home-made tart armandine (£1.90); deliberately, they serve most food simply, so that people who want to can eat standing up. The atmosphere is friendly and relaxed – locals drifting in with their dogs, sensible piped music (Handel on Palm Sunday), cosy open fires; welcoming landlord, good service. The sizeable garden is attractive, with a play area, chickens and rabbits, and popular Sunday barbecues; the pub tends to get crowded on summer weekends. *(Recommended by Robert Gomme, Pat and Tony Martin, Tom Evans, Nigel Clifton, Julian and Sarah Stanton, David Campbell, Vicki McLean, Sue Holland, Dave Webster)*

Hook Norton ~ Tenants Steve and Wendy Tindsley ~ Real ale ~ Meals and snacks (not Tues or Sun evenings) ~ (01608) 737482 ~ Children in eating area of bar till 9pm ~ Open 12-2.30(3 Sat), 6-11 ~ One bedroom: £20S/£35S

nr HOOK NORTON SP3533 Map 4

Gate Hangs High ♀

Banbury Rd; a mile N of village towards Sibford, at Banbury—Rollright crossroads

Very popular locally, this isolated country pub is well run and cared for by friendly licensees. The bar has joists in the long, low ceiling, a brick bar counter, stools and assorted chairs on the carpet (some tables set for diners), and a gleaming copper hood over the hearth in the inglenook fireplace. Popular freshly-prepared bar food includes soup (£1.65), ploughman's (£2.95), salads (from £5.50), honey-baked ham and egg (£5.50), home-made steak and kidney pie (£5.95), steaks (£8), daily specials such as carrot roulade with cream cheese and herb filling (£5.25), beef rogan josh (£5.50), and supreme of chicken with fresh tarragon sauce (£7.50). Well kept Hook Norton Best and a guest on handpump, a good wine list, malt whiskies, and dominoes. The broad lawn, under holly and apple trees, has swings for children to play on – though one reader told us the view has been a bit spoilt by caravans. Five miles south-west are the Bronze Age Rollright Stones – said to be a king and his army who were turned to stone by a witch. *(Recommended by John and Shirley Dyson, Graham and Karen Oddey, M Pearlman, Peter and Jenny Coombs, George Murdoch, Marjorie and David Lamb)*

Hook Norton ~ Tenant Stuart Rust ~ Real ale ~ Meals and snacks (not Sun evening) ~ Restaurant ~ (01608) 737387 ~ Children in eating area of bar and in restaurant ~ Open 11.30-3, 6.30-11

KELMSCOT SU2499 Map 4

Plough 🛏

NW of Faringdon, off A417 or A4095

This pretty inn was briefly called the Manor Inn – confusingly, as this peaceful hamlet by the upper Thames does include an altogether more famous building of that name, William Morris's summer home. However, the friendly new owners have restored order by bringing back the original name. They have refurbished the pub well, and it's now most enjoyable. There's an attractively traditional small bar, homely and warmly welcoming, with ancient flagstones and stripped stone walls, and a larger cheerfully carpeted back room with more Laura-Ashleyesque furnishings and yet no unnecessary gloss, a good woodburning stove, and prints on its uncluttered walls. A wide choice of reasonably priced good home-cooked food includes soup (£1.75), ploughman's (from £2.75), roast nut portugaise (£4.95), cat fish in basil sauce (£5.95), buckwheat pancakes filled with chicken, bacon and mushroom or smoked haddock and prawn or salami and peppers (from £5.95), caribbean chicken or beef and orange pie (£6.50),

Aberdeen angus steaks (from £7.95), and puddings like home-made cheesecakes or fresh fruit fools (from £2), with vegetarian dishes and a good value Sunday lunch. Well kept Bass and Morlands Original, a good range of malt whiskies, attentive service; darts, shove-ha'penny, cribbage, dominoes, fruit machine, trivia, occasional piped music. The pretty garden has tables and Aunt Sally, and there are Thames moorings a few minutes' walk away. *(Recommended by David and Jane Warren, P and J Shapley, Martin and Karen Wake, Roger Huggins, Tom McLean, Dave Irving, Ewan McCall, D C Humphreys, Peter and Audrey Dowsett)*

Free house ~ Licensees Trevor and Anne Pardoe ~ Real ale ~ Meals and snacks ~ Restaurant ~ (01367) 253543 ~ Children welcome ~ Live entertainment Sat evening ~ Open 11.30-3, 6-11; 11-11 Sat ~ Bedrooms: £35B/£45B

LEWKNOR SU7198 Map 4

Olde Leathern Bottle

Under a mile from M40 junction 6; just off B4009 towards Watlington

In a pretty village, this well run, bustling pub is popular with a good mix of people. The two rooms of the bar have heavy beams in the low ceilings, open fires, rustic furnishings and an understated decor of old beer taps and the like – and a warmly friendly atmosphere. The no-smoking family room is separated only by standing timbers, so you don't feel cut off from the rest of the pub. The dogs are called Penny (the doberman) and Charlie (the west highland white). Good home-made bar food using fresh local produce includes sandwiches (lunchtime, from £1.65), ploughman's (from £3.50), a late breakfast (£3.75), filled baked potatoes (from £3.95), salads (from £4.25), various curries (from £4.50), home-made steak and kidney pie (£4.95), gammon and egg (£5.50), steaks (from £7.25), daily specials like fish stew provençale (£5.25), and home-made puddings (£2); quick, obliging service. Well kept Boddingtons Bitter and Brakspears PA, SB and Old on handpump; dominoes and piped music. There are tables on the sizeable lawn alongside the car park; this is a very pretty village. *(Recommended by Graham Reeve, Gordon, Michael Sargent, Marjorie and David Lamb, C G and B Mason, D A Edwards, Dorothee and Dennis Glover, Lynn and Bill Capper, K H Frostick, TBB)*

Brakspears ~ Tenants Mike and Lesley Fletcher ~ Real ale ~ Meals and snacks (till 10pm Fri/Sat) ~ (01844) 351482 ~ Children in family room and lounge bar ~ Open 11-2.30(3 Sat), 6-11

LITTLE MILTON SP6100 Map 4

Lamb

3 miles from M40, junction 7; A329 towards Wallingford

One of the reasons why the rolling farmland around here is a conservation area is partly because of this honey-coloured stone pub. The old-fashioned and simple beamed bar has little windows in the stripped stone walls that are so low you have to stoop to look out, lots of tables with wheelback chairs, and soft lighting. Bass, Benskins, and Ind Coope Burton on handpump, and home-made food such as sandwiches, ploughman's, quail's eggs with ham and mozzarella, breast of duckling with cointreau and orange, and half a shoulder of lamb with blackcurrant and port. In summer the quiet garden is lovely: hanging baskets, tubs of flowers, roses, a herbaceous border, fruit trees, and swings. It can get quite crowded at lunchtimes. *(Recommended by A T Langton, TBB, M A and C R Starling; more reports please)*

Sycamore Taverns (Allied) ~ Tenant David Bowell ~ Real ale ~ Meals and snacks (till 10pm) ~ (01844) 279527 ~ Children in eating area of bar ~ Open 11-2.30, 6.30-11; closed evening 25 Dec

---

Planning a day in the country? We list pubs in really attractive scenery at the back of the book.

MAIDENSGROVE SU7288 Map 2

Five Horseshoes 🍴 ♈

W of village, which is signposted from B480 and B481; OS Sheet 175, map reference 711890

At weekends, the imaginative food here is so popular that booking is now essential. Their fish dishes are becoming very popular, and the fish is collected by the landlord from the markets twice a week (he then goes on to Smithfield). From a wide menu, the food might include soup (£2.50), baked potatoes filled with things like prawns in a tomato and brandy mayonnaise (from £4.75), home-made vegetarian or smoked salmon pâté (£4.95), filled pancakes (from £5.50, turkey and ham with cranberries in a cream sauce (£5.75), pasta with a pesto or tomato, mushroom and cream sauce (£5.75), steak and kidney pie (£5.90), tiger prawns in filo pastry with sweet chilli dip (£6.75), stir-fried chicken with ginger, nuts and crispy vegetables (£6.95), monkfish with herb mustard and honey sauce (£7.95), lovely rack of lamb, sea bass cooked in a parcel with fresh orange and lime butter, and steaks (from £10.95). Well kept Brakspears PA, SB and OBJ on handpump and 11 wines by the glass. The rambling bar is furnished with mostly modern wheelback chairs around shiny dark wooden tables – though there are some attractive older seats and a big baluster-leg table, as well as a good log fire in winter; the low ceiling in the main area is covered in bank notes from all over the world, mainly donated by customers. There's a separate bar for walkers where boots are welcome, and a dining conservatory. There are some picnic-table sets on the sheltered lawn, and the barbecue area has been rebuilt. *(Recommended by Andy Thwaites, Jean Gustavson, Michael Sargent, Brad Wilson, Chris Warne, Ian Phillips, Dr Gerald Barnett, Mark Hydes, David Warrellow, K Harvey, Mrs S Kirby, Mrs A Morrison, H Taylor, Neville Kenyon)*

Brakspears ~ Tenant Graham Cromack ~ Real ale ~ Meals and snacks ~ Conservatory restaurant ~ (01491) 641282 ~ Children in restaurant ~ Open 11.30-2.30, 6-11

MOULSFORD SU5983 Map 2

Beetle & Wedge 🍴 🛏

Ferry Lane; off A329, 1½ miles N of Streatley

Our excuse for keeping this very civilised and smart riverside hotel in our book is that you can still drop in for just a drink, if that is what you want; our reason is that this is one of the very few decent places on the river – and that we like it. The most pubby part is the informal Boathouse bar restaurant by the river, where there's a nice mix of old chairs around polished wooden tables, oak saddle-beams, a tiled floor, flint and brick walls, and a relaxed, chatty atmosphere; in fine weather this extends out onto the terrace where there are tables on the jetty. Food is either cooked on an open charcoal grill in the room or in the small kitchen: moules marinières (£5.50), duck and pork rillettes (£4.75), ploughman's with interesting cheeses or avocado salad with smoked chicken and prawns (£6.25), roast saddle of rabbit (£12.95), pan-fried Dover sole with scallops and baby onions (£13.95), calf's liver and bacon (£14.50), sirloin steak bearnaise (£14.95), and puddings like rhubarb crumble, pears poached in red wine or lemon tart with lemon ice cream (from £5.25). The main (no-smoking) dining room has been completely rebuilt this year with a lovely conservatory, and there is also the Watergarden outside restaurant and the Barge (St John's College Barge, moored off the Watergarden). Well kept Adnams Bitter, Badger Tanglefoot, and Wadworths 6X on handpump, an extensive wine list, and freshly squeezed orange juice. The waterside lawn, flanked by roses, has robustly old-fashioned garden furniture. Rowing boats are available nearby. *(Recommended by Dave Carter, Pippa Bobbett, Giles Bullard, R L and M B, Mrs S Kirby)*

Free house ~ Licensees Richard and Kate Smith ~ Real ale ~ Meals and snacks (till 10pm) ~ Restaurants (not Sun evening) ~ (01491) 651381 ~ Children welcome ~ Open 11.30-2.30, 6-11; closed 25 Dec ~ Bedrooms: £80B/£95B

MURCOTT SP5815 Map 4

Nut Tree ♀

Off B4027 NE of Oxford, via Islip and Charlton-on-Otmoor

In a lovely spot, this civilised low-thatched old house has colourful hanging baskets, ducks on a pretty front pond, trim lawns, and usually plenty of animals such as donkeys, peacocks and rabbits. Inside, you'll get a warm welcome from the friendly landlord – and some good food: sandwiches (from £2.50), locally-made sausages (£3.30), veal, ham and egg pie or home-made burgers using prime steak (the landlord is a master butcher, £3.50), quite a few fresh fish dishes (from £5.50), steak and kidney pie (£6.50), chicken dishes (from £9.50), daily specials and vegetarian dishes; the steaks are very good. Bass, Hook Norton, and Morrells Bitter and Varsity on handpump; a fair number of malt whiskies, and a decent range of wines. The beamed lounge is decorated in stylish shades of red, has fresh flowers on its tables (set for food), and a winter log fire; there's also a small back conservatory-style extension. Aunt Sally, darts, shove-ha'penny, cribbage and dominoes. There's an unusual collection of ten gargoyles (loosely modelled on some of the local characters) hanging in the garden – each carved into a magnificently grotesque form from a different wood; you can find nine of them in the walnut tree and one in a pillar overlooking the well. The pub's handy for walks through the boggy Otmoor wilderness, and from the M40 (junction 9). *(Recommended by Nigel Flook, Betsy Brown, Gordon, Michael Sargent, Alan and Margot Baker, N and J Strathdee, John Waller, S Demont, T Barrow, TBB, Sir Nigel Foulkes, Mayur Shah)*

Free house ~ Licensee Gordon Evans ~ Real ale ~ Meals and snacks (not Sun) ~ Restaurant (not Sun) ~ (01865) 331253 ~ Children in restaurant ~ Open 11-3.30, 6.30-11

NUFFIELD SU6687 Map 2

Crown ♀

A423/B481

Promptly served by consistently friendly staff, the food in this attractive little partly 17th-c brick-and-flint pub is still proving very popular. Everything (except the bread) is home-made and from a wide choice might include sandwiches, soup (£2.75), tuna pâté or a cheesy chilli dip (£3.75), sausage and chilli bean casserole or steak and kidney pie (£5.50), bacon chop with honey and topped with mustard and parsley butter (£5.75), rich leek tart (£5.95), salads (from £6.50), roast quail (£8.25), steaks (from £8.75), daily specials and lots of puddings. Well kept Brakspears PA, SB and OBJ on handpump, a good range of decent wines, and cappuccino and espresso coffee. The heavily beamed lounge has country furniture, roaring log fires in a fine inglenook fireplace, a relaxed atmosphere, and shelves of golf balls (there's an adjacent golf course); cribbage and dominoes. There's another big log fire in the public bar, and a third family room; friendly cat. There are tables out under cocktail parasols in the partly terraced back garden, with more in front; the pub's right on the Ridgeway Long Distance Path. There are no bedrooms but the pub will put you in touch with local people who do B&B, and Nuffield Place, the home of the late Lord Nuffield of Morris cars fame, is close by. *(Recommended by Joan Olivier, Dick Brown, R D Knight, David Dimock, Hazel Astley)*

Brakspears ~ Tenants Ann and Gerry Bean ~ Real ale ~ Meals and snacks 12-2, 7-9.45 (9.30 Sun) ~ (01491) 641335 ~ Children in small family room next to bar, lunchtimes only ~ Open 11-2.30(3ish Sat), 6-11; closed 25/26 Dec, and evening 1 Jan

OXFORD SP5106 Map 4

Turf Tavern

Bath Place; via St Helen's Passage, between Holywell Street and New College Lane

This is an unexpected little old-fashioned building in a quaint little old-fashioned courtyard that seems a million miles and a hundred years away from the bustle of the city. The two little rooms have a snug feel, dark beams, and low ceilings, and are still much as Hardy described it when Jude the Obscure discovered that Arabella the barmaid was the wife who'd left him years before; there's also a bar in one of the courtyards. Brakspears and Wadworths 6X on handpump or tapped from the bar with three guests like Boddingtons, Flowers Original or Morland Old Speckled Hen, and they hold four ale festivals a year – the summer one has over 100 different beers; winter mulled wine and Old Rosie farm cider. Bar food includes lots of filled baps, hot or cold, like bacon, egg and tomato or chicken tikka mayonnaise (from £1.45), vegetarian lasagne, traditional roasts, cotswold chicken or steak and mushroom pie (all £4.85). Outside, there are three attractive walled-in flagstoned or gravelled courtyards – and in winter there are braziers out here on which you can roast chestnuts. *(Recommended by Julian Bessa, Sue Demont, Tim Barrow, Mrs Pat Crabb, Gordon, Neil and Elaine Piper, N and J Strathdee, Walter Reid, Martin Jones, Eamon Green, Tim and Ann Newell, Jim and Maggie Cowell, Professor C MacCallum, Gill and Maurice McMahon)*

Whitbreads ~ Managers Biff and Pam Griffin ~ Real ale ~ Meals and snacks (12-3, 6-9) ~ (01865) 243235 ~ Children in back bar only ~ No nearby parking ~ Open 11-11

PISHILL SU7389 Map 2

Crown

B480 N of Henley

In winter, this mainly 15th-c red brick and flint pub is most appealing when its three fine fireplaces in the bar blaze their way through a ton of logs each week. There are old photographs on the partly panelled walls, an elegant corner cabinet of decorated plates, and a central black-beamed and red-and-gold carpeted part with little blocky country chairs and stools around wooden tables. The rear section is knocked-through, with standing oak timbers. Well kept Brakspears, Flowers Original, and a guest beer on handpump, and very attractively presented home-made bar food such as sandwiches (weekday lunchtimes), deep-fried brie with a peach dip or pâté (£3.50), filled baked potatoes (from £4), pasta dishes (from £5.25), steak and kidney pie (£5.95), liver stroganoff (£6.50), duck in orange (£8.95), steaks (from £9.50), and daily specials using fish and game. Picnic table sets on the attractive side lawn. The thatched barn they use for parties and functions is some 500 years old. No children – except see below. *(Recommended by Michael Sargent, Eamon Green, David Warrellow, S J Tasker, P A and M J White, Margaret and Michael Norris, Susan and John Douglas)*

Free house ~ Licensee Jeremy Capon ~ Real ale ~ Meals and snacks (till 10pm); not Sun or Mon evenings ~ Restaurant (not Sun evening) ~ (01491) 638364 ~ Children in restaurant Sun lunchtime only ~ Jazz Sun evening ~ Open 11.30-2.30, 6-11 ~ Bedrooms in separate cottage: £65

ROKE SU6293 Map 2

Home Sweet Home ★

Village signposted off B4009 Benson—Watlington

There's a good country atmosphere in this rather smart thatched and tiled old house – and good, popular food, too. The two smallish, bare-boarded and stone-walled rooms of the bar have heavy stripped beams, leather armed chairs, just a few horsey or game pictures such as a nice Thorburn print of snipe, and big log fires – one with a great high-backed settle facing it across a hefty slab of a rustic table. On the right, a carpeted room with low settees and armchairs, and an attractive corner glass cupboard, leads through to the restaurant. Bar food includes sandwiches, steak and kidney pudding (£6.50), fresh salmon fishcakes with parsley sauce (£6.95), calf's liver with crispy bacon or chicken roulade (£7.95), and puddings like terrific treacle pudding. Well kept Brakspears Ordinary and Special on handpump, and a good choice of malt whiskies. The low-walled garden at the front looks on to the quiet hamlet, and has lots of flowers around the tables out by the well. The licensees also run another of our main entries, the Old Boot at Stanford Dingley in Berkshire. *(Recommended by Mrs N Cooke, Nicholas Holmes, John Waller, David Wright, Eamon Green, Mrs S Kirby, J A Collins, Martin Cooke)*

Free house ~ Licensees Jill Madle, Peter and Irene Mountford ~ Real ale ~ Meals and snacks (till 10pm) ~ Restaurant ~ (01491) 838249 ~ Well behaved children welcome ~ Open 11-3, 5.30-11

SHENINGTON SP3742 Map 4

Bell ♀

Village signposted from A422 W of Banbury

The lucky village school get their meals cooked by the friendly staff of this 300-year-old pub. Readers remain delighted with their food too, which might include sandwiches, excellent home-made spinach soup, lovely leek and mushroom gratin, nice goat's cheese quiche, steak and kidney pie or almond, celery and nut bake (£5.75), lamb and lime casserole (£7.25), salmon in cucumber sauce (£7.50), duck breast with black cherries, and puddings such as good sticky toffee pudding. Well kept Boddingtons, Hook Norton Best and Websters Yorkshire on handpump, and a good choice of wines from Berry Bros; good, friendly service. The heavy-beamed and carpeted lounge has old maps and documents on the cream wall, brown cloth-cushioned wall seats and window seats, and vases of flowers on the tables; the wall in the flagstoned area on the left is stripped to stone and decorated with heavy-horse harness, and the right side opens into a neat little pine-panelled room (popular with locals) with decorated plates on its walls; darts, dominoes, coal fire. There's a tortoiseshell cat called Willow and a west highland terrier, Lucy. The tables at the front look across to the green. *(Recommended by Joan Olivier, Mr and Mrs W W Swaitt, Mr and Mrs C Moncreiffe, Alex Nicholls, Adele Faiers, G Diamond, R T and J C Moggridge, P D and J Bickley, Mr and Mrs Carlyle-Lyon, Sir Nigel Foulkes, Dr and Mrs Frank Rackow, John Bowdler, Peter and Erica Davis)*

Free house ~ Licensees Jennifer and Stephen Dixon ~ Real ale ~ Meals and snacks (12-3, 6.30-11.30; supper licence) ~ Restaurant ~ (01295 87274) ~ Children welcome ~ Open 12-2.30(3 Sat), 7(6.30 Sat)-11 ~ Bedrooms: £15(£18B)/£30

SHIPTON-UNDER-WYCHWOOD SP2717 Map 4

Lamb ★ ⑪ ♀ 🛏

Just off A361 to Burford

There's certainly quite an emphasis on food in this rather civilised and stylish old sandstone pub, but there's plenty of room for drinkers, too, in the relaxed beamed bar with its fine oak-panelled settle, nice mix of solid old farmhouse-style and captain's chairs on the wood-block floor, polished tables, cushioned bar stools, solid oak bar counter, pictures on old partly bared stone walls, and newspapers on rods to read. Popular choices on the bar menu (with prices unchanged since last year) include a good summer cold buffet, home-made soup, duck and orange pâté (£3.50), Loch Fyne gravadlax (£4.95), jugged hare (£7.75), roast duck (£10.50), lots of fresh fish like seafood tart, scallops, Dover sole, lobster and salmon, and puddings such as outstanding chocolate mousse or tipsy-making trifle; vegetables are well presented, salads well dressed, and breakfasts very good indeed. The restaurant is no smoking. Well kept Hook Norton Best and Wadworths 6X on handpump, several malt whiskies, carefully chosen wines and champagne by the glass. In summer, you can sit at tables among the roses at the back. No children. *(Recommended by Ewan McCall, Dave Irving, Roger Huggins, Tom McLean, S Demont, T Barrow, Martin Jones, the Monday Club, Michael Sargent, Mark and Toni Amor-Segan, Mrs J M Bell, Dr Stern, Miss Dawe, Adam and Elizabeth Duff, Mark Bradley, T R and B C Jenkins, George and Chris Miller, Frank W Gadbois, P Boot, Bill and Edee Miller, Pete and Rose Flower; also recommended by The Good Hotel Guide)*

Free house ~ Licensees Mr and Mrs L Valenta ~ Real ale ~ Meals and snacks ~ Restaurant (not Sun evening) ~ (01993) 830465 ~ Open 11-3, 6-11; closed Mon ~ Bedrooms: /£65B

Shaven Crown 🛏

The medieval courtyard garden behind this heavily stone-roofed pub is a tranquil place on a sunny day with its own lily pool, roses, and old-fashioned seats set out on the stone cobbles and crazy paving. Inside, there is a magnificent double-collar braced hall roof and lounge at the front with lofty beams and a sweeping double stairway down the stone wall. A fine beamed bar has a relief of the 1146 Battle of Evesham, as well as seats forming little stalls around the tables and upholstered benches built into the walls. Good bar food includes soup (£2.15), ploughman's (from £2.95), smoked haddock mousse or mushroom and walnut pancake (£3.95), a mild curried meat loaf, home-baked ham or salmon, cod and dill fishcakes (£5.25), steak, kidney and mushroom pie (£5.75), sirloin steak (£8.95), daily specials, and puddings like treacle tart, lemon soufflé or home-made ice creams (from £1.40); the restaurant is no smoking. Well kept Hook Norton and a guest such as Adnams Broadside or Morlands Old Speckled Hen on handpump, wines of the week, and very good service. The pub has its own bowling green. This was originally a hospice for the monastery of Bruern in the 14th c, and parts of it are said to have been used as a hunting lodge by Elizabeth I; the residents' lounge, the medieval hall, is lovely. *(Recommended by John Drew, Dr C I Haines, Peter and Iris Jones, T R and B C Jenkins, Peter and Anne Hollindale, Susan and John Douglas, R G Barton, Heather Thomas, Peter and Rosemary Ellis, David Campbell, Vicki McLean)*

Free house ~ Licensees Trevor and Mary Brookes ~ Real ale ~ Meals and snacks (not 25 Dec) ~ Restaurant ~ (01993) 830330 ~ Children welcome – but no under 5s in restaurant in evening ~ Open 12-2.30, 7-11 ~ Bedrooms: £33B/£68B

SIBFORD GOWER   SP3537   Map 4

Wykham Arms

Village signed off B4035 Banbury—Shipston on Stour

The comfortable and attractively renovated low-beamed lounge in this pretty stone-built neatly thatched cottage spreads through three open-plan areas around the central servery, with brocaded built-in wall seats and Windsor chairs, pictures on the bare stone walls, and one table consisting of a glassed-in ancient well. The smaller tap room has an inglenook fireplace, and the attractive, partly no-smoking restaurant was once the stables. Good bar food includes lunchtime sandwiches (from £1.50), broccoli and stilton soup (£1.85), chicken satay (£2.85), filled baked potatoes (from £2.85), lunchtime ploughman's (£4.50), chicken curry, home-cooked ham (in cider) and egg or spinach and mushroom lasagne (£4.95), beef and stout pie (£5.50), salmon steak (£7.25), steaks (from £8.75), daily specials like beef and Guinness casserole (£5.50), fish pie (£5.95), and puddings such as apple crumble or strawberry cheesecake (£1.95); children's dishes (£2.50); Sunday roast. Well kept Hook Norton Best and Old Hookey, Mansfield Old Baily, Morlands Old Speckled Hen, and Wadworths 6X on handpump, and lots of country wines. Darts and piped music. The black labrador is called Megan, the german shepherd Portia, and the two young farm cats Merlin and Ziggy. There's a rambling rose and well tended flower baskets and a big well planted garden with children's play area and views over the rolling countryside. *(Recommended by George Atkinson, Sir Nigel Foulkes, Julian and Sarah Stanton)*

Free house ~ David Faulkner and Rachel Neilson ~ Real ale ~ Meals and snacks (not Mon) ~ Restaurant ~ (01295) 780351 ~ Children welcome ~ Live music once a month ~ Open 12-3, 6.30-11; closed Mon lunchtime

SOUTH LEIGH   SP3908   Map 4

Mason Arms 🍸 🛏

Village signposted from A40 Witney—Eynsham

There may be peacocks and chickens pottering around the sweeping lawns behind this delightful old thatched country pub, some Cotswold sheep in the small field by the car park, and picnic-set tables in a small grove by some quite bizarrely-shaped trees and little bushes. Inside, the flagstoned lounge is separated into two halves by a wrought-iron divider, and has lots of polished copper and brass, built-in cushioned settles curving around the corners, a panelled bar counter, an open fire with stone hearth at one end, and a log-effect gas fire at the other. Home-made bar food includes sandwiches, smoked salmon pâté (£2.75), venison casserole (£6.45), pheasant in red wine, Old Peculier beef or prawns in filo pastry (£6.95), and fillet steak stuffed with stilton (£11.25); Sunday roasts and daily specials. Well kept Sow-lye (brewed for them) and Theakstons Best on handpump, a good range of cognacs and malt whiskies, and lots of wines; the bedrooms are well-equipped. Dylan Thomas used to pop in here while writing *Under Milk Wood* at the nearby Manor House, and the 12th-c church has the pulpit from where John Wesley preached his first sermon. *(Recommended by Harold and the Monday Club, Mr and Mrs J Brown, Dr P Mummery, Alys Daubney; more reports, please)*

Free house ~ Licensee Geoff Waters ~ Real ale ~ Meals and snacks (not Sun evening or Mon) ~ Restaurant (not Sun evening or Mon) ~ (01993) 702485 ~ Children in restaurant ~ Open 11-2.30, 6.30-11; closed Mon ~ Bedrooms: £34.50B/£48.50B

SOUTH STOKE SU5983 Map 2

Perch & Pike ♀

Off B4009 2 miles N of Goring

Since Mr and Mrs Robinson have re-opened this attractive flint pub after major internal renovations, its reputation has been going from strength to strength. With just a handful of dedicated staff, they have created a fine pubby atmosphere, have comfortable seats and a nice assortment of tables, and are perfectly happy for people to come for just a drink – though it would be a shame to miss Mrs Robinson's cooking. Everything is home-made and customers have linen table napkins in old napkins rings, bone-handled knives and spoons and forks gleaned from antique markets. From a menu that changes every couple of weeks, there might be soup (£2.50), fresh mussels in wine, garlic and cream (£4.25), stilton and mushroom tart (£4.50), home-made char-grilled burger with cheese bread and avocado salsa (£6.95), baked aubergine filled with roasted sweet peppers, mixed cheese and pine nuts (£8.95), honey-glazed lamb chops with mint yoghurt sauce (£9.50), strips of beef marinated in tahini sauce and char-grilled, steaks using Aberdeen Angus beef (from £9.95), daily specials such as three-storey sandwich with bacon, lettuce and tomato (£3.75), beef in garlic bread (£4.50), and beef, bacon and mushroom casserole in ale (£8.50), and puddings like treacle tart, fresh strawberry pavlova or luxury bread and butter pudding (£3.45). Well kept Brakspears PA and SB on handpump from an old oak bar, and around 15 good wines by the glass. The window boxes are pretty, and there are seats out in the large flower-bordered lawn. *(Recommended by Joan Olivier, Nick Holmes, Pippa Bobbett, Dick Brown, Gordon)*

Brakspears ~ Tenants Michael and Jill Robinson ~ Real ale ~ Meals and snacks (not Sun evening) ~ Restaurant ~ (01491) 872415 ~ Children in eating area of bar ~ Open 12-2.30, 6-11

STANTON ST JOHN SP5709 Map 4

Star

Pub signposted off B4027; village is signposted off A40 heading E of Oxford (heading W, the road's signposted Forest Hill, Islip instead); bear right at church in village centre

There's a pleasant, relaxed atmosphere in the little low-beamed rooms of this bustling pub, set out on two levels. One room has ancient brick flooring tiles and the other quite close-set tables, while up a flight of stairs (but on a level with the car park) is a busy and well refurbished extension with rugs on flagstones, pairs of bookshelves on each side of an attractive new inglenook fireplace, old-fashioned dining chairs and an interesting mix of dark oak and elm tables, shelves of good pewter, terracotta-coloured walls with a portrait in oils, and a stuffed ermine. A good choice of vegetarian dishes might include fruit and nut cutlet, ratatouille au gratin, broccoli and mushroom au gratin and vegetarian pie (£5.50), as well as chicken tikka, chilli con carne or beef curry (£4.85), and steak and kidney pie, sea trout and halibut pie or smoked haddock and bacon au gratin (£5.05). Well kept Badger Tanglefoot, Wadworths IPA, Farmers Glory, 6X and winter Old Timer on handpump, country wines and hot toddies; behind the bars is a display of brewery ties, beer bottles and so forth; shove-ha'penny, dominoes, cribbage, piped music. The family room is no smoking. The walled garden has picnic-table sets among the rockeries, and swings and a sandpit. There are annual classic car rallies, and it gets busy then. *(Recommended by Marjorie and David Lamb, Jon Carpenter, Mark Whitmore, S Demont, T Barrow, Joan Olivier, T G Brierly, Michael and Janet Hepworth, Robert Gomme, Walter Reid, Terry and Eileen Stott, D C T and E A Frewer)*

Wadworths ~ Tenants Nigel and Suzanne Tucker ~ Real ale ~ Meals and snacks (till 10pm) ~ (01865) 351277 ~ Children in family areas ~ Folk music first Sun of month ~ Open 11-2.30, 6.30-11; closed 25 and 26 Dec

STEEPLE ASTON SP4725 Map 4

Red Lion ♀
Off A4260 12 miles N of Oxford

For over 21 years, this lively and friendly old place has been run by Mr Mead, who is an exceptionally welcoming host. He is also very keen on his wines – the cellar contains over 100 different wines and they have regular tastings and themed promotions and events. The comfortable partly panelled bar has beams, an antique settle and other good furnishings, and a collection of rather crossword-oriented books under the window. Good, popular lunchtime bar food includes tasty stockpot soup (£1.35), sandwiches (from £1.70), beef and pork dumplings with caper sauce (£3.50), ploughman's with local farm cheese and crusty bread (£3.30), pâté or home-made taramasalata (£3.40), summer salads such as fresh salmon (around £5), and in winter various hot dishes and casseroles; the evening restaurant is more elaborate. Well kept Badger Tanglefoot, Hook Norton Best and Wadworths 6X on handpump, and a choice of 60 or so malt whiskies. The suntrap front terrace with its lovely flowers is a marvellous place to relax in summer. *(Recommended by B Pullee, Dr Ann Wintle, Roger Huggins, Dave Irving, Tom McLean, Ewan McCall, P A Reynolds, Lynn Sharpless, Bob Eardley, Margaret Dyke, A W Dickinson, Michael Sargent, Dorothee and Dennis Glover, R C Smail, D C Eastwood, Chris Raisin)*

Free house ~ Licensee Colin Mead ~ Real ale ~ Lunchtime bar meals and snacks (not Sun) ~ Evening restaurant (closed Sun and Mon and two weeks late Sept-early Oct) ~ (01869) 40225 ~ Children in restaurant ~ Open 11-3, 6-11

STEVENTON SU4691 Map 4

North Star
The Causeway; central westward turn off main road through village, which is signposted from A34

Marvellously unspoilt and simple, this village pub has a low half-hidden door leading through a porch and into the main bar with a high-backed settle facing a row of seats around a couple of elm tables; decorations include veteran steam engine pictures and a polished brass track gauge on the walls, and interesting local horsebrasses, and there's no bar counter – the Morlands Mild, Bitter and Best are tapped from gleaming casks and surrounded by lots of neatly stacked bottles, bars of chocolate, crisps and so forth; cheap ploughman's, and friendly, chatty licensees. There's also a simply furnished dining room, and a small parlourish lounge with an open fire; cribbage. The garden is entered from the road through a small yew arch, and grass at the side has some old-fashioned benches. *(Recommended by Gordon, Roger Huggins, Tom McLean, Ewan McCall, Pete Baker, Nic Armitage)*

Morlands ~ Tenant Mr R Cox ~ Real ale ~ Meals and snacks (weekday lunchtimes only) ~ (01235) 831309 ~ Open 10.30-2.30, 6.45-11

SUTTON COURTENAY SU5093 Map 4

Fish 🍴 ♀

Appleford Rd (B4016) S of Abingdon

Tables are laid for meals throughout this very popular pub/restaurant, yet those in the open-plan front bar seem largely for effect – if you just drop in for a drink (as many people do – they keep Morlands Original and Old Speckled Hen in good condition, as well as good wines by the glass and bottle), there's no feeling of being a second-class citizen, and the atmosphere is friendly and informal. However, there's no denying that it's the food which really counts in this solid late Victorian bay-windowed pub. It's by no means cheap, by pub standards, with even a ploughman's costing £5.25, but good fresh ingredients are put to good imaginative use in many fine dishes such as a lunchtime bacon and cheese sizzler (on request, £3.95), tagliatelle carbonara (£5.95), grilled tuna with roast tomatoes and fennel (£11.95), roast cod with pesto potato or roast rack of English lamb with risotto of sun-dried tomatoes (£12.50), fillet of turbot with samphire and chanterelles, calf's liver and bacon or angus entrecote steak with bearnaise sauce (£12.95), and roast baby sea bass with marinated chick peas (£14.25). There's always a vegetarian dish, such as a butter puff of contrasting vegetables cooked al dente, even if it's not listed on the board; puddings such as white chocolate quenelles with dark chocolate sauce or hazelnut meringue with raspberry sauce (£3.95). Appropriately enough, fish comes fresh daily from Brixham in Devon and Newlyn in Cornwall. On Sunday lunchtime, they do only booked restaurant meals – two-course Sunday lunch (£11.95). There are usually excellent nibbles on the bar counter (often crowded with people drooling over the blackboard before going to their tables), and staff are very friendly. The back eating area is no smoking. *(Recommended by A T Langton, Margaret Dyke, Sue Demont, Tim Barrow)*

Free house ~ Licensees Bruce and Kay Buchan ~ Real ale ~ Meals and snacks (till 10pm Fri/Sat) ~ Restaurant ~ (01235) 848242 ~ Children welcome ~ Open 11-3, 6.30-11; cl 26-29 Dec

SWINBROOK SP2811 Map 4

Swan

Back road 1 mile N of A40, 2 miles E of Burford

Close to the River Windrush and its bridge, this quietly traditional 400-year-old wisteria-covered place is a genuine country pub, with simple antique furnishings and a woodburning stove in the flagstoned tap room and the back bar; darts, shove-ha'penny, dominoes and cribbage. Popular bar food includes sandwiches, lunchtime dishes like home-made steak and kidney pie (£5.10), fish pie (£5.50), and a seafood platter (£6.20), with imaginative evening dishes like wiener schnitzel or roast poussin stuffed with stilton, spinach and chopped ham in cream and madeira sauce (£6.90) and assorted puddings. Morlands Bitter and Wadworths 6X on handpump, and Westons farm cider; there's an old english sheepdog. There are old-fashioned benches outside by the fuchsia hedge. No dogs or children and no muddy boots in the carpeted dining room. *(Recommended by Jerry and Alison Oakes, Tony Walker, John Waller, Gordon Smith, A K Rankin, Pete and Rose Flower, Tom Evans, E A Beulah, Ted George, Prof C MacCallum)*

Free house ~ Licensee H J Collins ~ Real ale ~ Meals and lunchtime snacks (12-1.30, 6.30-8.45; not Sun evening) ~ Dining room (not Sun evening) ~ (01993) 822165 ~ Open 11.30-2.30, 6-11; closed evening 25 Dec

TADPOLE BRIDGE SP3300 Map 4

Trout £

Back road Bampton – Buckland, 4 miles NE of Faringdon

Perhaps at its best in summer when the garden at this friendly 18th-c pub really makes the most of its Thames-side setting, and is quite a pleasant place to spend a couple of hours, with small fruit trees, pretty hanging baskets, and flower troughs;

you can fish on a 2-mile stretch of the river (the pub sells day tickets), and there are moorings for boaters. A wide choice of good, promptly served bar food includes very well priced sandwiches (from 90p; toasties from £1.30), ploughman's (from £3.50), beef and basil lasagne (£4.25), vegetable curry or home-cooked ham and egg (£4.50), sirloin steak (£8), specials such as rook casserole (£3), pigeon hotpot (£3.25), macaroni cheese (£3.50), rabbit stew (£4.25), liver and bacon casserole (£4.50), steak and kidney pie (£5), and 16oz T-bone steak (£10.50), with puddings (from £1.50). Service is friendly, with the landlord seeming genuinely pleased to see people; Archers Golden and Village, Gibbs Mew Bishops Tipple and Trout, Hook Norton Best, and Morlands Original on handpump. The small L-shaped bar has flagstones, attractive pot plants on the window sills and mantelpiece, and a good pubby atmosphere; darts, dominoes, shove-ha'penny, piped music and Aunt Sally. They offer overnight moorings and have a caravan and camping area. *(Recommended by Marjorie and David Lamb, George Atkinson, Joan Olivier, Dr M I Crichton, Comus Elliott, George Murdoch)*

Free house ~ Licensees Mick and Maureen Bowl ~ Real ale ~ Meals and snacks ~ (0136 787) 382 ~ Children welcome ~ Mainly 60s and country live music Friday evenings ~ Open 11.30-11 (11.30-3, 5.30-11 winter weekdays)

TOOT BALDON SP5600 Map 4

Crown

Village signed from A423 at Nuneham Courtenay, and B480

Bustling and friendly country pub with a warm welcome from the hard-working licensees. The simple beamed bar has a log fire, solid furnishings on the tiled floor, and a pleasant atmosphere. Good, homely and generously served bar food might include sandwiches and ploughman's as well as changing specials like creamy pasta with smoked salmon and prawns or beef carbonnade (£5.25), middle eastern lamb with spinach and lentils (£5.95), chicken supreme with coriander, ginger and cream (£6.50), lamb, asparagus and mint pie (£6.95), and mixed grill (£7.95); it may be best to book, especially in the dining room. Well kept Fullers London Pride, Morlands Original, and Charles Wells Bombardier on handpump, with guests like Adnams, Bass or Theakstons; shove-ha'penny, darts. The friendly cream labrador is called Ben. Aunt Sally, summer barbecues, and tables on the terrace. *(Recommended by Margaret and Roy Randle, Margaret Dyke, A T Langton, Canon and Mrs M A Bourdeaux, R C Watkins, Marjorie and David Lamb, R C Watkins, D C T Frewer)*

Free house ~ Licensees Liz and Neil Kennedy ~ Real ale ~ Meals and snacks (not Mon evening) ~ Restaurant ~ (01865) 343240 ~ Children welcome ~ Open 11-3, 6.30-11

WATLINGTON SU6894 Map 4

Chequers

2¼ miles from M40, junction 6; Take B4009 towards Watlington, and on outskirts of village turn right into residential rd called Love Lane which leads to pub

The wide choice of good bar food in the cheerful and cosy old pub is very popular at the moment and might include sandwiches, ploughman's, deep-fried camembert (£3.80), king prawns in filo pastry (£4), lentil and aubergine moussaka (£5), summer salads, cauliflower cheese and crispy bacon (£5.50), steak and kidney pie (£6.50), gammon steak (£7.50), salmon supreme (£8.50), steaks (from £9.50), and specials like honey-glazed king prawn and monkfish kebab (£8.20), chicken with apricot and ginger sauce (£8.50), and calf's liver with bacon (£9.50); vegetables are extra (which can make the main meals rather expensive). The rambling bar has a low panelled oak settle and character chairs such as a big spiral-legged carving chair around a few good antique oak tables, red-and-black shiny tiles in one corner with rugs and red carpeting elsewhere, and a low oak-beamed ceiling darkened to a deep ochre by the candles which they still use; steps on the right lead down to an area with more tables; a conservatory has been added. Brakspears PA and SB on handpump, and a pale grey cat. The notably pretty garden is quite refreshing after the bustle of the main street, with picnic-table sets under apple and pear trees, and sweet peas, roses, geraniums, begonias and rabbits. The cheese shop in Watlington itself is recommended. *(Recommended by TBB, I E and C A Prosser, Michael Sargent, Tony and Wynne Gifford, Sheila Keene, Dave Braisted, Susan and John Douglas)*

Brakspears ~ Tenants John and Anna Valentine ~ Real ale ~ Meals and lunchtime snacks ~ (01491) 612874 ~ Children in conservatory ~ Open 11.30-2.30, 6-11

WOODSTOCK SP4416 Map 4

Feathers 🍽 🛏
Market St

This rather smart and civilised Cotswold stone hotel has an old-fashioned garden bar at the back with a small bar in one corner, oils and watercolours on its walls, stuffed fish and birds (a marvellous live parrot, too), a central open fire, and a relaxed, tranquil atmosphere; it opens on to a splendid sunny courtyard with attractive tables and chairs among geraniums and trees. A short but thoughtful and imaginative menu might include tomato and basil or chilled cucumber and mint soup (£3.50), warm goat's cheese with chorizo and watercress or locally smoked mussels with shallot and chilli (£4.75), pastry leaves filled with Mediterranean vegetables (£5.95), confit of chicken with butter beans and smoked bacon (£6.25), smoked and cured meats with pickles and parmesan, char-grilled salmon with beetroot and walnut dressing or braised rump in ale and baby onions (£6.95), and puddings like raspberry terrine with warm blueberries or toasted marshmallow with berry compote (£4.25); ingredients are first-class and service courteous. Well kept (though *very* pricey) Wadworths 6X on handpump, a good choice of malt whiskies and home-made lemonade. Get there early for a table; no dogs. *(Recommended by Walter Reid, George Atkinson, Tim Barrow, Sue Demont, Marion and John Hadfield, Andrew and Ruth Triggs; also recommended by The Good Hotel Guide)*

Free house ~ Licensee Tom Lewis ~ Real ale ~ Bar meals (not Sat or Sun evening) ~ Restaurant (not Sun evening) ~ (01993) 812291 ~ Children welcome ~ Open 11-3, 6-10.30(11 Sat) ~ Bedrooms: £75B/£99B

WOOTTON SP4320 Map 4

Kings Head 🍽
Chapel Hill; off B4027 N of Woodstock

This year, the beamed lounge bar in this pretty 17th-c Cotswold stone house has had a bar counter added – as well as a nice mix of old oak settles and chairs around wooden tables, though the comfortable armchairs and chintzy sofas are still there, as is the open log fire, and old prints and ceramics on the pale pink walls; you can now eat in here, too. The neat and spacious restaurant leads off here. The emphasis is very much on the good, popular food which includes home-made soup (£2.25), home-made pâté (£2.95), ham and mushroom tagliatelle (£4.95), beef bourguignon (£6.95), rack of lamb with honey and rosemary sauce (£11.95), roast local duckling with mandarin and ginger sauce (£11.95), and home-made puddings (£2.45). The young French chef has made fresh fish something of a speciality, and it's outstanding here: lots of choice, perhaps salmon and asparagus (£7.95), halibut with parsley butter or sardines provençale (£8.95), crab mornay (£9.95), fresh lemon sole (£10.95), and king prawns in garlic butter (£12.95). Well kept Courage Directors, Hook Norton, and Wadworths 6X on handpump, freshly squeezed orange juice, and decent wines; attentive, friendly staff. Fruit machine, trivia, backgammon and piped music. *(Recommended by F M Bunbury, D C T and E A Frewer; more reports please)*

Free house ~ Licensee Tony Simmons ~ Real ale ~ Meals and snacks (till 10pm) ~ Restaurant ~ (01993) 811340 ~ Well behaved children in eating area of bar ~ Open 11-2.30, 6.30-11 ~ Bedrooms: £34.95B/£69.90B

WYTHAM SP4708 Map 4

White Hart

Village signposted from A34 ring road W of Oxford

Under a new manager, this picturesque creeper-covered pub has a partly panelled, flagstoned bar with high-backed black settles built almost the whole way round its cream walls, wheelback chairs, a shelf of blue and white plates, and a fine relief of a heart on the iron fireback; well kept Ind Coope Burton, Tetleys, Wadworths 6X and a guest beer on handpump, and a good choice of malt whiskies. Bar food from the food servery includeds help-yourself salads, filled baked potatoes (from £1.55), cheese and bread (£1.85), fish like red mullet, plaice or trout (from £5.50), steaks (from £6.10), mixed grill (£7.10), daily specials like steak and kidney pie, pasta dishes or chilli (£4.50), and puddings (£1.80); maybe summer barbecues in the lovely walled rose garden. The pub's name is said to have come from a badge granted to the troops of Richard II after the Battle of Radcot Bridge in 1390. *(Recommended by John Sanders, Prof A N Black, Joan Olivier, Julian Bessa, Peter and Anne Hollindale, Terry and Eileen Stott, Walter Reid, the Monday Club, Pat and Roger Fereday, Giles Bullard, Jenny and Brian Seller, D and H Broodbank)*

Ind Coope (Allied) ~ Manager Marcus Perrin~ Real ale ~ Meals and snacks (till 9.45) ~ (01865) 244372 ~ Children welcome ~ Open 11-11

Lucky Dip

Besides the fully inspected pubs, you might like to try these Lucky Dips recommended to us and described by readers (if you do, please send us reports):

☆ **Abingdon** [St Helens Wharf; SU4997], *Old Anchor*: Nice spot by Thames, little front bar looking across river, lovely panelled dining room (good Sun lunch) overlooking neat almshouse gardens, flagstoned back bar with shoulder-height serving hatch, bigger lounge; well kept Morlands on handpump, good atmosphere, usual range of bar food inc children's dishes, friendly service, attractive flower tubs *(Basil Minson, Geraint Roberts, Wayne Brindle, Mr and Mrs G D Amos)*
Abingdon [Milton], *Caltons*: Recently opened satellite of Fish at Sutton Courtenay, good food *(A T Langton)*
Adderbury [Tanners Lane, off Hornhill Rd (signed to Bloxham) towards W end of village; SP4635], *White Hart*: Friendly small heavy-beamed pub with decent food inc good toasties, Marstons Pedigree and Whitbreads West County PA, old-fashioned seats, pictures, good log fire; tables in garden *(George Atkinson, LYM)*
☆ **Alvescot** [B4020 Carterton—Clanfield – OS Sheet 163 map ref 273045; SP2604], *Plough*: Wide range of good standard food inc vegetarian and popular Sun lunch (must book) in welcoming and neatly kept pub with dining area at one end of lounge, friendly attentive staff, old maps, quiet piped music, well kept Wadworths and guest such as Adnams, decent wines, good coffee, log fire; separate public bar *(Mr and Mrs J Brown, Mr and Mrs W N Jeeves, Marjorie and David Lamb)*
Appleton [50 Eaton Rd; SP4401], *Thatched*: Attractive country pub with four real ales, mostly from small brewers, good value home-cooked food *(Simon Briston)*

☆ **Ardington** [off A417 Didcot—Wantage, signed 2 miles E of Wantage; SU4388], *Boars Head*: Good interesting restaurant-quality food at pub prices in former village local refurbished for new tenants as more upmarket dining pub, three well cared-for interconnecting bar/dining rooms, one primarily for eating with pine settles and big tables, the others with smaller country tables and chairs; fresh flowers, old pictures, affordable daily changing menu, pleasant welcoming staff, Morlands and Fullers London Pride *(JE, R C Watkins, Col A H N Reade)*
Ardley [B430 (old A43), just SW of M40 junction 10; SP5427], *Fox & Hounds*: Charming and hospitable licensees and staff, tastefully furnished room, courteous service, food inc delightful fish pie *(W L G Watkins)*
Ashbury [SU2685], *Rose & Crown*: Ideally placed for walkers doing the Ridgeway, good range of food inc good puddings; bedrooms *(Nick Cox)*
☆ **Asthall** [off A40 at W end of Witney bypass, then 1st left; SP2811], *Maytime*: Wide choice of well served food very popular with older people midweek, small back bar used by local regulars, slightly raised plush dining lounge neatly set with tables, airy upper conservatory restaurant (children allowed), Morrells and Wadworths 6X, prompt service; in tiny hamlet, nice views of Asthall Manor and watermeadows from garden, big car park; good bedrooms around striking courtyard *(C E Power, TGB, Pete and Rose Flower, BB)*
Bablock Hythe [W of Cumnor; off B4449 S

of Stanton Harcourt; SP4304], *Ferryman*:
Popular rebuilt riverside pub with well kept
beer and welcoming landlord and locals,
displays of old ferry equipment; terrace,
moorings and foot-ferry; well equipped
newly furnished bedrooms with river-view
balconies *(Noel Jackson, Louise Campbell,
Mr and Mrs Peter Dowsett)*

Bampton [Mkt Sq; SP3103], *Talbot*:
Quaint pub in lovely village, good food and
well kept Tetleys and Wadworths 6X;
bedrooms clean and old-fashioned *(Simon
Briston)*

☆ **Banbury** [47 Parsons St, off Market Pl;
SP4540], *Reindeer*: Splendid 17th-c beams
and old fireplaces in atmospheric place,
much refurbished but well done, with wide
floorboards, panelling, log fires, well kept
Hook Norton Best, country wines, good
coffee, snuffs, clay pipes, good food well
presented and served in generous helpings;
no under-21s, some live folk music *(Ted
George, George Atkinson, LYM)*

Banbury [Parsons St], *Wine Vaults*: Really
quaint old tucked-away pub with old-
fashioned layout, very basic fittings, dark-
partitioned areas; Morrells Varsity and
Graduate, coffee, wide range of bottled
beers *(George Atkinson)*

☆ **Barnard Gate** [off A40 E of Witney;
SP4010], *Boot*: Wide choice of well cooked
reasonably priced food and decent wine list
in thriving well decorated extended dining
pub, prompt friendly service, well kept
Boddingtons and Hook Norton, espresso
coffee, friendly staff, huge log fire, side
restaurant; children welcome *(Mark
Jackson, Louise Mee, Dr H Y Chan, David
Surridge, Michael Sargent)*

Blackthorn [signposted from A41, 3 miles E
of Bicester; SP6219], *Rose & Crown*:
Friendly characterful village pub, old
advertisements outside, lots of postcards
and photographs inside, well kept beers,
limited good value lunchtime bar food;
pleasant garden behind *(Peter Baker)*

☆ **Blewbury** [London Rd; SU5385], *Blewbury
Inn*: Charming character downland village
pub with two small beamed rooms, open
fires, rustic furniture, friendly and
comfortable; main draw under newish
licensees is surprisingly good food from
excellent chef inc ambitious though not
cheap evening set menu; bedrooms
(Lorraine Webster)

Bloxham [High St, off A361; SP4235],
Joiners Arms: Homely pub with very
friendly chatty staff, Home Bitter and four
Theakstons ales on handpump, carpeted
lounge, local radio, fruit machines, lots of
brasses, and two fires; good coffee, decent
wine *(George Atkinson, BB)*

Bodicote [Goose Lane/High St; off A4260 S
of Banbury; SP4537], *Plough*: Friendly old
squat pub, originally two cottages, notable
for its own-brewed Bodicote Bitter, with
three others kept well on handpump, a few
country wines, tea and coffee; two rooms
with old beams, pictures, brasses, two

friendly cats; wide choice of good food
running up to steaks *(CMW, JJW)*

☆ **Broadwell** [SP2503], *Five Bells*: Friendly
and attentive new owners in attractive
beamed and part-flagstoned pub with
dining area off lounge, tables also in several
smaller rooms, decent food, big open fires,
pleasant garden; disabled access; bedrooms
(Joan Olivier)

☆ **Buckland** [SU3497], *Lamb*: Plushly
refurbished and extended 18th-c stone
building in tiny village, clean, with good
changing real food (not Mon) inc some
memorable and imaginative dishes; friendly
service, real ale, decent wines *(J C Cetti, A
T Langton, HNJ, PEJ)*

☆ **Bucknell** [handy for M40 junction 10;
SP5525], *Trigger Pond*: Good atmosphere
and friendly service in quaint village pub
increasingly popular for good food at
reasonable prices; well kept beer, pleasant
garden *(Mrs A Purser, L M Miall)*

☆ **Burford** [High St; SP2512], *Bull*:
Comfortable sofas in long narrow beamed
and panelled hotel bar with Courage-
related ales and a guest such as Wadworths
6X, woodburner, good choice of wines by
the glass, wide choice of bar food, friendly
attentive service, restaurant; piped music;
children welcome, open all day; good value
comfortable bedrooms *(Gwen and Peter
Andrews, Andrew and Ruth Triggs, A D
Crafter, Mark Bradley, LYM)*

Burford [Sheep St], *Bay Tree*: Attractive old
village inn with good atmosphere, very
good food in bar and restaurant; bedrooms
(Joan and Ian Wilson); [A40], *Inn for All
Seasons*: Quite smart, but good pubby
atmosphere, with good food inc fish fresh
from Brixham, real ales inc Wadworths 6X,
decent wine, friendly staff; good bedrooms
(Peter and Audrey Dowsett); [Witney St],
Royal Oak: Stripped-stone pub with
popular generous food esp home-cooked
specials, welcoming staff, well kept Flowers
IPA, Wadworths 6X and Farmers Glory,
some home-made country wines, good
coffee, no music, interesting collection of
tankards and mugs; games bar with pool
table; small car park *(D C T and E A
Frewer, Mark Bradley, DH)*

Cassington [SP4510], *Red Lion*:
Welcoming new landlord in unspoilt low-
ceilinged mid-terrace pub, traditional
settles, old prints, well kept Marstons, farm
cider *(Gordon, R Huggins, D Irving, T
McLean, E McCall)*

☆ **Caulcott** [SP5024], *Horse & Groom*: Part-
thatched creeper-covered 16th-c pub, now a
free house, with limited good value food
esp sandwich platters, big log fire in stone
fireplace, beams, brasses, real ales; picnic-
table sets under cocktail parasols in garden
with good summer barbecues, well kept
outside lavatories *(CMW, JJW, D C T and
E A Frewer, JO)*

Chadlington [Mill End; off A361 S of
Chipping Norton, and B4437 W of
Charlbury; SP3222], *Tite*: Nice pub with

garden in pretty Cotswold village, comfortable welcoming atmosphere, lovely views, good value often original food, well kept real ales such as Badger Best, Palmers Tally Ho and Wadworths IPA on handpump; very professionally organised, children welcome *(M M Matthews, John Waller, G E de Vries)*

☆ **Chalgrove** [High St; SU6396], *Red Lion*: Good helpings of good value straightforward home-cooked food from sandwiches to steaks and well kept Brakspears, Fullers London Pride, Hook Norton Best and Ringwood in pleasantly restored old-fashioned streamside beamed pub with log fire and woodburner, part tiled floor, small restaurant, sizeable garden with Sun lunchtime barbecues; owned by local church trust for over 350 years; lavatory for disabled (but car park some way off); children welcome *(Joan Olivier, Graham Reeve)*

☆ **Charlbury** [SP3519], *Bell*: Small and attractive civilised bar, warm and friendly, with flagstones, stripped stonework, huge open fire, short choice of good interesting bar lunches (not Sun) from sandwiches up, well kept Hook Norton and Wadworths real ales, wide choice of malt whiskies, decent if pricey restaurant; children in eating area; good bedrooms with tasty breakfasts *(Steve Goodchild, Gordon, R and E Allison, Michael Sargent, LYM)*

☆ **Charlbury** [Sheep St], *Farmers*: Friendly and cosy 17th-c local, lounge split into several areas, oak beams, inglenook fireplace and original Victorian stove, traditional pub games, Ansells on electric pump, decent cheap food; quiz evenings *(George Atkinson, Hugh Datson)*

☆ **Checkendon** [OS Sheet 175 map ref 666841; SU6683], *Black Horse*: Classic Brakspears country pub tucked into woodland well away from main village, friendly, unpretentious and kept by the same family for many decades; three interconnecting old-fashioned rooms each with distinctive character, unfashionable armchairs, well kept ale tapped from the cask in a back room (ladies' beyond that); lunchtime opening can be erratic, antiquated gents'; fine walking country *(Pete Baker)*

☆ **Checkendon** [OS Sheet 175 map ref 663829], *Four Horseshoes*: Wide choice of good value popular food with good fresh veg from sandwiches to local game in attractive and welcoming partly thatched country pub, music-free stripped-floor dining lounge (where children allowed), local public bar with pool table and piped music; good friendly service, well kept Brakspears, good simple wine list; big garden with picnic-table sets, friendly dog Katie *(Lyn and Bill Capper)*

☆ **Chipping Norton** [High St; SP3127], *Fox*: Particularly good value well refurbished bedrooms in ancient pub with wide choice of well presented food inc Italian (Italian

landlord) and very well kept Hook Norton and other ales; character rambling lounge with some antique oak settles, open fire, upstairs restaurant (can be used for lunchtime bar food), friendly service; good views from back garden; children welcome *(David Campbell, Vicki McLean, Andy and Jill Kassube, LYM)*

☆ **Chipping Norton** [High St], *Blue Boar*: Wide range of well priced food in homely rambling bar divided by arches and pillars, and big back eating area with long flagstoned conservatory; Courage Directors and Marstons on handpump, good cider, quick friendly service even if busy, Sun bar nibbles *(John and Shirley Dyson)*

Chipping Norton [High St], *Crown & Cushion*: No recent reports on this fine old 16th-c hotel with attractive bar, some stripped stone and flagstones, flower-decked conservatory, tables in sheltered garden with suntrap terrace and coffee room, good bedrooms; has had well kept Donnington, Wadworths IPA and 6X and guest beers, bar food (may be restricted Fri/Sat evenings), and a welcome for children *(LYM)*; [High St], *White Hart*: Hotel with friendly attentive staff, well kept beers in well stocked bar; bedrooms *(Gwen and Peter Andrews)*

Chislehampton [B480 Oxford—Watlington, opp B4015 to Abingdon; SU5998], *Coach & Horses*: Pleasant 16th-c pub with well kept Flowers and Hook Norton, good choice of well prepared and served food, polished oak tables, padded chairs and wall seats, big log fire; bedrooms *(Mr and Mrs J Brown)*

Cholsey [39 Wallingford Rd; SU5886], *Red Lion*: Nicely refurbished dining room with decent food inc very fresh fish; quiet weekday lunchtimes, busy evenings and weekends *(DWAJ)*

Churchill [B4450 Chipping Norton—Stow; SP2824], *Chequers*: 18th-c two-roomed pub with nice garden, good if not cheap food; no dogs; bedrooms *(CW, JW)*

☆ **Clifton Hampden** [towards Long Wittenham, S of A415; SU5495], *Barley Mow*: Chef & Brewer a short stroll from the Thames, famous from *Three Men in a Boat;* very low beams, oak-panelled family room, flagstoned public bar, though decor now rather brewerified; usual food, Courage-related real ales, piped music, restaurant, tables in well tended garden; bedrooms *(Basil Minson, Eamon Green, Giles Bullard, Geraint Roberts, Martin Cooke, Joan Olivier, LYM)*

Coleshill [SU2393], *Radnor Arms*: Former smithy, interesting tools in cosy bar with two coal-effect gas fires; Flowers and Marstons Pedigree tapped from the cask, good choice of reasonably priced food, friendly quick service, garden behind; piped music; charming village, lots of good walks nearby *(Peter and Audrey Dowsett)*

☆ **Crawley** [OS Sheet 164 map ref 341120; SP3412], *Lamb*: 17th-c stone-built village pub on several levels, doing well under friendly and hard-working new owners; food particularly promising, all home-cooked using fresh ingredients, with good fresh lunchtime sandwiches too; well kept Eldridge Pope Dorchester and Wadworths 6X on handpump, short but good wine list, small family area, lots of tables in pleasant garden *(Joan Olivier, Andrew and Rachel Fogg)*

☆ **Crays Pond** [B471 nr junction with B4526, about 3 miles E of Goring; SU6380], *White Lion*: Clean and welcoming low-ceilinged pub with open fire, attractive conservatory, well kept Courage-related real ales, good inventive if not cheap food (not Tues evening), big garden with play area *(G B Longden)*

Crowell [was Catherine Wheel; B4009, 2 miles from M40 junction 6; SU7499], *Shepherds Crook*: Former tied house recently refurbished as free house by same landlord, sensitive use of brick and timber give warmth to traditional flagstoned bar, good cheap filling home-made food in carpeted raftered dining area (former sheep byre), decent wines, very friendly landlord, exemplary lavatories; views from tables out on green *(Nigel Henbest, Heather Couper, Gordon)*

Crowmarsh Gifford [72 The Street (A4130); SU6189], *Queens Head*: Dating back to 13th c, with good very attractively priced food, well kept John Smiths, friendly village atmosphere, tables in garden; children in dining area, no dogs *(David Dimock)*

Cuxham [Main Rd; B4009; SU6695], *Half Moon*: Good atmosphere in attractive and pleasantly refurbished largely 17th-c pub (older origins), Brakspears real ales, decent food, seats outside *(Marjorie and David Lamb, Graham Reeve, Michael Sargent, LYM)*

☆ **Denchworth** [SU3791], *Fox*: Pretty thatched pub with two really good log fires in low-ceilinged comfortable connecting areas, popular for good range of reasonably priced food (not Sun) inc good puddings, Morlands Bitter and Old Speckled Hen, pleasant helpful landlord, unobtrusive piped music, beamed restaurant; quiet pretty garden *(Marjorie and David Lamb, Joan Olivier)*

☆ **Dorchester** [High St; SU5794], *Fleur de Lys*: Wide choice of decent straightforward home cooking, all fresh (not Mon; no sandwiches), in pleasant small tastefully furnished village pub opp abbey, well kept Bass, Flowers IPA and Morlands, very friendly service; unobtrusive piped music, exemplary ladies' *(Wayne Brindle, P J Keen, R C Watkins, Tim and Ann Newell, Dorothy and Leslie Pilson)*

Dorchester, *Plough*: Particularly good English home cooking by the landlord, good atmosphere, pub games inc Aunt Sally, pictures and prints for sale, well kept Morlands; piped Radio 2 *(Bruce Pennell)*;

White Hart: Big beamed bar with attached restaurant, good range of beers; bedrooms *(David and Alison Walker)*

☆ **Drayton** [A422 W of Banbury; SP4241], *Roebuck*: Creeper-covered pub, comfortable and cosy, with well kept ales inc Boddingtons, Fullers London Pride and Hook Norton Best, good value bar food esp freshly cut double-decker sandwiches, solid fuel stove, attractive evening restaurant, friendly obliging staff *(I R Hewitt, F M Bunbury, George Atkinson)*

Drayton St Leonard [SU5996], *Catherine Wheel*: Friendly little refurbished village pub with food from decent filled rolls up in lounge bar, Morrells ales, friendly spaniel, games bar with pool *(Joan Olivier)*

Ducklington [just SE of Witney; SP3507], *Strickland Arms*: Welcoming and cosy, smart bar half for dining, extensive reasonably priced food, well kept beer, decent wine, low piped music; small no-smoking restaurant; small garden *(Peter and Audrey Dowsett)*

☆ **Duns Tew** [SP4528], *White Horse*: Beamed dining pub with glass wall to show the cooking, lovely flagstones, old oak panelling, stripped stonework, enormous inglenook, settles, sofas and homely stripped tables, good if not cheap bar food (more room in pretty dining area than bar itself), very popular evening meals and Sun lunch, well kept Bass and other real ales, open fires, helpful staff; pretty village; comfortable bedrooms in former stables *(Mrs B Sugarman, Marjorie and David Lamb, Daryl Gallacher, Amanda Flower, David and Anthea Hewitt, Sue Demont, Tim Barrow, D C T and E A Frewer; more reports please)*

☆ **East Hendred** [Orchard Lane; SU4588], *Plough*: Enjoyable straightforward bar food from good sandwiches and baked potatoes up in beamed village pub's attractive and airy main bar, Morlands ales, quick friendly service, farm tools; attractive garden with good play area *(Geraint Roberts, ABS, BB)*

Enstone [A44 Chipping Norton—Woodstock; SP3724], *Harrow*: Attractive Morrells pub with big hillside garden, tasty home-made food in separate dining room *(Frank W Gadbois)*

Ewelme [off B4009, about 5 miles SW of M40 junction 6; SU6491], *Ploughman*: Handsomely fitted-out bars, decent food; attractive village *(Paul McPherson)*; *Shepherds Hut*: Pleasant well run carpeted bar, good value food, Morlands Bitter and Old Masters on handpump, pot plants, darts and fruit machine; piped pop music; children welcome; tables and swing in garden *(JJW, CMJ, Nick Holmes)*

Eynsham [Newlands St; SP4309], *Newlands*: wide choice of good reasonably priced food in cosy flagstoned bar with stripped early 18th-c pine panelling, very busy and bustling weekends; friendly staff, decent wine, inglenook log fire, fairly unobtrusive piped music *(Wayne Brindle, Jenny and Brian Seller)*; [B4044 towards Swinford Bridge], *Talbot*: Good range of appetising food under current friendly management, long bar popular with staff from modern factory next door; pleasant walk along Thames towpath *(T G Brierly)*

☆ Faringdon [Market Pl; SU2895], *Crown*: Unpretentious English inn with flagstones, panelling, homely atmosphere, roaring log fires and lovely summer courtyard; imaginative inexpensive well presented food in bar or buttery, good value Sun lunch, good friendly staff, well kept Hook Norton and Morlands; children welcome; good bedrooms *(Comus Elliott, Gordon, D C Eastwood, Basil Minson, LYM)*

☆ Fifield [A424; SP2318], *Merrymouth*: New licensees yet again, new to the trade this time, in isolated rambling old pub with relaxed atmosphere, flagstones, lots of stripped stone, bay windows, farm tools on low beams, open fires, Donnington and perhaps other ales, unobtrusive piped music, food in bar and restaurant; tables on terrace and in back garden; children allowed one end; bedrooms *(Joan Olivier, LYM; more reports please)*

Filkins [village signposted off A361 Lechlade—Burford; SP2304], *Five Alls*: Good food from generous ploughman's through steak and kidney pudding to carvery meals with loads of vegetables at good competitive prices in bar or sizeable restaurant, interesting puddings such as pancake pie along with gateaux, profiteroles etc; real ale, decent house wine in good-sized glasses; cl Mon *(Mr and Mrs J Brown)*

Fritwell [signed off B4100, quite handy for M40 junction 10; SP5229], *George & Dragon*: Friendly service, limited range of bar snacks *(Dave Braisted)*

☆ Fulbrook [SP2513], *Masons Arms*: Friendly Cotswold stone village pub with relaxed chatty atmosphere, limited range of good value home cooking inc good puddings, nice open fire, small cosy bar, good service, bar billiards, locals with dogs *(John and Marianne Cooper, Tom and Ruth Rees, Tim Brierly)*

Goring [SU6080], *Catherine Wheel*: Genuine enjoyable local with good value restaurant, friendly licensee, L-shaped bar with good log fire *(Tony Merrill, D T Taylor)*; [Manor Rd], *John Barleycorn*: Friendly traditional village local, good food well priced (and displayed in price order), well kept Brakspears, pleasant atmosphere, helpful service; bedrooms *(Dick Brown, R C Davis)*

☆ Goring Heath [off A4074 NW of Reading – OS Sheet 175 map ref 664788; SU6679], *King Charles Head*: Charming small-roomed rambling country pub with lovely big garden and idyllic woodland setting, good walks nearby; good value home-cooked food, good range of well kept beers, relaxed atmosphere, friendly landlord;

furnishings and decor more modern than you'd expect from cottagey appearance *(Prof John White, Patricia White, Tim Brierly, Rob and Helen Townsend, ABS, LYM)*

☆ Great Milton [The Green; SP6202], *Bell*: Small friendly pub, tastefully and comfortably extended, with good interesting home-made food, well kept real ales inc Brakspears and interesting guests, log fire, aircraft memorabilia (friendly ex-pilot landlord); separate games bar *(G H M Hunt)*

☆ Grove [Station Rd (A338); by former Wantage Road stn; SU4191], *Volunteer*: Now a free house, open all day, comfortably modernised without losing refreshing local atmosphere; very attentive friendly staff happy to bring drinks over, down-to-earth family feel, nine real ales inc two guest beers, wide choice of good reasonably priced food inc several eastern dishes – Bangladeshi chef *(HNJ, PEJ, Rachel Hunter)*

Hailey [Whiteoak Green, B4022 Witney—Charlbury; SP3414], *Bird in Hand*: Friendly modern country inn with wide range of food in lounge or attractive restaurant, attentive service, Whitbreads-related real ales, nice views; comfortable cottage-style bedrooms *(Charles and Dorothy Ellsworth, Mr and Mrs P B Dowsett)*

Headington [London Rd; SP5407], *White Horse*: Busy but spacious, divided into smaller screened-off areas; popular reasonably priced straightforward bar food served all day inc children's, quick service, Morrells ales, good coffee, friendly staff; piped music, fruit machines *(George Atkinson)*

☆ Henley [Friday St; SU7882], *Anchor*: Easy-going place almost right on the Thames, lots of bric-a-brac in parlourish beamed front bar with soft lights, armchairs (one for Cognac the friendly boxer), elegant cat; darts, pool and TV in second room, caged birds in eating area, back dining room, charming back terrace with rabbit hutch; huge helpings of very reasonably priced food, well kept real ales, friendly and obliging landlady; here and there piles of the sort of stuff you might find dumped around a loosely run family home; children welcome *(Brian and Anna Marsden, JD, SD)*

Henley [Riverside], *Little White Hart*: Large comfortable civilised hotel bar with lots of regatta pictures and bric-a-brac relating to the regatta inc three racing skiffs hanging from ceiling, lots of shortened oars; gas lighting, friendly landlord; bedrooms *(Gordon, David Warrellow)*; [Bell St], *Old Bell*: Homely, comfortable and attractive heavily beamed bar, wall-length window filled with pot plants, back dining room, well kept Brakspears *(Gordon)*; [West St], *Row Barge*: Friendly local, its cosy low-beamed bar dropping down the hill in steps, good value home cooking, well kept Brakspears, darts, big back garden *(Brian and Anna Marsden, Gordon)*

☆ **Highmoor** [B481 N of Reading, off A423 Henley—Oxford; SU6984], *Dog & Duck*: Cosy low-beamed country cottage taken over 1994 by the Taylors who had previously made the Carpenters Arms at Nettlebed a popular main entry with their good food, extremely obliging service and well kept Brakspears; log fires in both attractive front bars, back dining room, tables in garden *(Christian Farmer, Gordon, Andy Petersen)*

Hook Norton [off A361; SP3533], *Sun*: Rather over-refurbished, but solidly, and the enormous helpings of good value food from sandwiches to exotic dishes and well kept Hook Norton ales are big draws; restaurant; bedrooms *(Helen Hazzard, Tom Evans, Philip and Debbie Haynes)*

☆ **Islip** [B4027; SP5214], *Red Lion*: Wide choice of well presented generous food in three cosy if not especially pubby eating areas inc main tankard-decorated dining room and conservatory, starters from the restaurant menu good value, Allied ales, decent wine, fast service; lavatories for the disabled, good garden with barbecue and play area (no children allowed in) *(Sir Nigel Foulkes, Dave Braisted, D C T and E A Frewer, P A Baxter)*

☆ **Kidmore End** [Chalkhouse Green Rd; signed from Sonning Common; SU6979], *New Inn*: Well run and popular country dining pub with good mainly home-cooked food, well kept Brakspears PA, SB and Old, decent wines, modern furnishings in beamed main room, efficient service, maybe piped music; small children's side room, tables in big pretty sheltered garden with pond and boules piste; can be busy weekends *(Mark Shutler, Clifford Payton, Mrs A Morrison, H Taylor, Brian and Anna Marsden)*

Kingston Bagpuize [1 Witney Rd; SU4098], *Hinds Head*: Quiet, basic and unpretentious local, two bars with well kept beers on handpump, small but good value menu; play area *(Brig J S Green)*

☆ **Kingston Lisle** [SU3287], *Blowing Stone*: Recently smoothly done up with neat traditional-style public bar, relaxing lounge bar, dining conservatory; impressive choice of decent food from generous sandwiches and good home-made soup up, good range of changing ales such as Fullers London Pride, Marstons Pedigree, Morlands Old Speckled Hen, Wadworths 6X, friendly efficient service; attractive village, handy for Ridgeway walks; pretty garden; bedrooms clean and pretty if small *(Elizabeth Chalmers, R T and J C Moggridge)*

Leafield [OS Sheet 164 map ref 316152; SP3115], *Old George*: Free house with L-shaped bar, Cotswold stone walls, cushioned rocking chair, big open hearth, tables and chairs on lawn overlooking

green, well kept beers, good range of bar food *(Frank Cummins)*

☆ **Letcombe Regis** [follow Village Only sign for ¼ mile; SU3886], *Sparrow*: Newish licensees doing a wider choice of food than formerly in relaxed and unpretentious local below Segsbury hillfort, well kept Morlands Bitter, Mild and Old Speckled Hen; good garden with play area *(Giles Bullard, LYM)*

Little Coxwell [just off A420 SW of Faringdon; SU2793], *Eagle*: Welcoming and friendly, with generous helpings of above-average straightforward bar food, Morlands beers, pleasantly refurbished airy bar kept spotless, small pool/games room *(HNJ, PEJ)*

Littleworth [A420 NE of Faringdon; SU3197], *Fox & Hounds*: Straightforward pub with generous food, well kept Morlands and (at low price) Hook Norton, friendly service, good log fire, small restaurant; garden with lawn and apple trees *(Tom Evans)*

Long Hanborough [A4095 Witney—Woodstock – OS Sheet 164 map ref 423143; SP4214], *Bell*: Good value food from sandwiches up, well kept Bass and Morrells, friendly service, heavy rustic tables, leatherette seats, small games room, upstairs evening restaurant, tables on back terrace; children in side room and restaurant *(Derek and Sylvia Stephenson, Andrew and Ruth Triggs)*

☆ **Long Wittenham** [SU5493], *Machine Man*: Good basic village pub with good choice of genuine food inc tasty fresh sandwiches using real sausages, good range of perfectly kept Eldridge Pope beers, guest beers such as Exmoor Gold and Hook Norton Best, decent wines; bedrooms *(John C Baker)*

☆ **Long Wittenham**, *Plough*: Good choice of reasonably priced prompt bar food in low-beamed lounge, rustic furniture, lots of brass, games in public bar, inglenook log fires, welcoming landlord, Courage-related real ales, pool and children's room; Thames moorings at bottom of long spacious garden; bedrooms *(Marjorie and David Lamb, Eamon Green)*

☆ **Longworth** [SU3899], *Blue Boar*: Cosy and welcoming local with two good log fires and unusual decor (skis on beams etc), usual reasonably priced food, well kept Morrells Best, piped music, friendly service *(Jed and Virginia Brown, P A Shewry, Audrey and Peter Dowsett)*

☆ **Lower Assendon** [B480; SU7484], *Golden Ball*: Friendly renovated pub with good food esp pies and casseroles, well kept Brakspears, log fire *(Mr and Mrs S Price, David Warrellow)*

☆ **Lower Heyford** [21 Market Sq; SP4824], *Bell*: Very welcoming beamed pub in sleepy village, good range of beers inc Greene King Abbot, good simple home-cooked food from home-made sausages in a cob up; charming building *(Chris Raisin, P Ware)*

☆ **Marsh Baldon** [the Baldons signed off

A423 N of Dorchester; SU5699], *Seven Stars*: Large open room with good interesting rather restaurranty food (no sandwiches), generous helpings, decent wines, good coffee; on attractive village green *(A T Langton)*

☆ **Marston** [Mill Lane, Old Marston – OS Sheet 164 map ref 520090; SP5208], *Victoria Arms*: Tucked away in quiet spot by River Cherwell, attractive waterside grounds inc spacious terrace, good play area, punt moorings; full range of Wadworths beers and guests such as Badgers Tanglefoot and Cains, generous good value food (not Sun evening in winter) from chunky sandwiches up, lots of tables in main room and smaller ones off, real fires; piped music, children and dogs allowed; lavatory for disabled; beware vicious sleeping policemen *(George Atkinson, Giles Bullard, Joan Olivier, BB)*

Marston [Church Lane, Old Marston], *Bricklayers Arms*: Decent food and well kept Tetleys and Wadworths 6X in handsomely neo-Victorian pub, generously refurbished; good current management, open all day *(JHBS)*

Middle Assendon [SU7385], *Rainbow*: Friendly local with good straightforward food, well served in pleasant setting; well furnished with small tables, limited number of chairs as opposed to stools *(Gordon)*

☆ **Middle Barton** [SP4325], *Red Fox*: Spacious yet cosy village pub with friendly Italian landlord, good value food inc Italian dishes (not Sun evening, restaurant only lunchtime then), plans for brewing own beer *(Hugh Datson, Frank W Gadbois)*

Middleton Stoney [A43/B4030; SP5323], *Jersey Arms*: Lovely cosy oak-beamed bar, comfortable adjoining panelled lounge, good reasonably priced bar food, Youngers Scotch ale; bedrooms *(Nigel Foster)*

Milton under Wychwood [High St; SP2618], *Quart Pot*: Good atmosphere in spotless pub with good choice of good value home-cooked food from very cheerful cook; garden, attractive Cotswold village *(Mrs J Burton)*

Minster Lovell [just N of B4047 – OS Sheet 164 map ref 314112; SP3111], *Old Swan*: Interesting and attractive old inn which has moved far upmarket since its days as a main entry – does do expensive sandwiches as well as light lunches, but not really a place to drop into for a casual drink now; bedrooms *(Bill and Edee Miller, Mrs G Teall, LYM)*

☆ **Nettlebed** [A423; SU6986], *White Hart*: Civilised rambling beamed bar on two levels, with handsome old-fashioned furnishings inc fine grandfather clock, discreet atmosphere, good log fires, well kept Brakspears, spacious restaurant; not cheap; children welcome; modernised bedrooms *(Gordon, Paul McPherson, LYM)*

Nettlebed [Crocker End, E of village], *Carpenters Arms*: The licensees who made this tucked-away open-plan Brakspears pub popular for good food and friendly kind service have now moved to the Dog & Duck at Highmoor *(LYM; news please)*

☆ **Newbridge** [A415 7 miles S of Witney; SP4101], *Maybush*: New management keeping this low-beamed little local's pleasantly unpretentious cheerful atmosphere, good range of decent bar food (no sandwiches) at sensible prices, well kept Morlands, interesting collection of old mangles and other machines; moorings, pretty and neatly kept terrace by Thames *(Wayne Brindle, Michael Sargent, Mr and Mrs R Stewart, A T Langton, LYM)*

☆ **Newbridge**, *Rose Revived*: Big pub well worth knowing for its lovely setting by the upper Thames, across the road from our other entry here; spacious sheltered riverside lawn, prettily lit at night (good overnight mooring free); inside now knocked through as Morlands Artists Fayre eatery – usual food all day, Morlands real ales; children welcome, bedrooms *(LYM)*

☆ **Noke** [signed off B4027 NE of Oxford; SP5413], *Plough*: Wide range of low-priced honest food in big helpings from cheerfully unpretentious small country local, quick friendly service, well kept Morlands, no dogs; tables in pretty garden, busy on a sunny day *(Joan Olivier, D C T and E A Frewer, Marjorie and David Lamb, LYM)*

☆ **North Leigh** [New Yatt Rd – OS Sheet 164 map ref 384132; SP3813], *Woodman*: Notable warm welcome and efficient service in roomy village pub with good choice of reasonably priced freshly prepared food, real ales such as Glenny Witney and Wychwood, Hook Norton Best and Wadworths 6X, decent wines, proper coffee; daily papers, big garden; bedrooms comfortable *(M E Gurr, Marjorie and David Lamb)*

☆ **North Newington** [High St; just W of Banbury; SP4139], *Roebuck*: Attractively refurbished pub with good individual furnishings, nice relaxed bistro feel, wide range of good value interesting home-made food from good filled rolls up (popular lunchtime with Banbury businessmen), several well kept real ales inc Morlands and unusual guests, country wines, open fires, lovely briards, friendly service, piped classical music; children very welcome, good garden with play area and animals *(George Atkinson, I R Hewitt, John Bowdler and others)*

☆ **Oxford** [Binsey Lane; narrow lane on right leaving city on A420, just before Self Operated Storage], *Perch*: Lovely thatched pub with low ceilings, flagstones, stripped stone, high-backed settles as well as more modern seats (plenty of space), log fires, bar food, no-smoking eating area, Wadworths 6X and Allied real ales, decent wine, friendly helpful staff, unobtrusive piped music; prices not low; pleasant setting with big garden off riverside meadow, particularly good play area, summer marquee and barbecues, landing stage, attractive waterside walks; no dogs (the pub dog's called Mr Chips); children allowed in eating area *(Jenny and Brian Seller, Jim and Maggie Cowell, Julian Bessa, Joan Olivier, Eamon Green, Ann and Bob Westbrook, Margaret Dyke, LYM)*

☆ Oxford [Alfred St], *Bear*: Thousands of ties decorating four friendly and busy little basic low-ceilinged and partly panelled rooms, simple food most days inc sandwiches (no puddings; kitchen may be closed Weds), good range of well kept Allied and other ales from centenarian handpumps on rare pewter bar counter, no games machines, tables outside; open all day summer, good place to take overseas visitors *(Gill and Maurice McMahon, Robert Gomme, W Fletcher, Walter Reid, Eamon Green, Gordon, Terry and Eileen Stott, Julian Bessa, Tim and Ann Newell, LYM)*

☆ Oxford [Holywell St], *Kings Arms*: Big front bar, half a dozen cosy and comfortably worn-in side and back rooms inc no-smoking coffee room, well kept Youngs and guest ales, decent bar food, papers provided, tables on pavement; very busy and popular with students, but civilised – no music or games, no attempt to hurry you *(JM, PM, Jim and Maggie Cowell, Walter Reid, Elizabeth and Klaus Leist, Gordon, Walter Reid, BB)*

☆ Oxford [St Giles], *Eagle & Child*: Friendly students' pub without being studenty, nice panelled front snugs, tiny mid-bars full of actors' and Tolkien/C S Lewis memorabilia, modern back extension with no-smoking conservatory, well kept Allied ales and Wadworths 6X, good cheap plain pub food inc huge doorstep sandwiches, piped classical music, newspapers; small roofed-in terrace *(John Waller, Julian Bessa, Gordon, Terry and Eileen Stott, Tim and Ann Newell, E McCall, D Irving, R Huggins, T McLean, BB)*

☆ Oxford [Broad St], *White Horse*: Perhaps the city's smallest pub, sandwiched between bits of Blackwells bookshop; busy unspoiled traditional interior, beautiful view of the Clarendon building and Sheldonian, well kept Wadworths 6X and Allied ales, friendly licensees *(Prof C MacCallum, Tim and Ann Newell, Gordon, Julian Bessa, Walter Reid, BB)*

☆ Oxford [North Parade Ave], *Rose & Crown*: Friendly and unspoilt old local with popular bar lunches inc middle eastern specialities and Sun roasts, Allied ales, decent wine; ref books for crossword buffs, no piped music or machines, piano available for good players, jazz Tues; traditional small rooms, pleasant back yard with motorised awning and big gas heaters – children not allowed here or inside unless with friends of landlord *(E McCall, D Irving, R Huggins, T McLean, S Demont, T Barrow, Gordon, Julian Bessa, John Waller, BB)*

☆ Oxford [39 Plantation Rd; 1st left after Horse & Jockey going N up Woodstock Rd], *Gardeners Arms*: Relaxed local and University atmosphere in large, comfortable open-plan pub, good value filling home-made food inc vegetarian in back room where children allowed, well kept Morrells, real cider, tables outside *(Giles Bullard, Jon Carpenter, LYM)*

Oxford [Iffley Rd], *Fir Tree*: Friendly unpretentious local, well kept Morrells, decent coffee, good food inc home-made pizzas; piano Sun evenings, traditional games, dogs on leads and children welcome until 8.30 *(Nick Thorn)*; [Iffley Lock; towpath from Donnington Bridge Rd, between Abingdon Rd and Iffley Rd], *Isis*: Beautiful location with lovely big garden (and play equipment) right by the river, crowded in good weather; well kept Morrells, decent lunchtime food inc vegetarian, roaring fire, lots of rowing mementoes and old photographs *(Jon Carpenter, Jim and Maggie Cowell)*; [Banbury Rd, Summertown – different from the more central pub of the same name], *Kings Arms*: Popular lunchtime for well presented reasonably priced food, esp filled baked potatoes, bacon baguettes, salads and steaks *(David Campbell, Vicki McLean)*; [14 Gloucester St, by central car park and Gloucester Green bus stn], *Oxford Brewhouse*: Very mixed furnishings and bric-a-brac on several rambling floors, dark but lively, with stripped brickwork and woodwork, lots of well kept real ales at a price, loud piped music, food (not Sat or Sun evenings) from well laid out servery, seats in small courtyard, monthly live music; children in upper levels *(Geraint Roberts, Eamon Green, S Demont, T Barrow, LYM)*; [Beaumont St], *Randolph*: Warm welcome and clubby decor in big hotel's comfortable Spires Bar; wide range of cocktails made with generous measures, Osbert Lancaster paintings of the Zuleika Dobson story; bedrooms *(Walter Reid)*; [Woodstock Rd], *Royal Oak*: Lots of little rambling rooms, celebrity pictures in front bars, separate food bar; games area with darts, pool etc *(E McCall, D Irving, R Huggins, T McLean, Gordon)*; [Friars Entry, St Michael St], *Three Goats Heads*: Cheap well kept Sam Smiths and good choice of quick generous bar food from sandwiches up in two good-sized bars with dark wood and booths, relaxed downstairs, more formal upstairs; Weds quiz night *(Alastair Campbell, K Regan, A Y Drummond)*

Pyrton [SU6896], *Plough*: Decent food inc interesting specials in 17th-c thatched pub with big log fire in stripped-stone beamed main bar, real ales inc Adnams and Brakspears; closed Mon evening *(Marjorie and David Lamb)*

☆ Radcot [Radcot Bridge; A4095 2½ miles N of Faringdon; SU2899], *Swan*: Well kept Morlands, log fire, straightforward food inc good value sandwiches and afternoon teas, piped pop music (may be loud), pub games, lots of stuffed fish; the star is for its pleasant Thames-side lawn, with boat trips from pub's camping-ground opp (lift to bring wheelchairs aboard); children in eating area; bedrooms clean and good value, with good breakfast *(S Demont, T Barrow, LYM)*

☆ **Ramsden** [SP3515], *Royal Oak:* Wide range of good generous sensibly priced food inc good Sun lunch, and well kept Hook Norton, in well run cosy and comfortable 17th-c pub; welcoming atmosphere, good log fire; cosy bedrooms in separate cottages *(Phil Russell, John Waller, Karin Rucker, D Jacobs, Rosemary Harris)*

Rotherfield Greys [SU7282], *Maltsters Arms:* Pretty and pleasantly modernised pub by church, Brakspears PA, SB and Old reasonably priced for area, wide choice of food inc children's menu, back garden with picnic-table sets; handy for Greys Court (NT), good walks nearby *(Brian and Anna Marsden, Mr and Mrs N Hazzard)*

Rotherfield Peppard [Gallowstree Rd; SU7181], *Greyhound:* Pretty and cottagey country pub with homely interior, friendly landlord and good choice of beers; some concentration on good home-made food, very popular for this with older people at lunchtime; attractive garden with boules piste *(Maysie Thompson, Gordon)*

☆ **Russells Water** [up track past duck pond; village signposted from B481 S of junction with B480; SU7089], *Beehive:* Warm relaxed atmosphere in attractive old-world pub with interesting furnishings, inglenook log fire, subdued lighting, wide choice of good home-made food (no sandwiches, not Sun evening) inc popular Sun lunch, well kept Brakspears, Flowers Original, Marstons Pedigree and Wadworths 6X, no piped music or machines; restaurant, family room, garden with duck pond, terrace and fairy-lit arbour; has been closed Mon/Tues *(Verity Kemp, Richards Mills, LYM)*

Sandford on Thames [Church Rd; SP5301], *Kings Arms:* Large but welcoming Thames-side pub with lots of good value food, well kept Courage ales, friendly efficient service, good garden – plenty for children; moorings *(Comus Elliott, Mr and Mrs G D Amos)*

☆ **Satwell** [just off B481, 2 miles S of Nettlebed; follow Shepherds Green signpost; SU7083], *Lamb:* Cosy and attractive 16th-c low-beamed farm cottage, very small (so can get cramped), with tiled floors, friendly licensees, huge log fireplace, well kept Brakspears, traditional games, bar food from sandwiches up inc good if not cheap ploughman's, tables outside *(Gordon, John Carter, LYM)*

☆ **Shilton** [SP2608], *Rose & Crown:* Good choice of well prepared home-cooked food at reasonable prices in friendly 17th-c stonebuilt village local with helpful staff, well kept Morlands Bitter, Old Masters and

Old Speckled Hen on handpump, darts in beamed and tiled public bar, tables in sizeable garden; pretty village *(Joan Olivier, Marjorie and David Lamb)*

Shiplake [Sonning Eye; A4155 towards Play Hatch and Reading – OS Sheet 175 map ref 746768; SU7476], *Flowing Spring:* Well kept Fullers ales in three cosy rooms of countrified pub with open fires and floor-to-ceiling windows overlooking the water meadows; big attractive garden *(Martin Kay, Andrea Fowler, LYM); Plowden Arms:* Neat friendly pub with good range of food lunchtimes and evenings, Brakspears Bitter and Mild; children's room *(P J Caunt, TBB)*

Sonning Common [Blounts Court Rd, just off B481 Reading—Nettlebed, NE of centre; SU7080], *Butchers Arms:* Well kept Brakspears Mild, PA and SB on handpump, big family room, decent food inc good Sun lunch, pleasant garden adjoining woodland with picnic-table sets, good play area with helterskelter, swings, roundabout swing, regular weekend entertainment like Punch & Judy; bedrooms *(Brian and Anna Marsden, LYM)*

☆ **Souldern** [SP5131], *Fox:* Charming beamed stone pub, well kept Hook Norton and other real ales, good interesting though not speedy bar food from ploughman's up, friendly German landlady, nice village location; comfortable bedrooms, good breakfasts *(George Atkinson, T A Bryan, Marjorie and David Lamb, N and J Strathdee)*

South Hinksey [SP5004], *Fishes:* Comfortable pub with new chef doing good food inc local produce and impaginative vegetarian dishes, well kept Morrells ales inc Graduate, pleasant sun room, big garden running down to river; path across fields towards Oxford, along causeway originally built by John Ruskin to give students experience of healthy outdoor labour *(Jon Carpenter)*

☆ **South Moreton** [SU5588], *Crown:* Good mostly home-produced food inc some interesting Spanish dishes in tastefully opened-out character country pub, particularly well kept Wadworths and guest ales tapped from the cask, friendly service; children allowed, discount scheme for OAPs *(John C Baker, Susie Northfield, R C Watkins)*

☆ **Sparsholt** [SU3487], *Star:* Small choice of good home-cooked food in friendly and relaxed old country local, comfortable furnishings, log fire, attractive pictures, welcoming landlord, attentive staff, real ales inc Fullers London Pride, Morlands Original, Worthington BB, daily papers, subdued piped music, back garden; pretty village *(HNJ, PEJ, Jed and Virginia Brown)*

Standlake [High St; SP3902], *Bell:* Well presented good food in plush surroundings, well kept Morlands *(S Holder)*

Stanford in the Vale [SU3493], *Red Lion:* Basic old low-beamed two-bar village local, friendly staff, limited choice of good well presented food at low prices with no frills; dogs allowed, occasional live music *(HNJ, PEJ)*

Stanton Harcourt [B4449 S of Eynsham; SP4105], *Harcourt Arms*: Wide choice of freshly cooked good food in pub/restaurant's three attractive, simply furnished and pleasantly informal dining areas, with Spy cartoons and huge fireplaces; good choice of wines, piped music, friendly service *(M E Gurr, ABS, LYM)*

☆ **Steventon** [SU4691], *Cherry Tree*: Eating-out village pub with spacious and relaxing interconnecting rooms, dark green walls, two or three old settles among more modern furnishings, unobtrusive piped music, film-star pictures, stuffed woodpecker and squirrel, nice bay window; Charles Wells Eagle, Morlands and Wadworths 6X, popular quick straightforward food, open fire *(R Huggins, T McLean, E McCall, D Irving, Gordon)*

Steventon, *Fox*: Good atmosphere and decent food in well kept bar and recently opened restaurant *(A T Langton)*

☆ **Stoke Lyne** [off B4100; SP5628], *Peyton Arms*: Classic unspoilt village pub, tiny snug, bigger public bar with good range of traditional games (no juke box or machines), pleasant garden with Aunt Sally, particularly welcoming landlord and customers, well kept Hook Norton tapped from the cask; no food *(Pete Baker, Phil and Sally Gorton)*

☆ **Stoke Row** [Newlands Lane; off B491 N of Reading – OS Sheet 175 map ref 684844; SU6784], *Crooked Billet*: Opened-up country pub/restaurant with no shortage of wine racks and wide choice of good interesting home-cooked meals; well kept Brakspears ales tapped from the cask (as well as decent wines), good log fires, but no longer a place for just a drink; big garden, by Chilterns beech woods *(TBB, Clifford Payton, LYM)*

Stoke Row, *Cherry Tree*: Basic local, four interconnecting rooms inc one like someone's drawing room, another with pool; friendly licensees and locals, Brakspears tapped from the cask in back stillage room *(Gordon)*; [Kingwood Common, a mile S of Stoke Row, signposted Peppard and Reading – OS Sheet 175 map ref 692825], *Grouse & Claret*: Attractive pub in nice quiet setting, several cosy and intimate nooks; well kept Morlands, decent wines, good changing choice of well priced good food, attentive welcoming staff; piped music *(the Monday Club)*

Stoke Talmage [signed from A40 at Tetsworth; SU6799], *Red Lion*: Friendly and unspoilt, basic bar, parlour-like lounge where cards and dominoes are popular, well kept Butcombe and Morlands on handpump; pleasant garden *(Pete Baker)*

☆ **Sutton Courtenay** [SU5093], *George & Dragon*: Plenty of character and interest in welcoming and attractive 16th-c pub with good choice of fair-priced home-made food from sandwiches upwards, well kept Morlands, good range of decent wines; relaxed atmosphere, candlelit restaurant; no dogs, picnic-table sets on back terrace overlooking cemetery where Orwell and Asquith are buried *(Wayne Brindle, Marjorie and David Lamb, Robert Dale, Stephen Bayley)*

Sutton Courtenay, *Swan*: Doing well under current management, with pleasant atmosphere, decent food, well kept beers *(A T Langton)*

Sydenham [SP7201], *Crown*: Cottagey Morrells pub, long rambling low-ceilinged bar with a little lamp in each small window, reasonable choice of interesting food, good choice of wines by the glass, very friendly welcome, at least two demonstrative cats, relaxed homely atmosphere, dominoes and darts; picturesque village, views of lovely church *(Heather Couper, Nigel Herbert, Gordon)*

☆ **Tackley** [SP4720], *Gardiners Arms*: Comfortable and welcoming lounge bar with well presented good value bar food inc good vegetarian choice and full meals even on Sun, attentive friendly staff, coal-effect gas fire, well kept Morrells ales; entirely separate public bar with darts and piped pop music, bookable bowling alley, picnic-table sets on grass by car park; handy for Rousham House *(Maureen Hobbs, Margaret Dyke, T G Brierly)*

☆ **Thame** [Cornmarket; SP7005], *Abingdon Arms*: Good doorstep sandwiches and other generous standard bar food, Bass, Brakspears, Fullers London Pride, good choice of well identified bottled beers, small no-smoking bar, bright and basic main bar with some character; piped music; tables in garden *(Lt Col E H F Sawbridge, N and J Strathdee, Tim Newell, Mr and Mrs M J Smith)*

☆ **Thame** [High St], *Rising Sun*: Flagstones and bare boards in three linked rooms, well kept Hook Norton and Morlands ales, good food inc huge rolls and notable burgers, real fire *(N and J Strathdee)*

Thame [High St], *Black Horse*: Traditional old inn with attractive panelled and chintzy back lounge, simple dining area, sunny covered basic back area, good range of standard food, well kept Bass, good coffee, friendly atmosphere; open for breakfast; bedrooms *(John Waller, George Atkinson, LYM)*; [Moreton, just SW; SP6904], *Royal Oak*: Attractively restored old building, recently refurbished under welcoming new licensees; well kept Whitbreads-related ales with a guest such as Brakspears *(Tim and Ann Newell)*; [High St], *Swan*: Busy, with good range of real ales, bar food from good sandwiches to interesting hot dishes, interesting mix of furniture *(T A Bryan)*

☆ **Thrupp** [SP4815], *Boat*: Good quiet atmosphere and lovely canalside surroundings for small friendly 16th-c stone-built local with quick good value home-cooked food, well kept Morrells, no piped music, waterside garden *(P Ware, Sue Demont, Tim Barrow, M Joyner, Geoff Lee)*

Thrupp [Banbury Rd], *Jolly Boatman*: Recently extended, with good cheap food, Morrells beers; children allowed in conservatory overlooking Oxford Canal *(Dick Brown)*

☆ **Towersey** [down drive nr Chinnor Rd/Manor Rd crossroads; SP7304], *Three Horseshoes*: Unpretentious flagstoned country pub with old-fashioned furnishings, good log fire, well kept Allied and guest real ales, bar food inc vegetarian, log fire, piped music, small restaurant; biggish garden with playthings among fruit trees; children allowed lunchtime *(John Waller, LYM)*

Uffington [SU3089], *Fox & Hounds*: Pubby old local, very friendly, with good log fire, decent wine, Morrells beer, wide choice of fairly priced straightforward food, lots of horse-related bric-a-brac, bottles and horse prints; garden with play area; charming village, interesting weekend museum; handy for White Horse Hill *(Audrey and Peter Dowsett, Tim Brierly)*

Wallingford [St Leonards Ln; SU6089], *Little House Around the Corner by the Brook*: Comfortable and civilised but welcoming, good well presented home-made food inc imaginative children's dishes in smallish tasteful bar with pews or (10% service charge added) adjacent raised dining area with antique furniture, fresh flowers, candles; changing real ales; piped music; next to church in beautiful spot by brook *(A P Seymour, Dominic and Sue Dunlop)*

☆ **Wantage** [Mill St; past square and Bell, down hill then bend to left; SU4087], *Lamb*: Delightful old low-beamed and timbered pub with choice of attractively and comfortably furnished seating areas, pictures, well kept Morlands, good choice of generous reasonably priced nicely presented freshly cooked bar food, friendly staff, good play area *(Marjorie and David Lamb, Giles Bullard, Geraint Roberts, LYM)*

Wantage [Market Pl], *Bear*: Old traditional hotel with comfortable chairs and settees in big bustling bar, Morlands ales, wide choice of food, no-smoking area, friendly and attentive staff, newspapers; piped music; restaurant; bedrooms *(George Atkinson, BB)*

☆ **Warborough** [Thame Rd (off A329 4 miles N of Wallingford); SU5993], *Cricketers Arms*: Good range of freshly prepared reasonably priced food (not Sun/Mon evenings) in welcoming and attractively decorated two-bar pub, prompt friendly service, well kept Morlands, tables and boules piste outside *(Marjorie and David Lamb)*

☆ **Warborough** [The Green South; just E of A329], *Six Bells*: Generous fair value home-made food in recently refurbished low-ceilinged thatched pub with country furnishings, big fireplace, separate dining area, Brakspears ales; tables in back orchard, cricket green in front, boules; children in eating area *(Marjorie and David Lamb, LYM)*

Wardington [Upper Wardington; off A361 Banbury—Daventry; SP4945], *Plough*: Pleasant old pub in pretty village, wide range of straightforward food, friendly landlord and staff, Adnams and Hook Norton beers *(George Atkinson)*

Watlington [SU6894], *Carriers Arms*: Outstanding choice of cheap well cooked food in giant helpings from sandwiches through enormous bargain omelettes to full meals; always full but copes with the crowds remarkably well; genial landlord *(Dick Brown)*

☆ **West Hanney** [SU4092], *Plough*: Friendly and welcoming newish licensees in attractive and genuinely old two-bar thatched pub, locally popular for good value simple tasty food inc good fresh ploughman's, quiches and omelettes; quietly congenial surroundings, original timbers and uneven low ceilings, homely panelled lounge with open fire in stone fireplace, unusual plates, brasses and butterflies; darts in public bar; Allied ales, interesting whiskies, back garden with aviaries; children welcome *(HNJ, PEJ, Rachel Hunter, R C Watkins)*

☆ **West Hendred** [Reading Rd; off A417 – OS Sheet 174 map ref 447891; SU4488], *Hare*: Civilised welcoming two-bar local very popular for generous good value food served till late evening; well kept Morlands, decent wine *(A T Langton, Giles Bullard, R C Watkins, Peter and Audrey Dowsett)*

Westcott Barton [Enstone Rd (B4030); SP4325], *Fox*: Friendly characterful stone pub, traditional English and home-made Italian dishes, five real ales, good wines *(Frank Gadbois)*

☆ **Weston on the Green** [A43, a mile from M40 junction 9; SP5318], *Chequers*: Busy thatched pub with good food cooked by Thai chef – you can see her doing it from the long comfortable raftered bar with its profusion of old jars, brasses, stuffed fox and ferrets etc; clean and friendly, Fullers ales, farm cider; tables under cocktail parasols in attractive garden with animals *(D C T and E A Frewer, Frank W Gadbois, Mrs Susan Gibson, Martin Kay, Andrea Fowler)*

☆ **Weston on the Green**, *Ben Jonson*: Friendly and enthusiastic young landlord in thatched pub with good generous popular food inc authentic Tex-Mex dishes, well kept Bass and Greene King, dark wood settles in beamed lounge bar, snug with roaring winter fire, discreet pool room; usually open all day; children welcome; sheltered garden with occasional barbecues *(David Campbell, Vicki McLean, D C T and E A Frewer)*

☆ **Whitchurch** [SU6377], *Greyhound*: Good value food and well kept Wadworths 6X and Allied ales in neat but relaxed low-beamed L-shaped bar with displays of miniatures and cricket bats, polite service, no music or machines; dogs on leads allowed, pleasant garden; nr Thames toll bridge in attractive village, good walks *(Frank Cummins, Dr Andrew Brookes, Mark and Diane Grist)*

☆ **Witney** [Corn St; SP3510], *Three Horseshoes*: Thriving little very well run 17th-c Cotswold stone inn, beautifully furnished bar with antiques, persian rug, two open fires, good value tasty popular food inc simple cheap lunches, bargain steaks Thurs evening, well kept Morlands and a guest ale such as Adnams Broadside or Charles Wells Bombardier, candlelit dining room *(J Waller, Tom Macdonald, Brian Heywood, Mrs J Burton)*

Witney [Corn St], *Eagle*: Comfortable, warm and cosy, several adjoining lounges, family room, back garden; Bass and Worthington BB, buffet meals *(Peter and Audrey Dowsett)*; [17 High St], *Royal Oak*: Small cosy lounge, larger bar, courtyard full of farm tools; Hook Norton beer, good value bar meals, friendly licensees, quiet piped music *(Peter Pocklington)*

Woodcote [Goring Rd; SU6481], *Red Lion*: Good food, friendly staff *(Tony Merrill)*

☆ **Woodstock** [Park St; SP4416], *Bear*: Fine old inn with pleasant bar on right, cosy alcoves, good fresh sandwiches and bar food, excellent service, interesting medley of well-worn wooden antique armchairs, chintz cushions, paintings, sporting trophies; Bass and Morrells Bitter; good bedrooms – Forte *(Mrs L Powys-Smith, Andrew and Ruth Triggs)*

☆ **Woodstock** [Market St], *Woodstock Arms*: 16th-c heavy-beamed stripped-stone pub which keeps its local atmosphere; good value food inc sandwiches and vegetarian, friendly prompt service, log-effect gas fires in splendid stone fireplaces, Bass and Morells real ale, decent wine, commendable housekeeping; tables out in yard; bedrooms *(Phil and Sally Gorton, F M Bunbury, Basil Minson, D C T Frewer)*

☆ **Woolstone** [SU2987], *White Horse*: Attractive partly thatched 16th-c pub in secluded downland valley village, good range of reasonably priced quickly served food, well kept Morells or Flowers and Wadworths 6X, two big open fires in spacious beamed and part-panelled room, children allowed in eating area; sheltered garden; lovely spot, handy for White Horse; four bedrooms *(Paul Randall, Dick Brown, HNJ, PEJ, Paul S McPherson)*

Wootton [Glympton Rd; B4027 N of Woodstock; the one at SP4320], *Killingworth Castle*: 17th-c inn with friendly new Canadian licensees, big helpings of good reasonably priced home-cooked food using fresh produce inc delicious puddings; improved garden; bedrooms cosy and comfortable *(Dick Little, Andrew Bill)*

☆ **Wroxton** [Church St; off A422 at hotel – pub at back of village; SP4142], *North Arms*: Pretty thatched stone pub behind attractive garden in quiet part of lovely village, good value wholesome bar food, simple but comfortable modernised lounge with lots of beer mugs and log fire, character restaurant (not Mon); well kept Morrells, cheerful service, darts, dominoes, fruit machine, weekly summer folk music *(I R Hewitt, N and J Strathdee, LYM)*

The Post Office makes it virtually impossible for people to come to grips with British geography, by using a system of post towns which are often across the county boundary from the places they serve. So the postal address of a pub often puts it in the wrong county. We use the correct county – the one the pub is actually in. Lots of pubs which the Post Office alleges are in Oxfordshire are actually in Berkshire, Buckinghamshire, Gloucestershire or the Midlands.

Shropshire

Two new entries here, both charming old buildings in attractive scenery, by lively streams, and both with virtually the same name, are the Horseshoe at Bridges and the Horse Shoe at Llanyblodwel. There's no shortage of good food in the county's pubs. We've noticed prices actually falling at some pubs here, and the area is now very good value indeed for pub food – especially as such a high proportion of our entries here have qualified for our Food Award. From among them we choose as Shropshire Dining Pub of the Year the remarkably welcoming Wenlock Edge Inn on Wenlock Edge, with the Crown at Hopton Wafers running it close. Drinks too are much cheaper than the national average here, with very little change over the last year: the cheapest pubs we found for beer here are the Three Tuns at Bishops Castle and Plough at Wistanstow, both brewing their own good beer, and the cheerful Lion of Morfe at Upper Farmcote (Banks's beers – and cheap food, too). Among Lucky Dip entries at the end of the chapter, we'd particularly commend the Railwaymans Arms in Bridgnorth, Feathers at Brockton, Crown at Claverley, Sun and White Horse at Clun, Bear at Hodnet, New Inn at Ironbridge, Green Dragon at Little Stretton, Old Three Pigeons at Nesscliffe, Stiperstones Inn at Stiperstones and Bell at Tong.

BISHOPS CASTLE SO3289 Map 6

Three Tuns 🗲

Salop Street

Across the yard is the many-storeyed Victorian brewhouse (it's a Grade I listed building) that produces their popular beers. It's unique for its traditional tower layout, with each stage of the brewing process descending floor by floor. From it comes the XXX Bitter, Mild, an old-fashioned dark somewhat stoutish ale called Steamer and winter Old Scrooge; brewery tours can be arranged. Inside the quirky atmospheric beamed pub there's a no-frills welcoming air. Low backed settles on vinyl flooring form three niches on one side with padded settles against the walls and comfortable chairs around heavy walnut tables. On the other side is a long wall settle and three big kitchen tables. Home-made bar food includes soup (£1.50), burgers (from £3), ploughman's (from £3.50), chilli con carne or cottage pie (£3.95), smoked mackerel pâté (£4), lasagne, home-made fisherman's pie, scampi or lemon sole (£4.95) and steaks (from £9), quite a few vegetarian dishes like bean and mushroom stroganoff, mushroom and cashew nut pilaf or three bean casserole (from £4.50) and lots of Indian dishes like onion bhajis (£2.50), beef madras, mixed vegetable curry or prawn curry (£5), lasagne (£4.20) and steaks (from £8); puddings like treacle tart. Hall's and Weston's ciders; malt whiskies; dominoes and quoits. There's a small garden and terrace, with a selection of plants for sale. *(Recommended by Frank Cummins, Nigel Woolliscroft, P Boot, Mike and Penny Sanders, Brian Kneale; more reports please)*

Own brew ~ Licensee Dominic Wood ~ Real ale ~ Meals and snacks ~ Restaurant ~ (01588) 638797 ~ Well behaved children welcome ~ Open 11.30-3, 6.30-11 (maybe longer in summer; closed 25 Dec)

Pubs staying open all afternoon are listed at the back of the book.

BRIDGES SO3996 Map 6

Horseshoe £

Near Ratlinghope, below the W flank of the Long Mynd

A real oasis in these deserted hills, this attractive old pub is delightfully placed by the little River Onny. It's an interesting building (especially the windows), and the single large bar, tidily comfortable and bright, has a good log fire and local paintings for sale. There is a small dining room off, and promptly served decent home-made food includes sandwiches, ploughman's with local cheese, and straightforward cooked dishes. The changing choice of well kept real ales is altogether better than you could expect out here, such as Adnams, Fullers ESB, Marstons Pedigree and Worthington Special, Weston's farm cider; friendly service, and the landlord's a real individual. There are tables outside, and the pub's very handy for walks on the Long Mynd itself and on Stiperstones – despite its isolation, it can get very busy in summer. *(Recommended by WHBM, Nigel Woolliscroft, Jenny and Brian Seller, Dave Braisted)*

Free House ~ Real ale ~ Meals and snacks ~ Children's room ~ Open 11-3, 6-11

CARDINGTON SO5095 Map 4

Royal Oak

Village signposted off B4371 Church Stretton—Much Wenlock, pub behind church; also reached via narrow lanes from A49

This pretty, welcoming wisteria-covered white stone house is reputedly Shropshire's oldest pub, first licensed back in the 15th c. Even today it remains one of the best placed, with lovely views over hilly fields from the tables beside roses in the front court, and a mile or so away – from the track past Willstone (ask for directions at the pub) – you can walk up Caer Caradoc Hill which also looks over scenic countryside. It's pleasant inside too, and the friendly rambling bar has low beams, old standing timbers of a knocked-through wall, hops draped along the bar gantry, a vast inglenook fireplace with its roaring winter log fire, cauldron, black kettle and pewter jugs, and gold plush, red leatherette and tapestry seats solidly capped in elm. Prices of the home-made lunchtime bar food are the same as last year and include sandwiches (£1.50; toasties £2.20), soup (£2), ploughman's (£2.90) and at least seven dishes – served without vegetables – such as macaroni cheese (£2.25), enjoyable fidget pie (£3.20), meaty or vegetarian lasagne (£3.75), steak and kidney pie (£4.50), with evening dishes like chicken (£4.80), gammon and egg (£5.90), and rump steak (£6.60); no chips at lunchtime. Well kept Bass on handpump under light blanket pressure and two others, usually Boddingtons, Hook Norton Old Hookey or Wadworths 6X; dominoes and cribbage in the main bar, there may also be two boxer dogs. *(Recommended by Jeff Davies, Wayne Brindle, Basil Minson, Paul Boot, Nigel Woolliscroft, D Hanley, A G Roby, the Monday Club; more reports please)*

Free house ~ Licensee John Seymour ~ Real ale ~ Meals and snacks (12-2, 7-8.30; not Sun evening) ~ Longville (01694) 771266 ~ Children welcome lunchtime; only if eating in evening ~ Open 12-2.30, 7-11; closed Mon except bank holidays ~ One self-contained double bedroom: £22S/£33S

HOPE SJ3401 Map 6

Stables ★ ⊕

Drury Lane, Hopesgate; pub signposted off A488 S of Minsterley, at the Bentlawnt ¾, Leigh 1¾ signpost – then take first right turn; or closer to Minsterley, turn off at Ploxgreen – but a mile and a half of single-track road

Originally built in the 1680s as a drovers' pub on what was once a busy road – now it's a quiet lane – between Montgomery and Shrewsbury, this small friendly country cottage has spectacular views over the Stiperstones and Long Mountain. The welcome is relaxed and friendly, the atmosphere particularly homely, and the food very good. The range of promptly served lunchtime dishes from the blackboard changes every day, but typically includes soup (£2), salads (from £2.80), local sausages (£3.80), mushroom and Shropshire blue hotpot (£5), chilli pork on rice (£5.50) and casseroles (£5.75). The evening menu is more extensive and includes taramasalata (£2.85), spinach roulade (£3.10), excellent local sausages (£3.80), cheesy tomato and aubergine bake (£5), Hungarian veal goulash (£5.95), chicken breast in garlic butter (£6.25), kidney and smoked sausage hotpot (£6.50), rabbit and cider stew (£6.85), fresh fish like plaice with fennel and green peppercorns (£7.25) and half roast guinea fowl with prune and armagnac sauce (£8.75); home-made puddings like bread and butter pudding, spiced plum crumble and hot chocolate fudge pudding (all £2.50); the home-made ice creams are highly recommended, vegetables are fresh. On Wednesday to Saturday evenings, the cottagey dining room is open with a more substantial menu. There are only four tables, so it's virtually essential to book; smoking is discouraged. The small black-beamed L-shaped bar with logs burning in a massive stone fireplace has comfortably cushioned or well polished wooden seats around attractive oak and other tables, hunting prints of varying ages and degrees of solemnity and well chosen china; in a back room are some big prints of butterflies and herbs. Well kept Felinfoel Double Dragon, Tetleys, Woods and one guest on handpump, with Addlestone's and Weston cider in summer, decent wines and spirits (they do a good kir, buck's fizz or black velvet, and Pimms), and half-a-dozen malt whiskies. Shove-ha'penny, cribbage, dominoes and a fruit machine; several cats and McEwan, a west highland terrier. *(Recommended by P and J Shapley, the Monday Club, Paul and Margaret Baker, Pat and John Millward, WAH, J Barnwell, M G Hart, Frank Cummins, W C M Jones, C A Brace, Basil Minson, Nigel Woolliscroft, A G Roby)*

Free house ~ Licensees Denis and Debbie Harding ~ Real ale ~ Meals and snacks (12-1.30, 7-8.30) ~ Restaurant (not Sun evening) ~ (01743) 891344 ~ Older children in eating area of bar ~ Open 11.30-2.30, 7-11; 12-2 in winter; closed Mon and a week in early summer

HOPTON WAFERS SO6476 Map 4

Crown 🛏 🍴

A4117

This year many readers have been telling us how delicious the food is at this attractive welcoming creeper-covered stone inn. There's an excellent imaginative choice from the menu – which isn't necessarily cheap, but can be considered as good value – which includes sandwiches (from £1.85), soup (£2.40), ploughman's (£3.80), spinach and stilton or seafood pancakes (£3.95), tagliatelle in a stilton cream sauce (£3.95), sautéed vegetables on pasta (£5.75), breaded plaice, braised beef pie or scampi (£6.25), salads (from £6.50), spicy Mexican sausages (£6.50), grilled gammon (£6.75), mixed grill (£9.25), steaks (from £9.75) and from the blackboard which might have moules marinières (£5), fresh fish (from £6), variety of madras curries (£7) and local venison steak (£7.50); home-made puddings on the board; children's menu, and small portions of some of the above (£3.25). The cosy, warmly decorated antique yellow beamed bar is neatly cared for and fairly smart. There's a large inglenook fire as well as a woodburning stove, various seats and flowery cushions on the black settles, oil paintings, and maybe fresh flowers. Well kept Boddingtons, Flowers Original and Marstons Pedigree on handpump, good house wines; wide variety of malt whiskies, and coffee; service is very friendly and efficient. There are tables under cocktail parasols on the terraces and in the streamside garden, with plenty of tubs of bright flowers and ducks on the pond. It's worth getting there early, as they do get busy; no-smoking area in restaurant; pretty, timbered bedrooms, one with lovely oak floor, another with woodburning stove. *(Recommended by R and S Bentley, KC, Graham Reeve, E A C and S J C Sutton, Miss R M Tudor, Rita Horridge, Bill and Beryl Farmer, the Monday Club, George Atkinson, A W and P McCully, Chris Wrigley, DAV, Basil Minson)*

Free house ~ Licensee John Price ~ Real ale ~ Meals and snacks (till 10pm Fri and Sat) ~ Restaurant; not Sun evening ~ Cleobury Mortimer (01299) 270372 ~ Children in eating area of bar and in restaurant ~ Open 12-3, 6-11 ~ Bedrooms: £37.50B/£60B

LLANFAIR WATERDINE SO2476 Map 6

Red Lion 🛏️

Village signposted from B4355 approaching eastwards; turn left after crossing bridge

In a part of the country renowned for beautiful walks (a good stretch of Offa's Dyke is nearby) and designated as an area of outstanding natural beauty, the licensee is keen to keep the pub's traditional feel intact – there are no machines or children here. At the back of this atmospheric old place tables look over the River Tene, the border of England and Wales, and there are more seats among the roses in the quiet lane at the front. The heavily beamed rambling lounge bar has cosy alcoves, easy chairs, some long, low settles and little polished wooden seats on its turkey carpet, and a woodburner. Perhaps even nicer is the small black-beamed taproom, with plain wooden chairs on its flagstoned floor, and table skittles, dominoes, cribbage, shove-ha'penny, and sensibly placed darts; quoits. Good home-made food includes sandwiches (from £1.50), home-made soup (£1.50), home-made ploughman's (from £2.95), chilli con carne or spaghetti bolognese (£4.40), chicken madras (£5.50), beef in garlic and red wine (£6.75), chicken stuffed with stilton (£7.20), rump steak (£7.70), breast of duck in orange and brandy sauce (£9.20) and some quite elaborate specials on the blackboard. Well kept Marstons Pedigree and Tetleys and a guest like Benskins Best or Friary Meux Best on handpump kept under light blanket pressure; good selection of whiskies and draft ciders; friendly service. No walking boots inside; piped music. *(Recommended by Basil Minson, R J Walden, Mike and Penny Sanders, N C Walker)*

Free house ~ Licensee Mick Richards ~ Real ale ~ Meals and snacks (12-1.30, 7-9, not Sun evening) ~ Knighton (01547) 528214 ~ Open 12-2, 7-11; closed Tues lunchtime ~ Bedrooms: /£33(£40B)

LLANYBLODWEL SJ2423 Map 7

Horse Shoe

Village and pub signposted from B4396

It's refreshing to paddle and watch children splash in a delightful stretch of the River Tanat which rushes around the boulders under a little red stone bridge in front of the tables outside this lovely early 15th-c inn. There's a mile of fly-fishing for trout or grayling which is free for residents; day tickets otherwise. The simple low beamed front bar with an old black range in the inglenook fireplace has traditional black built-in settles alongside more modern chairs around oak tables on a reclaimed maple floor and lots of brass and china. In the rambling rooms leading off you'll find darts, pool, shove-ha'penny, dominoes, cribbage, a space game and piped music. The dining room is oak panelled. Bar food – much improved under the new licensee – from the menu includes baguettes (from £2.25), salads (from £2.95), home-made liver pâté or ploughman's (from £3.25), king prawns or lasagne (from £4.50), home-made beef and ale pie with suet crust (£6.50), several vegetarian dishes like Mediterranean bean casserole or tagliatelle with stir-fried vegetables (from £4.50) and on the specials board dishes there might be fresh fish (£5.25) or chicken chasseur; puddings on the blackboard which changes every two days are home-made and might include lemon and treacle tart, profiteroles filled with Drambuie and cream, sticky toffee pudding or spotted dick – all served with fruit coulis and cream. Well kept Banks's Mild, Marstons Best and Pedigree. *(Recommended by Basil Minson, Paul McPherson; more reports please)*

Free House ~ Licensee Angela Lewis ~ Real ale ~ Meals and snacks (11.30-3; 7-10) ~ Restaurant ~ (01691) 828969 ~ Children in eating area ~ Open 11-11 (6.30 Mon) ~ Bedrooms: £25(£29.50B)/£35/(£45B)

LONGVILLE SO5494 Map 4

Longville Arms 🛏️

B4371 Church Stretton—Much Wenlock

A good mix of customers seem to like this large modernised big-windowed inn that you'll find in the midst of some really beautiful countryside. In fact it's fairly renowned for its very friendly atmosphere and warm welcome. Of the two spacious bars the left one is simpler with sturdy elm or cast-iron-framed tables, leatherette banquettes and a woodburning stove at each end. The right-hand lounge has dark plush wall banquettes and cushioned chairs, with some nice old tables. There's a wide range of good-value home-made bar food, including soup (£1.50), deep-fried camembert with home-made chutney (£3.30), fresh grilled trout with almonds (£5.85), sirloin steak (from £7.50), vegetarian dishes, as well as specials of the day; usual children's meals (from £2) and excellent puddings (from £1.80). Well kept Bass and Worthington BB on handpump and a guest in summer; selection of wines from the new world. There are picnic-table sets under cocktail parasols in a neat side garden, with a play area. Besides the good value bedrooms, there's a good self-contained flat in an adjacent converted barn; superb breakfasts. *(Recommended by Dave Braisted, Nigel Woolliscroft, the Whalley family, the Staughton family, Brian Congreve, Adrian and Karen Bulley, Mrs B Garmston, Dr and Mrs T O Hughes, Desmond and Rhona Crilly)*

Free house ~ Licensee Patrick Egan ~ Real ale ~ Meals and snacks (not Tues lunchtime) ~ (01694) 771206 ~ Children welcome ~ Open 12-3, 7-11; closed Tues ~ Bedrooms: £18.50/£30(£35B)

LUDLOW SO5174 Map 4

Church 🛏

Church Street, behind town centre Buttercross

Neatly and comfortably modernised, there's been some sort of inn on the site of this Georgian stuccoed building for seven centuries, though during that period it's also been anything from a blacksmith's to a druggist's. Inside, the friendly, airy bar is cosier than the exterior suggests. Divided into two by a stub wall, it has comfortably cushioned burgundy wall banquettes looping around the alcoves, cream walls, Liberty-print curtains swagged up to their rails, pink-fringed wall lamps, a delft shelf with some china and books, country and botanical prints, attractively engraved old song title-pages and paintings by local artists. Well served reasonably priced bar food includes lunchtime sandwiches (from £1.60; toasties from £2.20) and ploughman's (from £3), as well as soup (£2), quiche (£4) and steak (£7.95). Well kept Bullringer, Courage Directors, Ruddles County, Websters Yorkshire, and a changing guest (probably only in summer) on handpump. It opens behind on to a decorous walk by the red sandstone church; no-smoking area in restaurant; quiet piped music. *(Recommended by D Hanley, Rita Horridge, Richard and Maria Gillespie, A G Roby, Graham Reeve, A E and P McCully; more reports please)*

Free house ~ Licensees Stuart and Brenda Copland ~ Real ale ~ Meals and snacks (roast lunch or ploughman's only on Sun) ~ No-smoking restaurant ~ (01584) 872174 ~ Children in eating area of bar and in restaurant ~ Open 11-11 ~ Bedrooms: £28B/£40B

Unicorn

Lower Corve St, off Shrewsbury Rd

In contrast this traditional 17th-c inn is built in a row of black-and-white houses along the banks of the River Corve. The single large beamed and partly panelled bar has a big stone fireplace and pleasant, friendly atmosphere. There's a timbered, candlelit restaurant (where they prefer you not to smoke). Consistently good bar food (you can also choose from the restaurant menu) is written up on a blackboard and might include sandwiches (from £1.50), home-made vegetable soup (£2.25), filled baked potatoes (from £2.50), prawns in garlic or mushrooms in stilton sauce (£3.50), home-made liver pâté (£2.95), ploughman's (£3.75), mushroom and broccoli bake, bacon or mushroom and cauliflower bake or home-cooked ham salad (£4.25), breaded plaice (£4.75), grilled trout (£5.95), salmon with cucumber and lemon sauce or steaks (from £7.50), pork with brandy and rosemary (£7.75), Cumberland duck (£10.50) and a good choice of around ten home-made puddings (with lots of traditional English ones) (all £2.50); there's a fairly interesting selection of vegetarian and even vegan dishes like Moroccan orange salad (£2.75) or mushroom stroganoff (£4.95). Well kept Bass and Worthington BB on handpump; maybe piped popular classical music. Beyond the car park is a terrace with tables sheltering pleasantly among willow trees by the modest river. *(Recommended by Bill and Beryl Farmer, Mary N Davies, Bob and Maggie Atherton; more reports please)*

Free house ~ Licensees Alan and Elisabeth Ditchburn ~ Real ale ~ Meals and snacks ~ Restaurant ~ (01584) 873555 ~ Well behaved children welcome ~ Pianist Sun evening ~ Open 12-3, 6-11 ~ Bedrooms: £18(£20B)/£36(£40B)

MUCH WENLOCK SJ6200 Map 4

George & Dragon

High St

Hanging from the beams of this bustling, friendly unpretentious town local is probably the biggest pub collection of water jugs – about a thousand – in England. The cosy atmospheric rooms are lined with a fantastic collection of old brewery and cigarette advertisements, bottle labels and beer trays and some George-and-the-Dragon pictures. There's a few antique settles as well as conventional furnishings, and a couple of attractive Victorian fireplaces (with coal-effect gas fires). At the back, the quieter snug old-fashioned rooms have black beams and timbering, little decorative plaster panels, tiled floors, a stained-glass smoke room sign, a big George-and-the-Dragon mural as well as lots of smaller pictures (painted by local artists), and a little stove in a fat fireplace. The good choice of above average and quite filling bar food includes stilton and walnut pâté (£2.95), prawns in lime and ginger (£3), home-baked ham with parsley sauce (particularly recommended by readers), Thai chicken or spinach pancakes (£4.85) and a very good steak and stout pie; home-made puddings like hot sticky toffee pudding, meringues with fudge sauce or home-made ginger ice cream (£2.25); evening meals are served in Eve's Kitchen. Well kept Hook Norton Best and perhaps guest beers on handpump; eccentric landlord and friendly staff; music from vintage wireless. It can get busy and smoky. *(Recommended by Mr and Mrs J Back, H K Dyson, J S Rutter, Nigel Woolliscroft, Basil Minson, Alan and Heather Jacques, Denzil T Taylor, Mike and Wendy Proctor, Joy Heatherley, Paul Noble)*

Free house ~ Licensee Eve Nolan ~ Real ale ~ Lunchtime meals and snacks (not Sun evening) ~ Evening restaurant (not Sun evening) ~ (01952) 727312 ~ Well behaved children in restaurant ~ Open 11-2.30, 6(12-2.30, 7-11 winter weekdays)-11

Talbot 🍽 🛏

High Street

Fronting on to the historic bustling high street, this civilised inn – originally part of Wenlock Abbey – has its entrance through an archway that opens on to an attractive sheltered courtyard garden with white seats and tables. Inside the charming 14th-c building are several neatly kept areas with lovely flowers, comfortable button-back wall banquettes around highly polished tables, low ceilings with exposed beams, and two fires (one in an inglenook). The walls are decorated with prints of the town and surrounding areas and beer barrel paraphernalia, while the unusual piped music is from the characterful landlord's own collection; he's rather an expert on old music-hall records and bands. Very good food is prepared from local produce and served with fresh vegetables. The attractively presented range includes sandwiches (from £1.95), soup, smoked salmon mousse or black pudding bramley (£2.25), filled baked potatoes (from £2.95), Greek salad (£3.45), country lentil crumble or omelettes (from £5.25), very tasty home made spicy pancake (£5.50), fresh poached salmon (£8.25), sirloin steak (£8.50) and at least two daily specials such as chicken breast stuffed with stilton and pear, lamb and apricot casserole or steak and kidney pie (£5.50); puddings like bread and butter pudding and fruit crumble (£2.25); four-course

Sunday roast lunch (£8.95) in the restaurant where smoking is not allowed. Well kept Ruddles Best and Websters Yorkshire on handpump, good value wines, at least eight malts, good coffee and tea; very friendly helpful staff. *(Recommended by Dave Braisted, E H and R F Warner, WAH, Mrs K Williams, Neil Tungate, Basil Minson, Sue Holland, Dave Webster, Mike and Wendy Proctor, Roy and Mary Roebuck, Cyril Burton, P M Lane, C S Bickley, Martin Aust, D T Deas)*

Free house ~ Licensee Tim Lathe ~ Real ale ~ Meals and snacks (till 9.30) ~ Restaurant ~ (01952) 727077 ~ Well behaved children allowed (no babies or prams) ~ Open 10.30-2.30, 6-11; closed 25 and 26 Dec ~ Bedrooms: £35B/£70B

NORTON SJ7200 Map 4

Hundred House 🍽 🛏

A442 Telford—Bridgnorth

The wonderful gardens here are brimming with herbs, old-fashioned roses and flowers that are cut and piled up in the bars or dried and set cascading from the high beams or used in the excellent carefully prepared food – there's even a bunch of herbs on every table. Although not cheap, meals are carefully prepared from fresh ingredients and are of a consistently high standard. The bar snack menu has soup (£2.50), chicken liver pâté (£2.95), smoked trout mousse with orange and walnut salad or ploughman's (from £3.95), sausage and mash (£4.95), fisherman's pie, lasagne or vegetarian savoury pancake (£6.50), steak and kidney pie, cassoulet of lamb or chicken chasseur (£6.95), sirloin steak (£9.95) very good three-course Sunday lunches (£10.95); usual children's menu (£3.75). If the restaurant – which has a more elaborate menu – is very busy on a Saturday night, they may well stop doing bar meals. There's a spacious feel to this artfully refurbished civilised old place. The spotless bar is cleverly divided into several areas with old quarry tiles at either end, and modern hexagonal ones in the main central part. Steps lead up past a little balustrade to a partly panelled eating area with mellow old brickwork. Handsome fireplaces, one of which has a great Jacobean arch, have log fires or woodburners and are hung with fine old black cooking pots. Around sewing-machine tables are a variety of interesting chairs and settles with some long colourful patchwork leather cushions. Well kept Brains Mild, Flowers Original and guest ales on handpump, with Heritage (light and refreshing, not too bitter) and the stronger Ailrics Old Ale brewed for them by a small brewery; 30 wines, with an emphasis on English wine. Shove-ha'penny, dominoes, cribbage, darts and piped music; no dogs. The Victorian-style gents' has a blackboard for graffiti. *(Recommended by D Jones, M M Williams, M Handley, Frank Cummins, George Atkinson, G L Tong, the Monday Club, WHBM, Paul Cartledge, Chris Vallely, J Weeks, Julie Peters, Mr and Mrs P F Meadows, Nigel Hopkins)*

Free house ~ Licensees Henry, Sylvia and David Phillips ~ Real ale ~ Meals and snacks (12-2.30; 7-9.45) ~ Restaurant ~ (0195) 71353 ~ Children welcome ~ Open 11-3 , 6-11 ~ Bedrooms: £59B/£69B

PULVERBATCH SJ4202 Map 6

White Horse

From A49 at N end of Dorrington follow Pulverbatch/Church Pulverbatch signposts, and turn left at eventual T-junction (which is sometimes signposted Church Pulverbatch); OS Sheet 126 map reference 424023

Plenty of regulars crowd into the atmospheric bar at this cosy and character-filled inn, but there's a very warm welcome for strangers too. The several rambling areas (entry is from the back of the pub) have black beams and heavy timbering, as well as unusual fabric-covered high-backed settles and brocaded banquettes on its turkey carpet, sturdy elm or cast-iron-framed tables, and an open coalburning range with gleaming copper kettles. A collection of antique insurance plaques, big brass sets of scales, willow-pattern plates, and pewter mugs hang over the serving counter, and there's a good Thorburn print of a grouse among the other country pictures. The quarry-tiled front loggia with its sturdy old green leatherette seat is a nice touch. The very good value satisfying food in carefully cooked, huge helpings includes sandwiches (from £1.50), very popular hot roast beef with melted cheese on french bread (£2), tasty soup (from £1.10), filled baked potatoes (from £1.95), macaroni cheese (£2.95), burgers (from £3.10), ploughman's (from £3.25), lasagne (£3.95), tuna and mushroom casserole (£4.75), curries (from £4.95), scotch trout (£5.95), steak (from £6.75); home-made puddings such as apple pie (£1.85), pecan and treacle pie, a huge number of ice creams (from £1.25) and some wonderful ice cream sundaes (from £2.50); children's dishes (from £1.35). Well kept Boddingtons, Flowers Original, and Wadworths 6X on handpump, several decent wines by the glass, and over a hundred malt whiskies. Darts, juke box, pool and fruit machine; friendly efficient service. *(Recommended by C A Hall, the Monday Club, A P Jeffreys, Basil Minson, Dave Braisted; more reports please)*

Whitbreads ~ Lease: James MacGregor ~ Real ale ~ Meals and snacks (till 10pm) ~ (01743) 718247 ~ Children welcome ~ Open 11.30-3, 7-11 (closed 25 Dec)

UPPER FARMCOTE SO7792 Map 4

Lion of Morfe £
Follow Claverley 2½ signpost off A458 Bridgnorth—Stourbridge

Popular with strongly accented locals, the traditional core of this unpretentious and friendly tucked-away pub is the interesting public bar on the right which has wood-backed wall seats on red tiles, a game trophy over the coal fire with its big black kitchen range and a framed history of the place since the mid 19th c. In sharp contrast is the comfortable brown-carpeted lounge bar, which is altogether smarter with its pink plush button-back built-in wall banquettes in curving bays, and a good log fire. This room opens into the more modern no-smoking conservatory (decorated this year), which has comfortable cushioned cane chairs around glass tables on the red-tiled floor. There's a large pleasant garden, with picnic-table sets under cocktail parasols on a terrace, and a lawn spreading out into an orchard with a floodlit boules piste. Simple but well prepared, cheerfully served, very reasonably priced food might include a lunchtime choice of sandwiches (from £1.45), filled baked potatoes (£1.65), ploughman's (£2.60), salads (from £3.15), home-cooked hot dishes such as steak and kidney pie, cottage pie or chicken and mushroom in savoury sauce with breadcrumbs (£2.95), a vegetarian dish (£3.15), chicken curry with mango chutney (£3.25), and puddings (from £1.35) and a daily special on the blackboard. The evening menu is all from the changing blackboard and might include lasagne (£3.95), breaded sole (£4.95), gammon steak and egg (£5.75) and steaks (from £6.50). Well kept, very cheap Banks's Bitter and Mild on electric pump as is usual for these beers and Bass and a guest like Ruddles County, Stones or Wadworths 6X on handpump; carpeted pool room, dominoes, fruit machine on the public side; friendly service. *(Recommended by the Monday Club, Roger Taylor, Frank Cummins, Basil Minson, Pete Yearsley, DAV; more reports please)*

Free house ~ Licensees Bill and Dinah Evans ~ Real ale ~ Meals and snacks (not Fri, Sat evening or Sun) ~ (01746) 710678 ~ Children in eating area of bar and conservatory ~ live music Sat monthly and jazz second Thurs in the month ~ Open 11.30-2.30(4 Sat), 7-11

WENLOCK EDGE SO5796 Map 4

Wenlock Edge Inn ★ 🍴 🛏
Hilltop; B4371 Much Wenlock—Church Stretton, OS Sheet 137 map reference 570962
Shropshire Dining Pub of the Year

The delightful atmosphere and incredibly welcoming Waring family (they've now been joined by Jonathan) continue to mark this green-shuttered stone building as one of the friendliest pubs that many of our readers have ever visited. You're bound to be drawn into the cheerfully ceaseless banter and chat that goes on between the licensee – our landlord of the year in 1994 – and his friendly regulars. It's probably cosiest on story-telling night when the right-hand bar is packed with 'Tales at the Edge', an enthusiastic local group swapping tales. There's a big woodburning stove in an inglenook in here, as well as a shelf of high plates, and it leads into a little no-smoking dining room. The room on the left has pews that came from a Methodist chapel in Liverpool, a fine oak bar counter, and an open fire. It can get very busy and you will probably need to get there early to try the consistently excellent fresh home-made bar food which includes soups like tomato and sweet pepper, mushroom or celery and apple (£2.10), garlic mushrooms with cream and sherry (from £2.90), minced roast pork and apple pie, home-baked ham or steak and mushroom pie (£5.20), beef and venison pie, Elizabethan pork casserole or smoked chicken breast and broccoli gratin (£6.50); good old-fashioned puddings like wonderful lemon pudding, fruit crumbles or treacle tart (£2.10); no chips; excellent breakfasts for residents (try the sausage). Well kept ales like Hobsons, Websters Yorkshire and Woods Special on handpump, interesting whiskies (usually about twenty Scottish malts), decent wines by both glass and bottle, and no music – unless you count the deep-throated chimes of Big Bertha the fusee clock (or the serenading landlord). This is also a very popular place to stay, and your shower will be in mineral water from the pub's own 119-foot well. There are some tables on a front terrace and the side grass. The building is in a fine position just by the Ippikins Rock viewpoint, and there are lots of walks through the National Trust land that runs along the Edge. *(Recommended by David Eberlin, Brian Horner, Brenda Arthur, R M Bloomfield, TOH, M G Hart, John Greenwood, Gordon Mott, Dr Richard Fry, Martin Aust, C A Brace, Roy Smylie, BKA, M Cox, Andrew Stephenson, Diane Tailby, Bob and Maggie Atherton, Chris Vallely, Pat and John Millward, Dave Braisted, Roberta O'Neill, R and S Bentley, John and Beryl Knight, A G Roby, Mr and Mrs B Hobden, R J Walden, Paul and Margaret Baker, Graham Reeve, Basil Minson, R C Smail, Dick Brown, H O Dickinson, Lynn Sharpless, Bob Eardley, Dave Webster, Sue Holland, Mr and Mrs D Tapper, Paul McPherson, Mrs D Jones, Susan Holmes, R J Walden, DAV, Maureen and Keith Gimson, Wayne Brindle; also recommended by The Good Hotel Guide)*

Free house ~ Licensee Stephen Waring ~ Real ale ~ Meals (not Mon except Bank holidays) ~ Restaurant ~ (0174 636) 403 ~ Children in restaurant (not under 10 if after 8pm Sat) ~ Local story-telling club, second Mon each month 8.30pm ~ Open 11.30-2.30, 6(6.30 winter)-11; closed Mon lunchtime exc bank holidays; closed 24 and 25 Dec ~ bedrooms: £38S/£55S

WHITCHURCH SJ5345 Map 7

Willey Moor Lock

Pub signposted off A49 just under 2 miles N of Whitchurch; in fact this puts the pub itself just inside the Cheshire border

You have to cross a little footbridge over the Llangollen Canal and its rushing sidestream to get to this prettily placed family run lock keeper's cottage with its wonderful views of colourful narrowboats from white tables under cocktail parasols on the terrace and beer garden. Inside several neatly decorated carpeted rooms with low ceilings house the landlady's extensive and much talked-about collection of teapots. There's also a decorative longcase clock, a shelf of toby jugs, brick-based brocaded wall seats, stools and small chairs around dimpled copper and other tables, and two winter log fires. Bar food includes sandwiches, cheese and onion pasty or steak and kidney pie (£3.50), plaice or scampi (£4.30), home-made steak and kidney pie or lasagne (£4.80), salads (from £5), gammon steak or mixed grill (£6.50), steaks (from £6.75), several vegetarian dishes like vegetable chilli or vegetable stroganoff (£3.95); usual children's menu (from £2); puddings (from £1.50); well kept Theakstons Best and two guest beers like Batemans XXXB, Bushys Old Bush Tail, Butterknowle Conciliation and Black Diamond and Wadworths 6X on handpump; large selection of malt whiskies and liqueur coffees; fruit machine, piped music, and several dogs and cats. There's a children's play area with swings, slides and climbing frame. It's on the sandstone trail, a walk covering Cheshire. *(Recommended by Mr and Mrs Jones, Mr and Mrs R J Phillips, Martin Aust, Colin Davies, Kate and Robert Hodkinson, J and P Maloney, Mrs R Gregory; more reports please)*

Free house ~ Licensee Mrs Elsie Gilkes ~ Real ale ~ Meals and snacks 12-2, 6(6.30 winter)-9 ~ (01948) 663274 ~ Children in eating area of bar and in restaurant ~ Open 12-2.30, 6-11 (12-2,6.30-11 in winter)

WISTANSTOW SO4385 Map 6

Plough 🍴 ♀ 🍺

Village signposted off A49 and A489 N of Craven Arms

Apart from the really friendly licensees this isn't necessarily what you'd expect of a pub in a Shropshire village – it's modern, spacious, simple and brightly lit with lots of tables and chairs under the high rafters, but it's very well worth knowing for the tasty Woods Special, and the stong Wonderful, that are brewed in the separate older building next door. They also have a weekly changing guest. Equally good, and not as simple as the surroundings might suggest, is the popular well-priced lunchtime bar food which includes sandwiches, pâtés, baked mushrooms filled with stilton and leeks, green shell mussels in wine and cream (£4.20), tagliatelle with prawns and mushrooms in cream and garlic (£4.50) and local venison in red wine (£4.95) and lots more in the evening like loin of pork with a honey, orange and ginger sauce (£6.95), duck breast with fresh plum sauce (£7.20), scampi provençale (£7.50), fillet steak stuffed with stilton and wrapped in smoked bacon and four or five fish dishes like seabass baked in wine, cream and herbs (£9.50); all served with fresh vegetables, lots of genuinely home-made puddings, such as bread and butter pudding or chocolate and rum torte. They keep two farm ciders, there's a fine display cabinet of bottled beers and a remarkably wide choice of wines by the glass. The games area has darts, dominoes, pool, fruit machine, video games and juke box; maybe piped music; very friendly service. Outside there are some tables under cocktail parasols. *(Recommended by R and S Bentley, Jenny and Brian Seller, Pat and John Millward, K Baxter, A G Roby, Andrew Stephenson, R M Bloomfield, Basil Minson, Paul McPherson, L S Pay, A E and P McCully, M G Hart)*

Own brew ~ Tenant Robert West ~ Real ale ~ Meals and snacks (not Mon lunchtime exc bank holidays, or Sun night) ~ (01588) 673251 ~ Children in eating area of bar and games room; food served to under eights at lunchtime only ~ Open 12-2.30, 7-11; closed Mon lunch except bank holidays

---

Lucky Dip

Besides the fully inspected pubs, you might like to try these Lucky Dips recommended to us and described by readers (if you do, please send us reports):

☆ **All Stretton** [SO4695], *Yew Tree*: Quickly served good bar food in comfortable beamed bars with helpful service, well kept Bass and Worthington BB, quiet piped music, restaurant; children welcome; lovely walks on Long Mynd nearby *(M Watson, A G Roby)*

Astley [A53 Shrewsbury—Shawbury; SJ5319], *Dog in the Lane*: Reasonably priced good straightforward food and Wem (Allied) ales in beamed lounge with copper etchings; tables outside *(Dave Braisted, David Hanley)*

☆ **Bridgnorth** [stn; A458 towards Stourbridge; SO7293], *Railwaymans Arms*: Authentic re-creation of 1940s-style station bar nicely placed in Severn Valley steam railway terminus, busy and atmospheric on summer days, quiet evenings; four or five well kept changing Black Country and other interesting ales, simple summer snacks, coal fire, railway memorabilia inc lots of signs, superb mirror over fireplace, seats out on platform; children welcome; car-parking fee refundable against train ticket or what you spend here *(B M Eldridge, Nick and Alison Dowson, Pete Yearsley, Graham Reeve, Nigel Woolliscroft, LYM)*

☆ **Bridgnorth** [Northgate], *Bear*: Good food (not Sun) inc fresh beautifully served lunchtime specials and home-made puddings in friendly and relaxed town pub with Courage-related and changing guest real ales; Thurs gourmet dinners (booking needed), tables in sheltered enclosed garden *(Andrew Kerr, J C Joynson)*

Bridgnorth [St Johns St], *Falcon*: Good pubby atmosphere in big beamed hotel lounge bar with open fire, display of spirits miniatures, good food, well kept Bass *(A P Jeffreys)*; [Whitburn St], *Kings Head*: Old timbered pub with good value food *(Pete Yearsley)*; [High St], *Swan*: Pleasant old half-timbered town pub in middle of town, well kept unusual beers such as Batemans Salem Porter, pleasant service *(George Atkinson)*

nr **Bridgnorth** [old Ludlow Rd – B4364, 3 miles out], *Down*: Stonebuilt pub overlooking rolling countryside, very smart and clean, imaginative home-cooked food, super service *(Paul and Maggie Baker)*;
nr **Bridgnorth** [B4364, closer in], *Punch Bowl*: Decent generous food inc very wide vegetarian choice in unpretentious beamed and panelled 17th-c country pub, good range of real ales, superb views *(Peter and Jenny Quine)*

☆ **Brockton** [B4378 SW of Much Wenlock; SO5894], *Feathers*: Welcoming little upmarket country dining pub with good well presented interesting food inc children's dishes; good no-smoking area, well kept real ales; huge set of bellows from local smithy as one table, pretty little covered back terrace *(Dave Webster, Sue Holland, LYM)*

Bucknell [Chapel Lawn Rd; SO3574], *Baron of Beef*: Pleasant lounge with big open fire, lots of bits and pieces; welcoming service, good bar food inc some interesting and vegetarian dishes, largish upstairs restaurant with own bar, popular carvery Fri/Sat evening and Sun lunch, well kept beer inc guest such as Fullers London Pride, decent house wines *(Basil Minson)*

☆ **Burwarton** [B4364 Bridgnorth—Ludlow; SO6285], *Boyne Arms*: Pleasant and friendly no-nonsense Georgian country pub doing well under new landlady, generous reasonably priced home-made food, popular evenings; changing well kept real ales such as Bass, Ind Coope Burton and Woods; tables in garden; bedrooms *(J C Joynson, C S Bickley)*

Chelmarsh [SO7288], *Bulls Head*: Good bar food, well kept beer, very friendly helpful staff; bedrooms very pretty; lovely views *(G E Stait)*; *Kings Arms*: Lovely view over reservoir from cosy bar with old scullery off; good value food inc Sun lunch in lounge and little dining room, attentive welcoming owners *(Mr and Mrs H S Hill)*

☆ **Claverley** [High St; off A454 Wolverhampton—Bridgnorth; SO7993], *Crown*: Very picturesque pub in lovely village, interesting old-fashioned heavy-beamed bar, really friendly service, good competitively priced home-made food (not Sun-Weds evenings) cooked just as you ask, well kept Banks's, open fires, splendid family garden; dogs allowed, long Sat opening; children allowed in eating area *(Steve Bryant, LYM)*

Claverley, *Plough*: Busy, with genial and efficient service, good range of Allied beers, good simple bar food; separate bistro in converted outbuilding *(the Monday Club, Pete Yearsley)*

Cleehill [A4117; SO5975], *Royal Oak*: Friendly, with good value plain bar food, real ales such as Marstons Pedigree, Theakstons and Worthington; good view from the front *(Dave Braisted)*

☆ **Clun** [High St; SO3081], *Sun*: Friendly and individual pub in lovely village, Tudor timbers and beams, some sturdy antique furnishings; enormous open fire in flagstoned public bar, well kept real ales inc Banks's Bitter and Mild, Marstons Pedigree, Woods Special and several changing guest beers; children allowed in eating area; tables on sheltered back terrace; bedrooms simple but comfortable, with good breakfast *(Dave Irving, Bernard Phillips, David and Donna Burnett, Janet Pickles, Catherine Haynes, Steve Wheldon, LYM)*

☆ **Clun** [Market Sq], *White Horse*: Cosy, welcoming and neatly kept beamed L-shaped bar with inglenook and woodburner, well kept Bass, Woods and Worthington on handpump, decent straightforward bar food inc vegetarian, friendly efficient service; children welcome; tables in back garden; bedrooms *(Margaret Horner, Catherine Haynes, Steve Wheldon, Michael Hinkley)*

☆ **Coalport** [Salthouse Rd, Jackfield; nr Mawes Craft Centre, over footbridge by chinaworks museum – OS Sheet 127 map reference 693025; SJ6902], *Boat*: Simple cosy waterside pub in lovely quiet part of Severn Gorge, basic with some character, coal fire in lovely range, food inc very cheap roast meat baps and good value Sun lunch, Banks's ales inc excellently kept Mild, welcoming service, darts; summer barbecues on tree-shaded lawn *(Basil Minson, Roger and Judy Tame, BB)*

Corfton [B4368 Much Wenlock—Craven Arms; SO4985], *Sun*: Well kept ales Whitbreads-related ales and good value simple home cooking inc good veg, children's dishes and bargain Sun lunch, pleasant lounge bar, lively and cheery locals' bar, restaurant; tables on terrace and in good-sized garden with good play area; piped music *(Mr and Mrs D E P Hughes, BB)*

Cross Houses [A458 Shrewsbury—Bridgnorth; SJ5407], *Fox*: Long single room with good value straightforward food, well kept Burtonwood, friendly staff *(Dave Braisted)*

☆ **Ellesmere** [Scotland St; SJ4035], *Black Lion*: Marstons pub, reopened after refurbishment by the Louises, who ran the Queens Head at Tirril up in Cumbria as a popular main entry; should be one to watch, with good food and a very warm welcome *(Anon)*

Ellesmere [Birch Rd], *White Hart*: Ancient black and white pub, small and attractive, perhaps the oldest in Shrops, reopened under friendly new landlord; well kept Marstons ales, a few mins' walk from canal *(A D Marsh)*

Gledrid [A5 S of Chirk; SJ2937], *New Inn*: Good reasonably priced food, welcoming service *(A D Marsh)*

Goldstone [Goldstone Wharf; off A529 S of Mkt Drayton, at Hinstock; SJ7128], *Wharf*: Very pleasant gardens by Shropshire Union Canal, hot food, cold buffet, well kept beer; children welcome *(Nigel Woolliscroft)*

☆ **Hampton Loade** [SO7586], *Lion*: Fine old inn tucked away at end of road that's not much more than a rough track for the last ¼ mile, exposed stonework, lots of country wines, good interesting food such as duck in birchbark wine, good friendly service *(George Atkinson)*

☆ **Harley** [A458 NW of Much Wenlock; SJ5901], *Plume of Feathers*: Very cheerful efficient staff in friendly and comfortable beamed pub with big open fire, good reasonably priced bar food, well kept Courage-related and guest ales, darts; spacious dining room, tables outside; bedrooms with own baths *(F M Bunbury, Graham Reeve, David Hanley, Wayne Brindle)*

☆ **Hinstock** [just off A41 9 miles N of Newport; SJ6926], *Falcon*: Consistently good value food inc very popular cheap Sun lunch, good service, well kept beer, decent wines and malt whiskies, friendly atmosphere *(Basil Minson, R Ward)*

☆ **Hodnet** [SJ6128], *Bear*: Comfortable and civilised 16th-c beamed bar, spacious and welcoming, good range of reasonably priced food inc imaginative dishes, well kept Courage-related real ale, good service; attractive furnishings, giant framed jigsaw puzzles; restaurant with small no-smoking area and corner alcove with glass-tile floor over unusual sunken garden in former bear pit; opp Hodnet Hall gardens; four bedrooms, not big but comfortable and warm *(Julie Peters, R M Bloomfield, Jason Caulkin, John and Joan Holton, Mrs S Kellaway)*

Hope [A488 Shrewsbury—Bishops Castle, 2 or 3 miles S of village; SO3298], *More Arms*: Typical unspoilt country pub with good open fire, simple food from tasty burgers to steaks inc good value ploughman's; handy stop on interesting circular walk from Stiperstones car park *(Jenny and Brian Seller)*

☆ **Ironbridge** [Blists Hill Open Air Museum – follow brown museum sign from M54 exit 4, or A442; SJ6703], *New Inn*: Part of this good heritage museum, recreated working Victorian community (shares its opening hours); rebuilt Victorian pub run just as it might have been then, friendly staff in period dress, well kept Banks's ales, pewter measure of mother's ruin for 2½ d (money from nearby bank), gas lighting, traditional games, upstairs tearoom; back yard with hens, pigeon coop, maybe children in costume playing hopscotch and skipping; children welcome *(WHBM, A E and P McCully, George Atkinson, WAH, LYM)*

Ironbridge [Wesley Rd, off Madeley Hill – OS Sheet 127 map reference 678035], *Golden Ball*: Friendly local with interesting range of reasonably priced food, pleasant terraced walk down to river *(Mike and Wendy Proctor)*; [off Madeley rd], *Horse & Jockey*: Very good food inc good steak and kidney pie, duck and vegetarian dishes; Bass and Morlands *(Mike and Wendy Proctor, Dave Braisted)*; [Buildwas Rd], *Meadow*: Interesting good value home-cooked food, pleasant atmosphere; garden running down to Severn *(John Hughes, DH)*; *Olde Robin Hood*: Friendly pub by river bridge, good value standard food inc rolls and

sandwiches, interesting ornaments; handy for museums complex *(George Atkinson, Phil and Heidi Cook)*

Kinlet [B4363 Bridgnorth—Cleobury Mortimer; SO7280], *Eagle & Serpent*: Basic Banks's pub with surprisingly good value for money food in recently refurbished dining room *(C S Bickley)*

Knockin [Main St; SJ3422], *Bradford Arms*: Popular and busy, doing well under friendly newish owners, with good fresh food in relaxing not overdecorated bar *(Robert W Buckle)*

☆ **Leebotwood** [A49 Church Stretton—Shrewsbury; SO4898], *Pound*: Generous good value food in comfortable beamed bar and restaurant of attractive thatched roadside pub, pleasant atmosphere, friendly staff *(Mr and Mrs S Sugarman, D Hanley)*

☆ **Linley** [pub signed off B4373 N of Bridgnorth; SO6998], *Pheasant*: Unspoilt and relaxed country local in lovely spot, good honest food (not Sun if busy) maybe using their own free-range eggs, attractive prices, interesting choice of real ales; individual landlord *(Gerard Paris, Wayne Brindle, LYM)*

☆ **Little Stretton** [Ludlow Rd; village well signposted off A49; SO4392], *Green Dragon*: Neat and civilised dining pub quietly popular esp with older people at lunchtime for reasonably priced straightforward food, pleasant service; well kept Tetleys, Wadworths 6X, Woods and a guest such as Shepherd Neame Spitfire, decent wines and malt whiskies, children in eating area and restaurant; tables in prettily planted garden, handy for Long Mynd walks *(Miss R M Tudor, BKA, Brian Horner, Brenda Arthur, DAV, DC, Nigel Woolliscroft, LYM)*

☆ **Little Stretton** [Ludlow Rd], *Ragleth*: Comfortably worn-in bay-windowed lounge, huge inglenook in brick-and-tile-floored public bar, reasonably priced home-made standard food from sandwiches to steaks, quick service, well kept Ansells Mild and Best, Marstons Pedigree, Woods Parish and guest beers, tables on lawn by tulip tree; children welcome, restaurant *(Nigel Woolliscroft, Andrew and Barbara Sykes, LYM)*

Longdon upon Tern [SJ6215], *Tayleur Arms*: Greenalls Millers Kitchen family dining pub, decent bar food, very big lounge with children's area, jungle barn outside; piped music *(D Hanley)*

Loppington [B4397; SJ4729], *Dickin Arms*: Heavily beamed cosy pub with good atmosphere in bar, lounge and dining room, open fire, Bass, Wadworths and Youngers beers, good bar food inc good value Sun lunch *(David Hanley)*

☆ **Ludlow** [Broadgate/Lower Bridge St – bottom of Broad St; SO5175], *Wheatsheaf*: Nicely furnished traditional 17th c pub spectacularly built into medieval town gate; wide range of good value reliable food, well kept Bass, M&B and Ruddles County, choice of farm ciders, friendly owners, restaurant; attractive beamed bedrooms, warm and comfortable *(E W Lewcock)*

☆ Ludlow [Bull Ring/Corve St], *Feathers*: Hotel famous for glorious timbered façade, striking inside with Jacobean panelling and carving, period furnishings (for the decent bar food or a casual drink you may be diverted to a humbler side bar); efficient pleasant service, well kept Flowers Original and Wadworths 6X, restaurant, comfortable bedrooms; not cheap *(Lawrence Pearse, D Hanley, LYM)*

Ludlow [Ludford Bridge], *Carlton Arms*: Comfortable and friendly, well kept beers; bedrooms clean *(Michael Witte)*; [King St], *Olde Bull Ring*: Another striking timbered building; Allied ales, good food in bar and restaurant, pleasant friendly service *(Mrs P J Pearce, D Hanley)*

☆ Munslow [B4368 Much Wenlock—Craven Arms; SO5287], *Crown*: Generous helpings of good value home-made food with al dente veg and unusual dishes in traditional old country local, mix of furnishings in warm and friendly beamed lounge with flagstones, stripped stone, good open fire and friendly dog; small snug, games room; reasonably priced Bass, Marstons Mild and Wadworths 6X; children welcome; open all day summer *(Mr and Mrs J L Hall, Wayne Brindle, Sue Dean)*

Myddle [A528 7 miles N of Shrewsbury – OS Sheet 126 map reference 468239; SJ4724], *Red Lion*: Comfortable old-fashioned pub with cosy coal fire in winter, friendly staff and consistently good food cooked by welcoming licensee *(R M Tudor)*

☆ Nessscliffe [A5 Shrewsbury—Oswestry; SJ3819], *Old Three Pigeons*: Nice interior behind plain exterior, very popular – get there early for a seat, maybe book evenings; good choice of well cooked generous food esp fresh fish dishes, very friendly staff, Whitbreads-related ales, coffee all day, log fires, restaurant; opp Kynaston Cave, good cliff walks *(David Warrellow, Jason Caulkin, D Hanley, I A Wadman)*

☆ Newcastle [B4368 Clun—Newtown; SO2582], *Crown*: Good value usual bar food in quite spacious lounge bar with log fire and piped music, locals' bar with darts, pool and so forth in games room, well kept Bass and Worthington BB, decent wines, normally a good friendly welcome, friendly Great Dane called Bruno; tables outside; good reasonably priced bedrooms, attractive countryside *(RM, John Trenchard, Nigel Woolliscroft, LYM)*

☆ Newport [Chetwynd End (A41 N); SJ7519], *Bridge*: Good service, tasty reasonably priced simple home-cooked food and well kept Bass in small, cosy and friendly 17th-c black and white local with small separate restaurant; reasonably priced bedrooms *(A D Marsh)*

☆ Northwood [SJ4634], *Horse & Jockey*: Low oak-beamed pub with lots of horse and jockey memorabilia, good friendly service, good range of decent reasonably priced food, very well kept beer; children's play area *(Myke and Nicky Crombleholme, A Wilson)*

Oswestry [Cross St; SJ2929], *Fox*: Ancient

black and white timbered façade, little local entrance bar down a step, attractive low-beamed and panelled main room with dark oak furniture, well kept Marstons Pedigree, good plain decor, fox theme, open fire *(C Roberts, Roger Berry)*; *Wynnstay*: Friendly welcome, well kept beer, good food, very spacious and comfortable bar; nice bedrooms – a comfortable respite from Offa's Dyke Path *(N H and B Ellis)*

Picklescott [SO4399], *Bottle & Glass*: Typical country pub, pleasant bar with open fire, good range of food and beer *(D E P and I D Hughes)*

☆ Pipe Gate [A51 Nantwich—Stone; SJ7441], *Chetwode Arms*: Wide choice of good food in friendly and comfortably refurbished family pub, attractively priced good carvery restaurant with no-smoking area, pleasant efficient staff, Ansells ales with interesting guests such as Aston Manor and Gunpowder Mild, open fire; children's play area *(D Hanley)*

Quatford [A442 Kidderminster—Bridgnorth, a bit N of Shatterford; SO7491], *Danery*: Busy, with several rooms off central bar, open fires, good reasonably priced varied food, courteous pleasant landlord, Stones and Bass on handpump *(F M Bunbury)*

Ryton [SJ7603], *Fox*: Smart rural pub with good views, lots of interesting pictures, friendly landlord, wide range of food *(R M Bloomfield)*

☆ Shifnal [High St; SJ7508], *White Hart*: Good range of well kept ales inc several interesting changing guest beers in comfortable old-fashioned half-timbered pub in pretty village, good promptly served standard food inc fresh veg; very reasonable prices, very welcoming staff *(Bob Alton, A E and P McCully, W L G Watkins)*

Shifnal [Church St], *Old Bell*: Food inc very good value Sun lunch with wide choice *(Ann Griffiths)*

☆ Shrewsbury [New St/Quarry Park; leaving centre via Welsh Bridge/A488 turn into Port Hill Rd], *Boat House*: Half a dozen interesting changing real ales, good choice of lunchtime food, filled baguettes all day, in comfortably modernised pub by the Severn, river views from long lounge bar, tables out on sheltered terrace and rose lawn; friendly staff, children welcome, summer barbecues *(Alan Castle, LYM)*

Shrewsbury [Castle Gates], *Bulls Head*: Open all day, with Banks's beers, lunchtime food (not Sun); well decorated with pictures and books; no parking nr this or other central pubs *(D Hanley)*; [centre], *Butcher Row*: Bass, Boddingtons and M&B Brew XI in two-bar pub, some exposed brickwork, good bar food, darts and fruit machine, tables outside *(D Hanley)*; [16 Castle Gates, nr stn], *Castle Vaults*: Eight changing real ales inc a foreign one, with good choice of wines and other drinks, in friendly black and white pub with good landlord, unusual if worn decor; generous helpings of good food in adjoining Mexican restaurant, little roof garden with spiral staircase up towards castle; bedrooms good *(Richard Lewis, K Harvey, Ian Phillips)*; [Swan Hill/Cross Hill, nr old Square], *Coach & Horses*: Award-winning flower boxes outside, pine-panelled snug, pleasant bar and restaurant with carvery, well kept Bass and two rotating guest beers, good home-made food, attentive service *(R M Bloomfield, D Hanley)*; [48 St Michaels St (A49 ½ mile N of stn)], *Dolphin*: Five different weekly changing beers kept well; can be smoky, but interesting *(K Harvey)*; [Abbey Foregate], *Dun Cow Pie Shop*: Another addition to the Little pubs, eccentric inside with cheery food and Allied and Lumphammer ales; the big cow effigy on the porch has been there for over a century *(Patrick and Mary McDermott, Dave Braisted)*; [Bellstone], *Exchange*: Big split-level Greenalls pub in centre, good cheap lunchtime food, popular with young people evenings; closed Sun lunchtime *(D Hanley)*; [Church St], *Loggerheads*: Four rooms, one filled by old scrubbed wooden table; bar food, good atmosphere, Rugby football associations *(D Hanley)*; [Milk St, nr St Julians Craft Centre], *Old Post Office*: Marstons beers inc Owd Roger in big split-level bar/lounge, plenty of bric-a-brac and brassware, bar food; piped music *(D Hanley)*; [Mardol], *Pig & Truffle*: Interesting woodwork, lots of pig pictures, spacious atmosphere, well kept Marstons Best and Tetleys, interesting choice of good value food from sandwiches to steak inc outstanding potato soup, welcoming staff *(D Deas, DAV)*; [Fish St], *Three Fishes*: Recently refurbished with heavy beams and timbers, part stone floor; varied home-cooked bar food inc Sun lunches, several Whitbreads-related and enterprising guest beers, friendly welcome; open all day *(D Hanley, Neil Calver)*

☆ **Stiperstones** [village signed off A488 S of Minsterley – OS Sheet 126 map reference 364005; SO3697], *Stiperstones*: Open all day, with good simple food at attractive prices all day inc vegetarian; welcoming little modernised lounge bar with comfortable leatherette wall banquettes, lots of brassware on ply-panelled walls, well kept Woods Parish, pleasant service, darts in plainer public bar, restaurant, tables outside; good walking nearby; maybe pop music but not too loud *(Frank Cummins, BB)*

Telford [Long Lane (A442); SJ6710], *Bucks Head*: Smartly furnished hotel bar with well kept Davenports, good quick food inc good value Sun lunch and children's dishes in bar, family eating area and restaurant; piped music *(Phil and Heidi Cook, David Hanley)*

☆ **Tong** [A41 towards Newport, just beyond village; SJ7907], *Bell*: Friendly and efficient Milestone Tavern dining pub, popular weekday lunchtimes with older people, in attractive countryside nr Weston Park; good choice of reasonably priced food inc children's dishes and good value Sun lunch, well kept Banks's and Marstons Pedigree,

olde-worlde stripped brickwork, big family room, dining room, pleasant back conservatory, big garden; unobtrusive piped music, no dogs *(Mr and Mrs D T Deas, Michael and Margaret Norris, R M Bloomfield, M Joyner, the Monday Club, Jean and Douglas Troup)*

Trench [Trench Rd; SJ6913], *Duke*: Greenalls pub with big split-level lounge, big bar with pinball, pool, darts and piped music; bar food inc Sun lunches *(D Hanley)*

Uckington [B5061; SJ5810], *Horseshoes*: Decent spacious Brewers Fayre dining pub with Whitbreads-related beers, reasonable food, children's eating area and play area *(David Hanley)*

☆ **Upton Magna** [Pelham Rd; SJ5512], *Corbet Arms*: Good value cheap food and well kept Banks's ales in big L-shaped lounge bar with armchairs by log fire; darts and juke box in smaller public bar, friendly staff; handy for Attingham Park (NT), busy at weekends *(J and P Maloney)*

Wentnor [SO3893], *Crown*: Popular 16th-c dining pub (all tables may be reserved) with clean and attractive bar and cosy and pleasant restaurant; friendly dog, tables outside; four good bedrooms, fine views, caravan and camp site *(A Barker, David and Donna Burnett)*

Weston under Redcastle [off A49 N of Shrewsbury; SJ5729], *Hawkstone Park*: Good range of beers, tasty reasonably priced food; nr fascinating walks through wooded parkland; bedrooms *(Brenda and Derrick Swift)*

☆ **Whitchurch** [St Marys St; SJ5341], *Old Town Hall Vaults*: Attractive and civilised small 18th-c town pub, good reasonably priced home-cooked food, well kept Marstons Border Mild and Pedigree, cheerful quick service; piped light classics – birthplace of Sir Edward German *(Roger Reeves)*

Whittington [A495 Ellesmere rd, just off A5; SJ3331], *Olde Boot*: Comfortable pub attractively placed by 13th-c castle; good value food; bedrooms *(W L G Watkins)*

Whixall [Platt Lane; SJ5236], *Waggoners*: Young enthusiastic management, well kept beers, enterprising range of good food inc dishes served on sizzling platters; an easy walk from Llangollen Canal *(A D Marsh)*

Wollerton [A53 Shrewsbury—Mkt Drayton; SJ6230], *Squirrel*: Panelled bar, lounge, two open fires, Ansells and guest beers, good food, tables outside; restaurant *(David Hanley)*

☆ **Woore** [London Rd (A51); SJ7342], *Falcon*: Very wide choice of food, esp French, oriental and seafood, all using fresh produce, generous and well presented, in plain roadside building with good friendly service even when busy, well kept Marstons, interesting prints; nr Bridgemere garden centre *(Paul and Gail Betteley, Mr and Mrs D T Deas, WCMJ)*

Yockleton [SJ4010], *Yockleton Arms*: Particularly good food at the right price, good friendly service *(J B Oakley)*

Somerset and Avon

A good crop of new entries in this favoured area (or pubs bouncing back into the main entries after an absence) includes the welcoming good value King William at Catcott, the characterful Black Horse at Clapton in Gordano (currently doing very well), the Rudgleigh at Easton in Gordano (a useful food pub, handy for the motorway), the White Hart at Littleton upon Severn (a great find, very individual, tied to the small Smiles brewery in Bristol), the Fox & Badger at Wellow (free of its former brewery tie under a friendly new Australian landlord), the Blue Bowl at West Harptree (a lively country pub, popular for food) and the smart thatched Royal Oak at Winsford on Exmoor. Other pubs currently doing particularly well here include the unspoilt Globe at Appley, the lively Highbury Vaults in Bristol (another pub tied to Smiles), the delightfully traditional Crown at Churchill, the Strode Arms at Cranmore (very popular for eating out), the Bull Terrier at Croscombe (excellent all-rounder), the New Inn at Dowlish Wake (good cooking by its Swiss landlady), the very well run Poulett Arms at Hinton St George (gaining our Wine Award this year), the Royal Oak at Luxborough (currently prompting more enthusiastic reports than any other pub here – it gains a star award this year), the well liked Notley Arms at Monksilver (very welcoming to families), the grand old George at Norton St Philip (keen new licensees promise to make the most of its vast potential), the White Horse at Stogumber (gaining our Place to Stay Award this year), the White Hart at Trudoxhill (excellent own-brewed beers, decent food and a fine atmosphere), the Cotley at Wambrook (a real favourite with an increasing number of readers; another to gain our Place to Stay Award). There's excellent food to be had at the Bull Terrier at Croscombe, the New Inn at Dowlish Wake, the Three Horseshoes at Langley Marsh, and the Notley Arms at Monksilver; however, the pub which we choose as Somerset Dining Pub of the Year is the Strode Arms at Cranmore – such an enjoyable place for a meal out. Food prices in the area are rather lower than the national average, with plenty of attractive pubs where you can get a good main dish for well under £5 and a ploughman's for around £3. Drinks prices are around the national average, though pubs getting their beers from local breweries such as Butcombe, Exmoor, Hardington, Oakhill, Smiles and Wickwar produce significant savings: by far the best drinks prices we found were at the Fox & Badger at Wellow, White Hart at Trudoxhill (brewing its own) and Anchor at Oldbury on Severn. In the Lucky Dip section at the end of the chapter, pubs to note particularly include the Lamb at Axbridge, Princes Motto at Barrow Gurney, George in Bath, Crown at Bathford, Red Cow at Brent Knoll, Brewery Tap in Bristol, Manor House at Ditcheat, Old Mill at Haselbury Plucknett, Ring o' Bells at Hinton Blewett, Kingsdon Inn, Olde Kings Arms at Litton, Queens Head at Milborne Port, Panborough Inn, Masons Arms in Taunton, Fountain and City Arms in Wells, Lion and perhaps Apple Tree at West Pennard, Rest & Be Thankful at Wheddon Cross and Holman Clavel at Widcombe.

ALMONDSBURY (Avon) ST6084 Map 2

Bowl 🖎 ♀

1¼ miles from M5, junction 16 (and therefore quite handy for M4, junction 20; from A38 towards Thornbury, turn first left signposted Lower Almondsbury, then first right down Sundays Hill, then at bottom right again into Church Road

Brightly decked out in summer with flowering tubs, hanging baskets and window boxes, this very popular white cottage by the village church is a handy stop for travellers on the motorway. It's a friendly place, with the staff welcoming and keen to please, and the atmosphere pleasant and relaxed. A long neatly kept beamed bar has blue plush-patterned modern settles and pink cushioned stools and mate's chairs, elm tables, and quite a few horsebrasses; the walls are stripped to bare stone and there's a big winter log fire at one end, with a woodburning stove at the other. Well kept Courage Best and Directors, John Smiths, Wadworths 6X and a weekly changing guest on handpump, some enterprising bottled beers, good value wines, ten malt whiskies, freshly pressed fruit juices, tea or coffee. Good value home-made bar food includes sandwiches (£1.75), soup (£1.95), burgers (from £2.65), vegetarian pasta bake or filled baguettes (£2.95), ploughman's (£3.65), omelettes (from £4.25), pork and leek sausages (£4.65), chicken korma (£5.65), lamb and apricot casserole (£5.75), salads such as smoked chicken with grapes and walnuts in lemon mayonnaise or scampi (both £5.95), steak and kidney pie (£6.25) and puddings (£2.30); children's helpings. Fruit machine and piped music. The little restaurant is very attractive. At the back a patio area overlooks a field and can be booked for private parties, and there are some picnic-table sets across the quiet road. *(Recommended by John and Joan Wyatt, Mr and Mrs R J Phillips, Rona Murdoch, Jennifer Tora, Don Kellaway Angie Coles, Pat and John Millward, Simom and Amanda Southwell, Cdr Patrick Tailyour, Professor J R Leigh, Gill and Mike Cross, R W Brooks, Bob and Maggie Atherton)*

Courage ~ Lease: John Alley ~ Real ale ~ Meals and snacks (till 10) ~ Restaurant ~ Almondsbury (01454) 612757 ~ Children in eating area of bar and restaurant ~ Open 11-3, 5(6 Sat)-11; closed evening 25 Dec ~ Bedrooms: £38.50B/£48.50B

APPLEY (Somerset) ST0621 Map 1

Globe £

Hamlet signposted from the network of back roads between A361 and A38, W of B3187 and W of Milverton and Wellington; OS Sheet 181 map reference 072215

Nestling in the centre of a maze of pretty twisting lanes, and surrounded by graceful hilly pastures, this 500-year-old country pub is delightfully unspoilt and cheery. It's very popular for eating, but is still very much the sort of place that locals use for a drink, so there's usually quite a jolly atmosphere throughout its cosy, characterful rooms. This owes a lot to the fact that the two couples who run the place get on very well, and their enthusiasm does rub off. A stone-flagged entry corridor leads to a serving hatch from where Cotleigh Tawny (a local brew) and Furgusons Dartmoor Best are served on handpump (maybe kept under light blanket pressure), and they have farmhouse cider made in a neighbouring village. The simple beamed front room is relaxed and chatty, with benches and a built-in settle, bare wood tables on the brick floor, and pictures of magpies. What used to be a pool room at the back is now used mainly for eating, while a further room has easy chairs and other more traditional ones; darts, shove-ha'penny and alley skittles. Good generously served bar food might include filled rolls (from £1, the beef is especially recommended), delicious hot soup (£1.95), a choice of ploughman's (from £3.95, the beef is enormous), seafood pancake or lamb curry (£5.25), cashew nut paella or pasta and spinach in stilton sauce (£5.50), gammon (£6.95), steaks (from £8.50), specials like beef stroganoff (£6.25) and fresh salmon with a cream, white wine and chive sauce (£6.95) and puddings such as coconut grove, marinated pineapple cream, coconut and malibu with coconut ice cream – or hot chocolate fudge cake (£2.75); the vegetables are very good (as is the service); children's meals (from £2.95) and popular Sunday roast (£4.95). The restaurant is no smoking. Seats, climbing frame and swings outside in the garden; the path opposite leads eventually to the River Tone. *(Recommended by John Hazel, H and D Cox, John A Baker, Pete and Rosie Flower, Patrick Freeman, S G N Bennett, Richard Dolphin, F J Willy)*

Free house ~ Licensees A W and E J Burt, R and J Morris ~ Real ale ~ Meals and snacks (till 10) ~ Restaurant (not Sun evening) ~ Greenham (01823) 672327 ~ Children in eating area and restaurant ~ Open 11-3, 6.30-11; closed Mon lunchtime, except bank holidays

ASHCOTT (Somerset) ST4337 Map 1

Ashcott Inn

A39 about 6 miles W of Glastonbury

Under the newish managers this attractively refurbished and pleasantly atmospheric old pub is still a useful lunchtime food stop, though the menu doesn't have the same emphasis on fish dishes that it's been well known for in recent years. Instead a varied range includes sandwiches (from £1.75), soup (£1.65), deep-fried whitebait (£2.95), good ploughman's (from £3.75), vegetarian bake (£4.25), pork and local cider casserole (£4.95), beef, ale and mushroom pie (£5.25), grilled trout and almonds (£7.25), steak (£8.95), daily specials like salmon in dill sauce, and puddings. Well kept Butcombe Bitter, Flowers Original and a regularly changing guest on handpump; friendly service. The bar has stripped stone walls, beams, good oak and elm tables, some interesting old-fashioned seats among more conventional ones, and a log-effect gas fire in its sturdy chimney; darts, cribbage, dominoes, shove-ha'penny, fruit machine, alley skittles and piped classical music. Part of the eating area is no smoking. Seats on the terrace, and a pretty walled garden which the restaurant overlooks. The pub went through a rather uncertain period last year and reports rather reflected this, but things seem to be settling down a bit now. *(Recommended by Anthony Barnes, Ralf Zeyssig, Bill and Beryl Farmer, Mark and Diana Bradshaw, E H and R F Warner, Judith and Stephen Gregory, P H Brown, H F Cox, Brig J S Green, Alan Skull, Mr and Mrs G A Pepper, D H, Mr N R and Mrs L Y Gunn, Blair and Dinah Harrison, A J Frampton, A J Vermeuil, Rev A Nunnerley, Alan and Eileen Bowker)*

Heavitree (who no longer brew) ~ Managers Tony and Bernice Massey ~ Real ale ~ Meals and snacks ~ Restaurant (closed Sun evening) ~ Ashcott (01458) 210282 ~ Well behaved children in dining area ~ Open 11-11

nr ASHILL (Somerset) ST3217 Map 1

Square & Compass

Windmill Hill; turn left off A358 when see Stewley Cross Garage on a side road

Despite its nicely remote setting, you'll often find this pleasant place rather busy in the evenings, especially at weekends. Upholstered window seats overlook the rolling pastures around Neroche Forest, and the cosy little bar has other comfortable seating (there's extra room for eating) and an open fire in winter. Good hearty bar food includes sandwiches, home-made soup, filled baked potatoes, ploughman's, avocado filled with prawns (£3.25), mushroom stroganoff or chicken balti (£5.50), steak and mushroom casserole (£5.75), tagliatelle with a smoked salmon and cream sauce (£5.95), grilled swordfish steak (£6.95), and good daily specials; children's menu, Sunday roast. They have occasional themed food and music evenings, such as Italian, Irish or Spanish, and a well liked fish and chip evening on Thursday (£2.75). Well kept Bass, Boddingtons, Exmoor Bitter and Flowers Original on handpump; darts, shove ha'penny, cribbage, dominoes and piped music. Enthusiastic, friendly licensees. Outside on the grass are picnic-set tables and a good children's play area with badminton and volleyball. There's a touring caravan site. *(Recommended by John A Barker, Helen Taylor, Ian, Janet and Joanne James, Linda and Brian Davis, P H Brown, Derek Patey, Richard Dolphin, G H Burdge)*

Free house ~ Licensees Simon and Ginny Reeves ~ Real ale ~ Meals and snacks ~ Restaurant ~ Hatch Beauchamp (01823) 480467 ~ Children in eating area and restaurant ~ Fri folk night ~ Open 11.30-2.30, 6.30-11

AUST (Avon) ST5789 Map 2

Boars Head

½ mile from M4, junction 21; village signposted from A403

Unexpectedly rural considering its proximity to the motorway, this small-roomed village pub continues to be a well liked and reliable stop on the journey between Wales and England; it can fill up quickly at lunchtimes, but service is always warmly welcoming and efficient. The comfortable main bar has well polished country kitchen tables and others made from old casks, old-fashioned high-backed winged settles in stripped pine, some walls stripped back to the dark stone, decorative plates hanging from one stout black beam, big rugs on dark lino, and a log fire in the main fireplace. In another room is a woodburning stove, while a third has dining tables with lace tablecloths, fresh flowers and candles. Popular bar food includes home-made stock-pot soup (£2.20), ploughman's (£3.50), help-yourself salads (from £3), smoked salmon and scrambled eggs (£5.95), daily specials such as home-made pies like steak and kidney or chicken, a tasty beef casserole, venison and other game dishes or winter meals like braised oxtail (from £4.95), whole fresh plaice and Severn salmon (from £6), and good puddings (£2); Sunday lunch (from £5.50) and children's helpings; coffee. Part of the eating area is no smoking. Well kept Courage Best, a Whitbread beer and regularly changing guest like Ind Coope Burton on handpump. There's a medieval stone well in the pretty sheltered garden, which has an aviary and maybe rabbits, and a touring caravan site. When the pub was first recorded in the 18th c it stood next to a row of cottages built by the parish for unmarried mothers; even the vicar's daughter was there for a while, and when a rudimentary version of the CSA tracked down the fathers, they were fined 17/6. The nearby village church is unusual for having no name. *(Recommended by D G Clarke, C H Stride, G K Johns, A D Shore, Margaret Drazin, R Michael Richards, Michael, Alison and Rhiannon Sandy, T A Bryan, Peter and Rose Flower, R and E Allison, A E Brace, John Evans, Alan and Eileen Bowker)*

Courage ~ Lease Mary May ~ Real ale ~ Meals and snacks (till 10; not Sun eve) ~ Pilning (01454) 632278 ~ Children in eating area and family room till 9pm ~ Open 11-2.30, 6-11

BATH (Avon) ST7565 Map 2

Crystal Palace

Abbey Green; via Church Street, opposite end from abbey

A cheerful Georgian town pub in a quiet square with a tree-shaded green, well liked for its sheltered courtyard decorated with tubs of bright flowers and hanging baskets; there are plenty of tables both here and in the well furnished heated conservatory. Inside it's comfortably modernised, with promptly served good-value home-made food including sandwiches and baguettes (lunchtime only, from £2.35), filled baked potatoes (from £3.20), ploughman's (from £3.60), shepherd's pie or chilli (£4.25), and steak and mushroom pie (£4.50). Eldridge Pope Dorchester, Hardy's, Royal Oak and Blackdown Porter on handpump; a couple of fruit machines, video game, pinball and unobtrusive piped music. It may be popular with office-workers at lunchtime. *(Recommended by Steve Huggins, P M Lane, Michael, Alison and Rhiannon Sandy, Alastair Campbell, Adrian Pitts and others)*

Eldridge Pope ~ Manager J Duncan ~ Real ale ~ Meals and lunchtime snacks (not Sun evening, orders end 8.30, 8 Fri and Sat) ~ (01225) 423 944 ~ Children on patio ~ Nearby parking may be difficult, metered ~ Open 11-11; 11-3, 6-11 winter weekdays

Old Green Tree 🍺

12 Green St

Now a free house, this is a good smart but unpretentious town pub, cosy and chatty, and with a thriving genuinely old-fashioned atmosphere in the three oak-panelled little rooms. The main bar can get quite busy thanks to its size, but service always remains efficient, attentive and friendly; there's a comfortable lounge on the left as you go in, its walls decorated with wartime aircraft pictures, and the back bar is no-smoking. The big skylight lightens things up attractively. A short choice of decent home-made bar food includes a good ploughman's or large rolls with fillings such as crab (£3), salad (£3.50), at least three fresh pasta dishes (£4), sausages and mash, spanish omelette or chilli (£4.50) and daily specials like smoked trout open sandwich (£4.50) or seafood or beef platter (£5.60); helpings are usually quite generous. There are usually five well kept beers on handpump at a time, with some emphasis on ales from local breweries such as Hardington Best, Oakhill Bitter and Wickwar Brand Oak, and there's an eclectic choice of other drinks that includes some uncommon wines; they do a good Pimms in summer, and hot punches in winter. The pub is free from any distractions like music or machines. The lavatories, though good, are down steep steps. *(Recommended by Simon and Amanda Southwell, A Plumb, Bob Riley, Peter Churchill, Roger Huggins, Dave Irving, Ewan McCall, Tom McLean, Alan Skull, Roger Wain-Heapy, Pat and John Millward)*

Free house ~ Nick Luke ~ Real ale ~ Lunchtime meals and snacks (not Sun) ~ Children over 10 if eating, lunchtime only ~ Occasional live entertainment Weds ~ Open 11-11; closed Sun morning in winter

BLAGDON (Avon) ST5059 Map 2

New Inn

Church Street, off A368

A very nice spot, this neat and old-fashioned pub has lovely views from the picnic-table sets at the back, looking down over fields to wood-fringed Blagdon Lake, and to the low hills beyond. Inside, the two warm and individualistic rooms are spotless and full of character, and have some comfortable antique settles – one with its armrests carved as dogs – as well as little russet plush armchairs, mate's chairs and so forth. Big logs burn in both stone inglenook fireplaces, the ancient beams are decorated with gleaming horsebrasses and some tankards, and decorations include advertisements for Slades now-defunct ales from Chippenham. There's an elderly black labrador, and a plump cat (no dogs allowed in the garden). Well kept Bass and Wadworths IPA and 6X on handpump; darts, shove-ha'penny, fruit machine and piped music. Bar food (in big helpings) includes sandwiches, soup (£1.95), ploughman's, sausages (£3.40), home-made steak and kidney pie (£4.10), seafood platter (£4.75), specials like trout bake, chilli or filo parcels (£4.95), japanese butterfly prawns (£5.50), gammon (£6.25) and rump steak (£7.75); there may be a 30p charge for cheques under £10. The pub can get busy at weekends. Please note they don't allow children inside, a policy that doesn't vary, whatever the weather. *(Recommended by Brig J S Green, Roger Huggins, Mr and Mrs A E McCully, Joy Heatherley)*

Wadworths ~ Licensee M K Loveless ~ Real ale ~ Meals and snacks (till 9.45, 10.15 Fri and Sat) ~ (01761) 462475 ~ Open 11-2.30, 7-11

BRADLEY GREEN (Somerset) ST2538 Map 1

Malt Shovel 🏠

Pub signposted from A39 W of Bridgwater, near Cannington; though Bradley Green is shown on road maps, if you're booking the postal address is Blackmoor Lane, Cannington, BRIDGWATER, Somerset TA5 2NE; note that there is another different Malt Shovel on this main road, 3 miles nearer Bridgwater

Recent reports have all praised the warm welcome at this friendly family-run free house, nicely tucked away in a remote hamlet; it's the kind of place where they always seem genuinely pleased to see you. The homely no-frills main bar has window seats, some functional modern elm country chairs and little cushioned casks, sturdy modern winged high-backed settles around wooden tables, a black kettle standing on a giant fossil by the woodburning stove, and various boating photographs; there's also a tiny snug with white walls and black beams. The bar is in solid oak with a natural stone front and the floor is covered with red quarry tiles. Good value simple, tasty food includes lunchtime sandwiches (£1.25, crusty rolls £1.65) and ploughman's (from £2.80), as well as pasta and spinach mornay (£3.25), lamb and potato provençale or smoked haddock cheesy bake (£3.50), filled baked potatoes (from £3.75), steak and kidney pie (£3.95), salads (from £4), plaice or gammon (£4.25), fisherman's pie (£5.25), steaks (from £7.50) and daily changing starters and puddings; children's meals (from £1.95); occasional summer barbecues, and skittle alley. Good breakfasts. Well kept Butcombe, John Smiths and guest on handpump; farmhouse cider. The family room opens on to the garden, where there are picnic-table sets and a fishpond. The bedrooms fit in with the comfortable simplicity of the place. West of the pub, Blackmore Farm is a striking medieval building. *(Recommended by Steve Dark, the Shinkmans, Joan Coleman, Dr Bill Baker, John A Barker, Douglas Allen, G W A Pearce, Mr and Mrs K H Frostick, Tom and Sally Wilton, L and J, Mr and Mrs P A Jones, Theo Schofield, John Whitehead, David Holloway, Alison Burt, M K C Wills, Mark and Diane Grist)*

Free house ~ Licensees Robert and Frances Beverley ~ Real ale ~ Meals (not winter Sun evening) and lunchtime snacks ~ Restaurant (not winter Sun evenings) ~ Combwich (01278) 653432 ~ Children in family room, eating area of bar and restaurant ~ Live entertainment 31 Dec and possibly once in summer ~ Open 11.30-2.30(3 Sat), 6.30(7 winter)-11; closed 25 Dec ~ Bedrooms: £21.50(£30B)/ £30(£38B); family room £46

BRENDON HILLS (Somerset) ST0334 Map 1

Raleghs Cross

Junction of B3190 Watchet—Bampton with the unclassified but good E-W summit road from Elworthy to Winsford

A lonely white house nearly 1,200 feet up in the Bredon Hills, as welcome a sight to hungry travellers today as it must have been in its days as a coaching stop. In exceptionally clear weather you can see right over the Bristol Channel to Wales. The spacious comfortably-modernised bar has little red leatherette armchairs around the tables, button-back banquettes along the strip-panelled walls, a good collection of photographs of the old mineral railway, open fires and a preserved well rather incongruously popping up out of the carpet. Popular bar food includes sandwiches (from £1.50), soup (£1.50), crispy coated baby sweetcorn with dip (£2.75), ploughman's (£3.50), omelettes (from £4.75), beef or chicken curry (£5.50), broccoli and cream cheese bake (£5.75), local trout (£5.95), beef stroganoff (£6.75), mixed grill (£8.25), steak (16oz T-bone £9.95), and puddings such as pavlova or apple pie (from £2.25); Sunday lunch (£5.50), carvery (Wednesday lunch and evening, Friday and Saturday evenings – booking recommended, £5.75), summer cream teas, and children's menu (from £1.50); waitresses bring food to pre-booked tables on Saturday evenings. Well kept beers such as Flowers Original and Exmoor Ale on handpump; gentle piped music. It can get busy, especially in summer, but service always remains prompt. There's a children's play area in the garden. It's a handy base for exploring Exmoor, and you can walk from the spacious lawns to Clatworthy Reservoir, or, from the road about a mile west, down the track of the railway that used to take iron ore from the mines here to Watchet harbour. *(Recommended by Peter Watkins, Pam Stanley, Janet Pickles, John Hazel, Phil and Heidi Cook, R W Brooks)*

Free house ~ Licensees Roy and Wendy Guppy ~ Real ale ~ Meals and snacks ~ Restaurant Sat evening only ~ Washford (01984) 40343 ~ Children in restaurant ~ Open 11-2.30, 6-11, all day Jul-Sept; cl 25 Dec ~ Bedrooms: £25B/£36B

BRISTOL (Avon) ST5872 Map 2

Highbury Vaults £ 🍺

St Michaels Hill, Cotham; main road out to Cotham from inner ring dual carriageway

This classic atmospheric cornerhouse must be one of our best-loved town pubs. In early Georgian times it was a lock-up where condemned men ate their last meal, and some of the bars can still be seen on the windows. Today the character and welcome are altogether more hospitable, though it's still well liked for eating, mainly because the meals are such a bargain. There's a cosy and crowded front bar with the corridor beside it leading through to a long series of little rooms – wooden floors, green and cream paintwork, old-fashioned furniture and prints, including lots of period Royal Family engravings and lithographs in the front room. It's one of the handful of pubs tied to the local Smiles brewery, so has all their beers well kept on handpump at attractive prices, as well as Brains SA, Fullers London Pride and changing guests like Hopback Summer Lightning or Ringwood 49er; also local Long Ashton cider. Exceptionally well priced bar food may include filled rolls (from 60p) and hot meals like vegetable curry (£2), chilli (£2.20), nut roast in filo pastry or Moroccan lamb (£2.50) and pies like steak and kidney or chicken, leek and white wine (£2.75). Darts; friendly informal service. It's very popular with students in term time, and can get busy at weekends. They keep a crossword dictionary for quieter moments. A nice terrace garden has tables built into a partly covered flowery arbour – not large, but a pleasant surprise for the locality; they have good barbecues out here in the summer. *(Recommended by Paul Cartledge, Gwen and Peter Andrews, Simon and Amanda Southwell, Pat and John Millward, William Pryce, I R Jagoe, Paul Weedon, David Atkinson, Steve and Carolyn Harvey, J Boylan, Susan and John Douglas)*

Smiles ~ Manager Greg Duckworth ~ Real ale ~ Meals and snacks (12-2, 5.30-8.30; not Sat/Sun evenings) ~ 0117-973 3203 ~ Open 12-11; closed 25 and 26 Dec

CATCOTT   (Somerset) ST3939 Map 1

King William

Village signposted off A39 Street—Bridgwater

There's an instant feeling of welcome at this comfortable cottagey pub, very handy for the M5. Traditional furnishings in the spacious bar include kitchen and other assorted chairs, brown-painted built-in and other settles, window seats, stone floors with a rug or two, and Victorian fashion plates and other old prints; everywhere is notably clean and tidy. One of the big stone fireplaces has had its side bread oven turned into a stone grotto with kitsch figurines. Good value home-made bar food such as sandwiches (from £1.20), home-made soup (£1.60), ploughman's (from £2.85), salads (from £3.50), quiche (£3.40), steak and kidney pie, shepherd's pie or vegetable lasagne (£4.20), various curries (£4.35), smoked haddock in cider sauce (£4.40), seafood pie (£4.50), trout with almonds or pork tenderloin (£6.50), mixed grill (£7.20), lemon sole (£8.95), duckling in orange sauce (£9.95), specials and puddings (£1.90); friendly service, pleasant landlord. Bass, Eldridge Pope Dorchester and Royal Oak and Palmers BB on handpump, with Wilkin's farm cider and a good range of malt whiskies; fruit machine, and piped music. A large extension at the back includes a skittle-alley and a glass-topped well. *(Recommended by Adrian M Kelly, John A Barker, Ted George, Jonathan and Amanda Checkley, Ann Reeder, David Craine)*

Free house ~ Licensee Michael O'Riordan ~ Real ale ~ Meals and snacks (till 10) ~ (01278) 722374 ~ Children in eating area ~ Open 11.30-2.30, 6-11

CHURCHILL   (Avon) ST4560 Map 1

Crown ◗

Skinners Lane; in village, turn off A368 at Nelson Arms

At its most delightful and atmospheric on cosy winter evenings, this very popular, well run old cottage is full of charm and unspoilt rustic simplicity. It's one of those rare places where the only noise is the low chatter of other customers (or maybe the piano), and the only game you're likely to come across is dominoes. Those who like their comforts more on the modern side may feel a little out of place, but if, like us, you appreciate an old-fashioned friendly atmosphere and smiling, helpful service, then visiting the Crown is never less than a joy. Many people come just for the beer, as there's a constantly changing range of up to twelve well kept real ales such as Bass, Butcombe, Eldridge Pope Hardy, Greene King Abbot, Morlands Old Speckled Hen and Palmers IPA all tapped from casks at the back, along with a nice light but well hopped bitter brewed for the pub by Cotleigh; also a range of country wines, and local Axbridge wine. The small and local stone-floored and cross-beamed room on the right has built-in wall benches, a wooden window seat, and an unusually sturdy settle; the left-hand room has a slate floor, and some steps past the big log fire in a big stone fireplace lead to more sitting space. Generously served bar food includes a good home-made soup (in winter, £2.50), sandwiches (from £1.80), wholesome ploughman's with real lumps of butter and a pickle tray (£2.75), chilli or steak and kidney pudding (£3.50), rabbit casserole (£3.95) and lots of rare roast beef in sandwiches, salads, baked potatoes and popular trenchers; the choice may be limited on Sundays. They can be busy at weekends, especially in summer. There are garden tables on the front and a smallish but pretty back lawn with hill views; the Mendip Morris Men come in summer. Good walks nearby. *(Recommended by Sally Pidden, Simon and Amanda Southwell, David Holloway, Dr and Mrs B D Smith, Peter Lecomber, William Price, Pat and John Millward, P M Lane, Jerry and Alison Oakes, H O Dickinson, Alan and Heather Jacques and others)*

Free house ~ Licensee Tim Rogers ~ Real ale ~ Lunchtime meals and snacks ~ (01934) 852995 ~ Children in eating area ~ Open 11.30-3.30, 5.30-11

CLAPTON IN GORDANO (Avon) ST4773 Map 2

Black Horse

4 miles from M5 junction 19; A369 towards Portishead, then B3124 towards Clevedon; in N Weston opp school turn left signposted Clapton, then in village take second right, maybe signed Clevedon, Clapton Wick

The great charm of this fascinating 14th-c pub – known locally as the 'Kicker' – is the very good atmosphere and pretty much unaltered simplicity. The partly flagstoned and partly red-tiled main room has a big log fire with stirrups and bits on the mantelbeam, pleasant window seats, winged settles and built-in wall benches around narrow, dark wooden tables, amusing cartoons and photographs of the pub, and a relaxed, friendly atmosphere. A window in an inner snug is still barred from the days when this room was the petty-sessions gaol; high-backed settles – one a marvellous carved and canopied creature, another with an art nouveau copper insert reading *East, West, Hame's Best* – lots of mugs hanging from its black beams, and plenty of little prints and photographs. There's also a simply furnished children's room, just off the bar, with high-backed corner settles and a gas fire; darts, dominoes, cribbage and piped music. Good quickly-served bar food includes filled rolls and french sticks (from £1.50), ploughman's (from £2.80), and various changing hot dishes like sausage, bacon and mushroom casserole or garlic and coriander chicken (from £3.50). Well kept Courage Best, Smiles Best and Wadworths 6X tapped from the cask; farmhouse cider. The little flagstoned front garden is exceptionally pretty in summer with a mass of flowers in tubs, hanging baskets and flowerbeds, and some old rustic tables and benches, with more to one side of the car park and in the secluded children's play area with its sturdy wooden climber, slide, rope ladder and rope swing. Paths from here lead up Naish Hill or along to Cadbury Camp. It's an excellent stop from the M5. *(Recommended by WHBM, P A Neate, Heather and Howard Parry, Jerry and Alison Oakes, Pat and John Millward and others)*

Courage ~ Tenants Nicholas Evans and Alfonso Garcia ~ Real ale ~ Lunchtime meals and snacks (not Sun) ~ (01275) 842105 ~ Children in family room ~ Live music/Quiz night alternate Mon evenings ~ Open 11-3, 6-11, all day Sat

COMBE HAY (Avon) ST7354 Map 2

Wheatsheaf

Village signposted from A367 or B3110 S of Bath

A lovely spot in summer, this busy country pub has a very enterprising garden, with tables on the spacious sloping lawn looking down past the plunging plantings to the church and ancient manor stables; good nearby walks. The pleasantly old-fashioned rooms have low ceilings, brown-painted settles, pews and rustic tables, a very high-backed winged settle facing one big log fire, old sporting and other prints, and earthenware jugs on the shelf of the little shuttered windows. It's a very popular place for eating, and bar food might include dishes like home-made soup (£2.50), ploughman's (from £3.50), stuffed mushrooms with brie (£4.25), seafood bake (£4.50) lasagne or tasty pan-fried pigeon breast (£4.75), hot cooked ham (£5), lots of specials like venison, king prawns, stuffed lemon sole, scotch salmon, whole fresh crab or lobster and duck breast, with grouse in season, and puddings (from £2.25); occasional summer barbecues. Well kept Courage Best and a guest like Wadworths 6X tapped from the cask, and local Combe Hey village wine; friendly staff (and dog). The pub has three dovecotes built into the walls. *(Recommended by Michael and Janet Hepworth, R M Bloomfield, Paul Weedon, John Hazel, Barry and Anne, Chris Philip, Dr and Mrs D M Gunn)*

Free house ~ Licensee M G Taylor ~ Real ale ~ Meals and snacks ~ Restaurant ~ Bath (01225) 833504 ~ Children away from bar area ~ Open 11-3, 6.30-10.30(11 Fri and Sat)

COMPTON MARTIN (Avon) ST5457 Map 2

Ring o' Bells
A368 Bath—Weston

Another of those places that really comes into its own on quiet winter weekdays, when the snugly traditional front part has a wonderfully cosy feel that you should be able to appreciate relatively undisturbed. At this time of year there are usually rugs on the flagstones and inglenook seats right by the log fire, but in summer, when it's busier, you may prefer to go up the step to a cool and spacious carpeted back part, with largely stripped stone walls and pine tables. Good value food includes sandwiches (from £1.25), soup (£1.65), ploughman's (from £3.15), lasagne, hot steak sandwich or mushroom, broccoli and almond tagliatelli (all £3.95), grilled ham and eggs (£4.20), beef in beer (£4.95), and daily specials such as lamb and apricot casserole or skate wings (£4.95) or lamb in port and cherry sauce (£5.25); children's meals (from £1.50) or helpings. Well kept Bass, Butcombe, Wadworths 6X and guest on handpump; friendly helpful service, maybe quiet piped classical music. The public bar has darts, shove-ha'penny, dominoes and cribbage, and a spacious, no-smoking family room has table skittles, trivia, a rocking-horse, toys, and bar billiards just outside; the new licensees have added baby-changing facilities. There's a decent-sized garden with fruit trees, sturdy tables, and a good play area, and it's not far from Blagdon Lake and Chew Valley Lake. No dogs. *(Recommended by Tom Evans, Gwyneth and Salvo Spadaro-Dutturi, A R and B E Sayer, Ian and Nita Cooper, Graham and Belinda Staplehurst, Alan and Heather Jacques, R W Brooks)*

Free house ~ Licensee Roger Owen ~ Real ale ~ Meals and snacks (till 10 Fri/Sat) ~ Restaurant (not Sun evening) ~ Children in no-smoking family room ~ (01761) 221284 ~ Open 11.30-3, 6-11

CRANMORE (Somerset) ST6643 Map 2

Strode Arms ★ ♀
West Cranmore; signposted with pub off A361 Frome—Shepton Mallet
Somerset Dining Pub of the Year

Pleasantly placed overlooking the village duckpond, this well run spacious 15th-c farmhouse is doing rather well at the moment, highly praised by readers for its range of really good home cooking. Big helpings of attractively served dishes like sandwiches (from £1.50), soup (£2.20), spinach pancakes (£3), ploughman's (£3.50), filled baked potatoes (from £3.75), venison sausages with bubble and squeak (£4.25), juicy ham and eggs or pies like steak and kidney and chicken, ham and leek (£4.50), vegetarian crumble (£6), baked rainbow trout with almonds (£6.95), escalope of veal with mushrooms in a brandy cream sauce (£8.75), fresh fish, daily specials like stuffed lamb's hearts, oxtail, liver and bacon or seasonal game, and puddings such as home-made meringue with raspberries or very good treacle tart (from £2.10); Sunday roasts. Readers like the sauté potatoes with cheese that they do as a snack (£1.60). When they're busy service may slow down, but it's generally friendly and willing. The smartly relaxed bar has charming country furnishings, a grandfather clock on the flagstones, fresh flowers and pot plants, remarkable old locomotive engineering drawings and big black and white steamtrain murals in a central lobby, good bird prints, newspapers to read, and lovely log fires in handsome fireplaces. Well kept Devenish Royal Wessex, Flowers IPA, Marstons Pedigree and Wadworths 6X on handpump; an interesting choice of decent wines by the glass and lots more by the bottle, farm cider, and quite a few liqueurs and ports. There's a front terrace with some benches and a back garden. On the first Tuesday of each month, there's a vintage car meeting, and the pub is handy for the East Somerset Light Railway. *(Recommended by Donald Godden, John Hazel, Mrs Joan Harris, A Nunnerley, John and Tessa Rainsford, H F Cox, Pat and Robert Watt, Stephen Brown, D B Dockray, David Wright, R J Waldewn, David and Ann Pert, David Holloway, P M Lane, Joy Heatherley, G Pugh, Wayne Brindle, Alan Skull)*

Free house ~ Licensees Rodney and Dora Phelps ~ Real ale ~ Meals and snacks (till 10 Fri/Sat) ~ Cottagey restaurant ~ Cranmore (01749) 880 450 ~ Children in restaurant ~ Open 11.30-2.30, 6.30-11; closed Sun evening Oct-Feb

CROSCOMBE (Somerset) ST5844 Map 2

Bull Terrier ★ ⑪ 🛏 ♀ 🍺

A371 Wells—Shepton Mallet

We know of a couple who drive from Bristol to this comfortable and friendly pub just about every week. A handsome building by a medieval cross, it's one of Somerset's oldest inns, and easily up there amongst those we get most reports on. Readers like the excellent welcome and good range of varied drinks, but as ever, the main draw is the freshly prepared food, with a choice including sandwiches (from £1.40; toasted from £1.65), soup (£1.95), ploughman's (from £2.75), chicken liver pâté (£3.25), salads (from £3.95), vegan and vegetarian dishes such as tomato crumble or pancakes stuffed with spinach and peanuts (from £4.95), lasagne (£5.25), excellent home-made steak and kidney pie (£5.35), fried chicken with banana and sweetcorn (£6.25), trout with almonds (£6.75), steaks (from £9.95), and home-made specials like ginger chicken with noodles, turkey, ham and mushroom pie, cheese and asparagus quiche or salmon roulade; lovely puddings such as apple strudel, butterscotch and walnut fudge cake or chocolate brandy truffle. Hearty breakfasts. Very well kept Bull Terrier Best Bitter (a strongish beer brewed for the pub), as well as Butcombe, Greene King Abbot, Hook Norton Old Hookey, Palmers IPA and Smiles Best on handpump, as well as local cider brandy, lots of soft drinks, and a very good range of wines, both by the glass and the bottle; they also have an off sales price list. Warm, courteous service. Smart and spotlessly kept, the lounge ('Inglenook') bar has cushioned wooden wall seats and wheelback chairs around neat glossy tables, pictures on its white walls, attractively moulded original beams, a log-effect gas fire in a big stone fireplace with a fine iron fireback, and a red carpet on its flagstone floor. A communicating ('Snug') room has more tables with another log-effect gas fire, and there's a third in the parquet-floored 'Common Bar', by the local noticeboard; there's also a family room. Dominoes, chess, draughts, shove ha'penny and cribbage. At the back is an attractive walled garden, where you might find the pub's friendly bernese mountain dogs, Ross and Lotti. There's a two-mile footpath to Bishop's Palace moat in Wells. *(Recommended by Steve Goodchild, S H Godsell, Gwen and Peter Andrews, Brig J S Green, Martin Aust, Jenny and Brian Seller, Myroulla West, John and Phyllis Maloney, David Holloway, Andrew Shore, Pat and John Millward, Margaret and Douglas Tucker, Bill and Beryl Farmer, D and H Broodbank, Mr and Mrs G W Olive, J Ferguson, G V Price, A Honigmann, R J Whitaker, Caroline White, Dr D C Deeing, R J Saunders, Klaus and Elizabeth Leist)*

Free house ~ Licensees Stan and Pam Lea ~ Real ale ~ Meals and snacks (till 10 Fri/Sat; not winter Sun evenings or all day Mon) ~ Wells (01749) 343658 ~ Children in no-smoking family room ~ Open 12-2.30, 7-11; closed winter Mons ~ Bedrooms: £24B/£48B

DOULTING (Somerset) ST6443 Map 2

Poachers Pocket

Follow Chelynch signpost off A361 in village, E of Shepton Mallet

A warmly welcoming and friendly 17th-c pub popular mainly for its generously served meals. The modernised bar has some black beams, one or two settles, small wheelback or captain's chairs, gundog pictures on the white walls, flagstones by the bar counter (though it's mainly carpeted), and a crackling log fire in the end stripped-stone wall; there's a garden at the back, with pleasant views of the surrounding countryside. Popular dishes include soup (£1.40), sandwiches and rolls (from £1.50), ploughman's (from £2.60), home-made quiche or cauliflower cheese (£3.95), tasty steak and kidney pie (£4.10), home-cooked ham (£4.15), scampi (£4.40), gammon or poacher's pie (pheasant, rabbit and venison, £5.95), pork chops or steaks (from £6.10) and a mixed grill (£9.25); puddings (from £1.80). Well kept Butcombe Bitter, Oakhill, Wadworths 6X and a guest on handpump; farmhouse cider. They don't do bedrooms, but are happy to help with the good farmhouse B&B next door. *(Recommended by Bob Smith, W F C Phillips, R J Walden, Paul Jones)*

Free house ~ Licensees Ken and Stephanie Turner ~ Real ale ~ Meals and snacks (lunchtime service stops at 1.45, 1.30 Sun, evenings till 9.45, 10 Fri and Sat) ~ (01749) 880 220 ~ Children welcome ~ Open 12-3, 6-11

DOWLISH WAKE (Somerset) ST3713 Map 1

New Inn £ ⑰

Village signposted from Kingstone – which is signposted from old A303 on E side of Ilminster, and from A3037 just S of Ilminster; keep on past church – pub at far end of village

You can always rely on a good meal at this friendly old place, still very popular for its food, atmosphere and welcome. The Swiss landlady does the cooking, and you'll often find a few of her native dishes on the menu. Good value and efficiently served meals typically include sandwiches (from £1.25), ploughman's (from £2.50), Bellew sausage or omelettes (from £2.75), stuffed mushrooms (£2.95), scampi (£3), ham and egg (£3.25), vegetarian dishes like pasta (£3.25) or nut roast (£3.50), chicken tikka masala (£4.25) and a daily special such as steak and kidney pudding, with evening à la carte dishes like butterfly prawns (£3.25), Swiss specialities such as raclette (cheese and baked potatoes, £5.25) or a steak fondue (£7.95), duck mandarin or paella (£9.75), beef fillet stuffed with stilton in mushroom and wine sauce (£9.95), and a choice of puddings like excellent lemon brûlée or coconut sorbet; no credit cards. The bar is never less than spotless and even at its busiest remarkably smoke-free; its dark beams are liberally strung with hop bines, and there's a stone inglenook fireplace with a woodburning stove, and old-fashioned furnishings that include a mixture of chairs, high-backed settles, and attractive sturdy tables. Well kept Butcombe, Theakstons Old Peculier and Wadworths 6X on handpump; a decent choice of whiskies, and Perry's cider. This comes from just down the road, and the thatched 16th-c stone cider mill is well worth a visit for its collection of wooden bygones and its liberal free tastings (you can buy the half-dozen different ciders in old-fashioned earthenware flagons as well as more modern containers; it's closed on Sunday afternoons). In a separate area they have darts, shove-ha'penny, dominoes, cribbage, table skittles as well as alley skittles and a fruit machine; maybe piped music. In front of the stone pub there's a rustic bench, tubs of flowers and a sprawl of clematis; the pleasant back garden has flower beds and a children's climbing frame, and dogs are allowed here. *(Recommended by Guy Consterdine, John and Fiona Merritt, Pauline Bishop, TOH, Janet Pickles, Desmond and Pat Morris, Major and Mrs E M Warrick, David and Michelle Hedges, Dr G Buckton, Heather M N Robson, Major D A Daniels, Richard Dolphin)*

Free house ~ Licensees Therese Boosey and David Smith ~ Real ale ~ Meals and snacks (till 10; not Sun evening Nov-Mar) ~ Ilminster (01460) 52413 ~ Children in no-smoking family room ~ Open 11-3, 6-11

DUNSTER (Somerset) SS9943 Map 1

Luttrell Arms 🛏

A396

A rather civilised place with an old-fashioned style very much in keeping with the character of the old town and castle, this imposing old building, now a Forte hotel, is based around a great hall built for the Abbot of Cleeve some 500 years ago. It's been altered and modernised since then, and the comfortable back bar is the place to head for, with a good pubby feel and the added attractions of no piped music and friendly, attentive staff. Bottles, clogs and horseshoes hang from the high beams, and there's a stag's head and rifles on the walls above old settles and more modern furniture. Ancient black timber uprights glazed with fine hand-floated glass, full of ripples and irregularities, separate the room from a small galleried and flagstoned courtyard. Promptly served bar snacks include sandwiches (from £1.20), soup (£2), steak and kidney pie or plaice (£4.95) and a speciality mixed grill (£3.35), as well as imaginative evening meals; they do a good Sunday lunch. Well kept Bass, Flowers IPA and John Smiths on handpump. In the gardens there are cannon emplacements dug out by Blake in the Civil War when – with Praise God Barebones and his pikemen – he was besieging the castle for six months. The town, on the edge of Exmoor National Park, is pretty. *(Recommended by B M Eldridge, Basil J S Minson, Michael and Harriet Robinson, Mr and Mrs Hillman, John and Christine Vittoe, Jim and Maggie Cowell, Joan Olivier, Alan and Eileen Bowker, Roger and Judy Tame)*

Free house (Forte) ~ Manager Mr Mann ~ Real ale ~ Meals and snacks ~ Restaurant ~ Dunster (01643) 821555 ~ Children in eating area ~ Open 10.30-11 ~ Bedrooms: £70B/£90B, four-poster room from £110

EAST LYNG (Somerset) ST3328 Map 1

Rose & Crown

A361 about 4 miles W of Othery

Plenty of antiques in the traditional beamed lounge bar give this friendly and relaxed place a rather unchanging air, with the dates on the stack of old *Country Life*s and the gentle ticking of the clock the only reminders that time is indeed moving on. Warm and chatty, the open-plan room also has a corner cabinet of glass, china and silver, a court cabinet, a bow window seat by an oak drop-leaf table, and a winter log fire in its modernised fine old stone fireplace. Freshly prepared straightforward food, in good helpings, includes sandwiches (from £1.30), steak (£3.20), soup (£1.80), pâté (£2.60), ploughman's (from £2.85), ham and egg (£3.50), omelettes (from £4.10), salads (from £4.95), scampi or trout (£5.50), steaks (from £8.95), mixed grill (£9.95), duckling in orange sauce (£10.50), daily specials, with at least two vegetarian meals, and puddings such as butterscotch and walnut gateau (£2.35); pleasant waitress service. You have to book for the restaurant. Well kept Butcombe and Eldridge Pope Royal Oak and Hardy on handpump; coffee; unobtrusive piped light music. The back garden (largely hedged off from the car park) is prettily planted and there are picnic-table sets and a full skittle alley. *(Recommended by Shirley Pielou, Stephen Brown, Brig J S Green, John and Tessa Rainsford, Richard Dolphin)*

Free house ~ Licensee P J Thyer ~ Real ale ~ Meals and snacks (till 10) ~ Restaurant ~ Taunton (01823) 698235 ~ Children in restaurant and eating area of bar ~ Open 11-2.30, 6.30-11; Bedrooms: £25B/£40B

EASTON IN GORDANO (Avon) ST5276 Map 2

Rudgleigh

Martcombe Rd, a mile from M5 junction 19; follow Easton in Gordano signpost, but stay on A369 – don't take village turnoff

As the very good food is available all day here, it's naturally a popular place with motorists escaping the M5. There are masses of specials such as three roasts and a home-made nut one, chicken korma, liver and bacon, gammon, baked ham and cauliflower cheese, excellent steak and mushroom pie with lovely pastry (all £4.50), 6oz rump steak (£5.75), and puddings like plum crumble or bread and butter pudding with custard or cream (£1.75); very good chips. Well kept Courage Best, Smiles, and Websters Green Label on handpump. The atmosphere is happy and bustling and the service very friendly. The main bar is divided into two smallish rooms, with the area on the right beyond a dividing wall set for food and decorated with jugs on beams, a delft shelf, and blue and white plates on cream walls; the lounge area has lots of toby jugs hanging from the beams, and brocaded wall benches and some red plush stools round shiny tables on the red flowery carpet. On the left of the entrance is another room with more jugs on beams that leads through to a big family dining room. The back garden has quite a few orderly picnic-table sets, a big timber climber and swings, and a post-and-rail fence onto the cricket pitch; there are more picnic-table sets by the busy road. *(Recommended by Tom Evans, Donald Godden, J and F Gowes, Vivienne and Brian Joyner, Nigel Gibbs)*

Free house ~ Licensees Michael and Joyce Upton ~ Real ale ~ Meals and snacks (11am-10pm – not all day Sun) ~ Restaurant ~ (01275) 372363 ~ Children in family room ~ Open 11-11

EXEBRIDGE (Somerset) SS9224 Map 1

Anchor 🍺

B3222 S of Dulverton

A handsome three-arched bridge crosses over the Exe at this peaceful spot, and well spaced tables in the sheltered garden look down over the river and the trout or salmon swimming gently upstream through its shallow waters. The pub has fishing rights for those who don't mind interrupting the plump little creatures' idyllic wanderings, and they can organise a number of other local sports. Inside, the main front bar has individually chosen tables and seats such as a big winged settle and a nice old library chair among more orthodox furnishings, some carpet on its floor tiles, Cecil Aldin hunting prints and Exmoor pictures above the stripped wooden dado, some hunting trophies, and a warm woodburning stove. Bar food includes good sandwiches (from £1.35), home-made soup (£1.75), filled baked potatoes (from £1.95), sausage, egg and chips or local pasty (£2.95), cauliflower cheese (£3.50), ploughman's or omelettes (from £3.75), steak and kidney pie or curry (£3.95), moussaka or lasagne (£4.95), broccoli and cream cheese bake (£5.25), local trout (from £5.50), 8oz rump steak (£8.95) and quite a wide choice of children's dishes (£2.25). There's a back games bar with pool and two fruit machines divided by a flexiwall from a lounge bar with button-back leather chesterfields, modern oak tables and chairs, and french windows to the garden, which has a play area. Well kept John Smiths, Ruddles County, Ushers Best, Wadworths 6X and Websters Yorkshire (called 'Doone' here – the pub is mentioned in R D Blackmore's *Lorna Doone*); alley skittles, cribbage, darts, dominoes, fruit machine, video game, trivia, shove ha'penny, pool and piped light music, cheery staff. *(Recommended by Jed and Virginia Brown, Mr and Mrs Hillman, John Hazel, John Evans, H Hazzard, J E Davies, Shirley Pielou)*

Free house ~ Licensees John and Judy Phripp ~ Real ale ~ Meals and snacks (till 10) ~ Restaurant (not Sun evening) ~ Dulverton (01398) 23433 ~ Children in eating area of bar ~ Open 11-3, 5.30-11, though open for cream teas 3-6 ~ Bedrooms: £35B/£70B

FAULKLAND (Somerset) ST7354 Map 2

Tuckers Grave £

A366 E of village

One of our readers who's been to a good many pubs thinks this uniquely atmospheric and friendly little place is the best he knows. A basic and homely tiny west country cider house, it's for many years claimed the title of smallest pub in the *Guide*. A flagstoned entry opens into a teeny unspoilt room with casks of well kept Bass and Butcombe Bitter on tap and Cheddar Valley cider in an alcove on the left. Two old cream-painted high-backed settles face each other across a single table on the right, and a side room has shove-ha'penny. There's a skittle alley and tables and chairs on the back lawn, as well as winter fires and maybe newspapers to read. Food is limited to sandwiches (75p) and ploughman's at lunchtime. *(Recommended by Roger Huggins, Tom McLean, Dave Irving, Ewan McCall, J S Poulter, John and Phyllis Maloney, Pat and John Millward, Pete Baker, Simon Collett-Jones, George Murdoch, Chris Elias, Tracey and Kevin Stephens)*

Free house ~ Licensees Ivan and Glenda Swift ~ Real ale ~ Lunchtime snacks (not Sun) ~ Frome (01373) 834230 ~ Children welcome ~ Open 11.30-3, 6-11

FRESHFORD (Somerset) ST7859 Map 2

Inn at Freshford
Village signed off B3108

Good views over the valley from the pretty flower-filled gardens of this picturesque three-storeyed former coaching inn, in quiet countryside by an old stone bridge over the River Fromes. There are lots of seats out here and you may need them to think about what to eat – the menu is enormous. A huge daily changing choice includes good meals like sandwiches, home-made soup, around 40 main courses such as melon and prawns or steak and mushroom pie (£4.95), oak-smoked chicken (£6.45), salmon in tarragon sauce (£6.50), or fillet steak (£7.95), a dozen or so vegetarian dishes and lots of puddings like a good tiramisu (£1.95); friendly, helpful service, open fire, piped music. Part of the restaurant is no smoking. They get busy, so it's worth booking, or at least getting there early. The comfortably modernised and interestingly decorated bar has a relaxed, friendly atmosphere and well kept Bass, Courage Best, Ruddles County, Ushers, and Websters Yorkshire on handpump, and a decent wine list. Good walks along the riverbank that lead to the Kennet & Avon Canal. *(Recommended by Andrew Shore, Brig T I G Gray, Simon and Amanda Southwell, Peter Neate, Dennis and Joan Rouse, Brian Barefoot, Dave and Jules Tuckett and others)*

Courage ~ Lease: Stephen Turner ~ Real ale ~ Meals and snacks (till 10pm) ~ Restaurant (not Sun evening) ~ (01225) 722250 ~ Children welcome ~ Open 11-3, 6-11

HASELBURY PLUCKNETT (Somerset) ST4710 Map 1

Haselbury Inn ♀
A3066 E of Crewkerne

Good food and drink are what draw people to this well kept and inviting place: there's a wide range of attractively served meals and an extensive choice of liquid refreshment. They usually have six to eight well kept real ales on handpump at a time, with brews such as Bunces Pigswill, Butcombe, Charles Wells Bombardier, Flowers IPA, Morlands Old Speckled Hen, Smiles Best, Wadworths 6X, and Hickelbury (brewed for them) tapped from the cask, as well as imported draft German lagers, a good choice of up to 50 wines, country wines, freshly squeezed orange juice, espresso coffee and local real lemonade. Bar food usually includes soup (£1.50), ploughman's with five cheeses or home-made pâté (£3.50), interestingly-filled baked potatoes or pizzas (from £4), good pasta dishes (£4.50), lamb's kidney and bacon tagliatelle or seafood platter (£4), lemon sole (£8), charcoal-grilled steaks (from £9), around 10 daily specials like moules marinières in season or Hungarian goulash, and puddings like apple strudel, home-made fruit pies or treacle tart (from £2); they also do a barbecue platter for two people (£7.50 each). Service is welcoming and friendly, though you may have to wait a while for your meal at busy times. Booking is recommended for the attractive no-smoking restaurant on a Friday or Saturday; piped music. Plants and fresh or dried flowers in the windows, chintz armchairs and sofas around the fire and television set, and in one half candlelit wooden tables with unusually heavy red-cushioned cask seats. There are picnic-table sets on the side grass. *(Recommended by Major and Mrs E M Warrick, Derek and Iris Martin, P and J Rush, Guy Consterdine, Romey Heaton)*

Free house ~ Licensee James Pooley ~ Real ale ~ Meals and snacks all day ~
Restaurant ~ Crewkerne (01460) 72488 ~ Children welcome ~ Open 12-3, 7-12
(they have a supper licence); closed Mon

HINTON ST GEORGE (Somerset) ST4212 Map 1

Poulett Arms ♀

Village signposted off A30 W of Crewkerne; and off Merriott road (declassified – former
A356, off B3165) N of Crewkerne; take care – there is another pub of the same name a mile
or so away, at a roundabout on the former A30

The prettily planted back garden at this bustling pub has some white tables under
cocktail parasols, near a real rarity – a massive pelota wall. We haven't heard a
hint of criticism of the place for quite some time, with readers particularly praising
the pleasant, friendly service and the very popular and admirably-presented bar
food. The good choice includes sandwiches, soup (£2.50), ploughman's (£3.50),
deep-fried Somerset brie (£3.75), spinach and mushroom lasagne (£4.75), mussels
and prawn chowder (£4.95), steak, mushroom and Guinness pie (£5.50), chestnut
patties in red wine (£6.20), lemon sole bonne femme (£6.25), poached chicken
breast filled with leeks and stilton (£7.90), salmon Balmoral (£8.20), guinea fowl
in Cumberland sauce (£8.95), and puddings such as seven-fruit summer pudding
or lemon and lime mousse (£2.50); vegetables are good. They can get very busy,
especially mid-evening. Well kept Boddingtons, Butcombe Bitter and Cotleigh Barn
Owl and Old Bailey on handpump, and a compact but carefully chosen wine list,
with all the wines available by the glass; welcoming licensee. The larger dining
room has maroon plush chairs (and a couple of high-backed settles), matching
velvet curtains, big black beams, stripped masonry, an imposing stone fireplace, a
few pistols and brasses, and two cosy smaller rooms opening off, one with a big
disused inglenook fireplace; cribbage, dominoes, maybe unobtrusive piped music.
There's also a skittle alley, with darts and table skittles, and a friendly cream
labrador, Willow. Note they no longer do bedrooms. *Recommended by A Wood,
Desmond and Pat Morris, Guy Consterdine, J Weeks, A E and P McCully, Rev A Nunnerley,
Dr D C Deeing, R J Saunders)*

Free house ~ Licensee Ray Chisnall ~ Real ale ~ Meals and snacks ~ Restaurant ~
Crewkerne (01460) 73149 ~ Children in eating area ~ Open 11-3, 7-11

HUISH EPISCOPI (Somerset) ST4326 Map 1

Rose & Crown £

A372 E of Langport

Locals know this wonderfully unspoilt place better as Eli's, after the present
landlady's father, who, like his father before him, held the licence here for 55
years. Nothing much has changed in all the time the family have been in charge,
and it's become an unforgettable and quite remarkable survival, an old cider
house remaining in pretty much its original form. One reader tells us the last time
he went into a pub like it was in 1941. The atmosphere and character are
determinedly unpretentious, and while to most of us that only adds to the charm,
it may not suit those looking for a touch of sophistication. There's no bar as such
– to get a drink, you just walk into the central flagstoned still room and choose
from the casks of well kept Bass, Boddingtons, and changing guests, or the wide
choice of Somerset farm ciders and country wines which stand on ranks of shelves
all around (prices are very low); this servery is the only thoroughfare between the
casual little front parlours with their unusual pointed-arch windows and
genuinely friendly locals. Food is simple and cheap: pasties (£1.10), generously
filled sandwiches (from £1.20, toasted £1.50), soup (£1.40), beans on toast,
ploughman's (from £2.60) and salads (from £3.50), and is served just about all
day; good helpful service. There's a fruit machine in one of the front rooms, along
with shove-ha'penny, chess, dominoes and cribbage. A much more orthodox big
back extension family room has darts, pool, trivia, juke box and a pinball
machine; skittle alley. There are tables in a garden outside, and they've recently
added a second enclosed garden with a children's play area. George the dog will

welcome a bitch but can't abide other dogs. They belong to S.P.O.T, the Society for the Preservation of Outside Toilets, with some readers suggesting the lavatories that earned them their membership should be eligible for a grant from English Heritage. A real ale festival is held in the adjoining field every September, and on some summer weekends you might find the pub's cricket team playing out here. *(Recommended by Peter Baker, John Hazel, Stephen Brown, Bill Darpe, R J Walden, John and Phyllis Maloney, John Sanders, Alan and Eileen Bowker, Richard Dolphin)*

Free house ~ Licensee Eileen Pittard ~ Real ale ~ Snacks (11.30-2.30, 5.30-10.30)~ (01458) 250494 ~ Children welcome ~ Open 11.30-3, 5.30-11, all day Fri and Sat

KELSTON (Avon) ST7067 Map 2

Old Crown 🍺

Bitton Road; A431 W of Bath

Picnic-table sets under apple trees in the neat, sheltered back garden of this atmospheric old place look out towards distant hills; you'd hardly believe you were just four miles from Bath's city centre. Carefully restored and genuinely preserved, the four small rooms don't have have anything noisy or modern to jar the classily traditional feel. Logs burn in an ancient open range (there's another smaller, open range and a Victorian open fireplace – both with coal-effect gas fires), beams are strung with hops, and there are lovely tableau photographs, interesting carved settles and cask tables on polished flagstones – all appealingly lit in the evenings by candlelight. Well kept Bass, Butcombe, Smiles Best, and Wadworths 6X, Farmers Glory (summer only) and winter Old Timer on handpump, also Mendip cider; shove-ha'penny and dominoes. Lunchtime bar food includes home-made soup (£1.85), ploughman's (£3.65), a choice of salads (from £4.30), cottage pie (£4.70), ham and leek pie (£4.90), a daily vegetarian dish, beef and Guinness casserole (£5.90), steaks (from £8.95) and puddings like Dutch apple pie, crème de menthe sundae or chocolate profiteroles (£2.80); prices are higher in the waitress-served evening restaurant, and, as we say, they don't do any food on Sundays. Service is welcoming and helpful. The car park is over quite a fast road. Note they don't allow children. *(Recommended by Simon and Amanda Southwell, Dave and Jules Tuckett, Fiona Dick, A Plumb, Jenny and John Muscat, Dave Irving, Roger Huggins, Ewan McCall, Tom McLean, Charles Davies, Neale Davies)*

Free house ~ Licensees Richard Jackson and Michael Steele ~ Real ale ~ Lunchtime meals and snacks (not Sun) ~ Restaurant (not Sun) ~ Bath (01225) 423032 ~ Open 11.30-2.30, 5-11

KILVE (Somerset) ST1442 Map 1

Hood Arms 🛏 🍷

A39 E of Williton

Beautifully run and notably friendly, this popular village inn is always busy with people come to sample the good, tasty food – it's best to get here early to be sure of a table. The menu might typically include sandwiches (from £1.50), soup (£2.25), pâté (£2.25), good ploughman's (£3), substantial salads (from £3.75), hot daily specials such as steak and kidney pie, aubergine bake, venison casserole, chicken and prawn risotto or spinach and garlic lasagne (all £4.95), and tasty puddings like very good treacle tart (from £2); there are always at least four vegetarian meals available. It gets quite restauranty in the evenings. The straightforwardly comfortable and carpeted main bar has a woodburning stove in the stone fireplace (decorated with shining horsebrasses on their original leathers) and leads through to a little cosy lounge with red plush button-back seats. The restaurant is no-smoking. Well kept Boddingtons and Flowers Original on handpump, several malt whiskies, various wines and they do tea and coffee; attentive service; dominoes, cribbage, alley skittles and gentle piped music. A sheltered back terrace, by a garden with a prettily planted old wall behind, has white metal and plastic seats and tables. *(Recommended by Jim and Maggie Cowell, Mr and Mrs M A Steane, R and G Underwood, A Plumb, David and Mary Webb, John Hazel, Dorothee and Dennis Glover)*

Free house ~ Licensees Robbie Rutt and Neville White ~ Real ale ~ Meals and snacks (till 10) ~ Restaurant Weds-Sat evenings ~ Holford (01278) 741210 ~ Children in restaurant ~ Open 11-2.30, 6-11 ~ Bedrooms: £36B/£60B

KNAPP (Somerset) ST3025 Map 1

Rising Sun ♀

Lower Knapp – OS Sheet 182 map reference 304257; off A38/A358/A378 E of Taunton

A really lovely 15th-c Somerset longhouse, with fine country views from the suntrap terrace. The choice of fresh fish and seafood continues to be the widest you're likely to find in the area, with plenty of blackboards listing the enormous range they have available each day. A typical day might see starters like crab fish cakes or bouillabaisse (£3.50) and countless imaginative main courses such as black bream marinated in lemon and rosemary (£8.75), poached skate or bass grilled with ginger, brown sugar and soy sauce (£10), scallops poached in vermouth, red mullet niçoise or salmon in asparagus sauce (all £10.50), monkfish provençale (£10.75), brill with a prawn and mushroom filling (£11), john dory poached in a garlic, prawn, fennel and mussel sauce (£12.25), and red snapper in tangy wine, rum and herb sauce (£12.95); they also do good plain bar food like open sandwiches (from £3.10), Welsh rarebit (£2.50), ploughman's (£3.25), spicy pork sausages (£3.40), ham and egg (£4.10), cheesy pilchard pancakes (£4.25), and a well liked Sunday lunch. It was carefully restructured a few years ago to expose well moulded beams, woodwork, and some of the stonework of its massive rather tilting walls, but it's not been over-prettified, and apart from the two inglenook log fires the thing which marks out its single big room is an utterly peaceful friendliness. Well kept Bass, Boddingtons and Exmoor on handpump; decent wine list. The staff (and dogs – Pepi the poodle and Pompey, who weighs in at nine stone) are very welcoming; high chair available, background classical music. Part of the restaurant is no smoking. *(Recommended by Marion and John Hadfield, Stephen Brown, P Neate, John A Barker, Mr and Mrs P J Murphy, Mrs Marian Greenwood)*

Free house ~ Licensee Tony Atkinson ~ Real ale ~ Meals and snacks (not Sun evening)~ Restaurant (not Sun evening) ~ (01823) 490436 ~ Children welcome ~ Occasional live music Sun evenings ~ Open 11.30-2.30, 6.30-11 ~ Bedrooms: £23/£36

LANGLEY MARSH (Somerset) ST0729 Map 1

Three Horseshoes ★ ⑪ ◖

Village signposted off B3227 from Wiveliscombe

It's typical of the careful detail the licensees put into running this good honest pub, tucked away in the Somerset hills, that when they decided to fit a new bar counter they hunted round tirelessly until they found an 80-year old mahogany counter that would blend in perfectly. In fact everything about the place seems to fit together really well, and in addition to an enviable range of beers and often idiosyncratic choice of food, things readers especially like are the simple but spotless and neatly polished feel of the place, the absence of chips or fried food, and the way the butter comes in little pots. The constantly changing and often imaginative menu might feature filled rolls, home-made soup, a choice of salads or filled baked potatoes, chilli con carne or liver and onion casserole (£3.95), vegetarian meals such as butter bean and brandy stew or courgette and mushroom bake, spinach parcels with rice and mushrooms (£4.50), lamb in Pernod, pigeon breasts in cider and cream or somerset fish pie (all £4.95), and puddings such as mincemeat, apple and brandy pancakes or creamy cheese cake (all £1.85); booking is recommended, they do get busy. Most of the vegetables come from the garden. The wide choice of frequently unusual real ales tapped from the cask typically includes Butcombe, Palmers IPA, Wadworths 6X and continually changing guests like Brains, Harveys, Morlands, Morrells, Oakhill Best, Timothy Taylors, Thwaites or Youngs; also Perry's farmhouse cider. The back bar has low modern settles, polished wooden tables with plants, dark red wallpaper, model planes hanging from the ceiling, banknotes papering the wall behind the bar counter, a piano, and a local stone fireplace; the lively front room has sensibly placed darts, shove-ha'penny, table skittles, dominoes, cribbage and bar billiards; separate skittle alley; piped music. It is small, so they can get crowded. The restaurant area is now no smoking. The pub alsatian is called Guinness. You can sit on rustic seats on the verandah or in the sloping back garden, with a new children's climbing frame and a view of farmland. In fine weather there are usually vintage cars outside. *(Recommended by Debbie Jones, John Hazel, Pete and Rosie Flower, H F Cox, Alan Carr, Anthony Barnes, Richard Dolphin, D Cox, P Boot, H G Robertson, Roger Taylor)*

Free house ~ Licensee J Hopkins ~ Real ale ~ Meals and snacks ~ Small restaurant ~ Wiveliscombe (01984) 623763 ~ Well behaved children allowed away from bar ~ Occasional spontaneous 'fiddle/squeeze box' sessions with local Morris dancing musicians ~ Open 12-2.30(3 Sat), 7-11

LITTLETON UPON SEVERN (Avon) ST5990 Map 2

White Hart 🍺

3½ miles from M4 junction 21; B4461 towards Thornbury, then village signposted

Lovingly restored, this pantiled, partly white-rendered stone pub has three atmospheric main rooms with flagstones in the front, huge tiles at the back, and smaller tiles on the left, and some fine furnishings that include long cushioned wooden settles, high-backed settles, oak and elm tables, a loveseat in the big low inglenook fireplace, some old pots and pans, and a lovely old White Hart Inn Simonds Ale sign. By the black wooden staircase are some nice little alcove seats, there's a black-panelled big fireplace in the front room, and hops on beams, fresh flowers, and candles in bottles. An excellent no-smoking family room, similarly furnished, has some sentimental engravings, plates on a delft shelf, and a couple of high chairs, and a back snug has pokerwork seats, table football and table skittles; darts and cribbage. Good bar food includes creamy pea and ham soup (£1.05), filled rolls (from £2.25), home-made chicken liver pâté (£2.95), mozzarella salad or a vegetarian dish with stilton, cheddar, potato and onions (£3.95), curry (£4.25), chicken with tomatoes, tarragon and white wine or celery, haddock and stilton bake (£4.95), chicken and broccoli crumble (£5.15), steak and kidney pie (£5.95), and sirloin steak (£8.95). Well kept Smiles Bitter, Best, and Exhibition, Wadworths 6X and a guest like Brakspears OBJ tapped from the cask, espresso coffee machine, very pleasant staff – and the jet black cat is called Snowy. Picnic-table sets sit on the neat front lawn, intersected by interesting cottagey flowerbeds; by the good big back car park are some attractive shrubs and teak furniture on a small back brick terrace. Dogs are allowed if on a lead, and there are quite a few walks from the pub itself. *(Recommended by Steve and Carolyn Harvey, Dave and Jules Tuckett, Carolyn Eaton, Mark Watkins, Simon and Amanda Southwell, John Andrew)*

Smiles ~ Manager Howard Turner ~ Real ale ~ Meals and snacks (not 25/26 Dec, 1 Jan) ~ Children welcome ~ Trad jazz Thurs evenings ~ Open 11.30-2.30, 6-11; 11.30-11 Sat ~ Bedrooms: £29.50B/£39.50B

LUXBOROUGH (Somerset) SS9837 Map 1

Royal Oak ★ 🛏 🍺

Kingsbridge; S of Dunster on minor rds into Brendon Hills – OS Sheet 181 map reference 983378

Unspoilt and traditional, this nicely out of the way thatched pub is doing exceptionally well at the moment, and this year we've had more reports singing its praises than for any other pub in Somerset; because it really does seem to give so much pleasure to so many people we've decided to give it a star. Guarding the only direct road through a narrow pass in the Bredon Hills, it owes a lot of its popularity to its cheerful and enthusiastic young licensees, who've done a great deal of work on the building to restore it to its optimum old-fashioned charm, and continually manage to please with a good choice of dependable and hearty bar food. Served in very big helpings, tasty meals include huge sandwiches (from £1.95, not Sunday), tasty home-made soup with big hunks of bread and non-packet butter (£1.95), filled baked potatoes (from £2.85), good ploughman's (from £3.85), port and stilton pâté (£3.85), huge Cornish pasty, half meat and vegetables, half apple (£4.45), lamb curry or vegetable and stilton pie (£4.65), salads (from £4.95), beef and Beamish pie (£4.95), excellent specials such as turkey and tarragon pie (£5.95), a well liked rabbit stew (£6.50), pigeon breasts in gin and gooseberry sauce or roast wild boar with rowanberry sauce (£7.25) and fresh scallops on a dill, white wine and cream sauce (£8.25), and puddings like blackberry and apple pie or apricot crumble (£2.25); there's a wider choice in the evening (booking is recommended) and they do a Sunday lunch (from £4.95; a Sunday snack menu is also available) and children's meals (£2.45). Well kept real ales such as Batemans XXXB, Cotleigh Tawny, Exmoor Gold, Flowers IPA, and guest beers (often from quite some way away) mostly on tap with some on handpump, farm ciders, decent wines by the glass and some interesting ones by the bottle; attentive, friendly service. The three chatty and warmly atmospheric rooms have flagstones in the front public bar, beams and inglenooks, a real medley of furniture, and good log fires; pool, dominoes, cribbage, winter darts – no machines or music. Tables outside. The comfortable bedrooms fit in with the simple style of the place, and breakfasts are good. *(Recommended by Jean Gustavson, J Wedel, Jed and Virginia Brown, Peter and Audrey Dowsett, R Ward, John A Barker, Kevin and Katharine Cripps, Tim Barrow, Sue Demont, James Nunns, Colin Keane, Dagmar Junghanns, Basil J S Minson, Jan and Dave Booth, DC, Graham Pettener, John Hazel, H O Dickinson, Joan Coleman, Clem Stephens, John and Vivienne Rice, Pam and Bill Mills, J R Williams, G W A Pearce, P Boot, J E Davies, Gethin Lewis)*

Free house ~ Licensees Robin and Helen Stamp ~ Real ale ~ Meals and snacks (till 10) ~ Restaurant ~ (01984) 40319 ~ Children in back bar and dining room ~ Folk music Fri ~ Open 11-2.30, 6(6.30 winter)-11 ~ Bedrooms: £20/£26

MARSHFIELD (Avon) ST7773 Map 2

Catherine Wheel

Village signed off A420

Rather graceful in places, this is an interesting old pub, full of character and characters. The front part with its shelled hooded door was built in 1720, but the back part is 16th c. The carefully renovated bars are most attractive, especially the beautiful dining room, painted in authentic Georgian pastels, with a lovely fireplace and surrounding china cabinets; there's another big fireplace in the main bar, as well as plates and prints on the partly stripped stone walls, beams, a nice mix of chairs and settles around stripped pine tables, dried flowers, a warm atmosphere, and a really lovely clock that they discovered locked away in a cupboard in bits and pieces and dated 1720. The back bar is prettily cottagey. Good changing bar food might include sandwiches, soup, home-made steak and kidney pie, vegetarian dishes, chicken in a Portuguese-style tomato and garlic sauce (£7.65), pork tenderloin in stilton sauce or mussels, prawns and scallops in garlic and white wine (£7.95), and sea bass in lobster sauce (£8.25). Well kept Courage Best and Wadworths IPA and 6X on handpump, farm cider, and decent wine list; the golden labrador is called Elmer (after the licensees); darts, dominoes. The restaurant is no smoking. *(Recommended by Graham Fogelman, Susan and John Douglas, Peter and Rose Flower, Pat and John Millward, Chris Elias)*

Free house ~ Licensees Royston and Carole Elms ~ Real ale ~ Meals and snacks (till 10pm); not Mon lunch except bank holidays, or all day Sun ~ Restaurant (not Sun evening) ~ (01225) 892220 ~ Children in eating area and restaurant till 8.30 ~ Thurs evening sing-alongs ~ Open 11-3, 6-11; closed Mon lunchtime except bank holidays

MONKSILVER (Somerset) ST0737 Map 1

Notley Arms ★ ⊕

B3188

Several readers eager to visit this enduring favourite have had to go away disappointed, finding on arrival not a single car parking space empty. That's because the pub stands out as probably one of the best in the area, effortlessly combining much better than average food and service with a traditionally pubby atmosphere where drinkers are more than welcome. Relaxed and friendly, the characterful beamed and L-shaped bar has small settles and kitchen chairs around the plain country wooden and candle-lit tables, original paintings on the black-timbered white walls, a couple of woodburning stoves and maybe a pair of cats; dominoes, cribbage, table tennis, scrabble, draughts, trivial pursuit and alley skittles and well reproduced classical music. Regular dishes on the menu include sandwiches (from £1.35), soup (from £1.60), filled baked potatoes, very good ploughman's, home-made pasta dishes such as pasta with bacon, cheese and cream or an aubergine and courgette terrine (£3.75), vegetarian filo pie with feta cheese and pine nuts (£4.25), spicy baked Indian chicken (£4.95), lamb with apricots (£5.25) with puddings such as apricot bread and butter pudding (from £1.95). Well kept Courage Directors, Ushers Best, Wadworths 6X and a guest like Exmoor on handpump; country wines such as oak leaf or raspberry, home-made elder flower 'fizz' in the summer. Families are very well looked after – quite a few parents we know have been delighted with the colouring books and toys they've been provided with in the bright little family room. There are more toys outside in the immaculate garden, running down to a swift clear stream. *(Recommended by Clem Stephens, A Plumb, Dr R J Rathbone, M D Beardmore, Joan Olivier, John and Christine Vittoe, Kevin and Katharine Cripps, Jerry and Alison Oakes, Debbie Jones, J E Davies, Joy Heatherley, John and Helen Thompson, Richard Dolphin, P Bell, Pat and Roger Fereday, H O Dickinson, Chris and Sue Heathman, H G Robertson)*

Courage ~ Tenants Alistair and Sarah Cade ~ Real ale ~ Meals and snacks (not first two weeks of Feb) ~ (01984) 56217 ~ Children in eating area ~ Open 11-2.30, 6.30-11; closed 25 Dec and first two weeks in Feb

MONTACUTE (Somerset) ST4916 Map 2

Kings Arms

A3088 W of Yeovil

Always keeping up its high standards, this civilised early Georgian golden stone inn has a lovely peaceful atmosphere. Part of the walls at the front of the lounge bar are stripped back to the handsome masonry, and comfortable furnishings include grey-gold plush seats, soft armchairs, chintz sofas, and a high curved settle. Popular bar food includes sandwiches, an extensive cold buffet (from £4.30), and plenty of daily hot dishes like grilled swordfish in a creole sauce (£5.60), lemon chicken (£5.75) or Chinese gingered beef with noodles (£5.80). Bass, Wadworths 6X and a maybe a guest beer on handpump or tapped from the cask, good wines and farmhouse cider; welcoming and efficient service, cheery landlord. The restaurant is no smoking. The pretty village includes the stately Elizabethan mansion of the same name, and behind the hotel the wooded St Michael's Hill is owned by the National Trust. *(Recommended by Guy Consterdine, Ron and Anne Fowler, P J Caunt, David and Fiona Easeman, Major and Mrs E M Warrick, J L Alperin, Heather M N Robson, Maysie Thompson, Bernard Phillips, Mr and Mrs S Sugarman, Galen Strawson)*

Free house ~ Licensee Michael Harrison ~ Real ale ~ Meals and snacks (till 10) ~ Restaurant ~ Martock (01935) 822513 ~ Children in eating area and restaurant ~ Open 11-11 ~ Bedrooms: £46B/64B

The opening hours we quote are for weekdays; in England and most of Wales, Sunday hours are 12-3, 7-10.30.

NORTON ST PHILIP (Somerset) ST7755 Map 2

George ★

A366

A pub for nearly 600 years, this really is a remarkable old building, with a fine half-timbered and galleried back courtyard, an external Norman stone stair-turret, massive stone walls and high mullioned windows. The enthusiastic licensees who took over just after our last edition have been busy, beginning a sympathetic refurbishment that will see them smartening up the fittings and extending the dining area, without any alteration to the rather special feel of the place. They've also introduced a wide range of food that relies on home-made dishes and fresh local produce; on the rare occasions when they do buy things in (mustard, chutney and the like), they choose smaller companies who don't use any artificial colours, flavourings or preservatives. The choice typically includes soup (£2.25), chicken liver pâté (£2.95), cheese and leek pancakes (£3.25), filled baguettes or baked potatoes (£3.75), ploughman's (£3.95), meat or fish platters (from £5.50), tortellini and blue cheese bake with broccoli or escalope of pork coated in nuts and breadcrumbs (£5.95), steak and kidney pie or trout baked with bananas and almonds (£6.75), gammon (£6.95), daily specials like turkey parcels stuffed with ham and gruyere cheese (£6.95), prawn curry (£7.50) and pan-fried duck with plum sauce (£8.95), steaks with a peppercorn sauce (from £8.95), and puddings such as treacle tart (£2.75); Sunday roast (£6.95). Furnishings are simple: square-panelled wooden settles, plain old tables, wide bare floorboards, and lofty beams hung with hops. A long, stout table serves well kept Bass, and Wadworths IPA, 6X and seasonal beers on handpump, and a good range of wines and malt whiskies; good service. A panelled lounge is furnished with antique settles and tables; it's all perhaps more atmospheric in winter when the fires are lit. Darts, pool and dominoes; this year they plan to add a skittle alley. They hope to have bedrooms ready by Easter 1995 and at the time of going to press were negotiating this with English Heritage; it's several hundred years since these were last available. The Duke of Monmouth stayed here before the Battle of Sedgemoor, and after their defeat his men were imprisoned in what's now the Dungeon cellar bar. When a sympathetic customer held the courtyard gate open for them as they were led out to their execution, he was bundled along with them and executed too – whoever said manners cost nothing? *(Recommended by BHP, Wim Kock, Willem-Jan Kock, Hans Chabot, Pat and John Millward, Roger Huggins, Dave Irving, Tom McLean, Ewan McCall, G B Longden, Viv Middlebrook, John and Phyllis Maloney, Jerry and Alison Oakes, Bill Bailey, Angie Coles, Lynn Sharpless, Bob Eardley, Chris Elias, Tracey and Kevin Stephens, R D Greaves, Margaret Drazin, Alan Skull)*

Wadworths ~ Tenants Andrew and Juliette Grubb ~ Real ale ~ Meals and snacks (till 10 Sat; not evening 25 and 26 Dec) ~ Lunchtime restaurant ~ (01373) 834 224 ~ Children welcome ~ Open 11-3, 5.30(5 Sat)-11 ~ Bedrooms: £35.45B/£50.60B (though see above)

OLD SODBURY (Avon) ST7581 Map 2

Dog

Badminton Rd

A very friendly family-run pub, good for children, and with an enormous range of tasty food. The emphasis is on fresh fish, with plenty of dishes like plaice, red mullet, shark or tuna, whole fresh sole, Devon scallops or clam fries, and lots of different ways of serving squid (£4.50) and mussels (£4.95). A vast choice of other dishes includes sandwiches (from £1.75), soup, ploughman's (£3.50), cottage pie (£3.95), pizzas, steak and kidney pie or vegetarian moussaka (£4.50), hazelnut and brown rice roast (£4.75), sweet and sour pork (£5.25), curries (from £5.95), Hawaiian chicken creole (£5.95), steaks (from £6.50), puddings (from £1.95), children's menu (called 'puppy food', from £1.50), and daily specials (from £2.75). It's worth getting there early, they do get busy. The two-level bar and smaller no-smoking room both have areas of original bare stone walls, beams and timbering, low ceilings, wall benches and cushioned chairs, open fires, and a welcoming, cheery atmosphere. Well kept Boddingtons, Flowers Original, Wadworths 6X, and Wickwar Brand Oak on handpump, decent wine list, pimms and sangria by the glass or jug, vintage port, and malt whiskies; helpful, attentive staff. Darts, skittle alley, cribbage, pinball, dominoes, fruit machine and juke box. Trophy the border collie likes playing football with customers. There's a large garden with lots of seating, a summer barbecue area, pets' corner with rabbits, guinea pigs and so forth, climbing frames, swings, slides, football net, see-saws and so forth, and bouncy castle most bank holidays. Lots of good walks nearby. *(Recommended by Cdr Patrick Tailyour, Simon and Amanda Southwell, Don Kellaway, Angie Coles, Barry and Anne, R C Morgan, N and J Strathdee, Michael Wadsworth, KC)*

Whitbreads ~ Lease: John and Joan Harris ~ Real ale ~ Meals and snacks (till 10pm) ~ (01454) 312006 ~ Children welcome ~ Regular party nights ~ Open 11-11 ~ Bedrooms: £20B/£30B

OLDBURY-UPON-SEVERN (Avon) ST6292 Map 2

Anchor ◀

Village signposted from B4061

The good bar food at this neat and attractively-modernised peaceful village pub is still very popular indeed. Cooked by the landlord using fresh local produce, the chip-free choice changes daily and might include good salads (from £2.85, many of the ingredients coming from gardens in the village), a selection of cheeses (£2.95), a plate of rare beef with wholemeal bread and butter (£3.30) or full meals like leek and potato bake or sautéed mushrooms and onion topped with cheese and breadcrumbs (£3.95), chicken and pineapple curry (£4.35), filled Yorkshire pudding (£4.40), boozy beef pie (£4.50), local sausages (£4.95), poached fillets of plaice (£5.10), charcoal grilled chicken breast (£6.25), fillet of beef en croûte (£7.95), and well liked puddings such as apple crumble topped with caramel or sticky toffee pudding (£2.40); prompt and efficient waitress service in no-smoking dining room – best to get there early if you want a seat. Bass tapped from the cask, with Butcombe, Marstons Pedigree, Theakstons Best and Old Peculier and Wothingtons Best on handpump and well priced for the area; over 75 malts, decent choice of good quality wines, Inches cider, and freshly squeezed fruit juice; darts, shove-ha'penny, dominoes and cribbage and a good big boules area at the top end of the garden. The comfortably furnished beamed lounge has a curved high-backed settle facing an attractive oval oak gateleg table, winged seats against the wall, easy chairs, cushioned window seats, and a big winter log fire. There are seats in the pretty garden, and St Arilda's church nearby is interesting, on its odd little knoll with wild flowers among the gravestones (the primroses and daffodils in spring are lovely). Lots of paths over the meadows to the sea dyke or warth which overlooks the tidal flats. *(Recommended by A D Shore, Adrian M Kelly, John and Pat Smyth, D G Clarke, S Brackenbury, Margaret and Douglas Tucker, C H Stride, Nigel Foster, Dave and Jules Tuckett, Chris Elias)*

Free house ~ Licensees Michael Dowdeswell, Alex de la Torre ~ Real ale ~ Meals and snacks ~ Restaurant ~ Thornbury (01454) 413331 ~ Children in restaurant ~ Occasional live entertainment ~ Open 11.30-2.30(3 Sat), 6.30(6 Sat)-11; closed 25 Dec

OVER STRATTON (Somerset) ST4315 Map 1

Royal Oak ♀

Village signposted from former A303 Yeovil—Ilminster through Seavington St Michael, which itself is signposted off A303 at E end of new Ilminster bypass

Still managing to keep something of its old, traditional feel throughout the cosily extended dark-flagstoned bars, this 16th-c thatched pub is another where the food deserves attention. Well liked by readers and served in big helpings, the meals are often quite imaginative, with dishes like sandwiches (from £1.95), soup (£2.25), filled baked potatoes (£4.25), salads (from £5.75), deep-fried Somerset brie (£3.75 starter, £5.45 main), asparagus in hollandaise sauce (£3.95), moules marinières

(£4.75), steak and kidney pie, spare ribs or wild boar sausages (£5.95), chicken and lamb satay (£6.25), stuffed cabbage leaves (£7.95), roast spring chicken stuffed with apple and bacon or lamb in filo pastry (£8.95), salmon steak in vermouth (£10.95), sea bass in Thai sauce (£11.95) and puddings like strawberry crème brûlée or mango mousse (£2.95); children's dishes. The restaurant is no smoking. Simply but carefully furnished, the pub is decorated with a mixture of pews, settles or dining chairs, scrubbed deal farmhouse kitchen tables, plants in the windows, some hop bines, and a stuffed pheasant. The beams have been prettily stencilled with an oakleaf and acorn pattern, the walls are stripped to bare stonework or attractively ragrolled red, and log fires burn, sometimes even in summer. Well kept Badger Best, Hard Tackle and Tanglefoot on handpump; lots of malt whiskies and an extensive wine list. On a floodlit reconstituted-stone terrace sheltered by the back wings of the building are quite a few picnic-table sets, with more on a further sheltered gravel terrace with a barbecue; the play area is large and well equipped – there's even a big trampoline. *(Recommended by Major and Mrs E M Warrick, Andrew and Helen Latchem, Guy Consterdine, Helen Taylor, John and Vivienne Rice, Dr R J Rathbone, Peter and Lynn Brueton, M E and Mrs J Wellington, Paul and Gail Betteley, Richard Dolphin, Dr D C Deeing, R J Saunders)*

Badger ~ Manageress Lyn Holland ~ Real ale ~ Meals and snacks (till 10) ~ Restaurant (not Sun evening) ~ Ilminster (01460) 40906 ~ Children in restaurant ~ Open 11-3, 6-11

PORLOCK (Somerset) SS8846 Map 1

Ship ★
A39

Visited over the years by Coleridge, Wordsworth and countless photographers, this delightful partly 13th-c thatched cottage is idyllically set at the bottom of Porlock Hill, within easy walking distance of both sea and moor and with lovely views. The characterful low-beamed front bar is where most people head for first: traditional old benches on the tiled and flagstone floor, a sought-after window-ledge seat, an inglenook fireplace at each end, and hunting prints on the walls. At the back, the carpeted lounge has plush red banquettes, a Gothic settle, and a chimney seat. Well kept Bass, Cotleigh Old Buzzard, Courage Best, and a local guest beer on handpump, country wines (including local damson wine), choice of single malt whiskies and farmhouse cider. Bar food includes home-made soup, ploughman's (from £2.50), well liked deep-fried camembert with gooseberries, a good venison casserole, changing daily hot dishes like duck with spring herbs or pork with peppers (£4.75), and fresh crab and lobster when available; children's menu. Shove-ha'penny, cribbage, bar billiards, fruit machine and video game; a separate pool room (which has sensibly placed darts too), and a full skittle alley. The extended garden at the back seems almost higher than the thatched roof, and there's a children's play area. They can arrange hunting, pony trekking, fishing, tennis and golf. From here the hill climbs over 600 feet to the Exmoor plateau in little more than half a mile. *(Recommended by Joan Coleman, Jim and Maggie Cowell, Christopher and Sharon Hayle, Gwen and Peter Andrews, W A Wheeler, A Plumb, John Hazel, Jan and Dave Booth, Dorothee and Dennis Glover, John and Marianne Cooper, Jane Thompson)*

Free house ~ Licensees Mark and Judy Robinson ~ Real ale ~ Meals and snacks ~ Restaurant (not Sun evening) ~ Porlock (01643) 862507 ~ Children welcome away from bar ~ Morris dancing and occasional folk singers ~ Open 10.30-3, 5.30-11 ~ Bedrooms: £16.50(£21.50B)/£33(£39B)

SOUTH STOKE (Avon) ST7461 Map 2

Pack Horse £
Village signposted opposite the Cross Keys off B3110, leaving Bath southwards – just before end of speed limit

In good walking country, this is an unusual and unspoilt 500-year-old gabled pub clinging to the hillside. The entrance alleyway that runs through the middle is still a public right of way to the church, and used to be the route along which the dead were carried to the cemetery. It stops along the way at a central space by the serving bar with its well kept Courage Best, Founders Premium Beer and Ushers Best on handpump and a choice of ciders. The ancient main room has a good local atmosphere, a heavy black beam-and-plank ceiling, antique oak settles (two well carved), leatherette dining chairs and cushioned captain's chairs on the quarry-tiled floor, a cheery log fire in the handsome stone inglenook, some Royalty pictures, a chiming wall-clock, and rough black shutters for the stone-mullioned windows (put up in World War I); the cupboard in the fireplace used to be where they kept drunks until they sobered up. There's another room down to the left. Remarkably good value home-made bar food includes filled rolls (from 70p, the home-baked cider ham are good), mouth-watering pasties or sausage plait (80p), several ploughman's (from £2.70), fisherman's pie (£1.80) and steak pie, chips and peas (£1.85); friendly staff. Rather fine shove-ha'penny slates are set into two of the tables, and there are darts, dominoes, cribbage, fruit machine and piped music. The spacious back garden, with swings, looks out over the stolid old church and the wooded valley. *(Recommended by Roger Huggins, Dave Irving, Ewan McCall, Tom McLean, Nigel and Teresa Blocks; more reports please)*

Ushers (Courage) ~ Tenant Colin Williams ~ Real ale ~ Snacks ~ (01225) 832060 ~ Children in eating area ~ Open 10.30-4.30, 6-11; all day Sat

STANTON WICK (Avon) ST6162 Map 2

Carpenters Arms 🛏 ♟

Village signposted off A368, just W of junction with A37 S of Bristol

Converted from a row of old miners' cottages, this friendly tiled-roof inn is becoming quite a foody place, but still has a homely feel in places, particularly in the Coopers Parlour on the right, with one or two beams, red-cushioned wall pews around heavy tables, fresh flowers, and swagged-back curtains and houseplants in the windows; on the angle between here and the bar area there's a fat woodburning stove in an opened-through corner fireplace. The bar has a big log fire, wood-backed built-in wall seats and some red fabric-cushioned stools, stripped-stone walls and a good pubby atmosphere. Diners are encouraged to step down into a snug inner room (lightened by mirrors in arched windows'), or to go round to the sturdy tables angling off on the right (where a pianist may be quietly vamping his way through the favourite standards five nights a week). Note that most of these tables get booked at weekends. The well praised bar food (now waitress-served and thought to have gone slightly upmarket by some) includes home-made soup with a good chunk of wholemeal bread (£1.95), filled baguettes (from £2.50), spicy chicken wings in a hot chilli sauce or grilled goat's cheese with walnut dressing (£3.25), ploughman's (£3.55), mushrooms and bacon sautéed with sherry, cream and onions (£3.95), vegetable risotto or chilli (£4.75), cod in parsley sauce or fillet of beef and ginger stir-fry (£6.95), breast of chicken in a cream and grain mustard sauce (£7.75), salmon in hollandaise sauce (£7.50), steaks (from £9.25), specials like mussels or rack of lamb, and puddings (£2.25); tea and coffee. Well kept Bass, Boddingtons, Butcombe and Wadworths 6X, and a good wine list, strong on medium priced well made wines; efficient staff; cribbage, dominoes, fruit machine, boules, mousehole and trivia. The bedrooms are attractively furnished (all are non-smoking), and breakfasts are good. There are picnic-table sets on the front terrace. *(Recommended by Charles and Dorothy Ellsworth, L G Holmes, Peter Churchill, George Jonas, Dave and Jules Tuckett, Simon and Amanda Southwell, P M Lane, A R and B E Sayer, M G Hart, R A F Seymour, Richard W Chew, Adrian Kelly, R W Brooks, Dave Braisted, Neale Davies)*

Free house ~ Licensee Nigel Pushman ~ Real ale ~ Meals and snacks (till 10) ~ Restaurant (not Sun evening) ~ Compton Dando (01761) 490202 ~ Children welcome ~ Pianist Mon, Weds, Fri and Sat ~ Open 11-11 ~ Bedrooms: £45.50B/£59.50B

If we know a pub has an outdoor play area for children, we mention it.

STOGUMBER   (Somerset)   ST0937   Map 1

White Horse £ ⇔

From A358 Taunton—Williton, village signposted on left at Crowcombe

At any time of year visiting this delightful little pub in a quiet conservation village is a very relaxing affair; sit outside on a summer day and all is quiet except for rooks and lambs in the surrounding low hills, while in winter you can unwind in front of the coal fire and idly listen to the piped Mozart or Strauss. The spotless and well cared for long bar has old-fashioned built-in settles, other settles and cushioned captain's chairs around the heavy rustic tables on the patterned carpet, and a friendly, bustling feel. Good, well priced bar food includes sandwiches (from £1.10; toasted from £1.20), home-made vegetable soup (£1.50), burger (£1.70), salads, ploughman's or omelette (all from £3.10), vegetable casserole (£3.20), meat, vegetable or fish lasagne (£3.90), chicken curry (£4.60), somerset pork (£5.20), trout with almonds (£6.90), steak (from £8.80), and puddings such as excellent walnut tart or steamed sultana sponge (£1.30); booking is pretty much essential for the three-course Sunday lunch (£8.50). Service is helpful and attentive. Well kept Cotleigh Tawny and Exmoor on handpump, and farmhouse cider in summer. A side room has sensibly placed darts and a fruit machine; shove-ha'penny, dominoes, cribbage, video game and piped music, as well as a separate skittle alley. If you're staying, count on good breakfasts. *(Recommended by Alan Carr, Joan Coleman, Pat and Robert Watt, A Plumb, J R Williams, David and Fiona Easeman, Colin Keane, Dagmar Junghanns, John Hazel, Mrs F Smith, Dr B D Smith, Alan and Maggie Telford, P Boot)*

Free house ~ Licensee Peter Williamson ~ Real ale ~ Meals and snacks (till 10) ~ Restaurant (Sun lunch and party bookings only) ~ Stogumber (01984) 56277 ~ Children in restaurant ~ Open 11-2.30, 6-11 ~ Bedrooms: £25B/£35B

STOKE ST GREGORY   (Somerset)   ST3527   Map 1

Rose & Crown ⇔ ♀

Woodhill; follow North Curry signpost off A378 by junction with A358 – keep on to Stoke, bearing right in centre and right again past church

There's a really welcoming feel at this warmly friendly 17th-c cottage, something that's got a lot to do with the cheerful family in charge. It's obvious they all really care about the place, and their enthusiasm comes across in the food, service and even the decor – many of the wildlife paintings on the walls are the work of the landlady. Her two sons are responsible for the cooking (they bake their own bread and produce their own marmalade), with good use of fresh local ingredients; the eggs come from their own chickens. The neatly kept and rather jolly bar is decorated in a cosy and pleasantly romanticised stable theme: dark wooden loose-box partitions for some of the interestingly angled nooks and alcoves, lots of brasses and bits on the low beams and joists, stripped stonework, and appropriate pictures including a highland pony carrying a stag. There's an 18th-c glass-covered well in one corner. Very generous helpings of popular, good value food such as sandwiches (from £1.25), soup (£1.50), ploughman's with various English cheeses, pint of prawns (£3.35), omelettes (£4), grilled liver and bacon, stuffed sole with crabmeat, half a roast chicken or gammon (all £4.95), a good few vegetarian dishes like nut roast chasseur and stuffed peppers with wild rice or seafood risotto (all £5.75), fresh fish from Brixham, steaks (from £7.50), delicious mixed grill (£9) and puddings with local clotted cream or home-made ice cream; excellent breakfasts, and a good three-course Sunday lunch (£7.25). They do various set menus too. Service is prompt and obliging. One small dining area is no smoking. Well kept Eldridge Pope Hardy and Royal Oak, and Exmoor on handpump; large selection of Taunton ciders, decent wines; unobtrusive piped classical music, dominoes, fruit machine and popular skittle alley. Under cocktail parasols by an apple tree on the sheltered front terrace are some picnic-table sets. In summer residents have use of a heated swimming pool. The pub is in an interesting Somerset Levels village with willow beds still supplying the two basket works. *(Recommended by Mrs T Froud, John le Sage, John and June Hayward, John A*

Barker, Paul Collins, Anna Lindars, Mrs E M Downard, Peter D Keane, John and Fiona Merritt, Stephen Brown, Alan and Eileen Bowker, Y Cotterill, Gethin Lewis, Richard Dolphin, Beryl and Bill Farmer, Don and Thelma Beeson, Brig J S Green, J E Davies)

Free house ~ Licensees Ron and Irene Browning ~ Real ale ~ Meals and snacks (till 10) ~ Restaurant ~ North Curry (01823) 490296 ~ Children welcome ~ Open 11-3, 6.30-11 ~ Bedrooms: £22.50/£36

STOKE ST MARY (Somerset) ST2622 Map 1

Half Moon

2¾ miles from M5 junction 25; A358 towards Ilminster, then first right, then right at T-junction and follow the signs. Westbound turn left at sign ¾ mile after the traffic lights

Nicely off the beaten track, this extensively-modernised village pub is a very well liked place for a good value lunch. Efficient and friendly uniformed staff serve a wide range of tasty dishes like soup (£1.65), sandwiches, breaded mushrooms with stilton sauce or potato skins with beef chilli (£2.25), salads (from £4.50), haddock and prawn bake (£4.95), vegetarian dishes such as leek and stilton bake or vegetable lasagne (all £5.25), steak and ale pie (£5.25), pork stroganoff (£5.95), chicken chasseur, poached salmon or beef bourguignon (£6.95), steaks (from £7.95), and puddings such as toffee, apple and pecan pie (£2.45) or ice cream liqueurs (£3.45); children's meals (£3.95), coffee and tea. Well kept Boddingtons, Theakstons BB and Wadworths 6X on handpump, and a range of country wines. Despite the emphasis on eating, each of the five neat open-plan main areas is furnished and decorated with a good deal of character and individuality, and there's quite a roomy and relaxed feel. Picnic-table sets on a well kept lawn and more tables on a small gravel terrace. The restaurants are no smoking. The licensees run another pub, the Merry Monk, at Monkton Heathfield. *(Recommended by Professor A N Black, Richard R Dolphin, Shirley Pielou, Don and Thelma Beeson, A E Brace)*

Whitbreads ~ Lease: Pat and Jan Howard ~ Real ale ~ Meals and snacks (till 10) ~ Two restaurants ~ Taunton (01823) 442271 ~ Children in eating area ~ Open 11-2.30, 6-11

TRISCOMBE (Somerset) ST1535 Map 1

Blue Ball

Village (and pub) signposted off A358 Taunton—Minehead

A very friendly thatched and rather cottagey little pub up on the edge of the Quantocks. This is good walking country, and there are fine views of the Brendon Hills from the picnic-table sets on the narrow terraced lawns built into the steep and peaceful slope. It does get very busy in summer, but out of season the atmosphere is particularly relaxed and unhurried. The neat brown-beamed bar has sporting prints on the white walls, piped light classical music, and barely more than half a dozen tables – one tucked under the mantelbeam of what used to be a monumental brick and stone fireplace; the conservatory does relieve the seasonal pressure on space. Well kept Butcombe, Cotleigh Tawny, Exmoor and Morlands Old Speckled Hen on handpump; dominoes, cribbage, skittle alley, piped music. They have a cocker spaniel, Chadwick, and other dogs are welcome on a lead. Quickly served bar food might include sandwiches or soup (from £2), deep-fried camembert with mango chutney (£2.65), well sized ploughman's (£3.40), giant savoury pancakes (from £3.75), mushroom and cashew nut pasta bake (£4.95), pork in cider or scampi (£5.25), steak and kidney pie (£5.50), daily specials, and puddings like treacle tart or lime cream pie (from £1.75). The lavatories are in an unusual separate thatched building, and they've just added a bedroom. *(Recommended by Colin Keane, Dagmar Junghanns, Debbie Jones, A Plumb, Jed and Virginia Brown, Dr R J Rathbone, Dr and Mrs B D Smith, J E Davies, H G Robertson)*

Free house ~ Licensee Nanette Little ~ Real ale ~ Meals and snacks (not Sun evening) ~ (01984) 618242 ~ Children in eating area and conservatory ~ Open 11-2.30, 7-11; closed Sun evening ~ Bedroom: £22.50B/£35B

TRUDOXHILL (Somerset) ST7443 Map2

White Hart ◀

Village signposted off A361 Frome—Wells

One reader's visit to this cheery place on a freezing Sunday morning sounds like something close to perfection; as the snow flurried down past the window he sat contentedly by the fire in the inglenook, munching cheese and nuts from the bar and sipping one of their excellent own brew beers. The busy little Ash Vine Brewery (which they'll show you if they're not too pushed) produces several thousand pints of their six ales each week, from the well flavoured light Ash Vine Bitter and delicate Trudoxhill, through the smooth Challenger and Black Bess Porter to the stronger mid-brown Tanker and rich winter Hop & Glory. As well as these they serve a well kept guest like Bass or Butcombe Bitter, cheap Thatcher's farm ciders on handpump, and plenty of country wines. The long, attractively carpeted, stripped-stone bar, really two room areas, has beams supporting broad stripped ceiling boards and a thriving, relaxed atmosphere. It's mostly table seating, with a couple of easy chairs by the big log fire on the right (there's a second at the other end), and some seats in the red velvet curtained windows. A very wide choice of popular home-made bar food includes sandwiches (from £1.60, toasted from £1.70), soup (£1.75), burgers (from £2.10), ploughman's (from £3.50), kidneys braised in red wine (£3.75), several vegetarian meals like curry or stilton and celery pie, and quite a few fish dishes like plaice, kedgeree or tuna bake (from £4.25), ham and eggs (£4.75), lasagne or beef, Guinness and mushroom pie (£4.95), rabbit pie or venison casserole (£5.75), steaks (from £8.75), puddings like treacle tart and chocolate fudge cake (£2.50), a three-course Sunday lunch (£6.95), and a children's menu (from £1.95); piped music. There are picnic-table sets on a flower-filled sheltered side lawn. *(Recommended by Steve Goodchild, Brig J S Green, Mike and Sue Moss, Tony and Joan Walker, Derek and Sylvia Stephenson, David Eberlin, S G N Bennett, Chris Elias, Chris and Sue Heathman and others)*

Own brew ~ Licensee Adam and Shelly Rimmer ~ Real ale ~ Meals and snacks (till 10) ~ Restaurant (not Sun evening) ~ (01373) 836324 ~ Children welcome ~ Open 12-3, 7(6.30 Fri and Sat)-11

WAMBROOK (Somerset) ST2907 Map 1

Cotley 🛏

Village signposted off A30 W of Chard; don't follow the small signs to Cotley itself

Named after the local hunt, this is a very pleasant and civilised stone-built country pub, nestling amidst rather narrow Arcadian lanes and looking down over the peaceful valley village. It's a quietly welcoming and comfortable place, with a smart but unpretentious local atmosphere that readers really like. The food comes in big helpings and is excellent quality, with dishes like well garnished sandwiches (from £1.40), ploughman's or filled baked potatoes (from £2.50), mushroom fritters (£3.50), omelettes or salads (from £4.50), vegetarian dishes such as mushrooms stuffed with spinach and cheese (£5.50), chicken breast in sherry and mushroom sauce, salmon steak in tarragon and wine sauce or pork escalope with cider and apple (£6.50), up to ten fish courses like filleted plaice (£5.50) or seafood gratin (£7.25), pheasant breasts in blackberry and port sauce (£7.95), daily specials and puddings (£2.50); coffee and tea. They have a board listing meals for those with smaller appetites. Service is friendly and obliging; one family we know of arrived late after losing their way but were still cheerily served a meal. The simple flagstoned entrance bar opens on one side into a small plush bar, with beyond that a two-room dining area, one of which is no smoking; various open fires. An extension is often used for painting sessions, and the results (complete with price-tags in case you see something you like) can be seen around the walls of the various rooms. Well kept Boddingtons on hand pump, and a good choice of wines; pool table, fruit machine, video game, alley skittles, and piped middle-of-the-road music. Out in the garden below are some picnic-table sets, with a play area and goldfish pool. Quiet on weekday lunchtimes, it can be very busy at weekends. Breakfasts are good. Lots of lovely walks all around. *(Recommended by Clem Stephens, David Eberlin, Doug and Doris Nash, Major D A Daniels, Pauline Bishop, K R Harris, Mr and Mrs Bird, S G N Bennett)*

Free house ~ Licensee D R Livingstone ~ Real ale ~ Meals and snacks (till 10) ~ Restaurant ~ (01460) 62348 ~ Children in eating area and restaurant ~ Open 11.30-3, 7-11 ~ Bedrooms: £20B/£30B

WELLOW (Avon) ST7458 Map 2

Fox & Badger

Village signposted on left on A367 SW of Bath

Easily identified by its striking sign showing the two animals in Regency dress, this is a traditional pub of the old school, a simple, flagstoned place with a friendly rural atmosphere, and three welcoming open fires. Exmoor Ale is sold at the extraordinary price of just £1 a pint, and they also have well kept Butcombe Bitter, Morlands Old Speckled Hen and Wadworths 6X on handpump, along with a decent choice of wines. The attractively furnished flagstone-floored bar has seats built into snug alcoves, small winged settles with cushions to match the curtains, flowers on the tables, a handsome fireplace and a pleasantly chiming clock; log fires in winter. The cosy carpeted public bar has shove-ha'penny, table skittles, darts, dominoes, cribbage, trivia, fruit machine and piped music, there's also a conservatory, and a free skittle alley. Reasonably priced wholesome bar food includes sandwiches, several hot dishes like meat or vegetable lasagne, Cumberland sausage, poached mushroom in stilton sauce and several other vegetarian dishes (£4.85), steak pie (£4.90), steaks (from £6.95) and a Sunday roast (£4.25); there may be summer barbecues in the courtyard. The friendly Australian landlord who took over just as we went to press plans several sympathetic changes to the furnishings and decor over the next few months. *(Recommended by Bob Riley, Betty and Ken Cantle, S G N Bennett, Meg Hamilton, A Plumb, Mr and Mrs K Box, Roger Huggins, Dave and Jules Tuckett, MH)*

Grand Met ~ Tenant Ray Houston ~ Real ale ~ Meals and snacks ~ Restaurant ~ Bath (01225) 832293 ~ Children welcome except in public bar ~ Open 11-3, 6-11

WEST HARPTREE (Avon) ST5556 Map 2

Blue Bowl

Off A368 Bath—Weston

This extended stonebuilt country dining pub has an engaging series of separate rooms, with wheelback chairs around lots of tables, some traditional built-in wall seats, a delft shelf of decorative china. Unusually, it's the room where children are allowed, around the corner on the left, which tends to be the nicest when the pub's busy: another delft shelf, big windows, landscape pictures, a stripped panelling dado, and pews or sturdy light pine chairs around the tables. The very wide choice of good food, served generously, includes sandwiches (from £1.70), home-made soup (£1.85), ploughman's (from £3.50), home-baked ham and egg (£4.50), tagliatelle carbonara (£5.15), lamb with mushroom and peppers or chicken and leek pie (£5.45), smoked haddock pasta (£5.65) and specials such as stuffed courgettes (£4.95), monkfish provençale (£5.75) and massive Sunday roasts, with enormous helpings of home-made puddings such as spotted dick or bakewell tart (£2.10). Well kept Bass, Courage Best and Wadworths 6X on handpump; games area with sensibly placed darts, shove-ha'penny, table skittles, cribbage and dominoes; unobtrusive piped music. Service is friendly and efficient, and the atmosphere thriving and lively. Tables out on the back terrace look out over meadows, and there are picnic-table sets on quite a spacious stretch of safely fenced lawn; the new tenants have put up a big aviary, with zebra finches. We have not yet heard from readers who have stayed here. *(Recommended by Martyn G Hart, L Mercer, Peter Churchill)*

Courage ~ Lease: Mark Middleton ~ Real ale ~ Meals and snacks (12-2.30, 6.30-10) ~ (01761) 221269 ~ Children in family room ~ Open 11.30-11; cl evening 25 Dec ~ Bedrooms: £16.50/£33

WEST HUNTSPILL (Somerset) ST3044 Map 1

Crossways 🍺

2¾ miles from M5 junction 23 (A38 towards Highbridge); 4 miles from M5 junction 22 (A38 beyond Highbridge)

This spacious 17th-c dining pub is well worth the detour from the motorway, and at lunchtime is often full of people eating. The main part of the bar has dining-room chairs, a mixture of settles, seats built into one converted brick fireplace and good winter log fires in the others. At one end there's more of a dining room, prettily decorated with old farm machinery engravings, Albert and Chic cartoons (chiefly about restaurants), and 1920ish hunting prints, as well as neat red seats, and a brass colonial fan in its dark ceiling; on Friday and Saturday evenings this area becomes a bistro (£9.50 for three courses). The other end has an area with big winged settles making booths, and there's a family room with bamboo-back seats around neat tables. Bar food (listed on a rather handy pocket-sized menu) includes generous sandwiches (from £1.60), soup (£1.80), ploughman's (£3.20), vegetable bake (£3.80), ham and prawn mornay or moussaka (£4.50), steak and kidney pie or beef stroganoff (£4.80), steaks (from £8.50), daily specials and home-made puddings such as treacle tart, bitter sweet chocolate pudding or lemon cheesecake; children's menu. There might be a wait at busy times but they'll usually warn you. Well kept Boddingtons, Butcombe Bitter, Flowers IPA and Original, Eldridge Pope Royal Oak, Palmers IPA and Smiles Best on handpump, with a changing and often unusual guest; lots of malt whiskies, freshly squeezed orange juice and Rich's farmhouse cider. Darts, cribbage, dominoes, shove ha'penny, fruit machine, video game and skittle alley. There are picnic-table sets among fruit trees in quite a big garden. A few readers have this year come across slight hiccups in the generally high standards of food and service. If you're staying, the back rooms are quieter. *(Recommended by Bill and Beryl Farmer, Patrick Clancy, Dorothee and Dennis Glover, Jerry and Alison Oakes, Graham and Karen Oddey, H F Cox, Tom Evans, K R Waters, Don Kellaway, Angie Coles, Joan Coleman, E J Locker, Neale Davies, Richard Dolphin, E D Bailey, Joy Heatherley, John Radford, Dave Braisted)*

Free house ~ Licensees Michael Ronca and Tony Eyles ~ Real ale ~ Meals and snacks (till 10) ~ Restaurant (Fri/Sat only) ~ Burnham-on-Sea (01278) 783756 ~ Children welcome except in main bar ~ Occasional live music ~ Open 12-3, 5.30(6 Sat)-11; closed 25 Dec ~ Bedrooms: £24B/£34B

WINSFORD (Somerset) SS9034 Map 1

Royal Oak 🍺 ♀

In Exmoor National Park, village signposted from A396 about 10 miles S of Dunster

A beautiful thatched inn by the village cross, nicely placed beneath peaceful rolling fields and hills. The atmosphere is very relaxed in a smartly civilised sort of way, and it's hard to believe that in the 17th c customers were regularly plundered by the Exmoor highwayman Tom Faggus, exploits which R D Blackmore, a frequent visitor, worked into *Lorna Doone*. From the cushioned big bay-window seat in the cosy lounge bar you look across the road towards the village green and foot and packhorse bridges over the River Winn. Horsebrasses and pewter tankards hang from the beam above the attractively panelled bar counter, there are Windsor armed chairs and cushioned seats on the red carpet, and a splendid iron fireback in the big stone hearth (with a log fire in winter). Another similarly old-fashioned bar has good brass, copper, wall prints and darts. Home-made bar food includes soup (£1.95), sandwiches (from £2.25), a generous ploughman's (£3.95), asparagus pancake (£5.50), mushroom and nut strudel or good pies such as chicken and leek or steak and kidney (£5.75), evening extras like steak (£8.50) or local trout (£8.95), various daily specials, and a choice of home-made puddings (£2.25); tea and coffee; big breakfasts. The good (though pricey) restaurant has a special menu for vegetarians. Well kept Flowers IPA and Original on handpump, and an excellent range of other drinks, particularly liqueurs and brandies; friendly staff. As various prestigious awards testify, it is a very pleasant place to spend a night or two, and they do a useful guide to Exmoor National Park identifying places to visit. Good nearby walks – up Winsford Hill for magnificent views, or over to Exford. *(Recommended by T H G Lewis, John and Christine Vittoe, Peter and Audrey Dowsett, Neil and Anita Christopher, R W Brooks, Alec and Marie Lewery, Andrew Latchem, Helen Reed, John Allsopp)*

Free house ~ Licensee Charles Steven ~ Real ale ~ Meals and snacks ~ Restaurant (not Sun evening) ~ Winsford (0164 385) 455 ~ Children welcome except in front bar ~ Open 11-2.30, 6-11 ~ Bedrooms: £45B/£90B

WITHYPOOL (Somerset) SS8435 Map 1

Royal Oak 🛏 ♀
Village signposted off B4233

Another very well regarded place to stay, this stylish country inn nestles in the heart of some of Exmoor's best scenery. The smartly cosy beamed lounge bar, popular with locals, has a stag's head and several fox masks on its walls, comfortable button-back brown seats and slat-backed chairs, and a log fire in a raised stone fireplace; another quite spacious bar is similarly decorated. Acclaimed bar snacks include sandwiches (from £1.95), home-made soup (£1.85), snails grilled with garlic butter and parsley (£3.15), ploughman's or filled baked potatoes (from £3.65), salads (from £4.45), two large sausages (with a choice of garlic or herb or venison and bacon – £5.75), good steaks (from £6.30), half crispy duck (£9.90), lots of fish specials (including lobster in season), and puddings. Well kept Brians Bitter and Devenish Royal Wessex on handpump, as well as farm cider, a fair number of vintage brandies, quite a few malt whiskies, and unusual wines, several by the half bottle. Service is attentive and cheerful; Good coffee. It can get very busy (especially on Sunday lunchtimes), and is popular with the local hunting and shooting types; cribbage and dominoes. There are wooden benches on the terrace, and just up the road, some grand views from Winsford Hill, with tracks leading up among the ponies into the heather past Withypool Hill. The River Barle runs through the village itself, with pretty bridleways following it through a wooded combe further upstream. For guests, they can arrange salmon and trout fishing, riding (stabling also), clay pigeon shooting, rough shooting, hunting, sea fishing from a boat and trips to see wild red deer. This is another pub with a *Lorna Doone* connection; R D Blackmore stayed here while writing the book. *(Recommended by R J Walden, Jim and Maggie Cowell, Clem Stephens, Michael and Harriet Robinson, Dave and Louise Clark, Veronica Purcocks, H and D Payne, Gethin Lewis)*

Free house ~ Licensee Michael Bradley ~ Real ale ~ Meals and snacks ~ Restaurant ~ Exford (0164 383) 506 ~ Children in restaurant ~ Open 11-2.30, 6-11; closed 25 and 26 Dec ~ Bedrooms: £28(£40B)/£52(£68B)

WOOLVERTON (Somerset) ST7954 Map 2

Red Lion ♀
A36, at N end of village on E side of road

An attractive extended former farmhouse, said to be haunted by the ghost of a woman convicted for murder in the days when the building was the local court. The bar has beams, flagstones, old panelling, cushioned farmhouse chairs, and a winged high-backed settle by the big stone hearth with a log-effect gas fire, as well as lots of comfortably cushioned seats around decent elm tables, and an expanse of parquet flooring with oriental-style rugs. Consistently well kept Bass and Wadworths IPA and 6X on handpump, several bottled beers, mulled wine in winter and a notable choice of between 20 and 25 wines by the glass; good service. The range of bar food has changed, though there's still some emphasis on the popular filled baked potatoes, with various unusual stuffings like bacon, onion and stilton (£2.85), chicken, sweetcorn, pineapple and cheese (£3.15), and prawn, ham and asparagus (£3.55); other meals include burgers (£3.95), fresh plaice (£5.50), their good salads (around £4 – they don't do quite so many as before), substantial seafood or meat platters (£5.95), gammon (£6), steaks (£8.95) and various home-made daily specials; you can eat outside, under the trees. Piped music. *(Recommended by Dave and Jules Tuckett, M J D Inskip, Tracey and Kevin Stephens; more reports please)*

Wadworths ~ Tenant Barry Lander ~ Real ale ~ Meals and snacks (till 10) ~ (01373) 830350 ~ Children welcome except main bar ~ Open 11.30-11(10.30 Mon/Tues)

Lucky Dip

Besides the fully inspected pubs, you might like to try these Lucky Dips recommended to us and described by readers (if you do, please send us reports) Unless we say Av (for Avon), places outside Bath and Bristol are in Somerset:

Abbots Leigh, Av [Pill Rd; A369, between M5 junction 19 and Bristol; ST5473], *George*: Popular main-road dining pub with friendly prompt service, enormous choice of attractively presented food, real ales inc Marstons Pedigree; no children *(Alan and Heather Jacques, D Godden, Dave and Jules Tuckett, LYM)*

Alcombe [SS9845], *Britannia*: Good local run by friendly newish landlord, decent choice of food, interesting real ales *(John Hazel)*

Allerford [SS9047], *Victory*: Very popular recently extended pub with over half a dozen well kept ales inc guest beers, good value straightforward food inc substantial ploughman's and good steaks *(John and Fiona Merritt)*

☆ **Ashcott** [High St; ST4337], *Ring o' Bells*: Genuine three-room village local with good wide choice of food inc vegetarian, well kept Bass and Worthington BB, helpful service, comfortable seats, decent wines, good mix of customers, skittle alley, fruit machines, restaurant with soft piped music *(John A Barker, M E and Mrs J Wellington)*

☆ **Ashcott**, *Pipers*: Comfortable and roomy hotelish bar with good range of food in eating area (popular with lunching businessmen), Courage-related ales, prompt welcoming service, log fire, big fans, pleasant roadside garden *(Brig J S Green)*

☆ **Axbridge** [The Square; quite handy for M5; ST4255], *Lamb*: Rambling old pub with good generous food, welcoming service, well kept ales such as Butcombe and Wadworths 6X, farm cider, log fire, pub games, skittle alley, pretty little garden with cockatiels; children in eating area till 9; old-world spacious bedrooms; in attractive square *(Mr and Mrs A E McCully, Peter Cornall, Brig J S Green, LYM)*

☆ **Barrington** [ST3818], *Royal Oak*: Wide and unusual range of quickly changing real ales, lots of interesting foreign bottled beers, good choice of innovative bar food at reasonable prices and thriving chatty atmosphere in plain public bar and small cosy lounge; skittle alley, friendly landlord, attractive village; handy for Barrington Court *(Richard R Dolphin, Maj and Mrs J A Gardner)*

☆ **Barrow Gurney**, Av [Barrow St (B3130, linking A370/A38 SW of Bristol; ST5367], *Princes Motto*: Friendly little local with well kept Bass and other ales such as Boddingtons, Butcombe and Smiles Best; snug traditional tap room, long room up behind, a real welcome for visitors, cheap wholesome lunchtime snacks inc good value ploughman's *(Mr and Mrs A E McCully, Tim and Chris Ford, David Eberlin, LYM)*

☆ **Batcombe** [off A359 Bruton—Frome; formerly the Three Horse Shoes; ST6838], *Batcombe Inn*: Wide choice of good attractively presented home-made food inc vegetarian, not cheap but original, in 14th-c inn behind church in pretty village, low beams, big log fire and woodburning stoves, copper and brass, games room, new dining area, comfortable minstrel's gallery; well kept Flowers Original, Marstons Pedigree and Oakhill, service attentive without being intrusive, no music or machines, busy weekends; tables in walled garden, children welcome; two bedrooms with own bathrooms *(John and Joan Dawson, Mark Burne, R H Martyn)*

☆ **Bath** [Mill Lane, Bathampton (off A36 towards Warminster or A4 towards Chippenham)], *George*: Attractive creeper-covered canalside pub, friendly and efficient service even when busy (which it can be, esp weekends), wide choice of good quick food inc fish and vegetarian, not cheap, good log fires, well kept Bass and Courage Directors; dining room by towpath, no-smoking family room, tables on quiet safe spacious back terrace with garden bar (traffic noise at front); can get crowded, esp weekends *(Mrs M Hamilton, Bob Riley, Ralf Zeyssig, S G Brown)*

☆ **Bath** [The Paragon; junction with Guinea Lane], *Star*: Particularly well kept Bass, Butcombe and Wadworths 6X in jugs from the cask in good traditional pub with small rooms separated by glass and panelling, low prices, fresh filled rolls, friendly landlord *(Roger Wain-Heapy, Chris Elias, BB)*

Bath [Walcot St], *Bell*: Well kept Butcombe, Wadworths 6X and guest beers, superb value filled rolls, friendly efficient service, free music several times a week – very popular with musicians of all persuasions *(Bill Bailey)*; [Westgate Rd], *Mulligans*: Irish pub with small simple bar, good lunchtime snacks, lots of traditional Irish music, appropriate drinks inc impressive choice of Irish whiskeys, pleasant staff *(J Boylan, Mr and Mrs Staine)*; [Richmond Pl, Beacon Hill], *Richmond Arms*: Small 18th-c two-room local with good simple food, well kept beer, friendly staff, and interesting decor; front garden with tables *(Bob Riley)*; [42 Broad St], *Saracens Head*: Useful for wide choice of generous food (lower prices than in many places here) inc Sat cold table, well kept Courage, quick service; a bit dark inside, and atmosphere not its strongest point *(J Boylan, Caroline Wright)*

☆ **Bathford**, Av [2 Bathford Hill; signed off A363, Bath—Bradford-on-Avon; ST7966], *Crown*: Spacious and attractively laid out, with different furnishings in each of four or five linked areas inc no-smoking garden room, interesting decorations, good log fire; wide choice of generally good though rather pricy bar food from filled rolls up inc vegetarian dishes, though service can sometimes be slow; well kept Bass, Marstons Pedigree and Ushers Best, decent wines; good for families, tables on terrace, nice garden; cl Mon lunchtime exc bank hols *(Mrs M Hamilton, A Curry, Chris Elias, Alan and Eileen Bowker, Catherine Hamilton, Bob Riley, J E Rycroft, Adam and Elizabeth Duff, George Atkinson, Dr Andrew Brookes, Pat and John Millward, Joy Heatherley, LYM)*

Bathpool [ST2525], *Bathpool*: Welcoming family pub with lots of cosy seating, safe garden with bark-covered play park and bouncy castle, supervised indoor soft play area; good fresh and appetising food inc children's menu, high chairs; good choice of real ales *(Mrs Julia Apps)*

Bayford [ST7229], *Unicorn*: Very welcoming landlord, good value generous food, well kept Butcombe; beams and flagstones *(John Honnor)*

☆ **Biddisham** [off A38 Bristol—Bridgwater, not far from M5 junction 22; ST3853], *New Moon*: Large attractive family eating area in open-plan beamed pub with genuine well presented good value straightforward food, good friendly service; enclosed verandah, picnic-table sets in small garden *(K R Harris, Mr and Mrs D J Nash, Mark Undrill)*

☆ **Bishops Lydeard** [A358 towards Taunton; ST1828], *Kingfishers Catch*: Good choice of consistently good value food from lunchtime ploughman's and other snacks to steaks in neatly welcoming cottagey place, quiet and relaxing, with pleasant quick service; really run as a restaurant despite its pub licence *(Shirley Pielou, LYM)*

Bishops Lydeard [West St], *Bell*: Interesting pub in attractive village, children's room off big public bar with usual games, wide choice of good food in dining area of pleasant lounge, real ales inc Exmoor and

guests; very handy for West Somerset Rly *(B M Eldridge)*

Blagdon, Av [Bath Rd; A368; ST5059], *Live & Let Live*: Cosy partly panelled back bar with log fire and sporting prints, generous bar food maybe inc trout caught by landlord, good Sun lunch, well kept Ushers Founders, sensibly placed darts, pool and other pub games, restaurant; handy for fishing on Blagdon Lake; bedrooms *(Frank & Daphne Hodgson, LYM)*

Bleadon [Bridgwater Rd; ST3357], *Hobbs Boat*: Pleasant atmosphere, usual Brewers Fayre bar food all day, good young service, separate no-smoking dining area, family room with own entrance; play areas inside and out *(P H Brown, D Fitzgerald)*

☆ **Brent Knoll** [2 miles from M5 junction 22; right on to A38, then first left; ST3350], *Red Cow*: Sensibly short choice of good well priced food served promptly by pleasant staff in friendly and spotless dining lounge where children allowed, with well spaced tables; well kept Whitbreads-related ales, skittle alley, pleasant sheltered gardens *(Adrian and Gwynneth Littleton, Philip Brown, BB)*

☆ **Bristol** [Upper Maudlin St/Colston St], *Brewery Tap*: The tap for Smiles brewery with their beers kept well, also interesting Continental bottled ones; small but clean and attractive, with good atmosphere even when packed; filled rolls, real fire; drinks 11-8, closed Sun *(Barry and Anne, Simon and Amanda Southwell, R Marleyn)*

☆ **Bristol** [St Thomas Lane, off Redcliff St/Victoria St], *Fleece & Firkin*: Lively atmosphere in lofty dim-lit 18th-c wool hall stripped back to stone and flagstones, basic furniture, Allied and guest beers, lunchtime food (not Sun) inc gigantic filled baps, pleasant staff, live music Weds-Sat, children weekends *(J Boylan, Dave and Jules Tuckett, LYM)*

☆ **Bristol** [Sion Pl, off Portland St], *Coronation Tap*: Quaint and friendly little bustling old-fashioned low-ceilinged tavern famous for its fat casks of interesting farm ciders, also Courage Best and Directors, simple lunchtime food *(Barry and Anne, Gordon Mott, LYM)*

☆ **Bristol** [Victoria St], *Shakespeare*: Elegantly refurbished partly panelled 17th-c pub with wide choice of food all day, well kept Bass, Courage Best and Directors and Wadworths 6X, friendly quick service, open fire, good atmosphere *(Mike Walters, LYM)*

☆ **Bristol** [Lower Park Row], *Ship*: Several well kept real ales such as Smiles and Wadworths 6X and reasonably priced food in low-ceilinged long narrow bar with nautical memorabilia, dimly lit back balcony, spiral stairs down to lower area with pool table, small lounge and small sunny terrace; well reproduced piped music esp evening *(Simon and Amanda Southwell, J Boylan)*

Bristol [off Boyce's Ave, Clifton], *Albion*: Friendly and unpretentiously old-fashioned pub with unusual flagstoned courtyard off cobbled alley, well kept Courage real ales, simple snacks *(J Boylan, LYM)*; [Bell Hill, Stapleton; ST6176], *Bell*: Large high-ceilinged roadside pub with spotless lounge bar, well kept beers, friendly service, good home-made food *(Dr and Mrs A K Clarke, A E and P McCully)*; [Baltic Wharf, Cumberland Rd], *Cottage*: Converted customs house well placed in dockland redevelopment, fine views of Bath landmarks from tables on terrace, Boddingtons, Flowers IPA and Ruddles County on handpump, reasonably priced well cooked lunchtime food, efficient friendly staff, plenty of space; piped music; open all day *(Gwen and Peter Andrews, J Morrell, Bob Riley)*; [188 Church Rd (A420), Redfield], *Fire Engine*: Main rd suburban pub with good range of well prepared food inc bargain lunch *(K R Harris)*; [32 Park St], *Le Château*: Wonderful mix of real ale pub, wine bar, bistro, conservatory, Victorian memorial *(Dr and Mrs A K Clarke)*; [17-18 King St], *Naval Volunteer*: Well done re-creation of traditional city pub, long bar buzzing with conversation, real ales inc Bass and Smiles tapped from the cask, nice dark wood decor *(John and Phyllis Maloney)*; [51 Stokes Croft], *Old Pint & Pie*: Well refurbished with friendly atmosphere, good range of interesting beers *(Dr and Mrs A K Clarke)*; [Princess Victoria St, Clifton], *Quadrant*: Flourishing as free house under new management, pleasant atmosphere, well kept ales, sandwiches and coffee *(Patrick Godfrey)*; [Lower Redland Rd], *Shakespeare*: Well run Edwardian suburban local with quick friendly service, pleasant inexpensive bar food, well kept Bass and Wadworths 6X; no piped music *(A D Halls)*

☆ **Broomfield** [1½ miles outside, on Bishops Lydeard—Bridgwater rd; ST2033], *Travellers Rest*: Attractive two-room pub with three separate sitting areas in largest room; attentive staff, Flowers and Whitbreads real ales, wide choice of pleasantly served food inc good soups and pies, log fires; tables outside, well placed for Quantocks *(John A Barker)*

☆ **Bruton** [High St; ST6834], *Castle*: Good solid food value and changing choice of well kept real ales in friendly and unpretentious town pub, striking mural of part of town in skittle alley, tables in sheltered back garden; children in eating area and skittle alley *(Dorothy Pilson, LYM)*

Cannington [High St (A39); ST2539], *Kings Head*: Good reasonably priced food, separate dining area; bedrooms *(Rex Miller)*

Castle Cary [ST6332], *George*: Lovely thatched hotel in quiet market town, attractive dining room and lounge, cosy small front bar with big inglenook, well kept Bass and Butcombe, decent house wine, wide choice of bar food, good restaurant (not Sun), helpful hard-working owners and staff, good atmosphere; bedrooms comfortable *(Steve Goodchild)*

Catcott [ST3939], *Crown*: Popular and friendly local with decent food, well kept beer *(T J H Bodys)*

Charfield, Av [off M5 junction 14, via B4509; ST7191], *Huntingford Mill*: Welcoming and attractively unusual bars, Archers and Bass, bar food with good chips, OAP discount *(P Graham Woods)*

☆ **Charlton Musgrove** [B3081, 5 miles SE of Bruton; ST7229], *Smithy*: Welcoming new ex-Navy landlord doing well in neatly refurbished 18th-c pub, beautifully kept, with stripped stone, heavy beams, log fires, good atmosphere, home-cooked food inc Sun lunch, Butcombe, Fullers London Pride and Wadworths 6X; arch to small restaurant overlooking garden, skittle alley and pool table *(E J Wilde, WHBM)*

Chewton Magna [A38 Wells rd; ST5953], *Waldegrave Arms*: Very good range of reasonably priced home-cooked food, friendly efficient staff *(Hilary Aslett)*

☆ **Chilcompton** [ST6452], *Somerset Wagon*: Good popular food inc wide vegetarian choice in friendly and atmospheric pub with lots of books, stuffed animals and militaria *(Tracey and Kevin Stephens, Susan Bourton)*

☆ **Chilthorne Domer** [ST5219], *Carpenters Arms*: Comfortable and very welcoming country pub with good sensibly priced home-cooked bar food inc vegetarian, well kept Boddingtons, Marstons Pedigree and Wadworths 6X, service efficient even when busy, open fire, fresh flowers *(Matthew Phillips, Rebecca and Tom Hyde, Alan and June Lucas)*

Churchill, Av [Bristol Rd (A38); ST4560], *Churchill Inn*: Spacious and comfortable, with good prompt service, six real ales, usual bar food inc children's menu and Sun lunch *(Mr and Mrs Peter Woods)*

Churchingford [ST2112], *York*: Attractive decor, very welcoming landlord, very wide choice of well presented food worth waiting for, three real ales; bedrooms with own bathrooms *(Shirley Pielou)*

☆ **Clevedon**, Av [Elton Rd (seafront); ST4071], *Little Harp*: Spacious and popular recently refurbished pub, terrace and conservatory looking towards Exmoor and the Welsh hills, good helpings of food inc substantial beef sandwiches and vegetarian dishes, well kept Bass *(JCW, Tom Evans, Mr and Mrs A E McCully)*

☆ **Clevedon** [15 The Beach], *Moon & Sixpence*: Substantial seafront Victorian house with mezzanine bar, balconied upper floor with view to Brecon Beacons, well kept Bass and Smiles tapped from the barrel, good choice of good straightforward food, quick helpful service; children allowed downstairs *(Mr and Mrs A E*

McCully)

Clutton Hill, Av [King Lane; off A39 Bristol—Wells - OS Sheet 172 map ref 633601; ST6360], *Hunters Rest*: Carefully extended stonebuilt pub with wide choice of bar food from interestingly filled rolls and pastries, through ploughman's, steak and kidney pie, lasagne and so forth to steaks; several real ales, family room, no-smoking area, log fires, restaurant, gardens with weekend miniature railway and view to Mendips; facilities for disabled *(Anon)*

Cocklake [ST4349], *Trotters*: Character unspoilt pub with lots of interesting bric-a-brac, Butcombe, Eldridge Pope Royal Oak and Wadworths 6X, two friendly boxers and a cat roaming around *(Rupert Lecomber)*

Codrington, Av [handy for M4 junction 18, via B4465; ST7579], *Codrington Arms*: Welcoming, with good range of beers, well prepared food inc some unusual dishes and delicious fish and chips *(KC)*

Compton [B3151 S of Street; ST4933], *Castlebrook*: Recently refurbished keeping old flagstones etc, obliging landlord, well kept Morlands Old Speckled Hen and Worthington BB, bar food, skittle alley; caravan campsite behind *(John Sanders)*

☆ **Congresbury**, Av [St Pauls Causeway; off main rd; ST4363], *Old Inn*: Friendly and peaceful little local with well kept Bass, Marstons Pedigree, Smiles and Wadworths 6X, decent cheap food, open fire, ancient stove, hundred of matchboxes on low beams *(Mr and Mrs A E McCully, Ron Shelton, P M Lane)*

Congresbury [Brinsea Rd (B3133), *Plough*: Recent refurbishment after flood damage has enhanced old character; two open fires, well kept Bass and Wadworths 6X; tables outside in small garden *(Mr and Mrs McCully)*

Corton Denham [OS Sheet 183 map ref 634225; ST6322], *Queens Arms*: Warmly welcoming staff and hard-working owners in meticulously kept stonebuilt village inn with lots of fresh flowers and brasses, good range of well kept frequently changing often recherché guest beers, good reasonably priced food cooked by landlady; nr Cadbury Castle, bedrooms with good views *(Ian and Val Titman, John and Joan Nash)*

☆ **Dinnington** [ST4012], *Rose & Crown*: Good atmosphere in attractive country pub, unspoilt despite popularity, with good value home cooking esp seafood, good range of real ales, no juke box *(David and Fiona Easeman, Michael Duck)*

☆ **Ditcheat** [village signed off A37 and A371 S of Shepton Mallet; ST6236], *Manor House*: Really friendly welcome and very wide choice of good attractively priced food inc local cheddar sandwiches and unusual puddings in pretty village pub with arched doorways connecting big flagstoned public bar to comfortably relaxed lounge and close-tabled eating area; well kept

Butcombe and Youngers, open fires, skittle alley, tables on back grass *(Derek and Iris Martin, P and J Rush, Gwen and Peter Andrews, LYM)*

☆ **Dulverton** [High St; SS9127], *Lion*: Old-fashioned country-town hotel with warm, friendly and informal service, well kept Exmoor and Ushers on handpump, decent wine, good value food, decent cheap coffee *(Gwen and Peter Andrews)*

Dundry, Av [Church Rd; off A38 SW of Bristol; ST5567], *Dundry*: Comfortable country pub with outstanding views over Bristol, good quick lunchtime food, friendly service, well kept beer, tasteful prints, occasional summer barbecues *(P D Putwain, John Abbott)*

☆ **East Coker** [ST5412], *Helyar Arms*: Good well presented reasonably priced food esp fish, super service and good range of real ales in tastefully extended and nicely decorated oak-beamed pub; attractive village setting *(Wg Cdr J W Lovell)*

☆ **East Harptree** [ST5655], *Waldegrave Arms*: Unpretentiously comfortable and interesting, pleasant nooks and crannies, spotless brass and copper, friendly service, good food inc fresh veg, well kept Ushers, decent wine *(Alan and Heather Jacques)*

☆ **East Woodlands** [off Frome bypass; ST7944], *Horse & Groom*: Small country pub with decent food inc lots of fish under new owners, several mainly local well kept real ales, decent house wines, no music or machines, two good clean rooms (one allowing dogs) and new conservatory; not far from Longleat *(Mr and Mrs Paul Adams)*

☆ **Edington Burtle** [Catcott Rd; ST3943], *Olde Burtle*: Attractive and friendly local atmosphere, good food in bar and restaurant, very warm real fire *(M P Furmston)*

☆ **Exford** [B3224; SS8538], *White Horse*: Rustic-style open-plan bar, hunting prints and trophies, usual bar food and good generous Sun carvery, real ales such as Bass, Cotleigh Tawny, Exmoor and Worthington, log fire, pleasant safe garden by River Exe; children in eating area, dogs allowed; open all day summer, lovely Exmoor village setting; bedrooms comfortable *(Alec and Marie Lewery, Mr and Mrs K Box, Ian Smith, Dick Brown, LYM)*

☆ **Farleigh Hungerford** [A366 Trowbridge—Norton St Philip; ST8057], *Hungerford Arms*: Attractive smartly furnished pub with good views, decent food in main bar, more airy room off, and popular lower-level restaurant, well kept Courage-related ales, friendly service *(Ted George)*

Felton, Av [ST5265], *George & Dragon*: Plain and pleasant bar, decent straightforward food *(D G Clarke)*

Fitzhead [ST1128], *Fitzhead*: Village pub run by enthusiastic young couple, furniture made by landlord, good choice of real ales, popular food inc usual pub dishes and enterprising specials esp imaginative fish; friendly atmosphere, piped music mostly Irish, very busy weekends *(A Kersey-Brown)*

Frampton Cotterell, Av [Beesmoor Rd; ST6683], *Golden Lion*: Family dining pub with big helpings of reasonably priced nicely cooked food from varied menu inc good puddings, good friendly atmosphere, well kept Bass and Ind Coope Burton tapped from the cask; lots of tables but does get busy around 8pm *(Dennis Heatley, A D Shore)*

Frampton Cotterell [Bristol Rd], *Western Coach House*: Quiet, largish Courage local with good value dish of the day *(K R Harris)*

☆ **Glastonbury** [High St], *George & Pilgrims*: Magnificent medieval carved stone frontage, and front bar with handsome stone fireplace and 15th-c traceried stained-glass bay window; rest of pub, and food and service, more ordinary; well kept Bass and Wadworths 6X, children in buffet and pleasant upstairs restaurant; good clean bedrooms *(John and Phyllis Maloney, Gwen and Peter Andrews, LYM)*

☆ **Glastonbury** [Northload St; ST5039], *Who'd A Thought It*: Friendly landlord, good atmosphere in bar and separate no-smoking restaurant, lots of memorabilia inc ceilings decorated with events posters from 60s to present day, good often original food esp fish, well kept Bass, Eldridge Pope Blackdown Porter and Thomas Hardy and Palmers, decent wines, open fires; bedrooms cosy and comfortable, good breakfasts *(Dr and Mrs J D Abell, Andrew and Helen Latchem, P M Lane, Martin Copeman)*

Green Ore [A39 N of Wells; ST5750], *Plough Boy*: L-shaped bar with winter log fire, welcoming landlord and staff, and light piped music; generous helpings of well garnished food, well kept Bass, Smiles and changing guests *(Alistair Stanier)*

Hallatrow, Av [ST6357], *Old Station*: Decent food, simple model train layout hidden in formidable collection of bric-a-brac, garden behind *(D G Clarke)*

Hanham, Av [Hanham Mills; ST6472], *Chequers*: Large riverside pub well off the beaten track, good range of beers, friendly staff *(Dr and Mrs A K Clarke)*

☆ **Hardway** [rd to Alfreds Tower, off B3081 Bruton—Wincanton at Redlynch; pub named on OS Sheet 183 map ref 721342; ST7234], *Bull*: Neat and attractive country dining pub under new licensees, has been very popular locally esp with older people for weekday lunches and early reports suggest food still just as good; warm comfortable bar, character dining rooms, log fire, well kept Butcombe and Wadworths 6X, farm cider; piped music; tables in nice garden over road, handy for Stourhead Garden *(Pat and Robert Watt, Michael Porter, John and Joan Nash, W and S Jones; more reports please)*

☆ **Haselbury Plucknett** [off N side of A30 about 1½ miles from Crewkerne; ST4711], *Old Mill*: A real find, wonderful atmosphere, good bar food and good restaurant menu inc interesting dishes in superb dining room – the Bones who did so well at the Marquis of Lorne at Nettlecombe in Dorset have moved here; duck pond and tables outside *(Chris and Joan Woodward, Brian and Peggy Pinfold)*

Hatch Beauchamp [ST3220], *Hatch*: Good family-run village pub with lots of copper and brass in carpeted lounge bar with pleasant bow-window seats, good food cooked by daughter, well kept Bass, choice of farm ciders; quite separate pool room; bedrooms immaculate *(M D Green, BB)*

Henstridge [A30 Shaftesbury—Sherborne, junction with A357; ST7119], *Virginia Ash*: Big popular rambling pub, very handy stop, wide choice of food in large restaurant, particularly good puddings and ices, family area, no-smoking area, very accommodating service; morning coffee, tables outside with play area *(Frank Smith, Stephen Brown, Basil J S Minson)*

Hewish, Av [nr M5 junction 21; A370 towards Congresbury; ST4064], *Full Quart*: Good food and service, friendly atmosphere, pleasant beamed bar, reasonable choice of beers *(Mrs Redstone, D Fitzgerald)*

Hillfarance [ST1624], *Anchor*: Wide choice of good bar food inc children's helpings in friendly prettily placed country local with two good eating areas, family room with Wendy house, speedy service, well kept beers, garden with play area; bedrooms *(SP)*

Hinton Blewett, Av [signed off A37 in Clutton; ST5957], *Ring o' Bells*: Charming unspoilt low-beamed stone-built pub in small village, several well kept real ales inc Wadworths, friendly staff, good home-cooked food, log fire; children welcome; pleasant view from tables in sheltered front yard *(Robert Huddleston, LYM)*

Hinton Charterhouse, Av [off A36 S of Bath; ST7758], *Rose & Crown*: Well kept Bass, Butcombe, Smiles and Wadworths 6X tapped from barrels set in the wall behind the bar in good village pub with decent food in bar and restaurant *(M G Hart, David and Barbara Davies)*

Holford [A39; ST1541], *Plough*: Warmly welcoming busy local in little village, well served popular food inc lots of steaks, well kept beer, good landlord; handy for wonderful Quantocks walks *(David Wright, John Hazel)*

☆ **Holton** [ST6827], *Old Inn*: Interesting cheap snacks and other food in bar and restaurant of friendly 16th-c inn with beams, ancient flagstones, log fire; good service, real ales and ciders, tables on terrace *(Gethin Lewis)*

Holywell Lake [off A38; ST1020], *Holywell*: Welcoming landlord, pleasant efficient waitress, good food inc wide range of puddings, several real ales on handpump *(Alan Wheatley)*

☆ **Horsington** [village signposted off A357 S of Wincanton; ST7023], *Half Moon*: Well kept Adnams, Wadworths IPA and 6X and a guest beer, decent wines, good service and atmosphere; well presented home-made food inc good value full meals in knocked-through beamed bars with oak floors, inglenook log fires, stripped stone, dogs and cats; restaurant Thurs-Sat evening, big back garden with play area; good value bedrooms in chalets *(P and O Makower, Geraldine Berry, LYM)*

☆ **Howley** [ST2609], *Howley Tavern*: Beautifully kept spacious bar with wide choice of imaginative reasonably priced bar food inc vegetarian, Bass, Flowers Original and changing guest beers, decent wines, good happy service, attractive old-world restaurant; bedrooms *(M A J and Shirley Johnson)*

☆ **Ilchester** [The Square; ST5222], *Ivelchester*: Friendly inn with outstanding food in bar and restaurant inc sensational puddings; bedrooms extremely comfortable *(David Surridge, Nan and David Johnson)*

☆ **Keinton Mandeville** [off A37; ST5430], *Quarry*: Huge helpings of good sensibly priced food inc local seafood in popular pub, smart, comfortable and welcoming, with well kept real ales, friendly service, skittle room, cosy restaurant, attractive garden *(Nick Cox, Derek and Iris Martin, P and J Rush, Ted George)*

☆ **Keynsham**, Av [Bitton Rd; ST6568], *Lock Keeper*: Lovely spot by Avon with lock, marina and weir, good food inc good shellfish open sandwich and steak sandwich, well kept Wadworths 6X, impressive children's room in sort of cavern down steep stairway with murals; big riverside garden with boules *(Tom Evans)*

Keynsham, *New Inn*: Well placed local with well kept Bass, friendly helpful service, simple but decent good value bar food *(Steve Dark)*

Kingsbury Episcopi [ST4321], *Wyndham Arms*: Fine unspoilt village pub with flagstone floors, roaring log fire, well kept Bass, decent wines, good value food inc good steaks, good staff *(Stephen Brown, Clive Waldron)*

☆ **Kingsdon** [off A303 at Podimore Island; ST5126], *Kingsdon Inn*: Short choice of reliably good genuinely home-cooked food with plenty of fresh crispy veg, prompt courteous service; roomy and pretty pub, well kept Hook Norton and Smiles, decent wines, good coffee *(Mrs S H Richards, Pat and Robert Watt, Mr and Mrs J G Davies, Dr B Moyse)*

Langford Budville [off B3187; ST1022], *Martlet*: Simple unmodernised village pub with surprisingly wide choice of food inc unusual hot filled rolls; real ales, no piped music – beautifully peaceful *(Shirley Pielou)*

Lansdown, Av [N towards Dyrham; ST7269], *Blathwayt Arms*: Large

comfortable Whitbreads pub with well kept Boddingtons, good value generous food; open all day *(Dave Irving)*

☆ **Leigh upon Mendip** [ST6847], *Bell*: Comfortable 16th-c beamed village local updated without losing its country atmosphere; pleasant restaurant, wide range of good value home-cooked bar food inc some oriental dishes, good choice of well kept real ales, roaring log fire, efficient service; skittle alley *(J and R S Glover, M G Hart, Fiona Dick)*

☆ **Litton** [off A39 Bath—Wells; ST5954], *Olde Kings Arms*: Good new licensees doing wide range of good reasonably priced food in friendly and relaxed 15th-c pub with two big open fires and lots of tables in several small areas, well kept ales such as Butcombe and Wadworths 6X; pleasant terrace and lovely streamside garden with swings, slides and boules piste; unspoilt setting at bottom of tiny valley next to old cottages and interesting little church; bedrooms *(Steve Huggins, Martyn G Hart, Pete and Rose Flower)*

☆ **Long Sutton** [A372 E of Langport; ST4625], *Devonshire Arms*: Wide-ranging menu with unusual dishes, good specials and lots of fish; small unpretentious homely bar, two or three well kept real ales, restaurant; bedrooms spacious and clean, with good breakfasts *(Stephen Brown, Shirley Pielou)*

☆ **Long Sutton**, *Lime Kiln*: Very wide choice of good generous attractively presented food and friendly service in uncluttered pub with three well kept real ales, log fire, restaurant; good modern bedrooms *(Shirley Pielou, Mrs S Knight)*

Lower Langford, Av [ST4660], *Langford*: Refurbished as family dining pub by new landlord, good tasty food in charming spacious dining room, decent wines, fantastic children's room with lots of toys, accommodating staff; attractive terrace *(Belinda Seaton, Chris and Joan Woodward)*

Mark [ST3747], *White Horse*: Friendly new landlord and staff, well kept Flowers and guest beers on handpump, extended choice of good food, some decent malt whiskies; good garden with playground *(John Abbott, Philip Brown)*

☆ **Marshfield**, Av [A420 Bristol—Chippenham; ST7773], *Lord Nelson*: Spacious pub with enthusiastic newish licensees, well kept ales such as Bunces Pig Swill, Uley and Wickwar, wide choice of home-made food, unusual range of beamed bars with open fires, locals' games bar, bistro restaurant, charming small courtyard; bedrooms in cottage annexe *(Peter and Rose Flower, Adrian Kelly, KC)*

Marston Magna [Rimpton Rd; ST5922], *Red Lion*: Good reasonably priced food inc fresh fish, pleasant staff, good garden *(Anon)*

☆ **Mells** [ST7249], *Falcon*: Old-fashioned pub in lovely old-fashioned village with marvellous church, bars around central courtyard with little back alley; wonderful atmosphere, well kept ale tapped from the cask; little food *(Mike and Sue Moss)*

Mells, *Talbot*: 15th-c inn tastefully refurbished by newish owners, friendly stripped-stone beamed bar, well kept beer, good food, open fire, tables in courtyard and walled garden; six bedrooms *(Jed and Virginia Brown)*

Middlezoy [off A372 E of Bridgwater; ST3732], *George*: 16th-c country pub with low-ceilinged flagstoned bar, furnished with wooden tables, chairs and settles; well kept real ales, decent food, local landlord *(Mark Undrill)*

☆ **Midford**, Av [ST7560], *Hope & Anchor*: Spotlessly refurbished under welcoming new owners, interesting food in bar and restaurant end reflecting their northern Spanish and Polish origins, well kept Butcombe; tables outside *(Bill Bailey, N C Walker)*

☆ **Milborne Port** [A30 E of Sherborne; ST6718], *Queens Head*: Very good choice of generous good value home-cooked food in beamed lounge with good choice of well kept real ales and farm ciders, friendly service, games in public bar, skittle alley, quiet restaurant; tables in sheltered courtyard and garden with unusual playthings; children welcome (except in bars); three cosy bedrooms – good value *(Mr and Mrs K Box, LYM)*

☆ **Milton Clevedon** [High St (B3081); ST6637], *Ilchester Arms*: Homely and comfortable early 17th-c beamed and stripped-brick pub with friendly and genuine landlord, bar; rustic bric-a-brac, old-fashioned gas-style lamps in wall alcoves, wide choice of reasonably priced food, well kept Palmers and Wadworths 6X, piano, smaller restaurant bar; lovely hill views from garden and from conservatory with hanging plants; no food Sun, closed Mon lunchtime *(John Hazel)*

Minehead [Esplanade; SS9746], *Hobby Horse*: Good choice of good well cooked bar lunches, friendly service, Flowers IPA and Original *(D S Beeson)*; [Quay West], *Old Ship Aground*: Well kept Courage-related beers, good reasonably priced tasty food, pleasant harbour views *(Mark and Diana Bradshaw)*; *Queens Head*: Good food, well kept beer, real landlord; piped music may be loud *(John Hazel)*

Misterton [Middle St; ST4508], *White Swan*: Comfortable and friendly pub in quiet village, good reasonably priced food esp puddings, efficient service *(G C V Clifton, MK)*

Monkton Combe, Av [ST7762], *Wheelwrights Arms*: Small country inn with attractively laid out bar, lots of wheelwright and railway memorabilia, wide choice of reasonably priced wholesome food, well kept ales such as Adnams, Butcombe and Wadworths 6X, big open fire, tiny darts room at end, fruit machine, quiet piped music; well equipped small bedrooms in separate block *(Mike and Kathleen York, LYM)*

☆ **Montacute** [ST4916], *Phelips Arms*: Airy, relaxed and spacious old-fashioned pub with varied good freshly cooked fair-priced food, friendly service, well kept beers; tables in garden, lovely setting in delightful village, close to Montacture House *(Dr D C Deeing, R J Saunders, Maj and Mrs E M Warrick, Tony Gayfer, Donald Godden)*

Moorlinch [signed off A39; ST3939], *Ring of Bells*: Attractive lounge with open fires, masses of fresh flowers and friendly service; spotlessly kept, with some interesting personal memorabilia *(A E and P McCully)*

☆ **Nether Stowey** [Keenthorne – A39 E of village; not to be confused with Apple Tree Cottage; ST1939], *Cottage*: Warm and cheerful local with generous good value simple food, Butcombe and Flowers Original, friendly service, comfortable music-free dining lounge with woodburner, aquarium, interesting pictures; games room with two pool tables, juke box and machines (children allowed here); skittle alley, tables on terrace *(Dorothy and Leslie Pilson, John Hazel, LYM)*

☆ **North Brewham** [ST7236], *Old Red Lion*: Stone-floored low-beamed former farmhouse with good food, friendly and efficient service, good choice of real ales *(Dr and Mrs A K Clarke)*

North Cadbury [ST6327], *Catash*: Decent food and prices, happy local family atmosphere; bedrooms *(John Hazel)*

North Curry [Queens Sq; ST3225], *Old Coaching Inn*: Formerly the Bird in Hand, attractively transformed by new owners, big bar's old beams and timbers exposed, Gibbs Mew ales (rare around here), occasional promotional bargains such as half-price drinks; restaurant, conservatory *(Richard Dolphin)*

☆ **North Perrott** [ST4709], *Manor Arms*: Attractively modernised 16th-c pub on pretty village green, inglenook, beams and stripped stone, good value imaginative freshly made food from sandwiches up in bar and cosy restaurant, well kept Boddingtons and Smiles, decent wines, relaxed, friendly and interested service, pleasant garden with adventure play area; two good value comfortable bedrooms in coach house *(Ian and Rosemary Wood, Maureen Hobbs, Desmond and Pat Morris, J Dobson, G C V Clifton)*

☆ **North Wootton** [ST5641], *Three Elms*: Wide range of good reasonably priced food esp specials, well kept beers inc Boddingtons, Fullers London Pride and Hook Norton Mild, welcoming service, fine collection of Matchbox cars, also USA truck plates, milk bottles, champagne bottles, beer mats and books – and saucy postcards and humorous bottle labels in gents'; busy evenings; three bedrooms, good breakfasts *(Stephen and Julie Brown, Dr A and Dr A C Jackson)*

Northwick, Av [B4055 to Pilning; 2½ miles from M4 junction 21; ST5687], *White Horse*: Welcoming staff, well kept Courage-related ales, big colourful garden, good honest food *(J Morrell)*

Nunney [Church St; village signed off A361 Shepton Mallet—Frome; ST7345], *George*: Extensive rambling and much modernised open-plan bar with stripped stone walls, log fire, four well kept changing real ales such as Exmoor and Wadworths 6X, food majoring on steaks in bar and restaurant, afternoon teas, piped music; rare 'gallows' sign spanning road, in quaint village with stream (vociferous ducks) and ruined castle, bedrooms *(PM, JM, Mike and Sue Moss, LYM)*

☆ **Panborough** [B3139 Wedmore—Wells; ST4745], *Panborough Inn*: Wide range of unusual and generous food inc vegetarian dishes and splendid puddings in warm, friendly and spacious 17th-c village inn, several clean, comfortable and attractive rooms, inglenook, beams, brass and copper; good range of generous bar food, pleasant attentive service, real ales, unobtrusive piped music; skittle alley, small restaurant, tables in front terraced garden; bedrooms comfortable *(R W Brooks, K R Harris, Peter Cornall, Dono and Carol Leaman)*

☆ **Pitney** [ST4428], *Halfway House*: Recently extended sparsely furnished old-fashioned pub concentrating on some nine well kept real ales such as Cotleigh Tawney and Oakhill; very friendly atmosphere, three log fires, food inc speciality curries *(Arthur and Anne Frampton, Andy Jones)*

☆ **Polsham** [A39 N of Glastonbury; ST5142], *Camelot*: Well run roomy dining pub with wide choice of promptly served good food in 18th-c bar, restaurant and conservatory looking over fields; Palmers and a local beer brewed for the pub, big children's area, terrace; bedrooms *(Brig J S Green, Ann Reeder, David Craine, Mr and Mrs K Box)*

Porlock Weir [separate from but run in tandem with neighbouring Anchor Hotel; SS8547], *Ship*: Prettily restored old inn included for its wonderful setting by peaceful harbour, with tables in terraced rose garden and good walks; usual bar food and Courage-related and Exmoor ales in straightforward family Mariners Bar; bedrooms; not to be confused with the pub of the same name in nearby Porlock; restaurant *(James Nunns, David Wright, LYM)*

☆ **Priddy** [off B3135; ST5450], *New Inn*: Welcoming low-beamed pub, modernised but still traditional, simple and comfortable, with good log fire, spacious new conservatory; good sensibly priced food, Eldridge Pope Royal Oak and Wadworths 6X, good local cider and house wines, good welcoming service; bedrooms comfortable and homely, on quiet village green *(Joy Heatherley, Arthur and Anne Frampton, WHBM, Jim and Maggie Cowell)*

☆ **Priddy**, *Queen Victoria*: Relaxed country pub with flagstones and open fires, interesting bric-a-brac, friendly staff; well kept Butcombe and other ales tapped from the cask, organic beers, proper ciders and perries, reasonably priced standard food; good garden for children over road *(John and Phyllis Maloney)*

Pucklechurch, Av [ST7077], *Rose & Crown*: Good food well and promptly served, well kept beer, pleasant interior, simple but pleasant outside seating area *(P Neate)*

Roadwater [off A39 at Washford; ST0338], *Valiant Soldier*: Country pub with Bass and Stones, reasonably priced food, pool table, darts; children welcome, streamside garden with play area *(Keith Houlgate)*

Roundham [A30 Crewkerne—Chard; ST4209], *Travellers Rest*: Pleasant interior, with friendly staff and cat called Garfield, decent food inc enormous breakfasts (though not quick if busy), real ales such as Butcombe, Twelve Bore and Worthington BB *(Mrs C Luxton)*

Rowberrow [about ½ mile from A38 at Churchill; ST4558], *Swan*: Olde-worlde, with comic hunting prints and grandfather clock, well kept Bass and Wadworths 6X and a fine choice of not cheap snacks like rare beef sandwiches; good walking country *(Mr and Mrs A E McCully)*

Rudge [just off A36; ST8251], *Full Moon*: Friendly welcome in beautiful surroundings, good choice of real ales, good varied menu inc vegetarian, skittle alley; comfortable bedrooms *(Brian and Judith Young)*

Ruishton [Ilminster Rd (A358), just off M5 junction 25; ST2626], *Blackbrook*: Busy Country Carvery dining pub with wide choice of generous decent food inc children's in open-plan beamed bar with several roomy wooden-screened areas inc carvery and family area, quick efficient service, good-sized garden with play area, Courage-related ales; useful stop *(Gill and Keith Croxton, Prof A N Black)*

Seavington St Michael [signed from E side of A303 Ilminster bypass; ST4015], *Volunteer*: Comfortable much modernised dining pub with understated decor which has been well liked for friendly atmosphere and good home-cooked fresh food, with well kept Badger beers and good local Perry's cider; but no recent reports *(M E and Mrs J Wellington, LYM; news please)*

☆ **Shepperdine**, Av [off B4061 N of Thornbury; ST6295], *Windbound*: Good spot alone on the Severn estuary nr Wildfowl Trust, fine views from spacious upper lounge and sheltered fairy-lit lawn; usual bar food from cheap sandwiches up served very quickly, pleasantly pubby bar, welcoming staff *(John Honnor, Brian and Jill Bond, LYM)*

Shepton Beauchamp [The Shambles; ST4017], *Duke of York*: Decent well run free house with good range of meals, several real ales, skittle alley, darts and garden *(Michael Duck)*

Shepton Montague [off A359; ST6731], *Montague*: Really old-fashioned deep-country pub with brilliant views; no food *(M V Ward)*

Shipham [A38; ST4457], *Star*: Small and welcoming recently refurbished (not modernised) pub with new licensee, Bass, Flowers and Devenish Royal Wessex, wholesome food *(Mr and Mrs A E McCully)*

Somerton [Church Sq; ST4828], *Globe*: Friendly local with log fire, good bar food, well kept Bass and good choice of wine; no music *(D A C T Hancock)*

Staple Fitzpaine [ST2618], *Greyhound*: Interesting rambling country pub with antique layout, flagstones and inglenooks; friendly service, pleasant atmosphere, well kept real ales, food that's been inclined rather more to meals than snacks *(LYM; reports please)*

Staplegrove [junction A358/A361; ST2126], *Cross Keys*: Spacious yet cosy Chef & Brewer, good service, good range of well cooked food, wide choice of Courage-related beers *(K R Harris)*

Stoke sub Hamdon [ST4717], *Fleur de Lis*: Traditional well furnished village local with friendly landlady, well kept beers and local ciders, good well priced food; bedrooms *(Lisa Girling, Steven Robins)*

Street on the Fosse [A37; ST6139], *Portman Arms*: Village pub with wide range of real ales, good value well cooked food; very handy for Royal Bath & West Showground *(K R Harris)*

☆ **Taunton** [Magdalene St], *Masons Arms*: Busy and friendly oasis, landlord working hard to make everyone feel at home, good range of well kept ales inc Exmoor, good reasonably priced food from efficient food counter, comfortably basic furnishings, no music or pool tables; bedrooms *(James K McDonell, John Barker, M E and Mrs J Wellington, Bill and Beryl Farmer)*

Thornbury, Av [Chapel St; ST6390], *Wheatsheaf*: Home-cooked good value food, real veg, wide range of real ales *(K R Harris)*; [A38, handy for M5 junction 14], *White Horse*: Enjoyable reasonably priced usual bar food, well kept Bass and Theakstons ales, comfortable rooms with good-sized tables *(Paul and Gail Betteley)*

☆ **Thurloxton** [ST2730], *Maypole*: Pleasant Whitbreads pub, attractively renovated with several different areas in the early 1980s and still with the same friendly landlord; very wide choice of generous food from filled baps up, quick service, biggish no-smoking area, soft piped music; peaceful village *(Shirley Pielou, Richard Dolphin)*

Tickenham, Av [B3130 Clevedon—Nailsea; ST4571], *Star*: Big dining pub with log fire and pleasant atmosphere in comfortable main area, less character in games and children's area, wide choice of popular generous food, no-smoking conservatory,

good range of beers, decent wines, friendly landlord, piped music, high chairs; garden with good play area *(Joy Heatherley, M J V Kemp)*

Tockington, Av [ST6186], *Swan*: Attractive and spacious stone-built timbered pub in quiet village; wide choice of good value food in bar or no-smoking dining room, well kept Courage ales, tables in garden *(Dave and Jules Tuckett, R W Brooks)*

☆ **Tolldown**, Av [under a mile from M4 junction 18 – A46 towards Bath; ST7577], *Crown*: Useful relatively unspoilt off-motorway pub with usual food in heavy-beamed stone bar, no-smoking area, well kept Wadworths, log fire, dominoes, darts and fruit machine, piped music, good garden with play area; children in eating area and restaurant; bedrooms *(Barry and Anne, LYM)*

Tormarton, Av [under a mile from M4 junction 18; A46 towards Stroud, then first right; ST7678], *Compass*: Very extended off-motorway place with relaxed staff (can get a bit overwhelmed at weekends), choice of rooms inc basic conservatory, well kept ales (at a price) inc Smiles, decent ploughman's and day's specials, friendly labrador, restaurant, comfortable if expensive bedrooms; but not always on top form *(Gwen and Peter Andrews, Prof John White, Patricia White, Klaus and Elizabeth Leist, Nicholas Roberts, Neville Kenyon, W L G Watkins, LYM)*

Trull [Church Rd; ST2122], *Winchester Arms*: Welcoming lively local, consistently good lunchtime food from snacks to main meals inc good home-made soups and fresh veg, good value suppers in small dining room served by very cheerful young waitress *(Shirley Pielou)*

Tytherington [W Tytherington; ST7645], *Horse & Groom*: Good fish, pleasant newish licensees *(RHM)*

Tytherington, Av [ST6688], *Swan*: Well furnished big village pub, open fires, Courage-related ales, good food inc fish and chips and interesting pies; very busy weekends *(R W Brooks, A D Shore)*

☆ **Upton Cheyney**, Av [signed off A431 at Bitton; ST6969], *Upton Inn*: Immaculate plush and spacious bar with very wide choice of good reasonably priced home-cooked bar food (not Sat evening, Sun or Mon) inc vegetarian, attractive restaurant in nouveau rouge style, well kept Bass, Smiles and Wadworths 6X, decent wine and coffee, friendly staff; delightful surroundings, lovely Avon Valley views; closed Sun evening, Mon *(Paul Weedon, L Mercer, R W Brooks, Bob Smith)*

☆ **Upton Noble** [ST7139], *Lamb*: Adventurous good value food and lovely views in small comfortable stripped-stone village local; well kept beer, small restaurant, big garden; closed Mon *(Pat and Robert Watt)*

Wadeford [towards Combe St Nicholas; ST3010], *Haymaker*: Friendly and pleasant

pub, promising new licensees rethinking the food here; Whitbreads-related ales, separate games room; bedrooms *(Maj K W Johnson)*
Washford [ST0441], *White Horse:* Good local, good value food *(John Hazel)*
☆ Watchet [Swain St; ST0743], *West Somerset:* Good cheap food in unpretentiously attractive and welcoming pub with well kept Cotleigh Tawny and Courage-related ales, nice courtyard with rockery; bedrooms with own bathrooms *(Bob Smith)*
☆ Waterrow [A361 Wiveliscombe—Bampton; ST0425], *Rock:* Good welcoming service, wide choice of good value home-made food, well kept ales inc Cotleigh Tawny and Exmoor Gold, log fire in smallish bar exposing the rock it's built on, couple of steps up to civilised lunchtime dining room doubling as smart evening restaurant; small valley side bedrooms with own bathrooms *(Richard Dolphin, Patrick Freeman, Pete and Rosie Flower)*
Wedmore [ST4347], *George:* Traditional furnishings in interesting stripped-stone bar of rambling coaching inn with real ale, bar food, lively locals' bar, sheltered lawn; bedrooms *(Alan Skull, LYM)*; *New Inn:* Cosy olde-worlde charm, real ales inc Butcombe and guests, good wines by the glass, wholesome good home cooking esp speciality ham, vegetarian and children's dishes, friendly staff, jovial landlord and landlady *(Adrian Acton)*
☆ Wells [St Thomas St; ST5545], *Fountain:* Imaginative range of popular good value generous food from filled rolls through ploughman's with good local cheeses, children's and good vegetarian dishes and interesting starters to more elaborate main dishes, prices same in pleasantly pubby downstairs bar with roaring log fire and very popular straightforward upstairs restaurant – worth booking weekends, good Sun lunch; friendly quick staff, well kept Courage-related ales, farm cider, good choice of wines, piped music; right by cathedral; children welcome *(John and Phyllis Maloney, Dominic Barrington, Ivor Maw, Martyn G Hart)*
☆ Wells [nr St Cuthberts church], *City Arms:* Good choice of good food from sandwiches to alligator at reasonable prices in big L-shaped bar and upstairs restaurant of attractively converted largely early 18th-c building – some parts even older (said to have been a Tudor jail); Butcombe and Smiles ales, decent wines, friendly prompt service *(E H and R F Warner, John and Phyllis Maloney, M G Hart)*
☆ West Bagborough [ST1633], *Rising Sun:* Classic quiet local in tiny village well placed below Quantocks, friendly family service, short choice of fresh generous food cooked by granny, well kept Exmoor and Oakhill Farmers, unobtrusive piped music, darts, table skittles, big log fires; bedrooms comfortable, with own bathrooms *(Dr B and Mrs P B Baker, John A Barker)*

West Camel [ST5724], *Walnut:* Good service, most enjoyable food; bedrooms *(Mr and Mrs Copeland)*
West Monkton [ST2728], *Monkton:* Very big helpings of good value food from doorstep sandwiches up in comfortable country pub, spacious bar broken up into cosy and attractive areas, welcoming quick service; lots of tables in garden with play area, peaceful spot *(Shirley Pielou, R W Brooks)*
☆ West Pennard [A361 E of Glastonbury; formerly Red Lion; ST5438], *Lion:* Short choice of simple but particularly good home-made food in three neat and homely dining areas opening off small flagstoned and black-beamed core with log fire in big stone inglenook, second log fire in stripped-stone family area, well kept local real ales, real ginger beer, friendly staff; bedrooms comfortable and well equipped, in neatly converted side barn *(Mike and Sue Moss, W F C Phillips, BB)*
☆ West Pennard [A361], *Apple Tree:* Big roadside food pub comfortably renovated to a high standard, with flagstones, exposed brickwork, beams, good woodburner, thatch above the main bar; second bar and two eating areas; well kept Bass, the fine new Cotleigh Golden Eagle and Worthington BB, wide choice of impressive home-cooked food (worth the wait), pleasant staff, proper coffee; can get crowded lunchtime; tables on terrace *(Richard Dolphin, June and Tony Baldwin)*
Westbury on Trym, Av [Westbury Hill; ST5877], *Foresters Arms:* Good choice of good food (French chef) in lounge bar or oak-panelled dining room, four well kept real ales such as Bass, Courage Best, Marstons and Websters Green Label, tables in tastefully flower-decorated courtyard, barbecues in fine weather *(Peter Bush)*
Weston in Gordano, Av [B3124 Portishead—Clevedon; ST4474], *White Hart:* Very welcoming and helpful, good well priced straightforward food *(MK)*
Weston Super Mare, Av [seafront, N end; ST3261], *Claremont Vaults:* Good choice of lunchtime bar food and good sea and coast view in friendly, plushly comfortable pub with usual food, real ales, friendly service *(R W Brooks)*
Westport [B3168 Ilminster—Curry Rivel; ST3819], *Old Barn Owl:* Attractive tastefully decorated stripped-stone interior, long narrow main bar, three small dining areas and separate children's area; very peaceful; wide choice of good carefully cooked and presented food inc beautiful fresh vegetables and unusual dishes, well kept Boddingtons and Wadworths 6X; no piped music; bedrooms *(Shirley Pielou)*
☆ Wheddon Cross [A396/B3224, S of Minehead; SS9238], *Rest & Be Thankful:* Good food and quietly welcoming atmosphere in comfortably modern two-room bar with pleasant staff, well kept Courage-related real ales, also tea, hot

chocolate and so forth, log fire, aquarium and piped music; communicating games area, skittle alley, buffet bar, public lavatory for the disabled; children allowed in restaurant, with children's dishes; bedrooms *(Phil and Heidi Cook, Clem Stephens, A H Denman, LYM)*

Wickwar, Av [B4060 N of Chipping Sodbury; ST7288], *Buthay*: Good all-round pub with reasonably priced food inc good lasagne, well kept ales *(Andrew Shore)*

☆ **Widcombe** [Culmhead – OS Sheet 193 map ref 222160; ST2216], *Holman Clavel*: Very welcoming hard-working landlord in simple but comfortable and charming rustic pub named after its massive holly chimney-beam, good cheap home-cooked bar food (will try to cook you anything you want even if not on menu), well kept Cotleigh and Flowers Original, nice atmosphere; dogs welcome, handy for Blackdown Hills *(Richard Dolphin, BB)*

Williton [ST0740], *Egremont*: Friendly old coaching inn, good staff, generous reasonably priced food *(John Hazel)*

Wincanton [Mkt Pl; ST7028], *Red Lion*: Worth knowing for big helpings of cheap Sat lunchtime roast – they do only one joint so get there early *(Mr and Mrs Hillman)*

☆ **Winford**, Av [Crown Hill, Regil – pub signed from village; ST5262], *Crown*: Most obliging licensees in very interesting old pub, authentically old-fashioned, superb setting with lovely views from terrace; attractive restaurant, skittle alley *(G Hart, Mary Reed, Rowly Pitcher)*

Winsley, Av [B3108 W of Bradford-on-Avon; ST7961], *Seven Stars*: Attractive stripped-stone pub with lots of old tables and chairs, snug alcoves, wide choice of popular food, Courage-related ales and Wadworths 6X, log-effect gas fires, decent piped music, tables in garden; attractive village *(Viv Middlebrook)*

Winterbourne, Av [41 High St; ST6580], *Wheatsheaf*: Good value rather restaurant-y dining pub *(A D Shore)*

☆ **Winterbourne Down**, Av [Down Rd, Kendleshire; just off A432 Bristol—Yate, towards Winterbourne; ST6679], *Golden Heart*: Large well furnished welcoming pub with beams, open fires, inglenook, wide choice of reasonably priced food, good friendly service, well kept beer, country view from restaurant; fruit machines; children's room, huge lawns front and back, both with play equipment *(R W Brooks, P Neate)*

Witham Friary [signed from A361 – OS Sheet 183 map ref 745409; ST7441], *Seymour Arms*: Basic unspoilt local with two characterful rooms, central hatch servery, warm welcome, well kept Ushers on handpump, fine local cider; darts, cards, dominoes – no juke box or machines; pleasant garden behind *(Pete Baker)*

Yeovil [High St; ST5516], *Mermaid*: Spacious and friendly 17th-c beamed coaching inn doing well under new management, good food in bar and restaurant, well kept Palmers; bedrooms *(M A Vann)*

Please keep sending us reports. We rely on readers for news of new discoveries, and particularly for news of changes – however slight – at the fully described pubs. No stamp needed: *The Good Pub Guide*, FREEPOST TN1569, Wadhurst, E Sussex TN5 7BR.

Staffordshire *see* Derbyshire

Suffolk

Important changes to mention here include the return of the Grimwoods to the Old Chequers in Friston, which they originally made so popular; welcoming new licensees at the nice old Bell in Clare; our award of a star to the Ship at Dunwich (floods of enthusiastic reports in the last few months), and to the Angel in Lavenham (also extremely popular currently, especially with people eating there); the newish landlord at the Jolly Sailor in Orford settling in very well – a really thriving atmosphere now; and our Food Award newly granted to the Brewers Arms at Rattlesden, where the food's been on a definite upswing, and to the nice old Plough at Rede. Other pubs currently doing particularly well here include the very friendly Cross Keys in Aldeburgh, the Trowel & Hammer at Cotton (big helpings of authentic Greek food), the simple and unpretentious Victoria at Earl Soham (brewing its own good beers), the Crown at Great Glemham (transformed by its current licensees), the Beehive at Horringer (good food, in its licensees' tenth year there), the smart Golden Key at Snape, the Crown in Southwold (creative food and wines), the Angel at Stoke by Nayland (imaginative food in lovely surroundings), the busy Four Horseshoes at Thornham Magna, and the charmingly unspoilt Gardeners Arms at Tostock. Three pubs newly joining the ranks of the main entries here this year are the handsome old Queens Head at Dennington, flourishing under lively new owners; the Brewery Tap in Ipswich, the rather elegantly done new tap for the Tolly brewery; and the delightfully traditional Kings Head at Laxfield, carefully revived by new owners. There's no shortage of good food in the county – as shown by the many Food Awards gained by pubs here. For its great combination of attractive furnishings, good relaxed atmosphere and fine cooking of well chosen local ingredients, we choose the Angel at Stoke by Nayland as Suffolk Dining Pub of the Year. But you certainly need to choose your pub carefully: eating out in Suffolk pubs tends to be an expensive business. You are as likely to find a ploughman's costing £4 as you are to find one costing £3 here, and a good main dish may be nearer £6 than £5. Beer prices are close to the national average: high marks to the Four Horseshoes at Thornham Magna, the cheapest pub we found for beer here, for cutting its beer price sharply since last year. The next cheapest beers we found were those brewed on the premises at the Victoria at Earl Soham. In the Lucky Dip section at the end of the chapter, pubs we'd commend particularly include the Parrot & Punchbowl at Aldringham, Six Bells at Bardswell, Bell at Cretingham, Eels Foot at Eastbridge, Crown at Hartest, Star at Lidgate, Black Tiles at Martlesham, Plough & Sail and Crown at Snape and Black Horse at Thorndon. Southwold has a wonderful variety of good pubs for such a relatively small town – and it's here, near the brewery, that Adnams' fine beers tend to taste at their best.

Post Office address codings confusingly give the impression that some pubs are in Suffolk when they're really in Norfolk or Cambridgeshire (which is where we list them).

ALDEBURGH TM4656 Map 5

Cross Keys ◖

Crabbe Street

Looking particularly welcoming in summer months when the outside is decorated with a jungle of colourful hanging baskets, this is an attractive low-ceilinged old pub that seems to radiate friendly warmth. A gravel courtyard at the back opens directly on to the promenade and shingle beach, and there are wooden seats and tables out here to take in the view. Such a good spot does mean that the pub can get busy on sunny days, but there are enough staff to cope well and it always manages to keep its notably relaxed and good-humoured atmosphere. Inside, the two communicating rooms are divided by a sturdy central chimney with woodburning stoves on either side, and there are more flowers about. The well presented bar food is very well liked, and includes home-cooked dishes such as very good open sandwiches (from £2.80), ploughman's (£4.25), vegetarian meals such as spinach and mushroom lasagne, fisherman's pie, chicken curry or steak, kidney and ale pie (£5.25), scallops au gratin (£5.40), and shellfish platter (£8.50). Well kept Adnams Bitter, Broadside, Mild and Extra on handpump; efficient and enthusiastic service; dominoes, cribbage and fruit machine. It can get a little smoky at times. Traditionally the pub would remain open whenever the local lifeboat was out. *(Recommended by Basil J S Minson, R G Smedley, Anna Marsh, Neil Powell, Gwen and Peter Andrews, BKA, C G Bolton, Weston Sylvie)*

Adnams ~ Licensee Mr G Prior ~ Real ale ~ Meals and snacks (not winter Sun evenings) ~ (01728) 452637 ~ Children in eating area ~ Open 11-3, 6-11; all day Sat

BILDESTON TL9949 Map 5

Crown

104 High St (B1115 SW of Stowmarket)

A handsomely jettied black and white 15th-c inn, well liked for its good daily changing bar food. The comfortable beamed bars have latticed windows, an inglenook fireplace (and a smaller more modern one with dried flowers), old-fashioned prints and facsimiles of old documents on the cream walls, dark wood tables with armchairs and wall banquettes upholstered to match the floral curtains, and a friendly, relaxed atmosphere. Good food includes sandwiches (from £1.50, toasties from £1.75, super club sandwiches from £3.25), filled baked potatoes (from £2.50), ploughman's (from £3.50), seafood scramble (£3.65), omelettes (from £3.65), good fresh fish dishes, and daily specials such as spiced minced lamb, stuffed aubergine or avocado stroganoff (£4.95), various curries (£5.25), veal meatballs in a piquant sauce or cajun chicken (£6.25), and coufit of duck (£7.25). Well kept Adnams, Marstons Pedigree, Nethergate and a guest like Morlands Speckled Hen on handpump, elderflower or citrus pressé, several malt whiskies, local cider and decent wines. Darts, bar billiards, shove-ha'penny, table skittles, cribbage, dominoes, fruit machine and piped music. At the back an attractive two-acre garden has picnic-table sets sheltering among shrubs and trees. *(Recommended by Mrs P M Goodwyn, Mrs S A Greenwood, J G Smith; more reports please)*

Free house ~ Licensees Mr and Mrs E Henderson ~ Real ale ~ Meals and snacks ~ Restaurant ~ (01449) 740510 ~ Children in eating area ~ Trad jazz every 2nd Sun ~ Open 11-2.30, 6-11; closed evening 25 Dec ~ Bedrooms: £20(£32B)/£30(£39B); four-poster (£59)

BLYFORD TM4277 Map 5

Queens Head

B1123

Be careful entering this fine-looking thatched 15th-c village pub – the beams really are low and you could bang your head. Other aged features include the original well which, unusually, is not just for decoration: they still use the water from it. The attractively furnished, unfussy beamed bar has been redecorated after a bad fire, and has some antique settles, pine and oak benches built into its cream walls, heavy wooden tables and stools, and a huge fireplace filled with antique lamps; the atmosphere is very relaxed and pleasant. The good range of popular food includes lunchtime sandwiches, home-made quiche or ploughman's, moussaka, and vegetarian pasta, and in the evening more elaborate meals such as home-made venison and pheasant soup (£2.25), pâté (£2.95), pan-fried prawns in fresh garlic and peppercorn butter (£3.95), spinach and tomato cannelloni (£5.25), salmon and broccoli mornay (£5.95), battered cod from Lowestoft (£6.25), sirloin steak, kidney and mushroom pie or roast guinea fowl in port and peppercorn sauce (£6.35), quail stuffed with pâté and mushrooms in a red wine sauce (£6.45), Welsh lamb with apricots, Drambuie and peaches (£6.85), duck with mango and peach sauce (£8.95), sirloin steaks (£9.85), and good puddings like sticky toffee meringue (£2.30); children's menu or smaller helpings; booking recommended in the evenings. They do breakfasts from 8.30am, and afternoon teas. Well kept Adnams Bitter, Mild, Broadside and Extra on handpump. There are seats on the grass outside, and a good play area for children. The small village church is opposite, and another church a mile south at Wenhaston has a fascinating 15th-c wall-painting. *(Recommended by Mrs P J Pearce, Thomas Nott, D and B Carter, Mr and Mrs D J Carmichael, Derek R Patey, Dr S R Dando)*

Adnams ~ Tenant Tony Matthews ~ Real ale ~ Meals and snacks ~ Restaurant ~ Blyburgh (01502) 478404 ~ Children in eating area and no-smoking restaurant ~ Open 11-3, 6.30-11 ~ Bedrooms: /£35B

BRANDESTON TM2460 Map 5

Queens Head

Towards Earl Soham

The big rolling garden at this well run and friendly country pub is a delightful place to sit, with plenty of tables on the neatly kept grass among large flower-beds and a play tree, climbing frame and slide. There's always a nice lively local feel, and the pub is a real centre for village life, with various sports teams and the like. It's simply decorated with some panelling, brown leather banquettes and old pews in the open-plan bar, divided into separate bays by the stubs of surviving walls; shove ha'penny, cribbage, dominoes. Good value bar food includes sandwiches (from £1.10), soup (£1.80), long wholemeal rolls with different fillings (from £2), salads (from £3.50), ploughman's (from £3.95), chilli (£3.95), nut and mushroom pancake (£4), home-made sausage and onion pie or lasagne (both £4.95), evening extras like beef and mushroom casserole (£5.50) or Dover sole (£9.50), and tasty home-made puddings like apricot crumble or cold apple crunch (all £2); Sunday roast lunch (£5.50). Well kept Adnams Bitter, Broadside, and Mild on handpump, with good local cider; helpful staff; fruit machine and faint piped music (in a separate family room). The inn has a caravan and camping club site at the back. You can visit the nearby cider farm. *(Recommended by Dr and Mrs M Bailey; more reports please)*

Adnams ~ Licensee Tony Smith ~ Real ale ~ Meals and snacks (not Sun evening) ~ Earl Soham (01728) 685307 ~ Children in family room ~ Open 11.30-2.30, 6-11 ~ Bedrooms: £17/£34

nr CHELMONDISTON TM2037 Map 5

Butt & Oyster

Pin Mill – signposted from B1456 SE of Ipswich

Fine views over the River Orwell and the wooded slopes beyond from this simple old bargeman's pub, nicely set right on the waterfront, with plenty of seats to watch the boats going up and down. The same views can also be had from the bay window inside, where there's quite a nautical theme to match the surroundings. Cheerful and atmospheric, the half-panelled little smoke room is pleasantly worn and unfussy, with model sailing ships around the walls and high-backed and other old-fashioned settles on the tiled floor; spare a glance for the most unusual carving of a man with a woman over the mantelpiece. Good bar food includes tasty seafood dishes as well as sandwiches (from £1.10; not on Saturday or Sunday lunchtimes), ploughman's (from £2.60), home-made pies and quiches (from £3.85), popular self-service salads and weekend lunchtime buffet (from £4.50), home-made daily specials like steak and kidney pie, chicken casserole, seafood pots or mushroom stroganoff (all around £4.50), and a selection of puddings (all £2). Bass, Flowers IPA and Tolly Mild, Original and Shooter on handpump, with Bitter tapped from the cask, decent wines; winter darts, shove-ha'penny, dominoes and shut-the-box. A good time to visit the pub would be when the annual Thames Barge Race is held (end June/beginning July). No dogs. *(Recommended by David Peakall, Graham Reeve, Basil J S Minson, J L Phillips, MMD)*

Pubmaster ~ Tenants Dick and Brenda Mainwaring ~ Real ale ~ Meals and snacks (till 10pm in summer; not 25 Dec) ~ (01473) 780764 ~ Children welcome except in main bar ~ Occasional piano and folk dancing ~ Open 11-11; 11-3, 7-11 in winter; closed evening 25 Dec

CLARE TL7645 Map 5

Bell ♀
Market place

Splendidly carved black beams and old panelling and woodwork around the open fire give away the age of this attractive timbered hotel, well placed in the market square of an interesting village. The rambling lounge bar also has comfortable armchairs on the green carpet and village notices on the hessian walls, giving it a nicely relaxed local feel. Another room leads off, and to eat you go through to the Leggers Bar with masses of prints – mainly to do with canals – on its walls: food here includes sandwiches (from £1.50) and soup (£1.50), and a wide selection of hot dishes ranging from sausage, chips and beans (£3.95) through chicken in honey and mustard sauce (£4.95) to salmon, steaks or fresh lobster (around £9); lots of daily specials. A comfortable, light and airy conservatory has sofas and armchairs prettily covered in a burgundy Laura Ashley paisley. Well kept Greene King IPA and Nethergate Bitter and Old Growler on handpump, with several locally produced wines; darts, pool, fruit machine, trivia and piped music. There's a back terrace and attractive garden. Several other striking buildings in the village include the remains of the priory and the castle (which stands on prehistoric earthworks). *(Recommended by W H and E Thomas, Walter and Susan Rinaldi-Butcher, Dr and Mrs M Bailey, Heather Martin, Steve Goodchild, Mike and Joyce Bryant)*

Free house ~ Licensees Mr R Williams and Miss T Cole ~ Real ale ~ Meals and snacks ~ Restaurant ~ Clare (01787) 277741 ~ Children welcome ~ Occasional live music in the evenings ~ Open 11-11 ~ Bedrooms: £29.95(£39.95B)/ £39.95(£49.95B)

COTTON TM0766 Map 5

Trowel & Hammer
Mill Rd; take B1113 N of Stowmarket, then turn right into Blacksmiths Lane just N of Bacton

The oak panelling, thatch and tiles of this homely and welcoming place might make it seem like your average country local, but while the chatty atmosphere and decor are firmly traditional, the food marks it out as something a little more unusual, with many dishes heavily influenced by the Greek roots of the landlord. Favourites include very well flavoured dishes like hummus (£2.25), taramasalata (£2.50), kebabs (£3.10), moussaka (£4.75), and a popular kleftiko cooked with plenty of oregano (£5.75), as well as more straightforward pub fare like sandwiches (from £1.60), soup (£1.50), sausages and chips (£2.50), ham, egg and chips (£2.90), ploughman's (from £3), vegetable pancakes (£3.50), steak and kidney pie (£4.75), lasagne or curry (£4.90) and steaks (from £7.40); helpings are big. No credit cards. The spreading red-carpeted lounge has wheelback and one or two older chairs and settles around a variety of tables, lots of dark beamery and timber baulks, lantern lights, a big log fire and at the back an ornate woodburning stove; the windows have elaborately pelmeted and swagged velvet curtains. Service is very pleasant and friendly, and even when busy the landlord finds time to chat to customers. Well kept Adnams, Boddingtons and Greene King IPA and Abbot on handpump. The pretty back garden has neat climbers on trellises, picnic-table sets and a pool. It's quite difficult to find – but worth it. *(Recommended by John C Baker, Brian Jones, Dave Braisted, Gwen and Peter Andrews, D A Webb)*

Free house ~ Licensees George Kattos and Chris Frydas ~ Real ale ~ Meals and snacks (11.30-2, 6.30-11) ~ (01449) 781234 ~ Children in eating area ~ Open 11.30-2.30, 6.30-11

DENNINGTON TM2867 Map 5

Queens Head
A1120

The Bumsteads, who reopened this in late 1993 after some sympathetic refurbishments, are breathing new life into one of Suffolk's most attractive pub buildings. We and readers knew them well previously at the Queens Head in Brandeston, which had a particularly lively atmosphere in their time there. This new venture had been closed for a while after running with rather a low profile for some years: it's a Tudor building, set in gardens alongside the church, and for centuries – until quite recently – was owned by a church charity. Inside, you feel it may easily once have been a chapel: the arched rafters of the steeply roofed part on the right certainly give that impression. The main L-shaped room has some carpet and some traditional flooring tiles, carefully stripped wall timbers and beams – the great bressumer beam over the fireplace is handsomely carved. The new brick bar counters tone in well, and solid traditional furnishings suit the bill exactly. There are sandwiches (from £1.30) and a choice of ploughman's (from £3.25), and good value straightforward home cooking includes cheesy sausages in cottage pie (£2.95), kidneys in cream and mustard sauce or lamb and courgette bake (£3.95), very good fisherman's pie (£4.25), quiches (from £4.75), steak and kidney pie (£5.30), steaks (from £9.95), and puddings like fresh lemon cheesecake, treacle tart and coffee bombe (£2.50). They serve these dishes without vegetables, charging 60p to £1.80 extra if you want them to bulk out your meal. Well kept Adnams Bitter and Broadside and a guest beer on handpump; piped music. The side lawn, attractively replanted with flowers, is sheltered by some noble lime trees, and has picnic-table sets; this backs onto Dennington Park where there are swings and so forth for children. *(Recommended by C H and P Stride)*

Free house ~ Licensees Ray and Myra Bumstead ~ Real ale ~ Meals and snacks ~ Restaurant ~ (01728) 638241 ~ Children in family area ~ Open 11.30-2.30, 5.30(6 Sat)-11

DUNWICH TM4770 Map 5

Ship ★ 🛏 🍺

The combination of good food and drink, smiling unflappable service, lovely genuine atmosphere, and fresh sea breezes has long made this delightful old pub a favourite with readers. This year it seems to be more popular than ever, with a higher number of enthusiastic reports than any other place in the county, so we've at last given it the star we've been threatening for some time. Simple and relaxed with a pleasant bustling atmosphere, the traditionally furnished bar has benches, pews, captain's chairs and candle-lit wooden tables on the tiled floor, a woodburning stove (cheerfully left open in cold weather) and lots of old fishing nets and paintings on the walls. The reasonably priced, tasty, home-made bar food has a variety of fresh fish dishes, as well as lunchtime snacks like lovely soup (£1.30), cottage pie (£3.25), ploughman's (£3.50), a vegetarian meal like cauliflower, cheese, leek and potato pie (£3.75), beef and vegetable pie or lasagne (£4.10), and good fish and home-made chips, with evening dishes like mushrooms cooked in garlic, butter and cream (£3.25), home-made pâté (£3.75), pork escalope cordon bleu (£6.50) and fish dishes such as seafood pancake with a fresh fish, smoked haddock and prawn filling (£7.50) or salmon steak poached in wine (£7.75); the stir-fried buttered vegetables that accompany all the meals are well liked. Lunchtime service can stop promptly. Well kept Adnams Bitter, maybe Broadside and winter Old and Greene King Abbot and IPA on handpump at the handsomely panelled bar counter. The public bar area has darts, dominoes, cribbage, fruit machine, video game, trivia and piped music. It can be busy even at midweek lunchtimes, but this never causes any problems and the staff are still friendly and helpful. The conservatory has been rebuilt and the sunny back terrace prettily landscaped, and there's a well kept garden with an enormous fig tree. In summer a couple of theatre companies put on productions out here, and there may be Morris dancers. The pub is handy for the RSPB reserve at Minsmere. Dunwich today is such a charming little place it's hard to imagine that centuries ago it was one of England's major centres. Since then fairly rapid coastal erosion has put most of the village under the sea, and there are those who claim that on still nights you can sometimes hear the old church bells tolling under the water. *(Recommended by Helen Crookston, Mrs M A Mees, Mr and Mrs R P Begg, Brenda and Jim Langley, Mary and David Webb, Dr and Mrs P J Crawshaw, M J V Kemp, Basil Minson, Mr and Mrs G M Edwards, Rita Horridge, Nigel Woolliscroft, Jan and Peter Shropland, Neil Powell, Brian Viner, David Warrellow, Rob and Doris Harrison, Dr and Mrs M Bailey, George Atkinson, Katie and Steve Newby, Mrs S Burrows-Smith, Trevor Scott, P Bolton, M L and B S Rantzen)*

Free house ~ Licensees Stephen and Ann Marshlain ~ Real ale ~ Meals and snacks ~ Evening restaurant ~ Westleton (0172 873) 219 ~ Children welcome everywhere but bar ~ Open 11-3(3.30 Sat), 6(6.30 in winter)-11; closed evening 25 Dec ~ Bedrooms: £21/£42(£52S)

EARL SOHAM TM2363 Map 5

Victoria ★

A1120 Stowmarket—Yoxford

Popular mainly for its interesting range of beers brewed on the premises, this unspoilt pub is a simple, cheery place, totally free of any pretensions. You can visit the microbrewery that produces the Victoria Bitter, a mild called Gannet, and a stronger ale called Albert, and take some home with you. The bar has a very friendly atmosphere, along with well chosen traditional furnishings like kitchen chairs and pews, plank-topped trestle sewing-machine tables and other simple country tables with candles, tiled or board floors, stripped panelling, an interesting range of pictures of Queen Victoria and her reign, a piano, and open fires. Get there early to be sure of a seat, they do get busy. The good value bar food is very well liked, with a choice of straightforward dishes like sandwiches (from £1.50), excellent soup, ploughman's, burgers (£2.25), chilli (£3.50), pizzas (£3.75), vegetable lasagne (£4.25), and pork with apple and cider or beef curry (£4.50). Darts, shove ha'penny, cribbage, dominoes, cards and backgammon; seats out in front and on a raised back lawn. The pub is close to a wild fritillary meadow at Framlingham and a working windmill at Saxtead. *(Recommended by V and E A Bolton, Derek and Sylvia Stephenson, Dr and Mrs P J Crawshaw, Wayne Brindle, David Ball, Dr and Mrs M Bailey, Margaret Drazin, Dr S R Dando, D Cox, Frank W Gadbois)*

Own brew ~ Licensees Clare and John Bjornson ~ Real ale ~ Meals and snacks ~ (01728) 685758 ~ Impromptu folk music Tues and Fri evenings ~ Open 11.30-2.30, 5.30-11

EASTON TM2858 Map 5

White Horse

N of Wickham Market, on back road to Earl Soham and Framlingham

Nicely unspoilt and traditional, this attractive old pub is delightfully rickety-looking from the outside. Inside, the two enlarged rooms are neat and smartly simple, with country kitchen chairs, good small settles, cushioned stripped pews and stools, and open fires; the atmosphere is warmly welcoming, and there's a good mix of customers of all ages. The well presented food is popular, with a seasonally changing menu designed to cater to all tastes, including meals like char-grilled chicken kebabs in lime, chilli, garlic and ginger (£7.50), fillet of lamb with rosemary, honey and garlic (£8.50), sirloin steak with a brandy pepper sauce (£8.95), lots of fresh fish such as excellent salmon fillet in champagne sauce, and puddings like apple tart with butterscotch sauce; vegetables and potatoes come in separate dishes. Well kept Tolly Bitter, Shooter and Mild on handpump, good wines; polite, friendly service. There's also a separate games room, and a terrace with barbecue facilities, while the garden has a well equipped children's play area. Easton Farm Park is worth visiting. *(Recommended by Mrs P M Goodwyn, Mrs R Cotgreave, Neil Powell, C H Stride)*

Tolly ~ Lease Alan Done ~ Real ale ~ Meals and snacks (till 10) ~ Restaurant ~ Wickham Market (01728) 746456 ~ Children in eating area of bar ~ Live jazz 2nd and last Weds of month ~ Open 11-3(2.30 Sat), 6.30-11

ERWARTON TM2134 Map 5

Queens Head ♀

Village signposted off B1456 Ipswich—Shotley Gate; pub past the attractive church and manor house

One of those rare places where everything seems to gel, this remote and unspoilt pub is particularly well liked for its very good bar food. There's a nice homely feel and very relaxing atmosphere in the comfortably furnished bar, still showing signs of its age, with bowed 16th-c black oak beams in the shiny low yellowing ceiling; also a cosy coal fire and a cupboard of silver cups and trophies. The more modern restaurant has a good wide range of home-cooked food like sandwiches, soup (£1.90), ploughman's (£3.50), scampi platter (£4.85), three daily vegetarian meals, beef and ale casserole, lasagne, moussaka, curry or lamb chop in port and rosemary sauce (all £4.95), salmon in mussel sauce (£5.95), rump steak in tarragon and cream sauce (£8.50), several fresh fish dishes, game in season, and good puddings, particularly strong on unusual cheesecakes like banana and yoghurt (from £2.20). Well kept Adnams Bitter and Extra, Greene King IPA, Marstons Pedigree and Morlands Old Speckled Hen on handpump with Adnams Old and Tally Ho in winter; also occasionally Adnams barley wine, a decent wine list with several half bottles and a wide choice of malt whiskies; friendly service. The gents' have a fascinating collection of navigational maps. The orchard is now a car park. A patio has fine views over fields to ships on the Stour and the distant Parkeston Quay. Nearby Erwarton Hall with its peculiar gatehouse like an upturned salt cellar is an interesting place to visit. *(Recommended by Graham Reeve, Mrs P M Goodwyn, C H and P Stride; more reports please)*

Free house ~ Licensees Mr B K Buckle and Mrs Julia Crisp ~ Real ale ~ Meals and snacks ~ Restaurant (not Sun evening) ~ (01473) 787550 ~ Children in restaurant ~ Open 11-3(2.30 winter), 6(7 in winter)-11; closed 25 Dec

FRAMSDEN TM1959 Map 5

Dobermann 🛏 🍺

The Street; pub signposted off B1077 just S of its junction with A1120 Stowmarket—Earl Soham

There's a very pleasant tucked-away atmosphere at this charmingly restored old thatched pub, and the cheery licensees go out of their way to make you feel welcome. The two spotless and friendly bar areas are separated by a wonderful twin-facing fireplace and have very low, pale stripped beams, photographs of and show rosettes won by the owner's dogs on the white walls, a big comfy sofa, a couple of chintz wing armchairs, and a mix of other chairs, plush-seated stools and winged settles around polished rustic tables; there's a friendly tabby, Tinker. A good choice of well kept beers on handpump includes Adnams Bitter and Broadside and three constantly changing guests like Felinfoel Double Dragon, Arkells Kingsdown or other unusual brews, with a decent choice of spirits and malt whiskies; efficient service, piped music. Very well praised bar food includes sandwiches (from £1.35, maybe hot beef £1.90), home-made soup or deep-fried squid (£2.95), huge ploughman's (from £4.50), vegetable curry or mushroom stroganoff (£4.95), plaice stuffed with prawns (£5.95), rabbit pie, chicken breast sautéed in garlic with a cream and white wine sauce or game pie in season (all £7.95), sirloin steak (from £9.75) and lots of daily changing fish specials such as Dover sole (£10.50); good puddings like home-made apple pie or cordon bleu log (all £2.95). They play boules outside, where there are picnic-table sets by trees and a fairy-lit trellis, and lots of pretty hanging baskets and colourful window boxes. They host the Framsden pram race every year at the end of June. The river used to flood the nearby area so much that customers apparently had to enter the bar on horseback if they wanted to keep dry. *(Recommended by G E Rich, Sheila and Terry Wells, Simon Gay, Mr and Mrs D Wittekind)*

Free house ~ Licensee Susan Frankland ~ Real ale ~ Meals and snacks (11.30-2, 7-9.45) ~ Helmingham (01473) 890 461 ~ Open 11.30-2.30, 7-11 ~ Bedroom: £20/£30

FRISTON TM4160 Map 5

Old Chequers ♀

B1121 SE of Saxmundham; and village signposted off A1094

It's been a busy (if rather complicated) couple of years at this relaxed, friendly and very well liked place, but it looks like things have settled down now; the Grimwoods, who made the pub so popular with readers for the couple of years until they left in spring 1993, have now returned, and are running things much as they did before. Every lunchtime they have a popular hot and cold buffet with carefully prepared food such as cider-baked ham, game casserole, ratatouille crumble, baked cod, steak and kidney pie, and good help-yourself vegetables (£6.95), then in the evening meals are chalked up on a blackboard, with dishes like chicken supreme in a curry sauce, tenderloin of pork with fried apples and calvados, herb crusted chicken stuffed with a garlic and cream sauce, stilton, spinach and apple pancakes, and steaks. They also do themed nights, concentrating on dishes from various continents. Well kept Adnams and three guests on handpump, as well as good malt whiskies and an eclectic, thoughtfully-chosen range of wines, several by the glass. A small red-carpeted area by the bar, with a woodburning stove and stripped brickwork, opens on the left into an airy and spacious room decorated in cool greens and cream, with another big woodburner in one stripped wall, and well spaced chairs and country-kitchen tables (with fresh flowers) in pale wood. There are a few picnic-table sets in the small back yard. *(Recommended by Basil J S Minson, Paul and Ursula Randall, R C Morgan, Dr and Mrs P J S Crawshaw, C R Whitham, Mrs P M Goodwyn)*

Free house ~ Licensees David and Sally Grimwood ~ Real ale ~ Meals (not Sun evening) ~ Snape (01728) 688270 ~ Children welcome lunchtimes only ~ Open 11.30-2.30, 6.30(7 winter)-11

GREAT GLEMHAM TM3361 Map 5

Crown 🛏 ♀ ◀

Between A12 Wickham Mkt—Saxmundham, B1119 Saxmundham—Framlingham

Once again it's the atmosphere and nicely unspoilt air that people praise most at this pleasantly placed and well kept old brick house, though it's very well liked too as a place to stay. The credit for all this has to go to the Masons, who really do work hard at getting things just the way their customers want them. The open-plan lounge has beams, one or two big casks, brass ornaments or musical instruments, wooden pews and captain's chairs around stripped and waxed kitchen tables, two enormous fireplaces with logs blazing in winter, and contented chatter uninterrupted by any music. Local photographs and paintings decorate the white walls, and there are plenty of fresh flowers and pot plants, with more in a side eating room. Well kept Adnams Bitter, Broadside and winter Old, Bass and

Greene King Abbot, from old brass handpumps; good choice of malt whiskies and decent wines. Good promptly served bar food includes filled rolls (from £1.60), soup (£2.35), ploughman's (from £3), lasagne, beef enchiladas or vegetarian leek croutade (all £4.95), steak and kidney pie, fisherman's bake or chicken parmigiana (£5.95), and charcoal grills, with puddings like lemon cheesecake or cape brandy pudding (£2.45); children's meals (£2.95). Darts, shove-ha'penny, dominoes, chess, draughts, cards and a fruit machine. There's a neat, flower-fringed lawn, raised above the corner of the quiet village lane by a retaining wall; seats and tables under cocktail parasols out here. Breakfasts are good. *(Recommended by Derek and Sylvia Stephenson, G W H Kerby, Gwen and Peter Andrews, Basil J S Minson, Jeff Davies, W J Wonham, Rob and Doris Harrison, Wayne Brindle, Nicholas Cliffe)*

Free house ~ Licensee Roger Mason ~ Real ale ~ Meals and snacks (not Mon) ~ Restaurant ~ Rendham (01728) 663693 ~ Children in restaurant ~ Open 12-2.30, 7-11 ~ Bedrooms: £20S/£38B

HORRINGER TL8261 Map 5

Beehive 🍴
A143

The Kingshotts are just about to celebrate their tenth year at this pretty ivy-covered village pub, and during that period it seems to have gone from strength to strength. Doing particularly well at the moment, the pub is well liked for its good welcome and service, and especially for the good range of accomplished food. A typical choice of dishes might include sandwiches (from £2), soups such as lettuce and asparagus (£2.25), cream cheese and smoked fish mousse or home-made taramasalata with hot pitta bread (£3.95), ploughman's or whole avocado prawns (£4.50), curried vegetable pancake with toasted crumb topping or smoked salmon and scrambled egg (£4.95), chilli with several accompaniments or delicious local ham (£5.95), chicken and mushroom stroganoff in a cream, brandy and paprika sauce on a bed of wild rice or smoked salmon and prawn tagliatelle in a dill and vermouth sauce (£7.50), grilled fillet of oriental-style pork marinated in spices and served on a leaf salad (£7.95), fresh fish dishes, daily specials like pan-fried sweetbreads with lemon mayonnaise or lobster (£7.95), and giant rib steak (£10.95); eight good home-made puddings (£2.50); service remains prompt and friendly even at busy times. The little rambling rooms have stripped panelling or brickwork, some very low beams in some of the furthest and snuggest alcoves, carefully chosen dining and country kitchen chairs, one or two wall settles around solid tables, picture-lights over lots of 19th-c prints, and a woodburning stove. Their new dog Muffin is very good at making friends; other dogs aren't really welcome. The gents' has a frieze depicting villagers fleeing from stinging bees. Well kept Greene King IPA and Abbot on handpump and decent changing house wines. A most attractively planted back terrace has picnic-table sets, with more seats on a raised lawn. There's good B&B next door. *(Recommended by Sue and Dominic Dunlop, Dr and Mrs M Bailey, F M and A F Walters, Thomas Nott, Keith Wilson, N M Williamson, Wayne Brindle, Simon Morton, Lawrence Bacon, Martin and Pauline Richardson, Richard Balls, Charles Bardswell, Mike and Joyce Bryant, John C Baker, Heather M N Robson, Jeremy Williams, Anne Hyde, Mr and Mrs A Varnom, Clive Petts)*

Greene King ~ Tenants Gary and Dianne Kingshott ~ Real ale ~ Meals and snacks (not Sun evening) ~ Horringer (01284) 735260 ~ Children welcome ~ Open 11.30-2.30, 7-11

HOXNE TM1777 Map 5

Swan ♀
Off B1118; village signposted off A140 S of Diss

A carefully restored late 15th-c house, this is a magnificent old building, succesfully combining its recent popularity as a dining pub with its more traditional role as an atmospheric village inn. Evidence of its age isn't hard to find, with the ancient timber and mortar of the walls still visible; there are also two solid oak counters in its front bar, heavy oak floors, and a deep-set inglenook fireplace, with an armchair on either side and a long bench in front of it. A fire in the back bar divides the bar area and snug, and the dining room has an original wooden fireplace. Relaxed and peaceful, it's all very atmospheric. Very popular bar food includes burgers (from £1.10), sandwiches (from £1.30), ploughman's (from £2.35), a choice of omelettes (£2.75), tasty pancakes filled with mushrooms and cheese (£3.50), gammon (£3.80), plate of salamis with black olives (£3.95), scampi (£4.30), rump steak (£7.25), plus daily specials such as spinach and garlic terrine (£2.75), duck, bacon and walnut salad or spinach, chickpea and cumin parcels (£4.95), chicken breast in lemon, parsley and vermouth (£5.95) and pork fillet with rosemary and brandy cream sauce (£6.95); the vegetables are good. If you're sitting outside and waiting for your food order, keep your eye on the roof; rather than use a Tannoy, they briefly sound a buzzer and then prop scoreboard type numbers up there when your meal is ready. Service remains quick even at busy times. Well kept Adnams, winter Old and Tally Ho and Greene King Abbot on handpump or tapped from the cask, decent wines, and half-a-dozen malt whiskies; dominoes, pool, shove-ha'penny, cribbage and juke box. The extensive lawn behind is used for croquet, and is a very tranquil place to sit in summer on the hand-made elm furniture, sheltered by a willow and other trees and its shrub-covered wall. Nearby is the site of King Edmund the Martyr's execution; the tree to which he was tied for it is now reputed to form part of a screen in the neighbouring church. *(Recommended by Mr and Mrs D J Carmichael, Gwen and Peter Andrews, J Honner, Mrs P M Goodwyn, V and E A Bolton, M G Hart, George Atkinson, Nick Dowson, J E Rycroft, Dr S R Dando)*

Free house ~ Licensees Tony and Frances Thornton-Jones ~ Real ale ~ Meals and snacks (not Sat evening or all day Sun) ~ Restaurant (Sat evening and Sunday lunch) ~ Hoxne (01379) 668275 ~ Children in eating area ~ Open 12-2.30(3 Sat), 5.30-11; closed 25 Dec

HUNDON TL7348 Map 5

Plough 🛏

Brockley Green; on Kedington road, up hill from village

Perched atop one of the few hills in the area, this extended and modernised pub has fine views over miles of East Anglian countryside from its back terrace and gardens. A cosy place, especially in winter, the neat carpeted bar still has a double row of worn old oak timbers to mark what must once have been the corridor between its two rooms; there are also low side settles with Liberty-print cushions, spindleback chairs, and sturdy low tables on the patterned carpet, lots of horsebrasses on the beams, and striking gladiatorial designs for Covent Garden by Leslie Hurry, who lived nearby. The meals are very good, with an emphasis on fresh local produce; the daily changing bar menu might include lunchtime sandwiches or filled french bread, home-made soup, ploughman's, broccoli and camembert filo pie or vegetable tagliatelle (£4.95), steak and Guinness pie or pasta shells with parma ham (£5.95), home-cooked gammon in a mustard and cider sauce (£6.95), several succulent seafood dishes, the speciality, such as good mussels, dressed crab (£6.95), fresh salmon in a fennel butter sauce or sauté of monkfish (£10.50), and à la carte dishes like game pie (£8.75) or half pheasant poached in wine with celery and apple (£10.95); excellent sticky toffee pudding (£2.95). Changing beers such as well kept Greene King IPA, Mauldons Bitter, Nethergate and a guest on handpump, with freshly squeezed orange juice, local wine and a range of continental bottled beers; shove ha'penny, dominoes, cheerful piped music. Parts of the bar and restaurant are no smoking. There's a terrace with pergola and ornamental pool and a garden, popular with the two friendly retrievers, where there's croquet. It's also a certified location for the Caravan Club, with a sheltered site to the rear for tourers. The pub has been run by the same friendly family for three generations. *(Recommended by Frank W Gadbois, M J Morgan; more reports please)*

Free house ~ Licensees David and Marion Rowlinson ~ Real ale ~ Meals and snacks ~ Restaurant ~ Hundon (01440) 786789 ~ Children in eating area of bar only ~ Open 11-11; 12-2.30, 5.30-11 in winter ~ Bedrooms: £35B/£50B

ICKLINGHAM TL7772 Map 5

Red Lion

A1101, Mildenhall—Bury St Edmunds

A very well liked thatched and whitewashed old pub, standing out especially for its good choice of excellent bar food. You might find dishes like soup (£2.10), sandwiches, good cheese platter (£3.65), whole prawns in garlic butter (from £3.85), sausages in onion gravy (£4.05), shepherd's pie or a vegetarian dish of the day like mushroom stroganoff (£5.95), pork chops in apple and cider sauce (£6.85), warm chicken and pasta salad (£8.45), plenty of fresh fish such as local Larkwood trout (£7.25), fillet of codling (£7.95) and huge Torbay sole (£10.25), as well as daily specials, game in season, à la carte dishes like pork tenderloin in a black peppercorn sauce (£9.95), prawns and monkfish in a thermidor sauce (£10.65) or venison medallions in a port, chestnut and orange sauce (£11.05), very nice vegetables, and tasty puddings like ginger and lemon sauce pudding; the superb fresh fish is delivered from Lowestoft every day. The smartly refurbished bar has lots to look at under the heavy beams, such as antlers over the inglenook fireplace, old fishing rods and various stuffed animals, with a nice mixture of wooden chairs and tables, and decorated with lovely fresh flowers. Piped classical music and newspapers add to the civilised atmosphere. Well kept Greene King Abbot, IPA and Rayments and guest on handpump, and a good range of fruit wines; efficient attentive service; darts, dominoes, cribbage and a fruit machine. Pipe tobacco is available by the plug. Picnic-set tables on a raised back terrace face the fields – including an acre of the pub's running down to the River Lark, with Cavenham Heath nature reserve beyond. In front (the pub is well set back from the road) old-fashioned white seats overlook the car park and a flower lawn. A paddock has two pot-bellied pigs. It's close to West Stow Country Park and the Anglo-Saxon Village, and the same licensees also run the Pykkerel at Ixworth. *(Recommended by S Brackenbury, John and Elspeth Howell, Thomas Nott, Dr and Mrs M Bailey, R H Brown)*

Greene King ~ Licensees Ian Hubbert and Jonathan Gates ~ Meals and snacks (till 10) ~ Restaurant ~ (01638) 717802 ~ Children in eating area ~ Open 12-3, 6-11

IPSWICH TM1744 Map 5

Brewery Tap

Cliff Rd

This newish pub down by the waterfront makes a very handsome sight, an attractive pink-washed house nestling below the great Victorian bulk of the Tolly Cobbold brewery, saved from closure by a 1990 management buy-out. It's the ground floor of what might well have been an early 19th-c brewmaster's house. Inside, several very welcoming smallish room areas cluster around the main bar, with decently spaced solid small tables, some armchairs, rugs on polished boards. Some brickwork's been stripped back, and elsewhere some original lathework exposed. There are pictures of the docks and other local scenes, though the best picture is the real-life one framed by the heavy curtains around the big windows – the boats you can often see passing outside. The atmosphere is civilised, and the good range of food includes giant filled baps (from £2.25), filled baked potatoes (from £2.50), beef and tomato pasta or lasagne (£4.95), steak and kidney pie (£5.50) and vegetarian dishes from a daily specials board like pineapple paella (£4.95) and home-made puddings (1.95); they do Sunday lunches. Well kept Tolly Mild, Bitter, Original, Tolly-Shooter and Old Strong in winter, all on handpump, and the full range of Tolly bottled beers. A games area has darts, shove ha'penny, bar skittles and bar billiards. The back room looks into the brewery's steam-engine room, and a door from the pub leads straight into the brewery: there is usually one tour a day, ring for the time. *(Recommended by Ian Phillips, C H Stride, Neil Calver)*

Tolly ~ Manager Steve Palvey ~ Real ale ~ Meals and snacks 12-2.30, 6-9.30 ~ Restaurant (open all day Sun) ~ (01473) 281508/231723 ~ Children's room ~ Parking restrictions daytime ~ Open 11-11

IXWORTH TL9370 Map 5

Pykkerel

Village signposted just off A143 Bury St Edmunds—Diss

Run by the same people as the Red Lion at Icklingham (and currently drawing the same kind of enthusiastic reports), this friendly old place has had a slight name change since our last edition. It's an interesting building, sympathetically refurbished in keeping with the original character, with an assortment of panelling that's been gradually assembled since Tudor times. Several neatly kept small rooms lead off the central servery, and all have moulded Elizabethan oak beams, attractive brickwork, and big fireplaces, as well as antique tables and chairs and persian rugs on the gleaming floors; there's a similarly furnished dining area, and a small back sun lounge facing a sway-backed Elizabethan timbered barn across the old coach yard. The emphasis is on the generously served bar food, with the menu the same as at the Red Lion: sandwiches, soup (£2.10), good cheese platter (£3.65), whole prawns in garlic butter (from £3.85), sausages in onion gravy (£4.05), shepherd's pie or a vegetarian dish of the day like mushroom stroganoff (£5.95), pork chops in apple and cider sauce (£6.85), warm chicken and pasta salad (£8.45), plenty of very good fresh fish from Lowestoft such as local Larkwood trout (£7.25), fillet of codling (£7.95) and huge Torbay sole (£10.25), as well as daily specials, and à la carte meals like lamb's kidneys in a claret and mushroom sauce (£9.05), leg of lamb steak with mint and rosemary (£10.65) or roast duck in a port and wild black cherry sauce (£11.05). Well kept Greene King IPA and Rayments on handpump, with a collection of country wines, a dozen malt whiskies, clay pipes and snuff; pleasantly brisk service. On a goodish stretch of grass under a giant sycamore are some picnic-table sets. *(Recommended by Tony Gayfer, Andrew Scarr, Richard Balls, BHP, F C Johnston, Dr and Mrs M Bailey, Andrew McKeand, F M and A F Walters)*

Greene King ~ Lease: Ian Hubbert, Jonathan Gates ~ Real ale ~ Meals and snacks (till 10) ~ Restaurant ~ Pakenham (01359) 30398 ~ Children welcome ~ Open 12-3, 6-11

KERSEY TL9944 Map 5

Bell

Village signposted off A1141 N of Hadleigh

Well placed in a pretty village, just along the street from a ford filled with ducks and geese, this unusual timbered building is one of those places that seems especially cosy in winter. Dating back to Tudor times, it's just been taken over by the Old English Pub Company, and the friendly new managers don't plan any changes. The comfortable bar and lounge are divided by a brick and timber screen decorated with copper and brassware; the low-beamed public side has simple seating on its tiled floor and a log fire, while the lounge has comfortable red plush button-back banquettes, latticed windows, and a swirly red carpet. Corn dollies and other interesting ornaments decorate the walls; dominoes, cribbage, trivia, cards and piped music. Bar food includes sandwiches (from £2.10), soup (£2.25), ploughman's (£3.95), salads (from £4.50), steak and kidney pudding or chicken kiev (£5.95), and a good few imaginative daily specials like mille feuille of wild mushroom and leeks in a mushroom and Pernod sauce (£7.95) or medallions of pork baked in an orange crust with pineapple compote (£8.95); puddings such as apple pie or spotted dick (£2.50). Courage Directors, John Smiths, Ruddles Best and a regularly changing guest like Adnams or Wadworths 6X on handpump; also around a dozen malt whiskies and decent wines by the glass. Out on the sheltered back terrace and under a fairy-lit side canopy, there are white cast-iron tables and chairs. They are listed as a certified location for the Caravan Club (up to 3 units). *(Recommended by C H and P Stride, J N Child, V and E A Bolton, Tina nd David Woods-Taylor, W H and E Thomas, Basil J S Minson, Gwen and Peter Andrews)*

Free house ~ Managers James and Orla Cullen ~ Real ale ~ Meals and snacks ~ Restaurant ~ Ipswich (01473) 823229 ~ Children welcome ~ Open 10.30-5, 7-11

LAVENHAM TL9149 Map 5

Angel ★ ⊕ ⇔ ♀
Market Pl

Still encouraging more favourable reports than just about any other pub in Suffolk, this carefully-renovated Tudor inn is a delight to visit. Readers are so warmly enthusiastic about it (several going back time and time again), that this year we've decided to award it a star. The welcome, the food and the general air of thoughtfulness rarely fail to please, and there's a very civilised, relaxed and comfortable atmosphere, especially on those frequent occasions when Mr Whitworth is playing the piano (we praised his Chopin last year but readers seem to prefer his Schubert). The excellent changing bar food is carefully home-cooked, using mainly local ingredients, and includes dishes like tomato and tarragon or courgette and lentil soup (£2.25), fresh Suffolk asparagus or ploughman's (£3.95), smoked halibut and horseradish (£4.50), they do all their own smoking), broccoli and stilton tart (£5.75), excellent salads, steak and ale pie or roast rib of beef (£5.95), lamb in paprika and cream (£7.50), calf's liver, bacon and onions (£8.25) and good puddings and home-made ice cream (£2.75); in the evenings there are also more expensive, richly textured main dishes, such as escalope of veal with lemon and capers (£8.75) or fillet of brill with prawns and watercress sauce (£10.25). Several readers say they can't praise the meals too highly. One of the eating areas is no smoking. The green-carpeted main bar on the right feels very up-to-date, with piped light classics, lots of shelves of readable books, and blonde furniture including heavy kitchen tables and chairs; one table shaped like a piano-top occupies a bay window, with a nice polished wooden seat running around it to look out on the little market square of this pretty village, and its Guildhall (NT). The open-plan area loops around the servery to a more softly lit dark-beamed part on the left, with some sofas and mate's chairs around darker tables. There's a big log fire in the inglenook, under a heavy mantelbeam and the 16th-c pargeted ceiling. Well kept Adnams, Courage Directors, Mauldons White Adder, Nethergate, and Websters Yorkshire on handpump, quite a few malt whiskies, decent wines by the glass and a good choice by the bottle; the back area is a family room. Service is efficient and friendly even when busy, though we have heard of a couple of occasions when they've been less keen to see people who didn't want to eat. They have a good range of board games, and hold a chess night on Tuesdays, a bridge night Thursdays and a quiz on Sundays. The big ginger cat is called Dilly, the one without a tail is Stumpy. There are picnic-table sets out in front, and white tables under cocktail parasols in a sizeable sheltered back garden; it's worth asking if they've time to show you the interesting Tudor cellar. *(Recommended by Dougie Paterson, D A Edwards, H J Seddon, Alain and Rose Foote, C H and P Stride, Andy Thwaites, Rosemary Harris, David and Ruth Hollands, Eric and Jackie Robinson, John Baker, Joy Heatherley, R and S Bentley, Mr and Mrs R Leeds, Anne Campbell, Gina and Billy Olphert, Tina and David Woods-Taylor, Derek and Margaret Underwood, Gwen and Peter Andrews, Hugh Stewart, Paula Shillaw, Kevin Whitcombe, G E Rich, Keith Symons, J G Smith, Bill and Edee Miller, R C Wiles, John Evans, Susan and John Priestley)*

Free house ~ Licensees Roy and Anne Whitworth, John Barry ~ Real ale ~ Meals and snacks ~ Restaurant ~ Lavenham (01787) 247388 ~ Children in restaurant and eating area ~ Classical piano some lunchtimes and Fri evenings ~ Open 11-2.30(3 Sat), 6-11; closed 25 Dec ~ Bedrooms: £37.50B/£45B

Swan ★ ⇔

Lavenham is reckoned by many to be one of the country's nicest villages, and this handsome timbered Elizabethan inn is one of the striking buildings that gives it such charm. A touch too smart to please everyone, but ideal for those who need that extra bit of luxury, it's very much a hotel (and not a cheap one), but it does have a genuinely pubby and atmospheric little tiled-floor bar buried in its heart. From there it's an easy overflow into the drift of armchairs and settees that spreads engagingly through a network of beamed and timbered alcoves and more open areas. The bar itself has leather chairs and memorabilia of the days when this was the local for the US 48th Bomber Group in the Second World War (many Americans still come to re-visit old haunts); the set of handbells used to be employed by the local church bellringers for practice. Well kept Courage Directors, Greene King IPA and John Smiths on handpump, various malt whiskies and cognacs. Overlooking the well kept and sheltered courtyard garden is an airy Garden Bar, where at lunchtime a buffet counter serves freshly made sandwiches (£2.50 for tuna and cress to £3.95 for smoked salmon), a trio of pâtés, and mixed salads (ham and turkey £4.95); morning coffee (£3 for two) and afternoon tea (£4.50 per person). There is also a lavishly timbered no-smoking restaurant (with a minstrel's gallery) which serves a three course lunch (£12.95), and dinner (£19.95). Amongst the other fine buildings in this once-prosperous wool town is the Tudor Guildhall, which has a small folk museum. *(Recommended by Neville Kenyon, Spider Newth, Steve Goodchild, Gwen and Peter Andrews, Maysie Thompson and others; more reports please)*

Free house (Forte) ~ Licensee M R Grange ~ Real ale ~ Lunchtime meals and snacks ~ Restaurant ~ Lavenham (01787) 247477 ~ Children welcome ~ Pianist every night ~ Open 11-3, 6-11 ~ Bedrooms: £77B/£105B

LAXFIELD　TM2972　Map 5

Kings Head

Behind church, off road toward Banyards Green

Former friends of this thatched Tudor pub will be delighted to learn that it's been going from strength to strength in the couple of years since it reopened. There's always a welcoming local atmosphere, perhaps best of all on Tuesday lunchtimes, when they have old Suffolk songs and step dancing. The old-fashioned front room has a high-backed built-in settle on the tiled floor and an open fire, and a couple of other rooms have pews, old seats, scrubbed deal tables, and some interesting wall prints. The good bar food is cooked by the landlord using fresh local produce (plenty coming from nearby allotments), and includes dishes like hot roast beef sandwich with horseradish (£2.50), buck rarebit (£3.25), hot avocado and stilton (£3.75), and pork and onion dumplings or chicken pie (£4.95); Wednesday night is kipper night, with fresh kippers from Lowestoft served in newspaper. Friendly service, no piped music or machines, just a very nice traditional feel. Well kept Adnams Bitter, Broadside, Extra and winter Old and Tally Ho, Greene King Abbot and guests like Morlands Old Speckled Hen or Nethergate tapped from the cask, local cider and some country wines; darts, domimoes, shove ha'penny, cribbage. Going out past the casks in the back serving room, you find benches and a trestle table in a small yard. On your way try not to trip over Suzie the dog, who, old and ever so slightly deaf, seems not to notice people might want to get past her. From the yard, a honeysuckle arch leads into a sheltered little garden and the pub's own well kept and secluded bowling, badminton and croquet green; occasional Morris dancers on summer weekends. *(Recommended by David Alchin, Elizabeth and Klaus Leist, Derek and Sylvia Stephenson, David Ball and others)*

Free house ~ Licensees Ian and Sarah Macehiter ~ Real ale ~ Meals and snacks ~ Ubbeston (01986) 798395 ~ Children in eating area ~ Occasional folk nights ~ Open 11-3, 6-11

LEVINGTON　TM2339　Map 5

Ship

Gun Hill; village signposted from A45, then follow Stratton Hall sign

In summer you may find the other customers taking photographs of the magnificent hanging baskets outside this engaging traditional inn. It's popular with users of the local marina, and there's quite a nautical theme inside, with lots of ship prints and photos of sailing barges, beams and benches built into the walls, and in the middle room a marine compass set under the serving counter, which also has a fishing net slung over it. There are also a number of comfortably upholstered small settles, some of them grouped round tables as booths, and a big black round stove; one area is no-smoking. High quality home-made bar food includes a good ploughman's, kippers (£4.95), pork sausages in cider sauce (£5.25), and lots of other well presented hot dishes like braised peppered steak, chicken with lemon sauce, kidneys in red wine, salmon and broccoli bake, mussels in white wine and garlic butter and vegetable stroganoff (all £5.50), with interesting puddings such as raspberry cream flan or orange and ginger cheesecake. Service is friendly and professional. Well kept Bass, Flowers Original, Greene King IPA, and Tolly Cobold Bitter and Worthington Best tapped from the cask, and country wines; cribbage, dominoes. By the time this book is published they should have finished a planned restaurant extension. Note they don't allow dogs or children under 14. If you look carefully enough, there's a distant sea view from the benches in front. *(Recommended by C H and P Stride, Rita Horridge, J L Phillips, A Barker, Graham Reeve)*

Pubmaster ~ Tenants William and Shirley Waite ~ Real ale ~ Meals and snacks (not Sun or Mon or Tuesday evening) ~ (01473) 659573 ~ Folk music first Tues of month ~ Open 11.30-3, 6-11

LONG MELFORD   TL8645   Map 5

Bull 🛏

A134

Supporting the beautifully carved high main beam at this civilised old inn is a woodwose – the wild man of the woods that figures in Suffolk folk-tales. Originally a medieval manorial great hall, the black-and-white timbered building is an atmospheric place, with plenty of character and interesting original fittings. The soothing front lounge – divided by the remains of an oak partition wall – has big mullioned and leaded windows, lots of oak timbering, a huge brick fireplace with log fire, a longcase clock from Stradbrook, a rack of daily papers, and various antique furnishings. A more spacious back bar has armed brown leatherette or plush dining seats around antique oak tables, dark heavy beams, and sporting prints on the cream timbered walls; cribbage, dominoes, piped music. The Mylde lounge is no-smoking. Popular bar food includes sandwiches (from £1.25), soup (£1.95), traditional ploughman's (£3.50), a daily special pie, roast of the day (£5.50) and seafood platter (£5.95); it can be busy at lunchtimes. Well kept Adnams and Greene King IPA on handpump, natural fruit juices, various malt whiskies, country wines and cheerful, helpful staff. There are tables in the paved central courtyard. In 1648 a local man, arguing about Civil War politics, was murdered in a brawl just inside the front door (and buried in the yard of the magnificent church – look for the memorial to Richard Evered). Another murder was committed in 1739 and ghost-hunters hold these responsible for the old brass and copper supposedly rising out of the fireplace and floating around the ceiling. Nearby, the Elizabethan Melford Hall and moated Tudor Kentwell Hall are both fine buildings, in attractive grounds. *(Recommended by F M and A F Walters, Sidney and Erna Wells, Tony and Lynne Gifford, Marjorie and Bernard Parkin and others; more reports please)*

Free house (Forte) ~ Manager Peter Watt ~ Meals and snacks (limited menu Sun; not 25 Dec) ~ Restaurant (not Sun evening) ~ Sudbury (01787) 378494 ~ Children welcome ~ Open 11.30-3, 6-11 ~ Bedrooms: £65B/£80B

ORFORD   TM4250   Map 5

Jolly Sailor

The newish licensees at this unspoilt old smugglers' inn had to wait several years before they could achieve their ambition to run it – now they have, they're doing all they can to keep its rather special character and atmosphere. The sea is now some way away, but it used to run much closer, and the building itself was made from the timbers of ships wrecked nearby in the 17th c. The interesting inside, kept beautifully clean, has several cosily traditional rooms served from counters and hatches in an old-fashioned central cubicle. There's an uncommon spiral staircase in the corner of the flagstoned main bar, which also has a couple of brass door knockers and local photographs, and is warmed in winter by a good solid fuel stove; a small room is popular with the dominoes and shove-ha'penny players, and has draughts, chess and cribbage too. Well kept Adnams beers on handpump, friendly staff and locals. Straightforward bar food includes local fish and chips (£3.50), various roasts or omelettes (from £3.75), and home-cooked ham, egg and chips (£3.95). The dining room is no smoking. Tables and chairs in the big garden. The setting is very pleasant, by a busy little quay on the River Ore, opposite Orford Ness and close to marshy Havergate Island, where avocets breed. *(Recommended by Ian Phillips, Neil Powell, Basil Minson, M J Morgan, Wayne Brindle and others)*

Adnams ~ Tenant Philip M Attwood ~ Real ale ~ Meals and snacks (11.45-1.30, 6.30-8.30; not 25 Dec) ~ Orford (01394) 450243 ~ Children in dining room if eating ~ Open 11-2.30, 7-11 ~ Bedrooms: £20(no single rates at weekends)/£32

RATTLESDEN   TL9758 Map 5

Brewers Arms   🍴 ♀

Signposted on minor roads W of Stowmarket, off B1115 via Buxhall or off A45 via Woolpit

Very much the focal point of the quiet village, this cheery 16th-c local is a real favourite for eating, with an excellent range of imaginative and surprisingly cosmopolitan dishes cooked by the landlord, with the emphasis on fresh produce from the area. One reader tells us a rather well known chef is a regular satisfied customer. As well as filled rolls the choice might typically include soup like leek and potato (£1.85), hummus and pitta bread (£2.75), fresh asparagus mousse with cucumber sauce (£2.95), venison and pistacchio nut terrine with Cumberland sauce or prawns in a cheese fondue sauce (£3.25), and a dozen or so interesting daily changing main courses like spaghetti with mushrooms, coriander and stilton sauce (£4.85), spinach and ricotta cheese pancakes (£5.20), lamb and aubergine lasagne or chicken, tomato and pine-nut risotto (£5.50), lamb kofta meatballs (£6.25), delicious rabbit basque (£6.45), beef and Guinness pie or chicken stuffed with leeks and stilton in a sherry sauce (£7.25), with puddings such as apple and banana cinnamon filo pie with rum and fudge sauce (£2.65). Very welcoming and friendly service – Mr Cole in particular is quite a jolly old soul. The small but lively public bar on the right has backgammon, cribbage, dominoes, a good range of board games, and shove ha'penny. On the left, the pleasantly simple beamed lounge bar has horsebrasses, and individually chosen pictures and bric-a-brac on the walls. It winds back through standing timbers to the main eating area, which is partly flint-walled and has a magnificent old bread oven. French windows open on to a garden edged with bourbon roses, with a boules pitch. Well kept Greene King Abbot, IPA and Rayments on handpump, decent wines including some from a local vineyard, lots of malt whiskies and a good selection of spirits; very pleasant atmosphere. *(Recommended by Andrew McKeand, Gwen and Peter Andrews, Basil Minson, Donald and Margaret Wood, Caroline Shearer, Ian and Nita Cooper, J F M West, Mr and Mrs R Leeds, Brian Allt)*

Greene King ~ Tenant Ron Cole ~ Real ale ~ Meals and snacks (not Mon, Sun evening or all last week Jun/1st week Jul) ~ (01449) 736377 ~ Well behaved children welcome ~ Jazz every Thurs evening and monthly Sun lunchtimes ~ Open 12-2.30(3 Sat), 7-11; closed Mon and Sun evening

REDE   TL8055 Map 5

Plough   🍴 ♀

Village signposted off A143 Bury St Edmunds—Haverhill

Readers are often in two minds about which to praise first at this peaceful partly thatched pub, the excellent distinctive cooking or the warm personal welcome. The friendly licensees really seem to enjoy their work, and their enthusiasm shines through in everything they do – small wonder that people get so much pleasure from coming here. The imaginative menu changes every day, but typically includes first-rate dishes like wheat and walnut casserole (£4.95), turkey in a cream sauce with garlic and cheese topping (£5.25), lamb with artichokes and fennel or smoked pork chop in orange and melon sauce (£5.50), wild boar and venison pie (£5.95), chicken roulade filled with crab meat (£6.50), stuffed quail in soya sauce (£6.95), fresh fish and game in season, and puddings such as excellent lemon crush pie, lovely strawberry and raspberry mousses, or in winter the popular Wenceslas tart, a combination of mince, almonds and raisins. They also do ploughman's and salads (outstanding beef and Cromer crab), and the little evening restaurant does things like moules au gratin, poached salmon, and steaks, as well as a three course Sunday lunch. Service is efficient and obliging; decent wines. The simple and traditional cosy bar has decorative plates on a delft shelf and surrounding the solid fuel stove in its brick fireplace, copper measures and pewter tankards hanging from low black beams, and red plush button-back built-in wall banquettes; fruit machine, unobtrusive piped music. In front of the building are some picnic-table sets, with more in a sheltered cottage garden behind, where there's a little dovecote. *(Recommended by Gwen and Peter Andrews, Captain S Hood, J L Phillips, Wayne Brindle, Dr and Mrs M Bailey, J W Cockerton, PACW, Bill and Edee Miller)*

Greene King ~ Lease: Brian and Joyce Desborough ~ Meals and snacks (not Sun evenings) ~ Evening restaurant (not Sun evening, though they do Sun lunch) ~ Hawkedon (01284) 89208 ~ Well behaved children in eating area of bar and restaurant ~ Open 11-3, 6.30-11

SNAPE TM3959 Map 5

Golden Key ★
Priory Lane

Very comfortable and civilised, this quietly elegant pub is proving rather popular for its food at the moment, though it has a number of other charms. Prepared using only fresh ingredients and served in good sized helpings, well liked dishes include soup such as stilton (£2.95), filled rolls made to order, pâté (£2.95), meat or vegetable samosas (£3.75), sausage, egg and onion pie or smoked haddock quiche (£5.50), steak and mushroom or prawn and broccoli pie (both £6.50), grilled lamb chops or honey roast ham (both £6.75), plenty of fresh fish such as local crab, rainbow trout, and fresh lobster or Dover sole in season, steaks (from £8.95), and very good puddings. The low-beamed stylish lounge has a winter open fire, an old-fashioned settle curving around a couple of venerable stripped tables and a tiled floor, and at the other end there are stripped modern settles around heavy Habitat-style wooden tables on a turkey carpet, and a solid fuel stove in the big fireplace. The cream walls are hung with pencil sketches of customers, a Henry Wilkinson spaniel and so forth. A brick-floored side room has sofas and more tables. They keep the full range of Adnams beers on handpump, and have local cider and several malt whiskies; pleasant staff. They can get busy at weekends. The small sheltered garden behind is very well cared for, and a mass of colour in summer; there are plenty of white tables and chairs on the gravel from which you can enjoy the view. *(Recommended by Phil and Heidi Cook, J L Phillips, Wayne Brindle, R D Knight, Simon Cottrell, Derek and Sylvia Stephenson, Basil Minson, M A and C R Starling, GB, George Atkinson, Derek R Patey)*

Adnams ~ Tenants Max and Susie Kissick-Jones ~ Real ale ~ Meals and snacks ~ Snape (01728) 688 510 ~ Children in eating area ~ Open 11-3, 6-11, with afternoon and evening extensions during Aldeburgh Festival

SOUTHWOLD TM5076 Map 5

Crown 🍴 🛏 🍷 🍴
High Street

Still tremendously popular and with good reason – it's rare to find a place where the service, atmosphere, food and drink all blend together as successfully as they do at this smart old hotel. It's perhaps the latter two that stand out the most, with a range of meals and beverages that's as creative as it is satisfying. The wines in particular are carefully chosen, with a monthly changing choice of 20 interesting varieties by the glass or bottle kept perfectly on a cruover machine; they often have a common theme running through. Adnams brewery is nearby, and the Crown is understandably their flagship: they have the full range of Adnams wines by the bottle (well over 250, which you can get from the cash and carry by the mixed dozen round the corner), and perfectly kept Adnams Bitter, Broadside, Mild, and winter Old on handpump; also a good choice of malt whiskies, tea, coffee and herbal infusions. The very good, creative bar food changes every day, but might typically include starters like celery and stilton soup (£1.75), and Egyptian style devilled herring or pan-fried black pudding in a sweet onion sauce (£3.95), main courses such as broccoli, mushroom and cheese parcels in mustard sauce (£6), roast beef and Yorkshire pudding (£6.95), half a roast guinea fowl with an orange, ginger and mushroom sauce (£7.25), steamed wing of skate with lobster and tarragon butter or local plaice grilled with capers and lime (£7.50), and supreme of chicken with a leek and mushroom duxelle (£7.50), with puddings like banana fool with mango coulis or fruit crumble (£2.95); cheeses are thoughtfully selected, and breakfasts are good (although cooked are extra). The restaurant does a good three-course lunch for £14.75. The elegant main bar has a stripped curved high-backed settle and other dark varnished settles, a mix of kitchen pine tables and kitchen chairs, newspapers to read, large beams, a carefully restored and rather fine carved wooden fireplace, pretty fresh flowers, a big Act of Parliament clock, and a few bar stools; the small no-smoking restaurant with its white cloths and pale cane chairs leads off. The staff are friendly and helpful, even when under pressure, and the atmosphere cheerful and relaxed. The smaller back oak-panelled locals' bar has more of a traditional pubby atmosphere, red leatherette wall benches and a red carpet. Shove-ha'penny, dominoes and cribbage. There are some tables in a sunny sheltered corner outside. *(Recommended by V and E A Bolton, Michael Sargent, Anthony and Freda Walters, C Fisher, Nigel Woolliscroft, Dr and Mrs P J S Crawshaw, Mrs F M Halle, Thomas Nott, Simon Cottrell, Martin Richards, Anna Marsh, Hazel Morgan, Bernard Patrick, Rosemary Harris, Keith Symons, Evelyn and Derek Walter, Keith and Margaret Kettell, M J V Kemp, Sarah and Jamie Allan, Shirley Gofford, Quentin Williamson, Shirley Pielou, Susan and John Douglas; also recommended by The Good Hotel Guide)*

Adnams ~ Manager Anne Simpson ~ Real ale ~ Meals and snacks (12.15-1.45, 7.15-9.45) ~ Restaurant ~ Southwold (01502) 722275 ~ Children in eating area and restaurant ~ Open 10.30-3, 6-11; closed first week Jan ~ Bedrooms: £38B/£58B

STOKE BY NAYLAND TL9836 Map 5

Angel 🍴 🛏 �

B1068 Sudbury—East Bergolt; also signposted via Nayland off A134 Colchester—Sudbury
Suffolk Dining Pub of the Year

Another civilised old place with an unwavering chorus of glowing reports, this elegant dining pub is an exceptional place to eat, with an imaginative range of dishes that makes excellent use of fresh local meats and fish. A typical menu might feature dishes like soup (£2.45), fishcakes with remoulade sauce (£3.95), deep fried cambazola with cranberry sauce (£4.25), vegetarian filo parcels served with fresh tomato coulis (£5.75), home-made steak and kidney pudding or roast loin of pork with crackling, apple mousse and red cabbage (£5.95), supreme of chicken filled with brie and rolled in crushed hazelnuts or roast duckling with cassis sauce (£7.95), brochette of scallops wrapped in bacon (£9.50) and lovely puddings like home-made dark chocolate ganache gateau (£3); vegetables are crisply cooked and full of flavour. Considering the quality the meals are very reasonably priced; it's worth arriving early or booking in advance. Always busy but still relaxed, the comfortable main bar area has handsome Elizabethan beams, some stripped brickwork and timbers, a mixture of furnishings including wing armchairs, mahogany dining chairs, and pale library chairs, local watercolours and older prints, attractive table lamps, and a huge log fire. Round the corner is a little tiled-floor stand-and-chat bar - with well kept Adnams, Greene King IPA and Abbot and Nethergate Bitter and Old Growler on handpump, an extensive wine list and good coffee. One room has a low sofa and wing armchairs around its woodburning stove, and Victorian paintings on the dark green walls. There are cast-iron seats and tables on a sheltered terrace. *(Recommended by C H Stride, Mrs T Froud, John Evans, Gwen and Peter Andrews, Mr and Mrs G M Edwards, Sue Demont, Tim*

Barrow, Hazel Morgan, Bernard Patrick, Ian Phillips, M A and C R Starling, Richard
Fawcett, Andrew and Teresa Heffer)

Free house ~ Licensee Peter Smith ~ Real ale ~ Meals and snacks ~ Restaurant ~
Colchester (01206) 263245 ~ Open 11-2.30, 6-11; closed 25 and 26 Dec ~
Bedrooms: £44B/£57.50B

SUTTON TM3046 Map 5

Plough

B1083

All sorts of people seem to find their way across Sutton Common to this neat tiled
white house – locals, ramblers, birdwatchers, and tourists on their way to the site of
the Sutton Hoo ship burial a mile or so down the road to name a few. It's changed
hands since our last edition, but the menu still has some emphasis on fresh local
fish, along with sandwiches, and various home-made dishes like steak and kidney
pudding (£4.80), prawn piri-piri with pilau rice (£5.20), seasonal game pie (£5.50)
and lamb, honey and rosemary casserole (£5.90). The cosy little front room has
comfortable button-back wall banquettes, Flowers Original and IPA, and Tolly
Bitter and Mild on handpump, with a carefully chosen selection of wines, and five
different varieties of tea; darts, pool, dominoes, cribbage, fruit machine, video
game, juke box in the public bar and piped music in the restaurant. There are
picnic-table sets in front and more by the fruit trees. *(Recommended by Michael and*
Maggie Betton, A A Halliley, George Atkinson, George Rumsey; more reports please)

Pubmaster (Allied) ~ Tenant C J Matthews ~ Real ale ~ Meals and snacks ~
Restaurant (not Sun evening) ~ Shottisham (01394) 411785 ~ Children welcome
~ Open 11-3, 6-11

THORNHAM MAGNA TM1070 Map 5

Four Horseshoes 🛏

Off A140 S of Diss; follow Finningham 3¼ signpost, by White Horse pub

Well run and very popular, this handsome thatched pub is a very pleasant spot in
summer, when you can sit at the picnic-table sets beside the flowerbeds on a
sheltered lawn. Said to date back to the 12th c, the building has a lot of charm and
character, and, because it rambles round so much, a good deal of space. The
extensive bar is well divided into alcoves and distinct areas, and there are some tall
Windsor chairs as well as the golden plush banquettes and stools on its spread of
fitted turkey carpet, very low and heavy black beams, country pictures and farm
tools on the black-timbered white walls, and logs burning in big fireplaces; there's
also an inside well. It's popular mainly for eating, with generous helpings of good,
tasty food, quickly served by uniformed waitresses: sandwiches (from £1.60, home-
made chicken liver pâté £1.75, steak in french bread £2.95), soup (£1.95),
ploughman's (from £3.45), salads (from £3.95, honey baked ham £5.25), country
grill (using locally-made sausages, £4.25), vegetable and nut cutlets or spinach
canneloni (£4.95), home-made pies like chicken, ham, mushroom, apricot and
walnut or steak and kidney (£5.25), fisherman's hotpot or a seafood platter (£5.95),
a choice of prime steaks (from £7.50), puddings such as home-made cheesecake
(£3.25), or apple pie (£2.50), and children's menu (on request). Well kept Adnams
and Courage Best and Directors on handpump; as we went to press, the Courage
Best was at a very good price, nearly 10p below the regional average. Thornham
Country Park nearby has several walks, including the sponsored Horseshoe Country
Trail (a lovely pre-breakfast walk) and one suitable for the disabled, as well as a
walled herb garden, and a scented garden especially for the blind. The thatched
church at Thornham Parva is famous for its ancient wall paintings. *(Recommended by*
Andrew McKeand, A G Drake, Clare and Gordon Phillips, John C Baker, Basil Minson, John
Honnor, D J and P M Taylor, J E Rycroft, Andrew and Teresa Heffer)

Free house ~ Licensee Darren Holmes ~ Real ale ~ Meals and snacks (12-3, 6.45-
10) ~ Restaurant ~ Occold (01379) 678777 ~ Children welcome ~ Open
11(11.30 Sat)-11 ~ Bedrooms: £37B/£55B

TOSTOCK TL9563 Map 5

Gardeners Arms 🍺
Village signposted from A45 and A1088

In the heart of a pretty village, this delightfully unspoilt pub really is a friendly place. They get very busy but the service and smiles rarely falter, and they don't generally mind serving meals to hungry latecomers. The smart lounge bar has low heavy black beams, lots of what used to be called carving chairs (dining chairs with arms) around the black tables, and a bustling villagey atmosphere. Always home-made and good value, the very well liked bar food includes sandwiches (from £1.30; toasties from £2.25), tasty soup (£1.50), ploughman's with home-made granary rolls (from £3), salads (from £3.75, prawn and mayonnaise £4.75), quiche (£3.85), sausage, egg, chips and beans (£4), gammon steak (£4.50), specials such as chicken and vegetable stir-fry (£5.50), skate wing in brown butter (£6.75) or duck breast in ginger sauce (£8.75), and evening meals like grilled trout (£5.75), salmon steak (£6.75), or sirloin steak (£8.25); decent puddings (£1.90). Booking may be a good idea in the evenings. Very well kept Greene King Abbot, IPA and Rayments on handpump; welcoming licensees and staff. The lively tiled-floor public bar has darts, pool, shove-ha'penny, dominoes, cribbage, juke box and fruit machine. The picnic-table sets among the roses and other flowers on the sheltered lawn are a lovely place to sit and watch the local team playing steel quoits on the pitch. *(Recommended by J F M West, Wayne Brindle, Jenny and Michael Back, A H Thomas, Donald and Margaret Wood, Ian Phillips, Charles Bardswell, E Money, Dave Braisted)*

Greene King ~ Tenant Reg Ransome ~ Meals and snacks (not Mon or Tues evenings or Sun lunchtime) ~ Restaurant (not Sun lunchtime) ~ Beyton (01359) 270460 ~ Children in eating area of bar ~ Open 11.30(11 Sat)-2.30, 7-11

WALBERSWICK TM4974 Map 5

Bell
Just off B1387

A nice fresh spot close to the beach, with a well placed hedge sheltering the seats and tables on the sizeable flower-filled lawn from the worst of the sea winds. The pleasantly aged building still has the flooring bricks and oak beams that it had 600 years ago when the sleepy little village was a flourishing port. Bustling and characterful, the rambling bar has been redecorated since our last edition, and has curved high-backed settles on the well worn flagstones, tankards hanging from oars above the bar counter, and a woodburning stove in the big fireplace; to one side is a more conventionally comfortable area decorated with local photographs; maybe a friendly Irish wolfhound. Bar food includes soup, sandwiches (from £1.50), ploughman's (from £3), good local fish with chips (£4.50), and a good choice of summer help-yourself salads (from £4.50, the fresh Cromer crab is good); in winter they do a wide range of hot dishes; children's helpings. Well kept Adnams Bitter, Broadside and Extra on handpump; darts, cribbage, dominoes and fruit machine. It can get busy (and noisy) in summer, and service then can be rather haphazard. Most of the bedrooms look over the sea or the river. To really make the most of this very pleasant setting it's worth taking the little ferry from Southwold, and then enjoying the short walk along to the pub. *(Recommended by Evelyn and Derek Walter, Mrs F M Halle, BKA, D and B Carter, M J V Kemp, Derek and Sylvia Stephenson, MMD, Mrs M C Barrett, D J and R A Parish, Sarah and Jamie Allan, Brian Allt, John Townsend, Derek R Patey)*

Adnams ~ Tenant Mark Stansnall ~ Real ale ~ Lunchtime meals and snacks ~ Evening restaurant ~ Southwold (01502) 723109 ~ Children in small room off bar ~ Regular folk evenings or Greek dancing ~ Open 11-11; 11-4, 6-11 winter ~ Bedrooms: /£50(£60B)

Food details, prices, timing etc refer to bar food – not to a separate restaurant if there is one.

WESTLETON TM4469 Map 5

Crown 🛏 ♟

On B1125 Blythburgh—Leiston

Much more than the simple village pub it looks to be from the outside, this well liked place is rapidly becoming a rather smartly upmarket inn, though remaining, as ever, a quite delightful place to stay. The priest in charge of Sibton Abbey was the first to take in guests when he lived here in the 12th c, and the practice has continued virtually without a break ever since. Of course it's changed completely since then, and in the past few years particularly lots of time and effort has been spent on modernisation to cope with its ever-increasing popularity. The comfortably furnished bar has a growing collection of old photographs and postcards of Westleton, farm tools, pews, stools and settles, a couple of crab pots at one end, and a good open fire in winter; there's also a smart no-smoking dining conservatory. Excellent home-made bar food includes soup (£2.25), sandwiches (from £2.25, with home-made granary bread), smooth home-made duck pâté (£2.55), mushroom, onion and bacon fricassee (£2.95), various ploughman's (£3.95), salads (from £5.25), seafood lasagne (£5.25), vegetable and cashew bake (£5.35), steak and kidney pie with ale (£5.45), duck, venison, pork and port pie (£5.55), chicken breast filled with cheese and bacon (£5.65), grilled whole lemon sole (£5.75) and other fresh fish, plus mouth-watering puddings such as almond flan or raspberry and apple pudding (all £2.45); a decent children's menu with games and puzzles (from £2.50), Sunday roast beef. The evening restaurant (with quite an emphasis on seafood) is particularly well liked. Helpful courteous staff, though service can slow down at busy times. Well kept Adnams Bitter and Broadside, Greene King IPA, Marstons Pedigree, Morlands Old Speckled Hen and Tetleys on handpump, a very good well priced wine list, with a number of half bottles, around 50 malt whiskies, James White cider, coffee and fresh fruit juice. Dominoes, shove-ha'penny, table skittles, cribbage, and unobtrusive piped music. There's a very pretty landscaped garden (highly praised by readers) with an aviary, and outside bar, floodlit terrace and barbecue; all these areas have ramps for disabled access. Breakfasts are very good. Good walks nearby (the 'Westleton Walks') – perhaps over to our Lucky Dip entry at Eastbridge. Minsmere bird reserve is only a couple of miles away. *(Recommended by V and E A Bolton, Rosemary Harris, BKA, D and B Carter, Richard Balls, Mr and Mrs R P Begg, H R Bevan, Gwen and Peter Andrews, Dr and Mrs M Bailey, Basil Minson, Romey Heaton, Richard Alle, Mrs M C Barrett, Stephen and Jean Curtis, Rita Horridge, George Romsey, Dr S R Dando, Derek R Patey; also recommended by The Good Hotel Guide)*

Free house ~ Licensees Richard and Rosemary Price ~ Real ale ~ Meals and snacks (not Sat evening) ~ Evening restaurant ~ Westleton (0172 873) 777 ~ Children in restaurant ~ Trad jazz 2nd Fri each month ~ Open 11-3, 6-11; closed 25 and 26 Dec ~ Bedrooms: £49.50B/£69.50B; some have jacuzzis and 4-posters

---

Lucky Dip

Besides the fully inspected pubs, you might like to try these Lucky Dips recommended to us and described by readers (if you do, please send us reports):

Aldeburgh [The Parade; TM4656], *Brudenell*: Large palatial rather old-fashioned hotel right on the beach (sandbags by the doors), magnificent sea views from bar, attentive staff, good coffee; fine place to stay if you like the old style of hotel *(George Atkinson)*; [opp Moot Hall], *Mill*: Popular new landlord, ample reasonably priced good hot food in dining room, good service; local fishermen *(N Smith)*; *Railway*: Well kept Adnams, friendly staff and locals; comfortable bedrooms, good breakfasts – caters well for single people *(Anna Marsh)*;

[222 High St], *White Hart*: Nicely refurbished Victorian local, friendly, unspoilt, individual and unoppressive; well kept Adnams, remarkable range of spirits; good fish and chip shop next door; good comfortable bedrooms *(Neil Powell, Anna Marsh)*

☆ **Aldringham** [B1122/B1353 S of Leiston; TM4461], *Parrot & Punchbowl*: Three-level beamed pub very popular with Sizewell management, good food from downstairs servery, lots of decent wines, well kept Whitbreads-related real ales; piped music, dining-room meals Fri/weekend – when booking essential; children welcome; sheltered garden with a couple of swings, nice craft centre opp *(Mrs Romey Heaton, Mrs P M Goodwyn, BB)*

☆ **Badingham** [TM3068], *White Horse*: Old-fashioned pub with good wholesome reasonably priced bar food inc vegetarian and children's dishes, good friendly service, well kept Adnams, neat bowling green and nice rambling garden *(A H Thomas, LYM)*

☆ **Bardwell** [The Green; TL9473], *Six Bells*: Wide choice of good food inc fresh fish and good atmosphere in comfortably modernised beamed pub dating back to 16th c, well kept Adnams and Wadworths 6X, extensive wine list, log fires, restaurant; games evening Sun, folk music weekly, children and dogs welcome; garden with play area and Wendy house; attractive pine-furnished bedrooms *(John Baker, Charles Bardswell, Richard Balls, Mrs P M Goodwyn)*

Barham [TM1451], *Sorrel Horse*: Attractive pink-washed pantiled house with timber stables opp, and pleasant play area and gardens; beamed bar, lounge and two dining areas off; Tolly ales, bar food inc good daily specials *(Ian Phillips)*

☆ **Barton Mills** [A11, by Five Ways roundabout; TL7173], *Bull*: Pleasant local feel and helpful attentive staff in rambling old-fashioned bar with big fireplaces, well kept Adnams, Bass, Worthington BB and a guest beer, decent wines, reasonably priced standard bar food served noon-10 (not Sun), grill room, piped music; children allowed in eating area; simple bedrooms *(Ian Phillips, Thomas Nott, BB)*

Beccles [town centre; TM4290], *Swan*: Unusual bottled beers from all over the world, small but interesting reasonably priced menu, good friendly service *(Debby Hawkins, Mark Johnson)*

Beyton [TL9362], *Bear*: Totally unrefurbished with genuine Suffolk atmosphere, two or three ales in perfect condition, occasionally straight from the barrel *(John C Baker)*

Boyton [TM3747], *Bell*: Friendly local with good fish and enthusiastic chef for newish dining room *(Anon)*

☆ **Bramfield** [A144; TM4073], *Queens Head*: Friendly pub with particularly good service, good fresh food in pleasantly refurbished high-beamed lounge bar, big log fire, darts in public bar, well kept Adnams Bitter, Old and Broadside, piped music; restaurant *(Simon Wilmot-Smith)*

Bromeswell [Bromeswell Heath; TM3050], *Cherry Tree*: Good value bar food inc good vegetarian range in comfortably modernised neat beamed lounge with friendly staff, open fire and velvet curtains; seats outside, lounge with open fire and velvet curtains; seats outside, charming inn sign *(Bill and Wendy Burge, BB)*

☆ **Bury St Edmunds** [7 Out Northgate St, Station Hill; TL8564], *Linden Tree*: Wide choice of generous popular quickly served food in attractively renovated family dining pub with friendly willing service, well kept Greene King IPA and Rayments, wines in two glass sizes, nice atmosphere, popular conservatory restaurant, good well kept garden *(Frank Davidson, Richard Balls)*

☆ **Bury St Edmunds** [Whiting St], *Masons Arms*: Well kept Greene King IPA and good range of reasonably priced food in busy but comfortable and relaxing dining lounge with lots of oak timbering and prompt friendly service *(Nigel Woolliscroft, K D Day)*

☆ **Bury St Edmunds** [39 Churchgate St], *Queens Head*: Good choice of interesting real ales, cheap food in well decorated dining area and very quick service; much modernised, busy with professionals at lunchtime and young people Fri/Sat evening; may be open all day *(John C Baker, Richard Balls, F M and A F Walters)*

Bury St Edmunds [Risbygate St], *Falcon*: Cosy and clean little sidestreet pub with Greene King ales, limited cheap prompt tasty food, tables outside *(John Wooll)*; [Lower Baxter St], *Fleetwoods*: Curious part-pub part-café with five changing real ales, some rare, interesting food *(John C Baker)*;

☆ **Butley** [B1084; TM3651], *Oyster*: Informal furniture in small-roomed pub, modernised but pleasant, with varied fresh generous food, well kept Adnams, very friendly landlord, open fires; pleasant outside area with play area; folk nights *(Catherine Boardman, Dr and Mrs P J S Crawshaw, Pat and Robert Watt)*

Buxhall [Mill Green; village signed off B1115 W of Stowmarket, then L at Rattlesden sign; TM0057], *Crown*: Tucked-away country pub with snug little bar and side room, bar food, Adnams Broadside and Greene King IPA, open fires, games in separate public bar, restaurant; children allowed if eating *(Brian Allt, CB)*

Carlton [just N of Saxmundham; TM3864], *Poachers Pocket*: Good food at reasonable prices, friendly licensees, well kept beer inc guest ale; clean and welcoming *(N Smith)*

Cavendish [High St (A1092); TL8046], *Bull*: Attractive 16th-c beamed pub with nice fireplaces; bar, dining area, garden with barbecue, extensive good value menu lunchtime and evening, well kept Adnams beers on handpump; fruit machines, darts and pool, no piped music; children welcome; bedrooms *(JJW, CMW)*; *Five Bells*: Very warm and welcoming, with good choice of food inc good filled french sticks *(W H and E Thomas)*

☆ **Chelsworth** [The Street; near Bury St Edmunds; TL9848], *Peacock*: New management for attractive old pub in noted village, full of Tudor brickwork and exposed beams; central bar divided up into sections serving the various areas of the pub; several well kept changing real ales, decent coffee, usual food; nice small garden maybe with summer ice cream shop; children may be allowed in dining room; open all day Sat; bedrooms – the two at the back are quieter

(George Atkinson, J L Phillips, Wayne Brindle, LYM)

☆ **Chevington** [TL7860], *Greyhound*: Particularly good authentic curries as well as usual food, good cheerful service, big woodburner, interesting memorabilia, well kept Greene King IPA; restaurant, garden with good play area; close family connection with Queens Head at Great Wenham *(Wayne Brindle)*

Cockfield [Stows Hill; A1141 Lavenham Rd; TL9054], *Three Horseshoes*: Cosy and friendly village pub with good food from superb doorstep sandwiches to notable choice of puddings – weekly pudding club for trying at least six; Greene King ales *(Mrs Gill Janzen, Tony Hepworth)*

Cratfield [TM3175], *Cratfield Poacher*: Friendly local with well kept Adnams and Greene King IPA and Abbot, stuffed animals, bottle collection, character landlord *(Nick and Alison Dowson)*

☆ **Cretingham** [TM2260], *Bell*: Decent bar food from filled open baps through children's and vegetarian dishes to steaks in comfortably modernised attractive pub with striking 15th-c beams, timbers and big fireplace; simple furnishings, Adnams and changing guest beers, traditional games in public bar, family room, restaurant with good Sun lunch; may open all day in summer; seats out in rose garden and on front grass *(V and E A Bolton, LYM)*

Earl Soham [A1120 Yoxford—Stowmarket; TM2363], *Falcon*: Well kept Adnams and Greene King, very friendly landlord, good straightforward food; bedrooms *(Spider Newth)*

☆ **Eastbridge** [TM4566], *Eels Foot*: Generous basic home-made bar food (no winter evening meals) in simple unspoiled local, well kept Adnams, crisp varnish, red leatherette, bright carpet or lino; tables on quiet front terrace with unconventional plantholders alongside, children in eating area; pretty village, handy for Minsmere bird reserve and heathland walks *(Derek R Patey, LYM)*

Felixstowe Ferry [TM3337], *Ferry Boat*: Unpretentious 17th-c pub tucked away nr sand dunes, Martello Tower and harbour, pleasant staff, bar food, well kept Tolly ale tapped from the cask, interesting photographs of turn-of-the-century long-frock local bathing belles *(Rita Horridge, LYM)*

☆ **Fornham All Saints** [TL8367], *Three Kings*: Smart and spotless, nicely modernised in traditional style, Greene King IPA and Abbot, good value popular bar food inc six daily specials, friendly dining room, friendly staff *(W H and E Thomas)*

☆ **Framlingham** [Market Hill; TM2863], *Crown*: Old-fashioned heavy-beamed public bar opening into hall and comfortable character lounge with armchairs by log fire, decent bar food, Adnams on handpump, help-yourself morning coffee, restaurant; service can be slow; comfortable period bedrooms – traditional small Forte inn *(Ian*

Phillips, George Atkinson, LYM)

Great Barton [A143; TL8967], *Bunbury Arms*: Relaxing and spacious open-plan bar and separate restaurant, Greene King ales, interesting food (popular with business people lunchtime), landlord puts humorous political comments on blackboard by door; play area *(Richard Balls)*

☆ **Great Wenham** [The Row, Capel St Mary Rd; TM0738], *Queens Head*: Creative Indian food (not Mon evening) among other dishes in friendly and comfortable traditional country pub with four well kept interesting changing ales, good value wines; live soft rock alternate Thurs eve; families welcome in cosy snug; close family connection with Greyhound at Chevington *(John Baker, Richard Balls)*

Hadleigh [Mkt Pl; TM0242], *Ram*: Doing well under current management, good food from interesting menu, nice setting in old market town *(J D Burbidge)*

☆ **Hartest** [B1066 S of Bury; TL8352], *Crown*: Attractive and relaxed pub at end of nice village green, warm welcome, big log fire in impressive fireplace, good reasonably priced food from sandwiches to steaks inc notable soups and fish, well kept Greene King ales, decent house wine, log fire, quiet piped music, friendly quick service; pleasant family conservatory, good big garden *(Gwen and Peter Andrews, Brian Allt)*

☆ **Haughley** [Station Rd – out towards Old Newton by level crossing; TM0262], *Railway*: Unpretentious but individual traditional country local with popular well prepared straightforward cheap food (not Mon pm), well kept Greene King IPA, Mild, Abbot and a guest beer, log fire, lots of labrador pictures; children in neat back room *(John C Baker, BB)*

☆ **Haughley** [centre], *Kings Arms*: Lots of shiny dark tables in clean and brightly welcoming beamed dining lounge, smaller lounge and public bar with games; friendly prompt service, wide choice of fair-priced bar food from sandwiches through good curries to tender steaks, log fire, well kept Greene King ales, piped music; tables and play house on back lawn *(David and Mary Webb, Basil Minson, Ian and Nita Cooper, BB)*

☆ **Hawkedon** [Rede Rd; between A143 and B1066; TL7952], *Queens Head*: Lots of character, good sensibly priced home-made food inc really unusual dishes, well kept beers esp Nethergate, friendly staff *(Frank W Gadbois)*

Hepworth [A143 Bury—Diss; TL9874], *Duke of Marlborough*: Reasonably priced often adventurous food at sensible prices, four well kept local real ales, comfortable seating – suburban sitting-room rather than country cottage *(John C Baker)*

Hintlesham [George St; TM0843], *George*: Large refurbished stone-flagged bar, comfortable eating area extending to conservatory restaurant, a real welcome for children, good value food inc big filled baguettes and Yorkshire puddings, friendly landlord, Tetleys; garden with play area and animals *(Michael Betton, Steve and Sarah de Mellow)*

☆ **Holbrook** [Ipswich Rd; TM1636], *Compasses*: Popular for good value food in bar and restaurant, welcoming staff, log fire, well kept Tolly, garden with play area *(Mrs P M Goodwyn)*

Hollesley [TM3544], *Fox*: Much modernised, with well kept real ales *(Lorna and Bill Tyson)*

Horringer [TL8261], *Six Bells*: Friendly welcome, well kept Greene King ales, good range of attractively priced food; comfortable and uncluttered *(Andrew McKeand)*

☆ **Huntingfield** [TM3374], *Huntingfield Arms*: Quiet and pleasant pub overlooking green, good range of attractively presented bar food, well kept Adnams, pleasant combination of beams and stripped brickwork, handsome sectioned-tree-trunk tables and matching chairs, friendly service, restaurant, games area with pool beyond woodburner *(Gwen and Peter Andrews)*

Icklingham [62 The Street; TL7772], *Plough*: Friendly pub with interesting pictures inc a series of early cricketers, also cricket books; subdued piped music, good basic menu inc home-made dishes, good choice of beers; big garden with play area *(George B Spenceley)*

Ipswich [29 St Helens St; opp County Hall; TM1744], *County*: Entire range of Adnams beers, smart green Victorian lounge, lively pink bar with darts and pool, good value food inc imaginative vegetarian dishes; exemplary lavatories *(Tina Hammond)*; [Dogs Head St], *Plough*: Tastefully refurbished town-centre pub popular for its well kept real ales *(Tina Hammond)*; [St Helens St], *Tap & Spile*: Formerly the Dove, quite transformed, with six or more real ales from outside the area, big lounge, snug, games room *(Tina Hammond)*; [St Helens St], *Water Lily*: Bare but friendly local with Tolly and two guest beers, piano Sat *(Tina Hammond)*; [1 Tuddenham Rd, Westerfield Rd], *Woolpack*: Oldest pub here, with Tolly and two guest beers, smart lounge, room filled with settles, tiny locals' snug, games room *(Tina Hammond)*

Kesgrave [Grange Farm Estate; TM2245], *Farmhouse*: Very old beamed pub with fast very friendly service, no-smoking area, wide choice of food inc vegetarian and good puddings; outdoor tables *(Mrs Jackie Deale)*

Knodishall [TM4261], *Butchers Arms*: New licensees doing well in old pub with well kept Adnams, pleasant airy dining room, good reasonably priced home-cooked food, good lively local atmosphere *(N S Smith)*

Laxfield [TM2972], *Low House*: Popular pub with picnic-table sets in extended garden, food inc interesting ploughman's, Adnams Bitter, Broadside and Mild and a guest ale tapped from the cask *(Nick and Alison Dowson)*

Layham [Upper St, Upper Layham; TM0240], *Marquis of Cornwallis*: Beamed 16th-c pub with plush lounge bar, good food inc nice veg and home-made meringues, popular lunchtime with businessmen and retired locals; picnic-table sets in extensive riverside garden, open all day Sat in summer *(Mrs P M Goodwyn)*

Leiston [Main St; TM4462], *Engineers Arms*: Opp Long Shop Museum, bars seem almost an extension of that with all their memorabilia *(Dave Braisted)*

☆ **Lidgate** [TL7257], *Star*: Increasingly interesting food in quiet and homely old beamed pub with huge log fire (used for winter Sun spit-roasts), good fresh ingredients and often a Spanish emphasis; well kept Greene King IPA and Abbot under light CO2 blanket, decent wines by the glass, fresh coffee, welcoming service, no music; doubles as post office, lovely garden; children welcome *(Gwen and Peter Andrews, Wayne Brindle, Dr and Mrs M Bailey)*

Little Bealings [Sandy Lane; TM2347], *Admirals Head*: Welcoming licensees in reopened pub with good choice of food in restaurant and bar, well kept ales inc Adnams, Bass, Fullers Chiswick and Greene King; lovely atmosphere *(Frank W Gadbois, G Reeve)*

☆ **Long Melford** [Hall St; TL8645], *George & Dragon*: Well refurbished, with roaring log fires, good food in bar or separate dining room, no-smoking area; Greene King real ales, decent wines, good individual service, bar billiards; regular live jazz or blues (can be noisy weekends), sheltered garden and courtyard; open all day exc Sun; five comfortable bedrooms *(Richard Goss)*

Long Melford, *Hare*: Log fire in small back bar, larger front bar, dining area, upstairs dining room; helpful welcoming staff, good choice of mainly home-made food; nr church at end of village *(Hazel Morgan, H O Dickinson)*

☆ **Martlesham** [off A12 Woodbridge—Ipswich; TM2547], *Black Tiles*: Spacious expanded roadhouse, big woodburner in characterful old bar, wide choice of good inexpensive generous quick home-made food from sandwiches to steaks, quick service from smart attentive staff, well kept Adnams Bitter and Broadside and a guest such as McMullens AK Mild, garden tables; children allowed in pleasantly decorated bistro-style restaurant; has been open all day *(George Atkinson, Graham Reeve, Mrs Jacqueline Deale, LYM)*

Melton [Wilford Bridge; TM2851], *Wilford Bridge*: Friendly service, good food with plenty of local fish, spacious and light with lots of tables *(Hazel R Morgan)*

Metfield [The Street; B1123; TM2980], *Duke William*: Pretty village local with friendly staff, Adnams on handpump; tables outside *(Frank W Gadbois)*

Mettingham [B1062; TM3589], *Tally Ho*: Unpretentious comfortable roomy pub with good reasonably priced home-made lunches inc good sandwiches, Courage-related beers, pleasant quick service *(A H Thomas)*

☆ **Mildenhall** [Main St; TL7174], *Bell*: Spacious beamed bar in attractive old inn, open fires, friendly service, choice of good value generous food, pleasant dining room; well kept Courage Best and Directors, darts, juke box; comfortable bedrooms *(Clare Dawkins, Gordon Phillips, Frank W Gadbois)*

Mildenhall, *Half Moon*: Lovely flint pub close to air base, two bars recently refurbished; friendly welcome, well kept Greene King ales, good tender steaks; children's menu *(Stuart Dowden)*; *Riverside*: Extensively refurbished, good atmosphere, good range of bar meals in spacious attractive lounge, well kept Bass, dining area overlooking lawn down to River Lark; good bedrooms *(Anthony and Freda Walters)*

☆ **Monks Eleigh** [The Street; B1115 Sudbury—Stowmarket; TL9647], *Swan*: Clean and comfortably modernised lounge bar with highly polished chairs and tables, courteous efficient service, friendly landlord and staff, three real ales, open fire, pleasant dining extension, good home-cooked bar food and evening meals; bedrooms *(H R Bevan)*

☆ **Newmarket** [High St; TL6463], *Rutland Arms*: Good reasonably priced bar food and delightful comfortable atmosphere in elegant and spacious two-room Georgian bar, well kept Adnams, tucked-away fruit machine, exceptionally speedy service, restaurant; handy for National Museum of Horseracing; bedrooms good value – the ones overlooking the lovely cobbled yard are very quiet *(W H and E Thomas, R C Vincent)*

☆ **Norton** [Ixworth Rd (A1088); TL9565], *Dog*: Good value varied food in nice old pink-washed local with pretty hanging baskets, functional eating areas, relatively unspoilt lounge bar, Greene King ales *(Charles Bardswell)*

☆ **Orford** [Front St; TM4250], *Kings Head*: The Shaws who'd made this interesting old inn a long-standing main entry, with a very individual atmosphere and good food esp fish, left autumn 1994 with plans to start a local fish restaurant/bistro – too late for us to pass judgement on their successors; creakily quaint uneven-floored bedrooms *(LYM)*

☆ **Pakenham** [signed off A1088 and A143 S of Norwich; TL9267], *Fox*: Good relaxed local, well kept Greene King IPA, Abbot and Rayments, cheerful quick service, wide choice of decent food; beamed lounge with attractive Skegness advertising posters and so forth (can get smoky), flame-effect gas stove, games room, small neat dining room; tables in streamside garden with ducks, fieldful of motley animals behind; children welcome *(Charles Bardswell)*

☆ **Ramsholt** [off B1083 – OS Sheet 169 map ref 307415; TM3141], *Ramsholt Arms*: The star is for superb spot alone among pinewoods by Deben estuary, lovely views and walks along bank, big garden and sunny terrace, isolated from traffic; two bars, one with river view and maybe good winter log fire; usual bar food (may run short on bank hol), straightforward decor and furnishings, real ale *(Mrs Hilarie Taylor, Keith Archer, LYM)*

☆ **Rattlesden** [High St; TL9758], *Five Bells*: Basic village pub with super friendly atmosphere and perfectly kept and properly served Adnams, Charles Wells Eagle and Bombardier, Wadworths 6X and a guest beer; famous for its big dog Beamish, who really does drink his namesake stout *(John C Baker, Charles Bardswell)*

Redgrave [TM0477], *Cross Keys*: Nice friendly local, well kept beers, popular Sun quiz night *(Ann Reeder and friends)*

Reydon [Wangford Rd; TM4978], *Cricketers*: Adnams pub/hotel, formerly the Randolph, with ample helpings of well cooked changing food, friendly service, light and airy bar, tables in garden; bedrooms *(D and B Carter)*

Risby [TL7966], *Crown & Castle*: Congenial Greene King pub, well kept ales, friendly staff, interesting WWII intelligence map, home-cooked standard food inc good sandwiches; attractive village *(Richard Balls)*

☆ **Rumburgh** [TM3481], *Buck*: Pretty country local, clean, tidy and rambling, with cheap good food, lots of character, well kept ales such as Adnams Extra, friendly atmosphere, cards, juke box, fruit machine and pool table in end room; quiet back lawn *(Nick and Alison Dowson)*

Saxmundham [High St; TM3863], *Queens Head*: Nicely decorated town pub, no-smoking areas in restaurant and bar, big helpings of freshly cooked nicely presented food, cheerful quick service; children in dining room *(Mr and Mrs R P Begg)*

☆ **Saxtead Green** [B1119; TM2665], *Volunteer*: Nicely placed opp working windmill, with sizeable garden and pretty back terrace, and a main entry in our last edition for good value home cooking, well kept Greene King ales and good log fire in light and airy plush lounge bar; closed for refurbishment as we went to press, with reports of a possible change of name *(LYM; news please)*

Shotley Gate [end of B1456; TM2434], *Bristol Arms*: Welcoming, with pleasant view over Stour estuary and Parkeston Quay, fair choice of beers, food inc locally caught fish and crab, attentive service in restaurant; tables outside; children in restaurant *(Mr and Mrs Albert)*

☆ **Sibton** [Walpole rd; TM3669], *White Horse*: Comfortable and attractively laid out 16th-c pub with interesting furnishings, well kept Adnams Bitter and Broadside, decent limited bar food (not Sun evening or Mon lunchtime) from sandwiches to steak, attractive big garden with play area; restaurant, provision for children, simple but comfortable bedrooms in separate block, though breakfasts a bit regimented; closed Mon lunchtime exc bank hols; food service has stopped all too promptly at 1.30 on Sun *(Derek R Patey, LYM)*

Sicklesmere [TL8760], *Rushbrooke Arms*:
Well appointed and comfortable, very
popular locally for reasonably priced
straightforward bar food lunchtime and
evening; good restaurant *(W H and E
Thomas)*

☆ **Snape** [The Maltings; TM3959], *Plough &
Sail*: Cleanly modernised comfortable tiled-
floor bar with fireside settles, sturdy tables
and pale country-kitchen chairs, well kept
Adnams Bitter and Old, interesting
individual fresh-cooked bar food inc lovely
salads, good welcoming service even under
pressure, small restaurant, tables outside; the
Maltings also has quite an elaborate
crafts/plants/kitchenware complex *(Derek R
Patey, Keith and Janet Morris, BB)*

☆ **Snape** [B1069], *Crown*: Country pub
decorated in traditional cottage style with
low ceilings and lots of pictures, big L-
shaped bar with big fire, tall seating on old
hop tubs, front part supposed to be model
for the Boar in Britten's *Peter Grimes;*
smaller dining room with log-effect gas fire;
Adnams Bitter, Broadside and Old on
handpump, friendly bar staff, relaxed
atmosphere; big helpings of good if not
cheap food, often with Italian or Greek
emphasis, inc good seafood and puddings;
tables in sizeable garden with pond;
bedrooms well equipped *(Phil and Heidi
Cook, A H Thomas, C R Whitham, LYM)*

☆ **Southwold** [Market Pl; TM5076], *Swan*:
Quiet comfortable back hotel bar with good
choice of very tasty fresh interesting bar food
(not cheap), chintzy and airy front lounge,
good willing service, well kept Adnams and
Broadside on handpump and the full range
of their bottled beers, decent wines and malt
whiskies; ambitious restaurant; well
renovated bedrooms inc garden rooms
where (by arrangement) dogs can stay too
*(Susan and John Priestley, V and E A
Bolton, A Barker, Gwen and Peter Andrews,
Maysie Thompson, A H Thomas, Rob and
Doris Harrison, Pam and Tim Moorey,
LYM)*

☆ **Southwold** [7 East Green], *Sole Bay*: Homely
little Victorian local opp brewery (and the
lighthouse sharing its name), moments from
the sea; genuine and friendly, sparkling
clean, with particularly good value simple
lunchtime food (not Sun) esp local smoked
sprats, well kept Adnams, pleasant service,
friendly locals and dog (other dogs allowed),
tables on side terrace and with the budgies in
yard *(Anthony Barnes, Rob and Doris
Harrison, Graham Reeve, Thomas Nott, A
Barker, V and E A Bolton, Derek R Patey,
LYM)*

☆ **Southwold** [Blackshore Quay; from A1095,
right at Kings Head – pass golf course and
water tower], *Harbour*: Tiny low-beamed
front bar in basic local by the black
waterside net-sheds, upper back bar with
lots of nautical bric-a-brac – even ship-to-
shore telephone and wind speed indicator;
fish and chips in newspaper, other basic food
(not Tues or Thurs evening, cold things only

Sun lunchtime); well kept Adnams Bitter and
Broadside, darts, table skittles, tables outside
with play area, ducks and animals – can be a
bit untidy out here, and in general the pub
makes few concessions to outsiders but is
very friendly if you take it on its own terms;
occasional live music *(George Atkinson, V
and E A Bolton, Susan Kerner, Rob and
Doris Harrison, LYM)*

☆ **Southwold** [42 East St], *Lord Nelson*: Good
atmosphere and lively mix of customers in
cheerful low-ceilinged wood-panelled tiled-
floor local, small and well placed nr sea – so
can get crowded; well kept Adnams Mild,
Bitter, Broadside and Old on handpump,
good basic lunchtime food, lovely random
old furniture and lamps in nice nooks and
crannies, sheltered back garden; open all
day; children welcome *(Martin G Richards,
John McGee, Nigel Woolliscroft, Neil
Powell, BB)*

☆ **Southwold** [South Green], *Red Lion*: Tidy,
comfortable and relatively quiet recently
extended pale-panelled local with big
windows looking over green to sea, ship
pictures, brassware and copper, elm-slab
barrel tables; well kept Adnams Bitter,
Broadside and Mild, good range of good
value basic food (seafood recommended),
welcoming open-doors feel with family room
and summer buffet room, tables outside;
right by the Adnams retail shop; bedrooms
small but comfortable *(Thomas Nott,
George Atkinson, Jeff Davies, MJVK, BB)*

☆ **Southwold** [High St], *Kings Head*: Very wide
choice of promptly served good food esp fish
with good fresh veg in well run spacious
open-plan pub, lots of maroon and pink
plush, well kept Adnams, decent house
wines, efficient friendly staff; comfortable
family/games room with well lit pool table;
decent bedrooms in house owned by pub
across road *(Derek R Patey, A Barker,
Brenda and Jim Langley, BB)*

Southwold [High St], *Southwold Arms*:
Ordinary building, so less of a tourist target
than other pubs here, with good food in
dining bar inc imaginative game and fish
dishes and maybe terrific value bargain
winter lunches; pleasant service, well kept
Adnams *(D and B Carter, George Rumsey)*

Spexhall [Stone St; TM3780], *Huntsman &
Hounds*: Unpretentious exterior hiding very
generous good value food, warm welcome
and cosy village atmosphere *(Colin Mason)*

☆ **Sproughton** [Old Hadleigh Rd – from A45
Claydon interchange go through village then
left down unmarked dead end; TM1244],
Beagle: Particularly well kept ales such as
Adnams, Greene King IPA and Abbot and
Nethergate in plushly comfortable timber-
framed pub, wide choice of good plentiful
lunchtime food esp soups, kippers and
vegetarian chilli, good service, back
conservatory; under-5s not welcomed *(John
C Baker, C H Stride, Richard Balls)*

Stoke by Nayland [Polstead St; TL9836],
Black Horse: Well kept beer and friendly
service in town local with occasional curry

nights and surprisingly good Thai food most Thurs nights *(K Harvey)*; *Crown*: Spacious series of comfortably modernised rooms, straightforward food inc variety of reasonably priced steaks, Tolly on handpump, restaurant; good with children; bedrooms *(Hazel Morgan, LYM)*

Stradbroke [Wilby Rd; TM2374], *Ivy House*: Charming homely thatched pub with welcoming licensees, two bars, lounge and dining room, reasonably priced good food, well kept Adnams; pleasant garden and pond, quiet village; two comfortable bedrooms *(D Edwards)*

☆ **Stradishall** [A143; TL7452], *Cherry Tree*: Pleasant atmosphere in two small traditional beamed bars, good reasonably priced straightforward bar food inc vegetarian, pleasant atmosphere, open fires, Greene King beers under light pressure; friendly ducks and pond in huge rustic garden (dogs allowed here); outside gents' *(Gwen and Peter Andrews, BB)*

Stratford St Mary [TM0434], *Swan*: Very cosy olde-worlde beamed pub with good choice of generous food, well kept Tolly Original, log fire in big fireplace, quiet piped music, welcoming staff; beware steep step down to bars; some tables over road by River Stour; children welcome *(Gwen and Peter Andrews, D P Pascoe)*

Stutton [Manningtree Rd; TM1534], *Kings Head*: Atractive pub with real ales inc Adnams and Boddingtons, good generous food, not cheap but good value, friendly courteous staff, exposed timbers, woodburner; nr Alton Water reservoir and recreation area *(G E Rich)*

☆ **Sudbury** [Acton Sq; TL8741], *Waggon & Horses*: Comfortable welcoming local with great atmosphere, character landlord, good plain food, well kept Greene King ales, bar billiards *(Mike Simpson, Brian Allt)*

Sudbury [Walnut Tree Lane], *Mill*: Marvellous view over water meadows, good choice of good food, comfortable; bedrooms *(Mrs P M Goodwyn)*; [Bridge St], *Rose & Crown*: Civilised pub with emphasis on food; exposed beams, horsebrasses and wheelback chairs, back pool room *(Ian Phillips)*

☆ **Thorndon** [off A140 or B1077, S of Eye; TM1469], *Black Horse*: Friendly and individual country pub with good well presented food from sandwiches to unusual main dishes inc good puddings and restaurant Sun lunch; beams, timbers, stripped brick, ancient floor tiles, several well kept ales, tables on spacious lawn with country views; well behaved children in eating areas *(Dr S R Dando, LYM)*

Thurston [TL9365], *Victoria*: Well kept Greene King ales, separate eating area with wide choice of reasonably priced food inc good vegetarian choice; welcoming atmosphere, efficient service *(Richard Balls)*

☆ **Ufford** [Lower St; TM2953], *White Lion*;

Good reasonably priced home-cooked food and well kept Tolly in basic, clean, small and friendly pub; open central fireplace *(Dr and Mrs M Bailey)*

Walberswick [TM4974], *Anchor*: Good range of seafood, cosy winter log fires, well kept Adnams; bedrooms *(Keith Archer)*

☆ **Wenhaston** [TM4276], *Star*: Simple well run local with good reasonably priced home cooking (not Mon, landlady's day off), well kept Adnams and freshly squeezed orange juice; helpful landlord, suntrap lounge, games in public bar, tables on sizeable lawn *(Rob and Doris Harrison, LYM)*

West Row [NE of Mildenhall; TL6775], *Judes Ferry*: Well renovated pub with well kept Adnams Broadside and Greene King IPA on handpump, friendly new landlord, lots of farm animals, garden by River Lark *(Frank W Gadbois)*

Westleton [TM4469], *White Horse*: Warm friendly pub in beautiful vilage setting, good popular bar food inc children's dishes, well kept Adnams, garden with climbing frame; handy for Minsmere RSPB reserve *(M G and S M Keegan, H R Bevan, A H Thomas)*

Wetheringsett [Pages Green; TM1465], *Cat & Mouse*: This formerly most enjoyable country tavern has now closed

Withersfield [Thurlow Rd; nr Haverhill; TL6547], *Fox*: Good choice of beers inc changing guest, wide choice of bar food from rolls and sandwiches to home-cooked main dishes, friendly landlord, comfortable bar *(Joan and Russ Bowman)*

Witnesham [TM1851], *Barley Mow*: Character old pub with nice atmosphere, home-made food (separate room for meals), friendly staff, Greene Kinge IPA and Tolly Bitter and Mild *(Frank W Gadbois)*

☆ **Woodbridge** [73 Cumberland Rd; opp Notcutts Nursery, off A12; TM2749], *Cherry Tree*: Beamed central area with unusual back extension, light oak furnishings, good choice of well prepared food (not cheap but good value) from good doorstep sandwiches to vegetarian dishes, Flowers Original, Tetleys and Tolly, friendly helpful staff, stuffed fox, motley collection of books, 60s piped music, fruit machines; no dogs, garden with swings etc *(George Atkinson, Ian Phillips, Mrs Jackie Deale)*

☆ **Woodbridge** [Seckford St; TM2749], *Seckford Arms*: Both the interesting decor and the good food (which includes good doorstep sandwiches) owe much to Mexico – the Geordie landlord used to work there; well kept Adnams and often unusual guest beers, children welcome in garden lounge *(George Atkinson)*

Yaxley [A140 Ipswich—Norwich; TM1274], *Bull*: Friendly family service, well kept Adnams, Nethergate Old Growler and Woodfordes Wherry and occasional guest beers, good home-cooked food esp curry and fresh Friday seafood *(Trevor Moore)*

Surrey

From among a number of pubs in the Lucky Dip section which have been hovering on the fringe of the main entries, the pub which has stood out as having made the greatest advances recently is the Red Lion at Shamley Green, and we have this year promoted it to the main entries. Others currently well worth watching in the Lucky Dip section (almost all of them inspected by us, so we can vouch for them as good) are the Abinger Hatch on Abinger Common, Harrow in Charlton, Well House at Chipstead, Sun at Dunsfold, Woodcock at Felbridge (a really distinctive place), Sportsman at Mogador, Fox Revived at Norwood Hill, George in Oxted (very reliable dining pub), Swan on the Thames in Staines, Brickmakers Arms at Tandridge, another riverside Swan in Walton on Thames and Wotton Hatch at Wotton. There is a good, growing choice in Shepperton. Drinks prices in the area are quite a bit higher than the national average, but the difference is not as marked as we have found in previous years. Indeed, pubs in this area getting their beers from national brewers tended not to put their prices up in the more or less country-wide round of price increases in the summer of 1994, so their prices are virtually unchanged since last year. And pubs here getting their beers from smaller breweries have in some cases actually dropped their prices – on average, beers from the smaller breweries here cost about 15p a pint less than equivalent beers from the nationals. These results of our price survey, showing Surrey drinks prices going up less than the national average or even falling, are particularly interesting. Surrey was always a classic case of the national brewers' monopoly grip on pub pricing, with a particularly high proportion of pubs here in their hands. This year's price survey shows that the changes in the law designed to reduce the big brewers' hold on pricing have really started working here in Surrey. The two cheapest pubs we found for drinks here were the Donkey at Charleshill (tied to Morlands) and the Cricketers in Dorking (tied to Fullers): beer here was 40p cheaper than in pubs tied to the national chains. Pub food prices are rather lower than in most other parts of the south east (very low again in the case of the Dorking Cricketers, where most efficient new licensees are settling in well). The best pubs for eating out here are now the Plough at Blackbrook (excellent choice of wines, too), the Withies at Compton, and the Woolpack at Elstead: a very close-run thing between these last two, but it's the Withies which we choose as Surrey Dining Pub of the Year. Two pubs in the county qualify for our new Beer Award: the Plough at Coldharbour (an unconventional place, very untypical of Surrey) and the Royal Oak in Pirbright.

ALBURY TQ0547 Map 3

Drummond Arms

Off A248 SE of Guildford

Ducks and tame pheasants roam about among the tables and chairs in the pleasant, sunny streamside garden where they hold summer themed garden parties outside this well-run pub. It's come on in leaps and bounds since its successful refurbishment about four years ago; comfortable and attractively decorated, with a nice conservatory that overlooks the garden. Big helpings of popular changing bar food might include sandwiches (from £1.50, toasties from £1.75), soup (£1.95), sausages (£2.95), ploughman's (from £3.50), filled baked potatoes (from £3.95), salads (from £4.95), gammon and pineapple (£6.95), and sirloin steak (£9.95), with half-a-dozen daily specials that include good Chinese dishes. Well kept Courage Best and Directors, King & Barnes Festive, Broadwood and occasionally Bitter and Youngs Bitter on handpump; friendly service which can be a little slow when it gets busy; fruit machine and piped music. The village is rewarding to stroll through. *(Recommended by Father Robert Davies, M Veldhuyzen, John Pettit, Mrs Hilarie Taylor)*

Free house ~ Licensee David Wolf ~ Real ale ~ Meals and snacks (till 10pm Fri/Sat) ~ Restaurant ~ (01483) 202039 ~ Open 11-2.30(3 Sat), 7-11 ~ Bedrooms: £38B/£50B

ALBURY HEATH TQ0646 Map 3

King William IV

Little London; off A25 Guildford—Dorking to Albury, first left to Albury Heath; go over railway and take first left to Peaslake, then right towards Farley Green; OS Sheet 187 map reference 065468

Set in the heart of the county and surrounded by lovely walks, this is a genuinely traditional family-run pub. Three warmly friendly little rooms (which can get very busy) each have their own character; the main stone-floored bar has a big chunky elm table with a long pew and a couple of stools, beams in the low ochre ceiling, an enormous basket of dried flowers in the big brick fireplace (with a log fire in winter), several horse bits, traps and old saws, and an ancient baboon dressed in a jacket and hat in one corner. A tiny room leading off one end has an L-shaped elbow rest with a couple of stools in front of it, a table and settle; darts. Up a few steps at the other end of the main bar is a simple dining room with gingham-clothed tables, two glass cases with stuffed owls and a piano; shove-ha'penny. On the first Saturday evening of the month they hold a seafood evening, all the fish is bought fresh that day from Billingsgate by the licensee: green-lipped mussels (£4), whitebait or Mediterranean prawns (£4.50), Dover sole (£10), lobster (£14), while on the third Saturday in the month you could try some of the whole spit-roasted lamb or pig. The rest of the time the small but selective menu includes sensibly priced home-made dishes like sandwiches (not Sunday), generous ploughman's (from £3.60), cottage pie (£4.20), home-cooked ham, egg and chips or beef and Guinness pie (£4.50) and game pie or mutton casserole (£4.95) and puddings like treacle tart, banoffi pie or tiramisu (all £2.50); Sunday roast lunch (£5.60). Well kept Boddingtons, Greene King Abbot, Whitbreads Castle Eden and local Hogs Back under light blanket pressure; the friendly alsatian is called Major. The little garden in front has some picnic-table sets under umbrellas, and old cast-iron garden furniture. *(Recommended by J A Snell, Graham Pettener, M L Clarke, Mr and Mrs Williams, J N Tyler, Jenny and Brian Seller, Mr and Mrs C Moncreiffe, Tim Galligan, Mr and Mrs D E Powell, Susan and John Douglas, Don Mather, Martin Jones, D and J Tapper)*

Free house ~ Licensees Mike and Helen Davids ~ Real ale ~ Meals and snacks (12-2.30, 7-10) ~ Restaurant (not Sunday) ~ (01483) 202685 ~ Children welcome ~ Open 11-3, 5.30-11

BETCHWORTH TQ2049 Map 3

Dolphin

The Street; A25 W of Reigate, village signposted on left after 2½ miles, at Buckland

A wonderfully cosy little old village local, this is very much the sort of place people like to go back to time and time again. Still mostly unspoilt and with nostalgic touches like the three coal fires and well chiming longcase clock, it's particularly homely in winter. The atmospheric front room is furnished with kitchen chairs and plain tables on the 400-year-old scrubbed flagstones, and the carpeted back saloon bar is black-panelled with robust old-fashioned elm or oak tables. A wide range of consistently good, generous bar food with prices that haven't changed since last year includes sandwiches (from £1.50), filled baked potato (from £2.85, smoked salmon and asparagus £4.25), good ham on the bone with egg, calamari (£4.50), steak (£7.95), and daily specials such as steak and kidney or chicken ham and leek pie (£4.65). Very well priced Youngs Bitter, Special and Porter and, in the winter, Winter Warmer, on handpump, and a cruover machine guarantees that most wines can be served by the glass; very friendly and efficient service; darts, dominioes, cribbage, fruit machine and shove-ha'penny. There are some seats in the small laurel-shaded front courtyard and picnic-table sets on a lawn by the car park, opposite the church; they now also have a new back garden terrace. Get there early, as it doesn't take long for it to get busy. No children. *(Recommended by John Pettit, Gordon Smith, DWAJ, P Gillbe, E Burden; more reports please)*

Youngs ~ Manager: George Campbell ~ Real ale ~ Meals and snacks (12-2.30, 7-10) ~ (01737) 842288 ~ Open 11-3, 5.30-11; closed 25 Dec evening

BLACKBROOK TQ1846 Map 3

Plough 🍴 ♀

On byroad E of A24, parallel to it, between Dorking and Newdigate, just N of the turn E to Leigh

All good things are carefully combined at this popular light and airy pub with its cream and terracotta interior and white frontage a blaze of colourful and plentiful hanging baskets and window boxes. The welcoming landlord not only offers genuine pubby service and impressive food, but also has extremely well kept beers which year after year have won him best kept cellar awards. There are fresh flowers cut from the garden on the tables and sills of the large linen curtained windows in the no-smoking saloon characterful bar. Down some steps, the public bar has brass-topped treadle tables, a formidable collection of ties as well as old saws on the ceiling, and bottles and flat irons. Bar food comes in generous helpings and often with home-grown vegetables if available. The regular lunchtime menu includes hummus, taramasalata or pâté (£2.75), filled jacket potatoes (from £2.95), local spicy pork sausages (£3.45), roast breast of chicken (£3.65), ploughman's (£3.75), lasagne (£5.25), chilli con carne or moussaka (£5.25), prawn curry (£5.45) and rump steak (£9.45). There are lots of imaginative daily specials on the blackboard like tomato, orange and carrot soup (£2.45), asparagus baked with onion and cream (£3.45), steak and kidney pudding (£5.95), pork, sage and apple pie (£5.95) and seafood vol au vents with lobster sauce (£7.45), a few vegetarian dishes such as pear and stilton vol au vent or creamy vegetable and cheese pie (all £5.45) and puddings like hot carrot pudding, treacle tart, summer pudding, bakewell tart and apple and cinnamon pancake (all £2.45). A few tables can be booked for the more elaborate evening menu. King & Barnes Sussex, Broadwood, Festive and Summer in summer and in winter Old Ale kept on handpump; there are also 14 wines by the glass, including a wine of the month, vintage port by the glass, and about 20 country wines; pleasant, friendly staff; trivia machine and piped music. Tess the black labrador may put in an appearance after 10pm. At the back is a sizeable secluded cottage garden with a good few tables and children can play in the prettily painted Swiss playhouse furnished with tiny tables and chairs; there is further seating at the front of the pub. The countryside around here is a particularly good area for colourful spring and summer walks through the oak woods. *(Recommended by John Pettit, Ron Corbett, Sue Demont, Tim Barrow, A Plumb, Jenny and Brian Seller, Roger Taylor, D J Penny, David Ing, Tina and David Woods-Taylor, J S M Sheldon)*

King & Barnes ~ Tenants: Chris and Robin Squire ~ Real ale ~ Meals and snacks (not Mon evening) ~ (01306) 886603 ~ Only children over 14 in bar (must be eating) ~ Open 11-2.30(3 Sat), 6-11(10.30 in winter if weather is poor); closed 25 and 26 Dec and 1 Jan

---

We say if we or readers have seen dogs or cats in a pub.

CHARLESHILL SU8944 Map 2

Donkey

Near Tilford, on B3001 Milford—Farnham; as soon as you see pub sign, turn left

One reader describes this charming, old-fashioned 18th-c cottage as having a 'between the wars' feel to its neatly kept, slightly formal, civilised bars, and it has been in the same family for decades. Lots of polished stirrups, lamps and watering cans decorate the walls of the brightly cheerful saloon, furnished with prettily cushioned built-in wall benches and wheelback chairs, while the lounge has a lovely old high-backed settle and a couple of unusual three-legged chairs, as well as highly polished horsebrasses, a longcase clock, some powder pouches, swords on the walls and beams. Reasonably priced popular home-made bar food includes sandwiches and toasted sandwiches (from £2), filled baked potatoes (from £2.30) and four home-made daily specials like curries, lasagne and pies (all £4.75). A no-smoking conservatory, with blond wheelback chairs and stripped tables, fairy lights and some plants, has sliding doors into the garden. Well kept and very cheap for the area Morlands IPA, Old Speckled Hen and Charles Wells Bombardier on handpump kept under light blanket pressure; Gales country wines; may sometimes be piped music, shove-ha'penny, dominoes and cribbage. The garden is very attractive, with bright flowerbeds, white garden furniture, a tiny pond, an aviary with cockatiels and a big fairy-lit fir tree. Children's play area which we trust by now has had the maintenance it was due for. *(Recommended by Lyn and Bill Capper, Keith Widdowson, Phil and Sally Gorton, DAV, Peter and Lynn Brueton, Ron and Sheila Corbett, Susan and John Douglas, R B Crail, Mr and Mrs D E Powell, Ian Phillips, G B Longden)*

Morlands ~ Lease: Peter and Shirley Britcher ~ Real ale ~ Meals and snacks (not Sun evening) ~ (01252) 702124 ~ Children in conservatory lunchtimes only ~ Open 11-2.30, 6-11

COBHAM TQ1060 Map 3

Cricketers

Downside Common; 3¾ miles from M25 junction 10; A3 towards Cobham, 1st right on to A245, right at Downside signpost into Downside Bridge Rd, follow road into its right fork – away from Cobham Park – at second turn after bridge, then take next left turn into the pub's own lane

Sitting at one of the many tables overlooking the broad village green in front of this marvellously located, traditional pub or behind in the delightfully neat garden with its standard roses, dahlias, bedding plants, urns and hanging baskets is an exquisite way to pass a family summer afternoon. Larger than the superb characterful frontage suggests, the splendidly ancient spacious open plan interior has crooked standing timbers – creating comfortably atmospheric spaces – supporting heavy oak beams so low they have crash-pads on them. In places you can see the wide oak ceiling boards and ancient plastering lathes. Simple furnishings, horsebrasses and big brass platters on the walls, and a good winter log fire. The wide choice of popular bar food from the regularly changing menu includes soup and french bread or open sandwiches (from £1.85), a good range of salads (from £3.60), vegetable pasta (£4.15), moussaka (£4.35), chicken and prawn biryani or lamb stew (£4.65), fresh plaice, fresh red bream in garlic sauce or pork chops in apple and cider sauce (£4.85) and other seasonal fish; there's always an elaborate cold buffet. Well kept Ruddles Best and County, and Websters Yorkshire on handpump; fast friendly and accurate service. Get there early for a table, recent reports suggest many can have gone even by 12 o'clock and you'll probably need to book one of the smartly linen covered tables in the restaurant for Sunday lunch. Dogs welcome. *(Recommended by Guy Consterdine, Clem Stephens, Stephen G Brown, John Pettit, Mayur Shah, DWAJ, Doug Kennedy, A Plumb, Martin and Karen Wake, Ray Cuckow, John and Joan Calvert, H G M Osbourne, R C Vincent)*

Courage ~ Lease: Brian Luxford ~ Real ale ~ Meals and snacks (till 10pm) ~ Restaurant (not Sun evening) ~ (01932) 862105 ~ Children in Stable Bar ~ Open 11-2.30, 6-11

COLDHARBOUR TQ1543 Map 3

Plough ◧

Village signposted in the network of small roads around Abinger and Leith Hill, off A24 and
A29

There was no question about giving one of our new beer awards to this remote
pretty black-shuttered white house as one of its main attractions has always been
the excellent range of ten very well kept and reasonably priced beers, that might
include Adnams Broadside, Badger Best and Tanglefoot, Batemans XB, Charles
Wells Bombardier, Gibbs Mew Bishops Tipple, Ringwood Old Thumper,
Shepherd Neame Spitfire, Theakstons Old Peculier and Wadworths 6X on
handpump. They also have a short but interesting wine list, country wines and
Biddenden farm cider. As a pleasant alternative for this county it's busy with a
less conventional and younger crowd who are at home in the well worn interior.
The two bars have stripped light beams and timbering in the warm-coloured dark
ochre walls, with quite unusual little chairs around the tables in the snug red-
carpeted room on the left, and little decorative plates on the walls and a big open
fire in the one on the right – which leads through to the restaurant. Decent home-
made bar food includes bangers and mash or prawn creole (£4.95), fresh battered
cod or lasagne (£5.25), liver and smoky bacon casserole (£5.50), broccoli and
stilton flan (£5.75), steak, onion and Guinness pie or swordfish supreme (£5.95),
chicken breast in Dijonnaise sauce (£6.50) and fresh monkfish (£6.95), and
home-made puddings like gypsy tart or spotted dick (£2.20); they use butter for
all their pastry. The games bar on the left has darts, pool, cribbage, shove-
ha'penny, dominoes, and there is piped music. Outside there are picnic-table sets
by the tubs of flowers in front and in the the terraced garden with fishpond and
waterlilies; it's good walking country – walkers are welcome and dogs are
allowed if on a lead but not in the restaurant (which has a no-smoking area).
*(Recommended by Doug Kennedy, A Plumb, R B Crail, Sue Demont, Tim Barrow, Mr and
Mrs Holmes; more reports please)*

*Free house ~ Licensees Richard and Anna Abrehart ~ Real ale ~ Meals and snacks
~ Restaurant (not Sun evening) ~ (01306) 711793 ~ Children in eating area of
bar ~ Open 10.30-3, 6.30-11; 11.30-11 Sat; closed evening 25 Dec ~ Bedrooms:
/£50B*

COMPTON SU9546 Map 2

Harrow

B3000

A busy cheerful dining pub that's popular for its often unusual (although not
cheap) food, its fish specialities, and particularly for the excellent huge hot or
cold seafood platter (£11.50). The extensive menu also includes sandwiches,
lemon sole, monkfish and bacon kebabs or duck breast with port and orange
sauce (£8.75) and sirloin steak (£9.75). You will have to book on Friday and
Saturday evenings. Well kept but pricey Ind Coope Burton, Greene King IPA,
King & Barnes Sussex and Tetleys on handpump. The brightly lit main bar has
interesting racing pictures below the ancient ceiling – mostly portraits of horses,
jockey caricatures and signed race-finish photographs. Opening off here are more
little beamed rooms with latched rustic doors, and nice touches such as brass
horse-head coat hooks, photographs of the area, and a bas relief in wood of the
pub sign. You can sit outside in summer, round by the car park but looking out
to gentle slopes of pasture. In the pretty village the art nouveau Watts Chapel and
Gallery are interesting, and the church itself is attractive; Loseley House is nearby
too. *(Recommended by Jane and Laura Bailey, Tim Galligan, Derek and Margaret
Underwood, Dawn and Phil Garside, James Nunns, A and A Dale, Guy Consterdine; more
reports please)*

*Ind Coope (Allied) ~ Lease: Roger and Susan Seaman ~ Real ale ~ Meals and
snacks (12-3, 6-10; breakfast 7.30-12) ~ (01483) 810379 ~ Children welcome ~
Open 11-11 ~ Bedrooms: £30B/£35B*

Withies

Withies Lane; pub signposted from B3000

Surrey Dining Pub of the Year

A magnificent 16th-c family-run free house, smart yet atmospheric, with marked emphasis on the restaurant side, but still preserving a small genuinely pubby bar: settles (one rather splendidly art nouveau), beams, a massive inglenook fireplace which is lit with a roaring log fire even on summer evenings, and some attractive panels of 17th-c carving between the windows. The bar snacks are straightforward but excellent, and include soup (£2.50), Withies or smoked salmon pâté (£3.25), ploughman's (from £3.25), sandwiches (from £2.75), quiche (£3.50), filled baked potatoes (from £3.95) and seafood platter (£6.50). The pricier restaurant menu (also served outside under the arbour on warm days and evenings) concentrates on a traditional selection of simply cooked daily specials with lots of seafood; good Sunday lunch and a wonderful choice of really English home-made puddings like summer pudding or rice pudding. Well kept ales on handpump are Bass, King & Barnes and Friary Meux: draught cider. The delightfully immaculate garden overhung with weeping willows has tables under an arbour of creeper-hung trellises, more on a crazy-paved terrace and yet more under old apple trees, the neat lawn in front of the steeply tiled white house is bordered by masses of flowers. (*Recommended by M L Clarke, Christine and Geoff Butler, Susan and John Douglas, Jenny and Brian Seller, Guy Consterdine; more reports please*)

Free house ~ Licensee Mr O'Donnell-Thomas ~ Real ale ~ Meals and snacks (12-2.30, 7-10; not Sun evening) ~ Restaurant (not Sun evening)~ (01483) 421158 ~ Children in restaurant ~ Open 11-3, 6-11

DORKING TQ1649 Map 3

Cricketers £

81 South Street; from centre follow signs to Horsham (A2003)

Readers tell us that the new licensees and staff have settled with conspicuous efficiency at this busy little place which is one of Surreys few nice town pubs. There's a pleasant atmosphere in the comfortably modernised, attractive bar which has well cushioned sturdy modern settles, library chairs around cast-iron-framed tables, stripped-and-sealed brick walls decorated with various cricketing pictures, and a central servery with a big modern etched-glass cricketers mirror; there's a log-effect gas fire. Well kept, extremely cheap Fullers Chiswick, London Pride and ESB on handpump. Very good value promptly served pub food includes sandwiches, ham, egg and chips (£3.10), scampi and chips (£3.45), a selection of home-made daily specials (£3.25) and a barbecue throughout the summer months. Up some steps at the back there's a very pretty little sheltered terrace, interestingly planted with roses, a good red honeysuckle, uncommon shrubs and herbaceous plants, and gently floodlit at night. Daytime parking is limited but patience does pay off in the nearby car park. (*Recommended by John Kimber, Roger Taylor, John Pettit, D J Penny; more reports please*)

Fullers ~ Managers: Peter and Michelle Kalejs ~ Real ale ~ Meals and snacks (not Fri, Sat evening or Sunday lunch) ~ (01306) 889938 ~ Nearby daytime parking difficult ~ Open 11.30-11

EFFINGHAM TQ1253

Sir Douglas Haig

The Street; off A246 W of Leatherhead

In spite of renovations a couple of years ago that amounted to a virtually complete rebuild there's no sense of brashness or over-newness and this busy, roomy free house has quickly established itself as a popular and reliable place for a good value lunch. Straightforward home-cooked bar food served with a choice of up to five fresh vegetables includes sandwiches, ploughman's (£3.50), seafood platter (£3.95), huge steak and kidney pie (£4.50); Sunday roast lunch (£4.95). At one end of the long room there's an eating area with an open fire, small settles, banquettes and kitchen chairs, and at the other end, another open fire, a wood-stained floor, stools, an armchair, and shelves of books. Well kept Badger Tanglefoot, Boddingtons, Fullers London Pride, Gales HSB and King & Barnes Festive on handpump; quick, friendly service. There's a back lawn and terraced area with seats and tables; fruit machine and juke box. *(Recommended by DWAJ, A M Pickup, Mr and Mrs M Evans, John Pettit, WFL; more reports please)*

Free house ~ Licensee Laurie Smart ~ Real ale ~ Meals and snacks (not Sun evening) ~ (01372) 456886 ~ Open 11-3, 5.30-11; 11-11 Sat ~ Bedrooms: £45B/£55B

ELSTEAD SU9143 Map 2

Woolpack 🍽

The Green; B3001 Milford—Farnham

Without exception readers delightedly praise the superb home-made food at this cheerfully old-fashioned, warmly welcoming, spacious place, bustling with very contented, well-filled diners. The imaginative, extensive menu which is chalked up on a big board near the food servery changes daily and might include really generous helpings of avocado with mild curried crab or shell-on prawns in chilli and garlic (£4.50), several traditional home-made pies and casseroles like beef in orange and Guinness, chicken in stilton, whisky and thyme or pork in ginger and turmeric with spinach (£6.95), lamb steaks in Dijon, rosemary and wine sauce (£7.95) and guinea fowl breast in gin, orange and coriander (£8.95) and lots of tempting home-made puddings in large helpings made by Jill, the licensee's sister, like crème brûlée, chocolate and fruit scrunch or choux ring filled with cream and bananas (all £2.75); vegetables are good – beetroot in creamy sauce, leeks with crunchy topping and cheesy potatoes; Sunday lunch is busy, so arrive early; good attentive service in an informal warmly welcoming friendly atmosphere. There's a fair amount of wool industry memorabilia, such as the weaving shuttles and cones of wool that hang above the high-backed settles in the long airy main bar, which also has window seats and spindleback chairs around plain wooden tables. There are fireplaces at each end; the small brick one has copper pans on the mantelpiece and some pretty china on a shelf above it. The large dog basket tucked into a corner is the home of Taffy, a golden retriever. Leading off here is a big room decorated with lots of country prints, a weaving loom, scales, and brass measuring jugs; the fireplace with its wooden pillars lace frill is unusual. In the family room there are nursery-rhyme murals and lots of dried flowers hanging from the ceiling, and a door that leads to the garden with picnic-table sets and a children's play area. Well kept Greene King IPA and Wadworths 6X tapped from the cask; quite a few wines by the glass and bottle. Dominoes, cribbage, backgammon, fruit machine and trivia. *(Recommended by J M Campbell, Guy Consterdine, R Spens, Anna Marsh, Ray Cuckow, Martin and Karen Wake, Ron Corbett, Lyn Sharpless, Bob Eardley, Alex and Beryl Williams, Mr and Mrs G Turner, I E and C A Prosser, Stephen and Julie Brown, Tim Galligan, Ian Phillips, Phil and Sally Gorton, Martin Jones, Angela and Alan Dale)*

Friary Meux (Allied) ~ Lease: Jill Macready ~ Real ale ~ Meals and snacks (till 9.45) ~ Restaurant ~ (01252) 703106 ~ Children in restaurant and family room ~ Open 11-2.30(3 Sat), 6-11; closed 25 and 26 Dec

HASCOMBE TQ0039 Map 3

White Horse

B2130 S of Godalming

In a village tucked away among lovely rolling wooded country lanes on the Greensand way, you'll probably find the simple character-filled rooms of this rose-draped inn busy and bustling with a good pubby atmosphere. It's especially popular for generous helpings of interesting and varied bar food from the blackboard including huge sandwiches, home-made soup (£2.25), home-made pies (£4.50), home-made steak burgers or swordfish steaks (£6.95), whole seabass and charcoal grill specialities; all home-made puddings like bread and butter pudding and sticky toffee pudding (from £3); best to get there early for a table at lunchtime, especially at weekends; quick cheerful service. You can eat in a cosy inner beamed area with a woodburning stove and quiet small-windowed alcoves looking out on to roses and the gently sloping lawn, or in the light airy extension with blue check tablecloths and light bentwood chairs. There are plenty of tables in several places outside – on a little terrace by the front porch, in a bower and under a walnut tree. Well kept Friary Meux Best, Greene King IPA and Marstons Pedigree on handpump; quite a few wines. Darts, shove-ha'penny, dominoes, fruit machine and piped music. The National Trust's Winkworth Arboretum, with its walks among beautiful trees and shrubs, is nearby. *(Recommended by Brian and Jenny Seller, Liz and Ian Phillips, E G Parish, Nicola Thomas and Paul Dickinson, Michael Sargent, DAV, Mrs Hilarie Taylor; more reports please)*

Ind Coope ~ Lease: Susan Barnett ~ Real ale ~ Meals and snacks (12-2.20, 7-10; not 25 Dec) ~ Restaurant (not Sun evening) ~ (01483) 208258 ~ Children in eating area ~ Open 11-3, 5.30(6 Sat)-11

HEADLEY TQ2054 Map 3

Cock

Church Lane; village signposted off B2033 SE of Leatherhead

This congenial family run Tudor inn is reputedly the oldest house in the village and like many public houses has been a focal point to village life over the years in its varied roles as court of the manor, post office and even the setting for a sparrow shooting contest. It's not lost its local feel today, but there's always a good welcome for strangers. Unusually light and airy, the strikingly simple main bar has big windows, pews forming booths around its tables and a good log fire. On weekdays there's an overflow into an attractively spare well lit dining area with generously spaced tables (this functions as a restaurant, Friday to Sunday). The licensee tells us that the prices of the sensible-sized helpings of typical home-cooked bar food have not changed since last year: good soup (£1.65), ploughman's (from £3.25), lasagne (£4.50, they sometimes do a very nice chicken one in brandy sauce), pies (from £4.25), butterfly prawns (£6.75) and steak (£8.95), with puddings such as apple pie (£1.75), children's dishes (£2.65), and specials such as vegetable chilli, lamb and rosemary pie or Cumberland sausage; there are Sunday nuts and cocktail biscuits on the bar counter. Well kept Ind Coope Burton and Tetleys and one guest ale a month on handpump; a good choice of wines and efficient service. During the day there may be unobtrusive well reproduced piped music; in the evenings, as the atmosphere becomes more local, this is likely to be played a lot louder. The public end has darts, dominoes, draughts, chess, fruit machine, juke box and trivia. It's in an attractive setting, with tables and chairs outside giving pleasant views over rolling horsey countryside – good walking country. Dogs welcome and water provided. *(Recommended by Alan Blewitt, TOH, A Plumb, Julian Bessa, Jenny and Brian Seller, John Pettit, David Peakall, Ian S Morley, Ben Grose, TBB; more reports please)*

Ind Coope (Allied) ~ Managers Eric and Patricia Ford ~ Real ale ~ Meals and snacks (12-2, 6-9.15; not Sun evening) ~ Restaurant (closed Sun evening) ~ (01372) 377258 ~ Children in restaurant ~ Open 11-2.30(3 Sat), 6.00-11; closed evening 25 Dec

HURTMORE SU9545 Map 2

Squirrel

Hurtmore Rd; just off A3 nr Godalming, nestling under E embankment just by Hurtmore/Shackleford turn-off

Pleasantly spacious carefully refurbished white-painted pub. The licensees tell us that prices of the good range of home-cooked bar food have not changed since last year. You could try soup (£1.95), sandwiches (from £2.95; open toasted sandwiches, pizza, bacon or avocado from £3.95), potted shrimps (£2.95), filled baked potato skins or a choice of ploughman's (£3.25), unusual omelettes such as Persian, Spanish or Chinese (£4.50) and home-made steak and kidney pudding (£6.95). In the restaurant, there's a variety of things to cook yourself on a sizzle-stone, with kebab vegetables (from £7.95). The bar is spacious and comfortable, with pale country-kitchen tables and chairs and sofas matching the curtains, a fresh, airy decor – far from olde-worlde, but very much alive. At one end it leads into a restaurant with a no-smoking area, and there's a comfortable new conservatory. Well kept but pricey Ruddles Best and County and Websters Yorkshire, friendly service, unobtrusive piped music, no machines; facilities for the disabled. They have a library with books for children and adults, a children's playroom and a balloon room; trivial pursuit, cribbage, dominoes, chess and scrabble. There are picnic-table sets out in front, and under cocktail parasols in a spacious garden with swings and slides in the play area. The bedrooms are in a recently converted 17th-c cottage row; weekend bargains. *(Recommended by Alan Kilpatrick, Gwen and Peter Andrews, R B Crail, Mrs J A Blanks; more reports please)*

Free house ~ Licensees David and Jane Barnes ~ Real ale ~ Meals and snacks (12-2.30, 7-10) ~ Restaurant (not Sun evening) ~ (01483) 860223 ~ Children welcome ~ Open 11-3, 6-11 ~ guitarist and singer: Sun 7.30-10 ~ Bedrooms: 50B/£65B

LALEHAM TQ0568 Map 3

Three Horseshoes

Junction 1 of M3, then W on A308; village signposted on left on B376

Originally 13th-c, this busy old stone-flagged tavern is at its best on warm summer days when the façade is almost hidden by wisteria, hanging baskets and cartwheels. It does pull the crowds – just as it did when the likes of Lillie Langtry, Gilbert and his partner Sullivan, Marie Lloyd and Edward VII when he was Prince of Wales, all customers, boosted its popularity. It's been comfortably modernised, and the dusky open-plan bar has plush burgundy seats on the red carpet, lots of big copper pots and pans hanging from beams, interesting cock-fighting prints on the red walls, and blacksmith's tools hanging over the main fireplace. One small alcove has high-backed settles, and there's a small conservatory. Popular and highly praised bar food in big helpings served all day includes an excellent choice of sandwiches (from £1.60), soup (£1.95), ploughman's (from £4.25), a wide range of huge baked potatoes with hot or cold fillings (from £4.45), salads (from £5.95), a selection of daily specials such as wholefood lasagne, lamb and apricot pie or lamb in red wine (£6.50), plaice with prawns and mushrooms (£6.95), poached salmon or fried trout (£7.25), and puddings like sherry trifle, chocolate fudge cake or hot waffles and maple syrup (from £1.95); they may also prepare dishes on a more individual basis on request. Well kept Courage Best, Fullers London Pride, Ruddles Best and County, Wadworths 6X and Websters Yorkshire on handpump; decent wines, efficient service and piped music. There are plenty of tables in the rather distinctive creeper-filled garden, and just a short walk away is a grassy stretch of the Thames popular with picnickers and sunbathers. *(Recommended by Simon Collett-Jones, Clem Stephens, Ian Phillips, Stephen G Brown; more reports please)*

Courage ~ Lease: David Sword ~ Real ale ~ Meals and snacks (noon-9 Mon-Sat, 12-3, 7-9 Sun) ~ Restaurant (closed Sun evening)~ Staines (01784) 452617 ~ Children in conservatory ~ Open 11-11 (Sunday 12-3, 7-10.30); closed evening 25 Dec

LEIGH TQ2246 Map 3

Plough

3 miles S of A25 Dorking—Reigate, signposted from Betchworth (which itself is signposted off the main road); also signposted from South Park area of Reigate; on village green

Warmly welcoming pretty tiled and weatherboarded cottage in an attractive setting overlooking the village green. To the right is a very low beamed cosy white walled and timbered dining lounge and on the left, the more local bar has a good bow-window seat and an extensive listing of games from which customers can choose to play darts, shove-ha'penny, dominoes, table skittles, cribbage, trivia, the fruit machine, the video game, Jenca, chess or Scrabble; piped music. It's popular for bar food from the menu which includes sandwiches (from £1.75), soup (£1.95), pâté (£2.50), garlic mussels or ploughman's (from £3.95), filled baked potato (from £3.25), ham, egg and chips (£4.50), lasagne (£4.75) and sirloin steak (£9.50). There are daily blackboard specials which might include some good seafood, and puddings like hot chocolate fudge cake, apple pie and blackberry and apple pancake rolls (from £1.95). The restaurant menu offers a few further choices. Booking is recommended especially at weekends when it can get a bit cramped. Well kept King & Barnes Bitter, Festive, Mild and Broadwood and King & Barnes seasonal ales such as Old, Christmas, Easter, Summer and Harvest on handpump. There are picnic-table sets under cocktail parasols in a pretty side garden bordered by a white picket fence. Parking nearby is limited; no credit cards. *(Recommended by Andrew and Teresa Heffer, Nicola Thomas, Paul Dickinson, Jim and Maggie Cowell, Martin Jones, Richard Oxenham, Thomas Nott; more reports please)*

King & Barnes ~ Tenants Sarah Broomfield and Rob Long ~ Real ale ~ Meals and snacks (till 10) ~ Restaurant ~ Children in restaurant ~ (01306) 611348 ~ Open 11-2.30(3 Sat), 6-11

MICKLEHAM TQ1753 Map 3

King William IV

Byttom Hill; short but narrow steep track up hill just off A24 Leatherhead—Dorking by partly green-painted restaurant, just N of main B2289 village turn-off; OS Sheet 187 map reference 173538

Cut into the hillside – it's quite a climb up – this unusually placed thriving pub with panoramic views is especially popular for its wide range of good value varied food served with fresh vegetables and new potatoes – they don't do chips. The vast selection on the daily changing blackboard might include lamb's liver and onions (£4.95), baked smoked fish crumble with mozzarella cheese (£5.25), hot tandoori chicken salad with a mint yogurt dressing, rabbit pie or home-made steak and kidney pie cooked in Guinness (£5.50), fresh fish of the day (from £5.75) and melon, prawn and avocado salad (£5.75). Vegetarian dishes are a particular speciality, with at least five daily such as mushroom and aubergine bake or spinach and nut au gratin (£5.20); home-made puddings like hot butterscotch bananas, bread and butter pudding, hot chocolate fudge cake, fruit crumble or treacle tart (£2.20). In the evening there are also starters and additional specials like breast of chicken piri piri (£6.95), baked codling with prawn and saffron sauce (£7.50), rainbow trout with spring onions and ginger (£6.75) and salmon and broccoli bake (£5.25). There may be summer barbecues once a month with folk music (it's advisable to telephone beforehand to check). Relaxed and unpretentious, it dates mainly from the end of the 18th c. The snug plank-panelled front bar looks down the hill, and there's a rather more spacious quite brightly lit back bar with kitchen-type chairs around its cast-iron-framed tables; decent log fires and fresh flowers on all the tables. Well kept Adnams, Badger Best, Boddingtons, Hogs Back and a guest on handpump, with occasional guests and special offers; quick and friendly service; good coffee. Shove-ha'penny, dominoes, unobtrusive nostalgic piped pop music, and a serviceable grandfather clock. The interesting terraced garden, popular with families, is neatly filled with sweet peas, climbing roses and honeysuckle and plenty of tables (some in an open-sided wooden shelter). A path leads straight up into the open country. *(Recommended by Patrick and Patricia Derwent, Mark and Diane Grist, TBB, Father Robert Davies, Thomas Neate, Susan and Alan Buckland, David R Shillitoe, Mr and Mrs Gordon Turner, Tom and Rosemary Hall, G R Sunderland, Ian Phillips, Nic Armitage, N H and A H Harries, Rhoda and Jeff Collins)*

Free house ~ Licensees C D and J E Grist ~ Real ale ~ Meals and snacks (till 9.45, not Mon evening) ~ Restaurant ~ (01372) 372590 ~ Children in eating area of small bar and restaurant ~ Occasional folk/country groups in summer ~ Open 11-3, 6-11; closed 25 Dec

OUTWOOD TQ3245 Map 3

Dog & Duck

From A23 in Salfords S of Redhill take Station turning – eventually after you cross the M23 the pub's on your left at the T-junction; coming from the village centre, head towards Coopers Hill and Prince of Wales Road

Welcoming partly tile-hung country cottage with a comfortable and spacious bar that offers a good choice of well kept and reasonably priced real ales on handpump including Badger Best, Hard Tackle, Tanglefoot and winter Black Adder, Gribble Bitter and Reg's Tipple and Wadworths 6X. On the blackboard there is a popular range of mostly straightforward well prepared food served in generous helpings: sandwiches (from £1.50), soup (£1.95), ploughman's (from £3.50), salads (from £3.95), ham, egg and fries or local spicy sausage and mash (£4.25), steak and kidney pie or courgette layer bake (£5.25), cashew nut and parsnip bake (£5.45), chicken, leek and stilton pie (£5.75); Sunday roast lunch. The rambling bar has a good log fire, comfortable settles, oak armchairs and more ordinary seats, ochre walls, stripped dark beams, rugs on the quarry tiles, and daily newspapers to read. There's another huge fireplace in the restaurant area which leads off the bar. Comprehensive range of games that inclues darts, shove-ha'penny, table skittles, ring-the-bull, cribbage, chess, draughts, shut the box, dominoes, Scrabble, backgammon, and trivia; unobtrusive piped music. Picnic-table sets under cocktail parasols on the grass outside look over a safely fenced-off duckpond to the meadows. It's a nice walk to the village, with its old windmill, if you have an hour spare for the round trip. *(Recommended by A Church, R and S Bentley, B N J Tye, Andy and Jill Kassube, David Hedges, G S B G Dudley; more reports please)*

Badger ~ Manager Stephen Slocombe ~ Real ale ~ Meals and snacks (12-10) ~ Restaurant ~ Smallfield (01342) 842964 ~ Children in restaurant ~ Quiz night Sun ~ Open 11-11

PIRBRIGHT SU9455 Map 2

Royal Oak

Aldershot Rd; A324 S of village

Inside this neatly kept and pleasant Tudor cottage there's a rambling series of snug side alcoves with heavy beams and timbers, ancient stripped brickwork, and gleaming brasses set around the big low-beamed fireplace which roars in the winter. It's cosily furnished with wheelback chairs, tapestried wall seats and little dark church-like pews set around neat tables, decorated with fresh flowers in summer. This year they've extended their already good range of beers to include well kept Alford Arms Pickled Squirrel, Badger Best, Boddingtons, Flowers Original, Marstons Pedigree, Old Frithsden, Youngs Special, and a guest ale like Adnams, Fullers Hock or Timothy Taylors Landlord, the wine list is also improved with 15 wines by the bottle and glass; several malt whiskies. Bar food includes shell-on prawns (from £3.95), vegetable curry (£4.75), beef cooked in port with onions and walnuts or steak and ale pie (£5.25), chicken breast coated with stilton and mushroom sauce or pork chop with piquant sauce (£5.95), nut cutlet with cheese sauce and encased in puff pastry or lamb steak with orange and rosemary sauce (£6.95), spare ribs or rump steak (£7.95) and mixed grill (£8.50) and excellent puddings (from £2.25); Sunday lunch; coffee and newspapers all day; very friendly staff and service. In summer the huge front garden is a mass of colour and pretty in the evening with fairy lights although it can be a bit noisy with passing traffic; the large garden at the back is now open and once established should be a marvellous improvement. Interesting walks are accessible from the large car park, where walkers may leave cars if permission is gained from the licensee. *(Recommended by KC, Dr Paul Kitchener, Mike Davies, Ian Phillips, Mayur Shah, Guy Consterdine, Susan and John Douglas; more reports please)*

Whitbreads ~ Manager John Lay ~ Real ale ~ Meals and snacks ~ Restaurant ~ (01483) 232466 ~ Children in restaurant ~ Open 11-11 (including Sunday)

PYRFORD LOCK TQ0458 Map 3

Anchor

Lock Lane; 3 miles from M25 Junction 10; south on A3, then slip road signposted Ockham, Ripley and Send, past RHS Wisley Gardens to second bridge

Picnic-table sets on the big open terrace of this splendidly placed busy modern pub give a fine view of the narrowboats on the canal leaving the dock and edging under the steeply hump-backed road bridge and through the locks of the River Wey Navigation. The view is almost as good from the well positioned large new conservatory. The partly carpeted and partly brick-floored bar has big picture windows and comfortable furnishings; upstairs is full of narrowboat memorabilia. Good bar food (the licensee tells us prices haven't changed since last year) includes home-made specials (from £3.95), baked potato (from £2.50), basket meals (from £2.35), ploughman's (from £3.25), steak and kidney pie (£4.15), large salad selection (from £4) quiche (£3.95), scampi (£4.95), gammon steak (£4.95); daily vegetarian special (from £3), children's menu (from £1.80) and puddings, some home-made (from £1.50); coffee; lots of bustle and noise from the Tannoy system announcing food orders; friendly, efficient staff but you may have to queue to place your order; Courage Best and Directors on handpump and John Smiths under light blanket pressure; fruit machine, video games, piped music, pinball and juke box sometimes even outside. Always busy on a sunny day, partly owing to the pub's proximity to the Royal Horticultural Society's Wisley Gardens. (*Recommended by John Pettit, Doug Kennedy, Joy Heatherley, DWAJ, Douglas Jeffery, Stephen Barney, P Gillbe; more reports please*)

S & N ~ Manager Colin Dyke ~ Real ale ~ Meals and snacks (12-2.30, 6-9; 12-1.45, 7-9 Sunday) ~ (01932) 342507 ~ Open all day, (winter 11-3, 6-11)

REIGATE HEATH TQ2349 Map 3

Skimmington Castle ★

3 miles from M25 junction 8: through Reigate take A25 Dorking (West), then on edge of Reigate turn left past Black Horse into Flanchford Road; after ¼ mile turn left into Bonny's Road (unmade, very bumpy track); after crossing golf course fork right up hill

After 40 years here Andrew and Ann Fisher have handed over to a new licensee who acknowledges that they'll be a hard act to follow. There are bound to be a few changes at this characterful old cottage (certainly redecorating, carpeting and upgrading the lighting are planned) but we hope not too many, as its charm is the really traditional local atmosphere that makes it some people's ideal country pub. The bright main front bar leads off from a small central serving counter with dark simple panelling. There's a miscellany of chairs and tables, shiny brown vertical panelling decorated with earthenware bottles, plates, brass and pewter, and a brown plank ceiling. Flowers IPA, Greene King IPA and Abbot on handpump, and among a choice of eight ciders, Addlestones draught. Derek the stuffed fox is still sitting among the crisp packets. The cosy back rooms are partly panelled too, with old-fashioned settles and Windsor chairs; one has a big brick fireplace with its bread-oven still beside it. A small room down steps at the back has shove-ha'penny and dominoes; piped music. Reasonably priced bar food (now also served in the evening) includes sandwiches (from £1.30), ploughman's (from £2.95), home-made lasagne and seafood lasagne (£3.95), steak and kidney pie or cajun chicken (£4.50), gammon knuckle in spicy sauce (£4.95), steaks (from £5.50). There are nice views from the crazy-paved front terrace and tables on the grass by lilac bushes, with more tables at the back overlooking the meadows and the hillocks; surrounded by wooded countryside that is easily reached by winding paths. One bar area is no smoking. (*Recommended by David Peakall, Comus Elliott, Graham Pettener, M L Clarke, Ann Reeder, Dave Craine, Owen Upton, W J Wonham, Mark and Diane Grist, A Plumb; more reports on the new regime please*)

Allied ~ Tenants Guy and Rena Davies ~ Real ale ~ Meals and snacks (till 10; only sandwiches and pies Sun lunch, not Sun evening) ~ (01737) 243100 ~ Open 11-2.30, 5.30-11(11-11 Sat); closed 25 Dec evening

SHAMLEY GREEN TQ0343 Map 3

Red Lion
B2128 S of Guildford

Back in the *Guide* after a long absence the main draw here is the excellent (although not cheap) seasonal food from the menu and changing blackboard. There is a wide choice and the helpings are generous: starters like grilled stuffed mushrooms (£4.25), moules farcie (£4.95), giant prawns (£6.95), good winter soups, such as ham and lentil, mushroom with croûtons (£2.95), sandwiches (from £2.95), ploughman's (from £3.65), home-baked ham, eggs and chips (£5.85), ham and melon salad (£6.75), Dijon peppered chicken (£8.75), seafood salad or lamb medallions (£9.25), lamb cutlets (£11.45) and lemon sole Véronique (£12.95); vegetarian dishes like spinach and mushroom crêpes or mushroom tagliatelle (£5.85); usually they do a Sunday lunch, although not necessarily in summer (£7.95); children can have small portions of some dishes; home-made puddings (all £3.25) like sticky toffee pudding, strawberry and hazelnut roulade and hot chocolate fudge cake. On the cream walls are old photographs of cricket played on the opposite village green and the good mixture of furniture includes a handsome panel-back armed settle, red-brocaded high-backed modern settles forming booths around tables, some kitchen chairs and a couple of antique clocks. Well kept Abbot ale, Flowers Original and King and Barnes Sussex and a good selection of wines. *(Recommended by Steve Goodchild, Michael and Carol Meek, Tim Galligan; more reports please)*

Free house ~ Licensee: Ben Heath ~ Real ale ~ Meals and snacks ~ Restaurant ~ (01483) 892202 ~ Children welcome ~ Open 11-11 ~ Bedrooms: £30B/£35B

SHERE TQ0747 Map

White Horse
Village signposted on right on A25 3 miles E of Guildford

This fascinating and pretty half-timbered pub was constructed some 600 years ago, there are no foundations, just salvaged ships' timbers plunged into the ground. After careful restoration, there's still much evidence of the place's age, with uneven floors, massive beams, oak wall seats, old manuscripts and a huge inglenook fireplace; there's some elegant Tudor stonework in a second fireplace through in the Pilgrim's Bar. Renovations over the past few decades have also unearthed other interesting finds, such as casks of early 18th-c smugglers' brandy, and a pair of Elizabethan shoes put in the wattle and daub walls for luck. Good bar food includes sandwiches, coronation chicken salad, beef and venison pie or stuffed aubergines (£5) and cajun swordfish or fresh salmon with lime sauce (£5.75). Ruddles Best and County and Theakstons on handpump. There are seats outside on a sunny cobbled courtyard among carefully planted troughs of flowers and bright hanging baskets but they are a bit exposed to the traffic noise which you can avoid in the newly opened back garden; good walking in the beech woods on the road north towards East Clandon. The village is pretty, but it and the pub, one of its more striking features, do get busy at weekends, so parking can be difficult. *(Recommended by J S Mann, John Pettit, Ian Phillips, Maurice Southon, Sarah and Jamie Allan; more reports please)*

S & N ~ Manager Mike Wicks ~ Real ale ~ Meals and snacks ~ (01483 202161) ~ Children in eating area ~ Nearby parking may be difficult ~ Open 11.30-11

WALLISWOOD TQ1138 Map 3

Scarlett Arms ★
Village signposted from Ewhurst—Rowhook back road; or follow Oakwoodhill signpost from A29 S of Ockley, then follow Walliswood signpost into Walliswood Green Road

This relaxing and unspoilt red-tiled white building – once a pair of labourers' cottages – has long been popular for the charming straightforwad way it takes you back to old times. The original small-roomed layout has been carefully preserved, and the three neatly kept communicating rooms have low black oak beams, deeply polished flagstones, simple but perfectly comfortable benches, high bar stools with backrests, trestle tables, country prints, photographs of locals and two roaring log fires all winter. As it's a popular place there may be a wait for a seat. Well kept and very reasonably priced King & Barnes Sussex, Broadwood, Festive and Mild, and the seasonal Old, Easter, Summer, Harvest and Christmas ales on handpump. Good value bar food in hearty portions, mostly served with chips and peas, includes sandwiches, steak and kidney pie, rabbit pie, trout, ham and cheesy leek bake, chicken and mushroom with potato topping, ham, egg and chips, breaded plaice and macaroni, ham and mushrooms in cheese sauce (all £4.25), curries (£4.50) and roast beef or pork on Thursdays (£4.50). Darts, cribbage, shove-ha'penny, table skittles, dominoes and a fruit machine in a small room at the end. There are old-fashioned seats and tables with umbrellas in the pretty garden. Note that children are not allowed in the pub but well behaved dogs are. *(Recommended by Martin G Richards, R B Crail, Peter Locke, Peter Fraser, Graham Pettener, Steve Goodchild, Father Robert Davies, R Wilson, Andy and Jackie Mallpress, Mrs J M Aston, Martin Richards, J S M Sheldon, N H and A H Harries)*

King & Barnes ~ Tenant Mrs Pat Haslam ~ Real ale ~ Meals and snacks ~ (01306) 627243 ~ Open 11-2.30, 5.30-11

WARLINGHAM TQ3658 Map 3

White Lion
B269

Based on two 15th-c cottages, the friendly warren of black-panelled rooms in this unspoilt early Tudor coaching inn are full of nooks and crannies, an impressive old inglenook fireplace, low beams, and even tales of secret passages and ghosts. There's also plenty of deeply aged plasterwork, wood-block floors and high-backed settles, while a side room decorated with amusing early 19th-c cartoons has darts, a trivia machine and a fruit machine. It all amounts to quite an unusual find for the outer fringes of London, and it's good value too: beer is very cheap for the county, and the home-made bar food is well priced. Served in the bigger, brighter room at the end of the building, food includes sandwiches, beef curry or steak and kidney pie (£3.95); good service. Bass and Fullers London Pride and two constantly rotating guests on handpump; piped music in the eating area; no smoking during lunchtime meal-serving hours there. The well kept back lawn, with its rockery, is surrounded by a herbaceous border; there may be outside service here in summer. *(Recommended by Neil H Barker, Graham Pettener, E G Parish, Wayne Brindle, Helen Taylor, B B Morgan; more reports please)*

Charringtons (Bass) ~ Manager Julie Evans ~ Real ale ~ Meals and snacks ~ (01883) 624106 ~ Children in eating area of bar ~ Open 11-3, 5.30(6 Sat)-11; 11-11 Thurs, Fri

WEST CLANDON TQ0452 Map 3

Onslow Arms
The Street (A247)

Inside this well laid out spacious early 17th-c country inn the rambling heavy-beamed rooms have lots of nooks and crannies, polished brass and copper, leaded windows, carved settles on the flagstones or thick carpets, fresh flowers, log fires in inglenook fireplaces (one has an unusual roasting spit) and soft lighting. The establishment has an attractively well heeled and comfortable feel: there's a helicopter landing pad. A fine choice of around eight changing real ales well kept on handpump might include Bass, Boddingtons, Courage Best and Directors, Fullers London Pride, Flowers IPA, King & Barnes, Youngs Special and a guest. Beautifully prepared home-made bar food from the blackboard is served with fresh vegetables and includes sandwiches, coquille St Jacques (£3.85), tagliatelle niçoise (£4.50), chicken and mushroom pie (£5.25), steak, kidney and oyster pie (£5.85), cold meats carved from joints and help yourself salads and a popular carvery, and puddings; many, many more elaborate dishes in the stylish candlelit restaurant. Part of the eating area of the bar is no smoking. The village is pretty and in summer, the award-winning hanging baskets, flower filled tubs, shrubs and flower-laden cart outside on the flagged courtyard are a marvellous sight. *(Recommended by M L Clarke, R B Crail, Ian Phillips, John and Heather Dwane, A E and P McCully, Dr and Mrs A K Clarke; more reports please)*

Free house ~ Licensee Alan Peck ~ Real ale ~ Meals and snacks (till 10pm); not Sun evening ~ Partly no-smoking restaurant ~ (01483) 222447 ~ Children in eating area of bar and in restaurant ~ Open 11-2.30(3 Sat), 5.30-11

Lucky Dip

Besides the fully inspected pubs, you might like to try these Lucky Dips recommended to us and described by readers (if you do, please send us reports):

☆ **Abinger Common** [Abinger signed off A25 W of Dorking – then right to Abinger Hammer; TQ1145], *Abinger Hatch*: Lovely spot, esp for walkers, in clearing of rolling woods, nr pretty church and duck pond – they wander around the outside tables; half a dozen well kept real ales, current landlord working hard to bring in interesting ones such as Ringwood Fortyniner and Twelve Bore, in old-fashioned character bar with heavy beams, flagstones, basic furnishings, log fires; also country wines, wide choice of usual bar food, piped music, restaurant; provision for children; may have Sun afternoon teas, open all day bank hols and for village fair – around second weekend June *(Jenny and Brian Seller, Susan and John Douglas, John Pettit, Chris and Anne Fluck, LYM)*

Addlestone [138 Station Rd; TQ0464], *Crouch Oak*: Friendly pub with generous helpings of reasonably priced food inc children's dishes in bar and restaurant, Boddingtons, Flowers, Fullers ESB and London Pride and Theakstons Best and Old Peculier; bedrooms planned *(Peter and Lynn Brueton, Hugh Wood, Andy Davies)*

Ashtead [48 The Street (A24); TQ1858], *Leg of Mutton & Cauliflower*: Spaciously refurbished low-beamed pub with waitress-served usual food, Bass and Charrington IPA, no-smoking area, friendly efficient staff, fruit machines etc, barbecues in nice garden behind; very busy weekends *(John Pettit)*

Bagshot [Bagshott Lea; SU9163], *Crown*: Homely no-frilled Fullers local, big helpings of simple good value freshly cooked food *(Phil and Sally Gorton, Ray Cuckow)*

☆ **Banstead** [High St, off A217; TQ2559], *Woolpack*: Spotless Chef & Brewer with reliable reasonably priced food from sandwiches up inc children's dishes, good friendly service, well kept Courage-related ales, cosily decorated lounge, good no-smoking area; occasional free jazz, open all day *(DWAJ, John Pettit, P C Strange)*

Banstead, *Victoria*: Spacious well laid out lounges, attractive small conservatory, popular food from good choice of sandwiches up, good service, well kept Courage *(Maureen and Keith Gimson)*

☆ **Beare Green** [A24 Dorking—Horsham; TQ1842], *Dukes Head*: Good atmosphere and generous straightforward food in attractive roadside pub with good service, open fires, Allied real ales; pleasant garden *(John Evans, LYM)*

☆ **Betchworth** [TQ2049], *Red Lion*: Good food esp specials and well kept ales inc Bass in friendly old pub with smallish fairy-lit bar, helpful staff, not too much music; plenty of tables in rose-trellised garden with play area, squash court *(Al Blue, E D Bailey)*

☆ **Bletchingley** [11 High St; 2½ miles from M25 junction 6, via A22 then A25 towards Redhill; T250], *Whyte Harte*: A good deal of character in low-beamed open-plan bars with old prints, big inglenook log fire, plush settles, rugs and parquet; friendly staff, well kept Allied real ales and fair range of wines; big helpings of varied undemanding home-made bar food from sandwiches to steaks; seats outside; has been open all day Sat; children in dining room; bedrooms *(M D Hare, Alan Castle, Jenny & Brian Seller, LYM)*

☆ **Bletchingley** [Little Common Lane, off A25 on Redhill side of village], *William IV*: Reliably good bar food in prettily tile-hung and weatherboarded country local with comfortable little back dining room, well kept Bass, Worthington BB, good atmosphere, efficient friendly service; seats in nice garden with summer barbecues Sat evening and Sun lunchtime *(Julian Charman, David Hedges, LYM)*

☆ **Bletchingley** [2 High St], *Plough*: Generous helpings of good reasonably priced food in spacious bar or (no extra charge) popular restaurant of recently extended pub with well kept real ales such as King & Barnes, Tetleys and Wadworths 6X; friendly service, tables in big garden *(Chrystabel Austin, Doreen and Brian Hardham, DWAJ, David and Michelle Hedges)*

Bletchingley, *Prince Albert*: Remarkably wide choice of food in attractive pub with several nooks and corners, friendly and obliging staff, tables on terrace and in small pretty garden *(David and Michelle Hedges, TOH)*

Blindley Heath [Byers Lane; TQ3645], *Jolly*

Farmer: Good food (not Sun evening), nice staff, big dining area, fine garden; cl Mon *(Elizabeth and Klaus Leist)*

Bramley [High St; TQ0044], *Jolly Farmer:* Cheerful and lively, with wide choice of freshly prepared food (so may be a wait), Theakstons Old Peculier and Pilgrim Talisman served with a head as in a northern pub, two log fires, beer-mat collection, big restaurant; bedrooms *(Jacquie and Jon Payne, LYM)*

Brockham [Brockham Green; TQ1949], *Dukes Head:* Emphasis on wide range of good food in friendly pleasantly old-fashioned pub, in pretty spot by village green; real ale, log fire *(Jenny and Brian Seller, G B Longden)*

Buckland [A25 nr Reigate; TQ2150], *Jolly Farmers:* Recently refurbished, with decent usual food from lunchtime doorstep sandwiches, ploughman's and baked potatoes to steaks; Allied ales, Sun lunches, children's menu *(DWAJ)*

Burrowhill [B383 N of Chobham – OS Sheet 176 map ref 970633; SU9763], *Four Horseshoes:* Varied choice of well cooked food and Courage and Marstons ales in low cottagey pub overlooking village pump; lots of picnic tables, some under an ancient yew *(Ian Phillips, D P and J A Sweeney)*

☆ **Byfleet** [High Rd; TQ0661], *Plough:* Medley of furnishings in friendly and lively pub with good value straightforward bar food, well kept Courage and guest ales, lots of farm tools, brass and copper, log fire, dominoes; prices low for Surrey; picnic-table sets in big pleasant garden, several real ales inc guests *(Hugh Wood, Andy Davies, B and K Hypher)*

☆ **Charlton** [142 Charlton Rd, off B376 Laleham—Shepperton; TQ0869], *Harrow:* Particularly good pleasant service even when crowded in carefully modernised thatched 17th-c pub doing well under present tenant; short choice of generous interesting no-frills food (tables can be booked), well kept Courage-related real ales, friendly staff; extra room recently opened up, plenty of seats in and out *(W L G Watkins, Ian and Wendy Phillips, Simon Collett-Jones)*

Chelsham [Vanguard Way, over the common – OS Sheet 187 map ref 372590; TQ3759], *Bull:* Welcoming and hardworking newish landlord, wife does good fair-priced food inc lush steak and Guinness pie *(M D Hare)*; [Limpsfield Rd, Chelsham Common], *Hare & Hounds:* Good clean pub with Bass, Charrington IPA, Fullers London Pride and Highgate Mild, good reasonably priced bar food; locals' bar, lounge, pretty summer flowers, play area *(Jonathan and Gillian Shread)*

☆ **Chertsey** [London St (B375); TQ0466], *Crown:* Typical Youngs pub, relaxed atmosphere in attractively renovated Victorian-style bar, well kept real ales, back food area, restaurant, good service, conservatory, tables in courtyard and garden with pond; children welcome; smart 30-bedroom annexe *(M L Clarke, Comus Elliott, Ian Phillips, Richard Houghton)*

☆ **Chertsey** [Ruxbury Rd, St Anns Hill (nr Lyne)], *Golden Grove:* Friendly and very popular local with lots of stripped wood, good value straightforward home-made food from sandwiches up (not Sat-Mon evenings) in pine-tabled eating area, well kept Allied and Gales real ales; piped music, fruit and games machines; big garden with friendly dogs and goat, play area, wooded pond – nice spot by woods *(Clem Stephens, Ian Phillips, T A Bryan)*

☆ **Chiddingfold** [A283; SU9635], *Crown:* Some very recent promising reports on the food in this fine old inn's relatively simple side family bar, and through in the hotel part the ancient panelling, fine carving, massive beams and tapestried restaurant are worth seeing; real ales such as Badger Tanglefoot and Charles Wells, attractive surroundings, tables out on verandah; children allowed in some areas; has been open all day, very crowded 5 Nov (fireworks out on green); bedrooms *(Angela and Alan Dale, Paula Harrison, Jim and Maggie Cowell, John Evans, LYM)*

☆ **Chiddingfold** [A283 S], *Swan:* Very friendly service in cheery country local with spacious bar and tables set closely in small dining room, well kept Allied ales, good fairly priced straightforward food, Sun bar nibbles *(Jim and Maggie Cowell, Paula Harrison, LYM)*

☆ **Chilworth** [Dorking Rd; TQ0247], *Percy Arms:* Nicely refurbished Greene King pub with good choice of food, lunchtime bargains (not Sun), well kept ales and good pleasant service in spacious, clean and well lit bar; pretty views of vale of Chilworth from garden behind, pleasant walks *(Dr R B Crail, John and Heather Dwane)*

Chilworth [Blackheath; off A248 across the level crossing], *Villagers:* Pleasant atmosphere in lots of rooms with nooks and corners, very friendly and eager-to-please young staff, old pews (not comfortable for everyone), interesting if variable food, well kept Morlands Speckled Hen, decent wines and port; pleasant walks *(TOH)*

☆ **Chipstead** [3 miles from M25, junction 8; A217 towards Banstead, right at second roundabout; TQ2757], *Well House:* Good simple lunchtime food (not Sun) from sandwiches up inc good filled Yorkshire puddings in cottagey and comfortable partly 14th-c pub with lots of atmosphere, very welcoming efficient staff, log fires in all three rooms, well kept Bass and guest beers, good pot of tea; attractive garden with the old well, nice surroundings *(J G Smith, Maureen and Keith Gimson, Ian Phillips, Al Blue, Elizabeth and Klaus Leist, Beverley James, LYM)*

Chobham [High St, 4 miles from M3 junction 3; SU9761], *Sun:* Well kept low-beamed lounge bar in quiet timbered

Courage pub, a useful retreat *(Martin Richards, LYM)*

☆ **Cobham** [Pains Hill/Byfleet Rd, by Sainsburys; TQ1158], *Little White Lion*: Attractive and comfortable, two or three cottagey intercommunicating bars, friendly efficient service, good choice of interesting and appetising food showing some real flair, very reasonable prices; well kept ales, good choice of wines by the glass; some tables in small front garden, almost opp entrance to 18th-c Painshill Park *(Mrs J A Blanks)*

☆ **Cobham** [Plough Lane], *Plough*: Cheerful lively atmosphere in pretty black-shuttered local with comfortably modernised low-beamed lounge bar, well kept Courage ales, helpful staff, pine-panelled snug with darts, lunchtime food; piped pop music may be rather loud; seats outside *(John Sanders, Ian Phillips, LYM)*

☆ **Cox Green** [Baynards Station Yard; Baynards Lane (W off B2128 just N of Rudgwick) – OS Sheet 187 map ref 076349; TQ0934], *Thurlow Arms*: Interesting place full of paraphernalia relating largely to disused railway here, now Downs Link Path – busy summer weekends, when cyclists may turn up by the score; has had well kept real ales such as Badger, King & Barnes Broadwood and Marstons Owd Roger, good food and friendly staff, but we've not yet had reports on the new regime *(Andy and Jackie Mallpress)*

Dorking [45 West St; TQ1649], *Kings Arms*: Low half-timbered pub in antiques area, part-panelled lounge divided from bar area by timbers, back dining area, nice lived-in old furniture, warm relaxed atmosphere, good choice of home-cooked food, friendly service, six real ales inc King & Barnes; open all day *(Ian Phillips and others)*

Dormansland [High St; TQ4042], *Royal Oak*: Wide choice of good value home cooking inc unusual dishes and friendly service in pretty pub in quiet village, darts, character dogs, well kept garden; children welcome *(Lee Crozier, R and S Bentley)*

☆ **Dunsfold** [TQ0036], *Sun*: Genuine old-fashioned village-local atmosphere in elegantly symmetrical 18th-c beamed pub on attractive green, with interesting choice of good food, friendly helpful staff and well kept Allied real ales, log fires; separate cottage dining room; children welcome *(John Evans, D Sykes-Thompson, LYM)*

☆ **East Clandon** [TQ0651], *Queens Head*: Traditionally refurbished timbered pub with small connecting rooms, big inglenook log fire, fine old elm bar counter, bookcases, pictures, copperware, relaxed atmosphere; good choice of reasonably priced bar food, well kept ales, no lunchtime piped music; some tables outside *(P J Keen, J S Evans, Dr R B Crail, A Monte, G B Longden, M L Clarke, LYM)*

East Molesey [Bell Rd; TQ1267], *Bell*:

Masses of character in 15th-c beamed pub, stables still in use; antique surroundings, pleasant helpful staff, limited food; machines in left-hand area; big garden *(J S M Sheldon, Ian Phillips)*

☆ **Effingham** [Orestan Lane; TQ1253], *Plough*: Good value imaginative home cooking and efficient staff in civilised local with two coal-effect gas fires, beamery, panelling, old plates and brassware in long lounge, no-smoking extension, well kept Youngs; popular with older people – no dogs, children or sleeveless T-shirts inside, tables in nice garden with play area; convenient for Polesdon Lacey *(WFL, M G Hart, Mr and Mrs David Cure, John Evans, John Pettit, A Pickup, Mr and Mrs R J Foreman)*

Egham [34 Middle Hill; TQ0171], *Beehive*: Small, very friendly and often busy, with half a dozen well kept real ales, attractive food, nice garden *(Ian Phillips)*; [Egham Hill, A30 by roundabout], *Eclipse*: Recently smartly redecorated and modernised throughout, very pleasant L-shaped bar area, warm welcome, various real ales; bedrooms *(Mayur Shah)*

☆ **Englefield Green** [Bishopsgate Rd; SU9970], *Fox & Hounds*: Superb setting backing on to riding stables on edge of Windsor Great Park, short walk from Savile Garden, tables on pleasant front lawn and back terrace; wide choice of good food inc really good filled baguettes served in the bar, tantalising choice of freshly cooked dishes with al dente veg in candlelit dining room; friendly service, children welcome *(Caroline Raphael, Ian Phillips, Julian Bessa)*

Englefield Green [Northcroft Rd], *Barley Mow*: Very pleasant Chef & Brewer with good range of food (though no sandwiches), efficient service, lovely setting facing green, quiet secluded garden behind *(Shirley Pielou)*

Epsom [on green; TQ2160], *Cricketers*: Lovely setting, with canada geese on pond, by common with good walks; picnic-table sets outside; busy, popular food *(Romey Heaton, J S M Sheldon)*; *Tattenham Corner*: Big pub-restaurant next to racecourse, full even on a cold, wet weekday lunchtime; prompt friendly service *(E G Parish)*

Esher [71 High St; TQ1464], *Bear*: Spacious, smartly furnished and well ordered, with really good fresh food, good choice of beers *(David Logan)*

Ewell [High St; TQ2262], *Green Man*: Comfortable two-bar pub with good value bar food from sandwiches to char-grilled steaks; well kept beers, quiet piped music, darts, fruit machines; handy for riverside walks *(John Pettit)*

Ewhurst [Pitch Hill; a mile N of village on Shere rd; TQ0940], *Windmill*: Spacious series of hillside lawns give lovely views, as does conservatory restaurant; smart modern bar behind with decent but expensive snacks inc sandwiches and well kept ale such as Wadworths 6X, may sometimes be short-staffed; lovely walking country *(Belinda and Michael Lee-Jones, Alex and Beryl Williams, Jenny and Brian Seller, LYM)*

☆ **Farleigh** [Farleigh Common; on bus route 403 from Croydon; TQ3659], *Harrow:* Homely atmosphere in former barn with stripped-flint brickwork, rustic decoration inc farm tools and other bric-a-brac, even an owl high in the rafters; good lunchtime food from sandwiches up (not Sun), raised no-smoking area, well kept Bass, cheerful staff; separate locals' bar, tables on big lawn with pasture behind; popular with younger people evening *(Graham Pettener, Jean Bercelli, W J Wonham)*

☆ **Farncombe** [signed from Catteshall industrial estate on outskirts of Godalming beyond Sainsburys; SU9844], *Ram:* Attractive 16th-c timbered white pub in charming setting, huge carved wooden ram in big shaded garden through which stream runs, with lots of swings, slides and climbing frames, pretty flowered terrace and barbecue; three separate bars with coal-effect fires in old brick hearths, parquet floors, heavy beams, lots of fabric-covered pews, interesting choice of food lunchtime and evening inc good ploughman's, 23 varieties of cider, Fullers London Pride, very friendly staff, country wines inc sparkling apple, strange mixed drinks *(Giles Quick, Linda Adams)*

Farnham [Long Garden Walk; SU8446], *Hop Blossom:* Entertainingly idiosyncratic, with character landlord, well kept beer, good food, eclectic piped music *(Anna Marsh)*; [Tilford Rd, Lower Bourne; SU8544], *Spotted Cow:* Due for refurbishment, but wide choice of good food, well kept Courage-related and guest ales, decent wine, attentive friendly service, reasonable prices; play area in big garden *(Mr and Mrs R J Foreman)*; [Bridge Sq], *William Cobbett:* Cobbett's picturesque birthplace, low-beamed and dim-lit; popular with young people, friendly and welcoming, good range of food and drinks *(Philip Puddock, LYM)*

☆ **Felbridge** [Woodcock Hill – A22 N; TQ3639], *Woodcock:* Very interesting place, with busy flagstoned bar opening on to richly furnished room a bit like a film props department, spiral stairs up to another opulent room, candlelit and almost boudoirish, nice small Victorian dining room off; also roomy restaurant specialising (like the good bar food) in fresh seafood; well kept Harveys, Ringwood Old Thumper, Charles Wells Bombardier, piped music (can be loud and late), relaxed atmosphere – service can be very leisurely; children in eating area, open all day, some tables outside; bedrooms *(J E Lloyd, Chris and Anne Fluck, Rita Horridge, John and Janet Wigley, LYM)*

☆ **Fickleshole** [Featherbed Lane; off A2022

Purley Rd just S of A212 roundabout; TQ3860], *White Bear:* Rambling interestingly furnished partly 15th-c family country pub with lots of small rooms, well kept ales such as Felinfoel and Fullers, bar food, fruit machine, video game, piped music; children welcome, jazz Weds, open all day Sat; play area in sizeable garden *(Dave Lands, J S M Sheldon, Brian Hutton, Jenny and Brian Seller, G S B G Dudley, LYM)*

☆ **Forest Green** [nr B2126/B2127 junction; TQ1240], *Parrot:* All sorts of parrot designs in nicely placed rambling and quaint country pub with well kept Courage ales, good often interesting food (many tables reserved, giving it something of a restaurant feel in the evening), good cheerful service even when crowded; children welcome, open all day; plenty of space outside by cricket pitch, good walks nearby *(Brian Hutton, P Gillbe, Dr R B Crail, Peter Locke, Peter Fraser, LYM)*

☆ **Friday Street** [TQ1245], *Stephen Langton:* Country local behind cottages in secluded valley below Leith Hill (good walks), rather pricy usual food with real chips (no sandwiches), good log fire, attractive prints, welcoming service, Charrington IPA and Youngs, popular restaurant; bar lavatories down steps outside *(Martin G Richards, Dick Brown)*

☆ **Godalming** [Ockford Rd, junction Portsmouth Rd (A3100) and Shackstead Lane; SU9743], *Inn on the Lake:* Cosy and comfortable family bar with well presented reasonably priced bar food inc vegetarian, well kept Whitbreads-related and guest real ales, decent wines, log fire and friendly staff; elegant restaurant with indoor fishpond and grand piano, good choice of wines; tables out in lovely garden overlooking lake, summer barbecues; rather steep car park; bedrooms *(Ian Phillips)*

Godalming [High St (A3100)], *Kings Arms & Royal:* Good food and obliging service in friendly series of partitioned rooms in 18th-c coaching inn; the Tsar's Lounge is worth seeing if it's not booked for a funtion; bedrooms *(John and Joan Wyatt, BB)*; [off to right of top end of High St], *Rose & Crown:* Lovely old pub full of character with listed cellar – old bakery ovens still in situ; well kept Courage-related ales, good choice of sandwiches, unusual main dishes *(Anna Marsh)*

Godstone [128 High St; under a mile from M25 junction 6, via B2236; TQ3551], *Bell:* Spacious beamed and partly panelled main bar, big fires each end, character seats, also smaller timbered bar set out with bright check tablecloths like a Caribbean café; Allied real ales, restaurant (newish owners plan expansion of the food side), obliging service; good garden for children; Imaginatively decorated bedrooms in ancient core *(Dr C A Brace, E G Parish, LYM)*; [A25 towards Bletchingley], *Hare & Hounds:* Good food pub with wide choice, nice atmosphere *(Gordon Smith)*

☆ **Gomshall** [Station Rd (A25); TQ0847], *Compasses*: Well kept Gibbs Mew Bishops Tipple and Wiltshire and bar food from sandwiches and ploughman's to Sun roast in clean, cheerful and attractive pub with good staff; pleasant garden over duck stream with abundant weeping willows; walkers welcome *(Jenny and Brian Seller)*

Grayswood [A286 NE of Haslemere; SU9234], *Wheatsheaf*: Doing well under current owners, with well kept beers, friendly welcome, emphasis on food from good substantial sandwiches to generous roasts; bedrooms now *(Mr and Mrs R Halliday, Paula Harrison)*

Guildford [across car park from Yvonne Arnaud Theatre, beyond boat yard; SU9949], *Jolly Farmer*: Lovely setting esp in summer when can sit by the river, decent food *(D J and P M Taylor)*; [Trinity Churchyard], *Royal Oak*: Small Chef & Brewer pub tucked behind church, reasonably priced food inc triple decker sandwiches, Courage-related beers *(Ian Phillips)*; [46 Chertsey St], *Spread Eagle*: Lively town local with well kept Courage-related and changing guest beers, imaginative range of reasonably priced lunchtime food *(Phil and Sally Gorton, Anna Marsh)*; [2 Quarry St], *Star*: Modernised split-level pub with bric-a-brac, some interesting woodwork, reasonable food; popular with younger people, open all day *(Ian Phillips, Chris and Anne Fluck)*

Hersham [6 Queens Rd; TQ1164], *Bricklayers Arms*: Friendly atmosphere in well kept and clean pub, bigger than it looks, with good value genuinely home-cooked bar food, decent wines *(Ian and Liz Phillips)*

Holmbury St Mary [TQ1144], *Kings Head*: Food worth waiting for, well kept Ringwood Best and Fortyniner and local cider in friendly and cosy pub, popular weekends with walkers and cyclists; tables facing sloping back garden *(Jenny and Brian Seller, Andy Stone, Tom and Rosemary Hall)*

☆ **Horley** [Church Rd; quite handy for M23 junction 9, off Horley turn from A23; TQ2842], *Olde Six Bells*: Friendly unpretentious modernised town local notable for surviving signs of antiquity – not just heavy beams and timbers, but even traces of medieval chapel in one corner; Bass and Charrington IPA, open all day weekdays; children in raftered upstairs restaurant, conservatory *(J S M Sheldon, LYM)*

Horsell [Horsell Birch; SU9859], *Cricketers*: Fine setting, spacious well kept gardens a big draw in summer, with barbecues; wide choice of reasonably priced food inc Sun lunch, range of beers, friendly atmosphere *(Mr and Mrs D Lockwood, Mr and Mrs G Evans)*; SU9959], *Red Lion*: Well renovated, with good helpings of cheap food, warm welcome, pleasant

terrace (on wet days children can sit in picture-filled converted barn); good walks nearby *(A J Blackler, Ian Phillips)*; [The Anthonys, Horsell Common; Chertsey Rd (A320 Woking—Ottershaw)], *Bleak House*: Pleasant, friendly and comfortable pub opp good walks to the sandpits which inspired H G Wells's *War of the Worlds;* decent food, real ales, picnic-table sets and barbecues on back lawn *(Ian Phillips)*

Irons Bottom [Sidlow Bridge; off A217 – OS Sheet 187 map ref 250460; TQ2546], *Three Horseshoes*: Isolated but popular free house with five or six excellently kept real ales, good choice of well served decent food, rather sophisticated style *(Roger Byrne, Brian and Jenny Seller, Don Mather)*

☆ **Kenley** [Old Lodge Lane; left (coming from London) off A23 by Reedham Stn, then keep on; TQ3259], *Wattenden Arms*: Popular dark-panelled traditional country local nr glider aerodrome, well kept Bass and Charrington IPA, lunchtime bar food, prompt service, crisp-loving cat, patriotic and WWII memorabilia, seats on small side lawn; actually just inside London, but by long tradition we list it under Surrey *(Jenny and Brian Seller, Michael Wadsworth, B B Morgan, LYM)*

Kingswood [Waterhouse Lane; TQ2455], *Kingswood Arms*: Spacious and busy pub with airy conservatory dining extension, quick service, Courage-related ales, straightforward food; massive rolling garden with play area *(DWAJ)*

Laleham [The Broadway; TQ0568], *Feathers*: Reasonably priced generous straightforward food from well filled baps up, pub done up in traditional style, lots of hanging pewter mugs, beamed dining lounge, piped music, well kept Courage and guest beers, tables outside *(Ian Phillips, George Atkinson)*; [Broadway], *Turks Head*: Comfortable, busy and very welcoming, affordable well presented bar food, several real ales, various nooks and crannies, plenty of tables *(Ian Phillips)*

☆ **Leatherhead** [Chessington Rd; A243 nr M25 junction 9 – OS Sheet 187 map ref 167600; TQ1656], *Star*: Good choice of generous food inc good specials in friendly pub with good landlord, nice waitress service, log fire, well kept King & Barnes and Courage-related ales *(John Pettit, Ian Phillips, J S M Sheldon)*

Leatherhead [57 High St], *Dukes Head*: Busy and friendly, small front bar with pool and games machine leading to beamed, timbered and carpeted main bar with open fire and polished tables, steps to food servery and more seating; good range of bar food, good generous coffee; piped music; in pedestrianised street, convenient for good riverside walks *(John Pettit)*

☆ **Leigh** [S of A25 Dorking—Reigate; TQ2246], *Seven Stars*: Pretty country local with friendly landlord, bar food all week, Allied ales, inglenook fireplace, horse-racing pictures, darts alley in public bar;

flower-filled garden, maybe summer Sun barbecues; no children *(Derek and Maggie Washington, LYM)*

Lower Kingswood [Brighton Rd; A217, 1½ miles from M25 junction 8; TQ2453], *Fox*: Pleasantly decorated, with Allied real ales, decent coffee, friendly staff, good bar food; garden with bouncy castle, handy for Gatwick Airport; bedrooms *(Sir Simon Tilden)*

Lyne [Lyne Lane; TQ0166], *Royal Marine*: Limited but interesting choice of good reasonably priced unpretentious home cooking in small, friendly and cosy pub, neat as a new pin *(Clem Stephens, Ian Phillips)*

☆ **Martyrs Green** [Old Lane, handy for M25 junction 10 – off A3 S-bound, but return N of junction; TQ0957], *Black Swan*: Extensively enlarged, with simple furnishings, very good range of real ales, good service, generous if not cheap bar food, good restaurant, log fire; can get crowded with young people evenings, piped pop music may be loud then; open through afternoon (happy hour from 3), tables in woodside garden with play area; attractive setting, handy for RHS Wisley Garden *(M Owton, John Pettit, WFL)*

☆ **Merstham** [Nutfield Rd; off A23 in Merstham, or follow Nutfield Ch, Merstham 2 signpost off A25 E of Redhill – OS Sheet 187 map ref 303515; TQ3051], *Inn on the Pond*: Interestingly furnished rambling country local with good choice of bar food inc good vegetarian dishes (roast only, Sun), half a dozen well kept interesting ales, decent coffee, good service, piped radio; family conservatory, sheltered back terrace, views over scrubland (and small pond and nearby cricket ground) to N Downs *(Al Blue, Mrs G M E Farwell, BB)*

☆ **Mickleham** [Old London Rd; TQ1753], *Running Horses*: 16th-c beamed village pub attractively placed nr Box Hill, nice view from pretty courtyard garden; refurbished bars, new restaurant, wide choice of food, conservatory, well kept Allied real ales, two open fires, good clientele *(John Pettit, Ian Phillips)*

☆ **Mogador** [from M25 up A217 past 2nd roundabout, signed off; TQ2452], *Sportsman*: Interesting and welcoming low-ceilinged local said to date from 1500, though present building seems 18th c; currently doing well, with well kept Courage-related and a guest ale, good if not cheap food (bookable tables), darts, bar billiards; dogs welcome if not wet or muddy; tables out on common, on back lawn, and some under cover – quiet setting by Banstead Heath, popular with walkers and riders *(Al Blue, Jenny and Brian Seller, Owen Upton, W A Evershed)*

New Chapel [TQ3642], *Blacksmiths Head*: Fine old pub with nice atmosphere, good food, well kept beer *(J S M Sheldon)*

Newdigate [TQ2042], *Six Bells*: Popular local doing well under new management, good choice of usual food *(J and M Ratcliff)*; [Parkgate Rd – A24 S of Dorking, then left through Beare Green, first left fork after that], *Surrey Oaks*: Interesting layout, rustic lantern-lit booth seating off flagstoned beamed core with big log fire; good big garden with rockery and water feature; usual bar food, Sun carvery, Allied ales, games area; children welcome; new landlord *(K D and C M Bailey, LYM)*

Normandy [Guildford Rd E; SU9251], *Duke of Normandy*: Tasty home-made food, friendly helpful licensees, efficient service *(R Lake)*

☆ **Norwood Hill** [Leigh—Charlwood back rd; TQ2343], *Fox Revived*: Attractive cottagey old-fashioned furnishings in spacious bareboards country pub with big double conservatory and spreading garden; under previous tenants has been very popular for good value food, well kept real ales and decent wines, with a pleasant atmosphere and good service, but now taken back into Allied management – we've not yet had reports on the results *(LYM)*

Ockley [Stane St (A29); TQ1439], *Kings Arms*: Good generous food and well kept Fullers and Youngs in smart country pub with small restaurant *(Tom and Rosemary Hall)*; *Old School House*: Good value food, huge helpings, in bar and restaurant, specialises in good fresh fish; very friendly service, good wines, wonderful log fire *(Mrs R Maxwell)*

☆ **nr Ockley** [Oakwoodhill – signed off A29 S; TQ1337], *Punch Bowl*: Friendly, welcoming and cosy country pub with two bars and restaurant section; huge inglenook log fire, polished flagstones, lots of beams, Badger Best and Tanglefoot, Wadworths 6X, lots of traditional games, juke box (can be loud), decent bar food; children allowed in dining area, maybe weekend barbecues; can be quite a squash on winter Sun lunchtime; has been open all day *(DB, J S M Sheldon, LYM)*

☆ **Ottershaw** [222 Brox Rd; TQ0263], *Castle*: Comfortable and attractive recently extended pub popular for business lunches, good but not inexpensive bar menu, well kept changing Allied and other real ales, friendly, with profusion of agricultural and horticultural memorabilia among the mock beams and bare brick walls; open fire, no-smoking dining area; garden with tables in pleasant creeper-hung arbour *(Ian Phillips, Andy Giles, Martin Richards)*

☆ **Outwood** [off A23 S of Redhill; TQ3245], *Bell*: Fine view from country dining pub's well kept attractive garden, summer cream teas, good choice of well kept ales, children welcome; indoor barbecues, wide choice of food which can be eaten in bar or restaurant; has been open all day *(Mayur Shah, J G Smith, R and S Bentley, LYM)*

Outwood [Millers Lane], *Castle*: Friendly recently extended pub with good food and garden *(Mr and Mrs A L Budden)*

Oxshott [Leatherhead Rd (A244); TQ1460], *Bear*: Well kept beer, cheerful pleasant staff, occasional barbecues in small back garden; no music *(Richard Payne)*

☆ **Oxted** [High St, Old Oxted;TQ3951], *George*: Quiet and relaxing, with comfortable furnishings, attractive prints, wide choice of good generous food all day inc steaks cut to order in busy restaurant area, efficient friendly staff, no games or piped music, half a dozen well kept ales; tables outside *(Mrs P Harris, David and Michelle Hedges, Susan and Alan Buckland, Maureen and Keith Gimson, J S M Sheldon)*

☆ **Oxted** [High St, Old Oxted], *Crown*: Good choice of well kept ales and wide choice of good value food in stylish Elizabethan pub with classic Victorian panelling in upper dining bar; friendly efficient staff; can get crowded downstairs with young people and loud music evenings; children welcome weekends *(John Ingham)*

Pirbright [The Green; SU9455], *Cricketers*: Friendly welcome, pleasant service and food simple but nicely served, inc proper chips; well kept Ind Coope Burtons *(I D and W McCaw)*

Poyle [Poyle Rd; TQ0375], *Golden Cross*: Cosy and friendly, well kept Courage ales; quite handy for M25 and Terminal 4, Heathrow *(Dr and Mrs A K Clarke)*

☆ **Ranmore Common** [3 miles S of Effingham; TQ1451], *Ranmore Arms*: Lots of picnic-table sets and barbecues on terrace outside unusual building as if once café or bungalow, exceptional play area with wonderful play houses; olde-worlde inside, big log fire, quick service, decent bar snacks, well kept Courage-related ales *(Romey Heaton, WFL)*

☆ **Redhill** [St Johns; TQ2650], *Plough*: Small welcoming old-fashioned pub with interesting bric-a-brac, open fires, well kept Allied ales, reasonably priced food inc vegetarian, friendly efficient staff *(Andy and Jill Kassube)*

Redhill [Hatchlands Corner], *Hatch*: Interesting decor, good service, wide choice of country wines and real ales, four or five weekly changing guests *(Dave Snow, Maggie Stableford, David and Michelle Hedges)*

Reigate [High St; TQ2550], *Market*: Newly opened and quite smart, with good food inc good steak sandwiches, interesting choice of regularly changing real ales; open all day *(Owen Upton)*

Reigate Heath [A25; TQ2349], *Black Horse*: Clean and friendly with good unusual choice of inexpensive bar food, good service *(J J Booth)*

☆ **Ripley** [High St; TQ0556], *Half Moon*: Pleasant down-to-earth local with good atmosphere suiting the fine choice of changing real ales such as Boddingtons, Brakspears SB, Hogs Back TEA, Ringwood Fortyniner and Shepherd Neame Spitfire, darts, fruit machines, piped music not too loud; reasonably priced bar food, enormous friendly irish wolfhound *(Mike Davies, Ian Phillips, Alan and Maggie Telford)*

☆ **Ripley** [High St; TQ0556], *Ship*: Welcoming 16th-c local with wide choice of reasonably priced lunchtime bar food from sandwiches up, well kept Courage-related beers, low beams, flagstones, cosy nooks, window seats and log fire in vast inglenook; efficient service, small raised games area with bar billiards; small courtyard garden *(Stephen Barney, Ian Phillips)*

Runfold [B3000, off A31 just E of Farnham; SU8747], *Jolly Farmer*: Popular bar food, well kept Courage-related ales, pleasant garden with good adventure playground – nice retreat from trunk rd; children in restaurant, no dogs *(Dr and Mrs A K Clarke, LYM)*

Send [Cartbridge; TQ0155], *New Inn*: Charmingly placed by canal, cheerful staff (ditto landlord's children), decent bar food; piped music may be a bit loud *(Ian Phillips)*

Sendmarsh [Marsh Rd; TQ0454], *Saddlers Arms*: Good welcoming local with well kept Allied ales, good reasonably priced food, notable Christmas decorations *(Ian Phillips)*

Shalford [Broadguard Rd; TQ0047], *Parrot*: Very clean bar and restaurant, ample helpings of tasty good value food, friendly helpful staff *(Mrs H M T Carpenter)*; [The Street (A281 S of Guildford)], *Sea Horse*: Gales pub with well kept beer, good country wines, good range of reasonably priced food, friendly service; has had free drink if food ordered before 12.30 *(Dr R B Crail, Peter Locke, Peter Fraser)*

☆ **Shepperton** [Church Sq (off B375); TQ0867], *Kings Head*: Immaculately kept old pub in quiet and attractive square, inglenook fireplace, neat panelling, oak beams, highly polished floors and furnishings, various discreet little rooms, big conservatory extension with removable walls for summer; good value unpretentious bar food, well kept Courage-related and other ales, attentive service, sheltered back terrace; children welcome, open all day Sat *(Ian Phillips, Ron Corbett, John and Christine Simpson, LYM)*

☆ **Shepperton** [Russell Rd], *Red Lion*: Attractive old wisteria-covered pub in nice spot by Thames, plenty of tables on terrace among fine displays of shrubs and flowers, more on lawn over road with lovely river views and well run moorings; quick bar food, well kept Courage-related ales with a guest such as Fullers London Pride, restaurant, charming staff *(Phil Russell, David Sweeney)*

☆ **Shepperton** [152 Laleham Rd], *Bull*: Small friendly unassuming local with good simple food at sensible prices inc bookable Sun lunch, well kept beers; live music some nights; bedrooms with own bathrooms *(Ron Corbett, David Sweeney)*

Shepperton [Shepperton Lock, Ferry Lane

(off B375)], *Thames Court*: Busy 1930s pub with striking upper gallery overlooking Thames and moorings; quiet nooks and corners in low-lit lower panelled bar, roomy mezzanine, well kept Bass and Flowers IPA, bar food, children in eating area; popular with older people lunchtime, pleasant service, seats out under willow by water, more in big side garden *(Ron Corbett, P M Addison)*

☆ **South Godstone** [Tilburstow Hill Rd; TQ3648], *Fox & Hounds*: Consistently good low-beamed pub, cosy, friendly and comfortable, with welcoming staff, well kept Greene King, good generous reasonably priced bar food, old prints, some high-backed settles, relaxing garden *(BHP, Graham Pettener)*

☆ **Staines** [124 Church St; TQ0471], *Bells*: Reliably welcoming, with wide choice of consistently good value simple food – very popular with businessmen at lunchtime; attractive, with central fireplace, well kept Courage ales, darts and cribbage; plenty of seats in big garden *(Ian Phillips)*

☆ **Staines** [The Hythe; S bank, over Staines Bridge;], *Swan*: Splendidly set hotel on banks of Thames, well kept Fullers beers, friendly helpful staff, tables on pleasant riverside verandah, conservatory, good value food in bar and restaurant; moorings; bedrooms comfortable *(George Atkinson, M P Naworynsky, Martin Kay, Andrea Fowler, LYM)*

Staines [Leacroft], *Old Red Lion*: New young managers in clean, warm and welcoming pub with well cooked simple food, good atmosphere and service; seats outside, pretty spot by village green *(Ron and Sheila Corbett)*; [Moor Lane – different from the other Swan here], *Swan*: Welcoming pub on green, seeming deep in country, with lots of real ales such as Boddingtons, Camerons, Eldridge Pope Thomas Hardy, Wadworths 6X, good range of decent bar food, good garden with lots of picnic-table sets and big aviary *(Ian Phillips)*

☆ **Stoke Dabernon** [Station Rd; off A245; TQ1259], *Plough*: Homely and comfortable, with reasonably priced sensible bar food in airy conservatory, well kept Courage-related ales, big window seats, coal fire, helpful staff, sizeable garden *(Al Blue, BB)*

Sutton [B2126 – this is the Sutton near Abinger; TQ1046], *Volunteer*: Attractive good-sized terraced garden in lovely quiet setting, low-beamed traditional bar with bric-a-brac and military paintings, Allied and Courage-related ales, decent wines inc port, fast bar food *(Dr R B Crail, David Hedges)*

Sutton Green [Sutton Green Rd; TQ0054], *Fox & Hounds*: Attractive, cheerful and friendly, with good food and service, good value buffet, well kept Allied ales; restaurant more expensive but exceptionally good choice, reduced meal prices 5.30-7 *(Clem Stephens)*

Tadworth [Box Hill Rd; TQ2256], *Hand in Hand*: Well kept Courage, good simple bar food inc Sun lunch and friendly service in roomy extended country pub, big sheltered garden; handy for Box Hill *(John Pettit)*

☆ **Tandridge** [TQ3750], *Barley Mow*: Well managed free house with pleasant atmosphere, cheerful service, wide choice of beers, good choice of wines and food at reasonable prices, nice bar, separate restaurant, big garden; interesting church nearby, good walks to Oxted or Godstone *(W J Wonham, Mrs C S Clarke)*

☆ **Tandridge** [Tandridge Lane, off A25 W of Oxted], *Brickmakers Arms*: Good atmosphere in popular country dining pub, dating to 15th c but much extended and modernised, with wide choice of above-average food inc some German dishes and lots of fish (no cold snacks Sun), good range of well kept Whitbreads-related real ales, decent wines inc local ones, restaurant with good log fires, prompt friendly service *(Sir Simon Tilden, Mark and Nicola Willoughby, Mrs C S Clarke, Gordon Smith, Tamzie and Duncan Hollands, D and K Pinks)*

☆ **Thursley** [just off A3 SW of Godalming; SU9039], *Three Horseshoes*: Dark and cosy country pub with lovingly polished furniture, two good log fires, well kept Gales HSB and BBB, country wines, well presented if not cheap lunchtime food from sandwiches up inc good home-cooked soups and hot dishes (may be more limited evening), friendly landlord, tables in attractive back garden, with barbecues; restaurant; has been open all day Sat *(Doug Kennedy, Brenda Laing, Robert Sherriff, LYM)*

☆ **Tilford** [SU8743], *Barley Mow*: Idyllic setting between river and geese-cropped cricket green nr ancient oak, with waterside garden; decent mainly home-made food esp puddings, good welcoming service, well kept Courage ales, good open fire in big inglenook, comfortable traditional seats around scrubbed tables, interesting prints; small back eating area, weekend afternoon teas; darts, table skittles *(Lyn and Bill Capper, Mr and Mrs Williams, Jenny and Brian Seller, Tim Galligan)*

Upper Hale [just N of Farnham; SU8348], *Black Prince*: Good Fullers pub *(Martin Kay, Andrea Fowler)*

Upper Halliford [TQ0968], *Bugle*: Radically refurbished as Courage Trencherman dining pub, decent food, Best on handpump, attentive landlord; lively Fri night with trad jazz *(David Sweeney)*

Virginia Water [Trumps Green Rd; TQ0067], *Crown*: Chalet-bungalow-style pub, big garden with lots of tables, cheery landlord and wife, decent specials, Allied ales, roaring log fire *(Ian Phillips)*; [Christchurch Rd (B389) – formerly the Trottesworth], *Dog & Fireside*: Big lively young people's place, scrubbed tables, some sofas at one end, several real ales such as Morlands Old Speckled Hen and Wadworths 6X, decent wine; quiz nights, live music, tables outside *(Dr M Owton)*; [Callow Hill], *Rose & Olive Branch*: Comfortable Morlands pub with guest beer such as Theakstons, popular lunchtime for good range of interesting genuinely home-cooked food; friendly helpful service *(Ian Phillips, G B Longden)*

☆ **Walton on Thames** [50 Manor Rd; off A3050; TQ1066], *Swan*: Big riverside Youngs pub with lots of interconnecting rooms, huge garden on many levels overlooking Thames, well spread out and kept neat and tidy (shame about the loudspeaker food announcements), attractive restaurant, good generous food cooked to order, well kept ales, friendly service; moorings, riverside walks *(Mayur Shah, Richard Houghton, Ian Phillips, John and Christine Simpson)*

Walton on Thames [Riverside, off Manor Rd], *Anglers Tavern*: Unassuming ordinary pub mentioned for peaceful spot right by river, some tables across front track next to moored boats – peaceful; boat hire next door *(Mayur Shah)*; [Sunbury Lane], *Weir*: Interesting all-wood decor with masses of pictures, ceiling fans etc; overlooking river, moorings, inexpensive lunches, pleasant staff; busy summer *(Roger Taylor, Christine and Geoff Butler)*

☆ **Walton on the Hill** [Deans Lane; 3 miles from M25 junction 8; TQ2255], *Blue Ball*: Recently cosily refurbished and well managed, with some concentration on decent well priced food inc evening meals and theme nights, wide choice from sausage sandwich to alligator steak; good atmosphere, smart staff, five Courage-related and other ales, decent New World wines, big garden with barbecue; restaurant open all day Sun *(Sir Simon Tilden, Gordon Smith, A P Steer, D and B Thomas, Mr and Mrs D Thomas, A J Blunden)*

☆ **Walton on the Hill** [Chequers Lane], *Chequers*: Pleasant mock-Tudor Youngs pub with several rooms rambling around central servery, well kept ales, good value quick lunchtime bar food, restaurant (children allowed here), friendly service, terrace and neat sheltered garden with good summer barbecues; evenings busy with younger people; trad jazz Thurs *(Ian Phillips, LYM)*

Warlingham [Limpsfield Rd; TQ3658], *Botley Hill Farmhouse:* Newly converted from old farmhouse, wonderful views over North Downs, good walking country; ales (not cheap) inc Boddingtons, Flowers, Greene King, Pilgrims and Shepherd Neame, good changing bar food, good value restaurant *(D and J Tapper)*

☆ **West Clandon** [The Street; TQ0452], *Bulls Head*: Welcoming and spotless comfortably modernised country local with genial landlord, varied food in small raised inglenook dining area, bookable Sun lunch, Courage ales, decent wine, good waitress service, lantern-lit bar with another open fire and some stripped brick, old local prints, separate darts and pool areas; picnic-table sets in garden, convenient for Clandon Park, good walking country *(D P and J A Sweeney, Ian Phillips, John Pettit, DWAJ, A E and P McCully)*

West Horsley [TQ0753], *Barley Mow*: Good village local, well kept beers, decent wines and spirits, lunchtime food, small restaurant *(John and Heather Dwane)*; [The Street], *King William IV*: Comfortable seating, relaxing atmosphere with helpful and friendly staff, evening carvery, useful bar food, very low beams and door *(John Pettit)*

☆ **Westcott** [A25; TQ1448], *Crown*: Friendly busy local with attentive staff, interesting pictures and decor, lots of charity events, big helpings of freshly cooked food, good coffee, small back games room; lovely cottage garden *(S J Penford, T A Bryan)*; *Prince of Wales*: Friendly fairly modern pub, good value bar food, interesting cartoons *(Brian and Jenny Seller)*

☆ **Weybridge** [Cross Rd/Anderson Rd, off Oatlands Dr; TQ0764], *Prince of Wales*: Pretty pub, beautifully restored inside and warmly friendly, doing well under current management; good choice of reasonably priced bar food inc good home-made soup, well kept ales such as Adnams, Boddingtons, Fullers London Pride, Tetleys and Wadworths 6X, ten wines by the glass, coal-effect gas fires, imaginative restaurant menu *(James Nunns, Phil Russell, Dr R B Crail)*

Weybridge [Thames St], *Farnell Arms*: Particularly good value well cooked food inc generous roasts, well kept Badger Best and Tanglefoot and Wadworths 6X *(Dr R B Crail, Peter Locke, Peter Fraser)*; [Heath Rd], *Hand & Spear*: Lively, with unconventional atmosphere, good mix of customers, good choice of food; live jazz Sun, blues Weds *(Martin Bacon)*; [Thames St], *Lincoln Arms*: Comfortable extended pub with interesting inexpensive mix of English, Italian and Asian food; tables in garden *(Ian Phillips)*; [Thames St], *Old Crown*: Friendly straightforward waterside pub, Courage-related ales and Wadworths 6X, useful food *(Comus Elliott, Ian Phillips)*

☆ **Windlesham** [Chertsey Rd; SU9264], *Brickmakers Arms*: Popular dining pub with good interesting food in recently enlarged restaurant (well behaved children allowed here), some of these dishes also served in cheerful busy bar; well kept Courage and other ales, pleasant service, daily papers, tables in good garden with boules and barbecues *(Guy Consterdine, Mrs C A Blake, Mr and Mrs Damien Burke)*

☆ **Windlesham** [A30/B3020 junction], *Windmill*: Main attraction is bewildering array of reasonably priced well kept real ales inc unusual newcomers such as

Arundel Stronghold and Hampshire King Alfreds and Pendragon as well as better-known ones such as Brakspears, Hop Back Summer Lightning, Marstons Pedigree; largish, plain but attractively furnished, with one long bar, separate side room, welcoming atmosphere, youngish customers; friendly landlord, good range of country wines, improving range of food, unobtrusive piped music, occasional beer festivals; small front roadside terrace *(Mike Davies, Dr M Owton, Richard Houghton, Dr C P Dell)*

Windlesham [School Rd], *Bee*: Cosy Courage-related pub with darts, good range of bar food, small garden, discreet piped music *(Ian Phillips)*; [Church Rd], *Half Moon*: Lively, pleasant and friendly local, well kept real ales such as Fullers London Pride and Wadworths 6X, cheerful quick service, modern furnishings, log fires, piped music, silenced fruit machine, interesting WWII pictures; huge beautifully kept garden *(Mayur Shah, MD, Simon Collett-Jones, Dr M Owton, Mrs C A Blake)*

☆ **Wonersh** [The Street; TQ0245], *Grantley Arms*: Spacious and comfortable half-timbered 16th-c pub with good food in bar and restaurant, friendly staff *(P M Addison, Miss M Hankins)*

Wood Street [White Hart Lane; SU9550], *White Hart*: Big bar area very much set out for diners, but good changing range of well kept beers and quite a pubby atmosphere *(Richard Houghton)*

Worcester Park [Cheam Common; TQ2266], *Old Crown*: Formerly the Drill, much improved since Courage refurbishment in old farm style with beams, comfortable seating, restaurant; obligingly talkative staff, Directors, Wadworths 6X and Websters Green Label, food choice from sandwiches up inc plenty for vegetarians; garden *(John Sanders, DWAJ)*

☆ **Wotton** [A25 Dorking—Guildford; TQ1247], *Wotton Hatch*: Interesting well cooked food in bar, family restaurant, conservatory or garden with play area and impressive views towards Ranmore; well kept Fullers, friendly staff, decent wines, open fire in pleasantly traditional little low-ceilinged front bar, traditional games in central locals' bar *(Gwen and Peter Andrews, LYM)*

People don't usually tip bar staff (unlike in a really smart hotel). If you want to thank a barman – dealing with a really large party say, or special friendliness – offer him a drink. Common expressions are: 'And what's yours?' or 'And won't you have something for yourself?'.

Sussex

Good news here is that work to make good the fire damage to the Blackboys
Inn at Blackboys has been completed remarkably quickly – a good restoration
of what's always been one of the county's nicest pubs, so it can again take its
place among the main entries. Three other pubs which have been coming on
strongly recently, and this year join the main entries, are the very friendly old-
fashioned White Harte in Cuckfield, the Tiger in its lovely setting on the green
at Eastdean (much improved since it was last in these pages, and now
particularly good for wines), and the grand old Middle House in Mayfield.
Other pubs doing particularly well here at the moment include the welcoming
and traditional Rose Cottage at Alciston (good home cooking), the cheery and
lively Six Bells at Chiddingly, the friendly Old House At Home at Chidham,
the Elsted Inn at Elsted (excellent home cooking relying heavily on local
produce), the lovely old Juggs at Kingston near Lewes, the impressively well
run Halfway Bridge near Lodsworth, the bustling Golden Galleon near
Seaford (its Italian landlord now brews his own beer), the friendly old Bull at
Ticehurst (now The Good Pub Guide's local – and not just because it has the
cheapest beers we've found in the county this year) and the unpretentious
Richmond Arms at West Ashling. Almost all of these have qualified for our
new Beer Award; indeed, we have been struck by the very high proportion of
Sussex pubs which do. The county has two good local breweries, Harveys and
King & Barnes, which no doubt helps; and it has many old-school landlords
who are careful to keep their pubs the way they used to be – which seems
almost a guarantee of high beer quality, as at the Blue Ship near Billingshurst,
the Three Horseshoes at Elsted, the Three Cups near Punnetts Town and the
Royal Oak at Wineham. If part of our job is to record the things that happily
don't change, another is to point up the things that are new: a good new
manager for the fine old Star in Alfriston, the extended restaurant working
well at the Fountain at Ashurst, a vegetarian chef at the Cricketers in Brighton,
a new manager at the pretty Bell in Burwash, the friendly licensees who took
over the Black Horse at Byworth settling in really well, as are those who took
on the Merrie Harriers at Cowbeech, encouraging reports on the food under a
new regime at the Bull in Ditchling, new licensees for the Gribble at Oving,
the Chequers at Rowhook and the New Inn at Winchelsea, and a wider choice
of food, particularly seafood, at the tucked-away Crab & Lobster at
Sidlesham. In Sussex both drinks and food prices are markedly higher than the
national average. A pint of beer tends to cost 10p or 15p over the odds here,
and a good main dish is likely to set you back over £5 – but you can take some
comfort from the fact that pub food prices tend to be even higher in
neighbouring Hants and Kent. And there is a lot of good pub food here,
particularly at the Rose Cottage at Alciston, the Elsted Inn, the Griffin at
Fletching, the Half Moon at Kirdford (when it has fresh fish), and the rather
restauranty Crabtree at Lower Beeding. This year we choose the Crabtree as
Sussex Dining Pub of the Year, for Jeremy Ashpool's excellent inventive
cooking. In the Lucky Dip section at the end of the chapter, pubs we'd
currently draw special attention to include the Market Cross in Alfriston,
Black Horse at Amberley, Gardeners Arms at Ardingly, Cricketers at Berwick,
White Horse at Bodle Street Green, George & Dragon near Coolham, Old

Vine at Cousleywood, Lamb in Eastbourne, Foresters Arms at Fairwarp, Red Lion in Fernhurst, Swan at Fittleworth, Gallipot in Hartfield, Bent Arms in Lindfield, Plough & Harrow at Litlington, Sussex Ox at Milton Street, Hope in Newhaven, Jack Fullers at Oxleys Green, Lamb at Ripe, Sloop near Scaynes Hill, White Hart at Selsfield, Peacock at Shortbridge, Hare & Hounds at Stoughton, White Horse at Sutton, Horse Guards at Tillington, Crown at Turners Hill and Lamb near West Wittering; as we have inspected the great majority of these we can vouch for their quality.

ALCISTON TQ5005 Map 3

Rose Cottage 🍽

Village signposted off A27 Polegate—Lewes

A once-common Sussex custom now lives on only at this rustic little wisteria-covered cottage, where every Good Friday lunchtime you can still see locals long-rope skipping to make the crops grow faster. As this suggests it's a warmly traditional place, and the pub's genuinely old-fashioned charm has made it a real favourite with some readers. Small and cosy, it soon fills up, so get there early for one of the half-dozen tables with their cushioned pews in the relaxed and friendly bar – under quite a forest of harness, traps, a thatcher's blade and lots of other black ironware, with more bric-a-brac on the shelves above the dark pine dado or in the etched glass windows. In the mornings you may also find Jasper, the talking parrot. Most people come for the very good promptly served food, which includes wholesome soup, ploughman's (£3.50), ham and egg (£4.25), big salads (from £4.50, prawn with avocado £6.80), excellent home-made pies or vegetarian quiches (£4.50), specials like lasagne (£4.95), barbecue spare ribs (£5.85) and Thai-style curries or creamy tarragon chicken (£5.95), fish dishes when available including grilled plaice, brill meunière, and sea-bass in ginger and soy sauce (£10.25), and large steaks (from £7.95); evening extras such as whitebait (£2.95), smoked salmon cornet (£4.50), scampi (£5.50), and half a roast duckling (£9.25). They are licensed to deal in game (as well as selling local eggs), so this can work through into the menu, with their rabbit pie a special favourite (£4.50). There's a lunchtime overflow into the no-smoking restaurant area; service is welcoming and efficient, though may stop promptly. Well kept Harveys (sold as Beards) and a guest like John Smiths on handpump; Merrydown cider and decent wines, including a wine of the week – now usually English; log fires, maybe piped classical music. There are some seats under cover outside, and a small paddock in the garden has geese, ducks and a chicken. The pub has been run by the same clan for 35 years now. A family of house martins regularly returns to its nest above the porch, seemingly unperturbed by the people going in and out beneath them. *(Recommended by Colin Laffan, James Nunns, Alan Skull, R and S Bentley, Ben Grose, R J Walden, T A Bryan, Adrian and Gilly Heft, Michael and Merle Lipton, J E and A Jones, Mr and Mrs R D Knight, Tim and Pam Moorey, Mr and Mrs Moody, Dave Carter, Mr and Mrs W G Bryden, A Honigmann, J L Archambault, Father D Glover, Dr S Savvas, M Martin)*

Free house ~ Licensee Ian Lewis ~ Real ale ~ Meals and snacks (till 10, 9.30 Sun) ~ Evening restaurant (not Sun) ~ Alfriston (01323) 870377 ~ Children in eating area and restaurant ~ Open 11.30-2.30, 6.30-11; closed evening 25 Dec, all day 26 Dec

ALFRISTON TQ5103 Map 3

Star 🛏

Built in the 15th c by Battle Abbey as a guest house for pilgrims, this smart old place is these days a Forte hotel, but the front part remains wonderfully atmospheric and welcoming, and much as it must have looked for centuries. The façade is particularly worth a look, as it's studded with curious medieval carvings, mainly religious. The striking red lion on the corner – known as Old Bill – is more recent, and was probably the figurehead from a wrecked Dutch ship. Amongst the antiquities in the bustling heavy-beamed bar is a wooden pillar that was once a sanctuary post; holding it gave the full protection of the Church, and in 1516 one man rode a stolen horse from Lydd in Kent to take advantage of the offer – and so avoid the death penalty. Elegant furnishings include a heavy Stuart refectory table with a big bowl of flowers, antique Windsor armchairs worn to a fine polish and a handsome longcase clock; the fireplace is Tudor. Decent lunchtime bar food includes home-made soup (£1.95), cheddar cheese granary roll or Cumberland sausage with mash (both £2.95), ploughman's (from £3.50), vegetable lasagne (£3.95), and a cold meat salad buffet (£4.25); no bar meals on Sunday, but you can get a full lunch in the no-smoking restaurant. There's also a no-smoking lounge. Bass and Charringtons IPA on handpump, English wines; service is excellent, with nothing too much trouble. The bedrooms are in a comfortably up-to-date back part that you'd scarcely guess at from the ancient front inn. Board games are available, and if you're staying they can arrange a wide range of activities. *(Recommended by E G Parish, Mr and Mrs J E Hilditch, P Gillbe, Ian Phillips)*

Free house (Forte) ~ Manager Richard Hobden ~ Real ale ~ Lunchtime meals and snacks (not Sun) ~ Restaurant ~ Alfriston (01323) 870495 ~ Children in eating area ~ Open 11-2.30, 6-11 ~ Bedrooms: £78.50B/£102B

ASHURST TQ1716 Map 3

Fountain 🍺

B2135 N of Steyning

One reader had some American visitors who needed convincing that British pubs were as good as he claimed, so to settle the point he brought them to this unspoilt old place. As anyone who knows the Fountain would expect, they found it delightful – so much so they came back for another meal the next day. Behind the Georgian façade it's a charmingly rustic 16th-c country pub, quite foody at times, but with a strong local following that makes sure it never loses its relaxed traditional feel. The tap room on the right is the one to head for, with its scrubbed old flagstones, a couple of high-backed wooden cottage armchairs by the log fire in its brick inglenook, two antique polished trestle tables and usually six well kept real ales. The range typically includes Courage Best and Directors, Fullers London Pride, John Smiths, Youngs Special and a changing guest like Adnams Broadside or Charles Wells Bombardier. A bigger carpeted room with its orginal beams and woodburning stove is where most of the popular homecooked bar food is served: interesting soups (£2.25), oriental dim-sum (£3.75), Mediterranean king prawns or smoked salmon (£4.25), good vegetarian meals, cajun chicken (£6.95), duck breast in black cherry (£7.25), honey roast rack of lamb (£7.50), fillet steak (£9.75) and well praised koulibiac (poached salmon in a light pastry); regular theme evenings in winter. Service is cheery and efficient, but can slow down at busy periods; booking is advisable in the evenings. A gravel terrace has picnic-table sets by an attractive duckpond, and there are swings and a see-saw (and regular barbecues) in the pretty garden with fruit trees and roses. They have a cheery black labrador; shove-ha'penny, dominoes and cribbage. They've recently extended the restaurant, and an adjoining barn has been converted into a function room with skittle alley. *(Recommended by Dave Irving, David Holloway, Jenny and Brian Seller, John Beeken, Mrs S M Lee, Alison Burt, Pippa Bobbett, Tony and Wendy Hobden, R and S Bentley, Ron Tennant, J H L Davies, Mr and Mrs Moody, Howard Gregory)*

Free house ~ Licensee Maurice Caine ~ Real ale ~ Meals and snacks (till 10) ~ Restaurant ~ (01403) 710219 ~ Children in restaurant till 8pm ~ Open 11-2.30, 6-11; closed evenings 25 and 26 Dec

nr BILLINGSHURST TQ0925 Map 3

Blue Ship 🍺

The Haven; hamlet signposted off A29 just N of junction with A264, then follow signpost left towards Garlands and Okehurst

Tucked away down a remote country lane, this charmingly unpretentious pub is an idyllic spot on a summer evening, when you can relax at the tree-shaded side tables or by the tangle of honeysuckle around the front door, and contentedly take in the air of peaceful simplicity. Completely unspoilt, the beamed and brick-floored front bar has hatch service and an inglenook fireplace, and a corridor leads to a couple of similar little rooms; there may be a couple of playful cats. A decent little range of tasty home-made bar food includes dishes like sandwiches (from £1.60), a very good ham and vegetable soup (£2.10), ploughman's (from £2.80), macaroni cheese (£3.60), cottage pie (£3.90), ratatouille (£4.15), cod or plaice (£4.20), lasagne (£4.65), steak and kidney pie or scampi (£5.20), and puddings like fruit crumble or treacle tart (all £2.10); good helpings and service. Well kept King & Barnes Broadwood, Sussex and winter Old tapped from the cask. A games room has darts, bar billiards, shove-ha'penny, cribbage, dominoes and trivia. Good places rarely stay secret, and it can get crowded with young people at weekends. They still run their own shoot. *(Recommended by J S M Sheldon, Tony and Wendy Hobden, G Berneck, C Herxheimer, Dave Thomson, Margaret Mason, R Wilson, R and S Bentley, Mr and Mrs Moody and others)*

King & Barnes ~ Tenant J R Davie ~ Real ale ~ Meals and snacks (not evenings Sun or Mon) ~ (01403) 822709 ~ Children in two rooms without bar ~ Open 11-3, 6-11

BLACKBOYS TQ5220 Map 3

Blackboys

B2192 S edge of village

The atmospheric old-fashioned and unpretentious little rooms in this 14th-c weatherboarded pub were, luckily, little damaged by the fire that destroyed the top floor of the building in 1993. There are dark old beams, wooden chairs, stools and an unusual tree trunk rocking chair (carved by a local man) on the bare boards or parquet floors, masses of bric-a-brac and antique prints on the walls, and a good log fire in the inglenook fireplace. Decent bar food includes soup (£1.80), ploughman's (from £3.50), sausage and egg (£4.50), steak and kidney pie (£5), fresh plaice (£5.95), chicken and prawn pancake (£5.95), and half a lobster with garlic prawns and mussels (£8.50). Well kept Harveys PA and BB with winter warmers like XXXX or Armada on handpump; darts, fruit machine, trivia, juke box and their version of ring-the-bull – ring-the-stag's nose. In front of the pub there are plenty of seats overlooking the pretty pond, and to the side and behind extensive more informal grounds spread past the barn that was used for temporary bar quarters during the building works and may be brought back into use for families in the summer. *(Recommended by Dr S Savvas, M Martin, B R Shiner, Michael and Merle Lipton, Alan Skull)*

Harveys ~ Tenant Patrick Russell ~ Real ale ~ Meals and snacks (till 10pm; not Sun evening in winter) ~ Restaurant ~ (01825) 890283 ~ Children in restaurant ~ Open 11-3, 6-11; closed evening 25 Dec

BRIGHTON TQ3105 Map 3

Cricketers 🏆

15 Black Lion St; just on W edge of the Lanes

A very pleasant, down to earth cheery town pub, friendly and bustling, and not too far from the seafront. The two smallish rooms are full of Victorian furnishings such as old record sleeves, musical instruments, hot-water bottles, lots of engraved glass and red plush, and copper and brass, and even a stuffed bear. Under the new chef bar food is a little more imaginative than before, and as he's a vegetarian you're quite likely to find interesting meat-free daily specials; a typical menu might include sandwiches (from £1.55), ploughman's (from £2.60), filled baked potatoes (from £2.75), giant Yorkshire pudding (£3.75), steak and kidney pie (£4.25), fresh grilled plaice (£4.65), daily specials like pork and stilton pie or red bean and aubergine moussaka (around £4.50), and home-made puddings (from £1.75). Well kept Morlands Old Speckled Hen, Ruddles County and Youngs Special on handpump; efficient service. The pub is popular with students and young people in the evenings, but at lunchtimes the customers are a little more mixed, and the atmosphere and music nicely old-fashioned. The side courtyard is now covered and forms part of the eating area. When built in the 16th c it was called the Laste and Fishcart and used by the London fishbuyers from the nearby market. It got its new name when James Ireland had a cricket field nearby (now houses). *(Recommended by Chris and Anne Fluck, Gill Earle, Andrew Burton, R J Walden, Sheila Keene, Margaret and Roy Randle, Russell and Margaret Bathie, Barbara and Norman Wells, Simon Collett-Jones, David Shillitoe, Dr A K Clarke)*

Courage ~ Lease: Janice Jackson ~ Real ale ~ Meals and snacks (all day Weds-Sat, not Mon or Tues evening) ~ Restaurant (not evenings Sun or Mon) ~ Brighton (01273) 329472 ~ Open 11-11

BROWNBREAD STREET TQ6715 Map 3

Ash Tree ♀ 🍺

Village signposted off the old coach road between the Swan E of Dallington on B2096 Battle—Heathfield and the B2204 W of Battle, nr Ashburnham

A warmly welcoming 400-year-old pub nestling in a quiet spot where the air is full of gentle birdsong. It's blessed with particularly hard-working licensees, who really put that extra something into running the place, baking their own bread, grinding their own spices and growing many of their own vegetables. At Christmas the comfortably old-fashioned rooms are decked with really thoughtful decorations, and at other times there are plenty of flowers fresh from the garden. Candlelit at night, the bars also have three inglenook fireplaces (they get through 80 tons of wood a year), lots of oak beams, stripped brickwork, and nice old settles and chairs. Food is very good, home-made, and varied, with dishes like sandwiches (from £1.50), soup (£1.95), crab mousse (£3.50), beef curry or steak and kidney pie (£4.95), chicken, ham and mushroom pie (£5.25), diced beef with walnuts, pork and vegetables, lamb with rosemary, tomatoes and wine or chicken breast with Calvados (£5.50), seasonal game dishes (from £5.50), seafood parcel (£6.95), and puddings like boozy coffee pudding, apricot mousse and date and walnut flan (£2.35); every six weeks they hold a themed food evening. The beers on handpump are rotated from Boddingtons, Brakspears, Fullers London Pride, Harveys Best, Ind Coope Burton and Morlands Old Speckled Hen; six wines by the glass from a decent wine list. The springer spaniel is called Hoover, and the ginger cat, Cuthbert, is very partial to prawns. Darts, pool, shove-ha'penny, cribbage, dominoes, fruit machine, video game, discreet juke box, classical piped music. There's a pretty garden with picnic-table sets; they organise three shoots a week, host local beagle and fox hunt meets, also a mink hunt, and support two cricket teams and a tug-of-war team. *(Recommended by Mr and Mrs R D Knight, Alec and Marie Lewery, D L Barker; more reports please)*

Free house ~ Licensee Janice Lambird ~ Real ale ~ Meals and snacks (not Mon) ~ Restaurant ~ (01424) 892104 ~ Children in eating area and restaurant ~ Open 12-3, 7-11; closed Mon

BURPHAM TQ0308 Map 3

George & Dragon

Warningcamp turn off A27 a mile E of Arundel, then keep on up

Bright with window boxes, this smart and comfortable pub fits well into this charming hill village of thatch and flint, and tables in the garden have splendid views down to nearby Arundel Castle and the river. There've been a few changes since our last edition, but it looks like the new licensees are maintaining the emphasis on good food and drink that has made it so well liked by readers in recent years. There's a pleasant peaceful feel to the immaculately kept spacious open plan bar, which has good strong wooden furnishings, and a very interesting range of constantly changing beers such as Arundel Best, Belchers Best, Courage

Directors, Harveys Best and Spinaker Classic on handpump or electric pump. Good bar food includes sandwiches, soup, ploughman's, stuffed aubergines (£4.35), avocado with fresh Jersey crab (£4.90), lamb's liver and bacon (£5.25), duck and orange pie (£6.25), lots of fresh fish such as sea bass (£8.95), and various home-made puddings (£2.60). A busy place, it's popular with both locals and walkers. The partly Norman church has some unusual decoration, and there are good downland walks nearby. No dogs. *(Recommended by Derek and Sylvia Stephenson, TOH, Colin Laffan, Mr and Mrs Michael Boxford, Tony and Wendy Hobden, M A Gordon Smith, Derek and Maggie Washington, R W Tapsfield, N Bushby, W Atkins, David Holloway, Mr and Mrs A H Denman, Alison Burt, R T and J C Moggridge, Brian Kneale, Barry Roe, Wendy Mogose, Ian and Wendy McCaw, Mr and Mrs D E Connell)*

Courage ~ Tenants James Rose and Kate Holle ~ Real ale ~ Meals and snacks (not Sun evening) ~ Restaurant (not Sun evening) ~ Arundel (01903) 883131 ~ Occasional jazz or other live entertainment ~ Open 11-2.30, 6-11; closed winter Sun evenings

BURWASH TQ6724 Map 3

Bell

A265 E of Heathfield

Seats in front of this flower-covered mainly 17th-c local look across the road to the pretty village's church. Inside there's a nice genuinely pubby atmosphere in the friendly L-shaped bar on the right, which has an armchair by its big log fire (two fires if it's cold), all sorts of ironwork, bells and barometers on its ochre Anaglypta ceiling and terracotta walls, and well polished built-in pews around tables. The room on the left is broadly similar, but quieter (and greener). Well kept Adnams and Harveys on handpump, with two regularly changing guests such as Morlands Old Speckled Hen or Youngs Special, and farm cider. Shove-ha'penny, ring-the-bull and toad-in-the-hole, maybe unobtrusive piped music. Under the chirpy new manager bar food includes sandwiches (from £2.50), ploughman's (from £2.95), a couple of vegetarian meals like a huge salad (£3.50) or vegetable lasagne, hot dishes such as home-made steak and kidney pie, chilli or curry (around £4.50), fresh fish with crab and lobster in season, and puddings like home-made apple pie and cheesecake. Nearby parking may be difficult. The bedrooms (oak beams, sloping floors) can be recommended, but the bathroom is shared, and the road can be noisy at night. The pub is mentioned in Kipling's *Puck of Pook's Hill,* and is handy for Batemans, the lovely Jacobean ironmaster's house the writer made his home. *Good Walks Guide* Walk 67 starts close by. *(Recommended by D A Edwards, Fiona Dick, R D Knight, J E Hilditch, Dr S Savvas, M Martin, John Beeken, J E and A G Jones)*

Beards (who no longer brew) ~ Manager Colin Barrett ~ Real ale ~ Meals and snacks (not Sun evening) ~ Restaurant (not Sun evening) ~ Burwash (01435) 882304 ~ Children in restaurant ~ Open 11-11 ~ Bedrooms: £25/£35

BYWORTH SU9820 Map 2

Black Horse ◀

Signposted from A283

The garden at this busy old pub is particularly attractive, and the top tables on a steep series of grassy terraces, sheltered by banks of flowering shrubs, look across a drowsy valley to swelling woodland; a small stream runs along under an old willow by the more spacious lawn at the bottom. It's doing rather well under the current licensees, who seem to offer a winning combination of friendly service and tasty imaginative food. The wide choice of good seasonally changing bar meals includes sandwiches, french onion soup (£2), filled jacket potatoes, ploughman's, salads, and lots of imaginative daily specials like mushrooms stuffed with bacon and parmesan (£3.75), lamb, mint and cumin meatballs (£3.95), scallops with creamed celeriac (£4.50), pasta with a creamy pesto sauce (£4.50), supreme of chicken Véronique or spare ribs (£6.95), fillet of salmon with coriander hollandaise (£7.95), black bream with lime and water chestnuts (£8.25), and rack of lamb with port and rosemary gravy (£8.95); children's meals (£3.50). It can be busy at weekends, especially in summer, so it's worth booking then. The basic furnishings in the bar really add to the old-fashioned atmosphere and character of the place – the bare floorboards, scrubbed wooden tables and pews may at first look austere, but there's a real affability and informality that instead make them seem welcoming and cosy. Four well kept changing beers like Ballards Wassail, Flowers Original, Hopback Summer Lightning and Youngs Ordinary on handpump, good wines; efficient service; darts, shove ha'penny, cribbage. The pub was built on the site of a 15th-c friary. *(Recommended by Mrs M Rice, Viv Middlebrook, Dr M V Jones, W K Struthers, Mrs D M Gray)*

Free house ~ Paul Wheeler-Kingshott and Jenny Reynolds ~ Real ale ~ Meals and snacks (11.30-1.45 (2 weekends) 6-9.45) ~ Restaurant ~ Petworth (01798) 42424 ~ Children in restaurant ~ Open 11-3, 6-11

CHARLTON SU8812 Map 2

Fox Goes Free 🍺

Village signposted off A286 Chichester—Midhurst in Singleton, also from Chichester—Petworth via East Dean

A pub for nearly 500 years, this characterful old place has a very pleasant secluded back garden, with tables among fruit trees, one with seats built into its trunk, a notable Downland view, and a safe children's play area with sandpit; the barbecue area can be booked. Inside is a cosy series of separate rooms, one of which has a big brick fireplace and elm benches on the partly carpeted brick floors. A nice little low-beamed snug has a sturdy elm settle and a second big inglenook fireplace, and there are more tables in a no-smoking family extension, cleverly converted from horse boxes and the stables where the 1926 Goodwood winner was housed. Well kept Arundel Best, Ballards Best, Boddingtons and several weekly changing guests like Exmoor Gold, Morlands Old Speckled Hen and Ringwood Old Thumper on handpump; their own wine from a French auberge alongside a good range of country wines. Bar food (not perhaps quite as popular with readers as it has been) might include soup (£2), filled baguettes or deep-fried brie and cranberries (£2.50), filled baked potatoes or salads (£4.50), spinach and lentil pasta bake (£4.75), vegetable and broccoli lasagne or Cumberland sausage (£4.95), lamb rogan josh, chilli or pork chop in apple and herbs (£5.75), 10 oz sirloin steak (£8.95), and a children's menu (£2.50); fruit machine. The restaurant is no smoking. The pub has been the meeting place of various hunts for the last 300 years, and in 1915 was the site of the first Women's Institute meeting (though we've heard of a couple of instances when they haven't shown the same welcome to contemporary WI groups). Handy for the Weald and Downland Open Air Museum, the quiet village is busy on race days. *(Recommended by John Sanders, Jerry and Alison Oakes, Mrs M Rice, Eamon Green, J and P Maloney, Colin Harnett, Phil and Sally Gorton, Susan and John Douglas and others)*

Free house ~ Licensees Gil Battley and Irene Jenner ~ Real ale ~ Meals and snacks (till 10 weekends) ~ Restaurant ~ (01243) 811461 ~ Children in family room ~ Open 11-3, 6(7 winter)-11 ~ Bedrooms: £25/£39.50

CHIDDINGLY TQ5414 Map 3

Six Bells ★ £ 🍺

Village signed off A22 Uckfield—Hailsham

The cheerful landlord of this quirkily idiosyncratic pub is quite a music buff, and these days there seem to be good live bands most nights of the week, carefully segregated in an adjoining barn. At quieter times (say, midweek lunchtimes) the atmosphere is lively and chatty too, but the bustle rarely reaches the top bar where most of the incredibly low priced food is served. Well liked by readers, it's not what you'd call a smart place, but really is good fun, and the welcoming bars are full of character and atmosphere, with an intriguing and truly cosmopolitan mix of visitors that seem to go together really well. Dotted around are lots of old pictures, interesting bric-a-brac and fusty old artefacts, pews and antique seats – even a working pianola; the gents' has a fine collection of enamelled advertising signs. The tasty home-made food is consistently good value, with dishes like bargain french onion soup (75p), meat or vegetarian lasagne or shepherd's pie (£1.70), steak and kidney pie (£2.30), filled jacket potatoes (from £2.60), ploughman's (from £2.70), cheesy vegetable bake (£2.80), chilli con carne, chicken curry or spicy prawns mexicano (£3.50), spare ribs in barbecue sauce (£3.50), and generous puddings like raspberry pavlova and treacle tart (£1.70). Well kept Courage Directors and John Smiths on handpump; a good log fire; dominoes and cribbage. Outside at the back, there are some tables beyond a goldfish pond, and a new boules pitch; the church opposite has an interesting Jeffrey monument. Nicely set where the Weald Way crosses the Vanguard Way, it's a pleasant area for walks. There are vintage and Kit car meetings outside the pub once a month. *(Recommended by Nicola Thomas, Paul Dickinson, Mavis and John Wright, Alan Skull, Desmond L Barker, K and E Leist, P J Caunt, Michael Sargent, Mr and Mrs J E Hilditch, Rob and Doris Harrison, Mrs H Taylor, Dr S Savvas, M Martin, Mike and Joyce Bryant, Mr and Mrs Moody)*

Free house ~ Licensee Paul Newman ~ Real ale ~ Meals and snacks (12-2.30, 6-10.30) ~ (01825) 872227 ~ Jazz, blues and other live music in the barn Tues, Fri, Sat and Sun evenings, Sun lunch ~ Open 11-3, 6-11

CHIDHAM SU7903 Map 2

Old House At Home

Cot Lane; turn off A27 at the Barleycorn pub

Part of a peaceful cluster of farm buildings, this cosy old place is rather well liked by readers – indeed, those who've known it for some time say it's never been better than it is at the moment. Because it's quite out of the way it's rarely overrun by crowds, so you should be able to relax and take in the special atmosphere relatively undisturbed. An extensive range of very good food, in big helpings, includes sandwiches (from £1.40), soup (£2.25, the leek and potato is recommended), ploughman's (from £3.25), mussels in a cream and wine sauce (£3.75), omelettes (from £4), salads (from £4.25), fisherman's pie or liver and bacon (£4.75), steak and kidney pie (£4.95), roast rib of beef (£5.75), game pie (£6.50), grilled trout with almonds (£6.75), steaks (from £8), Dover sole (£13.50), and a healthy selection of vegetarian dishes like mushroom and asparagus pie (£5) and provençale nut Wellington (£5.95); children's meals (£2.25). Booking is recommended for summer evenings. Even if most other customers appear to be eating they still have plenty of time for people coming for just a drink: well kept real ales such as Badger Best, Ringwood Best and Old Thumper, their own Old House, and a guest beer on handpump, as well as a good selection of country wines and several malt whiskies. Warmly welcoming, the homely timbered and low-beamed bar has Windsor chairs around the tables, long seats against the walls, a welcoming log fire and a large friendly dog. It's quite handy for good walks by Chichester harbour, and in summer has a couple of picnic-table sets on its terrace, with many more in the garden behind. *(Recommended by Ann and Colin Hunt, David Eberlin, Derek and Margaret Underwood, Lawrence Pearse, T M Fenning, Barbara Hatfield, Miss A G Drake)*

Free house ~ Licensee Terry Brewer ~ Real ale ~ Meals and snacks (till 10) ~ Restaurant ~ (01243) 572477 ~ Children welcome ~ Open 11.30(12 Sat)-2.30(3 Sat), 6-11; closed evening 25 Dec

COWBEECH TQ6114 Map 3

Merrie Harriers

Village signposted from A271

Doing well under its current licensees, this is a cheery white clapboarded former farmhouse with an especially friendly and relaxed feel. The food is still well liked too, with the wide lunchtime menu including sandwiches (from £1.80), home-made soup (£2.25), filled cottage rolls, ploughman's (from £3.25), vegetarian quiche (£3.95), salads, steak and kidney pie (£6.50), various fresh local fish like grilled lemon sole (£8.95) and puddings like apple pie or summer pudding; in the evening they have dishes such as a mixed grill or steaks (from £8.95), and they do a good Sunday roast. You can eat either in the comfortable dining lounge, or in the back no-smoking conservatory, decorated in Victorian style with suitably attired waitresses; they take bookings. Well kept Boddingtons and Harveys Best on handpump, good choice of wines; friendly, professional service. The beamed and panelled public bar has a traditional high-backed settle by the brick inglenook as well as other tables and chairs, and darts, dominoes and cribbage. The terraced garden has rustic seats and a swing. *(Recommended by J H Bell, Colin Laffan, Robert Gomme, A E R Albert, Dr S Savvas, M Martin and others)*

Free house ~ Licensees J H and C P Conroy ~ Meals and snacks ~ Restaurant ~ Hailsham (01323) 833108 ~ Children in restaurant ~ Open 11-3, 6-11

CUCKFIELD TQ3025 Map 3

White Harte £ 🍺

South Street; off A272 W of Haywards Heath

This pretty partly medieval pub, tiled and tile-hung, has kept a most appealing traditional feel in its beamed bars, with polished floorboards, some parquet and ancient brick flooring tiles as well as the carpet in its split-level lounge, some standing timbers, and small windows looking out on to the road. Furnishings are sturdy and comfortable, and there's a roaring log fire in the inglenook. The mainly bare-boards public bar is also solidly traditional, with a fearsomely high standard of play on its sensibly placed darts board. The straightforward lunchtime food is good value, and includes ploughman's (from £2.80), salads, scampi and chips: what people tend to go for are the three to five home-cooked bargain specials (£3) such as fisherman's, chicken and mushroom, turkey or steak and kidney pies, stuffed marrow and stilton and celery quiche – there is always one vegetarian option. The specials tend to go by about 1.30, so it pays to be there early. Well kept King & Barnes Bitter, Broadwood and Festive on handpump, popular cheery landlord and pleasant friendly service; fruit machine, shove-ha'penny. The village is very pretty. *(Recommended by Terry Buckland, Mrs R D Knight, David Holloway, Andy and Jill Kassube)*

King & Barnes ~ Tenant Ted Murphy ~ Real ale ~ Meals and snacks (12-2; lunchtime only, not Sun) ~ (01444) 413454 ~ Children welcome lunchtime ~ Open 11-3, 6-11; cl evening 25 Dec

DITCHLING TQ3215 Map 3

Bull 🛏️

2 High St; B2112, junction with B2116

Law abiding readers will be interested to learn that in 1784 this atmospheric 14th-c pub was the founding place of the Society for Prosecuting Thieves, and there's still an old poster on the wall advertising its inaugural meeting. The beamed old building was already at the centre of local justice, for many years serving as a courthouse, even after it became a coaching inn. There's still plenty of evidence of these far off days in the main bar, with its old oak chests and settles, striking elm and mahogany tables, a longcase clock, and old prints and photographs above the wooden dado. The mood is very pleasant and relaxed, with the peaceful air undisturbed by music or machines. Another bar has simpler, neater furnishings; three inglenook fireplaces. Under the new licensees good bar food includes sandwiches, various ploughman's (from £3.80), homecooked gammon (£4.50), pies like steak and kidney or chicken and mushroom (£5.25), daily changing fresh fish such as smoked trout (£4.90), brill (£6.70), and Dover sole (£10.50), and puddings like apple pie or bakewell tart (£2.25). Boddingtons, Brakspears, Flowers Original, King & Barnes Sussex and Morlands Old Speckled Hen on handpump. The restaurant is no smoking. Picnic-table sets in a good-sized pretty garden look up towards Ditchling Beacon, and there are more tables on a suntrap back terrace. The charming old village is a popular base for the

South Downs Way and other walks. *(Recommended by Colin Laffan, David Holloway, R J Walden, D A Edwards, Mavis and John Wright, Sheila Keene, Peter Churchill, Frank Cummins, Dr and Mrs Rackow, Mrs C Archer)*

Whitbreads ~ Tenants John and Jannette Blake ~ Real ale ~ Meals and snacks ~ Restaurant (not Sun evening) ~ (01273) 843147 ~ Children in restaurant ~ Open 11-11 ~ Bedrooms: £30.50B/£42.50B

EARTHAM SU9409 Map 2

George

Signposted off A285 Chichester—Petworth; also from Fontwell off A27 and Slindon off A29

Set amidst some very attractive countryside, this is a bustling and friendly country pub standing out for its cheery atmosphere, personal service, and very good, well presented home-made food. Typical dishes might include home-made soup, open sandwiches (from £2.25), good home-made pâté, nice sardines, ploughman's (from £3.95), fresh fish dishes (from £6), lamb's liver and bacon (£6.95), their speciality sizzling platters (from £7.95), tiger prawns (£8.50), beef stroganoff (£9.25), and seven-boned rack of lamb in red wine and rosemary sauce (£9.50). They do various themed food nights or special events – the last few months have seen a lively Wild West night, an Oriental weekend and a French week. Well kept Courage Directors, Theakstons Best and Old Peculier and Wadworths 6X on handpump; quick service by very helpful, courteous staff. The cosy lounge is comfortable and pleasant without being fussily overdecorated, and there's a pubbier public bar; both have a relaxed atmosphere despite being busy. Piped music. Picnic-table sets in the pretty award-winning garden. *(Recommended by Mr and Mrs Hawkins, John and Joy Winterbottom, Ian Blackwell, Peter Robertson, R J and J C Moggridge, Eric G Kirby, Sylvia Kopelowitz)*

Free house ~ Licensees Stuart and Dawn Warren ~ Real ale ~ Meals and snacks ~ Restaurant ~ (01243) 814340 ~ Children welcome ~ Open 11-2.30, 6-11

EASEBOURNE SU8922 Map 2

Olde White Horse

A272, just N of Midhurst

Very welcoming and neatly cared for, this old stone local is a popular place, with a good pubby atmosphere. Leech and other prints on the walls of the modernised little lounge reflect local interest in polo, shooting or racing parties, but you'll be just as comfortable if your inclination is more towards the darts, dominoes, or cribbage found in the separate tap room, along with a juke box; there's also a bigger public bar. Well-liked promptly served bar food includes sandwiches (from £1.85), ploughman's (from £3.70), various well liked changing hot dishes like steak, Guinness and mushroom pie (£5.95), game in season, good fresh fish like red mullet, and puddings such as home-made crumbles or treacle tart (all £2.60); friendly service. Well kept Greene King IPA and Abbot, on handpump, and a few malt whiskies; a small log fire. There are tables out in a courtyard, with plenty more on the sheltered well kept back lawn. There's said to be the remains of a tunnel from smuggling days, connecting the pub to the church. *(Recommended by I D and W McCaw, Angela and Alan Dale, M A Gordon Smith, G Dobson)*

Greene King ~ Tenant Melanie Smith ~ Real ale ~ Meals and snacks ~ Restaurant ~ Midhurst (01730) 813521 ~ Open 11-2.30, 6-11; closed evening 25 Dec

EASTDEAN TV5597 Map 3

Tiger ♀

Pub (with village centre) signposted – not vividly – from A259 Eastbourne—Seaford

Several of our readers walking the South Downs Way make sure this low-beamed old-fashioned little local is the halfway point, so that they can relax on the seats outside and take in what really is a quite splendid setting. It's on the edge of a secluded, sloping green lined with low cottages, most of them – like the pub itself – bright with flowering climbers, roses and other flowers. The lane leads on down to a fine stretch of coast culminating in Beachy Head, and *Good Walks Guide* Walk 60 goes right past. It seems more idyllic than ever since the closure of the roads around the green, so not surprisingly it does get busy, especially in summer, when the green becomes a sort of overflow. Inside too, the ambience is perhaps the main attraction: smallish rooms, low beams hung with pewter and china, traditional furnishings including polished rustic tables and distinctive antique settles, old prints and so forth. The only music you're likely to hear will be from the visiting Morris dancers. Regularly changing beers might include well kept Adnams Broadside, Harveys Best, Morlands Old Speckled Hen, Timothy Taylors Landlord and Youngs Special on handpump; decent choice of wines by the glass and several interesting vintage bin-ends. Varying bar food, in good helpings, includes a short but good choice of home-made dishes such as brie-topped garlic mushrooms (£3.25), filled baked potatoes, ploughman's, macaroni cheese with stilton and tomatos (£4.75), fresh fish and chips (£4.95), and seasonal game like venison casserole with herb dumplings (£5.95). Efficient service from helpful staff. There's no problem parking here these days – there's a big walled car park next door. *(Recommended by Colin Laffan, Peter Churchill, Brian Jones, Ben Grose, Alec and Marie Lewery, Graham Pettener, Dr B A W Perkins, P Adsley and others)*

Free house ~ Licensee J Davies-Gilbert ~ Real ale ~ Meals and snacks (not Sun evening) ~ Open 11.30-2.30, 6.30-11

ELSTED SU8119 Map 2

Elsted Inn 🍴 🍺

Elsted Marsh; from Midhurst left off A272 Petersfield Rd at Lower Elsted sign; from Petersfield left off B2146 Nursted Rd at South Harting, keep on past Elsted itself

The kind of friendly and unpretentious place where everyone immediately feels at home, this really is a jolly old pub, rather out of the way, but very well liked indeed for the cheery welcome, excellent food and superb beer. The good range of carefully prepared meals relies heavily on fresh local produce, and as well as 18 different mustards might typically include dishes like tasty soup (£2.95), sandwiches (from £1.95), local asparagus (£2), crab and ginger filo parcels, Irish stew (with real mutton), braised oxtail, bacon pudding or spinach and walnut roulade (£6), venison casserole, rabbit saddle with mustard or steak and kidney pudding (£6.50), duck breast with honey and ginger (£8.75), fresh fish at weekends (from £7), and glorious home-made ice cream and puddings (from £1.95, the gooseberry and elderflower sorbet is recommended); children's helpings, and monthly curry, steak and pasta nights. There's a separate cottagey candlelit dining room, and they do now take credit cards. Once brewed here but now produced a couple of miles down the road, the full range of Ballards beers is perfectly kept on handpump (the landlord used to be one of the brewers), along with Fullers London Pride and two often unusual guests like Worldham Old Dray. The two cosy bars have simple country furniture on wooden floors, local photographs on the cream walls, an open fire in the Victorian fireplace, and two big friendly dogs; darts, dominoes, shove-ha'penny, cribbage, backgammon. Children are made very welcome. There are tables and boules out in a sizeable enclosed garden. *(Recommended by John and Joy Winterbottom, G Bint, Chris and Anne Fluck, Ian Jones, Lynn Sharpless, Bob Eardley, Alan Skull, Roger Berry, A, J and G, Dr Keats, Susan and John Douglas, Mr and Mrs Moody, Miss J F Reay, W K Struthers)*

Free house ~ Licensees Tweazle Jones and Barry Horton ~ Real ale ~ Meals and snacks (12-2.30, 7-10; not evening 25 Dec) ~ Restaurant ~ (01730) 813662 ~ Children in eating area and restaurant ~ Folk music first Sun of month, another monthly band, barn dances in summer ~ Open 11-3, 5.30-11(6 Sat); closed evening 25 Dec ~ Bedrooms: £17.50/£30

Planning a day in the country? We list pubs in really attractive scenery at the back of the book.

ELSTED SU8119 Map 2

Three Horseshoes ★ ◧

Village signposted from B2141 Chichester—Petersfield; also reached easily from A272 about 2 miles W of Midhurst, turning left heading W

The snug little rooms at this cosily old-fashioned 16th-c pub are full of rustic charm, with enormous log fires, antique furnishings, ancient beams and flooring, attractive prints and photographs, and night-time candlelight. Good regularly changing home-made food includes home-made soups (£2.95), generous ploughman's with a good choice of cheeses (£4.50), avocado with stilton and a mushroom sauce topped with bacon (£4.95), chicken and bacon casserole with celery and fennel, rabbit and pigeon casserole or steak and Guinness pie (£6.95), Scotch sirloin steak with spring onions, shallots and a red wine sauce and puddings like delicious treacle tart (you can take it away) or raspery and hazelnut meringue (£2.75). Well kept changing ales racked on a stillage behind the bar counter might include Ballards Best and Wassail, Cheriton Pots and Diggers Gold, Flowers Original, Fullers London Pride, and Gibbs Mew Bishops Tipple to name a few – they tend to concentrate on brews from smaller breweries; farmhouse ciders and summer Pimms. Service is friendly and obliging, and the staff stay smiling even when busy; darts, dominoes. The prettily planted garden with its free-roaming bantams has wonderful views over the South Downs; the essayist E V Lucas reckoned the site 'superior to that of many a nobleman's house'. *(Recommended by John Sanders, R D Knight, Lynn Sharpless, Bob Eardley, Gill and Mike Cross, A G Drake, Sue Demont, Tim Barrow, Angela and Alan Dale, A J Blackler, GAM)*

Free house ~ Licensees Andrew and Sue Beavis ~ Real ale ~ Meals and snacks (not winter Sun evenings) ~ Restaurant ~ Harting (01730) 825746 ~ Well behaved children in eating area ~ Open 11-3(2.30 winter), 6-11

FIRLE TQ4607 Map 3

Ram ⇔

Signposted off A27 Lewes—Polegate

A simple unfussy family-run village pub in good walking country, well liked for its friendly welcome and bustling atmosphere. The busy bars are still mainly unspoilt, with comfortable seating, soft lighting, a log fire (not always lit, but adding a lot to the mood when it is), and a nice, convivial feel; the snug is no-smoking. Well kept Charrington IPA and Harvey BB, and guest beers such as Hopback Summer Lightning and Otter Bitter on handpump, decent wines (including three produced locally), particularly good coffee. Cooked by the landlord's son, and relying heavily on local produce (especially free range eggs and poultry), the daily changing choice of bar food might include dishes like tomato and lentil soup (£2.35), various well sized ploughman's with warm bread (from £3.95), pitta bread with interesting fillings (from £4.95), local mackerel grilled in rolled oats or spicy carrot and chick peas on rice with onions, garlic, cashew nuts and chilli (£4.95), shepherd's pie (£5.25), salmon steak with cussy sauce (£7.85), chicken casserole (£7.95) and puddings like apple and cinnamon crumble (£2.85) or banana and toffee pie (£2.95). Darts, shove-ha'penny, dominoes, cribbage and toad in the hole. The gents' has a chalk board for graffiti, and there are tables in a spacious walled garden behind. Nearby Firle Place is worth visiting for its collections and furnishings, and the pub is handy for a particularly fine stretch of the South Downs, and for Glyndebourne. *(Recommended by D A Edwards, John Beeken, Mavis and John Wright, Adrian and Gilly Heft, Mr and Mrs Moody, R and S Bentley, Annette Tress, Gary Smith)*

Free house ~ Licensees Michael and Keith Wooller, Margaret Sharp ~ Real ale ~ Meals and lunchtime snacks ~ (01273) 858222 ~ Children in non-serving bars ~ Traditional folk music 2nd Mon in month, regular folk group 1st and 3rd Weds, another the 4th, and piano Sat evening ~ Open 11.30-3, 7(6 summer Sats)-11; closed evening 25 Dec ~ Three bedrooms: £25/£45(60S)

FLETCHING TQ4223 Map 3

Griffin ★ ⑪ 🛏 ♀

Village signposted off A272 W of Uckfield

Well placed on the edge of Sheffield Park, this old country inn is a satisfying and genuinely civilised place, which, despite its popularity, always remembers the essentials and resists the temptations of complacency. Readers like the enthusiastic service and the appealing atmosphere, but comment most of all on the good, often unusual food. The very popular range changes daily, but typically includes dishes like broccoli and asparagus soup (£2.50), filled baguettes, ploughman's or a warm pigeon breast salad (£3.95), home-cured gravadlax with dill sauce (£4.25), local sausage with onion gravy or three-cheese quiche (£4.95), haddock and spinach lasagne or jacket potato with garlic prawns (£5.95), poached haddock with Welsh rarebit crust (£6.95), stuffed fillet of pork or char-grilled Barnsley chop with fresh mint (£8.25), whole grilled lemon sole (£8.50), and puddings like summer fruit flan or crème brûlée (£2.95). The restaurant menu now merges with the bar menu on weekday evenings. They have regular fish and pasta evenings, as well as other occasional theme nights when the menu and attire of the staff are adjusted accordingly – on Beaujolais night for instance – and on Sundays there may be a barbecue. Badger Tanglefoot, Fullers London Pride, Harveys Best and a changing guest on handpump, around 70 good wines, including several New World, and various cognacs; pleasant friendly service. The beamed front bar has a cosy and relaxed 1930s feel – straightforward furniture, squared oak panelling, some china on a delft shelf, a big corner fireplace, and a small bare-boarded serving area off to one side. The landlord may be playing the piano. A separate public bar has darts, pool, fruit machine, video game and juke box. Picnic-table sets under cocktail parasols on the back grass have lovely rolling Sussex views; there are more tables on a sheltered gravel terrace, used for dining on warm evenings. Three of the four attractively individual bedrooms have four-posters. They can be terribly busy at weekends in summer, and, probably because they're so pushed, the generally high standards of food can wobble a little then. *(Recommended by R J Walden, David R Shillitoe, John and Tessa Rainsford, E D Bailey, Christopher P Glasson, R and S Bentley, Mr and Mrs A Dale, Alan Skull, Tony and Wendy Hobden, Tim Barrow, Sue Demont, Nicola Thomas, Paul Dickinson, D A Edwards, Joan and John Calvert, Mike and Joyce Bryant, WHBM, GB, Alec and Marie Lewery, J E and A G Jones, Dr S Savvas, M Martin, Dave Thompson, Margaret Mason, the Shinkmans)*

Free house ~ Licensees David and Nigel Pullan ~ Real ale ~ Meals and snacks ~ Restaurant (not Sun evening) ~ Newick (01825) 722890 ~ Children welcome ~ Piano Fri/Sat evenings, Sun lunchtime ~ Open 12-3, 6-11; closed 25 Dec ~ Bedrooms: £40B/£55B

FULKING TQ2411 Map 3

Shepherd & Dog

From A281 Brighton—Henfield on N slope of downs turn off at Poynings signpost and continue past Poynings

Superbly placed below a magnificent sweep of the downs, this charmingly atmospheric little pub used to sell illicit liquor to thirsty shepherds on their way to Findon sheep fair in the days before it became the more respectable – and licensed – drinking establishment it is now. In summer the garden is especially attractive: a series of prettily planted grassy terraces, some fairy-lit, with a little stream running down to the big stone trough, and an upper play lawn sheltered by trees. The partly panelled cosy bar has shepherds' crooks and harness on the walls, and antique or stoutly rustic furnishings around the log fire, with maybe fresh flowers on the tables. Popular bar food is not the cheapest in the area, but is tasty and well prepared, and comes in decent helpings; a changing choice might include sandwiches (from £3, smoked salmon £4), mussels steamed in white wine and garlic (£4.50), a wide choice of ploughman's (from £4.25), a vegetarian dish like vegetable pancakes, lasagne (£5.25), home-made beef and Guinness pie or big summer salads (£5.95), lemon sole (£6.50), trout (£6.95), a delightfully fresh whole wing of skate with whole grain mustard and capers (£7.50), tender sirloin steak (£8.50), and delicious home-made puddings such as chocolate torte or lemon and lime flan (all £2.75). Try and get there early, especially if you want a prime spot by the bow windows; service can slow down at the busiest times (summer weekends, maybe). Well kept Courage Directors, Harveys BB, and Websters Yorkshire on handpump, plus a couple of changing guests, often from smaller breweries; toad-in-the-hole. A path leads straight up to the South Downs Way (if you fancy a longer walk than the one back to your car parked down the lane). *(Recommended by Mark Percy, Mrs M Rice, David Eberlin, R Suddaby, Simon Small, Christopher P Glasson, Frank Cummins, J Dobson, David Holloway, R D Knight, Mike and Joyce Bryant, J E and A G Jones, E D Bailey, J G Smith)*

Free house ~ Licensees Anthony and Jessica Bradley Hull ~ Real ale ~ Meals and snacks ~ (01273) 857382 ~ Open 10-2.30, 6-11

GUN HILL TQ5614 Map 3

Gun 🏠

From A22 NW of Hailsham (after junction with A269) turn N at Little Chef

This beautiful old pub is another that's handy for walkers – in fact the Wealden Way runs through the lovely garden. They don't mind muddy boots, and indeed that sort of customer-comes-first thinking is very much the keynote of the place. Busy, well run and notably friendly, the 15th-c tiled and timbered house has a really nice country feel, and a welcoming frontage covered with clematis, honeysuckle and hanging baskets. There are plenty more flowers, and fairy-lit trees, in the big well hedged garden, which also has sensibly placed swings. Inside there's quite a warren of rooms and alcoves under the oak beams, and although most of the furnishings are aimed at eaters, there are some more individual pieces, with brasses, copper, pewter, prints and paintings on the panelled walls. In one corner is a venerable Aga, still used for cooking in the winter, and there are several open fires, one in a fine inglenook; a couple of areas are no smoking. Venerable oak floorboards were discovered by chance a couple of years ago when they took up the carpets. Well kept Boddingtons, Flowers IPA and Larkins Sovereign on handpump, a good choice of wines by the glass, farm ciders and country wines; cheery young service, with a good mix of ages among the many customers (they don't mind small children). Tasty good value food includes soup (£2.30), ploughman's and salads (from £3), well liked home-made steak and kidney pie (£4.90, made to the same successful recipe they've been using for 26 years), mushroom and nut fettucini or haddock and prawn tagliatelle (£5.20), fidget pie – diced pork in a creamy cider, sage and apple sauce (£5.40), fillet steak in puff pastry with pâté and sherry (£6.90), lots of fresh fish from Newhaven such as haddock, plaice or lobster and crab when available, various daily specials, local farm-made ice cream, and children's meals (from £3); they mark the healthiest dishes on the menu, and use wholesome, low-fat ingredients wherever possible. There may be a slight delay at busy periods. Cream teas in the afternoon. This is an ideal stop on the way to (or from) the ferry at Newhaven, 20 minutes away. *(Recommended by John Beeken, Mr and Mrs Albert, Roger Bellingham, W A Putland, Alec and Marie Lewery, Colin Laffan, T G Saul)*

Free house ~ Licensee R J Brockway ~ Real ale ~ Meals and snacks (till 10) ~ Chiddingly (01825) 872361 ~ Children welcome till 9pm ~ Open 11-11 (11-3 6-11 winter); closed 25 and 26 Dec ~ Bedrooms: £26(£30B)/£28(£34B)

HARTFIELD TQ4735 Map 3

Anchor 🍺

Church Street

One of the nice things about this welcoming old place is the way it seems to cater for so many tastes, with a broad cross-section of customers that might take in mothers with toddlers, the county set with their dogs, hefty local sportsmen and other disparate groups, all blending together really well. The front verandah soon gets busy on a warm summer evening, when the usual relaxed and contented atmosphere is even more evident than usual; there are further seats outside at the back. It's the food that understandably draws the crowds, especially their impressive seafood dishes like crab sandwiches (£2.50), fresh breaded plaice (£3.75), tagliatelle with shellfish and broccoli or salmon and spinach pancake (£4.75), prawn and crab curry (£5), wing of skate with black butter and capers (£8) and a giant seafood salad (£35 for two); other tasty food includes good home-made soup (£2), sandwiches (from £1.30, toasties from £1.50), filled baked potatoes (from £2.50), ploughman's (from £3), vegetarian cannelloni (£3.50), home-made pâté (£3.75), steak sandwich (£5), and grilled lamb or beef kebabs (from £8), with puddings (from £1.50), and children's meals (£2.50). The heavy-beamed bar rambles informally around the cheerful central servery, and the tables with their cushioned chairs and wall seats are set out in a way that lets you have a quiet conversation without ever feeling cut off. Old advertisements and little country pictures decorate the walls above the brown-painted dado, and there are houseplants in the brown-curtained small-paned windows. There's a good choice of beers, with very well kept Boddingtons, Flowers Original, Fremlins, Harveys Best, Marstons Pedigee and Wadworths 6X on handpump, in addition to guest ales such as Adnams Broadside, Larkins Porter, Palmers Tally Ho and Theakstons Old Peculier; warm woodburner; friendly quick service. Darts in a separate lower room; shove ha'penny, cribbage, dominoes and piped music. It's only been a pub since the last century, but dates back much further, with spells as a farmhouse and women's workhouse. The pub is on the edge of the Ashdown Forest, and near the start of the *Good Walks Guide* Walk 62. *(Recommended by Colin Laffan, the Shinkmans, D A Edwards, R T and C E Moggridge, A Kilpatrick, Gwen and Peter Andrews, Anthony John, R and S Bentley and others)*

Free house ~ Licensee Ken Thompson ~ Real ale ~ Meals and snacks (till 10) ~ Hartfield (01892) 770424 ~ Children welcome ~ Open 11-11; closed evening 25 Dec ~ Bedrooms: £30S/£35S

nr HEATHFIELD   TQ5920   Map 3

Star

Old Heathfield – head East out of Heathfield itself on A265, then fork right on to B2096; turn right at signpost to Heathfield Church then keep bearing right; pub on left immediately after church

As popular as ever under the new licensees, this tucked away 14th-c inn is a fascinating old place. Turner painted the view of rolling oak-lined sheep pastures that you get from the imaginatively planted sloping garden, and it really is impressive. Not surprisingly, it's this delightful spot that people head for in the summer months; there's a hedged-off children's play area and a floating population of rabbits, cats and birds – maybe even an owl and a couple of peacocks. The massive irregular stonework of the building dates back to the days when the pub served pilgrims following this high ridge across the Weald to Canterbury. The L-shaped beamed bar has a nicely old-fashioned atmosphere and furniture to match, murals depicting a connection with the founding of Jamestown in America, as well as window seats and tables by a huge inglenook fireplace – particularly cosy in cold weather. Bar food includes dishes like a dozen anchovy fillets with minced onion and crusty bread (£4.65), mussels in saffron, white wine, garlic and cream (£4.95), half a shoulder of lamb (£7.95) and lobster tails (£10.95). The restaurant is partly no smoking. Well kept Harveys Best, Hopback Summer Lightning, King and Barnes Sussex, and Youngs Special on handpump; darts, shove ha'penny, cribbage, dominoes and piped music. The neighbouring church is also rather interesting, with its handsome Early English tower. *(Recommended by Mr and Mrs J Stern, R D Knight, Jason Caulkin, Colin Laffan, A E R Albert)*

Free house ~ Real ale ~ Lease: Mike and Sue Chappell ~ Real ale ~ Meals and snacks (not Sun evening) ~ Restaurant (Fri/Sat evening, Sun lunchtime) ~ Heathfield (01435) 863570 ~ Children welcome ~ Jazz last Sun of month ~ Parking can be difficult (if so, park beyond church and walk through churchyard) ~ Open 11-3, 5.30(6.30 winter)-11

HOUGHTON TQ0111 Map 3

George & Dragon

B2139

This fine old building has changed hands since the last edition. It gets very busy in summer, when tables in the garden look down past the hardy walnut tree and the wishing well towards the Arun valley; for many the setting is the main attraction. The pub's origins go back some 700 years, but the building is mainly Elizabethan, and much as it must have been when Charles II stayed here escaping from the Battle of Worcester. The half-timbered bar is comfortably modernised, but still has handsome heavy oak beams and a formidable fireplace, as well as points of interest like a clockwork roasting-spit motor, and gourds given a glowing patina by rubbing with goosefat. Attractive antique tables lead into a back extension. A small area by the garden is no smoking – and also has the best indoor views. Bar food such as soup (£1.75), home-made pâté (£2.75), stilton ploughman's (£3.95), mushroom stroganoff (£4.25), ham, egg and chips or moules marinières (£4.50), lasagne (£4.95) and steak, kidney and ale pie (£5.95). Courage Directors, John Smiths, their own No Name Bitter brewed for them by a Hampshire brewery and a guest like Theakstons Best on handpump; Sussex pressed apple juice and country wines; piped music. To reach the South Downs Way, turn left off the side road to Bury. Well behaved dogs are now allowed in certain areas. *(Recommended by Dr K M Thomas, Dr M V Jones, A E and P McCully, David Holloway, Pippa Bobbett, J E and A G Jones, Mrs J E Hilditch, Roger Taylor)*

Free house ~ Managers Nigel Walker and Gill Kelly ~ Real ale ~ Meals and snacks ~ (01798) 831559 ~ Children welcome ~ Occasional live Irish music ~ Open 11-3, 6-11

KINGSTON NEAR LEWES TQ3908 Map 3

Juggs 🍺

The Street; Kingston signed off A27 by roundabout W of Lewes, and off Lewes—Newhaven road; look out for the pub's sign – may be hidden by hawthorn in summer

Very little disturbs the old-fashioned country feel of this lovely 15th-c cottage, brightly covered with climbing roses during the summer. It's perhaps at its most attractive and picturesque at this time of year, and there are a good many close-set rustic teak tables on the sunny brick terrace; a neatly hedged inner yard has more tables under cocktail parasols, and there are two or three out on grass by a timber climber and commando net. Inside, the medley of furnishings and decorations in the rambling beamed bar is one of the most interesting we know of in the area, with particularly good prints, pictures and postcards on the walls. The choice of bar food is not in itself unusual, and chips figure quite prominently, but the quality of the home cooking is well above average. It includes good open sandwiches (from £2.75), taramasalata or ploughman's (£2.95), local sausages (£2.95), pitta bread with grilled ham, tomato, mushrooms and cheese or chicken tikka (from £4.25), an interesting vegetarian dish (£4.50), very good huge steak and kidney pudding (£7.50), daily specials such as caramelised onion and parmesan cream quiche, mushroom roast with tomato sauce, three-cheese potato bake or chcken curry, good puddings (£2.50) and children's meals (£2); Sunday lunchtimes the choice is limited to a range of ploughman's. The restaurant and another small area are no smoking. An unusual and rather effective electronic bleeper system lets you know when meals are ready. Particularly well kept Harveys Sussex, King & Barnes Broadwood and a guest on handpump, with a wider choice than usual of non-alcoholic drinks; helpful, welcoming service; log fires, darts, shove-ha'penny. It's worth getting there early, they do get busy. *(Recommended by Julian Holland, R J Walden, Barbara and Norman Wells, David Holloway, Martin Jones, Frank Cummins, Alec and Marie Lewery, K R Flack, Colin Laffan, Mr and Mrs Moody, Michael and Marla Hipston)*

Free house ~ Licensee Andrew Browne ~ Real ale ~ Meals and snacks (limited Sun lunchtime) ~ Restaurant (not Sun lunchtime) ~ (01273) 472523 ~ Children in

two family areas ~ Open 11-2.30, 6-11; closed evening 25 and 27 Dec and 2 Jan, all day 26 Dec

KIRDFORD TQ0126 Map 3

Half Moon 🍴

Opposite church; off A272 Petworth—Billingshurst

There's something distinctly fishy about this 17th-c local. In fact the choice of very good meals relies heavily on fresh seafood, carefully chosen by the licensees who have links with Billingsgate going back 130 years (they have become the leading UK importer of fresh exotic species from around the world). Their menu would tie even a Brain of Britain in knots, delving as it does into tile fish, porgy, parrot fish, soft shell crabs, Morton Bay bugs, scabbard fish, razor shells, mahi mahi, and baramundi (all from around £5.50, though much higher for some of the more unusual dishes). They also do more familiar fish like lobster, crab, tiger prawns and snapper, as well as dishes like sandwiches (from £1.80), home-made soup (£2.50), ploughman's (£3.80), omelettes (from £3.90), good salads, home-made lasagne (£4.80), and home-made steak and kidney pie (£5.20). Do remember fresh fish is seasonal, so there may be times when the range isn't as big as you might hope. Well kept Arundel Best and Gold, Boddingtons, Flowers IPA and Original and Gales HSB; local wine and ciders. Service is friendly and welcoming, but can slow down at times. The simple partly flagstoned bars are kept ship-shape and very clean; darts, pool, cribbage, dominoes. The restaurant is no smoking. There's a big garden with swings, a large boules area and a barbecue area at the back, and more tables in front facing the pretty village's church. *(Recommended Clem Stephens, R D Knight, Mavis and John Wright, J S M Sheldon, M A Gordon Smith, R B Crail, Rosemary and Maine, Martin Richards, C H and P Stride, Brian Hutton)*

Whitbreads ~ Lease: Anne Moran ~ Real ale ~ Meals and snacks (not Fri or Sat evening except in restaurant) ~ Restaurant ~ (01403) 820223 ~ Children welcome till 9pm ~ Occasional live music ~ Open 11-3, 7-11; closed evening 25 Dec ~ One bedroom: /£35

LICKFOLD SU9226 Map 2

Lickfold Inn

Very handy for some lovely woods and countryside, this elegantly restored Tudor inn has a wonderful garden that spreads over several different levels, all with their own seating areas; interestingly planted, it's a very relaxing, characterful spot. There may be barbecues out here in summer. In contrast it's in winter that the bar seems to be at its most attractive, when the big log fires in the enormous brick fireplace create a lovely cosy atmosphere and cast subtly flickering shadows on the antique furnishings. In summer the fires are replaced by more tables, but at any time you'll still find the smart Georgian settles, heavy Tudor oak beams, handsomely moulded panelling, and ancient herringbone brickwork under rugs. Chalked up on a blackboard, the changing home-made bar food might include lunchtime sandwiches and ploughman's, tasty winter oxtail stew, lasagne, liver, bacon and onion or steak and kidney pie (all £5.75), fresh trout in season (around £6.75), good poached halibut in a creamy prawn sauce (£7.25), half roast shoulder of lamb (£7.75) or half a roast duck (£8.50), and puddings such as home-made ginger pear dumplings or treacle tart; good Sunday roast lunches. Usually six to eight well kept beers on handpump such as Adnams Best, Badger Best and Tanglefoot, Ballards Best, Fullers ESB and London Pride, and Harveys Best; good coffee. Some reports suggest the service could at times be a bit more friendly. Note they don't allow children. *(Recommended by Alec and Marie Lewery, David Holloway, Alison Burt, Mrs M Rice, J S M Sheldon, R B Crail, Peter Locke, Peter Fraser, B S Bourne, Mr and Mrs D E Connell, R and S Bentley and others)*

Free house ~ Licensees Ron and Kath Chambers ~ Real ale ~ Meals and lunchtime snacks (not Sun or Mon evenings) ~ (017985) 285 ~ Open 11-2.30(3 Sat), 6-11; closed Mon evenings

LODSWORTH SU9223 Map 2

Halfway Bridge ★ ♀ ◼

A272 Midhurst—Petworth

Deservedly doing rather well at the moment, this bright and roomy family-run pub is very well liked by readers, who like most of all the smartly civilised feel and range of very good food. It's been moving a little upmarket over the last few years, but not at the expense of the really impressive welcome and friendly atmosphere; the service is generally faultless, with good personal touches. The inventive home cooking comes in big helpings, with a choice of dishes like courgette and rosemary soup (£2.25), deep-fried camembert with gooseberry conserve or mushrooms in cream and tarragon (£2.95), soft roes on toast (£3.25), moules marinières(£3.95), leek and butterbean citron (£4.25), salads (from £4.95), chicken with cream, basil and peaches (£5.95), steak, kidney and Guinness pie (£6.25), provençale fish stew (£6.75), quails with an orange and Pernod sauce (£7.75), skate in black butter and capers (£8.50), roast half duck and honey (£8.95), grilled lemon sole (£12.50), home-made puddings like banana toffee pie or walnut and treacle tart (both £2.50) and various Sunday roasts; it gets busy at weekends so booking is advisable. The three or four comfortable rooms that loop around the central servery have attractive fabrics for their wood-railed curtains and pew cushions, with other furnishings running through good oak chairs and an individual mix of tables (many of them set for dining) to a dresser and longcase clock down steps in a charming country dining room; log fires include one in a well polished kitchen range. On the walls are paintings by a local artist. A good range of well kept beers includes well kept Ballards Best, Brakspears, Flowers Original, Fullers London Pride and Gales HSB on handpump, with Harveys Winter XXXX and Woodfordes Porter in winter, and maybe a couple of other local brews; farmhouse cider and a developing range of wines, with several by the glass and a few bin-ends; civilised family service. Dominoes, shove ha'penny, cribbage, backgammon, scrabble and mah jong. There are tables and chairs on the back patio. As we went to press they were still keeping up with their topical roadside blackboards, a popular practice which bizarrely the local Council don't seem to approve of. *(Recommended by M A Gordon-Smith, Larry Hansen, Angela and Alan Dale, J S M Sheldon, W K Struthers, Joe Jonkler, TOH, Mrs K I Burvill)*

Free house ~ Licensees Sheila, Edric, Simon and James Hawkins ~ Real ale ~ Meals and snacks (till 10) ~ Restaurant (not Sun evening) ~ Lodsworth (01798) 861281 ~ Children over 10 in restaurant ~ Open 11-3, 6-11; closed winter Sun evenings

LOWER BEEDING TQ2227 Map 3

Crabtree ⑪ ♀

A281 S of village, towards Cowfold

Sussex Dining Pub of the Year

The choice of food at this very welcoming 16th-c dining pub isn't huge, but the quality is excellent, with a half dozen or so really inventive and tasty main courses that are way better than your average bar meal. The choice changes every day, but as well as sandwiches (from £1.95) and ploughman's (from £3.25), both using their home-made bread, might include imaginatively prepared dishes such as watercress and potato soup (£2.75), marinated herrings with soured cream and dill (£4.15), duck liver and crispy bacon salad or feta cheese tart with olives and basil (£4.50), leek and mushroom pudding with ginger, garlic and limeleaf (£5.95), lamb rissoles with a redcurrant and mint sauce (£6.50), rabbit casserole in mustard sauce or chicken and ham pie (£6.95), grilled cod with herb butter (£7.25) and puddings like tropical fruit ice cream or Dutch apple pie (£2.75); they may also do a special three-course set meal (£9.50) or a selection of tapas (£5.50). They hope to have evening bar meals soon, but concentrate mainly on the attractive restaurant then. The cosy beamed bars have an air of civilised simplicity, and there's plenty of character in the back no-smoking restaurant. Well kept King & Barnes Sussex,

Broadwood, Festive and Mild on handpump (cheaper in the public bar), and various other seasonal brews, and good wines; prompt, friendly service. Darts, bar billiards, cribbage, dominoes and piped music. A pleasant back garden has seats, and there may be barbecues and live music out here on summer evenings. The pub is very handy for Leonardslee Gardens, which are closed in winter. *(Recommended by Martin and Catherine Horner, GB, CH, TOH, R J Walden, Terry Buckland, Mrs M Rice, David Holloway, Susan M Lee, Belinda Mead)*

King & Barnes ~ Tenants Jeremy Ashpool and Nicholas Wege ~ Real ale ~ Lunchtime meals and snacks, from 12.30 ~ Restaurant (not Sun evening) ~ (01403) 891257 ~ Children in restaurant ~ Occasional live entertainment Sun evenings ~ Open 11-3, 6-11

LURGASHALL SU9327 Map 2

Noahs Ark

Village signposted from A283 N of Petworth; OS Sheet 186 map reference 936272

Good home cooking is the main draw to this welcoming old pub, nicely set on the edge of the village green, though another attractive feature is the vividly coloured hanging baskets outside. There are more flowers in the two neatly furnished bars, replaced by warm log fires in winter (one in a capacious inglenook). The range of bar food includes sandwiches (from £2.25, toasties such as bacon and mushroom or garlic sausage £3.25), ploughman's (£3), chicken tikka (£4.90), good salads (from £4.95), steak and kidney pudding (£5.25), English lamb cutlets or calf's liver and bacon (£6.25), fresh fish, and home-cooked game and tongue, while the restaurant does more elaborate dishes like venison in red wine (£8.45) or escalope of veal with egg and anchovies (£8.50). Greene King Abbot, IPA and Raymons on handpump; friendly service. Sensibly placed darts and bar billiards, also shove-ha'penny, dominoes and cribbage. Tables on the front grass look across to a church with an unusual oak-built cloister running down the sunny side; it's said to have been designed as a sheltered spot for churchgoers from the far side of the parish to have their lunch in after service, so that they didn't have an excuse to visit the alehouse. *(Recommended by Mrs M Rice, J S M Sheldon, R D Knight, David Holloway, G B Longden, Mrs B M Spurr and others)*

Greene King ~ Tenant Kathleen G Swannell ~ Real ale ~ Meals and snacks (not Sun evening) ~ Restaurant (not Sun) ~ (01428) 707346 ~ Children in family room and restaurant ~ Occasional bands, theatre or concerts in garden on summer evenings ~ Open 11-2.30, 6-11

MAYFIELD TQ5827 Map 3

Middle House

High St; village signposted off A267 S of Tunbridge Wells

Built in 1575, this black-and-white timbered inn is Grade I listed – very rare for a pub or inn. The largely original L-shaped beamed main bar has a good mix of locals and visitors and a bustling, chatty atmosphere, good sturdy wooden tables, brocaded wall settles, captain's chairs, stools, hops around the bar gantry, plants along the window sills, and a log fire with a working spit in the large fireplace; there's also a restful separate lounge area with deep comfortable chesterfields and armchairs and another log fire in a fine ornate fireplace (attributed to Grinling Gibbons). A wide choice of regularly changing, good bar food includes ploughman's (£3.50), open sandwiches (from £4.25), steak and kidney pie (£6.50), pasta with salmon and prawns or grilled trout (£7.95), half roast duck or steak (£9.95), and puddings like fruit crumbles, brûlée or banoffi pie (£2.95); there's some handsome panelling in the restaurant. Well kept Greene King Abbot, Harveys Best, Wadworths 6X, and a guest like Fullers ESB on handpump; darts, fruit machine, trivia and piped music. The spacious back garden is prettily planted, has picnic-table sets, nice views, and a slide and a log house for children. We've not heard from readers who have stayed here, but would expect it to be comfortable. *(Recommended by Father D Glover, Donald Clay, Derek and Maggie Washington)*

Free house ~ Licensee Monica Blundell ~ Real ale ~ Meals and snacks ~ Restaurant (not Sun evening) ~ (01435) 782146 ~ Children welcome ~ Open 11-11; closed evenings 25/26 Dec ~ Bedrooms: £35(£45B)/£55B

Rose & Crown ★ 🛏 ♇

Fletching Street; off A267 at NE end of village

Once the village brewhouse, this pretty weather-boarded 16th-c inn is well liked as a place to stay, and has a very good varied range of thoughtfully prepared and presented food. On a typical day you might find lunchtime filled baguettes (from £3.95), ploughman's (from £4.50) and beef stew (£4.95), home-made soup (£2.50), smoked salmon quenelles (£3.45), stilton and crispy bacon salad (£3.85), pies such as steak and ale or spicy bean and vegetable (£5.95), chicken in a coriander, spinach and yoghurt sauce (£7.45), lamb in redcurrant and rosemary or poached salmon in a dill, vermouth and cucumber sauce (£7.95), duck in honey and ginger (£8.95), changing specials like game pie (£7.75), pheasant braised with chestnuts, juniper berries and bramble jelly (£8.65), or loin of pork in a leek and cider sauce (£8.85), fresh fish, and exceptional home-made puddings such as lemon brûlée or treacle and walnut tart (from £2.50). The most appealing parts are the two cosy little front rooms with low beam-and-board ceilings, some panelling and a handsome inglenook; there's a quieter side dining room, and an oak-beamed, candlelit restaurant. Well kept Adnams, Greene King Abbot, Harveys Best and more unusual twice-weekly changing guests on handpump, varied wines from around the world, and a growing range of malt whiskies; darts, bar billiards, shove-ha'penny, dominoes and cribbage, piped music at lunchtime. At weekends the bar may stay busy till late. The bedrooms are very pretty and comfortable. Outside there are rustic tables out among hanging baskets and flower tubs on the front terrace, and several picnic-table sets in the quiet and attractive back garden. *(Recommended by Penny and Martin Fletcher, Pam and Tim Moorey, Pauline Bishop, P J Sykes, Mrs Susannah Gooch, Edward Bace, Brenda and Ralph Barber, R Wilson, Neale Davies, E D Bailey; also recommended by* The Good Hotel Guide*)*

Free house ~ Licensees Peter and Jackie Seely ~ Real ale ~ Meals and snacks (12-2.30, 6.30-10.30, all day Sat) ~ Restaurant ~ Mayfield (01435) 872200 ~ Children over 7 in eating area and restaurant ~ Open 11-2.30, 5.30-11, all day Sat ~ Bedrooms: £44.95B/£54.95B

MIDHURST SU8821 Map 2

Spread Eagle 🛏

South St

A smart and very atmospheric old hotel, mostly mid 17th-c, but dating back in part to 1430. Most impressive is the spacious massively beamed and timbered lounge, with its dramatic fireplace, imposing leaded-light windows looking out on the most attractive part of this old town, and handsome yet quite unpretentious old armchairs and settees spread among the rugs on the broad-boarded creaking oak floor. There's apparently a secret room six feet up one chimney. The atmosphere is one of restful luxury, but despite the opulence it's a friendly, welcoming place. A concise lunchtime bar menu includes vegetable soup (£4.25), tomato, bacon and cheese tart or chicken liver parfait with a toasted brioche (£5.25), a daily special, smoked haddock topped with Welsh rarebit (£5.50), and puddings (£2.50); the well regarded restaurant has a wider choice. They do good cream teas at weekends. The lounge opens onto a secluded courtyard. Badger Best on handpump, not cheap but well kept; shove-ha'penny, cribbage, dominoes, trivia, maybe piped music. The pub was described in Hilaire Belloc's *The Four Men* as 'the oldest and most revered of all the prime inns of this world'. *(Recommended by Graham and Karen Oddey, Martin Jones, Ian Phillips, Mrs M Rice, Paula Harrison, John Sanders)*

Free house ~ Licensees Pontus and Miranda Carminger and Percy Hooper ~ Real ale ~ Lunchtime meals and snacks (not Sun) ~ Restaurant ~ Midhurst (01730) 816911 ~ Well behaved children welcome ~ Open 11-2.30, 6-11; closed evening 25 Dec ~ Bedrooms: £62B/£79B

NORMANS BAY TQ6805 Map 3

Star

Signposted off A259 just E of Pevensey; and from Cooden, off B2182 coast road W out of Bexhill

Particularly popular in summer, when you can relax in the hawthorn-sheltered treeside garden, this friendly old smugglers' pub is a consistently reliable place for a meal or a drink – though you might find it difficult to decide what to have. There are rarely less than 10 well kept real ales on handpump, with beers like Charles Wells Bombardier, Harveys Best, Hopback Summer Lightning, Marstons Owd Roger and a variety of other frequently changing brews from nearby or further afield. They also do lots of Continental bottled beers, good country wines (the local apple is recommended), and a wider range of lagers and ciders than you'll usually come across. The choice of bar food is big and so too are the helpings – they hand out doggy bags and warn on the menu of the things that might defeat even a smuggler-sized appetite. Especially popular are the half-dozen or more vegetarian dishes such as vegetable crumble, hot Boston beans, nut roast or pasta (from £3.75), and the good choice of fresh local fish (from £4.50 – the fishermen's huts are just down the road); other meals include a dozen or more starters like soup (£1.95), ploughman's (from £3.25), burgers (from £2.25), half shoulder of lamb (£5.75), ham and eggs, scampi or half a roast chicken with jumbo sausage (all £5.95), pork chops (£6.25), a whole spiced pheasant in prunes (£7.95), a good selection of steaks (from £8.25), and masses of puddings – people especially like their large waffles (from £2.50); children's dishes (£2.25). The atmosphere is notably welcoming and relaxed, especially in the spaciously modernised bar with comfortably cushioned seats spreading over the carpet of a brick-pillared partly timbered dining lounge; piped music, games in the children's room. Friendly staff cope admirably even when busy. There are tables on a small front terrace, and in the garden with its play area; there may be barbecues out here in summer. Paths inland quickly take you away from the caravan sites into marshy nature reserve. *(Recommended by Alec and Marie Lewery, R J Walden, E G Parish, R Wilson, Mrs C Archer, Colin Laffan)*

Free house ~ Licensee Francis Maynard ~ Real ale ~ Meals and snacks (till 10) ~ (01323) 762648 ~ Children in own room ~ Jazz Tues evening and other live music Sun lunchtime ~ Open 11-3, 6-11, maybe all day in summer

NUTHURST TQ1926 Map 3

Black Horse

Village signposted from A281 SE of Horsham

There's a warmly relaxed and welcoming feel to this cosy and old-fashioned black-beamed country pub, particularly in the main bar with its comfortable chairs on big Horsham flagstones in front of the inglenook fireplace. One end of the room opens out into other carpeted areas, one of which is the dining room, and there are interesting pictures on the walls, and magazines to read; cribbage, dominoes, piped music. A good range of well kept beers on handpump includes Adnams, Eldridge Pope Hardy, King & Barnes Sussex, Smiles Best, Tetleys and Wadworths 6X, and Gales country wines. Promptly served bar food such as soup (£2.25), doorstep sandwiches (from £2.50), ploughman's (from £3.50), filled baked potatoes (from £3.75), oriental vegetable parcels (£3.95), a pie of the day or vegetarian cannelloni romagna (£5.50), various curries (£5.95), and changing specials like chicken panang or prawns piri piri; they do good weekend barbecues in summer. The restaurant is no smoking. Service is friendly and efficient, and they're just as welcoming if you turn up wet and muddy after sampling one of the area's lovely woodland walks. *(Recommended by LM, R T and J C Moggridge, R J Walden, Mr and Mrs Hunns, Mavis and John Wright, B Fry, Mrs D Schopmann, Wendy Arnold, Alva and Mike Lockett, J H Purslow, Mrs P J Rand)*

Free house ~ Licensees Trevor and Karen Jones ~ Real ale ~ Meals and snacks (11.45-2.30, 6-9.45) ~ Restaurant ~ (01403) 891272 ~ Children in restaurant ~ Open 11-3, 6-11

OVING SU9005 Map 2

Gribble 🍺

Between A27 and A259 just E of Chichester, then should be signposted just off village road; OS Sheet 197 map reference 900050

The licensees who took over this attractive old thatched pub in December 1993 used to run the Jolly Sailor at Bursledon, a main entry in our Hampshire chapter. They've refurbished a little with new carpets and the like, but there's still the same emphasis on the tasty range of beers brewed in the pub's own microbrewery. Enduring favourites include the well kept Gribble Ale, Reg's Tipple, and Black Adder, with new varieties such as Pluckling Pheasant; they also have Badger Best and Tanglefoot on handpump, with country wines and Inch's farm cider. The garden has rustic seats among the apple trees, while the friendly bar is full of heavy beams and timbering and old country-kitchen furnishings and pews. Home-cooked bar food (still suffering a few teething troubles it seems) includes soup (£1.75), open sandwiches (from £2.25), ploughman's (from £3.75), ham and eggs (£3.75), ratatouille au gratin (£4.45), steak and mushroom pie (£5.25), salads (from £5.25), Mexican chicken, braised steak or grilled whiting fillets (£5.95), steaks (from £8.50) and puddings; they do smaller helpings of most meals, as well as children's dishes (£2.45) and a Sunday lunch (£5.35). On the left, a family room with pews provides perhaps the biggest no-smoking area we've so far found in a Sussex pub, and also has shove-ha'penny, dominoes, cribbage, and a separate skittle alley. *(Recommended by R J Walden, N E Bushby, Ted Burden, John Sanders, Colin Laffan, Eamon Green, Mr and Mrs D E Connell, M G Hart, Mr and Mrs Moody; more reports please)*

Own brew (Badger) ~ Managers Ron and Anne May ~ Real ale ~ Meals and snacks ~ (01243) 786893 ~ Children in family room ~ Open 11-2.30, 6-11, all day Sat

nr PUNNETTS TOWN TQ6220 Map 3

Three Cups 🍺

B2096 towards Battle

You feel at home in the peaceful long low-beamed bar of this unspoilt old pub as soon as you go in, thanks largely to the impressive log fire, full of what could just as well be called trunks as logs. The big fireplace stands under a black mantelbeam dated 1696, and there's also attractive panelling, and comfortable seats, including some in big bay windows overlooking a small green. All very traditional, it's the kind of old-fashioned and friendly country local that's becoming all too rare these days. A back family room leads out to a small covered terrace, with seats in the garden beyond – where you'll find chickens and bantams and a good safe play area. Good value unassuming food includes sandwiches, filled baked potatoes (from £2.75), prize-winning local giant sausages (£3.25), home-made steak or chicken pie (£4.50), half a roast chicken (£6.75) and steaks (from £7.50); part of the eating area is no smoking. Four well kept changing beers such as Adnams Broadside, Arkells Bitter, Gales HSB, or Harveys Best on handpump. Darts, table skittles, shove-ha'penny, dominoes and cribbage. There's space for five touring caravans outside. Good walks from here, on either side of this high ridge of the Weald. *(Recommended by DC, R D Knight, John Le Sage, James Nunns)*

Free house ~ Licensees Leonard and Irenie Smith ~ Real ale ~ Meals and snacks ~ (01435) 830252 ~ Children in eating area of bar and family room ~ Open 11-3, 6.30-11

ROWHOOK TQ1234 Map 3

Chequers

Village signposted from A29 NW of Horsham

Largely unchanged under its new licensees, this is a pleasantly rustic and genuinely old-fashioned place, unspoilt by the kind of modernisations that seem to blight so many of its type. A sunny little front terrace borders the quiet lane, and there are a good few tables in the peaceful and prettily planted side garden, with more on another crazy-paved terrace; good children's play area with swings, see-saw, Wendy house, slide and climbing frame. The snugly unpretentious beamed and flagstoned front bar has black beams in its white ceiling, upholstered benches and stools around the tables on its flagstone floor, and an inglenook fireplace; up a step or two, there's a carpeted lounge with a very low ceiling. Changing blackboard bar food includes filled cottage loaves (£2.95), Cumberland sausage (£4.95), steak and kidney pudding (£5.95), saddle of lamb (£8.95), char-grilled steaks such as venison (from £9.95) and various game and seafood dishes, which they plan on making the speciality. Well kept Brakspears, Flowers Original, Fullers London Pride and Morlands Old Speckled Hen on handpump, and a good range of wines with several by the glass; friendly service, piped music. Shove-ha'penny, dominoes and cribbage, and boules in the garden. *(Recommended by Martin Richards, J S M Sheldon, David Rule, C R and M A Starling, Angela and Alan Dale, Peter Adcock)*

Whitbreads ~ Tenant Tony Fulcher ~ Real ale ~ Meals and snacks ~ Restaurant ~ (01403) 790480 ~ Children welcome till 8.30pm ~ Open 11-3, 6-11

RYE TQ9220 Map 3

Mermaid 🛏

Mermaid St

Long one of Rye's most familiar images, with its distinctive sign hanging over the steeply cobbled street, this lovely black and white timbered inn looks much the same as when it was built in the 15th and 16th c. It's the same story in some of the rooms too, particularly a little back bar where a picture of the scene 70 years ago shows the detail of the furnishings has scarcely altered since. All that seems to have changed in the past couple of hundred years or so is the addition of electricity and a slight mellowing of the atmosphere: it used to be a favourite with gangs of notorious smugglers, who kept their loaded pistols by the side of their tankards while drinking, just in case. These days it's altogether more relaxed. Fine panelling, antique woodwork and rare frescoes fill the civilised rooms, and there are some unusual intricately carved antique seats, one in the form of a goat, as well as an enormous fireplace. The cellars date back seven centuries. Morlands Old Speckled Hen and local Potters Pride on handpump, and their own house wines, ports and sherries. Readers have enjoyed the restaurant, where there's a salad buffet (about £7), and simple dishes such as soup, sandwiches and ploughman's may also be requested; it's the kind of place where they'll ask you which colour bread you'd prefer and how you'd like the meat in your hot beef sandwich. Hearty breakfasts. There are seats on a small back terrace, and in summer there may be local brass band concerts in the car park. The ghost of a serving maid who lost her heart to a smuggler is said to return just before midnight. *(Recommended by Thomas Nott, Mrs M Rice, Mr and Mrs H and E Hanning, Jim and Maggie Cowell, Mr and Mrs P B Dowsett, Andrew and Ruth Triggs and others)*

Free house ~ Licensee Robert Pinwill ~ Real ale ~ Restaurant ~ Rye (01797) 223065 ~ Children welcome ~ Open 11-11 ~ Bedrooms: £54B/£88B, some rooms have four-posters

nr SEAFORD TV4899 Map 3

Golden Galleon 🍺

Exceat Bridge; A259 Seaford—Eastbourne, near Cuckmere

As they hoped last year, they've recently set up their own little microbrewery at this busy place, producing Brewery on Sea Best, Riptide and Cuckmere Haven. These slot rather comfortably into what was already a fine range of beers, with generally a half dozen or so other regularly changing ales such as Greene King Abbot, Harveys Armada and Tom Paine, HopBack Summer Lightning, Shepherd and Neame Bishops Finger and Timothy Taylor Landlord, on handpump or tapped from the cask; there's also freshly squeezed orange juice, a decent selection of malts, continental brandies and Italian liqueurs and cappuccino or espresso coffee. But it's the excellent food that draws most people here, and as the landlord is Italian, expect lots of properly prepared dishes from his homeland on the menu. Tasty and plentiful meals include home-made soup (£2.35), ploughman's, tonno e fagioli (tuna and butter beans with capers and onions dressed with olive oil, £3.15), Italian seafood salad (£3.95), deep fried chicken fillets (£5.50), various fresh local fish either steamed or deep fried (£5.50), specials such as lasagne, spaghetti carbonara, chicken in tomato and ginger sauce, popular deep-fried cod in garlic and dill batter or pork tenderloin, steaks (from 8oz sirloin £9.75) with an excellent selection of sauces, a good help-yourself salad counter (from £3.75), and half-helpings of most things for children. No credit cards. Inside around two-thirds of the turkey-carpeted bar and dining area with its neat rows of tables is no smoking; high trussed and pitched rafters give this quite an airy feel, and there's a nice little side area with an open fire. More space for eating has been created by the addition of a new conservatory. At most times of the year there's a cheerily bustling feel that some feel is more reminiscent of an Italian trattoria than a typical pub, and this is particularly the case in holiday periods. Very good friendly service, piped music. The pub is just ten minutes' stroll from the beach, and there are good views from the sloping garden towards Beachy Head and the Cuckmere estuary, with tables to take in the view; it gets very busy in summer. The Seven Sisters Country Park is just over the nearby Cuckmere River, and there are walks inland to Friston Forest and the downs. *(Recommended by John Beeken, Brian Jones, Alan Skull, Gerald Flanagan, A E R Albert, Dr S Savvas, M Martin)*

Own brew ~ Licensee Stefano Diella ~ Real ale ~ Meals and snacks (12-2, 6-9) ~ Seaford (01323) 892247 ~ Well behaved children welcome ~ Open 11-2.30(3 Sat), 6-11; closed Sun evenings mid Sept-Mar

SIDLESHAM SZ8598 Map 2

Crab & Lobster

Off B2145 S of Chichester, either Rookery Lane N of village (on left as you approach) or Mill Lane from village centre

One of the highlights of this nicely traditional place must be the lovely back garden, filled with sweet peas, gladioli, snapdragons, roses and so forth, and looking across a meadow to the coastal bird-reserve flats and silted Pagham Harbour. A bonus is that despite the lovely setting, it's well off the main tourist routes. The ochre-walled bar is straightforward and comfortable, with a good log fire, wildfowl and marine prints and maybe a few cheery locals; there's also a plusher side lounge. They've recently extended the range of bar food, with tasty meals now including sandwiches such as crab or prawn, leek and gruyere puff (£4.50), gammon and egg (£5.20), steak and kidney pie (£5.40), rack of lamb (£5.90), Selsey crab salad or oriental prawns (£6.20), mouth-watering crab and lobster mornay (from £7.50), and home-made puddings; as ever, the seafood is particularly good. Well kept Arundel Stronghold and Gales Best and BBB on handpump, various wines, Gales old country wines and a decent choice of other drinks. Darts, cribbage, dominoes, shut-the-box. *(Recommended by John and Tessa Rainsford, Mrs M Rice, John Beeken, R T and C E Moggridge, Susan and John Douglas, Miss A G Drake, John and Joy Winterbottom)*

Free house ~ Licensee Brian Cross ~ Real ale ~ Meals and snacks (not Sun evening) ~ (01243) 641233 ~ Open 11-2.30(3 Sat), 6-11; closed Sun evenings Jan and Feb

STOPHAM TQ0218 Map 3

White Hart ♀

Off A283 between village turn-off and Pulborough

The graceful seven-arched bridge at this attractive spot was constructed in 1309, and there's been some sort of building on the site of the pub for probably the same amount of time. The recent bypass has restored the peaceful air that a place like this is best suited for, and tables on the lawn across the road make the most of the striking setting. There are tree-lined grass walks down by the meeting of the Arun and Rother rivers, and a play area is across here too. The three relaxing cosy and comfortable beamed rooms are quite a draw in their own right, but the main focus of attention for most people is the good home-made food: sandwiches (from £1.10, smoked salmon £2.95), soup (£1.65), filled baked potatoes (from £2.60), various ploughman's and other platters (from £2.95), spicy sausages (£3.25), spinach ravioli (£3.95), fish pie (£4.50), and children's meals (£1.65). Best of all are probably the daily specials (served in the bar or the beamed and candlelit restaurant), where the emphasis is very much on often exotic fresh fish and seafood, with dishes such as fish soup (£2.25), sole and salmon roulade (£4.95), medallions of monkfish pan-fried in garlic and herbs (£5.50), smoked eel fillets or gravadlax (£5.75), plaice fillets filled with salmon mousse in a champagne sauce (£9.95), steamed red snapper with ginger and spring onions or shark steak in a peppercorn sauce (£10.50). Friendly staff and characterful spotted cat. Well kept Boddingtons and Flowers Original on handpump, and decent wines including several New World by the glass, half-bottle and bottle. Darts, shove-ha'penny, cribbage, dominoes, fruit machine, and piped jazz or big band music. The restaurant and usually one bar are no smoking. *(Recommended by J S M Sheldon, John and Tessa Rainsford, David Holloway, A H Denham, Mrs M Rice, Tony and Wendy Hobden, Mavis and John Wright, A C Morrison, DC, J E and A G Jones, R T and C E Moggridge)*

Whitbreads ~ Lease: John Palmer and Linda Collier ~ Real ale ~ Meals and snacks (not Sun evenings Oct-Apr) ~ Restaurant ~ Pulborough (01798) 873321 ~ Children welcome ~ Live entertainment in garden every other summer Sun ~ Open 11-3, 6.30(7 winter weekdays)-11

nr TICEHURST   TQ6830   Map 3

Bull 🍺

Three Legged Cross; coming into Ticehurst from N on B2099, just before Ticehurst village sign, turn left beside corner house called Tollgate (Maynards Pick Your Own may be signposted here)

Delightfully tucked away, this notably relaxed and peaceful old pub is based around a 14th-c Wealden hall, and the original core is still the place to head for. A series of small flagstoned, brick-floored or oak parquet rooms run together, with heavy oak tables, seats of some character, and the big focal fireplace (which the soft grey tabby heads for). A larger, more modern room is light and airy; darts, dominoes and cribbage. Even better in summer is the pretty sheltered garden, with tables beside an ornamental fishpond looking back at the building, covered in climbing roses and clematis. Not surprisingly it's a popular place, with the friendly rooms soon filling up. The food is very well liked (readers this year even raving about the gravy), and includes lunchtime dishes such as good sandwiches (from £1), home-made stilton soup (£1.65), tandoori chicken or spicy peeled prawns (£2.85), good ploughman's or smoked salmon and trout roulade (both £3.25), a well liked good-value summer buffet (from £3.95), garlic chicken en croute (£5.25), fresh whole trout or avocado and corn bake topped with a creamy cheese sauce (£5.75), steak, kidney and mushroom pie or Thai-style chicken breast cooked in a spicy peanut sauce (£6.50), fresh salmon with spinach wrapped in filo pastry in a watercress sauce (£6.95), sirloin steak (£7.95), shoulder of English lamb (for two, £13.95) and home-made puddings like apple strudel, summer pudding or hokey-pokey ice cream with honeycomb in it; in the evenings (when they prefer bookings), they do more elaborate meals. Service is friendly and efficient. Well kept Harveys Best and weekly changing guest like Morlands Old Speckled Hen or Robinsons Best on handpump (often at a very good price for the area) – and they make a good pot of tea. Children can escape to a big playing field, where at weekends they usually have a bouncy castle and maybe an outside bar and barbecue; they also have a couple of boules pitches. It's handy for visiting the gardens of Pashley Manor. *(Recommended by Ian Phillips, Mr and Mrs J Liversidge, Andy Thwaites, K and E Leist, R Suddaby, Penny and Peter Keevil, Colin Laffan, Maysie Thompson, C P and M G Stent, Mr and Mrs P B Dowsett)*

Free house ~ Licensee Josie Wilson-Moir ~ Real ale ~ Meals and snacks (not Sun or Mon evenings) ~ Restaurant ~ Ticehurst (01580) 200586 ~ Children in eating area and restaurant ~ Open 11-3, 6.30-11

WEST ASHLING SU8107 Map 2

Richmond Arms ◖

Mill Lane; from B2146 in village follow Hambrook signpost

You can get quite a shock when you see the astonishing range of well kept real ales at this unpretentious and notably friendly out-of-the-way village pub. There are usually ten of them on at a time, from all over the country, with a typical selection including Boddingtons, Brakspears, Greene King Abbot, Marstons Pedigree, Morlands Old Speckled Hen, Timothy Taylors Landlord, Youngs Special and a couple of more unusual brews you might not often find in this part of the world; also farm ciders, country wines, Belgian fruit beers and Continental bottled beers. The furnishings fit in well – the main room's dominated by the central servery, and has a 1930s feel, with its long wall benches, library chairs, black tables and open fire (maybe with a couple of black cats in front of it). Readers like the good choice of well priced no-nonsense food such as sandwiches (croque monsieur £3), excellent ploughman's, filled baked potatoes, home-made spinach and mushroom lasagne, vegetarian cannelloni, chilli con carne or curry (£4.20), game pie (£5.60) and salmon en croûte (£6.80). Service is consistently obliging and flexible, even when the pub is busy, as it often is, especially at weekends. Bar billiards, shove-ha'penny, dominoes, cribbage, and trivia and fruit machines in the games room; the skittle alley doubles as a function and family room. There's a pergola, and some picnic-table sets by the car park. *(Recommended by Derek and Sylvia Stephenson, John Beeken, Ann and Colin Hunt, Phil and Sally Gorton, Alan Kilpatrick, Barbara Hatfield)*

Free house ~ Licensees Bob and Christine Garbutt ~ Real ale ~ Meals and snacks (12-3, 6.30-10) ~ (01243) 575730 ~ Children welcome ~ Tues quiz night ~ Open 11-3, 5.30-11, all day Sat in summer; closed evening 26 Dec

WEST HOATHLY TQ3632 Map 3

Cat

Village signposted from either A22 or B2028 S of East Grinstead

Quite a summer favourite, this welcoming tiled pub is quite a busy place, but that just seems to fit in with the general cheeriness and friendly feel. Seats among the roses out in front are a good place to catch the sun, and there are fine views of the neighbouring old church nestling amongst its yew trees. Inside there are plenty of reminders of those long-gone days when it was a haunt of local smugglers. Ancient carvings decorate the inglenook on one side of the massive central chimney, and there are hefty blocks of stone masonry, some beams and panelling, and even some traces of wattle and daub plaster. The nicely presented well cooked bar food is popular, with a daily changing choice of home-made dishes that might include soup, tasty sandwiches, smoked salmon pâté, crab pâté or avocado prawn salad (£4.55), a pie of the day (£5.95), chicken livers with chipolatas (£6.95), beef stroganoff (£7.95) and various fresh fish; good-sized helpings. Well kept Boddingtons, Harveys BB and Wadworths 6X on handpump; prompt and attentive service, cheery Italian landlord. The pub is near the start of the *Good Walks Guide* Walk 64. *(Recommended by Graham Simpson, TOH, Sue Demont, Tim Barrow, Brian and Jenny Seller)*

Beards (who no longer brew) ~ Tenant Gonzalo Burillo ~ Real ale ~ Meals and snacks (not Sun evening) ~ Restaurant (not Sun evening) ~ (01342) 810369 ~ Children in eating area and restaurant ~ Open 11-2.30, 6-11

Anyone claiming to arrange or prevent inclusion of a pub in the *Guide* is a fraud. Pubs are included only if recommended by genuine readers and if our own anonymous inspection confirms that they are suitable.

WINCHELSEA TQ9017 Map 3

New Inn 🛏 🍺

Just off A259

Still a popular old pub in a nice setting, this is a rather friendly and well organised place, liked for its range of food and beers. The wide choice of rotated ales concentrates on beers from independent breweries, and might include such brews as Badger Tanglefoot, Everards Old Original, Harveys PA, Hatridges Nipper, Mitchells ESB, Palmers BB, Pilgrims Bitter, Smiles Bitter, Thwaites, or Wadworths 6X on handpump; they also do decent wines, several by the glass, and around 20 malt whiskies. There's an interesting set of rambling communicating rooms, with a comfortable variety of wall banquettes, settles and dining chairs around good sturdy tables, and a mix of bric-a-brac, interesting old photographs and other pictures on the walls, painted a deep and relaxing terracotta colour, and there's a good log fire; a third of the bar area is no-smoking. Popular, hearty bar food, as last year with a good emphasis towards seafood, includes sandwiches (from £2), home-made soup (£2), ploughman's (from £3.50), home-cooked ham and egg (£4.50), vegetarian meals including leek and mushroom bake, bean casserole or pasta ratatouille, plenty of fresh fish such as local plaice, brill, halibut, squid, red mullet, lemon sole or Dover sole (from £4.50), sumptuous home-made pies with fillings like lamb and apricot, wild boar, beef and mushroom, chicken and sweetcorn, and traditional steak and kidney (£5.50), steaks (£7.50), daily specials, children's meals (from £2.50) and puddings like home-made sherry trifle or bread and butter pudding; friendly, efficient waitress service. A quite separate public bar has darts, well lit pool, shove ha'penny, cribbage, fruit machine, trivia and unobtrusive piped music. There are picnic-table sets and swings in a sizeable neatly mown orchard. Once a favourite local of pre-Raphaelite artist John Everett Millais, the 18th-c pub is on the site of a much older building, whose medieval rib-vaulted cellar was used in Plantagenet times to store Gascon wine barrels. Some of the pretty bedrooms look across to the church among the lime trees opposite – particularly attractive in spring, with daffodils then drifts of bluebells; it has some interesting effigies and headstops in the graveyard. *(Recommended by D A Edwards, Maysie Thompson, David and Fiona Easeman, Dr T E Hothersall, Jack Taylor, Colin Laffan, Mr and Mrs P B Dowsett, Brian Kneale, Jim and Maggie Cowell, Andrew and Ruth Triggs)*

Beards (who no longer brew) ~ Manager Mrs Beverley Austen ~ Real ale ~ Meals and snacks ~ Restaurant ~ Rye (01797) 226252 ~ Children in eating area ~ Open 11-2.30, 6-11, all day summer Sats ~ Bedrooms: £30/£60(£72B)

WINEHAM TQ2320 Map 3

Royal Oak 🍺

Village signposted from A272 and B2116

The sort of charming and unchanging pub where the invention of snazzy tills, fruit machines and even beer pumps has gone by unnoticed. It's a nicely old-fashioned place, with the emphasis on drinking rather than eating, and can also pride itself on being one of the prettiest pubs in the county. The layout and style are commendably traditional, with very low beams above the serving counter, decorated with ancient corkscrews, horseshoes, racing plates, tools and a coach horn, along with basic old-fashioned furniture and logs burning in an enormous inglenook. It must have looked very like this when the current landlord first came here nearly 50 years ago. Well kept beers tapped from the cask in a still room on the way to a little snug include Boddingtons, Harveys BB, Wadworths 6X and Whitbreads Pompey Royal; darts, shove-ha'penny, dominoes, cribbage. A limited range of bar snacks such as fresh-cut or toasted sandwiches (from £1.25, roast beef £1.75 or smoked salmon £2.25) and home-made soup in winter (£1.50); good courteous service. The neat front lawn has wooden tables by a well. On a clear day male readers may be able to catch a glimpse of Chanctonbury Ring from the window in the gents'. The pub looks especially inviting at night. *(Recommended by Alec and Marie Lewery, Alan Skull, Mayur Shah, Comus Elliott, D E Clough, Terry Buckland)*

Whitbreads ~ Tenant Tim Peacock ~ Real ale ~ Snacks (available throughout opening hours) ~ (01444) 881252 ~ Children in family room ~ Open 11-2.30, 5.30(6 Sat)-11; closed evening 25 Dec

WITHYHAM TQ4935 Map 3

Dorset Arms

B2110

This unspoilt place is much older than its Georgian façade suggests, and actually dates back to the 16th c. It's rather unusual in that you have to go up a short flight of outside steps to enter the L-shaped bar, which at the end of the climb has sturdy tables and simple country seats on the wide oak floorboards, a good log fire in the stone Tudor fireplace, and a splendidly welcoming atmosphere. It's got quite a good reputation for food at the moment, with popular dishes such as sandwiches, soup (£2), ploughman's (£3.50), cheesy ratatouille bake (£3.50), steak, mushroom and Guinness pie (£4.25), home-cooked ham and eggs (£4.50), fresh plaice, cod or haddock (from £4.60), à la carte meals like chicken paprika (£6.95), tiger prawns in curry sauce (£7.50), or half a roast duckling with nut stuffing and brandy and orange sauce (£9.85), and puddings like apple and orange crumble (£2.20); they do a three course Sunday lunch. Well kept Harveys BB and PA, with their Porter in March, Tom Paine throughout July, and winter XXXX, all on handpump, and pleasant wines; friendly, efficient service. Darts, dominoes, shove ha'penny, cribbage, fruit machine and piped music. There are tables on a raised brick terrace outside. The road here used to be so muddy in winter that even oxen couldn't pull stuck waggons free. In nice countryside, the nearby church has a memorial to Vita Sackville-West. (*Recommended by R A Dean, Colin Laffan, Richard Waller, J S M Sheldon, M D Hare, Mr and Mrs G Lacey, Wayne Brindle*)

Harveys ~ Tenants John and Sue Pryor ~ Real ale ~ Meals and snacks (not Mon evening) ~ Restaurant (not Sun evening) ~ Hartfield (01892) 770278 ~ Children in restaurant and eating area of bar ~ Open 11.30(11 Sat)-3, 5.30(6 Sat)-11

Lucky Dip

Besides the fully inspected pubs, you might like to try these Lucky Dips recommended to us and described by readers (if you do, please send us reports):

Adversane, W Sus [TQ0723], *Blacksmiths Arms*: Food a cut above average, service extremely helpful and friendly *(Sally Edsall)*
Alfold Bars, W Sus [B2133 N of Loxwood – OS Sheet 186 map ref 037335; TQ0333], *Sir Roger Tichbourne*: Old-fashioned and welcoming beamed country pub with good relaxed atmosphere, friendly licensees and well kept King & Barnes, reasonably priced bar food (without its taking precedence), garden with children's play area *(Phil and Sally Gorton)*
☆ **Alfriston**, E Sus [TQ5103], *Market Cross*: Lots of olde-world atmosphere in low-beamed white-panelled bar with smuggling mementos, good value fair-priced bar food from sandwiches to steaks (snacks only, Sun lunch), well kept Courage Best and Directors, good choice of wines by the glass, friendly staff, tables in garden; children allowed in eating area and conservatory; can get crowded *(John and Joan Wyatt, Mark Percy, Brian Hutton, LYM)*
Alfriston [High St], *George*: Long, roomy and heavily beamed bar with huge fireplace, very extensive menu, warm welcome and efficient service, well kept Courage-related ales and King & Barnes, realistically priced wines, intimate candlelit dining area; comfortable attractive bedrooms, good breakfasts *(John Beeken)*
☆ **Amberley**, W Sus [off B2139; TQ0111], *Black Horse*: Unspoilt, attractive flagstoned village pub, up a flight of steps, its beams festooned with sheep and cow bells; wide choice of good simple home-cooked bar food from ploughman's to steaks, particularly good real chips, well kept Bass, Flowers and Worthington BB, farm cider, lovely open fires, friendly atmosphere, nice garden; children in eating area and restaurant, occasional folk music, two big dogs, sleepy cat *(John Beeken, Mr and Mrs Michael Boxford, Margaret Drazin, Mavis and John Wright, Mrs M Rice, LYM)*
☆ **Amberley** [Houghton Bridge, B2139], *Bridge*: Attractive, busy open-plan dining pub with pretty terrace garden, plenty of well presented fresh food from sandwiches up the local fish, well kept Gales ales, country wines, coffee (but no tea), interesting pictures, unobtrusive piped music; provision for children;

bedrooms; well placed by River Arun, get there early for space in the car park *(Howard Gregory, A E and P McCully, Susan M Lee, Russell and Margaret Bathie, N E Bushby, Mrs D Bromley-Martin)*

Amberley, *Sportsman*: Good small pub with three little rooms, back conservatory, fine views towards Pulborough from garden, well kept beers, decent wines and country wines, friendly welcome, good basic reasonably priced home-cooked food *(LM, Mrs M Rice)*

☆ **Angmering**, W Sus [TQ0704], *Spotted Cow*: Good straightforward food at proper tables and chairs – very popular weekdays with older people; cheerful attentive service even when busy, well kept beer, sensible prices, picnic-table sets in roomy garden with good separate play area; dogs allowed, at start of lovely walk to Highdown hill fort *(Ian Phillips, Brian Hutton)*

☆ **Ardingly**, W Sus [B2028 2 miles N; TQ5429], *Gardeners Arms*: Olde-worlde dining pub, very popular for its good reasonably priced home-made food from sandwiches up, inc good fresh fish and salads, till 3 even on Sun; welcoming and attractive if not exactly pubby bar with big log fire in inglenook, cheerful staff, well kept King & Barnes Festive, Theakstons and Courage-related real ales, morning coffee and tea, maybe soft piped music; plenty of space on big lawn (children not allowed in), handy for Borde Hill and Wakehurst Place *(Alain and Rose Foote, Mrs R D Knight, John and Judith Wells)*

Ardingly [Street Lane; TQ5427], *Ardingly Inn*: Should be well worth knowing, taken over 1994 by the Culvers who were so popular for their inventive food (with decent wines) and friendly service at the main-entry Chequers at Rowhook *(Anon)*; [Street Lane], *Oak*: Beamed 14th-c pub with well kept Courage-related and guest real ales, antique furnishings, lovely log fire in magnificent old fireplace, friendly staff, bar food; bright comfortable restaurant, pleasant tables outside; pool table in public bar *(Jean Minner, P Gillbe)*

☆ **Arlington**, E Sus [Caneheath, off A22 or A27; TQ5407], *Old Oak*: Popular reasonably priced food (not Mon; Tues is bangers and mash night) in 17th-c pub's big cosy L-shaped beamed bar and separate dining room; well kept Badger, Harveys and usually a guest beer tapped from the cask, pleasant staff, log fires, peaceful garden; children allowed, handy for Bluebell Walk *(A Albert, J H Bell, Dr S Savvas, M Martin, Alan Skull, Colin Laffan)*

☆ **Arlington**, *Yew Tree*: Welcoming village local, neatly modernised, decent straightforward bar food (even Sun evening), well kept Harveys and Courage ales, efficient service, subdued piped music, darts; restaurant, good big garden and play area by paddock with farm animals *(John Beeken, Peter Churchill, Jason Caulkin, Dr S Savvas, M Martin, Tony Albert, BB)*

☆ **Arundel**, W Sus [High St; TQ0107], *Arundel Brewery Tap*: Formerly the Swan, recently reopened after refurbishment as tap for new local brewery, with the full range of their good beers; pleasant L-shaped bar, rather more upmarket restaurant than previously; good well equipped bedrooms *(Derek and Sylvia Stephenson, Mrs M Rice, LYM)*

Arundel [Station Rd], *Arundel Park*: Small bar with well cooked tasty food, pleasant restaurant off, good service; motel-style bedrooms *(K and B Moore)*; [Mill Rd – keep on and don't give up!], *Black Rabbit*: Tranquil spot by River Arun, tables by river and on verandah with colourful hanging baskets and window boxes looking across to water meadows and castle, long picture-window bar; well kept Badger Best and Tanglefoot, bar food; busy in summer (open all day then), can be almost deserted winter, piped music may be loud; children in eating areas *(John Beeken, Andy and Jill Kassube, LYM)*; [Crossbush, A27 just SE], *Howards*: Elegant hotel bar with good views across the downs; bedrooms *(Dr and Mrs A K Clarke)*; [3 Queen St], *White Hart*: Two cosy lounges with old settles and books, comfortable dining area, quick friendly service, four well kept real ales, bar food *(Dr and Mrs A K Clarke)*

Balls Cross, W Sus [signposted off A283 N of Petworth; SU9826], *Stag*: 15th-c, flagstones, inglenook fireplace and more modern bar, reasonably priced food, seats outside *(Mrs M Rice)*

☆ **Barnham**, W Sus [OS Sheet 197 map ref 961043; SU9604], *Murrell Arms*: Genuine well preserved old pub with lots of pictures, old maps, notices and so forth; Gales tapped from the cask, good simple cheap food esp cheese or bacon doorsteps; several games inc ring-the-bull *(Tony and Wendy Hobden)*

☆ **Battle**, E Sus [25 High St; TQ7416], *George*: Upmarket but good value part pine-panelled bar and brasserie, clean and well run, with well kept Harveys, friendly staff, good teas; no music, open all day; bedrooms *(RB, P J Caunt)*

☆ **Battle** [Station Rd], *Senlac*: Good bar food at sensible prices, esp fish and puddings, well kept Whitbreads-related real ales, attractive layout; have to book for restaurant *(John Townsend)*

Battle [High St; sq by abbey], *1066*: Unpretentious old beamed pub nr Abbey with Whitbreads-related and other real ales kept well, pool area to left of entrance, fruit machine, piped music; several little seating areas, morning coffee and afternoon tea, open all day, friendly great dane *(Andrew and Ruth Triggs, Thomas Nott)*; [Mount St], *Olde Kings Head*: Well kept old pub with good medium-priced bar food, welcoming atmosphere, good Harveys as well as Courage; superb flower baskets outside, children welcome *(Graham Reeve, John Townsend)*

☆ **Berwick**, E Sus [Lower Rd, S of A27; TQ5105], *Cricketers*: Straightforward heavily beamed country pub, very busy weekends, with good traditional home-made food inc cheap specials and huge helpings of cheese and biscuits, well kept Harveys Bitter and Porter tapped from the cask, log fires, friendly service, beautiful olde-worlde garden with seats out in little segregated areas; well placed for walkers *(Paul and Heather Bettesworth, D L Barker, LM, Susie Northfield, John Beeken, Adrian and Gilly Heft)*

Bexhill, E Sus [Turkey Rd; TQ7407], *Rose & Crown*: Decent food inc good Sun lunches *(Alec and Marie Lewery)*

Billingshurst, W Sus [High St; A29; TQ0925], *Olde Six Bells*: Unspoilt partly 14th-c flagstoned and timbered pub with well kept King & Barnes real ales, generous food, inglenook fireplace, pretty roadside garden with proper tables and benches *(A N Black, LYM)*

Binstead, W Sus [Binstead Lane; about 2 miles W of Arundel, turn S off A27 towards Binstead – OS Sheet 197 map ref 980064; SU9806], *Black Horse*: 17th-c, with ochre walls and open fire in big bar, good range of real ales, darts and pool one end, welcoming young licensee, good choice of food in bar and reasonably priced restaurant; idyllic garden with country views; bedrooms *(Mrs M Rice, Tony and Wendy Hobden)*

Birling Gap, E Sus [TV5596], *Birling Gap*: Nicely decorated Thatched Bar, virtually separate from the hotel, with old tools for thatching and carpentry, pleasant atmosphere, nicely set just above seashore; usual bar food; bedrooms *(Peter and Lynn Brueton, E G Parish)*

Boarshead, E Sus [Eridge Rd, off A26 bypass; TQ5332], *Boars Head*: Unspoilt cosy old dim-lit stone-floored place next to pleasant farmyard, welcoming fire, simple good value food, very quiet weekday lunchtimes (piped music turned down then if asked) *(R D Knight, BB)*

Bodle Street Green, E Sus [off A271 at Windmill Hill; has been shut Mon Oct—Easter, opens 7pm; TQ6514], *White Horse*: Cheerily unpretentious simply modernised country pub with good value generous straightforward food, friendly service, well kept Harveys and King & Barnes Sussex and Festive, decent wines and malt whiskies, open fires, bar billiards, darts, cheery piped music; some tables outside *(N and M Foster, DC, BB)*

Bognor Regis, W Sus [56 London Rd; SZ9399], *Alex*: Friendly, warm and cosy, only ten mins' walk from Butlins but the welcoming landlord insists on proper dress; good value food in generous well cooked helpings inc Sun lunch, Courage-related and other ales such as King & Barnes, huge mug and jug collection hanging from ceiling *(J Wisden, Roger Byrne)*; [Steyne St], *Lamb*: Not that far from shops and sea, good range of well kept beers inc Arundel, Bass and Greene King Abbot, limited but useful food *(Derek and Sylvia Stephenson, Barbara Hatfield)*

Bosham, W Sus [High St; SU8003], *Anchor Bleu*: Star is for the lovely sea and boat views from this low-beamed waterside pub, in attractive village; well kept beer, log-effect gas fire, decent if pricy bar food; very popular with tourists, service can take a while in summer) *(Mrs M Rice, E M Hughes, David Dimmock, Brian Hutton, Eamon Green, LYM)*

Bosham, *Mill Stream*: Very pleasant setting nr estuary, good reasonably priced food, good wine list *(A and A Dale)*

Bramber, W Sus [TQ1710], *Bramber Castle*: Very efficient helpful staff, pleasant old-fashioned lounge, pretty garden, well kept beers and wide choice of reasonably priced food *(A E and P McCully)*

☆ **Brighton** [100 Goldstone Villas, next to Hove Rly Stn; TQ2805], *Hedgehog & Hogshead*: Bare floorboards, scrubbed tables, church pews, big windows, relaxed atmosphere; brews its own Brighton Breezy and strong Hogbolter, maybe Hedgehog or Hogswill – you can see the brewery; also two guest beers, good range of lunch and evening food, live music Fri, piped music may be loud other evenings; good service, very popular with young people Sat evening *(Dave Irving, Tony and Wendy Hobden, R Houghton, David Holloway)*

☆ **Brighton** [13 Marlborough Pl], *King & Queen*: Unusual and attractive building with medieval-style lofty and spacious main hall, generous good value food, pleasant cheerful service, well kept beer, pool table, flagstoned courtyard; good free jazz most evenings (when parking tends to be difficult) and Sun lunchtime evenings, aviary in flagstoned courtyard *(P Corris, LYM)*

☆ **Brighton** [59 Queens Rd; nr stn], *Royal Standard*: Well kept quickly changing guest beers tapped from the cask, brewery memorabilia, relaxed atmosphere, traditional tables with anti-spill rails; good varied menu with emphasis on fish *(Jim and Maggie Cowell)*

Brighton, *Battle of Trafalgar*: Good town pub, can get busy in the evenings, well kept Wadworths 6X and Youngs *(David Holloway)*; [New England Rd], *Cobblers Thumb*: Friendly happy local, obliging service, well kept Badger Tanglefoot, Fullers London Pride and Harveys, basic food; separate rooms for music, pool and conversation *(Caroline Driver)*; *Evening Star*: Impressive range of well kept real ales inc ones rare here such as Cotleigh Tawny in fairly basic backstreet pub *(R Houghton, David Holloway)*; [Boyces St, nr The Lanes], *Full Moon*: Good atmosphere, plenty of life on weekdays – no noisy music, but good company, good pub food, well kept real ales inc Badger and Wadworths 6X; quiet weekends, no food Sun *(Alan and Maggie Telford)*; [Southover St, Kemp Town], *Greys*: Worth knowing for good food inc adventurous puddings *(A M Pickup)*; [33 Upper St James's St, Kemp Town], *Hand in Hand*: Home of the Kemptown brewery, pleasant rather small local with a welcome for visitors; good service, food weekday lunchtimes *(R Houghton)*; [1 Hove Pl, Hove],

Mary Packs Cliftonville: U-shaped open-plan bar with restaurant off, good service, wholesome food inc good fish, Sun roast; can get busy and smoky *(Paul Weedon)*; [Market St, Lanes], *Pump House*: Light and airy pub, cosy and friendly, well kept ales *(Dr and Mrs A K Clarke)*; [Palace Pier], *Victorias*: Interesting bar with Victoriana suspended from walls and ceiling – prams, diving equipment, bicycles, model planes, clocks etc; good friendly service; good for pier views without the chill factor; Sky sports TV *(Barbara and Norman Wells)*

☆ **Broad Oak**, E Sus [A28/B2089 – the one N of Brede; TQ8220], *Rainbow Trout*: Attractive old pub, recently enlarged, very welcoming efficient staff, wide choice of good food but plenty of room for drinkers with wide range of beers, wines and spirits *(J H Bell, Leslie W Clark)*

Bucks Green, W Sus [TQ0732], *Fox*: Open-plan bar with wide choice of good bar food, well kept King & Barnes, inglenook, plenty of room for drinkers *(Steve Goodchild, Andy and Jackie Mallpress)*

☆ **Burwash**, E Sus [TQ6724], *Rose & Crown*: Timbered and beamed local tucked away down side street in pretty village, wide choice of real ales such as Bass, Charrington IPA and Shepherd Neame, decent wines, good log fire, friendly service, generous bar food, restaurant; tables on quiet lawn; bedrooms *(Rob Harrison, Joy and Arthur Hoadley, BB)*

Burwash Weald, E Sus [A265 2 miles W of Burwash; TQ6624], *Wheel*: Newish licensees doing decent straightforward food in open-plan local with good inglenook log fire, well kept Harveys and Ruddles Best and County, games bar up a step or two behind, tables outside; open all day; lovely walks in valley opp *(BB)*

Chailey, E Sus [Lewes rd; TQ5919], *Five Bells*: Free house with well stocked bar and food inc wide range of sandwiches; good service *(A H Denman)*; [South St (A275)], *Horns Lodge*: Clean well run free house with Badger Best, Harveys and Websters, good choice of popular food – get there early or book *(P J Keen)*

Chelwood Gate, E Sus [A275; TQ4129], *Red Lion*: Friendly new management doing good range of reasonably priced food, small choice of wines, well kept Courage-related ales and King & Barnes, green plush furnishings, small coal fire, dining room; delightful big sheltered garden with well spaced tables and barbecue; children welcome *(Martin and Catherine Horner, BB)*

☆ **Chilgrove**, W Sus [Hooksway; off B2141 Petersfield—Chichester, signed Hooksway down steep track without passing places – OS Sheet 197 map ref 814163; SU8214], *Royal Oak*: Smartly simple country tavern in very peaceful spot, beams, brick floors, country-kitchen furnishings, huge log fires; home-made standard food inc vegetarian, several well kept real ales, games, attractive seats outside; provision for children, has been cl winter Mons *(Peter Taylor, Eamon Green, LYM)*

☆ **Chilgrove**, *White Horse*: Smart dining pub in idyllic downland setting with small flower-filled terrace and pretty garden, lovely spot on a sunny day; very good food (must book restaurant), outstanding wines, welcoming landlord; lunches cheaper than evening *(Mrs M Rice, Mrs D Bromley-Martin)*

Cocking, W Sus [A286 Midhurst—Chichester; SU8717], *John Cobden*: Free house with warm welcome and well prepared and presented food *(Ian and Liz Phillips)*

☆ **Compton**, W Sus [SU7714], *Coach & Horses*: Good atmosphere in friendly spotless pub with well kept Broadwood, Fullers ESB and Gales HSB and Mild, traditional walkers' bar, plusher beamed lounge, good range of food in bars and restaurant; Flemish landlady *(Brian Bowden)*

Cooksbridge, W Sus [junction A275 with Cooksbridge and Newick rd; TQ5913], *Rainbow*: Welcoming tenants, good choice of good value food, pleasant atmosphere, attentive service *(J E and A G Jones)*

nr **Coolham**, W Sus [Dragons Green; TQ1423], *George & Dragon*: Charming small and ancient pub in huge garden, big inglenook, unusually low beams, King & Barnes ales, friendly atmosphere, usual bar food (not Sun evening) from sandwiches up inc fresh fish (may be a wait at busy times), pub games; children in eating areas *(Mark and Kate Porter, Gordon, WHBM, Mrs M Rice, LYM)*

Copsale, W Sus [signed off A24; TQ1725], *Bridge*: Modern pub popular with walkers, warm friendly welcome, basic food, King & Barnes beers, jazz Sun lunchtimes, garden with flowers, seats and play area; gets busy weekends *(Mrs M Rice, J E C Hobbs, BB)*

☆ **Cousleywood**, E Sus [TQ6533], *Old Vine*: Attractive dining pub with lots of old timbers and beams, wide range of generously served decent food, good house wine, well kept real ales; rustic restaurant decor on right, rather more pubby area by bar, a few tables out behind *(R and S Bentley, Jeff and Barbara Stratton, Tim and Pam Moorey, BB)*

Cowfold, W Sus [TQ2122], *Dog & Duck*: Well kept beer, wide choice of appetising food *(Dave Irving)*

Crawley Down, W Sus [J of A264/A2028; TQ5437], *Dukes Head*: Beefeater dining pub with Beards ales, reasonably priced food, friendly staff *(A H Denman)*

Crockerhill, W Sus [just off A27 Chichester—Fontwell; SU9207], *Winterton Arms*: Decent food in attractive old pub, pleasant service, open fire *(Mr and Mrs Hunns)*

Crowborough, E Sus [Beacon Rd (A26); TQ5130], *Blue Anchor*: Well run pub reopened after slight refurbishment, experienced new licensees, attractive garden *(Colin Laffan, JB)*

Dale Hill, E Sus [by Dale Hill golf club; junction A268 and B2099; TQ6930], *Cherry Tree*: Dining pub with big helpings of good reasonably priced food cooked to order with lots of veg – worth waiting for

(Christopher Day)

Danehill, E Sus [School Lane, Chelwood Common; off A275; TQ4128], *Coach & Horses*: Good home-cooked food inc vegetarian and well kept Harveys, Greene King and guest beers in unpretentious nicely placed pub with good atmosphere, pews in bar, decent house wine; ex-stables dining extension *(H R Taylor)*

Dell Quay, W Sus [SU8302], *Crown & Anchor*: Modernised 15th-c pub on site of Roman quay, yacht-harbour views from garden and comfortable bow-windowed lounge bar, panelled public bar with unspoilt fireplace, Courage-related ales, Marstons Pedigree and Wadworths 6X; good choice of popular food in bar and restaurant *(Ann and Colin Hunt, Eamon Green, BB)*

Devils Dyke, W Sus [TQ2511], *Devils Dyke*: Remarkable views night and day from touristy Brewers Fayre pub alone on downs above Brighton; decent food (served through Sun afternoon), efficient service, facilities for children and disabled *(Dr B A W Perkins, Julian Holland, Alec and Marie Lewery, LYM)*

Dial Post, W Sus [B2244, off A24; TQ1519], *Crown*: Comfortable free house with upmarket food in bar and restaurant, Courage-related and more local beers, log fires, no-smoking bar area *(E J and J W Cutting, Mrs M Rice)*

Donnington, W Sus [Selsey Rd (B2201); SU8502], *Blacksmiths Arms*: Excellent welcoming landlord, good choice of standard food in attractive dining extension, well kept ales such as Bass, Fullers London Pride, Marstons Pedigree and Wadworths 6X, decent wine, amazing collection of bric-a-brac, occasional live music, nice restaurant; children welcome, attractive garden *(John and Daphne Bowling, Ann and Colin Hunt, E M Hughes, John and Tessa Rainsford)*

Duncton, W Sus [set back from A285 N; SU9617], *Cricketers Arms*: Exhilarating atmosphere in friendly pub with genuine local feel despite some concentration on quickly served good original home-cooked food; well kept King and Barnes, lots of cricket memorabilia; some seats outside *(Dr L Kopelowitz)*

Eastbourne, E Sus [The Goffs, Old Town; TV6199], *Lamb*: Quite a classy feel in pretty Tudor pub's two main heavily beamed traditional bars off central oval servery, spotless antique furnishings, good inglenook log fire, well kept Harveys Best, Armada and Old, friendly polite service, usual food inc good ploughman's and toasties and good value Sun lunch from well organised food bar with upstairs dining room, no music or machines; children allowed in very modernised side room; by ornate church away from seafront; busy evenings, popular with students then *(R Wilson, Adrian and Gilly Haft, T G Thomas, Shirley Pielou, Pam Adsley, Brian Hutton, Kenneth Mason, M Veldhuyzen, Carol A Riddick, D L Barker)*

Eastbourne [Holywell Rd, Meads; just off

front below approach from Beachy Head], *Pilot*: Lively, comfortable and friendly, good range of prompt food inc good crab salad in season, pleasant landlady, well kept real ales, good ship photographs; garden *(Carol A Riddick, R Wilson, Mrs L M Tansley)*

Eastbourne [13/15 Carlisle Rd], *Cavalier*: Small pub with lively mix of customers, fun pictures, squabbling crayfish in fish tank; well kept Courage-related ales and King & Barnes, decent food, seats outside; good value bedrooms *(B R Shiner)*; [14 South St], *Dolphin*: Well refurbished intimate pub, coal fires, good well priced bar food, well kept Harveys; stylish restaurant with grand piano *(B R Shiner)*; [Kings Dr], *Rodmill*: Nicely set on outskirts, reasonably priced food in good helpings; summer barbecue and boules nights *(Alec and Marie Lewery)*; [Terminus Rd], *Terminus*: Not the smartest pub and may be smoky, but some character in its busy alcovey old-fashioned bar, with Harveys Mild and Best, varied lunchtime food, coffee, friendly helpful landlord, seats out in pedestrian precinct; children welcome *(Andrew and Ruth Triggs, Barbara and Norman Wells)*

Eridge Station, E Sus [TQ5434], *Huntsman*: Friendly landlady, well kept King & Barnes, food inc cheap well filled rolls *(Tony and Wendy Hobden)*

Ewhurst Green, E Sus [TQ7925], *White Dog*: Extensive and attractive partly 17th-c village pub in fine spot above Bodiam Castle, welcoming new licensees, interesting varied food inc good home-made game pie, good choice of real ales inc well kept Harveys; bedrooms *(Philip Rueff, LYM)*

☆ **Fairwarp**, E Sus [just off B2026, near Uckfield; TQ4626], *Foresters Arms*: Popular and well refurbished, with homely and welcoming atmosphere, good home cooking inc some unusual dishes and plenty of fresh veg, well kept King & Barnes Bitter, Festive, Broadwood and Old, good Polish staff, friendly fat dogs, pretty village setting nr Weald Way and Vanguard Way footpaths *(Colin Laffan, H R Taylor, Stella Knight, Alan Skull)*

☆ **Faygate**, W Sus [Wimland Rd, off A264 Horsham—Crawley; TQ2134], *Frog & Nightgown*: Attractively individual and relaxed old-fashioned local, very small, but clean, comfortable and friendly, with well kept Badger, King & Barnes and Shepherd Neame, bird prints, oldish record player; nice scenery *(Phil and Sally Gorton)*

☆ **Fernhurst**, W Sus [The Green, off A286 beyond church; SU9028], *Red Lion*: Well run old pub tucked quietly away by green nr church, good reasonably priced food from generously filled giant baps to braised rabbit in wine sauce, attractive layout and furnishings, friendly quick service, several well kept real ales, no-smoking area, good relaxed atmosphere; children welcome, pretty garden *(T Gillbe, Jenny and Brian Seller, BB)*

☆ **Findon**, W Sus [High St; off A24 N of Worthing; TQ1208], *Village House*: Good food from home-made soup to fish and local game in welcoming converted 16th-c coach house, oak tables, lots of racing silks and pictures, big open fire, wide range of alternating beers, good cheerful service, restaurant popular for Sun lunch, small attractive walled garden, pretty village below Cissbury Ring; bedrooms *(R Wilson, Mr and Mrs D E Powell)*

☆ **Findon**, *Gun*: Comfortably modernised low-beamed village local with good generous standard food with fresh veg, friendly service, well kept Whitbreads-related real ales; attractive sheltered lawn, quiet spot *(Mrs M Rice, LYM)*

Fishbourne, W Sus [A259; SU8404], *Black Boy*: Extraordinary decor inc farm tools, motorbicycles, Macbeth comic-strip, marble and statuary, even has had a live Vietnamese pot-bellied pig wandering around back conservatory; wide choice of food in bar and restaurant, Courage-related ales, children very welcome; motel-style bedrooms *(N Bushby, W Atkins)*

☆ **Fittleworth**, W Sus [Lower St (B2138); TQ0118], *Swan*: Prettily located 15th-c pub, now a Whitbreads Wayside Inn, with big inglenook log fire in friendly and comfortable lounge, good bar food with unusual specials and good Sun lunch in attractive panelled side room with landscapes by Constable's deservedly less-known brother George, courteous helpful staff, piped music; games inc pool in public bar, well spaced tables on big sheltered back lawn, good walks nearby; open all day Thurs-Sat, children in eating area; good value well equipped bedrooms *(Mrs M Rice, Ian Phillips, Helen and Stuart Dawson, LYM)*

Framfield, E Sus [The Street; B2012 E of Uckfield; TQ5020], *Hare & Hounds*: Clean, welcoming and spacious beamed country pub with well kept beers, wide range of other drinks, good changing choice of food, good service *(D L Barker)*

Frant, E Sus [A267 S of Tunbridge Wells; TQ5835], *Abergavenny Arms*: Some emphasis on restaurant in cosy pub with four well kept ales inc Harveys, good value bar food, log fire, bar billiards *(D L Barker)*; *George*: Five real ales inc Morlands Old Speckled Hen, good well priced food in bar and restaurant, friendly staff, beams and log fire; garden with barbecue *(M Buckingham)*

☆ **Funtington**, W Sus [SU7908], *Fox & Hounds*: Good atmosphere in welcoming old pub with imaginative choice of well cooked fresh food in bar with huge log fire or comfortable and attractive dining extension; Courage-related ales, farm cider, real ginger beer, reasonably priced wines, good coffee, no music, good waiter service *(Penny and Peter Keevil)*

Gatwick, W Sus [Airport; TQ2941], *Country Pub*: Remarkably successful imitation of a city pub given that there are no locals; decent straightforward food, real ale *(Gordon Mott)*

☆ **Glynde**, E Sus [TQ4509], *Trevor Arms*: Well kept Harveys, good range of food (though few puddings) from counter in saloon bar, small dining room, pleasant staff, sizeable

garden – very busy at weekends; nice spot, good walks (no muddy boots allowed) *(L M Miall, Adrian and Gilly Heft)*

Goddards Green, W Sus [TQ2820], *Sportsman*: Wide choice of reliable food inc good family Sun lunches, good waitress service in bar, garden and restaurant *(Desmond Curry)*

Graffham, E Sus [SU9217], *White Horse*: Pleasant family pub below South Downs with small dining room, conservatory with fine views, terrace and big garden; good choice of straightfoward bar food running up to steaks, very friendly staff, a welcome for walkers *(W K Struthers, Miss D J Hobbs)*

Halnaker, W Sus [A285 Chichester—Petworth; SU9008], *Anglesey Arms*: Smart simplicity in candlelit stripped-pine-and-flagstones dining room, locals' public bar with traditional games, well kept Friary Meux Best, Ind Coope Burton, King & Barnes Sussex and Tetleys, decent wines, tables in garden; children in restaurant *(J H L Davis, J and P Maloney, LYM)*

☆ **Hammerpot**, W Sus [A27 4 miles W of Worthing; TQ0605], *Woodmans Arms*: Welcoming low-ceilinged pub with interesting prints, horsey bric-a-brac, well kept King & Barnes ales, generous varied food inc giant Yorkshire puddings; seats in pleasant garden *(Andy and Jill Kassube, David Holloway, Brian Hutton, Tony and Wendy Hobden)*

Handcross, W Sus [High St; TQ2529], *Red Lion*: Quick friendly service in reliable Watneys Country Carvery *(A H Denman)*

☆ **Hartfield**, E Sus [Gallipot St; B2110 towards Forest Row; TQ4735], *Gallipot*: Good atmosphere in narrow but comfortable L-shaped bar with a couple of well kept real ales such as Fullers London Pride, obliging licensees, wide range of good genuine home-cooking (delicious choc pudding), no music, log fire, restaurant, dogs allowed if announced; on edge of attractively set village, good walks nearby *(Neil and Jenny Spink, Colin Laffan, R and S Bentley, R Spens)*

☆ **Hartfield** [A264], *Haywaggon*: Spacious and welcoming beamed pub with good bar food, well kept real ale, attractive restaurant, quick service *(Colin Laffan, R and S Bentley)*

☆ **Hastings**, E Sus [14 High St, Old Town; TQ8109], *First In Last Out*: Good reasonably priced beers brewed here, farm cider, good atmosphere – compartments formed by pews, no games or juke box; interesting lunchtime food, free Sun cockles, log fire *(T G Thomas, Rob and Doris Harrison, Sarah and Peter Adams)*

Haywards Heath, W Sus [TQ5324], *Fox & Hounds*: Friendly new owners, beer and food good *(Christopher Glasson)*

☆ **Hermitage**, W Sus [36 Main Rd (A259); SU7505], *Sussex Brewery*: Cosy atmosphere and good log fires in small friendly pub done out with bare bricks, boards and flagstones; sensibly priced real ales brewed for them, good value simple food from sandwiches up, no machines or piped music, small garden; can get very busy, open all day Sat *(Ann and*

Colin Hunt, Rob and Doris Harrison)

☆ Holtye, E Sus [A264 East Grinstead—
Tunbridge Wells; TQ4539], *White Horse*:
Generous food, very friendly and helpful
young staff and well kept ales inc Brakspears
in unpretentiously refurbished old village pub,
popular carvery restaurant with illuminated
aquarium set into floor; good facilities for the
disabled; bedrooms *(Chris and Anne Fluck,
the Shinkmans, Mrs R D Knight)*

☆ Hooe, E Sus [A259 E of Pevensey; TQ6809],
Lamb: Prettily placed dining pub, extensively
refurbished in uniform brick and flintwork
with added tile, flower pots, bottle bases etc;
extensive seating, also small eating area with
huge log fire; very wide choice of generous
popular food from well filled sandwiches up,
inviting open fire in snug original core, well
kept Harveys, quick friendly service *(A H
Denham, T G Saul)*

☆ Horsham, W Sus [31 North St; TQ1730],
Black Jug: Refurbished pub/restaurant with
pleasing panelled decor, good choice of food
inc fish, vegetarian and tasty puddings, well
kept ales such as Batemans, good changing
house wines *(Ken Hollywood, Belinda Mead)*
Horsham [Tower Hill – S, towards
Worthing], *Boars Head*: Good popular pub
food, welcoming landlord, half a dozen well
kept ales, back restaurant *(Mrs M Rice)*
Hurst Green, E Sus [A21; TQ7327], *Royal
George*: Friendly newish licensees,
Boddingtons, Courage Directors and Harveys,
decent bar food, restaurant; noisy road;
bedrooms *(N W Gill)*

☆ Icklesham, E Sus [TQ8816], *Queens Head*:
Generous helpings of varied appetising food
inc vegetarian, around a dozen changing real
ales and decent wines in friendly open-plan
beamed pub with lots of nooks, crannies and
different levels inc no-smoking area; log fires,
popular with families; views from garden
towards Rye *(P Corris, Amanda Hodges,
Anna and Aidan Walls)*
Iden, E Sus [Main St (B2082); TQ9123],
Conkers: Old pub with new name, soft
lighting, sumptuous leather chesterfields,
upmarket feel, open-plan layout with central
bar and dining tables either side;
straightforward bar food, good unusual
specialities in bistro, Courage-related real ales,
tables outside *(Mark Percy, E J Cutting)*

☆ Ifield, W Sus [Rusper Rd; TQ2437], *Gate*:
Quaint little country local which should do
very well as good value dining pub since being
taken on summer 1994 by tenants of Plough
at Leigh (see Surrey main entries); little side
garden with overhanging trees *(Anon)*
Isfield, E Sus [A m off A26; TQ4417],
Laughing Fish: Simply modernised Victorian
village local with well kept Harveys Best, PA
and Old, good honest home-cooked bar food,
tables in small garden with enclosed play area;
children welcome, right by Lavender Line
(John Beeken, BB)
Kingsfold, W Sus [Dorking Rd; A24
Dorking—Horsham, nr A29 junction;
TQ1636], *Dog & Duck*: Well kept King &
Barnes, good value tasty filling food,

comfortable *(Dave Irving)*
Lavant, W Sus [SU8508], *Royal Oak*: Gales
ales tapped from the cask in spacious bar,
cosy and dark, with good range of food, fresh
flowers; lovely setting right on seafront *(Viv
Middlebrook, Mike Forder, J H L Davis, Phil
and Sally Gorton)*

☆ Lewes, E Sus [Castle Ditch Lane/Mount Pl;
TQ4110], *Lewes Arms*: Old-fashioned
traditional local interestingly placed below
castle mound, cosy front lounge and two
larger rooms (one with pool), well kept
Harveys and other ales, limited range of basic
bar food, newspapers to read, warm
welcoming atmosphere *(John Beeken,
Margaret Drazin, Phil and Sally Gorton)*

☆ Lewes [22 Malling St], *Dorset Arms*: Good
bar food esp fresh fish Fri lunchtime in
popular, civilised and friendly 17th-c pub
with well kept Harveys, well equipped family
room, restaurant, outside terraces;
comfortable bedrooms *(Alan Skull)*
Lewes [Cliffe High St], *Gardeners Arms*:
Light and airy simple bar with good value
food and ever-changing range of eight or so
real ales *(Alan Skull)*; [South St/Malling St],
Snowdrop: Name grimmer than it sounds,
pub stands on site of cottages destroyed by
1836 avalanche which killed eight people;
caring and friendly licensees, well kept
Harveys and Fullers London Pride, interesting
food inc pizzas and vegetarian, eccentric
collection of gorgeous paraphernalia, relaxed
atmosphere *(Caroline Driver)*; [Bell Lane],
White Swan: Friendly local at end of
downland path from Brighton, generous
helpings of decent bar food, well kept
Harveys, courtyard with fishpond *(John
Beeken)*

☆ Lindfield, W Sus [98 High St (B2028);
TQ5425], *Bent Arms*: Spit-roasted beef
lunchtime Mon, Tues, Fri, Sat, spit driven by
model steam-engine, all sorts of other
interesting bric-a-brac, very individual antique
and art deco furnishings and stained glass;
wide choice of other good bar food, good
choice of well kept ales, friendly waitresses;
attractive garden, children in restaurant and
eating area; bedrooms *(Don Mather, LYM)*

☆ Litlington, E Sus [The Street; between A27
Lewes—Polegate and A259 E of Seaford;
TQ5201], *Plough & Harrow*: Friendly and
informal atmosphere in prettily placed and
attractively extended flint local's cosy beamed
front bar, six well kept changing real ales,
decent wines by the glass; consistently good
home-cooking from sandwiches to steaks inc
vegetarian in dining area done up as railway
dining car (children allowed here); back lawn
with children's bar, aviary and pretty views;
live music Fri evening inviting audience
participation *(Neil H Barker, A Plumb, LYM)*

☆ Littlehampton, W Sus [Wharf Rd; westwards
towards Chichester, opp rly stn; TQ0202],
Arun View: Comfortable and attractive
18th-c Inn right on harbour with river directly
below windows, Whitbreads-related ales,
wide choice of reasonably priced decent bar
food, restaurant (wise to book), flower-filled

terrace; summer barbecues evenings and weekends; bedrooms *(D H T Dimock, Mrs M Rice)*

Littlehampton [34 High St], *Dolphin*: Town-centre pub with bargain lunches, other bar food from sandwiches up; piped music *(P R Rainger)*

Lodsworth, W Sus [SU9223], *Hollist Arms*: Two small bars cosy in winter, varied range of food, good pubby atmosphere, darts, shove ha'penny etc *(Mrs M Rice)*

Lyminster, W Sus [Lyminster Rd; TQ0204], *Six Bells*: Above-average food, all home-made using fresh veg; well kept Allied ales *(J Wisden)*

Maresfield, E Sus [TQ4624], *Chequers*: Good food inc interesting pasta in smartly refurbished pub, friendly lively staff, well kept Harveys, good coffee, decent house wine *(Mrs R D Knight)*; [Piltdown (A272 Newick Rd)], *Piltdown Man*: Good welcome and atmosphere, wide range of food, piped music *(Mrs R D Knight)*

☆ **Midhurst**, W Sus [opp Spread Eagle; SU8822], *Bricklayers Arms*: Good new landlord doing good home-cooked food at reasonable prices in cosy early 17th-c pub with two bars, sturdy old oak furniture, well kept Greene King ales *(Mr and Mrs M Evans, R A Dean)*

☆ **Midhurst** [Petersfield Rd (A272 just W)], *Half Moon*: A Big Steak pub with Friary Meux Best, Ind Coope Burton and Tetleys, decent meals speedily served by friendly waitresses, prices very reasonable *(Colin Laffan)*

Midhurst [North St], *Angel*: Handsome partly 16th-c coaching inn with good reasonably priced food esp puddings, cosy welcoming atmosphere despite the plain tables and hard seats; comfortable bedrooms *(Mr and Mrs Michael Boxford, Mrs M Rice)*; [Wool Lane/Rumbolds Hill (A272)], *Wheatsheaf*: Attractive unpretentious pub with beams and brasses, very friendly staff, good range of real ales, wide choice of well cooked food at reasonable prices inc Sun lunch *(Brian Hutton)*

☆ **Milton Street**, E Sus [off A27 Polegate—Lewes, ¼ mile E of Alfriston roundabout; TQ5304], *Sussex Ox*: Attractive and individual family country pub beautifully placed below downs, with big lawn and marvellous play area; good atmosphere inside, well kept ales such as Harveys Best, popular food, pleasantly simple country furniture, brick floor, woodburner, one lively and one quieter family room; lots of good walks, busy weekends *(Dave Lands, LYM)*

☆ **Netherfield**, E Sus [Netherfield Hill, just off B2096 Heathfield—Battle; TQ7118], *Netherfield Arms*: Pleasant low-ceilinged village pub with warm and friendly service, good choice of well kept real ales and wines, good bar food from very wide choice, inglenook log fire, no-smoking area, restaurant, no music; lovely garden *(John and Vi Collins)*

New Bridge, W Sus [A272 W of Billingshurst; TQ0625], *Limeburners Arms*: Cosy and picturesque, friendly landlord, comfortable surroundings, good range of simple food; by well run modest-sized caravan and camping site, handy for Arun fishermen *(R Wilsono)*

☆ **Newhaven**, E Sus [West Quay; follow West Beach signs from A259 westbound – OS Sheet 198 map ref 450002; TQ4502], *Hope*: Welcoming and efficient new young managers in big-windowed pub overlooking busy harbour entrance, upstairs conservatory room and breezy balcony tables with even better view towards Seaford Head, well kept Flowers, Harveys and Wadworths 6X, reasonably priced simple food inc seafood specialities, unfussy decor with some nautical touches, darts and pool in airy public bar, waterside terrace *(Chris and Anne Fluck, Keith Mills, John Beeken, LYM)*

Newick, E Sus [A272 Uckfield—Haywards Heath; TQ4121], *Bull*: Roomy and attractive old Courage pub alongside village green, lots of beams and character, good relaxing pub atmosphere, reasonable choice of moderately priced food in sizeable eating area, good service, several well kept real ales *(Alec and Marie Lewery, Dave Irving, Colin Laffan)*

Ninfield, E Sus [TQ7012], *Red Lion*: A Brewers Fayre pub with good meals in pleasant setting; children welcome *(J LeSage)*

☆ **Northchapel**, W Sus [A285 Guildford—Petworth; SU9529], *Half Moon*: Big red David Brown tractor outside gives a clue to the masses of older but smaller agricultural bygones inside; beams and open fire, locally brewed beer, plenty of home-made food, live music last Mon of month; tame goose in the garden *(Ian Phillips, Sue Anderson, Phil Copleston)*

☆ **Oxleys Green**, E Sus [follow Brightling signs from Robertsbridge just off A21 N of Hastings; close to Brightling itself; TQ6921], *Jack Fullers*: Tucked-away country dining pub, two charming old rustic rooms with huge log fire, candlelit tables, good mix of old-fashioned furnishings, well kept Brakspears PA and a guest like Timothy Taylors, particularly good wines by the glass esp English ones, robust home cooking esp individual pies and meat puddings with interesting veg and old-fashioned steamed puddings, very attractive garden with unspoilt views – definite main-entry quality, but no longer a place for just a drink so this year has to return to the Dip; children welcome, cl Sun evening, Mon and Tues in winter *(Tim and Pam Moorey, Dr S Savvas, M Martin, LYM)*

Pagham, W Sus [Nyetimber Lane; SZ8897], *Lion*: Cosy 15th-c oak-beamed pub with two bars, wooden seating, uneven flooring, low ceilings, small restaurant, big terrace; very popular in summer, good in winter too *(Mrs M Rice)*

Peasmarsh, E Sus [TQ8822], *Horse & Cart*: Old beamed country pub very popular in summer, huge range of good reasonably priced food inc tasty home-cooked pies and chilli, pleasant staff *(Peter and Vivian Symes)*

☆ **Pett**, E Sus [TQ8714], *Two Sawyers*: Friendly pub with character main bar, small public bar, back snug, small oak-beamed back restaurant where children allowed; Whitbreads-related ales and others from distant small breweries, welcoming staff, reasonably priced standard bar food with some more interesting specials; big garden with swings and picnic-table sets, boules pitch; bedrooms *(P Corris, Alec and Marie Lewery, Andrew and Ruth Triggs)*

Petworth, W Sus [Market Sq; SU9721], *New Star*: Good reasonably priced food, friendly staff, pleasant little back restaurant, lots of Cyprus mementoes *(Rita and Derrick Barrey)*
nr **Petworth** [A283 towards Pulborough], *Welldiggers*: Stylishly simple low-ceilinged dining pub with good value restaurantish meals; plenty of tables on attractive lawns and terraces, lovely views *(Mrs M Rice, LYM)*
Pevensey, E Sus [TQ6304], *Smugglers*: Quiet and historic-feeling, with good value food inc tasty sandwiches, willing service *(E G Parish)*
Playden, E Sus [A268/B2082; TQ9121], *Peace & Plenty*: Small welcoming homely pub with roaring log fire in hop-hung lounge bar, well kept Greene King Abbot and Rayments, comfortable armchairs, wooden benches; wide range of good if not cheap food in softly lit dining room with protraits, esp home-cooked pies; odd dressed manikin in porch *(Mark Percy, Mr and Mrs C J Sanders, P Corris)*
Plumpton, E Sus [Ditchling Rd (B2116); TQ5613], *Half Moon*: Good varied choice of reasonably priced food (not Sun evening) and well kept King & Barnes and Wadworths 6X in picturesque pub with prompt friendly service, log fires and woodburner; evening restaurant, rustic seats in big garden with downs view, play area inc tractors *(Alec Lewery, Tony and Wendy Hobden, Mrs R D Knight)*
Polegate, E Sus [A27; TQ5805], *Old Polegate Station*: Useful standard food pub unusually sited in renovated station *(R Wilson)*
Poundgate, E Sus [A26 Crowborough—Uckfield – OS Sheet 199 map ref 493289; TQ4928], *Crow & Gate*: Wide choice of decent food inc OAP bargain lunches and well kept Bass, Harveys Best and Worthington BB; pleasant beamed bar with big copper-hooded fireplace, restaurant *(Colin Laffan)*
Poynings, W Sus [TQ2612], *Royal Oak*: Varied popular bar food inc home-cooked dishes, vegetarian choice and good fish; pleasant bar staff, cosy atmosphere in big bar around central servery, well kept Courage-related ales and a guest such as Harveys, attractive side garden – very popular in summer, parking on narrow rd can sometimes attract parking tickets *(Barry Roe, Wendy Mogose, Mrs M Rice, Alec and Marie Lewery, David Holloway, Alison Burt)*
Pulborough, W Sus [nr stn; TQ0418], *Waters Edge*: Good service, good choice of meals inc lots of puddings, lake views, no-smoking area, pet goat *(A and A Dale)*
Ringmer, E Sus [Uckfield Rd (off A26 just N of village turn-off); TQ4412], *Cock*: Heavily

beamed small bar with good inglenook log fire, piped music, no-smoking lounge, restaurant, Courage-related ales, good choice of wines by the glass, usual food, piped music, seats out on good terrace and in attractive fairy-lit garden; children allowed in overflow eating area; piped music *(Tony and Wendy Hobden, LYM)*
☆ nr **Ringmer** [outside village; A26 Lewes—Uckfield, S of Isfield turnoff], *Stewards Enquiry*: Good varied food inc good vegetarian, fish and steaks in tastefully refurbished olde-worlde beamed pub; good service, reasonable prices, three well kept real ales; some outside tables, play area *(Brian Hutton)*
☆ **Ripe**, E Sus [signed off A22 Uckfield—Hailsham, or off A27 Lewes—Polegate via Chalvington; TQ5010], *Lamb*: Character pub with interestingly furnished snug little rooms around central servery, attractive antique prints and pictures, nostalgic song-sheet covers, Victorian pin-ups in gents'; generous home-made food inc children's dishes and Sun roast, well kept Courage-related ales and a guest such as Harveys, several open fires, friendly service; pub games ancient and modern, pleasant sheltered back garden with play area and barbecues *(Emma and Dennis Dickinson, Anthony Barnes, LYM)*
Rogate, W Sus [A272 Midhurst—Petersfield; SU8023], *White Horse*: Rambling heavy-beamed local with flagstones and big log fire, step down to attractive dining area, well kept real ales, decent food, friendly licensees, no music or machines, some tables out behind *(A J Blackler, LYM)*
Rotherfield, E Sus [TQ5529], *George*: Pleasant atmosphere, comfortable, good popular home-cooked food *(Mrs R D Knight)*; *Rainbow Trout*: Former Kings Arms redone as dining pub, under same management as Brown Trout at Lamberhurst (see Kent main entries), with similar food concentrating on fresh fish; Whitbreads-related and other ales such as Morlands Old Speckled Hen and Wadworths 6X *(Colin Laffan)*
☆ **Rusper**, W Sus [High St; village signed from A24 and A264 N and NE of Horsham; TQ2037], *Plough*: Pleasant old village pub with padded very low beams, panelling and big inglenook, good range of real ales inc unusual and distant ones (Mansfield, Pilgrims), good choice of good value food; fountain in back garden, pretty front terrace, bar billiards and darts in raftered room upstairs, occasional live music; children welcome *(LM, Andy and Jackie Mallpress, Dr and Mrs A K Clarke, LYM)*
☆ **Rye**, E Sus [TQ9220], *Hope & Anchor*: Good value food esp fresh fish; friendly and pleasant *(Jeff and Barbara Stratton, Russell and Margaret Bathie, Rob and Doris Harrison)*
☆ **Rye** [Gun Gdn, off A259], *Ypres Castle*: Simple friendly pub in fine setting up the hill towards the tower, with great view, big lawn; wide choice of straightforward food using good ingredients, well kept ales such as

Morlands Old Speckled Hen, old yachting magazines, local event posters, piped music; winter opening may be limited *(Mr and Mrs P B Dowsett, Jay Voss, A Preston)*

Rye [The Mint, High St], *Bell*: Small comfortable two-roomed pub with Courage-related ales, good value simple menu, small garden with lovely wisteria; no dogs *(Neil and Jenny Spink, Jim and Maggie Cowell)*

Rye Harbour, E Sus [TQ9220], *Inkerman Arms*: Good fresh fish (grilled or fried), well kept Greene King ales and a changing guest, and friendly atmosphere; boules; nr nature reserve *(H R Taylor)*

☆ Salehurst, E Sus [½ mile off A21 T Wells—Battle – OS Sheet 199 map ref 748242; TQ7424], *Salehurst Halt*: Pleasantly renovated L-shaped bar in station building by dismantled line, good plain wooden furnishings, good log fire, old prints and photographs, well kept Harveys and Wadworths IPA and 6X, decent wines, imaginative generous food, good housekeeping, pleasant garden, pretty village with 14th-c church; bedrooms *(Robert Chown)*

Scaynes Hill, E Sus [TQ5623], *Farmers*: Picturesque-looking, with Fullers London Pride and Harveys ales, basic cheap generous food *(Alec and Marie Lewery)*

☆ nr Scaynes Hill, E Sus [Freshfield Lock; off A272 via petrol station at top of village, via Church Lane signpost; TQ5623], *Sloop*: Unpretentious tucked-away country pub with sofas and armchairs in long saloon, games room off basic public bar, lots of tables out in neat garden by derelict Ouse Canal; generous bar food inc children's dishes, well liked by most but sometimes a question-mark over value; well kept Harveys Best and guest beers, lots of country wines; piped music; children in eating area, handy for Bluebell steam railway, not far from Sheffield Park *(Alec and Marie Lewery, R J Walden, Mike and Joyce Bryant, P M Addison, Hilary Edwards, Tony and Wendy Hobden, M Veldhuyzen, John Beeken, Ron and Sheila Corbett, LM, LYM; more reports please)*

Seaford, E Sus [20 Church St; TV4899], *Old Plough*: 17th-c inn recently refurbished to a high standard; wide range of food at reasonable prices inc Sun lunch *(Brian Hutton)*

Sedlescombe, E Sus [TQ7718], *Queens Head*: Clean and comfortable country local opp village green, pleasant and welcoming with big inglenook log fire, Doulton toby jugs, hunting prints, limited good value bar food, Flowers, decent coffee; restaurant, attractive garden *(Rob and Doris Harrison, J H Bell, E G Parish)*

Selmeston, E Sus [on A27; TQ5006], *Barley Mow*: Long rambling bar nicely decorated with hunting prints, Bass, Flowers Original and Harveys beers, wide choice of food inc good steak pie and crab salad, attentive helpful staff, no-smoking children's area, restaurant; tables outside *(Michael and Jenny Back)*

☆ Selsfield, W Sus [Ardingly Rd; B2028 N of Haywards Heath, nr West Hoathly; TQ5434], *White Hart*: Big log fire, low 14th-c beams and timbers, wide choice of bar food inc some original dishes, well kept Gales, King & Barnes Sussex and Broadwood and Tetleys, good service; tastefully converted barn restaurant, picnic-table sets on side lawn above steep wooded combe, walks nearby; children welcome, handy for Wakehurst Place *(Dave Carter, Joan and John Calvert, David Holloway, LYM)*

☆ Shoreham by Sea, W Sus [Upper Shoreham Rd, Old Shoreham; TQ2105], *Red Lion*: Very welcoming staff in nice old low-beamed pub with log fire, generous well cooked bar food inc popular Sun lunch, Courage-related ales with a guest such as Wadworths 6X, decent wines, pretty sheltered garden; river walks, good South Downs views *(Paul Weedon, R T and J C Moggridge, Mrs M Rice)*

☆ Shortbridge, E Sus [Piltdown – OS Sheet 198 map ref 450215; TQ4521], *Peacock*: Attractive 16th-c beamed and timbered pub with big inglenook, turkey rugs on oak parquet, soft lighting, dining area with bar food from sandwiches up (salmon and king prawn pancake tipped), real ales such as Courage Directors, Flowers Original, Harveys Best and Larkins; tables out in impressive garden with playhouse, dominated by two majestic trimmed yews *(John Beeken, Caroline Alcock, A H Denman, GB, S R Knight, BB)*

Slaugham, W Sus [TQ2528], *Chequers*: Small bar, grill and restaurant, well kept King & Barnes Sussex and Festive, well cooked tasty if pricy food, cheaper lunchtime bar snacks, emphasis on seafood; enormous wine list; tables on front terrace, opp church among pretty cottages by bridleway to Handcross *(LM)*

Slindon, W Sus [Slindon Common; A29 towards Bognor; SU9708], *Spur*: 17th-c, attractive inside with enormous open fire, good choice of attractively presented properly cooked bar food, fresh veg in separate dish, sizeable restaurant *(TOH)*

Slinfold, W Sus [The Street; TQ1131], *Kings Head*: Pleasant pub with Whitbreads-related ales, wide choice of decent value food, tables in big garden; bedrooms *(LM)*

Sompting, W Sus [West St; TQ1605], *Gardeners Arms*: Handy stop just off main coast rd, generous good value lunches, Courage-related ales; bedrooms *(Mrs M Rice)*

☆ South Harting, W Sus [SU7819], *Ship*: Good value well served food inc good unlisted cheese and prawn toasted sandwich in traditional unspoilt local with quick cheerful service, Palmers and Eldridge Pope beers, unobtrusive piped classical music, dominoes, nice setting in pretty village *(Jenny and Brian Seller, John Evans)*

☆ South Harting [B2146], *White Hart*: Attractive old pub with good generous home cooking, lots of polished wood, big log fire, good service, well kept ales, decent coffee, cosy restaurant, separate public bar, well behaved dogs allowed *(Anna and Aidan Walls, Colin and Ann Hunt, Mrs M Rice)*

Southbourne, W Sus [A27 towards Emsworth; SU7806], *Harvest Home*: Large pub with two interconnecting bars and big restaurant; good service, generous good bar food all day inc Sun, children's menu, morning coffee and afternoon teas; Bass, Tetleys, Wadworths 6X; tables outside *(Ann and Colin Hunt)*; [A259], *Travellers Joy*: Very welcoming service and wide range of reasonably priced food inc Sun roasts and lots of puddings; garden *(Brian Hutton)*

St Leonards, E Sus [Mercatoria; TQ8009], *Horse & Groom*: Friendly local with usual food, well kept Courage, Harveys and Charles Wells Bombardier; nice town atmosphere *(Simon Green, Audrey Furnell)*

Staplefield, W Sus [Warninglid Rd; TQ2728], *Victory*: Particularly wide choice of food esp fish in charming whitewashed village pub opp village cricket green, dovecote in roof, picnic-table sets outside with play area; Gales and Courage-related ales *(TB, R J Walden)*

Stedham, W Sus [School Lane (off A272) – OS Sheet 197 map ref 856223; SU8522], *Hamilton Arms*: Straightforward English pub run by friendly Thai family, good reasonably priced Thai food in bar and restaurant; pretty hanging baskets, seats out by quiet lane, good walks nearby *(Mayur Shah, John Pearce, KC)*

Steyning, W Sus [41 High St; TQ1711], *Chequer*: Lots of character in handsome largely Tudor pub with labyrinth of bars and seating areas, friendly staff, good range of well kept Whitbreads-related beers, generous helpings of food from comprehensive menu *(David Dimock)*; [130 High St], *Star*: Flagstoned front bar, carpeted back one furnished in pine, rural memorabilia, welcoming service, well kept Wadworths 6X, good home-cooking *(Mike Elkerton)*

Stoughton, W Sus [signed off B2146 Petersfield—Emsworth; SU8011], *Hare & Hounds*: Much modernised pub below downs with reliably good home-cooked food in airy pine-clad bar, big open fires, half a dozen changing well kept ales such as Adnams Broadside and Boddingtons, friendly staff, winter restaurant, back darts room, tables on pretty terrace; nr Saxon church, good walks nearby; children in eating area and restaurant; one reader, lunching here in rising flood waters in early 1994, was lucky to leave when she did as from later that day the village was cut off for two weeks *(H A P Russell, Colin and Ann Hunt, Miss A G Drake, LYM)*

Sutton, W Sus [nr Bignor Roman villa; SU9715], *White Horse*: Inviting old-fashioned ivy-covered Georgian country pub in pretty downs-foot village, good choice of good value well presented generous food using local materials inc game and fish, pleasant simple decor, flowers on tables, well kept Batemans, Courage, Youngs and guest beers, log fire, friendly staff; tables in garden; good value bedrooms, comfortable and well equipped *(Brian Bowden, Sarah Quick, Tim Galligan)*

Thakeham, W Sus [TQ1017], *White Lion*: Two-bar village local, big friendly alsatian, warm welcome *(Mrs M Rice)*

☆ **Tillington**, W Sus [village signed off A272 Midhurst—Petworth OS Sheet 197 map ref 962221; SU9621], *Horse Guards*: Civilised upmarket dining pub with good if not cheap food (distinct restaurant mood Sat evenings), quick cheerful service, log fires and lovely view from bow window; well kept Badger Best and Wadworths 6X, decent wines, good coffee, no piped music, tables in sheltered garden; children welcome; bedrooms with own bathrooms *(J H Bell, Patricia Burvill, M A Gordon Smith, John and Tessa Rainsford, LYM)*

☆ **Trotton**, W Sus [A272 Midhurst—Petersfield; SU8323], *Keepers Arms*: Quickly served decent food and well kept ales such as Badger Best, Ballards and King & Barnes Festive in pleasant beamed and timbered pub with country views from latticed windows and from teak tables on narrow terrace *(BB)*

☆ **Turners Hill**, W Sus [East St; TQ5435], *Crown*: Wide choice of generous food in friendly and attractive dining pub with low settees as well as tables with dining chairs, log fire, steps down to bookable raftered dining area, pictures inc Victorian oils, books, china figurines; well kept Allied ales, decent wines, soft piped music, tables outside, pleasant valley views from back garden; children welcome; two bedrooms *(John Pettit, E G Parish, W J Wonham, LM, LYM)*

☆ **Upper Dicker**, E Sus [TQ5510], *Plough*: Wide choice of good generous bar food, Courage-related and King & Barnes real ales, log fire and quick friendly service in homely three-room pub, busy evenings; children's swings in big garden – which furnishes the plums for good summer crumbles *(Tony Albert, M F Goodwin)*

Wadhurst, E Sus [St James Sq (B2099); TQ6431], *Greyhound*: Pretty village pub strongly supported by local regulars, with wide choice of usual bar food (not Mon evening) and set Sun lunch in neat restaurant or pleasant beamed bar with big inglenook fireplace, real ales such as Bass, Fullers, Harveys, Ruddles County and Tetleys, no piped music; tables in well kept back garden; bedrooms planned *(BB)*

nr **Wadhurst**, E Sus [Mayfield Lane (B2100), Best Beech], *Best Beech*: Civilised well run dining pub, decent food; bedrooms *(G L Tong, J H Bell)*

☆ **Walderton**, W Sus [Stoughton rd, just off B2146 Chichester—Petersfield; SU7810], *Barley Mow*: Outstanding garden outside pretty village pub with warm and cosy flagstoned bar, comfortable and attractively furnished lounge, two log fires, huge helpings of good bar food inc notable ploughman's and Sun lunch, well kept Gales ales and country wines, cheerful staff, popular skittle alley; children welcome *(Viv Middlebrook, John Sanders, A J Blacker)*

Waldron, E Sus [Blackboys—Horam side road; TQ5419], *Star*: Pleasant panelled bar with restaurant off, fair range of standard pub food with some interesting specials, real ales inc Bass-related beers, Harveys and Wadworths 6X, no music, friendly and welcoming *(Tony Albert, R D and S R Knight)*

☆ **Warbleton**, E Sus [TQ6018], *Warbil in Tun*: Extended beamed dining pub, pleasantly worn in, with good freshly cooked food esp meat, fresh veg, wide choice of puddings, good friendly service, big log fire, well kept Flowers IPA and Harveys, relaxed civilised atmosphere, hard-working licensees; tables on roadside green *(S R Knight, J H Bell, Ian Louden, Tim Bishop, Revd and Mrs Michael Bishop)*

☆ **Warnham**, W Sus [Friday St; TQ1533], *Greets*: Friendly rambling 15th-c pub with well kept Whitbreads-related ales, decent wines, wide choice of good food inc unusual specials, delicious puddings and fine Sun lunch, uneven flagstones and inglenook fireplace; convivial locals' side bar *(B Perrotton)*

☆ **Washington**, W Sus [just off A24 Horsham—Worthing; TQ1212], *Franklands Arms*: Well kept, roomy and welcoming pub in quiet spot, yet busy weekends, with wide choice of good food esp pies and seafood mornay, several well kept ales, decent house wines, prompt service; big bar, smaller dining area, games area with pool and darts; tables in neat garden *(Jenny and Brian Seller, Alec and Marie Lewery, Mrs M Rice)*

☆ **West Chiltington**, W Sus [Smock Alley, just S; TQ0918], *Five Bells*: Consistently good reasonably priced freshly made food, full range of King & Barnes beers kept well and several other ales from small breweries, good prompt service, pleasant atmosphere *(M Morgan, H R Taylor)*

☆ **West Wittering**, W Sus [Chichester Rd; B2179/A286 towards Birdham; SU7900], *Lamb*: Friendly and relaxed 18th-c country pub, several small, clean and comfortable rooms, rugs on tiles, good range of well kept ales such as Bunces Best and Benchmark, Cheriton, Ind Coope Burton, Harveys Old, Ringwood, decent wines, interesting reasonably priced food, big log fire, welcoming efficient service; lots of tables out in front and in sheltered back garden – good for children, with outside salad bar on fine days; busy in summer *(Mrs D Bromley-Martin, Ted Burden, Caron Gilbert, E M Hughes, Ann and Colin Hunt)*

Wilmington, E Sus [TQ5404], *Giants Rest*: Imaginative range of home-made food reasonably priced, ales such as Adnams, Fullers and Harveys, friendly newish landlord, attractive furnishings; picnic-table sets outside; bedrooms *(Alan Skull, Rob and Doris Harrison)*

Winchelsea, E Sus [TQ9017], *Bridge*: Wide choice of good food inc home-made vegetarian dishes and local fish in bar and restaurant, friendly attentive service, relaxing atmosphere, well kept beers; free minibus service by arrangement *(T B and M E Tappenden)*

Winchelsea Beach, E Sus [TQ9017], *Ship*: Not so different from other seaside pubs, but the log fire's wonderfully welcoming if you've been caught in the rain, the Shepherd Neame Spitfire's well kept and the local plaice is good *(Jenny and Brian Seller)*

☆ **Wisborough Green**, W Sus [TQ0526], *Three Crowns*: Good reasonably priced food inc big ploughman's served very quickly in friendly refurbished stripped-brick-and-beams pub, very clean and polished; well kept real ales such as Greene King Abbot, efficient young staff *(A N Black, Colin Laffan, R Wilson)*

Worth, W Sus [TQ5036], *Cowdray Arms*: Large popular country pub (service can slow when crowded, though normally friendly and efficient); real ales with occasional festivals, playground with big plastic tree with swings and a slide *(Dave Irving)*

☆ **Worthing**, W Sus [High St; W Tarring; TQ1303], *Vine*: Self-effacing local, small, cosy, comfortable and welcoming, with excellent choice of well kept ales inc distant rarities (and yearly beer festival), good daily special and other food, friendly knowledgeable staff, attractive garden *(Ian Phillsy, Mrs M Rice)*

☆ **Worthing** [Montague St; TQ1402], *Rose & Crown*: Warm atmosphere, friendly staff, wide choice of reasonably priced well cooked food inc OAP bargains and three or four Sun roasts, cheap puddings *(Brian Hutton, K and B Moore)*

Worthing [Arundel Rd (A27 W)], *Coach & Horses*: Spotless 17th-c coaching inn, very much a friendly local, with good lunchtime food in pleasant well furnished dining area, well kept Allied ales, decent coffee, piped music, cosy back room, well kept garden with lots of tables *(John and Vi Collins)*; [Broadwater Green; TQ1504], *Cricketers*: Very comfortable, nice staff, good food *(Tony and Wendy Hobden)*; [Portland Rd, just N of Marks & Spencer], *Hare & Hounds*: Recently renovated friendly town-centre pub with good range of reasonably priced bar food; no car park but three multi-storeys nearby *(Brian Hutton)*; [77 Broadwater St], *Olde House At Home*: Small cosy pub with tidy comfortable lounge, good atmosphere, decent food, well kept beer; upmarket without being pretentious *(Graham Bush)*; [Richmond Rd], *Wheatsheaf*: Popular and comfortable open-plan pub with well kept real ales, good reasonably priced food, welcoming atmosphere *(Mike Appleton, Tony and Wendy Hobden)*

Yapton, W Sus [Maypole Lane; off B2132 – OS Sheet 197 map ref 977042; SU9703], *Maypole*: Welcoming country pub, lounge with two log fires, good value home-cooked food (not Sun or Tues evenings), good range of well kept real ales – four regulars, three guests *(Bruce Bird, Tony and Wendy Hobden)*

Tyne & Wear *see* Northumbria
Warwickshire *see* Midlands
West Midlands *see* Midlands

Wiltshire

Pub food in Wiltshire is now often very good indeed – though far from cheap, with a good main dish slightly more likely to cost near £6 than near £5. Some of the best pubs for a meal out now are the Red Lion at Axford (lots of fresh fish), the Quarrymans Arms just outside Box, the idyllically set Cross Guns near Bradford on Avon, the Three Crowns at Brinkworth (getting expensive now, but one of the most enjoyable), the White Hart at Ford (awarded a star this year), the Harrow at Little Bedwyn (owned by a consortium of villagers; not a wide choice of food, but very imaginative), the Wheatsheaf at Lower Woodford (huge choice), the relaxed Suffolk Arms in Malmesbury, the civilised Silver Plough at Pitton, the George & Dragon at Potterne (quite unpretentious and straightforward, but good), the quietly comfortable Bell in Ramsbury, and the Lamb near Semington (almost entirely geared to dining now – it gains our Food Award and Wine Award this year). Of these, it's the White Hart at Ford, doing exceptionally well at the moment, which we choose as Wiltshire Dining Pub of the Year. Several new entries here, or pubs back in these pages after an absence, are the Talbot at Berwick St John (much more of a dining pub than it used to be), the Compasses at Chicksgrove (doing very well since reopened under new owners – gains our Wine Award and Place to Stay Award), the Red Lion in Lacock (lots of food under cheery new licensees), the attractive thatched Hatchet at Lower Chute, and the lively and interesting Rattlebone in Sherston. Several pubs have gained our new beer award: the old-fashioned Two Pigs in Corsham (no food at all), the restful and unchanging Bear in Devizes, the consistently welcoming Horseshoe at Ebbesbourne Wake, the White Hart at Ford, the Rising Sun up above Lacock (new licensees doing well), the enjoyable Suffolk Arms in Malmesbury, and the George & Dragon at Potterne. Drinks prices in Wiltshire are a little higher than the national average; of the three pubs which we found clearly cheapest for beers, the Vine Tree at Norton and Rattlebone at Sherston both had beers specially brewed locally for them, and the Quarrymans Arms at Box had beer from the small Wickwar brewery in Avon. Beers from the dominant local brewer, Wadworths, are normally priced close to the area average, though a little cheaper than beers from the national chains. In the Lucky Dip section at the end of the chapter, pubs we'd note particularly include the Crown at Alvediston, Waggon & Horses at Beckhampton, Horse & Groom at Charlton, Mermaid at Christian Malford, Crown at Everleigh, Bell at Great Cheverell, Angel at Heytesbury, Who'd A Thought It at Lockeridge, George & Dragon at Rowde, Three Horseshoes at Stibb Green, Red Lion at West Dean and Golden Swan at Wilcot. As we have inspected most of these we can vouch for their quality. There are several good prospects in Marlborough and in Salisbury.

AXFORD SU2370 Map 2

Red Lion ⇐ ▉ ♀

Turn off in Marlborough A345/346 signposted Mildenhall and Ramsbury; Axford is between them

Although there's quite an emphasis on the very good food in this pretty flint-and-brick pub, drinkers are made just as welcome as those coming to enjoy a meal – and you are likely to be treated as a regular, even on your first visit. From an impressive range, bar food might include sandwiches, delicious courgette and tomato soup, lovely smoked salmon roulade, very good potted stilton in port, platters (£4.50), and lots of splendid fish dishes such as smoked prawns (£3.75), smoked trout (£4.50), lovely sardines or plaice (£7.25), river trout, mullet (£7.95), crayfish (£8.50), lemon sole (£9.95) and Dover sole (£12.50), lobster (£15.50), and also lamb fillet (£9.50), steaks (from £9.75) and local game such as pheasant or partridge (£10.50). Salads and vegetables are very fresh and crisp; no chips, but excellent sauté potatoes. The restaurant is no smoking. There are comfortable cask seats and other solid chairs on the spotless parquet floor of the beamed pine-panelled bar, with picture windows for the fine valley view. Well kept Archers Village, Flowers Original, Foxley Dog Booter (brewed about a mile away), Hook Norton, Marstons Pedigree and Wadworths 6X on handpump, and decent wines including local and New World ones; darts, shove-ha'penny, cribbage, dominoes, fruit machine and unobtrusive piped music; pleasant quick service. The sheltered garden has picnic-table sets under cocktail parasols, swings, and lovely views. *(Recommended by Colin Laffan, Derek and Sylvia Stephenson, Peter and Audrey Dowsett, R T and J C Moggridge, H Anderson, Nigel Clifton, JE, Chris Cook, June and Tony Baldwin)*

Free house ~ Licensee Mel Evans ~ Real ale ~ Meals and snacks (till 11) ~ Restaurant ~ (01672) 20271 ~ Children welcome ~ Open 11-3, 6-11; winter evening opening 6.30 ~ Bedrooms: £25B/£40B

BARFORD ST MARTIN SU0531 Map 2

Barford

Junction A30/B3089

The Israeli barbecues held on Friday evenings all year round at this neatly kept and friendly old place are proving very popular. And other well presented bar food includes soup (£1.50), basket meals (from £1.95), filled baked potatoes (from £2.25), big sandwiches (£2.50), ham and two eggs (£3.95), ploughman's (from £4.25), broccoli and mushroom casserole or cottage pie (£4.95), steak and kidney pie (£5.95), steaks (from £8.95), children's dishes (£2.95), and puddings (£1.75). The front bar has dark squared oak panelling, cushioned wall benches, dark seats and tables, and a big log fire in winter. Well kept Badger Best and Tanglefoot on handpump, and quite a few country wines; darts and piped music. Some of the restaurant is no-smoking; there are tables on a terrace outside. The bedrooms have been upgraded this year. *(Recommended by Dr and Mrs N Holmes, Mr and Mrs J M Hardman; more reports please)*

Badger ~ Tenant Mr Davids ~ Real ale ~ Meals and snacks (11.30-3, 7-10) ~ Restaurant ~ (01722) 742242 ~ Children welcome ~ Open 11.30-3, 7-11; 11.30-11 Sat ~ Summer folk duets and Morris dancers ~ Bedrooms: £28B/£40B

BERWICK ST JOHN ST9323 Map 2

Talbot

Village signposted from A30 E of Shaftesbury

The single long, heavy beamed bar in this well run and friendly Ebble Valley pub is simply furnished, with cushioned solid wall and window seats, spindleback chairs and a comfortable kitchen armchair (at the other end of the room there's a high-backed built-in settle), nicely shaped with bevelled corners, and a huge inglenook fireplace with a good iron fireback and bread ovens. Adnams Best and Broadside,

Bass, and Wadworths 6X on handpump. Carefully prepared bar food includes delicious home-made mushroom soup, excellent ploughman's, macaroni au gratin (£5.95), good curries or steak and kidney pie (£6.50), fresh skate, steaks, and lovely home-made puddings like treacle tart, chocolate and brandy biscuit cake or bread and butter pudding with real cream (£2.95). Cribbage, dominoes, fruit machine and piped music. Some tables on the back lawn, with swings for children. Very nice quiet village, full of thatched old houses. *(Recommended by H D Wharton, S G N Bennett, John Hazel, Tina and David Woods-Taylor)*

Free house ~ Licensees Mr and Mrs R H Rigby ~ Real ale ~ Meals and snacks (not Sun) ~ Restaurant ~ (01747) 828222 ~ Children in eating area of bar; no under 7s in evening ~ Open 11.30-2.30, 7(6.30 Sat)-11; closed Sun evening

BOX ST8268 Map 2

Quarrymans Arms

Box Hill; off A4 just W of Rudloe

Very popular locally, this friendly place has a growing reputation for good food – though it's still very much somewhere to enjoy a drink. From a new menu, bar food includes sandwiches, home-made soup (£1.75), baked avocado filled with walnut butter and wrapped in bacon (£2.95), vegetable stir-fry (£3.95), tagliatelle carbonara (£4.25), prawn and mussel bake (£4.75), steak and kidney pie or good stir-fry duck with plum sauce (£5.50), gammon and egg (£6.50), red mullet fillets with an orange and lemon butter sauce (£7.95), steaks (from £8.25), and daily specials. Well kept Bass, Butcombe, Wadworths 6X, and guests like Wickwar Brand Oak on handpump, and 40 malt whiskies. Darts, shove-ha'penny, cribbage, dominoes, fruit machine, trivia, boules, cricket and piped music. The bar's been much modernised with new furnishings, but does have interesting quarry photographs and memorabilia, and dramatic views over the valley. There are picnic-table sets outside and the pub is ideally situated for cavers, potholers and walkers, and runs interesting guided trips down the local Bath stone mine. *(Recommended by Roger and Jenny Huggins, Pat and John Millward, Peter Neate, Peter and Lynn Brueton, Paul Weedon, G J Evans, R H Crawcour, Chris Elias, P Gillett)*

Free house ~ Licensees John and Ginny Arundel ~ Real ale ~ Meals and snacks (11.30-3, 7-10) ~ Restaurant ~ (01225) 743569 ~ Children welcome ~ Open 11-4, 6-11; all day Thurs-Sat ~ Bedrooms: /£30

nr BRADFORD-ON-AVON ST8060 Map 2

Cross Guns

Avoncliff; pub is across footbridge from Avoncliff Station (road signposted Turleigh turning left off A363 heading uphill N from river in Bradford centre, and keep bearing left), and can also be reached down very steep and eventually unmade road signposted Avoncliff – keep straight on rather than turning left into village centre – from Westwood (which is signposted from B3109 and from A366, W of Trowbridge); OS Sheet 173 map reference 805600

It's best to book if you want to enjoy the good food at this idyllically-set and very popular old country pub. Generously served, there might be sandwiches (from £1.30), home-made pâté (£2), very good stilton or cheddar ploughman's (from £3.20), home-made steak and kidney pie (£4.30), various fish dishes including crab salad (£4.60), steaks (from £5.20; 32oz £11), lemon sole (£5.95), trout (£4.10), and duck in orange sauce (£5.95) with delicious puddings (from £1.50). Well kept Courage Best and Directors, John Smiths, Ushers Best and a guest beer on handpump. There's a nice old-fashioned feel to the bar, with its core of low 17th-c beams, rush-seated chairs around plain sturdy oak tables, stone walls, and a large ancient fireplace with a smoking chamber behind it; piped music; there may be a system of Tannoy announcements for meal orders from outside tables. From the pretty terraced gardens, floodlit at night, there are splendid views down to the wide river Avon, taking in the maze of bridges, aqueducts (the Kennet & Avon Canal) and tracks that wind through this quite narrow gorge. Quite a lot of walkers stop here – no muddy boots. *(Recommended by John and Christine Simpson, Peter Neate, Dr and Mrs R E S Tanner, Chris Elias, Paul Weedon, George Murdoch)*

Free house ~ Licensees Dave and Gwen Sawyer ~ Real ale ~ Meals and snacks (till 9.45) ~ (01225) 862335 ~ Children in eating area ~ Open 11-3, 6.30-11 (closed 25 and evening 26 Dec)

BRINKWORTH SU0184 Map 2

Three Crowns 🍴

The Street; B4042 Wootton Bassett—Malmesbury

Despite the fact that much of the emphasis in this bustling and friendly pub is on the particularly good, imaginative food, you won't be made to feel out of place if you just want a drink – and there's a good pubby atmosphere, too. Changing regularly, dishes might include home-made pies like steak and kidney or lamb and mint (£8.25), vegetarian tagliatelle (£8.50), apple and stilton parcels with fresh tomato and basil sauce (£8.95), half a locally smoked chicken with sherry and cream sauce (£11.45), steaks (from £11.95), roast duck thinly sliced with fresh watercress sauce and garnished with sautéed duck's liver (£12.25), whole fresh sea bass baked with prawns, capers, shallots and garlic (£12.95), and puddings such as home-made ice creams and sorbet or home-made puddings (£3.50); best to arrive early in the evening as they don't take bookings. Well kept Archers Village, Bass, Boddingtons, Gales HSB, and Wadworths 6X on handpump, and an expanding wine list. The small rambling bar has a very nice villagey atmosphere in all its little enclaves, big landscape prints and other pictures on the walls, some horsebrasses on the dark beams, a dresser with a collection of old bottles, log fires, tables of stripped deal (and a couple made from gigantic forge bellows), with green-cushioned big pews and blond chairs, and there's a conservatory extension; on the right there are sensibly placed darts, shove-ha'penny, dominoes, cribbage, chess, trivia and fruit machine; piped music. The garden stretches around the side and back, with well spaced tables, and looks over a side lane to the village church, and out over rolling prosperous farmland. *(Recommended by Roger Huggins, Dave Irving, Tom McLean, Ewan McCall, R M Bloomfield, Basil Minson, TBB, Sarah Rissone, J P Gale, Mrs S Smith, Mrs J M Bell, Jane Byrski, Michael Hunt, P C Russell, Chris Elias, M G Hart, Jeff Davies)*

Whitbreads ~ Lease: Anthony Windle ~ Real ale ~ Meals and snacks ~ Restaurant ~ (01666) 510 366 ~ Children in eating area of bar and in restaurant until 9pm ~ Open 10-2.30, 6-11

CHICKSGROVE ST9629 Map 2

Compasses 🛏 🍷

From A30 5½ miles W of B3089 junction, take lane on N side signposted Sutton Mandeville, Sutton Row, then first left fork (small signs point the way to the pub, but at the pub itself, in Lower Chicksgrove, there may be no inn sign – look out for the car park); OS Sheet 184 map reference 974294

Since Mr and Mrs Inglis re-opened this lovely thatched house, things have gone from strength to strength. Readers have very much enjoyed staying here, eating the carefully prepared food, and supping the well kept beers and good wines. The characterful bar has old bottles and jugs hanging from the beams above the roughly timbered bar counter, farm tools, traps and brasses on the partly stripped stone walls, and high-backed wooden settles forming snug booths around tables on the mainly flagstone floor. Using the best local produce, bar food might include courgette and stilton or carrot and tomato soup (£2.50), chicken liver and apple pâté (£3.75), asparagus and smoked salmon quiche (£4.50), vegetarian lasagne or home-cooked ham and eggs (£6.50), rabbit, prune and cider or fresh salmon and cod pies (£7.50), minty lamb, apricot and cashew nut casserole (£8.95), pork fillet cooked in a parcel with thyme and garlic (£10.50), turbot meunière (£11.50), and puddings like Jamaican lemon crunch pie or bread and butter pudding (£2.95), and summer Sunday lunchtime barbecues. Well kept Adnams, Bass, Wadworths 6X, and a guest beer on handpump; darts, shove-ha'penny, table skittles and shut-the-box; the dogs are called Bill, Ben and Otto. It's very peaceful and pleasant sitting in the garden or the flagstoned farm courtyard; lots to do nearby, and bike hire can be arranged. *(Recommended by D B McAlpin, Lawrence Bacon, Mr and Mrs R H Martyn, James Nason, Simon Harris, John E Rumney, Geoffrey Culmer, G M Betteridge, S K Robinson, Gordon, Jerry and Alison Oakes)*

Free house ~ Licensees Bob and Ann Inglis ~ Real ale ~ Meals and snacks (not Mon, Tues, Weds) ~ Restaurant ~ (01722) 714318 ~ Children in eating area of bar ~ Occasional live music ~ Open 12(11.30 Sat)-3, 6-11; closed Mon-Weds ~ Bedrooms: £35B/£45B

CORSHAM ST8670 Map 2

Two Pigs 🍺

A4, Pickwick

The emphasis in this characterful and old-fashioned pub is firmly on drinking, with well kept Pigswill (from local Bunces Brewery) and four changing guest beers on handpump like Foxleys Barking Mad, Hop Back Summer Lightning, Uley Pigs Ear and so forth; country wines. The very narrow long bar has stone floors, wood-clad walls and long dark wood tables and benches; a profuse and zany decor includes enamel advertising signs, pig-theme ornaments, and old radios, a bicycle, canoe and even tailor's dummy suspended from the ceiling. The atmosphere is lively and chatty (no games machines and only blues piped music), the landlord entertaining, and the staff friendly; a good mix of customers, too, though no under-21s. There's a covered yard outside, called the Sty. No food and no children. *(Recommended by Chris Elias, Nigel Gibbs; more reports please)*

Free house ~ Licensees Dickie and Anne Doyle ~ Real ale ~ (0249) 712515 ~ Live blues Mon evenings ~ Open 12-2.30, 7-11

DEVIZES SU0061 Map 2

Bear 🛏 🍺

Market Place

This rambling 17th-c old coaching inn is a very restful place to stay or spend some time in. The welcoming and pleasantly old-fashioned main bar has big winter log fires, fresh flowers, black winger wall settles, muted red button-back cloth-upholstered bucket armchairs around oak tripod tables, and old prints on the walls. The traditionally-styled Lawrence Room, separated from the main bar by some steps and an old-fashioned glazed screen, has dark oak-panelled walls, a parquet floor, shining copper pans on the mantelpiece above the big open fireplace, and plates around the walls. Straightforward bar food (there's a much wider choice in the Lawrence Room, which can also be eaten in the bar) includes sandwiches (from £1.60), home-made soup (£1.80), filled baked potatoes, three-egg omelettes or ploughman's (from £2.75), ham and egg (£3), filled giant Yorkshires (from £3.50), 8oz sirloin steak (£6.25), and home-made puddings (£1.95); part of the restaurant is no smoking. Well kept Wadworths IPA and 6X and a guest beer are served on handpump from an old-fashioned bar counter with shiny black woodwork and small panes of glass; it's brewed in the town, and from the brewery you can get it in splendid old-fashioned half-gallon earthenware jars. Freshly squeezed juices, and good choice of malt whiskies; prompt helpful service. *(Recommended by David Holloway, Colin and Ann Hunt, Dr M I Crichton, Wim Kock, Willem-Jan Kock, Hans Chabot, Jane Starkey, Ian and Nita Cooper, Gordon Mott, Gwen and Peter Andrews, I E and C A Prosser, Belinda Mead, George Atkinson)*

Wadworths ~ Tenant W K Dickenson ~ Real ale ~ Meals and snacks ~ Restaurant (closed Sun evening) ~ (01380) 722444 ~ Children in eating area of bar ~ Open 10am-11pm; 10-3, 6-11 in winter; closed 25/26 Dec ~ Bedrooms: £45B/£70B

Most pubs in the *Guide* sell draught cider. We mention it specifically only if they have unusual farm-produced 'scrumpy' or even specialise in it.

EBBESBOURNE WAKE ST9824 Map 2

Horseshoe 🍺

On A354 S of Salisbury, right at signpost at Coombe Bissett; village is around 8 miles further on

The barn opposite this lovely old pub has been done up this year and is now used as a pool room with darts and video game. Quite a few readers have a soft spot for this place – it is particularly welcoming to visitors and locals alike, has considerable character, well kept beer and enjoyable food. The beautifully kept bar has fresh garden flowers on the tables, lanterns, farm tools and other bric-a-brac crowded along its beams, and an open fire. Simple home-made bar food, with prices unchanged since last year, consists of sandwiches (£2.25), fresh trout pâté (£4.50), locally made faggots or lasagne (£5.25), fresh battered cod or home-made pies like fine venison, steak and kidney, fish or chicken and mushroom (all £5.95), lemon sole with crabmeat (£5.95), poached sole (£8.95) and excellent home-made puddings; good breakfasts and three course Sunday lunch (£8.95). Well kept Adnams Broadside, Hop Back HBS, Ringwood Best and Old Thumper, and Wadworths 6X tapped from the row of casks behind the bar, farm cider, and several malt whiskies. The pretty little garden has seats that look out over the small, steep sleepy valley of the River Ebble, and in a paddock at the bottom are two goats. Booking is advisable for the small no-smoking restaurant, especially at weekends when they can fill up quite quickly. *(Recommended by Jason Caulkin, Dennis Heatley, Ted Burden, John and Joan Nash, Jerry and Alison Oakes, Gordon, R and Mrs P F Shelton, S J Edwards, A Wagstaff)*

Free house ~ Licensees Anthony and Patricia Bath ~ Real ale ~ Meals and snacks (not Mon evening) ~ Restaurant ~ (01722) 780474 ~ Well behaved children in top bar and in restaurant ~ Open 11.30-3, 6.30-11; closed evening 25 Dec ~ Bedrooms: £25B/£40B

FORD ST8374 Map 2

White Hart ★ 🍽 🛏 🍷 🍺

A420 Chippenham—Bristol; follow Colerne sign at E side of village to find pub

Wiltshire Dining Pub of the Year

There's no doubt that this fine pub deserves a star this year. Readers are full of enthusiastic praise for the way the friendly licensees manage to remain attentive and cheerful – even when they are really busy, and for the fact that despite the exceptionally good, imaginative food, the atmospheric bar is very much a place for those wanting just a drink. And what could be nicer on a sunny day than to sit out on the terrace by the stone bridge and trout stream. There are heavy black beams supporting the white-painted boards of the ceiling, tub armchairs around polished wooden tables, small pictures and a few advertising mirrors on the walls, and a big log-burning stove in the ancient fireplace (inscribed 1553); the nicely decorated dining areas have been enlarged. Delicious home-made food includes fine leek and potato or broccoli soup (£2.50), rabbit and pigeon terrine or smoked trout pâté (£4.95), beef and mushrooms cooked in ale with pastry lid (£5.50), beef tomatoes filled with a risotto and wild mushrooms in white wine and chive butter sauce (£6.95), strips of chicken with tagliatelle, sweet peppers, tomato and garlic with soya glaze or whole grilled lemon sole with lemon butter (£7.95), good pork in Amaretto sauce or on a bed of apple purée with cider and sultana sauce (£8.50), lovely steak with sautéed wild mushrooms on bordelaise sauce or rack of spring lamb with tartlet of ratatouille on an orange and port wine sauce (£9.95), king prawns in garlic butter (£10.95), and puddings like heavenly banoffi pie or feather-light treacle tart. An excellent range of beers includes well kept Badger Tanglefoot, Bass, Boddingtons, Hook Norton Old Hookey, Flowers IPA, Marstons Pedigree, Smiles Best and Exhibition, and Theakstons Old Peculier on handpump; farm ciders, a dozen malt whiskies, and fine wines; piped music. It's a lovely place to stay and there's a secluded swimming pool for residents. *(Recommended by Paul Boot, Mrs Anne Parmenter, Simon and Amanda Southwell, Dr C E Morgan, Jane and Steve Owen, R C Morgan, Barbara*

Hatfield, Andrew Shore, Mrs M Lawrence, A R and B E Sayer, Paul Weedon, Susan and John Douglas, P Neate, Pat and John Millward, Dave Irving, Chris Elias, Dave and Jules Tuckett, June and Tony Baldwin, Pat and Tony Martin, John Knighton)

Free house ~ Licensees Chris and Jenny Phillips ~ Real ale ~ Meals and snacks ~ Restaurant ~ (01249) 782213 ~ Children welcome away from public bar ~ Open 11-2.30(2.45 Sat), 5.30(5 Sat)-11 ~ Bedrooms: £43B/£59B

HINDON ST9132 Map 2

Lamb

B3089 Wilton—Mere

This civilised solidly built old inn has a roomy long bar, split into several areas. The middle – and main – part has a long polished table with wall benches and chairs, and a big inglenook fireplace, and at one end there's a window seat with a big waxed circular table, spindleback chairs with tapestried cushions, a high-backed settle, brass jugs on the mantelpiece above the small fireplace, and a big kitchen clock; up some steps, a third, bigger area has lots of tables and chairs; shove-ha'penny. Bar food includes sandwiches, local mussels (£4.50), pork, ham and tomato bake (£4.95), venison and pigeon casserole or steak and kidney pie (£5.25), roast local pheasant (£5.95), and roast Sunday lunch (from £4.95); the restaurant is no smoking. Ash Vine, Boddingtons, Hook Norton, Oakhill, Ringwood Best, Wadworths 6X and Youngs IPA on handpump, and several malt whiskies. There are picnic-table sets across the road (which is a good alternative to the main routes west). No dogs. *(Recommended by John and Joan Nash, John and Christine Vittoe, David Surridge, M Owton, Joan and Ian Wilson, Joy Heatherley, F C Johnston, Patrick Clancy, S G Brown, Robert Tattersall, Colin Laffan)*

Free house ~ Licensees John and Paul Croft ~ Real ale ~ Meals and snacks (till 10pm) ~ Restaurant ~ Hindon (01747) 820573 ~ Children welcome ~ Open 11-11 ~ Bedrooms: £38B/£55B

KILMINGTON ST7736 Map 2

Red Lion 🛏

Pub on B3092 Mere—Frome, 2½ miles S of Maiden Bradley

A gate has been installed to let all the walkers who crowd into this unpretentious and friendly 400-year-old pub on to the lane which leads to White Sheet Hill where there is riding, hang gliding and radio-controlled gliders; picnic-table sets in the large garden. Inside, the bar is very cosy and comfortable, with an interesting display of locally-made walking sticks (popular with walkers), a curved high-backed settle and red leatherette wall and window seats on the flagstones, photographs on the beams, and a deep fireplace with fine old iron fireback and a second large brick fireplace, both with log fires in winter. A newer area has a large window and is decorated with brasses, a large leather horse collar and hanging plates. Good value bar food includes excellent home-cooked ham, home-made soup (£1.50), filled baked potatoes (from £2), toasties (from £2.50), ploughman's (from £2.95), steak and kidney or game pies (from £3.65), and meaty or vegetable lasagne (£4.50). Marstons Pedigree on handpump with a guest like Butcombe Bitter kept under light blanket pressure, farm cider and elderflower pressé; sensibly placed darts, dominoes, shove-ha'penny and cribbage. The charming labrador is called Kim. Stourhead Gardens are only a mile away. *(Recommended by Mrs R Humphrey, Brig T I G Gray, Guy Consterdine, Anthony Barnes, Mayur Shah, John Honnor, Dr J W Macleod, Colin and Jan Roe)*

Free house ~ Licensee Chris Gibbs ~ Real ale ~ Meals and snacks (not 25 Dec) ~ (01985) 844263 ~ Children in eating area of bar till 9pm ~ Open 11-3, 6.30-11; closed evening 25 Dec ~ Bedrooms: £15/£30

Waterside pubs are listed at the back of the book.

LACOCK   ST9168   Map 2

George

Village signposted off A350 S of Chippenham

One of the oldest buildings in this National Trust village and run by a courteous and friendly licensee. The atmospheric bar has a low beamed ceiling, upright timbers in the place of knocked-through walls making cosy corners, armchairs and Windsor chairs, seats in the stone-mullioned windows and flagstones just by the bar. The magnificent central fireplace with its roaring log fire still has a three-foot treadwheel set into its outer breast, originally for a dog to drive the turnspit. Well kept Wadworths IPA, 6X, and Farmers Glory on handpump, and bar food such as sandwiches, home-made lasagne (£4.95), home-made chicken and leek pie or home-made spinach roulade (£5.50), breaded lemon sole stuffed with crab meat and seafood sauce or spare ribs (£6.50), and puddings like spotted dick or rhubarb crumble (£2.25). Darts, shove-ha'penny, cribbage, dominoes and piped music. There are picnic-table sets with umbrellas in the back garden, and a bench in front that looks over the main street. It's a nice area for walking. The bedrooms are up at the landlord's farmhouse, and free transport to and from the pub is provided. *(Recommended by Colin and Ann Hunt, Stephen G Brown, P J Howell, Joan and Michel Hooper-Immins, Mrs B M Spurr, Tom McLean, Roger Huggins, Dave Irving, Ewan McCall, Joy Heatherley, Alan and Heather Jacques, Jeff Davies, George Atkinson, Simon Collett-Jones, Chris Elias)*

Wadworths ~ Tenants John and Judy Glass ~ Real ale ~ Meals and snacks (till 10pm) ~ Restaurant ~ (01249) 730263 ~ Children welcome ~ Open 11-11 ~ Bedrooms – see above; £18B/£35B

Red Lion

High Street

The long bar in this tall brick Georgian inn is divided into separate areas by cart shafts, yokes and other old farm implements, and the old-fashioned furniture includes a mix of tables and comfortable chairs, turkey rugs on the partly flagstoned floor, and a fine old log fire at one end; also, plates, paintings and tools cover the walls, and there are stuffed birds, animals and branding irons hanging from the ceiling. Under the new managers, the large choice of good bar food includes home-made filled rolls (from £2.50), basket meals (from £2.95), ham and egg (£3.50), filled baked potatoes (from £3.50), ploughman's (from £4.25), vegetarian dishes (£4.60), speciality sausages like Thai, leek and ginger or smoky New Orleans (£4.95), daily specials like steak and kidney or game pies or spicy lamb or turkey and apricot casseroles (£5.95), fresh fish like halibut, trout or sea bass (from £6.95), mostly home-made puddings like sticky toffee pudding (£2.25), and children's helpings or meals (from £1.95). Throughout the afternoon they serve light snacks and afternoon tea. Well kept Wadworths IPA, 6X, and Farmers Glory and a guest beer like Everards Tiger on handpump; darts. The bedrooms have been refurbished this year. The pub is close to Lacock Abbey and the Fox Talbot Museum. *(Recommended by Joy Heatherley, Mrs S Spevack, Alan and Heather Jacques, June and Tony Baldwin, Fiona Dick, Janet Pickles, Chris Elias)*

Wadworths ~ Managers Roger and Cheryl Ling ~ Real ale ~ Meals and snacks (all day in summer) ~ (01249) 730456 ~ Children welcome away from bar ~ Open 11-11; 11-3, 6-11 in winter ~ Bedrooms: £35B/£50B

nr LACOCK   ST9367   Map 2

Rising Sun 🍺

Bowden Hill, Bewley Common; on back road Lacock—Sandy Lane

The view from the seats on the two-level terrace outside this bustling pub is tremendous (especially at sunset) looking out over the Avon valley, some 25 miles or so away. Inside, the three little simply furnished, characterful rooms have a mix of old chairs and basic kitchen tables on stone floors, stuffed animals and birds, country pictures, and open fires. Well kept Bass, Moles IPA, Bitter, 97 and

Landlords Choice, and guest beers on handpump; friendly service. Under the new licensees, bar food now includes sandwiches, cheese and broccoli flan (£4.75), good chicken in red wine, tasty ham pancakes with cheese and chive sauce, chicken and asparagus in a big pastry case or braised shoulder of lamb with rosemary (£5.25), and fresh pineapple and prawn mayonnaise (£5.95). Darts, dominoes, shove-ha'penny, connect four, shut-the-box and cribbage. *(Recommended by Tom McLean, Roger Huggins, Dave Irving, Ewan McCall, Chris and Anne Fluck, John Willard, Alan and Heather Jacques, Joy Heatherley, P and J Shapley, Mrs Anne Parmenter, Stephen Brown, D Godden, Dorothy Pilson, Paul S McPherson, Chris Elias)*

Free house ~ Licensees John and Doreen Wiltshire ~ Real ale ~ Lunchtime meals and snacks (not Sun) ~ (01249) 730363 ~ Children in eating area of bar ~ Singer Weds evening ~ Open 11.30-3, 6(7 Tues)-11

LITTLE BEDWYN SU2966 Map 2

Harrow

Village signposted off A4 W of Hungerford

One of the things readers like about this friendly pub – actually owned by the villagers – is that there are no pub games at all and no piped music – just a relaxed chatty atmosphere in its three rooms. As you walk in there is a massive ship's wheel on the left, and a mixture of country chairs and simple wooden tables on its well waxed boards (one table in the bow window), a bright mural of scenes from the village, and a big woodburning stove; the two inner rooms have a fine brass model of a bull and locally done watercolours and photographs for sale. Good, often imaginative food might include tomato and basil soup (£2), marvellous bouillabaisse, Greek salad (£3.25), marinated baby squid salad (£3.50), black pudding, hash browns and marinated peppers or beetroot, mozzarella and soured cream crêpe (£3.95), delicious wild mushroom and spinach bubble and squeak, good meatballs in spicy sauce with melted cheese topping, smoked chicken and asparagus filo pie (£4.25), sirloin steak sandwich (£5.50), and lovely puddings like superb bramble brûlée, marmalade and whisky ice cream or chocolate gateaux; the restaurant is no smoking. Well kept Blackawton Forty-four, Foxley Best, and Hook Norton Best on handpump and lots of New World wines; service is good even when it's busy. There are seats out in the small, pretty garden, and the pub's a couple of hundred yards from the Kennet & Avon Canal. *(Recommended by P M Lane, TBB, JE, George Atkinson, Alan Kilpatrick, Miss Georgina Cole, Simon Reynolds, D J Clifton)*

Free house ~ Sean and Louize Juniper ~ Real ale ~ Meals (not Mon) ~ Restaurant ~ (01672) 870871 ~ Children welcome ~ Open 11-2.30, 5.30(6 Sat)-11; closed Mon lunchtime and 1 Jan ~ Bedrooms: £25B/£37B

LOWER CHUTE SU3153 Map 2

Hatchet

The Chutes well signposted via Appleshaw off A342, 2½ miles W of AnDover

This is a very attractive thatched 16th-c pub with a big winter log fire in front of a splendid 17th-c fireback in the huge fireplace, very low beams, and a mix of captain's chairs and cushioned wheelbacks set neatly around oak tables. Good bar food includes sandwiches, home-made soup (£2.25), ploughman's (£3.50), good moules marinières (£3.95), salads (from £3.95), cottage pie (£4.25), steak and Guinness pie (£4.95), tiger prawns in filo pastry (£5.95), and puddings. Well kept Bass, Bunces, Ind Coope Burton, Wadworths 6X and Youngs on handpump. Darts, shove-ha'penny, dominoes, cribbage and piped music. There are seats out on a terrace by the front car park, or on the side grass. *(Recommended by Brenda and Jim Langley, Mrs K Johnson, I E and C A Prosser)*

Free house ~ Licensee Jeremy McKay ~ Real ale ~ Meals and snacks ~ Restaurant ~ (01264) 730229 ~ Children in eating area of bar and in restaurant ~ Open 11-3, 6-11

LOWER WOODFORD SU1235 Map 2

Wheatsheaf

Leaving Salisbury northwards on A360, The Woodfords signposted first right after end of speed limit; then bear left

As we went to press, we heard that this welcoming 18th-c pub was about to undergo major changes: extensions to the bar, reception and dining room, new kitchens and lavatories (including a disabled one), reorganised terrace and garden, a new car park, and lots of refurbishment and redecoration. From a wide menu, the good, popular bar food includes home-made soup (£1.45), basket meals (from £2.15), ploughman's or filled baked potatoes (from £3.20), open sandwiches (from £3.30), salads (from £3.85), home-made chicken curry (£4.30), broccoli bake (£4.50), home-made lasagne (£5.15), home-made steak and kidney pie (£5.40), gammon and egg (£5.75), salmon or trout (£5.80), steaks (from £8.45), puddings (from £2.35), and children's dishes (from £1.55); they do summer afternoon cream teas; part of the dining room is no-smoking. Well kept Badger Best, Hard Tackle and Tanglefoot on handpump, and helpful, friendly staff; darts, dominoes and cribbage. The big walled garden has picnic-table sets, a climber and swings, and is surrounded by tall trees. *(Recommended by Ralf Zeyssig, Patricia Nutt, Joy Heatherley, W and S Jones, Mayur Shah, J E N Young, G Shannon, Don and Thelma Beeson)*

Badger ~ Tenants Peter and Jennifer Charlton ~ Real ale ~ Meals and snacks (till 10pm) ~ (01722) 73203 ~ Children in eating area of bar ~ Open 11-11; 11-2.30, 6.30-11 Mon and Tues and in winter (when pub shuts at 10.30); closed 25 Dec

MALMESBURY ST9287 Map 2

Suffolk Arms 🍺

Tetbury Hill; B4014 towards Tetbury, on edge of town

Consistently well run and friendly, this enjoyable creeper-covered old stone house has a softly lit, knocked-through bar with comfortable seats such as a chintz-cushioned antique settle, sofa and easy chairs, captain's chairs, and low Windsor armchairs, and copper saucepans and warming pans on the stripped stone walls; a stone pillar supports the beams, leaving a big square room around the stairs which climb up apparently unsupported. There's also a lounge, and flowers may decorate the tables. Very good, often imaginative bar food includes soup (£2.35), sandwiches (from £1.95), filled baked potatoes (from £3.25), ploughman's (from £3.45), tagliatelle topped with stilton and cream sauce (£4.95), pan-fried venison in Cumberland sauce (£5.95), at least three fresh fish dishes or several warm salads like duck and bacon, chicken and cashew nut or pigeon breast (from £5.95), chicken masala (£6.25), and up to ten home-made puddings like very popular banoffi pie or fruit pies and crumbles (£2.45). Well kept Wadworths IPA, 6X and one guest on handpump and a range of reasonably priced wines; very pleasant bar staff in long aprons. The neat lawns outside have some seats. The licensees also run the Northey Arms at Box. *(Recommended by Graham and Karen Oddey, TBB, Peter Neate, June and Tony Baldwin, Chris Elias, Brian Whittaker, Roderic Plinston; more reports please)*

Wadworths ~ Tenant John Evans ~ Real ale ~ Meals and snacks (till 10pm) ~ (01666) 824323 ~ Children in eating area of bar ~ Open 11-2.30, 6-11

NORTON ST8884 Map 2

Vine Tree

4 miles from M4 junction 17; A429 towards Malmesbury, then left at Hullavington, Sherston signpost, then follow Norton signposts; in village turn right at Foxley signpost, which takes you into Honey Lane

In pleasant countryside, this converted 18th-c mill house has picnic-table sets under cocktail parasols in a vine-trellised back garden with young trees and tubs of flowers, and a well fenced separate play area with a fine thatched fortress and so forth; they have stables at the back. Three smallish rooms open together – they are hoping to refurbish them soon – with plates, small sporting prints, carvings, hop bines, a mock-up mounted pig's mask (a game that involves knocking coins off its nose and ears), lots of stripped pine, candles in bottles on the tables (the lighting's very gentle), and some old settles. From a new menu there might be bar snacks such as ploughman's (from £2.65), basket meals (from £2.90), filled baked potatoes (from £3.70), home-made beefburger or nutburger (£4.60), and home-made lasagne (£5.25), as well as home-made soup (£2.60), a warm quiche of duck and fennel on a tangerine coulis (£2.90), fennel, vermouth and potato hotpot (£6.25), baked local trout with an orange and mint stuffing (£8.75), steaks (from £9.40), honey-roast duckling breast with an apricot and coconut cream sauce (£9.75), puddings like toffee apple and pecan pie (from £2.25), and children's melas (£2.05); best to book, especially at weekends. Well kept Wadworths 6X, a beer named for the pub, and a couple of guests like Archers Golden or Foxley Best on handpump. *(Recommended by Peter Neate, N K Kimber, Gwen and Peter Andrews, Vivien Lewis, Dave Irving, Roger Huggins, Tom McLean, Ewan McCall, Dr Sherriff)*

Free house ~ Licensees Ken Camerier ~ Real ale ~ Meals and snacks (till 10pm) ~ Restaurant ~ (01666) 837654 ~ Children in eating area of bar and in restaurant ~ Open 12-2.30, 6.30-11; closed Tues

PITTON SU2131 Map 2

Silver Plough ★ ⊗⊗ ⊉

Village signposted from A30 E of Salisbury

A farmhouse until after the Second World War, this civilised dining pub has jugs, glass rolling pins and curios hanging from the beamed ceilings in the main bar, paintings and prints on the walls, and oak settles; the skittle alley is next to the snug bar. But it's the very good food that readers like most here: soups like cream of tomato or game and ale (from £2.25), particularly good marinated dill herrings (£3.50), ploughman's (£3.95), chicken and apricot terrine (£4.25), ratatouille au gratin (£4.50), chilli con carne or fresh Dorset mussels (£4.75), vegetarian dishes, fillet steak sandwich (£6.75), game pie with hedgerow dressing (£8.95), marinated chicken kebabs (£9.95), and fillet of beef Diane (£11.95); two-course Sunday lunch (£11.95). Well kept Bass, Courage Best, Fullers London Pride, Gales HSB, Wadworths 6X and Websters Green Label on handpump, a fine wine list including 10 by the glass, a good range of country wines, and a worthy range of spirits; friendly, efficient service. There are picnic-table sets and other tables under cocktail parasols on a quiet lawn, with an old pear tree. *(Recommended by I E and C A Prosser, Tim Galligan, Joy Heatherley, Nic Armitage, Jerry and Alison Oakes, Dawn and Phil Garside, Martin and Karen Wake, W and S Jones, Lynn Sharpless, Bob Eardley, Jean-Bernard Brisset, Brian and Jill Bond, Marjorie and Bernard Parkin, Maysie Thompson)*

Free house ~ Licensee Michael Beckett ~ Real ale ~ Meals and snacks ~ Restaurant ~ (01722) 72266 ~ Children in restaurant ~ Open 11-3, 6-11

POTTERNE ST9958 Map 2

George & Dragon ⇔ ◖

A360 beside Worton turn-off

There's always a friendly welcome – both for visitors and locals alike, in this thatched old cottage. Furnishings include old bench seating and country-style tables, banknotes from around the world, and water jugs, and there's a pleasant traditional atmosphere. You can still see the fireplace and old beamed ceiling of the original hall. Very reasonably priced, good food includes sandwiches (from £1.35), baked potatoes (from £2.95), ploughman's (from £3.25), various omelettes (from £3.50), chilli con carne (£3.95), chicken curry (£4.25), salads (from £4.25), ham and egg (£4.50), 6oz rump steak (£5.50), and puddings (from £1.95); three-course Sunday lunch (£7.25). The dining room is no smoking. Well kept Wadworths IPA and 6X on handpump. A separate room has pool, darts, shove-ha'penny, dominoes, fruit machine and piped music, and there's a full skittle alley in the old stables. Through a hatch beyond the pool room there's a unique indoor .22 shooting gallery (available for use by visiting groups with notice to arrange marshalls and insurance). A museum of hand-held agricultural implements has been opened at the rear of the pub. There's a pleasant garden and a suntrap yard with a grapevine. *(Recommended by Mrs Anne Parmenter, John and Joan Nash, Mr and Mrs C R Saxby, Dr and Mrs C S Cox, David Logan, Derek and Trish Stockley, David Holloway, G Hart, Mr and Mrs N Hazzard, Gerrit and Martine)*

Wadworths ~ Tenants Richard and Paula Miles ~ Real ale ~ Meals and snacks (not Mon except bank holiday lunchtime) ~ (01380) 722139 ~ Children welcome ~ Open 12-2.30, 6.30(7 in winter)-11 (closed Mon lunch except bank holidays) ~ Bedrooms: £19.50/£35

RAMSBURY SU2771 Map 2

Bell

Village signposted off B4192 (still shown as A419 on many maps) NW of Hungerford, or from A4 W of Hungerford

Victorian stained-glass panels in one of the two sunny bay windows of this comfortable and civilised pub look out onto the quiet village street, and a big chimney breast with open fires divides up the comfortable bar areas, nicely furnished with polished tables with fresh flowers. The restaurant is incorporated into the bar, so that the same menu can be eaten in either area. Well prepared, the food might include soup (£2.25), seafood pancake topped with cheese (£3.25), ploughman's (from £3.95), a trio of locally-made sausages with bubble and squeak (£4.95), vegetable tikka masala (£5.25), chicken satay (£5.95), home-made beef and ale pie (£6.95), steaks (from £7.95), specials such as salmon and sweet potato fishcakes with a grain mustard sauce (£6.25), Moroccan lamb casserole (£6.95), venison steak with a madeira and vine fruits sauce (£8.75), and home-made puddings like treacle tart, apricot crumble or apple strudel; tables can be reserved in the restaurant. Well kept Wadworths 6X and IPA and guest beers like Bass and Eldridge Pope Royal Oak on handpump, and 20 malt whiskies; evening piped music. There are picnic tables on the raised lawn. Roads lead from this quiet village into the downland on all sides. *(Recommended by W K Struthers, R C Morgan, Evelyn and Derek Walter, Susie Northfield, Peter and Audrey Dowsett, Tom Evans, Rob and Helen Townsend)*

Free house ~ Licensee Graham Dawes ~ Real ale ~ Meals and snacks ~ Restaurant ~ (01672) 20230 ~ Children in eating area of bar and in restaurant ~ Open 12(11 Sat)-3, 6-11

SALISBURY SU1429 Map 2

Haunch of Venison ★

1 Minster Street, opposite Market Cross

It's this pub's venerable history that makes a visit here worthwhile. It goes back some 650 years to when it was the church house for the church of St Thomas, just behind, and there are massive beams in the ochre ceiling, stout red-cushioned oak benches built into its timbered walls, genuinely old pictures, a black and white tiled floor, and an open fire; a tiny snug opens off the entrance lobby. A quiet and cosy upper panelled room has a small paned window looking down onto the main bar, antique leather-seat settles, a nice carved oak chair nearly three centuries old, and a splendid fireplace that dates back to the building's early years; behind glass in a small wall slit is the smoke-preserved mummified severed hand of an unfortunate 18th-c card player. Well kept Courage Best and Directors on handpump from a unique pewter bar counter, with a rare set of antique taps for gravity-fed spirits and liqueurs; over 147 malt whiskies. Bar food, served in the lower half of the restaurant, includes sandwiches (from £1:70), pies (from £2.65), chicken kiev (£5.50), and sirloin steak (£7.95). *(Recommended by T A Bryan, Jenny and Brian Seller, Colin and Jan Roe, Wim Kock, Willem-Jan Kock, Hans Chabot, J L Alperin, Jerry and Alison Oakes, PWV, Wayne Brindle, Peter Neate, Susan and John Douglas, Paul S McPherson, Andy and Jill Kassube)*

Courage ~ Tenants Antony and Victoria Leroy ~ Real ale ~ Meals and snacks (not Sun evening) ~ Restaurant ~ Salisbury (01722) 322024 ~ Children away from bar area ~ Nearby parking may be difficult ~ Open 11-11 (closed 25 Dec)

Old Mill ♀

Town Path, W Harnham

Tucked away from the town centre, this old place was Wiltshire's first papermaking mill back in 1550, and in summer you can sit out by the mill pool; there's a lovely walk across the meadows with classic cathedral views (as painted by Constable. Inside, the two smallish square beamed bars are simply furnished with small polished wooden tables and comfortable settles and chairs, there's a collection of over 350 china and other ducks, and a friendly relaxed atmosphere. A fine choice of fresh fish and shellfish comes direct from local boats at Poole and from the west coast of Scotland – see daily specials for crab salad, langoustines, sea bass, salmon and so forth: moules marinières (£4.55), spicy cajun fish (£5.50), seafood special (£5.85), and salmon koulibiac (£7). Also, sandwiches (from £1.80; fresh crab £3.10), vegetable soup (£2.25), ploughman's (£3.65), creamy mushroom and courgette pasta (£5), steak and kidney pie (£5.50), and gammon (£5.95); well kept Boddingtons, Brakspears, and Hop Back GFB on handpump, and decent malt whiskies and wines; piped music. *(Recommended by W K Struthers, Tim and Felicity Dyer, Mr and Mrs N J Dorricott; more reports please)*

Free house ~ Licensees Roy and Lois Thwaites ~ Real ale ~ Meals and snacks (till 10.30pm) ~ Restaurant ~ (01722) 327517 ~ Children in eating area of bar ~ Open 11-2.30, 6-11 ~ Bedrooms: £40B/£60B

SEEND ST9461 Map 2

Barge

Seend Cleeve; signposted off A361 Devizes—Trowbridge, between Seend village and signpost to Seend Head

The picnic-table sets among former streetlamps in the neat waterside gardens by this splendidly restored and very popular pub are the perfect place for idly watching the barges and other boats on the Kennet and Avon Canal, and there are moorings by the humpy bridge. Inside, there's a strong barge theme in the friendly and relaxed bar, perhaps at its best in the intricately painted Victorian flowers which cover the ceilings and run in a waist-high band above the deep green lower walls. A distinctive mix of attractive seats includes milkchurns and the occasional small oak settle among the rugs on the parquet floor, while the walls have big sentimental engravings. The watery theme continues with a well stocked aquarium, and there's also a pretty Victorian fireplace, big bunches of dried flowers, and red velvet curtains for the big windows. Generous helpings of good bar food include soup (£1.50), home-made pâté (£2.95), ploughman's and filled baked potatoes (£3.25), chilli (£3.95), lasagne (£5.25), steak and mushroom in ale pie or wild mushrooms and garlic in a creamy saffron sauce topped with tarragon croûtons (£5.75), Chinese-style ribs (£6.25), steak and chicken kebabs with a sweet and sour sauce (£8.25), and 8oz sirloin steak (£8.95), children's dishes (£1.95), and puddings (from £2.50); the restaurant is no smoking. Well kept Badger Tanglefoot, Wadworths IPA and 6X, and a guest beer on handpump; mulled wine in winter; trivia. *(Recommended by John Hazel, Mrs C Archer, Gwen and Peter Andrews, P Neate, C H and P Stride, Pat and Robert Watt, I E and C A Prosser, Jerry and Alison Oakes, John and Tessa Rainsford, H Anderson, George Murdoch, Chris Elias)*

Wadworths ~ Tenant Christopher Moorley Long ~ Real ale ~ Meals and snacks (till 10pm Fri/Sat; not 25 Dec) ~ Restaurant (closed Sun evening) ~ (01380) 828230 ~ Well behaved children welcome ~ Open 11-2.30, 6-11

SEMINGTON ST9461 Map 2

Lamb ⊕ ♀

99 The Strand; A361 a mile E of junction with A350, towards Devizes

There's a sign just past this pub which says 'You have just passed us and missed a treat' – and readers would certainly agree with that. This is very much somewhere to come and enjoy the very good food rather than a casual drink, and it helps if you are a no-smoker as only five tables are allocated for those who wish to smoke. From a changing menu, the food might include home-made soup (£2.50), sauerkraut with chorizo sausage (£2.95), cold honey-baked ham or stilton, leek and bacon pie (£5.50), lamb and apricot casserole (£6.50), braised steak with sherry and mushrooms (£6.95), fresh fish of the day, noisette of lamb with a redcurrant sauce (£7.75), steaks (from £8.50), and home-made puddings such as white chocolate flan, chocolate and cherry roulade and bread pudding with a whisky sauce (£2.75). A series of corridors and attractively decorated separate rooms radiates from the serving counter, with antique settles, a woodburning stove, and a log fire. Well kept Eldridge Pope Hardy and Dorchester on handpump, and good, reasonably priced wines; friendly, helpful staff; maybe piped classical music. There is a very pleasant walled garden with tables and outside service when the weather is fine. *(Recommended by P C Wilding, Elizabeth Donnelly, Mr and Mrs H Roberts, Mr and Mrs Lionel Stone, Peter Neate, Wendy Bateman, David Leonard, A and J Carr, Lord Johnston of Rockport, Ken Frostick)*

Free House ~ Licensee Andrew Flahery ~ Real ale ~ Meals and snacks ~ Restaurant (not Sun evening) ~ (01380) 870236 ~ Children welcome ~ Open 12-2.30, 6.30(6 Sat)-10(10.30 Sat); closed Sun evenings in winter

SEMLEY ST8926 Map 2

Benett Arms 🛏 ♀

Turn off A350 N of Shaftesbury at Semley Ind Estate signpost, then turn right at Semley signpost

For the last 19 years, the sociable landlord has been making customers welcome at this little village inn, just across the green from the church. The two cosy rooms are separated by a flight of five carpeted steps, and have one or two settles and pews, deep leather sofas and armchairs, hunting prints, carriage lamps for lighting, a pendulum wall clock, and ornaments on the mantelpiece over the log fire. Down by the thatched-roof bar servery, the walls are stripped stone; upstairs, there's hessian over a dark panelling dado. Attractively presented bar food includes home-made soup (£2.35), ploughman's (£3.65), half-a-dozen Abbotsbury oysters (£3.95), omelettes, good leek and nut bake or home-made steak and kidney pie (£4.95), gammon with pineapple (£5.95), 8oz rump steak (£8.95), and puddings like home-made apple crumble or chocolate mousse (£2.50); also, daily specials using fish and game; big breakfasts. Well kept Gibbs Mew Bishops Tipple and Deacon on handpump, kept under light blanket pressure, farm cider, four chilled vodkas, 18 malt whiskies, and a thoughtfully chosen wine list; dominoes, cribbage. There are seats outside. Well behaved dogs welcome. *(Recommended by Nigel Clifton, Stephen Brown, Tim Barrow, Sue Demont, Mr and Mrs P Wildman, John and Beryl Knight, Robert McFarland, Paul Kitchener, R and S Knight)*

Gibbs Mew ~ Tenant Joe Duthie ~ Real ale ~ Meals and snacks (till 10pm) ~ Restaurant ~ (01747) 830221 ~ Children in eating area of bar and in restaurant ~ Open 11-2.30, 6-11; closed 25 and 26 Dec ~ Bedrooms: £29B/£44B

SHERSTON ST8585 Map 2

Rattlebone

Church St; B4040 Malmesbury—Chipping Sodbury

This 16th-c pub is named after John Rattlebone, a local hero, who fought bravely to help Edmund Ironside defeat Canute in the Battle of Sherston in 1016. He was mortally wounded and it's said that he bought this site to die. There are several rambling rooms and nooks and crannies with low beams, pink walls, pews, settles and country kitchen chairs around a mix of tables, big dried flower arrangements, and lots of little cuttings and printed anecdotes; the atmosphere is pleasant and relaxed; piped classical music. The public bar has a hexagonal pool table, darts, table skittles, fruit machine, cribbage, dominoes and juke box; alley skittles and three boules pitches. Good, popular bar food from a big menu includes home-made soup (£2.25), filled baps (from £2.50; minute steak with chips £3.70), lots of ploughman's (£3.50), home-made mushroom and chestnut stroganoff, a pasta dish or chilli (all £5.75), steak and kidney pie (£5.95), generous prawn salad (£6.25), pork tenderloin with cream, stilton and cashew nuts or lamb with a raspberry and mint coulis (£8.25), steaks (from £8.95), and puddings like fruit crumble (£2.50) or popular fresh fruit meringues (£2.75); good fresh vegetables. Well kept Smiles Best, Wadworths 6X, a beer named for the pub, and a regularly changing guest like Foxley Barking Dog (from Marlborough) on handpump, 50 malt whiskies, 20 rums, fruit wines, Westons cider, decent wines, and quick service. The smallish garden is very pretty with flowerbeds, a gravel terrace, boules, and picnic-table sets under umbrellas. The old core of the village is very pretty. *(Recommended by Simon and Amanda Southwell, Paul Weedon, Mrs Pat Crabb, N Cole, Dave and Jules Tuckett, Mr and Mrs R D King)*

Free house ~ Licensees Anne, David and Ian Rees ~ Real ale ~ Meals and snacks (till 10pm; not 25 Dec) ~ Restaurant ~ (01666) 840871 ~ Children in eating area of bar and in restaurant ~ Open 11.30-3, 5.30-11; 11.30-11pm Sat

WOOTTON RIVERS SU1963 Map 2

Royal Oak ♀

Village signposted from A346 Marlborough—Salisbury and B3087 E of Pewsey

Near the Kennet & Avon Canal, this pretty 16th-c thatched pub is mainly popular for its large choice of bar food. The friendly L-shaped dining lounge has slat-back chairs, armchairs and some rustic settles around good tripod tables, a low ceiling with partly stripped beams, partly glossy white planks, and a woodburning stove. The timbered bar is comfortably furnished, and has a small area with darts, pool, dominoes, cribbage, fruit machine and juke box. From the extensive menu, there might be soup (from £1.60), sandwiches (from £1.75), basket meals (from £2.50), quite a few ploughman's (from £3.75), lots of salads (from £3.50; avocado and prawn £5.50), herrings marinated in dill with apple and walnut salad (£4.75), home-made ratatouille with toasted brie topping (£5), local trout (£6.25), home-made steak and Guinness pie (£6.50), grilled pork with orange and lemon sauce (£7.50), gammon and egg or chicken with cajun spices (£8), fresh lemon sole (£9), steaks (from £10), and puddings such as home-made sticky treacle and almond tart or sherry trifle (£2.75); three-course Sunday lunch (£9.95). Booking is recommended in the evenings, and people may be quite smartly dressed. Well kept Boddingtons, Brakspears and guest beers tapped from the cask, and a good wine list (running up to some very distinguished vintage ones); good efficient service. There are tables under cocktail parasols in the back gravelled yard, by the car park. The thatched and timbered village is worth exploring, particularly the 13th-c church, and it's just a short walk to the Kennet and Avon Canal. The family also run the Tipsy Miller at Marten. *(Recommended by David Wright, A R and B E Wayer, Gwen and Peter Andrews, P M Lane, Jim and Maggie Cowell, Wim Kock, Willem-Han Kock, Hans Chabot, Mark and Toni Amor-Segan, Joy Heatherley, Brian Bannatyne-Scott, H Anderson, Mark and Diane Grist, Mrs C Watkinson, Ann and Colin Hart, JE, John and Sherry Moate, Paul S McPherson, Mr and Mrs J E C Hobbs, Peter and Audrey Dowsett, Jeff Davies)*

Free house ~ Licensees John and Rosa Jones ~ Real ale ~ Meals and snacks 12-2, 7-9.30 ~ (01672) 810322 ~ Children welcome ~ Open 10.30-3, 6(7 winter)-11 (closed 25 Dec and evening 26 Dec) ~ Bedrooms (in adjoining house): £20(£27.50B)/£30(£35B)

WYLYE SU0037 Map 2

Bell

Just off A303/A36 junction

Only four miles from Stonehenge and set in a peaceful village next to the church, this cosy country pub has three log fires in winter. The black-beamed front bar has sturdy rustic furnishings that go well with the stripped stonework and neat timbered herringbone brickwork. There are a good few tables in the side eating area, where straightforward food served in big helpings includes soup (£2.10), ploughman's (£3.25), ham, egg and chips (£4.95), steak and kidney pie (£5.35), sizzling skillet meals like cajun chicken, texas beef or Cantonese prawns (£6.95), fresh fish dishes, T-bone steak (£13.95), daily specials, children's dishes, and some several vegetarian meals; Sunday lunch (£5.25), and part of the restaurant is no-smoking. Badger Best, Wadworths 6X and a guest beer on handpump, a good range of country wines; friendly efficient service; the back area has dominoes and fruit machine. There is pleasant outdoor seating including a walled terrace; a friendly alsatian. We've not yet had reports on the bedrooms here. *(Recommended by W K Struthers, Tony and Joan Walker, Fiona Dick, E J Robinson, R J Walden, T A Bryan, Tim Bucknall, Tony Gayfer)*

Free house ~ Licensees Steve and Ann Locke ~ Real ale ~ Meals and snacks ~ Restaurant ~ (0198 56) 338 ~ Children in eating area of bar ~ Open 11.30-11; 11.30-2.30, 6-11 in winter ~ Bedrooms: £20(£25B)/£39B

Lucky Dip

Besides the fully inspected pubs, you might like to try these Lucky Dips recommended to us and described by readers (if you do, please send us reports):

☆ Aldbourne [The Green (off B4192); SU2675], *Blue Boar*: Spaciously refurbished Tudor pub in beautiful village-green setting, well kept Wadworths IPA and 6X, cheap Archers Village, wide choice of food from home-made soup and generous sandwiches up; picnic-table sets outside *(Simon Reynolds, R T and J C Moggridge)*

☆ Aldbourne, *Crown*: Friendly quick service, pleasant atmosphere, reasonably priced straightforward food inc good value sandwiches, spacious and well kept bar with interesting collections and slightly horsey overtones, well kept Courage-related ales, huge log fire, quiet piped music; tables under cocktail parasols in neatly refurbished courtyard *(R C Watkins, Ann and Colin Hart, P Neate)*

☆ Alderbury [Chute End, off A36; SU1827], *Green Dragon*: Lovely olde-worlde Tudor pub in delightful village setting, good bar snack and restaurant menus served by hatted and aproned chef, warm welcome, Badger ales, small public bar and comfortably modernised lounge; garden with big play area and weekly barbecues *(S J Penford, John Beeken, LYM)*

Alvediston [ST9723], *Crown*: Attractive thatched low-beamed country inn recently reopened under very promising new ownership, good enterprising inexpensive food, well kept Courage, Ringwood and Wadworths, friendly efficient service, comfortable surroundings and nice garden; good bedrooms *(Jerry and Alison Oakes, Pat and Robert Watt, G M Betteridge, S K Robinson, LYM)*

Ansty [ST9526], *Maypole*: The owners of this attractive pub, a very popular main entry up till now, have applied for planning permission to turn it into a private house; until that goes ahead, it's well worth knowing for good food in relaxed surroundings *(LYM)*

Ashton Keynes [SU0494], *White Hart*: Smart and pleasant village local with good reasonably priced food, well kept Flowers, good log fire, congenial and efficient landlord; piped music may be obtrusive; delightful village *(P A C Neate, Audrey and Peter Dowsett)*

Atworth [Bath Rd (A365); ST8666], *White Hart*: Reasonably priced food, friendly landlord, pleasant surroundings; bedrooms *(John Hazel)*

☆ Avebury [A361; SU0969], *Red Lion*: Much-modernised thatched Whitbreads pub in the heart of the stone circles; usual food from unpubby restaurant extension, original bar still pleasant *(Wim Kock, Willem-Jan Kock, Hans Chabot, LYM)*

Badbury [off A345 S of Swindon; SU1980], *Bakers Arms*: Two joined carpeted rooms with central fire, Arkells Bitter and BBB, decent food (not Mon), piped music, darts and games machine; children welcome, garden *(CW, JW)*

☆ Beckhampton [A4 Marlborough—Calne – OS Sheet 173 map ref 090689; SU0868], *Waggon & Horses*: Friendly stone-and-thatch pub handy for Avebury, with full range of Wadworths ales and a guest beer kept well, old-fashioned unassuming atmosphere, interesting Dickens connections; wide choice of reasonably priced generous bar food, family room (and children's helpings on request), pub games and machines, CD juke box, pleasant garden with good play area; parking over road, no dogs; bedrooms *(George Atkinson, WHBM, Brig J S Green, Paul S McPherson, Marjorie and David Lamb, D G Clarke, Mr and Mrs A L Budden, LYM)*

Beckington [Bath Rd/Warminster Rd; ST8051], *Woolpack*: Fairly recently reopened after thorough refurbishment, calm and historic old pub with good food, good reasonably priced wines, warm welcome; no-smoking area, nice quiet lounge, good village bar; comfortable bedrooms, delightfully furnished (*Mr and Mrs Paul Adams, Ian Jagoe*)

☆ Biddestone [The Green; ST8773], *White Horse*: Busy local, traditional and comfortable, dating back to 16th c, good generous well priced bar food, well kept Courage ales, welcoming landlord, small cosy carpeted rooms, shove-ha'penny, darts and table skittles; overlooks duckpond in picturesque village, tables in garden; bedrooms (*Paul Weedon, Peter Neate, Roger Huggins, Tom McLean*)

☆ Bishops Cannings [SU0364], *Crown*: Friendly and efficient new management, good range of food in huge helpings, Wadworths beers; next to handsome old church, walk to Kennet (*Marjorie and David Lamb, Miss Georgina Cole*)

Bishopstone [SU2483], *White Hart*: Good evening food, well kept Gibbs Mew real ale, good friendly service (*Dr and Mrs N Holmes, HNJ, PEJ*)

☆ Box [A4, Bath side; ST8268], *Northey Arms*: New tenants doing good food at attractive prices in relaxed open-plan pub with deep red walls, homely decor and lovely view; well kept real ales, decent wines, good service, restaurant, children welcome (*Chris Elias*)

☆ Bradford on Avon [Silver St; ST8261], *Bunch of Grapes*: Interesting and atmospheric pub, spotless converted shop on two levels, in picturesque steep street, with good choice of generously served interesting food, well kept Smiles Bitter, reasonably priced, and other ales; space is limited and it is very popular; friendly atmosphere, good service (*Mrs Joan Harris*)

Bradford on Avon [Frome Rd], *Canal*: Flagstones, plenty of character, well kept Bass, huge meals in bar and good value restaurant; children welcome (*Neil Andrews, Chris Elias*); [Masons Hill], *Dandy Lion*: Good pub/restaurant with Wadworths real ales and good wine list; pub part downstairs busy and favoured by teenagers, but nice atmosphere and friendly staff; upstairs restaurant with starters such as hot goat's cheese in olive oil, main courses such as spicy lamb, pork in cider or local duck (*G L Furguson, Paul Weedon*)

☆ Broad Chalke [SU0325], *Queens Head*: Particularly welcoming, with wide range of good home-cooked food inc unusual dishes at reasonable prices, well kept beer, decent wines and country wines, good coffee, attractive furnishings, no music; wheelchair access from back car park, tables in pretty courtyard; comfortable well equipped bedrooms (*Philip and Trisha Ferris, Buffy and Mike Adamson*)

☆ Broad Hinton [High St; off A4361 about 5 miles S of Swindon; SU1076], *Crown*: The atmosphere of a good unpretentious local but welcomes visitors too, pleasant and

roomy open-plan bar with well kept Arkells BB, BBB, Kingsdown and Mild, straightforward home-cooked food from sandwiches up, good friendly service, unobtrusive piped music; attractive restaurant, unusual gilded inn sign, spacious garden; bedrooms (*June and Tony Baldwin, Gwen and Peter Andrews, Nick and Meriel Cox, LYM*)

Brokenborough [ST9189], *Rose & Crown*: Colonial-style restaurant popular for generous well cooked food, served well – must book Fri/Sat night; pub part can be crowded and noisy (*Paul Weedon*)

☆ Bromham [ST9665], *Greyhound*: Outstanding puddings and other good food esp fish in two attractively lit bars with thriving atmosphere, lots of enjoyable bric-a-brac, blazing log fires, even a well; interesting real ales, decent wines, friendly landlord; skittle alley, pool and darts; big garden, small intimate restaurant (*James Fletcher, John Hazel*)

☆ Burton [B4039 Chippenham—Chipping Sodbury; ST8179], *Plume of Feathers*: Cosy old beamed pub with good well presented generous food, decent wines inc many Australian, well kept Bass, Smiles and Tetleys, relaxing atmosphere, log fire; bedrooms (*Margaret and Douglas Tucker, James Fletcher*)

☆ Castle Combe [signed off B4039 Chippenham—Chipping Sodbury; ST8477], *White Hart*: Pretty stone-built pub in famously picturesque village, attractive inside, with beams, flagstones and big log fire, also family room, games room and tables in sheltered courtyard; decent food, good range of beers (*Barry Roe, Wendy Mogose, LYM*)

☆ Castle Combe, *Castle Inn*: Old-world country inn recently reopened after refurbishment, clean and attractive, lounge overlooking village street, separate locals' bar, tables on terrace; open fires, good food and service, coffee and cream teas; bedrooms (*Nigel Gibbs, George Atkinson*)

nr Castle Combe [The Gibb; B4039 Acton Turville—Chippenham, nr Nettleton – OS Sheet 173 map ref 838791], *Salutation*: Comfortable lounge bar, good attractively served bar food, Whitbreads-related ales, raftered restaurant (*Mr and Mrs R Longbottom*)

☆ Castle Eaton [The Street; SU1495], *Red Lion*: Very unpretentious village pub, not at all smart and tends to be very quiet at lunchtime; limited simple food (service may be slow), well kept Courage-related ales and Ushers Founders, children allowed if eating; most notable for uncrowded informal shrubby garden by upper Thames, with caged chipmunks (*P Neate, Dr M I Crichton, LYM*)

☆ Charlton [B4040 toward Cricklade; ST9588], *Horse & Groom*: Good if not cheap well presented bar food, all home-cooked, in civilised pub with attractive and individual decor, relaxing atmosphere, good log fire, well kept Archers and Wadworths real ales, potent cider, decent wines; restaurant (good value Sun lunch), tables outside; has been closed Mon *(Mike Davies, R Huggins, D Irving, E McCall, T McLean, Chris and Linda Elston, P A C Neate, LYM)*

Chilton Foliat [B4192 N of Hungerford; SU3270], *Wheatsheaf*: Old-fashioned friendly village local with comfortable beamed lounge, separate dining room, well kept Morlands, good value decent food from well filled sandwiches up, pool room; big garden *(M E A Horler)*

Chippenham [ST9173], *White Horse*: Lovely setting on green with duckpond, delightful willing staff, delicious food inc fine Sun roast *(the Shinkmans)*

☆ **Christian Malford** [B4069 Lyneham—Chippenham, 3½ miles from M4 junction 17; ST9678], *Mermaid*: Recently redesigned under charming newish owners, long bar pleasantly divided into areas, mix of red plush and more interesting furnishings, some attractive pictures, well kept Bass, Courage Best, Wadworths 6X and Worthington BB, decent whiskies and wines, jelly-bean and nut machines, bar billiards, darts, fruit machine, good popular food from sandwiches to steaks inc some interesting dishes, piped music (live Thurs), tables in garden; bedrooms *(Tracy Madgwick, Patrick Godfrey, BB)*

Collingbourne Ducis [SU2453], *Last Straw*: Comfortably cottagey thatched pub with real ales, good home-made food, pleasant service *(P Freeman, Anthony and Freda Walters)*

☆ **Coombe Bissett** [Blandford Rd (A354); SU1026], *Fox & Goose*: Good choice of reasonably priced bar food inc interesting specials, very attentive staff and nice atmosphere in spacious and clean open-plan pub by green of delightful village; rustic wooden refectory-style tables, coal fires, old prints, hanging chamber-pots; real ales, good coffee, piped music (classical at lunchtime), children catered for, evening restaurant; tables in garden with play area; good access for wheelchairs *(W J Wonham, John Hazel, E A George)*

Corsley [A362 Warminster—Frome; ST8246], *White Hart*: Pleasantly furnished, with good food and well kept ales inc cheap Oakhill *(Don Mather)*

Crudwell [A429 N of Malmesbury; ST9592], *Plough*: Several rooms in lounge with open fire, bar with darts, pool room, dining area with comfortable well padded seats and more in elevated part; well kept ales such as Bass, Boddingtons, local Foxley, Morlands Old Specked Hen and Wadworths 6X *(Roger and Jenny Huggins)*

☆ **Dauntsey** [Dauntsey Lock; A420 – handy for M4 junctions 16 and 17; ST9782], *Peterborough Arms*: Welcoming landlord, good value generous food, good range of real ales, pool, skittle alley, garden with play area; nice spot by old Wilts & Berks Canal *(Jeff Davies)*

Derry Hill [ST9570], *Lansdowne Arms*: Wadworths pub refurbished under friendly and efficient newish licensees, well kept ales inc Farmers Glory and Old Timer, good range of country wines, popular food, open fire, restaurant, garden with good play area; nr Bowood House *(Chris and Anne Fluck)*

☆ **Devizes** [Monday Mkt St; SU0061], *White Bear*: Friendly and cosy relaxing 15th-c beamed pub with antiques and lots of atmosphere, well kept Wadworths IPA and 6X, good range of good value food, welcoming prompt service and entertaining newish landlord; good big bedrooms *(Ian and Ruth Prior, David Holloway, Joy Heatherley)*

☆ **Devizes** [Long St], *Elm Tree*: Wide choice of good food at most attractive prices in cheerfully welcoming local with well kept Wadworths IPA and 6X, decent house wines, heavy 16th-c beams, no-smoking area, friendly service; piped music; restaurant, bedrooms *(Joy Heatherley, John and Tessa Rainsford, John Hazel)*

Devizes [New Park St], *Castle*: Well kept Wadworths IPA, 6X and Henrys, good food such as filled pitta bread, well filled giant Yorkshire puddings, liver and bacon with fresh veg; bedrooms *(David Holloway)*; [nr brewery], *Crown*: Victorian atmosphere recreated with pine furnishing, comfortable, clean and relaxed; attentive staff, tasty food, three Wadworths Bitters and Mild; no machines *(Dieter Jebens)*

Dinton [SU0131], *Waggoners*: Good honest well run local with good value food *(John Hazel)*

Downton [A338 Salisbury—Fordingbridge; SU1721], *Bull*: Good largely home-made food from generous sandwiches up in straightforward long bar, dining area at one end (where juke box noise is muted), cheery staff; dogs allowed; bedrooms *(Harriet and Michael Robinson, LYM)*

☆ **East Knoyle** [The Green; ST8830], *Fox & Hounds*: In attractive spot with beautiful view, pleasant layout, big fire, six well kept real ales, good varied choice of well cooked appetising food *(M V Ward, Mrs D E Fryer)*

☆ **Everleigh** [A342 SE of Devizes; SU2054], *Crown*: Attractive mix of comfortable old-fashioned furnishings in open-plan bar with open fire and pictures on walls, good atmosphere, friendly staff, usual bar food from sandwiches up inc vegetarian, John Smiths and Wadworths 6X, piped music; children welcome, restaurant; spacious walled garden *(Brian Kneale, M J D Inskip, Valerie Coombs, Dr and Mrs N Holmes, LYM)*

☆ **Farleigh Wick** [A363 Bath—Bradford; ST8064], *Fox & Hounds*: Low-beamed rambling bar, neat and welcoming, highly polished old oak tables and chairs, gently rural decorations; good fresh food, attractive garden; can get packed weekends *(Maysie Thompson, Mrs M Hamilton)*

☆ **Fonthill Gifford** [2 miles from A303; ST9232], *Beckford Arms*: Friendly old stonebuilt pub doing well under newish landlord, attractive lounge bar with huge log fire, wide range of moderately priced bar food, pleasant relaxing atmosphere, well kept Ruddles Best, local country wines, nice conservatory; in lovely countryside; bedrooms *(John Dawson, Pat and Robert Watt, Steve Goodchild, G Fisher)*

Fovant [A30 Salisbury—Shaftesbury; SU0128], *Cross Keys*: Good well prepared food, good coffee and welcoming landlord in spotless pub with nice winter fire; bedrooms *(C and F M Watson)*; *Poplar*: French chef doing good food (inc takeaways), friendly staff *(John Hazel)*

Froxfield [A4; SU2968], *Pelican*: Charming and comfortable, with good food, monthly champagne casino nights for charity, back nightclub *(G Hart)*

☆ **Great Cheverell** [off B3098 Westbury—Mkt Lavington; ST9754], *Bell*: Spaciously extended village pub going great guns, very popular indeed for good robust food at relatively low prices, comfortable chairs and settles, cosy little alcoves, well kept Ansells, Benskins Best, Tetleys and a changing guest such as Greene King IPA on handpump, new upstairs dining room, good friendly service – same family as Cross Guns nr Bradford on Avon (see main entries) *(Gwen and Peter Andrews, Roger Wain-Heapy, Colin Laffan, JE)*

Great Hinton [3½ miles E of Trowbridge; ST9059], *Linnet*: Great local enthusiasm for freshly refurbished village pub with home-made food from sandwiches up, Wadworths IPA and 6X, keen young licensees, separate dining room, picnic-table sets outside, pretty village *(Anon)*

☆ **Grittleton** [High St; ST8580], *Neeld Arms*: Charming little pub recently reopened after renovation under very friendly helpful new owners, lovely atmosphere, good food; bedrooms neat and clean, with good breakfasts *(Joann Baker, Jenny and Denis Murphy)*

☆ **Hannington** [SU1793], *Jolly Tar*: Friendly village local with wide choice of good value honest food, well kept Arkells BB, BBB and Kingsdown, lounge bar with big log fire (when it's lit), ships' crests on beams, stripped stone and flock wallpaper; games bar, skittle alley, upstairs grill room; no machines, but piped music may obtrude; good robust play area in biggish garden, tables out in front too; pretty village *(G W A Pearce, Mr and Mrs P B Dowsett, Dave Irving, Jeff Davies, BB)*

Heddington [ST9966], *Ivy*: Low-key basic thatched village local, low beams and timbers, good inglenook fireplace, well kept Wadworths real ales tapped from the cask, children's room; seats outside, a pretty picture *(Jeff Davies, John Hazel, LYM)*

☆ **Heytesbury** [High St; ST9242], *Angel*: Some emphasis on wide choice of consistently good food inc interesting dishes in well kept and attractively refurbished pub, charming dining room opening on to secluded garden behind; Ash Vine, Marstons Pedigree and Border and Ringwood (the lovely dog's called Marston, too), friendly, helpful and relaxed landlady and staff, home-baked bread and cakes for sale; popular with army personnel and can sometimes be a bit noisy, though not off-putting; bedrooms comfortable and attractive *(David Surridge, John A Baker, BHP, Nigel Clifton, DP)*

Heytesbury [High St], *Red Lion*: Friendly and comfortable pub, with good range of food, well kept Courage-related ales, good bedrooms *(P M Woodger, John A Baker)*

☆ **Highworth** [Market Pl; SU2092], *Saracens Head*: Spacious more or less Victorian-style bar rambling interestingly through several distinct areas around great central chimney block; relaxed atmosphere, friendly service, wide choice of good value straightforward bar food (limited Sun) inc vegetarian and children's dishes, well kept Arkells BB and BBB, no piped music, tables in sheltered courtyard; open all day weekdays, children in eating area; comfortable bedrooms *(Mr and Mrs A F Walters, George Atkinson, LYM)*

Highworth [Swanborough; B4019, a mile W on Honnington turning – OS Sheet 174 map ref 184917], *Freke Arms*: Wide choice of good well prepared bar food inc good choice of toasties, children's dishes, Arkells ales *(Mr and Mrs Brown, GWAP)*; [High St], *King & Queen*: 17th-c coaching inn under newish management, with well kept Wadworths 6X and Whitbreads-related ales, good reasonably priced bar food; bedrooms comfortable and clean *(A Maundrell)*

☆ **Hindon** [High St; ST9132], *Grosvenor Arms*: Reopened with newish very hardworking and welcoming landlady, warm, friendly and pleasant bar, decent food inc some interesting dishes, well kept beers, good house wines, notable Irish coffee, good Sun bar nibbles – real competition for the Lamb now *(Geoffrey Culmer, J S Evans, Clifford Payton)*

☆ **Horningsham** [by S entrance to Longleat House; ST8141], *Bath Arms*: Smartly civilised old inn delightfully set in pretty village, modernised without being spoilt; good interesting food (though not cheap) in bar and restaurant, courteous staff, well kept Bass, Eldridge Pope Thomas Hardy and Wadworths 6X, lots of liqueurs and good malt whiskies, aircraft pictures, various dogs; extra charge for credit cards; attractive gardens front and back, dogs allowed on lead here; bedrooms well equipped, clean and comfortable *(Bill Bailey, Maysie Thompson, Alan Skull, Fiona Dick)*

☆ **Kington Langley** [handy for M4 junction 17; Days Lane; ST9277], *Hit or Miss*: Very clean pub with huge helpings of good food from interestingly filled baguettes to enterprising and unusual main dishes, large no-smoking area, restaurant with good log fire; well kept Courage ales and another such as Exmoor or Moles, darts in room by bar; closed Mon, attractive village *(Peter and Rose Flower, P J Caunt, Mrs M Hamilton)*

Kington Langley, *Plough:* Well kept beer, good food, friendly and efficient service *(B Haywood)*

Kington St Michael [handy for M4 junction 17; ST9077], *Jolly Huntsman:* Under very friendly new management, with good range of well kept ales esp Wadworths 6X, good value straightforward food, two roaring log fires; occasional live music *(John Clements)*

☆ **Lacock** [ST9168], *Carpenters Arms:* Good atmosphere in rambling pub with cosy local feel around serving bar, cottagey and old-fashioned rooms off inc eating area and restaurant; quickly served good standard bar food (no sandwiches), well kept Boddingtons and Ushers, friendly service, provision for children; bedrooms *(Nigel Gibbs, T McLean, R Huggins, D Irving, E McCall)*

☆ **Landford** [Hamptworth; village signed down B3079 off A36, then right towards Redlynch; SU2519], *Cuckoo:* Rustic and very unpretentious thatched cottage with well kept real ales such as Adnams Broadside, Badger Best and Tanglefoot, Bunces Best, Wadworths IPA and 6X, cheap filled rolls, pies and pasties, impromptu folk music Fri and maybe Sat and Sun; children in small room off bar; tables outside, big play area and bantams *(K Flack, LYM)*

Laverstock [Duck Lane; SU1631], *Duck:* Attractive pub with good food and service *(Mrs C Dasey)*

☆ **Liddington** [a mile from M4 junction 15, just off A419; SU2081], *Village Inn:* Wide choice of consistently good quickly served home-cooked lunchtime bar food in homely and cosy split-level bar, ungarish furnishings, helpful staff, three or more well kept real ales, farm cider tapped from the cask, log fire; particularly popular with older people, no children; bedrooms simple but clean *(Jeff Davies, K R Harris, HNJ, PEJ)*

Little Cheverell [Low Rd; B3098 Westbury—Upavon, W of A360; ST9853], *Owl:* Nice little pub, very friendly, with well kept beer, decent food (real chips, but only Fri-Sun in winter), beautiful streamside garden; owl collection *(Mr and Mrs G A Page, Colin Laffan)*

☆ **Lockeridge** [signed off A4 Marlborough—Calne just W of Fyfield; SU1467], *Who'd A Thought It:* Welcoming village pub, good choice of good value food, well kept Wadworths IPA and 6X and a guest beer such as Charles Wells Eagle, plush seats around pine and wood-effect tables, L-shaped lounge bar with eating area, separate public bar, log fire; family room, delightful back garden with children's play area *(Colin and Penny Campbell, Brig Green, Jeff Davies, Marjorie and David Lamb)*

Longbridge Deverill [A350/B3095; ST8740], *George:* Spacious quiet pub with very welcoming landlord, decent food inc good value Sun lunch, well kept if not cheap Gales; enormous cat *(D Baker)*

Malmesbury [Abbey Row; ST9287], *Old Bell:* Handsome old inn looking across churchyard to Norman abbey; traditionally furnished and decorated, with locals' bar chock-full on market day (good fires in here), usual pub food, Ushers Best and Wadworths 6X, attractively old-fashioned garden; bedrooms *(Bill Bailey, LYM)*; [High St], *Smoking Dog:* Cosy and unpretentious beamed and stripped stone pub with changing well kept ales such as Archers, Courage Best, Greene King Abbot, Smiles Best and Wadworths 6X, two farm ciders, open fire, good value appetising food, log fires in winter (can be smoky evenings), cool and dark in summer; small garden; bedrooms *(Geoff Summers, D Irving, R Huggins, T McLean, E McCall)*; [Market Cross], *Whole Hog:* Locally popular well converted former restaurant, well kept Archers and small-brewery guest beers, good value food all day, decent wine, tea, coffee, daily papers, individual landlord *(Anon)*

Manton [High St; SU1668], *Oddfellows Arms:* Fairly small, with very welcoming new management, well kept Wadworths ales, good straightforward pub food, big garden *(Paul Randall, Jeff Davies)*; [High St], *Up The Garden Path:* Welcoming landlord in largish carpeted beamed bar with wheelback chairs round the tables, train photographs, food inc good steak and kidney pie, no-smoking restaurant *(HNJ, PEJ, Mr and Mrs A L Budden)*

☆ **Marlborough** [1 High St; SU1869], *Bear:* Large Victorian inn doing well under new licensees who ran the Sun until recently, impressive log fire in centre of main bar, well kept Arkells Bitter, 3B, Kingsdown and Yeomanry, good reasonably priced bar food inc interesting specials prepared by landlady in smallish old-fashioned side bar with tables around central fireplace; small front restaurant facing main parade, medieval-style banqueting hall for special occasions; skittle alley being built; bedrooms inc good value family room *(Mr and Mrs C Holmes, Tom McLean, D Irving, E McCall, R Huggins)*

☆ **Marlborough** [High St], *Sun:* Fine old pub with heavy 16th-c beams, parquet floor and shiny black panelling, plainer lounge on left with open fire (children allowed here), well kept Bass and Hook Norton Best, good coffee, decent food, friendly staff; seats in small courtyard; piped music, live some nights; friendly staff; bedrooms simple but comfortable and reasonably priced *(George Atkinson, Kim Ryan Skuse, D G Clarke, Gordon, LYM)*

☆ **Marlborough** [High St], *Green Dragon:* Bustling well run straightforward pub with well kept Wadworths, wide choice of well prepared lunchtime bar food (plenty of eating areas), stripped brickwork, lots of blue and white plates, leatherette wall banquettes, steps down to back games room, back terrace; bedrooms, pretty little breakfast room *(Gordon, Ann and Colin Hart, D Irving, E McCall, R Huggins, T McLean)*

☆ **Marston Meysey** [SU1297], *Spotted Cow &*

Calf: Lovely Cotswold stone pub in picturesque village, good generous low-priced straightforward bar food, well kept Flowers IPA, Wadworths 6X and two guest beers, welcoming landlord, raised stone fireplace, candlelit restaurant (evening, also Sun lunch); fruit machine and piped music may be rather intrusive; spacious garden with lots of play equipment, even a sandpit, barbecue and summer marquee, backing on to fields *(Jan and Dave Booth, E McCall, D Irving, R Huggins, T McLean)*

Marten [S Head; SU2860], *Tipsy Miller*: The former Nags Head, recently taken over by the licensees of the Royal Oak at Wootton Rivers – see main entries; bedrooms *(Anon)*

Minety [SU0290], *White Horse*: Good value generous home-cooked food inc fresh fish in cosy and comfortably refurbished bars or restaurant, four real ales, welcoming service; pleasant lakeside setting *(M Tuohy, Mrs C Wise, Mrs P Green)*

☆ **Morgans Vale** [SU1921], *Apple Tree*: Lovely old pub with decent range of good food, Ringwood and Wadworths ales, log fires, very cosy and friendly atmosphere; one bar decorated with foreign coins and banknotes *(E W and S M Wills)*

☆ **Netherhampton** [SU1029], *Victoria & Albert*: Cosy and friendly low-beamed pub with antique furniture on polished flagstones, well kept Courage-related real ales, good choice of wines, limited range of good carefully cooked food, maybe unobtrusive piped music, fruit machine in side room; nice long garden behind with own serving hatch *(Jerry and Alison Oakes)*

☆ **Nettleton** [ST8178], *Nettleton Arms*: Very wide choice of good generous bar food in renovated 16th-c pub with no-smoking restaurant, interesting minstrels' gallery; good range of reasonably priced beers; bedrooms *(Peter and Rosie Flower, Paul Weedon, G A Gibbs)*

☆ **Newton Toney** [off A338 Swindon—Salisbury; SU2140], *Malet Arms*: Good imaginative food in bar and restaurant of very popular local, good atmosphere *(D H Buchanan, Jerry and Alison Oakes)*

☆ **North Newnton** [A345 Upavon—Pewsey; SU1257], *Woodbridge*: Useful well run pub open all day for food (afternoon teas etc), surprising variety of exotic Thai, Indian and especially Mexican dishes, good paella, well kept Wadworths 6X, good range of wines, well served coffee; very cosy on winter afternoons with blazing fire and lots of newspapers and magazines to read; big garden with boules, fishing available; bedrooms, small camping/caravan site *(George Atkinson, Howard and Margaret Buchanan)*

Oaksey [ST9893], *Wheatsheaf*: Honest village local with bar and lounge combined, one end for eating, Whitbreads PA on handpump, separate games room with pool and darts *(Roger and Jenny Huggins)*

Oare [SU1563], *White Hart*: Friendly country inn with good moderately priced food, well kept beers *(G W A Pearce, H Anderson)*

☆ **Odstock** [SU1526], *Yew Tree*: Fine old country inn with handsome thatch (inc owl), bewildering choice of good wholesome food (not cheap by pub standards, but good value), fresh fish and game a speciality; good range of real ales, nice unpretentious atmosphere *(Prof J M White, J V Dadswell)*

☆ **Ogbourne St Andrew** [SU1872], *Wheatsheaf*: Good bar food, friendly landlord, very pleasant atmosphere; tables in garden behind *(Dr and Mrs Nigel Holmes, Mr and Mrs K H Frostick)*

Pewsey [A345 towards Marlborough; SU1560], *French Horn*: Good choice of traditional food, well kept Wadworths 6X, log fire, good welcoming service, cheerful furnishings; interesting village *(Geoff and June Wade, A R and B E Sayer)*

☆ **nr Pewsey** [Bottlesford; Woodborough Rd 3 miles W; SU1159], *Seven Stars*: Combination of French restaurant focusing on fresh produce at value-for-money pub prices with charming thatched English country pub; delightful ambience, French owner, roaring log fires, well kept Badger Tanglefoot, Wadworths 6X and regular guest beer, good wine list, friendly atmosphere; pretty garden *(Colin Murray-Hill, Mr and Mrs S Larkin)*

Poulshot [SW of Devizes; ST9559], *Raven*: Nicely refurbished pub on long village green, Wadworths IPA and 6X tapped from the cask, decent choice of well cooked and presented slightly unusual food prepared by landlord, reasonable prices, good service, nice dining room *(Colin Laffan)*

Quidhampton [SU1030], *White Horse*: Small village pub with welcoming landlord and friendly locals, beers inc Bass and Gibbs Mew, good generous food; children welcome, garden safe for them too *(Gwyneth and Salvo Spadaro-Dutturi)*

Redlynch [N of B3080; SU2021], *Kings Head*: Comfortable cottagey 16th-c pub with good landlady, wide range of food from well filled fresh sandwiches up, four Ushers ales, farm cider *(WHBM)*

☆ **Rowde** [A342 Devizes—Chippenham; ST9762], *George & Dragon*: Good original upmarket food (not Mon), quite expensive but above pub standard, with plenty of ever-changing choice, fish a speciality; attractive rooms (though atmosphere not the strongest point), and they haven't forgotten the locals; booking almost essential Sat evening and Sun lunch *(F J and A Parmenter, I E and C A Prosser, A and J Carr, John Hazel, Mr and Mrs T F Marshall)*

☆ **Salisbury** [Castle St], *Avon Brewery*: Unpretentious long narrow bar, busy and friendly, with competitively priced food (not Sun evening), well kept Eldridge Pope real ales, maybe classical piped music, two open fires, simple but individual decor; children in eating area, pretty façade, long sheltered garden running down to river; open all day *(M A Watts, Wayne Brindle, Don Firmin,*

Mr and Mrs A P Reeves, LYM)

☆ Salisbury [Milford St], *Red Lion*: Mix of old-fashioned seats and modern banquettes in two-roomed panelled bar opening into other spacious and interesting areas, medieval restaurant, well kept Bass, Ushers, Wadworths 6X and a strong guest beer, lunchtime bar food, loggia courtyard seats; children in eating areas; bedrooms comfortable *(Jerry and Alison Oakes, LYM)*

☆ Salisbury [New St], *New Inn*: Entirely no-smoking, with ancient heavy beams and timbering, furniture to suit, well kept Badger beers, popular food; pleasant garden *(Mr and Mrs A F Walters, Wayne Brindle, Brian Bannatyne-Scott, BB)*

Salisbury [Castle St], *George & Dragon*: Consistently good fairly priced food, generous helpings with emphasis on home-cooking inc good home-made vegetable bake; welcoming landlord *(Dr and Mrs C S Cox)*; [33 Wilton Rd], *Village*: Several interesting changing well kept real ales, simple food, friendly landlord and locals, relaxed atmosphere; open all day (exc winter Mon-Weds) *(Callan Howarth, Andy and Jill Kassube)*

Sandy Lane [A342 Devizes—Chippenham; ST9668], *George*: Neat stonebuilt local with well kept Wadworths 6X and Old Timer, simple food inc Sun roast; car park on dodgy bend *(W H and E Thomas, LYM)*

Seend [A361; ST9461], *Bell*: Obliging newish landlord in unpretentious country pub, well kept Wadworths ales, small choice of food, small cosy lounge *(Gwen and Peter Andrews, John Hazel, Mr and Mrs N A Spink)*

☆ Sherston [B4040 Malmesbury—Chipping Sodbury; ST8585], *Carpenters Arms*: Cosy beamed village pub recently taken over by family who run Dog at Old Sodbury (see Somerset/Avon main entries), with extraordinarily wide choice of food inc lots of fresh fish, well kept Whitbreads-related ales tapped from the cask; scrubbed floors and tables, open fires, friendly efficient staff, dining area; tables in pleasant garden *(G Hart)*

South Marston [SU1987], *Carpenters Arms*: Good value food in recently extended pub with very friendly staff, well kept Arkells *(Dave Irving)*

Stapleford [Warminster Rd (A36); SU0637], *Pelican*: Very good value food, well kept Ringwood and guest beers, pleasant garden although near road *(R L Neame)*

Staverton [B3105 Trowbridge—Bradford-on-Avon; ST8560], *Old Bear*: Wide choice of good food – separate boards for meat/poultry, fish, vegetarian and puddings, long bar divided into sections, big fireplace, friendly helpful staff; booking recommended Sun lunchtime *(Meg and Colin Hamilton)*

☆ Stibb Green [SU2262], *Three Horseshoes*: Attractive and spotless old-world pub doing well under current youngish licensees, small beamed front bar with inglenook log fire, second smaller bar, wide range of good food,

well kept Wadworths ales, country wines, farm cider *(Gordon, Julie Ashton, A D Shore, Jeff Davies, H Anderson)*

☆ Stourton [Church Lawn; follow Stourhead signpost off B3092, N of junction with A303 just W of Mere; ST7734], *Spread Eagle*: Firmly managed National Trust pub in lovely setting at head of Stourhead lake (though views from pub itself not special), pleasant cool and spacious back dining room popular mainly with older people; standard food, Ash Vine, Bass and Wadworths 6X, waitress service, tables in back courtyard; bedrooms spacious and comfortable, with good residents' lounge *(Alan and Eileen Bowker, Janet Pickles, John A Barker, Fiona Dick, Christopher Gallop, WHBM, LYM)*

Swallowcliffe [ST9627], *Royal Oak*: Comfortable thatched pub with good food under new owners *(Jay Voss, Jerry and Alison Oakes)*

Swindon [Prospect Hill; SU1485], *Beehive*: Lively almost bohemian atmosphere – the posters and messages round the walls are a treat; particularly well kept Morrells, simple lunchtime food, Irish folk nights, basic furnishings *(Tom McLean)*; [Emlyn Sq], *Glue Pot*: Good town local in the heart of Swindon's historic railway village, full range of Archers beers on handpump, very efficient chatty staff; a bit rough and ready, esp evening *(N K Kimber, Tom McLean)*; [Drove Rd], *Grove*: Good example of Beefeater pub, good outdoor drinking area *(Dr and Mrs A K Clarke)*; [Toothill Centre], *Toot & Whistle*: Good split-level estate pub with lively atmosphere and lots of games; well kept beers, very friendly *(Dr and Mrs A K Clarke)*

Teffont Magna [ST9832], *Black Horse*: Pretty old stonebuilt pub in attractive village, comfortable and welcoming lounge, more basic public bar; wide choice of food, well kept Ushers, children's play area in pleasant garden *(LYM; more reports on new regime please)*

Tilshead [A360 Salisbury—Devizes; SU0348], *Rose & Crown*: Well kept beer, welcoming staff, friendly atmosphere, good reasonably priced food inc unusual dishes *(F C Wilkinson, Steve and Lindsey Colwill)*

Tisbury [Church St; ST9429], *Crown*: Beautiful recently enlarged old inn overlooking parish church, exceptional friendly service, good food *(John E Rumney)*

Upavon [A345/A342; SU1355], *Antelope*: Old-fashioned village pub with log fire in lounge bar, small bow-windowed games area, bar food inc some Greek dishes, restaurant, Wadworths real ales, roaming cats; bedrooms sharing bathroom *(Paul S McPherson, KC, Anthony Barnes, LYM)*

Upper Chute [SU2954], *Cross Keys*: Very welcoming, good value varied food, pleasant old-fashioned bar, well kept beers, friendly service, terrace with tables; interesting area for walking *(JE)*

Upper Woodford [SU1237], *Bridge*: Pleasant and welcoming, decent food *(Joy Heatherley)*

☆ **Upton Lovell** [ST9440], *Prince Leopold*: Unassuming but welcoming red brick building with lovely riverside garden, good varied food, decent good value wines, nicely decorated restaurant, cheerful staff; comfortable bedrooms – a quietly peaceful place to stay *(Mr and Mrs Paul Adams, Richard Chappelle, PC)*

Upton Scudamore [ST8647], *Angel*: Old whitewashed village pub with hens running about behind, stained glass in main bar; food now worth knowing *(Fiona Dick)*

☆ **Wanborough** [2 miles from M4 junction 15; Callas Hill, former B4507 towards Lower Wanborough and Bishopstone; SU2083], *Black Horse*: Small friendly inn on downs, lovely views, limited choice of good generous cheap food from doorstep sandwiches up (snacks only, Sun lunchtime), well kept low-priced Arkells BB and BBB on handpump, in winter Kingsdown tapped from the cask, welcoming landlord, simple character beamed bars, tiled floor, antique clock; lounge doubling as homely Mon-Sat lunchtime dining room; piped music; informal garden with adventure playground, aviary, pets' corner; children very welcome *(Robert and Jane Sherriff, Dr Peter Millington, Jeff Davies)*

☆ **Wanborough** [Foxhill; from A419 through Wanborough turn right, 1½ miles towards Baydon], *Shepherds Rest*: Friendly atmosphere in remote pub up on the Ridgeway, very busy in summer; good value well presented food, well kept Flowers IPA and Original and Marstons Pedigree, welcoming service, lots of tables in low-beamed lounge with hunting prints and brasses, two pool tables in bright and airy basic public bar, plain dining room; garden with play area; children and walkers welcome, camping *(Mrs Barker, Jeff Davies, I E and C A Prosser)*

Wanborough [High St, Lower Wanborough], *Plough*: Long low thatched stone pub, genuinely old but done out in ye-olde style, huge centrepiece log fire in one bar, another more or less for evening dining; quick good value bar food, well kept Archers, Flowers Original and Wadworths 6X, farm ciders, small terrace *(Tom McLean)*

Warminster [Mkt Pl; ST8744], *Old Bell*: Welcoming olde-worlde country-town hotel with good service, good traditional bar food inc Mexican dishes and lots of home-made pies, well kept real ale, good choice of wines; restaurant; bedrooms (some still being renovated), splendid breakfasts *(Ian and Nita Cooper)*

☆ **West Dean** [SU2527], *Red Lion*: Very relaxed but spotless country pub in lovely peaceful surroundings, with tables out by tree-sheltered village green running down to pretty stream-fed duckpond, play area; simple lounge with easy chairs and open fires, games inc bar billiards in small plain back bar; well kept real ales, good value home-cooking inc Sun lunch, no-smoking raised dining area, unhurried service; bedrooms spacious, light and fresh *(T A Bryan, Ann and Colin Hunt, LYM)*

West Lavington [Church St; SU0053], *Bridge*: Pretty flower-filled garden and beautifully decorated pink interior with big winter log fire; well kept beer, decent wines, good home-cooked food inc interesting fish dishes and outstanding nut roast *(Sue Stocks)*; *Wheatsheaf*: Nicely refurbished roadside free house with good tables and chairs in bar and adjoining well laid out dining room, good reasonably priced food, Burton Bridge and Tetleys *(Colin Laffan)*

Westbrook [A3102 about 4 miles E of Melksham; ST9565], *Westbrook Inn*: Small cleanly renovated pub, now a free house doing well under friendly and hardworking newish licensees; good generous food *(John Hazel, LYM)*

☆ **Westwood** [off B3109 S of Bradford-on-Avon; ST8059], *New Inn*: Cheerful beamed pub with wide choice of good value home-cooked food esp mixed grill, several rooms attractively opened together, lots of brasses, pleasant efficient staff, well kept Ushers, good fire; shame about the piped music; no-smoking in cellar bar *(W F C Phillips)*

☆ **Wilcot** [SU1360], *Golden Swan*: Very pretty old steeply thatched pub by Kennet & Avon Canal, unpretentiously welcoming, lots of china hanging from beams of two small rooms, well kept Wadworths IPA and 6X and in winter Old Timer, friendly retrievers and prize-winning cat; reasonably priced bar food, dining room; rustic tables on pretty front lawn, field with camping, occasional folk and barbecue weekends, children welcome; good value bedrooms, big and airy *(Colin and Ann Hunt, WHBM, H Anderson, BB)*

Wilton [SU0931], *Pembroke Arms*: Very good Sun carvery and evening meals at sensible prices; good snacks *(W and S Jones)*

Wingfield [ST8256], *Poplars*: Friendly country local with decent food esp Duke's sausage (baguette with long spicy sausage and spicy tomato dip), well kept Wadworths ales, no juke box or machines, own cricket pitch *(Fiona Dick, LYM)*

☆ **Winterbourne Monkton** [A361 Avebury—Wroughton; SU0972], *New Inn*: Small friendly redbrick village local with basic traditional bar, well kept Adnams, Wadworths 6X and a guest such as Hook Norton Old Hookey, decent cider, reasonably priced bar food, darts, fruit machine, subdued piped music; separate restaurant; comfortable bedrooms in converted barn, with good breakfasts *(Rona Murdoch)*

The telephone numbers we give include the new British Telecom codes.

Yorkshire

Again and again, readers' reports stress the size of food helpings in pubs here: extreme generosity seems to be the Yorkshire rule. Pub food prices are not low here – in fact, in the last year they've gone up by considerably more than the general rate of price inflation, so that it's all too common to have to pay more than £5 for a decent hot main dish, and £4 is now typical for a good ploughman's. But what you get for your money makes this very good value indeed. And it's not just quantity. In a high proportion of Yorkshire pubs, the food's quite special. Currently, the very best pubs here for an enjoyable meal out are probably the very atmospheric Crab & Lobster at Asenby, the Three Hares at Bilbrough (gaining a Food Award this year for its imaginative cooking), the characterful Abbey at Byland Abbey, the innovative Foresters Arms at Carlton (new licensees this year, going down very well indeed with readers), the beautifully kept Fox & Hounds at Carthorpe (a star award this year, for its fine service and lovely food), the stylish and individual Blue Lion at East Witton, the bustling Angel at Hetton, the unpretentious Buck at Thornton Watlass (currently doing very well indeed), and that friendly and attractively placed dining pub the Wombwell Arms at Wass. From among these, we choose as Yorkshire Dining Pub of the Year the Crab & Lobster at Asenby – an ideal combination of character surroundings with really good individual food. Among new entries here, the food's also a prime consideration at the civilised Kaye Arms up on Grange Moor, and the George & Dragon at Kirkbymoorside – quite transformed by its new owners, a very pleasant place to stay now, with lovely wines. Blind Jacks in Knaresborough, another new entry, is an excellent pastiche of an unspoilt Georgian town pub; the Beer Engine in Wakefield's main claim to fame is its unstuffy concentration on good beers from small independent brewers, though its food is surprisingly good value too. There are cheerful new licensees at the Green Tree at Hatfield Woodhouse (she's won lots of cooking awards), the charmingly placed old George at Hubberholme, the smart Yorke Arms at Ramsgill, and the Kings Head in Masham. It's in Masham that the independent Black Sheep brewery was started in 1992, in the former North of England Malt Roasting Works, by Paul Theakston – who left the family Theakstons brewing company, also based in Masham, when Scottish & Newcastle took it over. Black Sheep Bitter, a very fine beer, has really caught on in a big way, and this last year we've seen it moving into a great many Yorkshire pubs – readers have been very enthusiastic about it, and so have licensees. Drinks prices in Yorkshire are generally much lower than the national average; we found beer outstandingly cheap in the Kings Arms at Heath (tied to Clarks of Wakefield) and the Greyhound at Saxton (tied to Sam Smiths of Tadcaster). A point to be underlined is that the overall quality of pubs in Yorkshire, particularly in North Yorkshire, is very high indeed – buildings of character, with plenty of atmosphere, and really welcoming licensees. A consequence of this is that the standard of the Lucky Dip entries at the end of the chapter is higher than in many other areas: to do Yorkshire justice with all the main entries it deserves could fill a complete book. Though the list is very long, it's probably a help if we list

*those Dips currently showing really special merit: in North Yorkshire, the
White Swan at Ampleforth, Falcon at Arncliffe, Birch Hall at Beck Hole,
Crown at Bolton Percy, Bull at Broughton, Old Hill at Chapel Le Dale,
Bryherstones at Cloughton Newlands, Cross Keys at East Marton, Black
Bull at Escrick, Feversham Arms at Farndale East, Black Horse in
Grassington, Royal Oak in Great Ayton, Bridge at Grinton, both Helmsley
entries, Worsley Arms at Hovingham, Queens Head at Kettlesing, Forresters
Arms at Kilburn, Shoulder of Mutton at Kirkby Overblow, Red Lion at
Langthwaite, Lister Arms at Malham, Black Swan in Middleham, Black
Bull and Kings Arms at Reeth, Boars Head in Ripley, White Horse at
Rosedale Abbey, Royal at Runswick Bay, Hare at Scawton, Copper Horse
at Seamer, Royal Shepherd in Skipton, Hare & Hounds at Stutton,
Whitestoncliffe at Sutton under Whitestoncliffe, Angel & White Horse in
Tadcaster, Tan Hill Inn, Bull at West Tanfield, Wensleydale Heifer at West
Witton, and Hole in the Wall in York (which has plenty of other decent
pubs, too); in West Yorkshire, the White Swan at Aberford, Bingley Arms at
Bardsey, Griffin at Barkisland, Shears in Halifax, Sands House near
Huddersfield, Bulls Head at Linthwaite, Windmill at Linton, White Hart at
Pool, Three Acres at Shelley and Ring o' Bells at Thornton (there are lots of
decent pubs in Leeds – a particularly good place for real ales); in South
Yorkshire, the Stanhope Arms at Dunford Bridge, Cow & Calf at
Grenoside, Fountain at Ingbirchworth, Boat at Sprotbrough and Royal Oak
at Ulley. We have inspected a great many of these, and are confident that
they are well worth visiting.*

ALDBOROUGH (N Yorks) SE4166 Map 7

Ship 🍺

Village signposted from B6265 just S of Boroughbridge, close to A1

The neatly kept, heavily beamed bar in this very friendly 14th-c pub has some old-fashioned seats around heavy cast-iron tables, sentimental engravings on the walls, and a coal fire in the stone inglenook fireplace. A quieter back room (decorated with ship pictures) has lots more tables. Popular bar food includes soup (£1.40), well filled sandwiches (from £1.50), giant Yorkshire pudding with roast beef (£4.25), lasagne (£4.80), chicken curry (£4.95), vegetarian dishes, lamb cutlets (£5.10), scampi (£5.50), salads, battered cod (£5.75), weekly specials, and Sunday roast lunch. Well kept John Smiths, Tetleys, and Theakstons Old Peculier on handpump, lots of malt whiskies, and a wine of the week; dominoes, shove-ha'penny, and piped music; summer seats on the spacious grass behind. The ancient church is across the lane and beyond it is the Roman town for which the village is famous. *(Recommended by J L Cox, Beryl and Bill Farmer, Roger Bellingham, David Watson, Viv Middlebrook; more reports please)*

*Free house ~ Licensee Duncan Finch ~ Real ale ~ Meals and snacks (not Sun
evening) ~ Restaurant (not Sun evening) ~ (01423) 322749 ~ Children in
restaurant ~ Open 12-2.30(3 Sat), 5.30-11 ~ Bedrooms: £29S/£40S*

APPLETREEWICK (N Yorks) SE0560 Map 7

Craven Arms 🍷 🍴

Village signposted off B6160 Burnsall—Bolton Abbey

Picnic-table sets in front of this stone-built country pub look south over the green Wharfedale valley to a pine-topped ridge – and in summer, the pub is popular with walkers; there are more seats in the back garden. Inside, the small cosy rooms have roaring fires (one in an ancient iron range), attractive settles and carved chairs among more usual seats, and beams that are covered with banknotes, harness, copper kettles and so forth; the landlord is quite a character. Generous bar food includes home-made soup (£1.30), sandwiches (from £1.50), garlic mushrooms (£2.40), ploughman's (£3.50), Cumberland sausage and onion sauce (£4), salads (from £4), home-made steak and kidney pie (£4.15), vegetarian dishes, ham and egg (£5.25), steaks (from £7.95), and daily specials such as game pie (£4.50), pork (£5.20), and liver and onions (£5.75); quick table service in the charming small dining room. Well kept Theakstons Best, Old Peculier, and XB with a summer guest beer like Boddingtons, Tetleys or Youngers on handpump, 21 malt whiskies, and decent wines; darts, shove-ha'penny, cribbage, dominoes – no music. *(Recommended by J E Rycroft, K H Frostick, D Goodger, A Wilson, Mark Bradley, Paul Cartledge, Paul and Gail Betteley, Prof S Barnett, C Roberts, L Walker, M E A Horler, Nicola Thomas, Paul Dickinson)*

Free house ~ Licensees Jim and Linda Nicholson ~ Real ale ~ Meals and snacks (not 25 Dec) ~ (01756) 720270 ~ Children welcome ~ Open 11.30-3, 6.30-11

ASENBY (N Yorks) SE3975 Map 7

Crab & Lobster ★ ⑪ ♈

Village signposted off A168 – handy for A1
Yorkshire Dining Pub of the Year

Apart from excellent and imaginative food in this thatched dining pub, there's also a splendid atmosphere and a lot of character in the relaxed and rambling L-shaped bar. The menu is chalked over all the dark beams and joists – and might include soups such as wonderful lobster bisque, chicken, basil and bean or fish soup with croûtons (from £2.95), mouclade, upside-down tartlet of smoked salmon and garlic or baked scallops gruyère with lemon and garlic (£4.95), boned rabbit wrapped in sun-dried tomatoes on a bed of spinach or mustard rack of pork with black pudding and toffee apple (£8.95), medallions of monkfish and char-grilled vegetables with truffle oil and parmesan or salmon topped with crab crust, fresh pasta and lobster sauce (£9.95), and puddings such as brioche and white chocolate pudding, orange and mint terrine with citrus sorbets or chocolate and amaretto terrine and orange anglais (£3.75). Cooking is precise, using absolutely fresh ingredients, presentation is modern (large plates, pretty detailing, fresh herb garnishes, pools of sauces), and their bread is full of flavour. They do excellent sandwiches (from £3.50), and Sunday roast beef. Maybe nuts, dips and spicy sausages on the bar counter. Theakstons XB and Youngers Scotch and No 3 on handpump, good wines by the glass, with interesting bottles. Cosily cluttered, the bar has gnomelike carved and painted rustic figures on and over the counter, old hats and hat-boxes, an interesting jumble of seats from antique high-backed and other settles through settees and wing armchairs heaped with cushions to tall and rather theatrical corner seats and even a very superannuated dentist's chair; the tables are almost as much of a mix, and the walls and available surfaces are quite a jungle of bric-a-brac, with standard and table lamps keeping even the lighting pleasantly informal; well reproduced though not unobtrusive piped music. There are rustic seats on a side lawn, and out on a front terrace by tubs of flowers; maybe summer barbecues Friday and Saturday evenings and Sunday lunchtime, running to tiger prawns, lobster and suckling pig. *(Recommended by Robin and Lucy Harrington, W C M Jones, David Surridge, Tony Gayfer, P D and J Bickley, Geoffrey and Brenda Wilson, Prof J V Wood, Brian Bannatyne-Scott, C J Hartley, Andrew and Ruth Triggs, M J Marriage, David Wright, Dr Philip Jackson, Katie and Steve Newby, John Knighton, F J Robinson, Stephen Newell, Viv Middlebrook, Ronald Chapman, John Bestley, Pam and Bill Mills, Susan and John Douglas)*

Free house ~ Licensees David and Jackie Barnard ~ Real ale ~ Meals and snacks (not Sun evening) ~ Restaurant ~ (01845) 577286 ~ Children welcome ~ Jazz night first Tues in month ~ Open 11.30-3, 6.30-11; closed Sun evening

ASKRIGG (N Yorks) SD9591 Map 10

Kings Arms ⑪ ⇌ ♈

Village signposted from A684 Leyburn—Sedbergh in Bainbridge

Once a well-known horse-racing stud and then a coaching inn, this Georgian manor house has three atmospheric, old-fashioned bars – all with photographs of the filming of James Herriot's *All Creatures Great and Small* – the inn itself, in the series, is the Drovers Arms. The very high-ceilinged central room has an attractive medley of furnishings that includes a fine sturdy old oak settle, 19th-c fashion plates, a stag's head, hunting prints, and a huge stone fireplace; a curving wall with a high window shows people bustling up and down the stairs and there's a kitchen hatch in the panelling. The small low-beamed and oak panelled front bar has period furnishings, some side snugs, and a lovely green marble fireplace. A simply furnished flagstoned back bar has yet another fire, and a fruit machine and juke box. Darts, shove-ha'penny, dominoes and cribbage. Bar food includes good lunchtime sandwiches (from £1.85; filled french bread and open sandwiches from £3.25), soup (£2.25), stir-fried vegetables (£4), coq au vin or salmon with parsley sauce (£5.25), steak and kidney pie (£5.55), gammon and eggs (£5.95), grilled lamb cutlets, children's dishes (from £1.95), daily specials, and home-made puddings like sticky toffee pudding with butterscotch sauce (£2.50). Well kept Dent Bitter, McEwans 80/-, Theakstons XB and Youngers No 3 on handpump, quite a few malt whiskies, and a very good wine list (including interesting champagnes); pleasant, helpful staff. The two-level courtyard has lots of tables and chairs. *(Recommended by Annette Moore, Chris Pearson, Viv Middlebrook, Martin and Pauline Richardson, Andrew and Ruth Triggs, Mark Bradley, D Goodger, Margaret Mason, David Thompson, Paul Cartledge, M J Morgan, Dr David Webster, Sue Holland, Peter and Erica Davis, Mr and Mrs Peter B Dowsett, John Fazakerley, Bill and Edee Miller)*

Free house ~ Licensees Raymond and Elizabeth Hopwood ~ Real ale ~ Meals and snacks ~ Restaurant and partly no-smoking grill room ~ (01969) 50258 ~ Children welcome ~ Open 11-3(5 Sat), 6.30-11 ~ Bedrooms: £50B/£70B

AUSTWICK (N Yorks) SD7668 Map 7

Game Cock 🛏

Just off A65 Settle—Kirkby Lonsdale

This prettily placed inn is surrounded by good walks, and the crags and screes of the Dales National Park and the Three Peaks rise above the quiet village; fine views from the comfortable bedrooms. The cosy and simply furnished back bar has a friendly atmosphere, well made built-in wall benches and plain wooden tables, a few cockfighting prints on the butter-coloured wall, beams, and a good winter fire. Bar food, with prices unchanged since last year, includes soup (£1.40), sandwiches (from £2.20; toasties from £2.30), Cumberland sausage with gravy (£3.60), ploughman's (£3.95), salads (from £3.50), crispy haddock (£4.20), beef in ale pie (£4.20), gammon with egg and pineapple (£5.95), sweet and sour prawns (£4.50), 10oz sirloin steak (£8.50), gamecock mixed grill (£7.95), puddings such as spicy apple crumble (from £2.30), and children's menu (from £1.95); the restaurant is no smoking. Well kept Thwaites on handpump; darts, dominoes and shove ha'penny. There are some seats in a glass-enclosed sun loggia, and outside – where there's also an equipped children's play area. *(Recommended by Prof S Barnett, Derek and Margaret Underwood, Miss D Baker, Dr C A Brace; more reports please)*

Thwaites ~ Tenant Alex McGwire ~ Real ale ~ Meals and snacks (12-1.45, 7-8.30); not Mon evening ~ Restaurant ~ (0152 42) 51226 ~ Children in restaurant ~ Open 11-3, 6.30-11 ~ Bedrooms: £40

BAINBRIDGE (N Yorks) SD9390 Map 10

Rose & Crown 🛏

A684

Overlooking the wide village green with the old stocks, this long, white-painted stone inn is said to date from 1445. The beamed and panelled front bar has big windows, cushioned antique settles, stools and other old furniture, antlers and Highland cattle horns, horsebrasses, and a fire basket by the open fire (over which is a signed photograph of Christopher Timothy and a message from Jimmy

Saville; a snug with a caged cockatiel, a butterfly collection, and framed lines in praise of pubs by Samuel Johnson, and a locals' bar has green upholstered stools and pool table. Under the new chef, bar food now includes home-made soup (£2.25), sandwiches (from £2.25), filled baked potatoes (from £3.25), tagliatelle with mushrooms, peppers, broccoli and cream (£4.25), ploughman's (from £4.50), Whitby plaice with lime and chervil butter (£5.85), grilled Wensleydale lamb chops (£6.25), rump steak (£8.25), evening dishes like chicken breast with tomato and brandy sauce (£6.95) or grilled cod topped with Yorkshire rarebit (£7.25), children's meals (from £2.50), and puddings (from £2.75). John Smiths Magnet and Yorkshire Bitter on handpump; darts, shove-ha'penny, dominoes, cribbage, fruit machine, trivia, juke box and piped music. *(Recommended by Michael A Butler, Frank Cummins, M J Morgan, Geoff and Angela Jaques, Mark Bradley, J E Rycroft, Mr and Mrs Peter B Dowsett)*

Free house ~ Licensee Claire Jenkins ~ Real ale ~ Meals and snacks ~ Restaurant ~ (01969) 650225 ~ Children welcome ~ Open 11-11 ~ Bedrooms: £44B/£72B

BILBROUGH (N Yorks) SE5346 Map 7

Three Hares 🍽 ♀ 🍺

Off A64 York—Tadcaster

Run by particularly friendly people, this stylishly refurbished 18th-c pub serves very good and imaginative home-made food. As well as daily specials like lamb sausages on a bed of braised white cabbage with a cumin sauce (£6.25), fillet of whitby cod baked onto mousseline potato with a balsamic vinegar sauce (£6.95) or breast of chicken filled with a Somerset brie mousse and baked onto a chive cream sauce (£6.95), there might be lunchtime sandwiches (not Sunday), home-made soup, chicken and pistachio pâté with warm olive bread or tartlets of wensleydale cheese and watercress with a red onion salad (£2.95), fresh potted salmon with caper salad and lime mayonnaise (£3.95), field mushrooms stuffed with tofu and cashew nuts baked under a herb crust and served with a herb dressing (£5.75), casserole of local pork with leeks, fresh tarragon and cream (£5.95), steak and kidney pie (£6.25), Thai crab cakes with chilli dressing (£6.75), stir-fry of king prawns and vegetables flavoured with ginger and mint (£7.95), grilled sirloin steak (£9.50), and puddings like tipsy trifle soaked in Pimms, bread and butter pudding, and home-made ice creams (£2.75); they sell the recipes over the counter for charity; part of the restaurant is no smoking. Well kept on handpump, there are always two real ales like Black Sheep Bitter, John Smiths Bitter, Marstons Pedigree or Timothy Taylors Landlord, with guests such as Fullers London Pride, Rudgate Battleaxe of Theakstons XB; a good, interesting wine list (Mr Whitehead has started to wholesale the wines to customers). The old village smithy now forms part of the restaurant and the old forge and implement hooks are still visible, and the prettily wallpapered walls of the traditional bar are hung with pictures of the village (taken in 1904 and showing that little has changed since then), and polished copper and brass; darts, dominoes, cribbage, and piped music. The churchyard close to the pub is where Sir Thomas Fairfax, famous for his part in the Civil War, lies buried. *(Recommended by Caroline and Gerard McAleese, R Nish, David Watson; more reports please)*

Free house ~ Lease: Peter and Sheila Whitehead ~ Real ale ~ Meals and snacks ~ Restaurant ~ (01937) 832128 ~ Well behaved children in eating area of bar; must be over 10 in restaurant; prefer them to leave by 8pm ~ Open 12-2.30, 7(6.30 Fri/Sat)-11; closed Mon, 25 Dec, evenings 26 Dec and 1 Jan

BINGLEY (W Yorks) SE1039 Map 7

Brown Cow

Ireland Bridge; B6429, just W of junction with A650

In a spacious setting by the River Aire and woods of the St Ives estate (a large area of woodland open to the public) this unpretentious-looking place is warmly welcoming and popular for its very good value food. The friendly open-plan main bar is divided into smaller and snugger areas, with comfortable easy chairs and captain's chairs around the black tables on the carpet, a high shelf of toby jugs under the dark ceiling, and lots of pictures and some brass on the partly panelled walls. Bar food includes soup (£1.75), double-decker sandwiches (from £1.75), ploughman's (from £2.95), excellent filled Yorkshire puddings, steak and kidney pie (£4.95), daily specials such as lamb chops in rosemary sauce (£3.95), roast pork (£4.50) or large mixed grill (£7.95), and home-made puddings such as sticky toffee pudding with fudge sauce or sherry trifle (£1.75); the restaurant is no smoking. Well kept Timothy Taylors Bitter, Best, Ram Tam (in winter) and Landlord on handpump; coffee served all day; fruit machine, and piped music. Below a steep bluebell wood is a sheltered corner terrace behind with tables and chairs – some of them sturdy pews. There are several antique shops in the town. *(Recommended by Katie and Steve Newby, WAH, Roger Huggins, Tom McLean, Annette Moore, Chris Pearson, Bill and Lydia Ryan, Michael Wadsworth, P A and M J White, Alan Kilpatrick)*

Timothy Taylors ~ Tenants Simon and Madeleine Dibb ~ Real ale ~ Meals and snacks (12-2.30, 5.30-9); not Sun evening ~ Restaurant ~ (01274) 569482 ~ Children welcome ~ Trad jazz Mon evening ~ Open 11.30-3.30, 5.30-11

BLAKEY RIDGE (N Yorks) SE6799 Map 10

Lion 🛏 🍺

From A171 Guisborough—Whitby follow Castleton, Hutton le Hole signposts; from A170 Kirkby Moorside—Pickering follow Keldholm, Hutton le Hole, Castleton signposts; OS Sheet 100 map reference 679996

Readers love the contrast between the bleak moors outside and the warm cosiness in the characterful beamed and rambling bars here, with their open fires. There are a few big high-backed rustic settles around cast-iron-framed tables, lots of small dining chairs on the turkey carpet, a nice leather settee, stripped stone walls hung with some old engravings and photographs of the pub under snow (it can easily get cut off in winter), and dim lamps. Huge helpings of well cooked food include soup (£1.65), lunchtime sandwiches (from £1.95) and ploughman's (£4.25), macaroni cheese crumble, home-cooked ham and egg, home-made lasagne or steak and kidney pie or whitby cod in batter (all £5.25), butterbean and vegetable curry (£5.95), pork fillet (£6.25), and puddings (£1.95); Sunday roasts and good breakfasts; quick service even when busy – which it usually is. Well kept Bass, Tetleys, Theakstons Best, Old Peculier, XB and Mild, and Youngers No 3 on handpump; dominoes, fruit machine and piped music. During the late 19th-c coal-mining days, the mine here was linked to the railway at Rosedale by a tramway that ran within yards of the pub – it's now the course of the Cleveland Way, Coast to Coast path and Lyke Wake walk. The inn is said to be the fourth highest inn in England and the moorland views are spectacular. *(Recommended by John and Christine Simpson, Ian Boag, Fred Collier, Bronwen and Steve Wrigley, Tina and David Woods-Taylor, Andrew and Ruth Triggs, Rupert Lecomber, Andrew and Kathleen Bacon, R M Macnaughton, Mayur Shah, Jeff Davies, Mike Simpson, Frances Pennell, Graham Bush)*

Free house ~ Licensee Barry Crossland ~ Real ale ~ Meals and snacks (11-10) ~ Restaurant (all day Sun) ~ (01751) 417320 ~ Children welcome ~ Open 10.30am-11pm ~ Bedrooms: £15.50(£25.50B)/£43(£51B)

BREARTON (N Yorks) SE3261 Map 7

Malt Shovel 🍽 🍷

Village signposted off A61 N of Harrogate

People travel from near and far to enjoy the very good home-made food in this friendly and unpretentious pub. Several heavily-beamed rooms radiate from the attractive linenfold oak bar counter with plush-cushioned seats, sewing-machine and other tables, an ancient oak partition wall, both real and gas fires, and lively Nigel Hemming hunting prints. Reliably good, dishes might include spicy bean pot (£3.85), popular nut roast with tomato and mint sauce or steak and mushroom pie (£4.50), Trinidad prawn curry (£5.10), fresh haddock in batter (£5.50), fresh salmon with cucumber mayonnaise (£6.50), and imaginative salads; efficient service. They have decent wines, well kept Old Mill Traditional and Theakstons Best and two guest beers on handpump, farm cider, and malt whiskies; shove-ha'penny, darts, table skittles, cribbage and dominoes; quite a few cats who like to sit by the fires. There are tables behind, on the terrace and the grass leading to a discreet little caravan site; exemplary lavatories. *(Recommended by Catherine and Andrew Brian, Mayur Shah, G Dobson, Paul Boot, Mark Bradley, S Brackenbury, Ann and Bob Westerook, Viv Middlebrook, Derek and Sylvia Stephenson, Miss D Baker, S V Bishop, Michael Marlow)*

Free house ~ Licensee Leigh Trafford Parsons ~ Real ale ~ Meals and snacks (not Sun evening, not Mon) ~ (01423) 862929 ~ Children welcome ~ Open 12-3, 6.45(6.30 Sat)-11; closed Mon

BUCKDEN (N Yorks) SD9278 Map 7

Buck ♀
B6160

Surrounded by marvellous walks – there are good moorland views, too – this is a popular and professionally run place. Inside, the modernised and extended open-plan bar has local pictures, hunting prints, willow-pattern plates and the mounted head of a roebuck on the mainly buttery cream walls (one by the big log fire is stripped to bare stone), and upholstered built-in wall banquettes and square stools around shiny dark brown tables on its carpet – though there are still flagstones in the snug original area by the serving counter. Efficiently served by helpful uniformed staff, bar food includes home-made tomato and carrot soup (£1.95), home-made duck liver pâté (£2.95), baked eggs with blue cheese (£3.45), guinea fowl breast wrapped in bacon with tomato and leek sauce (£4.95), home-made beef bourguignon (£5.50), poached halibut or herb crêpe filled with vegetables and cheese (£5.95), good roast pork or plaice stuffed with spinach, pigeon breast with bacon, red wine and thyme sauce (£6.95), and 10oz sirloin steak (£9.95); the restaurant is no smoking. Well kept Black Sheep, Theakstons Best, Old Peculier and XB, Youngers Scotch, and a guest beer on handpump; good choice of malt whiskies and decent wines. Darts, dominoes, cribbage, trivia, and occasional piped music. *(Recommended by C Roberts, A Barker, E J and M W Corrin, Lee Goulding, P D and J Bickley, Ray and Liz Monk, M J Morgan, Annette Moore, Chris Pearson, TBB, Catheryn and Richard Hicks, Gordon Theaker, Prof S Barnett, Nick and Alison Dowson, Neil and Anita Christopher, WAH, Clive and Michele Platman, Mr and Mrs D Darby, G Dobson, Andrew Sykes)*

Free house ~ Licensee Nigel Hayton ~ Real ale ~ Meals and snacks ~ Evening restaurant ~ (01756) 760228 ~ Children in eating area of bar ~ Open 11-11 ~ Bedrooms: £31B/£62B

BURNSALL (N Yorks) SE0361 Map 7

Red Lion ♀
B6160 S of Grassington, on Ilkley road; OS Sheet 98, map reference 033613

This was originally a 16th-c ferryman's inn and stands on the bank of the River Wharfe looking across the village green towards Burnsall Fell; tables on the front cobbles enjoy the view, and there are more on a big back terrace; fishing permits for 7 miles of river are sold here. The bustling main bar has sturdy seats built in to the attractively panelled walls (decorated with pictures of the local fell races), Windsor armchairs, oak benches, rugs on the floor, and steps up past a solid-fuel stove to a back area with sensibly placed darts (dominoes players are active up here, too). The carpeted, no-smoking front lounge bar which is served from the same copper-topped counter through an old-fashioned small-paned glass partition, has a log fire. Good bar food includes home-made soup (£2), lunchtime sandwiches (£2.95), ratatouille and Wensleydale cheese (£5.25), salads (from £5.50), ploughman's or lamb's liver and bacon with onion gravy (£5.75), steak and kidney pie (£5.95), gammon with free range eggs (£6.50), sirloin steak (£8.95), daily specials such as hake, monkfish, lemon sole, crab, and seasonal game (pheasant, mallard, pigeon and partridge), and puddings such as sticky toffee pudding with caramel sauce or sherry trifle (from £2.95); the restaurant is no smoking. Well kept Tetleys Bitter and Theakstons Best and guest beers on handpump, malt whiskies, and a good wine list with several by the glass. Most of the bedrooms have views of the river and village green. *(Recommended by Gwen and Peter Andrews, JCW, Mark Bradley, Mary Moore, D Goodger, G Dobson, Wayne Brindle, Bill and Lydia Ryan, Simon Watkins)*

Free house ~ Licensee Elizabeth Grayshon ~ Real ale ~ Meals and snacks (12-2.30, 6-9.30) ~ Restaurant ~ (01756) 720204 ~ Children welcome ~ Open 11.30-3, 5.30(5 Sat)-11 ~ Bedrooms: £37B/£64B

BYLAND ABBEY (N Yorks) SE5579 Map 7

Abbey Inn ♟ ♍ ♗

The Abbey has a brown tourist-attraction signpost off the A170 Thirsk—Helmsley

Apart from the lovely setting opposite the abbey ruins, this attractive pub has characterful and friendly rambling rooms in which to enjoy the very good – and extremely popular – food. Served by neat and friendly waitresses this might include soup (£1.80), lunchtime sandwiches (£2.50), smoked salmon pâté or pear, stilton and bacon salad (£3.80), ploughman's (£4.30), vegetable moussaka (£6), devilled kidneys (£6.25), battered haddock (£6.50), rolled boned chicken filled with pork, ham and apricots (£6.60), and grilled plaice (£6.75), with evening dishes such as fresh crab and spinach timbale on a bed of dill and lobster sauce, broccoli and mushroom quiche (£6.50), pork fillet in a madeira sauce (£6.70), venison steak and Cumberland sauce (£9.50), sirloin steak with red wine sauce (£11.50), and puddings like chocolate roulade or strawberry cheesecake (£2.75); good vegetables. Well kept Black Sheep Bitter and Theakstons Best on handpump, and an interesting wine list. The rambling series of rooms have oak and stripped deal tables, settees, carved oak seats, and Jacobean-style dining chairs on the polished boards and flagstones, some discreet stripping back of plaster to show the ex-abbey masonry, big fireplaces, decorative bunches of flowers among the candles, various stuffed birds, cooking implements, little etchings, willow-pattern plates, and china cabinets. In a big back room an uptilted cart shelters a pair of gnomelike waxwork yokels, and there are lots of rustic bygones; piped music. No dogs. There's lots of room outside in the garden. *(Recommended by G Dobson, SS, Andrew and Ruth Triggs, The Mair Family, David Rogers, Pat Crabb, H Bramwell, Ann and Frank Bowman, Paul and Ursula Randall, Beryl and Bill Farmer, Mr and Mrs C Wright, Pat and Robert Watt, Mr and Mrs R M Macnaughton, John Lawrence, John and Christine Simpson, B B Pearce, Brian Bannatyne-Scott, Stephen Newell, W and S Rinaldi-Butcher, P Boot, D P Pascoe)*

Free house ~ Licensees Peter and Gerd Handley ~ Real ale ~ Meals and snacks (not Sun evening, not Mon) ~ (01347) 868204 ~ Children welcome ~ Open 11-2.30, 6.30-11; closed Sun evening and all day Mon

CADEBY (S Yorks) SE5100 Map 7

Cadeby Inn

3 miles from A1(M) at junction with A630; going towards Conisbrough take first right turn signposted Sprotbrough, then follow Cadeby signposts

The main lounge at the back of this popular pub has the caps of all seventeen County Cricket Clubs, an open fire in the big stone fireplace, comfortable seats around wooden tables as well as a high-backed settle made in the traditional style to fit around one stone-walled alcove, some stuffed animals and silver tankards, and lots of house plants. There's a quieter front sitting room, and decently out of the way, trivia and a fruit machine; also, an old each-way horse racing machine, shove-ha'penny, dominoes and cribbage; the snug is no smoking. Bar food includes a lunchtime salad bar, generous carvery or gammon steak (all £4.25), as well as soup (£1) and sandwiches (from £1.25), home-made steak and kidney pie (£3.45), and sirloin steak; Sunday roast lunch (£4.95). Well kept Courage

Directors, John Smiths Bitter and Magnet, Sam Smiths OB, Tetleys Bitter and a guest such as Ruddles County on handpump, and over 200 malt whiskies. There are seats in the front beer garden where they may hold summer barbecues. The licensee also runs the Mile Lodge at Marr. *(Recommended by David Ing, John and Elspeth Howell, Roy Bromell, Paul Cartledge, Mark Bradley, J M and K Potter)*

Free house ~ Licensee Walter William Ward ~ Real ale ~ Meals and snacks (till 10pm) ~ (01709) 864009 ~ Children in eating area of bar till 8.30pm ~ Open 11.30-3, 5-11; 11.30-11 Sat

CARLTON (N Yorks) SE0684 Map 10

Foresters Arms 🍽 🍷 🛏

Off A684 W of Leyburn, just past Wensley; or take Coverdale hill road from Kettlewell, off B6160

In a pretty village in the heart of the Yorkshire Dales National Park, this mid-17th-c stone coaching inn has friendly new licensees this year. It's a comfortable place with lots of atmosphere, open log fires, low beamed ceilings, and well kept Theakstons Best and XB and a guest beer on handpump. Very good and carefully prepared lunchtime bar food includes lots of daily specials like wood pigeon and black pudding warm salad or celestine of beef with Dijon sauce (£4.25) or apricot and pistachio nut risotto (£6.50), as well as sandwiches (from £2.25, home-made ox tongue £2.50, fillet steak with french mustard £4.95), potato and onion rosti (£4.50), ragout of wild mushrooms with cream and pasta or stir-fried chicken (£4.95), a bowl of home-made soup with assorted cheeses and pâtés (£5.25), pasta with smoked salmon in a white wine, chive and cream sauce (£5.50), a lovely paella, and fresh fish and local game (in season), with evening dishes such as ham and eggs (£5.45), sautéed scallops with saffron vinaigrette or baked crab and asparagus gateau with rosemary butter (£8.50), and grilled leg of lamb steak or poached wild Lune salmon with hollandaise sauce (£8.95); puddings like apple and cinnamon tart, chocolate terrine or hot baked soufflé (from £2.25); good wines. Part of the restaurant is no smoking; darts, cribbage, dominoes and piped music. There are some picnic-table sets among tubs of flowers. *(Recommended by J Durrant, E J Wilde, Mr and Mrs F J Parmenter, Alan Holmes; more reports on the new regime, please)*

Free house ~ Licensees Barrie Higginbotham and S J Thornalley ~ Real ale ~ Meals and snacks (not Sun evening, except for residents) ~ Restaurant (not Sun) ~ (01969) 40272 ~ Children in eating area of bar till 9.30pm ~ Open 12-3, 6.30-11; winter evening opening 7 ~ Bedrooms: £30S/£55S

CARTHORPE (N Yorks) SE3184 Map 10

Fox & Hounds ★ 🍽

Village signposted from A1 N of Ripon, via B6285

Readers have been so enthusiastic about this pretty little extended family-run village house this year, that we've decided to give it a star. Apart from the first-class, beautifully presented food, the service is excellent and the housekeeping exemplary. The cosy, L-shaped bar has quite a few mistily evocative Victorian photographs of Whitby, a couple of nice seats by the larger of its two log fires, dark red plush button-back built-in wall banquettes and chairs, blue patterned wallpaper with matching curtains on brass rails, plates on stripped beams, and some limed panelling. An attractive high-raftered restaurant leads off with lots of neatly black-painted farm and smithy tools. The menu is the same in the bar and no-smoking restaurant (best to book for the restaurant – they don't take bookings in the bar) and might include thick vegetable soup with croûtons or stilton cheese and onion soup (£2.25), terrine of duckling with home-made apple chutney (£3.95), seafood hors d'oeuvres (£4.95), steak and kidney pie (£6.25), fresh whole crab (from £6.95), baby chicken cooked in Theakstons beer (£7.45), fillet of salmon with hollandaise (£7.95), rack of English lamb (£8.95), and grilled whole Dover sole or fillet steak stuffed with mushrooms and garlic (£9.95); puddings such as apple and cinnamon flan, tipsy trifle or lemon sponge with tangy lemon sauce (from £2.65). They use local fish according to season and local meat and cheeses, and devote a good deal of care to their wines, with a wide choice by the bottle and half-bottle, decent wines by the glass, and some interesting bin-ends; well kept John Smiths and Theakstons Best on handpump. *(Recommended by Brian Kneale, Mrs E A Galewski, Malcolm Pettit, Mr and Mrs David J Hart, D Cummings, Mr and Mrs Pettit, Leonard Dixon, Janet and Peter Race, Frank Davidson)*

Free house ~ Licensee Howard Fitzgerald ~ Real ale ~ Meals and snacks (not Mon) ~ Restaurant ~ (01845) 567433 ~ Children welcome but no small ones after 8pm ~ Open 12-2.30, 7-11; closed Mon and first week of the year from 1 Jan

COXWOLD (N Yorks) SE5377 Map 7

Fauconberg Arms ★ 🛏 ♔

There's something for everyone in this civilised old stone pub – an old-fashioned back locals' bar for those wanting an informal drink and a chat, two cosy knocked-together rooms of the lounge bar with cushioned antique oak settles and other fine furniture, and a marvellous winter log fire in an unusual arched stone fireplace, a popular dining room – and very good home-made food. One menu serves both the bar and restaurant, and at lunchtime includes home-made soup (£1.95), sandwiches (from £2.25), smoked salmon and watercress mousse (£3.65), steak and kidney pie in ale (£5.75), salads (from £5.95), salmon and leek pancakes with tomato and herb sauce (£6.25), pan-fried lamb with an apple, mint and rosemary gravy (£6.75), and sirloin steak (£8.95), with evening dishes like smoked chicken and melon with an avocado dip (£3.25), stuffed aubergine (£5.25), vegetarian crêpes (£9.95), and half a roast duckling on buttered celeriac and apple with walnut gravy (£10.25); puddings such as white chocolate mousse or fresh fruit crumble (£2.95); three-course Sunday lunch (£10.45). Well kept John Smiths, Tetleys Bitter, and Theakstons Best on handpump, and an extensive wine list with blackboard bin ends available by the glass. Dominoes, fruit machine, juke box and piped music. The broad, quiet village street is pretty, with tubs of flowers and seats on its grass or cobbled verges. The inn is named after Lord Fauconberg, who married Oliver Cromwell's daughter Mary. *(Recommended by Andrew and Ruth Triggs, Joan Lawrence, H Bramwell, Bronwen and Steve Wrigley, Pat Crabb, Paul Wreglesworth, Paul Cartledge, Brian Kneale, Simon Collett-Jones, Janet Pickles, Gill Earle, Andrew Burton, W and S Rinaldi-Butcher, T Nott, Richard Waller, R M Macnaughton, Kim Schofield)*

Free house ~ Lease: Robin and Nicky Jaques ~ Real ale ~ Meals and snacks (not Mon evening in winter) ~ Restaurant ~ (01347) 868214 ~ Children welcome ~ Open 11-2.30(3 Sat), 6.30(6 Sat)-11; winter evening opening 7pm ~ Bedrooms: £24/£40

CRACOE (N Yorks) SD9760 Map 7

Devonshire Arms

B6265 Skipton—Grassington

Very popular locally and well run by friendly licensees, this stone village pub has low shiny black beams supporting creaky white planks, polished flooring tiles with rugs here and there, gleaming copper pans round the stone fireplace, and little stable-type partitions to divide the solidly comfortable furnishings into cosier areas: built-in wall settles, green plush cushioned dark pews and sturdy rustic or oak tripod tables. Above the dark panelled dado are old prints, engravings and photographs, with a big circular large-scale Ordnance Survey map showing the inn as its centre. Enjoyable bar food includes soup (£1.65), sandwiches (from £1.75), vegetarian lasagne (£3.75), ploughman's (£4.25), filled Yorkshire puddings (from £4.25), steak and mushroom pie (£4.95), daily specials like pasta dishes (£4.25), breast of duck or monkfish (£7.25), home-made puddings such as cheesecake or sticky toffee pudding (£2.50), and evening poached Scotch salmon (£5.50), and steaks (from £8.20). Well kept Theakstons Best and Old Peculier and Youngers Scotch and No 3 (summer only), malt whiskies and decent wines; a fruit machine and trivia are tucked discreetly away by the entrance; darts, dominoes and piped music. There are picnic-table sets on a terrace flanked by well kept herbaceous borders; and a small dog called Juno may watch you coming and going from his position on the roof. *(Recommended by Paul J Bispham, E A George, T M Dobby, E G Parish, Ann and Bob Westerook, Richard Waller, TBB, Geoff and Angela Jaques, Nick and Alison Dowson, Trevor Scott, Stephen, Julie and Hayley Brown)*

Free house ~ Licensees John and Jill Holden ~ Real ale ~ Meals and snacks ~ Restaurant ~ (01756) 730237 ~ Children in eating area of bar up to 9.30 ~ Open 11.30(11 summer Sats)-3, 6-11; winter evening opening 6.30; closed winter Sun evening and evening 25 Dec ~ Bedrooms: £25B/£40B

CRAY (N Yorks) SD9379 Map 7

White Lion ★ 🍺

B6160, Upper Wharfedale N of Kettlewell

This is a former drovers' hostelry and surrounded by some superb countryside. You can sit at the picnic-table sets above the very quiet, steep lane, or on the great flat limestone slabs in the shallow stream which tumbles down opposite. Inside, the simply furnished bar has a traditional atmosphere, a lovely open fire, seats around tables on the flagstone floor, shelves of china, iron tools and so forth, and a high dark beam-and-plank ceiling; there's also a no-smoking family snug. Good bar food includes good soup (£1.85), hoagies or large Yorkshire pudding with various fillings (from £2.50), locally-made Cumberland sausage (£4.75), vegetable lasagne (£5), evening dishes such as salads (from £5.25) and steaks (from £9.25), daily specials such as salmon steak with asparagus in a white wine sauce (£6.50) or Normandy chicken (£6.95), puddings (£1.95), and children's menu (£2.75); good breakfasts. Well kept Moorhouses Premier and Pendle Witches Brew, Tetleys Premier Bitter and a guest beer on handpump; dominoes, ring the bull and piped music. *(Recommended by Nicola Thomas, Paul Dickinson, Joanne Newton, David Wright, Neville Kenyon, Mr and Mrs K H Frostick, Andrew McKeand, Nick and Alison Dowson, Michael Marlow, Eric and Shirley Broadhead, Clive and Michele Platman, Greenwood and Turner)*

Free house ~ Licensees Frank and Barbara Hardy ~ Real ale ~ Meals and snacks ~ (01756) 760262 ~ Children welcome if pub quiet – in dining room only when busy ~ Limited parking ~ Open 11-11; 11-3, 6-11 winter weekdays ~ Bedrooms: £30B/£44B

CRAYKE (N Yorks) SE5670 Map 7

Durham Ox

Off B1363 at Brandsby, towards Easingwold

Both locals and visitors alike are made welcome at this carefully-run and relaxed village inn. The old-fashioned lounge bar has an enormous inglenook fireplace with winter log fires (flowers in summer), venerable tables and antique seats and settles on the flagstones, pictures and old local photographs on the dark green walls, a high shelf of plates and interestingly satirical carvings in its panelling (which are Victorian copies of medievel pew ends), and polished copper and brass. Some of the panelling here divides off a bustling public area which has a good lively atmosphere and more traditional furnishings; above the Victorian fire grate is a written account of the local history dating back to the 12th c, and on the opposite wall, a large framed print of the original famous Durham ox; the dogs are called Elsie and Nelson, and the cat, Henry. Darts and fruit machine. Good bar food includes sandwiches (£2, double deckers £2.80), large fresh grilled haddock (£5.50), lasagne, fish pot, steak and kidney pie or curry (all £4.95), 12oz sirloin steak (£8.95), and puddings (£2). Well kept Black Sheep, Marstons Pedigree, John Smiths, and Tetleys on handpump. The tale is that this is the hill which the Grand Old Duke of York marched his men up; the view from the hill opposite is wonderful. *(Recommended by Andrew and Ruth Triggs, W and S Rinaldi-Butcher, Stephen Newell, R T Moggridge; more reports please)*

Free house ~ Licensee Ian Chadwick ~ Real ale ~ Meals and snacks (not Sun evening) ~ Restaurant ~ (01347) 821506 ~ Children welcome ~ Open 12-3, 7-11 ~ Bedrooms: £25/£35

CROPTON (N Yorks) SE7588 Map 10

New Inn 🍺

Village signposted off A170 W of Pickering

The airy lounge bar in this comfortably modernised village inn has been refurbished this year with Victorian church panels, terracotta and dark blue plush seats, lots of brass, a small open fire, and a collection of teddies (made in the village) wearing Cropton Brewery T-shirts. The no-smoking family conservatory downstairs has farmhouse-style chairs around wooden tables. Their own robustly flavoured beers include Two Pints, Special Strong and Scoresby Stout (brewery trips are encouraged), with guests like King Billy (specially brewed for the King Billy in Hull) and Tetleys Bitter and Mild on handpump; several malt whiskies. Substantial helpings of good value bar food (with prices unchanged since last year) includes sandwiches (from £1.75; lunchtimes only and not on Sunday), home-made soup (£1.95), home-made pâté (£2.95), ploughman's (from £3.25), nut roast with barbecue sauce or salmon steak (£4.75), steak and kidney pie in stout (£5.25), sirloin steak with mushrooms (£6.95), popular duck with a weekly-changing sauce, puddings and children's meals (£2.95); they start serving early in the evening – popular with older people in the neighbourhood. Sunday carvery. The elegant small no-smoking restaurant is furnished with genuine Victorian and early Edwardian furniture. Pleasant service; darts, dominoes, fruit machine, pool room and juke box. There's a neat terrace and garden with pond. Comfortable, good value bedrooms. *(Recommended by D and J Johnson, Keith and Margaret Kettell, Joy Heatherley, Paul Wreglesworth, Martin Jones, Paul Cartledge, Paul Noble, Roger and Christine Mash, Andrew and Ruth Triggs)*

Own brew ~ Licensee Michael James Lee ~ Real ale ~ Meals and snacks ~ Restaurant ~ (01751) 417330 ~ Children in conservatory and in restaurant ~ Open 11-3, 6-11; 11-11 Sat; 12-2, 7-11 in winter ~ Bedrooms: £35B/£41B

EAST WITTON (N Yorks) SE1586 Map 10

Blue Lion 🍽️ 🛏️

A6108 Leyburn—Ripon

On the edge of the green in a pretty village, this stylish and characterful pub is very popular for its enterprising home-made bar food which might include sandwiches, home-made pasta dishes such as tagliatelle carbonara (£5.50), nice lamb steak in honey and nut sauce, grilled fillet of cod with bacon, garlic and thyme (£8.25), good chicken stuffed with goat's cheese in mustard sauce, wild boar casseroled in red wine (£8.95), and puddings such as treacle sponge, white chocolate mousse with orange, and apple crumble with brown-bread ice cream; good breakfasts; helpful, friendly staff. Well kept Boddingtons, Theakstons Best, and Timothy Taylor Landlord on handpump, decent wines, fruit wines in the summer, and old English liqueurs. The big squarish bar has high-backed antique settles and old Windsor chairs and round tables on the turkey rugs and flagstones, ham-hooks in the high ceiling decorated with dried wheat, teazles and so forth, a delft shelf filled with appropriate bric-a-brac, a couple of prints of the Battle of Omdurman, hunting prints, sporting caricatures and other pictures on the walls, log fire, and daily papers; the friendly black labrador is called Ben. Picnic-table sets on the gravel outside look beyond the stone houses on the far side of the village green to Witton Fell, and there's a big pretty back garden. *(Recommended by Michael A Butler, P D and J Bickley, M J Morgan, Frank Davidson, Jim Farmer, Walter and Susan Rinaldi-Butcher, John and Joan Nash, J Durrant, Annette Moore, Chris Pearson, Andrew Shore, Andrew and Ruth Triggs, P Bunbury, Jack Hill, Bill Edwards, Mayur Shah, Rob Noble, Paul and Gail Betteley, Peter and Erica Davis)*

Free house ~ Lease: Paul Klein ~ Real ale ~ Meals and snacks ~ Restaurant (closed Sun evening) ~ (01969) 24273 ~ Children welcome ~ Open 11-11 ~ Bedrooms: £35B/£60B

nr EAST WITTON (N Yorks) SE1586 Map 10

Cover Bridge

A6108 a mile N

The friendly little locals' bar on the left in this informally run 16th-c pub has lots of red-cushioned seats, as well as two elderly housekeeper's chairs that share the broad space under a fine arched stone chimneypiece with an old-fashioned grate complete with side kettle-rests; there's a labrador and a plump collie cross. The room on the right, no bigger, has attractive pews, unusual black cast-iron stools, a piano and a nice Victorian fireplace: it leads out into a biggish rather rough-hewn country garden by a small river and steep stone bridge, with several sheds and swings for children. Bar food includes good sandwiches or home-made soup (£1.75), sausage or egg with chips (£2), ploughman's (£3.75), vegetarian pasta bake (£4.25), home-made steak pie (£5.95), steaks (from £7.95), and puddings (£2) Well kept Black Sheep Bitter, John Smiths Bitter, and Theakstons Best on handpump, and country wines; darts, dominoes; a terrace and Wendy house. (*Recommended by M J Morgan, Andrew and Ruth Triggs, Bill Edwards, Brian Skelcher, Anthony Barnes, Jon Dewhirst, Roxanne Chamberlain, David Gaunt*)

Free house ~ Licensees Jim and June Carter ~ Real ale ~ Meals and snacks (till 10pm) ~ Restaurant ~ (01969) 23250 ~ Children welcome ~ Piano Sat evening ~ Open 11-11 ~ Bedrooms: £25B/£40B

EGTON BRIDGE (N Yorks) NZ8105 Map 10

Horse Shoe 🛏

Village signposted from A171 W of Whitby; via Grosmont from A169 S of Whitby

The setting here is lovely – some comfortable seats on a quiet terrace and lawn are set beside a little stream with ducks and geese, and the wild birds are so tame that they sit on your table waiting for food; a footbridge leads to the tree-sheltered residents' lawn which runs down to the river. Inside, the bar has a log fire, high-backed built-in winged settles, wall seats and spindleback chairs around the modern oak tables, a big stuffed trout (caught near here in 1913) and a fine old print of a storm off Ramsgate and other pictures on the walls. Good bar food served by very friendly staff includes lunchtime sandwiches, home-made soup, good bacon chops with peach sauce, tasty chicken breast in stilton sauce, ham and egg, vegetarian fettucine, and steaks, with daily specials such as liver and bacon casserole (£5.75), salmon and broccoli fishcakes (£6.20), beef cooked in ale (£6.40), and local monkfish in fresh breadcrumbs (£6.95); good fresh vegetables and nice breakfasts; children's dishes. Well kept Tetleys Bitter, Theakstons Best, Old Peculier and XB on handpump, and a weekly guest beer; English wines. Darts, dominoes and piped music. Perhaps the best way to reach this beautifully placed pub is to park by the Roman Catholic church, walk through the village and cross the River Esk by stepping stones. Not to be confused with a similarly named pub up at Egton. (*Recommended by Margaret Mason, David Thompson, Andrew and Ruth Triggs, Mayur Shah, B B Pearce, D L Parkhurst, Bronwen and Steve Wrigley, P D Kudelka, A W Dickinson, Giles Quick*)

Free house ~ Licensees David and Judith Mullins ~ Real ale ~ Meals and snacks (not 25 Dec) ~ Restaurant ~ (01947) 85245 ~ Children in eating area of bar ~ Open 11-3.30, 6.30-11; closed evening 25 Dec ~ Bedrooms: £26(£30B)/£38(£46B)

Postgate 🛏 🍺

This moorland pub is named after Father Nicholas Postgate, hanged, drawn and quartered at York 300 years ago for baptising a child into the Roman Catholic Church. The well kept and carpeted lounge bar has upholstered modern settles and seats in a sunny window, Windsor chairs, a high shelf of cups and bottles, an open fire, and a relaxed, informal atmosphere. Decent bar food includes sandwiches (from £1.50), soup (£1.60), salads (from £3.50), spicy bean and vegetable casserole (£3.95), tandoori chicken (£4.40), home-made steak in ale pie (£5), daily specials like tagliatelle with various sauces (£4.25), pork chop in honey and cider (£4.50), gammon (£5.95), and sirloin steak (£8.50), puddings, and children's meals (from £1.95). Well kept Camerons Lion and Strongarm, Flowers IPA, Ind Coope Burton, and Tetleys on handpump. The public bar has darts (several teams), dominoes, cribbage and piped music. Seats and big umbrellas on a sunny flagstoned terrace in front of the pub look down the steep twisty valley of the lovely River Esk. The tiny Egton Station (four little trains a day) is less than a minute's walk away – useful for local walkers. Salmon or trout fishing can be arranged, as can boat fishing – and horse riding. *(Recommended by Joy Heatherley, John Honnor, Kim Schofield, Andrew and Ruth Triggs)*

Camerons ~ Lease: David Mead ~ Real ale ~ Meals and snacks ~ Restaurant ~ (01947) 895241 ~ Children in eating area of bar and in restaurant until 9pm ~ Occasional music ~ Open 11-11 ~ Bedrooms: £18/£36(£50B)

ELSLACK (N Yorks) SD9249 Map 7

Tempest Arms 🍴 🛏 ♀

Just off A56 Earby—Skipton; visible from main road, and warning signs ¼ mile before

Well run and friendly, this 18th-c inn has a series of quietly decorated areas with a log fire in the dividing fireplace, quite a bit of stripped stonework, some decorated plates and brassware, small chintz armchairs, chintzy cushions on the comfortable built-in wall seats, brocaded stools, and lots of tables. Good, often delicious bar food includes home-made soup (£1.75), sandwiches (from £2.75, 6oz steak £4.50), lovely home-cured gravadlax (£3.75), vegetarian dishes (£4.75), cold seafood platter (£6), steak, kidney and mushroom pie in Guinness (£5.85), good tandoori chicken (£6.25), fresh fish dishes, sirloin steak (£8.25), specials such as good local venison casserole or grilled sea bream and orange butter, fresh lamb's liver with a Dubonnet sauce or prize-winning black pudding with white cabbage and sultanas, and children's meals (£3); cheerful and helpful staff. Well kept Tetleys Mild and Bitter, Thwaites Bitter and Craftsman, and Youngers Scotch on handpump, good house wines by the glass or bottle, and malt whiskies; darts, dominoes and piped music. Tables outside are largely screened from the road by a raised bank. *(Recommended by Prof S Barnett, Eric and Jackie Robinson, Karen Eliot, John and Joan Nash, Julie Peters, Hugh and Peggy Colgate, Stephen and Brenda Head, Paul McPherson, Mary Moore, Susan and Rick Auty, H K Dyson, Roger and Christine Mash, Doug Kennedy, WAH, Andrew Sykes)*

Free house ~ Licensee Francis Boulongne ~ Real ale ~ Meals and snacks (11.30-2.15, 6.30-10) ~ Restaurant ~ (01282) 842450 ~ Children welcome ~ Open 11.30-3, 6.30-11; 11.30-11 summer Sat; closed evening 25 Dec ~ Bedrooms: £46B/£52B

GOATHLAND NZ8301 Map 10

Mallyan Spout 🍴

Opposite church; off A169

Surrounded by good walks – and fine views – this ivy-clad stone hotel is in the centre of the moors, and there may even be sheep wandering through the streets. As well as three spacious lounges with winter log fires, the traditional bar has a relaxed atmosphere, well kept Malton PA and Theakstons Best on handpump, and imaginative, popular food such as sandwiches, home-made soup (from £1.95), home-made pâté (£3.75), ploughman's with home-made chutney and pickle (£3.95), poached fresh pear with blue and cream cheese (£4.25), spicy beef (£5.25), bean and leek gratin (£5.50), minced lamb, mushroom and chilli koftas (£5.80), escallope of wild boar with mushroom sauce (£6.50), poached Whitby salmon-trout mayonnaise (£7.50), grilled halibut fillet with lemon and parsley butter (£9.50), and puddings like home-made ice creams, fresh pear crumble or sticky toffee pudding (from £2.50); you can buy their home-made jams, sauces and chutneys to take home. 20 malt whiskies and good wines. One room is no smoking; dominoes, bar billiards. The Mallyan Spout waterfall is close by. Quite a lot of the filming for the *Heartbeat* TV series is done in the village and the cast stay here. *(Recommended by Jim and Maggie Cowell, Lawrence Bacon, Jean Scott, Andrew and Ruth Triggs, Geoff and Angela Jacques, Frank Davidson, David and Julie Glover, P D Kudelka, Mrs D Craig, Mike and Wendy Proctor, Kim Schofield)*

Free house ~ Licensee Judith Heslop ~ Real ale ~ Meals and snacks ~ Restaurant ~ (01947) 896206 ~ Children welcome till 8.30pm ~ Open 11-11 (may close earlier if weather is bad) ~ Bedrooms: £45B/£65

GOOSE EYE (W Yorks) SE0340 Map 7

Turkey

High back road Haworth—Sutton-in-Craven, and signposted from back roads W of Keighley; OS Sheet 104 map reference 028406

Though difficult to find, this pleasant place is well worth it when you do. The popular bar food is generously served and might include sandwiches such as hot roast beef (£2.50), cheese and onion quiche (£4.40), fillet of breaded haddock (£4.60), steaks (from £6.90; 32oz rump £13), daily specials like filled Yorkshire puddings (from £3.60), and puddings (from £1.90). Well kept Tetleys, Ind Coope Burton, Gooseye Bitter and Wharfedale (brewed by a local man) on handpump, and malt whiskies. The various cosy refurbished snug alcoves have brocaded upholstery and walls covered with pictures of surrounding areas, and the dining areas are no smoking; piped music. A separate games area has darts, dominoes, cribbage, space game, fruit machine, trivia and juke box. *(Recommended by Lorna and Antti Koskela, WAH, Jan and Dave Booth, Tony Hall, C A Hall)*

Free house ~ Licensees Harry and Monica Brisland ~ Real ale ~ Meals and snacks (not Mon) ~ Restaurant ~ (01535) 681339 ~ Children in eating area of bar and in restaurant ~ Open 12-3, 5.30-11; 12-5, 7-11 Sat; closed Mon evening

GRANGE MOOR (W Yorks) SE2215 Map 7

Kaye Arms 🍴 ♍

A642 Huddersfield—Wakefield

Family run and very civilised, this busy dining pub has a relaxed, easy-going atmosphere, and good, imaginative, totally home-made food. It's somewhere to come for a special occasion and people tend to dress accordingly. From a wide menu there might be sandwiches (rare beef £1.65; good open sandwiches from £3.30), home-made soup (£1.85), fresh salmon fishcake with parsley sauce or char-grilled venison sausages on braised red cabbage and apple (£3.20), a duo of chicken liver pâté and pigeon terrine (£3.25), good bresaola (£4.75), mature cheddar cheese soufflé with waldorf salad and provençal vegetable gratin (£5.95), hand-breaded Whitby scampi (£6.50), vegetable tagliatelle (£6.75), beef in Guinness and orange with horseradish dumplings and winter vegetables (£7.45), baked fillet of cod with mushroom duxelle (£7.90), roast corn-fed chicken with apple and Calvados sauce (£7.95), and good steaks (from £9.20); lovely home-made bread and fine vegetables. A thoughtful wine list with exceptional value house wines, several by the generous glass and wines of the month, and decent malt whiskies. The U-shaped dining lounge has black mate's chairs and black tables, panelled dado, quiet pastel-coloured wallpaper with decorative plates, a high shelf of hundreds of malt whisky bottles, and a brick fireplace; almost imperceptible piped music. The Yorkshire Mining Museum is just down the road. *(Recommended by Neil Townend, A Preston, Russell Hobbs, Geoffrey and Brenda Wilson, Mark Bradley, Stephen and Brenda Head, Alan Wilcock, Christine Davidson, Michael Butler, Mrs B Bridge)*

Free house ~ Licensee Stuart Coldwell ~ Meals and snacks (till 10pm) ~ (01924) 848385 ~ Children allowed at lunchtimes only ~ Open 11.30-3, 7(6.30 Sat)-11; closed Mon lunchtime

HARDEN (W Yorks) SE0838 Map 7

Malt Shovel £

Follow Wilsden signpost from B6429

The three rooms in this handsome dark stone building (one is no-smoking in the evening) are spotlessly clean and carefully kept and have red plush seats built into the walls, kettles, brass funnels and the like hanging from the black beams, horsebrasses on leather harness, and stone-mullioned windows; one has oak-panelling, a beamed ceiling, and an open fire. Good value bar food includes sandwiches, giant Yorkshire pudding with beef (£3), omelettes (from £3), steak pie (£3.50), and daily specials. Well kept Tetleys on handpump, and efficient service; dominoes and piped music. The pub is in a lovely spot by a bridge over Harden Beck, and the big garden is open to the public. *(Recommended by WAH, A Preston; more reports please)*

Tetleys (Allied) ~ Profit-sharing managers Keith and Lynne Bolton ~ Real ale ~ Lunchtime meals and snacks (not Sun) ~ (01535) 272357 ~ Children in eating area of bar until 8pm ~ Open 11.30-3, 5.30-11; 11.30-11 Sat

HAROME (N Yorks) SE6582 Map 10

Star

2 miles south of A170, near Helmsley

This is a particularly welcoming and friendly place with very good, popular food. The bar has a dark bowed beam-and-plank ceiling, heavy, deeply polished oak tables and cushioned old settles on the turkey carpet, a glass cabinet holding kepis, fine china and Japanese dolls, and a copper kettle on the well polished tiled kitchen range (with a ship in a bottle on its mantelpiece). Home-made food includes sandwiches (from £2.25), stilton pâté (£2.95), scallops, bacon and mushrooms (£4.95), home-made steak and Guinness pie (£5.95), seafood crêpe or lemon salmon (£7.95), duck in a cream, brandy and cherry sauce (£8.95), good daily specials and home-made puddings; there's a coffee loft up in the thatch. Well kept Tetleys, Theakstons Best and Old Peculier and Timothy Taylors Landlord on handpump. Darts, dominoes, trivia and piped music. On a sheltered front flagstoned terrace there are some seats and tables, with more in the garden behind which has an old-fashioned swing seat, fruit trees and a big ash. *(Recommended by Joy Heatherley, Andrew and Ruth Triggs, Mrs E H Hughes, Paul S McPherson, S Demont, T Barrow)*

Free house ~ Licensee Terry Rowe ~ Real ale ~ Meals and snacks (not Mon or Tues lunchtime or Sun-Weds evenings) ~ Evening restaurant (they do Sun lunch, closed Sun evening) ~ (01439) 770397 ~ Children welcome ~ Open 12-3, 6.30-11; winter evening open 7pm; closed Mon lunchtime

nr HARROGATE (N Yorks) SE2852 Map 7

Squinting Cat

Whinney Lane, B6162 W of Harrogate; turn at traffic lights down Pannel Ash Rd; at roundabout near sports centre, bear right along Whinney Lane; pub on left after about ¾ mile; OS Sheet 104 map reference 287525

As we went to press we heard that the partly no-smoking restaurant here is going to be made quite a lot bigger. The original rambling bar rooms have dark oak panelling, beam and plank ceilings, some copper warming pans and horsebrasses, and a stained-glass cat worked into a latticed bow window. The barn-like beamed extension has York stone walls (re-fashioned from an old railway bridge) hung with pictures, pine chairs and tables in one part with re-covered armchairs in another, old grain sacks, barrels and bottles, and nautical wooden pulley systems radiating out from a minstrel's gallery complete with boat. Under the new licensee bar food includes home-made soup (£1.75), sandwiches (from £2), home-made pâté (£2.50), burgers (from £2.85), vegetarian lasagne or stuffed pancakes (£4.50), steak and kidney pie or lasagne (£4.95), a buffet with home-cooked meats and so forth (£5), and evening dishes like chicken supreme, poached salmon and steaks (from £6.95). Well kept Tetleys Bitter on handpump; piped music, dominoes and fruit machine. There are tables outside. The North of England Horticultural Society's fine gardens on the curlew moors at Harlow Car are just over the B6162. *(Recommended by Geoffrey and Brenda Wilson, M J Marriage, Mayur Shah, Paul Cartledge, R M Sparkes, WD, David Watson)*

Tetleys (Allied) ~ Manageress Carol Blackburn ~ Real ale ~ Meals and snacks ~ Restaurant ~ (01423) 565650 ~ Open 12-3, 5.30-11; 11-11 Sat

HATFIELD WOODHOUSE (S Yorks) SE6808 Map 7

Green Tree

1 mile from M18 junction 5: on A18/A614 towards Bawtry

Friendly new licensees have taken over this neatly kept old pub and have introduced a new menu with vegetarian and vegan dishes and special prices for senior citizens – Mrs Wagstaff consistently wins awards for her home-made dishes: soups such as broccoli, mushroom, red pepper and courgette (£1.50), very good sandwiches, ploughman's (£2.95), steak and kidney pie or a roast of the day (£3.95), lots of fresh fish delivered three times a week from Grimsby such as halibut, haddock, cod, lobster, crab and salmon (from £3.95), vegetarian rogan josh or vegetable and tofu casserole (£4.50), and puddings like sticky toffee and date pudding or treacle sponge. The comfortably modernised series of connecting open-plan rooms and alcoves have banquettes and Windsor chairs around the tables, and well kept Thorne Bitter and Vaux Bitter and Samson on handpump; prompt service; piped music. *(Recommended by Paul Cartledge, Brian Horner, Brenda Arthur, Mr and Mrs P D Coombs; more reports on the new regime, please)*

Wards (Vaux) ~ Tenants Peter and Avril Wagstaff ~ Real ale ~ Meals and snacks ~ Restaurant (evenings and Sun lunch) ~ (01302) 840305 ~ Children in eating area of bar ~ Open 11-3, 5-11 ~ Bedrooms: £25S/£35S

HEATH (W Yorks) SE3519 Map 7

Kings Arms

Village signposted from A655 Wakefield—Normanton – or, more directly, turn off to the left opposite Horse & Groom

The new conservatory in this old-fashioned pub has now been opened (families are welcome) with direct access to the gardens. There are picnic-table sets on a side lawn, and the nice walled garden has a marvellous display of dahlias in late summer; more seats along the front of the building facing the village green. The dark-panelled original bar has plain elm stools and oak settles built into the walls, some heavy cast-iron-framed tables on the flagstones, a built-in cupboard of cut glass, and a fire burning in the old black range (with a long row of smoothing irons on the mantelpiece). A more comfortable extension has carefully preserved the original style, down to good wood-pegged oak panelling (two embossed with royal arms), and a high shelf of plates; there are also two other small flagstoned rooms. Good bar food includes Yorkshire pudding with rich onion gravy (£1.25), soup (£1.40), sandwiches (from £1.45; hot sausage with fried onions £1.75), omelettes or salads (from £3.25), home-made beef pie or vegetarian pancake (£3.50), daily specials, home-made puddings (from £1.50), and children's dishes (£1.45); the tables are cleared and cleaned promptly. As well as cheap Clarks Bitter and Festival, they also serve guests like Tetleys Bitter and Timothy Taylors Landlord on handpump. The new lavatories include one with disabled facilities. *(Recommended by Mark Bradley, J L Phillips, Gerry McGarry, Ian and Nita Cooper, Graham Reeves, Richard Waller, Paul Lightfoot, Derek and Sylvia Stephenson)*

Clarks ~ Managers Terry and Barbara Ogden ~ Real ale ~ Meals and snacks (12-2, 5.30-9.30) ~ Gas-lit restaurant (not Sun evening) ~ (01924) 377527 ~ Children welcome ~ Open 11.30-3, 5.30-11; closed evening 25 Dec

---

If we know a pub has a no-smoking area, we say so.

HECKMONDWIKE (W Yorks) SE2223 Map 7
Old Hall
New North Road; B6117 between A62 and A638; OS Sheet 104; map reference 214244

It's the building itself that readers like here. Dating from 1470, there are lots of old beams and timbers, brick or stripped old stone walls hung with pictures of Richard III, Henry VII, Catherine Parr and Priestley, comfortable furnishings that include cushioned oak pews and plush seats, some with oak backs, on a sweep of turkey carpet (flagstones by the serving counter), and latticed mullioned windows with worn stone surrounds. Snug low-ceilinged alcoves lead off the central part with its high ornate plaster ceiling, and an upper gallery room, under the pitched roof, looks down on the main area through timbering 'windows'. Decent waitress-served bar food includes sandwiches (from £1.85; not Sunday lunchtime), liver and onions, haddock or sausage and egg (£3.50), a pie of the day (£3.95), stuffed plaice (£4.50), and steaks (from £7.95). Well kept (and cheap) Sam Smiths OB on handpump; fruit machine, piped music. This was once the home of the Nonconformist scientist Joseph Priestley. *(Recommended by Paul Cartledge, Andrew and Ruth Triggs, Tony Hall, Mark Bradley, Mrs Gwyneth Holland, Mrs F Hart, Michael Butler, David Watson)*

Sam Smiths ~ Manager C W Mole ~ Real ale ~ Meals and snacks (not quiz nights) ~ (01924) 404774 ~ Children in small snug or at back away from bar area ~ Open 11.30-2.30, 6-11

HELMSLEY (N Yorks) SE6184 Map 10
Feathers ♀
Market Square

It's the medieval core that readers like in this handsomely solid three-storey inn: heavy medieval beams and dark panelling, unusual cast-iron-framed tables topped by weighty slabs of oak and walnut, a venerable wall carving of a dragonfaced bird in a grape vine, and a big log fire in the stone inglenook fireplace. The main inn has its own comfortable lounge bar. Well prepared bar food includes sandwiches, soup (£1.75), home-made salmon pâté (£2.75), home-made lasagne or broccoli quiche (£4.75), salads (from £4.75), home-made steak and kidney pie or battered prawns with sweet and sour sauce (£5.75), gammon and egg (£6), steaks (£9.75), and puddings (£2.50). Well kept Morlands Old Speckled Hen, John Smiths, Theakstons Best, Worthington Best, and Youngers Scotch on handpump, large choice of wines chalked on a blackboard, and some malt whiskies; friendly service, dominoes. There's an attractive back garden. Rievaulx Abbey (well worth an hour's visit) is close by. *(Recommended by J E Ryecroft, G C Brown, John and Christine Simpson, Peter Race, Ann Marie Stephenson, Alan Wilcock, Christine Davidson)*

Free house ~ Licensees Lance and Andrew Feather ~ Real ale ~ Meals and snacks ~ Restaurant ~ (01439) 770275 ~ Children in eating area of bar ~ Open 10.30-2.30, 6-11; all day Fri (market day); closed 25 Dec ~ Bedrooms: £22(£26.50B)/£44(£53B)

HETTON (N Yorks) SD9558 Map 7
Angel ★ 🍽 ♀
Just off B6265 Skipton—Grassington

As ever, this very well run, friendly dining pub remains one of our most popular Yorkshire entries, and it's essential to arrive early to guarantee a table. This is not somewhere to come for a cheap lunchtime snack, but in view of the quality, readers feel it is worth every penny: home-made soup (£2.45; lovely rustic fish soup with aioli £2.85), seafood baked in filo pastry served on lobster sauce (£3.85), fresh pasta with basil and fresh parmesan (£4.25), queen scallops baked with garlic and gruyère (£4.20; main course £6.85), an open sandwich of smoked salmon, cream cheese, smoked bacon and home-made chutney (£4.95), ploughman's or escalope fillet of pork baked with ham and cheese (£6.30), spring lamb steak char-grilled on a salad of rucola, parmesan and Italian vegetables

(£7.25), breast of chicken stuffed with prawns and smoked bacon with lemon sauce (£7.75), perfect confit of duck with braised Normandy red cabbage and orange and thyme sauce (£7.95), seafood hors d'oeuvre (£8.35), delicious salmon in lobster sauce, good calf's liver on fried parmesan polenta (£10.75), daily specials and fish dishes, and puddings like crème brûlée, sticky toffee pudding or chocolate mousse with a marquise base served with a rich chocolate sauce (£3.25); very helpful, hard-working uniformed staff. Well kept Black Sheep, Boddingtons, and Ruddles County on handpump, over 300 wines (24 by the glass) and quite a few malt whiskies. The four timbered and panelled rambling rooms have comfortable country-kitchen chairs or button-back green plush seats, Ronald Searle wine snob cartoons and older engravings and photographs, lots of cosy alcoves, log fires, a solid fuel stove, and in the main bar, a Victorian farmhouse range in the big stone fireplace; the snug is no smoking – as is part of the restaurant. Sturdy wooden benches and tables are built on to the cobbles outside. *(Recommended by E A George, Paul Boot, C Hedderman, Geoffrey and Brenda Wilson, Tony Hall, Stephen and Brenda Head, Mike and Jo, Annette Moore, Chris Pearson, Brian and Jill Bond, Neville Kenyon, Mark Bradley, John and Joan Nash, Nicola Thomas, Paul Dickinson, Karen Eliot, Gwen and Peter Andrews, Paul and Gail Betteley, Gill and Maurice McMahon, Dr and Mrs D M Gunn, Dr D K M Thomas, R M Sparkes, Stephen Newell, Alan Wilcock, Christine Davidson, David Atkinson, Mr and Mrs John Gilks, WD, Andrew Sykes)*

Free house ~ Licensee Denis Watkins ~ Real ale ~ Meals and snacks (till 10pm) ~ Restaurant (closed Sun evening) ~ (01756) 730263 ~ Well behaved children welcome ~ Open 12-2.30, 6-10.30(11 Sat)

HUBBERHOLME (N Yorks) SD9178 Map 7

George

Village signposted from Buckden; about 1 mile NW

New licensees had just taken over this remote pub as we went to press. The two small and well kept flagstoned bar-rooms have dark ceiling-boards supported by heavy beams, walls stripped back to bare stone and hung with antique plates, seats (with covers to match the curtains) around shiny copper-topped tables, and an open stove in the big fireplace. Bar food includes sandwiches, beef in ale pie (£5), mushroom and cream cheese bake (£5.25), pork fillet in mushroom and cream sauce (£6.25), and good steaks. Very well kept Youngers Scotch and No 3 on handpump, and around 20 malt whiskies. The dining room is no smoking. Darts, dominoes and cribbage. There are seats and tables overlooking the moors and River Wharfe – where they have fishing rights. This was J B Priestley's favourite pub. *(Recommended by J L Phillips, John and Joan Nash, M J Morgan, Bill and Lydia Ryan, Lee Goulding, Ray and Liz Monk, Andrew McKeand; more reports on the new regime, please)*

Free house ~ Licensees Jerry Lanchbury and Fiona Shelton ~ Real ale ~ Meals and snacks ~ Restaurant ~ (01756) 760223 ~ Children in eating area of bar ~ Open 11.30-4(3 in winter), 6.30-11; 11-11 Sat ~ Bedrooms: £18/£34(£44B); no children to stay under 8

KIRBY HILL (N Yorks) NZ1406 Map 10

Shoulder of Mutton

Signposted from Ravensworth road about 3½ miles N of Richmond; or from A66 Scotch Corner—Brough turn off into Ravensworth, bear left through village, and take signposted right turn nearly a mile further on

Converted from a farm some time in the 1830s, this friendly pub shares the crest of a ridge above ruined Ravensworth Castle with a tree-shaded churchyard. Inside, there's a stone archway between the lounge and public bar, open stone fireplaces, green plush wall settles around simple dark tables, and local turn-of-the-century photographs of Richmond. Decent bar food includes lunchtime sandwiches, lots of vegetarian dishes (from £4.25), steak and kidney pie (£4.50), good haddock (£4.95), steaks (from £7.95), and daily specials. Well kept Black Sheep Bitter, Courage Directors, John Smiths, and Websters Yorkshire on handpump; darts, dominoes and piped music. The yard behind has picnic-table sets and fine views. *(Recommended by Andrew McKeand, Neil and Angela Huxter, Roger Bellingham, John Allsopp; more reports please)*

Free house ~ Licensee Mick Burns ~ Real ale ~ Meals and snacks (not Mon lunchtime) ~ Restaurant ~ (01748) 822772 ~ Children in eating area of bar ~ Sing-along Mon evenings and bank hols ~ Open 12-3, 7-11; closed Mon lunchtime ~ Bedrooms: £25B/£39B

KIRKBYMOORSIDE (N Yorks) SE6987 Map 7

George & Dragon 🛏 ♀

Market place

Very well run by exceptionally helpful and friendly people, this handsome white-painted 17th-c coaching inn has a civilised, restful atmosphere in its convivial bar. There are fresh flowers and newspapers, brass-studded solid dark red leatherette chairs around polished wooden tables, horsebrasses along the beams, lots of photographs, prints, shields and memorabilia connected with cricket, rugby and golf on the walls (they have sporting celebrity dinners each quarter), and a blazing log fire. Very good bar food might include sandwiches in their own home-baked wholemeal buns, home-made soup (at least one is vegetarian, £1.95), stilton and walnut pâté (£2.95), fresh mussels in white wine with shallots (£3.90), venison sausages with onions and mustard (£3.95), mushroom provençal tagliatelle or mixed bean and vegetable hotpot (£4.95), strips of lamb's liver in peppercorn sauce and home-made pies such as steak and kidney or rabbit with ginger wine (£5.95), escalope of pork in lemon and ginger (£6.50), seafood hotpot (£6.90), grilled 10oz sirloin steak (£9.95) and puddings such as wild berry cheesecake, sherry trifle or banoffi pie (£2.50); fish is delivered three times a week and the game is locally caught; the attractive no-smoking restaurant was the old brewhouse until the early part of this century. Well kept Marstons Pedigree, John Smiths Bitter, Timothy Taylors Landlord and Theakstons XB on handpump, a fine wine list that includes nine house wines, seven cognacs, and over 30 malt whiskies; backgammon and piped classical music or jazz. There are seats under umbrellas in the back courtyard and a surprisingly peaceful walled garden for residents to use. The bedrooms are in a converted cornmill and old vicarage at the back of the pub. Wednesday is Market Day. *(Recommended by J R Smylie, W J E Smith, F M Bunbury, K A Barker, John and Joan Calvert, Anne and John Barnes; also recommended by* The Good Hotel Guide*)*

Free house ~ Licensees Stephen and Frances Colling ~ Real ale ~ Meals and snacks ~ Restaurant ~ (0751) 433334 ~ Children welcome until 9pm ~ Open 10-3, 6-11; 11-11 Weds (Market Day) ~ Bedrooms: £44B/£68B

KIRKHAM SE7466 (N Yorks) Map 7

Stone Trough

Kirkham Abbey

Attractive and comfortable beamed inn with several small, cosy and interesting rooms, a friendly atmosphere, log fires, and well kept Bass, Tetleys, Theakstons, and Timothy Taylors Landlord on handpump. Lunchtime bar food includes vetetable soup (£2.50), pâté (£3.75), filled Yorkshire puddings or steak and kidney pie (£5.25), fresh Whitby haddock, spinach pancake with tomato and cheese sauce, salmon and seafood pie (£6.10), breast of chicken stuffed with asparagus and cream cheese (£6.50), and puddings. The no-smoking farmhouse restaurant has a fire in an old-fashioned kitchen range. Pool, cribbage, fruit machine and piped music. There's a good outside seating area with lovely valley views; fine nearby walks. *(Recommended by Thomas Nott, F J and A Parmenter, Julian Price, R T Stanton, D P Pascoe, Roger Bellingham)*

Free house ~ Licensee Robert Ilsley ~ Real ale ~ Lunchtime bar meals and snacks (not Mon) ~ Restaurant ~ (01653) 618713 ~ Children in lounge, snug or restaurant ~ Open 12-3, 6.30-11; closed Mon lunchtime

KNARESBOROUGH (N Yorks) SE3557 Map 7

Blind Jacks ◖

Market Place

Named after Blind Jack, a well-known local character in the 18th c who is best known for his pioneer road building throughout the North of England. It's a listed Georgian building with two downstairs rooms – stripped brick on the left and dark panelling on the right, bare floorboards, pews (the one on the right as you go in has a radiator built in behind, which is lovely on a cold day), cast-iron long tables, brewery posters mainly from the south (Adnams, Harveys, Hook Norton, Shepherd Neame) and lots of framed beermats, and nice old-fashioned net half-curtains; upstairs restaurant. Well kept on handpump, there are usually six real ales such as Dale Side Old Leg Over, Exmoor Gold, Ind Coope Burton, Marston Moor Brewers Droop, Moorhouses Black Cat, and North Yorkshire Brewery Yorkshire Porter; country wines, foreign bottled beers and farm cider. Good bar food includes sandwiches (from £1.40), home-made soup (£1.50), mackerel pâté (£1.95), home-made burgers (from £2.50), filled baked potatoes (£2.75), salads (£3.75), and cheese and tomato quiche or chilli (£3.95), with evening dishes like button mushrooms with bacon and onions (£2.50), lamb and apricot hotpot (£4.75), seafood casserole (£5.25), gammon and eggs (£5.95), and steaks (from £6.95). No noisy games machines or piped music – just a chatty atmosphere. *(Recommended by CW, JW, Tim and Ann Newell, Tony and Pat Martin)*

Free house ~ Licensee L J Barrett ~ Real ale ~ Meals and snacks ~ Restaurant (not Sun) ~ (01423) 869148 ~ Children allowed away from main bar ~ Open 11-11; 11.30-3, 6-11 Mon/Tues

LASTINGHAM (N Yorks) SE7391 Map 10

Blacksmiths Arms ◖

Off A170 W of Pickering at Wrelton, forking off Rosedale rd N of Cropton; or via Appleton and Spaunton; or via Hutton-le-Hole

You're sure of a warm welcome in this cosy little village pub – and some good own-brewed beers as well: Church Bitter, Curate's Downfall, Amen and Celtic; they also keep well kept Bass and Websters Yorkshire, and guest beers on handpump. The comfortable, oak beamed bar has a good winter fire, an attractive cooking range with swinging pot-yards, some sparkling brass, and cushioned Windsor chairs and traditional built-in wooden wall seats; piped music. As well as bar food such as sandwiches (from £1.35), soup (£1.50), steak and kidney pie (£4.45), and steak (£8.95), they do a breakfast service for campers and caravanners in the area. A traditionally furnished, no-smoking dining area opens off the main bar, and serves Sunday roasts and bistro meals on Friday and Saturday; a good range of malt whiskies; friendly, helpful staff. There is a pool and games room as well as darts, dominoes, cribbage, fruit machine and video game. Good wheelchair access. The countryside all around here is lovely and there are tracks through Cropton Forest. The ancient nearby church has a Norman crypt. *(Recommended by Fred Collier, Paul Cartledge, Paul Wreglesworth, John Honnor)*

Free house ~ Licensees Mike and Sheila Frost ~ Real ale ~ Meals and snacks ~ Restaurant ~ (01751) 417247 ~ Well behaved children welcome ~ Open 11-11; Bedrooms: £17.50/£35

LEDSHAM (W Yorks) SE4529 Map 7

Chequers

Claypit Lane; a mile off A1 N of Pontefract

Several small, individually decorated rooms open off the old-fashioned little central panelled-in servery in this bustling and spotlessly kept creeper-covered pub. There are log fires, low beams, lots of cosy alcoves, a number of toby jugs, and well kept John Smiths, Theakstons Best, Youngers Scotch and Number 3 on handpump. Decent bar food includes soup (£1.55), sandwiches (from £2.45, steak £3.95), ploughman's (£3.95), scrambled eggs and smoked salmon (£4.25), lasagne or evening chilli con carne (£4.65), and gammon and eggs (£6.25); daily lunchtime specials could include chicken curry (£4.95), steak and mushroom pie (£5.45), poached lemon sole (£5.95), duck in orange sauce (£6.25) and fillet steak with red wine sauce (£8.50); there may be a loaf of crusty bread with bowls of dripping and sliced onion on the bar to help yourself to. A sheltered two-level terrace behind the house has tables among roses and is popular with families. *(Recommended by Mark J Hydes, Mark Bradley, F M Bunbury, John C Baker, Paul Cartledge, Mayur Shah)*

Free house ~ Licensee Chris Wraith ~ Real ale ~ Meals and snacks (not Sun) ~ Restaurant (not Sun) ~ (01977) 683135 ~ Children in separate room ~ Open 11-3, 5.30-11; 11-11 Sat; closed Sun

LEEDS (W Yorks) SE3033 Map 7

Garden Gate ★ ◖

37 Waterloo Road, Hunslet; leaving Leeds centre on A61, turn right at traffic lights signpost 'Hunslet Centre P, Belle Isle 1½, Middleton 3', take first right into Whitfield Way, first left into Whitfield Drive, then first right and park at rear of pub

Despite the unpromising surroundings (lots of modern redevelopment), this lively pub has a marvellously preserved Victorian layout. A high cool corridor with a tiled floor, deep-cut glass and mahogany panelling links four old-fashioned rooms. The finest, on the left as you enter, has a mosaic floor and a lovely free-flowing design of tiles coloured in subtle tones of buff, cream and icy green: the bar counter itself, the front of which is made from elaborately shaped and bowed tiles, has hatch service to the corridor too; some of the tables furthest from the bar have old push buttons for service. Perfectly kept Tetleys Bitter and Mild on handpump – the brewery is just up the Hunslet Road; pensioners get cheap rates; farm cider. They have darts, pool, dominoes (very popular here), juke box, and piped music. It's very much a working men's pub. No food. *(Recommended by Brian Jones, Eric Robinson, Andy and Jill Kassube, Lara H Cook)*

Tetleys (Allied) ~ Lease: Sharon Lamond-Ripley ~ Real ale ~ (0113) 270 0379 ~ Children welcome until 4.30 ~ Open 11-11

Whitelocks ★ £

Turks Head Yard; alley off Briggate, opposite Debenhams and Littlewoods; park in shoppers' car park and walk

There are few city centre pubs that remain as beautifully preserved as this atmospheric and bustling place – it has hardly changed since Victorian times. The long and narrow old-fashioned bar has polychrome tiles on the bar counter, stained-glass windows and grand advertising mirrors, and red button back plush banquettes and heavy copper-topped cast-iron tables squeezed down one side. Good, reasonably priced lunchtime bar food includes bubble and squeak, sausages and home-made scotch eggs (all 75p), sandwiches (£1.25) or Yorkshire puddings (£1.10), home-made quiche (£1.20), very good meat and potato pie (£2), and jam roly poly or fruit pie (95p); when it gets busy you may have to wait for your order, though the staff are very cheerful and pleasant. Well kept McEwans 80/-, Theakstons Bitter, Youngers IPA, Scotch and No 3 on handpump; quiz evenings every Tuesday in top bar. At the end of the long narrow yard another bar has been done up in Dickensian style. *(Recommended by Paul Cartledge, Annette Moor, Chris Pearson, Tony and Wendy Hobden, Mark Bradley, Tony Hall, Reg Nelson, Alan Reid, Brian Jones, Eric Robinson, Neale Davies, Prof S Barnett, Andrew Roberts, J E Rycroft)*

Youngers (S & N) ~ Manager Julie Cliff ~ Real ale ~ Meals and snacks (11-7.30; not Sun evening) ~ Restaurant (not Sun evening) ~ (0113) 245 3950 ~ Children in restaurant ~ Open 11-11

People **named** as recommenders after the main entries have told us that the pub should be included. But they have not written the report – we have, after anonymous on-the-spot inspection.

LEVISHAM   (N Yorks)   SE8391 Map 10

Horseshoe

Pub and village signposted from A169 N of Pickering

Even when this popular pub is busy at peak times, the staff remain very friendly and welcoming. It's set at the top of a lovely, unspoilt village, and there are picnic tables on the attractive village green – full of families, plentiful dog owners and walkers on warm days. Inside, the well kept bars have brocaded seats, a log fire in the stone fireplace, and bar billiards. Good bar food includes home-made soup (£1.95), sandwiches (from £1.95; the prawn is very generous and filling, £3.25), a good ploughman's (£4.25), salads (from £4.25), steak and kidney pie or lasagne (£4.95), prawn thermidor (£4.90), gammon and egg (£5.75), steaks (from £8.25), a big mixed grill (£8.95), daily specials, children's menu (£2.95), and puddings (£2.25); the restaurant is no smoking. Well kept Malton Double Chance, Tetleys Bitter, and Theakstons Best, XB and Old Peculier on handpump, and a good range of malt whiskies. Three to five times a day in spring and autumn, and seven times in summer, two steam trains of the North Yorks Moors Railway stop at this village. *(Recommended by Andrew and Ruth Triggs, Mark Whitmore, Simon Collett-Jones, P Boot, Mr J Brown, R M Macnaughton)*

Free house ~ Licensees Brian and Helen Robshaw ~ Real ale ~ Meals and snacks (not 25 Dec) ~ Restaurant ~ (01751) 460240 ~ Children welcome till 9.30pm ~ Open 10.30-3, 6.30-11 ~ Bedrooms: £23/£44(£46B)

LEYBURN   (N Yorks)   SE1191 Map 10

Sandpiper

Market Place – bottom end

This pretty, friendly and very neatly kept little 17th-c stone cottage is set away from the main bustle of the town. The bar has a couple of black beams in the low ceiling, a stuffed pheasant in a stripped-stone alcove, antlers, and just seven tables, even including the back room up three steps – where you'll find attractive Dales photographs, toby jugs on a delft shelf, and a collection of curious teapots. Down by the nice linenfold panelled bar counter there are stuffed sandpipers, more photographs and a woodburning stove in the stone fireplace. There's also a neat dining area on the left; dominoes and piped music. Bar food is home-made using fresh vegetables, and might include soups such as cauliflower and cheddar (£1.75), sandwiches (from £1.75), home-made pork and liver pâté (£3.25), ploughman's (£3.95), lasagne (£4.50), salads (from £4.50), puddings (£2), evening dishes like tuna fish pasta bake (£5.75), steaks (from £8.50), and halibut steak (£8.95), and daily specials such as Cumberland sausage (£3.25), fresh seafood pie or beef in ale (£4.50), and salmon en croûte with tarragon and caper sauce (£7.95); winter discounts on certain evenings. Well kept Theakstons Best and Old Peculier and Websters Yorkshire on handpump, around 100 malt whiskies (they have a whisky trail), bin-end wines, and cheerful service. The friendly English pointer is called Sadie – no other dogs allowed. There are award-winning hanging baskets, white cast-iron tables among the honeysuckle, climbing roses, cotoneaster and so forth on the front terrace, with more tables in the back garden. Please note that they now do bedrooms – news please; the beamed residents' lounge overlooks the Dale. *(Recommended by F and S Barnes, Geoff and Angela Jacques, M J Morgan, Andrew and Ruth Triggs, Jerry and Alison Oakes, M E A Horler, Noel Jackson, Louise Campbell, Mr and Mrs Peter Dowsett)*

Free house ~ Licensees Peter and Beryl Swan ~ Real ale ~ Meals and snacks ~ Evening restaurant ~ (01969) 622206 ~ Well behaved children welcome until 8pm ~ Open 11-2.30(3 Fri/Sat), 6.30-11 ~ Bedrooms: £20/£40

LINTHWAITE   (W Yorks)   SE1014 Map 7

Sair ◀

Hoyle Ing, off A62; 3½ miles after Huddersfield look out for two water storage tanks (painted with a shepherd scene) on your right – the street is on your left, burrowing very steeply up between works buildings; OS Sheet 110 map reference 101143

A fine range of very well kept own-brewed beers is the reason to visit this unspoilt rough-and-ready place: pleasant and well balanced Linfit Bitter, Mild and Special, Old Eli, Leadboiler, Autumn Gold, and the redoubtable Enochs Hammer; there's even stout (English Guineas) – and a guest beer; Thatchers farm cider, a few malt whiskies. The quaint cluster of rooms are furnished with pews or smaller chairs, bottle collections, beermats tacked to beams, rough flagstones in some parts and carpet in others, and several big stone fireplaces; one room is no smoking. The room on the right has darts, shove-ha'penny, cribbage, dominoes, and juke box; piano players welcome. There's a striking view down the Colne Valley – through which the Huddersfield Narrow Canal winds its way; in the 3½ miles from Linthwaite to the highest and longest tunnel in Britain, are 25 working locks and some lovely countryside. No food. *(Recommended by Bill and Lydia Ryan, H K Dyson, Reg Nelson, AT, RT, Paul Lightfoot, Dr I Pocsik, N Haslewood)*

Own brew ~ Licensee Ron Crabtree ~ Real ale ~ (01484) 842370 ~ Children in three rooms away from the bar ~ Open 7-11 only on weekdays; 12-3, 7-11 Sat, Sun and bank hols (not Good Fri)

LINTON IN CRAVEN (N Yorks) SD9962 Map 7

Fountaine

On B6265 Skipton—Grassington, forking right

Readers have very much enjoyed this welcoming pub over the last year. It's in a pretty setting in a lovely village with seats outside facing the green – you can eat out here on fine days. The little rooms are furnished with stools, benches and other seats, and lots of original watercolours and prints, several with sporting themes. Good, popular bar food includes tasty home-made soup (£2), sandwiches with chips (from £3), black pudding with a coarse-grain mustard (£2.25), good filled Yorkshire puddings (from £2.50), chilli con carne (£4.65), a pasta dish of the day (£4.95), home-made steak pie (£5.45), fish pie (£6.35), gammon and egg (£6.75), chicken breast with an orange and mushroom sauce (£8.45), steaks (£8.75), daily specials, and children's dishes (from £2.50). Well kept Black Sheep Bitter and Special, Jennings Bitter, and Youngers Scotch on handpump. Darts, dominoes, cribbage and ring the bull. The back of the dining area is no smoking. The pub is named after the local lad who made his pile in the Great Plague – contracting in London to bury the bodies. *(Recommended by Tony Hall, Prof Barnett, Geoffrey and Brenda Wilson, Wendy Arnold, C H Stride, C Roberts, R E and M Baggs, Wayne Brindle, Gwen and Peter Andrews, Sylvia Dutton, Dr and Mrs R E S Tanner)*

Free house ~ Licensee Frank Mackwood ~ Real ale ~ Meals and snacks ~ Restaurant ~ (01756) 752210 ~ Children away from bar ~ Open 12-3, 7-11

LITTON (N Yorks) SD9074 Map 7

Queens Arms

From B6160 N of Grassington, after Kilnsey take second left fork; can also be reached off B6479 at Stainforth N of Settle, via Halton Gill

Ideally situated for walkers – a track behind the inn leads over Ackerley Moor to Buckden and the quiet lane through the valley leads on to Pen-y-ghent – this friendly country pub has an attractive two-level garden with tables and stunning views over the fells. Inside, the main bar on the right has stools around cast-iron-framed tables on the stone and concrete floor, a seat built into the stone-mullioned window, a good coal fire, a brown beam-and-plank ceiling, stripped rough stone walls, signed cricket bats, and a large collection of cigarette lighters. On the left, the red-carpeted room has another coal fire and more of a family atmosphere with varnished pine for its built-in wall seats, and for the ceiling and walls themselves. Under the new licensees, decent bar food includes soup (£1.85), sandwiches (from £2.10; Danish ones from £2.95), filled baked potatoes (from £2.30), ploughman's (£3.65), vegetarian or meaty lasagne (£3.95), home-made steak and kidney in Guinness or rabbit pies (£4.95), gammon and egg (£5.25), and tuna pasta bake (£6.50). Well kept Youngers

Scotch on handpump; darts, dominoes, shove-ha'penny and cribbage. *(Recommended by John and Joan Nash, Mark and Toni Amor-Segan, Stephen Barney, TBB, John Cadman, Gwen and Peter Andrews, Clive and Michele Platman, Mike and Maggie Betton, Ann Marie Stephenson, Mr and Mrs J G Whitaker, Neil and Angela Huxter)*

Free house ~ Licensees Tanya and Neil Thompson ~ Real ale ~ Meals and snacks ~ (01756) 770208 ~ Children in eating areas and family room ~ Open 12(11.30 Sat)-3, 6.30-11; winter evening opening 7 ~ Bedrooms: £21.50(£21.50B)/ £32(£39B)

MASHAM (N Yorks) SE2381 Map 10

Kings Head 🛏

Market Square

On market day (Wednesday) this is a bustling place to be. The two opened-up rooms of the neatly kept and spacious lounge bar – one carpeted, one with a wooden floor – have green plush seats around wooden tables, a big War Department issue clock over the imposing slate and marble fireplace, and a high shelf of Staffordshire and other figurines. Under the new licensee bar food includes soup (£1.30), lunchtime sandwiches (from £1.75; not Sunday), ploughman's (£3.50), vegetarian samosa or vegetable bake (from £3.95), steak and kidney pie (£4.95), steaks (from £7.95), and puddings (£1.95); friendly, helpful service. Well kept Theakstons Best, XB and Old Peculier on handpump; fruit machine, dominoes, piped music. The broad partly tree-shaded market square in this lovely village is just opposite, and there are attractive hanging baskets and window boxes in front of this busy and handsome stone inn, and picnic-table sets under cocktail parasols in a partly fairy-lit coachyard. *(Recommended by Brian Horner, Brenda Arthur, Brian Kneale, M J Morgan, Fred Collier, F and S Barnes, Andrew and Marian Ruston, G Dobson, Paul and Ursula Randall, Murray Dykes, J and D Boutwood, Mrs K Williams, Peter Race, Martin Cooke)*

Theakstons (S & N) ~ Profit-sharing manager Paul Mounter ~ Real ale ~ Meals and snacks ~ Restaurant ~ (01765) 689295 ~ Children welcome ~ Open 11-11 ~ Bedrooms: £39B/£58B

MASHAM (N Yorks) SE2381 Map 7

White Bear ★ 🍴

Signposted off A6108 opposite turn into town centre

Not surprisingly, the Theakstons Best, XB, Old Peculier, and Mild on handpump here are very well kept – Theakstons old stone headquarters buildings are part of this pub and the brewery is on the other side of town; tours can be arranged at the Theakstons Brewery Visitor centre (01765 89057, extension 4317, Weds-Sun); morning visits are best. The traditionally furnished public bar is packed with bric-a-brac: Fairport Convention and Jethro Tull memorabilia, copper brewing implements, harness, pottery, foreign banknotes, and stuffed animals – including a huge polar bear behind the bar. A much bigger, more comfortable lounge has a turkey carpet. Bar food includes sandwiches (from £1.30), soup (£1.50), ploughman's (£3.25), curries or steak and kidney pie (£4.75), and daily specials. Shove-ha'penny, dominoes, cribbage, fruit machine and CD juke box. In summer there are seats out in the yard. *(Recommended by Margaret Mason, David Thompson, Andrew and Ruth Triggs, David and Julie Glover, Jan and Dave Booth, Andrew and Marian Ruston, Jim Farmer, Richard Houghton, Peter and Rhona Fear, Paul and Ursula Randall, Mr and Mrs Peter B Dowsett, Paul and Gail Betteley, Neil and Jenny Spink, Dr and Mrs B D Smith)*

Theakstons (S & N) ~ Tenant Mrs Lesley Cutts ~ Real ale ~ Meals and snacks (not Sat or Sun evenings) ~ (01765) 689319 ~ Children in lounge bar ~ Live music Sat evenings ~ Open 11-11 ~ Two Bedrooms: /£35

The details at the end of each main entry start by saying whether the pub is a free house, or if it's tied to a brewery (which we name).

MELTHAM (W Yorks) SE0910 Map 7

Will's o' Nat's £ ♀

Blackmoorfoot Road; off B6107

Very well run by friendly and efficient licensees and their staff, this moorland pub is always bustling with people keen to enjoy the wide choice of good value food. There might be soup (£1), sandwiches (from £1.30), deep-fried black pudding with apple fritters (£2.65), ploughman's (from £3.15), spicy bean casserole (£3.20), steak and kidney pie or deep-fried fresh haddock (£3.30), chicken curry (£3.50), vegetable moussaka or meaty lasagne (£3.70), home-cooked tongue with mustard sauce (£4.10), braised steak and onions (£4.20), grilled fresh whole baby plaice (£4.50), poached fresh salmon (£5.25), children's dishes (from £1.85), and several puddings (from £1.60) such as sherry trifle or a good treacle and orange tart served with a big jug of fresh cream; cheeses are traditionally made and are farmhouse or from a small dairy (£2.35). Well kept Oak Mill Bitter and Tetleys Bitter and Mild on handpump, a good little wine list, and a large collection of malt whiskies. By the bar there are heavy wooden wall seats cushioned comfortably in pale green corduroy around heavy old cast-iron-framed tables, and the cream walls have lots of interesting old local photographs and a large attractive pen and wash drawing of many local landmarks, with the pub as its centrepiece. A slightly raised, partly no-smoking dining extension at one end, with plenty of well spaced tables, has the best of the views. Dominoes, fruit machine and piped music (not obtrusive). The pub is situated on both the Colne Valley and Kirklees circular walks and close to Blackmoorfoot reservoir (birdwatching). The name of the pub means 'belonging to or run by William, son of Nathaniel'. *(Recommended by Stephen and Brenda Head, H K Dyson, Neil Townend, Andrew and Ruth Triggs, J L Phillips, Paul Lightfoot, Derek and Sylvia Stephenson, Frank Cummins, Andrew Roberts, Gillian Worrall)*

Tetleys (Allied) ~ Lease: Kim Schofield ~ Real ale ~ Meals and snacks (till 10pm) ~ Restaurant ~ (01484) 850078 ~ Children welcome until 9pm ~ Open 11.30-3(3.30 Sat), 6(6.30 Sat)-11; closed evening 25 Dec

MOULTON (N Yorks) NZ2404 Map 10

Black Bull ⊗

Just E of A1, 1 mile S of Scotch Corner

A favourite with several readers – this decidedly civilised place has a terrific atmosphere. The bar has an antique panelled oak settle, an old elm housekeeper's chair and built-in red-cushioned black settles and pews around the cast-iron tables (one has a heavily beaten copper top), silver-plate Turkish coffee pots and so forth over the red velvet curtained windows, copper cooking utensils hanging from black beams, and a huge winter log fire; decorations include three nice Lionel Edwards hunting prints, an Edwardian engraving of a big hunt meet, and a huge bowl of flowers. A nice side dark-panelled seafood bar has some high seats at the marble-topped counter. Excellent bar snacks include lovely smoked salmon: sandwiches (£2.50), pâté (£3.75), and smoked salmon plate (£5.25); they also do a very good home-made soup served in lovely little tureens (£2), fresh plump salmon sandwiches (£2.50), black pudding and pork sausage with caramelised apple (£3.75), memorable seafood pancakes or herb crumbed fishcakes (£4.25), hot tomato tart with anchovies and black olives or Welsh rarebit and bacon (£4.50), and fresh pasta with smoked chicken, bacon and sweetcorn (£4.75); you must search out someone to take your order – the bar staff just do drinks. In the evening, you can also eat in the polished brick-tiled conservatory with bentwood cane chairs or in the Brighton Belle dining car – they also do a three-course Sunday lunch (£15). Tetleys and Theakstons on handpump, good wine, a fine choice of sherries, and decent coffee. Service can seem a little unbending to first-time visitors, but most people quickly come to appreciate the dry humour and old-fashioned standards. There are some seats under trees in the central court. *(Recommended by Mike Farrell, G M Joyce, Ralph A Raimi, SS, Roger A Bellingham, Anthony Barnes, Comus Elliott)*

Free house ~ Licensee Audrey Pagendam ~ Real ale ~ Lunchtime bar meals and snacks (not Sun) ~ Restaurant (not Sun evening) ~ (01325) 377289 ~ Children over 7 in restaurant ~ Open 12-2.30, 6-10.30(11 Sat); closed Sun evening

MUKER (N Yorks) SD9198 Map 10

Farmers Arms ◨

B6270 W of Reeth

A genuinely enjoyable, unpretentious and friendly local, popular with walkers, and well placed both for nearby rewarding walks and for the interesting drives up over Buttertubs Pass or to the north, to Tan Hill and beyond. It's cosy and simply furnished with stools and settles around copper-topped tables, and a warm open fire. Promptly served, value-for-money food includes soup (£1.40), lunchtime filled baps (£1.55) and good toasties (£1.65), vegetable or meaty burgers (£1.70), filled baked potatoes (£2.10), ploughman's, omelettes or chicken curry (£3.85), steak pie or vegetable lasagne (£3.95), gammon and egg (£4.85), sirloin steak (£7.55), children's dishes (from £2.10) and puddings (£1.85). Well kept Butterknowle Bitter, Theakstons Best, XB and Old Peculier on handpump; darts and dominoes. *(Recommended by Peter and Lynn Brueton, Mrs B Garmston, Margaret Mason, David Thompson, Andrew and Ruth Triggs, Barbara and Dick Waterson, Peter Churchill, Martin and Pauline Richardson, M J Morgan, Bill Edwards, Pat and Tony Young, Mr and Mrs Peter B Dowsett, Nick and Alison Dowson, Andrew McKeand, Bill Sykes)*

Free house ~ Licensees Chris and Marjorie Bellwood ~ Real ale ~ Meals and snacks ~ (01748) 886297 ~ Children in eating area of bar ~ Open 11-3, 6.30-11; 11-11 Sat; winter evening opening 7

NEWTON ON OUSE (N Yorks) SE5160 Map 7

Dawnay Arms ♀

Village signposted off A19 N of York

This black-shuttered, 18th-c inn has picnic-table sets and other tables on the terrace, and at the bottom of the neatly kept lawn are moorings on the River Ouse; also, a children's play-house and see-saw. Inside, on the right of the entrance is a comfortable, spacious room with a good deal of beamery and timbering with green plush wall settles and brown plush chairs around wooden or dimpled copper tables. To the left is another airy room with red plush button-back wall banquettes built into bays and a good log fire in the stone fireplace; lots of brass and copper, coins, and an old cash register. Popular bar food includes home-made soup, sandwiches with chips, ploughman's, good salmon mousse, home-made lasagne, fresh local cod or haddock and a roast of the day (all £4.95), steak in ale pie (£5.95), and daily specials. Well kept John Smiths, and Theakstons Best, XB and Old Peculier on handpump, decent house wines and good sherry; maybe unobtrusive piped music. *(Recommended by H Bramwell, Mayur Shah, Rhoda and Jeff Collins, John Knighton, Murray Dykes, H K Dyson, R M Macnaughton)*

Free house ~ Licensees John and Angela Turner ~ Real ale ~ Meals and snacks ~ Restaurant ~ (01347) 848345 ~ Children in eating area of bar ~ Open 11.30(11 Sat)-3, 6.30-11 ~ Bedrooms: £20/£40

NUNNINGTON (N Yorks) SE6779 Map 7

Royal Oak ♈

Church Street; at back of village, which is signposted from A170 and B1257

This attractive little dining pub is always busy with people keen to enjoy the generous helpings of well presented food. And although all the dishes are good, it's the home-made daily specials that receive the most praise: steak and kidney casserole with herb dumpling, breast of chicken in orange and tarragon or fisherman's pot (£7.50), and roast duckling with orange sauce (£8.95); also, home-made soup, sandwiches, very good ploughman's, gammon and egg, and steaks; good Sunday lunch. Well kept Ind Coope Burton, Tetleys and Theakstons Old Peculier on handpump; friendly, efficient service. The carefully chosen furniture includes kitchen and country dining chairs or a long pew around the sturdy tables on the turkey carpet, and a lectern in one corner. The high black beams are strung with earthenware flagons, copper jugs and lots of antique keys, one of the walls is stripped back to the bare stone to display a fine collection of antique farm tools, and there are open fires. Near the car park there are a couple of tables on a little terrace with a good view. Handy for a visit to Nunnington Hall (National Trust). No children. *(Recommended by Patrick Renouf, John and Christine Simpson, Roger A Bellingham, Brian Kneale, Andy Thwaites, G S Jacques, John and Joan Wyatt)*

Free house ~ Licensee Anthony Simpson ~ Real ale ~ Meals and snacks (not Mon) ~ (01439) 748271 ~ Open 11.45-2.30, 6.30-11; closed Mon

nr OTLEY (W Yorks) SE2047 Map 7

Spite

Newall-with-Clifton, off B6451; towards Blubberhouses about a mile N from Otley, and in fact just inside N Yorks

Run by helpful and friendly people, this comfortable and neatly kept pub – known as the Roebuck until a century ago – has beamed ceilings, plain white walls hung with some wildfowl prints and a collection of walking sticks, wheelback chairs and plush or leatherette stools around the orderly tables, and a good log fire. At lunchtime, bar food includes delicious soup, sandwiches (the hot beef and fried onions is very good, £3), ploughman's (£4), home-made steak pie or Cumberland sausage with apple sauce and fried onions (£4.10), lasagne (£4.30), roast beef with Yorkshire pudding (£4.50), fresh salmon salad or mornay (£4.85), roast duck with orange sauce (£4.95), and home-made puddings (from £1.70); vegetables are fresh. Well kept Websters Yorkshire and a guest beer like Theakstons Best on handpump; dominoes and unobtrusive piped music. The neat, well-lit little rose garden has white tables and chairs. *(Recommended by Mark Bradley, Dave Davey, M and J Back, J L Phillips, J E Rycroft, David Watson)*

Courage ~ Lease: Jeremy Hollings ~ Real ale ~ Meals and snacks (not Sun or Mon evening) ~ Restaurant ~ (01943) 463063 ~ Children welcome until 9pm ~ Open 11.30-3, 6.30(5.30 Fri/Sat)-11

PENISTONE (S Yorks) SE2402 Map 7

Cubley Hall

Mortimer Road; outskirts, towards Stocksbridge

A children's adventure playground has now been opened here and by the time this book is published, bedrooms will have been added and the pub itself will have been refurbished. It was originally a grand Edwardian villa and the spreading bar has panelling, an elaborately plastered ceiling, and lots of plush chairs, stools and button-back built-in wall banquettes on the mosaic tiling or turkey carpet in the spreading bar. Leading off this spacious main area are two snug rooms and a side family sun lounge which gives a nice view beyond the neat tree-sheltered formal gardens to pastures in the distance; there's a second children's room, too. One room is no smoking. A wide choice of good value bar food is served efficiently by neat waitresses: good chip butties (£1.10), soup (£1.50), triple-decker sandwiches (from £1.95, steak and onions £2.50), meaty or vegetarian lasagne (£3.85), omelettes (from £3.95), salads (from £4.95), jumbo Whitby cod (£5.95), steaks (from £6.95), puddings (£1.95), and children's menu (£1.75); there's also a carvery. Well kept Ind Coope Burton, Tetleys Bitter, Rockside Barnsley, and a regular guest beer on handpump, quite a few malt whiskies and other spirits, and a fair choice of wines; cribbage, dominoes and piped music. Out on the terrace are some tables and the attractive garden has a good children's play house. *(Recommended by Geoffrey and Brenda Wilson, J F M West, Stephen and Brenda Head, JJW, CMW)*

Free house ~ Licensee John Wigfield ~ Real ale ~ Meals and snacks (not 25 Dec) ~ Restaurant ~ (01226) 766086 ~ Children in two family rooms, in eating area of bar and in restaurant ~ Open 11-3, 6-11

PICKHILL (N Yorks) SE3584 Map 10

Nags Head 🛏 ♀

Village signposted off A1 N of Ripon, and off B6267 in Ainderby Quernhow

It's the good food that draws most people to this popular dining inn. Served in large helpings, there might be home-made soup (£1.25), sandwiches (from £2.25), spicy vegetarian kebab (£3.25), moussaka (£4.50), cottage pie (£4.75), half roast chicken and bacon (£5.25), very good halibut and salmon fishcake with lobster sauce (£5.25), wild boar sausage with Cumberland sauce (£5.45), giant fish and chips (£6.50), and puddings like fresh raspberry cheesecake or chocolate and cappuccino mousse (£2.50); good breakfasts; the restaurant is no smoking. Well kept Theakstons Best, XB and Old Peculier, Youngers Scotch, and beers brewed only a mile away called Hambleton Bitter and Goldfield on handpump; over 30 malt whiskies, farm cider, and over 100 decent wines, including some by the glass; the friendly service does slow down under pressure. The busy tap room on the left has masses of ties hanging as a frieze from a rail around the red ceiling, and the beams are hung with jugs, coach horns, ale-yards and so forth; the comfortable beamed lounge has red plush button-back built-in wall banquettes around dark tables. One table's inset with a chessboard, and they also have cribbage, darts, dominoes, draughts, shove ha'penny, and faint piped music. A smarter bar with deep green plush banquettes and a carpet to match has pictures for sale on its neat cream walls. *(Recommended by John Allsopp, Jack Morley, David Surridge, June and Tony Baldwin, Paul Cartledge, Martin Jones, Noel Jackson, Louise Campbell, Beryl and Bill Farmer, Stephen and Brenda Head, Julie Peters, Peter and Lynn Brueton, R M Macnaughton)*

Free house ~ Licensees Raymond and Edward Boynton ~ Real ale ~ Meals and snacks (till 10pm) ~ Restaurant ~ (01845) 567391 ~ Well behaved children welcome ~ Open 11-11 ~ Bedrooms: £32B/£45B

RAMSGILL (N Yorks) SE1271 Map 7

Yorke Arms 🛏

Take Nidderdale rd off B6265 in Pateley Bridge; or exhilarating but narrow moorland drive off A6108 at N edge of Masham, via Fearby and Lofthouse

Behind the warm stone façade and the stately stone-mullioned windows of this well run small country hotel there are carefully refurbished bars with open log fires, two or three heavy carved Jacobean oak chairs, a big oak dresser laden with polished pewter and other antiques. As we went to press, we heard that a new licensee was about to take over. Bar food has included home-made soup (£1.75), sandwiches (from £1.85, open from £3.50), filled baked potatoes (from £2.95), black pudding thermidor topped with bacon (£3.25), smoked haddock with onions and chives in a cheese sauce (£3.50), ploughman's (from £4.50), salads (from £5.25), grilled Whitby plaice with parsley butter or seafood tagliatelle (£5.50), trout with grapes and almonds (£5.75), steaks (£7.95), and puddings (from £1.95). They prefer smart dress in the no-smoking restaurant in the evening. The inn's public rooms are open throughout the day for tea and coffee, and shorts are served in cut glass. You can walk up the magnificent if strenuous moorland road to Masham, or perhaps on the right-of-way track that leads along the hill behind the reservoir, also a bird sanctuary. *(Recommended by Gordon Theaker, J Peters, Andrew and Marian Ruston; more reports on the new regime, please)*

Free house ~ Licensee Colin MacDougall ~ Lunchtime bar meals and snacks ~ Restaurant ~ (01423) 755243 ~ Children in eating area of bar until 6.30; if over 7 yrs, can go in restaurant ~ Open 11-11; closed first full week of Feb ~ Bedrooms: £47B/£69B

REDMIRE (N Yorks) SE0591 Map 10

Kings Arms 🍺

Wensley—Askrigg back road: a good alternative to the A684 through Wensleydale

Tucked away in an attractive small village, this unpretentious and friendly local has a relaxed atmosphere in its neatly kept and simply furnished bar. Also, a woodburning stove, lots of interesting photographs of local filming for *All Creatures Great and Small* and old local scenes, a long soft leatherette wall seat and other upholstered wall settles, red leatherette café chairs or dark oak ones, round cast-iron tables, and a fine oak armchair (its back carved like a mop of hair). Popular, home-made bar food includes fine soup, sandwiches, excellent pâté in lovely brown terrine pot (£3.95), very good omelettes (£4.45), meaty or good vegetarian lasagne (£4.95), good steak and kidney pie (£6.15), grilled local trout (£6.45), chicken with garlic or stilton (£7.45), half a roast duck (£9.45), steaks (from £9.45), and daily specials like steak and mushroom pie (£5.95) or chicken with stilton (£7.45); Sunday roast lunch (£4.95, best to book), and there may be cheese and crackers on the bar; the restaurant is no smoking. Well kept Black Sheep, John Smiths, Theakstons Old Peculier, local Hambleton Bitter and two regularly changing guest beers on handpump, 53 malt whiskies, and decent wines. The Staffordshire bull terrier is called Kim. Darts, pool, dominoes, cribbage, board games and music quizzes. There are tables and chairs in the pretty garden, which has a superb view across Wensleydale; fishing nearby. Handy for Castle Bolton where Mary Queen of Scots was imprisoned. *(Recommended by P D and J Bickley, Paul S McPherson, Geoff and Angela Jaques, Jim Farmer, Ray and Liz Monk, Michael Butler, Andrew and Ruth Triggs, John Honnor, M J Morgan, Alan Holmes, Mr and Mrs Peter B Dowsett, Paul and Gail Betteley)*

Free house ~ Licensee Roger Stevens ~ Real ale ~ Meals and snacks ~ Restaurant ~ (01969) 22316 ~ Children in eating area of bar ~ Live music last Fri of month ~ Open 11-3, 5.30-11 ~ Two bedrooms: £18/£30

RIPPONDEN (W Yorks) SE0419 Map 7

Old Bridge 🍷

Priest Lane; from A58, best approach is Elland Road (opposite Golden Lion), park opposite the church in pub's car park and walk back over ancient hump-backed bridge

For 31 years this medieval house has been run by the same licensee who has carefully restored the fine structure. Some of the plasterwork has been stripped away to show the handsome masonry and ceilings have been removed to show the pitched timbered roof. The three communicating rooms are each on a slightly different level and have oak settles built into the window recesses of the thick stone walls, antique oak tables, rush-seated chairs, a few well-chosen pictures, a big woodburning stove, and a relaxed, welcoming atmosphere. On weekday lunchtimes, there's a popular cold meat buffet which always has a joint of rare beef, as well as spiced ham, quiche, scotch eggs and so on (£7.50, with a bowl of soup and coffee). In the evenings, and at lunchtime on Saturdays (when it's busy) dishes change quite often, but might include smoked trout pâté (£3.50), beef and lamb meatballs with spicy tomato sauce (£3.75), sauté of beef with walnuts, orange and ginger, fresh mild smoked haddock pancakes or chicken and broccoli lasagne (all £4.25), and puddings like sticky toffee pudding (£1.75); they will cut fresh sandwiches (from £1.80). Well kept Black Sheep Special, Ryburn Best, and Timothy Taylors Best and Golden Mild on handpump, several malt whiskies, and interesting wines, many by the glass. The pub has a good restaurant, across the very pretty medieval bridge over the little River Ryburn. *(Recommended by Roger and Christine Mash, Ann and Bob Westerook, Mark Bradley, Stephen and Brenda Head, Geoffrey and Brenda Wilson, Neville Kenyon, Annette Moore, Chris Pearson, J E Rycroft, Andrew and Ruth Triggs)*

Free house ~ Licensee Ian Beaumont, Manager Timothy Walker ~ Real ale ~ Meals and snacks ~ Evening restaurant (not Sun) ~ (01422) 822595 ~ Children in eating area of bar ~ Open 11.30-3.30, 5.30-11; 11-11 Sat

ROBIN HOODS BAY   (N Yorks)   NZ9505 Map 10

Laurel

Village signposted off A171 S of Whitby

Bustling with locals and visitors, this cosy white pub stands at the heart of one of the prettiest and most unspoilt fishing villages on the North East coast. The friendly beamed main bar is decorated with old local photographs, Victorian prints and brasses, lager bottles from all over the world, and there's an open fire. Bar food consists of lunchtime sandwiches (from £1.20) and winter soup. Well kept Marstons Pedigree, Ruddles Best, John Smiths, and Theakstons Old Peculier on handpump; darts, shove-ha'penny, table skittles, dominoes, cribbage, video game. In summer, the hanging baskets and window boxes are lovely. *(Recommended by Andrew Hazeldine, Mayur Shah, Mike and Wendy Proctor, Mrs D Craig, Trevor Scott, C J McFeeters, Prof R N Orledge)*

Free house ~ Lease: David Angood ~ Real ale ~ Lunchtime snacks ~ Whitby (01947) 880400 ~ Children in family room ~ Open 12-11 ~ Well equipped cottage to rent next to pub

ROSEDALE ABBEY   (N Yorks)   SE7395 Map 10

Milburn Arms 🛏 ♀

The easiest road to the village is through Cropton from Wrelton, off the A170 W of Pickering

The steep moorland surrounding this friendly 18th-c pub is very fine, and there are picnic-table sets on the terrace and in the garden area. Inside, the main bar is traditionally furnished and has well kept Bass, Stones, and Theakstons Best, XB and Old Peculier on handpump, 30 malt whiskies, and good house wines by the glass. Good enjoyable bar food includes sandwiches, home-made soup (£1.95), smoked kipper pâté (£2.95), tiger tail prawns in garlic butter (£3.25), lunchtime ploughman's or grilled black pudding on apples, onions and garlic (£3.95), filled home-made giant Yorkshire pudding (£4.50), home-made vegetarian lasagne (£4.75), local seafood tagliatelle (£4.95), home-made steak and kidney pie (£5.50), supreme of salmon (£6.75), 9oz sirloin steak (£8.95), puddings like home-made treacle tart or home-made raspberry and blackcurrant cheesecake (£1.95), and children's dishes (from £2.95); the restaurant is no smoking. Sensibly placed darts, winter pool table, cribbage and fruit machine. *(Recommended by Bronwen and Steve Wrigley, David Ing, Mike and Maggie Betton, Julie Peters, G S and A Jaques, Joyce and Stephen Stackhouse, Roger and Christine Mash, Joy Heatherley, John and Sheila Kettel, Dr and Mrs D A Everest, Carol and Phil Byng)*

Free house ~ Licensee Terry Bentley ~ Real ale ~ Meals and snacks ~ Restaurant ~ (01751) 417312 ~ Well behaved children in eating area of bar till 8.30 ~ Open 11.30-3, 6.30-11 ~ Bedrooms: £42.50B/£70B

SAWLEY   (N Yorks)   SE2568 Map 7

Sawley Arms ♀

Village signposted off B6265 W of Ripon

Owned by Mrs Hawes for 25 years, this rather smart and firmly-run pub has a refurbished little no-smoking area this year, with oak panelling and tables and a new kitchen; it came second in the Britain in Bloom competition for Yorkshire for its lovely gardens, flowering baskets and tubs. Inside, a series of small turkey-carpeted rooms have log fires and comfortable furniture ranging from small softly cushioned armed dining chairs and greeny gold wall banquettes to the wing armchairs down a couple of steps in a side snug; there may be daily papers and magazines to read. Good bar food includes home-made soup (£2.20), sandwiches, salmon and herb pancakes with a cheese glaze (£3.95), stilton, port and celery pâté (£3.90), plaice mornay, chicken in mushroom sauce or steak pie (£5.30), and quite a few puddings such as lovely bread and butter pudding; decent house wines. The pub is handy for Fountains Abbey (the most extensive of the great monastic remains – floodlit on late summer Friday and Saturday evenings, with a live choir on the Saturday). No dogs. *(Recommended by Gwen and Peter Andrews, Neville Kenyon, Maysie Thompson, Roger and Christine Mash, John and Joan Nash, A M McCarthy, Peter Race, Alison Dowson, D M and M Wood, Ann Marie Stephenson)*

Free house ~ Licensee Mrs June Hawes ~ Meals and snacks (not Sun or Mon evenings) ~ Restaurant ~ (01765) 620642 ~ Children in restaurant if over 9 ~ Open 11.30-3, 6.30-10.30; winter evening opening 7

SAXTON (N Yorks) SE4736 Map 7

Greyhound

Village signposted off B1217 Garforth—Tadcaster; so close to A1 and A162 N of Pontefract

This companionable local is much as village pubs used to be way back when – only a lot cleaner and better run. The unspoilt, cosy and chatty taproom on the left has a cushioned window seat by the mouth of the corridor as well as other simple seats, a coal fire burning in the Victorian fireplace in the corner, and ochre Anaglypta walls and a dark panelled dado; an etched-glass window looks into the snug with its sturdy mahogany wall settle curving round one corner, other traditional furniture, fancy shades on the brass lamps, and browning Victorian wallpaper. Down at the end of the corridor is another highly traditional room, with darts, shove-ha'penny and dominoes. Well kept (and very cheap) Sam Smiths OB tapped from casks behind the counter; during the week, they will make sandwiches on request – at the weekends they are on offer. In summer the pub is very pretty with a climbing rose, passion flower, and bedding plants, and a couple of picnic-table sets in the side courtyard; next to the church. Close to Lotherton Hall Museum. This is also the community Post Office (Monday, Tuesday and Thursday 8.45am to 10.45am). *(Recommended by Thomas Nott, Tony Gayfer, Dr I Pocsik, N Haslewood; more reports please)*

Sam Smiths ~ Managers Mr and Mrs McCarthy ~ Real ale ~ Sandwiches (lunchtime) ~ (01937) 557202 ~ Children in games room only ~ Open 12-3, 5.30-11; 11-11 Sat

SETTLE (N Yorks) SD8264 Map 7

Royal Oak 🛏

Market Place; town signposted from A65 Skipton—Kendal

The bar in this substantial low stone inn is almost one big open-plan room – though enough walls have been kept to divide it into decent-sized separate areas. There's usually an interesting mix of customers as well as plenty of tables, dark squared oak or matching oak-look panelling, a couple of elegantly carved arches and more carving above the fireplaces, and a relaxed atmosphere. Lights vary from elaborate curly brass candelabra through attractive table lamps and standard lamps with old-fashioned shades to unexpectedly modernist wall cubes. A wide choice of good bar food includes home-made soup (£1.95), sandwiches (closed, danish or warm french bread from £2.45, Jamaican with prawn, pineapple, banana and coleslaw £4.40), Morecambe Bay potted shrimps (£3.40), filled Yorkshire puddings (from £4), vegetable crumble (£4.40), salads (from £4.50), battered haddock (£5.80), steak and mushrooms in ale with pastry top (£6), gammon and egg (£6.40), 8oz sirloin steak (£9.30), children's dishes (£3), and puddings (from £2.25). Well kept Boddingtons, Flowers Original and Whitbreads Castle Eden on handpump, and a good range of malt whiskies; courteous service. Readers say the Settle & Carlisle railway (only 5 minutes away) is worth a trip, and the Tuesday market here is very good. Some road noise (absurdly heavy quarry lorries cut through the attractive small town – they should certainly be kept out).

(Recommended by Dave and Carole Jones, Lynn Sharpless, Bob Eardley, Mary Moore, Catheryn and Richard Hicks, Mark Bradley, Miss Woodsend, Mike and Maggie Betton, Brian Horner, Gill and Maurice McMahon, Dr S W Tham, Jon and Jacquie Payne)

Whitbreads ~ Tenants Brian and Sheila Longrigg ~ Real ale ~ Meals and snacks (noon-10pm) ~ Restaurant ~ (01729) 822561/823102 ~ Children welcome ~ Open 11-11; closed evening 25 Dec ~ Bedrooms: £29.95B/£49.75B

SHEFFIELD   (S Yorks)   SK3687 Map 7

Fat Cat   £   🍺

23 Alma St

The cheap own-brewed beer here – Kelham Island Bitter – is named after the nearby industrial museum; they also serve well kept Marstons Pedigree, Timothy Taylors Landlord, and Theakstons Old Peculier, and six interesting guest beers on handpump (usually including another beer from Kelham Island), and keep foreign bottled beers (particularly Belgian ones), country wines, and farm cider. Cheap bar food that changes weekly might include sandwiches, soup, and main dishes like pork and pepper casserole, pasta with nutty Cheshire sauce, salmon and potato pie (all £2.50), puddings such as creamy nectarine and chocolate crunch (80p); Sunday lunch; cribbage, dominoes and Monday evening quiz night 10pm. The two small downstairs rooms have coal fires and simple wooden tables and burgundy-coloured seats around the walls, with a few advertising mirrors and an enamelled placard for Richdales Sheffield Kings Ale; the one on the left is no smoking. Steep steps take you up to another similarly simple room (which may be booked for functions) with some attractive prints of old Sheffield; there are picnic-table sets in a fairlyit back courtyard. *(Recommended by R Holmes, F Reynolds, Terry Barlow, Paul Cartledge, P Butler)*

Own brew ~ Licensee Stephen Fearn ~ Real ale ~ Lunchtime meals and snacks ~ (01742) 728195 ~ Children allowed upstairs if not booked, until 8pm ~ Open 12-3, 5.30-11; closed 25/26 Dec

SICKLINGHALL   (N Yorks)   SE3648 Map 7

Scotts Arms

Leaving Wetherby W on A661, fork left signposted Sicklinghall

In summer, the hanging baskets, flowering tubs and neat garden here are a riot of colour. Inside, the friendly main bar is divided up by stubs of the old dividing walls which give it a cosy, less open-plan feel. Seats are built into cosy little alcoves cut into the main walls, there's a curious sort of double-decker fireplace with its upper hearth intricately carved, and a big inglenook fireplace. Decent bar food includes home-made soup (£1.75), garlic mushrooms (£2.75), ploughman's (£4.25), home-made curry (£4.60), steak, ale and mushroom pie (£4.85), salads with home-cooked meats or broccoli and cream cheese bake (£4.95), fresh haddock in batter (from £4.95), puddings, daily specials, and children's dishes (£2.50). Well kept Theakstons Best, XB and Old Peculier, and Youngers Scotch and No 3 on handpump; darts, dominoes, fruit machine, video game, CD juke box and unobtrusive piped music, and down steps a separate room has pool. There are tables in the garden, a children's play area with slide, climbing frame and wooden animals, and summer barbecues. *(Recommended by David Watson, Roy Bromell, Dr A and Dr A C Jackson, Paul Cartledge, Pat Crabb, Margaret Mason, David Thompson, Mark Bradley, H K Dyson, C J Westmoreland)*

S & N ~ Profit-sharing manager Carl Lang ~ Real ale ~ Meals and snacks (not 25 Dec) ~ Restaurant (not Sun evening) ~ (01937) 582100 ~ Children in family rooms ~ Live band Sun evenings ~ Open 11.30-3, 6(5.30 Sat)-11; winter lunchtime opening noon

SOWERBY BRIDGE   (W Yorks)   SE0623 Map 7

Moorings   🍺

Off Bolton Brow (A58) opposite Java Restaurant

This attractively converted ex-canal warehouse overlooks the basin where the Rochdale and Calder & Hebble canals meet and there are tables out on a terrace. Inside, the spacious beamed bar has big windows, bare floorboards, and stone walls and is decorated with a grain hopper, grain sacks and old pulley wheels and so forth; there's a separate eating area. The lounge bar is pleasantly furnished with rush-seated stools, tile-top tables and fabric-covered seats built against the stripped-stone walls (which are decorated with old waterways maps and modern canal pictures), and the big windows and very high ceiling give a relaxed and airy atmosphere. A lobby leads to a no-smoking family room alongside, similarly furnished; fruit machine, video game and piped music. Good, reasonably priced bar food includes home-made soup (from £1.50), filled granary cobs or filled baked potatoes (from £2.75), home-made chicken liver pâté (£2.95), gammon (from £4.75), salads (from £4.75), home-made pie (£4.95), vegetarian layer cake (£5.25), steaks (from £8.95), daily specials, puddings (£1.95), and children's dishes (£1.95). A wide range of drinks includes well kept Moorhouses Bitter, Theakstons Best and XB, Youngers Scotch and a regularly changing guest beer on handpump, over 90 bottled beers of the world including quite a few Belgian ones (also, fruit beer on draught), and 30 malt whiskies. *(Recommended by Mark Bradley, Andrew and Ruth Triggs, E J and M W Corrin, Paul Boot, J L Phillips, Patrick Clancy, Roxanne Chamberlain, Michael Butler, M L Clarke, Carl Travis)*

Free house ~ Lease: Miss Christine Krasocki ~ Real ale ~ Meals and snacks (11.45-2.30, 6.30-9.30; 12-7 Sun) ~ Restaurant (noon-7 on Sun) ~ (01422) 833940 ~ Children in no-smoking family room ~ Open 11.30-3, 5.30-11; 11.30-11 Sat

STARBOTTON (N Yorks) SD9574 Map 7

Fox & Hounds 🍴 🛏️

B6160 Upper Wharfedale rd N of Kettlewell; OS Sheet 98, map reference 953749

Walkers crowd into this whitewashed stone building, set at the foot of the hills; seats in a sheltered corner enjoy the view. The bar has traditional solid furniture on the flagstones, a collection of plates on the walls, whisky jugs hanging from the high beams supporting ceiling boards, a big stone fireplace (with an enormous fire in winter), and a warmly welcoming atmosphere. Very good, interesting bar food includes home-made soups such as courgette and broccoli or chicken and vegetable (£1.75), good devilled mushrooms (£2.50), stilton and walnut pâté (£2.85), almond risotto with peanut sauce, mixed bean casserole or pork and sage burger (£4.65), steak and mushroom pie (£5.40), chicken and leek crumble (£5.75), Moroccan-style lamb (£6.65), and puddings like honey and brandy cheesecake, fudgy nut and raisin pie or sticky toffee pudding (£2); at lunchtime they also offer filled french bread, ploughman's, filled Yorkshire puddings, with evening chicken and fish dishes, and daily specials; the dining area is no smoking. Well kept Black Sheep, Theakstons Best and guests like Marstons Pedigree and Moorhouses Premier on handpump, and around 24 malt whiskies. Dominoes, cribbage, chess, draughts, trivia and well reproduced, unobtrusive piped music. *(Recommended by A D Shore, Neil and Angela Hunter, TBB, John and Judith Wells, Paula Shillaw, Keven Whitcombe, Andrew McKeand, Prof S Barnett, Stephen, Julie and Hayley Brown, Carol Pritchard, Clive and Michele Platman, Peter and Kay Dines, T S O'Brien, Mike Whitehouse)*

Free house ~ Licensees James and Hilary McFadyen ~ Real ale ~ Meals and snacks ~ (01756) 760269 ~ Children welcome ~ Open 11.30-3, 6.30-11; closed Mon evening; closed all day Mon Nov-Mar ~ Bedrooms: £30S/£44S

SUTTON (S Yorks) SE5512 Map 7

Anne Arms

From A1 just S of Barnsdale Bar service area follow Askern, Campsall signpost; Sutton signposted right from Campsall

The generous helpings of remarkably good value food (no snacks) in this creeper-covered stone house are very popular, and include a fresh roast every day, their speciality rabbit pie, braised pork chops with apple sauce and stuffing, fresh battered haddock, and Barnsley chops with mint sauce (all £3.50), braised steak with Yorkshire pudding (£3.75), and puddings like home-made fruit pies (£1.50). John Smiths Magnet on handpump. The bar is crammed full of china: oak dressers filled with brightly coloured plates, fruit plates embossed with lifesize red apples, a throng of toby jugs collected over many years, lots of colourful five-litre and smaller Bavarian drinking steins, latticed glass cases thronged with china shepherdesses and the like, and wooden figures popping out of a Swiss clock when it chimes the quarter-hours. A separate room is filled with brass and copper, and there's a Victorian-style conservatory; fruit machine and piped music. Sadly, the licensees are leaving the pub in mid-1995. *(Recommended by David Ing, Mark Bradley, Michael Butler, Hilary Edwards, Richard Cole, Bill and Edee Miller; more reports please)*

Courage ~ Tenants John and Irene Simm ~ Real ale ~ Meals ~ (01302) 700500 ~ Children in conservatory ~ Open 10.30-11

SUTTON HOWGRAVE (N Yorks) SE3279 Map 7

White Dog 🍴 ♀

Village signposted from B6267 about 1 mile W of junction with A1

This must be virtually the only country pub which is open only at lunchtime. It's an immaculately kept pretty village cottage by a peaceful green – rather like a private home with a licence rather than a pub, and the two main rooms are furnished with comfortably cushioned Windsor chairs and flowers on the polished tables. On one side of the black-beamed bar there's an open kitchen range with a welcoming fire in cool weather; the brindle Staffordshire bull terrier is called Betsy. Very good bar lunches include lovely french onion soup (£1.95), smoked salmon sandwiches (£3.75), mariner's hotpot (£4.50), cheese or prawn omelette (£4.95), vegetarian casserole (£5.50), crunchy topped prawn and asparagus bake or curried smoked fish pasty (£5.95), steak and kidney pie (£6.50), ragout of lamb (£6.75), venison pie (£6.95), puddings (£2.25), and daily specials; small selection of New World wines; friendly service. In summer, the upper windows are almost hidden by the climbing rose (called Handel) and the flowers in the window boxes. *(Recommended by J R W Bune, Mrs E Mitchell, J E Rycroft, Mrs N J Clarke, W M and G M Greenhalgh)*

Free house ~ Licensees Basil and Pat Bagnall ~ Lunchtime meals and snacks (not Mon) ~ (01765) 640404 ~ Children allowed at licensees' discretion ~ Open 12-3; closed Mon, 25 Dec, 1 Jan

THORNTON WATLASS (N Yorks) SE2486 Map 10

Buck 🍴 🛏

Village signposted off B6268 Bedale—Masham

There's been a lot of warm praise from readers this year for this bustling country pub – for the friendly way the licensees welcome visitors and regulars alike, for the memorable food, and for the cheerful, relaxed atmosphere; it's also a smashing place to stay. The pleasantly traditional right-hand bar has handsomely upholstered old-fashioned wall settles on the carpet, a fine mahogany bar counter, a high shelf packed with ancient bottles, several mounted fox masks and brushes (the Bedale hunt meets in the village), and a brick fireplace. Particularly good – often delicious – food at lunchtime might include cheese or home-cooked meats in french bread (from £1.80), soups like watercress and orange, five-onions soup or cheese and ale (£1.95), a platter of melon, ham pâté and salad with french bread (£3.95), cauliflower and mushrooms baked with cheese and cashew nuts (£4.75), chick pea and potato curry (£4.95), steak and kidney pie or large deep-fried cod (£5.25), liver and bacon (£5.50), with evening extras such as aubergine and tomato charlotte (£4.95), grilled gammon with eggs (£6.75), lovely Whitby cod, tasty mussels in basil and cream sauce, good chicken curry, salmon fillet grilled with asparagus and lemon butter (£6.95), medallions of beef fillet with creamed mushrooms (£7.25), excellent seafood tagliatelle with scampi, scallops and prawns (£7.50), and sirloin steak (£8.95); good vegetables. The restaurant is no smoking; summer evening and Saturday afternoon barbecues. Well kept Black Sheep, John Smiths, Tetleys, Theakstons Best, and a guest beer on handpump, and around 40 malt whiskies. The beamed and panelled dining room is hung with large prints of old Thornton Watlass cricket teams. A bigger plainer bar has darts and dominoes. The low stone building – with its lovely hanging baskets – looks past a grand row of sycamores to the village cricket green (they have a team), and has two quoits pitches in the garden (with league matches on summer Wednesday evenings, practice Sunday morning and Tuesday evening; the world champion plays for one of their teams). Trout fishing on the Ure, and an equipped children's play area. Their walking holidays remain popular. *(Recommended by Philip and Elizabeth Hawkins, M J Morgan, E R Shlackman, G Roberts, Frank Davidson, Geoff and Angela Jaques, Tina and David Woods-Taylor, Allen Sharp, RB, M and J Back, Mr and Mrs Moody, S V Bishop, I T Parry, A Preston, R M Macnaughton, Geoffrey and Eddi Cowling, G Dobson, C F Walling)*

Free house ~ Licensees Michael and Margaret Fox ~ Real ale ~ Meals and snacks (not 25 Dec) ~ Restaurant ~ (01677) 422461 ~ Well behaved children welcome ~ Organ sing-along Sat evening, country & western Sun evening ~ Open 11-2.30, 6-11; 11am-midnight Sat ~ Bedrooms: £28S/£48S

THRESHFIELD (N Yorks) SD9763 Map 7

Old Hall ⓦ🍴 ◧

B6265, just on the Skipton side of its junction with B6160 near Grassington

This friendly dining pub is so popular that there are sometimes queues outside before the doors open. But even when busy there's still a stylish – though relaxed – atmosphere and the staff work hard to prevent delays. Changing daily and using fresh, seasonal ingredients, dishes might include a crispy pancake stuffed with ricotta cheese, leeks and mushrooms (£2.95), chicory wrapped in Bavarian smoked ham with gruyère cheese (£3.45), a vegetarian antipasta of artichokes, forest mushrooms, roasted peppers and Italian onion (£3.50), late breakfast (the home-made sausages are lovely), gado gado – stir-fried cabbage, chillis and peppers in a satay sauce – or nasi goreng (£5.95), pan-fried Scarborough woof with garlic, mushrooms and smoked bacon (£6.25), chicken breast marinated in grapefruit and honey (£6.75), sautéed venison in blackcurrant and cassis sauce, fillet of fresh haddock topped with herbed breadcrumbs with a fresh tomato and garlic sauce (£7.95), guinea fowl cooked in a coriander and cumin sauce or lovely individual lamb joint with redcurrant and mint sauce (£8.95), and puddings like brandy-snap baskets filled with amaretto ice cream, passion fruit torte, stilton and pear pie or bread and butter pudding (£2.25); get there early to bag a table. Well kept Theakstons Best, Timothy Taylors Bitter and Landlord and Youngers Scotch on handpump, with guest beers in summer and quite a few malt whiskies. The three communicating rooms have simple, cushioned pews built into the white walls, a high beam-and-plank ceiling hung with pots, unfussy decorations such as old Cadburys advertisements and decorative plates on a high delft shelf, and a tall well blacked kitchen range. Darts, dominoes, and maybe piped pop music. A neat side garden, partly gravelled, with young shrubs and a big sycamore has some tables and an aviary with cockatiels and zebra finches. This is, of course, a fine base for Dales walking; there's a 15th-c cottage behind the inn for rent. *(Recommended by Paul J Bispham, A D Shore, Dr and Mrs P J S Crawshaw, Prof S Barnett, Mary Moore, Brian Kneale, Stephen and Brenda Head, M E A Horler, Jim Paul, Andrew Shore, Neville Kenyon, Nicola Thomas, Paul Dickinson, Tony Hall, J E Rycroft, Ray Cuckow, Mr and Mrs John Gilks, P Boot, Amanda Dauncey, G Dobson, Gill and Maurice McMahon, Stephen Newell, Alan Wilcock, Christine Davidson, Viv Middlebrook, Mrs Ann Saunders, Michael and Isabel Richardson, Peter Race)*

Free house ~ Licensees Ian and Amanda Taylor ~ Real ale ~ Meals and snacks (not Sun evening, not Mon) ~ Restaurant (not Sun evening) ~ (01756) 752441 ~ Children welcome ~ Open 11.30-3, 5.30-11; winter evening opening 6; closed evening 25 Dec ~ Bedrooms: £20/£30

WAKEFIELD (W Yorks) SE3321 Map 7

Beer Engine ◧

77 Westgate End

There's a fine chatty and relaxed atmosphere in this traditional gas-lit pub – but it's the extraordinary range of up to 20 guest ales, all from independent brewers, that draws the mainly male customers here. There might by Burton Bridge Summer Ale, Hadrian Emperor, Hop Back Summer Lightning, Ringwood Old

Thumper, Rudgate Battleaxe, Sean Franklins, and Timothy Taylors Landlord on handpump; also, Biddenden farm cider. The home-made food using only fresh ingredients is very good and cheap and might include home-made soup (£1.75), sandwiches (from £1.75), liver and bacon casserole, seafood bake, pasta and vegetarian dishes, and home-made pies (all around £3.75). The main bar has flagstones, leatherette cushioned built-in wooden wall seats with high backs, a few snob-screens, Victorian-style flowery wallpaper, a honey-coloured vertical-planked dado, brewery mirrors, and several little rooms leading off the corridor; attractive Victorian fireplaces with tiled surrounds. No children. *(Recommended by Ian and Nita Cooper, Gerry McGarry, Mark Bradley, Dave and Carole Jones)*

Free house ~ Licensee Robert Hunter ~ Real ale ~ Meals and snacks (12-2 Tues-Fri, till 3 Sat; not Sun/Mon) ~ (01924) 375887 ~ Open 12-11; closed 25 Dec

WASS (N Yorks) SE5679 Map 7

Wombwell Arms 🅿️ 🛏️ 🍷

Back road W of Ampleforth; or follow brown tourist-attraction sign for Byland Abbey off A170 Thirsk—Helmsley

In a pretty village below the Hambleton Hills, this warmly welcoming inn is mainly popular for its particularly good food – and although there's a cosy and tasteful little central bar, it's the three comfortable and inviting low-beamed dining areas, incorporating a former 18th-c granary, that most people head for. Using fresh often local ingredients in interesting recipes, there might be standbys such as lunchtime sandwiches, lovely ploughman's with home-made pickles, and delicious prawns in garlic butter, as well as cod with a parsley crust (£6.95), excellent crab and avocado, ragged rabbit (£7.25), pan-fried beef (£7.50), a salmon baked in a lemon and dill sauce (£8.50), and puddings like bread and butter pudding, treacle tart or sticky toffee pudding (£2.95); lots of good crisp vegetables and vegetarian options. Well kept Black Sheep, Camerons, and Timothy Taylors Landlord on handpump, a good choice of wines (by glass or bottle) and decent malt whiskies. *(Recommended by Paul McPherson, W C M Jones, H Bramwell, Pat Crabb, John and Carol Holden, Wendy Arnold, G W H Kerby, CIJH, Andrew and Ruth Triggs)*

Free house ~ Licensees Alan and Lynda Evans ~ Real ale ~ Meals and snacks ~ (01347) 868280 ~ Children in eating area of bar (no under-5s evening) ~ Open 12-2.30, 7-11; closed Sun evening and all day Mon Oct-April, one week in Jan ~ Bedrooms: £24.50B/£49B

WATH-IN-NIDDERDALE (N Yorks) SE1467 Map 7

Sportsmans Arms 🅿️ 🛏️ 🍷

Nidderdale rd off B6265 in Pateley Bridge; village and pub signposted over hump bridge on right after a couple of miles

Although strictly speaking this is more of a hotel than a pub, readers are very happy to find it in this book – and there is a bar where locals do drop in for just a drink. But, of course, it's the superb food that most people come to this delightful 17th-c inn to enjoy. A choice of fresh fish might include moules marinières, fresh dressed crab, Scarborough woof sautéed in butter with prawns, almonds and capers, scallops tossed in garlic butter and glazed with mozzarella or fresh monkfish in a grape and mushroom sauce, delicious plaice Véronique, and Whitby turbot on a bed of spinach and sorrel with a wine, grape and mousseline sauce (all from £6.95-£7.50); also, good home-made soup (£2.70), ploughman's with locally-made cheeses (£4.50), prawns in wholemeal bread with a tomato flavoured mayonnaise (£5.50), breast of local chicken sautéed and served with garlic butter or marvellous loin of pork with spinach (good crackling; £6.90), and puddings like crème brûlée or chocolate roulade (£3) and a tremendous range of 18 cheeses (many local); excellent 3-course restaurant Sunday lunch (£11.75). To get the best of the excellent cooking, you should really stay overnight and enjoy a good leisurely dinner. There's a very sensible and extensive wine list with an emphasis on the New World, good choice of malt whiskies, several Russian vodkas, and attentive service; open fire, dominoes. Benches and tables outside. *(Recommended by Andrew and Marian Ruston, Geoffrey and Brenda Wilson, Nicola Thomas, Paul Dickinson, C H Stride, Peter Race, K and R Beaver, Andrew Shore, Stephen and Brenda Head, Ann Marie Stephenson, John Walker, Gwen and Peter Andrews, Stephen Newell, H K Dyson; also recommended by* The Good Hotel Guide)

Free house ~ Licensee Ray Carter ~ Meals and snacks ~ Evening restaurant (not Sun evening; they do Sun lunches) ~ (01423) 711306 ~ Children welcome until 9pm ~ Open 12-3, 6.30-11; closed 25 Dec ~ Bedrooms: £30(£32S)/£50(£55S)

WIDDOP (W Yorks) SD9333 Map 7

Pack Horse

The Ridge; from A646 on W side of Hebden Bridge, turn off at Heptonstall signpost (as it's a sharp turn, coming out of Hebden Bridge road signs direct you around a turning circle), then follow Slack and Widdop signposts; can also be reached from Nelson and Colne, on high, pretty road; OS Sheet 103, map reference 952317

High up on the moor, this cosy and friendly pub is busy all year with a good mix of people – though it's obviously popular with walkers. There are window seats cut into the partly panelled stripped stone walls that take in the moorland view, sturdy furnishings, and warm winter fires. Generous helpings of good bar food include sandwiches (from £1.30, double-deckers from £2.40, open sandwiches on french bread from £3), burgers (from £2.50), cottage hotpot (£2.95), ploughman's (£3.50), salads (from £4), home-made steak and kidney pie (£4.50), steaks (from £6.25), and specials such as haddock mornay (£5.95), poached Scotch salmon (£6.95), and rack of lamb (£8.95); vegetarian dishes and puddings. Well kept Theakstons XB, Thwaites Bitter and Craftsman, Youngers IPA and Scotch on handpump; around 100 single malt whiskies, and some Irish ones as well. There are seats outside. *(Recommended by Patrick Renouf, Cynthia Waller, Comus Elliott, G T Jones, Carl Travis, Andrew and Ruth Triggs)*

Free house ~ Licensee Andrew Hollinrake ~ Real ale ~ Meals and snacks (till 10pm) ~ (01422) 842803 ~ Children welcome until 8pm ~ Open 12-3, 7-11; closed weekday lunchtimes Oct-Easter and winter Mon evenings

WIGGLESWORTH (N Yorks) SD8157 Map 7

Plough 🛏

B6478

This relaxed, family-run country inn has acquired an American pit barbecue this year – probably the only one in the Dales – where the meat is cooked slowly over aromatic woods like hickory, mesquite and oak; they've also introduced an American-style diner menu for evening meals – though the conservatory will stick to English dishes: oak-smoked eggs with home-made mayonnaise (£1.95), sandwiches like hot beef or cajun chicken (from £4.25), filled savoury pancakes (from £3.95), hickory chicken (£4.95), salads (from £4.95), halibut steak smoked in mesquite (£6.50), a huge shoulder of lamb (£7.25), smoked steak (£9.45), puddings like pecan pie or cheesecake (£2.50), and children's dishes (from £2.50); lunchtime dishes such as sandwiches, gammon and eggs or chicken marengo (£5.50), good steak and kidney pie, and braised steak in ale (£5.95). Various little rooms surround the bar area – some spartan yet cosy, others smart and plush, including the no-smoking panelled dining room and snug; there's also a conservatory restaurant with fine panoramic views of the Dales and Ingleborough. Well kept Boddingtons and Tetleys on handpump and a decent wine list; good, friendly service; darts. An attractive landscaped garden is shaping up. *(Recommended by Roger and Christine Mash, Prof S Barnett, C J Parsons; more reports please)*

Free house ~ Licensee Brian Goodall ~ Real ale ~ Meals and snacks ~ Restaurant ~ (01729) 840243 ~ Children in eating area of bar ~ Open 11.30-2.30, 7-11 ~ Bedrooms: £32.45B/£46.40B

It's against the law for bar staff to smoke while handling food or drink.

WIGHILL (N Yorks) SE4746 Map 7

White Swan ★

Village signposted from Tadcaster; also easily reached from A1 Wetherby bypass – take
Thorpe Arch Trading Estate turnoff, then follow Wighill signposts; OS Sheet 105 map
reference 476468

The tiny front bar – popular with locals – has perhaps the most character in this
homely and unspoilt village pub. There's also a plainer bar opposite with lots of
racing prints, a small lobby that's also a favoured place for locals to gather, and a
back bar with a mix of old chairs and tables, and quite a few decorative plates,
and old theatrical memorabilia and sporting prints on the wall; a dining room
leads off this; open fires in most rooms. Bar snacks include sandwiches (from
£1.50 to jumbo ones at £3.30), pies such as steak, game, fish and chicken (from
£4.20), and puddings (£2.50). Well kept Stones, Tetleys Bitter, and Theakstons
Best and Old Peculier on handpump; piped music. There's a terrace overlooking
the garden where there are lots of seats. *(Recommended by B D Atkin, Paul Cartledge,
Mark Bradley, David Watson, C J McFeeters, Prof R N Orledge)*

*Free house ~ Licensee Mrs Rita Arundale ~ Real ale ~ Meals and snacks (not Sun
or Mon evenings) ~ Restaurant ~ (01937) 832217 ~ Children in restaurant or
family room ~ Open 12-3, 6-11*

WORMALD GREEN (N Yorks) SE3065 Map 7

Cragg Lodge

A61 Ripon—Harrogate, about half way

It's the extraordinary collection of malt whiskies that many people come to this
comfortably modernised dining roadhouse to sample. It probably houses the widest
choice in the world, and there are nearly 1,000 of them, including two dozen
Macallans going back to 1937. They have 16 price bands, between £1.15 and
£6.50, depending on rarity – with a 17th 'by negotiation' for their unique 1919
Campbelltown. Also, well kept Tetleys Bitter and Theakstons Best, XB and Old
Peculier on handpump, several distinguished brandies, and mature vintage port by
the glass. The big open-plan bar is laid out for eating and has Mouseman furniture
as well as little red plush chairs around dark rustic tables, horsebrasses and pewter
tankards hanging from side beams, a dark joist-and-plank ceiling, and a coal fire.
Bar food at lunchtime includes soup (£1.10), sandwiches (from £1.35),
ploughman's (£2.80), home-made steak and kidney pie (£3.50), vegetarian nut
cutlets (£3.90), lasagne (£3.90), salads such as Scotch salmon (£4.50), steaks and a
daily roast; in the evenings, there's a larger, more elaborate menu, with a new
emphasis on fish such as halibut, cod and fresh sardines; puddings (£1.90), and
morning coffee and snacks from 10am; the pub is partly no smoking. Shove-
ha'penny, cribbage, dominoes and piped music. There are picnic-table sets under
cocktail parasols on the side terrace, with more in a sizeable garden and pretty
hanging baskets in summer. The pub is popular with older people. *(Recommended by
Mary Moore, David Surridge, Kevin Potts, Paul Cartledge, Tony Bland, M L Clarke, K Harvey)*

*Free house ~ Licensee Garfield Parvin ~ Real ale ~ Meals and snacks ~
Restaurant ~ (01765) 677214 ~ Children in eating area of bar ~ Open 11.30-
2.30, 6-11 ~ Bedrooms: £30B/£45B*

YORK (N Yorks) SE5951 Map 7

Black Swan

Peaseholme Green; inner ring road, E side of centre; the inn has a good car park

As we went to press, this surprisingly uncommercialised pub told us that they
would be undergoing refurbishment early in 1995 and that they hoped to create an
extra room for drinkers, in keeping with the rest of the pub. The busy black-
beamed back bar has wooden settles along the walls, some cushioned stools, and a
throne-like cushioned seat in the vast brick inglenook, where there's a coal fire in a
grate with a spit and some copper cooking utensils. With its little serving hatch, the

cosy panelled front bar is similarly furnished but smaller and more restful. The crooked-floored hall that runs along the side of both bars has a fine period staircase (leading up to a room fully panelled in oak, with an antique tiled fireplace). Good bar food served by cheerful staff includes sandwiches, home-made soup (£1.50), generously filled giant Yorkshire puddings (from £1.95), ploughman's (from £4), home-made steak and onion pie or vegetable bake (£4.25), and half a roast chicken with stuffing (£4.95), with evening extras such as soup, gammon and egg, mixed grill and steaks. The dining area is no smoking. Well kept Bass, Stones, Timothy Taylors Landlord and Worthingtons on handpump; dominoes and fruit machine. If the car park is full, it's worth knowing that there's a big public one next door. The timbered and jettied façade here and original lead-latticed windows in the twin gables are very fine indeed. No children. *(Recommended by Trevor Scott, John Fazakerley, C J Westmoreland, Miss Woddsend, Bill and Edee Miller; more reports please)*

Bass ~ Manager Joseph Cahill ~ Meals and snacks (12-2, 6-8.15 Mon-Thurs; 12-2, 7-9 Fri/Sat) ~ (01904) 625236 ~ Folk Thurs evening, Blues Sun evening ~ Open 11-11 ~ Bedrooms: £45B

Olde Starre

Stonegate; pedestrians-only street in centre, far from car parks

This is York's oldest licensed pub (1644) and is very popular with visitors. The main bar has original panelling, green plush wall seats, a large servery running the length of the room, and a large leaded window with red plush curtains at the far end. Several other little rooms lead off the porch-like square hall – one with its own food servery, one with panelling and some prints, and a third with cream wallpaper and dado; the tap room is no smoking. Well kept Ruddles County, John Smiths Best and Magnet and Theakstons Best and XB on handpump, and decent whiskies; piped music, fruit machine and CD juke box. Bar food includes sandwiches, ploughman's, vegetarian lasagne, lamb's liver, sausage and onion or steak and kidney pie (£3.95), beef in ale or Highland mutton casserole (£4.25); helpful staff. Perhaps best visited at lunchtime. Parts of the building date back to 900 and the cellar was used as a hospital in the Civil War. *(Recommended by Mark Walker, Paul Cartledge, David Hedges, Neil and Jenny Spink)*

S & N ~ Managers Bill and Susan Embleton ~ Real ale ~ Meals and snacks (11.30-3, 5.30-8; not Fri-Sun evenings) ~ (01904) 623063 ~ Children in three areas away from bar until 8pm ~ Open 11-11

Spread Eagle 🍺

98 Walmgate

There's a fine choice of real ales in this narrow, popular pub, which includes quite a few from local micro breweries as well as Black Sheep Bitter, Theakstons Best, Old Peculier and XB, Timothy Taylors Landlord, and Youngers No 3 on handpump; country wines and malt whiskies. The main bar is a dark vault and two smaller, cosier rooms lead off – lots of old enamel advertisements and prints on the walls, and a friendly atmosphere. A wide choice of bar food might include sandwiches (from £1.70), vegetarian dishes, pasta in a tomato, cheese and seafood sauce or curries (£5), and cashew chicken (£6.10). Fruit machine, trivia, juke box and piped music. *(Recommended by P R Morley, C J Westmoreland; more reports please)*

Free house ~ Licensee Adrian Wilkinson ~ Real ale ~ Meals and snacks (noon-10pm Mon-Sat) ~ Restaurant ~ (01904) 635868 ~ Children welcome ~ Live Blues Sun lunchtime ~ Open 11-11

Tap & Spile £ 🍺

Monkgate

It's the fine choice of around ten well kept constantly changing real ales that draws people to this traditionally furnished pub; Big Lamp Bitter, Marston Moor Cromwell, Old Mill Bitter and Theakstons Old Peculier with seven constantly changing guests on handpump; fruit wines and some malt whiskies. The big split-level bar has bare boards, green leatherette wall settles right around a big bay window, with a smaller upper area with frosted glass and panelling; darts, shove-ha'penny, dominoes, fruit machine, video game and piped music. Simple cheap bar food includes sandwiches (from £1.25; bacon butty £1.80), filled giant Yorkshire puddings (from £2.10), meaty or vegetarian chilli (£3.20), daily specials, and children's dishes (£1.75). There are a few picnic-table sets outside. This is part of the small chain of pubs with this name. *(Recommended by Andrew Stephenson, Derek and Sylvia Stephenson; more reports please)*

Brent Walker ~ Managers Ian Kilpatrick and Vicky Office ~ Real ale ~ Meals and snacks (noon-7; till 2.30 Weds and Sun) ~ (01904) 656158 ~ Children in eating area of bar till 9pm ~ Live Blues Mon, quiz night Weds ~ Open 11.30-11 ~ Bedrooms: £30/£30

Lucky Dip

Besides the fully inspected pubs, you might like to try these Lucky Dips recommended to us and described by readers (if you do, please send us reports):

☆ **Aberford**, W Yor [Old North Rd; best to use A642 junction to leave A1; SE4337], *White Swan*: Amazing choice of good value generous food in very busy attractively refurbished dining pub, with lots of bric-a-brac, prints on walls, cosy layout, though pressure on tables makes for lively rather than relaxing atmosphere; well kept Tetleys and Whitbreads-related ales, generous glasses of wine, friendly staff, more upmarket upstairs restaurant; bedrooms *(Mark Bradley, C J Westmoreland, Anthony Barnes, Andy and Jill Kassube, Michael A Butler)*

Aberford [Old North Rd], *Arabian Horse*: Welcoming beamed village local with central bar, front lounge and back public bar, a few ornaments, relaxed friendly atmosphere; lunchtime food, open fires, Theakstons Best and Youngers Scotch and No 3; open all day Sat *(Mark Bradley, Michael A Butler, C J Westmoreland)*

Acaster Malbis, N Yor [SE5945], *Ship*: Pleasant riverside inn, tempting food, well kept Timothy Taylors Landlord, faultless friendly service, attractive garden; bedrooms clean and comfortable *(John C Baker, C J Westmoreland)*

☆ **Addingham**, W Yor [SE0749], *Craven Heifer*: Pleasant modernised lofty beamed lounge, two fireplaces, dark green plush, lots of rustic prints; nice efficient service, good choice of usual food, Ind Coope Burton, Tetleys and Youngers real ales, piped music; steep steps from car park *(Neil and Anita Christopher)*

Aislaby, N Yor [SE7886], *Huntsman*: Refurbished under new young landlord, well kept beers, friendly locals, good reasonably priced food; busy weekends and holidays *(R Williamson)*

Allerston, N Yor [A170 Pickering—Scarborough; SE8882], *Cayley Arms*: Good choice of good value bar food, well kept beers, friendly staff, pleasant furnishings *(C K Wilkins, Ken Smith)*

☆ **Almondbury**, W Yor [bear left up Lumb Lane; village signposted off A629/A642 E of Huddersfield – OS Sheet 110 map ref 153141; SE1615], *Castle Hill*: Perched high above Huddersfield on site of prehistoric hill fort, with terrific views of the moors dwarfing the mill towns, three coal fires in rambling part-panelled bar, well worn-in sturdy traditional furnishings, well kept Theakstons, Tetleys and Timothy Taylors; reasonably priced generous helpings of usual food (not Sun-Tues evenings), popular Sun lunch, partly no-smoking dining room; very spacious grounds *(Paul Lightfoot, LYM)*

☆ **Ampleforth**, N Yor [Main St; SE5878], *White Swan*: Extensive modern lounge/dining bar in small attractive village, wide choice of good value generous traditional food inc some good recipes, with crisp veg and traditional Sun lunch (very popular with older people then – should book); also front country bar with several real ales inc a guest beer, lots of malt whiskies, darts and a couple of fruit machines; decent wines, good friendly service; back terrace, huge car park *(DKC, Simon Collett-Jones, Paul Williams, H Bramwell, Pat Crabb)*

☆ **Appleton Roebuck**, N Yor [SE5542], *Shoulder of Mutton*: Popular and attractive beamed pub/steak bar overlooking village green, wide choice of good value food from sandwiches to steaks, Sam Smiths real ales, friendly service; bedrooms *(Neil O'Callaghan)*

☆ **Appletreewick**, N Yor [SE0560], *New Inn*: Welcoming stonebuilt pub with good value simple food, well kept beers inc interesting bottled imports, interesting photographs, pub games; in superb spot, with lovely views; garden; bedrooms *(Gwen and Peter Andrews, LYM)*

☆ **Arncliffe**, N Yor [off B6160; SD9473], *Falcon*: Basic genuinely unspoilt country tavern ideal for walkers, matchless setting on out-of-the-way moorland village green; absolutely no frills, Youngers tapped from cask to stoneware jugs in central hatch-style servery, limited but generous plain lunchtime bar snacks, open fire in small bar with elderly furnishings and humorous sporting prints, airy back sunroom (children allowed here lunchtime) looking on to garden; one reader speculates that the gents' may have been used by men commemorated in the local church for fighting at Flodden in 1513; run by same family for generations – they take time to get to know customers; closed winter Thurs evenings; bedrooms (not all year), good breakfasts and evening meals – real value *(Bill and Lydia Ryan, Mark Bradley, Neil and Angela Huxter, Gwen and Peter Andrews, Mark Undrill, TBB, Brian Wainwright, LYM)*

☆ **Askwith**, W Yor [3 miles E of Ilkley; SD1648], *Black Horse*: friendly new management and good choice of well cooked food in big family pub with L-shaped bar counter serving lounge and small public area; well kept Courage-related ales and Theakstons Best, good service, lots of tables reserved; attractive small village, extensive Wharfedale views esp from terrace *(Jon and Jacquie Payne, Mark Bradley, Alan Wilcock, Christine Davidson, Prof S Barnett)*

☆ **Aysgarth**, N Yor [SE0088], *George & Dragon*: Hotel with cosy and friendly separate bar, copper-topped tables, lots of bric-a-brac, portraits of locals by landlord, also spacious polished hotel lounge with antique china, grandfather clock; ample helpings of usual food well prepared and reasonably priced inc some vegetarian dishes and Sun roasts, five well kept ales inc Hambleton, good friendly service, a welcome for dogs, separate pool area; bedrooms *(C F Walling, Michael A Butler, Richard Houghton)*

Aysgarth, *Palmer Flatt*: Moorland hotel in great scenery nr broad waterfalls, medley of cheerful largely modernised bars but some interesting ancient masonry at the back recalling its days as a pilgrims' inn, good range of bar food, well kept beers, restaurant, seats outside, fishing rights; bedrooms *(H W Kennedy, LYM)*

☆ **Bardsey**, W Yor [A58; SE3643], *Bingley Arms*: Ancient pub and decorated to look it, full of interest and atmosphere; very wide range of good value bar food (stops 8) in spacious lounge divided into separate areas inc no smoking, Tetleys Bitter and Mild and Timothy Taylors Landlord, pleasant speedy service, smaller public bar, picturesque upstairs brasserie, charming quiet terrace with good interesting summer barbecues inc vegetarian; bedrooms comfortable *(Stephen Oxley, Anna Cwajna, Paul Cartledge, Annette Moore, Chris Pearson, Mark Bradley)*

☆ **Barkisland**, W Yor [Stainland Rd; SE0520], *Griffin*: Good value food and very well kept Ryburn and Worthington BB as well as a potent cheap ale brewed here, open fires and lots of old-fashioned woodwork in tastefully refurbished smart little rooms inc cosy oak-beamed parlour, friendly licensees and atmosphere, restaurant *(S Bradley, H K Dyson, LYM)*

☆ **Barkisland** [Bank Top, Elland Rd; B6113 towards Ripponden – OS Sheet 110 map ref 048199], *Fleece*: Oak beams and stripped

stone in 18th-c moorland pub with comfortable settles and copper-topped tables, wide choice of reasonably priced food till small hours, well kept Marstons Burton, John Smiths and Tetleys on handpump, central fireplace, separate restaurant, evening cellar wine bar with CD juke box; seats outside with barbecue and play area *(Paul Lightfoot, M L Clarke, BB)*

☆ **Barnsley**, S Yor [Cundy Cross; Grange Lane (A633); SE3706], *Mill of the Black Monks*: Tastefully converted three-storey watermill said to date back to 12th c, with split-level bar and restaurant, Theakstons Best, XB and Old Peculier and Youngers IPA and No 3 on handpump, candlelight, lovely old stonework; shame about the piped pop music, live music most nights; big garden with picnic-table sets, mature trees, swings, ducks and small animals in cages *(CW, JW, Mark Bradley, R Holmes, F Reynolds)*

☆ **Barnsley** [Hoyle Mill, 150 Pontefract Rd (A628); SE3606], *Old White Bear*: Friendly and pleasant straightforward pub popular for well kept real ales with up to six guests, open-plan communicating rooms inc one with darts and pool, wide choice of food till 8pm inc popular home-made pies and Yorkshire puddings, tables outside; bedrooms, though we have as yet no grounds for recommending them *(Mark Bradley, Richard Waller)*

Bawtry, S Yor [28 High St (A614); SK6593], *Turnpike*: Comfortable L-shaped bar with lots of wood, quiet piped pop music, good value food lunchtime and Tues-Thurs evening, cheap well kept local Stocks Bitter and Porter on handpump *(CMW, JJW, Des Pejko)*

☆ **Beck Hole**, N Yor [OS Sheet 94 map ref 823022; NZ8202], *Birch Hall*: Unique and unchanging pub-cum-village shop; hot and cold drinks inc keg Theakstons and perhaps even cask-conditioned Black Sheep, sandwiches using their own bread, hot pies and other refreshments served through hatch into small room with very simple furniture; ancient outside mural, benches out in front, steep steps up to charming little side garden with nice view; lovely spot by bridge over river in beautiful steep-valley village, nr Thomason Fosse waterfall, steam railway; best of all is to walk out here on the old railway track from Grosmont or Goathland *(C J Westmoreland, Elizabeth and Anthony Watts, Dr R M Williamson, Mayur Shah, Martyn and Mary Mullins)*

Bedale, N Yor [Market Pl; SE2688], *Olde Black Swan*: Nice old bustling beamed pub with well kept Theakstons, good value food inc substantial sandwiches in lovely brown bread, proper coffee with real milk; no intrusive music at least at lunchtime *(Robert W Buckle, Comus Elliott, Dr and Mrs A K Clarke)*

Bishop Thornton, N Yor [SE2664], *Drovers Arms*: Pleasant pub with friendly staff, good food and decent choice of drinks *(Stephen R Holman)*

Blubberhouses, N Yor [SE1755], *Hopper Lane*: Pleasant old-world interior, two or three connected areas served by one main bar, Black Sheep and Theakstons, varied and interesting bar food at reasonable prices, huge mixed grill; bedrooms *(Lawrence Pearse)*

☆ **Bolton Percy**, N Yor [SE5341], *Crown*: Basic cosy and unpretentious country local with Sam Smiths, cheap simple food (not Mon or Tues), friendly dogs, tables on sizeable terrace with pens of ornamental pheasants, quiet setting nr interesting 15th-c church and medieval gatehouse; children welcome *(Paul Cartledge, LYM)*

Boroughbridge, N Yor [St James Sq; SE3967], *Black Bull*: Friendly new owners doing good reasonably priced food, new kitchen and dining room, friendly atmosphere; new bedroom wing *(Mr MacGwire)*

☆ **Bradfield**, S Yor [Strines Reservoir; signed from A616 W of Stocksbridge, and A57 Sheffield—Ladybower – OS Sheet 110 map ref 222906; SK2692], *Strines*: Very relaxed take-us-as-you-find-us atmosphere in beautifully isolated ancient pub with three rooms (one candlelit), open fires, hunting pictures, lots of stuffed animals, wide choice of bar food from sandwiches up (not Sun evening, exc residents), upstairs restaurant; Whitbreads Castle Eden on handpump, decent wines and malt whiskies; children welcome; open all day – unless snowed in; simple bedrooms *(DC, LYM)*

☆ **Bradford** [Heaton Rd; SE1633], *Fountain*: Popular and pleasant, with good staff, hard-working landlord, good food and beer; probably one of the most civilised pubs in the first town where the police have offered their services to pubs as paid security guards *(J E Rycroft)*

☆ **Bradford** [Grattan Rd/Barry St], *Yorkshire Small Brewers*: Plain town local owned by group of small independent brewers, distinguished by its good collection of cheap well kept unusual real ales such as Goose Eye Bitter and Wharfedale, Griffin Lions, Merry Marker, Morlands Old Master, Riding Bitter and Mild, Ryburn, Timothy Taylors Golden Pale; basic cheap food, well reproduced piped music (maybe some live) *(Tony and Pat Martin, BB)*

☆ **Bradford** [Kirkgate/Ivegate], *Rams Revenge*: Well kept Clarks, Theakstons and guest beers in unpretentious pub with old pews, wooden floor, upper gallery, fine old Bradford prints; lunchtime bar food, folk music, relaxed atmosphere; clock from former gatehouse on this site in back room *(Bill and Lydia Ryan)*

Bradford [Preston St (off B6145)], *Fighting Cock*: Good choice of real ales such as Black Sheep, Exmoor Gold, Sam Smiths, Timothy Taylors, Theakstons in busy basic alehouse with hard benches and bare floors; farm ciders, foreign bottled beers, coal fires, snacks *(Susan and Nigel Wilson, Reg Nelson)*; [Easby Rd, nr Univ], *McCrorys*:

Popular cellar bar with local blues and folk bands, rather reminiscent of the late 1950s *(Reg Nelson)*; [28 Kirkgate], *Shoulder of Mutton*: Notable for its fine suntrap garden; cosy inside, with decent fresh food (not Sun), well kept Sam Smiths, low prices *(Bill and Lydia Ryan)*

Bramham, W Yor [The Square; just off A1 2 miles N of A64; SE4243], *Red Lion*: Good food from quite extensive reasonably priced menu and well kept Sam Smiths in warm and attractive former coaching inn *(C J Westmoreland, Paul Cartledge, K H Frostick)*

Bramhope, W Yor [SE2543], *Fox & Hounds*: Popular two-roomed pub in Leeds's stockbroker belt; Tetleys Mild and Bitter well kept, lunchtime food, open fire; children welcome; has been open all day *(Mark Bradley, Annette Moore, Chris Pearson)*

☆ **Brighouse**, W Yor [Brookfoot; A6025 towards Elland; SE1524], *Red Rooster*: Homely smallish drinking pub on sharp bend with single bar divided into separate areas which feel like separate rooms inc one with books to read or buy, good range of beers such as Old Mill, Marstons Pedigree, Moorhouses Pendle Witches Brew, Roosters Yankee, Timothy Taylors Landlord and several guest beers; brewery memorabilia, knowledgeable landlord, open fire *(Mark Bradley)*

☆ **Broughton**, N Yor [SD9351], *Bull*: Smartly modernised pub popular for good food inc children's meals in bar and restaurant; cosy and comfortable, pleasant busy atmosphere, friendly service, well kept John Smiths and Tetleys *(J E Rycroft, LYM)*

☆ **Burnt Yates**, N Yor [B6165, 6 miles N of Harrogate; SE2561], *Bay Horse*: 18th-c dining pub with friendly staff, welcoming log fires, low beams and brasses; wide range of bar meals lunchtime and evening, pleasant restaurant, welcoming traditional atmosphere; bedrooms in motel extension *(Roy Bromell, A B Dalton, Peter Marren)*

☆ **Burton Leonard**, N Yor [off A61 Ripon— Harrogate; SE3364], *Hare & Hounds*: Friendly attentive newish licensees doing solidly good value food in spotless bar and restaurant, cheerful atmosphere, cosy coffee lounge, good value French wines, four well kept real ales, no games or juke box *(Paul J Bispham, Peter Race)*

☆ **Calder Grove**, W Yor [just off M1 junction 39; A636 signposted Denby Dale, then first right into Broadley Cut Rd; SE3116], *Navigation*: Useful motorway break – cheery waterside local full of canalia, with well kept Tetleys, simple food, tables outside *(Paul Lightfoot, LYM)*

Carperby, N Yor [a mile NW of Aysgarth; SE0189], *Wheatsheaf*: Friendly local in quiet village, good atmosphere, well kept Theakstons, bar food inc good sandwiches and ploughman's, separate well furnished rooms, restaurant for residents; bedrooms *(Michael A Butler, Annette Moore, Chris Pearson)*

Castleton, N Yor [High St; NZ6908], *Downe Arms*: Well kept Ruddles, stone walls, small pews with leatherette seats, coal fire, electric organ, decent service; separate room with pool and fruit machine; bedrooms *(Simon Collett-Jones)*; *Moorlands*: Wonderful spot high above the Esk Valley, old stonebuilt hotel with good value meals – local Whitby fish particulary recommended; good choice of wines, keg beers; comfortable bedrooms *(Norma and Keith Bloomfield)*

Cawood, N Yor [SE5737], *Ferry*: Very old, cosy and friendly, with open fires, comfortable seats, good choice of beers inc well kept Riding, good reasonably priced bar food *(D R Clarke)*

☆ **Chapel le Dale**, N Yor [B5655 Ingleton—Hawes, 3 miles N of Ingleton; SD7477], *Old Hill*: Basic stripped-stone bar with potholing pictures and memorabilia of the Settle railway line and its viaduct, flagstone floors for wet-weather gear and muddy boots, old woodwork and partitions with waggon wheels; roaring log fire in cosy back parlour, well kept Dent and Theakstons Bitter, XB and Old Peculier, generous simple home-made food in separate room inc good beef sandwiches and pies, plenty of vegetarian dishes; juke box; children welcome; bedrooms basic but good, with good breakfast – wonderful isolated spot *(Jenni Mitchell-Gibbs, Nigel Woolliscroft, LYM)*

Chop Gate, N Yor [SE5699], *Buck*: Hospitable old-world stone pub with red plush seating, restaurant and garden, good range of meals and sandwiches; new bedrooms, handy for walks *(Paul and Margaret Baker, D M Caslaw)*

☆ **Clapham**, N Yor [off A65 N of Settle; SD7569], *New Inn*: Popular food from burgers and filled Yorkshire puddings to huge mixed grill with good puddings in riverside pub with small comfortable panelled lounge, public bar with games room, smart restaurant; friendly service, Dent, John Smiths, Tetleys and Youngers No 3, good welcoming service; bedrooms comfortable and reasonably priced, all with own bathroom; handy for walks *(D A Cash, T M Dobby, M and J Back)*

☆ **Clifton**, W Yor [Westgate; off Brighouse rd from M62 junction 25; SE1623], *Black Horse*: Wide choice of good food in smart village inn with cosy oak-beamed bars, well kept Whitbreads-related beers, good service, popular restaurant (weekend booking recommended); bedrooms comfortable *(Michael Butler, Mark Bradley, RJH)*

☆ **Cloughton**, N Yor [N of village; TA0096], *Hayburn Wyke*: Attractive old rose-covered pub nr NT Hayburn Wyke and Cleveland Way coastal path, lots of tables outside, red-cushioned settles in beamed L-shaped bar, restaurant and eating area beyond; good reasonable priced food, well kept John Smiths, Theakstons Best and Youngers, friendly efficient staff, well behaved children and babies welcome; bedrooms *(Andrew and Ruth Triggs, Giles Quick)*

☆ **Cloughton Newlands**, N Yor [A171; TA0196], *Bryherstones*: Particularly welcoming – on your first visit you feel like a regular; several interconnecting rooms, well kept Youngers, over 50 whiskies, big helpings of well prepared food inc fresh fish and veg, large collection of miniatures in cases; one room has two pool tables, quieter room upstairs; children welcome, delightful surroundings *(David and Julie Glover, Steve and Julie Cocking, Keith and Margaret Kettell, Mike and Wendy Proctor)*

Coley, W Yor [a mile N of Hipperholme; Lane Ends, Denholme Gate Rd (A644 Brighouse—Keighley) – OS Sheet 104 map ref 123269; SE1226], *Brown Horse*: Quietly welcoming, with good food promptly served, smart staff, decent house wines, golfing memorabilia *(A Preston)*

Constable Burton, N Yor [SE1791], *Wyvill Arms*: Comfortably converted and attractively decorated farmhouse with elaborate stone fireplace and fine plaster ceiling in inner room, good value bar food, well kept Theakstons, good service *(Dono and Carol Leaman, LYM)*

Cridling Stubbs, N Yor [between junctions 33 and 34 of M62 – easy detour – OS Sheet 105 map ref 520214; SE5221], *Ancient Shepherd*: Reasonably priced decent bar food (not Sat lunchtime or Sun evening), well kept Marstons Pedigree and Whitbreads Trophy, pleasant service and layout, comfortable banquettes – a refuge from M62/A1/A19; children in eating areas *(Mark Bradley, Thomas Nott, LYM)*

☆ **Dacre Banks**, N Yor [SE1962], *Royal Oak*: Cosy and comfortable open-plan village pub with beautiful valley views, wide choice of good food from sandwiches to well presented main dishes, Black Sheep, Tetleys and Theakstons, two lounge areas with interesting old photographs, open fire in front part, unusual piped music (Duke Ellington and the like), hospitable landlady, helpful and efficient young staff; restaurant; bedrooms *(Lawrence Pearse, Mrs B M Fyffe, Prof S Barnett, Andrew and Marian Ruston)*

☆ **Danby Wiske**, N Yor [off A167 N of Northallerton; SE3499], *White Swan*: Handy pub for coast-to-coast walk, friendly and informal, with good value home cooking inc own free range eggs; bedrooms undistinguished but cheap and comfortable *(David Varney)*

Denby Dale, W Yor [A635 to Barnsley; SK2208], *Dunkirk*: Small and cosy, good freshly cooked food under newish licensees *(F and Dorothy Twentyman)*

Dewsbury, W Yor [2 Walker Cottages; Chidswell Lane, Shaw Cross; SE2523], *Huntsman*: Converted cottages alongside urban-fringe farm, pleasant decor and atmosphere, lots of brasses and bric-a-brac, Stones, Worthington BB and maybe other ales; no food evening or Sun/Mon lunchtime, busy evenings *(Michael Butler, Paul Lightfoot)*; [Church St], *Market House*: Proper old well restored town centre pub, well kept Tetleys *(Comus Elliott)*

Doncaster, S Yor [Market Pl; SE5703], *Olde Castle*: Well kept beers, nice atmosphere, genuinely old-fashioned feel – no riff-raff *(Des Pejko)*

☆ **Dunford Bridge**, S Yor [Windle Edge Lane; off A628 Barnsley-M'ter – OS Sheet 110 map ref 158023; SE1502], *Stanhope Arms*: Decent good value straightforward food from sandwiches up with some more unusual specials in cheerful and nicely placed family pub below the moors around Winscar Reservoir, afternoon teas summer Suns, well kept John Smiths and Magnet; central hall servery for comfortable high-ceilinged dining lounge, little copper-tabled snug and plain pool room (with fruit machine); piped music can be a bit loud; sizeable garden with camping ground *(Lee Goulding, Gwen and Peter Andrews, BB)*

☆ **East Keswick**, N Yor [Main St; SE3644], *Duke of Wellington*: Tasty generous home-cooked straightforward food (not Mon) in big ornate Victorian dining room, convivial bar with big open fire *(C Lomas, C J Westmoreland)*

☆ **East Layton**, N Yor [A66 not far from Scotch Corner; NZ1609], *Fox Hall*: Wide choice of bar food and good friendly service in panelled bar with cosy booths, sporting prints, more open back part with big south-facing window, well kept Theakstons Best (more ales in summer), good range of malt whiskies and wines; games room, juke box, piped music; tables on back terrace; evening restaurant, Sun lunches; children and well behaved dogs welcome; bedrooms comfortable, good breakfasts *(Andrew and Ruth Triggs, LYM)*

☆ **East Marton**, N Yor [Marton Bridge; A59 Gisburn—Skipton; SD9051], *Cross Keys*: Wide and interesting choice of particularly good value bar food in welcoming nicely decorated pub with interesting and comfortable old-fashioned furnishings; well kept Black Sheep and Theakstons, friendly helpful staff, open fires, children's area (where the food counter is), evening restaurant; tables outside, lovely spot nr Leeds & Liverpool Canal *(Dr and Mrs D E Awbery, Kevin Potts, M E A Horler, LYM)*

Eccup, W Yor [off A660 N of Leeds; SE2842], *New Inn*: Isolated but popular Tetleys pub with big lounge and family room, good range of bar meals and sandwiches, friendly efficient service; children's play area at back; well placed for good walks, on Dales Way and nr Harewood Park *(D Stokes)*

Egton, N Yor [NZ8106], *Horseshoe*: Traditional low-beamed moorland village pub with good value basic food inc tasty starters and puddings, warm welcome, open fire; may be closed some winter lunchtimes; not to be confused with the Horse Shoe down at Egton Bridge *(Bronwen and Steve Wrigley, LYM)*

Eldwick, W Yor [The Green; SE1240], *Acorn*: Big main bar and surrounding open-plan seating with banquettes around the walls, well kept Bass and Stones, good lunchtime bar food at most attractive prices, friendly staff; open all day *(Ann and Bob Westbrook)*

Elland, W Yor [Park Rd, next to canal; quite handy for M62 junction 24; SE1121], *Barge & Barrel*: Friendly old-fashioned pub between canal and flyover, huge helpings of cheap food, wide changing range of well kept beers, particularly good family room (with air hockey), piped radio *(Lee Goulding)*

☆ **Embsay**, N Yor [Elm Tree Sq; SE0053], *Elm Tree*: Civilised well refurbished open-plan beamed village pub with good bar food inc good-sized children's helpings, good service, old-fashioned prints, log-effect gas fire; games area, well kept Whitbreads ales with an interesting guest beer, juke box; busy weekends esp evenings; comfortable bedrooms – handy for S Dales *(Alan Wilcock, Christine Davidson)*

☆ **Escrick**, N Yor [E of A19 York—Selby – OS Sheet 105 map ref 643425; SE6343], *Black Bull*: Well done up under warmly welcoming newish landlord, warm cosy atmosphere, well spaced tables in bar, good imaginative if not cheap food in good-sized dining area, decent wines; very popular weekends *(Roger Bellingham, Ian S Morley)*

☆ **Farndale East**, N Yor [Church Houses; next to Farndale Nature Reserve; SE6697], *Feversham Arms*: Really friendly walkers' pub, unspoilt though very popular weekends, in lovely quiet daffodil valley; two smallish rooms with flagstone floors and real fires, well kept Tetleys, staggering helpings of good cheap genuine home-cooked food, open fire, pleasant restaurant; nice small garden; good bedrooms, big breakfasts *(C J Westmoreland, Elizabeth and Anthony Watts, Ian Boag, Lee Goulding, Geoff and Angela Jaques)*

☆ **Farnley Tyas**, W Yor [signed off A629 Huddersfield—Sheffield – OS Sheet 110 map ref 165128; SE1612], *Golden Cock*: Wide range of good adventurous food, courteous professional service and smart decor – more what you'd hope for in a London hotel than a village pub; Tetleys Mild on handpump with a guest beer such as Timothy Taylors Best, good if pricy choice of wines *(Paul Lightfoot, Malcolm J Steward)*

☆ **Felixkirk**, N Yor [SE4785], *Carpenters Arms*: Comfortable 17th-c free house in picturesque little village handy for Sutton Bank, big helpings of decent food at a price, real ale, smart restaurant with own menu inc popular Sun lunch (should book), efficient service *(CIJH, F J and A Parmenter)*

Ferrensby, N Yor [A6055 N of Knaresboro; SE3761], *General Tarleton*: Wide choice of bar food, well kept beers *(Dr A and Dr A C Jackson)*

Finghall, N Yor [Akebar Park; off A684 E of Leyburn; SE1890], *Friars Head*: Attractively converted barn (was restaurant for caravan site), log fire, cosy nooks, large conservatory;

Black Sheep and other ales, good imaginative food; looks over bowling green and golf courses *(Dono and Carol Leaman)*

Flockton, W Yor [Barnsley Rd – OS Sheet 110 map ref 249153; SE2415], *George & Dragon*: Civilised old low-beamed local serving small village, very well kept with lots of brass and household bygones, well kept Stones and Worthington; sandwiches only *(Michael Butler, Paul Lightfoot)*; [Barnsley Rd; off A642 Wakefield—Huddersfield at Blacksmiths Arms – OS Sheet 110 map ref 235149], *Sun*: Welcoming newish landlord doing reasonably priced bar food in two comfortable little rooms with open fires, Stones and Worthington BB, tables outside *(Michael Butler, Paul Lightfoot)*

Follifoot, N Yor [OS Sheet 104 map ref 343524; SE3452], *Lascelles Arms*: Interesting reasonably priced food, good open fires, small and cosy lounge area, well kept Sam Smiths OB, decent wines *(Annette Moore, Chris Pearson)*

Friendly, W Yor [SE0524], *Brothers Grimm*: Well kept Tetleys, good value food at low prices *(J R Henderson)*

☆ **Galphay**, N Yor [off B6265 Ripon—Pateley Bridge; SE2573], *Galphay Inn*: Cosy dining pub, one side pine-panelled with matching solid tables and settles, adjoining larger more open area with pictures; very hospitable, good food inc speciality roasts, S&N beers on handpump, decent house wine, log fire; cl Mon evening and weekday lunchtimes *(Peter Churchill)*

☆ **Gargrave**, N Yor [A65 W of village; SD9354], *Anchor*: Popular and spacious canalside Brewers Fayre family pub with superb play area and waterside tables; good choice of decent bar food all day at least in summer, welcoming competent service, Marstons Pedigree and Whitbreads-related real ales, good wheelchair access; piped music; economically run bedrooms in modern wing *(E G Parish, Elizabeth and Anthony Watts)*

☆ **Gargrave** [Church St/Marton Rd], *Masons Arms*: Friendly well run local on Pennine Way, between river and church, well kept Whitbreads-related real ales, generous quick bar food inc vegetarian, copper-canopied log-effect gas fire dividing two open-plan areas; bowling green behind; children if well behaved *(R W Grey, Dave Braisted)*

Garsdale Head, N Yor [junction A684/B6259; nr Garsdale stn on Settle—Carlisle line – OS Sheet 98 map ref 798926; SD7992], *Moorcock*: Well kept Theakstons Best, good range of bar food, pleasant lounge bar, pool room, seats outside with views of viaduct and Settle—Carlisle railway *(Dono and Carol Leaman)*

Giggleswick, N Yor [Brackenbar Ln (A65); SD8164], *Old Station*: Handy stop on Settle bypass, huge helpings of straightforward home-made food from three-decker sandwiches up in L-shaped bar with brasses and railway prints, dining one end, locals and dominoes the other, separate no-

smoking restaurant; friendly staff, well kept John Smiths and Tetleys Mild and Bitter on handpump; bedrooms *(J L Phillips, John Allsopp)*

Gillamoor, N Yor [SE6890], *Royal Oak*: Good bar meals and sandwiches etc, comfortable uncongested bars, outstandingly clean, beams and panelling *(F M Bunbury)*

Gilling West, N Yor [just N of Richmond; NZ1804], *White Swan*: Friendly and efficient staff, Black Sheep, Tetleys and Theakstons, food (not Mon) up to huge mixed grill inc children's meals; cheap bedrooms, attractive village *(Andrew and Ruth Triggs)*

Goathland, N Yor [NZ8301], *Goathland*: Big bar, smaller lounge area and separate restaurant, well kept Camerons Bitter and Strongarm; seats out in front *(Andrew Hazeldine)*

☆ **Golcar**, W Yor [Scapegoat Hill; off A62 (or A640) up W of Huddersfield – OS Sheet 110 map ref 088163; SE0816], *Scapehouse*: Roomy and friendly, locally popular for food and for wide range of beers inc Tetleys, Theakstons Best and Timothy Taylors Landlord and Best *(Paul Lightfoot)*

Grantley, N Yor [off B6265 W of Ripon; SE2369], *Grantley Arms*: Attractive beamed stone pub in quiet Dales village, welcoming coal fires, good plain bar food running up to steaks, Tetleys and Theakstons, restaurant *(Roger Berry)*

☆ **Grassington**, N Yor [Garrs Lane; SE0064], *Black Horse*: Comfortable and friendly open-plan modern bar, very busy in summer, with generous straightforward home-cooked bar food inc children's dishes, reasonable prices, excellent service, well kept Black Sheep Bitter and Special, Tetleys and Theakstons Best and Old Peculier, darts in separate back room, open fires, sheltered terrace, small but attractive restaurant; bedrooms comfortable, well equipped and good value *(Paul J Bispham, G Olive, NT, PD, Charles Hall, Prof S Barnett, Ray Cuckow, BB)*

☆ **Grassington** [The Square], *Devonshire*: Busy and comfortable hotel under newish management, good window seats overlooking sloping village square, interesting pictures and ornaments, open fires, good range of well presented food in big well furnished dining room, good family room, friendly efficient service, McEwans 80/- and full range of Theakstons ales, tables in back garden; well appointed good value bedrooms, good breakfasts *(J R Smylie, Ray Cuckow, Jean and Douglas Troup, Andrew and Marian Ruston, Gwen and Peter Andrews, LYM)*

☆ **Great Ayton**, N Yor [High Green; off A173 – follow village signs; NZ5611], *Royal Oak*: Thoughtful service, wide range of generous good food from sandwiches to steaks and well kept Theakstons ales on handpump; friendly unpretentious bar with open fire in huge inglenook, beam-and-plank ceiling, bulgy old partly panelled stone walls, traditional furnishings inc antique settles, long dining lounge (children allowed); pleasant views of elegant village green from bay windows; bedrooms *(John Fazakerley, Geoff and Angela Jaques, LYM)*

Great Ouseburn, N Yor [SE4562], *Three Horseshoes*: Food inc well cooked and presented generous Sun lunch; nice friendly atmosphere *(Mr G Stockton)*

Greenhow Hill, N Yor [B6265 Pateley Bridge—Grassington; SE1164], *Miners Arms*: Good value food, well prepared and in generous helpings, inc good value Sun lunch; friendly and efficient service, S&N real ales, decent wines, beams and brasses, darts, fruit machine, woodburning stove and quiet piped music; children welcome; bedrooms *(Dr R M Williamson)*

☆ **Grenoside**, S Yor [Skew Hill Lane; 3 miles from M1 junction 35 – OS Sheet 110 map ref 328935; SK3394], *Cow & Calf*: Neatly converted farmhouse, three friendly connected rooms, one no smoking, high-backed settles, lots of brass and two copper pans hanging from beams, plates and pictures, butter churn, quite a wide choice of good value home-cooked weekday lunchtime bar food from sandwiches up inc children's dishes, well kept Sam Smiths OB and Museum on electric pump, tea and coffee; piped music; family room in block across walled former farmyard with picnic-table sets; splendid views over Sheffield, open all day Sat *(CMW, JJW, LYM)*

☆ **Grinton**, N Yor [B6270 W of Richmond; SE0598], *Bridge*: Unpretentious roadside inn in lovely spot opp charming church by River Swale, two bars, very friendly service, well kept Black Sheep Special, John Smiths Magnet and Theakstons, good range of good value food; attractive tables outside, front and back; bedrooms with own bathrooms; open all day *(Richard Houghton, Rhona and Peter Fear, Mr and Mrs Peter B Dowsett, Paul and Janet Waring, E G Parish, Andrew and Ruth Triggs)*

☆ **Halifax**, W Yor [Paris Gates, Boys Lane – OS Sheet 104 map ref 097241; SE0924], *Shears*: Down steep cobbled lanes among tall mill buildings, pleasantly dark unspoilt interior, warm welcome, well kept Marstons Pedigree, Timothy Taylors Landlord and unusual guest beers; very popular lunchtime for good cheap food from hot-filled sandwiches to home-made pies, curries, casseroles etc; sporting prints, local sports photographs, collection of pump clips and foreign bottles; seats out above the Hebble Brook *(Madeleine Cheung, Lee Goulding, Annette Moore, Chris Pearson)*

Halifax [New Rd, nr stn], *Pump Room*: Very popular drinking pub with up to a dozen or so changing real ales; basic, clean and friendly *(Ian Woodhead, Gayle Butterfield)*

☆ **Hampsthwaite**, N Yor [Main St; about 5 miles W of Harrogate; SE2659], *Joiners Arms*: Good atmosphere, well kept ales, reliable generous bar food from sandwiches

up *(J E Rycroft, Andrew and Marian Ruston)*

Harden, W Yor [Long Ln, off B6165; SE0838], *Golden Fleece*: Good atmosphere and warm welcome, lounge bar with local prints and plates on racks, small pool room, well kept Ruddles, Websters Green Label and Yorkshire and Worthington BB, bar food *(WAH)*

Harecroft, W Yor [B6144 Bradford—Haworth; SE0835], *Station*: Well kept Whitbreads-related ales with interesting guest beers in thriving pub, comfortable and friendly; real fires *(Bill and Lydia Ryan)*

Harewood, W Yor [SE3245], *Harewood Arms*: Busy former coaching inn opp Harewood House, three attractive, comfortable and spacious lounge bars with wide choice of good food – sandwiches and daily changing blackboard menu; friendly prompt service, well kept real ales inc Sam Smiths OB, decent wines by the glass, good friendly service; open for coffee and afternoon tea *(Janet Pickles, B M Eldridge)*

Harome, N Yor [SE6582], *Pheasant*: Lovely terrace, lawns with ducks from pond across lane; good food *(G S and A Jaques)*

☆ **Harrogate**, N Yor [31 Tower St; SE3155], *Tap & Spile*: Basic bare-boards stripped-stone decor in three clean and pleasant rooms, up to ten changing well kept and well described ales such as Big End Piston, Claydon SS, Daleside, Hambleton, Hull Mild, Mitchells and Marston Moor, helpful staff, cheap basic lunchtime bar food, newspapers to read; open all day Sat *(Mark Bradley, Derek and Sylvia Stephenson, Andrew and Marian Ruston, David Watson)*

☆ **Harrogate** [off E Parade], *Regency*: Comfortable straightforward town pub with well kept Bass and Tetleys, ad lib coffee, good service, good generous home-cooked bar food from sandwiches up *(Ian Boag)*

Harrogate [Swan Rd], *Studley*: Hotel not a pub, but worth knowing for pleasant civilised bar, good value three-course dinner, decent house wine, friendly service; bedrooms clean and comfortable *(Ray Cuckow)*

nr **Harrogate** [Burn; off A61 about 3 miles S], *Black Swan*: Big traditionally furnished country pub, wide-ranging good value menu, efficient service *(Ray Cuckow)*; [off Crag Lane, by Harlow Carr Gardens], *Harrogate Arms*: Quiet setting with tables outside and play area; wide choice of reasonably priced food (part of bar set out for eating), friendly and efficient service, choice of real ales *(Dono and Carol Leaman)*

Hawes, N Yor [High St; SD8789], *Crown*: Traditional local with a welcome for walkers, quickly served reasonably priced lunchtime bar food from good sandwiches up, well kept Theakstons Best, XB and Old Peculier on handpump, pleasant coal fires; children allowed away from bar; seats out on front cobbled forecourt *(Paul and Gail Betteley, Peter and Lynn Brueton)*; [High St], *White Hart*: Busy, friendly pub with one bar but two distinct areas; public feel around bar counter and lounge atmosphere in what is almost a separate room on left; wide choice of reasonably priced food in bar and restaurant, welcoming service, warm cosy feel; bedrooms good value *(Richard Houghton, G W Lindley)*

☆ **Hawnby**, N Yor [SE5489], *Hawnby*: Good choice of well cooked generous typical food in spotless stonebuilt inn, lovely location in village surrounded by picturesque countryside, a magnet for walkers; Vaux beers, good unhurried service, owl theme; tables in garden with country views; bedrooms well maintained *(W J E Smith, David and Margaret Bloomfield, Andrew and Ruth Triggs)*

☆ **Haworth**, W Yor [Main St; SE0337], *Fleece*: Small partly panelled rooms, not too touristy, with flagstones, some carpeting, plants in pots and hanging baskets, well kept Timothy Taylors ales on handpump, open fires, tasty reasonably priced food most lunchtimes, friendly staff; maybe piped disco/pop music *(Myke and Nicky Crombleholme, Paul Lightfoot)*

☆ **Haworth** [Sun St], *Old Hall*: Friendly and atmospheric 16th-c beamed and panelled building with several rooms, good value generous lunches in bar and restaurant, good service, well kept Bass, Stones and Tetleys, inoffensive piped music; five mins from centre, open all day Fri, Sat; bedrooms *(Anthony Bayes)*

Haworth [West Lane], *Old White Lion*: Very good value food esp home-made pâté and light game pie *(R MacDonald)*; [Main St], *White Lion*: Good restaurant food; bedrooms fine - if some a bit small *(Paul McPherson)*

Hebden Bridge, W Yor [Pecket Well; A6033 out towards Keighley; SD9928], *Robin Hood*: Four beautifully decorated, clean rooms with red wall seats and small polished tables, toby jugs, nice views; friendly landlord, fast service, good fairly priced food; nice views; bedrooms *(M E A Horler)*

☆ **Helmsley**, N Yor [Market Plq; SE6184], *Crown*: Wide choice of good value bar food esp roast beef and Yorkshire pudding, also good afternoon teas, in warm and friendly beamed front bar opening into bigger central dining bar; gracious service, nice unpretentious atmosphere, good choice of well kept beers, roaring fires, tables in sheltered garden behind with conservatory area; bedrooms pleasant *(H Bramwell, BB)*

☆ **Helmsley** [Market Pl], *Black Swan*: Smart Forte hotel, not a pub, but does have real ale in beamed and panelled bar with attractive carved oak settles and Windsor armchairs, cosy and comfortable lounges with a good deal of character, and charming sheltered garden; good place to stay - expensive, but comfortable and individual *(T Nott, BB)*

☆ **Helperby**, N Yor [SE4470], *Farmers*: Very friendly and unspoilt local with pine country furniture, good value food, small restaurant, Theakstons Best, XB and Old Peculier,

comfortable games room with fruit machine and darts, tables in garden; bedrooms *(Andrew and Ruth Triggs)*

Hemingbrough, N Yor [School Lane; SE6730], *Hemingbrough Hall*: Set in picturesque seven-acre grounds, friendly hotel with well kept varied beers, wide range of good restaurant dishes; comfortable bedrooms *(Stewart Awde)*

Heptonstall, W Yor [46 Towngate - OS Sheet 103 map ref 981287; SD9828], *Cross*: Pleasant three-roomed pub dating from early 17th-c, in ancient village up fearsomely steep cobbled lanes above Hebden Bridge; friendly chatty landlord, two big friendly dogs, quite a wide choice of good value freshly prepared straightforward food (maybe not winter weekday lunchtimes), well kept Timothy Taylors Best, Golden Best and Landlord on handpump, real fire, quiet piped music, fruit machine; furnishings oddly reminiscent of airport departure lounges, very low tables *(CMW, JJW, Paul Lightfoot)*

☆ **Hepworth**, W Yor [38 Towngate; off A616 SE of Holmfirth - OS Sheet 110 map ref 163069; SE1606], *Butchers Arms*: Good friendly feel in L-shaped bar with stone and partly panelled walls, open fire, Boddingtons, Tetleys and Timothy Taylors Landlord on handpump, bar food, evening restaurant; pool and darts at one end; open all day Fri/Sat *(Paul Lightfoot)*

☆ **High Hoyland**, S Yor [Bank End Lane - OS Sheet 110 map ref 273101; SE2710], *Cherry Tree*: Clean and attractive stone-built village pub, bar food, well kept John Smiths, friendly staff, small popular restaurant (best to book, esp Sun lunch); lovely views from front *(Michael Butler)*

☆ **Holme**, W Yor [SE1006], *Fleece*: Very welcoming landlord, efficient staff, plenty of locals and accents from all around the country and world - tucked in the hill below Home Moss TV mast, great walks; cosy pleasant rooms (inc one for pool and darts), lots of lifeboat memorabilia, well kept Tetleys, Theakstons and Youngers, freshly cooked decent pub food, quiet piped music *(Paul Lightfoot, Bill Sykes)*

☆ **Holmfirth**, W Yor [Victoria Sq; aka Rose & Crown - OS Sheet 110 map ref 143082; SD1408], *Nook*: Character local down by the stream, seats outside; flooring tiles, low beams and basic furnishings, friendly atmosphere, Timothy Taylors and many other well kept ales, fruit machine, video game *(Paul Lightfoot, Rupert Lecomber)*

Holmfirth [3 Victoria Sq], *Karbowskis*: New café/bar with good mix of customers and good reasonably priced food *(Janet Lee)*; *Old Bridge*: Friendly staff, comfortable surroundings, huge range of food; bedrooms *(Paul Cartledge)*; [134 Huddersfield Rd], *Post Card*: Comfortable friendly and obliging Victorian-style pub handy for the Bamforth postcard museum, well kept beers, popular good value food inc cheap Sun lunch, quiet piped music, two fruit machines *(CW, JW)*; [A6024], *Victoria*: Roadside pub with rooms off small entrance bar, popular food (huge mixed grill), Tetleys and Timothy Taylors Best (Andrew and Ruth Triggs)

Holywell Green, W Yor [just off M62; SE0820], Rock: Comfortably refurbished in Victorian style, with cosy bar areas, conservatory, good reasonably priced beers on handpump, decent bar food, open fire; bedrooms (Jim Cowell)

☆ Honley, W Yor [SE1312], Jacobs Well: Good value bar food with some imaginative dishes, good range of well kept beers inc Tetleys and Thwaites, decent whiskies and wines; friendly atmosphere, pleasant surroundings (J L Phillips, Stephen and Brenda Head)

Horton in Ribblesdale, N Yor [SD8172], Golden Lion: Fairly spacious village pub with generous well served bar food (G W Lindley)

☆ Hovingham, N Yor [SE6775], Worsley Arms: Good value well prepared food, interesting choice esp for vegetarians, in friendly and welcoming back bar comfortably furnished for eating, well kept John Smiths, Malton Double Chance, Tetleys and Theakstons Mild, good coffee, lots of Yorkshire cricketer photographs esp from 1930s and 40s; nice tables out by stream; pleasant bedrooms (F J and P Parmenter, BB)

Hovingham, Malt Shovel: Friendly two-roomed pub, good food with more adventurous evening menu, nice decor, good old-fashioned dining tables, well kept beers (Steve and Julie Cocking)

Hoyland Common, S Yor [nr M1 junction 36; SE3500], Hare & Hounds: Well kept John Smiths beers, good value house wine, relaxed and cosy atmosphere, spotlessly clean, friendly helpful staff, consistently good food (Cathy Scott, Richard Baker)

Hoyland Swaine, S Yor [Barnsley Rd (A628); SE2605], Lord Nelson: Brewers Fayre pub with lovely views, Whitbreads beers, useful food, braille menu; high chairs, lively indoor play area (CW, JW)

Huby, N Yor [the one nr Easingwold; SE5766], New Inn: Pub of the old type with RAF background, four bars, Theakstons Best and Old Peculier, obliging staff, fairly priced tasty bar meals, soft piped music, domino and darts teams (G and M Armstrong)

☆ Huddersfield, W Yor [Crosland Moor; SE1115], Sands House: The licensees, cheery staff and good value cook who made the Bulls Head at Linthwaite a popular main entry are now to be found here; Boddingtons and other ales on handpump in oblong bar with lots of woodwork and all sorts of disputaceous clocks and watches, wide choice of good value food, downstairs dining room (Malcolm J Steward, H K Dyson, Andrew and Ruth Triggs)

☆ Huddersfield [Chapel Hill, just outside ring rd – OS Sheet 110 map ref 143162], Rat & Ratchet: Very wide range of well kept ales inc Marstons Pedigree, Smiles, Timothy

Taylors Landlord and Best and lots of changing guest beers, bare boards in bar and adjoining room, two more comfortable rooms up steps, basic well cooked cheap bar food inc Weds curry night (Paul Lightfoot, Tony and Wendy Hobden, David Whitehead)

Huddersfield [Colne Bridge; B6118 off A62 NE – OS Sheet 110 map ref 178201], Royal & Ancient: Spacious, comfortable and popular, with log fires, good range of good imaginative bar food (A Preston); [1 Halifax Old Rd], Slubbers Arms: Warmly welcoming landlord in friendly V-shaped pub with good range of simple food (no chips), excellently kept Marstons Pedigree, Timothy Taylor Landlord and a guest beer, a dozen good malt whiskies (Andy and Jill Kassube, Andrew and Ruth Triggs)

Hunmanby, N Yor [TA0977], Royal Oak: Welcoming staff, roomy well furnished open-plan bar areas with stripped pews and cushioned stools, good reasonably priced snacks and cooked meals; John Smiths beers (Brian and Jill Bond)

☆ Hutton le Hole, N Yor [SE7090], Crown: Very wide choice of good if not cheap food from sandwiches up, well kept Tetleys, lots of whisky-water jugs, quick service, busy friendly atmosphere; children welcome; small pretty village with wandering sheep (Kim Schofield, I McCaskey, D M Kirke-Smith)

☆ Ilkley, W Yor [Stockel Rd/Stourton Rd; off Leeds—Skipton rd; SE1147], Ilkley Moor Vaults: Tastefully furnished lounge and public bars, well kept Tetleys and Timothy Taylors, good reasonably priced food, good atmosphere and service even when packed; games room upstairs, pleasant seats outside; aka The Taps (Prof S Barnett)

Ilkley [nr Old Bridge], Riverside: Good position by River Wharfe with pleasant outside area; well kept Sam Smiths (Gordon Smith); [Ben Rhydding; SE1347], Wheatley Arms: Pleasant family atmosphere under new landlord, high chairs, decent food, well kept Tetleys, efficient service; nice location (Jackie Davies)

☆ Ingbirchworth, S Yor [Welthorne Lane; off A629 Shepley—Penistone; SE2205], Fountain: Neat and cosy pub with comfortable family room, red plush banquettes in spacious turkey-carpeted lounge, quite snug front bar, open fires; generous bar food inc exotic salads and superb puddings, well kept Tetleys on handpump, well reproduced pop music, friendly service, tables in sizeable garden overlooking reservoir (Peter and Carolyn Clark, BB)

☆ Ingleby Cross, N Yor [NZ4501], Blue Bell: Cosy and friendly country local handy for coast-to-coast walk, well kept John Smiths and Theakstons Best, wide choice of good value often interesting bar food from sandwiches to steaks; simple but good bedrooms in converted barn (Dr Keith Bloomfield, David Varney)

Ingleby Greenhow, N Yor [NZ5806], *Dudley Arms*: Village pub with good food and real ale, friendly service *(K Flack)*
Ingleton, N Yor [SD6973], *Craven Heifer*: Long building divided into two by bar, wide choice of bar food inc snacks such as pizza and steak in a bun, Thwaites beer, games room *(M and J Back)*
nr **Ingleton**, N Yor [Low Bentham; SD6469], *Sundial*: Small village pub, popular with local holidaymakers; generous bar food *(Jenni Mitchell-Gibbs)*
☆ **Jackson Bridge**, W Yor [Scholes Rd; signed off A616; SE1607], *White Horse*: Low-ceilinged small-roomed pub with blue plush wall seats and dining chairs, simple home-cooked early lunches, well kept Bass and Stones, coffee from 9am, friendly landlord, *Last of the Summer Wine* photographs (front of pub used in series), pool room looking out on to charming waterfall and ducks behind *(Paul Lightfoot)*
☆ **Kettlesing**, N Yor [signed off A59 W of Harrogate; SE2256], *Queens Head*: Well run dining pub, popular weekday lunchtimes with older people, lots of quite close-set tables, good food; well kept Theakstons Best and XB, Youngers Scotch, decent wines, quick friendly service, unobtrusive piped music, attractive and interesting decorations *(J E Rycroft, Prof S Barnett, BB)*
Kettlewell, N Yor [SD9772], *Bluebell*: Roomy simply furnished knocked-through local with snug areas and flagstones, well kept beers (mainly S&N), reasonably priced straightforward food; pool room, piped music, children's room, tables on good-sized back terrace; well placed for Upper Wharfedale walks; bedrooms *(Gwen and Peter Andrews, Peter Churchill, BB)*; *Kings Head*: Character old local away from the tourist centre, changing well kept ales such as Black Sheep, Boddingtons and Youngs, good value food; pool room, bedrooms *(A Barker, John Cadman, Bill and Lydia Ryan, BB)*; *Racehorses*: Extensively refurbished in 1994, comfortable and civilised, with good value food well prepared and presented, Black Sheep, John Smiths and Theakstons on handpump, good choice of wines, log fires, professional service; well placed for Wharfedale walks; bedrooms good, with own bathrooms *(Geoff and Angela Jaques, A Barker, Bill and Lydia Ryan, Peter Churchill, BB)*
☆ **Kilburn**, N Yor [SE5179], *Forresters Arms*: Welcoming dim-lit two-level bar furnished in 'mouseman' Thompson oak furniture from next-door workshops (there's now a visitor centre opposite), big log fire, varied bar food from sandwiches to steaks, well kept Black Sheep and Theakstons Best, games and piped music; restaurant, well behaved children allowed, open all day; suntrap seats out in front; bedrooms clean, cheerful and bright *(Graham Bassett, Ian Boag, David Logan, Andrew and Ruth Triggs, Jim Farmer, Paul and Margaret Baker, Mrs R Humphrey, LYM)*

Killinghall, N Yor [SE3059], *Greyhound*: Newish landlord doing good hot well presented food in clean pub with comfortable banquettes, well kept Sam Smiths, friendly staff *(Mrs D Harrison, Andrew and Marian Ruston)*
☆ **Kilnsey**, N Yor [Kilnsey Crag; SD9767], *Tennant Arms*: Reliable, clean and pleasant pub in nice spot over road from River Wharfe, views over spectacular Kilnsey Crag from restaurant; open fires, Tetleys and Theakstons Best and Old Peculier, decent bar food, good service, piped music; weapon collection, maps and stuffed or skeleton animals and fish; good walks; comfortable bedrooms all with private bathrooms *(Andy and Julie Hawkins, D Stokes, Drs N R and A de Gay)*
☆ **Kirkby Malham**, N Yor [SD8961], *Victoria*: Pleasantly understated Victorian decor in down-to-earth real pub with good value generous food, friendly service, well kept Theakstons, juke box or piped music; lovely village with interesting church, quieter spot than nearby Malham though busy with walkers at lunchtime; bedrooms *(A N Rose, Prof S Barnett, Andrew McKeand)*
Kirkby Malzeard, N Yor [Galphay Moor; Pateley Bridge rd – OS Sheet 99 map ref 210720; SE2172], *Drovers*: Small and unpretentious with pleasant landlord and decent food – welcome oasis on edge of lonely moorland *(Roger Berry)*
☆ **Kirkby Overblow**, N Yor [SE3249], *Shoulder of Mutton*: Charming old pub with attractive layout, interesting decor, two log fires and tables in lovely garden with play area by meadows; after inspection was to have been promoted to the main entries, but popular landlord leaving just as this edition went to press; we hope his successor will keep up the wide choice of good reasonably priced home-cooked food, well kept Tetleys and other real ales, and better-than-average choice of wines by the glass; bedrooms *(Andrew and Marian Ruston, Annette Moore, Chris Pearson, Mark Bradley, C J Westmoreland, David Watson, BB)*
Kirkby Overblow, N Yor, *Star & Garter*: Cosy welcoming local with generous good value standard bar food, dining room for evening meals; well kept Camerons and Everards *(Margaret Watson, Michael and Merle Lipton)*
Kirkbymoorside, N Yor [SE6987], *Royal Oak*: Long low room with two real fires – very cosy and popular *(A and M Dickinson)*
Knaresborough, N Yor [by Beech Avenue, at Low Bridge end of riverside Long Walk; SE3557], *Mother Shipton*: Beams, antique furnishings inc 16th-c oak table, good low-priced food inc good sandwiches, efficient service, well kept beers; big terrace overlooking river *(Miss B Mattocks, Noel and Mo Turnbohm)*
Langdale End, N Yor [off A170 at East Ayton; or A171 via Hackness OS Sheet 101 map ref 938913; SE9491], *Moorcock*: Simple moorland village pub, refurbished

after long closure; traditional old-fashioned atmosphere, well kept beer *(Mark Whitmore, BB)*

☆ **Langsett**, S Yor [A616 nr Penistone; SE2100], *Waggon & Horses*: Spotlessly clean and comfortable stone pub in lovely moorland setting, pleasant helpful staff, blazing log fire, good plain home cooking inc popular Sun lunch, well kept Bass and Stones; fairly roomy but bar itself small, so service can slow when busy *(P Corris, Michael A Butler, Cynthia Waller)*

☆ **Langthwaite**, N Yor [just off Reeth—Brough rd; NZ0003], *Red Lion*: Lovely Arkengarthdale setting for unspoilt and relaxing village pub, spick and span, interesting and idiosyncratic, with local books and maps, basic cheap nourishing lunchtime food, Black Sheep, Theakstons XB and Youngers Scotch, country wines, tea and coffee; well behaved children allowed lunchtime in very low-ceilinged side snug, quietly friendly service; good walks all around, inc organised circular ones from the pub *(D T Taylor, Ray and Liz Monk, Andrew and Ruth Triggs, Peter Churchill, LYM)*

☆ **Lealholm**, N Yor [NZ7608], *Board*: Lounge with big log fire favoured by Billy the monster pub cat, good range of food inc big filled Yorkshire puddings and good puddings, Camerons real ale, riverside garden; nice spot *(Mike and Maggie Betton, Geoff and Angela Jaques)*

☆ **Leeds** [Gt George St], *Victoria*: Well preserved ornate Victorian pub with grand etched mirrors, impressive lampstands extending from the ornately solid bar; well kept Tetleys inc Mild, friendly smart bar staff, interesting mix of customers, reasonably priced food from end serving hatch *(Reg Nelson)*

☆ **Leeds** [Hunslet Rd], *Adelphi*: Well restored handsome Edwardian tiling, woodwork and glass, several rooms, impressive stairway; particularly well kept Tetleys (virtually the brewery tap), good cheap lunchtime bar food at reasonable prices, live jazz Sat *(Eric Robinson, Reg Nelson, C J Westmoreland)*

☆ **Leeds** [9 Burley Rd, junction with Rutland St], *Fox & Newt*: One of the first pubs to switch to the cheery neo-Victorian style of bright paintwork, dark wood and bare floorboards which has since become quite common; interesting choice of mainly Whitbreads-related ales as well as several brewed in the cellar here, good value limited standard lunchtime food, good interesting mix of customers, well reproduced piped music; open all day, children welcome, dogs allowed evening *(Thomas Nott, Roger A Bellingham, LYM)*

☆ **Leeds** [North St (A61)], *Eagle*: Well kept Timothy Taylors ales and several guest beers usually from distant smaller breweries in 18th-c pub with choice of basic or plush bars, helpful staff, photographs of old Leeds; pleasant for lunch, good bands in back bar weekends; bedrooms *(Miss B Mattocks, Dr I Pocsik, N Haslewood, LYM)*

☆ **Leeds** [Headrow, Kirkgate, by indoor mkt], *Duck & Drake*: BB basic two-bar pub notable for its dozen or more well kept and reasonably priced real ales well served by knowledgeable staff; bustling friendly atmosphere, limited range of good value bar food, open fire; loud live music Sun, Tues and Thurs nights, quieter back room *(Mark Bradley)*

☆ **Leeds** [86 Armley Rd, by Arkwright St], *Albion*: The original for the 00-gauge model railway pub, three well restored interesting rooms, separate pool room, well kept Boddingtons and Tetleys from superb brass handpumps, friendly staff, good service, wide range of filling snacks *(Eric Robinson)* **Leeds** [Great George St], *George*: Fine unspoilt and un-refurbished pub *(Reg Nelson)*; [Otley Rd, Headingley; SE2836], *Three Horseshoes*: Handsome pub with lots of hanging baskets, good choice of typical bar food inc good vegetarian specials, well kept beer; busy evenings *(Simon and Louise Chappell)*; [Otley Rd; 3 miles from centre, past university], *Woodies*: Regularly changing well kept real ales, busy friendly atmosphere, bare boards, wooden seats *(M J Murphy)*; [New Briggate], *Wrens*: Relaxing bar, daily papers, great chip butties *(Paul Cartledge)*

☆ **Leyburn**, N Yor [Market Pl; SE1191], *Golden Lion*: Relaxing rather genteel bay-windowed two-room bar with light squared panelling, armchairs, china on delft shelf; pale country tables and chairs in airy eating area with log-effect gas fire, good value generous straightforward bar food, evening restaurant; good beer brewed to their own recipe in Harrogate as well as Theakstons, decent coffee, friendly service, tables out in front; open all day, dogs allowed; bedrooms good value *(M J Morgan, BB)*

☆ **Linthwaite**, W Yor [31 Blackmoorfoot – off A62 Huddersfield—Marsden opp Coach & Horses; SE1014], *Bulls Head*: Cheerful extended two-roomed local which has had its ups and downs in the last couple of years, but doing well under current management, with good reasonably priced simple food esp Yorkshire pudding sandwich, well kept Boddingtons Mild and Bitter, Marstons Pedigree and guests such as Theakstons Old Peculier and XB, good service, piped music can be a bit loud; children very welcome, open all day weekdays *(Geoffrey and Brenda Wilson, Paul Lightfoot, Mark Bradley, Catheryn and Richard Hicks, Bill and Lydia Ryan, H K Dyson, Andrew and Ruth Triggs, WAH, Ann and Bob Westbrook, LYM)*

☆ **Linton**, W Yor [Main St; SE3947], *Windmill*: Good country atmosphere in carefully preserved small rooms with pewter tankards for the locals, polished antique settles, oak beams, longcase clock; generous helpings of good bar food (not Mon or Sun evening), well kept Theakstons Best and XB and Youngers Scotch, friendly staff; tables in pleasant garden, car park through interesting coaching entrance *(Mark Bradley, C M F Harrison, C J Westmoreland, J E Rycroft, LYM)*

Little Crakehall, N Yor [A684 2 miles NW of Bedale; SE2490], *Bay Horse*: Nice spot on village green, cheap imaginative bar food, good house wines, Black Sheep Bitter *(Frank Davidson)*

Long Marston, N Yor [B1224 Wetherby—Rufford; SE5051], *Sun*: Cheap Sam Smiths, good straightforward food, friendly staff, log fire; garden with play area *(Phil and Anne Smithson)*

☆ **Long Preston**, N Yor [A65 Settle—Skipton; SD8358], *Maypole*: Dining pub with spacious beamed dining room and comfortable lounge with copper-topped tables, stag's head, open fire; big helpings of good value food inc Sun lunch, well kept Timothy Taylors Landlord and Whitbreads-related real ales, very helpful service; bedrooms *(P Corris, Greenwood and Turner, P G Clissett)*

Lothersdale, N Yor [Dale End; SD9646], *Hare & Hounds*: Comfortable and welcoming village pub nicely off the beaten track, one of the few exactly on the Pennine Way; John Smiths and Tetleys, good prompt lunchtime food at competitive prices; quiet midweek, busy with families weekends *(A Preston, G W Lindley)*

☆ **Low Row**, N Yor [B6270 Reeth—Muker; SD9897], *Punch Bowl*: Useful youth-hostelish family bar, open all day in summer, with several well kept S&N beers and rows of malt whiskies, wide choice of good value food, efficient service, log fire, games room, lots of caving photographs; fine Swaledale views; tea shop 10-5.30 with home-made cakes, small shop, bicycle and cave lamp hire, folk music Fri; basic bedrooms, also bunkhouse *(Mark Bradley)*

Lower Dunsforth, N Yor [SE4465], *Angler*: Well kept Theakstons Bitter and XB and Websters Yorkshire, friendly staff, good food from good menu inc several vegetarian dishes and delicious puddings; modern building *(J L Cox)*

Luddenden Foot, W Yor [Burnley Rd (A646) – OS Sheet 104 map ref 038252; SE0325], *Coach & Horses*: Big comfortable open bar with friendly landlord, good standard reasonably priced food, wide range of ales inc Timothy Taylors and Theakstons, two bay-windowed alcoves, mature customers, occasional organist *(Paul Lightfoot, L G Milligan)*

☆ **Malham**, N Yor [SD8963], *Lister Arms*: Friendly and relaxed open-plan lounge with good reasonably priced bar food, well kept real ales inc Caledonian and Timothy Taylors, helpful staff, restaurant, games area with pool; seats outside the substantial stone inn overlooking green, more in back garden – nice spot by river, ideal for walkers; bedrooms *(Greenwood and Turner, Prof S Barnett, Mary Moore, Paul McPherson, Drs N R and A de Gay, R E and M Baggs)*

Malham, *Buck*: Large hikers' bar and

comfortable lounge bar with good range of attractively presented generous food, well kept Black Sheep; bedrooms *(C J Parsons, Steve Webb, Marianne Lantree)*

Malton, N Yor [SE7972], *Coach & Horses*: Cosy village atmosphere with brasses and nick-nacks, huge Yorkshire puddings, delicious home-made soup *(A and M Dickinson)*; [Commercial St, Norton], *Cornucopia*: Well run dining pub with good food in big helpings well served by friendly staff *(David Watson)*; [Old Malton], *Royal Oak*: Very friendly helpful service, good guest beers, good generous quickly served standard food inc Whitby seafood platter; tables in garden, children welcome *(Dr Philip Jackson, K J Hillier)*

Marr, S Yor [Barnsley Rd; A635 a mile W of A1(M); SE5105], *Marr Lodge*: Interesting collection of malt whiskies, well kept Courage-related ales and a guest beer, bar food inc old favourites and some imaginative dishes; now run by landlord of the Cadeby Inn (see main entries); open all day from 8am, so very useful A1 break *(Anon)*

☆ **Marton cum Grafton**, N Yor [signed off A1 3 miles N of A59; SE4263], *Olde Punch Bowl*: Attractive old pub with comfortable and roomy heavy-beamed open-plan bar, open fires, brasses, framed old advertisements and photographs; Tetleys and Youngers Scotch and No 3, decent wines, magazines to read, good bar food, no piped music, welcoming service, restaurant; picnic-table sets in garden, space for caravans; children welcome *(JJW, CMW, LYM)*

☆ **Masham**, N Yor [Silver St, linking A6168 with Market Sq; SE2381], *Bay Horse*: Good range of good value straightforward bar food, friendly staff, Black Sheep and Theakstons ales – both produced in this village; children allowed *(Andrew and Marian Ruston, Richard Houghton)*

Meltham, W Yor [A635; SE0910], *Ford*: Recently refurbished pub on edge of moors, long bar with old-fashioned fireplace at one end, comfortable settees and armchairs, Timothy Taylors Landlord and Wards, upstairs restaurant; big picture windows with views towards Holme Moss *(Andrew and Ruth Triggs)*

☆ **Middleham**, N Yor [SE1288], *Black Swan*: Very welcoming cheerfully civilised local atmosphere in heavy-beamed stripped-stone bar with very sturdy furniture inc high-backed settles built in by big stone fireplace, good attentive service, wide choice of reasonably priced filling and tasty bar food, well kept John Smiths, Theakstons Best, XB and Old Peculier; maybe piped pop music; separate dining room, tables on cobbles outside and in sheltered back garden; charming village in good walking country; bedrooms comfortable, clean and spacious, with own bathrooms *(Paul and Gail Betteley, Gordon Theaker, Philip da Silva, Michael A Butler, D Grzelka, Jim Paul, LYM)*

Middleham [Market Pl], *White Swan*: Very

good value food inc original vegetarian dishes and good choice of puddings, efficient friendly service, homely little dining room; bedrooms *(F and S Barnes)*

☆ nr **Midgley**, W Yor [signed from Hebden Br, with evening/Sun bus to pub; coming from Halifax on A646 turn right just before Hebden Bridge town centre on to A6033 towards Keighley, take first right up steep Birchcliffe Rd and keep on to the top – OS Sheet 104 map ref 007272; SE0027], *Mount Skip*: Wonderful spot by Calderdale Way footpath, spectacular views of Pennines and mill-town valleys (at night the necklaces of streetlamps far below look like the view from an aeroplane); very welcoming staff, well kept Tetleys and Timothy Taylors Bitter, Landlord and Golden Best, good log fire, lots of prints and old photographs, china and brasses, generous cheap food inc two sizes for children; games area, unobtrusive piped music, restaurant, benches outside; children allowed (not late); cl Mon lunchtime Oct–Easter, Tues lunchtime Jan–Easter *(Mark Bradley, C A Hall, Bruce Bird, LYM)*

Midhopestones, S Yor [off A616; SK2399], *Midhopestones Arms*: Character 17th-c stonebuilt pub, flagstones and stripped pine, three small rooms, woodburner, pictures, assorted chairs, tables and settles; eight well kept ales inc Courage-related ones, Timothy Taylors and Wards, friendly staff, log fires, bar food (not Sun evening) inc imaginative puddings, breakfasts; restaurant, seats outside; children welcome *(CMW, JJW, John B Dickinson)*

Mirfield, W Yor [105 Leeds Rd (A62); Mirfield Moor; SE2019], *White Gate*: Very popular with older people, Bass and Timothy Taylors Landlord, cheap food from plain but substantial menu, friendly staff; comfortably renovated in modern olde-worlde style *(Andrew and Ruth Triggs)*

Mytholmroyd, W Yor [Cragg Vale; SE0126], *Hinchcliffe Arms*: Remote old stonebuilt country pub on road that leads only to a reservoir, very popular with walkers, plenty of character, good value food in bar and restaurant inc carvery, S&N beers *(M L Clarke, Graham Reeve)*

Nether Silton, N Yor [SE4692], *Gold Cup*: Good food in bar and attached restaurant, Theakstons ales, pine decor, friendly service; lovely quiet village *(Andrew and Ruth Triggs)*

New Mill, W Yor [Penistone Rd (A635) – OS Sheet 110 map ref 180086; SE1808], *Crossroads*: Attractive roadside pub with bar area, family room and restaurant; efficient staff, Mansfield Riding and Old Bailey, good value bar food from hot beef sandwich up Tues-Sun, open fire in bar, kitchen range in smaller room leading off, adjoining restaurant; nice garden with country views; closed Mon *(Paul Lightfoot, Andrew and Ruth Triggs)*

Northallerton, N Yor [High St; SE3794], *Golden Lion*: Pleasant bar in Forte ex-coaching inn, good bar food in attractive eating area, well kept Hambleton Bitter; bedrooms *(Roger Bellingham)*

☆ **Nosterfield**, N Yor [B6267 Masham—Thirsk; SE2881], *Freemasons Arms*: Recently reopened under new owners, quite smart but warm and friendly beamed open-plan bar and dining area with central log fire, flagstones, bric-a-brac, well kept Black Sheep and Theakstons, decent wines, promising food; tables outside, very pleasant surroundings; children welcome *(Martin and Tracy Land, Mrs B J Head, Andrew and Kathleen Bacon)*

Nun Monkton, N Yor [off A59 York—Harrogate; SE5058], *Alice Hawthorn*: Modernised beamed bar with dark red plush settles back-to-back around dimpled copper tables, good value food, friendly service, open fire in big brick fireplace, darts; on broad village green with pond, nr River Nidd *(T A Bryan, BB)*

☆ **Oakworth**, W Yor [Harehills Lane, Oldfield; 2 miles towards Colne; SE0038], *Grouse*: Comfortable and interesting old pub packed with bric-a-brac, gleaming copper, lots of prints and pottery, attractively individual furnishings; good home-made lunchtime soup, sandwiches and home-roast salads (not Mon), charming evening restaurant, well kept Timothy Taylors, good range of spirits, entertaining landlord, excellent service, good Pennine views *(A and M Dickinson, WAH)*

Oldstead, N Yor [SE5380], *Black Swan*: Unpretentious inn in beautiful surroundings with pretty valley views from two big bay windows and picnic-table sets outside; reasonably priced good food, well kept Theakstons; service may sometimes suffer at busy times; children welcome; bedrooms in comfortable modern back extension *(Andrew and Ruth Triggs, BB)*

☆ **Osmotherley**, N Yor [SE4499], *Three Tuns*: Largely original layout with attractive coal fire in front lounge, clean and tidy simple bar, interesting choice of fresh-cooked food worth the wait in popular back dining room, excellent bread and real cheeses from small producers (though little else for vegetarians), friendly landlord, smart staff, well kept S&N ales; pleasant tables outside; children welcome; bedrooms *(Thomas Nott, Paul Williams, GSJ, AJ, Roger Berry, J N Child, RB)*

☆ **Osmotherley** [The Green], *Golden Lion*: Friendly family service, wide range of good bar food inc good puddings, well kept John Smiths Magnet, decent coffee, tables out overlooking village green; 44-mile Lyke Wake Walk starts here; may be closed Mon lunchtime *(Geoff and Angela Jaques)*

Ossett, W Yor [Low Mill Rd/Healey Lane – OS Sheet 104 map ref 271191; SE2719], *Brewers Pride*: Friendly basic local of character, wide range of constantly changing real ales, cosy front room and bar both with open fires, small games room, tasty reasonably priced bar food, big back garden with local entertainment summer weekends; open all day Fri/Sat *(Mark Bradley)*; [Spa St], *Fleece*: Increasingly popular, with strong local following, well kept Tetleys, good tap room, cheap food; country & western nights Thurs *(Michael Butler)*; [Manor Rd], *Victoria*: Roadside pub with surprising variety of reasonably priced food, game casserole, swordfish, lobster, carvery Sun; wide range of changing beers inc Greene King Abbot, Marstons and Tetleys; cl Mon-Thurs lunchtime *(Michael Butler)*

☆ **Oswaldkirk**, N Yor [signed off B1363/B1257 S of Helmsley; SE6279], *Malt Shovel*: Distinctive former 17th-c small manor house, heavy beams and flagstones, fine staircase, simple traditional furnishings, huge log fires, two cosy bars (one may be crowded with well heeled locals), family room, interestingly decorated dining room; well kept Sam Smiths OB and Museum, good simple well presented food (maybe not Mon/Tues, and may sometimes stop before 2) using good fresh ingredients, interesting garden; children may be allowed; no longer do bedrooms *(Dr J Johnson, M and J Back, LYM)*

Otley, W Yor [Main St; SE2045], *Fleece*: Pleasant market-town pub with goat and geese in garden, good lunchtime food inc wide choice of filled Yorkshire puddings, Theakstons and Tetleys on handpump *(Andy and Jill Kassube)*; [Bondgate], *Junction*: Warm and welcoming old-fashioned beamed pub with single small bar, bare floorboards, wall benches, open fire, well kept Tetleys, Theakstons XB and Old Peculier, Timothy Taylors Landlord and Best, interesting curios *(Mark Bradley, Reg Nelson)*

Outlane, W Yor [A640; SE0717], *Nonts Sarahs*: Redecorated moorland pub with Tetleys and Theakstons ales, big helpings of good meals; good views; children's room full of toys *(Andrew and Ruth Triggs)*

Overton, W Yor [204 Old Rd; off A642 Huddersfield—Wakefield; SE2617], *Reindeer*: Next to Mining Museum, increasing concentration on good value bar food; good service, Tetleys real ale, quiz nights *(Ann and Bob Westbrook, T F Wendon)*

☆ **Oxenhope**, W Yor [A6033 Keighley—Hebden Bridge; SE0335], *Waggon & Horses*: Warmly welcoming stripped-stone moorside pub with good views, good range of generous food till late evening, Tetleys and Theakstons, open fires, pleasant simple decor, cheerful service, separate dining room; children welcome *(A Preston, WAH, LYM)*

☆ **Oxenhope** [off B6141 towards Denholme], *Dog & Gun*: Well kept Timothy Taylors Landlord and Best in roomy bar with mock beams, coppers, brasses and delft racks of plates and jugs, open fire at each end, padded settles and stools, a couple of smaller rooms; warm and comfortable welcome; usual bar food from sandwiches up – service can slow when busy at lunchtime; bistro-

style restaurant, nice views *(WAH, J E Rycroft)*

Oxenhope [Denholme Rd, Lower Town], *Lamb*: Clean, tidy, light and modern-feeling, with well kept Timothy Taylors Best, Vaux Bitter and Samson and Websters Green Label, friendly welcome, good cheap bar food, open fires in small bar and second room; live band Weds, folk music Thurs; good views *(Charles Hall, Geoff and Angela Jaques)*

☆ **nr Pateley Bridge**, N Yor [Fellbeck; B6265, 3 miles E; SE2066], *Half Moon*: Cosy easy chairs around central woodburner, plush button-back banquettes, light wood chairs, low tables and spaciously airy decor; generous helpings of good quick bar food, well kept Timothy Taylors Landlord and S&N beers, welcoming staff, golden labrador called Maurice; piped music; children welcome; bedrooms in chalets; open all day, handy for Brimham Rocks; bedrooms *(Jeff Davies, Roger Berry, WAH, LYM)*

☆ **nr Pateley Bridge** [Nidderdale rd N – OS Sheet 99 map ref 148665], *Water Mill*: Generous helpings of good value straightforward food in roomy bar and eating areas of converted flax mill with one of the largest waterwheels in England, still working; well kept Marstons Old Peculier, Theakstons XB and Youngers Scotch, friendly efficient staff; open all day, inc for tea and coffee; picnic-table sets in big garden with good play area; bedrooms *(Lawrence Pearse)*

Patrick Brompton, N Yor [SE2291], *Green Tree*: Old stone pub with good friendly atmosphere, well kept Black Sheep, Hambleton and Theakstons beers, wide choice of good reasonably priced food; public bar, separate dining lounge with waitress service *(P A Shewry)*

☆ **Pecket Well**, W Yor [A6033 N of Hebden Bridge; SD9929], *Robin Hood*: Warmly welcoming extrovert landlord and locals, genuine home cooking, well kept Tetleys and Theakstons Best and Old Peculier *(Gwen and Peter Andrews)*

Penistone, S Yor [A616; SE2402], *Pennine*: Fine old pub with good atmosphere, well kept Wards, good value food, Turkish Cypriot landlord; bedrooms *(Comus Elliott)*

Pickering, N Yor [18 Birdgate; SE7984], *Black Swan*: Substantial former coaching inn, central bar with well kept Courage-related ales and an emphasis on food; bedrooms *(Andrew Hazeldine)*; *Forest & Vale*: Well stocked smart bar and cocktail bar, good food changing daily, cosy fire, good service; bedrooms *(Margaret and Fred Punter)*; [Park St], *Station*: Tastefully renovated, big back restaurant, good food, well kept Theakstons Best *(Andrew Hazeldine)*

Pontefract, W Yor [East Hardwick Rd; SE4622], *Carlton*: Wide choice of well presented food, big helpings, modern open-plan layout, plenty of seats; clean and well kept (D Illing)

☆ Pool, W Yor [SE2445], White Hart: Popular family dining pub, good generous food inc vegetarian and outstanding sandwiches all day, first-class service, good range of well kept beers, friendly atmosphere; flagstones, assorted old furniture, no-smoking area, children's corner (Wayne Brindle, Gerald and Su Mason, J E Rycroft)

☆ Potto, N Yor [Cooper Lane; NZ4704], Dog & Gun: Roomy pub with open fire in big L-shaped bar with plush alcove seating, charming lounge with interesting decor, wide choice of bar food inc delicious puddings, attractive evening restaurant; run by friendly outgoing family; bedrooms spacious and tidy, very homely (Jay Voss)

☆ Pudsey, W Yor [SE2233], Beulah: Comfortable and friendly old-fashioned pub with superb views, reasonably priced bar snacks, good interesting food cooked to order in small restaurant area, delicious puddings, good choice of cheese, well kept Tetleys, friendly efficient service (R B and H Rand, Brian Bannatyne-Scott)

Queensbury, W Yor [A644 towards Keighley; SE1030], Pineberry: Friendly, cosy and relaxed even when busy, with Courage-related and Theakstons ales, maybe a cheap local guest such as Clarks, home-made food inc good choice for vegetarians; popular with hikers (S Rushworth, Comus Elliott)

Rainton, N Yor [village green; under a mile from A1 Boroughbridge—Leeming Bar, N of A168; SE3775], Bay Horse: Three separate rooms off central bar, low beams, open fires, horsebrasses, farm tools and photographs; big helpings of good value food, well kept Theakstons (full range), very friendly owners and staff; bedrooms comfortable (John Allsopp)

Ravensworth, N Yor [off A66; NZ1408], Bay Horse: Attractive stone-built local with picnic-table sets facing village green, split-level bar, dining room, pump clips and jugs on beams, farm tools, good value food inc vegetarian and children's dishes, four real ales; darts, juke box, fruit machine, quiet piped pop music; children and dogs welcome (JJW, CMJ)

☆ Reeth, N Yor [just off B6270; SE0499], Black Bull: Genuine local feel in friendly and well laid out traditional beamed and flagstoned L-shaped bar, separate lounge, several well kept S&N real ales, reasonably priced usual bar food, open fires; children allowed till 8.30, pool and other games; at bottom of fine broad sloping green; bedrooms big and comfortable, with character and good facilities, good breakfasts (Michael A Butler, Margaret Mason, David Thompson, LYM)

☆ Reeth [Market Pl (B6270)], Kings Arms: Popular dining pub by green, with oak beams, pine pews around walls, log fire in big 18th-c stone inglenook, quieter room behind; good reasonably priced food, welcoming service, well kept Theakstons, John Smiths and Tetleys; children very welcome; bedrooms (Roger Bellingham, WD, Dr Keith Bloomfield)

Riccall, N Yor [A19 10 miles S of York; SE6238], Hare & Hounds: Very cheap straightforward bar food from sandwiches up, full Sun lunches (that's all, that day), well kept John Smiths on handpump, decent wines (Janet Pickles)

☆ Richmond, N Yor [Finkle St; NZ1801], Black Lion: Well kept real ales, good generous bar food, sensible prices, friendly service; lots of cosy separate rooms inc no-smoking lounge, good atmosphere, dark traditional decor; bedrooms reasonably priced (Mr and Mrs Peter B Dowsett)

☆ Ripley, N Yor [off A61 Harrogate—Ripon; SE2651], Boars Head: Beautiful old hotel with long flagstoned bar, neat and well run, in what may have been the stables – series of stalls, each with tables and chairs, popular at lunchtime for good value straightforward bar food from sandwiches up; good wines by the glass, well kept Theakstons, friendly and helpful young staff, plenty of tables in charming garden; good restaurant; comfortable if not cheap bedrooms (M G Hart, David Surridge, O K Smyth, DH, RH)

☆ Ripon, N Yor [Bridge Lane, off Bondgate Green (itself off B6265); or cross bridge nr cathedral and turn left along path; SE3171], Water Rat: Big helpings of good straightforward food inc wide vegetarian choice and good range of well kept real ales inc ones from small breweries in pleasantly bustling pub, unassuming but well furnished, prettily set by footbridge over River Skell with ducks and weir, charming view of cathedral from riverside terrace; friendly service (GSB, D H T Dimock, A Craig)

Ripon [Boroughbridge Rd (B6265), nr racecourse], Blackamoor: Simple pub worth knowing for good value popular fresh bar food; Stones Bitter (Frank Davidson); [Allhallow Gate, off Mkt Sq], Golden Lion: Small and cosy, well kept Theakstons, good reasonably priced food in bar and small back restaurant (Roger Berry)

☆ Robin Hoods Bay, N Yor [King St, Bay Town; NZ9505], Olde Dolphin: Roomy 18th-c inn stepped up above sea front in attractive little town; unpretentious furnishings, friendly service, convivial atmosphere, well kept cheap Courage, good open fire, bar food inc local seafood, popular back games room; dogs welcome in bar if well behaved, piped music, Fri folk club; can get crowded weekends, long walk back up to village car park; bedrooms basic but very cheap (Mike and Wendy Proctor, C J McFeeters, Prof R N Orledge)

Robin Hoods Bay [The Dock, Bay Town], Bay: Fine sea views from picture-window homely lounge, well kept Courage-related ales, log fires, generous decent food with separate dining area, firm management; maybe piped music, children may be allowed in room up steps if very well behaved – and again the long walk to the car park; tables outside; bedrooms (Amanda Dauncey,

Andrew Hazeldine, Mike and Wendy Proctor, C J McFeeters, Prof R N Orledge); [Station Rd], *Victoria*: Victorian hotel overlooking the bay, good views from garden, well kept Camerons; bedrooms *(Andrew Hazeldine)*

☆ **Rosedale Abbey**, N Yor [300 yds up Rosedale Chimney; SE7395], *White Horse*: Cosy and comfortable farm-based country inn with well kept Tetleys and Theakstons, quite a few wines and good choice of malt whiskies, good generous reasonably priced home-made bar food esp range of pies, good medley of furnishings and decorations in relaxing bar, friendly service, restaurant, lovely views from terrace (and from bedrooms); children allowed if eating, open all day Sat; a nice place to stay *(Ron Monk, J L Phillips, Paul Cartledge, Bronwen and Steve Wrigley, LYM)*

☆ **Runswick Bay**, N Yor [NZ8217], *Royal*: Welcoming pub with lovely views over fishing village and sea from big-windowed plain front lounge with interesting marine fishtank, limited choice of good value food inc huge helpings of fresh local fish, cheerful atmosphere and friendly young staff, well kept John Smiths, nautical back bar, terrace; bedrooms *(C J McFeeters, Prof R N Orledge, Mike and Wendy Proctor, LYM)*

Ruswarp, N Yor [NZ8909], *Bridge*: Old riverside pub by railway station, lounge and smoke room, well kept John Smiths and Courage Directors, reasonably priced meals *(Andrew Hazeldine)*

Sandal, W Yor [Barnsley Rd; junction with Chevet Lane; SE3418], *Three Houses*: Small bar with two small rooms around it, big separate dining room, John Smiths ales, open fire *(Mark Bradley)*

Sandsend, N Yor [A174; NZ8613], *Hart*: Good helpings of good food in shoreside pub with log fire in downstairs bar, friendly staff and well kept Camerons bitter *(Andrew Hazeldine)*

☆ **Saxton**, N Yor [B1217 Towton—Garforth about a mile outside; SE4736], *Crooked Billet*: Very reasonably priced popular food inc giant sandwiches, filled baked potatoes, enormous Yorkshire puddings, seafood and steaks – get there early for a seat *(Janet Pickles, C J Westmoreland)*

Saxton, *Plough*: Warm and comfortable lounge, well kept beers, delicious food inc excellently cooked fresh veg, separate public bar *(David Watson)*

☆ **Scarborough**, N Yor [Vernon Rd; TA0489], *Hole in the Wall*: Unassuming and friendly three-roomed local with one long central bar, well kept beers inc Malton Double Chance, Theakstons BB, XB and Old Peculier and guests, range of country wines, friendly landlord, no piped music or machines; cheap basic lunchtime food *(Andrew Hazeldine, Bill Black)*

Scarborough [31 Sandsend, opp harbour], *Golden Ball*: On the front with good harbour and bay views, well kept Sam Smiths OB; family room in summer *(Andrew*

Hazeldine); [15 The Esplanade (formerly Stresa Hotel)], *Highlander*: Home of North & East Riding Brewers, with their well kept Thistle (a Scotch ale), EB and 68 alongside Tetleys and Youngers IPA; tartan curtains and carpet, piped Scottish music, hundreds of whiskies; bedrooms *(Andrew Hazeldine)*; [Eastborough], *Jolly Rodger*: Interior decorated like a ship, well kept Theakstons beers; bedrooms *(Andrew Hazeldine)*

☆ **Scawton**, N Yor [SE5584], *Hare*: Low and pretty pub, much modernised, with a couple of cosy settees, simple wall settles, little wheelback armchairs, lots of air force memorabilia; friendly service, well kept Home, Theakstons Best and Old Peculier, decent straightforward food from sandwiches to big steaks in eating area on left, two friendly dogs, pool in room up steps; tables in big back garden with caged geese (they sell painted duck and goose eggs), nice inn-signs; children welcome, handy for Rievaulx *(Andrew and Ruth Triggs, BB)*

☆ **Scorton**, N Yor [B1263 Richmond—Yarm, just outside village – off A1 just N of Catterick; NZ2500], *St Cuthberts*: Friendly informal atmosphere, welcoming efficient service, expensive but good value wide and well presented range of imaginative freshly cooked food inc good generous Sun lunches and vast choice of puddings, well kept Theakstons; restaurant *(Paul and Ursula Randall, Sarah Thomas, Mr and Mrs C J Davey, Keith Davey)*

☆ **Seamer**, N Yor [Main St; TA0284], *Copper Horse*: Generous helpings of good food in friendly no-smoking dining areas off main bar, beams, brasses, bare stone, part wood-floored and part carpeted, with gold plush bar stools and wooden chairs around cast-iron-framed tables; pleasant helpful service, Youngers real ale, restaurant; cl Mon in winter; pretty village *(C A Hall, Ian Morley, WD)*

Settle, N Yor [SD8264], *Golden Lion*: Bright red plush in cheerful high-beamed lounge with enormous fireplace, well kept Thwaites ales, games in lively public bar, horses still stabled in coachyard; bedrooms *(Dave and Carole Jones, LYM)*

☆ **Sheffield** [Division St; corner of Westfield Terr], *Frog & Parrot*: Largely bare-boarded pub with lofty ceiling, huge windows, comfortable banquettes up a few steps, lively studenty café-bar atmosphere in evenings, interesting beers brewed on the premises – one fearsomely strong *(T Henwood, John Fazakerley, Paul Cartledge, LYM)*

Sheffield [Broad Lane], *Fagans*: Warm and welcoming, with friendly staff, well kept Tetleys, wide range of malt whiskies, no juke box, live music Fri *(Andrew Hilton)*; [Poole Rd, Darnall – off Prince of Wales Rd, not far from M1 junctions 33/34; SK3988], *Kings Head*: Basic but filling very cheap weekday lunches in comfortable, friendly three-room corner local, clean and tidy; Stones and Tetleys on handpump, TV on bar, piped music, fruit machine, small back terrace *(JJW, CMW)*; [Hemsworth Rd, nr Graves Pk], *New Inn*: Split-level Tetleys steak house, reasonable prices, friendly if not speedy service, good coffee *(JJW, CMW)*; [3 Crookes], *Old Grindstone*: Busy Victorian pub with good value food inc good Sun roast, Timothy Taylors Landlord and Wards, teapot collection, friendly black cat, games room with pool etc, no piped music *(JJW, CMW)*; [255 Ecclesall Rd], *Pomona*: Large comfortably modernised suburban pub with wide choice of good value food 11-9 (not Sun), Theakstons XB and Youngers Scotch and No 3 (no proper cider despite name), conservatory, snooker room, fruit and Monopoly machines *(JJW, CMW)*; [412 Glossop Rd], *West End*: Lively and studenty, occasional live music, well kept Tetleys *(Paul Cartledge)*

☆ Shelley, W Yor [Roydhouse; SE2112], *Three Acres*: 18th-c coaching inn in superb moorland setting, good out of the ordinary freshly prepared food from unusual sandwiches to dishes such as smoked chicken and Cumberland sausage salad with walnut or hazelnut dressing, pleasantly upmarket bar, restaurant; good service, well kept Timothy Taylors, exceptional choice of wines, good views; comfortable bedrooms, good breakfast *(Stuart Sutton, Stephen and Brenda Head, Michael Butler, John Allsopp, Keith and Margaret Kettell, Neil Townend)*

☆ Shepley, W Yor [Station Rd, Stocksmoor; Thunderbridge and Stocksmoor signed off A629 N; SE1810], *Clothiers Arms*: Good atmosphere in softly lit bar with conservatory extension, polite helpful staff and friendly landlord; bar food (not Sun or Mon evenings), downstairs carvery, tables out on balconies; quiet countryside *(Paul Lighfoot)*

☆ Shepley [Penistone Rd – OS Sheet 110 map ref 197088], *Sovereign*: Wide choice of popular good value freshly cooked unpretentious bar food in welcoming open-plan L-shaped dining lounge with beamery, red carpets and upholstery, yucca plants, restaurant leading off; Bass and Worthington BB, moderately priced wines, attentive service; garden, provision for children; very busy weekends *(Paul Lightfoot)*

Shipley, W Yor [Saltaire Rd; SE1537], *Victoria*: Tastefully redecorated Victorian local with friendly landlord, regularly changing guest beers, standard food *(Nick Bentley)*

☆ Sinnington, N Yor [SE7586], *Fox & Hounds*: Food not cheap but good, home-made and generous, in two clean and welcoming bar areas or dining area; impressive service even when busy, nice paintings and old artefacts, cosy fires, well kept Bass and Camerons, separate pool room; attractive village with pretty stream and lots of grass; bedrooms *(Steve and Julie Cocking, Elizabeth and Anthony Watts, Mr Rymer, Mrs Boothman, Miss Halse)*

☆ Skipton N Yor [Market Pl; SD 9852], *Black Horse*: Bustling and friendly beams-and-stripped-stone coaching inn opp castle, popular with cavers, climbers and Saturday-market people; good choice of usual food served quickly, S&N ales, huge log-effect gas fire in big stone fireplace; open all day, children welcome; bedrooms with own bathrooms *(Amanda Dauncey, C F Walling)*

☆ Skipton [Canal St; from Water St (A65) turn into Coach St, then left after canal bridge], *Royal Shepherd*: Unpretentiously old-fashioned local in pretty spot by canal, good busy atmosphere, good low-priced basic food served quickly, well kept Whitbreads-related ales with a guest such as Hartleys, decent wine, friendly service, unusual sensibly priced whiskies, open fires and old local pictures in big bar, snug and dining room, tables outside, games and juke box *(Roger Bellingham, Ray and Liz Monk, A Preston, Leonard Dixon)*

☆ Slaithwaite, W Yor [B6107 Meltham—Marsden; SE0813], *White Horse*: Good unusual home-cooked food in attractively set moorland inn with quick friendly service, Tetleys and Timothy Taylors Landlord, small bar with log fire, comfortable lounge on right, attractive restaurant area on left, tables out on flagstones in front; children welcome; two bedrooms sharing bath, huge breakfasts *(Andrew and Ruth Triggs, Louise Knowles, Sarah Harvey)*

Sleights, N Yor [180 Coach Rd; NZ8707], *Plough*: Stonebuilt pub with good country views, tasty food, well kept John Smiths and Theakstons *(Andrew Hazeldine)*

☆ Snape, N Yor [SE2784], *Castle Arms*: Enterprising if not cheap food in attractive small dining area of comfortable and homely pub, with cosy inglenooks, open fires, friendly licensees, well kept ale, wide choice of reasonably priced wines by the bottle; pleasant village *(Paul Wreglesworth)*

Sneaton, N Yor [Beacon Way; NZ8908], *Wilson Arms*: Well kept Theakstons Best, good range of snacks and meals, friendly landlord, real fire *(Andrew Hazeldine)*

South Otterington, N Yor [SE3887], *Short Horn*: Pleasant country pub with decent food inc huge mixed grill, well kept beers, friendly and chatty bar staff *(Andrew and Marian Ruston)*

☆ Sowerby, W Yor [Steep Lane; SE0423], *Travellers Rest*: Several little rooms, cosy with open fire (can feel a bit stuffy sometimes), good value generous bar food, friendly service; surrounded by fields and farms, good view over Halifax and Calderdale Valley from garden (lovely at night) *(Paul Lighfoot, L G Milligan)*

☆ Sowerby Bridge, W Yor [Hollins Mill Lane, off A58; SE0623], *Puzzle Hall*: Friendly, informal and relaxed old bar with benches, pews and settles, cast-iron-framed tables, open fire, darts, larger room off; good cheap lunchtime food using fresh local ingredients, evening snacks, well kept Wards/Vaux ales, quiet piped music, quiz machine, live music Thurs evenings, music weekend in summer;

open all day; children and dogs welcome (*Ian Richardson*)

☆ **Soyland**, W Yor [OS Sheet 110 map ref 012203; SE0423], *Blue Ball*: 17th-c attractively unmodernised moorland pub with consistently well kept real ales such as Bass, Bass Special, Stones, Timothy Taylors Landlord and Golden Best, good straightforward bar food, comfortable old pews; music room with piano and organ, seats out in big porch with good views over valley and reservoir; bedrooms (*M L Clarke*)

Spennithorne, N Yor [SE1489], *Old Horn*: Small cosy low-beamed 17th-c inn with well kept John Smiths and Theakstons Best and Old Peculier and John Smiths on handpump, good generous straightforward home-cooked food, dining room, friendly locals, unobtrusive piped music; bedrooms (*Mike and Penny Sanders, D Grzelka*)

☆ **Sprotbrough**, S Yor [Lower Sprotbrough; 2¾ miles from M18 junction 2; SE5302], *Boat*: Three roomy and interestingly furnished areas in busy ex-farmhouse in quiet spot by River Don, big stone fireplaces, latticed windows, dark brown beams, bar food inc good ploughman's and wide choice of hot dishes (no sandwiches), well kept Courage-related beers, farm cider, helpful staff; piped music, fruit machine, no dogs; big sheltered prettily tiled courtyard, river walks; restaurant (Tues-Sat evening, Sun lunch); open all day summer Sats (*JJW, CMW, Peter Marshall, LYM*)

☆ **Stainforth**, N Yor [B6479 Settle—Horton-in-Ribblesdale; SD8267], *Craven Heifer*: Friendly Upper Ribblesdale village pub, small, cosy and scrupulously clean, with well kept Thwaites, log fire, reasonably priced bar food inc well filled sandwiches; bedrooms simple but comfortable, fine breakfasts (*A N Ellis, M E A Horler*)

Staithes, N Yor [High St; NZ7818], *Black Lion*: Recently relicenced small and comfortable hotel bar with real fire, good choice of real ale, friendly staff; unspoilt fishing village; bedrooms (*Andrew Hazeldine*); [Top of Bank], *Captain Cook*: Comfortable and friendly with real fire in lounge, games room behind, good food, well kept John Smiths (*Andrew Hazeldine*); *Cod & Lobster*: Right by the water, at the foot of the sandstone cliff; well kept beers inc Camerons Best and Strongarm, lovely views from seats outside; quite a steep walk up to top car park (*Andrew Hazeldine, LYM*)

Stanbury, W Yor [SE0037], *Old Silent*: Moorland village pub rebuilt after a fire, beams, stone fireplaces and so forth, but now a rather modern clean open-plan feel, with conservatory, separate games room, juke box; straightforward food, open fire, welcoming service; bedrooms (*CW, WAH, LYM*)

☆ **Staveley**, N Yor [signed off A6055 Knaresborough—Boroughbridge; SE3663], *Royal Oak*: Good food in bar and restaurant of prettily laid out beamed and tiled-floor pub with Ind Coope Burton and Tetleys on

handpump, welcoming service, broad bow window; tables on front lawn (*Capt F A Bland, MM, LYM*)

☆ **Stokesley**, N Yor [1 West End; NZ5209], *White Swan*: Simple country pub with regularly changing interesting real ales, pizzas, no music (*G S and A Jaques, E J Cutting*)

☆ **Stutton**, N Yor [SE4841], *Hare & Hounds*: Wide choice of good food at sensible prices (inc good Sun lunch) in attractive and unspoilt low-ceilinged stone-built pub unusually done out in 1960s style; good welcoming service, well kept and priced Sam Smiths OB, decent wine; restaurant; lovely big fenced garden with toys for children; children allowed if eating (*Dr W J Reeves, Paul Cartledge, C J Westmoreland, Peter and Lois Haywood, David Watson*)

Sutton Bank, N Yor [A170 Thirsk—Scarboro; SE5282], *Hambleton*: Roadside pub with well kept Theakstons Best and Youngers No 3, good value bar food in three areas, caravan site behind; on Cleveland Way, popular with walkers (*Andrew and Ruth Triggs*)

Sutton on the Forest, N Yor [SE5965], *Crown*: Village dining pub with cheerful new licensees, recently taken over; two small rooms, tablecloths, Windsor chairs, prints; decent food from sandwiches up inc good puddings, good range of wines, good service (*Susan and Walter Rinaldi Butcher*)

☆ **Sutton under Whitestonecliffe**, N Yor [A170 E of Thirsk; SE4983], *Whitestonecliffe*: Beamed roadside pub with good value bar meals (can be eaten in small restaurant) inc fresh fish and good puddings, open fire in comfortable front lounge, back pool/family room with juke box and fruit machine, pleasant tap room with traditional games; John Smiths, Tetleys and Theakstons Best, decent wines, good friendly service; children welcome; back bedroom wing (*Andrew and Ruth Triggs, J E Rycroft*)

Swainby, N Yor [NZ4802], *Black Horse*: Well kept Camerons, good food esp Sun lunch; garden with children's play area (*E J Cutting*)

☆ **Tadcaster**, N Yor [1 Bridge St; SE4843], *Angel & White Horse*: Tap for Sam Smiths brewery, cheap well kept OB and Museum, friendly staff, big helpings of good simple lunchtime food (not Sat) from separate counter; longish brightly lit bar with alcoves at one end, fine oak panelling and solid furnishings but piped pop music; restaurant (children allowed there); the dappled grey dray horses are kept across the coachyard, and brewery tours can be arranged – tel Tadcaster (01937) 832225; open all day Sat (*C J Westmoreland, Susan and Nigel Wilson, Paul Cartledge, Brian Kneale, LYM*)

☆ **Tan Hill**, N Yor [Arkengarthdale (Reeth—Brough) rd, at junction with Keld/W Stonesdale rd; NY8906], *Tan Hill Inn*: Simple furnishings, flagstones and big open fires in Britain's highest pub, on the moors by the Pennine Way, nearly five miles from the nearest neighbour – the sheep up here have the best fleeces in Britain; well kept Theakstons Best, XB and Old Peculier (in winter the cellar does chill down – for warmth you might prefer coffee or whisky with hot water), good choice of hearty food from sandwiches up, some good old photographs, games room, occasional singalong accordion sessions, quite a heady atmosphere; children welcome, open all day at least in summer; bedrooms, inc some in newish extension; often snowbound, with no mains electricity (juke box powered by generator) *(G and M Stewart, M J Morgan, Mrs D Craig, Jim Farmer, Ben Grose, Richard Houghton, David Atkinson, Phil and Anne Smithson, Mr and Mrs Peter B Dowsett, LYM)*

☆ **Terrington**, N Yor [SE6571], *Bay Horse*: Cosy pub with good generous food inc vegetarian dishes, John Smiths and Youngers IPA and No 3 on handpump, open fire, dining room, tap room; delightfully unspoilt village; bedrooms *(A and M Dickinson)*

Thirn, N Yor [2 miles W of B6268 Masham—Bedale; SE2286], *Boot & Shoe*: Modest pub, popular locally for good cheap steaks and other fairly priced food; chatty landlord is serious about his limited range of wines – which are also good value; Tetleys and Theakstons *(Frank Davidson)*

Thirsk, N Yor [Market Pl; SE4382], *Golden Fleece*: Comfortable two-room bar with good reasonably priced food from sandwiches up, well kept Whitbreads-related ales, view across square from bay windows; restaurant, bedrooms *(Andrew and Ruth Triggs, Barbara and Norman Wells)*

Thixendale, N Yor [off A166 3 miles N of Fridaythorpe; SE8461], *Cross Keys*: Small pleasant village pub in deep valley below the rolling Wolds, single L-shaped room with fitted wall seats, relaxed atmosphere, well kept Jennings and Tetleys, good range of food inc interesting specials, pleasant garden behind *(Lee Goulding)*

Tholthorpe, N Yor [SE4767], *New Inn*: Really genuine, no-gimmick pub with good atmosphere and limited choice of good generous food; well kept beers; bedrooms *(John Knighton)*

Thoralby, N Yor [SE0086], *George*: Small Dales village pub, very friendly, with generous sensibly priced food, Black Sheep, John Smiths and Websters; bedrooms excellent, clean and cheap *(Ray and Liz Monk)*

Thornhill, W Yor [Combs Hill – OS Sheet 110 map ref 253191; SE2519], *Alma*: Good choice of reasonably priced food in popular new small restaurant and in bar, flagstones by counter, carpeting elsewhere, pink banquettes in partitioned bays, pleasant decor, well kept Bass, Stones, Theakstons and Worthington BB on handpump *(Paul Lightfoot, Michael Butler)*

☆ **Thornton**, W Yor [Hill Top Rd; SE0933], *Ring o' Bells*: Wide choice of intriguingly named and well presented good food inc

fresh fish, meat and poultry specialities and appetising puddings; Courage-related real ales, excellent attentive service *(Geoffrey and Brenda Wilson, Nick Haslewood, A D Shore, Stephen and Brenda Head)*

☆ **Thornton in Lonsdale**, N Yor [just NW of Ingleton; SD6976], *Marton Arms*: Quiet newly refurbished country pub with antique pine furniture, 15 well kept real ales, farm cider, lots of malt whiskies, good bar food inc good pizzas, enormous gammon and daily specials, efficient friendly service even when busy; children welcome, attractive Dales setting; bedrooms *(Paul J Bispham, John Hazel, Andy and Jill Kassube, Richard Houghton, Mr and Mrs J Connor)*

Thornton le Clay, N Yor [SE6865], *White Swan*: Particularly good food, very friendly staff, lovely country surroundings *(Eileen Walker)*

☆ **Thunder Bridge**, W Yor [village signed off A629 Huddersfield—Sheffield – OS Sheet 110 map ref 189114; SE1811], *Woodman*: Two roomy and spotless bars with attractive decor and not too many ornaments, good value food, upstairs restaurant, polite staff; well kept ales such as Marstons Pedigree, Tetleys, Timothy Taylors *(Paul Lightfoot)*

☆ **Thurlstone**, S Yor [OS Sheet 110 map ref 230034; SE2303], *Huntsman*: Well run old stone-built pub with good range of well kept Wards and other ales, welcoming atmosphere, lunchtime bar food, coal fire *(Michael A Butler)*

Tickhill, S Yor [Westgate; SK5993], *Carpenters Arms*: Well kept beers and straightforward food in clean, friendly and comfortable lounge bar, conservatory backing on to attractive garden, picturesque village, *(Des Pejko, Paul Cartledge)*

☆ **Todmorden**, W Yor [550 Burnley Rd, Knotts; A646 – OS Sheet 103 map ref 916257; SD9125], *Staff of Life*: Attractive partly flagstoned pub, formerly a main entry, reopened 1993 under new ownership, fully refurbished, with new stone-vaulted drinking area, home-cooked food inc vegetarian, Jennings real ales and ones brewed locally by Robinwood *(Annette Moore, Chris Pearson, LYM)*

Towton, N Yor [B1217 S of Tadcaster; between A1 and A162, away from village; SE4839], *Crooked Billet*: Tidy and well run extended pub, popular for good food esp pies and filled Yorkshire puddings, friendly comfortable atmosphere, efficient service *(David Watson, Thomas Nott, John Broughton, F and Dorothy Twentyman)*; [A162 Tadcaster—Ferrybridge], *Rockingham Arms*: Bright, friendly and welcoming recently renovated inn, well kept Vaux, varied home-cooked bar food inc good range of sandwiches, splendid home-baked ham, also popular fish and chips from 5pm *(John Broughton, C J Westmoreland)*

☆ **Ulley**, S Yor [Turnshaw Rd; 2 miles from M1 junction 31 – off B6067 in Aston; SK4687], *Royal Oak*: Friendly and cosy stonebuilt pub in lovely countryside, very popular for good range of good value bar food, attractive and intimate inexpensive restaurant (must book); well kept cheap Sam Smiths OB, stable-theme beamed lounge with rooms off, helpful service, quiet piped music, good children's room, big garden with play area; can get packed on warm summer evenings, esp Sat *(Glenys Cowham, JJW, CMW, WAH, Andy and Penny Vaughan, Gordon Theaker)*

Upper Poppleton, N Yor [A59 York— Harrogate; SE5554], *Red Lion*: Reasonably priced bar food inc good vegetarian dishes in dark and cosy olde-worlde bars and dining areas, spotless, quiet yet welcoming – popular with older people and businessmen; pleasant garden; bedrooms *(Roger Bellingham)*

☆ **Wainstalls**, W Yor [Lower Saltonstall – Pellon Lane/Pellon New Rd from Halifax, then left into Wainstalls Lane; OS Sheet 104 map ref 041285; SE0428], *Cat i' th' Well*: Three cosy rooms with lots of bric-a-brac and interesting pictures, wide range of beers, very cheerful licensees, good atmosphere, pleasant tree-sheltered garden with play area *(Paul Lightfoot)*

Wakefield, W Yor [Ferry Lane; entrance by Ship Inn – OS Sheet 104 map ref 354229; SE3522], *Ferryboat*: Much-extended popular family eating pub – seems more conservatory and extension than the original small canalside house; carvery, usual food with ethnic dishes recalling popular package holiday areas, Tetleys and Theakstons, very nautical decor *(TN)*; [58 Market St], *Graziers*: Authentic Yorkshire local with particularly well kept Tetleys, basic lunchtime food inc enormous chip butties *(Gerry McGarry)*

Walton, W Yor [nr Wetherby; SE4447], *Fox & Hounds*: Clean and happy pub quite handy for A1, good choice of reasonably priced food inc home-made puddings, good service, car park *(Eric Baker)*

☆ **Warthill**, N Yor [village signed off A64 York—Malton and A166 York—Great Driffield; SE6755], *Agar Arms*: Popular food pub specialising in all sorts and sizes of succulent steaks, other dishes inc lunchtime sandwiches and children's dishes; softly lit and nicely decorated welcoming L-shaped bar and extension, open fires, well kept Sam Smiths on electric pump, decent house wine, pleasant staff; pretty spot opp duckpond *(D Baker, BB)*

☆ **Welburn**, N Yor [SE7268], *Crown & Cushion*: Tidy stonebuilt village pub with two connecting rooms, good value home-cooked fish, pie, pasta and vegetarian dish of the day, well kept Camerons Bitter and Strongarm and Tetleys, welcoming staff, games in public bar, restaurant; piped music may obtrude; attractive small back garden with terrace and tables; children in eating areas, has been closed Mon lunchtime in winter *(Geoffrey and Brenda Wilson, J E Rycroft, F J and P Parmenter, LYM)*

Wentbridge, W Yor [Great North Rd (off

A1); SE4817], *Blue Bell*: Recently decorated 18th-c pub, several communicating rooms, beams, stripped stone, bric-a-brac and solid wooden tables, chairs and settles; wide choice of quick generous food inc Sun evening, friendly efficient service, well kept Tetleys, Theakstons Best and Timothy Taylors Landlord; family room, good view from garden *(Mark Bradley, John Watson, JC, JW, JJW, CMW)*

☆ **Wentworth**, S Yor [3 miles from M1 junction 36, village signed off A6135, pub on B6090; can also be reached from junction 35 via Thorpe; SK3898], *George & Dragon*: Popular rambling split-level bar with friendly new owners, home-cooked food in bar and restaurant, good choice of guest ales such as Morlands Old Speckled Hen, assorted old-fashioned furnishings, ornate stove in lounge, back small games room, benches in front courtyard *(Peter Marshall, Cathy Scott, Richard Baker, LYM)*

☆ **Wentworth** [village centre], *Rockingham Arms*: Friendly stripped-stone bar with settles, chairs and cast-iron-framed tables, hunting pictures, several rooms off inc dining room and family room, coal fires, good choice of reasonably priced food from sandwiches up (not Sun evening), well kept Theakstons Best, XB and Old Peculier and Youngers No 3 and Scotch, piped music; tables in attractive garden with own well kept bowling green; has been open all day; bedrooms *(Mark Bradley, Paul and Janet Waring, LYM)*

West Burton, N Yor [on green, off B6160 Bishopdale—Wharfedale; SE0186], *Fox & Hounds*: Unpretentious local in idyllic Dales village around long green; simple inexpensive food inc children's dishes, Black Sheep and Theakstons ales, residents' dining room, children welcome; nearby caravan park; good bedrooms *(Michael A Butler, Dr Philip Jackson, Patricia Heptinstall)*

☆ **West Tanfield**, N Yor [A6108 N of Ripon; SE2678], *Bull*: Open-plan but the best of two smallish rooms, comfortable pub furniture, popular food all day, well kept Black Sheep Best, Tetleys and Theakstons Best, decent wines, welcoming service, lollipop jar, unobtrusive piped music, small restaurant; tables in riverside garden *(Gillian M Chapman, Myke and Nicky Crombleholme, Peter Race, BB)*

☆ **West Witton**, N Yor [A684 W of Leyburn; SE0688], *Wensleydale Heifer*: Clean and comfortable low-ceilinged front lounge with small interconnecting areas, big attractive bistro, good helpings of carefully prepared food inc interesting dishes and seafood, good log fire, attractive prints, pleasant decor and civilised atmosphere; good service, small bar with Exmoor Gold and Theakstons; comfortable bedrooms in main building and nearby houses *(M J Morgan, Alan Wilcock, Christine Davidson, D Grzelka, Mr and Mrs Peter B Dowsett)*

Whiston, S Yor [Turner Lane; nr M1 junction 33; SK4590], *Golden Ball*: Well kept Tetleys, relaxed atmosphere *(Paul Cartledge)*

☆ **Whitby**, N Yor [Bagdale; off Stn Sq opp Pannett Pk; NZ9011], *Bagdale Hall*: Hotel in handsome and carefully restored medieval former manor, good inventive bar lunches, different each day, well kept Tetleys, good choice of spirits, piped classical music, fine restaurant, welcoming owners; six comfortable bedrooms, of character, huge breakfasts *(Mrs Margaret Mulgrew, Peter and Anne Hollindale, Consuelo Littlehales, D L Parkhurst)*

☆ **Whitby** [Flowergate], *Little Angel*: Friendly spotless local with well kept John Smiths and Tetleys, boating theme, good value generous lunchtime food, service friendly and quick even if busy, children allowed if well behaved *(Andrew Hazeldine)*

Whitby [41 Church St], *Black Horse*: Longest-serving pub here, tastefully refurbished to reflect its age (gas lights, stained glass); well kept Tetleys and Marstons Pedigree, well priced snacks and lunchtime meals; seafaring memorabilia *(Andrew Hazeldine)*; [Church St, nr 199 Steps, East Side], *Duke of York*: Comfortable beamed pub next to harbour, good views from lounge, friendly and lively atmosphere, good value bar food, well kept Courage-related ales; open all day summer *(Ken Smith, Simon Dale, Andrew Hazeldine)*; [Church St], *Fleece*: On harbour front, popular with local fishermen; lively but friendly, well kept Tetleys *(Andrew Hazeldine)*

Whitwood, W Yor [nr M62 junction 31; Altofts Lane – OS Sheet 104 map ref 399247; SE3723], *Bridge*: Recently built roomy rustic-feel pub – old bricks, reclaimed timber beams, some stone floors, sofas in no-smoking lounge; good choice of bar food (not Sun), Black Sheep Bitter and Champion, Theakstons Mild, Best, XB and Old Peculier, Tetleys, Timothy Taylors Landlord and John Smiths; open all day, adjoining motel *(Mark Bradley)*

Wilsden, W Yor [Main St; SE0935], *Bell*: Pleasant, clean and friendly local, lovely flowers, well kept Worthington BB *(Katie and Steve Newby)*; [B6144], *Ling Bob*: Friendly staff, particularly low-priced decent straightforward home-cooked food, well kept beer *(Elizabeth and Anthony Watts)*

☆ **Winksley**, N Yor [off B6265 Ripon—Pateley Bridge; SE2571], *Countryman*: Attractive heavily beamed stone-walled downstairs bar, bar food inc notable bookmaker's lunch and good puddings, Theakstons and Websters real ales, decent whiskies, coffee and tea, helpful staff, simple upstairs family/games room, tables on fairy-lit front terrace and out behind, restaurant; handy for Fountains Abbey and Studley Royal; has been closed Mon lunchtime (all day Mon in winter) *(Dr Philip Jackson, Patricia Heptinstall, LYM)*

Wragby, W Yor [Nostell Priory – OS Sheet 111 map ref 412172; SE4117], *Spread Eagle*: Homely beamed bar with Bass and

Stones, well presented generous bar food, evening restaurant *(D Isling)*

☆ **York** [High Petergate], *Hole in the Wall*: Good atmosphere in rambling open-plan pub handy for Minster, beams, stripped brickwork, turkey carpeting, plush seats, well kept Mansfield beers, good coffee, cheap simple food noon-8 inc generous Sun lunch, friendly efficient service, juke box, piped music not too loud; open all day *(D J and P M Taylor, C J Westmoreland, Roger A Bellingham, C H Stride, MJ, Michael Butler, George Atkinson, LYM)*

☆ **York** [18 Goodramgate], *Royal Oak*: Cosy black-beamed 16th-c pub with big helpings of good value imaginative bar food (limited Sun evening) served 11.30-7.30, quick friendly service, consistently well kept Camerons, Ind Coope Burton and Tetleys, wines and country wines, good coffee; prints, swords and old guns, no-smoking family room; can get crowded *(C J Westmoreland, Neil H Barker, JJW, CMW, C H Stride, BB)*

☆ **York** [Kings Staithe just below Ouse Bridge], *Kings Arms*: Fine riverside position with picnic-table sets out on cobbled waterside terrace; bowed black beams and flagstones inside, straightforward furnishings and bar food from sandwiches up, CD juke box can be loud; open all day *(Geoff and Angela Jaques, LYM)*

☆ **York** [26 High Petergate], *York Arms*: Snug little basic panelled bar, big refurbished no-smoking lounge, second cosier partly panelled lounge full of old bric-a-brac, prints, brown-cushioned wall settles, dimpled copper tables and an open fire; quick friendly service, well kept Sam Smiths OB, Sovereign and Museum, good value simple food lunchtime and early evening, no music; handy for Minster, open all day *(P R Morley, Paul Cartledge, BB)*

York [55 Blossom St], *Bay Horse*: Unspoilt Victorian-feel rambling local with low beams, old prints, tiled fireplace, bar hatches, buttoned leather settles, lots of nooks and alcoves *(C J Westmoreland, LYM)*; [Wellington Row], *Maltings*: Good range of guest beers, decent pub food with vast helpings of chips, chip butties, friendly service; handy for Rail Museum *(G P Wood)*; [7 Stonegate], *Punchbowl*: Attractive local with small public bar, helpful service, lunchtime food, ¼-gill spirits measures *(Mark Walker, C J Westmoreland)*; [Merchantgate, between Fossgate and Piccadilly], *Red Lion*: Well presented food inc fish and lots of steaks as well as usual pub food in low-beamed rambling rooms with some stripped Tudor brickwork, comfortable old-fashioned furnishings, well kept John Smiths; tables outside *(Ray Cuckow, Michael Butler, C J Westmoreland, LYM)*; [Nunnery Ln], *Trafalgar Bay*: Quiet traditional local just outside city walls; bar either side of front door, reasonably priced food, very cheap Sam Smiths OB and Museum *(Marjorie and David Lamb)*

London
Scotland
Wales
Channel Islands

London

Several new entries here, or pubs back in these pages after an absence, are the Westminster Arms, a thriving free house tucked between the Houses of Parliament and St James's Park (Central), the comfortable and relaxed Olde White Bear up in Hampstead (North), the big bustling Phoenix & Firkin (South) and its unpretentious sister pub the Ferret & Firkin (West), and (also West) the well preserved Windsor Castle up on Campden Hill, with its excellent tree-shaded terrace garden. Other pubs currenty doing particularly well in Central London are the cheerful and atmospheric Chandos, the charming little Dog & Duck (now opened an upstairs room), the Eagle (very good imaginative food), the quiet and relaxing Grouse & Claret, that striking Wetherspoons flagship the Hamilton Hall, the Lamb in Bloomsbury (probably readers' current Central London favourite), the busy Lamb & Flag, the interesting Princess Louise (good Thai food upstairs, good beers down), and the smart and ever-reliable little Red Lion in Waverton St (food even on Sunday). Outside the centre, current favourites include, in North London, the genuinely old-fashioned Spaniards; in South London, the engagingly individual Alma, the Crown & Greyhound (food better than average for London), and the riverside Cutty Sark; in West London, the smart yet relaxed Anglesea Arms, the Churchill Arms (splendid landlord, good Thai food), the riverside Dove (great atmosphere), the friendly and relaxed Kings Arms (unusual beers), and the very well run White Horse (good beers, wines and food, thriving atmosphere). From among all these, for the second year running we choose the Eagle in Farringdon Rd (EC1, Central) as London Dining Pub of the Year. In fact it's the only London pub which currently qualifies for our Food Award: others coming close are the Princess Louise (Central), the Front Page (Central) and Sporting Page (West), the Alma and Ship (South), and the Churchill Arms and White Horse (West). Though food quality is not generally strong in London pubs, food prices are attractive. Good main dishes more commonly cost around £4 than the £5 which is now the national average. By contrast, drinks prices are high – nearly 20p more than the national average for a pint in Central London. Free houses, very much in the minority in London, have held their prices virtually unchanged this last year – those in the Wetherspoons chain, which is growing very rapidly, were the pubs we found cheapest for beers. The two London breweries, Youngs and Fullers, are very useful sources of good value beer: it was Youngs beer in the Olde White Bear in NW3 which was the cheapest we found outside the Wetherspoons chain; and Fullers excellent light but well flavoured Chiswick beer stands out this year as a real bargain in pubs tied to that brewer. You may now come across London pubs labelled Highgate Brewery, and think you've found another local chain – don't be fooled, this is just a Midlands brand owned by Bass. But there certainly is now a much wider choice of beers available in London than there used to be. Smaller breweries such as Greene King, Sam Smiths and Vaux are making London inroads. And the national chains are bringing many more independent brewers' beers into their London pubs, particularly Allied in its Nicholsons pubs, and now Whitbreads in its new Hogshead pubs. In the Lucky Dip section at the end of the chapter, pubs we'd *currently single out for special mention (almost all inspected by us) include the Hand & Shears (EC1), Old Bell (EC4), Antelope (SW1), Red Lion (Duke of York St, SW1), Kings Head & Eight Bells (SW3), Bunch of Grapes (W1) and Salisbury (WC2), all Central; Island Queen (N1), Flask and Old Bull & Bush (NW3), Clifton and Crockers (NW8), all North; Woodman (SW11), Nightingale (SW12), Sun (SW13), Boaters (Kingston), White Cross and White Swan (Richmond), all South; Bulls Head and City Barge (W4), Britannia (W8), Ladbroke Arms (W11), Plough (Norwood Green), White Swan (Twickenham) and Load of Hay (Uxbridge), all West; and Alfred Hitchcock (E11) and Barley Mow (E14), East. The proliferating Wetherspoons pubs are reliably good value and civilised; one of the best is J J Moons in Ruislip, West London. Another London chain well worth knowing is the set of Davys wine bars: lots of character in these sawdust-floored imitations of ancient taverns, with decent beer as well as wines, and reliable food. And for a special drink it's always worth thinking about the grander hotel bars – we list the St Georges for its magnificent views – though you do then have to think in terms of £5 or so a drink.*

CENTRAL LONDON

Covering W1, W2, WC1, WC2, SW1, SW3, EC1, EC2, EC3 and EC4 postal districts

Parking throughout this area is metered throughout the day, and generally in short supply then; we mention difficulty only if evening parking is a problem too. Throughout the chapter we list the nearest Underground or BR stations to each pub; where two are listed it means the walk is the same from either

Argyll Arms (Oxford Circus) Map 13

18 Argyll St, W1; ⊖ Oxford Circus, opp tube side exit

They like to say they bring a breath of the country into the heart of the West End, and they're not far wrong – this busy place is a very handy retreat from the hordes of Oxford Street, and it's a nice surprise to find it still so traditional and full of character. The three cubicle rooms at the front are the most unusual – all oddly angular, and made by wooden partitions with frosted and engraved glass. A long mirrored corridor leads to the spacious back room, with the food counter in one corner; the blackboard menu includes good and unusual sandwiches like generously filled stilton and grape (£2.25) or smoked salmon and cream cheese (£2.50), ploughman's (£4.25) and main courses such as salads, a pie of the day such as steak and mushroom (£4.50) and roast beef (£5.50). The blackboard often also has topical cartoons chalked on it. Brains SA, Greene King IPA, Marstons Pedigree, Tetleys, Wadworths 6X and a couple of guests on handpump; welcoming, efficient staff; two fruit machines, piped pop music. The quieter upstairs bar, which overlooks the busy pedestrianised street, is divided into several snugs with comfortable plush easy chairs; swan's neck lamps, and lots of small theatrical prints along the top of the walls. A popular penned area outside has elbow-height tables, with good views of the pub's handsome frontage, liberally covered with plants and flowers. *(Recommended by Brian and Anna Marsden, Paul Cartledge, T Nott, TBB and others)*

Nicholsons (Allied; run as free house) ~ Managers Mike and Sue Tayara ~ Real ale ~ Meals and snacks (11-7; not Sun) ~ 0171-734 6117 ~ Children welcome ~ Open 11-11; closed Sun, 1 Jan

Black Friar 🍺 (City) Map 13

174 Queen Victoria Street, EC4; ⊖ Blackfriars

An inner back room of this well known pub has some of the best fine Edwardian bronze and marble art-nouveau decor to be found anywhere. It includes big bas-relief friezes of jolly monks set into richly coloured Florentine marble walls, an opulent marble-pillared inglenook fireplace, a low vaulted mosaic ceiling, gleaming mirrors, seats built into rich golden marble recesses, and tongue-in-cheek verbal embellishments such as Silence is Golden and Finery is Foolish. The whole place is much bigger inside than at first seems possible from the delightfully odd exterior, and that's quite a good thing – they do get very busy, particularly after work; lots of people spill over onto the front pavement in summer. See if you can spot the opium-smoking hints modelled into the fireplace of the front room. Bar food includes filled rolls (£2.50) and baked potatoes (£2.95), and a couple of hot dishes like mushroom lasagne or chilli con carne (£4.50); service is obliging and helpful. Well kept Adnams, Brakspears, Tetleys, Wadworths 6X and an Allied beer named for Nicholsons on handpump; fruit machine. There's a wide forecourt in front, by the approach to Blackfriars Bridge. If you're coming by Tube, choose your exit carefully – it's very easy to emerge from the network of passageways on the other side of the street or marooned on a traffic island. *(Recommended by A Plumb, David and Michelle Hedges, Andy Thwaites, Brian Jones, Dr and Mrs A K Clarke, David and Shelia)*

Nicholsons (Allied) ~ Manager Mr Becker ~ Real ale ~ Lunchtime meals (11.30-2.30; not Sat or Sun) ~ 0171-236 5650 ~ Open 11.30-10 weekdays; closed weekends and bank holidays

Chandos (Covent Garden) Map 13

29 St Martins Lane, WC2; ⊖ Leicester Square

Very well positioned for the motley attractions around Trafalgar Square, this impressive pub is a splendid meeting place. The downstairs part, with bare boards, alcoves and Dutch wall tiles, generally has a good, cheery bustling feel, with an interestingly varied mix of people, but it's the upstairs Opera Room that those in the know head for. Quieter and more atmospheric (as well as surprisingly spacious), it has secluded alcoves, wooden tables and panelling, and comfortable leather sofas, with opera memorabilia dotted around the walls; it's rather like a cross between a typical pub and a chattily civilised salon. Food is served up here, at lunchtime including dishes like soup (£1.95), chicken and tarragon or steak and kidney pies or stews (£4), salads (from £2.95), quiches, flans, or pizzas (£3.75), various pasta dishes (£4), puddings such as home-made spicy apple crumble (£2.25), and Sunday roasts; evening extras such as lasagne (£4.50), lamb or pork steak (£5.25), salmon steak (£5.50), and rump steak (£7.50). Well kept Sam Smiths OB and Museum on handpump, at a good price; darts, pinball, fruit machines, video game, trivia and piped music. Downstairs can get very busy in the evenings. On the roof facing the National Portrait Gallery they have an automaton of a cooper at work (10-2, 4-9). The Coliseum is just around the corner, so one reader often nips back in here during the interval (the theatre's own bar can be terribly slow). If you are going to the opera don't be tempted to dawdle – our research officer was enjoying the pub so much he almost lost track of the time, and even though he was only a minute late ended up having to stand up for the whole of the first half. *(Recommended by Andy Thwaites, Wayne Brindle, Susan and Nigel Wilson, John Fazakerley, John C Baker, J H Bell, Mick Hitchman, T Nott, Rob and Helen Townsend)*

Sam Smiths ~ Manager Neil Park ~ Real ale ~ Meals and snacks (11-2.45, 5.30-9.30) ~ 0171-836 1401 ~ Children in eating area of upstairs bar until 8pm ~ Open 11-11; closed 25 Dec

Cittie of Yorke ◪ (Holborn) Map 13

22 High Holborn, WC1; find it by looking out for its big black and gold clock; ⊖ Chancery Lane

The unique triangular Waterloo fireplace here, with grates on all three sides and a figure of Peace among laurels, used to stand in the Grays Inn Common Room until barristers stopped dining there. There's been a pub on the site since 1430, though the current building owes more to the 1695 coffee house which stood here behind a garden; it was reconstructed in Victorian times using 17th-c materials and parts. Rather like a huge baronial hall, the main back room is quite amazing when seen for the first time, the extraordinarily extended bar counter (the longest in Britain) stretching off into the distance, vast thousand-gallon wine vats above the gantry, and big bulbous lights hanging from the astonishingly high raftered roof. It does get packed at lunchtime and in the early evening, particularly with lawyers and judges, but most people tend to congregate in the middle, so you should still be able to bag one of the intimate, old-fashioned and ornately carved cubicles that run along both sides. A smaller, comfortable wood-panelled room has lots of little prints of York and attractive brass lights. There's a lunchtime food counter in the main hall with more in the downstairs cellar bar: filled baps, ploughman's (£3.60), salads (£4.50), and several daily changing hot dishes such as beef in red wine and mushroom pie, spicy chicken lasagne, paella, lamb in redcurrant sauce or seafood bake (all £3.95). Well-priced Sam Smiths OB and Museum on handpump; darts, pinball, dominoes, fruit machine, trivia and piped music. The ceiling of the entrance hall has medieval-style painted panels and plaster York roses. *(Recommended by Gordon, Tom Thomas; more reports please)*

Sam Smiths ~ Manager Stuart Browning ~ Real ale ~ Meals and snacks (12-2.30, 5.30-10) ~ 0171-242 7670 ~ Children in eating area ~ Open 11.30-11 weekdays; 11.30-3, 5.30-11 Sat; closed Sun

Dog & Duck (Soho) Map 13

Frith Street, W1; ⊖ Tottenham Court Rd/Leicester Square

There's a little bit more space at this delightful little corner house since they opened an upstairs bar. A cheery popular place, it's right in the heart of fashionable Soho, and in good weather especially there tend to be plenty of people spilling onto the bustling street outside. On the floor by the door is a mosaic of a dog, tongue out in hot pursuit of a duck, and the same theme is embossed on some of the shiny tiles that frame the heavy old advertising mirrors. The main bar really is tiny, and it's mostly standing room only, with some high stools by the ledge along the back wall, though there are seats in a roomier area at one end. The little bar counter is rather unusual, and serves well kept Ind Coope Burton, Morlands Old Speckled Hen, Tetleys, Timothy Taylor Landlord and an Allied beer brewed for Nicholsons on handpump; doorstep sandwiches (from £1.70). No machines or piped music though if you fancy a few tunes Ronnie Scott's Jazz Club is near by. *(Recommended by Gordon, Mark Walker, Gill Earle, Andrew Burton)*

Nicholsons (Allied) ~ Manageress Mrs Gene Bell ~ Real ale ~ Snacks (not weekends) ~ 0171-437 4447 ~ Open 12-11; closed Sat and Sun lunchtimes, opening 6 Sat evening

Eagle 🍴 (City) Map 13

Farringdon Rd, EC1; ⊖ Old Street

London Dining Pub of the Year

It's unusual to find a London pub where the food is the centre of attention, and even rarer to come across one with meals as good as these. Highly distinctive and made with the finest quality produce, the choice changes at least once every day, and there's quite an emphasis on Mediterranean dishes (particularly Spanish and Italian). On a typical day you might be able to sample gazpacho or a Portuguese chicken broth with rice, coriander, mint and lemon (£3.50), Greek or Lebanese style feta salads (£6), fettucini with barlotti beans and pancetta or pappardelle with chicken livers and sage (£6.50), clams and courgettes with saffron rice or Italian garlic and fennel sausages (£7.50), fabada (a Spanish stew with butter beans, chorizo, pork, ham and black pudding, £8), seafood and rabbit paella (Friday lunchtimes only, £8), sea bass with fennel, tomato, olives and basil (£9.50), and Spanish or Italian cheeses (£4.50). The open kitchen forms part of the bar, and furnishings are simple but stylish – school chairs, circular tables and a couple of sofas on bare boards, modern paintings on the walls (there's an art gallery upstairs, with direct access from the bar). The atmosphere is lively and chatty and although there's quite a mix of customers, it is popular with media people (a national newspaper is based just up the road); it's best to get here before 12.30 if you want a seat. Well kept Banks & Taylors Shefford and Ruddles County on handpump, decent wines, good coffee, and properly made cocktails; piped music. In the evenings it's more traditionally pubby. *(Recommended by Nicola Thomas, Paul Dickinson, Sarah King, Patrick Forbes, P Smith)*

Free house ~ Lease: Michael Belben and David Eyre ~ Real ale ~ Meals and snacks (12-2.30, 6.30-10.30) ~ 0171-837 1353 ~ Children welcome ~ Open 12-11; closed Sat, 2-3 weeks at Christmas, bank holidays

Front Page (Chelsea) Map 12

35 Old Church Street, SW3; ⊖ Sloane Square, but some distance away

It's a shame we don't get more reports about this smart place, to our minds one of the most stylish pubs in town. Relaxed and comfortable but with a smartly civilised air, it's generally busy but never full, chatty but rarely loud; you'll usually find a good mix of people around its heavy wooden tables or pews and benches. Huge windows with heavy navy curtains and big ceiling fans give the place a light and airy feel, and one cosy area has an open fire; lighting is virtually confined to brass picture-lights above small Edwardian monochrome pictures, and there are newspapers to read (if they see you're waiting for someone they quite often bring these across to you). Big blackboards at either end list the nicely presented bistro-style food: good soup of the day (£2.50), bangers, mash and beans, hot and cold salads (£4.75), various fresh fish, smoked salmon with scrambled eggs, or salmon fishcakes with hollandaise sauce (all around £5.50), cheese fondue (for two, £8), and puddings like baked bananas (£3). Well kept Boddingtons, John Smiths, Ruddles County and Websters Yorkshire on handpump; decent wines; quick, pleasant, smiling service. Outside, there are big copper gaslamps above pretty hanging baskets. The same people run the Sporting Page not too far away (also a main entry in this chapter), and a couple of other pubs, including the Chequers at Well (see Hampshire main entries). *(More reports please)*

Courage ~ Lease: Christopher Phillips and Rupert Fowler ~ Real ale ~ Meals (12-2.30, 7-10) ~ Well behaved children welcome lunchtimes ~ 0171-352 0648 ~ Open 11-3, 5.30(6 Sat)-11; closed for four days from 24 Dec

Glassblower (Piccadilly Circus) Map 13

42 Glasshouse Street, W1; ⊖ Piccadilly Circus

A useful retreat from the shops of Regent Street, this vibrant pub has an enormous copper and glass gaslight hanging from the centre of the ceiling in the main bar, flickering gently, with more gaslight-style brackets around the walls. There are also lots of untreated rough wooden beams with metal wheel-hoops hanging on them, plain wooden settles and stools, and sawdust on gnarled floorboards; lots of beer towels, framed sets of beer mats and bottle tops. The pub's position means it's well liked by visitors to London at lunchtime, and in the evenings it can get very busy – you might find it quieter in the lounge bar upstairs, and you're certainly more likely to find a table there. A wide range of real ales on handpump includes Courage Best and Directors, John Smiths, Theakstons Old Peculier and XB and Wadworths 6X; also a good few malt whiskies and Scrumpy Jack cider. Food such as filled baguettes (from £2.85), ploughman's, popular fish and chips and home-made daily specials (£4.85); table service upstairs. Fruit machine, video game, trivia, pinball, juke box and piped music. There are hanging flower-baskets outside. *(Recommended by Wayne Brindle, Mark Walker, Richard Waller, Professor S Barnett)*

S & N ~ Manager Mervyn Wood ~ Real ale ~ Meals and snacks (11.30-9 Mon-Thurs, 11-5.30 Fri and Sat; not Sun evening) ~ 0171-734 8547 ~ Children in eating area of bar ~ Open 11-11; closed 25 Dec

Grenadier (Belgravia) Map 13

Wilton Row, SW1; the turning off Wilton Crescent looks prohibitive, but the barrier and watchman are there to keep out cars; walk straight past – the pub is just around the corner; ⊖ Knightsbridge

Patriotically painted in red, white and blue, this is a lovely snug pub tucked away in a peaceful mews. It's particularly nice standing outside on a summer evening, watching the sky gradually darken behind the smart houses and forgetting for a while that you're anywhere near the centre of London. If you get there first you may be lucky enough to bag the bench. There's a similar lack of seating in the cramped front bar, but you should be able to plonk yourself on one of the stools or wooden benches, as despite the charms of this smart and characterful little place it rarely gets crowded. Friendly, helpful staff serve well kept Courage Best, Directors and John Smiths on handpump from the rare pewter-topped bar counter – or if you'd prefer it they will shake you a most special Bloody Mary. Reasonably priced bar food served straight from the kitchen includes soup (£2.30), ploughman's (£3.95), and hot dishes like sausage and beans (£4.40) or scampi (£4.90); they're usually quite happy to serve snacks like a bowl of chips. The pub is proud of its connection with Wellington, whose officers used to use it as their mess, and is also famous for its well documented poltergeist. *(Recommended by Gordon, M Clarke, Graham and Karen Oddey; more reports please)*

Watneys (Courage) ~ Licensee Peter Martin ~ Real ale ~ Meals and snacks 12-2.30, 6(7 Sun)-10 ~ Intimate candlelit restaurant ~ 0171-235 3074 ~ Children in restaurant ~ Open 12-3, 5-11; closed evening 24 Dec and all day 25, 26 Dec and 1 Jan

Grouse & Claret (Belgravia) Map 13
14 Little Chester St; ● Hyde Park Corner/Victoria

All sorts of plaudits have been raining down on this spotless and smartly friendly pub recently, and we can't pretend to be surprised; when the Coxes ran their previous pub the Crockers up in Hampstead they earned it not just a main entry but a star as well. Tucked into a discreet mews off Belgrave Square, this is a good solidly built modern pastiche of a gentlemanly old-fashioned tavern – snug areas around central servery, silvery-grey or claret-coloured plush, wood and etched glass forming booths, heavy panelling, big pictures, and attractive lamps. Bar food from a corner servery includes sandwiches, home-made scotch eggs (£1.90), salads (£4.90), Cumberland sausages (£5.40), pasta dishes, meatballs, and chicken Dijonnaise, beef carbonnade or seafood casserole (£5.65); the basement wine bar does a three-course lunch. A fine choice of well kept real ales on handpump such as Boddingtons, Brakspears, Greene King IPA, Wadworths 6X, Youngs Special and a monthly changing guest on handpump. Notably cheerful service; darts, shove-ha'penny, cribbage, dominoes, video game, trivia, shut-the-box and piped music. Quiet at night, with plenty of standing room for the lunchtime crowds. *(Recommended by Richard Waller, Susan and John Douglas, John Scarisbrick)*

Free house ~ Manager Mrs Rosalind Cox ~ Real ale ~ Meals and snacks ~ Restaurant (not Sun) ~ 0171-235 3438 ~ Children in eating area of bar and in restaurant ~ Open 11-11; 11.30-3, 6-11 Sat; closed Sun evening, bank holidays, and 3 or 4 days after Christmas

Hamilton Hall (Bishopsgate) Map 13
Liverpool Street Station, EC2; ● Liverpool Street

Pretty much the flagship of the Wetherspoon chain of pubs that you'll find all around London (and slowly but surely out of town too), this popular place was once the ballroom of the Great Eastern Hotel, and still has much of the original stunning Victorian baroque decor. Plaster nudes and fruit writhe around the ceiling and fireplace, and there are fine mouldings, chandeliers and mirrors; the upper level was added during the exemplary conversion, and part of it is no smoking. Comfortable small armchairs and stools are grouped into sensible-sized areas, and filled by a good mix of customers. As at other pubs in the chain good bar food includes filled granary baps (from £1.85), soup (£1.95), filled baked potatoes (from £2.25), burgers (from £3.25), fish and chips (£3.45), sausage hotpot (£3.75), chicken, ham and leek pie (£4.25), ham and courgette fusilli or avocado beanfeast (£4.75), daily specials and puddings like butterscotch cream pie (£1.95). Well kept Courage Directors, Greene King Abbot and IPA, Theakstons Best and XB, and Youngers Scotch on handpump, all at very good prices, the Youngers Scotch often on at 99p a pint; fruit machine. Friendly, efficient staff. Another Wetherspoons main entry is the White Lion at Mortimer up in Finsbury Park and there are more listed in the Lucky Dips – most share the same reliable standards of food, beer and service. *(Recommended by Neil Barker, John Fahy, Sue Demont, Tim Barrow, Derek Patey, Comus Elliott)*

Free house ~ Licensees Dave Chapman and Bernice Hartnett ~ Real ale ~ Meals and snacks (11-10pm) ~ 0171-247 3579 ~ Open 11-11

Lamb ★ ▇ (Bloomsbury) Map 13

94 Lamb's Conduit Street, WC1; ⊖ Holborn

Victorian London lives on at this unspoilt, atmospheric place, little changed since the last century and easily one of our more popular entries in the capital. It's famous for its cut-glass swivelling 'snob-screens' all the way around the U-shaped bar counter, but lots of sepia photographs on the ochre panelled walls of 1890s actresses, and traditional cast-iron-framed tables with neat brass rails around the rim very much add to the overall effect. Decimal currency doesn't quite fit in, and when you come out you almost expect the streets to be dark and foggy and illuminated by gas lamps. Sandwiches (£1.15, not Sunday), ploughman's (£3), and quite a few salads are available all day, and, until 2.30, they do hot dishes such as home-made pies or steak and kidney pudding (£3.95), and daily specials like curry or vegetable lasagne; Sunday carvery in restaurant (£4.95). Consistently well kept Youngs Bitter and Special on handpump, with Warmer in winter; prompt service, and a good mix of customers. There are slatted wooden seats in a little courtyard beyond the quiet room which is down a couple of steps at the back; dominoes, cribbage, backgammon. No machines or music. A small room at the back on the right is no smoking. It can get very crowded, especially in the evenings. *(Recommended by Margaret Whalley, Lindsley Harvard, Nicola Thomas, Paul Dickinson, Timothy Gee, Brian Jones, TBB, Gordon, A Plumb, P Smith, M Clarke, Tom Thomas, Olive Carroll, Nick Dowson, Gordon B Mott)*

Youngs ~ Manager Richard Whyte ~ Real ale ~ Meals and snacks (11.30-10) ~ 0171-405 0713 ~ Children in eating area of bar ~ Open 11-11; closed evening 25 Dec

Lamb & Flag ▇ (Covent Garden) Map 13

33 Rose Street, WC2; off Garrick Street; ⊖ Leicester Square

Still very much as it was when Dickens described the Middle Temple lawyers who frequented it when he was working in nearby Catherine Street, this popular old pub is a well liked place for Londoners to meet after work, and you'll almost always find plenty of people standing in the little alleyways outside, even in winter. It was out here on a December evening in 1679 that Dryden was nearly killed by a hired gang of thugs; despite several advertisements in newspapers he never found out for sure who was behind the dastardly deed, though the most likely culprit was Charles II's mistress the Duchess of Portsmouth, who suspected him of writing scurrilous verses about her. It's a lot safer these days (though watch out for the darts in the tiny plain front bar), but they still celebrate Dryden Night each year. Very well kept Courage Best and Directors, John Smiths, Morlands Old Speckled Hen and Wadworths 6X on handpump, and a good few malt whiskies. The busy low-ceilinged back bar has high-backed black settles and an open fire, and in Regency days was known as the Bucket of Blood from the bare-knuckle prize-fights held here. It fills up quite quickly, though you might be able to find a seat in the upstairs Dryden Room, which has a choice of several well kept cheeses and pâtés, served with hot bread or french bread, as well as doorstep sandwiches (£2.50), roast beef baps (Mon-Fri, £2.95), ploughman's (£2.95), and hot dishes like shepherd's pie or bangers and mash (£3.50). The pub is very handy for Covent Garden. *(Recommended by Bob and Maggie Atherton, Gordon, SRH, Margaret Whalley, Lindsley Harvard, Howard and Margaret Buchanan, Caroline Wright, Simon Collett-Jones, T Nott, M Clarke, Graham and Karen Oddey, David and Shelia)*

Courage ~ Lease: Terry Archer and Adrian Zimmerman ~ Real ale ~ Lunchtime meals (till 2.30) and snacks (12-5); not Sun ~ 0171-497 9504 ~ Live jazz Sunday evening ~ Open 11-11; closed 25 and 26 Dec and 1 Jan

Museum Tavern ♦ (Bloomsbury) Map 13

Museum Street, WC1; ✚ Holborn/Tottenham Court Rd

Karl Marx is fondly supposed to have had the odd glass at this old-fashioned Bloomsbury pub. On a corner opposite the British Museum, it has an 'Egyptian' inn sign, and gas lamps above the tables outside. Inside is simple but civilised, with high-backed benches around traditional cast-iron pub tables, and old advertising mirrors between the wooden pillars behind the bar. Good beers include well kept Courage Best and Directors, Greene King Abbot, John Smiths, Theakstons Best and Old Peculier and a couple more changing guests on handpump; they also have a wide range of wines by the glass, and several malt whiskies. Available all day from a servery at the end of the room, bar food might include salads (£3.80), ploughman's (£3.95), vegetarian meals like vegetable curry (£4.25), and hot dishes such as steak and ale or cottage pies (£4.95). Fruit machine. Unlike most other pubs in the area, and despite its popularity with lunchtime tourists, it generally stays pleasantly uncrowded in the evenings. *(Recommended by Andy Thwaites, Martin and Pauline Richardson, Prof S Barnett)*

Grand Met ~ Managers John and Carmel Keating ~ Real ale ~ Meals and snacks (11-10) ~ 0171-242 8987 ~ Children in eating area of bar till 5pm ~ Open 11-11; closed evening 25 Dec

Nags Head ♦ (Belgravia) Map 13

53 Kinnerton St, SW1; ✚ Knightsbridge

Walking into this friendly little gem is like being transported to an old-fashioned pub somewhere in a sleepy country village, right down to the friendly locals chatting around the unusual sunken bar counter. Cosy and homely, it feels almost rural, and really not like London at all – not least because it's rarely busy, even at weekends. The atmosphere is always relaxed and welcoming, and it's the kind of place where they'll greet you when you come in and say goodbye as you leave. Warmly traditional, the small, panelled and low-ceilinged front area has a wood-effect gas fire in an old cooking range, and a narrow passage leads down steps to an even smaller back bar with stools and a mix of comfortable seats. There's a 1930s What-the-butler-saw machine and a one-armed bandit that takes old pennies, as well as rather unusual piped music, generally jazz, folk or show tunes. Adnams, Benskins, Tetleys and Youngs pulled on attractive 19th-c china, pewter and brass handpumps; freshly squeezed orange juice. Served for most of the day, decent food includes sandwiches (from £2.50), filled baked potatoes (£2.95), ploughman's (£3.65), real ale sausage, mash and beans (£3.75), salads (from £3.85), chilli con carne or steak and mushroom pie (£3.95) and specials like roast pork or cod mornay (£4.50); there's a £1 service charge added to all dishes in the evenings. The pub is attractively placed in a quiet mews, with a bench outside. *(Recommended by Gordon, Steve and Carolyn Harvey, the Shinkmans, Graham and Karen Oddey, Paul Cartledge, and others; more reports please)*

Free house ~ Licensees Kevin and Peter Moran ~ Real ale ~ Meals and snacks (11-9) ~ 0171-235 1135 ~ Children welcome ~ Open 11-11

Old Coffee House (Soho) Map 13

49 Beak Street, W1; ✚ Oxford Circus

A friendly little cornerhouse that's often surprisingly peaceful at lunchtimes, when it's a useful place to know for a decent well priced meal. The downstairs bar is a busy jumble of stuffed pike and foxes, great brass bowls and buckets, ancient musical instruments (brass and string sections both well represented), a good collection of Great War recruiting posters, golden discs, death-of-Nelson prints, theatre and cinema handbills, old banknotes and so forth – even a nude in one corner (this is Soho, after all). Upstairs, the food room has as many prints and pictures as a Victorian study. The choice of lunchtime bar food is rather wider than you'll find in some other pubs in the area, with a range including sandwiches, filled baked potatoes (from £2.20), burgers (from £2.95), salads (£3.50), various hot dishes like chicken, ham and leek pie, seafood platter, macaroni cheese, lasagne, tuna and pasta bake, chicken tikka masala or winter stews and casseroles (all £3.95), and puddings (£1.70); on Sundays they only do toasted sandwiches. Well kept Courage Best, Marstons Pedigree and Ruddles Best on handpump; helpful, attentive service. *(Recommended by G Atkinson, Wayne Brindle, A Y Drummond, and others)*

Courage ~ Lease: Barry Hawkins ~ Real ale ~ Lunchtime meals and snacks (12-3; no meals Sun) ~ 0171-437 2197 ~ Children in upstairs food room 12-3pm ~. Open 11-11

Olde Cheshire Cheese (City)   Map 13

Wine Office Court; off 145 Fleet Street, EC4; ⊖ Blackfriars

This bustling 17th-c former chop house is one of London's most famous old pubs, its great cellar vaults dating to before the Great Fire; over the years Congreve, Pope, Voltaire, Thackeray, Dickens, Conan Doyle, Yeats and perhaps Dr Johnson have visited its unpretentious little rooms. Up and down stairs, these have bare wooden benches built in to the walls, sawdust on bare boards, and on the ground floor high beams, crackly old black varnish, Victorian paintings on the dark brown walls, and a big open fire in winter; darts, bar billiards, fruit machine and piped music. Surprisingly untouristy, it's now been extended in a similar style towards Fleet St. The stuffed parrot entertained princes, ambassadors and other figures from various countries here for over 40 years, and when she died in 1926 the news was broadcast on the BBC and obituary notices appeared in 200 newspapers all over the world. Snacks include sandwiches and filled rolls (from £1.20), and in the downstairs bar ploughman's (£3.50) or hot dishes such as lasagne, chilli or Old Brewery beef casserole (£3.95). Well kept (and, as usual for this brewery, well priced) Sam Smiths Old Brewery and Museum on handpump, friendly service. *(Recommended by Gordon, Dr and Mrs A K Clarke, John Fazakerley and others; more reports please)*

Sam Smiths ~ Licensee Gordon Garrity ~ Meals and snacks (not Sun evening) ~ Restaurant (not Sun) ~ 0171-353 6170 ~ Children welcome ~ Open 11.30-11; closed Sun evening and bank holidays

Olde Mitre £ (City)   Map 13

Ely Place, EC1; there's also an entrance beside 8 Hatton Garden; ⊖ Chancery Lane

The iron gates that guard Ely Place are a reminder of the days when this area made up the grounds of the palace belonging to the Bishops of Ely, who actually administered the law in the district. Even today it's still technically part of Cambridgeshire, and the interesting little pub certainly feels miles away from Holborn and the edge of the city, in reality of course just around the corner. The carefully rebuilt tavern with its quaint façade carries the name of an earlier inn built here in 1547 to serve the people working in the palace. The dark panelled small rooms have antique settles and – particularly in the back room, where there are more seats – old local pictures and so forth. An upstairs room, mainly used for functions, may double as an overflow at peak periods; on weekdays, the pub is good-naturedly packed between 12.30 and 2.15, with an interesting mix of customers. Good bar snacks include really good value sandwiches such as ham, salmon and cucumber or egg mayonnaise (from £1, including toasted) as well as sausages (40p), filled rolls (70p) and pork pies or scotch eggs (75p). Well kept Friary Meux, Ind Coope Burton and Tetleys on handpump; darts. There are some seats with pot plants and jasmine in the narrow yard between the pub and St Ethelreda's church. *(Recommended by Helen Hazzard, Gordon, A W Dickinson, Thomas Nott, D Cox)*

Taylor-Walker (Allied) ~ Manager Don O'Sullivan ~ Real ale ~ Snacks (all day) ~ 0171-405 4751 ~ Open 11-11; closed Sat, Sun, bank holidays

Orange Brewery (Pimlico)   Map 13

37 Pimlico Road, SW1; ⊖ Sloane Square

Every week the cellars of this lively and friendly pub produce over 500 gallons of their own brew beers – SW1, a stronger SW2, Pimlico Light and Pimlico Porter, and Victoria lager; they may also have a couple of guest beers on handpump. The cheery Pie and Ale Shop has lots of sepia photographs on the dark stained plank-panelling, plain wooden tables and chairs on the carpet, and a shelf full of old flagons and jugs above the counter where they serve a range of home-made food: sandwiches (from £1.75), salads, cold pies and quiches (£3.95), and hot dishes like steak and kidney pie (£4.25). The bar has more sepia photographs, decorative Victorian plates, and a stuffed fox above the nicely tiled fireplace; fruit machine, piped music. There are seats outside facing a little concreted-over green beyond the quite busy street. *(Recommended by Andy Thwaites, Ian Phillips, Richard Waller, A W Dickinson, Sue Demont, Tim Barrow, John Scarisbrick, A J Frampton, A Vermeul)*

Own brew (though tied to S & N) ~ Real ale ~ Meals and snacks (11.30-10.30; limited choice Sun) ~ 0171-730 5984 ~ Children welcome ~ Open 11-11

Princess Louise (Holborn) Map 13

208 High Holborn, WC1; Holborn

Some people consider this deservedly popular old-fashioned gin-palace to be the quintessential London pub, and it certainly has much in common with the city it represents so well – big, bustling, and full of a richly diverse assortment of people, grandly elegant but bang-up-to-date, with calmer corners away from the crowds, and despite all that seems familiar, enough that's individual to mark it out as unusual. Many people come just for the excellent spicy and authentic Thai food, cooked by a Thai couple and served in the quieter upstairs bar (from £4). Downstairs there's a fine range of regularly changing real ales, well kept on handpump, such as Bass, Brakspears SB and PA, Gales BBB, Theakstons Old Peculier, Wadworths 6X and a couple of more unusual guests; also several wines by the glass – including champagne. Neat, quick staff. They do sandwiches (from £1.75) down here just about all day. The elaborate decor includes etched and gilt mirrors, brightly coloured and fruity-shaped tiles, and slender Portland stone columns soaring towards the lofty and deeply moulded crimson and gold plaster ceiling; the green plush seats and banquettes are comfortable. The gents' are the subject of a separate preservation order. *(Recommended by David Wright, Howard and Margaret Buchanan, Stephen R Holman, Margaret Whalley, Lindsley Harvard, Gordon, Brian Jones, David and Shelia, T Nott, Prof S Barnett)*

Free house ~ Licensee Ian Phillips ~ Real ale ~ Meals and snacks (12.30-2.30, 5.30-9; no meals weekends) ~ 0171-405 8816 ~ Open 11-11; 12-3, 6-11 Sat

Red Lion (Mayfair) Map 13

Waverton Street, W1; Green Park

Quite a stylish place, this relaxed and civilised Mayfair pub has something of the atmosphere of a smart country pub. A very good range of well kept beers includes Courage Best and Directors, Greene King Abbot and IPA, John Smiths, Theakstons Best and XB and Wadworths 6X on handpump; they also do a special Bloody Mary. The little L-shaped bar has small winged settles on the partly carpeted scrubbed floorboards and London prints below the high shelf of china on its dark-panelled walls. Good food includes sandwiches (from £2.20), and main courses like Cumberland sausage, duck and venison pie or stuffed cabbage leaves (all £4.75); they home-cook all their meats; unusually for the area, food is served morning and evening seven days a week. It can get crowded at lunchtime. The gents' has a copy of the day's *Financial Times* at eye level. *(Recommended by Gordon, Mark Walker, Ian Phillips, Anthony Barnes, Bill and Edee Miller, TBB, G Walsh)*

S & N ~ Manager Raymond Dodgson ~ Real ale ~ Meals and snacks ~ Restaurant ~ 0171-499 1307 ~ Children in eating area of bar and in restaurant ~ Open 11-11; 12-3, 6-11 Sat

Star (Belgravia) Map 13

Belgrave Mews West, SW1 – behind the German Embassy, off Belgrave Sq; Knightsbridge

Service at this traditional pub is very obliging and helpful; they're quite happy being flexible with the menu or providing something slightly different if they can.

The whole feel of the place is very un-London, and though it can get busy at lunchtime and on some evenings, there's a pleasantly quiet and relaxed local feel outside peak times. The small entry room, which also has the food servery, has stools by the counter and tall windows; an arch leads to a side room with swagged curtains, lots of dark mahogany, stripped mahogany chairs and tables, heavy upholstered settles, globe lighting and raj fans. The back room has button-back built-in wall seats and there's a cosy room upstairs. Good value bar food such as sandwiches (£1.20), salads or hot specials like fish and chips, steak pie or corned beef hash (around £3.40) at lunchtime, and barbecue chicken (£4.90) and steaks (£5.90) in the evening. Very well kept and priced Fullers Chiswick, ESB and London Pride served by friendly staff. Outside in the attractive mews are pretty flowering tubs and hanging baskets. *(Recommended by Gordon, Ian Phillips, John Fazakerley, Richard Waller, M Clarke, T Nott, G Walsh)*

Fullers ~ Managers Bruce and Kathleen Taylor ~ Real ale ~ Meals and snacks (not Sat or Sun) ~ 0171-235 3019 ~ Children allowed if eating ~ Open 11.30-3, 5(6.30 Sat)-11, 11.30-11 Fridays and every day for two weeks before Christmas; closed 25 and 26 Dec

Sun (Bloomsbury) Map 13

63 Lamb's Conduit St, WC1; ✪ Holborn

Definitely one to head for if you're a beer drinker, this pleasantly spartan bare-boards pub has the biggest selection of real ales in London – and indeed we don't know of many other places in the whole country that can boast such a wide range. There can be anything between ten and 16 different brews on handpump, rotated from a much wider choice in the cellar from all over the country, and typically including Adnams Broadside, Badger Best and Tanglefoot, Brakspears, Courage Best and Directors, Ruddles Best and County, Theakstons XB and Old Peculier, and Wadworths 6X and Farmers Glory. The wall is taken up with an alphabetical listing of all the beers they have stocked, with details of their strengths. Furnishings are simple and basic, with a few tables around the U-shaped bar counter, and a couple of picnic-table sets in the street outside. Straightforward bar food includes toasted sandwiches (from £1.50), burgers (from £2.75), and basket meals or hot dishes like curry, lasagne or a pie (around £3.50); several malt whiskies, darts, fruit machine, video game, trivia, piped music, TV. Often filled with smart-suited City folk after work; they sometimes organise popular tours of the cellar. *(Recommended by Tina Hammond, Margaret Whalley, Lindsley Harvard and others; more reports please)*

Free house ~ Licensee Gary Brown ~ Real ale ~ Meals and snacks (12-2.30, 6-10) ~ 0171-405 8278 ~ Children in eating area of bar ~ Open 11-11

Westminster Arms ◗ (Westminster) Map 13

Storey's Gate, SW1; ✪ Westminster

Handily placed near Westminster Abbey and Parliament Square, this traditional local has a lot in common with any other place where nearby workers come for a drink at the end of the day – except that most of these people, one way or another, work in government. For many the main draw is the fine range of real ales on handpump, typically including Adnams, Bass, Brakspears, Theakstons Best, Wadworths 6X, Westminster Best brewed for them by Charringtons and unusual weekly changing guests like Archers Golden; they also do decent wines. Furnishings in the busy main bar are simple and old-fashioned, with proper tables on the wooden floors and a good deal of panelling; there's not a lot of room, and they do get very busy, so come early for a seat. Pleasant, courteous service. They do sandwiches and pasties in here (from £1.50), but most of the food is served in the downstairs wine bar, quite different in character with some of the tables in cosy booths: ploughman's and a few hot dishes like steak and kidney pie, scampi, or chicken stir-fry (around £4.50). Piped music in this area, and in the upstairs restaurant, but not in the main bar; fruit machine. There are a couple of tables and seats by the street outside. *(Recommended by Dr J R G Beavon, John Fazakerley, Richard Waller, Brian and Jenny Seller, Wayne Rossiter)*

Free house ~ Licensee Darren Truesdale ~ Real ale ~ Meals and snacks (11-10, weekends 11-6) ~ 0171-222 8520 ~ Children in downstairs wine bar and upstairs restaurant ~ Open 11-11; closed 25 and 26 Dec

NORTH LONDON

Parking is not a special problem in this area unless we say so

Compton Arms (Canonbury) Map 12

4 Compton Avenue, off Canonbury Lane, N1; ⊖ Highbury & Islington

Hidden away up a mews, this tiny local has a quiet little crazy paved back terrace, with benches and cask tables among flowers under a big sycamore tree. Well run by friendly staff, the low-ceilinged rooms are simply furnished with wooden settles and assorted stools and chairs, with local pictures on the wall, and there's a quiet, relaxed atmosphere. Well kept Greene King Abbot, IPA and Rayments on handpump, and good value bar food such as sandwiches (from £1.20), burgers (£2.50), salads (from £2.75), chicken kiev or ploughman's (£2.80), and gammon and egg (£3.20). *(Recommended Sue Demont, Tim Barrow; more reports please)*

Greene King ~ Managers W and P Porter ~ Real ale ~ Meals and snacks (11-10) ~ 0171-359 6883 ~ Children in eating area ~ Open 11-11

Holly Bush (Hampstead) Map 12

Holly Mount, NW3; ⊖ Hampstead

You'd hardly think this lovely place was so close to Hampstead High Street, as the peaceful little lanes in which it nestles are so tranquil and relaxed. The atmospheric front bar has real Edwardian gas lamps, a dark and sagging ceiling, brown and cream panelled walls (decorated with old advertisements and a few hanging plates), open fires, and cosy bays formed by partly glazed partitions. Slightly more intimate, the back room, named after the painter George Romney, has an embossed red ceiling, panelled and etched glass alcoves, and ochre-painted brick walls covered with small prints and plates. During the week bar food includes toasted sandwiches (from £1.40), ploughman's (£2.95), and pasta, chilli or shepherd's pie (around £3.25), with more imaginative weekend dishes such as home-made scouse (the cheery licensees are from Liverpool), a daily vegetarian dish, winter Singapore-style fish curry (£3.60), and traditional Sunday roasts (£4.75). Benskins, Ind Coope Burton, Tetleys and a frequently changing guest on handpump; darts, shove-ha'penny, cribbage, dominoes, fruit machine and video game. Good friendly service. It's worth taking a pleasant stroll around the area. *(Recommended by Gordon, Wayne Brindle, Margaret Whalley, Lindsley Harvard, Tom Thomas)*

Taylor-Walker (Allied) ~ Manager Peter Dures ~ Real ale ~ Meals and snacks (12.30-3, 5.30-11) ~ 0171-435 2892 ~ Children in coffee bar ~ Jazz Sun night, 60s guitarist Weds ~ Nearby parking sometimes quite a squeeze ~ Open 11-3(4 Sat), 5.30(6 Sat)-11; closed evening 25 Dec

Olde White Bear (Hampstead) Map 12

Well Road, NW3; ⊖ Hampstead

Once again in a nice part of Hampstead, this neo-Victorian pub is a friendly traditional place, well liked for its relaxing villagey feel. The dimly lit main room has lots of Victorian prints and cartoons on the walls, as well as wooden stools, cushioned captain's chairs, a couple of big tasselled armed chairs, a flowery sofa, handsome fireplace and an ornate Edwardian sideboard. A similarly lit small central room has Lloyd Loom furniture, dried flower arrangements and signed photographs of actors and playwrights. In the brighter end room there are elaborate cushioned machine tapestried pews, marble topped tables, a very worn butcher's table and dark brown paisley curtains. Good bar food includes soup (£1.80), sandwiches or filled baked potatoes (from £1.90), burgers (£3.25), ploughman's (£3.50), hot dishes like cottage pie or steak and kidney pie (£3.50) and the particularly popular Greek platter – a huge salad with olives and feta cheese (£3.90). Adnams, Ind Coope Burton, Greene King Abbot, Tetleys, Wadworths 6X and Youngs Bitter on handpump, a decent range of malt whiskies, and maybe winter mulled wine. Piped music. Parking may be a problem – it's mostly residents' permits only nearby. *(Recommended by Walter Reid, Wayne Brindle, Gordon, Don Kellaway, Angie Coles, Tom Thomas)*

Taylor Walker (Allied) ~ Tenant P W Reynolds ~ Real ale ~ Meals and snacks ~ 0171-435 3758 ~ Open 11-11

Spaniards Inn (Hampstead) Map 12

Spaniards Lane, NW3; ⊖ Hampstead, but some distance away

This popular former toll-house and a similar little whitewashed outbuilding opposite are responsible for the slight bottlenecks you sometimes come across driving around here; they jut out into the road rather like King Canute holding back the tide of traffic, and cars all have to slow down to squeeze past. It's a very atmospheric and comfortable place, authentically old-fashioned, with open fires, genuinely antique winged settles, candle-shaped lamps in pink shades, and snug little alcoves in the low-ceilinged oak-panelled rooms of the attractive main bar; the upstairs bar is quieter, though may not always be open. A very nice sheltered garden has slatted wooden tables and chairs on a crazy-paved terrace which opens on to a flagstoned walk around a small lawn, with roses, a side arbour of wisteria and clematis, and an aviary. Well kept Bass, Fullers London Pride, Hancocks BB and a guest like Robinsons Best on handpump; friendly service, piped music. Daily changing bar food includes sausage and chips (£2.25), ploughman's (from £3.25), ratatouille (£4.25), vegetable lasagne (£4.75), cottage bake (£4.95) and chicken and mushroom pie (£5.50); the dining area is no smoking at lunchtime. It's very handy for Kenwood, and indeed during the 1780 Gordon Riots the landlord helped save the house from possible disaster, cunningly giving so much free drink to the mob on its way to burn it down that by the time the Horse Guards got here the rioters were lying drunk and incapable on the floor. The pub is named after the Spanish ambassador to the court of James I who is said to have lived here. Dogs welcome. *(Recommended by Gordon, N and M Foster, S J Elliott, E G Parish, Paul Cartledge, Philip W Brindle)*

Charringtons (Bass) ~ Manager D E Roper ~ Real ale ~ Meals and snacks (12-3, 6-9.30; cold food all day Sat) ~ 0181-455 3276 ~ Children in eating area of bar and in upstairs bar ~ Open 11-11

Waterside (King's Cross) Map 13

82 York Way, N1; ⊖ King's Cross

Escape from the city bustle to this friendly pub's unexpectedly calm outside terrace overlooking the Battlebridge Basin, where on sunny days you might find a barbecue or jazz or folk music. The building really isn't very old but it's done out in firmly traditional style, with stripped brickwork, latticed windows, genuinely old stripped timbers in white plaster, lots of dimly lit alcoves (one is no smoking), spinning wheels, milkmaid's yokes, and horsebrasses and so on, with plenty of rustic tables and wooden benches. Some of the woodwork was salvaged from a disused mill. Boddingtons, Greene King Abbot, Marstons Pedigree and a guest on handpump, as well as wines on draught; bar billiards, pinball, fruit machine, video game, trivia and sometimes loudish juke box. Bar food includes filled rolls, ploughman's (£3.25), home-made beef or lamb burgers or filled baked potatoes (£3.50), spinach lasagne or steak and mushroom pie (£3.95), and daily specials such as beef and onion pie, garlic chicken in parmesan or vegetable lasagne (all £3.50); they do a good value Sunday roast. No dogs inside. *(Recommended by CW, JW, Ian Phillips, Don Kellaway, Angie Coles, Dr and Mrs A K Clarke, Russell Dawson, Paul Cartledge)*

Whitbreads ~ Manager John Gibson ~ Real ale ~ Meals and snacks (all day; not Sun evening) ~ 0171-837 7118 ~ Children in eating area of bar ~ Open 11-11; closed 25 and 26 Dec and 1 Jan

White Lion of Mortimer (Finsbury Park) Map 13

127 Stroud Green Road, N4; ⊖ Finsbury Park

Bustling but spacious, this easy-going and relaxed Wetherspoons pub is a reliable place for good value drinks and food. The carved island servery runs the length of the bar, which has cream tilework at the front, lion pictures on the partly panelled walls, and a medley of old tables. The cooking implements down the left-hand side contrast with the horse harness and farm tools on the right, which also has a public telephone with an old copper fireplace as its booth. Some alcoves have an old cast-iron fireplace and plush settees, and there's a restful conservatory area at the back, with hanging ivy plants; around a third of the pub is no-smoking. As usual in a Wetherspoons pub the beers are at a price few other London pubs can match, with Youngers Scotch at maybe 99p a pint, and the Courage Directors, Greene King Abbot, Theakstons Best and XB and guests also costing much less than you might expect; also country wines and farm cider. Decent bar food includes filled granary baps (from £1.85), soup (£1.95), filled baked potatoes (from £2.25), burgers (from £3.25), fish and chips (£3.45), sausage hotpot (£3.75), chicken, ham and leek pie (£4.25), ham and courgette fusilli or avocado beanfeast (£4.75), daily specials and puddings like butterscotch cream pie (£1.95); Sunday roast (£3.95). Dominoes, chess, fruit machine, video game. There are some wooden tables on the pavement outside. *(Recommended by Russell and Margaret Bathie; more reports please)*

Free house ~ Licensees Mark and Simone Gray ~ Real ale ~ Meals and snacks (11-10) ~ 0171-281 4773 ~ Open 11-11; closed evening 25 Dec

SOUTH LONDON

Parking is bad on weekday lunchtimes at the inner city pubs here (SE1), but is usually OK everywhere in the evenings – you may again have a bit of a walk if a good band is on at the Bulls Head in Barnes, or at the Windmill on Clapham Common if it's a fine evening

Alma (Wandsworth) Map 12

499 York Road, SW18; ⇌ Wandsworth Town

Stylish, civilised and just that little bit different, there's an authentic French café-bar feel to this bustling place. Even when it's very full – which it often is – service is careful and efficient, and you'll find a real air of chattily relaxed bonhomie and joie de vivre. There's a mix of chairs around cast-iron-framed tables, lots of ochre and terracotta paintwork, gilded mosaics of the Battle of the Alma, an ornate mahogany chimney-piece and fireplace, bevelled mirrors in a pillared mahogany room divider, and pinball and a fruit machine; the popular but less pubby dining room has a fine turn-of-the-century frieze of swirly nymphs. Youngs Bitter, Porter, Special and Winter Warmer on handpump from the island bar counter, decent house wines, freshly squeezed orange juice, good coffee, tea or hot chocolate, newspapers out for customers. Unusual and tasty, the good value bar food includes sandwiches (£1.20), soup (£2.50), croque monsieur (£2.35), filo parcels stuffed with ricotta cheese, ginger and vegetables (£3.65), toasted muffins with ham and poached egg (£4.20), smoked fishcakes in dill and mustard sauce (£4.25), lamb, lentil and spinach ragout (£5.25), chicken supreme poached with wine and tarragon in a creamy herb sauce (£5), daily fresh fish, and steak (£9.25). You can book and even specify a table in the dining room, where there's friendly waitress service. If you're after a quiet drink don't come when there's a rugby match on the television. They've recently introduced a new 'smart-card' for customers, which you can charge up with cash and then use at a discount here or at the management's other two pubs, the Ship at Wandsworth (see below) and the Coopers Arms, SW3. *(Recommended by Susan and John Douglas, Ian Phillips; more reports please)*

Youngs ~ Tenant Charles Gotto ~ Real ale ~ Meals and snacks (12-3, 7-10.45; not Sun evening) ~ Restaurant (not Sun evening) ~ 0181-870 2537 ~ Children in eating area and restaurant ~ Open 11-11; closed 25 Dec

Bulls Head ♀ (Barnes) Map 12

373 Lonsdale Road, SW13; ⇌ Barnes Bridge

Top-class modern jazz groups perform at this imposing riverside pub every night, and they're quite a draw. You can hear the music quite clearly from the lounge bar (and on peaceful Sunday lunchtimes from the villagey little street as you approach), but for the full effect and genuine jazz club atmosphere it is worth paying the admission to the well equipped music room. Back in the bustling bar alcoves open off the main area around the island servery, which has Youngs Bitter and Special on handpump and around a hundred or so malt whiskies. Around the walls are large photos of the various jazz musicians and bands who have played here; darts, Scrabble, chess, cards, fruit machine and video game in the public bar. All the food is home-made, including the bread, pasta, sausages and ice cream, and there are meals like sandwiches (from £1.80, hot roast meat £2), soup (£1.50), a pasta dish or home-baked pie (from £3), and a popular carvery of home-roasted joints (£3.50). Service is efficient and very friendly – one reporting couple arrived a little early, but they were quite happy to let them sit in a comfortable corner until opening time. Bands play 8.30-11 every night plus 12-2pm Sundays, and depending on who's playing prices generally range from £3.50 to £6. *(Recommended by Bob and Maggie Atheron, Susan and John Douglas, Malcolm Perkin; more reports please)*

Youngs ~ Tenant Dan Fleming ~ Real ale ~ Lunchtime meals and snacks ~ Evening restaurant (not Sun evening, though they do Sun lunch) ~ 0181-876 5241 ~ Children welcome ~ Jazz every night and Sun lunchtime ~ Nearby parking may be difficult ~ Open 11-11

Crown & Greyhound (Dulwich) Map 12

73 Dulwich Village, SE21; ⇌ North Dulwich

Rather well liked by readers at the moment, this imposing place is blessed with a very pleasant big two-level back terrace, with a good many picnic-table sets under a chestnut tree; just right for summer, when there's a salad bar and ice cream stall out here. Inside is grand and astonishingly spacious – it gets very busy in the evenings but there's enough space to absorb everyone without any difficulty. The most ornate room is on the right, with its elaborate ochre ceiling plasterwork, fancy former gas lamps, Hogarth prints, fine carved and panelled settles and so forth. It opens into the former billiards room, where kitchen tables on a stripped board floor are set for the rather good home-made bar food: popular doorstep sandwiches and toasties (from £1.95), filled baked potatoes (from £2), ploughman's (£3.25), vegetarian dishes such as nut roast or quiche, and a range of specials like shepherd's pie, pork and cheese filo parcels, chicken, leek and stilton crumble, good lamb fennel casserole or steak and mushroom pie (all around £4.75); popular Sunday carvery (£5.95) – get there early, they don't take bookings. Very efficient, friendly service. A central snug leads on the other side to the saloon – brown ragged walls, upholstered and panelled settles, a coal-effect gas fire in the tiled period fireplace, and Victorian prints. Well kept Ind Coope Burton, Tetleys, Youngs Bitter and unusual monthly changing guests like Arrols 80/- on handpump; fruit machines, video game and piped music. A family area on the right is no smoking. The pub is handy for walks through the park. *(Recommended by Sue Demont, Tim Barrow, David Wright, E G Parish, Lee Goulding, Andy Thwaites, Ian Phillips, Tom and Rosemary Hall)*

Taylor Walker (Allied) ~ Manager Bernard Maguire ~ Real ale ~ Meals and snacks (12-2.30, 5.30-9; not Sun evening) ~ Restaurant (not evenings Sun or Mon) ~ 0181-693 2466 ~ Children in restaurant and no-smoking family room ~ Open 11-11

Cutty Sark (Greenwich) Map 12

Ballast Quay, off Lassell St, SE10; from the river front walk past the Yacht in Crane St and Trinity Hospital; ⇌ Maze Hill, from London Bridge

Full of atmosphere and conjuring up images of the kind of London we imagine Dickens once knew, this attractive late 16th-c white-painted house is now probably one of London's best riverside pubs. Particularly striking as you approach is the big upper bow window jettied out over the pavement, which, from inside, offers good views across to the Isle of Dogs. Inside are flagstones, rough brick walls, wooden settles, barrel tables, open fires, low lighting and narrow openings to tiny side snugs – all very cosy, and, says one reader, just as it was in the 50s. A roomy eating area has efficiently served food such as burgers, ploughman's with home-made pickles and chutney, poached halibut with samphire sauce, grilled aubergine, pepper and artichoke salad and swordfish with tomato and fennel sauce (from £2.50-£7.95); there may be seafood nibbles at the bar on Sunday. Well kept Bass, Charringtons IPA, and Worthington Best on handpump, lots of foreign bottled beers; pleasant, helpful staff. An elaborate central staircase leads up to an upstairs area. Fruit machine, video game, juke box. There are waterside tables on a terrace across the narrow cobbled lane. The pub can be very busy with young people on Friday and Saturday evenings. *(Recommended by Robert Gomme, Eamon Green, Thomas Nott, Jenny and Brian Seller and others)*

Free house ~ Licensee David Rogers ~ Real ale ~ Meals and snacks every lunchtime and Tues-Fri evenings ~ 0181-858 3146 ~ Children in upstairs area 12-2.30 only ~ Live music Tues and Thurs evenings ~ Open 11-11; 11-3, 5.30-11 winter

Fox & Grapes (Wimbledon) Map 12
Camp Rd, SW19; ⊖ Wimbledon

This well placed pub changed hands just before we went to press, though the new licensee hopes to continue the emphasis on food that has made it so well liked over the past couple of years or so. Many dogs bring their owners here after a brisk stroll, as it's ideally located on the edge of Wimbledon Common, and it's especially pleasant on summer evenings when the doors are open and you can sit out on the grass. The neatly comfortable main bar has no surprises – traditional pub furniture, a bit of beamery, log-effect fire and so forth, with a good chatty atmosphere at lunchtimes. There's a step or two down to a rather cosier area. Service is notably quick and friendly. A wide choice of home-made bar food includes sandwiches, deep-fried brie (£3.95), steak and kidney pie (£5.95), sirloin steak (£8.95) and changing daily specials. Well kept Courage Best and Directors, John Smiths, Wadworths 6X and Youngs Special on handpump; varied wines, farm cider, mulled wine in winter; fruit machine, piped music. *(Recommended by Susan and John Douglas, Colin Pearson, D and B Thomas, John and Shirley Dyson, C H Ball, R Wilson, Ian Phillips; reports on the new regime please)*

Courage ~ Lease: Jacques Frankenberger ~ Real ale ~ Meals and snacks (12-9.30 Mon-Sat; 12-2.30, 7-9.30 Sun) ~ 0181-946 5599 ~ Open 11-11; closed evening 25 Dec

George ★ (Southwark) Map 13
Off 77 Borough High Street, SE1; ⊖ Borough/London Bridge

Southwark in the 17th c was described as a 'continuous ale-house', with 'no workers, but all drinkers'. This old coaching inn is the only one of those alehouses left, unchanged since it was rebuilt in its original style after the Southwark fire of 1676. Now owned by the National Trust, it's a splendid looking building with an appealingly rich history. The tiers of open galleries look down on a cobbled courtyard, where there are plenty of picnic-table sets and maybe in summer Morris men or performing players from the nearby Globe Theatre. It's just as unspoilt inside, the row of simple ground-floor rooms and bars all containing square-latticed windows, black beams, bare floorboards, some panelling, plain oak or elm tables and old-fashioned built-in settles, along with a 1797 'Act of Parliament' clock, dimpled glass lantern-lamps and so forth. The snuggest refuge is the simple room nearest the street, where there's an ancient beer engine (currently not in use) that looks like a cash register. Boddingtons, Flowers Original, Greene King Abbot, Whitbread Castle Eden and a changing guest on handpump; they have a beer festival on the third Monday of every month, when you may find up to 14 real ales. Also farm cider, and mulled wine in winter; darts, bar billiards, table skittles and trivia. A short choice of bar food might include soup (£2), filled bloomer sandwiches (from £2.25), ploughman's (£3), home-made pies like steak and mushroom (£3.75), and cold meats and salad (£4). A splendid central staircase goes up to a series of dining-rooms and to a gaslit balcony. Unless you know where you're going (or you're in one of the many tourist groups that flock here during the day in summer) you may well miss it, as apart from the great gates there's little to indicate that such a gem still exists behind the less auspicious looking buildings on the busy high street. The inn was mentioned by Charles Dickens in *Little Dorritt*. *(Recommended by Don Kellaway, Angie Coles, Sue Demont, Tim Barrow, Walter Reid, Howard and Margaret Buchanan, M Clarke)*

Whitbreads ~ Manager John Hall ~ Real ale ~ Lunchtime meals and snacks ~ Restaurant (not Sun; often used for groups only – check first) ~ 0171-407 2056 ~ Children in eating area of bar ~ Nearby daytime parking difficult ~ Globe Players, Morris dancers and Medieval Combat Society during summer ~ Open 11-11; closed 25 and 26 Dec, 1 Jan

Green Man £ (Putney) Map 12

Wildcroft Road, SW15; ⇌ Putney, but some distance away – take the No. 14 bus from the station and it stops right outside the pub

They've just relandscaped the pretty garden at this friendly old pub, nicely set on the edge of Putney Heath, and, many years ago, the birthplace of Thomas Cromwell. There are lots of seats as well as a swing, slide and see-saw among the flowering shrubs and trees on the good-sized lawn, with more tables on sheltered colonnaded side terraces. Every day from spring to autumn, weather permitting, there's a barbecue out here, with burgers (including vegetarian ones), sausages, kebabs, chicken, ribs or steak (£3-£7); in the winter they keep the steaks and burgers, and have a daily special as well, such as lamb casserole or spaghetti bolognese, and they also do filled rolls (£1). Inside, the cosy green-carpeted main bar opens into a quiet sitting room, and both have a sort of down-to-earth country pub feel that readers really like. Well kept Youngs Bitter and Special on handpump, reasonably priced for London, and several wines by the glass; ring the bull, dominoes, sensibly placed darts and a fruit machine. The staff work hard to keep everything just right. The pub used to be a haunt of ruthless young highwaymen like Jerry Avershawe, hanged at Kennington in 1795, and the rather pitiful footpads (the old equivalent of muggers) like Will Brown and Joseph Whitlock who were hanged after they'd stolen a baker's boy's silver buckle and a ha'penny. *(Recommended by Brad and Joni Nelson, Ian Phillips and others; more reports please)*

Youngs ~ Manager Karl Robson ~ Real ale ~ Meals and snacks (12-2.30, 7-10; not winter evenings) ~ 0181-788 8096 ~ Open 11-11

Hole in the Wall (Waterloo) Map 13

Mepham Street, SE1; ⊖ Waterloo

Don't be alarmed when the walls at this no-frills drinkers' pub start to shake and there's a loud rumbling accompaniment – it's just another train passing overhead. The deep red brick ceiling is in fact part of a railway arch, and the main bar is virtually underneath Waterloo Station. A wide range of well kept beers on handpump includes Adnams, Bass, Boddingtons, Everards Tiger, Greene King IPA, King and Barnes Sussex, Ruddles County, Theakstons Best, Websters Yorkshire and Youngs Ordinary and Special; they also stock various malt and Irish whiskies. The furnishings are very basic, and a good range of amusements includes a loudish juke box, pinball, two fruit machines, trivia and a couple of video games. Bar food includes sandwiches, home-made pies (£2.95), chilli con carne, home-cooked meats and salads. A smaller front bar is rather smarter. *(More reports please)*

Free house ~ Licensee Ulick Burke ~ Real ale ~ Meals and snacks all day ~ Week-day daytime parking difficult ~ 0171-928 6196 ~ Open 11-11; closed 25 Dec

Horniman (Southwark) Map 13

Hays Galleria, Battlebridge Lane, SE1; ⊖ London Bridge

Wonderful views of the Thames, HMS *Belfast* and Tower Bridge from the picnic-table sets outside this ambitiously designed pub. Terribly elaborate and rather smart-looking, the spacious and gleaming bar is rather like a cross between a French bistro and a Victorian local – and something else besides. There's a set of clocks made for Frederick Horniman's office showing the time in various places around the world, and the area by the sweeping bar counter is a few steps down from the door, with squared black, red and white flooring tiles and lots of polished wood. Steps lead up from here to various comfortable carpeted areas, with the tables well spread so as to allow for a feeling of spacious relaxation at quiet times but give room for people standing in groups when it's busy; part of the upstairs area is no-smoking. Bar food includes sandwiches (from £1.95), ploughman's and daily changing hot dishes such as steak and kidney pie (£4.95), and they do a four-course carvery (£12.75). Well kept Ind Coope Burton, Tetleys, Wadworths 6X, changing guests and a beer named for the brewery on handpump, and there's a tea bar serving coffee, chocolate and other hot drinks, and Danish pastries and so forth; a hundred-foot frieze shows the travels of the tea. Fruit machine, video game, unobtrusive piped music. The pub is at the end of the visually exciting Hays Galleria development, several storeys high, with a soaring glass curved roof, and supported by elegant thin cast-iron columns; various shops and boutiques open off. *(Recommended by D Cox, David and Michelle Hedges, Ian Phillips, Andy Thwaites, Thomas Nott and others)*

Nicholsons (Allied) ~ Managers Bette Bryant and Dennis Hayes ~ Real ale ~ Bar meals and snacks (12-5) ~ Carvery restaurant (not Sun evening) ~ 0171-407 3611 ~ Children welcome ~ Occasional live entertainment ~ Open 10-11 (till 4 Sat, 3 Sun); closed evenings 24 and 31 Dec and all day 25 and 26 Dec

Market Porter (Southwark) Map 13
9 Stoney Street, SE1; ⊖ London Bridge

Busy and atmospheric, this friendly pub near the market has a good range of well kept beers on handpump, which as well as the Market Bitter and Special brewed for them might offer a range of Boddingtons, Bunces Pigswill, Courage Best, Greene King Abbot, Hanby Black Magic Mild, Timothy Taylor Landlord and Young's Special. The main part of the long U-shaped bar has rough wooden ceiling beams with beer barrels balanced on them, a heavy wooden bar counter with a beamed gantry, cushioned bar stools, an open fire with stuffed animals in glass cabinets on the mantelpiece, several mounted stags' heads, and 20s-style wall lamps. A comparatively wide choice of bar food includes a range of 'quick dips' throughout the day such as chicken satay (£1.50) or calamari (£2.25), as well as sandwiches (from £1.85), filled baked potatoes (from £1.95), ploughman's (from £2.95), all day breakfast (£3.65), grilled turkey steak or rainbow trout (£3.95), seafood pancakes (£4.25), spinach and mushroom lasagne (£4.95), steaks (from £7.95), and changing daily specials; Sunday lunch. Obliging service; darts, cribbage, dominoes, fruit machine, video game, pinball and piped music. A small partly panelled room has leaded glass windows and a couple of tables. Part of the restaurant is no smoking. The company that own the pub have similar establishments in Reigate and nearby Stamford St. *(Recommended by Don Kellaway, Angie Coles, Sue Demont, Tim Barrow, David and Michelle Hedges, Brian and Jenny Seller, John Walker, Geoff Roynon)*

Free house ~ Licensee Steve Turner ~ Real ale ~ Meals and snacks (not Sat or evening Sun) ~ Restaurant (not Sun evening) ~ 0171-407 2495 ~ Children welcome ~ Open 11-11 (11-3, 7-11 Sat)

Mayflower (Rotherhithe) Map 12
117 Rotherhithe Street, SE16; ⊖ Rotherhithe

This carefully restored and atmospheric old place takes its name in honour of the ship that carried the Pilgrim Fathers to the New World from here in 1611: one side room has a set of pictures showing the way it would have been built and there's a model of the vessel too. The rather dark old-fashioned main bar has black ceiling beams, dark panelled walls, latticed windows, and high-backed winged settles and wheelback chairs around its tables. Decent bar food includes filled baguettes (£2), ploughman's (£3.50), vegetarian meals, changing specials such as cottage pie, steak and ale pie or filled Yorkshire puddings (from around £4.30), trout or grilled salmon (£5.95), and rump steak (£8.50). Well kept Bass and Greene King Abbot, IPA and Raymonts on handpump; friendly, welcoming service. Good river views from upstairs. Once upon a time the 18th-c pub was the only one in Britain licensed to sell postage stamps. The wooden jetty outside still feels very close to the Thames of days gone by, with its heavy piles plunging down into the water, converted high old warehouse buildings on either side and lighters swinging on their moorings. *(Recommended by K Flack, Jon Lyons, Nigel and Sue Foster, Joanna Whitehouse and others)*

Greene King ~ Manager Mr Fitzpatrick ~ Real ale ~ Meals and snacks (12-2.30, 6-9.30; not Sun night) ~ 0171-237 4088 ~ Children welcome ~ Open 11-11

Phoenix & Firkin ★ (Denmark Hill) Map 12

5 Windsor Walk, SE5; ⇌ Denmark Hill

An interesting conversion of a palatial Victorian railway hall but it's the vibrant atmosphere rather than the architecture that draws so many people here. A model railway train runs back and forth behind the food bar, and there are paintings of steam trains, old-fashioned station name signs, a huge double-faced station clock (originally from Llandudno Junction in Wales), solid wooden furniture on the stripped wooden floor, old seaside posters, Bovril advertisements, and plants. At one end there's a similarly furnished gallery, reached by a spiral staircase, and at the other arches lead into a food room; fruit machine. Their own Phoenix, Rail and Dogbolter on handpump, as well as two weekly guest beers like Tetleys or Golden Glory (from one of the other Firkin pubs), maybe kept under light blanket pressure. The piped music may be loud, especially in the evenings when it's quite a favourite with young people (it can be a little smoky then too). Straightforward food includes big filled baps (£2.10), a good cold buffet with pork pies, spring rolls, salads, quiche and so forth, and a couple of daily hot dishes (around £3.30). There are a couple of long benches outside, and the steps which follow the slope of the road are a popular place to sit. *(Recommended by Dr M Owton, Sarah King, Patrick Forbes, Andy Thwaites)*

Own Brew ~ Real ale ~ Meals and snacks ~ 0171-701 8282 ~ Children in eating area of bar ~ Live blues Mon and Thurs evenings ~ Open 11.30-11

Ship ♀ (Wandsworth) Map 12

41 Jews Row, SW18; ⇌ Wandsworth Town

The extensive riverside terrace of this immensely popular smart pub really comes into its own in summer. On two levels, partly cobbled and partly concrete, it has picnic table sets, pretty hanging baskets, brightly coloured flowerbeds, small trees, its own summer bar, and a Thames barge moored alongside. Inside, only a small part of the original ceiling is left in the main bar – the rest is in a light and airy conservatory style, with wooden tables, a medley of stools, and old church chairs on the wooden floorboards, and a relaxed, chatty atmosphere; one part has a Victorian fireplace, a huge clock surrounded by barge prints, and part of a milking machine on a table, and there's a rather battered harmonium, old-fashioned bagatelle, and jugs of flowers around the window sills. The basic public bar has plain wooden furniture, a black kitchen range in the fireplace and darts, bar billiards, pinball and a juke box. Youngs Bitter, Special and Winter Warmer on handpump, freshly squeezed orange juice, wide choice of wines, several by the glass. Very good, unusual bar food uses mostly free-range produce, and might include dishes like sandwiches, bouillabaisse (£3.50), New Zealand mussel salad (£4.50), Chinese spare ribs on a beansprout and fruit salad (£6) and duck kebabs with a quince and red onion sauce (£7); there's an al fresco restaurant on the terrace. Their annual firework display is incredibly popular and draws huge crowds of young people. The parking situation has been eased slightly by the addition of an adjacent car park, though this can get full pretty quickly in the summer. *(Recommended by Paul Cartledge, Wayne Brindle; more reports please)*

Youngs ~ Licensees Charles Gotto and D N Haworth ~ Real ale ~ Meals and snacks (12-3, 7-10) ~ Restaurant ~ 0181-870 9667 ~ Children in eating area of bar and restaurant ~ Open 11-11

Windmill ♀ (Clapham) Map 12

Clapham Common South Side, SW4; ⊖ Clapham South

A painting in the Tate by J P Herring has this fine old Victorian inn in the background, shown behind local turn-of-the-century characters returning from the

Derby Day festivities. Nicely placed right by the common, it's a smartly civilised place, busy and bustling, and still offering varied delights to locals and travellers. Drawing particular acclaim over the past year or so have been the entertaining Monday opera evenings in the conservatory, when the genre's rising stars perform various solos and arias; they also have good jazz nights in here, all nicely segregated from the comfortable domed main bar. Spacious and airy, this has as its centrepiece an illuminated aquarium, surrounded by colourfully upholstered L-shaped banquettes, and plenty of prints and pictures on the walls, including several of Dutch windmills. It's a big place, so although it often gets lively, you should usually be able to find a quiet corner. Bar food includes sandwiches and baguettes (from £1.50), soup (£1.75), ploughman's (from £3.50), vegetable lasagne or kedgeree (£3.75), salads (from £4.45), chicken satay (£5.25), barbecue spare ribs (£6.50), steak (£9.75) and home-made daily specials; service is friendly and cheerful. Youngs Bitter and Special on handpump, a good choice of wines by the glass and plenty more by the bottle; fruit machine and video game. They've recently added a barbecue area in the secluded front courtyard with tubs of shrubs, doing lunches every day in summer, and there's another courtyard at the opposite end. The inn can get packed in summer, when it seems to serve not just the pub but half the Common too. It's a particularly nice play to stay – they've spent a good deal of time and effort upgrading the accommodation side over the last couple of years. *(More reports please)*

Youngs ~ Manager Richard Williamson ~ Real ale ~ Meals and snacks (till 10) ~ Restaurant ~ 0181-673 4578 ~ Children in no-smoking conservatory ~ Live opera by up-and-coming artists Mon, jazz Sun, cabaret Fri ~ Open 11-11 ~ Bedrooms: £75B/£85B

WEST LONDON

During weekday or Saturday daytime you may not be able to find a meter very close to the Anglesea Arms or the Windsor Castle, and parking very near in the evening may sometimes be tricky with both of these, but there shouldn't otherwise be problems in this area

Anglesea Arms (Chelsea) Map 13
15 Selwood Terrace, SW7; ⊖ South Kensington

Not many places manage to be smart and cosy at the same time but this cheery pub pulls it off with ease. In summer especially it's popular with well heeled young people who spill out onto the terrace and pavement, and even in winter it's generally packed in the evenings, resulting in a very pleasant chatty feel. Inside, the bar has central elbow tables, leather chesterfields, faded turkey carpets on the wood-strip floor, wood panelling, and big windows with attractive swagged curtains; at one end several booths with partly glazed screens have cushioned pews and spindleback chairs, and down some steps there's a small carpeted room with captain's chairs, high stools and a Victorian fireplace. The old-fashioned mood is heightened by some heavy portraits, prints of London, a big station clock, bits of brass and pottery, and large brass chandeliers. Well kept Adnams, Boddingtons, Brakspears SB, Fullers London Pride, Greene King Abbot, Harveys, and Youngs Special on handpump, and several malt and Irish whiskies. Food from a glass cabinet includes doorstep sandwiches (from £1.50), ploughman's (£2.75), broccoli, cauliflower or macaroni cheese (£3.80), pies such as turkey and ham or steak and mushroom (all £3.90), sirloin steak (£6), and a Sunday roast (£4.95); in the late evening, you may get sandwiches for £1 or less. Good, quick service. *(Recommended by Quentin Williamson, Sue Demont, Tim Barrow, Graham and Karen Oddey; more reports please)*

Free House ~ Licensee Patrick Timmons ~ Real ale ~ Meals and snacks (not Sun evening) ~ 0171-373 7960 ~ Children welcome lunchtimes only ~ Daytime parking metered ~ Open 11-3, 5(7 Sat)-11; closed 25 and 26 Dec

Churchill Arms £ 🍴 (Kensington) Map 12
119 Kensington Church St, W8; ⊖ Notting Hill Gate/Kensington High Street

Winter is the time to come to this friendly pub, particularly around Halloween or the week leading up to Churchill's birthday (November 30th). That's when they really go to town, decorating the place with balloons, candles and appropriate oddities, serving special drinks and generally just creating a lively carefree atmosphere. All year round it feels very much like a village local, something that owes a lot to the character and enthusiasm of the good-natured Irish landlord, who obviously really cares about the pub and the people who come in it. He has quite a memory for faces and goes out of his way to offer an individual welcome. One of his hobbies is collecting butterflies, and you'll see a variety of prints and books on the subject dotted around the bar. There are also lamps, miners' lights, horse tack, bedpans and brasses hanging from the ceiling, a couple of interesting carved figures and statuettes behind the central bar counter, prints of American presidents, and lots of Churchill memorabilia. The spacious and rather smart plant-filled dining conservatory is where the landlord hatches his butterflies, but is better known for its big choice of really excellent Thai food: chicken and cashew nuts (£4.50) or Thai noodles, roast duck curry or beef curry (£4.75). They also do things like sandwiches (from £1.75), sausages (£2.15), ploughman's or home-made steak and kidney (£2.75), and Sunday lunch (£4.75). Well kept Fullers ESB, London Pride, Chiswick and Hock Mild on handpump; cheerful service; shove-ha'penny, fruit machine and unobtrusive piped music; they have their own cricket and football teams. *(Recommended by Stephen R Holman, Tony and Lynne Stark, Susan and John Douglas and others)*

Fullers ~ Manager Jerry O'Brien ~ Real ale ~ Meals and snacks (12-2, 6-9.30; not Sun evening) ~ Restaurant (not Sun evening) ~ 0171-727 4242 ~ Children welcome ~ Open 11-11; closed evening 25 Dec

Dove ★ (Hammersmith) Map 12

19 Upper Mall, W6; ⊖ Ravenscourt Park

One of the most famous of all the pubs that punctuate the banks of the Thames, this atmospheric and characterful old place is also one of the nicest. In summer most people head for the the tiny Thameside terrace at the back, where the main flagstoned area, down some steps, has a few teak tables and white metal and teak chairs looking over the low river wall to the Thames reach just above Hammersmith Bridge. A very civilised spot. In the evenings you'll often see rowing crews practising along this stretch of the water. By the entrance from the quiet alley, the main bar has black wood panelling, red leatherette cushioned built-in wall settles and stools around dimpled copper tables, old framed advertisements, and photographs of the pub; very well kept Fullers London Pride and ESB on handpump. Up some steps, a room with small settles and solid wooden furniture has a big, clean and efficiently served glass food cabinet, offering filled baked potatoes (£2.95), salads (£3.95), shepherd's pie or steak and kidney pie (£4.25), carbonnade of beef or ham, leek and mushroom pie (£4.65) and various daily specials; they also do a range of Thai meals, particularly in the evening (from £5.50). Most readers like the food, though a few this year have had slightly mixed experiences. No noisy games machines or piped music. Perhaps the best time to visit is at lunchtime when it's not quite so crowded, but even at its busiest, the staff remain briskly efficient. There's a manuscript of 'Rule Britannia' on the wall in one of the bars: James Thomson, who wrote it, is said to have written the final part of his less well known 'The Seasons' in an upper room here, dying of a fever he had caught on a trip from here to Kew in bad weather. Elsewhere a plaque marks the level of the highest-ever tide in 1928. Local people often still call it the Doves, the pub's name until 1948. This stretch of the river has a number of decent pubs all close together – this is the best. *(Recommended by Ian Phillips, Gordon, Martin Kay, Andrea Fowler, A W Dickinson, Andy Thwaites, Stephen and Julie Brown, Simon Collett-Jones, L Grant, Jenny and Brian Seller, M Clarke, A M McCarthy, M Quine)*

Fullers ~ Tenants Brian Lovrey and Dale Neal ~ Real ale ~ Meals and snacks (12-3, 6-10.30) ~ 0181-748 5405 ~ Children welcome ~ Open 11-11

Ferret & Firkin (Fulham) Map 12

Lots Road, SW10; ⊖ Fulham Broadway, but some distance away

Popular with a good mix of mostly young, easy-going customers, this is a determinedly basic place, with the same infectiously cheery atmosphere you'll find in most of the other Firkin pubs. A small, unusually curved corner-house, it has traditional furnishings well made from good wood on the unsealed bare floorboards, slowly circulating colonial-style ceiling fans, a log-effect gas fire, tall airy windows, and plenty of standing room in front of the long bar counter – which is also curved. Several readers feel it looks like a sort of anglicised Wild-West saloon. Well kept beers include their own Ferret and notoriously strong Dogbolter, Balloon from another of the Firkin pubs, and a guest like Felinfoel Double Dragon; with 24 hours' notice you may be able to collect a bulk supply of their own beers. Attentive friendly service. A food counter serves heftily filled giant meat-and-salad rolls (£2), salads (£3.50), and three daily hot dishes like chilli con carne, steak and kidney pie or casseroles (£3.50); Sunday roast (£4.25). Good – and popular – juke box. It's handy for Chelsea Harbour, which, to continue the Western analogies, sadly at times feels rather like a ghost town. *(Recommended by Susan and John Douglas, Simon Collett-Jones, Gordon, Dave Carter, Graham Reeve)*

Own brew ~ Manager Fergal Bolger ~ Real ale ~ Meals and snacks (till about 7 or 8) ~ 0171-352 6645 ~ Daytime parking is metered ~ Pianist or guitarist Fri-Sun evenings ~ Open 11-11

Kings Arms (Hampton Court) Map 12

Hampton Court Rd; next to Lion Gate; ≥ Hampton Court

An imposing, white-painted pub right on the edge of the grounds of Hampton Court, this is a friendly, comfortable place. One bar, leading off to the right, has a cosy atmosphere, black panelling, some seats and tables made from casks, and fine stained glass around the serving counter. The lounge bar on the left is mainly given over to food, and has one or two settles, bunches of dried flowers over an old cooking range and walls stripped back to the brick. Bar food, from an efficient servery, includes soup (£1.95), sandwiches, ploughman's (£3.95), smoked haddock and poached egg (£4.40), battered cod and chips (£4.95) and steak, mushroom and ale pie (£5.95). Well kept Badger Best, Hard Tackle and Tanglefoot, Gribble Black Adder, and Wadworths 6X on handpump; service is friendly and efficient. They also have a little tea shop, with several unusual varieties of the brew and light snacks. The public bar at the end is properly old-fashioned and notably relaxed, with good games – an old pin-ball machine that takes two-pence pieces (proceeds to the RNLI), and a good darts area; sawdust on the floor, dried hops hanging from the beams, a few casks, a fireplace with a stuffed pheasant above it, and some enamel adverts, one for Camp coffee; cribbage, dominoes, fruit machine, board games and unobtrusive piped music. There are several picnic-table sets outside by the road. Dogs welcome (free biscuits for them). Parking is metered nearby. *(Recommended by Ralf Zeyssig, Gill Earle, Andrew Burton, Ian Phillips, Susan and John Douglas, M Clarke)*

Badger ~ Managers Terri and Niall Williams ~ Real ale ~ Meals and snacks (11-10) ~ Upstairs restaurant; closed Sun evening, Mon ~ 0181-977 1729 ~ Children welcome till 8pm ~ Open 11-11; closed evening 25 and 26 Dec

Popes Grotto (Twickenham) Map 12

Cross Deep; ≥ Strawberry Hill

Well-run and spacious, this pleasantly low-key pub has a very relaxed and comfortable feel to its stroll-around main bar. There are lots of little round seats and armed chairs, and a quieter, more intimate fringe behind a balustrade at the back. Also, a snug and rather stylish bow-windowed front bar, and a public bar with darts, shove-ha'penny, dominoes, cribbage, fruit machine and video game. Good bar food includes soup (£1.70), sandwiches (from £2), filled baked potatoes (from £2.85), salads (from £3.80), chicken curry (£4), king prawns in herbs and garlic (£4.30), spinach and mushroom lasagne (£4.50), gammon (£5), sirloin steak (£8.30), puddings, daily specials and Sunday lunch (£4.95). Well kept Youngs Bitter and Special on handpump, with Winter Warmer in season; also a good range of malt and other whiskies. The back terraced garden has seats and tables under trees, with more on the front terrace. Public gardens opposite (closed at night) slope down to the Thames. The pub is named after the poet

Alexander Pope who had a villa nearby. (*Recommended by Derek and Sylvia Stephenson, M·Clarke; more reports please*)

Youngs ~ Manager Stephen Brough ~ Real ale ~ Meals and snacks ~ 0181-892 3050 ~ Children in eating area of bar till 9pm ~ Open 11-3, 5.30-11, all day Sat

Sporting Page (Chelsea) Map 12
6 Camera Place, SW10; ⊖ Sloane Square, but some distance away

Entertaining sporting decorations cover the walls of this unusual little place – old prints of people playing polo, Rugby football, cricket and so forth, and big painted-tile-effect murals of similar scenes. Determinedly smart but busy and relaxed, the pub has a rather crisp, airy feel thanks to its big windows and light paintwork, and the sturdy, cleanly cut tables around the walls leave plenty of room by the bar. Good interesting bar food might include soup or potato skins with cheese and sour cream (£2.50), a pasta of the day (£4.50), hot chicken, bacon and avocado salad (£4.95), smoked salmon and scrambled eggs or salmon fishcakes with hollandaise sauce (£5), sirloin steak sandwich (£5.25), chicken breast stuffed with avocado and garlic (£5.50) and puddings like banoffi pie (£3). Boddingtons, John Smiths, Wadworths 6X and Websters Yorkshire on handpump; decent house wines, espresso coffee; civilised service. They show all UK Rugby internationals on big screens. There are a couple of picnic-table sets outside, and the cars parked beside them should give a good indication to the overall style of the place. See also the Front Page (Central London). (*More reports please*)

Courage ~ Lease: Rupert Fowler, Michael Phillips ~ Real ale ~ Meals and snacks (12-2.30, 7-10.15) ~ 0171-376 3694 ~ Open 11-3, 5.30(6 Sat)-11

White Horse ♀ 🍺 (Fulham) Map 12
21 Parsons Green, SW6; ⊖ Parsons Green

Plenty to praise at this very well run and rather tastefully refurbished place overlooking the green – the atmosphere, food and service, and best of all perhaps the well chosen range of drinks. It's a favourite with smart young people, especially on summer evenings, when crowds of them relax at the white cast-iron tables and chairs on the quite continental-feeling front terrace; it's times like these that have led to locals affectionately dubbing the pub 'the Sloaney Pony'. It's no less popular earlier in the day, when it's generally busy with ladies lunching. At all times the atmosphere is comfortable and easygoing, and the service refreshingly helpful; they always greet you with a smile and take time to explain their eclectic choice of drinks. Particularly well kept and often unusual beers might include Adnams Extra, Bass, Harveys Sussex, Highgate Mild and a guest on handpump, with some helpful tasting notes; they also have 15 Trappist beers, a guest foreign lager on draught, a dozen malt whiskies, and a good, interesting and not overpriced wine list. They organise several themed beer evenings and weekends (often spotlighting regional breweries) – the best known is for strong old ale held on the last Saturday in November. You'll generally find lively celebrations too on American Independence Day or Thanksgiving. Well-liked weekday lunches might include soup (£2.25), spinach and lentil au gratin (£3.90), tagliatelle with squid (£4.50), steak and kidney pie (£4.95), spicy coconut chicken (£5.25) to salmon and dill fishcakes or venison marinated in beer (£5); in the evening there's a changing à la carte menu with dishes like tortilla (£2.95), smoked salmon scramble (£4.50), crispy bacon and spinach salad (£5.90), oriental vegetable stir fry (£6) and salmon fishcakes with tomato sauce or rabbit, walnut and prune casserole with a tarragon risotto (£6.75). Several of the high-backed pews at the side are often reserved for eating. They also do a very good Sunday lunch served in the old billiard room upstairs. The main part of the spacious U-shaped bar has big leather chesterfields and huge windows with slatted wooden blinds; to one side is a plainer area with leatherette wall banquettes on the wood plank floor, and a tiled Victorian fireplace; dominoes, cribbage, chess, cards, fruit machine. The manageress is efficient and friendly, and very much in evidence – you'll often see her organising her troops. (*Recommended by Sue Demont, Tim Barrow, Bob and Maggie Atherton, Wayne Brindle and others; more reports please)*

Bass ~ Manager Sally Cruickshank ~ Real ale ~ Meals and snacks (12-2.45, 5.30-10) ~ 0171-736 2115 ~ Children in eating area ~ Occasional jazz nights ~ Open 11.30-3, 5-11; all day summer Sats, 11-4, 7-11 winter Sats; closed 4 or 5 days over Christmas

Windsor Castle (Holland Park/Kensington) Map 12

114 Campden Hill Road, W8; ◒ Holland Park/Notting Hill Gate

It's said that in the early 19th c when this splendid pub was built you could see the real Windsor Castle from the top of this hill. The surroundings and view have changed almost beyond recognition since then, but the pub has stayed very much the same, a relaxing country-style tavern with a great deal of character and atmosphere. One of the features that marks it out at the moment is the food, an interesting range of dishes that's especially welcoming in a part of the world not renowned for unusual bar meals. Served all day, the changing choice might typically include sandwiches (from £2.25), seafood chowder (£2.95), salads such as spinach, stilton or walnut or riccotta and aubergine, or grilled goat's cheese (£3.95), vegetable couscous (£4.75), fish dishes such as tuna steak (£4.95), moules marinières (£4.50) or a half dozen oysters (£5), steak and kidney pudding, rack of lamb, game pie or rabbit pie (£5.95), and steaks; the Sunday lunch is popular. Over the bar they sell sausages made by the landlord's brother (75p); he has a sausage shop nearby. The series of little dark-panelled, old-fashioned rooms, have sturdy built-in elm benches, time-smoked ceilings and soft lighting; a snug little pre-war-style dining room opens off the bar. Adnams Extra, Bass, Charringtons IPA, Hancocks HB and a monthly guest on handpump; decent house wines, various malt whiskies, maybe mulled wine in winter. Helpful, enthusiastic staff. No fruit machines or piped music. An attractive summer feature is the big tree-shaded back garden which has lots of sturdy teak seats and tables on flagstones, knee-high stone walls (eminently sittable-on) dividing them, high ivy-covered sheltering walls, and soft shade from a sweeping, low-branched plane tree, a lime and a flowering cherry; there's a brick garden bar out here. Usually fairly quiet at lunchtime, the pub can be packed in the evenings, often with smart young people. The Camden bar is no smoking Sunday lunchtimes. *(Recommended by Annie Rolfe, Gordon, Ian Phillips, Nick Dowson, B Brown, Sue Demont, Tim Barrow, David Quirk, and others)*

Charringtons (Bass) ~ Manager Matthew O'Keefe ~ Real ale ~ Meals and snacks (11-11) ~ 0171-727 8491 ~ Children welcome ~ Daytime parking metered ~ Open 11-11

EAST LONDON

Grapes (Limehouse) Map 12

76 Narrow Street, E14; ◒ Shadwell, but some distance away

Dickens used this characterful 16th-c pub as the basis of his 'Six Jolly Fellowship Porters' in *Our Mutual Friend*, and it was from here that watermen used to row out drunks, drown them, then sell the salvaged bodies to the anatomists. Nicely off the tourist track, it's a relatively quiet place, and was a favourite with Rex Whistler who came here to paint the river (the results are really quite special). The back part is the oldest, and the glass-roofed back balcony is a fine place for a sheltered waterside drink. The partly panelled bar has lots of prints, mainly of actors, and some elaborately etched windows. Friary Meux, Ind Coope Burton, Tetleys and a guest beer on handpump (they hope to start having another soon). Bar food such as sandwiches (from £1.50), ploughman's (£3.75), and main courses with a fishy emphasis such as seafood risotto, fish and chips, lemon sole or seafood mornay (all around £4.50); the upstairs fish restaurant (with fine views of the river) is highly praised; piped music. *(Recommended by Andy Thwaites and others; more reports please)*

Taylor-Walker (Allied) ~ Managers Michele and Gary Wicks ~ Real ale ~ Meals and snacks (not Mon evening, Sun) ~ Restaurant (closed Sun) ~ 0171-987 4396 ~ Children in eating area of bar ~ Open 12-3, 5.30(7 Sat)-11

Hollands (Stepney) Map 12

9 Exmouth Street, E1; ⊖ Aldgate East, but some distance away

Much the same as it has been in all the time we've known it, and indeed a good deal longer, this is an unspoilt Victorian gem. Most of the decorations and furnishings are original, and the heavy bar counter has swivelling etched and cut glass snob screens, antique mirrors, *Vanity Fair* pictures, Victorian cartoons and photographs, and a clutter of trumpets, glass and brass ornaments hanging from the ochre painted and panelled ceiling in the main bar. Through an arched doorway and heavy brocade curtains is the split-level, red-tiled lounge bar, with its panelled and re-upholstered bench seats, old sepia photographs, brass pots hanging from the ceiling and a big Victorian fireplace with large china ornaments on its mantelpiece. Bar food consists of freshly made sandwiches (from £1.50), ploughman's, and hot dishes such as scampi, shepherd's pie (nothing more than £3.50). Youngs Bitter and Special on handpump; darts. *(More reports please)*

Youngs ~ Tenants Alan and Susan Jones ~ Real ale ~ Lunchtime snacks and meals ~ 0171-790 3057 ~ Open 11-11

Lucky Dip

Besides the fully inspected pubs, you might like to try these Lucky Dips recommended to us and described by readers (if you do, please send us reports). We have split them into the main areas used for the full reports – Central, North, and so on. Within each area the Lucky Dips are listed by postal district, ending with Greater London suburbs on the edge of that area.

CENTRAL LONDON
EC1

[Bunhill Row], *Artillery*: Good prompt friendly service, well kept Fullers, darts in small unspoilt public bar – rest kitted out in standard 'character'style *(Brian Jones)*

[56 Faringdon Rd], *Betsey Trotwood*: Decent enough pub with well kept Shepherd Neame ales, busy spot but well away from visitors *(T Nott)*

[St Martins Le Grand; entry via wine bar at NE exit from St Pauls tube stn], *City Pipe*: Davys tavern, good pastiche of ancient style with lots of bare wood, sawdust on floor, well kept Old Wallop in pewter tankards, good traditional English food in main room and lots of nooks and crannies off; cl weekends *(Tim Heywood, Sophie Wilne)*

☆ [115 Charterhouse St], *Fox & Anchor*: Good food esp tender meat in long, narrow bar with narrow tables; opens early for Smithfield workers' breakfasts *(Dr and Mrs A K Clarke)*

☆ [1 Middle St], *Hand & Shears*: Traditional Smithfield pub dating from 16th c and still much of the old layout; lively mixed clientele, well kept Courage ales, quick service, interesting bric-a-brac, reasonably priced food – evening too; open all day exc weekends, cl Sun *(Brian Jones, LYM)*

[33 Seward St], *Leopard*: Pleasant walled garden with picnic-table sets, reasonable choice of bar food inc competitively priced hot specials served promptly; Courage-related ales, gleaming copper pipework in lavatories *(Ian Phillips)*

☆ [166 Goswell Rd], *Pheasant & Firkin*: Very basic range of food and decent beer brewed on the premises in pubby bare-boards pub, fairly recently redecorated, with pleasant atmosphere (esp midweek evenings), congenial staff, good cheap CD juke box, cheerful Fri night guitarist *(Sue Demont, Tim Barrow, Ian Phillips, LYM)*

[Rising Sun Ct; Cloth Fair], *Rising Sun*: Formerly very popular good Sam Smiths pub, closed spring 1994 evidently for major refurbishment *(News please)*

[4 Leather Lane], *Sir Christopher Hatton*: Lively, with big cellar bar, well kept Bass, Worthington BB and other ales, popular lunchtime bar food; has been closed Sat evening and Sun *(Dr and Mrs A K Clarke)*

[Rosoman St], *Thomas Wethered*: Whitbreads pub with well kept Adnams, Flowers, Greene King Abbot, very reasonably priced well cooked standard Country Fayre food lunchtime and evenings, genial staff; jazz Tues *(G L Tong)*

[126 Newgate St], *Viaduct*: Interesting – pub forms a quarter-circle, opp Old Bailey; well kept real ales, welcoming regulars – many of them postmen; Victorian decor all the way up to the high ceiling *(Tim Heywood)*

EC2

[New St; off Liverpool St], *Bell*: Well kept ales such as Adnams Extra, Tetleys, Wadworths 6X *(D Cox)*

EC3

[St Michaels Alley, Cornhill], *Jamaica Wine*

House: Upstairs bare-boards bar divided by partitioning, wine bottles and intriguing collection of copper vessels behind bar; downstairs livelier with young city gents, on hot days spilling into alleys and garden around corner; good sandwiches (the roast beef takes some beating) and pies, friendly atmosphere *(Ian Phillips)*

EC4

[Lower Thames St, below Tower Bridge nr junction with Fish St], *City FOB*: Pubby and relaxing sawdust-floor bar with own good beer in half-gallon jugs or pewter tankards, efficient pleasant staff, bar nibbles, dining area; cl Sat/Sun *(G Walsh)*

[29 Knightrider St], *Horn*: Lots of little booths, well kept Eldridge Pope; said to be associated with Guy Fawkes *(Dr and Mrs A K Clarke)*

☆ [Fleet St, nr Ludgate Circus], *Old Bell*: Rebuilt by Wren as commissariat for his workers on St Brides Church (burnt down in 1940 air raid); largely unspoilt, small cosy flagstoned front bar with trap door to cellar, stained-glass window, nice window seat; back bar with cast-iron tables and unusual three-legged triangular stools on sloping bare boards; particularly well kept beer *(Gordon, Andy Thwaites)*

☆ [Ludgate Circus], *Old King Lud*: 10 to 15 changing reasonably priced real ales in busy pub recently renovated in 'beams and sawdust' style, no music, knowledgeable and helpful staff; yesterday's sports page from *The Times* framed in the gents'; *(Tim Heywood, Carl Stevenage)*

[22 Fleet St], *Olde Cock*: Remarkably friendly, with well kept beer *(Dr and Mrs A K Clarke)*

☆ [99 Fleet St], *Punch*: Warm, comfortable, softly lit Victorian pub, not too smart, ornate mirrors in entrance lobby, more mirrors in bar, dozens of *Punch* cartoons, ornate plaster ceiling with unusual domed skylight, good bar food, Allied and other ales such as Marstons and Wadworths *(Gordon, Dr and Mrs A K Clarke)*

[164 Queen Victoria St], *Sea Horse*: Well kept Courage Best and Directors, choice of food, seats outside; handy for Mansion House *(S C Brown)*

SW1

☆ [Victoria St], *Albert*: Handsome and colourful exterior set off against bleak surrounding cliffs of modern glass; solid and spacious inside, yet packed weekday lunchtimes, gleaming mahogany, original gas lamps, engraved glass; quick bar food, well kept Courage-related ales, friendly service, upstairs restaurant *(Richard Waller, Mark Walker, BB)*

☆ [Eaton Terr], *Antelope*: Cheery upmarket panelled local, well kept Allied and guest ales, decent wines, decent food; can get crowded evenings; open all day, children in eating area *(TBB, M Clarke, LYM)*

[104 Horseferry Rd], *Barley Mow*:

Comfortable and well kept, Courage-related ales, good value efficient self-service food counter, helpful staff, a few pavement tables in side street; piped music may be obtrusive *(John Fazakerley, BB)*

[62 Petty France], *Buckingham Arms*: Congenial Youngs local close to Passport Office and Buckingham Palace, unusual long side corridor fitted out with elbow ledge for drinkers, well kept ales, good value simple lunchtime food, service friendly and efficient even when busy *(Brian Jones, LYM)*

[20 The Broadway], *Feathers*: Large comfortable pub, a Scotland Yard local, bar food downstairs, restaurant up, well kept Bass and Charrington IPA *(Robert Lester, Stephen Savill, BB)*

[43 Vauxhall Bridge Rd], *Lord High Admiral*: Simple good food, real ales such as Shipstones, pool *(the Shinkmans)*

[Dean Bradley St], *Marquis of Granby*: Big open-plan Charringtons pub, with Fullers London Pride and Youngs too, rather restricted wines, lunchtime food, largely Australian staff; open all day, busy with civil servants lunchtime and early evening; cl weekends *(Dr J R G Beavon, Robert Lester)*

☆ [58 Millbank], *Morpeth Arms*: Early Victorian Youngs pub handy for the Tate, old prints, photographs, old books, earthenware jars and bottles; busy lunchtimes, quieter evenings – good roomy atmosphere, well kept ales, good choice of wines, food, helpful staff; seats outside (a lot of traffic) *(John Fazakerley, Dr J R G Beavon, Quentin Williamson, BB)*

☆ [153 Knightsbridge], *Paxtons Head*: Splendid Victorian pub, calm and unhurried, attractive period decor and furnishings (the glass and mirrors came from Paxton's Crystal Palace), decent steaks and so forth upstairs, nice little cellar overflow bar *(Ian Phillips)*

[23 Crown Passage; behind St James's St, off Pall Mall], *Red Lion*: Pleasant setting down narrow pedestrian alley nr Christies, small cosy local with panelling and leaded lights, decent lunchtime food, unobtrusive piped music *(Gordon, BB)*

☆ [D of York St], *Red Lion*: Busy little pub notable for dazzling mirrors, crystal chandeliers and cut and etched windows, splendid mahogany, ornamental plaster ceiling – architecturally, central London's most perfect small Victorian pub; good Australian service even when it's packed, minuscule eating area up an elegant cast-iron spiral staircase, decent sandwiches, snacks and hot dishes, well kept Allied ales *(Gordon, LYM)*

[Rutherford St; on corner with Regency St], *Royal Oak*: Very good wines and good food in unpretentious single bar, part bare boards *(Dr J R G Beavon)*

[33 Whitehall], *Silver Cross*: Small maybe crowded pub with suprisingly fine Italian waggon-vaulted ceiling; good lunchtime food from servery by entrance, pleasant atmosphere, Courage-related beers; said to have been a tavern since 1674, and to date back to 13th c *(Mark Walker, BB)*

☆ [Victoria Stn], *Wetherspoons*: Warm, comfortable, not overcrowded, with cheap real ale, reasonably priced food all day, individual atmosphere, usual lack of gimmicks and themes, good staff and housekeeping *(Comus Elliott, Neil Barker)*

[Horseferry Rd, corner Monck St], *White Horse & Bower*: Recently refurbished in ancient style, food at lunchtime (busy then), Fullers London Pride, Worthington BB, darts, TV, some seats outside *(Dr J R G Beavon)*

[71 Kinnerton St], *Wilton Arms*: Pleasant and comfortable civilised local with friendly atmosphere, Whitbreads-related ales, bar food; open all day *(T Nott, G Walsh)*

SW3

[17 Mossop St], *Admiral Codrington*: Solid panelled pub with well kept beers, friendly staff, vine in covered garden *(Dr and Mrs A K Clarke)*

☆ [87 Flood St], *Coopers Arms*: Unusual furnishings and decor inc lots of stuffed creatures keeping an eye on you (and not just the locals, either), relaxed atmosphere even when busy; food (not Sat/Sun evenings) inc some inventive hot dishes and attractive show of cheeses and cold pies on chunky deal table; well kept Youngs Bitter and Special, good choice of wines by the glass; under same management as Alma and Ship in South London (see main entries) *(George Atkinson, LYM)*

[Lawrence St], *Cross Keys*: Bustling Victorian local with island bar, interesting old-fashioned layout, sheltered back courtyard, well kept Courage ales, bar food; new restaurant *(Sarah King, Patrick Forbes, LYM)*

[43 Beauchamp Pl], *Grove*: Though much altered (bar along one side as opposed to in middle), still something of an oasis in a sea of feminine frippery; reasonably priced bar food *(Dave Braisted)*

☆ [50 Cheyne Walk], *Kings Head & Eight Bells*: Well worth knowing for attractive location, as if on Thames-side village green, with some tables and chairs outside; friendly cosy local, clean and comfortable, with decent food at reasonable prices in bar and restaurant, well kept ales inc Brakspears; well behaved dogs allowed *(Mark Walker, George Atkinson, Paul Bowden, David Dimock, Gordon, BB)*

W1

☆ [54 Old Compton St], *Admiral Duncan*: Friendly and efficient drinking pub with well kept Theakstons Best and Old Peculier, friendly quick service, bare bricks and floorboards, good busy atmosphere, piped music, fruit machine *(Mark Walker, P Smith)*

[Bathurst St, just behind Lancaster Gate Hotel], *Archery Tavern*: Homely three-room pub with pots and hanging baskets of dried flowers and herbs in front bars, games inc darts in back room, horses stabled in yard behind *(Gordon)*

[8 Dorset St], *Barley Mow*: Built in 1791, a pub when Marylebone was still a village; attractive, unspoilt and cosy, with panelling, old pictures, two unusual cubicles abutting on to serving bar in which the poor old farmers could pawn their watches to the landlord in private *(Gordon)*

☆ [Shepherd Mkt], *Bunch of Grapes*: Old-fashioned traditional pub, dimly lit friendly bar, good range of well kept ales, simple bar food; often packed with smartly dressed people evenings, surrounded by the bustle of this lively enclave; open all day, children welcome *(G Walsh, Bill and Edee Miller, Prof S Barnett, Gordon, Ian Phillips, LYM)*

[Kingly St], *Clachan*: Popular and comfortable, ornate plaster ceiling supported by two large fluted and decorated pillars; smaller drinking alcove up three or four steps *(Gordon)*

[Poland St], *Coach & Horses*: Small, with friendly staff, good choice of real ales such as Greene King Abbot, Marstons Pedigree, Morlands Old Speckled Hen and three or four others, good coffee and house wines, *Private Eye* cartoons and customers *(G Atkinson, Walter Reid)*

[another, in Romilly St], *Coach & Horses*: Crowded and lively, with great atmosphere, irregular regulars, decent food *(Michael Clarke, Nigel Woolliscroft)*

[27 Great Portland St], *Cock*: Large Victorian pub still with tiled floor and lots of wood inc good carving, some cut and etched glass, ornate plasterwork, velvet curtains; Sam Smiths OB and Museum *(Walter Reid)*

[151 Cleveland St], *De Hems*: Unusual pastiche of a Dutch pub, lots of old Dutch engravings, big continental founts; real ale *(Dr and Mrs A K Clarke)*

[43 Weymouth Mews], *Dover Castle*: Well kept real ales such as Adnams, Boddingtons and Wadworths 6X, quiet cosy atmosphere *(Sue Demont, Tim Barrow)*

[94A Crawford St], *Duke of Wellington*: Welcoming little local with interesting signed pictures, prints and beer bottles, salt beef speciality, outstanding Bass and other well kept beers inc a guest; tables outside *(Peter and Jenny Quine)*

☆ [55 Gt Portland St], *George*: Solid old-fashioned BBC local, lots of mahogany and engraved mirrors, friendly atmosphere, well kept Greene King ales, straightforward food; open all day, cl 6 Sat *(Brian and Anna Marsden, Mike and Wendy Proctor, LYM)*

[Bulstrode St], *Golden Eagle*: One-room local with choice of well kept real ales, decent lunchtime food in local sausages; piano music *(Catherine Boardman)*

☆ [2 Shepherd Mkt], *Kings Arms*: Lively and busy, minimalist bare wood and rough concrete decor, dim upper gallery, friendly young staff, good range of bar food all day, Courage-related ales and Wadworths 6X; CD juke box may be loud, and some evenings they allow only couples inside; summer pavement overflow *(Ian Phillips, LYM)*

[Barrett St/James St], *Lamb & Flag*: Pleasant bare-boards pub with panelling and low ribbed and bossed ceiling, local customers, Courage-related ales, attractive bar counter with barley-sugar pillars supporting coloured leaded glass *(Walter Reid)*

[7 Greek St], *Pillars of Hercules*: Ornate heavily painted plasterwork in largely unspoilt pub with good choice of real ales such as Batemans, Marstons Pedigree, Theakstons, Youngers, specialised range of bottled beers; food esp pies *(Walter Reid)*

[Wigmore St; corner with St Christopher Pl], *Pontefract Castle*: Friendly service, pleasant food and decor, well kept beer inc occasional beer festival with wide choice *(Richard Waller)*

☆ [Kingly St], *Red Lion*: Well kept Sam Smiths OB and Museum in relaxed and friendly pub, solidly modernised without being spoilt; reasonably priced good food upstairs, video juke box (may be loud evening) *(Mark Walker, Ian Phillips, LYM)*

[5 Charles St], *Running Footman*: Exceptionally friendly Australian bar staff *(Sally Edsall)*

[Wardour St], *Ship*: Remarkable value Fullers pub, friendly if perhaps a little twee, with well kept ales, decent generous lunchtime food *(Dr and Mrs A K Clarke, C J Parsons)*

☆ [Langham Pl; take express lift in far corner of hotel lobby], *St Georges Hotel*: Expensive but civilised Summit Bar has magnificent bird's-eye view of London from floor-to-ceiling picture windows, low gilt and marble tables, properly mixed cocktails, abundant good nibbles, good fresh sandwiches and other bar food; usually a pianist (not Sun), very handy for Broadcasting House; bedrooms *(TBB, LYM)*

[Poland St], *Star & Garter*: Friendly and interesting little Soho pub, popular with younger people; floor, ceiling and walls of bar all wooden; well kept Courage Best and Directors, handy for Oxford St *(Gordon, LYM)*

[1 Portman Mews S], *Three Tuns*: Very popular and busy; several interconnecting rooms, bare boards, beams with banknotes and coins *(Gordon)*

[26 Crawford St], *Turners Arms*: Wide choice of good Thai food, reasonably priced wines, good choice of well kept real ales, friendly attentive service; small back eating area *(Peter and Jenny Quine)*

[3 Piccadilly Pl; passage Vine St Police Stn—Piccadilly], *Vine*: More bar and grill than pub, but does have bottled beer and good sandwiches as well as more substantial food *(David Howse)*

[89 George St], *Worcester Arms*: Well worth knowing for half a dozen interesting real ales kept in good condition; can be very quiet evenings *(Richard Waller)*

W2

[Bathurst St; opp Royal Lancaster Hotel], *Archery*: Good choice of Badger and other ales in early Georgian pub with four seating areas around its horseshoe bar, good helpings of decent food; tables outside *(Stephen and Jean Curtis)*

[Edgware Rd; corner Bell St], *Green Man*: Friendly open-plan Chef & Brewer, good friendly service, friendly mixed clientele, bar food inc Sat, pool, fruit machine, good basic decor and furniture; no optics behind bar – everything hand-poured bistro-style *(Jim Penman)*

[Edgware Rd; under flyover], *London Metropole*: Large hotel bar, worth knowing (despite hotel prices) for good furniture and decor, professional service, maybe a pianist, seating on three levels; bedrooms *(Jim Penman)*

[32 Southwick St], *Monkey Puzzle*: Friendly landlord, wife and staff; own-label Monkey Puzzle real ale and a guest such as Harveys, good reasonably priced food inc Sun roast, candles and tablecloths; bar billiards *(the Shinkmans)*

☆ [66 Bayswater Rd], *Swan*: Pleasant tree-shaded courtyard looking across busy road to Kensington Gardens, old London prints inside, well kept Courage-related ales, busy food bar, quiet upper room at back *(Dr and Mrs A K Clarke, Frank W Gadbois, LYM)*

[10a Strathearn Pl], *Victoria*: Very individual corner pub, paintings of Queen Victoria and family, pillars over bar counter supporting overmantel with small paintings depicting royal Victorian events, mahogany panelling, tobacco-stained historical military paintings, two cast-iron fireplaces; Bass and Charrington IPA on handpump, picnic-table sets on pavement; upstairs (not always open) replica of Gaiety Theatre bar, all gilt and red plush *(Gordon, LYM)*

WC1

☆ [252 Grays Inn Rd], *Calthorpe Arms*: Consistently well kept Youngs Bitter, Special and Porter at sensible prices in relaxed and unpretentious pub with plush wall seats, big helpings of usual bar food upstairs *(K P Smith)*

[New Oxford St], *Crown*: Terrace out on small shady square looking down Shaftesbury Ave (an entrance from this side too); comfortable, usually reasonably quiet with relaxed atmosphere, good pub food, good range of beers inc Sam Smiths OB, Museum, Dark Mild and sometimes Taddy Porter *(Walter Reid)*

[Red Lion St], *Enterprise*: Recently reopened, with Bass, Fullers London Pride, Greene King IPA, Harveys Best, Highgate Mild, Morlands Old Speckled Hen and two changing guest beers, wide choice of bottled beers from around the world, food inc sandwiches and pork pies; pub memorabilia *(D Cox)*

☆ [1 Pakenham St], *Pakenham Arms*: Unspoilt corner pub with pleasant informal atmosphere in split-level bar, largely local customers and generally quiet at lunchtime; notable for well kept real ale inc imaginative guests such as Exmoor Gold as well as usual Adnams, Brakspears etc, big helpings of good value food *(Sue Demont, Tim Barrow, P Smith)*

[Rugby St], *Rugby*: Well kept Fullers ales and polite service in fairly big one-bar corner pub with good atmosphere and muted beige decor; a few framed cartoons *(Brian Jones)*

WC2

[236 Shaftesbury Avenue], *Bloomsbury*:

Pleasant and busy, with fans-cum-chandeliers, nice dark oak panelling and bar counter, cast-iron tables, stained-glass coats of arms; real ales such as Greene King IPA, Marstons Pedigree and Tetleys, billiard table in upper bar *(Gordon)*

[The Arches; off Villiers St], *Champagne Charlies*: Open weekdays, subterranean Davys bar with real ales such as Eldridge Pope Royal Oak and Old-Wallop (in half-gallon copper jugs if you like), good choice of wines and ports, small choice of good value bar food *(Chris Warne)*

[31 Endell St], *Cross Keys*: Tiny pub festooned with hanging baskets and window-boxes, inside packed with bric-a-brac inc lots of brasses and some interesting photographs and posters eg Beatles and Presley; friendly staff, basic lunchtime food, fruit machine, small upstairs bar *(Ian Phillips, Dr and Mrs A K Clarke)*

[Long Acre], *Freemasons Arms*: Roomy and relaxed, with interesting prints, chesterfields, well kept Greene King IPA, Abbot and Rayments; music some nights in upstairs club room, video juke box in lower bar *(Roger Byrne, David Wright, BB)*

[Betterton St/Drury Lane], *Hogshead*: Basic but busy, with pleasant atmosphere, well kept ales such as Adnams, Boddingtons, Exmoor Gold, Flowers Best, Fullers London Pride and Morlands Old Speckled Hen on handpump or tapped from the cask, very basic cheap food *(Alastair Campbell)*

[354 Strand], *Lyceum*: Pleasantly simple furnishings downstairs, with three small discreet snugs on the left, steps up to a bigger alcove with darts, food in much bigger upstairs lounge with deep button-back leather settees and armchairs; Sam Smiths OB and Museum served with a rich creamy head, two Milds *(Ian Phillips)*

☆ [39 Bow St], *Marquis of Anglesea*: Welcome haven from the tourists, well kept Youngs, reasonable choice of food inc vegetarian upstairs where bar-style seating looks over window-boxes to street below; good service even when busy – they try to serve quickly if you're going to the theatre (opp Royal Opera House); no loud music *(Gill Earle, Andrew Burton, Roger Byrne)*

[28 Leicester Sq], *Moon Under Water*: Well placed Wetherspoons pub, usual high standards, good staff, food always available, low prices *(Neil Barker)*

[10 James St], *Nags Head*: Etched brewery mirrors, red ceiling, mahogany furniture, some partitioned booths, popular lunchtime food, friendly service, well kept McMullens – unusual here; often crowded with what would have been called bright young things back in the days when this was a famous thespian pub *(T Nott)*

[Bull Ct, The Strand], *New Nell Gwynn*: Recently overhauled, great decor, friendly management, free house with good beer at low prices *(Edward Hoban)*

[191 Drury Lane], *Old White Hart*: Good food and well kept beer in clean pub with interesting history and quick friendly staff; prices reasonable for area *(Mick Coen)*

[St Martins Ct], *Round Table*: Very popular, with half a dozen excellently kept real ales and interesting Belgian and German beers on draught and in bottle *(John Baker)*

[corner of Bedford St with King St], *Roundhouse*: Handy for Covent Garden and Tesco Metro, particularly well kept real ales inc wide-ranging choice of interesting guest beers, good value bar food; few tables in this refurbished semi-circular bar *(Brian and Jenny Seller, T Nott)*

[Goslett Yd; off Charing X Rd], *Royal George*: Large, modern and functional, bars on two floors, good choice of ales such as Holts, Tetleys, Wadworths 6X, good range of sandwiches; pinball machine *(Walter Reid)*

☆ [90 St Martins Lane], *Salisbury:* Sumptuous Victorian pub with sweeps of red velvet, huge sparkling mirrors and cut glass, glossy brass and mahogany; decent food (confined to right-hand side evening; even doing Sun lunches over Christmas/New Year), well kept Allied ales and satisfactory house wines, no-smoking back room, acceptable piped music, friendly service *(Wayne Brindle, BB)*

☆ [53 Carey St], *Seven Stars*: Lovely little unspoilt early 18th-c pub just behind law courts, barrister caricatures, toby jugs, very steep stairs up to lavatories (warning notice), small cluttered layout with only one small table, friendly genuine landlord, well kept beer, sandwiches, no machines or music *(Gordon, Thomas Nott)*

☆ [66 Long Acre], *Sun*: Well kept Courage-related ales, several dozen malt whiskies and a good many blends, character landlady, decent food inc Sun lunches, good old photographs of Covent Gdn market, first-floor wine bar; not as smart as many pubs round here, but less touristy and more enjoyable *(David Wright, Andy Thwaites)*

[Sandford St], *Three Cups*: Relaxing atmosphere in nice little pub with well kept beer *(S C Brown)*

[Drury Lane], *White Hart*: Deeply penetrating series of rooms with an Elizabethan look, deep leather armchairs and club fenders (but juke box, pintables and pool tables); Bass, Fullers London Pride, Worthington BB and ambitious range of food (orders announced over loudspeakers) *(Walter Reid)*

[14 New Row], *White Swan*: Small pillared and mirrored front bar, corridor to roomier 17th-c panelled back part with comfortable and cosy genuine public-bar atmosphere *(Gordon, LYM)*

NORTH LONDON
N1

[179 Upper St], *179 Upper Street*: Reliable Wetherspoons pub with good staff, usual high standards, food always available, low prices, no-smoking area *(Neil Barker)*

☆ [10 Thornhill Rd], *Albion*: Interesting almost countrified unspoilt pub named for a long-distance coach, with lots of horsebrasses and trappings; room behind bar furnished like

someone's drawing room, cosy back hideaway on the right, back terrace and big garden with sun and shade; some old photographs of the pub, cosy fires, some gas lighting, real ales, food, very friendly landlord; interesting Victorian gents' *(Gordon, Neil H Barker)*
[24 York Way], *Duke of York*: Unspoiled oasis, with well kept beers *(Dr and Mrs A K Clarke)*
[156 Pentonville Rd], *George IV*: Basic traditional corner local with some lovely original details, esp the mirrors behind the bar *(Dr and Mrs A K Clarke)*
☆ [87 Noel Rd], *Island Queen*: Good freshly made and often unusual food in amiable character pub with eccentric life-size caricature fancy-dress figures floating from ceiling – personalities updated from time to time, well kept Bass and Worthington BB, upstairs restaurant; lively youngish welcoming atmosphere, good juke box; handy for Camden Passage antiques area; children welcome *(Sue Demont, Tim Barrow, LYM)*
[33 Caledonian Rd; Kings X end], *Malt & Hops*: Gibbs Mews' first London pub, with their beers and several others such as Bass, Ind Coope Burton and Wadworths 6X – 11 in all, well kept; reasonably small, a basic real local, with juke box and pinball; lunchtime food, pasties any time *(Ian Lock, Gabrielle Coyle, M L Hooper-Immins)*
☆ [Liverpool Rd], *Minogues*: Smart and lively traditional Irish bar with friendly efficient staff, good food to suit in adjoining restaurant, Irish newspapers and drinks inc real Dublin Guinness, folk music *(L Curran)*

N5
[26 Highbury Pk], *Highbury Barn*: Wide choice of beers and good hot food, super atmosphere; half-mile from Arsenal's ground *(Nigel Woolliscroft)*

N6
☆ [77 Highgate West Hill], *Flask*: Georgian pub much modernised in straightforward way, but has intriguing up-and-down layout, some old-fashioned features inc sash-windowed bar hatch, panelling and high-backed carved settle tucked away in snug lower area; usual food inc salad bar, Allied and Youngs ales, well behaved children allowed, tables out on spacious front courtyard *(Gordon, Shirley Gofford, Quentin Williamson, LYM)*
[1 North Hill], *Gate House*: Good Wetherspoons pub opened summer 1993, nicely done out with no-smoking area, tables in back yard, good value beer, good staff, food always available *(Don Kellaway, Angie Coles, Neil Barker)*

N14
[Arnos Grove], *Bankers Draft*: What a tourist pictures an English pub to be: individual feel, good lunches, friendly management, well kept beers *(Edward Hohan, Comus Elliott)*

N16
[145 High St], *Rochester Castle*: Reliable

Wetherspoons pub with good staff, usual high standards, food always available, low prices, no-smoking area *(Neil Barker)*

N17
[503 High Rd], *Elbow Room*: Yet another in the reliable Wetherspoons chain, all the usual virtues *(Neil Barker)*

N19
[17 Archway Rd], *Dog*: And another – more of the trustworthy Wetherspoons formula *(Neil Barker)*

N20
[Barnet High St], *King George*: Tastefully refurbished, with well kept Charrington IPA, friendly helpful bar staff, good range of lunchtime food *(S C W Taylor)*

N21
[18 Highfield Rd; Winchmore Hill], *Orange Tree*: Great atmosphere, fine choice of real ales, good food, fabulous garden *(James Holden)*

NW1
[Gloucester Ave], *Lansdown*: Spacious with some tables outside and in a courtyard, good Italian food, very relaxed, pleasant and spacious – the sort of pub one might prefer to a restaurant for dinner; good wines, attractively varied menu *(Sarah King, Patrick Forbes)*
[26 Tolmers Sq], *Square*: Friendly newish pub in redevelopment nr Euston Stn, framed *Beano* and *Dandy* in curious mix of modern and traditional decor, bar billiards, juke box (may be loud), well kept Brakspears and Youngs Bitter and Special *(Dr and Mrs A K Clarke)*

NW3
☆ [14 Flask Walk], *Flask*: Bustling and relatively unspoiled Hampstead local with carved wooden archway and stained-glass panels dividing the two front bars, interesting back part, partly arched and vaulted stone; popular with actors and artists as it has been for 300 years; well kept Youngs, decent coffee, friendly staff, good value food inc baked potatoes and several hot dishes more interesting than usual, friendly helpful service *(Gordon, Ian Phillips, Prof S Barnett, Paul Cartledge, Wayne Brindle, BB)*
[32 Downshire Hill], *Freemasons Arms*: Big pub with spacious garden right by Hampstead Heath, good arrangements for serving food and drink outside; good comfortable seating inside, well spaced variously sized tables, leather chesterfield in front of open fire; usual bar food inc Sun roast beef (no-smoking eating area, at lunchtime), Bass and Charrington IPA; children allowed in dining room, dogs in bar, open all day summer; front roadside tables catch the early afternoon sun nicely *(Wayne Brindle, Michael, Alison and Rhiannon Sandy, Ben Grose, LYM)*
[North End Way], *Jack Straws Castle*: 16th c coaching inn rebuilt after bomb damage in WW2, highest spot in London, on site of pre-Roman earthworks, with panoramic views

from upstairs restaurant; warm friendly bars, daily changing very varied menu, wide range of real ales; bedrooms *(Gordon B Thornton)*

☆ [North End Way], *Old Bull & Bush:* Period family-oriented pub attractively refurbished in Dickensian style, comfortable sofa and easy chairs, nooks and crannies, side library bar with lots of bookshelves and pictures and mementoes of Florrie Ford who made the song about the pub famous; friendly landlord, efficient staff, good food bar inc good Sun specials, good wine list *(Len and Fran Shaw, Gordon, Nigel Gursu, LYM)*

[28 Heath St], *Three Horseshoes:* Pleasant Wetherspoons pub in nice location, well kept sensibly priced beers, good staff, food always available, no-smoking area *(Neil Barker)*

[50 Englands Lane], *Washington:* Splendid black and gold exterior, decent bar food esp doorstep sandwiches, well kept real ales and wines *(E G Parish)*

[Well Rd/Church Hill], *Wells Tavern:* Cosy and villagey Hampstead local handy for the Heath, great atmosphere with roaring fires *(Don Kellaway, Angie Coles)*

NW4

[56 The Burroughs (A504)], *White Bear:* Reasonably priced good wholesome hot food, good changing choice, waiter service *(Keith Hollingworth)*

NW6

[Kilburn High Rd; corner Springfield Ave], *Old Bell:* Large open-plan Allied pub, one part carpeted, decor basic but functional and clean; TV, juke box, pool, stage for live music *(Anon)*

[1 Kilburn High Rd], *Queens Arms:* Large two-bar Youngs pub, weekday dining area with separate servery in main bar, pleasant furniture and decor in good clean condition, lots of clay pipes in glass case, old photographs, no music, Youngs real ales on handpump *(Jim Penman)*

NW7

[Highwood Hill], *Rising Sun:* Beautiful wisteria-covered local dating to 17th c, cheerful helpful staff, small main bar, big lounge, atmospheric side snug, lots of dark panelling and timber; well kept Ind Coope Burton, Tetleys, Youngs and occasional guest ales, simple but adequate bar food from sandwiches up *(R L Nelson, N and M Foster)*

NW8

[21 Loudoun Rd], *Blenheim Arms:* Large very friendly L-shaped bar, good for conversation – no piped music or juke box *(Dr and Mrs A K Clarke)*

☆ [96 Clifton Hill], *Clifton:* Attractive series of small individually decorated rooms around central servery, conservatory, leafy front terrace; open all day Fri, Sat, provision for children, bar food, Allied ales *(Nic Armitage, Peter Atkinson, LYM)*

☆ [24 Aberdeen Pl], *Crockers:* Ostentatious marble, decorated plaster and opulent woodwork in showy Victorian pub, relaxing and comfortable too, with Vaux, Wards and a wide range of other ales, friendly service, decent food inc vegetarian, generous Sun roasts; on Regents Canal walk *(Gordon, Dr and Mrs A K Clarke, Helen Chalmers, LYM)*

[23 Queens Grove], *Rossetti:* Elegant two-floor bar with marble tables, polished echoic floors, bentwood chairs, total lack of background music, Italian and other food *(Dr and Mrs A K Clarke, LYM)*

NW9

[553 Kingsbury Rd], *J J Moons:* Well above the area average, well laid out and well run Wetherspoons pub with all the usual solid ungimmicky virtues inc food all day *(Neil Barker)*

[10 Varley Par], *Moon Under Water:* Another reliable Wetherspoons pub, as above *(Neil Barker)*

Barnet

[St Albans Rd (A1081); nr M25], *Green Dragon:* Good choice of real ales inc well kept Flowers and changing guests, good reasonably priced food (though service can be slow) in conservatory overlooking fields *(Gareth Edwards)*

[18 Hadley Highstone; towards Potters Bar], *King William IV:* Very old small local with real fires, nooks and corners, cosy atmosphere; home-cooked food inc good fresh fish Fri, friendly staff *(Prof John White, Patricia White)*

☆ [58 High St], *Olde Mitre:* Small early 17th-c double-fronted pub, bay windows in low-ceilinged panelled front bar with fruit machines, three-quarter panelled back area on two slightly different levels, lots of dark wood, dark floral wallpaper, pleasant atmosphere, friendly service, well kept Wadworths 6X and Allied ales *(Brian Jones, LYM)*

Cockfosters

[Chalk Lane/Games Rd], *Cock & Dragon:* Was just the Cock, new name reflects Chinese food as well as more traditional dishes in bar and restaurant; popular for lunch, plentiful good food *(John Barker)*

Edgware

[122 High St], *Blacking Bottle:* Former freezer-supply shop tastefully converted into Wetherspoons pub with good food, sensible prices, bargain beer, good staff, no-smoking area *(Russell and Margaret Bathie, Neil Barker)*

[Whitewebbs Lane], *King & Tinker:* Typical country pub, not over-modernised, very friendly; good choice of beers, good lunches *(John Barker)*

Greenford

[19 The Broadwalk; Pinner Rd, N Harrow], *J J Moons:* Good Wetherspoons pub, well kept beer at favourable prices, among the best of the chain for food; splendid occasional beer festivals *(Barbara Hatfield, Neil Barker)*

Harrow

[111 Bessborough Rd], *Kingsfield Arms*:
Pleasant one-bar pub, quiet, with well kept
Courage beers *(Dr and Mrs A K Clarke)*
[373 Station Rd; nr underground stn], *Moon
on the Hill*: Busy Wetherspoons pub, very
varied mix of customers, good value and
good food; bargain beer, friendly efficient
staff *(Russell and Margaret Bathie, Myke
Crombleholme, Neil Barker)*

Harrow Weald

☆ [Old Redding; off A409 – OS Sheet 176 map
ref 144926], *Case is Altered*: Fine country
setting, peaceful views from remarkably big
sloping garden (good for children); villagey
inside, low ceiling, wooden wall benches,
olde-worlde prints, well kept Allied ales,
good friendly service, reasonably priced bar
food from sandwiches and burgers to big
steaks (only snacks weekends, no food Sun
evening); summer barbecues; children
welcome; easiest to park at neighbouring
viewpoint/picnic area *(Martin and Penny
Fletcher, LYM)*
[Uxbridge Rd (A410)], *Leafe Robinson VC*:
Cosy pleasant atmosphere in big well
decorated open-plan Beefeater with
Boddingtons and Flowers Original on
handpump, restaurant *(Robert Lester)*

Hatch End

☆ [250 Uxbridge Rd], *Moon & Sixpence*: Usual
Wetherspoons style, good service, well kept
beers, good value food, sensible prices
(Russell and Margaret Bathie)

New Barnet

[13 East Barnet Rd; A110 nr stn], *Railway
Bell*: Wetherspoons pub with superb service
and usual good value food and drink *(Philip
O'Loughlin)*

Pinner

[250 Uxbridge Rd], *Moon & Sixpence*:
Wetherspoons pub converted from former
bank, usual high standards, food always available, low prices, no-smoking area *(Neil Barker)*
[High St], *Queens Head*: Traditional pub
dating from 16th c, good food, Allied real
ales with changing guests such as Marstons
Pedigree and Wadworths 6X, very friendly
staff and landlord, no music so atmosphere
depends on conversation *(Mark Cottingham)*

Southgate

☆ [115 Chase Side], *Moon Under Water*:
Superb value Wetherspoons pub in lovely old
converted chapel, with good food, service
and beer, big barn of a place with some
slightly surreal decor inc a landau in the
lounge and unreachable library; separate
smoking and no-smoking areas *(Philip
O'Loughlin, Neil Barker)*

Wealdstone

[32 High St], *Sarsen Stone*: Good value
Wetherspoons pub, attractively priced food
and drink, well trained staff *(Neil Barker)*

SOUTH LONDON
SE1

☆ [34 Park St; Bankside, Southwark Bridge
end], *Anchor*: Rambling set of beamed and
black-panelled old-fashioned rooms (best by
front door), very commercial and much
photographed by tourists, but has kept some
high-backed settles, even bar billiards among
more usual pub games; usual food (service
can be slow for fitting into a lunch hour),
well kept Courage and other ales, terrace
overlooking Thames, restaurant; children
allowed in eating area, open all day Sat
*(David and Michelle Hedges, Dr and Mrs A
K Clarke, LYM)*

☆ [Bankside], *Founders Arms*: Sparkling view
of Thames and St Pauls from spacious glass-
walled plush-seat modern bar and big
waterside terrace; well kept Youngs Bitter
and Special, reasonable food, pleasant service
(Brian Jones, LYM)
[47 Borough Rd], *Goose & Firkin*: Basic
decor, good range of good basic food, good
range of well kept own brew beers and very
friendly staff *(Richard Waller, BB)*
[25 Roupell St], *Kings Arms*: Fine two-bar
London pub, friendly service, well kept beer
(Dr and Mrs A K Clarke)
[Union St/Nelson Sq], *Nelson*: Well kept
Fullers London Pride, good cheap food, good
atmosphere, very helpful staff *(Mal
Broadbent)*
[Waterloo Rd], *Old Fire Station*: In former
LCC central fire station: well kept real ale,
more exotic bottled beers, good food *(A W
Dickinson)*

☆ [St Mary Overy Wharf; off Clink St], *Old
Thameside*: Good pastiche of ancient tavern,
two floors – hefty beams and timbers, pews,
flagstones, candles; splendid river view
upstairs and from charming waterside terrace
by schooner docked in landlocked inlet; well
kept Boddingtons, Courage Directors,
Flowers and another ale, good generously
filled baps etc upstairs, more choice
downstairs *(Dr and Mrs A K Clarke, LYM)*
[24 Blackfriars Rd], *Paper Moon*: Single bar
with very interesting Shakespeare mural;
customers show you're on the fringes of the
City *(Dr and Mrs A K Clarke)*
[216 Blackfriars Rd], *Prince William Henry*:
Quiet and elegant modern Youngs estate
pub, quick pleasant service, well kept beers
(Dr and Mrs A K Clarke, BB)
[68 Borough Rd], *Ship*: Busy, with good
atmosphere, well kept Fullers, good food,
friendly Irish licensees and staff; a local for the
RPO *(Steve Merson, Dr and Mrs A K Clarke)*

SE3

[1a Eliot Cottages], *Hare & Billet*: Done out
in Victorian style a few years ago and now
settled in well, with popular food, well kept
Whitbreads-related real ales, good atmosphere
esp weekends *(Andy Thwaites, BB)*

★ [1 Montpellier Row], *Princess of Wales*:
Pleasant spot overlooking heath, with back
conservatory, fair choice of reasonably priced
straightforward food from sandwiches up, good

helpings, well kept real ales such as Adnams Extra, Bass, Fullers London Pride and Harveys, brisk service *(Tony Gayfer, Ian Phillips)*

SE5

[149 Denmark Hill], *Fox on the Hill*: Wetherspoons pub with tables in extensive grounds; usual high standards, food always available, low prices, good staff *(Neil Barker)*

☆ [Bromley Rd/Southend Ln], *Tigers Head*: Pleasant Wetherspoons pub festooned with hanging baskets in summer, growing local popularity for good inexpensive bar meals, impressive choice of ales (one very cheap), roomy inside with good layout and no music or machines; picnic-table sets on forecourt; can get loud at weekends, but pleasant staff stay well in control *(E G Parish, Andy Thwaites, A M Pring)*

SE9

[80 High St], *Bankers Draft*: Reliable Wetherspoons pub in former bank, consistently good value food and drink, no-smoking area *(Neil Barker)*

SE10

[opp Cutty Sark], *Gypsy Moth*: Comfortable split-level dining lounge, simple bar menu, good garden with picnic-table sets, well kept Adnams, Marstons and Ind Coope; polite efficient staff, not too crowded *(S R Howe)*
[King William Walk], *Kings Arms*: Courage ales, lots of wood, maps and boat pictures, friendly landlady, decent food, coal-effect gas fire; big room partitioned for snugger feel, central bar; handy for Cutty Sark and Museum *(Roger Huggins)*

☆ [52 Royal Hill], *Richard I*: Quiet and friendly no-nonsense proper pub, particularly well kept Youngs, bare boards, panelling, good range of traditional bar food inc outstanding sausages, well kept Youngs, good staff, no piped music; tables in back garden with barbecues, busy summer weekends and evenings *(Robert Gomme, GTW)*

☆ [Crane St], *Yacht*: Friendly, clean and civilised, with good river view from spacious upper room, light wood panelling, portholes, yacht pictures, cosy banquettes, reasonable food *(Thomas Nott, D C Eastwood)*

SE11

[48 Cleaver Sq], *Prince of Wales*: Hidden away in elegant and secluded square, oasis of tranquillity; good summer barbecues, Youngs beer, Sun roasts (not cheap); fairly handy for the Oval *(Andy Thwaites, BB)*

SE15

[Peckham Rye], *Clockhouse*: Youngs beers, and rare for keeping something of a country atmosphere – great in summer with wonderful hanging baskets; nice mixed crowd, no music *(Andy Thwaites)*

SE16

[Rotherhithe St], *Clipper*: Not old but has character, with welcoming landlord,

Boddingtons on handpump, bar food inc good range even Sun lunchtime, big well furnished bar, small room with games; children's playground next door, on Thames footpath *(Jenny and Brian Seller)*

SE17

[Brandon St], *Crown*: Small friendly backstreet pub, well kept Bass and Youngs Special on handpump, small side garden, reasonable prices, limited food; handy for East St market *(Mrs Christine Kennett)*

SE19

[41 Beulah Hill], *Beulah Spa*: Well placed and currently doing well, with friendly welcome and good service indeed, civilised bar food at reasonable cost, Morlands Old Speckled Hen and Worthington BB on handpump, well spaced tables, sedate lunchtime atmosphere; exceptionally good parking *(E G Parish)*

SE21

[Park Hall Rd], *Alleyns Head*: Currently has good bar food and outstanding service; comfortable furnishings, the book-lined walls of the saloon adding a collegey touch *(E G Parish)*

SE22

☆ [Dartmouth Rd, Forest Hl], *Bird in Hand*: Good Wetherspoons pub, solidly furnished and simply decorated, no piped music, good range of reasonably priced ales, good cheap pubby food inc substantial filled baps; spotless, with courteous efficient service *(Quentin Williamson)*
[Crystal Palace Rd], *Crystal Palace Tavern*: Typical Victorian local complete with tiny gas lights and Victorian bar; good friendly service, well kept Allied ales and a guest beer; tables outside *(Jon Lyons)*

SE23

[35 Dartmouth Rd], *Bird in Hand*: Good Wetherspoons pub, a real oasis for this area *(Neil Barker)*

SE25

[Selhurst], *Selhurst Arms*: Largish comfortable pub, good service, friendly atmosphere; nr station, handy for Crystal Palace *(R Wilson)*

SE26

☆ [39 Sydenham Hill], *Dulwich Wood House*: Victorian lodge gatehouse complete with turret – its position (for a suburban pub) could hardly be improved upon, with lots of tables in pleasant back garden and a wooded walk to Sydenham Hill rly stn; well kept Youngs ales, food increasingly popular at lunchtime with local retired people; barbecues *(Ian Phillips, E G Parish)*
[Sydenham Rd (A212)], *Golden Lion*: Very decorative exterior, flower tubs, white latticed seats on terrace; current friendly and hardworking landlord concentrating on good meals, pleasantly served in roomy and well

carpeted lounge and bars *(E G Parish)*
[Sydenham Rd (A212); junction Kirkdale],
Greyhound: Recently refurbished to a high
standard, quite eye-catching outside; good
atmosphere in several themed areas, good
choice of ales on handpump, increasingly
popular for lunch; no-smoking area *(E G
Parish)*

SW2

☆ [2 Streatham Hill, on South Circular], *Crown
& Sceptre:* Ornate and substantial
Wetherspoons pub, formerly J J Moons, with
good traditional decor, divided into sensible-
sized areas inc no-smoking; well kept
reasonably priced ales inc some unusual ones,
reasonably priced well organised food, good
service *(E G Parish, Sue Demont, Tim
Barrow, Neil Barker)*
[Acre Lane], *Hope & Anchor:* Large Youngs
pub with big colourful garden, good food inc
well priced daily pie and salads, friendly
landlord, games machines; often live busking-
style music *(Charles Davey)*

SW4

[Chalham Rd], *Eagle:* Good range of beers,
friendly landlord, great summer garden
(Rosie Lupton)

SW8

[43 St Stephens Terr; off S Lambeth Rd],
Royal Albert: Attractively refurbished
Regency pub, friendly and relaxed old-
fashioned atmosphere, five real ales, garden,
separate pool room; lunchtime bar food
*(Miss Joanna Whitehouse, Sue Demont, Tim
Barrow)*
☆ [16 Southville], *Surprise:* Friendly new
landlord, well kept Youngs and usual cheap
wholesome food in two cosy rooms
decorated in colourful Liberty prints; dried
flowers, real fire, friendly dog and cat, tables
out under leafy arbour overlooking small
park *(John Douglas, BB)*

SW9

[169 South Lambeth Rd], *Rebatos:* Not a
pub, but the crowded front tapas bar is an
excellent substitute in this dismal area, with
good wines and spirits by the glass and a
wide choice of interesting little dishes esp
seafood; restaurant, very good service *(E G
Parish, BB)*

SW11

[St Johns Hill], *Falcon:* Large three-roomed
pub with very welcoming friendly staff,
honest basic lunchtime food till 3, good range
of real ales such as Bass, Fullers London
Pride, Morlands Old Speckled Hen,
Worthington BB and Youngs Special; cheap
tea or coffee *(Graham Reeve)*
☆ [60 Battersea High St], *Woodman:* Most
attractive local, busy, friendly and individual,
with little panelled front bar, long turkey-
carpeted main room, log-effect gas fires; tied
to Badger, with their beers and those from
their own-brew pub at Oving in Sussex, also

several guests such as Wadworths 6X, at fair
prices; bar billiards, darts and trivia machine
at one end, picnic-table sets on terrace with
barbecue; provision for children; not to be
confused with Original Woodman next door
(Ted Burden, Sue Demont, Tim Barrow, BB)

SW12

[194 Balham High Rd], *Moon Under Water:*
Wetherspoons pub, reliable as ever *(Neil
Barker)*
☆ [97 Nightingale Lane], *Nightingale:* Very
friendly staff, good well priced bar food, well
kept Youngs – one of their nicest locals,
friendly, comfortable and civilised; sensible
prices, timeless cream and brown decor with
gallery of sponsored guide-dog pictures on
one wall, attractive back family conservatory;
children in useful small family area *(L G
Milligan, R Wilson, BB)*

SW13

☆ [2 Castelnau], *Red Lion:* Big smartly restored
Fullers pub with impressive Victorian
woodwork, three separate areas, good
service, well kept Fullers Chiswick, London
Pride and ESB, nice atmosphere, good choice
of lunchtime food inc children's helpings; big
garden with good play area, barbecue and
pets' corner *(Martin Kay, Andrea Fowler,
Richard K Blodgett, BB)*
☆ [7 Church Rd], *Sun:* Renovated well, so that
the spacious series of communicating room-
areas looped neatly around the central
servery gives a convincing feel of age and
solidity – esp the furniture; really pleasant,
with nice generally young crowd, Allied ales
such as Ind Coope Burton and Tetleys with a
guest such as Eldridge Pope, usual food,
benches and tables over road overlooking
duckpond *(Susan and John Douglas, Ian
Phillips)*

SW14

[Lower Richmond Rd], *Star & Garter:* Well
Kept Courage Directors and Tetleys, nice
river view, straightforward food *(Dave Irving)*
☆ [10 West Temple Sheen], *Victoria:* Large
friendly pub, often crowded, with generous
reasonably priced food, all home-made, well
kept Courage-related beers, helpful staff,
good conservatory and garden *(Roger
Sherman, P Gillbe)*

SW15

☆ [8 Lower Richmond Rd], *Dukes Head:* Classic
Youngs pub, spacious and grand yet friendly,
in great spot by Thames (Boat Race start); well
kept real ales, 20 wines by the glass; main bar
light and airy with big ceiling fans, very
civilised feel, good service, tables by window
with great Thames view, smaller more basic
locals' bar at the back; good freshly cooked
lunchtime food; lavatories below street level,
parking can be difficult *(BB)*
[61 Lacy Rd], *Jolly Gardeners:* Small warmly
furnished Fullers pub with basic bar food,
fairly priced well kept real ales, interesting
prints and decorative objects on the walls;

occasional live music *(Brad and Joni Nelson, Martin Kay, Andrea Fowler)*
[202 Upper Richmond Rd], *Railway*: Wetherspoons pub with good choice of sensibly priced ales, reliable food, good service and layout *(Neil Barker)*

SW16

☆ [151 Greyhound Lane], *Greyhound*: Big three-bar local with several beers brewed on the premises, food all day, efficient staff, well equipped games bar, spacious and attractive family conservatory, sizeable garden *(D Cox, L G Milligan, LYM)*
[1327 London Rd], *Moon Under Water*: Yet another civilised good value Wetherspoons pub *(Neil Barker)*

SW17

[56 Tooting High St; opp Tooting Broadway tube], *J J Moons*: Wetherspoons pub that should do very well here, good all round *(Neil Barker)*

SW19

☆ [6 Crooked Billet], *Hand in Hand*: Very well kept Youngs inc seasonal Winter Warmer, good straightforward food inc home-made pizzas and burgers, relaxed and cheerful U-shaped bar serving several small areas, some tiled, others carpeted, inc no-smoking family room with bar billiards, darts etc, log fires, children's room; tables out by edge of Wimbledon Common *(Ted Burden, BB)*
☆ [55 Wimbledon High St], *Rose & Crown*: Comfortably modernised old local, can get very busy, with well kept Youngs, friendly service, decent generous food from back servery at sensible prices, open fires, set of Hogarth's proverb engravings, green plush seats in alcoves; tables in former coachyard *(Ian Phillips, P Gillbe, LYM)*
☆ [Merton Abbey Mills; Merantum Way; next to Savacentre], *William Morris*: Lively and popular two-floor modern pub on site of the old Wm Morris/Liberty mills by R Wandle, lots of corners, seats outside; interesting Wm Morris materials and old bicycle posters, good range of ales inc Brakspears and Worthington BB, good choice of reasonably priced food inc some imaginative dishes and traditional puddings (just filled rolls Sat), brisk service; can get crowded *(Jenny and Brian Seller)*

Bexley

[Black Prince Interchange, Southwold Rd (A2)], *Black Prince*: Friendly reception, reliably good service, wide choice of bar food inc good value specials and Bass and Charrington IPA in cosy areas of traditional lounge bar, attached to but separate from Forte Post House; bedrooms *(E G Parish)*

Bexleyheath

[Mount Rd], *Royal Oak*: Courage pub with good choice of well kept real ales, malt whiskies and good lunchtime food; gardens good for children in summer *(T F Lendon)*

Carshalton

[High St], *Fox & Hounds*: Ind Coope Burton, Tetleys and Wadworths 6X, good food, friendly service, homely decor, comfortable seats, good free live jazz Sun and Weds evening; open all day *(P C Strange)*
☆ [by Carshalton Ponds], *Greyhound*: Large and handsome Youngs pub with several comfortable bars opp ponds in picturesque outer London 'village'; wide choice of good middling-priced food inc specials and lots of fish, well kept ales, good service, easy parking; bedrooms *(R Wilson, C J Parsons)*

Cheam

[Royal Parade], *Bulls Head*: Pleasant relaxed furnishings and decor, good service, well kept real ales *(M E A Horler)*

Croydon

[Cherry Orchard Rd; Addiscombe], *Cherry Orchard*: Nice functional interior, pleasant lounge bar, friendly service, lunchtime snacks such as rolls, sandwiches, ploughman's; karaoke evenings *(A M Pring)*
[Junction Rd; off Brighton Rd], *Crown & Sceptre*: Good Fullers pub *(Martin Kay, Andrea Fowler)*
[63 Brighton Rd], *Earl of Eldon*: Recently refurbished and reopened Greene King pub, under new management, with mahogany panelling, attractive red and burgundy decor, open fires in neo-Victorian fireplaces, two raised seating areas, woodblock flooring, persian rug, no-smoking and dining areas, books; food from sandwiches up, real ales; open all day *(E G Parish)*
[17 George St], *George*: Useful well run Wetherspoons pub *(Neil Barker)*
[Sumner Rd], *Nowhere in Particular*: Small refurbished corner local, nice atmosphere, good range of real ales, good lunches *(Neil Barker)*

Cudham

☆ [Cudham Lane], *Blacksmiths Arms*: Friendly welcome, good well thought-out reasonably priced food inc interesting soups, huge helpings, well kept Courage, good coffee; nearly always busy with plenty of tables, with cheerful cottagey atmosphere, soft lighting, blazing log fires, low ceiling; service friendly if not always very speedy; big garden, pretty window-boxes, nice walks and riding nearby *(John and Elspeth Howell, Mrs R D Knight)*

Keston

[Westerham Rd], *Keston Mark*: Handy for walks on Hayes Common and for nearby nursery, pleasant service, decent bar food; open all day, inc for food on Sun *(E G Parish)*

Kew

[Station Ave], *Flower & Firkin*: Actually in the Victorian station buildings (street and platform entrances), with good range of well kept own-brewed ales and guests, popular food at popular prices, pointedly unpretentious style and decor; open all day, tables out on big terrace by street *(John Fazakerley, R Houghton)*

Kingston
☆ [Canbury Gdns; park in Lower Ham Rd if you can], *Boaters:* Good Thames views, very wide choice of generous good value food inc Sun lunch, comfortable banquettes in quiet charming bar, floodlit tables in garden, Courage-related ales with a guest such as Wadworths 6X, friendly welcoming service, unobtrusive piped jazz (live Sun evening); in small park, ideal for children in summer *(Martin Jones, Mayur Shah)*
Cocoanut: Good Fullers pub *(Martin Kay, Andrea Fowler)*
[Clifton Rd], *Norbiton Arms:* Well kept real ale inc guests, pleasant garden an oasis on a hot day; good food *(Dr John Lunn)*
Wych Elm: Very good Fullers pub *(Martin Kay, Andrea Fowler)*

Leaves Green
Kings Arms: Attractive oldish two-bar pub with low beams and log fire, airy conservatory, wide range of good value lunchtime food, friendly staff, jovial landlord, Courage-related ales; by end of Biggin Hill aeroplane runway *(John and Elspeth Howell)*

Mitcham
[Mitcham Common], *Ravensbourne Arms:* Ind Coope Burton, Tetleys and Youngs, decent wine, hot and cold food, barbecues in big garden *(J A Snell)*
[223 London Rd], *White Lion of Mortimer:* Good solid Wetherspoons pub *(Neil Barker)*

Morden
[Central Rd], *Morden:* Currently doing well, with very Irish feel, Courage ales, Irish-sized helpings of reasonable food, huge TV screen brings in the locals on sporting occasions, restaurant (base of local Rotary Club), tables in big garden *(Brian and Jenny Seller)*

New Malden
[Coombe Rd], *Royal Oak:* Large, but crowded at lunchtime for its wide range of reliably good home-made food inc big helpings of fresh veg; good choice of well kept Allied and other real ales; big garden *(P Gillbe, Steve and Sarah de Mellow)*

Purley
[8 Russell Hill Rd], *Foxley Hatch:* Good value reliable Wetherspoons pub, formerly a bathroom centre though you'd never guess it now – its name recalls the tollgate which used to stand here long before that *(Neil Barker)*

Richmond
[345 Petersham Rd; Ham Common], *New Inn:* Well established but newly refurbished, bright and clean, in lovely position on Ham Common, with friendly atmosphere, comfortable banquettes and stools, good choice of hot and cold lunchtime food,

decent evening meals in pleasant dining area; a welcome even to young women on their own *(Brig T I G Gray, Jill Bickerton)*
☆ [Petersham Rd], *Rose of York:* Well refurbished in 1994, good design and materials; comfortable seats inc leather chesterfields, Turner prints on stripped pine panelling, old photographs, attractive layout inc no-smoking area; good choice of reasonably priced Sam Smiths ales, pleasant helpful service; high chairs, bar billiards, fruit machines, TV, piped pop music; lighting perhaps a bit bright; bedrooms *(Susan and John Douglas)*
☆ [Cholmondeley Walk; riverside], *White Cross:* Thriving open-plan pub with great Thames and bridge views from banquettes around big tables in deep bay windows; civilised and attractively decorated, with reasonably priced lunchtime bar food, well kept Youngs, no music or machines, friendly efficient service; spacious upstairs family dining room with river-view balcony, tables outside with summer garden bar *(M Clarke, R Wilson, K P Smith)*
☆ [25 Old Palace Lane], *White Swan:* Little rose-covered cottage with pretty paved garden, barbecues, dark-beamed open-plan bar, well kept Courage beers, good coal fires, usual bar food; children allowed in conservatory *(Susan and John Douglas, Mark Hydes, M Clarke, Dr and Mrs Rackow, JB, Ian Phillips, JS, BS, LYM)*

South Norwood
☆ *Goat House:* Outstanding Fullers pub, particularly good atmosphere *(Martin Kay, Andrea Fowler)*

Surbiton
[Victoria Rd], *Victoria:* Victorian, with good food such as steak and kidney pie or liver and bacon, lots of vegetables, some OAP bargains Weds lunchtime, quick service though can be crowded, well kept Youngs; open all day *(W L G Watkins)*

Sutton
[5 Hill Rd], *Moon on the Hill:* Huge Wetherspoons pub, but usual high standards, good staff, food always available, low prices *(Neil Barker)*

Thornton Heath
[Bensham Gr; corner Beulah Rd], *Lord Napier:* Most attractive, with good live jazz, popular bar lunches, well kept Youngs *(E G Parish)*

Wallington
☆ [25 Ross Parade; Woodmancote Rd], *Whispering Moon:* Very civilised Wetherspoons pub in former cinema with worm's-eye glimpse of trains at back, lots of well spaced tables in cosily divided area, good solid furnishings and pleasant decor, no music or machines, well kept real ales such as Courage Directors, Greene King, Wadworths 6X and Youngers Scotch, decent generous wines, good staff, good value unpretentious food all day served quickly *(Neil Barker,*

Chris and Anne Fluck, BB)

West Wickham

☆ [Pickhurst Lane], *Pickhurst*: Extremely popular esp with retired people, good value Sun lunches with two sittings; double-sitting evening meals too, worth booking Apr-Oct; food and service good *(E G Parish)*

WEST LONDON

SW7

[44 Montpelier Sq], *King George IV*: Brightly refurbished and welcoming, with reasonably priced well prepared and presented bar food, changing real ales, entertainer Thurs, disco Fri/Sat – quiet lunchtime *(Ian Phillips)*.

W3

[281 Acton High St], *Red Lion & Pineapple*: One of the first Wetherspoons pubs in this part of London, imposing building with usual high standards, though already so popular could do with more staff Sat evening *(Neil Barker)*

W4

[72 Strand on the Green], *Bell & Crown*: Big Fullers pub in good riverside location, happy efficient staff making for great atmosphere, local paintings and photographs, simple good value food inc sandwiches and lunchtime hot dishes, well kept Fullers, log fire, no piped music or machines *(Steven Tait, Susie Lonie, Dr Sherriff)*

☆ [15 Strand on the Green], *Bulls Head*: Lovely Thames-side spot for this unpretentious well worn in old pub with little rambling rooms, black-panelled alcoves, simple traditional furnishings, Courage-related ales, no-smoking eating area (not Sun or Mon evenings), no piped music, back games bar; picnic-table sets by river, children allowed in back conservatory *(Gordon, Dr Sherriff, LYM)*

☆ [27 Strand on the Green], *City Barge*: Small panelled riverside bars in picturesque partly 15th-c pub (this original part reserved for diners lunchtime), also airy newer back part done out with maritime signs and bird prints; usual lunchtime bar food (not Sun), Courage Best and Directors, back conservatory, winter fires, some tables on towpath *(Dr Sherriff, Graham and Belinda Staplehurst, LYM)*

☆ [185 Chiswick High St], *George IV*: Nice clean Fullers pub with pleasant staff, good if not cheap food eg pies really well filled with meat, well kept ales inc Chiswick, good friendly atmosphere *(Mrs S Jones, Martin Kay, Andrea Fowler, N Clack, Dr and Mrs A K Clarke)*

[80 Chiswick Rd], *J J Moons*: Wetherspoons pub, good as usual *(Neil Barker)*

[434 Chiswick High Rd], *Old Pack Horse*; Tastefully upgraded Fullers pub with music hall prints; friendly welcome *(Dr and Mrs A K Clarke)*

[214 Chiswick High Rd], *Windmill*; One of the better Fullers pubs *(Martin Kay, Andrea Fowler)*

W5

[124 Pitshanger Lane], *Duffys*: Civilised

atmosphere, not too wine-barish, with slightly separate small restaurant – appetising aromas infiltrating nicely; well kept Fullers London Pride and Wadworths 6X, reasonably priced bar food, friendly staff *(Andrew Stephenson)*

[Hanger Lane], *Fox & Goose*: Good Fullers pub *(Martin Kay, Andrea Fowler)*

W6

[2 South Black Lion Lane], *Black Lion*: Cosy and welcoming Chef & Brewer, staff pleasant and eager to please, food reasonably priced and quite imaginative, served evenings too; big log-effect gas fire separating off area with pool tables, machines etc *(Ian Phillips, BB)*

[Lower Mall], *Blue Anchor*: Useful food and well kept Courage in friendly panelled pub right on Thames, oars and other rowing memorabilia, pleasant river-view upstairs restaurant; busy weekends *(M Quine, BB)*

W8

☆ [1 Allen St; off Kensington High St], *Britannia*: Friendly local little changed since the 60s, good value fresh home-cooked food inc notable bacon rolls (it's the sort of place where they remember your favourite snack after a gap of months); well kept beer, friendly and helpful landlady, peaceful comfort – no music; attractive indoor 'garden' *(Prof S Barnett, Ian Phillips, BHP)*

[40 Holland St], *Elephant & Castle*: Basic two-bar open-plan pub, bigger than it looks, with friendly staff, well kept Bass and Worthington BB, good food inc pizzas (busy at lunchtime); good seats on small suntrap terrace with very pretty hanging baskets *(Stephen Savill)*

[Hillgate St, behind Gate Cinema], *Hillgate*: Well Victorianised, cosily partitioned high-ceilinged main bar with lots of pictures in cottagey room off, good lighting, well kept Fullers and Ruddles, pleasant service *(Susan and John Douglas)*

☆ [23a Edwardes Squ], *Scarsdale Arms*: Attractive Victorian building in lovely leafy square, stripped wooden floors, two or three fireplaces with good coal-effect gas fires, lots of nick-nacks like Staffordshire pottery dogs, ornate bar counter; well kept Courage-related ales, decent wines, cheerful service, back food servery with reasonably priced simple generous food; tree-shaded front courtyard *(Susan and John Douglas, LYM)*

W9

[5a Formosa St], *Prince Alfred*: Ornate Victorian pub with several separate bars, good range of well kept real ales, glass snob-screens *(Dr and Mrs A K Clarke)*

☆ [93 Warrington Cres], *Warrington*: Beautifully ornate, with luscious decor, well kept real ale, good pub food, also successful upstairs Thai restaurant *(Stephen Savill, Dr and Mrs A K Clarke)*

[6 Warwick Pl], *Warwick Castle*: Busy straightforward high-ceilinged Victorian local, good unspoilt atmosphere (dogs allowed), decent bar snacks, well kept Bass and Charrington IPA; benches out by quiet lane nr Little Venice (*S J Elliott, Sue Demont, Tim Barrow, LYM*)

W11

☆ [54 Ladbroke Rd], *Ladbroke Arms*: Good home cooking inc unusual dishes in comfortably refurbished pub with open fire in upper room, good attentive service, Courage-related and other ales; good Sun lunches (*Mrs Wyn Churchill*)

W13

[2 Scotch Common], *Kent*: Very good Fullers pub (*Martin Kay, Andrea Fowler*)

W14

[247 Warwick Rd], *Radnor Arms*: Nice interior, friendly landlord, well kept Everards and Shepherd Neame Bishops Finger; no food Sun (*Sally and Bill Hyde*)

Brentford

[3 High St; not the same as Mary O'Riordans], *O'Riordans*: Irish-theme pub with notable array of all sorts of jugs, oil lamps, bottles, chamber-pots etc hanging from beams; cosy and attractive, with small terrace overlooking river (*Gordon*)
[Ferry Lane], *Waterman*: Friendly little one-bar local, horseshoe-shaped with raised end, warm and relaxing (*Gordon*)

Cranford

[123 High St; Cranford Lane off A312], *Queens Head*: Good Fullers pub (*Martin Kay, Andrea Fowler*)

Feltham

[Poplar Way], *General Roy*: New big open-plan traditional-style pub with floorboards, flagstones, high beams, lots of photographs and interesting artefacts; Bass, Fullers London Pride, Worthington BB and a guest beer; tables outside (*R Houghton*)
[Ashford Rd], *Sawyers Arms*: One of the better Fullers pubs (*Martin Kay, Andrea Fowler*)

Hampton

☆ [70 High St], *White Hart*: Well run pub with interesting choice of well kept changing ales, quiet relaxed atmosphere, nice open fires, subdued lighting, good staff, small front terrace (*Debby Hawkins, Mark Johnson, R Houghton*)

Hampton Court

[Hampton Court Rd], *Mitre*: Comfortable new riverside Tavern Bar in extensively renovated hotel opp palace and gardens; a bit like a licensed conservatory, with flagstoned terrace (and landing stage), Thames view, traditional dark wood tables and chairs, simple bar foods, well kept Courage-related real ales, rather loud vaguely classical piped music; bedrooms (*Paul Randall, E G Parish*)

Hampton Wick

[Kingston Bridge], *White Hart*: Very good Fullers pub (*Martin Kay, Andrea Fowler*)

Harefield

☆ [Shrubs Rd/Harefield Rd; Woodcock Hill, off A404 E of Rickmansworth at Batchworth], *Rose & Crown*: Good atmosphere in attractive low-ceilinged country local, carefully refurbished, with good service, wide choice of good changing food, Allied ales, beautiful garden (*Mark J Hydes*)

Hillingdon

[Bath Rd (A4)], *White Hart*:Very obliging service in Courage pub with bar food (not weekends), family room with electric horse and video game, tables in back garden (*Roger and Jenny Huggins*)

Isleworth

[Church St], *London Apprentice*: Thames-side Chef & Brewer worth knowing for its position and attractive terrace; bar food, upstairs restaurant (open all Sun afternoon), Courage-related beers on handpump; children welcome, open all day; popular at weekends with Rugby fans (*John Saunders, E G Parish*)
[1 Swan St], *Swan*: One of the better Fullers pubs (*Martin Kay, Andrea Fowler*)

Norwood Green

☆ [Tentelow Lane (A4127)], *Plough*: Good Fullers pub with cheerful villagey feel, congenial staff, two log fires (one in cosy family room), even a bowling green dating to 14th c; fairly compact and does get crowded weekends, but good service and comfortable seats; well kept ales, good value bar food, occasional barbecues in pretty garden with play area, open all day (*Tom Evans, Martin Kay, Andrea Fowler*)

Osterley

☆ [Windmill Lane; B454, off A4], *Hare & Hounds*: Thriving open-plan suburban Fullers pub with soft lighting, reasonably priced straightforward bar lunches, good service, darts, piped music; good mature garden, nr Osterley Park (*Martin Kay, Andrea Fowler*)

Ruislip

☆ [12 Victoria Rd; opp Ruislip Manor tube], *J J Moons*: One of the best Wetherspoons pubs, good traditional style and atmosphere), very big but cosily divided, good value food all day and beer of consistently high standard yet prices very attractive (*Andrew Stephenson, Mark J Hydes, Nigel Gibbs, Neil Barker*)

Twickenham

[Hampton Rd], *Prince Albert*: Good open-plan Fullers local, friendly and busy, doing well under current regime; seats in enclosed garden, budgerigars, chickens etc behind (*Charles Owens, Catherine Almona, M Clarke*)
[The Green], *Prince Blucher*: One of the better Fullers pubs (*Martin Kay, Andrea Fowler*)

☆ [Riverside], *White Swan*: Attractive lunchtime buffet with reasonably priced hot food, real ales that do not seem as cheap, in relaxed pub tucked away in very quiet spot by the Thames, pleasant balcony overlooking Thames and tables outside right down to the water's edge; huge rough-looking tables, walls packed with Rugby memorabilia (other sports banned on TV), blazing fire; very busy for Sun lunchtime and events such as barbecues, raft races (*J Boylan, Ian Phillips, Sue Demont, M Clarke, LYM*)

Uxbridge

[90 Oxford Rd; A4020], *Crown & Old Treaty House*: Handsome pub with historic panelled room, extended range of guest beers currently doing well (*Andrew Stephenson*)

☆ [Villiers St; off Clevedon Rd opp Brunel University], *Load of Hay*: Good value generous food inc good soup and warm french bread, friendly staff, well kept Courage-related and genuine guest beers, choice of teas inc Earl Grey and Darjeeling, impressive fireplace in no-smoking back lounge-area part used by diners, more public-bar atmosphere nearer serving bar, another separate bar, local paintings, back garden (*John Barker, R Houghton, TBB, Bjorn Barton*)

EAST
E1

[St Katharines Way], *Dickens Inn*: Very commercial touristy pastiche of olde-worlde dockside tavern by smart docklands marina, heavy timbers, bare bricks and boards, hard benches, candles in bottles; open all day, usual bar food, Courage-related beers and a couple brewed for the pub just over the river; upstairs restaurant (*Wayne Brindle, LYM*)

☆ [62 Wapping High St], *Town of Ramsgate*: Interesting old-London Thames-side setting, with restricted but evocative river view; long narrow bar with squared oak panelling, bric-a-brac, old Limehouse prints, fine etched mirror of Ramsgate harbour, well kept Bass and Charrington IPA, usual bar food, open all day (*D Cox, LYM*)

[Wapping Lane], *White Swan & Cuckoo*: Bare-boards local with basic but good food, adventurous very cheap guest beers (*Tony and Lynne Stark*)

E2

[456 Bethnal Green Rd], *Camdens Head*: Small Wetherspoons local, usual high standards, food, low prices, good staff (*Neil Barker*)

E3

[Cadogan Terr, Bow], *Top of the Mornin'*: Relaxed atmosphere in Irish pub with very welcoming staff (*Eric Robinson*)

E4

[Larkshall Rd], *Larkshall*: Good value weekday lunchtime food in Chingford's only surviving farmhouse, extravagantly refurbished with one Victorian end and the other going back at least to the very early 16th c, with gallery over bar and various farm tools; friendly and pleasant, well kept Courage-related ales (*Joy Heatherley*)

☆ [Mott St; off Sewardstone Rd (A112) – OS Sheet 177 map ref 384983], *Plough*: Cosily countrified pub with friendly atmosphere, good value straightforward food, well kept Courage Directors, brisk service; bar billiards and darts in neat public bar; occasional live music Sun (*Joy Heatherley*)

[219 Kings Head Hill], *Royal Oak*: Spacious McMullens pub, popular, smart and clean, with panelled public bar, bar billiards in public bar, McMullens Country and AK Mild, good value lunches; seats outside, superb hanging baskets and window boxes (*Joy Heatherley*)

[94 Hatch Lane], *Wheelwrights*: Large Beefeater decorated with waggon wheels, photographs of old Chingford Hatch and of working wheelwrights; Flowers Original and Marstons Pedigree on handpump, restaurant, garden (*Robert Lester*)

E5

[Elderfield Rd], *Priory*: Welcoming and relaxing local, a decent proper pub, bar snacks rather than meals (*Eric Robinson*)

E6

[419 Barking Rd], *Millers Well*: Good Wetherspoons pub, an asset to the area (*Neil Barker*)

E8

☆ [Forest Road], *Lady Diana*: Comfortable and friendly local with good choice of well kept real ales, good atmosphere, good home-made pizzas; tables out on sheltered back terrace (*Will Podmore, NHB*)

E10

[557 Lea Bridge Rd], *Drum*: Typical Wetherspoons pub, recently enlarged, with friendly local atmosphere, drum decor, well kept ales such as Eldridge Pope, Greene King Abbot, Theakstons XB, Youngers Scotch (*Robert Lester*)

E11

☆ [off Whipps Cross Rd], *Alfred Hitchcock*: Much more atmosphere than usual for the area in this pleasant rather countrified pub, a free house with well kept and fairly priced real ales such as Boddingtons, Courage Best and Directors, Felinfoel Double Dragon, Wadworths 6X; useful Chinese restaurant (*Philip Calwell, Neil and Jenny Spink, Caroline Shearer*)

[63 New Wanstead; A113], *British Queen*: Courage-related ales in cosy and friendly open-plan pub with lunchtime food, good relaxing atmosphere (*Robert Lester*)

[36 High St], *Clutterbucks*: Panelling, character and good friendly atmosphere in free house with eight real ales, board games (*Robert Lester*)

[Wanstead High St], *George*: Nice

atmosphere in Wetherspoons pub, one of the best for food (straightforward, but well cooked and presented at low prices), with wide choice of well kept beer, no-smoking area, good staff; popular with older people at lunchtime *(Caroline Wright, Neil Barker)*

E14

☆ [44 Narrow St], *Barley Mow*: Former docklands pump house converted to substantial pub, clean and comfortable, well worth knowing for its breezy terrace overlooking Limehouse Basin, mouth of Regents Canal and two Thames reaches; lots of sepia Whitby photographs, food, Allied ales, conservatory *(Andy Thwaites, Neil Barker, Paul Haworth)* [1 Fishermans Walk; Canary Wharf], *Cat & Canary*: New Docklands pub with real pub feel, good lunches and good fat baps at attractive prices, well kept Fullers; closes 9 *(Miss C B Stone)* [114 Glengall Gr], *George*: Very cheery and pleasant, good food in bar and restaurant inc good value specials, real ales such as Ruddles, conservatory *(Ian Phillips)*

E15

[146 The Grove], *Goldengrove*: Wetherspoons pub with good staff, food always available, sensible prices, no-smoking area, well kept range of beers *(Neil Barker)*

E17

[Shernhall St], *Lord Brooke*: Good lunchtime home-cooked food, genial landlord, sensible beer prices, tables on terrace; big satellite TV, games room, weekend live entertainment, quizzes and karaoke *(A Stopforth)*

E18

[142 Hermon Hill; South Woodford], *Boar & Thistle*: Long, low cream-painted Edwardian-style pub with glass and wrought-iron canopy over front bay windows and door, very spick and span; reasonably priced lunchtime food, Courage-related ales, warm welcome; can be lively at night, with DJ *(Ian Phillips)*

Barking

[61 Station Par], *Barking Dog*: Recently opened Wetherspoons pub, quite large, with booth seating, Theakstons XB, Wadworths 6X and Youngers Scotch on handpump, good dining area *(Robert Lester, Neil Barker)* [15 Longbridge Rd (A124)], *Spotted Dog*: Davys Wine Lodge with lots of panelling and sawdust, Courage-related ales, restaurant (not Sun or Mon evenings) *(Robert Lester)*

Gidea Park

[main rd Gallows Corner—Romford], *Ship*:

Attractive building dating from 16th c, with Courage-related real ales, friendly golden retriever; in village centre *(D Cox)*

Harold Wood

[51 Station Rd; ½ mile from A12], *King Harold*: Spacious two-bar family pub with good friendly atmosphere, popular with nursing staff from nearby hospital; Allied ales, plenty of machines *(Robert Lester)*

Havering Atte Bower

Willow: Friendly helpful staff, good choice of particularly good value food, nice garden; clean and tidy, piped music in restaurant area *(S J Penford)*

Hornchurch

[46 High St], *Last Post*: Good reliable Wetherspoons pub *(Neil Barker)*

Ilford

[308 Ley St; nr A123], *Bell*: Smart and comfortable, with sporting caricatures, Courage-related ales; occasional Sun jazz *(Robert Lester)*

☆ [553 Ilford High Rd; A118], *Cauliflower*: Massive Victorian open-plan pub; good friendly atmosphere, regular live music, Courage-related ales *(Robert Lester)* [Aldborough Rd N; Newbury Pk, off A12], *Dick Turpin*: Dick Turpin theme in beamed and panelled Beefeater with Whitbreads-related real ales, good food and service *(Robert Lester)* [16 Ilford Hill; nr A406], *Rose & Crown*: Split-level Allied pub, lots of panelling, guests such as Adnams and Greene King, occasional beer festivals *(Robert Lester)*

Noak Hill

[Noak Hill Rd; nr A12], *Bear*: Large friendly refurbished pub with good children's facilities in big garden; Charrington IPA and Greene King on handpump *(Robert Lester)*

Romford

[260 London Rd (A110); Spring Gdns], *Crown*: Refurbished mock-Victorian open-plan pub nr dog track, Allied ales *(Robert Lester)* [South St], *Moon & Stars*: Very big new Wetherspoons pub with cubicles at one side, raised end area, usual range of beers with a regular guest, food *(D Cox)*

Woodford

[692 Chigwell Rd (A113)], *White Hart*: Large comfortable recently refurbished local with good friendly atmosphere; Allied ales, beams, darts, pool, crystal maze machine *(Robert Lester)*

Though lunchtime closing time is 3 on Sundays in England and Wales (with 20 minutes' drinking-up time), some pubs hope to close a bit earlier – please let us know if you find this happening.

Scotland

Three new main entries here, all comfortable places to stay in, are the
Creebridge House at Creebridge near Newton Stewart (a wide range of
good food), the bustling Traquair Arms in Innerleithen (unusual for the area
in doing decent food all through the afternoon, and very handy for Traquair
House whose splendid ales it sells), and the Tushielaw Hotel, a friendly little
wayside inn in lovely Ettrick Valley scenery. As these new entries suggest, in
much of rural Scotland it's the country hotel or inn which looks after
visitors and even locals in the way that in England a country pub would be
expected to. In the remoter places often even quite grand hotels have a
surprisingly pubby locals' bar, and on a lonely road you should never feel
shy of going into a hotel if all you want is a casual drink or just a snack.
Drinks prices tend to be higher than in England, with places selling Scottish
beers generally charging about 10p a pint less than those supplied by
English brewers. The cheapest places we found for drinks were the
interesting Four Marys in Linlithgow, the stylish Riverside Inn at Canonbie
(one of the best pubs in Scotland for good food), the friendly Fishermans
Tavern at Broughty Ferry (food cheap here too), and in Edinburgh
Bannermans Bar and the imposing Guildford Arms – which has a
remarkable range of Scottish beers. We've noticed Belhaven turning up
quite often as the cheapest beer stocked, incidentally – well worth looking
out for. Food seems to be improving in Scottish pubs and inns: we've
noticed more individual recipes this year, and more places using local fresh
ingredients. Among the best places for an enjoyable meal are the Byre at
Brig o' Turk, the Riverside Inn at Canonbie, the smartly refurbished Crinan
Hotel (sweeping sea and island views from its top-floor restaurant), the
lively and welcoming Babbity Bowster in Glasgow, the remote Kilberry Inn
on the West Coast, the upmarket and restauranty Wheatsheaf at Swinton,
the unpretentious Tayvallich Inn (good local seafood) and the restaurant of
the Morefield Motel in Ullapool (local seafood again). From among these
we choose the Wheatsheaf at Swinton as Scotland's Dining Pub of the Year.
Some pubs we'd particularly draw attention to in the Lucky Dip section at
the end of the chapter are, in the Borders, the Queens Head in Kelso and
Eagle in Lauder; in Central, the Castlecary House at Castlecary and
Inverarnan Drovers Inn; in Dumfries & Galloway, both Auchencairn
entries and the wide choice in Moffat; in Highland, the Badachro Hotel,
Lock in Fort Augustus and Cluanie in Glen Shiel; in Lothian, the Hawes at
Queensferry; in Strathclyde, the Ardentinny Hotel, Falls of Lora at Connel
and Cuilfail at Kilmelford; in Tayside, the Royal Oak in Dundee and
Kenmore Inn; on North Uist, the Claddach Kirkibost at Westford, and on
South Uist, the Pollachar. In Edinburgh the Peacock (for food) and Jolly
Judge stand out, though there's a very wide choice indeed of good pubs here
– far wider than in Glasgow, where the Ubiquitous Chip stands out. We
have inspected the great majority of these noted Dip entries, so can firmly
recommend them.

ABERDEEN (Grampian) NJ9305 Map 11

Prince of Wales £ 🍺

7 St Nicholas Lane

Standing in the narrow cobbled lane outside this individual old tavern, you easily forget that this is the very heart of Aberdeen's shopping centre, with Union Street almost literally overhead. A bustlingly cosy flagstoned area has the city's longest bar counter and is furnished with pews and other wooden furniture in screened booths, while a smarter main lounge has sensibly placed darts and fruit machine. Popular, good value and generously served lunchtime food includes soup (£1.20), chicken in cider sauce (£3.30) and home-made pies (£3.50). An excellent range of excellently kept beers includes Bass, Caledonian 80/-, Courage Directors, Orkney Dark Island, Theakstons Old Peculier, Youngers No 3 and several guests on handpump and tall fount air pressure. *(Recommended by Duncan and Vi Glennig, Les Mackay, Mark Walker, Julian Bessa)*

Free house ~ Licensee Peter Birnie ~ Real ale ~ Lunchtime meals and snacks (not Sun) ~ (01224) 640597 ~ Children in eating area of bar ~ No nearby parking ~ Open 11am-12pm

APPLECROSS (Highland) NG7144 Map 11

Applecross Inn

Off A896 S of Shieldaig

The exhilarating west coast drive to get here over the Beallach na Ba pass – the pass of the cattle – is one of the highest in Britain and not to be tried in bad weather. The alternate route, along the single-track lane winding round the coast from just south of Shieldaig, has equally glorious sea loch and then sea views nearly all the way. In a lonely setting against a breathtaking backdrop towards Raasay and Skye this refreshingly jolly and decidedly unsmart local is popular for very fresh local seafood, including cod or monkfish (£4.75), dressed crab or queen scallops in cream sauce (£5.95) and local oysters (six for £6.95); they also do good home-made soups (£1.40) and puddings such as fruit crumble or fudge cake, and other dishes such as venison burgers (£1.95) and chicken in herb and garlic butter (£4.95); children's menu. The simple bar is friendly and quite comfortable, with quite a lot of cheery regulars – especially as the evening wears on. The lively landlord is from Yorkshire. Musicians particularly are welcomed, and in the background there's usually piped folk music; darts, pool, dominoes and trivia; decent coffee, a good choice of around fifty malt whiskies, efficient service. There is a nice garden by the shore with tables. Bedrooms are small and simple but adequate, all with a sea view; booking for the seafood restaurant is essential. *(Recommended by Lee Goulding, N C Walker, A J and J A Hartigan, Ian and Deborah Carrington, Tony and Joan Walker; more reports please)*

Free house ~ Licensees Judith and Bernie Fish ~ Meals and snacks (12-9 in summer; 12-2, 7-9 in winter) ~ No-smoking restaurant ~ (01520) 744262 ~ Children welcome until 8.30pm ~ Open 11(12.30 Sun)-11 (till 12 Fri, 11.30 Sat); winter 11-2.30, 5-11 (11-11.30 Sat; closed Sun evening, Mon lunchtime) ~ Bedrooms: £20/£40

ARDFERN (Strathclyde) NM8004 Map 11

Galley of Lorne

B8002; village and inn signposted off A816 Lochgilphead—Oban

Ideally placed inn with marvellously peaceful views of the sea loch and yacht anchorage from the sheltered terrace and the big windows. The cosy main bar is decorated with old Highland dress prints and other pictures, big navigation lamps by the bar counter, and an unfussy assortment of furniture, including little winged settles and rug-covered window seats on its lino tiles. Very good bar food includes stilton and walnut pâté (£2.85), haggis with cream and whisky (£3.25), moules marinières (£4.85), fresh sole fillets (£7.25), fresh turbot (£11.25) and delicious Islay scallops (£11.95); home-made puddings like bread and butter pudding

(£1.95) and banoffi pie (£2.75) and assorted Scottish cheeses; children's helpings; spacious restaurant. A wide choice of malt whiskies and bin-end wines; darts, dominoes, fruit machine and piped music; no credit cards for meals. *(Recommended by J R and H Soulsby, Margaret and Fred Punter, Capt E P Gray; more reports please)*

Free house ~ Licensee Susana Garland ~ Meals and snacks ~ Restaurant ~ (01852) 500284 ~ Children in eating area of bar ~ Occasional live folk/Scottish music ~ Open 11-2.30, 5-11; 11am-12pm Sat; closed 25 Dec ~ Bedrooms: £25(£30B)/£50(£60B)

ARDUAINE (Strathclyde) NM7910 Map 11

Loch Melfort Hotel 🛏

A816 S of Oban and beside Luing

There's a magnificent view over the wilderness of the loch and its islands from the wooden seats on the front terrace of this comfortable hotel, and it's only a short stroll through grass and wild flowers to the rocky loch foreshore, where the licensees keep their own lobster pots and nets, serving up the catch for dinner that evening. The airy and modern bar has a pair of powerful marine glasses which you can use to search for birds and seals on the islets and on the coasts of the bigger islands beyond. The walls are papered with nautical charts, and there's a freestanding woodburning stove and dark brown fabric-and-wood easy chairs around light oak tables. There's quite an emphasis on seafood, and the lunchtime bar menu might include trout and salmon fishcakes with tomato coulis (£5.75), Ormsary venison sausages (£5.50) and large grilled langoustines (£8.95); seafood buffet on Sundays in the restaurant, and with a little notice they will prepare vegetarian meals and high teas for children. Darts and piped music. It's very popular with passing yachtsmen who are welcome to use their mooring facilities. From late April to early June the walks through the neighbouring Arduaine woodland gardens are lovely. *(Recommended by Mrs Pat Crabb, Roger and Christine Mash, Martin, Jane, Simon and Laura Bailey, Iain Grant, L Walker; more reports please; also recommended by* The Good Hotel Guide*)*

Free house ~ Licensee Philip Lewis ~ Meals and snacks (12-2.30, 6-9) ~ No-smoking restaurant (closed Sun lunchtime) ~ (01852) 200233 ~ Children welcome ~ Open 9.30(10 in winter)-11(11.30 Sat); between 5 Jan-25 Feb open only 12-2.30 ~ Bedrooms: £55.50B/£95B

ARDVASAR (Isle of Skye) NG6203 Map 11

Ardvasar Hotel 🍴 🛏

A851 at S of island; just past Armadale pier where the summer car ferries from Mallaig dock

Commanding views across the Sound of Sleat – an area often referred to as the Island's garden – and on to the dramatic mountains of Knoydart from this comfortably modernised 18th-c white stone coaching inn – which has some of the most dramatic summer sunsets in Scotland. It's run by friendly and obliging young owners and can get busy in the evening with locals gathering in the simple public bar which has stripped pews and kitchen chairs or the cocktail bar which is furnished with crimson plush wall seats and stools around dimpled copper coffee tables on the red patterned carpet (and Highland dress prints on the cream hessian-and-wood walls). In a room off the comfortable hotel lounge there are armchairs around the open fire (and a large TV); darts, dominoes, bar billiards, pool table, pinball, video game, juke box and fruit machine. Excellent home-made food from the evening restaurant menu might include mussels in garlic and cream (£3.80), braised rump of Scottish deer with herb dumplings (£6.80), goujons of fresh monkfish (£7.10), sauté pork chops with apple and cider cream (£9.80), fillet of guinea fowl with grapes and wine (£12.30) and pan-fried brill fillet with cashew nuts and Glayva (£12.50), and puddings like apple and bramble tart (£2.30), rhubarb and ginger creamy fool (£2.50) and a selection of Scottish cheeses (£3.80). The bar menu may be simpler, and beware, it is high tea so they stop serving food at 7pm; coffee. Handy for the Clan Donald centre.

(Recommended by Neale Davies, Capt E P Gray, James Nunns; more reports please; also recommended by The Good Hotel Guide*)*

Free house ~ Licensees Bill and Gretta Fowler ~ Meals and snacks (12-2, 5-7 bar food, restaurant 7-10) ~ Restaurant ~ (0147 14) 223 ~ Children in eating area of bar ~ Open 11-2.30, 5-11 ~ Bedrooms: £35B/£60B

BLANEFIELD (Central) NS5579 Map 11

Carbeth Inn

West Carbeth; A809 Glasgow—Drymen, just S of junction with B821

A relaxed and well kept old country pub that has been redecorated since last year and easily stands out in this area for the range and standard of its food. The cheerfully old-fashioned bar has heavy cast-iron-framed tables on the stone and tile floor, cushioned booths built from pine planking under a high frieze of tartan curtain and a high ceiling of the same brown wood. At one end, under the mounted stag's head, there's an open fire and at the other end, a woodburning stove. Generous helpings of good value bar food include home-made soup (£1.20), breaded mushrooms (£1.75), chicken liver pâté (£1.95), prawn cocktail (£2.25), macaroni cheese (£3.35), deep-fried haddock (£3.75), lasagne, country vegetable and cheese pie (£3.95), haggis with filo pasty and whisky and onion sauce, steak pie or scampi (£4.50), gammon steak (£4.95), rib eye steak (£6.50); home-made puddings like fruit crumbles (£2), banana boat special (£2.45); usual children's menu (from £1.75). Well kept Belhaven St Andrews and 80/- under light blanket pressure; fruit machine and piped music. On the front terrace outside there are lots of rustic benches and tables. *(Recommended by Andy and Jill Kassube; more reports please)*

Belhaven ~ Lease: Brian and Kate McDade ~ Real ale ~ Meals (12-2, 7-9; 12-9 Sat and Sun) ~ Restaurant ~ (01360) 770002 ~ Children welcome ~ weekend sing-alongs ~ Open 11(12 in winter)-11(midnight Sat) ~ Bedrooms £15/£30

BRIG O TURK (Central) SK8306

Byre 🍴 🍷

A821 Callander—Trossachs

They seem to be getting most things right at this carefully converted 18th-c cowshed (or byre in Scots). It's in a lovely setting on the edge of a network of forest and lochside tracks in the Queen Elizabeth Forest Park on the Killin – Loch Lomond cycle way – also much loved by walkers. The cosy, spotless beamed bar has comfortable brass-studded black dining chairs, an open fire, stuffed wildlife, some decorative plates, and rugs on the stone and composition floor, and there's a stylish dining room. Very good, imaginative food changes every 4-6 weeks (although the licensee tells us that prices haven't changed since last year) and at lunchtime might include chicken and stilton soup (£1.75), cheese frits with redcurrant jelly (£2.95), sandwiches or lentil, hazelnut and mushroom pâté (£3.25), peppered mackerel with horseradish cream (£3.55), haddock in their own breadcrumbs (£5.25), courgette and walnut loaf with orange and cranberry sauce or roast chicken with bacon and savoury stuffing (£5.95), and puddings like lemon cheesecake or walnut fudgecake (£2.55); evening dishes such as seafood chowder (£1.95), wild mushroom feuilletage (£3.25), vegetable quenelles (£7.95), honey-roast duckling with a plum and ginger sauce (£8.95), pan-fried monkfish with an orange sauce (£9.55), red mullet with citrus fruits (£9.75), sirloin steak with béarnaise sauce (£9.95), and puddings like profiteroles with chocolate sauce or bread and butter pudding (£2.55); pleasant, friendly service. Well kept Broughton Special Bitter and Greenmantle on handpump, several local and rare malt whiskies, and very good wines; piped music. The lovable cat is called Soda. There are tables and parasols outside. *(Recommended by D S Jay, Owen and Helen McGhee, Duncan and Vi Glennig, Mrs S Gillotti, Mr and Mrs J H Adam, Sue and Mike Grant)*

Free house ~ Licensee John Park ~ Real ale ~ Meals and snacks ~ No-smoking restaurant ~ (01877) 376292 ~ Children welcome lunchtime only ~ Open 12-2.30, 6-11; 12-11 Sat and Sun; closed 5 Jan – 5 Feb

BROUGHTY FERRY (Tayside) NO4630 Map 11

Fishermans Tavern 🛏 £ 🍺

12 Fort St; turning off shore road

Comfortably rambling old pub with an unusually good range of very well kept award winning real ales including Belhaven 60/-, 80/- and St Andrews, Maclays 80/- and daily changing guest beers like Courage Directors on handpump and tall fount air pressure; there's also a choice of around 30 malt whiskies and some local fruit wines by the glass. The diminutive brown carpeted snug has light pink soft fabric seating, basket-weave wall panels and beige lamps; in the carpeted back bar, popular with diners, there's a Victorian fireplace and brass wall lights; dominoes and fruit machine. Lunchtime bar food includes sandwiches (95p), soup (£1), steak roll (£1.90), home-made fisherman's pie or chicken and mushroom pie (£3.25), home-made steak pie, lasagne or Yorkshire pudding with roast beef (£3.90) and daily specials like fresh crab salad or navarin of lamb; efficient professional service. The nearby seafront gives a good view of the two long, low Tay bridges. Bedrooms are comfortable. *(Recommended by Julian Bessa, N J Mackintosh, Bill and Lydia Ryan; more reports please)*

Free house ~ Licensee Mr Jonathan Stewart ~ Real ale ~ Meals and snacks (12-2.30, 5-9; limited food Sunday)~ Restaurant (12.30-7 Sun) ~ (01382) 75941 ~ Children in eating area of bar ~ Folk music Thurs evening ~ Open 11-midnight ~ Bedrooms: £15/£28

CANONBIE (Dumfries and Galloway) NY3976 Map 9

Riverside ★ ★ 🍽 🛏 🍷

Village signposted from A7

Once again delighted readers' reports confirm our high opinion of this excellent, welcoming place. There's always that extra special bit of effort put into things, and the result is a comfort and style that you'd be lucky to find in most five star hotels. The comfortable and restful communicating rooms of the bar – set out for eating – have a charmingly peaceful atmosphere, stuffed wildlife, local pictures, good, sensitively chosen chintzy furnishings and open fires. The genuinely interesting seasonal bar menu of excellent home-cooked food is chalked up on two blackboards each lunchtime and might include soups like mushroom and mustard or chestnut, guinea fowl terrine, baked fresh sardines, herring in oatmeal (£4.55), a dozen langoustines (£5.25), cod fillets in beer batter (around £6.25), and (from their new char-grill) Barnsley chops, venison, corn-fed chicken or guinea fowl (£6.55); lots of puddings such as upside down pear gingerbread and toffee sauce, spiced brown bread and butter pudding with toffee sauce or baked rhubarb cheesecake with rhubarb and orange sauce. There are careful small touches like virgin olive oil for the salad dressings, bread baked on the premises or at the local bakery in Melmerby, and a concentration on 'organic' foods such as undyed smoked fish, wild salmon and naturally-fed chickens; they also have an award-winning range of cheeses; substantial and highly-praised breakfasts. Lunchtime service can stop quite promptly. Well kept and very reasonably priced for the area Black Sheep and regularly changing guest beers such as Morlands Old Speckled Hen, Greene King or Tetleys on handpump; a good range of properly kept and served wines; about 12 malt whiskies; organic wines and farm ciders; sympathetic service; dominoes; half of the bar is no smoking. In summer – when it can get very busy – there are tables under the trees on the front grass. Bedrooms are notably comfortable and well decorated. Over the quiet road, a public playground runs down to the Border Esk (the inn can arrange fishing permits), and there are lovely walks in the area. *(Recommended by Mrs S Gillotti, John Townsend, Richard W Chew, Gill and Maurice McMahon, G D and M D Craigen, Doug Kennedy, Dr I M Ingram, Alan Wilcox, Christine Davidson, N P Hopkins, Dr Wayne Scott, R C Wiles, Dr R H M Stewart, Mr and Mrs Richard Osborne, John and Joan Wyatt, Tim Barrow, Sue Demont, Stephanie Sowerby, WTF, JCW, Dr A N B Bradford, P O Harrop, R L Anderson, Dr and Mrs James Stewart, Dr Brian G Lake; also recommended by The Good Hotel Guide)*

Free house ~ Licensees Robert and Susan Phillips ~ Real ale ~ Meals and snacks (not Sun lunchtime) ~ Children welcome (all ages in bar, from 8 yrs in restaurant) ~ No-smoking restaurant (closed Sun) ~ (013878) 71512/71295 ~ Open 11-2.30, 6.30-11(12 Sat); closed Sun lunchtime, last 2 weeks Feb, first 2 weeks Nov, 25 and 26 Dec and 1 and 2 Jan ~ Bedrooms: £55B/£72B

CARBOST (Isle of Skye) NG3732 Map 11

Old Inn

This is the Carbost on the B8009, in the W of the central part of the island

It's the straightforward simplicity of this basically furnished stone house beside Loch Harport that makes it one of the most traditionally pubby places on the island. It's popular with climbers down from the harshly craggy peaks of the Cuillin Hills, which you can see from the lochside terrace, and is handy too for the Talisker distillery – where there are guided tours, with free samples, most days in summer. The pub stocks the whisky from here, plus a good few more malts. The three areas of the main, bare-board bar are knocked through into one, and furnished with red leatherette settles, benches, and seats, part-whitewashed and part-stripped stone walls, and a peat fire; darts, pool, cribbage, dominoes and piped traditional music. Sustaining and quickly served bar meals include chicken broth (£1.30), potato skins with garlic dip (£2.10), sausage hotpot and jacket potato with cheese (£4.45) and venison pie (£5.25) and puddings such as home-made apple crumble (£2); children's play area. Non-residents can come for the breakfasts if they book the night before. *(Recommended by Neale Davies, Mr and Mrs G Hart, Nigel and Helen Aplin, Mark Gillis, Nigel Woolliscroft; more reports please)*

Free house ~ Licensee Deirdre Cooper ~ Meals and snacks (12-2, 5.30-10) ~ (01478) 640205 ~ Children welcome in bar till 8pm (in other rooms till later) ~ Occasional live music ~ Open 11am-midnight(11.30 Sat); winter 11-2.30, 5-11 ~ Bedrooms: £21.50S/£43S

CAWDOR (Highland) NH8450 Map 11

Cawdor Tavern £

Just off B9090; Cawdor Castle signposted from A96 Inverness—Nairn

The eclectic mixture of styles here isn't really what you'd expect of a little Highland village pub. The exterior with its concrete terrace looks modern but there's a stately appearance to the substantial lounge and furnishings, largely due to the oak panelling and a chimney breast salvaged from the nearby castle. The public bar on the right has surprising elaborate wrought-iron wall lamps, chandeliers laced with bric-a-brac such as a stuffed mongoose wrestling a cobra, banknotes pinned to joists, a substantial alabaster figurine, and imposing pillared serving counter. The lounge has green plush button-back built-in wall banquettes and bucket chairs, a delft shelf with toby jugs and decorative plates (chiefly game), small tapestries, and attractive sporting pictures. Tasty and often quite unusual home-made bar food (the licensee tells us prices haven't changed since last year) such as very good value sandwiches (from £1), baked potatoes (from £2.50), lasagne, fresh Scotch salmon steak or various vegetarian dishes (£5.50), roasts (£5.75), chicken stuffed with leeks and stilton or duck breast in cherry sauce (£6.50). Well kept Charles Wells Bombardier, Fullers London Pride, Shepherd Neame Spitfire and Theakstons Best and a weekly guest beer on handpump; well over a hundred malt whiskies and some rare blends, a good choice of wines and decent coffee. There are tables on the front terrace, with tubs of flowers, roses, and creepers climbing the supports of a big awning; summer Saturday barbecues roughly once a fortnight. Darts, pool, cribbage, dominoes, juke box and video game in the public bar; no dogs; no-smoking area in restaurant. *(Recommended by Spider Newth, R M Macnaughton, Tony and Joan Walker; more reports please)*

Free house ~ Licensee T D Oram ~ Real ale ~ Meals and snacks ~ Restaurant ~ (01667) 404316 ~ Children welcome away from public bar until 9 ~ Open 11-2.30, 5-11

CLACHAN SEIL (Highland) NM7718 Map 11

Tigh an Truish

This island is linked by a bridge via B844, off A816 S of Oban

Splendid yachtsman's pub set next to the attractive old bridge which joins Seil Island to the mainland of Scotland, and near a lovely anchorage, this 18th-c inn has a thriving local atmosphere in its unpretentious L-shaped bar. It has a solid woody feel, with pine-clad walls and ceiling, some fixed wall benches along with the wheelback and other chairs, tartan curtains for the bay windows overlooking the inlet, prints and oil paintings, a woodburning stove in one room, and open fires in the others. Good bar food includes starters: home-made soup (£1.50), smoked meat platter (£2.95), local oysters (£3.95) and main courses: home-made beefburger (£2.95), nutburger (£3.25), home-made lasagne, chilli con carne or pork chop in coarse-grain mustard sauce (£4.50), seafood pie (£4.75), venison in pepper cream and Drambuie sauce, locally caught prawns or steak and ale pie (£6.50); children's menu (£2.50) and puddings like home-made treacle tart (£1.50) and more from the specials board. Well kept McEwans 80/- on handpump, and a good choice of malt whiskies; darts. There are some seats in the small garden, and they have their own filling station just opposite. *(Recommended by Capt E P Gray; more reports please)*

Free house ~ Licensee Miranda Brunner ~ Real ale ~ Meals and snacks (12-2, 6-8.30) ~ (01852) 300242 ~ Children in restaurant ~ Open 11(12.30 Sun)-11; 11-2.30, 5-11 in winter ~ Bedrooms: /£40B

CLEISH (Tayside) NT0998 Map 11

Nivingston House 🏠

1½ miles from M90 junction 5; follow B9097 W until village signpost, then almost immediately inn is signposted

Despite the smartness of this plushly comfortable country house hotel, it's very relaxed and friendly with an emphasis on attentive but unobtrusive service from the welcoming staff. The well presented, interesting and tasty bar lunches might include delicious tomato and orange soup (£1.75), home-made pâté with oatcakes (£3.95), venison burger (£4.75), tagliatelle carbonara (£4.95), hot smoked trout (£5.35), chicken tikka or croque madame (£5.45), Scotch smoked salmon and prawn platter (£5.75), minute steak (£5.85) and daily specials; home-made puddings (from £2). There's a restful warmly decorated, mainly modern L-shaped bar with bold wallpaper and a log fire and a library; Yorkshire Bitter on handpump and a good choice of malt whiskies and an extensive wine list. Set in 12 acres of landscaped gardens with benches looking out over a lawn sweeping down to shrubs and trees, with hills in the distance. *(Recommended by R F and M K Bishop, N J Mackintosh, Mr and Mrs Richard Osborne, June and Tony Baldwin, Tony and Joan Walker; more reports please)*

Free house ~ Licensee Allan Deeson ~ Real ale ~ Meals and snacks (not evenings) ~ Restaurant ~ (01577) 850216 ~ Children welcome ~ Open 12-2.30, 6-11(11.45 Sat) ~ Bedrooms: £70B/£90B

CREEBRIDGE (Dumfries and Galloway) NX4165 Map 9

Creebridge House 🏠

Minnigaff, just E of Newton Stewart

This sizeable country hotel has been pushing towards a main entry for some time now. It has a welcoming and neatly kept proper carpeted bar with that great rarity for Scotland, a bar billiards table, besides Arrols 80/-, Tetleys and a guest beer such as Ind Coope Burton or Jennings on handpump, a good range of malt whiskies, dominoes, and comfortably pubby furniture; maybe unobtrusive piped music. The main draw is the good food, which includes home-made soup (£1.60), sandwiches (from £2.50), a ramekin of smoked haddock pâté (£2.95), locally smoked salmon (£4.10), smoked scallops with avocado (£4.50), vegetarian dishes (£5.50), Galloway beef silverside with brandy and mushroom sauce (£6.95 – a long-standing favourite) and grilled lamb cutlets with rosemary (£7.10); meats are

local and well hung, presentation is careful with good attention to detail; they have excellent local fish on Fridays, and game in season. Home-made puddings might include chocolate roulade with coffee sauce and passionfruit pavlova (£2.10). There's a popular three-course Sunday carvery lunch (£8.95) in the airy and comfortable no-smoking restaurant. In fine weather, tables under cocktail parasols out on the front terrace look across a pleasantly planted lawn.
(Recommended by John Watson, MK, JP, J L Phillips, Neil Townend)

Free house ~ Licensees Susan and Chris Walker ~ Real ale ~ Meals and snacks ~ Restaurant ~ (01671) 402121 ~ Children welcome ~ Occasional folk Sun evening ~ Open 12-2.30, 6-11.30 (winter opening 12.30, 7; cl evening 25 Dec) ~ Bedrooms: £40B/£75B

CRINAN (Strathclyde) NR7894 Map 11

Crinan Hotel 🍽 🛏

A816 NE from Lochgilphead, then left on to B841, which terminates at the village

The stylish glass-enclosed cocktail bar on the roof commands a panoramic view of the village, lighthouse and comings and goings of the busy entrance basin of the Crinan Canal, with its fishing boats and yachts wandering out towards the Hebrides. It's been handsomely refurbished this year with a wooden floor, oak and walnut panelling, antique tables and chairs, sailing pictures of classic yachts framed in walnut on a paper background of rust and green paisley, matching the tartan upholstery, model boats in glass cases and a nautical chest of drawers. Downstairs the simpler wooden-floored public bar with cosy stove and kelims on the seats has similar marvellous views and there's a popular side terrace with seats outside. The popular food still includes lots of local fish like Arbroath smokies (£5.95), local sea loch mussels (£6.25), fillet of local trout (£6.95), Loch Fyne princess clams (£9.50), Loch Crinan seafood stew (£12.50) and a few examples of more usual bar food: home-made soup (£2.20), honey roasted ham with salad (£5.75), chicken filled with mushrooms and leeks with a coronation sauce (£6.95), salad (£7.50) and pudding of the day, and you can get sandwiches from their coffee shop or Lazy Jack's. Large wine list, Bass and Caledonian 80/-, a wide range of malt whiskies and freshly squeezed orange juice. The jacket-and-tie top floor evening restaurant, like its associated bar, has a wonderful view out over the islands and the sea; it's no smoking, and in the evenings the hotel's atmosphere, centred on the restaurant, does become relatively formal.
(Recommended by Mr Craddock, Walter Reid, Capt E P Gray; more reports please; also recommended by The Good Hotel Guide*)*

Free house ~ Licensee Nicholas Ryan ~ Real ale ~ Lunchtime meals ~ Children welcome ~ Restaurant ~ (0154 683) 261 ~ Children welcome in eating area of cocktail bar ~ Ceilidh Sat ~ Open 11-11 (winter 11-2.30, 5-11) ~ Bedrooms: £75B/£115B

EDINBURGH (Lothian) NT2574 Map 11

The two main areas here for finding good pubs, both main entries and Lucky Dips, are around Rose St (just behind Princes St in the New Town) and along or just off the top part of the Royal Mile in the Old Town. In both areas parking can be difficult at lunchtime, but is not such a problem in the evenings.

Abbotsford

Rose St; E end, beside South St David St

At lunchtime you'll usually find an eclectic mix of business people and locals in this small gently formal single bar pub that's long been an old favourite of the city folk. Soft orange lighting and a welcoming log-effect gas fire cast a warm glow on the dark wooden half-panelled walls and highly polished Victorian island bar counter, long wooden tables and leatherette benches. There are prints on the walls and a notably handsome ornate moulded plaster high ceiling. Well kept Boddingtons, Caledonian 80/- and R & D Deuchars IPA, Greenmantle and a guest on handpump, lots of malt whiskies; fruit machine, tucked well away. Good, reasonably priced food includes soup (90p), filled toasted croissant (from £2.95), ploughman's (£3.10), vegetable flan or haggis and neeps (£3.50), pan-fried liver and onions (£3.70), pork and cider casserole or curried chicken (£3.80), roast beef and Yorkshire pudding (£4.05), breast of chicken with mustard sauce or steak and Guinness pie (£4.15) and mixed grill (£4.95); puddings like rhubarb crumble (all £1.50); efficient service from dark-uniformed or white-shirted staff, although it can be slower in the restaurant when they are busy. *(Recommended by Dave and Jules Tuckett, Ian Phillips, John Fazakerley, Capt E P Gray, Chris and Anne Fluck; more reports please)*

Free house ~ Licensee Colin Grant ~ Real ale ~ Lunchtime meals and snacks ~ Restaurant (closed Sun) ~ 0131-225 5276 ~ Children in eating area of bar and restaurant ~ Open 11-2.30, 5-11; Fri, Sat 11-11; closed Sun

Athletic Arms £ 🍺

Angle Park Terr; on corner of Kilmarnock Rd (A71)

As this is the official home of McEwans 80/- you'll find it exceptionlly well kept and dispensed from a gleaming row of eleven tall air-pressure founts. Also known as the Diggers, thanks to its earlier popularity with workers from the nearby cemetery, this thoroughly unpretentious, plain but bustling pub is at its busiest when football or rugby matches are being played at Tynecastle or Murrayfield, and they generally have a team of up to 15 red-jacketed barmen serving then. Opening off the central island servery there are some cubicles partitioned in glossy grey wood with photographs of Hearts and Scotland football teams – a side room is crowded with keen dominoes players; fruit machine, cribbage; predominantly young customers. Good value filled rolls (60p), mince or steak pies (from 80p), and stovies (£1.20) all day. *(Recommended by Mark Walker; more reports please)*

S & N ~ Manager Scott Martin ~ Real ale ~ Snacks all day ~ 0131-337 3822 ~ Open 11-11(midnight Thurs-Sat); 12.30-6 Sun

Bannermans Bar £ 🍺

212 Cowgate

Simple but marvellously atmospheric warren of brightly lit rooms deep in the heart of the city. It's popular with students, and one of the best times to visit is during the Festival when it seems to hum with suppressed excitement and arty-looking characters are constantly flowing in and out. The crypt-like flagstoned rooms have barrel-vaulted ceilings, bare stone walls and strip lighting, wood panelling and pillars at the front, and theatrical posters and handbills in the rooms leading off. A huge mixture of purely functional furnishings includes old settles, pews and settees around barrels, red-painted tables and a long mahogany table. A no-smoking back area, with tables and waitress service, is open when they're busy. A very good choice of very reasonably priced, well kept beers includes Belhaven St Andrews, Boddingtons, Caledonian 80/- and IPA, Heather Ale (brewed independently in Taynault), McEwans 80/-, Theakstons Best, and Youngers No 3, all on handpump, with plenty of malt whiskies and Belgian fruit beers. Good value, straightforward food includes filled rolls (served all day, 80p), soup (80p), filled baked potatoes (£1.95), a budget special (£2.25), ploughman's (£2.50), vegetarian specials (£2.50-£3) and a meat dish (£2.95). Dominoes, cribbage, chess, draughts and backgammon. It's very popular with students. *(Recommended by N J Mackintosh, Capt E P Gray, Ian Phillips, David and Ruth Hollands; more reports please)*

Free house ~ Licensee Douglas Smith ~ Real ale ~ Lunchtime meals and snacks, evening snacks ~ 0131-556 3254 ~ Children in eating area of bar daytime only ~ Folk bands Sun-Thurs evenings ~ Open 11am-midnight(Sat till 1am); closed 25 Dec and 1 Jan

Bow Bar ★ £ 🍺

80 West Bow

You may see a couple of barmen with big white aprons standing outside this spartan, but good traditional drinker's pub which has 12 perfectly-kept real ales rotated from a range of about 80: Bass, Caledonian 70/-, 80/-, Deuchars IPA,

Courage Directors, Exmoor Gold, Golden Promise and Merman, their own Edinburgh Real Ale, Greenmantle, Ind Coope Burton, Mitchells Mild, ESB and Bitter, Orkney Dark Island and Raven, Tetleys, and Timothy Taylors Best and Landlord – all served on impressive tall founts made by Aitkens, Mackie & Carnegie, Gaskell & Chambers, and McGlashan, dating from the 1920s. The grand carved mahogany gantry has an impressive array of malts (over 140) including lots of Macallan variants and 'cask strength' whiskies, an exclusive supplier of Scottish Still Spirit, with a good collection of vodkas (nine) and gins (eight), and, particularly, rums (24). Splendidly redesigned a few years ago to catch the essence of the traditional Edinburgh bar, the rectangular room has a fine collection of appropriate enamel advertising signs and handsome antique trade mirrors, sturdy leatherette wall seats and heavy narrow tables on its lino floor, café-style bar seats, an umbrella stand by the period gas fire, a (silent) pre-war radio, a big pendulum clock, and a working barograph. Look out for the antiqued photograph of the present bar staff in old-fashioned clothes (and moustaches). Simple, cheap bar snacks – filled rolls (85p), mince and steak pies (from 70p), and forfar bridies (£1); no games or music – just relaxed chat, and the clink of glasses; quick and helpful service and friendly landlord. It's conveniently located just below the Castle. *(Recommended by TBB, John Fazakerley, Chris and Anne Fluck, Thomas Nott, Andy and Jill Kassube; more reports please)*

Free house ~ Licensee Bill Strachan ~ Real ale ~ Lunchtime snacks ~ 0131-226 7667 ~ Open 11am-11.15pm

Cafe Royal Circle Bar
West Register St

There's a sophisticated feel to this attractively refurbished Victorian-style café. One of the features is a series of highly detailed Doulton tilework portraits of Watt, Faraday, Stephenson, Caxton, Benjamin Franklin and Robert Peel (in his day famous as the introducer of calico printing). The gantry over the big island bar counter is similar to the one that was first here, the floor and stairway are laid with marble and there are leather covered seats, and Victorian-style chandeliers – recalling the days when this was a flagship for such modern fittings – hang from the fine ceilings. Marstons Pedigree, McEwans 80/-, Theakstons Best, Youngers No 3 and a weekly guest beer on handpump (some kept under light blanket pressure); over 40 malt whiskies. Simple bar food includes rolls such as brie and tomato or filled with a choice of three hot roasts (carved to order). Good choice of daily newspapers; fringe productions in the building during festival week. *(Recommended by David and Ruth Hollands, Ian Phillips, Walter Reid, Capt E P Gray, Susan and John Douglas; more reports please)*

S & N ~ Manager Maureen Diponio ~ Real ale ~ Lunchtime snacks ~ Restaurant ~ 0131-556 1884 ~ Children in restaurant ~ Open 11-11(till 12 Thurs, 1am Fri and Sat); closed Sun

Guildford Arms ◀
West Register St

There's always an extremely good choice of real ales on handpump at this well preserved Victorian pub, six of which are always Scottish – one of the largest choices of brews from north of the border that we know of. The range usually has beers like Bass, Belhaven 60/-, Caledonian R & D, Deuchers IPA, Harviestoun 70/-, 80/-, Orkney Dark Island, Traquair Bear and at least three rotating English ales. The bustling atmosphere is welcoming and friendly and there's a good mix of customers. The unique and breathtakingly decorated main bar has lots of mahogany, glorious colourful painted plasterwork, big original advertising mirrors, and heavy swagged velvet curtains at the arched windows. The snug little upstairs gallery restaurant gives a dress-circle view of the main bar (notice the lovely old mirror decorated with two tigers on the way up), and under this gallery a little cavern of arched alcoves leads off the bar. Good choice of malt whiskies; fruit machine, lunchtime piped jazz and classical music. Bar food under the new landlord includes filled baked potatoes, salads (from £3.50), three dishes of the day, (from £3.95) and char-grilled kebabs or burgers (£3.95), spare ribs (£4.05), tandoori chicken (£4.70) and steak (£7.55). It is very popular, but even at its busiest you shouldn't have to wait to be served. *(Recommended by David and Ruth Hollands, John Fazakerley, Ross Lockley, Mr and Mrs S Ashcroft, Chris and Anne Fluck, Susan and John Douglas, Andy and Jill Kassube, Mark Walker)*

Free house ~ Licensee John Durnan ~ Real ale ~ Lunchtime snacks and meals ~ 0131-556 4312 ~ No children ~ Open 11-11(12 Sat); 12.30-11 Sun

Kays Bar £

39 Jamaica St West; off India St

The cosy little bar in this charming reproduction of a Victorian tavern which is bigger than the exterior suggests has casks, vats and old wine and spirits merchant notices, gas-type lamps, well worn red plush wall banquettes and stools around cast-iron tables, and red pillars supporting a red ceiling. A quiet panelled back room leads off, with a narrow plank-panelled pitched ceiling; open coal fire in winter. Simple bar food includes baked potatoes, omelettes, haggis, neeps and tatties, chilli, mince and tatties, steak pie, beans and chips, chicken balti and Finnan haddock. A good range of changing beers, with nine being served at any one time, includes well kept Belhaven 80/-, Golden Promise, Marstons Pedigree, McEwans 80/-, Rogers Roger & Out, Smiles Exhibition, Theakstons Best and XB, Youngers No 3; up to 70 malts, between eight and 40 years old, and ten blended whiskies – they tell us they keep lager for visitors; cribbage, dominoes and Connect 4. *(Recommended by Ross Lockley, John Fazakerley, Capt E P Gray; more reports please)*

S & N ~ Tenant David W L Mackenzie ~ Real ale ~ Lunchtime snacks ~ 0131-225 1858 ~ Children in library area until 5pm ~ Open 11am-11.45pm; 12.30-11 Sun

Starbank ♀ ☕

67 Laverockbank Road, off Starbank Road

There are marvellous views (you can also look through a telescope) over the Firth of Forth from the picture windows in the neat and airy bar of this comfortably elegant pub. Like most of our main entries in the city, it's an excellent place for a wide range of rotating beers, with around ten well kept real ales on handpump that might include a combination from the brewers Belhaven, Broughton, Caledonian, Harviestoun, Maclays, Orkney and Tomintoul and a range from south of the border. A good choice of wines too, with usually around 12 by the glass, and 25 malt whiskies. Well presented good bar food could include home-made soup (£1.20), garlic mushrooms (£2.50), a vegetarian dish (£3.75), steak pie (£4.50), ploughman's (£4.75), baked haddock mornay (£5), supreme of chicken with tarragon cream (£5.25), and puddings like rhubarb and ginger pie and mandarin chocolate cake (from £2.50); service is helpful and friendly; sheltered back terrace. *(Recommended by R M Macnaughton, Capt E P Gray; more reports please)*

Free house ~ Licensee Valerie West ~ Real ale ~ Meals and snacks ~ No-smoking conservatory restaurant ~ 0131-552 4141 ~ Children welcome ~ Open 11-11 Mon-Wed (till midnight Thurs-Sat); Sun 12.30-11

ELIE (Fife) NO4900 Map 11

Ship

Harbour

Across the road from this welcoming and cosily old-fashioned harbourside pub, the well positioned garden has pretty views over the bay (which at low tide is mostly sand) to the pier and the old stone fish depot on the left, the little town on the right, and a grassy headland opposite; you can look more closely through a telescope positioned on the balcony of the restaurant. In summer there's a bar and barbecues in the garden, both lunchtime and evening (not Sunday evening). The villagey, unspoilt beamed bar with friendly locals and staff still has its lively nautical feel, as well as coal fires and winged high-backed button-back leather seats against the partly panelled walls, now studded with old maps; there's a snugger carpeted back room. Very good home-made bar food might include dishes such as carrot and butter bean or smoked haddock soup (£1.35), herring in oatmeal (£2.95), chicken liver pâté (£3.25), prawn and melon vinaigrette or haggis, neeps and tatties (£3.95), vegetable lasagne or poached haddock mornay (£4.95), seafood pie with up to seven types of fish or steak and Guinness pie (£5.25), Ship Inn roast ham (£6.95) grilled lamb cutlets in minted butter or rainbow trout with capers (£7.95), peppered salmon steak (£8.95) or half a pineapple filled with monkfish, lemon sole, prawns, and salmon in a cream and white wine sauce (£10.25), and puddings such as home-made lemon pavlova (£2.50); also children's menu or small portions from the main menu. The Belhaven 80/-, Boddingtons and Courage Directors on handpump are well kept and they do various wines and malt whiskies; darts, dominoes, captain's mistress, cribbage and shut-the-box. *(Recommended by Basil J S Minson, Dennis Dickinson, Gordon Smith, Paul and Ursula Randall; more reports please)*

Free house ~ Licensees Richard and Jill Philip ~ Real ale ~ Meals and snacks (12-9) ~ Restaurant (not Sun eve) ~ (01333) 330 246 ~ Children in restaurants and lounge bar ~ Occasional jazz in beer garden ~ Open 11am-midnight; 12.30-11 Sun (winter closed 2.30-5, Mon-Fri); closed 25 Dec

GATEHOUSE OF FLEET (Dumfries and Galloway) NX5956 Map 9

Murray Arms

Situated in a conservation area of lovely countryside a mile from the coast and Cardoness Castle, this coaching inn was once the home of the keeper of the ford across the river and the only house in the town. The pub was originally called the Gatehouse, and unusually the town that grew up here took its name from the inn. Sensitively modernised it retains the traditional whitewashed walls of the area and a striking clock tower. Always friendly, the exceptionally welcoming bar has a changing, well kept real ale on handpump such as Theakstons XB, and lots of malt whiskies. It opens into a room with comfortable easy chairs, Thorburn game bird prints and Victorian coaching prints, an antique box settle; the quite separate public bar has darts, pool, dominoes, fruit and trivia machines and juke box. There's a sunny sheltered side courtyard. Good bar food served all day in the Lunky Hole restaurant includes sandwiches and toasties (from £1.45), home-made soup (£1.55), salad selection £4.95), a hot daily special and vegetarian dish of the day (£3.95) and cold meats and salad (£6.50). A wider choice at lunchtime additionally includes filled baked potatoes (from £2.10), fried breaded fillet of haddock or chicken curry (£4.95), braised Galloway beefsteak with puff pastry topping (£5.55), lasagne (£5.75) and in the evening the full complement is made with the additions of a couple more meat and fish dishes; a fondue is available with 24 hours' notice; home-made puddings (£2.45). Children are very welcome, they can have smaller portions from the main menu or from the children's list (from £2.75). *(Recommended by Janet and Gary Amos, J M Watson, Ian Phillips, R E and P Pearce; more reports please)*

Free house ~ Licensee Mr R Raphael ~ Real ale ~ Meals and snacks 12-9.45 ~ One no-smoking restaurant ~ (01557) 814207 ~ Children welcome ~ Open 11-2.30, 5-12 (open for food all day) ~ Bedrooms: £39.50B/£70B

GIFFORD (Lothian) NT5368 Map 11

Tweeddale Arms 🛏
High St

In a lovely peaceful village below the Border foothills this civilised old inn looks across a green to the 300-year-old avenue of lime trees leading to the former home of the Marquesses of Tweeddale. The comfortably relaxed lounge has big Impressionist prints on the apricot coloured walls (there are matching curtains to divide the seats), modern stools on a muted red patterned carpet and brass lamps. The gracious dining room has unusual antique wallpaper. The tranquil hotel lounge has antique tables and paintings, chinoiserie chairs and chintzy easy chairs, an oriental rug on one wall, a splendid corner sofa and magazines on a table. Sandwiches are available all day, and the lunchtime bar food consists of a soup and dish of the day, and starters and snacks like coleslaw filled baked potato (£2.75), deep-fried smoked haddock strips in sweet and sour batter (£3), smoked rainbow trout fillet wrapped in smoked salmon (£3.75), and main courses such as deep-fried haddock, tagliatelle in cream sauce topped with stir-fried vegetables or creamed cauliflower, carrots and mushroom crêpe (£4.75), poached supreme of salmon in cucumber and parsley sauce (£5.25), curried lamb madras (£5.50), sauté noisettes of lamb in onion and mushroom sauce (£5.75) and puddings like lemon lush mousse cake or strawberry and whipped cream shortbread (all £2.25). In the evening you may be able to order dishes from the restaurant menu in the bar. Flowers IPA, Ind Coope Burtons, Greenmantle, Morlands Old Speckled Hen, Orkney Dark Island and Tetleys Bitter on hand-pump; lots of malt whiskies; charming, efficient service; dominoes, fruit machine and piped music. *(Recommened by Roger A Bellingham; more reports please)*

Free house ~ Licensee Chris Crook ~ Real ale ~ Meals and snacks ~ Restaurant ~ (01620) 810240 ~ Children in lounge and restaurant ~ Open 11-11(midnight Sat) ~ Bedrooms: £47.50B/£65B

GLASGOW (Strathclyde) NS5865 Map 11

Babbity Bowster 🍴 ♟

16-18 Blackfriars St

This Robert Adam town house down a quiet pedestrian-only street takes its name from *Bab at the Bowster*, a folk song which is illustrated in the pub by a big ceramic of a kilted dancer and piper, while the Scottische restaurant is also named after a traditional dance. Rather more like a continental bistro than a traditional British pub this jolly, warmly welcoming, chatty place with its varied and interesting clientele, usefully serves refreshments from 8am till 11pm, starting with good breakfasts (served 8am-10.30; till noon Sunday) – either a full Scottish one (£3.95, including Ayrshire bacon) or traditionally smoked Carradale kippers (£2.75). After midday the café bar and patio serve very good bar food with a Scottish bias, such as filled baguettes (from £2.75), baked potatoes (from £2.75), haggis, neeps and tatties (£3.35), vegetarian or beef chilli (£2.95 or £3.65), salad Lyonnaise (£3.75), and from the blackboard lots of seasonal fresh fish and shellfish with a basket of crusty bread, such as mussels in sauces like cream and white wine or tomato and garlic sauce (£4.75), grilled whole prawns in barbecue sauce (£5.75), half a dozen Loch Sween oysters (£6.50), grilled langoustine with garlic butter (£6.75); puddings such as cloutie dumpling, sticky toffee pudding or triple chocolate terrine (from £2.25); barbecued food in the spring and summer. There are more elaborate meals in the restaurant. Well kept Maclays 70/-, 80/-, Babbity Thistle beer (brewed for the pub by Maclays) and several guests beers on air pressure tall fount, a remarkably sound collection of wines, freshly squeezed orange juice and good tea and coffee. Enthusiastic service is consistently efficient and friendly, taking its example from the energetic landlord. The simply decorated interior has pierced-work stools and wall seats around dark grey tables on the stripped boards, an open peat fire, and fine tall windows; also, well lit photographs and big pen-and-wash drawings of Glasgow and its people and musicians. Piped Celtic music in the restaurant. A small terrace has tables under cocktail parasols; boules court; conveniently for the centre of the city, there is a car park. *(Recommended by Ian Phillips, Doug Kennedy, Stephen R Holman, Mark Bradley, J M Watson, Walter Reid, Owen McGhee; also recommended by* The Good Hotel Guide*)*

Free house ~ Licensee Fraser Laurie ~ Real ale ~ Meals and snacks (12-9, and breakfast) ~ Restaurant ~ 0141-552 5055 ~ Children in restaurant ~ Traditional live music Sun evenings ~ Open 8-midnight; closed 25 Dec and 1 Jan ~ Bedrooms: £40B/£65B

Bon Accord 🍺

153 North St

Recently refurbished in the style of a Victorian kitchen, this friendly and traditional busy pub is well known for its outstanding choice of about a dozen well kept real ales served from tall founts that might include Marstons Pedigree, McEwans 80/-, Theakstons Best and Old Peculier, Youngers No 3, and a good few guest beers on handpump; over 100 malt whiskies. Bar food includes snacks like filled baguettes and baked potatoes (£1.95 – £2.45), porkers, chips and beans (£2.95), haddock (£3.35) and traditional pies (from £2.25). *(Recommended by Ross Lockley, Alastair Campbell; more reports please)*

S & N ~ Manageress Anne Kerr ~ Real ale ~ Meals and snacks (till 9) ~ Restaurant (closed Sun) ~ 0141-248 4427 ~ Daytime parking restricted ~ Open 11am-11.45pm

Horseshoe £
17-19 Drury Street

Full of fine Victoriana, this bustling friendly city pub is listed in the *Guinness Book of Records* as having the longest bar counter in Britain. Still in authentic condition the bar has old-fashioned brass water taps and interesting pillared snob-screens. The horseshoe motif spreads through the place from the apposite promontories of the bar itself to the horseshoe wall clock and horseshoe-shaped fireplaces (most blocked by mirrors now); there's a great deal of glistening mahogany and darkly varnished panelled dado, a mosaic tiled floor, a lustrous pink and maroon ceiling, standing height lean-on tables, lots of old photographs of Glasgow and its people, antique magazine colour plates, pictorial tile inserts of decorous ladies, and curly brass and glass wall lamps. Bass, Belhaven 80/-, Broughton Greenmantle, a new Irish beer – Caffreys – Caledonian 80/- and Maclays 80/- on handpump, large selection of malts; fruit machines, trivia and three televisions. The upstairs bar is less special, though popular with young people. Amazingly cheap food includes filled rolls (from 40p), Scotch pie and peas (80p), lasagne (£1.80), and a three-course lunch with a choice of dishes such as haddock, roast beef or macaroni cheese (£2.40); part of the lounge is no smoking. Not far from Central station. *(Recommended by Michael Sandy, BB; more reports please)*

Tennents (Bass) ~ Manager David Smith ~ Real ale ~ Meals and snacks (11-7; not Sun) ~ 0141-221 3051 ~ Children welcome until 7 ~ Karaoke every eve and Sun afternoon ~ Open 11am-midnight; Sun 12-12; closed 1 Jan

GLENDEVON Tayside NN9904 Map 11

Tormaukin 🛏 ♀
A823

A smallish hotel in beautiful countryside with good walks over the nearby Ochils or along the River Devon. The softly lit bar has plush seats against stripped stone and partly panelled walls with gentle piped music. Bar food (which isn't necessarily cheap) includes soup (£1.70), chicken liver pâté (£2.95), potted salmon with lemon, cream and walnuts (£3.75), deep-fried haddock with home-made tartar sauce (£5.65), venison sausages with red wine and redcurrant jelly (£5.75), baked trout (£5.95), stir-fry chicken with lemon and lime (£6.45), char-grilled rump steak (£7.85), creamy vegetable pasties (£5.45), sweet and sour chicken (£5.65), pork meat balls braised in tangy sweet and sour sauce or salads (from £5.95), game bridie with port and juniper sauce (£6.25), salmon and seafood crêpe (£6.45), char-grilled breast of chicken marinated in chilli and garlic served on a bed of pasta with garlic and cream, steaks (from £7.25), collops of wild venison (£8.25) and daily specials like char-grilled whole fresh fish; vegetarian dishes like pasta with pesto and sun-dried tomatoes, vegetable korma with fresh spices (£5.85) and filo pastry parcel of spinach and blue cheese (£6.25); puddings such as bread and butter pudding (£2.85), choux bun filled with white chocolate ice cream (£2.95), hot summer fruit crêpes or sticky toffee pudding (£3.10) and a children's menu (from £2.65, sausage, chips and beans £3.45); good breakfasts. Well kept Harviestoun 80/- and Ind Coope Burton on handpump, 80 wines, and around 30 malt whiskies. Some of the bedrooms are in a converted stable block. Loch and river fishing can be arranged. *(Recommended by Colin Steer, Mark Hydes, Susan and John Douglas, R M MacNaughton, Katie Tyler; more reports please)*

Free house ~ Licensee Marianne Worthy ~ Real ale ~ Meals and snacks (12-2, 6.30-9.30; all day Sun) ~ (01259) 781252 ~ Restaurant (not Sun lunch) ~ Children welcome ~ Open 11-11; closed 25 Dec, two weeks in Jan after New Year ~ Bedrooms: £47B/£66B

INNERLEITHEN (Borders) NT3336 Map 9

Traquair Arms 🛏 🍺

Traquair Rd (B709, just off A72 Peebles—Galashiels; follow signs for Traquair House)

Last year we said the breakfasts here were nice: a reader promptly wrote in outrage saying that description bordered on the libellous as they should properly be called superb or outstanding – and other readers say the breakfasts are the best they've ever had. There's a bustling welcoming feel in the little bar, which stocks Traquair House Ale (very rare on handpump, as it's usually all bottled) from the fine brewhouse at nearby Traquair House, as well as Greenmantle, Theakstons Best and maybe Traquair Bear, all well kept. House wines are above average, and there's an interesting selection of bottled beers and of malt whiskies; there's a warm open fire. Good popular well served bar food in generous helpings includes sandwiches (from £1), home-made soup (£1.40), filled baked potatoes (from £2.50), omelettes (around £3), spicy chicken, venison casserole or steak in ale pie (£5), evening steaks (from £11.95), and puddings (from £2.50); there's usually a good choice of vegetarian dishes. A pleasant roomy dining room has an open fire and high chairs for children if needed. Good quick service, welcoming licensees, no music or machines. *(Recommended by I S Thomson, David Dolman, J M Potter, Roger Berry)*

Free house ~ Licensee Hugh Anderson ~ Real ale ~ Meals and snacks (midday-9pm) ~ Restaurant ~ (01896) 830229 ~ Children welcome ~ Story telling and singing 1st Sun evening of month ~ Open 11am-midnight; Sun opening midday; cl 2 days Christmas, 2 days New Year ~ Bedrooms: £58B/£74B

ISLE OF WHITHORN (Dumfries and Galloway) NX4736 Map 9

Steam Packet 🛏 £

The big picture windows of this comfortably modernised inn look out to a picturesque natural harbour sheltered by a long quay, with yachts, inshore fishing boats, fishermen mending their nets, and boys fishing from the end of the pier. Inside, the cheery low-ceilinged, grey carpeted bar is split into two: on the right, plush button-back banquettes, brown carpet, and boat pictures; on the left, green leatherette stools around cast-iron-framed tables on big stone tiles, and a wood-burning stove in the bare stone wall. Bar food can be served in the lower beamed dining room, which has a big model steam packet boat on the white wall, excellent colour wildlife photographs, rugs on its wooden floor, and a solid fuel stove, and there's also a small eating area off the lounge bar; dominoes, pool and piped music; friendly, welcoming service. Bar food includes home-made soup (80p), filled rolls (from 95p), venison pâté (£1.75), haggis (£2.85), dish of the day from the blackboard or fish and chips (£3), fried chicken and bacon (£3.50) and additional dishes in the evening such as salmon and broccoli cutlet (£4.50), chicken breast with coriander and garlic (£6.50), sirloin steak (£9.80); children's menu (from £1.35); fresh lobster is usually available from tanks at the back of the hotel – prices vary according to the market price and it's helpful if you can order in advance. Well kept Boddingtons and Theakstons XB on handpump. Good range of malt whiskies, and reasonably priced wine by the glass or bottle. White tables and chairs in the garden. Every 1½ to 4 hours there are boat trips from the harbour, and in the rocky grass by its mouth are the remains of St Ninian's Kirk. *(Recommended by M K and J P, Geoffrey and Brenda Wilson, David Bloomfield, Capt E P Gray, J L Phillips; more reports please)*

Free house ~ Licensee John Scoular ~ Real ale ~ Meals and snacks ~ Restaurant ~ Whithorn (01988) 500334 ~ Children welcome ~ Occasional live folk music Fri evenings ~ Open 11-11(closed 2.30-6 winter Mon-Thurs); closed 25 Dec ~ Bedrooms: £22.50B/£45B

ISLE ORNSAY (Isle of Skye) NG6912 Map 11

Tigh Osda Eilean Iarmain 🛏 🍷

Signposted off A851 Broadford—Armadale

Gaelic is truly the first language of the staff (even the menus are bilingual) at this

19th-c inn overlooking the sea harbour in this picturesque part of Skye. Currently winning many prestigious awards – and no wonder – this civilised, carefully managed and extremely welcoming hotel is a delightful place to stay. The big and cheerfully busy bar in this white inn has a swooping stable-stall-like wooden divider that gives a two-room feel: good tongue-and-groove panelling on the walls and ceiling, leatherette wall seats, brass lamps, a brass-mounted ceiling fan, and a huge mirror over the open fire. There are 34 local brands of blended and vatted malt whisky (including their own blend, Te Bheag, and a splendid vatted malt, Poit Dhubh Green Label, bottled for them but available elsewhere), and an excellent wine list; darts, dominoes, and piped music. With emphasis on seafood and game from the hills, bar food includes lunchtime sandwiches (from £1.50), soup (£1.50), smoked venison (£3.50), prawns (£4), herring in oatmeal or lamb casserole (£5.95), halibut with chives (£6.50), wild salmon steaks (£8.50), steak (£10.50), a daily special and puddings such as home-made lemon meringue pie (£1.75); usual children's menu. The pretty dining room has a lovely sea view past the little island of Ornsay itself and the lighthouse on Sionnach (you can walk over the sands at low tide). Some of the bedrooms are in a cottage opposite. The most popular room has a canopied bed from Armadale Castle. *(Recommended by Neale Davies, Annette Moore, Richard Dyson, Chris Pearson, Bill Bailey, Simon J Barber; more reports please)*

Free house ~ Licensee Sir Ian Noble, Manager Effie Kennedy ~ Meals and snacks ~ No-smoking restaurant ~ (0147 13) 332 ~ Children welcome but only till 8.30 in the bar ~ Folk and Scottish music Thurs and some Fri and Sat eves ~ Open 12-3, 5-12(11.30 Sat) ~ Bedrooms: £50B/£78B

KILBERRY (Strathclyde) NR7164 Map 11

Kilberry Inn 🍴 🛏️
B8024

Converted by the current owners, this white painted croft post office has been turned into a relaxed but high quality inn with remarkably varied and individually cooked country food prepared from fresh ingredients – some say it's the best in Scotland. Besides the ploughman's with home-baked bread (£4.75), current favourites include country sausage pie (£7.25), chicken breast with cheese and pineapple sauce or stilton and walnut pie (£7.95), beef cooked in Old Peculiar ale, venison in red wine and salmon fish pie, all served with vegetables cooked to order. Puddings are decidedly out of the usual run, too – maybe fresh strawberry fool with a hint of Cointreau, chocolate fudge, sticky toffee or lemon meringue pie, or an unusual Blackpool Rock ice cream (£3.50). They do children's helpings – and appreciate booking if you want an evening meal. The small dining bar is tastefully and simply furnished but warmly welcoming, with a good log fire. No real ale, but bottled beers and plenty of malt whiskies. The pub is on a delightful slow winding and hilly circular drive over Knapdale, from the A83 S of Lochgilphead, with breathtaking views over the rich coastal pastures to the sea and the island of Gigha beyond. *(Recommended by Geoff and Marjorie Cowley, L Walker, Mrs Pat Crabb; more reporets please)*

Free house ~ Licensees John and Kathy Leadbeater ~ Meals and snacks ~ (0188 03) 223 ~ Well behaved children in no-smoking family room ~ Open 11-2, 5-10; cl Sun ~ No-smoking bedrooms: £30B/£50B

KIPPEN (Central) NS6594 Map 11

Cross Keys 🛏️
Main Street; village signposted off A811 W of Stirling

Warmly welcoming little family run 18th-c hotel in an historic village. There's a good log fire, wildfowl prints and stuffed birds in the relaxed small straightforward lounge, a coal fire in the painted stone walled family dining room, and a separate public bar decorated with militaria. Decent waitress-served home-made bar food from fresh produce includes soup (£1.25), deep-fried brie with fresh fruit coulis (£1.95), bramble and port liver pâté (£2.25), smoked salmon and prawn cornets (£3.75), home-made lasagne (£4.15), fillet of haddock (£4.75), steak pie (£5.20),

Scottish salmon poached with a light lemon sauce (£5.25), chicken breast with mushroom and cream sauce (£5.50), sirloin steak (£9.95); a vegetarian dish; smaller portions for children; puddings like apple pie (£2.05), home-made cloutie dumpling (£1.95) and butterscotch and walnut fudge cake (£2.85); readers have been impressed by the nappy-changing facilities in the ladies'. Well kept Greenmantle and Youngers No 3 on electric and handpump, lots of malt whiskies, good tea or coffee; pool, darts, dominoes, fruit machine and juke box; simple bedrooms. *(Recommended by Brian Skelcher, G G Calderwood; more reports please)*

Free house ~ Licensees Angus and Sandra Watt ~ Real ale ~ Meals (12-2, 5.30-9.30; only 12.30-2 Sun) ~ Restaurant ~ (01786) 870293 ~ Children in restaurant ~ Open 12-2.30, 5.30-11(12 Sat); closed 1 Jan and eve of 25 Dec ~ Single bedrooms £19.50/£39

KIRKTON OF GLENISLA (Tayside) NO2160 Map 11

Glenisla Hotel 🛏

B951 N of Kirriemuir and Alyth

This lively 17th-c former posting inn is up one of the prettiest of the Angus glens and very much at the centre of local life. It's been cheerfully and attractively refurbished with a lot of stripped wood – both in the building and in its furniture. The simple but cosy carpeted pubby bar has an open fire, decent prints, a good few stuffed birds and a rather jolly thriving atmosphere, especially towards the end of the week. Good bar food using fresh local ingredients includes sandwiches, Orkney mussels in white wine and garlic or pan-fried Orkney scallops in herb butter (£3.25), fillet of pork in lime and juniper berries (£6.95), three grilled local lamb cutlets (£7.95), hot toffee or bread and butter puddings or the like, and cream teas in a sunny and comfortable lounge. Boddingtons, McEwans 80/- and Theakstons Best on handpump, a full range of island malt whiskies; caring and attentive service. A refurbished stable block has skittles, also darts and pool. The bedrooms are attractively individual, and the hotel has fishing and skeet shooting. *(Recommended by A Matthew, A P Jeffreys; more reports please)*

Free house ~ Licensee Michael Bartholomew ~ Real ale ~ Meals and snacks ~ Restaurant ~(0157 582) 223 ~ Children welcome ~ Open all day; closed 25 and 26 Dec ~ Bedrooms £28B/£50B

LINLITHGOW (Lothian) NS9976 Map 11

Four Marys 🍺

65 High St; 2 miles from M9 junction 3 (and little further from junction 4) – town signposted

This atmospheric pub is named after the Maids of Honour (all Marys) of Mary Queen of Scots who was born at nearby Linlithgow palace. The L-shaped, comfortable and friendly bar has masses of mementoes of the ill-fated queen, not just pictures and written records, but a piece of bed curtain said to be hers, part of a 16th-c cloth and swansdown vest of the type she'd be likely to have worn and a facsimile of her death-mask. Seats are mostly green velvet and mahogany dining chairs around stripped period and antique tables, there are a couple of attractive antique corner cupboards, and an elaborate Victorian dresser serves as a bar gantry, housing several dozen malt whiskies (they stock around 80 altogether). The walls are mainly stripped stone, including some remarkable masonry in the inner area. A very good choice of ten constantly changing, very reasonably priced well kept real ales includes Batemans Mild, Belhaven 60/-, 80/- and St Andrews, Black Sheep Special, Caledonian R & D Deuchars IPA, Harviestoun Ptarmigan, Orkney Dark Island, Timothy Taylors Ram Tam and Ushers Founders on handpump, with a twice-yearly beer festival and 80 malt whiskies; friendly and helpful staff; maybe piped pop music. Enjoyable waitress-served bar food, changing daily, includes good soups such as cream of fennel or cullen skink (£1.20), stilton, celery and port pâté (£2.50), braised oxtail, lamb's liver and bacon (£4) and beef goulash or chicken Basquaise (£4.50); good value Sunday lunch. When the building was an apothecary's shop David Waldie experimented in it with chloroform – its first use as an anaesthetic; parking difficult. *(Recommended by Dave Braisted, JJW, CMW, Duncan Small, Capt E P Gray, Ian Phillips, Brian Jones; more reports please)*

Free house ~ Licensee Gordon Scott ~ Real ale ~ Meals and snacks (not Sun eve) ~ (01506) 842171 ~ Children in eating area of bar ~ Open 12-2.30, 5-11; 12-midnight Sat

LYBSTER (Highland) ND2436 Map 11

Portland Arms 🛏️

A9 S of Wick

They are about to start refurbishing and extending this staunch old granite hotel which was built as a staging post on the early 19th-c Parliamentary Road. It's our most northerly main entry. Run by really friendly, obliging staff, it has a small but cosy and comfortable panelled lounge bar, and a wide choice of very generously served bar food including fish soup (£1.50), sandwiches, game terrine (£2.95), mousseline of fish (£3.90) and baked sole with prawns and cream (£4.95); the same dishes are served for high tea at slightly higher prices in the dining room. They keep 40 or more malt whiskies (beers are keg) and squeeze fresh orange juice. A separate plain public bar popular with locals has darts, pool and fruit machine, and there's a spacious residents' lounge; maybe unobtrusive piped music. They can arrange fishing and so forth, and the inn is a good base for the area with its spectacular cliffs and stacks; pets in bedrooms but not public rooms. *(Recommended by Alan Wilcock, Christine Davidson, Stephen R Holman, Christine Davidson; more reports please)*

Free house ~ Licensee Gerald Henderson ~ Meals and snacks (11-2.30, 5-10) ~ Restaurant ~ (015932) 208 ~ Children welcome ~ Occasional live entertainment ~ Open 11-11(11.45 Sat) ~ Bedrooms: £38.50B/£58B

MELROSE (Border) NT5434 Map 9

Burts Hotel 🍴 🛏️

A6091

Set in a picturesque 18th-c market square, this 200-year-old hotel is especially popular at the moment for well presented, imaginative and promptly served bar food with good vegetables. The range at lunchtime might include sandwiches (from £2) or open croissants (from £2.95), quenelles of chicken liver pâté (£2.80), smoked salmon pâté with a cucumber vinaigrette, parfait of local game with a Cumberland sauce or deep-fried brie on a pool of Cumberland sauce (£3.25), chicken and mozzarella strudel coated with a leek sauce, stir-fry beef with ginger and capsicums or stuffed escalope of chicken with garlic and brie (£4.90), breaded trout with almonds and remoulade sauce (£5.95); vegetarian dishes like home-made ravioli and agnolotti coated in mushroom and tarragon cream sauce (£4.60) and puddings like baked chocolate and fudge pudding with a chocolate fudge sauce or jam roly poly (£1.70); more elaborate evening dishes such as char-grilled Vienna steak coated in madeira wine sauce glazed with bacon and stilton (£6.25), supreme of chicken stuffed with a savoury pilaff rice wrapped in ribbons of flaky pastry (£6.50), grilled Ettrick trout with almond and orange butter (£6.50); extremely good breakfasts. Try and get there early, as the food's popularity means tables will go quickly. The comfortable and friendly L-shaped lounge bar has lots of cushioned wall seats and Windsor armchairs on its turkey carpet, and Scottish prints on the walls; Belhaven 80/- and Courage Directors on handpump; wide range of unusual malt whiskies, and a good wine list. There's a well tended garden (with tables in summer). An alternative way to view the abbey ruins is from the top of the tower at Smailholm. *(Recommended by J Goodwill, David Gittins, Mrs S Gillotti, Richard Davies, R M McNaughton, Capt E P Gray, E Evans, Eric and Jackie Robinson, J E Rycroft, RJH, Mrs Gwyneth Holland, Thomas Nott, Nick and Meriel Cox)*

Free House ~ Licensee Graham Henderson ~ Real ale ~ Meals and snacks (till 10.30 Fri and Sat) ~ Restaurant ~ (01896) 822285 ~ Children welcome ~ Open 11-2.30, 5-11; closed 26 Dec ~ Bedrooms: £43B/£72B

MOUNTBENGER (Border) NT3125 Map 9

Gordon Arms

Junction A708/B709

In an isolated spot on the splendid empty moorlands, this warmly welcoming little inn with its very friendly landlord is a walkers' haven. The comfortable public bar has an interesting set of period photographs of the neighbourhood, one dated 1865, there's a fire in cold weather and some well illustrated poems including a local 'shepherd song' and 'A Glorious Glout' on Scotland's 1990 Rugby Grand Slam are pinned on the wall. The literary traditions reach far back, as the inn was known to both Sir Walter Scott and James Hogg, the 'Ettrick Shepherd' and is said to be the last place they met. Well kept Greenmantle and a changing guest ale on air pressure tall fount as well as Scottish oatmeal stout and a choice of 55 malt whiskies. Good home-made bar food includes soup (£1.65), lunchtime sandwiches (£2.15), pâté and oakcakes (£3.50), filled baked potatoes (from £3.75), crispy garlic mushrooms (£3.95), all day breakfast (£4.75), breaded haddock or chicken portions (£5.50), grilled lamb chops or breaded scampi (£6.50), fresh local trout (£6.70) and favourite Scottish puddings like clootie dumpling, crannachan, Scotch trifle and border tart; usual children's dishes and smaller helpings at reduced prices for pensioners. The lounge bar serves high teas in summer – a speciality here. In addition to the hotel bedrooms, there's a bunkhouse which provides cheap accommodation for hill walkers, cyclists and fishermen, all of whom should find this area particularly appealing. The resident family of bearded collies are called Jura, Misty and Morah. (*Recommended by J D Maplethorpe, Nick and Meriel Cox, Keith Stevens, Andy and Jill Kassube*)

Free house ~ Licensee Harry Mitchell ~ Real ale ~ Meals and snacks (and high teas 4-6 Easter-Oct) ~ Restaurant (not Sun eve) ~ (01750) 82232 ~ Children in eating area of lounge bar and dining room until 8pm ~ Accordion and fiddle club third Weds every month ~ Open 11-11(midnight Sat); 11-3, 6.30-11 winter weekdays; closed Tues mid Oct-Easter ~ Bedrooms: £22/£36; bunkhouse £4.50

OBAN (Strathclyde) NM8630 Map 11

Oban Inn

Stafford St

The lively beamed downstairs bar of this late 18th-c inn overlooking the harbour has quite a mix of locals and visitors. On its uneven slate floor are small stools, pews and black-winged modern settles, blow-ups of old Oban postcards on the cream walls, and unusual brass-shaded wall lamps. The smarter, partly panelled upstairs bar (also overlooking the harbour) has button-back banquettes around cast-iron-framed tables, a coffered woodwork ceiling, and little backlit arched false windows with heraldic roundels in 17th-c stained glass. Well kept McEwans 80/- from tall fount, a large selection of whiskies. Good straightforward lunchtime bar food includes home-made soup (£1.10), garlic mushrooms (£1.50), smoked mackerel (£1.95), lasagne (£3.50), steak and ale pie (£4.05), haddock in batter (£4.20), breaded scampi or chicken kiev (£4.50) and a dish of the day on the blackboard; puddings (from £1.70); piped music can be a little loud. (*Recommended by Dave Braisted, Susan and John Douglas, Keith W Mills, N P Hopkins, Mr and Mrs J H Adam, Alec and Marie Lewery; more reports please*)

S & N ~ Manageress Jeanette Boyd ~ Real ale ~ Lunchtime meals and snacks (12-2.30, 5-8) ~ (01631) 62484 ~ Occasional music sessions Wed ~ Children welcome in small area till 8pm ~ Open 11-12.45am

nr PITLOCHRY (Tayside) NN9458 Map 11

Killiecrankie Hotel 🍴 🛏

Killiecrankie signposted from A9 N of Pitlochry

This pleasant and comfortable country hotel is splendidly set in lovely peaceful grounds with dramatic views of the mountain pass. The home-made food is still deservedly popular, with a typical choice at lunchtime including soup (£1.95), chicken liver pâté (£2.95), hot dishes of the day which might be grilled haddock or halibut, beef olives with haggis braised in a tomato sauce, venison casserole or braised pheasant in red wine sauce (all £5.95) and cold dishes like ploughman's (£4.75), lightly curried chicken mayonnaise (£5.95), freshly poached salmon or smoked salmon and prawn open sandwich (£6.95). In the evening there are more hot specials like grilled local trout (£6.95), grilled salmon steak with lime and parsley butter (£7.25), game casserole (£7.50), grilled breast of duck with apple and cranberry sauce (£9.95); puddings like hot syrup sponge pudding, banoffi pie, Scottish burnt cream with strawberries, chocolate mousse or cheese and biscuits (£2.75); generally helpful service. Decent wines and fair selection of malt whiskies, coffee and a choice of teas. The well furnished bar has mahogany panelling, upholstered seating and mahogany tables and chairs, as well as stuffed animals and some rather fine wildlife paintings; in the airy conservatory extension there are light beech tables and upholstered chairs, with discreetly placed plants and flowers; putting course and croquet lawn. *(Recommended by Robin and Anne Denness, Ralph A Raimi, Paul and Ursula Randall; more reports please; also recommended by* The Good Hotel Guide*)*

Free house ~ Licensees Colin and Carole Anderson ~ Meals and snacks ~ No-smoking evening restaurant ~ (01796) 473220 ~ Children welcome ~ Open 11-2.30, 6-11; closed Jan/Feb ~ Bedrooms: £48B/£92B

PLOCKTON (Highland) NG8033 Map 11

Plockton Hotel

Village signposted from A87 near Kyle of Lochalsh

After a long drive across the hills this National Trust village is a lovely surprise. With its dramatic mountainous backdrop, the hotel is set in a row of prettily elegant houses with a delightful outlook across the palm tree and colourful flowering shrub-lined shore and sheltered anchorage to the rugged mountainous surrounds of Loch Carron. The welcome and service are notably friendly, and the licensees go to great trouble to make sure things are right. The plush, comfortably furnished lively lounge bar has window seats looking out to the boats on the water, as well as green leatherette seats around neat Regency-style tables on a tartan carpet, an open fire, three model ships set into the woodwork, and partly panelled and partly bare stone walls. The separate public bar has darts, pool, shove-ha'penny, dominoes, cribbage and piped music; dogs welcome (except in lounge at mealtimes). Very well liked bar food includes home-made soup (£1.35), cream of fish soup (£2.50), home-made whisky or smoked fish pâté and basket meals (from £2.95), queen scallops in oatmeal (£3.50), smoked fish platter (£4.95), home-made lasagne (£5.75), venison casserole (£5.95), smoked fillet of haddock (£6.25), lobster tails (£7.50), grilled local trout (£7.65), kishorn clams in light wine sauce (£9.30), monkfish and prawn mornay (£9.85), jumbo prawn platter (£10.50); usual children's dishes (£1.95), good breakfasts. Caledonian and Tennents 70/- and 80/- on tall fount air pressure, a good collection of whiskies and a short wine list. *(Recommended by Spider Newth, Mark Gillis, J E Tong, Alan Reid, Capt E P Gray, David and Margaret Bloomfield, Darren Ford; more reports please)*

Free house ~ Licensees Tom and Dorothy Pearson ~ Real ale ~ Meals and snacks (12-2, 6-10) ~ Restaurant ~ (0159 544) 274 ~ Children in eating area of bar and restaurant till 9 ~ Local traditional band Thurs night ~ Open 11-2.30, 5-12 (till 11.30 Sat) ~ Bedrooms: £25(£28B)/£40(£46B)

PORTPATRICK (Dumfries and Galloway) NX0154 Map 9

Crown ★ 🛏

Perhaps the best day to visit this traditionally atmospheric harbourside inn is on Thursday when the fishing fleet comes in. You can sit outside on seats served by a hatch in the front lobby and make the most of the evening sun. Inside the bustling characterful old-fashioned bar has lots of rambling and dim little nooks, crannies and alcoves, and interesting old furnishings such as a carved settle with barking dogs as its arms, an antique wicker-backed armchair, a stag's head over the coal fire, and shelves of old bottles above the bar counter. The partly panelled butter-coloured walls are decorated with old mirrors with landscapes painted in their side panels. Bar food still has an emphasis on very fresh and beautifully cooked local seafood which is really popular with lots of our readers: moules marinières or fish kebab (£4.55), grilled scallops wrapped in bacon with garlic butter sauce (£4.95), crab salad (£6.45), whole grilled jumbo prawns (£11), lobster (from £18.15), as well as sandwiches (from £1.40, open sandwiches from £1.75), chicken (£3.85), haddock (£4.50) and roast beef salad (£6.55); puddings such as apple tart or brandy snaps (£2); excellent big breakfasts. Carefully chosen wine list, and quite a few malt whiskies. Piped music; sensibly placed darts in the separate public bar, and a fruit machine. An airy and very attractively decorated early 20th-c dining room opens through a quiet conservatory area into a sheltered back garden. Even when it's busy there still seems to be enough space. Unusually attractive bedrooms have individual touches such as uncommon Munch prints. *(Recommended by Eric and Jackie Robinson, Neil Townsend, Dr and Mrs R E S Tanner, Geoffrey and Brenda Wilson, Walter and Susan Rinaldi-Butcher, Nigel Woolliscroft)*

Free house ~ Licensee Bernard Wilson ~ Meals and snacks (till 10) ~ No-smoking conservatory restaurant ~ (01776) 810261 ~ Children welcome ~ Open 11am-11.30pm ~ Bedrooms: £35B/£70B

SHERIFFMUIR   (Central) NN8202 Map 11

Sheriffmuir Inn

Signposted off A9 just S of Blackford; and off A9 at Dunblane roundabout, just N of end of M9; also signposted from Bridge of Allan; OS Sheet 57 map reference 827022

This remotely placed white house, by a single-track road with spectacular views over a sweep of moorland uninhabited except for the sheep, cattle and birds, was built in the same year as the Battle of Sheriffmuir (1715), making it one of the oldest inns in Scotland. Inside the welcoming and neat family run L-shaped bar has pink plush stools and button-back built-in wall banquettes on a smart pink patterned carpet, polished tables, olde-worlde coaching prints on its white walls, and a woodburning stove in a stone fireplace. Well kept Arrols 80/-, Ind Coope Burton and Marstons Pedigree on handpump under light blanket pressure, good choice of whiskies, a range of wines, decent coffee; friendly, neatly uniformed staff, unobtrusive well reproduced piped 1960s music. The wide choice of promptly-served lunchtime bar food includes soup (£1.30), home-made pâté with oatcakes (£2.30), lunchtime filled baked potatoes (from £3), ploughman's (£3.50), home-made steak and Guinness pie or spaghetti bolognese (£4.65), haddock fillet (£4.95), scampi or prawn curry (£5.50), seafood platter (£5.60), chicken curry (£6.30), chicken kiev (£6.50), steaks (from £9.25); usual children's meals (£2.25); puddings such as apple pie (£1.95) or sticky toffee meringue (£2.55) and daily specials on the blackboard. There are tables and a children's play area outside. *(Recommended by Peter and Lyn Brueton, Capt E P Gray, Julian Holland, L Grant, Sara Price, the Shinkmans, Robin and Anne Dennes)*

Free house ~ Licensee Roger Lee ~ Real ale ~ Meals and lunchtime snacks (all day at weekends) ~ Restaurant ~ Dunblane (01786) 823285 ~ Children welcome ~ Open 11.30-2.30; 5.30-11 (Sat 11.30am-12pm); closed 25 Dec ~ Bedrooms: £22/£38

SHIELDAIG   (Highland) NG8154 Map 11

Tigh an Eilean 🛏

Village signposted just off A896 Lochcarron—Gairloch

The 19th-c village setting of this friendly hotel looking over the Shieldaig Island (a sanctuary for a stand of ancient Caledonian pines) to Loch Torridon and then out to the sea beyond, is without doubt one of the loveliest of all the Scottish pubs in the *Guide*. The simple side bar isn't that big, but is pleasantly atmospheric, with red brocaded button-back banquettes in little bays, picture windows looking out to sea and three picnic-table sets outside in a sheltered front courtyard; popular with locals. The residents' side is quite a contrast, with easy chairs, books and a well stocked help-yourself bar in the neat and prettily decorated two-room lounge, and an attractively modern comfortable dining room specialising in good value local shellfish, fish and game. Quickly served, simple well priced bar food includes soup (£1.20), sandwiches (all £1.35), macaroni cheese (£3.50), lasagne (£4.15), and fresh salmon salad (£6.35) with weekly specials such as chicken in white wine, pheasant, beef bourguignon or Highland rabbit (£4.50). Darts and dominoes. They have private fishing and can arrange sea fishing, while the National Trust Torridon estate or the Beinn Eighe nature reserve aren't too far away. *(Recommended by M L Clarke, Jeanne and Tom Barnes, David and Margaret Bloomfield, Mark Gillis; more reports please; also recommended by* The Good Hotel Guide*)*

Free house ~ Licensee Mrs E Stewart ~ Meals and snacks (not Sun evening) ~ Evening restaurant summer only with advance booking ~ Shieldaig (01520) 755251 ~ Children welcome till 8 ~ open 11-11, 11-2.30 Sun; winter 11-2.30, 5-11 (closed all day Sun); closed 25 Dec evening and all day 1 Jan ~ Bedrooms: £39.50B/£87B

SKEABOST (Isle of Skye) NG4148 Map 11

Skeabost House Hotel ★ 🛏

A850 NW of Portree, 1½ miles past junction with A856

This civilised and friendly family run late Victorian hotel stands in 12 acres of secluded woodland and gardens with glorious views over Loch Snizort. The bustling high-ceilinged bar has a pine counter and red brocade seats on its thick red carpet, and a fine panelled billiards room leads off the stately hall; there's a wholly separate public bar with darts, pool and juke box (and even its own car park). Popular lunchtime bar food includes good home-made soup (£1.20), chicken liver pâté (£1.50), haggis and oatcakes (£1.30), home-made pizza (£3.30), minute steak (£4.25), beef and beer pie (£4.80), smoked salmon platter (£5.50), scampi (£5.60), sauté scallops, mussels and scampi tails in white wine sauce with smoked salmon and tagliatelle (£6.50); assorted cold puddings; the spacious and airy no-smoking conservatory has an attractively laid out buffet table with lots of salads and an evening menu; good selection of over 85 single malt whiskies, including their own. Note that the hotel side is closed in winter. The loch has some of the best salmon fishing on the island. *(Recommended by Neale Davies, Richard Dyson, R C Wiles, Mark Gillis, Lee Goulding; more reports please)*

Free house ~ Licensee Iain McNab ~ Meals and snacks ; no bar food Sun; or in winter) ~ No-smoking evening restaurant ~ (01470) 532202 ~ Children welcome ~ Open 12-2, 6-11(midnight Sat); public bar closed Sun; hotel closed Oct-March ~ Bedrooms: £39(£43B)/£86B

ST MARY'S LOCH (Borders) NT2422 Map 9

Tibbie Shiels Inn 🛏

This fine down-to-earth old inn in its perfect tranquil setting beside a beautiful loch is named after the redoubtable woman who kept house here for 75 years until she died in 1878 aged 96. The wife of the local mole-catcher, she was a favourite character of Edinburgh literary society during the Age of Enlightenment in spite of her sharp intimate questions on the writings of some of her admirers – Scott, Stevenson and Hogg among them. 'When I'm dead and gone this place will still be ca'ed Tibbie Shiels's,' she once predicted, and so it is, with much of the place not too far removed from the way she knew it; her photograph hangs in the cosy stone back bar with its well cushioned wall benches or leatherette armed chairs. Good value straightforward waitress-served lunchtime bar food includes home-made soup (£1.50), beefburger (£2.20), ploughman's (£2.95), spicy chicken (£3.85), chilli or lovely fresh Yarrow trout (£4.50) and vegetarian dishes like cashew nut loaf, mushroom and hazelnut crumble or vegetable strudel (£3.75); puddings such as home-made cloutie dumpling, death-by-chocolate gateau and treacle sponge (£1.80). The lounge bar is no smoking. Well kept Belhaven 80/- and Broughton Greenmantle on handpump; about 52 malt whiskies, a choice of wines; darts, shove-ha'penny, cribbage and dominoes. The Southern Upland Way – a long-distance footpath – passes close by, and the Grey Mare's Tail waterfall is just down the glen. Day members are welcome at the sailing club on the loch, with fishing free to the inn's residents; it's very peaceful – except when low-flying jets explode across the sky. *(Recommended by P and K Lloyd, J and M Falcus, Dr Travers Grant, Capt E P Gray, Nick and Meriel Cox, D T Deas, Jean and Douglas Troup, June and Tony Baldwin, Andy and Jill Kassube, Thomas Nott, Mike and Penny Sanders)*

Free house ~ Licensees Jack and Jill Brown ~ Real ale ~ Meals and snacks (12-2.30, 3.30-8.30) ~ Restaurant ~ Selkirk (01750) 42231 ~ Children welcome ~ Open 11-11(midnight Sat); closed Mon Nov-Mar ~ Bedrooms: £22(£26B)/ £38(£46B)

nr STONEHAVEN (Grampian) NO8493 Map 11

Lairhillock ♀ ▪

Netherley; 6 miles N of Stonehaven, 6 miles S of Aberdeen, take the Durris turn-off from the A92; we listed this in previous editions under Peterculter, which is the closest sizeable settlement

Smart but very characterful and friendly, this much extended 18th-c pub is a popular place for very good and unusual home-cooked bar food, freshly prepared by the imaginative French and German chefs. Bar lunches, might include lunchtime baguettes (£3.25) or ploughman's (£4.95) and soup (£1.65), cullen skink (£2.85), pâté (£3.95), seafood filled pancakes with burgundy sauce, gratineed (£4.25), curry of the day (£6.25), chicken and chestnut lasagne (£6.50), potato and ham pie (£6.75), fish of the day, pan-fried escalope of pork, venison goulash, grilled chicken breast with paprika cream sauce (£6.95), and steak (from £10.75); about four vegetarian dishes like spinach and mushroom lasagne (£6.50) and pasta with wild mushroom cream sauce (£5.95); puddings on the blackboard (£2.75); Sunday bar lunch is a cold buffet. There are countryside views from the bay window in the cheerfully atmospheric beamed bar, as well as panelled wall benches and a mixture of old seats, dark woodwork, harness and brass lamps on the walls, and a good open fire. The spacious separate lounge has a central fire; the traditional atmosphere is always welcoming, even at its busiest. Well kept Boddingtons, Flowers IPA, Thwaites Craftsman and a changing guest ale all on handpump, over forty malt whiskies and a large wine list; friendly efficient staff; darts, cribbage, dominoes, a trivia game and maybe piped music. The restaurant in a converted raftered barn behind is cosy, with another log fire. Panoramic southerly views from the conservatory. *(Recommended by Sarah and John Douglas, Duncan and Vi Glennig, C Moncreiffe, Julian Bessa, Mark Walker; more reports please)*

Free house ~ Licensee Frank Budd ~ Real ale ~ Meals and snacks (12-2, 6-9.30; till 10 Fri-Sat) ~ Restaurant ~ (01569) 730001 ~ Children in eating area of bar, dining room or conservatory till 8pm ~ Live folk music Fri night, jazz in small function room last Fri of month ~ Open 11-2.30, 5-11(midnight Fri and Sat)

STRACHUR (Strathclyde) NN0901 Map 11

Creggans 🛏️

A815 N of village

The cosy and attractively tweedy lounge at this smart and charming little hotel has panoramic views overlooking the loch to hills on the far side with more seats in a conservatory; this and part of the cocktail bar are no smoking. The public bar, lively with locals, has pool, darts, fruit machine, dominoes and piped music. There's a good selection of malt whiskies, including their own vatted malt, as well as coffee and tea, a cappuccino bar and gift shop with home-baked goodies. Popular and quite restauranty bar food with emphasis on local seafood (the friendly, welcoming licensee tells us prices havn't changed since last year) includes home-made soup (£1.55), filled rolls and toasties (from £1.90), home-made game pâté (£3.60), vegetarian stroganoff with cream and paprika (£4.25), spiced beef and pickle (£4.30), beef or venison burgers (£4.85), half-a-dozen local oysters (£5.40), trout pan-fried in oatmeal (£5.65), Loch Fyne smoked salmon (£7.65), and puddings (from £2.25). In front are some white tables, and you can walk for hours from here on the owners' land; deerstalking as well as fishing and ponytrekking may be arranged for residents. *(Recommended by Duncan and Sheila McLaren, J Roy Smylie, John G Bockstoce, Walter Reid, Mrs S Woodburn, Michael and Harriet Robinson; more reports please)*

Free house ~ Licensee Sir Fitzroy Maclean ~ Meals and snacks ~ No-smoking evening restaurant ~ (0136 986) 279 ~ Children welcome ~ Occasional live entertainment Sat ~ Open 11am-midnight ~ Bedrooms: £49B/£98B

SWINTON (Borders) NT8448 Map 10

Wheatsheaf 🍴 🛏
A6112 N of Coldstream
Scotland's Dining Pub of the Year

The charming landlord here is also the head chef, so the emphasis at this smart restauranty sandstone hotel is very much on the superb, extremely good value food. A typical choice from the sensible length menu might include lunchtime sandwiches, omelettes and salads, home-made soup (£1.85), deep-fried aubergine (£3.40), chicken liver and brandy pâté (£3.45), baked avocado with seafood topped with cream and cheese (£4.20), spinach and pesto pancake in cheese sauce (£5.20), vegetable and pine nut stroganoff (£5.40), smoked haddock and cheese rarebit topped with crispy bacon (£5.90), fillet of pork with parma ham in light mustard sauce (£8.65), tiger prawns in lime butter with ginger and spring onions (£10.25), peppered sirloin steak (£11.65), medallions of scotch beef fillet in an oyster, mushroom and brandy sauce (£12.85) and plenty of daily changing specials; puddings like sticky toffee pudding (£2.75), crème brûlée laced with Drambuie (£2.85) and iced praline soufflé on a warm dark chocolate sauce (£3.25). Booking is advisable, particularly from Thursday to Saturday evening. Well kept Broughton Merlin and Greenmantle and a monthly changing guest like Jennings Cumberland from a tall air pressure fount; decent range of malt whiskies, good choice of wines, and coffee. The warmly welcoming and friendly service and decor all indicate tremendous attention to detail, and this year there have been some refurbishments. The main area has an attractive long oak settle and some green-cushioned window seats as well as the wheelback chairs around the tables, a stuffed pheasant and partridge over the log fire, and sporting prints and plates on the bottle-green wall covering; a small lower-ceilinged part by the counter has pubbier furnishings, and small agricultural prints on the walls – especially sheep. The quite separate side locals' bar has pool and fruit machine, and there's a no-smoking front conservatory with a vaulted pine ceiling and walls of local stone; dominoes. The garden has a play area for children. *(Recommended by E Evans, Thomas Nott, June and Tony Baldwin, P M Steeples, John Oddey, G W Lindley, Olive Carroll, Peter and Penny Keevil, RJH; also recommended by The Good Hotel Guide)*

Free house ~ Licensee Alan Reid ~ Real ale ~ Meals and snacks (12-2, 6-9.30) ~ Restaurant ~ (01890) 860257 ~ Children welcome ~ Open 11-2.30(3 Sat), 6-11 Tues-Sun; closed Mon; closed Sun evening Nov-Mar; closed middle two weeks Feb ~ Bedrooms: £28(£42S)/£40(£116S)

TAYNUILT (Strathclyde) NN0030 Map 11

Station £
A85 E of Oban

Very basic but fascinating (particularly to railway buffs) you'll find this small steam micro-brewery (West Highland Brewers) and its associated pub amongst the listed buildings of a working station and its platforms – you can view the brewery from one of them. The buildings have been carefully converted with plenty of simple character and even on one of those dismally damp West Highland afternoons the plainly furnished but engaging pub part has a thoroughly cheerful atmosphere. The very good value hoppy beers are Highland Heavy (OG 1038), Old Station Porter (OG 1048) and Highland Severe (OG 1052); lots of malt whiskies on optic, maybe a summer guest beer. The simple bar snacks are priced far more attractively than we usually find in Scotland: besides sandwiches, there are burgers (from £1.25) drover's pie, chilli, filled baked potato (with haggis or chilli) or spaghetti bolognese (£2). Dogs allowed. The surrounding scenery is lovely, with Highland cattle virtually on the doorstep. *(Recommended by Anna Marsh, David Warrellow; more reports please)*

Own brew ~ Licensee Richard Saunders ~ Real ale ~ Snacks all day ~ (018662) 246 ~ Children in family room till 8 ~ Folk, rock or traditional music Fri/Sat ~ Open 11am-1am; winter 11-3, 5-11.30

TAYVALLICH (Strathclyde) NR7386 Map 11

Tayvallich Inn 🍽

B8025, off A816 1 mile S of Kilmartin; or take B841 turn-off from A816 2 miles N of Lochgilphead

There's a lovely view from the garden of this pleasant and simply refurbished pub across the lane to the sheltered yacht anchorage and bay of Loch Sween. Frequented by locals and visitors, it's very popular at the moment for good food, with an emphasis on local seafood, especially shellfish, with the lunchtime menu featuring large helping of moules marinières (£3), fillet of haddock (£4), fusili with seafood in a cream sauce (£5.75), six Loch Sween oysters (£6), Loch Fyne smoked salmon (£6.50), fillet of salmon with cajun seasoning (£7), fried Sound of Jura scallops (£9.50) and seafood platter (£10.50). There are other dishes such as soup (£1.50), beef curry (£4.80), char-grilled ribs (£4.95), cajun chicken (£5), minced steakburger (£6.50) and sirloin steak (£9.50); vegetarian dishes like chilli beans (£4.20) or baked goat's cheese on bed of roasted pepper (£4.95) home-made puddings (£2.50); decent house wines, coffee in cafetière, several Islay malts. Service is friendly and helpful and people with children are very much at home here. There's a no-smoking dining conservatory. The small bar has cigarette cards and local nautical charts on brown hessian walls, exposed ceiling joists, and pale pine upright chairs, benches and tables on its quarry-tiled floor; sliding glass doors open on to a concrete terrace furnished with picnic-table sets. *(Recommended by Mrs Pat Crabb, Michael and Harriet Robinson, Iain Grant, L Walker, Miss Julie Clarke, Andrew and Helen Latchem, Mr and Mrs G Hart)*

Free house ~ Licensee John Grafton ~ Meals and snacks (12-2, 6-8) ~ Restaurant ~ (0154 67) 282 ~ Children allowed in eating area of bar ~ Open 11am-midnight(1am Sat); closed Mon Nov-March

THORNHILL (Central) NS6699 Map 9

Lion & Unicorn

A873

It's pleasant to sit in the garden (where they have summer barbecues) of this charming friendly inn and watch the bowling on the pub's own bowling green – it can be used by non-residents. There's a fairly extensive changing blackboard menu. Food is nearly all home-made unless the chef feels a frozen product is superior, and typically has meals like soup (£1.50), baked avocado with smoked venison and tarragon cream sauce (£3.50), sautéed breast of wood pegeon with pecan nut and asparagus sauce or open sandwiches (from £4), steak and Guinness pie or haddock in real ale batter (£5.25), roast pork in pineapple gravy or grilled peppered mackerel in Arran mustard sauce (£6), game pie (£6.25), scallops in mixed peppers and Pernod sauce or poached river salmon with whisky and crème fraîche (£7), rack of lamb with apricot and rosemary glaze (£8) and sirloin steak (£9); smaller portions available for children, or the usual children's dishes; puddings like chocolate and applemint mousse, raspberry crème caramel or cranachan. A changing range of beers might include Belhaven Best, Broughton Merlin and Greenmantle, Caledonian 80/- and R & D Deuchars IPA, Courage

Directors, Marstons Pedigree, McEwans 80/-, Morlands Old Speckled Hen, Ruddles County, and Tetleys Bitter on handpump, with a decent range of changing malt whiskies, and a good choice of wines. The bar (with new log fire) is made up of two communicating rooms, and there's also a family room; the public bar has darts, pool, cribbage, dominoes and a fruit machine. The no-smoking restaurant is in the original part of the building which dates from 1635 and contains the original massive fireplace (six feet high and five feet wide). Dogs welcome; piped music. *(Recommended by Peter and Lynn Brueton, Martin, Jane, Simon and Laura Bailey, Michael and Harriet Robinson; more reports please)*

Free house ~ Licensees Walter and Ariane MacAulay ~ Real Ales ~ Meals and snacks (12-2.30, 5-9.30; 12-10 Sat; 12.30-9.30 Sun and bank holidays) ~ Restaurant ~ (01786) 850204/850707 ~ Children welcome ~ Monthly live music ~ Open 12-12 (1am Fri and Sat) ~ Bedrooms: £25/£37.50

TURRIFF (Grampian) NJ7250 Map 11

Towie

Auchterless; A947, 5 miles S

This extended white pebble-dash dining pub has a carefully and comfortably furnished series of warmly welcoming rooms and an elegant dining room. Good, reasonably priced seasonal home-made food from monthly changing menu using local produce includes soup (£1.50), deep-fried mushrooms stuffed with cheese, spicy tomato sauce or chicken liver pâté with oatcakes, raisins or Cumberland sauce (£2.95), beef chilli (£5.25), fresh fillet of haddock in batter (£5.50), macaroni with smoked haddock, prawns, tomato, onion in cheese sauce (£5.75), chicken with ham sauce, tomato, pineapple cream sauce or deep-fried scampi (£6.75), and daily specials. Well kept Theakstons and a guest like Marstons Pedigree on handpump, decent wine list and over 60 malt whiskies; darts, pool, dominoes and piped music. Handy for Fyvie Castle (Scottish National Trust) and Delgatie Castle. *(Recommended by G D and M D Craigen, Duncan Glennie, John and Christine Deacon)*

Free house ~ Licensee Douglas Pearson ~ Real ale ~ Meals and snacks ~ No-smoking restaurant ~ (01888) 511201 ~ Children welcome ~ Open 11-2.30, 6-11 (midnight Sat)

TUSHIELAW (Borders) NT3018 Map 9

Tushielaw Hotel ⟺

Ettrick Valley, B709/B7009 Lockerbie—Selkirk

This very small country hotel is in a lovely spot, with pretty views over Ettrick Water; a good base for walkers or for touring, with its own fishing on Clearburn Loch up the B711. The unpretentious but comfortable little bar has decent house wines, a good few malts, and an open fire, and opens on to a terrace with tables for those who are lucky with the weather. Welcoming young owners, and a good range of changing home-cooked food such as home-made soup (£1.95), toasties (from £1.95), mushrooms stuffed with stilton and served with garlic mayonnaise (£2.95), ploughman's (£3), cheese and haggis fritters with Cumberland sauce (£3.25), steak in stout pie (£4.95), fresh fish such as sole, trout or salmon (from £7), fillet of pork en croûte with hazelnut and orange sauce (£8.95), steaks (from £8.95), and home-made puddings (from £2); piped music. *(Recommended by Gen and Dry, John and Molly Knowles, Nick Hyams)*

Free house ~ Licensees Steve and Jessica Osbourne ~ Real ale ~ Meals and snacks ~ Restaurant ~ (01750) 62205 ~ Children in eating areas ~ Open 12-2.30, 6-11; all day summer Sun; winter evening opening 7; closed Mon/Tues/Weds lunchtimes in winter ~ Bedrooms: £19(£21B)/£38(£42B)

We mention bottled beers and spirits only if there is something unusual about them – imported Belgian real ales, say, or dozens of malt whiskies; so do please let us know about them in your reports.

TWEEDSMUIR (Borders) NT0924 Map 9

Crook 🛏

A701 a mile N of village

On a lonely road through grand partly forested hills this atmospheric old drovers' inn was first licensed in 1604, making it one of Scotland's oldest inns. In the 17th c it was a clandestine meeting place for the Covenanters, and one landlady is well remembered for hiding a fugitive from the dragoons in her peat stack. Burns wrote his poem 'Willie Wastles Wife' here, and though it's been extended and modernised since there's still a cosy, old-fashioned look and feel to the place. The flagstoned back bar is cosy and simply furnished, with local photographs on its walls; one very thick wall, partly knocked through, has a big hearth, and opens into a large airy lounge with comfortable chairs around low tables and an open log fire; beyond is a sun lounge. The pub's various art-deco features are most notable in the lavatories – superb 1930s tiling and cut design mirrors. Well kept Greenmantle on handpump and a good choice of malt whiskies. Bar food includes sandwiches, home-made soup (£1.50), smoked salmon and prawn rolls marie rose (£3.95), deep-fried breaded haddock or chilli con carne (£4.25), grilled lamb's liver with bacon, onion and tomato (£4.50), local trout with almonds and lemon (£5.25), scampi or grilled lamb chops with gooseberry and mint sauce (£5.95), poached salmon steak with dill sauce (£6.95), rump steak (£7.95), mixed grill (£10.50); vegetarian dishes like vegetarian tikka (£4.75) or cashew and pine nut roast with tomato sauce (£5.25); high tea (£6.95); friendly service. A separate room has darts, dominoes, cribbage, shove-ha'penny, fruit machine and video game. There are tables on the grass outside, with a climbing frame and slide, and across the road the inn has an attractive garden, sheltered by oak trees; maybe pétanque here in summer. Trout fishing permits for about 30 miles' fishing on the Tweed and its tributaries are available from the pub at about £5 a day. They've just added a craft centre to the old stable block with displays and demonstrations of glassblowing. *(Recommended by Mr and Mrs R M Macnaughton; more reports please)*

Free house ~ Licensee Stuart Reid ~ Real ale ~ Meals and snacks (12-9) ~ Restaurant ~ (0189 97) 272 ~ Children welcome ~ Open 11am-midnight ~ Bedrooms: £36B/£52B

ULLAPOOL (Highland) NH1294 Map 11

Ceilidh Place

West Argyle St

Wonderfully unusual for this part of Scotland, the atmosphere in this pretty rose-draped white house is rather like that of a stylish arty café-bar, but with a distinctly Celtic character. There's an art gallery, lot's of live jazz, classical and folk music, dance and some experimental theatre in the auditorium, a bookshop and a coffee shop. It's set in a quiet side street above the small town, there are tables on a terrace looking over the other houses to the distant hills beyond the natural harbour. Inside there are bentwood chairs and one or two cushioned wall benches among the rugs on its varnished concrete floor, spotlighting from the dark planked ceiling, attractive modern prints and a big sampler on the textured white walls, piped classical or folk music, magazines to read, venetian blinds, houseplants, and mainly young upmarket customers, many from overseas. There's a woodburning stove and dominoes. The side food bar – you queue for service at lunchtime – does good hot dishes from fresh ingredients – there's always a good choice for vegetarians – such as savoury flans or stovies, vegetable curry (£3.45), chilli bean casserole (£3.85), beef and aniseed stew (£5.25) home-made ice cream and puddings. In the evening dishes such as lemon chicken casserole or kedgeree (£6.50) and a melange of seafood (£8.50) are served by efficient waitresses. Though the beers are keg they have decent wines by the glass (and pineau de charentes), some uncommon European bottled beers and Orkney bottled real ales, an interesting range of high-proof malt whiskies and a choice of cognacs that's unmatched around here. There's an attractive conservatory dining room and the bedrooms are comfortable and pleasantly decorated. *(Recommended by Andrew Stephenson, Ian and Deborah Carrington, Andrew Low; more reports please)*

Free house ~ Mrs Jean Urquhart ~ Meals and snacks (noon-9.30pm) ~ No-smoking restaurant (Wed-Sun, 7-9) and conservatory ~ Ullapool (01854) 612103 ~ Children in eating area of bar and restaurant ~ Regular ceilidhs, folk, jazz and classical music ~ Open 11-11 (closed two weeks mid Jan) ~ Bedrooms: £35(£48B)/£70(£96B)

Ferry Boat

Shore St

There are fine views to the tall hills beyond the attractive fishing port with its bustle of yachts, ferry boats, fishing boats and tour boats for the Summer Isles from this very traditional pub that's popular with visitors and locals alike. The simple, genuine two-roomed bar has brocade-cushioned seats around plain wooden tables, quarry tiles by the corner serving counter and patterned carpet elsewhere, big windows, and a stained-glass door hanging from the ceiling. The quieter inner room has a coal fire, a delft shelf of copper measures and willow-pattern plates. Well kept constantly changing real ales that might include Belhaven 80/- or Best, Boddingtons or McEwans 80/- on air-pressure tall fount, a decent choice of whiskies. Good value straightforward home-made bar lunches, changing daily, include soup (£1.25), vegetarian pâté (from £2.95) and meat pâtés (from £3.25), ploughman's (£3.25), haggis, neeps and tatties (£4.45), leek and mushroom croustade, liver and bacon casserole, aubergine bake, courgette, pepper and mushroom lasagne or fresh haddock (£5.25), roast beef salad (£5.50), smoked haddock gratinée (£5.75), chicken with white wine and mushroom sauce (£6.25) and home-made puddings like coffee and mandarin trifle, fresh raspberrry soufflé or chocolate, banana and raisin cheesecake (£1.70); small portions for children (£2.25). They do a wonderful afternoon tea with lots of scones, cakes and tea. Unobtrusive piped pop music; fruit machine; bedrooms have recently been upgraded. *(Recommended by Michael and Harriet Robinson, Jeanne and Tom Barnes, Mark Gillis, Ian, Kathleen and Helen Corsie, Mike and Penny Sanders; more reports please)*

Free house ~ Licensee Richard Smith ~ Real ale ~ Meals and snacks (lunchtime only, summer, but also 6-8.30 winter) ~ No-smoking evening restaurant (summer only) ~ (01854) 612366 ~ Children welcome till 8pm ~ sometimes live music Thurs eve ~ Open 11-11; closed four days over Christmas ~ Bedrooms: £31B/£56B

Morefield Motel 🍽

North Rd

The owners (themselves ex-fishermen and divers) have a ship to shore radio in the office which they use to corner the best of the day's catch before the boats have even come off the sea, and the superbly fresh seafood and fish they've served here for over thirteen years has built them a tremendous reputation. Served in large helpings and changing seasonally, the choice in the bar might include poached salmon cocktail (£3.25), mussels (£3.95), sesame prawn toasts (£3.65), butterfly split prawns (£4.25), haddock bake or beer battered haddock (£5.95), scampi (£6.50), local salmon (£6.75), sole and broccoli bonne femme (£6.95), scallops in the shell cooked with fresh lemon and coriander (£7.95), salmon steamed with prawns and mussels in seafood cream sauce (£8.25), split half lobster filled with sliced scallops and prawns cooked in creamy thermidor sauce (£9.95) and a high-heaped seafood platter (£12.95). Other dishes include home-made soup (£2.25), local haggis fried in batter (£3.30), roast Aberdeen rump of beef or lamb chops (£6.50), sirloin stroganoff or Singapore curry (£6.95), sirloin steak (£8.95, topped with prawns £10.95), curries (from £5.50), venison pie or roast rib of beef (£5.95), steaks (from £8.75); vegetarian dishes like vegetable curry, mushroom and onion stroganoff or steamed vegetable mornay (£5.50). You can also eat in the smarter Mariners restaurant which has a slightly more elaborate menu. In winter (from November to March) the diners tend to yield to local people playing darts or pool, though there's bargain food then, including a very cheap three-course meal. They now have well kept Belhaven Best and Broughton Greenmantle on handpump, and a very good range of over 80 malt whiskies, decent wines and friendly tartan-skirted waitresses; piped pop music, fruit machine. The L-shaped lounge, newly refurbished, is partly no smoking. There are tables on the terrace. The bedrooms are functional. *(Recommended by Ian and Deborah Carrington, Lee Goulding, Joan and Tony Walker; more reports please)*

Free house ~ Licensee David Smyrl ~ Meals and snacks (12-2, 5.30-9.30) ~ Partly no-smoking evening restaurant ~ (01854) 612161 ~ Children welcome ~ Occasional live music winter Fri ~ Open 11-11(closed 2.30-5 in winter); closed 25 and 26 Dec ~ Bedrooms: £25B/£40B

WEEM (Tayside) NN8449 Map 11

Ailean Chraggan
B846

There's an excellent view from the tables on the large terrace outside this comfortably friendly inn across the flat ground between here and the Tay to mountains beyond. This is another of those Scottish places that's highly recommended for its fish dishes. The well presented bar food includes soup (£1.55), cullen skink (£2.95), chicken liver pâté (£3.25), smoked ham salad (£5.95), grilled lamb chops (£6.15), beef curry (£6.25), grilled lemon sole (£6.95), creamy garlic chicken breast or venison casseroled in red wine and redcurrant jelly (£7.15), salmon fillet fried with lemon butter and tarrragon, (£7.50), garlic prawns (£9.50), sirloin steak (£10.50) or Sound of Jura seafood platter (£12.50), and puddings like pineapple upsidedown cake or chocolate cream cheese pie (£2.95). The menu is the same in the restaurant. The modern lounge has long plump plum-coloured banquettes, and Bruce Bairnsfather First World War cartoons on the red and gold Regency striped wallpaper; winter darts, dominoes and piped music; about 80 malt whiskies. Bedrooms are described by readers as spacious and comfortable. *(Recommended by Mr and Mrs R M Macnaughton, Susan and John Douglas, Paul and Ursula Randall, C Moncreiffe; more reports please)*

Free house ~ Licensee Alastair Gillespie ~ Meals and snacks ~ Restaurant ~ (01887) 820346 ~ Children welcome ~ Open 11-11; closed 25 Dec, 1,2 Jan ~ Bedrooms: £26B/£52B

WESTRUTHER (Borders) NT6450 Map 10

Old Thistle
B6456 – off A697 just SE of the A6089 Kelso fork

At the heart of village life this unpretentious local really comes into its own in the evenings, when local farmers, fishermen, gamekeepers and shepherds all come down from the hills and may even break into song when Andrew strikes up on the accordion. There's a tiny, quaint bar on the right with some furnishings that look as if they date back to the inn's 1721 foundation – the elaborately carved chimney piece, an oak corner cupboard, the little bottom-polished seat by the coal fire; some fine local horsebrasses. A simple back room with whisky-water jugs on its black beams has darts, pool, dominoes, fruit machine and video game, and doors from here lead out onto their terrace; there's a small, plain room with one or two tables on the left. On the food front, what really stands out is the quality of the evening steaks – fine local Aberdeen Angus, hung and cooked to perfection (8oz sirloin £8.50, 8oz fillet £10, 20oz T-bone £12.50). The menu is otherwise very simple, with soup (£1.50) and salads (from £5), the lunchtime menu is equally straightforward with sandwiches (from £1.30), sausages (£2.95), haddock (£4.25), lasagne (£5.50) and steak and eggs (£6.50). A more conventionally comfortable two-room lounge has flowery brocaded seats, neat tables and a small coal fire, leading into the restaurant. Piped music; according to one reader the bedrooms in a separate cottage have good facilities but no mirrors! *(Recommended by P M Steeples, R M Tudor, Stephen R Holman, E C Waterer; more reports please)*

Free house ~ Licensee David Silk ~ Meals and snacks (12-2, 5-10; no food Monday) ~ Restaurant ~ (01578) 740275 ~ Children welcome ~ Open 12-2.30, 5-11; 12-11 Sat-Sun; closed lunchtime Mon and Tues ~ Bedrooms: £20B/£40B

Lucky Dip

Besides the fully inspected pubs, you might like to try these Lucky Dips recommended to us and described by readers (if you do, please send us reports):

BORDERS

Auchencraw [NT8661], *Craw*: Decent well run pub with good atmosphere, well kept Greenmantle, guest beers *(H K Dyson)*

Blyth Bridge [A6094 Edinburgh—Galashiels; NT1345], *Old Mill*: Interesting old building with good welcome and adequate well cooked and reasonably priced food *(Jean and Douglas Troup)*

Bonchester Bridge [NT5812], *Horse & Hound*: Wide range of well cooked food, three well kept real ales, interesting building, good landlord; bedrooms *(Alison Bell, Michael Patterson)*

Carlops [NT1656], *Alan Ramsay*: Interesting late 18th-c pub, several interconnecting beamed rooms, eating areas each end (wide choice of good value food all day), two fires, lots of bric-a-brac, fresh flowers, witches' sabbat mural recalling local legend; well kept Belhaven 80/- and Sandy Hunter on handpump, good coffee; piped pop music, fruit machine and TV; service can slow when busy; children welcome *(JJW, CMW)*

Eyemouth [Harbour; NT9564], *Contented Sole*: Quick friendly bar and food service, good whitebait *(F A Noble)*

Gordon [NT6543], *Gordon Arms*: Friendly pub doing well under new licensees, good food, Greenmantle ale *(Bill Knight)*

☆ **Greenlaw** [NT7146], *Castle*: Straightforward pub distinguished by really good food inc good soups, well flavoured steak pie, good value Sun lunch; well kept Greenmantle, two dear old dogs *(E C Waterer, RMM)*

Jedburgh [NT6521], *Pheasant*: Very warm welcome, first-class service, fair choice of wine and whiskies, good food usefully served 12-2.30 and 6-9, inc amazing value pheasant in season; decor not its strongest point *(Jonathan Mann, Abigail Regan)*

☆ **Kelso** [Bridge St (A699); NT7334], *Queens Head*: Friendly helpful staff and wide choice of very good generous food inc imaginative dishes in old coaching inn, good mix of modern and traditional; reasonable prices, well kept ales such as Aitkens, Greenmantle, Tetleys and Theakstons, big back lounge, small streetside locals' tap room; children welcome; good value bedrooms, bright and clean *(Thomas Nott, Gerry McGarry, P Woodward, A D Lealan, Nigel Woolliscroft)*

☆ **Lauder** [Market Pl (A68); NT5347], *Eagle*: Dark wood and beams, pictures, plates, brass, plants, remarkably ornate bar counter, stone fireplace; decent bar food inc vegetarian, efficient smiling service, well kept McEwans 80/-, Theakstons and maybe Broughton Oatmeal Stout, games in public bar, summer barbecues in old stableyard, children welcome, open all day; bedrooms *(JJW, CMW, LYM)*

Lilliesleaf [B6400 SE of Selkirk; NT5325], *Cross Keys*: Small pleasant 200-year-old stone and plaster pub in attractive village, two clean and comfortable rooms with solid beams, real fires and old photographs, friendly landlord, good value menu and specials inc good soup, well kept Greenmantle and McEwans 80/-, fruit machine but no piped music *(JJW, CMW)*

Melrose [High St; NT5434], *George & Abbotsford*: Welcoming inn with well kept beers, quite a few malt whiskies, good reasonably priced bar food, friendly service; bedrooms *(Mike and Penny Sanders)*

Peebles [High St; NT2540], *Tontine*: Forte hotel with small bar and big comfortable lounge, good food in both, relaxing atmosphere, good helpful service, Greenmantle ale, reasonable prices; bedrooms *(A D Lealan)*

Reston [NT8862], *Wheatsheaf*: Good cheap place to stay, lovely welcome and well cooked generous food; bedrooms spotless and comfortable *(S Mowbray)*

Selkirk [28 West Port; NT4728], *Queens Head*: Open-plan beamed bar with copper-topped tables, navy banquettes, some timber-effect, Scott prints; freshly cooked food inc imaginative vegetarian dishes served till 9.30, friendly service, simpler public bar with games and so forth; children welcome, dogs allowed in public bar, open all day summer *(Graham and Belinda Staplehurst, LYM)*

☆ **St Boswells** [A68 just S of Newtown St Boswells; NT5931], *Buccleuch Arms*: Busy but civilised and spacious Georgian-style panelled bar in well established sandstone inn, wide choice of well prepared bar food (not Sun), sandwiches all day, no-smoking alcove, restaurant, tables in garden behind; children welcome; bedrooms *(J D Maplethorpe, Gordon Smith, David Logan, LYM)*

CENTRAL

☆ **Castlecary** [village signed off A80 Glasgow—Stirling; NS7878], *Castlecary House*: Generous quick low-priced decent food till 10 in handily placed cheerful pub, open all day, with well kept Bass, Belhaven 80/-, Jennings Cumberland, John Smiths Magnet and Stones on handpump, very friendly staff; restaurant specialising in steaks on hot metal platters; comfortable well equipped bedrooms, generous breakfasts *(Janet Brown, Karen Phillips, LYM)*

☆ **Dollar** [Chapel Pl; NS9796], *Strathallan*: Good bar food inc fine choice of fresh fish in pleasant, clean and welcoming pub with well kept local Harviestoun 70/-, 80/-, 85/- and Strong, also Belhaven 80/- and lots of malt whiskies inc bargain malt of the month; good service, thriving friendly atmosphere; bedrooms *(Jean and Douglas Troup)*

☆ **Drymen** [The Square; NS4788], *Clachan*: Small white cottage, licensed since 1734, friendly and welcoming; original fireplace with side salt larder, tables made from former bar tops, former Wee Free pews along one wall; good food, well kept beer, chatty landlord; on square of attractive village *(Ian Phillips, Robert Blundell)*

Drymen [The Square], *Winnock:* A hotel but has a popular bar with reasonably priced food, lots of English guest beers, big garden with picnic-table sets; bedrooms – very friendly and helpful place to stay *(Ian Phillips)*

Dunblane [NN7801], *Dunblane:* Nice decor, prompt lunchtime service; bedrooms *(P Corris)*

Gartmore [NS5297], *Black Bull:* 17th-c drovers' inn on edge of Trossachs with enthusiastic new young owner who's kept the simple atmosphere but added good choice of all-day food inc wonderful home-made pizzas (take-aways too); new garden; bedrooms *(Melanie Reid)*

☆ Inverarnan [A82 N of Loch Lomond; NN3118], *Inverarnan Drovers Inn:* Odd and interesting, with sporting trophies, other stuffed animals, armour, deerskins slung over the settles, Scots music (barmen sometimes in kilts), great collection of malt whiskies, farm cider; bar food, good earthy atmosphere, wandering dog, tables outside with miscellaneous animals; well behaved children allowed, open all day; the building has seen better days, and housekeeping can be a bit casual; bedrooms *(Julian Holland, Mary Moore, Annette Moore, Chris Pearson, LYM)*

☆ Kilmahog [A821/A84 just N of Callander; NN6108], *Lade:* Very wide range of straightforward food inc help-yourself salad, vegetarian and children's dishes, efficient casual service, good range of wines, all available by the glass, inc some good Antipodean ones, real ales, no-smoking area, pleasant garden with summer evening barbecues; bedrooms *(Ian and Freda Millar, Dave Davey, James Nunns)*

☆ Stirling [91 St Mary's Wynd; from Wallace Memorial in centre go up Baker St, keep right at top; NS7993], *Settle:* Early 18th-c, restored to show beams, stonework, great arched fireplace and barrel-vaulted upper room; bar games, snacks till 7, Belhaven 70/- and 80/- and Maclays on handpump, friendly staff; piped music, open all day *(Julian Holland, LYM)*

☆ nr Stirling [Easter Cornton Rd; Causewayhead; off A9 N of Stirling centre], *Birds & Bees:* Interestingly furnished ex-byre, dimly lit and convivial, very comfortable since thorough-going 1993 refurbishment and extension; Caledonian 80/-, Tennents Special and 80/-, guests such as Alloa 80/-, Marstons Pedigree and others, good if not particularly cheap food, friendly staff; decor includes milk churns, iron sculptures and re-fleeced sheep; live bands most weekends, open all day till 1am – very popular with young people, reliably well run; children welcome *(Julian Holland, LYM)*

DUMFRIES AND GALLOWAY

☆ Auchencairn [about 2½ miles off A711;

NX7951], *Old Smugglers:* Warmly welcoming popular 18th-c inn, comfortable and attractive with clean white woodwork, good pub food at sensible prices inc outstanding puddings and cakes, quick competent all-female staff, pretty garden and terrace; children welcome *(J L Phillips, Dr M I Crichton)*

☆ Auchencairn, *Balcary Bay:* Well ordered and comfortable hotel, lovely spot for eating outside with terrace and gardens in peaceful surroundings, magnificent sea views, civilised but friendly bar, well presented food from soup and open sandwiches up (inc huge child's helpings); reasonable prices, pleasant service; bedrooms *(Dr and Mrs R E S Tanner, Janet and Gary Amos, P and J Coombs, Roy R Bromell, MK, JP)*

Carsethorn [off A170 at Kirkbean; NX9959], *Steamboat:* Good home-made food with helpings so big that fries and veg come on a separate plate, estuary views from front dining room, seafaring items in adjoining little bar *(Paul and Ursula Roberts)*

Castle Douglas [Main St; NX7662], *Royal:* Plentiful good value food, long public bar, back room with pool and darts, well kept McEwans 80/-, friendly landlord; bedrooms *(Paul and Ursula Roberts)*

Crocketford [A75 N of Dumfries; NX8372], *Galloway Arms:* Well refurbished inn with particularly well prepared and presented food, very friendly and helpful staff; comfortable well equipped bedrooms, own bathrooms *(Colin and Lynn Dodd)*

☆ Dalbeattie [1 Maxwell St; NX8361], *Pheasant:* Good choice of bar food till 10 in simply modernised but comfortable upstairs lounge/restaurant; lively downstairs bar, children welcome till 6, open all day; bedrooms *(Paul and Ursula Roberts, LYM)*

☆ Gatehouse of Fleet [High St; NX5956], *Angel:* Warm and cosy hotel lounge bar, good friendly service, popular bar food, sensibly priced restaurant, McEwans ales; bedrooms comfortable and good value *(Maysie Thompson)*

Gatehouse of Fleet, *Masons Arms:* Lots of atmosphere, huge helpings of good food *(C Philip)*

☆ Glencaple [NX9968], *Nith:* Good quickly served reasonably priced food, esp smoked salmon and wild salmon; bedrooms *(Mr and Mrs Henry Stephens)*

Kippford [NX8355], *Anchor:* Wide range of generous bar food inc children's dishes (served all day in summer) in waterside inn facing quiet yacht anchorage, traditional back bar with lots of varnished woodwork, plush front dining bar with lots of prints on stripped stone walls, log fire, S&N real ales; games room, seats out facing water; open all day summer *(GW, BW, LYM; more reports on new management please)*

☆ Kirkcudbright [Old High St; NX6851], *Selkirk Arms:* Quiet modern decor in cosy and comfortable partly panelled lounge with good local flavour; good bar food inc fine fresh salmon pie, restaurant, evening steak bar, friendly efficient service, tables in good spacious garden; fishing; children in restaurant and lounge; good value bedrooms *(Maysie Thompson, LYM)*

Laurieston [NX6864], *Laurie Arms*: Small pub with lounge and public bars, Bass, Tetleys and a guest such as Ind Coope Burton, decent wine; usual food *(John Watson)*

☆ **Moffat** [1 Churchgate; NT0905], *Black Bull*: Quick friendly service and generous straight-forward bar food, friendly public bar with railway memorabilia and good open fire (may be only bar open out of season), plush softly lit cocktail bar, simply furnished tiled-floor dining room, side games bar with juke box; children welcome; open all day all week; bedrooms comfortable, with hearty breakfasts *(Jim Cowell, Gordon Smith, Cyril Burton, LYM)*

☆ **Moffat** [44 High St], *Star*: Amazingly narrow building yet has two surprisingly capacious bars inc quiet, comfortable and relaxing lounge; warm friendly atmosphere, swift service, reasonably priced interesting food, well kept S&N beers on tall fount, good coffee, moderately priced wine by the bottle; bedrooms *(Bob Smith, TBB)*

☆ **Moffat** [High St], *Moffat House*: Friendly well run extended Adam-style hotel with good range of good value food inc memorable steaks in large comfortable lounge bar, good service, very friendly atmosphere; usually has real ale (not always in winter); comfortable bedrooms with good breakfasts *(Norman Ellis, G P Fogelman)*

☆ **Moffat** [High St], *Balmoral*: Well kept ale and well cooked and presented simple food in fine main-street village pub; quick cheerful service, comfortable peaceful bar *(P Corris, Stephen R Holman)*

Moffat [High St], *Buccleuch Arms*: Georgian coaching inn with good reasonably priced home-made food inc generous charcoal grills with lots of veg, interesting choice of wines; friendly and accommodating licensees; modern bedrooms *(Angela Steele)*

☆ nr **Moffat** [hotel signposted off A74], *Auchen Castle*: Beautifully appointed country-house hotel (so dress appropriately) in lovely quiet spot with spectacular hill views, imaginative choice of good food in peaceful and comfortable bar, decent wines, good choice of malt whiskies, friendly service; trout loch in good-sized grounds; bedrooms superbly decorated, wonderful views *(Rev J E Cooper)*

Moniaive [High St (A702); NX7790], *George*: Good food and service in interestingly old-fashioned flagstoned bar of considerable character, in 17th-c Covenanters' inn; friendly staff and locals; bedrooms simple and comfortable *(Dr and Mrs Mitt, LYM)*

☆ **Port Logan** [NX0940], *The Inn*: Very popular for good well cooked beautifully presented food, immaculate table settings, very friendly landlord, hard-working staff; children very welcome *(Janet and Gary Amos)*

FIFE

Aberdour [A921; NT1985], *Aberdour*: Cosy nicely decorated hotel bar with open fire, red plush banquettes, friendly service, good

choice of whiskies, McEwans 80/- and Theakstons Best on handpump, papers out, food inc cauldron of scotch broth sitting on bar; restaurant; open all day Thurs-Sun; bedrooms *(Jim Penman)*; *Cedar*: Two bars – one very small and plain, the other smallish and very nicely decorated – and lounge and dining area; friendly service, fruit machine, pool *(Jim Penman)*; *Woodside*: Well furnished hotel bar with nautical flavour, good service, no piped music, standard bar food, Theakstons XB on handpump, restaurant; bedrooms *(Jim Penman)*

☆ **Anstruther** [Bankwell Rd; NO5704], *Craws Nest*: Well run hotel with good variety of reliably good generous food inc outstanding haddock and other fresh fish in straightforward lounge; good service; bedrooms *(Paul and Ursula Randall, R J Herd, Basil J S Minson)*

☆ **Ceres** [Main St; NO4011], *Meldrums*: Consistently good bar lunches inc unusual starters and popular traditional main courses in clean and attractive beamed dining lounge, pleasant waitresses; bedrooms *(Paul and Ursula Randall)*

☆ **Crail** [4 High St; NO6108], *Golf*: Good fresh low-priced food in cosy village inn with bustling little public bar, rather more restrained if not exactly smart lounge; well kept McEwans 80/-, good range of malt whiskies, good service, coal fire; bedrooms clean and comfortable though basic, with good breakfasts *(Basil J S Minson)*

Elie [NO4900], *18th Hole*: Charming pub with several rooms each with a different style, well kept beer, old-fashioned gas cigar-lighter on bar *(Dennis Dickinson)*

☆ **Lower Largo** [The Harbour; NO4102], *Crusoe*: Harbourside inn with good food from servery in beamed family bar with stripped stonework, comfortably cushioned settees in bays, open fire, S&N beers, quick service; separate lounge bar with Crusoe/Alexander Selkirk mementos, restaurant; bedrooms spacious and comfortable, with good sea views *(Andrew and Ruth Triggs)*

☆ **North Queensferry** [NT1380], *Queensferry Lodge*: Good well run hotel, included as useful motorway break with good views of Forth bridges and the Firth from light and airy lounge, tastefully decorated with lots of wood and plants; McEwans real ale, good value bar food running up to decent steaks 12-2.30, 5-10; bedrooms good, buffet breakfast *(Norman Ellis)*

☆ **St Andrews** [40 The Scores; NO5116], *Ma Bells*: By golf course, open all day, with big lively basement bar brimming with students during term-time, well kept Deuchars IPA and Theakstons XB with a couple of guest beers, lots of interesting bottled beers and malt whiskies, popular food, friendly service; no-smoking raised back area, bar mirrors, old enamel signs; well reproduced piped music, pleasant seafront views from outside *(Paul and Ursula Randall, John Fazakerley)*

St Andrews [32 Bell St], *St Andrews Wine*

Bar: Well kept beer in cellar bar, food from wine bar above can be served here if you wish; usually a good mix of customers *(N J Mackintosh)*

☆ nr **St Andrews**, [Grange Rd – a mile S], *Grange*: More restaurant than pub, in attractive setting, with good choice of generally very good if not cheap food in spotless small bar too, friendly service, good range of malt whiskies, decent wines (but keg beers), furniture in keeping with the age of the building, individual character *(Paul and Ursula Randall, Basil J S Minson, Brian Bannatyne-Scott)*

☆ **Wormit** [NO4026], *Sandford*: Good imaginative food in elegant and comfortable yet friendly bar of country house hotel, cushioned window seat overlooks pretty garden as does the terrace, friendly waitresses in Highland dress, welcoming landlord; good restaurant; bedrooms good *(Susan and John Douglas)*

GRAMPIAN

☆ **Aberdeen** [Bon Accord St], *Ferryhill House Hotel*: Well run small hotel with comfortable communicating spacious and airy bar areas, half a dozen well kept real ales, well over 100 malt whiskies, friendly staff, wide range of very generous bar food and cheap set lunches; lots of well spaced tables on neat sheltered lawns; open all day, children allowed in restaurant; bedrooms comfortable *(P Corris, Mark Walker, LYM)*
Aberdeen [121 Gallowgate; NJ9305], *Blue Lamp*: Small and dark, with modern flagstoned lounge, good friendly bar staff, McEwans 80/-, Theakstons Best and guest beers, free juke box, fruit machine, occasional band; popular with beer drinkers and students *(Mark Walker)*; [1 Backwynd], *Booths*: Good choice of tasty and inexpensive food, well kept beers *(John Howard)*; [Windmill Brae, Bath St], *Royal*: Comfortable and relaxing hotel lounge bar locally popular for wide choice of reasonably priced food all day, friendly quick service, well served Tennents, good wine; bedrooms *(Gerald and Nicola Neale)*; [Castle St], *Tilted Wig*: Comfortable open-plan central pub with Caledonian 80/-, Ind Coope Burton and Tetleys on handpump *(Julian Bessa)*

☆ **Braemar** [NO1491], *Fife Arms*: Welcoming and elegantly refurbished big Victorian hotel, comfortable sofas and tartan cushions, reasonably priced pub food, decent staff; children and dogs welcome (and on the coach routes); bedrooms warm and comfortable *(Susan and John Douglas, R M Macnaughton, Julian Bessa)*
Bridge of Alford [NJ5617], *Forbes Arms*: Family-owned fishing pub, good Aberdonian staff, good basic home-made food, well kept Ruddles County, spotlessly clean *(R M Macnaughton)*

☆ **Catterline** [NO8778], *Creel*: Warmly welcoming landladies, cosy bar with real fire, big lounge with friendly cat and plenty of tables, good generous food in bar and seaview restaurant, well kept Maclays 70/- and Tennents 80/-, all clean and comfortable; bedrooms *(Roger and Sheila Thompson, M D Farman)*
Elgin [Thunderton Pl; NJ2162], *Thunderton House*: Friendly and popular 17th-c town-centre pub, sympathetically refurbished in 19th-c style, real ales inc guests, good pub food, fast friendly service, children's room *(D Newth)*
Findhorn [NJ0464], *Crown & Anchor*: Useful family pub with usual food all day inc children's dishes, up to six changing real ales, big fireplace in lively public bar, separate lounge; bedrooms, good boating in Findhorn Bay (boats for residents) *(Spider Newth, DE, CM, LYM)*; *Kimberley*: Well kept and run by friendly staff, McEwans 80/-, Tetleys and guest beers, good food in huge helpings from sandwiches to steaks *(G Hooper)*
Kincardine O' Neil [A93 W of Aberdeen; NO5999], *Gordon Arms*: Public bar and unusual L-shaped panelled lounge/dining room with swords and piano, friendly service, wide choice of generous food, good coffee, Flowers and Theakstons on handpump, piped pop music; open all day every day; children welcome; bedrooms *(JJW, CMW)*

☆ **Monymusk** [signed from B993 SW of Kemnay; NJ6815], *Grant Arms*: Good choice of food, not the cheapest, from sandwiches to steaks inc seafood and game in comfortable and well kept inn with good fishing on the Don; log fire dividing dark-panelled lounge bar in two, lots of malt whiskies, S&N real ales, locals' bar, restaurant; children welcome, open all day weekends; bedrooms *(John Howard, LYM)*

☆ **Newburgh** [A975 N of Aberdeen; NJ9925], *Udny Arms*: Pleasant small hotel with attractively decorated lounge bar opening into wicker-furniture sun lounge; good simple bar lunches, more imaginative than usual, wider choice of evening food, Theakstons Best on handpump, lots of tables on sheltered back lawn, stroll over golf links to sandy beach; comfortable bedrooms *(Alastair Campbell, LYM)*
Old Aberdeen [Ellon Rd/Donmouth Rd; NJ9308], *Don View*: Modern pub with large pleasant bar and split-level eating area, good food, Marstons Pedigree and Tetleys on handpump, service attentive to a fault even when busy; open all day every day, food all day; children welcome *(JJW, CMW)*
Pennan [just off B9031 Banff—Fraserburgh; NJ8465], *Pennan*: Very small oasis, very popular with locals and visitors, good imaginative food inc fantastic fish soup – stop bar food 7pm to concentrate on restaurant; marvellous spot right by sea at foot of steep single street, tables out by the seagulls; bedrooms *(Margaret Kemp)*

☆ **Stonehaven** [Shorehead; NO8786], *Marine*: Basic unpretentious harbourside pub with seats outside and superb view; good reasonably priced food, five real ales inc McEwans 80/- and guests, coffee and tea, polite service, upstairs lounge and restaurant; lively downstairs, piped music may compete with TV, dogs allowed here; juke box, games machines and pool table in room past bar; open all day; bedrooms *(JJW, CMW, Mark Walker)*

HIGHLAND

Aultguish [NH3570], *Aultguish*: Isolated highland inn nr Loch Glascarnoch with friendly licensees and staff, decent food, a welcome for children and walkers (they'll put their gear out to dry); bedrooms inexpensive, simple but good *(Tim Galligan, LYM)*

Aviemore [Coylumbridge Rd; NH8912], *Olde Bridge*: Well kept and friendly inn with good bar food – char-grilled salmon, venison and Sun roast beef all recommended *(CJC, P G Topp)*

☆ **Badachro** [B8056; NG7773], *Badachro Hotel*: Superb waterside setting, nice garden and tables on terrace over Loch Gairloch; homely public bar, more comfortable than usual, friendly and relaxing; good wholesome hot basic bar food, good log fire, friendly helpful staff, children welcome; Nov-March open only Weds and Fri evenings, Sat lunch and evening; bedrooms *(J E Rycroft, Ron Corbett)*

Ballachulish [Oban Rd, S; NN0858], *Ballachulish*: Pleasant lounge bar with beautiful view and good food inc vegetarian dishes, interesting specials and children's dishes; Arrols 80/- and West Highland real ales, basic public bar; bedrooms *(P G Topp, Alan Reid)*

Bower [B876 11m NW of Wick; ND2462], *Bower*: Nearest thing to a typical country pub in the area, cosy lounge bar with open fires, good value no-frills food and more sophisticated dishes in restaurant, friendly service, interesting submarine memorabilia *(Alan Wilcock, Christine Davidson)*

☆ **Carrbridge** [NH9022], *Dalrachney Lodge*: Good menu, friendly staff, pleasant shooting-lodge-type hotel with simply furnished bar, quiet and comfortable lounge with books and log fire in ornate carved inglenook fireplace, decent malt whiskies, old-fashioned dining room; bedrooms, most with mountain and river views *(E J Wilde)*

Cromarty [Marine Terr; NH7867], *Royal*: Good food, drink and service, beautiful view across Cromarty Firth to Ben Wyvis; bedrooms *(L Grant)*

☆ **Dores** [B852 SW of Inverness; NH5934], *Dores*: Reasonably priced popular bar food in attractive traditional country inn in delightful spot by Loch Ness, splendid views; exposed stone walls, low ceilings, basic public bar, more comfortable lounge with open fire; well kept beer, friendly service, front garden and tables out behind *(Alan Wilcock, Christine Davidson)*

Dornie [NG8827], *Clachan*: Jolly, cheap and cheerful *(David and Margaret Bloomfield)*; [8 Francis St], *Loch Duich*: Nice lunchtime atmosphere, good food from fresh sandwiches up inc some interesting home cooking, friendly prompt service, good coffee; bedrooms *(Joan and Tony Walker)*

☆ **Fort Augustus** [NH3709], *Lock*: Very comfortable and homely, a real pub at the foot of the loch, opp start of flight of Caledonian Canal locks; big fire, lively cheerful atmosphere, good value substantial plain food served 12-3 and 6-9 (half the room reserved for this), pleasantly faded decor, hospitable character ex-Merchant sailor landlord, soft Scottish piped music, well kept McEwans 80/-, good choice of whiskies; open all day *(June and Tony Baldwin, Mark Gillis, Ann and Bob Westbrook)*

Fort William [High St; NN1174], *Ben Nevis*: Large bar with pool table, fruit machine, pinball and big lounge; live music in big lounge; Youngers No 3, Tennents 80/-, restaurant *(D Hanley)*

☆ **Gairloch** [just off A832 nr bridge; NG8077], *Old Inn*: Usefully placed over rd from small harbour, nr splendid beach; dimpled copper tables and so forth in two small and rather dark rooms of comfortable lounge, a good few malts, Youngers No 3 and maybe Bass, popular bar food, games in public bar; piped music may be loud; picnic-table sets out by stream; open all day; bedrooms *(Michael and Harriet Robinson, BB)*

☆ **Glen Shiel** [A87 Invergarry—Kyle of Lochalsh, on Loch Cluanie – OS Sheet 33 map ref 076117; NH0711], *Cluanie*: Nice place in wild setting by Loch Cluanie, big helpings of good simple freshly prepared bar food in three knocked-together rooms with dining chairs around polished tables, overspill into restaurant; friendly and efficient staff, no pool or juke box, and now has real ale such as Orkney; video library for residents (no TV – too many mountains); children welcome; interesting gift shop, big comfortable modern bedrooms nicely furnished in pine, stunning views and good bathrooms *(Derek and Maggie Washington, A P Jeffreys, Nigel Woolliscroft)*

☆ **Glencoe** [on old Glencoe rd, behind NTS Visitor Centre – OS Sheet 42 map ref 128567; NN1256], *Clachaig*: Great setting surrounded by soaring mountains, inn doubling as mountain rescue post and very popular indeed with outdoor people (service can slow when it's crowded); public bar with two woodburners and pool, pine-panelled snug, big modern-feeling lounge bar; simple food all day, wider evening choice, lots of malt whiskies, half a dozen well kept ales such as Arrols 80/-, Caledonian Golden Promise, Maclays 80/-, Tetleys, Theakstons Old Peculier and Youngers No 3; children in no-smoking restaurant; frequent live music; bedrooms *(Dave and Jules Tuckett, Capt E P Gray, John Hazel, LYM)*

Glencoe [off A82 E of Pass], *Kingshouse*: Some way off, also alone in this stupendous mountain landscape, with simple bar food inc children's dishes, well kept McEwans 80/-, back climbers' bar with very basic furnishings, loud pop music, pool and darts, central cocktail bar with cloth banquettes and other seats around wood-effect tables; open all day; bedrooms in inn itself, and in cheaper dormitory-style bunkhouse *(John Hazel, BB)*

Glenelg [unmarked rd from Shiel Bridge (A87) towards Skye – inn tucked away by bend at road junction and easily missed; NG8119], *Glenelg*: Overlooking Skye across own beach and sea loch; public bar/snack bar with open fire even in summer, plain solid furnishings, pool table, piped music, homely pictures; good simple food in bar and nice restaurant, lots of whiskies, decent wine list, tables on back terrace; steep, narrow road to inn has spectacular views of Loch Duich; there's a short summer ferry crossing from Skye, too; bedrooms good, superb views and sensitively modernised *(Peter Watkins, Pam Stanley)*

Grantown on Spey [NJ0328], *Garth*: Friendly service, good home-made food, tables overlooking green *(Simon Pyle)*

John o' Groats [ND3773], *John o' Groats*: Not strictly a pub, but worth knowing for good food in simple and straightforward bar, lounge bar and dining room, and for wonderful situation right on harbour overlooking Orkneys; welcoming staff; bedrooms *(Gordon Smith)*

Kingussie [High St; NH7501], *Royal*: Very good inexpensive sandwiches, range of other food, two real ales, no-smoking area; decor not a big draw; open all day; bedrooms *(Ian, Kathleen and Helen Corsie)*

☆ **Kinlochewe** [NH0262], *Kinlochewe*: Welcoming public bar and lounge, good food from toasties and ploughman's up, open fire, piped classical music, Tennents 80/-; stupendous scenery all around, especially Loch Maree and Torridon mountains; bedrooms comfortable and clean *(N C Walker, Jeanne and Tom Barnes)*

☆ **Kylesku** [A894; S side of former ferry crossing; NC2234], *Kylesku*: An oasis on remote NW coast, rather spartan local bar in glorious surroundings, short choice of reasonably priced good local seafood, also sandwiches and soup; happy mix of locals and visitors, restaurant; five comfortable and peaceful if basic bedrooms, good breakfast; boatman does good loch trips *(Howard Bateman, Jeanne and Tom Barnes, June and Tony Baldwin)*

Lochinver [NC0923], *Inver Lodge*: Largish modern plush hotel on hill overlooking Lochinver harbour and sea; good bar lunches, very friendly service, well furnished bar area; bedrooms *(June and Tony Baldwin)*

Mallaig [up hill from harbour; NM6797], *Tigh-a-Chlachain*: Friendly place with good food and atmosphere; children welcome *(P G Topp)*

☆ **Melvich** [A836; NC8765], *Melvich*: Good food inc fresh wild salmon in civilised lounge bar or restaurant, relaxed atmosphere, friendly staff, peat or log fire; lovely spot, beautiful sea and coast views; bedrooms *(Alan Wilcock, Christine Davidson)*

Mey [ND2873], *Castle Arms*: Former 19th-c coaching inn, tastefully refurbished in understated stripped pine and so forth; shortish choice of good usual bar food, wider choice for high teas and dinners in dining room, very pleasant helpful service; photographs of Queen Mother during her Caithness holidays; bedrooms in back extension, well placed for N coast of Caithness *(Alan Wilcock, Christine Davidson)*

☆ **Plockton** [Innes St; NG8033], *Creag Nan Darach*: Fresh well cooked food with real chips and veg done just right, McEwans 80/-, good service; bedrooms recently upgraded *(David and Margaret Bloomfield, John and Molly Knowles)*

Poolewe [fronting Corriness Guest House; NB8580], *Choppys*: Not a pub, a restaurant with simple modern bar (which has pool table), well worth knowing for good well presented food at attractive prices; very friendly service, plain decor *(Ian, Kathleen and Helen Corsie)*

Portmahomack [NH9184], *Caledonian*: Welcoming local with friendly cheerful service; keg beer, karaoke *(Paul and Ursula Randall)*

Shiel Bridge [NG9318], *Kintail Lodge*: Good food inc local game, wild salmon and own smokings, also children's helpings; restaurant in attractive conservatory with magnificent loch views; plain bar has own eating area, also well kept Theakstons Best on handpump, plenty of malt whiskies; good value big bedrooms *(Nigel and Helen Aplin)*

☆ **Spean Bridge** [A82 7 miles N; NN2491], *Letterfinlay Lodge*: Extensive comfortably modern main bar with popular lunchtime buffet and usual games, small smart cocktail bar, no-smoking restaurant; good malt whiskies, friendly service, children and dogs welcome, pleasant lochside grounds, own boats for fishing; clean and comfortable bedrooms, good breakfasts *(Tony and Joan Walker, P G Topp, Jeanne and Tom Barnes, LYM)*

Strathcarron [NG9442], *Strathcarron*: Spotlessly clean under new management, good beers, bar food; bedrooms *(N C Walker)*

Strathy [A836 Trugue—Thurso; NC8365], *Strathy*: New owners transforming this isolated wayside inn into a pleasant and welcoming pub – good stopover for fishermen and explorers; simply furnished and decorated small bars, Tennents 80/-, decent if limited freshly prepared bar food, restaurant, reasonable prices; bedrooms small but comfortable and clean *(Paul and Ursula Randall, E A George)*

Talladale [A832 Kinlochewe—Gairloch; NG8970], *Loch Maree*: Pleasant well stocked bar with marvellous old barman; bedrooms *(Jeanne and Tom Barnes)*

Tongue [A836; NC5957], *Ben Loyal*: Superb location with lovely views up to Ben Loyal and out over Kyle of Tongue; good value bar meals (stop 2 prompt), Tennents 80/-, restaurant serving taste of Scotland food, much of it home-grown; traditional live music in lounge bar in summer; comfortable good value bedrooms *(Alan Wilcock, Christine Davidson, E A George)*

LOTHIAN

Aberlady [NT4679], *Kilspindie House*: Bar lunches and high teas make good use of local produce, esp fish inc superb trout *(Bill and Sylvia Trotter)*

Balerno [Johnsburn Rd; NT1666], *Johnsburn House:* Handsome Scottish-baronial mansion with ornate ceiling by Robert Lorimer, log fire in beamed bar with Timothy Taylors Landlord, Theakstons Best and lots of quickly changing guest beers, panelled dining lounge with food inc shellfish, game and vegetarian, more formal evening dining rooms *(Anon)*

☆ **Cramond Bridge** [A90 N of Edinburgh; NT1875], *Cramond Brig:* Well run family stop recently bailed out in neo-Victorian books and bric-a-brac style, bar food all day, well kept McEwans 80/-, restaurant; children very welcome, piped music may be obtrusive; bedrooms *(Robert and Gladys Flux, LYM)*

☆ **Dirleton** [village green; NT5184], *Castle:* Good helpings of imaginative reasonably priced food esp fish and well filled sandwiches, and well kept real ale such as Belhaven or McEwans 80/-, in pleasant unpretentious but comfortable lounge; friendly service, restaurant; attractive spot in pretty village on green opp castle; bedrooms *(Ian Phillips)*

☆ **Dirleton**, *Open Arms:* Small comfortable hotel, not a place for just a drink, but good for bar food inc huge open sandwiches and well presented hot dishes such as tender venison casserole with good fresh veg; welcoming service, lovely little sitting room with good open fire, fine position facing castle; comfortable bedrooms *(Ian Phillips)*

☆ **East Linton** [5 Bridge St; NT5977], *Drovers:* Good imaginative bistro-style food inc fresh local fish and well cooked veg in small and attractive cleanly renovated pub dating back to 18th c; young, enthusiastic and welcoming licensees and staff, interesting changing real ales in good condition, unusual decor, upstairs restaurant *(R J Archbold, W F Coghill)*

☆ **Edinburgh** [Lindsay Rd, Newhaven; NT2574], *Peacock:* Good food esp fresh seafood in smart, stylish and plushly comfortable pub with conservatory-style back room leading to garden, well kept McEwans 80/-; very popular, best to book in evenings and Sun lunchtime; open all day; children welcome *(David Logan, LYM)*

☆ **Edinburgh** [James Ct; by 495 Lawnmarket], *Jolly Judge:* Interesting and comfortable pub in basement of 16th-c tenement, with traditional fruit-and-flower-painted ceiling; quickly served lunchtime bar meals and all-day snacks, Caledonian 80/- and Ind Coope Burton on handpump, changing malt whiskies, hot drinks, friendly service, lovely fire; piped music, games machine; children allowed at lunchtime in eating area; closed Sun lunchtime; space outside in summer *(Mark Walker, Mr and Mrs S Ashcroft, LYM)*

☆ **Edinburgh** [152 Rose St], *Kenilworth:* Friendly Edwardian pub with ornate high ceiling, carved woodwork, etched mirrors and windows, not many seats; central bar with Allied real ales and a guest such as Marstons Pedigree, hot drinks inc espresso, good generous bar food lunchtime and evening; quick friendly service; piped music, games machine, TV, maybe Sun papers, back family room; space outside in summer, open all day *(Mark Walker, John Fazakerley, Spider Newth, Ian Phillips)*

☆ **Edinburgh** [55 Rose St], *Rose Street Brewery:* Main attraction is the malt-extract beer they brew on the premises, mild-flavoured though quite potent Auld Reekie 80/- and stronger sticky 90/- – tiny brewery can be seen from comfortable partly panelled upstairs lounge (closed at quiet times); downstairs low-beams-boards-and-flagstones saloon, also panelled, open all day, with well reproduced pop music from its CD juke box, machines; usual bar food, good service, tea and coffee, live music some evenings *(Ross Lockley, Walter M Reid, David Warrellow, Nick and Meriel Cox, Bill and Lydia Ryan, Mark Walker, BB)*

☆ **Edinburgh** [Rose St, corner of Hanover St], *Milnes:* Large bar with another downstairs, done out 1992 in lots of dark wood, bare floorboards, cask tables and old-fashioned decor; lots of S&N real ales with a guest or two such as Burton Bridge and Marstons Pedigree, good range of snacks and hot food (not Sun evening) such as various pies charged by size; very busy but cheerful quick aproned staff; mixed customers, lively atmosphere *(Jim Penman, Spider Newth)*

Edinburgh [1 Princes St], *Balmoral:* Corner lobby of the former North British Hotel at the hub of the town, relaxing calm, thick carpets, deep armchairs, welcoming staff; good hot rolls filled with daily roast (by no means cheap); piped music a bit redundant; bedrooms *(Walter M Reid, Jim Penman)*; [Rose St], *Bar 37:* Small narrow bar with red flock wallpaper, banquettes, cheap snacks like pre-prepared rolls and pies warmed behind bar *(Jim Penman)*; [18-20 Grassmarket], *Beehive:* Good range of well kept real ales in civilised comfortable lounge with cheerful atmosphere, good value food noon-6pm, upstairs restaurant *(John Fazakerley, Bill and Lydia Ryan, P Woodward, LYM)*; *Bull & Bush:* Edwardian-style pub, red plush banquettes and stools, prints on walls, fake gas lamps, split-level food area *(Ian Phillips, Mark Walker)*; [Young St], *Cambridge:* Series of comfortable small rooms on quiet Georgian street, good food, decent range of beers like Arrols, Deuchars and Ind Coope Burton, not widely used by tourists *(Walter M Reid)*; [435 Lawnmarket], *Deacon Brodies:* Entertainingly commemorating the notorious councillor who was the model for R L Stevenson's Dr Jekyll and Mr Hyde, and like Dr Guillotine was eventually executed on his own brainchild; limited decent food inc some unusual home-made dishes, Arrols 80/-, comfortable leather-chair upstairs lounge *(Thomas Nott, BB)*; [Market St], *Doric:* Verging on being café/restaurant, but has full bar with well kept Deuchars and Maclays 70/- as well as wide range of good food, decent wines and good mix of customers; relaxing atmosphere on first floor *(Jenny and Brian Seller)*; [Royal Mile – last pub on right heading up to Castle], *Ensign Ewart*: Comfortable old-world pub with lots of pictures and theme on the eponymous soldier and Waterloo; Caledonian 80/-, Deuchars IPA, Orkney Dark Island and Alloa ales, large range of whiskies, decent helpings of usual food lunchtime and some summer evenings; juke box, fruit machine, folk music Thurs/Sun *(Mark Walker)*; [26-28 Shandwick Pl], *Grosvenor*: Tasteful modern decor, well kept McEwans 80/- on handpump, coffee; very busy Fri evening *(Spider Newth)*; [Cockburn St], *Malt Shovel*: At least ten Allied and other real ales, good helpings of reasonably priced lunchtime food in separate area; friendly service, lots of seats, though small serving area; piped music, machines, TV, occasional evening entertainment *(Mark Walker, Bill and Lydia Ryan)*; [Young St], *Oxford*: Unspoiled town pub with busy friendly front bar, quieter back room with tables and chairs for talking, reading or writing; lino floor, no gentrification, real Scottish pub food – mutton pies, pickled eggs, Forfar bridies; good range of beers inc Belhaven and Courage *(Walter M Reid)*; [Rose St], *Paddys*: Fair-sized open-plan pub with friendly service and locals, lunchtime food, Arrols 80/- *(Jim Penman)*; [Royal Mile], *Royal Mile Tavern*: Plush comfortable lounge bar good for a Royal Mile rest, good service if not rushed, friendly service, McEwans 80/- on tall fount and a guest ale, good reasonably priced food in upstairs restaurant, snacks in bar; piped music, fruit machine *(Mark Walker)*; [Giles St, Leith], *Scottish Malt Whisky Society*: Downstairs Vintners Room bar/restaurant, upstairs Members Room (theoretically members only, but smile); lunchtime sandwiches and maybe soup, a limited range of general drinks, but the Society is devoted to the provision of cask strength single malt whiskies of the highest quality *(Thomas Nott)*; [The Causeway, out at Duddingston], *Sheep Heid*: Old-fashioned rather upmarket ex-coaching inn in lovely spot beyond Holyroodhouse, below Arthur's Seat; interesting pictures and fine rounded bar counter in main room, Tennents 80/- on handpump, no-smoking area, newspapers; piped music; restaurant (children allowed here), pretty garden with summer barbecues, skittle alley; open all day, can get crowded *(Ian Phillips, JW, CW, LYM)*; [Northumberland St, by entrance to Dublin St Mews], *Star*: In heart of Georgian New Town, but local village atmosphere; homely interior in light oak panelling, guest beers such as Bass or Caledonian 80/-, maybe hot toddy or hot honey rum punch in cold weather *(Walter M Reid)*; [118 Biggar Rd (A702)], *Steadings*: Popular modern pub with good choice of Scottish beers and Timothy Taylors Landlord on handpump, good generous food *(Nigel Pritchard, Robert and Gladys Flux)*; [Waverley stn], *Talisman*: Fair-sized station bar open 7am-12.45am, friendly service, banquettes on tiled floor, bare bricks, all clean and pleasant; fruit machines and TV not obtrusive, juke box can be a bit loud *(Jim Penman)*;

☆ Gifford [NT5368], *Goblin Ha'*: Good village pub, welcoming and pretty, with well kept Bass and an S&N beer such as Theakstons in plainly furnished bar, good home cooking, quick service, jolly atmosphere; boules in good garden with Sat evening jazz; bedrooms *(Mrs J Ashley)*
Haddington [NT5174], *George*: Hotel bar with well kept Belhaven 80/- and Morlands Old Speckled Hen, above-average food inc interesting seafood and other dishes, friendly service; children welcome; comfortable bedrooms, pretty market town *(Mrs S le Bert-Francis)*
Longniddry [NT4476], *Longniddry Inn*: Series of three or four local stone cottages with various comfortable and welcoming bars, decent food *(Ian Phillips)*
☆ Queensferry [South Queensferry; NT1278], *Hawes*: Comfortably modernised lounge bar with fine views of the Forth bridges, featured famously in *Kidnapped*; good choice of good value standard food from efficient food counter, well kept Arrols 80/-, Ind Coope Burton and guest beers such as Caledonian 80/- from tall founts, games in small public bar, no-smoking family room, restaurant, children welcome; tables on back lawn with play area; bedrooms *(Ian Phillips, Robert and Gladys Flux, LYM)*
Ratho [NT1370], *Bridge*: Extended 18th-c pub by partly restored Union Canal, with own canal boats (doing trips for the disabled, among others) and waterside garden with good play area; open all day from noon, well kept Belhaven, decent range of food inc vegetarian, good children's dishes and tactful choice of food for those with smaller appetites, pleasant helpful and chatty staff *(Dave Irving, Roger Bellingham)*

STRATHCLYDE
☆ Ardentinny [NS1887], *Ardentinny Hotel*: Well run comfortable family hotel with lovely views of Loch Long from waterside bars and garden (dogs allowed out here), welcoming staff, consistently good often inventive home-made bar food inc local seafood, Belhaven real ale, own moorings, Harry Lauder bar with appropriate memorabilia; no-smoking evening restaurant, children allowed in eating area; lavatories labelled Gulls and Buoys; bedrooms, cl winter *(Walter Reid, Ian and Deborah Carrington, Michael and Harriet Robinson, LYM)*
Barrhead [Lochlibo Rd (A736); NS5058], *Dalmeny Park*: Pleasant gardens a real find in this largely built-up area, good choice of good value bar food, pleasant helpful staff; bedrooms pleasantly furnished, well cooked flexible breakfast *(M E and G C Cowley)*
☆ Bothwell [27 Hamilton Rd (B7071); a mile from M74 junction 5, via A725; NS7058], *Cricklewood*: Smartly refurbished dining pub with good bar food, S&N real ale, pleasant restful atmosphere, neat decorations inc old carved wooden trade signs on stairway, complete sets of cigarette cards in gents';

open all day; bedrooms *(P Corris)*

Bridge of Orchy [off A82; NN2939], *Bridge of Orchy*: Good service, good food, warm atmosphere, friendly welcome and particularly well kept Caledonian 80/- on handpump; bedrooms *(Tom Espley)*

Clachan of Glendaruel [A886 W of Dunoon; NR9985], *Glendaruel*: Welcoming old coaching inn in particularly attractive part of Argyll; small freshly decorated lounge bar, larger public bar; Tennents 70/- and 80/-, salmon and seasonal fishing on nearby River Rull; bedrooms *(Walter Reid)*

☆ **Connel** [NM9133], *Falls of Lora*: Small well run hotel with very good civilised pub facilities, across rd from Loch Etive; well presented food, several spacious and well kept bar areas inc no-smoking ones, sturdily comfortable cane armchairs, plush banquettes in bays, lots of brass and copper, tubs of plants forming booths, 1920s-style lamps, big watercolour landscapes, and free-standing Scandinavian-style log fire; bedrooms comfortable and good value *(Capt F A Bland, LYM)*

☆ **Connel** [North Connel; NM9134], *Lochnell Arms*: Attractive hotel with cosy public bar, small lounge, conservatory extension; decent straightforward food inc good seafood, friendly service, bric-a-brac, plants, beautiful view over Loch Etive; waterside garden; bedrooms *(Ian Baillie, Jean and Douglas Troup)*

Dalmally [NN1627], *Glenorchy Lodge*: Good hotel bar that welcomes non-residents, well liked by locals, good range of promptly served bar meals *(Mrs K E Cripps)*

Dunure [just off A719 SW of Ayr; NS2515], *Anchorage*: Well cooked reasonably priced food with splendid sauces *(F J Willy)*

☆ **Glasgow** [12 Ashton Lane], *Ubiquitous Chip*: Good busy public bar, minimal decoration apart from some stained glass, real ale, wide choice of malt whiskies, some decent wines by the glass, daily changing home-cooked lunchtime food in upstairs dining area inc vegetarian dishes, peat fire; wider choice in downstairs restaurant opening on to court-yard, with outstanding wines; quintessentially Glasgow, with lots of university staff and students *(Walter Reid, Ian Phillips)*

☆ **Glasgow** [83 Hutcheson St], *Rab Ha's*: Same family as Babbity Bowster – see main entries; civilised and friendly dark-panelled bar in sensitively converted Georgian town house, well cooked seafood in bar and basement restaurant, informal atmosphere, intermittent robust live music but otherwise relatively quiet; McEwans 80/- real ale, good service; bedrooms elegant and immaculate *(Michael Sandy)*

Glasgow [Pollok Park; NS5562], *Burrell Collection Bar*: Lunch room on ground floor of museum has a corner or end that might be called a pub, with surprisingly tasty fresh sandwiches, sufficient range of beer and wine, nice views of garden and no music *(Ralph A Raimi)*; [10 Kilmarnock Rd, Shawlands; NS5661], *Granary*: Trendy designer pub, recently refurbished, good Mexican food, overhead toy train and cognate idiosyncracies

(Christine and Malcolm Ingram); [266 Bath St], *Griffin*: Big Edwardian corner pub, cheap and cheerful bar food, fast efficient waitress service, very busy at lunchtime *(Ian Phillips)*; [North St, Charing Cross], *Mitchells*: At meal times more restaurant than pub, with good food; several Scottish ales and one or two English ones; open all day *(Ian Phillips)*; [154 Hope St], *Pot Still*: Comfortable tall pub with slender pillars and good split-level effect, good range of malt whiskies, usual bar food (lunchtime more extensive than evening), Youngers No 3 *(Michael Sandy, LYM)*; [11 Exchange Pl], *Rogano*: Not really a pub but a nice place to eat in Glasgow; lovingly restored and preserved 1930s art deco interior, good cocktails at Oyster bar on ground floor with good if slightly pricy restaurant, downstairs café cheaper but good too – emphasis on fish; good wines *(Walter Reid)*; [Airport], *Tap & Spile*: Concessions to traditional pub design blended with good use of space and light to create open and relaxing atmosphere; lots of real ales like Archers, Arrols, Caledonian, Greene King, Ind Coope Burton, Lees and so forth; filled french bread *(Walter M Reid)*

☆ **Houston** [Main St; NS4166], *Fox & Hounds*: Comfortable village pub with well kept Greenmantle and McEwans 70/- on handpump, clean plush hunting-theme lounge, comfortable seats by fire, attentive bar staff, wide range of food upstairs, good filled rolls downstairs, also sophisticated restaurant; separate livelier bar with video juke box and pool; open all day – busy evening, more civilised daytime *(Owen McGhee, Walter Reid)*

Hunters Quay [NS1879], *Royal Marine*: Large lounge bar in half-timbered building opp Western Ferries jetty, former HQ of Royal Clyde Yacht Club; good range of reasonably priced food all day inc good home-made soups, local salmon, good choice of malt whiskies, McEwans beers; very quick service even when busy; bedrooms *(Deborah and Ian Carrington)*

☆ **Inveraray** [A83 just S], *Loch Fyne*: Good clean family-run hotel, friendly and pleasant, good choice of beers, good basic bar food from sandwiches to steak; stunning views, big garden, pleasant comfortable bedrooms *(Brian Murphy)*

☆ **Johnstone** [High St; NS4263], *Coanes*: Thriving atmosphere in old-fashioned oak-balustered bar with well kept ales such as Bass, Boddingtons, Caledonian Merman, Orkney Dark Island and Shepherd Neame Spitfire, malt whiskies inc malt of the month, good friendly staff, above-average food; larger plush lounge popular with young *(Owen McGhee, Walter Reid)*

☆ **Kilchrenan** [B845 S of Taynuilt; NN0222], *Kilchrenan Inn*: Useful local with fresh pine decor, welcoming service, good home cooking using fresh ingredients, quiet relaxed atmosphere (no TV, darts, music or games); charming spot with magnificent views of nearby Loch Awe *(Anon)*

Kilcreggan [NS2380], *Creggan*: Enjoyable

atmosphere, effusive welcome; Bass, bar food (*J R Smylie*)

☆ Kilmartin [NR8398], *Kilmartin Hotel*: Unpretentious two-room bar with interesting decorations, medley of furnishings inc attractive carved settles, dozens of malt whiskies, usual bar food inc vegetarian, friendly service, children allowed till 8, folk music Fri/Sat, restaurant; open all day; bedrooms (*Iain Grant, LYM*)

☆ Kilmelford [NM8412], *Cuilfail*: Attractive old inn with cheerful stripped-stone pubby bar, welcoming family service, good value food inc imaginative home-cooked dishes in inner eating room with light wood furnishings, well kept McEwans and Youngers No 3, good range of malt whiskies, charming garden across road; comfortable bedrooms (*Peter J Gannon, David Mervin, Mrs Pat Crabb, Roger and Christine Mash, LYM*)

Larkhall [39 Millheugh; NS7651], *Apple Bank*: Pub pleasant and friendly, decent food inc good cheap home-made soup (*TBB*)

Lochaweside [B840; NN1227], *Portsonachan*: This lochside fishing inn, formerly highly rated by us, has now become too absorbed in the time-share development around it to be such an attractive stop for casual visitors (*LYM*)

Lochgilphead [Poltalach St; NR8687], *Comm*: Traditional west Highland bar with unique bar fittings in decorated glass and sycamore; two coal fires, friendly atmosphere, good range of whiskies (*C Platts*)

Lochwinnoch [Lares Rd; NS3558], *Mossend*: Standard Brewers Fayre family dining pub with efficient reasonably priced catering (good home-made soup), four rotating real ales such as Flowers, Greene King, Marstons Pedigree, Morlands Old Speckled Hen; playground; good walking area (*Tom McEwan, Walter Reid*)

Oban [Stephenson St; NM8630], *Lorne*: Well restored friendly Victorian pub with tile decoration and central bar with ornate brasswork; freshly prepared food inc wild salmon, haggis, local seafood and so forth, well kept McEwans 80/-, Theakstons and Youngers No 3 (*David Warrellow*)

Paisley [100 Neilson Rd; NS4864], *Tannahills*: Good lounge bar, good lunchtime food (no chips), real ale, malt whiskies (*Iain Wylie*)

☆ Symington [Main St; just off A77 Ayr—Kilmarnock; NS3831], *Wheatsheaf*: Charming and cosy 18th-c pub inc pretty village, consistently good original food esp fish and local produce, Belhaven beers, friendly quick service; tables in garden (*Christine and Malcolm Ingram*)

Tarbert [Bardmore Rd; NR8467], *Victoria*: Friendly and efficient pub overlooking harbour, imaginative well prepared food with starters like oak-smoked venison slices with melon, main courses such as home-made lasagne or lemon sole (*Mrs Pat Crabb*); [A83 a mile S], *West Loch*: Old white stone-fronted inn overlooking loch, convenient for Islay ferry; McEwans beers, good choice of reasonably

priced bar food, friendly service, restaurant using local produce; simple bedrooms (*Deborah and Ian Carrington, LYM*)

☆ Taynuilt [a mile past village, which is signed off A85; NN0030], *Polfearn*: Very picturesque setting by loch with Ben Cruachan towering over, well kept beers, relaxed atmosphere and friendly service, good food inc outstanding mussels; bedrooms (*J R and H Soulsby*)

TAYSIDE

☆ Bridge of Cally [NO1451], *Bridge of Cally*: Good atmosphere in straightforward friendly and comfortable bar, sensible choice of good value food inc outstanding ploughman's; bedrooms, attractive area (*John Oddey, John Whitehead*)

☆ Broughty Ferry [behind lifeboat stn; NO4630], *Ship*: Consistently good generous food in pretty upstairs dining room with fantastic view, upmarket decor, considerate staff; very friendly (*Susan and John Douglas*)

☆ Crieff [N, signed off A85, A822; NN8562], *Glenturret Distillery*: Not a pub, but good adjunct to one of the best whisky-distillery tours; good value whiskies in big plain bar/dining area with tasty sandwiches, good generous Highland soups, stews and pies, and knock-out Glenturret ice cream from self-service food counter; kindly staff, pleasant views, luxurious lavatories (*Ross Lockley, Joyce and Stephen Stackhouse, Susan and John Douglas, R M Macnaughton*)

☆ Dundee [Brook St; NO4030], *Royal Oak*: Friendly and unusual pub with sombre dark green decor and surprising range of really interesting reasonably priced food esp curries in bar and restaurant; well kept Allied ales inc Ind Coope Burton, courteous friendly staff (*Neil Townend, Paul and Ursual Randall*)

Dundee [142 Perth Rd], *McGonagalls*: Busy and lively, well kept Belhaven; popular with university students (*Chris and Anne Fluck*); [Commercial St], *Mercantile*: Old building in town centre, panelling, stand-up drinking area around bar, seating in sort of gallery overlooking it, good inexpensive food; very friendly helpful staff (*M J V Kemp*); [1 Constitution Rd/Wards Rd], *Number 1*: Friendly corner pub with comfortable banquettes in roomy if rather dark lounge, good cheap food (*Ian Phillips*)

Dunkeld [NO0243], *Atholl Arms*: Nice old-fashioned country hotel with hard-working welcoming new owners, food in relaxing lounge bar, keg beer; bedrooms (*Walter Reid*)

Glenfarg [A912; nr M90 junction 9; NO1310], *Bein*: Well kept McEwans and Theakstons beers, good varied menu with changing daily special; can be crowded weekends; bedrooms (*A Matthew*)

Harrietfield [A85 N of Methven; NN9829], *Drumtochty*: Wonderful untouched two-bar country inn with lots of bric-a-brac esp whisky advertising mirrors, own front bowling green (*Nic Armitage*)

☆ Kenmore [NN7745], *Kenmore*: Civilised and

quietly old-fashioned small hotel in very pretty village setting, long landscape poem composed here written in Burns' own handwriting on residents' lounge wall, clean, friendly and smart back bar, lively separate barn bar, lovely views from back terrace; good bar food, helpful staff, restaurant, Tay fishing, fine walks; comfortable bedrooms *(Susan and John Douglas, M E and G R Keene, LYM)*

Meikleour [on A984; NO1539], *Meikleour*: Relaxed friendly old coaching inn with comfortable public bar and attractive chintzy lounge, both with open fires; good bar food inc fine range of open sandwiches, Maclays 70/-; near famous 100ft beech hedge planted in 1746 *(Walter Reid)*

Memus [NO4259], *Drovers*: Warm and friendly pub with roaring old-fashioned fire and good food *(Mrs P Burvill)*

Montrose [George St; NO7157], *George*: Plush comfortable lounge, open fire, Flowers Original, Marstons Pedigree, Theakstons XB and Whitbreads Castle Eden on handpump, big helpings of reasonably priced good food, back no-smoking area, adjoining restaurant; piped music, TV; bedrooms *(Mark Walker)*

☆ **Perth** [15 South St; NO1123], *Greyfriars*: Welcoming simply decorated bar with prints of Perth, newspapers to read, unusual guest beers on handpump, reasonably priced bar food; small restaurant upstairs *(Julian Holland)*

Scone [A94; NO1226], *Scone Arms*: Welcoming local atmosphere, good value lunches; doing well under newish owners *(Neil Townend)*

St Fillans [NN6924], *Achray*: Stunning lochside position, good friendly service, good varied reasonably priced food esp puddings, extensive wine list; bedrooms *(John Doig)*

Stanley [NO1033], *Tayside*: Fishing hotel where staff take a genuine interest in the day's fishing news, banquette-lined bar with photographs of remarkable catches, remarkable stuffed fish in the hall; good current reports on food and bedrooms *(Walter Reid)*

THE ISLANDS

Arran

Brodick [Esplanade; NS0136], *Kingsley*: Well run bar with good home-made soup and other home-cooked dishes, good beers, around 40 malt whiskies, wide choice of wines, pleasant bay views; bedrooms *(Ken Richards)*; *Ormidale*: Large helpings of sensibly priced interesting food inc lots of daily specials, well kept McEwans 70/-, lots of malt whiskies; bedrooms *(Nick and Alison Davies)*

Benbecula

Creagorry [NF7948], *Creagorry*: Pleasantly refurbished modern hotel lounge, S&N beers, entertaining if rough-and-ready public bar, decent varied bar food, friendly bar staff; bedrooms *(Nigel Woolliscroft)*

Eriskay

Eriskay [NF7910], *Am Politician*: Virtual museum dedicated to the sinking of *The Politician* of *Whisky Galore* fame – the boat is still visible at low tide; good for drinking enthusiasts, good local seafood; original bottles of the salvaged whisky on show – they collect around £1,500 when they come up for sale *(Nigel Woolliscroft)*

Gigha

Gigha [NR6450], *Gigha Hotel*: The island's only pub, well kept, nicely furnished and clean, in lovely spot overlooking the Sound and Kintyre; pine-decor public bar, sofas in drawing-room bar, good service; bedrooms *(Margaret and Fred Punter, Mrs Pat Crabb)*

Harris

Tarbert [NB1400], *Isle of Harris*: Good value bar food served all day in pleasant front bar, modern furnishings, good prompt service; bedrooms *(Ian and Deborah Carrington)*

Islay

Bowmore [Shore St; NR3159], *Lochside*: Friendly family-run hotel, decent food inc local fish and lamb and home-made puddings in bar or restaurant, both with lovely views over Loch Indaal; good choice of malt whiskies, keg beers; bedrooms *(Deborah and Ian Carrington)*

Port Askaig [NR4268], *Port Askaig*: Glorious water views, excitement of ferry arriving; two basic bars, food inc good Sun lunch buffet, tables out on big stretch of grass; bedrooms, self-catering across road *(Mrs A Storm)*

Lewis

Stornoway [4 South Beach St; NB4233], *Caledonian*: Hotel bar with wide range of decent bar food, modern furnishings, pleasant staff; bedrooms *(Ian and Deborah Carrington)*

North Uist

☆ **Claddach Kirkibost** [NF7766], *Westford*: Very old inn in windswept desolate spot, great character with local concerts, fiddling and singing; good original home-made food inc local seafood in two small pine-fitted rooms, enterprising dinner menu; big back public bar; handy for RSPB reserve at Dalranald, landlord helpful about local walks and archaeology; bedrooms *(Nigel Woolliscroft, Mr MacGwire, Hayes Durlston)*

Orkney

Harray [HY2916], *Murkister*: Good pub and restaurant food, good friendly Scottish atmosphere, superb views; bedrooms *(Ian, Kathleen and Helen Corsie)*

☆ **Stromness** [HY2509], *Ferry*: Busiest pub here, very popular with locals and diving groups exploring the German fleet in Scapa Flow – so bar can be rather noisy and smoky; wide choice of good fast reasonably priced food inc good fish and steak, adjoining restaurant, McEwans 80/- and Orkney real ales, friendly staff and atmosphere; very handy for Scrabster ferry; bedrooms *(A and M Jones, Ian, Kathleen and Helen Corsie, Keith Stevens)*

Shetland
Bressay [HU5243], *Maryfield House*: Wide choice of good food inc lots of seafood, all reasonably priced; very welcoming and friendly; comfortable bedrooms *(Else Smaaskjaer, Kay Smith)*

Skye
Ardvasar [A851 towards Broadford; NG6203], *Clan Donald Centre*: More cafeteria/restaurant than pub, but good food, efficient friendly service and ubiquitous McEwans *(John and Elspeth Howell)*
Culnaknock [13 miles N of Portree on Staffin rd; NG5162], *Glenview*: Attractive whitewashed house in lovely position below the Old Man of Storr, recently reopened under new owners, with good food inc delicious fresh salmon and home-made ice cream, friendly efficient service, good view; cosy bar; bedrooms newly and very comfortably furnished, good filling breakfasts *(Richard Dyson)*
Dunvegan [NG2548], *Misty Isle*: Good location, friendly staff, well presented simple food, fine views; very busy summer evenings; bedrooms *(Ron Corbett, Nigel Woolliscroft)*
Flodigarry [nr Staffin; NG4572], *Flodigarry*: Superb views of sea and highlands, bar with Moorish design, conservatory, reasonably priced bar food all day every day inc fine haggis toastie, Bass on handpump; some live music, Flora MacDonald connections *(Mr and Mrs G Hart)*
Portree [on harbourside; NG4843], *Pier*:

Down-to-earth fishermen's bar on harbourside, very simple flagstoned bar, keg beers, restaurant meals fish-based and served in huge helpings; very welcoming landlord, occasional live music, pipers during Skye games week; bedrooms good value, clean; family rooms *(Nigel Woolliscroft)*
☆ **Sligachan** [A850 Broadford—Portree, junction with A863; NG4830], *Sligachan*: Remote inn, capacious, welcoming and comfortable, with fast food in huge new modern bar separating the original big basic climbers' and walkers' bar from the plusher more sedate hotel side; a real ale brewed for the pub, particularly fresh seafood, restaurant; very lively some nights; children welcome, big campsite opp; bedrooms good value; closed winter *(Bob Smith, Ian and Deborah Carrington, James Nunns, Nigel Woolliscroft, Tom Espley, John and Elspheth Howell, BB)*
Uig [NG3963], *Ferry*: Tiny but friendly saloon bar with reasonably priced varied food; good value bedrooms, comfortable and bright, overlooking pier and water *(John and Elspeth Howell, Nigel Woolliscroft, BB)*

South Uist
Loch Carnan [signed off A865 S of Creagorry; NF8044], *Orasay*: Good local seafood in modern lounge (drinks only if you're eating); bedrooms *(Nigel Woolliscroft)*
☆ **Pollachar** [NF7414], *Pollachar*: Incredible setting on seashore with dolphins, porpoises and seals; 17th-c inn now fully modernised, with big public bar, separate dining room, good bar meals; very friendly staff and locals (all Gaelic speaking), fantastic views to Eriskay and Barra; eleven bedrooms *(Nigel Woolliscroft)*

People don't usually tip bar staff (unlike in a really smart hotel). If you want to thank a barman – dealing with a really large party say, or special friendliness – offer him a drink. Common expressions are: 'And what's yours?' or 'And won't you have something for yourself?'.

Wales

Quite a few new entries here, or pubs bouncing back after an absence, include the friendly Black Lion in its fine setting at Abergorlech, the Carew Inn at Carew (good food – a more stylish place than when we knew it before), the friendly and individual old Harp up at Old Radnor (new people settling in well now), the lively Ferry on the waterside at Pembroke Ferry (good fresh fish), the civilised Clytha Arms near Raglan (good reliable food), the interesting new Armstrong Arms at Stackpole, and the enterprising Nantyffin Cider Mill near Crickhowell. Both these last two pubs qualify for our Food Award; other Welsh pubs and inns which stand out for a good meal are the Penhelig Arms in Aberdovey, the Ty Gwyn in Betws y Coed, the Bear in Crickhowell, the Walnut Tree at Llandewi Skirrid, the Queens Head at Llandudno Junction, and the Groes at Tyn y Groes. The quality of the food at the Walnut Tree does stand head and shoulders above the competition, and it can't be beaten for a meal of restaurant quality and style. However, for a really enjoyable bar meal in more interestingly pubby surroundings we choose the Bear in Crickhowell as Wales Dining Pub of the Year. Other pubs here currently doing particularly well include the engagingly old-fashioned Halfway Inn near Aberystwyth, the handsome Olde Bulls Head in Beaumaris, the ancient Blue Anchor at East Aberthaw, the cosy and friendly Britannia at Halkyn, the very individual Pen-y-Gwryd up in the mountains near Llanberis, the cheery Llanerch in Llandrindod Wells, the atmospheric and remote old Cerrigllwydion Arms at Llanynys, the Crown at Llwyndafydd (stands out in an otherwise unrewarding area), the well established Griffin at Llyswen, the very cheerful Grapes at Maentwrog, the warm-hearted and very well run Open Hearth in Pontypool, the well placed Ship on Red Wharf Bay, and the bustling Royal Hotel in Usk. A good few pubs here qualify for our new Beer Award. Drinks prices in Wales are just a shade below the national average, after rising slightly more than average this last year: the cheapest places we found were the interesting Old House at Llangynwyd and the Open Hearth at Pontypool (which has a splendid range). There are generally savings to be made in pubs getting beers from local smaller breweries such as Brains, Crown Buckley and Felinfoel rather than from the national chains. In general, food prices in Welsh pubs are rather higher than average, with good hot main dishes tending to cost at least £5, and a ploughman's nearer £4 than £3. The Llanerch in Llandrindod Wells stands out for its very low food prices. In the Lucky Dip sections at the end of the chapter, pubs currently standing out are, on Anglesey, the Liverpool Arms at Menai Bridge; in Clwyd, the Sportsmans Arms at Bylchau, Mountain View near Colwyn Bay, Boat at Erbistock, Hanmer Arms in Hanmer, White Lion at Llanelian yn Rhos, Druid at Llanferres, Red Lion at Llansannan and Sun at Rhewl; in Dyfed, the New Inn at Amroth, Druidstone near Broad Haven, Pendre at Cilgerran, Dyffryn Arms at Cwm Gwaun, Georges in Haverfordwest, Paxton Arms in Llanarthney, and Plough at Rhosmaen; in Glamorgan, the Pelican at Ogmore (Mid), Star in Dinas Powis (South), Joiners Arms at Bishopston, Greyhound at Oldwalls and King Arthur at Reynoldston (West); in Gwynedd, the White Horse at Capel Garmon, Llew Coch at

Dinas Mawddwy, Priory near Llanrwst, George III at Penmaenpool, Ship in Porthmadoc, Cwellyn Arms at Rhyd Ddu and Golden Fleece at Tremadog; and in Powys, the Dolfor Inn, Royal Oak at Gladestry, Old Black Lion in Hay, Dragons Head at Llangenny, Red Lion at Llangorse, Glansevern Arms near Llangurig (a favourite of many), Coach & Horses and Red Lion both at Llangynidr and Star at Talybont on Usk. As we have inspected the great majority of these we can vouch for their quality.

ABERDOVEY   (Gwynedd)   SN6296 Map 6

Penhelig Arms 🍴 ⇌ 🍷
Opp Penhelig railway station

Most people seem to come to this mainly 18th-c hotel in the summer, when you can sit outside by the harbour wall, and while this is quite understandable, it's a shame more people don't visit in winter too, when the views across the Dyfi estuary are just as dramatic but the atmosphere is altogether snugger. The friendly little original beamed bar has been refurbished this year but still has its warmly cosy feel, cheery locals and winter fires, as well as changing real ales such as Brains SA, Felinfoel Double Dragon, Morlands Old Speckled Hen, Smiles Best, Tetleys or Youngs Special on handpump. There's also a plusher cocktail bar. Food, both in the bar and restaurant, plays a big part here, and you can eat the lunchtime bar food in the restaurant if you prefer: sandwiches (from £1.75), vegetable soup (£1.95), game terrine (£4.25), omelettes (from £4.50), seafood pancakes, pizza or home-cooked ham and eggs (£4.95), tortellini with ham and mushroom sauce (£5.25), chicken in a creamy cardamom and cumin sauce (£5.50), daily specials such as liver and bacon, lots of daily changing fresh fish such as baked sea bass or grilled halibut, and puddings like chocolate and brandy truffle cake or pears in fudge sauce (£2.20); children's helpings on request. Three-course Sunday lunch (£11.50) in the restaurant. An excellent wine list, 24 malt whiskies, ordinary, fruit or peppermint teas, and coffee; friendly, helpful service. *(Recommended by J S M Sheldon, Martin and Mary Mullins; more reports please; also recommended by* The Good Hotel Guide*)*

Free house ~ Licensees Robert and Sally Hughes ~ Real ale ~ Meals and snacks (no bar food Sun lunchtime or maybe summer evenings, depending on how busy the restaurant is) ~ Restaurant (not Sun evening) ~ (01654) 767215 ~ Children in restaurant ~ Open 11-3, 6-11; closed 25 Dec ~ Bedrooms: £38B/£66B

ABERGORLECH   (Dyfed)   SN5833 Map 6

Black Lion
B4310 (a pretty road roughly NE of Carmarthen)

Well placed in the beautiful Cothi Valley with the Brechfa Forest around, this pleasant old black and white pub has picnic table sets and wooden seats and benches across the quiet road to take in the view. The garden slopes down towards the River Cothi where there's a Roman triple-arched bridge; the licensee has fishing rights and the river is good for trout, salmon and sea trout fishing. The atmospheric stripped-stone bar is traditionally furnished with plain oak tables and chairs, high-backed black settles facing each other across the flagstones by the log-effect gas fire, horsebrasses on the black beams, and some sporting prints; a restaurant extension has light-oak woodwork. Popular bar food includes sandwiches, soup (£1.75), escargots in garlic butter or various omelettes (£2.95), greenlip mussels (£3.25), ploughman's (from £3.25), ham, egg and chips or vegetable chilli (£3.95), sweet and sour pork or chicken tikka masala (£4.30), plaice stuffed with broccoli and cheese (£5.25), pink trout stuffed with asparagus and prawns (£6.25), chicken breast with leek and stilton sauce (£6.45), venison in redcurrant sauce with pears and mushrooms (£6.95), steaks (from £7.20), daily specials, and children's meals (from £1.45); in summer there may be afternoon teas with a selection of home-made cakes, and Saturday barbecues. Well kept Wadworths 6X and Worthingtons Best on handpump, and Addlestone's cider; good service from friendly licensees and staff. Sensibly placed darts, cribbage, dominoes, trivia, and unobtrusive piped music. Remy the Jack Russell loves to chew up beer mats. The car park is over the road, too. Lots of good walks nearby. *(Recommended by Mr and Mrs Bryn Gardner, Patrick Freeman, Helen Crookston, Martin and Pauline Richardson)*

Free house ~ Licensee Mrs Brenda Entwhistle ~ Real ale ~ Meals and snacks; afternoon teas in summer ~ Restaurant ~ Talley (01558) 685271 ~ Children welcome ~ Open 11.30-11; 12-3, 7-10.30 in winter

nr ABERYSTWYTH (Dyfed) SN6777 Map 6

Halfway Inn ★ 🛏 🍴

Pisgah (NOT the Pisgah near Cardigan); A4120 towards Devil's Bridge, 5¾ miles E of junction with A487

Several hundred feet above sea level, with panoramic views down over the Rheidol Valley, this enchanting old place is quite a favourite with some readers, who really appreciate its genuine old-fashioned charm. Unusually, they still let you tap your own beer from the cask, though they also keep Batemans XXXB, Eldridge Pope Royal Oak, Felinfoel Double Dragon, Flowers Original, Wadworths 6X, Whitbreads Castle Eden and plenty of changing guests on handpump for those who prefer their pint pulled rather more professionally; five draught ciders too, including Westons Old Rosie. It's particularly busy in summer, with both locals and visitors, and there may then be special events such as sheep shearing contests and Welsh choirs. Good bar food includes soup (£1.50), filled baked potatoes (from £1.50), sandwiches (from £2.25), breaded mushrooms with home-made garlic dip (£2.50), leek and double gloucester filo tartlet in a mustard sauce (£3.25), chicken liver pâté with Cointreau and orange (£3.45), ploughman's (£4), home-made spaghetti bolognese (£4.50), breaded plaice (£4.75), brie and broccoli pithivier (£5.50), home-made chicken, ham and mushroom pie (£6.75), char-grilled Scotch steaks (from £8), daily specials like dressed Cardigan Bay crab (£4.75) or steak in ale pie (£6), home-made puddings such as treacle tart (£2), and children's dishes; good friendly service. The beamed and flagstoned bar has stripped deal tables and settles, bare stone walls, and a dining room/restaurant area where tables can be reserved. Darts, pool and piped music (classical at lunchtimes, popular folk and country in the evenings). Outside, picnic-set tables under cocktail parasols have fine views of wooded hills and pastures; there's a play area, free overnight camping for customers and a paddock for pony-trekkers. The Friday night live music is good. Bedrooms are comfortable, but watch your head. *(Recommended by LD, JD, Gwyneth and Salvo Spadaro-Dutturi, M Joyner, Joan and Michel Hooper-Immins, P Neate)*

Free house ~ Licensees Raywood and Sally Roger ~ Real ale ~ Meals and snacks ~ Restaurant ~ (01970) 880631 ~ Children welcome except in serving bar ~ Live music Fri such as jazz, Welsh and folk ~ Open 11-11; 11.30-2.30, 6.30-11 winter weekdays ~ Bedrooms: £27B/£37B

BEAUMARIS (Anglesey) SH6076 Map 6

Olde Bulls Head ★ 🍷

Castle Street

Parts of this smartly cosy old inn date back to 1472, and in its time the place has been commandeered by Cromwellian forces and given shelter to illustrious figures like Samuel Johnson and Charles Dickens, neither of whom would look particularly out of place here now. The look and style of the building are genuinely old-fashioned, and the quaint rambling bar is decorated with plenty of reminders of its long and illustrious past; a rare 17th-c brass water clock, a bloodthirsty crew of cutlasses, and even the town's oak ducking stool. There's also lots of copper and china jugs, snug alcoves, low beams, low-seated settles, leather-cushioned window seats and a good open fire. The entrance to the pretty courtyard is closed by the biggest simple hinged door in Britain. Daily changing lunchtime bar food might include sandwiches (from £1.60), home-made vegetable, ham and barley soup (£1.85), good ploughman's (£3.10), Spanish omelette (£4.25), terrine of chicken with red onion marmalade (£4.50), pork and mushroom pie (£4.75), strips of rare roast sirloin beef with marinated peppers or baked fillet of codling with herb crust (£4.95), dressed crab or smoked trout and avocado salad (£5.50), and puddings such as mango cheesecake or warm almond tart (£1.75). The no-smoking restaurant does a good three-course Sunday lunch (£14.75). Very well kept Bass, Worthington Best and guest on handpump, a good comprehensive list of over 180 wines, with plenty of half bottles, and freshly squeezed orange juice; cheerful, friendly service. Dominoes, chess, draughts and cards. The charming bedrooms (with lots of nice little extras) are named after characters in Dickens' novels. *(Recommended by David and Ruth Hollands, Roy Smylie, Blair and Dinah Harrison, Roger and Christine Mash)*

Free house ~ Licensee David Robertson ~ Real ale ~ Lunchtime meals and snacks (not Sun – but restaurant open then) ~ Restaurant ~ Beaumaris (01248) 810329 ~ Children welcome until 8pm, no under 7s in dining room ~ Open 11-11; closed 25-26 Dec, 1 Jan ~ Bedrooms: £42B/£72B

BETWS-Y-COED (Gwynedd) SH7956 Map 6

Ty Gwyn 🛏

A5 just S of bridge to village

The atmosphere at this friendly family-run former coaching inn is very much like that of a private house, and people who come here often do end up feeling like welcome personal guests. The licence is such that you can only have a drink if you're eating or staying, but that shouldn't be a problem: the food is imaginative and well presented and it's a delightful place to spend a night or two, well placed for all the area's attractions but without a touristy feel. Highly regarded by readers, the promptly served dishes from the daily changing menu might include good soup (£1.95), generous helpings of sandwiches (lunchtime only, from £1.95), black pudding with mustard (£2.95), greenlip mussels cooked with tomato and sage butter (£3.50), wheat and walnut casserole or spaghetti bolognese (£5), gammon, whole plaice or home-made curry (£5.95), roast poussin and bacon with a bordelaise sauce (£6.50), plenty of fish such as salmon in a basil and vermouth sauce or monkfish bonne femme (£7.95), pheasant in a wine and wild mushroom sauce (£8.50), steaks (from £9.95), children's menu (highchair and toys available), excellent three-course Sunday lunch (£9.95) and well liked daily set three-course menu (£16.95). Helpings are generous, and service efficient and unhurried. The interesting clutter of unusual old prints and bric-a-brac in the beamed lounge bar aren't the usual inconsequential space-fillers you'll find in some pubs – carefully chosen and worth a close look, they reflect the fact that the owners run an antique shop next door. Theakstons Best on handpump. The bar has an ancient cooking range worked in well at one end and rugs and comfortable chintz easy chairs on its oak parquet floor. *(Recommended by Gordon Theaker, Dave and Jules Tuckett, David Heath, Peter and Jenny Quine, J L Moore, Nick Haslewood, Tina and David Woods-Taylor, KC, H K Dyson, J E Rycroft, Blair and Dinah Harrison, H Saddington, Canon Michael Bordeaux, Dave Thompson, Margaret Mason, P W Knatchbull-Hugessen)*

Free house ~ Licensees Jim and Shelagh Ratcliffe ~ Real ale ~ Meals and snacks ~ Restaurant ~ Betws y Coed (01690) 710383/710787 ~ Children welcome ~ Open 12-3, 7-11 ~ Bedrooms: £19/£35(£54B)

BODFARI (Clwyd) SJ0970 Map 6

Dinorben Arms ★ ♀

From A541 in village, follow Tremeirchion 3 signpost

They've just opened a new bar at this characterful and warmly welcoming place, mainly so that they can show off their impressive range of drinks to best advantage. As well as the Courage Directors, John Smiths, Ruddles County and

Websters Yorkshire on handpump, they keep around 150 whiskies (including the full Macallan range and a good few from the Islay distilleries), plenty of good wines (with several classed growth clarets), vintage ports and cognacs, and a few unusual coffee liqueurs. But it's the reliable bar food that readers seem to like best, particularly the good-value eat-as-much-as-you-like smorgasbord counter at lunchtimes (£7.50). Other snacks then include home-made vegetable soup (£1.45), filled rolls (£1.65), ploughman's (£3.40) or their popular Chicken Rough, with evening meals such as home-made steak and kidney pie (£4.50), vegetarian lasagne (£4.75), salads (from £4.75), fresh grilled salmon (£5.85), gammon (£5.95), steaks (from £6.95) and specials like veal cordon bleu or halibut mornay (£8.50); you choose starters and puddings from an attractive list by an ancient glassed-in well, and there's a children's menu. Upstairs, there's a carvery on Friday and Saturday evenings (£12.95) and a good help-yourself hot and cold buffet on Wednesday and Thursday evenings (£8.95). The three rooms which open off the heart of the carefully extended building have beams hung with tankards and flagons, high shelves of china, old-fashioned settles and other seats, and three open fires; there's also a light and airy garden room. Two parts (including one of the dining areas) are no-smoking; piped music. Lots of tables outside on the prettily landscaped and planted brick-floored terraces, with attractive sheltered corners and charming views, and there's a grassy play area which – like the car park – is neatly sculpted into the slope of the hills. *(Recommended by Michael and Janet Hepworth, Brian and Jill Bond, KC, Ian Morley, D J Poole)*

Free house ~ Licensee David Rowlands ~ Real ale ~ Meals and snacks (12-2.30, 6-10.30, Sun lunchtime only smorgasbord) ~ Restaurant (not Sun evening) ~ Bodfari (01745) 710309 ~ Children welcome ~ Open 12-3.30, 6-11; closed 25 Dec

BURTON GREEN (Clwyd) SJ3458 Map6

Golden Grove

Former A483 Chester—Wrexham through Pulford towards Rossett

A very pleasant, peaceful and old-fashioned half-timbered 13th-c coaching inn, the kind of place where everyone is welcomed as though they were a familiar local. Standing timbers and plaster separate the knocked-together rooms, which have two open fires, comfortable settees, settles and copper-topped tables, collections of plates and horsebrasses, figures carved in the beams, and a friendly, relaxed atmosphere. Decent home-made bar food might include soup, sandwiches, steak and ale pie, chicken curry or lasagne (£4.95), vegetarian dishes, scampi (£5.35), steaks (from £5.75) and a big mixed grill (£8.25); children's menu (£2.25), Sunday roast (£4.95). Well kept Marstons Best and Pedigree on handpump, and quite a few malt whiskies; fruit machine, piped music. Obliging service. The big back streamside garden has a barbecue area and children's adventure playground with lifesize plane, train and ship, climbing frame and bouncy castle. *(Recommended by David and Rebecca Killick, Sally Davies; more reports please)*

Marstons ~ Manager David Piner ~ Real ale ~ Meals and snacks (till 10pm) ~ Restaurant (not Sun evening) ~ (01244) 570445 ~ Children in eating area ~ Open 12-3, 6(7 winter)-11; 12-11 summer Sats

CAERPHILLY (Mid Glam) ST1484 Map 6

Courthouse

Cardiff Road; one-way system heading N, snugged in by National Westminster Bank – best to park before you get to it

There aren't many pubs we know of that have their own dairy, but this venerable place does, producing the caerphilly you may find in the ploughman's and other dishes. Originally built as a longhouse in the 14th c, the Courthouse still has much of its old character, with the stone walls and roof and the raftered gallery at one end all bearing witness to its great age. The view of the adjacent castle directly over its peaceful lake is splendid and can be enjoyed both from the tables out on the grassy terrace behind or from the light and airy modern café/bar at the back. The long bar has pews, comfortable cloth-upholstered chairs and window seats, rugs on ancient flagstones, shutters and curtains on thick wooden rails for the small windows and a formidably large stone fireplace. Well-priced lunchtime bar food includes home-made soup (£1.40), big filled baguettes (the hot beef is good), ploughman's (£1.95), omelettes or cod (£4.25), tuna and pasta bake, vegetarian nut cutlets or cheese and lentil rissoles (£4.45), salads, chicken with a variety of sauces (£4.95), a daily lunchtime carvery (from £4.45), and children's dishes (from £1.30); on the evenings when they serve food they add dishes like whole trout with almonds and prawns (£5.45) and beef Wellington (£7.95); prompt service. Part of the eating area is no smoking. Well kept Ruddles Best, Shepherd Neame Spitfire, Wadworths 6X and Websters Yorkshire on handpump, good coffee; cribbage, fruit machine and piped pop music (even outside). *(Recommended by Barbara Ann Mayer, Rachael Pole, Y M Rees, M J Laing, J E Lloyd)*

Courage ~ Lease: James Jenkins ~ Real ale ~ Lunchtime meals and snacks (until 5.30 Fri and Sat) ~ Restaurant (Tues-Thurs evenings only) ~ (01222) 888120 ~ Children in restaurant and café area ~ Open 11-11; closed 25 Dec

CAREW (Dyfed) SN0403 Map 6

Carew Inn 🛏
A4075 just off A477

In a good setting opposite the imposing ruins of Carew Castle, this simple old inn is a friendly place with a good deal of character. The snug little panelled public bar and comfortable lounge both have old-fashioned settles and scrubbed pine furniture, and interesting prints and china hanging from the beams, while a dining room has an elegant china cabinet, a mirror over the tiled fireplace and sturdy chairs around the well spaced tables; another dining room upstairs is no-smoking. The home-made bar food is good, fresh and generously served, from a range that includes sandwiches, soup (£1.50), pâté (£2.25), mussels provençale (£3.50), spaghetti bolognese or chilli (£3.95), salads (from £4.50 – the crab is recommended), steak and mushroom pie (£4.95), potato, leek and mushroom pie (£5.50), specials such as local dressed crab (£5.95), Welsh lamb, duck breast in orange sauce (£9.50) and local sea bass (£9.95), puddings (from £1.95) and children's meals; two-course Sunday lunch (£5.95). Well kept Buckleys Best and Reverend James, Worthington Best and locally brewed Main Street Bitter on handpump, as well as local wines and mineral waters; sensibly placed darts, dominoes, cribbage, piped music; swings and slide outside. Efficient friendly service. Dogs in the public bar only. There's a remarkable 9th-c Celtic cross in view of the sunny back courtyard, and more seats in the little flowery front garden look down to the river, where a tidal watermill (known as the French Mill – it was built by Napoleonic War prisoners) is open for afternoon summer visits. *(Recommended by S Watkins, P A Taylor, Bob ad Hilary Gaskin, M E Hughes, Patrick Freeman, David Wallington)*

Free house ~ Licensees Rob and Mandy Hinchcliffe ~ Real ale ~ Meals and snacks (not Sun lunch, or winter Mon evenings) ~ Restaurants ~ (01646) 651267 ~ Children in eating area ~ Live music Thurs evening ~ Open 11-11, 12-2.30, 4.30-11 weekdays Sept-Jun ~ Bedrooms: £15/£25

CARNO (Powys) SN9697 Map 6

Aleppo Merchant 🛏
A470 Newtown—Machynlleth

Notably friendly and welcoming, this reliably hospitable place was named by the sea captain who retired to open it in 1632. The beamed lounge bar is comfortably modernised with red plush button-back banquettes around its low wooden tables and plenty of tapestries on the partly stripped stone walls; more tapestries in the small adjoining lounge, which also has dining tables and an open fire in winter. Part of this area is no smoking. A wide choice of well liked bar food includes onion bhajees (£1.35), home-made sandwiches (from £1.45), stockpot soup (£1.75), ploughman's (from £2.55), vegetable tikka masala (£3.65), breaded plaice or lasagne (£4.45), home-made smoked fish pie (£5.15), steak and onion pie (£5.25), whole rack of ribs (£5.95), Welsh lamb chops (£6.35), steaks (from £7.95), and puddings like home-made sherry trifle or treacle nut tart (£1.95). Pool, darts, dominoes, fruit machine trivia, and juke box in the public bar. Well kept Boddingtons and guests on handpump, Welsh spirits, wines, and waters; piped music. Local girl Laura Ashley was in here the night before she died and is buried in the churchyard immediately opposite. *(Recommended by P Appleby, Derek and Cerys Williams, Ian Phillips, Barbara A Graham, Mrs S Plowright, A J Knight)*

Free house ~ Licensee John Carroll ~ Real ale ~ Meals and snacks (not 25 Dec) ~ Restaurant ~ Carno (01686) 420210 ~ Children in restaurant and garden only ~ Open 11.30-2.30, 6(7 winter Mon and Tues)-11 ~ Bedrooms: £20/£35

CILCAIN (Clwyd) SJ1865 Map 7

White Horse

Village signposted from A494 W of Mold; OS Sheet 116 map reference 177652

Part of an idyllic cluster of stone houses and marked out by its attractively naive inn-sign, this creeper-covered flower-decked pub is the sort of homely place where everything comes with a smile. The cosy parlour by the bar has exposed joists in the low ochre ceiling, mahogany and oak settles, a shelf of china and copper, and a snug inglenook fireplace; there are Lloyd Loom chairs, old local photographs and a goldfish tank in the room on the right, and beyond a further little room with a piano (and a grandfather clock), there's one more conventionally furnished with tables and chairs. A separate quarry-tiled bar at the back allows dogs. Well presented home-made food includes lunchtime filled rolls (from £1.50), omelettes (£4.80), various curries, home-baked ham, vegetable samosas, scampi, cannelloni or steak and kidney pie (all £5.40), rump steak (£8.20), specials such as lamb cobbler, bacon cassoulet or sausages braised in red wine, plenty of seasonal game dishes like venison casserole or devilled pheasant, and puddings like raspberry pie (£2.10); they rely a lot on local produce, using organically grown vegetables and free range eggs. Three well kept changing real ales on handpump such as Adnams, Batemans XXB, Felinfoel Double Dragon, Fullers London Pride, Greene King Abbot, Morlands Old Speckled Hen, Shepherd Neame Bishops Finger and Youngs Special; Addlestones cider, varied range of wines. Darts, dominoes, cribbage and fruit machine. There are picnic-table sets at the side. Note they don't allow children inside. *(Recommended by David and Rebecca Killick, Owen W Jones; more reports please)*

Free house ~ Licensee Peter Jeory ~ Real ale ~ Meals and snacks (till 10pm Fri and Sat) ~ (01352) 740142 ~ Open 12-3.30(4 Sat), 7-11

CRESSWELL QUAY (Dyfed) SN0406 Map 6

Cresselly Arms

Village signposted from A4075

Pubs rarely come as traditional as this unpretentious place. Covered in creepers and facing the tidal creek of the Cresswell River, it's simple and thoroughly old-fashioned – no food, children or dogs, just a good honest atmosphere and friendly welcome. There are seats out by the water, and, if the tides are right, you can get here by boat. Inside, the two comfortably unchanging communicating rooms have red-and-black flooring tiles, built-in wall benches, kitchen chairs and plain tables. There's an open fire in one room, and a working Aga in the other, a high beam-and-plank ceiling hung with lots of pictorial china, and a relaxed and jaunty feel. A third red-carpeted room is more conventionally furnished, with red-cushioned mate's chairs around neat tables. Well kept Flowers Original is tapped straight from the cask into glass jugs; helpful service, fruit machine and darts. *(Recommended by David Wallington, Simon and Amanda Southwell, Pete Baker, Mr and Mrs A Varnom)*

Free house ~ Licensees Maurice and Janet Cole ~ Real ale ~ (0646) 651210 ~ Open 11-3, 5-11

CRICKHOWELL (Powys) SO2118 Map 6

Bear ★ ⑪ 🛏 ⅋ ◖

Brecon Road; A40

Wales Dining Pub of the Year

We know of a couple who regularly travel 90 miles to this exceptional place just to sample the puddings. It's a pub that a good many really do like a lot and no wonder – the food, service, drinks and atmosphere all blend together in a way so natural it seems effortless. Beautifully presented bar food might include substantial sandwiches (from £1.95), home-made soup (£1.95), brandied chicken liver and pink peppercorn pâté (£2.95), chicken satay with a peanut sauce (£3.75), leek and cream cheese pancake (£3.95), deep-fried bread basket filled with scrambled eggs and smoked salmon (£4.25), smoked bacon, minced cockle and laverbread cake with mushroom sauce (£4.75), spiced venison sausages, tasty salmon fishcakes or good and often quite unusual vegetarian dishes like red bean, cinnamon and orange casserole (£4.95), Thai noodles with minced chicken and shrimps (£5.25), beef, mushroom and Guinness pie (£5.95), duck confit (£6.25), grilled local Welsh lamb cutlets (£7.50), steaks (from £9.50), and lovely puddings like home-made ice creams, bread and butter pudding (with bananas and rum-soaked raisins), and triple chocolate mousse (£2.95). The partly no-smoking restaurant has an à la carte menu with main courses that concentrate on Welsh produce (at about £11.50), though readers seem to prefer the bar food. Well kept Bass, Ruddles Best and County and Websters Yorkshire on handpump; malt whiskies, vintage and late-bottled ports, and unusual wines and liqueurs, with some hops tucked in amongst the bottles. The fascinating heavily beamed lounge has lots of little plush-seated bentwood armchairs and handsome cushioned antique settles and, up by the great roaring log fire, a big sofa and leather easy chairs are spread among the rugs on the oak parquet floor; antiques include a fine oak dresser filled with pewter and brass, a longcase clock and interesting prints. A window seat looks down on the market square. It can get terribly busy. Service is usually very welcoming and friendly, though one reader with a baby got short shrift when his family settled down in the wrong bar. The back bedrooms – particularly in the new block – are the most highly recommended, though there are three more bedrooms in the pretty cottage at the end of the garden. Lovely window boxes, and you can eat in the garden in summer. *(Recommended by Roy Y Bromell, John Cox, Dr and Mrs Richard Neville, A R and B E Sayer, Gwynne Harper, Alan and Heather Jacques, Brian and Jill Bond, Simon Collett-Jones, Mr and Mrs J Brown, Mrs S Segrove, Jenny and Brian Seller, Barry and Anne, Rita Horridge, A P Jeffreys, Julia Stone, Andrew Latchem, Helen Reed, D J and J R Tapper, Jonathan and Rachel Marsh, Maureen and Keith Ginson, Mr and Mrs H S Hill, Carol and Phil Byng, Graham Bush, John Nash, D J Underwood, J E and A G Jones, Andrew and Barbara Sykes, Gordon Theaker, Peter and Audrey Dowsett, Dr P D Putwain, Dave Irving, S H Godsell)*

Free house ~ Licensee Mrs Judy Hindmarsh ~ Real ale ~ Meals and snacks (till 10pm) ~ Restaurant (not Sun evening) ~ Crickhowell (01873) 810408 ~ Children in separate family bar (no-smoking at lunchtime) and in restaurant ~ Open 10.30-3, 6-11 ~ Bedrooms: £42B/£52B

nr CRICKHOWELL (Powys) SO2118 Map 6

Nantyffin Cider Mill ⑪

1½ miles NW, by junction A40/A479

In beautiful countryside, this rather handsome L-shaped pink-washed tiled stone dining pub faces an attractive stretch of the River Usk, and has charming views from the tables out on the lawn above its neat car park. The bar at one end of the main open-plan area has several real ales on handpump, drawn in rotation from a pool of Crown Buckley Reverend James, Felinfoel Double Dragon, Gibbs Mew Bishops Tipple, Marstons Pedigree, Mitchells Fortress, Morlands Old Speckled Hen and Smiles Best, with other guest beers, several farm ciders, and decent wines. The style is traditional, rather upmarket, with a warm woodburner in a fine broad fireplace, warm grey stonework, cheerful bunches of fresh and dried flowers, and good solid comfortable tables and chairs. The current owners have converted a raftered barn with a big cider press into quite a striking restaurant; the same menu is served throughout the pub. A wide choice of changing food, freshly prepared and beautifully presented, using some local supplies and fish and seafood from Cornwall, might include home-made soup (£2.25), quite a few snacky dishes such as hot honey-glazed melon kebab in bacon (£2.95), samosas filled with aubergine and chickpea dhal (£3.25), Welsh rarebit (£3.50), game terrine with onion marmalade (£3.50) or spiced crab cakes with red pepper salsa (£4.25), main dishes such as faggots and mushy peas (£5.25), steak and kidney pie (£5.95), vegetable and cashew korma (£6.65), rabbit and cider casserole (£7.45), chicken breast stuffed with crab and spinach (£8.25) and lamb steak with unusual sauces (£10.95), with some good unusual puddings (£2.95). Given the individual cooking, it's no surprise that there can be a wait for food. A ramp makes disabled access easy. *(Recommended by Anne Morris, M Stroud, N H E Lewis, Mrs M Clemenson, Mrs Joan Harris)*

Free house ~ Licensees Glyn Bridgeman, Sean Gerrard ~ Real ale ~ Meals and snacks (12-2.30, 6.30-10) ~ Restaurant ~ (01873) 810775 ~ Children welcome ~ Open 12-3, 6.30(7 winter)-11; cl Mon during Oct-Mar, cl 2 weeks Jan

EAST ABERTHAW (South Glamorgan) ST0367 Map 6

Blue Anchor ★ 🍷

B4265

Delightfully unspoilt, this lovely creeper-covered thatched pub can barely have changed since it was built in the late 14th c. Low-beamed cosy rooms still wriggle through massive stone walls and low doorways (watch your head!) and there are open fires everywhere, including one in an inglenook with antique oak seats built into its stripped stonework. Other seats and tables are worked into a series of chatty little alcoves, and in the more open front bar is an old lime-ash floor; darts, fruit machine and trivia. Good value bar food includes sandwiches (from £1.50), soup (£1.75), filled baked potatoes (from £2.25), Welsh rarebit or ploughman's (£3.50), lemon marinated sardines or salads (£3.75), grilled pork chop with apple, cider and cream sauce or faggots with onion gravy (£3.95), baked fish cocotte, a daily roast or curry and pies such as steak and kidney (all £4.20), plaice with avocado, orange and prawns (£5.25), and children's meals (£1.60); Sunday lunchtime they just do a three-course roast lunch (£9.45). The good restaurant is popular. Boddingtons, Buckleys Best, Flowers IPA, Marstons Pedigree, Theakstons Old Peculier, Wadworths 6X, and a regularly changing guest beer are kept carefully at a controlled temperature, and served by handpump. Rustic seats shelter peacefully among tubs and troughs of flowers outside, with more stone tables on a newer terrace. From here a path leads to the shingly flats of the estuary. The pub can get packed in the evenings and on summer weekends. *(Recommended by Patrick and Mary McDermott, Steve Thomas, L P Thomas, Gwynne Harper, David Lewis, Chris and Anne Fluck, J E Davies, Mr and Mrs Thomas, J E Lloyd)*

Free house ~ Licensee Jeremy Coleman ~ Real ale ~ Meals and snacks ~ Restaurant (not Sun evening) ~ Barry (01446) 750 329 ~ Children welcome till 8pm ~ Open 11-11

HALKYN (Clwyd) SJ2172 Map 6

Britannia 🍷

Pentre Rd, off A55 for Rhosesmor

One of the nice things about this cosy and friendly place is the way the old and new parts blend together so comfortably – it's very much a pub at ease with itself. The original stone-built back part dates back to the 15th c, when it was a farm; it has been extended many times since then, most recently with the dining conservatory and terrace that make the most of the great views right over the Dee estuary to the Wirral. The cosy unspoilt lounge bar has some very heavy beams, with horsebrasses, harness, jugs, plates and other bric-a-brac; there's also a games room with darts, pool, dominoes and fruit machine. Consistently good bar food includes sandwiches (from £1.55), home-made soups with rhes-y-cae bread (£1.85), burgers (from £2.95, including vegetarian), filled baked potatoes (£2.95), ploughman's (£4.20), all-day brunch (£4.60), steak and kidney pie (£5.80), vegetarian stir-fry (£5.95), chicken madras or gammon steak with their own fresh eggs (£6.20), grilled Welsh lamb chops with honey and rosemary sauce (£6.40), steaks (from £7.85), daily specials, puddings (from £2.25), and children's meals (£1.95); helpings are good and vegetables and butter generally come in little dishes. Best to book if you want the view. Service can slow down a little when busy but is always friendly and attentive, and the licensees really take pride in what they're doing. Lees Bitter and Moonraker Strong Ale on handpump, and a choice of coffees. *(Recommended by L G Milligan, KC, Andy and Jill Kassube, David Heath, Nick Haslewood, P Boot, Joan and Jim Griffiths)*

J W Lees ~ Tenant Terry O'Neill ~ Real ale ~ Meals and snacks (till 10pm) ~ Restaurant ~ (01352) 780272 ~ Children welcome ~ Open 11-3, 5.30-11; 11-11 Sat

KENFIG (Mid Glamorgan) SS8383 Map 6

Prince of Wales £ ◧

2¼ miles from M4 junction 37; A4229 towards Porthcawl, then right when dual carriageway narrows on bend, signposted Maudlam, Kenfig

This unspoilt and unpretentious old place still has a few reminders of the days when Kenfig was an important medieval port: the aldermen's mace kept upstairs (where, uniquely, they also hold Sunday school), and ghostly voices from the old town said to have become embedded in the walls. The town has long since become a victim of the relentless shifting sands, with the busy pub just about the only survivor. It's well liked for its good range of real ales, probably the best in the area. These might include brews like Bass, Camerons Strong Arm, Felinfoel Double Dragon, Fullers London Pride and ESP, Hancocks HB, Marstons Pedigree, Mitchells ESB, Morrells Varsity and Wadworths 6X on tap/gravity and Worthington BB on handpump. Its walls stripped back to the stone, the friendly main bar has heavy settles and red leatherette seats around a double row of close-set cast-iron-framed tables, an open fire, and small storm windows. The simple but good value home-made bar food is very popular, and quickly served, with dishes like scotch eggs (70p), pasties (75p), large filled baps (from 85p: the home-roasted meat is well done), faggots (from £1), cheese and potato pie or cottage pie (£1.50), steak and onion pie (£1.60) or lasagne (£2.50) – prices don't include potatoes or vegetables (which are grown in the garden). There's also a wide range of lunchtime daily specials such as bacon and laver bread (£3.75), chicken and mushroom pie (£3.95), braised steak and gravy, plenty of fish such as fresh cod fillet or skate wing (£4.25), a roast (£4.25), fresh salmon (£7.50), fisherman's platter (£10.50), and home-made puddings like apple pie or fruit crumble (from £1.50); 3-course Sunday lunch (£7.50), fresh eggs from their own hens. Dominoes, cribbage and card games. *(Recommended by Barbara Ann Mayer, John and Helen Thompson, Ian Phillips, R Michael Richards, Margaret Whalley, E M Davies)*

Free house ~ Licensee Jeremy Evans ~ Real ale ~ Meals and snacks (11.30-4, 7-10) ~ Restaurant ~ (01656) 740356 ~ Children in dining room ~ Open 11.30-4, 6-11; closed evening 25 Dec

LITTLE HAVEN (Dyfed) SM8512 Map 6

Swan

A welcoming place really making the best of the lovely views across the broad and sandy hill-sheltered cove – both from seats in the bay window or from the sea wall outside (just the right height for sitting on). The two communicating rooms have quite a cosily intimate feel, as well as comfortable high-backed settles and Windsor chairs, a winter open fire, and old prints on the walls that are partly stripped back to the original stonework. Cooked by the landlord, the compact choice of well liked lunchtime bar food includes home-made soup (£1.75), sandwiches (from

£1.25), ploughman's (£3.25), pâté (£3.50), crab and mayonnaise bake or sardines grilled with spinach, egg and mozzarella (£3.95), chicken or beef curry (£4.50), ham salad or prawns in garlic mousse (£5.25), locally smoked salmon or fresh local crab (£5.95), lobster in season, and a selection of home-made puddings (£1.95); this is another place where you won't often see plastic packets of butter, milk or sugar – the good coffee may come with a little jug of cream. Well kept Wadworths 6X and Worthington BB on handpump from the heavily panelled bar counter; pleasant, efficient service. Little Haven is one of the prettiest coastal villages in west Wales, and a footpath from the pub takes you down to the cove itself. *(Recommended by David Wallington, Gwynne Harper, Ewan and Moira McCall, Barbara Ann Mayer, H and D Payne, D J Underwood)*

James Williams (who no longer brew) ~ Tenants Glyn and Beryl Davies ~ Real ale ~ Lunchtime meals and snacks (not 25 Dec) ~ Tiny evening restaurant Weds-Sat in summer, bookings only in winter (and advisable in summer) ~ Broad Haven (01437) 781256 ~ Open 11-3, 6(7 winter)-11; closed evening 25 Dec

LLANBEDR-Y-CENNIN (Gwynedd) SH7669 Map 6

Olde Bull 🍺

Village signposted from B5106

A lovely spot, this 16th-c drovers' inn has splendid views down over the Vale of Conwy to the mountains beyond. A large wild garden has a waterfall and an orchard, as well as a fishpond and plenty of seats. It's doing well under the current licensee, certainly no local, and indeed one of the only Scandinavian landlords we've ever heard of. Inside, the knocked-through rooms are full of massive low beams (some salvaged from a wrecked Spanish Armada ship), elaborately carved antique settles, a close crowd of cheerfully striped stools, brassware, photographs, Prussian spiked helmets, and good open fires (one in an inglenook); there might be some subdued Sibelius in the background. The former lounge bar is now another dining area. The atmosphere is very friendly, and children are made welcome. Well kept Lees Bitter and Mild on handpump from wooden barrels, and several malt whiskies; pleasant service. A changing choice of good bar meals might include soup (£1.40), sandwiches (from £1.95), filled baked potatoes (from £2.80), sausage and egg (£3.25), ploughman's (from £3.95), steak, kidney and Guinness pie or sweet and sour chicken (£4.95), trout (£5.50), changing specials such as honey roast poussin (£6.95), breast of duck with black bean sauce (£8.75) or sirloin steak in Welsh whisky sauce (£9.25), and maybe a couple of the licensee's native dishes such as Finnish meatballs with the traditional accompaniments (£6.25). The pub is popular with walkers. Darts, cribbage, dominoes. Lavatories are outside. *(Recommended by Dave Braisted, Mary Ann Cameron and others; more reports please)*

Lees ~ Tenant Paavo Alexander Salminen ~ Real ale ~ Meals and snacks (not winter Mons) ~ Restaurant ~ Colwyn Bay (01492) 660508 ~ Children welcome till 8pm ~ Open 12-3, 7(6.30 Sat)-11; closed Sun evening

nr LLANBERIS (Gwynedd) SH6655 Map 6

Pen-y-Gwryd 🛏️ 🍺

Nant Gwynant; at junction of A498 and A4086, ie across mountains from Llanberis – OS Sheet 115 map reference 660558

Apart from its magnificent setting the main draw of this jovial climbers' inn must be the wonderful atmospere – simple, cheery and welcoming. The rugged slate-floored climbers' bar is like a log cabin and doubles as a mountain rescue post; there's also a smaller room with a collection of boots that have done famous climbs, and a cosy panelled smoke room with more climbing mementoes and equipment. The team that climbed Everest first in 1953, like many other mountaineers, used the inn as a training base, leaving their signatures scrawled on the ceiling. A snug little room with built-in wall benches and sturdy country chairs lets you contemplate the majestic surrounding mountain countryside – like precipitous Moel-siabod beyond the lake opposite. There's a hatch where you order lunchtime bar meals: good robust helpings of home-made food such as soup, sandwiches, ploughman's using home-baked french bread, quiche lorraine or pâté (£2.50) and a home-made pie of the day (£3), with casseroles in winter. In the evening residents sit down together for the hearty and promptly served dinner (check on the time when you book); the dining room is no smoking. They serve Bass and sherry from their own solera in Puerto Santa Maria, with mulled wine in winter; friendly, obliging service. Table tennis, darts, pool, bar billiards, table skittles, dominoes and shove-ha'penny for residents (who have a charmingly furnished, panelled sitting room too, and hopefully from next year a sauna in the trees). Bedrooms are clean and sensible rather than luxurious; one of them has long had an unusual Edwardian bath in it, and it's recently been joined by an older Victorian one colourfully decked out with raised fruit and flowers – the V & A apparently say they've never seen anything like it. It's becoming a very popular place to spend a night or two (especially after press reports describing it as one of the most romantic settings in the country), so it might be best to book ahead. *(Recommended by Andrew Stephenson, John Le Sage, Dave and Jules Tuckett, Lorrie and Mick Marchington, John Nash, Martin Howard Pritchard, Dr M G Yates, Mrs J S England, H K Dyson, Blair and Dinah Harrison, David Thompson, Margaret Mason, Klaus and Elizabeth Leist, E H and R F Warner, K R Flack; also recommended by* The Good Hotel Guide)

Free house ~ Licensee Jane Pullee ~ Real ale ~ Lunchtime meals and snacks ~ Evening restaurant ~ Llanberis (01286) 870 211 ~ Well behaved children welcome, except residents' bar ~ Open 11-11; no drinks on Suns except to residents; closed early Nov to New Year, open weekends only Jan and Feb ~ Bedrooms: £19(£23B)/£38(£43B)

LLANCARFAN (South Glamorgan) ST0570 Map 6

Fox & Hounds

Village signposted from A4226; also reached from B4265 via Llancadle or A48 from Bonvilston

A comfortably modernised old pub in a nice setting, blending in very well with the rest of the lovely village. Rambling through arches in thick Tudor walls the neatly kept carpeted bar has high-backed traditional settles as well as the plush banquettes around its copper-topped cast-iron tables, and a coal fire in winter. Reliable bar food includes sandwiches (from £1.20), soup (£1.50), burger (£1.80), ploughman's (from £3.50), pizzas (from £4.50, not lunchtime), steak and mushroom pie, lentil crumble or vegetable curry (all £4.50), gammon steak (£5.25), children's meals (£1.75), Sunday roast beef (£4.75) and bargain four-course meals (£4.95); summer Saturday barbecues. Well kept Brains Bitter, Felinfoel Double Dragon, John Smiths, Ruddles Best, and two regular guests on handpump; non-alcoholic elderflower spritz, espresso, cappuccino and decaffeinated coffee and hot chocolate; darts, fruit machine, unobtrusive piped music. At the back is an attractive crazy-paved terrace, beside a little stream overhung by a thicket of honeysuckle, with tables under flowering trees. The nearby churchyard is interesting. *(Recommended by Steve Thomas, David Lewis, Michael, Alison and Rhiannon Sandy; more reports please)*

Free house ~ Licensee Mike Evans ~ Real ale ~ Meals and snacks (not Sun evenings Sept-Mar) ~ Restaurant (not Sun or Mon evening) ~ (01446) 781297 ~ Children in eating area of bar ~ Open 11-3(2 winter), 6.30-11; all day Sat

LLANDEWI SKIRRID (Gwent) SO3416 Map 6

Walnut Tree ★ ⑪ ♀

B4521

Quite different from most of the places we recommend, this excellent establishment is now pretty much a restaurant, but the atmosphere still doesn't have the formality that that suggests – they still have a pub licence, and they're quite happy for people to come in and just have one course, or even a drink and a pudding. In fact the food is considerably better than in most restaurants, cooked with considerable skill by the licensee who's been here now for nearly 30 years; meals these days are pretty much faultless. As usual however, quality doesn't come cheap, so you'll probably need your cheque book (they don't take credit cards). A typical menu might include gazpacho soup (£3.95), crab pancake (£5.45), bruschetta with seafood (£6.75), tagliolini with courgette flowers and truffle paste or griddled squid (£6.95), half-a-dozen oysters (£8.75), vegetarian platter (£9.95), calf's liver with sweet and sour onions (£10.95), escalope of salmon with rhubarb and ginger (£12.85), roast guinea fowl with spinach, mushrooms and vin santo (£12.95), roast duck with figs and strawberries (£13.95), fricassee of lobster and monkfish (£14.95), and puddings such as coconut parfait with mango sauce (£4.25), chocolate brandy loaf and coffee bean sauce (£5.85), and torte with three liqueurs (£6). The attractive choice of wines is particularly strong in Italian ones (they import their own), and the house wines by the glass are good value, as is the coffee. Service is efficient and friendly. The small white-walled bar has some polished settles and country chairs around the tables on its flagstones, and a log-effect gas fire. It opens into an airy and relaxed dining lounge with rush-seat Italianate chairs around gilt cast-iron-framed tables. There are a few white cast-iron tables outside in front. *(Recommended by Rita Horridge, the Monday Club, Martin G Richards, Paul Williams, J E Lloyd; more reports please)*

Free house ~ Licensee Ann Taruschio ~ Meals and snacks (12-3, 7-10.15, not Sun or Mon) ~ Restaurant (not Sun or Mon) ~ Abergavenny (01873) 852797 ~ Children welcome ~ Open 12-3, 7-12; closed Sun and Mon

LLANDRINDOD WELLS (Powys) SO0561 Map 6

Llanerch £ 🍺

Waterloo Road; from centre, head for station

A cheerful 16th-c inn with peaceful mountain views from its back terrace; it feels very much like a country pub but is in fact in the middle of town. As well as the atmosphere it's the good value bar food that readers like, with popular lunchtime dishes like soup (£1.75), sandwiches (from £1.50, good hefty toasties £2.50), filled baked potatoes or Welsh rarebit (£2.25), sausages and chips (£2.50), fisherman's pie, lasagne, vegetable pancakes or gammon casserole (all £2.95), salads (from £4.25), steak and kidney pie (£4.50), mixed grill (£7.95), and children's meals (from £1.75), and evening extras like beef and venison casserole (£5.95) or salmon steak (£7.95). The squarish beamed main bar has old-fashioned settles snugly divided by partly glazed partitions and a big stone fireplace that's richly decorated with copper and glass; there are more orthodox button-back banquettes in communicating lounges (one of which is no smoking at lunchtime). Well kept Boddingtons, Hancocks HB and a guest beer on handpump; they have a Victorian Festival in late August with lots of real ales. Welcoming, friendly service; fruit machine, video game, trivia and piped music, while a separate pool room has darts, cribbage and dominoes. The back terrace has tables and a summer bar and leads on to a garden (where you can play boules), looking over the Ithon Valley; also, a play area and front orchard. *(Recommended by Joan and Michel Hooper-Immins, M Joyner, D J Underwood, Bernard Phillips)*

Free house ~ Licensee John Leach ~ Real ale ~ Meals and snacks ~ Restaurant ~ Llandrindod Wells (01597) 822086 ~ Children in eating area and games room ~ Open 12-3(2.30 winter weekdays), 6-11 ~ Bedrooms: £22.50(£27.50B)/ £38(£48B)

nr LLANDUDNO JUNCTION (Gwynedd) SH8180 Map 6

Queens Head 🍽 🍷

Glanwydden; heading towards Llandudno on A546 from Colwyn Bay, turn left into Llanrhos Road as you enter the Penrhyn Bay speed limit; Glanwydden is signposted as the first left turn off this

The thoughtfully prepared food at this modest village pub attracts people from quite some distance away, with quite a few making major detours just to have a meal. It's really not that surprising – the standards are invariably excellent. Fish and seafood is always a good bet, as are the puddings – a huge range, from traditional bread and butter pudding or treacle tart to more exotic orange and coffee liqueur trifle or lemon and wine syllabub (£2.20); the only complaint readers make is that they can rarely fit one of these in. Other carefully prepared and generously served home-made food might include soup such as fresh pea and mint (£1.75), open rolls (from £2.25), home-made pâtés such as smoked trout (£3.75), baked black pudding with apple and brandy (£4.50), lovely fat Conway mussels in garlic butter and topped with smoked cheese (£4.95), good quiches (£5.20), salads (from £5.50), vegetarian pancake with mushrooms and asparagus (£5.50), and daily specials like steak and mushroom pie (£5.50), grilled Welsh lamb cutlets in a redcurrant and port sauce (£6.50), or fresh dressed Conway crab (£6.95). Evening extras such as pork filled with apricots and orange zest in an apple and cider sauce (£7.95), a trio of local grilled fish in hollandaise and tarragon sauce on a bed of sea asparagus (£8.95), or rump steak (£9.75); excellent mayonnaise. Best to get there early to be sure of a table – it's very popular indeed. Service stands out too: drop a knife and you may find they've brought another before you've finished bending down to pick up the original. Well kept Benskins, Ind Coope Burton, Tetleys and maybe a guest like Youngs Bitter on handpump, decent wine list, several malts, and good coffee, maybe served with a bowl of whipped cream. The spacious and comfortably modern lounge bar has brown plush wall banquettes and Windsor chairs around neat black tables and is partly divided by a white wall of broad arches and wrought-iron screens; there's also a little public bar. There are some tables out by the car park. No dogs. *(Recommended by KC, J E Hilditch, Roy Smylie, W C M Jones, Mark Bradley, Mr and Mrs B Hobden, Blair and Dinah Harrison, Neville Kenyon, Maysie Thompson, Mr and Mrs N Sanders and others)*

Ansells ~ Lease: Robert and Sally Cureton ~ Real ale ~ Meals and snacks ~ (01492) 546570 ~ Children over 7 only ~ Open 11-3, 6.30-11; closed 25 Dec

LLANFIHANGEL CRUCORNEY (Gwent) SO3321 Map 6

Skirrid

Village signposted off A465

This is the oldest pub in Wales (and up there amongst the oldest in Britain), and many of the windows of this dark brown stone inn are medieval, while the oak beams were made from ships' timbers, and the panelling in the dining room is said to be from a British man o'war. The high-ceilinged bar has settles and wooden tables on its flagstones, walls stripped back to show ancient stonework, and a big open fire in the stone hearth. For many years the pub served as the area's courthouse, and between 1110 and the 17th c nearly 200 people were hanged here; you can still see the scorch and drag marks of the rope on the beam above the foot of the stairs which served as the traditional scaffold. Good popular bar food includes dishes like home-made soup, deep-fried camembert (£4.95), ploughman's with a range of Welsh cheeses, local sausages, excellent beef in ale pie (£5.95), wild rabbit with mushrooms, cream and garlic or filo pastry parcels with cream cheese and pine nuts (£6.50), and local lamb chops glazed with an apple and rosemary jelly (£6.95). Well kept Ushers Best, Founders and four seasonal brews on handpump, a range of malt whiskies; darts, pool and piped music. One reader was a little surprised to be charged for a glass of plain tap water, and a few others have found the generally friendly welcome can be a little variable – particularly if they're expecting big groups or coach parties in. A crazy-paved back terrace has white seats and tables, and there are more rustic ones on a small sloping back lawn. *(Recommended by R C Morgan, Gwynne Harper, Ian Jones, Gwen and Peter Andrews, Mr and Mrs P B Dowsett)*

Ushers ~ Lease: Steven and Heather Gant ~ Real ale ~ Meals and snacks (not Tues evening) ~ Restaurant ~ (01873) 890 258 ~ Children in restaurant till 9pm ~ Occasional folk or other live entertainment ~ Open 12-3, 7-11 ~ Bedrooms: £25B/£50B

LLANFRYNACH (Powys) SO0725 Map 6

White Swan ⬤

Village signposted from B4558, just off A40 E of Brecon bypass

The secluded terrace behind this pretty black and white pub is attractively divided into sections by roses and climbing shrubs, and overlooks peaceful paddocks; there are plenty of stone and other tables out here. Inside all is friendly and relaxed, and the lounge bar rambles back into a series of softly lit alcoves, with plenty of well spaced tables on the flagstones, a big log fire, and partly stripped stone walls; there may be piped classical music. Very good (though rather pricy) bar food includes french onion soup (£2.50), ploughman's (from £4), snails in garlic butter, lasagne or macaroni and broccoli cheese (£4.50), two eggs on garlic sausage, ham, peppers and green beans (£4.75), chicken curry or haddock and prawn pie (£6), lamb chops marinaded in garlic and herbs (£7.75), Welsh-style grilled trout with bacon (£8), beef and mushroom pie (£8.50), well hung steaks (from £9), puddings such as sherry trifle (£2.25), children's dishes (£3.75), and maybe weekend specials. Service is friendly and efficient; well kept Brains Bitter and Flowers IPA on handpump. The churchyard is across the very quiet village lane. *(Recommended by R T and J C Moggridge, C J Parsons, TBB, D J and J R Tapper, R C Morgan, P J Howell, A Kilpatrick, Andrew and Barbara Sykes)*

Free house ~ Licensee David Bell ~ Real ale ~ Meals and snacks (lunches stop 1.30 Sun) ~ (01874) 86276 ~ Children welcome ~ Open 12-2.30, 7-11; closed Mon (except bank hols), and last three weeks of Jan

LLANGATTOCK (Powys) SO2117 Map 6

Vine Tree

A4077; village signposted from Crickhowell

All the meals at this friendly dining pub seem to come with that little bit extra attention; they bake their own bread, most of their produce is carefully selected locally, and they even arrange children's meals to look like a funny face. Popular and generously served dishes include lunchtime filled baguettes and ploughman's (from £3.50), stock-pot soup (£1.55), home-made pâté (£2.95), garlic mushrooms with chilli butter (£2.95), cottage or fisherman's pie (£4.35), vegetable bake (£5.45), chicken cooked in spicy honey and tomato sauce (£6.55), fresh salmon or lamb chop with rosemary and garlic (£7.95), steaks (from £8.95), lots of puddings and Sunday roast beef, pork, lamb or chicken (£4.50); their fish comes twice a week from Cornwall, and they use local meat and vegetables. The front part of the bar has soft seats, some stripped stone, and brass ornaments around its open fireplace. The back part is set aside as a dining area with Windsor chairs, scrubbed deal tables, and decorative plates and highland cattle engravings on the walls; most of the tables are set out for eating. Well kept Bass, Boddingtons and Hook Norton Best on handpump. Tables under cocktail parasols give a view of the splendid medieval stone bridge over the River Usk, and a short stroll takes you to our Crickhowell main entry, the Bear. *(Recommended by Barry and Anne, P J Howell, Roger Danes, Brian Plowright; more reports please)*

Free house ~ Licensee I S Lennox ~ Real ale ~ Meals and snacks (12-2, 6-10) ~ Restaurant (not Sun evening) ~ (01873) 810514 ~ Children welcome ~ Open 12-3, 6-11

LLANGYNWYD (Mid Glamorgan) SS8588 Map 6

Old House

From A4063 S of Maesteg follow signpost Llan ¾ at Maesteg end of village; pub behind church

Known locally as Yr Hen Dy, this friendly thatched and thick walled pub dates back in part to 1147, making it among the oldest in Wales. It has quite a history – Wil Hopkin is said to have written *Bugeilio'r Gwenith Gwyn* here, and what's now the restaurant was originally the first nonconformist chapel in the Valleys.

It's been much modernised, but there are still comfortably traditional touches in the two cosy rooms of its busy bar, which have high-backed black built-in settles, lots of china and brass around the huge fireplace, shelves of bric-a-brac, and decorative jugs hanging from the beams. Generously served, good bar food includes soup (£1.70), sausages (£2.50), omelettes (from £3.50), aubergine lasagne (£3.80), home-made steak and kidney pie or beef curry (£3.95), salads (from £4.25), gammon and eggs (£5.95), hake cutlet or trout and almonds (£6.50), poached salmon (£7.75), steaks (from £9.40), puddings such as raspberry charlotte (£1.95), daily specials, and children's dishes (from £1.25). Well kept Brains SA, Flowers IPA and Original and a guest on handpump, good range of whiskies. An attractive conservatory extension (half no smoking) leads on to the garden with good views, play area, and a soft-ice-cream machine for children. At Christmas they still go in for the ancient Mari Lwyd tradition, where a horse's skull decorated with ribbons, on a stick, is paraded round the houses, with impromptu verses sung about the people in them. Not many places still do this, which is a great shame – abusing your neighbours using the excuse of an ancient custom strikes us as eminently enjoyable. *(Recommended by R Michael Richards, John and Joan Nash, JE Lloyd, John and Helen Thompson; more reports please)*

Whitbreads ~ Lease: R T and P C David ~ Real ale ~ Meals and snacks (till 10) ~ Restaurant ~ Maesteg (01656) 733310 ~ Children welcome ~ Open 11-11)

LLANNEFYDD (Clwyd) SH9871 Map 6
Hawk & Buckle
Village well signposted from surrounding main roads; one of the least taxing routes is from Henllan at junction of B5382 and B5429 NW of Denbigh

Seven hundred feet up in the hills, this welcoming village inn has remarkable views over Rhyl and Prestatyn to the Irish Sea from almost all its bedrooms (and its car park). In very clear weather you can see as far as the Lancashire coast, and on autumn evenings those with very keen sight may be able to pick out Blackpool Tower, 40 miles away, by its illuminations. The bar food is well above average, with a choice of home-made dishes like sandwiches, vegetarian meals (from £4.60), steak and kidney pie (£4.75), chicken madras or lasagne (£4.95), lemon sole (£6.50) and sirloin steak (from £7.95). The dining room is no smoking. The long knocked-through black-beamed lounge bar has comfortable modern upholstered settles around its walls and facing each other across the open fire, and a neat red carpet in the centre of its tiled floor, while a lively locals' side bar has darts and pool; good house wines. The landlord is friendly, as are the two cats and dog. There's an attractive mosaic mural on the way through into the back bedroom extension; the modern rooms here are comfortable and well equipped. *(Recommended by Daniel and Patricia Neukom, Ken and Monica Charlton, Maysie Thompson; more reports please)*

Free house ~ Licensee Bob Pearson ~ Meals and snacks (lunch service stops 1.30; no lunch winter weekdays) ~ Restaurant (closed Sun) ~ Llannefydd (0174) 579 249 ~ Children in eating area till 8 ~ Open 12-2(not winter weekdays), 7-11; closed 25 Dec ~ Bedrooms: £36B/£50B

LLANTHONY (Gwent) SO2928 Map 6
Abbey Hotel
Shortly after the abbey was founded here in the 12th c the site was described as 'a place truly fitted for contemplation', and despite the passing of time the same can still be said today. The pub, originally part of the prior's house, is lifted out of the ordinary by this lovely setting, one of the most unusual and atmospheric you're likely to come across; it's surrounded by and indeed really part of the abbey's graceful ruins, with lawns among the lofty arches and tranquil views towards the border hills. The dimly lit, vaulted crypt bar still has some of the atmosphere of its contemplative past – you can almost imagine the monks going about their daily business (if that's the right word). The main bar is basic and simply furnished with half-a-dozen wooden tables, spindleback chairs and wooden

benches on the flagstone floor, and serves well kept Bass, Brains SA, Hook Norton Best, Ruddles County, and Wadworths 6X on handpump or tapped from the cask, and farm cider in summer. Lunchtime bar food is simple too, with toasted sandwiches (£1.60), good home-made soups (£2.25), decent ploughman's (£3.95), and home-made meaty and vegetarian burgers (£3.95), with evening dishes like spicy bean goulash, (£4.95), nut roast with chestnut stuffing and wine sauce, casseroles or local lamb with garlic wine and mushrooms (all £5.95). Service can be a little indifferent at times. Note they don't allow children inside. On *Good Walks Guide* Walk 201. *(Recommended by Anthony Barnes, Patrick Freeman, John Nash, Sue Demont, Tim Barrow, Gwynne Harper, Barry and Anne)*

Free house ~ Licensee Ivor Prentice ~ Real ale ~ Meals and lunchtime snacks ~ Crucorney (01873) 890487 ~ Occasional live music ~ Open 11-3, 6-11; 11-11 Sat and summer hols; closed weekdays end Nov-end Mar except Christmas and New Year week ~ Bedrooms: £21(Sun-Thurs)/£41(£95 for Fri and Sat for two)

LLANWNDA (Gwynedd) SH4758 Map 6

Goat 🛏

Village (a couple of houses or so) signposted as short loop off A499 just S of junction with A487 S of Caernarfon

You often feel like a personal guest at this friendly village local, as the chatty Welsh speaking landlady really does make visitors welcome. For many the highlight has long been the excellent help-yourself lunchtime cold table, with well over twenty fresh and attractive dishes laid out on crisp linen: £5.50 for as much as you like, including starters such as fresh melon in ginger wine and sherry-marinated grapefruit, then over half a dozen fish like prawns, herring, or smoked mackerel, several cold meats like home baked ham, freshly baked quiche, and five different cheeses to finish. They no longer do this all through the summer, generally limiting it to high season and week or ten days around each bank holiday from Easter. The other food shows the same careful touch, with home-made soup like curried vegetable (£2), particularly good and rather different sandwiches (from £2), substantial ploughman's with two cheeses, home-cured ham and fruit (£3.95), and grilled farmhouse breakfast (£5, from 8am-10am). Well kept Bass and Boddingtons on handpump, some malt whiskies; good service. The main bar area at the back is divided into two rooms by the almost circular bar counter, which has an old-fashioned small-paned rounded screen complete with serving hatch, and an ancient cash register. Visitors go for the bright red plush chairs by the coal fire on the left and the Welsh speakers seem to gravitate to the red leatherette button-back built-in wall banquettes around the four tables on the right. A genteel front room on the right is reserved for non-smokers. In the evenings the buffet table's stripped down to reveal a pool table; also, dominoes, fruit machine and juke box. Tables on the sunny front terrace, another under a sycamore down in the garden. *Recommended by John Atherton, Michael and Janet Hepworth, Gordon Theaker, Simon Reynolds, E H and R F Warner)*

Free house ~ Licensee Anne Griffith ~ Real ale ~ Lunchtime meals and snacks (not Sun) ~ Caernarfon (01286) 830256 ~ Children welcome ~ Open 11-4, 6-11; closed Sun ~ Bedrooms: £15/£30

LLANYNYS (Clwyd) SJ1063 Map 7

Cerrigllwydion Arms ◖

Village signposted from A525 by Drovers Arms just out of Ruthin, and by garage in Pentre further towards Denbigh

A happy place in a wonderfully remote setting, this characterful old pub dates back in part some 600 years. Much loved by readers, it looks quite small from the outside but once through the door actually rambles about delightfully, its maze of atmospheric little rooms filled with dark oak beams and panelling, a good mix of seats, old stonework, interesting brasses, and a collection of teapots. Well kept Bass and Tetleys on handpump, and a decent choice of whiskies and liqueurs;

good coffee. Very pleasant service from chatty staff, maybe a big friendly labrador. Darts, dominoes and unobtrusive piped music. Good bar food using fresh local ingredients includes home-made soup (£1.70) and sandwiches, as well as changing hot dishes such as sizzling chicken and rice (£5.50), plaice with lobster and prawn sauce (£6.50) and grilled salmon steak with herb butter (£7.50). Across the quiet lane is a neat garden with teak tables among fruit trees looking across the fields to low wooded hills; the church is interesting. *(Recommended by R W Abel, G Richardson, E G Parish, G Hallett, Brian Kneale, Paul Boot, Jeanne and Tom Barnes, KC, D A Hasprey, Roger and Christine Mash, A P Jeffreys)*

Free house ~ Licensee Jennifer Anne Lee ~ Real ale ~ Meals and snacks ~ Restaurant ~ Llanynys (01745) 78247 ~ Children welcome ~ Open 11.30-3, 7-11

LLWYNDAFYDD (Dyfed) SN3755 Map 6

Crown 🏮

Coming S from New Quay on A486, both the first two right turns eventually lead to the village; the side roads N from A487 between junctions with B4321 and A486 also come within signpost distance; OS Sheet 145 map reference 371555

Firmly standing out in an otherwise undistinguished area for pubs, this attractive place is a popular choice for a family lunch, and even out of season it can be busy. The pretty tree-sheltered garden has won several awards, and there are picnic-table sets on a terrace above a small pond among shrubs and flowers, as well as a good play area for children. Well-liked home-made bar food includes decent lunchtime sandwiches, as well as home-made soup (£2.30), garlic mushrooms (£2.95), deep-fried haddock (£4.95), pizzas (from £5.25), vegetarian stuffed peppers or home-made pies such as lamb or steak and kidney (£5.45), salads (from £5.50), local trout (£5.95), steaks (from £7.55), and children's menu (from £2); the choice may be limited at Sunday lunchtime when they do a traditional roast. Notably well kept Boddingtons, Flowers IPA and Original and guest, a range of wines, and good choice of malt whiskies. The friendly, partly stripped-stone bar has red plush button-back banquettes around its copper-topped tables, and a big woodburning stove; piped music. It's best to get there early if you want a seat at the weekend. The side lane leads down to a cove with caves by National Trust cliffs. *(Recommended by Ian Phillips, G W and M C Brooke-Williams, J E and A G Jones; more reports please)*

Free house ~ Licensee Keith Soar ~ Real ale ~ Meals and lunchtime snacks (12-2, 6-9) ~ Restaurant ~ New Quay (01545) 560396 ~ Children in eating area and long room without bar ~ Open 12-3, 6-11; closed Sun evening Jan-March

LLYSWEN (Powys) SO1337 Map 6

Griffin ★ 🛏 ♀

A470, village centre

The friendly family that run this attractive ivy-covered inn have just celebrated their tenth year here. During that time the pub has become very highly regarded for its warmly old-fashioned character and good range of hearty country cooking, and it's not hard to see that the licensees really enjoy running the place and organising its varied activities. Relying firmly on local produce (some from their own gardens), the very good meals at lunchtime might include delicious home-made soup such as cream of caerphilly, onion and thyme (£2.90), home-made pâtés or cold curried chicken salad (£3.25), a selection of Welsh cheeses (£4.65), ratatouille pasta au gratin (£4.95), venison burger, shepherd's pie or salmon fishcakes (£5.75), lamb's liver and bacon, braised oxtail, fresh trout or wild rabbit stew (all £7.85), and home-made puddings like lemon crunch or banana and rum trifle (£2.85), with evening dishes such as stilton, celery and port terrine (£3.95), black-eyed bean and leek pie (£7.75), roast duckling with apple sauce (£10.50) and sirloin steak (£10.50). Most days after Easter they serve brook trout and salmon, caught by the family or by customers in the River Wye – just over the road – and they are particularly renowned for very good seasonal game dishes such as jugged hare or pheasant (around £8.50). In the evenings you may find a range of tapas, and they do regular theme nights and menus. Boddingtons and Flowers IPA on handpump, and a good varied wine list with several half bottles. The Fishermen's Bar is decorated with old fishing tackle and has a big stone fireplace with a good log fire, and large Windsor armchairs, leatherette wall benches and padded stools around its low tables; at lunchtime there's extra seating in the no-smoking dining room for bar meals. Quoits, a couple of resident cats, and huge dog, Amber; others are allowed. You can shoot or fish here and can have lessons (or courses) in both – they have a full-time ghillie and keeper. It's a particularly pleasant place to stay. The dining room is no smoking. Service is friendly and helpful, though can slow down at busy times. *(Recommended by Martin and Pauline Richardson, Sue Demont, Tim Barrow, Patrick Freeman, David J B Lewis, Dave and Jules Tuckett, Dr and Mrs A K Clarke, A K Thorlby, Wyn Churchill, Pat and John Millward, Cl G D Stafford, Mrs A Archer, Madeline and Ernest Knight, Mrs J Oakes)*

Free house ~ Licensees Richard and Di Stockton ~ Real ale ~ Meals and snacks (roast only Sun lunchtime, no food Sun evening except for residents) ~ Restaurant (not Sun evening) ~ Llyswen (01874) 754241 ~ Children welcome ~ Open 12-3, 7-11 ~ Bedrooms: £28.50B/£50B

MAENTWROG (Gwynedd) SH6741 Map 6

Grapes ★ 🛏️ ♇ 🍺

A496; village signposted from A470

Well geared up for families, this warmly welcoming and atmospheric old coaching inn is very popular with readers at the moment, and has long been a favourite with locals (always a good sign) – you'll often hear Welsh speakers mixed up with the visitors come to eat the consistently tasty bar food. Home-made, wholesome, and served in hearty helpings, the choice at lunchtime includes sandwiches and ploughman's, notably good soup (£1.60), filled tacos or pitta bread (£2.75), seafood crêpes or locally smoked mussels (£3.75), fried sliced beef with mushrooms in french bread (£3.85), burgers or salads (from £4.50), several vegetarian (and vegan) dishes like stilton and mushroom bake or vegetable croquettes (£5), steak and kidney pie (£5.25), pork schnitzel or beef balti (£5.75), rack of Welsh lamb (£6.75), 10oz steaks (from £8.50), and children's meals (£2.25); specials these days tend to concentrate on fresh fish, with tasty dishes like a very good fish pie (£5.75), monkfish tails in orange sauce (£6.25), grilled turbot with anchovy butter (£6.75), blackened redfish (£7) and john dory with a wine and asparagus sauce (£7.75). Big breakfasts. Quick, friendly service even at the busiest times, reliably well kept Bass, Morlands Old Speckled Hen, Worthingtons Best and a rotated guest beer on handpump, varied wine list (especially in the restaurant), decent selection of malts, and good coffee. All three bars are full of stripped pitch-pine usually salvaged from chapels – pews, settles, pillars and carvings, and the effect is very attractive and characterful. Good log fires – there's one in the great hearth of the restaurant where there may be spit-roasts. You shouldn't be able to hear the piped music in the lounge or dining room. Dominoes, cribbage and interesting juke box in the public bar, where there's also an intriguing collection of brass blowlamps. The good-sized, sheltered verandah (with a shellfish counter at one end) catches the evening sunshine and has lovely views over a pleasant back terrace and walled garden; there's a fountain on the lawn, and magnificent further views. The dining room is no smoking. *(Recommended by David Atkinson, the Mair family, David Rogers, Gordon Theaker, Mr and Mrs H Hobden, Michael and Janet Hepworth, Dave and Jules Tuckett, David J B Lewis, John Nash, Phil and Heidi Cook, Jay Voss, G Richardson, J E Hilditch, Roy Smylie, Roger Byrne, John Coatsworth, Dave Thompson, Margaret Mason, John Evans)*

Free house ~ Licensees Brian and Gill Tarbox ~ Real ale ~ Meals and snacks (12-2.15, 6-9.30) ~ Restaurant (not Sun evening) ~ Maentwrog (0176 685) 208/365 ~ Children in family room and verandah (with baby changing facilities ~ Open 11-11 ~ Bedrooms: £25B/£50B

Sunday opening is 12-3 and 7-10.30 in all Welsh pubs allowed to open that day (we mention in the text the few that aren't).

MARIANGLAS (Anglesey) SH5084 Map 6

Parciau Arms
B5110

Warmly cosy and welcoming, this friendly palce is a well liked lunchtime food
stop. There's plenty to look at around its gleaming bar, with local colour
photographs on the dark red hessian walls of the inner bar area, and miner's
lamps, horse bits, lots of brass (especially car horns), horsebrasses, a mounted
jungle fowl and other bric-a-brac dotted around. The main seating area has
comfortable built-in wall banquettes and stools around elm tables, a big settee
matching the flowery curtains, spears, rapiers and so forth on the elaborate
chimney-breast over the coal fire, and antique coaching prints. An airy family
dining room with little bunches of flowers on the tables has a series of prints
illustrating the rules of golf. Decent bar food includes sandwiches (from £1.65),
home-made soup (£2), lots of pizzas (from £3.25), filled baked potatoes or
vegetable curry (£4.50), ploughman's (from £4.95), turkey rogan josh (£5.25),
local plaice with parsley sauce or home-made steak and kidney pie (£6.25),
gammon and egg or a choice of salads (£6.50), fresh poached salmon (£6.95), 8oz
sirloin steak (£9.25), puddings like sherry trifle, children's meals (from £2.50),
and specials such as chicken provençale, fresh trout, liver and bacon or popular
lamb in cider (all £6.50); also morning coffee and afternoon tea. Well kept Bass,
Tetleys and changing guests like Marstons Pedigree or Youngs Special on
handpump, various wines and whiskies, freshly squeezed orange juice; obliging,
cheery service. Darts, pool, cribbage, dominoes, fruit machine, video game,
satellite tv, juke box and piped music; boules area. There are picnic-table sets on
a terrace, with pews and other tables under cocktail parasols in a good-sized
garden; it also has a good play area including a pensioned-off tractor, a camel-
slide, a climber and a children's cabin with video game. *(Recommended by M Joyner,
Mr and Mrs D C Shenton, Dr D H Jones, Richard Houghton, Mr and Mrs A E McCully)*

*Free house ~ Licensee Philip Moore ~ Real ale ~ Meals and snacks (11am-
9.30pm) ~ Restaurant ~ (01248) 853766 ~ Well behaved children in eating area
of bar till 8.30 ~ Open 11-11; only open 2 hours lunchtime 25 Dec*

MOLD (Clwyd) SJ1962 Map 7

We Three Loggerheads
Loggerheads; A494 3 miles towards Ruthin

Though there's still quite a pubby feel to this carefully refurbished old pub the
emphasis is very much on the food, with the menu featuring a good number of
rather unusual dishes and flavours. As well as sandwiches (£2.75), you might find
well presented dishes such as spicy Greek sausages with yoghurt and mint dip
(£3.25), a choice of ploughman's (£4.45), home-made chicken and mango curry
or pies like steak and kidney with Guinness or pumpkin and cheese (£5.25), and a
huge range of interesting daily specials like lamb samosas with yoghurt and mint
dip (£3.25), moules marinières (£4.25), Chinese-style Peking duck (£4.95),
popular spicy Mexican feast (nachos in melted cheese with jalapenos, sour cream,
chillis, salsa and taco dips, £6.95), and cajun or Thai spiced chicken in a coconut
shell with fresh pineapple salad (£7.25); home-made puddings might include spice
and cinnamon rice pudding or a brandy snap basket with fresh berries, fruit
coulis and crème anglais (from £2.25); children's dishes and half portions
available. It's on two levels, with on the right owl prints and other country
pictures, stuffed birds and a stuffed fox, and lighting by pretty converted paraffin
lamps. On the left a tiled-floor locals' bar has pool, dominoes, shove-ha'penny
and table skittles. The arched windows came from a former colliery winding
house. Up steps at the back is a really spacious area with high rafters, pillars, a
false ceiling holding farm machinery and carts, and comfortable green cloth
banquettes set around tables in stripped-wood stalls. Well kept Bass tapped from
the cask and maybe a guest beer or two; friendly, chatty service. Loudish juke
box, fruit machine and trivia. There are white tables and chairs on a side terrace.
The sign outside only has two faces – ask about the other and they point back at

you as the third. *(Recommended by David and Ruth Shillitoe, KC, Simon and Louise Chappell, Paul McPherson, Roy Cove, P Boot, Brian Kneale, P Neate)*

Bass ~ Manager Gary Willard ~ Real ale ~ Meals and snacks (till 10; not Sun evening) ~ Restaurant (not Sun evening) ~ (0135 285) 337 ~ Children welcome ~ Open 12-3, 5.30-11, all day Sat; closed evening 25 Dec

MONMOUTH (Gwent) SO5113 Map 6

Punch House

Agincourt Square

A good traditional market-town pub, this is a handsome place, the 17th-c building decked out with colourful hanging baskets. There are tables outside on the cobblestones overlooking the square. Inside, the spreading open-plan beamed bar has a chatty, relaxed atmosphere, red leatherette settles, lots of copper, brass and horse-tack, bound copies of early issues of *Punch* (even the dog is called Punch), a big fireplace, and the original oak gate from the town gaol. Big helpings of popular bar food such as lunchtime sandwiches, home-made soup (£1.50), steak and kidney pie (£4.75), mexican chicken, cod in parsley sauce on a bed of spinach or beef bourguignon (all £5), pork provençale or curried chicken (£5.50), and a roast of the day (£6.75); quick, friendly service. Well kept Bass, Hancocks HB, Wadworths 6X and Worthington Best on handpump; fruit machine, piped music. *(Recommended by Bryan Hicks, M A Cameron; more reports please)*

Free house ~ Licensee John Wills ~ Real ale ~ Meals and snacks ~ Restaurant (not Sun evening) ~ (01600) 713855 ~ Children welcome ~ Occasional live entertainment ~ Open 11-11; 11-3, 5-11 Mon-Thurs in winter; closed 25 Dec

MONTGOMERY (Powys) SO2296 Map 6

Dragon ◀

The Square

Friendly and characterful, a strikingly timbered 17th-c hotel in the centre of this peaceful county town, well placed for splendid walks and views. Many of the beams and much of the masonry are reputed to have come from the castle just up the hill after it was destroyed by Cromwell. Other interesting old features include a window in the restaurant signed by the hangman at his last public hanging in the market square, and an arch from the pub's days as a coaching inn now converted to an inside patio. It's a popular place for eating, with good bar meals such as sandwiches and toasties (from £1.85), soup (£1.95), ploughman's (from £3.50), fresh pasta with a sauce of the day (£2.50), filled baked potatoes (from £2.75), vegetable curry (£5.25), steak and kidney pie, lamb's liver in a bacon and walnut gravy or baked whole trout with capers and lemon (all £6.25), mixed grill (£8.95), and children's meals (£2.75); three course Sunday lunch (£7.50, more in restaurant). You can use the hotel swimming pool if you order a full meal in the bar or partly no-smoking restaurant; book the pool and the food will be ready when you come out. The friendly carpeted lounge bar has a window seat looking down to the market square and the old town hall (which has a very sweet-toned clock bell), tapestried stools and wall benches around dimpled copper tables, game bird and old England prints, and willow-pattern plates on a high shelf, up by the colonial ceiling fan. Efficient and welcoming licensees. Very well kept Felinfoel Double Dragon, Powells Old Sam and a weekly changing guest on handpump, and good coffee; there may be piped music. *(Recommended by R Ward, Joan and Michel Hooper-Immins, Margaret and Arthur Dickinson, G A and J E Gibbs, Hugh Spottiswoode, A Barker)*

Free house ~ Licensees Mark and Sue Michaels ~ Real ale ~ Meals and snacks (limited choice after 7.30pm Sat) ~ Restaurant (lunchtime bookings essential) ~ Montgomery (01686) 668 359/287 ~ Children welcome ~ Open 11-11 ~ Bedrooms: £41B/£67B

Sunday opening is 12-3 and 7-10.30; but pubs around Porthmadog and on the Lleyn Peninsula are not allowed to open for drinks that day.

NEVERN (Dyfed) SN0840 Map 6

Trewern Arms 🛏

B4582 – a useful short-cut alternative to most of the A487 Newport—Cardigan

It's the stripped-stone slate-floored bar that most people head for at this cosily extended inn, its high rafters strung with nets, ships' lamps, ancient farm and household equipment, shepherds' crooks and cauldrons, and with a couple of high-backed traditional settles, and comfortable plush banquette seating. Well kept Boddingtons, Flowers Original and Whitbreads Castle Eden and Pompey Royal on handpump; efficient service. A games room has sensibly placed darts, pool, fruit machine, video game, trivia, and a loudish juke box; beyond is a more spacious lounge. The lawn has tables set among shrubs and trees. Generous helpings of bar food such as sandwiches, ploughman's (£3.70), quarter chicken (£4.80), vegetarian dishes (£5.70), steak and kidney pie or lasagne (£5.90), trout and almonds or gammon (£6.90) and steaks (from £9), with children's dishes (from £2.80), and puddings; huge breakfasts. The pub is a welcoming sight as you come round the bend from the little medieval bridge over the River Nyfer. The pilgrims' church over the river has a notable Celtic cross and pre-Christian stones set into its windows, and is sheltered by fat yew trees which are said to weep tears of what local people say is blood if the priest is not Welsh-speaking. *(Recommended by Patrick Freeman, S P Bobeldijk, Roy and Bettie Derbyshire, Jed and Virginia Brown, Mac Tennick; more reports please)*

Free house ~ Licensee Mrs E A Jones ~ Real ale ~ Meals and snacks ~ Restaurant (Thurs-Sat and Sunday lunch) ~ Newport (01239) 820395 ~ Children in eating area and games room until 9pm ~ Open 11-3, 6-11 ~ Bedrooms: £28S/£45S

OLD RADNOR (Powys) SO2559 Map 6

Harp 🛏

Village signposted from A44 Kington—New Radnor just W of B4362 junction

Charles I was one of the few people left unmoved by the rather special setting and atmosphere of this old hilltop place – when he stayed here he complained about the food. Other people though seem to be won over straight away, with perhaps the new licensees as notable examples. They came here for their honeymoon two decades ago and liked it so much that when they heard last year it was on the market they bought it straight away. Settling down again after a few teething troubles, the pub guards the village green from its nice position beside the 15th-c turreted church (worth a look for its early organ screen), and has splendid views over the Marches; there's plenty of seating out here, under the big sycamore tree, and on the side grass, where there's a play area, and lots of resident geese and goslings, ducks, and Jersey cows. Inside, it's full of character, and the old-fashioned brownstone public bar has high-backed settles, an antique reader's chair and other elderly chairs around a log fire, as well as friendly locals; they play table quoits (Monday evenings) and cribbage (Fridays). The cosy slate-floored lounge has a handsome curved antique settle and a fine inglenook log fire, and there are lots of local books and guides for residents. Well kept Woods Bitter and Special, Wye Valley Hereford and guests on handpump. Simple bar food might include very good home-made soup (£1.75), garlic mushrooms (£2.95), club sandwiches (£3.95), and salad niçoise (£4.95). No dogs. Lots of good walks nearby, including *Good Walks Guide* Walk 93. *(Recommended by Sarah and Peter Gooderham, Margaret and Arthur Dickinson, John MacLean, James Skinner, Anthony Barnes, Pat and John Millward, Richard and Maria Gillespie, Peter Griffiths, L Walker, Drs G N and M G Yates, J G Quick, A P Jeffreys)*

Free house ~ Licensees Stephen and Dee Cope ~ Real ale ~ Meals and snacks (not Mon) ~ Restaurant ~ New Radnor (0154) 421 655 ~ Well behaved children welcome ~ Live entertainment Sat lunchtime ~ Open 11.30-11, maybe less in winter ~ Bedrooms: £25/£35

Post Office address codings confusingly give the impression that some pubs are in Gwent or Powys, Wales when they're really in Gloucestershire or Shropshire (which is where we list them).

PEMBROKE FERRY (Dyfed) SM9603 Map 6

Ferry

Nestled below A477 toll bridge, N of Pembroke

This former sailors' haunt has a nautical decor to suit its past, and its attractive setting right on the water can make for fascinating views. It has a very rewarding combination of a fine relaxed yet buoyantly pubby atmosphere with a good range of drinks and good tasty food that makes full use of local produce – particularly from the sea. Fish is cooked simply, so as not to mask the delicacy of its freshness: between cod and plaice (£4.25) and lobster (£8 to £11) there may be brill, turbot, Dover sole, local Carew oysters, crayfish or crab. Other dishes include scampi (£4.50), schnitzel with a creamy mushroom sauce (£4.95) and steak (£7.95), with a good choice of puddings, not all home-made (£2.25). They have well kept Bass, Hancocks HB and Worthington Dark Mild on handpump, with an interesting guest beer such as the new Caffreys Irish Ale, and a decent choice of malt whiskies. Booking is virtually essential for Sunday lunch. Efficient service, fruit machine, unobtrusive piped music. There are tables out on the waterside terrace. *(Recommended by Ian Jones, R and M Jones, Mr and Mrs R Franklin, R T and J C Moggridge, Linda and Brian Davis)*

Free house ~ Licensee David Henderson ~ Real ale ~ Meals and snacks (till 10) ~ Restaurant ~ (01646) 682947 ~ Children in restaurant lunchtime ~ Open 11.30-2.45, 6.30(7 Mon)-11

PONTYPOOL (Gwent) ST2998 Map 6

Open Hearth 🍺

The Wern, Griffithstown; Griffithstown signposted off A4051 S – opposite British Steel main entrance turn up hill, then first right

The stretch of the Monmouthshire & Brecon Canal which runs above this cheery and welcoming pub has recently reopened, and you can watch the comings and goings from the comfortable lounge bar. But the main attraction here is the excellent range of changing real ales on handpump, much better than you'll find anywhere else in the area, with usually 10 very well priced weekly changing brews such as Archers Best and Golden, Bass, Brains Dark and SA, Boddingtons, Bull Mastiff Best, Hancocks HB, Hook Norton and Smiles Bitter; they also have a good choice of wines and malt whiskies. Reliably tasty and good value bar food includes well liked filled rolls (from £1.30), soup (£1.50), filled baked potatoes (from £2.75), various curries (from £3.95), vegetable stir fry (£4.50), steak and Guinness pie or rainbow trout with almonds (£4.95), cheese filled tortellini with baby sweetcorn and mixed peppers (£5.25), gammon or lamb's kidneys in a creamy mustard and sherry sauce (£5.50), lamb cutlets grilled with mint butter (£5.95), and whole spring chicken with chasseur sauce (£6.50); three-course Sunday lunch (£7.50). They do their best to suit you if you want something not on the menu, and the downstairs restaurant is something of a local landmark; decent coffee, cheap tea, very friendly and efficient service. The smallish, comfortably modernised lounge has a turkey carpet and big stone fireplace; a back bar has more space and leatherette seating. Cribbage, dominoes and piped music; boules in summer. There are picnic-table sets, swings, and shrubs outside. *(Recommended by Mike Pugh, the Monday Club, Graham Reeve, J E Lloyd)*

Free house ~ Licensees Gwyn Philips and Roger MacMillan ~ Real ale ~ Meals and snacks (till 10) ~ Restaurant ~ Pontypool (01495) 763752 ~ Children in eating area and restaurant ~ Open 11.30-3(4 Sat), 6-11

PRESTEIGNE (Powys) SO3265 Map 6

Radnorshire Arms 🛏

High Street; B4355 N of centre

Renovations at this rambling timbered Forte inn have revealed secret passages and priest's holes, with one priest's diary showing he was walled up here for two years. It's probably now a good deal more comfortable than he'd remember it, though he'd recognise the venerable dark oak panelling, latticed windows and elegantly moulded black oak beams now decorated with horsebrasses; the old-fashioned charm and atmosphere never seem to change. Reasonably priced bar food might include good sandwiches, home-made soup (£1.95), Cumberland sausage and mash (£2.95), ploughman's (£3.50), vegetable lasagne (£3.95), a pie of the day (£4.45), minute steak in granary roll (£4.75), gammon steak with fried egg (£5.95) and puddings (£2.95); children's helpings (about £2.10), morning coffee, afternoon tea. Bass and Courage Directors on handpump, English wines by the glass, several malt whiskies, and welcoming, attentive service; separate no-smoking restaurant. Furnishings are discreetly modern. There are some well spaced tables on the sheltered flower-bordered lawn, which used to be a bowling green. The building was constructed by the brother of one of the men who signed Charles I's death warrant, though it wasn't actually licensed until 1792. This is a nice area for a quiet weekend. *(Recommended by Ian Jones, the Monday Club, Neville Kenyon, Pat and John Millward, A P Jeffreys, Lt Cdr L R Ball)*

Free house ~ Manager Aidan Treacy ~ Real ale ~ Meals and snacks ~ Restaurant (not Sun evening) ~ Presteigne (01544) 267406 ~ Children welcome ~ Open 11-11 ~ Bedrooms: £73.50B/£92B

nr RAGLAN (Gwent) SO3608 Map 6

Clytha Arms

Clytha, off Abergavenny road – former A40, now declassified

This fine old building has been carefully and tastefully refurbished by its new owners over the two years they've been there – bringing with them a good few admirers from the Beaufort Arms at Monkswood, where they'd previously built a strong reputation for good food in civilised yet pleasantly pubby surroundings. They've created the same sort of effect here on a rather broader scale, with good solidly comfortable traditional furnishings, log fires, and a warm welcome from cheerful helpful staff (and maybe quietly friendly dogs). They have half a dozen well kept ales on handpump including Hancocks HB, Hook Norton Best, Theakstons XB and interesting changing guest beers such as Dent Ramsbottom and Hardington Old Lucifer, Weston's farm ciders and freshly squeezed orange juice; darts, table skittles, cribbage, draughts and chess – no music or machines. The changing choice of fresh food, well prepared and presented, is increasingly the main draw, and besides sandwiches and a choice of ploughman's (£4.35), the menu chalked on the beams might include faggot and mushy peas (£3.20), Manx kippers (£3.35), leek laver bread and caerphilly cheese rissoles (£3.45), moules marinières (£3.75), venison sausages with potato pancakes (£3.95), scrambled eggs with smoked seatrout (£5.50), Caribbean fruit curry (£6.95), cajun spiced quail (£9.60) or Chinese-style bass (£12.20), with a good selection of often delicious home-made puddings (£3) and a good value Sunday lunch. There is a roomy no-smoking dining room. *(Recommended by Gwyneth and Salvo Spadaro-Dutturi, A R and B E Sayer, R and M Jones, Mike Pugh, Julia Stone)*

Free house ~ Licensees Andrew and Beverley Canning ~ Real ale ~ Meals and snacks (not Sun evening or Mon lunchtime) ~ Restaurant ~ (01873) 840206 ~ Children welcome away from bar till 8 ~ Open 11.30-3.30, 6-11; all day Sat; cl Mon lunchtime exc bank hols ~ Bedrooms: /£40B

RED WHARF BAY (Anglesey) SH5281 Map 6

Ship ◀

Village signposted off B5025 N of Pentraeth

Lovely fresh sea views from this solid, slate-roofed 16th-c house: tables on the front terrace look down over ten square miles of treacherous tidal cockle-sands, with low wooded hills sloping down to the broad bay. Inside is characterful and old-fashioned, with a big room on each side of the busy stone-built bar counter, both with long cushioned varnished pews built around the walls, glossily varnished cast-iron-framed tables, and quite a restrained decor including toby jugs, local photographs, attractive antique foxhunting cartoons and coal fires. Enterprising and well presented daily changing bar food might typically include sandwiches, chicken liver pâté (£3.95), ploughman's (£4.10), stilton and broccoli quiche or cold chicken and ham pie with home-made chutney (£4.30), braised oxtail (£4.85), spinach tart or mussels in garlic topped with cheese (£4.95), casseroled hake (£5.75), pepperpot beef with ginger or chicken balti (£5.80), roast duckling with black cherries (£9.20) and puddings like mincemeat meringue pie (£2.55); tea, various coffees. There may be delays at busy times, but service is always friendly and smiling; the cheery licensees have been here now for over 20 years. The dining room is no smoking. The well kept Tetleys Mild and Bitter, a beer brewed for the pub, and guests like Youngs Bitter are drawn by handpump with a tight spray to give a northern-style creamy head; a wider choice of wines than usual for the area, and quite a few malt whiskies. Pool, darts and dominoes in the back room, and a family room; piped music. There are rustic tables and picnic-table sets by an ash tree on grass by the side. *(Recommended by Mark Bradley, Philip Putwain, Brian and Jill Bond, L G Milligan, Mr and Mrs B Hobden, Simon Reynolds, David and Rebecca Killick, Margaret Mason, David Thompson)*

Free house ~ Licensee Andrew Kenneally ~ Real ale ~ Meals and snacks ~ (01248) 852568 ~ Children in family room ~ Open 11-11 Jul-Sept, otherwise 12-3.30, 7-11 weekdays and bank hols

ST HILARY (S Glamorgan) ST0173 Map 6

Bush ◀

Village signposted from A48 E of Cowbridge

Genuinely old-fashioned and friendly, this is a lovely old 16th-c thatched pub tucked away behind the village church, still said to be haunted by a notorious local highwayman and very close to Stalling Down, a hill rich in Welsh history. The comfortable and snugly cosy low-beamed lounge bar has walls stripped to the old stone, and Windsor chairs around copper-topped tables on the carpet, while the public bar has old settles and pews on aged flagstones, and darts, bar billiards, table skittles, cribbage and dominoes in a room leading off; piped music. Good bar food, using fresh ingredients, includes sandwiches (from £1.50), french onion soup (£1.95), laverbread and bacon (£2.35), Welsh rarebit (£2.95), spinach and cheese pancake (£3.35), ploughman's (£3.60), liver or sausages with onion gravy (£3.95), salads (from £3.95), steak and ale pie (£4.75), gammon (£5.25), mixed grill (£6.75) and good daily specials; the restaurant menu is available in the bar in the evenings, with meals like trout pan-fried in sherry with toasted almonds (£7.95) or medallions of pork Normandy (£8.50). Well kept Bass, Morlands Old Speckled Hen and a guest such as Crown Buckley Reverend James on handpump, with a range of malt whiskies; friendly and efficient service. There are tables and chairs in front, and more in the back garden. *(Recommended by Gwynne Harper, Brian and Gill Hopkins; more reports please)*

Bass ~ Lease: Sylvia Murphy ~ Real ale ~ Meals and snacks (till 10; not Sun evening) ~ Restaurant (not Sun evening) ~ (01446) 772745 ~ Children welcome ~ Open 11.30-11

STACKPOLE (Dyfed) SR9896 Map 6

Armstrong Arms ⊕

Village signposted off B4319 S of Pembroke

Though this rather Swiss-looking building on the Stackpole estate was converted some time ago, it was opened as a pub only a couple of years ago – and what's remarkable for such a new place is that the cooking is already very assured, giving extremely satisfying pub meals. Besides sandwiches (from £1.35) and ploughman's (from £3.45), cheerful black-and-white uniformed waitresses serve good soups such as watercress (£1.80), a changing selection of about 15 main courses such as grilled bacon chops (£5.45), mushroom stroganoff with brandy and cream sauce (£5.50), steak and kidney or parmesan-and-potato-topped fish pie (£5.95), pork loin with apple sauce (£6.45), supreme of chicken in apricot sauce (£7.45) and a good choice of fresh fish from cod (£5.50) and plaice (£6) to brill, baby turbot or Dover sole. There is a choice of chips, new or baked potatoes, and of first-class fresh vegetables or salad. The home-made puddings are often a high point – ginger cake pudding, blackberry and apple pie, crème brûlée, strawberry pavlova (all around £2). Coffee is good (it's a shame, given the high standards in other respects, that they use those irritating plastic pots of cream and portioned butter). One spacious area has darts, pool, fruit machine and juke box (with lower prices for the well kept Bass and Worthington BB), but the major part of the pub, L-shaped on four different levels, is given over to diners, with neat light oak furnishings, and glossy beams and ceilings to match. There are tables out in the attractive gardens, with colourful flowerbeds and mature trees around the car park. *(Recommended by David Wallington, Miss L Kassam, D Bruford)*

Free house ~ Licensees Senga and Peter Waddilove ~ Real ale ~ Meals and snacks (not winter Sun evenings) ~ (01646) 672324 ~ Children welcome ~ Open 11-3, 6-11

TREMEIRCHION (Clwyd) SJ0873 Map 6

Salusbury Arms ◀

Off B5429 up lane towards church

Some of the panelling in this neatly civilised country pub dates from the 14th c, and is said to have come originally from St Asaph's Cathedral. The current licensees are encouraging a good traditionally pubby feel and atmosphere – they even have community singing at weekends. The lower part of the smallish beamed bar has richly upholstered seats on the thick carpet, and there are three log fires. Well kept Marstons Pedigree, Morlands Old Speckled Hen and four monthly changing guests on handpump; attentive, friendly service. Home-made bar food includes dishes like soup (£1.50), sandwiches (from £1.75), filled baked potatoes, chicken curry (£5.75), steak and kidney pie (£5.95), gammon (£6.25), trout or chicken in white wine and cucumber sauce (£7.50), speciality steaks (from £7.95), and children's meals; on Sunday they do a main course and pudding for £5.50. A games room houses a pool table, darts, dominoes, cribbage, fruit machine, trivia, chess and sports television. Tables in the pretty gardens are set among flowers, shrubs and a pond with goldfish; there's also an under-cover barbecue. *(Recommended by Mr and Mrs R F Wright, John and Avian Withinshaw, G B Rimmer, E Riley, J E Rycroft, C F Walling, Ian Morley; more reports please)*

Free house ~ Licensees Heulwen and Jim O'Boyle ~ Real ale ~ Meals and snacks (not Sun evening) ~ Restaurant (not Sun evening) ~ Bodfari (01745) 710 262 ~ Children welcome ~ Organist and community singing Fri-Sat, quiz Sun ~ Open 11-11; 11-3, 6.30-11 winter

TUDWEILIOG (Gwynedd) SH2437 Map 6

Lion ⇔

Nefyn Rd; B4417, Lleyn Peninsula

This cheery 17th-c village inn is a friendly and helpful place to stay. A good choice of decent bar food, served in either the cosy and welcoming main bar or the no-smoking extension family dining room, includes home-made soup (£1.25), lunchtime sandwiches (from £1.75), filled baked potatoes (from £2.25) and ploughman's (£3.95), as well as burger in a bap (£2.35), home-made steak and kidney pie or lasagne (£4.35), Spanish-style chicken or spare ribs (£4.95), gammon and egg (£5), vegetarian dishes such as tagliatelle niçoise (£5.75) or wheat casserole (£5.95), chicken tikka masala (£5.85), sirloin steak (£7.95), and puddings (from £1.80; the hot chocolate fudge cake is a favourite); they do half helpings at half price. Well kept Boddingtons, Marstons Pedigree, Ruddles Best, and Theakstons Best and Mild on handpump, and several malt whiskies; prompt, efficient service. Darts, pool, dominoes, fruit machine and juke box in the separate lively public bar. The front garden, with some tables made from old stone mill wheels, has a children's play area, and from the back garden (which has had do-it-yourself barbecues) there are fine views. *(Recommended by H K Dyson, Margaret Brown, Joe Sutton, Estelle Budge; more reports please)*

Free house ~ Licensee Leonard Lee ~ Real ale ~ Meals and snacks (not Sun) ~ Restaurant ~ (01758) 770244 ~ Children in family dining room ~ Open 11-3, 5.30-11; 12-2, 7-11 winter; closed Sun ~ Bedrooms: £20(£22B)/£32(£34B)

TY'N Y GROES (Gwynedd) SH7672 Map 6

Groes ♨

B5106 N of village

Apparently the first Welsh pub to be properly licensed in 1573, this popular old family-run place really is a charming spot, especially in summer when it's decked out with colourful plants and flowers. Seats by the road in front have a good view of the River Conwy, and there are more in the pretty back garden with its flower-filled hayricks; an ideal spot for sampling one of their good afternoon teas (not winter weekdays). Inside is a homely series of rambling, low-beamed and thick-walled rooms with antique settles and an old sofa, old clocks, portraits, hats and tins hanging from the walls and a good welcoming atmosphere. A fine antique fireback is built into one wall, perhaps originally from the formidable fireplace which houses a collection of stone cats as well as winter log fires. A no-smoking conservatory has lovely mountain views. Very well liked, imaginative bar food might include sandwiches, kippers and bacon (£4.75), home-baked gammon with apricot sauce (£5.25), lavender chicken (£5.50), poached fresh Conwy salmon (£6.50), Aga-baked whole baby sea bass, local Welsh lamb, lots of seasonal game dishes and half-boned roast duckling (£7.50); Sunday lunch (£10.50). They do various theme nights (usually on the last Friday of the month, September-April) such as fish or game – the menus are up well in advance and booking is pretty much essential. Well kept Ind Coope Burton and Tetleys on handpump, a good few malt whiskies and a fruity fresh Pimms in summer; cribbage, dominoes and light classical piped music at lunchtimes (music from the 1930s-1950s at other times). It can get busy but this shouldn't cause any problems with the efficient, friendly service. The hard-working licensees now intend to add bedrooms, and the plans sound interesting. It's only a couple of miles from here to Conwy. *(Recommended by M G Lavery, John Roberts, David J B Lewis, Gordon Theaker, D W Jones-Williams, G R Sunderland, J E Hilditch, Canon Michael Bordeaux, Mrs J Oakes, H K Dyson)*

Free house ~ Licensees Dawn, Tony and Justin Humphreys ~ Real ale ~ Meals and snacks ~ Restaurant ~ (01492) 650545 ~ Children in eating area of bar; in restaurant if over 10 ~ Open 12-11.30; closed winter Sun evenings

USK (Gwent) SO3801 Map 6

Royal ♨

New Market Street (off A472 by Usk bridge)

Locals and visitors agree that when in Usk this characterful Georgian country-town pub is the place to head for, and there's usually a good mix of people filling up the two open-plan rooms of the homely and old-fashioned bar. Many of them are enjoying the good value bar meals, served in big helpings from a range that includes ploughman's (£2.50), very good chilli con carne, grilled lamb chops, or chicken kiev (£3.95), with evening beef in ale pie (£4.95; superb pastry), lovely tender steaks, and fresh salmon (£6.50); popular Sunday roasts. The left-hand room is the nicer, with a cream-tiled kitchen range flush with the pale ochre back wall, a comfortable mix of tables and chairs, a rug on neat slate flagstones, plates and old pictures on the walls, china cabinets, and a tall longcase clock. Particularly well kept Bass, Hancocks HB and a guest like Felinfoel Double Dragon on handpump; open fires, dominoes, cards, and piped music. There are some seats out in front, facing a cedar. *(Recommended by Mrs S Jones, Iris and Eddie Brixton; more reports please)*

Free house ~ Licensees Sylvia Casey and Anthony Lyons ~ Real ale ~ Meals and snacks; not Sun evening or Mon lunchtime ~ (01291) 672931 ~ Children in eating area of bar ~ Open 11-3, 7-11

Lucky Dip

Besides the fully inspected pubs, you might like to try these Lucky Dips recommended to us and described by readers (if you do, please send us reports):

ANGLESEY

Beaumaris [Church St; SH6076], *Sailors Return*: Good range of bar food from sandwiches to steaks inc vegetarian dishes, Whitbreads-related real ales, green banquettes and chairs, old prints and naval memorabilia in single bar with dining area (M Joyner)

☆ **Bodedern** [SH3281], *Crown*: Recently repainted quiet local, very pretty; friendly staff, well kept beer, good well served basic food; bedrooms (Margaret Mason, David Thompson, L G Milligan)

☆ **Menai Bridge** [St Georges Pier, by Menai Straits; SH5572], *Liverpool Arms*: Good happy old-fashioned atmosphere in chatty pub, popular with locals and visitors; well kept Greenalls, friendly attentive service, no music, good value above-average fresh straightforward food inc specials such as local salmon, panelled dining room (G Roberts, Dennis Dickinson, Richard Houghton)

Valley [SH2979], *Bull*: Good value bar food (also restaurant, often fully booked), well kept Greenalls, very busy esp with ferry passengers, despite plenty of space; big garden (Nigel Pritchard, L G Milligan)

CLWYD

☆ **Betws Yn Rhos** [SH9174], *Wheatsheaf*: Good range of food in well furnished old-fashioned two-bar 17th-c pub (also take-aways), very welcoming staff, well kept John Smiths and Thwaites, good log fires, restaurant; bedrooms good value (Colin Martin)

Broughton [The Old Warren; old main rd towards Buckley; SJ3263], *Spinning Wheel*: Pleasant roadside setting, traditional freshly prepared good value food, welcoming atmosphere (E G Parish)

☆ **Bylchau** [A543 3 miles S; SH9863], *Sportsmans Arms*: Good views from highest pub in Wales, decent if not cheap food with all fresh veg and vegetarian dishes, well kept Lees Traditional and Best Dark Mild, drinks cheaper than usual; Welsh-speaking locals, old-fashioned high-backed settles among more modern seats, darts and pool, no piped music, harmonium and Welsh singing Sat evening; children allowed in eating area, closed Mon/Tues lunchtimes in winter (and maybe other lunchtimes then) (Mr and Mrs B Hobden, LYM)

☆ **Chirk** [Chirk Bank, S; SJ3028], *Bridge*: Varied and interesting range of reasonably priced home-made food in big helpings, well kept beer, friendly staff; handy for canal (Jason Caulkin, A D Marsh, Roger Berry)

☆ **nr Colwyn Bay** [Chapel St, Mochdre; off link road between A470 and start of A55 dual carriageway – OS Sheet 116 map ref 825785; SH8578], *Mountain View*: Neatly kept and unexpectedly plush and spacious modern pub locally popular for good value generous food with plenty of well cooked veg, cheerful prompt if not always accurate service, discreet piped music, real ales, games area inc pool; seems to have lost its big no-smoking area (KC, Blair and Dinah Harrison, D J Roberts)

Cwm [S of Dyserth; SJ0677], *Blue Lion*: Very pleasant 16th-c free house with well kept beer and good malt whiskies, landlord behind bar, son as chef (food inc excellent steaks, separate restaurant); pleasant decor, over 200 chamber pots hanging from beams, inglenook log fire (Basil Minson)

☆ **Erbistock** [village signposted off A539 W of Overton, then pub signposted; SJ3542], *Boat*: Idyllic spot, tables in a pretty partly terraced garden sharing a sleepy bend of the River Dee with a country church; has been a very popular dining pub, mainly given over to food, with good interesting bar lunches and more restauranty evening meals, good malt whiskies in small flagstoned bar, comfortably plush beamed dining room, bigger summer dining annexe, a welcome for children; closed and for sale spring 1994, subsequently reopened but no reports since (LYM; news please)

Ffrith [B5101, just off A541 Wrexham—Mold; SJ2855], *Poachers Cottage*: Pleasant 18th-c two-bar pub doing well under newish owners, with good atmosphere in two bars and restaurant, real ales, decent changing wines, good reasonably priced home-cooked food inc vegetarian dishes and some Danish specialities cooked by landlady; cl lunchtime exc Sun (David Parry)

Glyn Ceiriog [SJ2038], *Golden Pheasant*: Intriguingly decorated bar, tables out in nicely planted garden; bedrooms (Paul McPherson)

Glyndyfrdwy [A5 W of Llangollen; SJ1542], *Bedwyn Arms*: Lovely setting above River Dee and what will be the next stretch of the Llangollen Railway; bar food, Burtonwood, several small rooms (Dave Braisted)

☆ **Gwaenysgor** [just S of Prestatyn; SJ0881], *Eagle & Child*: Original early 19th-c pub, spotless, with shining brasses and plates, great welcome and service, generous helpings of good freshly cooked good value food, Bass, exemplary lavatories; well kept floodlit gardens, in hilltop village with fine views (Derek and Cerys Williams, J E Hilditch)

☆ **Hanmer** [SJ4639], *Hanmer Arms*: Good range of reasonably priced straightforward food from sandwiches to steaks inc vegetarian dishes in relaxed and pleasantly uncrowded country inn with well kept bar, Allied real ales, big family dining room upstairs – good for Sun lunch; no music, neat and attractive garden, with church nearby making a pleasant backdrop; pretty village; comfortable good value bedrooms in former courtyard stable block *(Peter Burton, G Hallett, P Corris)*

Llanarmon D C [SJ1633], *West Arms:* Extended 16th-c beamed and timbered inn with inglenook log fires, picturesque upmarket lounge bar full of antique settles, sofas, even an elaborately carved confessional stall, good range of beers, wines and malt whiskies at fair prices, good welcoming service, big log fires, more sofas in old-fashioned entrance hall, comfortable back bar too; food, not cheap, inc good fresh fish; pretty lawn running down to River Ceiriog (fishing for residents); children welcome; bedrooms comfortable *(T A Smith, Paul McPherson, BJSM, LYM)*

Llanarmon DC, *Hand:* Civilised inn tucked away in lovely countryside, doing well under new manager (and chef), good value food in spacious side room next to bar and in restaurant, pleasant afternoon teas, helpful attentive staff, good log fires; children welcome, comfortable bedrooms *(Tom Linton, C E Power, Paul McPherson, LYM)*

✩ **Llanelian Yn Rhos** [S of Colwyn Bay; signed off A5830 (shown as B5383 on some maps) and B5381; SH8676], *White Lion:* Very well run old inn, well managed and attractively extended, an oasis for its wide choice of good reasonably priced bar food from sandwiches up in neat and spacious dining area, with broad steps down to traditional snug bar with flagstones, antique high-backed settles and big fire; well kept Courage-related beers, good wine list, lots of malt whiskies; can get busy with tourists in summer; dominoes, cribbage, piped music; rustic tables outside, good walking nearby; children in eating area; bedrooms *(F M Bunbury, LYM)*

✩ **Llanferres** [A494 Mold—Ruthin; SJ1961], *Druid:* Warmly welcoming new management in extended old inn with good hill and valley views from small bay-windowed plush lounge, some oak settles as well as plainer more modern furnishings in big friendly saloon, attractive dining room; well kept Burtonwood Best, good food, some live entertainment; good walking country; comfortable bedrooms *(Dr Bill Baker, J S Green, KC, BB)*

✩ **Llangedwyn** [B4396; SJ1924], *Green:* Clean well run country dining pub in lovely Tanat Valley surroundings, pleasant helpful service, good quickly served food esp fish in bar and evening restaurant, well kept Boddingtons, Whitbreads and Woods 2000 and Special, good choice of malt whiskies and wines, oak settles; beautiful garden over rd, own fishing *(C Roberts, Basil J S Minson, Paul McPherson, Nigel Woolliscroft)*

Llangollen [SJ2142], *Abbey Grange:* Converted from quarrymaster's house, in beautiful spot with superb views nr Valle Crucis Abbey; ales inc Theakstons, good wine list, moderately priced food all day (at least in summer), efficient courteous service; picnic table-sets outside; comfortable bedrooms with own baths *(Derek and Cerys Williams)*

✩ nr **Llangollen** [Horseshoe Pass; A542 N – extreme bottom right corner of OS Sheet 116 at overlap with OS Sheet 117, map ref 200454], *Britannia:* Lovely Dee Valley views from picturesque though well extended inn, straightforward food inc popular steak and kidney pie and bargain OAPs' meals, two quiet bars and brightly cheerful dining area; Whitbreads-related ales, pleasant efficient staff; well kept garden; bedrooms clean, pretty, well equipped and good value *(KC, Joan and Michel Hooper-Immins, D W Jones-Williams)*

✩ nr **Llangollen** [Trevor Uchaf, off A539; SJ2442], *Sun Trevor:* High up over Dee Valley with spectacular views, good food in bar and restaurant, friendly staff, well kept Courage-related ales *(P G Topp)*

✩ **Llanrhaeadr** [just off A525 Ruthin—Denbigh; SJ0863], *Kings Head:* Good value food, well kept beer, pleasant atmosphere; nice village – good Jesse window in church; bedrooms *(D W Jones-Williams, P Neate)*

Llanrhaeadr Ym Mochnant [from Oswestry on B4580, just before bend at junction in village; SJ1326], *Hand:* Two rooms on either side of door with longer room in middle leading up to bar, big inglenook on left, good lively atmosphere, outgoing staff, bar food; side garden up slope; bedrooms *(Paul McPherson)*

✩ **Llansannan** [A544 Abergele—Bylchau; SH9466], *Red Lion:* Intriguing little old-fashioned front parlour in friendly Welsh-speaking 13th-c hill-village local, other more straightforward bars; well kept Lees, obliging service, roaring fire, simple food inc children's dishes; normally cl Mon; seats in garden; bedrooms *(P Corris, Derek and Cerys Williams, LYM)*

Llansilin [B4580 W of Oswestry; SJ2128], *Wynnstay:* Pleasant and unpretentious with good food; bedrooms *(Roger Berry)*

Overton Bridge [A539; SJ3643], *Cross Foxes:* Very popular 17th-c coaching inn in attractive setting on Dee, good value home-cooked bar food, warm welcome *(E G Parish)*

✩ **Pontblyddyn** [A5104/A541, 3 miles SE of Mold; SJ2761], *Bridge:* Old and sympathetically restored, with lively traditional atmosphere, good log fires, bar food inc some interesting dishes, pleasant dining area with sensible tables and chairs, good Sun lunches, real ales; tables on roadside terrace, attractive gardens by River Alyn with ducks and geese – good for children *(P A Neate, KC)*

✩ **Rhewl** [the one on A525 Ruthin—Denbigh; SJ1160], *Drovers Arms:* Good value food inc children's dishes in three roomy and spotless eating areas of old-fashioned low-beamed pub, reasonable prices, good service, friendly locals, well kept beer, no piped music, pool room; attractive garden *(KC)*

✩ **Rhewl** [off A5 W of Llangollen; the one at SJ1744 – OS Sheet 125 map ref 176448; SJ1744], *Sun:* Friendly and unpretentious little cottage in good walking country just off

Horseshoe Pass, with relaxing views from terrace and garden; simple good value food from sandwiches to home-cooked hot dishes, well kept Felinfoel Double Dragon and cheap Worthington BB, malt whiskies, old-fashioned hatch service to back room, dark little lounge, portakabin games room – children allowed here and in eating area *(George Murdoch, Bill and Beryl Farmer, David Atkinson, Blair and Dinah Harrison, Jeff Davies, Andy and Jill Kassube, LYM)*
Ruthin [Rhos St; SJ1258], *Olde Anchor*: Friendly landlord, good food in bar and restaurant, well kept Bass and Courage Directors; bedrooms good and inexpensive, some walls a bit thin *(N H and B Ellis, Mrs A Taylor)*
St Asaph [The Waen; SJ0374], *Farmers Arms*: Super little country pub, good food esp home-made puddings, local beer tapped from the cask and served in a jug, friendly landlord (may play piano requests evening), efficient staff *(Mr and Mrs D Lawson)*
Trofarth [B5113 S of Colwyn Bay; SH8569], *Holland Arms*: Old-fashioned 17th-c former coaching inn, warm cosy atmosphere, plenty of stuffed owls, good food inc bargain lunches *(David Wynne Hughes)*

DYFED
Aberaeron [Quay Parade; SN4462], *Harbourmaster*: Popular local in lovely harbourside setting, well kept beer, wide choice of usual food; can be a bit noisy and smoky *(Gwyneth and Salvo Spadaro-Dutturi, LYM)*; [High St], *Royal Oak*: Reasonable range of nicely cooked well presented food inc interestingly filled baked potatoes, big bar, friendly prompt service, Ansells on handpump; back games area with pool, machines *(Ian Phillips, Madeline and Ernest Knight)*
Aberystwyth [Mill St; SN6777], *Mill*: Friendly local with well kept ales such as Ansells Mild, local Dinas Best, Felinfoel Double Dragon, Greenalls Original, Marstons Pedigree and Tetleys, lunchtime cold snacks; popular with local Welsh-speaking Rugby club *(Joan and Michel Hooper-Immins)*
☆ Amroth [SN1607], *New Inn*: Traditional beamed local by lovely beach, wide choice of good generous home cooking inc good soups, local seafood, real chips and children's dishes; open fires, no music and good atmosphere in three-roomed bar, upstairs lounge bar, children allowed in separate games room with pool tables and machines; well kept real ales inc Ind Coope Burton, relaxed helpful staff, picnic-table sets in good garden, holiday flat to let *(S and E Timerick, David Wallington)*
Bosherston [SR9694], *St Govans*: Big open-plan bar popular with locals and visitors, welcoming service, bar food (all day Sun in summer), Worthington BB on handpump, piped music, bar billiards, bedrooms; the eponymous hermit's chapel overlooking the sea is worth getting to, as are the nearby lilyponds *(Steve Thomas, LYM)*

Broad Haven [SM8614], *Galleon*: Popular seafront pub with softly lit small bar, rooms and alcoves leading off, friendly atmosphere and staff, simple bar food, Ansells, Tetleys and Worthington BB *(Gwen and Peter Andrews, Dave Braisted)*
☆ nr Broad Haven [N of village on coast rd, bear L for about 1½ miles then follow sign L to Druidstone Haven – inn a sharp left turn after another ½ mile; OS Sheet 157 map ref 862168, marked as Druidston Villa], *Druidstone*: A great favourite with many readers, very unusual and – if it suits you – a marvellous place to stay; its club licence means you can't go for just a drink and have to book to eat there (the food is inventively individual home cooking, with fresh ingredients and a leaning towards the organic; restaurant cl Sun evening); a very individual, lived-in and informal house alone in a grand spot above the sea, with terrific views, spacious homely bedrooms, erratic plumbing, a cellar bar with a strong 1960s folk-club feel, Worthington BB and good wines, country wines and other drinks, ceilidhs and Irish jamborees, chummy dogs (dogs welcomed), all sorts of sporting activities from boules to sand-yachting; cl Nov and Jan; bedrooms *(Michael Quine, Jed and Virginia Brown, Janet and Gary Amos, Mrs Cynthia Archer, Bob Riley, Paula Harrison, LYM)*
☆ Burry Port [Stepney Rd; SN4400], *George*: Civilised and outstandingly clean lounge bar and good coffee shop, cheap standard bar food, Felinfoel, lots of Amelia Earhart memorabilia, charming service; comfortable bedrooms *(George Atkinson, K Harvey)*
Capel Bangor [A44; SN6580], *Tynllidiart Arms*: Quaint roadside cottage, good friendly landlord, brasses on the walls, well kept beer *(Dr and Mrs A K Clarke)*
Cardigan [outside centre just beyond bridge; SN1846], *Eagle*: Good lively atmosphere, poems stuck up in one alcove, wide choice of food and beer *(Federico and Mario Cristini)*
☆ Cilgerran [off A478; SN1943], *Pendre*: Welcoming medieval pub with good value food (filled rolls only, Sun), massive stone walls, broad flagstones, high-backed settles, well kept Bass and Hancocks HB, old-fashioned atmosphere, friendly landlord; pool table, fruit machine and juke box in public bar, restaurant (not Sun lunchtime); children very welcome, tables out by modern extension in garden; nr romantic riverside fort *(S P Bobeldijk, Patrick Freeman, Barbara Ann Mayer, LYM)*
Cross Inn [B4337/B4577 – note this is not the one nr Newport; SN5464], *Rhos yr Hafod*: Friendly and traditionally furnished Welsh-speaking country pub with enjoyable food in bar and smart upstairs restaurant, well kept Flowers IPA, friendly service *(Madeline and Ernest Knight, LYM)*
☆ Cwm Gwaun [Pontfaen; Cwm Gwaun and Pontfaen signed off B4313 E of Fishguard; SN0035], *Dyffryn Arms*: Very basic and idiosyncratic Welsh-speaking country tavern

known locally as Bessie's, run by same family since 1840; plain deal furniture, well kept Bass and Ind Coope Burton served by jug through a hatch, good sandwiches if you're lucky, Great War prints, draughts-boards inlaid into tables, very relaxed atmosphere; pretty countryside *(Paul McPherson, Patrick Freeman, LYM)*

Cwmbach [B4308 Llanelli—Trimsaran; SN4802], *Farriers Arms*: Friendly country pub with well kept Felinfoel, McEwans and guest beers such as Ringwood Old Thumper, interesting country wines, quaint stone-walled bar with high wooden settles, big informal garden with play area and trout stream; may be shut Mon *(Huw and Carolyn Lewis; more reports on new regime please)*

Cynwyl Elfed [A484 N of Carmarthen; aka Rock & Fountain; SN3727], *Tafarn y Roc*: Plain but spotless, with scrubbed tables, accommodating service, usual bar food, well kept Buckleys; predominantly Welsh-speaking locals *(Michael Richards)*

Dinas [Pwllgwaelod; from A487 in Dinas Cross follow Bryn-Henllan signpost – OS Sheet 157 map ref 005399; SN0039], *Sailors Safety*: Superb position, snugged down into the sand by an isolated cove below Dinas Head with its bracing walks; unpretentious, unspoilt, even a bit scruffy in summer, when there's generally something to eat all day and there may be real ales tapped from the cask; winter food and opening more restricted, but welcoming log fires then; children welcome *(Lorrie and Mick Marchington, LYM)*; [A487; SN0139], *Ship Aground*: 18th-c smugglers' pub recently refurbished with nautical trappings, some interesting ropework, good value fresh bar food and good choice of evening restaurant food inc vegetarian and local fish and seafood; very friendly staff, well kept Buckleys, open all day in summer *(John Allsopp, BB)*

☆ **Dreenhill** [Dale Rd (B4327); SM9214], *Denant Mill*: 16th-c converted watermill with well kept real ales inc ones rare here such as Hook Norton Best, inexpensive wines, decent coffee, good informal stripped-stone restaurant with unusual freshly cooked food esp authentic Goan dishes; remote setting down narrow lane, big safe garden with ducks on millpond, extensive wood behind; bedrooms clean and reasonably priced *(R T and J C Moggridge, Paul Bachelor, Wendy Trineman)*

☆ **Fishguard** [Lower Town; SM9537], *Ship*: Lots of atmosphere in dimly lit fishermen's local nr old harbour, well kept Worthington BB and Dark Mild tapped from the cask, homely bar food (not weekends), friendly licensees; children welcome, toys provided *(Patrick Freeman, LYM)*

☆ **Fishguard** [The Square, Upper Town], *Royal Oak*: Pleasant atmosphere, decent standard food in bar and back restaurant, coal fire, Felinfoel, Tetleys and Worthington BB; military prints and pictures commemorating defeat here of second-last attempted French invasion *(R Michael Richards)*

☆ **Haverfordwest** [Old Quay, Quay St; from A40 E, keep left after crossing river, then first left; SM9515], *Bristol Trader*: Much modernised old pub in lovely waterside setting, friendly service, cheap generous home-made lunchtime food, well kept Ind Coope Burton, decent malt whiskies, CD juke box, maybe entertainment; children allowed if well behaved, tables out overlooking water; open all day Fri, Sat *(D J Underwood, Barbara Ann Mayer, LYM)*

☆ **Haverfordwest** [Market St], *George*: Very informal relaxing atmosphere and unusually wide choice of generous home-made food using fresh veg and good meat in attractive bar with character stable-like furnishings, good choice of well kept real ales such as Bass, Ind Coope Burton and Marstons Pedigree, more sophisticated evening restaurant, good friendly service; no dogs *(K F Glasby, Carole Fletcher, Jane Byrski, Michael Hunt, Gareth Coombe)*

Hubberston [just W of Milford Haven; SM8906], *Priory*: Charming atmosphere and friendly service in ancient monastic building, good value nicely served usual food, well kept Bass, lovely garden; children in lounge; bedrooms *(R T and J C Moggridge)*

Landshipping [SN0111], *Stanley Arms*: Nice little pub on lovely estuary, decent food inc vegetarian and children's, real ales such as Crown Buckley Reverend James and Worthington BB, two cats; weekend live music; tables in garden, afternoon cream teas *(S Watkin)*

☆ **Little Haven** [SM8512], *Castle*: Good fresh local fish and other food in friendly well placed pub by green nr attractive seafront, good bay view, well kept Worthington BB, good service; big oak tables, stone walls, oak beams in bar lounge and restaurant area, collection of castle prints, outside seating; children welcome, good facilities for them; the village has a paying car park *(Madeline and Ernest Knight, R T and J C Moggridge, Barbara Ann Mayer)*

☆ **Little Haven** [in village itself, not St Brides hamlet further W], *St Brides*: A short stroll from the sea, with Worthington BB and guest beers such as Courage Directors, pews in stripped-stone bar and communicating dining area (children allowed here), quite a wide choice of food, piped music; interesting well in back corner may be partly Roman; big comfortable bedrooms, some in annexe over rd *(Mrs K F Gogerty, Dave Braisted, David and Helen Wilkins, Mr Evans, LYM)*

☆ **Llanarthney** [B4300 E of Carmarthen (good fast alternative to A40); SN5320], *Paxton Arms*: Extraordinary main bar crammed chaotically with objets de non-art, balloons, flashing lights; more restrained restaurant; most obliging friendly service (chatty landlord may wear Victorian dress), wide choice of generous food as well as good value lunch, well kept Worthington BB and a guest such as Theakstons, good local farm cider, decent malt whiskies; very music-oriented – jazz, folk, blues and poetry, with occasional beer and music festivals; opp wood leading to Paxtons Tower (NT) *(Anne Morris, Gwyneth and Salvo Spadaro-Dutturi, Pete Baker)*

Llanarthney [B4300], *Golden Grove Arms*: Interestingly laid-out inn with huge lounge, open fire, well kept ales such as Boddingtons and Buckleys, decent food, children's play area; many Welsh-speaking customers, Tues folk night; bedrooms *(Gwyneth and Salvo Spadaro-Dutturi, LYM)*

☆ **Llanddarog** [SN5016], *Butchers Arms*: Good generous home cooking from sandwiches up inc quite sophisticated daily specials, well kept Felinfoel Double Dragon and other ales tapped from the cask, tiny low-beamed central bar with woodburner, brasses and old photographs, two mainly dining areas off, friendly very helpful staff; tables outside *(Ian Phillips, Anne Morris, Peter Rees)*

Llandovery [Market Sq; SN7634], *Red Lion*: One basic but welcoming room with spartan furniture and no bar, well kept Crown Buckley tapped from the cask, friendly and individual landlord; cl Sun, may close early evening if no customers *(Pete Baker, BB)*

☆ **Llandybie** [6 Llandeilo Rd; SN6115], *Red Lion*: Wide choice of reasonably priced good fresh food, very generous, in attractive inn's tastefully modernised, spacious and comfortable bar and restaurant; several well kept Whitbreads-related ales, welcoming efficient service, local pictures for sale; bedrooms *(Wyn Churchill)*

Llanelli [Park St; SN5000], *Stepney*: Friendly staff, good straightforward food inc gigantic puddings in roomy bar and separate restaurant, real ale; bedrooms *(G W Knights)*

☆ **Llangranog**, *Ship*: On edge of beach in pretty fishing village, with interesting varied home-cooked food inc vegetarian, good Sun carvery, well kept Whitbreads-related ales, good service, open fire; seats out by car park; can get busy summer, may be closed Mon in winter; bedrooms *(Anon)*

☆ **Llanwnnen** [village centre; A475 Lampeter—Newcastle Emlyn; SN5346], *Grannel*: Roomy and comfortably refurbished, with good personal service, particularly well kept Worthington BB, good value largely home-made straightforward food in bar and restaurant; clean and comfortable reasonably priced bedrooms *(R T and J C Moggridge)*

Marloes [OS Sheet 157 map ref 793083; SM7908], *Lobster Pot*: Friendly family pub with wide choice of food inc bargain children's dishes, in easy-going surroundings; fairly handy for coast walk and beautiful beach, has been open all day at least in summer *(Roy and Bettie Derbyshire, Lorrie and Mick Marchington)*

☆ **Mathry** [off A487 Fishguard—St Davids; SM8732], *Farmers Arms*: Welcoming local with well kept Bass and Worthington BB on handpump, small garden, very good food inc local fish and prawns; has been open all day, at least in summer *(C Driver)*

Meidrim [off B4298/A299, ¾ mile W of village; SN2820], *Maenllwyd*: Old-fashioned

unspoilt pub with lounge like 1940s parlour, games room with darts and cards, no bar counter – well kept Crown Buckley on handpump in back room, friendly landlord; cl lunchtime and Sun *(Pete Baker)*

Mynydd Y Garreg [NE of Kidwelly, follow signs to Industrial Museum; SN4308], *Gwenllian Court*: Riverside hotel with picnic areas and walking; bar food, carvery and restaurant meals, good choice of beers, big bar; by old tin-working museum; good value bedrooms *(Steve Thomas)*

Newcastle Emlyn [Bridge St; SN3040], *Bunch of Grapes*: Freshly pink-painted façade in attractive main street leading to bridge, solid oak round tables and chairs in roomy and welcoming bar, well kept Courage and guest beers, conservatory with grape vines *(Anne Morris, S P Bobeldijk)*; [Sycamore St (A475)], *Pelican*: 17th-c inn with varied menu, real ales, pews and panelling, and fireplace with bread oven still recognisable as the one where Rowlandson in 1797 sketched a dog driving the roasting spit; tables in garden, children welcome; bedrooms in adjoining cottage *(S P Bobeldijk, LYM)*

Newport [East St; SN0539], *Llwyngwair Arms*: Very good Indian food inc take-aways by Sri Lankan cook, as well as usual bar food; friendly locals, well kept Worthington, coal fire *(R Michael Richards)*

Pembroke [A4139 towards toll br; SM9801], *Watermans Arms*: Food inc good fresh sea trout, lovely outside balcony with castle and river views *(Barbara Ann Mayer)*

Penally [SS1199], *Cross*: Pleasant spot, friendly staff, good menu, Bass or Worthington BB *(Ian Phillips)*

☆ **Pont Ar Gothi** [6 miles E of Carmarthen on A40 Carmarthen—Llandeilo; SN5021], *Cresselly Arms*: Small old well furnished pub by river which provides its fresh sea trout and salmon, other more usual food from sandwiches and ploughman's up; good welcome, Whitbreads-related ales, bar full of fishing memorabilia, restaurant evenings and Sun *(Mr and Mrs S Thomas, Mark Bostock, Mike Thornton)*

Pont Ar Gothi, *Salutation*: Friendly traditional pub under new licensees, well kept Felinfoel Double Dragon, log fire, big settles in small flagstone-floored rooms, bar food, restaurant; bedrooms *(Huw and Carolyn Lewis, Pam and John Gibbon)*

Pontarsais [A485 Carmarthen—Lampeter; SN4428], *Stag & Pheasant*: Welcoming pub with good range of reasonably priced food, choice of real ales, pleasant decor, simple friendly atmosphere *(Dave and Judith Risley, I H Rorison)*

Pontfaen [some miles E; SN0634], *Gelli Fawr*: A country-house hotel, but has a proper bar with good food and very good service; bedrooms excellent *(Paul McPherson)*

☆ **Porthgain** [SM8132], *Sloop*: Old, unspoilt and friendly pub well placed overlooking green of interesting fishing/stone-exporting village, short walk from old harbour; good local atmosphere, dark bare stone, lots of alcoves, character old furniture, nautical and wreck memorabilia, newer family/eating extension; well kept Felinfoel Double Dragon and other ales, wide range of good value food inc nice full crab sandwiches, small seating area outside *(A A Turnbull, Laurie and Mick Marchington, Paul McPherson, Patrick Freeman)*

Pwll [Bassett Terr; A484 W of Llanelli; SN4801], *Tafarn y Sospan*: Doing well under welcoming newish owners, wide range of bar food, separate restaurant, pool room, good choice of beers and other drinks; Welsh spoken but warm welcome *(Mr and Mrs S Thomas)*

☆ **Rhosmaen** [SN6424], *Plough*: Deep-cushioned comfort and good value fresh bar food inc good puddings in smart lounge with picture-window views, well kept Bass, tiled front bar, separate restaurant; long-serving friendly licensees *(Tom Evans, Mrs S Wright, Wyn Churchill, LYM)*

☆ **Saundersfoot** [Wogan Terr; SN1304], *Royal Oak*: Very popular friendly and unspoilt local, well kept Bass, Boddingtons and Flowers Original, no music or machines, tasty food esp fresh fish, tables outside *(Miss S Lingard, Colin and Ann Hunt, L E Snellgrove, Simon and Amanda Southwell)*

☆ **Solva** [Main St, Lower Solva; SM8024], *Ship*: Simple, clean and cosy fishermen's pub quaintly set in attractive harbourside village, interesting low-beamed bar with lots of old photographs, nautical artefacts and bric-a-brac; big back family dining room with barn-like village hall atmosphere; well kept Bass, Brains, Felinfoel Double Dragon and Worthington BB, simple bar food generously served and reasonably priced, friendly service, maybe radio; little garden has play area over stream *(Roy and Bettie Derbyshire, M E and Mrs J Wellington, K R Flack)*

Solva [Lower Solva], *Cambrian Arms*: Attractive dining pub with popular bar food inc some unusual dishes and home-made pasta, decent Italian wines, well kept Allied ales, log fires; no dogs or children *(D J Underwood, Gwynne Harper)*; [Lower Solva], *Harbour House*: Good harbourside setting, warm friendly atmosphere, good range of beers and of reasonably priced freshly prepared unusual bar food inc local cheeses *(Gill Owen, David Green, Roy Y Bromell)*

St Davids [Goat St; SM7525], *Farmers Arms*: Genuine and cheerful pub, busy and well patronised, with good cheap food, well kept Worthington BB, cathedral view from tables in tidy back garden *(Roy and Bettie Derbyshire, I H Rorison, M E and Mrs J Wellington, Patrick Freeman)*; [centre], *Old Cross*: Good pub food inc delicious ploughman's, sensible prices, good position; bedrooms *(Miss E Evans)*

St Florence [SM0801], *Old Parsonage Farm*: Good pub for children with quick and easy food inc children's helpings, very pleasant

service; bedrooms *(R T and J C Moggridge)*

Tenby [Upper Frog St; SN1300], *Coach & Horses*: Good atmosphere and service, good choice of bar food inc at least two locally caught fish dishes *(Ian Phillips)*; *Five Arches*: Local stone walls, green tartan carpet, tan hessian seat covers and Bass or Worthington BB ales in the three bar areas; upstairs restaurant *(Ian Phillips)*

Trapp [OS Sheet 159 map ref 653189; SN6518], *Cennen Arms*: Small country pub with good choice of simple but well cooked food – good value *(Wyn Churchill)*

Tregaron [SN6759], *Talbot*: Friendly and thoughtful service, good bar food, lovely building – busy but not unpleasantly so; interesting town; bedrooms *(N W Alton)*

☆ **Wolfs Castle** [A40 Haverfordwest—Fishguard; SM9526], *Wolfe*: Wide choice of good popular home-made food (not Sun or Mon evenings in winter) in comfortable lounge, garden room and conservatory, well kept Ind Coope Burton and Tetleys, decent wines, attractively laid-out garden; simpler public bar with darts, restaurant; children welcome; bedrooms *(Gwynne Harper, LYM)*

GLAMORGAN – MID

Caerphilly [Groeswen, NW of town – OS Sheet 171 map ref 128869; ST1286], *White Cross*: Full range of well kept Theakstons ales and guests such as Hook Norton Old Hookey, Greene King Abbot and Morlands Old Specked Hen, good range of cheap bar food; separate dining room, very friendly atmosphere, children welcome; weekend evening barbecues in summer, play area *(Ian Fairweather)*

nr Caerphilly [Watford; Tongwynlais exit from M4 junction 32, then right just after church – OS Sheet 171 map ref 144846], *Black Cock*: Neat and comfortable blue-plush bar with particularly well kept Bass, wide range of good value food from cheap snacks up, open fire in pretty tiled fireplace; interesting brass-tabled public bar where children allowed; sizeable terracd garden among trees with play area and barbecue, restaurant extension; up in the hills, just below Caerphilly Common *(Michael, Alison and Rhiannon Sandy, BB)*

☆ **Llangeinor** [nr Blackmill; SS9187], *Llangeinor Arms*: Partly 15th-c beamed pub tastefully decorated with old Welsh china and bygones, coal fire, decent usual bar food, well kept Hancock HB, Brains SA and Worthington BB, evening restaurant; good hilltop position with front conservatory (where children allowed) overlooking Ogmore and Garw valleys and Bristol Channel beyond *(Peter Douglas, R Michael Richards, LYM)*

☆ **Nottage** [Heol y Capel (off A4229); handy for M4 junction 37; SS8178], *Rose & Crown*: Useful Chef & Brewer family dining pub in comfortably modernised old inn not far from coast, usual food in bar and restaurant, friendly service, well kept Courage-related ales, unobtrusive piped music, fruit machine; open all day Sat; children in eating area and restaurant; comfortable well equipped bedrooms *(George Atkinson, A Kilpatrick, Margaret Whalley, LYM)*

☆ **Ogmore** [B4524; SS8674], *Pelican*: Friendly old country local above ruined castle, functional main bar leading back to snug and cosy side area and pretty little side bistro, cheap popular bar food inc fresh fish, welcoming staff, well kept Courage-related ales; side terrace with swings beside, quite handy for the beaches *(John and Helen Thompson, Steve Thomas, LYM)*

Pontsticil [above A465 N of Merthyr Tydfil; SO0511], *Butchers Arms*: Bar with raised dining area and hidden-away pool table and machine room, food from filled rolls up, tables outside with stunning views, including mountain railway *(Ian Phillips)*; *Butchers Arms*: All food genuinely home-cooked, landlord doing his own venison and game in season besides more usual dishes such as curry, vegetable lasagne, home-cured gammon, sirloin steak *(Ian Phillips)*

nr **Pontypridd** [Eglwysilan; off A470 towards Rhydyfelin, then follow Superstore sign, then Eglwysilan sign – OS Sheet 171 map ref 107890; ST0690], *Rose & Crown*: Well off beaten track on mountainside, with good food inc good fresh fish, well kept Hancocks HB on handpump, children welcome; big play area behind *(Ian Fairweather)*

Rudry [ST1986], *Maenllwyd*: Comfortably furnished traditional lounge in low-beamed Tudor pub with well kept Youngers IPA, popular bar food, welcoming atmosphere, good service, spacious restaurant; provision for children, pleasant countryside nearby *(J E Lloyd, R Michael Richards, LYM)*

St Brides Major [SS8974], *Farmers Arms*: Opp lovely pond with swans and ducks, good reasonably priced food, helpful staff *(Mrs B Sugarman)*

Taffs Well [ST1283], *Fagins*: Vast range of real ales from handpump or tapped from the cask, friendly olde-worlde atmosphere, reasonably priced restaurant off bar *(S P Bobeldijk)*

Thornhill [A469 towards Caerphilly, on Caerphilly Mountain – OS Sheet 171 map ref 144846; ST1484], *Travellers Rest*: Wide choice of good cheap food and well kept Bass in attractive thatched pub with huge fireplace in atmospheric low-ceilinged bar on right; other bars more modernised; tables out on grass *(Peter Rees, Gwynne Harper, John Nash)*

Wick [SS9272], *Star*: Recently refurbished, with good freshly cooked food in lounge and dining room; Hancocks HB, Worthington BB and a guest beer; bedrooms planned *(Martin and Catherine Snelling)*

GLAMORGAN – SOUTH

Aberthin [A4222 nr Cowbridge; ST0075], *Farmers Arms*: Spotless, with good service and well kept beers *(G J Cardew)*

☆ **Cardiff** [St Marys St; nr Howells], *Cottage*: Carefully restored with lots of polished wood and glass, deceptively big behind its narrow façade; particularly well kept Brains SA, Bitter and Dark Mild, good value popular home-cooked lunches, good cheerful service, open all day *(Mike Pugh, Joan and Michel Hooper-Immins)*

Cardiff [Cathedral Rd], *Beverley*: Good atmospheric Victorian-style pub close to city centre, Hancocks HB on handpump, good value food; bedrooms *(P Corris)*; [Custom House St], *Golden Cross*: Well restored early Victorian pub with attractive tilework, fine woodwork and glass; Brains ales, some home cooking *(Mike Pugh)*; [Harrowby St, Butetown], *New Sea Lock*: Little changed since the heyday of the Docks, lots of nautical prints and photographs in two unspoilt basic rooms (one not always open), friendly atmosphere, well kept Brains Bitter and SA on handpump *(Pete Baker)*; [Penarth Rd], *Old Pump House*: Theme pub with specialised fish and chip restaurant, real ales, some live music *(S P Bobeldijk)*; [Atlantic Wharf], *Wharf*: Big newish Victorian-look pub on waterfront in now residential Bute East Dock; nautical theme and old prints and photographs of the area in downstairs bar, small lounge bar and restaurant upstairs; Brains and interesting guest beers; local bands Fri/Sat, sometimes Thurs *(Gwynne Harper, Mr and Mrs S Thomas)*

☆ **Cowbridge** [High St, signed off A48; SS9974], *Bear*: Neatly kept old coaching inn with Brains Bitter and SA, Hancocks HB, Worthington BB and a guest beer, decent house wines, good service, flagstones and panelling in beamed bar on left, quieter area with plush armchairs on right, log-effect gas fires, usual lunchtime bar food from sandwiches up; children welcome; bedrooms quiet and comfortable, good breakfasts *(Chris and Anne Fluck, M Barrell, Lyn and Bill Capper, LYM)*

Cowbridge [High St], *Duke of Wellington*: Old building newly refurbished with traditional games room, locals' bar, popular lounge, upstairs restaurant; food cheap and good, comfortable quiet surroundings, well kept Brains *(Mr and Mrs S Thomas, J E Lloyd)*

☆ **Dinas Powis** [Station Rd; ST1571], *Star*: Well kept Brains and good quick cheap food in spacious and well run four-room village pub with stripped stone walls, attractive panelling, heavy Elizabethan beams, two open fires and a no-smoking dining room; friendly licensees, cheerful locals, decent wines by the glass; best to book for Sun lunch *(Steve Thomas, LYM)*

nr **Lisvane** [follow Mill Rd into Graig Rd, then keep on – OS Sheet 171 map ref 183842; ST1883], *Ty Mawr Arms*: Country pub with attractive garden looking down over Cardiff, changing real ales, several comfortable rooms, one with big open fire *(Gwynne Harper, LYM)*

Llandaff [ST1578], *Butchers Arms*: Friendly welcome and well kept ales in no-nonsense pub in pretty area nr cathedral *(S P Bobeldijk)*

Morganstown [Ty Nant Rd; not far from M4 junction 32; ST1281], *Ty Nant*: Well run, busy and popular, with beamed lounge and basic bar; consistently well kept real ale, pool table, generous helpings of usual bar food, seats outside (*J E and A G Jones*)

Penarth [Sea Front; ST1871], *Inn at the Deep End*: Converted seafront swimming bath opp pier which has kept some of its previous features; good choice of bar food, upstairs restaurant (fish specialities), two-level bar with some live music; seaview terrace, open all day (*Steve Thomas*)

nr **Penarth** [Beach Rd, Swanbridge – signed off B4267 at Penarth end of Sully], *Captains Wife*: Sizeable pub right by sea, long a main entry, but taken over summer 1994 by Whitbreads who closed it for complete refurbishment – to open around December 1994; likely to keep same manager, but otherwise we don't yet know their plans for what's been a handsome and individual place, with exposed stonework, broad bare boards and several quite distinct areas; obvious possibilities for a fine family dining pub (*LYM; news please*)

☆ **Sigingstone** [SS9771], *Victoria*: Quickly served good value food in nice spotless neo-Victorian country pub, tending more towards being a restaurant that also serves beer (*Patrick and Mary McDermott, J E Lloyd*)

GLAMORGAN – WEST

Alltwen [Rhos Rd, Alltwen Hill; SN7203], *Butchers Arms*: Increasingly popular for evening meals (*G Reeve*); *Pen-yr-Allt*: Wide range of food in bar and restaurant, choose your own steak from the cool cabinet, good value Sun lunch, children's dishes, well kept Boddingtons and Brains SA and Old Original; bedrooms clean and comfortable (*Graham Reeve*)

☆ **Bishopston** [50 Bishopston Rd; off B4436; SS5789], *Joiners Arms*: Thriving local atmosphere in attractively restored village pub, clean and friendly, with quarry-tiled floor, traditional furnishings, local paintings and massive solid fuel stove; cheap simple food lunchtime and early evening, particularly well kept Courage-related ales, children welcome, open all day Thurs-Sat – the Rugby club's local on Sat nights; parking can be difficult (*George Atkinson, Graham Reeve, John and Helen Thompson, HK, Dave and Jules Tuckett, WLGW, J S M Sheldon, LYM*)

Bishopston [opp Joiners Arms], *Valley*: Horseshoe servery with bar either side, one a lounge with plush banquettes and brass and wood, the other smaller with TV; well kept Bass and Hancocks HB, basic good big basket-style meals and happy to do things not on menu; quiet at lunchtime in week (*Michael and Alison Sandy*)

Clydach [High St; SN6901], *Carpenters Arms*: Very clean cosy pub with friendly landlord, efficient staff, good bar and restaurant food, well kept Ansells Mild, Sky TV, juke box, games machine (*S Watkins*)

Glais [625 Birchgrove Rd; off A4067, a mile from M4 junction 45; SN7000], *Old Glais*: Traditional old two-bar pub in lovely surroundings, warm welcome, good atmosphere, good range of well kept beers, interesting varied reasonably priced food, quite a few antiques (*Andrew Lindell, Graham Reeve*)

Glyn Neath [Wellfield Ave (A465); SN8706], *Lamb & Flag*: Big roadhouse with good reasonably priced food, charming service, good view, seats outside (*Ian Phillips, J F Reay*)

Kittle [18 Pennard Rd; SS5789], *Beaufort Arms*: Lovely old pub sheltering below ancient chestnut tree, plenty of character in lower level, shortish choice of good food esp fish, also sandwiches, quick friendly service, well kept beers (*J S M Sheldon*)

Llanddewi [Henllys; SS4589], *Castell-y-Bwch*: Unspoilt bar with stone floor, log fire, big restaurant area, Wadworths 6x and guests like Whitbreads Pompey Royal; extensive views over Cwmbran and Newport, garden with play area (*Gwyneth and Salvo Spadaro-Dutturi*)

Llanmadoc [the Gower, nr Whiteford Burrows – NT; SS4393], *Britannia*: Lovely setting with fine estuary views from good gardens and terrace with play area, lots of ducks, geese and aviary; low beams, flagstones, well kept Wadworths 6X, big helpings of usual decent food, friendly service; piped music, may cl Tues lunchtime (*Gwyneth and Salvo Spadaro-Dutturi, George Atkinson*)

Llanrhidian [SS4992], *Welcome to Town*: Nicely placed small pub on green overlooking the cockle flats of the Loughor estuary, friendly staff, well kept ales such as Wadworths 6X, usual bar food, piped music and fruit machine; displays Dylan Thomas's typewriter (*George Atkinson, Gwyneth and Salvo Spadaro-Dutturi, John and Joan Nash, LYM*)

Llansamlet [Fendrod Way, Enterprise Park; SS6997], *Fendrod*: On busy estate with decent standard food (*Graham Reeve*)

Mumbles [Newton Rd, Oystermouth; SS6287], *White Rose*: Good reasonably priced food; can get very crowded – seems to serve sometimes as unofficial HQ for footballers (*W L G Watkins*)

☆ **Oldwalls** [SS4891], *Greyhound*: Reasonably priced popular bar food inc good local fish and ploughman's with choice of Welsh cheeses in busy but spacious, comfortable and convivial beamed and dark-panelled lounge bar, well kept Bass, Hancocks HB and a guest beer, good coffee inc decaf, good coal fire, good friendly service; back bar with display cases; restaurant popular at weekends; big tree-shaded garden with play area (*George Atkinson, Michael, Alison and Rhiannon Sandy, John and Joan Nash, Mr and Mrs S Thomas*)

Pontlliw [Swansea Rd; A48 towards Pontardulais from M4 junction 47; SN6100], *Buck*: Useful chain dining pub with good value food, tree-lined riverside garden with a few tables and climbing frame *(Michael, Alison, Rhiannon and Stuart Sandy)*

☆ Reynoldston [SS4789], *King Arthur*: Increasingly popular pub in long Georgian building, big log fire, prints, plate rack and warming pans, rugs on floorboards; plusher dining lounge, back games bar; good bar food changing daily inc fresh fish, well kept Bass and Felinfoel Double Dragon, friendly staff; newish back play garden; prettily set overlooking green and common, in good walking country; recently refurbished bedrooms *(Gwyneth and Salvo Spadaro-Dutturi, J S M Sheldon, A J Madel, Graham Reeve)*

☆ Swansea [Kingsway], *Hanbury*: Lots of dark panelling, prints of old Swansea, efficient staff, good choice of good value lunchtime food, well kept Courage-related ales *(Michael Sandy)*

Three Crosses [SS5794], *Poundffald*: Friendly 17th-c local with lots of beams, horse tack, separate dining room, Ansells and Tetleys beers, extensive cheap menu; several armchairs in lounge bar, cheerful and efficient staff, small pretty garden *(Jackie Welch)*

Ynystawe [634 Clydach Rd; A4067 just N of M4 junction 45; SN6800], *Millers Arms*: Real ales, huge meals, well decorated, good welcome *(Mrs S Wright)*

GWENT

☆ Abergavenny [Flannel St; SO3014], *Hen & Chickens*: Busy, welcoming and unspoilt local with tidy bar and cosy back room, good choice of wholesome cheap home-cooked food and thick lunchtime sandwiches, well kept ales inc Bass, friendly staff *(Gwyneth and Salvo Spadaro-Dutturi, Mike Pugh, Ted George)*

☆ Abergavenny [Mkt St], *Greyhound*: Enjoyable atmosphere, good interesting reasonably priced food, Boddingtons real ale, decent wines, good service, comfortable environment; particularly good evening meals – when it's more restaurant *(I H Rorison, Peter Yearsley)*

Abergavenny [37 Brecon Rd (not nr stn despite name), *Station*: Recently painted and refurbished, old-fashioned town pub with good variety of foreign lagers and real ale inc Bass, Crown Buckley Reverend James and Tetleys *(Gwyneth and Salvo Spadaro-Dutturi)*

☆ nr Abergavenny [Raglan Rd, Hardwick; B4598 (old A40), 2 miles SE], *Horse & Jockey*: Good range of well presented reasonably priced food in well furnished and attractive pub, extra plate for children without any fuss, nice family room, well kept Bass, good staff *(K R Harris, M A Watts)*

☆ nr Abergavenny [The Bryn, Penpergwm; B4598 (old A40) 3 miles SE; SO3310], *King of Prussia*: Well furnished and comfortable, with good food at reasonable prices well served by pleasant staff in an unspoilt traditional atmosphere; spotless housekeeping, well kept Bass; locally very popular *(Wg Cdr C F H Hudson)*

nr Abergavenny [well out on Brecon Rd (A40)], *Lamb & Flag*: Good straightforward pub with big helpings of good value food in bar or two dining rooms, well kept Brains SA and Dark and guest beers in big bar, good service; children welcome, high chairs; open all day in summer, looks out to Brecon Beacons – tables outside; newly refurbished bedrooms *(Joan and Michel Hooper-Immins)*; [Old Hereford Rd], *Crown*: Food-oriented, with decent beer, flagstoned bar, tables out in front, pets' corner in big car park; pleasant country location; children welcome *(Gwyneth and Salvo Spadaro-Dutturi)*

Caerleon [Llanhennock; ST3592], *Wheatsheaf*: Cosy, friendly country pub, three well kept beers inc Bass, well priced snacks; children welcome *(Robert Powell, Mike Pugh)*

☆ Chepstow [ST5394], *Bridge*: Civilised low-ceilinged pub beautifully placed opp Wye bridge, tables out in delightful garden with castle view; flagstoned entrance, carpeted main room with light pine tables and chairs, prints on walls, open fire; attractively served bar food inc good home-made soup and several daily specials, quietly friendly staff, well kept real ales *(John Boylan, JT)*

Chepstow [16 Bridge St], *Castle View*: Wide range of unusual bar food inc good vegetarian dishes in pleasant pub facing castle, delightful garden; bedrooms *(J Boylan)*; [Welsh St, just outside Town Arch], *Coach & Horses*: A drinkers' pub with very well kept Bass, Brains, Crown Buckley Reverend James and so forth, but comfortable and well appointed, attracting all ages; split-level rooms, fine old etched windows, open fire, prints *(Andrew and Liz Roberts, J Boylan)*

Clydach [SO2213], *Drum & Monkey*: Old pub with pleasant bar in scenic spot, cheerful helpful staff, good reasonably priced food in bar and restaurant, real ale *(M E Hughes)*; [Old Black Rock Rd], *Rock & Fountain*: Good generous straightforward bar food at attractive prices, lovely mountainside spot, friendly owners, well kept Brains SA; good value clean bedrooms, good traditional breakfasts *(Mike and Trew Mehaffy, LYM)*

☆ Gilwern [High St; SO2414], *Bridgend*: Small welcoming pub in former sawmill offices, grassy bank leads from tiled terrace to towpath and line of moored boats, canal-related prints on walls, good range of well kept changing beers and of nicely presented food inc unusual burgers, friendly staff and sleepy red setter; children welcome *(Roger Danes, C H Stride, Mike Dickerson)*

☆ Llangattock Lingoed [SO3620], *Hunters Moon*: Attractive beamed and flagstoned country pub with two character bars dating from 13th c, very friendly atmosphere, good reasonbaly priced food; landlord plays the bagpipes, wife does the cooking *(R G Stephenson, BB)*

Llantarnam [Newport Rd (A4042 N of M4 junction 26); ST3093], *Greenhouse*: Welcoming and roomy old pub very popular with businessmen at lunchtime for wide choice of good value decent food from good sandwiches up; well kept Courage-related ales, beautiful big garden; folk nights *(M Barrell, John and Joan Nash)*

Llanthony [SO2928], *Half Moon*: Basic country inn mirroring the character of this undeveloped valley with all its walks and pony-trekking centres, decent plain food, real ales such as Bull Mastiff Son-of-a-Bitch and Flowers Original; bedrooms not luxurious but clean and comfortable *(John Nash, Dave Braisted, John Cox)*

Llantrisant [off A449; ST3997], *Greyhound*: Good hill views from attractive country pub with well presented reasonably priced reliable home-cooked bar food inc vegetarian, spacious open-plan rooms, friendly service; bedrooms in small attached motel – lovely setting *(Mac Tennick, R Michael Richards, the Monday Club)*

Llanvetherine [B4521 ENE of Abergavenny; SO3617], *Kings Arms*: Old whitewashed inn with good value bar food inc vegetarian, several well kept beers such as Bass, Butcombe, Morlands Old Speckled Hen and Thwaites Coachman, helpful staff, pool table at back; garden; children welcome *(Dave Braisted)*

Mamhilad [SO3003], *Star*: Friendly, comfortable and straightforward, 200 yards from canal, coal fire in one bar, woodburner in another, good range of usual bar food *(Mike Dickerson)*

Monmouth [Lydart; B4293 towards Trelleck; SO5009], *Gockett*: Attractive bar, two big well furnished dining areas, good food inc good Sun lunch with plenty of choice, good wine list, plenty of different beers, cheerful efficient service; pleasant garden; children welcome; bedrooms with own bathrooms *(Mr and Mrs A R Hawkins)*; [Cinderhill St; SO5113], *Riverside*: Civilised and well run inn with decent food; comfortable bedrooms *(DG)*

Pontypool [Greenhill Rd, Sebastopol; ST2998], *Crown*: Large old-fashioned pub, big lounge with pool table and juke box, smaller bar and second lounge; welcoming landlord, well kept real ale; children welcome; opp very good fish and chip shop *(Gwyneth and Salvo Spadaro Dutturi)*

Raglan [High St; SO4108], *Ship*: Friendly old coaching inn with three well kept changing real ales, three open fires, good food in bars and restaurant area, friendly staff *(Richard Waller, Robert Huddleston)*

Rhyd Y Meirch [up cul-de-sac off A4042 S of Abergavenny – OS Sheet 161 map ref 289073; SO2807], *Goose & Cuckoo*: Tiny very friendly unspoilt country pub run by Scottish couple, lots of malt and blended whiskies, good home-cooked food esp vegetarian, well kept Penarth Bullmastiff, Wadworths 6X and more esoteric ales; near hill walks, Vietnamese pot-bellied pigs in field behind; dogs allowed if on lead *(Gwyneth and Salvo Spadaro-Dutturi, John and Daphne Elphinstone, Mike Pugh)*

☆ **Shirenewton** [B4235 Chepstow—Usk; ST4893], *Carpenters Arms*: Quaint series of four small well refurbished rooms off central bar, log fires, warm atmosphere, welcoming staff, seven well kept ales inc guests such as Bass, Hook Norton Best, Theakstons XB, wide choice of good reasonably priced food from sandwiches up; beautiful hanging baskets in summer; children may be tolerated *(Jane and Ian Williams, A R and B E Sayer)*

St Brides Wentlooge [Beach Rd; ST2982], *Lighthouse*: Good range of weekly-changing guest beers, good food upstairs, outstanding view of Severn estuary *(Anon)*

☆ **Talycoed** [B4233 Monmouth—Abergavenny; SO4115], *Halfway House*: Well run unspoilt 16th-c character inn in pleasant countryside, good home-cooked food (not Sun evening) using local and even own produce, polite friendly licensees, well kept real ale, good atmosphere, log fires, timbers and stripped stone; tables in well kept garden, charming views; bedrooms *(Paul and Heather Bettesworth, W W Swait)*

Tintern [Devauden Rd, off A446; SO5301], *Cherry Tree*: Well kept Hancocks PA and farm cider in quaint little unspoilt country tavern with no food but great garden; children welcome *(E Money, Paul and Heather Bettesworth)*

☆ **Trelleck** [B4293 6 miles S of Monmouth; SO5005], *Lion*: Good interesting meat dishes, veg a delight, not a chip in sight; quiet and unpretentious country pub with very pleasant lounge bar *(Terry and Pat Scott)*

☆ **Trelleck**, *Village Green*: Sensitively preserved old building, really a restaurant/bistro, but a bar too (with well kept beers as well as its mainstay wine); comfortable, with prints, lots of dried flowers on beams, friendly landlord, good food *(R Michael Richards, Paul Weedon, R G and M P Lumley)*

Usk [Bridge St; SO3801], *Cross Keys*: 14th-c inn with oak beams, log fire, good range of good food and drink, restaurant *(J C Hathaway)*; *Greyhound*: Pleasant landlord and staff, fair choice of reasonably priced good food *(M E Tennick)*; [Old Market St], *Kings Head*: Busy pub with fine choice of real ales, superb fireplace; open all day; bedrooms *(Graham Reeve)*; [The Square], *Nags Head*: Relaxed and pleasant, good landlord, unusual food esp home-made pies and game in season, interesting decor *(Mike Pugh)*; [Llangeview; outside town, off A449/A472 junction; first right off B4235 – OS Sheet 171 map ref 396005], *Rat Trap*: Good restaurant and bar meals, Bass and Tetleys, cheerful staff, tasteful surroundings; bedrooms in motel wing *(Mac Tennick)*

GWYNEDD

☆ **Aberdovey**, [SN6296], *Britannia*: Good range of good value generous bar food in busy and friendly pub, superb position with great view over Dovey estuary to mountains of N Cardigan from upstairs with summer balcony; well kept Bass, good service, children in side room *(J E and A G Jones)*

Abergynolwyn [Tywyn—Talyllyn pass; SH6807], *Railway*: Friendly pub, good food, lovely setting *(D Evans)*

Abersoch [OS Sheet 123 map ref 320264; SH3128], *Porth Tocyn*: Genial welcoming landlord, landlady seems to live for cooking – delicious food, marginal use of herbs and sauces, range of breads, sumptuous 5-course or shorter meal, a challenge to have seconds; bedrooms *(Nick Haslewood)*

Bala [High St; SH9336], *Olde Bulls Head*: Oldest inn in town, comfortably refurbished bar, food, Whitbreads ale; bedrooms *(Blair and Dinah Harrison, LYM)*; [High St], *Ship*: Spacious but cosy low-beamed room with ship motif, generous fresh good value food, Allied ales, good service and welcome *(Derek and Cerys Williams)*

Bangor [nr harbour; SH5973], *Nelson*: Well kept beer, friendly landlady, limited choice of decent bar food *(L G Milligan)*

☆ **Barmouth** [Church St; SH6116], *Last Inn*: Harbourside local with low beams, flagstones, ship's lamps, intriguing watery grotto, wide choice of good cheap bar lunches, particularly well kept Marstons Pedigree, friendly service *(Richard Houghton)*

☆ **Betws Y Coed** [A5 next to BP garage and Little Chef; SH7956], *Waterloo*: Wide choice of generous food inc interesting soups and hot dishes, good generous veg; efficient service, unobtrusive piped music; bedrooms *(KC)*

Bontnewydd [SH4860], *Newborough Arms*: Friendly and comfortable recently redecorated local, welcoming to visitors, with well kept Burtonwood and other ales, fair range of decent food, dining room; juke box can be loud; bedrooms *(Dave Thompson, Margaret Mason, Michael Back)*

Caernarfon [Northgate St; SH4863], *Black Boy*: Bustling local by castle walls, beams from ships wrecked here in 16th c, bare floors, cheery fire, homely and cosy atmosphere, good choice of real ales inc Bass, good value well presented food in bar and restaurant, pleasant service; TV in main bar *(Richard Houghton, W A D Hoyle, M G Lavery)*; [opp Castle], *Palace Vaults*: Friendly town pub with good mix of locals and visitors (and children), limited menu with daily specials, Marstons Pedigree and other guest beers *(Keith and Ann Dibble)*

☆ **Capel Curig** [SH4682], *Cobdens*: At foot of Moel Siabod, back bar has bare rockface in it; good varied satisfying food inc good home-made bread and some interesting vegetarian dishes, well kept Courage-related beers, friendly old english sheepdog and border collie cross, very pleasant service; lovely river scene across road, good walks all around; bedrooms *(Mr and Mrs D J Tapper, KC, Nick Haslewood)*

☆ **Capel Curig**, *Bryn Tyrch*: Prompt friendly service even when busy, good choice of interesting food esp vegetarian dishes, well kept ales such as Marstons Pedigree and Whitbreads Castle Eden; bedrooms simple but good value, with good breakfasts *(Dave Braisted, C M Charlton, N K Musgrave, Neal Marsden)*

☆ **Capel Garmon** [signed from A470 just outside Betws-y-coed, towards Llanrwst; SH8255], *White Horse*: Unspoilt character low-beamed inn dating from 16th c, comfortable and homely, with warmly welcoming new licensees, log fires, games in public bar, wide choice of good value generous mostly home-cooked bar food, well kept Bass, Stones and Worthington BB, refurbished restaurant; bedrooms simple but comfortable, fine countryside with magnificent views *(Peter Burridge, Mr and Mrs D Tapper, D A Hasprey)*

Clynnog Fawr [SH4249], *Bryn Eisteddfod*: Pleasant surroundings, welcoming staff and good food *(Mrs D Williams, Miss P Williams)*

☆ **Corris** [village signed off A487 Machynlleth—Dolgellau; SH7608], *Slaters Arms*: Very pleasant small pub in interesting and beautifully placed ex-slate-mining village; good fire in cosy slate inglenook, high-backed antique settles, good value simple bar food, well kept Banks's Bitter and Mild at attractive prices, friendly service; nearby forest walks *(Ann Griffiths, LYM)*

☆ **Dinas Mawddwy** [SH8615], *Llew Coch*: Genuine old-style country local with charming front bar dripping with sparkling brasses, well kept Bass, food inc trout or salmon from River Dovey just behind; plainer inner family room lively with video games, pool and Sat evening live music; surrounded by steep fir forests *(Paul McPherson, LYM)*

Dolgellau [A487/A470 3 miles E – OS Sheet 124 map ref 766168; SH7318], *Cross Foxes*: Good food inc fine doorstep sandwiches, two roaring fires, comfortable atmosphere, interesting ornaments *(R and S Bentley, D Evans, M Joyner)*

☆ **Ganllwyd** [SH7224], *Tyn-y-Groes*: Old inn owned by National Trust in lovely Snowdonia setting, fine forest views, old-fashioned furnishings in partly panelled lounge, Boddingtons, Felinfoel Double Dragon and Flowers IPA, quite a few malt whiskies, generous bar food and (not Sun evening) no-smoking restaurant, public bar with games; comfortable well equipped bedrooms, salmon and seatrout fishing *(J S Green, G W H Kerby, Mr and Mrs K H Frostick, H Saddington, LYM)*

☆ **Llanbedr** [A496; SH5827], *Victoria*: Pleasant riverside pub, big refurbished lounge (has kept old-fashioned inglenook), useful choice of decent food from counter in dining area, well kept Robinsons Best; attractive garden with big adventure slide; children welcome – even a nappies bin in ladies'; bedrooms *(M Joyner, Klaus and Elizabeth Leist, LYM)*

☆ **Llandudno** [Old St, behind tram stn; SH7883], *Kings Head*: Interesting rambling pub, much extended around 16th-c core, spaciously open-plan, with comfortable traditional furnishings, red wallpaper, dark pine, good reasonably priced bar food, several Allied real ales, children allowed, open all day in summer *(LYM)*

Llandwrog [SH4456], *Harp*: Friendly and attractive, in pretty village, with well kept Whitbreads-related real ales, comfortable straightforward furnishings, good range of good food esp salads, welcoming new Scots licensees; good bedrooms *(D W Jones-Williams, Dave Thompson, Margaret Mason, Anne and Tony Parry)*

☆ Llanengan [Lleyn Peninsula; SH2927], *Sun*: Good pub in small village near spectacular Hells Mouth beach, wide range of drinks inc well kept Ind Coope Burton and Tetleys on handpump, good food inc wholesome ploughman's, friendly service; bedrooms *(Nicholas Wright, Ian J Clay)*

☆ nr Llanrwst [Maenan (A470 N); SH7965], *Priory*: Formerly the Maenan Abbey Hotel, steep-gabled substantial Victorian building with battlemented tower in charming stately grounds, lots of tables outside and good play area; good bar food from sandwiches to steaks in elegant and airy back dining lounge, welcoming if sometimes rather cramped-feeling front bar with Websters Choice and Yorkshire on handpump, good service, unobtrusive piped music and Welsh singing Sat night; partly no-smoking restaurant, children welcome; good comfortable bedrooms, good as a place to stay *(H K Dyson, KC, Brian and Jill Bond, Dave and Jules Tuckett, Eric and Jackie Robinson, Mrs Thomas, LYM)*

☆ Morfa Nefyn [A497/B4412; SH2840], *Bryncynan*: Modernised pub concentrating (particularly in summer) on quickly served well presented good value bar food inc vegetarian and local fish and seafood; quiet in winter with good log fire; above-average summer choice of well kept Allied ales, restaurant, rustic seats outside, children allowed; cl Sun *(Simon Reynolds, Michael and Janet Hepworth, LYM)*

☆ Morfa Nefyn, *Cliff*: Good choice of reasonably priced bar food and friendly service in tastefully furnished pub, popular with locals; attractive conservatory dining area in lovely setting overlooking sea *(D Jones-Williams, Mrs D M Everard)*

☆ Penmaenpool [SH6918], *George III*: Attractive inn with cheery 17th-c beamed and flagstoned holidayish bottom bar and civilised partly panelled upstairs bar opening into cosy and chintzy inglenook lounge; lovely setting on Mawddach estuary, sheltered terrace, good walks; home-cooked food in bar and restaurant inc some interesting dishes esp good lamb and seafood, Courage-related ales under light CO_2 blanket, children in eating area, open all day; bedrooms inc some in interesting conversion of former station on disused line *(Jeff Davies, Mr and Mrs R F Wright, FMB, Canon Michael Bordeaux, LYM)*

Pentir [SH5767], *Vaynol Arms*: Plushy pub with decent food inc good veg and children's helpings, friendly service, children very welcome; Theakstons Old Peculier and a guest ale *(MM, DT)*

☆ Porth Dinllaen [beach car park signed from Morfa Nefyn, then a good 15-min walk – which is part of the attraction; SH2741], *Ty Coch*: Right on curving beach, far from the roads, with stunning view along coast to mountains; pub itself full of attractive salvage and RNLI memorabilia; beach drinks in plastic glasses, service may be slow, beer keg and food ordinary – so it's the position which appeals, and the coffee's decent; may be closed much of winter, but open all day summer *(Neil and Elaine Piper, Klaus and Elizabeth Leist)*

☆ Porthmadog [Lombard St; SH5639], *Ship*: Welcoming local with wide choice of mostly fresh generous nicely cooked food with good choice of veg at sensible prices, popular upstairs evening oriental restaurant, well kept Ind Coope Burton, Tetleys and a weekly guest beer; huge open fireplace in lounge (mainly eating in here), long comfortable public bar; children allowed till 8 in small gated back room with video games/fruit machines, beyond pool room *(Nigel and Teresa Blocks, A P Jeffreys, Richard Houghton, David J B Lewis)*

☆ Rhyd Ddu [A4085 N of Beddgelert; SH5753], *Cwellyn Arms*: Very busy and efficient stone-built pub, good sensibly priced food inc salad bar, vegetarian dishes, popular steaks and home-made puddings, Courage-related ales; flagstones, log fire in huge ancient fireplace, small games bar with pool, darts and TV, restaurant; children and walkers welcome, fine Snowdon views from garden tables with barbecue *(KC, Richard Houghton, Gordon Theaker, Lorrie and Mick Marchington)*

Tal Y Bont [B5106 6 miles S of Conwy, towards Llanrwst; SH7669], *Black Lion*: Good choice of home-made food inc river trout in season, pleasant welcoming staff *(D Jones-Williams)*; *Lodge*: Good food esp fish and seafood, some veg from own garden; very friendly staff *(Anon)*

Tal Y Cafn [A470 Conway—Llanrwst; SH7972], *Tal y Cafn*: Handy for Bodnant Gardens, cheerful and comfortable lounge bar with big inglenook, simple bar meals, Greenalls on handpump, seats in spacious garden; children welcome *(H K Dyson, LYM)*

Talysarn [SH4953], *Halfway*: Well kept Banks's Mild and Marstons Pedigree *(A C Page)*

Trawsfynydd [SH7136], *White Lion*: Genuine unspoilt village pub, well kept Burtonwood *(Dr and Mrs A K Clarke)*

☆ Tremadog [SH5640], *Golden Fleece*: Stonebuilt inn on attractive square, good value standard bar food inc vegetarian, well kept Bass, Mild and Marstons Pedigree, friendly service, cosy partly partitioned rambling beamed lounge with open fire, nice

little snug, separate bistro (children allowed
here and in small family room), games room,
intriguing cellar bar, tables in sheltered inner
courtyard; closed Sun (A P Jeffreys, LYM)

POWYS

☆ **Beulah** [A483 Llanwrtyd Wells—Builth
Wells – OS Sheet 147 map ref 931513;
SN9151], *Trout*: Friendly, well kept nicely
refurbished front lounge, spacious well lit
dining area with wide choice of reasonably
priced home-cooked food (limited
Mon/Tues) inc good puddings, public bar
and pool, Hancocks HB, Youngers IPA and
Worthington BB; very busy at weekends; six
comfortable bedrooms (D J Underwood, M
and J Back)

☆ **Bleddfa** [A488; SO2168], *Hundred House*:
Friendly, comfortable and attractively
furnished stripped-stone lounge bar with
good log fire in very fine fireplace, good
home cooking, well kept real ale, separate
bar and games room – walkers welcome;
tables in garden with barbecue, lovely
countryside; bedrooms (Lyn Juffernholz,
Alan Ruttley)
Brecon [George St; SO0428], *George*: Good
range of good value food, attractive dining
room, pleasant staff (James Morrell)
Builth Wells [SO0351], *Greyhound*: Friendly
welcome, warm atmosphere, good value bar
food, real ale (D Millichap); *Lion*: Roomy
hotel bar with well kept Bass on handpump,
wide range of reasonably priced bar food;
bedrooms (C J Parsons)

☆ **Coedway** [B4393 W of Shrewsbury; SJ3415],
Old Hand & Diamond: Log fire in roomy
pleasant bar with well kept beers, variety of
good reasonably priced food in dining area
and restaurant, smaller back bar, friendly
service, no music (C E Power, D E P and I D
Hughes)

☆ **Crickhowell** [New Rd; SO2118], *Bridge End*:
Spacious and attractive pub in good spot by
many-arched bridge over weir of river Usk,
nice warmly local chatty feel, good
straightforward food, gleaming furniture,
well kept Bass and Worthington BB on
handpump; open all day (Barry and Anne;
more reports on new regime please)

☆ **Cwmdu** [A479 NW of Crickhowell;
SO1823], *Farmers Arms*: Welcoming and
plushly comfortable pub, decent
straightforward food, well kept Bass, Brains
and Worthington BB, pleasant landlady,
friendly staff, flagstones and attractive prints,
tables in big garden and out in front;
bedrooms with good breakfasts – handy for
pony-trekkers and Black Mountains (M A
Watts, Mr and Mrs Peter B Dowsett)

☆ **Derwenlas** [A487 Machynlleth—
Aberystwyth; SN7299], *Black Lion*: Quaint
450-year-old pub doing well under new
owners, huge log fire in low-beamed cottagey
bar divided by oak posts and cartwheels,
good home-cooked food in dining area, well
kept Marstons Pedigree on handpump,
decent wines, unobtrusive piped music;
garden up behind with adventure playground

and steps up into woods (Derek and Cerys
Williams)

☆ **Dolfor** [inn sign up hill off A483 about 4
miles S of Newtown; SO1187], *Dolfor Inn*:
Welcoming much modernised hillside inn
with easy chairs in beamed lounge opening
into neatly modern dining area, very well
prepared generous standard food, well kept
ales, unobtrusive piped music, good views
from behind; bedrooms comfortable and
good value (W F C Phillips, LYM)

☆ **Garthmyl** [SO1999], *Nags Head*: An oasis in
this under-served area, pleasant and friendly,
with good choice of generous home-cooked
food (even properly cured home-cooked ham
for the sandwiches), well kept beers (J E
Davies, Col A H N Reade)

☆ **Gladestry** [SO2355], *Royal Oak*: Relaxing
unpretentious beamed and flagstoned inn
handy for Offa's Dyke Path, friendly service,
well kept Bass and Felinfoel Double Dragon,
good simple bar food inc home-cooked ham,
gammon and fish, reasonable prices – lunch
opening 12-2; refurbished lounge, separate
bar, children allowed, picnic-table sets in
lovely secluded garden behind, safe for
children; bedrooms clean, well equipped and
good value, with good breakfasts (Mrs B
Sugarman, C J Parsons, Ian Jones)

☆ **Glasbury** [B4350 towards Hay, just N of
A438; SO1739], *Harp*: Snug log-fire lounge
and airy games bar with picture windows
over garden sloping to River Wye, usual bar
food inc children's dishes (children very
welcome), well kept Robinsons and
Whitbreads-related ales; good value simple
bedrooms, good breakfasts (Alan P Carr,
LYM)
Guilsfield [3 miles N of Welshpool; SJ2212],
Kings Head: Spotless old pub with good new
licensees, well kept beers, genuine home
cooking, friendly atmosphere, attractive
garden with hanging baskets (Brenda and
Derrick Swift)

☆ **Hay on Wye** [26 Lion St; SO2342], *Old
Black Lion*: Low-beamed partly oak-
panelled traditional bar with candles and soft
lighting, wide choice of bar food inc some
interesting cooking and a lot for vegetarians,
candlelit restaurant (last orders may be 8 if
business slack), usually Flowers Original or
Worthington BB and Fullers London Pride
well kept; children welcome in eating areas;
comfortable good value bedrooms, Wye
fishing rights; in general very well up to main
entry standards, but should perhaps
sometimes be more flexible (P D Putwain,
Sue Demont, Tim Barrow, Annette and
George Series, Bill and Beryl Farmer, John
and Beryl Knight, John Gorman, David J B
Lewis, D J Underwood, DAV, George
Atkinson, Dorothy Pilson, A Kilpatrick, Mrs
D Nisbet, LYM; more reports please)

☆ **Hay on Wye** [Bull Ring], *Kilvert Court*: Small
well furnished hotel bar with flagstones and
candles, friendly staff, well kept Bass on
handpump, good range of good food in bar
and restaurant; live music Thurs; outside
tables overlooking small town square;

bedrooms immaculate and well equipped *(Mr and Mrs T J Anslow, Katie and Steve Newby)*

Hay on Wye, *Three Tuns*: One for lovers of the unspoilt, tiny little quarry-tiled bar with chatty landlady, wall benches and Edwardian bar fittings; no food *(Phil and Sally Gorton)*

Howey [off A483 S of Llandrindod Wells; SO0559], *Drovers Arms*: Clean, tidy and genuine, lots of character, good mostly home-made food *(Mr and Mrs Lorusso)*

☆ **Hundred House** [SO1154], *Hundred House*: Particularly good friendly licensees in attractive, clean and interesting pub full of intriguing artefacts, well kept Bass and Hancocks HB with interesting guest beers such as Woods Christmas Cracker in season, good wine list, decent food in small dining room, big garden with play area; children welcome *(Pat and John Millward, Mrs J Holding)*

Kerry [A489; SO1589], *Kerry Lamb*: Useful country pub with obliging service and decent food inc outstanding trifle *(Susanne Bertschinger)*

Knighton [Broad St; SO2972], *Knighton*: Friendly welcome, well kept Ansells, inexpensive bar snacks, beautiful staircase and galleried layout; bedrooms; handy for Offa's Dyke Path *(N H and B Ellis)*

Llanbrynmair [junction A470/B4518; SH9003], *Wynnstay Arms*: Decent straightforward village local with public bar, smaller lounge, helpful staff; bedrooms *(Paul McPherson)*

Llanfair Caereinion [High St, off A458; SJ1006], *Goat*: Relaxed local with settees and easy chairs in inglenook lounge, good value straightforward bar food inc vegetarian in back dining area, well kept Felinfoel and Hancocks on handpump, games room, garden *(Derek and Cerys Williams)*

Llanfyllin [High St (A490); SJ1419], *Cain Valley*: Old coaching inn with good food inc fresh veg and well kept beers in hotelish panelled lounge bar, friendly helpful service; handsome Jacobean staircase to comfortable bedrooms, good breakfasts *(A N Ellis, Richard Houghton)*

☆ **Llangenny** [off A40 Abergavenny—Crickhowell; SO2417], *Dragons Head*: Well kept beer, good food and exceptionally pleasant staff in low-beamed bar with big log fire, pews, housekeeper's chairs and a high-backed settle among other seats, restaurant, tables outside; lovely spot in little riverside hamlet tucked below the Black Mountains *(P J S Goward, LYM)*

☆ **Llangorse** [SO1327], *Red Lion*: Efficient friendly service, wide range of well kept Welsh and other beers, good farm cider, good straightforward food at sensible prices, attractive position by stream through village; bedrooms *(Anne Morris, P J S Goward, LYM)*

☆ **Llangurig** [Pant Mawr; A44 Aberystwyth rd, 4½ miles W — OS Sheet 135 map ref 847924, SN8482], *Glansevern Arms*: Very civilised, with cushioned antique settles and open fire in high-beamed bar, yet manages to preserve something of a local atmosphere; well kept Bass and Worthington Dark Mild on handpump, decent malt whiskies and wines, lunchtime sandwiches and hot soup (not Sun) with maybe cold wild salmon in season; good value seven-course dinners (not Sun evening; must book); in a smashing remote position over 1,000 ft up, with well equipped comfortable bedrooms *(Ann Marie Stephenson, D W Jones-Williams, Roger Entwistle, LYM)*

☆ **Llangynidr** [B4558, Cwm Crawnon; SO1519], *Coach & Horses*: Friendly new management doing well in spacious pub with safely fenced pretty sloping waterside garden by Brecon—Monmouth Canal across road, wider choice of generous well presented straightforward bar food, well kept changing Courage-related ales, open fire, pub games, restaurant; children welcome, lovely walks *(Chris and Sue Heathman, Steve Thomas, Ross Lockley, Mike Dickerson, Roger Danes, K W J Wood)*

☆ **Llangynidr** [off B4558], *Red Lion*: Creeper-covered 16th-c inn reopened under new owners, attractively furnished traditional bow-windowed bar with good range of real ales inc Theakstons Best and XB on handpump, good sandwiches and interesting range of unusual hot dishes, sheltered pretty garden; comfortable bedrooms *(Jenny and Brian Seller, LYM)*

☆ **Llanwddyn** [SJ0219], *Lake Vyrnwy*: Comfortable old-feeling well done pub in new extension among smart country hotel overlooking lake, friendly staff, two real ales, good food, darts, great view from big windows or balcony; bedrooms *(Dr and Mrs A K Clarke, W F C Phillips)*

Llanyre [SO0462], *Bell*: Old but modernised inn, very comfortable, with wide choice of good food well presented by efficient staff in stylish restaurant; bedrooms *(C E Power)*

☆ **Llowes** [A438 Brecon—Hereford – OS Sheet 161 map ref 192416; SO1941], *Radnor Arms*: Well run and attractive country inn with good choice of superb food from good filled rolls and inventive soups to fine restaurant-style dishes; ancient cottagey bar, very welcoming, with well kept Felinfoel and log fire, tables in imaginatively planted garden looking out over fields towards the Wye; closed Sun pm, at weekends it's wise to book *(Brian Plowright)*

☆ **Machynlleth** [Heol Pentrerhedyn; A489, nr junction with A487; SH7501], *White Lion*: Welcoming atmosphere, dark oak and copper-topped tables, dark pink plush seats, well kept Banks's Bitter and Mild and Marstons Pedigree, big log fire, wide range of food inc good vegetarian choice, adjacent dining area, service brisk and pleasant; best to book for 3-course Sun lunch; pretty views from picnic-table sets in garden; neatly modernised stripped pine bedrooms *(Iris and Eddie Brixton, Merym and Zilpha Read)*

☆ **Montgomery** [Pool Rd; B4388 towards Welshpool], *Cottage*: Mix of old-fashioned furnishings and decorations in several small rooms, quiet atmosphere, freshly made bar food inc Sun lunch, evening restaurant, well kept Tetleys, decent wines, unobtrusive piped music; tables on neat grass behind, children in eating area, cl Mon exc bank hols *(George Murdoch, LYM)*

Nant Ddu [A470 Merthyr Tydfil—Brecon; SO0015], *Nant Ddu*: Useful food stop *(A K Thorlby)*

Neuadd Fawr [SO2322], *Stables*: Hotel high in the hills with superb views, character and atmosphere in bar and dining room, huge log fire, good home-made food, friendly licensees, lovely garden; cottagey bedrooms *(Peter and Audrey Dowsett)*

☆ **Newbridge on Wye** [SO0158], *New Inn*: Friendly village inn in upper Wye Valley, well kept Flowers IPA, decent standard bar food running up to steaks, spacious carpeted back lounge with button-back banquettes in big bays, good local atmosphere in straightforward public bar with darts and pool, third snug with cushioned wall benches, restaurant; clean fresh well equipped bedrooms, good breakfasts *(N W Kingsley, J S M Sheldon, BB)*

Pen y Cae [Brecon Rd; SN8413], *Ancient Briton*: Reasonably priced good meals inc takeaways, good service; handy for Dan-yr-Ogof caves and Carig y Nos country park *(S Watkins)*

Pentre Bach [off A40 in Sennybridge; SN9032], *Shoemakers Arms*: Individual welcoming local in the middle of nowhere, good value enjoyable food; phone (01874) 636508 winter weekday lunchtime and they'll normally open up if not otherwise planning to *(LD, JD)*

Rhayader [SN9768], *Bear*: Warm welcome, attractively served food with helpings just right for elderly people *(Dr Dave Morgan)*; [Llangurig Rd (A470)], *Castle*: Old beams, inglenook, plush seats and comfortable chairs; Boddingtons, Flowers and Worthington BB, decent choice of sensibly priced generous food inc children's helpings, children allowed in lounge; restaurant beyond public bar; bedrooms *(M and J Back)*

St Harmon [B4518; SN9973], *Sun*: Interesting pub, main part over 300 years old, interconnecting rooms with partitions, beams, flagstones, woodburner, obliging service, real ales inc Hook Norton *(Mr and Mrs J Back)*

☆ **Talybont on Usk** [B4558 – OS Sheet 161 map ref 114226; SO1122], *Star*: No-frills take-us-as-you-find-us pub specialising in a dozen or so well kept ales, inc unusual ones, and good farm ciders; several plainly furnished rooms radiating from central servery, cheery unpretentious atmosphere, quick generous simple good value food, seats in pleasant garden by aqueduct; children allowed, though scarcely suitable for them; live blues Weds, jazz Thurs, open all day Sat; bedrooms *(Gillian and Jamie Cole, Dr P D Putwain, M Joyner, A P Jeffreys, David and Kate Jones, LYM)*

☆ **Talybont on Usk**, *Usk*: Unspoilt traditional character inn, one bar with log fire, flagstones with scattered rugs, panelling and sporting prints, another with fishing prints and memorabilia – fishing available; varied adventurous food inc game, friendly staff, antiques shop; bedrooms good value, big breakfasts *(Peter Bond, Mrs Rhian Oliver)*

Talybont on Usk, *White Hart*: Stone coaching inn with big bar, beamed dining room, open fires, well presented bar food, well kept real ales; on Taff Trail next to canal; bedrooms *(Mike Dickerson)*

Trecastle [SN8729], *Castle*: Recently refurbished and reopened Georgian inn, sparklingly clean, with friendly licensees, good bar snacks, imaginative restaurant; bedrooms comfortable *(Ron and Pat Grace)*

Welshpool [Raven Sq – OS Sheet 126 map ref 223081; SJ2207], *Raven*: Very wide choice of food in lounge bar/restaurant inc good vegetarian choice, some real ale, friendly licensee *(R C Morgan, Paul McPherson)*; *Royal Oak*: Friendly welcome, well kept Bass and Worthington BB, good bar food; bedrooms *(N H and B Ellis)*

Please keep sending us reports. We rely on readers for news of new discoveries, and particularly for news of changes – however slight – at the fully described pubs. No stamp needed: *The Good Pub Guide*, FREEPOST TN1569, Wadhurst, E Sussex TN5 7BR.

Channel Islands

The Old Portelet at St Brelade on Jersey has reopened after a very attractive refurbishment, still under the same good landlady as when it was last in these pages; it's a good addition to this year's main entries. The best pub food we've found on the islands this year is at the Fleur du Jardin at Kings Mills on Guernsey. Not quite enough of a pub to qualify as a main entry (and therefore listed with the Lucky Dips at the end of the chapter), the Rocquaine Bistro at Rocquaine Bay on the same island also has excellent food – in its case, outstanding fish. Other pubs on the islands currently doing particularly well include the roomy Admiral in St Helier (Jersey), with lots of atmosphere and a very wide choice of very cheap meals; and the Star & Tipsy Toad at St Peter (Jersey), good all round, and especially attractive for its very cheap own-brewed real ales. In the Lucky Dip sections at the end of the chapter, other pubs we'd particularly mention include, on Jersey, the Smugglers at St Brelade, Lamplighters in St Helier and Les Fontaines at St John (though its long-standing tenant was to retire at the end of 1994), and on Sark the Stocks Hotel. Drinks prices on the islands are lower than on the mainland, though not by such a wide margin as in the past; we have this year found lower prices in a few mainland pubs than we found in any on the Channel Islands. Even so, a pint of beer is typically about 35p cheaper here than it is on the mainland. Food prices, scarcely increased at all here this year, generally offer excellent value by mainland standards – a good hot dish in a pub here now typically saves over 50p, compared with a mainland equivalent. Pubs on Guernsey close on Sundays; those on Jersey have a break between 1 and 4.30 that day.

CASTEL (Guernsey)

Hougue du Pommier 🍺

Route de Hougue du Pommier, off Route de Carteret; just inland from Cobo Bay and Grandes Rocques

In a pleasant setting, this friendly and well equipped hotel – called 'Apple Tree Hill' – was a cider mill in the 18th c, and plenty of fruit trees still stand shading the tables on its neatly trimmed lawn, as well as by the swimming pool in the sheltered walled garden, and in a shady flower-filled courtyard. Inside, the most prized seats are perhaps those in the snug area by the big stone fireplace with its attendant bellows and copper fire-irons. The rest of the oak-beamed bar is quite roomy, with leatherette armed chairs around wood tables, old game and sporting prints, guns, sporting trophies and so forth. As well as a wide variety of daily specials, very good bar food in generous helpings includes home-made soup (£1.35), ploughman's (from £2.85), sandwiches (from £2.25; good open sandwiches from £3.50), vegetarian dishes like mushroom stroganoff (from £3.95), salads (from £4.45), plaice (£4.95), chicken and ham pancake rolls, steak and kidney pie or gammon and egg (£4.95), chicken kiev (£5.95), entrecote steak (£7.55), usual children's dishes (£2.55), and from the carvery, roast sirloin of scotch beef (£5.35 and £4.45 for the second carvery of the day) and daily specials (from £3.95 – £8), puddings from the trolley (£2.55), good coffee and decent wines. Pool, ring the bull and maybe unobtrusive piped music; no-smoking areas in bar and in the good quality restaurant. Good leisure facilities include a pitch-and-putt golf course and a putting green (for visitors as well as residents). For residents there's free temporary membership to the Guernsey Indoor Green Bowling Association, the stadium is next door and rated as one of the best in Europe, and a daily courtesy bus into town. No dogs. *(Recommended by Mrs P Davies, Mike and Pam Simpson, Sharon and Laurie Gepheart, John Evans; more reports please)*

Free house ~ Licensee Tracy Hudson-Pestana ~ Meals and snacks 12-1.45; 6.45-8.30 (not Sun eve) ~ Restaurant ~ Guernsey (01481) 56531 ~ Children welcome ~ Open 11-2.30, 6-11.45 ~ Bedrooms: £43B/£86B

GREVE DE LECQ   (Jersey)   OS 583552 Map 1

Moulin de Lecq

This place is well worth a visit just to see the massive reconstructed waterwheel turning outside this serenely placed black-shuttered old mill, with its formidable gears remorselessly meshing in their stone housing behind the bar. But far from being a touristy gimmick, this is a very proper pub, with plenty of local custom and a warm and pleasant atmosphere. Well kept Ann Street Ann's Treat and Old Jersey and Guernsey Bitter on handpump. There's a good log fire, toasting you as you come down the four steps into the cosy bar; besides plush-cushioned black wooden seats against the white-painted walls; piped music. Good bar food is from the daily specials board or menu and includes soup (£1.20), filled baked potatoes (from £2.75), ploughman's (£3.25), lasagne (£4.25), steak and kidney or fish pie (£4.50), vegetarian dishes like stir-fry vegetables or ratatouille filled pancakes (£4.25), usual children's menu (£1.50). In winter they serve traditional Jersey dishes such as bean crock, rabbit casserole and beef in red wine. Service is welcoming and helpful. The terrace has picnic-table sets under cocktail parasols, with swings and a climber in the paddock and this year they've built a children's adventure playground. The road past here leads down to one of the only north-coast beaches; the valley and nearby coast have pleasant walks. *(Recommended by John and Karen Day, Andrew Roberts, Steve and Carolyn Harvey, Alan and Sandra Holdsworth, Stephen and Julie Brown, Bob and Maggie Atherton)*

Ann Street ~ Manager Shaun Lynch ~ Real ale ~ Meals and snacks (12-2.30, 6-8.30, not Sun eve) ~ (01534) 482818 ~ Children welcome ~ Open 11-11

KINGS MILLS   (Guernsey)

Fleur du Jardin 🍴 🛏

Kings Mills Rd

A stone house set in two acres of beautiful gardens, nestling in the centre of this delightful conservation village, among some of the island's most delightful scenery. Picnic-tables are surrounded by flowering cherries, shrubs, colourful borders, bright hanging baskets, and unusual flower barrels cut lengthwise rather than across. Inside it's attractive too: sensitive refurbishments aimed at taking the steep-tiled inn's character and appearance closer to its origins have exposed the low-beamed ceilings and thick granite walls, and there's a nice cosy feel to the place. The friendly public bar has cushioned pews and other suitable seats and a good log fire. The lounge bar on the hotel side has individual country furnishings. Excellent varied bar food includes sandwiches (from £1.75, hot char-grilled steak £4.95), lasagne or chilli con carne (£3.95), steak and kidney pie (£4.25), salads (from £4.95), vegetarian dishes (from £3.95), plaice (£5.50), children's meals (from £1.95), and lots of daily specials that always include a fresh fish or game dish according to the season like swordfish steak grilled with green peppercorns and white wine (£5.95), braised half a guinea fowl with redcurrants and rosemary or grilled fillet of fresh mackeral on a tomato and basil sauce (£6.25), braised wood pigeon with port, rosemary and wild mushrooms or red bream fillet on a white wine and fresh herb sauce (£7.25). There is a slightly bigger selection in the lounge bar and a really grand evening menu in the restaurant, although it isn't too expensive (£12.50 for three courses). Well kept Guernsey Bitter on handpump, and maybe other guest beers, decent wines by the glass or bottle; friendly efficient service; unobtrusive piped music; darts. Part of the restaurant is no smoking, and there's a play area in the garden. *(Recommended by Dr J C Harrison, Mike and Pam Simpson, J T Charman, Stephen and Jean Curtis; more reports please)*

Free house ~ Licensee Keith Read ~ Real ale ~ Meals and snacks ~ Restaurant ~ (01481) 57996 ~ Children welcome ~ Open 11-11.45 ~ Bedrooms: £36B/£72B

ROZEL (Jersey)

Rozel Bay

On the edge of a sleepy little fishing village, this idyllic little pub is positioned just out of sight of the sea and the delightful harbour. There is a genuinely snug and cosy feel to the interior of the small dark-beamed back bar where the locals drink, and which has old prints and local pictures on its cream walls, dark plush wall seats and round stools around its low tables. The simple serving bar has a little shelf of toby jugs above it, and its clock claims that 'Guinness es bouan por te'; a pool room leads off. There's an open fire in the lounge. Straightforward good value lunchtime bar food includes sandwiches (from £1.50), fish and chips (£3.50), ploughman's (from £3.50), salads (from £3.50, prawn and crab £4), scampi (£3.50) and pies in winter (£2.25). Bass on handpump; darts, pool, fruit machine, video game, trivia, juke box and piped music, cheerful landlord. There are tables under cocktail parasols by the quiet lane past the pub, and more behind in the attractive gardens steeply terraced up the hillside. *(Recommended by Bob and Maggie Atherton, Stephen and Julie Brown, John and Karen Day; more reports please)*

Randalls ~ Tenant John Holmes ~ Real ale ~ Lunchtime meals and snacks (not Sun) ~ (01534) 863438 ~ Children welcome ~ Occasional live entertainment ~ Open 10-11

ST AUBIN (Jersey) OS 607486

Old Court House Inn 🛏

There are fine sea views from this charming 15th-c inn across the tranquil harbour to St Aubin's fort, and right across the bay to St Helier. The restaurant still shows signs of its time as a courtroom and the front part of the building used to be the home of a wealthy merchant, whose cellars stored privateers' plunder alongside more legitimate cargo. The upstairs cocktail bar is elegantly (and cleverly) crafted as the aft cabin of a galleon, with a transom window and bowed varnished decking planks on the ceiling. The atmospheric main basement bar has cushioned pale wooden seats built against its stripped granite walls, low black beams and joists in a white ceiling, heavy marble-topped tables on a turkey carpet and an open fire, a dimly lantern-lit inner room with an illuminated rather brackish-looking deep well, and beyond that a spacious cellar room open in summer. Bar food includes plenty of fish such as excellent moules marinières, grilled prawns, crab, lobster mayonnaise and fisherman's platter as well as soup, ploughman's, sausage and mash, lasagne or spare ribs and steaks; Flowers IPA, Fullers London Pride, Gales Pompey Royal, Marstons Pedigree and Theakstons Old Peculier on handpump or on gravity; darts, and bar billiards in winter. The bedrooms, individually decorated and furnished, are small but comfortable, and you might get one on the harbour front. *(Recommended by Stephen and Julie Brown, Beverley James, Steve and Carolyn Harvey, Bob and Maggie Atherton; more reports please)*

Free house ~ Licensee Jonty Sharp ~ Meals and snacks 12-2.30; 7.30-9.30 (not Sun evening) ~ Restaurant ~ Jersey (01534) 46433 ~ Children welcome ~ Open 11-11 ~ Bedrooms: £40B/£80B

ST BRELADE (Jersey) OS 603472

Old Portelet Inn

Portelet Bay

This 17th-c clifftop farmhouse has recently been extensively and cleverly refurbished. The heart of the old inn has been retained and the additions sensitively blended into the original features. The upstairs wooden floored loft bar commands magnificent views across Portelet, Jerseys' most southerly bay. The low ceilinged, beamed downstairs bar has a stone bar counter on bare oak boards and quarry tiles, a huge open fire, gas lamps, old pictures, etched glass panels from France and a nice mixture of old wooden chairs. The big, timber ceilinged restaurant with standing timbers is similar. Outside there are picnic-table sets on the partly covered flower-bower terrace by a wishing well, with more in a sizeable landscaped garden with lots of scented stocks and other flowers (the piped music may follow you out here). Right below, there's a sheltered cove, reached by a long flight of steps with glorious views on the way down. Decent well priced bar food (the same menu is available in the restaurant) includes sandwiches, home-made soup and dishes of the day such as rack of ribs (£2.90), spinach and riccotta cannelloni (£3.60), moules marinières (£4.50), salmon and plaice rolled with creamy dill and prawn sauce (£5.50), rolled pork fillet stuffed with grape and walnuts (£5.95), and specials like half a lobster with prawn salad (£7.50); children's menu (£2) and Sunday cream teas; friendly neatly dressed staff are quick and well drilled. Well kept cheap Boddingtons, Flowers Original, McEwans Export and Theakstons Best on handpump and very reasonably priced house wine; darts, pool, cribbage, dominoes, video games, fruit machine, piped music and plenty of board games in the loft bar; no-smoking area; baby changing room; children's playroom. *(Recommended by Steve and Carolyn Harvey, Mark Hydes; more reports please)*

Randalls ~ Manageress Tina Lister ~ Real ale ~ Meals and snacks ~ Restaurant ~ (01534) 41899 ~ Children welcome, over ten only in Loft bar ~ sing-along accordionist five nights a week in summer ~ Open 10-11

ST HELIER (Jersey) Map 1

Admiral £
St James St

Inside this big atmospheric and carefully renovated dark wood panelled candlelit pub you'll find attractive and solid country furniture, heavy beams (some of which are inscribed with famous quotations), interesting decorations such as old telephones, a clocking-in machine, copper milk churn, enamel advertising signs (many more in the small back courtyard which also has lots of old pub signs), and nice touches such as the daily papers to read and an old penny 'What the Butler Saw' machine. Extremely good value food includes fresh seafool pasta bake, chicken masala, spicy cajun jambala, stir-fries, chicken in oyster sauce and egg noodles or tagliatelle in a blue cheese sauce (£2.95), various steak pies, spiced ribs, honey coated gammon steak or Cumberland sausages (£3), braised rump steak in red wine or broccoli and camembert roulade, (£3.20) and cod fillet in ale batter or supreme of chicken au poivre (£3.50); three course Sunday lunch (£5.95). Well kept Boddingtons, Fullers London Pride, Morlands Old Speckled Hen and Theakstons XB; efficient, friendly staff; cribbage and chess; plastic tables outside on flagged terrace. *(Recommended by Steve and Carolyn Harvey, Stephen and Julie Brown; more reports please)*

Free house ~ Licensee: Les de la Haye (Manager: Richard Evans) ~ Real ale ~ Meals and snacks (12-2, 6-8) ~ (01534) 30095 ~ Children allowed Sundays only until 6pm ~ Open 11-11

ST LAWRENCE (Jersey)

British Union
Main Rd

There are new licensees at this bustling lively roadside pub which is in the centre of the island, opposite St Lawrence church. The busy friendly lounge bar is decorated in a cottagey style with pretty wallpaper, beams and panelling, *Punch*-style cartoons, and royal prints, and a large ceiling fan; leading off here is an interconnecting snug, largely set out for diners, with a woodburning stove, and toy cupboard full of well loved toys, books and games. Locals tend to favour the quieter little bar with cigarette card collections, gun cartridges, and brass beer spigots on the walls, and darts. Children are welcome in the plainly furnished games room with pool, trivia and video games, cribbage and dominoes and juke box and there is even a child-sized cat flap leading out to a small enclosed terrace with a playhouse. Good bar food includes soup (£1.30), vegetarian dishes (from £3.10), steak sandwich (£3), home-cooked ham and egg (£4), salads or lasagne (£4.80), swordfish steak (£6.30) or chicken Wellington (£6.50), half-a-dozen king prawns (£6.80), steaks (from £5.80), daily specials such as fresh haddock and beer pie (£4.20) and steak in ale pie (£5), and children's meals (£1.50). Well kept Sunbeam (previously called Guernsey Bitter) on handpump; efficient, thoughtful service; piped music. *(Recommended by Steve and Carolyn Harvey; more reports please)*

Ann Street ~ Manager: Mary Boschat ~ Real ale ~ Meals and snacks (12-2, 6-8.30, not Sun eve in winter) ~ (01534) 861070 ~ Children in family room or lounge ~ Live entertainment Sun eve ~ Open 10am-11pm; closed 25 Dec eve, Sun hours on Good Fri)

ST PETER (Jersey) OS 595519 Map 1

Star & Tipsy Toad ◀

In village centre

There are tours and tastings every day at this pub's own brewery – the only one on the island – and if it's closed you can still see the workings through a window in the pub. As well as their own brews, Horny Toad and JB Bitter, they have several mainland guest beers like Bass, Fullers, Morlands Old Speckled Hen, Theakstons Old Peculier and Worthington, all on handpump. You'll find the licensees and their staff are very welcoming. It's a popular, place sensitively refurbished, with cottagey decor, panelling, exposed stone walls, tiled and wood-panelled floors, a good family conservatory, and children's playground and terraces. Good bar food includes home-made soup (£1.40), filled rolls (from £1.85), home-made pâté with Cumberland sauce (£2.80), ploughman's (£3.50), vegetarian cutlet (£4), burgers (from £3.95), home-cooked ham and egg (£4), chicken in port wine sauce or steak and ale pie (£4.50), fresh cod in their own beer batter (£4.90), salads (£4.80), seafood pancakes (£5), melon with prawns (£5.50), grilled tuna steak (£5.75), steaks (from £5.90), and children's dishes (£1.50). A small games room has darts, pool, bar billiards, cribbage, dominoes, video game, football table and piped music; wheelchair access and disabled lavatories. *(Recommended by Andrew Roberts, Andy and Jill Kassube, Steve and Carolyn Harvey)*

Own brew ~ Licensees Steve and Sarah Skinner ~ Real ale ~ Meals and snacks (12-2.15, 6-8.15; not Sun) ~ (01534) 485556 ~ Children welcome ~ Karaoke Weds night; Blues, jazz and folk Fri, Sat and Sun ~ Open 10am-11.30pm

Lucky Dip

Besides the fully inspected pubs, you might like to try these Lucky Dips recommended to us and described by readers (if you do, please send us reports):

ALDERNY

☆ **St Anne** [Victoria St], *Georgian House*: Relaxing and welcoming civilised bar with Ringwood Best and Old Thumper, good interesting food in bar and restaurant, charming staff; nice back garden with barbecue and summer food servery; comfortable bedrooms *(Steve and Carolyn Harvey)*
St Anne, *Belle Vue*: Dimly lit ship's-theme bar with especially good pizzas and other standard dishes; bedrooms *(Steve and Carolyn Harvey)*; *Bounty Bar*: Cosy pub attached to hotel, good value food, superb views of the harbour only a few minutes'

walk away *(G Hutton)*; *Moorings*: Lovely spot overlooking beach with terrace bar, seats outside and Victorian-style gazebo; wide choice of international bottled beers, a real ale labelled for the inn, Coors American on draught; straightforward bar food inc some Mexican dishes, separate restaurant; bedrooms *(Steve and Carolyn Harvey)*; [Le Huret], *Rose & Crown*: Straightfoward food but also interesting South African potjiekos – food cooked very slowly in its own juices with some interesting ingredients such as sweet potatoes, bananas, waterblommetjies (water lilies – a plant grown in the Cape);

Wadworths 6X, extensive choice of wines, also specialist off-licence with over 500 wines; nice back garden *(Steve and Carolyn Harvey)*

GUERNSEY

Castel [Rue du Friquet], *Le Friquet:* Good value carvery with help-yourself veg, well kept Randalls; bedrooms *(Julian Charman)*

Grande Havre [Rte de Picquerel; (part of Houmet du Nord Hotel)], *Houmet:* Recently reopened with good value straightforward bar meals, friendly atmosphere, well kept Guernsey real ale, big picture windows overlooking rock and sand beach; bedrooms *(Mike and Pam Simpson, BB)*

☆ **Rocquaine Bay**, *Rocquaine Bistro:* Good if not cheap fresh well presented fish and seafood (they have their own outdoor live tanks) in cool, quietly stylish and civilised bar/bistro with decent wines, welcoming service; superb views of islet-dotted sea from terrace tables with cocktail parasols; part no smoking, children welcome, cl winter *(Mrs E Malcolm, P J Caunt, LYM)*

☆ **St Martin** [Jerbourg, nr SE tip of island], *Auberge Divette:* Glorious view of coast and Herm from fairy-lit garden high above sea; unpretentious picture-window saloon and lounge both with button-back banquettes, sensibly placed darts and bar billiards in back public bar; has had good value food inc children's, well kept Guernsey Bitter and Mild and very friendly staff, but tenant responsible for its previous main entry has now moved to the Prince of Wales in Manor Pl, St Peter Port *(LYM; news please)*

St Martin, *La Villette:* Generous bar meals, short wine list with some nice reasonably priced wines *(J S Rutter)*

Martin [La Fosse], *Les Douvres:* Civilised if busy Tudor-style bar with generous well prepared food, well kept Theakstons; lots of beautiful walks nearby; bedrooms *(J S Rutter);* [by church], *Royal:* Boddingtons, Marstons Pedigree and Theakstons Old Peculier and generous helpings of well priced popular food inc Sun lunch and good choice of children's meals in straightforward public bar and comfortable recently extended lounge with big eating area; small electronic games room, upstairs restaurant; outside play area *(Steve and Carolyn Harvey); Saints Bay:* An oasis for refreshment on cliff walk, good sandwiches and good choice of other reasonably priced food *(P J Caunt)*

☆ **St Peter Port** [North Esplanade], *Ship & Crown:* Cosy atmosphere with good harbour view from bay windows in busy old pub sharing building with Royal Guernsey Yacht Club; interesting ship photographs, fair-priced bar food from sandwiches to steak, well kept Guernsey Bitter, welcoming service *(Chris Cook, Frank Gadbois, Michael L Richardson, LYM)*

St Peter Port [South Esplanade], *Yacht:* Pleasant, comfortable and quiet, with good bar food and well kept Randalls *(Barrie and Pat Noonan, Chris Cook)*

St Prave Du Bois [rue de Quanteraine], *Café du Moulin:* Good light lunches, charming surroundings, competent service *(J S Rutter)*

☆ **St Sampsons** [Grand Fort Rd, Les Capelles], *Pony:* Good cheap straightforward food in friendly modern local, lounge done up in shades of brown, with russet plush armchairs and booth seats; well kept Guernsey Mild and Bitter; public bar with games and juke box; tables out by front car park *(P J Caunt, Mike and Pam Simpson, A Craig, LYM)*

HERM

Ship: Excellent local seafood, attractive wines and friendly service; charming surroundings on idyllic island, distant sea view if you choose your viewpoint carefully; bedrooms *(J S Rutter, A Craig)*

JERSEY

☆ **Gorey** [The Harbour; OS map ref 714503], *Dolphin:* Busy local across rd from quayside and harbour, basic fishing theme (nets etc), unpretentious pubby atmosphere; particularly good fish and seafood inc scallops, big prawns, grilled sardines, seafood platter; restaurant, children in eating area; piped music, Spanish or Portuguese waiters; comfortable bedrooms *(Alan and Sandra Holdsworth, Michael L Richardson, LYM)*

☆ **Grouville** [La Rocque; coast rd St Helier—Gorey], *Seymour:* Comfortable and popular local in attractive spot, clean and well looked-after, friendly staff, wide choice of simple pub food, well kept Guernsey Bitter and Mild; views over road to sea from tables outside *(Andrew Roberts)*

Jersey Airport [take lift up from Departures building], *Aviator Bar:* Friendly helpful service, surprisingly good food, very wide choice of spirits, good view of the runway *(John Evans, BB)*

☆ **St Brelade** [Ouaisne Bay; OS map ref 595476], *Smugglers:* Recently extended thick-walled black-beamed pub, friendly and comfortable, with open fires, cosy black built-in settles, well kept Bass and Marstons Pedigree, good value quickly served bar food inc good seafood and children's dishes, sensibly placed darts; just above lovely Ouaisne beach, pretty public gardens further along; children allowed *(Bob and Maggie Atherton, Steve and Carolyn Harvey, LYM)*

St Brelade [le Boulevard, OS map ref 581488], *La Marquanderie:* Big granite pub, comfortable beamed old-fashioned lounge, good range of bar food, restaurant with some spit-roasting; roomy terrace outside with lots of picnic-table sets among roses and cistuses *(Steve and Carolyn Harvey, BB)*

☆ **St Helier** [Mulcaster St], *Lamplighter*: Good gas-lit atmosphere in atmospheric pub with heavy timbers, rough panelling and scrubbed pine tables; good value simple food, well kept Bass, open 14 hours a day *(Steve and Carolyn Harvey, Penny and Peter Keevil, LYM)*

☆ **St Helier** [Halkett Pl], *Cock & Bottle*: Period-feel pub, smart and busy, with lots of woodwork; bars upstairs (with zinc-topped counter) and downstairs, good range of beers inc Old Jersey Ale, good value bar food, fast friendly service; well placed on distinguished old leafy square *(Andrew Roberts)*

St Helier, *Chambers:* Opened 1993 by landlord of nearby Admiral (see main entries); similar but bigger, with a law theme *(Anon)*

☆ **St John** [Le Grand Mourier, OS map ref 620565], *Les Fontaines*: The back bar of this extended pub has stood out as the island's most genuine traditional tavern, fascinating atmosphere in ancient surroundings; the long-serving tenant retired at the end of 1994 and the pub is to revert to Randalls brewery management *(LYM)*

☆ **St Mary**, St Marys: Inviting and well appointed country inn with unusual English-country-pub feel, comfortable beamed granite-walled bar with big open fire, old photographs, decent lunches (not Sun), sandwiches and evening meals Fri/Sat, friendly atmosphere, Bass on handpump,

even bar billiards; good children's room; bedrooms *(Andrew Roberts)*

☆ **Trinity** [Bouley Bay; OS map ref 669546], *Waters Edge*: Spacious and comfortable modern hotel with well kept waterside grounds and picture-window sea views; it includes 17th-c core with relaxed stripped-stone Black Dog bar (no view from here), with lots of panelling and ornate carvings, old-world furnishings and decor, Mary Ann and Whitbreads beers, neat staff, lunchtime bar food (not Sun) inc fresh local seafood and more standard items; decent wines, open all day; comfortable bedrooms *(Steve and Carolyn Harvey, LYM)*

Trinity [OS map ref 663539], *Trinity Arms*: True Jersey country local, spacious and comfortable turkey-carpeted lounge and rambling quarry-tiled public bar with pool, video game and juke box; Guernsey and Old Jersey real ale, cheap simple food, cheery atmosphere, piped music; tables outside *(Andrew Roberts, BB)*

SARK

☆ **Stocks:** Welcoming family-run hotel with stormy sailing-ship prints in comfortably snug stone-and-beams bar, prompt friendly service, good conservatory bistro with wide choice of decent food here, in sheltered courtyard and on poolside terrace, good cream teas, good value good fresh set evening meals in candlelit partly no-smoking restaurant; comfortable bedrooms in elegant old extended country house *(Melinda Pople, LYM)*

If a service charge is mentioned prominently on a menu or accommodation terms, you must pay it if service was satisfactory. If service is really bad you are legally entitled to refuse to pay some or all of the service charge as compensation for not getting the service you might reasonably have expected.

Overseas Lucky Dip

We're always interested to hear of good bars and pubs overseas – or, more desirably, their genuine local equivalents. These are ones recently recommended by readers. We start with ones in the British Isles, then work alphabetically through other countries. We mark with a star the few pubs that we can be confident would qualify as main entries.

IRELAND

A general point here is that in contrast to Great Britain it's bad form to offer a drink to the barman or other customers.

Agivey, *Brown Trout*: Well worth knowing for good food, drink and atmosphere – even has its own golf course *(I MacG Binnie)*

☆ **Belfast** [Gt Victoria St; opp Europa Hotel], *Crown*: 19th-c gin palace with pillared entrance, opulent tiles outside and in, elaborately coloured windows, almost church-like ceiling, handsome mirrors, individual snug booths with little doors and bells for waiter service, gas lighting, mosaic floor – wonderful atmosphere; good lunchtime meals inc oysters, Hilden real ale, open all day; National Trust; would certainly be a main entry if we had them in Ireland *(Greg Parston, I MacG Binnie)*

Castleroe, *Salmon Leap*: Of real historic interest *(I MacG Binnie)*

Crawfordsburn [Main St], *Old*: Wonderful atmosphere, good well priced food, Bass; bedrooms *(W G Hall, Jr)*

Dervock, *North Irish Horse*: Pub of character, inexpensive menu, riverside garden, collection of militaria *(I MacG Binnie)*

Dublin [21 Fleet St], *Palace*: Good beer in character pub *(Graham Bush)*

Kilcolgan, *Morans o' the Weir*: In all the guidebooks, but really worth visiting – pleasant relaxed atmosphere, very good food (even if you don't like oysters) and Guinness, friendly service *(Dr M Owton)*

Midleton [Main St], *Mary O's*: Mary O'Farrell (big bouncy beautiful and a psychotherapist as well) has run this little pub since her father the local undertaker bought it for her 12 years ago as a birthday present; claims to be oldest pub in town and is certainly the smallest, jolliest and most welcoming; separate snug for women that's the size of an airing cupboard *(Graham Tayar)*

Schull [Upper Main St], *Bunrattys*: Attractive, comfortable pub with nice garden, good welcome, good choice of drinks and a fresh crab salad to kill for; evening restaurant menu too, dogs welcome; gets crowded in summer *(Kim Ryan Skuse)*

ISLE OF MAN

Glenmaye [S of Peel – OS Sheet 95 map ref 236798; SC2480], *Waterfall*: At top of lovely tree-lined glen down to beach, 10 mins away, past a waterfall; attractive warm brick interior, corn ears and dried flowers, open fire, Bass and Okells beers inc Mild, wide range of good interesting food inc local seafood and vegetarian dishes, pleasant staff; open all day, no food Sun evening; minibus for parties of six or more *(Dr J P Cullen, Stephen R Holman, Gill Hardinge)*

Laxey [Tram Station – OS Sheet 95 map ref 433846; SC4484], *Mines Tavern*: Beamed pub in lovely woodland clearing where Manx electric railway and Snaefell mountain railway connect, just below the Lady Isabella wheel (largest working water wheel in the world); splendid old tram photographs, advertisements and other memorabilia in one bar with counter salvaged from former tram, other bar dedicated to mining; fresh sandwiches and reasonably priced home cooking, well kept Bass Mild, Okells and Tetleys ales; piped music, darts, fruit machines (public bar not lounge); can sit outside and watch Victorian trams *(Dave Craine, W F C Phillips, A Craig, Barry and Lindsey Blackburn, Bill Sykes)*

Peel [Station Pl; NX2484], *Creek*: Okells ales andreasonably priced food such as local kippers and queen scallops in low-ceilinged and atmospheric pub overlooking castle and harbour; quick friendly service *(Dave Craine, Dr J P Cullen)*

Sulby Glen [A14 below Snaefell; NX3793], *Tholt-e Will*: Swiss chalet in forest below Snaefell, good choice of local and other beers inc Smithwicks, good bar food inc good generous Manx cheese with the ploughman's; very popular with the locals *(Stephen R Holman)*

LUNDY

Marisco: One of England's most isolated pubs and very much at the centre of island life; brews its own beer, has Lundy spring water on tap, and food based around island produce; decorated with shipwreck relics; souvenir shop, and doubles as general store for the island's few residents *(B M Eldridge)*

AUSTRALIA

★ **Adelaide** [Pultney St; corner with Carrington St], *Earl of Aberdeen*: Well kept Coopers beers, some brewed here, in mahogany, brass and mirrors Victorian pub, very young and lively, with CD juke box or live band, friendly staff, unusual rolling ceiling fans *(Tony and Lynne Stark)*

Adelaide [King William St], *Bull & Bear*: Brews own beers inc Highland Ale (said to include Drambuie), and has local Old Lion keg and bottled beers; share prices on board – next to Stock Exchange *(Tina Hammond)*

Atherton Tablelands [nr Yungaburra; N Queensland], *Peeramon*: Typical tin-roof and wooden-verandah 'hotel', built 1908 and said to be oldest in area; cold Powers beer, quiet and friendly by day, lively at night with great atmosphere and food *(Martyn and Mary Mullins)*

Melbourne [Collins St; Victoria], *Dickens on Collins*: Below street level, entered from shopping arcade; lots of English pub literature, and what's reputed to be the only 5-10-15-20 dart board in Australia; bar food, English keg beers such as Bass, Stones, Tetleys *(Tina Hammond)*; [Collins St; Victoria], *Sherlock Holmes*: Bar snacks, full meals in back dining room, English keg beers such as Stones and Tetleys; below street level *(Tina Hammond)*; [St Kilda Rd; Victoria], *Sherlock Holmes.*: Modern pub set back from rd, a newer version of the one on Collins St; Holmes memorabilia, English keg beers such as Tetleys, bar snacks *(Tina Hammond)*

★ **Sydney** [Argyle Pl, The Rocks], *Lord Nelson*: Solid stone, with beams and bare floorboards – the city's oldest pub; brews its own Nelsons Revenge, Three Sheets, Trafalgar and Victory, and has tastings first Weds of month (not Jan); good choice of other Australian beers, nautical theme, upmarket atmosphere, pine furniture; open all day, gets touristy *(Tina Hammond, Wayne Wheeler)*

Sydney [Lower Fort St, The Rocks], *Hero of Waterloo*: Another stone building, also old – touristy, but good atmosphere (even in the haunted basement function room, scene of several murders in the old days); ten beers on tap inc Bass and Guinness, English singalong Sun evening, strolling cat *(Wayne Wheeler, Tina Hammond)*; [Paddington], *Royal*: Classic Victorian pub with thoroughly Australian atmosphere in great bare-boards bar – boisterous but never intimidating; usual beers from Castlemaine to Coopers with rotating choice of lesser-known ones, good restaurant upstairs *(Tony and Lynne Stark)*; [Watsons Bay], *Watsons Bay*: Large garden overlooking Sydney Harbour, seafood and barbecues *(Sally Edsall)*

BARBADOS

St Lawrence Gap [nr Bridgetown], *Ship*: Fairly modern in style, claims to be an English pub but where in England would you find such laid-back service with a gleaming smile, regular reggae evenings, good rum punch – and that courtyard with its palm trees and tropical plants; local lager-style Banks beer, good reasonably priced carvery *(Jenny and Brian Seller)*

★ **St Philip**, *Lantern*: Formerly owned by Sam Lords Castle and just outside its gates, now belongs to friendly British couple; nice relaxed informal atmosphere in small bar on the right, and further drinking area past the restaurant; good local Banks beer, great martinis and rum-based cocktails, modest but good snack menu such as flying-fish sandwiches, very good English or continental breakfasts, evening meals with fresh-caught king fish, grilled chub and so forth, lots of lovely puddings inc home-made apple pie; great cocktails; good service, wide windows, bright colours and fans make it seem cool; small drinking area outside *(Fiona Sellors)*

BELGIUM

Ghent [17 bis St Jacobs], *Trollekelder*: Multi-level pub with some 140 beers; trolls everywhere *(Dr and Mrs A K Clarke)*; [6 Graslei], *Witte Leeuw*: Excellent old bar overlooking castle, excellent range of some 120 Belgian beers *(Dr and Mrs A K Clarke)*

Leuven [Tiensestraat], *Erasmus*: Sizeable bar, not too studenty, with wide range of wonderful Belgian beers and good choice of food; similar sister bar, the Domus, in the same street, and about 30 other more or less studenty bars in the Oude Markt, all friendly, cheap, with a splendid range of good beers *(Michael and Derek Slade)*

BELIZE

Caye Caulker, *Reef Bar*: Sand-floored thatched-roof bar on offshore coral island, portrait of the Queen, police notice on consequences of throwing glass, Caribbean view, floor-to-ceiling loudspeakers starting with Bob Marley and blasting into heavy dub; Belikan beer, but rum and Coke (and 'herbal' cigarettes) more in keeping; great atmosphere until the larger locals get somewhat volatile towards midnight *(Tony and Lynne Stark)*

Western Highway [Mile Marker 33], *JBs Watering Hole*: A welcoming break from the heat and monotonous highway; noisier than Caesars Palace, with a more boisterous crowd; good barbecue chicken and fruit juices; usual range of Belikan beer; local ruins *(Patrick and Mary McDermott)*

BERMUDA

Hamilton [Hamilton Princess Hotel], *Colony*: English-style panelled hotel theme bar useful for decent snacks and food inc pasties and very good steaks; evening pianist; not cheap, service charge added to food orders and drinkers expected to tip barman *(John Evans)*

Somerset [Mangrove Bay Rd], *Loyalty*: Tables out overlooking bay, huge interesting menu inc amazing Sunday brunch, friendly local staff *(June and Malcolm Farmer)*; [Mangrove Bay Rd], *Somerset Country Squire*: Very English, dark, with old prints, long bar, piano; wide choice of food inc sandwiches, also fish chowder and wahoo; reasonable prices, seats outside *(June and Malcolm Farmer)*

St Georges [Kings Sq], *Murphys Bar*: Guinness and Murphys, Watneys and Heineken; more bar than pub *(June and Malcolm Farmer)*; [Kings Sq], *White Horse*: Good atmosphere in very large popular pub right on the waterfront in beautiful old square, Watneys and other beers, many local seafood specialities, not too expensive; tables on big waterside verandah, which can get hot *(June and Malcolm Farmer, John Evans)*

CANADA

Toronto [14 College St, nr Yonge St; Ontario], *Hop & Grape*: Pleasant and genuine, away from the city bustle, with Irish beers and maybe keg Fullers ESB as well as their own Bitter, good food, Rugby football connections; upstairs wine bar with good choice of wines, panelled dining rooms *(Terry Buckland)*

Waterloo [33 Erb St W; Ontario], Duke of *Wellington*: Warm and friendly, with traditional pub decor, Iron Duke memorabilia, huge worldwide beer-bottle collection, well kept domestic and imported real ales inc Wellington County, separate glassed-in dining room, outstanding staff; live entertainment Thurs-Sat evenings – can get very busy *(George Greer)*

CANARY ISLANDS

Lanzarote [Ave de las Playas; Puerto del Carmen], *Sports Bar Up & Down*: Seaside bar with 5,000 sporting autographs from 50 sports, open all year 9.30 am to 3.30 am; great atmosphere, good cocktails as well as beers and cider, great staff, good home-cooked food, great value *(Rosie Lupton)*

FIJI

☆ **Levuka**, *Ovalau Club*: Old colonial haunt now local-run, visitors very welcome; Victorian snooker table, Fiji Bitter (rather a good lager) brewed under licence from VB in Melbourne *(Tony and Lynne Stark)*

FINLAND

Tampere [Salhojankatu], *Salhojanadus*: The locals claim this is the most English pub in Europe – not so, but well worth visiting; bench seating in alcoves around central bar, pictures and flock wallpaper, darts, back pool room, sandwiches, good wide range of beers inc many interesting bottled ones as well as keg Fullers London Pride and Guinness; doorman expects a small coin for minding your coat *(Stephen George Brown, Veikko Silmu)*

FRANCE

Arras [off Grandè Place], *Taverne d'Ecu*: English-style but not synthetic, superb range of French, Belgian and English beers on draught and in bottles, good food, excellent service, pleasant atmosphere *(D Stokes)*

GERMANY

☆ **Trier** [Fleischstrasse 12], *St Gangolfstubchen*: Very well appointed part pavement café, part Viennese Konditorei, part Anglo-French brasserie, part good German Hofbrauhaus – owned by Bitburger brewery, excellent Pils in all sizes from 20 ml to one-litre stone tankards; very good moderately priced food sometimes inc Eiffel area specialities; named after nearby church *(John C Baker)*

ITALY

Rimini [via Regina Elena, just off Tripoli Sq], *Rose & Crown*: Wonderful 'English pub' on seafront, opened 1964, much appreciated by members of the Royal Philharmonic Orchestra whose Guinness expert reckons the Guinness – imported from Dublin – is the best outside Ireland or Mulligans (next to Carnegie Hall, New York); very good bacon and eggs, steak pies, lasagne etc served 11 am right through to 4 am, very accommodating Italian owners and staff, wide choice of beers, nightly competitions from bingo to beer-drinking *(Steve Merson)*

MADEIRA

Portela [nr Machico], *Portela a' Vista*: A restaurant, but with a really pubby feel; three attractive dark pine-panelled front rooms with good view down to coast, centre one with bar, two cosy side ones for eating, with quarry-tiled floors, green shutters and log fire on left; simple dark pine furniture, good choice of drinks inc local Coral lager brewed by English firm, three rustic soups, three main courses – delicious charcoal-grilled steak kebab *(Susan and John Douglas)*

NETHERLANDS

☆ **Amsterdam** [Spuistraat 18], *Café Hoppe*: Probably Amsterdam's most famous 'brown café', its huge old-fashioned bar busy from early morning till late at night, with staggering range of gins and whiskies as well as fine beers from Delft handpumps; one part traditional, with sand on floor, heavy leather portière and standing only, the other with tables and chairs; in good weather most customers are out on pavement *(G E De Vries, Debby Hawkins)*

NEW ZEALAND

Christchurch [by Arts Centre market], *Dux de Lux*: Busy modern pub with wide choice of vegetarian food and fish, own-brewed beers as well as international brands *(Neil O'Callaghan)*

OMAN

Muscat [Al Bustan Palace Hotel], *Al Bustan Bar*: Friendly, welcoming and relaxing bar with imported beers, free nibbles and local fish caught by staff's families, in sumptuous and exotic surroundings of national guest palace, run as hotel when not needed for visiting heads of state; breathtakingly opulent central domed area with national treasures around main fountain, several good restaurants; bedrooms sumptuously comfortable *(Bill Bailey)*

RUSSIA

Moscow [9 Znamenka], *Rosie O'Gradys*: Lively Irish-style pub, Irish as well as Russian staff, Guinness and continental beers, food inc stews and dish of the day, good atmosphere; open all day, very busy evenings *(I and F Lacey)*

SINGAPORE

Singapore [Beach Rd], *Raffles*: Magnificent colonial monument, lavishly restored: Long Bar well worth a visit for its atmosphere, Singapore slings and underfoot peanut shells, sedate Billiards Bar, Tiffin Room with elaborate changing buffets, more expensive meals in the Writer's Room, and five other food outlets each with its own style of cooking; cultural and Raffles displays; prices can be astronomical if you stay *(Debby Hawkins)*

SOUTH AFRICA

Babanango [Natal], *Babanango Hotel*: Perhaps the closest thing to a British pub in Northern Natal; genial Anglo-German landlord, tiny bar crammed with interest inc militaria (the display of women's underwear and somewhat smutty cards may not please everyone), good beer, mainly lagers, and wide range of other drinks, very good food at low cost, lovely Great Dane, friendly locals – a welcome drinking hole in a remote area *(Ted Brown, ACM)*

Cape Town [Adelaide St], *Red Lion*: Just off Parliament St, with very British feel, Castle and Lion beers, excellent bar food inc Cape steaks and succulent salads; friendly barman, spittoons *(Alan Gough)*

SWEDEN

Harstena Island [Blakust Archipelago], *Fisk Rokeri*: Smoked fish business expanded into pub by retired fisherman owner, shop and café by day, legendary boatmen's drinking spot by night, popular with yachtsmen, fishermen and sea traders from all over the Baltic, beers maybe from Denmark, Finland, Germany and Poland, Russian vodkas, very warm welcome, Swedish folk music and dance; bedrooms basic, traditional sauna, moorings *(Bill Bailey)*

USA

Alexandria [121 S Union St; on Potomac River just S of Washington DC; Virginia], *Union Street*: Airy and high-ceilinged, with lots of character, dark wood and wide range of interesting beers inc several brewed specially for it, others from US microbreweries, maybe some from UK; reasonably priced sandwiches, pastas and salads *(Dawn and Tom Farmer, Wayne Brindle)*

Buckingham [Pennsylvania], *Wookey Hole*: Established a few years ago below a high-class steakhouse – name comes from owners'

connections with that area of England; authentic English-pub style with telephone kiosk outside the door, beers inc Bass, Batemans, Courage, Double Diamond, Fullers, Newcastle Brown, Watneys, Whitbreads and Youngs, with Harp and Guinness (you can have your own tankard), home-cooked pasties, steak and kidney pie etc *(Jim Love)*

Cincinnati [6104 Montgomery Rd; Ohio], *Gas Light Café*: Traditional American bar, friendly staff, good value food (esp home-made chilli), local and imported beers, good collection of wines and mixers; pinball, darts *(Helen and Bill Frost, Marie and Brian Leadbeater)*

Cloverdale [Redwood Highway (Highway 101, about 80 miles N of San Francisco); California], *Red Tail Brewery*: Good atmosphere in 'brewing boutique' with particularly good beer, also food *(Stephen R Holman)*

Georgetown [1264 Wisconsin Ave NW; Washington DC], *Billy Martins*: Subdued lighting, opened 1933, draught beers inc Sam Adams; friendly, with attractive decor – mirrors, stuffed animals etc *(Dr and Mrs A K Clarke)*; [3150 M St NW], *Nathans*: Vast range of spirits, draught beers too; genuine old feel *(Dr and Mrs A K Clarke)*

Gettysburg [Pennsylvania], *Dobbin House*: In what used to be the root/storage cellar of the oldest house in town, with a running spring in the corner; named for the Revd Dobbin, original owner and a co-founder of the town – wounded cared for here in both the Revolutionary and Civil Wars; dates from 1700s, with well preserved colonial atmosphere (servers in period garb), fine upstairs dining room; American food, beer from nearby Red Feather microbrewery *(Jim Love)*

Great Falls [Georgetown Pike/Walker; Virginia], *Old Brogue*: Irish pub not far from Dulles Int Airport, Irish and other imported beers, fine spirits, good choice of pub food at reasonable prices, harpist sometimes at Sun lunch *(Lisa Witherspoon, Les Downes)*

Larkspur [Larkspur Landing; mall next to Larkspur/San Francisco ferry terminal; California], *Marin Brewery*: Welcoming microbrewery which claims more awards than any other in US for its good, interesting and even eccentric beers; good restaurant with standbys like ploughman's, bangers and mash, outstanding burgers, two dartboards, young friendly staff; interesting 50-min ferry trip past Alcatraz and San Quentin, footbridge from ferry – the mall is lovely *(Jones o' the Outback, Stephen R Holman)*

Moab [Utah], *McStiffs*: Brews its own beers from stout to lager, inc Amber Ale (similar to Bitter): sampler tray with brewing details; great pizzas, good atmosphere, enthusiastic staff; in archetypal clean and spacious Mid-West town in marvellous scenery nr Arches NP *(Tony and Lynne Stark)*

☆ **New York** [93 South St Seaport], *North Star*: Good imitation English pub with dark green lincrusta ceiling, wall mirrors, oak furniture, handpumps for the Bass and Fullers ESB and London Pride, good choice of English bottled beers and Scotch malt whiskies, fish and chips, steak and kidney pie, good bangers and mash; obliging and friendly staff; attractive location in group of restored warehouses and quays with a couple of full-rigged ships as background *(Dawn and Tom Farmer)*

New York [914 3rd Ave/55th St], *Old Stand*: Lively Irish bar, smart but very good value, with super food to go with the Guinness; very friendly *(Wayne Brindle)*

Philadelphia [2nd St/Pine St; Pennsylvania], *Dickens Inn*: Upstairs in historic old colonial terrace house, wooden floors, beams, Youngs, Watneys and other English beers, food such as steak and kidney pie, darts, cheerful customers – mainly young professionals; FA Cup Final live on TV with traditional English breakfast; overlooks courtyard where one of colonies' first open-air markets held *(Jim Love)*

Plymouth [Summer St; Mass], *John Carver*: Warm and genuine, like a 'Cheers' bar, excellent bar nibbles, Samuel Adams and other beers, restaurant with good clam chowder and puddings with mountains of cream *(Penny and Martin Fletcher)*

Prestcott [Gurley St; Arizona], *Hassayampa Inn*: Bar on left reminiscent of quietly smart English coaching inn – expect to be seated and served; gleaming floor tiles, painted ceilings, period furniture – all very 1926; enormous hall with fire if temperature much below 80°F *(Ian Phillips)*

Reston [2331 Hunters Woods Plaza; Virginia], *Fritzbes*: Typical American bar/restaurant, American, Cajun, Italian and Mexican food, seafood, wide range of drinks inc Adnams; popular after-work happy-hour spot, not far from Dulles Int Airport *(Les Downes)*

Sacramento [1001 R St; California], *Fox & Goose*: Good for a replica British pub – and they import Fullers London Pride instead of Double Diamond and Red Barrel *(Tony and Lynne Stark)*

San Diego [beach rd N towards La Jolla; California], *Pacific Beach Brewhouse*: Brews its own Amber Ale; buzzing with great juke box and Californian beach life in all its glory *(Tony and Lynne Stark)*

☆ **San Francisco** [155 Columbus Ave; California], *San Francisco Brewing Co*: Unusual for brewing lagers as well as top-fermented beers such as great Barbary Coast ESB; good food such as hot Louisiana sausage and pepper sandwich, turn-of-the-century stained glass, mahogany and brass; hums with activity lunchtime and early evening; facing one of the few old wooden buildings left here (dwarfed by Trans-Am Pyramid), handy for Chinatown *(Tony and Lynne Stark)*

San Francisco [11th St, nr Folsom; California], *21 Tank Brewery*: Very good beers in brew-pub with limited but funky

menu of snacks, soups and so forth, haunt of touring motorcyclists and other offbeat types *(Stephen R Holman)*

Santa Cruz [California], *Front Street Pub*: Open and airy, with lots of space, good food inc bangers and mash, beers brewed on premises inc superb Lighthouse Amber; young staff working hard, proud of their pub and enjoying themselves *(Tony and Lynne Stark)*

South Lake Tahoe [3542 Lake Tahoe Bvd; California], *Brewery at Lake Tahoe*: No smoking bar surrounded by microbrewery producing its own Pale Ale, Amber, Porter, Bad Ass and specials *(Graham Bush)*

Stowe [Stoweflake Inn, Mountain Rd; Vermont], *Charlie Bs*: Large split-level 1970s lounge bar with log fire, wide choice of well prepared food, excellent wine list inc good value house wine, stimulating conversation, live music weekends; comfortable bedrooms in the inn *(Penny and Martin Fletcher)*; [Mountain Rd], *Mr Pickwicks Polo Club*: Beamed home counties English village pub created by English couple here for last decade, Watneys and Guinness as well as Samuel Adams and 100 world-wide bottled beers, darts, American food as well as steak and kidney pie, bangers and mash etc; tables out on covered deck, good staff *(Penny and Martin Fletcher)*

Tempe [Arizona], *Bandersnatch*: Brews three real ales inc a stout, with small choice of good value food; bar and split-level seating area, not a conscious copy of an English pub but a very relaxed pubby feel in appropriate western style; rustic mainly wooden decor, glass panels showing the modern stainless brewery; handy for Arizona State Univ *(Dave Irving)*

☆ **Washington** [1523 22nd St, NW; DC], *Brickskeller*: Marvellous collection of over 550 beers from all over the world, the more obscure and distant microbrews not priced appreciably higher than national US brands; good cosy atmosphere, friendly service, quick good value food and gingham tablecloths in stripped-brick and flagstone dining room, smartly informal games bar *(Wayne Brindle)*

Washington [22nd and M Sts], *Déjà Vu*: Popular very high-ceilinged bar with interlocked upper floors and stained-glass windows, square central servery, US beers; connected with Blackies Restaurant and Jules Café *(Ian Phillips)*; [Massachussetts Ave, nr Union Stn], *Dubliner*: Very good authentic big-city Irish pub, Bass and Guinness as well as American beers, typical pub food inc excellent Irish stew; big, with several mostly dark-panelled rooms, but can still get quite crowded *(Gordon B Mott)*

ZIMBABWE

Lake Kariba, *Bulls Hills Hotel*: Excellent lake views, superb bar, very good service, tremendous value food, bottled beer very good and cheap; bedrooms very good but quite expensive – UK visitors use hard currency *(Fred and Margaret Punter)*

Special Interest Lists

OPEN ALL DAY
(AT LEAST IN SUMMER)
*We list here all the pubs that
have told us they plan to stay
open all day, even if it's only
on a Saturday. We've included
the few pubs which close just
for half an hour to an hour,
and the many more, chiefly in
holiday areas, which open all
day only in summer. The
individual entries for the pubs
themselves show the actual
details. A few pubs in England
and Wales, allowed to stay
open only in the last two or
three years, are still changing
their opening hours – let us
know if you find anything
different.*

Berkshire
Brimpton Common, Pineapple
Sonning, Bull
Yattendon, Royal Oak

Buckinghamshire
Brill, Pheasant
Chalfont St Peter, Greyhound
Cheddington, Old Swan
Easington, Mole & Chicken
Great Missenden, George
Ley Hill, Swan
Stoke Green, Red Lion
Waddesdon, Five Arrows
West Wycombe, George &
Dragon

Cambridgeshire and Bedfordshire
Cambridge, Anchor, Eagle,
Mill
Etton, Golden Pheasant
Stretham, Lazy Otter
Wansford, Haycock

Cheshire
Barbridge, Barbridge
Barthomley, White Lion
Burleydam, Combermere
Arms
Church Minshull, Badger
Great Budworth, George &
Dragon
Macclesfield, Sutton Hall
Mobberley, Bird in Hand

Cornwall
Falmouth, Quayside
Helford Passage, Ferryboat
Helston, Blue Anchor
Lanner, Fox & Hounds
Mousehole, Ship
Mylor Bridge, Pandora
Pendoggett, Cornish Arms
Polruan, Lugger
Port Isaac, Golden Lion
Porthallow, Five Pilchards

St Agnes, Railway, Turks
Head
St Just in Penwith, Star
Trebarwith, Port William
Treen, Logan Rock
Tresco, New Inn

Cumbria
Ambleside, Golden Rule
Bowness on Windermere,
Hole in t' Wall
Braithwaite, Coledale
Buttermere, Bridge
Cartmel, Cavendish Arms,
Kings Arms
Chapel Stile, Wainwrights
Coniston, Sun
Dent, Sun
Dockray, Royal
Elterwater, Britannia
Eskdale Green, Bower House
Grasmere, Travellers Rest
Hawkshead, Kings Arms,
Queens Head
Heversham, Blue Bell
Kirkby Lonsdale, Snooty Fox,
Sun
Langdale, Old Dungeon Ghyll
Little Langdale, Three Shires
Loweswater, Kirkstile
Lowick Green, Farmers Arms
Seathwaite, Newfield
Sedbergh, Dalesman
Troutbeck, Queens Head
Ulverston, Bay Horse
Wasdale Head, Wasdale Head

Derbyshire and Staffordshire
Acton Trussell, Moat House
Ashbourne, Smiths Tavern
Ashford in the Water, Ashford
Derby, Brunswick
Foolow, Barrel
Grindleford, Maynard Arms
Hayfield, Lantern Pike
Holmesfield, Robin Hood
Monsal Head, Monsal Head
Shardlow, Hoskins Wharf
Shraleybrook, Rising Sun
Wardlow, Three Stags Heads

Devon
Bishops Tawton, Chichester
Arms
Budleigh Salterton, Salterton
Arms
Burgh Island, Pilchard
Cockwood, Anchor
Combeinteignhead, Coombe
Cellars
Dartmouth, Royal Castle
Exeter, Double Locks, White
Hart
Exminster, Turf
Haytor Vale, Rock
Kenn, Ley Arms
Lustleigh, Cleave

Moretonhampstead, White
Hart
Newton St Cyres, Beer Engine
Postbridge, Warren House
Stoke Gabriel, Church House
Stokenham, Church House
Topsham, Passage
Welcombe, Old Smithy

Dorset
Abbotsbury, Ilchester Arms
Bridport, George
Cerne Abbas, Royal Oak
Chideock, Anchor
Corfe Castle, Greyhound
Dorchester, Kings Arms
Osmington Mills, Smugglers
Shaftesbury, Ship
Tarrant Monkton, Langton
Arms
West Bexington, Manor
Worth Matravers, Square &
Compass

Essex
Coggeshall, Fleece
Dedham, Marlborough Head
Lamarsh, Red Lion
Littlebury, Queens Head
Stock, Hoop

Gloucestershire
Ampney Crucis, Crown of
Crucis
Bibury, Catherine Wheel
Chipping Campden, Kings
Arms, Noel Arms
Clearwell, Wyndham Arms
Coates, Tunnel House
Coln St Aldwyns, New Inn
Ewen, Wild Duck
Ford, Plough
Great Barrington, Fox
Lechlade, Trout
Parkend, Woodman
Redbrook, Boat
Sheepscombe, Butchers Arms
Stanton, Mount
Woodchester, Ram

Hampshire
Bentley, Bull
Bursledon, Jolly Sailor
Droxford, White Horse
Langstone, Royal Oak
Portsmouth, Still & West
Rotherwick, Coach & Horses
Sopley, Woolpack
Southsea, Wine Vaults
Upham, Brushmakers Arms
Wherwell, Mayfly
Winchester, Wykeham Arms

Hereford and Worcester
Bewdley, Little Pack Horse
Defford, Monkey House
Knightwick, Talbot
Ledbury, Feathers

Lugwardine, Crown & Anchor
Ombersley, Kings Arms

Hertfordshire
Aldbury, Valiant Trooper
Barley, Fox & Hounds
Bourne End, Three Horseshoes
Great Offley, Green Man
St Albans, Fighting Cocks, Garibaldi
Watton at Stone, George & Dragon

Humberside
Beverley, White Horse
Hull, Minerva, Olde White Harte
Pocklington, Feathers
Skidby, Half Moon
Sutton upon Derwent, St Vincent Arms

Isle of Wight
Chale, Clarendon (Wight Mouse)
Cowes, Folly
Niton, Buddle
Shanklin, Fishermans Cottage
Ventnor, Spyglass

Kent
Bough Beech, Wheatsheaf
Boughton Aluph, Flying Horse
Chiddingstone, Castle
Groombridge, Crown
Speldhurst, George & Dragon
Tunbridge Wells, Sankeys

Lancashire
Bilsborrow, Owd Nells
Blacko, Moorcock
Darwen, Old Rosins
Dukinfield, Globe
Liverpool, Philharmonic Dining Rooms
Lytham, Taps
Manchester, Dukes 92, Lass o' Gowrie, Marble Arch, Mark Addy, Royal Oak, Sinclairs Oyster Bar
Marple, Romper
Newburgh, Red Lion
Newton, Parkers Arms
Ribchester, White Bull
Summerseat, Waterside
Uppermill, Cross Keys
Yealand Conyers, New Inn

Leicestershire, Lincolnshire and Nottinghamshire
Dyke, Wishing Well
Empingham, White Horse
Kimberley, Nelson & Railway
Lincoln, Wig & Mitre
Loughborough, Swan in the Rushes
Normanton on Trent, Square & Compass
Nottingham, Fellows Morton & Clayton, Olde Trip to Jerusalem
Retford, Market
Stamford, George of Stamford
Stretton, Ram Jam

Wellow, Olde Red Lion

Midlands (including Warwickshire and Northants)
Ashby St Ledgers, Olde Coach House
Badby, Windmill
Brierley Hill, Vine
Himley, Crooked House
Lapworth, Navigation
Lowsonford, Fleur de Lys
Oundle, Ship
Southam, Old Mint
Stratford upon Avon, Slug & Lettuce

Norfolk
Aldborough, Black Boys
Blakeney, Kings Arms
Kings Lynn, Tudor Rose
Norwich, Adam & Eve
Scole, Scole
Snettisham, Rose & Crown
Swanton Morley, Darbys
Thornham, Lifeboat
Tivetshall St Mary, Old Ram
Winterton-on-Sea, Fishermans Return

Northumberland, Durham, etc
Corbridge, Wheatsheaf
Matfen, Black Bull
New York, Shiremoor House Farm
Newcastle upon Tyne, Cooperage, Crown Posada, Tap & Spile
North Shields, Chain Locker, Wooden Doll
Piercebridge, George

Oxfordshire
Bampton, Romany
Blewbury, Red Lion
Burford, Mermaid
Clifton Hampden, Plough
Cropredy, Red Lion
Cumnor, Bear & Ragged Staff
Deddington, Kings Arms
Faringdon, Bell
Finstock, Plough
Godstow, Trout
Henley-on-Thames, Three Tuns
Kelmscot, Plough
Oxford, Turf Tavern
Tadpole Bridge, Trout
Wytham, White Hart

Shropshire
Llanyblodwel, Horse Shoe
Ludlow, Church

Somerset and Avon
Ashcott, Ashcott
Bath, Crystal Palace, Old Green Tree
Brendon Hills, Raleghs Cross
Bristol, Highbury Vaults
Clapton in Gordano, Black Horse
Dunster, Luttrell Arms
Easton in Gordano, Rudgleigh
Exebridge, Anchor
Huish Episcopi, Rose & Crown
Montacute, Kings Arms

Norton St Philip, George
Old Sodbury, Dog
South Stoke, Pack Horse
Stanton Wick, Carpenters Arms
West Harptree, Blue Bowl
Woolverton, Red Lion

Suffolk
Aldeburgh, Cross Keys
Chelmondiston, Butt & Oyster
Clare, Bell
Hundon, Plough
Ipswich, Brewery Tap
Thornham Magna, Four Horseshoes

Surrey
Coldharbour, Plough
Compton, Harrow
Dorking, Cricketers
Effingham, Sir Douglas Haig
Laleham, Three Horseshoes
Outwood, Dog & Duck
Pirbright, Royal Oak
Pyrford Lock, Anchor
Reigate Heath, Skimmington Castle
Shamley Green, Red Lion
Shere, White Horse
Warlingham, White Lion

Sussex
Brighton, Cricketers
Ditchling, Bull
Fulking, Shepherd & Dog
Gun Hill, Gun
Hartfield, Anchor
Mayfield, Middle House, Rose & Crown
Normans Bay, Star
Oving, Gribble
Rye, Mermaid
West Ashling, Richmond Arms
Winchelsea, New Inn

Wiltshire
Barford St Martin, Barford
Box, Quarrymans Arms
Devizes, Bear
Hindon, Lamb
Lacock, George
Salisbury, Haunch of Venison
Sherston, Rattlebone
Wylye, Bell

Yorkshire
Bainbridge, Rose & Crown
Blakey Ridge, Lion
Buckden, Buck
Cadeby, Cadeby
Cray, White Lion
Cropton, New Inn
East Witton, Blue Lion, Cover Bridge
Egton Bridge, Postgate
Elslack, Tempest Arms
Goathland, Mallyan Spout
Harden, Malt Shovel
Harrogate, Squinting Cat
Helmsley, Feathers
Hubberholme, George
Kirkbymoorside, George & Dragon

Knaresborough, Blind Jacks
Lastingham, Blacksmiths
  Arms
Ledsham, Chequers
Leeds, Garden Gate,
  Whitelocks
Masham, Kings Head, White
  Bear
Muker, Farmers Arms
Pickhill, Nags Head
Ramsgill, Yorke Arms
Ripponden, Old Bridge
Robin Hoods Bay, Laurel
Saxton, Greyhound
Settle, Royal Oak
Sicklinghall, Scotts Arms
Sowerby Bridge, Moorings
Sutton, Anne Arms
Thornton Watlass, Buck
Wakefield, Beer Engine
York, Black Swan, Olde
  Starre, Spread Eagle, Tap &
  Spile

London, Central
EC1, Eagle, Olde Mitre
EC2, Hamilton Hall
EC4, Black Friar, Olde
  Cheshire Cheese
SW1, Grouse & Claret, Nags
  Head, Orange Brewery, Star
W1, Argyll Arms, Dog &
  Duck, Glassblower, Old
  Coffee House, Red Lion
WC1, Cittie of York, Lamb,
  Museum Tavern, Princess
  Louise, Sun
WC2, Chandos, Lamb & Flag

London, North
N1, Compton Arms,
  Waterside
N4, White Lion of Mortimer
NW3, Spaniards

London, South
SE1, George, Hole in the
  Wall, Horniman, Market
  Porter
SE5, Phoenix & Firkin
SE10, Cutty Sark
SE16, Mayflower
SE21, Crown & Greyhound
SW4, Olde Windmill
SW13, Bulls Head, Alma
SW18, Ship
SW19, Fox & Grapes
Putney, Green Man

London, West
SW6, White Horse
SW10, Ferret & Firkin
W6, Dove
W8, Windsor Castle
Hampton Court, Kings Arms
Twickenham, Popes Grotto

London, East
E1, Hollands

Scotland
Aberdeen, Prince of Wales
Applecross, Applecross
Ardfern, Galley of Lorne
Arduaine, Loch Melfort
Blanefield, Carbeth
Brig o Turk, Byre

Broughty Ferry, Fishermans
  Tavern
Carbost, Old Inn
Clachan Seil, Tigh an Truish
Crinan, Crinan
Edinburgh, Abbotsford,
  Athletic Arms, Bannermans
  Bar, Bow Bar, Caf_ Royal,
  Guildford Arms, Kays Bar,
  Starbank
Elie, Ship
Gifford, Tweeddale Arms
Glasgow, Babbity Bowster,
  Bon Accord, Horseshoe
Glendevon, Tormaukin
Innerleithen, Traquair Arms
Isle of Whithorn, Steam
  Packet
Kirkton of Glenisla, Glenisla
Linlithgow, Four Marys
Lybster, Portland Arms
Mountbenger, Gordon Arms
Oban, Oban
Portpatrick, Crown
Sheriffmuir, Sheriffmuir
Shieldaig, Tigh an Eilean
St Mary's Loch, Tibbie Shiels
Strachur, Creggans
Taynuilt, Station Tap Bar
Tayvallich, Tayvallich
Thornhill, Lion & Unicorn
Tushielaw, Tushielaw
Tweedsmuir, Crook
Ullapool, Ceilidh Place, Ferry
  Boat, Morefield Motel
Weem, Ailean Chraggan
Westruther, Old Thistle

Wales
Abergorlech, Black Lion
Aberystwyth, Halfway
Beaumaris, Olde Bulls Head
Burton Green, Golden Grove
Caerphilly, Courthouse
Carew, Carew
East Aberthaw, Blue Anchor
Halkyn, Britannia
Llanberis, Pen-y-Gwryd
Llancarfan, Fox & Hounds
Llangynwyd, Old House
Llanthony, Abbey
Maentwrog, Grapes
Marianglas, Parciau Arms
Mold, We Three Loggerheads
Monmouth, Punch House
Montgomery, Dragon
Old Radnor, Harp
Presteigne, Radnorshire Arms
Raglan, Clytha Arms
Red Wharf Bay, Ship
St Hilary, Bush
Tremeirchion, Salusbury
  Arms
Tudweiliog, Lion
Tyn y Groes, Groes

Channel Islands
Greve de Lecq, Moulin de
  Lecq
Kings Mills, Fleur du Jardin
St Aubin, Old Court House
St Brelade, Old Portelet
St Helier, Admiral
St Lawrence, British Union
St Peter, Star & Tipsy Toad

NO-SMOKING AREAS
*So many more pubs are now
making some provision for the
majority of their customers –
that's to say non-smokers –
that we have now found it is
worth listing all the pubs
which have told us they do set
aside at least some part of the
pub as a no-smoking area.
Look at the individual entries
for the pubs themselves to see
just what they do: provision is
much more generous in some
pubs than in others.*

Berkshire
Cookham, Bel & the Dragon
East Ilsley, Swan
Frilsham, Pot Kiln
Hare Hatch, Queen Victoria
Woolhampton, Rowbarge

Buckinghamshire
Adstock, Old Thatched
Amersham, Queens Head
Chalfont St Peter, Greyhound
Cheddington, Old Swan
Fawley, Walnut Tree
Fingest, Chequers
Forty Green, Royal Standard
  of England
Great Missenden, George
Ley Hill, Swan
Little Hampden, Rising Sun
Marlow, Hare & Hounds
Skirmett, Old Crown
Stoke Green, Red Lion

**Cambridgeshire and
Bedfordshire**
Barnack, Millstone
Barrington, Royal Oak
Bythorn, White Hart
Cambridge, Eagle, Free Press,
  Live & Let Live
Gorefield, Woodmans Cottage
Hinxton, Red Lion
Holywell, Olde Ferry Boat
Horningsea, Plough & Fleece
Keysoe, Chequers
Keyston, Pheasant
Stretham, Lazy Otter
Sutton Gault, Anchor
Swavesey, Trinity Foot
Wansford, Haycock
Woodditton, Three Blackbirds

Cheshire
Barbridge, Barbridge
Church Minshull, Badger
Great Budworth, George &
  Dragon
Higher Burwardsley, Pheasant
Langley, Leathers Smithy
Marbury, Swan
Mobberley, Bird in Hand
Over Peover, Whipping Stocks
Peover Heath, Dog
Weston, White Lion
Wrenbury, Dusty Miller

Cornwall
Chapel Amble, Maltsters
  Arms
Constantine, Trengilly Wartha

Lanner, Fox & Hounds
Lerryn, Ship
Ludgvan, White Hart
Mylor Bridge, Pandora
Pendoggett, Cornish Arms
Pillaton, Weary Friar
Polruan, Lugger
Port Isaac, Port Gaverne
Scorrier, Fox & Hounds
St Agnes, Turks Head
St Mawgan, Falcon

Cumbria
Appleby, Royal Oak
Bassenthwaite, Pheasant
Braithwaite, Coledale
Buttermere, Bridge
Cartmel, Kings Arms
Casterton, Pheasant
Chapel Stile, Wainwrights
Cockermouth, Trout
Coniston, Sun
Dent, Sun
Dockray, Royal
Elterwater, Britannia
Eskdale Green, Bower House
Eskdale Green, King George IV
Grasmere, Travellers Rest
Hawkshead, Drunken Duck, Kings Arms, Queens Head
Hesket Newmarket, Old Crown
Heversham, Blue Bell
Ings, Watermill
Little Langdale, Three Shires
Melmerby, Shepherds
Outgate, Outgate
Scales, White Horse
Seathwaite, Newfield
Ulverston, Bay Horse
Wasdale Head, Wasdale Head

Derbyshire and Staffordshire
Acton Trussell, Moat House
Ashford in the Water, Ashford
Birchover, Druid
Brassington, Olde Gate
Butterton, Black Lion
Cresswell, Izaak Walton
Derby, Brunswick
Froggatt Edge, Chequers
Hartington, Jug & Glass
Melbourne, John Thompson
Monsal Head, Monsal Head
Over Haddon, Lathkil
Shardlow, Hoskins Wharf
Tutbury, Olde Dog & Partridge
Wardlow, Three Stags Heads
Woolley Moor, White Horse

Devon
Ashprington, Watermans Arms
Axmouth, Harbour
Berrynarbor, Olde Globe
Branscombe, Fountain Head, Masons Arms
Churchstow, Church House
Cockwood, Anchor
Dartington, Cott
Dartmouth, Royal Castle
Doddiscombsleigh, Nobody
East Down, Pyne Arms

Exminster, Turf
Hatherleigh, Tally Ho
Haytor Vale, Rock
Holne, Church House
Kenn, Ley Arms
Kilmington, Old Inn
Kingston, Dolphin
Knowstone, Masons Arms
Lustleigh, Cleave
Lydford, Castle
Lynmouth, Rising Sun
Moretonhampstead, White Hart
Noss Mayo, Old Ship
Plymouth, China House
Sidford, Blue Ball
Stokenham, Church House
Tipton St John, Golden Lion
Topsham, Bridge
Torcross, Start Bay
Totnes, Kingsbridge
Trusham, Cridford
Welcombe, Old Smithy

Dorset
Abbotsbury, Ilchester Arms
Askerswell, Spyway
Bishops Caundle, White Hart
Bridport, George
Burton Bradstock, Three Horseshoes
Cerne Abbas, New Inn
Chideock, Anchor
Christchurch, Fishermans Haunt
Church Knowle, New Inn
Corfe Castle, Greyhound
East Chaldon, Sailors Return
East Knighton, Countryman
Kingston, Scott Arms
Lyme Regis, Pilot Boat
Osmington Mills, Smugglers
Plush, Brace of Pheasants
Powerstock, Three Horseshoes
Tarrant Monkton, Langton Arms
West Bexington, Manor

Essex
Castle Hedingham, Bell
Clavering, Cricketers
Gosfield, Green Man
Hatfield Broad Oak, Cock
Lamarsh, Red Lion
Littlebury, Queens Head
Pleshey, White Horse
Rickling Green, Cricketers Arms
Saffron Walden, Eight Bells
Tillingham, Cap & Feathers
Widdington, Fleur de Lys

Gloucestershire
Amberley, Black Horse
Ampney Crucis, Crown of Crucis
Bledington, Kings Head
Brimpsfield, Golden Heart
Great Rissington, Lamb
Gretton, Royal Oak
Hyde, Ragged Cot
Kingscote, Hunters Hall
Little Washbourne, Hobnails
Parkend, Woodman

Sapperton, Daneway
Southrop, Swan
St Briavels, George
Stanton, Mount
Stow on the Wold, Coach & Horses

Hampshire
Boldre, Red Lion
Bursledon, Jolly Sailor
Chalton, Red Lion
Droxford, White Horse
Ibsley, Old Beams
Portsmouth, Still & West
Winchester, Wykeham Arms

Hereford and Worcester
Bransford, Bear & Ragged Staff
Bretforton, Fleece
Fownhope, Green Man
Ombersley, Crown & Sandys Arms
Weobley, Olde Salutation
Woolhope, Crown

Hertfordshire
Aldbury, Valiant Trooper
Ayot St Lawrence, Brocket Arms
Barley, Fox & Hounds
Bourne End, Three Horseshoes
Rushden, Moon & Stars
St Albans, Garibaldi
Watton at Stone, George & Dragon

Humberside
Beverley, White Horse
Hull, Minerva
Pocklington, Feathers
Skidby, Half Moon
Sutton upon Derwent, St Vincent Arms

Isle of Wight
Niton, Buddle
Seaview, Seaview
Ventnor, Spyglass

Kent
Boyden Gate, Gate
Conyer Quay, Ship
Smarden, Bell
Tunbridge Wells, Sankeys
Whitstable, Pearsons Crab & Oyster House

Lancashire
Bilsborrow, Owd Nells
Darwen, Old Rosins
Goosnargh, Bushells Arms
Liverpool, Philharmonic Dining Rooms
Manchester, Sinclairs Oyster Bar
Yealand Conyers, New Inn

Leicestershire, Lincolnshire and Nottinghamshire
Braunston, Blue Ball, Old Plough
Drakeholes, Griff
Empingham, White Horse
Grantham, Beehive
Greatford, Hare & Hounds
Hose, Rose & Crown

Knipton, Red House
Nottingham, Sir John Borlase
  Warren
Old Somerby, Fox & Hounds
Redmile, Peacock
Stretton, Ram Jam
Wellow, Olde Red Lion

**Midlands (including
Warwickshire and Northants)**
Alderminster, Bell
Ashby St Ledgers, Olde Coach
  House
Himley, Crooked House
Ilmington, Howard Arms
Oundle, Mill, Ship
Southam, Old Mint
Twywell, Old Friar

Norfolk
Blakeney, Kings Arms
Blickling, Buckinghamshire
  Arms
Burnham Market, Hoste Arms
Burnham Thorpe, Lord
  Nelson
Cawston, Ratcatchers
Kings Lynn, Tudor Rose
Norwich, Adam & Eve
Reedham, Ferry
Ringstead, Gin Trap
Snettisham, Rose & Crown
Stow Bardolph, Hare Arms
Titchwell, Manor
Tivetshall St Mary, Old Ram
Upper Sheringham, Red Lion
Warham, Three Horseshoes
Woodbastwick, Fur &
  Feather

Northumberland, Durham, etc
Carterway Heads, Manor
  House
Cotherstone, Fox & Hounds
Eglingham, Tankerville Arms
Matfen, Black Bull
Newton on the Moor, Cook
  & Barker Arms
North Shields, Wooden Doll
Romaldkirk, Rose & Crown
Seaton Sluice, Waterford
  Arms
Stannersburn, Pheasant

Oxfordshire
Adderbury, Red Lion
Bampton, Romany
Blewbury, Red Lion
Burcot, Chequers, Angel,
  Lamb, Mermaid
Church Enstone, Crown
Clanfield, Clanfield Tavern
Clifton Hampden, Plough
Cumnor, Bear & Ragged Staff
Faringdon, Bell
Finstock, Plough
Fyfield, White Hart
Godstow, Trout
Great Tew, Falkland Arms
Moulsford, Beetle & Wedge
Shipton-under-Wychwood,
  Lamb, Shaven Crown
Sibford Gower, Wykham
  Arms
Stanton St John, Star
Sutton Courtenay, Fish

Tadpole Bridge, Trout

Shropshire
Hope, Stables
Hopton Wafers, Crown
Ludlow, Church, Unicorn
Much Wenlock, Talbot
Upper Farmcote, Lion of
  Morfe
Wenlock Edge, Wenlock Edge

Somerset and Avon
Appley, Globe
Ashcott, Ashcott
Aust, Boars Head
Bath, Old Green Tree
Brendon Hills, Raleghs Cross
Compton Martin, Ring o'
  Bells
Croscombe, Bull Terrier
Dowlish Wake, New Inn
Dunster, Luttrell Arms
Haselbury Plucknett,
  Haselbury
Kilve, Hood Arms
Langley Marsh, Three
  Horseshoes
Montacute, Kings Arms
Old Sodbury, Dog
Oldbury-on-Severn, Anchor
Over Stratton, Royal Oak
Stoke St Gregory, Rose &
  Crown
Stoke St Mary, Half Moon
Wambrook, Cotley

Suffolk
Blyford, Queens Head
Hundon, Plough
Kersey, Bell
Lavenham, Angel, Swan
Levington, Ship
Long Melford, Bull
Orford, Jolly Sailor
Southwold, Crown
Sutton, Plough
Westleton, Crown

Surrey
Blackbrook, Plough
Charleshill, Donkey
Coldharbour, Plough
Hurtmore, Squirrels
Reigate Heath, Skimmington
  Castle
Warlingham, White Lion
West Clandon, Onslow Arms

Sussex
Alciston, Rose Cottage
Alfriston, Star
Charlton, Fox Goes Free
Cowbeech, Merrie Harriers
Ditchling, Bull
Firle, Ram
Gun Hill, Gun
Heathfield, Star
Houghton, George & Dragon
Kingston near Lewes, Juggs
Kirdford, Half Moon
Lower Beeding, Crabtree
Nuthurst, Black Horse
Oving, Gribble
Punnetts Town, Three Cups
Seaford, Golden Galleon
Stopham, White Hart

Winchelsea, New Inn

Wiltshire
Axford, Red Lion
Barford St Martin, Barford
Devizes, Bear
Ebbesbourne Wake,
  Horseshoe
Hindon, Lamb
Little Bedwyn, Harrow
Lower Woodford, Wheatsheaf
Malmesbury, Suffolk Arms
Potterne, George & Dragon
Seend, Barge
Semington, Lamb
Wylye, Bell

Yorkshire
Askrigg, Kings Arms
Austwick, Game Cock
Bilbrough, Three Hares
Bingley, Brown Cow
Buckden, Buck
Burnsall, Red Lion
Cadeby, Cadeby
Carlton, Foresters Arms
Carthorpe, Fox & Hounds
Cray, White Lion
Crayke, Durham Ox
Cropton, New Inn
Goathland, Mallyan Spout
Goose Eye, Turkey
Harden, Malt Shovel
Harrogate, Squinting Cat
Hetton, Angel
Hubberholme, George
Kirkbymoorside, George &
  Dragon
Kirkham, Stone Trough
Lastingham, Blacksmiths
  Arms
Levisham, Horseshoe
Linthwaite, Sair
Linton in Craven, Fountaine
Meltham, Will's o' Nat's
Penistone, Cubley Hall
Pickhill, Nags Head
Ramsgill, Yorke Arms
Redmire, Kings Arms
Rosedale Abbey, Milburn
  Arms
Sawley, Sawley Arms
Sheffield, Fat Cat
Sicklinghall, Scotts Arms
Sowerby Bridge, Moorings
Starbotton, Fox & Hounds
Thornton Watlass, Buck
Wath-in-Nidderdale,
  Sportsmans Arms
Wigglesworth, Plough
Wormald Green, Cragg Lodge
York, Olde Starre

London, Central
EC2, Hamilton Hall
W1, Argyll Arms
WC1, Lamb

London, North
N1, Waterside
N4, White Lion of Mortimer
NW3, Spaniards

London, South
SE1, Horniman, Market
  Porter

SE5, Phoenix & Firkin
SE21, Crown & Greyhound

Scotland
Applecross, Applecross
Arduaine, Loch Melfort
Brig o Turk, Byre
Broughty Ferry, Fishermans Tavern
Canonbie, Riverside
Cawdor, Cawdor Tavern
Creebridge, Creebridge House
Edinburgh, Starbank
Gatehouse of Fleet, Murray Arms
Glasgow, Horseshoe
Isleornsay, Tigh Osda Eilean Iarmain
Kilberry, Kilberry
Pitlochry, Killiecrankie
Plockton, Plockton
Portpatrick, Crown
Skeabost, Skeabost House
St Mary's Loch, Tibbie Shiels
Strachur, Creggans
Swinton, Wheatsheaf
Tayvallich, Tayvallich
Thornhill, Lion & Unicorn
Turriff, Towie Tavern
Ullapool, Ceilidh Place, Ferry Boat, Morefield Motel

Wales
Beaumaris, Olde Bulls Head
Bodfari, Dinorben Arms
Carew, Carew
Carno, Aleppo Merchant
Crickhowell, Bear
Llanberis, Pen-y-Gwryd
Llandrindod Wells, Llanerch
Llangynwyd, Old House
Llannefydd, Hawk & Buckle
Llanwnda, Goat
Llyswen, Griffin
Maentwrog, Grapes
Montgomery, Dragon
Presteigne, Radnorshire Arms
Raglan, Clytha Arms
Red Wharf Bay, Ship
Tudweiliog, Lion
Tyn y Groes, Groes

PUBS WITH GOOD GARDENS
The pubs listed here have bigger or more beautiful gardens, grounds or terraces than are usual for their areas. Note that in a town or city this might be very much more modest than the sort of garden that would deserve a listing in the countryside.

Berkshire
Aldworth, Bell
Chaddleworth, Ibex
Cookham Dean, Jolly Farmer
Hamstead Marshall, White Hart
Holyport, Belgian Arms
Hurley, Dew Drop
Marsh Benham, Water Rat
West Ilsley, Harrow
Woolhampton, Rowbarge

Buckinghamshire
Amersham, Queens Head
Bledlow, Lions of Bledlow
Bolter End, Peacock
Fawley, Walnut Tree
Fingest, Chequers
Ford, Dinton Hermit
Hambleden, Stag & Huntsman
Lacey Green, Pink & Lily
Little Horwood, Shoulder of Mutton
Marsh Gibbon, Greyhound
Northend, White Hart
Skirmett, Old Crown
Waddesdon, Five Arrows
West Wycombe, George & Dragon
Whitchurch, White Swan
Worminghall, Clifden Arms

Cambridgeshire and Bedfordshire
Bolnhurst, Olde Plough
Eltisley, Leeds Arms
Fowlmere, Chequers
Horningsea, Plough & Fleece
Madingley, Three Horseshoes
Riseley, Fox & Hounds
Stretham, Lazy Otter
Swavesey, Trinity Foot
Ufford, Olde White Hart
Wansford, Haycock

Cheshire
Barbridge, Barbridge
Brereton Green, Bears Head
Broomedge, Jolly Thresher
Church Minshull, Badger
Lower Peover, Bells of Peover
Macclesfield, Sutton Hall
Over Peover, Whipping Stocks
Weston, White Lion

Cornwall
Helford, Shipwrights Arms
Philleigh, Roseland
St Agnes, Turks Head
St Mawgan, Falcon
Tresco, New Inn

Cumbria
Barbon, Barbon
Bassenthwaite, Pheasant
Cockermouth, Trout
Eskdale Green, Bower House

Derbyshire and Staffordshire
Acton Trussell, Moat House
Buxton, Bull i'th' Thorn
Grindleford, Maynard Arms
Little Longstone, Packhorse
Melbourne, John Thompson
Onecote, Jervis Arms
Rushton Spencer, Crown
Shardlow, Hoskins Wharf
Tatenhill, Horseshoe
Tutbury, Olde Dog & Partridge
Woolley Moor, White Horse

Devon
Berrynarbor, Olde Globe
Broadhembury, Drewe Arms
Cornworthy, Hunters Lodge
Dartington, Cott
Doddiscombsleigh, Nobody

Exminster, Turf
Haytor Vale, Rock
Poundsgate, Tavistock
Sidford, Blue Ball
South Zeal, Oxenham Arms
Stokenham, Church House
Torbryan, Old Church House
Welcombe, Old Smithy
Weston, Otter

Dorset
Child Okeford, Saxon
Christchurch, Fishermans Haunt
Farnham, Museum
Osmington Mills, Smugglers
Plush, Brace of Pheasants
Shave Cross, Shave Cross
Tarrant Monkton, Langton Arms
West Bexington, Manor

Essex
Castle Hedingham, Bell
Chappel, Swan
Coggeshall, Fleece
Great Yeldham, White Hart
Littlebury, Queens Head
Mill Green, Viper
Peldon, Rose
Stock, Hoop
Toot Hill, Green Man
Wendens Ambo, Bell
Woodham Walter, Cats

Gloucestershire
Amberley, Black Horse
Ampney Crucis, Crown of Crucis
Bibury, Catherine Wheel
Brockhampton, Craven Arms
Chipping Campden, Kings Arms
Ewen, Wild Duck
Great Rissington, Lamb
Gretton, Royal Oak
Kilkenny, Kilkeney
Kingscote, Hunters Hall
Lechlade, Trout
North Nibley, New Inn
Oddington, Horse & Groom
Redbrook, Boat
Sapperton, Daneway
Southrop, Swan

Hampshire
Battramsley, Hobler
Bramdean, Fox
Lymington, Chequers
Ovington, Bush
Petersfield, White Horse
Steep, Harrow
Stockbridge, Vine
Tichborne, Tichborne Arms

Hereford and Worcester
Berrow, Duke of York
Bretforton, Fleece
Fownhope, Green Man
Much Marcle, Slip Tavern
Sellack, Lough Pool
Woolhope, Butchers Arms

Hertfordshire
Ayot St Lawrence, Brocket Arms
Great Offley, Green Man

Old Radnor, Harp
Presteigne, Radnorshire Arms
St Hilary, Bush
Stackpole, Armstrong Arms
Tremeirchion, Salusbury Arms
Tudweiliog, Lion
Tyn y Groes, Groes

Channel Islands
Castel, Hougue du Pommier
Kings Mills, Fleur du Jardin
Rozel, Rozel Bay

WATERSIDE PUBS
*The pubs listed here are right
beside the sea, a sizeable river,
canal, lake or loch that
contributes significantly to
their attraction.*

Berkshire
Great Shefford, Swan
Woolhampton, Rowbarge

**Cambridgeshire and
Bedfordshire**
Cambridge, Anchor, Mill
Holywell, Olde Ferry Boat
Odell, Bell
Stretham, Lazy Otter
Sutton Gault, Anchor
Wansford, Haycock

Cheshire
Barbridge, Barbridge
Wrenbury, Dusty Miller

Cornwall
Falmouth, Quayside
Helford, Shipwrights Arms
Helford Passage, Ferryboat
Mousehole, Ship
Mylor Bridge, Pandora
Polkerris, Rashleigh
Polruan, Lugger
Port Isaac, Port Gaverne
Porthallow, Five Pilchards
Porthleven, Ship
St Agnes, Turks Head
Trebarwith, Port William
Tresco, New Inn

Cumbria
Cockermouth, Trout
Ulverston, Bay Horse

Derbyshire and Staffordshire
Fradley, Swan
Onecote, Jervis Arms
Shardlow, Hoskins Wharf,
  Old Crown

Devon
Ashprington, Watermans
  Arms
Burgh Island, Pilchard
Combeinteignhead, Coombe
  Cellars
Dartmouth, Royal Castle
Exeter, Double Locks
Exminster, Turf
Lynmouth, Rising Sun
Lynton, Rockford
Noss Mayo, Old Ship
Plymouth, China House
Topsham, Passage
Torcross, Start Bay
Tuckenhay, Maltsters Arms

Weston, Otter

Dorset
Chesil, Cove House
Chideock, Anchor
Lyme Regis, Pilot Boat

Essex
Chappel, Swan
Leigh on Sea, Crooked Billet
North Fambridge, Ferryboat

Gloucestershire
Ashleworth Quay, Boat
Great Barrington, Fox
Lechlade, Trout
Redbrook, Boat

Hampshire
Bursledon, Jolly Sailor
Langstone, Royal Oak
Ovington, Bush
Portsmouth, Still & West
Wherwell, Mayfly

Hereford and Worcester
Knightwick, Talbot
Wyre Piddle, Anchor

Hertfordshire
Berkhamsted, Boat
Bourne End, Three
  Horseshoes

Humberside
Hull, Minerva

Isle of wight
Cowes, Folly
Seaview, Seaview
Shanklin, Fishermans Cottage
Ventnor, Spyglass

Kent
Conyer Quay, Ship
Whitstable, Pearsons Crab &
  Oyster House

Lancashire
Bilsborrow, Owd Nells
Garstang, Th'Owd Tithebarn
Manchester, Dukes 92, Mark
  Addy
Whitewell, Inn at Whitewell

**Midlands (including
Warwickshire and Northants)**
Lapworth, Navigation
Lowsonford, Fleur de Lys
Netherton, Little Dry Dock
Oundle, Mill

Norfolk
Reedham, Ferry

Northumberland, Durham, etc
North Shields, Chain Locker
Piercebridge, George

Oxfordshire
Godstow, Trout
Moulsford, Beetle & Wedge
Tadpole Bridge, Trout

Shropshire
Llanyblodwel, Horse Shoe
Ludlow, Unicorn
Whitchurch, Willey Moor
  Lock

Somerset and Avon
Exebridge, Anchor

Freshford, Inn at Freshford

Suffolk
Aldeburgh, Cross Keys
Chelmondiston, Butt &
  Oyster
Ipswich, Brewery Tap

Surrey
Pyrford Lock, Anchor

Sussex
Stopham, White Hart

Wiltshire
Bradford-on-Avon, Cross
  Guns
Salisbury, Old Mill
Seend, Barge

Yorkshire
Newton on Ouse, Dawnay
  Arms
Sowerby Bridge, Moorings

London, North
N1, Waterside

London, South
SE1, Horniman
SE10, Cutty Sark
SE16, Mayflower
SW13, Bulls Head
SW18, Ship

London, West
W6, Dove

London, East
London E14, Grapes

Scotland
Ardfern, Galley of Lorne
Arduaine, Loch Melfort
Carbost, Old Inn
Clachan Seil, Tigh an Truish
Crinan, Crinan
Edinburgh, Starbank
Elie, Ship
Isle of Whithorn, Steam
  Packet
Isleornsay, Tigh Osda Eilean
  Iarmain
Plockton, Plockton
Portpatrick, Crown
Shieldaig, Tigh an Eilean
Skeabost, Skeabost House
St Mary's Loch, Tibbie Shiels
Strachur, Creggans
Tayvallich, Tayvallich
Ullapool, Ferry Boat

Wales
Aberdovey, Penhelig Arms
Abergorlech, Black Lion
Cresswell Quay, Cresselly
  Arms
Little Haven, Swan
Nevern, Trewern Arms
Pembroke Ferry, Ferry
Pontypool, Open Hearth
Red Wharf Bay, Ship

Channel islands
St Aubin, Old Court House

**PUBS IN ATTRACTIVE
SURROUNDINGS**
*These pubs are in unusually
attractive or interesting places –*

ovely countryside, charming
illages, occasionally notable
own surroundings. Waterside
ubs are listed again here only
 their other surroundings are
pecial, too.

Berkshire
Aldworth, Bell
Frilsham, Pot Kiln
Hurley, Dew Drop
Waltham St Lawrence, Bell

Buckinghamshire
Bledlow, Lions of Bledlow
Gotley, Five Bells
Brill, Pheasant
Frieth, Prince Albert
Hambleden, Stag &
  Huntsman
Little Hampden, Rising Sun
Littleworth Common,
  Blackwood Arms
Northend, White Hart
Turville, Bull & Butcher

**Cambridgeshire and
Bedfordshire**
Barrington, Royal Oak

Cheshire
Barthomley, White Lion
Bottom of the Oven, Stanley
  Arms
Great Budworth, George &
  Dragon
Langley, Leathers Smithy
Lower Peover, Bells of Peover
Marbury, Swan
Sutton, Ryles Arms

Cornwall
Boscastle, Cobweb
Chapel Amble, Maltsters
  Arms
Lerryn, Ship
Morwenstow, Bush
Penelewey, Punch Bowl &
  Ladle
Pillaton, Weary Friar
Porthallow, Five Pilchards
St Agnes, Turks Head
St Breward, Old Inn
St Kew, St Kew
St Mawgan, Falcon
Tresco, New Inn

Cumbria
Alston, Angel
Askham, Punch Bowl, Queens
  Head
Bassenthwaite, Pheasant
Braithwaite, Coledale
Cartmel, Cavendish Arms,
  Kings Arms
Chapel Stile, Wainwrights
Coniston, Sun
Dent, Sun
Dockray, Royal
Elterwater, Britannia
Eskdale Green, King George
  IV
Garrigill, George & Dragon
Grasmere, Travellers Rest
Hawkshead, Drunken Duck,
  Kings Arms
Hesket Newmarket, Old

Crown
Ings, Watermill
Langdale, Old Dungeon Ghyll
Little Langdale, Three Shires
Loweswater, Kirkstile
Melmerby, Shepherds
Scales, White Horse
Seathwaite, Newfield
Troutbeck, Queens Head
Ulverston, Bay Horse
Wasdale Head, Wasdale Head

Derbyshire and Staffordshire
Alstonefield, George
Ashford in the Water, Ashford
Brassington, Olde Gate
Froggatt Edge, Chequers
Hayfield, Lantern Pike
Holmesfield, Robin Hood
Kirk Ireton, Barley Mow
Little Hucklow, Old Bulls
  Head
Little Longstone, Packhorse
Monsal Head, Monsal Head
Over Haddon, Lathkil
Rushton Spencer, Crown
Woolley Moor, White Horse

Devon
Blackawton, Normandy Arms
Branscombe, Fountain Head
Burgh Island, Pilchard
Chagford, Ring o' Bells
Exminster, Turf
Haytor Vale, Rock
Holbeton, Mildmay Colours
Holne, Church House
Horndon, Elephants Nest
Horsebridge, Royal
Iddesleigh, Duke of York
Kingston, Dolphin
Knowstone, Masons Arms
Lustleigh, Cleave
Lydford, Castle
Lynmouth, Rising Sun
Lynton, Rockford
Meavy, Royal Oak
Postbridge, Warren House
Rattery, Church House
Slapton, Tower

Dorset
Abbotsbury, Ilchester Arms
Askerswell, Spyway
Burton Bradstock, Three
  Horseshoes
East Chaldon, Sailors Return
Farnham, Museum
Milton Abbas, Hambro Arms
Osmington Mills, Smugglers
Plush, Brace of Pheasants
Powerstock, Three
  Horseshoes
Worth Matravers, Square &
  Compass

Essex
Leigh on Sea, Crooked Billet
Mill Green, Viper
North Fambridge, Ferryboat

Gloucestershire
Amberley, Black Horse
Ashleworth Quay, Boat
Bibury, Catherine Wheel
Bisley, Bear

Bledington, Kings Head
Brockhampton, Craven Arms
Brockweir, Brockweir
Chedworth, Seven Tuns
Coates, Tunnel House
Cold Aston, Plough
Coln St Aldwyns, New Inn
Great Rissington, Lamb
Guiting Power, Olde Inne
Nailsworth, Weighbridge
Newland, Ostrich
North Nibley, New Inn
Sapperton, Bell
Sapperton, Daneway
St Briavels, George
Stanton, Mount
Stow on the Wold, Queens
  Head

Hampshire
Crawley, Fox & Hounds
Lymington, Chequers
Ovington, Bush
Petersfield, White Horse
Tichborne, Tichborne Arms

Hereford and Worcester
Broadway, Crown & Trumpet
Hanley Castle, Three Kings
Knightwick, Talbot
Much Marcle, Slip Tavern
Ruckhall, Ancient Camp
Sellack, Lough Pool
Weobley, Olde Salutation
Woolhope, Butchers Arms

Hertfordshire
St Albans, Fighting Cocks
Westmill, Sword in Hand

Isle of Wight
Chale, Clarendon (Wight
  Mouse)

Kent
Boughton Aluph, Flying
  Horse
Brookland, Woolpack
Chiddingstone, Castle
Groombridge, Crown
Lamberhurst, Brown Trout
Newnham, George
Sole Street, Compasses

Lancashire
Blacko, Moorcock
Blackstone Edge, White
  House
Marple, Romper
Newton, Parkers Arms
Uppermill, Cross Keys
Whitewell, Inn at Whitewell

**Leicestershire, Lincolnshire
and Nottinghamshire**
Exton, Fox & Hounds
Glooston, Old Barn
Hallaton, Bewicke Arms
Laxton, Dovecote
Lyddington, Marquess of
  Exeter

**Midlands (including
Warwickshire and Northants)**
Alveston, Ferry
Himley, Crooked House
Priors Marston, Holly Bush
Warmington, Plough

Norfolk
Blickling, Buckinghamshire Arms
Burnham Market, Hoste Arms
Castle Acre, Ostrich
Thornham, Lifeboat
Woodbastwick, Fur & Feather

Northumberland, Durham, etc
Blanchland, Lord Crewe Arms
Craster, Jolly Fisherman
Diptonmill, Dipton Mill
Haltwhistle, Milecastle
Matfen, Black Bull
Romaldkirk, Rose & Crown
Stannersburn, Pheasant

Oxfordshire
Brightwell Baldwin, Lord Nelson
Burford, Angel, Mermaid
Chinnor, Sir Charles Napier
Christmas Common, Fox & Hounds
Cropredy, Red Lion
Great Tew, Falkland Arms
Hailey, King William IV
Kelmscot, Plough
Maidensgrove, Five Horseshoes
Oxford, Turf Tavern
Pishill, Crown
Shenington, Bell
Shipton-under-Wychwood, Shaven Crown
Swinbrook, Swan

Shropshire
Bridges, Horseshoe
Cardington, Royal Oak
Hope, Stables
Llanfair Waterdine, Red Lion
Wenlock Edge, Wenlock Edge

Somerset and Avon
Appley, Globe
Blagdon, New Inn
Brendon Hills, Raleghs Cross
Combe Hay, Wheatsheaf
Cranmore, Strode Arms
Luxborough, Royal Oak
Stogumber, White Horse
Triscombe, Blue Ball
Wambrook, Cotley
Winsford, Royal Oak

Suffolk
Dennington, Queens Head
Dunwich, Ship
Easton, White Horse
Kersey, Bell
Lavenham, Angel
Levington, Ship
Long Melford, Bull
Sutton, Plough
Walberswick, Bell

Surrey
Albury, Drummond Arms
Blackbrook, Plough
Cobham, Cricketers
Headley, Cock
Mickleham, King William IV
Reigate Heath, Skimmington Castle
Shere, White Horse

Sussex
Billingshurst, Blue Ship
Brownbread Street, Ash Tree
Burpham, George & Dragon
Burwash, Bell
Ditchling, Bull
Eartham, George
Eastdean, Tiger
Fletching, Griffin
Fulking, Shepherd & Dog
Heathfield, Star
Kirdford, Half Moon
Lickfold, Lickfold
Lurgashall, Noahs Ark
Mayfield, Middle House
Seaford, Golden Galleon
Sidlesham, Crab & Lobster
West Hoathly, Cat
Wineham, Royal Oak

Wiltshire
Axford, Red Lion
Bradford-on-Avon, Cross Guns
Ebbesbourne Wake, Horseshoe
Lacock, Rising Sun
Wootton Rivers, Royal Oak

Yorkshire
Appletreewick, Craven Arms
Askrigg, Kings Arms
Bainbridge, Rose & Crown
Blakey Ridge, Lion
Buckden, Buck
Burnsall, Red Lion
Byland Abbey, Abbey
Cray, White Lion
East Witton, Blue Lion
Heath, Kings Arms
Hubberholme, George
Kirby Hill, Shoulder of Mutton
Lastingham, Blacksmiths Arms
Levisham, Horseshoe
Linton in Craven, Fountaine
Litton, Queens Arms
Masham, Kings Head
Meltham, Will's o' Nat's
Muker, Farmers Arms
Ramsgill, Yorke Arms
Robin Hoods Bay, Laurel
Rosedale Abbey, Milburn Arms
Starbotton, Fox & Hounds
Sutton Howgrave, White Dog
Thornton Watlass, Buck
Wath-in-Nidderdale, Sportsmans Arms
Widdop, Pack Horse
Wigglesworth, Plough

London, Central
EC1, Olde Mitre

London, North
NW3, Spaniards

London, South
SE1, Horniman
SE21, Crown & Greyhound
SW4, Olde Windmill
SW19, Fox & Grapes
Putney, Green Man

London, West
Hampton Court, Kings Arms

Scotland
Applecross, Applecross
Arduaine, Loch Melfort
Brig o Turk, Byre
Clachan Seil, Tigh an Truish
Crinan, Crinan
Kilberry, Kilberry
Mountbenger, Gordon Arms
Pitlochry, Killiecrankie
Sheriffmuir, Sheriffmuir
St Mary's Loch, Tibbie Shiels
Strachur, Creggans
Taynuilt, Station Tap Bar
Tushielaw, Tushielaw
Tweedsmuir, Crook

Wales
Abergorlech, Black Lion
Aberystwyth, Halfway
Caerphilly, Courthouse
Carew, Carew
Cilcain, White Horse
Crickhowell, Nantyffin Cider Mill
Kenfig, Prince of Wales
Llanbedr-y-Cennin, Olde Bull
Llanberis, Pen-y-Gwryd
Llanthony, Abbey
Maentwrog, Grapes
Monmouth, Punch House
Old Radnor, Harp
Red Wharf Bay, Ship

Channel Islands
St Brelade, Old Portelet

PUBS WITH GOOD VIEWS
These pubs are listed for their particularly good views, either from inside or from a garden or terrace. Waterside pubs are listed again here only if their view is exceptional in its own right – not just a straightforward sea view, for example

Berkshire
Chieveley, Blue Boar

Buckinghamshire
Brill, Pheasant
Great Brickhill, Old Red Lion

Cheshire
Higher Burwardsley, Pheasant
Langley, Hanging Gate, Leathers Smithy
Overton, Ring o' Bells

Cornwall
Polruan, Lugger
St Agnes, Turks Head

Cumbria
Braithwaite, Coledale
Cartmel Fell, Masons Arms
Eskdale Green, King George IV
Hawkshead, Drunken Duck
Langdale, Old Dungeon Ghyll
Loweswater, Kirkstile
Troutbeck, Queens Head
Ulverston, Bay Horse
Wasdale Head, Wasdale Head

Derbyshire and Staffordshire
Foolow, Barrel
Monsal Head, Monsal Head

Over Haddon, Lathkil
Rushton Spencer, Crown

Devon
Burgh Island, Pilchard
Postbridge, Warren House

Dorset
Kingston, Scott Arms
West Bexington, Manor
Worth Matravers, Square &
Compass

Gloucestershire
Amberley, Black Horse
Gretton, Royal Oak
Kilkenny, Kilkeney
Sheepscombe, Butchers Arms
Stanton, Mount
Woodchester, Ram

Hampshire
Beauworth, Milbury's

Hereford and Worcester
Ruckhall, Ancient Camp
Wyre Piddle, Anchor

Hertfordshire
Great Offley, Green Man

Isle of Wight
Niton, Buddle
Ventnor, Spyglass

Kent
Penshurst, Spotted Dog
Ulcombe, Pepper Box

Lancashire
Blacko, Moorcock
Blackstone Edge, White
House
Darwen, Old Rosins
Marple, Romper
Tockholes, Rock
Uppermill, Cross Keys

**Leicestershire, Lincolnshire
and Nottinghamshire**
Knipton, Red House

Northumberland, Durham, etc
North Shields, Wooden Doll
Seahouses, Olde Ship

Shropshire
Hope, Stables

Somerset and Avon
Blagdon, New Inn
Brendon Hills, Raleghs Cross

Suffolk
Erwarton, Queens Head
Hundon, Plough
Levington, Ship

Sussex
Burpham, George & Dragon
Byworth, Black Horse
Elsted, Three Horseshoes
Fletching, Griffin
Houghton, George & Dragon

Wiltshire
Axford, Red Lion
Box, Quarrymans Arms
Lacock, Rising Sun

Yorkshire
Appletreewick, Craven Arms

Blakey Ridge, Lion
Kirby Hill, Shoulder of
Mutton
Kirkham, Stone Trough
Litton, Queens Arms
Meltham, Will's o' Nat's

Scotland
Applecross, Applecross
Ardvasar, Ardvasar
Crinan, Crinan
Edinburgh, Starbank
Isleornsay, Tigh Osda Eilean
Iarmain
Kilberry, Kilberry
Pitlochry, Killiecrankie
Sheriffmuir, Sheriffmuir
Shieldaig, Tigh an Eilean
St Mary's Loch, Tibbie Shiels
Strachur, Creggans
Tushielaw, Tushielaw
Ullapool, Ferry Boat
Weem, Ailean Chraggan

Wales
Aberdovey, Penhelig Arms
Aberystwyth, Halfway
Bodfari, Dinorben Arms
Caerphilly, Courthouse
Halkyn, Britannia
Llanbedr-y-Cennin, Olde Bull
Llanberis, Pen-y-Gwryd
Llangynwyd, Old House
Llannefydd, Hawk & Buckle
Old Radnor, Harp
Tudweiliog, Lion
Tyn y Groes, Groes

Channel Islands
St Aubin, Old Court House

**PUBS IN INTERESTING
BUILDINGS**
*Pubs and inns are listed here
for the particular interest of
their building – something
really out of the ordinary to
look at, or occasionally a
building that has an
outstandingly interesting
historical background.*

Berkshire
Cookham, Bel & the Dragon

Buckinghamshire
Forty Green, Royal Standard
of England

Cornwall
Morwenstow, Bush

Derbyshire and staffordshire
Buxton, Bull i'th' Thorn
Derby, Abbey

Devon
Dartmouth, Cherub
Harberton, Church House
Rattery, Church House
Sourton, Highwayman
South Zeal, Oxenham Arms

Hampshire
Beauworth, Milbury's

Hereford and Worcester
Bretforton, Fleece

Humberside
Hull, Olde White Harte

Lancashire
Garstang, Th'Owd Tithebarn
Liverpool, Philharmonic
Dining Rooms

**Leicestershire, Lincolnshire
and Nottinghamshire**
Nottingham, Olde Trip to
Jerusalem
Stamford, George of Stamford

**Midlands (including
Warwickshire and Northants)**
Himley, Crooked House
West Bromwich, Manor
House

Norfolk
Scole, Scole

Northumberland, Durham, etc
Blanchland, Lord Crewe Arms

Oxfordshire
Fyfield, White Hart

Somerset and Avon
Norton St Philip, George

Suffolk
Lavenham, Swan
Long Melford, Bull

Surrey
Shere, White Horse

Sussex
Alfriston, Star
Rye, Mermaid

Wiltshire
Salisbury, Haunch of Venison

London, Central
EC2, Hamilton Hall
EC4, Black Friar
WC1, Cittie of York

London, South
SE1, George
SE5, Phoenix & Firkin

London, East
E1, Hollands

Scotland
Edinburgh, Café Royal,
Guildford Arms
Glasgow, Horseshoe

Wales
Llanfihangel Crucorney,
Skirrid
Llanthony, Abbey

**PUBS THAT
BREW THEIR OWN BEER**
*The pubs listed here brew
their own brew on the
premises; many others not
listed have beers brewed for
them specially, sometimes to
an individual recipe (but by a
separate brewer). We mention
these in the text.*

Cornwall
Helston, Blue Anchor

Cumbria
Cartmel Fell, Masons Arms
Dent, Sun
Hesket Newmarket, Old
Crown

Derbyshire and Staffordshire
Burton on Trent, Burton
Bridge
Derby, Brunswick
Melbourne, John Thompson
Shraleybrook, Rising Sun

Devon
Ashburton, London
Hatherleigh, Tally Ho
Holbeton, Mildmay Colours
Horsebridge, Royal
Newton St Cyres, Beer Engine

Essex
Gestingthorpe, Pheasant

Hertfordshire
Barley, Fox & Hounds

Humberside
Hull, Minerva

Lancashire
Manchester, Lass o' Gowrie

Leicestershire, Lincolnshire and Nottinghamshire
Burrough on the Hill, Stag &
Hounds
Nottingham, Fellows Morton
& Clayton

Midlands (including Warwickshire and Northants)
Brierley Hill, Vine
Langley, Brewery

Norfolk
Woodbastwick, Fur &
Feather

Shropshire
Bishops Castle, Three Tuns
Wistanstow, Plough

Somerset and Avon
Trudoxhill, White Hart

Suffolk
Earl Soham, Victoria

Sussex
Chidham, Old House At
Home

Yorkshire
Cropton, New Inn
Linthwaite, Sair
Sheffield, Fat Cat

London, Central
SW1, Orange Brewery

London, South
SE5, Phoenix & Firkin

London, West
SW10, Ferret & Firkin

PUBS CLOSE TO MOTORWAY JUNCTIONS
The number at the start of each line is the number of the junction. Detailed directions are given in the main entry for

each pub. In this section, to help you find the pubs quickly before you're past the junction, we give in abbreviated form the name of the chapter where you'll find them in the text.

M1
18: Crick (Midlands), 1 mile
Ashby St Ledgers
(Midlands), 4 miles
24: Shardlow (Derbys/Staffs),
3¼ miles
Kegworth (Leics/Lincs/
Notts), under a mile
26: Kimberley (Leics/Lincs/
Notts), 2 miles

M2
7: Selling (Kent), 3½ miles

M3
5: Mattingley (Hants),
3 miles
Rotherwick (Hants), 4 miles
7: Dummer (Hants), ½ mile

M4
9: Holyport (Berks), 1½ miles
12: Stanford Dingley (Berks),
4 miles
13: Chieveley (Berks), 3½ miles
14: Great Shefford (Berks),
2 miles
18: Old Sodbury
(Somerset/Avon), 2 miles
21: Aust (Somerset/Avon),
½ mile
Littleton upon Severn
(Somerset/Avon), 3½ miles
37: Kenfig (Wales), 2¼ miles

M5
2: Langley (Midlands),
1½ miles
9: Bredon (Herefs & Worcs),
4½ miles
16: Almondsbury
(Somerset/Avon), 1¼ miles
19: Easton in Gordano
(Somerset/Avon), 1 mile
Clapton in Gordano
(Somerset/Avon), 4 miles
23: West Huntspill
(Somerset/Avon), 2¾ miles
25: Stoke St Mary
(Somerset/Avon), 2¾ miles
28: Broadhembury (Devon),
5 miles
30: Topsham (Devon), 2 miles
Woodbury Salterton
(Devon), 3½ miles
Exeter (Devon), 4 miles

M6
2: Withybrook (Midlands),
4 miles
9: West Bromwich
(Midlands), 2 miles
13: Acton Trussell
(Derbys/Staffs), 2 miles
16: Barthomley (Cheshire),
1 mile
Shraleybrook (Derbys/
Staffs), 3 miles

Weston (Cheshire),
3½ miles
17: Brereton Green (Cheshire),
2 miles
19: Plumley (Cheshire),
2½ miles
Great Budworth
(Cheshire), 4½ miles
29: Brindle (Lancs etc), 3 miles
31: Balderstone (Lancs etc),
2 miles
32: Goosnargh (Lancs etc),
4 miles
35: Yealand Conyers (Lancs
etc), 3 miles
40: Stainton (Cumbria),
3 miles
Askham (Cumbria),
4½ miles
41: Newton Reigny
(Cumbria), 2 miles

M9
3: Linlithgow (Scotland),
2 miles

M11
10: Hinxton (Cambs/Beds),
2 miles

M18
5: Hatfield Woodhouse
(Yorks), 2 miles

M25
8: Reigate Heath (Surrey),
3 miles
Betchworth (Surrey),
4 miles
10: Pyrford Lock (Surrey),
3¼ miles
Cobham (Surrey), 3¾ miles
Flaunden (Herts), 4 miles
18: Chenies (Bucks), 2 miles

M27
8: Bursledon (Hants), 2 miles

M40
2: Beaconsfield (Bucks),
1 mile
Forty Green (Bucks),
3½ miles
5: Bolter End (Bucks), 4 miles
6: Lewknor (Oxon), ½ mile
Watlington (Oxon),
2¼ miles
7: Little Milton (Oxon),
2½ miles
8: Worminghall (Bucks),
4½ miles

M55
1: Broughton (Lancs etc),
3½ miles

M56
12: Overton (Cheshire),
2 miles

M66
1: Summerseat (Lancs etc),
1½ miles

M90
5: Cleish (Scotland), 1½ miles

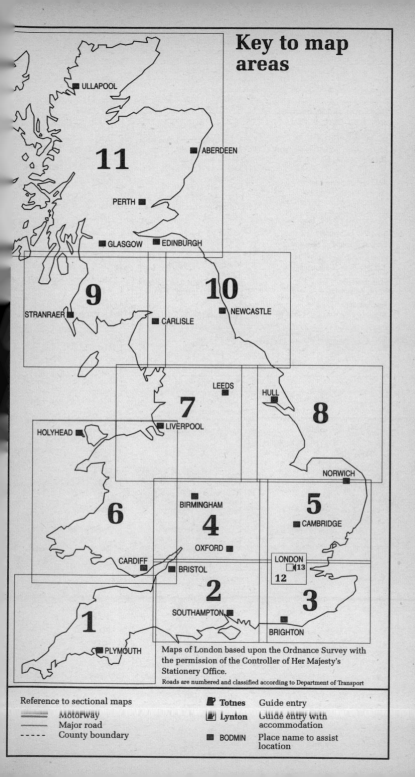

Key to map areas

ULLAPOOL

11

ABERDEEN

PERTH

GLASGOW EDINBURGH

9 **10**

STRANRAER CARLISLE NEWCASTLE

LEEDS HULL

7 **8**

HOLYHEAD LIVERPOOL

NORWICH

BIRMINGHAM **5**

6 **4** CAMBRIDGE

OXFORD

CARDIFF LONDON **13**
BRISTOL **12**

2 **3**

1 SOUTHAMPTON

BRIGHTON

PLYMOUTH

Maps of London based upon the Ordnance Survey with
the permission of the Controller of Her Majesty's
Stationery Office.

Roads are numbered and classified according to Department of Transport

Reference to sectional maps

       Motorway
       Major road
- - - - -   County boundary

Totnes   Guide entry

Lynton   Guide entry with
          accommodation

BODMIN   Place name to assist
          location

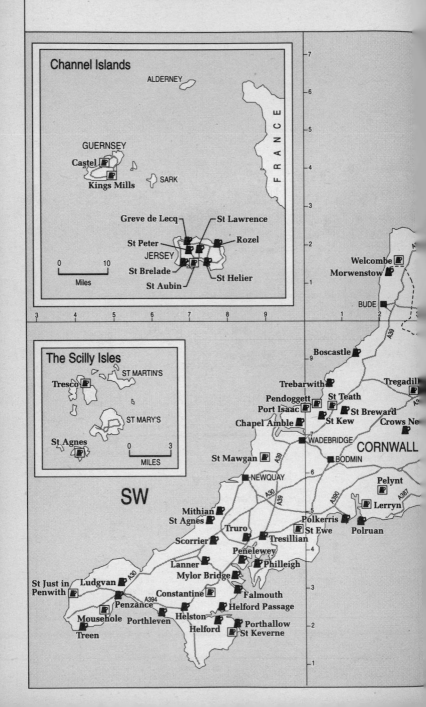

1

Channel Islands

ALDERNEY

GUERNSEY

Castel

Kings Mills

SARK

FRANCE

Greve de Lecq — St Lawrence

St Peter — Rozel

JERSEY

St Brelade

St Aubin — St Helier

0   10
Miles

The Scilly Isles

ST MARTIN'S

Tresco

ST MARY'S

St Agnes

0   3
MILES

SW

Welcombe

Morwenstow

BUDE

Boscastle

Trebarwith

Tregadil

St Teath

Pendoggett

Port Isaac   St Breward

Chapel Amble   St Kew   Crows Ne

WADEBRIDGE   **CORNWALL**

St Mawgan   BODMIN

NEWQUAY

Pelynt

Lerryn

Mithian

St Agnes

Truro   Polkerris

Tresillian   St Ewe   Polruan

Scorrier

Penelewey

Lanner   Philleigh

Mylor Bridge

St Just in   Ludgvan

Penwith   Constantine   Falmouth

Penzance   Helford Passage

Mousehole   Porthleven   Helston

Treen   Helford   Porthallow
                                St Keverne

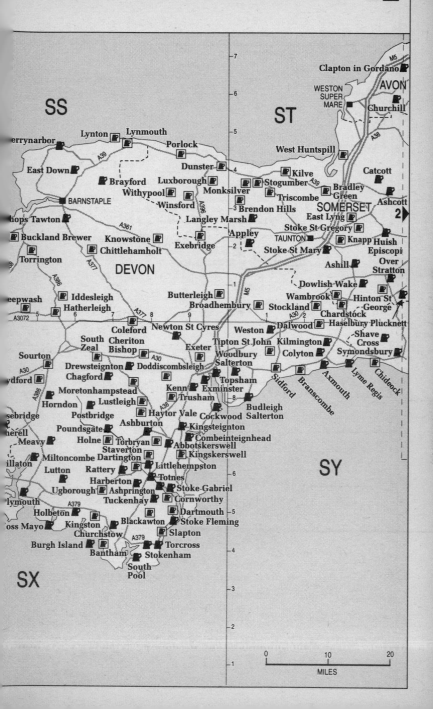

1

SS

ST

SY

SX

DEVON

SOMERSET

AVON

BARNSTAPLE

TAUNTON

WESTON SUPER MARE

Clapton in Gordano

Churchill

Catcott

Ashcott

West Huntspill

Kilve

Stogumber

Triscombe

Bradley Green

Stoke St Gregory

Knapp Huish Episcopi

Over Stratton

Hinton St George

Haselbury Plucknett

Shave Cross

Symondsbury

Chideock

Lyme Regis

Axmouth

Branscombe

Sidford

Budleigh Salterton

Cockwood

Topsham

Exminster

Kingsteignton

Combeinteignhead

Kingskerswell

Abbotskerswell

Littlehempston

Stoke Gabriel

Cornworthy

Dartmouth

Stoke Fleming

Slapton

Torcross

Stokenham

South Pool

Bantham

Burgh Island

Churchstow

Kingston

Blackawton

Tuckenhay

Ashprington

Harberton

Ugborough

Totnes

Rattery

Staverton

Dartington

Miltoncombe

Lutton

Holne

Torbryan

Ashburton

Poundsgate

Meavy

Postbridge

Holbeton

Horndon

Lustleigh

Moretonhampstead

Chagford

Drewsteignton

Sourton

South Zeal

Cheriton Bishop

Coleford

Doddiscombsleigh

Kenn

Trusham

Haytor Vale

Exeter

Newton St Cyres

Tipton St John

Woodbury Salterton

Colyton

Kilmington

Weston

Dalwood

Stockland

Chardstock

Wambrook

Dowlish Wake

Ashill

Stoke St Mary

Appley

Langley Marsh

Brendon Hills

Monksilver

Luxborough

Dunster

Porlock

Lynmouth

Lynton

East Down

Brayford

Withypool

Winsford

Exebridge

Butterleigh

Broadhembury

Knowstone

Chittlehamholt

Buckland Brewer

Torrington

Iddesleigh

Hatherleigh

eepwash

Bishops Tawton

errynarbor

South Pool

Burgh Island

A39

A361

A377

A386

A396

A30

A38

A39

A379

M5

MILES

0   10   20

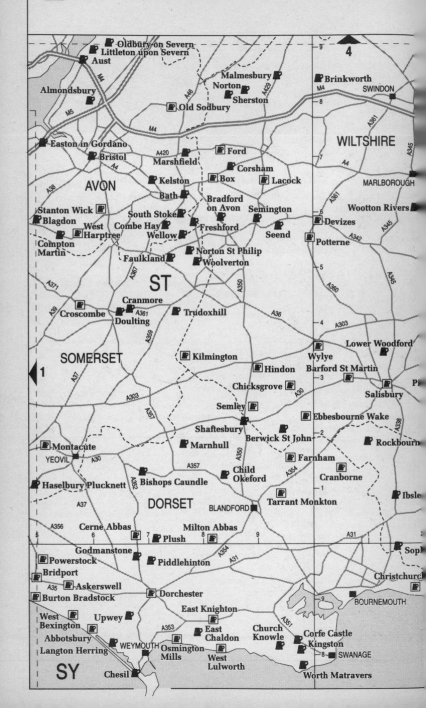

2

4

Oldbury on Severn
Littleton upon Severn
Aust
Almondsbury
Malmesbury
Norton
Sherston
Brinkworth
SWINDON
Old Sodbury
WILTSHIRE
Easton in Gordano
Bristol
Ford
Marshfield
Corsham
MARLBOROUGH
AVON
Kelston
Box
Lacock
Bath
Bradford on Avon
Semington
Stanton Wick
Blagdon
South Stoke
Devizes
West Harptree
Combe Hay
Freshford
Potterne
Compton Martin
Wellow
Seend
Faulkland
Norton St Philip
Woolverton
ST
Cranmore
Trudoxhill
Croscombe
Doulting
Lower Woodford
SOMERSET
Kilmington
Wylye
Hindon
Barford St Martin
Chicksgrove
Salisbury
Semley
Ebbesbourne Wake
Shaftesbury
Montacute
Marnhull
Berwick St John
Rockbourn
YEOVIL
Farnham
Haselbury Plucknett
Bishops Caundle
Child Okeford
Cranborne
Ibsle
DORSET
Tarrant Monkton
BLANDFORD
Cerne Abbas
Milton Abbas
Plush
Sop
Godmanstone
Powerstock
Piddlehinton
Christchurc
Bridport
Askerswell
Dorchester
Burton Bradstock
East Knighton
BOURNEMOUTH
West Bexington
Upwey
East Chaldon
Church Knowle
Corfe Castle
Abbotsbury
WEYMOUTH
Kingston
Langton Herring
Osmington Mills
West Lulworth
SWANAGE
SY
Chesil
Worth Matravers

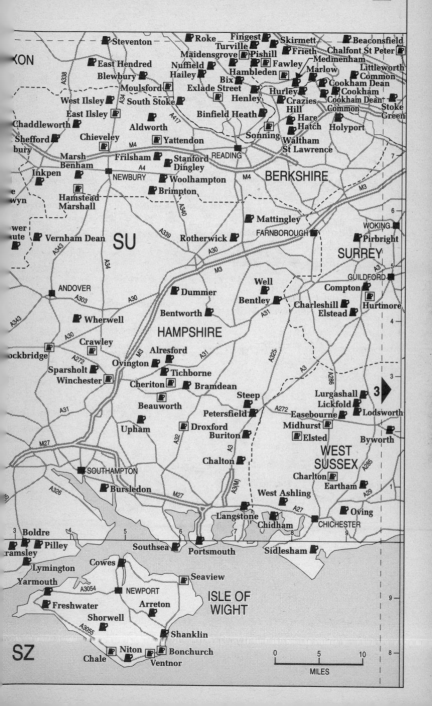

2

Steventon
Roke
Fingest
Skirmett
Beaconsfield
Turville
Frieth
Chalfont St Peter
Maidensgrove
Pishill
East Hendred
Nuffield
Fawley
Medmenham
Littleworth
Blewbury
Hailey
Hambleden
Marlow
Common
Moulsford
Bix
Cookham Dean
West Ilsley
South Stoke
Exlade Street
Hurley
Cookham
Cookham Dean
East Ilsley
Henley
Crazies
Common
Stoke
Chaddleworth
Binfield Heath
Hill
Green
Aldworth
Sonning
Hare
Holyport
Shefford
Chieveley
Yattendon
Hatch
bury
Waltham
Marsh
Frilsham
Stanford
READING
St Lawrence
Benham
Dingley
BERKSHIRE
Inkpen
NEWBURY
Woolhampton
Hamstead
Brimpton
Marshall
wyn
Mattingley
WOKING
wer
Vernham Dean
SU
Rotherwick
FARNBOROUGH
Pirbright
aute
A30
SURREY
GUILDFORD
ANDOVER
Dummer
Well
Compton
Hurtmore
Bentley
Charleshill
Wherwell
Bentworth
Elstead
HAMPSHIRE
Crawley
Alresford
Sparsholt
Ovington
Tichborne
Lurgashall
ockbridge
Cheriton
Bramdean
Lickfold
Lodsworth
Winchester
Steep
Easebourne
Beauworth
Petersfield
Midhurst
Byworth
Upham
Droxford
Elsted
Buriton
WEST
SOUTHAMPTON
Chalton
SUSSEX
Bursledon
Charlton
Eartham
West Ashling
Oving
Langstone
CHICHESTER
Boldre
Chidham
Pilley
Southsea
Portsmouth
Sidlesham
ramsley
Lymington
Cowes
Yarmouth
Seaview
NEWPORT
Freshwater
Arreton
ISLE OF
Shorwell
WIGHT
Shanklin
SZ
Niton
Bonchurch
Chale
Ventnor

0   5   10
MILES

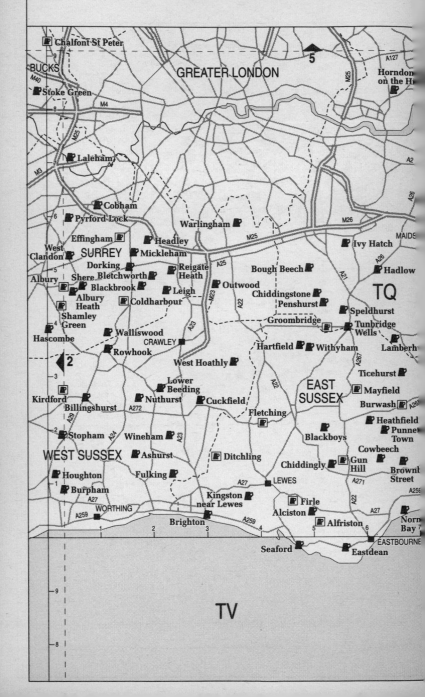

Chalfont St Peter

9

BUCKS
M40

Stoke Green

GREATER LONDON

5

A127

Horndon
on the Hi

M25

A2

Laleham

M3

M25

8

M4

A26

6

Cobham

Pyrford Lock

Warlingham

M26

MAIDS

Ivy Hatch

A26

Effingham

Headley

SURREY

Mickleham

M25

Hadlow

TQ

West
Clandon

Dorking

Reigate
Heath

A25

Bough Beech

A21

Albury

Shere Bletchworth

Blackbrook

Outwood

Chiddingstone

A22

Penshurst

Speldhurst

Albury
Heath

Leigh

Coldharbour

M23

Groombridge

Tunbridge
Wells

Shamley
Green

Hascombe

Walliswood

A23

Hartfield

Withyham

Lamberh

Rowhook

CRAWLEY

West Hoathly

EAST
SUSSEX

Ticehurst

2

3

Lower
Beeding

A22

Mayfield

Kirdford

Nuthurst

Cuckfield

Burwash

A26

Billingshurst

A272

Fletching

Heathfield

A29

Wineham

A23

Blackboys

Punne
Town

Stopham

A24

Cowbeech

WEST SUSSEX

Ashurst

Ditchling

Chiddingly

Gun
Hill

Brownl
Street

Houghton

Fulking

A271

A259

Burpham

Kingston
near Lewes

LEWES

Firle

A22

A27

Norn
Bay 7

A27

WORTHING

Alciston

Alfriston

A259

Brighton

A259

5

6

EASTBOURNE

Seaford

Eastdean

9

8

TV

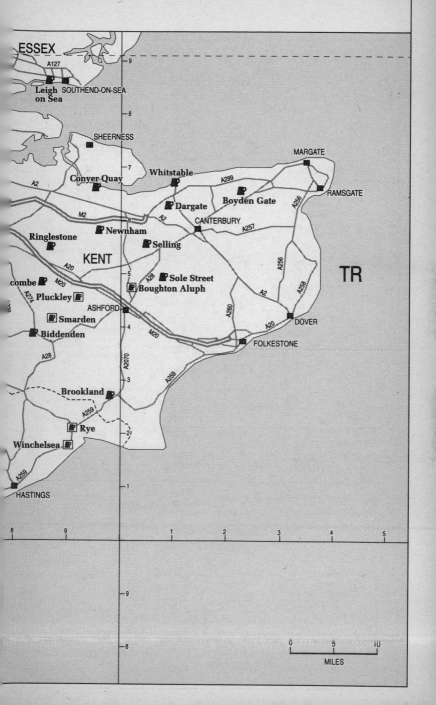

3

ESSEX

A127

Leigh
on Sea SOUTHEND-ON-SEA

SHEERNESS

A2

Conyer Quay Whitstable MARGATE

A299 RAMSGATE

Boyden Gate A256

Dargate

M2 A2 CANTERBURY

Ringlestone Newnham

A257

KENT Selling

A256

A20 TR

combe A28 Sole Street

M20 Boughton Aluph

A274 Pluckley ASHFORD A259

Smarden M20 A2

Biddenden DOVER

A28 A260

A2070 FOLKESTONE

M20

Brookland A259

A259

Rye A259

Winchelsea

A259

HASTINGS

ESSEX 9
8
7
6
5
4
3
2
1

9
8

0   5   10

MILES

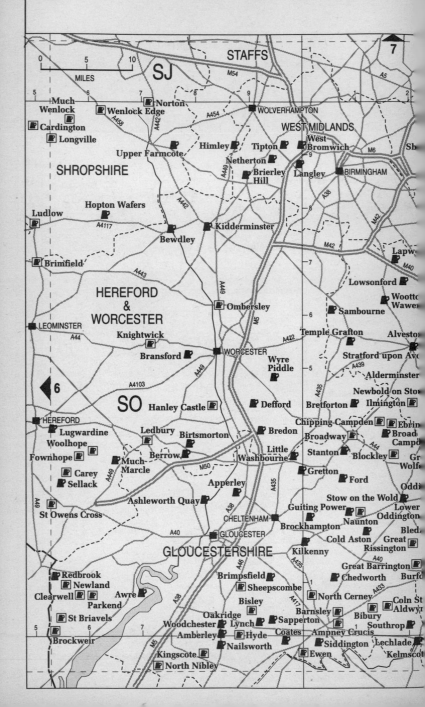

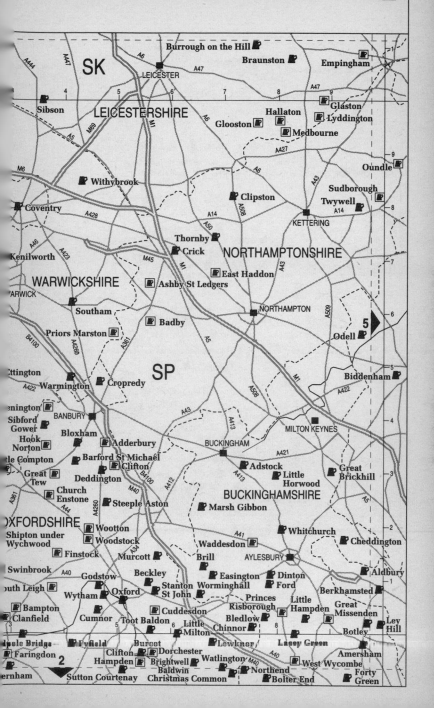

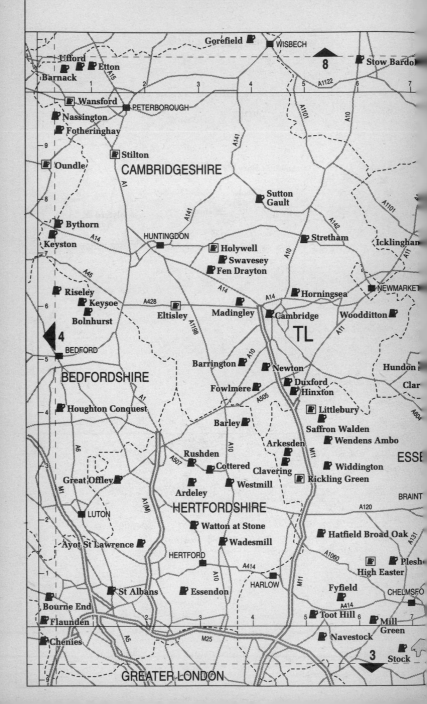

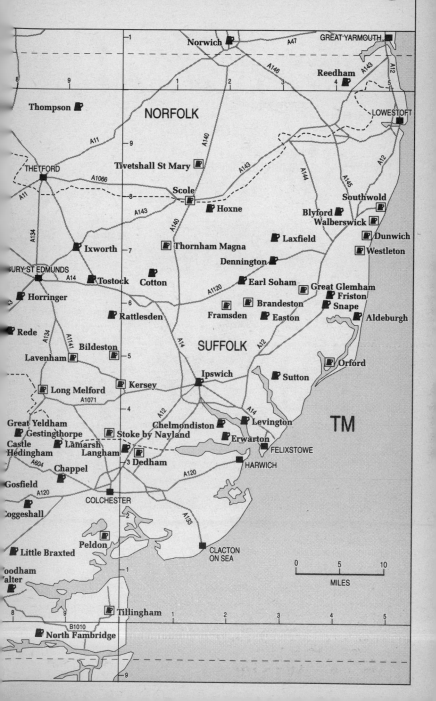

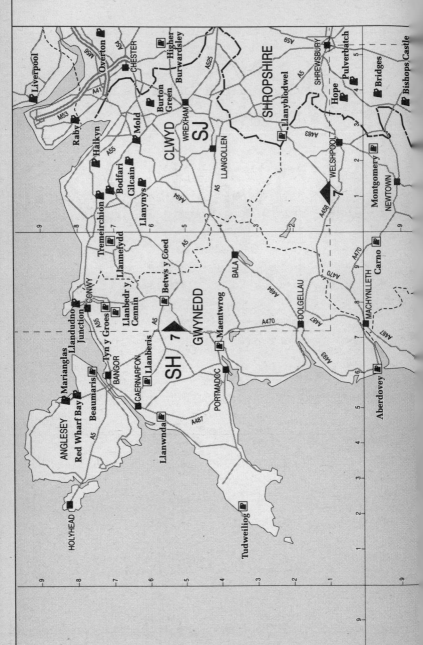

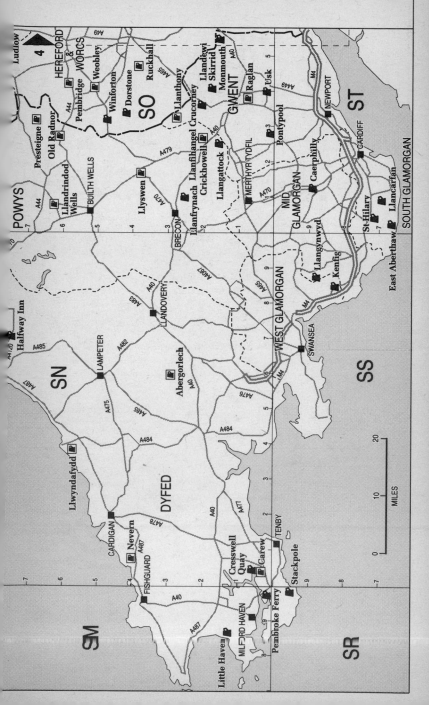

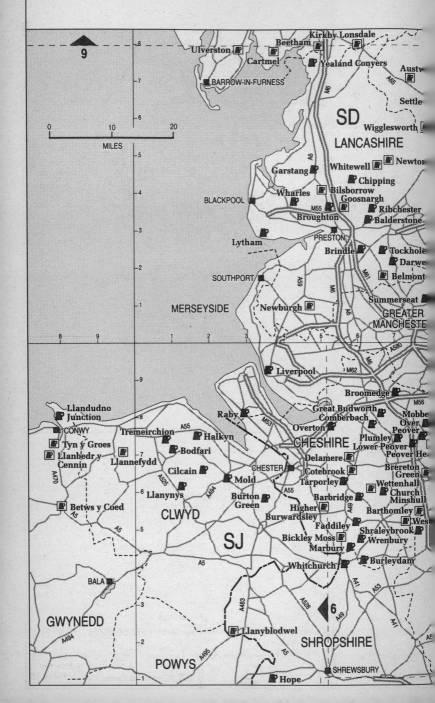

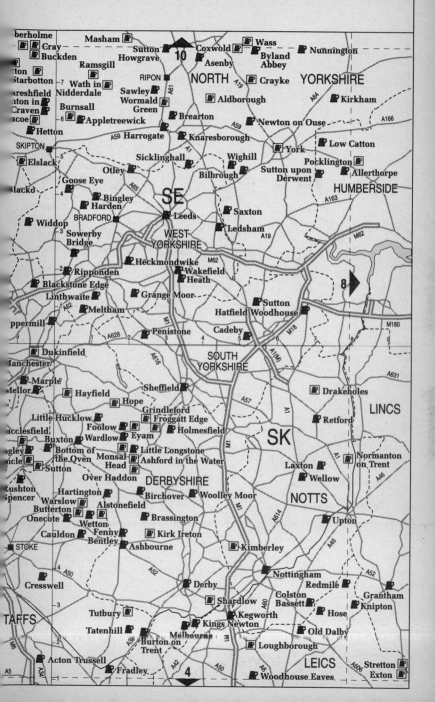

7

Aberholme
Cray
Buckden
Starbotton
Staton
Staton in Craven
Cracoe
Hetton
SKIPTON
Elslack
Blacko
Goose Eye
Widdop
Bingley
Harden
BRADFORD
Sowerby Bridge
Ripponden
Blackstone Edge
Linthwaite
Meltham
ppermill
Dukinfield
Manchester
Marple
Mellor
Macclesfield
Little Hucklow
Buxton
ngley
ncle
Sutton
Rushton Spencer
Hartington
Warslow
Butterton
Onecote
Cauldon
STOKE
Cresswell
TAFFS
Tutbury
Tatenhill
Acton Trussell
Fradley

Masham
Sutton Howgrave
Ramsgill
RIPON
Wath in Nidderdale
Sawley
Wormald Green
Burnsall
Appletreewick
Harrogate
Otley
Sicklinghall
Leeds
WEST YORKSHIRE
Heckmondwike
Wakefield
Heath
Grange Moor
Penistone
SOUTH YORKSHIRE
Hayfield
Hope
Grindleford
Froggatt Edge
Foolow
Wardlow
Eyam
Holmesfield
Bottom of the Oven
Monsal Head
Little Longstone
Ashford in the Water
Over Haddon
Birchover
Alstonefield
Brassington
Wetton
Fenny Bentley
Kirk Ireton
Ashbourne
Derby
Shardlow
Melbourne
Kings Newton
Burton on Trent
Woodhouse Eaves

Coxwold
Asenby
Wass
Byland Abbey
Crayke
NORTH YORKSHIRE
Aldborough
Brearton
Knaresborough
Newton on Ouse
Wighill
Bilbrough
York
Sutton upon Derwent
Saxton
Ledsham
Sutton
Hatfield Woodhouse
Cadeby
Sheffield
SK
DERBYSHIRE
Woolley Moor
Laxton
Wellow
NOTTS
Upton
Kimberley
Nottingham
Colston Bassett
Kegworth
Old Dalby
Loughborough

Nunnington
Kirkham
A166
Low Catton
Pocklington
Allerthorpe
HUMBERSIDE
Drakeholes
LINCS
Retford
Normanton on Trent
Redmile
Grantham
Knipton
Hose
Stretton
Exton
LEICS

10
8
4

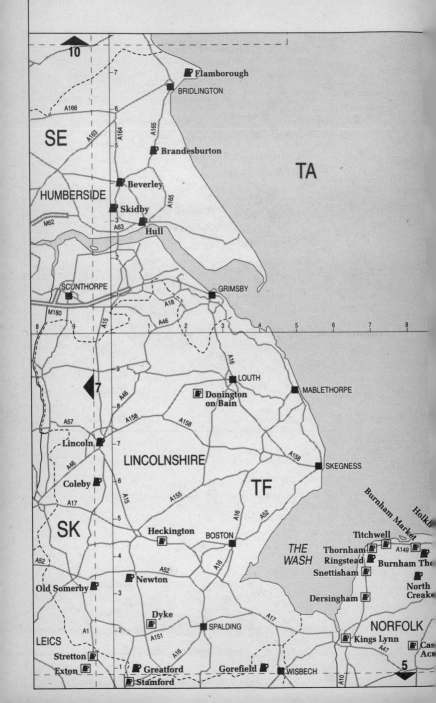

10

7

A166

SE

A165

A164

A163

A165

Flamborough

BRIDLINGTON

Brandesburton

TA

HUMBERSIDE

Beverley

A165

Skidby

M62

A63

3

Hull

2

SCUNTHORPE

GRIMSBY

M180

A18

A15

A46

M180   9   1   1   2   3   4   5   6   7   8

8   9

A16

9

LOUTH

7

A46

Donington
on Bain

MABLETHORPE

A57

8

A158

A158

Lincoln

A46

7

LINCOLNSHIRE

A158

SKEGNESS

Coleby

6

A155

TF

A17

A15

A16

A52

SK

5

Heckington

BOSTON

Burnham Market

Holkh

A52

4

A52

THE
WASH

Titchwell

Thornham

A149

Newton

3

A52

A16

Ringstead

Burnham Tho

Old Somerby

A52

Snettisham

North
Creake

Dyke

Dersingham

LEICS   A1

2

A52

A151

SPALDING

A17

NORFOLK

Stretton

A16

Kings Lynn

Cas
Acr

Exton

1

Greatford

Gorefield

WISBECH

A47

Stamford

A10

5

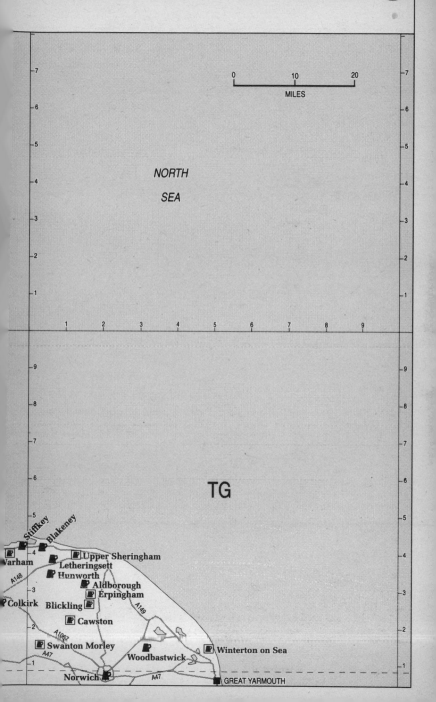

8

0   10   20
MILES

NORTH

SEA

7

6

5

4

3

2

1

1   2   3   4   5   6   7   8   9

9

8

7

6

TG

5

Stiffkey Blakeney

Warham Upper Sheringham

Letheringsett

A148 Hunworth Aldborough

Erpingham

Colkirk Blickling

A149

Cawston

A1067

Swanton Morley Winterton on Sea

A47 Woodbastwick

Norwich A47 GREAT YARMOUTH

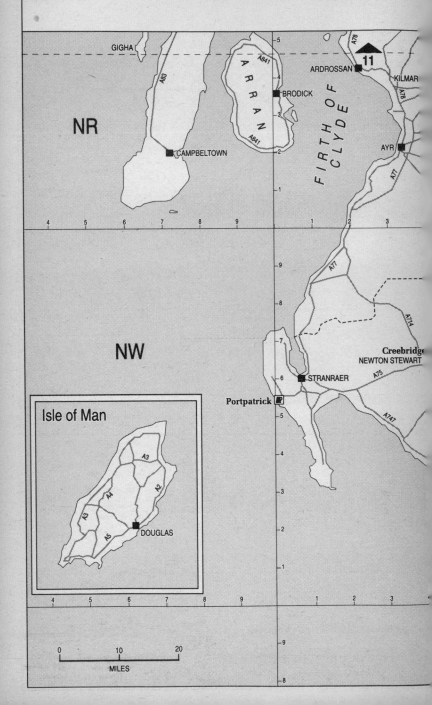

GIGHA

ARRAN

A841

A83

5

A78

11

4

ARDROSSAN

KILMAR

BRODICK

3

A78

NR

2

CAMPBELTOWN

FIRTH OF CLYDE

AYR

A841

1

A77

4   5   6   7   8   9   1   2   3

9

A77

8

A714

NW

7

Creebridge

NEWTON STEWART

6

STRANRAER

A75

Portpatrick

5

A747

Isle of Man

4

A3

3

A4

A2

2

A3

A5

DOUGLAS

1

4   5   6   7   8   9   1   2   3

9

8

0   10   20

MILES

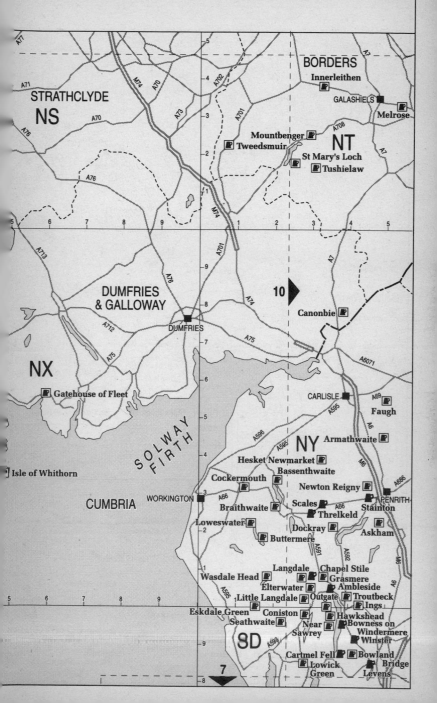

9

STRATHCLYDE
NS

BORDERS

Innerleithen

GALASHIELS
Melrose

NT

Mountbenger
Tweedsmuir

St Mary's Loch
Tushielaw

10

DUMFRIES
& GALLOWAY

DUMFRIES

Canonbie

NX

Gatehouse of Fleet

CARLISLE

Faugh

NY

Armathwaite

Isle of Whithorn

SOLWAY FIRTH

Hesket Newmarket

Bassenthwaite

Cockermouth

Newton Reigny

CUMBRIA

WORKINGTON

Braithwaite

Scales

PENRITH

Stainton

Threlkeld

Loweswater

Dockray

Askham

Buttermere

Wasdale Head

Langdale

Chapel Stile

Elterwater

Grasmere

Little Langdale

Ambleside

Eskdale Green

Outgate

Troutbeck

Coniston

Ings

Seathwaite

Hawkshead

Near
Sawrey

Bowness on
Windermere

SD

Winster

Cartmel Fell

Bowland
Bridge

Lowick
Green

Levens

7

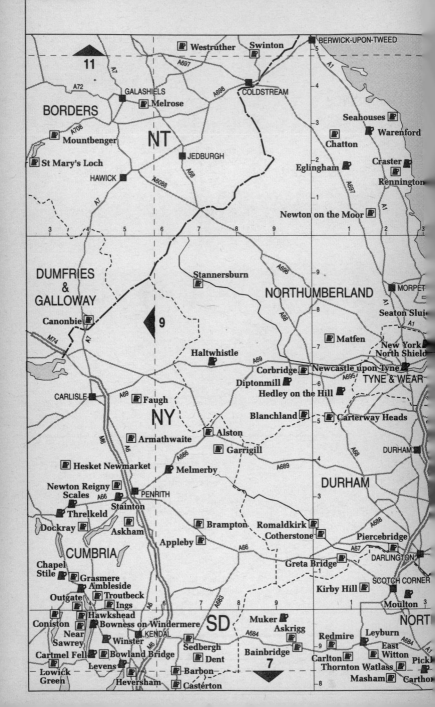

10

BORDERS

Westruther · Swinton · BERWICK-UPON-TWEED

Galashiels · Melrose · COLDSTREAM

NT

Mountbenger

Seahouses · Warenford

Chatton

St Mary's Loch

JEDBURGH

Eglingham · Craster

HAWICK

Rennington

Newton on the Moor

DUMFRIES & GALLOWAY

Stannersburn

NORTHUMBERLAND · MORPET

Canonbie

9

Seaton Slui

Matfen

New York
North Shield

Haltwhistle

Corbridge · Newcastle upon Tyne

CARLISLE

Diptonmill

TYNE & WEAR

Hedley on the Hill

Faugh

Blanchland · Carterway Heads

NY

Armathwaite · Alston

DURHAM

Garrigill

Hesket Newmarket

Melmerby

A689

DURHAM

Newton Reigny
Scales · PENRITH
Stainton

Brampton · Romaldkirk
Cotherstone

Piercebridge

Threlkeld

DARLINGTON

Dockray · Askham

Appleby

Greta Bridge

SCOTCH CORNER

CUMBRIA

Chapel Stile

Kirby Hill

Moulton

NOR

Grasmere
Ambleside

Outgate · Troutbeck
Ings

SD · Muker
Askrigg

Coniston · Hawkshead
Bowness on Windermere

Redmire · Leyburn

Near Sawrey

Winster · KENDAL

Sedbergh

Bainbridge · East
Witton · Pick

Cartmel Fell · Bowland Bridge
Levens · Dent

Carlton
Thornton Watlass

Lowick Green

Barbon

Masham · Cartho

Heversham · Casterton

7

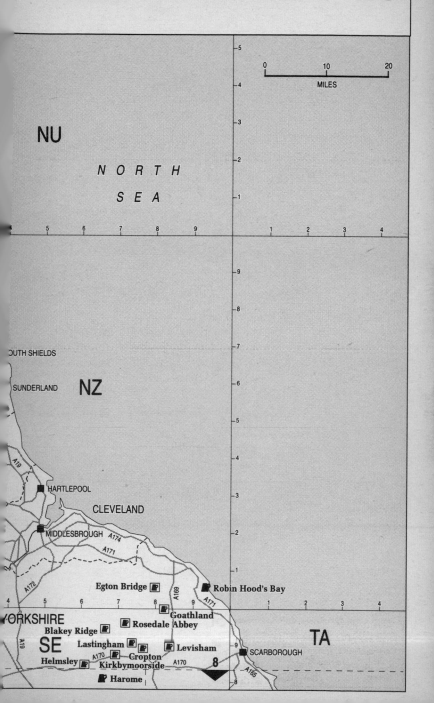

NU

N O R T H

S E A

0   10   20
MILES

OUTH SHIELDS

SUNDERLAND   NZ

HARTLEPOOL

CLEVELAND

MIDDLESBROUGH A174

A171

A172

Egton Bridge 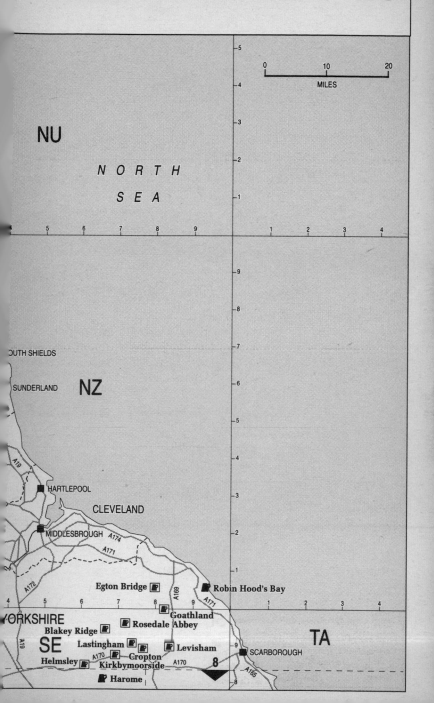   Robin Hood's Bay

YORKSHIRE

Blakey Ridge   Rosedale Abbey

Goathland

Lastingham   Levisham

Helmsley   Cropton

Kirkbymoorside   A170   SCARBOROUGH

Harome   TA

8

SE

A19

A170

A169

A171

A165

A19

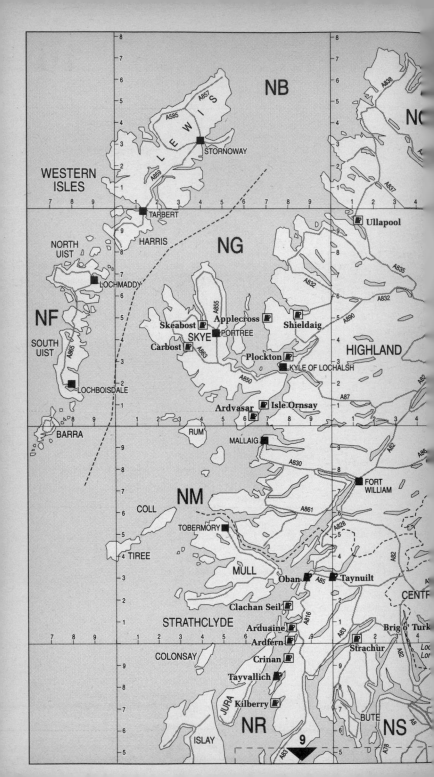

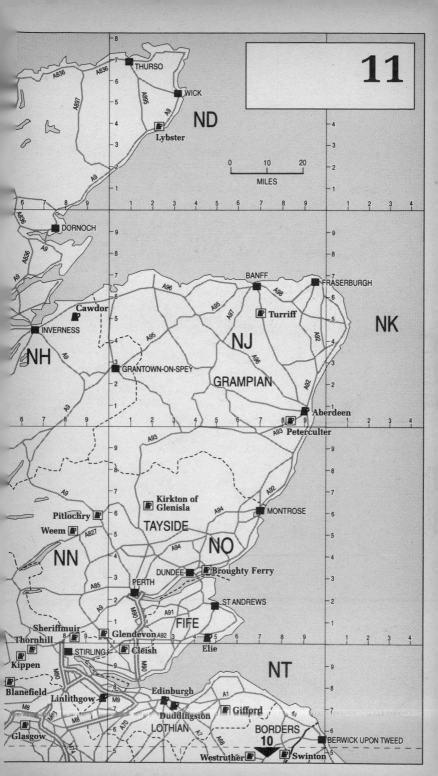

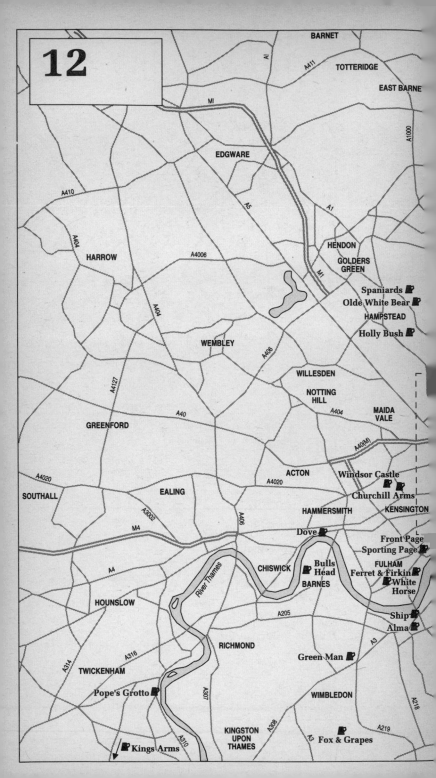

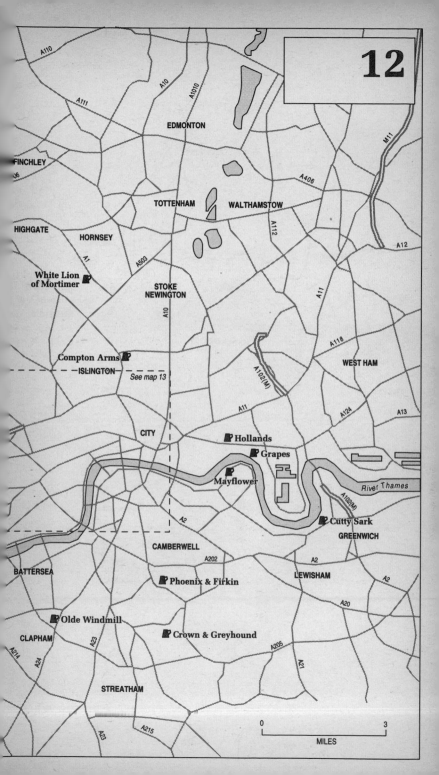

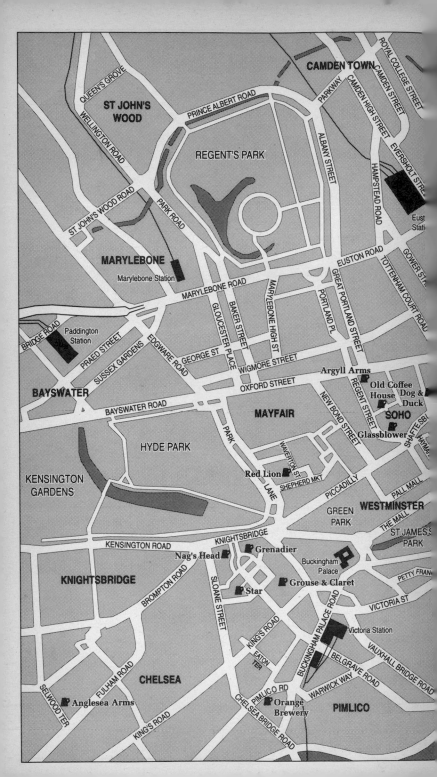

Report forms

Please report to us: you can use the tear-out forms on the following pages, the card in the middle of the book, or just plain paper – whichever's easiest for you. We need to know what you think of the pubs in this edition. We need to know about other pubs worthy of inclusion. We need to know about ones that should not be included.

The atmosphere and character of the pub are the most important features why it would, or would not, appeal to strangers. But the bar food and the drink are important too – please tell us about them.

If the food is really quite outstanding, tick the FOOD AWARD box on the form, and tell us about the special quality that makes it stand out – the more detail, the better. And if you have stayed there, tell us about the standard of accommodation – whether it was comfortable, pleasant, good value for money. Again, if the pub or inn is worth special attention as a place to stay, tick the PLACE-TO-STAY AWARD box.

Please try to gauge whether a pub should be a main entry, or is best as a Lucky Dip (and tick the relevant box). In general, main entries need qualities that would make it worth other readers' while to travel some distance to them; Lucky Dips are the pubs that are worth knowing about if you are nearby. But if a pub is an entirely new recommendation, the Lucky Dip may be the best place for it to start its career in the *Guide* to encourage other readers to report on it, and gradually build up a dossier on it; it's very rare for a pub to jump straight into the main entries.

The more detail you can put into your description of a Lucky Dip pub that's only scantily described in the current edition (or not in at all), the better. This'll help not just us but also your fellow-readers gauge its appeal. A description of its character and even furnishings is a tremendous boon.

It helps enormously if you can give the full address for any new pub – one not yet a main entry, or without a full address in the Lucky Dip sections. In a town, we need the street name; in the country, if it's hard to find, we need directions. Without this, there's little chance of our being able to include the pub. And with any pub, it always helps to let us know about **prices** of food (and bedrooms, if there are any), and about any lunchtimes or evenings when food is **not** served. We'd also like to have your views on drinks quality – beer, wine, cider and so forth, even coffee and tea; and do let us know if it has bedrooms.

If you know that a Lucky Dip pub is open all day (or even late into the afternoon), please tell us – preferably saying which days.

When you go to a pub, don't tell them you're a reporter for the *Good Pub Guide;* we do make clear that all inspections are anonymous, and if you declare yourself as a reporter you risk getting special treatment – for better or for worse!

Sometimes pubs are dropped from the main entries simply because very few readers have written to us about them – and of course there's a risk that people may not write if they find the pub exactly as described in the entry. You can use the form opposite just to list pubs you've been to, found as described, and can recommend.

When you write to *The Good Pub Guide*, FREEPOST TN1569, WADHURST, East Sussex TN5 7BR, you don't need a stamp in the UK. We'll gladly send you more forms (free) if you wish.

Though we try to answer letters, there are just the four of us – and with other work to do, besides producing this *Guide*. So please understand if there's a delay. And from June till August, when we are fully extended getting the next edition to the printers, we put all letters and reports aside, not answering them until the rush is over (and after our post-press-day late summer holiday). The end of May is pretty much the cut-off date for reasoned consideration of reports for the next edition.

We'll assume we can print your name or initials as a recommender unless you tell us otherwise.

I have been to the following pubs in *The 1995 Good Pub Guide* in the last few months, found them as described, and confirm that they deserve continued inclusion:

Continued overleaf
PLEASE GIVE YOUR NAME AND ADDRESS ON THE BACK OF THIS FORM

Pubs visited continued...

Your own name and address *(block capitals please)*

Please return to
The Good Pub Guide,
FREEPOST TN1569,
WADHURST,
East Sussex
TN5 7BR

REPORT ON _(pub's name)_

....

Pub's address

....

☐ **YES MAIN ENTRY**   ☐ **YES** _Lucky Dip_   ☐ NO don't include
Please tick one of these boxes to show your verdict, and give reasons and
descriptive comments, prices etc

☐ Deserves FOOD award   ☐ Deserves PLACE-TO-STAY award   95:1

PLEASE GIVE YOUR NAME AND ADDRESS ON THE BACK OF THIS FORM

REPORT ON _(pub's name)_

....

Pub's address

....

☐ **YES MAIN ENTRY**   ☐ **YES** _Lucky Dip_   ☐ NO don't include
Please tick one of these boxes to show your verdict, and give reasons and
descriptive comments, prices etc

☐ Deserves FOOD award   ☐ Deserves PLACE-TO-STAY award   95:2

PLEASE GIVE YOUR NAME AND ADDRESS ON THE BACK OF THIS FORM

Your own name and address *(block capitals please)*

DO NOT USE THIS SIDE OF THE PAGE FOR WRITING ABOUT PUBS

Your own name and address *(block capitals please)*

DO NOT USE THIS SIDE OF THE PAGE FOR WRITING ABOUT PUBS